Williams on Wills

Editors of previous editions

First edition	1952	W J Williams
Second edition	1961	W J Williams
Third edition	1967	W J Williams
Fourth edition	1974	C H Sherrin and R F D Barlow
Fifth edition	1980	C H Sherrin, R F D Barlow and R A Wallington
Sixth edition	1987	C H Sherrin, R F D Barlow and R A Wallington
Seventh edition	1995	C H Sherrin, R F D Barlow and R A Wallington

Williams on Wills

Eighth edition

C H SHERRIN
LLM Ph D
Professor of Law,
Department of Professional Legal Education,
University of Hong Kong

R F D BARLOW
MA (Oxon)
Barrister
A Bencher of Lincoln's Inn

R A WALLINGTON
MA (Cantab)
of the Middle Temple and
Lincoln's Inn, Barrister

SUSANNAH L MEADWAY
MA (Oxon)
of the Middle Temple and
Lincoln's Inn, Barrister

MICHAEL WATERWORTH
MA (Cantab)
of Lincoln's Inn, Barrister

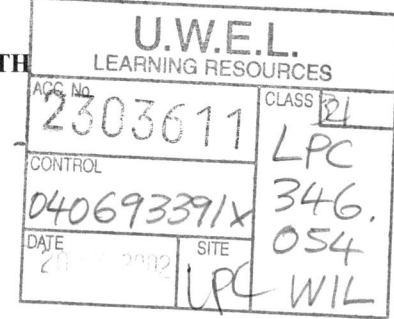
Volume 1
The Law of Wills

Butterworths
London • Dublin • Edinburgh
2002

United Kingdom   Butterworths, a Division of Reed Elsevier (UK) Ltd, Halsbury House,
                  35 Chancery Lane, LONDON WC2A 1EL and
                  4 Hill Street, EDINBURGH EH2 3JZ

Australia   Butterworths, a Division of Reed International Books Australia Pty Ltd,
                  CHATSWOOD, New South Wales

Canada   Butterworths Canada Ltd, MARKHAM, Ontario

Hong Kong   Butterworths Asia (Hong Kong), HONG KONG

India   Butterworths India, NEW DELHI

Ireland   Butterworth (Ireland) Ltd, DUBLIN

Malaysia   Malayan Law Journal Sdn Bhd, KUALA LUMPUR

New Zealand   Butterworths of New Zealand Ltd, WELLINGTON

Singapore   Butterworths Asia, SINGAPORE

South Africa   Butterworths Publishers (Pty) Ltd, DURBAN

USA   Lexis Law Publishing, CHARLOTTESVILLE, Virginia

A CIP Catalogue record for this book is available from the British Library

VOLUME 1 BARCODE/ISBN
ISBN 0-406-93392-8

9 780406 933928

COMPLETE SET BARCODE/ISBN
ISBN 0-406-93391-X

9 780406 933911

Typeset by Thomson Litho Ltd, East Kilbride, Scotland
Printed and bound in Great Britain by Clays Ltd, St Ives plc

Visit Butterworths LEXIS *direct* at: http://www.butterworths.com

PREFACE

Volume One continues the long established policy of the work by providing a concise and practical text on the law of wills with a comprehensive exposition of the substantive law and extensive cross-referencing to the precedents and commentary in Volume Two. Readers familiar with the previous editions of the book will notice that paragraph numbering has been introduced throughout both volumes with cross-referencing to the paragraphs so numbered. The new format has enabled footnotes to be appended to each numbered paragraph. While this represents a significant break from the continuous numbering of references in recent editions it is thought that the new format will render the work more accessible to the user. The previous sub-division of Volume One into Parts A to P has been retained. Volume One has been extensively revised and updated with the addition of new text reflecting the developments and changes to the law of wills and always with an eye to the elimination of otiose cases and materials.

The most significant developments in the law of its subject-matter have been legislative. The period since the previous edition has seen the enactment of three important Acts of Parliament. The Trusts of Land and Appointment of Trustees Act 1996 has radically affected the previous law relating to settled land and trusts for sale of land replacing them prospectively by the new trusts of land. The same Act has precluded the future creation of entails; abolished the doctrine of conversion and provided a new regime for the appointment of trustees. These changes have been reflected principally in Chapters 7, 26, 27, 37, 78 and 84. The Trustee Delegation Act 1999 affects the subject-matter of its title requiring revisions in Chapter 27. A third major piece of legislation affecting *Williams on Wills* has been the Trustee Act 2000, which by virtue of s 35 'applies in relation to a personal representative administering an estate according to the law as it applies to a trustee carrying out a trust for beneficiaries, and so that references to the trust instrument are to be read as references to the will'. The Act makes significant reforms and changes to the law by introducing a new duty of care for trustees, new powers of trustee investment, extensions to the power to appoint agents, and new provisions on remuneration (including interesting amendments to the effect of s 15 of the Wills Act 1837 and to s 34(3) of the Administration of Estates Act 1925). The changes made by the Trustee Act 2000 have been principally reflected in Chapters 9, 25, 26 and 27.

There has been the usual flow of case law notably on conditional wills (where the Court of Appeal decision in *Corbett v Newey* [1996] 2 All ER 914 has been included), mutual wills (*Re Goodchild (decd)* [1997] 3 All ER 63, rectification (*Walker v Geo H Medlicott & Son* [1999] 1 All ER 685), the forfeiture rule (*Dunbar v Plant* [1997] 4 All ER 289 and *Re DWS* [2000] 2 All ER 83), formalities (*Couser v Couser* [1996] 3 All ER 256), disclaimers (*Re Smith, Smith v Smith* [2001] 3 All ER 552), ademption (*Re Cameron* [1999] 2 All ER 924), appropriation (*Re Kane, Kane v Radley-Kane* [1998] 3 All ER 753), estoppel (*Gillett v Holt* [2000] 2 All ER 289), intestacy (*Re DWS* [2001] 1 All ER 97) and family provision (*Re Goodchild (decd)* [1997] 3 All ER 63 and *Re B*

v

[2000] 1 All ER 665). In keeping with the traditions of the work as a common law authority significant recent cases from Commonwealth jurisdictions which follow the English tradition, have been added.

Williams on Wills has an established reputation as an authoritative source and statement of the law of wills and has been frequently cited as such in both English and Commonwealth courts – there are some 36 such references in footnotes to the text. We are pleased to note that this judicial citation has continued since the publication of the previous edition, two examples being *Re Goodchild* [1996] 1 All ER 670 at p 677 and *Gibson Estate v Ashbury College Inc* (1999) 179 DLR (4th) 557 at p 562.

Volume Two is divided into seven parts as in the previous edition. Part A contains an Introductory Note, now much expanded to take account, in particular, of the reform of the law relating to the holding of land in trust effected by the Trusts of Land and Appointment of Trustees Act 1996. Part A draws attention to a number of practical matters and potential traps which are not infrequently encountered by the will draftsman. The main parts containing drafting precedents are, as formerly, Part B (Clauses in wills) and Part C (Complete wills). Forms for codicils are separately contained in Part D and E and an extended Part F contain, as previously, the statutory will forms and forms for non-testamentary instruments (such as deeds of appointment and deeds of variation). Finally, Part G contains the statutory material which is much expanded in consequence of the legislative developments mentioned below.

The two previous editions saw radical changes in the content and layout of Volume Two, in particular of Parts B and C. This edition has consolidated those changes in a new format and it has been updated throughout to take account of recent developments. Principal among these are the Trusts of Land and Appointment of Trustees Act 1996 and the Trustee Act 2000. Both these statutes have important implications for will drafting. The text of both Acts is included in Section 3 of Part G and an outline of their principal provisions is contained in Part A. A more detailed account of the impact of the 1996 Act on rights of occupation and on administration trusts is given in the Preliminary Notes to B8 and B14 and the precedents contained in those sections have been revised to take account of the changes made by the Act. The effect of both statutes on administrative powers and provisions is considered in the explanatory notes in B20 dealing with the investment powers and powers of management in relation to land of personal representatives and trustees and is reflected in the revisions to the forms contained in that section. The effect of the two Acts on other provisions affecting personal representatives and trustees, eg indemnities, the appointment of new trustees and the power of professional personal representatives and trustees to charge, is considered in the explanatory notes in B21 and is reflected in the revisions to the precedents contained in that section.

Whereas Part B continues, as in previous editions, to be arranged by the lawyer's classification of types of clause – eg specific gifts of chattels, legacies, annuities, administration trusts etc – Part C is divided, as in the previous edition, into sections according to the circumstances of the testators – eg married couples with young children, married couples with older children, families where there is a disabled person, testators with more than one family, sole parents with young parents, testators who are unmarried or childless etc. One casualty of the recent reforms has been the strict settlement of the landed estate contained in Form C13.2 in the previous edition. Since strict settlements and entailed interests can now no longer be created, the retention of this precedent cannot now be justified even for reference purposes. It is replaced by a form which contains a settlement of a mansion house and landed estate and which attempts, as nearly as the 1996 Act will allow, to recreate the trusts of a strict settlement and to confer on the life tenant the powers of a tenant for life under a strict settlement. In addition the new Form C13.2 contains a gift of a maintenance fund for the upkeep of the mansion house.

A further innovation is the inclusion, in addition to forms for nil-rate band discretionary legacies (designed to give a surviving spouse access to the income of the nil-rate band legacy without it forming part of his or her estate), forms for debt or charge nil-rate band discretionary legacies (for use where the principal asset is the matrimonial home or a share of it and there are insufficient funds to constitute an investment fund of the appropriate value). The elements of such schemes are discussed in the Preliminary Note to B18. Form B18.2 is one precedent for such a scheme. Others are to be found in the complete will precedents Form C3.4 and C3.5. In addition precedents for the appropriate post-death instruments implementing such a scheme are contained in F5.

The introductory notes which appear throughout Volume Two have been updated. Important amongst these are the notes on the inheritance tax implications of will drafting generally which are to be found in Part A and on the availability and exploitation of business and agricultural property reliefs and their interaction with the spouse exemption which are to be found in the Preliminary Notes to C11 and C12. Forms for deeds of variation are, as before, contained in F3.

In the precedents contained in Volume Two, in particular those contained in complete will forms in Part C, we have retained the moderately conservative drafting style adopted in former editions. We try to avoid excessive and unnecessary verbiage, or the use of archaisms where a more modern word will do equally well, but we do not favour abandoning all the traditional vocabulary of the will draftsman where it has a useful function, even though it may sound old-fashioned to some. A good example is the use of words such as 'herein' and 'hereinafter'. They are not words used in spoken English, at any rate outside the legal profession. On the other hand their meaning should be perfectly clear to the non-lawyer, and there are no words with the same concision and precision to be found in idiomatic spoken English. We are not ashamed to use them.

We are always pleased to hear from our readers, and we make careful notes of all points made to us by them. We think that this edition takes account of all the points made to us in correspondence since the last edition, and we are most grateful to those who have written to us. If any reader has an example of a clause or a complete will or codicil which provides a solution to a practical problem and is not represented in Volume Two, we would be interested to hear about it. We would also be interested to hear whether the disk is found useful.

We are most grateful to the publishers for their exceptional patience at the manuscript preparation stage and their thoroughness and general helpfulness in getting it through the press.

Preface

As usual Professor Sherrin has concentrated on Volume One and the four other editors on Volume Two.

The law is stated as at 1 November 2001.

November 2001

C.H.S.
R.F.D.B.
R.A.W.
S.L.M.
M.W.

Contents

Volume 1
THE LAW OF WILLS

Part D
FORM OF WILL AND EXECUTION

24 Wills with a foreign element: essential validity and construction and exercise of powers of appointment

Part G
EXECUTORS, TRUSTEES AND GUARDIANS

28 Appointment of guardians

Part H
CONTENTS OF WILLS

29 Appropriation

30 Legacies

31 Abatement and refunding of legacies

Part I
FAILURE OF GIFTS

Part J
CONSTRUCTION OF WILLS: GENERAL PRINCIPLES

Part K
CONSTRUCTION OF WILLS: PARTICULAR RULES RELATING TO PROPERTY

Part L
CONSTRUCTION OF WILLS: PARTICULAR RULES RELATING TO PERSONS

Part M
CONSTRUCTION OF WILLS: PARTICULAR RULES RELATING TO BENEFICIAL INTERESTS

Contents

Part N
CHARITIES

Part O
INTESTACY

Volume 1 – Table of Statutes

References in this Table to *Statutes* are to Halsbury's Statutes of England (Fourth Edition) showing the volume and page where the Act will be found.
References in the right hand column are to paragraph.

Volume 1 – Table of Cases

A

B

1

Table of Cases

Table of Cases

Table of Cases

K

Table of Cases

PARA

PARA

PARA

PARA

PARA

PARA

PARA

PARA

PARA

PARA

PARA

PARA

PARA

PARA

PARA

King v Farley (1828) 1 Hag Ecc 502 .... 4.19

King v Farley (1828) 1 Hag Ecc 502 .... 4.19
King v Frost (1890) 15 App Cas 548, 60 LJPC 15, 63 LT 422, 6 TLR 443, PC 67.4, 67.5
King v George (1877) 5 Ch D 627, 36 LT 759, sub nom Re George's Estate, King v George
  46 LJ Ch 670, 25 WR 638, CA 38.10
King v King (1864) 15 I Ch R 479... 42.4
King v King (1885) 13 LR Ir 531...42.4, 57.19
King v King [1942] P 1, [1941] 2 All ER 103, 111 LJP 90, 167 LT 241, 57 TLR 529 .... 35.23
King v Malcott (1852) 9 Hare 692, 22 LJ Ch 157, 16 Jur 237, 19 LTOS 19 .... 29.4, 30.33
King v Melling (1671) 1 Vent 225; on appeal (1671) 1 Vent 232, Ex Ch 76.1
King v Mullins (1852) 1 Drew 308, 20 LTOS 178 .... 30.42
King v Perpetual Trustee Co Ltd (1955) 94 CLR 70 .... 87.1
King v Rymill (1898) 67 LJPC 107, 78 LT 696 .... 50.2
King v Tootel (1858) 25 Beav 23... 66.20, 91.6
King v Withers (1735) Cas temp Talb 117, 3 P Wms 414; affd sub nom Wither v King
  (1735) 3 Bro Parl Cas 135, HL.. 93.44
King's College Hospital v Wheildon (1854) 18 Beav 30, 23 LJ Ch 537, 2 WR 202.................... 57.15
King's Estate, Re (1888) 21 LR Ir 273 .... 36.3
King's Goods, Re (1875) 23 WR 552 .... 14.10, 14.11
King's Proctor v Daines (1830) 3 Hag Ecc 218.. 10.1
King's Trusts, Re (1892) 29 LR Ir 401 .... 33.20, 34.3
King's Will Trusts, Re, Assheton v Boyne [1964] Ch 542, [1964] 1 All ER 833, [1964] 2
  WLR 913, 108 Sol Jo 335, 189 Estates Gazette 879 .... 27.15
King-Harman v Cayley [1899] 1 IR 39.. 32.21
Kingdon, Re, Wilkins v Pryer (1886) 32 Ch D 604, 55 LJ Ch 598, 34 WR 634, 54 LT 753 .... 18.8
Kingham, Re, Kingham v Kingham [1897] 1 IR 170.. 94.13
Kingsbury v Walter [1901] AC 187, 70 LJ Ch 546, 84 LT 697, HL...................... 47.30, 47.31, 47.34,
                                                                                                                50.20, 57.14
Kingston (Earl) v Lady Elizabeth Pierepont (1681) 1 Vern 5 .... 34.12, 35.47
Kinleside v Harrison (1818) 2 Phillim 449 .... 4.13, 4.19
Kinnaird v Allen (1898) 24 VLR 609 .... 72.6
Kinnear, Re, Kinnear v Barnett (1904) 90 LT 537 .... 66.6
Kinsella v Caffrey (1860) 11 I Ch R 154; affd (1860) 13 Ir Jur 277... 101.10
Kipping, Re, Kipping v Kipping [1914] 1 Ch 62, 83 LJ Ch 218, 109 LT 919, CA 30.36, 66.13
Kirby, Re (1982) 3 FLR 249, 11 Fam Law 210... 105.16
Kirby v Potter (1799) 4 Ves 748 .... 30.8
Kirby's Goods, Re [1902] P 188, 71 LJP 116, 87 LT 141.. 25.2
Kirby-Smith v Parnell [1903] 1 Ch 483, 72 LJ Ch 468, 51 WR 493, 47 Sol Jo 279 .... 49.5, 50.17,
                                                                                                                51.1, 60.2
Kirk, Re, Kirk v Kirk (1882) 21 Ch D 431, 31 WR 94, 47 LT 36, CA 47.7, 91.2
Kirk, Re, Nicholson v Kirk (1885) 52 LT 346.. 74.1
Kirk, Re, Wethey v Kirk (1915) 85 LJ Ch 182, 113 LT 1204..54.2, 68.9
Kirk v Eddowes (1844) 3 Hare 509, 13 LJ Ch 402, 8 Jur 530.................... 44.5, 44.14, 57.30, 100.7
Kirk v Kirk (1896) 40 NSR 147... 42.6
Kirkbank v Hudson (1819) Dan 259, 7 Price 212.. 102.18
Kirkbride's Trusts, Re (1866) LR 2 Eq 400, 14 WR 728, 15 LT 51 .... 50.16, 56.8, 96.1
Kirkby v Phillips [1948] Ch 109, [1947] 2 All ER 777, 92 Sol Jo 11, 63 TLR 631 .... 33.12
Kirkley, Re, Halligey v Kirkley (1918) 87 LJ Ch 247, 62 Sol Jo 364, 119 LT 304 ....93.4, 93.6, 93.31
Kirkman v Miles (1807) 13 Ves 338... 37.8
Kirkman's Trust, Re (1859) 3 De G & J 558 .... 68.11
Kirkpatrick, Re, Ferguson v Kirkpatrick (1912) 29 WN 56, 12 SRNSW 282 .... 68.6
Kirkpatrick v Bedford (1878) 4 App Cas 96, HL 88.2
Kirs Estate, Re (1990) 55 SASR 61 .... 14.2
Kitcat v King [1930] P 266, 99 LJP 126, 74 Sol Jo 488, 143 LT 408, 46 TLR 617 .... 9.8, 18.9
Kiver v Oldfield (1859) 4 De G & J 30.. 82.2
Kleinwort Benson (Hong Kong) Trustees Ltd v Wong Foon Hang [1993] 1 HKC 649............... 27.15
Knaggs, Re, Knaggs v Knaggs (1905) 49 Sol Jo 314 .... 64.54
Knapman, Re, Knapman v Wreford (1881) 18 Ch D 300, 50 LJ Ch 629, 30 WR 395, 45 LT
  102, [1881–5] All ER Rep Ext 1758, CA 30.11
Knapp, Re, Spreckley v A-G [1929] 1 Ch 341, 98 LJ Ch 95, 140 LT 533 .... 95.12, 102.26
Knapp v Noyes (1768) Amb 662 .... 35.14

clii

Table of Cases

Table of Cases

S

Table of Cases

Table of Cases

Table of Cases

Z

VOLUME 1

The law of wills

Nature of wills

CHAPTER 1

Nature of a will

[1.1]

Testamentary power. The unbridled testamentary freedom which English law had permitted since 1891[1] was ended in 1938 by the enactment of the Inheritance (Family Provision) Act which for the first time, gave statutory recognition to a man's responsibility to maintain his wife and children even after his death. That Act was replaced by the more far reaching Inheritance (Provision for Family and Dependants) Act 1975 (I(PFD)A 1975) which enables a spouse, and a wider class of dependants who are inadequately provided for by the deceased's will, to apply to the court for reasonable financial provision to be made for them out of the deceased's estate.[2] Such provision for applicants other than a spouse is limited to maintenance, but a spouse can be awarded ... such financial provision as it would be reasonable in all the circumstances of the case for a husband or wife to receive, whether or not that provision is required for his or her maintenance'.[3] In order to make such an award in appropriate cases the court has power to make wide-ranging orders and consequential directions. It will thus be appreciated that the I(PFD)A 1975 can constitute a severe indirect limitation on a person's testamentary freedom. However, subject to this jurisdiction and to particular rules of law, such as perpetuities, a person has complete testamentary freedom to dispose of his property in whatever manner he pleases. If a person dies leaving a will which effectively disposes of all his property, then his whole estate will be distributed in accordance with the intentions expressed in the will. If the will is effective to dispose of part only of his property, then the person will be said to die 'partially intestate', and the estate will be distributed in accordance with the will so far as it extends, and as to the rest, according to the rules of intestacy.[4] If a person dies without leaving any valid will then his estate will be distributed according to the statutory rules relating to intestacy.[5]

1   The Mortmain and Charitable Uses Act 1891 removed restrictions on devises for charitable purposes.
2   As amended by the Law Reform (Succession) Act 1995, s 2. The jurisdiction conferred by the I(PFD)A 1975 is fully discussed in Chapter 105.
3   I(PFD)A 1975, s 1(2)(a).
4   Formerly a person did not in law die intestate unless both the dispositions and the appointment of executors totally failed: *Re Roby, Howlett v Newington* [1908] 1 Ch 71; *Re Ford, Ford v Ford* [1902] 2 Ch 605; *Re Cuffe, Fooks v Cuffe* [1908] 2 Ch 500. Now there is a statutory definition of 'intestate' stating that it includes a person who leaves a will but dies intestate as to some beneficial interest in his property: Administration of Estates Act 1925, s 55(1)(vi); 17 *Halsbury's Statutes* (4th edn) 467. See Chapter 104.
5   Administration of Estates Act 1925, Pt IV; see Vol 2, Part G, para **[244.59]**.

[1.2]

The advantages of making a will. Many people are apparently content that their property should be distributed on intestacy but it is advisable to make a formal will since precise dispositions can be made of particular property according to individual needs and preferences. Thus a testator can, if he wishes,[1] disposes of his property in a manner totally different from the intestacy rules. Even if the paramount intention of the testator is to benefit his wife and children, a will enables small legacies and bequests to be given to non-relatives and friends. Further, although the primary purpose of most wills is to dispose of property, many beneficial ancillary functions can also be performed; thus a testator can appoint executors, and trustees, and guardians of his children,[2] revoke former wills, alter or augment statutory provisions regarding powers of administration or management of the estate and give directions as to burial or cremation.[3] If there is a business involved, the testator can consider what arrangements should be made for carrying on the business after his death. It might be appropriate at the time of making a will for an aged or infirm testator, to consider whether to create an enduring power of attorney. Such powers are made under the Enduring Powers of Attorney Act 1985 (as amended by the Trustee Delegation Act 1999[4]) and can be used as an ordinary power initially and then as an enduring power if there is subsequent incapacity.

1   Subject to the possibility of a claim under the I(PFD)A 1975; see Chapter 105.
2   Under the previous law an appointment of a guardian had to be by deed or will. Guardians now can only be appointed in accordance with the Children Act 1989, s 5. This enables such an appointment to be made by any dated written instrument provided that it is signed by the appointor in the presence of two witnesses. It will still be appropriate in many cases to make the appointment by will, which from 14 October 1991, will not be dependent on the formal validity of the will. See Chapter 28.
3   See para [7.33] infra and Vol 2. It is, however, essential that any such instructions should be immediately available, and so it might be preferable for them to be contained in a separate document.
4   Enduring Powers of Attorney Act 1985, ss 4, 6, and sub-ss 2(8), 3(3), have been repealed by the Trustee Delegation Act 1999.

[1.3]

Inheritance tax. At the time of making a will it will obviously be appropriate, in many cases, for a testator to consider the fiscal position at his death and perhaps take some steps to mitigate inheritance tax. Those aspects of this tax which have most relevance to the making of wills, and to the position on death, are fully discussed in the introductory note to Volume 2 (Part A, para **[200.1]** et seq) to which reference should be made. It can be pointed out at this stage that if it is desired to minimise the amount of inheritance tax payable on death, then the will should form part of a considered scheme, of which inter vivos dispositions and arrangements will play an important part.

[1.4]

Making a will. Wills can be made with or without legal assistance and, subject to formalities, can be made in any form.[1] Only persons with recognised legal capacity can make a will.[2]

1   See Chapter 10.
2   See Chapter 4.

[1.5]

Liability for preparation of a will. A solicitor instructed by his client to carry out a transaction to confer a benefit on an identified third party, such as making a will in favour of that person, owes a duty of care to that third party to use proper care in carrying out instructions.[1] This duty extends in law to an intended beneficiary who is reasonably foreseeably deprived of his intended legacy as a result of the solicitor's negligence in circumstances in which there was no confidential or fiduciary relationship and neither the testator nor his estate has a remedy against the solicitor.[2] A solicitor, when preparing a will, owes a duty of care to an intended beneficiary to ensure that effect is given to the testator's testamentary intentions so that the beneficiary receives what the testator intended he should receive.[3] A solicitor instructed to draw up a will must ensure that the will is presented for execution by the client within a reasonable time.[4] The Court of Appeal has held that a solicitor who is instructed to prepare a will for a client is liable in damages to a disappointed beneficiary when the client dies before the will has been prepared or signed.[5] It has been held that a solicitor could owe a duty of care to a beneficiary named in a will in respect of advice given to a testator.[6] But a solicitor who had acted for a testator in preparing his will owed no duty of care to a beneficiary under that will when acting in a subsequent transaction for the testator which adversely affected the value of an asset which formed part of the beneficiary's potential interest under the will.[7] If the mistake in the will is one that is capable of being cured by rectification of the will, that remedy must be pursued before a negligence action against the draftsman will be entertained.[8]

1   *Ross v Caunters* [1980] Ch 297, [1979] 3 All ER 580. Solicitor liable in negligence for failing to warn testator that attestation by beneficiary's spouse would invalidate the testamentary gift to that beneficiary. See *Watts v Public Trustee for Western Australia* [1980] WAR 97; *Seale v Perry* [1982] VR 193; *Whittingham v Crease & Co* (1978) 88 DLR (3d) 353; *Sutherland v Public Trustee* [1980] 2 NZLR 536; *Allied Finance and Investments Ltd v Haddow & Co* [1983] NZLR 22, NZCA.
2   *White v Jones* [1995] 1 All ER 691, HL, affirming [1993] 3 All ER 481, CA; solicitor liable in negligence for delay that effectively deprived the beneficiaries of their legacies. The general tortious cases of *Headley Byrne & Co Ltd v Heller & Partners* [1963] 2 All ER 575 and *Caparo Industries plc v Dickman* [1990] 1 All ER 568, amongst others, followed. See also *Esterhuizen v Allied Dunbar Assurance plc* [1998] 2 FLR 668 and *Ryan v Public Trustee* [2000] 1 NZLR 700.
3   *Carr-Glynn v Frearsons (a firm)* [1998] 4 All ER 225, CA; reversing Lloyd J [1997] 2 All ER 614 (failing to ensure testatrix severed her joint tenancy in property disposed by will), applying *White v Jones* [1995] 1 All ER 691. The duty was owed notwithstanding that the testator's estate might also have a remedy against the solicitor for breach of duty, since the duties owed by the solicitor to the testator and to the beneficiary were complementary, and extended to ensuring that the relevant property formed part of the testator's estate: *White v Jones* supra at p 710.
4   *Gartside v Sheffield, Young and Ellis* [1983] NZLR 37 (NZCA), solicitor instructed by elderly testatrix in poor health to draw up a will. Seven days later she died, the solicitors having failed to present the new will to her for execution. Probate of a previous will granted. Solicitors held to be liable to person who would have been a beneficiary under the new will. Similarly in *White v Jones* [1995] 1 All ER 691.
5   *White v Jones* [1995] 1 All ER 691. See also *Murphy v Brentwood District Council* [1991] 1 AC 398, [1990] 2 All ER 908 and *Smith v Claremont Haynes & Co* (1991) Times, 3 September.

6   *Kecskemeti v Rubens Rabin & Co* (1992) Times, 31 December.
7   *Clarke v Bruce Lance & Co (a firm)* [1988] 1 All ER 364, [1988] 1 WLR 881, CA.
8   *Walker v Geo H Medlicott & Son (a firm)* [1999] 1 All ER 691; the plaintiff must seek to
    mitigate his (alleged) loss by bringing proceedings for rectification of the will under the
    Administration of Justice Act 1982, s 20 (if appropriate) and to exhaust that remedy before
    bringing proceedings for negligence against the solicitor. It will be appreciated that rectification
    will only be an appropriate remedy in certain circumstances; see Chapter 6; thus the mistakes of
    the solicitors in *Ross v Caunters* [1979] 3 All ER 580 and *White v Jones* [1995] 1 All ER 691
    would not be susceptible to rectification.

[1.6]
Definition of a will. In common with many legal concepts it is difficult to
formulate an exhaustive definition of a will, and both the legislature and the
judiciary have refrained from making any definitive statement. However in
general terms it can be noted that a will is a document in writing executed in
accordance with certain formalities[1] which is generally subject to probate and
which contains statements regarding the disposition of a person's property on
death. One of the learned editors of this text has described a will as follows: 'A
will is a privilege which the law grants to a person of sound mind, enabling him,
subject to certain limits, to dispose of his estate as he pleases'.[2] The Annex to
the Trustee Act 2000 (Glossary of Terms) defines a will as 'a document by
which a person (called the testator) appoints executors to administer his estate
after his death and directs the manner in which it is to be distributed to the
beneficiaries he specifies'.

It can alternatively or additionally appoint executors, trustees or guardians and
revoke previous wills.[3] It is a characteristic document which is testamentary,
ambulatory and revocable. A reference to a person's will can mean the
expression of a person's testamentary wishes but more commonly refers to the
document itself.

Though the word 'will' is sometimes used to mean all the unrevoked
testamentary documents left by the testator,[4] it is more usual to speak of wills as
a different class of instruments from codicils, which are documents adding to,
varying or revoking the provisions of a will previously made. It is, too, not
uncommon for a testator to make quite separate wills in respect of his property
in different countries[5] and, by the use of suitable expressions, other documents
may be incorporated in a will.[6] The fact that the testator calls a document his
'last will' is of no significance.[7]

1   Subject of course to the exception of privileged wills, see Chapter 16.
2   Francis Barlow as counsel in *Re DWS, Re EHS, TWGS v JMG* [2000] 2 All ER 83 at 92;
    affirmed [2001] 1 All ER 97, CA.
3   Although these are the main functions of wills it is of course recognised that a will can also
    have other purposes, eg to give directions as to burial, or to exercise testamentary powers of
    appointment.
4   *Lemage v Goodban* (1865) LR 1 P & D 57 at 62; *Green v Tribe* (1878) 9 Ch D 231 at 234; *Re
    Elcom, Layborn v Grover Wright* [1894] 1 Ch 303 at 314, CA. However many unrevoked
    testamentary writings a man may leave, they together constitute but one will in the strict sense
    (*Douglas-Menzies v Umphelby* [1908] AC 224 at 233, PC, where the testator executed separate
    Scottish and Australian wills to be construed according to the law of those countries
    respectively); and see *Re Smith, Prada v Vandroy* [1916] 2 Ch 368, CA ('by this my will' held
    not to exclude codicils).
5   See Chapter 23.
6   See Chapter 15.

7   'Last Will' and similar phrases mean, as a rule, no more than 'will' (*Lord Walpole v Earl Cholmondeley* (1797) 7 Term Rep 138 at 146, 150); and, on construction, a reference by a testator to his 'last will', or a description of a document as such, may merely allude to or describe the last of a series of testamentary documents (*Thomas d Jones v Evans* (1802) 2 East 488 at 496; *Stoddart v Grant* (1852) 1 Macq 163 at 171, HL; *Cutto v Gilbert* (1854) 9 Moo PCC 131; *Freeman v Freeman* (1854) 5 De G M & G 704; *Pettinger v Ambler, Bunn v Pettinger* (1866) LR 1 Eq 510; *Re De la Saussaye's Goods* (1873) LR 3 P & D 42 at 44 ('last and deliberate will'); *Simpson v Foxon* [1907] P 54 ('last and only will')). As to the effect on prior testamentary instructions, see Chapter 18, para **[18.8]** infra.

[1.7]
Distinguishing features of a will. A will is a document which is of no effect until the testator's death and until then is a mere declaration of his intention[1] and is at all times until such death subject to revocation or variation.[2] The execution of a will leaves the testator free during his life to dispose of his property as he pleases and operates subject to any such disposition inter vivos;[3] and on the other hand, a person named as a beneficiary in a will takes no interest whatever under it until the death of the testator and he will not then take any interest unless he is alive at that time.[4] A will subjects the assets of the testator, from the moment of its execution, to a series of dispositions which, unless revoked, will operate at his death; these dispositions will remain inchoate until his death, but they operate immediately as ambulatory provisions varying in range or subject matter according as the assets in the ownership of the testator during his lifetime may change in nature value or extent.[5]

Though wills are now commonly drawn in a well-settled form, no particular form or wording is necessary. All that is necessary is that the document shall be testamentary ie not taking effect until death, and that the document, or such part of it as is testamentary, shall be executed in accordance with the statutory requirements.[6] The following propositions were thought to be established by authority in a Court of Appeal decision. First, an instrument cannot be a 'provable will' (by which expression is meant the type of instrument which will be admitted to probate in the English courts) unless it contains a revocable ambulatory disposition of the maker's property which is to take effect on death. Secondly, an instrument cannot be a 'provable will' unless the maker had an '*animus testandi*'. Thirdly, this expression does not mean that a document cannot be a 'provable will' unless the maker has addressed his mind to the question whether the instrument will be capable of admission to probate in the English court, and wishes that it shall be so. Rather, it conveys only that the maker must intend that his document shall effect the kind of disposition referred to above. Fourthly, it is possible to make a 'provable will', whatever its form or appearance or mode of expression and irrespective of the language in which it is written, so long as it combines the requirements above mentioned, the necessary intention and execution as required by the Wills Act 1837 (if the circumstances are such as to require execution). Fifthly, if the document has the necessary dispositive effect, and is duly executed, the necessary *animus* will be presumed. This presumption is however rebuttable, either by other terms of the document itself, such as the statement that the document is intended for guidance only, or by strong extrinsic evidence.[7]

1   *A-G v Jones and Bartlett* (1817) 3 Price 368 at 391; *Re Llanover, Herbert v Freshfield No (2)* [1903] 2 Ch 330 at 335; *Re Thompson, Thompson v Thompson* [1906] 2 Ch 199 at 202.

2   As Morritt J stated in *Re Dale, Proctor v Dale* [1993] 4 All ER 129 at 132, 'The survivor (of a mutual will) may thereafter alter his will, because a will is inherently revocable …'. The case was concerned with mutual wills (as to which see Chapter 2). As to variation by codicil, see Chapter 20.

3   See *Bullock v Bennett* (1855) 7 De G M & G 283. The position of a will in this respect is usually described by the words that the will is ambulatory until the testator's death. See, however, the effect of contracts relating to wills, Chapter 3.

4   *Re Currie's Settlement, Re Rooper, Rooper v Williams* [1910] 1 Ch 329 at 334. As to the nature of a beneficiary's interest under a will, see para [1.12] infra.

5   Per Waite LJ in *Corbett v Newey* [1996] 2 All ER 914 at 921.

6   See Sir Denys Buckley in *Re Berger* [1989] 1 All ER 591 at 602, CA; *Whyte v Pollok* (1882) 7 App Cas 400; *Re Slinn's Goods* (1890) 15 PD 156; *Oldroyd v Harvey* [1907] P 326; *George v Daily* (1997) 143 DLR (4th) 273. See, further, Chapter 11.

7   Per Mustill LJ in *Re Berger* [1989] 1 All ER 591 at 599. In that case a document described as a *zavah* and correctly executed as an English will, was admitted to probate; see also *Corbett v Newey* [1996] 2 All ER 914, fully discussed in para [1.10] infra.

[1.8]

Other documents. The fact that a document is executed as a will does not make it testamentary and the whole document will not be so if it has any operation before the death of the testator,[1] but a severable part which has no operation until death may be testamentary while the remainder is not.[2] A will must be distinguished from other revocable instruments which may take effect only on the death of the maker, eg a voluntary settlement with a power of revocation[3] or an appointment on death without issue[4] or a deed covenanting that something shall be done on or after death,[5] or a nomination to receive contributions to a pension scheme, in the event of the employee's death before entitlement to a pension,[6] or indorsements on deposit receipts in respect of bank accounts.[7] The difference between such instruments and a will is perhaps best shown by taking a non-testamentary instrument which settles property on the testator for life and then on A absolutely and a will giving the property to A absolutely. Provided A survives the testator the practical effect of these two instruments is the same, but if A does not survive the testator his estate takes nothing under the will, but under the settlement A takes a vested interest from the date of its execution and his estate will take on his death.[8] Where a deed is executed, it can, apart from a special reservation of a power of revocation, be revoked only by the agreement of all parties, but a will can be revoked by the testator alone without the concurrence of any other party.

1   *Fletcher v Fletcher* (1844) 4 Hare 67; *Cock v Cooke* (1866) LR 1 P & D 241.

2   *Doe d Cross v Cross* (1846) 8 QB 714; *Wolfe v Wolfe* [1902] 2 IR 246; *Re Anziani, Herbert v Christopherson* [1930] 1 Ch 407 at 424.

3   *Tompson v Browne* (1835) 3 My & K 32.

4   *Majoribanks v Hovenden* (1843) Drury temp Sug 11.

5   *Fletcher v Fletcher* (1844) 4 Hare 67. A disposition in a deed was found to be testamentary in nature in *Re White* (1987) 38 DLR (4th) 631. See also *Re Watson's Estate* (1986) 43 SASR 15; and *Glynn v Glynn* [1987] ILRM 589.

6   *Re Danish Bacon Co Ltd Staff Pension Fund, Christensen v Arnett* [1971] 1 All ER 486, [1971] 1 WLR 248, applied in *Baird v Baird* [1990] 2 AC 548, [1990] 2 All ER 300, PC. It is, of course, axiomatic that an essential characteristic of a will is that, during the lifetime of the testator, it is a mere declaration of his present intention and may be revoked or altered. It does not follow that every document intended to operate on death and containing a power of revocation is necessarily testamentary in character. Per Lord Oliver, at 305. See para [18.4] infra.

7   *Grays Trustees v Murray* 1970 SLT 105; *Young v Sealey* [1949] Ch 278, [1949] 1 All ER 92.

8   It is, of course, possible so to draft a will as to provide against lapse, so that on the death of the legatee, the property passes under his will or intestacy or to some substituted person or persons. As to this, see Chapter 47, paras **[47.22]–[47.23]** infra.

[1.9]
Revocable nature of will. A will is always revocable even though it be expressed to be irrevocable[1] and a covenant not to revoke a will does not make it irrevocable. It may be revoked despite the covenant and, even in cases where specific performance of the covenant is granted, the operation of the remedy is not to reinstate the earlier will, but to require the personal representatives (or the beneficiaries under the later will if the property has been vested in them) to execute such documents that effect is given to the former will.[2]

1   *Vynior's Case* (1609) 8 Co Rep 81 b.
2   See para **[1.13]** infra.

[1.10]
Instruments conditionally testamentary. The operation of a will may be conditional in the sense that the execution of the will is unconditional but its terms make it conditional in its operation.[1] Thus a reference in a will to a particular event may cause the will to have effect only on the happening of that event;[2] in other cases it may only express the motive for the gift, in which case the will is not conditional.[3] In deciding this question, evidence of the testator keeping the will carefully after the event cannot be relied on,[4] but subsequent declarations of the testator may be.[5] A conditional will is inoperative if the contingency does not occur, [6] but it may become operative free from the condition by being republished or re-executed after failure to satisfy the condition.[7] But although it is possible to have a will that is on its face conditional, it is not possible to have a will that, though unconditional on its face, purports, through some direction imposed externally by the testator at the time of its execution, to be made conditional in its operation.[8] A document which is conditionally executed cannot take effect as a valid will since a will cannot be executed in escrow.[9] Thus there cannot be a valid will if the execution of the document is conditional. The reason being that in such a situation the testator will lack the necessary *animus testandi* since at the moment when he signs the will he will not intend to bring into being a document which would operate with unconditional effect.[10] Further, a purported will that is subject to an extrinsic condition would be contrary to the policy and requirements of the Wills Act 1837, s 9, which makes it impossible for any condition to be introduced into a will that the testator had neither stated in writing nor signed.[11]

1   Per Morritt LJ in *Corbett v Newey* [1996] 2 All ER 914 at 925, CA; reversing [1995] 1 All ER 570. See the facts set out in n 8 infra.
2   *Parsons v Lanoe* (1748) 1 Ves Sen 189; *Re Winn's Goods* (1861) 2 Sw & Tr 147; *Re Porter's Goods* (1869) LR 2 P & D 22; *Roberts v Roberts* (1862) 2 Sw & Tr 337; *Re Robinson's Goods* (1870) LR 2 P & D 171; *Re Hugo's Goods* (1877) 2 PD 73; *Edmondson v Edmondson* (1901) 17 TLR 397 (all relating to death on journeys or during absence); *Re Govier* [1950] P 237 ('In the event of our two deaths' in joint will held to confine will to simultaneous death by enemy action); *Re Da Silva's Goods* (1861) 2 Sw & Tr 315 (testator surviving wife); *Re O'Connor's Estate* [1942] 1 All ER 546 (conditional on predeceasing sister). Where the will is

executed or re-executed after return from absence, it is not conditional: *Re Hobson's Goods* (1861) 7 Jur NS 1208; *Re Cawthron's Goods* (1863) 3 Sw & Tr 417. But a conditional codicil which republishes an earlier will may be admitted to probate although the condition fails: *Re Da Silva's Goods*. The condition must appear in the will; *Corbett v Newey* [1996] 2 All ER 914.

3   *Strauss v Schmidt* (1820) 3 Phillim 209 ('In case I should die'); *Burton v Collingwood* (1832) 4 Hag Ecc 176 ('lest I should die before the next sun'); *Re Hobson's Goods* (1861) 7 Jur NS 1208; *Re Thorne's Goods* (1865) 4 Sw & Tr 36; *Re Dobson's Goods* (1866) LR 1 P & D 88 ('in case of any fatal accident, being about to travel' etc); *Re Martin's Goods* (1867) LR 1 P & D 380 ('in event of my death during' a time of removal to hospital ship'); *Re Spratt's Goods* [1897] P 28 (where these cases are considered and compared); *Halford v Halford* [1897] P 36; *Re Heubner* (1974) 53 DLR (3d) 730.

4   *Roberts v Roberts* (1862) 2 Sw & Tr 337.

5   *Re Vines's Estate* [1910] P 147. It would seem that the condition must be intrinsic, ie set out in the terms of the will and executed with due formality, and not extrinsic to be proved by extrinsic evidence; see *Corbett v Newey* [1996] 2 All ER 914.

6   *Parsons v Lanoe* (1748) 1 Ves Sen 189; *Re Winn's Goods* (1861) 2 Sw & Tr 147; *Robert v Roberts* (1862) 2 Sw & Tr 337; *Re Robinson's Goods* (1870) LR 2 P & D 171; *Re Wright, Burrows v Honeysette* [1937] 3 WWR 452 (will stating 'as I have no relations'. Testator had in fact a wife and daughter living. Will inoperative and wife and daughter took as on intestacy). For a case where the contingency could still arise when the testator died, see *Re Cooper's Goods* (1855) Dea & Sw 9. In the case of *Re Vines's Estate, Vines v Vines* [1910] P 147 the court distinguished between 'If I die tomorrow' and 'lest I die tomorrow' but the decision was aided by declarations by the testator. A conditional will which revokes all former wills is inoperative to revoke such wills if the contingency does not happen; *Re Hugo's Goods* (1877) 2 PD 73.

7   *Re Cawthron's Goods* (1863) 3 Sw & Tr 417. See also *Re Gillies* [1991] 1 NZLR 760, a conditional codicil in respect of which the condition had not been fulfilled, was nevertheless admitted to probate. As to republication, see Chapter 22.

8   Per Waite LJ in *Corbett v Newey* [1996] 2 All ER 914 at 921, CA; the testatrix signed an undated will intending that the will should take effect on completion of specified inter vivos gifts. This intention was not expressed in the will; the inter vivos gifts were subsequently made. It was held that the will was not valid for want of *animus testandi* and as not conforming with the Wills Act 1837, s 9.

9   Per Morritt LJ in *Corbett v Newey* [1996] 2 All ER 914 at 925.

10   Per Morritt LJ in *Corbett v Newey* [1996] 2 All ER 914 at 920, 926.

11   Per Morritt LJ in *Corbett v Newey* [1996] 2 All ER 914 at 922–923, 962.

[1.11]
Will now takes effect in equity only. A deceased person's personal estate (including leaseholds) has always vested in his personal representatives on death.[1] However, before 1898, the real estate vested immediately in the heir or devisee as the case might be, and thus a will could pass a legal or equitable estate in realty directly to a devisee.[2] This position was changed by the Land Transfer Act 1897, which provided that on death both realty and personalty vested in the personal representatives. This position was confirmed by the Administration of Estates Act 1925, s 1(1). After due administration of the estate the personal representatives will pass title to the beneficiaries under the will by means of an assent or conveyance.[3] Thus, the position is now that the will cannot pass a legal estate directly to the beneficiary and thus the will is said 'to take effect in equity only'.[4]

1   Wills Act 1837, s 3; see Vol 2, Part G, para **[244.4]**.

2   Wills Act 1837, s 1(1); the Act did not extend to legal interests in copyholds. On intestacy the legal estate in realty vested in the heir until an administrator was appointed. Now, by virtue of the Administration of Estates Act 1925, s 9 (17 *Halsbury's Statutes* (4th edn) 427) where a

person dies intestate, until administration is granted in respect thereof, the legal estate now vests in the Public Trustee (Law Reform Miscellaneous Provisions) Act 1994, s 14.

3   See Chapter 25.

4   Law of Property (Amendment) Act 1924, Sch 9; 37 *Halsbury's Statutes* (4th edn) 119; see para [25.18] infra.

[1.12]

Nature of the beneficiary's interest under a will. Although the title to the assets vests in the personal representative and the will is said to take effect in equity only, the property is not held on trust for the beneficiary under the will so as to vest any equitable interest in him.[1] It is in fact a fallacy to seek for the separate existence of the equitable beneficial interest in the assets during the period of administration.[2] As Viscount Radcliffe commented in *Stamp Duties Comr v Livingston*:[3]

'When the whole right of property is in a person, as it is in an executor, there is no need to distinguish between the legal and equitable interest in that property, any more than there is for the property of a full beneficial owner. What matters is that the court will control the executor in the use of his rights over assets that come to him in that capacity: but it will do it by the enforcement of remedies which do not involve the admission or recognition of equitable rights of property in those assets.'

Thus the legatee of a share of residue has no interest in any of the property of the testator until the residue has been ascertained. His right is to have the estate properly administered and applied for his benefit when the administration is complete.[4] It has been held that this right in the nature of a chose in action[5] is transmissible and can be made the subject of specific bequest.[6] Likewise, persons entitled on intestacy have no interest in the deceased's assets during administration.[7] However, once the estate has been fully administered by the executors and the net residue ascertained, then the position is different and the residuary legatee might well have a definable interest in the property, since he is entitled to have the residue, as so ascertained, with accrued income, transferred and paid to him.[8]

It has been suggested that a specific legatee or specific devisee has an equitable interest in the property from the date of the testator's death.[9] This is consistent with the rule that specific legacies and devises carry income from the death of the testator and, conversely, that the legatee or devisee is responsible for any expenses incurred in storing or preserving the property from the date of the death. However, at best, the specific legatee or devisee has a defeasible interest, since the asset might be required for the purposes of administration. It is suggested that the better view is that until a personal representative assents to a specific gift, the specific legatee or devisee (like any other beneficiary) has, during the period of administration, only a chose in action to have the deceased's estate properly administered.[10]

1   *Stamp Duties Comr v Livingston* [1965] AC 694, [1964] 3 All ER 692 at 708 and 700 respectively, PC (a widow entitled to her husband's residuary estate which was still unadministered at her death. Held: she had no beneficial interest in any particular property comprised in his residuary estate and therefore Queensland succession duty was not exigible); applying *Lord Sudeley v A-G* [1897] AC 11; not following dicta in *Cooper v Cooper* (1874) LR 7 HL 53 at 65; *McCaughey v Stamp Duties Comrs* (1945) 46 NSWR 192 at 204; and *Smith v Layh* (1953) 90 CLR 102 at 108, 109.

2   Per Viscount Radcliffe in *Stamp Duties Comr v Livingston* [1965] AC 694, [1964] 3 All ER 692
    at 712 and 699 respectively, PC; followed in *Re Curlett Estate* [1996] 3 WWR 545. See also
    Trustee of the Property of Law Ip Po (a bankrupt) v Yuen Yip Kan [1994] 3 HKC 493; *Chan
    Chun Wah v Chan Chun Wai, Patrick* [1987] 2 HKC 397 and *Wu Koon Tai v Wu Yau Loi*
    [1995] 2 HKC 732, HKCA; revsd [1996] 3 HKC 559, PC.
3   *Stamp Duties Comr v Livingston* [1964] 3 All ER 692 at 699 applied in *Re K* [1985] 2 All ER
    833 at 837, CA; affirming [1985] 1 All ER 403.
4   Per Viscount Finlay in *Barnardo's Homes v Income Tax Special Comrs* [1921] 2 AC 1 at 8.
    Likewise Viscount Cave in *Barnardo's Homes v Income Tax Special Comrs* [1921] 2 AC 1 at
    10; and Lord Sterndale MR, in the Court of Appeal decision in the *Barnardo's case* [1920] 1
    KB 468 at 479. See also *Corbett v IRC* [1938] 1 KB 567 at 575–577.
5   Per Buckley J, in *Re Leigh's Will Trusts, Handyside v Durbridge* [1970] Ch 277, [1969] 3 All
    ER 432.
6   *Re Leigh's Will Trusts, Handyside v Durbridge* [1970] Ch 277, [1969] 3 All ER 432 (widow the
    sole administratrix and sole beneficiary under her husband's intestacy. His unadministered
    estate included shares in SMP Ltd. The widow made a will specifically bequeathing the shares.
    The gift was held effective by recognising the chose in action vested in the wife as beneficiary,
    to ensure due administration of the husband's estate).
7   *Eastbourne Mutual Building Society v Hastings Corpn* [1965] 1 All ER 779, [1965] 1 WLR 861
    (where only site value compensation was payable for a house compulsorily purchased because
    the husband, who was entitled to the house under his wife's intestacy and was in fact occupying
    it, was held not to have an 'interest' in the house whilst administration was incomplete: *Stamp
    Duties Comr v Livingston* [1964] 3 All ER 692 followed); *Lall v Lall* [1965] 3 All ER 330,
    [1965] 1 WLR 1249 (held that a mother who had a right to claim a house as part of her share in
    intestacy had no locus standi to resist an action for possession: *Stamp Duties Comr v Livingston*
    [1964] 3 All ER 692 applied). See JL Pinkerton, 42 Conv 213; *Kavanagh v Best* [1971] NI 89.
8   Per Viscount Cave in *Barnardo's Homes v Income Tax Special Comrs* [1921] 2 AC 1 at 10,
    referred to by Viscount Radcliffe in *Stamp Duties Comr v Livingston* [1965] AC 694 at 711,
    [1964] 3 All ER 692 at 699, PC, who also seems to distinguish completely administered and
    unadministered estates.
9   *IRC v Hawley* [1928] 1 KB 578 at 583; *Re Neeld, Carpenter v Inigo-Jones* [1962] Ch 643 at
    687–688, 691.
10 JB Clark, *Parry and Clark: The Law of Succession* (10th edn) p 478. See Ungoed-Thomas J, in
    Re Hayes' Will Trusts, Pattinson v Hayes [1971] 1 WLR 758 at 764.

[1.13]

Will substitutes. A will is in general the appropriate document to govern the
disposition of property on death but the transfer of property on the death of the
owner can in effect be achieved by forms of disposition other than wills. Thus
the owner can execute a revocable inter vivos settlement reserving to himself a
life interest with remainders over.[1] Where property is held on joint tenancy then
on the death of the other party or parties the property will automatically accrue
to the survivor.[2] In respect of some property, originally small monetary sums in
savings accounts, there is a power to nominate the person who is to receive the
property on the owner's death.[3] *Donationes mortis causa* can also effect the
transfer of property on death.[4]

1   See Cross J in *Re WJGL* [1965] 3 All ER 865 at 870 referring to the execution of such
    settlements as will substitutes by the Court of Protection on behalf of mentally disordered
    patients. The court now has power to execute wills on behalf of such persons, see paras **[4.21]–
    [4.24]** infra. It will be appreciated that revocable inter vivos settlements are not very tax
    effective.
2   Typically the joint ownership by a husband and wife of the matrimonial home; or a joint bank
    account; *Young v Sealey* [1949] Ch 278, [1949] 1 All ER 92.
3   For example, money in friendly societies, see para **[7.9]** infra. In *Re Danish Bacon Co Ltd Staff
    Pension Fund, Christensen v Arnett* [1971] 1 All ER 486, [1971] 1 WLR 248, the member of a
    company pension fund was allowed by the rules to nominate a person to receive the benefits on
    his death. See also *Baird v Baird* [1990] 2 AC 548, [1990] 2 All ER 300, PC.
4   See para **[1.14]** infra.

[1.14]

Donatio mortis causa. Property may also pass on death under a *donatio mortis causa* which has been described[1] as a singular form of gift, which is of an amphibious nature, being a gift which is neither entirely inter vivos nor testamentary. It is an act inter vivos by which the donee is to have the absolute title to the subject of the gift, not at once, but if the donor dies. If the donor dies the title becomes absolute, not under, but as against, the executor. In order to make the gift valid it must be made so as to take complete effect on the donor's death.[2] The essentials of a *donatio mortis causa* are that it is a gift made in contemplation of,[3] and conditional on,[4] death, and that before death the deceased should have either handed over the subject matter of the gift[5] or some essential indicia of title to the gift.[6] A valid *donatio mortis causa* cannot be revoked by will.[7]

Where a testatrix wished to give certain jewellery to a donee, some of which was in safe deposits, there was held to be sufficient delivery by the handing over of the key to the trunk, in which was the key to one safe deposit, which in turn contained the key to the other safe deposits. The fact that the key alone was not sufficient to gain entry to the safe deposits (a signed authority and a pass word being also required) was irrelevant.[8] Similarly handing over a post office savings bank book, a trustee savings bank book, and deposit pass books of two joint stock banks was held to be a sufficient delivery.[9] It has now been decided by the Court of Appeal that real property, a house in this case, can be the subject of a valid *donatio mortis causa*.[10] It was thought that the title deeds are the essential *indicia* of title to unregistered land and that the handing over of the deeds could amount to a parting with the dominion over the land.[11] Nourse LJ commented:

'Let it be agreed that the doctrine is anomalous. Anomalies do not justify anomalous exceptions. If due account is taken of the present state of the law in regard to mortgages and choses in action, it is apparent that to make a distinction in the case of land would be to make just such an exception. A *donatio mortis causa* of land is neither more nor less anomalous than any other. Every such gift is a circumvention of the Wills Act. Why should the additional statutory formalities for the creation and transmission of interests in land be regarded as some greater obstacle? The only step which has to be taken is to extend the application of the implied or constructive trust arising on the donor's death from the conditional to the absolute estate.'[12]

1 Per Buckley J in *Re Beaumont, Beaumont v Ewbank* [1902] 1 Ch 889 at 892. Such gifts should be distinguished from wills since, for example, the subject-matter of a *donatio mortis causa* does not vest in the personal representatives on the deceased's death, but passes retroactively to the donee. But see the Inheritance (Provision for Family and Dependants) Act 1975, s 8(2); Chapter 105.

2 Per Buckley J in *Re Beaumont, Beaumont v Ewbank* [1902] 1 Ch 889 at 892–893. In *Re Beaumont, Beaumont v Ewbank* [1902] 1 Ch 889 the gift of a cheque drawn by the deceased was held not to be a good *donatio mortis causa* because a person's cheque is not property; it is only a revocable order such that if the banker acts on it the donee will have the money to which it relates, following *Hewitt v Kaye* (1868) LR 6 Eq 198; and *Re Beak's Estate, Beak v Beak* (1872) LR 13 Eq 489.

3 *Re Craven's Estate, Lloyds Bank Ltd v Cockburn* [1937] Ch 423 at 426 (the donor must contemplate death in the near future; what may be called death for some reason believed to be impending); *Wilkes v Allington* [1931] 2 Ch 104 (immaterial that death occurs from different cause); *Re Dudman, Dudman v Dudman* [1925] Ch 553 (but not contemplation of suicide).

4   *Gardner v Parker* (1818) 3 Madd 184 (can be implied); *Treasury Solicitor v Lewis* [1900] 2 Ch
    812; *Re Ward, Ward v Warwick* [1946] 2 All ER 206.

5   *Re Craven's Estate, Lloyds Bank Ltd v Cockburn* [1937] Ch 423 at 427.

6   *Sen v Headley* [1991] Ch 425, [1991] 2 All ER 636, CA; reversing Mummery J [1990] Ch 728,
    [1990] 1 All ER 898; *Birch v Treasury Solicitor* [1951] Ch 298, [1950] 2 All ER 1198 (a post
    office savings bank book held to be sufficient even though all the terms of the contract between
    the saver and the bank were not included). The giving of a power of attorney was not alone
    sufficient: *Re Craven's Estate, Lloyds Bank Ltd v Cockburn* [1937] Ch 423. The following have
    been held good subjects of donation as amounting to *indicia* of title: a promissory note payable
    to the deceased's order but not indorsed (*Veal v Veal* (1859) 27 Beav 303); bills of exchange in
    favour of the deceased on his order (*Rankin v Weguelin* (1832) 27 Beav 309); bills of exchange
    payable to order and which had not been indorsed (*Re Mead, Austin v Mead* (1880) 15 Ch D
    651); a cheque drawn payable to the donor's order and not indorsed (*Clement v Cheeseman*
    (1884) 27 Ch D 631); a banker's deposit note (*Re Dillon, Duffin v Duffin* (1890) 44 Ch D 76).
    But not the deceased's own cheque: *Re Beaumont, Beaumont v Ewbank* [1902] 1 Ch 889.

7   *Jones v Selby* (1710) Prec Ch 300.

8   *Re Lillingston, Pembery v Pembery* [1952] 2 All ER 184, following *Re Wasserberg* [1915] 1 Ch
    195 at 202, 205; and *Delgoffe v Fader* [1939] Ch 922 at 927. See also *Ward v Turner* (1752) 2
    Ves Sen 431; compare *Re Johnson, Sandy v Reilly* (1905) 92 LT 357 at 358. In *Woodard v
    Woodard* [1995] 3 All ER 980 the handing over the keys to a car was thought to be a sufficient
    parting with the dominion in the car to constitute a valid donatio mortis causa; *Re Craven's
    Estate, Lloyds Bank Ltd v Cockburn* [1937] Ch 423 and *Sen v Headley* [1991] 2 All ER 636
    followed.

9   *Birch v Treasury Solicitor* [1951] Ch 298, [1950] 2 All ER 1198, applying *Re Dillon, Duffin v
    Duffin* (1890) 44 Ch D 76 (banker's deposit note), and *Moore v Darton* (1851) 4 De G & Sm
    517 (debt), distinguishing *Delgoffe v Fader* [1939] Ch 922 and *Reddel v Dobree* (1839) 10 Sim
    244 (cash box not fully handed over).

10 *Sen v Headley* [1991] Ch 425, [1991] 2 All ER 636, CA; reversing Mummery J [1990] Ch 728,
    [1990] 1 All ER 898. The nearest previous authority was that of Lord Eldon's in *Duffield v
    Elwes* (1827) 1 Bli NS 497, HL where it was held that there could be a *donatio* of a gift of
    money secured by a mortgage of land, by delivery of the mortgage deed.

11 Analogous to the handing over of the savings bank books in *Birch v Treasury Solicitor* [1951]
    Ch 298, [1950] 2 All ER 1198, CA.

12 *Sen v Headley* [1991] 2 All ER 636 at 647. It was noted that both *Re Dillon, Duffin v Duffin*
    (1890) 44 ChD 76, CA and *Birch v Treasury Solicitor* [1950] 2 All ER 1198 had extended the
    doctrine. The essential requirements for the application of the doctrine, noted above, were
    affirmed.

CHAPTER 2

Joint and mutual wills

[2.1]

Nature of joint will. Before speaking of joint wills it is perhaps necessary to say that so far as English law is concerned they have nothing whatever to do with joint property, ie property held by beneficial joint tenants. Such property (provided always that the joint tenancy is subsisting at death and has not been severed) cannot be subject to any will but passes automatically to the survivor or surviving joint tenants.[1] By joint will is meant a will attempting in one disposition to dispose of property belonging to two or more testators. Such a will is in general inconvenient but can be appropriate, first, to exercise a joint power of appointment,[2] and secondly, where the intention is to make mutual wills.[3]

---

1   The general rule is that severance of a joint tenancy cannot be effected by a will, but where all the joint tenants make joint or mutual wills upon an agreement that the joint will or their mutual wills shall be irrevocable and deal with their property held in joint tenancy, such will or wills and the agreement will operate to sever the joint tenancy and it must be administered on the footing that it is held as tenants in common: *Re Wilford's Estate, Taylor v Taylor* (1879) 11 Ch D 267; and *Re Heys' Estate, Walker v Gaskill* [1914] P 192.
2   *Re Duddell, Roundway v Roundway* [1932] 1 Ch 585.
3   See Chapter 2.

[2.2]

How far joint will operative. A single disposition by two or more persons jointly cannot take effect as one will.[1] Two or more persons may, however, join in making a single instrument which becomes operative as their separate wills and on the death of each and every one of such persons will be admitted to probate as their respective wills.[2] A joint will may by its terms show that it was intended to be irrevocable[3] but the mere fact of the execution of a joint will is not sufficient to establish an agreement not to revoke.[4] In the case of a joint mutual will, on the death of the first to die the survivor becomes a trustee of all the assets of both spouses at that date for the benefit of those named in the joint will.[5] On the death of one the will becomes effective to control the disposition of a one-half interest in any property which was at that time jointly held.[6]

---

1   This seems still to be the law but a joint will may clearly take effect as the exercise of a joint power of appointment by will and will so take effect on the death of the survivor provided it is still unaltered: *Re Duddell, Roundway v Roundway* [1932] 1 Ch 585 (where a joint will was confirmed by the testator's separate will). See also *Re Stracey's Goods* (1855) Dea & Sw 6 (where a joint will by husband and wife was held to operate as an exercise of a power of appointment by the wife). A joint will commencing 'In the event of our two deaths' is conditional on the simultaneous deaths of the parties and, if that does not happen, is inoperative: *Re Govier* [1950] P 237.

2   *Re Duddell, Roundway v Roundway* [1932] 1 Ch 585; *Re Stracey's Goods* (1855) Dea & Sw 6;
       Re Lovegrove's Goods (1862) 2 Sw & Tr 453; *Re Miskelly's Goods* (1869) 4 IR Eq 62; *Re*
       Piazzi-Smyth's Goods [1898] P 7; *Re Heys' Estate, Walker v Gaskill* [1914] P 192 at 196; *Re*
       Fletcher's Goods (1883) 11 LR Ir 359 (separate will recognising joint will); *Re Crofton's*
       Goods (1897) 13 TLR 374 (joint codicil to separate will). Where there was a joint will and a
       separate will and the latter was held conditional on a condition that failed and, therefore,
       inoperative, pursuance a grant of administration with the joint will annexed was made: *Re*
       O'Connor's Estate [1942] 1 All ER 546. As to joint wills in jurisdictions where there is
       community of property, see *Denyssen v Mostert* (1872) LR 4 PC 236; *Dias v De Livera* (1879)
       5 App Cas 123; *Natal Bank Ltd v Rood* [1910] AC 570. As to such wills being impressed with a
       trust so as to be irrevocable by subsequent marriage or later will, see *Re Kerr* [1948] 3 DLR
       668; affd [1949] 1 DLR 736.
3   *Re Kerr* [1948] 3 DLR 668; affd [1949] 1 DLR 736; *Re Johnson's Estate* (1957) 8 DLR (2d)
       221; affd (1959) 16 DLR (2d) 385. In the case of mutual wills an agreement not to revoke must
       be clearly proved: see para **[2.5]** infra.
4   *Pratt v Johnson* (1959) 16 DLR (2d) 385 (where the agreement was proved by affidavit). But
       see *Re Gillespie* (1969) 3 DLR (3d) 317 (where it is suggested that the fact that both testators
       sign the same will as a joint document may itself be sufficient to prove the existence of the
       agreement).
5   *Re Hagger, Freeman v Arscott* [1930] 2 Ch 190 at 195; *Re Kerr* [1948] 3 DLR 668.
6   *Benjamins v Chartered Trust Co* (1965) 49 DLR (2d) 1; *Szabo v Boros* (1967) 60 DLR (2d)
       186.

[2.3]
Mutual wills. In England a joint will is practically never executed at the present
time, but what are called mutual wills, where two or more persons each agree to
execute a separate will conferring, with or without other provisions,[1] usually,
reciprocal benefits on each other, have become more common in recent times.[2]
    Mutual wills embrace the twin concepts of an agreement by the two parties to
make such wills and the enforcement of that agreement after the death of the
first to die by means of a constructive trust. Such wills can lead to difficulties in
the proof of the agreement and to uncertainties and complexities relating to the
nature, scope and effect of the trust imposed on the estate of the second to die.
These difficulties centre on questions such as whether the trust is constructive or
implied; whether the trust is fixed or floating; when the trust is imposed, ie at the
death of the first to die, or the death of the second to die; and what property is
affected by the trust, ie all the joint property or only the property inherited by the
second to die from the first to die. Depending on the answer to these questions,
problems can arise as to the powers of the survivor to deal or dispose of the joint
property or his own property, after the death of the first to die. The will of the
survivor will remain revocable but the property will none the less still be
affected by the trust imposed to give effect to the agreement. Mutual wills can
thus have the effect of restricting the freedom of the survivor to effectively deal
with both his own property and the property inherited from the first to die. For
these reasons professional advisors often advise that mutual wills are not
recommended.

1   The origin of the doctrine of mutual wills is the decision of Lord Camden LC in *Dufour v*
       Pereira (1769) 1 Dick 419; see Morritt J in *Re Dale* [1993] 4 All ER 129 at 133 where the
       authorities are reviewed. The usual form of mutual wills includes reciprocal benefits given to
       each party, which may be either absolute interests in each other's property (*Stone v Hoskins*
       [1905] P 194) with alternative provisions in case of lapse (*Re Oldham, Hadwen v Myles* [1925]
       Ch 75; *Re Heys' Estate, Walker v Gaskill* [1914] P 192 at 196; *Re Cleaver, Cleaver v Insley*
       [1981] 2 All ER 1018, [1981] 1 WLR 939) or life interests with the same ultimate disposition
       on the death of the survivor (*Gray v Perpetual Trustee Co Ltd* [1928] AC 391; *Re Hagger,*

Freeman v Arscott [1930] 2 Ch 190). The other provisions are usually pecuniary legacies or specific gifts of a personal nature and these will generally be outside the mutual provisions or the provisions intended to be irrevocable where an agreement as to revocability is made. Though perhaps the most common case of mutual wills is that of husband and wife, they are can also be made by persons having common interests, such as unmarried brothers or sisters or persons engaged to be married.

2   For recent illustrations see *Re Cleaver, Cleaver v Insley* [1981] 2 All ER 1018, *Re Dale* [1993] 4 All ER 129, and *Re Goodchild* [1996] 1 All ER 670; affd [1997] 3 All ER 63, CA. To the contrary, the Law Reform Committee 22nd Report on The Making and Revocation of Wills (1980) (Cmnd 7902) paras 3.50–3.52 thought that mutually binding wills were 'extremely rare' and created a number of problems, but they did not recommend their abolition; see Carnwath J in *Re Goodchild* [1996] 1 All ER 670 at 677.

[2.4]

Form of Mutual Wills. Although the wills usually provide for reciprocal benefits it is not necessary for the doctrine of mutual wills to apply that the second testator to die should have obtained a personal financial benefit under the will of the first testator to die.[1] Since the first testator to die has performed his part of the contract the subsequent refusal by the second testator to perform his or her part of the bargain amounts to fraud not only when the second testator benefited under the first testator's will but also when the testators had left their property to others rather than to each other, since in each case there was a binding contract.[2] Mutual wills, though distinct wills , are sometimes contained in a single document, but they are generally in separate documents. Though such wills may be executed with reference to death in a common disaster, they are not confined to such cases[3] and they may or may not be executed in pursuance of an express agreement as to their revocation or non-revocation.[4] The mere execution of mutual wills does not imply any agreement either as to revocation or non-revocation.[5] Execution of such wills has been held to sever a joint tenancy of property.[6]

1   See *Re Dale* [1993] 4 All ER 129, where the second to die received no benefits under the will of the first to die; applying *Dufour v Pereira* (1769) 1 Dick 419 and *Lord Walpole v Lord Orford* (1797) 3 Ves 402; distinguishing *Re Cleaver, Cleaver v Insley* [1981] 2 All ER 1018. But it must be stated that this is not the usual case in mutual wills.

2   *Re Dale* [1993] 4 All ER 129.

3   They can be made by unmarried persons with the idea that the property shall go to the survivor or survivors and ultimately to a charity in which they are all interested.

4   Although the reported cases deal mostly with cases where there is a mutual agreement against revocation, in modern times some such wills have expressly negatived any such agreement and have left the survivor free to deal as he likes both with his own property and with that received from the first to die.

5   See cases cited in para **[2.5]**, n 4. In cases where in error the husband executed the wife's will and the wife executed the husband's will, the necessary corrections were made and probate granted accordingly: *Re Brander Estate* (1952) 4 DLR 688; *Re Thorleifson Estate* (1954) 13 WWR NS 515; *Re Knott's Estate* (1959) 27 WWR 382; but in a similar case the court refused to grant probate on the ground that the testator did not intend to leave his estate to his 'husband X' and striking out words would make the clause nugatory: *Re Foster* [1956] NZLR 44, distinguishing *Guardian Trusts Executors Co of New Zealand Ltd v Inwood* [1946] NZLR 614, where by striking out the word 'Jane' the disposing intentions of the testator were exactly expressed; *Re Bohachewski Estate* (1967) 60 WWR 635 (similar case, and on the death of the first to die the will incorrectly signed by him was admitted to probate subject to certain changes). See now the power to rectify wills in the Administration of Justice Act 1982, s 20, fully discussed in Chapter 6.

6   *Re Wilford's Estate* (1879) 11 Ch D 267; *Re Heys' Estate, Walker v Gaskill* [1914] P 192.

[2.5]

Agreements relating to mutual wills. In order for the doctrine of mutual wills to apply there has to be, what amounts to, a contract at law between the two testators that both wills will be irrevocable and will remain unaltered.[1] A mere mutual desire that both wills should remain unaltered could not, in the absence of an express agreement, of itself prevent the survivor from resiling from the arrangement.[2] Such agreements vary according to the circumstances of particular cases and the wishes of the parties. The wills may be executed upon an agreement that they shall not be revoked or altered.[3] On the other hand, they may be made in pursuance of an agreement that they shall be freely revocable by any party.[4] In a modern case such wills and the accompanying agreement were construed so that as to one part of the residuary estate revocation was allowed, but not as to the other part.[5] In some cases no agreement at all is made, or at least none is proved.[6]

1   *Re Goodchild* [1997] 3 All ER 63, CA; affirming Carnwath J [1996] 1 All ER 670; applying *Gray v Perpetual Trustee Co Ltd* [1928] All ER Rep 758 at 762 and *Re Dale, Proctor v Dale* [1993] 4 All ER 129 at 133. In *Re Goodchild* the absence of proof of such an agreement meant that the mutual wills were not established.

2   *Re Goodchild* [1997] 3 All ER 63.

3   Such an agreement was held proved in *Stone v Hoskins* [1905] P 194. In *Re Oldham, Hadwen v Myles* [1925] Ch 75, it was only proved that the parties agreed to make mutual wills and nothing was proved as to any agreement to revoke.

4   This is commonly evidenced by making the gift to the other 'absolutely and beneficially and without any sort of trust or obligation'. It may also be evidenced by a recital that the will though made as a mutual will is made without any agreement that it or any of its provisions shall be irrevocable and that the intention is that either party shall have full liberty to revoke or alter all or any of the provisions of his or her will. This clearly leaves it open to the survivor to revoke his will and make other provisions, which, indeed, may often be necessary in altered circumstances, such as re-marriage, or the marriage of some children while others remain unmarried. It is apprehended that an agreement not to revoke leaves the testator free to dispose of his property during his lifetime (see para **[2.3]**, n 1), and this is clearly so where there is no such agreement. Where the agreement is in special terms (see eg *Re Green, Lindner v Green* [1951] Ch 148, [1950] 2 All ER 913, more fully discussed in n 5) it may be that the terms of the agreement prevent his disposing of his own property or property coming from the first to die or some other specified source. If the agreement relates to specific property, the right of disposition is fettered as to that property, but, if the agreement has been ignored, it may be that only a remedy in damages is available against the estate of the testator so ignoring it: see Chapter 3.

5   *Re Green, Lindner v Green* [1950] 2 All ER 913. In this case the survivor re-married and made a new will giving the whole of the residue to his second wife. Certain property which by his former will he had disposed of as property belonging to his first wife was held to be taken by the personal representatives upon trust to give effect to the first will. Certain legatees were given pecuniary legacies under both wills but not of identical amounts. As these legacies had in the first will been given out of property notionally regarded as the first wife's property, the legatees were entitled to take under both wills. Apparently the legacies under the first will were in the special circumstances of the case subject to abatement.

6   *Re Oldham, Hadwen v Myles* [1925] Ch 75; *Gray v Perpetual Trustee Co Ltd* [1928] AC 391; *Garioch's Trustees v Garioch's Executors* 1917 SC 404. In such case the will may be revoked by one of the parties by a holograph will: *Saxby v Saxby Executors* 1952 SC 352.

[2.6]

Proof of agreement. The agreement may be incorporated in the will by recital or otherwise,[1] or it may be proved outside the will.[2] It may be oral or in writing,[3] but it would seem that in so far as such agreement affects a disposition of land, it must be in writing.[4] The mere simultaneity of the wills and the similarity of their terms are not enough taken by themselves to establish the necessary agreement,[5] which must be established by clear and satisfactory evidence on the balance of probabilities.[6] Proof of the precise terms of the agreement is essential, for any subsequent limitation of the powers of disposition of any party is dependent upon the precise restriction being proved to have been agreed between the parties.[7]

1   *Re Hagger, Freeman v Arscott* [1930] 2 Ch 190. This is certainly the better course because, if any question arises, it may well arise many years after the execution of the will and evidence of an oral agreement may be either unobtainable or it may be difficult to establish its precise terms. See *Re Ohorodnyk* (1980) 102 DLR (3d) 576 on proof of the agreement.
2   *Re Heys' Estate, Walker v Gaskill* [1914] P 192 at 194.
3   See *Stone v Hoskins* [1905] P 194; *Re Oldham, Hadwen v Myles* [1925] Ch 75; *Gray v Perpetual Trustee Co Ltd* [1928] AC 391.
4   It would seem that this must be so since 1989 by virtue of the Law Reform (Miscellaneous Provisions) Act 1989, s 2. As to cases before that Act see *Humphreys v Green* (1882) 10 QBD 148. It seems there is no distinction between the law applicable to an ordinary agreement not to revoke a will and a mutual agreement not to revoke a mutual will; indeed, it was said in *Dufour v Pereira* (1769) 1 Dick 419, as reported in 2 Hargrave Juridicial Arguments 304 at 309, that 'there is no difference between promising to make a will in such a form and making a will with a promise not to revoke it', and this has been cited with approval in *Stone v Hoskins* [1905] P 194 at 196, 197; *Re Oldham* [1925] Ch 75 at 84, and in *Gray v Perpetual Trustee Co Ltd* [1928] AC 391 at 399.
5   *Gray v Perpetual Trustee Co Ltd* [1928] AC 391 at 399–400 per Viscount Haldane; *Dufour v Pereira* (1769) 1 Dick 419, cited with approval by Nourse J in *Re Cleaver, Cleaver v Insley* [1981] 2 All ER 1018 at 1022. See also *Re Oldham, Hadwen v Myles* [1925] Ch 75 at 87; *Re Skippen, Hodgson v Armstrong and MacInnes* [1947] 1 DLR 858; *Re Gillespie* (1969) 3 DLR (3d) 317.
6   Per Nourse J in *Re Cleaver, Cleaver v Insley* [1981] 2 All ER 1018 at 1024, applying *Birmingham v Renfrew* (1937) 57 CLR 666; clear and satisfactory evidence of the agreement was found in *Re Cleaver, Cleaver v Insley* [1981] 2 All ER 1018. See *Re Goodchild* [1997] 3 All ER 63 where these points were emphasised by Leggatt LJ at 67–72: a 'common understanding' will not suffice, 'clear and satisfactory evidence' is required. The crucial difference between *Re Cleaver* and *Re Goodchild* was that in the former case there was specific evidence as to the testator's mutual intentions at the time the wills were made, whereas in the latter case there was not: *Re Goodchild* [1997] 3 All ER 63 at 71c.
7   This seems to follow from the decision in *Re Oldham*, where it was held that an agreement to make mutual wills was proved but there was no proof of an agreement not to revoke such wills. In *Re Green, Lindner v Green* [1951] Ch 148, [1950] 2 All ER 913, the agreement was set out in the wills which were in identical terms *mutatis mutandis*. At the time of making the wills the parties had little property but were entitled in reversion to a substantial estate given to them in equal shares or to the survivor as the case might be. The wife died and the husband succeeded to the whole of her estate, then the reversionary interest fell in. The husband remarried, made a subsequent will and later died. It was held that the effect of the mutual wills was that the wife's moiety was impressed with a trust binding on the testator, while the testator's moiety remained at his free disposition; *Dufour v Pereira* (1769) 1 Dick 419 applied; *Re Oldham, Hadwen v Myles* [1925] Ch 75, distinguished. See also *Re Grisor* (1980) 101 DLR (3d) 728. See also, para **[2.8]**, n 1.
    The principle has been extended to the case where the agreement is that if one party makes a change in his will, the other will make a corresponding change and the court will compel him to do so: *Re Fox* [1951] 3 DLR 337.

[2.7]
Effect of first to die not abiding by agreement. Where there is an agreement not to revoke and the first party to die has revoked or altered his will, the survivor, if he has notice of such alteration or revocation, cannot claim to have

effect given to the will without such alteration or revocation, because he has been given the chance of altering or revoking his own will as regards his own property; notice of the death of the first to die is sufficient notice for this purpose.[1]

1   *Stone v Hoskins* [1905] P 194. Where, however, the wife had no independent means and invested the husband's funds paid into a joint account in certain assets which by a subsequent will she bequeathed to persons not beneficiaries under the mutual will, the subsequent will was not allowed to stand and the property vested in the husband who survived: *McGeachy v Russ* [1955] 3 DLR 349. In *Re Hobley* (1997) Times, 16 June, the first to die had altered his will and it was held that the survivor was not bound by the mutual will agreement.

[2.8]
Effect of first to die abiding by agreement. Where the first to die has left his will unaltered and unrevoked in pursuance of the agreement, the survivor is bound by the agreement, and, though it is not strictly true to say that he cannot alter or revoke his will, the court, if asked, will ultimately refuse to give effect to such alteration or revocation.[1] The agreement is enforced by means of a constructive trust. Nourse J has stated the position as follows:[2]

> 'The principle of all these cases[3] is that a court of equity will not permit a person to whom property is transferred by way of gift but on the faith of an agreement or clear understanding that it is to be dealt with in a particular way for the benefit of a third person, to deal with that property inconsistently with that agreement or understanding. If he attempts to do so after having received the benefit of the gift equity will intervene by imposing a constructive trust on the property which is the subject matter of the agreement or understanding.'[4]

In a more recent case the principles were expressed as follows. The doctrine of mutual wills is to the effect that where two individuals have agreed as to the disposal of their property and have executed mutual wills in pursuance of the agreement, on the death of the first (T1) the property of the survivor (T2), the subject matter of the agreement, is held on an implied trust for the beneficiary named in the wills. The survivor may thereafter alter his will, because a will is inherently revocable, but if he does so his personal representatives will take the property subject to the trust.[5] The agreement or understanding must be such as to impose on the donee a legally binding obligation to deal with the property in the particular way and certainty as to the subject matter of the trust and the persons intended to benefit under it must be present.[6] Giving effect to such a mutual will is an indirect process because probate must be granted of a testator's last will. If, therefore, the survivor has revoked the mutual will by making a new will, it is the new will which is admitted to probate.[7] If he has altered the will by duly executing a codicil, the codicil must be admitted to probate with the will.[8] It is, however, open to those benefiting under the mutual will to apply to a court of construction,[9] and then in a proper case an order will be made upon the personal representatives to hold the estate upon trust to give effect to the provisions of the mutual will.[10] Where the trusts are for the survivor for life with absolute remainders over, the remainders vest on the first death and the remainderman's interest does not lapse where he survives the first deceased but dies before the death of the second.[11] The parties might intend that the mutual wills should only affect those assets which are in existence before the death of the first party to the agreement.[12]

1   *Re Heys' Estate, Walker v Gaskill* [1914] P 192 at 200. The doctrine is not confined to cases in which the surviving testator receives a benefit under the will of the first to die but extends to cases where both testators leave their estates to beneficiaries other than themselves: *Re Dale, Proctor v Dale* [1994] Ch 31, [1993] 4 All ER 129.

2   In *Re Cleaver, Cleaver v Insley* [1981] 2 All ER 1018 at 1024; see also Clauson J in *Re Hagger, Freeman v Arscott* [1930] 2 Ch 190 at 195, on the authority of Lord Camden in *Dufour v Pereira* (1769) 1 Dick 419. See also *Re Dale, Proctor v Dale* [1993] 4 All ER 129, where the fraud giving rise to a constructive trust approach was followed.

3   *Birmingham v Renfrew* (1936) 57 CLR 666; *Ottaway v Norman* [1972] Ch 698, [1971] 3 All ER 1325.

4   Nourse J equated mutual wills with analogous situations such as secret trusts, in which a court of equity will intervene to impose a constructive trust, referring to *Ottaway v Norman* [1971] 3 All ER 1325, and *Re Pearson Fund Trusts* (21 October 1977, unreported).

5   Per Morritt J in *Re Dale, Proctor v Dale* [1993] 4 All ER 129 at 132. The judge continued: 'The basic doctrine is not in dispute. The dispute is as to the circumstances in which the doctrine applies.' In *Re Goodchild* [1996] 1 All ER 670, Carnwath J referred to the trust as a 'floating trust'; see affirmed [1997] 3 All ER 63, CA but mutual wills were not made out: see para **[2.4]** supra.

6   *Re Goodchild*, n 5 supra. It was held in *Re Dale, Proctor v Dale* [1993] 4 All ER 129, that the doctrine will apply not only where the parties each take a benefit but also where both leave their property to particular beneficiaries.

7   *Hobson v Blackburn and Blackburn* (1822) 1 Add 274; *Re Heys' Estate, Walker v Gaskill* [1914] P 192. In the case of *Re O'Connor's Estate* [1942] 1 All ER 546, it was part of the agreement to make separate wills after the execution of the joint will and one testatrix dying very shortly after the other, the court made a grant of the joint will and ignored the separate will of the second to die as conditional on her predeceasing the first to die.

8   See n 7.

9   That is the Chancery Division of the High Court.

10 *Stone v Hoskins* [1905] P 194; *Re Hagger, Freeman v Arscott* [1930] 2 Ch 190; *Re Green, Lindner v Green* [1951] Ch 148, [1950] 2 All ER 913 as in *Re Cleaver, Clever v Insley* [1981] 2 All ER 1018, [1981] 1 WLR 939.

11 *Re Hagger, Freeman v Arscott* [1930] 2 Ch 190.

12 *Re Gillespie* (1969) 3 DLR (3d) 317.

[2.9]

Re-marriage. A will unless it is made in expectation of a particular marriage is revoked by the marriage or re-marriage of the testator or testatrix.[1] If the survivor of mutual testators remarries the question arises as to the effect of the marriage on the earlier mutual will. Vaisey J in *Re Green, Lindner v Green* thought the position to be as follows:[2]

'Nothing could prevent the testator from revoking the will, as he in fact did by his second marriage. The only question is over what property any subsequent will operates. In my view, it can only operate as regards the moiety which was under the testator's control at his death. With regard to the other moiety, which was notionally the property of his wife, the first will must take effect, not as a will, but as evidence of a trust which is plainly to be discerned in the two wills.'

However, it has already been shown that an agreement not to revoke has been construed as relating to revocation otherwise than by marriage.[3] Accordingly, until the death of the first mutual testator, when the trust will arise, a mutual will will be revoked by marriage. The further point arises that any agreement in restraint of marriage generally is contrary to public policy but an agreement restraining re-marriage is not looked upon with such severity as one against marriage generally.[4] Where, therefore, a mutual will is made by an unmarried person, an agreement not to revoke it might be contrary to public policy as in restraint of marriage.[5]

1   Wills Act 1837, s 18, as substituted by the Administration of Justice Act 1982, s 18; 50 *Halsbury's Statutes* (4th edn) 586; see Chapter 17; see Vol 2, Part G, para **[244.15]**. As Morritt J commented in *Re Dale* [1993] 4 All ER 129 at 132: 'The survivor may hereafter alter his will, because a will is inherently revocable, but if he does his personal representatives will take the property subject to the trust.' Cited with approval by Carnwath J in *Re Goodchild* [1996] 1 All ER 670 at 674.

2   In *Re Green, Lindner v Green* [1951] Ch 148 at 155, where the husband remarried after the death of his wife, the other mutual testatrix, and effect was given to the mutual will in so far, it seems, as the agreement extended. The agreement in this case was merely to give effect to the wishes expressed in the will and that did not necessarily prevent re-marriage. Revocation was allowed as to the testator's moiety, but not as to the other moiety which he had inherited from his wife, the other mutual testatrix, which was deemed to be subject to a trust to carry out the agreement. See also *Re Oldham, Hadwen v Myles* [1925] Ch 75, where there was a remarriage but there was no proof of an agreement not to revoke.

3   *Re Marsland, Lloyds Bank Ltd v Marsland* [1939] Ch 820, [1939] 3 All ER 148, not a case of mutual wills; see Chapter 3. This passage of the text was cited with approval by Carnwath J in *Re Goodchild* [1996] 1 All ER 670 at 677. The judge considered the question whether a mutual will is revoked by marriage with reference to this passage of text, the views of the Law Reform Committee on The Making and Revocation of Wills (1980) (Cmnd 7902), and the cases of *Re Marsland, Lloyds Bank Ltd v Marsland* [1939] 3 All ER 148 and *Re Green, Lindner v Green* [1951] Ch 148. He concluded that whether the mutual wills are simply expressed to be 'irrevocable', or are expressed to be subject to an obligation to give effect to their terms, the intention is presumably the same: that is, that the underlying trust is to be respected and the law will give effect to that intention.

4   See Chapter 35, paras **[35.1]–[35.8]** infra.

5   *Robinson v Ommanney* (1883) 23 Ch D 285, CA, where it was held that in so far as the covenant not to revoke was in restraint of marriage, it was void, but the covenant was severable and was enforceable in so far as it did not involve restraint of marriage. In this case there was no marriage.

[2.10]

Taking the benefit of the agreement. In the earlier cases[1] on this subject, the remedy given by the court was obviously based on the fact that the survivor had taken the benefit of the agreement, but subsequent cases have at least made it clear, that taking such benefit is not sufficient to bind the court to declare a trust of the property subject to the mutual wills or some part thereof[2] though it has so far never been said that a refusal to take such benefit releases the survivor from his or her agreement.

1   *Dufour v Pereira* (1769) 1 Dick 419, 2 Har Jur Arg 304 at 310; sufficiently cited for this purpose in [1930] 2 Ch 190 at 194, 195; *Lord Walpole v Lord Orford* (1797) 3 Ves 402.

2   *Re Oldham, Hadwen v Myles* [1925] Ch 75 (where the benefit had been taken but the agreement as proved did not extend beyond an agreement to make mutual wills). In this case, also, the wife re-married, so that any revocation may be said to be by operation of law and not by breach of any agreement (see *Re Marsland, Lloyds Bank Ltd v Marsland* [1939] Ch 820, [1939] 3 All ER 148). In *Gray v Perpetual Trustee Co Ltd* [1928] AC 391, it was said that in the absence of a definite agreement, it is immaterial that the benefits under the will of the first to die have been accepted. See also *Re Dale* [1993] 4 All ER 129, para **[2.3]**, n 2 where it was emphasised that, conversely, it is not necessary for the survivor to take a benefit under the first will for the trust to be imposed. It would appear from the facts in *Re Green, Lindner v Green* [1951] Ch 148, [1950] 2 All ER 913, that a trust was imposed upon property of far greater value than that received from the first to die, but in this case the property was largely derived from a bequest to the makers of the mutual wills as tenants in common.

CHAPTER 3

Contracts relating to wills

[3.1]

General statement. Although a will is by its nature always revocable, yet a testator may bind himself personally as to the contents of his will and may bind his assets so that his personal representative, whether he dies testate or intestate, must give effect to such agreement at the expense of the beneficiaries under the will or intestacy. There must, however, in any such case, be a binding agreement by the testator to dispose of his property in a certain way, and this involves two certainties. It must be shown that there was an agreement in law and not a mere statement of intention or a mere representation. It must also be shown with certainty what the subject-matter of the gift by the will was to be. Further, if the agreement relates to real property it must comply with the formalities prescribed by the Law of Property (Miscellaneous Provisions) Act 1989.[1] It can be noted that apart from contract it may be possible to base a claim against the deceased estate on the principles of proprietary estoppel.[2]

1   37 *Halsbury's Statutes* (4th edn) 658.
2   See *Re Basham* [1987] 1 All ER 405, [1986] 1 WLR 1498 which indicates an alternative approach to a claim to a house, based on proprietary estoppel. Similarly in *Gillett v Holt* [2000] 2 All ER 289, CA (reversing [1998] 3 All ER 917) the deceased made repeated inter vivos assurances to the plaintiff that in return for his work on the deceased's farm he would leave him the farm in his will. The deceased did not do so. The court allowed the plaintiff's claim to an equity in the farm, under the doctrine of proprietary estoppel arising from reliance on the latter's assurances causing the plaintiff detriment. See further discussed in Chapter 43.

[3.2]

Certainty of subject-matter. The gift must be clearly ascertainable ie its description must not be too vague. Some matters are clearly within the requirements eg a legacy of stated amount,[1] a gift of specific freehold or leasehold property,[2] or of the whole or a specific share of residue,[3] or a promise to provide for the payment of a debt of ascertained amount.[4] The following less specific descriptions have been held sufficiently certain: a promise to give as much as any of his children;[5] to enable a person to purchase property at £1,500 cheaper than the best purchaser;[6] to leave a sum for the maintenance of a school.[7] The following have been held uncertain and, therefore, unenforceable: to recognise son in common with the rest;[8] to make ample provision.[9]

1   *Hammersley v Baron de Biel* (1845) 12 Cl & Fin 45; *Eyre v Monro* (1857) 3 K & J 305; *Graham v Wickham* (1863) 1 De GJ & Sm 474 (a legacy of not less than £2,500); *Walker v Boughner* (1889) 18 OR 448. Where there is a covenant to give a pecuniary legacy, it constitutes a specialty debt and is provable accordingly in the administration of the testator's

25

estate. For cases where relief was refused because no specific sum was mentioned, see *Moorhouse v Colvin* (1851) 15 Beav 341; and *Kay v Crook* (1857) 3 Sm & G 407.

2   See *Synge v Synge* [1894] 1 QB 466; *Maddison v Alderson* (1883) 8 App Cas 467; *Wakeham v Mackenzie* [1968] 2 All ER 783, [1968] 1 WLR 1175; *Schaefer v Schuhmann* [1972] AC 572, [1972] 1 All ER 621, PC.

3   *Bennett v Houldsworth* (1877) 6 Ch D 671; *Re Vernon, Garland v Shaw* (1906) 95 LT 48. 'One full fourth part' means a fourth share in value and not specie: *Bell v Clarke* (1858) 25 Beav 437. 'Equal share' means that advances to other children are to be brought into account: *Willis v Black* (1828) 4 Russ 170. It has been said that the covenantee is, for many purposes, in the position of an ordinary legatee: *Jervis v Wolferstan* (1874) LR 18 Eq 18, ie he takes subject to debts, duties and administration expenses and to the fact that he may predecease the testator and lose the legacy by lapse. But see *Schaefer v Schuhmann* [1972] 1 All ER 621 which suggests the contrary at least so far as claims under the Family Provision legislation are concerned; see Chapter 105.

4   *Wells v Horton* (1826) 4 Bing 40.

5   *Silvester's Case* (1619) Poph 148.

6   *Bromley v Fettiplace* (1700) Freem Ch 245.

7   *Re Soames, Church Schools Co Ltd v Soames* (1897) 13 TLR 439.

8   *Kay v Crook* (1857) 3 Sm & G 407.

9   *Macphail v Torrance* (1909) 25 TLR 810.

[3.3]

Certainty of obligation. The law requires for the formation of a contract an offer and acceptance[1] accompanied by consideration or in the form of a covenant, ie an agreement under seal. As to the latter no more need be said, but, where there is no such formal agreement, it has sometimes been held that what is set up as an agreement amounts to no more than a statement of intention or a representation. The mere representation that a person intends to do something in the future is not, though the person to whom it is made relies upon it, sufficient to entitle the latter person to specific performance or damages. There must be a contract to entitle that person to relief,[2] ie the representation must amount to a positive undertaking. Thus the following were held sufficiently positive to be enforceable: 'at my decease she shall be entitled to her share of whatever property I may die possessed of';[3] 'I will take care that my property shall be properly secured upon her and her children';[4] intention to leave £10,000 by will to be settled on daughter and her children, or if she has no children as the father should prescribe;[5] proposal to leave house and lands to induce a party to marry the proposed devisee;[6] contract whereby a person gave up her tenancy to come and live with another, to look after the other's house in consideration of living there rent-free during their joint lives and a promise to leave the house to that person by her will;[7] execution of codicil devising testator's house and contents to a housekeeper, 'if she should still be employed by me as a housekeeper at the date of my death'; thereafter no more wages paid to the housekeeper.[8] Vague statements, on the other hand, have been held unenforceable: eg no intention to alter will unless unforeseen events occur;[9] an unattested document which the maker thought operated as a present gift;[10] 'she will have a share of what I leave' accompanied by an assertion that on account of the testator's large family it could not be much;[11] a statement that testator had made a will leaving his property equally among his children;[12] a promise to reward services by a gift by will.[13]

1   The acceptance in most of the cases here considered is marriage, see eg *Re Broadwood, Edwards v Broadwood (No 2)* (1912) 56 Sol Jo 703, CA (letter followed by marriage). For a

case where the acceptance was held not sufficiently connected with the offer, see *Dashwood v Jermyn* (1879) 12 Ch D 776 (consent to marriage where the arrangement was not made with the person consenting).

2   *Schaefer v Schuhmann* [1972] 1 All ER 621 at 627, PC; *Hammersley v De Biel* (1845) 12 Cl & Fin 45; *Re Fickus, Farina v Fickus* [1900] 1 Ch 331; *Maddison v Alderson* (1883) 8 App Cas 467, HL, not following *Loffus v Maw* (1862) 3 Giff 592; *Legeas v Trusts and Guarantee Co* [1912] 5 DLR 389; *Barnes v Cunningham* [1933] 3 DLR 653; *Briese v Dugard (No 2)* [1936] 1 DLR 723; *Lahay v Brown* (1958) 12 DLR (2d) 785. Even an expression to leave a certain sum to charity is not effective after death unless it amounts to a binding contract: *Re Hudson* (1885) 54 LJ Ch 811; *Sinnett v Herbert* (1871) (as reported in LR 12 Eq 201 at 206 (deposit of money in savings bank in trust for charitable purposes but such purposes not named)).

3   *Laver v Fielder* (1862) 32 Beav 1. This and the cases in nn 4–12, are necessarily decisions on questions of fact and dependent on all the circumstances of each particular case.

4   *Coverdale v Eastwood* (1872) LR 15 Eq 121.

5   *Hammersley v De Biel* (1845) 12 Cl & Fin 45.

6   *Synge v Synge* [1894] 1 QB 466; *Wakeling v Ripley* (1951) 15 SRNSW 183.

7   See earlier proceedings reported in *Re Edwards, Macadam v Wright* [1958] Ch 168, [1957] 2 All ER 495. See also *Parker v Clark* [1960] 1 All ER 93; *Balkwill v Smith* (1957) 21 WWR 474.

8   *Schaefer v Schuhmann* [1972] AC 572, [1972] 1 All ER 621, PC. Contract created by execution of codicil which housekeeper had previously read coupled with testator telling housekeeper that as he had left her the house by will he was not going to pay her any more wages and her acquiescence with that arrangement. The contract could be regarded as a contract not to revoke the gift provided that the housekeeper continued to serve the testator until his death, and no memorandum would have been necessary, [1972] 1 All ER 621, PC at 627. Alternatively, the codicil could be regarded as a sufficient memorandum, [1972] 1 All ER 621, PC at 627. But see Lord Simon's dissenting judgment in the case, [1972] 1 All ER 621, PC at 624–635, and *Maddison v Alderson* (1883) 8 App Cas 467, HL. As to the effect of contracts to leave property by will on Family Provision claims, see para **[3.12]** and Chapter 105.

9   *Maunsell v White* (1854) 4 HL Cas 1039.

10   *Vincent v Vincent* (1887) 56 LT 243.

11   *Re Fickus, Farina v Fickus* [1900] 1 Ch 331.

12   *Re Allen, Hincks v Allen* (1880) 49 LJ Ch 553; *Walker v Claridge* (1968) 207 Estates Gazette 341.

13   See cases in n 2.

[3.4]

Unenforceable contract. The covenant or agreement must not be unenforceable by reason of non-compliance with the Law of Property Act 1925, s 40[1] or, in the case of contracts entered into after 27 September 1989, with the provisions of the Law of Property (Miscellaneous Provisions) Act 1989, s 2. Thus the contract if it relates to land, must be in writing. The doctrine of part performance can be applied to pre-1990 contracts[2] but not to contracts entered into after the coming into force of the Law of Property (Miscellaneous Provisions) Act 1989. An alternative possibility is to claim against the estate based on the doctrine of unjust enrichment,[3] or on the equitable principles of proprietary estopple.[4]

1   Previously the Statute of Frauds.

2   *Humphreys v Green* (1882) 10 QBD 148; *Maddison v Alderson* (1883) 8 App Cas 467, HL; *Horton v Jones* (1934) 34 SRNSW 356; *Damphousse v Damphousse* [1943] OWN 349, but a verbal acceptance of a written offer is sufficient; *Parker v Clark* [1960] 1 All ER 93.

3   See *Foster v Royal Trust Co* [1951] 1 DLR 147; *Deglman v Guaranty Trust Co of Canada* [1954] SCR 725, and cases there cited. In *Wakeham v Mackenzie* [1968] 2 All ER 783, it was suggested that even if there had not been part performance, the promisee would have been entitled to specific performance on the footing that it would have been fraudulent for the testator immediately before his death, to have repudiated the oral contract for want of writing, [1968] 2 All ER 783 at 788.

4   See *Yaxley v Gotts* [2000] Ch 162 and *Gillett v Holt* [2000] 2 All ER 289, CA and the cases
     discussed in the judgment of Sir Robert Walker LJ in the latter; see para **[3.1]**, n 1.

[3.5]
Ante-nuptial contract. Where the deceased entered into an ante-nuptial contract
with a woman whom he subsequently married and later made a will giving his
property otherwise than in accordance with the agreement, the court enforced the
agreement and the will so far as it dealt otherwise with the testator's property
was void.[1] A woman executed a deed giving up her rights under the family
provision legislation upon consideration of a covenant by her then intended
husband to pay her £600 on his death. The marriage was later celebrated and the
husband died intestate. This deed was not enforceable since it was executed
without a full knowledge of the rights the woman was giving up. She was not
told the extent of her husband's estate, that the marriage would revoke his will,
nor of the possibility of future testamentary dispositions.[2]

1   *Haque v Haque* [1963] WALR 15.
2   *Zamet v Hyman* [1961] 3 All ER 933.

[3.6]
Enforcement. The promisee's rights do not arise under the will; they arise
contractually and exist independently of the will.[1] If the contract is to devise or
bequeath specific property then the agreement is enforceable by way of damages
for its breach[2] and the remedy by way of damages may be claimed immediately
the covenantor has put it out of his power to perform his obligation, even during
his life.[3] If the promisee can intervene before a purchaser for value without
notice obtains an interest in the property he can obtain a declaration of his right
to have it left to him by will and an injunction to restrain the testator from
disposing of it in breach of contract.[4] If the property is land he could also
register the contract or a caution against the title.[5] It may also be enforced by
specific performance where there is valuable consideration and the other
circumstances are such that the court will specifically enforce it,[6] but when this
remedy is granted the court does not set aside a will not in accordance with the
contract, but orders the personal representatives or possibly the devisees to
convey the property according to the contract or otherwise to give effect to it.[7]
The agreement may also be given effect to upon the principle that the law
imposes an obligation upon the estate to compensate a person who has rendered
services to the deceased based upon the principle of unjust enrichment.[8] In such
proceedings, the statute of limitations runs from the death of the deceased.[9]

1   *Coffill v Stamp Duties Comr* (1920) SRNSW 278; *Re Syme* [1933] VLR 282; *Re Richardson's
     Estate* (1935) 29 Tas LR 149, followed and approved in *Schaefer v Schuhmann* [1972] 1 All ER
     621 at 629–631, overruling *Dillon v Public Trustee of New Zealand* [1941] AC 294, [1941] 2
     All ER 284.
2   *Hammersley v De Biel* (1845) 12 Cl & Fin 45; *Synge v Synge* [1894] 1 QB 466, CA.
3   *Synge v Synge* [1894] 1 QB 466, CA (covenant to leave specific realty, which the covenantor
     sold in his lifetime). If the testator sells the property during his lifetime the promisee can treat
     the sale as a repudiation of the contract and recover damages at law which will be assessed
     subject to a reduction for the acceleration of the benefit, and also if the benefit of the contract is
     personal to the promisee, subject to a deduction for the contingency of his failing to survive the
     promisor: *Schaefer v Schuhmann* [1972] 1 All ER 621 at 628.

4   *Synge v Synge* [1894] 1 QB 466, CA; *Schaefer v Schuhmann* [1972] 1 All ER 621 at 628.
5   *Schaefer v Schuhmann* [1972] 1 All ER 621 at 628.
6   *Goilmere v Battison* (1682) 1 Vern 48; *Dufour v Pereira* (1769) 1 Dick 419; *Coverdale v Eastwood* (1872) LR 15 Eq 121.
7   *Schaefer v Schuhmann* [1972] 1 All ER 621 at 636. The will is a valid will of which probate must be granted and the court granting probate is not concerned with the contract. The contract, therefore, can be enforced only in the administration of the estate, ie by order upon the personal representatives to convey the property so as to give effect to the contract and not to the gift in the will.
8   See *Balkwill v Smith* (1957) 21 WWR 474 (agreement to provide maintenance in consideration of being compensated by gift by will); *Deglman v Guaranty Co of Canada* [1954] SCR 725.
9   See n 8 supra.

[3.7]

Inheritance tax. The general rule applicable to inheritance tax is that in determining the value of a person's estate at any time his liabilities are taken into account[1] but a liability incurred by the deceased is only to be taken into account to the extent that it was incurred for consideration in money or money's worth.[2] It is expressly provided that where the right to dispose of any property has been excluded or restricted by a contract made at any time then in determining the value of the property the exclusion or restriction is taken into account only to the extent of the consideration in money or money's worth given for it.[3]

1   Inheritance Tax Act 1984 (ITA 1984), s 5(3).
2   ITA 1984, s 5(5).
3   ITA 1984, s 163(1)(a).

[3.8]

Dispositions tending to defeat covenant. Where the covenantor does not contract with reference to any specific property but contracts to leave all or a share of the property he may die possessed of, he is at liberty to spend or dispose of all or any of his property during his life,[1] but, if it is personalty and he lays it out in land, the land is charged with a sum equal to the purchase money in favour of the covenantee.[2] If the contract is to leave the promisee the residue of the estate then the property intended is the net residue after payment of creditors and expenses.[3] The covenantor cannot defeat the covenant by testamentary disposition,[4] nor can he settle the property on himself for life with remainders over ie by a disposition inter vivos having practically the same effect as a testamentary disposition.[5]

1   *Cochran v Graham* (1811) 19 Ves 63 at 66; *Needham v Smith* (1828) 4 Russ 318. This includes subsequently acquired realty and personalty: *Needham v Kirkman* (1820) 3 B & Ald 531.
2   *Lewis v Madocks* (1803) 8 Ves 150; *Cochran v Graham* (1811) 19 Ves 63 at 66.
3   *Jervis v Wolferstan* (1874) LR 18 Eq 18 at 24; *Legeas v Trusts and Guarantee Co* [1912] 5 DLR 389; *Schaefer v Schuhmann* [1972] 1 All ER 621 at 628. Where a share of residue is promised, the testator will not be permitted fraudulently (in the sense used by equity) to render his promise nugatory by making substantial gifts inter vivos or by way of specific legacies: *Gregor v Kemp* (1722) 3 Swan 404; *Schaefer v Schuhmann* [1972] 1 All ER 621 at 638.
4   *Harmore v Brook* (1674) Cas *temp* Finch 183.
5   *Jones v Martin* (1798) 3 Anst 882; *Fortescue v Hennah* (1812) 19 Ves 67 (explained by the High Court of Australia in *Palmer v Bank of New South Wales* (1975) 133 CLR 150); *Logan v Wienholt* (1833) 7 Bli NS 1, HL.

[3.9]

Insolvency. If the covenantor dies insolvent then, whether or not he has left the legacy by his will, the covenantee is entitled to claim as a creditor for the amount of the legacy.[1] If the contract is to devise or bequeath specific property and the covenantor had retained the property in question until his death but has died insolvent, then the property would form part of his general estate available for the payment of debts, but the covenantee would be entitled to rank as a creditor for the value of the property as at the death in competition with other creditors of the same degree.[2]

1   *Graham v Wickham* (1863) 1 De G J & Sm 474; *Schaefer v Schuhmann* [1972] 1 All ER 621 at 627, 628.
2   *Graham v Wickham* (1863) 1 De G J & Sm 474; *Schaefer v Schuhmann* [1972] 1 All ER 621 at 627, 628.

[3.10]

Lapse. The covenant may be defeated by the lapse of a testamentary gift. Where the covenantor was bound to leave all his real estate to his children in equal shares, only children living at his death were entitled to the benefit of the covenant.[1] The covenantor is not in his will bound to guard against the defeat of an interest by lapse.[2]

1   *Needham v Smith* (1828) 4 Russ 318; *Jones v How* (1850) 9 CB 1.
2   *Re Brookman's Trust* (1869) 5 Ch App 182; *McDonald v McDonald (No 2)* (1935) 35 SRNSW 463. The general rule being that in so far as lapse is concerned the covenantee stands in the same position as any other legatee: *Jervis v Wolferstan* (1874) LR 18 Eq 18. As to lapse, see Chapter 47, and for provisions against lapse, see Vol 2. But see, however, *Schaefer v Schuhmann* [1972] 1 All ER 621 at 637.

[3.11]

Intestacy. If the covenantor dies intestate and the covenantee is a beneficiary under the intestacy, his share under the intestacy will be a satisfaction of the whole or pro tanto of the liability under the covenant as the amount received under the intestacy is on the one hand equal to or more than the amount covenanted to be bequeathed or on the other hand falls short of that amount.[1] If the covenant is to leave an annuity, a benefit under the intestacy is no satisfaction of the covenant.[2] The covenant may on its proper construction only be referable to intestacy and leave the covenantor free to dispose of all his property by will.[3]

1   *Wilcocks v Wilcocks* (1706) 2 Vern 558; *Blandy v Widmore* (1715) 2 Vern 709; *Garthshore v Chalie* (1804) 10 Ves 1.
2   *Couch v Stratton* (1799) 4 Ves 391; *Salisbury v Salisbury* (1848) 6 Hare 526; *James v Castle* (1875) 33 LT 665 (where a sum was to be paid to trustees on trust for the wife for life).
3   *Stocken v Stocken* (1838) 4 My & Cr 95 (where the covenant was to settle on particular persons all personal estate subject only and without prejudice to other dispositions made by will of, or concerning, the same or any part thereof).

[3.12]

Inheritance (Provision for Family and Dependants) Act 1975 (I(PFD)A 1975). In order to prevent avoidance of the family provision legislation[1] the deceased's net estate can be deemed, for the purposes of that legislation, to include property which is the subject of contracts relating to wills.[2] It is provided by the I(PFD)A 1975, s 11 that certain contracts whereby the deceased agreed to leave by his will a sum of money or other property to any person, or by which he agreed that a sum of money or other property would be paid or transferred to any person out of his estate, may be made the subject of an order by the court.[3] The contract must have been made otherwise than for full valuable consideration with the intention of defeating an application for financial provision under the I(PFD)A 1975.[4] The court can make one of the following orders.[5] First, if any money has been paid or any other property has been transferred to or for the benefit of the donee in accordance with the contract, an order directing the donee to provide a specified sum of money or other property.[6] Second, if the money or all the money has not been paid or the property or all the property has not been transferred in accordance with the contract, an order directing the personal representatives not to make any such payment or transfer.[7]

1   See the Privy Council's decision in *Schaefer v Schuhmann* [1972] AC 572, [1972] 1 All ER 621, on New South Wales family provision legislation. In that case there was a devise of a house to a housekeeper if she should still be employed as the testator's housekeeper at his death; thereafter housekeeper paid no more wages. After the testator's death the burden of an award under family provision legislation fell to be determined. Held, that the housekeeper's contractual rights prevailed over the dependant's statutory rights, and so was not liable to bear any part of the award. *Coffill v Stamp Duties Comr* (1920) SRNSW 278; *Re Syme, Union Trustee Co of Australia Ltd v Syme* [1933] VLR 282 and dictum of Nicholls CJ in *Re Richardson's Estate* (1935) 29 Tas LR 149 at 155, approved and applied, *Dillon v Public Trustee of New Zealand* [1941] AC 294, [1941] 2 All ER 284, HL, not followed.
2   I(PFD)A 1975, s 25(1).
3   I(PFD)A 1975, s 11(1), (2)(a); more fully discussed in Chapter 105.
4   I(PFD)A 1975, s 11(2)(b), (c).
5   I(PFD)A 1975, s 11(2)(d), where it would facilitate the making of financial provision under the I(PFD)A 1975.
6   I(PFD)A 1975, s 11(2)(i).
7   I(PFD)A 1975, s 11(2)(ii).

[3.13]
Covenant not to revoke. A covenant not to revoke a will or a particular gift or clause in a will is binding upon the covenantor.[1] It applies only to revocation by the act of the covenantor and does not apply to revocation by operation of law, ie on marriage or on lapse.[2] In the case of mutual wills, if the one party dies without having altered his will, the will of the other becomes irrevocable[3] otherwise than by re-marriage,[4] but, if the party dying first has revoked his will, the survivor cannot have a later will set aside or modified, but he is released from his obligation not to alter his will.[5] A covenant may be wider than one against mere revocation. Thus a covenant not to 'do or commit any act deed matter or thing by means whereof the said will should be revoked, annulled, cancelled or affected in any manner whatsoever' has been held to prevent the making of a further will after remarriage.[6]

1   *Robinson v Ommanney* (1883) 23 Ch D 285; *Re Marsland, Lloyds Bank Ltd v Marsland* [1939] Ch 820, [1939] 3 All ER 148; *Benn v Hawthorne* [1925] 4 DLR 400; *Gertzbein v Winer* (1971) 13 DLR 692.
2   *Re Marsland, Lloyds Bank Ltd v Marsland* [1939] Ch 820, [1939] 3 All ER 148; *Clausen v Denson* [1958] NZLR 572.
3   *Stone v Hoskins* [1905] P 194, and see Chapter 2.

4   *Re Oldham, Hadwen v Myles* [1925] Ch 75.
5   *Stone v Hoskins* [1905] P 194 at 197. As to joint and mutual wills, see further, Chapter 2.
6   *Robinson v Ommanney* (1883) 23 Ch D 285. In that case the covenant was held void as against public policy in so far as it prevented re-marriage, but was severable and was broken by the making of another will. In respect of the making of the further will damages were awarded. In *Re Marsland, Lloyds Bank Ltd v Marsland* [1939] Ch 820, [1939] 3 All ER 148, where the covenant was simply 'not to revoke or alter' a will, it was held that that covenant was not broken by re-marriage and, although a further will was made, no relief was given.

[3.14]
Covenant to exercise a power by will in a particular way. If the power is a general power and the covenant is for valuable consideration, damages are recoverable for its breach, but the remedy of specific performance is not available.[1] If the power is a special power, such a covenant is altogether unenforceable,[2] but a will in pursuance of the covenant is a valid exercise of the power.[3]

1   *Re Parkin, Hill v Schwarz* [1892] 3 Ch 510; *Beyfus v Lawley* [1903] AC 411; *Robinson v Ommanney* (1883) 23 Ch D 285.
2   *Re Bradshaw, Bradshaw v Bradshaw* [1902] 1 Ch 436; *Re Cooke, Winckley v Winterton* [1922] 1 Ch 292.
3   *Palmer v Locke* (1880) 15 Ch D 294.

[3.15]
Covenant not to exercise special power by will. The donee of a special power can release the power or covenant not to exercise it.[1] He can also by such negative covenant fetter his exercise of the power and, so far as such fetter extends, the property will go in default of appointment,[2] thus it may be released so that the power cannot subsequently be exercised in favour of a particular object of the power.[3]

1   *Re Evered, Molineux v Evered* [1910] 2 Ch 147; *Re Brown's Settlement, Public Trustee v Brown* [1939] Ch 944, [1939] 3 All ER 391.
2   *Re Coake, Winckley v Winterton* [1922] 1 Ch 292.
3   *Re Brown's Settlement, Public Trustee v Brown* [1939] Ch 944, [1939] 3 All ER 391.

Capacity and disposing intent

CHAPTER 4

Testamentary capacity

I. IN GENERAL

[4.1]

General position. At the present time, the question of capacity has become of small importance except in the case of persons who are minors and of persons who are not of sound mind, memory and understanding. Such incapacity as formerly existed in the case of married women, aliens and convicts has been removed. It goes without saying that corporate bodies are incapable from their very nature of making a will, though they may benefit under the will of an individual person. To some extent two or more individuals may make a joint will.[1]

1   See Chapter 2.

[4.2]

Testamentary capacity and domicile. Questions of testamentary capacity have to be determined by the law of the domicile of the testator at the time of the making of the will.[1]

1   *Re Fuld's Estate (No 3), Hartley v Fuld* [1968] P 675, [1965] 3 All ER 776.

[4.3]

Supervening incapacity. A will made by a person of full capacity is not revoked by the fact that he subsequently becomes incapable of making a will and a will made by a sane person is not revoked by his subsequent insanity.[1]

1   *Forse and Hembling's Case* (1588) 4 Co Rep 60 b.

[4.4]

Removal of disability. A will made at a time when the testator or testatrix is incapable of making a will is not rendered valid by the fact that the incapacity ceases during his or her lifetime, unless the will has been re-executed after such cesser.[1]

1   *Bunter v Coke* (1707) 1 Salk 237; *Willock v Noble* (1875) LR 7 HL 580.

II. ALIENS

[4.5]
No disability since 1870. By virtue of the Naturalization Act 1870 an alien has been under no disability with regard to disposing by will of any property acquired after the coming into force of the Act.[1]

1   Naturalization Act 1870, s 2(3). As to wills of persons with foreign domicile, see Chapter 23, similarly as to the disposition of immovable property situate outside England and Wales.

III. CRIMINALS

[4.6]
Present position. The Criminal Justice Act 1948, s 70, repealed the provisions of the Forfeiture Act 1870,[1] and from 18 April 1949, a criminal has been subject to no disabilities affecting his property and no administrator is now appointed.

1   12 *Halsbury's Statutes* (4th edn) 115; see Statute Law (Repeals) Act 1977; 41 *Halsbury's Statutes* (4th edn) 575.

IV. MINORS

[4.7]
General disability. Wills executed before 1 January 1970, are governed by the Wills Act 1837, s 7,[1] which provides that no will (except for the special provisions affecting soldiers in actual military service and mariners or seamen at sea[2]) made by a person under the age of twenty-one years is valid. This rule applies notwithstanding that the will has been confirmed by a codicil executed on or after that date.[3] However, wills made on or after that date by persons who are aged eighteen years or over are valid.[4] A person attains a particular age at the commencement of the relevant anniversary of the date of his birth.[5] A will made on a person's eighteenth birthday is therefore valid.

1   Wills Act 1837, s 7; see Vol 2, Part G, para **[244.5]**.
2   See Chapter 16.
3   Family Law Reform Act 1969, s 1(7); 6 *Halsbury's Statutes* (4th edn) 121.
4   FLRA 1969, s 3(1); 50 *Halsbury's Statutes* (4th edn) 613.
5   Family Law Reform Act 1969, s 9(1), replacing the common law rule that a person attained a particular age on the eve of his birthday: *Herbert v Turball* (1663) 1 Keb 589; *Howards Case* (1699) 2 Salk 625; *Re Shurey, Savory v Shurey* [1918] 1 Ch 263, all cases concerned with attaining twenty-one.

V. MARRIED WOMEN

[4.8]
No disability. A married woman is now under no disability in disposing by will of her property.[1]

1   Law Reform (Married Women and Tortfeasors) Act 1935, ss 1, 2(1); 27 *Halsbury's Statutes* (4th edn) 738. See also the Married Women's Property Act 1893, s 2.

VI.   SOUND DISPOSING MIND

[4.9]
The relevant time. It must be shown that the testator was of sound disposing mind at the time when the will or codicil was made.[1] The law requires that there should be sound disposing mind both at the time when the instructions for the will are given and when the will is executed, but it would appear that if the will is shown to have been drawn in accordance with instructions given while the testator was of sound disposing mind, it is sufficient that, when he executes it, he appreciates that he is being asked to execute as his will a document drawn in pursuance of those instructions though he is unable to follow all its provisions.[2] Supervening insanity will not revoke the will[3] nor will a recovery validate a will or codicil made during absence of testamentary capacity.[4] A will has been admitted to probate although a codicil made shortly after has been refused on the ground of want of sound disposing mind at the time of its execution.[5]

1   *Arthur v Bokenham* (1708) 11 Mod Rep 148; *Palmer and Brown v Dent* (1850) 2 Rob Eccl 284 (where a later will made while not of sound mind was rejected).
2   *Perera v Perera* [1901] AC 354; *Kenny v Wilson* (1911) 11 SRNSW 460; *Wilkie v Wilkie* (1915) 17 WALR 156; *Thomas v Jones* [1928] P 162; *Battan Singh v Amirchand* [1948] AC 161, [1948] 1 All ER 152. This is so even though the testator is unable to remember the instructions previously given and his signature was affixed by another person on his behalf: *Parker v Felgate* (1883) 8 PD 171. See *Re Flynn, Flynn v Flynn* [1982] 1 All ER 882, [1982] 1 WLR 310, per Slade J at 890, 891 and *Re Rodziszewski's Estate* (1982) 29 SASR 256. As to cases where testator is too ill to sign, see para **[11.21]** infra.
      Forse and Hembling's Case (1588) 4 Co Rep 60 b at 61 b; *Warn v Swift* (1832) 1 LJ Ch 203 (incapacity developing shortly after execution); *Re Crandon's Goods* (1901) 84 LT 330. Since any testamentary disposition must be made while the testator is of sound disposing mind, supervening insanity will ex hypothesi prevent his varying any will made while sane, and since the same sound disposing mind is required for revocation (see Chapter 18, para **[18.4]** infra) it also prevents any revocation of a will made while sane.
3   *Arthur v Bokenham* (1708) 11 Mod Rep 148 at 157; *Public Trustee v Prisk* (1896) 14 NZLR 306.
4   *Brouncker v Brouncker* (1812) 2 Phillim 57.
5   *Harwood v Baker* (1840) 3 Moo PCC 282; *Banks v Goodfellow* (1870) LR 5 QB 549 at 569; *Re Sever's Will* (1887) 13 VLR 572; *Boreham v Prince Henry Hospital* (1955) 29 ALJ 179. See also *Baker Estate v Myhre* [1995] 6 WWR 410 and *Webb v Webb Estate* [1995] 6 WWR 52. There is a simple statement of the essentials in a very early case; *Re Marquess Winchester's Case* (1598) 6 Co Rep 23a, in these words:
      'It is not sufficient that the testator be of memory when he makes his will to answer familiar and unusual questions, but he ought to have a disposing memory, so that he is able to make a disposition of his lands with understanding and reason.'

[4.10]
Criterion of sound disposing mind. Sound testamentary capacity means that three things must exist at one and the same time: (i) The testator must understand that he is giving his property to one or more objects of his regard; (ii) he must understand and recollect the extent of his property; (iii) he must also understand the nature and extent of the claims upon him both of those whom he

is including in his will and those whom he is excluding from his will.[1] The testator must realise that he is signing a will and his mind and will must accompany the physical act of execution.[2] It is said that perversion of moral feeling does not constitute unsoundness of mind in this respect,[3] but this is really a matter of degree.[4] The criterion to be applied has been thus stated by Cockburn CJ, in *Banks v Goodfellow*:[5]

> 'It is essential to the exercise of such a power that a testator shall understand the nature of the act and its effects; shall understand the extent of the property of which he is disposing; shall be able to comprehend and appreciate the claims to which he ought to give effect; and with a view to the latter object, that no disorder of the mind shall poison his affections, pervert his sense of right, or prevent the exercise of his natural faculties—that no insane delusion shall influence his will in disposing of his property and bring about a disposal of it which, if the mind had been sound, would not have been made.'

The mere fact that the testator was eccentric or was subject to one or more delusions is not of itself sufficient.[6] It must be shown that the delusion had, or was calculated to have, an influence on testamentary dispositions.[7] A will has been held good subject to the deletion of a clause affected by a delusion.[8]

1   For a statement of the essentials by the Supreme Court of Canada, see *Re Poirier Estate, Leger v Poirier* [1944] 3 DLR 1.
2   *Langlais v Langley* [1952] 1 SCR 28.
3   *Frere v Peacocke* (1846) 1 Rob Eccl 442 at 456.
4   *Sutton v Sadler* (1857) 3 CBNS 87; *Burdett v Thompson* (1873) LR 3 P & D 72n.
5   LR 5 QB 549 at 565; applied most recently in *Wood v Smith* [1993] Ch 90, [1991] 2 All ER 939, affirmed on this point by Court of Appeal [1993] Ch 90, [1992] 3 All ER 556, where capacity was lacking. See para **[11.10]** infra on the formalities aspect of this case. See also *Brown v Pourau* [1995] 1 NZLR 352 where a number of points relating to capacity are set out, *Banton v Banton* (1998) 164 DLR (4th) 176 (lacked capacity) and *Longmuir v Holland* (2000) 192 DLR (4th) 62 (will invalid on grounds incapacity).
6   *Banks v Goodfellow* (1870) LR 5 QB 549; *Murfelt v Smith* (1887) 12 PD 116. It had been laid down at one time that a mind unsound on one subject could not be called sound on any subject (*Waring v Waring* (1848) 6 Moo PCC 341) and that proof of such unsoundness of mind on one subject, though quite irrelevant to any testamentary disposition, completely negatived testamentary capacity, but this doctrine has long been not only departed from but definitely overruled.
7   *Boughton v Knight* (1873) LR 3 P & D 64; *Smee v Smee* (1879) 5 PD 84; *Montreal Trust Co v McKay* (1957) 21 WWR 611. This passage of the text was cited with approval by White J in *O'Connell v Shortland* (1989) 51 SASR 337, at 350, 351, where despite the near approach of death and no medical evidence of the testator's capacity at the time, the testator was held to have capacity.
8   *Re Bohrmann's Estate, Caesar and Watmough v Bohrmann* [1938] 1 All ER 27 l. There are two old decisions in which part of a will was admitted to probate: *Billinghurst v Vickers* (1810) 1 Phillim 187; *Wood v Wood* (1811) 1 Phillim 357.

[4.11]

Mental disorder. The law relating to persons suffering from mental disorders has been consolidated by the Mental Health Act 1983 (MeHA 1983),[1] and the provisions of that Act now govern the classification and treatment of such persons, including ... the management of their property'.[2] The MeHA 1983 defines four categories of mental impairment,[3] namely: 'mental disorder', means mental illness, arrested or incomplete development of mind, psychopathic disorder and any other disorder or disability of mind; 'severe mental impairment', means a state of arrested or incomplete development of mind which includes severe impairment of intelligence and social functioning and is associated with abnormally aggressive or seriously irresponsible conduct on the part of the person concerned; 'mental impairment', means a state of arrested or incomplete development of mind (not amounting to severe mental impairment) which includes significant impairment of intelligence and social functioning and is associated with abnormally aggressive or seriously irresponsible conduct on the part of the person concerned;[4] and 'psychopathic disorder', means a persistent disorder or disability of mind (whether or not including significant impairment of intelligence) which results in abnormally aggressive or seriously irresponsible conduct on the part of the person concerned.[5] However, simply because a person is deemed to be suffering from mental disorder within the meaning of the MeHA 1983, or even that he is detained pursuant to the powers contained in the MeHA 1983, does not necessarily mean that he is incompetent to make a will. Each case must, it seems, be considered with reference to the general definitions noted above, and medical and psychiatric evidence will be important.[6]

1 28 *Halsbury's Statutes* (4th edn) 829; the MeHA 1983 came into force on 30 September 1983 repealing and consolidating the previous legislation, notably the Mental Health Act 1959.
2 See the power to make wills for mentally disordered persons: MeHA 1983, ss 96 and 97, paras **[4.21]–[4.23]** infra.
3 MeHA 1983, s 1(2), which derives from the Mental Health (Amendment) Act 1982, ss 1, 2; 28 *Halsbury's Statutes* (4th edn) 834.
4 A new category introduced by the Mental Health (Amendment) Act 1982.
5 It is expressly provided by the MeHA 1983, s 1(3), that a person shall not be deemed to be suffering from any form of mental disorder as described above, by reason only of promiscuity or other immoral conduct, sexual deviancy or dependence on alcohol or drugs.
6 This passage of the text was cited with approval by White J in *O'Connell v Shortland* (1989) 51 SASR 337.

[4.12]
Presumption of sound disposing mind. It is presumed that the testator was sane at the time when he made his will[1] but, if the question of his sanity is contested, the onus is on the person propounding the will to prove that the testator was of sound disposing mind at the time when he made his will.[2] While there must be a vigilant examination of all the evidence, if the court feels there is no doubt substantial enough to defeat a grant of probate, the grant must be made. Complete proof of capacity or even proof beyond reasonable doubt is not essential.[3] A will not irrational on its face,[4] duly executed, is admitted to probate without proof of competence unless such competence is contested.[5] The law presumes that a state of things shown to exist continues to exist unless the contrary is proved and thus a testator, when there is no suggestion of insanity, is presumed to have remained sane;[6] and, on the other hand, if there is evidence of insanity at a time prior to the making of the will, the person propounding the will must prove competence at the relevant time.[7]

In the latter case the presumption in the first instance is against sanity especially where the will contains dispositions which are prima facie not such as an ordinary testator would make.[8] Such presumption as there is, is always affected by the provisions of the will itself. If these are such as a sane person would make, and, still more, if the will is drawn by the testator himself, the will can be held valid.[9] If the dispositions are irrational, the presumption is against the will.[10]

1   *Wellesley v Vere* (1841) 2 Curt 917.
2   *Re Flynn, Flynn v Flynn* [1982] 1 All ER 882 at 890. See also *Sutton v Sadler* (1857) 3 CBNS 87, where the fundamental proposition is stated that a party propounding a will is bound to show that the testator was of sound disposing mind, but it is agreed that, if there is no evidence of incompetency the will must be found for. This last proposition was upheld in *Turner v Penny* (1843) 1 LTOS 412 (where there was a plea of insanity but no evidence). See *Chambers and Yatman v Queen's Proctor* (1840) 2 Curt 415 (will found for where there had been previous delusions and testator committed suicide on the day following the execution of the will). Where the will is sought to be proved in solemn form, the onus is still on the person propounding it although there has been a grant in common form: *Robins v National Trust Co* [1927] AC 515. See also *Royal Trust Co v Ford* (1971) 20 DLR (3d) 348 and *Re Schwartz* (1970) 10 DLR (3d) 15; on appeal (1971) 20 DLR (3d) 313; *Vout v Hay* (1995) 125 DLR (4th) 431.
3   *Worth v Clasohm* (1952) 86 CLR 439. This passage of the text was cited with approval by White J in *O'Connell v Shortland* (1989) 51 SASR 337.
4   As to the weight to be given to the nature of the dispositions, see *Levy v Lindo* (1817) 3 Mer 81 (reasonable will by person found to be insane); *Re Watt's Goods* (1837) 1 Curt 594 (a similar case); *Nichols and Freeman v Binns* (1858) 1 Sw & Tr 239; *Evans v Knight and Moore* (1822) 1 Add 229 (slight evidence needed to support reasonable dispositions); *Re Sample's Estate* [1955] 3 DLR 199 (gifts to friends rather than to nephews); *Re Breidenbach Estate, Yaerger v Breidenbach* (1956) 19 WWRNS 109 (gifts to strangers in blood insufficient in itself).
5   *Sutton v Sadler* (1857) 3 CBNS 87.
6   *Chambers and Yatman v Queen's Proctor* (1840) 2 Curt 415.
7   *Smee v Smee* (1879) 5 PD 84; *Groom v Thomas* (1829) 2 Hag Ecc 433; *Banks v Goodfellow* (1870) LR 5 QB 549; *Guerin v Guerin* [1962] SCR 550.
8   *Harwood v Baker* (1840) 3 Moo PCC 282 at 291; *Re Davis* (1963) 40 DLR (2d) 801.
9   *Cartwright v Cartwright* (1793) 1 Phillim 90 at 100; *Rutherford v Maule* (1832) 4 Hag Ecc 213 at 226; *Clarke v Leare and Scarwell* (1791) cited in 1 Phillim at 119; *Symes v Green* (1859) 1 Sw & Tr 401. This passage of the text was cited with approval by White J in *O'Connell v Shortland* (1989) 51 SASR 337.
10 See cases cited in nn 2 and 3, but mere foolishness or eccentricity of a disposition is not sufficient; see para **[4.18]** infra.

[4.13]
Lucid interval. Where the testator is shown to have been insane prior to the date of the will, it must be shown that the will was made during a lucid interval.[1] Even a person of unsound mind so found could make a will during a lucid interval.[2] To establish the existence of a lucid interval is not necessary to prove complete mental recovery.[3] It is sufficient if it is shown that the testator understands that he is making a testamentary disposition and what is required of him in making the disposition[4] and that any delusion from which he is still suffering does not affect such disposition.[5] A person may suffer from intermittent insanity and perhaps the burden of proving a lucid interval is then less than where it is sought to prove an isolated interval, but, once insanity is established, it is for the person setting up the lucid interval to prove the lucid interval and that the testamentary act was done during the interval.[6]

1   *Hall v Warren* (1804) 9 Ves 605 at 610; *Rodd v Lewis* (1755) 2 Lee 176; *Cartwright v Cartwright* (1793) 1 Phillim 90; *Groom v Thomas* (1829) 2 Hag Ecc 433; *Bannatyne v Bannatyne* (1852) 2 Rob Eccl 472; *Re Walker* [1905] 1 Ch 160 at 172. The burden of proof is upon the party alleging the lucid interval: *A-G v Parnther* (1792) 3 Bro CC 441; *Cartwright v Cartwright* (1793) 1 Phillim 90.

2 *Hall v Warren* (1804) 9 Ves 605; *Re Watts' Goods* (1837) 1 Curt 594; *Levy v Lindo* (1817) 3
   Mer 81; *Cooke v Cholmondeley* (1849) 2 Mac & G 18; *Prinsep and East India Co v Dyce
   Sombre* (1856) 10 Moo PCC 232; *Re Walker* [1905] 1 Ch 160.
3 *Ex p Holyland* (1805) 11 Ves 10 at 11; *Creagh v Blood* (1845) 8 I Eq R 434 at 439; *Prinsep and
   East India Co v Dyce Sombre* (1856) 10 Moo PCC 232. A lucid interval has been established
   where the patient destroyed himself the following day: *Chambers and Yatman v Queen's
   Proctor* (1840) 2 Curt 415.
4 *Bennet v Duke of Manchester* (1854) 23 LTOS 331; *Cleare v Cleare* (1869) LR 1 P & D 655.
   The fact that dispositions are in accordance with former intentions has told in favour of the will:
   Coghlan v Coghlan (circa 1790) cited in 1 Phillim at 120, or that the will is a rational one:
   Nichols and Freeman v Binns (1858) 1 Sw & Tr 239; *Agar v Chatham Public General Hospital*
   [1955] 1 DLR 401 (testator able without advice or suggestion to make reasonable dispositions
   and remembered earlier will and appreciated altered circumstances).
5 *Dimes v Dimes* (1856) 10 Moo PCC 422; *Re Walker's Estate, Watson v Treasury Solicitor*
   (1912) 28 TLR 466.
6 *Cartwright v Cartwright* (1793) 1 Phillim 90; see also *Steed v Calley* (1836) 1 Keen 620;
   Tatham v Wright (1832) 2 Russ & M 1; *Borlase v Borlase* (1845) 4 Notes of Cases 106;
   Kinleside v Harrison (1818) 2 Phillim 449.

[4.14]

Delusions. A delusion is a belief in the existence of something which no rational
person could believe and, at the same time, it must be shown to be impossible to
reason the patient out of the belief.[1] To avoid a will, the delusion must be such
as to influence the testator in making the particular disposition made.[2] The
existence of a delusion is quite compatible with the retention of the general
powers and faculties of the mind.[3] It is a question of fact whether the delusion
affects the disposition, and, even where the delusion is connected with the
subject-matter of the disposition, it is not a necessary conclusion that the
delusion affected it.[4] A parent may take a harsh view of the character and
conduct of his children or relations without being subject to such a delusion as
will avoid a will, but there is a point where such a view ceases to be a harsh
unreasonable judgment and must be held to proceed from some mental defect.[5]
For the will to stand the testator's mind must not be dominated by an insane
delusion so as to overmaster his judgment to such an extent that he is incapable
of disposing of his property reasonably and properly or of taking a rational view
of the matters to be considered in making a will.[6] The well-trusted legal
decision, that best of all guides on this question,[7] is the following statement of
Cockburn CJ in *Banks v Goodfellow*:[8]

> 'Here, then, we have the measure of the degree of mental power which should
> be insisted on. If the human instincts and affections, or the moral sense,
> become perverted by mental disease; if insane suspicion, or aversion, take the
> place of natural affection; if the reason and judgment are lost, and the mind
> becomes a prey to insane delusions calculated to interfere with and disturb its
> functions, and to lead to a testamentary disposition, due only to their baneful
> influence—in such a case it is obvious that the condition of the testamentary
> power fails, and that a will made under such circumstances ought not to
> stand.'

It cannot be said that there are people who are not suffering from delusional
insanity but are incapable of making a will.[9] A testator may be stated by medical
evidence to have recovered from delusions, and yet the will be pronounced
against on the ground that the onus of proof has not been discharged, even where

the dispositions are probable.[10] The court may grant probate of will and codicil with the deletion of one clause from the codicil which has been affected by a delusion.[11] A pretended delusion assumed for the purpose of deception will not invalidate a will.[12]

1   *Dew v Clark and Clark* (1826) 3 Add 79. This paragraph was cited with approval by White J in *O'Connell v Shortland* (1989) 51 SASR 337 at 351.
2   *Jenkins v Morris* (1880) 14 Ch D 674; *Frere v Peacocke* (1846) 1 Rob Eccl 442; *Smith v Tebbitt* (1867) LR 1 P & D 398; *Boughton v Knight* (1873) LR 3 P & D 64; *Smee v Smee* (1879) 5 PD 84; *Murfett v Smith* (1887) 12 PD 116; *Pare v Cusson* (1921) 60 DLR 105; *O'Neil v Royal Trust Co and McClure* [1946] 4 DLR 545.
3   *Boughton v Knight* (1873) LR 3 P & D 64; *Banks v Goodfellow* (1870) LR 5 QB 549; *Beal v Henri* [1951] 1 DLR 260; but a will has been found against even where it was sensible on the face of it and contained no trace of any reference to or connection with the testator's then subject of delusion: *Symes v Green* (1859) 1 Sw & Tr 401; *Smith v Tebbitt* (1867) LR 1 P&D 398.
4   *Jenkins v Morris* (1880) 14 Ch D 674; *Smith v Tebbitt* (1867) LR 1 P&D 398, and see *Greenwood v Greenwood* (1790) 3 Curt App 1; *Dew v Clark and Clark* (1826) 3 Add 79; *Fowlis v Davidson* (1848) 6 Notes of Cases 461.
5   *Boughton v Knight* (1873) LR 3 P & D 64; *Thamer v Jundt* [1912] 4 DLR 753; *Royal Trust Co v Ford* (1971) 20 DLR (3d) 348.
6   *Banks v Goodfellow* (1870) LR 5 QB 549; *Hope v Campbell* [1899] AC 1; *Re Walker's Estate, Watson v Treasury Solicitor* (1912) 28 TLR 466; *Re Belliss, Polson v Parrott* (1929) 141 LT 245; *Ballantyne v Evans* (1886) 13 R (Ct of Sess) 652; *Sivewright v Sivewright's Trustees* 1920 SC (HL) 63; *Re Mitchell's Estate (Man)* [1924] 1 DLR 1039; *Re Onofrichuk, Onofrichuk v Onofrichuk* [1974] 2 WWR 469.
7   Per Langton J in *Re Bohrmann's Estate, Caesar and Watmough v Bohrmann* [1938] 1 All ER 271 at 278. The decision in *Re Bohrmann's Estate* was not followed in *Woodhead v Perpetual Trustee Co Ltd* (1981) 11 NSWLR 267.
8   (1870) LR 5 QB 549 at 565.
9   *Re Bohrmann's Estate* [1938] 1 All ER 271 at 279.
10 *Johnson v Blane* (1848) 6 Notes of Cases 442.
11 *Re Bohrmann's Estate, Caesar and Watmough v Bohrmann* [1938] 1 All ER 271. This is a singular decision which should, perhaps, be treated with caution.
12 *Ditchburn v Fearn* (1842) 6 Jur 201.

[4.15]
Religious belief and delusions. Religious beliefs may amount to delusions which justify a finding of incapacity[1] but where a person held a belief that he was commanded by the Deity to carry out particular work, this did not show his incapacity to make a will.[2] Superstitious terrors have been stated to be sufficient to set aside a will where they deprive a man of the exercise of his free judgment.[3]

1   *Smith v Tebbitt* (1867) LR 1 P & D 398; *Hope v Campbell* [1899] AC 1; *Re McDonald's Estate (NS)* (1914) 14 ELR 109 (where the bulk of the estate was left to religious uses and family not properly provided for).
2   *Hope v Campbell* [1899] AC 1;. See *Re Grant's Estate* [1944] 1 WWR 71 and *Faucher v Tucker* (1993) 109 DLR (4th) 699.
3   *Middleton v Sherburne* (1841) 4 Y & C Ex 358; on appeal, sub nom *Sherburne v Middleton* (1842) 9 Cl & Fin 72, HL.

[4.16]
Senile decay and illness. Unsoundness of mind may be occasioned by physical infirmity or advancing years as distinguished from mental derangement and the resulting defect of intelligence may be a cause of incapacity, but the intelligence

must be reduced to such an extent that the proposed testator does not appreciate the testamentary act in all its bearings.[1] In particular, the instructions for the will may have been given when the testator was of far better understanding than when the will was actually executed, and in these cases the will is generally pronounced for.[2] Where it is shown that the testator was incapable of reading the will and it is not read over to him, it is generally rejected but the criterion in such cases is whether he was really aware of the contents.[3] A will has been found for where the testatrix could only answer the drawer by means of nods and pressure of the hand in answer to questions as to her intentions,[4] but where the testatrix had suffered from delusions, the dispositions being probable and made when her medical attendant stated that she had recovered from her delusions, it was held that the onus of showing capacity had not been discharged.[5] The infirmity of the testator will strengthen certain presumptions which arise against the will in any case, eg where the will is contrary to the previously expressed intentions of the testator as to his testamentary dispositions[6] or where the will is drawn by the propounder and is wholly or largely in his favour.[7] Old age, or the near approach of death at any age, lend strength to suggestions that the testator had no proper knowledge of the contents of the will,[8] or that there was undue influence,[9] or the suspicion arising from the fact that the will is largely in favour of the person drawing or procuring it.[10] A desirable safeguard in such circumstances is for the will to be witnessed by a medical practitioner who satisfies himself as to the capacity and understanding of the testator and makes a record of his examinations and findings.[11] This has been described as the 'golden rule'.[12] It has been said that the grand criterion by which to judge whether the mind is injured or destroyed is to ascertain the state of the memory, for without memory the mind cannot act.[13]

1 *Banks v Goodfellow* (1870) LR 5 QB 549 at 566; *Emes v Emes* (1865) 11 Gr 325 (there must be some evidence of mental incapacity); *Re Munn, Hopkins v Warren* [1943] SASR 304; *Re Smith's Estate* [1945] 3 WWR 216; *Re Schwartz* (1970) 10 DLR (3d) 15; on appeal (1971) 20 DLR (3d) 313.
2 *Parker v Felgate* (1883) 8 PD 171; *Perera v Perera* [1901] AC 354; *Thomas v Jones* [1928] P 162; *Re Wallace's Estate, Solicitor of the Duchy of Cornwall v Batten* [1952] 2 TLR 925; *Re Flynn, Flynn v Flynn* [1982] 1 All ER 882, [1982] 1 WLR 310.
3 *Mitchell v Thomas* (1847) 6 Moo PCC 137; *Durnell v Corfield* (1844) 1 Rob Eccl 51. For a case where the will was read over to the testatrix but was not admitted to probate, see *Tyrrell v Painton* [1894] P 151. See also *Fulton v Andrew* (1875) LR 7 HL 448; *Re Martin, MacGregor v Ryan* (1965) 53 DLR (2d) 126. For a case where the will was not read over but admitted to probate, see *Re Wallace's Estate, Solicitor of the Duchy of Cornwall v Batten* [1952] 2 TLR 925.
4 *Re Holtham's Estate, Gillett v Rogers* (1913) 108 LT 732. See also *Re Souch* [1938] 1 DLR 563 (loss of power of speech and writing due to epileptic fit).
5 *Johnson v Blane* (1848) 6 Notes of Cases 442; *Batten Singh v Amirchand* [1948] AC 161, [1948] 1 All ER 152 (testator stating he had no relations when in fact he had nephews); *Re Morrison's Estate* [1953] 3 DLR 274 (changes in dispositions made on advice of solicitor); *Re Nightingale, Green v Nightingale (No 2)* (1974) 119 Sol Jo 189 (testator suffering from cancer made a second will shortly before he died excluding his son, who was the principal beneficiary under the first will, from benefiting. This exclusion was prompted by a belief founded on fanciful evidence that the son was trying to kill him. Held, executors had failed to discharge onus of proof of capacity and first will pronounced for).
6 *Harwood v Baker* (1840) 3 Moo PCC 282.
7 *Reece v Pressey* (1856) 2 Jur NS 380; *Mackenzie v Handasyde* (1829) 2 Hag Ecc 211.
8 *Durnell v Corfield* (1844) 1 Rob Eccl 51.

9   *Ashwell v Lomi* (1850) LR 2 P & D 477.
10   See cases cited in n 3.
11   *Re Simpson, Schaniel v Simpson* (1977) 121 Sol Jo 224; *Kenward v Adams* [1975] CLY 3591, and *Buckenham v Dickinson* [1997] CLY 4733; see para **[4.20]** infra.
12   See n 11.
13   *Murphy v Lamphier* (1914) 20 DLR 906.

[4.17]

Eccentricity and foolishness. Eccentricity or mere foolishness is insufficient to show want of capacity to make a will.[1] It has, however, been said that what may be mere eccentricity in one person may be shown to amount to incapacity in another.[2] Foolishness like eccentricity must be judged on a review of the whole life of the testator and the life and habits of a person may make what would be mere foolishness in one, incapacity in the case of another.[3] Both eccentricity and foolishness must be disregarded unless accompanied by evidence of general conduct amounting to insanity.[4]

1   *Wellesley v Vere* (1841) 2 Curt 917; *Mudway v Croft* (1843) 3 Curt 671; *Frere v Peacocke* (1846) 1 Rob Eccl 442; *Pilkington v Gray* [1899] AC 401.
2   *Mudway v Croft* (1843) 3 Curt 671.
3   *Austen v Graham* (1854) 8 Moo PCC 493; *Mudway v Croft* (1843) 3 Curt 671.
4   *Wellesley v Vere* (1841) 2 Curt 917; *Arbery v Ashe* (1828) 1 Hag Ecc 214; *Earl Sefton v Hopwood* (1855) 1 F & F 578 (foolishness may amount to harshness, capriciousness or injustice without showing incapacity); *Hobart v Merryfield* (1844) 2 LTOS 518.

[4.18]

Drunkenness. Habitual drunkenness giving rise to acts very like those of a madman or to deterioration of the mental faculties is not per se proof of incapacity.[1] It may be shown that the testator was not under the influence of liquor at the time the will was made.[2]

1   *Ayrey v Hill* (1824) 2 Add 206; *Handley v Stacey* (1858) 1 F & F 574; *Wheeler and Batsford v Alderson* (1831) 3 Hag Ecc 574 (where the will was admitted though greatly in favour of the solicitor who drew it); *Brunt v Brunt* (1873) LR 3 P & D 37 (where a duly executed will was destroyed in a fit of delirium tremens: held no revocation); *Campbell v Campbell* (1906) 5 WLR 59 (person affectionate to wife when sober but the reverse when drunk).
2   See cases cited in n 1, in all of which (except the last which is a revocation case) the will was held good.

[4.19]

Evidence of sound disposing mind. Both oral and documentary evidence is admissible to show that the testator was of sound disposing mind at the relevant time.[1] All statements made by him at the time of making the will or preparatory thereto are admissible to prove that he knew the character of the act he was undertaking.[2] The fact that the will is in his own handwriting is strongly in favour of his capacity.[3] The evidence of an attesting witness, since it must impeach his own act of attestation, is admissible but in general requires corroboration.[4] Evidence of the manner in which the act of making the will was performed is admissible, and also evidence of its accord with natural affection and moral duty, and its conformity to past and subsequent declarations of intention.[5] Evidence of conduct before and after the actual making of the will is admissible,[6] but it carries little weight where there is satisfactory evidence of sound disposing mind at the actual time of making the will,[7] and its importance varies with the nature of the mental disease from which the testator is alleged to be suffering.[8] Generally, evidence of the general habits and course of life is of a greater weight than that of particular acts.[9] It has been doubted whether the fact that unsoundness of mind has existed or exists in the testator's family is admissible.[10] The treatment of the testator by his friends and relations is admissible as for or against them, but not as against third parties, such evidence being admissible to introduce what the testator did with regard to it but not otherwise.[11] General reputation that a person is suffering from unsoundness of mind is not admissible.[12] The evidence of a medical witness who has attended the testator is admissible but such a witness cannot be asked to give his opinion as to the existence of facts which he has not himself observed.[13] The evidence of experts, however, has been held not to outweigh that of eye-witnesses who had opportunities for observation and knowledge of the testatrix[14] but a scientific witness who did not see the testator may be asked his opinion upon the facts proved in evidence.[15]

1   *Wheeler and Batsford v Alderson* (1831) 3 Hag Ecc 574; *Jenkins v Morris* (1880) 14 Ch D 674; *Bannatyne v Bannatyne* (1852) 2 Rob Eccl 472; *Snook v Watts* (1848) 11 Beav 105. Subsequent letters are admissible but of little value: *Bootle v Blundell* (1815) 19 Ves 494. This paragraph of the text was cited with approval by White J in *O'Connell v Shortland* (1989) 51 SASR 337 at 353.

2   *Hall v Warren* (1804) 9 Ves 605 at 610; *Levy v Lindo* (1817) 3 Mer 81; *Filmer v Gott* (1774) 4 Bro Parl Cas 230; *Fane v Duke of Devonshire* (1718) 6 Bro Parl Cas 137; *Wheeler and Batsford v Alderson* (1831) 3 Hag Ecc 574; *Butlin v Barry* (1837) 1 Curt 614 at 629; *Durling and Parker v Loveland* (1839) 2 Curt 225.

3   *Cartwright v Cartwright* (1793) 1 Phillim 90 at 100; *Rutherford v Maule* (1832) 4 Hag Ecc 213 at 216; *Clarke v Leare and Scarwell* (1791), cited in 1 Phillim at 119.

4   *Bootle v Blundell* (1815) 19 Ves 494 at 504; *Howard v Braithwaite* (1812) 1 Ves & B 202; *Kinleside v Harrison* (1818) 2 Phillim 449 at 499; *Young v Richards* (1839) 2 Curt 371; *Pennant v Kingscote* (1843) 3 Curt 642.

5   *Wrench v Murray* (1843) 3 Curt 623; *Boughton v Knight* (1873) LR 3 P & D 64; *Arbery v Ashe* (1828) 1 Hag Ecc 214; *Brouncker v Brouncker* (1812) 2 Phillim 57; *Evans v Knight and Moore* (1822) 1 Add 229; *Brydges v King* (1828) 1 Hag Ecc 256. But a change in dispositions may be accounted for: *Williams v Goude* (1828) 1 Hag Ecc 577. In *King v Farley* (1828) 1 Hag Ecc 502, there was a change of dispositions and a subsequent reversion to the former dispositions.

6   *Rodd v Lewis* (1755) 2 Lee 176; *Re Watts' Goods* (1837) 1 Curt 594; *Beavan v M'Donnell* (1854) 10 Exch 184.

7   *Ferguson v Borrett* (1859) 1 F & F 613; *Prinsep and East India Co v Dyce Sombre* (1856) 10 Moo PCC 232.

8   *Mudway v Croft* (1843) 3 Curt 671.

9   *Snook v Watts* (1848) 11 Beav 105; *Smith v Tebbitt* (1867) LR 1 P&D 398; *Boughton v Knight* (1873) LR 3 P&D 64 at 75.

10   *M'Adam v Walker* (1813) 1 Dow 148; *Doe d Mather v Whitefoot* (1838) 8 C & P 270.

11   *Re Windham* (1862) 4 De G F & J 53; *Wright v Doe d Tatham* (1834) 1 Ad & El 3; *Wheeler and Batsford v Alderson* (1831) 3 Hag Ecc 574; *Bannatyne v Bannatyne* (1852) 2 Rob Eccl 472.

12   *Greenslade v Dare* (1855) 20 Beav 284.

13   *Doe d Bainbrigge v Bainbrigge* (1850) 16 LTOS 245; *Martin v Johnston* (1858) 1 F & F 122; *Lovatt v Tribe* (1862) 3 F & F 9 (evidence of medical men who gave certificates on which person confined. Such medical men should give the grounds on which they base their certificates). As to the advisability of having a medical man at hand to hear a person critically ill approve the contents of a will, see *Re Johnson's Estate* [1946] 3 WWR 424.

14   *O'Neil v Royal Trust Co and McClure* [1946] 4 DLR 545; *Boughton v Knight* (1873) LR 3 P&D 64.

15   *Papijans v Gudowski* [1963] Tas SR 183; *Re Schwartz* (1970) 10 DLR (3d) 15; on appeal (1971) 20 DLR (3d) 313.

[4.20]
Solicitor's duty. It has been suggested that a solicitor taking instructions for a will or supervising the execution of a will, has a duty to satisfy himself that the client has testamentary capacity.[1] Where such capacity is in doubt it might be useful for the solicitor to record his or her impressions of the testator's state of mind, at the time.[2] It has been suggested that solicitors should follow the 'golden rule' that a medical practitioner should be present where there are doubts about the testator's capacity.[3] As to possible negligence action against the solicitor in connection with wills, see Chapter 1.[4]

1   *Murphy v Lamphier* (1914) 31 OLR 287; affd 32 OLR 19; *Re Carvell Estate* (1977) 21 NBR (2d) 642; *Re Worrell* (1970) 8 DLR (3d) 36.
2   *Maw v Dickey* (1974) 52 DLR (3d) 178 at 190–191; *Ross v Caunters* [1980] Ch 297, [1979] 3 All ER 580; *Whittingham v Crease & Co* (1978) 88 DLR (3d) 353; *Orles and Kruger v R* (1958) 38 Sask LR 38.
3   *Kenward v Adams* [1975] CLY 3591 followed in *Re Simpson* (1977) 121 Sol Jo 224. Solicitors should ask open questions where the capacity is in doubt, such as 'why, what, who or where', to establish that a testator could know and understand the contents of his will; *Buckenham v Dickinson* [1997] CLY 4733 (testator very old, partially blind and deaf, held not to have capacity).
4   See para **[1.5]** supra.

VII.   POWER TO MAKE WILLS FOR MENTALLY DISORDERED PERSONS

[4.21]
The jurisdiction. The Mental Health Act 1959 (MHA 1959) conferred in s 102 a wide general power on the court with respect to the property and affairs of a mentally disordered person ('a patient') to do all such things as appear necessary or expedient in order to provide maintenance for the patient or his or her family, or otherwise for administering the patient's affairs. Without prejudice to this general provision s 103(1) conferred specific powers to manage and deal with the patient's property in the patient's name; and to make settlements and gifts of the patient's property.[1] However, the MHA 1959 did not confer the power to make a will for the patient a deficiency which was remedied by the Administration of Justice Act 1969, s 17, which added a new provision, as paragraph (dd), to this effect to the MHA 1959, s 103(1).[2] This new power was considered in a number of reported decisions[3] and guidelines relating to the law and practice were laid down by Vice-Chancellor Megarry in *Re D(J)*.[4] The MHA 1959 has been repealed and the legislation consolidated in the Mental Health Act 1983 (MeHA 1983)[5] and the jurisdiction is now to be found in the MeHA 1983, ss 93 to 97.[6] The previous MHA 1959, s 103(1)(dd) is now reproduced as the MeHA 1983, s 96(1)(e), which empowers the court to order:

'The execution for the patient of a will making any provision (whether by way of disposing of property or exercising a power or otherwise) which could be made by a will executed by the patient if he were not mentally disordered.'

The jurisdiction cannot be exercised where the patient is a minor, and in other cases, only where the judge has reason to believe that the patient is incapable of making a valid will for himself.[7] It will be appreciated that it is possible for a person subject to the Court of Protection to have capacity to make a personal will and in such cases that should be done subject to guidance and advice.

The details relating to the formalities governing the exercise of this jurisdiction are to be found now in the MeHA 1983, s 97.[8] This provides that the will should be signed by the authorised person with the name of the patient and with his own name, in the presence of two or more witnesses present at the same time, and these witnesses attest and subscribe in the usual way and the will is then authenticated with the official seal of the Court of Protection.[9] Where these formalities are complied with then it is provided that the will shall have the same effect for all purposes as if the patient were capable of making a valid will and the will had been executed by him in the manner required by the Wills Act 1837 (WA 1837).[10]

With the exception, of course, of s 9, the WA 1837 applies to such wills.[11] The will so made, often referred to as a 'statutory will' (although judicial will would seem more apt) becomes the patient's will for all purposes and thus precludes the Court of Protection from jurisdiction to make a different distribution.[12]

1 It was this power to make settlements for the patient which was invoked in *Re L(WJG)* [1966] Ch 135, [1965] 3 All ER 865, to provide, in effect, a substitute for a will; an inter vivos settlement was ordered by the court on behalf of a sixty-eight-year-old bachelor patient, who would otherwise have died intestate with assets of over £130,000.
2 The new jurisdiction came into effect on 1 December 1969 (SI 1969/607).
3 See *Re HMF* [1976] Ch 33, [1975] 2 All ER 795, and *Re Davey* [1980] 3 All ER 342, [1981] 1 WLR 164.
4 [1982] Ch 237, [1982] 2 All ER 37; see post.
5 28 *Halsbury's Statutes* (4th edn) 829; with effect from 30 September 1983, MeHA 1983, s 149(2).
6 The MeHA 1983 is a consolidating measure which in the main reproduces without significant alteration the provisions of the MHA 1959 relevant to this discussion. However, whereas the MHA 1959 jurisdiction was expressed with reference to 'a nominated judge' the MeHA 1983 enables the powers to be exercised additionally by 'nominated officers', ie Masters of the Court of Protection, MeHA 1983, s 93.
7 MeHA 1983, s 96(4), previously the MHA 1959, s 103(3). Thus in many cases the court will require a report from one of the Lord Chancellor's visitors as to this and such further medical evidence as the Master may direct; *Practice Direction* [1983] 3 All ER 255.
8 Previously the MHA 1959, s 103A.
9 MeHA 1983, s 97(1)(a), (b) and (c).
10 MeHA 1983, s 97(3).
11 MeHA 1983, s 97(2); such a will will not affect immovable property outside England and Wales; see MeHA 1983, s 97(4).
12 This can be achieved by revoking the statutory will and making a new will in its place—which is impossible if (as in *Re Davey* [1980] 3 All ER 342, [1981] 1 WLR 164; see FOX J at 349) the patient were then dead since it is not possible to make a will for, or to revoke the will of, a deceased person.

[4.22]
Guidelines governing the exercise of the jurisdiction. The Vice-Chancellor in *Re D(J)*[1] has stated the factors or considerations which should guide the court when exercising the power. These guidelines will assist not only the masters concerned with making the order but more importantly the patient's relatives and their legal advisers in formulating a set of agreed proposals that can form the basis of the application. The crucial consideration is that the court will regard the

disposition of the estate subjectively from the patient's point of view and will, so to speak sit in his armchair and make for him a will that he or she is likely to have made.[2] The other stated guidelines are as follows. It is to be assumed that the patient is having a brief lucid interval at the time when the will is made. Secondly, during the lucid interval the patient has a full knowledge of the past and a full realisation that as soon as the will is executed he or she will relapse into the actual mental state that previously existed with the prognosis as it actually is. These two propositions although recognised to be somewhat curious assumptions are consistent with the accepted practice regarding making of settlements for the patient.[3] The court will assume, thirdly, that during the hypothetical lucid interval the patient is to be envisaged as being advised by a competent solicitor. Finally, the patient will be assumed to take a fairly broad view of any claims upon his bounty and the court will not be concerned with examinations analogous to a profit and loss account. Although, recognised by the judge not to be either exhaustive or precise these principles for factors do provide useful guidance on the judicial attitude to the power vested in them.[4]

1   [1982] Ch 237, [1982] 2 All ER 37. Although expressed with reference to the jurisdiction in the MHA 1959 the comments are equally applicable to the consolidating MeHA 1983.
2   See Sir Robert Megarry, VC, [1982] Ch 237, [1982] 2 All ER 37 at 43; disagreeing with the previous remarks of Fox J in *Re Davey* [1980] 3 All ER 342 at 348, [1981] 1 WLR 164. It should be noted that the making of a statutory will by the court does not preclude an application under the Inheritance (Provision for Family and Dependants) Act 1975 (I(PFD)A 1975) and as Fox J emphasised in *Re Davey*, any objective unfairness can be remedied by an application under that Act. However, on the other hand it is not helpful for the court to make a totally unreasonable will consistent perhaps with the arbitrary prejudices of the patient when sane, if that will inevitably gives rise to an immediate application under the I(PFD)A 1975 on the death. It is inevitable perhaps that the court will try to effect ... the will which the actual patient, *acting reasonably*, would have made ...' per Sir Robert Megarry VC, [1982] Ch 237, [1982] 2 All ER 37 at 43.
3   See Cross J in *Re WJGL* [1965] 3 All ER 865 at 871–872.
4   Sir Robert Megarry VC, [1982] Ch 237, [1982] 2 All ER 37 at p 43.

[4.23]
Illustrations of the exercise of the jurisdiction. The power can be invoked to remedy an injustice caused by effect of ademption on a specific devise[1] or an emergency or salvage jurisdiction to avoid an undesirable intestacy.[2] The court has exercised the jurisdiction to make a will for a person who had been mentally disabled since birth and who had inherited a substantial estate. The will made provision for such persons and purposes for whom/which the patient might have been expected to provide if she had not been mentally disordered on the assumption that she would have been a normal decent person who would have acted in accordance with contemporary standards of morality.[3]

1   See *Re D(J)* [1982] Ch 237, [1982] 2 All ER 37 which was concerned with an elderly woman patient whose mental condition had deteriorated to such an extent that her affairs were made subject to the control of the Court of Protection. Whilst of full capacity the patient had devised the house in which she lived to one of her daughters and the residue of her estate to her five children in equal shares. Subsequently, the patient moved in with the daughter and remained with her, selling her own house and thus adeeming the devise. The patient purchased a new house near to her daughter but never lived in that house but remained with her daughter and her husband. The daughter (and another daughter who had been appointed to be patient's receiver) applied to the Court of Protection under the MHA 1959, s 103(1)(dd) for the execution of a

codicil to the original will specifically devising the new house to the daughter in place of the adeemed legacy of the old house and contents. The patient's new house was then sold for £22,000 and her estate was likely to be valued at about £50,000. The daughter was, no doubt, now looking for a legacy equal to the sale price of the house but the deputy master was less generous, ordering the execution of a will giving her a legacy of £10,000 with an equal share with the other children in the residue. The daughter appealed to the Vice-Chancellor, who decided that he did have a power of review, and ordered a new will which increased the legacy to £15,000.

2   A striking illustration is provided by *Re Davey* [1980] 3 All ER 342, [1981] 1 WLR 164, where a 92-year-old woman described as suffering from senile mental deterioration to a degree which rendered her incapable of properly managing her affairs, went through a ceremony of marriage with a much younger male employee of the nursing home in which she resided. That marriage, though voidable, had the effect of revoking an earlier will which the woman had made in favour of her two nephews who were her nearest relatives (see *Re Roberts, Roberts v Roberts* [1978] 3 All ER 225, [1978] 1 WLR 653, CA and Chapter 17). Her affairs were made subject to the Court of Protection and the Official Solicitor applied to the court for an order for the execution under the MHA 1959, s 103(1)(dd) of a will for the woman in the same terms as the earlier will that had been revoked by the marriage. The matter was regarded as one of great urgency (which, in fact, proved to be the case since the woman died six days later) and the will was made by the deputy master without notice being given to the other party to the marriage or to the beneficiaries under the earlier will. The court (Fox J) decided that, in the circumstances, this was an acceptable procedure since although normally notice should be given to parties adversely affected by the exercise of the jurisdiction, the urgency of the matter precluded that course in this case. The judge thought that any delay might result in an undesirable intestacy and that any unfairness to the other party to the marriage could be remedied by an application by him to the court, during the patient's lifetime, for a new statutory will, or, after her death, for provision out of her estate under the Inheritance (Provision for Family and Dependants) Act 1975. See also the Administration of Justice Act 1982, s 49 which facilitates the presentation of petitions for matrimonial relief on behalf of the patient and thus might provide an alternative, although more protracted, solution to cases like *Re Davey* [1980] 3 All ER 342, [1981] 1 WLR 164.

3   *Re C (a patient)* [1991] 3 All ER 866. On that basis it was thought that the patient would have felt a moral obligation to show recognition to the community and to her family since she had spent the whole of her life in the care of the community, as embodied in the national health service, the hospital and voluntary mental health charities, and had derived her fortune from being a child of a family. *Inter vivos* gifts of £100,000 to charity and £400,000 to her family were made, with a will drawn leaving her estate equally divided between charity and the family. The difficulty in such a case where the patient has been disabled since birth is that there is no subjective indication of her wishes. See also *Re S* [1997] 1 FLR 96 where inter vivos dispositions under the MeHA 1983, s 95, and a statutory will under the MeHA 1983, s 103, were made for a mental patient.

[4.24]

Practice Direction. Procedural guidelines regarding the exercise of the jurisdiction are to be found in the Court of Protection Rules[1] and in a recent practice direction.[2] Applications will be heard and determined by the master unless he decides because of the complexity of the matter, the size of the estate, or dispute between the parties to refer the matter to a nominated judge.[3] The application should be made by one or more of the persons who seek to benefit and the receiver, if not the applicant, should be joined as a party.[4] In general all persons whose interests will be materially affected by the application should be joined as parties, but exceptionally where the matter is one of great urgency, the court can proceed on the application of the receiver without notice to affected parties.[5]

The application should be supported by evidence of reasonably detailed information as to the size of the estate, the income, and the expenses of maintaining the patient.[6] Other relevant matters include the nature or character of the patient when of testamentary capacity and the financial or other circumstances of all those who claim to receive benefits under a will. Thus full particulars as to age, family fortune, needs and general circumstances of the patient and the general background of his affairs in addition to the facts directly relating to the application need to be provided.[7] Further the evidence should state the patient's domicile and regard should also be paid to any immovable property outside England and Wales (which is not subject to the will, section 97(4) of the Mental Health Act 1983.[8] Where the patient has been incapable since birth the court will not have any subjective indications of the testator's wishes and thus will have to make assumptions as to these.[9]

1   Court of Protection Rules 2001, SI 2001/824, r 18.
2   [1983] 3 All ER 255, superseding the previous, and similar, *Practice Direction* [1970] 1 All ER 15, sub nom *Practice Note* [1970] 1 WLR 228.
3   *Practice Direction* [1983] 3 All ER 255; see Sir Robert Megarry VC, in *Re D (J)* [1982] 2 All ER 37 at 50, 51.
4   [1983] 3 All ER 255, para 1.
5   As in *Re Davey* [1980] 3 All ER 342, [1981] 1 WLR 164, per Fox J at 348; see also *Re HMF* [1976] Ch 33, [1975] 2 All ER 795.
6   Referred to by Sir Robert Megarry VC in *Re D (J)* [1982] 2 All ER 37 at 49, as the hard facts of the case.
7   *Practice Direction* [1983] 3 All ER 255, para 1.
8   [1983] 3 All ER 255, para 2(b).
9   As was the case in *Re C (a patient)* [1991] 3 All ER 866; see para **[4.24]**, n 3.

CHAPTER 5

Knowledge and approval

I. KNOWLEDGE AND APPROVAL

[5.1]

Knowledge and approval. Before a paper is entitled to probate[1] the court must be satisfied that the testator knew and approved of the contents at the time he signed it.[2] It has been said[3] that this rule is evidential rather than substantive and that in the ordinary case proof of testamentary capacity and due execution suffices to establish knowledge and approval,[4] but that in certain circumstances the court requires further affirmative evidence.[5] It was at one time thought that the fact that the will had been duly read over to a capable testator on the occasion of its execution, or that its contents had been brought to his notice in any other way, should when coupled with his execution thereof, be held conclusive evidence that he approved as well as knew the contents thereof.[6] However, the better view now seems to be that such a circumstance raises but a prima facie presumption of knowledge and approval.[7] In some cases where the testator employs an expert draftsman to provide the appropriate wording to give effect in law to the testator's intentions, the testator has to accept the phraseology selected by the draftsman without himself really understanding its esoteric meaning and in such a case he adopts it and knowledge and approval is imputed to him.[8] This principle is carried further by the so-called rule in *Parker v Felgate*[9] to the effect that a will which has been prepared in accordance with previous instructions given when the testator fully understands the contents and effect thereof is valid, notwithstanding that at the time of execution the testator does not in fact have that understanding.[10]

---

1 As to which see *Tristram and Coote's Probate Practice* (27th edn).
2 *Guardhouse v Blackburn* (1866) LR 1 P & D 109 at 116; *Barry v Butlin* (1838) 2 Moo PCC 480; *Wintle v Nye* [1959] 1 All ER 552, [1959] 1 WLR 284; *Re Morris, Lloyds Bank Ltd v Peake* [1971] P 62, [1970] 1 All ER 1057.
3 *Re Fuld's Estate (No 3), Hartley v Fuld* [1968] P 675 at 697, [1965] 3 All ER 776 at 781.
4 As to the presumption of the execution see Chapter 13.
5 *Barry v Butlin* (1838) 2 Moo PCC 480, at 490; *Re Ireland* (1963) 147 DLR (3d) 480 at 482. Where a major beneficiary gave instructions to a solicitor to draft a will for an elderly aunt with failing eyesight it was held that a suspicion was raised which had to be removed before the will could be admitted to probate: *Re Hall* (1988) 50 DLR (4th) 51. *Tyrrell v Painton* [1894] P 151, CA; *Fulton v Andrew* (1875) LR 7 HL 448 and *Barry v Butlin* (1838) 2 Moo PCC 480 referred to.
6 Per Lord Penzance in *Guardhouse v Blackburn* (1866) LR 1 P & D 109; *Atter v Atkinson* (1869) LR 1 P & D 665; *Harter v Harter* (1873) LR 3 P & D 11 at 22.
7 *Re Morris, Lloyds Bank Ltd v Peake* [1971] P 62, [1970] 1 All ER 1057, tracing the progressive erosion of the rule; *Fulton v Andrew* (1875) LR 7 HL 448 at 449, 460, 461, 469; *Martell v*

Consett Iron Co Ltd [1955] Ch 363 at 414, [1955] 1 All ER 481 at 498; *Gregson v Taylor* [1917] P 256 at 261; *Crerar v Crerar* (1956) unreported, see 106 Law Journal 694. See also *Re Ticehurst, Midland Bank Executor and Trustee Co v Hankinson* (1973) Times, 6 March; *Re Schwartz* (1971) 20 DLR (3d) 313 (change of solicitor not a suspicious circumstance that could lead to inference that the testator might not have known and approved of the contents of the will); and *Re Fenwick* [1972] VR 646.

8   *Rhodes v Rhodes* (1882) 7 App Cas 192 at 199, 200; *Re Morris, Lloyds Bank Ltd v Peake* [1971] P 62, [1970] 1 All ER 1057 at 79 and 1066 (respectively). But see *Re Ticehurst, Midland Bank Executor and Trustee Co v Hankinson* (1973) Times, 6 March.

9   (1883) 8 PD 171.

10 See also, *Perera v Perera* [1901] AC 354; *Thomas v Jones* [1928] P 162; *Re Wallaces' Estate, Solicitor of the Duchy of Cornwall v Batten* [1952] 2 TLR 925; *Re Flynn, Flynn v Flynn* [1982] 1 All ER 882 at 890, 891.

[5.2]

When evidence required. The cases referred to above, when affirmative evidence of knowledge and approval of the contents of a will will be required include the following: testators who are deaf and dumb,[1] or blind,[2] and when the person who prepared the will received a benefit under the will.[3]

1   The question is a matter of fact in each case, see *Dickenson v Blisset* (1754) 1 Dick 268; *Re Harper* (1843) 6 Man & G 732; *Re Owston's Goods* (1862) 2 Sw & Tr 461; *Re Geale's Goods* (1864) 3 Sw & Tr 431; *Re Biddulph's Trusts, Re Poole's Trusts* (1852) 5 De G & Sm 469; *Re Souch* [1938] 1 DLR 563; *Re Sellwood's Estates, Heynes v Sellwood* (1964) 108 Sol Jo 523.

2   To establish the will of a testator wholly blind, or so nearly as to be incapable of discerning writing, it must be shown to the satisfaction of the court that the will was read over to him in the presence of the witnesses or that he was otherwise acquainted with its contents: *Fincham v Edwards* (1842) 3 Curt 63; affd 4 Moo PCC 198; *Re Axford* (1860) 1 Sw & Tr 540; *Re Sellwood* (1964) 108 Sol Jo 523. See also *Re Hall* (1988) 50 DLR (4th) 51.

3   *Barry v Butlin* (1838) 2 Moo PCC 480; *Fulton v Andrew* (1875) LR 7 HL 448; *Wintle v Nye* [1959] 1 All ER 552; *Re Stott, Klouda v Lloyds Bank Ltd* [1980] 1 All ER 259; see next sections.

[5.3]

The evidence in support of the plea. It has been said that where a question is raised concerning knowledge and approval of the contents of a will the circumstances which are held to excite the suspicions of the court must be circumstances attending or at least relevant to, the preparation and execution of the will itself,[1] but it is accepted that the allegations could also be relevant to the testamentary capacity of the deceased or to a plea of undue influence.[2] It is open to a party alleging want of knowledge and approval to cross-examine the person propounding the will on matters which may result in establishing fraud or undue influence on the part of such person, even though fraud or undue influence are not pleaded.[3] Further there is authority to the effect that the failure or deliberate omission of a party, who had raised a plea of want of knowledge and approval in a probate action, also to plead undue influence, does not preclude such a party from introducing in support of his plea matters of fact which would also, at least in a broad sense, be relevant in support of a plea of undue influence.[4] However the defence of want of knowledge and approval is not to be used 'as a screen behind which one man is to be at liberty to charge another with fraud or dishonesty without assuming the responsibility for that charge in plain terms'.[5]

1   Per Willmer J in *Re R* [1951] P 10, [1950] 2 All ER 117 where allegations irrelevant to the plea of want of knowledge and approval were struck out.

2   Per Willmer J in *Re R* [1951] P 10, [1950] 2 All ER 117; see Slade J in *Re Stott, Klouda v Lloyds Bank Ltd* [1980] 1 All ER 259 at 262.
3   See Lord Simonds in *Wintle v Nye* [1959] 1 All ER 552 at 560; Slade J in *Re Stott, Klouda v Lloyds Bank Ltd* [1980] 1 All ER 259 at 264.
4   Scarman J in *Re Fuld's Estate, Hartley v Fuld (No 3)* [1965] 3 All ER 776 at 783. Thus in *Re Stott, Klouda v Lloyds Bank Ltd* [1980] 1 All ER 259, there was an attempt to strike out many of the allegations pleaded in support of a defence of want of knowledge and approval as contravening RSC Ord 76, r 9(3) in that the allegations would also be relevant in support of a plea of undue influence which the defendant had not pleaded. The attempt failed because the judge thought that there will often be an inevitable overlap between evidence in support of want of knowledge and approval and evidence in support of undue influence.
5   Willmer J in *Re R* [1950] 2 All ER 117 at 123. The risk as to costs of a party opposing a will is reduced if he puts his opponent to proof of knowledge and approval instead of making positive allegations of fraud or undue influence which he himself has the burden of proving.

[5.4]
Will prepared by a beneficiary. It is not the law that in no circumstances can a solicitor or other person who has prepared a will for a testator take a benefit under it.[1] But that fact creates a suspicion that must be removed by the person propounding it.[2] Baron Parke expressed the rule as follows in *Barry v Butlin:*[3]

... if a party writes or prepares a will, under which he takes a benefit, that is a circumstance that ought generally to excite the suspicion of the court, and calls upon it to be vigilant and jealous in examining the evidence in support of the instrument, in favour of which it ought not to pronounce unless the suspicion is removed, and it is judicially satisfied that the paper propounded does express the true will of the deceased.'

The degree of suspicion will vary with the circumstances of the case,[4] and the burden of dispelling that suspicion[5] may be slight or 'so grave that it can hardly be removed'.[6]

1   Per Viscount Simonds in *Wintle v Nye* [1959] 1 All ER 552 at 557; see Slade J in *Re Stott* [1980] 1 All ER 259 at 262. See also *Low v Guthrie* [1909] AC 278; *Fulton v Andrew* (1875) LR 7 HL 448; *Re Harmes Estate, Hinkson v Harmes* (1946) 62 TLR 445; *Langlais v Langley* [1952] 1 SCR 28; *Re Moore's Estate, Cooke v Walsh* (1965) 52 WWR 449; *Re Timlick's Estate, Timlick v Crawford* (1965) 53 WWR 87; *Russell v Fraser* (1980) 118 DLR (3d) 733 (bank manager); *Re Emanuel* [1981] VR 113.
2   See n 1. See also *Vout v Hay* (1995) 125 DLR (4th) 431; *McKinnon v Voight* [1998] 3 VR 543; and *Roos v Karpenkow* (1998) 71 SASR 497.
3   (1838) 2 Moo PCC 480 at 482, 483.
4   It has been said that where the propounder obtains only a small legacy suspicion is confined to that gift: *Re Mackay's Estate* (1935) 8 MPR 526.
5   Proof that the testator read, or had read over, the will before execution is not now considered to be conclusive. See *Re Morris, Lloyds Bank Ltd v Peake* [1970] 1 All ER 1057; see para **[5.1]** supra.
6   The burden was not discharged in *Wintle v Nye* [1959] 1 All ER 552, where the solicitor who prepared the will was the substantive beneficiary to the large estate. See *Vout v Hay* (1995) 125 DLR (4th) 431 (suspicious circumstances removed). In *Re Ticehurst, Midland Bank Executor and Trustee Co v Hankinson* (1973) Times, 6 March, the will was prepared by correspondence with a solicitor conducted by an amanuensis, who was the wife of one of the beneficiaries. The court thought that the circumstances created a suspicion which was not dispelled and pronounced against the will.

[5.5]
Solicitors. Where the will is prepared by a solicitor under which he takes a benefit, it has been held that the solicitor has a duty not merely to tell the client

that he should obtain independent advice but, if the client declines to do so, to refuse to act further in the matter.[1] The Law Society has published rules regarding this matter in The Guide to the Professional Conduct of Solicitors.[2] A gift to a solicitor of an insignificant amount is permitted provided the client does not feel obliged to make such a gift. There is no need for independent advice where the solicitor takes under a secret trust or communication by the client to him provided that the solicitor cannot benefit personally or financially from the gift to him.[3]

1   In *Re a Solicitor* [1975] QB 475, [1974] 3 All ER 853 (where a solicitor had prepared a will for two sisters under which he and his family were substantive beneficiaries), in disciplinary proceedings against the solicitor the Law Society held that a solicitor in whose favour a client wished to make a will was bound to tell her that she must be separately advised and if she refused to go to another solicitor it was his duty to forgo the benefit. As the solicitor in the case had failed to comply with that standard of conduct, he was found guilty of professional misconduct and struck off the Roll of Solicitors.
2   See the current edition of the Guide.
3   In such cases the solicitor should preserve the instructions from which the gift was drawn and should see that the terms of such secret trust are embodied in a written document signed or initialled by the testator.

II. MISTAKE

[5.6]
Introduction. Where it is alleged that the testator did not know and approve of particular words or clauses in the will on the grounds of mistake, there are three possible remedies available. First, the court of probate has always had power to omit (but not to add) words from probate and this jurisdiction will remain applicable to wills of testators who die before 1 January 1983. Second, in the case of testators who die on or after that date, the Administration of Justice Act 1982, s 20 has conferred additional power on the court (in specified circumstances) to rectify defective wills.[1] Third, omissions or errors in wills can sometimes be cured by a court of construction as a matter of construction.[2]

1   See Chapter 6 where this jurisdiction is fully discussed.
2   See para **[5.7]** infra.

[5.7]
Mistake in will: power to omit words from probate. Where the testator is shown to have known and approved of a particular word or clause in the will, it cannot be excepted out of the probate.[1] The court will, however, except out of the grant a word or clause which has been introduced into the will inadvertently, without the knowledge or instructions of the testator,[2] and will refuse probate of a document executed by mistake.[3] The court will omit from the probate words shown to have been introduced by mistake[4] and has power to revoke a probate containing a mistake,[5] but cannot omit a word where to do so would alter the meaning of what remains.[6] The fact that the testator read and executed the will raises a prima facie inference that he knew and approved of its contents, but the court is free to consider the possibility of fraud or mistake in the light of all the possible evidence.[7] Although a testator who had delegated to a draftsman the

task of drafting an instrument and had executed it as drafted might in some circumstances be bound by a mistake which the draftsman had made, this would not be so where the mind of the draftsman had never really been applied to the words introduced and never adverted to their significance and effect and there was a mere clerical error on his part.[8] In the case of deaths on or after 1 January 1983, the power to rectify such clerical errors would now be available.[9]

1   *Re Horrocks, Taylor v Kershaw* [1939] P 198 at 216; *Re Beech's Estate, Beech v Public Trustee* [1923] P 46 at 53.

2   *Re Morris, Lloyds Bank Ltd v Peake* [1971] P 62, [1970] 1 All ER 1057 (solicitor drew up codicil revoking cl 7 of a will which was executed by testatrix; codicil only intended to revoke cl 7 (iv) of the will; held—court would omit the numeral '7' from the probate, enabling the court of construction to interpret the blank). Followed in *Re Phelan* [1972] Fam 33, [1971] 3 All ER 1256 (revocation clauses omitted); *Re Oswald's Goods* (1874) LR 3 P & D 162; *Morrell v Morrell* (1882) 7 PD 68; *Re Moore's Goods* [1892] P 378; *Re Boehm's Goods* [1891] P 247; *Re Reade's Goods* [1902] P 75; *Re Smith* [1956] NZLR 593; *Re Luck* [1977] WAR 148. Words inserted by a clerical error will be omitted: *Re Schott's Goods* [1901] P 190; *Jane v Jane* (1917) 33 TLR 389; *Re Clark* (1932) 101 LJP 27 (exclusion of wrong description of legatee); *Re Zurowski* [1928] 1 DLR 357; *Re Veres, Pirot v Veres* [1942] 3 DLR 770; but see *Re McKittrick Estate* [1934] 1 DLR 422 (where only seven parts of residue were disposed of and reference was made in each case to 'one-eighths'. The will having obviously been drawn with care, held an intestacy as to one-eighth); *Re Reynette-James, Wightman v Reynette-James* [1975] 3 All ER 1037, [1976] 1 WLR 161 (words omitted by a typist which significantly altered the construction of one clause of the will. Held; the gifts in the clause must be omitted from the probate). Such a will could now, in the case of a post 1982 death, be rectified, see Chapter 6.

3   *Re Meyer's Estate* [1908] P 353; *Re Swords' Goods* [1952] P 368, [1952] 2 All ER 281 (where testatrix thought a draft in her possession was a true copy of the will and revoked a clause which in fact had been omitted from the will). It was pointed out in *Corbett v Newey* [1996] 2 All ER 914 that apparently regular wills which were shams (*Lister v Smith* (1863) 3 Sw & Tr 282 and *Ferguson-Davie v Ferguson-Davie* (1890) 15 PD 109) or executed by the wrong person (*Re Hunt's Goods* (1875) LR 3 P&D 250 and *Re Meyer's Estate* [1908] P 353) were refused probate. See also *O'Leary v Douglass* (1878) 3 LR Ir 323 (where an executed draft and the subsequently executed engrossment were in identical terms and the question was whether both documents should be admitted to probate or only the engrossment).

4   *Re Morris, Lloyds Bank Ltd v Peake* [1971] P 62, [1970] 1 All ER 1057; *Vaughan v Clerk* (1902) 87 LT 144; *Marklew v Turner* (1900) 17 TLR 10; *Re Wrenn's Goods* [1908] 2 IR 370.

5   *Brisco v Baillie and Hamilton* [1902] P 234, and *Re Tatham, Huxtable v Princess Margaret Children's Hospital* (1951) 81 CLR 639.

6   *Re Horrocks, Taylor v Kershaw* [1939] P 198, [1939] 1 All ER 579; *Osborne v Smith* [1961] ALR 831 (so long as the omission does not alter the sense of what remains).

7   *Re Morris, Lloyds Bank Ltd v Peake* [1971] P 62, [1970] 1 All ER 1057, not following Lord Penzance's formulation in *Guardhouse v Blackburn* (1866) LR 1 P & D 109 at 116, or *Harter v Harter* (1873) LR 3 P & D 11; following *Fulton v Andrew* (1875) LR 7 HL 448 and *Crerar v Crerar* (unreported), but see (1956) 106 Law Journal 694, 695.

8   *Re Morris, Lloyds Bank Ltd v Peake* [1971] P 62, [1970] 1 All ER 1057; see *Rhodes v Rhodes* (1882) 7 App Cas 192; *Re Horrocks, Taylor v Kershaw* [1939] P 198, [1939] 1 All ER 579, CA applied in *Re Walker* [1973] 1 NZLR 449; *Crerar v Crerar* (unreported), but see (1956) 106 Law Journal 694, 695; *Collins v Elstone* [1893] P1; *Gregson v Taylor* [1917] P 256; *Re Beech's Estate, Beech v Public Trustee* [1923] P 46. This part of the text was cited in *Re Hess* [1992] 1 Qd R 176 at 192.

9   Administration of Justice Act 1982, s 20; 50 *Halsbury's Statutes* (4th edn) 615; see Vol 2, Part G, para **[244.96]**. Rectification is fully discussed in Chapter 6.

[5.8]

Construction of the will. The jurisdiction of the court of construction is much more limited in the case of an alleged mistake in a will; for this court has no jurisdiction to correct the probate and must be satisfied on the construction of the will alone that there is a mistake or omission in it.[1] In the case of a mere matter of doubt the court adheres to the words of the will.[2] A mistake in a name or description or in the insertion or the omission of any words, whether by the testator or by the draftsman, can be corrected by the court of construction[3] but only on inferences obtained from the whole will, and from any permissible extrinsic evidence.[4]

1   *Taylor v Creagh* (1858) 8 I Ch R 281 at 287; *Re Bywater, Bywater v Clarke* (1881) 18 Ch D 17 at 22.
2   *Mellish v Mellish* (1798) 4 Ves 45 at 50 (the mistake must be clearly inconsistent with the intention upon the whole will); *Thompson v Whitelock* (1859) 4 De G & J 490 at 500, 501; *Morgan v Thomas* (1882) 9 QBD 643 (stronger context required than when the court has to decide which of two meanings of a word the testator intended).
3   See Chapter 50.
4   Including now the power to admit evidence in accordance with the Administration of Justice Act 1982, s 21; 50 *Halsbury's Statutes* (4th edn) 616; see Vol 2, Part G, para **[244.97]**.

III.   UNDUE INFLUENCE AND FRAUD

[5.9]
Undue influence and fraud. Fraud and undue influence are really questions of knowledge and approval rather than of testamentary capacity since what has first to be proved is not the lack of capacity of the testator, but the acts of others whereby the testator has been induced to make dispositions which he did not really intend to make. Although undue influence is not impossible in the case of a testator of sound health and understanding, it is far more common in the case of a testator of weak or impaired mental capacity or in failing health. A gift obtained by undue influence or fraud is liable to be set aside upon proof of the undue influence or fraud.[1] Undue influence means coercion to make a will in particular terms.[2] The principle has thus been stated by Sir J P Wilde in *Hall v Hall:*[3]

'Persuasion is not unlawful, but pressure of whatever character if so exerted as to overpower the volition without convincing the judgment of the testator, will constitute undue influence, though no force is either used or threatened.'

The proof of motive and opportunity for the exercise of such influence is required but the existence of such coupled with the fact that the person who has such motive and opportunity has benefited by the will to the exclusion of others is not sufficient proof of undue influence. There must be positive proof of coercion overpowering the volition of the testator.[4] The mere proof of the relationship of parent and child, husband and wife, doctor and patient, solicitor and client, confessor and penitent, guardian and ward, or tutor and pupil does not raise a presumption of undue influence sufficient to vitiate a will[5] and although coupled with, for example, the execution of the will in secrecy, such relationship will help the inference, yet there is never in the case of a will a presumption of undue influence.[6] There is no presumption of undue influence, which must be proved by the person who sets up that allegation. The onus of proof resting upon a party propounding a will where circumstances of suspicion are disclosed does not extend to the disproof of an allegation of undue influence or fraud, the burden of establishing which always rests upon the parties setting it up.[7] The person who affirms the validity of the will must show that there was no force or coercion depriving the testator of his judgment and free action[8] and that what the testator did was what he desired to do.[9] The act of the testator in making the will or gift must be inconsistent with any hypothesis of undue influence.[10] Exaggerated description of the conduct of a proposed beneficiary is insufficient.[11] Where the testator is influenced by immoral considerations, there is no undue influence provided the will expresses his wishes.[12] Much less influence will induce a person of weak mental capacity or in a weak state of health to do any act and in such cases the court will the more readily find undue influence[13] and where a legatee for a large amount or one where a fiduciary relationship is found to exist between the testator and the beneficiary propounds a will prepared by himself more than ordinary proof of the authenticity of the will is called for[14] and this is so where the will is signed by a mark instead of the testator's usual signature.[15]

Undue influence has been found to be exercised by a person who was dead at the date of the execution of the will,[16] and, in a rare case, exercised on a person other than the testator.[17] Undue influence exerted for the benefit of someone other than the person exerting the influence is equally subject to the rules concerning undue influence as influence exerted by someone for his own benefit.[18] The party setting up a case of undue influence must give the particulars of the acts alleged in exercise of it with necessary dates[19] but not the means of the persons present.[20] Evidence of a statement of the party exerting the undue influence though not made in the presence of the testator is admissible.[21] A plea of undue influence ought never to be put forward unless the person who pleads it has reasonable grounds to support it.[22]

1   *Wingrove v Wingrove* (1885) 11 PD 81. The onus of proof is upon the party asserting undue influence or fraud: *Hutley v Grimstone* (1879) 5 PD 24; *Craig v Lamoureux* [1920] AC 349; *Re Hodgins* (1978) 85 DLR (3d) 705; *Maw v Dickey* (1974) 52 DLR (3d) 178; *Winter v Crichton* (1991) 23 NSWLR 116; *Baker Estate v Myhre* [1995] 6 WWR 410; *Robertson v Smith* [1998] 4 VR 144.

2   *Williams v Goude* (1828) 1 Hag Ecc 577; *Wingrove v Wingrove* (1885) 11 PD 81; *Hall v Hall* (1868) LR 1 P & D 481.

3   LR 1 P & D 481 at 482.

4   *Craig v Lamoureux* [1920] AC 349; *Pocock v Pocock* [1952] OR 155; *Re Montone* [1955] OWN 799; *Banton v Banton* (1998) 164 DLR (4th) 176 (onus of proving wife exercised undue influence over husband satisfied).

5   These relationships raise a presumption of undue influence in the case of contracts, but, in the case of a will, these relationships (or most of them) are naturally the source and reason of the testator's bounty and no such presumption is made. See *Parfitt v Lawless* (1872) LR 2 P & D 462; *Nye v Sewell* (1894) 15 NSWLR 18. Nor does the doctrine of fiduciary relationship, gifts to executors and trustees as such, excite any suspicion. However, in *Re Howell* [1955] OWN 85, a will prepared by a parish priest leaving nearly all the estate to the priest's church was held to be obtained by undue influence.

6   *Wheeler and Batsford v Alderson* (1831) 3 Hag Ecc 574; *Wyatt v Ingram* (1832) 3 Hag Ecc 466; *Walker v Smith* (1861) 20 Beav 394; *Croft v Day* (1838) 1 Curt 782; *Tuckwell v Cornick* (1844) 2 LTOS 336; *Wintle v Nye* [1959] 1 All ER 552, [1959] 1 WLR 284; *Fulton v Andrew* (1875) LR 7 HL 448 at 462, all cases where the solicitor largely benefited under the will; *Barry v Butlin* (1838) 2 Moo PCC 480, a similar case where the will was found for; see also *Re Fuld's Estate (No 3), Hartley v Fuld* [1968] P 675, [1965] 3 All ER 776; *Tilley v Berg and Berg (No 2)* [1945] 4 DLR 179 (where a solicitor was sole beneficiary, but the will was drawn by another solicitor it was held that there was no evidence of fraud or undue influence); *Greville v Tylee* (1851) 7 Moo PCC 320 (medical attendant); *Ashwell v Lomi* (1850) LR 2 PD 477 (medical attendant); *Re Stott, Klouda v Lloyds Bank Ltd* [1980] 1 All ER 259, [1980] 1 WLR 246 (manageress of nursing home); *Parfitt v Lawless* (1872) LR 2 P & D 462 (confessor); *Aimers v*

Taylor (1897) 15 NZLR 530; *Eady v Waring* (1974) 43 DLR (3d) 667; *Goldsworthy v Thompson* (1974) 46 DLR (3d) 237; and *Re Bailey* (1974) 47 DLR (3d) 670.

7   *Boyse v Rossborough, Boyse v Colclough* (1857) 6 HL Cas 2; *Low v Guthrie* [1909] AC 278; *Tyrrell v Painton* [1894] P 151; *Re R* [1951] P 10, [1950] 2 All ER 117 (the circumstances which are held to excite the suspicions of the court must be circumstances attending, or at least relevant to, the preparation and execution of the will itself); *Craig v Lamoureux* [1920] AC 349; *Riach v Ferris* [1934] 1 DLR 118; *Re Kaufman, Anderson and Houge v Walkey and Mason* (1961) 27 DLR (2d) 178; *Vout v Hay* (1995) 125 DLR (4th) 431.

8   *Williams v Goude* (1828) 1 Hag Ecc 577; *Earl Sefton v Hopwood* (1855) 1 F & F 578; *Lovett v Lovett* (1857) 1 F & F 581 (where it is said that gratitude, affection and esteem do not give rise to undue influence); *Leach v Smith* (1859) 23 JP 168.

9   *Wingrove v Wingrove* (1885) 11 PD 81.

10   *Boyce v Rossborough, Boyse v Colclough* (1857) 6 HL Cas 2; *Re Boyd's Will, Miller v Farr* (1872) 3 VR 46.

11   *Browning v Budd* (1849) 6 Moo PCC 430.

12   *Wingrove v Wingrove* (1885) 11 PD 81.

13   *Hampson v Guy* (1891) 64 LT 778.

14   This passage was cited with approval in *Ma Shiu-lim's Estate, Ma Po-chim v Ma Lok-shan* [1992] 2 HKLR 286 at 290, where it was held that although there were well-founded suspicions surrounding the preparation and execution of a will there was no case of actual coercion in which pressure was made to bear on or was otherwise exercised, to overpower the volition of the deceased in making the will, and thus no undue influence.

15   *Donnelly v Broughton* [1891] AC 435.

16   *Radford v Risdon* (1912) 28 TLR 342.

17   *Chennells v Bruce* (1939) 55 TLR 422.

18   See *Naidoo v Naidu* (2000) Times, 1 November and *Huguenin v Baseley* (1807) 14 Ves 273 at 289.

19   RSC Ord 18, r 12.

20   *Re Earl of Shrewsbury's Estate, McLeod v Earl of Shrewsbury* [1922] P 112; but to the contrary *Jackson v Hillas* (1869) 18 WR 216.

21   *Radford v Risdon* (1912) 28 TLR 342. The question is one of fact and an appellant court will not reverse concurrent findings of the courts below: *Larámee v Ferron* (1909) 41 SCR 391.

22   Per Slade J in *Re Stott, Klouda v Lloyds Bank Ltd* [1980] 1 All ER 259 at 264, where it was alleged, unsuccessfully, that what was in effect being raised was a plea of undue influence under cover of a plea of want of knowledge and approval; see also *Re Fuld's Estates, Hartley v Fuld (No 3)* [1968] P 675 at 722, [1965] 3 All ER 776 at 783; and *Re R* [1951] P 10 at 19, [1950] 2 All ER 117 at 123.

[5.10]
Will prepared by a beneficiary. See para **[5.4]** supra.

CHAPTER 6

Rectification

[6.1]

Rectification. Although the law of probate permits the court to omit words from a will in certain circumstances,[1] the general equitable doctrine of rectification was not previously available as a remedy in the law of wills.[2] Although it is beyond the scope of this work to consider rectification in detail one or two important characteristics can be noted.[3] Rectification is an equitable discretionary remedy[4] primarily available to remedy mistakes in written instruments recording the terms of contracts.[5] The remedy is however generally available and has always been applicable to unilateral documents such as voluntary settlements.[6] Wills, have hitherto, been one of the very few types of document which could not be rectified. The point was expressed by Templeman J in *Re Reynette-James, Wightman v Reynette-James*.[7]

> 'Any document other than a will could be rectified by inserting the words which the secretary omitted, but in this respect the court is enslaved by the Wills Act 1837. Words may be struck out but no fresh words may be inserted. ...'[8]

The Administration of Justice Act 1982 (AJA 1982)[9] has now conferred a limited power to rectify wills to remedy two types of mistake; first, those caused by clerical errors, and secondly those arising from a failure to understand the testator's instructions. The power to rectify applies only to the wills of testators who die on or after 1 January 1983.[10]

1   See previous Chapter for illustrations.
2   The reason for the exclusion has always been somewhat obscure since analogous unilateral documents such as voluntary settlements could be rectified, see, for example, *Re Butlin's Settlement Trusts, Butlin v Butlin* [1976] Ch 251, [1976] 2 All ER 483. The true explanation seemed to relate to the strict formal requirements for the execution of wills for it could be said that words varied or added by the court could not properly have been executed in accordance with the formalities. However, this is hardly convincing and modern cases such as *Re Morris, Lloyds Bank Ltd v Peake* [1971] P 62, [1970] 1 All ER 1057 and *Re Reynette-James, Wightman v Reynette-James* [1975] 3 All ER 1037, [1976] 1 WLR 161, had illustrated the necessity for a change in the law, at least in so far as patent clerical errors (of the sort apparent in those two cases) are concerned. In *Re Jensen* [1992] 2 NZLR 506 a judge rectified a codicil even though there was no statutory power in the jurisdiction to do so: '... the time has come to review that assumption' commented Fisher J at 511.
3   For a full exposition see *Snell's Principles of Equity* (28th edn), pp 610–619.
4   *Whiteside v Whiteside* [1950] Ch 65, [1949] 2 All ER 913.
5   *Joscelyne v Nissen* [1970] 2 QB 86, [1970] 1 All ER 1213, CA, a useful modern case where the remedy is considered.
6   *Re Butlin's Settlement Trusts, Butlin v Butlin* [1976] Ch 251, [1976] 2 All ER 483, where it was decided that the court had power to rectify a voluntary settlement notwithstanding that the

mistake had arisen not in omitting, or using, words intended or not intended to be included, but in ascribing the wrong interpretation to words intended to be used; applying *Lackersteen v Lackersteen* (1860) 30 LJ Ch 5; *Jervis v Howle and Talke Colliery Co Ltd* [1937] Ch 67, [1936] 3 All ER 193; *Whiteside v Whiteside* [1950] Ch 65, [1949] 2 All ER 913; and *Joscelyne v Nissen* [1970] 2 QB 86, [1970] 1 All ER 1213, CA. Rectification ordered, after some hesitation, despite the opposition of one trustee.

7   *Re Reynette-James, Wightman v Reynette-James* [1975] 3 All ER 1037, [1976] 1 WLR 161, words accidentally omitted changing sense of clause; clause omitted although mistake clear.

8   Referring to *Re Schott's Goods* [1901] P 190; *Re Horrocks, Taylor v Kershaw* [1939] P 198, [1939] 1 All ER 579; *Re Boehm's Goods* [1891] P 247.

9   Administration of Justice Act 1982, s 20; 50 *Halsbury's Statutes* (4th edn) 615; (Vol 2, Part G, para **[244.96]**) following the recommendations of the Law Reform Committee's 19th Report on the Interpretation of Wills, 1973 Cmnd 5301. For a general discussion of the jurisdiction under s 20, see Mummery LJ's judgment in *Walker v Geo H Medlicott & Son (a firm)* [1999] 1 All ER 685 at 699–670 where the previous cases are reviewed.

10   Administration of Justice Act 1982, ss 73(6)(c) and 76(11); and the provision applies only to England and Wales, s 77(1). For statutory provisions in other jurisdictions, see, for example, *Re Hess* [1992] 1 Qd R 176.

[6.2]
Clerical errors. The Administration of Justice Act 1982, s 20[1] provides as follows:

'If a court is satisfied that a will is so expressed that it fails to carry out the testator's intentions, in consequence—
(a)   of a clerical error . . . it may order that the will shall be rectified so as to carry out his intentions.'

It has been stated that the term 'clerical error' means an inadvertent error made in the process of recording the intended words of the testator in drafting or in the transcription of his will. Thus where a solicitor failed to include a clause in a later will which was intended to mirror a clause in an earlier will which it replaced, it was held to be an error made in the process of recording the intended words of the testatrix. The will was rectified to include the omitted clause.[2] The introduction of a clause which is inconsistent with the testator's instructions in circumstances in which the draftsman has not applied his mind to its significance or effect is also a 'clerical error' for the purposes of this provision.[3]

This provision seems apt to cover cases such as *Re Morris*,[4] where it will be recalled the codicil as written revoked 'clause 7 of the will' whereas the admitted intention had been to revoke 'clause 7(iv) of the will'. The omission of the Roman numeral (iv) was accepted on all sides as a clerical error, and such a case would now be simply resolved by the addition of the missing number, or words as the case might be. In many of these cases the error will be that of the draftsman, typist or amanuensis but the section is not so limited.[5]

1   See Vol 2, Part G, para **[244.96]**.
2   *Wordingham v Royal Exchange Trust Co Ltd* [1992] Ch 412, [1992] 3 All ER 204.
3   *Re Segelman* [1995] 3 All ER 676 at 686 (in which the offending clause was deleted).
4   [1971] P 62, [1970] 1 All ER 1057.
5   The Law Reform Committee 19th Report on the Interpretation of Wills (1973, cmnd 5301), para 19, saw no difference in principle between a slip made by the testator himself, his solicitor or the typist: and there is nothing in the wording in s 20 to introduce such a distinction. This view has been confirmed, obiter, by Nicholls J in *Re Williams, Wiles v Madgin* [1985] 1 All ER 964 at 969.

[6.3]
Failure to understand the testator's instructions. The second situation where the AJA 1982, s 20(1)[1] introduces a power of rectification is as follows:

'If a court is satisfied that a will is so expressed that it fails to carry out the testator's intentions, in consequence—
(a) ...
(b) of a failure to understand his instructions,
it may order that the will shall be rectified so as to carry out his intentions.'

It will be noticed that this provision is confined to cases where a draftsman fails to understand instructions and thus has a limited scope. The section does not cover the more common type of mistake, ie cases where the testator (and possibly his solicitor as well) fails to understand the legal effect of the words actually used, and thus produces the wrong result although using the intended expression; where in effect, all concerned may know what the testator wants but fail to use the right technique to achieve it.[2]

But where it can be established first, that the will fails to embody the testator's instructions, and secondly, what those instructions were, then it is now open to the court to rectify the will so as to make it embody them.[3] An example of such a case is where for instance, the testator has instructed his solicitor to draw his will in such a way as to leave certain property to X; the solicitor failing to understand what is wanted draws the will in such a way as to leave the property to Y, and the testator, not appreciating the mistake executes the will. Such a will could be rectified under the power in section 20.

It is apparent from the wording, '... a failure to understand his instructions . . .', that the power of rectification in this second context is available only where there has been the intervention of another person. This will typically be where the testator has instructed another to draft his will, whether that person be a solicitor or a lay person, or where the testator dictates his will to an amanuensis. Thus this power would not be available in the much more common cases where mistakes occur, where a lay testator writes out his whole will using inappropriate or unsatisfactory language.

Further in order for the remedy to be available it must be established not only that the will fails to carry out the testator's instructions but also what those instructions were.[4] This will be a matter of proof and there is no guidance in the section as to the admissibility of the evidence in support. Section 21, which provides for the admissibility of extrinsic evidence as an aid in a will's interpretation, does not assist here, but clearly extrinsic evidence must be admitted to aid rectification since by definition the instructions for a will are not to be found within the will.[5]

1 See Vol 2, Part G, para **[244.96]**.
2 Rectification in such circumstances is sometimes possible in relation to eg settlements: see *Re Butlin's Settlement Trusts, Butlin v Butlin* [1976] Ch 251, [1976] 2 All ER 483. But the Law Reform Committee did not think the power of rectification appropriate to wills in such cases, op cit, para 20.
3 Law Reform Committee, 19th Report on the Interpretation of Wills (1973, cmnd 5301), para 21.
4 See *Walker v Geo H Medlicott & Son (a firm)* [1999] 1 All ER 685 where the plaintiff failed to prove by convincing evidence that the testatrix had instructed the solicitor defendants to include in her will a gift of a house to the plaintiff as alleged. See also *Racal Group Services Ltd v Ashmore* [1995] STC 1151, CA, upholding Vinelott J [1994] STC 416 (case concerning the equitable remedy to rectify a deed of covenant).

5 The Law Reform Committee (n 3 supra, para 28–30) considered the question and concluded that although the standard of proof should be high, there should be no rigid restrictions on the nature of the evidence admissible (or on its weight) on a claim of rectification of a will (n 3 supra, para 65). In the absence of anything in the section to the contrary this is probably the position.

[6.4]

Rectification and negligence actions. Where a disappointed beneficiary sues a solicitor draftsman alleging negligence in the drafting of the will, the court would expect the plaintiff in such circumstances to mitigate his damage by bringing proceedings for rectification of the will under the AJA 1982, s 20, where such an action would be an appropriate remedy.[1]

1 *Walker v Geo H Medlicott & Son (a firm)* [1999] 1 All ER 685. In this case the plaintiff had failed to mitigate his damages by first issuing proceedings for rectification of the will and therefore his claim for negligence against the solicitor draftsman had to fail. In fact both the negligence and any possible rectification claim were held to fail in any event due to insufficiency of proof. It will be appreciated that rectification will not be an appropriate remedy in all circumstances where negligence in the drafting or the preparation of the will is alleged. As to negligence claims against solicitors in connection with wills, see para **[1.5]** supra.

[6.5]

Supplementary. An application for rectification must be made within six months of the date when representation is first taken out (except with the permission of the court).[1] In computing this period certain limited grants (settled land, trust property etc) are left out of account.[2] There is an express provision protecting personal representatives in that they will not be liable for any distribution of the estate, after the six months' period has elapsed, ... 'on the ground that they ought to have taken into account the possibility that the court might permit the making of an application for an order under this section after the end of that period'.[3] However, this is without prejudice to the power of the court to recover any part of the estate so distributed.[4]

1 AJA 1982, s 20(2); Vol 2, Part G, para **[244.96]**.
2 AJA 1982, s 20(4).
3 AJA 1982, s 20(3).
4 AJA 1982, s 20(3).

[6.6]

Procedure. If no probate action has been commenced, an application for rectification of a will may be made to a Registrar.[1] Such an application must be supported by an affidavit setting out the grounds, together with such evidence as can be adduced as to the testator's intentions and identifying which of the paragraphs of the AJA 1982, s 20(1) are claimed to be satisfied.[2] Notice must be given to any person interested under the will whose interest might be affected by the rectification and such persons given opportunity to comment. Where this has been done and the application is unopposed, the Registrar may make the order for rectification.

1 Non-Contentious Probate Rules 1987, SI 1987/2024, r 55(1).
2 SI 1987/2024, r 55(2).

What dispositions may be made

CHAPTER 7

What may be disposed of by will

[7.1]
In general a testator may dispose of any property vested in him at the time of his death for an interest not ceasing on his death.[1] Since the general rule is that every kind of property and interest in property may be the subject of a gift by will, it is proposed to consider first the exceptions to that general rule, that is property or interests in property which cannot be disposed of by will.

1   Interests ceasing on death are life interests (other than interests *per autre vie*) or interests held as a joint tenant (ie as one of two or more joint tenants). An estate or interest held as a joint tenant, whether legal or equitable, passes by survivorship to the other joint tenant or joint tenants. See infra. The power of testamentary disposition cannot be delegated: see para **[9.45]** infra.

[7.2]
Entailed interests. It is not possible to create entailed interests on or after 1 January 1997.[1] Where a person purports by instrument to create an entailed interest after that date, the instrument is not effective to grant an entailed interest but takes effect as a declaration that the property is held in trust absolutely for the grantee.[2] Where there is an existing estate tail, by a will executed on or after 1 January 1926, a tenant in tail of full age can dispose by will of all property of which he is tenant in tail in possession at his death, and of money (including proceeds of property directed to be sold), subject to be invested in the purchase of property, of which, if the money had been so invested, he would have been tenant in tail in possession at his death. Such a gift by will operates as if he had barred the entail and was tenant in fee simple or absolute owner of such property. The devise or bequest must refer either specifically to the property or the instrument under which it was acquired or to entailed property generally. Unless he so disposes of such property, it devolves according to the limitations of the estate tail.[3] In this provision a tenant in tail includes an owner of a base fee in possession who has power to enlarge the base fee into a fee simple without the concurrence of any other person.[4] The provision applies to both entailed interests in land and to entailed interests of personalty.[5]

1   Trusts of Land and Appointment of Trustees Act 1996, s 2(6), Sch 1, para 5. See Vol 2, Part G, para **[246.87]**.
2   Trusts of Land and Appointment of Trustees Act 1996, s 2(6), Sch 1, para 5(1).
3   Law of Property Act 1925, s 176(1); 37 *Halsbury's Statutes* (4th edn) 344; see Vol 2, Part G, para **[244.53]**. If the tenant in tail disposes of part only of the property, the rest of the property devolves according to the estate tail, and similarly if he disposes of part only of his interest as such owner in fee or absolute owner, the interest undisposed of passes according to the entail. The entail takes effect subject to and in default of the disposition by will. A reference to the

property is sufficient although the entailed interest is only in an undivided share of it: *Acheson v Russell* [1951] Ch 67, [1950] 2 All ER 572.

4   Law of Property Act 1925, s 176(3); see Vol 2, Part G, para **[244.53]**.

5   An entailed interest in personalty could not be created before the coming into force of the Law of Property Act 1925, s 130; 37 *Halsbury's Statutes* (4th edn) 288.

[7.3]

Joint tenancy. Property held under a joint tenancy survives to the surviving joint tenant or joint tenants and one of two or more joint tenants has no power to dispose of his interest by will.[1] The rule is applicable to both legal and equitable joint tenancies and a purely legal joint tenancy (ie where the joint tenant has no beneficial interest and which must be a trust estate) is also governed by the rule that a testator cannot now dispose of a trust estate.[2] A joint tenancy may be severed during the lifetime of the joint tenant,[3] but he cannot sever it by any disposition made by his will.[4] Since, however, the will speaks from the death of the testator and he is expressly empowered to devise or bequeath any real or personal estate 'which he shall be entitled to, either at law or in equity, at the time of his death', it is clear that, if there is a severance during the testator's lifetime, a gift in his will made before severance will pass the severed interest in the property and of course a gift made after severance will pass that interest. If there is no severance but the testator by the death of the other joint tenant or tenants becomes the sole survivor, the will can pass the whole interest in the property.[5]

1   *Swift d Neale v Roberts* (1764) 1 Wm Bl 476; *Low v Carter* (1839) 1 Beav 426; *Turner v A-G* (1876) 10 IR Eq 386; *Renouf's Trustees v Haining* 1919 2 SLT 15. The matter is now settled so far as England and Wales is concerned by the Administration of Estates Act 1925, s 3(4); 17 *Halsbury's Statutes* (4th edn) 423, which provides that the interest of a deceased person under a joint tenancy where another tenant survives the deceased is an interest ceasing on his death. It can be noted that by the Trusts of Land and Appointment of Trustees Act 1996, Sch 2, para 4, trusts for sale of land, whether created before or after 1 January 1997, now become trusts of land; statutory trusts for co-owners under Law of Property Act 1925, s 34 (tenants in common) and s 36 (joint tenants) cease to be trusts for sale and become trusts of land.

2   See n 1.

3   Severance would be effected by an assignment of the joint tenant's interest: *Partriche v Powlet* (1740) 2 Atk 54; *Daly v Aldworth* (1863) 15 I Ch R 69; or by a mortgage or charge of his share: *Re Pollard's Estate* (1863) 3 De G J & Sm 541; or by the bankruptcy of the joint tenant: *Re Butler's Trusts, Hughes v Anderson* (1888) 38 Ch D 286; or by a notice in writing given to the other joint tenant or tenants under the Law of Property Act 1925, s 36(2) (as amended by the Trusts of Land and Appointment of Trustees Act 1996, Sch 2, para 4). See *Nielson-Jones v Fedden* [1975] Ch 222, [1974] 3 All ER 38; *Burgess v Rawnsley* [1975] Ch 429, [1975] 3 All ER 142, CA; and *Harris v Goddard* [1983] 3 All ER 242, [1983] 1 WLR 1203, CA; *Goodman v Gallant* [1986] Fam 106, [1986] 1 All ER 311, CA.

4   2 Cru Dig tit 18 Joint Tenancy, c 2, s 19; but an agreement to devise his share in a mutual will followed by a will carrying out the agreement severs the joint tenancy: *Re Hey's Estate, Walker v Gaskill* [1914] P 192.

5   *Re Horton, Lloyd v Hatchett* [1920] 2 Ch 1; *Re Russell, Russell v Chell* (1882) 19 Ch D 432; and see Wills Act 1837, s 24; Vol 2, Part G, para **[244.24]**. Possibly it is necessary that the wording of the gift shall not be such as can only refer to a share in the property.

[7.4]

Statutory tenancies. The scheme of succession to statutory tenancies contained in the Rent Act 1977, Sch 1, Pt 1 has been modified with effect from 15 January 1989 by the Housing Act 1988.[1] Succession to a statutory tenancy is only permitted now where the deceased tenant was the original tenant, not a successor to the original tenant, and there is a surviving spouse.[2] Other members of the tenant's family cannot take a statutory tenancy by succession. But a person who was living with the original tenant as his or her wife or husband is to be treated as a spouse for this purpose. Such a person is now included as a spouse and not as a member of the original tenant's family, as under the old law, and does not need to show any period of residence with the tenant.[3]

Statutory succession by other members of the original tenant's family can still occur but will give the successor an assured periodic tenancy rather than a statutory tenancy. The residence requirement for such a successor is now two years and the residence must be in the dwelling house subject to the tenancy.[4]

On the death after 14 January 1989 of a statutory tenant who was a successor to the original tenant, there can be a second succession to the tenancy by a person residing with the first successor provided the residence was for a two year period and the person was a member of the original tenant's family and of the first successor's family, immediately before both deaths. But the successor will take an assured periodic tenancy rather than a statutory tenancy.[5]

The Rent Act 1977 does not apply to a residential tenancy granted on or after 15 January 1989, such a tenancy may be an assured tenancy. Succession to such tenancies by a spouse or a cohabitee can take place. But there is no provision either for a second succession or for succession by a person other than a spouse or deemed spouse of the deceased tenant.[6]

1   See the Housing Act 1988, ss 17(1), 39. The law is complex and this is not intended to be a full discussion; reference should be made to standard texts on Landlord and Tenant.
2   See the Housing Act 1988, ss 17(1), 39. See 139 NLJ 252.
3   See the Housing Act 1988, ss 17(1), 39. As to what constitutes residence, see *Hedgedale Ltd v Hards* [1991] 1 EGLR 118, CA. Succession to public sector tenancies is governed by the Housing Act 1985, ss 87–90. For a case considering the 'residence' requirement, see *Waltham Forest London Borough Council v Thomas* [1992] 2 AC 198, [1992] 3 All ER 244, HL. In *Fitzpatrick v Sterling Housing Association Ltd* [1999] 4 All ER 705, HL, it was held that a homosexual partner could not be a 'spouse' for this purpose but could succeed as a member of the tenant's family.
4   See n 3.
5   See n 3.
6   See n 3. It can be noted that on the death of a tenant intestate the tenancy now vests in the Public Trustee, Law of Property (Miscellaneous Provisions) Act 1994, s 14, repealing Law of Property Act 1925, s 55(1).

[7.5]

Agricultural tenancies. In the case of tenancies created before 12 July 1984[1] there was a statutory scheme for the succession to an agricultural holding on the death of the tenant embodied in the Agricultural (Miscellaneous Provisions) Act 1976.[2] This scheme was abolished for tenancies created after that date by the Agricultural Holdings Act 1984,[3] which preserved a number of exceptions. The rules relating to succession, both on death and retirement, which are complex but of major importance to both landlords and tenants alike, are now to be found in the Agricultural Holdings Act 1986.[4] Although protected tenancies being tenancies of agricultural holdings as defined by the Agricultural Holdings Act 1986 can no longer be created since 1 September 1995, exceptions are provided in the Agricultural Tenancies Act 1995, s 4. These include succession tenancies as therein defined. The succession legislation contained in the Agricultural

Part C   What dispositions may be made

Holdings Act 1986, Part IV, is preserved and remains applicable to those tenancies falling within the Agricultural Holdings Act 1986 which carry with them succession rights.[5]

1   The date when the Agricultural Holdings Act 1984 came into force.
2   See the Agricultural (Miscellaneous Provisions) Act 1976, ss 18–23.
3   For a full discussion, see *Scammell and Densham's Law of Agricultural Holdings* (8th edn) (1997, Butterworths), Part IV.
4   Agricultural Holdings Act 1986, ss 34–48, which repealed and re-enacted the Agricultural (Miscellaneous Provisions) Act 1976 and the Agricultural Holdings Act 1984.
5   Sentences quoted from Scammell and Densham, op cit, see n 3, *Introduction to Part IV* (8th edn), to which reference should be made.

[7.6]

Trust estates. A testator who is a sole or sole surviving trustee has an indirect and limited power over the devolution of the trust estate, without being able in any way to affect the beneficial interests. If he appoints executors of his will, the trust estate will, notwithstanding any testamentary disposition, devolve upon the executors[1] and the executors may follow one of two courses. They have statutory power to exercise the trusts affecting the property themselves,[2] or, if they do not desire to do so, the person expressly nominated to appoint trustees or the executors where no such person is nominated, can appoint a new trustee or trustees of the trust.[3] Thus a testator-trustee can to a limited extent control the devolution of the trust property, but, when the testator is one of two or more trustees, he has no control over the devolution of the trust.

1   Trustee Act 1925, s 18(2); 48 *Halsbury's Statutes* (4th edn) 469; as amended by the Trustee Act 2000.
2   See n 1. They have power to exercise the trust until the appointment of new trustees. Presumably in doing so they are acting as trustees and, if the trust is a trust for sale, the requirement of s 14(2) (as amended by the Trusts of Land and Appointment of Trustees Act 1996, Sch 3, para 3) applies and there must be two trustees.
3   See n 1. Where there is a person nominated by trust for the appointment of trustees, such person has power, even against the wishes of the personal representative, to oust him from the trust and appoint others in his place: *Re Routledge's Trusts* [1909] 1 Ch 280. But see now the Trusts of Land and Appointment of Trustees Act 1996, ss 19–21.

[7.7]

Trust property purchased by trustee. Where trust property is purchased by a nominee of the trustee, although such a purchase can be set aside upon proceedings brought by the beneficiaries under the trust, the trustee, until such proceedings are brought, has an equitable interest in the purchased property of which he can dispose by will.[1] The rights of the beneficiaries do not prevent the trustee disposing of such interest if he dies before such proceedings are brought. The beneficiary under the trustee's will, however, is entitled to receive the purchase money received by the trustee in lieu of the property and also to receive interest on the purchase money accruing after the trustee's death. Interest accruing before death is part of the personal estate of the trustee.[2] The purchase money paid by the trustee becomes part of the trust funds and the beneficiaries are allowed to set the transaction aside only upon repaying from the trust funds the purchase money with interest from the time of its receipt.

68

1   *Re Sherman, Trevenen v Pearce* [1954] 1 All ER 893; *Holder v Holder* [1968] Ch 353, [1968] 1 All ER 665.
2   *Re Sherman, Trevenen v Pearce* [1954] 1 All ER 893.

[7.8]
Confirmation of voidable transaction by will. A voidable transaction may be confirmed by will or codicil provided the testator knew when making the will or codicil that the transaction was voidable;[1] but it is otherwise where there is ignorance of that right.[2]

1   *Stump v Gaby* (1852) 2 De G M & G 623; *Gresley v Mousley* (1859) 4 De G & J 78 (sales by client to solicitor); *Seale v Lowndes* (1868) 17 LT 555 (voidable settlement).
2   *Waters v Thorn* (1856) 22 Beav 547.

[7.9]
Nominations. In the case of certain property, mostly small monetary sums in savings accounts, statute has provided a power of nomination which if exercised will mean that the property will not pass under a will.[1] Such nominations can, in some cases, be made by a person of 16 years of age and are subject to simple rules regarding execution;[2] as such they can provide an informal alternative to a will in respect of the property in question. Indeed the power was originally created to enable persons of modest means to effectively dispose of their small savings without the necessity of executing a formal will.[3] Although more recently larger sums could be nominated in the National Savings Bank,[4] this power has now been removed,[5] and in general the power to nominate is limited to sums not exceeding £5,000.[6] It can also be noted at the outset that the power to nominate savings certificates and stock on the National Savings Stock Register was withdrawn in 1981[7] and the power to nominate sums in the Trustee Savings Bank was removed in 1979.[8]

A nomination may be made in a will, but for it to be effective as a nomination of money in a friendly society for instance, the original will must be left in the custody of the society.[9] For this reason it is usually made as a separate document. On the other hand, an invalid nomination if executed in accordance with the Wills Act 1837, may operate as a will.[10] A nomination has all the elements of a testamentary disposition and all the characteristics of a testamentary document;[11] thus the nomination is ambulatory and is governed by the ordinary principles of lapse and so, if the nominee dies before the nominator, the nomination fails and the money is part of the estate of nomination.[12]

1   See, for example, the Friendly Societies Act 1974, s 66; 19 *Halsbury's Statutes* (4th edn) 93; *A-G v Rowsell* (1844) 36 Ch D 67n; *Re Phillips' Insurance* (1883) 23 Ch D 235; *Urquhart v Butterfield* (1887) 37 Ch D 357; *Bennett v Slater* [1899] 1 QB 45.
2   See the rules governing Friendly Society nominations in para **[7.10]** infra.
3   See Lord Mersey in *Eccles Provident Industrial Co-operative Society v Griffiths* [1912] AC 483 at 490.
4   This was because the power to nominate was limited only by the total permissible investment in the National Savings Bank.
5   The National Savings Bank (Amendment) Regulations 1981, SI 1981/484.
6   See the Administration of Estates (Small Payments) (Increase of Limit) Order 1984, SI 1984/539; the limit was previously £1,500; see SI 1975/1137 and the figure is liable to change.
7   SI 1981/485, 486.
8   SI 1979/259.

9   *Fielding and Lord v Rochdale Equitable Pioneers Society* (1892) 92 LT Jo 431; production of
     the will or the probate to the society is not sufficient; *M'Kee v Meikle* (1893) 27 ILT 100.
10   *Re Baxter's Goods* [1903] P 12.
11   Per Farwell J in *Re Barnes, Ashenden v Heath* [1940] Ch 267 at 273.
12   Per Farwell J in *Re Barnes, Ashenden v Heath* [1940] Ch 267 at 273.

[7.10]
Friendly society nominations. A member of a friendly society, if of the age of
16 upwards, can by nomination specify the person to whom money in the
society is to be paid on his death.[1] This provision does not apply to a member of
a benevolent society or a working men's club.[2] The sum must be one payable on
the death of the member and the total amount which may be so nominated is
subject to rules.[3] Similar provisions apply to industrial and provident societies[4]
and to trade union funds payable on death.[5] It must be in writing,[6] signed by the
nominator,[7] and delivered at or sent to the registered office of the society or
branch or given to its secretary[8] and recorded.[9] All these formalities must be
effected during the life of the nominator.[10] Alternatively, it may be made in a
book kept at the registered office of the society.[11]
    A nomination cannot be revoked by will unless the original will is left in the
custody of the society at the registered office as in the case of a nomination by
will;[12] but it is revoked by the subsequent marriage of the nominator.[13]

1   See now the Friendly Societies Act 1974 (FSA 1974), ss 66–69; 19 *Halsbury's Statutes* (4th
     edn) 93–96.
2   FSA 1974, s 66(4).
3   See the Administration of Estates (Small Payments) (Increase of Limit) Order 1984,
     SI 1984/539, £5,000; previously £1,500, see SI 1975/1137, and the figure is liable to change.
4   Industrial and Provident Societies Act 1965, ss 23, 24, 21 *Halsbury's Statutes* (4th edn) 1084,
     also subject to the amending SI 1975/1137, and SI 1984/539, supra.
5   Trade Union and Labour Relations (Consolidation) Act 1992, s 17(1); 16 *Halsbury's Statutes*
     (4th edn) 205. A member of a trade union can nominate a person to become entitled to the
     whole or part of the moneys payable at his death out of the funds of the trade union of which he
     is a member; see the Trade Union (Nominations) Regulations 1977, SI 1977/789.
6   Friendly Societies Act 1974, s 66; 19 *Halsbury's Statutes* (4th edn) 93. It may be printed;
     Interpretation Act 1978, Sch 1; 41 *Halsbury's Statutes* (4th edn) 592.
7   Signature by mark has been said to be insufficient even where attested by two witnesses:
     Morton v French 1908 SC 171. But see *Re Gill* (1920) CR Rep 63 (mark held sufficient).
8   Friendly Societies Act 1974, s 66; *Hughes v Hardy* (1885) Diprose & Gammon 402.
9   Friendly Societies Act 1974, s 66; *Hughes v Hardy* (1885) Diprose & Gammon 402.
10   *Fielding and Lord v Rochdale Equitable Pioneers Society* (1892) 92 LT Jo 431.
11   FSA 1974, s 66.
12   FSA 1974, s 66(6); *M'Kee v Meikle* (1893) 27 ILT 100; *Fielding and Lord v Rochdale
     Equitable Pioneers Society* (1892) 92 LT Jo 431; *Lavin v Howley* (1897) 102 LT Jo 560;
     Bennett v Slater [1899] 1 QB 45.
13   FSA 1974, s 66(7).

[7.11]
Savings bank nominations. The power to nominate sums in the National
Savings Bank was removed in 1981, so that a nomination made after 30 April
1981 is of no effect.[1] However, nominations made before that date remain
effective and thus the provisions can be shortly noted.[2] A depositor of sixteen
years and more could nominate any person to receive any sum due to him at his
death, subject to the discretionary power of the Director of Savings to refuse to
accept a nomination.[3] The amount that could be so nominated was limited only

by the maximum that could be invested in ordinary and investment accounts.[4] Every nomination had to be in writing in the prescribed form, and signed by the nominator in the presence of a witness and the witness had to attest the signature.[5] A nomination was of no effect unless it was sent to the Director of Savings during the lifetime of the nominator; on receipt he had to register it and return it to the nominator.[6] A person who attested the signature of a nominator could not benefit under the nomination.[7] A nomination could be in favour of one or more persons, and where there was more than one nominee it could direct that specific sums should be paid to one or more of the nominees or that the nominees should take the money nominated in specified shares, or it could give directions to both effects.[8] A nomination was revoked by any of the following: by the death of the nominee, or all the nominees, in the lifetime of the nominator; by a written notice of revocation, sent to the Director of Savings in the lifetime of the nominator, signed by the nominator in the presence of a witness who had attested his signature; by a subsequent nomination either wholly or pro tanto; by the marriage of the nominator.[9] Apart from these situations a nomination was not revoked by a will. Where the sum in the National Savings Bank which forms part of the personal estate of a deceased person, does not exceed £5,000,[10] then probate or other proof of the title of the personal representative of the deceased person may be dispensed with and the amount due may be paid to certain specified persons.[11]

Similar provisions, again restricted to nominations made before 1 May 1981, apply to savings certificates.[12]

Nominations of money in the Trustee Savings Bank were possible before 1 May 1979 when the power was withdrawn.[13] Similar rules to those noted above governed such nominations.[14]

---

1   The National Savings Bank (Amendment) Regulations 1981, SI 1981/484.
2   The National Savings Bank Act 1971, s 8; 39 *Halsbury's Statutes* (4th edn) 283; see the National Savings Bank Regulations 1972, SI 1972/764, regs 33–38.
3   The National Savings Bank Act 1971, s 8; 39 *Halsbury's Statutes* (4th edn) 283; see the National Savings Bank Regulations 1972, SI 1972/764, regs 33–38.
4   See the National Savings Bank (Investment Deposits) (Limits) Order 1977, SI 1977/1210, as amended by SI 1981/108, which increased the limit for investment deposits to £200,000.
5   SI 1981/484.
6   SI 1981/484.
7   SI 1981/484.
8   SI 1981/484.
9   SI 1981/484.
10   Administration of Estates (Small Payments) (Increase in Limit) Order 1984, SI 1984/539.
11   See n 10, as amended by the National Savings Bank (Amendment) Regulations 1975, SI 1975/1190. A nomination of money in a savings bank could amount to an advancement for the purposes of Administration of Estates Act 1925, s 47(1)(iii): *Re Hayward, Kerrod v Hayward* [1957] Ch 528, [1957] 2 All ER 474, although not so held in that case.
12   The Savings Certificate Regulations 1972, SI 1972/641, as amended by the Savings Certificates (Amendment) (No 2) Regulations 1981, SI 1981/486. See also the National Savings Stock Register Regulations 1976, SI 1976/2012, power to nominate likewise withdrawn from 1 May 1981, SI 1981/485.
13   The Trustee Savings Bank (Amendment) Regulations 1979, SI 1979/259. See now the Trustee Savings Bank Act 1985, reorganised as a company.
14   See the Trustee Savings Bank Regulations 1972, SI 1972/583, as amended by SI 1975/1802 which increased the limit on the amount that could be nominated to £1,500, and the figure is liable to change.

[7.12]

Insurance policies. In general the policy moneys payable on a policy effected by the testator on his own life are his own and he can dispose of them as he pleases by his will.[1] The terms of the policy may, however, provide otherwise.[2] In the case of a policy effected under the Married Women's Property Act 1882 the proceeds of a policy taken out by a spouse on his or her life and expressed to be for the benefit of the other spouse or the children or the other spouse and the children or any of them are, so long as any object of the trust remains unperformed, held upon those trusts and do not form part of the estate and are not subject to the deceased's will.[3] The terms of a policy may make the money payable thereunder not subject to disposition by the will of the person taking out such insurance[4] and such limitations are valid not only against persons beneficially entitled on his death but also against his creditors.[5]

1   *Re Phillips Insurance* (1883) 23 Ch D 235 at 247.
2   Policies are now issued for so many different purposes that the terms can often earmark the policy moneys for some special purpose. For cases see *Re Davies, Davies v Davies* [1892] 3 Ch 63, and case cited in n 1, supra.
3   Married Women's Property Act 1882, s 11; 27 *Halsbury's Statutes* (4th edn) 733, as amended by the Family Law Reform Acts 1969 and 1987; see Chapter 72.
4   See case cited in n 1.
5   *Re Flavell, Murray v Flavell* (1883) 25 Ch D 89. See *Gold v Hill, Hill v Gold* [1999] 1 FLR 54 (nomination of beneficiary under life assurance policy).

[7.13]

Pension schemes. The terms of a pension scheme may empower an employee to nominate the person entitled to receive an amount equal to his contributions in the event of his death before entitlement to his pension. The nature of such nominations have been stated by MegarryJ[1] in a passage approved by the Privy Council[2] as follows:

'First, although a nomination had certain testamentary characteristics, and not least that of being ambulatory, it took effect as a contractual arrangement and not as a disposition by the deceased. The contributions and interest did not come to the deceased and then pass on from him by force of his will or the nomination; they went directly from the fund to the nominee, and formed no part of the estate of the deceased. I may say that I think that *Bennett v Slater*[3] and *Eccles Provident Industrial Co-operative Society Ltd v Griffiths*[4] provide some support for this view. Despite certain testamentary characteristics, the nomination takes effect under the trust deed and rules, and the nominee in no way claims through the deceased. Secondly, there is a vast difference, it was said, between a testamentary paper and a disposition of a testamentary nature. A testamentary paper must satisfy the Wills Act 1837; but a disposition might have certain testamentary characteristics without the paper containing it being a testamentary paper. Indeed, counsel for the plaintiffs urged that a nomination was sui generis, with some of the characteristics of an appointment under a power, some of the characteristics of a will, and some of the characteristics of a donatio mortis causa. As Alice said, curiouser and curiouser. I appreciate the force of these arguments. Non-statutory nominations are odd creatures, and the cases provide little help on their nature. I do not, however, think that a nomination under the trust deed and rules in the present case requires execution as a will. It seems to me that such a nomination operates by force of the provisions of those rules, and not as a testamentary disposition by the deceased. Further, although the nomination has certain testamentary characteristics, I do not think that these suffice to make the paper on which it is written a testamentary paper. Accordingly, in my judgment the requirements of the Wills Act 1837 have no application.'

In that case a nomination signed in the presence of a single witness was held to be effective since it was not in the nature of a testamentary disposition required to be executed as a will. In the later case[5] the deceased had nominated, in accordance with the rules of a pension scheme, his brother as beneficiary in the event, which happened, of his death in service. Subsequently he married but did not vary or revoke the nomination of his brother as beneficiary. His widow argued that the nomination was a testamentary disposition which was only valid if it was executed with the formalities required for a will, which it was not. The first instance judge ruled in favour of the brother and the widow's appeal was dismissed by both the Court of Appeal of Trinidad and Tobago and by the Privy Council. By becoming party to the scheme each employee constituted himself both a beneficiary and (quoad his contributions to the trust fund from which benefits are payable) a settlor. He retained no proprietary interests in his contributions but received instead such rights, including the right to appoint interests in the fund to take effect on the occurrence of specified contingencies, as the trusts of the fund conferred on him. Thus the power to appoint death in service benefits was no different from any power of appointment. As such it was not testamentary in character. This was confirmed in the present case by the fact that the nomination lacked the essential characteristic of being freely revocable since it could be made and revoked or altered only with the consent of the management committee.

1   *Re Danish Bacon Co Ltd Staff Pension Fund, Christensen v Arnett* [1971] 1 All ER 486 at 493.
2   *Baird v Baird* [1990] 2 AC 548 at 558, [1990] 2 All ER 300 at 307, PC.
3   [1899] 1 QB 45, CA.
4   [1912] AC 483 at 490, HL.
5   *Baird v Baird* [1990] 2 AC 548 at 558, [1990] 2 All ER 300 at 307, PC.

[7.14]
Shares in a company. If the articles of a company so provide, a testator may have no power or only a restricted power of disposing of his shares in the company,[1] but apart from such restriction, such shares are as freely disposable by will as any other form of property. A sole administrator who is the sole beneficiary of an intestate can dispose by will of shares forming part of the intestate's estate, even though the shares are still registered in the intestate's name and even though the administrator has made no formal assent in his own favour in respect of any part of the intestate's estate.[2]

1   Companies Acts; 8 *Halsbury's Statutes* (4th edn) 1999 Reissue. Reference should be made to specialist texts on company law for a full discussion.
2   *Re Leigh's Will Trusts, Handyside v Durbridge* [1970] Ch 277, [1969] 3 All ER 432, applying *Stamp Duties Comr v Livingston* [1965] AC 694, [1964] 3 All ER 692, and dictum of Lord Hatherley in *Cooper v Cooper* (1874) LR 7 HL 53 at 71.

[7.15]
Partnership interests. It has been held in an Australian case that even if a partnership has been dissolved by the testator's death, the testator's interest in the partnership did not thereby cease to exist and so might validly be bequeathed by will.[1]

1   *Re Miller* [1991] 1 Qd R 359.

[7.16]
Mortgage estates. The legal estate held by the mortgagee has since 1881 devolved on the personal representative of a sole or sole surviving mortgagee,[1] but the mortgagee may dispose by will of the debt, and then the personal representative will be bound to transfer the mortgage to the beneficiary subject to his rights in due administration of the estate. In the case of a contributory mortgage, each mortgagee can dispose of his share in the debt where such a debt is held in separate shares.[2]

1   The relevant statutory enactment is now the Administration of Estates Act 1925, ss 1, 3; 17 *Halsbury's Statutes* (4th edn) 421, 423.
2   The legal term is held in joint tenancy (Law of Property Act 1925, s 36, as amended by the Trusts of Land and Appointment of Trustees Act 1996; 37 *Halsbury's Statutes* (4th edn) 164), and will pass on the death of one of the contributors to the survivor or survivors who are trustees bound to give effect to the disposition. If there is any reason to suppose that there may be any difficulty in securing such disposition, the legal estate may be vested in a trust corporation. For full security of the beneficiary under a disposition of the share, the surviving mortgagee or mortagees should transfer the mortgage to themselves and the beneficiary and execute a new memorandum as to the right to the individual shares.

[7.17]
Property not belonging to testator. The will can only dispose of property, or an interest in property belonging to the testator at the time of his death, except in so far as he has a testamentary power of appointment over property. Any disposition of property in which the testator has never had an interest or of property in which he had an interest at the date of his will but has since disposed of in his lifetime must fail.[1]

1   As to the first branch of this statement, it does happen from time to time that testators attempt to dispose of property in which they have never had any interest at all, and such a disposition clearly fails, but may raise a case of election on the part of the donee; see Chapter 42. As to the second branch, the disposition may be saved by the exceptions to the doctrine of ademption; see Chapter 41. In some few cases the property or interest in property may cease to exist and so become subject to the doctrine of ademption. It has already been shown that a gift of property held in beneficial joint tenancy at the date of the death must fail.

[7.18]
General rule allowing testamentary disposition. Subject as already stated, a testator of full capacity may dispose by will of the equitable interest[1] in any property[2] to which he is entitled at the time of his death,[3] always subject to the paramount interest in such property which by law devolves on the personal representative for the purpose of due administration[4] and to the possibility of an application under the Inheritance (Provision for Family and Dependants) Act 1975.[5] Some special classes of property require a little further consideration.

1   Prior to 1926 the testator could dispose by will of both the legal and equitable interest: Wills
     Act 1837, s 3; see Vol 2, Part G, para **[244.4]**, but by the Law of Property (Amendment) Act
     1924, Sch 9, No 3 (37 *Halsbury's Statutes* (4th edn) 119) the Wills Act 1837 takes effect to
     enable equitable interests to be disposed of subject and without prejudice to the estate and
     powers of a personal representative. Since 1926 the legal estate passes to the personal
     representative by statute (Administration of Estates Act 1925, s 1; 17 *Halsbury's Statutes* (4th
     edn) 421), and it is apprehended that the personal representative also takes by virtue of the
     statute, the equitable or beneficial interest for he takes the property in like manner as chattels
     real devolved on the personal representative and in the case of chattels real and personalty
     generally the personal representative takes the whole legal and beneficial interest and can
     dispose of the same in due course of administration without reference to the persons entitled
     under the will.
2   Both real and personal estate pass, but for many practical purposes the distinction is between
     land and other property. For this purpose the 'land' is defined in the Administration of Estates
     Act 1925, s 3 (17 *Halsbury's Statutes* (4th edn) 423), and includes both freeholds and chattels
     real and such property held in trust (including settled land) or by way of mortgage or security,
     but not money to arise under a trust for sale of land nor money secured or charged on land.
3   That is, for an interest not ceasing at his death or passing by survivorship.
4   The nature of this paramount interest is stated in n 2.
5   As to the Inheritance (Provision for Family and Dependants) Act 1975, see Chapter 105. An
     application under the Act must be made within six months of the date on which representation
     with respect to the estate of the deceased is first taken out, unless the court gives leave for a
     later application; s 4. After the expiration of this period the personal representative will not be
     liable for having distributed any part of the estate on the ground that he ought to have taken into
     account the possibility of an application under the Act; s 20.

[7.19]

Estates pur autre vie. An interest in property held for the life of another is
devisable so long as the 'other' survives the testator.[1] The interest will pass to
the personal representative of the testator and he will assent to the land vesting
in the devisee as a person having the powers of a tenant for life.[2] Such property
was formerly settled land and subject to the Settled Land Act 1925,[3] but no new
settlements under that Act can be created after 1 January 1997.[4]

1   Wills Act 1837, s 3; 50 *Halsbury's Statutes* (4th edn) 577; see Vol 2, Part G, para **[244.4]**.
2   Settled Land Act 1925, s 20(1)(v); 48 *Halsbury's Statutes* (4th edn) 282. If the 'other' does not
     survive the testator, the gift fails, for it ceases on the death of the 'other'. An estate *pur autre vie*
     can now be created only under a settlement or by the assignment of a life interest under a
     settlement. A lease for the life of another is now a lease for 90 years (or if created after 1925,
     for some such fixed term) determinable by notice after the death of the 'other'. If not
     determined, the lease may continue for the stated period and if the testator dies within that
     period, the interest (which is a leasehold one) will pass under an appropriate gift or as part of
     the residue in the will. Such an interest was not settled land.
3   Being property which was settled land under a settlement not ceasing on the death of the
     testator. This land will normally be the subject of a special or limited grant, and the assent will
     be in the form of a vesting deed under the Settled Land Act, properly called a 'vesting assent' as
     distinct from an 'assent'; see the Settled Land Act 1925, s 117(1)(xxxi); 48 *Halsbury's Statutes*
     (4th edn) 424.
4   By virtue of the Trusts of Land and Appointment of Trustees Act 1996, s 2(1); see Vol 2,
     Part G, para **[246.87]**. Existing settlements are preserved for so long as there is 'relevant
     property': Trusts of Land and Appointment of Trustees Act 1996, s 2(2).

[7.20]

Contingent and future interests. All contingent executory and future interests
in any property are devisable and this is so whether the testator may or may not
be ascertained as the person or one of the persons in whom the same may
become vested[1] and whether he may be entitled thereto under the instrument by

which the same were created or under any disposition thereof by deed or will.[2] Such interests include a possibility coupled with an interest.[3]

1   Wills Act 1837, s 3, 50 *Halsbury's Statutes* (4th edn) 577; see Vol 2, Part G, para **[244.4]**; *Ingilby v Amcotts* (1865) 21 Beav 585; *Re Shannon* [1968] NZLR 852.
2   Wills Act 1837, s 3; see Vol 2, Part G, para **[244.4]**.
3   *Jones v Roe* (1789) 3 Term Rep 88. The possibility must by the time of the death of the testator have ripened into an interest by the death of the named person before the death of the testator (*Re Parsons, Stockley v Parsons* (1890) 45 Ch D 51; *Re Earl of Midleton's Will Trusts, Whitehead v Earl of Midleton* [1969] 1 Ch 600, [1967] 2 All ER 834). But a mere *spes successionis* is not disposable; *Izard v Tamahau Mahupuku* (1902) 22 NZLR 418.

[7.21]
Rights of entry. Rights of entry for condition broken and rights of reverter are devisable.[1]

1   Wills Act 1837, s 3; see Vol 2, Part G, para **[244.4]**. As to devisability of a right of reverter, see *Pemberton v Barnes* [1899] 1 Ch 544.

[7.22]
Interest given under will of another. A testator may devise an interest given to him under the will of another, even where such other person survives him, provided the gift does not lapse.[1]

1   *Re Scott* [1901] 1 KB 228; *Johnson v Johnson* (1843) 3 Hare 157; *Winter v Winter* (1846) 5 Hare 306.

[7.23]
Leaseholds. It has generally been held that the ordinary covenant against assignment without consent does not apply to a specific or a general bequest of leaseholds.[1] In any case it would not now apply to a gift by will as that can only pass an equitable interest,[2] and the only question can be whether the executor on assenting to the property vesting in the legatee requires the consent of the lessor.[3] A decision in 1949, though not concerned with gifts by will, has cast some doubt upon the position.[4]

1   *Fox v Swann* (1655) Sty 482; *Crusoe d Blencowe v Bugby* (1771) 3 Wils 234 at 237; *Doe d Goodbehere v Bevan* (1815) 3 M & S 353 at 360.
2   Law of Property (Amendment) Act 1924, Sch 9; 37 *Halsbury's Statutes* (4th edn) 119.
3   It depends upon the wording of the covenant whether an equitable assignment is a breach; but a covenant 'not to assign' is only broken by a legal assignment (*Gentle v Faulkner* [1900] 2 QB 267), but a covenant 'not to assign or part with the possession of' forbids an equitable assignment: *Jackson v Simons* [1923] 1 Ch 373.
4   *Re Wright, ex p Landau v Trustee* [1949] Ch 729, [1949] 2 All ER 605. This case deals with the lease passing to a trustee in bankruptcy, but is based on the holding that *Doe d Goodbehere v Bevan* (1815) 3 M & S 353 turned upon the construction of the particular covenant and does not support (as it has been regarded as supporting for nearly 150 years) the proposition that such a covenant does not apply to involuntary assignments and gifts by will. So far as a gift by will is concerned, the law prima facie is not altered, but doubt is clearly cast upon it.

[7.24]
Rent. A rent reserved on a lease may be devised apart from the lease itself.[1]

1   *Ards v Walkin* (1598) Cro Eliz 637; *Re Daveron, Bowen v Churchill* [1893] 3 Ch 421.

[7.25]

Emblements. A testator may devise emblements to which he is entitled by reason of his interest in the land.[1]

1   Growing crops generally pass to the devisee of the land but a contrary intention may be shown by a specific gift of stock on the farm (*Re Roose, Evans v Williamson* (1880) 17 Ch D 696) or of live and dead stock (*Rudge v Winnall* (1849) 12 Beav 357), but a contrary intention is not shown by a mere gift of the residuary personal estate (*Re Roose, Evans v Williamson* (1880) 17 Ch D 696).

[7.26]

Incorporeal hereditaments. These may be devised except in so far as (eg in the case of an easement) they are inseparable from the tenement, when they can be devised only so as to go with the tenement.[1] If they are devised to the owner of the servient tenement, they are extinguished.[2]

1   Wills Act 1837, s 1; 50 *Halsbury's Statutes* (4th edn) 576; see Vol 2, Part G, para **[244.3]**; *Whalley v Tompson* (1799) 1 Bos & P 371 (effect of devise with appurtenances); *Pearson v Spencer* (1863) 3 B & S 761; *Bolton v Bolton* (1879) 11 Ch D 968; *Phillips v Low* [1892] 1 Ch 47; *Schwann v Cotton* [1916] 2 Ch 459.
2   *Whalley v Tompson* (1799) 1 Bos & P 371.

[7.27]

Property agreed to be purchased or sold. The testator's interest in property agreed to be purchased may be devised[1] and also the right to the purchase money where property has been agreed to be sold.[2]

1   *Morgan v Holford* (1852) 1 Sm & G 101; *Re Rix, Steward v Lonsdale* (1921) 90 LJ Ch 474 (gift bad where no enforceable contract).
2   Where there is a binding agreement for sale, the specific devise of the land fails and the purchase money passes as personalty (*Farrar v Lord Winterton* (1842) 5 Beav 1), and see *Lysaght v Edwards* (1876) 2 Ch D 499. The devise being ineffective, the testator may by a new will or codicil bequeath the purchase money to a particular legatee or let it pass as residuary personalty. A specific devise is saved, however, where the devise is subsequent to the binding agreement for sale (*Drant v Vause* (1842) 1 Y & C Ch Cas 580; *Emuss v Smith* (1848) 2 De G & Sm 722; *Re Calow, Calow v Calow* [1928] Ch 710), and in such case the devisee is entitled to the purchase money. Where the will was confirmed by a codicil on the same day as the agreement, the devise was held to carry the proceeds of sale (*Re Pyle, Pyle v Pyle* [1895] 1 Ch 724). The devisee is entitled to the rents and profits until completion: *Collingwood v Row* (1857) 26 LJ Ch 649.

[7.28]

Choses in action. These whatever their nature may be bequeathed by will but a bequest of a debt does not entitle the legatee to sue. The right to sue is in the personal representative and not in the legatee, unless he happens also to be the personal representative.[1]

1   *Bishop v Curtis* (1852) 18 QB 878; *Re Leigh's Will Trusts, Handyside v Durbridge* [1970] Ch 277, [1969] 3 All ER 432 (testatrix as sole administrator and sole beneficiary of intestate entitled to money owing to intestate; held she could dispose of the benefit of the debt by her will).

[7.29]

Rights of action. Such rights vested in the testator at his death may be devised in so far as they do not cease on the death of the testator and remain enforceable by the personal representative.[1]

1   *Twycross v Grant* (1878) 4 CPD 40.

[7.30]
State of testator's title. The state of the testator's title has no effect on the power to devise or bequeath, but he can only devise or bequeath, and the devisee or the legatee can only get, what the testator had at the time of his death. A mere possessory title is devisable.[1]

1   *Asher v Whitlock* (1865) LR 1 QB 1; *Clarke v Clarke* (1868) IR 2 CL 395; *Calder v Alexander* (1900) 16 TLR 294.

[7.31]
Co-owners. Tenants in common can bequeath their share in the proceeds of sale of land and their interest in other property. Joint tenants, however, as already stated,[1] cannot devise their shares. The power to give partnership property by will is often controlled by the terms of the partnership deed.[2] Where a testator made a gift of all his livestock and all his real estate and the only livestock and real estate he had was his interest in a partnership including such property, it was held that the gift passed the interest in such property which was part of his share of the partnership.[3]

1   See para [7.3] supra.
2   *Robertson v Quiddington* (1860) 28 Beav 529.
3   *Hendry v Perpetual Executors and Trustees Association of Australia Ltd* (1961) 106 CLR 256.

[7.32]
Contract to leave specific property to specific person. It has already been shown that a testator may restrict his power of disposition by contract.[1]

1   See Chapter 3.

[7.33]
Funeral and burial wishes. A binding disposition of the dead body of the testator cannot be made by will so as to oust the executors' rights and duties as to its disposal[1] but statutes have allowed some qualification of this position.
    Cremation is not unlawful at common law unless it is done so as to create a nuisance or to prevent the coroner holding an inquest.[2] A direction, therefore, for cremation is valid apart from the statute[3] and, although under the statute and the regulations made thereunder it is not necessary that written directions for cremation should be given, it is not unlawful to cremate the body of a person who has left written directions to the contrary,[4] and cremation must take place in a recognised crematorium.[5] Although it is a common practice for such directions to be included in a will, it is not the most convenient method of giving such directions as the will may not be found or not be opened before the funeral.
    The testator can if he so desires give directions as to funeral[6] or the erection of tombstone or other monument[7] and provide for the maintenance of his grave.[8] He may, where he desires to be cremated, arrange for the disposal of his ashes. These may be buried or scattered on consecrated ground[9] or under a church even after it has been closed for burial subject to a faculty from the ordinary.[10] A fortiori they may be scattered or kept in an urn in any unconsecrated place. In the absence of a direction by the testator, the person who applies for cremation may arrange for such disposal[11] and in the absence of any such direction they

will be decently interred in a burial ground or land adjoining the crematorium or scattered thereon.[12]

1   *Williams v Williams* (1882) 20 Ch D 659. The doubt expressed in this case as to the legality of cremation has been departed from; see cases in n 13: *Hunter v Hunter* [1930] 4 DLR 255.
2   *R v Price* (1884) 12 QBD 247; *R v Stephenson* (1884) 13 QBD 331.
3   Cremation Act 1902; 5 *Halsbury's Statutes* (4th edn) 840; Cremation Regulations 1930, SR & O 1930/1016, as amended by the Cremation Regulations 1965, SI 1965/1146. The procedure relating to cremation is slightly amended by the Cremation Act 1952, and regulations made thereunder.
4   Formerly there was such a prohibition by virtue of reg 4 of the Cremation Regulations, but this regulation has now been revoked: Cremation Regulations 1965, SI 1965/1146.
5   Cremation Regulations 1930, SR & O 1930/1016, reg 3.
6   Such directions are in general better given in a separate writing to be opened immediately on death; but, if the testator desires any specific arrangement which is likely to increase the funeral expenses beyond what is reasonable for a person of his rank, he should also include them in his will with an authority to pay out of his estate all such expenses as the proper carrying out of such directions shall entail and the executor's decision as to what is reasonable and proper in accordance with the direction should be made conclusive on all parties; see *Re Read, Galloway v Harris* (1892) 36 Sol Jo 626. Where an executrix was directed to spend £300 on the funeral and grave, it was held she was entitled to spend that sum or any smaller sum she thought proper: *Re Pearce* [1946] SASR 118.
7   See *Re Dean, Cooper-Dean v Stevens* (1889) 41 Ch D 552. It would appear that the cost of a monument is not funeral expenses (*Hart v Griffith-Jones* [1948] 2 All ER 729); but as to a tombstone, see *Goldstein v Salvation Army Assurance Society* [1917] 2 KB 291, where the question is said to be one of fact.
8   See para **[9.29]** infra.
9   *Re Dixon* [1892] P 386.
10   *Re Kerr* [1894] P 284.
11   Cremation Regulations 1930, SR & O 1930/1016, reg 16.
12   Cremation Regulations 1930, SR & O 1930/1016, reg 16.

[7.34]

Anatomical examination and therapeutic use. The testator may in writing, or by the declaration in the presence of two witnesses during the illness from which he dies, direct the anatomical examination of his body after death.[1] If the person lawfully in possession of the body after death has no reason to believe that the request was withdrawn, he may authorise the use of the body in accordance with the request.[2] Further the person lawfully in possession of a body may authorise it to be used for anatomical examination if having made such reasonable inquiry as may be practical he has no reason to believe that the deceased has formally expressed an objection or that the surviving spouse or any surviving relatives of the deceased object to the body being so used.[3]

The testator may desire to direct such examination of his body by skilled persons as may ensure that he shall not be buried alive. Any such direction as above should authorise the executor to pay all reasonable expenses incurred thereby out of the estate.[4]

By the Human Tissue Act 1961, a deceased may authorise the use of his eyes or his body or any part thereof for therapeutic purposes.[5] The removal and use of any part of the body may be authorised by the person lawfully in possession of the body where the deceased has orally or in writing in the presence of witnesses indicated that his body may be used for therapeutic purposes and there is no reason to believe that this request was subsequently withdrawn, or where the person lawfully in possession of the body has no reason to believe that the deceased had expressed an objection to such use and that the surviving spouse or any surviving relative does not object to such use.[6] It is desirable that express written permission for anatomical examination or for therapeutic use should be included in the will where this is desired. Donor cards can be useful in addition.

1   Anatomy Act 1984 (AA 1984), s 4(1); see Vol 2, paras **[202.8]** to **[202.17]**.
2   AA 1984, s 4(2).
3   AA 1984, s 4(3). The AA 1984 came into force on 14 February 1988.
4   Such expenses are no doubt properly paid by the executor out of the estate without such an authority, but an express power will avoid any question.
5   The Human Tissue Act 1961, s 1 appears to be unaffected by the AA 1984 which repeals the Human Tissue Act 1961, s 2(1) and s 3.

CHAPTER 8

Interests which may be created by will

[8.1]
General nature of power of disposition. The power of disposition by will is
not at the testator's caprice, but extends only to the creation of those interests
which are recognised by law,[1] and is limited by the extent of the testator's
interest in the property the subject of the disposition. Thus, as examples of the
former class of restriction the testator cannot create an easement in gross or a
disposition offending the rule against perpetuities,[2] and as examples of the latter,
a testator possessed of property for a leasehold interest can dispose of the
property only for the residue of such period as the lease grants[3] and a testator
holding property for the life of another can dispose of it only for the period of
that life and provided he predeceases the *cestui que vie.*

1   *Egerton v Earl of Brownlow* (1853) 4 HL Cas 1 at 242; *Re Elliot, Kelly v Elliot* [1896] 2 Ch 353
     at 356; *Re Wallace, Champion v Wallace* [1920] 2 Ch 274.
2   As to the rule of perpetuities and wills, see Chapter 94.
3   Or such shorter period as the lease subsists where it is determinable under an option, power of
     re-entry or notice to quit.

[8.2]
Form of creation of interests. No new settlements can be created after 1
January 1997,[1] under the Settled Land Act 1925.[2] Further trusts for sale of land,
whether created before or after 1 January 1997,[3] now become trusts of land.
Trusts of sale are not abolished, but the Trusts of Land and Appointment of
Trustees Act 1996 seeks to create a set of rules under which it makes no
practical difference whether or not there is a trust for sale, by providing a
common set of powers and provisions which apply to all 'trusts of land' whether
or not there is a trust for sale.[4] Consequently, there is no longer any necessity for
gifts of land by will to be by way of disposition on trust for sale in order to avoid
the land becoming settled land.[5]
    Provided the interests are known to the law, it is not essential that they should
be created in the form in which the law now requires them to be held.
    The testator may give a beneficiary such rights to secure his legacy as the law
allows. Thus a legacy may be charged upon specific land and in addition the
legatee may be given a right of entry upon the land to enforce the payment of his
legacy.[6]
    A gift may be given subject to conditions but the law will in certain cases
disregard the conditions where these are illegal or contrary to public policy.[7] In
some cases, in place of inserting a condition, the gift may be made for a period.

Then, if the period is to be determined by the consideration of matters which the law considers contrary to public policy, the gift may be void.[8]

1   The date when the Trusts of Land and Appointment of Trustees Act 1996 came into force.
2   Trusts of Land and Appointment of Trustees Act 1996, s 2(1). Existing settlements are preserved so long as there remains 'relevant property' subject to the settlement: Trusts of Land and Appointment of Trustees Act 1996, s 2(2).
3   See n 1.
4   See Trusts of Land and Appointment of Trustees Act 1996, s 4. Implied trusts for sale become trusts of land: Trusts of Land and Appointment of Trustees Act 1996, s 5. In both cases with a power but not a duty to sell: ss 4, 5.
5   This is the consequence of the prospective abolition of Settled Land Act settlements and the reformulation of trusts for sale into trusts of land; Trusts of Land and Appointment of Trustees Act 1996, ss 2, 3, 4 and 5. See Vol 2, Part G, para **[246.87]** et seq.
6   *Wigg v Wigg* (1739) West *temp* Hard 677; *Emes v Hancock* (1743) 2 Atk 507; *Sherman v Collins* (1745) 3 Atk 319. Now it will probably be sufficient to say that the beneficiary shall have all the remedies for securing payment of the legacy as if it were an annual sum charged upon land. As to such remedies, see Law of Property Act 1925, s 121; 37 *Halsbury's Statutes* (4th edn) 284. If the legacy is a mere equitable charge on the land, the enforcement is regulated by the Law of Property Act 1925, s 90; 37 *Halsbury's Statutes* (4th edn) 242, or by obtaining the appointment of a receiver, both of which entail applications to the court.
7   As to conditions and the effect of their being illegal or void, see Chapter 34, para **[34.17]** infra.
8   *Re Moore, Trafford v Maconochie* (1888) 39 Ch D 116. If the period is indefinite, the gift may be void for uncertainty; see para **[34.9]** infra. If the words are not part of the limitation but impose a condition, it may be possible to reject them: *Re Lovell, Sparks v Southall* [1920] 1 Ch 122.

[8.3]
Gifts of chattels not consumed in use for successive interests. Such gifts are more conveniently made by vesting the chattels in trustees;[1] but they can be made by will without the intervention of trustees as executory bequests so as to confer legal rights on the second and subsequent donees[2] indefeasible by any act or default on the part of the first donee.[3] The courts will protect the interests of the ulterior legatee in specific chattels the loss of which cannot be compensated for in damages, by compelling the legatee for life to give an inventory.[4]

1   Such goods are in the usual case household furniture and effects and it is necessary to provide for their repair and insurance against fire and burglary and possibly other risks. Repair is the liability of the tenant for life but he is under no liability to insure apart from a special provision in the will. Since the tenant for life is usually the widow, it is better to vest the furniture in trustees and make them responsible for both repairs and insurance, the cost of which is commonly charged against the income of the widow. The trustees will be required to apply all insurance moneys received in replacement or re-instatement of the chattels. It is, however, still quite common to vest the chattels in the widow for life and then the trustees are relieved by the terms of the will from all liability in respect of them.
2   *Vachel v Vachel* (1669) 1 Cas in Ch 129; *Clarges v Albemarle* (1691) 2 Vern 245; *Hyde v Parrat* (1696) 1 P Wms 1; *Tissen v Tissen* (1718) 1 P Wms 500. The subsequent donees may sue in trover for the chattels: *Hoare v Parker* (1788) 2 Term Rep 376. The first donee has been said to take in trust or as bailee for the subsequent donees and to be liable to make good any loss caused by improper use (*Re Swan, Witham v Swan* [1915] 1 Ch 829). The interest of a subsequent donee during the continuance of the interest of the first donee is a transmissible interest (*Doe d Roberts v Polgrean* (1791) 1 Hy Bl 535).
3   *Cotton v Heath* (1638) Poll 26; *Fonnereau v Fonnereau* (1745) 3 Atk 315.
4   *Foley v Burnell* (1783) 1 Bro CC 274 at 279; *Conduitt v Soane* (1844) 1 Coll 285; *Temple v Thring* (1887) 56 LJ Ch 767. For a case where compensation for loss was awarded to the subsequent donee, see *Re Swan, Witham v Swan* [1915] 1 Ch 829.

[8.4]

Gifts of chattels consumed in use for successive interests. Generally an attempt to limit successive interests in such chattels will fail, and, upon the ground that the chattels and their use have no separate existence[1] the gift will be construed as an absolute gift to the first taker.[2] There are, however, exceptions to this rule.[3] Where, by the terms of the will or the circumstances of the case, such chattels are given to successive donees in the character of money's worth, personal use or consumption is not intended.[4] Where such chattels are included in a residuary gift, they must be sold and the proceeds treated as capital of the residuary gift,[5] unless by the terms of the will, the first taker is given the right to enjoy them in specie.[6] The first taker may be made responsible for the value of such chattels[7] and the testator may in express terms give the first taker a right to consume so much as he shall require and make a gift over of the amount remaining.[8]

1   *Randall v Russell* (1817) 3 Mer 190 at 195.
2   *Randall v Russell* (1817) 3 Mer 190 (corn and hay); *Andrew v Andrew* (1845) 1 Coll 686 (wine and spirits); *Montresor v Montresor* (1845) 1 Coll 693 (wine and provisions); *Bryant v Easterson* (1859) 32 LTOS 352 (farming stock); *Phillips v Beal* (1862) 32 Beav 25 (wine for household consumption); *Breton v Mockett* (1878) 9 Ch D 95 (live and dead stock). The fact that a gift of personal estate for successive interests may include such articles has been considered in the construction of the gift and has operated to exclude such articles: see *Porter v Tournay* (1797) 3 Ves 311; *Manning v Purcell* (1855) 7 De GM & G 55 at 61; *Randfield v Randfield* (1860) 8 HL Cas 225 at 236; *Re Moir's Estate, Moir v Warner* [1882] WN 139. A testator can, however, limit the first donee's interest to the amount consumed and make a valid subsequent gift of the amount not consumed: *Re Colyer, Millikin v Snelling* (1886) 55 LT 344.
3   An unusual exception was a gift of male clothing to a female tenant for life; see *Re Hall's Will* (1855) 1 Jur NS 974.
4   The cases mostly concern farming or live stock intended to be kept up by the tenant for life; *Montresor v Montresor* (1845) 1 Coll 693; *Groves v Wright* (1856) 2 K & J 347; *Cockayne v Harrison* (1872) LR 13 Eq 432; *Myers v Washbrook* [1901] 1 KB 360; *Griffin v McCabe* (1918) 52 ILT 134; *Beresford v Preston* (1920) 54 ILT 48. The first taker in such cases must keep up the value of the stock but he is entitled to any increased value as profits: *Re Powell, Dodd v Williams* [1921] 1 Ch 178. For the application of the role to wine of a wine merchant's business, see *Phillips v Beal* (1862) 32 Beav 25, and to deer in a park; see *Maynard v Gibson* [1876] WN 204; *Paine v Warwick* [1914] 2 KB 486. For its application to pigeons in a dovecote, see *Maynard v Gibson* [1876] WN 204. It may be that the growing crops on a farm are taken in absolutely by the first taker: *Steward v Cotton* (1777) 5 Russ 17n; but in *Bryant v Easterson* (1859) 32 LTOS 352, this conclusion was reached because the testator had not ordered a valuation, and in *Myers v Washbrook* [1901] 1 KB 360, the opposite conclusion was reached.
5   That is the rule in *Howe v Earl of Dartmouth* (1802) 7 Ves 137; *Randall v Russell* (1817) 3 Mer 190; see para **[38.17]** infra.
6   *Re Bagshaw's Trusts* (1877) 46 LJ Ch 567.
7   *Deering v Hanbury* (1687) 1 Vern 478; *Connolly v Connolly* (1887) 56 LT 304; *Re Powell, Dodd v Williams* [1921] 1 Ch 178.
8   *Re Colyer, Millikin v Snelling* (1886) 55 LT 344.

[8.5]

Assent to first taker is assent to all. The property in such chattels will be vested in the legatee or legatees by the assent of the executor. Not being an interest in land to which the Administration of Estates Act 1925, s 36 applies, the old common law rules will regulate such assent. Not only will it not be required to be in writing, but also an assent to the gift to the first taker will, without more, also be an assent to the gifts to the subsequent donees (if, under the authorities already referred to, they take any interest in the chattels).[1] The executor is not, therefore, so far as the assent is concerned, obliged to consider or to decide whether or not the subsequent donees have any interest in the chattels, but, of course, if he is also a trustee, he will at some time have to resolve this problem.

1   *Foley v Burnell* (1789) 4 Bro Parl Cas 34; *Stevenson v Liverpool Corpn* (1874) LR 10 QB 81.

[8.6]
Options. The testator may give a donee a mere option to purchase property.[1]

1   See Chapter 92.

[8.7]
Rights of selection. A testator having several properties of the same description may give a donee a right of selection of one or more of such properties[1] or he may give the donee a right to select from them property to a stated amount or value.[2] The right to select may be expressly stated or may appear by inference.[3] If no limit is placed on the selection, the donee may take all the properties if he so desires.[4] Where a number of similar properties are given to an equal number of beneficiaries, the selection is to be made by the beneficiaries in the order in which they are named in the will[5] and where in such a case some beneficiaries are collectively referred to, such as children or nephews or nieces, then the order of selection must be determined by lot.[6] Where by the imperfect wording of the will a testator gives one of several similar properties to a donee and the court is unable to say from the will itself or from extrinsic evidence which of the properties the testator intended the donee to take, the gift fails for uncertainty and the donee cannot select one of the properties.[7] Where a right of selection is given to one donee, and a second donee is to take the residue of the property, and if the first donee predeceases the testator so that he cannot make the selection, the gift to the second donee fails.[8] The right of selection is purely personal to the donee, and, if he dies without having made the selection, the right does not pass to his personal representatives[9] and a donee, once having made a selection, has no power to give up the selected property and make a second selection and any permission by trustees for him to do so is ultra vires.[10]

1   *Asten v Asten* [1894] 3 Ch 260; *Harby v Moore* (1860) 3 LT 209; *Re Collin's Settlement Trusts, Donne v Hewetson* [1971] 1 All ER 283, [1971] 1 WLR 37; *Re Sapusak* (1984) 8 DLR (4th) 158; *Re Barlow's Will Trusts* [1979] 1 All ER 296, [1979] 1 WLR 278.
2   *Earl of Bandon v Moreland* [1910] 1 IR 220.
3   *Hobson v Blackburn* (1883) 1 My & K 571 (grant of 10 acres adjoining or surrounding a particular house); *Tapley v Eagleton* (1879) 12 Ch D 683 (two houses in a street where testator owned three); *Duckmanton v Duckmanton* (1860) 5 H & N 219 (one close in the field); *Jacques v Chambers* (1846) 2 Coll 435 (gift of 30 shares out of 120, legatee entitled to select and to select fully-paid shares rather than partly-paid shares); *Millard v Bailey* (1866) LR 1 Eq 378 (similar case); *O'Donnell v Welsh* [1903] 1 IR 115 (similar case where shares of unequal value). In *Re Cheadle, Bishop v Holt* [1900] 2 Ch 620, CA it was held on the construction of the will that the legatee had no right of selection between fully-paid and partly-paid shares, but in *Re Eager* [1952] St R Qd 105, where the testator held 20,000 shares of different kinds in each of two companies and bequeathed 4,000 shares to A, it was held that this was a specific gift and A had a right to select what shares he would take. In *Wilson v Wilson* (1847) 1 De G & Sm 152, a legatee was given £500 or an annuity of £25 for life and it was held that the choice lay not with

the legatee but with those interested in the property subject to the annuity. *Re Boddington, Boddington v Clairat* (1884) 25 Ch D 685, was a similar case but the annuity was given to the legatee so long as she should continue to be the widow of the testator. As a decree of nullity of the marriage had been made, the legatee could not be the widow and as the annuity failed for this reason, it was held that the legatee had no right to the alternative sum of money. To some extent a will may grant a right of selection of beneficiaries to trustees; *Re Johnson* [1928] SASR 490; but this must not be such a delegation that the trustees have in effect to make testator's will for him. *Houston v Burns* [1918] AC 337 at 342; *A-G v National Provincial Bank* [1924] AC 262; *Re Abrahams' Will Trusts, Caplan v Abrahams* [1969] 1 Ch 463, [1967] 2 All ER 1175 (a power for trustees to settle moneys for the benefit of certain specified persons and 'with such ulterior or ultimate trusts' as the trustees should think fit was not void as amounting to a delegation of the testator's power of making a will); *Re Flavel's Will Trusts, Coleman v Flavel* [1969] 2 All ER 232; *Lutheran Church of Australia, etc v Farmers Cooperative Executors and Trustees Ltd* (1969–70) 121 CLR 628; *Buckle v Bristow* (1864) 5 New Rep 7; *Yeap Cheah Neo v Ong Cheng Neo* (1875) LR 6 PC 381; *Re Matthews* [1920] NZLR 135. As to curing uncertainty by selection: see para **[9.46]**, n 1.

4   *Arthur v Mackinnon* (1879) 11 Ch D 385; *Re Sharland, Kemp v Rozey (No 2)* (1896) 74 LT 664; *Re Wavertree, Rutherford v Hall-Walker* [1933] Ch 837. To the contrary, see *Kennedy v Kennedy* (1853) 10 Hare 438, followed in *Re Gillespie, Gillespie v Gillespie* (1902) 22 NZLR 74 (where it was also held that the selection could be made five years after the death of the testator and the legatee had had possession of the furniture).

5   *Re Knapton, Knapton v Hindle* [1941] Ch 428, [1941] 2 All ER 573; *Guild v Mallory* (1983) 144 DLR (3d) 603.

6   *Re Knapton, Knapton v Hindle* [1941] Ch 428, [1941] 2 All ER 573; *Guild v Mallory* (1983) 144 DLR (3d) 603.

7   *Asten v Asten* [1894] 3 Ch 260 at 263; *Re Cheadle, Bishop v Holt* [1900] 2 Ch 620, CA.

8   *Boyce v Boyce* (1849) 16 Sim 476.

9   *Re Madge, Pridie v Bellamy* (1928) 44 TLR 372, approved in *Skelton v Younghouse* [1942] AC 571, [1942] 1 All ER 650.

10   *Littledale v Bickersteth* (1876) 24 WR 507.

[8.8]

Uncertainty. The court must be able to ascertain with sufficient certainty the property and the interest therein the donee is to take, otherwise the gift must fail.[1] Care is needed where the gift comprises part or a specific number out of a larger mass or amount; such a gift can be valid if all the components of the mass are all exactly the same[2] but not if they can not be so regarded.[3]

1   See para **[34.9]** infra.

2   *Hunter v Moss* [1994] 1 WLR 452 (shares).

3   *Re Goldcorp Exchange Ltd* [1995] 1 AC 74 (gold bullion); and *Re London Wine Co (Shippers) Ltd* [1986] Palmer's Company Cases 121.

CHAPTER 9

Who may benefit under a will

[9.1]

Capacity to benefit. Incapacity to benefit under a will does not follow the usual lines of incapacity, but is principally concerned with cases of incapacity peculiar to gifts by will. These are persons dead at the date of the death of the testator, attesting witnesses, the murderer of the testator and persons who have obtained their gifts by fraud or undue influence. The usual forms of incapacity, however, may prevent the donee from being able to give a good discharge for the gift. The gift in such cases is good, the only difficulty being the obtaining of a proper receipt or discharge by the personal representative, and the difficulties thus arising have now been largely provided for by statute.[1]

---

1 Chiefly by the Trustee Act 1925, s 63; 48 *Halsbury's Statutes* (4th edn) 535, enabling a personal representative to pay the legacy or fund into court. See also the Administration of Estates Act 1925, s 42, (s 42(6)(a) has been amended by the Trustee Act 2000, Sch 2, para 37); 17 *Halsbury's Statutes* (4th edn) 448. Special provision may be made in the will for such discharge and in the case of small estates it is especially advisable to insert such a provision.

I. BENEFICIARY PREDECEASING TESTATOR

[9.2]

Persons dead at the death of the testator. In general a gift cannot be made by will to a person dead at the date of the will,[1] and the gift also fails if the donee dies before the testator, even though he is alive at the date of the will.[2] Apart from the statutory exceptions from lapse and apart from the addition of a substitutional gift, the personal representatives of the donee take no interest under such gifts.[3] If any question arises whether the donee survived the testator, the burden of proof is on those claiming the gift;[4] but where it is proved that for a period of seven years no news of a person has been received by those who would naturally hear of him if alive, and that such inquiries and searches as the circumstances suggest have been made, there is a legal presumption of death, but not that such person died at any particular time nor that he continued alive up to the end of the seven years.[5] In appropriate cases the executors or trustees may be given leave to distribute the estate in the *Re Benjamin*[6] form on the basis that a specified person or persons have predeceased the testator. Such an order does not vary or destroy the beneficial interests, it merely enables the property to be distributed in accordance with the practical probabilities.[7] Furthermore whether such an order should be made does not depend on the testator's intentions or on the administrative inconvenience caused to the executors or trustees but simply on the question whether the beneficiaries should be allowed to enjoy their apparent interests, at the present rather than a future time.[8] By the use of a proper clause, however, the property may be made to pass as if the donee had survived the testator, or may be made to form part of his estate.[9]

1   Substitutionary gifts have sometimes been construed to include children of persons dead at the date of the will: see *Re Smith's Trusts* (1875) 5 Ch D 497n; *Re Lucas's Will* (1881) 17 Ch D 788; and see Chapter 68. A gift to M, his executors, administrators and assigns where M was dead at the date of the will has been held to fail: *Maybank v Brooks* (1780) 1 Bro CC 84.
2   As to exceptions from the doctrine of lapse, see Chapter 47.
3   *Browne v Hope* (1872) LR 14 Eq 343, and see Chapter 47, as to lapse.
4   *Re Phené's Trusts* (1870) 5 Ch App 139; *Re Lewes' Trusts* (1871) 6 Ch App 356; *Re Walker* (1871) 7 Ch App 120; *Re Benjamin, Neville v Benjamin* [1902] 1 Ch 723; *Re Aldersey, Gibson v Hall* [1905] 2 Ch 181; *Dowley v Winfield* (1844) 14 Sim 277; *Mason v Mason* (1816) 1 Mer 308. As to presumption where death is in a common disaster, see Chapter 70.
5   *Re Callicott's Goods* [1899] P 189; *Re Bowden's Goods* (1904) 21 TLR 13; *Wills v Palmer* (1904) 53 WR 169; *Lal Chand Marwari v Mahant Ramrup Gir* (1925) 42 TLR 159; *Re Dolling* [1956] VLR 535. The Presumption of Death (Scotland) Act 1977 provides in the law of Scotland for the presumed death of missing persons. Where it has to be shown that the legatee was alive at the testator's death, seven years must have elapsed before that death: see *Thomas v Thomas* (1864) 2 Drew & Sm 298. This case is said to have been overruled by *Re Phené's Trusts* (1870) 5 Ch App 139 but they both seem to have been decided on the principle that one has to decide on whom the burden of proof lies and, if he fails, the decision must be against him. Thus, where the seven-year period has not elapsed at the material time those who have to prove survival will succeed and those who have to prove death will fail. Where a person was last heard of in 1920, leave was given in 1962 to presume that he was then dead: *Re Newson-Smith's Settlement, Grice v Newson-Smith* [1962] 3 All ER 963n.
6   *Re Benjamin, Neville v Benjamin* [1902] 1 Ch 723; applied in *Re Green's Will Trusts, Fitzgerald-Hart v A-G* [1985] 3 All ER 455. In the New Zealand case of *Re Plato, AMP Perpetual Trustee Co Ltd v Shalders* [1990] NZLJ 3, a Benjamin Order was used in a situation other than the usual missing or presumed dead beneficiary. It was not clear on the evidence or the facts whether a particular person had been formally adopted or not, although the probability was that he had been. If he had, then the estate was to be distributed on the statutory trusts; if not, then the Crown was entitled to bona vacantia. The administrators were given leave to distribute on the former basis, the court noting that the *Re Benjamin* type of order had been used in a variety of circumstances. The case of *Re Evans, Evans v Westcombe* [1999] 2 All ER 777 illustrates other ways of dealing with the problem of the missing beneficiary. First, the personal representatives can invoke the protection of the Trustee Act 1925, s 27. Second, the personal representatives can set aside and retain such part of the estate as the missing beneficiary might be entitled to. Third, the personal representatives can take out a missing beneficiary insurance policy to cover the risk of the missing person subsequently reappearing; this was the method adopted in *Re Evans*.
7   Per Nourse J in *Re Green's Will Trusts, Fitzgerald-Hart v A-G* [1985] 3 All ER 455 at 462.
8   *Re Green's Will Trusts, Fitzgerald-Hart v A-G* [1985] 3 All ER 455. Such an order was made in that case to enable a gift to a charity to be accelerated.
9   See para **[47.22]** infra.

II.   ATTESTING WITNESSES

(i)   In general

[9.3]
Statutory provision. The attesting witnesses, and the husbands and wives of attesting witnesses, cannot take under a beneficial gift contained in the testamentary instrument so attested.[1] The disability extends only to a beneficial

devise, legacy, estate, interest, gift or appointment[2] and only those of whom it can be predicted at the time of attestation (or possibly at the time of the testator's death) that the gift was given to an attesting witness.[3] It does not include charges[4] or directions for the payment of debts, nor does it affect the competency of the witness to prove the validity or invalidity of the execution.[5]

1   Wills Act 1837, s 15; 50 *Halsbury's Statutes* (4th edn) 584; see Vol 2, Part G, para **[244.12]**. *Re Doland, Westminster Bank Ltd v Phillips* [1970] Ch 267, [1969] 3 All ER 713 (gift to the husband of an attesting witness). A solicitor who failed to warn the testator of the effect of s 15 has been held liable in tort to the disappointed beneficiary: *Ross v Caunters* [1980] Ch 297, [1979] 3 All ER 580, see Chapter 1, para **[1.5]** supra.
2   That is, appointment by the will. Where there was a gift to the wife for life with remainder to the children as the wife should appoint, and the wife appointed to all the children, one child did not lose her share because her husband had witnessed the original testator's will: *Re Koch v Koch* [1931] VLR 263. Where the testator directed a house to be sold to E for less than its value and the purchase price was not to be paid if E was disabled by sickness or accident, and E's wife attested the will, the gift was void: *Re Cumming* (1963) 38 DLR (2d) 243.
3   *Re Royce's Will Trusts, Tildesley v Tildesley* [1959] Ch 626, [1959] 3 All ER 278; *Burns Philp Trustee Co Ltd v Elliott* [1976] 1 NSWR 14.
4   As to solicitor's power of charging, see para **[9.11]** infra.
5   Wills Act 1837, ss 15, 16; 50 *Halsbury's Statutes* (4th edn) 584, 585.

[9.4]

Trust gifts. A gift to a witness merely as a trustee is not beneficial and is, therefore, valid.[1] A gift to a person to be held upon a secret trust for a witness is valid[2] and it seems immaterial whether or not the witness at the time of the attestation is aware of the secret trust in his favour.[3]

1   *Cresswell v Cresswell* (1868) LR 6 Eq 69; *Re Ryder's Goods* (1843) 2 Notes of Cases 462; *Re Ray's Will Trusts, Re Ray's Estate, Public Trustee v Barry* [1936] Ch 520, [1936] 2 All ER 93 (gift to abbess at death of testator in trust for convent).
2   *Re Young, Young v Young* [1951] Ch 344, [1950] 2 All ER 1245, not following *Re Fleetwood, Sidgreaves v Brewer* (1880) 15 Ch D 594; and *Sullivan v Sullivan* [1903] 1 IR 193, but following *O'Brien v Condon* [1905] 1 IR 51; *Cullen v A-G for Ireland* (1866) 14 WR 869; and *Re Gardner, Huey v Cunningham* [1923] 2 Ch 230.
3   See cases cited in n 2.

[9.5]

Gifts by codicil. A gift by a will to a beneficiary is not rendered invalid by the fact that the beneficiary attests a codicil to the will, even though the codicil confirms the will[1] unless he also receives a benefit under the codicil.[2] There is a benefit under the codicil when a contingent benefit is made absolute[3] but not when, by revoking other gifts, the residue in which the beneficiary shares is increased.[4] A codicil duly executed by other witnesses and confirming a will containing a gift to the witness to the will, validates the gift in the will[5] and the gift remains valid, although the beneficiary is witness to a subsequent codicil.[6] The gift is avoided only where the beneficiary has attested the instrument under which he takes[7] and a gift in a will written on several sheets of paper separately attested may be good if the beneficiary has not attested the sheet on which his gift appears.[8]

1   *Re Fleetwood, Sidgreaves v Brewer* (1880) 15 Ch D 594; *Gurney v Gurney* (1855) 3 Drew 208; *Tempest v Tempest* (1856) 2 K & J 635; *Re Marcus, Marcus v Marcus* (1887) 56 LJ Ch 830.

2   *Gaskin v Rogers* (1866) LR 2 Eq 284. In *Re White, Barker v Gribble* [1991] Ch 1, [1990] 3 All ER 1, a beneficiary was a witness to amendments to a will but was not a witness to the original will. He accordingly argued for probate of the original will to be granted despite the fact that the amendments purported to increase his share. He also argued that if the amended will was admitted to probate he was still entitled to take the share given to him in the original will albeit that he could not take the increased share. Held, will in original form admitted to probate, because the testator had failed to sign the amendments, and beneficiary entitled to original share.

3.   *Gaskin v Rogers* (1866) LR 2 Eq 284.

4   *Gurney v Gurney* (1855) 3 Drew 208.

5   *Anderson v Anderson* (1872) LR 13 Eq 381; *Re Trotter, Trotter v Trotter* [1899] 1 Ch 764; *Re Elcom, Layborn v Grover Wright* [1894] 1 Ch 303, CA. But republication does not validate a gift in a codicil void by being in favour of an attesting witness; *Burton v Newberry* (1875) 1 Ch D 234; *French v Hoey* [1899] 2 IR 472.

6   *Re Trotter, Trotter v Trotter* [1899] 1 Ch 764.

7   *Re Trotter, Trotter v Trotter* [1899] 1 Ch 764.

8   *Re Craven, Crewdson v Craven* (1908) 99 LT 390.

[9.6]

Conditional revocation of earlier will. Where a beneficiary was not a witness to the original will which contained the gift to him, but was a witness to two subsequent wills which repeated the gift to him and purported to revoke the first will, it was held that conditional revocation applied, so that the gift in the first will was not revoked.[1]

1   *Re Finnemore* [1992] 1 All ER 800, [1991] 1 WLR 793. Thus the beneficiary was able to take his gift under the first will despite being a witness to the second and third wills. See discussion of dependent relative revocation, Chapter 19.

[9.7]

Subsequent marriage of witness. The marriage must be subsisting at the date of the attestation and a subsequent marriage of the beneficiary to a witness does not affect the validity of the gift.[1]

1   *Thorpe v Bestwick* (1881) 6 QBD 311.

[9.8]

Superfluous attestation. Under the Wills Act 1837 (WA 1837) it was established that a gift to an attesting witness was void, even if there were two other witnesses to the will who were not beneficiaries.[1] However, in respect of persons dying after 30 May 1968 (whether the will was executed before or after that date) the attestation of a will by a person to whom or to whose spouse a beneficial interest is given, shall be disregarded if the will is duly executed without his attestation and without that of any other such person.[2] Alternatively it may be shown that a superfluous signature was not added as an attestation and thus save a gift to that witness or his or her spouse.[3] There is a presumption, however, that persons who so sign their names do so as witnesses[4] and it must be shown by evidence that the signature was not put to the attestation thereof.[5] If the question is raised on the application for the grant, the court will, in a proper case, omit the signature from the probate.[6] If, after execution is complete, a third person adds his name, the court requires cogent evidence that he did so as a witness.[7]

Part C   What dispositions may be made

1   *Doe d Taylor v Mills* (1833) 1 Mood & R 288; *Randfield v Randfield* (1863) 2 New Rep 309; *Fell v Biddolph* (1875) LR 10 CP 701 (where it was suggested that, if the witness in question did not sign in the presence of the testator, the gift might be good); *Re Brush* [1943] 1 DLR 74 (three witnesses, two of whom were beneficiaries: both gifts failed); *Re Bravda's Estate* [1968] 2 All ER 217, [1968] 1 WLR 479 (two independent witnesses, then two beneficiaries signed 'to make it stronger': gift to beneficiaries were void). The maxim *omnia praesumuntur rite esse acta* is not applicable on this point; *Re Bravda's Estate* [1968] 2 All ER 217 at 223.

2   Wills Act 1968, s 1; 50 *Halsbury's Statutes* (4th edn) 612; Vol 2, Part G, para **[244.82]**. It may be noted that the Wills Act 1968 preserves an attesting beneficiary's benefit only when the will is sufficiently executed without the attestation of any beneficiary (or beneficiary's spouse). Thus, if a will was attested by one independent witness and any number of beneficiaries, or their spouses, none of those beneficiaries could take under the will.

3   *Re Purssglove's Goods* (1872) 26 LT 405; *Re Murphy's Goods* (1873) 8 IR Eq 300. Where a legatee attested, but the solicitor then realising the difficulty, procured two other witnesses to sign but failed to have the legatee's signature deleted, the gift was held good: *Re Sturgis, Webling v Van Epery* (1889) 17 OR 342.

4   *Re Bravda's Estate* [1968] 2 All ER 217, [1968] 1 WLR 479; *Wigan v Rowland* (1853) 11 Hare 157; *Cozens v Crout* (1873) 42 LJ Ch 840; *Re Mitchell's Goods* (1841) 2 Curt 916; *Re Forest's Goods* (1861) 2 Sw & Tr 334; *Re Raine's Goods* (1865) 34 LJPM & A 125.

5   See cases in n 1. In *Re Bravda's Estate* [1968] 2 All ER 217, [1968] 1 WLR 479, it was said that the strength of the presumption varies according to the position of the signature ([1968] 2 All ER 217 at 225) and to the time of signing ([1968] 2 All ER 217 at 221).

6   *Re Sharman's Goods* (1869) LR 1 P & D 661; *Re Smith's Goods* (1889) 15 PD 2; in both cases there was clear and unequivocal express evidence that the beneficiaries signed in some other capacity; see *Re Bravda's Estate* [1968] 2 All ER 217 at 225; *Kitcat v King* [1930] P 266 (adversely commented on in *Re Bravda's Estate* [1968] 2 All ER 217 at 225). The court will require notice to be served on interested parties before making the order.

7   *Randfield v Randfield* (1860) 8 HL Cas 225 at 228; *Re Sharman's Goods* (1869) LR 1 P & D 661; *Re Murphy's Goods* (1873) 8 IR Eq 300; *Re Smith's Goods* (1889) 15 PD 2; *Kitcat v King* [1930] P 266.

[9.9]

Construction of will where gift fails. That part of the will which contains the nullified gift is not disregarded if it is necessary to have regard to it for the purpose of ascertaining what is the nature of other gifts in the will, or in what event other gifts are intended to take effect.[1] But the gift as regards the person who attests the will or his or her spouse or anyone claiming through them, is utterly null and void, so that so far as conferring any beneficial interest on any such person, the will is treated as though it did not contain that disposition at all. Therefore, a nullified gift cannot pass by virtue of a proviso governing gifts which 'fail', but results in an intestacy.[2] If the gift is a life interest, the subsequent interests are accelerated.[3] Where the gift is to A and his children and, if A has no children, the gift is to go over and if at the death of the testator A is still living but has no children, the gift over is not accelerated but must await his death without children. Until A has children or dies, there is an intestacy as to income.[4] Where there is an absolute gift to A or B and the gift to A fails because her husband has attested the will, the gift to B also fails.[5] Where the gift is to joint tenants and the gift to one fails as a gift to a witness, the other joint beneficiary takes the whole.[6] Similarly, where members of a class are excluded for this reason, the other members of the class take the whole between them.[7]

1   *Aplin v Stone* [1904] 1 Ch 543; *Re Doland, Westminster Bank Ltd v Phillips* [1970] Ch 267, [1969] 3 All ER 713; *Re Parker* (1982) 139 DLR (3d) 292.

2   *Re Doland, Westminster Bank Ltd v Phillips* [1970] Ch 267, [1969] 3 All ER 713.

3   *Jull v Jacobs* (1876) 3 Ch D 703; *Re Clark, Clark v Randall* (1885) 31 Ch D 72; *Burke v Burke* (1899) 18 NZLR 216.

4   *Re Townsend's Estate, Townsend v Townsend* (1886) 34 Ch D 357. The income is not accumulated for the benefit of those taking when the event is decided.
5   *Aplin v Stone* [1904] 1 Ch 543. In this case the alternative gift was to the children of A.
6   *Young v Davies* (1863) 2 Drew & Sm 167; *Re Fleetwood, Sidgreaves v Brewer* (1880) 15 Ch D 594; *Re Cotton* (1923) 19 Tas LR 57.
7   *Fell v Biddolph* (1875) LR 10 CP 701.

(ii)   Soldiers' wills

[9.10]
Will of member of forces. In the case of what is commonly called a 'soldier's will', which requires no attestation,[1] the section[2] invalidating a gift to a witness is not applicable even in the case where such a will is attested and there is a gift to an attesting witness.[3]

1   Wills Act 1837, s 11; see Chapter 16 and Vol 2, Part G, para **[244.9]**.
2   Wills Act 1837, s 15; see Vol 2, Part G, para **[244.12]**.
3   *Re Limond, Limond v Cunliffe* [1915] 2 Ch 240.

(iii)   Power of charging

[9.11]
Solicitor's power of charging. The inclusion in a will of a power for a solicitor or other professional trustee to charge his profits costs has been traditionally regarded as being in the nature of a legacy to that person and is rendered inoperative if such person attests the will,[1] but attestation by the solicitor's clerk will not have this effect.[2] The power to charge may be saved where the will is republished by a codicil referring to the will and not attested by the solicitor, and this benefit is not lost where the solicitor is a witness only to a subsequent codicil,[3] nor is it lost where the solicitor is a witness and is appointed a trustee subsequent to the death of the testator and on the death of one of the trustees appointed by the will.[4] The WA 1837, s 15 does not apply to a solicitor witnessing a will containing a solicitor-trustee clause in favour of his partner.[5] But the position has been changed in respect of wills of testators who die after the commencement of the Trustee Act 2000 (TrA 2000)[6]. By the TrA 2000, s 28 any payments to which a trustee is entitled in respect of services are to be treated as remuneration for services and not as a gift for the purposes of the WA 1837, s 15.[7]

1   *Re Barber, Burgess v Vinnicome* (1886) 31 Ch D 665; *Re Pooley* (1888) 40 Ch D 1, CA.
2   *Re Oberg* [1952] QWN 38.
3   *Re Trotter, Trotter v Trotter* [1899] 1 Ch 764.
4   *Re Royce's Will Trusts* [1959] Ch 626, [1959] 3 All ER 278. See *Cordery on Solicitors* (9th edn), p 262.
5   *Re Bunting* [1974] 2 NZLR 219.
6   See the TrA 2000, s 33. The TrA 2000 does not affect the operation of the WA 1837, s 15 in relation to deaths occurring before the commencement of the WA 1837.
7   TrA 2000, s 28(3). Similarly such payments are to be treated as debts not gifts for the purposes of the Administration of Estates Act 1925, s 34(3). The TrA 2000, Pt V, has made new provisions for the more effective remuneration of trustees (which includes personal

representatives for this purpose) who are (inter alia) acting in a professional capacity. As to the effect of revocation of the probate on a power to charge in the will see *Gray v Richards Butler* [1996] 29 LS Gaz R 29. See Chapter 27.

(iv)   Foreign wills

[9.12]
Will executed abroad. Where the testator, domiciled in England, made a holograph will in Scotland, which did not require attestation, but it was in fact attested by one of the beneficiaries, it was held that the gift failed.[1] This is in accordance with the rule that the law of the domicile governs the material validity of a will of movables.[2]

1   *Re Priest, Belfield v Duncan* [1944] Ch 58, [1944] 1 All ER 51.
2   See Chapter 23.

III.   UNLAWFUL KILLINGS: RULE OF PUBLIC POLICY

[9.13]
Introduction. The rule of public policy which precludes a person who has unlawfully killed another from acquiring a benefit in consequence of the killing has been modified in respect of deaths on or after 13 October 1982 by the Forfeiture Act 1982 (FoA 1982).[1] The FoA 1982 enables the court to grant relief in some cases from the consequences of the rule.[2] The rule is a wholly judge made creation but the FoA 1982 gives statutory recognition to it by stating that the 'forfeiture rule' means, 'the rule of public policy which in certain circumstances precludes a person who has unlawfully killed another person from acquiring a benefit in consequence of the killing'.[3] A useful modern judicial statement of the rule is as follows:[4]

'Under this rule, so far as relevant, a person who murders another cannot take, or enforce, any right or benefits resulting from his crime. The rule applies to rights and benefits arising under the victim's intestacy, just as much as it does to rights and benefits arising under the victim's will.'

The case law principles will be considered initially in the next paragraph.

1   12 *Halsbury's Statutes* (4th edn) 754.
2   See para **[9.20]** infra.
3   FoA 1982, s 1(1). Generally speaking, however, no person is of so unmeritorious a character that he is debarred from benefiting under a will (*Thellusson v Woodford* (1799) 4 Ves 227 at 312, 329) and the disqualification of the slayer of the testator must be taken as an exception made to that general rule by reason of public policy (*Re Hall's Estate, Hall v Knight and Baxter* [1914] P 1).
4   See Blackburne J in *Re DWS, Re EHS, TWGS v JMG* [2000] 2 All ER 83 at 86; affd [2001] 1 All ER 97, CA.

[9.14]
General principle. A person who is proved guilty of the murder or manslaughter of the testator and is not found to have been insane at the time cannot benefit under his will.[1] The basis of the law on this point was stated by

Fry LJ, in *Cleaver v Mutual Reserve Fund Life Association*,[2] in the following words:

'It appears to me that no system of jurisprudence can with reason include among the rights which it enforces rights directly resulting to the person asserting them from the crime of that person. If no action can arise from fraud, it seems impossible to suppose that it can arise from felony or misdemeanour.'

Where a person has been convicted of manslaughter the rule applies,[3] and the question whether he was deserving of punishment or morally blameworthy is irrelevant. However, the rule does not apply to a person found 'not guilty by reason of insanity', because the verdict amounts to an acquittal.[4]

1   *Cleaver v Mutual Reserve Fund Life Association* [1892] 1 QB 147; *Re Hall's Estate, Hall v Knight and Baxter* [1914] P 1; *Re Crippen's Estate* [1911] P 108; *Re Medaini* [1927] 4 DLR 1137; *Re Johnson* [1950] 2 DLR 69; *Re Giles, Giles v Giles* [1972] Ch 544, [1971] 3 All ER 1141. As to a finding of insanity taking the case out of the rule, see *Re Houghton, Houghton v Houghton* [1915] 2 Ch 173; *Re Pitts, Cox v Kilsby* [1931] 1 Ch 546; *Re Plaister* (1934) 34 SRNSW 547; *Re Batten's Will Trusts* (1961) 105 Sol Jo 529. But in the absence of a finding of insanity, the killing is held to be murder: *Re Pollock, Pollock v Pollock* [1941] Ch 219, [1941] 1 All ER 360. The same rule applies to an intestacy: *Re Sigsworth, Bedford v Bedford* [1935] Ch 89. In *Re S' Estate* [1968] P 302, [1967] 2 All ER 150, a wife was appointed sole executrix and beneficiary of her husband's will; she was convicted of manslaughter of her husband and sentenced to life imprisonment. It was held that these were special circumstances within the Supreme Court of Judicature (Consolidation) Act 1925, s 162(1), provision (b), enabling the court to pass over the executrix, and letters of administration with the will annexed were granted to the daughters. See now the Supreme Court Act 1981, s 116; 17 *Halsbury's Statutes* (4th edn) 540.
2   [1892] 1 QB 147 at 156. In *Permanent Trustee Co Ltd v Freedom from Hunger Campaign* (1991) 25 NSWLR 140 the judge held that the rule did not apply where the killing was not intended to bring about a benefit from the estate of the deceased. There is no support for this view in the authorities.
3   *Re Giles, Giles v Giles* [1972] Ch 544, [1971] 3 All ER 1141 (a wife who was the sole beneficiary under her husband's will killed her husband; she pleaded guilty to manslaughter by reason of diminished responsibility and was sent to Broadmoor Hospital); Criminal Procedure (Insanity) Act 1964; s 1; 12 *Halsbury's Statutes* (4th edn) 302. See also *Jones v Roberts* [1995] 2 FLR 422, applying *Royse v Royse* [1985] Ch 22.
4   *Re Giles, Giles v Giles* [1972] Ch 544, [1971] 3 All ER 1141.

[9.15]
Crimes within the principle. The principle extends both to the crimes of murder[1] and manslaughter.[2] It has been judicially stated that the rule will not apply to all manslaughters but only perhaps to those in which there has been violence or a threat of violence[3] but this no longer seems to represent the correct view.[4] It would appear that the motive and degree of moral guilt are not important,[5] save that where unsoundness of mind or justifiable homicide is proved the gift will stand.[6] It has been stated that the gift stands where the will is made in the interval of time between the wound and death.[7] The rule has been held to apply to the survivor of a suicide pact.[8]

1   *Cleaver v Mutual Reserve Fund Life Association* [1892] 1 QB 147; *Re Crippen's Estate* [1911] P 108; but relief under the Forfeiture Act 1982 is not available to a person convicted of murder, see para **[9.20]** infra.

2   *Re Hall's Estate, Hall v Knight and Baxter* [1914] P 1; *Lundy v Lundy* (1895) 24 SCR 650; *Jones v Roberts* [1995] 2 FLR 422.
3   *Re K* [1985] Ch 85, [1985] 1 All ER 403 at 412, 413, per Vinelott J; affd [1985] 2 All ER 833, CA; applying *R v Chief National Insurance Comr, ex p Connor* [1981] QB 758, [1981] 1 All ER 769 and *Gray v Barr* [1970] 2 QB 626, [1970] 2 All ER 702, considering *Re Giles, Giles v Giles* [1971] Ch 544, [1971] 3 All ER 1141. See also *Re H* [1990] 1 FLR 441 (forfeiture rule held not to apply where the killing was not deliberate), a decision not followed in *Jones v Roberts* [1995] 2 FLR 422. The rule was applied in *Re K*, but relief under the Forfeiture Act 1982, see para **[9.20]** infra, granted. The rule can apply also where there is no conviction but the only conclusion reasonably possible is that the beneficiary killed the testator: *Re Dellow's Will Trusts, Lloyds Bank Ltd v Institute of Cancer Research* [1964] 1 All ER 771, [1964] 1 WLR 451; *Clift v Clift* [1964–5] NSWR 1896.
4   *Dunbar v Plant* [1997] 4 All ER 289, disapproving *Re H* [1991] 1 FLR 441.
5   See *Re Giles, Giles v Giles* [1972] Ch 544, [1971] 3 All ER 1141.
6   See para **[9.14]**, n 1.
7   *Lundy v Lundy* (1895) 24 SCR 650.
8   *Dunbar v Plant* [1997] 4 All ER 289, CA, but with the forfeiture fully relieved under the Forfeiture Act 1982, see para **[9.20]** infra. See also *Re Jones, Jones v Midland Bank Trust Co Ltd* [1997] 3 FCR 697, CA.

[9.16]
Proof of the slaying. The proof generally offered will be the conviction, and proof of the conviction upheld by the Court of Appeal renders the fact indisputable.[1] The incapacity, however, does not depend on the trial or conviction, but on the fact of the murder or manslaughter itself and this may be proved although the slayer has not been tried. There is no principle which prevents a defendant from alleging that the plaintiff's claim is vitiated by the plaintiff's own act.[2] Where there is no evidence whether or not the slayer was sane, it is presumed that the killing is criminal and any gift is void.[3]

1   *Re Hall's Estate, Hall v Knight and Baxter*, see para **[9.15]**, n 1.
2   *Re G's Estate, M v L* [1946] P 183, [1946] 1 All ER 579.
3   *Re Pollock, Pollock v Pollock* [1941] Ch 219, [1941] 1 All ER 360.

[9.17]
Effect of the incapacity. It has been stated that where the rule applies, the interest of the criminal passes as if there has been a 'lapse', and in other cases it has been said that the name of the wrongdoer must be treated as 'struck out'.[1]
    The property bequeathed to the murderer under the will does not pass to the Crown as bona vacantia but passes to the other beneficiaries under the will in accordance with the plain construction of the will.[2] The property does not pass as if the murderer had predeceased the deceased.[3] Thus on intestacy if the murdered is disqualified from benefiting under the rule of public policy, the murderer's son cannot take as issue under the statutory trusts as if the murderer had predeceased the deceased,[4] but the next class of intestate beneficiary is entitled to take.[5]

1   Per Vaisey J in *Re Callaway, Callaway v Treasury Solicitor* [1956] Ch 559 at 563 [1956] 2 All ER 451 at 453.
2   *Re Callaway, Callaway v Treasury Solicitor* [1956] Ch 559 at 563 [1956] 2 All ER 451. Thus in *Re Callaway*, where the whole estate had been given to a son and a daughter and the daughter murdered the mother, the whole estate passed to the son. See also *Re Sigsworth, Bedford v Bedford* [1935] Ch 89,104 LJ Ch 46; *Cleaver v Mutual Reserve Fund Life Association* [1892] 1 QB 147; *Re Peacock, Midland Bank Executor and Trustee Co Ltd v Peacock* [1957] 2 All ER 98; *Hunter's Executors, Petitioners* 1992 SLT 1141; and *Re Jones, Jones v Midland Bank Trust Co Ltd* [1997] 3 FCR 697.

3   *Re DWS, Re EHS, TWGS v JMG* [2000] 2 All ER 83; affd [2001] 1 All ER 97, CA; applying *Re Sinclair, Lloyds Bank plc v Imperial Cancer Research Fund* [1985] Ch 446, [1985] 1 All ER 1066, a case on the effect of failure of a gift to a spouse by reason of divorce under the Wills Act 1837, s 18A. See also *Re Scott, Widdows v Friends of the Clergy Corpn* [1975] 2 All ER 1033, a case on the effect of a disclaimer under intestacy. It can be noted that the reasoning in *Re DWS* is different from that in *Re Scott*, which could lead to a different conclusion in certain situations; see para **[46.1]**, n 1 and para **[48.8]**, n 5, where the point is explained. See also *Re Robertson's Estate, Marsden v Marsden* (1963) 107 Sol Jo 318.

4   As set out in the Administration of Estates Act 1925, ss 46 and 47.

5   *Re DWS, Re EHS, TWGS v JMG* [2000] 2 All ER 83; affd [2001] 1 All ER 97, CA, where it was stated that the murderer is treated as having survived the deceased with the consequence that the disqualification operates as a personal bar so that, in the result, the share in question is undisposed of; per Blackburne J at 93. This is because the issue only take their deceased parent's share and the murderer has not predeceased the deceased, merely been disqualified as a living person from taking. In that case the son of the murderer was held not to be entitled but the deceased's sister's estate, being the next class of intestate beneficiary entitled under the Administration of Estates Act 1925, was held to be entitled.

[9.18]

The application the rule.[1] Not only is the slayer incapacitated from benefiting under the will, but where he dies at about the same time, his personal representatives are also excluded.[2] Where the donee is responsible for the murder of the testator, the donee can take no benefit.[3] If the donee is one of a class, he or she is excluded from the class and the others take an augmented share.[4] The incapacity is restricted to the donee and his personal representatives claiming for him but rights bona fide acquired by third parties can be enforced against the estate of the deceased.[5] In some cases the result may be to bring into effect a resulting,[6] or constructive,[7] trust in favour of the estate of the slain. Where the murderer was sole legatee under the will and with one other was entitled on the intestacy of the deceased, the murderer took nothing under the will or intestacy, but the other person entitled on intestacy took the whole to the exclusion of the Crown taking as bona vacantia.[8] The unlawful killing and the resultant disqualification from benefiting under the will does not entitle the court to rewrite the will, in effect speculating as to what the testatrix's wishes might have been.[9] It has been decided in a case,[10] to which the Forfeiture Act 1982 was not applicable, that a person convicted of the unlawful killing of the testator was not able to apply for financial provision out of the estate under the Inheritance (Provision for Family and Dependants) Act 1975.[11]

1   Subject, where applicable to the relief under the Forfeiture Act 1982, see para **[9.20]** infra.

2   *Re Sigsworth, Bedford v Bedford* [1935] Ch 89 (where the slayer committed suicide after murdering the testatrix, his mother). See also *Re Dreger* (1976) 69 DLR (3d) 47. In the case of a suicide pact where the wife died but the husband survived, it was held that the husband could take no benefit under the will of his wife; *Whitelaw v Wilson* [1934] 3 DLR 554 and *Re Dunbar, Dunbar v Plant* [1997] 4 All ER 289. See also *Re Pollock, Pollock v Pollock* [1941] Ch 219, [1941] 1 All ER 360. A husband while insane killed his wife and then killed himself. Under the wife's will the husband was sole executor and beneficiary. Administration with the wife's will annexed was granted to the husband's executors: *Re Beiers* [1953] QWN 9.

3   Per Southin J in *Dhaliwall v Dhaliwall* (1986) 30 DLR (4th) 420 at 424, following *Cleaver v Mutual Reserve Fund Life Association* [1892] 1 QB 147 and *Re Giles, Giles v Giles* [1972] Ch 544, [1971] 3 All ER 1141; not following *Re Dellow's Will Trusts* [1964] 1 All ER 771, [1964] 1 WLR 451. See also *Public Trustee v Fraser* (1987) 9 NSWLR 433 where it was thought that an intestacy resulting from the application of the forfeiture rule will involve the disentitled beneficiary being treated as notionally not in existence, so that the other next-of-kin take the estate; *Davitt v Titcumb* [1990] Ch 110, [1989] 3 All ER 417 (one tenant in common unable to

profit indirectly from his murder of the other tenant in common where a joint life insurance policy was used by their building society to pay off the mortgage).

4   *Re Peacock, Midland Bank Executor and Trustee Co Ltd v Peacock* [1957] Ch 310, [1957] 2 All ER 98.
5   See *Cleaver v Mutual Reserve Fund Life Association* [1892] 1 QB 147.
6   *Cleaver v Mutual Reserve Fund Life Association* [1892] 1 QB 147.
7   *Schobelt v Barber* (1966) 60 DLR (2d) 519 (one of two joint tenants murdered the other. On the question of entitlement to the deceased's interest, held: (i) that the normal rule of survivorship applied, and the full interest accrued to the survivor; (ii) that the court would impose a constructive trust so that the survivor held the property as to an undivided one-half interest for the benefit of the deceased joint tenant's estate).
8   *Re Callaway, Callaway v Treasury Solicitor* [1956] Ch 559, [1956] 2 All ER 451.
9   *Re Jones, Jones v Midland Bank Trust Co Ltd* [1997] 3 FCR 697, CA following *Re Sinclair* [1985] Ch 446 and *Re Hunter's Executors, Petitioners* 1992 SLT 1141. The testatrix had left her estate on trust for her son and in the event of his predeceasing her 'for such of her nephews ... as shall be living at the date of my death'. The son unlawfully killed the mother and it was held that the gift over in favour of the nephews could not take effect as the event specified by the testatrix had not occurred and that her estate accordingly devolved on her next of kin.
10 *Re Royse, Royse v Royse* [1985] Ch 22, [1984] 3 All ER 339 (because the absence of reasonable financial provision for the applicant could not be attributed to the deceased's will or intestacy but was solely because of the rule of public policy; discussed in Chapter 105).
11 Where the WA 1982 applies the position could be different: see Chapter 105.

[9.19]
Property owned jointly. The question arises as to the effect of the rule on property owned jointly by the victim and the killer. In *Re K*[1] where a matrimonial home was so owned, it was held to have been rightly conceded that the effect of the forfeiture rule was to sever the joint tenancy, so that the beneficial interest vested in the deceased and the survivor as tenants in common. The deceased's share can then be made subject to relief under the FoA 1982 if appropriate.[2]

1   [1985] Ch 85, [1985] 1 All ER 403; affd by Court of Appeal [1985] 2 All ER 833. There was previously no English authority on the point. Under Commonwealth cases it had been held that the law imports a constructive trust of an undivided one half share for the benefit of the next of kin of the deceased other than the offender; see *Shobelt v Barber* (1967) 60 DLR (2d) 519, discussed above in para **[9.18]**, n 7, and *Re Pechar; Re Grbic* [1969] NZLR 574.
2   As was done in *Re K* [1985] Ch 85, [1985] 1 All ER 403, see para **[9.21]** infra.

[9.20]
Relief under the Forfeiture Act 1982. The FoA 1982 came into force on 13 October 1982[1] and enables the court to grant discretionary relief from the effects of the rule of the public policy,[2] which the FoA 1982 refers to as the 'forfeiture rule'.[3] Where the court determines that the rule would apply to preclude a person who has unlawfully killed another from acquiring any 'interest in property', then the court may make an order under the FoA 1982 modifying the effect of the rule.[4] If there has been a conviction, the application must be brought within three months of the date of conviction.[5] The court has no power to modify the rule in favour of a person who stands convicted of murder,[6] and the jurisdiction is thus limited to offenders convicted of other forms of unlawful killing.[7] Whether relief is granted or not is a matter for the court's discretion, governed by the terms of the FoA 1982, s 2(2), which states that an order is not to be made unless the court is satisfied that, having regard to the conduct of the offender and of the

deceased and to such other circumstances as appear to the court to be material, the justice of the case requires the effect of the rule to be so modified in that case.

The 'interests in property' referred to above include all benefits by way of succession, expressly including beneficial interests acquired under the deceased's will, or intestacy, or a nomination, or a *donatio mortis causa* or benefits under a trust. The FoA 1982, s 2(1) states that in respect of such an interest the court may make an order modifying the effect of the rule. The FoA 1982, s 2(5) then enlarges this provision by stating that the modification may be done in either or both of the following ways:

'(a) where there is more than one such interest, by excluding the application of the rule in respect of any (but not all) of those interests; and

(b) in the case of any such interest in property, by excluding the application of the rule in respect of part of the property.'

At first sight this would seem to preclude the court from relieving the beneficiary from the consequences of the rule altogether. However, both Vinelott J and the Court of Appeal in *Re K*[8] thought that such a result would be bizarre and concluded that subsection (5) was intended to enlarge the power conferred by subsection (1) by making it clear that the court is not bound either to relieve against the operation of the forfeiture rule altogether or not to relieve against the operation of the rule at all. Subsection (1) empowers the court to relieve an applicant from the operation of the rule in respect of the entirety of all interests affected by the rule. But the FoA 1982, s 2(7) provides that the court cannot make an order under the section modifying the effect of the forfeiture rule in respect of any interest in property which, in consequence of the rule, has been acquired before the coming into force of the section (13 October 1982) by a person other than the offender or a person claiming through him. In *Re K*[9] it was held that this applied to property which had actually been transferred to the person entitled to it and did not include property which at the time the FoA 1982, s2(7) came into force, was held by a personal representative who had not completed the administration of the estate.

1   FoA 1982, s 7(2); 12 *Halsbury's Statutes* (4th edn) 759.
2   FoA 1982, s 2.
3   FoA 1982, s 1(1). See *Re Cross, Petitioner* 1987 SLT 384.
4   FoA 1982, s 2(1).
5   FoA 1982, s 2(3).
6   FoA 1982, s 5.
7   There seems little doubt that the provision was prompted by unease over cases such as *Re Giles, Giles v Giles* [1972] Ch 544, [1971] 3 All ER 1141, where the rule was applied although the court recognised that no great moral blameworthiness attached to the killing likewise; in cases of mercy killings, provided the conviction is for manslaughter not murder. Full relief was granted under the FoA 1982 to a person convicted of complicity in a suicide pact, *Dunbar v Plant* [1997] 4 All ER 289, CA.
8   [1985] 1 All ER 403 at 414; affd [1985] 2 All ER 833, CA.
9   [1985] 1 All ER 403 at 414; affd [1985] 2 All ER 833, CA at 839.

[9.21]
Exercise of the discretion. The FoA 1982 as interpreted by Vinelott J in *Re K*[1] confers an unfettered discretion on the court to relieve the person responsible for

the unlawful killing (other than a person who stands convicted of murder)[2] from the consequences of the forfeiture rule. In *Re K*, a wife who had been subjected to repeated violence at the hands of her husband killed him when a shotgun she was threatening him with went off. She was convicted of manslaughter and made subject to a two-year probation order. The estate was worth £412,000 (and in addition there was a jointly owned matrimonial home valued at £80,000) and by his will the husband left the whole estate to his widow for life and after her death to four residuary beneficiaries. Vinelott J and the Court of Appeal held that the rule applied, but that relief under the FoA 1982 was appropriate. In view of the fact that she had been a loyal wife who had suffered grave violence at the hands of the husband and having regard to the fact that there were no other persons for whom the testator was under any moral duty to provide, the judge thought that full relief was appropriate so that she took the entirety of her interests under the will.[3] The Court of Appeal affirmed the decision.[4]

Other cases where relief might be regarded as appropriate include so called mercy killings, and where the offender commits suicide shortly after the killing, his family who are prima facie excluded from benefit as claiming through the offender, might obtain relief.[5]

1   [1985] 1 All ER 403 at 414; affd [1985] 2 All ER 833, CA.
2   FoA 1982, s 5.
3   Including the interest in the residuary estate of the husband's severed half share in the matrimonial home, see para **[9.20]** supra.
4   [1986] Ch 180, [1985] 2 All ER 833.
5   As where a wife kills her husband and then commits suicide and by her will or intestacy her children are entitled to her estate, which includes the husband's estate.

[9.22]
Family provision. It is expressly provided by way of clarification, that the forfeiture rule is not to be taken as precluding any person from making an application under the Inheritance (Provision for Family and Dependants) Act 1975 (I(PFD)A 1975).[1] Such a person can also apply for variation of periodical payments orders, or maintenance agreements under the Matrimonial Causes Act 1973.[2] At first sight this would seem to indicate that the forfeiture rule no longer applies to disentitle a person from making a successful application under the FoA 1982. However the decision in *Re Royse, Royse v Royse*[3] casts doubts on this. It was decided in that case that a woman who was convicted of the unlawful killing of her husband and who was thus disinherited by the effect of the rule of public policy was not able to apply for financial provision out of his estate under the I(PFD)A 1975. The reason being that the absence of reasonable financial provision could not be attributed to the deceased's will under which the woman was the sole beneficiary but was solely due to the operation of the public policy rule which had disentitled her from acquiring the testamentary benefit.[4] The FoA 1982 did not in fact apply in that case because the events had taken place before that Act came into force. However there are dicta[5] that suggest that the result would have been the same even if the FoA 1982 applied because the essential precondition in the I(PFD)A 1975, s 2(1) would still not have been satisfied. The solution is to apply initially for relief under the FoA 1982 and then if the will or intestacy makes inadequate provision for the person concerned to apply under

the I(PFD)A 1975 for provision. Where the will fails to make any provision for the killer then the FoA 1982 will not be applicable and the person disentitled will have to rely entirely on an application under the I(PFD)A 1975.

1   FoA 1982, s 3(1), (2).
2   FoA 1982, s 31(6); s 36(1).
3   [1985] Ch 22, [1984] 3 All ER 339.
4   See Ackner LJ in *Re Royse, Royse v Royse* [1984] 3 All ER 339 at 342; Slade LJ at 344.
5   See Ackner LJ in *Re Royse, Royse v Royse* [1984] 3 All ER 339 at 343; Slade LJ at 344, 345.
    See also Ackner LJ in *Re K* [1985] 2 All ER 833 at 842.

IV.   UNDUE INFLUENCE AND FRAUD

[9.23]
This has already been considered.[1]

1   See para **[5.9]** supra.

V.   ILLEGITIMATE CHILDREN

[9.24]
As object of gift. This section deals only with the question whether an illegitimate child can be the object of a valid testamentary gift and not with the question whether on its proper construction a gift includes illegitimate children.[1] It is necessary to differentiate between pre-1970 wills and post-1970 wills.

1   See Chapter 72.

[9.25]
Pre-1970 wills. The following rules apply to any will or codicil executed before 1 January 1970, notwithstanding that the will or codicil is confirmed by codicil executed after that date.[1] A gift to an illegitimate child is valid: (i) if the child was alive or *en ventre sa mère* at the date of the will; and (ii) in certain special cases hereinafter stated, if the child was alive or *en ventre sa mère* at the date of the testator's death. This is an exception to the legal rule that there could be no gift to a future illegitimate child since such a gift would be contrary to public policy as an encouragement of immorality. Where the child was alive at the date of the will, there could be no question of such a future gift; but where the child was not then alive, there was at first glance what may be said to be a future gift. The rules governing the validity of such a gift are as follows: (i) The law allows such a gift to a child of reputed paternity provided the paternity is reputed or acknowledged[2] but not where the child is described solely by reference to paternity, as the child or children of A by B;[3] (ii) Where the child is described by reference to maternity alone;[4] (iii) A child *en ventre sa mère* cannot obtain a reputation of paternity[5] and such a gift is only valid where there is no reference to any person as the father.[6] The law is said to have decided these matters on the ground that it is more in accordance with public policy that provision should be

made for such unfortunate offspring, than that they should become a burden on public funds.[7] The fact that the donees, including some excluded by the above rules, were to take as a class, does not prevent the remainder who are not so excluded from taking.[8]

1   Family Law Reform Act 1969, s 15(7) and (8), see Vol 2, Part G, para **[245.39]**.
2   *Occleston v Fullalove* (1874) 9 Ch App 147; *Re Hyde, Smith v Jack* [1932] 1 Ch 95.
3   *Re Du Bolton, Brown v Bolton* (1886) 31 Ch D 542; *Re Shaw, Robinson v Shaw* [1894] 2 Ch 573; *Re Bochet, Mansell v Allen* [1901] 2 Ch 441; *Re Pearce, Alliance Assurance Co Ltd v Francis* [1914] 1 Ch 254; *Re Homer, Cowlishaw v Rendell* (1916) 86 LJ Ch 324.
4   *Re Frogley's Estate* [1905] P 137; *Re Loveland, Loveland v Loveland* [1906] 1 Ch 542.
5   *Occleston v Fullalove* (1874) 9 Ch App 147; *Re Bolton, Brown v Bolton* (1886) 31 Ch D 542; *Re Shaw, Robinson v Shaw* [1894] 2 Ch 573.
6   *Gordon v Gordon* (1816) 1 Mer 141; *Evans v Massey* (1819) 8 Price 22.
7   *Re Loveland, Loveland v Loveland* [1906] 1 Ch 542 at 548.
8   *Hill v Crook* (1873) LR 6 HL 265; *Ebbern v Fowler* [1909] 1 Ch 578. In some cases a gift to a future illegitimate child would have been void also for uncertainty. This was where the gift was to children defined by reference to paternity, for the law did not allow enquiry into the question of actual paternity, *Re Bolton, Brown v Bolton* (1886) 31 Ch D 542; *Re Shaw, Robinson v Shaw* [1894] 2 Ch 573; *Re Du Bochet, Mansell v Allen* [1901] 2 Ch 441.

[9.26]
Post-1970 wills. The rules discussed above with reference to gifts to future illegitimate children have been abolished with respect to dispositions in wills or codicils executed after 1 January 1970.[1] See now the Family Law Reform Act 1987 which effectively abolishes the status of illegitimacy.[2]

1   Family Law Reform Act 1969, s 15(7), see Vol 2, Part G, para **[245.39]**. Notwithstanding any rule of law, a disposition made by will or codicil before 1 January 1970 is not to be treated for the purposes of the section as made on or after that date by reason only that the will or codicil was confirmed by a codicil executed on or after that date; Family Law Reform Act 1969, s 15(8).
2   See Volume 2, Part E, Division 11, discussed at para **[72.14]**.

VI.   CHILD BORN AS A RESULT OF FERTILISATION TECHNIQUES

[9.27]
Status of such children. The status of children born as a result of artificial insemination or other fertilisation techniques is now governed by the Human Fertilisation and Embryology Act 1990 (HFEA 1990). The provisions of the HFEA 1990 are discussed in Chapter 74.

VII.   CHARITIES

[9.28]
Gifts of land. Any estate or interest in land can now be assured by will to or for any charitable use.[1]

1   See the Charities Act 1993; 5 *Halsbury's Statutes* (4th edn) 942.

VIII.   GIFTS FOR UPKEEP OF GRAVES, ETC

[9.29]

Tombs and graves. Gifts for building or repairing tombs or monuments which are not part of the fabric of the church are not charitable,[1] and are accordingly void if they exceed the limits of remoteness. A bequest to trustees to provide 'so far as they legally can do so and in any manner that they may in their discretion arrange' for the care and upkeep of certain graves, a vault, and certain monuments is valid for 21 years from the death of the testator.[2] The addition of the words 'that is to say until the period of twenty-one years from the death of the last survivor of all persons who shall be living at my death' makes the bequest void for uncertainty.[3] But a gift of a fund to trustees upon trust to pay the income to a cemetery company during such period as the company should continue to keep specified graves in order with a gift over in the event of the graves not being kept in order was held not to infringe the rule against perpetuities or the rule against inalienability and was a valid gift.[4] Similarly, a perpetual condition for this purpose, not constituting a trust, imposed on a charity with a gift over on failure to comply with it to another charity is valid,[5] but if the gift over is not to a charity, such gift is void and the original charitable bequest takes effect freed from the condition.[6] The original gift must impose only a moral obligation to repair and if such gift shows that no mere moral obligation was intended, it will be invalid.[7] A gift of residue to a charity subject to a condition that a sum of £100 set apart therefrom shall be applied in keeping a grave in repair in perpetuity is good as to the gift of residue, but bad as the condition which is avoided and the gift of residue takes effect free from the condition.[8]

A gift for the perpetual repair of a monument in a church may be held good, on the ground that it is an ornament although not part of the fabric.[9] A gift for the upkeep of a monument, burial ground and churchyard has been held to be valid, and as the churchyard was closed and a cemetery had been opened adjoining it, one-half of the legacy was ordered to be paid to the local authority as the proprietors of the cemetery.[10]

---

1   *Fowler v Fowler* (1864) 33 Beav 616; *Hoare v Osborne* (1866) LR 1 Eq 585; *Re Rigley's Trusts* (1866) 36 LJ Ch 147; *Fisk v A-G* (1867) LR 4 Eq 521; *Hunter v Bullock* (1872) LR 14 Eq 45; *Re Williams* (1877) 5 Ch D 735; *Re Birkett* (1878) 9 Ch D 576; *Re Rogerson, Bird v Lee* [1901] 1 Ch 715; *Re Dalziel, Midland Bank Executor and Trustee Co Ltd v St Bartholomew's Hospital* [1943] Ch 277, [1943] 2 All ER 656; *Re Martin, Barclays Bank v Board of Governors of St Bartholomew's Hospital* [1952] WN 339. If the gift can be construed as contributing to the maintenance or improvement of the fabric of a church, it is charitable and good: *Re Ross* [1964] Qd R 132.
2   *Re Hooper, Parker v Ward* [1932] 1 Ch 38, following *Pirbright v Salwey* [1896] WN 86.
3   *Re Moore, Prior v Moore* [1901] 1 Ch 936.
4   *Re Chardon, Johnston v Davies* [1928] Ch 464. But see now Perpetuities and Accumulations Act 1964, s 12, which subjects such gifts to the rule against perpetuities.
5   *Christ's Hospital v Grainger* (1849) 1 Mac & G 460; *Re Tyler, Tyler v Tyler* [1891] 3 Ch 252; *Re Martin,* supra.
6   *Re Davies, Lloyd v Cardigan County Council* [1915] 1 Ch 543.
7   *Re Dalziel, Midland Bank Executor and Trustee Co Ltd v St Bartholomew's Hospital,* supra.
8   *Re Elliott* [1952] Ch 217, [1952] 1 All ER 145.
9   *Hoare v Osborne* (1866) LR 1 Eq 585.
10   *Re Eighmie, Colbourne v Wilks* [1935] Ch 524.

[9.30]

Statutory power. The Parish Councils and Burial Authorities (Miscellaneous Provisions) Act 1970 (PCBA(MP)A 1970)[1] has now provided an alternative method of maintaining a grave. A burial authority or a local authority may agree with any person in consideration of the payment of a sum by him to maintain a grave, vault, tombstone, or other memorial in a burial ground or crematorium provided or maintained by the authority, or a monument or other memorial to any person within the area of the authority to which the authority have a right of access.[2] The maximum period of such an agreement is 100 years from the date of the agreement.[3] A testator can accordingly direct his executors to enter into such an agreement although it must be pointed out that the power is merely permissive on the authority and not obligatory.[4]

1   5 *Halsbury's Statutes* (4th edn) 846, for regulations see SI 1977/204.
2   PCBA(MP)A 1970, s 1. Such powers had previously been available in some areas under the provisions of local Acts, which are now otiose.
3   PCBA(MP)A 1970; in so far as the PCBA(MP)A 1970 avoids any perpetuity problems, it is simpler than the sort of provisions discussed above.
4   For a precedent, see Form B2.11, Vol 2, para **[202.34]** and the notes at paras **[202.18]** to **[202.30]**.

IX.   ANIMALS

[9.31]

A gift for the maintenance of particular animals has been held to be a valid form of gift.[1] Such a gift, however, is not charitable, and it is conceived that it must be restricted in time within the perpetuity rule,[2] and that the life of the animal is not a life in being for the purposes of that rule.[3] There are other gifts for the welfare and protection of animals which are clearly charitable and so valid;[4] but they must be shown to be for purposes beneficial to the community.[5]

1   *Pettingall v Pettingall* (1842) 11 LJ Ch 176; *Re Dean, Cooper-Dean v Stevens* (1889) 41 Ch D 552, where it was held that a trust for the maintenance of animals so long as they shall live is not a charitable trust, and is good although there is no one who can enforce the trust. Needless to say this decision has been severely criticised, but it still stands for what it is worth. In practice, such trusts are usually restricted in time within the perpetuity rule, eg for 21 years from the date of death if the animals or any of them shall so long live. In *Re Thompson, Public Trustee v Lloyd* [1934] Ch 342, a trust for the promotion and furthering of fox-hunting was held good. See also *Re Kelly, Cleary v James* [1932] IR 255.
2   *Re Dean, Cooper-Dean v Stevens* (1889) 41 Ch D 552.
3   *Re Kelly, Cleary v James* [1932] IR 255 (where the gift was upheld for 21 years only).
4   *Re Moss, Hobrough v Harvey* [1949] 1 All ER 495; *Re Grove-Grady, Plowden v Lawrence* [1929] 1 Ch 557; *Re Douglas, Obert v Barrow* (1887) 35 Ch D 472; *Marsh v Means* (1857) 30 LTOS 89; *Re Cranston, Webb v Oldfield* (1898) 1 IR 431; *Swifte v A-G for Ireland (No 2)* [1912] 1 IR 133; *Re Wedgwood, Allen v Wedgwood* [1915] 1 Ch 113. Gifts for the promotion of prosecutions for cruelty to animals have been upheld: *Re Vallance* (1876) 2 Seton's Judgments & Orders (7th edn) 1304; *Re Herrick, Colohan v A-G* (1918) 52 ILT 213, but a gift providing rewards for police obtaining convictions was held bad: *Re Hollywood, Smyth v A-G* (1917) 52 ILT 51. The gift is good, although the protection is to be given in a foreign country: *Re Jackson, Bell v Adlam* (1910) Times, 11 June: *Armstrong v Reeves* (1890) 25 LR Ir 325. A society the main object of which is the total abolition of vivisection is not charitable: *National Anti-Vivisection Society v IRC* [1948] AC 31, [1947] 2 All ER 217, overruling *Re Foveaux, Cross v London Anti-Vivisection Society* [1895] 2 Ch 501, and in effect, though the case was apparently not cited, *Armstrong v Reeves* (1890) 25 LR Ir 325; see also *Re Recher's Will Trusts, National*

Westminster Bank Ltd v National Anti-Vivisection Society Ltd [1972] Ch 526, [1971] 3 All ER 401.

5   *National Anti-Vivisection Society v IRC* [1948] AC 31, [1947] 2 All ER 217: where *Re Grove-Grady, Plowden v Lawrence* [1929] 1 Ch 557, is fully discussed. In *Re Grove-Grady, Plowden v Lawrence* the trust was held not to be for the benefit of the community, an essential of a charitable trust which has received more attention since the judgment in *Re Compton* [1945] Ch 123, [1945] 1 All ER 198; see para **[102.9]** infra.

X.   CORPORATIONS

[9.32]

Corporations in general. A gift of land to a corporation is now good by statute.[1] Personal property to any amount may be bequeathed to a corporation.[2] A gift to a corporation sole or to corporation aggregate is valid notwithstanding a vacancy in the office of the corporation sole or in the office of the head of a corporation aggregate, at the time of the gift.[3]

1   Charities Act 1993; 5 *Halsbury's Statutes* (4th edn) 942, 1998 Reissue.
2   *Fulwood's Case* (1591) 4 Co Rep 64b.
3   Law of Property Act 1925, s 180(2).

XI.   COMPANIES

[9.33]

Limited companies. In general, companies registered under the Companies Acts have power to hold land to any amount[1] and a bequest or devise may be made to a registered company.[2]

A bequest may be made to a company of shares in the company, but they must be vested in nominees for the company.[3]

1   See Companies Acts; 8 *Halsbury's Statutes* (4th edn) 1999 Reissue.
2   See Companies Acts; 8 *Halsbury's Statutes* (4th edn) 1999 Reissue.
3   *Re Castiglione's Will Trusts, Hunter v Mackenzie* [1958] Ch 549, [1958] 1 All ER 480. Where the company is a private company with the usual restrictions on transfer, the nominees must be persons to whom the shares can be transferred under the articles of association.

XII.   LOCAL AUTHORITIES

[9.34]

Local authorities. Local authorities may accept, hold and administer gifts of property, whether real or personal, made either for the purpose of discharging any of their functions or for the benefit of the inhabitants of their area or of some part of it.[1]

1   Local Government Acts 1972 to 2000; 25 *Halsbury's Statutes* (4th edn) 178 to 1470. See *Re Armitage, Ellam v Norwich Corpn* [1972] Ch 438, [1972] 1 All ER 708 (eleemosynary charity).

XIII.   GIFTS TO INSTITUTIONS, SOCIETIES, CLUBS, TRADE UNIONS

[9.35]

Institutions. A gift of land or personal property may be made to a perpetual institution or society, whether corporate or unincorporated, but, where it is not upon a charitable trust, it must be limited within the perpetuity rule.[1] The rule is avoided, however, where the members may dispose of the gift as they think fit, ie all the money may be spent as income[2] or it can be construed as a gift to the individual members.[3] An unincorporated non-charitable association is not a separate entity in law and the validity of gifts to such an institution will depend on the construction of the gift.[4] Absolute and beneficial gifts to non-charitable unincorporated associations have been upheld as gifts to the members of the association at the date of the gift as joint tenants, so that any member could sever his share and claim it whether or not he continued to be a member.[5] Alternatively, it has been suggested that the gift could be regarded as being to the members of the association at the date of the gift not as joint tenants, but subject to their contractual rights and liabilities towards one another as members of the association.[6] In such a case, a member cannot sever his share, which will accrue to the other members on his death or resignation. However, if the terms or circumstances of the gift or the rules of the association show that the subject of the gift is not to be at the disposal of the members for the time being but is to be held in trust for, or applied for the purposes of, the association, then the gift will fail unless the association is charitable.[7] But notwithstanding this rule a deed conferring on employees a right to use and enjoy land as a sports ground has been upheld, on the grounds that the rule against enforceability of non-charitable 'purpose or object' trusts was confined to those which were abstract or impersonal in nature where there was no beneficiary or *cestui que trust*; a trust which though expressed as a purpose was directly or indirectly for the benefit of an individual or individuals was valid provided those individuals were ascertainable at any one time and the trust was not otherwise void for uncertainty.[8] This case was applied in a later decision upholding the validity of a testamentary trust for the benefit of an unincorporated non-charitable association, the funds to be used 'solely in the work of constructing new buildings'.[9]

---

1   *Thomson v Shakespear* (1860) 1 De GF & J 399; *Carne v Long* (1860) 2 De GF & J 75; *Re Dutton, ex p Peake* (1878) 4 Ex D 54; *Re Amos, Carrier v Price* [1891] 3 Ch 159; *Re Swain, Phillips v Poole* (1908) 99 LT 604; *Re Bland-Sutton's Will Trusts, National Provincial Bank Ltd v Middlesex Hospital* [1951] Ch 485, [1951] 1 All ER 494; *Neville Estates Ltd v Madden* [1962] Ch 832 at 849, [1961] 3 All ER 769 at 779.

2   *Re Clarke, Clarke v Clarke* [1901] 2 Ch 110; *Cocks v Manners* (1871) LR 12 Eq 574; *Morrow v McConville* (1883) 11 LR Ir 236; *Re Wilkinson's Trusts* (1887) 19 LR Ir 531; *Bradshaw v Jackman* (1887) 21 LR Ir 12; *Re Delany, Conoley v Quick* [1902] 2 Ch 642.

3   Where, eg, the individual members are expressly referred to or indicated in the terms of the gift: *Re Delany's Estate* (1882) 9 LR Ir 226; *Henrion v Bonham* (1844) Drury *temp* Sug 476, see *O'Leary on Charitable Uses*, p 89; *Bradshaw v Jackman* (1887) 21 LR Ir 12; *Re Smith, Johnson v Bright-Smith* [1914] 1 Ch 937, and not for the institution simpliciter: *Morrow v McConville* (1883) 11 LR Ir 236; *Re Amos, Carrier v Price* [1891] 3 Ch 159; *Leahy v A-G for New South Wales* [1959] AC 457, [1959] 2 All ER 300, applied in *Re Metcalfe* (1973) 29 DLR (3d) 60; *Neville Estates Ltd v Madden* [1962] Ch 832, [1961] 3 All ER 769.

4   *Leahy v A-G for New South Wales* [1959] AC 457 at 477, [1959] 2 All ER 300 at 306; see
    Conservative and Unionist Central Office v Burrell (Inspector of Taxes) [1980] 3 All ER 42 on
    requirements of an unincorporated association.
5   *Re Clarke, Clarke v Clarke* [1901] 2 Ch 110 (a gift to the Corps of Commissionaires); *Re Smith,
    Johnson v Bright-Smith* [1914] 1 Ch 937 (gift to the Society of Franciscan Friars of Somerset);
    Re Drummond, Askworth v Drummond [1914] 2 Ch 90 (gift to the Old Bradfordians Club); *Re
    Turkington, Owen v Benson* [1937] 4 All ER 501 (gift to a Masonic lodge); *Re Taylor, Midland
    Bank Executor and Trustee Co Ltd v Smith* [1940] Ch 481, [1940] 2 All ER 637 (gift to the
    Midland Bank Staff Association); *Re Price, Midland Bank Executor and Trustee Co Ltd v
    Harwood* [1943] Ch 422, [1943] 2 All ER 505 (gift to the Anthroposophical Society); *Re
    Ogden, Brydon v Samuel* [1933] Ch 678. See Cross J in *Neville Estates Ltd v Madden* [1962]
    Ch 832 at 849, [1961] 3 All ER 769 at 778.
      Accordingly, 'the prudent conveyancer provides that a receipt by the treasurer or other proper
    officer of the recipient society for a legacy to the society shall be a sufficient discharge to
    executors'; per Viscount Simonds in *Leahy v A-G for New South Wales* [1959] AC 457 at 477,
    [1959] 2 All ER 300 at 306.
6   Cross J in *Neville Estates Ltd v Madden* [1962] Ch 832, [1961] 3 All ER 769, followed in *Re
    Recher's Will Trusts, National Westminster Bank Ltd v National Anti-Vivisection Society Ltd*
    [1972] Ch 526 at 540, [1971] 3 All ER 401 at 408, 409 (residuary estate to 'The Anti-
    Vivisection Society', held, had the society continued its separate existence, the legacy to it
    would have been a valid legacy to the members beneficially, as an accretion to the funds of the
    society subject to the contract the members had inter se as set out in the rules of the society).
7   *Leahy v A-G for New South Wales* [1959] AC 457, [1959] 2 All ER 300 (land to be held upon
    trust for 'such order of nuns of the Catholic Church or the Christian Brothers as my executors
    and trustees shall select'; invalid); *Re Macaulay's Estate, Macaulay v O'Donnell* [1943] Ch
    435n; *Bacon v Pianta* (1965) 40 ALJR 187 (the Communist Party of Australia). See also
    Morrow v McConville (1883) 11 LR Ir 236; *Re Amos, Carrier v Price*, supra; *Re Metcalfe*
    (1973) 29 DLR (3d) 60; *Hogan v Byrne* (1862) 13 ICLR 166; *Stewart v Green* (1870) 5 IR Eq
    470; *Re Grant's Will Trusts* [1979] 3 All ER 359, [1980] 1 WLR 360.
8   *Re Denley's Trust Deed, Holman v H H Martyn & Co Ltd* [1969] 1 Ch 373 at 382–384, [1968]
    3 All ER 65 at 69.
9   *Re Lipinski's Will Trusts, Gosschalk v Levy* [1976] Ch 235, [1977] 1 All ER 33 (the Hull
    Judeans Maccabi Association). These two first instance cases should be treated somewhat
    cautiously as they could be regarded as inconsistent with the decision in *Leahy v A-G for New
    South Wales* [1959] AC 457, [1959] 2 All ER 300.

XIV.   RELIGIOUS DISABILITIES

[9.36]
These have all been removed.[1] A Roman Catholic can be a beneficiary and it
makes no difference that he or she is a member of a society under vows as to the
property of its members.[2] A gift cannot, however, be made to superstitious uses
and this prevents a gift to a contemplative order or society of the Church of
Rome bound by religious or monastic vows[3] as distinct from individual
members of such a society.[4] A gift for the saying of masses for the dead is
valid.[5]

1   Roman Catholic Relief Act 1829, s 28; 14 *Halsbury's Statutes* (4th edn) 1143.
2   *Re Metcalfe's Trusts* (1864) 2 De GJ & Sm 122.
3   *Cussen v Hynes* [1906] 1 IR 539; *Re Smith, Johnson v Bright-Smith* [1914] 1 Ch 937.
4   *Re Wilkinson's Trusts* (1887) 19 LR Ir 531; *Roche v M'Dermott* [1901] 1 IR 394; *Bradshaw v
    Jackman* (1887) 21 LR Ir 12; *Bourne v Keane* [1919] AC 815.
5   *Bourne v Keane* [1919] AC 815; *Re Caus, Lindeboom v Camille* [1934] Ch 162, and *Re
    Hetherington* [1990] Ch 1, [1989] 2 All ER 129 distinguishing *Gilmour v Coats* [1949] AC 426,
    [1949] 1 All ER 848. See Chapter 102.

XV.   ALIENS

[9.37]
Aliens were always capable of taking a gift by will of personalty and the common law disability of taking a gift of land has long been removed by statute.[1] An enemy alien or a person resident in enemy or enemy-occupied territory could not in time of war receive a gift by will because it would vest in the custodian of enemy property.[2]

1   Naturalization Act 1870; see now the British Nationality Act 1981; 31 *Halsbury's Statutes* (4th edn) 157.
2   Trading with the Enemy Act 1939; 50 *Halsbury's Statutes* (4th edn) 342. See *Re Bulwilowicz* [1957] SASR 252. It is possible that an enemy alien could take an interest which did not vest until after the termination of the war as officially declared.

XVI.   DISCRIMINATION

[9.38]
Apart from statute, it would seem that a trust which discriminated against potential beneficiaries on the grounds of colour[1] or religion[2] was not void as being contrary to public policy. Acts of discrimination against sections of the community are now governed by the Race Relations Act 1976[3] and the Sex Discrimination Act 1975.[4] The relevant provisions of these Acts are discussed post in the context of charitable gifts.[5]

1   *Re Dominion Students' Hall Trust* [1947] Ch 183.
2   *Re Lysaght, Hill v Royal College of Surgeons of England* [1966] Ch 191, [1965] 2 All ER 888.
3   7 *Halsbury's Statutes* (4th edn) 115.
4   7 *Halsbury's Statutes* (4th edn) 36.
5   See Chapter 102.

XVII.   MINORS

[9.39]
Gifts to minors. A gift to a minor whether of realty or personalty is good, but two problems arise. First, it is not possible to vest a legal estate in a minor.[1] Since a will operates only in equity[2] this does not of itself matter, but the form of the gift may affect the nature of the interest which the minor takes.[3] Second, it is not generally possible for personal representatives to obtain a valid receipt and discharge from the minor until he attains full age,[4] as a minor cannot give a valid receipt for a legacy[5] unless the will expressly so provides.[6]

The provisions of the Trusts of Land and Appointment of Trustees Act 1996 must be noted in relation to conveyances or gifts of land to minors after 1 January 1997. Where after that date a person purports to convey legal estate in land to a minor, or to two or more minors, alone, the conveyance will not be effective to pass a legal estate but will operate as a declaration that the land is held in trust for the minor or minors.[7] Where there is a purported conveyance to a minor and another person who is of full age, then the conveyance will operate to vest the land in the person of full age in trust for the minor and the other person.[8] In the circumstances where previously a conveyance to a minor would have been deemed to operate as an agreement to execute a settlement in favour of the minor[9] the conveyance will now take effect as a declaration of a trust of land.[10] In all other circumstances, including cases of intestacy where on or after 1 January 1997, a legal estate in land would vest in a person who is a minor if that person were of full age, the land is deemed to be held in trust for the minor.[11]

1   The previous position was governed by the Settled Land Act 1925. But see now the Trusts of Land and Appointment of Trustees Act 1996, s 2 , to the effect that no new settlements can be created after 1 January 1997 under the Settled Land Act 1925. By the Family Law Reform Act 1969, s 1(2): 'infant' or 'minor' means under 18 years of age.
2   Law of Property (Amendment) Act 1924, Sch 9, para 3; 37 *Halsbury's Statutes* (4th edn) 119.
3   See now the Trusts of Land and Appointment of Trustees Act 1996 (TLATA 1996) on the previous position of trusts for sale and on the creation of entailed interests. The previous effect of the Administration of Estates Act 1925, s 51 (3) has been amended by the TLATA 1996. Now if the minor dies under age, unmarried and without issue, he is deemed by the TLATA 1996 to have had a life interest; TLATA 1996, s 25(2), Sch 3, para 4. See the Family Law Reform Act 1969, s 1(2), 6 *Halsbury's Statutes* (4th edn) 121 and *Re Taylor, Pullan v Taylor* [1931] 2 Ch 242.
4   *Philips v Paget* (1740) 2 Atk 80. Where the minor is abroad the legacy is payable when the minor attains full age under English law or the law of the domicile, whichever first happens: *Re Hellmann's Will* (1866) LR 2 Eq 363.
5   *Philips v Paget* (1740) 2 Atk 80; *Ledward v Hassells* (1856) 2 K & J 370.
6   *Re Denekin, Peters v Tanchereau* (1895) 72 LT 220, the executor is not obliged to pay unless the will also provides that the receipt of the minor is to be a sufficient discharge: *Re Robertson* (1908) 17 OLR 568; *Re Somech, Westminster Bank Ltd v Phillips* [1957] Ch 165, [1956] 3 All ER 523.
7   TLATA 1996, Sch 1, paras 1 and 2. See para 1(1).
8   TLATA 1996, Sch 1, para 1(2).
9   Under the Settled Land Act 1925, s 27.
10 TLATA 1996, Sch 1, para 1(3).
11 TLATA 1996, Sch 1, para 2.

[9.40]
Receipts on behalf of minors—former law. Under the previous law personal representatives were not discharged by paying the legacy to the father[1] or any person other than his guardian[2] unless the will expressly or impliedly authorises such payment,[3] or unless the minor ratifies such payment on attaining his majority.[4] In the absence of such an authority the personal representative can obtain a full discharge only by payment of the legacy into court or by creating a trust under the Administration of Estates Act 1925, s 42.[5] Before 1925, if an executor desirous of distributing the residue set aside and invested in proper securities an ample sum to answer a minor's legacy, he was nevertheless personally liable for any loss by reason of the investment proving insufficient when the minor attained his majority.[6] The executor had, however, as now, a statutory power to pay a minor's legacy into court.[7] Now, where a minor is absolutely entitled, under the will or on the intestacy of a person, whether dying before or after 1925, to a devise or legacy or to the residue of the estate of the deceased, or any share under the will, if any, of the deceased devised or bequeathed to trustees for the minor, the personal representatives of the deceased may appoint a trust corporation or two or more individuals not exceeding four (whether or not including the personal representatives or one or more of them) to

be the trustee or trustees of such devise, legacy, residue or share for the minor, and to be trustees of any land devised or any land being or forming part of such residue or share for the purposes of the Settled Land Act 1925, and of the statutory provisions relating to the management of land during a minority, and may execute, or do any assurance or thing required for vesting such devise, legacy, residue or share in the trustee or trustees as appointed.[8] On such appointment the personal representatives as such are discharged from all further liability in respect of such devise, legacy, residue or share, and the same may be retained in its existing condition or state of investment, or may be converted into money, and such money may be invested in any authorised investment.[9]

1   *Dagley v Tolferry* (1715) 1 P Wms 285; *Rotherham v Fanshaw* (1748) 3 Atk 628; *Cooper v Thornton* (1790) 3 Bro CC 96; *Re Nakauchi Estate* [1927] 3 DLR 1087. A small legacy has been ordered by the court to be paid to the father: *Walsh v Walsh* (1852) 1 Drew 64; and a legacy given to a parent for himself and his child may be paid to the parent: *Cooper v Thornton* (1790) 3 Bro CC 96; *Robinson v Tickell* (1893) 8 Ves 142.

2   *Dobbs v Brain* [1892] 2 QB 207. A good receipt can be given by the guardian for capital: *M'Creight v M'Creight* (1849) 13 I Eq R 314; *Huggins v Law* (1887) 14 AR 383; *Sime v Hume* (1901) 20 NZLR 191; or the income of the legacy, *Re Long, Lovegrove v Long* [1901] WN 166. A married minor can give a receipt for income: Law of Property Act 1925, s 21; see Vol 2, Part G, para **[246.39]**. Where the minor is not in England, it must be shown that the guardian's receipt is a full discharge by the local law: *Re Crichton's Trust* (1855) 24 LTOS 267.

3   *Cooper v Thornton* (1790) 3 Bro CC 96; *Robinson v Tickell* (1893) 8 Ves 142; *Re Parton, Parton v Parton* (1911) 131 LT Jo 106.

4   *Cooper v Thornton* (1790) 3 Bro CC 96.

5   Trustee Act 1925, s 63; 48 *Halsbury's Statutes* (4th edn) 535.

6   *Re Salomons, Public Trustee v Wortley* [1920] 1 Ch 290.

7   Trustee Act 1925, s 63; 48 *Halsbury's Statutes* (4th edn) 535 (as amended by the Family Law Reform Acts 1969 and 1987).

8   Administration of Estates Act 1925, s 42(1); 17 *Halsbury's Statutes* (4th edn) 448. A number of minor and consequential amendments have been made to the Settled Land Act 1925 and ss 27 and 29 have been repealed, all with effect from 1 January 1997, by the Trusts of Land and Appointment of Trustees Act 1997, s 25(1), (2), Sch 3, para 2 and Sch 4. An appointment may be made under this section by an attorney administrator: *Re Kehr, Martin v Foges* [1952] Ch 26, [1951] 2 All ER 812. In some cases a sum has been set aside to answer the legacy, but this has not freed the residue from liability, *Rimell v Simpson* (1848) 18 LJ Ch 55; *Re Hall, Foster v Metcalfe* [1903] 2 Ch 226 at 233. But such a sum could now be deposited or invested in redeemable government security so that loss of capital would be next to impossible, and in a proper case the executors become free from liability: *Re Hall, Foster v Metcalfe* [1903] 2 Ch 226 at 233. The court has on occasion allowed small sums to be paid into the National Savings Bank to the account of the infant: *Elliott v Elliott* (1885) 54 LJ Ch 1142.

9   Administration of Estates Act 1925, s 42(1) (s 42(6)(a) has been amended by the Trustee Act 2000, Sch 2, para 37). The section does not apply if the minor is not absolutely entitled: *Re Yerburgh, Yerburgh v Yerburgh* [1928] WN 208.

[9.41]

Minor domiciled abroad. A legacy may be paid to a minor domiciled abroad on his attaining full age by the lex loci, though not of age by English law.[1] The court will not, however, pay a legacy to the father of a minor domiciled abroad as of right, and without evidence as to the application for the benefit of the minor, even if by the lex loci the father is entitled to receive the money as legal guardian.[2]

1   *Re Hellmann's Will* (1866) LR 2 Eq 363; *Re Schnapper* [1928] Ch 420.

2   *Re Chatard's Settlement* [1899] 1 Ch 712.

[9.42]
Receipts on behalf of minors—new law. Under the Guardianship Act 1973, s 7 a guardian of a minor had the statutory power to receive or recover in his own name for the benefit of the minor any property which the minor was entitled to receive or recover, and there was a similar power under the previous law. The Children Act 1989, section 3(3)[1] has now re-enacted this power, and, more importantly, extended it so that it is conferred on any person having 'parental responsibility' for a minor, a term which includes parents as well as guardians[2]. Accordingly, a parent with parental responsibility for a minor can now give a good receipt for a legacy to which that minor is entitled, and, moreover, may require it to be paid to him.[3]

1   Printed in Vol 2, Part G, para **[244.119]**. It came into force on 14 October 1991. For the former law see para **[9.40]** supra.
2   See Chapter 28 on the Appointment of Guardians.
3   See Michael Waterman 'Minor Solutions: Receipt Clauses Under the Children Act 1989 Regime' [1997] Private Client Business 37.

[9.43]
Trust. A minor cannot be appointed a trustee.[1]

1   Law of Property Act 1925, s 20; 37 *Halsbury's Statutes* (4th edn) 143, as amended by the Family Law Reform Acts 1969 and 1987.

XVIII.   CRIMINALS

[9.44]
Capacity to receive. Under the old law a gift to a 'felon' was in much the same position as one to a minor. Such a gift vested in the 'felon' but the property had to be paid to or vested in his administrator under the provisions of the Forfeiture Act 1870.[1] These provisions have, however, now been repealed and the 'felon' can receive and give a good discharge for the gift.[2]

1   See the Forfeiture Act 1870, ss 9, 10; since repealed.
2   Criminal Justice Act 1948, s 70; 12 *Halsbury's Statutes* (4th edn) 215. The Criminal Law Act 1967, ss 1; 12 *Halsbury's Statutes* (4th edn) 316, abolished the old classification of felonies and misdemeanours.

XIX.   PERSONS OF UNSOUND MIND

[9.45]
Capacity to receive. There is no objection to a person of unsound mind being a beneficiary under a will, but the personal representatives of the testator will not get a good discharge unless they have no notice of the unsoundness of mind. If they have such notice, they have the choice of several courses. They may pay the legacy into court.[1] If in the case of an adult person of unsound mind they appropriate and set apart the legacy and accumulate the dividends, they will be free from liability.[2] They may pay the legacy to the receiver appointed, by a nominated judge, or master of the Court of Protection, to acquire the property in the name or on behalf of the patient.[3]

1   Trustee Act 1925, s 63; 48 *Halsbury's Statutes* (4th edn) 535.
2   *Pothecary v Pothecary* (1848) 2 De G & Sm 738.
3   Mental Health Act 1983, ss 99, 100, 101; 28 *Halsbury's Statutes* (4th edn) 968, 969, 970, *Re Oppenheim's Will Trusts, Westminster Bank Ltd v Oppenheim* [1950] Ch 633, [1950] 2 All ER 86. As to the limited circumstances in which the Chancery Court has jurisdiction, see *Re K's Settlement Trusts* [1969] 2 Ch 1, [1969] 1 All ER 194.

XX.   DELEGATION OF TESTAMENTARY POWER

[9.46]
The fundamental principle is that an intending testator cannot delegate to another the task of deciding how his property shall be willed.[1] As it was put in a leading case, ... he cannot leave it to someone else to make a will for him ... '.[2] Equally, he cannot leave to another a power to revoke his will after his death.[3] However, powers of appointment may be created by will so that a testator may provide that a special class of persons, or of institutions invested by law with the capacity of persons to hold property, are to take in such shares as a third person may determine, but this is only because the testator has disposed of the beneficial interest in favour of that class as his beneficiaries.[4] The class must not be described in terms so vague and indeterminate that the trustees are afforded no guidance as to the ambit of their selection.[5] On this basis a wide ranging power of appointment has recently been upheld.[6] The judge refused to accept that the non-delegation rule cast doubts on the validity of powers of appointment created by will, whether special, general or hybrid. Such powers have been upheld in a number of modern cases.[7] The judge thought that the non-delegation rule was confined to the content of gifts for purposes which were expressed in conceptually vague language so that it would be impossible for the court to say whether any specific application was within the terms of the will or not.[8] A true exception to the non-delegation rule applies in the case of charitable gifts, where the testator may confer a wide discretion to select particular charities provided he declares a charitable purpose.[9]

1   Per Latey J in *Re Morris, Lloyds Bank Ltd v Peake* [1970] 1 All ER 1057 at 1066; see *Hastilow v Stobie* (1865) LR 1 P & D 64 at 67. He can, of course, entrust someone else with the task of *drafting* his will. It is also possible for some other person in the testator's presence and by his direction to sign the will on the testator's behalf; Wills Act 1837, s 9; 50 *Halsbury's Statutes* (4th edn) 578; see Vol 2, Part G, paras **[244.6]** and **[244.7]**.
2   Viscount Haldane in *A-G v National Provincial and Union Bank of England* [1924] AC 262 at 268; Lord Macmillan in *A-G (New Zealand) v New Zealand Insurance Co* [1936] 3 All ER 888 at 890; and in *Chichester Diocesan Fund and Board of Finance Inc v Simpson* [1944] AC 341 at 349; Lord Penzance in *Re Smith's Goods* (1869) LR 1 P & D 717; Lord Robertson in *Blair v Duncan* [1902] AC 37 at 47; Lord Halsbury LC in *Grimond (or MacIntyre) v Grimond* [1905] AC 124 at 126; Lord Haldane in *Houston v Burns* [1918] AC 337 at 342; CROSS J in *Re Abraham's Will Trusts, Caplan v Abrahams* [1969] 1 Ch 463, [1967] 2 All ER 1175; *Lutheran Church of Australia etc v Farmers' Co-operative Executors and Trustees Ltd* (1969–70) 121 CLR 628; *Gerhardy v Bible Society* (1982) 30 SASR 12; *Heran v James* [1982] 2 NSWLR 376; Templeman J in *Re Manisty's Settlement, Manisty v Manisty* [1973] 2 All ER 1203 at 1206; *Re Lysiak* (1975) 55 DLR (3d) 161.
3   *Re Smith's Goods* (1869) LR 1 P & D 717 at 719 ('I give my wife the option of adding this codicil to my will or not, as she may think proper or necessary'; invalid).
4   Per Viscount Haldane in *Houston v Burns* [1918] AC 337 at 342, 343; Lord Macmillan in *Chichester Diocesan Fund and Board of Finance Inc v Simpson* [1944] AC 341 at 349; and in *A-G (New Zealand) v New Zealand Insurance Co* [1936] 3 All ER 888 at 890; *Re Weekes'*

Settlement [1897] 1 Ch 289; *Re Combe, Combe v Combe* [1925] Ch 210. In *Re Park, Public Trustee v Armstrong* [1932] 1 Ch 580, Clauson J held valid an intermediate power conferred by a testator on an individual to appoint to anyone in the world except the donee of the power. Likewise, in *Re Abraham's Will Trusts, Caplan v Abrahams* [1969] 1 Ch 463, [1967] 2 All ER 1175; Cross J held valid an intermediate power conferred by a testator on trustees to appoint to anyone in the world except the trustees; *Whishaw v Stephens* [1970] AC 508, [1968] 3 All ER 785, special power upheld; *Re Manisty's Settlement, Manisty v Manisty* [1973] 2 All ER 1203 at 1206, power conferred on trustees to nominate and add to a class of beneficiaries in a settlement, upheld; applied in *Re Hay's Settlement Trusts* [1981] 3 All ER 786, [1982] 1 WLR 202. But in *Lutheran Church of Australia, etc v Farmers' Co-operative Executors and Trustees Ltd* (1969–70) 121 CLR 628, the court was divided on the validity of a discretionary power to transfer. The latitude shown in respect of wide-ranging powers of appointment created by will is somewhat anomalous since this exception tends to consume the rule.

5   Lord Macmillan in *Chichester Diocesan Fund and Board of Finance Inc v Simpson* [1944] AC 341 at 349, referring to Viscount Haldane in *Houston v Burns* [1918] AC 337 at 342, 343; Lord Simonds [1918] AC 337, at 371.

6   *Re Beatty's Will Trusts* [1990] 3 All ER 844, [1990] 1 WLR 1503. In that case a testatrix bequeathed her personal estate and a legacy of £1.5m to her trustees to 'allocate ... to or among such person or persons ... as they think fit' and by another clause she requested the trustees 'to give effect to any memorandum ... which may be deposited with ... my will or left among my papers ... or ... to any wishes of mine of which they shall be aware ...' The residuary beneficiaries challenged the validity of distributions made by the trustees under the clause on the ground that the gifts infringed the cardinal rule noted above. The power was held to be valid, citing *Williams on Wills* (6th edn) at p 850.

7   *Re Abrahams' Will Trusts, Caplan v Abrahams* [1969] 1 Ch 463, [1967] 2 All ER 1175; *Re Park, Public Trustee v Armstrong* [1932] 1 Ch 580 and *Re Jones, Public Trustee v Jones* [1945] Ch 105.

8   Per Hoffman J in *Re Beatty's Will Trusts* [1990] 3 All ER 844 at 849. If an application of money in accordance with such a gift was upheld, it would not be giving effect to the will of the testator because that, *ex hypothesi*, was incapable of being enforced. It would be giving effect to the autonomous act of the executor. In that sense it would be truly a delegation of the testamentary power. But in contrast, Hoffman J thought that the execution of an otherwise valid general, special or intermediate power, was giving effect to the testator's will and not making a will for a testator who had failed to do so himself. In a bold conclusion the judge stated:

'It seems to me, however, that a common law rule against testamentary delegation, in the sense of a restriction on the scope of testamentary powers, is a chimera, a shadow cast by the rule of certainty, having no independent existence.' (at p 849).

Accordingly the judge concluded that since the clauses in the will would have been valid powers of appointment if they had been inserted in a settlement and gave effect to the testatrix's will, rather than permitting the trustees to make a will when she had failed to do so, the distributions made by the trustees under the clauses were valid. *Williams on Wills* was referred to in support of the validity of a wide power of appointment.

See also *Re Nicholls* (1987) 34 DLR (4th) 321; *Gregory v Hudson* (1998) 45 NSWLR 300 (not a breach of the rule against delegation to give property by will to a pre-existing trust).

9   Viscount Simon LC, in *Chichester Diocesan Fund and Board of Finance Inc v Simpson* [1944] AC 341 at 348; per Lord Porter at 364; Lord Cane in *A-G v National Provincial and Union Bank of England* [1924] AC 262 at 264.

Form of will and execution

CHAPTER 10

Form of will

I. IN GENERAL

[10.1]
Formalities required. Wills must be executed in accordance with the statutory formalities.[1] English law has no doctrine of substantial compliance[2] and with the exceptions of privileged wills[3] and foreign wills[4] there is no power to relax the statutory stipulations. Subject to that a will may be in any form[5] provided (i) it is in writing,[6] (ii) it is executed in accordance with the statutory provisions,[7] and (iii) it is clear that the deceased intended that the document should operate after his death.[8] Such intention must be fixed and final[9] and may be proved by extrinsic evidence.[10] A document which is in terms an instruction for a more formal document may be admitted to probate if it is clear that it contains a record of the deliberate and final expression of the testator's wishes as to the disposition of his property.[11] Where the document is unfinished, there must be shown a fixed and final intention as to the disposition of property and that its completion was prevented by act of God.[12]

---

1 See the next succeeding chapters.
2 As in some Commonwealth jurisdictions such as South Australia for example; see Wills Act 1936–1975, s 12(2); *Re Dale's Estate* (1984) 32 SASR 215 and other cases reported at pp 227, 413, and 473 in the same volume of the reports; *Re Williams' Estate* (1985) 36 SASR 423; *Re Smith's Estate* (1985) 38 SASR 30; *Re Roberts' Estate* (1985) 38 SASR 324; *Re Lynch's Estate* [1986] SASR 131. On the analogous Queensland Succession Act 1981–1983, s 9, see *Re Johnston* (1985) 1 Qd R 516. See also the Hong Kong provisions in s 5(2) of the Wills Ordinance providing for probate of a will which fails to satisfy the usual requirements of s 5(1). But see the Administration of Justice Act 1985, s 49 providing for a simplification of procedure for approving a compromise of a probate action which can relate to the validity of one or more wills.
3 See Chapter 16.
4 See Chapter 23.
5 *Whyte v Pollok* (1882) 7 App Cas 400 at 409; *Masterman v Maberly* (1829) 2 Hag Ecc 235; *Oldroyd v Harvey* [1907] P 326; *Re Somers* [1941] 1 DLR 674. However, the Principal Registry of the Family Division has reminded solicitors that it is desirable that wills should be prepared in a form which lends itself to being easily photocopied. The ideal is for the will to be foolscap or A4 size, typed in black on white paper; [1974] CLY 4013. Requests for copies of wills by post are now dealt with in York Probate Sub-Registry, and requests sent to the Principal Registry will be forwarded to York: see *Practice Direction* [1990] 3 All ER 734, [1990] 1 WLR 1510. As to form of will made outside the United Kingdom, see Chapter 23. As to holograph wills, see para **[10.18]** infra.
6 Wills Act 1837, s 9, as substituted in the case of deaths on or after 1 January 1983, by the Administration of Justice Act 1982, s 17; 50 *Halsbury's Statutes* (4th edn) 578; see Vol 2, Part G, para **[244.93]**. As to wills of members of the forces, see Chapter 16.

7   Wills Act 1837, s 9. As to execution of will, see Chapters 10 and 11, and as to attestation, see Chapter 12. A gift by placing money or securities in joint names though only intended to have effect after death does not require execution as a will: *Young v Sealey* [1949] Ch 278, [1949] 1 All ER 92.

8   *Nichols v Nichols* (1814) 2 Phillim 180; *King's Proctor v Daines* (1830) 3 Hag Ecc 218; *Re Webb's Goods* (1864) 3 Sw & Tr 482; *Milnes v Foden* (1890) 15 PD 105. It must, however, contain a disposition of property: *Re Warin* [1919] NZLR 555. A document duly executed as a will stating that if anything happens to the maker he wants certain named persons 'to take possession of anything that belongs to me' has been held not to be a will: *Re Rodger Estate* [1943] 2 WWR 700. See the propositions stated by Mustill LJ in *Re Berger* [1989] 1 All ER 591 at 599 on the fundamental requirements of English wills. Refer also to Sir Denys Buckley's comments at 602 in the same case.

9   *Theakston v Marson* (1832) 4 Hag Ecc 290; *Whyte v Pollok* (1882) 7 App Cas 400; *Godman v Godman* [1920] P 261; *Re Benton's Will* (1959) 20 DLR (2d) 737. If what is produced is held to be two alternative drafts, there is no such intention: *Boughton-Knight v Wilson* (1915) 32 TLR 146.

10 *Re English's Goods* (1864) 3 Sw & Tr 586; *Cock v Cooke* (1866) LR 1 P & D 241; *Re Coles' Goods* (1871) LR 2 P & D 362. Evidence may be given that a document in form testamentary was not intended to be so: *Trevelyan v Trevelyan* (1810) 1 Phillim 149; *Lister v Smith* (1863) 3 Sw & Tr 282 applied in *Corbett v Newey* [1995] 1 All ER 570. *Re Nosworthy's Goods* (1865) 4 Sw & Tr 44 (where there were two incorporated wills, one of which it was proved was executed by mistake); *Re Horner* [1965] VR 177 where two documents executed on the same day and one later destroyed; remaining document not a will because not finally intended as such at the time of execution). A statement in the document that it is 'not meant as a legal will' is, it seems, conclusive: *Ferguson-Davie v Ferguson-Davie* (1890) 15 PD 109. A document will not be granted probate if it cannot be carried out as a will, although there is evidence of testamentary intention: *Re Watt's Estate* (1890) 8 NZLR 72. A document partly testamentary has been admitted to probate: *Wolfe v Wolfe* [1902] 2 IR 246.

11 *Godman v Godman* [1920] P 261 at 271; *Re Gray* [1958] SCR 392 (where a letter to a solicitor showed that the testatrix did not want it to operate as a will). See also n 4, para **[10.18]** infra, and the text thereto.

12 *Theakston v Marson* (1832) 4 Hag Ecc 290.

[10.2]
Date. There is no requirement in law that a will should be dated and the lack of a date or the inclusion of a wrong date cannot invalidate a will.[1] A will is made when the formalities of proper execution are completed not necessarily at the date it is dated.[2] It can be noted that dating is required for an appointment of guardians, even when by will.[3]

1   *Corbett v Newey* [1996] 2 All ER 914; see further discussed in para **[10.4]** infra.
2   *Corbett v Newey* [1996] 2 All ER 914.
3   Children Act 1989, s 5(5).

[10.3]
International will. The form of an international will[1] must be in accordance with the uniform law agreed at the Convention on International Wills.[2] The Convention published an Annex to the Convention which set out a number of detailed regulations relating to the manner of execution of the international will and included the form of an authenticating certificate to be completed by an 'authorised person'. The Administration of Justice Act 1982 (AJA 1982), s 27 simply provides that this Annex 'shall have the force of law in the United Kingdom', and the Annex is published as Sch 2 of the AJA 1982.[3]

The formalities prescribed in the Annex envisage a central and crucial role to be played by the 'authorised person' who in continental countries would be a notary. English law has no exact equivalent and the AJA 1982, s 28 provides that the persons authorised to act in the United Kingdom in connection with international wills will be solicitors and notaries public. International wills executed in accordance with these formalities (which are in fact similar but more stringent than the formalities demanded in English law by the Wills Act 1837, s 9) will be acceptable in addition to the forms recognised by the Wills Act 1963.[4]

1   See the Administration of Justice Act 1982, s 27(3); 50 *Halsbury's Statutes* (4th edn) 620; see Vol 2, Part G, para **[244.103]**.
2   Concluded at Washington on 26 October 1973, AJA 1982, s 27(3).
3   The provisions of the AJA 1982, namely ss 27 and 28, relating to international wills are to come into force on such a day as the Lord Chancellor and the Secretary of State may by order jointly appoint, AJA 1982, s 76(5), (6).
4   See Chapter 23.

II.   TESTAMENTARY INTENTION

[10.4]
Animus testandi. An instrument cannot be a provable will unless the maker had an *animus testandi*.[1] This means that the maker must intend that his document shall take effect as a revocable ambulatory disposition of his property which is to take effect on death.[2] The document in whatever form, must disclose the intention of the maker respecting the posthumous disposition of his property.[3] Subject to this it is not necessary that the testator should intend to perform or be aware that he has performed a testamentary act,[4] but there must be the intention that the document is dependent on the death of the person who executes it.[5] The position is put thus by Sir James Hannen P:[6]

'The true principle appears to be that if there is proof, either in the paper itself or from clear evidence *dehors*, first that it was the intention of the writer of the paper to convey the benefits by the instrument which would be conveyed by it if considered as a will; secondly, that death was the event which was to give effect to it, then whatever may be its form it may be admitted to probate as testamentary. It is not necessary that the testator should intend to perform or be aware that he has performed a testamentary act.'

If it is shown by extrinsic evidence that a document which appears to be a will was not intended by the maker to operate with unconditional effect then it will not be admitted to probate.[7]

1   Per Mustill LJ in *Re Berger* [1989] 1 All ER 591 at 599, a zavah, executed in accordance with the required formalities of English law, admitted to probate, see para **[10.12]** infra.
2   Per Mustill LJ in *Re Berger* [1989] 1 All ER 591 at 599.
3   Per Buckley LJ, *Re Berger* [1989] 1 All ER 591 at 602.
4   *Milnes v Foden* (1890) 15 PD 105, at 107; *Re Kemp Estate* [1954] 2 DLR 451.
5   *Cock v Cooke* (1866) LR 1 P & D 241 (distinction between will and present gift); *Robertson v Smith* (1870) LR 2 P & D 43 (the same); *Re Slinn's Goods* (1890) 15 PD 156 (deed poll shown by extrinsic evidence to be intended as a will); *McMurty v Scarrow and Scarrow* (1938) 20 DLR 270.
6   *Milnes v Foden* (1890) 15 PD 105 at 107.
7   *Corbett v Newey* [1996] 2 All ER 914, CA applying *Re Berger* [1989] 1 All ER 591. See the case further discussed above in Chapter 1, para **[1.10]** supra, on Conditional Wills.

III.   VARIOUS DOCUMENTS ADMITTED AS WILLS

[10.5]

Deeds. A document in the form of a deed may be considered a will if it bears upon its face a testamentary intention[1] or if it is not intended to have any operation or effect until the maker's death it is testamentary.[2] All these documents must be executed as a will.[3]

1   *Green v Andrews* (1877) 41 JP 105.
2   *Re Montgomery's Goods* (1846) 5 Notes of Cases 99; *Re Morgan's Goods* (1866) LR 1 P & D 214; *Robertson v Smith* (1870) LR 2 P & D 43; *Re Anziani, Herbert v Christopherson* [1930] 1 Ch 407 (deed of appointment expressed to operate both inter vivos and as will); *Fielding v Walshaw, Re Walshaw's Goods* (1879) 48 LJP 27; *Green v Andrews* (1877) 41 JP 105, (deed poll); *Milnes v Foden* (1890) 15 PD 105 (deed poll). The court will not act on such a deed unless a grant of probate has been obtained: *Consett v Bell* (1842) 1 Y & C Ch Cas 569. An imperfect voluntary gift, though it refers to the donor's death, will not be enforced after death: *Dillon v Coppin* (1839) 4 My & Cr 647; *Re McDonald* (1911) 30 NZLR 896 (power of attorney). A deed acknowledging debt and making it payable after death out of a certain fund must be executed as a will to be operative: *Re Carile, Dakin v Trustees etc Co* [1920] VLR 263; *Conyers v Orr and Skelton* [1944] 1 DLR 201 (transfer of land); *Bessette v Toronto General Trusts Corpn (No 3)* (1953) 7 WWRNS 673 (transfer of land). It cannot, however, be regarded as a will if the disposition is irrevocable and takes immediate effect; *Re Halpin's Goods* (1873) 8 IR Eq 567; *Beyer v Beyer* [1960] VLR 126.
3   *Re Williams, Williams v Ball* [1917] 1 Ch 1; *Boyko v Jendzyjowski* (1958) 16 DLR (2d) 464; *Carson v Wilson* (1961) 26 DLR (2d) 307 and see para **[12.3]**, n 4.

[10.6]

Voluntary settlement. To be admitted as a will the document must have no operation as a document inter vivos or be clearly intended to operate after death.[1] In the reported cases, documents of this nature which have failed to fulfil the conditions have been held not to be testamentary.[2]

1   *Patch v Shore* (1862) 2 Drew & Sm 589; *Glynn v Oglander* (1829) 2 Hag Ecc 428; *Fletcher v Fletcher* (1844) 4 Hare 67; *Re Robinson's Goods* (1867) LR 1 P & D 384 (lease providing for application of rent after death).
2   *Tompson v Browne* (1835) 3 My & K 32; *Jeffries v Alexander* (1860) 8 HL Cas 594; *Patch v Shore* (1862) 2 Drew & Sm 589.

[10.7]

Instructions for will. These can be admitted only if executed as a will[1] and must be something more than mere heads of instructions.[2]

1   *Guardhouse v Blackburn* (1866) LR 1 P & D 109; *Re Barnes* [1954] NZLR 714, explaining *Re Gilmour* [1948] NZLR 687; *Re Treloar* (1984) 36 SASR 41.
2   *Torre v Castle* (1836) 1 Curt 303. The fact that it is called 'Heads' or 'notes' will not prevent its being a will unless, either upon the face or by extrinsic evidence, it is shown that it was intended only as a memorandum of a future will: *Whyte v Pollok* (1882) 7 App Cas 400; *Re Meynell* (1949) 93 Sol Jo 466; *White v White* (1908) 28 NZLR 129; *George v Daily* (1997) 143 DLR (4th) 273.

[10.8]

Letters. Letters and parts of letters duly attested have been admitted to probate,[1] but though admitted to probate, the terms of the letter must be sufficiently certain for the court to enforce, especially where the letter is to operate as a codicil and vary a gift in a previous will.[2] Where there is an earlier formal will, a letter of instructions will not generally be admitted.[3]

1   *Re Wedge's Goods* (1842) 2 Notes of Cases 14; *Re Mundy's Goods* (1860) 2 Sw & Tr 119; *Re Mitchell Estate (Man)* [1924] 1 DLR 1039; *Re Bathern* [1941] SASR 266. But it must be executed as a will: *Baker v Simes* (1902) 21 NZLR 184; except in jurisdictions where unattested holograph wills are accepted: *Re Stobie Estate* [1942] 3 WWR 414. See also *Permanent Trustee Co v Milton* (1995) 39 NSWLR 330 (letter held not to be a will). A few phrases in a letter will not alter a formal will: *Re Austin's Estate, Sullivan and Lee v Cameron* [1949] 1 WWR 1041. See also Holograph Will, para **[10.18]** infra.
2   *Re Pinckard's Trust* (1858) 27 LJ Ch 422; *Molinari v Winfrey* [1961] SCR 91 (letter must dispose of property).
3   *Re Gray Estate* (1957) 22 WWR 241.

[10.9]

Memoranda. As in the case of all informal documents, these must be duly executed and shown to be testamentary.[1] Subject to this memoranda have been admitted to probate.[2] Unsigned memoranda are not admissible.[3] Incorporation of documents in wills is dealt with elsewhere.[4]

1   *Thorncroft and Clarke v Lashmar* (1862) 2 Sw & Tr 479; *Kreh v Moses* (1892) 22 OR 307 (attempted bequest of insurance policy).
2   *Tapley v Kent* (1846) 1 Rob Eccl 400; *Cock v Cooke* (1866) LR 1 P & D 241; *Re Coles' Goods* (1871) LR 2 P & D 362; *Warwick v Warwick* (1918) 34 TLR 475.
3   *Re Sharp, Sharp v Sharp* (1887) 3 TLR 806; *Hamilton's Trustees v Hamilton* 1901 4 F (Ct of Sess) 266; *Re Willmott's Goods* (1858) 1 Sw & Tr 36 (where the memorandum was below the signature to the will and before a duly executed codicil on the same paper).
4   See Chapter 15.

[10.10]

Orders on banker. These may be admitted to probate if duly executed.[1] Signed mandates to a bank, of themselves non-testamentary, have been held to be ineffective notwithstanding a reference in the will to informal dispositions.[2]

1   *Jones v Nicolay* (1850) 2 Rob Eccl 288; *Re Patterson's Estate, Mitchell v Smith* (1864) 4 De GJ & Sm 422 (a direction to pay promissory note which failed because insufficiently executed); *Re Marsden's Goods* (1860) 1 Sw & Tr 542 (direction to Savings Bank); *Hill v Hill* (1904) 5 OWR 2 (deposit receipt).
2   *Grays Trustees v Murray* 1970 SLT 105 (two signed deposit receipts indorsed to named persons; trustees in will directed to pay such legacies as the testator might leave by any writings under his hand).

[10.11]

Nomination. A nomination under the Industrial and Provident Societies Acts was invalid if it purported to dispose of more than £500, but being duly executed in the presence of two witnesses, it was held operative as a will.[1]

A nomination under a pension trust, although having certain testamentary characteristics, has been held not to be a testamentary disposition subject to the Wills Act 1837.[2]

1   *Re Baxter's Goods* [1903] P 12; *Re Barnes, Ashenden v Heath* [1940] Ch 267; *McFadden v Public Trustee for Victoria* [1981] 1 NSWLR 15, and see para **[1.8]** supra.
2   *Re Danish Bacon Co Ltd Staff Pension Fund, Christensen v Arnett* [1971] 1 All ER 486, [1971] 1 WLR 248; *Baird v Baird* [1990] 2 AC 548, [1990] 2 All ER 300.

[10.12]

A Zavah. A form of Jewish will known as a Zavah recognised by Jewish religious law, which was executed with the formalities required for an English will, has been admitted to probate.[1]

Part D   Form of will and execution

1   *Re Berger* [1989] 1 All ER 591. See Mustill LJ, at 596, for comment on the nature of the
     document.

IV.   WRITING ESSENTIAL

[10.13]

Statutory provision. No will is valid unless it be in writing and executed in the
manner stated in the statute.[1] There is an exception in the case of members of the
forces on actual military service and mariners at sea.[2]

1   Wills Act 1837, s 9, as substituted, in the case of deaths on or after 1 January 1983, by the
     Administration of Justice Act 1982, s 17; 50 *Halsbury's Statutes* (4th edn) 578; see Vol 2,
     Part G, para **[244.93]**.
2   Wills Act 1837, s 11. See Chapter 16.

[10.14]

Any kind of writing or print valid. A will may be written on any material and
may be typed, printed or lithographed,[1] either in whole or in part.[2] Blanks in a
will printed or typed may be filled in in ordinary writing,[3] either in ink or
pencil.[4] A will may be altered in pencil[5] though such alterations must be shown
to be intended as final alterations.[6] A will may be made wholly in pencil.[7]

1   Interpretation Act 1978, Sch 1; 41 *Halsbury's Statutes* (4th edn) 592.
2   *Re Moore's Goods* [1892] P 378; *Re Smithers, Watts v Smithers* [1939] Ch 1015 at 1020,
     [1939] 3 All ER 689 at 692. In *Re Slavinsky's Estate* (1989) 53 SASR 221, the will admitted to
     probate had been written on a wall in the presence of witnesses. *Re Barnes Goods, Hodson v
     Barnes* (1926) 43 TLR 71, where the will was written on an eggshell, was referred to.
3   See *Re Smithers, Watts v Smithers* [1939] Ch 1015.
4   *Re Adams' Goods* (1872) LR 2 P & D 367 (where the ink writing extended over the pencil and
     the pencil writing was ignored as intended to be ink writing).
5   *Re Lawson's Goods* (1842) 6 Jur 349; *Re Hall's Goods* (1871) LR 2 P & D 256; *Re Tonge's
     Goods* (1891) 66 LT 60 (where a printed revocation clause was struck through in pencil).
6   *Re Adams' Goods* (1872) LR 2 P & D 367; *Re Hall's Goods* (1871) LR 2 P & D 256. As to
     alterations, see Chapter 14.
7   *Goods of Usborne* (1909) 25 TLR 519; *Rymes v Clarkson* (1809) 1 Phillim 22; *Simson v Simson*
     (1883) 10 R 1247; *Muir's Trustees* (1869) 8 M 53. If both pencil and ink wills are found, it may
     be inferred that the pencilled one is deliberative (that is, subject to further consideration), and
     the ink one final (*Rymes v Clarkson* (1809) 1 Phillim 22). Where a will appeared to have been
     first written in pencil and then inked over, words only in pencil were not admitted to probate:
     Re Bellamy's Goods (1866) 14 WR 501, and *Re Adams' Goods* (1872) LR 2 P & D 367.

[10.15]

Writing or printing need not be continuous. Testators often use printed or
even written forms prepared in blank and leaving spaces which may or may not
be required to be filled in, or the space left may be too large for what the testator
ultimately decides to put in. In such cases it is immaterial that the will is not
continuous and that the spaces are not ruled through but left completely blank.[1]
A whole page left blank has been accepted.[2] Legacies have been held good when
included in a schedule at the end of the will.[3]

1   *Re Corder's Goods* (1848) 1 Rob Eccl 669; *Corneby v Gibbons* (1849) 1 Rob Eccl 705.
2   *Re Gore's Goods* (1843) 3 Curt 758; *Re Corder's Goods* (1848) 1 Rob Eccl 669.
3   *Re Burnett's Goods* (1884) 2 LTOS 317. As to matters after signature see Chapter 11.

[10.16]
Use of signs. It seems no objection that the testator uses common signs, such as ditto marks[1] or code letters which can be explained by extrinsic evidence.[2]

1   *Murray v Haylow* [1927] 3 DLR 1036.
2   *Kell v Charmer* (1856) 23 Beav 195.

[10.17]
Omission to cancel printed words not required. Printed words clearly not required but not crossed out may be neglected as a matter of construction.[1]

1   *Re Spencer, Hart v Manston* (1886) 54 LT 597; but it has been said that this was not the basis of the decision, see per Harman J in *Re Gare* [1951] 2 All ER 863 at 864, though in the latter case the learned judge came to much the same decision, holding on construction that a prior residuary gift in handwriting carried the whole residue and a partly printed residuary clause was inoperative.

V.   HOLOGRAPH WILL

[10.18]
Nature of holograph will. A holograph will is one written entirely in the handwriting of the testator and signed by him.[1] There can be holograph wills in any jurisdiction, but in some jurisdictions, where the law is derived from the Roman law, unattested holograph wills are valid, the fact that the will is in the handwriting of the testator taking the place of the necessity for the formalities of attestation.[2] English law does not accept the validity of holograph wills unless duly executed in accordance with the requirements of the Wills Act 1837, s 9.[3] A holograph will is not testamentary unless it contains a fixed, final and deliberate expression of intention as to the disposal of property on death.[4]

1   See *Re Brown Estate* (1953) 10 WWRNS 163, where the last three pages were also in the handwriting of the testator but only the first page was signed. Where the evidence showed that the signature was written before the dispositive parts, the will was not admitted to probate: *Re Coughlan Estate* (1955) 16 WWRNS 14.
2   Such jurisdictions are those of Scotland and Quebec, and by modern legislation unattested holograph wills are now valid in most parts of Canada. See *Re James' Estate* [1934] 3 WWR 364; *Re Scott Estate* [1938] 3 WWR 278 (attestation does not deprive the will of its privileges as a holograph will).
3   As substituted, in the case of deaths on or after 1 January 1983, by the Administration of Justice Act 1982, s 17, 50 *Halsbury's Statutes* (4th edn) 578, see Vol 2, Part G, para **[244.93]**.
4   *Whyte v Pollock* (1882) 7 App Cas 400; *Re Beech's Estate, Beech v Public Trustee* [1923] P 46; *Re Gray* [1958] SCR 392; *Canada Permanent Trust Co v Bowman* [1962] SCR 711.

VI.   FORM OF CODICILS

[10.19]
A codicil is executed and attested in the same way as a will.[1]

1   Wills Act 1837, s 9, as amended. See Chapter 20.

VII.   DEPOSIT AND REGISTRATION OF WILLS

[10.20]

A system of voluntary deposit for safe custody of wills has been in operation since 1925[1] and this facility will be extended under provisions in the Administration of Justice Act 1982 (AJA 1982).[2] Under the existing scheme deposit may be made on personal attendance by the testator, or by an agent authorised in writing by the testator to do so, at any registry, or may be sent by post for deposit by the testator or any agent so authorised to the Principal Registry.[3] Such will can be withdrawn, and regulations provided for the procedure on death of the testator.[4]

The AJA 1982 provides that specified registering authorities[5] shall provide and maintain safe and convenient depositories for the custody of the wills of living persons, and that any person may deposit his will therein subject to regulations[6] it will be the duty of the registering authority to register any deposited will[7] and any will required to be registered in accordance with the European Convention on the establishment of a scheme of registration of wills.[8] Regulations, to be drawn up, will provide as to the conditions for the deposit of a will, and as to the manner and procedure for withdrawal or cancellation.[9]

1   Supreme Court of Judicature (Consolidation) Act 1925, s 172; 13 *Halsbury's Statues* (3rd edn) 109; see now the Supreme Court Act 1981, s 126; 17 *Halsbury's Statutes* (4th edn) 546.
2   See AJA 1982, ss 23–26; see Vol 2, Part G, para **[244.99]**; these sections will come into force on such day as the Lord Chancellor and the Secretary of State may jointly appoint, AJA 1982, ss 76(5), (6).
3   Wills (Deposit for Safe Custody) Regulations 1978, SI 1978/1724.
4   SI 1978/1724, regs 8 and 9.
5   Namely, the Principal Registry of the Family Division of the High Court of Justice; the keeper of the Registers of Scotland; and the Probate and Matrimonial Office of the Supreme Court of Northern Ireland, AJA 1982, s 23.
6   AJA 1982, s 23(2), (3).
7   AJA 1982, s 23(4)(a).
8   AJA 1982, s 23(4)(b); the Convention was concluded at Basle on 6 May 1972; AJA 1982, s 24(1).
9   AJA 1982, s 25.

CHAPTER 11

Signature

I. IN GENERAL

[11.1]

Statutory provisions. It is necessary to differentiate between wills of testators who died before 1 January 1983 and wills of testators who die on or after that date.[1] The former are governed by the provisions of the Wills Act 1837 (WA 1837), s 9[2] as originally enacted, and as amended by the Wills Act Amendment Act 1852,[3] which required that the will must be signed 'at the foot or end thereof'. There is no longer any such requirement under the new s 9 as substituted by the Administration of Justice Act 1982 (AJA 1982), s 17[4] but there is the additional requirement that 'it must appear that the testator intended by his signature to give effect to the will'.[5]

The other requirements of the WA 1837, s 9 relating to the testator's signature, namely that the will should ... be signed ... by the testator, or by some other person in his presence and by his direction' and that such ... signature shall be made or acknowledged by the testator in the presence of two or more witnesses present at the same time', are unaffected by the AJA 1982.[6]

---

1   This is the date when the provisions of the AJA 1982, relevant to this discussion, came into effect, AJA 1982, s 73(6); s 76(11).
2   See Vol 2, Part G, para **[244.6]**.
3   See Vol 2, Part G, para **[244.7]**.
4   See Vol 2, Part G, para **[244.93]**; the Wills Act Amendment Act 1852 is repealed, AJA 1982, s 75(1); s 79(5); and Pt I of Sch 9. This applies to the wills of testators who die on or after 1 January 1983. See n 1.
5   New WA 1837, s 9(b); AJA 1982, s 17; 50 *Halsbury's Statutes* (4th edn) 578.
6   See original WA 1837, s 9, and substituted provision.

II. PLACE OF SIGNATURE: DEATHS BEFORE 1 JANUARY 1983

[11.2]

Statutory provisions. The validity of wills of testators who die before 1 January 1983[1] is determined by reference to the WA 1837, s 9[2] as originally enacted subject to the Wills Act 1852.[3] The WA 1837[4] required the signature to be at the foot or end of the will by the testator or by some other person in his presence and by his direction, but this provision was so strictly construed by the courts that an amending Act was passed in 1852.[5] The wording of the later Wills Act

1852 is very particular and may seem needlessly so, but it was designed to nullify the effects of decisions construing the WA 1837 which the legislature disapproved. In view of the repeal of the WA 1852 by the AJA 1982 it is not thought necessary to discuss it in detail,[6] however, some general points can be made.[7] The court in general leant towards validity rather than invalidity and thus a generous attitude towards the position of the signature was adopted.[8]

It has been said[9] that provided the court was satisfied that the whole document was written before the signatures were made and that the dispositive part of the document may be fairly read as preceding and leading up to the part containing the signatures, then strict proof that the several parts of the document were written in a particular order should not be insisted on. Thus in *Re Little, Foster v Cooper*[10] the court did not think that the fact that at the time of execution, a blank space intervened between the body of the will and the signature of the deceased rendered the will invalid, since it appeared that the intention of the deceased was to give effect to the document as a testamentary disposition immediately, although he intended before long to add something to it in the nature of a codicil.[11] Likewise a will has been pronounced valid although part of the dispositive provisions extended below the signature.[12] However, where the will was quite clearly signed at the top and not at the bottom it has been pronounced invalid.[13] Further where there is clear evidence that the part of the will in question was written after signature, the court must exclude it.[14]

1   Which is the date when the relevant provisions of the AJA 1982 take effect, see the AJA 1982, s 73(6); s 76(11).
2   WA 1837, s 9; see Vol 2, Part G, paras **[244.6]** and **[244.7]**.
3   Wills Act Amendment Act 1852; see Vol 2, Part G, para **[244.7]**; repealed in respect of post 1982 deaths by the AJA 1982, , s 75(1) and Pt 1, Sch 9; see AJA 1982, s 73(6).
4   WA 1837, s 9, as originally enacted.
5   See n 3 supra.
6   For a detailed discussion see the fifth edition of this work, pp 78–81.
7   This discussion will concentrate in the main, on the modern English authorities.
8   See for example, *Re Wotton's Goods* (1874) LR 3 P & D 159; *Re Coombs's Goods* (1866) LR 1 P & D 302; compare *Royle v Harris* [1895] P 163; *Re Gee's Goods* (1898) 78 LT 843.
9   Per Sir Boyd Merriman, in *Re Long's Estate* [1936] P 166 at 173; see also *Re Little, Foster v Cooper* [1960] 1 All ER 387, [1960] 1 WLR 495.
10 *Re Little, Foster v Cooper* [1960] 1 All ER 387, [1960] 1 WLR 495.
11 The testator wrote his name on the reverse of the back sheet some eight inches down the page and the attesting witnesses signed below. On death it was found that a disposition of specific chattels had been added in the blank space above the signatures. The will was admitted to probate excluding the gift of the chattels.
12 *Re Ainsworth's Goods* (1870) LR 2 P & D 151 (words written below signature); *Re Hornby's Goods* [1946] P 171, [1946] 2 All ER 150 (box reserved in body of will for signature); *Re Roberts's Estate* [1934] P 102 (will signed in margin at right angles to text).
13 *Re Stalman, Stalman v Jones* (1931) 145 LT 339, followed in *Re Beadle, Mayes v Beadle* [1974] 1 All ER 493, [1974] 1 WLR 417; *Re Harris, Murray v Everard* [1952] P 319, [1952] 2 All ER 409; and this is so although witnesses sign at the bottom: *Re Wright* [1962] OWN 122. Where there was a signature of the testator and those of two witnesses with an attestation clause at the top and the testator signed again at the bottom it was also held that there was not sufficient compliance with the statutory conditions: *Re Bercovitz's Estate, Canning v Enever* [1962] 1 All ER 552, [1962] 1 WLR 321.
14 *Re Arthur's Goods* (1871) LR 2 P & D 273; *Re Little, Foster v Cooper* [1960] 1 All ER 387, [1960] 1 WLR 495; *Royle v Harris* [1895] P 163; but will try to admit parts proved to have been written before signature, see *Re Long's Estate* [1936] P 166, [1936] 1 All ER 435.

[11.3]

Signature constructively at end of will. Words, either wholly or in part, physically beneath the signature have been considered to be above it either by reason of the mode of writing[1] or by reason of the use of an asterisk[2] or other sign of interpolation.[3] Where the court is satisfied that the signature really follows the dispositions, though it may appear above some part thereof, the whole may be admitted to probate.[4] The fact that the executed part of the will terminates with an incomplete sentence has not always been enough to justify the admission to probate of the following words.[5]

1   *Re Ainsworth's Goods* (1870) LR 2 P & D 151; *Re Wilkinson's Goods* (1881) 6 PD 100.
2   *Re Birt's Goods* (1871) LR 2 P & D 214; *Re Greenwood's Goods* [1892] P 7.
3   *Re Kimpton's Goods* (1864) 3 Sw & Tr 427. Where there were the words 'See other side for completion,' the later part was held valid: *Palin v Ponting* [1930] P 185. See also *Re Hammond's Goods* (1863) 3 Sw & Tr 90.
4   *Re Gilbert's Goods* (1898) 78 LT 762; but in some cases the court has admitted only the part preceding the signature: *Re Anstee's Goods* [1893] P 283; *Royle v Harris* [1895] P 163; *Millward v Buswell* (1904) 20 TLR 714; *Re Brown's Estate* (1953) 10 WWRNS 163 (where the first page was a complete will and the signature was at the foot of that page). But the signature must have been made for the purposes of execution and not merely for identification or the avoidance of interpolation: *Ewen v Franklin* (1855) Dea & Sw 7; *Re Dilkes' Goods* (1874) LR 3 P & D 164; *Phipps v Hale* (1874) LR 3 P & D 166; *Sweetland v Sweetland* (1865) 4 Sw & Tr 6. See also n 13, para **[11.2]** supra. For extreme cases where this principle was applied, see *Re Long's Estate* [1936] P 166, [1936] 1 All ER 435; *Re Wagner Estate* (1959) 29 WWRNS 34.
5   *Re Gee's Goods* (1898) 78 LT 843. This decision was, in effect confirmed by *Practice Direction* [1953] 1 WLR 689 which stated that in such cases the continuation on the second page should not be admitted to probate unless there is also a reference above the signature on the first page, which effects incorporation.

[11.4]

Will on several sheets. It is not necessary that the testator should sign every sheet but it was at one time held that for the prevention of fraud the sheets must at the time of execution be attached in some way.[1] The rule was subsequently relaxed to allow that holding the sheets together with finger and thumb was sufficient annexation.[2] It has been held that a paper and its enclosing envelope are sufficiently connected to be admitted to probate together if otherwise duly executed.[3] The presumption, where several sheets constituting a connected document disposing of property are found together, is that they all form the will of the deceased[4] and that any apparent alteration in their order was made before execution.[5] If the will is written on several separate and disconnected sheets of paper and the last only is attested it has been said generously, that it should be admitted to probate on the presumption that the whole will was in the room and under the control of the testator at the time of execution.[6]

1   *Lewis v Lewis* [1908] P 1 at 5; *Cook v Lambert* (1863) 3 Sw & Tr 46 (sheets attached by wafers); *Re West's Goods* (1863) 32 LJPM & A 182 (no evidence whether addendum attached before execution); *Re Horsford's Goods* (1874) LR 3 P & D 211 (attached by string); *Re Gausden's Goods* (1862) 2 Sw & Tr 362 (strip bearing execution pasted on). Where separate sheets are signed, it is merely for the prevention of interpolation and it is the signature on the last sheet which must be attested: *Ewen v Franklin* (1855) Dea & Sw 7; *Sweetland v Sweetland,* supra. Where a second sheet contained only the attestation clause and signatures of witnesses and the sheets were not attached in any way, probate was refused although the first sheet containing the dispositive clauses was signed by the testator: *Re Ryan's Estate* [1955] VLR

316; but where all three sheets were signed but the attestation clause was only on the third sheet, probate was granted: *Re Vergers' Will* [1956] VLR 94.

2 *Lewis v Lewis* [1908] P 1; *Re Little, Foster v Cooper* [1960] 1 All ER 387; *Sterling v Bruce* [1973] NI 255; see also *Re Horsford's Goods* (1874) LR 3 P & D 211 where the attestation clause with the signature was on a separate paper attached to dispositive paper by string; held on the evidence of the witnesses, sufficient.

3 *Re Mann's Goods* [1942] P 146, [1942] 2 All ER 193. See also *Re Dytrych* [1928] VLR 144; *Re De Gruchy* (1941) 56 BCR 271 (signature as endorsement of printed form though witnessed in usual place); *Re Eaglestone* [1950] SASR 257 (similar case); *Re Nicholls, Hunter v Nicholls* [1921] 2 Ch 11 (signature at end of will, signature and attestation on envelope); *Re Haselgrove* [1950] SASR 99 (will on four sheets, only last sheet signed and attested, will enclosed in envelope). But see *Re Bean's Estate* [1944] P 83, [1944] 2 All ER 348; and *Re Beadle, Mayes v Beadle* [1974] 1 All ER 493, [1974] 1 WLR 417 where it was pointed out that a signature on an envelope may be intended as an authentication of the will or as an identification only; held to be the latter in this case.

4 *Marsh v Marsh* (1860) 1 Sw & Tr 528; *Re O'Brien's Goods* [1900] P 208; *Re M'Key's Goods* (1876) 11 IR Eq 220 (where the whole will was on one sheet except signatures, and the sheets, though enclosed in an envelope, were unattached, and there was no evidence that the first sheet was produced to the witnesses at the time of execution).

5 *Rees v Rees* (1873) LR 3 P & D 84; *Re Madden's Goods* [1905] 2 IR 612 (where the sheets were pinned together but out of order and it was assumed that the misplacement was inadvertent); *Re Moir Estate* [1942] 1 DLR 337 (wherever possible the sheets are read so that the signed sheet is last).

6 Per Hanna J in the Irish case *Re Tiernan's Goods* [1942] IR 572, after a close consideration of the English authorities, cited with apparent approval by Sachs J in *Re Little, Foster v Cooper* [1960] 1 All ER 387, [1960] 1 WLR 495 at 499; see also *Re Smith's Will* [1965] Qd R 177.

[11.5]

Declarations by testator. These whether made before or after execution are admissible to show what were the constituent parts of the will.[1]

1 *Gould v Lakes* (1880) 6 PD 1; *Re Hutchison's Goods* (1902) 18 TLR 706.

[11.6]

Signature in attestation or testimonium clause. A signature has been accepted though it appears in the attestation or testimonium clause both where the will is a holograph document[1] and where it is not[2].

1 In attestation clause: *Weatherhill v Pearce* [1995] 2 All ER 492; *Re Woodington's Goods* (1839) 2 Curt 324; *Re Walker's Goods* (1862) 2 Sw & Tr 354; *Re Torre's Goods* (1862) 8 Jur NS 494; *Re Huckvale's Goods* (1867) LR 1 P & D 375; *Re Pearn's Goods* (1875) 1 PD 70; *Re Moore's Goods* [1901] P 44; *Re Casmore's Goods* (1869) LR 1 P & D 653; *Re Harris's Goods* (1875) 23 WR 734. In testimonium clause: *Re Gunning's Goods* (1846) 1 Rob Eccl 459; *Re Dinmore* (1853) 2 Rob Eccl 641; *Re Mann's Goods* (1858) 28 LJP & M 19.

2 See *Re Mann's Goods* (1858) 28 LJP & M 19.

[11.7]

Signature on envelope or as indorsement. This has been accepted where the testator's name on the envelope or indorsement has been held to be a signature[1] but not where the signature on the envelope has been regarded merely as a label to identify the document.[2]

1 See the cases cited in n 3, para **[11.4]** supra.

2 *Re Bean's Estate* [1944] P 83, [1944] 2 All ER 348 and *Re Beadle, Mayes v Beadle* [1974] 1 All ER 493, [1974] 1 WLR 417 where the testatrix signed her will at the top with the signature of one witness, and then enclosed it in an envelope which she signed together with the two witnesses. Held that the signature on the envelope was not put there to authenticate the will, but merely as a label to identify the document inside; thus will improperly executed.

[11.8]

Unfinished signature. Where only the first page was signed with an unfinished signature and the testator died before he could sign the second page, a grant of administration with only the first page annexed (which was duly attested) was made.[1]

1   *Re Smith* [1955] SASR 227.

III.   PLACE OF SIGNATURE: DEATH ON OR AFTER 1 JANUARY 1983

[11.9]

Statutory provision. The AJA 1982 substitutes a new s 9 of the WA 1837[1] and repeals the Wills Act Amendment Act 1852.[2] The new s 9 is applicable to determine the validity of the will of a testator who dies on or after 1 January 1983[3]. The new formulation re-iterates the requirements that wills should be 'signed by the testator or by some other person in his presence and by his direction' and that '[4] the signature is made or acknowledged by the testator in the presence of two or more witnesses present at the same time'[5] but there is no longer any formal requirement that the signature should be at the foot or end of the will. Instead the legislation provides that it must appear ... that the testator intended by his signature to give effect to the will'.[6]

The original WA 1837, s 9[7] did not contain any such express wording, but it is clear from the Wills Act Amendment Act 1852 and from the 'envelope cases'[8] that such a requirement was essential for valid execution under the previous law. Thus the Wills Act Amendment Act 1852 stated[9] that a will was to be deemed to be valid ... if the signature shall be so placed at, or after, or following, or under, or beside, or opposite to the end of the will, that it shall be apparent on the face of the will that the testator intended to give effect by such signature to the writing signed as his will'.[10]

1   AJA 1982, s 17; see Vol 2, Part G, para **[244.93]**; the legislation gives effect to the recommendations of the Law Reform Committee, 22nd Report on the Making and Revocation of Wills 1980 (Cmnd 7902).
2   AJA 1982, s 75(1) and Pt I of Sch 9: see also the AJA 1982, s 77(5).
3   AJA 1982, s 73(6); AJA 1982, s 76(11).
4   WA 1837, s 9(a).
5   WA 1837, s 9(c).
6   WA 1837, s 9(b).
7   50 *Halsbury's Statutes* (4th edn) 578.
8   *Re Mann's Goods* [1942] P 146, [1942] 2 All ER 193; *Re Bean's Estate* [1944] P 83, [1944] 2 All ER 348; and *Re Beadle, Mayes v Beadle* [1974] 1 All ER 493, [1974] 1 WLR 417; see n 3, para **[11.4]** supra.
9   For a full commentary, see 5th edn of this work, pp 78–81.
10 See, for example, *Re Hornby's Goods* [1946] P 171, [1946] 2 All ER 150 (space reserved for signature); *Re Roberts* [1934] P 102 (signed in margin); *Lewis v Lewis* [1908] P 1; *Re Walker's Goods* (1862) 2 Sw & Tr 354; *Burke v Moore, Re Moore's Goods* (1875) IR 9 Eq 609; and *Dunn v Dunn* (1866) LR 1 P & D 277.
    Some wills, however, which were previously invalid might now be acceptable. See, for example, cases where the will was signed at the top, such as *Re Stalman, Stalman v Jones* (1931) 145 LT 339; and *Re Harris, Murray v Everard* [1952] P 319, [1952] 2 All ER 409.

[11.10]

Signature to will. It is essential that the document propounded as the will should be signed. A signature on the document will not be accepted if it was a signature to some earlier will, or to an earlier and different, form of the document.[1] Where the testator signed his will and then made alterations to it witnessed by two witnesses, but did not re-sign, he could not rely on the earlier signature as a signature to what was in effect, a later will, although on the same document.[2] The Court of Appeal has held that paragraphs (a) and (b) of section 9 are complementary and that a written name is capable of being a signature for the purposes of paragraph (a) even though it is not a normal signature. Thus the testator's name written at the top of a paper before any of the dispositive provisions had been written out, has been held to be a valid signature to the will.[3]

1   *Re White, Barker v Gribble* [1991] Ch 1, [1990] 3 All ER 1.
2   *Re White, Barker v Gribble* [1991] Ch 1, [1990] 3 All ER 1. Ferris J thought the position analogous to where the testator finds a sheet of paper on which he wrote his signature months ago, he crosses out all the original text, writes his will on the paper above his signature and gets two witnesses to sign. Will not correctly executed. Likewise where the testator makes an earlier will, crosses out the whole text and writes a new will on the same paper, and gets his original signature witnessed by two witnesses. Not correctly executed; see Ferris J [1991] Ch 1 at 5, 6.
3   *Wood v Smith* [1993] Ch 90, [1992] 3 All ER 556, CA; reversing on the formalities point [1991] 2 All ER 939. The first instance judge had taken the view that until the dispositive provisions were written, there could not be said to be 'a will' so that the initial signature could not be said to be a signature to the will. This view is persuasive. The Court of Appeal's view depends on regarding the signing of the name and the writing out of the dispositive provisions as all part of one contemporaneous operation. And see *Weatherhill v Pearce* [1995] 2 All ER 492, [1995] 1 WLR 592 following the 'practical approach' to the application of the WA 1837, s 9 advocated by Scott LJ in *Wood v Smith* [1993] Ch 90, [1992] 3 All ER 556, CA.

[11.11]

The intention. The 'intention' in the section refers to the act of signing not to the presence on the document of the testator's signature.[1] Thus it will not suffice where the testator signed the document as an earlier will and then made alterations to it, in effect making a new will, to argue that his earlier signature was intended to give effect to the later will.[2] It cannot be said that when the testator signed the earlier will he was intending to give effect to the later will.[3] In contrast the Court of Appeal,[4] reversing the first instance decision, has held where the deceased signed his name at the top of the paper before he had written out the dispositive provisions, that this could be sufficient because the testator intended his name as his signature.[5] Examples of circumstances where the testator's intention in relation to his signature is problematic are the 'envelope cases', ie cases where the testator has enclosed the will in an envelope and has signed the envelope. In the most recent of these[6] the testatrix had signed her will, at the top, and had also written her name on the envelope in which the will was enclosed. The court held that on the facts, the testatrix had not intended her name on the envelope to be a signature to her will, since she had already signed it, but was more in the nature of a label or identification.[7] However the signature on the will was invalid since it was at the top and not the bottom, and thus the will was invalid. Under the new provisions the attitude to the signature on the envelope would be the same but the signature on the will might now be acceptable.[8]

The new WA 1837, s 9 requires that it should 'appear' that the testator intended by his signature to give effect to the will. In most cases the intention (or lack of it) will appear from the will or alleged will itself, but the section does not require that it should appear from the will. It is thought that extrinsic evidence will be admissible to show the testator's intention, just as it was admissible under the previous law, and as it normally is admissible to show matters relevant to the validity of a will.[9]

The intention to give effect to the will, will govern those cases where the will is written on several sheets and the testator only signs one; such cases[10] were generously treated under the old law, and it is thought will be unaffected by the new provisions. Similarly where there is an interpolation or interlineation in the will.[11]

1   *Re White, Barker v Gribble* [1991] Ch 1, per Ferris J at 6.
2   *Re White, Barker v Gribble* [1991] Ch 1.
3   *Re White, Barker v Gribble* [1991] Ch 1. Probate was granted of the earlier, not the later will.
4   *Wood v Smith* [1993] Ch 90, [1992] 3 All ER 556, CA; reversing on the formalities point [1991] 2 All ER 939. The will was held to be invalid due to lack of testamentary capacity of the deceased at the time of execution. This 'practical' approach was followed in *Weatherhill v Pearce* [1995] 2 All ER 492.
5   See n 4 supra.
6   *Re Beadle, Mayes v Beadle* [1974] 1 All ER 493, [1974] 1 WLR 417.
7   See also *Re Bean's Estate* [1944] P 83, [1944] 2 All ER 348 and contrast *Re Mann's Goods* [1942] P 146, [1942] 2 All ER 193.
8   Provided, of course, it is correctly attested, which it was not in *Re Beadle, Mayes v Beadle* [1974] 1 All ER 493, [1974] 1 WLR 417.
9   See Chapter 57.
10 See para **[11.4]**, n 1.
11 See para **[11.3]**, n 3.

[11.12]
Professional practice. There is, of course, nothing in the new formulation to affect the fundamental rule that the whole of the will must be authenticated by the signature; the will must be complete before it is signed and no subsequent unexecuted additions to the will will be admitted to probate.[1] The clearest way of avoiding any doubt in this respect is for the signature of the testator to follow close after the end of the dispositive parts of the will, ie to be at the foot or end of the will.[2] Accordingly, it is not thought that the new WA 1837, s 9 will occasion any change in professional practice in the formal execution of wills. Existing standard forms of testimonium[3] will clearly be fully adequate to show this intention, and no change in the form of testimonium clauses is implied by the new s 9(b).

1   See para **[11.2]**, n 12.
2   Although it was established that a gap between the end of the narrative and the signature did not invalidate the will, such a situation is, for obvious reasons, best avoided. See the cases cited in para **[11.2]** supra; and *Re Little, Foster v Cooper* [1960] 1 All ER 387; *Hunt v Hunt* (1866) LR 1 P & D 209 (will on three and a half pages then half a page blank and signature on fourth page); and see *Re Young* (1915) 34 NZLR 950 (a similar case); *Re Archer's Goods* (1871) LR 2 P & D 252 (signature on back though blank space on front); *Re Fuller's Goods* [1892] P 377 (will on first sheet, second and third sheets blank, signature on fourth sheet).
3   See Vol 2.

IV. FORM OF SIGNATURE

[11.13]

Mark. A mark is a sufficient signing of a will and proof of inability to write is unnecessary;[1] where a testator is prevented by illness from signing, he may sign by a mark.[2] A mark has been held a sufficient signature where there is no name of the testator, or even the wrong name of the testator, in the will.[3] Where the will is open to suspicion (eg as being prepared and propounded by the principal donee) it has been said that the onus of proof is greater by reason of the signature being by mark.[4] The mark need not be a cross, although that is the usual form, but any shape of mark is sufficient[5] and even a thumb mark has been accepted.[6]

1   *Lemaine v Staneley* (1681) Freem KB 538; *Baker v Dening* (1838) 8 Ad & El 94; *Hindmarsh v Charlton* (1861) 8 HL Cas 160; *Re Kieran* [1933] IR 222.
2   *Wilson v Beddard* (1841) 12 Sim 28 (hand guided when making the mark); *Re Holtam's Estate, Gillett v Rogers* (1913) 108 LT 732; *Re Hodgins* (1978) 85 DLR (3d) 705. He may even be assisted in making the mark: *Re White* [1948] 1 DLR 572.
3   *Re Bryce's Goods* (1839) 2 Curt 325 (no name); *Re McNamee* (1912) 31 NZLR 1007 (no name); *Re Clarke's Goods* (1858) 1 Sw & Tr 22 (wrong name); *Re Douce's Goods* (1862) 2 Sw & Tr 593 (wrong first name).
4   *Donnelly v Broughton* [1891] AC 435.
5   *Re Kieran* [1933] IR 222. In one case a seal bearing the initials of the testator was impressed: *Re Emerson's Goods* (1882) 9 LR Ir 443.
6   *Re Finn's Estate* (1935) 105 LJP 36.

[11.14]

Unfinished signature. Where through feebleness the testator is unable to finish his signature, a signing of part only of his name has been accepted[1] though the mere writing of part of the Christian name was in the case of a witness held insufficient.[2] A part of a name will not be sufficient if it is merely the commencement of the full signature which is completed.[3]

1   *Re Chalcraft's Goods, Chalcraft v Giles and Rance* [1948] P 222, [1948] 1 All ER 700 and see *Re Smith* [1955] SASR 227.
2   *Re Maddock's Goods* (1874) LR 3 P & D 169.
3   *Re Colling, Lawson v Von Winckler* [1972] 3 All ER 729, [1972] 1 WLR 1440 (testator commenced to sign his name in the presence of two witnesses, one of whom was called away; the testator completed his signature in the witness's absence; held, not signed in the presence of both witnesses).

[11.15]

Initials. The signature should preferably be a full signature, but initials are sufficient provided they are intended to authenticate the whole will.[1]

1   *Re Savory's Goods* (1851) 18 LTOS 280; *Re Schultz* (1984) 8 DLR (4th) 147. A seal stamped with the testator's initials has been accepted: *Re Emerson's Goods* (1882) 9 LR Ir 443.

[11.16]

Stamp. Signature by a stamp has been accepted.[1]

1   *Jenkins v Gaisford and Thring, Re Jenkins' Goods* (1863) 3 Sw & Tr 93 (where an aged person had a stamp made of his signature).

[11.17]
Signature in pencil. A signature in pencil has been accepted where the remainder of the will was written in ink.[1]

1   *Bateman v Pennington* (1840) 3 Moo PCC 223.

[11.18]
Signature by dry pen. Passing a dry pen over a signature already written is not a good subscription of a will;[1] but it may amount to an acknowledgment of the signature by the testator.[2]

1   *Playne v Scriven* (1849) 1 Rob Eccl 772; *Kevil v Lynch* (1874) IR 9 Eq 249; *Re Maddock's Goods* (1874) LR 3 P & D 169.
2   *Playne v Scriven* (1849) 1 Rob Eccl 772; *Lewis v Lewis* [1908] P 1 at 5; but it has been said that a signature pencilled by a third person to show the place of signature cannot be acknowledged: *Reeves v Grainger* (1908) 52 Sol Jo 355.

[11.19]
Seal. Mere sealing is clearly not sufficient since the WA 1837.[1]

1   There are a number of cases before the WA 1837 deciding that sealing a will was not sufficient: see English and Empire Digest Repl, Vol 48, p 102. Where a seal included the initials of the testator, it was held a sufficient signature: *Re Emerson's Goods* (1882) 9 LR Ir 443, but this decision may be supported either as a signature by a mark or by initials.

[11.20]
Wrong or assumed name. Provided that it is intended as the name of the testator, a wrong or an assumed name is accepted.[1] Thus, a signature by a widow in her maiden name,[2] or a signature by a woman in the name of her first husband after second marriage[3] has been accepted. Where a woman signed in an assumed name, then erased that name and signed in her true name, but the witnesses did not subscribe the will as altered, the will was granted probate as it originally stood, treating the assumed name as a mark.[4] Similarly it is sufficient where a testator puts his mark to a will in which he is wrongly named.[5] In the case of a holograph will the words 'your loving mother' were accepted as a signature.[6]

1   *Re Glover's Goods* (1847) 5 Notes of Cases 553; *Re Redding's Goods* (1850) 2 Rob Eccl 339; *Re Clarke's Goods* (1858) 1 Sw & Tr 22. In Saskatchewan a holograph will signed 'Mother' was accepted; *Re Smith's Estate* [1948] 2 WWR 55, and see n 5.
2   *Re Weston's Goods* (1844) 3 LTOS 140.
3   *Re Glover's Goods* (1847) 5 Notes of Cases 553.
4   *Re Redding's Goods* (1850) 2 Rob Eccl 339. See also *Re Hurd's Will* (1883) 9 VLR 23.
5   *Re Douce's Goods* (1862) 2 Sw & Tr 593.
6   *Re Cook's Estate, Murison v Cook* [1960] 1 All ER 689, [1960] 1 WLR 353.

[11.21]
Signature on testator's behalf. When the signature is written by another on behalf of the testator it must be made in his presence and by his direction.[1] The person so signing may be one of the attesting witnesses.[2] The person so signing on the testator's behalf may sign his own name so long as it is expressly stated to be on behalf of the testator.[3] The testator must in some way indicate to the witnesses that the signature has been put there at his request and this may be evidenced by his conduct.[4]

1   WA 1837, s 9, as substituted by the AJA 1982, s 17, 50 *Halsbury's Statutes* (4th edn) 578; see
    Vol 2, Part G, para **[244.93]**, which makes no change in this respect. *Re Kevil's Goods* (1873)
    IR 8 Eq 244.
2   *Re Bailey's Goods* (1838) 1 Curt 914; *Smith v Harris* (1845) 1 Rob Eccl 262; *Re Ullersperger's
    Goods* (1841) 6 Jur 156.
3   *Re Clark's Goods* (1839) 2 Curt 239; *Smith v Harris* (1845) 1 Rob Eccl 262; *Jenkins v Gaisford
    and Thring, Re Jenkins' Goods* (1863) 3 Sw & Tr 93; *Re Blair's Goods* (1848) 6 Notes of Cases
    528; *Re Deeley and Green* [1930] 1 DLR 603 (signature by notary in own name); *Re Fiszhaut
    Estate* (1966) 56 DLR (2d) 381.
4   *Re Marshall's Goods* (1866) 13 LT 643. The testator may by subsequent declarations show that
    the signature was on his behalf: *Re Elcock's Goods* (1869) 20 LT 757. All that is required is
    mere consent to the signature being appended and no instructions in writing are necessary:
    Parker v Felgate (1883) 8 PD 171; *Parker v Parker* (1841) Milw 541. For a case where the
    testatrix was incapable of speech or writing, see *Re Holtman's Estate, Gillett v Rogers* (1913)
    108 LT 732.

V.   SIGNATURE BY BLIND OR ILLITERATE TESTATOR

[11.22]
The Non-Contentious Probate Rules 1987[1] provide for this case in rule 13 in the
following terms:

Before admitting to proof a will which appears to have been signed by a blind
or illiterate testator or by another person by direction of the testator, or which for
any other reason gives rise to doubt as to the testator having knowledge of the
contents of the will at the time of its execution, the registrar shall satisfy himself
that the testator had such knowledge.[2]

1   SI 1987/2024.
2   Previously r 11 of the Non-Contentious Probate Rules 1954, SI 1954/796. The Registrar is
    usually satisfied where the attestation clause is in one of the special forms as in Vol 2. See *Re
    Sellwood's Estate, Heynes v Sellwood* (1964) 108 Sol Jo 523, and *Tristram and Coote's
    Probate Practice* (28th edn).

VI.   SIGNATURE IN PRESENCE OF WITNESSES

[11.23]
The cases upon this part of the statutory provision[1] are considered elsewhere.[2]

1   WA 1837, s 9; see Chapter 12. The AJA 1982 makes no change in this respect.
2   See Chapter 12.

VII.   ACKNOWLEDGMENT OF SIGNATURE

[11.24]
Sufficiency of acknowledgment. The testator must sign his will or
acknowledge his signature in the presence of two or more witnesses present at
the same time.[1] It is not sufficient for the testator to acknowledge his signature
to each witness in turn; the acknowledgment must be made in the joint presence
of the witnesses.[2] Nor is it sufficient to commence a signature in the presence of
both witnesses, one of whom then departs to return when the testator's and the
other witness's signature are on the will.[3] The acknowledgment may be by

gesture[4] or made in answer to a question[5] but the witnesses must at the time of the acknowledgment see, or have the opportunity of seeing, the signature of the testator, and if what takes place involves an acknowledgment by the testator that the signature is his, that is enough.[6] It has been held that a witness sufficiently acknowledged her signature by protesting throughout the transaction as to her signature's validity.[7] The signature to be acknowledged may be made either by the testator or by another for him;[8] but it must be a signature and it is not enough that the name of the testator is pencilled to show where the signature should be.[9]

1   Wills Act 1837, s 9 as substituted by the AJA 1982; 50 *Halsbury's Statutes* (4th edn) 578, which makes no change in this respect. It is the signature and not the will which has to be acknowledged: *Re Shewchuk* (1968) 1 DLR (3d) 288. No express declaration of acknowledgment is necessary to satisfy the WA 1837, s 9(c): *Weatherhill v Pearce* [1995] 2 All ER 492, [1995] 1 WLR 592.
2   *Re Groffman, Groffman and Block v Groffman* [1969] 2 All ER 108, [1969] 1 WLR 733.
3   *Re Colling, Lawson v von Winckler* [1972] 3 All ER 729, [1972] 1 WLR 1440 (the part of the name that had been subscribed before the witness departed was neither the name itself nor some mark intended to represent the name).
4   *Re Davies' Goods* (1850) 2 Rob Eccl 337; *Re Owston's Goods* (1862) 2 Sw & Tr 461 (testator deaf and dumb). Going over testator's own signature with a dry pen may be an acknowledgment or a re-execution: *Lewis v Lewis* [1908] P 1.
5   *Kelly v Keatinge* (1871) IR 5 Eq 174; in *Re Groffman, Groffman and Block v Groffman* [1969] 2 All ER 108, [1969] 1 WLR 733, the signed will was in the testator's inside coat pocket and it was held that gesturing towards that pocket was not a sufficient acknowledgment since the witnesses could not see the signature.
6   *Re Gunstan's Goods, Blake v Blake* (1882) 7 PD 102; *O'Meagher v O'Meagher* (1883) 11 LR Ir 117; *Clery v Barry* (1887) 21 LR Ir 152; *Daintree v Butcher and Fasulo* (1888) 13 PD 102 (document not stated to be a will); *Whiting v Turner* (1903) 89 LT 71; *Re Swift's Goods* (1900) 17 TLR 16, and see *Brown v Skirrow* [1902] P 3; *Re Groffman, Groffman and Block v Groffman* [1969] 2 All ER 108, [1969] 1 WLR 733; *Re Colling, Lawson v von Winckler* [1972] 3 All ER 729, [1972] 1 WLR 1440. See *Re White, Barker v Gribble* [1990] 3 All ER 1, at 7 where *Daintree v Butcher and Fasulo* (1888) 13 PD 102, was referred to.
7   *Couser v Couser* [1996] 3 All ER 256, applying *Brown v Skirrow* [1902] P 3 and *Casson v Dade* (1781) 1 Bro CC 99..
8   *Re Regan's Goods* (1838) 1 Curt 908; *Parker v Parker* (1841) Milw 541. It is not enough that the witnesses see the signature written if they are not present when the testator directs the signature to be made: *Burke v Moore, Re Moore's Goods* (1875) IR 9 Eq 609.
9   *Reeves v Grainger* (1908) 52 Sol Jo 355. Nor, in a case where the signature was not written by the testator, was it enough where the testator affixed a seal and said that the document was his act and deed: *Re Summers' Goods* (1850) 2 Rob Eccl 295.

[11.25]
Presence of witnesses. The WA 1837[1] requires acknowledgment in the presence of two witnesses present at the same time, but, unless it is proved that the witnesses did not see, or could not have seen, the signature, it is presumed in the absence of fraud and where there is a proper attestation clause or where it is shown that the testator knew the requirements of the law, that the attesting witnesses saw the acknowledged signature. Even where the attestation clause is informal and the witnesses have no recollection of the circumstances in which the will was executed, there is a presumption of proper execution, if the witnesses identify the testator's and their own signatures.[2]

1   AJA 1982, s 17; 50 *Halsbury's Statutes* (4th edn) 578; see Vol 2, Part G, para **[244.93]**, makes no change in this respect.

2   *Blake v Knight* (1843) 3 Curt 547; *Gwillim v Gwillim* (1859) 3 Sw & Tr 200; *Re Huckvale's Goods* (1867) LR 1 P & D 375; *Re Janaway's Goods* (1874) 44 LJP & M 6. See, further, Presumption of Due Execution, Chapter 13.

[11.26]

Acknowledgment by production of signed will. The production of a will by the testator with his signature upon it, and a request by him, or by someone for him in his presence,[1] to the witness to attest it, is a sufficient acknowledgment of the signature.[2] Where the witnesses are familiar with the signature of the testator, it is sufficient if they see the will.[3] There need not be positive evidence from the attesting witnesses that the testator's signature was on the will when they signed it,[4] but the mere calling in of witnesses, who had no opportunity of seeing the testator's signature, without giving them any explanation of the instrument they were signing, is not an acknowledgment.[5] It is not, however, absolutely necessary that the witnesses should know that the instrument is a will provided they are told that it is a document requiring attestation by two witnesses.[6] On the re-execution of a will acknowledgment of the original signature is sufficient.[7]

1   *Inglesant v Inglesant* (1874) LR 3 P & D 172; *Re Bishop's Goods* (1882) 46 JP 392. It seems that the testator must be aware of the request of the third party: *Morritt v Douglas* (1872) LR 3 P & D 1; *White v Tunnicliffe* (1897) 13 TLR 469.
2   *Ilott v Genge* (1842) 3 Curt 160; *Gaze v Gaze* (1843) 3 Curt 451; *Keigwin v Keigwin* (1843) 3 Curt 607; *Leech v Bates* (1849) 1 Rob Eccl 714; *Wright v Sanderson* (1884) 9 PD 149; *Daintree v Butcher and Fasulo* (1888) 13 PD 102; *Lewis v Lewis,* supra; *Weatherhill v Pearce* [1995] 2 All ER 492, [1995] 1 WLR 592.
3   *Re Gibson* [1953] NZLR 122.
4   *Blake v Knight* (1843) 3 Curt 547.
5   *Ilott v Genge* (1842) 3 Curt 160; *Gaze v Gaze* (1843) 3 Curt 451; *Keigwin v Keigwin* (1843) 3 Curt 607; *Re Rees' Goods* (1865) 34 LJPM & A 56; *Fischer v Popham* (1875) LR 3 P & D 246; *Wright v Sanderson* (1884) 9 PD 149; *Daintree v Butcher and Fasulo* (1888) 13 PD 102; *Patterson v Benbow* (1889) 7 NZLR 673. This is especially so where there is no evidence that the testator's signature was on the will at the time: *Re Swinford's Goods* (1869) LR 1 P & D 630; *Pearson v Pearson* (1871) LR 2 P & D 451.
6   *Daintree v Butcher and Fasulo* (1888) 13 PD 102.
7   *Re Dewell's Goods* (1853) 1 Ecc & Ad 103.

[11.27]

Second signature to will. A testatrix had signed her will, but it was unattested. She signed it again in the presence of two witnesses, who signed above her later signature after the words 'Signed again in the presence of', etc. It was held that there was a good acknowledgment of the first signature.[1]

1   *Re Pattison's Goods, Henderson v Priestman* [1918] 2 IR 90.

CHAPTER 12

Attestation

I. STATUTORY PROVISIONS

[12.1]

Administration of Justice Act 1982 (AJA 1982). The AJA 1982[1] substitutes a new provision for the Wills Act 1837 (WA 1837), s 9 which will apply to determine the formal validity of wills of testators who die on or after 1 January 1983.[2] In the case of deaths before that date the requirements of attestation will be subject to the provisions of the WA 1837, s 9 as originally enacted.[3] The provisions of the AJA 1982 do not in fact affect the main features of the WA 1837, s 9; thus the testator must sign or acknowledge in the presence of two or more witnesses present at the same time,[4] and the witnesses must attest and sign (or now acknowledge a prior signature) in the presence of the testator.[5] There never was any formal requirement that the witnesses should sign in the presence of each other (although this was invariably so where the execution was professionally supervised)[6] and this point is now expressed in the AJA 1982.[7] Likewise there was never any formal requirement as to the position of the witnesses' signature in the will (although invariably placed after the testator's signature at the end of the will where the execution was professionally supervised),[8] and the AJA 1982 does not contain any positive requirement on this point.[9] No form of attestation was or is, required.[10] Further there is nothing in the AJA 1982 to affect the provisions of the Wills Act 1968 or the WA 1837, s 15. The one significant change introduced to the requirements of attestation introduced by the AJA 1982 is that it is now possible for a witness to acknowledge his signature, which was not permitted under the original WA 1837, s 9.[11] This change is of course a relaxation of the old law and tends to validate rather than invalidate; for this reason, and because of the minor nature of the change effected it is not thought necessary for this discussion to expressly differentiate between the position before and after 1 January 1983.

---

1 AJA 1982, s 17; see Vol 2, Part G, para **[244.93]**, which applies only to England and Wales, AJA 1982, s 77(1).
2 AJA 1982, s 73(6), 76(11).
3 50 *Halsbury's Statutes* (4th edn) 578.
4 See the new WA 1837, s 9(c).
5 See the new WA 1837, s 9(d).
6 And such a course is recommended.
7 See the new WA 1837, s 9(d).
8 And such a course is recommended.
9 See the new WA 1837, s 9(d).

10   WA 1837, s 9(d).
11   See the new WA 1837, s 9(d).

[12.2]
Professional practice. There is nothing in the provisions of the AJA 1982 that will necessitate a change in professional practice when supervising the formal execution of wills. Existing attestation clauses in common form[1] can continue to be used without change. Although the formal acceptance of an acknowledgment by a witness may save some previously invalid 'home-made' wills,[2] it is not recommended that witnesses should be encouraged to acknowledge. Where the circumstances require a re-attestation by witnesses the professional adviser should recommend that they would re-sign, as was the practice before 1983.[3]

1   See Vol 2, paras **[216.12]** to **[216.22]**.
2   Cases such as *Re Colling, Lawson v von Winckler* [1972] 3 All ER 729, [1972] 1 WLR 1440, see para **[12.13]** infra. See Law Reform Committee's 22nd Report on the Making and Revocation of Wills 1980 (Cmnd 7902) paras 2.7–2.8. It seems however unlikely that the power to acknowledge will save many wills because laymen who make a mistake in the formal execution of wills are unlikely to be aware that the defect might be covered by an acknowledgement.
3   This is because a re-signing will be apparent on the face of the will and will, hopefully, dispel any doubts as to the correctness of the execution. An acknowledgement will obviously not be so apparent and will depend upon proof by affidavit evidence that it was done, which may not be forthcoming on death. It is as a matter of practicality just as easy and quick to re-sign as it is to acknowledge.

II.   MODE OF ATTESTATION

[12.3]
Signature in presence of both witnesses. The signature of the testator must be made or acknowledged in the presence of two witnesses,[1] and such witnesses must attest and subscribe the will,[2] or acknowledge a prior signature,[3] in the presence of the testator.[4] Both attesting witnesses must be present at the same time[5] and both witnesses must attest and subscribe,[6] or acknowledge,[7] after the testator's signature has been made or acknowledged in their presence.[8] Each witness should be able to say that he knows of his own knowledge that the testator had signed the document.[9] There is no sufficient acknowledgment unless the witnesses either saw or had the opportunity of seeing the signature,[10] even though the testator should expressly declare that the paper to be attested is his will or should state that his signature is inside the will.[11] A blind person cannot be a witness.[12]

1   The presence of one witness is not enough: *Re Garner's Goods* (1861) 25 JP 183; *Re Swift's Goods* (1900) 17 TLR 16; *Brown v Skirrow* [1902] P 3 (a second witness near but not really cognisant of the signing); *Re Groffman, Groffman and Block v Groffman* [1969] 2 All ER 108, [1969] 1 WLR 733 (witnesses called in one after the other). For a case where the execution was seen by neither witness, see *Ilott v Genge* (1842) 3 Curt 160; *Re Hammond's Goods* (1863) 3 Sw & Tr 90 (no evidence of any writing on paper when witnesses signed); *Re Trinder's Goods* (1844) 3 Notes of Cases 275 (witnesses saw only blank space where they signed); *Hudson v Parker* (1844) 1 Rob Eccl 14 (will and testator's signature purposely concealed); *Shaw v Neville* (1855) 2 Ecc & Ad 203 (perfect signature and attestation clause, but attesting witnesses saw nothing whatever except the space where they wrote); *Re Pearsons' Goods* (1864) 33 LJPM & A 177 (a similar case).

2   In the case of testators who die before 1 January 1983; WA 1837, s 9; see Vol 2, Part G, para
    [244.6].

3   As an additional alternative in the case of testators who die on or after 1 January 1983; WA
    1837, s 9 as substituted by the Administration of Justice Act 1982, s 17; see Vol 2, Part G, para
    [244.93].

4   WA 1837, s 9, as substituted by the AJA 1982, s 17. *Hudson v Parker* (1844) 1 Rob Eccl 14;
    Betts v Gannell (1903) 19 TLR 304. As to what amounts to a signature, see, ante, and as to what
    amounts to an acknowledgment of signature, see ante. As to documents which cannot take
    effect as wills for want of attestation, see *Re Hughes* (1888) 59 LT 586; *Re Williams, Williams v
    Ball* [1917] 1 Ch 1.

5   *Wyatt v Berry* [1893] P 5; *Hindmarsh v Charlton* (1861) 8 HL Cas 160; *Re Morgan's Will*
    [1950] VLR 335; *Re Groffman, Groffman and Block v Groffman* [1969] 2 All ER 108, [1969] 1
    WLR 733. If only one is present on the first occasion, then the signature of the testator must be
    acknowledged and both subscribe on the second occasion: *Re Allen's Goods* (1839) 2 Curt 331;
    Moore v King (1842) 3 Curt 243. But where there was a proper attestation on the first occasion
    but, one of the witnesses being an executor, it was wrongly supposed to be invalid, and it was
    amended by erasing his name and adding another, the will was held good, as it had been
    properly attested on the first occasion and the subsequent actions would not invalidate it: *Re
    Hannam's Goods* (1850) 7 Notes of Cases 437. Where the second witness came within view of
    the document while the first witness was completing his signature, it was held that such witness
    came too late to validate the execution: *Re Linley, McDonnell v Linley* (1949) 207 LT Jo 372,
    CA. In *Gray v Richards Butler* (1996) 140 Sol Jo LB 194, the will on which the professional
    executor relied to justify the retention of his firm's charges had been held invalid in previous
    proceedings because the witnesses had not witnessed it at the same time.

6   See n 1.

7   See n 4.

8   *Moore v King* (1842) 3 Curt 243; *Cooper v Bockett* (1843) 3 Curt 648; *Hindmarsh v Charlton*
    (1861) 8 HL Cas 160; *Wyatt v Berry* [1893] P 5; *Brown v Skirrow* [1902] P 3 at 7; *Re Davies'
    Estate* [1951] 1 All ER 920; *Re Groffman, Groffman and Block v Groffman* [1969] 2 All ER
    108, [1969] 1 WLR 733; *Hudson v Bower* (1968) 67 WWR 564, 1 DLR (3d) 288; *Re Colling,
    Lawson v von Winckler* [1972] 3 All ER 729 [1972] 1 WLR 1440; see para **[12.5]**, n 3.

9   *Brown v Skirrow* [1902] P 3 at 5; but it is not necessary that an attesting witness should know
    that the document signed is a will: *Re Benjamin's Estate* (1934) 150 LT 417.

10 *Re Gunstan's Goods, Blake v Blake* (1882) 7 PD 102; it is sufficient if the witnesses see the
    testator write what the court presumes to be the signature: *Smith v Smith* (1866) LR 1 P & D
    143.

11 See cases cited in n 6, para **[11.24]** supra.

12 *Re Gibson's Estate* [1949] P 434, [1949] 2 All ER 90.

[12.4]

Witness must attest the will. It is essential that the witnesses in signing should
attest the will and not merely some alteration to it.[1]

1   *Re White, Barker v Gribble* [1990] 3 All ER 1 at 7. Where a will was validly executed in 1981
    and alterations were made to it in 1984 which the witnesses signed, it was held that they did not
    attest the document as the 1984 will but merely as alterations to the 1981 will. Applying *Re
    Martin's Goods* (1849) 1 Rob Eccl 712 and *Re Shearn's Goods* (1880) 50 LJ P 15.

[12.5]

Signature of testator must precede attestation. The testator must sign or
acknowledge his signature before either of the witnesses subscribes the will.[1]
This requirement was not expressed in the WA 1837, s 9 but was thought to be
implicit in the wording.[2] Thus it will not suffice if the testator signs in the
presence of the witness who signs, and then the testator acknowledges his
signature in the presence of both witnesses, and the second witness signs.[3]
Although the testator has acknowledged his signature in the presence of both
witnesses, and both witnesses have signed in the testator's presence, the

operative signature or acknowledgment has not been subsequently attested by two witnesses.[4] The AJA 1982 does not change this basic rule relating to the order of signing and attestation but the invalidity illustrated above could now be remedied by the first witness acknowledging his prior signature after the testator acknowledges his, with the second witness then signing.[5] It is in fact preferable and simpler in such cases for the first witness to resign.[6] It is not necessarily assumed, however, that where the testator's signature is placed after the witnesses' signature he signed after them.[7] One of the witnesses may sign the testator's signature for him before either attest.[8]

1   See the cases cited in n 8, para **[12.3]**, and *Re Olding's Goods* (1841) 2 Curt 865; *Re Hoskins' Goods* (1863) 1 New Rep 569; *Re Dilkes' Goods* (1874) LR 3 P & D 164; *Re Winter* [1926] VLR 300; *Chesline v Hermiston* [1928] 4 DLR 786. This sentence of the text was applied in *Re Young* [1969] NZLR 454 at 458.
2   See *Moore v King* (1842) 3 Curt 243 at 253.
3   See *Re Colling, Lawson v von Winckler* [1972] 3 All ER 729, [1972] 1 WLR 1440 where the testator commenced his signature in the presence of two witnesses one of whom was called away before he had completed his signature; the first witness signed, the other witness returned, the testator acknowledged his signature in the presence of both and the second witness signed; held invalid execution. In so far as the first witness acknowledged his signature after the testator's acknowledgment, such a case would now be valid by virtue of the new WA 1837, s 9. It was the facts and decision in *Re Colling* which prompted the change in the law permitting witnesses to acknowledge; see Law Reform Committee's 22nd Report on the Making and Revocation of Wills 1980 (Cmnd 7902), paras 2.7 and 2.8.
4   *Re Colling, Lawson v von Winckler* [1972] 3 All ER 729, [1972] 1 WLR 1440.
5   See the new WA 1837, s 9 substituted by the AJA 1982, s 17; see Vol 2, Part G, para **[244.93]**.
6   For the reasons given in n 3. The attestation could also be corrected by the subsequent execution of a codicil even on the same paper, *Re Claringbull's Goods* (1844) 3 Notes of Cases 1.
7   *Re O'Neill's Goods* (1916) 50 ILT 180.
8   *Doe d Caldwell v Lee* (1852) 19 LTOS 49.

[12.6]
Attestation in presence of testator. It is not necessary that the testator should actually see the witnesses sign, it is sufficient if he might have seen them if he cared to look.[1] The witnesses may be in an adjoining room, but only in such part of that room as is visible by the testator.[2] The testator must be mentally capable of recognising the act of attestation, and conscious of the transaction in which the witnesses are engaged and, if the testator becomes insensible before the witnesses subscribe, the attestation is insufficient.[3]

1   *Tod v Winchelsea (Earl)* (1826) 2 C & P 488; *Jenner v Ffinch* (1879) 5 PD 106; *Carter v Seaton* (1901) 85 LT 76. But where the testator is incapable of turning to see the witnesses sign, even if he cares to do so, the attestation is bad: *Tribe v Tribe* (1849) 1 Rob Eccl 775; *Re Wozciechowiecz Estate* [1931] 4 DLR 585.
2   *Re Trimnell's Goods* (1865) 11 Jur NS 248; *Re Piercy's Goods* (1845) 1 Rob Eccl 278 (testator might have seen, but was blind). For cases where the will was rejected because the position in the adjoining room was not visible by the testator, see *Re Killick's Goods* (1864) 3 Sw & Tr 578 (where testatrix might have seen by raising herself but there was no evidence that she did so); *Carter v Seaton* (1901) 85 LT 76 (impossible to see); *Betts v Gannell* (1903) 19 TLR 304 (impossible to see); *Jenner v Ffinch* (1879) 5 PD 106 (testator unaware witnesses were signing); *Norton v Bazett* (1856) Dea & Sw 259 (testator could have seen by shifting position but evidence that he did not); *Winchilsea v Wauchope* (1827) 3 Russ 441 (where seeing possible, presumption in favour of will if no evidence).

3   *Right v Price* (1779) 1 Doug KB 241. Where testator blind, see *Re Piercy's Goods* (1845) 1
    Rob Eccl 278. A testator may be losing his facilities, yet they may be sufficient to validate the
    execution: *Re Chalcraft's Goods, Chalcraft v Giles* [1948] P 222, [1948] 1 All ER 700.

[12.7]

Attestation by witnesses in presence of each other. This is not essential[1] but it
is usual for them to do so.[2]

1   See the new WA 1837, s 9 as substituted by the AJA 1982; see Vol 2, Part G, para **[244.7]**.
2   *Re Webb's Goods* (1855) Dea & Sw 1; *Sullivan v Sullivan* (1879) 3 LR Ir 299; *O'Meagher v
    O'Meagher* (1883) 11 LR Ir 117; *Brown v Skirrow* [1902] P 3 at 5.

[12.8]

Superfluous attestation: Wills Act 1968. For the purposes of the WA 1837,
s 15 (avoidance of gifts to attesting witnesses and their spouses) the attestation
of a will by a person to whom or to whose spouse there is given or made any
such disposition as is described in that section shall be disregarded if the will is
duly executed without his attestation and without that of any other such person.[1]

1   WA 1968, s 1(1); 50 *Halsbury's Statutes* (4th edn) 612; see Chapter 9.

III.   FORM OF ATTESTATION

[12.9]

Attestation clause. Though no special form of this clause is essential,[1] there are
two well-recognised forms of this clause, showing that the requirements of the
statute have been complied with, and one of them should always be used[2] in
order to avoid any difficulty in securing a grant in common form.

1   WA 1837, s 9, as originally enacted; 50 *Halsbury's Statutes* (4th edn) 578; and as substituted by
    the AJA 1982; see Vol 2, Part G, para **[244.6]** et seq. *Bryan v White* (1850) 2 Rob Eccl 315. The
    attestation clause is not strictly part of the will: *Re Atkinson's Goods* (1883) 8 PD 165 (an
    erroneous statement in the attestation clause of a codicil that a previous codicil has been
    cancelled is of no effect).
2   There is a longer form, which is the usual form, and a shorter form: 'Signed by the above-
    named testator in the joint presence of us who in his presence and that of each other have
    hereunto subscribed our names as witnesses.' Either form may be used. In *Re Selby-Bigge*
    [1950] 1 All ER 1009, an even shorter form was allowed: 'Signed by the testatrix in our
    presence and attested by us in the presence of her and each other.' The point in this case being
    that it is not essential to use the word 'subscribe' as 'attest' includes it. For special forms where
    there are alterations or the testator is infirm or illiterate and other special cases, see Vol 2, para
    [216.12] et seq.

[12.10]

Absence of formal attestation clause. Where there is no such clause or the
clause does not show beyond doubt that the statutory requirements were
observed, there must be an affidavit by one of the attesting witnesses or by
someone who can depose to the facts before probate will be granted on the
executor's oath alone.[1] There must, of course, in all cases be the signatures of
two witnesses, but that they signed as witnesses and in accordance with the
above conditions may be proved by evidence. If, however, there is a proper

attestation clause, no such evidence is required and the will so far as attestation is concerned is admitted to probate without further questions.[2]

1   Non-Contentious Probate Rules 1987, SI 1987/2024, r 12; see *Tristram and Coote's Probate Practice* (28th edn).
2   See Presumption of Due Execution, see Chapter 13.

[12.11]

Position of attestation in will. The WA 1837, s 9[1] does not specify where the witnesses are to sign,[2] and the signatures may therefore be placed on any part of the will, if it is clear that they were placed there with the intention of attesting the signature of the testator.[3] The attestation may be on the sheet next to where the testator has signed, ie overleaf,[4] or on a separate sheet so long as it is attached.[5] Where the will is signed on more than one sheet, it seems that the signature on the last sheet should be duly attested but the decisions on the point are not uniform.[6] It is clear, however, that no part of the will which is shown to be written after attestation is valid.[7]

1   See n 2, para **[12.9]** supra.
2   *Re Chamney's Goods* (1849) 1 Rob Eccl 757.
3   *Re Streatley's Goods* [1891] P 172; *Re Ellison's Goods* [1907] 2 IR 480 (where the signatures were in the body of the will); *Byles v Cox* (1896) 74 LT 222.
4   *Re Davis' Goods* (1843) 3 Curt 748; *Re Chamney's Goods* (1849) 1 Rob Eccl 757; *Re Braddock's Goods* (1876) 1 PD 433; *Roberts v Phillips* (1855) 4 E & B 450 (signature of one witness overleaf); *Re Wilson's Goods* (1866) LR 1 P & D 269 (where the court concluded that the names were not for the purpose of attestation). *Re Denning, Harnett v Elliott* [1958] 2 All ER 1, [1958] 1 WLR 462 (where there were merely two signatures on the back of a single sheet will).
5   *Re Childes' Goods* (1845) 4 Notes of Cases 36 (attestation attached by pin). Such attestation has been refused where there was no evidence that the attachment was before execution; see *Re West's Goods* (1863) 32 LJPM & A 182.
6   Where the signature on the last sheet is not attested, probate has been refused in *Ewen v Franklin* (1855) Dea & Sw 7; *Re Dilkes' Goods* (1874) LR 3 P & D 164; *Phipps v Hale* (1874) LR 3 P & D 166. In other cases the court has admitted to probate such sheets as were duly signed and attested; *Re Malen's Goods* (1885) 54 LJP 91; *Re Pearse's Goods* (1867) LR 1 PD 382; *Re Dearle's Goods* (1878) 47 LJP 45.
7   *Re Jones' Goods* (1842) 1 Notes of Cases 396; *Cooper v Bockett* (1843) 3 Curt 648; but where there was no definite evidence that the testator, whose signature was below the attestation, signed after the attestation, the will was held valid: *Re O'Neill's Goods* (1916) 50 ILT 180.

[12.12]

Signature. The attestation should be by the usual signature but it may be by initials,[1] or by a mark,[2] or by a stamp which puts the testator's name on the paper, whether or not the stamp produces his signature in facsimile or otherwise.[3] It is no objection to a mark that the witness is able to write.[4] It is usual to notice alterations and interlineations by the initials of the witnesses to show that they had been made at the time of execution, and such initials are not a proper attestation.[5] It must be shown that the initials were intended as an attestation of the whole will and not to note certain alterations.[6] Alterations and interlineations are more properly noticed in the attestation clause and the clause also mentions the fact that the testator is illiterate or blind, when it is usual to add that the will has been read over to the testator and that he appeared to understand and approve its contents.

While it is most advisable that the witness should sign his real and proper name, yet it is only necessary that the attestation should identify him as the person attesting the will.[7] Thus it is, in exceptional cases, no objection that the attestation is in a wrong name[8] or a mere description of the witness.[9] If but part of a name is signed, it will not be sufficient unless it is shown that it was intended for the whole.[10] In the case of an illiterate witness the pen may be guided by another person.[11] The passing of a dry pen over an existing signature has been held insufficient[12] and the witness himself must sign and not someone else for him.[13] A purported witness whose name had been stamped on the will by his wife in his presence has been held not to have complied with the statutory provisions.[14]

1   *Re Christian's Goods* (1849) 2 Rob Eccl 110, and see n 7.
2   *Hindmarsh v Charlton* (1861) 8 HL Cas 160; *Re Amiss' Goods* (1849) 2 Rob Eccl 116; *Re Eynon's Goods* (1873) LR 3 P & D 92. It has been said that marks are injudicious on account of the difficulty of proving their identity: *Doe d Counsell and Parker v Caperton* (1839) 9 C & P 112, but such attestation is well recognised.
3   *Re Bulloch's Estate* [1968] NI 96 (but the witness must himself participate by some physical act in the affixing of his name by means of the stamp). See *Firstpost Homes Ltd v Johnson* [1995] 4 All ER 355 on the meaning of 'sign' and 'subscribe' in the context of contracts for the sale of land.
4   *Re Amiss' Goods* (1849) 2 Rob Eccl 116.
5   *Re Cunningham's Goods* (1860) 4 Sw & Tr 194.
6   *Re Cunningham's Goods* (1860) 4 Sw & Tr 194; *Re Christian's Goods* (1849) 2 Rob Eccl 110.
7   *Re Sperling's Goods* (1863) 3 Sw & Tr 272; *Re Eynon's Goods* (1873) LR 3 P & D 92.
8   *Re Olliver's Goods* (1854) 2 Ecc & Ad 57; *Re Sperling's Goods* (1863) 3 Sw & Tr 272. A witness must not, however, sign her husband's or his wife's name: *Re White's Goods* (1843) 2 Notes of Cases 461; *Pryor v Pryor* (1860) 29 LJPM & A 114; *Re Leverington's Goods* (1886) 11 PD 80; *Re Cope's Goods* (1850) 2 Rob Eccl 335. Where a witness wrote her wrong surname and then wrote over it her right surname not wholly obliterating the former, probate was granted: *Re Powell's Goods* (1848) 6 Notes of Cases 557.
9   *Re Sperling's Goods* (1863) 3 Sw & Tr 272.
10 *Re Maddock's Goods* (1874) LR 3 P & D 169 and see n 1, para **[11.14]** supra.
11 *Lewis v Lewis* (1861) 2 Sw & Tr 153; *Harrison v Elvin* (1842) 3 QB 117; *Re Frith's Goods* (1858) 1 Sw & Tr 8; *Re Kileher's Goods* (1848) 6 Notes of Cases 15 (name written by drawer of will, witness holding top of pen insufficient).
12 *Playne v Scriven* (1849) 1 Rob Eccl 772; *Re Savory's Goods* (1851) 18 LTOS 280; *Re Mobbs' Goods* (1854) 2 Ecc & Ad 59; *Cunningham's Goods* (1860) 4 Sw & Tr 194 (where the will has already been attested, but the additional tracing of the signature was meant to give effect to certain alterations: the alterations were refused probate); *Re Maddock's Goods* (1874) LR 3 P & D 169.
13 *Re Duggins' Goods* (1870) 39 LJP & M 24; *Re Mead's Goods* (1842) 1 Notes of Cases 456.
14 *Re Bulloch's Estate* [1968] NI 96.

[12.13]
Acknowledgment by witness. The AJA 1982 includes an additional alternative to the requirement that each witness 'attests and signs the will', namely, 'or acknowledges his signature'.[1] This change applies to the wills of testators who die on or after 1 January 1983.[2] This power will enable wills which are incorrectly attested because of the order of signing to be remedied by the witness acknowledging a prior signature after the testator has signed or acknowledged,[3] although a re-signing is preferable.[4] The section makes it clear, by providing for signature or acknowledgment in the alternative that one witness can sign and the other acknowledge.[5] It is thought that so far as the sufficiency of an act of

acknowledgment is concerned, the position would be analogous to the rules governing a testator's acknowledgment.[6]

1   Wills Act 1837, s 9, as substituted by the AJA 1982, s 17, 50 *Halsbury's Statutes* (4th edn) 578; see Vol 2, Part G, para [244.93].
2   AJA 1982, s 73(6); s 76(11).
3   See para [12.12] supra; and *Re Colling, Lawson v von Winckler* [1972] 3 All ER 729.
4   For the reasons given in para [12.5], n 3.
5   The wording of the provision was expressly changed in order to make this clear.
6   See para [11.24] supra. Where there has been a subsequent addition to the will it is possible for this to be authenticated by the testator and witnesses collectively acknowledging their prior signatures; however, for obvious reasons, this is not recommended and it is better to re-sign in full.

IV.   INTENTION TO ATTEST

[12.14]

General rule. Apart from the subscription of the signature, it must be shown that the signatures were added to the document with the intention of attesting the testator's signature.[1] Whether a person signed as an attesting witness is a question of fact depending on the circumstances of each case and is to be determined without regard to what the consequences might be.[2] In the absence of any evidence the intention to attest might be presumed.[3]

1   *Re Wilson's Goods* (1866) LR 1 P & D 269; *Re Sharman's Goods* (1869) LR 1 P & D 661; *Re Streatley's Goods* [1891] P 172; *Re Beadle, Mayes v Beadle* [1974] 1 All ER 493, [1974] 1 WLR 417.
2   *Re Bravda's Estate* [1968] 2 All ER 217, [1968] 1 WLR 479.
3   *Re Bravda's Estate* [1968] 2 All ER 217, [1968] 1 WLR 479. See Presumption of Due Execution, Chapter 13.

[12.15]

How intention ascertained. Where there is no attestation clause and there is on the will some doubt as to the intention to attest the will, oral evidence is admissible to prove the intention.[1] Where there are more signatures than necessary, it may be shown that some were added not for the purpose of attesting the will.[2] A signature purporting to attest the signatures of the witnesses has been held sufficient to attest the execution of the will by the testator.[3]

1   *Re Sharman's Goods* (1869) LR 1 P & D 661. *Re Streatley's Goods* [1891] P 172; *Robert v Phillips* (1855) 4 E & B 450.
2   This is generally required where a beneficiary has signed and it can be shown that he did not sign as witness: see para [9.8] supra.
3   *Mason v Bishop* (1883) Cab & El 21.

V.   WITNESS

[12.16]

Who may be witnesses. A blind person cannot be a witness.[1] A will is not invalid because at the time of execution or at any time afterwards any person attesting the execution is incompetent to be admitted a witness to prove its execution.[2] No person is, therefore, too incapable of credit to prove its execution, but care should be taken in the selection of witnesses to choose persons of good credit and known honesty and, if possible, persons who could have no likelihood of being beneficiaries under the will or on an intestacy,[3] in order that no suspicions may be raised as to due execution. Where possible persons of some standing and position should be chosen so that they may be more readily traced if difficulties arise in securing a grant of probate. Executors,[4] creditors and their wives or husband[5] and beneficiaries and their wives or husbands (but a beneficiary who or whose wife or husband witnesses a will will lose his or her gift under the will) are all admissible witnesses to prove the execution of a will or the validity or invalidity thereof.[6] Where there is a possibility of the testamentary capacity of the testator being called in question, it is advisable to have a medical man or a solicitor as one of the witnesses.[7]

1   *Re Gibson's Estate* [1949] P 434, [1949] 2 All ER 90.
2   WA 1837, s 14; 50 *Halsbury's Statutes* (4th edn) 584; see Vol 2, Part G, para **[244.11]**. There may be a conflict between this section and the law that requires an intention in the witness to attest a will. Clearly the witness must be of sufficient mental capacity to understand the act of attestation. The enactment appears to go to credibility rather than capacity, but it has not so far as is known been the cause of any difficulty. Perhaps some light is thrown upon this by the judgment in *Re Gibson's Estate* [1949] P 434, [1949] 2 All ER 90.
3   No one who is a witness can take a gift under a will: see paras **[9.3]–[9.9]** supra. A person who can take on an intestacy has an interest in defeating the will.
4   WA 1837, s 17; 50 *Halsbury's Statutes* (4th edn) 586; see Vol 2, Part G, para **[244.14]**. An executor can take no benefit under a will to which he is a witness and would lose the benefit of a charging clause in his favour: see para **[9.11]** supra.
5   WA 1837, s 16; 50 *Halsbury's Statutes* (4th edn) 585; see Vol 2, Part G, para **[244.13]**.
6   WA 1837, s 15; 50 *Halsbury's Statutes* (4th edn) 584; see Vol 2, Part G, para **[244.12]**.
7   See Chapter 4, but the court may prefer the evidence of non-professional witnesses, see the text to n 13, para **[4.19]** supra.

[12.17]
Witnesses—professional privilege. A witness whose evidence relates to the execution of a will is the court's witness[1] and the existence of legal professional privilege does not avail to prevent the production of documents so privileged. The court will order that, notwithstanding their privileged character, such documents must be produced so far as they appertain to the execution of a will or codicil.[2]

1   *Re Fuld's Estate (No 2), Hartley v Fuld* [1965] 2 All ER 657.
2   *Re Fuld's Estate (No 2), Hartley v Fuld* [1965] 2 All ER 657.

CHAPTER 13

Presumption of due execution

[13.1]
The presumption. If a will, on the face of it, appears to be duly executed, the presumption is in favour of due execution, applying the principle *omnia præsumuntur rite esse acta.*[1] The force of the presumption varies with the circumstances. If the will is entirely regular in form, it is very strong, but if the form is irregular and unusual the maxim does not apply with the same force.[2] If the witnesses are entirely ignorant of the details of the execution the presumption is the same.[3] If they profess to remember and state that the will was not duly executed, and this negative evidence is not rebutted by showing that the witnesses are not to be credited, or, taking their statement of the facts, that their memories are defective, the will must be pronounced against.[4] The court does not require direct affirmative evidence of due execution.[5]

1   *Re Musgrove's Estate, Davis v Mayhew* [1927] P 264, CA; *Byles v Cox* (1896) 74 LT 222; *Re Ferreira* [1927] VLR 90; *Re Denning, Harnett v Elliott* [1958] 2 All ER 1, [1958] 1 WLR 462; *Chester v Baston* (1980) 118 DLR (3d) 323. It is said in an Irish case that it is only where witnesses or persons present at the execution of the will are dead or cannot give evidence or their evidence is unreliable, that the doctrine can be called in: *Rolleston v Sinclair* [1924] 2 IR 157. When the deceased had lived alone leaving a will, wholly in the deceased's handwriting and witnessed apparently by two witnesses of whom nothing was known, the maxim was not applied to establish the will: *Re Robertson's Estate* [1964] NSWR 1087; *Re Sims, Sims v Faulkner* (1972) 116 Sol Jo 356.
2   *Re Bercovitz's Estate, Canning v Enever* [1962] 1 All ER 552, [1962] 1 WLR 321; *Re Lucas* [1966] VR 267; *Re Haverland* (1975) 55 DLR (3d) 122. This passage of the text was applied in *Re Young* [1969] NZLR 454 at 458.
3   *Re Moriaty's Will* [1956] VLR 400.
4   *Burgoyne v Showler* (1844) 1 Rob Eccl 5; *Keating v Brooks* (1845) 4 Notes of Cases 253; *Brenchley v Still* (1850) 2 Rob Eccl 162; *Re Amos* [1954] 2 DLR 574 (where the will was found in irregular order of pages). For cases where the evidence of the two attesting witnesses was not accepted, see *Bailey v Frowan* (1871) 19 WR 511; *Dayman v Dayman* (1894) 71 LT 699; *Re Collins* [1955] OWN 603.
5   *Gregory v Queen's Proctor* (1846) 4 Notes of Cases 620; *Blake v Knight* (1843) 3 Curt 547; *Leech v Bates* (1849) 1 Rob Eccl 714. It has been suggested that a solicitor who has taken instructions for a will should furnish a statement of evidence to any one interested in challenging or upholding the will; 56 Law Society's Gazette 619.

[13.2]
Attestation clause. Where there is a proper attestation clause, even though the witnesses have no recollection of having witnessed the will, the presumption applies.[1] In the absence of such a clause a will which on the face of it is duly executed is accepted, although no evidence is forthcoming.[2] Where there is such a clause, the court requires the strongest evidence before deciding that the will was not duly executed.[3]

1   *Lloyd v Roberts* (1858) 12 Moo PCC 158; *Wright v Sanderson* (1884) 9 PD 149; *Wright v Rogers* (1869) LR 1 P & D 678; *Woodhouse v Balfour* (1887) 13 PD 2 (witnesses having no recollection of having seen the paper before); *Vinnicombe v Butler* (1864) 3 Sw & Tr 580; *Harris v Knight* (1890) 15 PD 170, CA. Where the attestation does not say that the signature was made by the direction of the testator, the omission may be passed over in cases where everything is otherwise in order: *Re Cooper's Goods* (1847) 5 Notes of Cases 618.

2   *Re Peverett's Goods* [1902] P 205; *Clarke v Clarke* (1879) 5 LR Ir 47; *Re Malins' Goods* (1887) 19 LR Ir 231; *Vinnicombe v Butler* (1864) 3 Sw & Tr 580; *Re Rees' Goods* (1865) 34 LJPM & A 56; *Scarff v Scarff* [1927] 1 IR 13; *Re Griffiths* [1955] NZLR 127; *Re Laxer* (1963) 37 DLR (2d) 192; *Re Strong's Estate, Strong v Hadden* [1915] P 211. In *Re Denning, Harnett v Elliott* [1958] 2 All ER 1, [1958] 1 WLR 462, there were only two signatures on the back of a single sheet will.

3   *Wright v Rogers* (1869) LR 1 P & D 678; *Whitting v Turner* (1903) 89 LT 71; *O'Meagher v O'Meagher* (1883) 11 LR Ir 117; *Goodisson v Goodisson* [1913] 1 IR 31, 218; *Dubourdieu v Patterson* (1919) 54 ILT 23. The decision in *Re Swinford's Goods* (1869) LR 1 P & D 630, seems out of line with the general run of the cases. Where it was suggested that the signature was a traced forgery the court accepted the positive evidence of the witnesses: *Re Kryskiw* [1954] OWN 717.

[13.3]

Evidence rebutting presumption. This must be positive and reliable[1] and the court must not give undue weight to the circumstances on which the presumption is founded and on the other hand must not lose sight of them.[2] The burden of proving due execution, whether by presumption or by positive evidence rests on the propounder.[3] The direct evidence of both attesting witnesses unless discounted rebuts the presumption[4] and the evidence of one of the witnesses has been held to do so.[5]

1   *Glover v Smith* (1886) 57 LT 60; *Wyatt v Berry* [1893] P 5; *Pilkington v Gray* [1899] AC 401, DC; *Re Moore's Goods* [1901] P 44.

2   *Cooper v Bockett* (1846) 4 Moo PCC 419 at 439; *Re Bladen* [1952] VLR 82 (presumption applied in spite of conflicting evidence); *Re Gramp* [1952] SASR 12 (presumption rebutted).

3   *Brenchley v Still* (1850) 2 Rob Eccl 162; *Clery v Barry* (1887) 21 LR Ir 152; *Loftus v Harris* (1914) 19 DLR 670.

4   *Croft v Croft* (1865) 4 Sw & Tr 10; *Glover v Smith* (1886) 57 LT 60; *Pennant v Kingscote* (1843) 3 Curt 642; *Re Michnik Estate* [1945] 4 DLR 521. See *Dayman v Dayman* (1894) 71 LT 699; *Neal v Denston* (1932) 147 LT 460, for cases where the evidence was discounted. Since the reason for the provisions of the Wills Act 1837, s 9, was the prevention of fraud, evidence is admissible to show that the two attesting witnesses are wrong: *Re Vere-Wardale* [1949] P 395, [1949] 2 All ER 250.

5   *Cregeen v Willoughby* (1860) 24 JP 408; *Noding v Alliston* (1850) 14 Jur 904. To the contrary: *Keating v Brooks* (1845) 4 Notes of Cases 253 (where the presumption prevailed although one witness said her signature was forged); *Re Thomas' Goods* (1859) 1 Sw & Tr 255 (incomplete recollection); *Wright v Rogers* (1869) LR 1 P & D 678 (perfect attestation clause rebutted only by strongest evidence). See also *Reeves v Grainger* (1908) 52 Sol Jo 355 (execution by illiterate testator: evidence of clerk writing testator's name as guide where signature should be, in ignorance of the fact that testator was too illiterate to sign); *Pattie v Fry* (1911) 30 NZLR 581; *Re Irwin* [1920] NZLR 440. The will was held good where one witness would not deny proper execution: *Re Johnson* [1953] 4 DLR 777.

[13.4]

Signature affixed by direction of testator. The presumption of due execution applies both where the testator has himself signed the will and where it has been signed by his direction.[1]

1   *Clery v Barry* (1887) 21 LR Ir 152.

CHAPTER 14

Alterations, interlineations and erasures

[14.1]
Statutory provisions. The Wills Act 1837 (WA 1837), s 21[1] provides as follows:

'No obliteration, interlineation[2] or other alteration made in a will after the execution thereof shall be valid or have any effect, except so far as the words or effect of the will before such alteration shall not be apparent, unless such alteration shall be executed in like manner as hereinbefore is required for the execution of the will; but the will, with such alteration as part thereof, shall be deemed to be duly executed if the signature of the testator and the subscription of the witnesses be made in the margin or on some other part of the will opposite or near to such alteration, or at the foot or end of or opposite to a memorandum referring to such alteration, and written at the end or some other part of the will.'

It is essential that any alterations made to a will should be correctly executed in accordance with the requirements of the WA 1837, s 9.[3]

The above statutory provision applies only where the alterations, interlineations or erasures are made after the execution of the will and, where it can be shown that they were made before execution, the statute does not apply and no execution or attestation of such alterations, interlineations or erasures is necessary.[4] There is a presumption that alterations are made after execution,[5] but that presumption does not apply to the mere filling in of gaps or matters left vacant, such as names and addresses or the amount of a sum of money and it is immaterial that these are in different ink or in a different handwriting.[6] The Probate Rules[7] provide that where there appears in a will any obliteration, interlineation or other alteration which is not authenticated in the manner prescribed by the WA 1837, or by the re-execution of the will or by the execution of a codicil, the registrar shall require evidence to show whether the alteration was present at the time the will was executed and shall give directions as to the form in which the will is to be proved.[8] Provided that this paragraph shall not apply to any alteration which appears to the Registrar to be of no practical importance.

Where the alteration is of no effect under the above statutory provision and the original words are apparent, probate is granted of the will as it originally stood.[9] Where the original words are not apparent, probate is granted in blank,[10] that is, without the altered part or the obliterated words.

---

1 50 *Halsbury's Statutes* (4th edn) 591. See Vol 2, Part G, para **[244.21]**.
2 As to obliterations or interlineations, see Chapter 14.

146

3   The importance of strictly complying with the requirements of the WA 1837 has been re-emphasised by *Re White, Barker v Gribble* [1991] Ch 1, [1990] 3 All ER 1. Alterations were made to a will, the testator wrote, 'Alterations to Will dated 14-12-84' on the will and asked two witnesses to sign it. The testator did not sign the alterations or the will again. It was held that the will could not be admitted to probate in its altered form. Nor could the original signature on the will be said to have been intended to give effect to the will in its amended form within the requirements of the WA 1837, s 9(b). Further the witnesses to the alterations had not attested a new will but merely the alterations to the original will and therefore the requirement of the WA 1837, s 9(d) that each witness 'attests ... the will' had not been satisfied. It followed that the will in its original form, which was correctly executed, would be admitted to probate. See also *Re Gill's Estate* [1988] 6 WWR 726; *Olson v Olson* [1988] 6 WWR 631 and *James v Burdekin* in [1990] 3 WAR 299.

4   *Greville v Tylee* (1851) 7 Moo PCC 320; *Maule v Maule* (1890) 62 LT 702 (where it was admitted that the alterations were made before execution).

5   See para **[14.3]** infra.

6   *Greville v Tylee* (1851) 7 Moo PCC 320.

7   Non-Contentious Probate Rules 1987, SI 1987/2024, r 14(1). See *Tristram and Coote's Probate Practice* (28th edn).

8   Erased words were omitted where it was shown that the will was placed before the testatrix with the words crossed through, there was no further evidence that the testatrix approved the crossing out: *Re Baker's Will, ex p Cochrane* [1964–5] NSWR 1805. See further paras **[14.10]** and **[14.11]** infra.

9   *Re Beavan's Goods* (1840) 2 Curt 369; *Soar v Dolman, Re Rippin's Goods* (1842) 3 Curt 121 (original amount of legacy restored); *Re Harris' Goods* (1860) 1 Sw & Tr 536 (appointment of original executor restored); *Strurton v Whetlock* (1883) 52 LJP 29.

10 *Re Livock's Goods* (1838) 1 Curt 906; *Re Ibbetson's Goods* (1839) 2 Curt 337; *Re James' Goods* (1858) 1 Sw & Tr 238.

[14.2]

Apparent. The original words are apparent where they can be ascertained on inspection of the document and not when they are made known by extrinsic evidence.[1] Words are apparent where experts by use of a magnifying glass can decipher them and satisfy the court that they have done so[2] but resort cannot be made to any physical interference with the document so as to render clearer what may have been written upon it[3] nor can resort be had to infra-red photography to render the original words apparent.[4] Where obliteration or erasure has rendered the words not apparent, such alteration or erasure, though not attested, is rendered valid by the Act and there is pro tanto entire destruction of the will, and therefore, so far as such alteration or erasure extends, a revocation in part of the will.[5]

1   *Re Ibbetson's Goods* (1839) 2 Curt 337; *Re Horsford's Goods* (1874) LR 3 P & D 211; *Ffinch v Combe* [1894] P 191; *Re Itter's Goods, Dedman v Godfrey* [1950] P 130, [1950] 1 All ER 68; *Re McCabe's Goods* (1873) LR 3 P & D 94 at 96; *Re Hamer's Estate* (1943) 113 LJP 31 (where the words 'two hundred and' in the amounts of legacies had been completely obliterated, there was a revocation of the legacies).

2   *Re Ibbetson's Goods* (1839) 2 Curt 337; *Re Brasier's Goods* [1899] P 36; *Ffinch v Combe* [1894] P 191 (surrounding obliteration by brown paper and holding against window pane) applied in *Re Adams* [1990] Ch 601, [1990] 2 All ER 97 where the signatures to a will were so heavily scored out with a ball point pen that they could not be read and were held to be 'not apparent'. Will held revoked, see Chapter 18. See also *Re Kirs Estate* (1990) 55 SASR 61.

3   *Re Horsford's Goods* (1874) LR 3 P & D 211. Where the doctrine of dependent relative revocation applies the court has allowed the removal of paper pasted over a word or disposition: ibid, and see *Re Itter's Goods, Dedman v Godfrey* [1950] P 130, [1950] 1 All ER 68; see para **[19.3]** infra.

4   *Re Itter's Goods, Dedman v Godfrey* [1950] P 130, [1950] 1 All ER 68. The use of infra-red photography creates a new document, namely the photography, which is not the will. But where

the amounts of legacies only had been obliterated, and no new amounts substituted, it was held that the revocation was intended to take effect only on the substitution of new amounts. The will would therefore be proved with the old amounts, to be discovered either by infra-red photography or the removal of the slips pasted over the original amounts.

5   *Townley v Watson* (1844) 3 Curt 761; but see *Lushington v Onslow* (1848) 6 Notes of Cases 183.

[14.3]

Presumption that alterations etc made after execution. There is a presumption that unattested alterations, interlineations and erasures were made after execution,[1] and if the original words before alteration are apparent, probate is granted with those words included in the will and the alterations, interlineations or erasures are ignored, but if the original words are not apparent, then probate is granted in blank, ie neither the original nor the altered or added or erased words are included in the probate.[2]

1   *Cooper v Bockett* (1846) 4 Moo PCC 419, which is generally regarded as establishing this presumption, but it has been stated many times since. In the case of deeds the presumption is the other way, ie that alterations were made before execution. The reason given for the difference is that a deed could not be altered after execution without fraud or wrong, but a testator may alter his will without fraud or wrong: *Doe d Tatum v Catomore* (1851) 16 QB 745. The presumption is a rebuttable presumption and not an irrebuttable one or what is called a presumption of law: see the next following paragraphs. See *Re Samson* (1966) 59 DLR (2d) 132 (presumption applied where word 'money' interlineated but word 'estate' implied in its place and effect given to clear intention to make a residuary bequest).
2   See cases cited in nn 9 and 10, para **[14.1]** supra, and see *Re Holden Estate* [1945] 3 WWR 564 (although erasure after execution does not alter the will, it is some evidence of the intention of the testator).

[14.4]

Onus of proof. The burden is upon the person seeking to rely upon the alteration, interlineation or erasure to prove that it was made before the execution of the will,[1] but slight evidence will rebut the presumption.[2]

1   *Doe d Shallcross v Palmer* (1851) 16 QB 747; *Greville v Tylee* (1851) 7 Moo PCC 320; *Williams v Ashton* (1860) 1 John & H 115; *Re Hawkins Estate, Carlson and Pendray v Hawkins and Ellery* [1941] 2 WWR 469.
2   *Re Duffy's Goods* (1871) IR 5 Eq 506.

[14.5]

Evidence to rebut presumption in attestation clause. Where alterations, interlineations or erasures have been made, the practice is to notice them in the attestation clause referring to the page and line in the will where they occur and stating that such were made prior to execution. It is a common practice also to place the signatures and initials of the testator and the witnesses in the margin near to the alterations, interlineations or erasures; but, where the alterations or similar matters are sufficiently identified in the attestation clause, this is not necessary[1]. In such cases the presumption is rebutted and probate is granted with the alterations, interlineations or erasures.[2] In the case, however, where the interlineations or addition extend beyond and below the execution, the will should be re-executed below the addition.[3]

1   It is shown in the next paragraph that signatures or initials against the alteration amount in law to a re-execution and as such are sufficient to establish the alteration without any addition to the usual attestation clause.

2   The addition to the attestation makes the acceptance of the alterations, etc., automatic just the same as a proper attestation makes the grant of probate automatic so far as due execution is concerned. The matter is neatly stated in the headnote to *Re Stevens* [1918] NZLR 940. Where the attestation clause speaks of 'some alterations' it may be concluded that all alterations were prior to execution: *Doherty v Dwyer* (1890) 25 LR Ir 297.

3   See nn 1 and 2, para **[4.10]**, and the text thereto.

[14.6]

Signatures or initials of testator and witnesses near alterations. Without any reference to the alterations or similar matters in the attestation clause, the signatures or initials of the testator and witnesses near to the alterations, interlineations or erasures are sufficient to render them valid whether they were made before or after the execution of the will.[1] Where they are made before execution the signatures or initials are evidence that the alterations were so made, and where they were made after execution the signatures or initials amount to a re-execution. There must, however, be the signatures or initials of the testator and of the two witnesses[2] and the signatures or initials of the testator and one witness[3] or those of two witnesses without that of the testator[4] are insufficient. Retracing signatures with a dry pen is not sufficient.[5] An alteration in a holograph will need only be signed or initialled by the testator, but even in jurisdictions where holograph wills are permitted, an alteration to a formal will must be signed or initialled by the testator and two witnesses.[6]

1   *Re Wingrove's Goods* (1850) 16 LTOS 347; *Greville v Tylee* (1851) 7 Moo PCC 320; *Re Hinds' Goods* (1852), 20 LTOS 264; *Re Blewitt's Goods* (1880) 5 PD 116; *White v Grier* (1841) Milw 602; *Smith v Meriam* (1878) 25 Gr 383; *Re Brown's Will* (1895) 13 NZLR 645; *Re Pugh* (1889) 15 VLR 833; *Re Pattulla Estate* (1955) 17 WWR 666.

2   See cases cited in n 1; *Re McVay Estate* (1955) 16 WWR 200. In one case it was held that the initials of the witnesses opposite the alterations and an acknowledgment of his previous signature by the testator was sufficient: *Re Dewell's Goods* (1853) 1 Ecc & Ad 103; but this should not be relied on in practice as it involves proving that acknowledgment by oral evidence, see also *Re Shearn's Goods* (1880) 50 LJP 15. It is now possible for both the testator and the witnesses to acknowledge their prior signatures and thus authenticate an alteration: see the new WA 1837, s 9, substituted by the AJA 1982, s 17; 50 *Halsbury's Statutes* (4th edn) 578; Vol 2, Part G, para **[244.93]**; see also para **[12.1]** ante. This course is not recommended for the reason just given; see also n 3, para **[12.2]** ante.

3   *Re Parr's Goods* (1859) Sea & Sm 146.

4   *Re Martin's Goods* (1849) 1 Rob Eccl 712; *Re Shearn's Goods* (1880) 50 LJP 15; *Re Cunningham's Goods* (1860) Sea & Sm 132; *Re Delves* (1875) 1 VLR 33. In the case of *Re Martin's Goods*, the testator also retraced his signatures with a dry pen, and in the case of *Re Cunningham's Goods*, both the testator and witnesses did so, but probate with the alterations was refused in both cases.

5   See n 4.

6   *Re Cottrell Estate* [1951] 4 DLR 600, but see *Equitable Trust Co v Doull* (1958) 25 WWR 465.

[14.7]

What will render subsequent alterations valid. Clearly such alterations, interlineations or erasures may be rendered valid by re-execution of the will;[1] but the fact of the testator and the witnesses going over their previous signatures with a dry pen does not amount to re-execution.[2] The placing of the signatures of the testator and two witnesses near the alteration or similar matter, however, has been held to amount to re-execution, as has already been stated.[3] It remains to consider how such alterations may be rendered valid by a subsequent codicil and by evidence that they were made before execution.

1   *Re Treeby's Goods* (1875) LR 3 P & D 242. A partial re-execution is not sufficient: *Locke v James* (1843) 11 M & W 901 (where only one witness signed the re-execution).
2   *Re Martin's Goods* (1849) 1 Rob Eccl 712; *Re Cunningham's Goods* (1860) Sea & Sm 132.
3   See para [14.6] supra.

[14.8]
Effect of subsequent codicil. A codicil is a republication of a will and validates it (including unattested alterations in it mentioned in the codicil) as from the time of the execution of the codicil;[1] but, if the codicil takes no notice of the alterations in the will, the presumption is that they were made after the date of the codicil and are ineffective;[2] but this is only a presumption and may be rebutted by evidence.[3] Unattested alterations can in this way be validated by a subsequent codicil subject to three conditions: (i) the codicil must refer to the alterations; (ii) if no reference is made there must be proof that they were made before the date of the codicil; and (iii) the alterations must not be shown by the codicil or otherwise to have been deliberative.[4]

1   *Re Mills' Goods* (1847) 10 LTOS 230; *Re Hall's Goods* (1871) LR 2 P & D 256; *Re Heath's Goods* [1892] P 253; *Oldroyd v Harvey* [1907] P 326.
2   *Lushington v Onslow* (1848) 6 Notes of Cases 183; *Re Sykes' Goods* (1873) LR 3 P & D 26; *Christmas and Christmas v Whinyates* (1863) 3 Sw & Tr 81 at 89; *Rowley v Merlin* (1860) 24 JP 824; *Doherty v Dwyer* (1890) 25 LR Ir 297.
3   *Re Bradley's Goods* (1846) 5 Notes of Cases 187; *Re Sykes' Goods* (1873) LR 3 P & D 26.
4   *Re Heath's Goods* [1892] P 253; *Tyler v Merchant Taylors' Co* (1890) 15 PD 216; *Re Hay, Kerr v Stinnear* [1904] 1 Ch 317. As to distinction between final and deliberative alterations, see *Francis v Grover* (1845) 5 Hare 39; *Doe d Strickland v Strickland* (1849) 8 CB 724; *Lamont v Glasgow Magistrates* (1887) 14 R 603.

[14.9]
Rebuttal of presumption by evidence. In the absence of any evidence when the alterations, interlineations or erasures were made, the presumption prevails and they are taken as made after execution and not admitted to probate.[1] In exceptional cases, however, the fact that the testator knew the statutory requirements has been accepted as sufficient to rebut the presumption.[2] The evidence in rebuttal may be internal furnished by the document itself or external furnished by declarations of the testator or the evidence of the attesting witnesses.

1   *Cooper v Bockett* (1846) 4 Moo PCC 419; *Re Parfitt's Goods* (1842) 1 Notes of Cases 533; *Burgoyne v Showler* (1844) 1 Rob Eccl 5; *Re Brennan's Will* [1952] QWN 1 (words added in margin: no evidence as to when added: excluded from grant).
2   *Re Jacob's Goods* (1842) 1 Notes of Cases 401 (will of barrister); *Re Thomson's Goods* (1844) 3 Notes of Cases 441 (testator with knowledge of proper mode of execution and correct in transacting business). See also *O'Meagher v O'Meagher* (1883) 11 LR Ir 117.

[14.10]
Internal evidence. Any document must, if possible, be constructed so as to give it some effect and, if a will is meaningless without the alteration, interlineation or erasure, effect is given to the alteration, interlineation or erasure.[1] Of this kind

are the filling in of blanks left for the names of legatees[2] or for the amount of the legacies.[3] Interlineations and erasures apparently written with the same pen and the same ink as the rest of the will (especially but not necessarily supplying a blank in the sense) are accepted as written before execution.[4] Expert evidence in this connection has been accepted.[5]

1 *Re Heath's Goods* [1892] P 253; *Re Cadge's Goods* (1868) LR 1 P & D 543; *Dench v Dench* (1877) 2 PD 60.
2 *Greville v Tylee* (1851) 7 Moo PCC 320; *Birch v Birch* (1848) 1 Rob Eccl 675 (objection that ink is different); *Moore v Moore* (1872) IR 6 Eq 166.
3 *Greville v Tylee* (1851) 7 Moo PCC 320; *Kell v Charmer* (1856) 23 Beav 195 (amounts inserted in pencil and in code).
4 A revocatory clause inconsistent with the rest of the will struck out in pencil was omitted where its omission was consistent with a statement by the testator in *Re Tonge's Goods* (1891) 66 LT 60; *Re Purvis's Will* (1877) 3 VLR 37; *Re Oates' Estate, Callow v Sutton* [1946] 2 All ER 735.
5 *Re Rushout's Goods* (1849) 13 LTOS 264; *Re Hindmarch's Goods* (1866) LR 1 P & D 307; *Re King's Goods* (1875) 23 WR 552; *Re Riddell's Will* (1880) 6 VLR 5.

[14.11]
External evidence. This has generally consisted of declarations made by the testator before or at the time of execution.[1] Declarations by him after the time of execution have been held inadmissible.[2] The evidence of the person drawing the will has been accepted.[3] Special provisions apply to obliterations.[4]

1 *Doe d Shallcross v Palmer* (1851) 16 QB 747; *Re Foley's Goods* (1855) 2 Ecc & Ad 206; *Re Sykes' Goods* (1873) LR 3 P & D 26; *Re King's Goods* (1875) 23 WR 552; *Dench v Dench* (1877) 2 PD 60; *Re Tonge's Goods* (1891) 66 LT 60; *Re Jessop* [1924] P 221; *Re Oates' Estate, Callow v Sutton* [1946] 2 All ER 735.
2 *Re Hardy's Goods* (1861) 30 LJPM & A 142; *Re Sykes' Goods* (1873) LR 3 P & D 26; *Re Adamson's Goods* (1875) LR 3 P & D 253; *Re Jessop* [1924] P 221.
3 *Keigwin v Keigwin* (1843) 3 Curt 607.
4 See para **[14.13]** infra.

[14.12]
Interlineation. This is not confined to something written between the lines but is equally applicable to something inserted on the lines or carried in by a cross or asterisk.[1] Words written following the executed part of the will have been refused to be treated as an interlineation even where they completed an otherwise incomplete sentence in the executed part.[2]

1 *Re Birt's Goods* (1871) LR 2 P & D 214 (words on second sheet with 'see over'); and see *Re Martin's Will* (1899) 17 NZLR 418; *Re Greenwood's Goods* [1892] P 7 (executors appointed below attestation referred to by asterisk); *Re White's Goods* (1860) 30 LJPM & A 55 (bequest referred to by mark excluded); *Leonard v Leonard* [1902] P 243 (interpolation of two new sheets making remainder unworkable held to be revocation of whole); *Re Samson* (1966) 59 DLR (2d) 132 (word 'money' inserted by mark).
2 *Re Malen's Goods* (1885) 54 LJP 91; *Re Anstee's Goods* [1893] P 283; *Re White's Goods* [1896] 1 IR 269; *Re Gee's Goods* (1898) 78 LT 843.

[14.13]
Obliterations. Where the words of a will have been erased by the testator so as to be no longer apparent, and other words have been written over them which are not admissible to probate because they are not duly attested, extrinsic evidence of the original words may be received if the obliteration is referable

wholly and solely to the testator's intention to substitute the other words for them. The testator's intention must be ascertained from his declarations and surrounding circumstances. Where the intention as thus established would be defeated by the restoration of the original words, it may be held that the original words have been revoked although the other words have been ineffectually substituted.[1]

Where a testator has pasted over a whole legacy a piece of paper on which at some time he has written a new bequest, the court will not order the upper paper to be removed and will direct the probate to issue in blank as to that legacy; but if the testator has covered over the amount of the legacy only, leaving the legatee's name untouched, the court will consider it a case which comes under the principle of a dependent relative revocation and will endeavour to discover the amount of the legacy originally bequeathed by removing the upper paper.[2]

1   *Re Zimmer's Estate* (1924) 40 TLR 502. See *Re Bedford's Goods* (1847) 5 Notes of Cases 188 (erasure of executor's name and substitution of another, complete revocation), and cf *Brooke v Kent* (1841) 3 Moo PCC 334 (alteration of amount of legacy; original amount restored); *Re Adams* [1990] Ch 601, [1990] 2 All ER 97 and see Chapter 18.
2   *Re Horsford's Goods* (1874) LR 3 P & D 211; *Ffinch v Combe* [1894] P 191; *Re Itter's Goods, Dedmam v Godfrey* [1950] P 130, [1950] 1 All ER 68.

[14.14]

Alterations by persons other than testator. Alterations made after execution by persons other than the testator even though made to correct errors in drawing the will, have been rejected and probate granted as the document originally stood.[1]

1   *Re Rolfe's Goods* (1846) 4 Notes of Cases 406; *Re Escott's Goods* (1842) 1 Notes of Cases 571; *Fligelstone v Fligelstone* (1902) 46 Sol Jo 451. Needless to say, an alteration made after the death of the testator was rejected: *Re North's Goods* (1842) 6 Jur 564.

CHAPTER 15

Incorporation of unattested documents

[15.1]
Conditions of incorporation. Subject to certain conditions being complied with, documents referred to in a testator's will or codicil, though not themselves duly executed in accordance with the Wills Act 1837,[1] may be incorporated in the will and included in the probate.[2] First, the document must be referred to in the will.[3] Second, such reference in the will must be sufficient to identify the document.[4] Oral evidence is admissible for the purpose of identification.[5] Lastly, the document must be an existing document, and not one which is to come into existence at a future date.[6] It is, therefore, improper to incorporate a document 'or any substitution therefor or modification thereof'.[7] An existing document can be incorporated, though the incorporated document gives power to make a future unattested disposition, but in so far as that power is concerned, the incorporated document becomes invalid since, when incorporated in the will, the will contains a provision not allowed by law. However, all other parts of the incorporated document may be valid and take effect.[8] If the will can be construed as referring equally to an existing or future document, oral evidence is not admissible as to which class of document is referred to.[9] The onus of proving the identity of the document and its existence at the date of the will lies upon the party seeking to establish it.[10]

1   Wills Act 1837, s 9; as substituted by the Administration of Justice Act 1982, s 17; 50 *Halsbury's Statutes* (4th edn) 578; see Vol 2, Part G, para **[244.93]**. The incorporated document need not be of a testamentary form or character: *Re Mardon's Estate* [1944] P 109, [1944] 2 All ER 397. In *Re Berger* [1990] Ch 118, [1989] 1 All ER 591 (noted more fully at para **[1.8]** ante) an English will which was invalidly executed was incorporated into a Hebrew *zavah* which was correctly executed. There was a reference in the *zavah* to the English will and it was clear on the facts that the former was a document in existence when the *zavah* was signed and so was capable of incorporation into it. See *Practice Direction (Fam D) (Incorporation of Standard Forms and Clauses in Wills)*, 10 April 1995.
2   In some cases such documents have been omitted from the probate on the ground of reasonableness; see eg *Re Balme's Goods* [1897] P 261 (reference to a library catalogue of considerable length). Cf *Re Lansdowne's (Marquis) Goods* (1863) 3 Sw & Tr 194; *Re Battersbee's Goods* (1852) 2 Rob Eccl 439 (where trustees refused to bring in the deeds); *Re Jones' Goods* (1920) 123 LT 202 (special circumstances justifying exclusion).
3   *Smart v Prujean* (1801) 6 Ves 560; *Re Norris* (1866) 14 WR 348; *Re Jones' Goods* (1920) 123 LT 202; *Re Saxton's Estate, Barclays Bank Ltd v Treasury Solicitor* [1939] 2 All ER 418 (where the will without the document had no dispositive effect and the will said 'I give and bequeath to the following persons' and the document commenced 'I wish to leave the following amounts'; held a sufficient cross-reference); *Re Poole, Stewart v Poole (PEI)* [1929] 1 DLR 418.
4   Certainty and identification is the very essence of incorporation: *Croker v Marquis of Hertford* (1844) 4 Moo PCC 339 at 366. General description or mere reference has been held

insufficient: *Croker v Marquis of Hertford* (1844) 4 Moo PCC 339; *Re Pembroke's Goods* (1856) Dea & Sw 182; *Re Hubbard's Goods* (1865) LR 1 P & D 53; *Re Watkins' Goods* (1865) LR 1 P & D 19 ('hereunder' not sufficient reference to second & third pages of will of which only first page was duly executed'); *Re Dallow's Goods* (1866) LR 1 P & D 189 (appointment of executors below execution); *Re Williamson's Goods* (1902) 46 Sol Jo 552. Reference sufficient to identify documents: *Re Norris* (1866) 14 WR 348; *Re Jones' Goods* (1920) 123 LT 202; *Paton v Ormerod* [1892] P 247 (testatrix confused between previous will and deed: no sufficient reference); *Re Garnett's Goods* [1894] P 90 (papers numbered 1 to 6 stated by testator to be signed by himself in the presence of witnesses: denial of witnesses); *Eyre v Eyre* [1903] P 131 (draft will not proved to exist is not incorporated by being referred to in a codicil as a duly executed will); *Re Mihalopulos Estate* (1956) 19 WWR 118 (document not proved to be in existence at date of will); *Gray's Trustees v Murray* 1970 SLT 105 (insufficient identification of signed deposit receipts).

5 *Allen v Maddock* (1858) 11 Moo PCC 427; *Re Gorton's Will* (1910) 29 NZLR 733 (evidence of identification). But there must be a reference to the paper before evidence of intention to incorporate is admissible: *Re Luke's Goods* (1865) 34 LJPM & A 105; *Re Dallow's Goods* (1866) LR 1 P & D 189 (where the evidence offered was to show that the document was written before the will); *Re Sunderland's Goods* (1866) LR 1 P & D 198 (evidence that document existing at date of will); *University College of North Wales v Taylor* [1908] P 140 (where evidence was excluded that an existing document was intended because the words used in the will could refer to future documents); *Re Beveridge's Will* (1905) 6 SRNSW 125; *Re Kehoe's Goods* (1883) 13 LR Ir 13.

6 *Re Berger* [1990] Ch 118, [1989] 1 All ER 591; *Re Keen, Evershed v Griffiths* [1937] 1 All ER 452; *Re Bateman's Will Trusts, Brierley v Perry* [1970] 3 All ER 817, [1970] 1 WLR 1463 (direction as to sealed letter invalid as relating to a future non-testamentary instrument); see Chapter 35 on Secret Trusts. *Singleton v Tomlinson* (1878) 3 App Cas 404; *Re Sunderland's Goods* (1866) LR 1 P & D 198; *Re Phillips' Estate, Boyle v Thompson* (1918) 34 TLR 256 (will stating document in existence and document found with will); *Re Currie* (1978) 91 DLR (3d) 559. See also *Re Norman's Goods* (1847) 5 Notes of Cases 550; *Stuart v Clemons* [1951] Tas LR 23.

7 *Re Jones, Jones v Jones* [1942] Ch 328, [1942] 1 All ER 642, but see Chapter 20, as to effect of a codicil.

8 *Re Edwards' Will Trusts, Dalgleish v Leighton* [1948] Ch 440, [1948] 1 All ER 821 (where the incorporated document was a settlement).

9 *University College of North Wales v Taylor* [1908] P 140; *Re Jones, Jones v Jones* [1942] Ch 328, [1942] 1 All ER 642.

10 *Singleton v Tomlinson* (1878) 3 App Cas 404.

[15.2]
Documents coming into existence after will and before codicil. A document not in existence at the date of the will, but which comes into existence before the execution of a subsequent codicil, may be included in the probate, if the will read as speaking at the date of the codicil contains language which would operate as an incorporation of that document[1]; but even so the language of the will must point to an existing document.[2]

1 *Re Truro's (Lady) Goods* (1866) LR 1 P & D 201; *Re Reid's Goods* (1868) 38 LJP & M 1; *Re Rendle's Goods* (1899) 68 LJP 125; *Re Phillips' Estate, Boyle v Thompson* (1918) 34 TLR 256, but see cases cited in next note.

2 *Re Reid's Goods* (1868) 38 LJP & M 1; *Durham v Northen* [1895] P 66; *Re Smart's Goods* [1902] P 238. In the case of *Re MacGregor's Goods* (1889) 60 LT 840, a document coming into existence after the will and before the codicil was excluded because the will required it to be signed by the testatrix and it was not so signed.

[15.3]
Effect of incorporation. By incorporation the document becomes testamentary and must be construed with the will[1] and anything therein which would be

invalid if included in a will becomes inoperative.[2] Where a deed is said to be incorporated but in fact the document described as a deed never becomes operative, the incorporation is of no effect and the estate is not to be administered by reference to the inoperative instrument.[3]

1   *A-G v Jones and Bartlett* (1817) 3 Price 368; *Watson v Arundel* (1876) IR 11 Eq 53.
2   *Re Edwards' Will Trusts, Dalgleish v Leighton* [1948] Ch 440, [1948] 1 All ER 821 (incorporation of settlement containing a power to nominate beneficiaries by future memorandum under hand).
3   *Re Hurdle, Blakeney v Hurdle* [1936] 3 All ER 810.

[15.4]
Further incorporation by the incorporated document. The incorporated document may itself incorporate other documents and these will be incorporated in the will provided the above conditions as to reference identity and existence at the date of the will or codicil are satisfied throughout the whole procedure of incorporation,[1] but if any alteration has been made in any such document after the execution of the will, the alteration is ineffective unless the will has been confirmed by a codicil specifically referring to it.[2]

1   *Symes v Appelbe* (1887) 57 LT 599, and see the judgment of Lord Greene MR, in *Re Edwards' Will Trusts, Dalgleish v Leighton* [1948] 1 All ER 821 at 823, 824. Once incorporation is held valid, the will and the document incorporated then become the will and so on each incorporation. But words in the will may be held merely descriptive of the incorporated document, so that an offending clause is not incorporated: *Re Schintz's Will Trusts, Lloyds Bank Ltd v Moreton* [1951] Ch 870, [1951] 1 All ER 1095.
2   *Re Smart's Goods* [1902] P 238.

[15.5]
Document not found after death of testator. A document said to be incorporated which cannot be found after the testator's death cannot be incorporated in the will and generally the provision in the will fails.[1]

1   *Re Barton, Barton v Bourne* (1932) 48 TLR 205, but see *Willoughby v Storer* (1870) 22 LT 896. Where the document was proved to have been in existence at the date of the will, secondary evidence is admissible as to its contents: *Sugden v Lord St Leonards* (1876) 1 PD 154.

[15.6]
Declaration against incorporation in will. Where there is an express declaration against incorporation or that the document is not to be considered testamentary, the document cannot be incorporated.[1]

1   *Re Louis, Louis v Treloar* (1916) 32 TLR 313, and cf *Re Falkiner, Mead v Smith* [1924] 1 Ch 88.

CHAPTER 16

Wills of soldiers, sailors and airmen

[16.1]

Statement of the privilege. Since the Statute of Frauds the wills of soldiers in actual military service, and of mariners or seamen at sea, have not been required to be in writing, or, if in writing, they were not after 1837 required to follow the requirements of the Wills Act 1837 (WA 1837) as to execution,[1] so far as they disposed of personal estate.[2] These privileges have been extended to members of the Royal Naval and Marine Forces, not only when at sea, but also when so circumstanced that, if soldiers, they would be 'in actual military service',[3] and to members of the Royal Air Force[4] in actual military service,[5] and to real estate in England or Ireland as well as personal estate.[6] These extended privileges apply whenever the will was made.[7] Any appointment, made after 6 February 1918, in a will so privileged of any person as guardian of the infant children of the testator is valid.[8] A member of the forces in actual military service or marine or seaman at sea may make a valid will though under the age of 18 years[9] if the will is made after 1 January 1970,[10] or under the age of 21 years in the case of wills made before that date.

1 For such requirements, see Chapters 10–13. Wills of members of the forces are specially exempted by the WA 1837, s 11; see Vol 2, Part G, para **[244.9]**.
2 The provisions have been extended to real estate, see n 6.
3 Wills (Soldiers and Sailors) Act 1918 (W(SS)A 1918), s 2; 50 *Halsbury's Statutes* (4th edn) 604.
4 W(SS)A 1918, s 5(2).
5 See para **[16.2]** infra.
6 W(SS)A 1918, s 3 as amended by the Family Law Reform Act 1969, s 3(1); 50 *Halsbury's Statutes* (4th edn) 604.
7 *Re Yates' Estate* [1919] P 93.
8 W(SS)A 1918, s 4, reversing the effect of the decision in *Re Tollemache's Estate* [1917] P 246, on this point.
9 W(SS)A 1918, s 1, as amended by the Family Law Reform Act 1969, s 3(1); and see *Re Wernher, Wernher v Bret* [1918] 2 Ch 82.
10 Family Law Reform Act 1969, s 3(1); 50 *Halsbury's Statutes* (4th edn) 613.

[16.2]

Soldier in actual military service. The term 'actual military service' was said to be the equivalent of the Latin term 'in expeditione'.[1] Before the war of 1939–1945 it was generally defined as including the case of a member of the forces who has taken some step towards joining the forces in the field, and involved mobilisation,[2] and the mere fact that a soldier was in barracks was held insufficient.[3] Recently, the term has been given a wider meaning. Most members of the forces in England during the 1939–1945 war were considered to be in actual military service as being in a beleaguered fortress or war base from which active offensive or defensive operations are being conducted.[4] The rule was also applied to a member of the Royal Air Force in training in Canada who was killed in an accident while training, and in actual military service was then dissociated from the Latin term 'in expeditione' and described as active military service, that is, service directly concerned with operations in a war which is or has been in progress[5] or is imminent.[6] A proclamation by a Governor-General of a Dominion that persons in the position of the testator were 'on active service' has been held to validate such a will;[7] a similar case is that of a soldier under orders to proceed to Malaya at the time when a state of emergency in that country had been declared.[8] A soldier stationed in Northern Ireland as part of the armed forces deployed there at the request of the civil authorities to assist in the maintenance of law and order has been held to be in actual military service.[9] The fact that there was not a state of war or that the enemy was not a uniformed force engaged in regular welfare or an insurgent force organised on conventional lines has been held to be irrelevant in deciding whether the deceased was in actual military service.[10] The term 'soldier' includes officers and every rank and service,[11] but does not include a civilian engineer employed by the army but having no military status.[12]

1   *Drummond v Parish* (1843) 3 Curt 522; but it is now held that the Roman law test is inapplicable: *Re Wingham, Andrews v Wingham* [1949] P 187, [1948] 2 All ER 908.
2   *Re Hiscock's Goods* [1901] P 78; *Gattward v Knee* [1902] P 99; *Stopford v Stopford* (1903) 19 TLR 185; *Re Booth, Booth v Booth* [1926] P 118; but it is now held that a state of war is not essential and a member of the forces ordered to rejoin his unit to be in readiness for war is entitled to make such a will: *Re Rippon's Estate* [1943] P 61, [1943] 1 All ER 676.
3   *Drummond v Parish* (1843) 3 Curt 522; *White v Repton* (1844) 3 Curt 818; *Re Hill's Goods* (1845) 1 Rob Eccl 276; but this case has been said to be no longer of any authority: *Re Wingham, Andrews v Wingham* [1949] P 187, [1948] 2 All ER 908. Cases in which it was held that a soldier was ordered to go abroad or intending to go abroad (*Re Gossage's Estate, Wood v Gossage* [1921] P 194, and *Gattward v Knee* [1902] P 99) have been approved and extended: *Re Wingham, Andrews v Wingham* [1949] P 187, [1948] 2 All ER 908.
4   *Re Spark's Estate* [1941] P 115, [1941] 2 All ER 782 (soldier in camp in England killed in air raid); *Re Rowson's Estate* [1944] 2 All ER 36 (member of Women's Auxiliary Air Force in charge of depot); *Re Anderson's Estate* [1944] P 1, [1943] 2 All ER 609; *Re Gibson's Estate* [1941] P 118n, [1941] 2 All ER 91, where a contrary decision was reached were said not to be any longer good law in *Re Wingham, Andrews v Wingham* [1949] P 187, [1948] 2 All ER 908, but in both these cases the member of the forces was living in his home though engaged in military duties nearby.
5   *Re Colman's Estate* [1958] 2 All ER 35, [1958] 1 WLR 457 (soldier on leave in England from army of occupation in Germany).
6   *Re Wingham, Andrews v Wingham* [1949] P 187, [1948] 2 All ER 908.
7   *Re Graham's Estate* (1949) 67 WNNSW 23.
8   *Re Anderson's Will* (1953) 75 WNNSW 334.
9   *Re Jones* [1981] Fam 7, [1981] 1 All ER 1 (soldier shot on patrol and on return to hospital stated 'if I don't make it, make sure Anne gets all my stuff'; held valid nuncupative will).
10   Following *Re Anderson's Will* (1953) 75 WNNSW 334; see also *Re Booth* [1926] P 118.
11   *Re Hayes' Goods* (1839) 2 Curt 338; *Re Donaldson's Goods* (1840) 2 Curt 386 (surgeon); *Re Cory's Goods* (1901) 84 LT 270 (irregular); *May v May* [1902] P 103n (quarter-master); *Re Stanley's Estate* [1916] P 192 (military nurse); *Re Gibson's Estate* [1941] P 118n, [1941] 2 All ER 91 (regular officer in Army Dental Corps); *Re Rippon's Estate* [1943] P 61, [1943] 1 All ER 676 (officer in Territorial Army); *Re Anderson's Estate* [1944] P 1, [1943] 2 All ER 609 (home guard); *Re Rowson's Estate* [1944] 2 All ER 36 (member of Women's Auxiliary Air Force); *Re*

Wingham, Andrews v Wingham [1949] P 187, [1948] 2 All ER 908 (airman in training); and see *Blyth v Lord Advocate* [1945] AC 32, [1944] 2 All ER 375. The privilege is not limited to persons of little education; *May v May* [1902] P 103n.

12   *Re Lewis' Estate* [1974] 2 NSWLR 323 (but quaere whether persons serving as soldiers in the military forces of another country would be included).

[16.3]

Mariner or seaman. The privilege to make an informal will extends to 'any mariner or seaman being at sea'.[1] In these circumstances there is no requirement of actual military service and the privilege is of wide scope. In a recent case[2] it has been said that the privilege can be invoked if the following conditions are satisfied. First, it has to be shown that the testator was serving, or employed, in, or by, the Royal Navy[3] or the Merchant Navy,[4] on service of whatever nature, that could be regarded as sea-service.[5] It matters not whether the person be a man or a woman.[6] Secondly, the testator must be 'on maritime service' in the sense that the testator either, (a) is already (that is at the time of signing the document in question or making the nuncupative will) in post as a ship's officer[7] or (b) is already a member of a particular ship's company serving in that ship[8] or on shore leave,[9] or on long leave ashore[10] or (c) being employed by owners of a fleet of ships and having been discharged from one such, is already under orders to join another ship in that fleet.[11] But the privilege will not apply to the will of a seaman made whilst on shore on leave, at a time when he is not a member of the compliment of a particular ship and when he has not yet received orders to join a ship.[12]

1   WA 1837, s 11.
2   Per Judge Finlay QC in *Re Rapley's Estate, Rapley v Rapley* [1983] 3 All ER 248, [1983] 1 WLR 1069; but see Havers J in *Re Newland's Estate* [1952] P 71 at 75, [1952] 1 All ER 841 at 843 who doubted whether any principle of universal application could be extracted from the cases.
3   *Re M'Murdo's Goods* (1868) LR 1 P & D 540 (mate in HMS Excellent); *Re Lay's Goods* (1840) 2 Curt 375 (mate in HMS Calliope).
4   *Re Newland's Estate* [1952] P 71 at 75, [1952] 1 All ER 841 (apprentice); *Re Wilson's Estate, Wilson v Coleclough* [1952] P 92, [1952] 1 All ER 852 (chief officer); *Re Hayes's Goods* (1839) 2 Curt 338 (purser).
5   Per Judge Finlay QC in *Re Rapley's Estate, Rapley v Rapley* [1983] 3 All ER 248 at 251, [1983] 1 WLR 1069 at 1071; see for example, *Re Hale's Goods* [1915] 2 IR 362 (female typist on Lusitania); *Re Saunders's Goods* (1865) LR 1 P & D 16 (naval surgeon); *Re Stanley's Goods* [1916] P 192 (female nurse) but not the will of an admiral living ashore, *Euston v Seymour* (1802) cited in 2 Curt 339, 340, nor of a canal pilot, *Re Barnes' Goods, Hodson v Barnes* (1926) 96 LJP 26, nor of the captain of a cross-Channel ferry, *Barnard v Birch* [1919] 2 IR 404.
6   *Re Rapley's Estate, Rapley v Rapley* [1983] 3 All ER 248, [1983] 1 WLR 1069.
7   *Re M'Murdo's Goods* (1868) LR 1 P & D 540; *Re Lay's Goods* (1840) 2 Curt 375.
8   *Re Patterson's Goods* (1898) 79 LT 123.
9   *Re Lay's Goods* (1840) 2 Curt 375.
10 *Re Newland's Estate* [1952] P 71 at 75, [1952] 1 All ER 841.
11 *Re Hale's Goods* [1915] 2 IR 362; *Re Wilson's Estate, Wilson v Coleclough* [1952] P 92, [1952] 1 All ER 852.
12 *Re Rapley's Estate, Rapley v Rapley* [1983] 3 All ER 248, [1983] 1 WLR 1069; distinguishing, *Re Hale's Goods* [1915] 2 IR 362; *Re Newland's Estate* [1952] P 71 at 75, [1952] 1 All ER 841 and *Re Wilson's Estate, Wilson v Coleclough* [1952] P 92, [1952] 1 All ER 852 where the deceased was under orders to join another ship. The mere contemplation of another voyage will not suffice.

[16.4]

Informal and nuncupative wills. Any form of words, whether written or spoken by the testator, will suffice to constitute a soldier's or sailor's or airman's will, provided that it is a deliberate expression of his wishes as to the disposition of his property in the event of death,[1] but not where the words are a mere casual conversation not intended to be testamentary.[2] It is not necessary that the member of the forces should think he is making a will,[3] but a letter which states that the member has made a will to a certain effect cannot be admitted as the will.[4] When a will is made orally it is called nuncupative. The will, whether formal or informal, may be revoked by a letter or other informal act expressing such intention, without any new will, provided that the conditions at the time of the revocation are the same as are required to validate a soldier's or sailor's or airman's will.[5] Neither lapse of time nor return to civil life will revoke such a will,[6] but it has been held that subsequent marriage will revoke the will.[7] Such a will can revoke a former will although that will was executed in accordance with the WA 1837, s 9.[8]

1   *Drummond v Parish* (1843) 3 Curt 522; *Re Vernon's Estate* (1916) 33 TLR 11; *Selwood v Selwood* (1920) 125 LT 26; see *Re Jones* [1981] Fam 7, [1981] 1 All ER 1. But where the deceased, speaking about making a will and told that if he died without making one everything would go to his mother, said 'That is just what I want. I want my mother to have everything', it was held that these words did not show an intention of making a will: *Re Donner's Estate* (1917) 34 TLR 138; *Re Butcher* [1920] VLR 166. On the other hand where wishes as to what was to happen to property on death are expressed, those spoken words are a will despite the fact that those present may have thought that such wishes were written in the pay book which the soldier took out at the time and which could not be found after his death; *Re Spicer's Goods, Spicer v Richardson* [1949] P 441; [1949] 2 All ER 659.
2   *Re Knibbs' Estate, Flay v Trueman* [1962] 2 All ER 829, [1962] 1 WLR 852.
3   *Re Stable, Dalrymple v Campbell* [1919] P 7.
4   *Re MacGillivray's Estate* [1946] 2 All ER 301, CA.
5   *Re Gossage's Estate, Wood v Gossage* [1921] P 194, CA; *Re Beech's Estate* [1923] P 46 (letters, which were not expressions of what the testator wished to be done with his property but were merely statements, partly erroneous, of what he thought he had done, were not admitted to probate). See *Re Jones* [1981] Fam 7, [1981] 1 All ER 1, where a privileged nuncupative will revoked a written will.
6   *Re Leese's Goods* (1853) 21 LTOS 24; *Re Booth, Booth v Booth* [1926] P 118; *Re Coleman's Goods* [1920] 2 IR 332.
7   *Re Wardrop's Estate* [1917] P 54. This has been doubted as contrary to the reasoning in *Re Gossage's Estate, Wood v Gossage* [1921] P 194, CA. A will made in contemplation of marriage is not revoked by the contemplated marriage: Law of Property Act 1925, s 177; see Vol 2, Part G, para **[244.54]**; repealed and replaced by a slightly differently worded provision by the Administration of Justice Act 1982, s 18; 50 *Halsbury's Statutes* (4th edn) 586; see Vol 2, Part G, para **[244.94]**, which applies to wills made on or after 1 January 1983; see para **[17.5]** infra.
8   *Nixon v Prince* (1918) 34 TLR 444. Before 6 February 1918, it could not revoke such a will so far as it disposed of real property or exercised a power of appointment over real property.

[16.5]

Will written but lost. If the will is written but lost, the court requires cogent evidence of its contents, which must generally show not only the beneficiaries but the shares they are to take.[1] A certified copy from army base records has been accepted.[2]

1   *Re MacGillivray's Estate* [1946] 2 All ER 301. In this case the evidence suggested there were special provisions as to the shares in which the estate was to be taken and so was insufficient as

the shares were left uncertain. See also *Re Spicer's Goods, Spicer v Richardson* [1949] P 441, [1949] 2 All ER 659.
2   *Re Murphy* [1953] QWN 36.

[16.6]
Exercise of power of appointment. Such a will can exercise a power of appointment vested in the testator whether the power be a general power[1] or a special power[2] and whether or not it affects real property.[3] It is immaterial in such a case that the testator is a minor.[4]

1   *Re Wernher, Wernher v Beit* [1918] 2 Ch 82.
2   *Re Chichester's (Earl) Will Trusts, Pelham v Countess Chichester* [1946] Ch 289, [1946] 1 All ER 722.
3   *Re Chichester's (Earl) Will Trusts, Pelham v Countess Chichester* [1946] Ch 289, [1946] 1 All ER 722.
4   *Re Wernher, Wernher v Beit* [1918] 2 Ch 82.

[16.7]
Gifts to witnesses. Since no attestation by witnesses is required, a gift to a witness in a soldier's or sailor's or airman's will is effective.[1]

1   *Re Limond, Limond v Cunliffe* [1915] 2 Ch 240.

[16.8]
Proof by affidavit. In order to prove a soldier's or sailor's privileged will, an affidavit should be sworn showing that at the time of its making the testator was 'in actual military service'.[1] If it is a written will and signed with the testator's mark, an affidavit must show that he had knowledge of its contents.[2] If the document be unattested, an affidavit of two disinterested persons to prove that the signature is that of the testator is required,[3] and alterations and interlineations by the testator necessitate similar proof.[4] If the will is attested, evidence of alterations must follow the requirements of the Wills Act 1837.

1   Chapter 14.
2   *Re Hackett's Goods* (1859) 4 Sw & Tr 220; *Re Thorne's Goods* (1865) 4 Sw & Tr 36. See *Tristram and Coote's Probate Practice* (28th edn).
3   *Re Hackett's Goods* (1859) 4 Sw & Tr 220; *Re Neville's Goods* (1859) 4 Sw & Tr 218.
4   *Re Tweedale's Goods* (1874) LR 3 P & D 204.

[16.9]
Words excluded. Where a soldier's will, as, for example, a letter, contains matter in reference to military operations, to the inclusion of which in the probate the military authorities object, the court may grant probate only of the part of the letter which is of a testamentary character without including in the probate the rest of the letter.[1]

1   *Re Heywood's Estate* [1916] P 47.

[16.10]
Revocation. Since such a will requires no formalities for its execution, it requires none for its revocation in whole[1] or in part.[2] A privileged will made by a minor may be revoked by the testator even though he is still a minor and even

though he has returned to civilian life, and so ceased to be in circumstances entitling him to privilege.[3] A privileged will, will be revoked by a subsequent marriage.[4]

1   *Re Gossage's Estate* [1921] P 194, where a soldier on actual military service wrote to his son asking him to burn an earlier formal will; held sufficient revocation, see para **[16.4]**, n 5.
2   *Re Newland's Goods* [1952] P 71, [1952] 1 All ER 841 (where one bequest was struck out).
3   Family Law Reform Act 1969, s 3(3); 50 *Halsbury's Statutes* (4th edn) 613; this provision is necessary to enable a minor who has made a privileged will to revoke it, otherwise the will would be irrevocable until he reached the age of eighteen years. It is probable however that if the minor is no longer in privileged circumstances, that the usual formalities should be observed.
4   *Re Wardrop* [1917] P 54: see para **[17.2]**, n 2.

[16.11]
Naval seamen or marines. A seaman or marine can now make a privileged will disposing of all his assets whether civilian or naval.[1]

1   Navy and Marines (Wills) Act 1953; 50 *Halsbury's Statutes* (4th edn) 607, which applies to deaths after 14 August 1953, there were formerly limitations.

Revocation, republication and revival of wills

CHAPTER 17

Revocation by marriage

I. STATUTORY PROVISIONS

[17.1]
The Wills Act 1837 (WA 1837), s 18[1] embodies the general rule that a will is revoked by the subsequent marriage of the testator or testatrix, subject to the exception relating to powers of appointment and to the provisions of the Law of Property Act 1925, s 177[2] relating to wills in contemplation of marriage. The WA 1837, s 18 as originally enacted will continue to apply to wills made before 1 January 1983.[3] In the case of a will made on or after that date the position will be governed by the new s 18 of the WA 1837 as substituted by the Administration of Justice Act 1982 (AJA 1982), s 18(1).[4] These new provisions reiterate the basic rule but reformulate the exception in favour of powers of appointment and contain new provisions governing wills made in expectation of marriage, repealing the Law of Property Act 1925, s 177.[5] These new provisions embody new tests to be applied to the wording of wills and thus it is appropriate to confine their operation to post-Act wills.[6] Accordingly it is necessary to differentiate between wills made before and wills made after, 1 January 1983.

The AJA 1982 also contains a new provision which appears as the WA 1837, s 18A dealing with the effect of dissolution or annulment of marriage on wills.[7] This provision will apply to the will of a testator who dies on or after 1 January 1983[8] and will be considered in Chapter 47.

1 50 *Halsbury's Statutes* (4th edn) 586. See Vol 2, Part G, paras **[244.15]** and **[244.16]**.
2 See Vol 2, Part G, para **[244.54]**.
3 The date when the AJA 1982 came into force, s 76(11).
4 See Vol 2, Part G, para **[244.94]**.
5 But only as respects wills made on or after 1 January 1983, AJA 1982, s 73(7).
6 In contrast to the other relevant provisions under the AJA 1982, which apply to wills whenever made of testators who die on or after 1 January 1983, AJA 1982, s 73(6); s 76(11).
7 AJA 1982, s 18(2); see Vol 2, Part G, para **[244.94]**.
8 See the AJA 1982, s 73(6); s 76(11).

II. WILLS MADE BEFORE 1 JANUARY 1983

[17.2]
The general rule. The WA 1837, s 18 as originally enacted[1] provided that 'Every will made by a man or woman shall be revoked by his or her marriage ...'.[2] This is a rule of law independent of any question of intention of the testator

and evidence of intention is inadmissible to avoid such revocation.[3] The marriage must be a lawful marriage[4] and the onus of proving the marriage is on the person who seeks to set aside the will.[5] A will is not revoked by a void marriage, within the meaning of the Matrimonial Causes Act 1973 (MCA 1973), s 11.[6] But a marriage which is voidable on the grounds set out in the MCA 1973, s 12[7] will revoke a prior will, irrespective of whether a decree of nullity has been obtained or not.[8] The reason is simply that a voidable marriage is a valid marriage until declared void, and by virtue of the MCA 1973, s 16 a decree of nullity does not have retrospective effect.[9]

1   See Vol 2, Part G, para **[244.15]**.
2   The section applies to the will of a soldier, sailor or airman although such a will is privileged in other respects: *Re Wardrop's Estate* [1917] P 54. As to such wills see Chapter 16.
3   *Marston v Roe d Fox* (1838) 8 Ad & El 14; *Israell v Rodon* (1839) 2 Moo PCC 51.
4   *Mette v Mette* (1859) 1 Sw & Tr 416; *Warter v Warter* (1890) 15 PD 152; *Pilot v Gainfort* [1931] P 103 (second marriage relying upon legal presumption of death from disappearance of first wife).
5   *Re Fitz Ray Estate* (1966) 57 WWR 77. There is a presumption of marriage which arises in certain circumstances: *Re Taylor, Taylor v Taylor* [1961] 1 All ER 55, [1961] 1 WLR 9. In *Rumsey v Sterne* (1967) 111 Sol Jo 113 a prior will was revoked by a marriage presumed valid by virtue of a ceremony followed by cohabitation.
6   See Lord Greene MR in *de Reneville v de Reneville* [1948] P 100 at 111, [1948] 1 All ER 56 at 60; *Re Fleming's Estate* [1987] 1 LRM 638; and *Re Roberts, Roberts v Roberts* [1978] 3 All ER 225, [1978] 1 WLR 653.
7   The grounds, shortly, are: non-consummation; wilful refusal to consummate; lack of consent due to duress, mistake, unsoundness of mind or otherwise; mental disorder rendering the person unfitted for marriage; venereal disease; existing pregnancy.
8   *Re Roberts, Roberts v Roberts* [1978] 3 All ER 225, [1978] 1 WLR 653, where it was alleged that a marriage was voidable on the grounds that the man was suffering from senile dementia and other mental illness at the time of the marriage to the extent that he was unable to understand the nature of the ceremony or its effects or to consent to the marriage; held, even if so proved, the marriage being merely voidable was effective to revoke a previous will. See the similar case of *Re Davey* [1980] 3 All ER 342, [1981] 1 WLR 164 where *Re Roberts, Roberts v Roberts* was applied. The MCA 1973 consolidates the provisions of the Nullity Act 1971 in this respect, which effected a change in the law. Before 1971 the law was that a voidable marriage revoked a prior will of either party, except where a decree of annulment was obtained when the marriage was treated as never having existed and thus had no effect on prior wills.
9   *Re Roberts, Roberts v Roberts* [1978] 3 All ER 225, [1978] 1 WLR 653 per Buckley LJ at 231; per Goff LJ at 233. The consequences of this rule can be unsatisfactory because if no decree is obtained inter vivos (and the disabled party is unlikely to apply for it, and the other party has every interest not to apply for it) then the marriage will revoke all previous wills, resulting in an intestacy to the advantage of the new spouse. The solution adopted in *Re Davey* [1980] 3 All ER 342, [1981] 1 WLR 164 was to apply to the court for a statutory will to be made for the disabled party under the jurisdiction in the Mental Health Act 1959 (see now the Mental Health Act 1983), see para **[4.21]** supra, which effectively excluded the new spouse. However, such a course will not be possible in all cases and the only recourse then will be to the jurisdiction under the Inheritance (Provision for Family and Dependants) Act 1975 which is unlikely to achieve a satisfactory result, see Chapter 105.

[17.3]
Will in contemplation of marriage. The Law of Property Act 1925, s 177[1] stated that a will expressed to be made in contemplation of a marriage shall not be revoked by the solemnisation of the marriage contemplated.[2] It was essential that the will expressed a contemplation of a particular marriage and not marriage in general.[3] The crucial consideration was that it was the will and not merely some gift in it, that had to be expressed to be made in contemplation of a

marriage.[4] However, it would probably suffice if all, or substantially all, the beneficial dispositions in the will were so expressed.[5] It can be taken as established that a testamentary gift to a named person described in the will as being the testator's fiance normally would express a sufficient contemplation of marriage to that person for the purposes of the section.[6] A gift to a person described in the will as being the testator's wife may well not satisfy the section.[7] The operation of the section was a matter of construction on which extrinsic evidence of intention or purpose was inadmissible.[8]

1   27 *Halsbury's Statutes* (4th edn) 345. This provision is repealed in respect of wills made on or after 1 January 1983 by the AJA 1982, ss 75(1), 73(7), 76(11). In view of this fact only a short discussion of the provision will be included here.

2   Much of the law relating to the section was reviewed by Megarry J in *Re Coleman, Coleman v Coleman* [1976] Ch 1, [1975] 1 All ER 675 to which reference should be made.

3   *Sallis v Jones* [1936] P 43; *Re Hamilton* [1941] VLR 60; see Megarry J in *Re Coleman, Coleman v Coleman* [1975] 1 All ER 675 at 677, 678.

4   Per Megarry J in *Re Coleman, Coleman v Coleman* [1976] Ch 1, [1975] 1 All ER 675 at 680. See *Layer v Burns Philip Trustee Co Ltd* (1986) 6 NSWLR 60 where Megarry J's approach in *Re Coleman, Coleman v Coleman* was considered but not followed. The statute is not framed in terms of a will 'in which a contemplation of a marriage is expressed', or a will 'containing a disposition expressed to be made in contemplation of a marriage'. The desired result was best achieved by an express clause such as 'This will is made in contemplation of my marriage to X'.

5   See Megarry J in *Re Coleman, Coleman v Coleman* [1976] Ch 1, [1975] 1 All ER 675.

6   Per Megarry J in *Re Coleman, Coleman v Coleman* [1975] Ch 1 at 11, [1975] 1 All ER 675 at 683; *Re Knight* (1944) (unreported, but mentioned in *Re Langston's Estate* [1953] P 100 at 103) (testator's will gave all his property to X 'my future wife'; held, sufficient); *Re Chase* [1951] VLR 477 (gift of two-thirds of the testator's net estate to X 'my fiance at present travelling to Australia on board the SS Stratheden due in Fremantle on June 8, 1948', will made 6 June 1948; held, within statutory provision analogous to s 177). *Re Langston's Estate* [1953] P 100 (entire estate 'unto my fiance X' who was appointed sole executor; held, within the section); cf *Burton v McGregor* [1953] NZLR 487 (testator gave his whole estate 'unto my fiance X'; held, not expressed to be made in contemplation of a marriage), and *Re Whale* [1977] 2 NZLR 1.

    In *Re Natusch, Pettit v Natusch* [1963] NZLR 273, a will which made a gift to an 'intended wife' and contained a declaration that it was made in anticipation of the intended marriage was held good, though the marriage was never solemnised because a divorce from the donee's husband was not obtained.

7   Per Megarry J in *Re Coleman, Coleman v Coleman* [1975] Ch 1 at 11, [1975] 1 All ER 675 at 683. In *Pilot v Gainfort* [1931] P 103, a gift to X 'my wife' was held to satisfy the section. The testator's wife had disappeared three years before he began to live with X, six years before he made his will, and seven years before he married X. This decision has not been well received and was not followed in *Re Taylor* [1949] VLR 201, or in *Burton v McGregor* [1953] NZLR 487. The decision in *Re Gray's Estate* (1963) 107 Sol Jo 156, is usually preferred. There the will gave everything to 'my wife' X, whom the testator had previously 'married' bigamously. Subsequently the true wife died and the testator married X; held, not within the section since the expression 'my wife' in the will could not be said to indicate an intention to legally marry X, in view of the testator's existing marriage.

8   Per Megarry J in *Re Coleman, Coleman v Coleman* [1975] Ch 1 at 11, [1975] 1 All ER 675 at 83 (refusing to admit evidence to the effect that in giving instructions for his will the testator was concerned to make provision for his fiance until the marriage took place, but he had said that he intended to make a new will as soon as he was married).

[17.4]

Will in exercise of power of appointment. A will made before 1 January 1983, exercising a power of appointment is not revoked by the testator's subsequent marriage unless the persons to take in default of appointment take in the capacity of the testator's heir executor or administrator or next of kin under the Statute of

Distribution.[1] Next of kin under the Statute of Distribution includes a widow, and, if those to take in default of appointment exclude the widow, the will is not revoked.[2] The exception in the second part of the above provision does not apply where the gift in default of appointment in fact goes to the statutory next of kin but is given in the deed creating the power in another capacity, as for example to the children of the appointer,[3] or issue[4] or simply as the next of kin and not as the statutory next of kin of the appointer.[5] Where the gift in default of appointment was to the testator, his heirs and assigns, the appointment in the will was revoked.[6]

1   WA 1837, s 18; 50 *Halsbury's Statutes* (4th edn) 586; see Vol 2, Part G, para **[244.15]**. So long as the persons to take in default of appointment do not fill the description, the will is not revoked so far as it appoints under the power; *Re Paul, Public Trustee v Pearce* [1921] 2 Ch 1; *Re Stone* [1959] QWN 2. The expression 'next of kin under the Statute of Distribution' may not fit the persons now entitled on intestacy under the Administration of Estates Act 1925, ss 46, 47, and it may be that that part of the WA 1837, s 18 has no reference to those sections. The matter has never been decided, but reference should be made to *Re Brigden, Chaytor v Edwin* [1938] Ch 205, [1937] 4 All ER 342, where a rule of convenience was so adapted. It should be noticed that the Administration of Estates Act 1925, s 50 applies only to instruments inter vivos and wills and not to statutes. See *Re Russell's Goods* (1890) 15 PD 111; *Re Poole's Estate, Poole v Poole* [1919] P 10.
2   *Re Gilligan* [1950] P 32, [1949] 2 All ER 401 (where the persons to take in default were those who would take on death intestate and unmarried, which obviously excluded a widow).
3   *Re Fitzroy's Goods* (1858) 1 Sw & Tr 133; *Re Fenwick's Goods* (1867) LR 1 P & D 319. What is here referred to as an exception is often called a sub-exception, because it is an exception from an exception to the rule that marriage revokes a will.
4   *Re Worthington's Goods* (1871) 25 LT 853.
5   *Re McVicar's Goods* (1869) LR 1 P & D 671.
6   *Vaughan v Vanderstegen, Annesley Case* (1854) 2 Drew 165 at 194.

III.   WILLS MADE ON OR AFTER 1 JANUARY 1983

[17.5]
The new section 18: the general rule. There is no change to the general rule that 'a will shall be revoked by the testator's marriage'.[1]

1   The WA 1837, s 18(1), as substituted by the AJA 1982, s 18(1), Vol 2, Part G, para **[244.16]**, applicable to wills made on or after 1 January 1983, AJA 1982, s 73(7); s 76(11). For precedents see Vol 2, paras **[201.5]** to **[201.9]**. In particular the rule relating to voidable marriages embodied in the *Re Roberts, Roberts v Roberts* [1978] 3 All ER 225, [1978] 1 WLR 653, decision is unaffected by the new legislation.

[17.6]
Wills in expectation of marriage. In the case of wills made on or after 1 January 1983[1] the AJA 1982 repeals the Law of Property Act 1925, s 177[2] and substitutes a new provision governing wills made before marriage. The legislation covers two situations. First, the AJA 1982, s 18(3)[3] provides:

'where it appears from a will that at the time it was made the testator was expecting to be married to a particular person and that he intended that the will should not be revoked by the marriage, the will shall not be revoked by his marriage to that person.'

This provision refers to an intention with respect to the will and provides that the whole will is not to be revoked. The second situation relates to the more difficult case (and the more commonly met situation with home-made wills) where the intention relates only to a disposition or to a part of the will. Such a case is provided for by the AJA 1982, s 18(4) as follows:

'where it appears from a will that at the time it was made the testator was expecting to be married to a particular person and that he intended that a disposition in the will should not be revoked by his marriage to that person—
(a)   that disposition shall take effect notwithstanding the marriage; and
(b)   any other disposition in the will shall take effect also unless it appears from the will that the testator intended the disposition to be revoked by the marriage.'[4]

It will be noticed that both subsections embody the dual tests of the expectation of marriage to a particular person, and the intention that the will, or the disposition, should not be revoked by the marriage to that person.[5] Three points can be made; first, both the expectation and the intention are subjective to the testator; it is what he thought which is crucial not an objective view of the circumstances. Second, it is submitted that this subjective expectation and intention must appear from the will, ie the evidence in support of each must be intrinsic not extrinsic. Third, that both the expectation and the intention must be present at the time the will is made.[6]

The effect of the latter provision is that an expectation and intention in any clause of the will not only save that disposition but will also tend to preserve the whole will.[7] The effect of subsection (4)(b) set out above is to reverse the burden of proof; previously it was necessary to find positive evidence supporting the non-revocation of the will; now the will will only be revoked if there is positive evidence in favour of revocation. Since in most cases there will be no indication either way in the clauses of the will other than the gift to eg the fiance, the effect will be to preserve the whole will. Thus an express indication of expectation of marriage in one part of the will will tend to colour the whole; a change surely to be welcomed as not only tending to preserve rather than revoke wills, but also as being most likely to be consistent with most testators' intentions.

1   AJA 1982, s 73(7); s 76(11).
2   AJA 1982, s 75(1) and Sch 9, Pt 1.
3   Strictly WA 1837, s 18(3), as substituted by the AJA 1982, s 18(1); see Vol 2, Part G, para **[244.94]**.
4   The provisions are based on the recommendations of the Law Reform Committee, 22nd Report on The Making and Revocation of Wills, 1980 (Cmnd 7902). See paras 3.13–3.18.
5   The proof of these matters will therefore be found in the inclusion of express statements of expectation and intention and in professionally drawn wills such as an introductory clause should be included in appropriate cases; see Volume 2.
6   Strictly WA 1837, s 18(3) and (4), as substituted by the AJA 1982, s 18(3) and (4).
7   Thus if the facts of *Re Coleman, Coleman v Coleman* [1976] Ch 1, [1975] 1 All ER 675, were to recur in a post-1982 will, the whole will would be likely to be held to survive the marriage. This is because the word 'fiance' would probably suffice to indicate the required expectation and intention; see the cases in para **[17.3]**, n 7.

[17.7]

Wills conditional on marriage. It is possible that the will could be framed on condition of marriage, in which case it will not take effect unless the condition is satisfied.[1]

1   See Chapter 1, on Conditional Wills.

[17.8]

Will in exercise of a power of appointment. The new section 18[1] preserves the exception in favour of the exercise of powers of appointment but restates the provision in more modern wording as follows:[2]

'... A disposition in a will in exercise of a power of appointment shall take effect notwithstanding the testator's subsequent marriage unless the property so appointed would in default of appointment pass to his personal representatives.'

This does more than bring the previous rule up to date; it causes a wider class of testamentary appointments to be saved from revocation by marriage than the provision it replaces.

1   WA 1837, s 18(2), as substituted by the AJA 1982, s 18(1); see Vol 2, Part G, para **[244.94]**.
2   Applicable to wills made on or after 1 January 1983; AJA 1982, ss 73, 76(11).

IV.   THE EFFECT OF DISSOLUTION OR ANNULMENT OF MARRIAGE ON WILLS

[17.9]

This aspect of the law is considered in Chapter 47 on lapse.

CHAPTER 18

Voluntary revocation

I. GENERAL PRINCIPLES GOVERNING REVOCATION

[18.1]
The subject of revocation of a will divides itself quite neatly into involuntary and voluntary revocation. Involuntary revocation, or revocation by operation of law, is confined to revocation by subsequent marriage. Voluntary revocation on the other hand is not at all easy to divide into watertight compartments. The first point is that throughout voluntary revocation the question of revocation or no revocation or part revocation is governed by the question of the intention of the testator. This is largely a question of fact and that no doubt explains why it is difficult to classify the cases with complete satisfaction. There is, of course, a distinction between express and implied revocation, but a great number of cases show that even an express clause of revocation has very often been treated as inoperative. Again the question of revocation overlaps to some extent the question of alteration of a will and to a still greater extent the question of obliteration and erasure. In the following pages, therefore, the subject is divided into sections dealing with the methods by which voluntary revocation may be effected as being the division which is the most practical from the point of view of the inquirer who desires to ascertain whether or not what has happened in his particular case amounts to revocation.

The subject of conditional revocation is dealt with separately. This, of course, is more usually known as dependent relative revocation and is a subject of known difficulty.

II. MODES OF VOLUNTARY REVOCATION

[18.2]
Three methods. Voluntary revocation can now be effected only in one or other of the following ways: (i) by a later will or codicil duly executed; or (ii) by some writing declaring an intention to revoke the will and duly executed as a will; or (iii) by burning, tearing or otherwise destroying the will by the testator or someone in his presence and by his direction, with the intention of revoking the same.

[18.3]

No delegation of power to revoke. The testator cannot delegate his power of revocation so as to authorise the revocation of his will after his death.[1]

1   *Stockwell v Ritherdon* (1848) 1 Rob Eccl 661.

III.   INTENTION TO REVOKE

[18.4]

Will generally revocable. Though the testator make his will irrevocable in the strongest terms, the law regards it as of its nature revocable but irrevocability can be secured to the extent already discussed either by contract or covenant[1] or agreement associated with the execution of joint or mutual wills.[2]

1   See Chapter 3.
2   See Chapter 2.

[18.5]

Intention to revoke. The intention of the testator is the sole guide as to whether words amount to a revocation of a will[1] and revocation is not proved by mere accidental words or by inference or by the form of the testamentary document or by implication where the circumstances do not accord with such an intention.[2] If, however, anything is done by the testator or by his direction which, if there was an intention to revoke, would amount to a revocation, then, if there is no further evidence, an intention to revoke is assumed, but, if there is further evidence, it may rebut that presumption and the inference of revocation is not to be made.[3] An act which is not shown to have the intention to revoke, is wholly ineffectual for that purpose, even though it results in the total destruction of the will.[4] There is no revocation where, for example, the testator destroys the will through inadvertence,[5] or under the belief that it is useless,[6] or invalid,[7] or has already been revoked,[8] or on any assumption of fact which proves false where the revocation is based on the assumption being correct[9], or where he is drunk at the time of the alleged revocation[10], or insane at the time though he afterwards recover.[11] The fact that the testator destroyed the will in error may be inferred from a statement by him shortly before his death that he thought it was still in existence.[12]

1   Wills Act 1837 (WA 1837), s 20; 50 *Halsbury's Statutes* (4th edn) 589; see Vol 2, Part G, para **[244.20]**; *Smith v Cunningham* (1823) 1 Add 448; *Powell v Powell* (1866) LR 1 P & D 209; *Re Barker, Nemes v Barker* [1995] 2 VR 439.
2   WA 1837, s 70; *Symson v Kirton* (1606) Cro Jac 115.
3   *Onions v Tyrer* (1716) 1 P Wms 343; *Burtenshaw v Gilbert* (1774) 1 Cowp 49; *Kennedy v Peikoff* (1966) 56 WWR 381, and see Proof of Intention.
4   *Clarkson v Clarkson* (1862) 2 Sw & Tr 497; *Re Thornton's Goods* (1889) 14 PD 82; *James v Shrimpton* (1876) 1 PD 431; *Cheese v Lovejoy* (1877) 2 PD 251.
5   *Burtenshaw v Gilbert* (1774) 1 Cowp 49; *Re Booth, Booth v Booth* [1926] P 118; and as to revocation by destruction, see Chapter 18.
6   *Beardsley v Lacey* (1897) 67 LJP 35.
7   *Giles v Warren* (1872) LR 2 P & D 401; *Re Thornton's Goods* (1889) 14 PD 82.
8   *Scott v Scott* (1859) 1 Sw & Tr 258; *Clarkson v Clarkson* (1862) 2 Sw & Tr 497.

9   *Campbell v French* (1797) 3 Ves 321; *Newton v Newton* (1861) 12 I Ch R 118; *Re Faris, Goddard v Overend (No 2)* [1911] 1 IR 469; *Re Southerden's Estate, Adams v Southerden* [1925] P 177.
10 *Brunt v Brunt* (1873) LR 3 P & D 37; *Re Brassington's Goods* [1902] P 1.
11 *Scruby and Finch v Fordham* (1822) 1 Add 74; *Borlase v Borlase* (1845) 4 Notes of Cases 106 at 139; *Re Shaw's Goods* (1838) 1 Curt 905; *Re Downer's Goods* (1853) 18 Jur 66; *Brunt v Brunt* (1873) LR 3 P & D 37; *Re Hine's Goods* [1893] P 282; *Sprigge v Sprigge* (1868) LR 1 P & D 608; *Re Beattie Estate* [1944] WWR 727; *Eaton (Norris Estate) v Heyman* [1946] 3 WWR 98; *Re McGinn Estate* (1969) 70 WWR 159.
12 *Re Templemore's Estate* (1925) 69 Sol Jo 382.

[18.6]
Proof of intention. The intention must be clearly proved.[1] It must be a present not a future intention to revoke,[2] but a present intention of revocation accompanied by a statement of intention to make a new will which is not in fact made is an effective revocation.[3] Declarations by the testator, especially if contemporaneous with the act of revocation, are admissible.[4] The intention may also be inferred from the nature of the act done.[5]

1   *Kellett v Kellett* (1868) LR 3 HL 160; *Re Wilcock, Kay v Dewhirst* [1898] 1 Ch 95; *Doe d Hearle v Hicks* (1832) 8 Bing 475; *Re Ince's Goods* (1877) 2 PD 111; *Re Freeman, Hope v Freeman* [1910] 1 Ch 681; *Randfield v Randfield* (1860) 8 HL Cas 225; *Van Grutten v Foxwell* [1897] AC 658 at 694.
2   *Cleoburey v Beckett* (1851) 14 Beav 583; *Burton v Gowell* (1593) Cro Eliz 306; *Thomas d Jones v Evans* (1802) 2 East 488.
3   *Toomer v Sobinska* [1907] P 106.
4   *Clark v Scripps* (1852) 2 Rob Eccl 563. It has been said that such declarations are admissible only to prove his state of mind towards the document: *Re Moore* [1941] 2 DLR 112.
5   *Clarke v Scripps* (1852) 2 Rob Eccl 563; *North v North* (1909) 25 TLR 322.

[18.7]
Burden of proof. The party setting up the revocation must prove it and, in the absence of proof, revocation is not presumed.[1] Where the testator has become insane since the execution of the will, and the will is found mutilated or not found at all, the burden lies on the party setting up revocation to prove that it was intentionally mutilated or destroyed while the testator was of sound mind.[2] In all these cases the execution of a valid will must first be shown.[3]

1   *Harris v Berrall* (1858) 1 Sw & Tr 153; *Sprigge v Sprigge* (1868) LR 1 P & D 608; *Benson v Benson* (1870) LR 2 P & D 172.
2   *Re Hine's Goods* [1893] P 282; *Allan v Morrison* [1900] AC 604.
3   *Allan v Morrison* [1900] AC 604. Where the will is executed in duplicate, see *Jones v Harding* (1887) 58 LT 60 (testator's duplicate not forthcoming, presumed revocation); *Topham and Tombs v Norris* (1857) 29 LTOS 346 (similar case but no presumed revocation because testator subsequently became insane).

IV.   LATER WILL OR CODICIL

[18.8]
Revocation clause in will or codicil. An earlier will is revoked by an express clause of revocation in a subsequent will or codicil[1] and no particular form of words is necessary for this purpose.[2] An express clause of revocation is not essential[3] but, if inserted in general terms, may operate to revoke all

testamentary instruments previously executed[4] including testamentary appointments.[5] Such a clause is not, however, conclusive, for it may be shown that it was inserted by mistake and without the approval of the testator[6] or the two wills may be dealing with property in different jurisdictions.[7] But if the language of the revoking clause is unambiguous the revoked clause cannot be resorted to.[8]

1   WA 1837, s 20 (see Vol 2, Part G, para **[244.20]**).
2   *Birks v Birks* (1865) 4 Sw & Tr 23; *Cottrell v Cottrell* (1872) LR 2 P & D 397. Insertion in the attestation clause of words revoking a previous testamentary document is of no effect because that clause is not part of the will: *Re Atkinson's Goods* (1883) 8 PD 165. If the later will is not forthcoming, but there is evidence that it was drawn by a solicitor, it will be presumed that it contained a revocation clause and probate of an earlier will will not be granted: *Re Hampshire's Estate* [1951] WN 174, not followed in *Re Dear* [1975] 2 NZLR 254, where the principle in *Cutto v Gilbert* (1854) 9 Moo PCC 131 was preferred. See also *Re Archibald* [1992] 2 NZLR 109.
3   *Dempsey v Lawson* (1877) 2 PD 98 (revocation in accordance with general tenor of later will). See also *Jenner v Ffinch* (1879) 5 PD 106; *Re Bryan's Estate* [1907] P 125.
4   *Sotheran v Dening* (1881) 20 Ch D 99; *Cottrell v Cottrell* (1872) LR 2 P & D 397; but the general rule is that an express revocation clause shall operate only so far as is necessary to effectuate the intention of the testator: *Re Lewis' Goods* (1850) 7 Notes of Cases 436; *Doe d Evers v Ward* (1852) 18 QB 197.
5   *Sotheran v Dening* (1881) 20 Ch D 99; *Re Kingdon, Wilkins v Pryer* (1886) 32 Ch D 604; *Lowthorpe-Lutwidge v Lowthorpe-Lutwidge* [1935] P 151; *Smith v Thompson* (1931) 47 TLR 603.
6   *Dempsey v Lawson* (1877) 2 PD 98; *Robinson v Clarke* (1877) 2 PD 269; *O'Leary v Douglass* (1878) 1 LR Ir 45; *Re Oswald's Goods* (1874) LR 3 P & D 162; *Barclay v Maskelyne* (1858) John 124 (erroneous belief as to persons benefiting under will). A mere misunderstanding of the testator was held not sufficient to warrant the omission of the clause from the probate: *Collins v Elstone* [1893] P 1 but this case has been adversely criticised in *Lowthorpe-Lutwidge v Lowthorpe-Lutwidge* [1935] P 151, and in *Re Wayland's Estate* [1951] 2 All ER 1041; *Re Moore's Goods* [1892] P 378 (revocation clause in will form omitted); *Marklew v Turner* (1900) 17 TLR 10 (revocation clause in codicil omitted); *Re Phelan* [1972] Fam 33, [1971] 3 All ER 1256 (four wills, all on printed will forms, admitted to probate, with the omission of the revocation clauses from three); *Re Crannis' Estate, Mansell v Crannis* (1978) 122 Sol Jo 489. As to the power of the court to omit words inserted in a will see para **[5.7]**. As to the power to rectify wills, see Chapter 6. A revocation founded on a false assumption of fact takes effect unless the truth of that fact was a condition of the revocation: *Re Faris, Goddard v Overend (No 2)* [1911] 1 IR 469.
7   *Begin v Bilodeau* [1951] SCR 699 (one will dealing with property in Quebec, the other with property in United States of America).
8   *Choa Eng Wan v Choa Giang Tee* [1923] AC 469.

[18.9]
'Last will.' The insertion of such words as 'last and only will' does not necessarily work a revocation of all previous testamentary instruments.[1] It is only where it is clear from the general tenor of the last will that the testator did not intend the earlier will to remain in operation that it is revoked.[2]

1   *Simpson v Foxon* [1907] P 54; *Pepper v Pepper* (1870) IR 5 Eq 85; *Kitcat v King* [1930] P 266. The express confirmation of a will and one only of two previous codicils does not revoke the other codicil: *Follett v Pettman* (1883) 23 Ch D 337. See Chapter 20.
2   *Richards v Queen's Proctor* (1854) 1 Ecc & Ad 235; *Re Howard's Goods* (1869) LR 1 P & D 636; *Lemage v Goodban* (1865) LR 1 P & D 57 (two wills both stated to be the last will); *Re Petchell's Goods* (1874) LR 3 P & D 153 (question of construction whether former will revoked); *Re De La Saussaye's Goods* (1873) LR 3 P & D 42 ('last and deliberate will'); *Pepper v Pepper* (1870) IR 5 Eq 85 ('last will'); *Cutto v Gilbert* (1854) 9 Moo PCC 131 (it

must be proved that the contents of the later will differ from the former: later will not forthcoming at death and contents unknown except that it was described as 'last will and testament'), overruling *Plenty v West and Budd* (1845) 1 Rob Eccl 264; *Re Dear* [1975] 2 NZLR 254; *Re Wyatt* [1952] 1 All ER 1030, applying the decision in *Cutto v Gilbert* (1854) 9 Moo PCC 131; *Freeman v Freeman* (1854) 5 De GM & G 704 ('last will and testament'); *Moorhouse v Lord* (1863) 8 LT 212 (will disposing of all testator's property); *Dempsey v Lawson* (1877) 2 PD 98 (general tenor of later will showed intention to revoke); *Leslie v Leslie* (1872) IR 6 Eq 332 (words not entitled to any weight); *Re O'Connor's Goods* (1884) 13 LR Ir 406; *Re Christie's Will* (1883) 9 VLR 46; *Jones v Treasury Solicitor* (1932) 147 LT 340 (former will stated to be cancelled); *Re Hawksley's Settlements, Black v Tidy* [1934] Ch 384 (similar case); *Re Henderson* [1996] 1 Qd R 249.

[18.10]
Subsequent inconsistent will. A later unambiguous will dealing with all the testator's property revokes all earlier wills whether or not it contains a clause of revocation.[1] A later will covering practically the same ground as an earlier one must be taken as in substitution for it, and probate of the later one only is granted.[2] This may be so where the whole ground is not completely covered, if the language shows an intention on the part of the testator to dispose of his property in a manner different from that in the earlier will.[3] The mere fact of making a subsequent disposition does not, however, work a total revocation of an earlier disposition, unless the later one expressly or in effect revokes the former, or the two are incapable of standing together.[4] A later inconsistent disposition not valid in itself does not revoke an earlier disposition;[5] but a codicil altering and confirming a first will may thereby revive that will and revoke a will made after the first will but before the last codicil.[6] The fact that a document has been admitted to probate even after consideration of the construction of that and other testamentary instruments does not prevent a court of construction from coming to the conclusion that the document has no operative effect.[7]

1   *Re Palmer's Goods, Palmer v Peat* (1889) 58 LJP 44; *Cadell v Wilcocks* [1898] P 21; *Re Bryan's Estate* [1907] P 125 (residue left undisposed of); *Re Fitzsimmons* [1939] 2 DLR 50.
2   *Henfrey v Henfrey* (1842) 4 Moo PCC 29; *Dempsey v Lawson* (1877) 2 PD 98; *Re Turnour's Goods* (1886) 56 LT 671; *Re Palmer's Goods, Palmer v Peat* (1889) 58 LJP 44; *O'Leary v Douglass* (1878) 3 LR Ir 323; *M'Ara v M'Cay* (1889) 23 LR Ir 138; *Cadell v Wilcocks*, supra; *Chichester v Quatrefages* [1895] P 186 (two codicils, one a virtual repetition of the other).
3   *Dempsey v Lawson* (1877) 2 PD 98; *Re Bryan's Estate* [1907] P 125.
4   *Lemage v Goodban* (1865) LR 1 P & D 57; *Re Petchell's Goods* (1874) LR 3 P & D 153; *Re Summers' Goods* (1901) 84 LT 271 (one treated as codicil of the other); *Townsend v Moore* [1905] P 66; *Simpson v Foxon* [1907] P 54; *Reeves v Reeves* [1909] 2 IR 521; *Re Bund, Cruikshank v Willis* [1929] 2 Ch 455; *Busteed v Eager* (1834) Milw 345; *Clarke v Clarke* 1925 SC 431 (English and Scottish wills); *Re Allen Estate* [1935] 1 WWR 584 (one will dealing with Canadian property, later will excepting such property, but revocation upheld); *Re Owens Estate* (1956) 2 DLR (2d) 144 (second will bequeathing only certain personal chattels and with revocation clause struck out but not initialled); *Re Mitchell Estate, Bradshaw v Pidgeon* (1954) 33 MPR 359 (two holograph wills with no revocation clause). The same rules applies to a codicil: *Pilsworth v Mosse* (1862) 14 I Ch R 163; *O'Leary v Douglass* (1878) 3 LR Ir 323; *Re Wray* [1951] Ch 425, [1951] 1 All ER 375; *Re Spensley's Will Trusts* [1952] Ch 886, [1952] 2 All ER 49, and a codicil may be revoked by a similar disposition in a later codicil: *Re Buckley* [1952] VLR 107, where the second codicil repeated the disposition but made it conditional on the general residuary beneficiary under the will predeceasing the testator and if both should perish in the same disaster.

5   *Re Fleetwood, Sidgreaves v Brewer* (1880) 15 Ch D 594; *Duguid v Fraser* (1886) 31 Ch D 449; *Morley v Rennoldson* [1895] 1 Ch 449; *Vencatanarayana Pillay v Subammal* (1915) 32 TLR 118; *Ward v Van der Loeff* [1924] AC 653; *Alexander v Kirkpatrick* (1874) LR 2 Sc & Div 397; *Re Gardner* [1935] 1 DLR 308; *Baker v Story* (1874) 31 LT 631, was not followed in *Ward v Van der Loeff* [1924] AC 653, and in *Re Robinson, Lamb v Robinson* [1930] 2 Ch 332 (where it is said that the rule that a second will will revoke an earlier one though it is ineffective to confer any gift, if such failure is due to the incapacity of the devisee or legatee and not to any infirmity in the will itself, is no longer acceptable).

6   *Re Baker, Baker v Baker* [1929] 1 Ch 668; followed in *Re Pearson, Rowling v Crowther* [1963] 3 All ER 763, [1963] 1 WLR 1358; *Re Alford's Estate* (1939) 83 Sol Jo 566; but in *Goldie v Adam* [1938] P 85, [1938] 1 All ER 586, it was held that where there are no words of revival an earlier will was not revived, see Chapter 21.

7   *Re Hawksley's Settlement, Black v Tidy* [1934] Ch 384 at 396; approved in *Re Resch's Will Trusts, Le Cras v Perpetual Trustee Co Ltd* [1969] 1 AC 514, [1967] 3 All ER 915.

[18.11]

Wills of the same date or undated. Where there are two valid but inconsistent testamentary documents of the same date, or undated, and it cannot be ascertained which was executed first, neither can be admitted to probate,[1] but, if they both contain a revocation clause, they operate to revoke a previous will.[2]

1   *Biddles v Biddles* (1843) 3 Curt 458; *Townsend v Moore* [1905] P 66; *Loftus v Stoney* (1867) 17 I Ch R 178. Where there is no consistency and no revocation clause both wills have been admitted: *Re Mitchell Estate, Bradshaw v Pidgeon* (1954) 33 MPR 359.

2   *Re Howard, Howard v Treasury Solicitor* [1944] P 39.

[18.12]

Lost will. Where a testamentary document has been lost or destroyed in such a way as not to effect a revocation[1] probate may be granted of the contents thereof upon proof of such contents and due execution and attestation of the instrument.[2] Where the person setting up an alleged will cannot produce any copy or draft of any written evidence of its contents, he must prove all these matters so as to remove all reasonable (but not all possible) doubt on these points.[3] The evidence of a solicitor that he had made the will and that it was not informal establishes due execution and attestation.[4] The contents may be proved from the instructions given to the solicitor[5] or by the evidence of a witness, although he is an interested party, but his evidence must be unimpeached.[6] An alleged draft will be considered side by side with the oral evidence.[7] There has been doubt about the admission of declarations made by the testator after the making of the will,[8] but almost certainly for the reason that evidence of such declarations would be hearsay;[9] if that is the reason, such evidence will now be admissible under Civil Evidence Act 1968, s 1, or the replacement of it now going through Parliament. The fullest enquiries must be made in any such case.[10]

1   As to the position where the loss effects a revocation, see para **[18.27]** infra.

2   *Brown v Brown* (1858) 8 E & B 876; *Sugden v Lord St Leonards* (1876) 1 PD 154, 238, CA; *Allan v Morrison* [1900] AC 604, PC; *Re Crandon's Goods* (1901) 84 LT 330; *Re Spain* (1915) 31 TLR 435 (where the testator, attesting witnesses and the will were lost in an explosion); *Re Phibbs' Estate* [1917] P 93; *Re Queen Marie of Roumania* (1950) 94 Sol Jo 673; *Re Davies, Panton v Jones* [1978] CLY 3095.

3   *Harris v Knight* (1890) 15 PD 170 at 179; *Re Wipperman's Estate* [1953] 1 All ER 764 at 766; *Re MacGillivray's Estate* [1946] 2 All ER 301. As to the contents of the affidavit to lead to probate of a lost will, see *Tristram and Coote, Probate Practice* (28th edn). For a case where the evidence was insufficient, see *Re Plunkett* [1965] VR 118.

4   *Re Hannah* [1954] NZLR 836.
5   *Fincham v Edwards* (1842) 3 Curt 63; on appeal 4 Moo PCC 198.
6   *Sugden v Lord St Leonards* (1876) 1 PD 154, 238, CA; *Re Yelland, Broadbent v Francis* (1975) 119 Sol Jo 562 (will proved by daughter's recollection of contents).
7   *Burls v Burls* (1868) LR 1 P & D 472 at 474; *Re Webb Smith v Johnston* [1964] 2 All ER 91, [1964] 1 WLR 509 (a draft will was admitted because the inclusion of a proper attestation clause led to the presumption that the will had been duly executed).
8   *Atkinson v Morris* [1897] P 40; but they were admitted in *Sugden v Lord St Leonards* (1876) 1 PD 154, 238, CA.
9   This seems clear from *Atkinson v Morris* [1897] P 40, but *Barkwell v Barkwell* [1928] P 91 at 97 seems to suggest that the rule is based on the requirement of Wills Act 1837, s 9 that a will must be in writing.
10 See *Re Ferguson-Smith Estate* (1954) 13 WWR NS 387; on appeal (1955) 15 WWR 237, Sask CA.

[18.13]

Lost subsequent will. Where a subsequent will is not forthcoming, the person alleging that it revoked an earlier will must strictly prove his allegation[1] and there must be proof of difference of disposition.[2] If the person alleging revocation succeeds there is an intestacy,[3] otherwise the earlier will is entitled to probate.[4]

1   See cases cited in para **[18.7]**, n 1; *Re Trelease* (1911) 30 NZLR 226; *West Australian Trustee, Executor and Agency Co Ltd v O'Connor* (1955) 57 WALR 25 (later will prepared by competent and careful solicitor not proof of revocation of former will).
2   *Cutto v Gilbert* (1854) 9 Moo PCC 131; applied in *Re Dear* [1975] 2 NZLR 254; *Re Debac's Goods, Sanger v Hart* (1897) 77 LT 374; *Brown v Brown* (1858) 8 E & B 876; *Wood v Wood* (1867) LR 1 P & D 309; *Re Steward's Will* [1964] VR 179; *M'Ara v M'Cay* (1889) 23 LR Ir 138 (no revocation clause in subsequent will but additional legacy otherwise the same: held, first will revoked).
3   *Wood v Wood* (1867) LR 1 P & D 309.
4   *Hellier v Hellier* (1884) 9 PD 237; *Dickinson v Stidolph* (1861) 11 CBNS 341.

[18.14]

Partly inconsistent wills. Where there are several testamentary instruments which are not wholly inconsistent, they are read together to constitute the last will of the testator[1] for any number of documents whatever their date or form can be so admitted to probate.[2] The prior disposition is not to be disturbed further than is absolutely necessary to give effect to the later one.[3] The presumption against implied revocation is greater where the testator has used words showing an intention only to alter the dispositions in certain specific respects.[4] The general rule is that a revocation by subsequent will or codicil shall operate only so far as is necessary to effectuate the intention of the testator.[5] Therefore, an apparent inconsistency in the testamentary instruments may be rebutted by oral evidence that the testator did not intend revocation[6] or by extrinsic evidence of the surrounding circumstances.[7] It is incumbent upon those who contend that a gift in one testamentary instrument is not to take effect by reason of some subsequent instrument, to show that the intention to revoke is as clear and free from doubt as the original intention to give.[8] Extrinsic evidence, including evidence of the testator's intention, is admissible if the relevant wording is ambiguous on its face, or extrinsic evidence, other than evidence of intention, shows the wording to be ambiguous in the light of surrounding circumstances.[9]

177

1   *Re Budd's Goods* (1862) 3 Sw & Tr 196; *Birks v Birks* (1865) 4 Sw & Tr 23; *Lemage v Goodban* (1865) LR 1 P & D 57; *Re Fenwick's Goods* (1867) LR 1 P & D 319; *Re Griffith's Goods* (1872) LR 2 P & D 457; *Re Petchell's Goods* (1874) LR 3 P & D 153; *Re Hartley's Goods* (1880) 50 LJP 1; *Re Hodgkinson's Goods* [1893] P 339; *Reeves v Reeves* [1909] 2 IR 521.

2   *Lemage v Goodban* (1865) LR 1 P & D 57; *Townsend v Moore* [1905] P 66.

3   *Farrer v St Catharine's College, Cambridge* (1873) LR 16 Eq 19; *Young v Hassard* (1841) 1 Dr & War 638; *Wallace v Seymour* (1872) 20 WR 634.

4   *Follett v Pettman* (1883) 23 Ch D 337.

5   *Doe d Evers v Ward* (1852) 18 QB 197. The question is what disposition the testator intended, not what papers did he desire to be admitted to probate: *Dempsey v Lawson* (1877) 2 PD 98 at 107.

6   *Busteed v Eager* (1834) Milw 345; *Fawcett v Jones, Coldrington and Pulteney* (1810) 3 Phillim 434 at 478.

7   *Jenner v Ffinch* (1879) 5 PD 106; *Paton v Ormerod* [1892] P 247; *Re Brian's Estate* [1974] 2 NSWLR 231; *Re Bryan's Estate* [1907] P 125.

8   *Follett v Pettman* (1883) 23 Ch D 337; *Doe d Hearle v Hicks* (1832) 8 Bing 475; approved in *Re Resch's Will Trusts, Le Cras v Perpetual Trustee Co Ltd* [1967] 3 All ER 915 at 925.

9   See the AJA 1982, s 21. See also *Thorne v Rooke* (1841) 2 Curt 799. See full discussion on admission of extrinsic evidence, Chapter 57.

[18.15]

Codicils. Where a will is revoked by a subsequent codicil, the question whether an intermediate codicil is also revoked is one of construction. If the revoking codicil distinguishes between the will and subsequent codicils, as, for instance, by date, the latter are not revoked.[1]

The revocation of a will by loss, destruction or other means does not now revoke a codicil to it by implication,[2] for a properly executed testamentary paper can only be revoked by the methods prescribed by statute;[3] but upon proof that a testator by cutting off his signature to his will intended to revoke a codicil to it written on the same piece of paper, the codicil may also be revoked.[4] An intermediate codicil is not impliedly revoked by a later codicil itself confirming the will.[5]

If a codicil contains not only words of revocation but also superadded words of construction susceptible of being read as relating to the same subject-matter directing the will to be construed in a particular way, then prima facie those words will be restrictively construed and the court will lean towards regarding them as doing no more than reinforcing the words of revocation. Thus, where certain bequests are revoked by codicil with a direction that the will should be read 'as if' those bequests had not been made, then the hypothesis should not be read as affecting anything save those words.[6] Accordingly, where a will is by a codicil directed to be read as if a certain person's name has been omitted, the revocation is confined to that person's beneficial interests under the will, and interests given to the issue of that person are not affected.[7]

1   *Farrer v St Catharine's College, Cambridge* (1873) LR 16 Eq 19. See *Bunny v Bunny* (1840) 3 Beav 109; *Pratt v Pratt* (1844) 14 Sim 129; *Cartwright v Shepheard* (1853) 17 Beav 301 (codicil revoking appointment as executor and trustee); *Patch v Graves* (1855) 3 Drew 347; *Re Hastings' Goods* (1872) 26 LT 715; *Follett v Pettman* (1883) 23 Ch D 337.

2   *Black v Jobling* (1869) LR 1 P & D 685 (loss of will); *Re Turner's Goods* (1872) LR 2 P & D 403 (destruction of will); *Re Clements' Goods* [1892] P 254 (loss of will); *Paige v Brooks* (1896) 75 LT 455. But where the will is destroyed under a wrong impression that it is useless, the will and codicil are both admitted: *Beardsley v Lacey* (1897) 67 LJP 35.

3   WA 1837, s 18, as substituted, with reference to wills made on or after 1 January 1983 by the AJA 1982; see Vol 2, Part G, para **[244.18]**; and s 20; *Re Savage's Goods* (1870) LR 2 P & D 78; *Gardiner v Courthope* (1886) 12 PD 14.

4   *Re Bleckley's Goods* (1883) 8 PD 169, but cf *Beardsley v Lacey* (1897) 67 LJP 35, where the opposite result was reached.

5   *Green v Tribe* (1878) 9 Ch D 231; *Follett v Pettman* (1883) 23 Ch D 337; approved in *Re Resch's Will Trusts* [1969] 3 All ER 915 (a third codicil described as a 'first codicil' and ending with a statement that in all other respects the testator confirmed his will did not revoke earlier codicils).

6   *Re Lawrence's Will Trusts, Public Trustee v Lawrence* [1971] 3 All ER 433 at 445, [1971] 3 WLR 188 at 202–3 ('in all respects my said will shall be construed as if the bequests to Helen had not been made'). See also *Harris v Davis* (1844) 1 Coll 416; *Sykes v Sykes* (1868) 3 Ch App 301; and *IRC v Cookson* [1975] 3 All ER 590.

7   *Re Spensley's Will Trusts* [1952] Ch 886, [1952] 2 All ER 49 (a special power of appointment is beneficial to the donee of the power and is revoked by saying that his or her name is to be omitted); *Re Wray* [1951] Ch 425, [1951] 1 All ER 375 (where a will appointed G one of the executors and gave him a legacy if he accepted the office and also gave the residue to C with a provision that if C predeceased the testator, the residue should go as part of C's estate. Under C's will G became tenant for life of C's estate. The testator then by codicil revoked the appointment of G and directed that the will should be read as if G's name was omitted from the will and as if G were dead. It was held that the codicil did not effect a revocation of the referential trusts and G was entitled to the life estate in the residue).

[18.16]

Instrument of revocation. A writing declaring an intention to revoke a will must, to be effectual, be executed in the manner in which a will is required to be executed.[1] Such a writing may be a codicil;[2] a memorandum on the will;[3] a letter;[4] a settlement;[5] declaration of intention to revoke,[6] or a mere obliteration of the testamentary document[7] or a statement in a will qualifying a bequest.[8] A technical point arises in such cases as to whether the grant should be one of probate or of administration. Unless there remains an effective disposition it seems that the grant should be one of administration with a note that it is so made in consequence of the execution of the paper revoking the earlier will.[9]

1   WA 1837, s 20; 50 *Halsbury's Statutes* (4th edn) 589; see Vol 2, Part G, para **[244.20]**. The testator must at the time of revocation be of testamentary capacity, see Chapter 4.

2   *Brenchley v Still* (1850) 2 Rob Eccl 162.

3   *Re Hicks' Goods* (1869) LR 1 P & D 683.

4   *Re Durance's Goods* (1872) LR 2 P & D 406 (letter to brother); *Re Spracklan's Estate* [1938] 2 All ER 345 (letter to bank manager); *Re Eyre's Goods* [1905] 2 IR 540 (letter to daughter).

5   See *Thompson v Simpson* (1881) 50 LJ Ch 461.

6   *Toomer v Sobinska* [1907] P 106, and see *Hawksley v Barrow* (1866) LR 1 P & D 147.

7   *Re Gosling's Goods* (1886) 11 PD 79 (where a codicil was obliterated and subscribed: 'We are witnesses to the erasure of the above' and signed by the testator and two witnesses).

8   *Re Brown Estate* (1953) 9 WWRNS 27 (direction in will for obliteration of part if a beneficiary survived the testatrix).

9   *Toomer v Sobinska* [1907] P 106, departing from *Re Durance's Goods* (1872) LR 2 P & D 406, but apparently where the revoking document is a will or codicil, a grant of probate may be made.

V.   BY DESTRUCTION

[18.17]

Destruction with intention to revoke. A will may be revoked by burning,[1] tearing[2] or otherwise destroying it,[3] by the testator or by some person in his presence and by his direction, with the intention of revoking it.[4] For this purpose there must be both an act of destruction[5] and an intention[6] to revoke, and the will must be actually injured.[7] A symbolical destruction is not sufficient.[8] Nor is a will revoked by being destroyed by mistake[9] or in a fit of madness,[10] since all the destroying in the world without intention does not revoke a will.[11] A testator must have the same standard of mind and memory and the same degree of understanding when destroying his will as when he made it.[12] Subsequent acquiescence does not amount to intention.[13] The destruction of the will even with the intent to revoke will not revoke a codicil thereto.[14]

1 *Stephens v Taprell* (1840) 2 Curt 458; *Cheese v Lovejoy* (1877) 2 PD 251 (symbolical burning insufficient) both cases referred to in *Re Adams* [1990] Ch 601, [1990] 2 All ER 97.
2 *Stephens v Taprell* (1840) 2 Curt 458; *Elms v Elms* (1858) 1 Sw & Tr 155 (where there was a partial tearing and insufficient evidence to revoke); *Cheese v Lovejoy* (1877) 2 PD 251 (symbolical tearing insufficient). Tearing includes cutting: *Hobbs v Knight* (1838) 1 Curt 768; *Re Cooke's Goods* (1847) 5 Notes of Cases 390.
3 A memorandum of revocation and cancellation of the signature is insufficient unless duly signed and attested as required by the WA 1837, s 20 (see Vol 2, Part G, para **[244.20]**): *Re Brewster's Goods* (1859) Sea & Sm 108. As to cancellation, see para **[18.25]** infra.
4 WA 1837, s 20, and see *Burtenshaw v Gilbert* (1774) 1 Cowp 49 at 52.
5 *Cheese v Lovejoy* (1877) 2 PD 251 (in this case the testator drew his pen through various parts of the will and wrote on the back: 'This is revoked'; whatever the testator intended, the will had not been actually injured); *Andrew v Motely* (1862) 12 CBNS 514 (there must be some unequivocal act of cancellation or obliteration in the presence and by the direction of the testator).
6 *Powell v Powell* (1866) LR 1 P & D 209 at 212. (All acts of destruction are equivocal. They may be accidental or intentional and, if intentional, of various intentions. The intention must be completely to revoke and not to revoke upon the fulfilment of some condition.) As to dependent relative revocation, see Chapter 19, post.
7 *Giles v Warren* (1872) LR 2 P & D 401. The object of the statutory provision was to prevent revocation depending on oral evidence: *Doe d Reed v Harris* (1837) 6 Ad & El 209.
8 See nn 1 and 2.
9 *Onions v Tyrer* (1716) 1 P Wms 343; *Scott v Scott* (1859) 1 Sw & Tr 258; *Clarkson v Clarkson* (1862) 2 Sw & Tr 497; *Giles v Warren* (1872) LR 2 P & D 401; *Re Thornton's Goods* (1889) 14 PD 82; *Beardsley v Lacey* (1897) 67 LJP 35.
10 *Brunt v Brunt* (1873) LR 3 P & D 37; *Re Hine's Goods* [1893] P 282 (softening of the brain); *Re Downer's Goods* (1853) 1 Ecc & Ad 106; *Re Brassington's Goods* [1902] P 1 (intoxication). The testator must be of sound mind at the time of revocation and the onus is on the person setting up revocation to prove that destruction or mutilation occurred while he was of sound mind.
11 *Cheese v Lovejoy* (1877) 2 PD 251 at 253.
12 *Re Sabatini* (1969) 114 Sol Jo 35.
13 *Re Booth, Booth v Booth* [1926] P 118.
14 *West Australian Trustee Executor and Agency Co Ltd v O'Connor* (1955) 57 WALR 25.

[18.18]
Evidence of intention. The intention to revoke a will wholly or in part may be evidenced by proof of the expressed intention of the testator in doing the act,[1] or of circumstances from which the intention may be inferred,[2] or by the state and condition to which the instrument has been reduced by the act itself.[3]

1 *Re Maley's Goods* (1887) 12 PD 134; *Clarke v Scripps* (1852) 2 Rob Eccl 563 at 567.
2 *Christmas and Christmas v Whinyates* (1863) 3 Sw & Tr 81; *Bruce's Judicial Factor v Lord Advocate* 1969 SLT 337.
3 *Williams v Jones* (1849) 7 Notes of Cases 106; *Bell v Fothergill* (1870) LR 2 P & D 148; *Treloar v Lean* (1889) 14 PD 49; *Re Witham* [1938] 3 DLR 142.

[18.19]

Destruction of duplicate. The destruction with intention to revoke of one part of a will executed in duplicate amounts to a revocation, whether only one part or both parts were in the possession of the testator;[1] and the presumption generally is that by such destruction the testator intended complete revocation.[2] This presumption is not so strong where the testator destroys one of two duplicates both in his own possession, especially if he has previously made alterations on the part so destroyed.[3]

1   *Gregory v Gregory* (1849) 13 Jur 843; *Re Lady Slade's Goods* (1869) 20 LT 330; *Jones v Harding* (1887) 58 LT 60; *Paige v Brooks* (1896) 75 LT 455 (retained duplicate missing at testator's death).
2   *Luxmoore v Chambers* (1885) cited in 58 LT at 61.
3   *Re Hains' Goods* (1847) 5 Notes of Cases 621; *Roberts v Round* (1830) 3 Hag Ecc 548 (partial destruction of one, careful preservation of other duplicate).

[18.20]

Incomplete destruction. The intention to revoke must continue until the destruction of the document is complete. If a testator leaves unfinished the work of destruction which he had commenced, either in consequence of the remonstrance or interference of a third person or by his own voluntary change of purpose, the will is unrevoked, the intention to revoke being itself revoked before the act was complete.[1] Similarly, probate is granted of a will the signature to which has been partially erased and rewritten,[2] or where the testator was cut out but replaced the part containing the signatures of the witnesses,[3] but not where the testator's signature has been cut out and pasted on in the previous position.[4] Partial tearing which leaves all the words legible does not necessarily show an intention to revoke.[5]

1   *Elms v Elms* (1858) 1 Sw & Tr 155.
2   *Re Kennett's Goods* (1863) 2 New Rep 461 (this seems to have been because the court thought the original signature was 'apparent'): see Chapter 14, para **[14.2]** supra.
3   *Re Eeles' Goods* (1862) 2 Sw & Tr 600. As to conditional revocation, see Chapter 19.
4   *Bell v Fothergill* (1870) LR 2 P & D 148; *Magnesi v Hazelton* (1881) 44 LT 586 (signature and attestation clause cut out and folded inside will). These cases appear to be decided on the footing that there was no sufficient rebuttal of the presumption of intention to revoke.
5   *Re Cowling, Jinkin v Cowling* [1924] P 113. See also *Re McGinn Estate* (1969) 70 WWR 159.

[18.21]

Destruction by stranger. Destruction by a third person in the presence and by the direction of the testator is effectual.[1] On the other hand destruction by the testator's direction, but not in his presence, is ineffectual;[2] nor can the testator revoke his will by subsequent ratification of a previous unauthorised act of destruction by a third person.[3] Where a will was torn in pieces after the testator's death and pasted together again, though there were still some blanks, probate was granted of the will and a copy.[4]

1   WA 1837, s 20 (see Vol 2, Part G, para **[244.20]**); *Rooke v Langdon* (1844) 2 LTOS 495.
2   *Re Dadds' Goods* (1857) Dea & Sw 290; *Re Bacon's Goods* (1859) 23 JP 712 (destruction after testator's death on instructions given in his lifetime).
3   *Gill v Gill* [1909] P 157 (the intention to revoke must be manifested at the time of the act of destruction); *Mills v Millward* (1889) 15 PD 20; *Re Simkin* [1950] VLR 341.
4   *Re Leigh's Goods* [1892] P 82.

[18.22]
Extent of destruction. There must be such an injury, with intent to revoke, as destroys the entirety of the will;[1] but it is sufficient if its essence as a will, though not the materials of which it is composed, destroyed.[2] Thus, cutting off the testator's signature[3] or scratching it out,[4] unless done under a mistaken belief as to the effect of the will,[5] or cutting off by the testator of the signature of attesting witnesses, if done with intention to revoke, works a revocation[6] unless otherwise explained,[7] but the erasure by the witnesses of their own signatures does not revoke the will.[8]

1   *Price v Powell* (1858) 3 H & N 341 (tearing off seal, but intention to revoke proved); *Re Drury's Will* (1882) 22 NBR 318.
2   *Hobbs v Knight* (1838) 1 Curt 768 (cutting out signature); applied in *Re Adams* [1990] Ch 601, [1990] 2 All ER 97 where the signatures of the testator and the witnesses had been very heavily scored out by a ball point pen so that they were impossible to read. Held revoked. The test to be applied in such cases was whether the original signatures were 'apparent', analogous to the tests applied to that word in the WA 1837, s 21; *Ffinch v Combe* [1894] P 191 applied.
3   *Re Jones, Evans v Harries* [1976] Ch 200, [1976] 1 All ER 593 (will held to be revoked where the signatures of the testatrix and of the attesting witnesses were cut off and never found again; also cut off were dispositive clauses of the will). See also Chapter 19; *Hobbs v Knight* (1838) 1 Curt 768; *Re Simpson's Goods* (1859) 5 Jur NS 1366 (where the cut-off signatures were preserved); *Re Marshall's Goods* (1869) 17 WR 687 (where it may have been that only revocation of an appointment of an executor was intended); *Re Lady Slade's Goods* (1869) 20 LT 330 (where only the original was mutilated by cutting off signature: a complete copy remained out of the possession of the testatrix).
4   *Re Morton's Goods* (1887) 12 PD 141; *Re Adams* [1990] Ch 601, [1990] 2 All ER 97; *Doe d Reed v Harris* (1837) 6 Ad & El 209. But *Re Godfrey's Goods* (1893) 69 LT 22, is to the contrary, but there the signature was still legible. See also Cancellation, infra.
5   *Stamford v White* [1901] P 46 (belief that will useless founded on mistaken view of effect of settlement).
6   *Re Wheeler's Goods* (1879) 49 LJP 29; *Re Dallow's Goods* (1862) 31 LJPM & A 128; *Abraham v Joseph* (1859) 5 Jur NS 179; *Re Marshall's Goods* (1869) 17 WR 687 (where both the testator's and witnesses' signatures were cut off); *Re White's Goods* (1879) 3 LR Ir 413 (only portion with no dispositions found after decrease).
7   *Re Wheeler's Goods* (1879) 49 LJP 29; *Re Taylor's Goods* (1890) 63 LT 230 (where the signature was accidentally cut through in removing a later addition to the will).
8   *Margary v Robinson* (1886) 12 PD 8.

[18.23]
Partial destruction. Where a portion of a will not necessary to its validity as a testamentary instrument is destroyed, the question is whether the portion destroyed is so important as to raise the presumption that the rest cannot have been intended to stand without it, or whether it is unimportant and independent of the rest of the will.[1] Where a testator destroys some sheets of a will and substitutes others, but does not re-execute the whole will, there is a revocation;[2] but merely tearing off a part of no dispositive character[3] or of the commencement of a will,[4] or a clause containing legacies[5] or appointing executors[6], does not necessarily revoke the rest of the will.[7]

1   *Re Lambert's Goods* (1841) 1 Notes of Cases 131; *Clarke v Scripps* (1852) 2 Rob Eccl 563; *Leonard v Leonard* [1902] P 243; *Re Anderson* [1933] 1 DLR 581.
2   *Treloar v Lean* (1889) 14 PD 49; in *Gullan v Grove* (1858) 26 Beav 64 (only the two intermediate sheets were found and were rejected).
3   *Re Nunn's Estate* [1936] 1 All ER 555.

4   *Re Woodward's Goods* (1871) LR 2 P & D 206; applied in *Re Everest* [1975] Fam 44, [1975] 1
     All ER 672 (mutilations not such as to give rise to an inference that it had been done with the
     intention of revoking the will in toto); see also *Re Cooke's Goods* (1847) 5 Notes of Case 390.
5   *Re Nelson's Goods* (1872) IR 6 Eq 569; *Re Talbot* [1925] SASR 100; but where the alteration is
     merely of the amount of the legacies, the doctrine of dependent relative revocation usually
     applies: see Chapter 19.
6   *Re Leach's Goods* (1890) 63 LT 111; *Re Maley's Goods* (1887) 12 PD 134.
7   As to destruction of a book containing a list of advances to children and specifically referred to
     in the will, see *Re Coyte, Coyte v Coyte* (1887) 56 LT 510 (after such destruction the advances
     had not to be brought into account).

[18.24]

Destruction of will but not of codicil. Where after a will of codicil was
executed giving a specific bequest and confirming the will, and later the testator
destroyed the will with the intention of revoking it, it was held that the special
bequest in the codicil was good, but the will was revoked and ineffective.[1]

1   *Re Formaniuk Estate* (1963) 44 WWR 686, and see also para **[18.23]**, nn 2 and 3, and the text
     thereto.

[18.25]

Cancellation. A will or codicil is not destroyed by being struck through with a
pen,[1] even though done with intention to revoke,[2] nor by the word cancelled
being written across it,[3] for cancelling is not now one of the modes of
revocation.[4]

1   *Stephens v Taprell* (1840) 2 Curt 458; *Re Barrett's Will* (1876) 2 VLR 98; *Re Shephard's
     Estate* (1982) 29 SASR 247; *Cheese v Lovejoy* (1877) 2 PD 251 and *Re Adams* [1990] Ch 601,
     [1990] 2 All ER 97.
2   *Re Brewster's Goods* (1859) Sea & Sm 108; *Benson v Benson* (1870) LR 2 P & D 172.
3   *Sakzewski Will and Codicil* [1943] QWN 38.
4   'Otherwise destroying' in the WA 1837, s 20; see Vol 2, Part G, para **[244.20]**, means
     destruction by method ejusdem generis with burning or tearing, the other methods therein
     stated: see *Stephens v Taprell* (1840) 2 Curt 458.

[18.26]

Evidence of revocation. Declarations by the testator that he had destroyed his
will are not admissible to prove the fact of destruction, but they are admissible to
prove his intention to revoke it, from which the fact of destruction may be
inferred.[1] It has been said that such declarations are of little weight since they
may be misunderstood, misremembered or not repeated in the exact words of the
deceased.[2]

1   *Keen v Keen* (1873) LR 3 P & D 105 at 107; *Re Sykes, Drake v Sykes* (1907) 23 TLR 747; *Re
     Maley's Goods* (1887) 12 PD 134; *Re Templemore's Estate* (1925) 69 Sol Jo 382; *Re Barker,
     Nemes v Baker* [1995] 2 VR 439 (extrinsic evidence admissible to show intention to revoke).
     See *North v North* (1909) 25 TLR 322.
2   *Williams v Jones* (1849) 7 Notes of Cases 106.

[18.27]

Presumption of intention to revoke—destruction or mutilation of will.
Where a will is destroyed or found mutilated, in a place in which the testator
would naturally put it, the presumption is that the testator destroyed it, and that it
was destroyed with the intention of revoking it,[1] and if there is a codicil, after

the execution of the codicil,[2] but this presumption is only prima facie and may be rebutted.[3]

1   This passage of the text was cited with approval by Ferris J in *Re Adams* [1990] 2 All ER 97 at 99. *Re Lewis' Goods* (1858) 1 Sw & Tr 31; *Elms v Elms* (1858) 1 Sw & Tr 155; *Magnesi v Hazelton* (1881) 44 LT 586; *Re Gullan's Goods* (1858) 1 Sw & Tr 23; *North v North* (1909) 25 TLR 322. See also *Re Weeks* (1972) 28 DLR (3d) 452 (presumption applied). A blank sheet was found substituted for the will in *Abbott and Bearman v Willstead* (1885) 2 TLR 23, and in *Treloar v Lean* (1889) 14 PD 49, three new sheets had been substituted but though signed the new sheets were not attested and the will was not admitted to probate. See also *Leonard v Leonard* [1902] P 243 (where the will was rendered unintelligible).
2   *Christmas and Christmas v Whinyates* (1863) 3 Sw & Tr 81.
3   *Patten v Poulton* (1858) 1 Sw & Tr 55; *Boddy v Carpenter* [1931] 4 DLR 927 (where the evidence so attenuated the presumption that it became negligible).

[18.28]
Presumption of intention to revoke—will not forthcoming. If a will was last traced to the possession of the testator and is not forthcoming at his decease, there is a prima facie presumption, in the absence of circumstances tending to a contrary conclusion, that the testator destroyed it with intention to revoke it.[1] This does not, however, involve a presumed intention to revoke duly executed codicils to such will which are forthcoming at the testator's death, even though such codicils contain references to the will[2] which is known to have been destroyed by the testator.[3]

1   *Allan v Morrison* [1900] AC 604; *Re Sykes, Drake v Sykes* (1907) 23 TLR 747; *McCauley v McCauley* (1910) 10 CLR 434; *Re Perry* [1925] 1 DLR 930; *Re Paget's Goods* (1913) 47 ILT 284; *Re Welbrock* [1920] NZLR 1; *Re Robinson Estate* [1930] 2 WWR 673; *Re Morrison* [1942] 1 DLR 273; *Re Podger's Will* [1957] VLR 275; *Re Riordan* [1961] VR 271; *Gordon v Beere* [1962] NZLR 257; *Bruce's Judicial Factor v Lord Advocate* 1969 SLT 337. In *Re Davies, Panton v Jones* (1978) Times, 23 May, a lost will was found for and letters of administration were revoked.
2   *Black v Jobling* (1869) LR 1 P & D 685; *Gardiner v Courthope* (1886) 12 PD 14; *Re Ellice's Goods* (1863) 33 LJPM & A 27; *Re Clements' Goods* [1892] P 254.
3   *Re Turner's Goods* (1872) LR 2 P & D 403.

[18.29]
Rebuttal of presumption. The presumption may, however, be rebutted by evidence, but the evidence must be clear and satisfactory.[1] Recent declarations by a testator of satisfaction at having settled his affairs,[2] or of goodwill towards the persons benefited by the will, or of adherence to the will and to the contents of the will itself,[3] may be used for this purpose. A declaration by the testator of adherence to a will may be answered by his declarations to a contrary effect.[4] The presumption may, it seems, also be rebutted by a consideration of the contents of the will itself,[5] or by showing that the testator had no opportunity of destroying the will, or that it had been lost or destroyed without his privity or consent.[6]

1   *Eckersley v Platt* (1866) LR 1 P & D 281; *Battyll v Lyles and Phillips* (1858) 4 Jur NS 718; *Eaton (Norris Estate) v Heyman* [1946] 4 DLR 441.
2   *Whiteley v King* (1864) 17 CBNS 756.
3   *Keen v Keen* (1873) LR 3 P & D 105; *Patten v Poulton* (1858) 1 Sw & Tr 55; *Re Mackenzie's Estate* [1909] P 305. See also *Sugden v Lord St Leonards* (1876) 1 PD 154; *Unwin v Unwin* (1914) 20 BCR 77; *Public Trustee v Kells* (1904) 23 NZLR 605; *Re Matt Estate* (1954) 11

WWRNS 28; *Re Boyd's Will, ex p Whelan* [1959] SRNSW 369 (where the testator was asked shortly before his decease as to the whereabouts of the will and said it was in a bag beside his bed and there appeared to be no one who could benefit other than the named beneficiary); *Brown v Woolley* (1959) 27 WWR 425; *Re Keluga Estate* (1956) 64 Man R 138.

4   *Keen v Keen* (1873) LR 3 P & D 105; *Re Sykes, Drake v Sykes* (1907) 23 TLR 747. But it seems that oral declarations of destruction are not admissible: *Atkinson v Morris* [1897] P 40.

5   *Sugden v Lord St Leonards* (1876) 1 PD 154, where the contents of a codicil and the testator's papers were also given weight. In *Re Witham* [1938] 3 DLR 142, the cutting out was so carefully done and an intelligible will left properly executed that the resulting will was admitted.

6   *Finch v Finch* (1867) LR 1 P & D 371.

[18.30]

Fraudulent abstraction. There is a presumption against fraudulent abstraction of a will either before or after the death of the testator, but circumstances making such abstraction possible must be given due weight.[1]

1   *Allan v Morrison* [1900] AC 604.

[18.31]

Burden of proof. Where there is proof that a will was duly executed, the onus of proof is first upon the party setting up revocation to prove such revocation,[1] but when the above presumption of revocation arises from the will being mutilated or not forthcoming at the death of the testator, the onus lies upon those propounding the will to rebut that presumption.[2] Where the will is said by the testator to have been destroyed but is in fact in existence after his death, effect must be given to it.[3] If the testator becomes insane after the execution of the will, those relying upon mutilation or destruction as a revocation must prove mutilation or destruction while the testator was of sound mind.[4]

1   *Stoddart v Grant* (1852) 1 Macq 163; *Pennefather v Lloyd* [1917] 1 IR 337.
2   *Welch v Phillips* (1836) 1 Moo PCC 299; *Re Sykes, Drake v Sykes* (1907) 23 TLR 747.
3   *Re Jones Estate* (1955) 16 WWR 78.
4   *Harris v Berrall* (1858) 1 Sw & Tr 153; *Sprigge v Sprigge* (1868) LR 1 P & D 608; *Benson v Benson* (1870) LR 2 P & D 172; *Re Hine's Goods* [1893] P 282; *Allan v Morrison* [1900] AC 604; *Gill v Gill* [1909] P 157. *Re Taylor's Estate, National and Provincial and Union Bank of England v Taylor* (1919) 64 Sol Jo 148; *Re Beattie Estate* [1944] WWR 727; *Re Broome Estate, King and Ewens v Broome* (1961) 29 DLR (2d) 631.

VI.   PARTIAL REVOCATION

[18.32]

Statutory provision. The Wills Act 1837 itself recognises that revocation may extend either to the whole will or only to some part thereof.[1]

1   WA 1837, s 20; see Vol 2, Part G, para **[244.20]**.

[18.33]

Intention. Since revocation is wholly a matter of intention and the intention is the sole guide as to whether there is an operative revocation,[1] it is clear that the intention must govern the extent and measure of operation to be attributed to an act of revocation and such act may operate to revoke only a part or the whole of the will according to the proved intention of the testator.[2] Revocation of part which leaves the remainder of the will unintelligible will result in total revocation.[3]

Where there are different gifts of residue in the will and in a codicil, that in the codicil prevails and that in the will is revoked, even though the codicil merely purports to deal with the residue of property not disposed of by the will.[4] But where there is a gift of residue to several legatees, a revocation by codicil of the gift to one of several of them does not, in the absence of an indication of intention to that effect, carry the shares to the other legatees, but results in an intestacy,[5] but there is no intestacy where the shares are given to a class or to joint tenants.[6] Where the shares are not given to a class or to joint tenants, the mere confirming of the will in all other respects does not, it now seems, prevent an intestacy as to the revoked share,[7] and a confirmation except as to any lapsed legacy has the same effect.[8]

1   See para **[18.4]** supra.
2   *Re White's Goods* (1879) 3 LR Ir 413. Where the revocation of part is in its words an absolute revocation, it is not limited in operation by a recital showing that absolute revocation was not intended; *Holder v Howell* (1803) 8 Ves 97 (codicil setting out trusts again with the omission of one where a recital suggested that such omission was not intentional), but see *Hill v Walker* (1858) 4 K & J 166.
3   *Leonard v Leonard* [1902] P 243.
4   *Earl Hardwicke v Douglas* (1840) 7 Cl & Fin 795; *Re Pereira, Worsley v Society for the Propagation of the Gospel in Foreign Parts* (1912) 28 TLR 479; *Re Stoodley, Hooson v Locock* [1916] 1 Ch 242.
5   *Re Forrest, Carr v Forrest* [1931] 1 Ch 162; and where the codicil gave all the residue to named persons this was held to apply to the revoked portion: *Re Ockley Estate* (1953) 10 WWRNS 282; but it is otherwise where the codicil gives a special direction as to the distribution of residue; *Re Wilkins, Wilkins v Wilkins* [1920] 2 Ch 63. As to revocation by codicil of a share of residue, see Chapter 20.
6   See Chapter 47, paras **[47.28]–[47.34]** infra.
7   *Re Wilkins, Wilkins v Wilkins* [1920] 2 Ch 63; *Re Forrest, Carr v Forrest* [1931] 1 Ch 162. It seems that *Re Whiting, Ormond v De Launay* [1913] 2 Ch 1 to the contrary, would not now be followed.
8   *Re Wood's Will* (1861) 29 Beav 236.

CHAPTER 19

Conditional revocation and dependent relative revocation

[19.1]

Conditional revocation in general. Revocation by destruction, or obliteration, or by subsequent will or codicil, may be conditional, and if the condition in question is unfulfilled the revocation fails and the will, as made before such revocation, remains operative.[1] A clause in a will which, on its face, revoked all previous wills could be read distributively so as to relate absolutely to some dispositions but only conditionally to others.[2] But the revocation of a will is prima facie absolute unless it is shown to be conditional, and the burden of proof lies on the person seeking to show that a revocation is conditional.[3]

In all cases of revocation by destruction or obliteration, the question whether revocation is conditional is a question of fact,[4] to be considered in connection with the circumstances in which revocation occurred and the declarations of the testator with which it may have been accompanied,[5] which are accordingly admissible in evidence.[6] A revocation grounded on an assumption of fact which is false takes effect unless, as a matter of construction, the revocation is conditional on the fact being true.[7]

---

1   *Re Faris, Goddard v Overend (No 2)* [1911] 1 IR 469; *Re Southerden's Estate, Adams v Southerden* [1925] P 177 at 185.

2   *Re Finnemore* [1992] 1 All ER 800, [1991] 1 WLR 793. The doctrine of conditional revocation was applied to save a gift in a later will which was subject to the Wills Act 1837 (WA 1837), s 15. It was appropriate to give a revocation clause in the testator's last will a distributive reading in order to carry out the clear intention of the testator determined by the construction of the last will (which contained a revocation clause and the legacy subject to the WA 1837, s 15) in the light of the surrounding circumstances including the existence of earlier wills (where the legacy was not subject to the WA 1837, s 15). A useful authority where all the previous authorities on the subject were reviewed.

3   *Re Surridge, Sparks v Kingdom* (1970) 114 Sol Jo 208, CA; *Re Irvine's Goods* [1919] 2 IR 485; *Re Southerden's Estate, Adams v Southerden* [1925] P 177.

4   *Dixon v Treasury Solicitor* [1905] P 42.

5   *Powell v Powell* (1866) LR 1 P & D 209 (dependent on validity of new provision to be brought into existence or belief in the revival of an old disposition); *Cossey v Cossey* (1900) 69 LJP 17.

6   *Re Zimmer's Estate* (1924) 40 TLR 502.

7   *Re Faris, Goddard v Overend (No 2)* [1911] 1 IR 469; *Re Southerden's Estate, Adams v Southerden* [1925] P 177 (testator destroyed his will with the intention of revoking it, but under the misapprehension that by doing so his wife, if she survived him, would become entitled to the whole of his property absolutely under his intestacy; assumption incorrect and will stood). See also *Thomas v Howell* (1692) 1 Salk 170; *Re Jones, Evans v Harries* [1976] Ch 200 at 209, [1976] 1 All ER 593 at 599; *Re Carey* (1977) 121 Sol Jo 173 (where the testator destroyed his will under the belief that he had no longer anything to leave and conditional on that belief).

[19.2]

Revocation by subsequent will or codicil. In cases, however, of revocation by subsequent will or codicil, the question is a question of construction,[1] revocation is not conditional unless it appears to be such on the face of the subsequent will or codicil.[2] The circumstances of the case must be considered,[3] but extrinsic evidence of the testator's intention to make the revocation conditionally is inadmissible.[4]

1   *Re Finnemore* [1992] 1 All ER 800, [1991] 1 WLR 793; *A-G v Lloyd* (1747) 1 Ves Sen 32 at 34; *Re Hawksley's Settlements, Black v Tidy* [1934] Ch 384.
2   *Nevill v Boddam* (1860) 28 Beav 554; *Tupper v Tupper* (1855) 1 K & J 665; *Quinn v Butler* (1868) LR 6 Eq 225; *Re Churchill, Taylor v Manchester University* [1917] 1 Ch 206; *Re Murray, Murray v Murray* [1956] 2 All ER 353, [1954] 1 WLR 605.
3   *Re Gentry's Goods* (1873) LR 3 P & D 80.
4   *Re Churchill, Taylor v Manchester University* [1917] 1 Ch 206; *Newton v Newton* (1861) 12 I Ch R 118. Where the subsequent will cannot be found the doctrine does not apply; *Re Watson* [1957] NZLR 544.

[19.3]

Dependent relative revocation. In particular, revocation may be relative to another disposition which has already been made or is intended to be made, and so dependent thereon that revocation is not intended unless that other disposition takes effect.[1] Such a revocation is known as a dependent relative revocation,[2] and if from any cause,[3] the other disposition fails to take effect, the will remains operative as it was before the revocation.[4] This conditional revocation must take effect. Thus, a testator made three wills, and wrote to his solicitor that the second will would be found at his bank and that the third one had been destroyed. Only the first will was found at the bank. It was held that there was evidence of the destruction of the third will which was intended to validate the second will. Thus there was a revocation of the third will on the condition that the second will was validated. In the circumstances this condition was not fulfilled, and the third will was admitted to probate.[5]

1   *Powell v Powell* (1866) LR 1 P & D 209; but see *Eckersley v Platt* (1866) LR 1 P & D 281 (no intention to set up former will); *Re Weston's Goods* (1869) LR 1 P & D 633. There may be no intention to deprive the original donee of benefit but merely to impose trusts upon the gift. If the trusts fail, the original gifts stand: *Re Bernard's Settlement, Bernard v Jones* [1916] 1 Ch 552, but where no intention to revive is shown there is no revival of the original provisions; *Re Murray, Murray v Murray* [1956] 2 All ER 353, [1956] 1 WLR 605. For a case where the new will was never made, see *Re Bromham's Estate* [1952] 1 All ER 110n; *Re Jones, Evans v Harries* [1976] Ch 200 at 209, [1976] 1 All ER 593.
2   The doctrine has its historical origin in a judgment of Cowper LC in *Onions v Tyrer* (1716) 1 P Wms 343.
3   *Re Fleetwood, Sidgreaves v Brewer* (1880) 15 Ch D 594 at 609.
4   *Re Southerden's Estate, Adams v Southerden* [1925] P 177.
5   *Re Bridgewater's Estate* [1965] 1 All ER 717, [1956] 1 WLR 416; *Re Finnemore* [1992] 1 All ER 800, [1991] 1 WLR 793; see also *Re Ott* (1972) 24 DLR (3d) 517 (destruction of second will only in the belief that the act of destruction would revive earlier will).

[19.4]

Instances. The question may thus arise in the case of destruction of a will as part of the act of making a fresh will, which is not in fact made,[1] or is ineffectually made for want of due execution,[2] or destruction in order to set up a prior will which needs revival,[3] or obliteration of the amount of a legacy, and the substitution, without proper formalities, of a different amount,[4] or obliteration and substitution, in a similar manner, of a different donee,[5] or other person,[6] or of a different event upon which the gift is to take effect,[7] or where the legacy in the second will failed by reason of the WA 1837, s 15.[8] The doctrine does not apply unless the revocation is dependent on the effectiveness of the new provisions.[9]

In all these and other cases, however, the question is whether the disposition revoked is intended not to operate whatever happens, or is only to be destroyed if the provisions of the substituted instrument operate in its stead.[10] Thus, where a testator mutilated or destroyed a will with the intention of making a new will but failed to carry out that intention, it did not necessarily follow that the mutilation or destruction was ineffective to revoke the existing will.[11] That would only follow if the testator intended that the revocation should only take effect when a new will was executed.[12] The question is not determined by the presence or absence of express words of revocation.[13] The court must be satisfied that the testator did not intend to revoke the original will except conditionally, in so far as the other disposition could be set up,[14] and the court must be similarly satisfied that the testator intends to make a new will; merely contemplating to do so is not sufficient;[15] and failure to do so prevents the revocation of the original will.[16] If there is an intention to set up another will, it is immaterial that the destruction of the former will results from a desire to exclude a particular beneficiary.[17]

1 *Re Cockayne's Goods* (1856) Dea & Sw 177; *Re Eeles Goods* (1862) 2 Sw & Tr 600; *Dixon v Treasury Solicitor* [1905] P 42. Where a former valid will is not forthcoming, that is sufficient evidence of destruction with intent to revoke, and if another valid will is made, there is evidence unless the contrary is proved that the destruction was conditional on the new will being effective: *Re Botting's Estate* [1951] 2 All ER 997, explaining the decision in *Homerton v Hewitt* (1872) 25 LT 854.

2 *Dancer v Crabb* (1873) LR 3 P & D 98; *Re Irvin's Estate* (1908) 25 TLR 41; *Re Bunn, Durber v Bunn* (1926) 134 LT 669; *Re Davies' Estate, Russell v Delaney* [1951] 1 All ER 920; *Sterling v Bruce* [1973] NI 255. In the case of *Re Hope Brown's Goods* [1942] P 136, [1942] 2 All ER 176, the second will was in part good though incomplete and the doctrine was applied, and similarly in *Re Cocke's Estate* [1960] 2 All ER 289, [1960] 1 WLR 491 (where a charging clause was omitted in the second will), applied in *Re McKenzie, McKenzie v Thomas* [1968] NZLR 493.

3 *Powell v Powell* (1866) LR 1 P & D 209; *Cossey v Cossey* (1900) 82 LT 203; *Re Irvine's Goods* [1919] 2 IR 485; *West v West* [1921] 2 IR 34; *Re Wenborn* [1923] NZLR 27; *Re Taylor* [1924] NZLR 1109. The court refused to apply the doctrine because a legatee was deprived of her legacy by reason of her husband being a witness to the later will: *Re Bourke* [1923] VLR 480.

4 *Re Horsford's Goods* (1874) LR 3 P & D 211; *Re Nelson's Goods* (1872) IR 6 Eq 569. But the obliteration of part of the amount has sometimes been held effectual: *Re Nelson's Goods* (1872) IR 6 Eq 569. Where the obliteration is effectual the original amount may be proved by infra-red photography or by removal of the slips pasted on: *Re Itter's, Dedman v Godfrey* [1950] P 130, [1950] 1 All ER 68.

5 *Re McCabe's Goods* (1873) LR 3 P & D 94.

6 *Re Parr's Goods* (1859) Sea & Sm 146; *Re Harris' Goods* (1860) 1 Sw & Tr 536.

7 *Sturton v Whetlock* (1883) 52 LJP 29 (gift to children at 21 changed to gift at 25).

8 *Re Finnemore* [1992] 1 All ER 800, [1991] 1 WLR 793; *Re Cocke's Goods* [1960] 2 All ER 289, [1960] 1 WLR 491; *Re Rich* [1947] SASR 98; *Re Mills* (1968) 70 SR NSW 36; *Re Crannis' Estate* (1978) 122 Sol Jo 489.

9 *Re Feis, Guilliaume v Ritz-Remorf* [1964] Ch 106, [1963] 3 All ER 303 (codicil revoking disposition purported to be effected by power of attorney which was ineffective by German law).

10 *Dancer v Crabb* (1873) LR 3 P & D 98; *Welch and Freeman v Gardner* (1887) 51 JP 760;
      Ward v Van der Loeff, Burnyeat v Van der Loeff [1924] AC 653; *Re Hawksley's Settlement,*
      Black v Tidy [1934] Ch 384; *Sacks v Gridiger* (1990) 22 NSWLR 502.
11 *Re Jones, Evans v Harries* [1976] Ch 200, [1976] 1 All ER 593 (will held revoked and testatrix
      died intestate).
12 *Re Jones, Evans v Harries* [1976] Ch 200, [1976] 1 All ER 593.
13 *Re Hawkesley's Settlements, Black v Tidy* [1934] Ch 384; *Re Owens Estate* (1956) 2 DLR (2d)
      144.
14 *Re Mitcheson's Goods* (1863) 32 LJPM & A 202.
15 *Re Bolton Estate, Bolton and Hess v Toronto General Trusts Corpn* (1961) 29 DLR (2d) 173.
16 *Re Service* [1964] 1 OR 197.
17 *Re Lindrea* [1953] VLR 168.

[19.5]

Mistake. A revocation which is shown to be upon a mistake either of fact,[1] or of law,[2] and is considered by the court not to be intended by the testator except conditionally on the mistaken assumption being correct,[3] is inoperative.

1 *Doe d Evans v Evans* (1839) 10 Ad & El 228 (belief that person dead without issue); *Thomas v*
      Howell (1874) LR 18 Eq 198 (belief that estate of specified value).
2 Belief that prior will no longer of use: *Scott v Scott* (1859) 1 Sw & Tr 258; *Beardsley v Lacey*
      (1897) 67 LJP 35; or that such will was inoperative: *Giles v Warren* (1872) LR 2 P & D 401;
      James v Shrimpton (1876) 1 PD 431; *Re Thornton's Goods* (1889) 14 PD 82; or has already
      been revoked: *Clarkson v Clarkson* (1862) 2 Sw & Tr 497; or that the cancellation of an entire
      will was a necessary pre-condition of making a new one: *Dixon v Treasury Solicitor* [1905] P
      42; or in the legal rights of the widow which, however, was treated as a mistake of fact: *Re*
      Southerden's Estate, Adams v Southerden [1925] P 177. See also *Re Hope Brown's Goods*
      [1942] P 136, [1942] 2 All ER 176. If the mistake is that another instrument or disposition is
      substituted, the case is one of dependent relative revocation: see *Re Middleton's Goods* (1864) 3
      Sw & Tr 583; *Stamford v White* [1901] P 46; *Newton v Newton* (1861) 12 I Ch R 118.
3 *Re Faris, Goddard v Overend (No 2)* [1911] 1 IR 469; *Re Phelan* [1972] Fam 33, [1971] 3 All
      ER 1256, and cases noted at para **[18.8]**, n 2.

[19.6]

A matter of construction. It appears from the most recent case on the subject that the question whether conditional or dependent revocation applies, is a matter of construction of the second will in the light of the circumstances surrounding the testator in his armchair when that will was made.[1] Strong confirmatory extrinsic evidence of the testator's intention is not needed where the intention is clear from the wills themselves.[2]

1 Per Judge Micklem in *Re Finnemore* [1992] 1 All ER 800 at 828, [1991] 1 WLR 793 at 830.
2 *Re Finnemore* [1992] 1 All ER 800 at 828, [1991] 1 WLR 793.

CHAPTER 20

Codicils

[20.1]

Use of codicil. Codicils which in form and execution are similar to a will are useful for the purpose of making slight alterations to a will, such as a change of executors or deleting some specific gift. Codicils may be used for making any alteration in a will, but it is so easy to fail to see that a substantial alteration so made will affect parts of the will other than that intended to be affected, that it is a wise practical rule to execute a new will whenever any substantial alteration is intended. In particular, 'as if' revocatory clauses are perilous devices since it is a rare draftsman who can foresee all the possible consequences of the hypothetical state of affairs that he is bringing into being.[1] However, it may, in cases of urgency, be more practical to execute a codicil than to prepare a new will.

1   Per Megarry J in *Re Lawrence's Will Trusts, Public Trustee v Lawrence* [1971] 3 All ER 433 at 445, [1971] 3 WLR 188 at 202; see para **[18.15]** supra.

[20.2]

Form of codicil. A codicil takes much the same form as a will. It commences with a statement that it is a codicil to a will, identifying the will by its date,[1] and in the case of a woman who has been married or re-married since the execution of her former will, an explanation of the change in her surname. There follows a recital of the provisions of the will it is proposed to alter or revoke with the reasons for such alteration or revocation. The operative part of the codicil effects the alterations and revocations with the new provisions which are to be operative. After a statement that in all other respects the will is confirmed, the codicil is executed and attested in the same way as a will.

1   A document described as a 'last will' which was obviously intended to be a codicil has been admitted to probate as a codicil along with the former will: *Re Luffman's Goods* (1847) 5 Notes of Cases 183; *Re Langhorn's Goods* (1847) 5 Notes of Cases 512; *Re Barry* (1911) 30 NZLR 1192. A codicil will be admitted to probate although the will referred to is not found and although the reference to the will in the codicil is quite indefinite: *Re Coulthard's Goods* (1865) 11 Jur NS 184; *Black v Jobling* (1869) LR 1 P & D 685; *Gardiner v Courthope* (1886) 12 PD 14; *Re Clements' Goods* [1892] P 254. Instructions for a codicil duly attested will be admitted to probate and treated as a codicil of a will therein wrongly described as to date: *Re White, Knight v Briggs* [1925] Ch 179. Where the testator left two holograph wills and there was no revocation clause, the two were treated as one testamentary disposition: *Re Mitchell Estate* (1954) 33 MPR 359.

[20.3]

Construction and effect in general. The codicil takes effect as annexed to the will. The will and all the codicils thereto are construed together as one

testamentary disposition,[1] although not as one document'[2] and the same
principles in general apply to the construction of a codicil as of a will. For the
purpose of explaining the will or any codicil, the court may and is bound to look
at the will and at all the other codicils.[3] Thus, the will and codicils read together
may indicate a consistent scheme of benefit for a family, which will govern the
construction of a particular codicil[4]. The court may, for example, look at a recital
of a will contained in a codicil, and may alter the construction of the will by it[5]
unless the recital is obviously erroneous.[6] A will is not altered by a codicil
further than is necessary to give effect to the intentions of the testator shown by
the will and codicil taken together, and similarly as to a will and a later will or
series of codicils,[7] and the court has looked at an unattested codicil, directed to
form part of a will, to arrive at the testator's intention.[8] A valid codicil does not
validate an invalid will if there is no evidence that the testator's attention was
not directed to the contents of the will. Such a codicil has an independent
existence and can be a valid testamentary instrument.[9]

1   *Re Hardyman, Teesdale v McClintock* [1925] Ch 287; *Re Wilcock, Kay v Dewhirst* [1898] 1 Ch
    95; *Morely v Rennoldson* [1895] 1 Ch 449; *Re Smith, Prada and Vandroy* [1916] 2 Ch 368. The
    language of the will may be interpreted by that of the codicil: *Darley v Martin* (1853) 13 CB
    683; *Jenkins v Stewart* (1906) 3 CLR 799 (the language of the will must be open to two
    constructions). The execution of a codicil assumes the continued existence of the will: *Re
    Smith, Bilke v Roper* (1890) 45 Ch D 632.
2   *Re Towry's Settled Estate, Dallas v Towry* (1889) 41 Ch D 64. Where an intention is expressed
    that two properties shall go together, effect is given to that intention. Where no such intention is
    expressed, it ought not to be inferred from the mere fact that, under the will, the two properties
    are in fact devised in the same way and so in fact united.
3   *Hartley v Tribber* (1853) 16 Beav 510; *Re Townley, Townley v Townley* (1884) 53 LJ Ch 516.
    See also *Re Timson, Harper v Timson* [1953] 2 All ER 1252, [1953] 1 WLR 1361 (codicil
    giving real and personal estate on trust for sale made legacies payable out of realty and
    personalty).
4   *Re Resch's Will Trusts, Le Cras v Perpetual Trustee Co Ltd* [1969] 1 AC 514, [1967] 3 All ER
    915, where there were identical legacies in the first and third codicils, and it was held that
    although the third codicil did not revoke the first codicil the legacies were not cumulative; see
    also *Bagots Executors and Trustees Co Ltd v Bathern* (1982) 15 NTR 3.
5   *Re Venn, Lindon v Ingram* [1904] 2 Ch 52.
6   *Re Smith* (1862) 2 John & H 594. A recital that a particular person is entitled to a gift under
    another instrument does not amount to a gift by the instrument containing the recital, because
    the testator supposes the gift to have been already given and therefore cannot intend then to
    create it. It is otherwise where the testator states in the same instrument that he has made the
    gift by that instrument: *Re Venn, Lindon v Ingram* [1904] 2 Ch 52.
7   *Re Resch's Will Trusts, Le Cras v Perpetual Trustee Co Ltd* [1969] 1 AC 514, [1967] 3 All ER
    915; *Doe d Hearle v Hicks* (1832) 1 Cl & Fin 20; *Re Bund, Cruikshank v Wills* [1929] 2 Ch
    455; *Wallace v Seymour* (1872) IR 6 CL 219; *Pennefather v Lloyd* [1917] 1 IR 337; *Re
    Florence, Lydall v Haberdashers' Co* (1917) 87 LJ Ch 86; *Re Atkinson, Atkinson v Weightman*
    [1925] WN 30; *Re Kappele* [1954] OR 456; affd [1955] 1 DLR 29. Thus where a codicil
    appointed a new trustee of a will which had appointed one person as executor and trustee, it was
    held that the person originally appointed executor was still the executor: *Re Overand* (1963) 42
    WWR 625.
8   *Green v Marsden* (1853) 1 Drew 646.
9   *Re Gray* [1956] NZLR 981.

[20.4]
Confirmation of will by codicil. The effect of a confirmation of the will[1] by a
codicil is for many purposes[2] to bring the dispositions of the will down to the
date of the codicil and to effect the same disposition of the testator's estate as if

the testator had at the date made a new will containing the same dispositions as the original will.[3] This, however, is subject to any contrary intention being shown[4] and without prejudice to the original effect of the will and intermediate codicils,[5] and the will is brought down to date with the alterations introduced by the various codicils,[6] except such codicils as are inoperative without being themselves expressly confirmed or incorporated,[7] or are expressly or impliedly revoked.[8] Particularly, descriptions of property not referring to particular objects but to a class of objects capable of increase or decrease are prima facie referred not to the date of the will, but to the date of the codicil,[9] so as to pass all the testator's interest[10] in the property then so described,[11] unless the gift in the meantime lapses,[12] or is revoked,[13] or, under the presumption against double portions, is adeemed or satisfied;[14] but such confirmation need not affect the conditions of a gift. Thus, where advances 'already' made are to be brought into hotchpot, this condition does not affect advances made after the date of the will;[15] where marriage is to be with consent, the condition does not apply only to marriage after the execution of the codicil.[16] But where legacies were to be subject to certain duties, that condition applied to duties substituted between the date of the will and codicil,[17] and a condition relating to residence during a specified lease was not discharged by the renewal of the lease before the date of the codicil.[18] Where a legacy given by the will was subject to a condition, which had been dispensed with by the subsequent acts of the testator, and the will was confirmed by a codicil, the condition was not thereby re-attached to the legacy.[19]

The confirmation by codicil need not affect the question of who is the donee, where the description may apply to different persons at different times.[20] Thus, where there are illegitimate children in esse at the time of the will, a gift to the children 'I may have by' A, the mother of the illegitimate children, is not confined to future legitimate children of A by the testator although at the time of the will he may have contemplated marriage with A after the death of his then wife.[21] But it has been held that a gift to 'my youngest son J' did not fail where there was a youngest son J at the date of the will who died but another son J was born before the date of the codicil,[22] and the words 'to whom I have given legacies' have been held to apply both to those to whom legacies are given by the will and to those to whom legacies are given by the codicil.[23]

Furthermore, where a gift in a will would be revoked by the effect of a different disposition in a codicil and the disposition in the codicil for any reason fails, the gift in the will may stand.[24]

The codicil has no such effect where it is executed for a limited purpose only, and does not purport to confirm the will or bring its terms down to the date of the codicil.[25] The date of original execution of the will remains as a factor for determining the construction, for example when it is necessary to determine the date to which expressions of time occurring in the will are referable.[26]

---

1   Confirmation for this purpose amounts to republication of the will: Wills Act 1837, s 34 (see Vol 2, Part G, para [244.35]). The confirmation does not operate as a re- execution of the will so as to make the gifts in the will effective only from the date of codicil: *Re Moore, Long v Moore* [1907] 1 IR 315 (confirmation of charitable gift).
2   *Doe d Biddulph v Hole* (1850) 15 QB 848.
3   *Re Rayer, Rayer v Rayer* [1903] 1 Ch 685; *Re Northcliffe, Arnholz v Hudson* [1925] Ch 651; *Grealey v Sampson* [1917] 1 IR 286; *Re Hardyman, Teesdale v McClintock* [1925] Ch 287; *Re Reeves, Reeves v Pawson* [1928] Ch 351, *Re Yates, Singleton v Povah* (1922) 128 LT 619

(legacy increased to amount mentioned in codicil). A valid conditional codicil which expressly referred to the earlier will had the effect of republishing the will, *Re Gillies* [1991] 1 NZLR 760.

4   *Doe d Biddulph v Hole* (1850) 15 QB 848; *Re Farrer's Estate* (1858) 8 ICLR 370.
5   See *Stilwell v Mellersh* (1851) 20 LJ Ch 356 at 361; *Re Moore, Long v Moore* [1907] 1 IR 315; *Re Beirnstein, Barnett v Beirnstein* [1925] Ch 12 (no extension of meaning of 'mortgage' as used in will).
6   *Wedgwood v Denton* (1871) LR 12 Eq 290; *Capron v Capron* (1874) LR 17 Eq 288; *Re Fraser, Lowther v Fraser* [1904] 1 Ch 726; *Re Michell, Thomas v Hoskins* [1929] 1 Ch 552 (two codicils of same date held to be duplicates of same instrument).
7   *Green v Tribe* (1878) 9 Ch D 231; *Re Steele's Goods* (1868) LR 1 P & D 575; *Burton v Newbery* (1875) 1 Ch D 234.
8   *McLeod v McNab* [1891] AC 471; *Re Resch's Will Trusts, Le Cras v Perpetual Trustee Co Ltd* [1969] 1 AC 514, [1967] 3 All ER 915.
9   Assuming the first rule making descriptions referable to the death of the testator has been displaced by the context: *Lady Langdale v Briggs* (1855) 3 Sm & G 246; *Re Champion, Dudley v Champion* [1893] 1 Ch 101; *Re Fraser, Lowther v Fraser* [1904] 1 Ch 726.
10 Thus the purchase money passed where the will contained devise of land over which the testator afterwards granted a lease with an option to purchase which was exercised after his death: *Re Pyle, Pyle v Pyle* [1895] 1 Ch 724; and see *Re Steele, Steele v Steel* [1913] 1 IR 292.
11 As to ademption, see Chapter 41.
12 *Winter v Winter* (1846) 5 Hare 306.
13 *Powys v Mansfield* (1837) 3 My & Cr 359.
14 *Montague v Montague* (1852) 15 Beav 565; *Cowper v Mantell (No 2)* (1856) 22 Beav 231; *Hopwood v Hopwood* (1859) 7 HL Cas 728; *Sidney v Sidney* (1873) LR 17 Eq 65; *Re Aynsley, Kyrle v Turner* [1914] 2 Ch 422; *Re Richards, Jones v Rebbeck* (1921) 90 LJ Ch 298. Where there is a serious doubt whether or not there has been ademption, the fact that there is a subsequent codicil may be important: *Re Aynsley, Kyrle v Turner* [1914] 2 Ch 422; *Re Warren, Warren v Warren* [1932] 1 Ch 42.
15 *Stilwell v Mellersh* (1851) 20 LJ Ch 356.
16 *Re Park, Bott v Chester* [1910] 2 Ch 322.
17 *Re Rayer, Rayer v Rayer* [1903] 1 Ch 685.
18 *Wedgwood v Denton* (1871) LR 12 Eq 290. See also *Re Taylor, Dale v Dale* [1909] WN 59 (gift over to issue of deceased children).
19 *Violett v Brookman* (1857) 26 LJ Ch 308.
20 *Stilwell v Mellersh* (1851) 20 LJ Ch 356 at 361, 362; *Re Park, Bott v Chester* [1910] 2 Ch 322 at 328.
21 *Wilkinson v Adam* (1823) 12 Price 470.
22 *Perkins v Micklethwaite* (1715) 1 P Wms 274.
23 *Re Donald, Moore v Somerset* [1909] 2 Ch 410, where Warrington J refused to follow *Anon* cited in *Pattison v Pattison* (1832) 1 My & K 12 at 14.
24 *Doe d Murch v Marchant* (1843) 6 Man & G 813; *Ward v Van der Loeff* [1924] AC 653; *Re Davies, Thomas v Thomas-Davies* [1928] Ch 24, but see *Re Murray, Murray v Murray* [1956] 2 All ER 353, [1956] 1 WLR 605 (there must be shown an intention to revise the original gift).
25 *Hughes v Turner* (1835) 3 My & K 666; *Monypenny v Bristow* (1832) 2 Russ & M 117 (the general rule is that a codicil makes the will speak as at the date of the codicil but it may be so framed as to operate only as a partial republication or to work no republication at all); *Ashley v Waugh* (1839) 9 LJ Ch 31; *Re Taylor, Whitby v Highton* (1888) 57 LJ Ch 430. Where a codicil is executed for a specific purpose which fails the provisions incidental to that specific purpose fail also: *Re Jeffs, Brown v Jeffs* (1912) 31 NZLR 156.
26 *Earl Mountcashell v Smyth* [1895] 1 IR 346 at 360; *Re Moore, Long v Moore* [1907] 1 IR 315. It must be established that the intention of the testator is that the provisions of the will are to apply to circumstances existing at the date of the will.

[20.5]
Revocation by codicil of share of residue. If by a will a residuary estate is given to a number of persons as individuals and not as a class, and as tenants in common and not as joint tenants, and by a codicil the share of one such person is revoked, then that share devolves as on the testator's intestacy,[1] unless it is

otherwise disposed of.[2] The intention that the others of the named persons should take may be shown by a direction that that share should fall into residue[3] or by other means.[4] If the named persons are to take as a class[5] or as joint tenants,[6] the others of them take the revoked share.

1   *Ramsay v Shelmerdine* (1865) LR 1 Eq 129, dissented from in *Re Dunster, Brown v Heywood* [1909] 1 Ch 103 (a case of a class gift); *Sykes v Sykes* (1868) 3 Ch App 301; *Re Forrest, Carr v Forrest* [1931] 1 Ch 162.
2   *Re Palmer, Palmer v Answorth* [1893] 3 Ch 369. See also para **[7.31]** supra, and notes thereto.
3   *Re Palmer, Palmer v Answorth* [1893] 3 Ch 369; *Re Allan, Dow v Cassaigne* [1903] 1 Ch 276 (direction that lapsed shares should become part of the residuary estate); *Re Wand, Escritt v Wand* [1907] 1 Ch 391 (forfeiture of share).
4   *Vaudrey v Howard* (1853) 2 WR 32; *Re Radcliffe, Young v Beale* (1903) 51 WR 409 (where there was a survivorship clause but on the construction of the codicil it was to be read as if the beneficiary was not one of the residuary legatees); *Re Whiting, Ormond v De Launay* [1913] 2 Ch 1; *Re Wood's Will* (1861) 29 Beav 236; *Re Wilkins, Wilkins v Wilkins* [1920] 2 Ch 63.
5   *Shaw v M'Mahon* (1843) 4 Dr & War 431; *Clark v Phillips* (1853) 17 Jur 886; *Re Dunster, Brown v Heywood* [1909] 1 Ch 103; *M'Kay v M'Kay* [1900] 1 IR 213; *Re Gibson's Will* [1922] VLR 165.
6   *Humphrey v Tayleur* (1752) Amb 136.

[20.6]
Execution of codicil. The same rules apply as in the case of wills.[1]

1   Chapter 11.

[20.7]
Revocation of codicil. This has been considered with the revocation of wills and the same considerations apply.[1]

1   Chapters 17, 18.

[20.8]
Subsequent codicil operating as revocation of intermediate codicil. This has already been considered.[1]

1   Chapter 18.

[20.9]
Revival of will or codicil by codicil. This is considered in the next following chapter.

CHAPTER 21

Revival

[21.1]

Modes of revival. The only modes in which a revoked will or codicil can be revived are either by re-execution[1] or by a codicil duly executed, and showing an intention to revive it. It is provided by the Wills Act 1837[2] (WA 1837) that every will re-executed, or republished or revived by any codicil, shall, for the purposes of the Act, be deemed to have been made at the time at which it was so re-executed, republished or revived. Where a will or codicil which has been partly revoked and afterwards wholly revoked is revived, such revival does not extend to the part first revoked, unless an intention to the contrary is shown.[3] A codicil may revive in its altered state a will or previous codicil to which unattested additions have been made.[4]

1   As to what amounts to re-execution, see Chapter 22.
2   WA 1837, s 34; 50 *Halsbury's Statutes* (4th edn) 601; see Vol 2, Part G, para **[244.35]**.
3   Wills Act 1837, s 22; 50 *Halsbury's Statutes* (4th edn) 592; see Vol 2, Part G, para **[244.22]**; *Skinner v Ogle* (1845) 1 Rob Eccl 363; *Re Brown's Goods* (1858) 1 Sw & Tr 32; *Re Hodgkinson's Goods* [1893] P 339. The revocation of a revoking will or codicil does not revive a will revoked thereby: *Boulcott v Boulcott* (1853) 2 Drew 25.
4   *Neate v Pickard* (1843) 2 Notes of Cases 406.

[21.2]

Incorporation in later will. A will or codicil which has been revoked, or a part thereof, may, without revival, have a validity given to it by incorporation in a subsequent valid testamentary disposition.[1]

1   *Jorden v Jorden* (1843) 2 Notes of Cases 388; *Re Terrible's Goods* (1858) 1 Sw & Tr 140; *Re Bangham's Goods* (1876) 1 PD 429; *Lothian's Trustees v Back* 1918 SC 401. See *Paton v Ormerod* [1892] P 247 (where there was not sufficient reference to the revoked wills to incorporate it in the later will and oral evidence was not admissible to explain the intention of the testatrix).

[21.3]

Form. For the purpose of reviving a will no precise form of words is necessary, nor need the reviving instrument be annexed to or indorsed on the will.[1] But for a will to be revived, it must be in existence; hence a will which has been destroyed cannot be revived.[2]

1   *Potter v Potter* (1750) 1 Ves Sen 437.
2   *Rogers and Andrews v Goodenough and Rogers* (1862) 2 Sw & Tr 342; *Re Reade's Goods* [1902] P 75.

[21.4]

Lost will. Evidence may be given to show that a lost will revoked a former one,[1] and where a lost will is not shown to have been destroyed with intent to revoke it, it may be revived by codicil although there is in existence an intermediate will inconsistent with the former one.[2]

1   *Barkwell v Barkwell* [1928] P 91.
2   *Re Watson* (1887) 13 VLR 599.

[21.5]

Express intention. Where a will which has been revoked is re-executed,[1] the fact of re-execution shows that the testator intends to revive it. Where it is revived by codicil the statutory requirement[2] that there shall be an intention to revive it must be satisfied. For this purpose the intention must appear on the face of the codicil,[3] either by express words referring to a will as revoked and importing an intention to revive it, or by a disposition of the testator's property inconsistent with any other intention, or by some other expressions showing, with reasonable certainty, the existence of the intention,[4] but this does not mean that evidence of surrounding circumstances is inadmissible.[5]

1   Where the revocation was by cutting out the signature, pasting a new signature on is not a re-execution and will not revive the will: *Bell v Fothergill* (1870) LR 2 P & D 148.
2   Wills Act 1837, s 22; see Vol 2, Part G, para **[244.22]**.
3   *Marsh v Marsh* (1860) 1 Sw & Tr 528; *Re Steele's Goods* (1868) LR 1 P & D 575, applied in *Re Dear* [1975] 2 NZLR 254 (reference in a codicil to an earlier will by its date was insufficient to revive an earlier will); *Purcell v Bergin* (1893) 20 AR 535. See also *Re Archibald* [1992] 2 NZLR 109 (codicil reviewed earlier will and revoked later will) where several of the cases cited on this page, were discussed.
4   *Re Steele's Goods* (1868) LR 1 P & D 575; *Re Brian's Estate* [1974] 2 NSWLR 231; *Re Dear* [1975] 2 NZLR 254; *Macdonell v Purcell* (1896) 23 SCR 101; *Re Courtenay's Goods* (1891) 27 LR Ir 507. Although extrinsic evidence of the testator's intention is excluded, the court ought always to receive evidence of surrounding circumstances in order to place it in the position of the testator and so enable it to arrive at the true meaning of the words he has used; *McLeod v McNab* [1891] AC 471; *Re Mulock's Goods* [1933] IR 171 (where the cases are reviewed); *Re Davis' Goods* [1952] P 279, [1952] 2 All ER 509. Declaration of testator's intention made at time of destroying later will: *Ward v Crook* (1896) 17 NSWLR (B) 64.
5   *Re Davis' Goods* [1952] P 279, [1952] 2 All ER 509.

[21.6]

Confirmation by codicil of revoked will. If a codicil refers by date to an existing will and expressly confirms it, that sufficiently shows an intention to revive it;[1] and this is so, even though the codicil itself takes effect on a contingency,[2] and the contingency may not have happened at the death of the testator.[3] But the intention of revival must appear from the contents of the codicil,[4] or otherwise be shown by that document.[5] The mere physical annexation of a codicil to a revoked will is not sufficient to revive it,[6] nor is a mere reference by recital in the codicil to such will by date.[7]

1   *McLeod v McNab* [1891] AC 471; *Re Dyke's Goods* (1881) 6 PD 205. A fortiori where in addition to confirming certain terms are expressly referred to: *Re Van Cutsem's Goods* (1890) 63 LT 252; *Re Baker, Baker v Baker* [1929] 1 Ch 668; *Re Alford's Estate* (1939) 83 Sol Jo 566; *Re Killick's Will* [1960] VLR 98; *Re Pearson, Rowling v Crowther* [1963] 3 All ER 763, [1963] 1 WLR 1358. 'Ratify' has the same effect and it is sufficient to ratify without reference to date where there can be no doubt as to the will to which reference is made: *Neate v Pickard* (1843) 2

Notes of Cases 406, or where the codicil treats the will as subsisting: *Re Earl Caithness* (1891) 7 TLR 354.

2   *Re Da Silva's Goods* (1861) 2 Sw & Tr 315; *Re Colley's Goods* (1879) 3 LR Ir 243.

3   *Re Bangham's Goods* (1876) 1 PD 429.

4   *Marsh v Marsh* (1860) 1 Sw & Tr 528.

5   *Re Harper's Goods* (1849) 7 Notes of Cases 44; *Re Terrible's Goods* (1858) 1 Sw & Tr 140, applied in *Re Brian's Estate* [1974] 2 NSWLR 231.

6   *Marsh v Marsh* (1860) 1 Sw & Tr 528; but see *Re Davis' Goods* [1952] P 279, [1952] 2 All ER 509, where a will revoked by marriage was revived by writing on the envelope: 'The herein-named [sole beneficiary] is now my lawful wedded wife,' duly signed and attested. This was held to be a codicil reviving the will.

7   *Re Dennis' Goods* [1891] P 326. A mere statement that a codicil is a codicil to a revoked will is not sufficient to revive it since the Wills Act 1837, s 22 (see Vol 2, Part G, para **[244.22]**). It requires some further indication of the testator's intention: *Re Steele's Goods* (1868) LR 1 P & D 575; *Re Reynolds's Goods* (1873) LR 3 P & D 35; *Goldie v Adam* [1938] P 85, [1938] 1 All ER 586.

[21.7]
Reference to will by date. A codicil is part of the testamentary disposition of the testator and when a will is revived then, in the absence of a contrary intention, the revival extends to the will with all previous codicils,[1] and the mere fact that a testator described his will by reference to its original date does not exclude the inference that the will thus referred to is the will as modified by a previous codicil.[2] But where a codicil in its original form was ineffectual, it will not be revived and made effectual without distinct reference to it.[3] Where a codicil purports to revive a will without mentioning its date, evidence of facts and circumstances outside the codicil is admissible for the purpose of identifying it,[4] and only if the result is to disclose an ambiguity is evidence of the testator's intention allowed.[5] Where the will is referred to by date, parol evidence that the date was stated erroneously is inadmissible;[6] but if it appears on a comparison of successive testamentary instruments that the date is a mistake it will be disregarded,[7] though this will not be done where the mind of the draftsman (which must be treated as that of the testator) was actually applied to the provisions of the wrong document, and he based the reviving codicil upon it.[8]

1   *Stewart v MacLaren* 1920 SC (HL) 148; *Green v Tribe* (1878) 9 Ch D 231. For cases where revival was confined to original will, see *Re Reynolds's Goods* (1873) LR 3 P & D 35; *McLeod v McNab* [1891] AC 471; *French v Hoey* [1899] 2 IR 472; *Re Carritt's Goods* (1892) 66 LT 379.

2   *McLeod v McNab* [1891] AC 471.

3   *Burton v Newbery* (1875) 1 Ch D 234.

4   *Re McCabe's Goods* (1862) 2 Sw & Tr 474.

5   *Paton v Ormerod* [1892] P 247.

6   *Re Chapman's Goods* (1844) 1 Rob Eccl 1; *Payne and Meredith v Trappes* (1847) 1 Rob Eccl 583.

7   *Re Turner's Goods* (1891) 64 LT 805; *Re Gordon's Goods* [1892] P 228; *Re Snowden's Goods* (1896) 75 LT 279; *Jane v Jane* (1917) 33 TLR 389; *Goldie v Adam* [1938] P 85; *Re Rhodes* (1914) 34 NZLR 190.

8   *Re Stedham's Goods* (1881) 6 PD 205; *Re Chilcott's Goods* [1897] P 223; but see *Re Dear* [1975] 2 NZLR 254. In *Goldie v Adam* [1938] P 85, the earlier will was not revived, the court coming to the conclusion that, in all the circumstances, the testator did not intend to revive it. In the case of *Re Carleton's Goods* [1915] 2 IR 9, a duly executed codicil was endorsed on and referred to a revoked will and was held to revive it. See also *Stewart v MacLaren* 1920 SC (HL) 148; *Re Mulock's Goods* [1933] IR 171.

[21.8]
Revocation of revoking will. The methods prescribed by the Wills Act 1837, s 22[1] (namely re-execution or a codicil showing an intention of revival) being the only methods by which a will can be revived, it follows that, where a will has been revoked by a later will, the revocation of the second will, whether by destruction or by codicil, does not have the effect of reviving the first will.[2] Where the first will has been partly revoked by the second either expressly, or impliedly, in consequence of a different disposition of part of the testator's property, the cancellation of the second will does not revive the revoked part of the first.[3] Where by reason of the Wills Act 1837, the revocation of a revoking will fails to revive the first will, there is prima facie an intestacy,[4] but evidence can be given that the second will was revoked solely with the intention of validating the earlier will and the revocation of the second will is then treated as conditional. The condition not having been fulfilled, the doctrine of dependent relative revocation[5] applies, and the second will is not revoked.[6] Where an earlier will, which has been revoked by a later will, is revived by a codicil, the question arises whether the second will is revoked. It may be expressly revoked by the codicil, or it may be impliedly revoked by reason of dispositions inconsistent with it being contained in the codicil;[7] but otherwise it stands and all three documents will be admitted to probate, their effect being left for a court of construction to determine.[8] The mere fact that a codicil is described as a codicil to an earlier will does not impliedly revoke a later one, though it may have this effect.[9]

1   See Vol 2, Part G, para **[244.22]**.
2   *Major and Mundy v Williams and Iles* (1843) 3 Curt 432; *Re Brown's Goods* (1858) 1 Sw & Tr 32.
3   *Stride v Sandford* (1853) 21 LTOS 24; *Re Hodgkinson's Goods* [1893] P 339.
4   *Re Brown's Goods* (1858) 1 Sw & Tr 32.
5   See Chapter 19.
6   *Powell v Powell* (1866) LR 1 P & D 209.
7   See para **[18.8]** supra.
8   *Re Stedham's Goods* (1881) 6 PD 205; *Re Mardon's Estate* [1944] P 109, [1944] 2 All ER 397; *Re Perdue* [1943] 1 DLR 46.
9   *Re Stedham's Goods* (1881) 6 PD 205; *Re Reynold's Goods* (1873) LR 3 P & D 35; *Re Baker, Baker v Baker* [1929] 1 Ch 668.

CHAPTER 22

Republication

[22.1]
Distinguished from revival. The distinction between revival and republication is that the former restores a revoked will or codicil, while the latter merely confirms an unrevoked testamentary instrument so as to make it operate as if executed on the date of republication.[1]

1   *Skinner v Ogle* (1845) 1 Rob Eccl 363.

[22.2]
Modes of republication. Republication may be either express or constructive.[1] The former takes place where a testator re-executes his will, with the necessary formalities of attestation,[2] for the express purpose of republishing it. Constructive republication occurs when a testator makes a codicil to his will or some testamentary instrument from which the inference can be drawn that he wishes it to be read as part of his will. No precise form of words is necessary,[3] nor need the codicil expressly republish the will.[4] Thus, if the instrument is described as 'codicil to my will',[5] or if the codicil is written on the same paper as the will and refers to 'my executors above named', it operates as a republication of the will.[6] A reference which would be sufficient to revive a revoked instrument[7] is sufficient to republish an earlier unrevoked instrument so as to shift its date;[8] but the converse does not hold, for a codicil described as a codicil to a will republishes it, though it might not revive the will if it has been revoked.[9]

1   *Re Smith, Bilke v Roper* (1890) 45 Ch D 632.
2   See Chapter 12. But in the absence of an intention to bring the will down to the later date, re-execution does not amount to republication. Going over the signatures with a dry pen is not republication: *Re Cunningham's Goods* (1860) 4 Sw & Tr 194. As to re-execution without intention of republication, see *Dunn v Dunn* (1866) LR 1 P & D 277.
3   *Potter v Potter* (1750) 1 Ves Sen 437 at 442.
4   *Barnes v Crowe* (1792) 1 Ves 485; *Pigott v Waller* (1802) 7 Ves 98; *Grealey v Sampson* [1917] 1 IR 286.
5   *Re Champion, Dudley v Champion* [1893] 1 Ch 101; *Re Taylor, Whitby v Highton* (1888) 57 LJ Ch 430.
6   *Serocold v Hemming* (1758) 2 Lee 490; *Potter v Potter* (1750) 1 Ves Sen 437; *Re Cotton's Goods* [1923] 2 IR 52. It has been said that the codicil must refer in its body to the will even if on the same paper: *Re Eteson's Will* (1927) 27 SRNSW 119.
7   See Chapter 21.
8   *Re Champion, Dudley v Champion* [1893] 1 Ch 101.
9   *Re Smith, Bilke v Roper* (1890) 45 Ch D 632.

[22.3]
Effect of republication. The effect of republishing a will is for many purposes to shift its date to the date of the republishing instrument,[1] as if the testator at that date had made a will in the words of the will so republished,[2] but with the alterations made by the various codicils,[3] including unattested additions.[4] Republication does not, however, necessarily make the will operate for all purposes as if it had originally been made at the date of the republishing instrument; a contrary intention may be shown.[5] The rule is subject to the limitation that the intention of the testator is not to be defeated thereby.[6] The effect of republication on the application of statutory provisions expressed to apply to 'dispositions made', or 'provisions contained in instruments made', before or after a specified date, depends on the wording of the statute. Thus, where a will made before the statutory date is confirmed by a codicil made after the statutory date, there are decisions to the effect that, for the purposes of the particular statutory provision, the operative date is the date of the will,[7] the date of the codicil,[8] and the testator's death.[9]

1 See Wills Act 1837, s 34; 50 *Halsbury's Statutes* (4th edn) 601; Vol 2, Part G, para **[244.35]**. *Stilwell v Mellersh* (1851) 20 LJ Ch 356; *Re Fraser, Lowther v Fraser* [1904] 1 Ch 726. For a case where republication nullified the effect of revocation by marriage, see *Cooper v Cooper* (1856) 6 I Ch R 217.
2 *Hamilton v Carroll* (1839) 1 I Eq R 175; *Re Fraser, Lowther v Fraser* [1904] 1 Ch 726.
3 *Re Fraser, Lowther v Fraser* [1904] 1 Ch 726; *Green v Tribe* (1878) 9 Ch D 231; *Follett v Pettman* (1883) 23 Ch D 337. But republication does not validate a gift in an intermediate codicil void by being in favour of an attesting witness; *Burton v Newbery* (1875) 1 Ch D 234; *French v Hoey* [1899] 2 IR 472. What documents form a will is to be settled by a consideration of all the circumstances as showing the intention of the testator: see *Smith v Cunningham* (1823) 1 Add 448; *Greenough v Martin* (1824) 2 Add 239; *McLeod v McNab* [1891] AC 471.
4 *Re Wollaston's Goods* (1845) 3 Notes of Cases 599; *Re Barke's Goods* (1845) 4 Notes of Cases 44; *Re Tegg's Goods* (1846) 4 Notes of Cases 531.
5 *Re Champion, Dudley v Champion* [1893] 1 Ch 101; *Hopwood v Hopwood* (1859) 7 HL Cas 728; *Earl Mountcashell v Smyth* [1895] 1 IR 346; *Re Park, Bott v Chester* [1910] 2 Ch 322.
6 *Doe d Biddulph v Hole* (1850) 15 QB 848; *Re Moore, Long v Moore* [1907] 1 IR 315.
7 *Rolfe v Perry* (1863) 3 De GJ & Sm 481; *Re Elcom, Layborn v Grover Wright* [1894] 1 Ch 303; *Re Moore, Long v Moore* [1907] 1 IR 315; *Re Waring, Westminster Bank Ltd v Awdry* [1942] Ch 309; on appeal [1942] Ch, 426, CA; *Re Sebag-Montefiore, Sebag-Montefiore v Alliance Association Co Ltd* [1944] Ch 331; *Re Heath's Will Trusts, Hamilton v Lloyds Bank Ltd* [1949] Ch 170, [1949] 1 All ER 199.
8 *Re Tredgold, Midland Bank Executor and Trustee Co Ltd v Tredgold* [1943] Ch 69, [1943] 1 All ER 120.
9 *Berkeley v Berkeley* [1946] AC 555, [1946] 2 All ER 154. The Family Law Reform Act 1969, s 1(7), expressly provided that republication was not to make a will subject to the Act. See now Family Law Reform Act 1987.

[22.4]
Effect of legacies. Republication does not revive a legacy which has been revoked, adeemed or satisfied[1] in the interim, nor does it revive a lapsed gift[2] or substitute a new legatee.[3]

1 *Powy's v Mansfield* (1837) 3 My & Cr 359; *Hopwood v Hopwood* (1859) 7 HL Cas 728; *Montague v Montague* (1852) 15 Beav 565; *Sidney v Sidney* (1873) LR 17 Eq 65. See the qualification on this doctrine in *Re Warren, Warren v Warren* [1932] 1 Ch 42 at 50; *Re Aynsley, Kyrle v Turner* [1914] 2 Ch 422; on appeal [1915] 1 Ch 172, CA (where there is a serious doubt as to whether there has been ademption or not, the fact of there being a subsequent codicil confirming the will may be important); *Re Richards, Jones v Rebbeck* (1921) 90 LJ Ch 298; *Re*

Dolamore, Hammond v Dolamore (1897) 13 TLR 487 (bequest of shares: reconstruction of company before republication).
2   *Hutcheson v Hammond* (1790) 3 Bro CC 128; *Doe d Turner v Kett* (1792) 4 Term Rep 601.
3   *Drinkwater v Falconer* (1755) 2 Ves Sen 623; *Doe d Turner v Kett* (1792) 4 Term Rep 601; *Perkins v Micklethwaite* (1714) 1 P Wms 274.

[22.5]
Effect of intermediate wills. The republication of a will does not necessarily revoke any intermediate will or codicil.[1]

1   *Re Rawlins' Goods* (1879) 48 LJP 64; *Re Stedham's Goods, Re Dyke's Goods* (1881) 6 PD 205; *Re Chilcott's Goods* [1897] P 223.

Wills with foreign element

CHAPTER 23

Form of wills where foreign property or domicile is involved

[23.1]
General statement. Where a will is made in England by a testator domiciled in England at the date of his death, all matters, other than disposition of immovables (ie generally speaking land) situated outside England, will be governed by English law. In other cases questions of locality and domicile may arise and these questions are of importance because England law persists in applying different rules of succession to movables, which are governed by the law of domicile (lex domicilii) and to immovables, which are governed by the law of the country in which they are situate (lex situs). The meaning of these terms is thus crucial to an understanding of the rules of private international law governing succession. It is beyond the scope of this work to consider these concepts in detail[1] but some brief reference can be made.

1 For full accounts see the specialist works, Cheshire and North, *Private International Law* (13th edn); and Dicey and Morris, *The Conflict of Laws* (12th edn).

I. DEFINITIONS

[23.2]
Domicile. It is axiomatic that every person has a single domicile which is essentially that of the country in which he or she has his or her permanent home.[1] Every person has a domicile of origin by operation of law but this can be affected subsequently by the adoption of a domicile of choice or, in the case of children under the age of sixteen or of mentally disordered persons, by the acquisition of a domicile of dependency.[2]

The domicile of children and married woman has been affected by the Domicile and Matrimonial Proceedings Act 1973 (DMPA 1973) to which reference should be made.[3] Unmarried children under the age of sixteen years take the domicile of their father, except that an illegitimate child assumes the domicile of his or her mother.[4] But the domicile of a dependent child whose parents are living apart, and who lives with his or her mother, can be that of the mother.[5] A child on attaining the age of sixteen years or marrying can acquire an independent domicile.[6] The domicile of a married woman is no longer regarded as automatically that of her husband but is ascertained by reference to the same factors as in the case of any other individual having an independent domicile.[7]

1   See Cheshire and North, *Private International Law* (13th edn), Chapter 7; and Dicey and Morris, *The Conflict of Laws* (12th edn), Chapter 7; *Whicker v Hume* (1858) 7 HL Cas 124 at 160; *Re Fuld's Estate (No 3), Hartley v Fuld* [1968] P 675 at 682.
2   See Cheshire and North, n 1 supra.
3   Which came into effect on 1 January 1976.
4   See the texts in n 1.
5   DMPA 1973, s 4; 6 *Halsbury's Statutes* (4th edn) 200.
6   DMPA 1973, s 3.
7   DMPA 1973, s 5.

[23.3]

Immovables and movables. Though in English law the main distinction is between reality and personalty, and for the present purposes this distinction is still important, there is also a distinction between immovables and movables,[1] ie roughly between land and other property. The main point to notice is that leaseholds, which are personalty in English law, are for present purposes immovables, but the matter must be examined in a little more detail.

1   These terms are no part of English law but are conveniently used in considering questions between English law and foreign systems: *Re Hoyles, Row v Jagg* [1911] 1 Ch 179.

[23.4]

Immovables. These include all estates and interests in freehold,[1] including freeholds subject to a statutory trust for sale,[2] and leasehold land;[3] a rentcharge and an annuity payable out of rents and profits of land;[4] fixtures, if they go with the freehold.[5] The general rule is that the proceeds of sale of immovables are immovables[6] but this is not so in the case where such proceeds are part of the assets of a partnership[7] or where the land is sold under an agreement to sell or under a trust for sale.[8] But until sale the immovable is regarded as such.[9]

Where the property is not of necessity to be classed as an immovable, the local law must be followed as to its nature,[10] but where peculiar attributes are ascribed to property by the local law for specific purposes or for purely local reasons, such attributes will be recognised in England only for such specific purposes or special reason[11] and where English law has such peculiarities the courts will not extend them to foreign property.[12] The restrictions applying to money to be laid out in land do not apply where the land to be acquired is in a foreign country which has no such restrictions.[13]

1   *Allen v Anderson* (1846) 5 Hare 163; *Chatfield v Berchtoldt* (1872) 7 Ch App 192.
2   *Re Berchtold, Berchtold v Capron* [1923] 1 Ch 192; the doctrine of conversion does not turn immovables into movables. Compare *Re Cutliffe's Will Trusts, Brewer v Cutliffe* [1940] Ch 565. See now the abolition of the doctrine of conversion by the Trusts of Land and Appointment of Trustees Act 1996, s 3; Chapter 37.
3   *Freke v Lord Carbery* (1873) LR 16 Eq 461; *Duncan v Lawson* (1889) 41 Ch D 394; *De Fogassieras v Duport* (1881) 11 LR Ir 123; *Pepin v Bruyere* [1902] 1 Ch 24.
4   *Chatfield v Berchtoldt* (1872) 7 Ch App 192; *Whitaker v Forbes* (1875) LR 10 CP 583; on appeal 1 CPD 51, CA.
5   *Forbes v Adams* (1839) 9 Sim 462; *Re Rea, Rea v Rea* [1902] 1 IR 451 at 461; *Re Moses, Moses v Valentine* [1908] 2 Ch 235. The nature of fixtures is determined by the law of the place where the land is situated.
6   *Waterhouse v Stansfield* (1851) 9 Hare 234; *Re Cutliffe's Will Trusts, Brewer v Cutliffe* [1940] 2 All ER 297.
7   *Forbes v Steven* (1870) LR 10 Eq 178.
8   *Re Stokes, Stokes v Ducroz* (1890) 62 LT 176.

9   *Re Piercy, Whitwham v Piercy* [1895] 1 Ch 83; *Murray v Champernowne* [1901] 2 IR 232.

10   *Chatfield v Berchtoldt* (1872) 7 Ch App 192; *Elliott v Lord Minto* (1821) 6 Madd 16 (Scottish heritable bond); *Jerningham v Herbert* (1829) 4 Russ 388 (Scottish heritable bond with addition of personal security); *Monteith v Monteith's Trustees* (1882) 9 R 982 (mortgage money in England being personal property held to be a movable in Scotland); *Re Hoyles, Row v Jagg* [1911] 1 Ch 179 (mortgage debts secured on foreign land held to be an immovable).

11   *Chatfield v Berchtoldt* (1872) 7 Ch App 192.

12   *Beaumont v Oliveira* (1868) LR 6 Eq 534.

13   *Mackintosh v Townsend* (1809) 16 Ves 330.

[23.5]

Movables. Such things as are not immovables are movables.[1] Mortgage money secured on land is a movable[2] unless the local law regards it as an immovable,[3] and it is thought that, where a testator has a power of absolute disposition over land and orders it to be sold, he can dispose of the proceeds as a movable, ie in any manner authorised by the law of his domicile.

1   As to the meaning of 'movables' in an English will, see para **[64.42]** infra.

2   *Monteith v Monteith's Trustees* (1882) 9 R 982; *Re Gauthier* [1944] OR 401.

3   See para **[23.4]**, n 10. A mortgage has been held to be an immovable: *Re Landry and Steinhoff* [1941] 1 DLR 699.

II.   FORMALITIES: MOVABLES

[23.6]

The wills of testators who died before 1 January 1964, which raise conflict on points of law are governed by the Wills Act 1861.[1] That Act applied only to the wills of British subjects and was confined to the disposition of personal estate.[2] The Wills Act 1861 was repealed by the Wills Act 1963 (WA 1963), which applies to the wills of persons (whenever executed) who die on or after 1 January 1964.[3] The WA 1963 is not confined to British subjects, and extends to govern the disposition of both real and personal property. The WA 1963 has facilitated the validity of wills by widening the choices of law that will be regarded as rendering the will valid.[4] Further although the Wills Act 1861 is repealed that is not to invalidate any will executed in accordance with its provisions before 1 January 1964.[5] The pre-1964 position will be considered initially.

1   See Vol 2, Part G, para **[244.41]**.

2   Wills Act 1861, s 1.

3   WA 1963, s 7(3); 50 *Halsbury's Statutes* (4th edn) 611; see Vol 2, Part G, para **[244.81]**.

4   Except that the provision in the Wills Act 1861 validating wills executed by a British subject in accordance with the laws then in force in that part of Her Majesty's dominions where he had his domicile of origin, s 1, does not appear in the WA 1963.

5   WA 1963, s 7(4); so that a will executed before that date by a testator who dies after that date can be valid according to either the Wills Act 1861 or the WA 1963.

[23.7]

Pre-1964 law: wills made out of the United Kingdom. A will or other testamentary instrument made out of the United Kingdom by a British subject whatever his domicile at the time of making the will or at his death, is, for the purposes of disposition of personal estate,[1] well executed for the purpose of being admitted to probate if it is made according to the forms required either by the law of the place where it was made,[2] or by the law of the place where the testator was domiciled when it was made,[3] or by the laws then in force in that part of Her Majesty's dominions where he had his domicile of origin.[4] A will of a British subject having an English domicile of origin may be proved in England if executed in accordance with English law although not executed in accordance with the law of the domicile and of which proof has there been refused.[5]

1   For the purposes of the WA 1963, personalty includes leaseholds; *Re Watson, Carlton v Carlton* (1887) 35 WR 711; *Re Grassi, Stubberfield v Grassi* [1905] 1 Ch 584; *Lyne v De La Ferte and Dunn* (1910) 102 LT 143; the proceeds of land held on trust for sale: *Re Lyne's Settlement Trusts, Re Gibbs, Lyne v Gibbs* [1919] 1 Ch 80; *Re Grassi, Stubberfield v Grassi* [1905] 1 Ch 584; but not capital money or investments representing capital money under the Settled Land Act 1925; *Re Cartwright, Cartwright v Smith* [1939] Ch 90, [1938] 4 All ER 209. Note that trusts for sale and settled land have been affected by the Trusts of Land and Appointment of Trustees Act 1996, ss 1–5; see Chapters 26 and 37.
2   Wills Act 1861, s 1; see Vol 2, Part G, para **[244.41]**. See *Lyne v De La Ferte and Dunn* (1910) 102 LT 143. The English courts will apply the principle that, if the courts of the place where the will was made regard the courts of another country as being the courts primarily entitled to pronounce, any pronouncement by those courts as to the validity of the form of the will is followed by the English courts: see *Collier v Rivaz* (1841) 2 Curt 855; *Re Trufort, Trafford v Blanc* (1887) 36 Ch D 600; *Re Brown-Séquard's Goods* (1894) 70 LT 811. Presumably in such a case there is no question of domicile and *Re Rippon's Goods* (1863) 3 Sw & Tr 177, applies and the court will not inquire as to domicile but it must be noted that that case concerned a will made in England.
3   Wills Act 1861, s 1; *Re Lacroix's Goods* (1877) 2 PD 94.
4   Wills Act 1861, s 2. See n 2 as to pronouncements by courts of the domicile.
5   *Re Manifold, Slater v Chryssaffinis* [1962] Ch 1, [1961] 1 All ER 710.

[23.8]
Will made in United Kingdom. A will or other testamentary instrument made within the United Kingdom[1] by a British subject (whatever his domicile at the time of making the same or at the time of his death) is, for the purposes of disposition of personal estate,[2] well executed and entitled to be admitted to probate if executed according to the forms recognised by the laws for the time being in force in that part of the United Kingdom where the same was made.[3]

1   See para **[23.4]**, n 10, and text thereto.
2   A holograph will disposing of realty and personalty executed in Scotland, where such a will is only valid if the estate consists wholly of personalty, is not well executed within this section and a gift to the wife of an attesting witness failed: *Re Priest, Belfield v Duncan* [1944] Ch 58, [1944] 1 All ER 51.
3   Wills Act 1861, s 2. *Re Rippon's Goods* (1863) 3 Sw & Tr 177; *Re Watson, Carlton v Carlton* (1887) 35 WR 711; *Re Cocquerel* [1918] P 4 (a grant will not be made which will conflict with an order already made by a foreign court). Where the court of the domicile has pronounced whether the deceased died testate or intestate, the English courts must follow them; *Re Cosnahan* (1866) LR 1 P & D 183; *Doglioni v Crispin* (1866) LR 1 HL 301; *Re Trufort, Trafford v Blanc* (1887) 36 Ch D 600.

[23.9]
Wills of testators dying on or after 1 January 1964. The formal validity of wills (whenever executed) of persons dying on or after 1 January 1964, will be determined by reference to the WA 1963.[1] The WA 1963 does not differentiate between British subjects and foreigners, nor is the application of the Act

confined to movables but is largely confined to the formalities for the execution of wills.[2] The WA 1963 provides that the execution of a will (which includes any testamentary instrument or act) must conform to the internal law[3] either where it is executed, or where the testator is domiciled, or had his habitual residence at the time of its execution or his death, or where at either of those times he was a national.[4] This wide choice of jurisdiction would seem effectively to exclude any application of the doctrine of *renvoi*. In addition and without prejudice to the above the execution of a will on a vessel or aircraft is sufficient if it conforms to the law of the registration of the vessel or aircraft.[5] Where a law in force outside the United Kingdom falls to be applied to a will, any requirement as to execution by testators of a particular description or as to witnesses possessing certain qualifications shall be treated as formal.[6]

1   WA 1963, s 7(2); see Vol 2, Part G, para **[244.81]**; by the WA 1963, s 6(1) 'will' includes any testamentary instrument or act, and 'testator' is construed accordingly.
2   The WA 1963, s 4 is however concerned with the construction of wills; see Chapter 24.
3   'Internal law' means the law which would apply in a case where no question of the law in force in any other territory or state arose. 'State' means a territory or group of territories having its own law of nationality: WA 1963, s 6(1).
4   WA 1963, s 1. This, of course, significantly widens the provision beyond domicile.
5   WA 1963, s 2(1)(a).
6   WA 1963, s 3. The conflict of laws rules relating to wills were discussed at the Hague Convention on succession and a Consultative Paper was published in February 1990.

[23.10]
Capacity. The WA 1963 does not expressly deal with capacity and thus the general rule that capacity to make a will is founded by the law of the testator's domicile would seem to apply.[1]

1   See Scarman J in *Re Fuld's Estate (No 3), Hartley v Fuld* [1968] P 675 at 696.

III.   FORMALITIES: IMMOVABLES

[23.11]
Realty in England, pre-1964. Previously, wills of real estate in England, whether made by a British subject or a foreigner, had to be executed in accordance with English law if they were to be admitted to probate,[1] and the same rule applied to wills of leaseholds and chattels real in England where the testator was not a British subject and died domiciled abroad.[2]

1   *Freke v Lord Carbery* (1873) LR 16 Eq 461.
2   *De Fogassieras v Duport* (1881) 11 LR IR 123; *Pepin v Bruyere* [1902] 1 Ch 24; *Re Von Brentano's Estate* [1911] P 172.

[23.12]
Immovables wherever situate, post-1964. Now, by virtue of the WA 1963, a will of immovables wherever situate must be made either in the form required by the law of the place where they are situate,[1] or according to the formalities of any of the alternatives applicable to movable property set out above. Such a will must not violate restrictions placed upon the disposition of immovables by that

law,[2] such as, in the case of English land, the perpetuity rule,[3] and the law relating to accumulations.[4]

1   WA 1963, s 2(1)(b), which is stated to be without prejudice to s 1, supra; *Coppin v Coppin* (1725) 2 P Wms 291; *Pepin v Bruyere* [1902] 1 Ch 24; *De Fogassieras v Duport* (1881) 11 LR Ir 123. An executor can sell land before probate and this applies to foreign land so long as the will is executed according to the law of the country where the land is situated and there is nothing to prevent it in that law: *National Trust Co v Mendelson* [1942] 1 DLR 438.
2   As to capacity to make the will, see *Re Hernando, Hernando v Sawtell* (1884) 27 Ch D 284. As to material validity, see *Freke v Lord Carbery* (1873) LR 16 Eq 461; *Duncan v Lawson* (1889) 41 Ch D 394; *Re Piercy, Whitwham v Piercy* [1895] 1 Ch 83.
3   *Re Grassi, Stubberfield v Grassi* [1905] 1 Ch 584 at 592.
4   *Re Grassi, Stubberfield v Grassi* [1905] 1 Ch 584; *Re Moses, Moses v Valentine* [1908] 2 Ch 235.

IV.   REVOCATION

[23.13]
By a later will. A will that is valid in accordance with the rules in the WA 1963, s 1, set out above, will be effective to revoke a previous will.[1] Further, without prejudice to this general proposition, it is provided that a will, so far as it revokes a will which would be treated as properly executed under the 1963 Act, or revokes a provision which would be treated as comprised in a properly executed will under the 1963 Act, shall be treated as properly executed if the execution of the later will conformed to any law by reference to which the revoked will or provision would be so treated.[2] It seems that a disposition of real estate in an English will made in accordance with English law is not revoked by a revocation clause in a foreign will made according to foreign law.[3] With regard to property other than English real estate revocation is governed by the law of the place where the deceased died domiciled.[4]

1   By virtue of the definition of will in the WA 1963, s 6.
2   WA 1963, s 2(1)(c); *Cottrell v Cottrell* (1872) LR 2 P & D 397; *Velasco v Coney* [1934] P 143; *Re Barker, Nemes v Barker* [1995] 2 VR 439 (the question of whether a German will was intended to affect an Australian will was to be determined as a matter of evidence according to the lex fori).
3   *Re Alberti's Estate* [1955] 3 All ER 730n, [1955] 1 WLR 1240.
4   *Re Martin, Loustalan v Loustalan* [1900] P 211; *Re Annesley, Davidson v Annesley* [1926] Ch 692; *Re Reid's Goods* (1866) LR 1 P & D 74.

[23.14]
By destruction. Whether a will is revoked by destruction depends on the law of the testator's domicile at the time of the alleged act of destruction.[1] If there has been a change in the domicile between the alleged act of destruction and the death, the better view is that the law of the domicile at the date of the act should apply.[2]

1   See Dicey and Morris, *The Conflict of Laws* (12th edn), p 1034.
2   See *Velasco v Coney* [1934] P 143.

[23.15]
By marriage. The WA 1963 contains no express provision relevant to revocation by marriage, which is thus subject to the general laws. Where,

however, by the law of the domicile, marriage does not revoke a testamentary disposition, a subsequent change of the domicile of the testator or testatrix does not affect its validity.[1]

1   See *Westerman's Executor v Schwab* (1905) 8 F 132 (woman domiciled in England made a will and married a man domiciled in Scotland, the will was governed by Scots law and was not revoked); *Re Reid's Goods* (1866) LR 1 P & D 74 (man domiciled in Scotland made a will and married, will was not revoked, although he later gained an English domicile); *Re Groos' Estate* [1904] P 269 (testatrix domiciled in Holland at date of will and married a man domiciled in Holland, will not revoked although subsequently she became domiciled in England and so died). Only the domicile at the time of the marriage is of importance and the will is revoked or not according as the law of the domicile provides for revocation of a will by marriage or does not so provide.

V.   INTESTATE SUCCESSION

[23.16]

Movables. The succession to the movables of a person who dies intestate[1] is governed by the law of the deceased's domicile at the time of his death.[2] The entitlement of the Crown or the State to intestate estates where there is no heir is likewise governed by the law of the domicile provided the Crown or the State takes as *ultimus haeres*[3] and not as *jus regale*.[4]

1   See generally Sherrin and Bonehill, *The Law and Practice of Intestate Succession* (2nd edn), Chapter 16.
2   *Re Maldonado's Estate, State of Spain v Treasury Solicitor* [1954] P 223 at 245. The rule has been established for over 200 years, see Barnard J [1954] P 223 at 266; *Pipon v Pipon* (1744) Amb 25; *Duncan v Lawson* (1889) 41 Ch D 394; *Freke v Lord Carbery* (1873) LR 16 Eq 461; *Balfour v Scott* (1793) 6 Bro Parl Cas 550; *Ewing v Orr Ewing* (1885) 10 App Cas 453; *Re Ralston* [1906] VLR 689; *Re Collens, Royal Bank of Canada (London) Ltd v Krogh* [1986] Ch 505, [1986] 1 All ER 611; *Re Barnett's Trusts* [1902] 1 Ch 847 at 856, 857.
3   See *Re Maldonado's Estate, State of Spain v Treasury Solicitor* [1954] P 223, and *Re Mitchell, Hatton v Jones* [1954] Ch 525, [1954] 2 All ER 246.
4   The older pre-1925 view was that the Crown or State took by virtue of a *jus regale* and thus took the property within its jurisdiction whatever the domicile of the deceased, see *Re Barnett's Trusts* [1902] 1 Ch 847; *Re Musurus's Estate* [1936] 2 All ER 1666.

[23.17]

Immovables. Intestate succession to immovables is governed by the *lex situs* or *lex loci*.[1]

1   *Duncan v Lawson* (1889) 41 Ch D 394; *Freke v Lord Carbery* (1873) LR 16 Eq 461; *Gentili's Goods* (1875) IR 9 Eq 541; *Balfour v Scott* (1793) 6 Bro Parl Cas 550; *Re Osoba, Osoba v Osoba* [1978] 2 All ER 1099, [1978] 1 WLR 791; *Re Collens, Royal Bank of Canada (London) Ltd v Krogh* [1986] Ch 505, [1986] 1 All ER 611, *Re Rea, Rea v Rea* [1902] 1 IR 451.

VI.   PREPARATION OF THE WILL

[23.18]

Foreign testator. If the intending testator has a foreign domicile then, in accordance with the rules above, any will of movable property should be made according to the law of the person's domicile. In most cases English practitioners will not feel competent to undertake this task and the client will be referred to a lawyer in the country of his domicile or a foreign lawyer will be appointed as agent for this purpose. If the intending testator has an English domicile but immovable property situated in a foreign jurisdiction then the English will should clearly be confined to movable property and immovable property situated in England and Wales.[1] A separate will or wills should be prepared by a foreign lawyer restricted to the immovable property situated within that jurisdiction. If there is evidence that such an intending testator previously made a will or wills then care must be exercised to ensure that the previous will or wills, are correctly revoked according to the rules set out above. Advice will need to be sought where foreign elements are involved, as to the effect on the will of the rules of essential validity and construction which might be applicable to the will.

1   *Re Osoba, Osoba v Osoba* [1978] 1 WLR 791 at 796.

VII.   OBTAINING GRANTS

[23.19]
Deceased domiciled in England and Wales. If the deceased has left a separate will to deal with assets which are situated abroad, then such a will will normally be in the form of the foreign jurisdiction and a local practitioner should be instructed to obtain formal proof of the will in accordance with local procedures.

[23.20]
Deceased domiciled outside England and Wales. Where there are assets in England and Wales then a grant should be obtained here so that they can be effectively dealt with. The Non-Contentious Probate Rules 1987, r 30[1] will apply as to which reference should be made to specialist texts.[2]

1   SI 1987/2024.
2   See *Tristram and Coote's Probate Practice* (28th edn, Butterworths).

VIII.   INTERNATIONAL WILL

[23.21]
The Administration of Justice Act 1982 (AJA 1982)[1] gives legislative effect in the United Kingdom to the Convention Providing a Uniform Law on the Form of an International Will.[2] The statutory provisions are to come into force on a day to be appointed jointly by the Lord Chancellor and the Home Secretary.[3] It will be appreciated that this form of international will is to be acceptable in addition to the existing forms of wills in each country.[4] Such a will might be advantageous where the testator has assets in more than one of the signatory countries.[5]

The formal requirements of an international will are to be found in the Annex[6] to the Convention and if complied with it is stated that such a will shall be valid as regards form irrespective particularly of the place where it is made, of the location of the assets and of the nationality, domicile or residence of the testator.[7] The formalities prescribed are that the will shall be in writing in any language by hand or any other means, but that it need not be written by the testator himself.[8] The testator must declare in the presence of two witnesses and of a person authorised to act in connection with international wills that the document is his will and that he knows the contents but it is not necessary for the witnesses or the authorised person to know the contents of the will.[9] In the presence of the authorised person and the witnesses, the testator must sign, or, acknowledge a previous signature.[10]

The witnesses and the authorised person there and then attest the will by signing in the presence of the testator.[11] The signatures must be placed at the end of the will and where there is more than one sheet, the sheets are to be numbered and each signed.[12] It will be noticed that these formalities envisage a central and crucial role to be played by 'the authorised person' who in continental countries would be a notary. The AJA 1982, s 28 provides that the persons authorised to act in the United Kingdom in this capacity are solicitors and notaries public. Such persons can under the Convention draw up a certificate in prescribed form which will establish that the formalities prescribed above have been complied with.[13] International wills are subject to the ordinary rules of revocation of wills.[14] These wills can be deposited and registered under the provisions of the AJA 1982[15] and in accordance with regulations thereunder to be drawn up.[16]

1 AJA 1982, ss 27, 28 and Sch 2; 50 *Halsbury's Statutes* (4th edn), 620, 621, 624; see Vol 2, Part G, para **[244.103]**.
2 Drawn up in Washington DC in October 1973 under the auspices of the International Institute for the Unification of Private Law.
3 AJA 1982, s 76(5), (6).
4 The invalidity of the will as an international will is not to affect its formal validity as a will of another kind, Article 2, Annex to Convention.
5 A number of countries have ratified the Convention but each must incorporate the Uniform Law into its own law (as the AJA 1982, s 27 does in the United Kingdom) before the international will will be accepted in those countries.
6 Which is set out in the AJA 1982, Sch 2 and incorporated by s 27.
7 Article 1.
8 Article 3. It would appear from Articles 5 and 6 that another person may sign on his behalf.
9 Article 4.
10 Article 5. Where the testator is unable to sign he must indicate the reason therefor to the authorised person who makes note of this on the will. Moreover the testator may be authorised by the law under which the authorised person was designated to direct another person to sign on his behalf.
11 Article 5.
12 Article 6. There are provisions relating to the date in Article 7, and to the safekeeping of the will in Article 8.
13 Articles 9, 10, 11, 12. The absence of a certificate does not however affect the formal validity of a will under these provisions; Article 13.
14 Article 14.
15 AJA 1982, s 28(3), (4), referring to s 23.
16 AJA 1982, s 28(5), (6), referring to s 25.

CHAPTER 24

Wills with a foreign element: essential validity and construction and exercise of powers of appointment

I. ESSENTIAL VALIDITY

[24.1]
Material or essential validity. The rules set out in the previous chapter and largely embodied in the Wills Act 1963, govern only the formal validity of the will. Once the will has been admitted to proof as a matter of form it will become subject to the principles of the relevant jurisdiction governing the essential validity of the dispositions it contains. An obvious example is the restriction on testamentary freedom provided by jurisdictions embracing systems of fixed rights of inheritance, as in Scotland, or *la reserve*, as in French law. A person domiciled in England may make a will valid as to form according to English law but which will be subject to the effects of the operation of these principles according to the foreign law.[1]

1 See Dicey and Morris, *The Conflict of Laws* (12th edn), p 1034 citing *Thornton v Curling* (1824) 8 Sim 310; *Campbell v Beaufoy* (1859) John 320; *Re Annesley, Davidson v Annesley* [1926] Ch 692; *Whicker v Hume* (1858) 7 HL Cas 124; *Re Adams, Bank of Ireland Trustee Co Ltd v Adams, Hutchings and Parker* [1967] IR 424.

[24.2]
Rules applicable. The essential validity of a will of movables, or of a gift of movables is governed by the law of the testator's domicile at the time of his death.[1] The essential validity of a will of immovables or of a gift of immovables, is governed by the law of the country where the immovables are situated, the *lex situs*.[2] It is the domicile at the time of death, not at the time of the will, which is applicable, so that a change of domicile after the will is made can affect the essential validity of the dispositions contained in the will.[3]

1 See Dicey and Morris, *The Conflict of Laws* (12th edn), p 1034 citing *Whicker v Hume* (1858) 7 HL Cas 124; *Thornton v Curling* (1824) 8 Sim 310; *Campbell v Beaufoy* (1859) John 320; *Macdonald v Macdonald* (1872) LR 14 Eq 60; *Re Groos, Groos v Groos* [1915] 1 Ch 572; *Re Annesley, Davidson v Annesley* [1926] Ch 692; *Re Ross, Ross v Waterfield* [1930] 1 Ch 377; *Re Priest, Belfield v Duncan* [1944] Ch 58; *Philipson-Stow v IRC* [1961] AC 727, [1960] 3 All ER 814; *Re Levick's Will Trusts, Ffennell v IRC* [1963] 1 All ER 95, [1963] 1 WLR 311; *Haque v Haque* (1962) 108 CLR 230; and *Re Adams, Bank of Ireland Trustee Co Ltd v Adams, Hutchings and Parker* [1967] IR 424. See also *Re Berger* [1990] Ch 118, [1989] 1 All ER 591.

2   See Dicey and Morris, *The Conflict of Laws* (12th edn), p 1037 citing *Earl Nelson v Lord Bridport* (1846) 8 Beav 547; *Freke v Lord Carbery* (1873) LR 16 Eq 461; *Duncan v Lawson* (1889) 41 Ch D 394; *Re Moses, Moses v Valentine* [1908] 2 Ch 235; *Re Hoyles, Row v Jagg* [1911] 1 Ch 179; *Re Miller, Bailie v Miller* [1914] 1 Ch 511; *Re Ross, Ross v Waterfield* [1930] 1 Ch 377 and *Haque v Haque* (1962) 108 CLR 230.

3   *Re Groos, Groos v Groos* [1915] 1 Ch 572.

[24.3]

Matters of essential validity. Example of such essential validity include the following: restrictions on testamentary freedom[1] and the application of the English Inheritance (Provision for Family and Dependants) Act 1975 (I(PFD)A 1975);[2] whether a gift to charity is valid;[3] the application of rules of perpetuity and accumulation;[4] whether a gift to an attesting witness is void;[5] rules governing commorientes[6] and rules governing the enjoyment of property *in specie*.[7]

1   See the cases cited in para **[24.1]**, n 1 supra.
2   The statute limits its application to persons who die domiciled in England, I(PFD)A 1975, s 1(1); see *Mastaka v Midland Bank Executor and Trustee Co Ltd* [1941] Ch 192, sub nom *Re White* [1941] 1 All ER 236.
3   *Macdonald v Macdonald* (1872) LR 14 Eq 60.
4   *Freke v Lord Carbery* (1873) LR 16 Eq 461.
5   *Re Priest, Belfield v Duncan* [1944] Ch 58, [1944] 1 All ER 51.
6   *Re Cohn* [1945] Ch 5.
7   *Re Moses, Moses v Valentine* [1908] 2 Ch 235.

[24.4]

Legatee. It has been stated, in the absence of authority, that the law of the legatee's domicile should determine whether he or she is of full age and capacity to receive a legacy.[1]

1   See Dicey and Morris, *The Conflict of Laws* (12th edn), p 1028.

[24.5]

Validity of testamentary trusts. The initial validity of a trust contained in a will depends on the validity of the will, so that if for any reason the will is not recognised as valid any purported constitution of a trust by vesting the trust property in the trustees also fails.[1] An attempted constitution of a trust may be affected by matters relating to the essential validity of the will; for example, if the applicable jurisdiction restricts the freedom of testamentary disposition, a disposition on trust in the will, will likewise be restricted and may fail for that reason.[2]

But once the trust has been successfully constituted by the will, ie once the property has been vested in the trustees then questions relating to the validity and operation of the trust provisions are governed by the Convention on the Law Applicable to Trusts and on their Recognition which was brought into force by the Recognition of Trusts Act 1987.[3] The Convention is concerned with the recognition of trusts, including testamentary trusts, but not with the recognition of wills per se.

A trust is governed by the law chosen by the settlor if any,[4] alternatively by the law with which it is most closely connected.[5] For the latter purpose regard is had to the place of administration of the trust designated by the settlor; the situs of the assets of the trust; the place of residence or business of the trustee and the objects of the trust and the places where they are to be fulfilled.[6] Article 8 of the Convention provides that the law specified by Article 6 or 7 is to govern the validity of the trust, its construction, its effect and the administration of the trust.[7]

1   See Dicey and Morris, *The Conflict of Laws* (12th edn), p 1090.
2   Dicey and Morris, *The Conflict of Laws* (12th edn), p 1090.
3   Following the Hague Convention 15th Session of the Hague Conference, 1986. For a full explanatory note see Dicey and Morris, *The Conflict of Laws* (12th edn), pp 1088–1097.
4   Article 6 of the Convention. See the cases noted in Dicey and Morris, *The Conflict of Laws* (12th edn), p 1090.
5   Article 7. See the cases noted, Dicey and Morris, *The Conflict of Laws* (12th edn), p 1091.
6   Article 7. See the cases noted, Dicey and Morris, *The Conflict of Laws* (12th edn), pp 1091–1092.
7   See Dicey and Morris, *The Conflict of Laws* (12th edn), p 1092.

II. CONSTRUCTION

[24.6]
Law governing construction. As a general rule, wills of movables must be construed with reference to the law of the place which was the domicile of the testator at his death.[1] Where, however, there appears on the face of the will an intention that it should be construed by reference to some other law, that law will govern the construction.[2] For example, where technical expressions peculiar to a foreign law are used, that law and not the law of the domicile may determine the construction,[3] but the presence of a few such technical expressions may not by itself be a sufficient indication of the testator's intention to induce the court to construe the will with reference to the law to which such expressions belong,[4] and where it is shown that no technical rules of construction are applied to words by the law of the domicile, no reference to that law is necessary, and the will must be construed according to English rules of construction.[5] The construction of a will is not altered by reason of any change in the testator's domicile after the execution of the will.[6]

1   *Nisbett v Murray* (1799) 5 Ves 149; *Bradford v Young* (1884) 26 Ch D 656; on appeal (1885) 29 Ch D 617, CA; *Re Price, Tomlin v Latter* [1900] 1 Ch 442; *Re Lewal's Settlement Trusts, Gould v Lewal* [1918] 2 Ch 391; *Re Levick's Will Trusts, Ffennell v IRC* [1963] 1 All ER 95, [1963] 1 WLR 311; *Re Lord Cable, Garratt v Waters* [1976] 3 All ER 417, [1977] 1 WLR 7. Where a testator domiciled in Quebec made a will in English form it was to be construed according to the law of Quebec and the English rule that the later of two incompatible clauses is to prevail could not be applied: *Bayer v Montreal Trust Co* [1953] Que SC 89. In a gift of personalty to a person or his heirs, the persons taking under the words 'heirs' must be determined by the law of the domicile of the testator: *Re Collishaw* [1953] 3 DLR 829; *Re Cunnington, Healing v Webb* [1924] 1 Ch 68.
2   *Re Price, Tomlin v Latter* [1900] 1 Ch 442.
3   *Studd v Cook* (1883) 8 App Cas 577; *Re Cliff's Trusts* [1892] 2 Ch 229; *Re Cunnington, Healing v Webb* [1924] 1 Ch 68 (where the rule was not applied); *Re Allen's Estate, Prescott v Allen and Beaumont* [1945] 2 All ER 264 (reference to English law).
4   *Bradford v Young* (1884) 26 Ch D 656.
5   *Bernal v Bernal* (1838) 3 My & Cr 559. As to translations of foreign will, see para **[57.6]** infra.
6   Wills Act 1963, s 4; 50 *Halsbury's Statutes* (4th edn) 610; see Vol 2, para **[244.78]**.

[24.7]
Capacity and knowledge and approval. Where it is necessary to show that the testator knew and approved the contents of the will and that the will was that of a free and capable testator, the law of England must be applied.[1]

1   *Re Fuld's Goods (No 3), Hartley v Fuld* [1968] P 675, [1965] 3 All ER 776.

[24.8]
Immovable property. The Wills Act 1963 (WA 1963), s 4 applies to immovables as well as movables and so it is the law of the domicile at the time of the execution of the will which will govern the construction of the will.[1] This applies notwithstanding a change in the testator's domicile after the execution of the will.[2] But the use of technical language of the *lex situs* may indicate an intention that the construction is to be governed by that law.[3] However, matters of essential validity[4] must be distinguished from matters of construction. Thus whether a child is to be regarded as legitimate or illegitimate is a matter of essential validity; whether illegitimate children can take is a matter of construction.

1   *Philipson-Stow v IRC* [1961] AC 727, [1960] 3 All ER 814.
2   *Philipson-Stow v IRC* [1961] AC 727, [1960] 3 All ER 814.
3   *Bradford v Young* (1885) 29 Ch D 617.
4   See para **[24.1]** supra.

[24.9]
Debts and gifts. In construing a will, debts are usually considered as situated where the debtor is resident,[1] but whether or not a gift in a will is to be construed as being in satisfaction of a previous obligation depends on the testator's domicile, and not on the law governing the obligation.[2]

1   *Arnold v Arnold* (1834) 2 My & K 365. A gift of property in England passes debts due from persons resident in England; *Guthrie v Walrond* (1883) 22 Ch D 573.
2   *Campbell v Campbell* (1866) LR 1 Eq 383; *Re Ogilvie, Ogilvie v Ogilvie* [1918] 1 Ch 492.

[24.10]
Election. Under a will of movables the application of the doctrine of election between testamentary and non-testamentary gifts is governed by the law of the testator's domicile at the date of his death.[1] This is because the doctrine of election is usually regarded as affecting essential validity rather than construction.[2] An heir claiming against the will which purports to make a gift of an immovable, but is valid to bequeath movables, will be put to his election, wherever the law of the testator's domicile so provides,[3] irrespective of the law of the place where the immovable is situated,[4] but where, if the heirs of a foreign land were to elect for the testamentary disposition, it would be impossible according to the lex rei sitae to give effect, or compel legal effect to be given, to such disposition, no election can be imposed.[5]

1   See Dicey and Morris, *The Conflict of Laws* (12th edn), pp 1044–1045; *Re De Nicols, De Nicols v Curlier* [1898] 1 Ch 403; *Re Mengel's Will Trusts, Westminster Bank Ltd v Mengel* [1962] Ch 791, [1962] 2 All ER 490.
2   *Cooper v Cooper* (1874) LR 7 HL 53. Contrast *Re Allen's Estate, Prescott v Allen and Beaumont* [1945] 2 All ER 264.

3   Most of the cases deal with wills of domiciled Englishmen which were invalid to pass Scots real estate. Words referring specifically or by necessary implication to real estate are necessary to put the heir to his election: *Dundas v Dundas* (1830) 2 Dow & Cl 349; *Orrell v Orrell* (1871) 6 Ch App 302. For cases of insufficient indication of intention, see *Maxwell v Maxwell* (1852) 2 De GM & G 705; *Maxwell v Hyslop* (1867) LR 4 Eq 407; *Dewar v Maitland* (1866) LR 2 Eq 834.
4   When the land is out of England, the law of the domicile applies and the heir may be compelled to elect: *Re Ogilvie, Ogilvie v Ogilvie* [1918] 1 Ch 492.
5   *Brown v Gregson* [1920] AC 860.

III.   EXERCISE OF POWER OF APPOINTMENT

[24.11]
Exercise of power by English law. A will exercising a power of appointment must be executed in the manner required for the due execution of the will,[1] and a will so executed, so far as respects execution and attestation, is a valid exercise of the power although other solemnities required by the instrument creating the power are not observed.[2]

1   Wills Act 1837, s 10; 50 *Halsbury's Statutes* (4th edn) 581; see Vol 2, para **[244.8]**. But although the power is well exercised by a will so executed, such will if the testator is domiciled abroad may be revoked without complying with English law and then the exercise of the power fails: *Velasco v Coney* [1934] P 143.
2   WA 1837, s 10. The provision is useful as it empowers a testator by his ordinary will to exercise powers arising under various instruments. The provision applies to testamentary powers only, so that if there is not time to examine the instrument creating the power, it may be advisable to execute the will under seal to give validity to the exercise of the power, if it should turn out to be exercisable only by deed.

[24.12]
Donee domiciled abroad. Where the provisions of the Wills Act 1837 do not apply (eg where the donee is not domiciled in England),[1] then, so far as it exercises a power of appointment, the power shall be treated as validly exercised if the execution of the will conforms with any of the alternatives set out in the WA 1963, s 1 or if it conforms to the law governing the essential validity of the power.[2] Further a will so far as it exercises a power of appointment shall not be treated as improperly executed by reason only that its execution was not in accordance with any formal requirements contained in the instrument creating the power.[3] If an appointment under a special power is valid by English law, no restrictions placed by the law of the testator's domicile on the power of disposition can have any effect, the reason being that such restrictions apply to property and a power of appointment is not property.[4] But in the case of a general power, if by blending the settled funds with his free estate the testator has shown an intention that the settled funds should be treated as part of the free estate, then the settled funds are subject to the law of the testator's domicile.[5] Thus any restrictions placed by the law of the domicile on the power of disposition will apply.[6]

1   *Bremer v Freeman* (1857) 10 Moo PCC 306; *Re Price, Tomlin v Latter* [1900] 1 Ch 442.
2   WA 1963, s 2(1)(d); 50 *Halsbury's Statutes* (4th edn) 609; see Vol 2, para **[244.76]**. This statute only applies to wills of testators who die after 1 January 1964, WA 1963, s 7(4).
3   WA 1963, s 2(2). Formerly an appointment by will had to comply with the terms of the power: *Barretto v Young* [1900] 2 Ch 339. But where in such cases the terms of the power had been complied with or no special formalities had been prescribed, it would seem that the power, whether general or special (*Re Price, Tomlin v Latter* [1900] 1 Ch 442; *Pouey v Hordern* [1900] 1 Ch 492) might have been well exercised by the donee's will, if that was intended to take effect according to English law; *Re D'Este's Settlement Trusts, Poulter v D'Este* [1903] 1 Ch 898; *Re Simpson, Coutts & Co v Church Missionary Society* [1916] 1 Ch 502; *Re Wilkinson's Settlement, Butler v Wilkinson* [1917] 1 Ch 620; *Re Strong, Strong v Meissner* (1925) 95 LJ Ch 22.
4   *Pouey v Hordern* [1900] 1 Ch 492 and cases in the next footnote. For further comment on the essential validity of an exercise by will of a power of appointment, see Dicey and Morris, *The Conflict of Laws* (12th edn), pp 1060–1063.
5   *Re Pryce, Lawford v Pryce* [1911] 2 Ch 286 (testatrix domiciled in Holland had a general power of appointment by will over funds in England subject to an English settlement; she made a will in Dutch form exercising the power in such a manner as to make the property her assets for all purposes; held, to be subject to a restriction under Dutch law limiting the power of disposition to seven-eighths), distinguishing *Re Mégret, Tweedie v Maunder* [1901] 1 Ch 547, where all the property was not dealt with as one mass. Followed in *Re Khan's Settlement, Coutts & Co v Senior Dowager Begum of Bhopal* [1966] Ch 567, [1966] 1 All ER 160 (testator of foreign domicile executed a settlement in England under which he reserved to himself a general power of appointment by will; exercised the power in favour of his heirs under domiciliary law; held, that the testator had blended the settled funds with his free estate, therefore, the settled funds were subject to the law of his domicile) considering *Re Pinede's Settlement* (1879) 12 Ch D 667; *Coxen v Rowland* [1894] 1 Ch 406; *Re Marten, Shaw v Marten* [1902] 1 Ch 314, CA; *Re Hadley, Johnson v Hadley* [1909] 1 Ch 20; *O'Grady v Wilmot* [1916] 2 AC 231, HL. Not following *Re Waite's Settlement Trusts, Westminster Bank Ltd v Brouard* [1958] Ch 100, [1957] 1 All ER 629, where it was held that restrictions imposed by the domiciliary law did not affect the appointed property even though that property had been blended with his free estate.
6   *Re Pryce, Lawford v Pryce* [1911] 2 Ch 286; *Re Khan's Settlement, Coutts & Co v Senior Dowager Begum of Bhopal* [1966] Ch 567, [1966] 1 All ER 160.

[24.13]
Immovables. But the material or essential validity of an exercise by will of a power of appointment over immovables depends on the law of the country where the immovables are situated, the *lex situs*.[1]

1   *Re Pryce, Lawford v Pryce* [1911] 2 Ch 286, citing *Re Hernando, Hernando v Sawtell* (1884) 27 Ch D 284.

[24.14]
Revocation. The revocation of the exercise of a testamentary power is governed by the law applicable to the execution of the later will or to the manner of revocation, by for example, destruction.[1]

1   See para **[23.13]** supra; *Velasco v Coney* [1934] P 143.

[24.15]
Capacity of the testator. If the testator has capacity by the law of his domicile when he makes the will, then the will can validly exercise a power of appointment over English property, even though the testator has no capacity to make a will under English law.[1]

1   *Re Lewal's Settlement Trusts, Gould v Lewal* [1918] 2 Ch 391.

[24.16]

Effect of general residuary bequest. By the Wills Act 1837, s 27,[1] a general residuary bequest will operate as an execution of a general power of appointment unless a contrary intention appears. A general residuary bequest in an ordinary English will, therefore, duly exercises a general power of appointment without reference to the power of the property subject to the power. In the case of foreign wills it was at one time held that a general residuary bequest was insufficient for this purpose unless it specifically referred to the power or indicated that it was to be construed according to English law, but modern decisions have established that a foreign will valid according to the law of the domicile is governed by the Wills Act 1837, s 27, and is, therefore, a valid exercise of a general power of appointment unless the contrary appears.[2] The correct approach is first to interpret the will according to its proper law, and then, having ascertained the donee's intention, to consider as a matter of English law whether the effect of that intention is that the donee has made a 'bequest' of personalty within the meaning of the Wills Act 1837, s 27. Thus, where under the proper law the will's provisions are of a restrictive character and no positive rights have been conferred on anyone, the will contains no 'bequest' within the meaning of s 27 and therefore a power of appointment would not have been exercised.[3] It now seems the better view that in a will admitted to probate only by virtue of Lord Kingsdown's Act[4] or the Wills Act 1963, a general residuary bequest is a valid exercise of a general power of appointment.[5]

1   See Vol 2, Part G, para **[244.27]**.
2   *Re Simpson, Coutts & Co v Church Missionary Society* [1916] 1 Ch 502; *Re Wilkinson's Settlement, Butler v Wilkinson* [1917] 1 Ch 620; *Re Lewal's Settlement Trusts, Gould v Lewal* [1918] 2 Ch 391; *Re Strong, Strong v Meissner* (1925) 95 LJ Ch 22; *Re Harman, Lloyd v Tardy* [1894] 3 Ch 607; *Re Waite's Settlement Trusts, Westminster Bank Ltd v Brouard* [1958] Ch 100, [1957] 1 All ER 629, where the decision in *Re Lewal's Settlement Trusts* was considered and distinguished. *Re Waite's Settlement Trusts*, was not followed in *Re Khan's Settlement, Coutts & Co v Senior Dowager Begum of Bhopal* [1966] Ch 567, [1966] 1 All ER 160.
3   *Re Fenston's Settlement, Max-Muller v Simonsen* [1971] 3 All ER 1092, [1971] 1 WLR 1640 (donee, a Danish subject, made a will in Danish form held not to exercise a power of appointment given to the donee under an English settlement) applying *Re Simpson, Coutts & Co v Church Missionary Society* [1916] 1 Ch 502.
4   Wills Act 1861; see Vol 2, Part G, para **[244.41]**.
5   See also Chapter 39.

[24.17]

Document purporting to be a will. A document purporting to be a will, executed in accordance with the form required by the instrument creating the power, is valid as an execution of the power, though it may be invalid as a will by the law of the domicile.[1] Such a document (unless saved by statute) is admissible to probate only for the purpose of executing the power and for no other purpose.

1   *Re Huber's Goods* [1896] P 209; *Murphy v Deichler* [1909] AC 446.

[24.18]

Evidence. The question whether or not the power had been validly exercised cannot be determined by evidence not admissible by English law, although such evidence would have been admitted by the law of the testator's domicile.[1]

1   *Re Scholefield, Scholefield v St John* [1905] 2 Ch 408 (where it was sought to introduce documents showing an intention to deal with the property subject to the power). The case was compromised on appeal [1907] 1 Ch 664, CA.

Executors, trustees and guardians

CHAPTER 25

Executors

[25.1]
Appointment of executor.[1] An executor is the person appointed by the will to administer the property of the testator and to carry into effect the provisions of the will.[2] The ordinary method of appointing an executor is for the testator to name in his will a specific person to be his executor. The clause or provision appointing the executor or executors must be in the body of the will and a direction beneath the testator's signature has been held to be ineffective.[3] If any question arises as to the identity of a person so named, the court can have regard to extrinsic evidence to resolve such a question.[4] This could include evidence of intention to resolve but not to create the ambiguity if latent.[5] Where the description can be regarded as a patent ambiguity, as being applicable in all its parts to two or more persons, then extrinsic evidence, including evidence of intention can be adduced.[6] Where there is a person exactly answering the name and description, the court will not admit evidence to show that some other person was intended.[7] The court has power where, by reason of the insolvency of the estate of the deceased or of any other special circumstances, it appears necessary or expedient, to pass over the executor named in the will and grant letters of administration with the will annexed to such person as the court thinks expedient.[8] Thus the court, acting under this provision, has passed over the testator's widow, who had been convicted of his manslaughter and sentenced to life imprisonment, and made a grant to his daughters.[9] There may be such uncertainty as to the person intended that the appointment is entirely void on the ground of uncertainty.[10] A corporation may be named as executor. A testator may authorise another to nominate an executor of his will, and effect will be given to such nomination;[11] and the person to nominate may nominate himself.[12] The number of executors is limited to four.[13]

The expression 'executor de son tort' (although it should perhaps more properly be an administrator de son tort) is applied to a person who takes possession of, or intermeddles with, any of the deceased's assets as if he were an executor or administrator but without taking out any grant of probate or letters of administration.[14]

---

1   See *Tristram and Coote's Probate Practice* (28th edn), Chapter 4. The Non-Contentious Probate Rules 1987 (SI 1987/2024) replaced the 1954 Rules with effect from 1 January 1988. The new rules reflect changes in the law and practice over the past thirty years and include a provision to ensure that executors not joining in an application for a grant of probate are nevertheless notified of the application: SI 1987/2024, r 27. There is also a provision for the grant of administration to a person acting as attorney under a registered enduring power of

attorney: SI 1987/2024, r 35. Provision is no longer made requiring a guarantee as a condition of granting letters of administration.

See *Practice Direction* [1988] 1 All ER 192, [1988] 1 WLR 195; notice of application where power reserved.

2 A personal representative is not the agent of the deceased; he derives his powers not on the authority given to him by the deceased but on the authority given to him by law to stand in the place of the deceased: *Rickless v United Artists Corpn* [1988] QB 40, [1987] 1 All ER 679.

3 *Re Woods' Goods* (1868) LR 1 P & D 556; *Re Dallow's Goods* (1866) LR 1 P & D 189. See also cases in note r p 80, 5th Edition.

4 See the Administration of Justice Act 1982 (AJA 1982), s 21, fully discussed in Chapter 57. For pre-AJA 1982 case law see: *Grant v Grant* (1869) LR 2 P & D 8; *Re De Rosaz's Goods* (1877) 2 PD 66; *Re Twohill's Goods* (1879) 3 LR Ir 21; *Re Brake's Goods* (1881) 6 PD 217.

5 AJA 1982, s 21. For pre-AJA 1982 case law see *Re Twohill's Goods* (1879) 3 LR Ir 21; *Re Chappell's Goods* [1894] P 98.

6 AJA 1982, s 21 For pre-AJA 1982 case law see: *Re Ashton's Goods* [1892] P 83; *Re Hubbuck's Estate* [1905] P 129.

7 *Re Peel's Goods* (1870) LR 2 P & D 46.

8 Supreme Court of Judicature (Consolidation) Act 1925, s 162; 13 *Halsbury's Statutes* (3rd edn) 101–102; see now the Supreme Court Act 1981, s 116; 17 *Halsbury's Statutes* (4th edn) 540. See for example, *Re Clore, IRC v Stype Instruments (Jersey) Ltd* [1982] Ch 456, [1982] 3 All ER 419; *Re Mathew* [1984] 2 All ER 396, [1984] 1 WLR 1011.

9 *Re S's Estate* [1968] P 302, [1967] 2 All ER 150.

10 *Re Baylis' Goods* (1862) 2 Sw & Tr 613; *Re Blackwell's Goods* (1877) 2 PD 72. The court will not accept a shifting appointment, as the manager for the time being of a company: *Re Were's Will* (1886) 12 VLR 271.

11 *Re Cringan's Goods* (1828) 1 Hag Ecc 548; *Re Deichman's Goods* (1842) 3 Curt 123. This power is unaffected by the Wills Act 1837; *Jackson and Gill v Paulet* (1851) 2 Rob Eccl 344; *Bradley v Saunders* (1906) Cout 380; *Re Hadden's Will* (1879) 5 VLR 91; *Re Macgregor's Will* (1901) 1 SRNSW 50; *Re Cleghorn* [1931] 2 DLR 865.

12 *Re Ryder's Goods* (1861) 2 Sw & Tr 127.

13 There is no actual limitation on the number who may be appointed but probate will not be granted to more than four in respect of any one part of the estate: Supreme Court Act 1981, s 114; 17 *Halsbury's Statutes* (4th edn) 539. Where four general and one literary executors were appointed, it was held under the Supreme Court of Judicature (Consolidation) Act 1925, s 160(1) that the grant could only go to four and one must renounce: *Re Holland's Estate* [1936] 3 All ER 13. In view of the change in wording in the Supreme Court Act 1981, s 114, this decision is now obsolete.

14 See most recently *James v Williams* [1999] 3 All ER 309 where the authorities are discussed. It is interesting to note that on the facts of that case the court found a constructive trust so that the intermeddler became a trustee. See also *Pollard v Jackson* (1993) 67 P & CR 327.

[25.2]

Implied appointment—executor according to the tenor. Where a testator fails to nominate a person to be his executor, any person who upon the terms of the will has been appointed to perform the essential duties of an executor is called an executor according to the tenor and is entitled to a grant of probate.[1] The following have been held to be executors according to the tenor: a residuary legatee who was also appointed to discharge all lawful demands against the estate;[2] a person given the personal estate upon trust for conversion and division among children where the will also contained a direction that all just debts and funeral and testamentary expenses were to be satisfied as soon as conveniently may be after the decease of the testator;[3] a person appointed to pay all just debts of the testator;[4] a person appointed 'trustee', where that word is used in a loose sense, but it must be implied from the will that the person named as trustee is required to pay the debts of the testator and generally to administer his estate;[5] a person appointed guardian of infant children.[6] A person may be executor according to the tenor even in a case where there are persons expressly appointed executors.[7]

1   *Re Collett's Goods* (1857) Dea & Sw 274; *Re Adamson's Goods* (1875) LR 3 P & D 253; *Re Brown's Goods* (1910) 54 Sol Jo 478. The essential duties are: getting in the estate, payment of funeral expenses and debts and the discharge of legacies: *Re Adamson's Goods* (1875) LR 3 P & D 253. An executor according to the tenor is entitled to a grant of probate: *Wankford v Wankford* (1699) 1 Salk 299 at 309.

2   *Grant v Leslie* (1819) 3 Phillim 116; *Re Brown's Goods* (1912) 31 NZLR 272; *Re Zei's Will* (1877) 3 VLR 110. The universal legatee without any such direction is only entitled to a grant of administration with the will annexed: *Re Oliphant's Goods* (1860) 1 Sw & Tr 525; *Re Pryse's Goods* [1904] P 301; *Re McMillan* [1925] 3 WWR 584.

3   *Re Baylis' Goods* (1865) LR 1 P & D 21. A direction to pay debts is not indispensable: *Re M'Kane's Goods* (1887) 21 LR Ir 1. A person appointed to 'see that wishes are carried out' is not a person appointed to carry them out and so not executor according to the tenor: *Re Branson* (1911) 31 NZLR 79.

4   *Re Cook's Goods* [1902] P 114; *Re Wilkinson's Goods* [1892] P 227; *Re Way's Goods* [1901] P 345. A direction to legatee to pay debts has been held only to make the legacy subject to debts and not to make the legatee executor according to the tenor; *Re Murphy's Goods* (1868) 18 LT 63.

5   *Re Leven's and Earl Melville's Goods* (1889) 15 PD 22; *Re Russell's Goods* [1892] P 380; *Re Kirby's Goods* [1902] P 188; *Re Shaw's Goods* (1895) 73 LT 192; *Re Nussey's Goods* (1898) 78 LT 169; *Re Love's Goods* (1881) 7 LR Ir 178; *Re Mackenzie's Estate* [1909] P 305; *Re Drumm's Goods* [1931] NI 12; *Re Broderick* (1913) 32 NZLR 1193 (no duty assigned to trustee, not executor); but see *Re Thompson* (1943) 44 WALR 75 (sole beneficiaries named as trustees but no mention of executors).

6   *Re Burns' Will* (1903) 4 SRNSW 257.

7   *Re Brown's Goods* (1877) 2 PD 110; *Re Lush's Goods* (1887) 13 PD 20; *Re Wright's Goods* (1908) 25 TLR 15.

[25.3]
Conditional and substituted appointments. A testator may appoint his widow to be executrix so long as she remains his widow. He may appoint his child to the office upon attaining his or her majority. The appointment may be made conditional upon the happening of a certain event.[1] The testator may appoint that upon the happening of a certain event a new executor shall be substituted for one already acting.[2] While the legality of such appointments is not in any doubt, they lead to practical difficulties and so far as possible should be avoided.[3] It is, however, a common and reasonably problem-free practice to include an alternative appointment in case a chosen executor predeceases the testator, or otherwise fails to prove the will.[4]

1   *Re Langford's Goods* (1867) LR 1 P & D 458. Conditions and limitations on the appointment should be resorted to only in the most special circumstances.

2   *Re Johnson's Goods* (1858) 1 Sw & Tr 17 (death in testator's lifetime); *Re Betts' Goods* (1861) 30 LJPM & A 167 (declining to act); *Re Lane's Goods* (1864) 4 New Rep 253 (absence abroad); *Re Foster's Goods* (1871) LR 2 P & D 304 (appointment of wife and 'in default of her' two others).

3   See *Re Hair Estate* [1941] 2 WWR 159.

4   See eg, Vol 2, Form B3.1, para **[203.7]**.

[25.4]
Who may be appointed executor. No restriction whatever has been placed upon the choice of an executor,[1] but probate will not be granted to a minor[2] or a person of unsound mind.[3] If such a person is the sole executor, then a grant of

administration with the will annexed is to a guardian or other person on his behalf; if he be one of several executors, power will be reserved to him to come in and prove after the cesser of the disability. In the case of supervening insanity, the original grant is revoked and a fresh grant issued to the remaining executor.[4] Where any appointed executor to whom a grant has been made is out of the jurisdiction at the expiration of twelve months from the testator's death, a special form of grant of administration is made,[5] and the court has a discretion whether or not to grant probate to a person resident outside the jurisdiction of the court and this discretion is particularly directed to the payment of debts.[6]

1   *Smethurst v Tomlin and Bankes* (1861) 2 Sw & Tr 143 at 147; *Smithson v Smithson* (1915) 33 WLR 230 (alien); *Schulze's Case* 1917 SC 400 (alien enemy); *Re Crolla* 1942 SC 21 (interned British subject). Probate will not be refused on the ground of ill will between the person appointed executor and beneficiaries: *Re Agnew, Brown v Agnew* [1941] 4 DLR 653.
2   See now the Supreme Court Act 1981, s 118; 17 *Halsbury's Statutes* (4th edn) 542. The age of 18 years was substituted for 21 years by the Family Law Reform Act 1969, Sch 1, Pt I; 6 *Halsbury's Statutes* (4th edn) 125.
3   Where an application is made for a grant of representation for the use and benefit of a person incapable of managing his affairs but not resident in an institution, the probate registrars will normally accept a certificate by the patient's doctor certifying the disability: *Practice Direction* [1969] 1 All ER 494, [1969] 1 WLR 301. Where the appointed executor has become of unsound mind, the grant goes to the receiver or a grant with will is made to the residuary legatee.
4   *Re Shaw's Estate* [1905] P 92.
5   See now the Supreme Court Act 1981, s 119; 17 *Halsbury's Statutes* (4th edn) 542. For an Australian case see *Re Yearwood's Estate* (1982) 30 SASR 169.
6   *Re Knox Estate* (1963) 40 DLR (2d) 397.

[25.5]

Appointment of a firm. A partnership firm, eg of solicitors, may be appointed executor, in which case, without more, the appointment will take effect as an appointment of those individuals who are partners in the firm at the date, prima facie, of the will, rather than of the testator's death.[1] For this reason it is usually thought desirable to specifically refer the appointment to the partners of the firm at the date of the death.[2] The usual power to charge professional fees should be included in such an appointment.[3] Where there is such an appointment, without naming the partners, and not all of them are applying for a grant, the executors' oath need not set out who all the partners were at the relevant time. It may show that the applicant or applicants are among those who were appointed executors simply by stating that they are or were partners in the firm at the appropriate date, and need not state that the other partners to whom power is to be reserved have been given notice of the application.[4]

1   *Re Fernie's Goods* (1849) 6 Notes of Cases 657; *Re Horgan* [1971] P 50, [1969] 3 All ER 1570.
2   See n 1 supra.
3   See Vol 2, paras **[203.14]** to **[203.23]** and Forms B21.32 to B21.35. On the construction of a professional charging clause see *Re Orwell's Will Trusts, Dixon v Blair* [1982] 3 All ER 177, [1982] 1 WLR 1337.
4   See *Practice Direction* of the Senior Registrar dated 12 June 1990, at [1990] 2 All ER 576 and Non-Contentious Probate Rules 1987, SI 1987/2024, r 27(1A).

[25.6]

Appointment of a corporation. A trust corporation may be appointed as executor either alone or jointly with others, and probate or administration may now be granted to the corporation. Where it is desired to appoint a bank or other trust corporation then the institution's own published clause of appointment should be used, to ensure acceptance.[1]

1   See Vol 2, paras [203.24] to [203.31].

[25.7]

Appointment of a spouse. An appointment by a testator of his spouse to be an executor or trustee is ineffective if the marriage has been dissolved or annulled after the will was made but before the testator's death (subject to any contrary intention appearing in the will).[1] Where a testator dies on or after 1 January 1996, an appointment in the alternative to such an appointment of the former spouse which is worded so as to take effect in the event of the former spouse predeceasing the testator will have effect even if the former spouse has in fact survived him.[2]

1   Wills Act 1837, s 18A(1) added by the AJA 1982, s 18(2), see Vol 2, Part G, para [244.17].
2   By virtue of the amendment made to Wills Act 1837, s 18A(1) by Law Reform (Succession) Act 1995, s 3 (the amended text is printed in Vol 2, Part G, para [244.18]), which deems the former spouse to have died when the marriage was dissolved or annulled. In relation to deaths before 1 January 1996 the appointment of the former spouse was merely treated as omitted, and an alternative appointment of this kind did not have effect: see para [47.2] infra.

[25.8]

The Public Trustee. The Public Trustee may be appointed executor either alone or jointly with others,[1] but this is subject to the statutory provision that the Public Trustee may decline either absolutely or except upon the prescribed conditions to accept any executorship or trust, save that he may not decline on the ground only of the small value of the estate.[2] He may be appointed by the name of Public Trustee or any other sufficient description[3] and, although no appointment is effective until he has sealed a formal consent to act,[4] he does not require previous notification of his appointment either as executor or trustee in the case of a will.[5] Whether or not there has been a previous notification and consent, the position is reviewed upon the will becoming operative and it is not till then that any consent to act is sealed.[6] It is the duty of any person appointed to act with the Public Trustee as executor and trustee and not renouncing the office or disclaiming the trust to give notice in writing of the appointment to the Public Trustee as soon as practicable after it has come to his knowledge.[7] A will may contain a clause prohibiting the appointment of the Public Trustee as a trustee thereof,[8] but such a clause is not binding on the court which may in the exercise of its power to appoint new trustees appoint the Public Trustee.[9] The Public Trustee may act as attorney of the executor of a testator who has died domiciled outside England and Wales and as such attorney obtain a grant to administer the property of the testator in England and Wales. The Public Trustee can renounce an appointment as executor in the same way as an ordinary executor. The Public Trustee is forbidden to act in Scottish, Irish,[10] colonial or foreign trusts;[11] in trusts involving the carrying on of a business for an indefinite period except where specially authorised by the Treasury;[12] in trusts where his appointment is forbidden by the creator of the trust;[13] in trusts exclusively for religious or charitable purposes.[14] The Public Trustee will normally decline to act in a trust containing a power to remove the trustee. The Public Trustee will accept an appointment as guardian of infant children.[15] Provision is made by statute for grants of probate and letters of administration.[16] Provision is made for the charging of administration and withdrawal of fees.[17]

1   Public Trustee Act 1906 (PTA 1906), s 2(2); 48 *Halsbury's Statutes* (4th edn) 232.
2   PTA 1906, s 2(3). See SI 1980/370, as amended by SI 1991/324; SI 1982/316.
3   PTA 1906, s 5(1); 48 *Halsbury's Statutes* (4th edn) 237.
4   Public Trustee Rules 1912, SI 1912/348, rr 8(2), 10. See *Re Shaw, Public Trustee v Little* (1914) 110 LT 924.
5   Public Trustee Rules 1912, SI 1912/348, r 10.
6   Public Trustee Rules 1912, SI 1912/348, r 10.
7   SI 1912/348, r 8(3).
8   PTA 1906, s 5(3); 48 *Halsbury's Statutes* (4th edn) 237.
9   PTA 1906, s 5(3); 48 *Halsbury's Statutes* (4th edn) 237.
10 Where a testator domiciled in the Irish Free State appointed the Public Trustee to be his executor and trustee, it was held that neither the Irish nor the English Public Trustee could accept the appointment: *Re Leeson's Goods* [1928] IR 168.
11 *Re Hewitt's Settlement, Hewitt v Hewitt* [1915] 1 Ch 228; but if a person dies domiciled in England and Wales, the Public Trustee can administer the whole estate even though it includes assets locally situate outside the jurisdiction of the English courts: [1915] 1 Ch 228 at 234. Where the law of the domicile permits, the Public Trustee may be appointed trustee of a fund which is an English trust, but the will must contain a clause that the Public Trustee is to be subject only to the jurisdiction of the English courts.
12 PTA 1906, s 2(4), and SI 1912/348, r 7.
13 PTA 1906, s 5(3); 48 *Halsbury's Statutes* (4th edn) 237.
14 PTA 1906, s 2(5); 48 *Halsbury's Statutes* (4th edn) 232.
15 SI 1912/348, r 6(b)(i).
16 PTA 1906, s 6; 48 *Halsbury's Statutes* (4th edn) 238.
17 See the Public Trustee (Fees) (Amendment) Order 1988, SI 1988/571, consequential to the Public Trustee (Fees) (Amendment) Order 1987, SI 1987/403, art 4, and the Public Trustee (Fees) (Amendment) Order 1992, SI 1992/724.

[25.9]

Duration of the office of executor. Distinction must be made between the duration of the office of executor itself and the duration of the powers of executor over property which comes into his hands as such. 'Once an executor, always an executor' is the rule so far as the office itself is concerned[1] and an executor remains such unless he has renounced[2] or the grant of probate has been revoked.[3] The executor's powers over property which becomes vested in him as such continue only until either he has executed an asset in respect of that property[4] or the position is such that an assent will be implied[5] or, the estate having been cleared, the property then vested in him becomes vested in him as trustee and not as executor.[6] Thus, while the powers of the executor over property vested in him may cease so that he becomes what may be called a bare executor, he still remains such and is available, during his life (and after his death any executor by representation[7] is available) to receive a reversionary interest in property which falls in many years after the death of the testator, or to exercise some power of appointment of new trustee vested in the testator, or for any other purpose for which representation of the testator's estate is required.

1   *Attenborough v Solomon* [1913] AC 76 at 85.
2   See para **[25.13]** infra.
3   See para **[25.16]** infra.

4   See Administration of Estates Act 1925, s 36.
5   See Administration of Estates Act 1925, s 36.
6   See Chapter 26.
7   See para **[25.10]** infra.

[25.10]
Devolution of the office of executor. In the main this is now settled by statute.[1] An executor of a sole or last surviving executor of a testator is the executor of that testator, but this provision does not apply to an executor who does not prove the will of his testator,[2] and, in the case of an executor who on his death leaves surviving him some other executor of his testator who afterwards proves the will of that testator, it ceases to apply on such probate being granted. So long as the chain of such representation is unbroken, the last executor in the chain is the executor of every preceding testator. The chain is broken by (i) an intestacy; (ii) the failure of a testator to appoint an executor; or (iii) the failure to obtain probate of a will; but is not broken by a temporary grant of administration if probate is subsequently granted. A full executor of a limited executor sufficiently represents the estate of the original testator[3] but not a limited executor of a full executor.[4] The office does not devolve on the administrator of an executor,[5] nor on the executor of an administrator.[6]

1   Administration of Estates Act 1925, s 7; 17 *Halsbury's Statutes* (4th edn) 425.
2   The executor must either by himself (*Wankford v Wankford* (1699) 1 Salk 299 at 308; *Twyford v Trail* (1834) 7 Sim 92) or by his attorney (*Re Bayard's Goods* (1849) 1 Rob Eccl 768) obtain probate or letters of administration which will be annexed (*Re Murguia's Goods* (1884) 9 PD 236) to his testator's estate in England.
3   *Re Beer's Goods* (1851) 2 Rob Eccl 349. A full executor is more usually called a general executor, being an executor to whom a general grant is made and therefore competent to deal with the whole estate whereas a limited executor can deal only with that part of the estate to which the grant to him is limited.
4   *Re Bayne's Goods* (1858) 1 Sw & Tr 132; *Re Bridger's Goods* (1878) 4 PD 77.
5   The chain is broken by an intestacy: Administration of Estates Act 1925, s 7(3)(a) (17 *Halsbury's Statutes* (4th edn) 425). When the chain is broken, the usual means of obtaining representation to the deceased is by a grant of administration de bonis non, but in several cases an executor who has renounced has been allowed in such circumstances to withdraw his renunciation and take a grant of administration either with the will annexed or de bonis non: *Re Rayner's Goods* (1908) 52 Sol Jo 226; *Re Bullock's Goods* (1845) 1 Rob Eccl 275; *Re Richardson's Goods* (1859) 1 Sw & Tr 515; *Re Blisset's Goods* (1881) 44 LT 816; *Re Morrison's Goods* (1861) 2 Sw & Tr 129; *Re Wheelwright's Goods* (1878) 3 PD 71; *Re Toscani's Estate* [1912] P 1.
6   *Maddock v Victoria Register of Titles* [1915] VLR 152; *Larence v Larence* (1911) 17 WLR 197.

[25.11]
Cesser of right of executor to prove. Where an executor (i) survives the testator but dies without taking out probate; or (ii) is cited to take out probate and does not appear; or (iii) renounces probate of the will, his rights as executor wholly cease and a grant is made as if that person had not been appointed executor.[1] Note also that an appointment of a spouse as executor will normally fail if there is a divorce.[2]

1   Administration of Estates Act 1925, s 5; 17 *Halsbury's Statutes* (4th edn) 424.
2   Wills Act 1837 s 18A(1)(*a*), added by the AJA 1982, s 18(2) and amended for deaths on or after 1 January 1996 by the Law Reform (Succession) Act 1995, s 3. See paras **[25.7]** supra and **[47.2]** infra.

[25.12]

Acceptance of the office. Apart from accepting the office by taking out a grant, an executor may do such acts with reference to the testator's estate as constitute an acceptance of the office.[1] Such acts include the release of a debt of the testator,[2] the application, even though unsuccessful, for the payment of money owing to the testator[3] or a statement that the will has been proved and that the maker of the statement is one of the executors.[4] But the mere performance of an act of necessity or of charity,[5] or an examination of the position of the estate to determine whether acceptance will be burdensome,[6] is not an acceptance. An act showing acceptance is final and the executor cannot afterwards renounce,[7] and he cannot accept in part and refuse in part. But minimal acts as executor such as concurrence in opening an executor's bank account, endorsing insurance policies, payment of funeral expenses and redemption of land tax, are not sufficient to constitute intermeddling so as to prevent a person renouncing his executorship.[8] An executor by representation having accepted the executorship of his own testator cannot renounce that of the earlier testators.[9] The acceptance involves the acceptance of trusts which the testator has imposed upon his executors as such, though an executor who is also appointed trustee may either accept the executorship and disclaim the trusteeship or renounce the executorship without disclaiming the trusts.[10]

1   No one can be compelled to accept, even though he has promised to do so in the lifetime of the testator (*Doyle v Blake* (1804) 2 Sch & Lef 231 at 239).
2   *Pytt v Fendall* (1754) 1 Lee 553.
3   *Re Stevens, Cooke v Stevens* [1897] 1 Ch 422.
4   *Vickers v Bell* (1864) 4 De GJ & Sm 274.
5   *Long and Feaver v Symes and Hannam* (1832) 3 Hag Ecc 771. Such acts are: giving directions for funeral: *Harrison v Rowley* (1798) 4 Ves 212 at 216; appropriating a reasonable sum for that purpose out of the assets: *Camden v Fletcher* (1838) 4 M & W 378; placing goods of the testator in a place of safety and making an inventory of them: *Re Fitzpatrick's Goods* (1892) 29 LR Ir 328; ordering necessities for the household or animals or payment of medical fees: *Long and Feaver v Symes and Hannam* (1832) 3 Hag Ecc 771. Under the Trustee Act 1925, s 36(5); 48 *Halsbury's Statutes* (4th edn) 500, executors intending to renounce may exercise a power of appointment of new trustee without thereby accepting the office of executor.
6   Taking possession of the books of account is an acceptance: *Clark v Phillips* (1854) 2 WR 331.
7   *Rogers v Frank* (1827) 1 Y & J 409; *Long and Feaver v Symes and Hannam* (1832) 3 Hag Ecc 771; *Re Badenach's Goods* (1864) 3 Sw & Tr 465. See, however, *Re Fitzpatrick's Goods* (1892) 29 LR Ir 328, where more leniency was shown to the executor.
8   *Holder v Holder* [1968] Ch 353, [1968] 1 All ER 665.
9   *Re Perry's Goods* (1840) 2 Curt 655; *Brooke v Haymes* (1868) LR 6 Eq 25; *Re Delacour's Goods* (1874) 9 IR Eq 86; *Re Pirie's Wills* (1884) 10 VLR 43.
10 *Mucklow v Fuller* (1821) Jac 198; *Ward v Butler* (1824) 2 Mol 533; *Stiles v Guy* (1832) 4 Y & C Ex 571; *Re Marsden, Bowden v Layland* (1884) 26 Ch D 783.

[25.13]

Renunciation. An executor is quite free to choose whether or not he will accept the office, but, if he decides not to do so, he should renounce the office in writing.[1] A renunciation need not be under seal but is not effective unless it is filed in the proper court.[2] Until it is filed, it may be withdrawn,[3] but after filing it can be withdrawn only by leave of the court.[4] Upon renunciation the executor's rights in respect of the executorship wholly cease and representation devolves as if he had not been appointed.[5] If he be allowed to withdraw his renunciation and take a grant, such grant takes effect without prejudice to the previous acts and dealings of and notices to any other personal representatives who have previously taken a grant and a note of the subsequent grant is made on the original grant.[6] Without actually renouncing an executor may refrain from joining in the application for the grant and then the grant reserves a power to him to come in and prove. He will in such circumstances have none of the powers of an executor unless he does come in and prove and the reservation of the power does not prevent a subsequent renunciation. A third case is where the appointed executor stands altogether aside from the application for the grant, when he will be cited to take out probate. If he does not do so, his rights and powers as executor wholly cease.[7] Although an executor has acted in good faith in carrying out the terms of the will, if he refuses to take out probate, the court has power to declare that the executor's interest in the executorship has wholly ceased and to grant letters of administration.[8]

1   *Re Boyle's Goods* (1864) 3 Sw & Tr 426. He may defer his decision, when power will be reserved for him to come in and prove. He may renounce in England and accept in Ireland: *Re Houghton's Goods* (1870) 18 WR 767; but an executor by representation who has accepted the executorship of his testator's will, cannot renounce executorship of any earlier will.
2   *Re Morant's Goods* (1874) LR 3 P & D 151.
3   *Re Morant's Goods* (1874) LR 3 P & D 151; *Melville v Ancketill* (1909) 25 TLR 655.
4   *Re Stiles' Goods* [1898] P 12; but renunciation cannot be withdrawn where all executors have renounced and a grant of administration has been made. See also *Re Foster* [1930] NZLR 60. He must show that the retraction is for the benefit of the estate or of those interested under the will: *Re Gill's Goods* (1873) LR 3 P & D 113.
5   Administration of Estates Act 1925, s 5; 17 *Halsbury's Statutes* (4th edn) 424. Where, as a compromise in an action for revocation of a grant of probate, the executor renounced probate, he was not entitled to a release from all liability; *Tiger v Barclays Bank Ltd* [1951] 2 KB 556, [1951] 2 All ER 262. As to delivery up of documents and especially inspection of a bank-trustee's records and accounts, see the same case on appeal [1952] 1 All ER 85, CA.
6   Administration of Estates Act 1925, s 6.
7   Administration of Estates Act 1925, s 5.
8   *Re Biggs' Estate* [1966] P 118, [1966] 1 All ER 358.

[25.14]
Acts before probate. Since the executor derives his title from the will[1] and all the estate and interest in the testator's property vests in him on the testator's death,[2] he can do any act before probate, which is a mere authentication of his title.[3] The only legal limitation upon this is that the court will not allow him to prove his title as executor otherwise than by the production of a grant of probate,[4] but in practice no one will deal with an executor as such unless he produces a grant and the matter is of little more than theoretical interest except as to matters which must be done before probate, when, in any proper case, acts may be done and agreements entered into upon an undertaking to obtain a grant without delay.

1   *Comber's Case* [1721] 1 P Wms 766.
2   *Woolley v Clark* (1822) 5 B & Ald 744. Contrast the position of an administrator although a limited doctrine of 'relation back' can apply: see *Mills v Anderson* [1984] QB 704, [1984] 2 All ER 538.
3   *Smith v Milles* (1786) 1 Term Rep 475 at 480; *National Trust Co v Mendelson* [1942] 1 DLR 438. Thus an executor who has not proved his testator's will is entitled to exercise the power of

appointing a new trustee confirmed by the Trustee Act 1925, s 36(1), whether or not he intended, or was able, to renounce probate: *Re Crowhurst Park, Sims-Hilditch v Simmons* [1974] 1 All ER 991, [1974] 1 WLR 583.
4   Probate is the sole and conclusive proof of the title of the personal representative provided the testator is dead. As to its being the sole proof: see *Pinney v Pinney* (1828) 8 B & C 335; *Pinney v Hunt* (1877) 6 Ch D 98. As to its being conclusive, see *Allen v Dundas* (1789) 3 Term Rep 125.

[25.15]
Effect of a grant. A grant of probate or letters of administration so long as it remains unrevoked is conclusive evidence of the will and its validity[1] and any action taken under such an unrevoked grant is protected by statute.[2] Executors of a will who, having obtained probate with notice of the fact that the next of kin intended or contemplated applying for revocation of the grant of probate on the ground of want of testamentary capacity, paid out pecuniary legacies to persons and institutions not entitled to share in the estate on an intestacy, were held liable to the estate for such terms, when probate was recalled.[3] A grant once made in solemn form will not be questioned.[4] Similarly a grant of administration is conclusive so long as it stands unrevoked that the deceased died intestate, or, in other words, that he left no effective will,[5] and no person can act as executor of a person in respect of whose estate such a grant has been made and not revoked.[6] So far as the court is concerned, the grant is conclusive evidence only of these matters. It is not conclusive evidence of the domicile of the deceased[7] nor is it strictly even prima facie evidence of his death.[8] A grant of probate does not prevent the courts from entertaining and deciding proceedings where it is alleged that the will is a forgery.[9] Where probate has been obtained by a fraud practised upon the persons entitled on intestacy, a court of equity has jurisdiction to declare the wrong-doer a trustee in respect of such probate,[10] but it cannot set aside a will which has been admitted to probate on account of fraud practised on the testator,[11] nor ought it to declare a person who has fraudulently obtained a benefit under the will a trustee for the persons defrauded.[12] A court of equity has power to look at the original will for the purpose of construing it,[13] even though the probate copy be in facsimile;[14] but it is not entitled to look at the original will with a view to correcting an inaccuracy in the probate copy.[15] Probate granted of a will and codicil is conclusive of the fact that there are two instruments, though they are written on the same paper.[16]

Though the general rule is that a will is proved by production of the grant of probate, a will twenty[17] years' old produced from the proper custody proves itself when required to be given in evidence in support of title.[18]

1   *Whicker v Hume* (1858) 7 HL Cas 124; *Re Barrance, Barrance v Ellis* [1910] 2 Ch 419.
2   Administration of Estates Act 1925, s 37 (17 *Halsbury's Statutes* (4th edn) 443), giving statutory effect to the decision in *Hewson v Shelley* [1914] 2 Ch 13, which overruled the decision in *Ellis v Ellis* [1905] 1 Ch 613, and earlier cases.
3   *Guardian Trust and Executors Co of New Zealand Ltd v Public Trustee of New Zealand* [1942] AC 115, [1942] 1 All ER 598, on the principle that if a trustee or other person in fiduciary capacity has received notice that a fund in his possession is, or may be, claimed by A, he will be liable to A if he deals with the fund in disregard of that notice should the claim subsequently prove to be well founded.
4   *A-G v Partington* (1964) 3 H & C 193 at 204; *Whyte v Rose* (1842) 3 QB 493 at 507; *Bond v Graham* (1842) 1 Hare 482; *Lasseur v Tyrconnel* (1846) 10 Beav 28.
5   *Tourton v Flower* (1735) 3 P Wms 369.

6   Administration of Estates Act 1925, s 15; 17 *Halsbury's Statutes* (4th edn) 428.

7   *Whicker v Hume* (1858) 7 HL Cas 124 at 144; *Bradford v Young* (1884) 26 Ch D 656; *Concha v Concha* (1886) 11 App Cas 541.

8   A grant of probate or letters of administration is made upon the oath of the person applying which states that the deceased died on a certain day. A certificate of registration of the death is not required. The grant, therefore, though commonly accepted as good conveyancing evidence of death is not in any way conclusive of the death or date of death. It is, however, and should be, accepted as such in the absence of evidence to the contrary. As to validity of things done under an unrevoked grant, see n 2 supra, and the text thereto. See *French v French* (1755) 1 Dick 268 at 271; *Loyd v Finlayson* (1797) 2 Esp 564; *Bateman v Butler* (1843) 1 LTOS 167.

9   *Ex p Jolliffe* (1845) 8 Beav 168; *Priestman v Thomas* (1884) 9 PD 210; *Re Payne Estate* [1934] 1 DLR 474.

10   *Barnesly v Powel* (1748) 1 Ves Sen 119; *Barnesly v Powel* (1749) 1 Ves Sen 284; *Meadows v Duchess of Kingston* (1775) Amb 756 at 762.

11   *Gingell v Horne* (1839) 9 Sim 539; *Allen v M'Pherson* (1847) 1 HL Cas 191; *Meluish v Milton* (1876) 3 Ch D 27.

12   *Meluish v Milton* (1876) 3 Ch D 27 at 33.

13   *Re Harrison, Turner v Hellard* (1885) 30 Ch D 390. The court may look at a foreign original even where an English translation has been proved: *Re Cliff's Trusts* [1892] 2 Ch 229.

14   *Shea v Boschetti* (1854) 18 Beav 321. No doubt this rule still applies although the probate copy is now a photocopy, for the original may show something that is not clear in the photocopy.

15   *Oppenheim v Henry* (1853) 9 Hare 802n.

16   *Baillie v Butterfield* (1787) 1 Cox Eq Cas 392.

17   Evidence Act 1938, s 4; 17 *Halsbury's Statutes* (4th edn) 159. Before the Evidence Act 1938 was passed the will or other instrument had to be thirty years' old; see also the Evidence Act 1938, s 3.

18   *Man v Ricketts* (1844) 7 Beav 93. Attesting witnesses are presumed after a lapse of thirty years (now presumably twenty years) to be dead: *Doe d Ashburnham v Michael* (1851) 17 QB 276.

[25.16]

Revocation of grant.[1] A grant in common form may be revoked upon any party interested requiring the will to be proved in solemn form. Where a grant in common form has been obtained, a person wishing the will to be proved in solemn form must issue a writ making the executor defendant and alleging invalidity of the will.[2] Where proceedings have been taken for a grant in solemn form, a person cognisant of those proceedings who has failed to intervene in them in his representative capacity cannot bring subsequent proceedings as that would be an abuse of the process of the court.[3] Although there is jurisdiction to set aside a grant in solemn form, such a grant will not be set aside where the failure to intervene is due to compromise and not to mistake.[4] Any grant may be revoked where it has been obtained on a false suggestion, whether made fraudulently[5] or in ignorance: for example, that the person entitled thereto is dead,[6] by a woman claiming to be the widow of the deceased but who was not legally married;[7] or by those entitled on intestacy where there is a valid residuary bequest;[8] or where a grant has been obtained to the will of a living person.[9] Where a will has been discovered after a grant of administration or a later will after a grant of probate, the original grant will be revoked.[10] A codicil discovered after a grant of probate, if it does not vary the appointment of executors, may be proved alone; but if it does vary such appointment, the original grant must be revoked. A grant containing a wrong name of the deceased must be revoked. An executor who has obtained a grant of probate cannot himself take steps to have it revoked, but he may propound the will in solemn form.[11] A revocation will not affect any act or thing bona fide done under the grant.[12] A grant may be impounded and a limited grant made during the incapacity of the executor through illness.[13] A professional executor who has acted under a will which is subsequently revoked cannot rely on the revoked probate to retain his own charges for acting, but the court may allow him to retain reasonable remuneration for work which would have been done anyway.[14]

1   See also *Tristram and Coote's Probate Practice* (28th edn), Chapter 17.
2   *Re Jolley, Jolley v Jarvis and Sands* [1964] P 262, [1964] 1 All ER 596.
3   *Re Langton's Estate* [1964] P 163, [1964] 1 All ER 749.
4   *Re Barraclough, Barraclough v Young* [1967] P 1, [1965] 2 All ER 311.
5   The grant may be revoked not only against the person committing or procuring the fraud but irrespective of that person as a will must either be good or bad as against all the world: *Birch v Birch* [1902] P 130, but the court refused to revoke a grant of administration where the Inland Revenue affidavit was shown to be false: *Re Cope's Estate* [1954] 1 All ER 698, [1954] 1 WLR 608. An executor can have a grant to creditors revoked where it has been obtained by non-disclosure of material facts: *Re Leguia's Estate* (1936) 105 LJP 72. Revocation is in discretion of the court: *Re Lamont's Will* (1881) 7 VLR 87.
6   *Harrison v Weldon* (1731) 2 Stra 911.
7   *Re Moore's Goods* (1845) 3 Notes of Cases 601; *Re Langley's Goods* (1851) 2 Rob Eccl 407.
8   *Warren v Kelson* (1859) 1 Sw & Tr 290.
9   *Re Napier's Goods* (1809) 1 Phillim 83.
10   *Priestman v Thomas* (1884) 9 PD 210.
11   *Re Chamberlain's Goods* (1867) LR 1 P & D 316; *Re Byrne's Goods (No 2)* (1910) 44 ILT 192. Any person not a party to the proceedings is bound by them only if he knew of them and had a right to intervene: *Young v Holloway* [1895] P 87.
12   *Hewson v Shelley* [1914] 2 Ch 13. *McParland v Coulson* [1930] NI 138, but a purchaser for value may be protected under the Law of Property Act 1925, s 204; 37 *Halsbury's Statutes* (4th edn) 367, re-enacting a provision which originally appeared in the Conveyancing Act 1881, s 70. The rights of the party accepting the disposition may also be saved under the Limitation Acts, but this point has never been decided. Compare the case of *Re West, West v Roberts* [1909] 2 Ch 180, where a later will was found some years after the grant of probate. At any rate, acts which an administrator is compellable to do stand good after revocation: see *Ellis v Ellis* [1905] 1 Ch 613 at 619, but there is a doubt about the extension of this principle to acts done in the due course of administration. It is submitted that, in the case of a purchaser for value, protection is afforded by the Law of Property Act 1925, s 204, referred to above. The section was applied in *Re Bridgett and Hayes' Contract* [1928] Ch 163. See the Administration of Estates Act 1925, ss 27, 37; 17 *Halsbury's Statutes* (4th edn) 434, 443.
13   *Re Knott's Goods* [1920] 2 IR 397. A grant has been revoked where both surviving executors were of advanced age and physically and mentally infirm: *Re Galbraith's Goods* [1951] P 422, [1951] 2 All ER 470n. A grant of administration has been revoked in New Zealand on account of the immorality of the administratrix: *Galloway v Galloway* (1877) 3 JRNS (CA) 29.
14   *Gray v Richards Butler* (1996) 140 Sol Jo LB 194. It is not thought that this position has been affected by the Trustee Act 2000, ss 28(4), 35(3); see Chapter 27, para **[27.10]** infra.

[25.17]
Substitution or removal of personal representative. In addition to the Trustee Act 1925 powers, the Administration of Justice Act 1985,[1] confers power on the High Court to appoint a person to act as personal representative in place of the existing personal representative or to remove one or more but not all of the personal representatives. This power can be invoked for example, where there has been excessive dilatoriness in winding up the estate.

1   Administration of Justice Act 1985, s 50.

[25.18]

Estate taken by the executor. At common law the executor obtained the whole estate and interest, both legal and equitable, which was vested in the testator at the time of his death in the testator's personal property, including leaseholds.[1] Such estate and interest was taken by the personal representative notwithstanding any testamentary disposition[2] and indeed in addition to any estate taken under a testamentary disposition.[3] By the Wills Act 1837, s 3[4] the testator had, until the end of 1925, power to devise or bequeath both the legal and equitable estate and interest to a beneficiary and the beneficiary derived his interest from the will and not from any conveyance or assignment from the personal representative. As the old authorities put it, the devisee or legatee was in under the will.[5] Of these two interests in the property the personal representative's was paramount and the beneficiary's interest was said to be inchoate until the executor indicated by an assent that he did not require the subject of the devise or bequest for the purposes of administration.[6] A change was made, however, in 1925 and the beneficiary was then by statute[7] prevented from obtaining the legal estate under the will.[8] Since 1925 the beneficiary can only obtain the legal estate by an assent or conveyance by the executor.[9] As already stated at common law the personalty vested in the personal representative but in 1897[10] the real estate of the testator was by statute made to vest in the personal representative in the same way as the personalty had always done at common law.[11] The position now is, therefore, that the personal representative obtains the whole interest in the property vested in the testator at the time of his death for an interest not ceasing at his death and the devisee or legatee has, during the period of administration, only a chose in action to have the deceased's estate properly administered.[12]

---

1 *Brazier v Hudson* (1836) 8 Sim 67; *Whale v Booth* (1784) 4 Term Rep 625n; *Ewer v Corbet* (1723) 2 P Wms 148; *Andrew v Wrigley* (1792) 4 Bro CC 125; *McLeod v Drummond* (1810) 17 Ves 152.

2 The beneficiaries under the will obtained only an inchoate interest in any legacy or bequest until the executor assented to it: see *Stamp Duties Comr (Queensland) v Livingston* [1965] AC 694, PC.

3 An express disposition in favour of executors was of some importance in the case of realty before 1898, but since then all realty (with now unimportant exceptions before 1926) has vested in the personal representative and (this must be carefully noted) in the like manner as chattels real devolved on the personal representative from time to time of the deceased. Thus the powers of a personal representative over the estate of the deceased are in every case the old common law powers. For authorities on these powers and their extent, see *Re Chaplin and Staffordshire Potteries Waterworks Co's Contract* [1922] 2 Ch 824; *Re Kemnal and Still's Contract* [1923] 1 Ch 293.

4 See Vol 2, Part G, para [244.4].

5 *Westwick v Wyer* (1591) 4 Co Rep 28a. For this reason the probate was not on the title before 1926.

6 *Mead v Lord Orrery* (1745) 3 Atk 235 at 240; *George Attenborough & Son v Solomon* [1913] AC 76 at 82, 83.

7 Law of Property (Amendment) Act 1924, Sch 9, para 3.

8 The precise provision is that the Wills Act 1837 takes effect to enable equitable interests to be disposed of subject and without prejudice to the estate and powers of a personal representative.

9 As to assent, see Administration of Estates Act 1925, s 36(4); 17 *Halsbury's Statutes* (4th edn) 442. Though the assent is convenient, it in no way lessens the right or power of the executor to convey the legal estate and the curtain provided by the Administration of Estates Act 1925, s 36(7), applies to conveyances as well as assents.

10   Land Transfer Act 1897, s 1, now re-enacted in the Administration of Estates Act 1925, s 1; 17 *Halsbury's Statutes* (4th edn) 421.
11   This shows the importance of ascertaining with precision the interest taken by the personal representative at common law in personalty (which in this case included leaseholds).
12   *Stamp Duties Comr (Queensland) v Livingston* [1965] AC 694 at 708, PC. See para **[1.12]** supra.

[25.19]

Gifts to executor. See the discussion at paras **[30.14]–[30.18]** and **[83.3]** infra.

CHAPTER 26

Special administrators for settled land

[26.1]

The Trusts of Land and Appointment of Trustees Act 1996 (TLATA 1996).
By virtue of the TLATA 1996 it is not possible to create a settlement of land
taking effect under the Settled Land Act 1925 on or after 1 January 1997.[1] Nor
will any property be deemed to be settled land under the Settled Land Act 1925.[2]
Instead such a disposition will take effect as a 'trust of land' within the TLATA
1996, s 1(1)(a) and the trustees will be 'trustees of land' as defined by s 1(1)(b).
The devolution of the land on death would thus follow the usual pattern of trust
property.[3] Strict settlements created before 1 January 1997 continue to be subject
to the Settled Land Act 1925 regime,[4] but there will be a gradual phasing out of
the Settled Land Act 1925 as existing strict settlements come to an end, or cease
to include land or heirlooms.[5] The discussion in the succeeding paragraphs of
text in this Chapter thus apply only to continuing settlements existing at 1
January 1997.

1   By virtue of the TLATA 1996, s 2(1), (2).
2   By virtue of the TLATA 1996, s 2(1), (2).
3   By virtue of the TLATA 1996, s 2(1), (2).
4   By virtue of the TLATA 1996, s 2(1), (2). By way of exception to this, existing settlements of
    land held on charitable, ecclesiastical or public trusts are converted by the TLATA 1996 into
    trusts of land, s 2(5).
5   TLATA 1996, s 2(4).

[26.2]

Devolution of legal estate in settled land.[1] A general executor or person
entitled to a general grant must now[2] take out a grant which excludes any settled
land which was vested in the deceased at his death which remained settled after
it.[3] Since 1925 in a properly constituted[4] settlement of land[5] the legal estate[6] is
vested in the tenant for life or the person or persons entitled by statute to
exercise the powers of a tenant for life.[7] Such persons will be either the tenant or
joint tenants for life[8] or the persons entitled to exercise the powers of a tenant for
life[9] or the statutory owner or owners.[10] Where there is more than one tenant for
life or statutory owner, the legal estate on the death of one passes by
survivorship to the survivor or survivors without any grant of representation.[11]
Upon the death of sole or sole surviving statutory owner the legal estate passes
as an ordinary trust to his general personal representative.[12] On the death of a
sole or sole surviving tenant for life, the legal estate passes to his general or
special personal representative in accordance with the rules hereinafter
expressed.

1   See also *Tristram and Coote's Probate Practice* (28th edn).
2   See the new r 29 of the Non-Contentious Probate Rules 1987, SI 1987/2024, in particular
    r 29(3), which came into force with effect from 14 October 1991 (by virtue of SI 1991/1876).
    For the previous law see the 6th edn of this work, Chapter 25.
3   Where there is settled land which continued to be settled land after the death of the testator, the
    general personal representative cannot deal with such settled land though he can deal with
    settled land which ceased to be such on the death of the testator. The powers of the executor
    depend on the nature of the grant made, which is conclusive by virtue of the Law of Property
    Act 1925, s 204; 37 *Halsbury's Statutes* (4th edn) 367); see *Re Bridgett and Hayes' Contract*
    [1928] Ch 163 (see the judgment at 168). Where the general executor takes a grant save and
    except it necessarily follows that someone else must take a grant to what is excepted from his
    grant, ie a limited grant.
4   See the Settled Land Act 1925 (SLA 1925), ss 4, 5; 48 *Halsbury's Statutes* (4th edn) 257, 259.
    A settlement is properly constituted only where there is a vesting instrument vesting the
    property in the tenant for life or declaring it to be so vested upon the trusts of the settlement.
5   See the SLA 1925, s 1(7), added by the Law of Property (Amendment) Act 1926, Sch; 37
    Halsbury's Statutes (4th edn) 536. It can be noted that trusts for sale are also affected by the
    TLATA 1996; see ss 3, 4 and 5. Land in this connection includes leaseholds.
6   In a settlement of freeholds this will be the fee simple and in a settlement of leasehold the term
    of years absolute (Law of Property Act 1925, s 1(1)); 37 *Halsbury's Statutes* (4th edn) 124.
7   For these persons, see SLA 1925, ss 19–23; 48 *Halsbury's Statutes* (4th edn) 280–291.
8   SLA 1925, s 19.
9   SLA 1925, ss 20–22.
10 SLA 1925, s 23.
11 See Administration of Estates Act 1925, s 3(4); 17 *Halsbury's Statutes* (4th edn) 423.
12 See SLA 1925, s 7(1); 48 *Halsbury's Statutes* (4th edn) 261.

[26.3]
When settled land grant necessary. The necessity for a settled land grant arises
only when the legal estate is vested in a sole or sole surviving tenant for life, and
in such cases only when the land continues to be settled land after his death.[1]
Where the land ceases to be settled land on the death of the tenant for life[2] it
passes under the ordinary general grant of the free estate to the general personal
representative.[3]

1   It was originally thought that the land remained technically settled land until actually vested in
    absolute owners or trustees for sale. It was held, however, in *Re Bridgett and Hayes' Contract*
    [1928] Ch 163, that it ceased to be such on the death of the tenant for life. This point is only the
    subject of a dictum in *Re Bridgett and Hayes' Contract*, but the dictum was adopted in *Re
    Bordass's Estate* [1929] P 107, and has always been acted on by the Probate Registry. Where,
    however, after ceasing to be settled land under one settlement, the property immediately
    becomes settled land under another settlement, a settled land grant is necessary (*Re Taylor's
    Estate* [1929] P 260). Where the land ceases to be settled land after 1 January 1997, the
    provisions of the TLATA 1996 apply. See para **[26.1]**, nn 1–5.
2   As to the duration of settlements, see SLA 1925, s 3; 48 *Halsbury's Statutes* (4th edn) 257. But
    see now the final sentence to n 1 above.
3   *Re Bridgett and Hayes' Contract* [1928] Ch 163.

[26.4]
Settled land grants on death of tenant for life. Where the land continues after
the death of the tenant for life to be settled land, two distinct cases arise: (i)
where the tenant for life dies testate,[1] and (ii) where he dies wholly intestate.
Upon the death of the tenant for life testate two further alternatives occur in that
there may or may not be trustees of the settlement[2] living at his death and

surviving at the time the grant is applied for. Where the trustees were such at the time of the death of the tenant for life, they are, in default of express appointment, by statute deemed to be appointed his special executors in regard to settled land.[3] Such trustees are therefore entitled to a grant of administration[4] limited to the settled land of which they are the trustees for the purposes of the Settled Land Act 1925.[5] Where the settlement, under which the deceased was tenant for life, was created by will or has arisen under an intestacy, and there are no other trustees, the personal representative of the settlor, being by statute[6] a trustee of the settled land, is entitled to a grant.[7] Trustees appointed after the death of the tenant for life are not appointed under the statute,[8] and are entitled to a grant of administration second in order after the statutorily appointed executors.[9] Where the deceased tenant for life dies wholly intestate, administration limited to the settled land may be granted to the trustees of the settlement whether the same be appointed before or after the death of the tenant for life.[10]

A grant of administration in respect of settled land is not a grant with the will annexed, and the only circumstances in which the will (if any) of the deceased tenant for life needs to be produced in support of an application for a grant in respect of settled land which continues to be settled is where an application is made by statutorily appointed executors who are not the trustees of the settlement at the time of the grant. The statutorily appointed executors and the trustees at the time of the application may apply together for a grant, but if the only applicants for a grant are the trustees at the time of the application and they are not the same persons as the statutorily appointed executors, they must clear off the latter first. The persons with a prior right to a grant of administration may be cleared off by death or renunciation in the same way as other persons entitled to a grant.[11] If there are no statutorily appointed executors or trustees of the settlement to take a grant, the general personal representatives may take one, but it will still be a separate grant of administration limited to the settled land.[12]

---

1   It is submitted that for these purposes the testator dies testate although there be no appointment of executors in the will or where for any reason, including renunciation, the appointment fails.
2   Trustees of the settlement means trustees for the purposes of the SLA 1925. As to who are such, see SLA 1925, s 30; 48 *Halsbury's Statutes* (4th edn) 299, as amended by the TLATA 1996, Sch 3, para 2(9).
3   Administration of Estates Act 1925, s 22; 17 *Halsbury's Statutes* (4th edn) 430. For this section to operate there must be a will, trustees of the settlement at the death of the tenant for life, and the settled land must have been vested in the tenant for life. The special executors constituted by s 22 have a prior right to a grant of administration limited to settled land, see the Non-Contentious Probate Rules 1987, SI 1987/2024, r 29(2).
4   It will usually be necessary for there to be two grantees in accordance with the Supreme Court Act 1981, s 114; 17 *Halsbury's Statutes* (4th edn) 539, formerly the Supreme Court of Judicature (Consolidation) Act 1925, s 160(1).
5   Non-Contentious Probate Rules 1987, SI 1987/2024, r 29(2)(i). Where there are different trustees of different settlements of which the deceased was the tenant for life, the grant to each set of trustees is limited to the land included in the particular settlement.
6   SLA 1925, s 30(3); 48 *Halsbury's Statutes* (4th edn) 299.
7   *Re Gibbings' Estate* [1928] P 28.
8   Such trustees could not be deemed to be appointed by the tenant for life as special executors within the meaning of the Administration of Estates Act 1925, s 22; 17 *Halsbury's Statutes* (4th edn) 430.
9   Such grants are made under the Supreme Court Act 1981, s 116; 17 *Halsbury's Statutes* (4th edn) 540. The person or persons entitled to a grant of administration limited to settled land are,

firstly, the statutorily appointed executors, secondly, the trustees of the settlement at the time of the application for the grant, and thirdly, the personal representatives of the deceased, see Non-Contentious Probate Rules 1987, SI 1987/2024, r 29(2).

10   Non-Contentious Probate Rules 1987, SI 1987/2024, r 29(2). It makes no difference whether the trustees are appointed before or after the death because, being a grant of administration, the grantees derive their authority wholly from the grant and not in any way from a will, and the only necessity is that they should be such trustees at the time of the grant.

11   Such renunciation is allowed in practice. The Administration of Estates Act 1925, s 23(1) (17 *Halsbury's Statutes* (4th edn) 431), contains an express provision enabling a personal representative, who is not a trustee of the settlement, to renounce before grant or apply for revocation after a grant has been made in regard to continuing settled land and without regard to other property. This subsection appears to assume that continuing settled land would vest in a general personal representative under a general grant; but where a general grant was intended so to operate, the Registry used to add to the grant the words 'including settled land'. This addition made it doubtful whether a general grant not so worded would enable personal representatives to deal with settled land continuing to be such, but it is submitted that the decision in *Re Bridgett and Hayes' Contract* [1928] Ch 163, clearly gave them such power. These points cease to be relevant from 14 October 1991 as a result of the requirement from that date of a separate grant of administration for settled land under the substituted r 29 of the Non-Contentious Probate Rules 1987, SI 1987/2024.

12   SI 1987/2024, r 29(2) and (3), and Probate Registry *Secretary's Circular (2)* 26 September 1991.

[26.5]

Discretionary grants. Where settled land ceases to be such on the death of the tenant for life and there is no one entitled to a grant of representation to his estate, the previous practice was for the court to make a discretionary grant to the remainderman.[1] Similar grants have been made after citation[2] and without citation of the next of kin.[3]

1   *Re Dalley* (1926) 136 LT 223 (a case decided before the ruling in *Re Bridgett and Hayes' Contract* [1928] Ch 163). The discretionary grant is made under the Supreme Court Act 1981, s 116; 17 *Halsbury's Statutes* (4th edn) 540. Where the land ceases to be settled land after 1 January 1997, the provisions of the TLATA 1996 apply; see para **[26.1]** supra.

2   See *Re Bordass's Estate* [1929] P 107.

3   See *Re Birch's Estate* [1929] P 164.

[26.6]

Renunciation and revocation. An appointed executor, not being a trustee of the settlement, may renounce probate in respect of the settled land, or he may obtain revocation, limited to the settled land, of probate already granted.[1]

1   Administration of Estates Act 1925, s 23; 17 *Halsbury's Statutes* (4th edn) 431.

[26.7]

Special or additional representatives. Whether such renunciation or revocation is made or not, the trustees of the settlement, or any person beneficially interested thereunder, may apply to the High Court for an order appointing a special or additional personal representative in respect of the settled land. In the absence of special considerations, the court in making such order will appoint such persons as may be necessary to secure that the persons to act as representatives in respect of the settled land shall be the trustees of the settlement, if willing to act.[1]

1   Administration of Estates Act 1925, s 23(3). Such order must be indorsed on the original probate or letters of administration (Administration of Estates Act 1925, s 23(3)).

[26.8]

Limitation of grant. A grant of administration to the trustees of the settlement may be limited in any way that the court thinks fit.[1]

1   Supreme Court Act 1981, s 116(2); 17 *Halsbury's Statutes* (4th edn) 540.

[26.9]

Disposing of settled land. Personal representatives appointed to act for the purposes of settled land, including any original personal representative who is to act with an additional personal representative for these purposes, can dispose of the settled land without the concurrence of the general personal representatives, who may likewise dispose of the other property without the concurrence of the special personal representatives.[1]

1   Administration of Estates Act 1925, s 24; 17 *Halsbury's Statutes* (4th edn) 432.

CHAPTER 27

Trustees

[27.1]

Introduction. The law relating to trustees has been affected by three recent statutes; the Trusts of Land and Appointment of Trustees Act 1996 (TLATA 1996),[1] the Trustee Delegation Act 1999 (TDA 1999) and the Trustee Act 2000.[2] This legislation has made significant amendments to the law by repealing, replacing, or amending, many of the provisions in the previous legislation, notably those contained in the Trustee Act 1925, the Trustee Investments Act 1961, the Settled Land Act 1925 and the Law of Property Act 1925.[3] It is beyond the scope of this work to set out the whole of the law of trusts, or of the provisions in the new Acts, but some reference to those aspects of the law relating to trustees which most closely concerns wills, will be considered in this Chapter and in the appropriate commentaries in Volume 2.

The whole of the Trustee Act 2000 (TrA 2000) (so far as it was not already in force) came into force on 1 February 2001.[4] It can be said that generally the provisions of the TrA 2000 are default provisions which will apply to existing trusts where there is no provision to the contrary in the trust instrument. An important point to note is that the provisions of the TrA 2000 apply in relation to a personal representative administering an estate according to the law as it applies to a trustee carrying out a trust for beneficiaries.[5] It is provided that the TrA 2000 is to be read with the appropriate modifications and thus references to 'the trust instrument' are to be read as references to 'the will';[6] references to a beneficiary are to be read as references to a person interested in the due administration of the estate[7] or under the law relating to intestacy.[8] Similarly the provisions of the substituted Trustee Act 1925, s 25, by the Trustee Delegation Act 1999, apply to a personal representative.[9]

1   See Vol 2, Part G, para **[246.85]**.
2   See Vol 2, Part G, para **[246.115]**.
3   For the full exposition of the sections amended and repealed by the TLATA 1996, see Schs 1, 2, 3 and 4. Similarly see the TDA 1999, Sch and the TrA 2000, Schs 2 and 4.
4   The Trustee Act 2000 (Commencement) Order 2001; SI 2001/49.
5   TrA 2000, s 35 (1). Similarly see the TLATA 1996, s 10.
6   TrA 2000, s 35 (2)(a).
7   TrA 2000, s 35 (2)(b).
8   TrA 2000, s 35 (2)(c).
9   See the Trustee Act 1925, s 25(10), as substituted by the TDA 1999, s 5.

[27.2]

Appointment of trustees. The provisions in the Trustee Act 1925, Pt III relating to the appointment and discharge of trustees are well known and will not be further set out here. Suffice it to note that these provisions remain in force but have been subject to significant amendment by the TLATA 1996.[1] The TLATA 1996 contains new provisions relating to the appointment of trustees.[2] Where no person is nominated for the purpose of appointing new trustees and the beneficiaries under the trust are of full age and capacity and between them absolutely entitled to the settled property, the beneficiaries may give a written direction to a trustee to retire from the trust, or give a written direction to the trustees to appoint as a trustee or trustees the person or persons specified in the direction.[3] Further beneficiaries who are of full age and collectively entitled to the beneficial interest, are given power, where a trustee is mentally incapacitated and there is nobody with power to appoint a new trustee under the Trustee Act 1925, to direct the trustee's receiver or attorney under an enduring power, to appoint a new trustee or trustees specified by the beneficiaries, thus effecting the appointment of a substitute trustee for an incapable trustee.[4]

The Trustee Act 1925, s 36 has been further amended by the TDA 1999. This now provides that a person who is either a trustee and attorney, or an attorney under a registered power may, subject to conditions,[5] make an appointment of a new trustee under the Trustee Act 1925, s 36(6)(b).[6]

1   See the TLATA 1996, Sch 3, para 4.
2   With effect from 1 January 1997.
3   TLATA 1996, s 19. This reverses the decision in *Re Brockbank, Ward v Bates* [1948] Ch 206, [1948] 1 All ER 287. The beneficiaries must act unanimously.
4   TLATA 1996, s 20. Sections 19 and 20 may be excluded in relation to new settlements and wills, see the TLATA 1996, s 21(5). There are detailed provisions relating to the manner in which the 'direction' may be given; TLATA 1996, s 21, and other supplementary provisions in the TLATA 1996, ss 22–26.
5   See new subsections in the Trustee Act 1925, s 36(6B), (6C) and (6D) added to s 36(6) by the TDA 1999, s 8.
6   TDA 1999, s 8, adding provisions to the Trustee Act 1925, s 36(6).

[27.3]

Persons who may be appointed trustees. Subject to the exception that a minor[1] may not be appointed a trustee,[2] any fit and proper person may be appointed a trustee. It was formerly thought undesirable to appoint a person beneficially interested in the trust property on the ground that he would be placed in a position in which his interest and duty would conflict.[3] It has, however, always been admitted that there is no inherent invalidity in such appointment,[4] and, in recent times, owing to the difficulty of obtaining individual persons to act as trustees, it has been the common practice to appoint beneficiaries to the office. It has been held that the court will not interfere with an appointment made by a person able and willing to appoint provided only that the person appointed was a fit and proper person to be appointed although the appointment was against the wishes of the beneficiaries.[5] Now that trustees can be subject to the direction of the beneficiaries,[6] testators would be well advised in selecting trustees who will work harmoniously with the beneficiaries and with one another, and where this is impossible to appoint a bank or insurance company or other trust corporation. In this connection it may be mentioned that a bank may be appointed a trustee although some or even all the beneficiaries are its customers.[7] Under the statutory power, the appointor may appoint himself,[8] but under an express power to appoint 'other persons', the appointment of the appointor has been held to be excluded.[9] There is no absolute bar to the appointment of a foreign resident as trustee of an English trust. Persons having power to appoint may therefore make such an appointment in exceptional circumstances, for instance, when the beneficiary is himself resident abroad.[10]

1   Under 18 years: Family Law Reform Act 1969, s 1; 6 *Halsbury's Statutes* (4th edn) 121.
2   Law of Property Act 1925, s 20; 37 *Halsbury's Statutes* (4th edn) 143.
3   See *Passingham v Sherborn* (1846) 9 Beav 424; *Re Clissold's Settlement* (1864) 10 LT 642; and *Re Lightbody's Trusts* (1884) 52 LT 40. These, however, were appointments by the court, and where the appointment of a beneficiary was duly made out of court it was not the practice of the court to interfere although the appointment was not one which the court would itself have made: see *Re Norris, Allen v Norris* (1884) 27 Ch D 333; *Re Coode, Coode v Foster* (1913) 108 LT 94. An appointment of a tenant for life was upheld to be a proper exercise of a power out of court in *Forster v Abraham* (1874) LR 17 Eq 351; *Tempest v Lord Camoys* (1888) 58 LT 221.
4   See *Forster v Abraham* (1874) LR 17 Eq 351.
5   *Re Higginbottom* [1892] 3 Ch 132, on the previous position where trustees consulted the beneficiaries. See now the TLATA 1996, ss 19–20 and para **[27.2]** supra.
6   TLATA 1996, Pt II, see the discussion in para **[27.2]** supra. The Law of Property Act 1925, ss 25 and 26 are repealed; see the TLATA 1996, Sch 4.
7   *Re Northcliffe's Settlements* [1937] 3 All ER 804. The fact that the beneficiaries have overdrafts at the time of the appointment is not material.
8   Trustee Act 1925, s 36(1); 48 *Halsbury's Statutes* (4th edn) 500; subject to minor amendments by the TLATA 1996, s 25(1), Sch 3, para 3(11). But not where he appoints an additional trustee under the Trustee Act 1925, s 36 (6), (as amended) *Re Powers Settlement Trusts* [1951] Ch 1074, [1951] 2 All ER 513.
9   *Re Skeats' Settlement, Skeats v Evans* (1889) 42 Ch D 522. There was a suggestion that the power was a fiduciary one and, therefore, the appointor could not appoint himself, but this suggestion has been repudiated: *Montefiore v Guedalla* [1903] 2 Ch 723 at 726. There is some authority for saying that the appointment is undesirable: see *Tempest v Lord Camoys* (1888) 58 LT 221; *Montefiore v Guedalla* [1903] 2 Ch 723.
10   The fact that the Trustee Act 1925, s 36(1), provides that a trustee who remains out of the United Kingdom for more than 12 months may be supplanted, does not make foreign residents ineligible to be appointed as new trustees: *Re Whitehead's Will Trusts, Burke v Burke* [1971] 2 All ER 1334.

[27.4]
Trust corporation. A trust corporation is the Public Trustee or a corporation either appointed by the court in any particular case to be a trustee or entitled by rules made under the Public Trustee Act 1906, s 4(3), to act as a custodian trustee.[1] Where a trust corporation is appointed trustee, it will usually require certain special clauses to be inserted in the will and will on request supply a print of those clauses.

1   Law of Property Act 1925, s 205(1)(xxviii); 37 *Halsbury's Statutes* (4th edn) 368. For the Public Trustee Act 1906, s 4(3), see 48 *Halsbury's Statutes* (4th edn) 235, and as to the Public Trustee, see Chapter 25.

[27.5]
Acceptance of the trust. There is no need for a written acceptance of a trust, and it is in practically every case accepted orally[1] or, more usually, by merely acting in the trust.[2] In general some acting in the trust has been required before acceptance will be presumed,[3] but although such a presumption has in fact been made where the trustee has not acted in the trust,[4] the modern view seems to be that inactivity over a long period of time is evidence of disclaimer rather than of

acceptance.[5] An acceptance of part of the trust operates as an acceptance of the whole and an acceptance of part and disclaimer of the remainder also operates as an acceptance of the whole.[6]

1   *Doe d Chidgey v Harris* (1847) 16 M & W 517.
2   *Conyngham v Conyngham* (1750) 1 Ves Sen 522; *White v Barton* (1854) 18 Beav 192. The retention of the trust deed for safe custody is not an acceptance: *Evans v John* (1841) 4 Beav 35.
3   See cases cited in n 1.
4   *Re Uniacke* (1844) 1 Jo & Lat 1; *Re Needham* (1844) 1 Jo & Lat 34.
5   *Re Clout and Frewer's Contract* [1924] 2 Ch 230 (thirty years' inactivity held to amount to a disclaimer), applying, *Re Gordon, Roberts v Gordon* (1877) 6 Ch D 531 and *Re Birchall, Birchall v Ashton* (1889) 40 Ch D 436, doubting *Re Uniacke* (1844) 1 Jo & Lat 1, and *Re Needham* (1844) 1 Jo & Lat 34. The law was considered in *Re Sharman's Will Trusts, Public Trustee v Sharman* [1942] Ch 311 at 317, [1942] 2 All ER 74 at 78. While as Bennett J, there does not go so far as to state any general principles, he seems to agree that it will not be presumed that the trustee has accepted the trusts merely because he has done nothing over a long period but has never formally disclaimed. He also seems to accept the proposition that where the office of executor is clothed with trusts, the taking out of probate acts as an acceptance of the trusts. Where a person takes out probate and does not wish to act in the trusts, he should either execute a deed of disclaimer of the office of trustee or secure the appointment of another person in his place.
6   *Re Lord and Fullerton's Contract* [1896] 1 Ch 228 (an attempt to disclaim as to English property and to accept as to property abroad); *Re v Garland* (1870) LR 5 QB 269, but see *Malzy v Edge* (1856) 2 Jur NS 80. But where another trustee is appointed a trustee may be discharged from the part of the trusts or powers: see Trustee Act 1925, s 36(1); (48 *Halsbury's Statutes* (4th edn) 500). The Trustee Act 1925, s 36(6) and (9) are amended in a minor way by the TLATA 1996, s 25(1), Sch 3, para 3(11).

[27.6]

Disclaimer of the trust. A person cannot be compelled to undertake the duties and responsibilities of a trustee against his wishes and, provided that he has not accepted the trust,[1] on the same principle as an executor is allowed to renounce, the trustee may disclaim; though unlike renunciation, which must be in writing and filed in the court, disclaimer of a trust, though it should as a practical precaution be in writing,[2] may be inferred from the fact that the person named as trustee has never acted in the trust.[3] Although at one time the presumption seems to have been in favour of acceptance,[4] it now seems to be in favour of disclaimer, and acceptance is not now presumed unless the trustee has in some way acted in the trust.[5] The expiration of nine years without acting in the trusts was held sufficient in a case where there was some evidence of a disclaimer in conversations.[6] Where a person had done nothing in the trust for thirty years, it was held that mere lapse of time was sufficient evidence of disclaimer.[7] Renunciation of probate is strong evidence of disclaimer of the trust where the same person is appointed to both offices, but it is not conclusive.[8] Where the office of trustee was disclaimed, the trust property did not vest in the trustee,[9] and, if there was another person who accepted the trust, then the whole trust estate vested in him.[10] Since 1925, however, the trustee will generally acquire the legal estate only by an assent. The trustee cannot disclaim the office and retain the estate,[11] nor can he disclaim as to part of the property even when part is in a foreign country.[12] The disclaimer involves renunciation of any benefit attached to the office,[13] but does not involve the renunciation of any benefit not annexed to the office.[14] A person who has disclaimed the office cannot act in it even to the extent of appointing a new trustee[15] and he does not become a trustee by subsequently acting as agent of the accepting trustees[16] or as adviser to the beneficiaries.[17]

1 *Re Sharman's Will Trusts, Public Trustee v Sharman* [1942] Ch 311, [1942] 2 All ER 74.
2 *Stacey v Elph* (1833) 1 My & K 195, where as Leach MR said at 199: 'It is most prudent that a deed of disclaimer should be executed by a person named as trustee, because such a deed is clear evidence of the disclaimer and admits of no ambiguity.' There is considerable authority that a disclaimer by deed is convenient and proper; *Nicloson v Wordsworth* (1818) 2 Swan 365; *Townson v Tickell* (1819) 3 B & Ald 31 at 39; *Stacey v Elph* (1833) 1 My & K 195; *Begbie v Crook* (1835) 2 Bing NC 70. But the deed operated as a disclaimer of the trust property as well as of the trust and it was held that a deed of release of the trust property was improper as purporting to accept and deal with the trust property (*Crewe v Dicken* (1798) 4 Ves 97; *Urch v Walker* (1838) 3 My & Cr 702) but it is not fatal to the disclaimer if the intention to disclaim is otherwise clear (*Nicloson v Wordsworth* (1818) 2 Swan 365; *Sharp v Sharp* (1819) 2 B & Ald 405; *Lord Wellesley v Withers* (1855) 4 E & B 750 at 757). Though the authorities speak of a deed of disclaimer, now that the trustee can take only an equitable interest under the will until an assent is made, possibly a disclaimer not under seal is sufficient where it is clear that there has been no assent. The deed seems to have been necessary because the disclaimer disclaimed the property as well as the trust. However, in so important a matter, the solemnity of a deed is not out of place. It has been said that a disclaimer by parol is sufficient: *Bingham v Lord Clanmorris* (1828) 2 Mol 253.
3 *White v M'Dermott* (1872) IR 7 CL 1; *Re Birchall, Birchall v Ashton* (1889) 40 Ch D 436.
4 See para **[27.5]**, n 1.
5 *Re Sharman's Will Trusts, Public Trustee v Sharman* [1942] Ch 311 at 317, [1942] 2 All ER 74 at 78.
6 *Re Birchall, Birchall v Ashton* (1889) 40 Ch D 436.
7 *Re Clout and Frewer's Contract* [1924] 2 Ch 230.
8 *Re Gordon, Roberts v Gordon* (1877) 6 Ch D 531; *Re Birchall, Birchall v Ashton* (1889) 40 Ch D 436; *Re Clout and Frewer's Contract* [1924] 2 Ch 230. It is a convenient practice to add a disclaimer of the trusts to the instrument of renunciation, but in such a case the instrument should be executed in duplicate because the renunciation has to be filed in court.
9 *Doe d Chidgey v Harris* (1847) 16 M & W 517 at 520; *Re Birchall, Birchall v Ashton* (1889) 40 Ch D 436.
10 *Bonifaut v Greenfield* (1587) Cro Eliz 80; *Crewe v Dicken* (1798) 4 Ves 97.
11 *Re Martinez' Trusts* (1870) 22 LT 403.
12 *Re Lord and Fullerton's Contract* [1896] 1 Ch 228; but, if he acts in the trust, he can now retire from part; see now the Trustee Act 1925, s 36(1); 48 *Halsbury's Statutes* (4th edn) 500. The Trustee Act 1925, s 36 has been amended, see para **[27.5]**, n 6.
13 *Slaney v Watney* (1866) LR 2 Eq 418; *Lewis v Mathews* (1869) LR 8 Eq 277.
14 *Pollexfen v Moore* (1745) 3 Atk 272; *Andrew v Trinity Hall, Cambridge* (1804) 9 Ves 525; *Talbot v Earl Radnor* (1834) 3 My & K 252; *Warren v Rudall, ex p Godfrey* (1860) 1 John & H 1.
15 *Re Birchall, Birchall v Ashton* (1889) 40 Ch D 436; but see the Trustee Act 1925, s 36(5) (48 *Halsbury's Statutes* (4th edn) 500), whereby a sole or last surviving executor intending to renounce, or all the executors where they all intend to renounce, may, at any time before renouncing probate, exercise the power of appointment of new trustee given by that section if willing to act for that purpose and without thereby accepting the office of executor.
16 *Lowry v Fulton* (1839) 9 Sim 104 at 115, 124.
17 *Stacey v Elph* (1833) 1 My & K 195.

[27.7]

Devolution of trusts. Trustees are joint tenants of the trust property and, on the death of any one of a number of trustees, the property and all the powers, authorities and discretions given to the original trustees devolve on the survivors or survivor.[1] There is, however, a statutory restriction on the right of a sole trustee to give a receipt for the proceeds of sale or other capital money arising under any trust of land.[2] This devolution is also subject to the fact that the creator of the trust may express a contrary intention.[3] On an appointment of new trustees under a power contained in the instrument creating the trust, the new trustee or trustees can exercise all the powers, authorities and discretions given to the original trustees; and in all cases where the appointment is made under the statutory power[4] every new trustee, as well before as after the trust property becomes vested in him by law, assurance, or otherwise, has all the powers, authorities and discretions of the original trustees, and may in all respects act as if he had been originally appointed a trustee by the instrument, if any, creating the trust.[5] The same rule applies where the trustee is appointed by a court of competent jurisdiction.[6] The personal representative of a sole or last surviving or continuing trustee is, until the appointment of new trustees,[7] capable of exercising or performing any power or trust which was given to, or capable of being exercised by, the sole, or last surviving or continuing trustee.[8]

Where all the original trustees of a will, or the sole trustee, disclaim[9] or predecease the testator, and no person is nominated to appoint new trustees, it is necessary to have new trustees appointed by the court.[10] In such a case the personal representative takes the property subject to the trust but cannot exercise the trust,[11] except in the case of settled land, where by statute[12] the personal representatives are until other trustees are appointed[13] authorised to exercise the trust and are made by virtue of the Settled Land Act 1925 trustees of the settlement, but, if there is only one trustee, he is required to appoint an additional trustee to act with him.[14]

1   Trustee Act 1925, s 18(1); 48 *Halsbury's Statutes* (4th edn) 469.
2   Trustee Act 1925, s 14(2); 48 *Halsbury's Statutes* (4th edn) 465. As amended by the TLATA 1996, s 25(1), Sch 3, para 3 so as to refer to capital money under any trust of land (within the meaning of the TLATA 1996) instead of under a trust for sale.
3   The creator may provide that the trust shall not be exercised by less than a certain number of trustees. This is very unusual except in the case of charitable trusts. The Trustee Act 1925, s 36(6); 48 *Halsbury's Statutes* (4th edn) 500 (as amended by the TLATA 1996) notices the possibility of such a provision.
4   Trustee Act 1925, s 36; 48 *Halsbury's Statutes* (4th edn) 500. This section has been amended by the TLATA 1996. See the amended form of the section in Vol 2, Part G, para **[246.31]**. Sections 19, 20 and 21 of the TLATA 1996 reverse the effect of *Re Brockbank* [1948] Ch 206 and gives beneficiaries who are sui juris and together entitled to the entire beneficial interest power to control the trusteeship without winding up the trust. As to the exercise of the statutory power by personal representatives of trustees, see TLATA 1996, s 18.
5   Trustee Act 1925, s 36(7); 48 *Halsbury's Statutes* (4th edn) 500 (as amended, see nn 3 and 4).
6   Trustee Act 1925, s 43; 48 *Halsbury's Statutes* (4th edn) 515. And see the provisions in the TLATA 1996, ss 19 and 20; see para **[27.2]** supra.
7   Two points have to be noted on this wording of the section (Trustee Act 1925, s 18(2); 48 *Halsbury's Statutes* (4th edn) 469). The first is in the nature of a technicality or trap. Since the personal representative can act only until the appointment of new trustees, he ceases to be a trustee upon the appointment of a new trustee or new trustees. If he wishes to appoint a second trustee to act with him (as he often must in order to be able to give a valid receipt for purchase money), he must not as an ordinary trustee would appoint an additional trustee to act with him, for, by reason of the words 'until the appointment of new trustees', the appointor himself ceases to be a trustee on the execution of the appointment. In such a case he must appoint himself and the new trustee to be trustees of the trust. The second point is that where there is a person nominated to appoint new trustees, the personal representative is completely at his mercy, for such person can at any time appoint new trustees without in any way consulting the personal representative; *Re Routledge's Trusts* [1909] 1 Ch 280.
8   Trustee Act 1925, s 18(2); 48 *Halsbury's Statutes* (4th edn) 469.
9   As to disclaimer, see para **[27.6]** supra.
10   *Nicholson v Field* [1893] 2 Ch 511.

11 *Robson v Flight* (1865) 4 De GJ & Sm 608 at 613.
12 Settled Land Act 1925, s 30(3); 48 *Halsbury's Statutes* (4th edn) 299; but see n 14 as to the effect of the TLATA 1996.
13 See n 7 supra.
14 In the case of settled land, two trustees for the purposes of the Settled Land Act 1925, are necessary under the Settled Land Act 1925, s 94; 48 *Halsbury's Statutes* (4th edn) 391, unless the trustee is a trust corporation. Though s 94 applies only to the giving of receipts for capital money, s 30(3) requires a sole personal representative in any case to appoint an additional trustee to act with him. In this case the wording of the subsection appears to allow the personal representative to continue to be a trustee after appointment and it is not essential that, as stated in connection with the Trustee Act 1925, s 18(2), in n 4, the personal representative should appoint himself and the new trustee to be the trustees of the settlement for the purposes of the Settled Land Act 1925. The Settled Land Act 1925 cannot apply to any trust created on or after 1 January 1997 by virtue of the TLATA 1996, see s 2.

[27.8]

Duty of care. The Trustee Act 2000 (TrA 2000)[1] creates a new precisely defined statutory duty of care applicable to trustees when carrying out their functions under the TrA 2000 or equivalent functions under the trust instrument.[2] The duty is defined as requiring a trustee to show such skill and care as is reasonable in the circumstances of the case, making allowance for his or her special knowledge, experience, or professional status.[3] But it seems that the duty of care may be limited by express provision in the trust instrument since it is provided that: 'The duty of care does not apply to powers conferred by a trust instrument if and so far as it appears from the trust instrument that the duty is not meant to apply'.[4] The duty of care also applies to trustees of land when exercising the powers conferred by the TLATA 1996.[5]

1 The TrA 2000, ss 1 and 2 and Sch 1. This duty will take effect in addition to the existing fundamental duties of trustees in the TrA 2000 but will exclude any common law duty of care which might otherwise have applied.
2 The duty is a default provision and may be excluded or modified by the terms of the trust; TrA 2000, s 26.
3 TrA 2000, s 1(1)(a) and (b). The TrA 2000, s 2 incorporates Sch 1 which sets out the application of the duty of care. Generally it will apply to the exercise of a power of investment or of acquisition of land; likewise to a decision to appoint agents, nominees and custodians or to insure trust property.
4 See the TrA 2000, Sch 1, para 5.
5 TrA 2000, Sch 2, para 38 adding the TLATA 1996, s 6(9). A new TLATA 1996, s 9A is added by the TrA 2000, Sch 2, para 40, relating to the duties of trustees in connection with delegation.

[27.9]

Power of delegation. The power of delegation has been enlarged and facilitated by new provisions in the Trustee Delegation Act 1999 (TDA 1999) and by the TrA 2000.[1] The TDA 1999 makes new provisions governing the delegation and exercise of trustee functions by power of attorney. The TDA 1999, s 1 states that the donee of a power of attorney is not prevented from doing acts in relation to land, capital proceeds of a conveyance of land or income from land by reason only that the act involves the exercise of a trustee function of the donor if, at the time when the act is done, the donor has a beneficial interest in the land, proceeds, or income.[2]

The Trustee Act 1925, s 25 is substituted with a new provision stating that a trustee may, by power of attorney, delegate the execution or exercise of all or any of the trusts, powers and discretions vested in him as trustee, either alone or jointly with any other person.[3] The previous rule that the donor of a power of attorney given under the section is liable for the acts or defaults of the donee as if they were the acts or defaults of the donor, is repeated.[4] Such a power can be an enduring power of attorney and can be registered as such.[5]

The TrA 2000 provides trustees with a wide power to collectively delegate their functions in the absence of an express power, or where an express power does not provide to the contrary.[6] These provisions do not relate to delegation by individual trustees which continue to be governed by the Trustee Act 1925, s 25 and the TDA 1999, s 1. The TrA 2000, s 11 states that (subject to the provisions of Part IV of the Act) the trustees of a trust may authorise any person to exercise any or all of their delegable functions as their agent.[7] Under this provision not all functions may be delegated but the new law will permit the delegation of discretionary functions that do not relate to the distribution of the trust assets.[8] In practice the new power will be useful to appoint an agent for the purpose of asset management. Subsequent sections impose a duty on trustees to keep any delegation under review and to take appropriate action where necessary.[9] An important new provision states that a trustee is not liable for any act or default of the agent[10] unless he has failed to comply with the duty of care applicable to him under Sch 1, para 3 of the TrA 2000 which relates to the application of the duty of care to delegation.[11]

1   With reference to the main provisions of the Trustee Act 1925 previously applicable to delegation, the TDA 1999 substitutes the Trustee Act 1925, s 25; the TrA 2000 repeals and replaces the Trustee Act 1925, ss 23 and 30.
2   TDA 1999, s 1(1). This is subject to any contrary intention expressed in the instrument creating the power of attorney, s 1(3) or in the trust instrument, s 1(5).
3   TDA 1999, s 5(1). There are further supplemental provisions in the next five subsections including a form of power of attorney.
4   TDA 1999 s 5(7).
5   TDA 1999, s 4. The Powers of Attorney Act 1971, s 9 and the Enduring Powers of Attorney Act 1985, ss 2(8) and 3(3) are repealed.
6   The TrA 2000, Pt IV sets out the new provisions. They are default provisions. The TrA 2000, ss 11–27 include matters relevant to agents, nominees and custodians. It is beyond the scope of this text to discuss these provisions in detail for which reference should be made to texts on trusts.
7   Thus repealing and replacing the Trustee Act 1925, s 23. Section 11(2) of the TrA 2000 states that the delegable functions consist of any function except four specified exclusions. But the principle of *delegatus non potest delagare* is preserved; Trustee Act 1925, s 25(8) as substituted by the TrA 2000, s 5.
8   See TrA 2000, s 11(2)(a)–(d), for the exclusions.
9   See TrA 2000, ss 21–22.
10 Or nominee or custodian.
11 TrA 2000, s 23(1); thus repealing and replacing the Trustee Act 1925, s 30 which referred to 'wilful default'. There are various further and supplemental provisions in ss 23–27 of the TrA 2000 which will not be noted here.

[27.10]

Remuneration of trustees. The Trustee Act 2000, Pt V makes better provision for the remuneration of trustees. There are new rules of construction of express professional charging clauses in trust instruments.[1] Second, the TrA 2000 in effect creates an implied professional charging clause applicable to all non-charitable trusts which do not make provision for the remuneration of professional trustees.[2] Where the trust instrument makes no provision for remuneration then trust corporations and trustees acting in a professional capacity will be entitled to charge reasonable remuneration for any services they provide for the trust.[3] This is so even if the services provided are capable of being provided by a lay trustee.[4] It can be noted that any payments to which a trustee is entitled in respect of services are to be treated as remuneration for services and not as a gift, for the purposes of the Wills Act 1837, s 15.[5]

1   TrA 2000, s 28(1)(a) and (b). By para (c) the payment of remuneration under the section must not be inconsistent with the terms of the trust instrument.
2   TrA 2000, s 29.
3   TrA 2000, s 29(1) reasonable remuneration is defined in s 29(3).
4   TrA 2000, s 28(2). See also ss 29–33 which contain further supplemental provisions relating to remuneration.
5   TrA 2000, s 28(3). Thus such remuneration would not be rendered void if the recipient was a witness to the will; see para **[9.11]** supra. Likewise for the Administration of Estates Act 1925, s 34(3).

[27.11]
Powers relating to investment. The Trustee Act 2000 repeals (most of) the Trustee Investments Act 1961[1] replacing the powers under that Act with a new general power of investment for trustees, giving them the same power of investment as an absolute owner other than in land (which is dealt with by a new power in the TrA 2000, s 8), subject to appropriate safeguards.[2] There are new and additional duties on the trustees to consider standard investment criteria and to take proper advice in exercising any power of investments.[3] The general power of investment is a default power for trustees who do not have specific powers of investment under the trust instrument and can operate as additional to, or alternative to, specific powers of investment under the trust instrument which are not contrary to the new statutory powers.[4] It can be noted that the 'duty of care' set out in the TrA 2000, s 1 will apply to the exercise of this new power of investment.[5]

1   See the TrA 2000, Schs 2, 3 and 4, for the extent of the repeal.
2   See the TrA 2000, s 3, where the power is set out.
3   See the TrA 2000, ss 4 and 5.
4   TrA 2000, s 6. See Vol 2, Part G, para **[246.121]**.
5   In the TrA 2000, s 1; see para **[27.8]** supra.

[27.12]
Power to acquire land. The Trustee Act 2000 (replacing provisions in the Trusts of Land and Appointment of Trustees Act 1996 (TLATA 1996))[1] creates a new power for trustees, whether of real or personal property, to acquire and deal with land on behalf of the trust.[2] But the power is limited to the acquisition of freehold or leasehold land as an investment.[3] The trustees are given the powers to deal with any land so acquired, of an absolute owner, analogous to the powers of a trustee of land under the TLATA 1996.[4]

1   TrA 2000, s 8, replacing s 6(4) of the TLATA 1996.
2   See the TLATA 1996, s 6(3) and (4).

3   TrA 2000, s 8(1).
4   TrA 2000, s 8(3). See para **[27.13]** infra.

[27.13]

Powers of trustees of land. The powers of trustees of land[1] in relation to the land are now by virtue of the TLATA 1996, those of an absolute owner.[2] Thus express enlargement of the trustees' powers is now much less necessary and the statutory powers[3] can be excluded or restricted by express provision.[4] Previously it had been the general practice to enlarge their powers so that they can carry out any transaction which an absolute owner could carry out.[5]

1   As to the meaning of the term see the TLATA 1996, s 1.
2   TLATA 1996, s 6(1). But having regard to the rights of the beneficiaries, TLATA 1996, s 6(5). This confers the widest discretion in respect of such matters as sale, insurance, repair, improvement, mortgaging and leasing and applies to all trusts of any kind involving land created on or after 1 January 1997 and all created before that date apart from ones to which the Settled Land Act 1925 continues to apply.
3   See the commentary in Vol 2.
4   The powers conferred by the TLATA 1996, see n 2, can be restricted or excluded, TLATA 1996, s 8(1), or made subject to consents, s 8(2). It is thought that in relation to trusts created before 1 January 1997, the trustees will have the full s 6 powers notwithstanding any express restrictions on the trustees' powers in the disposition creating the trust.
5   See Vol 2.

[27.14]

Power to insure. The Trustee Act 1925, s 19 has been substituted by the Trustee Act 2000.[1] A trustee may insure property which is subject to the trust against risks of loss or damage due to any event and may pay the premiums out of the trust funds.[2] The 'duty of care' applies to the exercise of this power.[3]

1   TrA 2000, s 34.
2   TrA 2000, s 34 (1)(a) and (b).
3   TrA 2000, s 1; see para **[27.8]** supra.

[27.15]

Trustees distinguished from personal representatives.[1] It is the common practice to appoint the executors also trustees of the will, but their respective functions are quite distinct. The function of the executors is to get in the estate and to clear it of debts, duties, and testamentary expenses, and, when those liabilities have been satisfied, it has been said that they cease to hold the estate as personal representatives and hold it as trustees;[2] but in the case of realty, even though the estate is to be held by the same person but in a different capacity, an assent in writing is necessary.[3] If the will contains no specific trusts upon which the property is to be held, they hold on trust for the beneficiaries according to their rights and interests under the will, and, where there are specific trusts, they hold upon those trusts.[4] In some cases the will appoints trustees who are different persons from the executors (though this is now rarely done) and then the executors must, when they have cleared the estate, vest the property in the trustees by an appropriate assent. The position is not complicated in the case of executors,[5] but where the grant is one of administration with the will annexed, it is complicated by the fact that the Administration of Estates Act 1925, s 33[6] makes the administrators trustees from the time of their appointment, but it is now generally accepted that they are in fact personal representatives until the estate is cleared.[7] Section 33 has been amended with effect from 1 January 1997 by the replacement of the 'trust to sell' by a 'power to sell', so that trustees under the section cease to be trustees for sale and become trustees of land with a power to sell but without any duty to sell.[8]

It is necessary to note the transition from personal representative to trustee because although the offices are analogous, they are distinct and can have consequences relating to the appointment of additional or substituted holders of the office;[9] the power to act severally;[10] the power to give receipts for purchase money on the sale of land[11] and the availability of the powers conferred by the Administration of Estates Act 1925, s 39.[12] The nature of the beneficial interest is also different under an incompletely administered estate on the one hand and a trust on the other.[13]

1   See also *Underhill and Hayton, Law of Trusts and Trustees* (15th edn), Div IV.
2   *Re Ponder, Ponder v Ponder* [1921] 2 Ch 59; *Toates v Toates* [1926] 2 KB 30. See also *Re Pitt, Pitt v Mann* (1928) 44 TLR 371; *Re Cockburn, Cockburn v Lewis* [1957] Ch 438, [1957] 2 All ER 522; *Re Real, McDowell v Real* (1914) 33 NZLR 1342. It is submitted that there is nothing in *Re Yerburgh, Yerburgh v Yerburgh* [1928] WN 208, to the contrary, but see now *Re King's Will Trusts, Assheton v Boyne* [1964] Ch 542, [1964] 1 All ER 833; *Re Edwards' Will Trusts, Edwards v Edwards* [1982] Ch 30, [1981] 2 All ER 941. See also the Hong Kong case of *Kleinwort Benson (Hong Kong) Trustees Ltd v Wong Foonang* [1993] 1 HKC 649.
3   *Re King's Will Trusts, Assheton v Boyne* [1964] Ch 542, [1964] 1 All ER 833; *Re Edwards' Will Trusts, Edwards v Edwards* [1982] Ch 30, [1981] 2 All ER 941. In the case of personalty no written assent is necessary and the transition will be automatic; see cases in n 2.
4   Whatever the legal position is as to the necessity for an assent, the transition from personal representative to trustee will properly be marked by the execution of an assent: see *Re Trollope's Will Trusts, Public Trustee v Trollope* [1927] 1 Ch 596; *Re Yerburgh, Yerburgh v Yerburgh* [1928] WN 208. The duties of personal representatives are commonly called 'clearing the estate', and when this is done their functions as executors cease. See also *Re Cavanagh* [1938] 2 DLR 761. Where a testator appoints executors but does not appoint them or any one else to be trustees, the executors are the persons referred to later in the will where the testator speaks of his 'trustees': *Re Robinson* [1951] Ch 198.
5   Otherwise than by the question whether an assent in writing is necessary to vest the legal estate in the trustees as such.
6   See Vol 2, Part G, para **[244.58]**. As amended by the TLATA 1996; see n 9.
7   See *Re Yerburgh, Yerburgh v Yerburgh* [1928] WN 208.
8   By the TLATA 1996, s 2(6), Sch 2, para 5. It is not thought that this change affects the points made in the text on the transition of a personal representative to a trustee.
9   An administrator can be appointed only by the court, whereas a trustee can be appointed by a trustee or by a person nominated to appoint trustees or by the beneficiaries under the TLATA 1996; see para **[27.2]** supra. A personal representative as such has no power to appoint a trustee, though as personal representative of a deceased sole or last surviving trustee he can appoint a new trustee of the trust of which the deceased was a trustee: Trustee Act 1925, s 36(1)(b); 48 *Halsbury's Statutes* (4th edn) 500.
10   As a general principle executors and presumably administrators can act severally: see *Fountain Forestry Ltd v Edwards* [1975] Ch 1, [1974] 2 All ER 280; trustees must act jointly. But executor's powers to act severally have been reduced by the amendments made to the Administration of Estates Act 1925, s 2(2) by the Law of Property (Miscellaneous Provisions) Act 1994, s 16(1). The Administration of Estates Act 1925, s 2(2) now requires that all the personal representatives, who for the time being have taken out a grant of probate, must concur in the conveyance or transfer of real estate, and in any contract for such a conveyance or transfer.
11   A sole personal representative can give a receipt for purchase money on the sale of land, a sole trustee cannot.

12   Personal representatives have the powers conferred by this section but not trustees. This section
has been amended by the TLATA 1996. The Administration of Estates Act 1925, s 39(1)(i) now
refers to 'as respects the personal estate'. The Administration of Estates Act 1925, s 39(1)(ii)
now reads, 'as respects the real estate, all the functions conferred on them by Part 1 of the
Trusts of Land and Appointment of Trustees Act 1996'. The section has been further amended
by the Trustee Act 2000, Sch 2, para 23 adding a new subsection (1A) to the Administration of
Estates Act 1925, s 39 to the effect that 39(1) is without prejudice to the powers conferred on
personal representatives by the Trustee Act 2000.

13   See discussion in para **[1.12]** supra.

[27.16]

Trustees for sale: pre-1 January 1997. Trustees for sale of land have been
converted to simple trustees by the Trusts of Land and Appointment of Trustees
Act 1996, whether the trust was created before or after 1 January 1997. The
position before the TLATA 1996 came into force will be considered in this
paragraph since many of the provisions previously applicable to trustees for sale
will likewise apply to trusts of land. There were first restrictions on the
maximum and minimum number of trustees who could hold land on trust for
sale. The maximum number was restricted to four and, if more than four were
appointed, only the first four named (who were able and willing to act) were to
be trustees; any others were not trustees unless and until they were appointed as
such on a vacancy.[1] The limitation applied not only to the original appointment,
but also to any subsequent appointment, and at no time could the number of
trustees be increased beyond four.[2] The minimum was fixed, not by a definite
restriction on the number of trustees for sale that could be appointed, but by a
provision that a valid receipt for the purchase money arising on a sale or for any
capital money arising under the trust could not be given by less than two
trustees.[3] It will be noted, therefore, that there was no prohibition of one trustee
conveying the legal estate in the land and thus, where a valid receipt could be
given otherwise than by the trustees, a sole trustee could convey the legal estate
and the receipt given by those entitled to the purchase money.[4] An exception,
too, was made in the case of a trust corporation,[5] which could in all cases act as
a sole trustee for sale.[6] The restriction as to the giving of valid receipts did not
apply to a personal representative acting as such.[7] A trustee with a mere power
of sale as distinct from a trust for sale could give a valid receipt, but this was of
little practical importance as under the law the power would fall to be exercised
by a tenant for life under the Settled Land Act 1925 and there being settled land
there would of necessity have to have been two trustees of the settlement.[8] The
exercise of a trust for sale was often made subject to the consent of the tenant for
life or other person or persons. Where the consent of more than two persons was
required, then in favour of a purchaser the consent of any two such persons was
sufficient.[9] Where the consent of a person was so made necessary and such
person was a minor, the consent of the parent or the testamentary or other
guardian was sufficient in favour of a purchaser, and where such person was of
unsound mind, then the consent of his receiver was in favour of a purchaser
sufficient.[10] In framing clauses requiring such consents, therefore, only in cases
where the matter was of real importance would the consent of more than two
persons be made necessary except where the consent of an unascertained class of
persons was thought to be desirable.

Trustee Act 1925, s 34; 48 *Halsbury's Statutes* (4th edn) 498. This provision (like many of the other sections of the Trustee Act 1925 and the Law of Property Act 1925, cited in this paragraph) has been amended by the TLATA 1996; see s 25(1) and Sch 3, para 3(9) and Sch 4, para 4. See para **[27.17]** infra for the post-1997 position.

2   Trustee Act 1925, s 34.

3   Trustee Act 1925, s 14(2) (48 *Halsbury's Statutes* (4th edn) 465), repeated in the Law of Property Act 1925, s 27(2), but with the addition that this did not affect the right of a sole personal representative (presumably acting as such and not when exercising a trust under the Trustee Act 1925, s 18(2); 48 *Halsbury's Statutes* (4th edn) 469) to give a receipt; and that it did not prevent a sole individual trustee from acting in a trust where no receipt for capital money was involved.

4   This was only suitable in simple cases where the bringing of the equities on the title really discloses no more than is otherwise known concerning the property. If there have been dealings with the equities, it is safer to appoint a new trustee. It has been pointed out that the Trustee Act 1925, s 18(2) does not make the personal representative in terms a trustee, but it is submitted that the section gives him the option of refusing or consenting to act in the trusts, and if he does act in the trusts, he becomes a trustee. It will also be noted that he can only exercise the powers which could have been exercised by the sole or last surviving or continuing trustee and, as these would not have included a power to give a valid receipt for capital moneys in the case of a trust for sale, it seems that there must be an appointment of new trustees before such a receipt can be given; sed quaere whether this is necessary where there are two personal representatives who have proved, although, on the strict wording of the section, they have only the powers of the sole trustee.

5   See para **[27.4]** supra.

6   See the Trustee Act 1925, s 14(2) (48 *Halsbury's Statutes* (4th edn) 465), and the Law of Property Act 1925, s 27(2); 37 *Halsbury's Statutes* (4th edn) 150.

7   See n 3.

8   Settled Land Act 1925, s 94; 48 *Halsbury's Statutes* (4th edn) 391. See para **[27.7]**, n 14.

9   Law of Property Act 1925, s 26; 37 *Halsbury's Statutes* (4th edn) 148.

10   Law of Property Act 1925, s 26; 37 *Halsbury's Statutes* (4th edn) 148.

[27.17]

Trustees for Sale: post-1 January 1997. With effect from this date all trusts for the sale of land (whether created before or after 1 January 1997) now become trusts of land as defined by the TLATA 1996.[1] The TLATA 1996 defines 'trustees of land' as trustees of a trust of land.[2] The propositions in para **[27.16]** supra continue to apply to all trustees of land, including trustees for sale of land, subject as follows. First, the limitations on the number of trustees who may hold land continue to apply to all trusts of land, including trusts for sale.[3] Second, the provisions regarding receipts for proceeds of sale of land have been amended to apply to all trusts of land, including trusts for sale.[4] Accordingly, a receipt from two persons or a trust corporation acting as trustee, is now needed for a purchaser to get a good receipt from trustees of land of any kind, whether the trustees are exercising a power of sale or executing a trust for sale.[5] Third, the rules relating to the requirements of consent[6] remain the same.[7]

1   See the TLATA 1996, s 1(1)(a).

2   TLATA 1996, s 1(1)(b).

3   Under the Trustee Act 1925, s 34(2) as amended by the TLATA 1996.

4   See TLATA 1996, s 25(1), Sch 3, para 4.

5   So that the sentence to which para **[27.16]**, n 8, refers no longer states the law.

6   See the text to para **[27.16]**, n 9.

7   Save that the Law of Property Act 1925, s 26 referred to in nn 9 and 10 to para **[27.16]** supra, has been replaced in materially identical terms by the TLATA 1996, s 10; see Vol 2, Part G, para **[246.96]**.

[27.18]

Trustees for the purposes of the Settled Land Act 1925. It is not possible on or after 1 January 1997 to create new settlements under the Settled Land Act 1925 (other than derivative settlements) although existing settlements subject to the Settled Land Act 1925 continue to be so subject so long as land or heirlooms are retained.[1] Such existing and continuing settlements are governed by the Settled Land Act 1925, s 30,[2] to which reference should be made.[3]

The Settled Land Act 1925, s 94,[4] requires that there shall be at least two trustees to receive any capital money, so that, if the number of trustees is reduced to one, an appointment of new trustees is required except where the trustee is a trust corporation.

1   TLATA 1996, ss 1 and 2.
2   48 *Halsbury's Statutes* (4th edn) 299. Subject to the provisions in the TLATA 1996, s 2 referred to above.
3   See also *Re Coull's Settled Estates* [1905] 1 Ch 712; *Re Garnett Orme and Hargreaves' Contract* (1883) 25 Ch D 595; *Re Carne's Settled Estates* [1899] 1 Ch 324; *Re Jackson's Settled Estate* [1902] 1 Ch 258; *Re Davies and Kent's Contract* [1910] 2 Ch 35.
4   48 *Halsbury's Statutes* (4th edn) 391.

CHAPTER 28

Appointment of guardians

I. APPOINTMENT OF GUARDIANS ON OR AFTER 14 OCTOBER 1991

[28.1]
The appointment of guardians on or after 14 October 1991 is governed by the Children Act 1989 (ChA 1989),[1] the relevant parts of which commenced from that date.[2] From 14 October 1991 guardians may only be appointed in accordance with the ChA 1989, s 5,[3] but appointments made before that date and valid under the law prevailing at the time can continue in force or take effect (as the case may be) under the ChA 1989.[4] Guardians can only be appointed in relation to a child under the age of 18 years, and references to a child or children in the account below must be understood as referring only to children under that age.[5] For the power of a guardian or parent with parental responsibility for a child under 18 to receive or recover his property see para **[9.42]** supra.[6]

1 See Vol 2, Part G, para **[244.117]**.
2 By virtue of Children Act 1989 (Commencement and Transitional Provisions) Order 1991, SI 1991/828.
3 ChA 1989, s 5(13).
4 ChA 1989, Sch 14, paras 12 and 13.
5 ChA 1989, s 105(1).
6 For precedents of appointments of guardians see Vol 2, Note and Forms B3.26 to B3.32, paras **[203.55]** to **[203.61]**.

[28.2]
Who may appoint guardians—parental responsibility. The Children Act 1989, s 5 gives the power to appoint a guardian to the parent or parents with parental responsibility for a child, and to a guardian of a child.[1] Parental responsibility means all the rights, duties, powers, responsibilities and authority which by law a parent of a child has in relation to the child and his property, and includes the rights, powers and duties which a guardian of the child's estate appointed before the ChA 1989 came into force would have had in relation to the child.[2]

Both parents of a legitimate child[3] have equal parental responsibility for him.[4] In the case of an illegitimate child the mother has parental responsibility,[5] and the father only acquires it if there is an order of the relevant court that he shall have it or it is conferred by a parental responsibility agreement between him and the mother,[6] or he marries the mother. A parental responsibility agreement only has effect if it is in the form prescribed by regulations made by the Lord Chancellor,[7] and once made it can only be terminated by an order of the court,[8] ie the mother cannot revoke it at will. A guardian of a child whose appointment has taken effect also has parental responsibility for that child,[9] but power is expressly conferred on a guardian to appoint someone else to take his place in the event of his death, independently of the provisions about parental responsibility.[10] It is arguable that this power of a guardian to appoint his successor may be exercised by someone who has been appointed a guardian before that appointment has taken effect,[11] but on balance it is thought that such an argument is incorrect.[12] The court also has power to appoint a guardian.[13] There are no further categories of persons empowered to appoint guardians.[14]

1   ChA 1989, s 5(3) and (4).
2   ChA 1989, s 3(1) and (2).
3   This includes a child legitimated by the subsequent marriage of his parents, an adopted child, and a child otherwise treated in law as legitimate: see the Family Law Reform Act 1987, s 1(2) and (3) (Vol 2, Part G, para **[245.70]**) and ChA 1989, ss 2(1) and (3).
4   ChA 1989, s 2(1), (4) and (5).
5   ChA 1989, s 2(2)(a).
6   ChA 1989, s 4(1). Where an order made under Family Law Reform Act 1987, s 4(1) giving a father parental rights and duties in relation to a child was in force immediately before 14 October 1991 it has effect from then as an order under ChA 1989, s 4 giving the father parental responsibility, and an order in force immediately before that date under previous legislation giving the father custody or care and control has effect under the Children Act 1989 from then as an order conferring parental responsibility on him: ChA 1989, Sch 14, paras 4 and 6(2) and (4).
7   ChA 1989, s 4(2). For the prescribed form see the Parental Responsibility Agreement Regulations 1991, SI 1991/1478 as amended by SI 1994/3157. The ChA 1989, s 4(2) also requires such an agreement to be recorded in the prescribed manner if the relevant regulations so require; SI 1991/1478 requires recording of a parental responsibility agreement in the Principal Registry of the Family Division of the High Court as a precondition of it taking effect.
8   ChA 1989, s 4(3).
9   ChA 1989, s 5(6).
10 See ChA 1989, s 5(4).
11 Because the reference in ChA 1989, s 5(8) to s 5(4) of that Act would appear to have no function if it is only a guardian whose appointment has taken effect who can appoint another guardian.
12 The wording of the power in ChA 1989, s 5(4) 'a guardian of a child may appoint ... to take his place as the child's guardian in the event of his death' suggests it is a power only exercisable after a guardian has taken up the office. Also a guardian is not really a guardian until his appointment has taken effect, and an appointment of a guardian is always revocable during the life of the appointor.
13 ChA 1989, s 5(1) and (2).
14 In particular, a person who is not the child's parent and in whose favour a residence order is made has parental responsibility but does not have power to appoint a guardian: see the ChA 1989, s 12(2) and (3)(c).

[28.3]
Who may be appointed guardians. Only individuals may be appointed.[1] It is not possible, for example, to appoint a trust corporation as a guardian.

1   See the ChA 1989, s 5(1), (3), and (4), referring throughout to the appointment of individuals as guardians.

[28.4]
The scope of the powers and deferral of the appointment until both parents are dead. The ChA 1989, s 5(3) empowers a parent with parental responsibility for his child to appoint another individual to be the child's guardian in the event

of his death. The ChA 1989, s 5(4) empowers a guardian of a child to appoint another individual to take his place as the child's guardian in the event of his death. An appointment of a guardian will only take effect when a death leaves the child without a parent with parental responsibility for him,[1] unless the death is of the parent (or guardian) making the appointment and there was a residence order[2] in favour of that parent or guardian in force immediately before his death,[3] not being a residence order made in favour of a parent of the child who is surviving after that death.[4]

This can be illustrated by an example. H and W are parents with parental responsibility for their child C. H appoints G1 as C's guardian in the event of H's death, and W appoints G2 as C's guardian in the event of W's death. H then dies. Because W is a surviving parent with parental responsibility, H's appointment of G1 does not take effect on H's death.[5] W then dies. On her death the appointments of both G1 and G2 as guardians will take effect.[6] It would probably have been a more sensible arrangement for H to have made an appointment taking effect only in the event of H dying after W, so that there would have been only one guardian of C at a time. Continuing the example, if G1 dies having appointed G3 as his successor, G3 will take office as C's guardian on G1's death even though G2 is still alive and acting as C's guardian, since the deferral of appointments mentioned above is only until the death of the last *parent* with parental responsibility. If there had been a residence order in force in favour of H (but not W) at H's death, then the appointment of G1 as C's guardian would have taken effect on H's death.

The wording of the powers in the ChA 1989, s 5(3) and (4) might be thought to permit only one person to be appointed as a guardian, but it is arguable that the rule of statutory interpretation that the singular includes the plural[7] is not excluded, particularly as the ChA 1989,[8] expressly contemplates that the same person may appoint more than one guardian of the same child. It is not clear whether the ChA 1989, s 5(3) gives power to appoint a guardian to act after the death of the appointor's first choice of guardian after the latter's appointment has taken effect (the most sensible practical course would seem to be to leave it to the guardian to appoint his own successor), although there is nothing to prevent an alternative appointment being made which is to take effect if the first choice predeceases the appointor or disclaims. It should also be noted that a joint appointment by two or more persons is expressly permitted,[9] so that, for example, where both parents have parental responsibility they can make a joint appointment of the same person to be guardian in the event of them both dying.

Another question is whether a parent must have parental responsibility both when making an appointment of a guardian and immediately before his death. The wording of the power conferred by the ChA 1989, s 5(3) makes it reasonably plain that he must have parental responsibility at the time of the appointment, but there is no clear implication that he must also have parental responsibility at his death.[10] It will not be common for a parent who has acquired parental responsibility to lose it subsequently, but it is possible in the case of a father of an illegitimate child.[11]

Because a guardian of a child may only be appointed in accordance with the provisions of the ChA 1989, s 5,[12] it is submitted that a person with power to appoint a guardian of a child cannot confer power on any other person to appoint a guardian of that child.

1 ChA 1989, s 5(7) and (8).
2 This is an order of the court settling the arrangements to be made as to the person with whom a child is to live: ChA 1989, s 8(1). It also includes for this purpose an order giving custody and control of the child made before 14 October 1991: ChA 1989, Sch 14, para 8(2).
3 ChA 1989, s 5(7)(b).
4 ChA 1989, s 5(9).
5 ChA 1989, s 5(8).
6 ChA 1989, s 5(7)(a) and (8).
7 Interpretation Act 1978, s 6(c).
8 See ChA 1989, s 6(1); Vol 2, Part G, para **[244.122]**.
9 ChA 1989, s 5(10).
10 Contrast Guardianship of Minors Act 1971, s 4(7)(b) (added by Family Law Reform Act 1987) and s 14(3) (before its repeal by Family Law Reform Act 1987) where it was expressly provided that a father of an illegitimate child must have the relevant parental rights at his death, as well as at the time of making the appointment, for an appointment by him of a guardian to be effective.
11 ChA 1989, s 4(3) empowers the court to terminate the parental responsibility of the father of an illegitimate child either where he acquired it under an order of the court or where he acquired it under a parental responsibility agreement.
12 ChA 1989, s 5(13).

[28.5]
Formal requirements. By virtue of the ChA 1989, s 5(5)[1] an appointment of a guardian will only be effective if it is in writing, is dated, and is either signed by the person making the appointment, or signed at his direction before two witnesses—if it is a will, in accordance with the Wills Act 1837, s 9,[2] and if it is not, in his presence and in the presence of two witnesses who each attest the signature. Accordingly, where a person appointing a guardian signs the instrument of appointment himself there is no requirement that it be witnessed, and it is thus possible for a will which is dated and signed by the testator and made after 14 October 1991, which contains the appointment of a guardian, to be valid as an appointment of that guardian even if it is invalid as a will because, eg, the correct procedure for execution of it as a will was not followed. The ability to make an appointment by a relatively informal written instrument is an innovation of the ChA 1989, but if a person is making a will it is still advisable to put the appointment of a guardian in his will rather than in an informal written instrument, because a will is less likely to be lost or overlooked at his death.

The requirement that the instrument should be dated is worthy of note. It is a general requirement of an appointment of a guardian, whether it is by will or other written instrument. Apart from this provision there is no requirement of wills that they be dated.[3] As wills almost invariably are dated, it might be thought that this provision will be readily complied with in relation to wills. However problems could arise if the will bears the wrong date, ie not the date of execution, or has been dated after execution. It is submitted that the ChA 1989, s 5(5) will not be satisfied unless (i) the instrument is dated when it is executed and (ii) the date is the day on which it is executed, and that if these requirements are not satisfied the appointment of a guardian will not be effective (even though the rest of the will may be valid). Where the date is wrong through a clerical error, eg the testator mistook what the date was when executing the will, it might be possible for it to be rectified by the court under Administration of Justice Act 1982, s 20.[4]

1 See also para **[28.4]** supra.

2   See Chapter 11, and Vol 2, Part G, paras **[244.6]** and **[244.7]**. It can be noted that the Wills
    (Soldiers and Sailors) Act 1918, s 4 confers a power to appoint guardians by informal will
    rendered valid by the Wills Act 1837, s 11 but it is thought that this is subject to the
    requirements of the ChA 1989, s 5(5) so that the Wills (Soldiers and Sailors) Act 1918, s 4 does
    not render valid anything which would not be valid anyway as an appointment of a guardian
    within the ChA 1989, s 5(5). As to privileged wills see Chapter 16.
3   See *Corbett v Newey* [1996] 2 All ER 914.
4   See Chapter 6, and Vol 2, Part G, para **[244.96]**.

[28.6]
Revocation of an appointment. All appointments of guardians are revocable
during the life of the appointor. There are various methods of revocation, and
this is a subject of some elaboration because of the liberal rules as to how the
appointments may be made in the first place. The possible ways in which an
appointment of a guardian by will may be revoked are as follows:

(a)   revocation of the will in any of the ways this may occur;[1]
(b)   revocation of the appointment by a written and dated instrument, signed
      by the maker of the appointment or at his direction in the presence of two
      witnesses who each attest the signature (ie a non-testamentary instrument
      which satisfies the same formal requirements as for an appointment of a
      guardian, witnessing not being necessary where the appointor signs it);[2]
(c)   by a later appointment of a guardian (by will or otherwise) by the same
      person in respect of the same child, unless it is clear (whether as a result
      of an express provision in the later appointment or by any necessary
      implication) that the purpose of the later appointment is to appoint an
      additional guardian;[3]
(d)   where the death is on or after 1 January 1996, and the appointment is of
      the appointor's spouse, by the dissolution or annulment of the marriage.[4]

The possible ways in which an appointment of a guardian by a non-
testamentary written instrument may be revoked are the same, except that (i)
revocation as a will under the Wills Act 1837 is naturally not applicable, but (ii)
such an appointment is revoked by destruction of the instrument by the person
who made the appointment or by someone else in his presence, the person who
made the appointment doing so with the intention of revoking it.[5]

Two particular points to note are that an appointment of a guardian in a will
can be revoked by an instrument which does not satisfy the requirements of the
Wills Act 1837 for the revocation of wills, and that an appointment of a guardian
contained in a will (not made in expectation of the marriage) is revoked by the
subsequent marriage of the person who made the appointment,[6] but such an
appointment in a non-testamentary instrument is not revoked in these
circumstances.

1   ChA 1989, s 6(4). This would include revocation by marriage. For revocation of wills see
    Chapters 17 to 19.
2   ChA 1989, s 6(2).
3   ChA 1989, s 6(1).
4   ChA 1989, s 6(3A), added by the Law Reform (Succession) Act 1995, s 4. This is of course
    only relevant where the appointor's spouse is not the other parent of the child.
5   ChA 1989, s 6(3).
6   For revocation of wills by marriage see Chapter 17.

[28.7]
Disclaimer of guardianship. A person who is appointed a guardian, either by a parent with parental responsibility or by a guardian, as described above, may disclaim his appointment by an instrument in writing signed by him and made within a reasonable time of his first knowing that the appointment has taken effect.[1] There are two elements to this knowledge: knowledge that the appointment has been made, and knowledge of the relevant death. These two pieces of information will often arrive together, but may not do so where the appointment was made by the first to die of two parents with parental responsibility, because in that case the appointment takes effect only on the death of the second to die of those parents (unless there was a residence order which did not apply to the survivor).[2] Regulations may be made by the Lord Chancellor to prescribe a manner of recording a disclaimer of an appointment as a guardian, and if there are such regulations such a disclaimer does not have effect until it is so recorded,[3] but so far no such regulations have been made and so there is no requirement at the moment that a disclaimer of guardianship be recorded. If an appointment of a guardian has taken effect and has not been validly disclaimed in accordance with this provision, it can only be terminated by an order of the court.[4]

1 ChA 1989, s 6(5).
2 ChA 1989, s 5(7) and (8) and see para **[28.4]** supra.
3 ChA 1989, s 6(6).
4 ChA 1989, s 5(7).

[28.8]
Transitional provisions relating to appointments made before 14 October 1991. Any appointment of a guardian made under the previous law which had taken effect before 14 October 1991 is deemed to be an appointment under the ChA 1989, s 5.[1] Among other things this means that a guardian so appointed will be able to appoint a successor as guardian under the ChA 1989, s 5(4).[2] An appointment of a guardian made under Guardianship of Minors Act 1971, ss 3 to 5[3] which had not taken effect immediately before 14 October 1991 takes effect in accordance with the ChA 1989, s 5.[4] This apparently means that the provisions as to when an appointment of a guardian takes effect,[5] the power of a guardian to appoint his successor,[6] and the revocation of an appointment,[7] all of which are innovations of the ChA 1989, will apply in relation to an appointment under the Guardianship of Minors Act 1971.

1 ChA 1989, Sch 14, para 12(1), where the relevant earlier law is specified. Where the appointment was under Sexual Offences Act 1956, s 38(3) the appointment does not have effect for longer than was specified in the order (para 12(2)).
2 See para **[28.4]** supra.
3 See para **[28.9]** infra.
4 ChA 1989, Sch 14, para 13.
5 See ChA 1989, s 5(7) and (8) and para **[28.4]** supra.
6 ChA 1989, s 5(4), and see para **[28.2]** supra.
7 ChA 1989, s 6(1) to (4), and see para **[28.6]** supra.

II.   APPOINTMENT OF GUARDIANS BEFORE 14 OCTOBER 1991

[28.9]

This is a topic which remains relevant as appointments made under pre-14 October 1991 legislation can continue to have effect (see above). The relevant legislation was the Guardianship of Minors Act 1971 with effect from 17 March 1971.[1] It was amended in relation to illegitimate children by the Family Law Reform Act 1987 with effect from 1 April 1989.

The mother and father of a child under 18 each had power to appoint by deed or will any person to be guardian of that child in the event of the appointor's death.[2] Thus, in contrast to the position on or after 14 October 1991, a guardian appointed by one parent would become a guardian of the child on the appointor's death even if the other parent was still living, and would act jointly with the surviving parent unless the court ordered otherwise.[3] In the case of an illegitimate child his mother had power to appoint a guardian to act in the event of her death, but his father had power to make an appointment of a guardian only if entitled to custody of the child at the time of the appointment and also immediately before his death,[4] or, where the appointment and/or the father's death occurred on or after 1 April 1989, the father had all the parental rights and duties with respect to the child by virtue of an order under the Family Law Reform Act 1987, s 4 or the right to custody, legal or actual custody or care and control of the child by virtue of an order made under any other enactment, both at the date of the appointment and at his death.[5] There was no statutory power of a guardian to appoint his own successor in the event of his death, and it is not clear whether a parent could, when making an appointment of a guardian, confer power on that guardian to appoint another guardian.[6]

1   The date of its commencement as provided by the Guardianship of Minors Act 1971, s 20(5). It in fact consolidated a number of earlier statutes going back to the Guardianship of Infants Act 1886.
2   Guardianship of Minors Act 1971, s 4(1) and (2).
3   See the Guardianship of Minors Act 1971, s 4(3) and (4).
4   Guardianship of Minors Act 1971, s 14(3).
5   Guardianship of Minors Act 1971, s 3(4) and 4(7), as added by Family Law Reform Act 1987, s 6.
6   *Re Parnell's Goods* (1872) LR 2 P & D 379 has been thought to be authority that this could be done, but it was a decision on the very different wording of the Tenures Abolition Act 1660.

Contents of wills

CHAPTER 29

Appropriation

I. COMMON LAW POWERS

[29.1]

Vested legacy immediately payable. Where the legacy is vested and immediately payable, an executor[1] may appropriate some particular property[2] to be taken in satisfaction[3] of the legacy or of part of it. Where this is fairly done[4] and the legatee receives no more than he is entitled to, the appropriation cannot be impeached[5] and it does not require the consent of other legatees though the executor must obtain the consent of the legatee in whose favour the appropriation is made,[6] who must be sui juris.[7] Such an appropriation may be made in favour of a legatee who is also an executor.[8] Where the executor is a legatee in trust for a person absolutely entitled and the legacy is allowed to remain mixed with the residue the legatee is entitled to share in any increase in the residuary estate[9] but this is not so in the case of a settled legacy where the tenant for life receives only interest at the basic rate, even though the executor is one of the residuary legatees.[10]

---

1   For the purposes of appropriation at common law the classes of legacies to be considered are (i) vested legacies, as to which different rules are applicable where they are immediately payable and where they are payable only in the future; (ii) contingent legacies, as to which different rules are applicable where they carry some part of the intermediate income or the whole of it and where they do not carry the intermediate income at all; and (iii) settled shares of residue.

2   As to what properties may be appropriated, see para **[29.9]** infra.

3   As to effect of appropriation, see para **[29.14]** infra.

4   As to valuation for appropriation, see para **[29.11]** infra.

5   *Re Lepine, Dowsett v Culver* [1892] 1 Ch 210.

6   *Baker v Farmer* (1868) 3 Ch App 537; *Re Salaman, De Pass v Sonnenthal* [1907] 2 Ch 46.

7   See n 6 supra. At common law no appropriation can be made in the case of a minor (*Rimell v Simpson* (1848) 18 LJ Ch 55; *Re Salaman, De Pass v Sonnenthal* [1907] 2 Ch 46; *Re Salomons, Public Trustee v Wortley* [1920] 1 Ch 290). As to payment where a pecuniary legatee is a minor, see para **[9.39]** supra. As to payment into court, see the Trustee Act 1925, s 63; 48 *Halsbury's Statutes* (4th edn) 535. As to appointment of special trustees of the fund and transfer to them, see the Administration of Estates Act 1925, s 42, (the Administration of Estates Act 1925, s 42(6)(a) has been slightly amended by the Trustee Act 2000, Sch 2, para 37); 17 *Halsbury's Statutes* (4th edn) 448. No such appropriation can be made where the legatee cannot be found: *Re Hall, Foster v Metcalfe* [1903] 2 Ch 226 at 233, and see *Re Salomons, Public Trustee v Wortley* [1920] 1 Ch 290 at 294. The executor may, however, appropriate a sufficient sum or invested fund to meet the legacy in order to be able to divide the residue but unless that is done under an express or implied power in the will, the appropriation did not at common law bind the legatee and he could claim any deficiency from residue, though not from the executor if he had acted fairly, *Re Hall, Foster v Metcalfe* [1903] 2 Ch 226, but under the statutory power the legatee is now bound: Administration of Estates Act 1925, s 41(1)(iii), (4); 17 *Halsbury's Statutes* (4th edn) 446.

8   *Barclay v Owen* (1889) 60 LT 220; *Re Richardson, Morgan v Richardson* [1896] 1 Ch 512; but he cannot appropriate to his own legacy property which has no market value: *Re Bythway, Gough v Dames* (1911) 80 LJ Ch 246; *Kane v Radley-Kane* [1998] 3 All ER 753.

9   *Re Chadwin* (1818) 3 Swan 380 (it is not in effect appropriated).

10 *Re Campbell, Campbell v Campbell* [1893] 3 Ch 468.

[29.2]

Vested legacy payable in the future. Where the legacy is vested[1] the legatee has an absolute right to require the amount to be invested by the executor and upon such investment being made there is an appropriation in the strict sense of the word,[2] that is to say, the legatee takes the investments in satisfaction of the whole (or part where that is the intention) of his legacy and takes the benefit of any increase in the value of the property appropriated and, on the other hand, has to bear any reduction in its value. This appropriation again requires that the legatee was sui juris and consented to it.[3]

1   The legacy must be vested, though payable in the future. It must not be contingent.

2   *Johnson v Mills* (1749) 1 Ves Sen 282; *Re Hall, Foster v Metcalfe* [1903] 2 Ch 226; *Barclay v Owen* (1889) 60 LT 220; *Re Waters, Preston v Waters* [1889] WN 39; *Re Tredwell, Jaffray v Tredwell (No 2)* (1891) 65 LT 742.

3   *Sitwell v Bernard* (1801) 6 Ves 520 at 544; *Re Lepine, Dowsett v Culver* [1892] 1 Ch 210; *Re Beverly, Watson v Watson* [1901] 1 Ch 681; *Re Salaman, De Pass v Sonnenthal* [1907] 2 Ch 46. A beneficiary not sui juris could give no proper consent.

[29.3]

Contingent legacy directed to carry intermediate income. Where, in the case of a contingent legacy, the testator has directed the intermediate income or part of it to be paid to or applied for the benefit of the legatee, it is inferred that the testator intended a fund to be set apart and invested to answer the legacy and in such a case an executor may set apart and invest a sum to carry out the testator's intentions.[1]

1   *Green v Pigot* (1781) 1 Bro CC 103; *Re Hall, Foster v Metcalfe* [1903] 2 Ch 226.

[29.4]

Contingent legacy not directed to carry intermediate income. In this case[1] in the absence of direction in the will to appropriate or set aside a fund[2] there is no power to appropriate and the legatee cannot require any such appropriation to be made.[3] The executor may, however, set aside a fund amply sufficient to answer the legacy and then proceed to distribute the residue without rendering himself personally liable to make good any loss, if it should turn out that the sum set aside is not sufficient.[4]

1   It seems insufficient that the legatee is entitled to the intermediate income apart from a specific direction in the will.

2   *Re Oswald, Oswald v Oswald* (1919) 64 Sol Jo 242.

3   *Webber v Webber* (1823) 1 Sim & St 311; *King v Malcott* (1852) 9 Hare 692; *Re Hall, Foster v Metcalfe* [1903] 2 Ch 226 at 235.

4   *Re Hall, Foster v Metcalfe* [1903] 2 Ch 226. Such a setting aside of a fund will not bind the legatee unless he consents to it, and his remedy against the residuary estate for any insufficiency will remain good. In *Re Rivers, Pullen v Rivers* [1920] 1 Ch 320, a sum set aside by order of the court to provide for an annuity proved insufficient to pay a pecuniary legacy payable on the death of the annuitant. The residuary legatees had obtained orders from the court for the

payment of various sums and of these applications and orders the pecuniary legatee had not had notice. The residuary legatees were ordered to make good the deficiency in the sum available for the pecuniary legatee.

[29.5]
Minor's legacies. These are dealt with later.[1]

1   See Chapter 30, paras **[30.19]–[30.22]** infra.

[29.6]
Settled shares of residue. Executors who are also trustees of settled shares of residue or of a settled legacy may appropriate to any share specific assets which are investments of an authorised nature,[1] and they may appropriate to any share or shares without appropriating to others.[2]

1   *Re Waters, Preston v Waters* [1889] WN 39; *Re Richardson, Morgan v Richardson* [1896] 1 Ch 512; *Re Craven, Watson v Craven* [1914] 1 Ch 358; *Re Wragg, Wragg v Palmer* [1919] 2 Ch 58. As to property authorised to be retained being an authorised investment, see para **[29.9]**, n 4, and the text thereto. In a case of difficulty the court has power to authorise an appropriation of unauthorised investments to settled shares (*Re Cooke's Settlement, Tarry v Cooke* [1913] 2 Ch 661).
2   *Re Nickels, Nickels v Nickels* [1898] 1 Ch 630; *Re Brooks, Coles v Davis* (1897) 76 LT 771.

[29.7]
Express power in will. This clearly justifies an appropriation in all cases and the appropriation may then be made although it is not possible to determine the exact amount to be appropriated[1] and although the stock to be appropriated, although it has a market value, cannot be sold at that value.[2] The executor or trustee can be compelled to comply with such a power.[3]

1   *Defflis v Goldschmidt* (1816) 1 Mer 417.
2   *Re Daniels, London City and Midland Executor and Trustee Co Ltd v Daniels* (1918) 87 LJ Ch 661.
3   *Prendergast v Prendergast* (1850) 3 HL Cas 195.

[29.8]
Implied power of appropriation. A power to appropriate can be implied from the terms of a will where the testator directs a sum to be invested in trust for persons in succession.[1] So also where a contingent legacy is directed to carry some intermediate income.[2]

1   *Ames v Parkinson* (1844) 7 Beav 379; *Kidman v Kidman* (1871) 40 LJ Ch 359.
2   See para **[29.3]**, n 1, and text thereto.

[29.9]
What may be appropriated. The property to be appropriated may be any form of personalty,[1] including leaseholds, and, it seems, freeholds where there is a trust for sale;[2] but where the appropriation is in respect of a settled legacy or share or residue only authorised investments may be appropriated.[3] Where there is a power in the will to retain part of the deceased's property in its then form of investment throughout the trust, that power is a power to invest in that class of property and constitutes that class of property an authorised investment for the

purpose of appropriation to a settled share of residue or a settled legacy,[4] but a
mere power to postpone conversion has not that effect.[5] No appropriation can be
made of or affecting property specifically devised or bequeathed.

1   Both executors and trustees have power of appropriation of personal estate for the purpose of
     paying out vested shares or sums of money: *Re Ruddock, Newberry v Mansfield* (1910) 102 LT
     89. For examples of different classes of personalty, see *Elliott v Kemp* (1840) 7 M & W 306
     (furniture); *Barclay v Owen* (1889) 60 LT 220; *Re Lepine, Dowsett v Culver* [1892] 1 Ch 210
     (mortgage debt); *Re Richardson, Morgan v Richardson* [1896] 1 Ch 512; *Re Brooks, Coles v
     Davis* (1897) 76 LT 771 (shares in company); *Re Nickels, Nickels v Nickels* [1898] 1 Ch 630
     (stock); *Re Waters, Preston v Waters* [1889] WN 39 (mortgages and other securities). But
     caution is needed when seeking to appropriate assets, such as shares in a private company,
     which are not cash or the equivalent of cash, and raise difficult questions of valuation; see *Kane
     v Radley-Kane* [1998] 3 All ER 753 (discussed in para **[29.20]** infra) where an appropriation of
     such shares was set aside when the shares were subsequently sold by the appropriatee for a
     much greater value.
2   *Re Beverly, Watson v Watson* [1901] 1 Ch 681.
3   *Re Brooks, Coles v Davis* (1897) 76 LT 771; *Re Wragg, Wragg v Palmer* [1919] 2 Ch 58.
4   *Fraser v Murdoch* (1881) 6 App Cas 855; *Re Brooks, Coles v Davis* (1897) 76 LT 771; *Re
     Cooke's Settlement, Tarry v Cooke* [1913] 2 Ch 661.
5   *Re Craven, Watson v Craven* [1914] 1 Ch 358; *Re Beverly, Watson v Watson* [1901] 1 Ch 681.

[29.10]
Appropriation in respect of two or more shares or legacies. A single
appropriation may be made in respect of two or more shares or legacies, and
then the beneficiaries will share the appropriated property rateably according to
their interests,[1] but, if the appropriated property is turned into money, it must
then be divided and separately invested.[2]

1   *Re Walker, Walker v Walker* (1890) 59 LJ Ch 386; *Re Murray's Trusts* (1868) 18 LT 747; *Re
     Waters, Preston v Waters* [1889] WN 39.
2   *Re Walker, Walker v Walker* (1890) 59 LJ Ch 386.

[29.11]
Valuation for appropriation. An appropriation must be fairly[1] made at a
valuation taken at the date of the appropriation,[2] and an executor or trustee who
makes an appropriation which is not fair according to such valuation of the
appropriated property is guilty of a breach of trust. A beneficiary who takes the
appropriated property with knowledge of such breach of trust is also liable to
make good the breach of trust.[3] Not only must the appropriated property be
valued but, where the person to whom property is appropriated is not entitled to
a specific sum of money, the other property of the estate must be valued at the
same time to ensure he is receiving a proper share and receiving no more than he
is entitled to.[4]

1   Thus in case of a mortgage debt it must be shown that the property is an adequate security for
     the debt: *Re Brookes* [1914] 1 Ch 558.
2   *Re Lepine, Dowsett v Culver* [1892] 1 Ch 210; *Re Brooks, Coles v Davis* (1897) 76 LT 771; *Re
     Nickels, Nickels v Nickels* [1898] 1 Ch 630; *Re Charteris, Charteris v Biddulph* [1917] 2 Ch
     379. Where a dwelling-house is appropriated in favour of an intestate's spouse in or towards
     satisfaction of the spouse's interest under the intestacy, the dwelling-house is valued at the date
     of appropriation, not at the date of the intestate's death: *Robinson v Collins* [1975] 1 All ER
     321, [1975] 1 WLR 309.
3   *Re Lepine, Dowsett v Culver* [1892] 1 Ch 210, applied in *Kane v Radley-Kane* [1998] 3 All ER
     753 (discussed in para **[29.20]** infra) where the self-dealing rule was applied to render an

appropriation under the Administration of Estates Act 1925, s 41, by a personal representative in favour of herself, voidable. See paras **[29.17]–[29.24]** infra.

4   *Fenwick v Clarke* (1862) 4 De GF & J 240; *Peterson v Peterson* (1866) LR 3 Eq 111; *Re Winslow, Frere v Winslow* (1890) 45 Ch D 249; *Re Hurst, Addison v Topp* (1892) 67 LT 96. On intestacy, a surviving spouse can require appropriation of the matrimonial home partly in satisfaction of his or her interest in the intestate spouse's estate and partly in return for the payment of money: *Re Phelps, Wells v Phelps* [1980] Ch 275, [1979] 3 All ER 373.

[29.12]

Consent. The consent of the legatee is necessary to an appropriation[1] and where the interest is settled that of the trustee is necessary.[2]

1   See para **[29.1]** supra.
2   *Re Beverly, Watson v Watson* [1901] 1 Ch 681.

[29.13]

Appropriation in favour of executor or trustee. This is allowable upon the same conditions of an appropriation in favour of any other legatee but the matter will be examined more strictly[1] and it is said that in such a case the appropriated property must have a market value[2] or as in the case of a mortgage an ascertained value, that is to say, that the mortgage must be shown to be a sufficient security for the debt or outstanding part thereof.[3]

1   *Elliott v Kemp* (1840) 7 M & W 306; *Barclay v Owen* (1889) 60 LT 220; *Re Richardson, Morgan v Richardson* [1896] 1 Ch 512.
2   *Re Bythway, Gough v Dames* (1911) 80 LJ Ch 246.
3   *Barclay v Owen* (1889) 60 LT 220.

[29.14]

Effect of appropriation. As soon as an appropriation has been made, the executor ceases to hold the property as executor and, if he does not immediately deliver or transfer it to the beneficiary, he holds it as trustee for the beneficiary and not as part of the assets of the testator's estate.[1] The appropriated property is thus separated from the testator's estate and, provided the appropriation is fair, it cannot be made liable to contribute to the costs and other liabilities affecting that estate. From this principle the following results. The beneficiary takes the appropriated property for better or worse and any increase or decrease in value of the property or the investments representing the same belongs to or falls on the beneficiary,[2] and any loss due to a breach of trust or misapplication of the appropriated property has to be borne by the beneficiary.[3] On the other hand the beneficiary is not affected by any subsequent decrease in value of the remainder of the testator's estate or any part of it.[4] The beneficiary on a subsequent division of the estate brings in the appropriated property at its value at the time of appropriation and not at any increased value or decreased value it may have at the time of the division.[5] Costs and expenses and liabilities of the estate other than the appropriated fund cannot affect the fund,[6] but the fund must bear the whole burden of costs, expenses and liabilities in respect of the fund itself.[7]

1   *Re Smith, Henderson-Roe v Hitchins* (1889) 42 Ch D 302; *Re Gompertz's Estate, Parker v Gompertz* (1910) 55 Sol Jo 76; *Re Wedgwood, Allen v Public Trustee* [1921] 1 Ch 601.

2 *Burgess v Robinson* (1817) 3 Mer 7; *Willmott v Jenkins* (1838) 1 Beav 401; *Kimberley v Tew* (1843) 4 Dr & War 139; *Ballard v Marsden* (1880) 14 Ch D 374; *Fraser v Murdoch* (1881) 6 App Cas 855.
3 *Baker v Farmer* (1867) LR 4 Eq 382.
4 *Fraser v Murdoch* (1881) 6 App Cas 855; *Peterson v Peterson* (1866) LR 3 Eq 111; *Re Winslow, Frere v Winslow* (1890) 45 Ch D 249; *Re Lepine, Dowsett v Culver* [1892] 1 Ch 210. But the appropriation may be held to be subject to the self-dealing rule and thus voidable; see *Kane v Radley-Kane* [1998] 3 All ER 753, discussed para [29.20] infra.
5 *Re Richardson, Morgan v Richardson* [1896] 1 Ch 512; *Re Nickels, Nickels v Nickels* [1898] 1 Ch 630; *Re Gollin's Declaration of Trust, Turner v Williams* [1969] 3 All ER 1591, [1969] 1 WLR 1858 (in 1947 a beneficiary received a one-third share of a trust fund in the form of stocks; subsequently decided that she should have received a five-ninths share. In assessing the amount now due to her, the transfer made in 1947 was treated as a transfer of the cash value of the stocks as at the date of transfer, not as a transfer of a one-third share of the whole fund).
6 *Fraser v Murdoch* (1881) 6 App Cas 855.
7 *Jenour v Jenour* (1805) 10 Ves 562; *Wilson v Squire* (1842) 13 Sim 212; *A-G v Lawes* (1849) 8 Hare 32; *Martineau v Rogers* (1856) 8 De GM & G 328; *Re Towry's Settled Estate, Dallas v Towry* (1889) 41 Ch D 64 at 87; *Re Hall-Dare, Le Marchant v Lee Warner* [1916] 1 Ch 272.

[29.15]

Mode of appropriation. An appropriation does not require any writing to carry it into effect so far only as it is an appropriation,[1] but in so far as an appropriation requires for its complete effect a transfer of property, the necessary transfer must be made in the appropriate way, either by delivery or writing under hand or by deed as the nature of the property requires.[2] The appropriation may thus be evidenced by oral statements, by letters, by implication from the acts of the parties concerned, or by a recital in a subsequent instrument.[3] The right of the executor or trustee to appropriate must be proved; thus, where an executrix purported to appropriate in respect of a debt due to her from her testator and no evidence of the existence of the debt was forthcoming, the appropriation was held insufficient.[4] A person setting up an appropriation must prove the date at which the appropriation took place.[5]

1 *Hutcheson v Hammond* (1790) 3 Bro CC 128; *Gray v Gray* (1852) 2 Sim NS 273; *Barclay v Owen* (1889) 60 LT 220.
2 The deed will necessarily attract a 50p stamp duty and both the deed and the instrument under hand may attract stamp duty under some heading such as a conveyance on sale, a voluntary disposition or other heading if the transaction can be shown to be of that nature: see Stamps on Appropriation, infra.
3 *Hutcheson v Hammond* (1790) 3 Bro CC 128 (statements in letters of trustees explaining purpose of investment); *Governesses' Benevolent Institution v Rusbridger* (1854) 18 Beav 467 (setting aside exact amount of legacies and distributing estate); *Re Nickels, Nickels v Nickels* [1898] 1 Ch 630 (setting aside stock at its then value); *Re Lepine, Dowsett v Culver* [1892] 1 Ch 210 (handing over mortgage debt though no transfer executed); *Barnett v Sheffield* (1852) 1 De GM & G 371 (recital in subsequent deed). But no appropriation is implied by carrying to a separate blended account moneys belonging to several legatees: *Willmott v Jenkins* (1838) 1 Beav 401; nor where a legacy is laid out in funds and the legatee is to receive the surplus interest: *Cooper v Douglas* (1787) 2 Bro CC 231. As to leaving legacies mingled with the residue where the executor is the trustee, see para [29.1], nn 9 and 10, and the text thereto.
4 *Neale v Davies* (1854) 5 De GM & G 258.
5 *Rogers v Rogers* (1855) 25 LTOS 262.

[29.16]

Stamps on appropriation. An appropriation pure and simple, even though evidenced in writing, requires no stamp, unless the document is a deed, when it must be stamped as a deed; but an instrument giving effect to an appropriation may attract ad valorem stamp duty.[1] It has been held that an appropriation in respect of a pecuniary legacy amounted to a sale of the property to the legatee and thus was liable to stamp duty[2] but this no longer applies in view of the new relief introduced by the Finance Act 1985, s 84(4). Nor is there now any necessity for stamp duty save to dispense with consents to appropriations but such dispensation will be desirable to make the administration easier and reduce the risk of a capital gains tax charge.[3] Where, however, the residue of an estate is divided up in specie among the residuary legatees, no one legatee receiving any more than he is entitled to under the will, it is understood that no ad valorem duty is charged, there being in such case nothing of the nature of a sale, and, indeed, it may be doubted whether there is in law an appropriation since the transaction partakes more of the nature of a partition.[4]

1   See also *Sergeant and Sims on Stamp Duties* (12th edn); *Dawson v IRC* [1905] 2 IR 69.
2   *Jopling v IRC* [1940] 2 KB 282, [1940] 3 All ER 279.
3   The Finance Act 1985, s 84(4) provides relief against the stamp duty charge on such an appropriation, and thus removes what was perhaps the main reason for dispensing with consents. The reasoning that when an appropriation is made in respect of a pecuniary legacy the effect is that the legacy is paid to the legatee who then purchases the appropriate asset is based on the judgments in *Re Lepine, Dowsett v Culver* [1892] 1 Ch 210, and *Re Beverly, Watson v Watson* [1901] 1 Ch 681.
4   If a legatee receives more than his share in such a case, he pays equality money and is charged ad valorem duty on such equality money.

II. STATUTORY POWER

[29.17]
The Administration of Estates Act 1925[1] gives certain statutory powers of appropriation to personal representatives which, of course, includes administrators as well as executors to whom the common law powers are in general restricted.[2] The statutory power extends to any part of the real or personal estate,[3] including things in action, of the deceased in the actual condition or state of investment thereof at the time of the appropriation[4] in or towards satisfaction of any legacy bequeathed by the deceased, or of any other interest or share in his property, whether settled or not,[5] as to the personal representative may seem just and reasonable, according to the respective rights of the persons interested in the property of the deceased. This general power is subject to the following provisos: (i) no appropriation can be made under this section so as to affect prejudicially any specific devise or bequest; (ii) an appropriation of property, whether or not being an investment authorised by law or by the will, if any, of the deceased for the investment of money subject to the trust, cannot (save as hereinafter mentioned) be made under the section except with the following consents; (a) when made for the benefit of a person absolutely and beneficially entitled in possession, the consent of that person; (b) when made in respect of a settled legacy share or interest,[6] the consent of either the trustee thereof, if any (not being also the personal representative), or the person who may for the time being be entitled to the income (if the person whose consent is so required is a minor[7] or incapable through mental disorder, the consent shall be given on his behalf by his parent, testamentary or other

guardian, receiver, or if, in the case of a minor there is no such parent or guardian, by the court on the application of his next friend); (iii) no consent (save of such trustee as aforesaid) shall be required on behalf of a person who may come into existence after the time of appropriation, or who cannot be found or ascertained at the time;[8] (iv) if no receiver of a person incapable through mental disorder has been appointed, then, if the appropriation is of an investment authorised by law or by the will, if any, of the deceased for the investment of money subject to the trust, no consent shall be required on his or her behalf; (v) if, independently of the personal representative, there is no trustee of a settled legacy, share or interest, and no person of full age and capacity entitled to the income thereof, no consent shall be necessary to an appropriation in respect of such legacy, share or interest, provided that the appropriation is of an investment authorised as aforesaid. Any property duly appropriated under these powers is thereafter to be treated as an authorised investment, and may be retained or dealt with accordingly.

1   Administration of Estates Act 1925, s 41; 17 *Halsbury's Statutes* (4th edn) 446. Sub-section (6) has been amended with effect from 1 January 1997 by the Trusts of Land and Appointment of Trustees Act 1996, s 25(1), Sch 3, para 6(3).

2   Before 1926 administrators had little need of a power of appropriation since the interests of the next of kin were immediately vested and either the next of kin being sui juris could agree to divide the estate in specie or it had to be turned into money and the proceeds divided between them. As to the nature of the interests of the next of kin, see *Cooper v Cooper* (1874) LR 7 HL 53, and *Vanneck v Benham* [1917] 1 Ch 60. In the case of gifts by will, as in all other cases, where all the persons entitled to the property in question are sui juris, of full age, and have not encumbered their interests or rendered them subject to subsidiary trusts, they can deal with such property (whether it is the whole estate or any part of it) as they desire. This, however, is the right of the parties as owning all the beneficial interests in the property and is more in the nature of a partition than an appropriation, but it is an absolute right of such parties and does not require the support of any power to partition or to appropriate.

3   The common law power applied to real estate only where it was held upon trust for sale—now upon trust of land.

4   Compare the cases relating to common law appropriation, para [29.1] et seq.

5   The common law power to appropriate to settled shares or legacies is narrower than that in the cases of an immediately vested interest.

6   A settled legacy, share or interest includes any legacy share or interest to which a person is not absolutely entitled in possession at the date of the appropriation, and also an annuity.

7   Under 18: Family Law Reform Act 1969, s 1; 6 *Halsbury's Statutes* (4th edn) 121.

8   No appropriation can be made at common law where a legatee cannot be found: see para [29.1], n 7. But when acting under the statutory power the personal representative must have regard to the interests of persons not in existence or who cannot be found and of all persons whose consent is required, but these matters will not concern purchasers of the appropriated property; Administration of Estates Act 1925, s 41(5) and (7), the substance of which is set out in the text at para [29.23] infra.

[29.18]

Valuation. For the purposes of the statutory appropriation, the personal representative may ascertain and fix the value of the respective parts of the real and personal estate and the liabilities of the deceased as he may think fit, and may for that purpose employ a duly qualified valuer in any case where such employment may be necessary; and may make any conveyance (including an assent) which may be requisite for giving effect to the appropriation.[1] Caution is needed when seeking to appropriate assets which are not cash or the equivalent of cash, since they may raise difficulties of valuation.[2]

1   Administration of Estates Act 1925, s 41(3). See *Robinson v Collins* [1975] 1 All ER 321, [1975] 1 WLR 309; see para **[29.11]**, n 2 ante; *Re Phelps, Wells v Phelps* [1980] Ch 275, [1979] 3 All ER 373.

2   See *Kane v Radley-Kane* [1998] 3 All ER 753 (discussed in para **[29.20]** infra) where the asset appropriated was shares in a private company and the appropriation was set aside.

[29.19]

Binding effect of appropriation. The Administration of Estates Act 1925 (AEA 1925), s 41(4) states that any appropriation made pursuant to the statutory provisions binds all persons interested in the property of the deceased whose consent is not necessary under the section.[1] But in so far as there is nothing impliedly or expressly in s 41 relieving the personal representatives from observing the self-dealing rule[2] which was applicable to them under the law before the AEA 1925 provision, it has been held that this provision does not affect the application of the self-dealing rule to appropriations.[3]

1   Administration of Estates Act 1925, s 41(4), 17 *Halsbury's Statutes* (4th edn) 447.
2   See para **[29.20]** infra.
3   Per Sir Richard Scott V-C in *Kane v Radley-Kane* [1998] 3 All ER 753 at 758. The Vice-Chancellor then considered the pre-1925 law with reference to *Elliott v Kemp* (1840) 7 M & W 306; *Barclay v Owen* (1889) 60 LT 220 and *Re Bythway, Gough v Dames* (1911) 80 LJ Ch 246.

[29.20]

Appropriation and the self-dealing rule. There is no express prohibition in the AEA 1925, s 41 against a sole personal representative appropriating assets under the section in favour of herself[1] and there is no reference express or implied to the so-called 'self-dealing rule'.[2] But it has been held that the rule does apply to a personal representative appropriating assets in her own favour in satisfaction of a pecuniary legacy to herself,[3] and such a purported appropriation has been held to be voidable under the rule in a decided case.[4] The matter might have been otherwise if the sanction of the court or the consent of the other beneficiaries had been obtained, or another personal representative had been appointed to join in the act.[5]

1   Sir Richard Scott V-C in *Kane v Radley-Kane* [1998] 3 All ER 753 at 758.
2   This rule has been expressed by Megarry V-C in *Tito v Waddel (No 2)* [1977] 3 All ER 129 at 240–241 as follows: 'The self-dealing rule is (to put it very shortly) that if a trustee sells the trust property to himself, the sale is voidable by any beneficiary ex debito justitiae however fair the transaction'. The provisions of the AEA 1925, s 41 are in contrast to the power to appropriate the matrimonial home conferred on a spouse by the Intestates Estates Act 1952, Sch 2 which contains a reference to the rule in para 5(1). Sir Richard Scott V-C in *Kane v Radley-Kane* [1998] 3 All ER 753, thought that the self-dealing rule did apply to appropriations pre-1925 and found nothing in the AEA 1925, s 41 which abrogated the continued application of the rule.
3   *Kane v Radley-Kane* [1998] 3 All ER 753, where an administrator appropriated private shares in satisfaction of her statutory legacy under intestacy. The shares were valued for the purposes of the appropriation at £50,000. They were subsequently sold for over £1,000,000. The beneficiaries obtained a declaration that the appropriation was voidable under the self-dealing rule.
4   *Kane v Radley-Kane* [1998] 3 All ER 753. It should be noted that the decision was strictly limited to an appropriation of an asset which was not cash or the equivalent of cash, referring to *Re Lepine, Dowsett v Culver* [1891-4] All ER Rep 945 and *Re Richardson, Morgan v Richardson* [1896] 1 Ch 512.
5   *Kane v Radley-Kane* [1998] 3 All ER 753.

[29.21]
Persons not in existence or who cannot be found. In making the appropriation the personal representative must have regard to the rights of any person who may thereafter come into existence or cannot be found or ascertained at the time of the appropriation, and of any other person whose consent is not required by the section.[1]

1   AEA 1925, s 41(5).

[29.22]
Without prejudice to other powers. The statutory powers are without prejudice to any other power of appropriation conferred by law or by the will. Where an appropriation is made pursuant to the statutory power in respect of a settled legacy, share or interest, the property appropriated remains subject to all trusts for sale and powers of leasing, disposition, and management or varying investments which would have been applicable thereto, or to the legacy, share or interest in respect of which the appropriation is made, if no such appropriation had been made.[1]

1   AEA 1925, s 41(6), as amended (minor) by the Trusts of Land and Appointment of Trustees Act 1996, s 25(1), Sch 3, para 6(3).

[29.23]
Protection of purchaser. If any real estate has been appropriated in purported exercise of the statutory power and the person to whom it was conveyed disposes of it or of any interest therein, then, in favour of a purchaser, the appropriation is deemed to have been made in accordance with the requirements of the section and after all requisite consents, if any, had been given.[1]

1   AEA 1925, s 41(7); real estate here includes leaseholds.

[29.24]
Extent of power. This statutory power extends to property over which a testator exercises a general power of appointment, including the statutory power to dispose of entailed interests, and authorises the setting aside of a fund to answer an annuity by means of the income of that fund or otherwise.[1]

1   AEA 1925, s 41(9).

CHAPTER 30

Legacies

I. KINDS OF LEGACIES

[30.1]

The term 'legacy' or 'bequest' in its ordinary sense is applied only to a gift of money or some chattel[1] but within a proper controlling context it is capable of meaning a devise of land.[2]

---

1   *Beckley v Newland* (1723) 2 P Wms 182; *Ansley v Cotton* (1846) 16 LJ Ch 55; *Windus v Windus* (1856) 6 De GM & G 549. The word 'legacy' may or may not include annuity according to the context: *Sibley v Perry* (1802) 7 Ves 522; *Cornfield v Wyndham* (1845) 2 Coll 184; *Heath v Weston* (1853) 3 De GM & G 601; *Ward v Grey* (1859) 26 Beav 485; *Mullins v Smith* (1860) 1 Drew & Sm 204; *Gaskin v Rogers* (1866) LR 2 Eq 284; *Re Fitch's Will Trusts, Public Trustee v Nives* (1928) 139 LT 556, and therefore, in some cases, the word 'legatee' includes 'annuitants'. 'Residue' is not a legacy in the ordinary sense of the term, though a person taking it or a share in it is a 'residuary legatee': *Ward v Grey* (1859) 26 Beav 485.

2   *Beckley v Newland* (1723) 2 P Wms 182; *Brady v Cubitt* (1778) 1 Doug KB 31 at 40; *Whicker v Hume* (1851) 14 Beav 509 at 518; *Gyett v Williams* (1862) 2 John & H 429 at 436; *Re Shepherd, Mitchell v Loram* [1914] WN 65.

[30.2]

Kinds of legacies. Legacies are ordinarily divided into three classes, namely, specific legacies, general legacies, and demonstrative legacies. A general legacy of money is commonly called a pecuniary legacy.[1]

---

1   But the Administration of Estates Act 1925, s 55(1)(ix); 17 *Halsbury's Statutes* (4th edn) 467, defines a 'pecuniary legacy' as including 'an annuity, a general legacy, a demonstrative legacy so far as it is not discharged out of the designated property, and any other general direction by a testator for the payment of money, including all death duties free from which any devise, bequest, or payment is made to take effect'.

    This seems a special definition for the purposes of the Act and seems to have been held to be so in *Re O'Connor, Westminster Bank Ltd v O'Connor* [1948] Ch 628, [1948] 2 All ER 270, where a direction to pay pecuniary legacies out of residue was held not to include a general legacy of shares. See also *Re Cushing* [1943] 2 WWR 606. A gift of a share of residue is not a pecuniary legacy: *Re Jones* [1955] NZLR 917. Clearly the meanings of pecuniary legatee and pecuniary legacy are to be determined upon a consideration of all the provisions of a will.

[30.3]

Specific legacies. A specific legacy is a legacy of something forming part of the testator's estate, which is by the will distinguished and separated from the whole of his personal property or from the whole of the general residue of his personal estate. It must be identified by a sufficient description, and separated in favour of the particular legatee from the general mass of the testator's personal estate.[1]

The importance of the distinction is that, so far as compatible with the payment and satisfaction of the testator's liabilities, the specific gifts are secured to the specific legatee or devisee. Apart from property appointed by the will under a general power of appointment, the specific gifts come last in the order of application of assets to the payment of liabilities except property specifically devised or bequeathed for the payment of debts.[2] The following have been held specific legacies:[3] legacy payable out of money on mortgage or similar security;[4] bequest of all property at specified place;[5] bequest of money in bag;[6] a bequest of the proceeds of the sale of a house;[7] a gift of a specific fund in aliquot proportions;[8] bequest of residue of specified sum;[9] forgiveness of debts due to testator;[10] and a bequest of farm stock.[11] It has been held that a residuary devise of real estate is specific,[12] but these cases have not been followed in a modern case where it was held that a gift of 'all my real estate' was a residuary gift.[13]

Generally a residuary bequest is of the nature of a general legacy, but, if part is specially made subject to a trust for certain named persons, the latter part must be treated as a specific gift,[14] and, though the term 'residuary legatee' is in common use, a direction by the testator as to legacies applies only to those which are legacies in the strict sense of the term and does not include residue, nor does the term 'legatee' include a residuary legatee.[15] The will, however, must be construed as a whole and, from the context of other parts of the will, it may appear that the testator's intention was otherwise and such legacies or legatees are included.[16] A residuary bequest is a legacy within the Limitation Act.[17]

The question whether gifts of stock and shares are specific, general or demonstrative is dealt with elsewhere.[18]

1 *Bothamley v Sherson* (1875) LR 20 Eq 304 at 308; *Robertson v Broadbent* (1883) 8 App Cas 812; *Dawson v Reid* (1915) 113 LT 52. A specific gift may be given as a general legacy and then for purposes of abatement and ademption it must be treated as a general legacy: *Re Compton, Vaughan v Smith* [1914] 2 Ch 119 (a gift of stocks, bonds and shares).
2 See Administration of Estates Act 1925, Sch 1; 17 *Halsbury's Statutes* (4th edn) 472.
3 See also Chapter 31, para **[31.4]**, nn 1–4.
4 *Smallbone v Brace* (1677) Cas *temp* Finch 303; *Chambers v Jeoffery* (1709) 2 Eq Cas Abr 541; *Lawson v Stitch* (1738) 1 Atk 507; *Gardner v Hatton* (1833) 6 Sim 93; *Sidebotham v Watson* (1853) 11 Hare 170; *Re Bridle* (1879) 4 CPD 336. A bequest of a sum on a specified note or bond; *Chaworth v Beech* (1799) 4 Ves 555; *Innes v Johnson* (1799) 4 Ves 568; *Ashburner v Macguire* (1786) 2 Bro CC 108; *Davies v Morgan* (1839) 1 Beav 405.
5 *Sayer v Sayer* (1714) 2 Vern 688; *Re Newcombe* (1918) 42 OLR 590.
6 *Lawson v Stitch* (1738) 1 Atk 507.
7 *Re Bennett* [1955] OWN 211.
8 *Page v Leapingwell* (1812) 18 Ves 463.
9 *Nelson v Carter* (1832) 5 Sim 530 (part of specified debt); *Walpole v Apthorp* (1867) LR 4 Eq 37; but a bequest of the residue of proceeds of sale of leaseholds has been held not to be specific: *Re Green, Baldock v Green* (1888) 40 Ch D 610. A general residuary bequest is not specific even when the income is earmarked to be applied to the support of a lunatic for life: *Chambers v Chambers* (1846) 15 Sim 183, and see nn 12 to 16 infra, and the text thereto.
10 *Re Wedmore, Wedmore v Wedmore* [1907] 2 Ch 277, and see *Smallman v Goolden* (1787) 1 Cox Eq Cas 329; *Sidney v Sidney* (1873) LR 17 Eq 65. See infra.
11 *Rudd v Harper* (1888) 16 OR 422; *Augustine v Schrier* (1889) 18 OR 192; *Kavanagh v Kelly* (1903) 37 ILT 71.
12 *Hensman v Fryer* (1867) 3 Ch App 420; *Lancefield v Iggulden* (1874) 10 Ch App 136; *Re Ridley* [1950] Ch 415, [1950] 2 All ER 1; *Re Eve* [1956] Ch 479, [1956] 2 All ER 321; *Re Rowe, Bennetts v Eddy* [1941] Ch 343, [1941] 2 All ER 330.
13 *Re Wilson, Wilson v Mackay* [1967] Ch 53, [1966] 2 All ER 867. The Administration of Estates Act 1925, Sch 1, Pt II, para 2; see Vol 2, Part G, para **[246.54]**, speaks of property not

specifically bequeathed but included in a residuary gift, and Pennycuick J at 69 and at 873 respectively, did not think it correct to hold that for the purposes of this paragraph there could be no such thing as a residuary gift of realty; followed in *Franguesco v Shaw* [1977] 1 NSWLR 660.

14   *Re Maddock, Llewelyn v Washington* [1902] 2 Ch 220, and see n 9 supra.
15   *Re Aiken, Bolon v Gilliland* [1898] 1 IR 335; *Re Elcom, Layborn v Grover Wright* [1894] 1 Ch 303 (pecuniary legacies).
16   *Ward v Grey* (1859) 26 Beav 485.
17   Limitation Act 1939, s 20; 19 *Halsbury's Statutes* (3rd edn) 80; *Re Davis, Evans v Moore* [1891] 3 Ch 119; see now the Limitation Act 1980, s 22; 24 *Halsbury's Statutes* (4th edn) 724.
18   See paras [30.8]–[30.9] infra.

[30.4]

Release of a debt. A debt can only be truly released and extinguished by agreement for valuable consideration or under seal. A will 'giving' or 'forgiving' or 'releasing' a debt to the debtor is construed as leaving a legacy of the amount of the debt.[1] The testator cannot by such purported release remove the asset from the claims of creditors of the estate and the requirements of funeral and administration expenses; the testator can give to his benefaction no other status than that of a specific legacy of the value of the debt.[2] The debt remains outstanding as an asset of the estate; but the debtor is in a position to deny an obligation to pay it to the extent that the specific legacy is effective as such.[3]

1   Per Lord Russell in *Stamp Duties Comr v Bone* [1976] 2 All ER 354 at 360.
2   Per Lord Russell in *Stamp Duties Comr v Bone* [1976] 2 All ER 354 at 360.
3   Per Lord Russell in *Stamp Duties Comr v Bone* [1976] 2 All ER 354 at 360. See also *Izon v Butler* (1815) 2 Price 34; *Sidney v Sidney* (1873) LR 17 Eq 65; *Re Wedmore, Wedmore v Wedmore* [1907] 2 Ch 277; *A-G v Holbrook* (1823) 12 Price 407; *A-G v Hollingworth* (1857) 2 H & N 416.

[30.5]

General legacies. A general legacy has no reference to the actual state of the testator's property. It is a gift of something which, in the event of the testator leaving sufficient assets, must be raised by his executors out of his general personal estate.[1] In this case the words 'general personal estate' include, where the ordinary personal estate is insufficient to pay the legacies, personal estate over which the testator had a general power of appointment.[2] Whether or not anything forms part of the testator's personal estate is a pure question of fact,[3] but whether or not it has been separated from the general personal estate depends upon the construction of the will which is a question of mixed law and fact or a pure question of law. Provided it has been separated, anything which was the property of the testator at the time of his death is capable of being specifically bequeathed and thus becoming a specific legacy.[4]

1   *Hawthorn v Shedden* (1856) 3 Sm & G 293.
2   *Hawthorn v Shedden* (1856) 3 Sm & G 293; *Re Seabrook, Gray v Baddeley* [1911] 1 Ch 151 (the testator will be taken to have exercised the power to the extent necessary for the payment not only of the legacies but also of the debts).
3   *Fontaine v Tyler* (1821) 9 Price 94; *Stephenson v Dowson* (1840) 3 Beav 342. As to legacies of stock, see para [30.8] infra.
4   See para [30.3], nn 12 and 13.

[30.6]
Demonstrative legacies. There is a third kind of legacy called a demonstrative legacy, which consists of a pecuniary legacy payable out of a particular fund.[1] Such a legacy has the following advantages—namely (1) it is not adeemed by the total or partial failure at the testator's death of the fund out of which it was directed to be paid, but becomes payable out of the general personal estate to the extent of such failure, pari passu with ordinary general legacies;[2] and (2) it does not abate with the general legacies until after the particular fund is exhausted.[3]

1   *Fowler v Willoughby* (1825) 2 Sim & St 354; *Dawson v Reid* (1915) 113 LT 52 (preference expressed by testator that legacy be paid from insurance moneys), but cf *Barker v Rayner* (1826) 2 Russ 122, where the insurance moneys were paid in testator's lifetime and invested by him. Though the investments were still in existence at the testator's death, it was held that the legacies failed; *Bevan v A-G* (1863) 4 Giff 361 (direction for legacies to be paid out of capital employed in partnership); *Day v Harris* (1882) 1 OR 147 (same); *Re Webster, Goss v Webster* [1937] 1 All ER 602 (legacy to be paid out of capital in partnership and, if legatee accepted as partner, not to be withdrawn from partnership assets until the expiration of one year from the testator's death); *Walford v Walford* [1912] AC 658 (legacies to be paid out of reversionary fund); *Re Jeffery, Nussey v Jeffery* (1913) 110 LT 11 (legacy to be paid out of debentures); *Re Atkins* (1912) 21 OWR 238 (sum to be paid from amount in named bank); *Re Culbertson* (1966) 59 DLR (2d) 381 (legatees to be 'paid out of money realised from sale of farm lands, and if the amount recovered should not be sufficient then each person shall take a proportionate share'; farm sold before death and one third of price still owing; held, legacies not adeemed, payable primarily out of farm proceeds and remainder out of the general assets of the estate).
2   *Roberts v Pocock* (1798) 4 Ves 150; *Mann v Copland* (1817) 2 Madd 223; *Fowler v Willoughby* (1825) 2 Sim & St 354; *Re Culbertson* (1966) 59 DLR (2d) 381.
3   *Mullins v Smith* (1860) 1 Drew & Sm 204.

[30.7]
Failure of legacy. A legacy may fail for a number of reasons, eg uncertainty,[1] illegality,[2] death of the legatee in the testator's lifetime,[3] ademption,[4] satisfaction,[5] attestation of the will by the legatee,[6] disclaimer,[7] and non-fulfilment of a condition.[8]

1   See Chapter 34.
2   See Chapter 34.
3   See Chapter 47.
4   See Chapter 41.
5   See Chapter 44.
6   See Chapter 9.
7   See Chapter 46.
8   See Chapter 34.

II.   LEGACIES OF STOCKS AND SHARES

[30.8]
A legacy of stock or shares is prima facie a general legacy, although the testator may have had the exact amount of the stock or number of shares at the date of the will.[1] The rule, however, only furnishes a general guide and yields to any indications in the will construed with reference to such surrounding circumstances as may be legitimately taken into account.[2] It is generally thought that the words 'now standing in my name' make the gift specific,[3] but even these words can be controlled by the context of the will.[4]

The courts have generally regarded the word 'my' or any possessive word as significant of a specific gift[5] and also the testator in order not make the gift specific should have at least the amount of stock or number of shares given by the will.[6] A gift of shares in a private company whose transfer must be restricted is more easily construed as specific than as general.[7]

The following facts have been given the significance in this connection shown in the notes below: (i) where the amount of stock or shares given is smaller than that possessed by the testator;[8] (ii) where the amount given is precisely the same as that possessed by him;[9] (iii) where the amount given is larger than that possessed by him;[10] (iv) where the amount given is described as 'all my' stock or shares of a stated kind;[11] (v) where the amount given is the remainder of 'all my' stock or shares.[12]

It seems immaterial from this point of view that the stock is misdescribed if the stock actually held can be considered to answer the description.[13] If the legacies are expressly stated to be given as general and not as specific legacies, they must be treated as general legacies.[14] A bequest of a sum to be paid out of named stock is not specific.[15]

A specific legacy of shares carries the dividends from the death of the testator but a general legacy carries only interest from the expiration of one year after such death and the legatee is not entitled to the dividends until the legacy is satisfied.[16] Where certain shares were given to beneficiaries after the death of the widow, the gift carried bonus shares and other increments to the specified shares.[17]

Shares can be bequeathed to a company.[18] A direction in a will to sell testator's shares for cash and to offer them first to the person or persons holding other shares in the company does not give a person who in fact holds all the other shares in the company a right of first refusal.[19]

1   *Re Willcocks, Warwick v Willcocks* [1921] 2 Ch 327. See also *Re Curry, Curry v Curry* (1908) 53 Sol Jo 117; *Re Gage, Crozier v Gutheridge* [1934] Ch 536 (where testator held the War Loan at the date of his will but on conversion elected to be repaid: the legacy was held general); *Re Borne, Bailey v Bailey* [1944] Ch 190, [1944] 1 All ER 382 (where the stock was acquired by the Treasury).

2   *Re Hawkins, Public Trustee v Shaw* [1922] 2 Ch 569 (where the stocks were particularised in schedules and corresponded exactly with what the testatrix had at the time of her will). See also *Re O'Connor, Westminster Bank v O'Connor* [1948] Ch 628, [1948] 2 All ER 270; *Re Millar* [1927] 3 DLR 270; *Re Ganong Estate, Ganong v Belyea* [1941] 1 DLR 433.

3   *Re Willcocks, Warwick v Willcocks* [1921] 2 Ch 327; but this was not so where the stock was given to trustees upon trust for several beneficiaries: *Re Howell-Shepherd, Churchill v St George's Hospital* [1894] 3 Ch 649.

4   *Auther v Auther* (1843) 13 Sim 422.

5   *Re O'Connor, Westminster Bank Ltd v O'Connor* [1948] Ch 628, [1948] 2 All ER 270; *Re Rose, Midland Bank Executor and Trustee Co Ltd v Rose* [1949] Ch 78, [1948] 2 All ER 971; *Sleech v Thorington* (1754) 2 Ves Sen 560; *Ashburner v Macguire* (1786) 2 Bro CC 108; *Bothamley v Sherson* (1875) LR 20 Eq 304.

6   *Re O'Connor, Westminster Bank Ltd v O'Connor* [1948] Ch 628, [1948] 2 All ER 270; but see the cases cited in n 5 supra.

7   *Re O'Connor, Westminster Bank Ltd v O'Connor* [1948] Ch 628, [1948] 2 All ER 270; *Re Rose, Midland Bank Executor and Trustee Co Ltd v Rose* [1949] Ch 78, [1948] 2 All ER 971.

8   Held to be specific in *Oliver v Oliver* (1871) LR 11 Eq 506; *Richardson v Brown* (1798) 4 Ves 177; *Fontaine v Tyler* (1821) 9 Price 94; *Re Eager* [1952] St R Qd 105; but held upon the construction of the will as a whole to be general in *Simmons v Vallance* (1793) 4 Bro CC 345; *A-G v Grote* (1827) 2 Russ & M 699. In *Re Eager* [1952] St R Qd 105 the shares were of differing values and the beneficiary had a right of selection, see para **[8.7]** ante.

9   This case was specifically stated to be a general legacy unless there was something else in the
will to lead to its construction as specific: *Re Willcocks, Warwick v Willcocks* [1921] 2 Ch 327.
It was held to render the legacy specific in *Jeffreys v Jeffreys* (1743) 3 Atk 120, but this case
was not followed in *Re Willcocks, Warwick v Willcocks* [1921] 2 Ch 327. The matter was also
discussed in *Mullins v Smith* (1860) 1 Drew & Sm 204, where as Kindersley V-C said at 209,
210: 'Testator gives certain legacies of stock and then says that if he has no such stock at his
decease, then he gives the value in money. That is tantamount to saying that if he has stock of
that denomination at his decease, then he gives so many sums of stock out of it, but that if he
has no such stock, then he gives so many sums of money out of his general estate. As the
testator had stock to answer the bequest at his decease, those legacies were specific; but if he
had had no such stock at his decease, then the bequests of the money would have been not
specific, but general legacies.'

10   Held to be specific in *Ashton v Ashton* (1735) 3 P Wms 384; *Sleech v Thorington* (1754) 2 Ves
Sen 560 (but only where the word 'my' occurred in the bequest); *Sawrey v Rumney* (1852) 5 De
G & Sm 698 (where the stock was wrongly described); *Gordon v Duff, Re Ward* (1861) 3 De
GF & J 662; *Queen's College, Oxford v Sutton* (1842) 12 Sim 521 (where there was a direction
to make up the deficiency out of residue); *Palin v Brooks* (1878) 48 LJ Ch 191.

11   Held to be specific in *Bothamley v Sherson* (1875) LR 20 Eq 304; *Stephenson v Dowson* (1840)
3 Beav 342. A gift of specified stocks as to which testatrix had a power of appointment was
held specific in *Kampf v Jones* (1837) 2 Keen 756, and in *Davies v Fowler* (1873) LR 16 Eq
308 (where the stock was given in separate parcels).

12   *Vincent v Newcombe* (1832) You 599 (specific); *Parrott v Worsford* (1820) 1 Jac & W 594
(general); *Re McLean, Larlee v Earle* (1969) 4 DLR (3d) 617 ('balance of my class B stock':
specific).

13   *Re Pratt, Pratt v Pratt* [1894] 1 Ch 491 (held specific: 2Æ per cent consols described as 2 per
cent consols).

14   *Re Compton, Vaughan v Smith* [1914] 2 Ch 119.

15   *Kirby v Potter* (1799) 4 Ves 748; *Gillaume v Adderley* (1808) 15 Ves 384; *Mytton v Mytton*
(1874) LR 19 Eq 30.

16   *Re Hall* [1951] 1 All ER 1073.

17   *Re Turland, Permanent Trustee Co v Macready* [1964] NSWR 414.

18   *Re Castiglione's Will Trusts* [1958] Ch 549, [1958] 1 All ER 480. Shares of a company cannot
be vested in the company itself but must be transferred to nominees in trust for the company.

19   *Widrig v Strazer* [1964] SCR 376.

[30.9]
Shares: aliquot share. The general rule can be stated that a person entitled to an
aliquot share of an estate is entitled to insist on a corresponding part of the estate
property being distributed to him intact if it is readily divisible rather than the
whole property being sold and the proceeds distributed. But this rule was not
applied where an aliquot division of shares would have resulted in a
disproportionate division of value.[1]

1   *Lloyds Bank plc v Duker* [1987] 3 All ER 193, [1987] 1 WLR 1324: a testator owned 999 of the
1000 shares in a company, the remaining share being owned by his wife. The shares formed
part of his residuary estate which was bequeathed to his wife and other beneficiaries in
specified proportions, the wife's share being 46/80ths. This resulted in the wife being entitled to
574 shares. The wife died before the shares could be transferred to her and she left her whole
estate to Duker who thus claimed the 574 shares. The other beneficiaries of the husband's will
objected to the transfer of these shares since, because they constituted a majority shareholding
in the company were worth more than 46/80ths of the total value of the estate. The court agreed
and ordered a sale of the shares and a division of the proceeds in the specified proportions. *Re
Marshall, Marshall v Marshall* [1914] 1 Ch 192 (cited in text para **[30.36]**, n 3); *Re Sandemans'
Will Trusts, Sandeman v Hayne* [1937] 1 All ER 368 (cited in text para **[30.36]**, n 5) and *Re
Weiner's Will Trusts, Wyner v Braithwaite* [1956] 2 All ER 482, [1956] 1 WLR 579
distinguished.

III.   TO A DEBTOR

[30.10]

General principle. A legatee is not entitled to receive out of the testator's estate any benefit without bringing into account money owing by him to the testator.[1] This is in the nature of a right of set-off,[2] and, as prima facie only money can be set off against money, the principle applies only to money legacies, ie general legacies and not to specific legacies, unless the latter happen to be specific legacies of a sum of money.[3] The debt to be brought into account must be one due and payable at the time the legacy is payable and must be owing to the testator in his own right and not in a fiduciary or representative capacity. There are thus two questions to be considered: (i) against what benefits the legatee has to bring the debts into account, and (ii) what debts have to be brought into account. The matter of the effect of bankruptcy is also dealt with separately.

1   For a statement of the right, see *Turner v Turner* [1911] 1 Ch 716 at 719. For precedents see Vol 2, paras **[210.27]** to **[210.32]**.

2   The right has been variously called a right of set-off, a right of retainer, a lien, but none of these terms is technically correct; see *Cherry v Boultbee* (1839) 4 My & Cr 442 at 447; *Smith v Smith* (1861) 3 Giff 263 at 270, 271; *Re Akerman, Akerman v Akerman* [1891] 3 Ch 212 at 219; *Turner v Turner* [1911] 1 Ch 716.

3   *Re Taylor, Taylor v Wade* [1894] 1 Ch 671 (profits arising from business); *Knight v Davis* (1833) 3 My & K 358 (share of a legacy bequeathed to testator).

[30.11]

Against what benefits debts have to be brought into account. The legatee must bring his debt into account against such of the following gifts as he receives under the will: pecuniary legacies;[1] a gift of the residuary personal estate or a share thereof;[2] a gift of the residuary estate or a part thereof consisting of personalty and the proceeds of sale of realty;[3] a specific legacy consisting of a sum of money;[4] a gift of personalty as to which there is a partial intestacy;[5] a gift of the proceeds of sale of residuary realty given on trust for sale where the personal estate is insufficient for the payment of debts.[6] The debt must be brought into account against such interests in the estate not only when they are original and immediate interests under the will, but also when they are reversionary interests,[7] interests acquired from other beneficiaries either by purchase,[8] or as a beneficiary on the death of a beneficiary under the will.[9] An assignee for value of any interest under the testator's will takes it subject to the payment of a debt due to the testator by the assignor.[10]

1   *Jeffs v Wood* (1723) 2 P Wms 128.

2   *Ballard v Marsden* (1880) 14 Ch D 374 at 377.

3   *Willes v Greenhill* (1860) 29 Beav 376; *Re Akerman, Akerman v Akerman* [1891] 3 Ch 212.

4   See para **[30.10]**, n 3.

5   *Re Cordwell's Estate, White v Cordwell* (1875) LR 20 Eq 644; *Re Wheeler, Hankinson v Hayter* [1904] 2 Ch 66; *Re Milnes, Milnes v Sherwin* (1885) 53 LT 534. Realty so descending did not have to bear any part of the debt before 1926 (*Re Milnes, Milnes v Sherwin* (1885) 53 LT 534), but this point seems to be overruled now by the Administration of Estates Act 1925 (AEA 1925), s 33; see Vol 2, Part G, para **[244.58]**. The AEA 1925, s 33 has been amended with reference to the trust for sale by the Trusts of Land and Appointment of Trustees Act 1996, s 2, Sch 2, para 5; see Vol 2, Part G, para **[244.58]**.

6   *Re Moore, Moore v Moore* (1881) 45 LT 466; *Re Melton, Milk v Towers* [1918] 1 Ch 37.

7   *Re Palmer, Palmer v Clarke* (1894) 13 R 220; *Re Watson, Turner v Watson* [1896] 1 Ch 925.
8   *Burridge v Row* (1842) 1 Y & C Ch Cas 183.
9   *Stammers v Elliott* (1868) 3 Ch App 195; *Re Dacre, Whitaker v Dacre* [1916] 1 Ch 344.
10 *Re Knapman, Knapman v Wreford* (1881) 18 Ch D 300.

[30.12]
What debts have to be brought into account. The debts which must be brought into account include debts statute-barred at the death of the testator;[1] a debt of which the testator was only the equitable owner;[2] a debt arising under a guarantee by the testator and not accruing due until after the testator's death;[3] a debt which is due but of which the amount is unascertained;[4] a debt due from an estate of which the legatee is the executor.[5] The debt must be owing by the legatee and not by a partnership of which he is a member;[6] it must be payable at the time when the legacy becomes payable,[7] and must be due to the testator personally and not in a representative or fiduciary capacity.[8] It is essential, in short, that the relationship of creditor and debtor exists between the testator and the legatee at the time the legacy falls to be paid.[9] It seems needless to add that a debt which has been expressly or impliedly released by the testator in his lifetime or by his will has not to be brought into account.[10]

1   *Courtenay v Williams* (1844) 3 Hare 539; *Rose v Gould* (1852) 15 Beav 189; *Coates v Coates* (1864) 33 Beav 249; *Gee v Liddell (No 2)* (1866) 35 Beav 629; *Re Milnes, Milnes v Sherwin* (1885) 53 LT 534; *Re Akerman, Akerman v Akerman* [1891] 3 Ch 212; *Dingle v Coppen* [1899] 1 Ch 726; *Re Cordwell's Estate, White v Cordwell* (1875) LR 20 Eq 644; *Re Wheeler, Hankinson v Hayter* [1904] 2 Ch 66; *Re Marshall Estate* (1963) 38 DLR (2d) 181.
2   *Bousfield v Lawford* (1863) 1 De GJ & Sm 459 (the sole residuary legatee of an estate bequeathed a share of the residue to a debtor to that estate. It was held that the debt must be brought into account although the estate yielded a clear residue without the debt).
3   *Willes v Greenhill* (1860) 29 Beav 376; *Re Whitehouse, Whitehouse v Edwards* (1887) 37 Ch D 683; *Re Watson, Turner v Watson* [1896] 1 Ch 925; *Re Binns, Lee v Binns* [1896] 2 Ch 584; *Re Mitchell, Freelove v Mitchell* [1913] 1 Ch 201; *Re Melton, Milk v Towers* [1918] 1 Ch 37; *Re Eiser's Will Trusts, Fogg v Eastwood* [1937] 1 All ER 244 (where the legatee had a protected life interest, the court allowed the trustees to pay such sum as they thought necessary for the legatee's support and maintenance notwithstanding that the debt or some part thereof might remain unpaid). Where the testator was a surety for the legatee, then, although neither testator nor his executor has been called upon to pay under the guarantee and the legatee's liability has not ripened into a debt, the legatee must clear off the guarantee before he can be paid his legacy: *Re Binns, Lee v Binns* [1896] 2 Ch 584; *Re Mitchell, Freelove v Mitchell* [1913] 1 Ch 201; *Re Melton, Milk v Towers* [1918] 1 Ch 37.
4   *Re Rhodesia Goldfields Ltd, Partridge v Rhodesia Goldfields Ltd* [1910] 1 Ch 239.
5   *Irby v Irby (No 3)* (1858) 25 Beav 632 (but there was also the point that the estate would be able to pay the debt if the legatee-executor paid his debts to the latter estate).
6   *Turner v Turner* [1911] 1 Ch 716; *Jackson v Yates* [1912] 1 IR 267.
7   *Re Rees, Rees v Rees* (1889) 60 LT 260 (debt not accruing due until after time for payment of legacy); *Re Abrahams, Abrahams v Abrahams* [1908] 2 Ch 69 (debt payable by instalments, only instalments due at one year after death of testator can be claimed).
8   *Richardson v Richardson* (1867) LR 3 Eq 686 at 695.
9   *Re Morley, Morley v Saunders* (1869) LR 8 Eq 594; *Re Bruce, Lawford v Bruce* [1908] 2 Ch 682 (legatee was executor and entitled to residue of person who owed money to testator and that debt was statute barred before death of debtor); *Avison v Holmes* (1861) 1 John & H 530; *Smee v Baines* (1861) 29 Beav 661.
10 As to release of debt, see *Stamp Duties Comr v Bone* [1977] AC 511, [1976] 2 All ER 354, see para **[30.4]** supra. See also *Re Neville* [1925] Ch 44; and *Midland Bank Executor and Trustee Co Ltd v Yarners Coffee Ltd* [1937] 2 All ER 54.

[30.13]

Effect of bankruptcy. Where the legatee becomes bankrupt after the death of the testator, the trustee in bankruptcy is in no better position than that of the legatee.[1] The executor can exercise the right in full,[2] unless he has proved in the bankruptcy.[3] Where the legatee becomes bankrupt before the death of the testator, the right cannot be exercised except to the extent of dividends declared or ascertained before the legacy is payable,[4] or, where a composition deed is executed in the lifetime of the testator, except for the amount of the composition in respect of the debt.[5]

1   *Bousfield v Lawford* (1863) 1 De GJ & Sm 459; *Re Batchelor, Sloper v Oliver* (1873) LR 16 Eq 481; *Re Watson, Turner v Watson* [1896] 1 Ch 925.
2   *Re Watson, Turner v Watson* [1896] 1 Ch 925.
3   *Stammers v Elliott* (1868) 3 Ch App 195; *Armstrong v Armstrong* (1871) LR 12 Eq 614; *Re Watson, Turner v Watson* [1896] 1 Ch 925. If the executor has no right of proof, he cannot retain the debt: *Re Binns, Lee v Binns* [1896] 2 Ch 584; but if he does prove, the right to retain the debt is lost: *Armstrong v Armstrong* (1871) LR 12 Eq 614; *Stammers v Elliott* (1868) 3 Ch App 195; *Re Watson, Turner v Watson* [1896] 1 Ch 925. The right to retain is unaffected by valuing a secured debt, but if the executors prove without valuing, they abandon the right to retain: *Stammers v Elliott*; *Re Watson, Turner v Watson*; *Re Melton, Milk v Towers* [1918] 1 Ch 37.
4   *Cherry v Boultbee* (1839) 4 My & Cr 442; *Re Hodgson, Hodgson v Fox* (1878) 9 Ch D 673; *Re Rees, Rees v Rees* (1889) 60 LT 260; and see *Re Pink, Pink v Pink* [1912] 1 Ch 498. The right to deduct may be affected by the rule against double proof: *Re Fenton (No 2), ex p Fenton Textile Association* [1932] 1 Ch 178.
5   *Re Orpen, Beswick v Orpen* (1880) 16 Ch D 202.

IV.   TO AN EXECUTOR

[30.14]

Legacy to executor.[1] The presumption is that a legacy to a person appointed executor is given to him in that character and is attached to the office, and, if he claims it otherwise than as attached to the office, it is incumbent on him to show something in the nature of the legacy, or other circumstances arising on the will, to rebut that presumption.[2] Where in the gift the testator has designated the executor-legatee as a friend[3] or as a relation,[4] or where the legacy is expressed to be given as a mark of respect[5] or as a remembrance,[6] the presumption is rebutted. So, too, where the legacy is one of residue,[7] or it is given to the executor after the death of the tenant for life under the will,[8] or it is a contingent additional gift.[9] But a difference either in the nature or amounts of the legacies given to executors is not as a general rule of itself sufficient to show that the gift is not attached to the office.[10]

1   See also para **[79.7]** infra.
2   *Stackpoole v Howell* (1807) 13 Ves 417; *Re Appleton, Barber v Tebbit* (1885) 29 Ch D 893 at 895; *Re Steele* (1915) 15 SRNSW 247. For cases where the legacy was held to be annexed to the office, see *Piggott v Green* (1833) 6 Sim 72; *Calvert v Sebbon* (1841) 4 Beav 222. The contrary decision was reached in *Wildes v Davies* (1853) 1 Sm & G 475; *Brand v Chaddock* (1871) 24 LT 347; *Re Bunbury's Trusts* (1876) 10 IR Eq 408. A request to give the executor a handsome gratuity is void for uncertainty: *Jubber v Jubber* (1839) 9 Sim 503.
3   *Re Denby* (1861) 3 De GF & J 350; *Bubb v Yelverton* (1871) LR 13 Eq 131; *Re Russell, Public Trustee v Campbell* (1912) 56 Sol Jo 651.
4   *Compton v Bloxham* (1845) 2 Coll 201; *Dix v Reed* (1823) 1 Sim & St 237.

5   *Burgess v Burgess* (1844) 1 Coll 367.
6   *Bubb v Yelverton* (1871) LR 13 Eq 131. See *National Trustees Executors and Agency Co of Australasia Ltd v Doyle* (1898) 24 VLR 626 (where it was shown that he was given a legacy in a previous will of which he was not executor).
7   *Re Maxwell, Eivers v Curry* [1906] 1 IR 386, following *Griffiths v Pruen* (1840) 11 Sim 202.
8   *Seley v Wood* (1804) 10 Ves 71; *Re Reeve's Trusts* (1877) 4 Ch D 841.
9   *Wildes v Davies* (1853) 1 Sm & G 475, and see *Brand v Chaddock* (1871) 24 LT 347.
10 *Re Appleton, Barber v Tebbitt* (1885) 29 Ch D 893, commenting on *Jewis v Lawrence* (1869) LR 8 Eq 345. Where there was both a difference in amount and one was given over in the event of the executor predeceasing the testatrix, the presumption was rebutted: *Re Wolff Estate* (1960) 32 WWR 550.

[30.15]
When executor entitled to legacy. Where the legacy is attached to the office, an executor whose appointment is revoked by codicil[1] or who does not act is not entitled to the benefit[2] even though he be prevented from acting by age or infirmity.[3] It is not, however, absolutely necessary to prove the will; it is sufficient if the executor has in fact done something showing an intention to act as executor.[4] An annuity given to an executor for his trouble does not cease by reason of the institution of administration proceedings.[5] Where a will appoints a solicitor as one of the executors and contains both a professional charging clause and a gift to the solicitor if he should prove the will, the latter gift has been interpreted as intending to reward the solicitor for his non-professional work as executor; the professional services being remunerated under the charging clause.[6]

1   *Walne v Hill* [1883] WN 171; *Re Russell, Public Trustee v Campbell* (1912) 56 Sol Jo 651. See *Re Mellor, Dodgson v Ashworth* (1912) 28 TLR 473 (where the legacy to a substituted executor was varied).
2   *Abbott v Massie* (1796) 3 Ves 148; *Slaney v Watney* (1866) LR 2 Eq 418; *Stackpoole v Howell* (1807) 13 Ves 417 (executor renouncing).
3   *Hanbury v Spooner* (1843) 5 Beav 630; *Re Hawkin's Trusts* (1864) 33 Beav 570.
4   *Harrison v Rowley* (1798) 4 Ves 212; *Lewis v Mathews* (1869) LR 8 Eq 277 (where the will was proved by the executor's attorney). An executor who proves without any intention of acting has been allowed the legacy: *Harford v Browning* (1787) 1 Cox Eq Cas 302, but now that legacies are often substantial in amount and given because of the arduous nature of the work of an executor, a different view might be taken. An executor who renounced but afterwards came in and proved was held entitled in *Angermann v Ford* (1861) 29 Beav 349. See also *Re Sharman* [1942] Ch 311, [1942] 2 All ER 74.
5   *Baker v Martin* (1836) 8 Sim 25.
6   *Re Parry, Dalton v Cooke* [1969] 2 All ER 512, [1969] 1 WLR 614. As to the provisions of the Trustee Act 2000 regarding remuneration to professional trustees and the effect of such remuneration on the Wills Act 1837, s 15, see Chapter 27.

[30.16]
Legacy liable to duty and to abatement. A legacy to an executor, though attached to the office, stands upon the same footing as ordinary legacies; it was subject to legacy duty[1] and is liable to abatement.[2]

1   *Re Thorley, Thorley v Massam* [1891] 2 Ch 613. See now inheritance tax.
2   *Duncan v Watts* (1852) 16 Beav 204; *Debney v Eckett* (1858) 4 Jur NS 805. See Chapter 31.

[30.17]
Lien on defaulting executor's interest. Where an executor, who is also a beneficiary, is in default to his testator's estate, the estate is entitled to a lien

upon his beneficial interest.[1] This lien is good not only against the executor himself, but against his assignee,[2] even though the wasting of the assets took place subsequently to the assignment;[3] and it applies not only to the beneficial interest taken by the executor directly under the will but to any interest to which he may have become entitled derivatively, eg as being one of the next of kin of a *cestui que trust* who has died intestate.[4] But an unpaid beneficiary has no lien upon a specific legacy given as an executor,[5] and the lien will be discharged by the acceptance of a composition in the bankruptcy of the defaulting executor.[6]

1   *Barnett v Sheffield* (1852) 1 De GM & G 371; *Cole v Muddle* (1852) 10 Hare 186; *Re Carew, Carew v Carew* [1896] 1 Ch 527; affd [1896] 2 Ch 311, CA.
2   *Irby v Irby (No 3)* (1858) 25 Beav 632.
3   *Morris v Livie* (1842) 1 Y & C Ch Cas 380.
4   *Jacubs v Rylance* (1874) LR 17 Eq 341; *Doering v Doering* (1889) 42 Ch D 203; *Re Dacre, Whitaker v Dacre* [1916] 1 Ch 344.
5   *Geary v Beaumont* (1817) 3 Mer 431.
6   *Re Sewell, White v Sewell* [1909] 1 Ch 806.

[30.18]
Appointment as executor of donee of incomplete gift. Upon a similar principle the appointment as an executor of a person to whom the testator has during his lifetime attempted to make a gift, which being incomplete fails on technical considerations, is sufficient to perfect the gift.[1] This principle is known as the rule in *Strong v Bird*.[2] For the rule to apply the donee must show a continuing intention on the part of the donor to make the gift.[3] The principle is not to be extended to a case where the testator has merely announced an intention of making a gift at some future time.[4]

1   *Re Stewart, Stewart v McLaughlin* [1908] 2 Ch 251; *Re Stoneham, Stoneham v Stoneham* [1919] 1 Ch 149. In *Re Gonin, Gonin v Garmeson* [1977] 2 All ER 720, it was assumed on the authority of *Re James, James v James* [1935] Ch 449, that this doctrine applied to administrators as well as to executors; Walton J, however clearly had doubts; see [1977] 2 All ER 720 at 734.
2   (1874) LR 18 Eq 315. A similar principle has been applied where the donee has been appointed a trustee: *Re Ralli's Will Trust, Ralli's Marriage Settlement* [1964] Ch 288, [1963] 3 All ER 940.
3   *Re Gonin, Gonin v Garmeson* [1979] Ch 16, [1977] 2 All ER 720; *Re Pink, Pink v Pink* [1912] 2 Ch 528.
4   *Vavasseur v Vavasseur* (1909) 25 TLR 250; *Re Innes, Innes v Innes* [1910] 1 Ch 188; *Re Freeland, Jackson v Rodgers* [1952] Ch 110, [1952] 1 All ER 16. See also *Re James, James v James* [1935] Ch 449, where the donee became administrator.

V. TO A MINOR

[30.19]
The main points which are relevant to gifts to minors are considered elsewhere.

[30.20]
Receipt for payment and discharge of executor. See paras **[9.40]–[9.42]** supra.

[30.21]
Intermediate income. See Chapter 32.

[30.22]
Powers of maintenance. See Volume 2.

VI.   TO EMPLOYEES

[30.23]
Description. Where the donees are described by their employment and not by name the persons taking are prima facie those filling the character at the date of the will, and it is not essential that the employment should continue until the date of the death of the testator;[1] but, if it appears from the will that the donees are a class to be ascertained in accordance with the ordinary rules,[2] the will may by its terms require the donees to fill the particular character required at the date of the will,[3] or at the death of the testator,[4] or for some specified length of time.[5] Most of the authorities on legacies to employees are old cases concerning domestic servants. Such gifts will obviously be less common in modern wills, but the construction adopted in these cases can be noted shortly as providing some general guidance.

1   *Parker v Marchant* (1842) 1 Y & C Ch Cas 290 at 299 (the circumstance that the description is by employment and not by name does not import continuance of employment); *Re Miller, Galloway v Miller* (1913) 135 LT Jo 10. For precedents, see Vol 2, paras **[210.57]** to **[210.62]**.
2   *Re Marcus, Marcus v Marcus* (1887) 56 LJ Ch 830 (office and warehouse employees to receive six months' full salary held to refer to employees at time of death). As to rules for determining classes, see Chapter 66, post, but in this connection the class will almost certainly be ascertained at the date of the death.
3   *Parker v Marchant* (1842) 1 Y & C Ch Cas 290; *Re Strombeck Estate* (1956) 2 DLR (2d) 109. See *Jones v Henley* (1685) 2 Rep Ch 361 (where the will on its construction was held to refer to servants at the date of the will who continued to be such until the date of the testator's death).
4   *Re Marcus, Marcus v Marcus* (1887) 56 LJ Ch 830; *Re Bell, Wright v Scrivener* (1914) 58 Sol Jo 517.
5   *Re Sharland, Kemp v Rozey* [1896] 1 Ch 517 (servant in employ for over ten years; servant who had been employed for the requisite period, but left before the date of the will held entitled); *Re Miller, Galloway v Miller* (1913) 135 LT Jo 10 ('at least three years'; apprenticeship for five years but salaried for less than three years).

[30.24]
Servants. The servants entitled to benefit as fulfilling the description is a question of construction in each case.[1] Servants living with the testator at the time of his death are not confined to those living in the same house with him[2] and the same construction has been applied to servants in the service of the testator at the time of his death.[3] Such servants, however, must be wholly in the testator's service and not free to serve others.[4] If the servant leaves the service, either voluntarily[5] or even upon wrongful dismissal,[6] he is not entitled to share in the gift, though a temporary absence is immaterial if the relationship of master and servant continues.[7] Where a housekeeper was required to be in the service of a surviving husband, the service did not determine on her marriage to the surviving husband where a special contract of service was made before marriage and fully implemented after marriage.[8] Domestic or household servants are generally indoor servants.[9]

1   *Sleech v Thorington* (1754) 2 Ves Sen 560 (legacy to two servants who should live with testatrix at the time of her death held to refer to a class and, therefore, to include a third such servant). In *Burchett v Woolward* (1823) Turn & R 442, a servant was given an annuity so long as she was in the service of the testator's wife, to cease when she left the service. The testator's wife predeceased him and the servant was held entitled to an annuity for life.

2   *Townshend v Windham* (1706) 2 Vern 546; *Blackwell v Pennant* (1852) 9 Hare 551 (but where they were required to have served three years, servants not hired by the year were excluded).

3   *Bulling v Ellice* (1845) 9 Jur 936 (farm bailiff); *Thrupp v Collett (No 2)* (1858) 26 Beav 147 (gardener entitled but not a boy occasionally employed); *Armstrong v Clavering* (1859) 27 Beav 226 (land agent).

4   *Feake v Brandsby* (1674) 2 Rep Ch 101; *Townshend v Windham* (1706) 2 Vern 546; *Chilcot v Bromley* (1806) 12 Ves 114; *Howard v Wilson* (1832) 4 Hag Ecc 107; *Thrupp v Collett (No 2)* (1858) 26 Beav 147; *Armstrong v Clavering* (1859) 27 Beav 226; *Re Lawson, Wardley v Bringloe* [1914] 1 Ch 682 (absence with consent for four months); *Re Travers, Hurmson v Carr* (1916) 86 LJ Ch 123 (nurse).

5   *Re Serres' Estate, Venes v Marriott* (1862) 8 Jur NS 882; *Re Benyon, Benyon v Grieve* (1884) 53 LJ Ch 1165.

6   *Darlow v Edwards* (1862) 1 H & C 547; *Re Hartley's Trusts* (1878) 47 LJ Ch 610 (dismissal by order in lunacy); *Re King, Jackson v A-G* [1917] 2 Ch 420 (servants in employ of committee), but see *Re Silverston, Westminster Bank Ltd v Kohler* [1949] Ch 270, [1949] 1 All ER 641, where an order in lunacy continued the employment and released them from all duties, a retaining fee being paid and it was held that the servants were still in the employment at the death of testatrix.

7   *Herbert v Reid* (1810) 16 Ves 481; *Re Lawson, Wardley v Bringloe* [1914] 1 Ch 682; *Re Cole, Cole v Cole* [1919] 1 Ch 218 (military service). In *Re Drake, Drake v Green* [1921] 2 Ch 99, it was held that the period of military service could not be counted in the period of service, but service prior to and after military service could be aggregated. But this aggregation depends upon it being shown that there was an agreement between the employer and employed that the employment should continue: *Re Marryat, Westminster Bank Ltd v Hobcroft* [1948] Ch 298, [1948] 1 All ER 796. The service was not broken where, after the employee was called up, his wife continued his work for him and the employee when on leave performed such duties as his employee assigned to him and paid him extra wages: *Re Feather, Harrison v Tapsell* [1945] Ch 343, [1945] 1 All ER 552.

8   *Re Kendrew, Hird v Kendrew* [1953] Ch 291, [1953] 1 All ER 551.

9   *Ogle v Morgan* (1852) 1 De GM & G 359; *Vaughan v Booth* (1852) 16 Jur 808; *Re Drax, Savile v Yeatman* (1887) 57 LT 475; *Re Ogilby, Cochrane v Ogilby* [1903] 1 IR 525; *Re Lawson, Wardley v Bringloe* [1914] 1 Ch 682. The word 'servants' in a legacy ordinarily means domestic servants, though not necessarily employed only in the testator's house, who minister in some way to his personal comfort or wants: *Re Forrest, Bubb v Newcomb* [1916] 2 Ch 386 (farm labourers not servants); see also *Re Jackson, Jackson v Hamilton* [1923] 2 Ch 365 (a chauffeur and a gardener included); *Re Forbes, Public Trustee v Hadlow* (1934) 78 Sol Jo 336; *Re Countess Rosse, Parsons v Earl Rosse* (1923) 93 LJ Ch 8; *Re Earl Brownlow, Tower v Sedgwick* (1924) 69 Sol Jo 176; *Re Drake, Drake v Green* [1921] 2 Ch 99; *Re Cassel, Public Trustee v Ashley* (1922) 39 TLR 75.

[30.25]
Gift of a year's wages. Where a testator gives servants wages for one year or a number of years, he generally means servants hired at yearly wages, and the nature of the gift explains the class of servants intended.[1] The mere fact of splitting up a year's remuneration into weekly payments does not exclude a servant from such a legacy,[2] and the class may be extended where the servants are further described as, eg, indoor and outdoor servants.[3] The general meaning is excluded wherever the will shows that the reference to a year is introduced merely to fix the amount of the legacy.[4] In this connection 'wages' is confined to wages in cash and does not include other benefits.[5]

1   *Blackwell v Pennant* (1852) 9 Hare 551; *Breslin v Waldron* (1855) 4 I Ch R 333; *Re Ravensworth, Ravensworth v Tindale* [1905] 2 Ch 1.

2   *Ogle v Morgan* (1852) 1 De GM & G 359.
3   *Re Earl of Sheffield, Ryde v Bristow* [1911] 2 Ch 267 (all indoor and outdoor servants included irrespective of whether they were hired by the year or the week).
4   *Re Earl of Sheffield, Ryde v Bristow* [1911] 2 Ch 267.
5   *Re Peacock, Public Trustee v Birchenough* (1929) 45 TLR 301.

[30.26]

Employed. The usual meaning of 'employed' is well understood, but a person may be affected by changes in the nature of a firm. Where the testator secretly formed a partnership but continued to run the business himself, it was held that there was no break in the employment.[1] On the other hand, where the employees were required to be in the service of a limited company for a stated period before the death of the testator, service with the testator before the formation of the company (though substantially the same business) did not count[2] and interruption by service in the armed forces of the Crown prevented any aggregation of service before enlistment and after discharge.[3] 'A period of five years' does not necessarily mean a continuous period of five years and not an aggregate of shorter periods amounting to five years.[4]

1   *Re Howell's Trusts, Barclays Bank Ltd v Simmons* [1937] 3 All ER 647. See also *Ryan v Smith* (1972) 22 DLR (3d) 1 (condition that beneficiaries be employees of business).
2   *Re Marryat, Westminster Bank Ltd v Hobcroft* [1948] Ch 298, [1948] 1 All ER 796.
3   *Re Marryat, Westminster Bank Ltd v Hobcroft* [1948] Ch 298, [1948] 1 All ER 796. The basis of this decision is that there was no agreement with the company for the continuation of the employment.
4   *Re Bedford* [1951] Ch 905, [1951] 1 All ER 1093, but see *Re Marryat, Westminster Bank Ltd v Hobcroft* [1948] Ch 298, [1948] 1 All ER 796, to the contrary. See also *Re Hartley's Trusts* (1878) 47 LJ Ch 610; *Re Silverston, Westminster Bank Ltd v Kohler* [1949] Ch 270, [1949] 1 All ER 641; *Re King, Jackson v A-G* [1917] 2 Ch 420.

[30.27]

Apprenticeship. Apprenticeship is employment for the purposes of such a legacy.[1]

1   *Re Marryat, Westminster Bank Ltd v Hobcroft* [1948] Ch 298, [1948] 1 All ER 796. See also *Re Miller, Galloway v Miller* (1913) 135 LT Jo 10.

[30.28]

Proof. The onus of proof of employment and continuance of employment is on the legatee.[1] A statement by the testator that the legatee was on a certain date still in his employment can be accepted as corroborative evidence of the statement by the employee that such was the case, but it is not evidence of the intention of the testator to continue the employment.[2]

1   *Re Feather, Harrison v Tapsell* [1945] Ch 343, [1945] 1 All ER 552.
2   *Re Feather, Harrison v Tapsell* [1945] Ch 343, [1945] 1 All ER 552; and see *Herbert v Reid* (1810) 16 Ves 481.

[30.29]

Redundancy payments. Refer to the current Employment Legislation[1] which may be relevant to the giving and drafting of legacies to employees.[2]

1   16 *Halsbury's Statutes* (4th edn), 2000 Revision.
2   See the Forms and Notes in Vol 2.

VII. PAYMENT OR DELIVERY

[30.30]

Time for payment. The time for payment of legacies may be fixed by the will,[1] by the rule known as the executor's year,[2] or by the general duty of executors to act with diligence in the administration of the estate, which in general requires that debts shall be paid before beneficiaries are put in possession of their interests.[3] While there is nothing to prevent a legacy being paid where the executor is satisfied that all the liabilities of the estate can be met despite such payment, his proper course must be that debts must be paid first.[4]

1 If this is within the executor's year, it will be unenforceable, see infra, and this principle will also apply where there is a possibility of an application under the Family Provision legislation; but it has been said that where a legacy is made payable immediately after the testator's death, the legatee is entitled to immediate payment: *Re Riddell* (1936), as reported in 155 LT 247; *Re Pollock* [1943] Ch 338, [1943] 2 All ER 443. Where a legacy is payable on a minor attaining majority and the minor is domiciled abroad, it is payable on his attainment of majority by English law or of that of the domicile whichever first happens: *Re Hellmann's Will* (1866) LR 2 Eq 363; *Re Schnapper* [1928] 1 Ch 420.

2 See para **[30.31]** infra.

3 *Re Tankard, Tankard v Midland Bank Executor and Trustee Co Ltd* [1942] Ch 69, [1941] 3 All ER 458. There is no rule of law that it is the duty of executors to pay debts within a year. Apart from any provisions of the will which expressly or impliedly deal with the payment of debts, it is the duty of executors as a matter of the due administration of the estate to pay debts with due diligence, having regard to assets in their hands which are properly applicable for the purpose. In determining whether due diligence has been shown, regard must be had to all circumstances of the case. Due diligence may require that payment be made before the expiration of the year, but the circumstances affecting the estate and the assets comprised in it may justify non-payment within the year. If debts are not paid within the year, the onus is on the executors to justify the delay. The duty to show due diligence is owed not only to the creditors but also to beneficiaries, for the ultimate object of the administration of an estate is to place the beneficiaries in possession of their interests and that cannot be fully achieved unless all debts are satisfied. As against creditors, the provisions of the will which relate to the realisation of the assets or otherwise bear upon the payment of debts are irrelevant. Beneficiaries, however, take their interest under the will only on the terms of the will, and, as respects them, full effect has to be given to any provisions which, either expressly or impliedly, modify the executor's duty to pay debts with due diligence. Thus a power to retain assets in the form of investment at the death of the testator may be exercisable notwithstanding that debts are outstanding and that there is not sufficient cash in hand to meet them.

4 *Re Tankard, Tankard v Midland Bank Executor and Trustee Co Ltd* [1942] Ch 69, [1941] 3 All ER 458, and see cases cited in nn 4 and 5.

[30.31]

The executor's year. The executor has a year from the date of the death of the testator within which fully to inform himself of the state of the testator's property, and during that period he cannot be required to pay any legacies, even though they are expressly directed by the testator to be paid within the year.[1] Problems arise if there is, or is likely to be, an application under the Inheritance (Provision for Family and Dependants) Act 1975.[2] Such an application must be made within six months of representation to the estate being taken out.[3] After this six month period the personal representatives can safely distribute the estate and are protected against the possibility of a late application or a variation of a previous order.[4] If an application has been made, there is no rigid rule that the personal representatives can make no disposition of any sort to beneficiaries until the determination of the application.[5] It was suggested in a case on the Inheritance (Family Provision) Act 1938[6] that in the majority of cases in which the applicant is given a benefit under the will, there would be no good reason for withholding it pending the hearing of the summons. So far as other beneficiaries under the will are concerned, the court indicated that executors should form their own view what interim payments should properly be made: if they were not prepared to make such payments on their own responsibility the executors should ask the persons who might be affected by them for their consent, and if consent was not forthcoming the executors could apply to the court for leave to make the payments. The executor, is, however, entitled to pay legacies within the year if he chooses.[7] No delay in payment affects the vesting of the legacy.[8] The subject of the postponement of payment and the payment of annuities is dealt with later.[9]

1   Administration of Estates Act 1925, s 44; 17 *Halsbury's Statutes* (4th edn) 450; *Pearson v Pearson* (1802) 1 Sch & Lef 10; *Wood v Penoyre* (1807) 13 Ves 325; *Re Livingston's Estate* [1922] 2 WWR 408; *Benson v Maude* (1821) 6 Madd 15 (where the legacy was directed to be paid as soon as convenient); *Beddy v Smith* (1843) 1 LTOS 390; *Re Smith, Dowzer v Dowzer* (1914) 48 ILT 236; *Re Lord Llangattock, Johnson v Church of England Central Board of Finance* (1918) 34 TLR 341 (legacy to relieve temporary lack of income). Where a legacy of a monthly sum to be paid for twenty-five consecutive months was given, it was held that the first payment was to be made at the expiration of one year from the testator's death: *Re Brown, Cavanagh v Cronin* [1940] QSR 154. As to legacies payable out of reversionary fund, see para **[30.32]**, n 1. It has been said that the executor is not entitled to delay payment beyond the year where funds are ample: *Cullen v McNeil* (1908) 42 NSR 346.
2   17 *Halsbury's Statutes* (4th edn) 505.
3   Inheritance (Provision for Family and Dependants) Act 1975 (I(PFD)A 1975), s 4.
4   I(PFD)A 1975, s 20(1).
5   *Re Ralphs, Ralphs v District Bank Ltd* [1968] 3 All ER 285, [1968] 1 WLR 1522; not following dictum of Vaisey J in *Re Simson* [1949] 2 All ER 826 at 829.
6   *Re Ralphs, Ralphs v District Bank Ltd* [1968] 3 All ER 285 at 288, [1968] 1 WLR 1522 at 1525, per Cross J.
7   *Re Palmer, Palmer v Palmer* [1916] 2 Ch 391 at 401; *Wilson v Spencer* (1732) 3 P Wms 172; *Garthshore v Chalie* (1804) 10 Ves 1; *Angerstein v Martin* (1823) Turn & R 232. The executor incurs some risk in paying legacies not expressly given priority by the will, since even a legacy stated to be given to the widow for immediate necessities has no priority apart from express provision: *Re Schweder's Estate, Oppenheim v Schweder* [1891] 3 Ch 44.
8   *Re Charteris, Charteris v Biddulph* [1917] 2 Ch 379; *Re Trollope's Will Trusts, Public Trustee v Trollope* [1927] 1 Ch 596 at 605; *Garthshore v Chalie* (1804) 10 Ves 1; *Whaley v Cox* (1736) 2 Eq Cas Abr 549; *Lewis v Moore* (1896) 24 AR 393.
9   For postponement of payment, see para **[30.36]** infra; for payment of annuities, see Chapter 33.

[30.32]
Condition attached to payment. An executor is under no obligation to give notice to a legatee of a condition attached to his legacy, even though he may derive a personal benefit on the breach of the condition by the legatee.[1]

1   *Re Lewis, Lewis v Lewis* [1904] 2 Ch 656; *Re Mackay, Mackay v Gould* [1906] 1 Ch 25. There is a general rule that ignorance of a condition attached to a devise or legacy does not protect the beneficiary from the consequences of non-performance; see para **[34.24]** infra. For cases independent of the executor's benefit, see *Powell v Rawle* (1874) LR 18 Eq 243; *Re M'Mahon, M'Mahon v M'Mahon* [1901] 1 IR 489; *Hawkes v Baldwin* (1838) 9 Sim 355 (where the legacy was to go over if not claimed within the year). The rule applies to a legacy payable out of a reversionary interest in the sense that interest is payable thereon and runs from one year after the testator's death although the reversion has not then fallen in: *Walford v Walford* [1912] AC

658; *National Trust Co Ltd and Bond v Crafts* [1939] 2 WWR 487; *Re Lightfoot* [1948] 2 DLR 418, but see *Re Lord's Estate, Lord v Lord* (1867) 2 Ch App 782.

[30.33]
Contingent legacies. The only right of a contingent legatee is to have security for the payment of his legacy if the contingency arises.[1] If an executor, without going to the court, can prove that he has acted reasonably, and that he has set apart an ample sum to answer the legacy and has invested it, and has then proceeded to distribute the residue, he will not be held personally liable to make good the loss if it should turn out that the sum so retained is not sufficient to answer the contingent legacy.[2]

1   *Webber v Webber* (1823) 1 Sim & St 311; *King v Malcott* (1852) 9 Hare 692.
2   *Re Hall, Foster v Metcalfe* [1903] 2 Ch 226; *Re Oswald, Oswald v Oswald* (1919) 64 Sol Jo 242.

[30.34]
Delivery of specific legacies. An executor should as far as possible preserve articles specifically bequeathed, and unless compelled, he ought not to apply them in payment of debts.[1] Where a specific bequest is in a country outside England and Wales, the executor is under no duty to bring the specific bequest into England and Wales in order to put the legatee into possession of the article or articles bequeathed.[2] He can, if he chooses, assent to the bequest and then his responsibility ceases and, if the legatee requires the gift to be brought in England and Wales, he must do so at his own expense and this includes the payment of all death duties payable in respect of the specific bequest.[3] It seems that where the executor gets in such a bequest, the cost of doing so is borne by the general estate,[4] whether the legacy is in the British Commonwealth[5] or in a foreign country,[6] including the payment of any duties payable to the country where the legacy is situated.[7] The cost of warehousing and preserving such a legacy pending the distribution of the estate must, however, in the absence of a contrary direction in the will, be borne by the specific legatee,[8] unless the title of the beneficiaries stems from an act of selection, when the costs prior to the selection have to be borne by the residuary estate.[9] A direction that the testator's testamentary expenses shall be borne by his general personal estate is sufficient to throw such expenses on the general estate.[10] After executors have assented to a specific legacy, any further costs are borne by the specific legatee even though they are the costs of vesting the property in the specific legatee.[11] The costs of packing and transporting specific gifts to legatees who are abroad may be borne by the general estate,[12] but, if that estate is insufficient to pay the pecuniary legacies in full, such costs must be borne by the specific legatees.[13]

1   *Clarke v Earl of Ormonde* (1821) Jac 108. Where a specific legacy was retained for assets but was not wanted and suffered depreciation, it was held that the legatee was entitled to the original value: *Chaworth v Beech* (1799) 4 Ves 555.
2   *Re Scott, Scott v Scott* [1915] 1 Ch 592. This was the case of the gift of a specific article (a picture). The position is different where land outside England and Wales is directed to be sold and the proceeds distributed between specified persons. In some countries the executor is not recognised and the specific gift will be given only to the legatee; see *Re Scott, Scott v Scott* [1915] 1 Ch 592; *Re Fitzpatrick* [1952] Ch 86, [1951] 2 All ER 949, not following *Re Hewett, Eldridge v Hewett* (1920) 90 LJ Ch 126.

3   *Re Scott, Scott v Scott* [1915] 1 Ch 592; *Re Sommery, Coelenbier v De Sommery* [1912] 2 Ch
    622, and see *Re Grosvenor, Grosvenor v Grosvenor* [1916] 2 Ch 375; *Re Fitzpatrick* [1952] Ch
    86, [1951] 2 All ER 949.
4   *Perry v Meddowcroft* (1841) 4 Beav 197, but this case was said in *Re Scott, Scott v Scott* [1951]
    1 Ch 592 at 607, not to be a case of 'great (if any) authority'. At the same time it would seem
    only right where the specific gift is brought to England for the purpose of clearing the liabilities
    of the estate, that the expenses should be borne by the general estate.
5   *Martin v Fear* (1832) 2 LJ Ch 21 (in the colonies); *Peter v Stirling* (1878) 10 Ch D 279 (in
    Victoria); *Re Maurice, Brown v Maurice* (1896) 75 LT 415 (in Australia). These cases were
    distinguished in *Re Brewster, Butler v Southam* [1908] 2 Ch 365, where land in Victoria was
    directed to be sold and the proceeds to be brought to England and held upon specific trusts. The
    English property was directed to bear the 'debts' which were held not to include the local death
    duty in Victoria although by the local law that was deemed a debt of the testator. The death
    duties and costs of realisation fell on the specific gifts and not on residue. In *Re Hewett,
    Eldridge v Hewett* (1920) 90 LJ Ch 126, the cost of packing, shipping and delivering a specific
    gift from Hong Kong to England were payable by the executors out of the general estate but this
    case was not followed in *Re Fitzpatrick* [1952] Ch 86, [1951] 2 All ER 949.
6   *Re De Sommery, Coelenbier v De Sommery* [1912] 2 Ch 622 (shares of French company). In
    this case, however, the property was given to the trustees (who were also the executors) and it
    was held that the executors must have assented to the property vesting in themselves as trustees
    while the property was still abroad and the costs (including succession duty) fell upon the
    specific legatees, applying the principle that after assent, all costs and expenses fall upon the
    legatees.
7   See nn 5 and 6.
8   *Re Rooke, Jeans v Gatehouse* [1933] Ch 970, following *Re Pearce, Crutchley v Wells* [1909] 1
    Ch 819, and not following *Sharp v Lush* (1879) 10 Ch D 468.
9   *Re Collins' Will Trusts, Donne v Hewetson* [1971] 1 All ER 283, [1971] 1 WLR 37
    (beneficiaries given a right to select items from amongst furniture and personal effects).
10 *Sharp v Lush* (1879) 10 Ch D 468; *Re Townend, Knowles v Jessop* [1914] WN 145. As to what
    are testamentary expenses, see para **[55.7]** infra.
11 *Re Grosvenor, Grosvenor v Grosvenor* [1916] 2 Ch 375, where the property was shares in a
    company and had to be vested in the legatee by a transfer. The costs of the transfer fell on the
    legatee.
12 *Re Hewett, Eldridge v Hewett* (1920) 90 LJ Ch 126, but this case was not followed in *Re
    Fitzpatrick, Bennett v Bennett* [1952] Ch 86, [1951] 2 All ER 949. Phillimore LJ in *Re Scott,
    Scott v Scott* [1915] 1 Ch 592 at 610, said that it was the practice where the expense was small
    for executors to pay it, but declined to go further.
13 *Re Sivewright, Law v Fenwick* (1922) 128 LT 416, and *Re Leach, Milne v Daubeny* [1923] 1 Ch
    161.

[30.35]
Absolute legacy with directions as to application. Where there is a bequest of
money to or in trust for a legatee absolutely but with a direction for the
enjoyment or application of the money in a particular mode, as towards
purchasing a residence, the legatee is entitled to receive the money regardless of
the particular mode directed for its enjoyment or application.[1]

1   *Knox v Lord Hotham* (1845) 15 Sim 82; *Lassence v Tierney* (1849) 1 Mac & G 551; *Re
    Skinner's Trusts* (1860) 1 John & H 102.

[30.36]
Payment of vested gift not to be postponed. Similarly, where a legatee takes
an absolute vested interest in a sum of money on attaining full age, a direction
that the sum is not to be paid to him,[1] or is to be accumulated[2] until a subsequent
period, is to be disregarded, unless during the interval the property is given to
another.[3] The principle is equally applicable where the legatee is a charity,
corporate or unincorporate,[4] and, at least in the case of personal estate, to part of

a legacy where the other part is settled or where there is power to postpone conversion or the property is shares in a private company.[5]

1 *Curtis v Lukin* (1842) 5 Beav 147; *Rocke v Rocke* (1845) 9 Beav 66; *Re Johnston, Mills v Johnston* [1894] 3 Ch 204; *Re Couturier, Couturier v Shea* [1907] 1 Ch 470.

2 *Josselyn v Josselyn* (1837) 9 Sim 63; *Saunders v Vautier* (1841) 4 Beav 115; *Gosling v Gosling* (1859) John 265; *Re Cresswell, Lineham v Cresswell* (1914) 58 Sol Jo 360. In *Re Marshall, Marshall v Marshall* [1914] 1 Ch 192, a legatee absolutely entitled was entitled to be paid despite trustees' power to postpone conversion.

3 The power of beneficiaries absolutely entitled to control their trustees embodied in the rule in *Saunders v Vautier* (1841) 4 Beav 115, has been enlarged in respect of the appointment and retirement of trustees by the Trusts of Land and Appointment of Trustees Act 1996, ss 19–20. See Chapter 27, para **[27.2]** supra.

4 *Harbin v Masterman* [1894] 2 Ch 184, CA; affd sub nom *Wharton v Masterman* [1895] AC 186, HL.

5 *Re Weiner's Will Trusts, Wyner v Braithwaite* [1956] 2 All ER 482, [1956] 1 WLR 579, where *Re Kipping, Kipping v Kipping* [1914] 1 Ch 62; *Re Horsnaill, Womersley v Horsnaill* [1909] 1 Ch 631; *Re Marshall, Marshall v Marshall* [1914] 1 Ch 192 and *Re Sandeman's Will Trusts, Sandeman v Hayne* [1937] 1 All ER 368, are considered. The last two mentioned cases were distinguished in *Lloyds Bank plc v Duker* [1987] 3 All ER 193, [1987] 1 WLR 1324.

[30.37]

Limitation of proceedings for recovery of legacy. Proceedings for the recovery of a legacy are barred after the expiration of twelve years next after a present right to receive the same has accrued to a legatee capable of giving a discharge for or release of the legacy; in the case of part payment or acknowledgment a further period of twelve years from the date of such part payment or acknowledgment is allowed.[1] In the case of an immediate legacy to a person sui juris, time begins to run from the death of the testator, and not from the expiration of one year after the death[2] but time does not begin to run in respect of reversionary interests belonging to the testator until they have come into the possession of the representative.[3]

1 Limitation Act 1980, s 22; 24 *Halsbury's Statutes* (4th edn) 724. This applies to a residuary gift, which is a legacy for this purpose: *Re Richardson, Pole v Pattenden* [1920] 1 Ch 423; but where executors hold a share of residue upon express trusts, there is no legacy within the section: *Re Oliver, Theobald v Oliver* [1927] 2 Ch 323.

2 *Waddell v Harshaw* [1905] 1 IR 416, and see the English cases there discussed.

3 *Adams v Barry* (1845) 2 Coll 285; *Re Ludlam, Ludlam v Ludlam* (1890) 63 LT 330.

[30.38]

Legacy held by executor upon express trust. The twelve-year limitation does not apply to a legacy held by an executor upon an express trust; but it is necessary for the legatee to make out that the executor is an express trustee. The fact that the legacy is subject to some implied trust does not deprive the executor of the benefit of the twelve years' limitation.[1] A claim against an executor in respect of a fund of which he is in law an express trustee, and being one to which no Statute of Limitation applies, is barred at the expiration of six years, except where it is founded upon any fraud or fraudulent breach of trust to which he was party or privy, or is to recovery trust property or the proceeds thereof still retained by him, or previously received by him and converted to his use.[2]

1 *Re Davis, Evans v Moore* [1891] 3 Ch 119; *Re Barker, Buxton v Campbell* [1892] 2 Ch 491; *Re Oliver, Theobald v Oliver* [1927] 2 Ch 323.

2   Limitation Act 1939, s 19; see now the Limitation Act 1980, s 21; 24 *Halsbury's Statutes* (4th edn) 722. See *Re Swain, Swain v Bringeman* [1891] 3 Ch 233; *Re Page, Jones v Morgan* [1893] 1 Ch 304; *Re Timmis, Nixon v Smith* [1902] 1 Ch 176; *Re Blow, St Bartholomew's Hospital (Governors) v Cambden* [1914] 1 Ch 233; *Re Oliver, Theobald v Oliver* [1927] 2 Ch 323; *Re Richardson, Pole v Pattenden* [1920] 1 Ch 423. However it can be argued that the 12-year limitation period is still applicable even where the personal representative has become a trustee. This view is based on the fact that the Limitation Act 1939, s 20 is more widely worded than the corresponding provision of the Real Property Limitation Act 1874, and derives some support from *Re Diplock, Diplock v Wintle* [1948] Ch 465, [1948] 2 All ER 318; affd sub nom *Ministry of Health v Simpson* [1951] AC 251, [1950] 2 All ER 1137; see now the Limitation Act 1980, s 22; 24 *Halsbury's Statutes* (4th edn) 724 which is virtually identical to the Limitation Act 1939, s 20.

[30.39]
Remedy against land charged with legacy. As against the land upon which a legacy may be secured, whether by charge or by an express trust, the remedy of the legatee is barred at the expiration of twelve years,[1] notwithstanding that throughout that period the testator's interest in the land may have been reversionary,[2] or subject to prior incumbrances.[3]

1   Limitation Act 1980, s 15(1); s 38(1).
2   *Re Owen* [1894] 3 Ch 220.
3   *Proud v Proud* (1862) 32 Beav 234.

[30.40]
Payment to bankrupt legatee without notice. Payment of a legacy without notice of his bankruptcy to a bankrupt legatee before the trustee in bankruptcy has intervened is good.[1]

1   *Re Ball* [1899] 2 IR 313.

[30.41]
Payment to person of unsound mind, etc. Payment of a legacy cannot safely be made to a person of whose unsoundness of mind the executor has notice.[1] A legacy should not be paid to a minor.[2]

1   Executors obtain a good discharge by payment into court: *Re Parker's Will* (1888) 39 Ch D 303. If they properly and honestly set apart the legacy and invest and accumulate the income after appropriation, they are free from responsibility in the case of an adult legatee of unsound mind: *Pothecary v Pothecary* (1848) 2 De G & Sm 738. See also statutory power of appropriation, Chapter 29.
2   See para **[9.39]** et seq.

[30.42]
Receipt. An executor is entitled to a receipt on payment of a legacy, but is not usually entitled to a formal deed of release.[1]

1   The position in law is obscure: see *Munro v Fitzgerald* (1844) 3 LTOS 3; *Chadwick v Heatley* (1845) 2 Coll 137; *King v Mullins* (1852) 1 Drew 308; *Re Wright's Trusts* (1857) 3 K & J 419; *Re Roberts' Trusts* (1869) 38 LJ Ch 708; *Re Earl of Stamford, Payne v Stamford* [1896] 1 Ch 288 at 301. Where trust funds are re-settled, see *Re Cater's Trusts (No 2)* (1858) 25 Beav 366. As to right of executor on revocation of his grant, see *Tiger v Barclays Bank Ltd* [1951] 2 KB 556, [1951] 2 All ER 262. In practice a legacy is handed over upon an ordinary receipt being given, a share of residue is handed over upon the beneficiary signing a receipt attached to the residuary accounts or a copy thereof. It is only in the case of settled legacies or shares of residue

that a release under seal is desirable and then the executors will have become trustees and receive a release as such. On discovery of further assets after a release has been given, the beneficiary is entitled to his share therein: *Anon* (1862) 31 Beav 310; *Turner v Turner, Hall v Turner* (1880) 14 Ch D 829. Where the legatee is a foreign national resident outside England, the consular officer can give a receipt for a legacy of other interest under a will provided no one has been given a power of attorney by the executor to take a grant: Consular Conventions Act 1949, ss 1, 6; 10 *Halsbury's Statutes* (4th edn) 577, 579. This provision is an addition to and in place of the ordinary law in such cases, and seems intended to be acted on only in exceptional cases.

[30.43]
Currency in which legacy payable. What currency a legacy is to be paid in is a matter of intention. Prima facie the currency is that of the domicile of the testator,[1] but where a different currency is expressly indicated in the will, the legacy must be paid in that currency.[2] Where the testator makes a separate distribution of property in different countries, charging legacies on each, such legacies must be paid respectively in the currency of the country in which the property on which they are charged is situated.[3] The mere fact that the testator owns properties situated in different countries does not, however, without such separate distribution, exclude the currency of the domicile.[4] Where some legacies are given in a currency different from that of the domicile, and in others no reference to currency is made, the latter are payable in the currency of the domicile.[5] The rate of exchange to be taken apart from express direction in the will is that prevailing on the first anniversary of the testator's death,[6] but where a legacy is given 'free of exchange', it must be paid in the currency of the country in which it is payable.[7] Where a legacy is payable in a foreign currency, its value must be computed according to the value of the currency in that country without regard to the rate of exchange and without any deduction for the cost of remittance;[8] but where such a legacy is payable out of assets in England, its value must be computed according to the rate of exchange, and not according to the actual value in the foreign country itself.[9]

In the British Commonwealth the meaning of such phrases as 'sterling', 'English pounds' and 'Australian pounds' depends on the date at which the question has to be answered.[10] Annuities are payable at the rate of exchange prevailing at the time of each payment.[11] The question of interest in such cases is dealt with elsewhere.[12]

1 *Saunders v Drake* (1742) 2 Atk 465. Sometimes the matter appears to have been decided according to the place where the will was made (*Malcolm v Martin* (1790) 3 Bro CC 50; *Pierson v Garnet* (1786) 2 Bro CC 38), but in these cases the place where the will was made and the testator's domicile appear to have been the same. Where the legacy is charged on an immovable, it is the currency of the place where the immovable is situated: *Lansdowne v Lansdowne* (1820) 2 Bli 60; *Holmes v Holmes* (1830) 1 Russ & M 660; *Wallis v Brightwell* (1722) 2 P Wms 88. In *Stapleton v Conway* (1750) 1 Ves Sen 427, it had been said to be in the discretion of the court. In Canada it has been held that where the will has nothing to indicate the rate to be chosen, the bequests will be paid at the rate showing the greatest benefit to the legatee: *National Trustee Co Ltd v Fleury* [1965] SCR 817; *Re Stilborn Estate* (1966) 58 DLR (2d) 575. As to that rate of exchange chosen; see n 6.
2 *Raymond v Brodbelt* (1800) 5 Ves 199.
3 *Pierson v Garnet* (1786) 2 Bro CC 38; *Saunders v Drake* (1742) 2 Atk 465.
4 *Saunders v Drake* (1742) 2 Atk 465.
5 *Malcolm v Martin* (1790) 3 Bro CC 50; *Saunders v Drake* (1742) 2 Atk 465.

6   *Re Eighmie, Colbourne v Wilks* [1935] Ch 524. In *Re Tatham* (1949) 51 WALR 39, the rate of
    exchange at the testator's death was taken.
7   *Thompson v Wylie* (1938) 38 SRNSW 328.
8   *Cockerell v Barber* (1810) 16 Ves 461; and see *Re Schnapper, Westminster Bank Ltd v
    Schnapper* [1936] 1 All ER 322.
9   *Campbell v Graham* (1831) 1 Russ & M 453; on appeal (1834) 2 Cl & Fin 429 at 450, HL.
10 *Bonython v Commonwealth* [1948] 1 ALR 185; *Goldsbrough Mort & Co Ltd v Hall* [1948]
    VLR 145, [1948] 1 ALR 201; *Payne v Federal Comr of Taxation* (1935) 51 CLR 197.
11 *Kornatzki v Oppenheimer* [1937] 4 All ER 133.
12 See para **[32.33]** infra.

CHAPTER 31

Abatement and refunding of legacies

I. ABATEMENT

[31.1]

General legacies. If the estate is insufficient to pay all the legacies in full, the general legacies must, in the absence of a contrary direction by the testator, abate in equal proportions.[1] The onus of proving that his legacy was intended by the testator to be paid in priority lies on the party seeking priority, and the proof must be clear and conclusive[2] on the language of the will. Near relationship to the testator does not of itself give a legatee priority over other legatees.[3] A mere direction to pay a legacy immediately, or within one month, or within three months after a testator's decease, is no evidence of any intention on the part of the testator to give priority to that particular legacy in case of a deficiency in the estate.[4] A direction to pay legacies out of a particular fund makes them payable out of that fund and, if it is insufficient, they abate and no recourse can be made to residue to supply the deficiency.[5] A legacy given to a testator's widow to be paid immediately after his death for her immediate wants is liable to abatement with the other legacies.[6] Nor is a legacy to an executor entitled to any priority.[7] Earlier cases on legacy duty established that where a legacy is given free from duty, the duty must be treated as an additional legacy and be added to the legacy for the purpose of abatement.[8] In those exceptional cases where a pecuniary legacy bore capital transfer tax (eg where the legacy is payable out of foreign realty[9]) it would seem that a similar principle would apply. A charging clause in favour of a solicitor-executor or solicitor-trustee is a legacy and his profit costs must abate with other general legacies.[10] After appropriation in respect of his legacy, the legatee cannot be called upon to contribute to a deficiency[11] but where further assets come in after an abatement, the legatees are entitled to have the benefit of those further assets and time runs against them only from the date of the coming in of those assets.[12]

---

1 *Re Whitehead, Whitehead v Street* [1913] 2 Ch 56; *Re Daniels, London City and Midland Executor and Trustee Co Ltd v Daniels* (1918) 87 LJ Ch 661; *Re Waddell's Estate* (1896) 29 NSR (17 R & G) 19.
2 *Miller v Huddlestone* (1851) 3 Mac & G 513 at 523 ('the rule is that in cases of deficiency of assets all annuities and legacies abate rateably and that the onus lies on the party seeking priority to make out clearly and conclusively that such priority was intended'). See also *Re Leach, Milne v Daubeny* [1923] 1 Ch 161. Where a gift of shares was charged with payment of an annuity, it was held that for the purposes of abatement the shares must be valued without deduction of the annuity: *Re Sloan, Stevens v Sloan* [1943] VLR 63.
3 *Re Schweder's Estate, Oppenheim v Schweder* [1891] 3 Ch 44.

4   *Re Schweder's Estate, Oppenheim v Schweder* [1891] 3 Ch 44; *Blower v Morret* (1752) 2 Ves
    Sen 420; *Re Hardy, Wells v Borwick* (1881) 17 Ch D 798; *Cazenove v Cazenove* (1889) 61 LT
    115 (all legacies to testator's wife). Nor will the putting of the word 'first' before one legacy,
    give it priority: *Re Barker* [1964] NZLR 299.
5   *Re Boyd Estate, Boyd v Boyd* [1928] NI 14 (the fund in this case was insufficient at the date of
    the will as well as at the date of death).
6   In practice such a legacy is made payable in priority to all other legacies and then no question of
    abatement can arise.
7   *Duncan v Watts* (1852) 16 Beav 204; *Roche v Harding* (1858) 7 I Ch R 338; *O'Higgins v Walsh*
    [1918] 1 IR 126; *Re Brown, Wace v Smith* (1918) 62 Sol Jo 487; *Re Leach, Milne v Daubeny*
    [1923] 1 Ch 161; *Anderson v Dougall* (1868) 15 Gr 405. To the contrary: *Allen v Edmonds*
    (1886) 12 VLR 789; *Re Dunn* (1904) 24 CLT 295 (where a co-executor had misappropriated
    part of the assets).
8   *Re Turnbull, Skipper v Wade* [1905] 1 Ch 726. Where the legacy is specific, the duty ranks as a
    pecuniary legacy and abates with other pecuniary legacies: *Farrer v St Catharine's College,
    Cambridge* (1873) LR 16 Eq 19.
9   For example where the legacy is payable out of foreign assets. As to the rules regarding the
    incidence of tax on realty, see para **[55.7]** infra.
10 *Re Brown, Wace v Smith* (1918) 62 Sol Jo 487; *O'Higgins v Walsh* [1918] 1 IR 126. Subject
    now to the Trustee Act 2000, s 29(4).
11 *Knight v Knight* (1846) 15 LJ Ch 363.
12 *Re Thompson* [1955] OWN 521; *Re Clarke* [1966] VR 321.

[31.2]
Legacy in satisfaction of a debt. There appears to be some doubt whether a
legacy given in satisfaction of a debt abates with legacies given to volunteers. In
a case where the debt was an ascertained debt, and the legatee had elected to
take under the will a legacy far in excess of his debt, it was held that his legacy
must abate rateably with the other pecuniary legacies;[1] but there are statements
to be found that legacies to creditors are not liable to abatement with legacies to
volunteers.[2] A creditor with whom the testator has compounded cannot be
treated as a purchaser of his legacy.[3]

1   *Re Wedmore, Wedmore v Wedmore* [1907] 2 Ch 277; *Re Whitehead, Whitehead v Street* [1913]
    2 Ch 56.
2   *Davies v Bush* (1831) You 341 at 343 (actual existence of debt not established); *Re Lawley,
    Zaiser v Lawley* [1902] 2 Ch 799, CA; on appeal [1903] AC 411, HL.
3   *Coppin v Coppin* (1725) 2 P Wms 291 at 296.

[31.3]
Demonstrative legacies. Demonstrative legacies[1] do not abate with general
legacies except so far as the fund provided is insufficient for their payment.[2]

1   As to what are demonstrative legacies, see para **[30.6]** ante.
2   *Roberts v Pocock* (1798) 4 Ves 150 at 160; *Mann v Copland* (1817) 2 Madd 223; *Fowler v
    Willoughby* (1825) 2 Sim & St 354; *Mullins v Smith* (1860) 1 Drew & Sm 204; *Re Turner,
    Armstrong v Gamble* [1908] 1 IR 274; *Re Culbertson* (1966) 59 DLR (2d) 381.

[31.4]
Specific legacies. Specific legacies do not abate with general legacies, but where
the general estate is insufficient to pay all the debts, they must abate rateably
inter se.[1] The rule applies to a gift of a specific fund in aliquot proportions,[2] but
where fixed sums are given out of a particular fund, and the balance is disposed
of as residue, and not as an aliquot proportion, the residue must be first
exhausted.[3] The forgiveness of a debt by will amounts to a specific legacy of the
debt.[4]

1   *Duke of Devon v Atkins* (1726) 2 P Wms 381; *Re Compton, Vaughan v Smith* [1914] 2 Ch 119;
    Re Cohen, National Provincial Bank Ltd v Katz [1960] Ch 179, [1959] 3 All ER 740; *Re West*
    [1942] 1 DLR 754; *Re Pharazyn* (1897) 15 NZLR 709.
2   *Page v Leapingwell* (1812) 18 Ves 463.
3   *Petre v Petre* (1851) 14 Beav 197; see also *De Lisle v Hodges* (1874) LR 17 Eq 440; *Re Tunno,
    Raikes v Raikes* (1890) 45 Ch D 66.
4   *Re Wedmore, Wedmore v Wedmore* [1907] 2 Ch 277; *Stamp Duties Comr v Bone* [1977] AC
    511, [1976] 2 All ER 354; see para **[30.4]** supra. A forgiveness of 'all debts ... up to the time of
    my decease' does not include the liability of the testator's estate under a guarantee of the
    legatee's banking account: *Re Mitchell, Freelove v Mitchell* [1913] 1 Ch 201.

[31.5]
Abatement of annuities. Annuities are dealt with separately.[1]

1   See Chapter 33.

II.   REFUNDING

[31.6]
Between executor and legatee. An executor who has voluntarily paid a legacy
cannot call upon the legatee to refund,[1] except in the case of a deficiency of
assets where he has made the payment under compulsion of an action.[2] Nor is an
executor-trustee who has severed a portion of the estate in favour of a particular
legatee entitled to have recourse to the severed portion to indemnify himself
against a liability which he has been called upon to discharge in respect of
another portion of the estate.[3]

1   *Hilliard v Fulford* (1876) 4 Ch D 389; *Herbert v Badgery* (1894) 15 NSWLR 236. As to
    executor's right to refuse payment unless a covenant or security to refund is given, see
    para **[31.19]** infra.
2   *Newman v Barton* (1690) 2 Vern 205.
3   *Knight v Knight* (1846) 15 LJ Ch 363; *Fraser v Murdoch* (1881) 6 App Cas 855; *Re Craven,
    Watson v Craven* [1914] 1 Ch 358. As to appropriation, generally, see Chapter 29.

[31.7]
Where executor has parted with residuary estate. Where the executor with
notice of a debt has parted with the residue to the residuary legatee he cannot
call upon the latter to refund;[1] but where he has parted with the residue without
knowledge of anything that interferes with the right of the residuary legatee to
receive it, and debts are subsequently discovered which he is obliged to pay, he
can call on the residuary legatee to refund it.[2] Notice at the time of distribution
of a mere liability which does not constitute a debt does not prevent him from
subsequently calling upon the residuary legatee.[3] He can, however, only recover
the capital paid to the legatee without interest.[4]

1   *Jervis v Wolferstan* (1874) LR 18 Eq 18 at 25.
2   *Whittaker v Kershaw* (1890) 45 Ch D 320 at 325.
3   *Jervis v Wolferstan* (1874) LR 18 Eq 18; *Whittaker v Kershaw* (1890) 45 Ch D 320.
4   *Jervis v Wolferstan* (1874) LR 18 Eq 18.

[31.8]

Right to equalise out of future payments. An executor-trustee who has overpaid one beneficiary is entitled in the future administration of the trusts to equalise the payments at the expense of the overpaid beneficiary;[1] and there is no general rule that he cannot claim such an adjustment in his own favour where he is the person responsible for the mistake which has been made.[2]

1   *Livesey v Livesey* (1827) 3 Russ 287; *Dibbs v Goren* (1849) 11 Beav 483. Where the executors are dead, the court and its officers may carry out such equalisation; *Re Drummond* (1912) 22 OWR 554.
2   *Re Ainsworth, Finch v Smith* [1915] 2 Ch 96; *Re Reading, Edmonds v Reading* (1916) 60 Sol Jo 655; *Re Horne, Wilson v Cox Sinclair* [1905] 1 Ch 76 (no claim where executor responsible for mistake).

[31.9]

As between legatees. Where the executor is solvent, a legatee who has been voluntarily paid cannot be called upon to refund at the instance of an unpaid legatee.[1] Where the executor becomes insolvent, it would appear that the legatee cannot be compelled to refund, if the estate was sufficient in the first instance to satisfy all the legacies.[2] A residuary legatee who institutes administration proceedings can be compelled in those proceedings to refund, for the purpose of paying legacies, money paid to him by the executor before action.[3]

1   *Orr v Kaines* (1750) 2 Ves Sen 194.
2   *Fenwick v Clarke* (1862) 4 De GF & J 240.
3   *Prowse v Spurgin* (1868) LR 5 Eq 99.

[31.10]

As between residuary legatees. Where one of several residuary legatees has received his share of the estate, the others cannot call upon him to refund if the estate is subsequently wasted; but they can do so if the wasting has taken place before the share was received.[1] It lies upon the person requiring the money to be refunded to show that the payment was made in excess.[2]

1   *Peterson v Peterson* (1866) LR 3 Eq 111; *Re Winslow, Frere v Winslow* (1890) 45 Ch D 249; *Re Rivers, Pullen v Rivers* [1920] 1 Ch 320 (sum set aside in administration action to pay annuity proving insufficient to pay legacy left to annuitant's children on the death of the annuitant, the residuary legatees held liable to refund deficiency).
2   *Peterson v Peterson* (1866) LR 3 Eq 111 at 114.

[31.11]

Mistake as to persons entitled. Where an intestate's estate has been distributed under an order of the court amongst the persons found to be next of kin and another person subsequently established his title to the next of kin, he can compel the persons amongst whom the estate has been distributed to refund what has been paid to them in excess of their shares.[1]

1   *David v Frowd* (1833) 1 My & K 200, approved by the House of Lords in *Ministry of Health v Simpson* [1951] AC 251, [1950] 2 All ER 1137; *Sawyer v Birchmore* (1837) 2 My & Cr 611.

[31.12]
Between creditor and legatees. A creditor has no legal right to recover payment of his debt against a legatee: but the court, in order to do justice and to avoid the evil of allowing one man to retain what is really and legally applicable to the payment of another man, has devised a remedy by which, where the estate has been distributed either out of court or in court without regard to the rights of a creditor, it has allowed the creditor to recover back what has been paid to the beneficiaries or to the next of kin.[1] The right of the creditor being, however, purely equitable may be met by any answer which affords a good equitable defence,[2] such as laches, acquiescence, or other conduct which would render it unjust for the court to allow him to assert any right against the legatee.[3]

1   *Harrison v Kirk* [1904] AC 1 at 4; *National Assurance Co v Scott* [1909] 1 IR 325. As to equitable right against persons wrongly paid, see *Ministry of Health v Simpson* [1951] AC 251, [1950] 2 All ER 1137 (which, however, was an administration action).
2   *Blake v Gale* (1886) 32 Ch D 571.
3   *Ridgway v Newstead* (1860) 2 Giff 492 at 501; *Re Eustace, Lee v McMillan* [1912] 1 Ch 561 (delay not amounting to laches).

[31.13]
Right of creditor against general fund in court. Where the estate is being administered by the court the creditor can at any time, upon such terms as the court may think fit to impose, come in and claim against a fund in court standing to the general credit of an administration action.[1]

1   *Harrison v Kirk* [1904] AC 1; *Browne v Browne* [1919] 1 IR 251.

[31.14]
Against fund carried to a separate account. As against a fund which has been carried to a separate account in an administration action, the creditor whose claim has not been previously established has not a right to have the whole of the debt paid out of the fund, but only such proportion thereof as the fund bears to the whole of the assets distributed by the court.[1]

1   *Gillespie v Alexander* (1827) 3 Russ 130; *O'Neill v M'Grorty* [1915] 1 IR 1 (funds carried to separate credits not freed from liabilities of fund carried to general credit).

[31.15]
When estate administered out of court. Where the estate has been administered out of court, the creditor is entitled to proceed against a legatee for the whole of his debt, and not merely for a proportionate part,[1] notwithstanding that the legatee has received payment of his legacy in entire ignorance of the creditor's claim.[2] He is entitled to attack any legatee he chooses; and the person attacked is entitled to contribution from his co-legatees.[3]

1   *Davies v Nicolson* (1858) 2 De G & J 693.
2   *March v Russell* (1837) 3 My & Cr 31.
3   *Davies v Nicolson* (1858) 2 De G & J 693; *Worthington & Co Ltd v Abbott* [1910] 1 Ch 588.

[31.16]

Insolvent contributories. Where the court has directed contribution amongst the beneficiaries for payment of debts and costs, and one of the beneficiaries is insolvent, it will direct an additional contribution amongst the solvent beneficiaries.[1]

1   *Conolly v Farrell* (1846) 10 Beav 142; *Re Peerless, Peerless v Smith* (1901) 45 Sol Jo 670.

[31.17]

When estate of undischarged bankrupt. The trustee in bankruptcy of an undischarged bankrupt intestate whose estate has been distributed by the administrator among the next of kin can call upon the latter to refund the shares they have received.[1]

1   *Re Bennett, ex p Official Receiver* [1907] 1 KB 149.

[31.18]

Right to follow a legacy. Unsatisfied creditors have a right to follow a legacy against volunteers claiming through the legatee, but they have no such right against a bona fide purchaser from the legatee.[1] Where the executor has not parted with control over the assets, or where the legacy is represented by a fund in court, the purchaser from the legatee takes subject to the rights of unsatisfied creditors, though their claim be established after the purchase.[2]

1   *Dilkes v Broadmead* (1860) 2 Giff 113; *Spackman v Timbrell* (1837) 8 Sim 253; Administration of Estates Act 1925, s 32(2); 17 *Halsbury's Statutes* (4th edn) 436. Presumably no assent is necessary for the protection of such a transaction, see *Re Atkinson, Proctor v Atkinson* [1908] 2 Ch 307 (equitable alienee protected).
2   *Noble v Brett* (1858) 24 Beav 499; *Hooper v Smart* (1875) 1 Ch D 90; *Jennings v Bond* (1845) 8 IR Eq 755.

[31.19]

Right of executor to require covenant to refund. An executor is not bound to pay a legacy without a covenant or security to refund if the assets should prove insufficient[1] or the liabilities prove greater than expected,[2] but after assent the executor cannot insist on the retention of a fund or provision of security[3] and cannot claim a refund where he has paid voluntarily[4] or appropriated assets to a particular legacy or bequest.[5]

1   *Nelthrop v Hill* (1669) 1 Cas in Ch 135; *Bailey v Hammond* (1802) 7 Ves 590; *Warren v Warren* (1829) 3 Ir L Rec 1st ser 85; *Re Moore, Moore v Moore* (1881) 45 LT 466 (executor's right to retain sum out of residue where the legatee who has been paid is also a residuary legatee).
2   Administration of Estates Act 1925, s 36(10); 17 *Halsbury's Statutes* (4th edn) 443.
3   *Re Bennett, Midland Bank Executor and Trustee Co Ltd v Fletcher* [1943] 1 All ER 467.
4   *Hilliard v Fulford* (1876) 4 Ch D 389.
5   See para **[31.6]**, n 3.

[31.20]

Will held invalid or later will found. Where, some years after the grant of probate, a later codicil was found which revoked a bequest of shares to A and gave the shares to B, it was held that B could recover from A not only the shares, but all the income therefrom from the date of the testator's death.[1] Where the probate is revoked, the executor can in a proper case recover back legacies he has paid.[2]

1   *Re West, West v Roberts* [1909] 2 Ch 180.
2   *Haldan v Beatty* (1876) 40 UCR 110.

[31.21]

Interest. A legatee who is not otherwise interested in the estate apart from his own legacy is not liable to pay interest when refunding; but where, under an erroneous construction of the will, a legatee was entitled to other funds making interest in the hands of the court, he was charged with interest on the amount required to be refunded.[1]

1   *Gittins v Steele* (1818) 1 Swan 199; *Duane v Lee* (1884) 14 LR Ir 56.

CHAPTER 32

Interest and income on legacies

I. GENERAL POSITION

[32.1]
In the case of specific legacies the question of the right of the legatee to income or interest arises only where the legacy is of an income-bearing nature, and the question is whether the legatee is entitled to the income from the date of the death of the testator or not at all. It is impossible for the testator to make special provisions in his will as to such income and to dispose of it to some person other than the legatee either for a time or altogether. Questions arising in the case of general or demonstrative legacies are questions as to interest payable and for the most part turn on the date from which interest is payable. Exceptionally, a gift of a debt may include arrears of interest outstanding at the testator's death.[1]

1   See Chapter 64 under 'Money due or owing'.

II. SPECIFIC LEGACIES

[32.2]
Vested legacies. A vested specific legacy in cases where it is of an income-bearing nature carries the income from the death of the testator.[1] Generally speaking, these consist of stock and shares and the legatee is entitled to all dividends from the testator's death[2] and to all bonuses and other benefits arising thereafter, including both those of an income and those of a capital nature, but are subject to apportionment under the Apportionment Act 1870 unless there is an express direction to the contrary.[3] Partnership profits are dealt with in the same way.[4] Where the specific legacy is vested but the enjoyment is postponed to some future date, the legatee is entitled to the income from the death of the testator.[5]

1   *Barrington v Tristram* (1801) 6 Ves 345; *Bristow v Bristow* (1842) 5 Beav 289 (gift of specific sums in funds to be paid within twelve months of the testator's death: held that the legatee was entitled to all dividends accruing during those twelve months); *Chester v Urwick* (1856) 23 Beav 404 (executors having option to grant legatee one of two different stocks); *Jacques v Chambers* (1846) 2 Coll 435; *Re Jeffery's Trusts* (1866) LR 2 Eq 68 (where the income of stock was apportioned between different legatees); *Re Marten, Shaw v Marten* [1901] 1 Ch 370; *Re Jacob, M'Coy v Jacob* [1919] 1 IR 134.
2   Arrears of preference dividends though stated to be in respect of profits earned in stated years are treated as income of the year in which they are declared: *Re Joel, Johnson v Joel* [1936] 2 All ER 962; *Re McCutcheon's Will* [1960] VLR 289.

3   *Re Edwards, Newbery v Edwards* [1918] 1 Ch 142; *Re Bate, Public Trustee v Bate* [1938] 4 All
     ER 218. The converse proposition also holds good, namely that the specific legatee is liable for
     all payments due in respect of the specific legacy, such as calls on shares: *Clive v Clive* (1854)
     Kay 600; *Re Pharazyn* (1897) 15 NZLR 709.
4   *Browne v Collins* (1871) LR 12 Eq 586.
5   *Long v Ovenden* (1881) 16 Ch D 691; *Guthrie v Walrond* (1883) 22 Ch D 573.

[32.3]

Contingent legacies. By section 175 of the Law of Property Act 1925,[1] a
contingent specific legacy now carries the intermediate income except is so far
as such income is otherwise disposed of by the will. Before that enactment a
contingent specific legacy did not in general carry the intermediate income, but
only in cases where it had to be set apart or was subject to a prior vested limited
interest.[2]

1   Vol 2, Part G, para **[244.52]**; and see *Re Buxton, Buxton v Buxton* [1930] 1 Ch 648.
2   See *Dundas v Wolfe Murray* (1863) 1 Hem & M 425; *Re Clements, Clements v Pearsall* [1894]
     1 Ch 665; *Re Woodin, Woodin v Glass* [1895] 2 Ch 309; *Kiersey v Flahavan* [1905] 1 IR 45.
     Where the legacy does not carry the interest, the interest falls into residue: *Re Inman, Inman v
     Rolls* [1893] 3 Ch 518; *Guthrie v Walrond* (1883) 22 Ch D 573. It was said in *Re Eyre, Johnson
     v Williams* [1917] 1 Ch 351, that it was segregated only where there was a prior vested limited
     interest, or the legacy was invested in trustees. Where an infant to whom the testator stood in
     loco parentis was contingently entitled to a farm, it was held that he was entitled to the
     accumulated rents: *Re Ferguson, Curry v Bell* (1915) 49 ILT 110.

III.   GENERAL AND DEMONSTRATIVE LEGACIES

[32.4]

When no time fixed for payment. Where no special time is fixed for the
payment of a general legacy, it carries interest at 6 per cent per annum[1] from the
expiration of one year after the testator's death,[2] although expressly made
payable out of a particular fund which does not fall in until after a longer
period.[3]

1   RSC Ord 44, r 10; SI 1982/1111; see also CCR 1981 Ord 23, r 2; the rate of 6 per cent is
     substituted for the previous 5 per cent with effect from 1 October 1983 by RSC (Amendment
     No 2) Order 1983, SI 1983/1181. The rate is liable to change and should be checked to ascertain
     the prevalent rate at any one time. The rule states 'where an account of legacies is directed by
     any judgment, then, subject to any directions contained in the will or codicil in question and to
     any order made by the court, interest shall be allowed on each legacy at the rate of 6 per cent
     per annum beginning at the expiration of one year after the testator's death.' Although the rule
     is thus strictly limited to accounts taken under judgment it is submitted that, in the absence of
     any other statutory provision or rule of court, it should be taken as governing also the rate of
     interest generally on legacies. The learned author of this text clearly thought the rates of interest
     in both circumstances were the same since the rule of court was the only authority cited with
     reference to interest rates generally on legacies. See also Williams, Mortimer & Sunnucks,
     Executors, Administrators and Probate, and Parry and Clarke, *The Law of Succession* (10th
     edn) Chapter 19. The point is however, surprisingly, not free from doubt; thus 17 *Halsbury's
     Laws* (4th edn) 1255, refers to 4 per cent per annum as being the correct rate payable unless
     under a judgment, when, by virtue of the rule of court, 5 per cent would have been ordered.
     Other relevant rates of interest are 5 per cent, under the Trustee Act 1925, s 21(3), and 6 per
     cent now payable on statutory legacies: (Intestate Succession (Interest and Capitalisation) Order
     1983, SI 1983/1374); previously the rate was 7 per cent, after 1977; and 4 per cent, after 1952.
     All these rates of interest are liable to change by statutory instrument and should be checked to
     ascertain the prevalent rate at any one time.

2   *Re Lord's Estate, Lord v Lord* (1867) 2 Ch App 782 at 789; *Webster v Hale* (1803) 8 Ves 410 (direction in will to pay as soon as possible), but see para **[32.5]**, n 5, where legacy is immediately payable; *Bourke v Ricketts* (1804) 10 Ves 330 (legacy in currency of Jamaica where testator resided); *Wood v Penoyre* (1807) 13 Ves 325 (payment out of mortgage debt when recovered); *Marquis of Hertford v Lord Lowther* (1846) 9 Beav 266 (delay in payment); *Re Barr* [1947] 3 DLR 784. As to directions which do not amount to a direction for payment at a special time, see *Re Yates, Throckmorton v Pike* (1907) 96 LT 758; *Re Whiteley, Whiteley v Bishop of London* (1909) 101 LT 508; *Walford v Walford* [1912] AC 658. See, further, as to legacy payable at a future date, para **[32.10]** infra. The interest is payable out of the residuary personal estate: *Greene v Flood* (1885) 15 LR Ir 450, and is subject to deduction of income tax at the current rate: *Hamilton v Linaker* [1923] 1 IR 104.

3   *Walford v Walford* [1912] AC 658.

[32.5]

Immediate general legacies. An immediate general legacy except as herein-after stated carries interest only from the expiration of a year after the testator's death,[1] even though it be directed to be paid as soon as possible,[2] but where it was directed to be paid to a wife immediately after the testator's death, it was held that the widow was entitled to immediate payment and interest ran from the testator's death.[3] Where the testator was the parent of, or stood in loco parentis to, a legatee who is a minor, the legacy carries interest from the date of his death.[4] This favour is not extended to an adult child,[5] nor to the testator's wife.[6]

1   *Wood v Penoyre* (1807) 13 Ves 325; *Re Palfreeman, Public Trustee v Palfreeman* [1914] 1 Ch 877 (legacies to children at age of twenty-three, some children attaining twenty-three in lifetime of testator).
2   *Webster v Hale* (1803) 8 Ves 410; *Benson v Maude* (1821) 6 Madd 15.
3   *Re Riddell, Public Trustee v Riddell* [1936] Ch 747, [1936] 2 All ER 1600; *Re Pollock, Pugsley v Pollock* [1943] Ch 338, [1943] 2 All ER 443.
4   *Wilson v Maddison* (1843) 2 Y & C Ch Cas 372; *Re Stokes, Bowen v Davidson* [1928] Ch 716.
5   *Raven v Waite* (1818) 1 Swan 553; *Wall v Wall* (1847) 15 Sim 513.
6   *Stent v Robinson* (1806) 12 Ves 461; *Re Whittaker, Whittaker v Whittaker* (1882) 21 Ch D 657, but see n 3, and text thereto.

[32.6]

To an executor who is a minor. A legacy given to a minor as executor does not carry interest until he attains full age and agrees to act.[1]

1   *Re Gardner, Long v Gardner* (1892) 67 LT 552. Where executor is an adult, see *Angermann v Ford* (1861) 29 Beav 349, and para **[30.14]** supra.

[32.7]

In satisfaction of debt. A legacy amounting to a satisfaction of a debt carries interest from the date of death.[1]

1   *Clark v Sewell* (1744) 3 Atk 96 at 99.

[32.8]

Legacies charged on land. In the case of legacies charged upon land, where no time is fixed for payment, interest runs from the death.[1]

1   *Pearson v Pearson* (1802) 1 Sch & Lef 10; *Spurway v Glynn* (1804) 9 Ves 483; *Shirt v Westby* (1808) 16 Ves 393.

[32.9]

Legacy payable out of proceeds of sale of land. Where the legacy is made payable out of the proceeds of sale of real estate, interest runs only from the end of a year after the testator's death,[1] but where the land is to be sold on the death of a tenant for life, interest is payable on a legacy charged on the proceeds from the death of the tenant for life.[2]

1   *Gough v Bult* (1848) 16 Sim 323; *Turner v Buck* (1874) LR 18 Eq 301; *Re Hull, Melhuish v Fletcher* (1896) 40 Sol Jo 257 (where there was power to postpone the sale).
2   *Re Waters, Waters v Boxer* (1889) 42 Ch D 517; *Re White, White v Shenton* (1909) 101 LT 780 (where the residuary estate was to be sold and the tenant for life died within a month of the testator).

[32.10]

Vested legacy payable at future date. Vested legacies payable at a future date carry interest from that date[1] and not before.[2] The date may be a date certain or dependent on some uncertain event,[3] or even an event which may happen before the death of the testator.[4] It is perhaps the better view that, if it happens before the death of the testator, the legacies become ordinary immediate legacies and interest runs from the expiration of one year from the death of the testator.[5] The general rule that interest runs from the time fixed for payment may not apply if the legacy is severed from the estate. If the severance is for some reason connected with the legatee and not for reasons connected with the more convenient administration of the estate, the interest runs from one year after the testator's death.[6] On the other hand, if the severance is for the more convenient administration of the estate, interest is payable only from the time fixed for payment.[7] Special rules apply to legacies to minors.[8]

1   *Re Gyles, Gibbon v Chaytor* [1907] 1 IR 65; *Re White, White v Shenton* (1909) 101 LT 780; *Donovan v Needham* (1846) 9 Beav 164. Interest is given for delay in payment, and, therefore, until the day of payment arrives, no interest is, in general, demandable: *Re Scadding* (1902) 4 OLR 632.
2   *Thomas v A-G* (1837) 2 Y & C Ex 525. But there may be a legacy payable at a future date where the intermediate interest is also given or ordered to be applied to the legatee's benefit. This amounts to an immediate legacy: *Re Miller* (1957) 8 DLR (2d) 170.
3   *Holmes v Crispe* (1849) 18 LJ Ch 439; *Re Lord's Estate, Lord v Lord* (1867) 2 Ch App 782 (legacies not payable until the conclusion of certain litigation); *Re Gyles, Gibbon v Chaytor* [1907] 1 IR 65; *Re White, White v Shenton* (1909) 101 LT 780 (death of life tenant of residue within executor's year).
4   *Pickwick v Gibbes* (1839) 1 Beav 271; *Coventry v Higgins* (1844) 14 Sim 30; *Re Palfreeman, Public Trustee v Palfreeman* [1914] 1 Ch 877.
5   *Re Palfreeman, Public Trustee v Palfreeman* [1914] 1 Ch 877. To the contrary: *Pickwick v Gibbes* (1839) 1 Beav 271; *Coventry v Higgins* (1844) 14 Sim 30.
6   *Dundas v Wolfe Murray* (1863) 1 Hem & M 425 at 431. In the circumstances of this particular case the legacy carried interest from the testator's death, the severance having to be made at that date, but the general rule is as stated in the text. See *Morpeth v Williamson* [1926] NZLR 39. Where a legacy was payable when and how the executor liked, it was held that interest did not run from the end of the year after testator's death: *Planta v Greenshields (No 2)* [1932] 3 DLR 423.
7   *Festing v Allen* (1844) 5 Hare 573.
8   See para **[32.18]** infra.

[32.11]

Legacy payable out of reversionary or specified property. Where from the circumstances of the estate the only property out of which the legacy can be paid is reversionary and cannot be profitably realised before it falls in, the general rule applies.[1] If it is contended that the legacy is payable only when the reversion falls in, some express direction in the will to this effect must be shown, and only if this is shown does interest run from the date when the reversion falls in.[2] Thus, where the direction was that the legacy was to be paid out of property 'inherited from my mother', the interest ran from the expiration of one year from the testator's death,[3] but where the legacy was made payable only when the reversionary interest fell in,[4] or not until there were sufficient assets for its payment,[5] the interest did not run until the direction was fulfilled.

1   *Re Blachford, Blachford v Worsley* (1884) 27 Ch D 676.
2   *Earle v Bellingham (No 2)* (1857) 24 Beav 448.
3   *Walford v Walford* [1912] AC 658.
4   *Re Lord's Estate, Lord v Lord* (1867) 2 Ch App 782.
5   *Holmes v Crispe* (1849) 18 LJ Ch 439.

[32.12]
Legacy payable within particular period exceeding one year. Where the legacy is made payable within a particular period exceeding one year from the testator's death, it carries interest from the end of a year from the testator's death, if the discretion to postpone is merely for the convenience of the estate, and there are sufficient assets to pay it;[1] but not until the expiration of the period, if the discretion to postpone is given for the personal benefit of the residuary legatee.[2]

1   *Varley v Winn* (1856) 2 K & J 700; *Re Olive, Olive v Westerman* (1884) 53 LJ Ch 525. As to legacy to be paid as soon as possible, see para **[32.4]**, n 2.
2   *Thomas v A-G* (1837) 2 Y & C Ex 525. See also *Lloyd v Williams* (1740) 2 Atk 108; *Re Robinson, McDonnell v Robinson* (1892) 22 OR 438; *McMylor v Lynch* (1894) 24 OR 632.

[32.13]
Legacy payable within the year. A positive direction for a legacy to be paid at a definite time within the year makes interest run from that time,[1] but a negative direction that a legacy shall not be legally payable until a period of less than a year from the testator's death does not alter the general rule.[2]

1   *Harrison v Rhodes* (1753) 1 Lee 197; *Lord Londesborough v Somerville* (1854) 19 Beav 295. This was held to be so where a wife was given a legacy to be paid 'immediately after my death and for her immediate requirements': *Re Pollock, Pugsley v Pollock* [1943] Ch 338, [1943] 2 All ER 443. As to legacy payable on an uncertain event which happens before the death of the testator, see para **[32.15]**, n 1.
2   *Jauncey v A-G* (1861) 3 Giff 308.

[32.14]
Defeasible legacy. The interest on a vested legacy liable to be divested on the happening of a particular event belongs to the legatee until the happening of the defeasance.[1]

1   *Re Buckley's Trusts* (1883) 22 Ch D 583. This was a legacy to an infant with a gift over on death under 21. The infant died before attaining 21, and it was held that the accumulations of income belonged to the infant and not to remainderman who became entitled to the capital on the failure of the infant to attain 21. See, however, para **[32.15]**, n 1.

[32.15]

Contingent general legacies. A contingent general legacy does not, as a rule, carry interest until the happening of the contingency.[1] Where, however, a contingent general legacy is directed to be set aside for the benefit of the legatee it carries the intermediate income,[2] but not where the severance is merely for the convenience of administering the estate.[3]

1   *Wyndham v Wyndham* (1789) 3 Bro CC 58; *Rawlins v Rawlins* (1796) 2 Cox Eq Cas 425 (gift to unborn child does not carry interest until it is born); *Re Gertsman* [1966] VR 45. A gift contingent on a person attaining twenty-one carries no interest until that age is attained (*Re George* (1877) 5 Ch D 837; *Re Dickson, Hill v Grant* (1885) 29 Ch D 331; *Re Inman, Inman v Rolls* [1893] 3 Ch 518); but a different rule applies where the legatee is a child of the testator or someone to whom he stands in loco parentis, see para **[32.20]** infra.
2   *Kidman v Kidman* (1871) 40 LJ Ch 359; *Re Medlock, Ruffle v Medlock* (1886) 55 LJ Ch 738; *Re Inman, Inman v Rolls* [1893] 3 Ch 518; *Re Clements, Clements v Pearsall* [1894] 1 Ch 665; *Re Snaith, Snaith v Snaith* (1894) 71 LT 318; *Re Woodin, Woodin v Glass* [1895] 2 Ch 309. A legacy is not set aside unless it is preceded by a vested limited interest or vested in trustees: *Re Eyre, Johnson v Williams* [1917] 1 Ch 351.
3   *Re Judkins Trusts* (1884) 25 Ch D 743.

[32.16]

Contingent gifts of residue. A contingent gift of residuary personalty, or of a blended fund of real and personal estate,[1] or of residuary realty if the will came into operation on or after 1 January 1926,[2] carries the intermediate income;[3] but this rule does not apply to surplus income arising after the expiration of a trust for accumulation,[4] nor in such a case can the income be claimed under the Trustee Act 1925, s 31(1)(ii),[5] when there is a trust for accumulation—such a trust, although it has ceased as exceeding the limits imposed by the Law of Property Act 1925, s 164,[6] being a direction to the contrary within the Trustee Act 1925, s 69(2).[7] A contingent life interest in residue now carries the intermediate income for the maintenance of minors.[8]

1   *Re Dumble, Williams v Murrell* (1883) 23 Ch D 360; *Re Burton's Will, Banks v Heaven* [1892] 2 Ch 38; *Re Taylor, Smart v Taylor* [1901] 2 Ch 134; *Re Mellor, Alvarez v Dodgson* [1922] 1 Ch 312.
2   A contingent gift of residuary realty under a will which came into operation before 1926 did not carry the intermediate income: *Hodgson v Earl of Bective* (1863) 1 Hem & M 376; on appeal (1864) 10 HL Cas 656.
3   Law of Property Act 1925, s 175; see Vol 2, Part G, para **[244.52]**. A contingent pecuniary legacy does not carry the intermediate interest: *Re Raine, Tyerman v Stansfield* [1929] 1 Ch 716.
4   *Re Ransome's Will Trusts, Moberley v Ransome* [1957] Ch 348, [1957] 1 All ER 690. See further as to residuary gifts subject to annuities, at para **[33.24]** infra.
5   See Vol 2, Part G, para **[246.26]**.
6   See Vol 2, Part G, para **[246.42]**.
7   See Vol 2, Part G, para **[246.37]**.
8   *Re Leng, Dodsworth v Leng* [1938] Ch 821, [1938] 3 All ER 181 (decision under the Trustee Act 1925, s 31).

[32.17]

Future gifts of residue. A future indefeasible gift of residue does not, apart from express provision in the will, or necessary implication therefrom, carry the intermediate income.[1] A future defeasible gift of residue is subject to the same rule and in both these cases, unless the intermediate income is disposed of by the will, it is undisposed of and passes as on an intestacy.[2] Where in a will there is a vested interest made payable at a future date with a direction to accumulate the income and pay it with the principal, the court will not enforce the accumulation and order immediate payment to the beneficiary.[3] The right to accumulations of income and income after the period allowed for accumulation has expired is dealt with elsewhere.[4]

1   *Bective v Hodgson* (1864) 10 HL Cas 656.
2   *Re Gillett's Will Trusts, Barclays Bank Ltd v Gillett* [1950] Ch 102, [1949] 2 All ER 893; *Re Geering, Gulliver v Geering* [1964] Ch 136, [1962] 3 All ER 1043; *Re Power Estate* (1964) 48 WWR 250. In such cases the wording of the residuary gift may be such as to include such income, eg 'after the death of' the tenant for life shows an intestacy, whereas 'subject to the interest of' the tenant for life leaves the residuary legatees entitled to the surplus income; *Re Wragg, Hollingsworth v Wragg* [1959] 2 All ER 717, [1959] 1 WLR 922. Where the deferred gift was of the trust fund 'and the income thereof' these words showed that the gift carried the intermediate income: *Re Geering, Gulliver v Geering* [1964] Ch 136, [1962] 3 All ER 1043.
3   *Wharton v Masterman* [1895] AC 186.
4   See Chapter 95.

IV.   INTEREST ON LEGACY TO A MINOR

[32.18]
Family Law Reform Act 1969. In the case of wills made on or after 1 January 1970, references in this discussion to minors mean persons under the age of eighteen years; in the case of wills made before that date, under twenty-one.[1] A difficulty arises with reference to wills made after the above date but where the gift is none the less made contingent on attaining twenty-one years. Such gifts are analogous to gifts under the old law made contingent on attaining an age greater than twenty-one years and it would seem that they would be subject to similar rules.[2]

1   Family Law Reform Act 1969, s 1; 6 *Halsbury's Statutes* (4th edn) 121.
2   See the cases noted in para **[32.20]**, nn 11,12 and 13.

[32.19]
Maintenance out of income of legacy. There are three cases to be considered in this connection: (i) where the minor legatee is the child of the testator or is some one to whom he stood in loco parentis;[1] (ii) where the minor legatee is not the child of the testator or someone to whom he stood in loco parentis; (iii) where the legacy is expressly given for maintenance.

1   As to who is in loco parentis, see paras **[32.20]** and **[44.8]** infra. A mother is not in loco parentis unless she is actually supporting the minor, even in the case of her own child: *Re Eyre, Johnson v Williams* [1917] 1 Ch 351.

[32.20]
Legacy to minor child of testator or by person in loco parentis. The law in this case is based upon a rule of equity or, as it is sometimes called, the practice of the court.[1] The doctrine, whereby a legacy to a minor payable only on the minor attaining full age or marrying thereunder and given by a parent or a person in loco parentis carries the intermediate interest from the date of the

death of the testator,[2] is based upon the natural obligation which the father would be under, if living, to maintain the child during minority.[3] Therefore prima facie, when the natural obligation to maintain ceases, the basis of the rule is gone; and where the contingency is some event other than the attainment of full age or marriage thereunder, it is much more difficult to find an intention upon the part of the testator that the legatee should be maintained out of the income of the legacy, but it is not impossible to find or presume such an intention.[4] If the contingency is one which must happen long after the attainment of full age the court will be very slow, and would in most cases find it impossible, to draw such an inference, but the court is not precluded from doing so.[5] The essentials of the rule are therefore, (i) the testator must be the father of the minor or a person standing in loco parentis;[6] (ii) the will must not contain some other provision entitling the minor to be maintained out of the estate,[7] but the fact that such a provision is implied by statute[8] does not prevent the operation of the rule,[9] nor does a power to raise part of the minor's share and apply the sum so raised for his advancement, preferment or benefit,[10] nor the bequest of a share of residue;[11] (iii) the contingency must be the attainment of full age or marriage or such that, read with the will as a whole, the court can presume that the testator intended the minor to be maintained out of the income of the legacy;[12] (iv) the legacy must be for the minor and not to trustees upon trust for the minor.[13] Where the testator has provided another fund for the maintenance of the minor, the interest is not required for that purpose and is payable only upon the happening of the contingency or at the time when the legacy is payable.[14]

1   The practice is stated in *Re Bowlby, Bowlby v Bowlby* [1904] 2 Ch 685 at 697, 698, and *Re Boulter, Capital and Counties Bank v Boulter* [1918] 2 Ch 40 at 44, and is fully considered in *Re Jones, Meacock v Jones* [1932] 1 Ch 642.

2   In the case of a posthumous child, the interest runs only from the birth of the child: *Rawlins v Rawlins* (1796) 2 Cox Eq Cas 425.

3   *Re Breed's Will* (1875) 1 Ch D 226.

4   *Re Jones, Meacock v Jones* [1932] 1 Ch 642.

5   *Re Jones, Meacock v Jones* [1932] 1 Ch 642, where the will read as a whole showed that the parent intended the children to be maintained.

6   *Green v Belchier* (1737) 1 Atk 505 at 507; *Re George* (1877) 5 Ch D 837 at 843.

7   *Wynch v Wynch* (1788) 1 Cox Eq Cas 433; *Donovan v Needham* (1846) 9 Beav 164; *May v Potter* (1877) 25 WR 507; *Re West, Westhead v Aspland* [1913] 2 Ch 345. See *Re Stewart, Stewart v Bosanquet* (1913) 57 Sol Jo 646 (where the other fund for maintenance is liable to determine on a contingency, no interest can be paid to the legatee so long as the contingency has not happened).

8   The statutory provision is now the Trustee Act 1925, s 31; see Vol 2, Part G, para **[246.26]**, as amended by the Family Law Reform Act 1969, s 1(3), substituting 18 for 21 in the section: Sch 1, Part I; 6 *Halsbury's Statutes* (4th edn) 122.

9   *Re Moody, Woodroffe v Moody* [1895] 1 Ch 101. This case is considered in *Re Raine, Tyerman v Stansfield* [1929] 1 Ch 716 at 720, 721 where it was held that the incorporation of the statutory power of maintenance does not evidence an intention on the part of the testator that the minor shall be maintained out of the legacy within the decision in *Re Churchill, Hiscock v Lodder* [1909] 2 Ch 431.

10   *Re Churchill, Hiscock v Lodder* [1909] 2 Ch 431. The power shows an intention that the minor shall be maintained and is not without provision for maintenance.

11   *Re Abrahams, Abrahams v Bendon* [1911] 1 Ch 108.

12   In *Re Abrahams, Abrahams v Bendon* [1911] 1 Ch 108, Eve J, refused to extend the rule (or rather the exception to the rule, for the doctrine here considered is an exception to the general rule relating to contingent legacies; see para **[32.15]** supra) to contingencies other than the

attainment of full age and marriage, but in *Re Jones, Meacock v Jones* [1932] 1 Ch 642, it was decided that, so long as the court could find an intention in the will that the legatee should be maintained, the contingency might be the attainment of a greater age than twenty-five or any other contingency consistent with such an intention. The matter is essentially a question of construction and it has been suggested that the headnote is wrong in treating it as a question for the discretion of the court..

13   *Re Medlock, Ruffle v Medlock* (1886) 55 LJ Ch 738 (where the legacy was to vest at twenty-one), and *Re Pollock, Pugsley v Pollock* [1943] Ch 338, [1943] 2 All ER 443 (where the legacy was to vest at twenty-five). In such a case, the legacy will be set apart and so will carry interest from one year after the testator's death under the general law relating to contingent legacies.

14   *Hearle v Greenbank* (1749) 3 Atk 695 at 716; *Wynch v Wynch* (1788) 1 Cox Eq Cas 433; *Donovan v Needham* (1846) 9 Beav 164; *Re George* (1877) 5 Ch D 837; *Re West, Westhead v Aspland* [1913] 2 Ch 345.

[32.21]
Legacy to minor not the child of testator. In the case of a minor, not being either the child of the testator or one to whom the testator stood in loco parentis, a legacy given contingently upon his attaining full age stands upon the same footing as an ordinary contingent legacy; it does not (save as otherwise provided by statute)[1] carry the intermediate income, unless there is a direction in the will that it should be set apart,[2] which direction must be for the benefit of the minor and not for the convenience of administration.[3] But a direction to set aside will not secure the income for the minor life tenant of a fund where there is an express trust to accumulate the income.[4]

1   See Trustee Act 1925, s 31; Vol 2, Part G, para **[246.26]**.

2   *Dundas v Wolfe Murray* (1863) 1 Hem & M 425; *Re Judkin's Trusts* (1884) 25 Ch D 743; *Re Medlock, Ruffle v Medlock* (1886) 55 LJ Ch 738; *Re Clements, Clements v Pearsall* [1894] 1 Ch 665; *Re Snaith, Snaith v Snaith* (1894) 71 LT 318; *Re Woodin, Woodin v Glass* [1895] 2 Ch 309.

3   *Re Judkin's Trusts* (1884) 25 Ch D 743; *Re Medlock, Ruffle v Medlock* (1886) 55 LJ Ch 738; *Re Snaith, Snaith v Snaith* (1894) 71 LT 318; *Re Inman, Inman v Rolls* [1893] 3 Ch 518; *Re Carfrae* [1905] VLR 641.

4   *Re Reade-Revell, Crellin v Melling* [1930] 1 Ch 52, followed in *Re Stapleton, Stapleton v Stapleton* [1946] 1 All ER 323, but there the life interest was in residue. For a case where the minor life tenant obtained maintenance, see *Re Leng, Dodsworth v Leng* [1938] Ch 821, [1938] 3 All ER 181, but in that case there was no trust for accumulation and the decision is on the provisions of the Trustee Act 1925, s 31. See also *King-Harman v Cayley* [1899] 1 IR 39. The court has jurisdiction to grant maintenance where the legacy is vested: *Stretch v Watkins* (1816) 1 Madd 253; *Re Wilson* (1891) 14 PR 261, but does not go against express directions in, or provisions of, the will: *Re Giles* (1878) 4 VLR 37.

[32.22]
Legacy given for maintenance carries interest from testator's death. Where the income of a legacy is given for the maintenance or for the education[1] of a minor the legacy carries interest from the testator's death, even where the minor is not a child of the testator.[2] A power to advance is not a provision for maintenance within this rule but a power to advance or to apply 'otherwise for the benefit of' the minor is within it.[3] Where maintenance is provided for during part of the minor's minority, interest is allowed during the remainder.[4] A contingent legacy to a minor on attaining full age 'with interest' carries no interest before the minor attains full age but upon the minor attaining that age the legacy is payable with interest from the expiration of one year from the testator's death.[5] Where the income is given to an adult person to enable him to

support himself and his children[6] or subject to an obligation of maintaining minors,[7] the legacy does not in general carry interest from the death of the testator, but it may do so where the testator is in loco parentis to the minors and there is an intention to provide for their maintenance as well as that of the adult.[8]

1   This rule has always been held to apply where the legacy is given for maintenance and was held to apply where the legacy was given for education in *Re Selby-Walker, Public Trustee v Selby-Walker* [1949] 2 All ER 178.
2   *Re Richards* (1869) LR 8 Eq 119; *Re Churchill, Hiscock v Lodder* [1909] 2 Ch 431; *Re Stokes, Bowen v Davidson* [1928] Ch 716; *Leslie v Leslie* (1835) L & G *temp* Sugd 1. It is sufficient if it clearly appears from the will that the legacy is intended for the support of the child: *Re Stokes, Bowen v Davidson* [1928] Ch 716. But the mere fact that the right to maintenance under the statute is incorporated in the will does not bring the case within this rule: *Re Raine, Tyerman v Stansfield* [1929] 1 Ch 716 at 721. Where a wife made a gift by will for maintenance of her child and the husband and father of the child surviving was well able to maintain the child out of his own moneys, it was held that the father was entitled to apply the wife's gift for maintenance: *Malcolmson v Malcolmson* (1885) 17 LR Ir 69.
3   *Re Churchill, Hiscock v Lodder* [1909] 2 Ch 431 at 433, 434.
4   *Chambers v Goldwin* (1805) 11 Ves 1; *Martin v Martin* (1866) LR 1 Eq 369.
5   *Knight v Knight* (1826) 2 Sim & St 490.
6   *Raven v Waite* (1818) 1 Swan 553 at 559; *Re Ramsay, Thorpe v Ramsay* [1917] 2 Ch 64.
7   *Re Crane, Adams v Crane* [1908] 1 Ch 379.
8   *Re Ramsay, Thorpe v Ramsay* [1917] 2 Ch 64.

[32.23]
Vested defeasible legacy to a minor. A vested legacy to a minor defeasible on the happening of a contingency carries interest until the contingency happens.[1]

1   *Taylor v Johnson* (1728) 2 P Wms 504 (gift over on death under 21); *Mills v Robarts* (1830) 1 Russ & M 555 (similar gift where the children were illegitimate). On death under full age and before the happening of the contingency the accumulations of income belong to the minor and pass to his personal representatives: *Re Buckley's Trusts* (1883) 22 Ch D 583; *Re Wells, Wells v Wells* (1889) 43 Ch D 281; and see *Re Humphreys, Humphreys v Levett* [1893] 3 Ch 1 (where the minor's interest was not defeasible).

[32.24]
Right to income not applied in maintenance. This is now in many cases settled by statutory provision.[1] Where the interest of the minor is a vested interest merely payable on attaining eighteen or marriage under that age and also where he becomes entitled to the property out of which the income arose in fee simple, absolute or determinable, or absolutely or for an entailed interest on attaining eighteen or marriage under that age, the accumulations of income go to the beneficiary absolutely unless he has during his minority made a settlement of such property.[2] In any other cases, notwithstanding that the beneficiary has a vested interest, the accumulations go as an accretion to capital and as one fund with the capital for all purposes.[3] Under the Trustee Act 1925 (TA 1925), however, trustees may during the minority apply the accumulations or any part thereof as income arising in the current year.[4] Where a share of residue is given absolutely[5] to a minor contingently on his attaining eighteen, the minor on attaining that age is entitled to both capital and accumulations of income,[6] but where he obtains a life interest on attaining full age, the accumulations are added to the capital.[7] In the case of interest arising under wills made on or after 1

January 1970,[8] where property is held by trustees upon trust for any beneficiary (whether he is entitled to a vested or to a contingent interest) the power of the trustees to apply income for his maintenance, education or benefit and to accumulate the surplus continues only while he remains under eighteen. After he has attained that age, and even though his interest may still be contingent, the trustees must pay the whole of the income to him. This can have tax disadvantages.[9] However, these disadvantages can be mitigated by ousting the TA 1925, s 31 and including in the will a full express power for the trustees to apply income for the beneficiary and to accumulate the surplus until he reaches twenty-one. Alternatively, the will could provide that the provisions of the TA 1925, s 31 should apply to the gift in question as though the Family Law Reform Act 1969 had never been enacted.

In respect of gifts contained in wills made before 1 January 1970, to which the TA 1925, s 31 applies in its unamended form, the trustees have merely a power to pay the income to the beneficiary himself once he has attained eighteen.[10]

1   TA 1925, s 31(2); as amended by the Trustee Act 2000, Sch 2, para 21; see Vol 2, Part G, para **[246.26]**, and for a fuller discussion of the TA 1925, s 31 see Vol 2, B18 at para **[218.1]**. The Family Law Reform Act 1969, Sch 1, Pt I has substituted 18 for 21 in the TA 1925, ss 31(1)(ii) and 31(2)(i)(a) and (b).
2   TA 1925, s 31(2)(i); as amended, see n 1.
3   TA 1925, s 31(2)(ii).
4   TA 1925, s 31(2).
5   'Absolutely' here means that the minor's interest is not a life interest. Where it is a life interest, see n 7. Where the interest is vested but defeasible, see para **[32.23]**, n 1.
6   *Re Bowlby, Bowlby v Bowlby* [1904] 2 Ch 685 at 711.
7   *Re Bowlby, Bowlby v Bowlby* [1904] 2 Ch 685; *Re Mellor, Alvarez v Dodgson* [1922] 1 Ch 312; and the TA 1925, s 31(2).
8   Family Law Reform Act 1969, s 1(2)(a), (3), Sch 1, and s 1(4), Sch 3; 6 *Halsbury's Statutes* (4th edn) 125, 127.
9   Income tax, see the Taxes Act 1988, s 686; capital gains tax, see the Taxation of Chargeable Gains Act 1992, ss 4, 5; inheritance tax, see the Inheritance Tax Act 1984, s 71.
10 Family Law Reform Act 1969, s 1(4) and Sch 3, para 5(2); 6 *Halsbury's Statutes* (4th edn) 127.

[32.25]
Rate of interest allowed. In any case in which the testator is (i) the parent of, or (ii) in loco parentis to, the minor, or (iii) the legacy carries interest under the general law, the rate allowed is 5 per cent per annum, if the income is sufficient to pay it and the statutory powers of maintenance are applicable.[1]

1   TA 1925, s 31(3).

[32.26]
Statutory powers. Both executors[1] and administrators[2] who hold property belonging to a minor are trustees for the purpose of exercising the statutory powers of trustees relating to maintenance of minors.[3]

1   *Re Smith, Henderson-Roe v Hitchins* (1889) 42 Ch D 302.
2   *Re Adams, Verrier v Haskins* (1906) 51 Sol Jo 113.
3   TA 1925, ss 31, 68(17).

[32.27]
Powers of maintenance. See Volume 2.

V.   INTERMEDIATE INCOME AND CLASS GIFTS

[32.28]
Rights of members of class. Where a gift carrying intermediate income such as a gift of residuary personal estate,[1] is made to a contingent class, if members of the class attain a transmissible interest on coming into existence, whether subject or not to being diminished in any event, the members for the time being in existence share the income,[2] while, if members attain a transmissible interest on attaining a certain age or satisfying some other description or condition, a member of a class attaining a transmissible interest takes only the income of the share to which he would be entitled if the other members of the class for the time being in existence[3] have transmissible interests;[4] but if a gift not carrying intermediate income,[5] such as a gift of real estate, is made to such a class, the members of the class whose interests are transmissible for the time being take the whole income.[6] The investments representing accumulations of income belonging contingently to a beneficiary dying before attaining a vested interest are added to, and thereafter dealt with as part of, the entire capital of the estate.[7]

1   See para **[32.17]** supra.
2   *Shepherd v Ingram* (1764) Amb 448.
3   If the class is enlarged by the birth of a further child, that further child has no right to share in the interest or income which has arisen prior to his birth: *Mills v Norris* (1800) 5 Ves 335; *Scott v Earl of Scarborough* (1838) 1 Beav 154.
4   *Re Holford, Holford v Holford* [1894] 3 Ch 30 (by which decision the rule was settled resolving previous doubts); *Re Jeffery, Arnold v Burt* [1895] 2 Ch 577; *Re Faux, Taylor v Faux* (1915) 84 LJ Ch 873; *Re Maber, Ward v Maber* [1928] Ch 88; *Re King, Public Trustee v Aldridge* [1928] Ch 330. If, however, on attaining that age the interest is still contingent, the beneficiary is not entitled to be paid the income: *Re Ransome's Will Trusts, Moberley v Ransome* [1957] Ch 348, [1957] 1 All ER 690; nor can he be paid the income under the TA 1925, s 31 (Vol 2, Part G, para **[246.26]**), if there is an express direction for accumulation, and this is so notwithstanding that such direction has then failed as transgressing the applicable period under the Law of Property Act 1925, s 164 (Vol 2, Part G, para **[246.42]**).
5   It must be remembered that the right to the intermediate income was enlarged by the Law of Property Act 1925, s 175, which, in the case of wills coming into operation after 1925, provided that (i) a future or contingent devise or bequest of property whether real or personal, and (ii) a contingent residuary devise of freeholds to trustee upon trust for persons whose interests are contingent or executory, carried the intermediate income from the death of the testator subject to any trust for accumulation and to any express disposition of such income. As to right to intermediate income, see paras **[32.1]–[32.17]** supra.
6   *Re Averill, Salsbury v Buckle* [1898] 1 Ch 523; *Re Walmsley's Settled Estates* (1911) 105 LT 332; but in *Re Stevens, Stevens v Stevens* [1915] 1 Ch 429 (followed in *Re Bird, Watson v Nunes* [1927] 1 Ch 210), where under the gift the donees were to be entitled to the income as well as the corpus, each donee was entitled to an equal share of the rents on becoming entitled to the corpus. See, however, n 3 supra. Where the income is to be applied to the education of the beneficiaries at the direction of the trustees, they may apply more to one beneficiary than to another, but cannot accumulate income: *Re Bukowski* [1954] QSR 286. Where the shares have vested on the death of the testator and there is a provision for maintenance out of income, the income is payable to the beneficiaries and the personal representatives of beneficiaries who have died after the death of the testator: *Re Wilson* [1954] NZLR 880.
7   *Re Joel's Will Trusts, Rogerson v Brudenell-Bruce* [1967] Ch 14, [1966] 2 All ER 482, not following *Re King, Public Trustee v Aldridge* [1928] Ch 330, on this point.

VI. GENERAL POINTS

[32.29]

Appropriation of payments to interest. Where there are insufficient funds for the payment of legacies when due, the legatees are entitled, when payment is later made, to appropriate such payment first to interest due before appropriating to capital.[1]

1 *Re Prince, Hardman v Willis* (1935) 51 TLR 526; *Re Morley's Estate, Hollenden v Morley* [1937] Ch 491, [1937] 3 All ER 204 (the right is subject to any direction in the will or in an order of court). Where two legacies were directed by the will to abate if necessary so that all others might be paid in full, this did not mean that, having abated for payment of principal in full, they should further abate for payment of interest: *Re Wyles, Foster v Wyles* [1938] Ch 313, [1938] 1 All ER 347.

[32.30]

Arrears of interest recoverable. Only six years' arrears of interest can be recovered in respect of a legacy,[1] but legatees who wait for the payment of their legacies until after the falling in of a reversionary interest are entitled to interest from the expiration of one year after the testator's death.[2] The six years' limitation applies as against land to arrears of interest on legacies charged upon or payable out of any land or rent, and secured by an express trust.[3]

1 Limitation Act 1980, s 22; 24 *Halsbury's Statutes* (4th edn) 724.
2 *Re Blachford, Blachford v Worsley* (1884) 27 Ch D 676.
3 Limitation Act 1980, s 20; 24 *Halsbury's Statutes* (4th edn) 720; but it appears from *Re Jordison, Raine v Jordison* [1922] 1 Ch 440, that if the land or the proceeds of sale out of which the claim is payable remains vested in the trustee, no limitation is applicable.

[32.31]

Rate of interest. In general, the rate of interest on legacies is 6 per cent;[1] interest is not allowed at a higher rate, even though the residuary estate has been producing interest at a higher rate.[2]

1 RSC Ord 44, r 10; SI 1982/1111; the rate of 6 per cent was substituted for the previous 5 per cent by RSC (Amendment No 2) Order 1983, SI 1983/1181 with effect from 1 October 1983; see para **[32.4]**, n 1.
2 *Re Campbell, Campbell v Campbell* [1893] 3 Ch 468.

[32.32]

Nature of interest payment. Interest payable on a legacy is not part of the legacy but a sum paid in administration to prevent injustice arising from delay in payment and consequently a legacy will not abate to provide interest on other legacies.[1]

1 *Re Wyles, Foster v Wyles* [1938] Ch 313, [1938] 1 All ER 347.

[32.33]

Legacy in foreign currency. Unless the will provides to the contrary, a legacy in a foreign currency carries interest at the local rate,[1] though possibly the true rule is that the interest is calculated at the rate of the country in which the fund is situated.[2] Where there were two funds and the beneficiaries elected to take payment out of the English fund only English interest was allowed.[3] Where the legacy is charged on foreign land, so much of the sum as remains unraised carries interest at the local rate.[4] Where the legacy is charged partly on English and partly on foreign land, the English rate of interest is payable.[5] This, however, is subject to the intention of the testator as expressed in or implied from the will.[6] Where the beneficiaries and trustees reside in England and the will is made in England, the English rate is payable.[7] No deduction is made for the difference in the exchange.[8]

1   *Saunders v Drake* (1742) 2 Atk 465; *Raymond v Brodbelt* (1800) 5 Ves 199. In *Malcolm v Martin* (1790) 3 Bro CC 50, only English interest was allowed.
2   *Malcolm v Martin* (1790) 3 Bro CC 50 at 54; *Raymond v Brodbelt* (1800) 5 Ves 199.
3   *Bourke v Ricketts* (1804) 10 Ves 330.
4   *Balfour v Cooper* (1883) 23 Ch D 472.
5   *Young v Lord Waterpark* (1842) 13 Sim 199, as explained in *Balfour v Cooper* (1883) 23 Ch D 472.
6   *Phipps v Earl of Anglesea* (1721) 1 P Wms 696; *Wallis v Brightwell* (1722) 2 P Wms 88; *Lansdowne v Lansdowne* (1820) 2 Bli 60.
7   *Wallis v Brightwell* (1722) 2 P Wms 88; *Stapleton v Conway* (1750) 1 Ves Sen 427. Where the beneficiaries were resident in Ireland, interest was payable at 5 per cent per annum in Irish currency; *Denny v Denny* (1866) 14 LT 854.
8   *Phipps v Earl of Anglesea* (1721) 1 P Wms 696.

CHAPTER 33

Annuities

I. DEFINITION AND CREATION

[33.1]

Definition. An annuity is a sum of money payable yearly and out of personal estate,[1] but this word is also commonly used where the sum is payable periodically.[2] Prima facie an annuity is itself personal estate,[3] and even where it is directed to be paid out of real and personal estate, the annuity is still prima facie personalty.[4] An annuity is a legacy and annuities are generally included in the term 'legacies'[5] and even in 'pecuniary legacies'.[6] A bequest of such a sum as fairly represents the capital value of a perpetual annuity of a stated amount is a bequest of an amount necessary to produce that income of the government security of the country where the matter falls to be decided which is the most permanent and least likely to be redeemed.[7]

1   *Savery v Dyer* (1752) Amb 139; *Bignold v Giles* (1859) 4 Drew 343 at 346; *Re Townshend* [1938] 3 DLR 767 (legacy of certain sum per annum); see Vol 2, Form B.11 at para **[211.1]** et seq.
2   *Bignold v Giles* (1859) 4 Drew 343. A gift of a portion of dividends stands on a different footing from an annuity simpliciter, being a gift of an aliquot part of a capital fund. A gift to executors of £400 a year for five years is an annuity out of income and not a legacy out of capital: *Scholefield v Redfern* (1863) 2 Drew & Sm 173. A gift of a certain sum payable every six months until the legatee dies or has received a certain sum is not an annuity: *O'Connor v Minister of National Revenue* [1943] 4 DLR 160.
3   *Wiltshire v Rabbits* (1844) 14 Sim 76.
4   *Parsons v Parsons* (1869) LR 8 Eq 260; *Re Trenchard, Trenchard v Trenchard* [1905] 1 Ch 82.
5   *Mullins v Smith* (1860) 1 Drew & Sm 204; *Re Thompson, Public Trustee v Husband* [1936] Ch 676, [1936] 2 All ER 141.
6   *Gaskin v Rogers* (1866) LR 2 Eq 284 at 291.
7   *Gilmour v Gilmour* (1930) 31 SRNSW 83.

[33.2]

Creation by simple bequest. Where the annuity is created by a simple bequest the annuitant, where the estate is sufficient, cannot claim to be paid in cash the value of the annuity.[1] He can, however, require such a sum or such securities to be set apart as will make it practically certain that the annuity will be paid.[2] Where the estate is insufficient, the annuitant can require that the annuity shall be valued, and the amount of the valuation, subject to an abatement in proportion to the abatement of the pecuniary legacies, shall be paid to him in cash.[3]

1   *Re Ross, Ashton v Ross* [1900] 1 Ch 162.
2   *Harbin v Masterman* [1896] 1 Ch 351 at 355.

3   *Wroughton v Colquhoun* (1847) 1 De G & Sm 357; *Re Ross, Ashton v Ross* [1900] 1 Ch 162. If
the annuity is liable to forfeiture, the capital must be paid to trustees: *Re Dempster, Borthwick v
Lovell* [1915] 1 Ch 795. Though the estate may be insufficient to pay the annuity as such, it
may in some cases be sufficient to pay the value of the annuity and other legacies in full and
then there is no abatement: see para **[33.35]** infra.

[33.3]
Simple bequest with direction or power to set aside a fund. Where there is a
direction or power, and the estate is sufficient, to set apart a fund, the annuitant
is entitled to have any deficiency of income made up out of capital, but he
cannot claim to have the value of the annuity paid over to him.[1] Where the estate
is insufficient to set apart the requisite fund and to pay in full any pecuniary
legacies bequeathed by the will, but is sufficient to pay in full the legacies and
the value of the annuity as at the testator's death, the general rule is that they
should be valued as at the death according to the government scale, and the
valuation may either be paid to the annuitant or invested in the purchase of an
annuity.[2] This rule, however, does not apply where the expectation of life of the
annuitant is so short that it is clear that the annuity can be paid in full out of
income without a resort to capital,[3] nor does it apply where the will shows a
contrary intention.[4] Where a widow took advantage of the rule and there was a
partial intestacy as to residue undisposed of, she was required to forgo her right
to the income of that residue, which was applied to recoup the capital taken out
of the estate by the application of the rule.[5] For this purpose a person entitled to
the income of a fixed sum or fund is treated as an annuitant.[6] Where the estate is
insufficient to pay in full the legacies and the value of the annuity as at the
testator's death, the amount of the valuation of the annuity should be treated as a
legacy, and, all legacies abating proportionately, the abated amount of the
annuity should be paid to the annuitant,[7] but this rule does not apply where the
will gives interests in the annuity fund after the cesser of the annuity and the
persons to whom such interests are given have a claim against residue in respect
of them although no fund is set aside.[8] If the annuity is liable to forfeiture during
the life of the annuitant, the annuity is to be purchased in the names of trustees
and the annuitant is not entitled to be paid the amount of the valuation.[9]

1   *Wright v Callender* (1852) 2 De GM & G 652; *Re Cottrell, Buckland v Bedingfield* [1910] 1 Ch
402 at 407.
2   *Re Cottrell, Buckland v Bedingfield* [1910] 1 Ch 402 at 407.
3   *Re Hill, Westminster Bank Ltd v Wilson* [1944] Ch 270, [1944] 1 All ER 502.
4   *Re De Chassiron, Lloyds Bank Ltd v Sharpe* [1939] Ch 934, [1939] 3 All ER 321 (direction to
resort to capital).
5   *Re Vardon, Brown v Vardon* [1938] 4 All ER 306.
6   *Re Richardson, Richardson v Richardson* [1915] 1 Ch 353; *Re Ellis, Nettleton v Crimmins*
[1935] Ch 193.
7   See *Re Thomas, Public Trustee v Falconer* [1946] Ch 36, [1945] 2 All ER 586, where other and
conflicting authority on this point is considered. These cases are all in the court of first instance,
and the matter is, therefore, still in some doubt.
8   *Re Thomas, Public Trustee v Falconer* [1946] Ch 36, [1945] 2 All ER 586.
9   *Re Dempster, Borthwick v Lovell* [1915] 1 Ch 795. Purchase in the name of the annuitant makes
him absolutely entitled and the forfeiture clause becomes void: *Hunt-Foulston v Furber* (1876)
3 Ch D 285; *Re Mabbett, Pitman v Holborrow* [1891] 1 Ch 707.

[33.4]
Power to purchase. A simple bequest of an annuity, followed by a power to trustees to purchase, gives the annuitant the right, but only when the trustees have decided to purchase and have provided the money for the purchase, to have the value of the annuity paid over to him.[1] If, however, the annuitant dies before the money has been provided, his personal representatives are not entitled to the money.[2]

1   *Re Mabbett, Pitman v Holborrow* [1891] 1 Ch 707.
2   *Re Mabbett, Pitman v Holborrow* [1891] 1 Ch 707.

[33.5]
Direction to purchase. Where there is a simple bequest of an annuity followed by a direction to purchase,[1] or a direction to purchase standing alone,[2] or if the annuitant elects to take a capital sum, the capital value should be calculated by reference to the government annuity tables,[3] and not the price at which the annuity could be purchased from an insurance company,[4] unless the executors are given a direction to purchase from any public company.[5] In these cases the annuitant has a right to claim in cash the price to be paid for the annuity, and, if he dies before the purchase, his representatives have a similar right, even when his death occurs immediately after that of the testator.[6]

1   *Stokes v Cheek* (1860) 28 Beav 620; *Re Brunning, Gammon v Dale* [1909] 1 Ch 276.
2   *Yates v Compton* (1725) 2 P Wms 308; *Dawson v Hearn* (1831) 1 Russ & M 606; *Ford v Batley* (1852) 17 Beav 303; *Re Robbins, Robbins v Legge* [1907] 2 Ch 8.
3   The sale of government annuities was discontinued in 1962, but tables for calculating their cost remain in force. These tables can be varied and the tables now in force are those laid down in the Government Annuity Table Order 1963, SI 1963/1178, as amended by Government Annuity Table Order 1977, SI 1977/1536.
4   *Re Castle, Nesbitt v Baugh* [1916] WN 195.
5   *Re Smith, Royal Exchange Assurance Co v Lee* (1923) 130 LT 185.
6   *Re Robbins, Robbins v Legge* [1907] 2 Ch 8; *Re Brunning, Gammon v Dale* [1909] 1 Ch 276; *Re Gildersleeve* [1934] OWN 51; *Re Garnett Estate* (1954) 12 WWRNS 617 (where the testator and the annuitant died in the same accident).

[33.6]
Direction to invest a stated sum. Where there is a direction to invest a stated sum in the purchase of an annuity for the annuitant's benefit, the annuitant is entitled to the sum;[1] and, if he dies before appropriation, his representatives have the same right.[2] Where the direction is to invest a sum to produce a stated income, the court has generally directed the sum to be invested in consols,[3] refusing to exercise a discretion given to the trustees.

1   *Barnes v Rowley* (1797) 3 Ves 305; *Bayley v Bishop* (1803) 9 Ves 6; *Palmer v Craufurd* (1819) 3 Swan 483.
2   *Barnes v Rowley* (1797) 3 Ves 305; *Bayley v Bishop* (1803) 9 Ves 6; *Palmer v Craufurd* (1819) 3 Swan 483.
3   *Re Hollins, Hollins v Hollins* [1918] 1 Ch 503, and see *Re Thomas, Public Trustee v Falconer* [1946] Ch 36, [1945] 2 All ER 586. For a case in which the court exercised a discretion, see *Re Marsh, Rhys v Needham* (1917) 62 Sol Jo 141. The amount to be set aside is in the discretion of the trustees, *Re Martin's Estate* [1958] SASR 365.

[33.7]

How right to payment of value negatived. The right to have the cash value of a life annuity can be prevented only by the inclusion of a gift over of the annuity fund on the cesser of the annuity[1] or a provision for cesser on alienation.[2] It is not prevented by a power given to trustees to apply the annuity for the annuitant's personal benefit,[3] or by a mere declaration that the annuitant shall not be entitled to receive the value of the annuity.[4]

1   *Power v Hayne* (1869) LR 8 Eq 262; *Re Draper* (1888) 57 LJ Ch 942; *Roper v Roper* (1876) 3 Ch D 714 at 721; and as to the importance and effectiveness of a gift over, see *Re Thomas, Public Trustee v Falconer* [1946] Ch 36, [1945] 2 All ER 586.
2   *Hatton v May* (1876) 3 Ch D 148; but such a provision is void if the annuity is purchased in the name of the annuitant for he then becomes absolutely entitled to it: *Hunt-Foulston v Furber* (1876) 3 Ch D 285. See, further, n 4 infra, and the text thereto.
3   *Re Browne's Will* (1859) 27 Beav 324.
4   *Stokes v Cheek* (1860) 28 Beav 620; *Re Nunn's Trusts* (1875) LR 19 Eq 331; *Hatton v May* (1876) 3 Ch D 148; *Hunt-Foulston v Furber* (1876) 3 Ch D 285; *Re Mabbett, Pitman v Holborrow* [1891] 1 Ch 707 at 713.

[33.8]

Right of personal representatives of annuitant to payment of value. Personal representatives of the annuitant have no right to receive the value of the annuity where it is given by a simple bequest with or without a direction or power to set aside a fund. Where there is power to purchase, they have a right to the money if the money has been provided before the death of the annuitant. Where there is a direction to purchase or to invest a stated sum in the annuity the personal representatives are entitled to the money in any event where the annuitant himself has not received it. These matters have been dealt with in the preceding paragraphs, but there remains one special case. When the trustees are directed to purchase in their own names an annuity to commence some time after the death of the testator (eg on the death of a tenant for life) and the annuity is subject to forfeiture on alienation, the personal representatives are not entitled to the value of the annuity if the annuitant dies before the annuity is purchased.[1]

1   *Power v Hayne* (1869) LR 8 Eq 262; *Re Draper* (1888) 57 LJ Ch 942; *Re Strange, Lamb v Bossi Leu* (1916) 60 Sol Jo 640. *Day v Day* (1853) 1 Drew 569, to the contrary has never been followed. In the first two cases cited, the annuitant predeceased the tenant for life.

[33.9]

Perpetual annuity amounting to a gift of corpus. The creation by will of a perpetual annuity may take the form of an unlimited gift of the income of a particular fund, and, in such a case amounts to a gift of the corpus of the fund or property from which the annuity arises, and the annuitant is entitled to the corpus accordingly.[1]

1   *Blight v Hartnoll* (1881) 19 Ch D 294 at 296; *Re Morgan, Morgan v Morgan* [1893] 3 Ch 222 at 229; *Bent v Cullen* (1871) 6 Ch App 235 at 238; *Re Jones* [1950] 2 All ER 239 (gift of sums to unincorporated body); *Re Fenwick* [1957] NZLR 709 (gift of £50 per annum to Dominion Government).

[33.10]
Cumulative and substitutional annuities. Two annuities of the same amount given by the same testamentary instrument[1] to the same person are prima facie substitutional,[2] but where they are given by different testamentary instruments, they are prima facie cumulative.[3] Where the amounts are different, the presumption is that they are cumulative,[4] but the will may show by its provisions that the annuities are substitutional.[5] Gifts of the same or different amounts to the same person but in different instruments are cumulative.[6] The question of satisfaction of a previous liability by a testamentary gift is dealt with elsewhere.[7]

1 For the purposes of this paragraph a codicil to a will is a different testamentary instrument to the will itself.
2 *Holford v Wood* (1798) 4 Ves 76 at 90; *Brine v Ferrier* (1835) 7 Sim 549. For a case where the instrument showed that the annuities were successive, see *Baylee v Quin* (1842) 2 Dr & War 116.
3 *Roch v Callen* (1848) 6 Hare 531; *A-G v George* (1836) 8 Sim 138.
4 *Yockney v Hansard* (1844) 3 Hare 620; *Hartley v Ostler* (1856) 22 Beav 449.
5 *Yockney v Hansard* (1844) 3 Hare 620; *Adnam v Cole* (1843) 6 Beav 353.
6 *Barclay v Wainwright* (1797) 3 Ves 462; *Spire v Smith* (1839) 1 Beav 419; *Radburn v Jervis* (1841) 3 Beav 450, but the two instruments may be shown to be duplicates if executed at about the same time: *Re Michell, Thomas v Hoskins* [1929] 1 Ch 552.
7 See Chapter 44.

II. COMMENCEMENT AND DURATION

[33.11]
Commencement of annuity. An annuity given by will commences prima facie from the death of the testator.[1] Where an annuity is to be paid monthly or weekly, the first payment is to be made at the expiration of one month from the testator's death.[2] If it is to be quarterly, a proportionate part is payable on the first quarter day.[3] If merely the first payment is to be made within one month of the testator's death, a year's payment is due within a month, but the second payment is not due until the expiration of two years from the testator's death.[4] Where a lump sum is payable it becomes due at the expiration of the executor's year.[5] The main rule applies where the annuity is charged upon a reversionary interest.[6] The will may, however, direct a different time for payment.[7] Arrears of an annuity under a will do not carry interest.[8]

1 *Re Robbins, Robbins v Legge* [1906] 2 Ch 648 at 653; *Re Brunning, Gammon v Dale* [1909] 1 Ch 276.
2 *Houghton v Franklin* (1823) 1 Sim & St 390; *Byrne v Healy* (1828) 2 Mol 94 (weekly payment); *Irvin v Ironmonger* (1831) 2 Russ & M 531.
3 *Williams v Wilson* (1865) 5 New Rep 267.
4 *Irvin v Ironmonger* (1831) 2 Russ & M 531.
5 *Re Friend, Friend v Young (No 2)* (1898) 78 LT 222.
6 *Re Williams, Williams v Williams* (1895) 64 LJ Ch 349.
7 *Storer v Prestage* (1818) 3 Madd 167; *Ingham v Daly* (1882) 9 LR Ir 484; *Harvey v Harvey* (1915) 50 ILT 12.
8 *Re Hiscoe, Hiscoe v Waite* (1902) 71 LJ Ch 347; *Re Kappele* [1954] OR 456.

[33.12]
Duration of annuity. An annuity given by will to a person simpliciter without words of limitation is for life only.[1] This being the general rule the annuitant

must establish an exception if the annuity is claimed for any longer period.[2] A gift by will to one person for life and then to another simply, is a gift to each of an annuity for life only.[3] A gift of an annuity is perpetual where there are express words to that effect. Generally these words will denote the continuance of the annuity after the death of the annuitant.[4] Such words include: a power to leave the annuity by will;[5] an annuity given for ever;[6] a gift of certain sums per month so long as funds remain;[7] an annuity with a gift over if the annuitant dies without issue;[8] an annuity given to several without survivorship with a direction for sale at a particular period of the annuity in its entirety.[9] A direction to purchase an annuity in government securities to the amount of so much a year may pass a perpetual annuity.[10] An annuity is perpetual when the words amount to a gift of the income of a particular fund without limit of time.[11] The limitation of an annuity to 'A and his heirs' or to 'A or his heirs' gives a perpetual annuity;[12] but an annuity to 'A and the heirs of his body' gives a conditional fee which becomes absolute on the birth of issue,[13] though now an entailed interest can be created in any personal property and therefore in an annuity.[14] A gift to 'A or his descendants', on the contrary, has been held to give an annuity for life to A and a substitutional gift to his descendants for life.[15] An unlimited gift of an annual sum 'being the interest on' certain stock carries the principal,[16] but a mere charge of an annuity on a particular fund does not render it perpetual,[17] nor does a charge on land devised in fee simple.[18] A charge on leasehold property may cause an annuity to continue during the lease.[19]

1   *Savery v Dyer* (1752) Amb 139; *Blight v Hartnoll* (1881) 19 Ch D 294 at 296; *Re Taber, Arnold v Kayess* (1882) 51 LJ Ch 721; *Re Forster's Estate* (1889) 23 LR Ir 269. Where annuities were given to each of four donees for life, that gift was not cut down by a direction that the fund on which the annuities were charged was to be distributed on the death of the testator's wife (one of the annuitants) but the annuities continued throughout each of the four lives: *Re Wood* [1943] 3 DLR 84.
2   *Yates v Maddan* (1851) 3 Mac & G 532 at 543; *Hill v Rattey* (1862) 2 John & H 634 at 639; *Re Jackson, Day v Atkin* [1946] 1 All ER 327 (gift of annual sum to be derived from War Loan to be applied for education and maintenance until donee attained twenty-one is a gift of a life annuity).
3   *Blight v Hartnoll* (1881) 19 Ch D 294 at 296; *Lett v Randall* (1860) 2 De GF & J 388.
4   *Mansergh v Campbell* (1858) 3 De G & J 232; *Pawson v Pawson* (1854) 19 Beav 146.
5   *Townsend v Ascroft* [1917] 2 Ch 14; but in *Kirkby v Phillips* [1948] Ch 109, [1947] 2 All ER 777, where the words were: 'for her to give away by will to any child or children she may have in marriage', the annuity was not perpetual, but limited to the lives of such children. An appointment to such children and after death of any or either of them to the survivor or survivors, was good as to the children, but bad as to the survivor or survivors, such limitation offending the rule against perpetuities.
6   *Taylor v Martindale* (1841) 12 Sim 158; *Joynt v Richards* (1882) 11 LR Ir 278; *Ashton v Adamson* (1841) 1 Dr & War 198. For a case where it was unsuccessfully contended that an annuity was perpetual, see *Re Jackson, Day v Atkin* [1946] 1 All ER 327.
7   *Re Steinberg's Will* (1968) 63 WWR 649 (held that these 'annuities' were not intended to last only for life but must be construed as gifts of a proportionate part of the corpus of the estate, which the donees could immediately claim). See also the similar Canadian case of *Torney v Lawrence* (1867) 61 WWR 510.
8   *Hedges v Harpur* (1858) 3 De G & J 129; *Robinson v Hunt* (1841) 4 Beav 450; *Warren v Wright* (1861) 12 I Ch R 401; *Fielding v Preston* (1857) 1 De G & J 438; *Barden v Meagher* (1867) 1 IR Eq 246; *Ward v Ward* [1903] 1 IR 211.
9   *Mansergh v Campbell* (1858) 3 De G & J 232 at 241.
10   *Ross v Borer* (1862) 2 John & H 469; *Kerr v Middlesex Hospital* (1852) 2 De GM & G 576; but see *Re Grove's Trusts* (1859) 1 Giff 74, and *Re Taber, Arnold v Kayess* (1882) 51 LJ Ch 721 at 723.

11 *Blewitt v Roberts* (1841) Cr & Ph 274 at 280; *Blight v Hartnoll* (1881) 19 Ch D 294 at 296;
    Hicks v Ross (1872) LR 14 Eq 141; *Re Fenwick* [1957] NZLR 709 (gift of £50 per annum to
    Dominion Government entitles Government to a capital sum to produce £50 per annum at an
    appropriate rate of interest).
12 *Aubin v Daly* (1820) 4 B & Ald 59; *Radburn v Jervis* (1841) 3 Beav 450, where the word was
    'and', and *Parsons v Parsons* (1869) LR 8 Eq 260, where the word was 'or'.
13 *Re Rivett-Carnac's Will* (1885) 30 Ch D 136 at 141.
14 Law of Property Act 1925, s 130; 37 *Halsbury's Statutes* (4th edn) 288.
15 *Re Morgan, Morgan v Morgan* [1893] 3 Ch 222.
16 *Engelhardt v Engelhardt* (1878) 26 WR 853.
17 *Re Morgan, Morgan v Morgan* [1893] 3 Ch 222 at 229; *Blight v Hartnoll* (1881) 19 Ch 294 at
    297; *Re Jackson, Day v Atkin* [1946] 1 All ER 327.
18 *Mansergh v Campbell* (1858) 3 De G & J 232 at 237.
19 *Courtenay v Gallagher* (1856) 5 I Ch R 154, 356; *Re Finlay's Estate* [1907] 1 IR 24; *Re
    Cunningham, Dulcken v Cunningham* [1914] 1 Ch 427.

[33.13]
Annuity for period other than life. A gift of an annuity for a period other than
the life of the annuitant, or for some purpose which may last only during some
such definite period, gives an annuity for that period only. The following are
examples: an annuity for a term or *pur autre vie* is a gift to the annuitant for the
term or for the duration of the life mentioned;[1] an annuity given to A for the life
of B continues for the life of B, although A predeceases him;[2] an annuity given
to the testator's son from his coming of age until the death or second marriage of
the testator's widow continues during that period notwithstanding that the son
dies before the widow, the annuity being payable after the son's death to his
personal representatives.[3]

1 *Re Ord, Dickinson v Dickinson* (1879) 12 Ch D 22 at 25.
2 *Savery v Dyer* (1752) Amb 139; *Re Ord, Dickinson v Dickinson* (1879) 12 Ch D 22; *Re
   Cannon, Cannon v Cannon* (1915) 114 LT 231; *Reid v Reid* [1944] AC 91, [1944] 1 All ER
   134; *Young's Trustees v Shelton's Executors* 1937 SC 28; *M'Donald's Trustees v M'Donald's
   Executors* 1940 SC 433.
3 *Re Ord, Dickinson v Dickinson* (1879) 12 Ch D 22; *Re Drayton, Francis v Drayton* (1912) 56
   Sol Jo 253; *Sutcliffe v Richardson* (1872) LR 13 Eq 606; *Re Cannon, Cannon v Cannon* (1915)
   114 LT 231.

[33.14]
One annuity to two persons. A single annuity given to two persons during their
lives continues to the death of the survivor who, after the death of the first to die,
takes the whole,[1] but a direction to purchase an annuity 'for the life of A and B'
to be equally divided between them, gives an annuity for the joint lives only.[2] In
such a case, however, a gift over after the deaths of the two parties may cause
the annuity to continue for the survivor's benefit during his life.[3] An annuity
given to A and B during their lives and the life of the survivor in equal shares
continues during that period, but without survivorship, the share of the first to
die going to his personal representatives;[4] but where there is a gift to A and B
during their lives and the life of the survivor with a gift over on the death of the
survivor, the survivor is entitled to receive the whole of the annuity.[5]

1 *Alder v Lawless* (1863) 32 Beav 72; *Moffatt v Burnie* (1853) 18 Beav 211.
2 *Grant v Winbolt* (1854) 2 Eq Rep 539.
3 *Re Telfair, Garrioch v Barclay* (1902) 86 LT 496.

4   *Bryan v Twigg* (1867) 3 Ch App 183; *Jones v Randall* (1819) 1 Jac & W 100.
5   *Cranswick v Pearson* (1862) 31 Beav 624. See *Re Hobson, Barwick v Holt* [1912] 1 Ch 626 at 631.

[33.15]
Separate annuities to two persons. A gift of separate annuities to two persons for their lives and the life of the survivor gives each an annuity for their joint lives and the life of the survivor;[1] but if such a bequest contains the additional words 'for their or her absolute use and benefit' the annuity of the first to die survives to the survivor for his life;[2] and in the case of a gift to each of two persons of an annual sum so long as each shall live, the annuitants each take an annuity for his or her life.[3] An annuity to several persons during their lives, without words of survivorship, gives each a separate annuity equal to an aliquot share of the whole, and upon the death of each his or her separate annuity ceases.[4]

1   *Eales v Earl of Cardigan* (1838) 9 Sim 384; and see *Re Ross, Ashton v Ross* [1900] 1 Ch 162.
2   *Hatton v Finch* (1841) 4 Beav 186.
3   *Lill v Lill* (1857) 23 Beav 446.
4   *Re Evans, Thomas v Thomas* (1908) 77 LJ Ch 583.

[33.16]
Annuities for the maintenance of animals. An annuity to an executor for the upkeep of the testator's mare is a valid gift during the life of the mare.[1] An annuity may be charged on land for a term of fifty years if any of his horses so long live and the annuity is applicable to the maintenance of the horses.[2] The duration of such an annuity should be limited by reference to human lives.[3]

1   *Pettingall v Pettingall* (1842) 11 LJ Ch 176.
2   *Re Dean, Cooper-Dean v Stevens* (1889) 41 Ch D 552; *Re Howard* (1908) Times, 30 October.
3   It has been questioned whether the lives of animals are 'lives' within the perpetuity rule, and *Re Dean, Cooper-Dean v Stevens* (1889) 41 Ch D 552, if and so far as it decides the contrary, has been the subject of criticism.

[33.17]
Annuity to executor or trustee. Such an annuity given 'for his trouble'[1] or 'so long as he executes the office'[2] continues so long as duties or trusts remain to be performed, and are performed by the annuitant.[3] It does not cease on judgment in an administration action.[4] Where, however, the annuities were for their services and collecting rents and the trustees employed a collector whose expenses to an amount exceeding the annuities were allowed to the trustees in an administration action, the trustees were not entitled to the annuities.[5]

1   *Baker v Martin* (1836) 8 Sim 25; *Henrion v Bonham* (1844) Drury *temp* Sug 476; *M'Dermot v O'Conor* (1876) 10 IR Eq 352 at 357; *Clay v Coles* [1880] WN 145.
2   *Hull v Christian* (1874) LR 17 Eq 546.
3   *Hull v Christian* (1874) LR 17 Eq 546.
4   *M'Dermott v O'Connor* (1876) 10 IR Eq 352; *Baker v Martin* (1836) 8 Sim 25.
5   *Re Muffet, Jones v Mason* (1887) 56 LJ Ch 600.

[33.18]
Annuities for maintenance and education of children. A gift of an annuity to
a testator's widow during a daughter's minority for the daughter's maintenance
and education does not cease on the death of the widow during the minority.[1] A
gift of an annuity for the maintenance of A is, whether A is an adult,[2] or a
minor,[3] a general trust for his benefit, which amounts to an absolute gift.[4] Such a
gift during the life of another person accordingly may continue after A's death[5]
and such a gift, where A is a minor, is not confined to his minority.[6] A gift for
the 'maintenance and education' of children, where no definite period is
mentioned, amounts to a gift for the joint lives of the children and the survivor
of them, the children for the time being entitled taking as joint tenants until they
sever.[7] A gift to a widow for a definite period 'for her own benefit and for the
maintenance and education' of a class of children may create a trust not limited
to children under twenty-one or unmarried.[8] Under such a trust the widow is
entitled to a separate interest.[9]

1   *Re Yates, Yates v Wyatt* [1901] 2 Ch 438. For a case where the gift was conditional on the
     religious education of the children, see *Re Gunn* (1912) 32 NZLR 153.
2   *Younghusband v Gisborne* (1844) 1 Coll 400; *Lewes v Lewes* (1848) 16 Sim 266; *Williams v
     Papworth* [1900] AC 563.
3   *Re Jackson, Day v Atkin* [1946] 1 All ER 327 (but this case was decided upon the construction
     of the will in question); *Holmes v Taggart* (1862) 1 NSWSCR (eq) 27.
4   *Webb v Kelly* (1839) 9 Sim 469 at 472.
5   *Webb v Kelly* (1839) 9 Sim 469; *Lewes v Lewes* (1848) 16 Sim 266; *Bayne v Crowther* (1855)
     20 Beav 400; *Attwood v Alford* (1866) LR 2 Eq 479.
6   *Soames v Martin* (1839) 10 Sim 287; *Alexander v M'Cullock* (1787) 1 Cox Eq Cas 391; *Farr v
     Hennis* (1881) 44 LT 202.
7   *Wilkins v Jodrell* (1879) 13 Ch D 564; *Williams v Papworth* [1900] AC 563.
8   *Longmore v Elcum* (1843) 2 Y & C Ch Cas 363; *Re Booth, Booth v Booth* [1894] 2 Ch 282.
9   *Re G (Infants)* [1899] 1 Ch 719.

[33.19]
Annuities for indefinite periods. Annuities for so long as the annuitant should
be a Roman Catholic,[1] or so long as the annuitant resides in a named house[2]
have been held good.

1   *Re May, Eggar v May* [1932] 1 Ch 99.
2   *Re Wilkinson, Page v Public Trustee* [1926] Ch 842.

[33.20]
Annuities during widowhood or spinsterhood. An annuity during widowhood
is good.[1] An annuity to a person 'so long as she continues my widow' ceases on
death or re-marriage.[2] The remarriage must be a valid ceremony,[3] but where at
the testator's death the annuitant is not his wife the gift is inoperative,[4] unless it
is shown that the testator used the word 'widow' in a sense which would include
the annuitant.[5] An annuity to a single woman until she shall die or be married is
good and ceases upon death or marriage,[6] but a gift to a person so long as she
remains unmarried, there being no gift over, requires marriage to determine it,
and, if she dies unmarried, her executor is entitled to the fund producing the
annuity,[7] but if there is a gift over on marriage, then the gift over takes effect on
marriage or on death unmarried.[8] A bequest of an annuity to a wife 'so long as
she continues unmarried' may not be prevented from taking effect by a divorce.[9]

1   *Scott v Tyler* (1788) 2 Dick 712 at 721; *Morley v Rennoldson* (1843) 2 Hare 570.
2   *Rishton v Cobb* (1838) 5 My & Cr 145 at 152; *Re Boddington, Boddington v Clairat* (1884) 25 Ch D 685.
3   *Re M'Loughlin's Estate* (1878) 1 LR IR 421; *Re Rutter, Donaldson v Rutter* [1907] 2 Ch 592; *Re Dewhirst* [1948] Ch 198, [1948] 1 All ER 147.
4   *Re Boddington, Boddington v Clairat* (1884) 25 Ch D 685 (nullity); *Re Hammond, Burniston v White* [1911] 2 Ch 342 (bigamous marriage); *Re Eaves, Eaves v Eaves* [1940] Ch 109, [1939] 4 All ER 260 (later marriage a nullity); *Re Dewhirst* [1948] Ch 198, [1948] 1 All ER 147 (nullity). See as to mistress: *Re Gale, Gale v Gale* [1941] Ch 209, [1941] 1 All ER 329; *Re Lynch, Lynch v Lynch* [1943] 1 All ER 168.
5   *Re Wagstaff, Wagstaff v Jalland* [1908] 1 Ch 162, and see *Re Lynch, Lynch v Lynch* [1943] 1 All ER 168. Where the gift is to a widow other than the widow of the testator, the gift fails on re-marriage in the testator's lifetime unless the bequest shows an intent that she shall have the annuity in that event: *West v Kerr* (1853) 23 LTOS 24.
6   *Heath v Lewis* (1853) 3 De GM & G 954; *Webb v Grace* (1848) 2 Ph 701; *Re King's Trusts* (1892) 29 LR IR 401; *Potter v Richards* (1855) 24 LJ Ch 488; *Re Hewett, Eldridge v Iles* [1918] 1 Ch 458.
7   *Rishton v Cobb* (1839) 5 My & Cr 145; *Re Howard, Taylor v Howard* [1901] 1 Ch 412.
8   *Re Mason, Mason v Mason* [1910] 1 Ch 695; *Re Tredwell, Jeffray v Tredwell* [1891] 2 Ch 640 at 647; *Re Barklie, M'Calmont v Barklie* [1917] 1 IR 1; *Re Henry Will Trust, Mussett v Smith* [1953] 1 All ER 531, [1953] 1 WLR 376 (where the gift fell into residue).
9   *Knox v Wells* (1883) 48 LT 655.

[33.21]
Failure of annuity. The failure of the annuity by the death of the annuitant in the lifetime of the testator will not defeat the gift over of a sum directed to be set aside to answer the annuity.[1]

1   *Re Clarke, Sheldon v Redrup* [1942] Ch 434, [1942] 2 All ER 294.

[33.22]
Conditions in restraint of marriage or tending to separate husband and wife. While a gift of an annuity until marriage may be good, the law is in general against any restraint on marriage and anything tending to the separation of spouses. This matter is dealt with later when considering the subject of conditions.[1]

1   See Chapter 35, para **[35.1]** et seq. See also *Re Jones, Midland Bank Executor and Trustee Co Ltd v Jones* [1953] Ch 125, [1953] 1 All ER 357 (condition reducing annuity on association with named person: void for uncertainty).

III.   OUT OF WHAT INCOME OR CAPITAL ANNUITY PAYABLE

[33.23]
Primarily a question of construction. The question of what moneys are to be resorted to for the payment of an annuity is one of construction and depends entirely on the words of the particular will construed according to their ordinary grammatical meaning.[1] An annuity created by covenant creates a debt which is subject to the ordinary rule that a testator's debt must be paid out of the capital of his estate and no beneficiary under the will can receive anything except when this has been done.[2] A debt by deferred instalments such as an annuity is no exception to the rule in *Allhusen v Whittell*,[3] and it has become the practice that where an estate is settled on successive interests, then, in relief of capital,

income will be called on to pay a share of each instalment of a covenanted annuity, or indeed a debt, increasing from year to year according to the principle set out in *Re Perkins, Brown v Perkins*.[4] This is so with respect to a covenanted annuity even though the will gives a further annuity payable out of income, of an amount sufficient in each year to make up the covenanted annuity to a specified sum.[5] The fact that the covenanted annuity is a factor, both directly, and indirectly through the tax element, in the quantification of the testamentary annuity, is not sufficient to render the covenanted annuity payable out of income. As to what capital may be resorted to there are two cases. The annuity may be charged upon the whole estate of the testator[6] or it may be a charge only upon a particular fund or property.[7] Where the annuity is payable only out of a particular fund, the further question arises whether or not it is in the nature of a settled legacy and subject to the ordinary rule applicable to tenant for life and remainderman that the capital must be kept intact for the remainderman. If this is the case, then the annuity is payable only out of income; if this is not the case, then the annuitant will be entitled to resort to capital to make up any deficiency of income. This is the case (i) where the gift is not of a sum of money specifically mentioned, but only the income of the capital sum set aside which accrues during the life of the donee;[8] (ii) where there is a direction to set aside a sum sufficient to produce a stated annual sum provided the sum is not left to fall into residue, but is specifically disposed of;[9] (iii) where the annuity is charged upon particular property and the property is given over to other persons upon the cesser of the annuity;[10] (iv) where there is a gift over of surplus income;[11] (v) where the residue is given to trustees to pay the annuity out of the income of the residue and there is no gift otherwise of the annuity.[12] In some cases the annuitant is to receive the income of a fund or of the residue up to or to the extent of a stated amount and then no resort to capital is allowed.[13] Where the annuity is payable out of income only, a last question arises whether, if in any year or years there is a deficiency of income, the annuitant can have that deficiency made up out of the surplus in other years.[14] The cases can also be considered from the point of view of the form of the gift as hereunder.

1   *Re Coller's Deed Trusts* [1937] 3 All ER 292 at 293, 294, where Romer J points out that all the cases are not reconcilable. It must not be thought, however, that, though the decisions present many real difficulties, there is any real difficulty in drafting clauses which put the matters here considered beyond dispute. In fact the Statutory Will Forms provide such a clause.
2   *Re Earl Berkeley, Inglis v Countess of Berkeley* [1968] Ch 744, [1968] 3 All ER 364.
3   (1867) LR 4 Eq 295; discussed at para **[38.26]** infra.
4   [1907] 2 Ch 596; discussed at para **[38.27]** infra.
5   *Re Earl Berkeley, Inglis v Countess of Berkeley* [1968] Ch 744, [1968] 3 All ER 364.
6   This is the general case and in all the forms of granting an annuity considered hereunder it is the prima facie rule that the whole estate is charged. If this is not to be so, then some special words must be found restricting the right of the annuitant to resort only to a particular fund or property or to the income thereof. While it is fundamental that a gift of residue includes everything not specifically disposed of by the will, at the same time the law requires that full effect shall be given to every other gift before the residue is determined. Therefore apart from some special restriction an annuity must be satisfied not only out of the income of the estate, but also by resorting to the capital thereof. This right to resort to the capital or corpus of the estate (or, as it is called, charging the annuity on the corpus) results wherever there is a simple gift of the annuity followed by a residuary gift or what is termed a direct gift of the annuity, see cases cited in para **[33.24]**, n 1, and it makes no difference that there is a direction to set aside a fund to answer the annuity, see cases in para **[33.24]**, n 9, unless, of course, the direction, as it should

in a properly drawn will, goes on to say that when a fund has been appropriated the annuity shall be wholly charged on the appropriated fund in exoneration of the rest of the estate.

7   *Re Earl Berkeley, Inglis v Countess of Berkeley* [1968] Ch 744, [1968] 3 All ER 364 (annuities charged firstly on settled estates, and secondly on heirlooms, so far as the residuary estate was insufficient). The same principles apply where the annuity is charged upon a particular fund or property except that only that fund or property can be resorted to in case of deficiency: see *Hickman v Upsall* (1860) 2 Giff 124. As to where income only is charged with the annuity, see para **[33.26]**, nn 6–8.

8   *Re Mason, Mason v Robinson* (1878) 8 Ch D 411; *Mitchell v Wilton* (1875) LR 20 Eq 269; *A-G v Poulden* (1844) 3 Hare 555. So, too, where the fund is given to pay an annuity out of the annual dividends or income of a fund: *Hindle v Taylor* (1855) 20 Beav 105; *Miller v Huddlestone* (1851) 3 Mac & G 513; *Heneage v Lord Andover* (1829) 10 Price 316; *Forbes v Richardson* (1853) 11 Hare 354; *Re Struthers* (1980) 114 DLR (3d) 492; but not where the fund is given in trust to pay the annuity: *Hickman v Upsall* (1860) 2 Giff 124.

9   *Baker v Baker* (1858) 6 HL Cas 616; *Tarbottom v Earle* (1863) 11 WR 680; *Mitchell v Wilton* (1875) LR 20 Eq 269.

10 *Foster v Smith* (1846) 1 Ph 629; *Earle v Bellingham* (1857) 24 Beav 445; *Sheppard v Sheppard* (1863) 32 Beav 194; *Re Wilson's Will* [1954] 3 DLR 161.

11 *Stelfox v Sugden* (1859) John 234; *Taylor v Taylor, Re Taylor's Estate Act* (1874) LR 17 Eq 324; *Salvin v Weston* (1866) 35 LJ Ch 552; *Wormald v Muzeen* (1881) 50 LJ Ch 776, and see *Re Coller's Deed Trusts, Coller v Coller* [1939] Ch 277, [1937] 3 All ER 292. If the surplus income is to be accumulated and the accumulations are to be held for the benefit of persons other than the annuitant, the annuitant has no claim on the accumulations: *Darbon v Rickards* (1845) 14 Sim 537.

12 *Re Boden, Boden v Boden* [1907] 1 Ch 132.

13 *Re Carey, Wardle v Carey* [1950] 1 All ER 726; *Re Wilson's Will* [1954] 3 DLR 161.

14 This class of gift is known as a continuing charge on income and is considered later at para **[33.30]** infra.

[33.24]
Gift of annuity followed by residuary gift. Where a simple gift of an annuity is followed by a residuary gift, the annuitant must be paid in preference to the residuary legatee, who takes nothing until the annuitant is paid in full.[1] This principle if applied in strictness would in every such case hold up the distribution of the estate until the death of the annuitant, but the executors may make a partial distribution of the estate where in all reasonable probability the undistributed part is more than sufficient to provide for the annuity.[2] The simplest case within this class is the simple will where, after some specific gifts and pecuniary legacies, an annuity is given without any provision for its payment followed by a residuary gift. Such a case is obviously within this class and so is a case where the residuary gift is made subject to or charged with the annuity.[3] The position is the same where an annuity is or annuities are given followed by an annuity given to be paid out of residue.[4] Indeed, where there is a simple gift of an annuity in the first place, the right of the annuitant to have recourse to the corpus of the estate is not easily negatived, though, as has already been said, the whole question is one of construction of the will as a whole. The right is not taken away by a direction to pay the annuity out of income;[5] nor as a general rule is it taken away by a direction to trustees to set aside a fund.[6] As a matter of practice, and independent of construction of the provisions of the will, the court will in any case order a sufficient fund to be set apart to answer the annuity and the surplus residue to be paid to the residuary legatee; but such setting apart will not affect the annuitant's right to resort to the capital of the sum so set apart if necessary for the complete payment of his annuity.[7] The

appropriation of a fund to answer the annuity does not discharge the rest of the estate whether it is made by the court[8] or by the executor.[9]

1   *Croly v Weld* (1853) 3 De GM & G 993; *Re Tootal's Estate, Hankin v Kilburn* (1876) 2 Ch D 628 at 633; *Re Webb, Leedham v Patchett* (1890) 63 LT 545; *Re Coller's Deeds Trusts, Coller v Coller* [1939] Ch 277, [1937] 3 All ER 292; *Re Kelly* (1964) 43 DLR (2d) 23.
2   *Harbin v Masterman* [1896] 1 Ch 351; but any such distribution is without prejudice to the annuitant's right to be paid in full out of the whole estate.
3   *Miner v Baldwin* (1853) 1 Sm & G 522; *Birch v Sherratt* (1867) 2 Ch App 644; *Re Mason, Mason v Robinson* (1878) 8 Ch D 411; *Re Howarth, Howarth v Makinson* [1909] 2 Ch 19; *Re Watkin's Settlement, Wills v Spence* [1911] 1 Ch 1; *Re Young, Brown v Hodgson* [1912] 2 Ch 479; *Re Cunningham, Dulcken v Cunningham* [1914] 1 Ch 427. This is the case, too, where the whole estate is charged with the annuity: *Stamper v Pickering* (1838) 9 Sim 176, and where legatees are given a life interest in specific funds which on their deaths is to fall into residue: *Re Richardson, Richardson v Richardson* [1915] 1 Ch 353 (where there was no mention of annuity in the will).
4   *Haynes v Haynes* (1853) 3 De GM & G 590.
5   *Re Mason, Mason v Robinson* (1878) 8 Ch D 411; *Davies v Wattier* (1823) 1 Sim & St 463; *Picard v Mitchell* (1851) 14 Beav 103; *Pearson v Helliwell* (1874) LR 18 Eq 411. The annuity is, however, primarily payable out of income: *Re Robertson* [1948] 4 DLR 606
6   *Re Taylor, Illsley v Randall* (1884) 53 LJ Ch 1161; *Upton v Vanner* (1861) 1 Drew & Sm 594; *Carmichael v Gee* (1880) 5 App Cas 588; *Re Mason, Mason v Robinson* (1878) 8 Ch D 411 at 413. The wording of the will may be such that, upon a fund being set aside, the residue is released from liability: *Kendall v Russell* (1830) 3 Sim 424.
7   *Harbin v Masterman* [1896] 1 Ch 351.
8   *Re Parry, Scott v Leak* (1889) 42 Ch D 570; *Davies v Wattier* (1823) 1 Sim & St 463; *Re Evans and Bettell's Contract* [1910] 2 Ch 438 (where it was held that a purchaser of part of the estate not set aside might object to the title on the ground that it was subject to the annuities).
9   *Gordon v Bowden* (1822) 6 Madd 342.

[33.25]
Surplus income after payment of annuity. Words added in a subsequent clause empowering the trustees to make payments during the life of the annuitant on account of the respective shares of the trust fund and the income thereof, prevented an individual beneficiary in the capital of the residue receiving the intermediate income during the life of the annuitant. Therefore surplus income (ie income not required for the payment of the annuity) must be accumulated for 21 years if the annuitant should live so long.[1] Whether or not the intermediate income falls into residue is governed by the terms of the will. Where the residuary gift carries the intermediate income the surplus income after satisfying an annuity is accumulated pending the possible vesting of the gift, and the accumulations fall into residue.[2] But where the testator has not applied his mind as to the destination of any surplus it will pass as on an intestacy.[3] It is not a necessary conclusion that surplus income will pass as on intestacy. Where there is no express trust declared of the income of a trust fund, it follows the destination of, and is an accretion to, the fund from which it is derived, unless there be words in the will excluding that implication.[4] Thus where a testator gives the estate to trustees to pay certain persons certain income for their care and maintenance and on the death of the last survivor of such persons to pay the income therefrom to a charity, surplus income belongs to the charity.[5] A devise and pecuniary legacy were declared by the will not to take effect until after the death of the testator's wife if she should survive him and in the event of the beneficiary's prior death then the issue should take by

substitution. The declaration that the devise should not take effect deferred the vesting in possession but not the vesting in interest. The devise was a future specific gift within the Law of Property Act 1925, s 175 and accordingly carried the intermediate income, but as the devise was subject to defeasance during the life of the testator's wife, the income should be accumulated for the shorter of the two periods, viz: the life of the testator's wife or 21 years from his death. The beneficiary was not entitled to payment of the income under the Trustee Act 1925, s 31(1) because the will showed a contrary intention within s 69(2) of that Act. If the beneficiary survived the testator's wife she would get the income eventually or, in the event of his earlier death leaving issue, the issue would take.[6] Where annuities were to be paid during the lives of three persons and then the trust was to be wound up and the estate distributed to two persons or their heirs, any surplus income after payment of the annuities was to be accumulated for 21 years or until the death of the last annuitant to die and such accumulations fell into residue. If the trust continued after the twenty-one years, the income passed as on an intestacy.[7] Where the residue does not vest until the death of the annuitant, surplus income must be accumulated for 21 years or the life of the annuitant if he dies within that period and falls into residue.[8] If the residuary gift is to charity, the surplus income falls to the charity as there is no intention of intestacy.[9]

1   *Re Geering, Gulliver v Geering* [1964] Ch 136, [1962] 3 All ER 1043.
2   *Watson v Conant* [1964] SCR 312.
3   *Re Amodeo* (1962) 33 DLR (3d) 24.
4   *Wharton v Masterman* [1895] AC 186 at 198; *Re Power Estate* (1964) 48 WWR 250.
5   *Re Passmore Estate* (1964) 49 WWR 588.
6   *Re McGeorge, Ratcliffe v McGeorge* [1963] Ch 544, [1963] 1 All ER 519.
7   *Re Nash, Miller v Allen* [1965] 1 All ER 51, [1965] 1 WLR 221; but see now *Re Berkleley, Inglis v Countess of Berkeley* [1968] Ch 744, [1968] 3 All ER 364; *Re Hammond's Estate* [1935] SCR 550.
8   *Re Hammond's Estate* [1935] SCR 550; *Watson v Conant* [1964] SCR 312.
9   *Re Passmore Estate* (1904) 49 WWR 588.

[33.26]
Direction to trustees to whom general estate is given to pay annuity out of income. There are two cases for consideration. In the first case there is what has been called a legacy and a residuary bequest, and the annuity is charged on the corpus.[1] In such cases, where a testamentary annuity is charged on both income and capital of the estate, the annuitant is entitled to require the executors not to part with any income or capital of residue lest it should turn out later that the estate is in fact otherwise insufficient to meet the annuity.[2] The right is not, however, absolute and distribution is not held up where it could not prejudice the annuitant.[3] It is not clear whether the trustees owe a similar duty to the remainderman to retain surplus income for the protection of capital.[4] If part of the capital has been realised to provide the annuity, the tenant for life of the fund subject to the annuity cannot be required to replace the capital out of surplus in a subsequent year.[5] In the second case the position is treated as one of tenant for life and remainderman and the annuity is not charged on the corpus. In this class falls a gift of an annuity followed by a gift over of surplus income during the life of the annuitant[6] or a gift over subject to the trusts aforesaid.[7] In some cases

where the will contains a direction to trustees of the general estate to pay an annuity out of the income of such general estate, the annuity is a continuing charge on the income after the death of the annuitant for the purpose of recovering arrears, though not charged on the corpus of the estate.[8]

1   This is the case where the residue is given subject to the annuity: see the cases cited in para **[33.24]**, n 3. But in all these cases it is a question of construction whether the testator means to give the residue subject to the complete satisfaction of the annuity or merely to refer to the previous gift of the annuity: see *Re Boden, Boden v Boden* [1907] 1 Ch 132; *Re Bigge, Granville v Moore* [1907] 1 Ch 714; *Re Buchanan, Stephens v Draper* [1915] 1 IR 95. An annuity payable out of the income or 'proceeds' of property is charged on the corpus unless the will shows that 'proceeds' has been used in some restricted sense: *Beal v Eastern Trust Co* (1914) 14 ELR 432, Can.

2   *Re Earl Berkeley, Inglis v Countess of Berkeley* [1968] Ch 744, [1968] 3 All ER 364, per Russell LJ citing *Re Coller's Deed Trusts, Coller v Coller* [1939] Ch 277 at 281, 282, [1937] 3 All ER 292 at 294, 295; see also *Re Clothier* [1971] NZLR 745; and *Re Chambers* [1971] NZLR 703.

3   *Re Earl Berkeley, Inglis v Countess of Berkeley* [1968] Ch 744, [1968] 3 All ER 364, per Russell LJ citing *Re Coller's Deed Trusts, Coller v Coller* [1939] Ch 277 at 281, 282, [1937] 3 All ER 292 at 294, 295; see also *Re Clothier* [1971] NZLR 745; and *Re Chambers* [1971] NZLR 703.

4   Dictum of Romer LJ in *Re Coller's Deed Trusts* [1939] Ch 277 at 283–285, [1937] 3 All ER 292 at 296, 297, would seem to suggest that there is such a power. However, *Re Platt, Sykes v Dawson* [1916] 2 Ch 563, indicates that there is no such power (Sargeant J authorised the distribution of surplus income although there was a 'reasonable probability' that future income might prove insufficient to pay the annuity in full). See *Re Earl Berkeley, Inglis v Countess of Berkeley* [1968] Ch 744, [1968] 3 All ER 364.

5   *Re Croxon, Ferrers v Croxton* [1915] 2 Ch 290; followed in *Re Earl Berkeley, Inglis v Countess of Berkeley* [1968] Ch 744, [1968] 3 All ER 364, although Harman LJ described the result as 'illogical': see also *Bathurst v Burke* [1946] IR 214.

6   *Stelfox v Sugden* (1859) John 234, and see *Miller v Huddlestone* (1851) 3 Mac & G 513; *Re Boden, Boden v Boden* [1907] 1 Ch 132 (a direction to pay out of income).

7   *Re Boulcott's Settlement, Wood v Boulcott* (1911) 104 LT 205; *Re Young, Brown v Hodgson* [1912] 2 Ch 479.

8   *Booth v Coulton* (1870) 5 Ch App 684. This construction will be resisted where after the death of the annuitant the trustees will not be in receipt of the income: *Re Boden, Boden v Boden* [1907] 1 Ch 132; *Re Bigge, Granville v Moore* [1907] 1 Ch 714. In *Re Young, Brown v Hodgson* [1912] 2 Ch 479, it was doubted whether there was any difference between a continuing charge on income and a charge on corpus. In theory there may be none, but in practice the result may be very different.

[33.27]
Direction to set apart sufficient property and out of income to pay annuity.
These cases also fall into two classes. In the first the direction to set apart is not the testator's main object, but merely the means by which his main object of bestowing an annuity is to be secured. In these cases the annuity is charged on the corpus of the estate.[1] In other cases, the testator makes it clear that he intends the corpus to remain intact and to go over to some other beneficiary or to fulfil some further trusts on the death of the beneficiary. In the latter cases, the annuity is charged on the income only and the annuitant cannot resort to the capital.[2]

1   *May v Bennett* (1826) 1 Russ 370; *Mills v Drewitt* (1855) 20 Beav 632; *Ingleman v Worthington* (1855) 25 LJ Ch 46; *Carmichael v Gee* (1880) 5 App Cas 588.

2   *Re Baker's Estate, Baker v Baker* (1858) 6 HL Cas 616; *Tarbottom v Earle* (1863) 11 WR 680; *Michell v Wilton* (1875) LR 20 Eq 269; *Trustees, Executors and Agency Co v Dimock* (1892) 18 VLR 729; *Re Amodeo* [1958] NZLR 787. If part of the capital is invested to provide the annuity, subsequent surplus income or accretions may be liable to make good the capital: *Re Street, Vevers v Holman* [1922] WN 291.

[33.28]
Direction to set apart specific property and out of income to pay annuity.
The same rules apply in this case and the annuity is charged on the corpus[1]
unless there is a gift over of the fund in its entirety,[2] or upon a new trust[3] or in
some cases where the property is to be sold on the death of the annuitant.[4]

1   *Hickman v Upsall* (1860) 2 Giff 124, and see cases in para **[33.30]**, n 7.
2   A gift over subject to the annuity is not sufficient, eg a gift over 'subject as aforesaid' (*Hindle v
    Taylor* (1855) 20 Beav 109, but see *Booth v Coulton* (1870) 5 Ch App 684) or 'subject to the
    annuity' (*Re London, Brighton and South Coast Rly Co, ex p Wilkinson* (1849) 3 De G & Sm
    633) or 'after performance of the antecedent trusts' (*Phillips v Gutteridge* (1862) 3 De GJ & Sm
    332; *Re Buchanan, Stephens v Draper* [1915] 1 IR 95). Where, on the death of the annuitant,
    the sum was to fall into residue, the gift was treated as an ordinary annuity: *Re Richardson,
    Richardson v Richardson* [1915] 1 Ch 353; and see also *Re Ellis, Nettleton v Crimmins* [1935]
    Ch 193, but both of these are cases on questions of abatement.
3   *Foster v Smith* (1846) 1 Ph 629; *A-G v Poulden* (1844) 3 Hare 555; *Earle v Bellingham* (1857)
    24 Beav 445; *Sheppard v Sheppard* (1863) 32 Beav 194. The distinction in these cases has been
    said to be that the fund is given over after the annuitant's death and not after the satisfaction of
    the prior trust, ie payment of the annuity.
4   *Darbon v Rickards* (1845) 14 Sim 537, where the leases expired during the life of the annuitant
    and it was held that the annuity was not payable out of the surplus rents.

[33.29]
Direction giving one annuity priority. Where annuities are charged on the
whole of the estate, but it is directed by the will that, in case of insufficiency,
one is to abate, in favour of the other, this direction does not in any way deprive
the one so given priority from having the corpus applied to make good any
insufficiency of income.[1]

1   *Pearson v Helliwell* (1874) LR 18 Eq 411.

[33.30]
Continuing charge on income. While the question is always one of the proper
construction of the instrument creating the annuity, a testator who desires that an
annuitant shall be paid out of income only, will probably also desire that
deficiencies in any year shall be made up out of surpluses in other years, but he
will probably intend that, on the death of the annuitant, all liability for the
annuity shall cease and, in so far as it has not then been paid out of income, it
shall to that extent fail and that unpaid arrears shall not be payable either out of
future income or corpus. In some cases, however, the annuitant's estate has been
held to be entitled to have arrears made up out of income accrued after his death[1]
but this construction cannot be adopted where trustees who are to pay the
annuity will not, after his death, be in receipt of the income.[2] As to procedure
during the annuitant's life, consent by the annuitant in past years to the
distribution of surplus income will not necessarily operate as a waiver of the
right to have surplus income in future years applied to arrears;[3] a deficiency in
any past years is payable in priority to payment of the current annuity.[4] A gift of
surplus income after payment of the annuity indicates that the annuity is not
meant to be a continuing charge on the income of the fund and so prevents the
trustees applying the surplus in one year in making good deficiencies in other

years[5] and, if the surplus is to be accumulated for the benefit of persons other than the annuitant, he cannot have the accumulation applied for arrears.[6] Trustees have power to retain surplus income for the benefit of the annuitant and to guard against a possible deficiency in future years.[7] But this power is not to be exercised blindly throughout the life of the annuitant but extends only to the retention from time to time, as a precautionary measure, of such sums as may foreseeably be required to meet deficiencies of income in future years.[8] Where surplus income is retained to protect an annuitant by securing payment of an annuity constituting a continuing charge on the income, such retention after the expiration of the statutory period of 21 years allowed for accumulation of income by the Law of Property Act 1925, s 164(1)(b) does not contravene s 164(1), for it is not an 'accumulation' of income 'for a period' within s 164(1)(b).[9] Where a continuing charge on income is restricted to the life of the annuitant it is clearly not rendered void by the rule against perpetuities, but, if the charge is to continue indefinitely after his death, clearly the question arises, though when the point was raised, a decision was avoided because on the construction of the will the charge did not continue after the death of the annuitant.[10]

1   *Booth v Coulton* (1870) 5 Ch App 684 (where further gifts were made 'subject as aforesaid'); *Re Rose, Rose v Rose* (1915) 85 LJ Ch 22 (no portion of corpus or capital to be made over so as to affect or prejudice due payment of annuity. It was held that there was nothing in the ultimate gift to indicate a fresh start or create any trusts inconsistent with the continuance of arrears of annuities as a charge on future income).
2   *Foster v Smith* (1846) 1 Ph 629; *Re Boden, Boden v Boden* [1907] 1 Ch 132; *Re Bigge, Granville v Moore* [1907] 1 Ch 714; *Re Boulcott's Settlement, Wood v Boulcott* (1911) 104 LT 205; *Re Barrett* [1955] SCR 93.
3   *Re Barrett* [1955] SCR 93.
4   *Re Barrett* [1955] SCR 93. Where, however, the annuity was to be paid in shares to several beneficiaries, a beneficiary in respect of whose share there was no deficiency is to be paid in full although there is a deficiency in respect of other shares.
5   *Re Coller's Deeds Trust, Coller v Coller* [1939] Ch 277, [1937] 3 All ER 292, applied in *Re Carey* [1950] 1 All ER 726, where a beneficiary was to be paid up to £1,000 per annum for life out of the income of the residue. The remainder of the income was given to others, but any surplus over £1,500 was to be divided between all these persons. It was held that there was no right to have any deficiency in one year made up out of a surplus in a later year. Where there was a gift of one-third of the income of the residuary estate to be made up to £6,500 if one-third was less than that sum, it was held that this was not a continuing charge on income and the beneficiary was not entitled to have deficiencies made up out of surpluses in succeeding years. This decision was largely based on a reference in the will to the beneficiary's interest in 'part of the income' of the trust fund: *Re Cameron, Currie v Milligan* [1955] 1 All ER 424. See also *Re Chance, Westminster Bank Ltd v Chance* [1962] Ch 593, [1962] 1 All ER 942; *Re Nash, Miller v Allen* [1965] 1 All ER 51, [1965] 1 WLR 221.
6   *Darbon v Rickards* (1845) 14 Sim 537.
7   *Re Earl Berkeley, Inglis v Countess of Berkeley* [1968] Ch 744, [1968] 3 All ER 364; *Re Coller's Deed Trusts, Coller v Coller* [1939] Ch 277, [1937] 3 All ER 292. But see *Re Platt, Sykes v Dawson* [1916] 2 Ch 563; *Re Chance, Westminster Bank Ltd v Chance* [1962] Ch 593, [1962] 1 All ER 942.
8   *Re Earl Berkeley, Inglis v Countess of Berkeley* [1968] Ch 744 at 779, [1968] 3 All ER 364 at 383, per Widgery LJ.
9   *Re Earl Berkeley, Inglis v Countess of Berkeley* [1968] Ch 744, following *Re Earle, Tucker v Donne* (1923) 131 LT 383; not following on this point *Re Coller's Deed Trusts, Coller v Coller* [1939] Ch 277, [1937] 3 All ER 292; *Re Robb's Will Trusts, Marshall v Marshall* [1953] Ch 459, [1953] 1 All ER 920; *Re Nash, Miller v Allen* [1965] 1 All ER 51, [1965] 1 WLR 221.
10   *Re Griffiths, Haworth v Welton* [1945] 1 All ER 610.

[33.31]
Interest on arrears. Where an annuity has fallen into arrears, the annuitant is not entitled to interest on those arrears, unless the non-payment was attributable to the fault of the person bound to pay it.[1]

1   *Re Earl Berkeley, Inglis v Countess of Berkeley* [1968] Ch 744, [1968] 3 All ER 364 (cause of the annuity remaining unpaid for many years was the gift of a prior annuity free of income tax and surtax; testator's estate now sufficient to pay off arrears with interest); following *Torre v Brown* (1855) 5 HL Cas 555.

[33.32]
Inheritance tax. If a testator by his will directs his estate or part of it to be charged with payment to an annuity, the assets so charged will be settled properly[1] and the annuity will be treated as being an interest in possession in a part of those assets.[2]

1   Inheritance Tax Act 1984, s 43(2)(c).
2   Inheritance Tax Act 1984, s 50(2).

IV.   PRIORITY BETWEEN ANNUITANTS

[33.33]
Property on which charged. An annuity charged on or directed to be paid out of residue may thereby be postponed to other annuities given by the will.[1]
Where a property is charged by the will with an annuity and by codicil the same property is charged with further annuities the annuity given by will has priority if the property is by the will given subject to the annuity.[2] The words 'in the first place' or '*imprimis*'[3] or 'to be paid without abatement'[4] give no priority.

1   *Haynes v Haynes* (1853) 3 De GM & G 590.
2   *Graves v Hicks* (1833) 6 Sim 391.
3   *Blower v Morret* (1752) 2 Ves Sen 420; *Thwaites v Forman* (1844) 1 Coll 409.
4   *Re Evan's Charities* (1858) 10 I Ch R 271.

[33.34]
Direction as to time of payment. Such a direction gives no priority. An annuity deferred as to its time of payment ranks equally with annuities directed to be paid immediately;[1] and an annuity payable immediately has no priority over one payable on the death of a tenant for life,[2] nor over annuities directed to be paid after certain legacies,[3] but a power to increase an annuity may give priority over legacies.[4]

1   *Nickisson v Cockill* (1863) 3 De GJ & Sm 622; *Roche v Harding* (1858) 7 I Ch R 338; *Ashburnham v Ashburnham* (1848) 16 Sim 186.
2   *Miller v Huddlestone* (1851) 3 Mac & G 513; *Street v Street* (1863) 2 New Rep 56.
3   *Ingham v Daly* (1882) 9 LR Ir 484.
4   *Toronto General Trusts Corpn v Fodey* (1953) 9 WWRNS 660.

V. ABATEMENT OF ANNUITIES

[33.35]
Rule for valuation. Where immediate annuities are given by will and the estate is insufficient for their payment in full, the general rule is that the annuities must be valued and abate rateably and the abated sum be paid to each annuitant.[1] For this purpose an annuity is a pecuniary legacy and annuities must abate with pecuniary legacies, so that the rule applies not only in the case where there is more than one annuity, but also where there are one or more pecuniary legacies and one or more annuities.[2] The rule, however, is not of universal application and in some few cases, where it is clear that the annuities can be paid in full, the rule is not applied.[3] Thus, where the expectation of life of the annuitants was so short that the annuities could be paid in full by resorting to capital to make up the deficiency of income and that was allowable under the provisions of the will, the rule was not applied.[4] Nor was it applied where before the annuities were finally valued some of the annuitants died and it then became possible to pay the sums due to the estates of the deceased annuitants and to provide for the annuities of the surviving annuitants in full.[5]

1   *Long v Hughes* (1831) 1 De G & Sm 364; *Wright v Callender* (1852) 2 De GM & G 652; *Re Cottrell, Buckland v Bedingfield* [1910] 1 Ch 402.
2   *Miller v Huddlestone* (1851) 3 Mac & G 513; *Re Hill, Westminster Bank Ltd v Wilson* [1944] Ch 270, [1944] 1 All ER 502.
3   *Re Hill, Westminster Bank Ltd v Wilson* [1944] Ch 270, [1944] 1 All ER 502.
4   *Re Hill, Westminster Bank Ltd v Wilson* [1944] Ch 270, [1944] 1 All ER 502.
5   *Re Thomas, Public Trustee v Falconer* [1946] Ch 36, [1945] 2 All ER 586. Cf the actual order made in *Re Bradberry, National Provincial Bank Ltd v Bradberry* [1943] Ch 35, [1942] 2 All ER 629.

[33.36]
Date of valuation. It is said that the normal date of valuation is the date of the death of the testator,[1] but where at the time when the court makes the order for valuation, or where the executors are proceeding out of court they proceed to a valuation and apportionment, some material change has occurred in the position, the valuation will be as at the date of the order or the valuation.[2] The death of an annuitant is such a material change in the position, but it is not the only change which may be material.[3] In practice the date of valuation is now the date of the order or valuation by executors.

1   *Todd v Bielby* (1859) 27 Beav 353; *Re Bradberry, National Provincial Bank Ltd v Bradberry* [1943] Ch 35, [1942] 2 All ER 629. See also *Potts v Smith* (1969) LR 8 Eq 683; *Re Ellis, Nettleton v Crimmins* [1935] Ch 193; *Re Ball, Lucas v Ball* [1940] 4 All ER 245; *Re Cox, Public Trustee v Eve* [1938] Ch 556, [1938] 1 All ER 661; *Re Twiss, Barclays Bank Ltd v Pratt* [1941] Ch 141, [1941] 1 All ER 93.
2   *Re Bradberry, National Provincial Bank Ltd v Bradberry* [1943] Ch 35, [1942] 2 All ER 629.
3   *Re Bradberry, National Provincial Bank Ltd v Bradberry* [1943] Ch 35, [1942] 2 All ER 629, and see *Re Ball, Lucas v Ball* [1940] 4 All ER 245. Alterations in the tax law may now cause a material change.

[33.37]
The valuation. The valuation is an actuarial valuation, but circumstances such as the health of the annuitant and the risks attendant to his vocation are

disregarded.[1] The sum which the annuity can be sold for is, therefore, not material and the amount is that at which a government annuity of the sum specified by the testator can be purchased.[2]

1   *Re Bradberry, National Provincial Bank Ltd v Bradberry* [1943] Ch 35, [1942] 2 All ER 629.
2   *Ex p Thistlewood* (1812) 19 Ves 236; *Re Bradberry, National Provincial Bank Ltd v Bradberry* [1943] Ch 35, [1942] 2 All ER 629. The sum would now be determined by reference to the Government Annuity Table Order 1963, SI 1963/1178, as amended by the Government Annuity Table Order 1977, SI 1977/1536.

[33.38]

Death of annuitant. It has already been shown that the death of an annuitant before valuation and apportionment may render valuation unnecessary.[1] Where the period of distribution is deferred, the valuation must take account of the position as it then is.[2] If all the annuitants are still alive, the value of each annuity is the arrears then due and the then present value of future payments.[3] If the annuitants are all dead, the value is the amount of the arrears then due.[4] If some are dead and some surviving the values are ascertained as follows. The value of the annuity of each deceased annuitant is fixed at what he would have received had the estate not been insufficient. The value of the annuity of each survivor is ascertained by adding to the arrears then due the then present value of future payments.[5]

1   See para [33.36] ante.
2   *Re Bradberry, National Provincial Bank Ltd v Bradberry*, supra; see [1942] 2 All ER 629 at 634–637. The annuitant cannot be said to have a vested right in his annuity at the death of the testator or at the date of the order so that he is entitled to its value at that date. His only right is to what he is entitled in due course of administration, which takes into account all facts known at the date of such order or valuation. See *Potts v Smith* (1869) LR 8 Eq 683 at 686, and *Re Bradberry, National Provincial Bank Ltd v Bradberry* [1943] Ch 35, [1942] 2 All ER 629.
3   *Heath v Nugent* (1860) 29 Beav 226; *Re Wilkins, Wilkins v Rotherham* (1884) 27 Ch D 703; *Delves v Newington* (1885) 52 LT 512.
4   *Todd v Bielby* (1859) 27 Beav 353.
5   *Todd v Bielby* (1859) 27 Beav 353.

[33.39]

Tax adjustments. In valuing annuities the fact that these are given free of tax must be taken into consideration, as must all allowances due to the annuitants. The rate of tax and amount of the allowances are those prevailing at the date of the order.[1]

1   *Re Ball, Lucas v Ball* [1940] 4 All ER 245; followed in *Re Twiss, Barclays Bank Ltd v Pratt* [1941] Ch 141, [1941] 1 All ER 93.

[33.40]

Minors and foreigners. A person absolutely entitled can elect whether he will take a sum of money, being the amount of the valuation (abated, if necessary), or have it laid out in the purchase of an annuity;[1] but any person under disability cannot so elect and the personal representatives should purchase an annuity from an insurance company.[2]

1   *Re Bradberry* [1943] Ch 35 at 41, [1942] 2 All ER 629 at 634, but this is the ordinary right of a person absolutely entitled.

2   *Re Twiss, Barclays Bank Ltd v Pratt* [1941] Ch 141, [1941] 1 All ER 93; *Re Dempster, Borthwick v Lovell* [1915] 1 Ch 795. A foreigner of full age absolutely entitled can, of course, elect to take the value if he so desires.

[33.41]

Defeasible annuities. Where the annuity is defeasible upon the happening of an event in the lifetime of the annuitant, there is a conflict of opinion whether the capital value of the annuity ought to be paid to the annuitant:[1] it should not, it is submitted, be paid to him if there is a gift over of the annuity upon the happening of the event.

1   *Carr v Ingleby* (1831) 1 De G & Sm 362, followed in *Gratrix v Chambers* (1860) 2 Giff 321, and *Re Richardson, Mahony v Treacy* [1915] 1 IR 39. To the contrary, see *Re Sinclair, Allen v Sinclair* [1897] 1 Ch 921; followed in *Re Viscount Rothermere, Mellor, Basden & Co v Coutts & Co* [1945] Ch 72, [1944] 2 All ER 593, but distinguished in *Re Beecham's Settlement* [1934] Ch 183 (annuity for life but other persons who might become interested in it in due course; provision made for them). An annuity forfeitable on bankruptcy does not vest in the beneficiary at all if he is an undischarged bankrupt at the date of the testator's death, although he obtains his discharge before the date for the first payment: *Re Walker* [1939] Ch 974, [1939] 3 All ER 902.

[33.42]

Valuation of reversionary annuities. Where there is a bequest of an immediate pecuniary legacy and also a bequest of a reversionary annuity and the estate is ascertained at the date of the death of the testator to be insufficient, the court values the annuity on the basis of its being a reversionary interest, and the valuation must abate rateably with that of the immediate interest.[1] Where in the case of a reversionary annuity the estate is ascertained to be insufficient only at some time after the death of the testator and before that time the reversionary annuity has fallen into possession, the value of the reversionary annuity must be ascertained by adding the amount of the arrears accrued since the annuity fell into possession to the then present value of the future payments.[2]

1   *Re Metcalf, Metcalf v Blencowe* [1903] 2 Ch 424; *Innes v Mitchell* (1846) 1 Ph 710.
2   *Potts v Smith* (1869) LR 8 Eq 683.

[33.43]

Division between immediate and reversionary annuitants. Where a testator bequeaths two annuities, one immediate and the other reversionary, and the immediate annuity is for some time paid in full, but the estate is subsequently found to be insufficient, and such annuity remains for some time unpaid, then, in the division between the reversionary and immediate annuitants of the funds ultimately available, the immediate annuitant is not bound to bring into hotchpot his early payments in full.[1]

1   *Re Metcalf, Metcalf v Blencowe* [1903] 2 Ch 424.

[33.44]

Abatement. The abatement may proceed in two steps. Where the testator has required his executors to set aside a sum to pay the annuity out of the income thereof, the estate is often found to be insufficient to set aside such a sum, but quite sufficient to pay the capital value of the annuity. Where it is sufficient to pay the capital value of all annuities and all pecuniary legacies no real abatement is necessary, for, while the estate cannot be administered in the way the testator intended, yet all beneficiaries receive what they were intended to be given.[1] If, however, it is not so sufficient, all annuities and pecuniary legacies must abate proportionately.[2] Once the abated amount has been paid, the matter is closed and cannot be reopened by the early death of an annuitant who has in fact received more than he would have received if his annuity had been paid to him in full.[3] Where there is no trust or direction to set apart a fund to answer the annuities, the first question here considered does not arise. Such is the case where annuities are to be paid out of the income of residue. If the testator states that the trustees are to have resort to capital to implement any deficiency of income and that no surplus income is to be paid to the annuitants, then it has been said that the testator has made his own provision for insufficiency and the rules here stated do not apply.[4] The precise line of demarcation between cases where the above rules apply and where it is to be said that the testator has himself provided for deficiency is not as the cases now stand very clear.

1   This was the case in *Re Cottrell, Buckland v Bedingfield* [1910] 1 Ch 402, and *Re Cox, Public Trustee v Eve* [1938] Ch 556, [1938] 1 All ER 661.
2   For a case of this sort, see *Wroughton v Colquhoun* (1847) 1 De G & Sm 357.
3   *Wroughton v Colquhoun* (1847) 1 De G & Sm 357.
4   *Re de Chassiron, Lloyds Bank Ltd v Sharpe* [1939] Ch 934, [1939] 3 All ER 321.

[33.45]
Where annuity fund given over on death of annuitant. Where the fund to be set apart is directed to fall into residue, the general rule prevails and until the annuitant is paid in full, the residuary legatee takes nothing.[1] The only other case in this connection is where the fund is given over to a reversioner on the death of the annuitant. In this case there has been a conflict in the decisions of the court. It seems reasonable to assume in such a case that the testator intended the reversioner to take something and presumably the estate should be so administered that something is left for him to take, and there has been some attempt to avoid a form of administration which would leave him nothing. The cases are as follows. A sum was directed to be set aside with power to resort to capital, and the fund, or so much thereof as was not used as capital to make up deficiencies of income was given over subject to the payment of the annuity, and it was held the annuitant must be paid the actuarial value abated if necessary rateably with the pecuniary legacies, even if that resulted in the reversioner receiving nothing.[2] Under this form of administration, the reversioner would receive nothing unless the estate was more than enough to pay the actuarial value and the legacies in full. In similar circumstances, however, it has been held that the annuity must not be taken at its actuarial value, but at the amount of the fund to be set aside, and that that sum must be abated rateably with the pecuniary legacies. This abated sum would not, of course, be handed over to the annuitant or used in the purchase of an annuity, but must be invested in the ordinary way which trusts funds are invested and the income applied in discharge of the annuity. It is unlikely that such income will meet the annuity in full, and, in so far as there is any deficiency, resort must be made to capital. This method of administration may result in the whole sum set aside being applied to

the payment of the annuity and then the reversioner will receive nothing, but, if the annuitant dies before the sum is exhausted, the reversioner will receive what remains of it.[3] In the other case decided upon this point there was a gift of residue to be held on trust to pay certain legacies and two annuities of £500 each, and after the death of each annuitant the capital representing his annuity was to be held upon trust for such persons as the annuitant should appoint with a trust in default of appointment. This gift was construed as creating settled legacies of a sum sufficient when invested in 2 per cent consols to produce £500 per annum and those legacies must abate rateably with the other legacies. The annuitants in this case received only the income of the invested sums and had no resort to capital.[4]

1   See para [33.34] supra.
2   *Re Farmer, Nightingale v Whybrow* [1939] Ch 573, [1939] 1 All ER 319; *Re Wilson, Hartley v Marie Curie Hospital* [1940] Ch 966, [1940] 4 All ER 57; *Re Esmonde, Synnott v McGonigal* [1946] IR 551. See also *Re Richardson, Richardson v Richardson* [1915] 1 Ch 353.
3   *Re Nicholson, Chadwyck-Healey v Crawford* [1938] 3 All ER 270; *Re Thomas, Public Trustee v Falconer* [1946] Ch 36, [1945] 2 All ER 586.
4   *Re Carew, Channer v Francklyn* [1939] Ch 794, [1939] 3 All ER 200.

VI.   TAX-FREE ANNUITIES

[33.46]
Incidence of tax. The rules governing the incidence of tax on annuities are contained in complex statutory provisions which are subject to frequent change.[1] Reference should be made to up-to-date books on tax.[2]

1   Reference should be made to the current Income and Corporation Taxes Acts.
2   Such as *Simon's Taxes*, Vol A, Div A3.4.

[33.47]
Power to grant tax-free annuity. A gift of an annuity without deduction of tax can be made quite lawfully by will, in which case the full amount should be paid.[1] In the first place it is settled that the word 'deduction' without more does not refer to income tax[2] and that word can only include such tax where there are other words in the will which show that the testator intended it to include that tax.[3] Thus, while 'free of all deductions' does not free the annuitant from liability to pay income tax,[4] 'free of all deductions in respect of tax' has been held to include income tax,[5] and the testator may show that he has treated income tax as coming under the head of deductions;[6] but even where, in the case of a particular will, 'deductions' must either refer to income tax or be meaningless, it has been held not to include this tax,[7] and where it could refer only to the Public Trustee fees,[8] or the cost of raising the annuity out of capital,[9] this word was held not to include income tax. A 'clear annuity' is not construed as an annuity free of income tax;[10] nor is an annuity 'free of all duties'[11]. In order to exempt an annuity from income tax (where income tax is not specially mentioned), not only must 'taxes' be mentioned, but the context must show that income tax is intended to be included in 'taxes'.[12] Where trustees were directed to set aside out of the residuary estate such proportion thereof as would be

sufficient to produce a specified income 'without deduction of tax', they ought to set aside such a sum as would produce a net annuity for the beneficiary of the stated sum, the expression used having the same meaning as 'free of tax'.[13] Where a sum was to be set aside sufficient to produce a 'net income of £10 per week', there was no context to show that the annuity was to be free of tax.[14]

1   *Ferguson v IRC* [1970] AC 442, [1969] 1 All ER 1025.
2   *Re Wells' Will Trusts, Public Trustee v Wells* [1940] Ch 411, [1940] 2 All ER 68; *Re Skinner, Milbourne v Skinner* [1942] Ch 82, [1942] 1 All ER 32 (where a general statement of the position was made by Morton J). See *Gleadow v Leetham* (1882) 22 Ch D 269 at 272; *Re Parker-Jarvis, Salt v Locker* [1898] 2 Ch 643 at 652.
3   *Turner v Mullineux* (1861) 1 John & H 334; *Re Buckle, Williams v Marson* [1894] 1 Ch 286.
4   *Abadam v Abadam* (1864) 33 Beav 475; *Gleadow v Leetham* (1882) 22 Ch D 269; *Re Crawshay, Crawshay v Crawshay* (1915) 60 Sol Jo 275; *Re Musgrave, Machell v Parry* [1916] 2 Ch 417 (without deduction); *Re Hooper, Phillips v Steel* [1944] Ch 171, [1944] 1 All ER 227 (free of all deductions whatsoever).
5   *Festing v Taylor* (1862) 3 B & S 217; *Lord Lovat v Duchess of Leeds* (1862) 2 Drew & Sm 62; *Re Bannerman's Estate, Bannerman v Young* (1882) 21 Ch D 105.
6   *Turner v Mullineux* (1861) 1 John & H 334; *Re Buckle, Williams v Marson* [1894] 1 Ch 286.
7   *Re Best, Belk v Best* [1942] Ch 77, [1941] 3 All ER 315; *Re Hooper, Phillips v Steel* [1944] Ch 171, [1944] 1 All ER 227; *Re Cowlishaw, Cowlishaw v Cowlishaw* [1939] Ch 654, which was thought to decide the contrary, was explained by Bennett J, who decided it in his later decision in *Re Best, Belk v Best* [1942] Ch 77, [1941] 3 All ER 315.
8   *Re Wells' Will Trusts, Public Trustee v Wells* [1940] Ch 411, [1940] 2 All ER 68.
9   *Re Best, Belk v Best* [1942] Ch 77, [1941] 3 All ER 315.
10 *Re Loveless, Farrer v Loveless* [1918] 2 Ch 1.
11 *Re Saillard, Pratt v Gamble* [1917] 2 Ch 401; *Re Hooper, Phillips v Steel* [1944] Ch 171, [1944] 1 All ER 227.
12 *Re Shrewsbury Estate Acts, Shrewsbury v Shrewsbury* [1924] 1 Ch 315.
13 *Re Williams, Williams v Templeton* [1936] Ch 509, [1936] 1 All ER 175. Where a testator granted an annuity to be considered as a continuation of the alimony he had been paying and the alimony had been paid without deduction of tax, the annuity was free of tax; *Re Batley, Public Trustee v Hert* [1951] Ch 558.
14 *Re Wright, Barclays Bank Ltd v Wright* [1952] 2 All ER 698.

CHAPTER 34

Conditions generally

I. IN GENERAL

[34.1]

General power to attach conditions. A testator may in the case of conditions as in all else make his will in any terms he likes, but the conditions may be void, fail to take effect, or the donee may for some reason be excused from the performance of the condition.[1] A condition may be void (i) by being against public policy; (ii) by being either (a) repugnant to the interest given to the beneficiary; or (b) repugnant to or inconsistent with other gifts in or provisions of the will; (iii) by being too uncertain to be enforced; (iv) because the law allows it to be disregarded; (v) because it is illegal. The court may, however, avoid the whole question of the validity of the words as a condition by construing those words as not being a condition, but a limitation or a trust.[2]

1   As to wills wholly conditional, see para **[1.10]** supra. As to conditions contained in documents other than the will, see Chapter 15, (incorporation of documents), and Chapter 36, (secret trusts). No precise form of words is necessary to create a condition: *Re Cleghorn* (1919) 48 DLR 511; *Re Meagher, Trustees, Executors and Agency Co Ltd v Meagher* [1910] VLR 407. A condition that the legatee learn to play the piano has been held good: *Re Whittaker, Whittaker v Whittaker* (1882) 21 Ch D 657, and also a condition to keep testator out of a lunatic asylum: *Re Archbold, McKee v Archbold* [1933] NI 47; *Ormiston's Executor v Laws* 1966 SC 47 (legacies to 'my fiancee Mrs M'; held that words descriptive and did not impose a condition).
2   *Page v Hayward* (1705) 11 Mod Rep 61; and see para **[34.3]** infra.

[34.2]

Conditions precedent or subsequent. A condition is always either precedent or subsequent to the vesting of the interest given by the will, and whether it is a condition precedent or subsequent is determined by the construction of the will.[1] If, upon the proper construction of the will, there is no gift intended until the condition has been fulfilled, the condition is a condition precedent.[2] Where a gift is contingent on an event, and until that event does take place there is no vested gift, the condition is a condition precedent.[3] For a condition to be subsequent the gift must already have vested and the condition is intended to put an end to the gift.[4] Where it is doubtful whether a condition is a condition precedent or subsequent, the court leans towards a construction which will hold it to be a condition subsequent, for that construction will lead to the early vesting of the gift and there is always a presumption in favour of early vesting.[5] If the condition is void and is a condition precedent, the gift fails,[6] but in the case of a condition subsequent the effect of the condition being void is that the gift takes effect free from the conditions.[7] The gift will also take effect free from the condition where the condition is merely voidable and is avoided by the donee or is repugnant to the gift or fails to take effect as being in terrorem,[8] and this is so whether the condition is precedent or subsequent.

The following are some considerations which may help to decide whether a condition is precedent or subsequent. If the condition is capable of being performed instanter[9] it will probably be precedent, whereas if time is requisite for its performance[10] it is more likely to be subsequent. If the nature of the interest is such as to allow time for the performance of the act before the interest can be enjoyed, it is generally precedent,[11] whereas if it is reasonable to suppose that the interest must vest in possession before the donee can be expected to comply with the condition, it will be subsequent.[12] Where a specific time is mentioned for the performance of the condition but not for the vesting of the estate or interest, the condition will in general be subsequent.[13]

1 *Edgeworth v Edgeworth* (1869) LR 4 HL 35; *Yates v University College, London* (1895) LR 7 HL 438. The court will construe a condition as subsequent rather than precedent as the law prefers early vesting: *Re Greenwood, Goodhart v Woodhead* [1903] 1 Ch 749; *Sifton v Sifton* [1938] AC 656 at 676, [1938] 3 All ER 435 at 446. It was said in *Robinson v Comyns* (1736) Cas *temp* Talb 164, that there are no technical words to distinguish a condition precedent from a condition subsequent and the same may indifferently be either according to the intent of the testator. See also *Doe d Planner v Scudamore* (1800) 2 Bos & P 289, to the same effect. This paragraph of the text was referred to in *Re Porter, Logan v Northern Bank Ltd* [1975] NI 157. The question whether a particular clause created a condition precedent or subsequent was considered in *Re Tepper's Will Trusts* [1987] Ch 358, [1987] 1 All ER 970 with reference to the test of certainty to be applied. The testator was a devout Jew who left a share of income on trust for the children of one of his children 'Provided that they shall remain within the Jewish faith and shall not marry outside the Jewish faith'. The residuary estate was left amongst all of his grandchildren 'Provided however that they shall not marry outside the Jewish faith'.

  Scott J considered the status and character of the provisos in question with reference to their language and to the context in which they appeared in the will, and concluded, despite argument in favour of the alternative construction, that in substance both clauses operated as conditions of defeasance.

2 *Reynish v Martin* (1746) 3 Atk 330 at 332; *Egerton v Earl of Brownlow* (1853) 4 HL Cas 1 at 74.

3 *Ellis v Ellis* (1802) 1 Sch & Lef 1; see Lord Denning MR in *Re Gulbenkian's Settlement Trusts; Hacobian v Maun* [1968] Ch 126 at 133, [1967] 3 All ER 15 at 18; but a condition the non-fulfilment of which will put an end to a contingent interest is a condition subsequent, even though the event to which the condition refers is not subsequent to the happening of the contingency, so that the condition in that case prevents the gift from taking effect: *Egerton v Earl of Brownlow* (1853) 4 HL Cas 1.

4 *Re Boulter, Capital and Counties Bank v Boulter* [1922] 1 Ch 75; *Sifton v Sifton* [1938] AC 656 at 676, [1938] 3 All ER 435; see Lord Denning in *Re Gulbenkian's Settlement Trusts, Hacobian v Maun* [1968] Ch 126 at 132, [1967] 3 All ER 15 at 17.

5 *Egerton v Earl of Brownlow* (1853) 4 HL Cas 1 at 182; *Woodhouse v Herrick* (1855) 1 K & J 352; *Lady Langdale v Briggs* (1856) 8 De GM & G 391; *Re Greenwood* [1903] 1 Ch 749 at 755; *Re Blackwell* [1926] Ch 223; *Bickersteth v Shanu* [1936] AC 290; *Sifton v Sifton* [1938] AC 656; *Re Lysiak* (1975) 55 DLR (3d) 161. But this is only so where the matter is not clear: *Hickling v Fair* [1899] AC 15 at 27; and see *Re Tuck's Settlement Trusts, Public Trustee v Tuck* [1978] Ch 49, [1978] 1 All ER 1047, where no ambiguous clause was construed as a condition precedent.

6 *Egerton v Earl of Brownlow* (1853) 4 HL Cas I; *Re Turton, Whittington v Turton* [1926] Ch 96; *Re Going* [1951] OR 147; and see para **[34.3]** infra.

7 *Morley v Rennoldson* (1843) 2 Hare 570; see also *Re Ross Estate* (1967) 59 WWR 572.

8 See *Re Moore, Trafford v Maconochie* (1888) 39 Ch D 116 at 128; and see para **[34.5]** infra.

9 *Gulliver d Corrie v Ashby* (1766) 4 Burr 1929. The following is taken from *De Hoherty, Quinn v Clarke* [1950] NI 83. The condition is precedent if it requires only a single act, is capable of

being performed instantly, a time limit for its performance is allowed, and it is drafted in the present tense. But in *Ackers v Phipps* (1835) 3 Cl & Fin 665, a condition for the execution of a deed to secure annuities charged on the land devised was held not to be a condition precedent. See also *Fitzgerald v Ryan* [1899] 2 IR 637 at 646, 647.

10 *Popham v Bampfield* (1682) 1 Vern 167; *Peyton v Bury* (1731) 2 P Wms 626; but see *Horrigan v Horrigan* [1904] 1 IR 29; *Kiersey v Flahavan* [1905] 1 IR 45.

11 *Acherley v Vernon* (1739) Willes 153. The setting of a time limit for performance may show that it is a condition precedent: *Re Doherty, Quinn v Clarke* [1950] NI 83; see, however, n 13, and text thereto.

12 *Re Greenwood, Goodhart v Woodhead* [1903] 1 Ch 749; *Re Fry, Reynolds v Denne* [1945] Ch 348, [1945] 2 All ER 205; *Lundy v Lundy* (1895) 24 SCR 650.

13 *Walker v Walker* (1860) 2 De GF & J 255.

[34.3]
Words construed as a limitation and not as a condition. The words so construed have in the majority of cases been words relating to marriage though the principle is by no means confined to such cases. It is well settled that marriage may be made the ground of a limitation ceasing or commencing.[1] The following gifts have been held good as limitations, whether or not they would be good as conditions: a gift to a person so long as that person remains unmarried;[2] a gift subject to marriage with consent;[3] a gift during widowhood or while remaining a widower, though this it is conceived is good whether the words amount to a limitation or a condition;[4] a gift of an annuity to a person if living and unmarried at the death of a prior annuitant;[5] a reduction of an annuity on marriage;[6] the cesser of an interest on re-marriage;[7] a gift to a mistress with a provision for cesser or reduction on marriage.[8] The following gifts not concerned with marriage or re-marriage have been held good as limitations: a proviso against alienation;[9] a devise to a person on condition that he marry a named person and have issue which form of devise has been construed to give an estate in special tail,[10] as has a devise on condition that a man marry a fit and worthy gentlewoman and have issue.[11] Words have been held to be properly construed to be a limitation with the result that the gift was void, where, if construed as a condition, the gift would have been good. Thus a periodic sum given to a woman so long as she lived apart from her husband was construed as a limitation and, being illegal as such, the gift was void; whereas, had it been construed as a condition, the illegal condition could have been ignored and the gift would have stood.[12] Similarly, a gift of income during spinsterhood and of the capital of a fund on marriage to a person of the Jewish faith and the child of Jewish parents is not a gift on condition but a limitation, and where upon any other marriage the legatee is to have only a part of the fund that also is a limitation and not a condition.[13] Such a form of words has, however, been construed as a legal limitation where the purpose of the gift was to maintain a woman until she returned to her husband or re-married and the gift held good[14] and a devise subject to the devisee maintaining a sister until marriage.[15]

1 *Godfrey v Hughes* (1847) 1 Rob Eccl 593; *Webb v Grace* (1848) 2 Ph 701.

2 *Webb v Grace* (1848) 2 Ph 701; *Meeds v Wood* (1854) 19 Beav 215; *Jones v Jones* (1876) 1 QBD 279 (there is no distinction between a condition subsequent and a conditional limitation in restraint of marriage to provide for the devisee while single); *Re Mason, Mason v Mason* [1910] 1 Ch 695; *Re King's Trusts* (1892) 29 LR IR 401.

3 *Fry v Porter* (1670) 1 Mod Rep 300.

4 *Evans v Rosser (or Rossall)* (1864) 2 Hem & M 190; *Dudding v Gauss* (1886) 2 TLR 465.

5   *Heath v Lewis* (1853) 3 De GM & G 954.
6   *Brown v Cutler* (1683) 2 Show 152.
7   Such a limitation has been held good as a condition: see para **[35.8]** infra.
8   *Potter v Richards* (1855) 24 LJ Ch 488.
9   *Newis v Lark* (1571) 2 Plowd 408; *Re Nilen's Will, Kidd v Nilen* [1908] VLR 332 (alienation of property adjoining that devised). See further Chapter 99.
10 *Page v Hayward* (1705) 2 Salk 570.
11 *Pelhams-Clinton v Duke of Newcastle* [1903] AC 111.
12 *Re Moore, Trafford v Maconochie* (1888) 39 Ch D 116.
13 *Re Wolffe's Will Trusts, Shapley v Wolffe* [1953] 2 All ER 697, [1953] 1 WLR 1211 (the beneficiary having married a person not of the Jewish faith before the gift vested in possession, it was held she was entitled only to part of the capital).
14 *Re Lovell, Sparks v Southall* [1920] 1 Ch 122.
15 *Hogden v Hogden* [1957] SRNSW 269.

[34.4]
Words construed as a trust and not as a condition. There are cases of sums of money charged upon a devise or legacy but expressed in the will as a condition of the devise. A gift of property on condition that the beneficiary pays certain sums to certain persons does not create a condition which, if not fulfilled by the donee, causes a forfeiture, but a trust which can be enforced against the property leaving the donee with the property after the sums and the expenses of recovery have been raised.[1]

1   *Wright v Wilkin* (1862) 2 B & S 259; *Re Oliver, Newbald v Beckitt* (1890) 62 LT 533 (where it was held that no trust was created but simply a charge). In such cases it seems that a gift 'subject to' certain payments creates a charge and not a trust: *Re Cowley, Souch v Cowley* (1885) 53 LT 494.

II.   REPUGNANT CONDITIONS

[34.5]
Nature of repugnant conditions. A repugnant condition is one which attempts to make the enjoyment of a vested gift contrary to the principles of law affecting the gift.[1] The usual type of such a gift is a gift of capital to an adult subject to a condition that it is not to be paid to him until he attains an age greater than eighteen.[2] A condition of this nature can be imposed only by giving the income until he attains that age to another person or by so clearly taking away the income from the donee that the court will hold that there is an intestacy as to the income.[3] A gift may be made contingent on a donee attaining an age greater than eighteen with a gift over on his dying under that age,[4] and the income till the attainment of such age can be secured to the donee with vesting at that age by means of a discretionary trust.[5] Any condition limiting the power of alienation of property given absolutely is repugnant and void.[6] A condition may also be repugnant because it is impossible of performance.[7]

1   *Saunders v Vautier* (1841) Cr & Ph 240; *Harbin v Masterman* [1894] 2 Ch 184; *Re Couturier, Couturier v Shea* [1907] 1 Ch 470; *Re Brodribb, Queensland Trustees Ltd v Brodribb* [1942] QSR 263; *Re Townshend* [1941] 3 DLR 609; *Re Burger Estate* [1949] 1 WWR 280. A restraint on alienation is repugnant to a gift in fee: *Re Rosher, Rosher v Rosher* (1884) 26 Ch D 801;

Hood v Oglander (1865) 34 Beav 513. As to conditions restraining alienation, see Chapter 99. As to repugnancy of words purporting to limit a clear absolute gift, see Chapter 82.

2   *Gosling v Gosling* (1859) John 265; *Re Hendy's Will, Hayes v Hendy* [1913] VLR 559; *Re Bickerdike's Will, Bickerdike v Hill* [1918] VLR 191; *Re Carter, Harding v Carter* (1903) 21 NZLR 227; *Wells v Woods* (1861) 4 LT 768 (where £1,000 was given to a legatee to be paid in instalments of £50 per annum for 20 years after the testator's death: the gift vested at once); *Re Squire* (1962) 34 DLR (2d) 481 (gift at 30, intermediate income given, no gift over in event of death under 30: absolutely vested interest at 21); *Re Price Estate, Shultz v Price* (1965) 55 DLR (2d) 458; *Re Beresford Estate* [1966] 56 WWR 248.

3   *Gosling v Gosling* (1859) John 265.

4   The gift over prevents the gift indefeasibly vesting in the beneficiary, so that the gift is either contingent or vested subject to defeasance on death under the stated age.

5   A gift of all the income until a beneficiary attains a greater age than 18 followed by a gift of the capital on attaining that age gives the beneficiary an absolute interest at latest on attaining 18: *Saunders v Vautier* (1841) Cr & Ph 240; but this effect may be avoided by giving the income to trustees with a discretion to pay it to the beneficiary or to others or by a gift over of the capital on the beneficiary dying under that age.

6   *Re Dugdale, Dugdale v Dugdale* (1888) 38 Ch D 176; *Corbett v Corbett* (1888) 14 PD 7; *Re McKay, McKay v McKay* (1904) 22 NZLR 121; *Lucas v Goldie* [1920] NZLR 28; *Doherty v Doherty* [1936] 2 DLR 180; *Re Wilcox, Wilcox v Wilcox* [1978] Tas SR 82. Such a condition has been held valid as a limitation; see para **[34.3]**, n 9.

7   See para **[34.7]** infra.

[34.6]
Various repugnant conditions. Where a gift was given absolutely to be paid at twenty-eight years of age and to be reduced if the beneficiary embraced a religious life, it was held that the provision for reduction was repugnant to the absolute gift.[1] Sums to be invested until sons attained twenty-one years of age and then to be applied as the trustees should decide in the advancement in life of the sons are absolute gifts to the sons at twenty-one and must be paid over free from the exercise of the discretion on the part of the trustees.[2] A testator cannot grant an absolute interest in property with a gift over in case the grantee shall die intestate,[3] or dies without disposing of his interest by will or appointment,[4] or dies mentally unfit,[5] or embraces a religious life.[6] A gift over on a previous gift being void is good[7] but where there is a devise of 'all my property' to one and a gift of residue to another, the latter provision is repugnant.[8]

1   *Re Thompson, Griffith v Thompson* (1896) 44 WR 582.

2   *Re Johnston, Mills v Johnston* [1894] 3 Ch 204.

3   *Holmes v Godson* (1856) 8 De GM & G 152; *Barton v Barton* (1857) 3 K & J 512; *Re Babcock* (1892) 9 Gr 427; *Re Dixon, Dixon v Charlesworth* [1903] 2 Ch 458 (beneficiary dying without a will and childless); *Re Ashton, Ballard v Ashton* [1920] 2 Ch 481 (absolute donee dying mentally unfit); *Re Gee* (1973) 41 DLR (3d) 317. Such gifts tend to contravene the law by providing a devolution of property different from that prescribed by law in the event of an absolute owner dying intestate; see *Re Wilcock's Settlement* (1875) 1 Ch D 229; *Re Ashton, Ballard v Ashton* [1920] 2 Ch 481. Gifts of the kind here considered were common at one time and were an attempt to keep the property from passing to the husband of a married woman.

4   *Hales v Margerum* (1796) 3 Ves 299; *Bull v Kingston* (1816) 1 Mer 314; *Re Yalden* (1851) 1 De GM & G 53; *Watkins v Williams* (1851) 3 Mac & G 622; *Re Mortlock's Trusts* (1857) 3 K & J 456; *Henderson v Cross* (1861) 29 Beav 216. See, however, *Comiskey v Bowring-Hanbury* [1905] AC 84, where the gift over was construed as an executory gift.

5   *Re Ashton, Ballard v Ashton* [1920] 2 Ch 481.

6   *Re Thompson, Griffith v Thompson* (1896) 44 WR 582.

7   *De Themmines v De Bonneval* (1828) 5 Russ 288; *Carter v Green* (1857) 3 K & J 591.

8   *Re Jenkins' Trusts* (1889) 23 LR IR 162.

III.   IMPOSSIBLE CONDITIONS

[34.7]

What amounts to impossibility. Impossibility consists in a state of facts which does not or cannot exist. It depends on the intention shown by the testator in his will whether the proper construction of the condition is that it operates only on the state of affairs existing, and, therefore, in the circumstances does not take effect at all,[1] or, on the other hand, operates in any event and so is impossible to perform.[2] The impossibility must be in the nature of things,[3] and, therefore, a condition is not impossible because its performance is highly improbable,[4] or because it is out of the power of the donee, or even out of any human power,[5] to ensure its performance.

1   *Yates v University College, London* (1873) 8 Ch App 454 at 461; affd (1875) LR 7 HL 438. An originally impossible condition may make the condition void as repugnant to the gift: *Lowther v Cavendish* (1758) 1 Eden 99 at 117. See *Re Jones, Williams v Rowlands* [1948] Ch 67, [1947] 2 All ER 716, where one set of trustees was to provide a hall and another to carry it on. Owing to the war, no sufficient sum of money to purchase a site was available and, if it had been available, building could not have been carried out. The condition was held impossible. See also *Watson v National Children's Home* [1995] 37 LS Gaz R 24, condition that the donee should care for the deceased's domestic pets was impossible to perform because the pets had predeceased the testator; held did not defeat the gift.
2   *Re Knox, Von Sheffler v Shuldham* [1912] 1 IR 288 (where a condition for naturalisation was not impossible because a private Act might be obtained); *Re Williams, Taylor v University of Wales* (1908) 24 TLR 716 (where the gift was held to be absolute); *Re Robinson, Wright and Tugwell* [1892] 1 Ch 95 (use of black gown in pulpit not impossible); *Re Hollis's Hospital Trustees and Hague's Contract* [1899] 2 Ch 540 (where it is stated that conditions once thought to be impossible may now be possible).
3   *Francos v Alvares* (1746) 3 Atk 342; *Egerton v Earl of Brownlow* (1853) 4 HL Cas 1 at 94. A gift of land 'until I am able to live there and enjoy it myself': *Bunbury v Doran* (1857) IR 9 CL 284.
4   *Egerton v Earl of Brownlow* (1853) 4 HL Cas 1 at 76.
5   *Egerton v Earl of Brownlow* (1853) 4 HL Cas 1 at 22, 23, but it seems a condition to do something which cannot be effected in law, eg to assume a Christian name by deed poll, is an impossible condition: *Re Parrott, Cox v Parrott* [1946] Ch 183, [1946] 1 All ER 321.

[34.8]

Effect of impossibility. A condition precedent obviously impossible[1] or a condition becoming impossible by operation of law before the date of the will, is repugnant and void and the gift remains.[2] If a condition, intended to be operative in any event, is precedent, and is possible of performance at the date of the will, but afterwards becomes impossible by an act of God or circumstances over which neither the donee nor the testator had any control,[3] the performance of the condition is not excused, and accordingly the gift does not vest;[4] where, however, in such a case the condition is subsequent the gift takes effect free from the condition.[5]

1   *Lowther v Cavendish* (1758) 1 Eden 99.
2   *Re Thomas' Will Trusts, Powell v Thomas* [1930] 2 Ch 67 (condition made impossible by imposition of statutory trusts on undivided shares in 1925). This sentence was cited with approval in the Canadian case, *Re Macdonald* (1971) 18 DLR (3d) 521 at 525 (condition impossible of performance failed, and gift free of condition).
3   *Boyce v Boyce* (1849) 16 Sim 476; *Earl of Shrewsbury v Hope-Scott* (1859) 6 Jur NS 452 at 462.

4   *Roundel v Currer* (1786) 2 Bro CC 67; *Egerton v Earl of Brownlow* (1853) 4 HL Cas 1 at 120;
     Priestley v Holgate (1857) 3 K & J 286 (gift conditional on return to England, donee
     shipwrecked); *Dawson v Oliver-Massey* (1876) 2 Ch D 753 at 755.
5   *Bunbury v Doran* (1857) IR 9 CL 284; *Re Bird, Bird v Cross* (1894) 8 R 326; *Re Greenwood,
     Goodhart v Woodhead* [1903] 1 Ch 749; *Re Edwards, Lloyd v Boyes* [1910] 1 Ch 541; *Re
     Grove, Public Trustee v Dixon* [1919] 1 Ch 249; *Re Croxon, Croxon v Ferrers* [1904] 1 Ch 252;
     Re Berens, Re Dowdeswell, Berens-Dowdeswell v Holland-Martin [1926] Ch 596 (condition to
     obtain coats of arms already granted to another).

IV.   UNCERTAIN CONDITIONS

[34.9]
Different rules affecting conditions precedent and conditions subsequent.
The question whether a condition is void for uncertainty differs in the case of a
condition precedent from that of a condition subsequent. In the case of a
condition subsequent the condition must be such that the court or the persons
affected can see from the beginning, precisely and distinctly, upon the
happening of what event the preceding vested interest is to determine. In the
case of a condition precedent no such general or academic test is called for.[1]
Conditions precedent will be valid if the condition is couched in language that
permits a particular individual to come with evidence before the court and show
that he satisfies or does not satisfy, as the case may be, that condition.[2] If the
condition is such as to involve questions of degree, the beneficiary will take if he
can satisfy any, or at least any reasonable, test. It is not right for the court to
declare a condition precedent void for uncertainty unless its terms are such that
it is impossible to give them any meaning at all or such that they involve
repugnancies or inconsistencies in the possible tests which they postulate as
distinct from mere problems of degree.[3] Thus where there is a condition or
qualification attached to one or more individual gifts then the gift is valid if it is
possible to say of one or more persons that he or they undoubtedly qualify, even
if it may be difficult to say of others whether or not they qualify.[4] The
underlying principle seems to be that, as the court prefers to hold a gift vested
rather than that it should fail, it will construe a condition precedent more
leniently on the question of uncertainty than it will construe a condition
subsequent, which if held certain would cause the divesting of a vested gift or a
forfeiture, two matters which the court will hesitate to enforce.[5]

1   In *Re Tuck's Settlement Trusts, Public Trustee v Tuck* [1978] 1 All ER 1047 at 1052, Lord
     Denning MR criticised the distinction on the grounds that the problem is essentially one of
     construction of words, and if the words are conceptually uncertain so as to avoid a condition
     subsequent, they are just as conceptually uncertain in a condition precedent and should avoid it
     also. The Master of the Rolls and Lord Russell at 1056, accepted however that *Re Allen, Faith v
     Allen* [1953] Ch 810, [1953] 2 All ER 898, established the distinction and that the Court of
     Appeal was bound by that decision. See also *Blathwayt v Lord Cawley* [1976] AC 397, [1975] 3
     All ER 625; and *Re Barlow's Will Trusts* [1979] 1 All ER 296, [1979] 1 WLR 278.
2   Per Scott J in *Re Tepper's Will Trusts, Kramer v Ruda* [1987] 1 All ER 970 at p 976–977 citing
     Re Allen, Faith v Allen [1953] Ch 810, [1953] 2 All ER 898; *Re Selby's Will Trusts, Donn v
     Selby* [1965] 3 All ER 386 and *Re Tuck's Settlement Trusts* [1978] Ch 49, [1978] 1 All ER
     1047. But a stricter test applies to conditions subsequent as laid down in *Clayton v Ramsden*
     [1943] AC 320, [1943] 1 All ER 16, as to which see, para **[34.10]** infra. See also *Re Lowry's
     Will Trusts, Barclays Bank Ltd v United Newcastle-upon-Tyne Hospitals Board of Governors*

[1967] Ch 638, [1966] 3 All ER 955; see Lord Denning MR in *Re Gulbenkian's Settlement Trusts, Hacobian v Maun* [1968] Ch 126 at 132, 133, [1967] 3 All ER 15 at 17, 18.

3   *Re Allen, Faith v Allen* [1953] 2 All ER 898 at 900, 901. See also *Re Mercer* [1953] OWN 765.

4   This is the test laid down by the Court of Appeal in *Re Allen, Faith v Allen* [1953] Ch 810, [1953] 2 All ER 898, and applied in *Re Tuck's Settlement Trusts* [1978] Ch 49, [1978] 1 All ER 1047; and in *Re Barlow's Will Trusts* [1979] 1 All ER 296, [1979] 1 WLR 278 Thus in the latter a provision enabling 'any member of my family and any friends of mine who may wish to do so' to purchase a painting at less than the current market price, was held to be valid as a series of individual gifts subject to a condition precedent. Cases such as *McPhail v Doulton* [1971] AC 424, [1970] 2 All ER 228 concerned with the tests of certainty applicable to trusts and powers were distinguished.

5   *Re Jones, Midland Bank Executor and Trustee Co Ltd v Jones* [1953] Ch 125, [1953] 1 All ER 357.

[34.10]

Conditions subsequent: the test of certainty. It has been stated that conceptual uncertainty may avoid a condition subsequent but not a condition precedent,[1] a comment based on the distinction which has arisen in recent years[2] between 'conceptual uncertainty' and 'evidential uncertainty'. Lord Denning MR (although himself very critical of the test) has stated the approach as follows:[3]

' "Conceptual uncertainty" arises when a testator or settlor makes a bequest or gift on a condition in which he has not expressed himself clearly enough. He has used words which are too vague and indistinct for a court to apply. They are not sufficiently precise. So the court discards the condition as meaningless. It makes it of no effect, at any rate when it is a condition subsequent. "Evidential uncertainty" arises where the testator or settlor, in making the condition, has expressed himself clearly enough. The words are sufficiently precise. But the court has difficulty in applying them, in any given situation because of the uncertainty of the facts. It has to resort to extrinsic evidence to discover the facts, for instance to ascertain those whom the testator or settlor intended to benefit and those whom he did not. Evidential uncertainty never renders the conditions meaningless. The court never discards it on that account. It applies the conditions as best it can on the evidence available.'

It seems clear that this test, although open to criticism,[4] underlies many of the recent decisions on uncertainty.[5] Other tests have been stated; thus it has been said that, in the case of conditions subsequent, the court must be able to see from the beginning precisely and distinctly upon the happening of what event the preceding vested interest is to determine.[6] Then it has been said that whether the condition has or has not taken effect must be capable of ascertainment at any moment.[7] In a Privy Council case, on appeal from Canada but in a judgment based on English decisions, it was said that the beneficiary must know clearly what it is he may do and what he may not do.[8] The difference between these statements may be slight, but it has an important practical bearing. Where there is an obvious difficulty in deciding whether a particular event has happened, draftsmen have attempted to avoid the uncertainty by making the decision of the trustees whether or not it has happened final and binding upon all parties. It is quite possible that, where the uncertainty is to be decided by the court, it may be sufficient for the decision to be left to the trustees, but, if the beneficiary is to be able to know beforehand what he may and may not do, he cannot know what view the trustees may take and it may well be that this drafting strategem will not render certain a condition subsequent which would otherwise be uncertain.[9] Thus, where an annuity was to be halved if in the uncontrolled discretion of the trustees the beneficiary had social or other relationship with a named person, the condition was held void for uncertainty and was not saved by the trustees being given an absolute discretion in the matter.[10] However, where trustees had a discretion to withhold a gift if they were satisfied in their sole and absolute discretion that a hospital had been taken over by the state or a local authority, the question whether such taking over had in fact occurred was for the trustees and their decision was final so long as it was arrived at reasonably and honestly,[11] and where an act had to be done within six months with such further period as the trustees should think reasonable the condition was sufficiently certain.[12] Many of the conditions upon which the question of their certainty arises concern a state of mind and some difference of opinion has been expressed as to how far the court can inquire into this.[13] There is a distinction between uncertainty as to the events prescribed by the testator as those in which the condition is to operate, which, generally speaking, is fatal to the validity of the condition, and difficulty in ascertaining whether those events have happened or not, which is not necessarily fatal to such validity.[14] Conditions in which uncertainty has been considered are conditions requiring residence;[15] concerning the religious faith of a person,[16] the beneficiary's behaviour[17] or fitness for a stated position in life.[18]

1   Per Lord Denning MR in *Re Tuck's Settlement Trusts, Public Trustee v Tuck* [1978] 1 All ER 1047 at 1052.
2   The dichotomy was stated by Jenkins J in *Re Coxen* [1948] Ch 747 at 760–762, [1948] 2 All ER 492 at 501, 502. See also Lord Upjohn in *Whishaw v Stephens* [1970] AC 508, 524, 525; Lord Wilberforce in *McPhail v Doulton* [1971] AC 424 at 457, [1970] 2 All ER 228 at 247; and *Re Baden's Deed Trusts (No 2)* [1973] Ch 9, [1971] 3 All ER 985.
3   *Re Tuck's Settlement Trusts, Public Trustee v Tuck* [1978] 1 All ER 1047 at 1051.
4   Thus the test would invalidate a condition that a person be 'of Jewish blood', but not a condition that a person be 'of Jewish faith': *Re Tuck's Settlement Trusts, Public Trustee v Tuck* [1978] 1 All ER 1047 at 1051–1052, per Lord Denning MR.
5   *Whishaw v Stephens* [1970] AC 508, [1968] 3 All ER 785; and *McPhail v Doulton* [1971] AC 424, [1970] 2 All ER 228; see Lord Denning MR in *Re Tuck's Settlement Trusts, Public Trustee v Tuck* [1978] 1 All ER 1047 at 1051.
6   *Clayton v Ramsden* [1943] AC 320 at 326, [1943] 1 All ER 16 at 18; *Clavering v Ellison* (1859) 7 HL Cas 707, applied in *Re Tepper's Will Trusts, Kramer v Ruda* [1987] Ch 358, [1987] 1 All ER 970. Applying this test the clauses in *Re Tepper* were held to be void for uncertainty. But the judge being clearly reluctant to come to that conclusion without more, decided to adjourn the summons and invited the parties to file further evidence as to the meaning in this will of the expression 'the Jewish faith'. See also *National Mutual Trustees Ltd v Gooding* [1990] VR 791: 'provide a home for him' too uncertain to have any legal effect; *Re Viscount Exmouth, Exmouth v Praed* (1883) 23 Ch D 158 (the condition must be certain, not only in expression, but also in operation and it is essential to its validity that whether the condition has or has not taken effect should be capable of ascertainment at any given moment of time); *Re Krawitz's Will Trusts, Krawitz v Crawford* [1959] 3 All ER 793. This sentence was referred to in *Re Porter, Logan v Northern Bank Ltd* [1975] NI 157.
7   *Re Viscount Exmouth, Exmouth v Praed* (1883) 23 Ch D 158.
8   *Sifton v Sifton* [1938] AC 656, [1938] 3 All ER 435.
9   See *Re Coxen, MacCallum v Coxen* [1948] Ch 747 at 759, [1948] 2 All ER 492 at 502 (where Jenkins J suggested that, if the condition were itself not sufficiently certain, merely making the decision of the trustees the criterion would not save it: in this case, however, the condition itself was held sufficiently certain); *Re Hains, Hains v Elder's Trustee and Executor Co Ltd* [1942] SASR 172 (where a similar decision was reached, where the condition was held uncertain). In *Re Tuck's Settlement Trusts, Public Trustee v Tuck* [1978] 1 All ER 1047 at 1053, Lord Denning MR saw no reason why the settlor should not provide for the resolution of doubts by the executors, trustees or a third person. In that case the settlor provided that in case of dispute

or doubt whether a person qualified as an 'approved wife', the decision of the Chief Rabbi was to be conclusive. Lord Denning MR thought that if there was any conceptual uncertainty in the provisions of the settlement it was cured by this clause; *Re Tuck's Settlement Trusts, Public Trustee v Tuck* [1978] 1 All ER 1047 at 1054.

10 *Re Jones, Midland Bank Executor and Trustee Co Ltd v Jones* [1953] Ch 125, [1953] 1 All ER 357.
11 *Dundee General Hospitals Board of Management v Walker* [1952] 1 All ER 896.
12 *Re Burton's Settlements, Scott v National Provincial Bank Ltd* [1955] Ch 82, [1954] 3 All ER 193.
13 In *Clayton v Ramsden* [1943] AC 320, [1943] 1 All ER 16, however, the House of Lords said that it did not find any real difficulty in this respect.
14 *Re Coxen, MacCallum v Coxen* [1948] 2 All ER 492 at 501, 502; and see *Re Wilkinson, Page v Public Trustee* [1926] Ch 842 at 849. In *Re Lanyon, Lanyon v Lanyon* [1927] 2 Ch 264, it was held that, if the condition is clearly expressed it is not necessary that the donee shall be in a position at all times to know whether he is committing a breach of it.
15 See para **[35.18]** infra.
16 See para **[35.29]** infra.
17 See para **[35.45]** infra.
18 *Re Hains, Hains v Elder's Trustee and Executor Co Ltd* [1942] SASR 172 (fitness to manage the residuary estate which was mainly the business of a limited company); *Re Wecke's Will* (1958) 26 WWR 164 (understanding farming and willing to emigrate).

[34.11]
Conditions which have been held sufficiently certain. Conditions as to the behaviour of the beneficiary have sometimes been held sufficiently certain.[1] Conditions as to residence were formerly often held sufficiently certain but in recent times such conditions have sometimes been held void for uncertainty.[2]

The following conditions have been supported as being sufficiently certain: a condition not to dispute the will;[3] a condition for forfeiture on alienation;[4] a condition against marriage with specified persons where the description is inaccurate;[5] a condition for marriage with person of ample fortune able to maintain her in comfort and affluence;[6] a condition against becoming or marrying a Roman Catholic;[7] a gift over if number of employees subscribing to a sports ground should fall below a certain percentage.[8] The following conditions have been rejected as too uncertain to be enforced: a condition not to associate with specified relatives;[9] a condition to retain testator's name as an addition to husband's name;[10] a condition to 'assume' testator's name;[11] a condition that a child should live free from parents' direct influence or control;[12] a condition subsequent terminating a beneficiary's interest in a house if 'she is not residing therein personally';[13] beneficiary not to adopt or carry on any profession or professional calling whether for gain or otherwise;[14] renewing acquaintance with named person;[15] beneficiary not to marry any one not of the Jewish faith;[16] beneficiary to marry any one not of Jewish parentage;[17] beneficiary to be of the Jewish faith and to be married to an approved wife.[18] Where there are two limbs to the condition, the condition is ineffective if one of the limbs is too uncertain to enforce.[19] A gift over of residue on the death of the legatee before actually receiving the legacy is void for uncertainty.[20] Conditions requiring residence are dealt with separately.[21]

1 *Tattersall v Howell* (1816) 2 Mer 26 (to give up low company); *Wynne v Wynne* (1840) 2 Man & G 8 (woman to be 'discreet'). Where the decision is left to trustees or executors and they decline to exercise their discretion, the condition has been ignored and the gift held good despite the condition: *Re Coe's Trusts* (1858) 4 K & J 199; *Maud v Maud* (1860) 27 Beav 615; but on this point, see, further, *Re Coxen, MacCallum v Coxen* [1948] Ch 747 at 759, [1948] 2

All ER 492 at 502. 'To such children as may in the opinion of my trustees be likely to use the same profitably'; held, not void for uncertainty; *Re Kozminsky* [1966] VR 299.

2   *Dunne v Dunne* (1855) 7 De GM & G 207 (to reside in mansion and make it principal place of abode held certain); *Wynne v Fletcher* (1857) 24 Beav 430 (a similar case); *Re Wilkinson, Page v Public Trustee* [1926] Ch 842 (until female beneficiary should voluntarily cease to make dwelling-house her permanent home: this condition was not void for uncertainty; and a married woman who ceased to make the place her home in pursuance of her husband's injunction would not 'voluntarily' cease to make it her permanent home); *Re Boulter, Capital and Counties Bank v Boulter* [1922] 1 Ch 75 (infants not to reside abroad for periods exceeding six weeks in each year not void for uncertainty, but void as tending to separate parent and child); *Sifton v Sifton* [1938] AC 656, [1938] 3 All ER 435 (to reside in Canada held too uncertain to be enforced); *Re Coxen, MacCallum v Coxen* [1948] Ch 747, [1948] 2 All ER 492 (cease permanently to reside in named house held sufficiently certain); *Re Talbot-Ponsonby's Estate, Talbot-Ponsonby v Talbot-Ponsonby* [1937] 4 All ER 309 (condition to make place the beneficiary's home and further not to allow a named person to set foot upon the property held sufficiently certain). See, further, para **[35.18]** infra.

3   *Evanturel v Evanturel* (1874) LR 6 PC 1. Bona fide proceedings as to construction or in defence of rights of a beneficiary will not cause a forfeiture under such a condition: *Adams v Adams* [1892] 1 Ch 369; *Re Raven, Spencer v National Association for the Prevention of Consumption and other forms of Tuberculosis* [1915] 1 Ch 673.

4   *Re Goulder, Goulder v Goulder* [1905] 2 Ch 100 (gift over in event of beneficiary being unable at any time prior to actual payment to give a receipt by reason of his having committed or suffered any act whereby he had deprived himself of the benefit to his share). As to forfeiture clauses, see Chapter 99.

5   *Re Bathe, Bathe v Public Trustee* [1925] Ch 377 (condition against marriage with named persons the names being inaccurate or incomplete but the persons identified by affidavit).

6   *Re Moore's Trusts, Lewis v Moore* (1906) 96 LT 44.

7   *Re Morrison's Will Trusts, Walsingham v Blathwayt* [1940] Ch 102, [1939] 4 All ER 332; *Re Evans, Hewitt v Edwards* [1940] Ch 629.

8   *Re Denley's Trusts, Holman v HH Martyn & Co Ltd* [1969] 1 Ch 373, [1968] 3 All ER 65. See also *Re Balkind* [1969] NZLR 669 (condition precedent requiring membership of the Hebrew congregation).

9   *Jeffreys v Jeffreys* (1901) 84 LT 417.

10   *Re Gassiot, Brougham v Rose-Gassiot* (1907) 51 Sol Jo 570 (further directions as to how the surname should be used were essential).

11   *Re Parrott, Cox v Parrott* [1946] Ch 183, [1946] 1 All ER 321. See also *Re Fry, Reynolds v Denne* [1945] Ch 348, [1945] 2 All ER 205.

12   *Re Sandbrook, Noel v Sandbrook* [1912] 2 Ch 471. Such a condition is void as against public policy apart from uncertainty.

13   *Re McColgan* (1969) 4 DLR (3d) 572.

14   *Re Reich, Public Trustee v Guthrie* (1924) 40 TLR 398.

15   *Re Lowe, Westminster Bank v Lowe* (1939) 83 Sol Jo 421.

16   *Re Blaiberg, Blaiberg and Public Trustee v De Andia, Yrarrazaval and Blaiberg* [1940] Ch 385, [1940] 1 All ER 632; *Clayton v Ramsden* [1943] AC 320 at 334, [1943] 1 All ER 16 at 23, per Lord Romer; *Re Donn, Donn v Moses* [1944] Ch 8, [1943] 2 All ER 564; *Re Moss's Trusts, Moss v Allen* [1945] 1 All ER 207. But in *Re Abraham's Will Trusts, Caplan v Abrahams* [1969] 1 Ch 463, [1967] 2 All ER 1175, where a power was to arise 'in the event of the testator's son becoming engaged to be married to a person professing the Jewish faith', it was held that this was a condition precedent and, less certainty being required in the case of such a condition, it was not void for uncertainty. See also *Re Tepper's Will Trusts, Kramer v Ruda* [1987] Ch 358, [1987] 1 All ER 970, 'Jewish faith' held to be too uncertain in condition subsequent. See also *Re Balkind* [1969] NZLR 669.

17   *Clayton v Ramsden* [1943] AC 320, [1943] 1 All ER 16; *Re Donn, Donn v Moses* [1944] Ch 8, [1943] 2 All ER 564.

18   *Re Tuck's Settlement Trusts, Public Trustee v Tuck* [1978] Ch 49, [1978] 1 All ER 1047. The settlement defined an 'approved wife' and provided that in case of doubt or dispute as to whether a person so qualified the decision of the Chief Rabbi was to be conclusive.

19   *Clayton v Ramsden* [1943] AC 320, [1943] 1 All ER 16.

20   *Re Hudson* [1912] VLR 140.

21   See para **[35.18]** infra.

354

V. PUBLIC POLICY

[34.12]
Conditions against public policy. A condition is against public policy if it is in the interest of the state that it should not be performed.[1] What is contrary to public policy has varied from time to time, and many conditions are now upheld which in former days would have been declared to be contrary to the policy of the law. The rule remains, but its application varies with the principles which for the time being guide public opinion.[2] The prevalent judicial-attitude to questions of public policy in testamentary gifts was stated by Lord Simon in *Blathwayt v Lord Cawley,*[3] as follows:

'I must not be taken thereby to be implying that it is for courts of law to embark on an independent and unfettered appraisal of what they think is required by public policy on any issue. Courts are concerned with public policy only in so far as it has been manifested by parliamentary sanction or embodied in rules of law having binding judicial force. As to such rules of law your Lordships have the same powers to declare, to bind and to loose as in regard to any other judicial precedent. Rules of law expressing principles of public policy therefore fall to be treated with the same respect and circumspection, the same common sense and regard for changing circumstances, as any other rules of law.'

In that case the court also emphasised the balancing rule of public policy that a testator should be free, subject to the rights of his surviving spouse and children, to dispose of his property as he pleases.[4]

The following conditions attached to a gift in a will have been held to be contrary to public policy and void: a condition inciting the beneficiary to commit a crime[5] or to do any act prohibited by law;[6] a condition requiring the beneficiary to exert his influence in any political matter, such as obtaining a title;[7] a condition tending to induce the future separation of husband and wife;[8] an unreasonable restraint of marriage,[9] or of trade or industry;[10] a condition forbidding service for the defence of the realm,[11] or any other public duty;[12] a condition tending to deprive a parent of the control of children;[13] a condition which requires a change of religion during infancy;[14] a condition which will operate beyond the limit imposed by the rule against perpetuities;[15] a gift for the mother of the largest number of children born during a certain period;[16] extravagant, wasteful or futile directions.[17]

---

1 *Cooke v Turner* (1846) 15 M & W 727.
2 *Evanturel v Evanturel* (1874) LR 6 PC 1 at 29. See Lord Wilberforce in *Blathwayt v Lord Cawley* [1975] 3 All ER 625 at 636 (forfeiture clause if the person entitled 'be or become Roman Catholic'; not void for public policy despite the Race Relations Act 1968; public policy does not require that testators may not prefer one branch of the family to another on religious grounds).
3 [1975] 3 All ER 625 at 637.
4 See Lord Wilberforce, [1975] 3 All ER 625 at 636, and Lord Frazer of Tulleybelton, [1975] 3 All ER 625 at 650. The rights of other 'dependants' under the Inheritance (Provision for Family and Dependants) Act 1975 would also now have to be considered; see Chapter 105.
5 *Mitchel v Reynolds* (1711) 1 P Wms 181 at 189; *Earl of Shrewsbury v Hope–Scott* (1859) 6 Jur NS 452 at 456.
6 *Mitchel v Reynolds* (1711) 1 P Wms 181; *Re Piper, Dodd v Piper* [1946] 2 All ER 503.

7   *Earl of Kingston v Pierepont* (1681) 1 Vern 5; *Egerton v Earl of Brownlow* (1853) 4 HL Cas 1;
   Re Wallace, Champion v Wallace [1920] 2 Ch 274 (where it was held that a condition to
   acquire the title of baronet was not against public policy since the title involved no duties other
   than those of every good citizen). A condition that if a person should not succeed to a peerage
   the lands should go over has been held valid in Scotland: *Earl of Caithness v Sinclair* 1912 SC
   79, and a similar gift was held good in Ireland where the condition was: 'if the House of Lords
   will allow his right' to be Viscount N: *Earl of Fingal v Blake* (1829) 2 Mol 50.

8   See para **[35.35]** infra.

9   See para **[35.1]** infra.

10 Though restraint of trade or industry has been one of the most discussed topics in connection
   with public policy, there appears to be no English decision on the point so far as a condition in a
   will is concerned apart from references in the judgments in *Cooke v Turner* (1846) 15 M & W
   727 at 736, and *Egerton v Earl of Brownlow* (1853) 4 HL Cas 1 at 18, 144, 241. This note was
   referred to in *Re Cowley* [1971] NZLR 468 at 472, where it was stated to be doubtful as to how
   far, if at all, the requirements of public policy could invalidate conditions in wills tending to
   restrict the freedom of trade of a beneficiary: referring to *Cooke v Turner* (1846) 15 M & W
   727; *Egerton v Earl of Brownlow* (1853) 4 HL Cas 1: *Permanent Trustee Co v Dougall* (1931)
   34 SRNSW 83; and *Esso Petroleum Co Ltd v Harper's Garage (Stourport) Ltd* [1968] AC 269,
   [1967] 1 All ER 699. In *Re Cowley*, it was held that a provision tending to encourage grandsons
   to become farmers was not contrary to public policy in New Zealand.

11 See Chapter 35.

12 See Chapter 35.

13 See Chapter 35.

14 See Chapter 35.

15 See Chapter 94.

16 *Re Millar* [1938] 2 DLR 164.

17 *Sutherland's Trustee v Verschoyle* 1968 SLT 43 (trust fund for maintenance of unimportant
   art collection).

VI.   CONDITIONS IN TERROREM

[34.13]

Nature of a condition in terrorem. Certain conditions, if attached to a legacy
of specific personal property or a legacy charged on personal estate only,[1] may
be void against the donee as made in terrorem, that is to say, as a mere idle
threat to induce the donee to comply with the conditions, but not to affect the
bequest,[2] unless the testator shows that his intention was not merely to threaten
or enjoin the donee by the condition,[3] but to make a different disposition of the
property in the event of non-compliance with the condition.[4] The conditions to
which this doctrine is ordinarily applied[5] are conditions in partial restraint of
marriage,[6] or forbidding the donee to dispute the will.[7]

1   The rule is said to have derived from the civil law as administered in the ecclesiastical courts
   (which could deal only with personalty) but with modifications: *Bellairs v Bellairs* (1874) LR
   18 Eq 510 at 515, 516; *Re Whiting's Settlement, Whiting v De Rutzen* [1905] 1 Ch 96 at 115. In
   the case of mixed gift of real and personal estate, without any trust for conversion, or a legacy
   charged on such a mixed fund, different rules are applied according to the nature of the property
   concerned: *Reynish v Martin* (1746) 3 Atk 330 at 335; *Duddy v Gresham* (1878) 2 LR IR 442,
   but see *Re Pettifer, Pettifer v Pettifer* [1900] WN 182; *Re Schmidt Estate* [1949] 2 WWR 513.

2   *Re Dickson's Trust, ex p Dickson* (1850) 1 Sim NS 37 at 43; *Duddy v Gresham* (1878) 2 LR IR
   442 at 464.

3   See *Harvey v Lady Aston* (1737) 1 Atk 361 at 377, 378; *Bellairs v Bellairs* (1874) LR 18 Eq
   510 at 516.

4   *Re Kent* (1982) 139 DLR (3d) 318, provision that benefits revoked if beneficiary commenced
   litigation in connection with provisions of will; held not in terrorem; gift over. Where there is

no gift over the condition is ineffective: *Harvey v Lady Aston* (1737) 1 Atk 361; *Re Catt's Trusts* (1864) 2 Hem & M 46; *Re Pashak Estate* [1923] 1 DLR 1130.

5   Though other conditions were at times said to be subject to the doctrine, it seems now well settled (see *Re Hanlon, Heads v Hanlon* [1933] Ch 254) that it applies only in the cases mentioned. However on the construction of particular wills other conditions have been construed as inducements or threats addressed to the donee personally and not as affecting the gift where the context so requires: *Byng v Lord Strafford* (1843) 5 Beav 558 at 571, 572; affd sub nom *Hoare v Byng* (1844) 10 Cl & Fin 508; *Re Meagher, Trustees, Executors and Agency Co Ltd v Meagher* [1910] VLR 407 (donee to learn a profession). In *Re Hanlon, Heads v Hanlon* [1933] Ch 254, it was held that a condition not to marry a named person or live with him as his wife or leave home with that intention or misconduct herself with him or be delivered of a child or children of which the named person was the father was not a condition in partial restraint of marriage and not a condition in terrorem and without a gift over was enforceable on the happening of any of the stated events. In this case it was said that if a testator desires and expressly intends a gift to be revoked on the happening of certain events, the absence of a gift over will not prevent that revocation. But the event not having happened, the beneficiary was entitled to continue to enjoy the income subject to forfeiture on the happening of the event and on her death without having married the named person, her interest would become absolute.

6   *Bellasis v Ermine* (1663) 1 Cas in Ch 22; *Jarvis v Duke* (1681) 1 Vern 19 at 20; *Semphill v Bayly* (1721) Prec Ch 562, and see para **[35.1]** et seq.

7   See para **[35.38]** infra.

[34.14]

Validity where condition subsequent. In cases where such a condition is a condition subsequent, a gift over on non-compliance with the condition is essential to[1] and sufficient for[2] the validity of the condition. Such a gift over may be made by a direction that on such non-compliance the gift is to fall into residue,[3] but not by a mere residuary gift without more.[4] A separate provision for the donee on non-compliance with the condition is sufficient to prevent it being in terrorem.[5]

1   *Lloyd v Branton* (1817) 3 Mer 108 at 117; *Leong v Lim Beng Chye* [1955] AC 648, [1955] 2 All ER 903.
2   *Strattons v Grymes* (1698) 2 Vern 357; *Aston v Aston* (1703) 2 Vern 452; *Daley v Desbouvrie* (1738) 2 Atk 261; *Re Whiting's Settlement, Whiting v De Rutzen* [1905] 1 Ch 96; *Re Kozminsky* [1966] VR 299.
3   *Lloyd v Branton* (1817) 3 Mer 108; and see *Pullen v Ready* (1743) 2 Atk 587 at 590.
4   *Wheeler v Bingham* (1746) 3 Atk 364.
5   *Bellasis v Ermine* (1663) 1 Cas in Ch 22; *Garret v Pritty* (1693) 2 Vern 293.

[34.15]

Validity where condition precedent. In cases where such a condition is a condition precedent, the testator may show that the condition is not in terrorem by a gift over on non-compliance with the conditions,[1] or a mere residuary gift[2] or by providing for the donee in both events, ie whether the condition is performed or not.[3] If property is given on marriage with consent as a condition precedent, and the condition is in terrorem, the gift takes effect on marriage even without consent,[4] but not until marriage.[5]

1   *Malcolm v O'Callaghan* (1817) 2 Madd 349; *Gardiner v Slater* (1858) 25 Beav 509. In the case of a condition for marriage with consent, a gift over on death under twenty-one or marriage without consent is not sufficient for this purpose: *Gray v Gray* (1889) 23 LR IR 399.
2   *Amos v Horner* (1699) 1 Eq Cas Abr 112, pl 9; *Harvey v Lady Aston* (1737) 1 Atk 361. See *Creagh v Wilson* (1706) 2 Vern 572; *Gray v Gray* (1889) 23 LR IR 399 (where the gift itself was residuary).

3 *Creagh v Wilson* (1706) 2 Vern 572; *Re Nourse, Hampton v Nourse* [1899] 1 Ch 63 at 71; *Gillet v Wray* (1715) 1 P Wms 284.
4 *Underwood v Morris* (1741) 2 Atk 184, but the actual decision in this case has not been accepted on account of the gift over: see *Hemmings v Munckley* (1783) 1 Bro CC 304, and *Scott v Tyler* (1788) 2 Bro CC 431 at 488.
5 *Garbut v Hilton* (1739) 1 Atk 381; *Elton v Elton* (1747) 3 Atk 504; *Gray v Gray* (1889) 23 LR IR 399.

[34.16]

Not applicable to freeholds. This doctrine does not apply to freeholds,[1] nor to legacies charged on freeholds,[2] or on personalty directed to be laid out in the purchase of land.[3]

1 *Duddy v Gresham* (1878) 2 LR IR 442 at 457, 465; *Jenner v Turner* (1880) 16 Ch D 188 at 196. As to mixed funds, see para **[34.12]**, n 17.
2 *Reynish v Martin* (1746) 3 Atk 330 at 335.
3 *Pullen v Ready* (1743) 2 Atk 587 at 590.

VII. EFFECT OF INVALIDITY

[34.17]

Effect of invalidity in general. If the condition is void,[1] the effect on the gift is that, if the condition is precedent, the gift fails.[2] If the condition is subsequent, the gift takes effect free from the condition.[3] If, however, the condition is only voidable and is avoided by the donee, or is repugnant to the gift to which it is attached, or fails to operate on the gift as being in terrorem or otherwise, then, whether the condition is precedent or subsequent, the gift takes effect free from the conditions.[4]

1 The condition may be void as contrary to public policy, repugnant to a prior gift, illegal or uncertain. Where the condition is a condition precedent and is illegal and is attached to a gift of personal property, the gift fails only where the illegality is malum in se. Where the illegality is merely malum prohibitum, the condition is avoided and the gift takes effect free from the condition: *Re Elliott* [1952] Ch 217, [1952] 1 All ER 145, applying *Reynish v Martin* (1746) 3 Atk 330, and *Re Moore* (1888) 39 Ch D 116 at 131.
2 Since the condition must be fulfilled before the gift vests and being void cannot be fulfilled. See cases cited in para **[34.2]**, n 5.
3 *Egerton v Earl of Brownlow* (1853) 4 HL Cas 1; *Re Gassiot, Fladgate v Vinters' Co* (1901) 70 LJ Ch 242.
4 As to the doctrine of in terrorem, see para **[34.13]** supra.

[34.18]

Malum in se and malum prohibitum. Where a condition precedent is invalid as being malum in se[1] both the gift and the condition are void and the gift fails,[2] but where such a condition is invalid as being malum prohibitum[3] the condition only is void and the gift becomes absolute.[4]

1 The distinction between malum in se and malum prohibitum has never been precisely stated.
2 See *Re Wolffe's Will Trusts, Shapley v Wolffe* [1953] 2 All ER 697 at 700.
3 Recent examples of malum prohibitum are *Re Piper* [1946] 2 All ER 503, separation of parent and child; *Re Elliott* [1952] Ch 217, [1952] 1 All ER 145, perpetuity; *Re Wolffe's Will Trusts, Shapley v Wolffe* [1953] 2 All ER 697, marriage within a certain religion.

4   *Re Piper* [1946] 2 All ER 503; *Re Elliott* [1952] Ch 217, [1952] 1 All ER 145; *Re Wolffe's Will Trusts, Shapley v Wolffe* [1953] 2 All ER 697. The rule as to malum prohibitum being derived from the civil law applies only to personalty.

[34.19]
Conditions nullified or dispensed by the testator. The donee may not be bound[1] by a condition imposed by the will on account of acts of the testator or other events, subsequent to the date of the will, where the effect is that, substantially, the condition is performed or nullified in the testator's lifetime, or that, substantially, the testator has dispensed with the condition or has put performance out of the power of the donee.[2]

1   See *Wedgwood v Denton* (1871) LR 12 Eq 290 at 296, where it is suggested that the effect in such cases is that the condition has become impossible. As to impossible conditions, see paras **[34.7]** and **[34.8]** supra.
2   *Darley v Langworthy* (1774) 3 Bro Parl Cas 359 (bequest of chattels conditional on residence at a property which the testator conveyed away during his lifetime); *Smith v Cowdrey* (1825) 2 Sim & St 358 (condition against marriage with a person where such marriage was made with consent of the testator in his lifetime); *Re Park, Bott v Chester* [1910] 2 Ch 322 (similar case) (as to conditions requiring consent to marriage; see para **[35.9]** infra); *Gath v Burton* (1839) 1 Beav 478 (payment of debt, satisfied by testator accepting composition); *Violett v Brookman* (1857) 26 LJ Ch 308 (condition not to dispute will of testator's father, acquiescence by testator in revaluation of the father's estate); *Walker v Walker* (1860) 2 De GF & J 255 (condition requiring conveyance by donee, purchase of donee's interest by testator); *Re Wolffe's Will Trusts, Shapley v Wolffe* [1953] 2 All ER 697 (gift of capital on marriage to person of Jewish faith and child of Jewish parents and a gift of part only of the capital if the marriage was not with a Jewish person; *held* that although the first gift was one upon an impossible condition, the second was good: it was suggested that in this form of gift there was not a condition but a limitation which failed).

[34.20]
Present position. The gift fails not only where the illegality is malum in se, but also where the performance of the condition is the sole motive of the bequest, or its impossibility was unknown to the testator, or a condition which was possible at the time of its creation has since become impossible by act of God. Where the condition is originally impossible, or is made so by act or default of the testator, or is illegal as involving malum prohibitum, only the condition fails and the gift becomes absolute.[1]

1   See cases cited in para **[34.18]**, n 4.

VIII.   PERFORMANCE OF CONDITIONS

[34.21]
Substantial performance. In many cases, particularly with regard to conditions requiring a consent to marriage, the court may hold a condition satisfied where it has been complied with substantially,[1] though not in terms,[2] whether the condition is precedent or subsequent,[3] but does not in general do so in the case of conditions divesting an estate that has become vested.[4] There may be cases where, in the circumstances, an attempted or inchoate performance is sufficient,[5] but this is not the general rule, even though the completion of the performance is prevented by the death of the donee or other act of God.[6] The general rule is that

where there is a gift over upon a certain contingency, it will not take effect unless the exact contingency happens.[7] Thus where the terms of a condition are clear and literal performance possible, the court may require literal performance,[8] and strict compliance is required where time is of the essence of the condition and the parties could not, in the case of non-compliance, be placed in the same position as if strict compliance had been made.[9]

1   *Re Moir, Warner v Moir* (1884) 25 Ch D 605 (condition as to residence complied with by staffing house with servants, paying outgoings and occasional residence); *Re Sax, Barned v Sax* (1893) 62 LJ Ch 688 ('cease to carry on business'; sale to company, donees serving as managing directors, amounts to ceasing to carry on); *Galwey v Barden* [1899] 1 IR 508 (entering on a calling, becoming teacher in Jesuit College); *Schnell v Tyrrell* (1834) 7 Sim 86 (remaining in England, joining regiment abroad); *Re Stone's Trusts* (1866) 14 LT 542 (claim to be made within specified time, beneficiary abroad, claim made on his behalf although his whereabouts were uncertain); *Re Arbib and Class's Contract* [1891] 1 Ch 601 (return to England, temporary visit sufficient); *Browne v Browne* [1912] 1 IR 272 (legatee to act as trustee) and compare *Re Sharman's Public Trustee v Sharman* [1942] Ch 311, [1942] 2 All ER 74; *Re Crumpe, Orpen v Moriarty* [1912] 1 IR 485 (annuitant not to return to or reside in England); *Re Cole, Cole v Cole* [1919] 1 Ch 218 (employment with company not broken by military service); *Re Drake, Drake v Green* [1921] 2 Ch 99 (service with testator); *Re Orchard, Carpenter v Lauer* [1948] 1 All ER 203 (conclusion of armistice with Germany: unconditional surrender sufficient). A condition requiring a donee to claim a legacy may be sufficiently complied with by an order in an administration action, even though the donee is not a party: *Tollner v Marriott* (1830) 4 Sim 19, but not, it seems, by a mere order on an originating summons not asking for general administration: *Re Hartley, Stedman v Dunster* (1887) 34 Ch D 742. A condition requiring a donee to give a good discharge may similarly be complied with by bringing an action: *Franco v Alvares* (1746) 3 Atk 342; *Ledward v Hassells* (1856) 2 K & J 370. As to literal performance, see para **[34.22]**, n 3.
2   A literal compliance may be required by the will and may be inferred where the terms are clear and literal compliance is possible: *Caldwell v Cresswell* (1871) 6 Ch App 278, and see para **[34.22]**, n 3. In cases where a gift is subject to a condition for marriage with consent, and no particular form or manner is prescribed for such consent, the court treats the consent as a matter of substance and not as a matter of form and if consent is substantially given, it will not look minutely at the form in which it is given: *Re Smith, Keeling v Smith* (1890) 44 Ch D 654. Substantial compliance is accepted where there would be difficulty in strict compliance, eg where beneficiaries were to appear before the executors and establish identity, the court was satisfied where in the case of an aged beneficiary one of the executors visited the beneficiary in order to obtain such proof: *Tanner v Tebbutt* (1843) 2 Y & C Ch Cas 225.
3   *Worsley v Wood* (1796) 6 Term Rep 710 at 719, 722; *Dawson v Oliver-Massey* (1876) 2 Ch D 753.
4   *Hervey-Bathurst v Stanley* (1876) 4 Ch D 251 at 272. See also *Re Hinckes, Dashwood v Hinckes* [1921] 1 Ch 475 (where the effect of a shifting clause was defeated by a conveyancing device).
5   *Priestley v Holgate* (1857) 3 K & J 286 at 288 (return to England where condition amounts to penalty or forfeiture may be satisfied by embarkation if the donee is lost on the voyage); *Re Connington's Will* (1860) 2 LT 535 (gift on condition certain church services were held which parishioners failed to attend).
6   *Tulk v Houlditch* (1813) 1 Ves & B 248 (where the legatee was to prove his existence in a certain way, strict proof was required); *Roundel v Currer* (1786) 2 Bro CC 67 (obvious intention to bar entail, but disentail not in fact effected).
7   Per Peter Gibson J in *Re Koeppler's Will Trusts, Barclays Bank Trust Co v Slack* [1984] 2 All ER 111 at 126; this is subject to the limited exception known as the rule in *Jones v Westcomb* (1711) Prec Ch 316; see Chapter 93, para **[93.9]** infra.
8   *Caldwell v Cresswell* (1871) 6 Ch App 278, *Brown v Peys* (1594) Cro Eliz 357; *Tulk v Houlditch* (1813) 1 Ves & B 248. Where the condition is to defeat a vested interest, it will be construed strictly and must be strictly complied with: *Clavering v Ellison* (1859) 7 HL Cas 707. Where an annuity was given to a woman on separation from her husband, separation merely by reason of the husband's infirmity was held sufficient: *Bedborough v Bedborough (No 2)* (1865) 34 Beav 286.

9   *Re Avard, Hook v Parker* [1948] Ch 43, [1947] 2 All ER 548 (option to purchase within three
     months of the death of a named person: the beneficiary died in the lifetime of the named person
     and his personal representative gave the notice a few days out of time: the gift failed though no
     one was prejudiced); *Re Goldsmith's Will Trust, Brett v Bingham* [1947] Ch 339, [1947] 1 All
     ER 451 (where the parties could not be put into the same position as if the condition had been
     complied with—the widow, who was interested, had died—the conditional gift failed).

[34.22]

Time of performance. Where the testator has prescribed a period within which
a condition must be performed, this period must be observed,[1] subject to the
jurisdiction of the court to grant relief from forfeiture;[2] but where there is no gift
over, the court considers what the condition is intended to guard against.[3] If,
however, the testator has not prescribed such a period and the condition is to be
performed by the donee personally, not requiring the intervention or concurrence
of any other person, the period for the performance of the condition is
necessarily the life of the donee and no longer, and the condition is not complied
with if the donee dies without having performed it.[4] Where persons other than
the donee are benefited, the period allowed as a rule is a reasonable period.[5]

1   *Simpson v Vickers* (1807) 14 Ves 341 (release to be given within specified time); *Brooke v
     Garrod* (1857) 2 De G & J 62 (option to purchase); *Austin v Tawney* (1867) 2 Ch App 143
     (option to beneficiaries to purchase with time limited to enter into agreement for completion);
     Re Glubb, Bamfield v Rogers [1900] 1 Ch 354 (charities to prove within four years that they
     have obtained additional subscriptions by reason of the testator's legacies); *Re Knox, Von
     Scheffler v Shuldman* [1912] 1 IR 288 (naturalisation within two years); *Re Jones, Williams v
     Rowlands* [1948] Ch 67, [1947] 2 All ER 716 (building to be built within five years). In
     computing time the day of the testator's death is included or excluded according to the
     circumstances: *Lester v Garland* (1808) 15 Ves 248; *Miller v Wheatley* (1891) 26 LR IR 144;
     Gorst v Lowndes (1841) 11 Sim 434; *Re Figgis, Roberts v Maclaren* [1969] 1 Ch 123, [1968] 1
     All ER 999.
2   See Chapter 99.
3   *Re Packard, Packard v Waters* [1920] 1 Ch 596 (legacy to be settled within a year, time not of
     essence of contract, no gift over on non-compliance); *Re Finlay, Dinsmore v Finlay* [1933] NI
     89 (assuming a name). Where there is no gift over, the court considers what the condition is
     intended to guard against: *Re Goodwin, Ainslie v Goodwin* [1924] 2 Ch 26; *Re Selinger's Will
     Trusts, Midland Bank Executor and Trustee Co Ltd v Levy* [1959] 1 All ER 407; *Elcock v
     Campbell* [1931] NZLR 1060 (condition for convenience of distribution).
4   *Patching v Barnett* (1881) 51 LJ Ch 74; *Re Greenwood, Goodhart v Woodhead* [1902] 2 Ch
     198 at 204, 205. Thus where the condition is of marriage to a particular person, or with the
     consent of a person or persons, the donee has his whole life in which to comply and it is
     immaterial that he marries someone else for that marriage may end in his lifetime and he may
     afterwards comply with the condition: *Johnson v Smith* (1749) 1 Ves Sen 314; *Randal v Payne*
     (1779) 1 Bro CC 55; *Fitzgerald v Ryan* [1899] 2 IR 637; and see *Beaumont v Squire* (1852) 17
     QB 905, the decision in which appears preferable to the suggestion in *Clifford v Beaumont*
     (1828) 4 Russ 325.
5   *Huckstep v Mathews* (1856) 1 Vern 362; *Davies v Lowndes* (1835) 1 Bing NC 597 at 618.

[34.23]

Enforcement of condition. The person entitled under a gift over on non-
performance of the condition may release the donee from the condition,[1] but as a
rule without prejudice to the rights of others.[2] No one can take advantage of the
non-performance of a condition who intentionally prevented the condition from
being performed.[3] If a legacy is given on a valid condition subsequent that the
donee does or abstains from doing any specified act, the court orders payment of
the legacy to the donee, but requires security for the observance of the

condition.[4] If, on the other hand, the condition refers to no act or default of the donee, he may be entitled to payment without giving security.[5] In each case, however, the court gives effect to the intentions of the testator which may modify or exclude these rules.[6]

1   *Ex p Palmer* (1852) 5 De G & Sm 649.
2   *Wynne v Fletcher* (1857) 24 Beav 430.
3   *Viscount Falkland v Bertie* (1698) 2 Vern 333; *Simpson v Vickers* (1807) 14 Ves 341 at 346.
4   *Aston v Aston* (1703) 2 Vern 452; *Colston v Morris* (1821) 6 Madd 89.
5   *Griffiths v Smith* (1790) 1 Ves 97; *Fawkes v Gray* (1811) 18 Ves 131; *Madill v Madill* (1907) 26 NZLR 737.
6   There may in the will be an express direction that security be given: *Roche v M'Dermott* [1901] 1 IR 394; *Re Lester, Burton v Lester* (1906) 7 SRNSW 58. Where trustees have the legal estate and active duties to perform, transfer to the legatee may be impossible: *Polson v Polson* (1900) 21 NSWLR Eq 90.

[34.24]
Excuses for non-performance. A married person may be excused from the performance of the condition on the ground that performance would separate the spouses[1] or prevent the proper supervision of the children.[2] A minor cannot choose where he will reside,[3] nor can he have any volition where the law requires that he shall obey or be subject to the direction of his parents or his properly appointed guardians.[4] The requirements of military service have been held a valid excuse for non-performance.[5] The performance of the condition may be rendered impossible by the acts of the testator.[6] On the other hand, ignorance of the condition is no excuse for not fulfilling it.[7] If he is required to claim the legacy within a certain time, he must do so.[8] A legatee is not entitled to notice of the condition,[9] unless the terms of the condition expressly provide that an interested party is to give him notice thereof. Impossibility is no excuse for non-performance where such impossibility arises from the acts of the beneficiary himself,[10] and, except as mentioned above, incapacity is no excuse.[11]

1   *Woods v Townley* (1853) 11 Hare 314; *Wilkinson v Wilkinson* (1871) LR 12 Eq 604; and see para **[35.35]** infra.
2   *Re Sandbrook, Noel v Sandbrook* [1912] 2 Ch 471, and see para **[35.36]** infra.
3   *Parry v Roberts* (1871) 25 LT 371; *Partridge v Partridge* [1894] 1 Ch 351. See para **[35.18]** infra.
4   *Parry v Roberts* (1871) 25 LT 371; *Partridge v Partridge* [1894] 1 Ch 351. See para **[35.18]** infra.
5   *Re Adair* [1909] 1 IR 311; *Schnell v Tyrrell* (1834) 7 Sim 86; *Re Cole, Cole v Cole* [1919] 1 Ch 218.
6   *Rajendra v Mrinalini* (1921) ILR 48 Calc 1100 (where it was held that the gift failed).
7   *Astley v Earl of Essex* (1874) LR 18 Eq 290; *Re M'Mahon, M'Mahon v M'Mahon* [1901] 1 IR 489.
8   See para **[35.48]** infra. See also *Re Hodge's Legacy* (1873) LR 16 Eq 92, where the beneficiary was required to execute a release within a certain time and failed to do so because he was in India.
9   The executor is under no duty to give notice even though he benefits by not doing so: *Re Lewis, Lewis v Lewis* [1904] 2 Ch 656; *Chauncey v Graydon* (1743) 2 Atk 616; *Powell v Rawle* (1874) LR 18 Eq 243; *Re Mackay, Mackay v Gould* [1906] 1 Ch 25.
10 *Carter v Carter* (1857) 3 K & J 617; *Middleton v Windross* (1873) LR 16 Eq 212; but it is otherwise where the impossibility arises under regulations preventing building and obtaining of a site for the building: *Re Jones, Williams v Rowlands* [1948] Ch 67, [1947] 2 All ER 716 (a charity case).

11   A minor has been held bound to comply with the following conditions: name and arms clause: *Whittingham's Case* (1603) 8 Co Rep 42b; *Bevan v Mahon-Hagan* (1892) 27 LR Ir 399; condition to give a discharge: *Ledward v Hassells* (1856) 2 K & J 370. In the case of a mental defective the court will order the receiver to perform the condition: *Re Earl of Sefton* [1898] 2 Ch 378; but mental deficiency may be an act of God preventing the performance and then in the case of a condition subsequent, the mental defective's personal representatives take free from the condition: *Re Greenwood, Goodhart v Woodhead* [1903] 1 Ch 749; see now the Mental Health Act 1983, ss 99–102; 28 *Halsbury's Statutes* (4th edn) 968–972. See also *Re Crumpe, Orpen v Moriarty* [1912] 1 IR 485.

IX.   RELIEF AGAINST CONDITIONS

[34.25]

When relief granted. A court will grant relief against a condition precedent,[1] or against forfeiture under a condition subsequent,[2] in the case of any condition on the usual equitable grounds of such relief, eg where performance has been prevented by the contrivance of the executors,[3] or of other persons interested,[4] and by no fault of the donee,[5] or where the condition is in the nature of a penalty.[6] The court also grants relief in the case of conditions relating to the payment of legacies or other sums[7] or the release of claims,[8] where performance has not been made within the time required by the testator, and generally where time is not of the essence of the condition and it is capable of being adequately performed at any time,[9] on compensation being made for the delay.[10] The court, however, does not give relief in such cases where there is a gift over to any other person other than the person who would take by operation of law.[11] Except in such cases, the court cannot give relief.[12]

1   *Wallis v Crimes* (1667) 1 Cas in Ch 89; *Woodman v Blake* (1691) 2 Vern 222; *Hayward v Angell* (1683) 1 Vern 222; *Viscount Falkland v Bertie* (1698) 2 Vern 333.
2   *Hayward v Angell* (1683) 1 Vern 222; *Hollinrake v Lister* (1826) 1 Russ 500.
3   See *Brooke v Garrod* (1857) 2 De G & J 62.
4   *D'Aguilar v Drinkwater* (1813) 2 Ves & B 225 (beneficiary under gift over); *Hayes v Hayes* (1674) Cas *temp* Finch 231 (beneficiary under a prior gift).
5   *Clarke v Parker* (1812) 19 Ves 1 at 17.
6   *Wallis v Crimes* (1667) 1 Cas in Ch 89; *Priestley v Holgate* (1857) 3 K & J 286 at 288.
7   *Paine v Hyde* (1841) 4 Beav 468. Where the heir had entered on the failure of the devisee to pay a legacy charged on the land, relief was granted on payment of the legacy by the devisee: *Underwood v Swain* (1649) 1 Rep Ch 161; *Barnardiston v Fane* (1699) 2 Vern 366; *Grimston v Lord Bruce* (1707) 1 Salk 156.
8   *Hayward v Angell* (1683) 1 Vern 222; *Taylor v Popham* (1782) 1 Bro CC 168; *Simpson v Vickers* (1807) 14 Ves 341; *Hollinrake v Lister* (1826) 1 Russ 500.
9   *Perpetual Trustee Co Ltd v Waddell* (1949) 49 SRNSW 266.
10   By payment of interest from the time when the payment should have been made: *Grimston v Lord Bruce* (1707) 1 Salk 156.
11   *Simpson v Vickers* (1807) 14 Ves 341.
12   Thus there is no relief against forfeiture under a condition for marriage with consent: *Dashwood v Lord Bulkeley* (1804) 10 Ves 230 at 239; *Clarke v Parker* (1812) 19 Ves 1; nor where the condition forbids the legatee to become a nun: *Re Dickson's Trust, ex p Dickson* (1850) 1 Sim NS 37. This paragraph of the text was referred to in *Re Porter, Logan v Northern Bank Ltd* [1975] NI 157.

CHAPTER 35

Particular conditions

I. RESTRAINT OF MARRIAGE

[35.1]
General points. Conditions in restraint of marriage may be in general or partial restraint thereof, and while the former in general are void, the latter are in general valid.

[35.2]
General restraint of marriage. Although it has been said that all general restraints upon marriage are void by the law and practice of the courts of this country, as being against the policy of the law,[1] yet the better view is that a condition subsequent in a will in restraint of the marriage of a single person is not absolutely but only prima facie void; and, if the intention of the testator is to promote, not celibacy, but some other lawful object, the condition may be valid.[2] A distinction has in this connection been taken between a condition precedent and a condition subsequent.[3] Where a gift of a certain duration is abridged by a condition subsequent in restraint of marriage, the condition is prima facie void and the original gift remains,[4] but property may be given to a person until she marries and when she marries then over and such a condition is valid.[5] A condition of this nature will be supported if the intention of the testator is to protect or to provide for a child of his even though the child be illegitimate.[6] The condition may also be personal to the donee herself as a provision that she marry only a man able to provide for her or to induce the donee to remain single for the benefit of her children.[7] In these cases, however, there is also a distinction between gifts of realty and personalty. In the case of gifts of real estate or legacies charged on real estate, an intention to restrain marriage is not shown by a gift on marriage,[8] but in the case of legacies payable out of personalty or the proceeds of sale of realty such a provision does show an intention to restrain marriage and is consequently void.[9] A distinction must be drawn between a condition against marriage or requiring marriage with a particular person[10] or one of a particular class of persons[11] and gifts where the words relating to marriage merely describe the interest to be taken by the donee.[12] There is no objection to gift to endure so long as the donee remains unmarried for marriage may be made the ground of a gift commencing or ceasing.[13] In such a case the words constitute not a condition but a limitation.[14]

It seems that a general restraint of marriage, subject as above stated, being against public policy, such a condition is void both in gifts of real and personal estate^{15} even where the condition is a condition precedent.^{16} The better view appears to be that such a condition is not within the in terrorem doctrine.^{17}

1   *Godfrey v Hughes* (1847) 1 Rob Eccl 593, but even in this case it was agreed that a gift until marriage is good. It may be, however, that such a condition is always void in the case of a gift of an entailed interest because it is of the nature of the interest that the donee shall marry and have issue: see *Anon* (1574) Jenk 243; but the condition is void for repugnancy rather than illegality. But the fact that different gifts are made on the death of a person married and on his death unmarried may not be a restraint on marriage at all: *Re Fentem, Cockerton v Fentem* [1950] 2 All ER 1073. As to restraint on re-marriage, see para **[35.8]** infra.

2   *Jones v Jones* (1876) 1 QBD 279; *Carrodus v Carrodus* [1913] VLR 1; *Re Haythornwaite's Estate* [1930] 3 DLR 235. In *Re Fentem, Cockerton v Fentem* [1950] 2 All ER 1073, after a life interest to a son, it was provided that, if he had not married, the gift was to become absolute, but, if he had married, there was a gift over to a servant for life, then for charity. It was held that the testatrix had not meant to prevent the son from marrying but merely that, after his death, the property should be dealt with in a particular way and the condition was valid. Where restrictions on persons allowed to reside on the property excluded a husband or issue, the gift was in restraint of marriage and void: *Re Snadden's Will* [1962] VR 571. A condition against re-marriage where the testator knew the beneficiary was a spinster may be construed as a condition against marriage: *Re Fowler* [1963] VR 639.

3   *Morley v Rennoldson* (1843) 2 Hare 570.

4   *Morley v Rennoldson* (1843) 2 Hare 570; *Lloyd v Lloyd* (1852) 2 Sim NS 255. As to condition against re-marriage of widow, see para **[35.8]** infra.

5   *Morley v Rennoldson* (1843) 2 Hare 570; *Godfrey v Hughes* (1847) 1 Rob Eccl 593; *Webb v Grace* (1848) 2 Ph 701.

6   *Potter v Richards* (1855) 24 LJ Ch 488; *Re Hewett, Eldridge v Iles* [1918] 1 Ch 458.

7   *Re Greene, Greene v Kirkwood* [1895] 1 IR 130 at 142; *Re Moore's Trusts, Lewis v Moore* (1906) 96 LT 44. See also *Long v Dennis* (1767) 4 Burr 2052 (not to marry without portion or consent: held condition performed by having portion only without consent).

8   *Jones v Jones* (1876) 1 QBD 279.

9   *Lloyd v Lloyd* (1852) 2 Sim NS 255; *Morley v Rennoldson* (1843) 2 Hare 570; *Bellairs v Bellairs* (1874) LR 18 Eq 510 (mixed fund); *Re Bellamy, Pickard v Holroyd* (1883) 48 LT 212; *Ree Wright, Mott v Issott* [1907] 1 Ch 231.

10 See para **[35.7]** infra.

11 See para **[35.4]** infra.

12 As in the case of gifts ceasing on re-marriage.

13 *Morley v Rennoldson* (1843) 2 Hare 570; *Godfrey v Hughes* (1847) 1 Rob Eccl 593; *Webb v Grace* (1848) 2 Ph 701; *Re Davies, Davies v Public Trustee* [1954] NZLR 520 (gift to daughter so long as she remained unmarried, gift over on marriage: gift to daughter valid: the gift over was vested and took effect in possession on marriage or death of the daughter); *Crown Trust Co v McKenzie* (1958) 66 Man R 294. A person given a gift for life or until remarriage has the ordinary powers of a life tenant and no power to commit waste: *Fullarton v Humble* (1958) 42 MPR 118.

14 *Webb v Grace* (1848) 2 Ph 701; *Heath v Lewis* (1853) 3 De GM & G 954; *Potter v Richards* (1855) 24 LJ Ch 488; *Evans v Rosser (or Rossall)* (1864) 2 Hem & M 190.

15 There seems to be no precise authority on this point.

16 *Keily v Monck* (1795) 3 Ridg Parl Rep 205; *Scott v Tyler* (1788) 2 Bro CC 431; *Younge v Furse* (1857) 8 De GM & G 756.

17 It has been held that these conditions are within the rule in *Marples v Bainbridge* (1816) 1 Madd 590, and *Bellairs v Bellairs* (1874) LR 18 Eq 510, but the better view seems to be that where these conditions are within the rules as stated above, they are to promote celibacy and are against public policy and void on that account. They are not rendered valid by a gift over: *Morley v Rennoldson* (1843) 2 Hare 570; *Lloyd v Lloyd* (1852) 2 Sim NS 255.

[35.3]

General restraint of marriage under a specified and reasonable age. These conditions have always been considered valid and an age as high as 28 has been held to be a reasonable age.^{1} This applies to a simple condition as to the age at which the beneficiary may marry, but where the marriage is to be with consent, any age whatever may be prescribed and the condition is valid.[2]

1   *Younge v Furse* (1857) 8 De GM & G 756; *Stackpole v Beaumont* (1796) 3 Ves 89 at 97.
2   See para **[35.9]** infra.

[35.4]
Condition against marriage with a particular class of persons. These conditions have in general been upheld as being only in partial restraint of marriage, but the condition must not be so framed as to amount in effect to a general restraint of marriage.[1] Thus a condition against marriage with a Scotsman[2], or with a domestic servant[3] or against a person marrying beneath her have been held good.[4] Where the prohibition was against marriage with a New Zealand native it was held that there was not sufficient evidence to prove that the person in question was not a New Zealand native.[5] Where the condition was against marriage with a blood relation, it was held that, since a person could never be certain that he was marrying someone to whom a common ancestor could not be traced, the condition was of a nature as would lead to a total prohibition of marriage and was void though in terms only a partial restraint was imposed.[6] A partial restraint must not be joined with a further condition relating to cohabitation.[7]

1   *Keily v Monck* (1795) 3 Ridg Parl Rep 205 (persons not seised of freehold of £500 yearly value); but cf *Long v Dennis* (1767) 4 Burr 2052 (marriage without a competent fortune, which seems to have been thought partial and valid).
2   *Perrin v Lyon* (1807) 9 East 170.
3   *Jenner v Turner* (1880) 16 Ch D 188.
4   *Re Greene, Greene v Kirkwood* [1895] 1 IR 130.
5   *Armitage v Armitage* (1868) 16 WR 643.
6   *Re Lanyon, Lanyon v Lanyon* [1927] 2 Ch 264; but a condition against marriage with a cousin german has been held good: *Welply v Cormick* (1864) 16 I Ch R 74.
7   *Poole v Bott* (1853) 11 Hare 33 at 39 (condition against marrying or illegally cohabiting with certain cousins and requiring beneficiaries to enter into bond not to do so: the execution of the bonds could not be insisted on and beneficiaries were entitled to their interests).

[35.5]
Condition against marriage with a person of a particular religion. Though there are authorities upholding such conditions, they must now be carefully considered with recent authorities deciding that the court cannot determine what is a person's faith and holding such conditions void for uncertainty.[1] Where, however, there was a condition precedent that a beneficiary should be married to an 'approved wife' the condition was upheld because the phrase was defined and it was provided that in case of doubt or dispute the matter should be determined by a specified individual.[2]

1   See para **[35.29]** infra.
2   *Re Tuck's Settlement Trusts, Public Trustee v Tuck* [1976] Ch 99, [1976] 1 All ER 545 (an 'approved wife' was defined as 'a wife of Jewish blood by one or both of her parents and who has been brought up in and has never departed from and at the date of her marriage continues to worship according to the Jewish faith as to which facts in case of dispute or doubt the decision of the Chief Rabbi in London or either the Portuguese or Anglo-German Community ... shall be conclusive'.

[35.6]
Condition against marriage with a particular person. Such a condition being only in partial restraint of marriage is valid,[1] and, in the case of a gift of personalty, is one of the conditions to which the doctrine of in terrorem applies.[2] There are, however, several ways in which such a condition can be attacked. It may be invalid for uncertainty owing to the imperfect description of the named person[3] or combined with a question of cohabitation into which the court declines to enquire.[4] It may become impossible owing to the death of the named person[5] but not by the marriage of that person to a person other than the beneficiary or by the marriage of the beneficiary to some person other than the named person, for the other party to such a marriage may die before either the named person or the beneficiary is dead so that a marriage in the terms of the condition is possible.[6] Provided the condition is subsequent, as it almost invariably is, the result of such a condition is that if the prohibited marriage is effectively[7] celebrated before the death of the named person or the beneficiary the gift fails, but until the gift so fails the beneficiary is entitled to the income of the gift;[8] and on the death of the person named during the lifetime of the beneficiary without the marriage having taken place,[9] the beneficiary is entitled to the gift according to its terms,[10] and on the death of the beneficiary in the lifetime of the person named without the marriage having taken place, the gift will vest in the persons entitled to it provided it is an interest which does not cease on the death of the beneficiary.[11] Where the beneficiary contracted the forbidden marriage during the testator's lifetime and with his consent, the beneficiary was held to be entitled to the legacy.[12]

1   *Re Bathe, Bathe v Public Trustee* [1925] Ch 377; *Jarvis v Duke* (1681) 1 Vern 19; *Lester v Garland* (1808) 15 Ves 248; *Blake v Jones* (1811) 1 Hud & B 227n.
2   *Marples v Bainbridge* (1816) 1 Madd 590; but the doctrine was not applied to gifts of realty: *Haughton v Haughton* (1824) 1 Mol 611; and possibly not to a mixed gift of personalty and realty: *Duddy v Gresham* (1878) 2 LR IR 442. See para **[34.13]** supra. In the case of real estate a gift to A and the heirs of her body on condition that she marry B gives an estate in special tail to A, the condition operating as a limitation: *Page v Hayward* (1705) 2 Salk 570.
3   *Re Bathe, Bathe v Public Trustee*, supra; where, however, the condition was rendered certain by evidence identifying the person concerned.
4   *W—— v B——* (1849) 11 Beav 621, as explained in *Cooke v Cooke* (1864) 11 Jur NS 533 at 535. This case has, however, been severely criticised.
5   *Re Bathe, Bathe v Public Trustee* [1925] Ch 377.
6   *Randall v Payne* (1779) 1 Bro CC 55. See, however, *Re Sharp, Canty v Sharp* (1904) 4 SRNSW 155.
7   See *Allen v Wood* (1834) 1 Bing NC 8; *Knox v Wells* (1883) 48 LT 655; *Re Boddington, Boddington v Clairat* (1884) 25 Ch D 685; *Re Dewhirst, Flower v Dewhirst* [1948] Ch 198, [1948] 1 All ER 147.
8   *Re Bathe, Bathe v Public Trustee* [1925] Ch 377.
9   See n 7, as to the law requiring an effective marriage.
10 *Collett v Collett* (1866) 35 Beav 312; *Re Greenwood, Goodhart v Woodhead* [1903] 1 Ch 749.
11 *Re Park, Bott v Chester* [1910] 2 Ch 322.
12 *Smith v Cowdery* (1825) 2 Sim & St 358.

[35.7]
Condition for marriage with particular person. This condition has been up held and has been construed as a condition precedent so that on non-compliance the gift fails although there is no gift over.[1] Where the legatee married someone else during the lifetime of the testator with his consent, it was held that the gift

failed.[2] Gifts for marriage with a particular class of persons are mostly concerned with marriage within a particular religion and are mentioned under the heading.[3]

A devise to A if he marries a fit and proper gentlewoman and has issue male to such issue and their male descendants is not upon its true construction a devise on a condition but a limitation in special tail.[4]

1   *Davis v Angel* (1862) 4 De GF & J 524 (where in fact the beneficiary married another in the lifetime of the testator and with his consent, but, the condition being precedent, the consent did not absolve the beneficiary from complying with the condition and the gift failed: in this case the gifts in reversion on the beneficiary's life interest as well as that interest failed); *Kiersey v Flahavan* [1905] 1 IR 45 (where the named person refused to marry the beneficiary: the condition being precedent, the gift failed, but it is in suspense during the joint lives of the parties). See also *Blake v Jones* (1811) 1 Hud & B 227n (where the gift was to two persons provided they married each other which they did).
2   *Davis v Angel* (1862) 4 De GF & J 524.
3   See para **[35.29]** infra.
4   *Pelham-Clinton v Duke of Newcastle* [1903] AC 111.

[35.8]
Conditions against re-marriage. The law has always recognised that a husband has such an interest in his wife's widowhood as to make it lawful for him to impose a condition that any provision made by him shall cease or be diminished on a second or subsequent marriage,[1] and such a condition may be annexed by a wife to a gift in favour of her husband.[2] Further, such a condition may be imposed by anyone, that is by a person who is not the husband or wife of the donee.[3] However, if the gift is of personalty such a condition is a condition in terrorem and is, therefore, invalid if there is no gift over.[4] Cohabitation with a man under an illegal marriage where the man holds himself out as the husband of the beneficiary does not bring the condition into operation.[5] Where a widow had, at the date of the will, secretly re-married but the second husband was out of England, had not been heard of for some years and the widow still passed as such, the gift was held good as the condition was subsequent and the beneficiary had not misrepresented the position in order to induce the testator to make it.[6] To defeat the widow's interest the re-marriage must be an effective re-marriage and, where the second marriage was made the subject of a decree of nullity, it has been held that the marriage must be treated as never having happened and the gift remained.[7] However, the Matrimonial Causes Act 1973, s 16[8] provides that where a decree of nullity of marriage is granted on or after 1 August 1971, on the ground that the marriage is voidable (as distinct from void), the decree operates to annul the marriage 'only as respects any time after the decree has been made absolute, and the marriage shall, notwithstanding the decree, be treated as if it had existed up to that time'. It seems clear therefore that in these circumstances the annulled marriage would no longer be treated as never having happened, and it would follow that in these situations the gift would be lost. Where such a condition is attached to a gift to a spinster, it may amount to a condition against marriage.[9]

1   *Lloyd v Lloyd* (1852) 2 Sim NS 255; *Newton v Marsden* (1862) 2 John & H 356; *Re Power, O'Leary v Power* [1904] St R Qd 93; *Re Heppner, Heppner v Heppner* (1913) 14 SRNSW 173; *Re Bowles' Will, Keam v Bowles* [1921] VLR 506; *Re Muirhead Estate* [1919] 2 WWR 454;

Russell v Durie (1920) 39 NZLR 91; *Re Jackson Estates, Houston v Western Trust Co (No 2)* [1940] 1 WWR 65, and *Re Gilbert* [1959] OWN 294 (where the gift was held absolute but defeasible on re-marriage); *Re Ferguson* [1942] 2 DLR 332, and *Re McLean* [1957] OWN 11 (where the more usual construction was applied making the gift either for life or widowhood); *Re White* [1957] OWN 465 (condition that widow shall not remarry: widow entitled free from the condition); *Stewart v Murdoch* [1969] NI 78.

2   *Allen v Jackson* (1875) 1 Ch D 399; *Re Muirhead Estate* [1919] 2 WWR 454; *Re d'Altroy's Will Trusts, Crane v Lowman* [1968] 1 All ER 181, [1968] 1 WLR 120 (such a gift is capable of taking effect if the widower remarries but has his marriage annulled on the ground of his failure to consummate the marriage).

3   *Evans v Rosser (or Rossall)* (1864) 2 Hem & M 190 (gift to son-in-law, the daughter being dead at date of will, to cease on remarriage); *Allen v Jackson* (1875) 1 Ch D 399.

4   *Marples v Bainbridge* (1816) 1 Madd 590; *Re Pettifer, Pettifer v Pettifer* [1900] WN 182; *Leong v Lim Beng Chye* [1955] AC 648, [1955] 2 All ER 903; *Duddy v Gresham* (1878) 2 LR IR 442 at 466, 467; *Re Schmidt Estate* [1949] 2 WWR 513. Where the gift is one of mixed realty and personalty. and there is no gift over and no trust for conversion, there has been a difference of opinion whether the whole gift is void, as decided in the last three of the authorities cited above, or whether it is void only as to the personalty, see *Reynish v Martin* (1746) 3 Atk 330 at 335, and *Duddy v Gresham* (1878) 2 LR IR 442 at 458; but the modern trend seems to favour the invalidity of the whole gift. As to the conditions in terrorem, see para **[34.13]** supra.

5   *Allen v Wood* (1834) 1 Bing NC 8.

6   *Rishton v Cobb* (1839) 5 My & Cr 145.

7   *Re Dewhirst, Flower v Dewhirst* [1948] Ch 198, [1948] 1 All ER 147 (where the question was left open whether the widow was entitled to recover income accrued during the period of the annulled marriage).

8   27 *Halsbury's Statutes* (4th edn) 947; see *Re Roberts, Roberts v Roberts* [1978] 3 All ER 225, [1978] 1 WLR 653.

9   *Re Fowler* [1963] VR 639.

II.   MARRIAGE WITH CONSENT

[35.9]

Statutory necessity for consent. Many of the cases on this subject were decided when the statute law relating to consent to marriage was different from what it now is. At the present time no one can contract a valid marriage under the age of 16 in any circumstances,[1] and a person under 18 in general requires the consent of parents or guardians unless such consent is dispensed with by an order of the court.[2]

1   Marriage Act 1949, s 2; 27 *Halsbury's Statutes* (4th edn) 626, as amended by the Family Law Reform Act 1969, s 2; 27 *Halsbury's Statutes* (4th edn) 702.

2   Marriage Act 1949, s 3. Where banns are published, there must be dissent. These provisions do not apply to a person who is a widow or widower. As is shown later, where a gift vests at a specified age, the condition is construed as referring only to marriage under that age: see para **[35.14]**, n 1. Though the courts have at times confined consents to marriages at an early age, it is clear that a condition requiring consent is applicable to marriage at any age: *Re Whiting's Settlement, Whiting v De Rutzen* [1905] 1 Ch 96.

[35.10]

Different rules applicable to real and personal property. Different rules are applied on the one hand to freehold land, money charged thereon and money to be laid out in such land, and on the other hand to personal property, money payable out of personal property and the proceeds of sale of land. The condition is one subject to the doctrine of conditions in terrorem, and as this doctrine does

369

not apply to conditions attached to gifts of freehold land,[1] it follows that in the first class of cases mentioned above—that is, gifts of freeholds and gifts treated as such—such a condition is a valid one and must be complied with whether it is a condition precedent or subsequent and whether or not there is a gift over.[2] In the other set of cases—that is, in the case of personal property and property treated as such—with the exception of a few special cases,[3] the condition in the absence of a gift over is treated as a mere idle threat and is not enforceable, with the result that the gift takes effect whether or not it is complied with.[4] Where the gift is charged on both real and personal estate—that is, a mixed fund—the condition is valid so far as the gift is payable out of real estate and void so far as the gift is payable out of personalty.[5]

1   *Duddy v Gresham* (1878) 2 LR Ir 442; *Jenner v Turner* (1880) 16 Ch D 188 at 196; *Reynish v Martin* (1746) 3 Atk 330 (legacy charged on real estate); *Pullen v Ready* (1743) 2 Atk 587 (personalty to be laid out in land).
2   See cases cited in n 1.
3   These are where the condition is a condition precedent and there is a gift over on non-compliance: *Malcolm v O'Callaghan* (1817) 2 Madd 349; *Gardiner v Slater* (1858) 25 Beav 509: but not where condition is on death before twenty-one or marriage with consent: *Gray v Gray* (1889) 23 LR Ir 399; or a mere residuary bequest: *Harvey v Lady Aston* (1737) 1 Atk 361; or by making an alternative gift on marriage without the prescribed consent: *Creagh v Wilson* (1706) 2 Vern 572; *Re Nourse, Hampton v Nourse* [1899] 1 Ch 63 at 71.
4   As to cases on the doctrine of in terrorem, see para **[34.13]** et seq.
5   *Reynish v Martin* (1746) 3 Atk 330 at 335; *Duddy v Gresham* (1878) 2 LR Ir 422 at 458; *Re Pettifer, Pettifer v Pettifer* [1900] WN 182.

[35.11]
Gift over. The effect of a gift over to displace the doctrine of in terrorem and what amounts to a gift over in such cases has already been dealt with in treating of conditions in terrorem.[1] It must be stressed, however, that a gift to take effect on marriage with consent does not take effect until marriage even though the condition of consent is dispensed with as being in terrorem—that is, where the condition is a condition precedent, marriage is essential to the vesting of the gift though consent is not.[2] Where there is a gift over, marriage without the necessary consent will not vest the legacy,[3] but the legatee has his or her whole life during which to fulfil the condition and the legacy is not forfeited by the marriage without consent.[4]

1   See para **[34.13]** et seq.
2   *Underwood v Morris* (1741) 2 Atk 184; *Garbut v Hilton* (1739) 1 Atk 381; *Elton v Elton* (1747) 1 Ves Sen 4; *Gray v Gray* (1889) 23 LR Ir 399.
3   *Harvey v Lady Aston* (1737) 1 Atk 361; *Malcolm v O'Callaghan* (1817) 2 Madd 349; subsequent proceedings (1833) Coop *Temp* Brough 73; *Gardiner v Slater* (1858) 25 Beav 509.
4   *Randal v Payne* (1779) 1 Bro CC 55; *Beaumont v Squire* (1852) 17 QB 905.

[35.12]
Consent of named person. A condition, whether precedent or subsequent, requiring the consent of a named person to a marriage is generally construed as operative only during the life of the named person,[1] and, if that person dies during the life of the testator or before any marriage, the gift takes effect free from the condition in cases where the condition is subsequent.[2] If the named person is the testator, the condition is restricted to marriage during his lifetime[3]

and the consent of the testator in his lifetime satisfies the condition whether it is precedent or subsequent.[4]

1   *Mercer v Hall* (1793) 4 Bro CC 326; *Grant v Dyer* (1813) 2 Dow 73; *Green v Green* (1845) 2 Jo & Lat 529; *Curran v Corbet* [1897] 1 IR 343; *Booth v Meyer* (1877) 38 LT 125. Where a condition subsequent becomes impossible by Act of God, it is dispensed with, or, it seems, for other reasons; see *Watson v National Children's Home* (1995) Times, 31 October.
2   *Peyton v Bury* (1731) 2 P Wms 626; *Aislabie v Rice* (1818) 3 Madd 256; *Collett v Collett* (1866) 35 Beav 312.
3   *Booth v Meyer* (1877) 38 LT 125; *Curran v Corbet* [1897] 1 IR 343.
4   *Tweedale v Tweedale* (1878) 7 Ch D 633; *Re Park, Bott v Chester* [1910] 2 Ch 322; *Re Grove* [1919] 1 Ch 249.

[35.13]
Consent by trustee or guardian. Where the person who is to give the consent is the holder of a certain office, the giving of consent is of a fiduciary nature[1] and is effective so long as any one holds or can be appointed to that office.[2] In the case of executors the consent of those renouncing is not required,[3] and in the case of trustees the consent of all is required unless the will provides otherwise.[4] The court will only interfere if the consent is withheld from a corrupt, vicious, or unreasonable cause,[5] and will exercise the right of the trustee to give or withhold consent where the trustee refuses either to consent or to dissent.[6] In such cases the condition is satisfied by the testator's unqualified[7] previous consent to or subsequent approbation of the marriage.[8] The condition does not apply to the case where the donee marries with the testator's consent or approbation during the testator's lifetime and the other party to the marriage dies before the testator's death,[9] but where the testator's consent is to a marriage to take place after his death, the consent of persons named in the will is necessary.[10] If upon the proper construction of the will the consent of trustees for the time being of a will is a necessary condition of the beneficial enjoyment, the circumstance that a new trustee has a direct interest in refusing consent will make the condition inequitable as a condition precedent.[11]

1   The consent of all is necessary unless the testator provides otherwise: *Clarke v Parker* (1812) 19 Ves 1 at 17, 22; *Goldsmith v Goldsmith* (1815) 19 Ves 368. It seems doubtful whether the consent of the survivor or survivors is sufficient. It has been held that on the death of one the condition becomes void; see *Peyton v Bury* (1731) 2 P Wms 626; *Graydon v Hicks* (1739) 2 Atk 16; and in *Re Wilmot's Trusts* (1864) 10 LT 563, it was held that where one trustee had died and the other had not expressed any decisive opinion, it was no longer of the essence of the beneficial enjoyment that there should be an express consent. In *Mercer v Hall* (1793) 4 Bro CC 326, where the consents of parents was required, an opposite conclusion seems to have been reached, and this point was definitely decided in *Dawson v Oliver-Massey* (1876) 2 Ch D 753, holding that consent of survivor is sufficient. Perhaps the former cases assume that the executors are named persons, so that in a will drafted at the present time with the usual interpretation clause, there would be no question of the consent of the survivor being sufficient.
2   *Re Brown's Will* (1881) 18 Ch D 61; distinguished in *Watson v National Children's Home* (1995) Times, 31 October (impossible condition). Thus where the consent of guardians is required, guardians must be appointed if there are none in existence at the material time.
3   *Worthington v Evans* (1823) 1 Sim & St 165; *Boyce v Corbally* (1834) L & G *temp* Plunk 102; *Ewens v Addison* (1858) 32 LTOS 103. The same rule applies to trustees who disclaim: *White v M'Dermott* (1872) IR 7 CL 1. It has been said that the power of consenting does not pass to the personal representative of a sole or last surviving executor or trustee: per Lord ELDON in *Grant v Dyer* (1813) 2 Dow 73 at 84.
4   See n 1.
5   *Clarke v Parker* (1812) 19 Ves 1 at 18.

6   *Goldsmith v Goldsmith* (1815) 19 Ves 368.
7   See *Lowry v Patterson* (1874) IR 8 Eq 372.
8   *Coventry v Higgins* (1844) 14 Sim 30; *Tweedale v Tweedale* (1878) 7 Ch D 633; *Re Park, Bott
    v Chester* [1910] 2 Ch 322 at 325, 326; *Wheeler v Warner* (1823) 1 Sim & St 304 (subsequent
    approbation).
9   *Crommelin v Crommelin* (1796) 3 Ves 227 (the legatee may then contract a subsequent
    marriage without consent).
10 *Lowry v Patterson* (1874) IR 8 Eq 372.
11 *Re Wilmot's Trusts* (1864) 10 LT 563.

[35.14]

Gift vesting at specified age. Where the gift vests at a specified age, the condition is construed as referring to marriage under that age.[1] There is no such restriction where no age is expressly specified or implied.[2]

1   *Desbody v Boyville* (1729) 2 P Wms 547; *Pullen v Ready* (1743) 2 Atk 587; *Knapp v Noyes*
    (1768) Amb 662; *Laird v Tobin* (1830) 1 Mol 543; *Gray v Gray* (1889) 23 LR Ir 399.
2   *Lloyd v Branton* (1817) 3 Mer 108.

[35.15]

Alternative provision for marriage without consent. Where the will contains alternative gifts, one to be taken on marriage with consent and another to be taken on marriage without such consent, the condition applies only to a first marriage,[1] but the condition must be complied with if the legatee is to take the provision made for her on marriage with consent.[2]

1   *Lowe v Manners* (1822) 5 B & Ald 917.
2   *Holmes v Lysaght* (1733) 2 Bro Parl Cas 261; *Re Nourse, Hampton v Nourse* [1899] 1 Ch 63.

[35.16]

Nature of consent. The consent must be a free consent, and not one wrung from the parent or guardian by the misconduct of one or both of the parties. The consent is a matter of substance and not of form,[1] but where the will prescribes a certain form, the court does not require strict compliance with those provisions, and, if the consent is given substantially, it will not look very minutely at the form in which it is given.[2] Thus the following forms of consent have been held to be sufficient: a general consent, that is a consent for the beneficiary to marry anyone he or she pleases;[3] a consent evidenced by conduct[4] or presumed from the circumstances;[5] a conditional consent where the condition has been afterwards performed;[6] or a subsequent approbation.[7] A consent given unconditionally cannot be withdrawn except on grounds affecting the propriety of the consent.[8]

1   *Re Stephenson's Trusts* (1870) 18 WR 1066; *Dillon v Harris* (1830) 4 Bli NS 321.
2   *Worthington v Evans* (1823) 1 Sim & St 165, and *White v M'Dermott* (1872) IR 7 CL 1
    (consent of non-acting trustees not necessary); *Re Smith, Keeling v Smith* (1890) 44 Ch D 654
    (no particular form prescribed by will: in this case the general position is stated); *Holton v
    Lloyd* (1827) 1 Mol 30 (will requiring written consent, oral consent sufficient).
3   *Mercer v Hall* (1793) 4 Bro CC 326; *Pollock v Croft* (1816) 1 Mer 181.
4   *D'Aguilar v Drinkwater* (1813) 2 Ves & B 225; *Burleton v Humfrey* (1755) Amb 256; *Harvey v
    Lady Aston* (1737) 1 Atk 361.
5   *Re Birch* (1853) 17 Beav 358.
6   *Le Jeune v Budd* (1834) 6 Sim 441; *Re Smith, Keeling v Smith* (1890) 44 Ch D 654. Consent
    once given may not be withdrawn by adding terms which do not go to the propriety of the
    assent: *Dashwood v Lord Bulkeley* (1804) 10 Ves 230.

7   *Burleton v Humfrey* (1755) Amb 256. This, however, is exceptional especially where the vesting of an estate in real property is in question: see *Clarke v Parker* (1812) 19 Ves 1 at 21; *Reynish v Martin* (1746) 3 Atk 330; *Malcolm v O'Callaghan* (1817) 2 Madd 349; *Duffield v Elwes* (1823) 1 Sim & St 239. Subsequent approbation has been held sufficient where a consent in writing is required by the terms of the will; *Worthington v Evans* (1823) 1 Sim & St 165; *Holton v Lloyd* (1827) 1 Mol 30.

8   *Le Jeune v Budd* (1834) 6 Sim 441 at 455; *Lord Strange v Smith* (1755) Amb 263; *Merry v Ryves* (1757) 1 Eden 1; *Dashwood v Lord Bulkeley* (1804) 10 Ves 230 at 242; *Re Brown, Ingall v Brown* [1904] 1 Ch 120, where it is stated that a person *in loco parentis* is justified in altering his mind and withdrawing his consent if circumstances subsequently come to his knowledge which, if known at the time, would have caused the withholding of the consent. This power of retraction, however, is not unlimited and cannot be exercised by mere caprice or without just and exceptional reasons. In this case a mother and her daughter (whose marriage was in question) disagreed about the terms of a settlement and the daughter left the mother's house and married. The mother having originally given her consent, withdrew it immediately before the marriage and it was held that such withdrawal was of no effect in the circumstances and the condition was fulfilled.

[35.17]

Proof of consent. Where the question of consent to a marriage was raised by a beneficiary under a gift over 28 years after the marriage and after the deaths of those to give the consent and of the legatee, due consent to the marriage was presumed.[1] It has been said that a trustee is not bound to show his reason for dissent, but that it rests upon the legatee to show that he has unreasonably withheld his consent.[2]

1   *Re Birch* (1853) 17 Beav 358. Everything is to be presumed to avoid a forfeiture, though in this case the acts of the trustees after the marriage were consistent with consent.
2   *Clarke v Parker* (1812) 19 Ves 1.

III.   RESIDENCE

[35.18]

General points. Conditions relating to residence have to be considered from the following points of view: the construction of the condition as to what amounts to residing or ceasing to reside within the terms of the condition; whether the condition is void for uncertainty; whether it is void as tending to separate husband and wife or parent and child; how far the condition is allowed in the case of women and children.

The effect of the Trusts of Land and Appointment of Trustees Act 1996 (TLATA 1996) on conditions relating to residence can be stated. Although a beneficiary beneficially entitled to an interest in possession in land,[1] subject to a trust of land, is given a statutory right of occupation of that land if certain other conditions are fulfilled,[2] the TLATA 1996 places no constraints on the circumstances in which the beneficiary's interest in possession may come to an end. It is therefore thought that under a trust of land there is no difficulty about a beneficiary's interest being subject to a condition which causes it to come to an end in the event of him giving up residence.[3] But it is thought that any attempt to cause the right of occupation to cease while the interest in possession continued would be ineffectual.[4] As the Settled Land Act 1925 cannot apply to any trust of land created on or after 1 January 1997[5] the Settled Land Act 1925 can no longer operate so as to render ineffective conditions as to residence imposed by such trusts.[6]

1   The phrase 'interest in possession in land' is not defined by the TLATA 1996 but is used in s 19 (power of delegation), s 11 (consultation with beneficiaries) and s 12 (right of occupation).
2   TLATA 1996, s 12; see Vol 2, Part G, para **[246.98]**.
3   See the Form in Vol 2.
4   As being inconsistent with the right of occupation conferred by the TLATA 1996, s 12.
5   By virtue of the TLATA 1996, ss 2(1) and (2).
6   By virtue of the TLATA 1996, ss 2(1) and (2).

[35.19]

Nature of residence required. Where premises were given to a beneficiary 'provided he chooses to reside therein', the condition was held to be satisfied by an intention to reside there.[1] Where a person has several houses in which he can reside, the condition is satisfied by occasional visits and does not entail the beneficiary sleeping there so long as he keeps up an establishment[2] but, in the case of a gift of a single house to a married woman, it is not satisfied by her retaining one room and letting the others although she sleeps in the one room three or four nights a week.[3] The condition is not satisfied by spending one night on the premises and never returning to them.[4] Where a beneficiary left England on account of his military duties, there was no breach of a condition to reside in England[5] and, in the case of such a condition, temporary absence is not a breach,[6] while permanent settlement abroad is obviously so.[7] 'To cease permanently to reside in a house' means to leave it without any intention of returning.[8] To live or reside on premises with another person implies personal association with that person and is not satisfied by the occupation of separate accommodation in the same house,[9] and a reversionary gift dependent on the remainderman living with the tenant for life does not imply that the remainderman had a right to reside in the house irrespective of the wishes of the tenant for life.[10] Where a gift is subject to a condition to occupy a house, personal residence is required and the house cannot be let.[11]

1   *Roe d Sampson v Down* (1787) 2 Chit 529; *Re Down* (1968) 68 DLR (2d) 30 (providing he stays on the farm); *Re McColgan* (1969) 4 DLR (3d) 572 (condition subsequent terminating a beneficiary's interest in a house if 'she is not residing therein personally' was held void for uncertainty).
2   *Walcot v Botfield* (1854) Kay 534 (daily visit, no necessity to sleep on premises); *Wynne v Fletcher* (1857) 24 Beav 430; *Re Moir, Warner v Moir* (1884) 25 Ch D 605 (where a tenant for life spent on the average alternate week-ends in the principal mansion house), but this decision was not followed by the Court of Appeal in *Re Vivian, Vivian v Swansea* (1920) 36 TLR 657, where it was held that personal residence for the minimum period is necessary under such a condition. Where the tenant for life is a minor such conditions are not binding during his minority: *Parry v Roberts* (1871) 25 LT 371; *Partridge v Partridge* [1894] 1 Ch 351.
3   *Re Wright, Mott v Issott* [1907] 1 Ch 231 (this was not a case of a settled estate, but where a leasehold house was devised to trustees upon trust to permit his wife to reside).
4   *Re Doherty, Quinn v Clarke* [1950] NI 83.
5   *Schnell v Tyrrell* (1834) 7 Sim 86. As to not residing in England, see *Re Crumpe, Orpen v Moriarty* [1912] 1 IR 485.
6   *Woods v Townley* (1853) 11 Hare 314.
7   *Woods v Townley* (1853) 11 Hare 314.
8   *Re Coxen, McCallum v Coxen* [1948] Ch 747, [1948] 2 All ER 492; *Re Wilkinson, Page v Public Trustee* [1926] Ch 842 (no voluntary cesser where matrimonial home of married woman is changed).
9   *Re Paskins' Will Trusts, Paskins v Underwood* [1948] 2 All ER 156.

10   *Re Paskins' Will Trusts, Paskins v Underwood* [1948] 2 All ER 156.
11   *Maclaren v Stainton* (1858) 27 LJ Ch 442; *Stone v Parker* (1860) 1 Drew & Sm 212; *Re Anderson, Halligey v Kirkley* [1920] 1 Ch 175; *May v May* (1881) 44 LT 412, but see *Mannox v Greener* (1872) LR 14 Eq 456; *Re Stewart, Stewart v Hislop* (1905) 23 NZLR 797; *Macklem v Macklem* (1890) 19 OR 482.

[35.20]
Voluntary and involuntary cesser of residence. It depends upon the terms of the condition whether a cesser of residence incurs a forfeiture of the gift. If the condition is only against voluntary cesser, a cesser by the act of a third party, as on bankruptcy or execution, will not affect the gift, but, unless some such words are included, such cesser causes a forfeiture.[1] Similarly if two persons are to reside together, the death of one does not avoid the gift.[2]

1   *Doe d Duke of Norfolk v Hawke* (1802) 2 East 481; *Doe d Shaw v Steward* (1834) 1 Ad & El 300; *Re Wilkinson, Page v Public Trustee* [1926] Ch 842, but where the beneficiary is old at any rate performance will be relaxed having regard to the age and health of the beneficiary: *Re Veres, Pirot v Veres* [1942] 3 DLR 770.
2   *Sutcliffe v Richardson* (1872) LR 13 Eq 606; but the gift may be void for uncertainty: *Re Crabtree* [1954] VLR 492.

[35.21]
Condition to provide a home. Such a condition is not susceptible of any such clear and definite interpretation as enables the court to say what it means and what obligation it involves and being a condition subsequent is void for uncertainty.[1] In the absence of an express gift over such words are precatory rather than a condition subsequent but on that view they are still ineffective.[2] If the person to provide the home is a tenant for life within the Settled Land Act 1925, the condition is void so far as it prevents the exercise of the statutory power of sale and the property can be sold under the Act.[3]

1   *Re Brace, Gurton v Clements* [1954] 2 All ER 354, [1954] 1 WLR 955; the words concerned in this case were held to be merely precatory and did not impose a condition subsequent. It is suggested in this case that the addition of the words 'free of cost or charge' to the person for whom the home is to be provided may save the condition ([1954] 2 All ER 354 at 359).
2   *Re Brace, Gurton v Clements* [1954] 2 All ER 354, [1954] 1 WLR 955. *National Mutual Trustees Ltd v Gooding* [1990] VR 791, 'provide a home with him for my son while he remains single', void as a condition subsequent, no legally enforceable obligation, words no more than a recommendation, or expression of hope.
3   Settlements of land subject to the Settled Land Act 1996 can no longer be created after 1 January 1997 (see the general points made in para **[35.18]** supra) and so the text refers to existing settlements. As to which see *Richardson, Richardson v Richardson* [1904] 2 Ch 777, and see para **[35.22]** infra. In the Dominions it is not unusual to find a devise made conditional upon the devisee providing a home for the widow or other relative and such conditions have usually been upheld: see *Gill v Gill* (1921) 21 SRNSW 400; *Grant v McLennan* (1866) 16 C & P 395; *Westhaver v Flett* (1917) 51 NSR 235; *McDonald v McLeod* (1921) 54 NSR 379; *Re Hamilton, Hamilton v Hamilton* (1907) 25 NZLR 218; *Re Duncan Estate* (1953) 10 WWRNS 289; *Re Wooddisse* [1943] 3 DLR 385; *Royal Trust Co v Moore* (1955) 16 WWR 204. As to a condition to 'care for' a relative, see *Re Dolebar* [1958] OWN 36.

[35.22]
Uncertainty. On a question of title, a condition to live and reside in a house has been held to be too uncertain and an order for specific performance was made on the ground that no forfeiture had been incurred,[1] but in the case of a tenant for

life of settled property a condition to reside in the mansion house of the estate has been held good[2] and this has been so held where the tenant for life was a female.[3] A condition to pay income so long as the legatee shall continue to reside in Canada has been held uncertain,[4] but a condition not to reside abroad is not too uncertain.[5] A condition for a gift to cease if the beneficiary ceased permanently to reside in a house, being construed to mean the cesser of permanent residence, was not void as uncertain.[6] Similarly, a condition not to cease to make a house the permanent home has been held not to be uncertain.[7] A condition that tenants for life should make the principal house their usual and common place of abode and residence is not void for uncertainty;[8] though a condition for devisees abroad to return to the country of the testator has generally been considered too uncertain to be enforced.[9] It seems that a condition must not use the words 'reside' or 'occupy' simply, for by themselves they are uncertain as it is impossible to say the nature or amount of the residence or occupation which will satisfy such a condition,[10] but the addition of 'permanent' or 'permanently' may save the condition.[11]

1   *Fillingham v Bromley* (1823) Turn & R 530, but this case might not be now followed as such conditions have been in the varying circumstances of cases sometimes held uncertain and sometimes sufficiently certain. In *Perpetual Trustees Executors and Agency Co Ltd v Walker* [1953] ALR 397, a condition for a widow to reside in a specified house was held too uncertain.
2   *Dunne v Dunne* (1855) 7 De GM & G 207, and see cases cited in para [35.19], n 2.
3   *Dunne v Dunne* (1855) 7 De GM & G 207; *Royal Trust Co v Moore* (1955) 16 WWR 204 (where a condition to permit beneficiaries to have the use and enjoyment of certain property as long as either of them should occupy the same was held sufficiently certain).
4   *Sifton v Sifton* [1938] AC 656, [1938] 3 All ER 435; considered in *Re Down* (1968) 68 DLR (2d) 30.
5   *Re Boulter, Capital and Counties Bank v Boulter* [1922] 1 Ch 75. Abroad means anywhere outside the British Isles and now presumably includes the Republic of Ireland. In this case children were to be maintained in England and not to reside abroad and this condition was held to be a condition placed upon the parents and any non-compliance would be non-compliance by the parents; see para [35.23], n 4, and text thereto.
6   *Re Coxen, MacCallum v Coxen* [1948] Ch 747, [1948] 2 All ER 492.
7   *Re Wilkinson, Page v Public Trustee* [1926] Ch 842. But a condition to reside on the devised property for the rest of one's natural life is uncertain: *Re Ross* (1904) 7 OLR 493.
8   *Wynne v Fletcher* (1857) 24 Beav 430.
9   *Re M'Cleary, Moffatt v M'Cleary* [1923] 1 IR 16; *Croskery v Ritchie* [1901] 1 IR 437.
10 *Sifton v Sifton* [1938] AC 656, [1938] 3 All ER 435; *Re Field's Will Trusts, Parry-Jones v Hillman* [1950] Ch 520, [1950] 2 All ER 188.
11 See *Re Coxen, MacCallum v Coxen* [1948] Ch 747, [1948] 2 All ER 492; *Re Gape's Will Trusts* [1952] 2 All ER 579 (permanent residence in England).

[35.23]

Separation of husband and wife. A gift subject to a woman making a house her permanent home and ceasing on her voluntary ceasing to do so is not valid either as being against public policy or as being uncertain, but in the case of a married woman the gift would not be defeated if she, at the injunction of her husband, made some other house the matrimonial home, because the cesser would not then be voluntary.[1] Indeed, in such a case the condition operates only while she is capable of residing, ie while she is a spinster.[2] A condition that a married woman should cease to reside at her husband's place of business has been held void for this reason.[3] Apart from this, however, a clause designed to separate persons other than husband and wife or parent and child is not illegal.[4]

376

1   *Re Wilkinson, Page v Public Trustee* [1926] Ch 842. As to the husband's right to say where a
    matrimonial home shall be, see *Mansey v Mansey* [1940] P 139, [1940] 2 All ER 424; and as to
    agreements to change it, see *King v King* [1942] P 1, [1941] 2 All ER 103.
2   *Re Wright, Mott v Issott* [1907] 1 Ch 231.
3   *Wilkinson v Wilkinson* (1871) LR 12 Eq 604. See para **[35.35]** infra.
4   See *Ridgway v Woodhouse* (1844) 7 Beav 437 (clause designed to separate wife and her sister).

[35.24]

Separation of parent and child. Separation of children from their parents is
against the policy of the law and conditions requiring them to reside away from
one or both have been held to be void.[1]

1   *Re Boulter, Capital and Counties Bank v Boulter* [1922] 1 Ch 75; *Re Morgan, Dowson v Davey*
    (1910) 26 TLR 398 (children to live with mother in case of separation); but a condition for
    separation of an adult from her mother is good: *McDonald v Trustees, Executors and Agency
    Co Ltd* (1902) 28 VLR 442. See para **[36.36]** infra.

[35.25]

Women and children. These conditions are in general inapplicable to minors
and to married women, for in the one case they must live with their parents[1] and
in the other case there is a duty to reside in the matrimonial home[2] and that is
chosen by the husband.[3]

1   Thus a gift over on an infant refusing or neglecting to reside in a house is ineffective while the
    devisee is an infant for he cannot choose to refuse and cannot neglect: *Parry v Roberts* (1871)
    25 LT 371; *Partridge v Partridge* [1894] 1 Ch 351; and see *Re Boulter, Capital and Counties
    Bank v Boulter* [1922] 1 Ch 75; *Re Morgan, Dowson v Davey* (1910) 26 TLR 398.
2   *Re Wilkinson, Page v Public Trustee* [1926] Ch 842.
3   See para **[35.23]**, n 3.

[35.26]

Discharge of condition. If the testator conveys the property away during his
lifetime a condition of residence is dispensed with and a gift of other property,
eg furniture, with a condition of residence in the property, takes effect free from
the condition.[1]

1   *Darley v Langworthy* (1774) 3 Bro Parl Cas 359. See also *Wedgwood v Denton* (1871) LR 12
    Eq 290, where the house to be resided in was leasehold and the testatrix surrendered the lease.
    In this case also the condition of residence was dispensed with and the gift held good.

[35.27]

Ignorance of condition. The ignorance of the condition attached to a gift does
not discharge the beneficiary from the consequences of not complying with it.[1]

1   *Astley v Earl of Essex* (1874) LR 18 Eq 290.

[35.28]

Effect of Settled Land Act 1925. In this connection it is necessary to
distinguish the position before and after 1 January 1997 when the TLATA 1996,
came into force. After that date settlements subject to the Settled Land Act 1925
can no longer be created and so that Act can no longer render ineffective
conditions in trusts created on or after that date.[1] In the case of settlements
existing at and continuing after that date the following propositions apply. A

condition for residence attached to settled land is void so far as it purports, or attempts, or tends, or is intended to prohibit or prevent the tenant for life exercising his statutory powers under the Settled Land Act 1925.[2] A condition for the interest of the tenant for life to cease on his ceasing to reside in the property does not prevent his leaving the property and letting it or selling it under the statutory powers.[3] The condition, however, is void only so far as it is a fetter on the exercise of the statutory powers, and the tenant for life, where the condition is for residence until the statutory powers are exercised, must fulfil the condition[4] and, if he fails to do so, his interest is forfeited.[5] The limitation on the powers of the tenant for life need not be in the settlement itself, but may be in a separate personalty settlement. But for the provision to be void under the Settled Land Act 1925, s 106[6] there must be a benefit for the tenant for life inducing him not to sell the settled property. This is not the case where moneys are provided for the upkeep of the settled property and the application and administration of those moneys are not determined by the tenant for life. Thus where the moneys were to be received by trustees and applied in their absolute discretion to the upkeep of the settled land, the provision was not void under the above section.[7]

1   TLATA 1996, s 2(1) and (2).
2   Settled Land Act 1925, s 106; 48 *Halsbury's Statutes* (4th edn) 406. A condition that a tenant for life during occupation shall be free from all outgoings is not such a condition, though on a sale that benefit would be lost: *Re Simpson, Clarke v Simpson* [1913] 1 Ch 277; *Re Patten, Westminster Bank v Carlyon* [1929] 2 Ch 276; *Re Burden* [1948] Ch 160, [1948] 1 All ER 31 (lump sum vested in trustees for maintenance). In *Re Herbert, Herbert v Lord Bicester* [1946] 1 All ER 421, the life tenant was held entitled to the income of the maintenance fund after sale.
3   *Re Freme, Samuel v Freme* (1912) 56 Sol Jo 362; *Re Patten, Westminster Bank v Carlyon* [1929] 2 Ch 276; *Re Acklom, Oakeshott v Hawkins* [1929] 1 Ch 195. Thus a gift over may be defeated by the exercise of the statutory powers: *Re Paget's Settled Estates* (1885) 30 Ch D 161; *Re Dalrymple, Bircham v Springfield* (1901) 49 WR 627; *Re Adair* [1909] 1 IR 311; *Re Acklom, Oakeshott v Hawkins* [1929] 1 Ch 195; *Re Orlebar, Orlebar v Orlebar* [1936] Ch 147. In *Re Fitzgerald, Brereton v Day* [1902] 1 IR 162, not only the gift over of the house was made void, but also the gift over of the income of a fund also given on condition of residence in that house.
4   *Re Trenchard, Trenchard v Trenchard* [1902] 1 Ch 378; *Re Patten, Westminster Bank v Carlyon* [1929] 2 Ch 276; *Re Bellew, O'Reilly v Bellew* [1924] 1 IR 1.
5   *Re Haynes, Kemp v Haynes* (1887) 37 Ch D 306; *Re Edwards' Settlement* [1897] 2 Ch 412; *Re Trenchard, Trenchard v Trenchard* [1902] 1 Ch 378.
6   48 *Halsbury's Statutes* (4th edn) 406.
7   *Re Aberconway's Settlement Trusts, McLaren v Baron Aberconway* [1953] Ch 647, [1953] 2 All ER 350, following the cases cited in n 2, supra. A gift of a guest-house for life with power to carry on the business subject to permitting a named person to reside therein so long as she shall desire is valid, but the named person can have no interest under the gift if the property is sold either in due course of administration or under the Settled Land Acts: *Re Johnson* [1955] VLR 198.

IV.   RELIGION

[35.29]

Uncertainty. There has been considerable difference of judicial opinion as to whether a requirement that a person be of a particular faith or religion is void for uncertainty. In the House of Lords case of *Clayton v Ramsden*[1] the House were unanimously of the opinion that a condition not to be of 'Jewish parentage' was void for uncertainty and a majority thought likewise of a condition not to be 'of the Jewish faith'.[2] At one time it was thought, following this authority, that a condition subsequent expressed with reference to a particular religion was void for uncertainty.[3] However, *Clayton v Ramsden*[4] has been considered by the House of Lords more recently and, after careful consideration, Lord Wilberforce[5] concluded that the earlier House of Lords decision 'was a particular decision on a condition expressed in a particular way about one kind of religious belief or profession' and that the case did not lay down a new general principle as to the invalidity on grounds of uncertainty of all subsequent conditions whatsoever relating to all varieties of religious belief.

Subsequent cases had in any event limited the decision in *Clayton v Ramsden* to conditions subsequent.[6] Every condition must obviously be considered on its own wording, but the present judicial tendency illustrated by the decisions in *Blathwayt v Lord Cawley*[7] and *Re Tuck's Settlement*[8] seems to be against invalidating religious conditions on the ground of uncertainty. A condition that otherwise might be void for uncertainty can be rendered valid if the resolution of any doubt or dispute is to be determined by the opinion of a third person.[9] Where a convert to a particular religion is received with a particular ceremony, such as baptism or the like, that ceremony is an act which the court can ascertain with certainty and in a proper case the condition is valid.[10]

1   [1943] AC 320, [1943] 1 All ER 16. See also *Re Donn, Donn v Moses* [1944] Ch 8, [1943] 2 All ER 564; *Re Moss's Trusts, Moss v Allen* [1945] 1 All ER 207; *Public Trustee v Gower* [1924] NZLR 1233; *Re Laudry Estate* [1941] 1 WWR 280; *Re Tarnpolsk, Barclays Bank Ltd v Hyer* [1958] 3 All ER 479, [1958] 1 WLR 1157.
2   Lord Wright took the opposite view—as had Lord Greene MR delivering the judgment of the Court of Appeal: [1941] 3 All ER 196. Lord Cross agreed with Lord Wright in *Blathwayt v Lord Cawley* [1976] AC 397 at 429, [1975] 3 All ER 625 at 639. In *Re Tepper's Will Trusts* [1987] Ch 358, [1987] 1 All ER 970 a condition subsequent forfeiting the interests of beneficiaries who remained outside 'the Jewish faith' was held (in the absence of admissible evidence of the Jewish faith as practised by the testator and his family) to be void for uncertainty; the proceedings were adjourned to enable such evidence to be filed: *Re Tuck's Settlement Trusts* [1978] Ch 49, [1978] 1 All ER 1047 applied. See para **[34.9]** ante.
3   See the fourth edition of this book, at p 305.
4   *Re Samuel, Jacobs v Ramsden* [1941] Ch 1.
5   *Blathwayt v Lord Cawley* [1976] AC 397 at 425, [1975] 3 All ER 625 at 636.
6   *Re Allen, Faith v Allen* [1953] Ch 810, [1953] 2 All ER 898; *Re Selby's Will Trusts, Donn v Selby* [1965] 3 All ER 386, [1966] 1 WLR 43; *Re Tuck's Settlement Trusts* [1978] Ch 49, [1978] 1 All ER 1047 (where Lord Denning MR criticised the distinction in approach to conditions subsequent on the one hand and conditions precedent on the other). See also *Re Barlow's Will Trusts* [1979] 1 All ER 296, [1979] 1 WLR 278.
7   See n 5 supra.
8   See n 6 supra.
9   *Re Tuck's Settlement Trusts* [1978] Ch 49, [1978] 1 All ER 1047, which provided in effect that the Chief Rabbi should decide whether a wife was of 'Jewish blood' and had been brought up 'according to the Jewish faith'. The argument, based on the decisions in *Re Coxen* [1948] 1 Ch 747 at 761, 762, [1948] 2 All ER 492 at 502, and *Re Jones, Midland Bank Executor and Trustee Co Ltd v Jones* [1953] Ch 125, [1953] 1 All ER 357, that if the words were not clear enough for the court they were not clear enough for the Rabbi either, was rejected by Lord Denning MR. As Eveleigh LJ put it, the Chief Rabbi knew what he meant by 'Jewish faith' and the testator had said that he meant the same thing. *Id certum est.* Furthermore, such a direction by the testator or settlor did not oust the jurisdiction of the court, for if the appointed third party found difficulty in interpreting the will or settlement the executors or trustees could apply to the court for directions to assist him in his interpretation. The evidence point was applied in *Re Tepper's Will Trusts* [1987] Ch 358, [1987] 1 All ER 970, where the judge was prepared to hear evidence as to how the testator practised his faith, thus showing what he meant by 'Jewish faith'.
10   *Re Evans, Hewitt v Edwards* [1940] Ch 629.

[35.30]

Roman Catholics. A forfeiture clause to operate should a beneficiary 'be or become a Roman Catholic' has recently been held to be not void for uncertainty, and the court after reviewing the cases concluded that the balance of authority was strongly in favour of validity.[1] Nor, despite the Race Relations Act 1968, was the clause void for public policy.[2] A condition against entering a convent or associating with Roman Catholics is good and, on entry into a Roman Catholic convent, the interest of the legatee ceases as from the time of entry,[3] but where the gift is absolute in the first instance, a condition cutting down the gift on embracing a religious life has been held repugnant to the absolute gift and void.[4] A condition against joining a religious society to which the legatee would be under an obligation to give his or her property is good, but where the society requires only that its members shall give to the society the income of their property and leaves them free to dispose of the capital there is no breach.[5] A condition not to become or marry a Roman Catholic is good, but this condition may upon its proper construction be confined to breaches before the death of the testator.[6] A gift to grandchildren who were Roman Catholics and not married to Protestants has been upheld as sufficiently certain,[7] and a condition not to marry a Roman Catholic or the child of Roman Catholic parents or parent or a scholar of a Roman Catholic school or institution was held sufficiently certain and a condition precedent.[8] Conditions requiring a child to be educated in the Roman Catholic faith or requiring a child not to be educated in a Roman Catholic school have been held bad as a fetter on the parent's right to choose the education he thinks best for a child.[9] However to say that any condition is void which in any way might affect or influence the way in which a child is brought up, or in which parental duties are exercised is to state the rule too widely.[10] A condition requiring a minor to be or become or cease to be a Roman Catholic does not in general become operative until he attains the age of 18,[11] but on attaining full age the condition has been held good.[12]

1 *Blathwayt v Lord Cawley* [1975] 3 All ER 625 at 635, distinguishing *Clayton v Ramsden* [1943] AC 320, [1943] 1 All ER 16.
2 *Blathwayt v Lord Cawley* [1975] 3 All ER 625 at 635, distinguishing *Clayton v Ramsden* [1943] AC 320, [1943] 1 All ER 16. See now the Race Relations Act 1976; 7 *Halsbury's Statutes* (4th edn, 1999 Reissue) 115.
3 *Re Dickson's Trust, ex p Dickson* (1850) 1 Sim NS 37; *Wainwright v Miller* [1897] 2 Ch 255. Entering a convent means taking final vows and no forfeiture is incurred by becoming a novice or a postulant, still less by being a boarder in a convent school: *Re Madore Estate* [1936] NLR 215; *Maguire v Boylan* (1870) 5 IR Eq 90.
4 *Re Thompson, Griffith v Thompson* (1896) 44 WR 582.
5 *Re Bell, Bell v Agnew* (1931) 47 TLR 401.
6 *Re Wright, Public Trustee v Wright* (1937) 158 LT 368; *Re Morrison's Will Trusts, Walsingham v Blathwayt* [1940] Ch 102, [1939] 4 All ER 332. Where the ban was on those who 'will have become or become a Roman Catholic or marry or shall have married a Roman Catholic', it applied only to those who became or married Roman Catholics before the testator's death: *Re Wright, Public Trustee v Wright* (1937) 158 LT 368. Cf *Saywell v Saywell* (1932) 32 SRNSW 155. The marriage may, on the construction of the whole will, be confined to marriage during infancy: *Duggan v Kelly* (1848) 10 I Eq R 473; *Re McKenna, Higgins v Bank of Ireland* [1947] IR 277. In *Re Morrison's Will Trusts, Walsingham v Blathwayt* [1940] Ch 102, [1939] 4 All ER 332, the will expressly provided that the condition was to apply during the lifetime of the testatrix and after her death and it was decided that on the life tenant becoming a Roman Catholic, not only her interest ceased, but that of a child of hers who had become a Roman Catholic and also those of two other children who had not become Roman Catholics. In *Re*

Evans, Hewitt v Edwards [1940] Ch 629, any child or grandchild who at any time became a convert to the Roman Catholic religion was ipso facto to forfeit the right to any income or capital of the estate. The words ipso facto showed that the person forfeiting must have a right at the time of becoming a Roman Catholic; the clause applied only after the death of the testator and the beneficiaries having been baptised in that church before the testator's death did not forfeit their interests under the will. Such a condition has, however, been held to operate to restrain parents from doing their duty in the matter of religious instruction of their children and on that ground to be void: *Re Borwick, Borwick v Borwick* [1933] Ch 657; and see *Re AT St George, Perpetual Trustee Co Ltd v St George* [1964] NSWR 587. In *Re Orr* [1940] SASR 395, this condition was held void for uncertainty, and such a condition may now be subject to the decision in *Clayton v Ramsden* [1943] AC 320; and see *Re Borwick, Borwick v Borwick*, supra. In *Grayson v Grayson* [1922] St R Qd 155, and *Re Found, Semmens v Loveday* [1924] SASR 301, such a condition had been held good, and in the last case it was held immaterial that the wife had changed her religion after marriage. A condition against ceasing to practise the Roman Catholic religion has been held uncertain: *Burke and O'Reilly v Burke and Quail* [1951] IR 216.

7   *Re Kearney* [1957] VLR 56.
8   *Re Whiting* [1957] VLR 400.
9   *Re Borwick, Borwick v Borwick* [1933] Ch 657; *Re Tegg, Public Trustee v Bryant* [1936] 2 All ER 878; *National Trustees, Executors and Agency Co Ltd v Keast* (1896) 22 VLR 447; *Birtwhistle v Myers* (1899) 25 VLR 306. As to a condition requiring a child to be educated for the priesthood, see *Re Regan* (1957) 8 DLR (2d) 541.
10 *Blathwayt v Lord Cawley* [1975] 3 All ER 625 at 637.
11 *Re May, Eggar v May* [1917] 2 Ch 126; *Patton v Toronto General Trusts Corpn* [1930] AC 629.
12 *Re May, Eggar v May* [1932] 1 Ch 99.

[35.31]
Jewish religion. A condition that a beneficiary should be of the Jewish faith and married to an 'approved wife', who was to be of Jewish blood and worship according to the Jewish faith, has been upheld.[1] A condition against marriage out of the Jewish religion is not void as against public policy,[2] but may be void for uncertainty[3] or as contravening the rule against perpetuities.[4] Where a beneficiary was to forfeit the benefit on marriage with a person not of Jewish parentage and of the Jewish faith it was held that this was only one condition of forfeiture and not two alternative conditions, and the whole would be void if one limb of the condition was void; in this case both limbs were void for uncertainty.[5] Where a daughter was married to a Jew and was not to take until she ceased to be the wife of a Jew, the condition was held void.[6]

1   *Re Tuck's Settlement Trusts, Public Trustee v Tuck* [1978] 1 All ER 1047; the relevant clause is set out supra at para **[35.8]**, n 2. See also *Re Tepper's Will Trusts, Kramer v Ruda* [1987] Ch 358, [1987] 1 All ER 970, discussed para **[35.29]** supra.
2   *Hodgson v Halford* (1879) 11 Ch 959; *Re Moss, Fox v Moss* [1919] VLR 192. It is, however, a condition in terrorem and in the absence of a gift over is ineffective: *Re Berens* (1888) 5 TLR 473.
3   *Re Blaiberg, Blaiberg and Public Trustee v De Andia Yrarrazaval and Blaiberg* [1940] Ch 385, [1940] 1 All ER 632; *Clayton v Ramsden* [1943] AC 320, [1943] 1 All ER 16; *Re Donn, Donn v Moses* [1944] Ch 8, [1943] 2 All ER 564; *Re Moss's Trusts, Moss v Allen* [1945] 1 All ER 207; *Re Tarnpolsk, Barclays Bank Ltd v Hyer* [1958] 3 All ER 479; *Re Krawitz's Will Trusts, Krawitz v Crawford* [1959] 3 All ER 793; *Re Selby's Will Trusts, Donn v Selby* [1965] 3 All ER 386 (where the condition was held valid); *Re Solomon, Solomon v Solomon* [1946] ALR 195; *Perpetual Trustee Co Ltd v Wansey* (1945) 46 SRNSW 226; *Re Abraham's Will Trusts, Caplan v Abrahams* [1969] 1 Ch 463, [1967] 2 All ER 1175 (condition precedent as to marriage to a person professing the Jewish faith is sufficiently certain).
4   See para **[35.52]**, n 4.

5   *Clayton v Ramsden* [1943] AC 320, [1943] 1 All ER 16. But see now *Re Tuck's Settlement Trusts, Public Trustee v Tuck* [1978] 1 All ER 1047; and *Blathwayt v Lord Cawley* [1975] 3 All ER 625.
6   *Re Hurshman* (1956) 6 DLR 615.

[35.32]

Church of England. A condition to conform to and be members of the Church of England is not void for uncertainty.[1] A condition to be a member of the Church of England and an adherent to the doctrine of that church is not void for uncertainty where it is a qualification or limitation or condition precedent and, where it is a condition precedent, it is open to the beneficiary to prove that he is a member of that church and to prove his adherence to the doctrine of that church.[2] Where a will provided for payment of legacies at 25 years and that they should not be paid until the legatees had been confirmed as members of the Church of England, and included a gift over in the case of legatees who attained 25 without having been so confirmed, it was held that the condition was a condition precedent, and, even if it were a condition subsequent, it was not against public policy or void as being impossible of performance.[3] A condition that certain legacies for Church of England missions should be void if a particular person was employed by or held Holy Orders in the Church of England has been held valid and not against public policy.[4]

1   *Re Mills' Will Trusts, Yorkshire Insurance Co Ltd v Coward* [1967] 2 All ER 193, [1967] 1 WLR 837 (proviso that if a grandchild should not be a 'member of the Church of England or of some Church abroad professing the same tenets' then share to be forfeited; held, the description was not void for uncertainty since the tenets of the Church of England, being part of the law of England by virtue of the Act of Uniformity 1662, were not uncertain. The Methodist Church of Australia was not within this definition. But see *Re Tegg, Public Trustee v Bryant* [1936] 2 All ER 878, where a similar condition was void for uncertainty since it was open to grave doubts whether any particular act or omission in the future would bring about a forfeiture; *Clavering v Ellison* (1859) 7 HL Cas 707 (educated in England and in the Protestant faith according to the rites of the Church of England, but in this case it was only held that the condition was to be construed strictly).
2   *Re Allen, Faith v Allen* [1953] Ch 810, [1953] 2 All ER 898; *Re Mills' Will Trusts, Yorkshire Insurance Co Ltd v Coward* [1967] 2 All ER 193, [1967] 1 WLR 837. See also *Re Cowley* [1971] NZLR 468.
3   *Re Forbes, Harrison v Commis* [1928] 3 DLR 22. In this case it was also held that a legatee who was so confirmed at the age of thirty-one had not substantially complied with the condition.
4   *Re Rice, Turner v Rice* [1920] VLR 44.

[35.33]

Protestant faith. A condition that children shall be brought up in the Protestant faith is void both as being uncertain and as interfering with the duty of the parent to bring children up in such religion as he deems best for their moral and spiritual welfare.[1] A condition precedent that a minor shall be educated in the Protestant faith and power given to trustees of the will to determine in their absolute discretion whether or not that is so does not prevent the trustees contributing to the cost of such education during the contingency of the gift, for it is still possible that the condition might be fulfilled.[2] Where the condition is a condition precedent and has not been complied with, it is immaterial to inquire whether or not it is a valid condition.[3] A condition that a legatee should marry a Protestant wife, the daughter of Protestant parents, has been held good,[4] but this might now perhaps be held uncertain.[5] 'Protestant' means a church or sect separated from the Roman Communion in the sixteenth century or the subsequent offshoots of any such sect which professes Christianity.[6]

1   *Clavering v Ellison* (1859) 7 HL Cas 707; *Re Cross, Law v Cross* [1938] VLR 221; *Perpetual Trustee Co v Hogg* (1936) 36 SRNSW 61.
2   *Re Mercer* [1953] OWN 765.
3   *Re Going* [1951] 2 DLR 136.
4   *Re Knox's Goods* (1889) 23 LR Ir 542; *Mainwaring v Mainwaring* (1923) 23 SRNSW 531.
5   See *Clayton v Ramsden* [1943] AC 320. In Australia a condition for forfeiture on marrying anyone not of the Protestant religion or following any religion other than the Protestant religion has been held to be two independent conditions. The first was held certain and valid but the second is uncertain and void: *Re Winzar* (1953) 55 WALR 35.
6   *Re Winzar* (1953) 55 WALR 35.

[35.34]
Conditions as to solemnisation of marriage. A condition that marriages of legatees should be solemnised according to the rites of any church recognised by the local law has been held a valid condition,[1] and so was a condition forbidding marriage contrary to the order and established rules of the people called Quakers.[2]

1   *Renaud v Lamothe* (1902) 32 SCR 357. This will also directed that the children of any such marriage should be educated according to the teachings of such church and this condition was held good, but at the present time this condition would probably be held invalid as against the rights of parents in this respect.
2   *Haughton v Haughton* (1824) 1 Mol 611.

V.   SEPARATION OF HUSBAND AND WIFE

[35.35]
Generally invalid. A condition that a married woman shall live apart from her husband is void as contrary to public policy[1] and any condition contemplating a voluntary separation of husband and wife is void for this reason;[2] but a trust for a wife so long as she shall cohabit with her present husband is valid[3], and so is a gift to a husband to vest indefeasibly at 35 years of age if he is then living amicably with his wife.[4] At one time a condition that an annuity given to a married woman separated from her husband at the date of the will was to cease on a return to cohabitation was held void,[5] but more recently the condition has been held good, partly on the ground that it is a limitation rather than a condition, and partly on the ground that it is intended to provide for her until she returns to her husband.[6] Where a will provides for an increase in benefit on the break-up of a marriage it should be treated as providing for the larger benefit with a provision cutting it down so long as the marriage endures, which is then struck out as contrary to public policy, so that the larger benefit is payable throughout.[7] But a similar gift to a son has been held to invade the sanctity of the marriage bond and to be invalid.[8] A provision for a daughter on the contingency of her being divorced by her husband is not against public policy.[9] A condition that a wife shall not reside at her husband's place of business is bad as tending to separate the spouses.[10] Apparently a provision for the separation of beneficiaries

383

or other persons who are not either husband and wife or parent and child is unobjectionable and valid.[11]

1 *Brown v Peck* (1758) 1 Eden 140; *Re Anderson* [1908] VLR 593; *Re Hepplewhite's Will Trusts* (1977) Times, 21 January.
2 *H v W* (1857) 3 K & J 382.
3 *Re Hope Johnstone, Hope Johnstone v Hope Johnstone* [1904] 1 Ch 470; and in *Re Ramsay* [1948] VLR 347, a gift to a husband of income so long as the marriage subsisted and on its termination the capital to vest in him absolutely was held good.
4 *Re Jones, Royal Trust Co v Jones (No 2)* (1934) 49 BCR 204.
5 *Wren v Bradley* (1848) 2 De G & Sm 49; *Bean v Griffiths* (1855) 1 Jur NS 1045.
6 *Re Moore, Trafford v Maconochie* (1888) 39 Ch D 116, and *Re Lovell, Sparks v Southall* [1920] 1 Ch 122 (where it was held to be a limitation); *Re Charleton, Bracey v Sherwin* (1911) 55 Sol Jo 330 (where the wife was already deserted by her husband at the date of the will); *Shewell v Dwarris* (1858) John 172 (where the condition merely referred to the state of the parties existing at the testator's death and could not influence the conduct of the parties in question).
7 *Re Johnson's Will Trusts, National Provincial Bank v Jeffrey* [1967] Ch 387, [1967] 1 All ER 553; not following *Re Thompson, Lloyds Bank Ltd v George* [1939] 1 All ER 681 (object not to separate spouses, but to keep funds out of husband's hands); *Re Lovell, Sparks v Southall* [1920] 1 Ch 122 distinguished.
8 *Re Caborne, Hodge and Nabarro v Smith* [1943] Ch 224, [1943] 2 All ER 7 (gift invalid as tending to invade the sanctity of the marriage bond), followed in *Re Johnson's Will Trusts, National Provincial Bank Ltd v Jeffrey* [1967] Ch 387, [1967] 1 All ER 553.
9 *Wacker v Bullock* [1935] NZLR 828.
10 *Wilkinson v Wilkinson* (1871) LR 12 Eq 604.
11 *Ridgway v Woodhouse* (1844) 7 Beav 437 (separation of sisters).

VI.   SEPARATION OF PARENT AND CHILD AND RESTRAINING PERFORMANCE OF PARENTAL DUTIES

[35.36]

Generally invalid. Conditions tending to the separation of parent and child are invalid as against public policy.[1] Where a testator whose daughter was living separate from her husband restricted the benefit to such of the daughter's children as should reside with her, the condition was unenforceable and the children were entitled in any event.[2] Similarly a condition not to live with or be under the control of a father is void.[3] Conditions requiring either parents or children to reside in a certain place or country may, if they entail such separation, be void.[4] It is unlikely that conditions would be void under this head as hindering or preventing the parent in the choice or supervision of the child's education. Thus a request for the benefit of a child to help with paying his school fees payable on condition of his going to a particular school, would be upheld.[5] Likewise a bequest on condition of his not going to a particular type of school, ought not to be contrary to public policy.[6] The same approach would apply to a requirement that a child be educated in a religious denominational school.[7] In special circumstances a condition that a father should not interfere with the education of his children was enforced.[8]

1 *Re Sandbrook, Noel v Sandbrook* [1912] 2 Ch 471; *Re Ellis, Perpetual Trustee Co Ltd v Ellis* (1929) 29 SRNSW 470; but a condition that an adult child shall not live with her mother has been held good: *McDonald v Trustees, Executors and Agency Co Ltd* (1902) 28 VLR 442.
2 *Re Morgan, Dowson v Davey* (1910) 26 TLR 398.
3 *Re Sandbrook, Noel v Sandbrook* [1912] 2 Ch 471; *Re Piper, Dodd v Piper* [1946] 2 All ER 503 (where the father was already divorced).

4   *Re Boulter, Capital and Counties Bank v Boulter* [1922] 1 Ch 75.
5   *Blathwayt v Lord Cawley* [1976] AC 397, [1975] 3 All ER 625, per Lord Cross at 644, and
    Lord Fraser at 650.
6   *Blathwayt v Lord Cawley* [1976] AC 397, [1975] 3 All ER 625, per Lord Cross at 644, and
    Lord Fraser at 650.
7   *Blathwayt v Lord Cawley* [1976] AC 397, [1975] 3 All ER 625, not following *Re Borwick,
    Borwick v Borwick* [1933] Ch 657; and *Re Tegg, Public Trustee v Bryant* [1936] 2 All ER 878.
8   *Colston v Morris* (1821) Jac 257n. It appeared that the parents were separated and the father a
    man of small means compared with the mother. The legacy was given by the grandfather and
    the trustees of the will were appointed guardians of the infant.

VII.   CONDITIONS AGAINST ALIENATION

[35.37]
These conditions are dealt with in the consideration of forfeiture on alienation.[1]

1   See Chapter 99.

VIII.   NOT TO DISPUTE WILL

[35.38]
Beneficiary's rights protected. A condition not to dispute a will is not void for
uncertainty, nor as being contrary to good morals or public policy, nor
prohibited by any positive law,[1] but, on the other hand, it is not broken if the
proceedings taken by the legatee are necessary for the protection of his rights.[2]
Proceedings for the revocation of probate are a breach[3] and so presumably are
frivolous proceedings.[4] Such a condition is a condition in terrorem and in the
case of personalty is void unless there is a gift over.[5]
Where, however, the clause attempts to oust the jurisdiction of the court, it is
both repugnant and contrary to public policy.[6] Thus a clause making the
trustees' decision final and binding upon all questions of doubt arising in the
execution of the trusts of the will is invalid,[7] and so is a clause which makes the
trustees' decision final as to the identity of a beneficiary.[8]

1   *Evanturel v Evanturel* (1874) LR 6 PC 1; *Cooke v Turner* (1846) 15 M & W 727; *Stevenson v
    Abington* (1863) 9 LT 74.
2   *Powell v Morgan* (1688) 2 Vern 90; *Rhodes v Muswell Hill Land Co* (1861) 29 Beav 560;
    Warbrick v Varley (No 2) (1861) 30 Beav 347; *Phillips v Phillips* [1877] WN 260; *Wallace v
    Wallace* (1898) 24 VLR 859; *Re Kent* (1982) 139 DLR (3d) 318.
3   *Stevenson v Abington* (1863) 9 LT 74.
4   *Nutt v Burrell* (1724) Cas *temp* King 1; *Adams v Adams* [1892] 1 Ch 369. This was a gift of an
    annuity with a proviso for cesser if the annuitant should in any way intermeddle or interfere or
    attempt to intermeddle or interfere in the management of the estate. The annuitant brought a
    frivolous action against the trustees for a receiver. This was an attempt to interfere and caused
    the annuity to cease, but an action in defence of the annuity, it was said, would not have been
    within the proviso.
5   *Morris v Burroughs* (1737) 1 Atk 399; *Lloyd and Jobson v Spillet* (1741) 2 Atk 148; *Warbrick v
    Varley (No 2)* (1861) 30 Beav 347; *Re Gaynor's Will* [1960] VLR 640 (where an application
    made under the Family Maintenance Acts was held to be in order as the condition was void). As
    to conditions in terrorem, see para **[34.13]** supra.
6   *Re Raven* [1915] 1 Ch 673; *Re Wynn* [1952] Ch 271, [1952] 1 All ER 341.
7   *Re Wynn* [1952] Ch 271, [1952] 1 All ER 341.

8   *Re Raven* [1915] 1 Ch 673. But where the executors had a discretion to withhold a gift if they were satisfied that a hospital had been taken over by the state or a local authority, their decision was final so long as it was arrived at reasonably and honestly; *Dundee General Hospital v Walker* [1952] 1 All ER 896.

IX.   NAME AND ARMS CLAUSE

[35.39]
On whom clause binding. A name and arms clause indicates the persons on whom the obligation is binding, and here the word 'entitled' means entitled in possession and not in interest to the rents and profits of the property.[1] A person is entitled in possession, however, although at the time there are no rents to receive.[2] Where the beneficiary was given the income of a trust fund to be met out of residue, such beneficiary, although he assumed the name, was not entitled to the income until the fund was set apart nor was he entitled to arrears or accumulations of income from the death of the testator.[3] The condition is not a condition precedent for it cannot be complied with instantly.[4] If a reasonable time is not specified in the condition, it must be allowed for[5] or the condition may be void as transgressing the rule against perpetuities.[6] Where the beneficiary is a minor the condition is usually drafted to require compliance only on attaining full age. Where the clause is not so drafted, a minor who does not assume the name cannot be said to neglect or refuse to do so.[7] Similarly where the beneficiary neglects to assume the name through ignorance of the condition, there is no forfeiture.[8] The general principle is that a breach of the condition is dependent upon its wording. If the condition is to take effect if the donee 'omit' or 'fail' to take the name and arms, every case of non-compliance is a breach.[9] The word 'refuse', however, if introduced into the condition, implies a conscious act of volition, so that ignorance of the condition or disability is an excuse for non-compliance.[10] 'Neglect', when used alone, prima facie covers only omissions which are negligent,[11] but when used in certain contexts it may mean no more than 'fail'.[12] The expression 'neglect or refuse', however, implies a conscious act of volition.[13] In these cases where there is a time limit for the assumption of name or arms or both, and the words of the condition require a conscious act of volition, the condition becomes ineffective on the lapse of the specified period in the case of ignorance or minority.[14] It must be remembered, however, that this is in the nature of a benevolent modification of the general rule, which is that ignorance on the part of the beneficiary is no excuse for failure to comply and the beneficiary is not entitled to any notice of the condition in the will.[15]

1   *Lady Langdale v Briggs* (1856) 8 De GM & G 391; *Abbiss v Burney Re Finch,* (1880) 17 Ch D 211; *Re Greenwood, Goodhart v Woodhead* [1903] 1 Ch 749. Generally 'entitled' in a shifting clause means entitled in possession and beneficially: *Chorley v Loveband* (1863) 33 Beav 189; *Umbers v Jaggard* (1870) LR 9 Eq 200. A person is not so entitled by being entitled in remainder for a life interest (*Monypenny v Dering* (1852) 2 De GM & G 145; *Curzon v Curzon* (1859) 1 Giff 248), or in tail (*Bagot v Legge* (1864) 4 New Rep 492), nor by possession as a purchaser for value, a mortgagee, a tenant from year to year, a lessee, a judgment creditor or tenant by elegit (*Taylor v Earl of Harewood* (1844) 3 Hare 372), nor by a release by life tenant where the beneficiary is to be entitled under the limitations of the settlement (*Re Petre's Settlement* [1910] 1 Ch 290; *Re Howard's Will Trusts* [1961] 2 All ER 413). Where trustees are

entitled to manage the estate for an infant, the infant is not in possession under a shifting clause: *Leslie v Earl of Rothes* [1894] 2 Ch 499; *Re Hinckes, Dashwood v Hinckes* [1921] 1 Ch 475.

2   *Re Varley, Thornton v Varley* (1893) 62 LJ Ch 652 (where the rents went in satisfaction of charges on the property).

3   *Re Leslie* [1954] OWN 472.

4   *Gulliver d Corrie v Ashby* (1766) 4 Burr 1929; *Vandeleur v Sloane* [1919] 1 IR 116; *Woodhouse v Herrick* (1855) 1 K & J 352.

5   *Davies v Lowndes* (1835) 1 Bing NC 597.

6   *Bennett v Bennett* (1864) 2 Drew & Sm 266; *Re Fry, Reynolds v Denne* [1945] Ch 348, [1945] 2 All ER 205.

7   *Re Edwards, Lloyd v Boyes* [1910] 1 Ch 541; *Re Quintin Dick, Lord Cloncurry v Fenton* [1926] Ch 992. The clause or condition is usually worded so as not to require compliance while the beneficiary is under the age of majority but, where the condition is construed as a condition precedent (which is exceptional), a minor it seems might incur a forfeiture on mere non-compliance: *Bevan v Mahon-Hagan* (1893) 31 LR Ir 342, and see *Whittingham's Case* (1603) 8 Co Rep 42b at 44b.

8   *Re Hughes, Rea v Black* [1943] Ch 296, [1943] 2 All ER 269.

9   *Astley v Earl of Essex* (1874) LR 18 Eq 290; *Re Quintin Dick, Lord Cloncurry v Fenton* [1926] Ch 992; and cf *Partridge v Partridge* [1894] 1 Ch 351.

10 *Doe d Kenrick v Lord Beauclerk* (1809) 11 East 657 at 657; *Re Quintin Dick, Lord Cloncurry v Fenton* [1926] Ch 992; *Re Hughes, Rea v Black* [1943] Ch 296, [1943] 2 All ER 269. If a person is aware of the condition a refusal need not be express, but may be implied: *Doe d Duke of Norfolk v Hawke* (1802) 2 East 481 at 487.

11 *Re Connington's Will* (1860) 2 LT 535; *Re Quintin Dick, Lord Cloncurry v Fenton* [1926] Ch 992; *Re Hughes, Rea v Black* [1943] Ch 296, [1943] 2 All ER 269.

12 *Hawkes v Baldwin* (1838) 9 Sim 355; *Re Hodge's Legacy* (1873) LR 16 Eq 92; *O'Higgins v Walsh* [1918] 1 IR 126; *Re Quintin Dick, Lord Cloncurry v Fenton* [1926] Ch 992.

13 *Partridge v Partridge* [1894] 1 Ch 351; *Re Edwards, Lloyd v Boyes* [1910] 1 Ch 541; *Re Quintin Dick, Lord Cloncurry v Fenton* [1926] Ch 992.

14 *Re Hughes, Rea v Black* [1943] Ch 296, [1943] 2 All ER 269. In the computation of time, the day of the death of the predecessor in title is not included: *Miller v Wheatley* (1891) 28 LR Ir 144. In the case of a specific devise the time runs from the death of the testator, but in the case of a residuary gift it runs from the completion of the administration: *Re Neeld, Carpenter v Inigo-Jones* [1962] Ch 643, [1962] 2 All ER 335.

15 See para **[34.21]** supra.

[35.40]
Assumption of name. If the condition does not state the method by which the name is to be assumed, a voluntary assumption of the name is sufficient.[1] There seems to have been some difference of opinion as to whether a minor can voluntarily change his name.[2] A minor can change his name by deed poll but, if the minor is not of the age of 16 years, the deed poll must be signed by the guardian on behalf of the minor. After his sixteenth birthday the minor can himself sign or the guardian can sign on his behalf, but if the minor signs, the guardian should witness the signature in order to show his consent.[3] A Christian name, it has been said, cannot be changed by deed poll.[4] If the condition requires the devisee to take the new name for himself and his heirs it has been said that a grant from the Queen or an Act of Parliament is necessary,[5] though changes by deed poll in practice adopt the name for the person executing the deed poll and his minor children (who need not be named in the deed) and, where they are named and execute the deed also for his adult children,[6] the condition as generally drafted requires the beneficiary to 'take and use' the name and this means that the use of the name is to be continued and a discontinuance involves a forfeiture.'[7] A direction for use 'upon all occasions' is not void for uncertainty;[8] nor is such a clause contrary to public policy merely because it is

so drawn as to impose an obligation of change of name on a husband to whom a woman is married or whom she may thereafter marry.[9] The beneficiary is not now usually directed as to how he is to acquire the new name[10] and then all methods of acquiring the new name are open to him.[11]

1   *Doe d Luscombe v Yates* (1822) 5 B & Ald 544; *Davies v Lowndes* (1835) 1 Bing NC 597; *Earl of Cowley v Countess of Cowley* [1901] AC 450; *Re Earl of Midleton's Will Trusts, Whitehead v Earl of Midleton* [1969] 1 Ch 600, [1967] 2 All ER 834 (gift of income to the person who shall succeed to a peerage on the death of the present holder is ineffective since that person cannot be ascertained until such death); *Blathwayt v Lord Cawley* [1976] AC 397, [1975] 3 All ER 625 (where the requirement was 'either with or without his or her own proper surname'). But see *Littras v Littras* [1995] 2 VR 283, where a names clause was regarded as anachronistic and as infringing the right of an individual to use the surname of his own choosing.
2   See *Re Talbot* [1932] IR 714.
3   This is believed to be the practice of the Enrolment Office of the High Court.
4   *Re Parrott, Cox v Parrott* [1946] Ch 183, [1946] 1 All ER 321. But a Christian name may be changed by Act of Parliament or at confirmation, and an additional name may be added on adoption. It is submitted, however, that this principle must be limited to baptismal names. First names of persons other than Christians may, it is submitted, be changed in the same manner as surnames, and where the only change is to anglicise a foreign form of the Christian names there seems to be no objection to it. There is also no authority to say that a new name cannot be obtained at common law by use. In general it is intended, though not generally so stated, that the change of name shall be effected by deed poll.
5   *Gulliver d Corrie v Ashby* (1766) 4 Burr 1929 at 1940.
6   Where adult children so execute the deed; it must be stamped with an additional 50p stamp for each adult child so executing.
7   *Re Drax, Dunsany v Sawbridge* (1906) 75 LJ Ch 317; *Blagrove v Bradshaw* (1858) 4 Drew 230. The condition usually makes provision for the beneficiary to be excused from taking the name when he would thereby forfeit some other property.
8   *Re Neeld, Carpenter v Inigo-Jones* [1962] Ch 643, [1962] 2 All ER 335; overruling *Re Lewis' Will Trust, Whitelaw v Beaumont* [1951] WN 591; *Re Bouverie, Bouverie v Marshall* [1952] Ch 400, [1952] 1 All ER 408; *Re Wood's Will Trusts, Wood v Donnelly* [1952] Ch 406, [1952] 1 All ER 740; and *Re Kersey, Alington v Alington* [1952] WN 541.
9   *Re Neeld, Carpenter v Inigo-Jones* [1962] Ch 643, [1962] 2 All ER 335, overruling *Re Fry, Reynolds v Denne* [1945] Ch 348, [1945] 2 All ER 205; and *Re Kersey, Alington v Alington* [1952] WN 541, approving *Re Lewis' Will Trust, Whitelaw v Beaumont* [1951] WN 591.
10 The usual form is 'to use and bear the name and arms of'. In *Re Parrott, Cox v Parrott* [1946] Ch 183, [1946] 1 All ER 321, the beneficiary was directed 'by deed poll' to assume the name, but this, it is thought, is unusual; and it is thought that the older form 'apply for and endeavour to obtain a licence from the Crown to take use and bear' the specific name and arms is not now used. The arms, however, cannot be borne without proper authority; see para **[35.42]** infra.
11 *Davies v Lowndes* (1835) 1 Bing NC 597 (the name may be acquired by use).

[35.41]
Position of name when acquired. If the will does not expressly provide for the assumption of the name as a surname, it is sufficient compliance that the beneficiary has the name as a Christian name.[1] If it is assumed as a surname, it must be used as the last name,[2] but if it is to be used 'alone or together with' the beneficiary's name, it may be used before the family name.[3]

1   *Bennett v Bennett* (1864) 2 Drew & Sm 266.
2   *D'Eyncourt v Gregory* (1876) 1 Ch D 441 at 455; *Re Llangattock, Shelley v Harding* (1917) 33 TLR 250; *Re Berens, Re Dowdeswell, Berens-Dowdeswell v Holland-Martin* [1926] Ch 596.
3   *Re Eversley, Mildmay v Mildmay* [1900] 1 Ch 96; *Blathwayt v Lord Cawley* [1976] AC 397, [1975] 3 All ER 625.

[35.42]
Assumption of arms. There is no reason why the word 'arms' should be used merely ancestrally and, therefore, arms which are granted to a person can properly be described as that person's own family arms; further, the requirement as to arms is not confined to those which a person might have had on becoming entitled, but will include any arms as soon as they come into existence. Accordingly a requirement that a beneficiary should take a particular name and quarter the arms of that family with his own family arms is construed as a requirement on the beneficiary to obtain a grant of arms.[1] Arms can only be legally assumed by a royal licence granted through the College of Arms, and a mere assumption of them without such a licence is not a compliance with the condition unless the beneficiary is entitled by descent to bear them.[2] If the proper royal licence cannot be obtained, the condition is ineffective.[3] A grant from the College of Arms is sufficient though the arms are not identical with those mentioned in the condition provided the condition is that the beneficiary use his best endeavours to obtain a grant.[4]

1   *Re Neeld, Inigo-Jones v Inigo-Jones (No 3)* [1969] 2 All ER 1025.
2   *Bevan v Mahon-Hagan* (1893) 31 LR Ir 342; *Re Berens, Re Dowdeswell, Berens-Dowdeswell v Holland-Martin* [1926] Ch 596.
3   *Re Croxon, Croxon v Ferrers* [1904] 1 Ch 252; *Re Berens, Re Dowdeswell, Berens-Dowdeswell v Holland-Martin* [1926] Ch 596.
4   *Austen v Collins* (1886) 54 LT 903; *Re Berens, Re Dowdeswell, Berens-Dowdeswell v Holland-Martin* [1926] Ch 596.

[35.43]
How clause may be ineffective. In general a name and arms clause following the language of established precedent is not void for uncertainty merely because it imposes an obligation to 'take and use' or to 'assume' or 'use upon all occasions' a surname or because it provides for defeasance if the propositus 'disuses' or 'discontinues to use' the surname.[1] Failure to insert a gift over on non-compliance makes the gift ineffective.[2] The clause should generally be construed as a condition subsequent though it has been construed as a condition precedent[3] and where the gift is an entailed interest the execution of a disentailing deed operates to put an end to the condition.[4] Where personal estate was settled with reference to the limitations of real estate, the tenant in tail of real estate did not become indefeasibly entitled to the personalty by barring the state tail.[5] The condition may be impossible where the arms required to be borne are not recognised by the College of Arms or are already granted to a third party.[6] The court is not justified in reading words into or re-modelling the clause so as to assist a forfeiture. It must be clear from the beginning (in this case when the first tenant for life entered into possession) precisely and distinctly on the happening of what event the estate of the tenant for life is to be determined.[7]

1   *Re Neeld, Carpenter v Inigo-Jones* [1962] Ch 643, [1962] 2 All ER 335.
2   *Gulliver d Corrie v Ashby* (1766) 4 Burr 1929; *Vandeleur v Sloane* [1919] 1 IR 116 (not a limitation but at most a condition subsequent); *Re Evan's Contract* [1920] 2 Ch 469 (if a condition, a common law condition which was ineffective until the heir entered, and on a sale under the Settled Land Acts before the heir entered a good title was shown).
3   *Re Greenwood, Goodhart v Woodhead* [1903] 1 Ch 749; *Bennett v Bennett* (1864) 2 Drew & Sm 266; *Re Talbot* [1932] IR 714; *Re Fry, Reynolds v Denne* [1945] Ch 348, [1945] 2 All ER 205.

4   *Earl of Scarborough v Doe d Savile* (1836) 3 Ad & El 897; *Milbank v Vane* [1893] 3 Ch 79; *Re Hind, Bernstone v Montgomery* [1933] Ch 208.

5   *Re Cornwallis, Cornwallis v Wykeham-Martin* (1886) 32 Ch D 388.

6   *Re Croxon, Croxon v Ferrers* [1904] 1 Ch 252; *Re Berens, Re Dowdeswell, Berens-Dowdeswell v Holland-Martin* [1926] Ch 596.

7   *Re Murray, Martins Bank Ltd v Dill* [1955] Ch 69, [1954] 3 All ER 129. In this case the beneficiary was to 'assume' the surname, but this provision was followed by a later clause saying that it was the testator's earnest wish and desire that he should continue to use the name so long as he was entitled to possession. The beneficiary was to assume the surname either alone or in substitution of his usual surname. Here there was clearly something left out, and the court refused to amend it as amendment would cause a forfeiture and the necessary amendment was not so clear as to be beyond doubt. The words 'shall refuse or neglect to assume the arms or to make such application' were also held uncertain without amendment.

[35.44]
Cost of compliance. The tenant for life under a will must bear the costs and expenses of taking the testator's name and arms as directed by the will.[1]

1   *Re Mercer, Drewe-Mercer v Drewe-Mercer* (1889) 6 TLR 95.

X.   BEHAVIOUR OF DONEE

[35.45]
Generally valid. Conditions relating to the behaviour of the donee have in general been treated as sufficiently certain and enforceable. Thus conditions 'to give up low company',[1] for 'discreet conduct' in the case of a female beneficiary,[2] and to conduct himself 'steadily',[3] and to 'follow the paths of virtue' and obey the wishes of the wife and executors in a gift to a daughter[4] have all been upheld by the court. Abstention from intoxicating drink has also been upheld.[5] A condition that a widow shall neither directly nor indirectly keep or have any concern or interest in a public or licensed victualling house or any other kind of business is good, but is not broken by becoming a servant at wages and having no interest in the profits or emoluments otherwise than by her wages.[6] If the condition requires the behaviour of the donee to be to the satisfaction of the executors, the court apparently will not exercise their discretion and the fund and interest is free from forfeiture if the trustees refuse to exercise their power;[7] but a condition that an annuity should be halved if in the uncontrolled discretion of the trustees the beneficiary had social or other relationship with a named person was void for uncertainty and was not saved by the trustees being given such uncontrolled discretion.[8]

1   *Tattersall v Howell* (1816) 2 Mer 26.
2   *Wynne v Wynne* (1840) 2 Man & G 8.
3   *Re Coe's Trust* (1858) 4 K & J 199.
4   *Maud v Maud* (1860) 27 Beav 615.
5   *Jordan v Dunn* (1887) 13 OR 267.
6   *Jones v Bromley* (1821) 6 Madd 137. In *Re Quay* (1907) 14 OLR 471, the donee was restrained from trading in intoxicating liquor or running a gambling business.
7   *Re Coe's Trust* (1858) 4 K & J 199; *Maud v Maud* (1860) 27 Beav 615; but in neither of these cases did it appear that there was any misbehaviour on which to ground a forfeiture.
8   *Re Jones, Midland Bank Executor and Trustee Co Ltd v Jones* [1953] Ch 125, [1953] 1 All ER 357.

XI.   OTHER CONDITIONS

[35.46]
Relating to fighting services. A condition for forfeiture of a gift on the legatee entering the naval, military or other services of the country is void as against public policy.[1]

A condition provided for forfeiture if the legatee entered Parliament or any other public office prior to a certain date. The legatee took a commission in the Territorial Army. This was held to be a breach, but the condition itself was void as being against public policy.[2] It was contended that a gift on leaving the army was invalid as an inducement for the beneficiary improperly to obtain a discharge, but this contention was rejected and the gift construed as one for the beneficiary at a time when he would most need help.[3]

1   *Re Beard, Reversionary and General Securities Co Ltd v Hall* [1908] 1 Ch 383.
2   *Re Edgar, Cohen v Edgar* [1939] 1 All ER 635.
3   *Re Pape Estate* [1946] 4 DLR 700.

[35.47]
Acquisition of dignity. A condition against the acquisition of a dignity is void as against public policy[1] unless the dignity be such that it entails no duties to the state or the public beyond those cast upon every good citizen.[2] A gift may, however, be made subject to the House of Lords allowing the donee's right to be a nobleman holding a particular title, and if the House reject this claim, then over.[3]

1   *Earl of Kingston v Pierepont* (1681) 1 Vern 5; *Egerton v Earl of Brownlow* (1853) 4 HL Cas 1.
2   *Re Wallace, Champion v Wallace* [1920] 2 Ch 274 (baronetcy).
3   *Earl of Fingal v Blake* (1829) 2 Mol 50.

[35.48]
Claiming bequests. The validity of a condition requiring the beneficiary to claim a bequest seems not to have been in question, the only matter discussed being whether strict compliance is essential or whether substantial compliance is sufficient – and substantial compliance has generally been held to be sufficient. On the question of what is a claim, it has been held that commencing an administration action is equivalent to a claim.[1] A claim may be made by an agent.[2] But where it was recited that a legatee had gone abroad and it was doubtful whether he was living and provided that, if he did not return to England and claim within seven years, he should be presumed dead and the legacy should fall into residue, the condition for claim to be made in England and the proof of his existence to be made in a special way was binding and it was not sufficient that it appeared otherwise that he in fact survived the testator and died abroad;[3] and where legacies were to be claimed within twelve months of the death of the testatrix, ignorance of the condition did not excuse the legatee.[4]

1   *Tollner v Marriott* (1830) 4 Sim 19. But where an order for limited administration was made on summons shortly after the testator's death, including an inquiry as to next of kin, the next of kin had to bring in a claim within the year where the will required that they should establish their right within a year from the testator's death: *Re Hartley, Stedman v Dunster* (1887) 34 Ch D 742.

2   *Tanner v Tebbutt* (1843) 2 Y & C Ch Cas 225 (where in the case of an aged and infirm
     beneficiary another attended with proof of identity); *Re Stone's Trusts* (1866) 14 LT 542 (where
     one cousin asked a solicitor to put in a claim for another whose address was not known). As to
     performance of conditions, see para [34.21] et seq.
3   *Tulk v Houlditch* (1813) 1 Ves & B 248.
4   *Hawkes v Baldwin* (1838) 9 Sim 355 (where a legatee who had not been heard of for upwards
     of twenty years claimed her legacy within a short time after having first heard of the death of
     the testatrix); *Burgess v Robinson* (1817) 3 Mer 7 (similar case where three years was allowed
     for claim); *Horrigan v Horrigan* [1904] 1 IR 29; *Powell v Rawle* (1874) LR 18 Eq 243. As to
     absolute gift of residue with gift over on beneficiary dying overseas, see *Re Holt* [1952] 3 DLR
     426, and Chapter 97.

[35.49]
To carry on testator's business. A condition to carry on the testator's business
is not fulfilled if the legatees turn the business into a limited company of which
they are managing directors,[1] though they would not be said to cease to carry on
the business if one of the legatees sold his share to the others who then continue
to carry on the business.[2] To carry on a business is generally to be engaged in it
as a principal. Where the condition was that the devisee should neither directly
nor indirectly keep or have any concern or interest in a licensed victualling
business, it was held that there was no breach where the devisee kept and took
care of a public-house belonging to others as their servant at regular wages with
no further interest in the profits of the business whatever.[3] Where a will
appointed a solicitor as trustee and executor and included a charging clause, it
was held that a gift of residue to the solicitor 'if he shall prove this my will and
act in the trusts thereof' denoted doing those acts which a non-professional
trustee was obliged to do in the execution of his trust including the exercise of
powers and discretions which could not be delegated to others.[4]

1   *Re Sax, Barned v Sax* (1893) 62 LJ Ch 688.
2   *Re Sax, Barned v Sax* (1893) 62 LJ Ch 688.
3   *Jones v Bromley* (1821) 6 Madd 137.
4   *In Re Parry, Dalton v Cooke* [1969] 2 All ER 512; distinguishing *Re Sharman's Will Trusts,
     Public Trustee v Sharman* [1942] Ch 311, [1942] 2 All ER 74 ('accept the trusteeship thereof');
     considering *Wilkinson v Wilkinson* (1825) 2 Sim & St 237 ('for their trouble in the execution of
     his will') and *Re Muffett, Jones v Mason* (1886) 55 LT 671.

[35.50]
To settle property. A condition that the gift to the beneficiary shall be
dependent on the execution of a settlement of other property is good;[1] but where
the terms of the proposed settlement are of doubtful validity and effect, a
substantial compliance with the condition is sufficient.[2] A condition to settle
hereditaments has been held to include capital money invested in land,[3] and one
to settle after-acquired property of which the beneficiary was possessed or to
which the beneficiary was entitled has been construed as meaning both property
of which the beneficiary is possessed and property to which he is entitled and,
therefore, a vested reversionary interest had to be settled if forfeiture was to be
avoided.[4]

1   *Duke of Montagu v Duke of Bealieu* (1767) 3 Bro Parl Cas 277.
2   *Scarlett v Lord Abinger* (1865) 34 Beav 833.
3   *Re Gosselin, Gosselin v Gosselin* [1906] 1 Ch 120.
4   *Re Brook, Brook v Hirst* (1914) 111 LT 36.

[35.51]

To execute a release. A condition to execute a release is enforceable, and upon refusal to do so the legatee forfeits the gift[1] unless the release tendered for execution is improper.[2] Where the legatee is to release an annuity, the release should include arrears due at the death of the testator.[3] It has been held that where the release is to be executed within a stated time this must be complied with.[4]

1 *Taylor v Popham* (1782) 1 Bro CC 168.
2 *Williams v Knipe* (1842) 5 Beav 273 (where the release included an inaccurate recital and its contents were not explained to the legatee).
3 *Philby v Philby* (1866) 15 WR 98.
4 *Simpson v Vickers* (1807) 14 Ves 341.

[35.52]

Perpetuity. Conditions which offend the rule against perpetuity are void if they are conditions subsequent and, if they are conditions precedent, they prevent the vesting of the gift within the period and the gift in consequence fails under the rule.[1] Conditions subsequent of this nature are those requiring a beneficiary to adopt a name or bear arms where the beneficiary is not a life in being at the testator's death and has more than the period allowed by the rule in which to satisfy the condition,[2] those requiring the beneficiary to execute a release in similar circumstances,[3] or those providing for forfeiture on a beneficiary forsaking a named faith.[4] The application of the perpetuity rule to conditions is now subject to the 'wait and see' principle introduced by the Perpetuities and Accumulations Act 1964.[5]

1 As to conditions precedent of this nature, see *Boughton v Boughton* (1848) 1 HL Cas 406 at 433; *Re Wrightson, Battie-Wrightson v Thomas* [1904] 2 Ch 95. As to conditions subsequent, see para **[34.2]** ante.
2 *Bennett v Bennett* (1864) 2 Drew & Sm 266; *Fry, Reynolds v Denne* [1945] Ch 348, [1945] 2 All ER 205.
3 *Re Staveley, Dyke v Staveley* (1920) 90 LJ Ch 111.
4 *Re Spitzel's Will Trusts, Spitzel v Spitzel* [1939] 2 All ER 266 (where the condition took effect only on the forsaking being proved to the satisfaction of the trustees, and it was held that such proof might not be given until after the expiration of the period allowed by the rule against perpetuities and the condition was for that reason void).
5 See Vol 2, Part G, para **[246.59]**; and Chapter 94.

[35.53]

Exhibit without charge. Artistic and other collections are sometimes left to a gallery or museum on condition that they be exhibited to the public. Certain museums and galleries are empowered to charge admission fees for public entry, and so a bequest to such an institution should no longer stipulate that the collection should be exhibited free of charge.[1]

1 The Museums and Galleries Admission Charges Act 1972; 24 *Halsbury's Statutes* (4th edn) 243. Whether charges are levied in pursuance of the Museums and Galleries Admission Charges Act 1972 is liable to change.

[35.54]

Impossible conditions. See para **[34.7]** et seq.

CHAPTER 36

Secret trusts

[36.1]

Two kinds of secret trusts. There are two kinds of secret trusts[1] in common use. In the first the property is given to the apparent beneficiary for an absolute interest though he secretly acquiesces with the testator that he will hold it on certain trusts.[2] The other class is where in the will the apparent beneficiary is by the terms of the will a mere trustee but the nature of the trusts upon which he is to hold the property are not disclosed or not fully disclosed.[3]

1 See the statement of the law in *Re Karsten, Edwards v Moore* [1953] NZLR 456. These pages of the text were referred to in *Re Armstrong* (1970) 7 DLR (3d) 36 at 43.
2 This form of the trust, though used from quite early times, was finally approved by the House of Lords in *McCormick v Grogan* (1869) LR 4 HL 82. After this decision, there was considerable discussion as to whether the second class of secret trusts (where the will shows that the apparent beneficiary is a trustee for others) was valid in law, and the validity of this class was finally established in *Re Blackwell, Blackwell v Blackwell* [1929] AC 318. There is a type of gift which is perhaps intermediate between these two forms, ie where the testator requests the beneficiary to deal with certain property in a way communicated or to be communicated to him, but such request is not to create any trust or legal obligation. This form of gift creates no enforceable trust and the donee takes absolutely: *Re Falkiner, Mead v Smith* [1924] 1 Ch 88. As to the inheritance tax position with reference to such gifts see the Inheritance Tax Act 1984, ss 143, 144. For precedents of such gifts, see Vol 2. Where a testatrix stated that it was her wish that a lease should be granted, these words created no binding obligation to grant the lease but merely a power to do which was not void as a delegation being certain as to obligation and subject-matter. A further desire that the trustees should before selling the property offer it to the lessee at a reasonable price also did not create a binding obligation: *Re Alston* [1955] VLR 281. Another allied form of disposition is the case where the particulars of the gift are stated in a document incorporated in the will. This has already been dealt with: see Chapter 15.
3 This form of secret trust was fully discussed in *Re Blackwell, Blackwell v Blackwell* [1929] AC 318. Where the residuary legatee is shown to have been party to a will being drawn in a particular way which has the effect of increasing the liabilities payable out of residue, the court has construed the will accordingly: *Re Applebee, Leveson v Beales* [1891] 3 Ch 422.

I. GIFT IN WILL ABSOLUTE

[36.2]

Where gift in terms absolute. The law requires every testamentary disposition to be duly executed and attested as a will or codicil,[1] but this requirement of the law is not carried to the length at which it would enable an apparent donee to act fraudulently. Therefore, where a testator makes, or leaves unrevoked, a disposition on the faith of a promise, whether express or tacit, on the part of the donee that he will carry out the testator's intentions with respect thereto,[2] equity will admit evidence[3] as to the testator's intentions and the communication thereof to the donee and his acquiescence therein, and will compel the donee, as being a trustee, to carry out the testator's intentions,[4] unless they are such as are prohibited by law.[5] Thus the essential elements of a secret trust are: the intention of the testator to subject the primary donee to an obligation in favour of the secondary donee; the communication of that intention to the primary donee; and the acceptance of that obligation by the primary donee either expressly or by acquiescence.[6] The method by which the primary donee is to carry out the obligation, whether by making a will in favour of the secondary donee or by some form of inter vivos transfer, is immaterial.[7]

1   Wills Act 1837, s 9; as substituted by the Administration of Justice Act 1982, s 17; 50 *Halsbury's Statutes* (4th edn) 586; Vol 2, Part G, para **[244.93]**; see also Part D.

2   Though the language used sometimes seems to point to a basis of implied contract, this doctrine has always been explained as the prevention of an act of fraud on the part of the apparent beneficiary. The word 'fraud' in this connection must not be construed in the *Derry v Peek* (1889) 14 App Cas 337 sense, but as something which equity will prevent as being unconscionable. Cf the case of *Tharp v Tharp* [1916] 1 Ch 142, where a testator was induced to revoke a codicil and thus revive a power of appointment upon an undertaking that the power would be exercised in a certain way and the same equitable doctrine was applied to enforce the power being exercised in that way. The case, however, went to appeal and was settled on terms, [1916] 2 Ch 205.

3   If a will contains a gift which is in terms absolute, clear evidence is needed before the court will assume that the testator did not mean what he said but intended that the gift should be held by the beneficiary subject to a secret trust. The standard of proof is perhaps analogous to that which the court requires before it will rectify a written instrument; per Brightman J in *Ottaway v Norman* [1972] Ch 698 at 712, [1971] 3 All ER 1325 at 1333.

4   *Wallgrave v Tebbs* (1855) 2 K & J 313; *McCormick v Grogan* (1869) LR 4 HL 82; *Moss v Cooper* (1861) 1 John & H 352; *Jones v Badley* (1868) 3 Ch App 362; *McDonald v Moran* (1938) 12 MPR 424; *MacMillan v Kennedy* [1942] 3 DLR 170; *Re Pugh's Will Trusts, Marten v Pugh* [1967] 3 All ER 337, [1967] 1 WLR 1262; it is easier to infer an intention that a sole trustee should take beneficially than that two or more trustees should do so, but that indication is not sufficient alone. Where a deceased spouse has bequeathed property to a surviving spouse and it is sought to prove a secret trust in favour of a particular person, the surviving spouse can be compelled to give evidence as to communications made between the spouses during the marriage: *Shenton v Tyler* [1939] Ch 620, [1939] 1 All ER 827, and see para **[36.13]** infra.

5   Most of the cases turn upon gifts or charities being illegal under the Mortmain Acts: *Muckleston v Brown* (1801) 6 Ves 52; *Stickland v Aldridge* (1804) 9 Ves 516; *Russell v Jackson* (1852) 10 Hare 204; *Springett v Jenings* (1871) 6 Ch App 333; *Tee v Ferris* (1856) 2 K & J 357; *Rowbothan v Dunnett* (1878) 8 Ch D 430. As to the effect of a trust being illegal, see note 2, para 36.4, post, and text thereto. The Mortmain Acts have now been repealed by the Charities Act 1960, s 38.

6   *Ottaway v Norman* [1972] Ch 698, [1971] 3 All ER 1325.

7   *Ottaway v Norman* [1972] Ch 698, [1971] 3 All ER 1325 (primary donee's executor obliged to hold a bungalow on trust for secondary donee in accordance with the terms of a secret trust that the primary donee would, on his death, devise the bungalow to the secondary donee).

[36.3]

Tacit acquiescence. A person accepts such a trust not only when he expressly accepts it either orally or in writing, but also when he silently acquiesces in it when communicated to him in the lifetime of the testator.[1]

1   *Paine v Hall* (1812) 18 Ves 475; *Lomax v Ripley* (1855) 3 Sm & G 48 at 73; *Tee v Ferris* (1856) 2 K & J 357; *Rowbotham v Dunnett* (1878) 8 Ch D 430; *Re King's Estate* (1888) 21 LR Ir 273 at 277. See also *Voges v Monaghan* (1954) 94 CLR 232 (where the question of communication was contested and the decision turned on the acts of the trustee after the death of the testator).

[36.4]
Conditions with which secret trust must comply. The trust itself must not be for an object which is prohibited by law, for in that case the gift itself in addition to the trust is void.[1] The trust but not the gift itself will fail where the intended trust, though not void in law: (i) cannot take effect;[2] (ii) is not communicated to the donee in the lifetime of the testator;[3] or (iii) is not assented to by the donee in the lifetime of the testator.[4]

1   *Muckleston v Brown* (1801) 6 Ves 52; *Stickland v Aldridge* (1804) 9 Ves 516; *Russell v Jackson* (1852) 10 Hare 204; *Tee v Ferris* (1856) 2 K & J 357; *Springett v Jenings* (1871) 6 Ch App 333; *Rowbotham v Dunnett* (1878) 8 Ch D 430.
2   *Burney v Macdonald* (1845) 15 Sim 6.
3   *Jones v Badley* (1866) LR 3 Eq 635; revsd (1868) 3 Ch App 362; *Re Stead, Witham v Andrew* [1900] 1 Ch 237. No declaration made by the testator and not communicated to the legatee (unless executed as a will) can impose a trust upon him, and a letter or similar document which he receives only after the death of the testator (unless so executed) will not affect him: see *Re Boyes, Boyes v Carritt* (1884) 26 Ch D 531. Apparently it is otherwise where the letter is handed to him and he is told that it contains the trusts but that it is only to be opened after the testator's death: see *Re Keen, Evershed v Griffiths* [1937] Ch 236, [1937] 1 All ER 452.
4   *Russell v Jackson* (1852) 10 Hare 204.

[36.5]
Effect of failure of trusts. If the secret trust is illegal, the apparent beneficiary holds the property on trust for those who would have taken if the gift had not been contained in the will.[1] Where, however, the trust is not illegal, but fails because, though not void in law, it cannot take effect,[2] or because it is not communicated to the donee,[3] or because it is not assented to by the donee during the lifetime of the testator,[4] the donee takes the gift absolutely and free from the trust.[5] If, therefore, in any such circumstances the donee does in fact apply the gift to the object indicated by the testator, he does so as a voluntary gift from himself.[6] Where the trusts fail as to part of the gift or where they relate in the first instance to part only of the gift the donee takes absolutely subject to the performance of the trusts, the benefits under the trusts being treated as legacies carrying interest at 6 per cent per annum after the expiration of one year from the testator's death.[7]

If there is any question as to what part of the property is affected by the trust, the onus is on the donee to show what part is not affected by it and to this extent the usual role of certainty of the subject of the trust does not apply.[8]

1   That is to say it falls into residue or passes on intestacy according to the circumstances: see Chapter 48.
2   *Russell v Jackson* (1852) 10 Hare 204.
3   *Carter v Green* (1857) 3 K & J 591.
4   *Podmore v Gunning* (1836) 7 Sim 644; *Jones v Badley* (1868) 3 Ch App 362.
5   *Russell v Jackson* (1852) 10 Hare 204; *Re Gardom, Le Page v A-G* [1914] 1 Ch 662 at 672; revsd sub nom *Le Page v Gardom* (1915) 84 LJ Ch 749.
6   *Lomax v Ripley* (1855) 3 Sm & G 48 at 78; *Geddis v Semple* [1903] 1 IR 73.
7   *Irvine v Sullivan* (1869) LR 8 Eq 673; RSC Ord 44, r 10; SI 1982/1111; The rate of 6 per cent is substituted for the previous 5 per cent with effect from 1 October 1983 by RSC (Amendment No 2) Order 1983, SI 1983/1181.
8   *Russell v Jackson* (1852) 10 Hare 204; *Re Huxtable, Huxtable v Crawfurd* [1902] 2 Ch 793.

[36.6]
Communication to donee not to create a trust. A testator can make an absolute gift to a donee with a desire that he will dispose of the gift in a certain way or in accordance with a memorandum adding that such desire is not to create a trust or legal obligation.[1] In such a case the donee takes absolutely for his own benefit and the law will not interfere if he applies the whole gift for his own benefit. If he gives effect to the desire, it will amount to a voluntary gift from himself.[2]

1   *Re Falkiner, Mead v Smith* [1924] 1 Ch 88; *Re White, Knight v Briggs* [1925] Ch 179; *Re Louis, Louis v Treloar* (1916) 32 TLR 313.
2   Cf cases in n 1, supra, and *Re Stirling, Union Bank of Scotland Ltd v Stirling* [1954] 2 All ER 113 (where the bank took absolutely although a memorandum indicating the testator's wishes was found among the testator's papers after his death).

[36.7]
Communication of secret trust. The trust must be communicated to the donee in the lifetime of the testator and, if no such communication is made, the donee takes the property for his own benefit.[1] No declaration made by the testator unless communicated to the donee in the latter's lifetime or unless executed as a will[2] can affect him with a trust.[3] An intermediate position is created where the testator tells the donee that he is to be a trustee of the property but does not inform him in his lifetime of the details of the trust, although the testator may leave a document or documents stating his wishes which are found only after the death of the testator.[4] In this case the donee cannot take beneficially but will hold the property in trust for the persons entitled to the residue or on intestacy as the case may require;[5] but, if the fact that the legatee was to hold as a trustee is not clearly established, he will take beneficially.[6] The communication to the donee cannot create more than a personal obligation on the donee which he is free, if he so desires, to renounce or disclaim, and such obligation will altogether cease on the death of the donee in the lifetime of the testator. It has been said that, in the event of any one of these things happening, the beneficiaries under the trust will have no claim against the testator's estate or any person entitled to an interest therein either under the will or under an intestacy.[7]

1   See para **[36.5]**, n 3.
2   *Re Boyes, Boyes v Carritt* (1884) 26 Ch D 531.
3   *Jones v Badley* (1866) LR 3 Eq 635; revsd (1868) 3 Ch App 362; *Re Stead, Witham v Andrew* [1900] 1 Ch 237.
4   *Re Boyes, Boyes v Carritt* (1884) 26 Ch D 531.
5   *Re Boyes, Boyes v Carritt* (1884) 26 Ch D 531.
6   *Jones v Badley* (1868) 3 Ch App 362 (no evidence of communication or acceptance); *McCormick v Grogan* (1869) LR 4 HL 82 (legatee merely told there was a will and he would find a letter); *Re Downing's Residuary Estate* (1888) 60 LT 140 (where it was held that the words 'in full confidence that they will carry out my wishes in respect thereof' created no trust whatever following *Irvine v Sullivan* (1869) LR 8 Eq 673); *Re Pitt Rivers, Scott v Pitt Rivers* [1902] 1 Ch 403; *Re Snowden, Smith v Spowage* [1979] 2 All ER 172 (civil standard of proof required to establish trust).
7   *Re Maddock, Llewellyn v Washington* [1902] 2 Ch 220 at 231; but it is submitted that, if it is possible by evidence to establish the acceptance and the terms of the secret trust, neither the disclaimer, renunciation or death of the trustee can prevent the court from enforcing the trust. Of course there will generally be considerable difficulty in proving the communication to and the acceptance of the trust by the donee and, unless the communication was in writing, the terms of the trust.

[36.8]

Gift to more than one on secret understanding with one. Where the property is given to more than one on an understanding or undertaking with one of them that it shall be held in trust for some particular person or object, the question whether the interest of the other donee under the gift is bound by the trust depends upon the time when the understanding was given, and it may also depend upon whether the gift is to the donees as joint tenants or as tenants in common. Both donees are bound if the understanding or undertaking was entered into by or on behalf of both before or at the time of the execution of the will, although it was given without the knowledge or consent of the other donee,[1] but the other is not bound if it is entered into after the will has been executed.[2] The fact that the gift is to the donees as tenants in common strengthens the case that the other is not bound, and this, of course, is only material where the understanding or undertaking was given before or at the time of the execution of the will.[3]

1   *Russell v Jackson* (1852) 10 Hare 204; *Jones v Badley* (1868) 3 Ch App 362; *Re Stead, Witham v Andrew* [1900] 1 Ch 237 at 240.
2   *Burney v Macdonald* (1845) 15 Sim 6; *Moss v Cooper* (1861) 1 John & H 352; *Re Stead, Withams v Andrew* [1900] 1 Ch 237.
3   *Tee v Ferris* (1856) 2 K & J 357; *Rowbotham v Dunnett* (1878) 8 Ch D 430; *Geddis v Semple* [1903] 1 IR 73.

[36.9]

Beneficiaries under the secret trust predeceasing testator. An ordinary beneficiary under a will must survive the testator to be entitled to the gift, but the beneficiary under the secret trust takes *dehors* the will and not under it, and, if he dies in the testator's lifetime, his personal representatives are entitled to the gift.[1]

1   *Re Gardner, Huey v Cunningham* [1923] 2 Ch 230. Likewise it is immaterial that a beneficiary under the secret trust is a witness to the will: *Re Young, Young v Young* [1951] Ch 344, [1950] 2 All ER 1245. See also *O'Brien v Condon* [1905] 1 IR 51. If the trustee predeceases the testator or disclaims, the position is unclear: see *Re Maddock, Llewelyn v Washington* [1902] 2 Ch 220, CA; and *Re Blackwell, Blackwell v Blackwell* [1929] AC 318.

II.   GIFT IN FORM OF INDEFINITE TRUST

[36.10]

Gift refers to but does not define trusts. Where the property is given by will to persons upon trusts which are referred to in, but not defined by, the will, the trustees cannot take beneficially[1] and the trustees hold the property either for the secret beneficiaries or, if the trusts fail, for those entitled to residue or on intestacy as the case may be. The trustees hold the property for the secret beneficiaries if the trusts are described in the will as having been defined and communicated to the trustees prior to or contemporaneously with the will[2] and it is also proved that they were so defined and so communicated to some, even though not to all, the trustees.[3]

1   *Re Boyes, Boyes v Carritt* (1884) 26 Ch D 531. It is a recognised principle that the person to whom property is given in trust cannot take beneficially and in the absence of beneficiaries he

takes as trustee for those entitled on intestacy. In *Re Rees, Williams v Hopkins* [1950] Ch 204, [1949] 2 All ER 1003, the gift was to 'my trustees absolutely they well knowing my wishes concerning the same'; the gift was held to be a gift on trust and not a gift conditional on the wishes being carried out. The trustees therefore were trustees for beneficiaries who were named to them by the testator and, in so far as that did not exhaust the fund, it must be held for those entitled on intestacy. Sir R. Evershed MR [1950] Ch 204 at 211, [1949] 2 All ER 1003 at 1007, commented that in the general public interest it is desirable that if a testator wishes his property to go to his solicitor and the solicitor prepares the will, that intention should be plainly expressed in the will, and should not be arrived at by the more oblique method of secret trusts. This case was followed in *Re Karsten* [1953] NZLR 456 (where, although the direction was that the trustee should have certain shares and a motor car, the trustee was held not to take the shares and motor car, which, if not caught by a residuary devise, passed as on an intestacy), but distinguished in *Re Tylers' Fund Trusts, Graves v King* [1967] 3 All ER 389, [1967] 1 WLR 1269. See also *Re Pugh's Will Trusts, Masten v Pugh* [1967] 3 All ER 337, [1967] 1 WLR 1262 ('unto my trustee absolutely and I direct him to dispose of the same in accordance with any letters or memoranda which I may leave with this my will and otherwise in such manner as he may in his absolute discretion think fit'; the testator left no letters or memoranda; held, a trust imposed which was void for uncertainty; therefore for the benefit of the persons entitled on intestacy).

2   *Re Blackwell, Blackwell v Blackwell* [1929] AC 318, though the point did not arise in that case as the trusts were defined and communicated contemporaneously with the execution of a codicil; *Re Keen, Evershed v Griffiths* [1937] Ch 236, [1937] 1 All ER 452; *Re Cooper, Le Neve-Foster v National Provincial Bank Ltd* [1939] 2 All ER 192 (where it was unsuccessfully attempted to increase the amount of the legacy by a communication to the trustees). The testator cannot reserve a power to alter the communication in any way after the date of the execution of the testamentary instrument in which the trusts are referred to.

3   *Re Keen, Evershed v Griffiths* [1937] Ch 236 at 248.

[36.11]

Trusts not defined and communicated at date of will. If the beneficial trusts are not defined and communicated to the trustees on or before the execution of the will, the trusts are unenforceable, as being an attempt to empower the testator to make unwitnessed dispositions by naming trustees and leaving the details of the trusts to be supplied afterwards.[1]

1   *Johnson v Ball* (1851) 5 De G & Sm 85; *Riordan v Banon* (1876) IR 10 Eq 469; *Re Boyes, Boyes v Carrit* (1884) 26 Ch D 531; *Re Hetley, Hetley v Hetley* [1902] 2 Ch 866; *Re Keen, Evershed v Griffiths* [1937] Ch 236; *Guest v Webb* [1965] VR 427 (letter expressing trusts retained for alteration and not found after death: intestacy). *Re Bateman's Will Trusts, Brierley v Perry* [1970] 3 All ER 817, [1970] 1 WLR 1463 (fund should be set aside and the income from it paid to such persons 'as shall be stated by me in a sealed letter ...'; held, that the direction relating to future non-testamentary instruments was invalid). Also referring to *Re Jones' Will Trusts, Jones v Jones* [1942] Ch 328, [1942] 1 All ER 642. Further, that a subsequent direction as to payment of income, being a direction to take effect on an event to be determined in the future by a non-testamentary instrument, was also invalid, as was a final gift over to residue. The principle applies in any case where it is clear from the will that the testator had not at the time of the testamentary instrument decided what the beneficial trusts are to be.

[36.12]

How far personal fraud a necessary element. Where there is nothing in the will disclosing any trust, it is the element of personal fraud which gives the court jurisdiction to enforce the trusts which the legatee has accepted.[1] Where, however, the donee cannot take beneficially since the gift is expressly stated to be subject to trusts, there can be no question of personal fraud on the part of the donee, and the fraud, if any, is a fraud on the testator; in such case those entitled on intestacy or the residuary legatees cannot take advantage of and thus make themselves parties to such fraud.[2]

399

1   *McCormick v Grogan* (1869) LR 4 HL 82; *Re Fleetwood, Sidgreaves v Brewer* (1880) 15 Ch D
      594 at 607.
2   *Re Blackwell, Blackwell v Blackwell* [1929] AC 318 at 341, 342; *Re Fleetwood, Sidgreaves v
      Brewer* (1880) 15 Ch D 594.

[36.13]

Evidence of secret trusts. Where the gift is absolute[1] and it can be proved[2] that
either before or after the date of the will but during the testator's lifetime[3] the
donee received from the testator a communication of certain trusts or conditions
to be attached to the gift and to be binding on the donee[4] and that the donee
accepted such trusts either by express acceptance or his silence[5] and thereby
induced the testator to make the gift or leave it unrevoked, then evidence of
these trusts or conditions is admissible except in so far as such evidence would
contradict the will.[6] Where the gift is upon trusts not disclosed by the will, such
evidence is admissible but must be restricted to trusts declared before or at the
execution of the will.[7] Such evidence is not evidence of the testator's intention
but of the obligation accepted by and binding on the donee[8] and is admitted to
prevent fraud on his part.[9] It is admissible although the will states that the gift is
not by way of trust,[10] but no evidence is admissible to prove that the trustee
takes any part of the estate beneficially.[11]

1   *Burney v Macdonald* (1845) 15 Sim 6; *Russell v Jackson* (1852) 10 Hare 204; *Re Spencer's
      Will* (1887) 57 LT 519.
2   This proof may be a confession by the donee: *Re Maddock, Llewellyn v Washington* [1902] 2
      Ch 220; *Re Huxtable, Huxtable v Crawfurd* [1902] 2 Ch 793; or evidence aliunde: *Podmore v
      Gunning* (1836) 7 Sim 644; but it must show the acceptance of the trust by the donee: *French v
      French* [1902] 1 IR 172; *Le Page v Gardom* (1915) 84 LJ Ch 749; *Re Gardner, Huey v
      Cunnington* [1920] 2 Ch 523.
3   *Moss v Cooper* (1861) 1 John & H 352 at 366; *Morrison v M'Ferran* [1901] 1 IR 360; but not
      after the testator's death: *Re Boyes, Boyes v Carritt* (1884) 26 Ch D 531.
4   For cases where the communication was not intended to be binding, see *Re Pitt Rivers, Scott v
      Pitt Rivers* [1902] 1 Ch 403; *Sullivan v Sullivan* [1903] 1 IR 193; *Re Falkiner, Mead v Smith*
      [1924] 1 Ch 88 (where the will expressly stated that any communication was not to create any
      trust or legal obligation).
5   If silent acceptance is relied on, the evidence must leave no doubt in the mind of the tribunal:
      French v French [1902] 1 IR 172 at 213; *Re Gardner, Huey v Cunnington* [1920] 2 Ch 523; *Re
      Williams, Williams v All Souls, Hastings (Parochial Church Council)* [1933] Ch 244.
6   *Re Huxtable, Huxtable v Crawfurd* [1902] 2 Ch 793; *O'Brien v Condon* [1905] 1 IR 51 (where
      the trusts were completely disclosed by the will); *Re Wright, Hegan v Bloor* [1920] 1 Ch 108 at
      118; *Re Ellis, Owen v Bentley* (1918) 53 ILT 6.
7   *Re Keen, Evershed v Griffiths* [1937] Ch 236, [1937] 1 All ER 452; and see *Re Cooper, Le Neve
      Foster v National Provincial Bank Ltd* [1939] Ch 811, [1939] 3 All ER 586; *Re Jones' Will
      Trusts, Jones v Jones* [1942] Ch 328, [1942] 1 All ER 642.
8   *Re Spencer's Will* (1887) 57 LT 519 at 521; *Re Ellis, Owen v Bentley* (1918) 53 ILT 6. The test
      in such a case is to consider the matter as unaffected by the Statute of Frauds and the Wills Act
      1837, and to inquire whether there is a trust imposed by the testator and binding on the donee
      such as a court of equity will enforce: *Jones v Badley* (1868) 3 Ch App 362 at 364. As to
      communications between husband and wife, see para **[36.2]**, n 4.
9   *McCormick v Grogan* (1869) LR 4 HL 82; *Re Stead, Witham v Andrew* [1900] 1 Ch 237; *Re
      Pitt Rivers, Scott v Pitt Rivers*, supra; *Tharp v Tharp* [1916] 1 Ch 142.
10   *Russell v Jackson* (1852) 10 Hare 204; *Re Spencer's Will* (1887) 57 LT 519.
11   *Re Rees, Edwards v Moore, Williams v Hopkins* [1950] Ch 204, [1949] 2 All ER 1003; *Re
      Karsten* [1953] NZLR 456.

CHAPTER 37

Conversion

[37.1]

General points. The doctrine of conversion is abolished in relation to trusts for sale of land, and in relation to trusts to invest personalty in the purchase of land, by the Trusts of Land and Appointment of Trustees Act 1996 (TLATA 1996),[1] except in relation to trusts for sale created by will where the testator died before 1 January 1997.[2] From that date an undivided share of land is either an equitable interest in land directly (ie without the imposition of a trust for sale) or it is an interest under a trust for sale but with the doctrine of conversion abolished.[3] Thus an interest under a trust for sale of land will apparently now pass under a gift of residuary realty, and not under a gift of residuary personalty.[4] But the doctrine remains applicable to contracts for the sale of land.[5] The discussion which follows is expressed as representing the previous law, but may have some relevance and effect to the residual exceptional cases where the doctrine can still operate.[6]

1 TLATA 1996, s 3(1) abolishes the doctrine of conversion in relation to express trusts for sale, whether made before or after the commencement of the TLATA 1996, s 3(3), with the consequence that land held on trust for sale is no longer to be regarded as personalty.
2 TLATA 1996, s 3(2).
3 TLATA 1996, s 3(2).
4 By the effect of the provisions in the TLATA 1996, s 3. The subject of conversion had in any event, lost much of its importance since 1925. Its main importance before 1926 was to decide whether undisposed-of property was land and passed to the heir, or was personalty and passed to the next of kin. The doctrine may still operate to decide whether property passes under a residuary gift of realty or a residuary gift of personalty, but as there is now an almost universal practice of including both realty and personalty in one residuary gift, it can seldom be of any significance.
5 Which is unaffected by the TLATA 1996.
6 For a fuller discussion see the 6th edn of this text, Chapter 37.

[37.2]

Direction for conversion must be imperative. Conversion took place when land was devised on trust for sale or money was bequeathed to be laid out in land, but in either case the direction had to be imperative, that is to say, one which the trustee had to perform unless an absolute owner of the property or those who together had the absolute ownership required the trustees not to give effect to the direction.[1] Thus, a mere power to sell land or to invest money in land,[2] a direction which left it optional whether the money was invested in realty or personalty,[3] or a mere declaration that personalty should devolve as realty or vice versa,[4] did not effect a conversion. If for any reason the direction was void, there was no conversion.[5]

1   *Walker v Denne* (1793) 2 Ves 170; *Buchanan v Angus* (1862) 4 Macq 374; *Atwell v Atwell* (1871) LR 13 Eq 23; *Re Bird, Pitman v Pitman* [1892] 1 Ch 279; *Re Walker, Macintosh-Walker v Walker* [1908] 2 Ch 705; *Re Newbould, Carter v Newbould* (1913) 110 LT 6. A direction for conversion and a further provision that the trustee was to have any profit on conversion: the trustee took absolutely the amount by which the proceeds of sale exceed the value at the testator's death: *Re Espie, Maffey v Espie* [1956] VLR 605.

2   *Re Hotchkys, Freke v Calmady* (1886) 32 Ch D 408; *Re Dyson, Challinor v Sykes* [1910] 1 Ch 750; *Re Newbould, Carter v Newbould* (1913) 110 LT 6; *Re Woods* [1947] 4 DLR 386 (the result was the same whether there was an absolute discretion to convert or not).

3   *Re Newbould, Carter v Newbould* (1913) 110 LT 6; *Glover v Heelis* (1875) 32 LT 534 (sale at such time as most beneficial: no conversion); but see *Re Raw, Morris v Griffiths* (1884) 26 Ch D 601; *Robinson v Robinson* (1854) 19 Beav 494 (sale whenever it should appear most advantageous: conversion).

4   *Hyett v Mekin* (1884) 25 Ch D 735; *Re Walker, Macintosh-Walker v Walker* [1908] 2 Ch 705; *Re Twopeny's Settlement, Monro v Twopeny* [1924] 1 Ch 522.

5   *Goodier v Edmunds* [1893] 3 Ch 455; *Re Garnham, Taylor v Baker* [1916] 2 Ch 413 (void for remoteness).

[37.3]

Implied conversion. The direction to convert did not need to be express but could be collected from the will as a whole. Thus though there might be an apparent option to invest money in land or in personalty, yet, if the limitations applicable to the investment were suitable only for real estate, the money would be treated as converted into land[1] and a mere power to sell land would operate as an imperative trust if the trusts were such that the power had to be exercised.[2] If both real and personal property were given for division in such a way as could be effected only by sale, a trust for conversion would be implied.[3]

1   *Cowley v Hartstonge* (1813) 1 Dow 361. A limitation to heirs was not sufficient to convert money into realty: *Atwell v Atwell* (1871) LR 13 Eq 23.

2   *Re Crips, Crips v Todd* (1906) 95 LT 865; *Gresham Life Assurance Society v Crowther* [1915] 1 Ch 214; *Re Johnson, Cowley v Public Trustee* [1915] 1 Ch 435.

3   *Mower v Orr* (1849) 7 Hare 473; *Greenway v Greenway* (1860) 2 De GF & J 128.

[37.4]

Conversion at request of a specified person. Where such a trust was exercisable only at the request of a specified person, the request was treated not as a condition of conversion but as intended to secure the performance of the trust. The trust in such a case was imperative and operated as a conversion, and similarly where there was provision for a specified consent or approbation of the exercise of the trust.[1]

1   *Thornton v Hawley* (1804) 10 Ves 129; *Burrell v Baskerfield* (1849) 11 Beav 525; *Re Wagstaff's Settled Estates* [1909] 2 Ch 201; *Re Ffennell's Settlement, Re Ffennell's Estate, Wright v Holton* [1918] 1 Ch 91; *Re Goswell's Trusts* [1915] 2 Ch 106.

[37.5]

Effect of conversion. The result of conversion was to make personalty liable to be included in a residuary devise of land on the one hand[1] and land in a residuary bequest of personalty on the other;[2] but, although conversion had taken place, the gift in the will of the beneficiary might be in terms which will, on the one hand, included the proceeds of sale of land in the devise or, on the other hand, included money to be laid out in land in the bequest.[3]

1   *Biddulph v Biddulph* (1806) 12 Ves 161; *Chandler v Pocock* (1881) 16 Ch D 648.
2   *Stead v Newdigate* (1817) 2 Mer 521; *Gover v Davis* (1860) 29 Beav 222.
3   *Cross v Addenbroke* (1719), cited in 3 P Wms at 222.

[37.6]
Date of conversion. The conversion took place at the death of the testator even though the sale was expressed to be had within a fixed period or was subject to a discretionary postponement,[1] but, if the sale was to be had on the happening of a future contingent event, the conversion did not take place until the event happens.[2] Where the sale was postponed after the time when it was deemed to take place, the intermediate income went to the person entitled to the proceeds of sale.[3]

1   *Hutcheon v Mannington* (1791) 1 Ves 366.
2   *Ward v Arch* (1846) 15 Sim 389 (in case of insufficiency of assets to pay annuity).
3   *Re Searle, Searle v Baker* [1900] 2 Ch 829. For the rule in *Howe v Dartmouth* (1802) 7 Ves 137, see para **[38.17]** et seq.

[37.7]
Failure of purpose of conversion. If the purposes for which conversion was directed failed either wholly or in part, then the property was treated, so far as the purposes failed, as reconverted, it being assumed that the conversion was directed for those purposes only.[1] This was so whether or not conversion had actually taken place[2] and although the real and personal property had been blended to form a mixed fund.[3] The testator could avoid this by declaring the conversion to be absolute and that the land should be treated as personalty or vice versa.[4] Where the purposes wholly failed before the death of the testator, the property passed to the beneficiary as unconverted, so that, if he was already dead, it had to be treated as property of that nature.[5] The result was otherwise where there was but a partial failure.[6]

1   *Hill v Cock* (1813) 1 Ves & B 173 at 175. The failure might be due to lapse: *Ackroyd v Smithson* (1780) 1 Bro CC 503; or failure to obtain a vested interest: *Jessopp v Watson* (1833) 1 My & K 665; or to accumulations being void: *Re Perkins, Brown v Perkins* (1909) 101 LT 345; *Re Walpole, Public Trustee v Canterbury* [1933] Ch 431; or to surplus proceeds of sale being undisposed of: *Naismith v Boyes* [1899] AC 495.
2   *Ackroyd v Smithson* (1780) 1 Bro CC 503; and see *Bective v Hodgson* (1864) 10 HL Cas 656 at 667.
3   *Jessopp v Watson* (1833) 1 My & K 665.
4   *Cruse v Barley* (1727) 3 P Wms 19 at 22.
5   *Re Hopkinson, Dyson v Hopkinson* [1922] 1 Ch 65.
6   *Re Richerson, Scales v Heyhoe* [1892] 1 Ch 379; *M'Dermott v A-G (No 2)* [1923] 1 IR 142.

[37.8]
Reconversion. When the proceeds of sale of land subject to a trust for conversion became vested in an absolute owner, he could elect to take the land as land. Such an election operated to determine the hypothetical conversion of the property or, in other words, it operated as a reconversion.[1] It was sufficient if such owner showed an intention to take the property in its actual state and it was immaterial whether he knew that he was effecting a reconversion.[2] Where several owners together have the absolute ownership they had to all concur in a reconversion and must not have encumbered or settled their shares or interests in

the property.[3] Once land could not be held in undivided shares, a reconversion to be fully effective had to take the form of a partition among such owners, though they could obtain control by having it vested in themselves (so long as there were not more than four of them) on trust for sale.[4] The person so electing to reconvert had to be of full age and sound mind, but in either case the court could elect on his behalf.[5] An election to reconvert was implied where the person entitled retained possession of the land for a considerable time;[6] or paid off a charge upon it;[7] or took possession of the title deeds;[8] or granted a lease;[9] or entered into a partition agreement.[10] A devise of land describing it as such operated as a reconversion.[11] The presumption of an election to reconvert in the case of money to be laid out in land was not so strong, but, if the money came into the hands of the absolute owner, it was discharged from the trust for conversion.[12] Even without actual receipt of the money, he might so deal with it as to show that he regarded it as personalty and then reconversion was effected.[13]

1   *Cookson v Cookson* (1845) 12 Cl & Fin 121. A person did not become an absolute owner if his interest was a contingent interest in personalty and so could not reconvert: *Re Sturt, De Bunsen v Hardinge* [1922] 1 Ch 416. As to reconversion by foreclosure of mortgage, see *Re Bogg, Allison v Paice* [1917] 2 Ch 239.
2   *Harcourt v Seymour* (1851) 2 Sim NS 12 at 46.
3   *Re Douglas and Powell's Contract* [1902] 2 Ch 296. See previously the Law of Property Act 1925, s 23, repealed by the TLATA 1996, s 25(2), Sch 4; see now the TLATA 1996, s 16 (purchaser protection).
4   See Law of Property Act, 1925, s 3(1)(b); 37 *Halsbury's Statutes* (4th edn) 428.
5   As to minors, see *Harrop's Estate* (1857) 3 Drew 726; *Robinson v Robinson* (1854) 19 Beav 494; as to persons of unsound mind, see *Re Jump, Galloway v Hope* [1903] 1 Ch 129; *Re Douglas and Powell's Contract* [1902] 2 Ch 296.
6   *Re Davidson, Martin v Trimmer* (1879) 11 Ch D 341. Two years may be too short a time: *Kirkman v Miles* (1807) 13 Ves 338; *Brown v Brown* (1864) 33 Beav 399.
7   *Re Davidson, Martin v Trimmer* (1879) 11 Ch D 341.
8   *Potter v Dudeney* (1887) 56 LT 395.
9   *Re Gordon, Roberts v Gordon* (1877) 6 Ch D 531; but not if the lease contains an option to purchase: *Re Lewis, Foxwell v Lewis* (1885) 30 Ch D 654.
10 *Sharp v St Sauveur* (1871) 7 Ch App 343.
11 *Meek v Devenish* (1877) 6 Ch D 566.
12 *Pulteney v Earl of Darlington* (1783) 1 Bro CC 223. See also *Rich v Whitfield* (1866) LR 2 Eq 583.
13 *Harcourt v Seymour* (1851) 2 Sim NS 12; *Cookson v Reay* (1842) 5 Beav 22; affd sub nom *Cookson v Cookson* (1845) 12 Cl & Fin 121.

[37.9]
Ademption. The question of conversion is also dealt with in the consideration of ademption and for that purpose conversion may be effected by a sale of land, a purchase under compulsory powers, the exercise of an option to purchase, the exercise of statutory powers, by order of the court, or by the operation of statutory provision.[1]

1   See Chapter 41.

CHAPTER 38

Residuary gifts

I. WHAT A RESIDUARY GIFT COMPRISES

[38.1]
Property not specifically disposed of. A general residuary gift after payment of debt and administration expenses,[1] passes everything not specifically disposed of, whether the testator has attempted to dispose of it and failed or whether the disposition fails by lapse or other event.[2] There is a distinction between a gift of residuary estate and a gift of the residue of the residuary estate, for if the latter gift lapses, there is an intestacy and the gift does not go to enlarge the other shares of residue.[3] The fact that the testator wrongly believes that certain property does not belong to him and is not his to dispose of and says so in his will does not exclude it from the residue.[4]

1   *Shuttleworth v Howarth* (1841) Cr & Ph 228; *Re Brooks' Will* (1865) 2 Drew & Sm 362; *Trethewy v Helyar* (1876) 4 Ch D 53.
2   *Re Bagot, Paton v Ormerod* [1893] 3 Ch 348; *Easum v Appleford* (1840) 5 My & Cr 56; *Bernard v Minishull* (1859) John 276; *Blight v Hartnoll* (1883) 23 Ch D 218. Where the testator is dealing with a definite ascertained sum, the word residue refers only to the amount remaining after the prior amounts have been taken out, and will not catch a share which has failed: *Bagge v Bagge* [1921] 1 IR 213, and see *Southmolton Corpn v A-G* (1854) 5 HL Cas 1; *Bland v Lamb* (1820) 2 Jac & W 399. Where a testator provides for the lapse of a gift by saying that it shall be disposed of in due course of administration, the gift falls into residue: *Scott v Moore* (1844) 14 Sim 35. If a residuary gift disposes of everything, a second inadvertently inserted (as in the case of a printed form of will) is ineffective: *Re Gare, Filmer v Carter* [1952] Ch 80, [1951] 2 All ER 863; and so where there is a gift of 'all my property' followed by a gift of residue, the second gift is redundant and repugnant and fails: *Re Jenkins' Trusts* (1889) 23 LR IR 162.
3   *Re Whitrod, Burrows v Base* [1926] Ch 118. See further para **[47.6]** infra.
4   *Re Bagot, Paton v Ormerod* [1893] 3 Ch 348 at 349; *Re Maber, Armsby v Maber* (1896) 12 TLR 267; *Re Lee, Gibbon v Peele* (1910) 103 LT 103. The earlier decisions to the contrary effect on this point would presumably not now be followed: see *Circuitt v Perry* (1856) 23 Beav 275; *Harris v Harris* (1869) 17 WR 790; *Hawks v Longridge* (1873) 29 LT 449; *Clibborn v Clibborn* (1857) 2 IR Jur 386. Where the testator has stated the amount of the residue and it is in fact greater, the whole passes: *Danvers v Manning* (1786) 2 Bro CC 18; *Page v Young* (1875) LR 19 Eq 501; and where in a clause beginning 'the residue of my estate' he gives specific sums, the residue is distributable in shares proportionate to those specific sums: *Re MacArthur Estate* [1953] 1 DLR 380.

[38.2]
Property subject to general power of appointment. A general devise of real estate or a general bequest of personal estate and, therefore what is now the more usual form, a general residuary gift of all the residue of the testator's real and personal property is to be construed to include any real or personal property

over which the testator may have a general power of appointment, and operates as an execution of such power in the absence of a contrary intention.[1] The testator must have the power at the time of his death and, therefore, if A by his will gives B a general power of appointment which B executes by his will, such execution will fail if B predeceases A,[2] but it is immaterial that the power is created after the execution of the will but before the death of the testator. Thus if A makes his will, and B at a later date by his will gives A a general power of appointment, A's will is a good execution of the power provided B predeceases A.[3]

1   Wills Act 1837, s 27; 50 *Halsbury's Statutes* (4th edn) 595; see Vol 2, Part G, para **[244.27]**. 'It is now absolutely necessary to show a contrary intention to exclude the execution of the power': per Lord St Leonards C in *Lake v Currie* (1852) 2 De GM & G 536 at 548.
2   *Jones v Southall (No 2)* (1862) 32 Beav 31; *Re Young, Public Trustee v Walker* [1920] 2 Ch 427; *Re Baker, Steadman v Dicksee* [1934] WN 94. The Wills Act 1837, s 33, as substituted by the Administration of Justice Act 1982, s 19; Vol 2, Part G, para **[244.95]** (providing against lapse), would validate such an appointment: see *Eccles v Cheyne* (1856) 2 K & J 676.
3   *Re Old's Trusts, Pengelley v Herbert* (1886) 54 LT 677. The rule is the same where the power is not created by will: *Patch v Shore* (1862) 2 Drew & Sm 589; *Boyes v Cook* (1880) 14 Ch D 53.

II.   WHAT AMOUNTS TO A GIFT OF RESIDUE

[38.3]
Words sufficient to pass residue. Many words are, in a suitable context, capable of denoting the whole or the residue of the real and personal estate of the testator,[1] but, however it is expressed, the effect must be that it is intended to compromise all that is not disposed of by will. It is not true residue if there is some part not disposed of at all.[2] The following words have been construed as a sufficient residuary gift: 'what shall be left';[3] 'whatever part shall be unappropriated';[4] 'rest or residue';[5] 'all other' with following words as shown in the note below;[6] 'what remains' and similar expressions;[7] 'what else testator may die possessed of';[8] 'all personal estate';[9] 'all my real estate';[10] 'property not disposed of by the will';[11] 'all I am worth';[12] 'balance';[13] 'surplus';[14] 'any residue remaining'.[15] A comprehensive gift followed by a direction to the legatee to pay debts and legacies is a gift of residue.[16] Where there is a gift of residue and, if it exceeds a certain sum, a further gift of the excess is made, the original is still a residuary gift;[17] but where, after a number of specific gifts, the testatrix stated that, if she had omitted naming anything, it was for her sisters, this was held not to be a residuary gift.[18] A residuary gift may, however, divide the remainder of the estate among the specific legatees in proportion to their legacies or the value of their legacies, for, in such a case, a legatee of a specific article, such as a ring, takes a proportionate part,[19] and similarly it may divide the remainder of the estate among legatees, the value of whose legacies does not exceed a stated sum.[20]

1   *Blight v Hartnoll* (1883) 23 Ch D 218 at 222; followed in *Re Barnes' Will Trusts, Prior v Barnes* [1972] 2 All ER 639, [1972] 1 WLR 587 ('any other personal property'; in the absence of contrary directions in the will, the law imputes a comprehensive sweeping-up effect to the residuary gift, so that any particular gift which fails, whether for lapse or illegality or otherwise, is caught up and goes with the residue).

2   *Blight v Hartnoll* (1883) 23 Ch D 218. Thus a gift of 'all my estate except my gold watch and leasehold house etc' is not a true residue, if the will does not give the gold watch and the leasehold to someone else. But for many purposes, such a gift is treated as a residuary gift.

3   *Duhamel v Ardovin* (1751) 2 Ves Sen 162; *Re Brown's Will* [1948] QWN 425 ('if there is any cash left'); *Leighton v Bailie* (1834) 3 My & K 267 ('I think there will be something left to give to A').

4   *Jackson v Kelly* (1751) 2 Ves Sen 285.

5   *Bradshaw v Bradshaw* (1756) 2 Lee 270; *Doe d Wall v Langlands* (1811) 14 East 370; *Boys v Morgan* (1838) 3 My & Cr 661 (residue); *Martin v Glover* (1844) 1 Coll 269 ('all other the rest and residue' where testator after enumerating several objects such as household furniture and the like goes on and bequeaths the rest and residue of his personal estate); *Re Craven, Crewdson v Craven* (1908) 99 LT 390; affd (1909) 100 LT 284 (rest of my investments); *Foxen v Foxen* (1864) 5 New Rep 1 (rest of his consols after debts and funeral expenses paid and what was found on his person and in his house). But a gift, after specific gifts of plate and furniture and legacies, of the 'residue of my things' was held not to be residuary: *Re Ludlow's Goods* (1858) 1 Sw & Tr 29; *Re Prout* [1943] 2 DLR 125. See also *Cogswell v Armstrong* (1855) 2 K & J 227 (all other my real and personal estate); *Smyth v Smyth* (1878) 8 Ch D 561 (all rest residue and all other effects); *Re Schott's Will Trust, Prause v Malmcrantz* (1968) 112 Sol Jo 335 (the rest and residue of my belongings); *Attree v Attree* (1871) LR 11 Eq 280 (all the rest); *Corballis v Corballis* (1882) 9 LR IR 309; *Re Aiken, Bolon v Gilliland* [1898] 1 IR 335; *Spearing v Hawkes* (1857) 6 I Ch R 297. Where all the estate was subject to a trust for sale a gift of the rest and residue of the proceeds of sale included the ready money of the testator: *Wilkinson v O'Sullivan* (1953) 27 ALJ 541.

6   *Bennett v Batchelor* (1789) 1 Ves 63 (all other unbequeathed goods and chattels); *Haerne v Wigginton* (1821) 6 Madd 119 (all my other effects); *Hodgson v Hodgson* (1876) 24 WR 575 (and other effects, following all furniture, plate and linen); *Re Shepheard's Goods* (1879) 48 LJP 62 (similar words adding 'whatsoever and wheresoever'); *Re Jupp's Goods* [1891] P 300 (all furniture, jewellery, pictures, wearing apparel and other effects); *Re Melnyk Estate, Lazaruk v Zelenko* [1936] 1 WWR 666 (all other articles); *Parker v Marchant* (1842) 1 Y & C Ch Cas 290 (jewels, plate, linen, china, carriages, wines and other goods, chattels and effects); *Wrench v Jutting* (1841) 3 Beav 521 (where the words 'all other goods of whatever kind' after enumerating certain articles failed to make the bequest a residuary one of personalty); *Martin v Glover* (1844) 1 Coll 269 (all other the rest and residue of personal estate); *Sargent v Roberts* (1848) 17 LJ Ch 117 (other personal estate not hereinbefore bequeathed); *Cogswell v Armstrong* (1855) 2 K & J 227 (all other real and personal estate of which testator might die possessed); *Re Sharman's Goods* (1869) LR 1 P & D 661 (all other chattels); *Powell v Riley* (1871) LR 12 Eq 175 (all household goods and furniture, farming stock, money, goods, chattels and effects and all other his personal estate held not to be residuary; but this decision has been doubted in *Re Ovey, Broadbent v Barrow* (1882) 51 LJ Ch 665); *Hutchinson v Rough* (1879) 40 LT 289 (all other real and personal estate); *Everall v Browne* (1853) 1 Sm & G 368 (any other property, goods and chattels); *Ayer v Benton* (1967) 204 Estates Gazette 359 (not otherwise disposed of). All worldly goods and chattels both real and personal is a residuary gift of both real and personal estate: *Re Young* [1951] Ch 344, [1950] 2 All ER 1245. But a gift of 'all other contents of my home or at the bank' is not residuary: *Re Abbott* [1944] 2 All ER 457; nor is a gift of 'my books furniture and other personal belongings at A or elsewhere': *Re Hynes* [1950] 2 All ER 879.

7   *Crooke v De Vandes* (1805) 11 Ves 330; *Dawson v Gaskin* (1837) 1 Jur 669; *Rogers v Thomas* (1837) 2 Keen 8 (all which may remain of my money); *Wrench v Jutting* (1841) 3 Beav 521 (whatever remaining sum or sums); *Re Bloomfield's Goods* (1861) 31 LJPM & A 119 (remainder of money, goods and debts); *Johnson v Johnson* (1846) 2 Coll 441 (remainder of my property); *Re Isaac, Harrison v Isaac* [1905] 1 Ch 427 (same words); *Gaffney v Hevey* (1837) 1 Dr & Wal 12 (if anything remains); *Re Edwardes* (1951) 95 Sol Jo 382 (all remaining things); *Re Stinson* (1973) 30 DLR (3d) 519.

8   *Fleming v Burrows* (1826) 1 Rus 276; *Wilce v Wilce* (1831) 7 Bing 664; *Re Hayter, Hayter v Tranter* [1937] 2 All ER 110: *Re Brace, Gurton v Clements* [1954] 2 All ER 354 ('any possessions I may have').

9   *Robertson v Broadbent* (1883) 8 App Cas 812; *Re Wolfe's Goods* [1919] 2 IR 491; *Re Scarborough's Goods* (1860) 30 LJPM & A 85 (all personal effects); *Re Garrett's Goods* (1872) 26 LT 984 (all household goods, furniture, clothes, moneys and securities for money); *Re Dutton, Herbert v Harrison* (1869) 20 LT 386 (a similar case).

407

10   *Re Wilson, Wilson v Mackay* [1967] Ch 53, [1966] 2 All ER 867, distinguishing *Re Rowe, Bennetts v Eddy* [1941] Ch 343, [1941] 2 All ER 330; considering *Re Ridley, Nicholson v Nicholson* [1950] Ch 415, [1950] 2 All ER 1.

11   *Taylor v Taylor* (1833) 6 Sim 246; *Sargent v Roberts* (1848) 17 LJ Ch 117; *Re Aston's Goods* (1881) 6 PD 203; *Green v Dunn* (1855) 20 Beav 6 (all my freeholds not hereinbefore devised).

12   *Huxtep v Brooman* (1785) 1 Bro C C 437; *Re Hayter, Hayter v Tranter* [1937] 2 All ER 110 ('Everything I die possessed of').

13   *Re Andrew, Andrew v Andrew* [1934] NZLR 526; *Re Biden* (1906) 4 WLR 477; *Re Wood* [1952] VLR 450 ('balance of my real estate'; 'real' omitted, testator having no real property at date of will or death): *Re Balakian* [1952] Argus LR 781 (balance means residue); *Re Cameron* (1967) 62 DLR (2d) 389; *Re Stinson* (1973) 30 DLR (3d) 519 (balance of cash, not residuary).

14   *Lockhart v Ray* (1880) 20 NBR 129.

15   *Re Steel, Public Trustee v Christian Aid Society* [1979] Ch 218, [1978] 2 All ER 1026 (gift of 'any residue remaining to be divided between those beneficiaries who have only received small amounts'; held that the latter words were merely words of explanation and referred to all the legatees and the residue was to be divided equally between them); *Re Sparrow* [1984] 1 NZLR 750.

16   *Chapman v Chapman* (1876) 4 Ch D 800.

17   *Duke v Hinxman* (1833) 2 LJ Ch 185; *Watt v Wood* (1862) 2 Drew & Sm 56.

18   *Barrett v White* (1855) 24 LJ Ch 724; *Re Capel, Arbuthnot v Capel* (1914) 59 Sol Jo 177; but 'any money left' after payment of debts, etc is a residuary gift: *Re Egan, Mills v Parton* [1899] 1 Ch 688.

19   *Nannock v Horton* (1802) 7 Ves 391. Where there was an intention to dispose of everything and the aggregate gifts did not dispose of all, the surplus was divided proportionally among the legatees: *Re Wilson's Will* [1935] 2 WWR 111; *Re Stevenson* [1944] 1 DLR 267; *Re MacArthur Estate* [1953] 1 DLR 380. See also para **[58.8]** infra, 'Enumeration of Particulars'.

20   *Nicholson v Patrickson* (1861) 3 Giff 209.

[38.4]

Words sufficient to pass realty. Prior to 1926 there was a disinclination to disinherit the heir[1] and residuary words which did not expressly refer to real property were not construed to include real property unless the trusts and context of the will pointed to real property as well as to personal property and showed that real property was present to the mind of the testator.[2] Since 1925 the reason for this disinclination has gone with the abolition of 'heir' and the distinction between real and personal property in the case of intestacy and there is little difficulty in the court now holding, as indeed it had often held from the earliest times, that realty could be included in a residuary gift containing no words specifically applicable to real estate.[3] Even before 1926 it had long been the practice of the courts to give more effect to the presumption that a man who makes a will does not intend to die intestate as to any of his property[4] than to show any disinclination to disinherit the heir.

1   *Doe d Hick v Dring* (1814) 2 M & S 448; *Midland Counties Rly Co v Oswin* (1844) 1 Coll 74 at 78, where Knight-Bruce V-C said 'It lies in the first instance on those who say that real estate has not descended, to show that it has not descended; but when they produce a will ... the burden is shifted. ...' The disinclination was, however, seriously weakened long before 1926.

2   *Coard v Holderness* (1855) 20 Beav 147; *Jones v Robinson* (1878) 3 CPD 344; *Re Rigetti Estate* [1950] 1 WWR 529; but the real estate passed in *Re Greenwich Hospital Improvement Act* (1855) 20 Beav 458; *Cogswell v Armstrong* (1855) 2 K & J 227; *Philips v Beal* (1858) 25 Beav 25; *Attree v Attree* (1871) LR 11 Eq 280; *Evans v Jones* (1877) 46 LJQB 280; *Lines v Lines* (1869) 22 LT 400; *Smyth v Smyth* (1878) 8 Ch D 561; *Re Andrew's Estate, Creasy v Graves* (1902) 50 WR 471.

3   *Jackson v Hogan* (1776) 3 Bro Parl Cas 388.

4   See Chapter 51. As to meaning of particular words, see further Chapter 64.

[38.5]

'Estate'. The word 'estate' used by itself was at one time thought to be sufficient in itself to pass real estate[1] but modern cases show that this word includes personal property unless the context clearly restricts it to one kind of property,[2] and it has been held to extend to real property notwithstanding the context.[3]

1   The well-known dictum of Kindersley V-C in *D'Almaine v Moseley* (1853) 1 Drew 629 at 632, has long been departed from: *Loftus v Stoney* (1867) 17 I Ch R 178; *Smyth v Smyth* (1878) 8 Ch D 561.
2   *Hamilton Corpn v Hodson* (1847) 6 Moo PCC 76.
3   *Stein v Ritherdon* (1868) 37 LJ Ch 369.

[38.6]
'Property'. This also is a word of such general import that it can be construed to include real or personal property according to the context and in general real estate will be included unless there is a distinct context restricting its meaning to personal property.[1]

1   *Doe d Wall v Langlands* (1811) 14 East 370; *Morrison v Hoppe* (1851) 4 De G & Sm 234; *Thomas v Phelps* (1828) 4 Russ 348; *Clancarty v Clancarty* (1892) 31 LR IR 530; *Re Guthrie, Trustees, Executors and Agency Co of New Zealand Ltd v Guthrie* [1925] NZLR 379. For cases where property has been restricted to personalty, see *Doe d Bunny v Rout* (1816) 2 Marsh 397; *Jauncey v A-G* (1861) 3 Giff 308.

[38.7]
'Effects'. This is a word commonly associated with personal property and clearly requires some context to extend its meaning to real estate.[1] Thus 'effects real and personal' will include real estate, and where the will has dealt with some real estate, a residue of 'effects' has been held to include realty.[2] A gift of 'all remaining effects, furniture, etc' followed by other gifts is not a residuary gift.[3]

1   *Doe d Haw v Earles* (1846) 15 M & W 450; *Michell v Michell* (1820) 5 Madd 69; *Hodgson v Jex* (1876) 2 Ch D 122; *Hall v Hall* [1891] 3 Ch 389 ('effects' without more will not pass real estate).
2   *Hogan v Jackson* (1775) 1 Cowp 299; *Doe d Chillcote v White* (1800) 1 East 33; *Marquis of Titchfield v Horncastle* (1838) 7 LJ Ch 279; *Re Wass, Re Clark* (1906) 95 LT 758.
3   *Re Brems* (1963) 36 DLR (2d 218; *Re Collins Settlement Trusts, Donne v Hewetson* [1971] 1 All ER 283. See also paras **[64.15]–[64.18]** infra.

[38.8]
Executorship. At one time it was thought that the fact the beneficiary was appointed executor showed that the words of the will were confined to personal property because an executor at that time took only the personal estate, but now that all property vests in the personal representative this construction has lost any force it formerly had.[1]

1   See *Doe d Gillard v Gillard* (1822) 5 B & Ald 785; *Murphy v Donnelly* (1870) IR 4 Eq 111.

[38.9]
Residuary legatee. These words have been held in a home-made will sufficient to pass realty.[1]

1   *Hughes v Pritchard* (1877) 6 Ch D 24; *Re Bailey, Barclay's Bank Ltd v James* [1945] Ch 191, [1945] 1 All ER 616. See, however, *Re Methuen and Blore's Contract* (1881) 16 Ch D 696, where a different conclusion was reached in a case where all the real property was acquired after the date of the will. See para **[38.12]** infra.

[38.10]

Ejusdem generis rule. Under this rule general words following particular words are restricted to articles or property of the same kind as those already enumerated or mentioned. The rule in general is subject to two important qualifications which restrict its general application and to one which restricts its application in the particular case of wills. In general, the particular words must, for the rule to apply, have some common characteristic which constitutes them a class or genus and then the rule applies to sweep in all other things of the same class, for the real purpose of the rule is to guard against accidental omissions.[1] The other general qualification, much less important, is that, if the particular words exhaust the whole class, there is nothing upon which the rule can operate and the general words then must refer to some larger class.[2] In the case of wills, the rule is commonly overridden by the presumption that, if a person makes a will, he does not intend to die intestate as to any part of his property, and, therefore, the will must be construed so as to prevent that result.[3] For this reason where general words occur in a clause in the nature of a residuary gift, the rule is not generally applied because the general words are often used for the very purpose of preventing the bequest from being so restricted.[4] This consideration, however, is not applied where the general words would in the wider meaning carry a residuary estate which is dealt with by another clause in the will;[5] nor where there is an intention to deal with a particular portion of the estate or property referred to as being in a particular locality.[6] From the general statement of the rule it applies only where the general words followed the specific enumeration, and it has been generally held not to apply where the general words precede the particular enumeration, so that, if the general words are such as would pass the residuary estate, they have that effect.[7] Again the testator may by express exception from a general description show that he intends to include that class of property in the gift, and, if that class of property is beyond a construction according to the ejusdem generis rule, the testator thus shows that the rule is not to apply. Then the disposition must be taken to carry all which has not been expressly excluded.[8]

---

1   *Lambourn v McLellan* [1903] 2 Ch 268; *Re Turner, Arnold v Blades* (1891) 36 Sol Jo 28. Where it is shown that there is no class or genus, the general words receive the widest interpretation; see, for example: *National Association of Local Government Officers v Bolton Corpn* [1943] AC 166, [1942] 2 All ER 425. Where there is only one particular word followed by general words, it has been said that the rule does not apply: see *Arnold v Arnold* (1834) 2 My & K 365; *Swinfen v Swinfen (No 4)* (1860) 29 Beav 207; *Campbell v M'Grain* (1875) IR 9 Eq 397 at 400; though this principle was not applied in *Northey v Paxton* (1888) 60 LT 30 (all household furniture and effects in residence held not to include jewellery), and there is no rule that general words cannot be so cut down: *Northey v Paxton* (1888) 60 LT 30; *Re O'Brien, O'Brien v O'Brien* [1906] 1 IR 649 at 653. The principle has been applied to investment clauses: see *Edwards v Thompson* (1868) 38 LJ Ch 65, and *Re Castlehow, Lamonby v Carter* [1903] 1 Ch 352 (companies restricted to English companies); but see *Re Stanley, Tennant v Stanley* [1906] 1 Ch 131, where the context showed that no restriction was intended. The following are examples of general words: 'etc': see para **[38.11]** infra; 'other things': *Trafford v Berrige* (1729) 1 Eq Cas Abr 201; *Re Smith's Goods* (1864) 3 Sw & Tr 589; *Stuart v Marquis of Bute* (1813) 1 Dow 73; 'all other societies': *Marks v Solomons* (1850) 2 H & Tw 323; 'other articles of a like nature': *Stone v Parker* (1860) 1 Drew & Sm 212; 'other articles': *Dutton v Hockenhull* (1874) 22 WR 701; 'all other goods of whatever kind': *Wrench v Jutting* (1841) 3 Beav 521. The general words may be restricted by one of themselves to a particular class of property: thus the words 'all other my personal estate property chattels and effects whatsoever

and wheresoever to which I am now seised possessed or entitled to or may hereafter acquire and can hereby dispose of', despite their generality in some respects, were restricted by the word 'personal' occurring in them and realty did not pass under them: *Jones v Robinson* (1878) 3 CPD 344, and cf *Lampheir v Despard* (1842) 2 Dr & War 59. In *Re Resch's Will Trusts. Le Cras v Perpetual Trustee Co Ltd, Far West Children's Health Scheme v Perpetual Trustee Co Ltd* [1969] 1 AC 514, [1967] 3 All ER 915, PC, it was held that a gift to a boy of 'my cameras projectors films and other photographic appliances and my watches (other than my calendar watch) chain studs and other personal jewellery' did not include the valuable jewellery which the testator had inherited from his deceased wife, since the words 'other personal jewellery' should be construed ejusdem generis with the description that preceded them.

2   *Fenwick v Schmalz* (1868) LR 3 CP 313 at 315.

3   *Bridges v Bridges* (1729) 2 Eq Cas Abr 330; *Chalmers v Stroil* (1813) 2 Ves & B 222; *Re Kendall's Trusts* (1851) 14 Beav 608; *Gibbs v Lawrence* (1860) 30 LJ Ch 170; *Dean v Gibson* (1867) LR 3 Eq 713 (cases of enumeration of particulars, 'viz', 'consisting of' and the like), applied in *Re Johnston* (1970) 7 DLR (3d) 256; *Shepherd v Nottidge* (1862) 2 John & H 766; *Re Parrott, Parrott v Parrott* (1885) 53 LT 12.

4   *Parker v Marchant* (1842) 1 Y & C Ch Cas 290; *Everall v Browne* (1853) 1 Sm & G 368; *Harris v James* (1864) 12 WR 509; *Hodgson v Jex* (1876) 2 Ch D 122; *Re Parrott, Parrott v Parrott* (1885) 53 LT 12.

5   *Woolcomb v Woolcomb* (1731) 3 P Wms 112; *Mullins v Smith* (1860) 1 Drew & Sm 204; *Smith v Davis* (1866) 35 LJ Ch 874; *Campbell v M'Grain* (1875) IR 9 Eq 397; *Hutchinson v Rough* (1879) 40 LT 289; *Re Miller, Daniel v Daniel* (1889) 61 LT 365; *MacPhail v Phillips* [1904] 1 IR 155; *Trustees, Executors and Agency Co Ltd v Ramsey* (1920) 27 CLR 279. Similarly, it may appear from other parts of the will that the clause is not intended to be a residuary gift: see *Rawlings v Jennings* (1806) 13 Ves 39; *Re Curling's Goods* [1928] IR 521; or the same may appear from a codicil: *Sutton v Sharp* (1826) 1 Russ 146; or where the residuary property cannot be required for a particular purpose to which the will would, construing it as a residuary gift, require it to be put: *Borton v Dunbar* (1860) 2 De GF & J 338.

6   *Gibbs v Lawrence* (1860) 30 LJ Ch 170.

7   *Re Kendall's Trust* (1851) 14 Beav 608; *Fisher v Hepburn* (1851) 14 Beav 626; *Drake v Martin* (1856) 23 Beav 89; *Nugee v Chapman (No 2)* (1860) 29 Beav 290; *Dean v Gibson* (1867) LR 3 Eq 713; *Re Maberly's Settlement Trusts* (1871) 24 LT 262; *King v George* (1877) 5 Ch D 627; *Re Fleetwood, Sidgreaves v Brewer* (1880) 15 Ch D 594; *Re Roberts, Kiff v Roberts* (1886) 55 LT 498; *Re Duffell, Equity Trustees, Executors and Agency Co Ltd v Duffell* [1926] VLR 489; *Tighe v Featherstonhaugh* (1883) 13 LR IR 401; *Re Recknell, White v Carter* [1936] 2 All ER 36. But the subsequent particular words may be a qualifying and defining statement substituted for the antecedent generality, when the gift will be confined to the particular words: *Sutton v Sharp* (1826) 1 Russ 146 (where the subsequent words were in a codicil); *Re Fletcher* (1914) 19 DLR 624.

8   *Hotham v Sutton* (1808) 15 Ves 319 ('other effects, money excepted': the gift included all property except money); but see *Cross v Wilks* (1866) 35 Beav 562 ('effects' controlled by the rule and real estate excluded).

[38.11]

The use of 'etc'. In early times there was a tendency to hold that the heir could not be deprived of his inheritance by the use of this word after the enumeration of a number of things not necessarily real estate,[1] but later cases seem to show an opposite tendency.[2] Where personal property only is concerned there are decisions both that its significance is restricted by the ejusdem generis rule, and others that it is to be given a wider import.[3]

1   *Timewell v Perkins* (1740) 2 Atk 102.

2   *Chapman v Chapman* (1876) 4 Ch D 800; *Re Andrew's Estate, Creasey v Greaves* (1902) 50 WR 471.

3   It was restricted in *Hertford v Lowther* (1843) 7 Beav 1; *Newman v Newman (No 2)* (1858) 26 Beav 220; *Barnaby v Tassell* (1871) LR 11 Eq 363; *Milne's Trustees v Davidson* 1956 SC 81. For the wider meaning, see *Kendall v Kendall* (1828) 4 Russ 360; *Twining v Powell* (1845) 2 Coll 262; *Gover v Davis* (1860) 29 Beav 222.

[38.12]

Appointment of person to be residuary legatee. Such an appointment will in the ordinary way give the legatee only the residue of the personal property,[1] but, where the context or the circumstances require it, it may pass residuary realty. This will be so where the will shows an intention to dispose of the whole real and personal estate;[2] where parts of the real estate are specifically devised,[3] but not where the residuary legatee is one of the specific devises,[4] nor where the real estate is directed to be sold for the general purposes of the will.[5] The fact that the testator either had no real estate at the date of his will[6] or made complete disposition of all such real estate by will[7] is against the residuary legatee taking, but not conclusive on the point.[8]

1   *Re Gibbs, Martin v Harding* [1907] 1 Ch 465 at 468; *Kellett v Kellett* (1815) 3 Dow 248; *Lea v Grundy* (1855) 25 LTOS 287; *Windus v Windus* (1856) 6 De GM & G 549; *Re Methuen and Blore's Contract* (1881) 16 Ch D 696.
2   *Pitman v Stevens* (1812) 15 East 505 (where the residuary legatee was to deal with the estate generally); *Day v Daveron* (1841) 12 Sim 200; *Davenport v Coltman* (1842) 12 Sim 588; *Evans v Crosbie* (1847) 15 Sim 600; *Singleton v Tomlinson* (1878) 3 App Cas 404; *Re Salter, Farrant v Carter* (1881) 44 LT 603; *Re Greally, Travers v O'Donoghue* [1910] 1 IR 239; *Re Pereira, Worsley v Society for the Propagation of the Gospel in Foreign Parts* (1912) 28 TLR 479; *Re Wightman Estate* (1945) 4 DLR 754.
3   *Hughes v Pritchard* (1877) 6 Ch D 24; *Re Bailey, Barclays Bank Ltd v James* [1945] Ch 191, [1945] 1 All ER 616.
4   *Hillas v Hillas* (1847) 10 I Eq R 134; *Re Morris, Morris v Atherden* (1894) 71 LT 179; *Re Gibbs, Martin v Harding* [1907] 1 Ch 465 at 468.
5   *Singleton v Tomlinson* (1878) 3 App Cas 404, and see *Re Gibbs, Martin v Harding* [1907] 1 Ch 465.
6   *Re Methuen and Blore's Contract* (1881) 16 Ch D 696.
7   *Re Gibbs, Martin v Harding* [1907] 1 Ch 465.
8   *Re Stephen, Stephen v Stephen* [1913] WN 210; *Re Fetherston-Haugh-Whitney's Estate* [1924] 1 IR 153.

III.   FAILURE OF SHARE

[38.13]

Failure of share of residue. Where the gift of a share in residue fails, prima facie the lapsed share does not go to increase the other shares of residue but passes on an intestacy;[1] but the will may direct that any such share, whether lapsed or revoked, shall fall into residue and such direction operates as a gift of that share to the other residuary legatees,[2] or the will may direct that all are to receive an equal participation in the property.[3] There is no intestacy where the residuary gift is to a class[4] or given in joint tenancy.[5] A mere confirmation of the will by a codicil in all other respects is, however, insufficient for this purpose[6] and so is a confirmation except as to any lapsed legacy.[7]

1   *Re Wood's Will* (1861) 29 Beav 236 (where only part of share failed); *Sykes v Sykes* (1868) 3 Ch App 301; *Re Bentley, Podmore v Smith* (1914) 110 LT 623; *Re Forrest, Carr v Forrest* [1931] 1 Ch 162. Where the residue is given in aliquot parts and there follows a gift introduced by the words 'and the rest', this rule applies: *Re Whitrod, Burrows v Base* [1926] Ch 118. Such a failure occurs where the residue is given on the trusts of a settlement with an ultimate trust for the testator which becomes effective: *Re Currie's Settlement, Re Rooper, Rooper v Williams* [1910] 1 Ch 329; *Re Powell, Bodvel Roberts v Poole* [1918] 1 Ch 407.

2   Lapsed share: *Re Palmer, Palmer v Answorth* [1893] 3 Ch 369, overruling *Humble v Shore* (1847) 7 Hare 247. Revoked share: *Re Allan, Dow v Cassaigne* [1903] 1 Ch 276 (considered as to a second and further accruer in *Re Lybbe's Will Trusts, Kildahl v Bowker* [1954] 1 All ER 487); *Re Wilkins, Wilkins v Wilkins* [1920] 2 Ch 63. Where in such a case the residue is given between two classes, a revoked share is divided proportionately between the classes: *Re Wand, Escritt v Wand* [1907] 1 Ch 391.
3   *Vaudrey v Howard* (1853) 2 WR 32.
4   *Clark v Phillips* (1853) 17 Jur 886; *Re Dunster, Brown v Heywood* [1909] 1 Ch 103; *Re Woods, Woods v Creagh* [1931] 2 Ch 138.
5   *Willing v Baine* (1731) 3 P Wms 113.
6   *Re Wilkins, Wilkins v Wilkins* [1920] 2 Ch 63; *Re Forrest, Carr v Forrest* [1931] 1 Ch 162, not following *Re Whiting, Ormond v De Launay* [1913] 2 Ch 1.
7   *Re Wood's Will* (1861) 29 Beav 236.

[38.14]
Failure of legacy given out of share of residue. If a legacy given out of a share of residue fails, it goes on an intestacy;[1] but where the will contains a gift over operating on the share of residue as a whole, the gift of the remaining part of that share carries such a legacy in the event of failure.[2] However, where a part of residue is given to an attesting witness, the effect of the Wills Act 1837, s 15[3] is to render such a gift null and void and the will must be treated as though it did not contain the offending disposition at all.[4]

1   *Lloyd v Lloyd* (1841) 4 Beav 231; applied in *Green v Pertwee* (1846) 5 Hare 249, but doubted in *Re Judkin's Trusts* (1884) 25 Ch D 743 at 750. See also *Re Parker, Stephenson v Parker* [1901] 1 Ch 408.
2   *Re Parker, Stephenson v Parker* [1901] 1 Ch 408; *Re Parnell, Ranks v Holmes* [1944] Ch 107 (where after the legacy given out of the residuary trust fund, there was a gift of 'all the remainder of the residuary trust fund').
3   See Vol 2, Part G, para **[244.12]**; and see para **[9.3]** supra.
4   *Re Doland's Will Trusts, Westminster Bank Ltd v Phillips* [1970] Ch 267, [1969] 3 All ER 713; accordingly such a gift was not covered by a proviso 'if the trusts of any of the shares aforesaid of my residuary estate shall fail' but was undisposed of, and passed as an intestacy.

IV.   RIGHTS OF RESIDUARY LEGATEE

[38.15]
Right of residuary legatee to have residue ascertained. A residuary legatee is in a peculiar position in that he has no right to anything until the residue is ascertained. It is, therefore, necessary that there shall be no undue delay in ascertaining the residue. At one time it was considered that in most cases a year was more than ample for this purpose and it was said that there was an executor's year during which he must clear the estate and ascertain the residue. However, there never was a rule of law that executors must clear the estate within a year of the testator's death.[1] The only duty is one of due diligence, and it may be that due diligence may require the clearing of the estate within the year.[2] The residuary legatee, however, takes under the will and must, therefore take the residue subject to all the terms of the will which modify the executor's duty to clear the estate with due diligence.[3] Thus a power to retain assets unconverted may justify a delay in realising those assets before the expiration of the executor's year and, if such retention is in all the circumstances reasonable, any loss resulting must be borne by the residuary legatee.[4]

413

1   *Re Tankard, Tankard v Midland Bank Executor and Trustee Co Ltd* [1942] Ch 69 at 73, [1941]
    3 All ER 458 at 464; *Wightwick v Lord* (1857) 6 HL Cas 217 (within a year, if possible).
2   *Re Tankard, Tankard v Midland Bank Executor and Trustee Co Ltd* [1942] Ch 69 at 73, [1941]
    3 All ER 458 at 464; *Wightwick v Lord* (1857) 6 HL Cas 217 (within a year, if possible), and
    see *Grayburn v Clarkson* (1868) 3 Ch App 605 at 606.
3   *Re Tankard, Tankard v Midland Bank Executor and Trustee Co Ltd* [1942] Ch 69.
4   *Re Tankard, Tankard v Midland Bank Executor and Trustee Co Ltd* [1942] Ch 69.

[38.16]
No right to any particular asset. The right of a residuary legatee is not to any
particular asset of the testator's estate. The only right of such a beneficiary is to
have the clear residue ascertained and such residue or the beneficiary's share of
it paid over.[1] Despite this, however, there is authority that an executor can
properly let a residuary legatee into possession of part of the estate before the
residue is finally ascertained,[2] and it is quite a common practice, where the
residuary legatees are absolutely entitled and the estate is obviously more than
sufficient to meet liabilities, to make a partial distribution of residue from time
to time as administration proceeds.

1   *Lord Sudley v A-G* [1897] AC 11, and see *Vanneck v Benham* [1917] 1 Ch 60; *Re Holmes,
    Villiers v Holmes* [1917] 1 IR 165; *Barnardo's Homes v Income Tax Special Comrs* [1921] 2
    AC 1; *IRC v Smith* [1930] 1 KB 713.
2   See *Austin v Beddoe* (1893) 41 WR 619.

V.   WHERE THE RESIDUARY ESTATE IS SETTLED—RULE IN HOWE V DARTMOUTH

[38.17]
Rule in *Howe v Dartmouth*.[1] Where the residuary personal estate[2] is settled it is
assumed, unless the will shows a contrary intention, that the testator intended his
trustees to hold an even hand between the beneficiaries entitled for life and those
interested in remainder. In order that the tenant for life shall not take too much
out of the estate by way of income, the rule requires that wasting assets and
hazardous securities[3] shall be either converted or treated as converted into
payment investments of a recognised character, ie trustee investments authorised
by the will. In order that the remainderman shall not enjoy property which is in
effect not available to the tenant for life, the rule requires that reversionary
interests[4] shall be sold,[5] and the proceeds invested in permanent investments of
the kinds already referred to. Other parts of the rule (and these are more
commonly required than those above stated) provide for the administration of
the estate on the footing that the rule has been complied with.

1   See Vol 2, Form B14. The rule in *Howe v Earl of Dartmouth* (1802) 7 Ves 137 strictly applies
    only in the case where the residue is not subject to a trust for sale and conversion. Where there
    is a trust for sale or conversion, the relevant rule is more strictly described as the rule in *Gibson
    v Bott* (1802) 7 Ves 89, but these rules have now for so long been referred to as the rule in
    Howe v Dartmouth that it is convenient so to describe them. The third rule in *Re Chesterfield's
    Trusts* (1883) 24 Ch D 643, has generally been considered a separate rule, but is properly
    included in the expression 'the rule as in *Howe v Dartmouth*'. At times the rules in *Gibson v
    Bott* and *Re Chesterfield's Trusts* are described as branches of the rule in *Howe v Dartmouth*

and a will sometimes excludes the application of the rule in *Howe v Dartmouth* in all its branches. See further, para **[38.22]** infra.

2   The rule applies only to personal estate and has no application to freeholds: *Re Woodhouse, Public Trustee v Woodhouse* [1941] Ch 332, [1941] 2 All ER 265; *Lottman v Stanford* (1980) 107 DLR (3d) 28. Its application to leaseholds was varied by the 1925 legislation: see para **[38.22]**, n 8. It has no application to any gifts whether by will or inter vivos other than residuary gifts.

3   Wasting and hazardous securities now include all securities not either trustee securities or investments authorised by the will. The modern tendency to give trustees wide investment powers necessarily narrows the scope of the rule and, indeed, it is a very common practice to exclude the rule by express words in the will. It is sometimes said that every well-drawn will should exclude the rule and *Re Norrington, Brindley v Partridge* (1879) 13 Ch D 654, is cited for this proposition, but this is not precisely what James LJ said at 655, though in effect it may be the same.

4   Reversionary interests include interests where the reversion is upon the life of the tenant for life of the residue: *Johnson v Routh* (1857) 27 LJ Ch 305; *Countess of Harrington v Atherton* (1864) 2 De GJ & Sm 352; *Rowlls v Bebb* [1900] 2 Ch 107. Where a person is entitled to property subject to the right of the trustees at their discretion to pay the whole or part of the income thereof to a widow, the interest is not a reversionary interest: *Re Holliday, Houghton v Adlard* [1947] Ch 402, [1947] 1 All ER 695. Where a policy provides for annual payments after the death of the insured, such payments are not reversionary interests: strictly so called but the *Re Chesterfield* rule can still apply to them: *Re Fisher, Harris v Fisher* [1943] Ch 377, [1943] 2 All ER 615. But where the deceased was entitled under a service contract to certain sums to be paid after his death, these were reversionary interests to be apportioned under the rule in *Re Chesterfield's Trusts; Re Payne, Westminster Bank Ltd v Payne* [1943] 2 All ER 675, and the same result was reached as to instalments of the purchase price of a business some of which fell to be received after the death of the testator and were to be apportioned to capital and income according to the rule: *Re Hollebone, Hollebone v Hollebone* [1919] 2 Ch 93.

5   *Johnson v Routh* (1857) 27 LJ Ch 305; *Rowlls v Bebb* [1900] 2 Ch 107. The testator may show by the terms of his will that he does not intend the reversion to be sold before it falls into possession: *Re Flower, Matheson v Goodwyn* (1890) 63 LT 201.

[38.18]

Trust for conversion. The rule applies whether or not there is a trust for conversion[1] but, where there is no trust for conversion, an express power to retain existing investment is sufficient to exclude the rule[2] and for this purpose there is no distinction between unauthorised securities of a wasting and those of a permanent character.[3] A discretionary power of sale, as opposed to a trust for sale or a direction to convert, excludes the application of the rule.[4] Where certain property is expressly excluded from the trust for conversion, that does not necessarily exclude the rule as to that property.[5]

1   See, however, para **[38.17]**, n 1. A trust to invest is a trust for conversion: *Re Fawcett, Public Trustee v Dugdale* [1940] Ch 402.

2   *Gray v Siggers* (1880) 15 Ch D 74; *Re Sheldon, Nixon v Sheldon* (1888) 39 Ch D 50; *Re Bates, Hodgson v Bates* [1907] 1 Ch 22; *Re Wilson, Moore v Wilson* [1907] 1 Ch 394; *Re Nicholson, Eade v Nicholson* [1909] 2 Ch 111. As to a trust either to retain or sell land, see now the Trusts of Land and Appointment of Trustees Act 1996, ss 1–5.

3   *Re Nicholson, Eade v Nicholson* [1909] 2 Ch 111.

4   *Simpson v Lester* (1858) 33 LTOS 6; *Re Pitcairn, Brandreth v Colvin* [1896] 2 Ch 199; *Re Bentham, Pearce v Bentham* (1906) 94 LT 307; *Re Mitchell Estate, National Trust Co Ltd v Carson* [1936] 3 WWR 249. The rule can be excluded by a discretionary power to sell when the trustees think fit; *Re Pitcairn, Brandreth v Colvin* [1896] 2 Ch 199. For this reason and as a result of the Trusts of Land and Appointment of Trustees Act 1996, it is now practical to draft residuary administration trusts in this form instead of providing a trust for sale.

5   *Arnold v Ennis* (1835) 2 I Ch R 601.

[38.19]

Power to postpone conversion. The usual power to postpone conversion and to retain existing securities does not in general exclude the rule,[1] but where the power of postponement amounts to a power to postpone and retain permanently for the benefit of the tenant for life the rule is excluded.[2] The rule is also excluded by the more usual provision that the tenant for life shall have actual income derived from the property pending conversion,[3] but where there is a power to postpone conversion, this provision in the will operates only from the time when the trustees determine to postpone.[4]

1   *Re Carter* (1892) 41 WR 140; *Re Woods, Gabellini v Woods* [1904] 2 Ch 4; *Re Chaytor, Chaytor v Horn* [1905] 1 Ch 233; *Re Berry, Lloyds Bank Ltd v Berry* [1962] Ch 97, [1961] 1 All ER 529; *Royal Trust Co and MacMurray v Crawford* [1955] SCR 184 (the rule might be excluded if a power to invest in the shares of certain companies, such shares being included in the estate, was inserted solely for the purpose of enabling the trustees to dispose of the shares more advantageously).
2   *Re Thomas, Wood v Thomas* [1891] 3 Ch 482; *Re Inman, Inman v Inman* [1915] 1 Ch 187; *Re Rogers, Public Trustee v Rogers* [1915] 2 Ch 437.
3   *Mackie v Mackie* (1845) 5 Hare 70; *Re Thomas, Wood v Thomas* [1891] 3 Ch 482; *Re Elford, Elford v Elford* [1910] 1 Ch 814; *Re Sherry, Sherry v Sherry* [1913] 2 Ch 508; *Re Godfree, Godfree v Godfree* [1914] 2 Ch 110; *Re Slater, Slater v Jonas* (1915) 85 LJ Ch 432. But it seems that the trustees cannot postpone conversion otherwise than as a matter of management for the general benefit of the estate and not so as to alter the rights of the parties: *Rowlls v Bebb* [1900] 2 Ch 107 at 117; nor is a clause excluding the rule operative unless the executors or the trustees, as the case may be, determine to postpone the sale. Until they so determine the rules must be applied, but after they have so determined the rules are not applied: *Re Hey's Settlement Trusts and Will Trusts, Hey v Nickell-Lean* [1945] Ch 294, [1945] 1 All ER 618, following *Rowlls v Bebb*, and applying *Re Fisher, Harris v Fisher* [1943] Ch 377, [1943] 2 All ER 615. The rule is not applied so long as the trustees postpone conversion, but trustees owe a duty to act impartially as between tenant for life and remainderman: *Re MacNaughton* [1955] NZLR 45.
4   See last part of preceding n 3.

[38.20]

Power to retain investments. Where there is a trust for conversion, this has been dealt with in the preceding paragraph. Where there is no trust for conversion, an express power to retain existing investments is sufficient to exclude the rule[1] and for this purpose there is no distinction between unauthorised securities of a wasting and those of a permanent nature,[2] but a power to invest in such securities as the executor may deem advisable is only a power to invest in authorised securities[3] and in this case the rule applies.[4]

1   See cases cited in para **[38.18]**, n 2.
2   *Re Nicholson, Eade v Nicholson* [1909] 2 Ch 111.
3   *Re Hazeldine, Public Trustee v Hazeldine* [1918] 1 Ch 433.
4   *Re Lennox Estate* [1949] SCR 446.

[38.21]

Adjustment where property not converted. The rule requiring the sale of unauthorised securities is seldom complied with even within one year of the testator's death and the problem is to give effect to the rule by adjustments between capital and income in the estate accounts. If some part of the estate consists of authorised investments, the tenant for life is entitled to the income from such investments from the date of the testator's death whether that income is more or less than 4 per cent per annum.[1] The unauthorised investments may in fact be sold during the year following the testator's death or after the expiration of that year. Where they are sold within the year, the tenant for life is entitled to receive interest at 4 per cent per annum on the net proceeds of sale from the date of death to the date of completion.[2] Where they are sold after the expiration of that year, the tenant for life is entitled to receive interest at 4 per cent per annum from the date of the death of the testator until the date of realisation on the value of such assets at the expiration of one year from the testator's death.[3] Special accounting rules apply to the income from unauthorised investments. Such investments are to be taken *en bloc* as one aggregate for the purpose of applying the rule[4] and no apportionment is to be made as at the death of the testator or as at the end of an accounting period. Any surplus income from such investments over the amount payable to the tenant for life in any accounting period is to be invested and treated as capital, but the tenant for life is entitled to the subsequent income earned by such invested income. In the case of deficiency (that is where the income from unauthorised investment is less than the amount payable to the tenant for life) interest is payable out of the proceeds of realisation. But while some unauthorised investments are still retained, any arrears of payments to the tenant for life (with added interest calculated at simple interest) are payable out of the subsequent income of the unauthorised investments so retained or out of the proceeds of their realisation when realised. No such deficiency can be made up out of surplus income in any previous year (for that should have been invested) nor out of the proceeds of sale of unauthorised investments sold before the deficiency arose (that is to say a deficiency cannot be made up out of the capital of authorised investments). After realisation the tenant for life is entitled only to the income from the authorised investments, whether that be at a rate above or below 4 per cent per annum.[5] Where the realisation is of part only this applies only to the part realised and the retained unauthorised investments and their income are dealt with as already stated.

There are two rules as to the time when the value of the unauthorised investments is computed. Where there is no trust for conversion or a trust for conversion with no power to postpone conversion, the date is as above stated one year from the testator's death.[6] Where, however, there is a trust for conversion and a power to postpone[7] the valuation is made as at the testator's death and it seems that the special rule above stated[8] as to unauthorised investments sold within a year from the testator's death will not apply.[9]

---

1   *Verner v General and Commercial Investment Trust* [1894] 2 Ch 239 at 258; *Re Fawcett, Public Trustee v Dugdale* [1940] Ch 402. The tenant for life is, of course, also entitled to the income from authorised investments resulting from the investment of the proceeds of sale of unauthorised investments and to all such income even if it exceeds 4 per cent per annum and not only to such income where it is less than 4 per cent per annum. It is only to the income of unauthorised investments while retained unconverted that these rules apply.

2   This and the following rules are taken from *Re Fawcett, Public Trustee v Dugdale* [1940] Ch 402. The rate of 4 per cent is still invariably cited as the correct rate of interest but is now out of line with other comparable rates and it could be that it would be proper to seek a direction of the court to pay a higher rate. It is submitted, however, that this part of the rule is not applicable where, as in *Re Parry, Brown v Parry* [1947] Ch 23, [1946] 2 All ER 412, the valuation has to be made at the death of the testator: see infra.

3   *Re Fawcett, Public Trustee v Dugdale* [1940] Ch 402. See *Re Kerrigan, National Trustees, Executors and Agency Co of Australasia v Kerngan* [1916] VLR 516, for a case where property was not immediately realisable and when sold would probably be sold upon a contract for payment by instalments.

4   *Re Owen, Slater v Owen* [1912] 1 Ch 519; *Re Fawcett, Public Trustee v Dugdale* [1940] Ch 402.
5   *Re Fawcett, Public Trustee v Dugdale* [1940] Ch 402.
6   *Howe v Dartmouth* (1802) 7 Ves 137; *Re Fawcett, Public Trustee v Dugdale* [1940] Ch 402.
7   It must be an ordinary power to postpone. A power amounting to a power to retain unauthorised investments will exclude the rule: see para **[38.20]** supra.
8   See n 2 supra.
9   *Re Parry, Brown v Parry* [1947] Ch 23, [1946] 2 All ER 412.

[38.22]
Reversionary interests—rule in *Re Chesterfield's Trusts.* In the case of reversionary interests there are two branches of the rule in *Howe v Dartmouth.* The first is the rule as it is ordinarily stated and provides, so far as reversionary interests are concerned, that they shall be sold and the proceeds invested in authorised securities[1]. The other is commonly known as the rule in *Re Chesterfield's Trusts*[2] and though often stated as a separate rule is now settled to be a part or branch of the earlier rule.[3] A clause in a will excluding the rule in *Howe v Dartmouth* also excludes the rule in *Re Chesterfield's Trusts.*[4] This second rule provides for the case where the reversionary interest has not been sold in accordance with the terms of the first rule and has fallen into possession after the death of the testator. When this happens it is clear that to do justice between the tenant for life and the remainderman, such an interest must not be treated wholly as capital, for it ought to have been sold at the commencement of the administration and the tenant for life should have been receiving from time to time income derived from the proceeds of sale. To remedy this position the amount of the reversionary interest is apportioned between capital and income. The apportionment is made by ascertaining the sum which, if put out at interest at 4 per cent per annum on the day of the testator's death and accumulated at compound interest with deduction for income tax, would with the accumulations of interest have produced the amount actually received in respect of the interest when it fell in.[5] The sum so ascertained is treated as capital and the remainder as income.[6] The rule does not apply to freehold land,[7] and , under the previous law, it may be that it did not apply to land subject to a trust for sale.[8] It is doubtful, too, whether it applies on an intestacy.[9] The complexity and difficulty of the calculation involved makes it very advisable to exclude it in the case of all wills, except possibly where there is known to be a reversionary interest of considerable value likely to fall into possession some long time after the death of the testator.[10] Not every sum that falls to be paid after the death of the testator is a reversionary interest.[11]

1   See para **[38.17]** supra.
2   (1883) 24 Ch D 643.
3   *Re Hey's Settlement Trusts and Will Trusts, Hey v Nickell-Lean* [1945] 1 All ER 618.
4   *Re Hey's Settlement Trusts and Will Trusts, Hey v Nickell-Lean* [1945] 1 All ER 618 at 627.
5   *Re Earl Chesterfield's Trusts* (1883) 24 Ch D 643.
6   If the tenant for life is dead, his estate is entitled to a proportionate part of the income.
7   *Re Woodhouse, Public Trustee v Woodhouse* [1941] Ch 332, [1941] 2 All ER 265; *Lottman v Stanford* (1980) 107 DLR (3d) 28.
8   That is the law before the coming into force of the Trusts of Land and Appointment of Trustees Act 1996 (TLATA 1996). The TLATA 1996 replaces trusts for sale with trusts of land ; see ss 1–5. Consequently the Law of Property Act 1925, ss 28–30 are repealed. On the effect of the Law of Property Act 1925, s 28 (2), (37 *Halsbury's Statutes* (4th edn) 151) on the rule in *Howe*

v Earl of Dartmouth (1802) 7 Ves 137, and on the rule in *Re Chesterfield's Trusts* (see n 5 supra), see *Re Brooker, Brooker v Brooker* [1926] WN 93 and *Re Woodhouse, Public Trustee v Woodhouse* [1941] Ch 332, [1941] 2 All ER 265. It is submitted that the true view is that the rule in *Howe v Dartmouth* was excluded in the case of land held upon trust for sale only so far as the statute expressly stated, ie that the tenant for life was entitled to the rents and profits of the land until sale, and not further, so that reversionary interests fell to be dealt with as the rule (including its *Re Chesterfield's Trusts* branch) required.

9   The Administration of Estates Act 1925, s 33; 17 *Halsbury's Statutes* (4th edn) 437 Vol 2, Part G, para **[244.58]** previously stated that reversionary interests were not to be sold. This section has been amended by the TLATA 1996, s 25, Sch 2, para 5 so as to no longer provide for a trust for sale and the direction not to sell a reversionary interest has been repealed. The rule in *Re Chesterfield's Trusts* probably does not apply where the trustees have a power to sell when they think fit.

10   It seems better to exclude the rule by stating in express terms that such interests shall not be sold and not be treated as producing income rather than excluding the rule by name.

11   See para **[38.17]**, n 4.

[38.23]

Exclusion of rule.[1] The rule prevails unless there can be gathered from the will some expression of intention that the property is to be enjoyed in specie, ie that the tenant for life is to receive the actual income of the property in the state in which it is found at the testator's death,[2] and the onus is on those resisting the application of the rule to show an intention.[3] The specific enumeration of property in the residuary gift can lead to the exclusion of the rule,[4] but this is not so where some of the specific things enumerated are not of such a nature that they can be left outstanding.[5] Directions for the property to be dealt with in a certain way after the death of the tenant for life[6] and even during the lifetime of the tenant for life[7] exclude the rule. Where the trust for conversion is only to arise on the death of the tenant for life (usually evidenced by a direction to divide the estate on the death of the tenant for life), the usual conclusion has been that the rule is to be applied.[8] A direction to pay rents to the tenant for life appears to exclude the rule where the residue does not include freehold property but to leave the rule effective where such property is included.[9] A direction or power to retain wasting securities coupled with a gift of the income of the residuary estate,[10] and discretionary power to sell when trustees shall think fit, since it negatives an immediate duty to sell, excludes the rule.[11] It goes without saying that if the testator has directed that income of the residue before conversion shall until conversion be treated as if it were income arising from the proceeds of conversion, then the rule is unquestionably excluded.[12] Indeed this is the general form used in wills for effecting such exclusion; and a direction that no property not actually producing income shall be treated as producing income negatives the application of the rule to reversionary interests,[13] but, where trustees took a mortgage in respect of a debt due to the estate and afterwards realised the mortgage, this was not property not actually producing income and the proceeds of realisation had to be apportioned between the tenant for life and remainderman in the proportions in which they represented interest and capital.[14] But, where there is a power to postpone the sale and an express clause excluding the rule, such a clause excluding the rule operates only if the executors in the property exercise of their discretion decide to postpone the sale.[15] The rule is not generally applicable to an absolute interest in residue subject to an executory limitation.[16]

1   For drafting aspects see Vol 2, Form B14.
2   *Simpson v Lester* (1858) 33 LTOS 6; *Alcock v Sloper* (1833) 2 My & K 699; and there are a number of authorities where it was held that the tenant for life was entitled to the income produced by long annuities, though there was much authority that these ought to be converted into consuls where the rule applied: *Howe v Howe* (1849) 14 LTOS 290 (leaseholds); *Solomon v Solomon* (1864) 33 LJ Ch 473 (leaseholds); *Cotton v Cotton* (1850) 14 Jur 950 (where furniture in a cottage was directed to be retained although the will only specifically mentioned the cottage); *Skirving v Williams* (1857) 24 Beav 275 (where partnership articles directed the retention of testator's capital for 18 months and the tenant for life was held entitled to the profits for that period); *Stroud v Gwyer* (1860) 28 Beav 130 (where the part of the profits of a partnership was to be ploughed back); *Stranier v Hodgkinson* (1903) 73 LJ Ch 179 (where the period of division was to be at the widow's death and the estate was given for her use); and for cases where the will directs conversion at the death of the tenant for life, see *Lane v Brown* (1871) 25 LT 152; *Greaves v Smith* (1874) 29 LT 798. See also *Collins v Collins* (1833) 2 My & K 703 (where the widow was given leaseholds in every shape for life and with power to dispose of half at her death); *Re Hendrie* (1969) 3 DLR (3d) 590.
3   *Morgan v Morgan* (1851) 14 Beav 72; *Macdonald v Irvine* (1878) 8 Ch D 101; *Re Slater, Slater v Jonas* (1915) 85 LJ Ch 432; *Re Barratt, National Provincial Bank Ltd v Barratt* [1925] Ch 550.
4   *D'Aglie v Fryer* (1841) 12 Sim 1; affd 12 Sim 328n (gift in remainder specifically referred to); *Vaughan v Buck* (1841) 1 Ph 75 (bulk of residue specifically enumerated); *Walker v Tillott* (1835) 4 LJ Ch 232; *Oakes v Strachey* (1843) 13 Sim 414; *Cockran v Cockran* (1844) 14 Sim 248; *Hubbard v Young* (1847) 10 Beav 203 (in the last four cases public funds were specifically referred to and formed the major part of the residuary estate: the two parts of the estate being separately stated in the will appears to lend support to the conclusion that that part specifically referred to is to be enjoyed in specie.
5   *Sutherland v Cooke* (1844) 1 Coll 498 (where enumeration included securities for money and outstanding debts).
6   *Goodenough v Tremamondo* (1840) 2 Beav 512 (power to apply rents after death of tenant for life in maintenance of remainderman); *Daniel v Warren* (1843) 2 Y & C Ch Cas 290 (direction for sale on happening of specific event); *Cafe v Bent* (1845) 5 Hare 24 (direction to retain percentage of rents); *Harris v Poyner* (1852) 1 Drew 174 (where the property was specifically given to remainderman). In *Lane v Brown* (1871) 25 LT 152, and *Greaves v Smith* (1874) 29 LT 798, the rule was excluded by a direction to convert at the death of the tenant for life.
7   *Harvey v Harvey* (1842) 5 Beav 134 (power to retain sum for renewal of leaseholds); *Re Bentham, Pearce v Bentham* (1906) 94 LT 307 (power to tenant for life to sell); *Re Rogers, Public Trustee v Rogers* [1915] 2 Ch 437 (sale only with consent of tenant for life).
8   *Hunt v Scott* (1847) 1 De G & Sm 219; *House v Way* (1848) 18 LJ Ch 22; *Marshall v Bremner* (1854) 2 Sm & G 237; *Holgate v Jennings* (1857) 24 Beav 623; *Boys v Boys* (1860) 28 Beav 436 (where the testator directed that the principle was to remain untouched); *Rowe v Rowe* (1861) 29 Beav 276; *Greaves v Smith* (1874) 29 LT 798; *Re Barratt, National Provincial Bank v Barratt* [1925] Ch 550. See to the contrary, *Re Evans Will Trusts, Pickering v Evans* [1921] 2 Ch 309. The effect of making the trust for sale subject to the consent of the tenant for life makes the position the same as where the trust is to arise only on the death of the tenant for life: *Re Rogers, Public Trustee v Rogers* [1915] 2 Ch 437.
9   The two cases of *Re Game, Game v Young* [1897] 1 Ch 881, and *Re Wareham, Wareham v Brewin* [1912] 2 Ch 312, are generally considered as stating the position correctly. Apparently the earlier decisions in *Burton v Mount* (1848) 2 De G & Sm 383, and *Blann v Bell* (1852) 2 De GM & G 775, remain unaffected for there was no freehold property included in the residue in those cases. The rule has never applied to freeholds: *Re Woodhouse, Public Trustee v Woodhouse* [1941] Ch 332, [1941] 2 All ER 265. But a direction is strictly construed. Thus the words 'no part of any dividends rents interest or moneys of the nature of income' did not make the rule inapplicable to the profits and loss of a business: *Re Berry, Lloyds Bank Ltd v Berry* [1962] Ch 97, [1961] 1 All ER 529.
10   *Re Bates, Hodgson v Bates* [1907] 1 Ch 22; *Re Wilson, Moore v Wilson* [1907] 1 Ch 394; *Re Nicholson, Eade v Nicholson* [1909] 2 Ch 111; *Porter v Baddeley* (1877) 5 Ch D 542 (no direction for conversion but authority to retain as long as trustees thought fit); *Gray v Siggers* (1880) 15 Ch D 74 (power to sell or retain).
11   *Burton v Mount* (1848) 2 De G & Sm 383; *Re Sewell's Estate* (1870) LR 11 Eq 80; *Re Schneider, Kirby v Schneider* (1906) 22 TLR 223; *Re Levien, Trustees, Executors and Agency*

Co Ltd v Levien [1937] VLR 80; *Miller v Miller* (1872) LR 13 Eq 263 (here there was a trust for sale to be exercised when advisable); *Lean v Lean* (1875) 32 LT 305 (similar case); *Re Leonard, Theobald v King* (1880) 43 LT 664; *Re Sheldon, Nixon v Sheldon* (1888) 39 Ch D 50; *Re Burrage, Burningham v Burrage* (1890) 62 LT 752; *Re Thomas, Wood v Thomas* [1891] 3 Ch 482 (trust for conversion, power to postpone and retain); *Re Pitcairn, Brandreth v Colvin* [1896] 2 Ch 199; *Re Bates, Hodgson v Bates* [1907] 1 Ch 22 (power to retain only); *Re Sherry, Sherry v Sherry* [1913] 2 Ch 508 (trust for sale with power to retain); *Re Godfree, Godfree v Godfree* [1914] 2 Ch 110 (trust for sale with widest powers of postponement); *Re Inman, Inman v Inman* [1915] 1 Ch 187 (trust for sale with power to postpone and power to retain) and *Re Pitcairn, Brandreth v Colvin* [1896] 2 Ch 199. The rule can thus be excluded by providing a discretionary power of sale over all residuary assets. For this reason, and as a result of the TLATA 1996, it is now practical to draft residuary administration trusts in the form of a power to sell when they think fit, instead of providing a trust for sale. Apparently the usual power to postpone sale in a trust for sale is insufficient to exclude the rule: *Re Carter* (1892) 41 WR 140. Leaseholds on trust for sale are not now subject to the rule: see para **[38.25]** infra.

12 *Johnston v Moore* (1858) 27 LJ Ch 453; *Lean v Lean* (1875) 32 LT 305: *Re Chancellor, Chancellor v Brown* (1884) 26 Ch D 42; *Re Elford, Elford v Elford* [1910] 1 Ch 814; *Re Sherry, Sherry v Sherry* [1913] 2 Ch 508. Where the direction was in the usual form but with the addition of the words 'without apportionment', the rule was excluded; but the provisions of the Apportionment Act 1870 must be applied: *Re Bate, Public Trustee v Bate* [1938] 4 All ER 218.

13 *Re Hubbuck, Hart v Stone* [1896] 1 Ch 754; *Re Canada Permanent Trust Co and McGregor* (1980) 115 DLR (3d) 697. It is usual to provide that a reversionary interest shall not be sold unless the trustees see good reason for such sale. The Administration of Estates Act 1925, s 33, previously included this provision as to sale, but this has been amended by the TLATA 1996, s 25, Sch 2, para 5, so as to no longer provide for a trust for sale and the direction not to sell a reversionary interest is repealed. The rule in *Re Chesterfield's Trusts* (see para **[38.22]** supra) does not apply where the trustees have a power to sell when they think fit.

14 *Re Hubbuck, Hart v Stone* [1896] 1 Ch 754.

15 *Re Rowlls* [1900] 2 Ch 107; *Re Hey's Settlement Trusts and Will Trusts, Hey v Nickell-Lean* [1945] Ch 294, [1945] 1 All ER 618; followed in *Re Guinness Settlement, Guinness v S G Warburg (Executor and Trustee) Ltd* [1966] 2 All ER 497, [1966] 1 WLR 1355.

16 *Re Bland, Miller v Bland* [1899] 2 Ch 336 (absolute gift to wife with provision that if she died without issue leaving an adopted daughter surviving, the adopted daughter should take).

[38.24]
Avoidance of direction in will by disclaimer or intestacy. Where a will directed that royalties, included in the residue, were to be treated as capital, it was held that the widow, who was entitled to a life interest in the residue, could disclaim the gift under the will and take the royalties under the provisions applicable on the resulting intestacy, when by the statutory exclusion of the rule in *Howe v Dartmouth* they would be income and wholly payable to the widow.[1] A direction, whether it be a direction for the application or the exclusion of the rule, is applicable only to the provisions of the will and in the carrying out of those provisions in due course of administration, and does not apply to an intestacy or partial intestacy arising from the failure of the will to take effect in whole or in part.[2]

1 *Re Sullivan, Dunkley v Sullivan* [1930] 1 Ch 84.
2 *Re Thornber, Crabtree v Thornber* [1937] Ch 29, [1936] 2 All ER 1594. Where a partial intestacy takes effect on the death of the widow, the widow's interest is a reversionary interest this previously did not have to be realised, by virtue of the Administration of Estates Act 1925, s 33 (1); 17 *Halsbury's Statutes* (4th edn) 437 (see Vol 2, Part G, para **[244.58]**). See *Re McKee, Public Trustee v McKee* [1931] 2 Ch 145. See now para **[38.23]**, n 13, on the amendment to the Administration of Estates Act 1925, s 33 by the TLATA 1996.

[38.25]
Residue to which the rules do not apply. Neither the rule in *Howe v Dartmouth* nor that in *Re Chesterfield's Trusts* applies to frechold land,[1] nor to such land directed by the will to be sold,[2] nor to land comprised in a mixed fund of realty and personalty so devised,[3] nor to money directed to be laid out in land,[4] nor to leaseholds held for a term having more than sixty years to run at the death of the testator and held as settled land.[5] In the case of a trust for sale of land coming into operation before or after 1925, the rule in *Howe v Dartmouth* was excluded by statute.[6] Where there is a discretionary power to postpone conversion and the residuary estate is stated to include investments for the time being remaining unconverted pursuant to a power therein contained the rule is not excluded if the trustees had not exercised their discretion to convert, but if they exercised their discretion the rule would be excluded thereafter. 'Land' in this connection includes both freeholds and leaseholds,[7] but the rule still remains applicable to pure personalty held on trust for sale.[8] The rules are excluded by statute in the case of property of which a deceased dies wholly or partially intestate,[9] but in the case of partial intestacy the rule applies so far as the estate is disposed of by will and not thereby subjected to a trust for sale.[10]

1   *Re Woodhouse, Public Trustee v Woodhouse* [1941] Ch 332, [1941] 2 All ER 265; *Lottman v Stanford* (1980) 107 DLR (3d) 28.
2   *Casamajor v Strode* (1809) 19 Ves 390n; *Yates v Yates* (1860) 28 Beav 637; *Spencer v Harrison* (1879) 5 CPD 97; *Hope v d'Hedonville* [1893] 2 Ch 361; *Re Searle, Searle v Baker* [1900] 2 Ch 829; *Re Oliver, Wilson v Oliver* [1908] 2 Ch 74.
3   *Re Searle, Searle v Baker* [1900] 2 Ch 829; *Re Oliver, Wilson v Oliver* [1908] 2 Ch 74; *Re Earl Darnley, Clifton v Darnley* [1907] 1 Ch 159.
4   *Sitwell v Bernard* (1801) 6 Ves 520; *Kilvington v Gray* (1825) 2 Sim & St 396; *Tucker v Boswell* (1843) 5 Beav 607; *Macpherson v Macpherson* (1852) 19 LTOS 221.
5   *Re Gough, Phillips v Simpson* [1957] Ch 323, [1957] 2 All ER 193 (where leaseholds became vested in four persons, two of them minors, for life and it was held on the true construction of the will that they were entitled to enjoy the land in specie and it was settled land and not subject to a trust for sale).
6   Law of Property Act 1925, s 28 (2); (37 *Halsbury's Statutes* (4th edn) 151). Now repealed; see para **[38.22]**, n 8. On the previous law see *Re Brooker, Brooker v Brooker* [1926] WN 93; *Re Berton, Vandyk v Berton* [1939] Ch 200, [1938] 4 All ER 286.
7   *Re Guinness's Settlement, Guinness v S G Warburg (Executor and Trustee) Ltd* [1966] 2 All ER 497, [1966] 1 WLR 1355.
8   Law of Property Act 1925, s 205 (1) (ix); 37 *Halsbury's Statutes* (4th edn) 368.
9   *Re Trollope's Will Trusts, Public Trustee v Trollope* [1927] 1 Ch 596.
10 Administration of Estates Act 1925, s 33 (5); (7) 17 *Halsbury's Statutes* (4th edn) 438: see Vol 2, Part G, para **[244.58]**; *Re Sullivan, Dunkley v Sullivan* [1930] 1 Ch 84. On the amendment to the Administration of Estates Act 1925, s 33(1), by the Trusts of Land and Appointment of Trustees Act 1996, see para **[38.23]**, n 13.

[38.26]
Adjustment in respect of debts, legacies, etc, between tenant for life and remainderman—rule in *Allhusen v Whittell*. This rule is based upon the assumption that it is inequitable that the debts and legacies should be paid wholly out of capital. Properly speaking, the residue is what is left after payment of debts, legacies and other liabilities payable out of residue (as they are termed) and, therefore, the money expended in the payment of debts, etc, is not strictly residue at all. The rule has not always been applied in the terms stated in[1] *Allhusen v Whittell*.[2] It is said that the rule is not to be universally applied, but

that the court should in adjusting accounts deal equitably between the tenant for life and the remainderman.[3] The rule as originally stated is that the executors are at liberty when making such payments to make them out of any of the estate moneys in their hands, but when adjusting the residuary account they must be treated as having paid such sums not out of capital, only, nor out of income only, but with such portion of capital as, together with the income of that portion, is sufficient for the purpose.[4] The adjustment is made at the time each debt or set of expenses is paid whether that be within or beyond the executor's year.[5] The rule applies to debts, legacies, administration and funeral expenses and death duties payable out of residue.[6] Where real estate is charged with debts, and recourse is had to such real estate, the tenant for life must, as from the testator's death, keep down the interest upon all interest-bearing debts which are paid by recourse to realty.[7] In applying the rule, the income is the net income after deduction of income tax,[8] and the average rate of interest earned in each year should be adopted for the calculation.[9] While it has been said that the rule in *Howe v Dartmouth* should be excluded, it has seldom been said that this rule ought to be excluded, but it is obvious that in any but estates of large money value the many intricate calculations involved to give effect to this rule are not really worthwhile and draftsmen ought to exclude it. A will may contain special provisions as to the payment of debts. Where it provides for debts to be paid out of income and they are in fact paid out of capital, the tenant for life does not have to recoup the capital so applied[10] and, if in such a case the income has been accumulated for payment of debts, the tenant for life is also entitled to the accumulated fund.[11] A direction to pay debts out of income does not create a charge on the corpus of the estate.[12] A direction 'that the income of such of the same premises as for the time being shall remain unsold shall as well during the first year ... as afterwards be applied as ... income' does not exclude the rule.[13] Where annual payments have to be made out of the income of residue which the testator has not entered into a covenant to make the rule does not apply.[14]

1   *Trollope's Will Trusts, Public Trustee v Trollope* [1927] 1 Ch 596.
2   (1867) LR 4 Eq 295; see Vol 2, para **[214.1]** et seq.
3   *Re McEuen, McEuen v Phelps* [1913] 2 Ch 704; *Re Wills, Wills v Hamilton* [1915] 1 Ch 769. The rule applies only between tenant for life and remainderman and has no application to a case where an absolute gift is given in the first place with an executory gift over: *Re Hanbury, Comiskey v Hanbury* (1909) 101 LT 32.
4   *Allhusen v Whittell* (1867) LR 4 Eq 295; *Lambert v Lambert* (1873) LR 16 Eq 320 (where the income was taken for one year after the death of the testator although the debt was paid before the expiry of the year but this is not now generally applied).
5   *Re McEuen, McEuen v Phelps* [1913] 2 Ch 704; *Re Wills, Wills v Hamilton* [1915] 1 Ch 769.
6   *Re McEuen, McEuen v Phelps* [1913] 2 Ch 704; but although the rule applies to contingent debts (*Re Perkins, Brown v Perkins* [1907] 2 Ch 596; *Re Poyser, Landon v Poyser* [1910] 2 Ch 444) it does not apply to continent legacies: *Allhusen v Whittell* (1867) LR 4 Eq 295; *Re Fenwick's Will Trusts, Fenwick v Stewart* [1936] Ch 720, [1936] 2 All ER 1096.
7   *Marshall v Crowther* (1874) 2 Ch D 199.
8   *Re Oldham, Oldham v Myles* (1927) 71 Sol Jo 491.
9   *Re Wills, Wills v Hamilton* [1915] 1 Ch 769.
10 *Tewart v Lawson* (1874) LR 18 Eq 490.
11 *Norton v Johnstone* (1885) 30 Ch D 649; *Re Brandon, Samuels v Brandon* (1932) 49 TLR 48.
12 *Re Green, Baldock v Green* (1888) 40 Ch D 610.
13 *Re Ullswater, Barclays Bank Ltd v Lawther* [1952] Ch 105, [1951] 2 All ER 989. For the form of such a clause excluding the rule, see Vol 2.

14 *Re Darby* [1939] Ch 905, [1939] 3 All ER 6 (residue subject to annuity charged by the will of
    the father of the testatrix); *Re Popham, Butler v Popham* (1914) 111 LT 524 (residue subject to
    rentcharge created by settlement). As to annuities given out of residue, see the next following
    paragraph.

[38.27]

Adjustment in respect of annuities. Where an annuity is payable out of settled
residue either of two courses may be adopted.[1] The successive instalments of the
annuity may be borne by income and capital in proportion to the actuarial values
of the life estate and the reversion at the testator's death;[2] or the sum required for
each instalment may be apportioned by calculating what sum set aside at the
testator's death and accumulated at compound interest would have produced the
particular payment, the sum so ascertained being attributed to capital and the
remainder of the payment to income.[3] A more convenient course, and one which
has on occasion been adopted,[4] is to pay each instalment out of capital, when the
sole contribution of the tenant for life is the consequent reduction of future
income, but this course does not appear to be technically correct.

1   The position here dealt with is where the annuity is given otherwise than by the will which is
    being administered, that is to say that the annuity is in the nature of a debt and not of a gift.
2   *Yates v Yates* (1860) 28 Beav 637; *Re Dawson, Arathoon v Dawson* [1906] 2 Ch 211.
3   *Re Perkins, Brown v Perkins* [1907] 2 Ch 596; applied in *Re Berkeley, Inglis v Countess of
    Berkeley* [1968] Ch 744, [1968] 3 All ER 364, CA; *Re Poyser, Landon v Poyser* [1910] 2 Ch
    444. Four per cent per annum has been stated to be the correct rate; see *Re Fawcett* [1940] Ch
    402, but a higher rate might now be considered appropriate.
4   *Re Harrison, Townson v Harrison* (1889) 43 Ch D 55; *Re Bacon, Grissel v Leathes* (1893) 62
    LJ Ch 445; *Re Henry, Gordon v Gordon* [1907] 1 Ch 30.

[38.28]

Other rights of tenant for life of residue. Where funds are set aside to answer
legacies or annuities, the tenant for life of residue is entitled to the income of
them which is not otherwise disposed of or by law payable to those entitled to
the fund.[1] Where trustees enter into possession of mortgaged property being part
of the residue, the tenant for life is entitled to so much of the rents as is equal to
the interest on the mortgage and, if the rents be less, he is entitled to have this
made up on a sale of the property, but without interest on arrears of income.[2]
Where an authorised investment has in breach of trust been sold and the
proceeds of sale invested in an unauthorised investment, the whole transaction is
reopened whether or not the tenant for life has been a party to the breach of
trust.[3] Payments due to the estate such as annual sums payable under an
insurance policy for some years after the death of the testator or on the failure of
a trust for accumulation are not income to which the tenant for life is entitled but
capital which must be invested.[4] Where the reversion on a lease is purchased
under compulsory powers, the tenant for life is entitled to the income from the
invested compensation moneys up to the amount of the rent until the time when
the lease would have expired, and from that date he is entitled to the whole
income and the income from any accumulations in the earlier period.[5] Where the
lease is purchased compulsorily, the tenant for life is entitled to such an annuity,
to be fixed by an actuary, as would exhaust the compensation in the number of
years of the unexpired part of the term whether that be greater or less than the
rent.[6] Where a sum charged on freeholds and leaseholds is not raised until the

leaseholds have decreased in value, an adjustment has been made,[7] but no adjustment is made where debts are directed to be paid out of income but are in fact paid out of capital.[8] Where sums are paid under a scheme of arrangement in respect of debentures the interest on which has not been paid for some time, an apportionment is made.[9] Where sums are received by the trustees of a will and the person paying those sums describes them as capital or income, the trustees must inquire into the source of those sums to establish their true nature.[10]

1   *Crawley v Crawley* (1835) 7 Sim 427; *Fullerton v Martin* (1860) 1 Drew & Sm 31; *Re Whithead, Peacock v Lucas* [1894] 1 Ch 678; *Re Fenwick's Will Trusts, Fenwick v Stewart* [1936] Ch 720, [1936] 2 All ER 1096.
2   *Re Moore, Moore v Johnson* (1885) 54 LJ Ch 432; *Re Walker's Settlement Trusts, Watson v Walker* [1936] Ch 280 (debentures). The latter case shows the method of apportionment where the amount realised is insufficient to meet capital and interest.
3   *Re Bird, Re Evans, Dodd v Evans* [1901] 1 Ch 916.
4   *Re Fisher, Harris v Fisher* [1943] Ch 377, [1943] 2 All ER 615; and see para **[38.17]**, n 4.
5   *Re Wootton's Estate* (1866) LR 1 Eq 589; *Re Mette's Estate* (1868) LR 7 Eq 72; *Re Wilkes' Estate* (1881) 16 Ch D 597; *Cottrell v Cottrell* (1885) 28 Ch D 628.
6   *Re Phillips' Trusts* (1868) LR 6 Eq 250; *Askew v Woodhead* (1880) 14 Ch D 27.
7   *Blake v O'Reily* [1895] 1 IR 479.
8   *Tewert v Lawson* (1874) LR 18 Eq 490; *Norton v Johnstone* (1885) 30 Ch D 649, and see *Re Brandon, Samuels v Brandon* (1932) 49 TLR 48.
9   *Re Morris's Will Trusts, Public Trustee v Morris* [1960] 3 All ER 548, [1960] 1 WLR 1210; and see *Re Pennington, Pennington v Pennington* [1914] 1 Ch 203.
10 *Re Whitehead's Will Trusts, Public Trustee v White* [1959] Ch 579, [1959] 2 All ER 497.

CHAPTER 39

Exercise of powers by will

I. CLASSIFICATION OF POWERS

[39.1]
Powers of appointment have generally been divided into three categories: general, special and hybrid.[1] The distinction between general and special powers and the status of hybrid powers may be of importance for a variety of purposes. Thus there is the question whether a particular power falls within the Wills Act 1837, s 27;[2] further, questions may arise in relation to the rule against perpetuities,[3] in relation to the doctrine of fraud on a power,[4] in relation to whether the property concerned constitutes assets in the administration of estates,[5] and in relation to the exercise of the power.[6] A classification for one purpose is by no means decisive or even a guide to the classification for another purpose.[7]

1   See Megarry J in *Re Lawrence's Will Trusts, Public Trustee v Lawrence* [1972] Ch 418 at 427, [1971] 3 All ER 433 at 439.
2   50 *Halsbury's Statutes* (4th edn) 595: see Vol 2, Part G, para **[244.27]**; see also para **[39.11]** infra.
3   See para **[94.41]** et seq.
4   See para **[40.14]** infra.
5   Administration of Estates Act 1925, s 32; 17 *Halsbury's Statutes* (4th edn) 436.
6   See para **[39.10]** infra.
7   Per Megarry J in *Re Lawrence's Will Trusts, Public Trustee v Lawrence* [1972] Ch 418 at 427, [1971] 3 All ER 433 at 439.

II. GENERAL POWERS

[39.2]
Definition of a general power. General powers have been defined as 'such as the donee can exercise in favour of such person or persons as he pleases, including himself'.[1] There are also several statutory definitions of general powers, although such definitions should strictly be confined to the subject matter of each statutory provision. The Wills Act 1837, s 27[2] refers to powers which may be appointed ... in any manner he may think proper ...'. The Perpetuities and Accumulations Act 1964, s 7[3] provides that for the purposes of the rule against perpetuities, a power of appointment is a general power if it is expressed to be exercisable by one person only[4] and it can at all times during its currency,[5] when that person is of full age and capacity, be exercised by him so as immediately to transfer the whole interest governed by the power without the

consent of any other person or compliance with any other condition not being a formal condition relating only to the mode of exercise of the power.[6] For the purpose of determining whether a disposition under a power of appointment exercisable by will only is void for remoteness, the power shall be treated as a general one where it would have been so treated if exercisable by deed.[7]

This definition is confined to the purposes of the rule against perpetuities and does not necessarily apply where no question of that rule arises. However, the rule as to what is a general power as stated in recent decided cases[8] is, apart from the subject of consent, stated in much the same terms. As to consent, it has been held that the requirement of the consent of a person is only possible in the case of a general power where the person to give the consent is not in a fiduciary position so that he must have regard to the trusts in exercising his consent.[9] Where the person to consent holds a fiduciary position the power has been held to be a special power,[10] but it would seem that the real basis of this decision was that it would not be right to hold that, upon the terms of the powers contained in a marriage settlement, the settlor (the donee of the power) was in substance the owner of the property, so that she was free to deal with it as she pleased.[11] A power unrestricted as to class of objects but exercisable jointly is, for the purposes of the rule against perpetuities, a special power.[12] This is because such a power cannot be equated with an absolute interest in the property which is the subject-matter of the power. The distinctive feature of a general power is that the donee may exercise it in favour of any person he may think fit including himself or his personal representatives.[13]

If a power is exercisable by a document witnessed by two witnesses, then if exercised by a document which is in terms testamentary that document must be executed as a will and in compliance with the Wills Act 1837.[14] A power may be created which is exercisable by will or by a document purporting to be a will. In the latter case the document will not be a will within the Wills Act 1837, but where it creates a general power, that power can be exercised by will by the operation of the Wills Act 1837, s 27.[15]

1   *Farewell On Powers* (1916), 3rd edn, p 8. See *Re Beatty's Will Trusts, Hinves v Brooke* [1990] 3 All ER 844, [1990] 1 WLR 1503, for a discussion of the validity of wide-ranging powers of appointment. See para **[9.46]** supra.
2   50 *Halsbury's Statutes* (4th edn) 595. For an example see *Re Fong, Yee Charles* [1997] 1 HKC 348 (general power not restricted to donee's lifetime and exercised by a residuary gift under a provision analogous to the Wills Act 1837, s 27).
3   See Vol 2, Part G, para **[246.65]**.
4   *Re Churston Settled Estates, Freemantle v Churston* [1954] Ch 334, [1954] 1 All ER 725, where it was decided that a joint power to appoint was a special power; applied in *Re Earl of Coventry's Indentures, Smith v Earl of Coventry* [1974] Ch 77, [1973] 3 All ER 1.
5   This would exclude a power exercisable only by will, but see the proviso to the section.
6   Such a formal condition would be a requirement that the power should be exercised by a deed witnessed by at least two persons or any similar provision. Compare the Law of Property Act 1925, s 158.
7   That is to say, it must be exercisable by one person only and in favour of such persons as the appointor pleases including himself or his personal representatives. This follows the decision in *Re Flower, Edmonds v Edmonds* (1885) 55 LJ Ch 200 and the cases there cited. As stated in *Re Churston Settled Estates, Freemantle v Churston* [1954] Ch 334, [1954] 1 All ER 725, there must be someone who for all practical purposes can be treated as the owner.
8   *Re Churston Settled Estates, Freemantle v Churston* [1954] Ch 334, [1954] 1 All ER 725.
9   *Re Dilke, Re Dilke's Settlement Trusts, Verey v Dilke* [1921] 1 Ch 34.
10   *Re Watts, Coffey v Watts* [1931] 2 Ch 302; but see *Re Dilke, Re Dilke's Settlement Trusts, Verey v Dilke* [1921] 1 Ch 34, and *Re Phillips, Lawrence v Huxtable* [1931] 1 Ch 347.

11   Compare n 7.
12   *Re Earl of Coventry's Indentures, Smith v Earl of Coventry* [1974] Ch 77, [1973] 3 All ER 1, applying *Re Churston Settled Estates, Freemantle v Churston* [1954] Ch 334, [1954] 1 All ER 725. This case was concerned with a pre-1964 settlement, and so the position according to the common law rules had to be considered. It was held that an appointment in exercise of a joint power of appointment was, for the purposes of the perpetuity rule, special, and so had to be read back to the instrument creating the power, and was void.
13   That is to say there is no limitation upon the objects of the power. In the case of a special power, as the term is usually defined, there is either a number of named persons or a distinct class of objects in favour of whom or some of whom only the power can be validly exercised.
14   *Re Barnett, Dawes v Ixer* [1908] 1 Ch 402.
15   See *Re Broad, Smith v Draeger* [1901] 2 Ch 86. A testamentary power cannot be exercised by deed: *Re Evered, Molineux v Evered* [1910] 2 Ch 147.

[39.3]

Nature of general powers. The generality of a power is destroyed if it is exercisable subject to exceptions, though a power limited in its inception may by reason of subsequent events become a general power.[1] A power is not general where it must be exercised for the benefit of special persons;[2] nor is a power to create a charge on realty and to appoint the sum raised a general power within the meaning of the Wills Act 1837, s 27;[3] but if the charge is created by an instrument and then by the same instrument a power is given to appoint the sum charged, a general bequest is an effectual appointment within the statutory provision.[4]

1   *Re Byron's Settlement, Williams v Mitchell* [1891] 3 Ch 474; *Re Harvey* [1950] 1 All ER 491 (a power for a spinster to appoint to anyone other than a husband she may marry was treated, while she remained unmarried, as a general power).
2   *Cloves v Awdry* (1850) 12 Beav 604 (children); *Re Caplin's Will* (1865) 2 Drew & Sm 527 (relations); but a power to appoint for such person or persons at such ages or times and in such manner as the donee thinks fit is a general power, the words not being a limitation of the class but a specification of the mode of exercise: *Kiel v Berghofer* (1949) 49 SRNSW 363.
3   See Vol 2, Part G, para **[244.27]** fully considered in para **[39.11]** infra. The statutory provision presupposes the prior existence of the property appointed and, therefore, a power to appoint the property or any part thereof does not extend to the creation of property at the expense of another or to the imposition of an otherwise non-existent charge upon the property of another or to the conversion pro tanto of the estate of another into a money charge, which if when charged will be personal estate which the testator will have to appoint as he may think fit, but which has no existence unless and until the testator creates it; *Re Salvin, Marshall v Wolseley* [1906] 2 Ch 459 at 464; *Re Wallinger's Estate* [1898] 1 IR 139 at 148.
4   *Re Jones, Greene v Gordon* (1886) 34 Ch D 65; *Re Wilkinson, Thomas v Wilkinson* [1910] 2 Ch 216 (charge on real and personal estate so that the power was an overriding one to appoint a fund of mixed realty and personalty).

[39.4]

Will made before power created. A will containing a general devise or bequest, made before the creation of a general power to appoint by will, and allowed by the testator to remain his will until his death, is a good execution of the power.[1] A power created by will lapses unless the donee survives the testator, even though in his will the donee refers to the power and purports to exercise it.[2]

1   *Boyes v Cook* (1880) 14 Ch D 53.
2   *Jones v Southall (No 2)* (1862) 32 Beav 31; *Sharpe v M'Call* [1903] 1 IR 179; *Re Young, Public Trustee v Walker* [1920] 2 Ch 427; *Re Baker, Steadman v Dicksee* [1934] WN 94. But the appointment may be good where the Wills Act 1837, s 33, as substituted by the Administration

of Justice Act 1982, 50 *Halsbury's Statutes* (4th edn) 599, see Vol 2, Part G, para **[244.34]** (statutory exceptions from lapse) applies: *Eccles v Cheye* (1856) 2 K & J 676.

[39.5]

Effect of appointment. An appointee under a power derives title from the instrument conferring the power and not from the appointment.[1] Nevertheless property, whether real or personal, with the exception of foreign property,[2] appointed by will under a general power of appointment passes to the appointor's personal representatives, and becomes assets for the payment of the appointor's debts after his own property has been exhausted.[3] An appointment does not operate as an appointment of funds which, subsequently to the appointment, are transferred or bequeathed upon the trusts of the settlement or will[4] unless words by which the additional funds are transferred or bequeathed clearly make them an addition to the original trust funds.[5] Upon the execution of the power the interests given in default of appointment are defeated. This is carried to its logical conclusion, so that an assignment of property by a person entitled in default of appointment may be defeated if the power of appointment is afterwards exercised even in favour of the assignor.[6]

1 *Beyfus v Lawley* [1903] AC 411; *Re Earl of Devon's Settled Estates, White v Earl of Devon* [1896] 2 Ch 562. As to the rule against perpetuities, see Chapter 94.
2 *Re Bald, Bald v Bald* (1897) 66 LJ Ch 524.
3 *Re Philbrick's Settlement* (1865) 11 Jur NS 558; *Hayes v Oately* (1872) LR 14 Eq 1; *Re Hoskin's Trusts* (1877) 5 Ch D 229; on appeal 6 Ch D 281; *O'Grady v Wilmot* [1916] 2 AC 231; Administration of Estates Act 1925, ss 3(2), 32; 17 *Halsbury's Statutes* (4th edn) 423, 436.
4 *Re Walpole's Marriage Settlement, Thomson v Walpole* [1903] 1 Ch 928.
5 *Re Paul's Settlement Trusts, Paul v Nelson* [1920] 1 Ch 99; *Re Campbell's Trusts, Public Trustee v Campbell* [1922] 1 Ch 551.
6 *Sweetapple v Horlock* (1897) 11 Ch D 745; *Lovett v Lovett* [1898] 1 Ch 82.

[39.6]

Appointor an undischarged bankrupt. If the appointor at the date of his death is an undischarged bankrupt, the appointed fund does not become divisible among the creditors as part of the bankrupt's property, but is payable to his executors for the benefit of subsequent creditors.[1]

1 *Re Guedalla, Lee v Guedalla's Trustee* [1905] 2 Ch 331; *Re Benzon, Bower v Chetwynd* [1914] 2 Ch 68.

[39.7]

Ineffectual appointment. Where an appointment under a general testamentary power is ineffectual, the property concerned, whether real or personal,[1] devolves as part of the testator's estate, or, in default of appointment, according to the intention of the donee of the power.[2] Thus, a testator shows an intention to make the property his own for all purposes by giving it to his executors or trustees,[3] or by dealing with the settled property and his other property as one mass, without making the appointment either to his executors or trustees, or to any individual object.[4] No such intention is shown, however, where the donee of a general power makes a will dealing only with the settled property,[5] or expressly distinguishes between his own and the settled property.[6] An express direction to pay debts, coupled with the appointment of an executor, takes the fund from the persons entitled in default of appointment only so far as it is required to pay debts.[7]

1   *Re Van Hagan, Sperling v Rochfort* (1880) 16 Ch D 18.
2   *Re De Lusi's Trusts* (1879) 3 LR Ir 232; *Re Pinede's Settlement* (1879) 12 Ch D 667; *Re Boyd, Kelly v Boyd* [1897] 2 Ch 232.
3   *Brickenden v Williams* (1869) LR 7 Eq 310; *Re Keown's Estate* (1867) IR 1 Eq 372.
4   *Re Pinede's Settlement* (1879) 12 Ch D 667; *Re Marten, Shaw v Marten* [1902] 1 Ch 314.
5   *Re Thurston, Thurston v Evans* (1886) 32 Ch D 508; *Bristow v Skirrow* (1870) IR 10 Eq 1.
6   *Re De Lusi's Trusts* (1879) 3 LR Ir 232; *Re Boyd, Kelly v Boyd* [1897] 2 Ch 232; *Re Creed, Thomas v Hudson* [1905] WN 94; *Re Doherty-Waterhouse, Musgrave v De Chair* [1918] 2 Ch 269.
7   *Laing v Cowan* (1857) 24 Beav 112.

[39.8]

Exercise by joint will. A general power of appointment by will given to two persons can be exercised by the joint will of those persons.[1]

1   *Re Duddell, Roundway v Roundway* [1932] 1 Ch 585. In this case the first to die made a separate will and confirmed the joint will. Both these will were admitted to probate. It was held that, if the other did not revoke the joint will and on her death it was admitted to probate, it would be a good execution of the joint power. See Chapter 2.

[39.9]

Exercise of power by will of testator domiciled abroad. See the discussion in Chapter 24.

[39.10]

Exercise of the power. In determining whether a power of appointment has been exercised, the width of the range of objects is not a relevant consideration;[1] the rule to be applied in all cases, whether the power be general, hybrid or special, is that a power will be validly exercised if, but only if, the purported exercise sufficiently indicated an intention to exercise it.[2] Thus, any prescribed conditions, for instance that the power is exercisable only by an instrument expressly referring to the power,[3] have to be complied with. If the instrument displays no indication whether a power was intended to have been exercised or not, then prima facie, the power has not been exercised.[4]

1   Apart from statutory provisions such as the Wills Act 1837, s 27; see Vol 2, Part G, para **[244.27]**. See para **[39.11]** infra.
2   Per Megarry J in *Re Lawrence's Will Trusts, Public Trustee v Lawrence* [1972] Ch 418 at 430, [1971] 3 All ER 433 at 442.
3   *Re Lane, Belli v Lane* [1908] 2 Ch 581 ('expressly referring to this power or the property subject thereto'); *Re Rolt, Rolt v Burdett* [1908] WN 76 ('expressly referring to the present power'); *Re Waterhouse, Waterhouse v Rylen* (1907) 98 LT 30 (... unless it expressly purported to exercise such power'); *Re Priestley's Will Trusts, Hambros Bank Executor and Trustee Co Ltd v Rabagliati* [1971] Ch 858, [1971] 2 All ER 817, CA ('expressly referring to this power as though it were a special power'; specific reference not necessary, the words merely excluded an implied exercise under the Wills Act 1837, s 27; words meant in effect 'this power of appointment is to be exercised by express reference to it and by that I mean a reference which shows that the donee of the power had directed her mind to this particular power': this was not satisfied by a residuary clause referring only to 'including any property over which I may have any general power of appointment exercised by will').
4   Per Megarry J in *Re Lawrence's Will Trusts* [1972] Ch 418 at 430, [1971] 3 All ER 433 at 442, where a hybrid power was held to have been duly exercised despite certain indications to the

contrary; applying *Re Ackerley, Chapman v Andrew* [1913] 1 Ch 510, [1911–13] All ER Rep 183; considering *Re Waterhouse, Waterhouse v Ryley* (1907) 98 LT 30 ('over which I have or shall have any disposing power', held sufficient to exercise a general power); and *Re Lane, Belli v Lane* [1908] 2 Ch 581 ('over which I shall have any power of disposition by will', held sufficient to exercise a general power).

[39.11]
Statutory provision – Wills Act 1837, s 27. By this section a general devise[1] of the real estate of the testator, or of such real estate in any place or in the occupation of any person mentioned in the will, or otherwise described in a general manner,[2] is construed to include any real estate to which such descriptions shall extend which he may have power to appoint in any manner he may think proper[3] and shall operate as an execution of that power,[4] unless a contrary intention[5] shall appear in the will. In like manner a bequest of the personal estate of the testator shall be construed to include any personal estate, which he may have power to appoint in any manner he may think proper and shall operate as an execution of such power, unless a contrary intention shall appear in the will.[6] The power of appointment must be capable of being exercised by will even though such power is contingent.[7] A general power may be exercised in this way by a minor soldier, airman, etc, in a soldier's will.[8]

1   While it is important to notice that the statute only requires a gift in general terms, it most commonly applies to a general residuary gift. As to what is a general devise or bequest, see para **[39.12]** infra.
2   See para **[39.12]** infra.
3   A general devise in favour of an object of a special power, the testator having no real estate of his own at the date of the will, does not raise a presumption of an intention to execute the power: *Re Williams, Foulks v Williams* (1889) 42 Ch D 93.
4   That is to say he must have a general power of appointment. See para **[39.2]** supra.
5   See para **[39.14]** infra.
6   Wills Act 1837, s 27.
7   See para **[39.13]** infra.
8   See Chapter 16.

[39.12]
General gifts. General pecuniary legacies are bequests of personal property and subject to any contrary direction may be paid out of money over which the testator has a general power of appointment.[1] A gift of 'stocks shares and securities' or of 'all stocks shares and securities which I possess or to which I am entitled'[2] is within the provision and so is a gift of 'all my shares' in a certain undertaking.[3] A gift of 'my real estate' or 'my personal estate' is none the less general because the testator uses the word 'my',[4] but realty subject to a general power of appointment will not pass under a general bequest, nor will personalty subject to such a general power pass under a general devise.[5] Where property is subject to a right of conversion by someone other than the testator, it will be treated as converted for the purpose of deciding whether it passes under a general devise or bequest.[6] Land subject to a trust for sale is treated as personalty[7] and a general gift of personalty does not pass money to be laid out in land.[8] The appointment of a residuary legatee, without any words of gift, is equivalent to a general residuary bequest and has the same operation as such a bequest.[9] The appointment of an executor, coupled with a gift of pecuniary legacies, operates as the appointment of a fund subject to a general power of

appointment to the extent required for the payment of the legacies,[10] and also of debts which must be discharged before the legacies are paid[11] and a direction for the payment of debts without more is sufficient.[12]

1 *Re Wilkinson's Settlement Trust* (1869) LR 8 Eq 487 (affd (1869) 4 Ch App 587); *Hawthorn v Shedden* (1856) 3 Sm & G 293; *Wilday v Barnett* (1868) LR 6 Eq 193; *Hurlstone v Ashton* (1865) 11 Jur NS 725; *Re Davies' Trusts* (1871) LR 13 Eq 163 at 166; *Re Seabrook, Gray v Baddeley* [1911] 1 Ch 151.

2 *Turner v Turner* (1852) 21 LJ Ch 843; *Re Jacob, Mortimer v Mortimer* [1907] 1 Ch 445; *Frankcombe v Hayward* (1845) 9 Jur 344.

3 *Re Doherty-Waterhouse, Musgrave v De Chair* [1918] 2 Ch 269.

4 *Chandler v Pocock* (1880) 15 Ch D 491; affd (1881) 16 Ch D 648; *Freme v Clement* (1881) 18 Ch D 499 (but see *Holyland v Lewin* (1884) 26 Ch D 266); *Francombe v Hayward* (1845) 9 Jur 344; *Re Priestley's Will Trusts, Hambros Bank Executor and Trustee Co Ltd v Rabagliati* [1971] Ch 858, [1971] 2 All ER 817, CA; *Re Lawrence's Will Trusts, Public Trustee v Lawrence* [1972] Ch 418, [1971] 3 All ER 433.

5 *Clifford v Clifford* (1852) 9 Hare 675; *Chandler v Pocock* (1880) 15 Ch D 491; affd (1881) 16 Ch D 648.

6 *Re Greaves' Settlement Trusts* (1883) 23 Ch D 313.

7 *Adams v Austen* (1829) 3 Russ 461; *Stead v Newdigate* (1817) 2 Mer 521.

8 *Gillies v Longlands* (1851) 4 De G & Sm 372; *Re Greaves' Settlement Trusts* (1883) 23 Ch D 313; but such money will pass under a general gift of land: *Re Duke of Cleveland's Settled Estates* [1893] 3 Ch 244; *Re Harman, Lloyd v Tardy* [1894] 3 Ch 607.

9 *Re Spooner's Trust* (1851) 2 Sim NS 129; *Hawthorn v Shedden* (1856) 3 Sm & G 293 at 304. The appointment of a 'residuary legatee' may be tantamount to a residuary devise if aided by the context; see *Singleton v Tomlinson* (1878) 3 App Cas 404 at 418; cf *Re Featherstone–Haugh–Whitney's Estate* [1924] 1 IR 153 at 160.

10 *Hawthorn v Shedden* (1856) 3 Sm & G 293; *Re Davies' Trust* (1871) LR 13 Eq 163 at 166; *Re Seabrook, Gray v Baddeley* [1911] 1 Ch 151; *Re Guedalla, Lee v Guedalla's Trustee* [1905] 2 Ch 331.

11 *Re Seabrook, Gray v Baddeley* [1911] 1 Ch 151.

12 *Laing v Cowan* (1857) 24 Beav 112; *Re Davies' Trusts* (1871) LR 13 Eq 163. An appointment of executor without more is insufficient.

[39.13]

Restrictions on exercise of power. A power to appoint by will specifically referring to the power[1] is not a general power within the Wills Act 1837, s 27,[2] but a power to appoint only by will[3] or a power to direct by will that a sum of money shall be raised and paid[4] are within the section. Hybrid powers[5] are not within the section and are thus not exercised by a general devise or bequest.[6]

1 *Phillips v Cayley* (1889) 43 Ch D 222; *Re Davies, Davies v Davies* [1892] 3 Ch 63; *Re Tarrant's Trust* (1889) 58 LJ Ch 780; *Re Priestley's Will Trusts, Hambros Bank Executors and Trustee Co Ltd v Rabagliati* [1971] Ch 858, CA, [1971] 2 All ER 817. But if the residuary gift is expressed to extend to property over which the testator has 'any disposing power', that is sufficient reference to the power: *Re Waterhouse, Waterhouse v Ryley* (1907) 77 LJ Ch 30.

2 See Vol 2, Part G, para **[244.27]**.

3 *Hawthorn v Shedden* (1856) 3 Sm & G 293; *Re Powell's Trusts* (1869) 39 LJ Ch 188.

4 *Re Jones, Greene v Gordon* (1886) 34 Ch D 65; *Re Wilkinson, Thomas v Wilkinson* [1910] 2 Ch 216, but see *Re Salvin, Marshall v Wolseley* [1906] 2 Ch 459.

5 As to which see para **[39.31]** infra.

6 *Re Byron's Settlement, Williams v Mitchell* [1891] 3 Ch 474; *Re Lawrence's Will Trust, Public Trustee v Lawrence* [1972] Ch 418 at 428, [1971] 3 All ER 433 at 439; *Perpetual Executors and Trustee Association of Australia v Adams* [1975] VR 462.

[39.14]

Contrary intention. The contrary intention sufficient to counteract this statutory provision must be clearly expressed or implied in the will.[1] There is no contrary intention within the meaning of the statute unless there is something in the will inconsistent with the view that the general devise was meant as an execution of the power,[2] and the fact that a testator exercises other general powers of appointment is no evidence of a contrary intention in respect of another power not referred to in the will.[3] The gift of part of an estate may fairly be considered as inconsistent with a gift of the whole.[4] A clear intention to except the subject-matter of the power from an earlier appointment in the will is not such a contrary intention as to prevent it from passing by a residuary bequest to the same person.[5] The qualification 'which I possess or to which I am entitled' added to the subject-matter does not show a contrary intention.[6] The words 'including all property over which at my death I may have an absolute power of appointment' in a residuary gift are not evidence of such a contrary intention as to prevent the application of the section to an antecedent bequest;[7] nor is the revocation by codicil of an appointment under a general testamentary power sufficient to prevent its application to a residuary bequest.[8] The specific exercise of a power which in the events which happen does not arise, or the omission of all mention of a power which does arise, does not show such a contrary intention to prevent a residuary bequest from operating as an appointment under a power which does arise.[9] No contrary intention is shown because a special power is expressly exercised in favour of the same beneficiary and the testator is careful in his will to distinguish between his own property and the settled funds over which the general power is to operate.[10] A restriction of the general bequest of residue to property not otherwise effectually disposed of has been held to show a contrary intention in the case of property effectually disposed of apart from the will.[11] The suggestion[12] that a general gift in a will, in order to defeat the provisions in default of appointment in a settlement made by the testator himself, would require some indication of his intention to defeat his own settlement, conflicts with the statute and is not borne out by the cases. It makes no difference whether the settlement was made by the testator himself or by a stranger.[13] To prevent the general gift in the will operating as an exercise of the power the will itself must show an intention that the limitations of the settlement are not to be disturbed.[14] An ineffectual exercise of the power of appointment does not exclude the statutory provision, and the property passes under the general bequest, just as property specifically bequeathed passes, on failure of the disposition, under a residuary bequest.[15] Under this statutory provision property over which the testator has a general power of appointment is treated as if it were his own property, and it is unnecessary for the testator to refer to the instrument creating, or to the subject-matter of, a general power,[16] or to use technical language in executing it.[17]

1   The real effect of this provision is that, if it is to be held that the power is not well exercised by the general gift, the burden is on those so stating to prove by some provision in the will itself that it is not exercised: see *Re Box's Settlement, Box v Plaut* [1945] 1 All ER 547 at 549. Of course, if it has already been otherwise fully exercised (eg by deed) the power itself is gone and the residuary or general gift can have no such effect. Further the exercise of the power may by the instrument creating it be subject to special formalities: eg it may be exercisable only by will or codicil expressly referring to the power; then, if the will or codicil includes no such express reference, the general gift will not exercise the power: *Phillips v Cayley* (1889) 43 Ch D 222, overruling *Re Marsh, Mason v Thorne* (1888) 38 Ch D 630; *Re Priestley's Will Trusts, Hambros Bank Executors and Trustee Co Ltd v Rabagliati* [1971] Ch 858, CA, [1971] 2 All ER 817. An unnecessary direction in the will does not show a contrary intention: *Re Stapleton* [1938] 3 DLR 752.

2   *Scriven v Sandom* (1862) 2 John & H 743 at 744; *Lake v Currie* (1852) 2 De GM & G 536;
     Hutchins v Osborne (1858) 4 K & J 252; *Thomas v Jones* (1862) 2 John & H 475.
3   *Re Thirlwell's Will Trusts, Evans v Thirlwell* [1958] Ch 146, [1957] 3 All ER 465.
4   *Scriven v Sandom* (1862) 2 John & H 743 at 745, but in *Re Stokes, Public Trustee v Brooks*
     [1922] 2 Ch 406, there was held to be no inconsistency merely because of duplication of a life
     interest under a special and general power intended to meet different contingencies, the subject-
     matter of each appointment not being necessarily the same.
5   *Bernard v Minshull* (1859) John 276.
6   *Re Jacob, Mortimer v Mortimer* [1907] 1 Ch 445; *Re Tidy* [1949] 2 OLR 302 ('my estate').
7   *Re Doherty-Waterhouse, Musgrave v De Chair* [1918] 2 Ch 269.
8   *Re Jarrett, Re Vrenegroor, Bird v Green* [1919] 1 Ch 366.
9   *Re Andrews, Public Trustee v Vincent* [1922] WN 34.
10 *Re Box's Settlement, Box v Plaut* [1945] 1 All ER 547.
11 *Moss v Harter* (1854) 2 Sm & G 458.
12 By Lord St Leonards in Sugden, *Powers*, pp 305, 306.
13 *Re Clark's Estate, Maddick v Marks* (1880) 14 Ch D 422; *Boyes v Cook* (1880) 14 Ch D 53;
     Airey v Bower (1887) 12 App Cas 263, and see *Re Wallinger's Estate* [1898] 1 IR 139. In *Moss
     v Harter* (1854) 2 Sm & G 458, there was a general power which was exercised as to part of the
     property by deed. The will contained a general disposition of all property not otherwise
     effectually disposed of. It was held that this disposition did not exercise the power so far as
     regards the remaining property because that passed according to the trusts declared in default of
     appointment. Reference can be made to surrounding circumstances at the date of the will but
     not at the date of the settlement: *Boyes v Cook* (1880) 14 Ch D 53 (where the settlement was
     made after the will).
14 It has never in effect been decided that a confirmation of the settlement by the will prevents the
     exercise of a power though such may be the result of *Lake v Currie* (1852) 2 De GM & G 536
     (settlement comprising two properties, one not being subject to the power of appointment; the
     settlement was confirmed as to the property not subject to the power and it was held that a
     general devise operated as an appointment of the other property). The better view seems,
     however, to be that an express confirmation extends only to that part of the settlement which the
     testator has no power to disturb.
15 *Re Spooner's Trust* (1851) 2 Sim NS 129, and *Bush v Cowan* (1863) 32 Beav 228 (failure of
     appointment by lapse); *Re Elen, Thomas v McKechnie* (1893) 68 LT 816 (contingent
     appointment); *Bernard v Minshull* (1859) John 276 (failure through uncertainty); *Re Andrews,
     Public Trustee v Vincent* (1922) 66 Sol Jo 284; *Re White Trust* [1952] 4 DLR 711. See also
     Hickson v Wolfe (1858) 9 I Ch R 144; *Freme v Clement* (1881) 18 Ch D 499 at 512 (doubted
     apparently on another point in *Holyland v Lewin* (1884) 26 Ch D 266).
16 *Re Wilkinson* (1869) 4 Ch App 587 at 590.
17 Any language capable of being construed as a residuary gift is sufficient: *Re Spooner's Trust*
     (1851) 2 Sim NS 129; *Re Wilkinson* (1869) 4 Ch App 587. For words which have been
     construed as a sufficient residuary gift, see para **[38.1]** supra, and n 15.

[39.15]
Exceptions from statutory provision. A general devise or bequest does not,
however, operate as an exercise of a power vested in the testator to revoke
existing trusts and appoint other trusts, except, it seems, where the gift would
otherwise be inoperative.[1] The general gift must be effective and where it fails,
eg because the husband of the donee has witnessed the will, the power of
appointment is not exercised.[2]

1   *Re Brace, Welch v Colt* [1891] 2 Ch 671.
2   *Re Vander Byl, Fladgate v Gore* [1931] 1 Ch 216.

III.   SPECIAL POWERS

[39.16]
Exercise of special powers. The exercise of a special power of appointment by
will is purely a question of intention,[1] the burden of proof being on those who

434

assert affirmatively the exercise of the power.[2] A mere general devise or bequest does not operate as an execution of a special power.[3] Thus, a general devise by a testator possessed of no real estate, but having a special power to appoint real estate, to persons some of whom are objects,[4] or even to a sole object of the power,[5] is not a valid exercise of the power.

1   In order to exercise a special power of appointment there must be a sufficient expression or indication of intention in the will or other instrument alleged to exercise it; and either a reference to the power or a reference to the property subject to the power constitutes in general a sufficient indication for the purpose. Where, however, two powers exist in reference to the same property, it may well be that a reference to the property will not indicate any intention to exercise more than one of the powers: *Re Ackerley, Chapman v Andrew* [1913] 1 Ch 510; applied in *Re Priestley's Will Trusts, Hambros Bank Executor and Trustee Co Ltd v Rabagliati* [1971] Ch 858, [1971] 2 All ER 817, CA; and in *Re Lawrence's Will Trusts, Public Trustee v Lawrence* [1972] Ch 418, [1971] 3 All ER 433 (where it was held that a will disclosed a sufficient intention to exercise a hybrid power although there were certain indications to the contrary); *Re Knight, Re Wynn, Midland Bank Executor and Trustee Co Ltd v Parker* [1957] Ch 441, [1957] 2 All ER 252.
2   *Re Mills, Mills v Mills* (1886) 34 Ch D 186.
3   *Re Hayes, Turnbull v Hayes* [1901] 2 Ch 529.
4   *Re Mills, Mills v Mills* (1886) 34 Ch D 186.
5   *Harvey v Harvey* (1875) 32 LT 141; *Re Williams, Foulkes v Williams* (1889) 42 Ch D 93.

[39.17]
Essentials of exercise of special power. To exercise a special power there must be either (1) a reference to the power, or (2) a reference to the property subject to the power, or (3) an intention otherwise expressed in the will to exercise the power.[1]

1   *Re Weston's Settlement, Neeves v Weston* [1906] 2 Ch 620; *Hicks v Hirst* (1907) 26 NZLR 1376; *Sharp v Eastern Trust Co* [1949] 1 DLR 557. As to the particular methods of showing intention, see para **[39.20]** infra.

[39.18]
Reference to power. Any reference to a special power, however slight, is sufficient.[1] Thus, an indirect reference to the power,[2] or even a reference to the instrument creating the power, may be enough.[3] The reference must be specific;[4] but, if the intention to exercise the special power is clear, an inaccurate or incomplete reference to it may suffice.[5] A reference to a 'beneficial' power may be treated as a reference to a special power.[6] On the other hand a mere reference to any power is not necessarily sufficient.[7] Likewise, an erroneous recital by a donee of a special power that another is entitled to the property subject to the power does not amount to an execution of the power;[8] nor does a statement, following an appointment to one object of the power, that the donee makes no further appointment as she wishes the fund to pass directly to two named objects of the power amount to an appointment by implication to the latter.[9]

1   *Re Williams, Foulkes v Williams* (1889) 42 Ch D 93; *Saunders v Carden* (1891) 27 LR Ir 43 (reference to any disposing power).
2   *Re Comber's Settlement* (1865) 11 Jur NS 968 (reference in another part of will); *Harvey v Stracey* (1852) 1 Drew 73 (reference in another part of will dealing with another power created by the same settlement); *Disney v Crosse* (1866) LR 2 Eq 592 (gift of legacies to objects followed by an appointment of the settled property charged with the legacies); *Lees v Lees* (1871) IR 5 Eq 549 (recital).

3   *Hunloke v Gell* (1830) 1 Russ & M 515; *Peirce v M'Neale* [1894] 1 IR 118.
4   *Re Walsh's Trusts* (1878) 1 LR Ir 320.
5   *Carver v Richards* (1859) 27 Beav 488 (where the intention is established to pass property
      subject of a power, the property, passes under the disposition although the intention to dispose
      of it by means of the power is not shown); *Re Wilmot* (1861) 29 Beav 644 (reference to power
      as created by settlement of 1819 instead of 1839); *Harvey v Stacey* (1852) 1 Drew 73; *Bruce v
      Bruce* (1871) LR 11 Eq 371 (will showing that testatrix thought power extinguished and
      purporting to be in execution of an invalid power: this case is more concerned with the principle
      that equity will in certain cases aid a defective execution of a power).
6   *Von Brockdorf v Malcolm* (1885) 30 Ch D 172 (no reference to power but gift of all property
      over which testator had any beneficial disposing power by his will); *Ames v Cadogan* (1879) 12
      Ch D 868 (similar but referred to property of or to which testator was seised or entitled or over
      which he might have any beneficial power of disposition).
7   *Re Knight, Re Wynn, Midland Bank Executor and Trustee Co Ltd v Parker* [1957] Ch 441,
      [1957] 2 All ER 252 ('including any property over which I may have any power of disposition
      at the date of my death'); applied in *Re Priestley's Will Trusts, Hambros Bank Executor Co Ltd
      v Rabagliati* [1971] Ch 858, [1971] 2 All ER 817, CA; see Pennycuick V-C [1971] Ch 562 at
      572, [1970] 3 All ER 1025 at 1032. Compare *Re Lawrence's Will Trusts, Public Trustee v
      Lawrence* [1972] Ch 418, [1971] 3 All ER 433 (exercise of hybrid power).
8   *L'Estrange v L'Estrange* (1890) 25 LR Ir 399; *Pennefather v Pennefather* (1873) IR 7 Eq 300;
      Haverty v Curtis [1895] 1 IR 23.
9   *Re Jack, Jack v Jack* [1899] 1 Ch 374. To deprive a person of an unappointed fund it must be
      shown that there has been an actual appointment: *Langslow v Langslow* (1856) 21 Beav 552;
      Carver v Richards (1859) 27 Beav 488. But see *Foster v Cautley* (1855) 6 De GM & G 55,
      where the appointment to one of three was made in lieu of all claims and demands of the
      appointee to or for any original or principal share and this was held by implication to be an
      appointment to the other two.

[39.19]
Reference to property. Where a testator describes and disposes of specific
property, over which he has a special power of appointment, in favour of
objects,[1] or of persons some of whom are objects[2] without mentioning the
power, the inference is that he intended to exercise it,[3] even though he
misdescribes the property,[4] but the intention of the testator to dispose of the
specific property subject to the power must be clear.[5] A gift in general terms of
property similar to that subject to the power, such as specific stock[6] or of
legacies equal to the fund subject to the power,[7] does not sufficiently evidence
an intention to exercise the power where the testator has property of his own
which will satisfy the gift; but if he expressly excepts from the general gift part
of the property subject to the power, the exception will make the residue of the
property subject to the power pass under that general gift.[8] If the gift is prima
facie specific,[9] evidence as to the testator's property is admissible in order to
show whether he intended to exercise the power.[10] If the testator possesses
property of his own answering the description the usual inference is that he did
not intend to exercise the power;[11] and a reference to property of the kind which
is subject to the power coupled with an attempt to dispose of it in an
unauthorised manner may rebut a presumption of intention to exercise the
power.[12]

1   *Forbes v Ball* (1817) 3 Mer 437; *Davies v Davies* (1858) 28 LJ Ch 102; *Elliott v Elliott* (1846)
      15 Sim 321; *Re Davids' Trusts* (1859) John 495; *Re Mackenzie, Thornton v Huddleston* [1917]
      2 Ch 58.
2   *Re Gratwick's Trusts* (1865) LR 1 Eq 177; *Bruce v Bruce* (1871) LR 11 Eq 371.
3   *Re Jonathan, Jonathan v Ward* [1962] NZLR 536.
4   *Mackinley v Sison* (1837) 8 Sim 561; *Bruce v Bruce* (1871) LR 11 Eq 371.

5   *Bennett v Aburrow* (1803) 8 Ves 609 (part of will would be wholly inoperative unless construed
      as execution of power); *Re Mattingley's Trusts* (1862) 2 John & H 426 (where the trust fund
      was a sum of consols and the testator had no money invested in the funds); *Re Huddleston,
      Bruno v Eyston* [1894] 3 Ch 595 (gift in will of all property of every kind but no express
      reference to the power: the gift being general no evidence of state of testator's property was
      admissible).

6   *Webb v Honnor* (1820) 1 Jac & W 352; *Re Wait, Workman v Petgrave* (1885) 30 Ch D 617.

7   *Jones v Tucker* (1817) 2 Mer 533; *Forbes v Ball* (1817) 3 Mer 437; *Davies v Thorns* (1849) 3
      De G & Sm 347.

8   *Reid v Reid* (1858) 25 Beav 469 (a general gift expressed to be of residue of property but with
      an exception of certain property which was in fact the subject-matter of a special power: it was
      held that the exception of part of the property subject to the power had the effect of making the
      general gift of residue pass the remaining property subject to the power). See also *Walker v
      Mackie* (1827) 4 Russ 76.

9   *Bennett v Aburrow* (1803) 8 Ves 609; *Re Mattingley's Trusts* (1862) 2 John & H 426.

10   *Re Huddleston, Bruno v Eyston* [1894] 3 Ch 595; *Innes v Sayer* (1851) 3 Mac & G 606;
      Humphery v Humphery (1877) 36 LT 91; *Peirce v M'Neale* [1894] 1 IR 118; *Re Herdman's
      Trusts* (1893) 31 LR Ir 87. The evidence admissible is only that which goes to show whether
      the testator had any such property of his own.

11   *Noel v Noel* (1859) 4 Drew 624; *Reid v Reid* (1858) 25 Beav 469; *Re Wait, Workman v
      Petgrave* (1885) 30 Ch D 617, doubted in *Re Nicholl, Re Perkins, Nicholl v Perkins* (1920) 125
      LT 62. In *Re Waldron's Settlement, Waldron v Errington-Wales* [1940] 3 All ER 442, the
      authorities on this matter were considered and it was there held that there was an appointment
      as to property of which the testatrix had none but no appointment as to property of which she
      possessed some of her own.

12   *Wildbore v Gregory* (1871) LR 12 Eq 482; *Re Rickman, Stokes v Rickman* (1899) 80 LT 518.

[39.20]

Intention to exercise power. The intention of a testator to exercise a special
power, if not expressed, can be inferred only from the words of his will and the
circumstances at the time of executing it which were known to him, and to
which the court, putting itself in his place, is bound to have regard.[1] Two matters
must be gathered from the construction of the will: (i) that the testator had the
power in mind at the time of making his will, and (ii) that he wished to exercise
it.[2] An intention to exercise a power is not generally inferred if there is a gift
over in default of appointment.[3] In particular, it requires very clear indications in
the language of a will to infer an intention to exercise a special power which was
not in existence at the date of the will.[4]

1   *Re Knight, Re Wynn, Midland Bank Executor and Trustee Co Ltd v Parker* [1957] Ch 441,
      [1957] 2 All ER 252 (where the decision was against the exercise of the power based on the fact
      that the general fund was made liable for debts, duties, etc). Compare *Re Priestley's Will Trusts,
      Hambros Bank Executor and Trustee Co Ltd v Rabagliati* [1971] Ch 858, [1971] 2 All ER 817,
      CA (power not exercised), with *Re Lawrence's Will Trusts, Public Trustee v Lawrence* [1972]
      Ch 418, [1971] 3 All ER 433 (hybrid power exercised). See also *Re Mills, Mills v Mills* (1886)
      34 Ch D 186; *Re Williams, Foulkes v Williams* (1889) 42 Ch D 93; *Re Mackenzie, Thornton v
      Huddleston* [1917] 2 Ch 58; but see *Re Morgan* (1857) 7 I Ch R 18, to the contrary.

2   *Wrigley v Lowndes* [1908] P 348.

3   *Henderson v Constable* (1842) 5 Beav 297.

4   *Re Hayes, Turnbull v Hayes* [1901] 2 Ch 529; not following *Stillman v Weedon* (1848) 16 Sim
      26. It is doubtful whether property appointed under a limited power can be said to be comprised
      in the will within the Wills Act 1837, s 24; 50 *Halsbury's Statutes* (4th edn) 593 (see Vol 2,
      Part G, para **[244.24]**); *Re Bower, Bower v Mercer* [1930] 2 Ch 82 (where a special power
      created after the execution of the will was referred to in the will and the intention to exercise it
      expressed and the will was subsequently by a codicil executed after the creation of the power
      confirmed inter alia as to the exercise of the power; but it was also held that a special power
      created after the execution of the codicil was not exercised); see also *Re Wells' Trusts, Hardisty
      v Wells* (1889) 42 Ch D 646; *Doyle v Coyle* [1895] 1 IR 205.

[39.21]
Partial exercise. A will containing an express but partial exercise of a special power and a residuary gift prima facie applicable only to the testator's property does not operate as an appointment of the balance of the property subject to the power,[1] unless such intention can be implied.[2]

1   *Hughes v Turner* (1835) 3 My & K 666; *Butler v Gray* (1869) 5 Ch App 26; *Re Nicholl, Re Perkins, Nicholl v Perkins* (1920) 125 LT 62.
2   *Elliott v Elliott* (1846) 15 Sim 321; *Davies v Fisher* (1842) 5 Beav 201; *Harvey v Stracey* (1852) 1 Drew 73.

[39.22]
Universal gifts. A gift leaving everything the testator has power to dispose of to an object of the power can indicate an intention to exercise a special power,[1] and the more so where the testator has no other power.[2] This rule applies even though the bequest includes the testator's own property,[3] or the testator purports to create interests in excess of the power, such as an absolute interest in lieu of a life interest,[4] but not where the power was not in existence at the date of the will.[5]

1   *Re Richardson's Trusts* (1886) 17 LR Ir 436; *Re Mayhew, Spencer v Cutbush* [1901] 1 Ch 677, *Re Milner, Bray v Milner* [1899] 1 Ch 563; *Re Welford's Will Trusts, Davidson v Davidson* [1946] 1 All ER 23; *Re Liverton* [1951] NZLR 351. The words 'over which I shall have any disposing power at the time of my decease' do not necessarily refer to a power acquired after the execution of the will, but include a power the testator already possesses at that time: *Re Welford's Will Trusts, Davidson v Davidson* [1946] 1 All ER 23. See also *Paykel v Guardian Trust and Executors Co of New Zealand Ltd* [1963] NZLR 168 (where the evidence of surrounding circumstances rebutted the rule).
2   *Wrigley v Lowndes* [1908] P 348; *Re Blackburn, Smiles v Blackburn* (1889) 43 Ch D 75; *Re Swinburne, Swinburne v Pitt* (1884) 27 Ch D 696 (where part of the property subject to the powers purported to be given to non-objects); *Gainsford v Dunn* (1874) LR 17 Eq 405; *Re Boyd, Nield v Boyd* (1890) 63 LT 92 (attempt to create illegal interests); *Thornton v Thornton* (1875) LR 20 Eq 599; *Ferrier v Jay* (1870) LR 10 Eq 550; *Re Welford's Will Trusts, Davidson v Davidson* [1946] 1 All ER 23.
3   *Byrne v Cullinan* [1904] 1 IR 42.
4   *Re Teape's Trusts* (1873) LR 16 Eq 442.
5   See para **[39.19]**, n 12.

[39.23]
Residuary gifts to objects. A residuary gift to persons who are objects of a special power may operate as an appointment to them of a fund wrongly appointed to a person who is not an object.[1]

1   *Re Hunt's Trusts* (1885) 31 Ch D 308.

[39.24]
Co-existing general and special powers. The fact that the testator possesses a general and a special power does not by itself prevent a general reference to powers from being sufficient to exercise a special power, but may be taken into consideration in arriving at the testator's intention.[1]

1   *Re Rickman, Stokes v Rickman* (1899) 80 LT 518 (special power not exercised); *Thornton v Thornton,* supra (special and general powers exercised); *Ferrier v Jay* (1870) LR 10 Eq 550 (special power exercised); *Re Ackerley, Chapman v Andrew* [1913] 1 Ch 510; *Re Milner, Bray v Milner* [1899] 1 Ch 563; *Re Sharland, Re Rew, Rew v Wippell* [1899] 2 Ch 536.

[39.25]

Use of word 'appoint'. Where the word 'appoint' is used, an intention may be gathered that the testator intends to exercise a special power,[1] especially if he has no general power.[2] Extrinsic evidence is admissible where the word 'appoint' is used to show that the testator possessed no other power of appointment at his death.[3] It is no objection that the testator, although he uses the words 'appoint', is dealing with his own property and the property he is appointing as one mass,[4] nor that non-objects are included among the beneficiaries either originally[5] or by substitutional gifts.[6]

1   *Re Latta's Marriage Settlement Trusts, Public Trustee v Latta* [1949] Ch 490, [1949] 1 All ER 665; *Re Mayhew, Spencer v Cutbush* [1901] 1 Ch 677; *Re Milner, Bray v Milner* [1899] 1 Ch 563; *Kent v Kent* [1902] P 108; *Pidgely v Pidgely* (1844) 1 Coll 255. In the following cases special powers were held not exercised by general words: *Re Cotton, Wood v Cotton* (1888) 40 Ch D 41; *Cooke v Cunliffe* (1851) 17 QB 245; *Sykes v Carroll* [1903] 1 IR 17; *Re Weston's Settlement, Neeves v Weston* [1906] 2 Ch 620; *Re Sanderson, Sanderson v Sanderson* (1912) 106 LT 26; *Re Beresford's Will Trusts, Sturges v Beresford* [1938] 3 All ER 566; *Re Holford's Settlement, Lloyds Bank Ltd v Holford* [1945] Ch 21, [1944] 2 All ER 462. It seems that the special power is not exercised where the property subject to the power is blended in one mass with the testator's own property and the whole made subject to debts, duties, legacies, trust for conversion and investment and the like, all of which are inapplicable to appointed property. But failure to use the word 'appoint' does not show an intention not to exercise a special power: *Re Welford's Will Trusts, Davidson v Davidson* [1946] 1 All ER 23; *Re Knight, Re Wynn, Midland Bank Executor and Trustee Co Ltd v Parker* [1957] Ch 441, [1957] 2 All ER 252; *Paykel v Guardian Trust and Executor Co of New Zealand Ltd* [1963] NZLR 168.
2   *Re Richardson's Trusts* (1886) 17 LR Ir 436.
3   *Re Mayhew, Spencer v Cutbush* [1901] 1 Ch 677; *Re Huddleston, Bruno v Eyston* [1948] 3 Ch 595.
4   *Re Latta's Marriage Settlement Trusts, Public Trustee v Latta* [1949] Ch 490, [1949] 1 All ER 665; *Re Mayhew, Spencer v Cutbush* [1901] 1 Ch 677; *Re Swinburne, Swinburne v Pitt* (1884) 27 Ch D 696.
5   *Re Swinburne, Swinburne v Pitt* (1884) 27 Ch D 696.
6   *Re Latta's Marriage Settlement Trusts, Public Trustee v Latta* [1949] Ch 490, [1949] 1 All ER 665.

[39.26]

Direction to pay debts. A direction to pay debts and general and testamentary expenses out of a fund which ex hypothesi includes the fund subject to the special power is not in itself sufficient to negative a presumption of intention to exercise the power otherwise established.[1]

1   *Cowx v Foster* (1860) 1 John & H 30; *Re Teape's Trusts* (1873) LR 16 Eq 442; *Re Swinburne, Swinburne v Pitt* (1884) 27 Ch D 696; *Re Milner, Bray v Milner* [1899] 1 Ch 563; *Re Welford's Will Trusts, Davidson v Davidson* [1946] 1 All ER 23. For decisions to the contrary, see *Clogstoun v Walcott* (1843) 13 Sim 523; *Re Mackenzie, Thornton v Huddleston* [1917] 2 Ch 58; and see the second line cases cited in para **[39.25]**, n 1, particularly *Re Holford's Settlement, Lloyds Bank Ltd v Holford* [1945] Ch 21, [1944] 2 All ER 462 at 468, 469, and *Re Knight, Re Wynn, Midland Bank Executor and Trustee Co Ltd v Parker* [1957] Ch 441, [1957] 2 All ER 252.

[39.27]

Exercise by both deed and will. Where the appointor exercises the power by will and then by deed with power of revocation, the will, unless it expressly revokes the appointment by deed, does not operate as a revocation of the appointment by deed, which, since it takes effect before the will which becomes operative only on the death of the appointor, is the operative appointment.[1]

1   *Re Butler's Settlement Trusts* [1942] Ch 403, [1942] 2 All ER 191. Where there is a power of
     appointment and of revocation, an appointment in exercise of the power of appointment, and
     every or any other power does not refer to the power of revocation and a plain appointment in
     those terms without revocation does not operate to revoke a previous appointment: *Re
     Thursby's Settlement, Grant v Littledale* [1910] 2 Ch 181 at 186.

[39.28]

Power of revocation. Where a person has a special power of appointment and
also a power of revocation and new appointment, an appointment expressed in
general words does not extend to property which the appointor cannot appoint
without the exercise of the power of revocation, if there is other property to
which the appointment can apply.[1] Similarly, a will exercising a special power,
which is afterwards exercised by deed reserving a power of revocation, does not
affect the property appointed by deed.[2] Where a power of revocation is to be
exercised by a trustee with the consent of a beneficiary, the consent may be
given while the beneficiary is a minor, if such appears to be the intention of the
testator.[3] Where a will gave the net revenue of an estate to a brother and sister
for their lives and at their deaths to go to charities as they may have selected
during their lives, it was held that having regard to the facts that a selection
between charities might require to be reviewed as circumstances changed, and
that appointments under the power were not made by deed, each appointment
was revocable although there was no power of revocation and an earlier
appointment made jointly was revocable by the survivor.[4] It was also held that
the will showed no intention on the part of the testator that confidence was
imposed only in the selection by both donees jointly and accordingly the power
was exercisable by the survivor.

1   *Pomfret v Perring* (1854) 5 De GM & G 775; *Re Barker's Settlement, Knocker v Vernon Jones*
     [1920] 1 Ch 527. See also *Re Hambro's Marriage Settlements, Hambro v Hambro* [1949] Ch
     484, where the appointment by deed was recoverable only by deed and was not revoked by an
     appointment by will.
2   *Re Wells' Trusts, Hardisty v Wells* (1889) 42 Ch D 646. A power of revocation may be
     impliedly exercised: *Quin v Armstrong* (1876) IR 11 Eq 161.
3   *Re Sutton, Boscawen v Wyndham* [1921] 1 Ch 257.
4   *Re Beesty's Will Trusts, Farrar v Royal Alfred Merchant Seaman's Society* [1966] Ch 223,
     [1964] 3 All ER 82.

[39.29]

Lapse. An appointment by will in exercise of a special power in favour of an
object of the power is not preserved from lapse in the event of the object
predeceasing the testator and leaving issue living at the latter's death.[1]

1   *Holyland v Lewin* (1884) 26 Ch D 266, disapproving *Freme v Clement* (1881) 18 Ch D 499. See
     further, Chapter 47.

[39.30]

Failure to exercise power of appointment. Where the power is in the nature of
a trust and there is no gift over in default of appointment, the court may imply a
gift to the objects equally.[1]

1   This complex subject is dealt with elsewhere; see Chapter 101.

IV.   HYBRID POWERS

[39.31]

Hybrid powers. The term 'hybrid powers', if not ideal, is a convenient expression, *faute de mieux*,[1] to cover an intermediate group of powers where the donee can appoint to anyone with certain exceptions, for example an exception of himself or an exception of named persons or classes of persons.[2] Examples from the decided cases are: a power to appoint to anyone except 'her said present husband or any friend or relative of his';[3] a power to appoint to anyone except the donee;[4] a power to a wife to appoint to anyone except her relations;[5] a testamentary power for the owner of a life interest to appoint to persons living at his death.[6] It will be noted from the definitions given at the beginning of this Chapter[7] that the statutory definitions of powers usually differentiate only between general and special powers and do not admit of an intermediate category. The status of a hybrid power in such cases must be considered specifically with regard to the statute or principle in point, and because a hybrid power has to be regarded as special for one purpose, it does not follow that the power is necessarily special for all purposes.[8] It would seem that hybrid powers will not generally be within the Wills Act 1837, s 27,[9] since they cannot satisfy the requirement that the power should be exercisable 'in any manner he may think proper'.[10] A power in a settlement in favour of a specified class subject to a specified excepted class, together with wide powers given to the donees to nominate and add to the class of beneficiaries, at their discretion, has been upheld notwithstanding arguments based on the principle of non-delegation and uncertainty.[11]

---

1   Per Megarry J in *Re Lawrence's Will Trusts, Public Trustee v Lawrence* [1972] Ch 418 at 428, [1971] 3 All ER 433 at 441. These powers are also sometimes referred to as 'intermediate powers'; see, for example, Templeman J in *Re Manisty's Settlement, Manisty v Manisty* [1974] Ch 17, [1973] 2 All ER 1203.

2   *Re Park, Public Trustee v Armstrong* [1932] 1 Ch 580 at 584, per Clausen J; see also *Re Hay's Settlement Trusts* [1981] 3 All ER 786, [1982] 1 WLR 202 (power to appoint to anyone in the world except specified class).

3   *Re Byron's Settlement, Williams v Mitchell* [1891] 3 Ch 474.

4   *Re Park, Public Trustee v Armstrong* [1932] 1 Ch 580; *Re Harvey, Banister v Thirtle* [1950] 1 All ER 491, a power for a spinster to appoint to anyone other than a husband she might marry was treated, whilst she was unmarried, as a general power.

5   *Re Lawrence's Will Trusts, Public Trustee v Lawrence* [1972] Ch 418, [1971] 3 All ER 433.

6   *Re Jones, Public Trustee v Jones* [1945] Ch 105.

7   See para **[39.1]** et seq.

8   Per Megarry J in *Re Lawrence's Will Trusts, Public Trustee v Lawrence* [1972] Ch 418 at 427, [1971] 3 All ER 433 at 439.

9   See Vol 2, Part G, para **[244.27]**.

10   See para **[39.11]** supra.

11   *Re Manisty's Settlement, Manisty v Manisty* [1974] Ch 17, [1973] 2 All ER 1203, applying *Re Park, Public Trustee v Armstrong* [1932] 1 Ch 580, [1931] All ER Rep 633, and *Re Abrahams' Will Trusts, Caplin v Abrahams* [1969] 1 Ch 463, [1967] 2 All ER 1175, on the delegation point; and *Re Gulbenkian's Settlement Trusts, Whishaw v Stephens* [1970] AC 508, [1968] 3 All ER 785; *McPhail v Doulton* [1971] AC 424, [1970] 2 All ER 228; *Re Baden's Deed Trusts (No 2), Baden v Smith* [1973] Ch 9, [1972] 2 All ER 1304 and *Re Hay's Settlement Trusts* [1981] 3 All ER 786, [1982] 1 WLR 202, on the uncertainty point. In the last mentioned case it was held that the duties of a trustee in exercising a hybrid power of appointment were (a) to ensure that any appointment was within the powers, (b) to consider periodically whether to exercise the power, (c) to consider the range of objects of the power and (d) to consider the appropriateness of individual appointments.

CHAPTER 40

Powers of appointment—miscellaneous matters affecting the exercise of the power

[40.1]

Illusory and exclusive appointments. Under the Law of Property Act 1925, s 158,[1] no appointment made in the exercise of a power to appoint among two or more objects is invalid on the ground that an insubstantial, illusory or nominal share only is appointed to, or left unappointed to devolve on, any one or more of the objects of the power, or on the ground that any object of the power is thereby altogether excluded. Every such appointment is valid notwithstanding that any one or more of the objects is not thereby, or in default of appointment, to take any share in the property. The section does not affect any provision in the instrument creating the power which declares the amount of any share from which any object is not to be excluded.

1 37 *Halsbury's Statutes* (4th edn) 332.

[40.2]

Appointment among a class. A power of appointment among a class, if on its true construction it is nothing more than a power to limit the proportions in which the members of the class are to take, cannot be exercised if there is only one object to whom the property is limited in default of appointment.[1] The power, however, may be so worded as to enable the appointor to make the property pass by, and not in default of appointment,[2] and such a power may be well exercised although there is but one object and that object takes in default of appointment.[3] A limitation in default of appointment to the only object of a power cannot be defeated by an appointment which fails in the event which happens. The estate in default of appointment can only be defeated by an appointment which takes effect, and only to the extent to which such appointment does take effect.[4]

1 *Campbell v Sandys* (1803) 1 Sch & Lef 281; *Folkes v Western* (1804) 9 Ves 456.
2 *Boyle v Bishop of Peterborough* (1791) 1 Ves 299 at 309.
3 *Bray v Bree* (1834) 2 Cl & Fin 453; *Noel v Lord Walsingham* (1824) 2 Sim & St 99 at 112; *Woodcock v Renneck* (1841) 4 Beav 190; *Re Cotton, Wood v Cotton* (1888) 40 Ch D 41.
4 *Roe d Buxton v Dunt* (1767) 2 Wils 336.

[40.3]

Appointment by successive instruments. A power may in general be executed by different appointments made at various times, and a partial execution, even though the power is non-exclusive, need not give a share to every object.[1] A power to appoint by one instrument may be exercised by several instruments provided that the whole series was intended to be and can be considered to be one document.[2] Where there is a primary power and, in default of its execution, a secondary power, a partial exercise of the primary power does not preclude an exercise of the secondary power over the portion of the fund which remains unaffected by the exercise of the primary power.[3] A power may be fully exercised at law by one appointment but not thereby exhausted in equity, as where a general power was exercised by way of mortgage in fee and the equity of redemption was subsequently appointed.[4]

1   *Wilson v Piggott* (1794) 2 Ves 351; *Colston v Pemberton* (1836) Donnelly 19; *Cunninghame v Anstruther* (1872) LR 2 Sc & Div 223; *Re Tenney's Goods* (1881) 45 LT 78 (complete exercise by later will which revoked former will also exercising power). The donee of a power making a partial appointment cannot alter, in respect of the part left unappointed, the range of investments authorised by the instrument creating the power: *Re Falconer's Trusts, Property and Estates Co Ltd v Frost* [1908] 1 Ch 410.
2   *Lord Braybrooke v A-G* (1861) 9 HL Cas 150.
3   *Mapleton v Mapleton* (1859) 4 Drew 515 at 519.
4   *Ruscombe v Hare* (1828) 2 Bli NS 192; *Heather v O'Neil* (1858) 2 De G & J 399; *Re Byron's Settlement, Williams v Mitchell* [1891] 3 Ch 474.

[40.4]
Exercise of powers of appointment: the creation of new administrative powers. It has been held[1] that a power of appointment in a fairly standard form authorised the creation of an additional administrative power.

1   *Re Rank's Settlement Trusts, Newton v Rollo* [1979] 1 WLR 1242. The decision depended on the precise wording of the power of which the material part was as follows:
'upon trust for all or any one or more exclusively of the others or other of the issue of Mrs Newton whether children or remoter descendants at such time and if more than one in such shares with such provisions for maintenance, education and advancement *and otherwise at the discretion of any person* and with such gifts over *and generally in such manner* for the benefit of such issue of some or one of them as Mrs Newton during her life shall by deed or deeds revocable or irrevocable appoint ...'
The italicised words were those which were regarded by the court as authorising the creation of additional administrative powers.

[40.5]
Delegation of powers. A power involving the exercise of personal discretion by the donee cannot be delegated.[1] An attempted delegation is a mere nullity.[2] It makes no difference whether or not the objects of the delegated power are objects of the original power.[3] A person cannot delegate the power to consent to the execution of a power,[4] unless a right to delegate can be implied on construction from the obvious impossibility at the date of the deed creating the power that the donee can always act in person.[5] An appointment on protective trusts is void as a delegation of the power as regards the disposition of the income after the act of forfeiture.[6] Where there is a power to appoint to issue, an appointment to a child for life after the death of the child to that child's children as the child shall appoint is bad as to the power given to the child,[7] but where the power is to appoint to children, an appointment can validly be made to a child for life, and after the death of such child to such persons generally as the child may by deed or will appoint, this being in effect an absolute appointment.[8] If the donee attempts to delegate his power, but does not appoint in contravention of the terms of the power and appoints, in default of execution of the delegated

power, to proper objects of this power, this appointment is valid, the words delegating the power being struck out.[9] Where the delegation is an intermediate part of the exercise of the power, as where a life interest is given on protective trusts, the ultimate limitation is accelerated.[10] But if the child was unborn at the date of the creation of the power, the appointor cannot give him a general power of appointment by will only.[11] If a power contains wide general terms authorising an appointment to the objects in such manner and form in all respects for the benefit of the objects as the donee shall appoint, an ordinary power of advancement can validly be bestowed upon trustees by the exercise of the power, whether the appointment be of vested[12] or contingent[13] interests; but a power given to trustees in effect so to alter the limitations under the appointment as to make contingent interests vested is an unlawful delegation,[14] and so is a power extending the range of persons to be benefited beyond those in whose favour an appointment has been made by the appointor.[15] A general power is equivalent to absolute ownership and can be delegated.[16] An unlimited power to appoint to anybody except a specified number of class of persons has been held not to be invalid merely by the width of the power and the number of objects.[17] But it could be void as amounting to a delegation of the testator's power of making the will for himself.[18] In the case of both general and special powers a purely administrative act, such as the execution of a document already approved, may be delegated.[19]

1   *Re Hay's Settlement Trusts* [1981] 3 All ER 786, [1982] 1 WLR 202; applying dictum of Viscount Radcliffe in *Re Pilkington's Will Trusts, Pilkington v Pilkington* [1962] 3 All ER 622 at 630; *Williamson v Farwell* (1887) 35 Ch D 128; *Re Greenslade, Greenslade v McCowen* [1915] 1 Ch 155; *Re Joicey, Joicey v Elliot* [1915] 2 Ch 115.
2   *Carr v Atkinson* (1872) LR 14 Eq 397.
3   *Williamson v Farwell* (1887) 35 Ch D 128.
4   *Hawkins v Kemp* (1803) 3 East 410, and see para **[40.6]** infra.
5   *Stuart v Norton* (1860) 14 Moo PCC 17.
6   *Re Boulton's Settlement Trust, Stewart v Boulton* [1928] Ch 703. For the statutory protective trusts, see Trustee Act 1925, s 33; 48 *Halsbury's Statutes* (4th edn) 496. But a power may be so worded that a protected interest may be given. In *Re Hunter's Will Trusts, Gilk v Harris* [1963] Ch 372, [1962] 3 All ER 1050, the words of the power were: 'in such shares and with such trusts for their respective benefit and such provisions for their respective advancement maintenance and education at the discretion of my trustees or any other person or persons'; the delegation of discretion was limited to advancement, maintenance and education and did not extend to benefit. The words 'with such trusts for their respective benefit' did not authorise the creation of an immediate discretionary trust for a class of appointees.
7   *Webb v Sadler* (1873) 8 Ch App 419; *Williamson v Farwell* (1887) 35 Ch D 128.
8   *Bray v Bree* (1834) 2 Cl & Fin 453; and see *Re McLean* [1929] Argus LR 216.
9   *Carr v Atkinson* (1872) LR 14 Eq 397; *Webb v Sadler* (1873) 8 Ch App 419; *Williamson v Farwell* (1887) 35 Ch D 128; and see *Re Finch and Chew's Contract* [1903] 2 Ch 486.
10   *Re Boulton's Settlement Trust, Stewart v Boulton* [1928] Ch 703.
11   *Wollaston v King* (1869) LR 8 Eq 165.
12   *Re May's Settlement, Public Trustee v Meredith* [1926] Ch 136.
13   *Re Mewburn's Settlement, Perks v Wood* [1934] Ch 112; but see *Re Greenslade, Greenslade v McCowen* [1915] 1 Ch 155, and the remarks on that case by Maugham J in *Re Mewburn's Settlement, Perks v Wood*. As to exercise of a power of advancement and the settlement of the sum advanced, see Vol 2.
14   *Re Joicey, Joicey v Elliot* [1915] 2 Ch 115.
15   *Re Morris' Settlement Trusts* [1951] 2 All ER 528.
16   *White v Wilson* (1852) 1 Drew 298; *Smith v Chishome* (1888) 15 AR 738.
17   *Re Hay's Settlement Trusts* [1981] 3 All ER 786; *Re Manisty's Settlement, Manisty v Manisty* [1974] Ch 17, [1973] 2 All ER 1203.

18   *Re Abrahams' Will Trusts, Caplan v Abrahams* [1969] 1 Ch 463, [1967] 2 All ER 1175; *Re Park, Public Trustee v Armstrong* [1932] 1 Ch 580, [1931] 1 All ER Rep 633; *Re Eyre v Eyre* (1883) 49 LT 259; *Lutheran Church of Australia South Australian District Inc v Farmers' Cooperative Executors and Trustees Ltd* (1969–70) 121 CLR 628. But see *Re Beatty's Will Trusts, Hinves v Brooke* [1990] 3 All ER 844, [1990] 1 WLR 1503 where a wide ranging power of appointment was not held to be void as a delegation of testamentary power; the cases cited in this footnote were referred to. On delegation of testamentary power, see para **[9.46]** supra.

19   *Re Airey, Airey v Stapleton* [1897] 1 Ch 164.

[40.6]

Consent to exercise. Where the consent of any person is required to the exercise of a power, that consent must be given during the life of the donee of the power and, if the person whose consent is required dies, the power cannot be exercised,[1] and if the consent of more than one person is required and any one of such persons dies, the power is gone.[2]

1   *Hawkins v Kemp* (1803) 3 East 410; *Offen v Harman* (1859) 1 De GF & J 253. See Law of Property Act 1925, s 159(2); 37 *Halsbury's Statutes* (4th edn) 333.

2   *Hutton v Simpson* (1716) 2 Vern 722.

[40.7]

Power to be exercised on a contingency. A power to be exercised on a contingency can be exercised before the contingency happens, and will take effect on the happening of the contingency,[1] but a power which is given to arise on a contingency cannot be exercised until the event happens.[2] A general power of appointment can be exercised by a contingency person provided that person proves to be the person entitled to exercise the power,[3] but a special power of appointment given to a contingency person cannot be exercised until the person to exercise it is determined.[4] A power which is to be determined on the happening of a particular event must be exercised before the event happens.[5]

1   *Hanbury v Bateman* [1920] 1 Ch 313; *Wandesforde v Carrick* (1871) IR 5 Eq 486. If, before the contingency happens, the donee covenants for valuable consideration to exercise the power, the court will aid the defective execution, but, if the power is exercisable by will only, the only remedy will be in damages: *Affleck v Affleck* (1857) 3 Sm & G 394; *Re Evered, Molineux v Evered* [1910] 2 Ch 147.

2   *Want v Stallibrass* (1873) LR 8 Exch 175; *Earle v Barker* (1865) 11 HL Cas 280; *Wilkinson v Thornhill* (1889) 61 LT 362; *Christie v Saunders* (1856) 5 Gr 464; *Re Verscholye's Trusts* (1879) 3 LR Ir 43.

3   *Thomas v Jones* (1862) 1 De GJ & Sm 63. A power to a married woman to be exercised during coverture cannot be exercised after the death of the husband: *Morris v Howes* (1845) 4 Hare 599; but it can be exercised by will made during coverture, even though the wife survives the husband: *Re Safford's Settlement, Davies v Burgess* [1915] 2 Ch 211.

4   *Re Blackburn, Smiles v Blackburn* (1889) 43 Ch D 75; *Re Walpole's Marriage Settlement, Thomson v Walpole* [1903] 1 Ch 928. A general testamentary power given to the survivor of two persons, may be exercised by will during the joint lives, but a special power exercisable 'after the decease of the other' cannot be so exercised unless confirmed by codicil after the death of the first.

5   *Potts v Britton* (1871) LR 11 Eq 433.

[40.8]

Donee of special power only controls beneficial interests. A donee of a special power of appointment has power to designate only the persons who are to take the beneficial interest in the property subject to the power, and in what shares and proportions. He cannot, in the absence of an express power to do so, appoint new trustees of the property.[1]

1   *Bush v Aldam* (1874) LR 10 Eq 16; *Scotney v Lomer* (1886) 31 Ch D 380; *Re Tyssen, Knight-Bruce v Butterworth* [1894] 1 Ch 56; *Von Brockdorff v Malcolm* (1885) 30 Ch D 172.

[40.9]

Appointment of land as money. A donee of a special power of appointment over land can validly appoint the land to trustees upon trust to sell the same and to divide the proceeds of sale among the objects of the power,[1] and can also charge the land subject to the power with a capital to annual sum in favour of one or more objects of the power.[2]

1   *Kenworthy v Bate* (1802) 6 Ves 793; *Re Paget, Re Mellor v Mellor* [1898] 1 Ch 290; *Re Redgate, Marsh v Redgate* [1903] 1 Ch 356; *Re Adams' Trustees' and Frost's Contract* [1907] 1 Ch 695.
2   *Ricketts v Loftus* (1841) 4 Y & C Ex 519.

[40.10]

Release of power. A person to whom any power, whether coupled with an interest or not, is given may by deed release it or contract not to exercise it,[1] but a power coupled with a duty or in the nature of a trust cannot be released.[2] The exercise of a power must be bona fide for the end designed by the donor of the power,[3] but this doctrine does not apply to the release of a special power[4] nor to the release of a power or revocation contained in the instrument exercising the power.[5] The power may be released wholly or in part by the donee,[6] and any dealing with the property inconsistent with the exercise of the power releases it wholly or pro tanto.[7] An absolute release of a power is irrevocable and any attempt to exercise the power after the release is void.[8] The following propositions are said to be established by authority:[9]

(i)   If a power is granted to appoint among a class of objects and in default of appointment there is a trust, express or implied, in favour of the members of that class, the donee of the power cannot, by failure to appoint or by purporting to bind himself not to appoint, or by purporting to release his power, defeat the interest of the members of the class of objects.

(ii)   Such a power cannot be released, for the donee is under a duty to exercise it notwithstanding that the court may not be able to compel him personally to perform that duty and can only remedy his default by executing the trust in default of appointment.

(iii) Where a power is conferred on trustees virtute officii in relation to their trust property they cannot release it or bind themselves not to exercise it in the absence of words in the trust deed authorising them so to do.[10]

(iv)   The same is true if the power is conferred on persons who are in fact trustees of the settlement by name or not by reference to their office, if on the true view of the facts they were selected as donees of the power because they were the trustees.

(v)   Where a power is conferred on someone who is not a trustee of the property to which the power relates or, if he is such a trustee, the power is not conferred on him in that capacity, then, in the absence of a trust in favour of the objects of the power in default of appointment, the donee is prima facie not under any duty recognisable by the court to exercise the power such as will disable him from releasing it.

In pursuance of a power to revoke trusts relating to a school the trustees of the trust (who were not the trustees of the property affected) revoked those provisions and appointed the fund to the issue of the founder and any wives, husbands, widows and widowers of any such issue or any charitable bodies as the trustees of the settlor's will should appoint, and in default of appointment to be held on the previous trusts. The question arose whether this last power of appointment could be released. It was held that this was not a power coupled with a duty or trust and could, therefore, be released because the donees of the power were not the trustees of the property to which the power related. Further as the deed contained an express trust in default of appointment there could be no trust for the objects in default of appointment. The power to appoint was given to each successive trustee of the settlor's will and no trustee for the time being could in any way prevent a later trustee from exercising it, but any trustee by completely exercising the power could exhaust it so that there was nothing for any successor to exercise.[11]

1   Law of Property Act 1925, ss 155, 160; 37 *Halsbury's Statutes* (4th edn) 329, 334. Every power reserved by a grantor for his own benefit, whether he has reserved an estate in the land or not, and whether the power relates to real or personal property, can release it: *Bird v Christopher* (1653) Sty 389; *Noel v Lord Henley, ex p Schwench and Mannwk* (1825) M'Cle & Yo 302; *Re Chambers* (1847) 11 I Eq R 518; *Palmer v Locke* (1880) 15 Ch D 294; *Nottidge v Dering* [1910] 1 Ch 297; *Re Brown's Settlement, Public Trustee v Brown* [1939] Ch 944, [1939] 3 All ER 391. As to contract not to exercise powers, see infra.
2   *Re Eyre, Eyre v Eyre* (1883) 49 LT 259; *Saul v Pattinson* (1886) 55 LJ Ch 831; *Re Dunne's Trusts* (1878) 1 LR Ir 516; *Re Mills, Mills v Lawrence* [1930] 1 Ch 654.
3   An appointment not so designed is called a fraudulent appointment: see para **[40.14]** infra.
4   *Smith v Houblon* (1859) 26 Beav 482; *Re Radcliffe, Radcliffe v Bewes* [1892] 1 Ch 227; *Re Somes, Somes v Somes* [1896] 1 Ch 250.
5   *Re Somes, Smith v Somes* [1896] 1 Ch 250.
6   Where the power is wholly released, the release will commonly take the form of a deed of release. A release in part, while it may take the same form, is more usually a covenant not to exercise the power in respect of a particular person or persons or in respect of a particular property or properties (property including securities or a fund or part of a fund). See, further, as to such a covenant, infra. The power may be released as to part of the settled property, leaving it intact as to the remainder: *Re Evered, Molineux v Evered* [1910] 2 Ch 147 at 157.
7   *Re Brown's Settlement, Public Trustee v Brown* [1939] Ch 944, [1939] 3 All ER 391. There is an implied release of the power as distinct from an express release by deed of release or covenant not to exercise it. See para **[40.13]** infra, under 'Implied Release'.
8   *Re Mills, Mills v Lawrence* [1930] 1 Ch 654; *Smith v Plummer* (1848) 17 LJ Ch 145. This result of a release is now statutory: see Law of Property Act 1925, s 155(1); 37 *Halsbury's Statutes* (4th edn) 329.
9   *Re Will's Trust Deed, Wills v Godfrey* [1963] 1 All ER 390 at 400.
10   *Muir v IRC* [1966] 3 All ER 38 at 45, [1966] 1 WLR 1269 at 1283 (where trustees were authorised to release the power, distinguishing *Re Will's Trust Deed, Wills v Godfrey* [1963] 1 All ER 390, where there was no such power).
11   *Muir v IRC* [1966] 3 All ER 38.

[40.11]
Covenant not to exercise power. A covenant not to exercise a power operates in the same way as a release and such a covenant is enforced whether or not it be given for value,[1] but a covenant to exercise in a certain way and not to revoke or alter it is not binding on the donee of the power and creates no fetter on its

exercise.[2] The negative covenant is binding, and may take the form of a covenant not to exercise the power in favour of one or more of the objects of the power,[3] or not to exercise it in any way that will result in a certain beneficiary receiving less than a stated share or amount.[4]

1   The covenant must be negative: *Re Evered, Molineux v Evered* [1910] 2 Ch 147; *Re Coake, Winckley v Winterton* [1922] 1 Ch 292; *Re Brown's Settlement, Public Trustee v Brown* [1939] Ch 944, [1939] 3 All ER 391.
2   See Chapter 3.
3   *Re Evered, Molineux v Evered* [1910] 2 Ch 147.
4   *Re Evered, Molineux v Evered* [1910] 2 Ch 147 at 157, where Cozens-Hardy MR said: 'Thus he may covenant that a particular beneficiary shall not have less than a certain share. In such a case he will retain his power over the whole fund, but he will be restricted as to use of that power. He will remain at liberty to exercise the power by appointing by will to that beneficiary the named sum or share, or by so appointing to other beneficiaries as that there shall remain unappointed such a sum as, with the assistance of a hotchpot clause if any, shall result in the particular beneficiary receiving the named sum or share. But he will by reason of his covenant be precluded from so exercising the power as that his covenant shall be defeated. Any act purporting to be an exercise of the power which will defeat the covenant will be an invalid exercise of the power to the extent to which the covenant will be defeated.' In this case the power of appointment was by will only.

[40.12]
Disclaimer of power. A power may also be disclaimed and upon such disclaimer being made the donee disclaiming becomes incapable of exercising the power or of joining in its exercise;[1] but where the power is given to more than one person the donees other than the one disclaiming, or the survivors or survivor of them, can exercise the power.[2]

1   A release is often called a disclaimer and a deed of release is commonly worded so that the party releasing both 'releases and disclaims' the power. There can, however, be a disclaimer by one of a number of donees of the power. The power to disclaim and the effect of such disclaimer is now statutory: see Law of Property Act 1925, s 156; 37 *Halsbury's Statutes* (4th edn) 331.
2   Law of Property Act 1925, s 156(2).

[40.13]
Implied release. Any dealing or concurrence in a dealing with the property by the donee of the power inconsistent with the exercise of that power releases it either wholly or pro tanto.[1] A promise not to exercise a power which induces a testator to revoke a codicil (which would have destroyed the power) and leave the original will (with the power) standing prevents the donee from exercising the power and amounts to an implied release;[2] but mutual wills made simultaneously but without any agreement that they are to be irrevocable do not, where there is no case for election, prevent the survivor from exercising a power which has not been released.[3]

1   *Foakes v Jackson* [1900] 1 Ch 807 (assignment of property); *Nottidge v Dering* [1910] 1 Ch 297 (mortgage of property); *Walford v Gray* (1865) 5 New Rep 235 (representation by father on treaty for marriage of daughter that he would not exercise the power of appointment); *Re Hancock, Malcolm v Burford-Hancock* [1896] 2 Ch 173 (prior to exercise of power with intention to exhaust it).
2   *Tharp v Tharp* [1916] 1 Ch 142; on appeal [1916] 2 Ch 205, CA.
3   *Gray v Perpetual Trustee Co* [1928] AC 391. As to mutual wills, see Chapter 2.

[40.14]
Fraudulent appointments. A person having a limited power of appointment must exercise it bona fide for the purpose for which it was created; otherwise the appointment is void as a fraud on the power.[1] Fraud in this sense does not necessarily imply any moral turpitude, but is used to cover all cases where the purpose of the appointor is to effect some bye or sinister object,[2] whether such purpose be selfish, as giving the appointor himself some advantage, or, in the appointor's belief, a more beneficial mode of disposition of the property, more consonant with that which he believes would be the real wish of the creator of the power in the circumstances existing at the date of the appointment.[3] In simpler language, the appointment is void if made with the object of obtaining a benefit for the appointor himself or some other person not an object of the power.[4] The doctrine is an equitable one and will be applied in any circumstances where the interference of the court is warranted because the appointment would offend the ordinary principles on which equitable jurisdiction is founded, namely, that the appointment is against conscience. Thus, where the donee in the testator's lifetime promised not to exercise the power so as to defeat the interests of those entitled in default of appointment, and thus induced the testator to revoke a codicil and to revive an earlier will creating the power, it was held that the donee could not exercise the power so as to defeat the interests of those entitled in default of appointment.[5] The doctrine does not apply to the release of a power nor to the revocation of an appointment.[6]

1   *Aleyn v Belchier* (1978) 1 Eden 132. The doctrine of fraud on the power has no application to general powers of appointment; *Dowdle v Coppel* [1987] VR 1024.
2   *Duke of Portland v Lady Topham* (1864) 11 HL Cas 32.
3   *Duke of Portland v Lady Topham* (1864) 11 HL Cas 32; *Vatcher v Paull* [1915] AC 372 at 378.
4   The doctrine applies to all limited powers including powers of advancement: *Lawrie v Bankes* (1858) 4 K & J 142. However, in *Blausten v IRC* [1972] Ch 256, [1972] 1 All ER 41, an appointment made with the motive of enabling the settlor to avoid surtax on his income was held to be good, applying *Muir v IRC* [1966] 3 All ER 38, [1966] 1 WLR 1269. In the case of an appointment by joint appointors, the fraudulent intention of one vitiates the whole appointment. An appointment to two persons may be severable where the fraudulent intention affects only one of the appointees: *Harrison v Randall* (1851) 9 Hare 397; and see para **[40.20]** infra. A person having a power to appoint to a class of which he is one can appoint to himself. *Taylor v Allthusen* [1905] 1 Ch 529; *Re Penrose, Penrose v Penrose* [1933] Ch 793; but this was questioned in *Tharp v Tharp* [1916] 1 Ch 142. The person affected by a fraudulent appointment may give effect to it: *Skeleton v Flanagan* (1867) IR 1 Eq 362; *Preston v Preston* (1869) 21 LT 346. The person making the fraudulent appointment is liable to make good to the estate the whole loss occasioned, and not merely the profit made by himself: *Re Deane, Bridger v Deane* (1889) 42 Ch D 9 at 19.
5   *Tharp v Tharp* [1916] 1 Ch 142; on appeal [1916] 2 Ch 205, CA.
6   *Re Greaves' Will Trusts, Public Trustee v Ash* [1954] Ch 434, [1954] 1 All ER 771, overruling *Re Jones' Settlement, Stunt v Jones* [1915] 1 Ch 373. See para **[40.17]**, n 1.

[40.15]
Grounds of fraud. There are three main grounds of fraud:
(1) Where the power is exercised for a corrupt purpose.[1] Examples of this are: where the intention is to benefit the appointor himself;[2] an appointment made to facilitate the divorce of the appointor;[3] a bargain with the appointees for the purchase of their expectant shares.[4] A covenant not to revoke an appointment in

no way vitiates an appointment,[5] nor is a covenant not to exercise the power open to objection on the ground that it may benefit the appointor.[6] The appointment is not bad simply because the appointor may derive some benefit from it,[7] though it is bad if exercised with the avowed object of benefiting the appointor.[8] Where the appointor is a minor, the appointment may indirectly benefit the appointor, and this is not necessarily an objection,[9] nor is it an objection where the appointor being the parent of the appointee purchases the interest of the appointee. Such an appointment is good unless its object is to benefit the appointor or a non-object of the power.[10] The burden of proof of corrupt motive is on the person who seeks to avoid the appointment.[11]

(2) Where the appointment is made in pursuance of an antecedent agreement by the appointee to benefit persons not objects of the power, even though the agreement itself is unobjectionable.[12] It is not necessary in such a case to show that there was such moral suasion on the part of the appointor that the appointee was to find it irresistible to carry out the appointor's wishes. It is sufficient if it is shown that the deliberate intention of the appointor in making the appointment was to benefit persons not objects of the power.[13] This is so where the appointor bargains for some benefit for himself,[14] or for some stranger to the power other than himself.[15] Mere suspicion of such a bargain is not enough,[16] but, on the other hand, the fact that the appointor believes in the existence of such a bargain is enough even if there is in fact no such bargain.[17] An appointment to a child who is an object of the power and a contemporaneous settlement by him of the appointed fund is not a fraud on the power unless it can be shown that the appointment was made in pursuance of an agreement inducing the appointment.[18] The fact that the appointor knows that the object intends to dispose of the fund in favour of a stranger to the power is not enough to vitiate the appointment unless the appointment would not have been made but for the agreement to dispose of the fund.[19] The question in each case is whether the appointment is for the benefit of the appointee. If this is not the appointor's purpose, the appointment is bad.[20] An appointment to the children of an object (such children not themselves being objects) has been upheld where the parent of the children (being an object of the power) has consented to the appointment.[21] An appointment in favour of an object and the making of a memorandum expressed to be without imposing any trust or legal obligation and expressing a desire that provision would be made for non-objects is a fraud on the power although the appointee had no knowledge of the memorandum until after the appointor's death and such memorandum was not found.[22] Merely to attach to an appointment a condition intended to compel the appointee to settle the appointed fund on new objects is not a fraudulent appointment.[23]

(3) Where the appointment is made for purposes foreign to the power, although such purposes are not communicated to the appointee before the appointment and although the appointor gets no personal benefit.[24]

1 *Aleyn v Belchier* (1758) 1 Eden 132.
2 *Askham v Barker* (1850) 12 Beav 499; *Harrison v Randall* (1851) 9 Hare 397; *Rowley v Rowley* (1854) Kay 242; *Lady Wellesley v Earl of Mornington* (1855) 2 K & J 143; *Re Chadwick's Trusts, Shaw v Woodward* [1939] 1 All ER 850 (where the subject of how far a later appointment is affected by the fraud of an earlier appointment is discussed).
3 *Cochrane v Cochrane* [1922] 2 Ch 230.

4   *Cunninghame v Anstruther* [1872] LR 2 Sc & Div 223.
5   *Robinson v Ommanney* (1882) 21 Ch D 780; *Re Parkin, Hill v Schwarz* [1892] 3 Ch 510; *Beyfus v Lawley* [1903] AC 411.
6   *Re Little, Harrison v Harrison* (1889) 40 Ch D 418; *Re Radcliffe, Radcliffe v Bewes* [1892] 1 Ch 227; *Re Somes, Smith v Somes* [1896] 1 Ch 250; *Re Evered, Molineux v Evered* [1910] 2 Ch 147.
7   *Re Huish's Charity* (1870) LR 10 Eq 5 at 9; *Pickles v Pickles* (1861) 31 LJ Ch 146.
8   *Re Jones' Settlement, Stunt v Jones* [1915] 1 Ch 373.
9   *Beere v Hoffmister* (1856) 23 Beav 101; *Butcher v Jackson* (1845) 14 Sim 444; *Hamilton v Kirwan* (1845) 2 Jo & Lat 393; *Domville v Lambe* (1853) 1 WR 246; *Fearon v Desbrisay* (1851) 14 Beav 635. Fraud is not shown by the appointment making the shares vest at an early age.
10   *Re Merton's Settlement, Public Trustee v Wilson* [1953] 2 All ER 707.
11   *Campbell v Home* (1842) 1 Y & C Ch Cas 664; *Topham v Duke of Portland* (1869) 5 Ch App 40 at 57. The burden may shift where, eg it is suggested that the improper motive has been abandoned: *Re Wright, Hegan v Bloor* [1920] 1 Ch 108; *Re Chadwick's Trusts, Shaw v Woodward* [1939] 1 All ER 850 (where a further appointment was tainted with the fraud of a previous one). Trustees have a duty to see that funds are properly administered and must refuse to act on an obviously fraudulent appointment: *Harrison v Randall* (1851) 9 Hare 397; *Mackechnie v Majoribanks* (1870) 39 LJ Ch 604. Trustees must not raise untenable objections, but they must be vigilant: *Re Metcalfe's Trusts* (1864) 2 De GJ & Sm 122; and the court will support the action of the trustees unless they have acted improperly.
12   *Daubeny v Cockburn* (1816) 1 Mer 626 at 644; *Jackson v Jackson* (1840) 7 Cl & Fin 977; *Duggan v Duggan* (1880) 5 LR IR 525; *Salmon v Gibbs* (1849) 3 De G & Sm 343; *Lee v Fernie* (1839) 1 Beav 483; *Knowles v Morgan* (1909) 54 Sol Jo 117.
13   *Re Dick, Knight v Dick* [1953] Ch 343, [1953] 1 All ER 559.
14   See the first three cases cited in n 12.
15   See the last three cases cited in n 12.
16   *Re Boileau's Will Trusts* [1921] WN 222; *Hamilton v Kirwan* (1845) 2 Jo & Lat 393; *Re Nicholson's Settlement, Molony v Nicholson* [1939] Ch 11, [1938] 3 All ER 532.
17   *Re Wright, Hegan v Bloor* [1920] 1 Ch 108 at 118; *Vatcher v Paull* [1915] AC 372 at 378.
18   *Thompson v Simpson* (1841) 1 Dr & War 459 at 487; *Goldsmid v Goldsmid* (1842) 2 Hare 187; *Birley v Birley* (1858) 25 Beav 299; *Re Boileau's Will Trusts* [1921] WN 222.
19   *Pryor v Pryor* (1864) 2 De GJ & Sm 205; *Daniel v Arkwright* (1864) 2 Hem & M 95; *Re Foote and Purdon's Estate* [1910] 1 IR 365.
20   *Cooper v Cooper* (1869) LR 8 Eq 312; *Roach v Trood* (1876) 3 Ch D 429; *Re Turner's Settled Estates* (1884) 28 Ch D 205.
21   *Wright v Goff* (1856) 22 Beav 207; *Cunninghame v Anstruther* (1872) LR 2 SC & Div 223 at 234.
22   *Re Dick, Knight v Dick* [1953] Ch 343, [1953] 1 All ER 559.
23   *Re Burton's Settlements, Scott v National Provincial Bank Ltd* [1955] Ch 82, [1954] 3 All ER 193. Such a condition is an excessive exercise of the power and must be rejected. In this case the appointees were not to receive a share of residue unless they settled appointed funds. The appointees were put to their election to accept the share of residue or to comply with the condition.
24   *Hay v Watkins* (1843) 3 Dr & War 339 at 343 (condition annexed); *Weir v Chamley* (1850) 1 I Ch R 295; *Lady Wellesley v Earl of Mornington* (1855) 2 K & J 143 (appointee very ill); *Re Marsden's Trust* (1859) 4 Drew 594 (appointee ignorant of fraud); *Topham v Duke of Portland* (1863) 1 De GJ & Sm 517 at 568; *D'Abbadie v Bizoin* (1871) IR 5 Eq 205 (appointment to induce residence abroad); *Re Crawshay, Crawshay v Crawshay* (1890) 43 Ch D 615 (appointment on trusts foreign to power); *Re Perkins, Perkins v Bagot* [1893] 1 Ch 283 (appointment subject to condition of giving up certain benefits); *Re Cohen, Brookes v Cohen* [1911] 1 Ch 37 (appointment for payment of appointor's debts); *Re Simpson* [1952] Ch 412, [1952] 1 All ER 963 (appointment treating funds of marriage settlement as appointor's own property). Where an appointment is subject to a condition foreign to the power, the condition may be severable, then the appointment stands and the condition is disregarded; *Re Holland, Holland v Clapton* [1914] 2 Ch 595. In *Re Walker and Elgee's Contract* (1918) 53 ILT 22, trusts for non-objects were struck out. See also *Vatcher v Paull* [1915] AC 372, where the condition was ineffective by the law of place where certain real property was situated.

[40.16]

Variation of trusts. If there is a fair case for investigation whether a proposed arrangement involves a fraud on a power and that question remains unresolved, the court will not give approval under the Variation of Trusts Act 1958, s 1(1)[1] to the proposed arrangement.[2] Where, in contemplation of the division between the tenant for life and persons interested subject to his life interest of a fund held on the trusts of a settlement, an arrangement varying the trusts is proposed for the court's approval on behalf of persons not sui juris on the basis of an appointment of the trust fund by the tenant for life in exercise of a special power, and under the proposed arrangement the tenant for life will become entitled absolutely to a sum no greater than the value of his life interest, the appointment is not invalid as a fraud on the power merely because it is made in contemplation of the division of the fund. On the other hand the fact that the tenant for life will take no more than the value of his life interest does not ipso facto make the appointment valid; but the question whether the motive for the appointment was an ulterior purpose, such as putting money in the pocket of the tenant for life, which, being a purpose not permitted by the settlement, would invalidate the appointment as a fraud on the power, is in each case a question of fact.[3] Thus where one of the objects for which the appointment was made was to obtain a benefit for the appointor which he might not otherwise have had by creating a position in which the interests of unborn children would be defeated and under which the court might be expected to approve a division more favourable to the appointor as tenant for life than if the division had to be shown to be also for the benefit of future children, the court held that the appointment was invalid as a fraud on a power and declined to approve the proposed variation.[4]

1   48 *Halsbury's Statutes* (4th edn) 561.
2   Per Megarry J in *Re Wallace's Settlements* [1968] 2 All ER 209 at 214, [1968] 1 WLR 711 at 718, 719.
3   Per Stamp J in *Re Brook's Settlement, Brook v Brook* [1968] 3 All ER 416 at 421, [1968] 1 WLR 1661 at 1666.
4   *Re Brook's Settlement, Brook v Brook* [1968] 3 All ER 416, [1968] 1 WLR 1661, distinguishing *Re Wallace's Settlements* [1968] 2 All ER 209, [1968] 1 WLR 711, since in that case the life tenants were receiving no more than the value to them of their life interests.

[40.17]
Doctrine not applicable to revocation of appointment. A power to revoke an appointment means that the appointor can wholly recall what he has done and place himself in all respects as if he had never made the appointment. Since the power of revocation is free from obligation there can be no fraud on the power by the exercise of such power. It is not so much a power as a right.[1] It is fundamental to the vice which constitutes a fraud on a power that the appointor shall have assumed the burden of making an appointment, a thing he is never bound to do, and should then have distorted its stated purpose, so defrauding the persons entitled in detail of appointment.[2]

1   *Re Greaves' Will Trusts, Public Trustee v Ash* [1954] Ch 434, [1954] 1 All ER 771, overruling *Re Jones' Settlement, Stunt v Jones* [1915] 1 Ch 373.
2   *Re Greaves' Will Trusts, Public Trustee v Ash* [1954] Ch 434, [1954] 1 All ER 771, where an appointment was revoked to enable the property to be appropriated to the interests of the life tenant and her children, thus ending the settlement.

[40.18]
Ascertainment of intention of the donor. The intention of the donor of the power can be ascertained only from the words of the instrument creating it, and

can only be dealt with as expressed therein.[1] This is the case even where the appointor himself is the settlor.[2]

1 *Lee v Fernie* (1839) 1 Beav 483; *Hutchins v Hutchins* (1876) IR 10 Eq 453; *Re Russell's Will Trusts* [1955] 2 DLR 721 (power to appoint to children provided that if the beneficiary left a widow, he might appoint in her favour. An appointment to widow although there was no child was good).
2 *Lee v Fernie* (1839) 1 Beav 483.

[40.19]

Protection of purchasers. An appointment to a person over the age of twenty-five at the time of his dealing with the purchaser, and who is a member of the class entitled in default of appointment, is not void on the ground of fraud on the power as against a purchaser for value without notice actual or constructive of the fraud, to the extent of the share to which the appointee was presumptively entitled in default of appointment immediately before the execution of the power, having regard to any advance in his favour and to any hotchpot provision.[1] This protection applies to persons deriving title through the purchaser.[2]

1 Law of Property Act 1925, s 157(1); 37 *Halsbury's Statutes* (4th edn) 331. Before 1926 a purchaser from an appointee who obtained the legal estate without notice of the fraud was not affected by it, but where the appointee did not obtain the legal estate the purchaser could rely on such equitable defences as were open to a purchaser for value without the legal estate: *Cloutte v Storey* [1911] 1 Ch 18.
2 Law of Property Act 1925, s 157(3).

[40.20]

Severance of appointments. Severance of appointments is allowed only where some consideration has been given which cannot be restored, or the court can sever the intentions of the appointor and distinguish the good from the bad.[1] Where severance is allowed, the appointment is good to the extent to which it is a bona fide exercise of the power.[2]

1 *Daubeny v Cockburn* (1816) 1 Mer 626; *Farmer v Martin* (1828) 2 Sim 502; *Askham v Barker* (1850) 12 Beav 499; *Tophams v Duke of Portland* (1863) 1 De GJ & Sm 517.
2 *Ranking v Barnes* (1864) 3 New Rep 660; *Harrison v Randall* (1851) 9 Hare 397.

[40.21]

Appointments to objects and non-objects. The rule as to excess in the execution of powers is that, where there is a complete execution of the power and something is added which is improper, the execution is good and the excess is bad, but where there is not complete execution, or where the boundaries between the excess and the execution are not distinguishable, the whole appointment fails.[1] The appointment must be absolute and distinct to prevail.[2] Thus an appointment to an object and non-object is good as to the object and fails as to the non-object.[3] Where the appointment is to a number of persons, even where the appointment is to a class, it is severable so long as the persons take as tenants in common.[4] An appointment to an object subject to a charge in favour of a non-object is good but the charge fails.[5] A provision for settlement is void only so far as it may apply to non-objects.[6] An appointment to an object in trust for a non- object is void either as being indivisible,[7] or on the ground that there was no intention to benefit objects.[8] Where there is a gift over to a non-object by way of executory limitation, the original gift, although distinct from such gift over, fails on the occurrence of the event on which the executory gift is to take effect, notwithstanding that the gift over is void as being to a non-object.[9] Where there is an appointment to an object followed by an appointment to a non-object absolutely with an executory appointment to an object, this executory appointment takes effect if the event upon which it is to arise happens, but, if not, it fails.[10] An appointment to a non-object for life with remainder to an object is a good appointment to the object in remainder but the interest of the object is not accelerated unless a contrary intention appears in the instrument executing the power.[11] An appointment by will to an object for life with remainder in tail to his first and other sons who are not objects is construed as an estate to the appointee.[12] Where a settlement gave trustees power to appoint to 'such persons' as they thought fit and the trustees executed a deed of appointment empowering themselves to appoint to 'such persons' as they thought fit, the appointment was void as an excessive execution of the power to appoint contained in the settlement.[13]

---

1   *Re Holland, Holland v Clapton* [1914] 2 Ch 595; *Re Cohen, Brookes v Cohen* [1911] 1 Ch 37. As to disregarding conditions, see para **[40.15]**, n 24 and as to severance; see para **[40.20]** supra.

2   *Rucker v Scholefield* (1862) 1 Hem & M 36; *Reid v Reid* (1858) 25 Beav 469; *Re Oliphant's Trusts, Re Dixon's Will, Phillips v Phelps* (1916) 86 LJ Ch 452.

3   *Alexander v Alexander* (1755) 2 Ves Sen 640; *Harvey v Stracey* (1852) 1 Drew 73; *Bruce v Bruce* (1871) LR 11 Eq 371; *Re Kerr's Trusts* (1877) 4 Ch D 600. The fund is divisible into as many parts as there are objects and non-objects and the objects do not divide the whole fund between them. Thus if there are three objects and three non-objects, the fund is divided into sixths and each object takes one-sixth of the fund: *Re Farncombe's Trusts* (1878) 9 Ch D 652; *Re Witty, Wright v Robinson* [1913] 2 Ch 666. For cases where the gift was held not severable, see *Harvey v Stracey* (1852) 1 Drew 73; *Re Brown's Trusts* (1865) LR 1 Eq 74.

4   *Harvey v Stracey* (1852) 1 Drew 73.

5   *Re Jeffreson's Trusts* (1866) LR 2 Eq 276; *Dowglass v Waddell* (1886) 17 LR Ir 384.

6   *Re Witty, Wright v Robinson* [1913] 2 Ch 666; *Re Leahy, Leahy v Payne* [1920] 1 IR 260.

7   *Rucker v Schofield* (1862) 1 Hem & M 36; *Gerrard v Butler* (1855) 20 Beav 541; *Tomkyns v Blane* (1860) 28 Beav 422.

8   *Re Cohen, Brookes v Cohen* [1911] 1 Ch 37; *Re Swinburne, Swinburne v Pitt* (1884) 27 Ch D 696.

9   *Doe d Blomfield v Eyre* (1848) 5 CB 713; *Re Staples* [1933] IR 126; *Re Jones, Last v Dobson* [1915] 1 Ch 246. The decision in *Doe d Blomfield v Eyre*, supra, has been generally followed though often with reluctance. It was decided in *Re Rooke's Will Trusts, Taylor v Rooke* [1953] Ch 716, [1953] 2 All ER 110, that the primary gift remained vested where the gift was to issue of the primary donee and was thus merely substitutionary. In the latter case the gift was to a brother and three sisters and, if any predeceased the tenant for life, their respective share was given to their respective issue. A sister having predeceased the tenant for life, her personal representatives took. If the gift over transgresses the rule against perpetuities, the gift over fails and the first gift remains: *Re Brown and Sibly's Contract* (1876) 3 Ch D 156; and see *Re Staveley, Dyke v Staveley* (1920) 90 LJ Ch 111.

10 *Alexander v Alexander* (1755) 2 Ves Sen 640; *Long v Ovenden* (1881) 16 Ch D 691; *Re Enever's Trusts, Power v Power* [1912] 1 IR 511; *Williamson v Farwell* (1887) 35 Ch D 128. Appointments to a contingent class or to take effect in futuro within due limits are good: *Harvey v Stracey* (1852) 1 Drew 73 at 136; *Re Farncombe's Trusts* (1878) 9 Ch D 652; *Re Coulman, Munby v Ross* (1885) 30 Ch D 186; *Re Witty, Wright v Robinson* [1913] 2 Ch 666 (where the method of distribution where some of the class are not objects is discussed). The appointment of a share of a fund to an object on the happening of a certain event carries the intermediate accretions to the share: *Long v Ovenden* (1881) 16 Ch D 691; *Re Lambert, Lambert v Lambert* [1910] 1 IR 280.

11   *Craven v Brady* (1867) LR 4 Eq 209; *Line v Hall* (1873) 43 LJ Ch 107; *Re Finch and Chew's Contract* [1903] 2 Ch 486; *Crozier v Crozier* (1843) 3 Dr & War 353; *Re Loughhead* [1918] 1 IR 227.

12   *Pitt v Jackson* (1786) 2 Bro CC 51; *Stackpoole v Stackpoole* (1843) 4 Dr & War 320.

13   *Re Hay's Settlement Trusts* [1981] 3 All ER 786, [1982] 1 WLR 202.

PART I

Failure of gifts

CHAPTER 41

Ademption

I. GENERAL PRINCIPLES

[41.1]

Nature of ademption. A specific gift[1] may be adeemed by the subject-matter of the gift, between the date of the will and that of the testator's death, ceasing to be part of his estate or ceasing to be subject to his right of disposition[2] or ceasing to conform to the description by which it is given.[3] This may result from the testator's own disposition or change of investment[4] or other events subsequent to the will and prior to the death of the testator.[5] A gift is also said to be adeemed where the testator during his lifetime and subsequent to the execution of the will gives the donee by gift inter vivos what he would obtain under the will. This is dealt with under the heading of satisfaction.[6]

1 As to specific general and demonstrative legacies see paras **[30.1]**–**[30.7]** supra.
2 *Lee v Lee* (1858) 27 LJ Ch 824 (property ceasing to be part of estate by stock being sold and the proceeds mixed with the testator's property and spent). Ademption is a destruction or cesser of existence of the thing given; *Purse v Snaplin* (1738) 1 Atk 414 (particular chattel not found after death); *Trustees, Executors and Agency Co Ltd v Scott* (1898) 24 VLR 522; *Durrant v Friend* (1852) 5 De G & Sm 343 (particular chattels lost in shipwreck: legatee not entitled to insurance money), applied in *Re Hunter* (1975) 58 DLR (3d) 175.
3 *Re Dowsett, Dowsett v Meakin* [1901] 1 Ch 398. If the gift be given by a description of the subject-matter as it exists at the date of the will, it will be adeemed if there is nothing of that description at the testator's death, but if there is something at the testator's death representing the property which still fits the description in the will, there is no ademption, and see *Re Hutton, Allen v Hutton* [1916] VLR 546.
4 *Re Slater, Slater v Slater* [1907] 1 Ch 665; *Re Kuypers, Kuypers v Kuypers* [1925] Ch 244.
5 *Durrant v Friend* (1852) 5 De G & Sm 343 (loss), and see nn 2 and 3. No ademption is caused by transfer from trustees to testator, see para **[41.22]** infra; or by unauthorised acts of third parties, see *Basan v Brandon* (1836) 8 Sim 171; *Jenkins v Jones* (1866) LR 2 Eq 323; *Re Jeffery* (1974) 53 DLR (3d) 650; nor can the legacy be increased by an unauthorised act of an agent: *Re Larking. Larking v Larking* (1887) 37 Ch D 310 (unauthorised discharge of liability affecting gift).
6 See Chapter 44.

[41.2]

Change in nature of property. Where a change has occurred in the nature of the specific property given, even though effected by Act of Parliament, ademption follows,[1] unless the change is a change in name or form only, and the property exists as substantially the same thing although in a different shape.[2] Whether the property exists substantially the same at the death of the testator is a question of fact.[3]

1   *Frewen v Frewen* (1875) 10 Ch App 610 (advowson affected by Irish Church Act 1869); *Re Slater, Slater v Slater* [1907] 1 Ch 665 (water company acquired by Metropolitan Water Board); *Re Lane, Luard v Lane* (1880) 14 Ch D 856 (debentures into debenture stock).

2   *Oakes v Oakes* (1852) 9 Hare 666; *Re Pilkington's Trusts* (1865) 6 New Rep 246; *Humphreys v Humphreys* (1789) 2 Cox Eq Cas 184; *Re Dorman* [1994] 1 All ER 804.

3   *Re Bridle* (1879) 4 CPD 336 at 341; *Re Slater, Slater v Slater* [1906] 2 Ch 480 at 484 (where the effect of the Wills Act 1837, s 24; 50 *Halsbury's Statutes* (4th edn) 593 (Vol 2, Part G, para [**244.24**]), which makes the will speak and take effect as if executed immediately before the death, is considered, and the description of a particular thing as 'my ring' is contrasted with a generic description of property, in this case 'the interest arising from money invested in the Lambeth Waterworks Co', the latter company having before the death of the testator been taken over by the Metropolitan Water Board: it was held that there was an ademption); *Re Jameson, King v Winn* [1908] 2 Ch 111 at 115 (where on an amalgamation of banks there was held to be no ademption). See also *Re Sikes, Moxon v Crossley* [1927] 1 Ch 364, and *Re Wilson* [1958] Qd R 559; and *Re Puczka Estate* (1970) 10 DLR (3d) 339.

[41.3]
Effect of codicil. Where a gift has been adeemed, it will not be set up again by a codicil confirming the will;[1] at least where the ademption has been affected by a subsequent gift. In the case of ademption effected by a change in the nature of the property, the codicil may prevent ademption.[2]

1   *Powys v Mansfield* (1837) 3 My & Cr 359; *Cowper v Mantell* (1856) 22 Beav 223; *Re Aynsley, Kyrle v Turner* [1914] 2 Ch 422; on appeal [1915] 1 Ch 172, CA.

2   See *Re Warren, Warren v Warren* [1932] 1 Ch 42; *Re Reeves* [1928] Ch 351; but see *Re Galway's Will Trusts* [1950] Ch 1, [1949] 2 All ER 419.

[41.4]
Ademption a question of construction. The first question in a case where the question of ademption is raised is one of construction: what the testator is describing or dealing with, or, in other words, what it is that is bequeathed.[1] The court may, on the words of the particular will, construed according to the usual rules in cases of description,[2] find that the testator contemplated a change of investment,[3] and that the thing bequeathed is the property which for the time being represents the property which the testator formerly had;[4] and the gift in that case is not dependent on the specific investments representing the gift at the date of the will, but includes re-investments into which they can be traced.[5]

1   *Re Bridle* (1879) 4 CPD 336 at 341; *Re Slater, Slater v Slater* [1906] 2 Ch 480 at 484; *Re Jameson, King v Winn* [1908] 2 Ch 111 at 115.

2   See Chapter 59. The case of generic descriptions is in point.

3   *Sidebotham v Watson* (1853) 11 Hare 170 at 174; *Earl of Thomond v Earl of Suffolk* (1718) 1 P Wms 461.

4   *Re Moses, Beddington v Beddington* [1902] 1 Ch 100 at 102, CA; affd sub nom *Beddington v Baumann* [1903] AC 13, HL. A bequest of specified investments may pass money on deposit representing the same: *Re Lewis's Will Trusts, O'Sullivan v Robbins* [1937] Ch 118, [1937] 1 All ER 227; and a bequest of 'all my rights' in a play will pass the purchase money if the play is sold after the death of the testator: *Re Bancroft, Bancroft v Bancroft* [1928] Ch 577. Where the gift in the will is of the proceeds of sale, see para [**41.3**] supra.

5   *Lee v Lee* (1858) 27 LJ Ch 824.

II. PARTICULAR CASES

[41.5]
Sale of devised land by testator. Where specifically devised land is sold by the testator in his lifetime the devise is adeemed,[1] and where such land is both sold and mortgaged to the testator to secure part of the purchase price, the devise is also adeemed.[2] There is ademption also where the contract for sale is complete at the time of the testator's death although the sale is not completed by conveyance,[3] but where the contract for sale is not complete, for example, where there is an offer to buy which has not been accepted, the devise is not adeemed.[4] Similarly if the agreement for sale is conditional on the purchaser succeeding in acquiring other lands, the agreement may be regarded merely as an option, which if not exercised will not adeem the subject-matter.[5] A sale of part of the devised land where that part is the right to certain minerals under the land is not an ademption.[6] In the same way a compulsory acquisition of the property causes an ademption,[7] even where the compulsory acquisition was before the execution of the will and the gift was of 'all my interest in the estate' and the purchase money remained deposited in the bank.[8] A bequest of a sum to carry on collieries sold to the devisee has been held not to be adeemed.[9] By the Wills Act 1837, s 23,[10] subject to the doctrine of ademption,[11] no conveyance or other subsequent act of the testator relating to property comprised in a will, except an act revoking the will, prevents the will from operating with respect to the estate or interest in property of which the testator has the power of disposing by will at the time of his death.[12] Thus a gift by will of four houses for the residue of the terms of years held by the testator was followed by the purchase of the reversion and assumed merger and was held to pass the freehold.[13] A devise of a rentcharge is adeemed by the merger arising on the purchase of the property out of which the rentcharge issues[14] and a devise of real property to be purchased by the testator is adeemed if the vendors repudiate the contract and the devisee is not entitled to the purchase money although it is directed to be paid out of the personal estate[15] or deposited with trustees.[16] Where a trustee purchases trust property in breach of trust, the devisee of the trustee is entitled to the purchase money in lieu of the property and interest thereon from the date of the trustee's death.[17] Interest accruing before death is part of the personal estate of the trustee.[18]

---

1 *Arnald v Arnald* (1784) 1 Bro CC 401; *Whiteway v Fisher* (1861) 9 WR 433; *Manton v Tabois* (1885) 30 Ch D 92; *Re MacDougall* [1927] 3 DLR 464; *Re Gardner* [1938] 2 DLR 772; *Re Barnard Estate* [1948] 2 WWR 879 (where no part of the purchase money had been received). Strictly speaking the term ademption applies only to personalty. In the case of realty, disposal by the testator in his lifetime operated before 1838 as a revocation of the will pro tanto, but since 1837 the effect of the Wills Act 1837 is to bring the case of realty into line with personalty and it is more convenient to treat a devise as adeemed. A gift of land including mines and minerals did not pass compensation money where the royalties were nationalised even where the will was confirmed by codicil after the valuation date: *Re Galway's Will Trusts* [1950] Ch 1, [1949] 2 All ER 419.
2 See para **[41.6]** infra.
3 *Farrar v Earl of Winterton* (1842) 5 Beav 1; *Gale v Gale* (1856) 21 Beav 349; *Watts v Watts* (1873) LR 17 Eq 217 (sale under compulsory powers where it was held that the devisee was, despite ademption, entitled to rents from the testator's death until completion); *Guiry v Condon* [1918] 1 IR 23; *Miley v Carty and Miley* [1927] 1 IR 541; *Re Morton* [1963] VR 40. For a case

where a testatrix contracted for valuable consideration to devise a house to one of the residuary legatees, see *Re Edwards, Macadam v Wright* [1958] Ch 168, [1957] 2 All ER 495. The abolition of conversion in relation to trusts for sale of land by the Trusts of Land and Appointment of Trustees Act 1996, s 3, does not affect ademption by a contract of sale which has been concluded before the testator's death, but not yet completed by conveyance or transfer.

4   *Re Pearce, Roberts v Stephens* (1894) 8 R 805.
5   *Re Rodger* (1966) 60 DLR (2d) 666 (Ont HC).
6   *Berkheiser v Berkheiser and Glaisler* [1957] SCR 387. Lease of petroleum and natural gas held not to be a sale, distinguishing *McColl-Frontenac Oil Co Ltd v Hamilton* [1953] 1 SCR 127.
7   *Re Manchester and Southport Rly Co* (1854) 19 Beav 365; *Re Bagot's Settlement* (1862) 31 LJ Ch 772; *Ex p Hawkins* (1843) 13 Sim 569; *Watts v Watts* (1873) LR 17 Eq 217; *Re Tarca* (1981) 29 SASR 152.
8   *Manton v Tabois* (1885) 30 Ch D 92.
9   *Parsons v Coke* (1858) 27 LJ Ch 828 (a gift of collieries, sold to the devisee before testator's death, and a gift of a sum of £10,000 enabling the devisee to carry on the collieries). See *Re Galway's Will Trusts* [1950] Ch 1, [1949] 2 All ER 419, for a case affected by coal nationalisation.
10 See Vol 2, Part G, para **[244.23]**.
11 *Moor v Raisbeck* (1841) 12 Sim 123.
12 The result of this provision is that the cases in which it was formerly held that a will was revoked by an alteration of the estate of the testator are no longer law. The section does not apply where the thing meant to be given is gone, ie where the interest devised has been sold: *Moor v Raisbeck* (1841) 12 Sim 123; *Blake v Blake* (1880) 15 Ch D 481 at 487. Where land specifically devised is sold, the purchase-money, if not otherwise disposed of by the will, passes as part of the general personal estate: *Moor v Raisbeck* (1841) 12 Sim 123. See also *Watts v Watts* (1873) LR 17 Eq 217, where the sale is before and the completion is after the testator's death.
13 *Struthers v Struthers* (1857) 5 WR 809; likewise *Cox v Bennett* (1868) LR 6 Eq 422; and *Saxton v Saxton* (1879) 13 Ch D 359. These cases were applied in *Re Fleming's Will Trust, Ennion v Hampstead Old People's Housing Trust Ltd* [1974] 3 All ER 323, [1974] 1 WLR 1552, where the freehold passed. Templeman J thought that the intention of the testator was more important than the test of merger.
14 *Re Bick, Edwards v Bush* [1920] 1 Ch 488.
15 *Re Rix, Steward v Lonsdale* (1921) 90 LJ Ch 474.
16 *Gilfoyle v Wood-Martin* [1921] 1 IR 105.
17 *Re Sherman, Trevenen v Pearce* [1954] 1 All ER 893, [1954] 2 WLR 903, and see para **[7.7]** supra.
18 *Re Sherman, Trevenen v Pearce* [1954] 1 All ER 893, [1954] 2 WLR 903.

[41.6]
Sale where part of purchase money left on mortgage. Where on the sale of devised land part of the purchase money is left on mortgage to the vendor the devise is adeemed[1] and no part of the mortgage debt passes under the devise.[2]

1   *Moor v Raisbeck* (1841) 12 Sim 123; *Re Clowes* [1893] 1 Ch 214; *Re Richards, Jones v Rebbeck* (1921) 90 LJ Ch 298. The gift was still adeemed although the purchase-money was deposited with trustees: *Gilfoyle v Wood-Martin* [1921] 1 IR 105.
2   *Re Foley* [1955] NZLR 702; see also *Hicks v McClure* (1922) 64 SCR 361.

[41.7]
Sale of land subjected by will to trust for sale before 1 January 1997. The Trusts of Land and Appointment of Trustees Act 1996 (TLATA 1996) has abolished the doctrine of conversion in relation to trusts for sale of land but not in relation to contracts for the sale of land.[1] The previous law was that where the will included a devise of land upon trust for sale, there was no ademption if it was sold during the testator's lifetime[2] but a specific devise upon trust for sale was adeemed[3] unless the gift was expressed in such wide terms as to carry not

only the original property but also property arising from the testator's dealing with it.[4]

1   The TLATA 1996, s 3, abolishes the doctrine of conversion in relation to trusts for sale of land, except in relation to trusts for sale arising under wills of persons who have died before 1 January 1997.
2   *Re Hughson* [1955] SCR 498 (no ademption because gift was construed as a legacy of an amount equal to the proceeds of the sale of the property).
3   *Re Stevens* [1946] 4 DLR 322 (direction to sell a particular property and hold the proceeds on certain trusts; testator sold the property before death but gift was held to be adeemed because the proceeds had been mixed with other property).
4   *Hicks v McClure* (1922) 64 SCR 361 (direction to sell a particular farm and divide proceeds among particular beneficiaries; the testator sold it during his life, some of the purchase money remained outstanding on the mortgage; held not adeemed as regards the mortgage).

[41.8]
Mortgage of devised land. A mortgage after the execution of the will only adeems the devise pro tanto and the devisee takes the land subject to the mortgage.[1]

1   *Brain v Brain* (1821) 6 Madd 221; *Plowden v Hyde* (1852) 2 De GM & G 684. Cf *Oakes v Oakes* (1852) 9 Hare 666 (mortgage of stock). But a gift of 'all monies owing' on a mortgage will not be adeemed merely by reason of the fact that the lender has obtained judgment foreclosing the mortgage and giving him possession of the property and a judgment on the covenant to pay: *Re Britt* [1968] 2 OR 12 (Can).

[41.9]
Bequest of mortgage debt. A bequest of a mortgage debt described as such is generally a specific bequest and is adeemed by payment off of the debt.[1]

1   *Re Robe, Slade v Walpole* (1889) 61 LT 497; *Phillips v Turner* (1853) 17 Bev 194; *Re Brazier Creagh's Trusts, Holmes v Langley* [1913] 1 IR 232; *Re Ashdown* [1943] 4 DLR 517; *Re Swick* [1944] 4 DLR 55 (where mortgage was foreclosed). See further, para **[41.19]**, nn 1 and 2.

[41.10]
Bequest of leaseholds. It is a matter of construction whether a bequest of leaseholds is adeemed by subsequent operations. A bequest of 'my leasehold house' has been held to pass the subsequently acquired freehold even though there was no merger of the leasehold and freehold interests.[1] A subsequent surrender and renewal has been held to be an ademption;[2] but a bequest of all the testator's leasehold property is still effective although the testator subsequently purchases the reversion and then leases it to a new tenant.[3]

1   *Re Fleming's Will Trusts, Ennion v Hampstead Old People's Housing Trust Ltd* [1974] 3 All ER 323, [1974] 1 WLR 1552; see para **[41.5]**, n 13.
2   *Hone v Medcraft* (1783) 1 Bro CC 261; but see *Re Reeves* [1928] Ch 351 (where there was a codicil after renewal and the renewed lease passed).
3   *Minifie v Hall* (1867) 1 CA 421.

[41.11]
Sale of stock or shares. A specific legacy of stock or shares is adeemed by sale of the securities in the lifetime of the testator.[1] This may be so even when similar stock or similar shares is or are purchased with the proceeds of sale,[2] but where a sale and re-investment was made under a power to do so in a settlement, the

change did not effect an ademption.[3] Where there was a specific legacy of stock, and other specific property was directed to be sold and the proceeds applied in discharge of a mortgage, and the testator sold part of the stock and discharged the mortgage with the proceeds, it was held that the specific legacy of the stock was adeemed pro tanto and that the specific legatees of the stock could have no relief from the funds appropriated for the discharge of the mortgage.[4] A testator in Jamaica directed his agents in England to sell certain stock which they did after his death but without knowledge of his death. It was held that neither the direction nor the sale effected an ademption.[5] A testator bequeathed all his share in a certain estate which share included certain stock. The testator sold that stock and applied the proceeds to his own purposes, and it was held that the sale effected an ademption of the bequest.[6] A bequest of policies is adeemed by the policies being paid in the lifetime of the testator and the proceeds otherwise invested.[7]

1   *Ashburner v Macguire* (1786) 2 Bro CC 108; *Hayes v Hayes* (1836) 1 Keen 97 (sale of shares and proceeds invested in mortgage); *Re Sayer, McClellan v Clark* (1884) 53 LJ Ch 832; *Re Tyler, Tyler v Tyler* (1891) 65 LT 367 (where there were both specific and general legacies). Where there is a general legacy of stock or shares, and many such legacies are so construed (see para **[30.8]** ante), and the stock or shares are paid off or otherwise redeemed, the legatee is entitled to a sum of money which would purchase equivalent stock or shares: *Re Gage, Crozier v Gutheridge* [1934] Ch 536; *Re Borne, Bailey v Bailey* [1944] Ch 190, [1944] 1 All ER 382.
2   *Pattison v Pattison* (1832) 1 My & K 12; *Macdonald v Irvine* (1878) 8 Ch D 101.
3   *Jones v Southall (No 2)* (1862) 32 Beav 31, and *Re Johnstone's Settlement* (1880) 14 Ch D 162, as explained in *Re Moses, Beddington v Beddington* [1902] 1 Ch 100.
4   *Humphreys v Humphreys* (1789) 2 Cox Eq Cas 184.
5   *Harrison v Asher* (1848) 2 De G & Sm 436.
6   *Lee v Lee* (1858) 27 LJ Ch 824.
7   *Barker v Rayner* (1826) 2 Russ 122.

[41.12]

Disposals under the Mental Health Act 1983. Where any property of a person of unsound mind has been disposed[1] of pursuant to the powers under the Mental Health Act 1983, and under that person's will or intestacy,[2] any other person would have taken an interest in the property but for the disposal, he shall take the same interest, if and so far as circumstances allow, in any property belonging to the estate of the deceased which represents the property disposed of.[3]

1   Disposal of property means sale, exchange, charging or other dealing, otherwise than by will.
2   Or by any gift perfected or nomination taking effect on his death.
3   Mental Health Act 1983, s 101 (28 *Halsbury's Statutes* (4th edn) 970), reproducing the Mental Health Act 1959, s 107, which itself embodied previous legislation.

[41.13]

Change of investment by Act of Parliament. If the Act effects a change in the nature of the property, ademption follows,[1] but not where the change is one of form only and the property exists as substantially the same thing though in a different shape.[2] Thus in the first class are: advowson in effect destroyed by the operation of the Irish Church Act 1869;[3] water company's shares affected by the establishment of the Metropolitan Water Board;[4] railway shares affected by the Railways Act 1921;[5] statutory scheme affecting gas shares;[6] exchange under statutory Treasury Rules of bonds for war loans.[7] In the second class are old decisions relating to the South Sea stock,[8] and some recent cases where hospitals have been nationalised.[9] The conversion of undivided shares in land into shares in the proceeds of sale of the land under the Law of Property Act 1925 is dealt with separately.[10]

1   *Frewen v Frewen* (1875) 10 Ch App 610; *Re Slater, Slater v Slater* [1907] 1 Ch 665; *Re Anderson, Public Trustee v Bielby* (1928) 44 TLR 295.
2   *Oakes v Oakes* (1852) 9 Hare 666 at 672; *Re Pilkington's Trusts* (1865) 6 New Rep 246.
3   *Frewen v Frewen* (1875) 10 Ch App 610.
4   *Re Slater, Slater v Slater* [1907] 1 Ch 665.
5   *Re Anderson, Public Trustee v Bielby* (1928) 44 TLR 295. See also *Re Jenkins* [1931] 2 Ch 218.
6   *Re Loveman, Watson v Watson* (1879) 48 LJ Ch 565.
7   *Re Macartney, Brookhouse v Barman* (1920) 36 TLR 394.
8   *Partridge v Partridge* (1736) Cas *temp* Talb 226; *Bronsdon v Winter* (1738) Amb 57; *Wingfield v Newton* (1739) 2 Coll 520n.
9   *Re Hunter* [1951] Ch 190, [1951] 1 All ER 58; *Re Morgan's Will Trusts, Lewarne v Minister of Health* [1950] Ch 637, [1950] 1 All ER 1097; *Re Glass, Public Trustee v South-West Middlesex Hospital Management Committee* [1950] Ch 643, [1950] 2 All ER 953n; *Re Meyers* [1951] Ch 534, [1951] 1 All ER 538; *Re Little, Barclays Bank Ltd v Bournemouth and East Dorset Hospital Management Committee* [1953] 2 All ER 852. See also *Re Galway's Will Trusts, Lowther v Viscount Galway* [1950] Ch 1, [1949] 2 All ER 419 (coal nationalisation).
10   See para **[41.18]** infra.

[41.14]

Change of investment by act of company or corporation. The same general rule applies here as in the case of change by Act of Parliament.[1] The following examples have been decided: exchanges of debentures for debenture stock;[2] conversion of railway bonds into shares;[3] subdivision of shares;[4] allotment of different stock on a transfer of an undertaking to a statutory board;[5] substitution of shares on reconstruction of company;[6] issue of additional shares on reduction of dividends and reorganisation of capital;[7] stock paid off.[8]

1   See para **[41.13]** supra.
2   *Re Lane, Luard v Lane* (1880) 14 Ch D 856 (held to be an ademption).
3   *Re Pilkington's Trusts* (1865) 6 New Rep 246 (held not to be an ademption although testator need not have joined in the arrangement).
4   *Re Greenberry, Hops v Daniell* (1911) 55 Sol Jo 633 (no ademption); *Re Clifford, Mallan v McFie* [1912] 1 Ch 29 (no ademption, subdivision on amalgamation of banks); *Re O'Brien* (1946) 115 LJ Ch 340 (no ademption by subdivision, but part ademption by sale); *Re Lloyd* [1960] VLR 63.
5   *Re Slater, Slater v Slater* [1907] 1 Ch 665 (water company taken over by Metropolitan Water Board; gift adeemed).
6   *Re Leeming, Turner v Leeming* [1912] 1 Ch 828 (no ademption).
7   *Re Kuypers, Kuypers v Kuypers* [1925] Ch 244 (additional shares did not pass by specific devise), and see *Re Lloyd* [1960] VLR 63.
8   *Harrison v Jackson* (1877) 7 Ch D 339 (ademption). See also para **[41.11]**, n 1.

[41.15]

Change in shares of partnership. Where a partnership is continued by the same parties but an alteration is made in the shares of profits to be taken by the partners, a legacy of one-ninth part of a share was not adeemed and the legatee took a one-ninth share of the testator's interest in the partnership at his death.[1] A gift of a share of a partnership valued at £600 is a legacy of that amount and is not adeemed by the testator ceasing to be a partner.[2] A gift of a business or practice of a professional man is not adeemed by the testator taking the legatee into partnership.[3]

1   *Backwell v Child* (1755) Amb 260.
2   *Hayes v Williams* [1918] 1 IR 6.
3   *Re Rhagg, Easten v Boyd* [1938] Ch 828, [1938] 3 All ER 314.

[41.16]
Gift of what testator may receive from the estate of another: investment of money received. In such a case, the investments have been assumed to replace the money received and the bequest of the share in the estate has been held not to be adeemed.[1] Where part of the investments were sold, the legacy was still not adeemed.[2] These cases have been decided on the principle that the gift in the will includes investments and reinvestments into which the subject-matter of the gift can be traced.[3]

1   *Moore v Moore* (1860) 29 Beav 496; *Morgan v Thomas* (1877) 6 Ch D 176; *Re Kenyon's Estate, Mann v Knapp* (1887) 56 LT 626 (so far as the investments representing the estate could be traced). See *Toole v Hamilton* [1901] 1 IR 383, where charges on the property were paid off.
2   *Clark v Browne* (1854) 2 Sm & G 524; but see the remarks on this case in *Harrison v Jackson* (1877) 7 Ch D 339, and *Manton v Tabois* (1885) 30 Ch D 92; but in *Oliver v Oliver* (1871) LR 11 Eq 506, the whole of the investments were sold and mixed with other moneys and the bequest was held to have been adeemed.
3   See cases cited in para **[41.2]**, n 2.

[41.17]
Removal of gift. The effect of the removal of the gift where the will describes the property as situated in a certain place is considered elsewhere.[1]

1   See Chapter 63.

[41.18]
Undivided shares in land. The TLATA 1996 contains provisions which alter the nature of an undivided share. The TLATA 1996, s 3 provides that an undivided share of land under a trust for sale is now an interest in land, not an interest in personal property, and by virtue of the amendments to the Law of Property Act 1925, s 34,[1] the trust imposed on dispositions to tenants in common without an express trust by the Law of Property Act 1925, s 34 is no longer a trust for sale, with the consequence that where the disposition which created the tenancy in common (whether before or after the TLATA 1996 came into force) did not contain an express trust for sale, the tenant in common's beneficial interest is now in the land and not the proceeds of sale.[2] Before the TLATA 1996 came into force, an undivided share of freehold land counted as personalty, since it was an interest in the proceeds of sale of land held on trust for sale and was thus treated as an interest in personalty by virtue of the doctrine of conversion.[3] Following the coming into force of the TLATA 1996 (1 January 1997) an undivided share of land is either an equitable interest in land directly under the Law of Property Act 1925, s 34 (ie without the interposition of a trust for sale), or it is an interest under a trust for sale, but with the doctrine of conversion abolished. The reversion to the pre-1926 position is less than total, because an undivided share remains an equitable interest, not a legal interest.[4]

The question of the ademption of a devise of an undivided share of land in a will executed before 1926 is a question of construction in every case.

1   Made by the TLATA 1996, Sch 2, para 3.
2   By virtue of the amendments made by the TLATA 1996 to the Law of Property Act 1925, ss 34 and 36.
3   *Re Kempthorne* [1930] 1 Ch 268.
4   However, there is a remote possibility of ademption by reverse application of *Re Newman, Slater v Newman* [1930] 2 Ch 409, either because a gift in a pre-1 January 1997 will, of a testator dying on or after that date, of an undivided share under an express trust for sale is phrased as a bequest of personalty and the interest is now an interest in realty, or, perhaps more likely, because a gift in such a will of such a testator is worded as a gift of his interest, the proceeds of sale of the property and his undivided share of that property was not under an express trust for sale but is governed by the Law of Property Act 1925, s 34.
5   See *Newman, Slater v Newman* [1930] 2 Ch 409 at 417; *Re Price* [1928] Ch 579; *Re Kempthorne, Charles v Kempthorne* [1930] 1 Ch 268; *Re Mellish* (1927) 164 LT Jo 23; *Re Wheeler, Jameson v Cotter* [1929] 2 KB 81n; *Re Warren, Warren v Warren* [1932] 1 Ch 42. Where there is a codicil executed after 1925 confirming the devise, the devisee takes even though the language of the will treats the gift as one of freehold property; *Re Warren, Warren v Warren*. This decision was applied in a case where the codicil did no more than place on record the destruction of a former codicil: *Re Harvey, Public Trustee v Hosken* [1947] Ch 285, [1947] 1 All ER 349.

[41.19]
Payment of debt. A bequest of a debt is adeemed by the whole debt being paid to the testator in his lifetime, whether the payment is compulsory or voluntary,[1] and whether the sum is expressed in the bequest or the debt is bequeathed generally.[2] Payment of part of the debt adeems the gift pro tanto.[3]

1   *Stanley v Potter* (1789) 2 Cox Eq Cas 180; *Lawson v Stitch* (1738) 1 Atk 507; *Drinkwater v Falconer* (1755) 2 Ves Sen 623; *Ashe v Berry* (1829) Beat 255; and see para **[41.11]**, n 1.
2   *Stanley v Potter* (1789) 2 Cox Eq Cas 180; *Rider v Wager* (1725) 2 P Wms 328; *Re Shortts* [1954] 2 DLR 817, OWN 481.
3   *Ashburner v Maguire* (1786) 2 Bro CC 108 (payment of dividends on bankruptcy); *Fryer v Morris* (1804) 9 Ves 360.

[41.20]
Exercise of option. There must be first stated what is known as the rule in *Lawes v Bennett*[1] which has long been regarded with disfavour by the courts but has been recognised as binding by reason of its having stood for so long. In this case the facts were as follows: (i) a lease granted by a testator seised in fee before the date of his will included an option to purchase the freehold, (ii) the will contained a general devise of real estate to one person and a general bequest of personal estate in equal shares to that person and one other, (iii) the option was exercised after the death of the testator. It was held that the exercise of the option dated back to the grant thereof and the freehold property was converted into personalty before the death of the testator and passed as such under his will to those entitled under the general bequest of personalty. It must be noted that in this case there was a general devise and not a specific one so that the case does not directly concern the question of ademption as here considered which is concerned only with the failure of a specific gift, the question at issue being not whether any gift failed, but whether the particular property passed under the general devise or the general bequest which is strictly speaking a question of conversion. The rule was later applied to a specific devise but in this case the

option was created after the date of the will.[2] The question was one of ademption as here considered. It is thus clear that so far as questions of ademption and conversion are concerned the exercise of the option relates back to the giving of the option so that a complete contract is formed at that earlier date.[3] The law may therefore be stated as follows. The exercise of an option, created by the testator after the date of the will, to purchase the property specifically given by the will adeems the gift,[4] unless the context of the will or the circumstances of the case show that the testator had the option present in his mind at the date of the will,[5] or otherwise that the donee was intended to take the whole interest of the testator.[6] Where the option is created before the date of the will, its exercise does not adeem the gift, since the property in the state in which it is given is subject to the option.[7] An agreement to sell land subject to a condition will be treated in the same way.[8]

1   (1785) 1 Cox Eq Cas 167. Applied in *Re Sweeting, Sweeting v Sweeting* [1988] 1 All ER 1016, noted infra, note 8. But was held to be excluded by a contrary intention in *Re Miller* [1991] 1 Qd R 359. The principles stated in this paragraph are not affected by the abolition of the doctrine of conversion in relation to trusts for sale by the TLATA 1996, s 3, as in so far as these principles depend on the doctrine of conversion it is conversion by entering into a contract of sale.

2   *Weeding v Weeding* (1861) 1 John & H 424.

3   The relation back of a notice exercising an option was recently considered in *Baker v Merckel* [1960] 1 QB 657, [1960] 1 All ER 668, but in circumstances which would not affect the authorities here cited.

4   *Lawes v Bennett* (1785) 1 Cox Eq Cas 167; *Weeding v Weeding* (1861) 1 John & H 424; *Re Carrington, Ralphs v Swithenbank* [1932] 1 Ch 1. Notice to exercise an option effects a conversion, though not followed by completion: *Re Blake, Gawthorne v Blake* [1917] 1 Ch 18. The determination after the death of the testator of a lease containing a provision for compensation on the exercise of the power to determine does not deprive the specific legatee of the right to the compensation: *Coyne v Coyne* (1876) IR 10 Eq 496.

5   *Re Pyle, Pyle v Pyle* [1895] 1 Ch 724 at 729.

6   *Re Calow, Calow v Calow* [1928] Ch 710; *Re Isaacs, Isaacs v Reginall* [1894] 3 Ch 506 at 510, explaining *Emuss v Smith* (1848) 2 De G & Sm 722 (option exercisable only after death).

7   *Drant v Vause* (1842) 1 Y & C Ch Cas 580; *Emuss v Smith* (1848) 2 De G & Sm 722 (codicil after date of contract); *Re Pyle, Pyle v Pyle* [1895] 1 Ch 724; *Re Albery* [1946] 1 OR 342; *Re Lewis* [1964] VR 537. The donee is in such a case entitled to the purchase-money payable on the exercise of the option.

8   *Re Rodger* (1966) 60 DLR (2d) 666 (Ont HC); *Re Sweeting, Sweeting v Sweeting* [1988] 1 All ER 1016. It was argued in the case that the rule should not apply to conditional contracts but Nicholls J was reluctant to draw the bounds of the rule arbitrarily and preferred to rely on dicta of Pickford and Warrington LJJ in *Re Marlay* [1915] 2 Ch 264 at 278, 281 to the effect that the rule applied. The facts of the case were that the testator devised a plot of land adjacent to his house to specific devisees under two separate gifts. Shortly before his death the testator exchanged two contracts of sale, one for the sale of the house, the other for the sale of the plot of land but he died before either contract could be completed. Both contracts were conditional—the land on the simultaneous completion of the house—the house on obtaining certain consents; both these conditions were fulfilled. It was held that the completion of the land contract had the effect of converting the land into personal property, the specific gifts of the land in the testator's will were adeemed and the proceeds of sale fell into the testator's residuary estate. See also *Re Dawson* [1987] 1 NZLR 580, and *Re Hurzin and Neumeyer Estate* (1990) 69 DLR (4th) 18. The presumption against ademption and the leaning against specific legacies was applied in *Public Trustee for Saskatchewan v Montreal Trust Co of Canada* (1989) 57 DLR (4th) 742.

[41.21]

Appointment by will. The doctrine of ademption applies to the exercise of a power of appointment by will whether made under a general or a special power.[1]

Thus where the appointed property is converted before the death of the testator there is ademption;[2] but it may be shown that the appointment is to take effect whatever the state of the property.[3] The mere acquiring of the legal estate where the equitable interest so far as the property was appointed was already in the appointor does not adeem the appointment.[4]

1   *Re Dowsett, Dowsett v Meakin* [1901] 1 Ch 398; *Re Moses, Beddington v Beddington* [1902] 1 Ch 100.
2   *Gale v Gale* (1856) 21 Beav 349 (where the purchase-money had not been received and the conveyance not executed by one of the trustees); *Blake v Blake* (1880) 15 Ch D 481. In *Beddington v Baumann* [1903] AC 13, the appointed property was leased and premiums taken and it was held that the appointments did not pass the premiums.
3   *Bullock v Thomas* (1838) 9 Sim 634; *Re Johnstone's Settlement* (1880) 14 Ch D 162.
4   *Dingwell v Askew* (1788) 1 Cox Eq Cas 427; *Clough v Clough* (1834) 3 My & K 296; *Re Oakes' Will Trusts, Lloyds Bank Ltd v Barker* [1948] WN 110 (property already notionally converted at date of appointment).

[41.22]
Transfer by trustees into testator's name. This form of transfer being merely a transfer of the legal right to the property when the beneficial interest has vested in the testator does not adeem a gift;[1] but the opposite operation, a transfer to trustees on the creation of a settlement may operate as an ademption.[2]

1   *Dingwell v Askew* (1788) 1 Cox Eq Cas 427; *Clough v Clough* (1834) 3 My & K 296; *Lee v Lee* (1858) 27 LJ Ch 824; *Re Vickers, Vickers v Mellor* (1899) 81 LT 719.
2   See *Williams v Owens* (1794) 2 Ves 595; *Rawlins v Burgis* (1814) 2 Ves & B 382; *Grant v Bridger* (1866) LR 3 Eq 347.

[41.23]
Money in a bank account. It has been held that a gift by will of the credit balance at the death of the testator in a specifically identified bank deposit account amounted on special facts of the case, to the gift of a fund, and that the transfer of the money during the lifetime of the testatrix to a new account which yielded a higher rate of interest and required 30 days' notice for any withdrawal, but was otherwise at the same bank branch and on the same terms as the former account, was a change in name and form only and did not adeem the gift.[1]

1   *Re Dorm* [1994] 1 All ER 804, [1994] 1 WLR 282.

[41.24]
Ademption of a legacy by a portion. This topic is dealt with in Chapter 44.

CHAPTER 42

Election

[42.1]
Statement of the doctrine. It has already been pointed out that a testator cannot, except in the proper exercise of a power of appointment,[1] dispose of property not vested in him at the time of his death or for any greater interest than is so vested in him.[2] Normally, therefore, a gift by the testator to a donee of property in which he has no interest fails altogether, but in the special case where the true owner of the property so given also receives a benefit under the same will, such owner is put to his election whether he will give up such benefit or will give effect to the disposition by the testator which has failed.[3] Thus, if the testator gives to A property which in fact belongs to B and by the same will makes a gift to B, then B will not be allowed to take such gift unless he undertakes to give effect to the gift to A or, in the usual phrase, he is prepared to carry into effect the whole of the testator's dispositions.[4] He is put to his election to take under the will or against it and, if he elects to take under the will, he will be ordered to convey his own property to the beneficiary under the will[5] or give effect to a provision in the will which is contrary to his own interests under a prior contract or settlement.[6] On the other hand he may elect to take against the will, ie he will keep his own property, but, if he does so, he must either give up his benefit under the will, or, since this would hardly be fair where there is great disparity between the value of the two gifts, the owner of the property which the testator has wrongly disposed of is given the opportunity of retaining his gift under the will provided he compensates the beneficiary by giving him the value of the property of which he is disappointed.[7] Where the gift of the property not belonging to the testator fails, because the beneficiary is unable to take, that gift falls into residue, and the residuary legatee profits by the election, and takes either the property wrongly disposed of or the compensation.[8]

1   In the case of property subject to a power of appointment, the property is usually vested in trustees and the exercise of a power of appointment varies the trusts upon which they hold the property. Where the trusts thus become absolute interests, the beneficiaries are entitled to demand a transfer of the property from the trustees. In such cases, therefore, a testator can properly dispose of property not vested in him at the time of his death.
2   See para **[7.30]** supra.
3   *Dillon v Parker* (1818) 1 Swan 359 at 394; *Blake v Bunbury* (1792) 1 Ves 514 at 523. See *Jay v Jay* [1924] 1 KB 826 (limitation of action). In a case of mutual wills of husband and wife, the doctrine does not apply so as to prevent the surviving spouse taking a benefit under the will of the deceased spouse and also making a new will, in the absence of a definite agreement to the contrary: *Gray v Perpetual Trustee Co Ltd* [1928] AC 391.
4   *Re Brooksbank, Beauclerk v James* (1886) 34 Ch D 160. The gift under the will must be bounty. A legacy in discharge of a statute-barred debt is bounty: *Re Fletcher's Settlement Trusts, Medley v Fletcher* [1936] 2 All ER 236.

5   *Blake v Bunbury* (1792) 1 Ves 514 at 527; *Gretton v Hayward* (1819) 1 Swan 409. For a
     discussion of the doctrine that a person cannot both 'approbate and reprobate', see *Lissenden v
     CAV Bosch Ltd* [1940] AC 412, [1940] 1 All ER 425.
6   *Re Fletcher's Settlement Trusts, Medley v Fletcher* [1936] 2 All ER 236, where under a
     settlement a settlor covenanted to take out a policy for £2,000 payable on his death to the
     trustees and to bequeath to the trustees all his copyrights. By his will he bequeathed £2,000 to
     the trustees in satisfaction of his obligation to effect a policy for that sum contained in the
     settlement (but the obligation under the covenant in the settlement was then statute- barred) and
     gave his copyrights to his widow. It was held that, if the trustees took the £2,000, they must
     allow the widow to take the benefit of the gift of the copyrights.
7   *Re Gordon's Will Trusts, National Westminster Bank Ltd v Gordon* [1978] 2 All ER 969 at 973,
     per Buckley LJ; *Brown v Gregson* [1920] AC 860 at 868–870, per Viscount Haldane; *Gretton v
     Haward* (1819) 1 Swan 409; *Pickersgill v Rodger* (1876) 5 Ch D 163; *Re Macartney,
     Macfarlane v Macartney* [1918] 1 Ch 300. If the property wrongly given by the testator is such
     that it cannot be assigned, as heirlooms or foreign property which cannot be made subject to the
     trusts of the will, the owner of such property is not put to his election, but can retain his gift
     under the will without assigning the property or giving compensation: *Re Lord Chesham,
     Cavendish v Dacre* (1886) 31 Ch D 466; *Brown v Gregson* [1920] AC 860. Property brought
     into the estate by reason of an election to take under the will is liable to contribute to the
     payment of debts: *Re Williams, Cunliffe v Williams* [1915] 1 Ch 450.
8   *Re Brooksbank, Beauclerk v James* (1886) 34 Ch D 160.

[42.2]
When doctrine applied. The doctrine of election requires that there shall be a
claim under the will and a claim outside the will and adverse to it. It is not
applied as between two clauses in the same will,[1] though in some cases a
beneficiary may reject onerous property and accept beneficial property, but this
is really a matter of disclaimer,[2] nor is it applied where the property is taken out
of the will by the doctrine of ademption.[3] It applies though part of the benefits in
the testator's own property may fail.[4] Where two wills of the same testator,
disposing of properties in different countries, form one testamentary disposition,
a beneficiary electing against one will can claim under the other only on terms
that his interest under the other must be applied to compensate those
disappointed by his election.[5]
The doctrine applies to all cases of property and to all classes of devisees and
legatees and in some few cases to the persons entitled on an intestacy.[6]

1   *Wollaston v King* (1869) LR 8 Eq 165 at 174. See *Re Irwin's Estate* (1910) 44 ILT 50.
2   See Chapter 46.
3   *Re Edwards, Macadam v Wright* [1958] Ch 168, [1957] 2 All ER 495 (where the testatrix orally
     agreed with a beneficiary, for consideration which was given, to devise to that beneficiary
     certain property which would otherwise have passed under the gift of residue and which was
     expressly stated in the will to be included in the residue).
4   *Newman v Newman* (1783) 1 Bro CC 186 (will not duly attested to pass real estate).
5   *Douglas-Menzies v Umphelby* [1908] AC 224.
6   *Cooper v Cooper* (1870) 6 Ch App 15 at 21; on appeal (1874) LR 7 HL 53, dictum at 71
     applied in *Re Leigh's Will Trusts, Handyside v Durbridge* [1970] Ch 277, [1969] 3 All ER 432.
     The doctrine applies where a testator purports to release a debt due to a third party upon whom
     he confers a benefit: *Synge v Synge* (1874) 9 Ch App 128, but it does not now apply to creditors
     in whose favour there is a devise in trust for payment of their debts. It applies where the
     beneficiary takes under a trust for sale, eg as tenant in common: *Re Dicey, Julian v Dicey*
     [1957] Ch 145, [1956] 3 All ER 696. Where there is a devise of land outside England which
     fails for non-compliance with the local law and the person taking is a beneficiary under the will,
     the doctrine applies: *Dewar v Maitland* (1866) LR 2 Eq 834; *Orrell v Orrell* (1871) 6 Ch App
     302; *Harrison v Harrison* (1873) 8 Ch App 342; but the land must be specifically described, for
     a general devise operates only on the land capable of passing under it: *Maxwell v Maxwell*
     (1852) 2 De GM & G 705. In cases where by foreign law a widow has a claim on her husband's

property which he cannot defeat by will, she may be put to her election: *Douglas-Menzies v Umphelby* [1908] AC 224; *Re Allen's Estate, Prescott v Allen and Beaumont* [1945] 2 All ER 264. Where there is incapacity to make a will, the will is void and there is no case of election: *Blaiklock v Grindle* (1868) LR 7 Eq 215; *Re Anderson, Pegler v Gillatt* [1905] 2 Ch 70. As to a husband being put to election where he might take under his marital right and under the will, see *Re Harris, Leacroft v Harris* [1909] 2 Ch 206. Where by foreign law a widow has a claim on her husband's property (eg by community of assets) the doctrine applied: *Re Mengel's Will Trusts, Westminster Bank Ltd v Mengel* [1962] Ch 791, [1962] 2 All ER 490; *Re Beauchamp* (1975) 56 DLR (3d) 644 (doctrine not applied where property was not acquired until after the testator's death).

[42.3]
Doctrine not dependent on testator's knowledge that he has no title. The application of the doctrine does not depend on whether or not the testator knows he has not title to the property he purports to dispose of. If he knows that he has no title and that it belongs to a person who is otherwise a beneficiary under his will, he is supposed to intend to put the beneficiary to his election,[1] but it is not essential that the testator should have this equitable principle in mind.[2] The doctrine is not excluded by the fact that the testator has expressly required legatees to take their legacies in satisfaction of sums due to them.[3]

Where, however, the testator has shown that he meant election to be confined to a particular property, it will not extend to other property.[4] The principle is equally applicable where he is in error as to his power of disposition and thinks that he is disposing of his own property.[5] The court does not consider whether, had he realised the property was not his own, he would have made a different disposition, but takes the will as it is and insists on the beneficiaries giving effect to it.[6]

1   *Wilkinson v Dent* (1871) 6 Ch App 339 at 341. The opposite statement of the rule in *Forrester v Cotton* (1760) 1 Eden 531, has not represented the accepted rule for very many years now.
2   *Cooper v Cooper* (1874) LR 7 HL 53 at 67.
3   *Wilkinson v Dent* (1871) 6 Ch App 339.
4   *East v Cook* (1750) 2 Ves Sen 30.
5   *Swan v Holmes* (1854) 19 Beav 471; *Woolaston v King* (1869) LR 8 Eq 165.
6   *Whistler v Webster* (1794) 2 Ves 367; *Thellusson v Woodford* (1806) 13 Ves 209.

[42.4]
Election under exercise of power. The doctrine applies also to the erroneous exercise of a special power of appointment, whereby property is appointed to a stranger, a benefit being at the same time conferred by the appointor out of his own property on an object of the power. The object of the power cannot claim this benefit and at the same time exclude the stranger and take in default of appointment.[1] There is no distinction between an invalid gift of property which a testator believed to be his own and an invalid gift of property which a testator knew not to be his own but over which he erroneously thought he had a power of appointment.[2] Where, however, there has been a proper appointment to an object of the power, invalid modifications of that appointment are altogether void, and do not raise a case of election.[3] Thus precatory words added to an appointment will not put the appointee to election,[4] unless the benefit conferred by the will is subject to forfeiture on non-compliance.[5] The doctrine is not available for curing illegality; hence an appointment to a stranger which is in its

nature void for illegality – eg where it infringes the rule against perpetuities –
does not raise a case of election.[6]

1   *Whistler v Webster* (1794) 2 Ves 367.
2   *Cooper v Cooper* (1870) 6 Ch App 15; *Re Brooksbank, Beauclerk v James* (1886) 34 Ch D 160.
3   *Carver v Bowles* (1831) 2 Russ & M 301; *Woolridge v Woolridge* (1859) John 63. See also
    King v King (1885) 13 LR Ir 531.
4   *Blacket v Lamb* (1851) 14 Beav 482; *Langslow v Langslow* (1856) 21 Beav 552; *Churchill v
    Churchill* (1867) LR 5 Eq 44.
5   *King v King* (1864) 15 I Ch R 479.
6   *Re Nash, Cook v Frederick* [1910] 1 Ch 1; *Re Handcock's Trusts* (1889) 23 LR Ir 34; *Re
    Oliver's Settlement, Evered v Leigh* [1905] 1 Ch 191; *Re Beales' Settlement, Barrett v Beales*
    [1905] 1 Ch 256; *Re Wright, Whitworth v Wright* [1906] 2 Ch 288. See also *Re McCormick,
    Hazlewood v Foot* [1915] 1 IR 315; *Re Ogilvie, Ogilvie v Ogilvie* [1918] 1 Ch 492 (where
    beneficiaries were 'obligatory heirs' under Paraguayan law).

[42.5]
Intention to dispose of particular property. To raise a case of election under a
will upon the ground that the testator has attempted to dispose of property over
which he had no disposing power, it must be clearly shown that the testator
intended to dispose of the particular property;[1] and this intention must appear on
the face of the will, either by express words or by necessary conclusion from the
circumstances disclosed by the will.[2] The presumption is that a testator intends
to dispose only of his own property;[3] and general words will not be construed so
as to include other property,[4] nor will oral evidence be admitted to show that the
testator believed such other property to be his own so as to allow it to be
comprised in general words.[5] Similarly, where a testator has a limited interest in
property, and purports to dispose of the property itself, the presumption is that
he intends to dispose only of his limited interest;[6] and, if it is sought to carry the
disposition further, it must be shown that he intended to dispose of more than
that interest. But for this purpose positive declaration is not necessary. Regard
may be had to the context of the will, and to the inaptitude of the testamentary
limitations if applied to the testator's actual interest.[7] But a devise of an estate
which is subject to incumbrances does not by itself import an intention to devise
it free from incumbrances, so as to put incumbrancers who take under the will to
their election.[8] Where it appears from a recital that a testator has disposed of his
own property under an erroneous belief as to the interests in other property of
certain beneficiaries under his will, giving less to some on the footing that they
would be compensated by their interests in the other property, such a recital is
not equivalent to a disposition of such other property, so as to raise a case of
election against the persons who unduly benefit under the will.[9]

1   *Lord Rancliffe v Lady Parkyns* (1818) 6 Dow 149; *Wintour v Clifton* (1856) 8 De GM & G 641.
2   *Blake v Bunbury* (1792) 4 Bro CC 21; *Minchin v Gabbett* [1896] 1 IR 1; and see *Re Sullivan,
    Sullivan v Sullivan* [1917] 1 IR 38; *Re Goodwin* (1905) 5 SRNSW 576; *Re Dicey, Julian v
    Dicey* [1957] Ch 145, [1956] 3 All ER 696 (omission of numbers of houses but identity
    otherwise proved). In *Re Edwards, Macadam v Wright* [1958] Ch 168, [1957] 2 All ER 495, the
    property was specifically mentioned as part of the residue but here it was held that the doctrine
    of ademption applied and no case for election arose.
3   *Pickersgill v Rodger* (1876) 5 Ch D 163; *Cosby v Ashtown* (1859) 10 I Ch R 219; *Thornton v
    Thornton* (1861) 11 I Ch R 474.
4   *Miller v Thurgood* (1864) 33 Beav 496; *Re Bidwell's Settlement Trusts* (1862) 1 New Rep 176.

5   *Dummer v Pitcher* (1833) 2 My & K 262; *Clementson v Gandy* (1836) 1 Keen 309; *Galvin v Devereux* [1903] 1 IR 185. It has been said that evidence is admissible where the devise or bequest is specific: *Graham v Clark (Dorland Estate) and Dorland* [1949] 3 DLR 539.
6   *Dummer v Pitcher* (1833) 2 My & K 262; *Howells v Jenkins* (1863) 1 De GJ & Sm 617; *Henry v Henry* (1872) 6 IR Eq 286. If the testator has only a life interest and the intention on the face of the will is to dispose of his interest (if any), there is no case of election; *Galvin v Devereux* [1903] 1 IR 185. Where a testator disposed of the residue of his property and the will was governed by English law, it was the residue according to English law, and as this included property of his wife to which community of goods applied, the wife must elect: *Re Allen's Estate, Prescott v Allen* [1945] 2 All ER 264.
7   *Wintour v Clifton* (1856) 8 De GM & G 641; *Usticke v Peters* (1858) 4 K & J 437. A bequest to a third person of stock standing in the joint names of the testator and his wife, where benefits are conferred on the wife by the will, puts the wife to her election (*Grosvenor v Durston* (1858) 25 Beav 97). Where a testator agreed to settle property on his niece and then left her a legacy on condition that she gave up her claim to a settlement, she was put to her election: *Central Trust and Safe Deposit Co v Snider* [1916] 1 AC 266.
8   *Stephens v Stephens* (1857) 1 De G & J 62; *Henry v Henry* (1872) 6 IR Eq 286. A devise inconsistent with the continuance of the incumbrance will put the incumbrancers to their election if they are beneficiaries under the will: *Blake v Bunbury* (1972) 1 Ves 514, and cf *Sadlier v Butler* (1867) IR 1 Eq 415; *Re Williams, Cunliffe v Williams* [1915] 1 Ch 450.
9   *Box v Barrett* (1866) LR 3 Eq 244. There is no case for election where a testator, erroneously reciting that a hotchpot clause will apply, refrains from appointing the unappointed residue of a fund: *Langslow v Langslow* (1856) 21 Beav 552.

[42.6]
Election depends on compensation. In applying the doctrine of election, equity proceeds upon the principle not of forfeiture, but of compensation;[1] that is, the beneficiary who elects against the instrument and keeps his own property is not required to abandon all the benefits which are conferred upon him by the instrument. Such benefits are treated in equity as a fund out of which compensation must be made to the disappointed beneficiary; and, after such compensation, the electing beneficiary is entitled to any surplus which may remain.[2] The amount of compensation payable is to be ascertained, in the case of a will, as at the date of the testator's death, and not at the time when the election is made.[3]

1   Per Buckley LJ in *Re Gordon's Will Trusts, National Westminster Bank Ltd v Gordon* [1978] 2 All ER 969 at 979; applying *Brown v Gregson* [1920] AC 860, and *Rogers v Jones* (1876) 3 Ch D 688, not following *Carter v Silber* [1891] 3 Ch 553.
2   *Rogers v Jones* (1876) 3 Ch D 688; *Pickersgill v Rodger* (1876) 5 Ch D 163; *Smith v Lucas* (1881) 18 Ch D 531; *Re Vardon's Trusts* (1884) 28 Ch D 124; *Re Lord Chesham, Cavendish v Dacre* (1886) 31 Ch D 466; *Public Trustee v Beckman* (1914) 15 SRNSW 6; *Gregg v Perpetual Trustee Co* (1918) 18 SRNSW 252; *Kirk v Kirk* (1896) 40 NSR 147. The fund for compensation will where necessary be appointed among the disappointed legatees rateably according to their interests: *Howells v Jenkins* (1863) 1 De GJ & Sm 617. The duty to pay compensation is a personal liability which may be pursued against the estate of the electing beneficiary: *Rogers v Jones* (1877) 7 Ch D 345; *Greenwood v Penny* (1850) 12 Beav 403. Where the person to elect dies and the properties go in different directions, the obligation to compensate falls on those who succeed to the benefits out of which, according to the above rule, compensation ought to have been made: *Pickersgill v Rodger* (1876) 5 Ch D 163.
3   *Re Hancock, Hancock v Pawson* [1905] 1 Ch 16.

[42.7]
No election unless fund for compensation. The doctrine of election cannot be applied, except where, if an election is made contrary to the will, the interest that would pass by the will can be laid hold of to compensate the beneficiary who is

disappointed by the election. Where the beneficial interest of a person who is sought to be made to elect is such that for any reason he cannot be made to submit to that interest being applied in compensating the disappointed parties, the circumstances are such that the doctrine cannot apply.[1] Therefore, in all cases there must be some free disposable property given by the will to the person whom it is sought to put to his election.[2] Thus the doctrine was inapplicable where the interest given to the beneficiary was a determinable life interest on protective trusts because any attempt to make compensation out of that interest would cause a forfeiture of the interest and thus render the fund unavailable for compensation.[3] Where a testator purports to exercise a limited power of appointment by appointing to a stranger, and appoints also to an object of the power, the latter may claim to participate, as in default of appointment, in the share appointed to the stranger, without compensating the stranger out of the properly appointed share. To raise a case of election the testator must both make a direct appointment to a stranger to the power and a gift of the testator's free property to an object of the power.[4]

1   Per Buckley LJ in *Re Gordon's Will Trusts, National Westminster Bank Ltd v Gordon* [1978] 2 All ER 969 at 979.
2   *Re Fowler's Trust* (1859) 27 Beav 362; *Re Aplin's Trust* (1865) 13 WR 1062.
3   *Re Gordon's Will Trusts, National Westminster Bank Ltd v Gordon* [1978] 2 All ER 969, reversing Goulding J's decision [1976] 2 All ER 577. Goulding J had thought himself bound by *McCarogher v Whielden* (1867) LR 3 Eq 236, but that case was concerned with the doctrine of satisfaction, not that of election. The fact that the other beneficiaries were included among the beneficiaries who would be objects of the discretionary trust which would come into play if the elector's determinable life interest was terminated, and thus might benefit from such termination by the acceleration of their interests under the discretionary trust, was immaterial. Anything that such beneficiaries might receive would not be by way of compensation but by virtue of the exercise of the trustee's discretion; per Buckley LJ [1978] 2 All ER 969 at 979.
4   *Whistler v Webster* (1794) 2 Ves 367. An appointment to an object of the power subject to a request to him to give the property to a stranger is insufficient, as the request is void: *Blackett v Lamb* (1851) 14 Beav 482.

[42.8]
Person taking under derivative title. Where a testator purports to dispose of property which is not his own, no case of election arises against a person who take such property by a derivative title (eg under the true owner's will or intestacy) after the testator's death, and who is also a beneficiary under the will.[1] At the date when the will comes into operation he must be in a position to claim in his own right an interest in the property.[2] A beneficiary is not put to his election, because he has a derivative title under another person who was the true owner at the time of the death.[3] Where such other person was also a beneficiary under the will and elected against it, paying compensation, there is the additional consideration that the payment has freed the property from the obligation of further election.[4]

1   *Grissell v Swinhoe* (1869) LR 7 Eq 291. But where a husband conveys property to his wife by deed and then devises the same with other property to her by his will the wife must elect: *Stratford v Powell* (1807) 1 Ball & B 1.
2   It is sufficient if the true owner dies before the testator even though the property at the death of the testator is still subject to the payment of the true owner's debts: *Cooper v Cooper* (1870) 6 Ch App 15; on appeal (1874) LR 7 HL 53.

3   *Cooper v Cooper* (1870) 6 Ch App 15; on appeal (1874) LR 7 HL 53; *Armstrong v Lynn* (1875) IR 9 Eq 186.
4   *Lady Cavan v Pulteney* (1795) 2 Ves 544.

[42.9]

Person electing entitled to information. No person can be required to elect without a clear knowledge of both the funds or properties between which he has to elect.[1] Hence, he is entitled to be allowed time to consider as to his election,[2] and, if necessary, the election will be postponed till accounts of the property concerned have been taken.[3] If there is an action pending, the necessary accounts and inquiries can be taken and made in the action;[4] otherwise, the person who wishes to decide as to election can commence an action to ascertain the value of the properties.[5] An election made before the party has had an opportunity of ascertaining his rights and the value of them,[6] or under a mistake as to matters on which those rights depend,[7] will not be binding; though, if election has once been deliberately made, persons claiming under the electing party are bound thereby without distinct evidence being given that he was aware of his rights.[8]

1   *Whistler v Webster* (1794) 2 Ves 367.
2   *Re Hancock, Hancock v Pawson* [1905] 1 Ch 16 at 19.
3   *Boynton v Boynton* (1785) 1 Bro CC 445.
4   *Douglas v Douglas* (1871) LR 12 Eq 617.
5   *Butricke v Broadhurst* (1790) 1 Ves 171, and see *Douglas v Douglas* (1871) LR 12 Eq 617 at 637.
6   *Pusey v Desbouvrie* (1734) 3 P Wms 315.
7   *Kidney v Coussmaker* (1806) 12 Ves 136.
8   *Dewar v Maitland* (1866) LR 2 Eq 834.

[42.10]

Election where several persons interested. Where several persons are interested in the property disposed of by the testator, and are also beneficiaries under his will, an election by one does not bind the others; and this is so whether they are entitled simultaneously as co-owners,[1] or in succession as tenant for life and remaindermen.[2] All the persons interested have a right to exercise their judgment as to the way in which they will elect.[3] Compensation may be payable inter se by persons electing against the will, that is, by some persons electing against the will to others so electing, and such compensation must then be included by the latter in the benefits taken by them under the will.[4]

1   *Fytche v Fytche* (1868) LR 7 Eq 494.
2   *Hutchison v Skelton* (1856) 2 Macq 492.
3   *Fytche v Fytche* (1868) LR 7 Eq 494.
4   *Re Booth, Booth v Robinson* [1906] 2 Ch 321.

[42.11]

Time for election. A person required by the court to elect within a specified time will, if he does not elect within that time, be treated as having elected against the instrument.[1] But otherwise no definite time limit can be assigned for election; and, if the party is neither required to elect, nor does any acts from which election can be inferred, his right to elect will remain open until it becomes inequitable to assert it.[2] This will be the case if he has allowed the

property devised away from himself to be enjoyed for a long time by the
devisee.[3]

1   *Streatfield v Streatfield* (1735) 1 Swan 436n.
2   *Butricke v Broadhurst* (1790) 1 Ves 171; *Brice v Brice* (1828) 2 Mol 21. The election will relate
     back to the death and the person electing may be liable to account for sums received under the
     will where he or she elects against the will: *Davis v Davis* (1896) 27 OR 532.
3   *Tibbits v Tibbits* (1816) 19 Ves 656 (where the period of time was ten years).

[42.12]

Implied election. Election is a question of fact.[1] It may be express, or may be
implied from the acts of the person bound to elect. To constitute an implied
election there must be clear proof that the person put to his election was aware
of the nature and extent of his rights; and that, having that knowledge, he
intended to elect.[2] Where there has been ignorance of the right, an enjoyment of
the benefits conferred by the will for a considerable time will not prevent the
party from claiming to elect.[3] But where, with knowledge of his obligation to
elect, a person enjoys property given by the will or exercises acts of ownership
over it, he will be held to have elected to confirm the will, and will be debarred
from keeping his own property as well.[4] Similar acts in relation to his own
property will show an election against the will.[5] It is necessary, however, to have
regard to the history of both the properties between which election was to be
made, and possession of or acts of ownership over both will raise no
presumption of election.[6] An implied election is binding on the representatives
of the person electing,[7] though, if, notwithstanding the acceptance of benefits,
the election has been left doubtful, the representative may, perhaps, elect on
renouncing the benefits and paying compensation.[8]

1   *Roundel v Currer* (1786) 2 Bro CC 67. Where the will required a party to execute a settlement
     and while the interests to be settled were still in reversion, the party wrote to the trustees of the
     will saying he intended to execute the settlement, it was held that he had not bound himself so
     as to make an irrevocable election: *Re Shepherd, Harris v Shepherd* [1943] Ch 8, [1942] 2 All
     ER 584.
2   *Worthington v Wiginton* (1855) 20 Beav 67; *Spread v Morgan* (1865) 11 HL Cas 588;
     Sweetman v Sweetman (1868) IR 2 Eq 141.
3   *Wake v Wake* (1791) 3 Bro CC 255; *Reynard v Spence* (1841) 4 Beav 103; *Rathborne v Lord
     Aldborough* (1831) Hayes 207; *Fidelity Trust Co of Ontario v Purdham and Northern Life
     Assurance Co of Canada* [1930] SCR 119.
4   *Worthington v Wiginton* (1855) 20 Beav 67; *Whitley v Whitley* (1862) 31 Beav 173.
5   A sale of the property; for example, see *Rogers v Jones* (1876) 3 Ch D 688, or granting a lease;
     see *Martin v Martin* (1904) 8 OLR 462.
6   *Padbury v Clark* (1850) 2 Mac & G 298; *Morgan v Morgan* (1853) 4 I Ch R 606; *Spread v
     Morgan* (1865) 11 HL Cas 588 at 613.
7   *Dewar v Maitland* (1866) LR 2 Eq 834. Cases of implied election generally occur after the
     death of the party to elect, because while he is alive, he can contradict the implication.
8   *Dillon v Parker* (1818) 1 Swan 359 at 385.

[42.13]

Persons of unsound mind. The Court of Protection has power to direct a
committee or Receiver to elect on behalf of a person of unsound mind, if
satisfied after due enquiry that such a course would be for the benefit of the
patient.[1]

1   Mental Health Act 1983, s 99; 28 *Halsbury's Statutes* (4th edn) 968.

[42.14]

Minors. Where the person to elect is a minor, the court, if there is no doubt as to what is for his benefit, elects for him at the hearing of the matter in which the question arises;[1] if there is doubt, an inquiry is directed to ascertain what course is for the benefit of the minor, and the court elects in accordance with the result of the inquiry.[2]

1   *Re Montagu, Faber v Montagu* [1896] 1 Ch 549; *Morrison v Bell* (1843) 5 I Eq R 354.
2   *Bennett v Houldsworth* (1877) 6 Ch D 671 at 680.

[42.15]

Wills not made in England. Where a will is invalid as to immovables but valid as to movables, the heir claiming against the will is put to his election, wherever the law of the testator's domicile so provides[1] irrespective of the law of the place where the immovable is situate,[2] but where the latter law prevents legal effect being given to any such election when made, no election can be imposed.[3]

1   Provided the law of the domicile recognises the principle of election in such a case, this becomes a mere matter of construction. Most cases are concerned with wills of domiciled Englishmen invalid to pass Scots real estate, and it appears that words referring specifically or by necessary implication to the real estate are required before the heir can be put to election. For cases where the intention has been sufficiently shown, see *Dundas v Dundas* (1830) 2 Dow & Cl 349; *Orrell v Orrell* (1871) 6 Ch App 302; and for cases where it has been insufficiently proved, see *Johnson v Telford* (1830) 1 Russ & M 244; *Maxwell v Maxwell* (1852) 2 De GM & G 705; *Maxwell v Hyslop* (1867) LR 4 Eq 407; *Dewar v Maitland* (1866) LR 2 Eq 834; *Baring v Ashburton* (1886) 54 LT 463. Where the will contemplates application of English law, the doctrine is applicable: *Re Allen's Estate, Prescott v Allen and Beaumont* [1945] 2 All ER 264.
2   *Re De Virte, Vaiani v De Virte* [1915] 1 Ch 920; *Re Ogilvie, Ogilvie v Ogilvie* [1918] 1 Ch 492.
3   *Brown v Gregson* [1920] AC 860 (impossible by the law of the Argentine, which recognised no trusts of land, for the beneficiaries to render the land in the Argentine subject to the trusts of the will).

[42.16]

Mutual obligation. Analogous to the doctrine of election applicable to wills, there is also a form of election under a deed that can be noted shortly under the heading of mutual obligation.[1] Where A and B enter into a mutual settlement under which A settles property on trust under which B has a beneficial interest, and B covenants to settle property on trusts under which A or C will be entitled to a beneficial interest, and if for some reason (as, for example, that B was a minor at the date of the covenant) B can repudiate his or her obligation to bring property into the settlement and does so, equity will compel B to submit to A or C, as the case may be, being compensated out of B's beneficial interest in A's trust fund, so far as practicable, for being deprived of his, A's or C's beneficial interest in B's intended trust fund.[2] Although the circumstances in which equity intervenes in such a case are different from the circumstances of election under a will, the equitable remedy is of the same character in each case for equity lays hold of B's beneficial interest under the disposition for the purpose of compensating the disappointed party thereout, but only interferes with B's enjoyment of it to the extent necessary to achieve compensation.[3]

1   *Re Gordon's Will Trusts, National Westminster Bank Ltd v Gordon* [1978] 2 All ER 969 at 973, per Buckley LJ.

2   *Re Gordon's Will Trusts, National Westminster Bank Ltd v Gordon* [1978] 2 All ER 969 at 973, per Buckley LJ.

3   *Re Gordon's Will Trusts, National Westminster Bank Ltd v Gordon* [1978] 2 All ER 969 at 973, per Buckley LJ. See *Vardon's Trusts* (1885) 31 Ch D 275; and *Carter v Silber* [1891] 3 Ch 553. In the former case the doctrine of election was held not to operate because, by reason of the restraint on anticipation attached to the wife's beneficial interest, the wife could not divest herself of the right to receive each instalment of income as it accrued. The latter case was criticised in *Re Gordon's Will Trusts, National Westminster Bank Ltd v Gordon* [1978] 2 All ER 969, since the decision seemed to ignore the feature that the equitable doctrine of election is concerned with compensating disappointed parties out of some beneficial interest of the elector, but is not concerned with forfeiting his beneficial interest. See also *Codrington v Lindsay* (1873) 8 Ch App 578; *Anderson v Abbott* (1857) 23 Beav 457; and *Brown v Brown* (1866) LR 2 Eq 481.

CHAPTER 43

Estoppel

I. PROPRIETARY ESTOPPEL

[43.1]
General principles. It is beyond the scope of this text to set out in detail the principles relating to proprietary estoppel as they have been developed in the modern law. But it can be noted that the doctrine can operate to affect a testamentary gift of property which is claimed by another relying on proprietary estoppel. The principles of proprietary estoppel are founded on representation, reliance and detriment[1] and can be stated in broad terms as follows. Where one person (A) has acted to his detriment on the faith of a belief which was known to and encouraged by another person (B) that he has or is going to be given a right in or over B's property, B cannot insist on his strict legal rights if to do so would be inconsistent with A's belief.[2] This has been applied to a situation where a claimant worked on the testator's farm for 40 years (for allegedly less than full remuneration) on the reliance of repeated assurances by the testator that he would leave the claimant the bulk of his estate including the farm, by his will on his death.[3] The testator made a new will excluding the claimant entirely from inheriting. The claimant succeeded in an action against the estate, claiming an equity in the testator's property under the doctrine of proprietary estoppel, arising from reliance in the testator's assurances causing him detriment.[4] The doctrine has also been applied in favour of a claimant in a case of intestacy.[5]

---

1 See, for example, *Plimmer v Mayor of Wellington* (1884) 9 App Cas 699, at 714; *Crabb v Arun District Council* [1975] 3 All ER 865 at 880; *Greasley v Cooke* [1980] 3 All ER 710 and *Grant v Edwards* [1986] Ch 638, [1986] 2 All ER 426.

2 Per Balcombe LJ in *Wayling v Jones* (1993) 69 P & CR 170 at p 172, citing Mr Nugee's statement of principle in *Re Basham* [1987] 1 All ER 405 at 410.

3 *Gillett v Holt* [2001] Ch 210, [2000] 2 All ER 289, Court of Appeal reversing Carnwath J at first instance [1998] 3 All ER 917 who had rejected the claim. This was a case where the facts supporting an estoppel were strong; it is not every promise or assurance of inheritance which will give rise to a successful claim under this head.

4 *Re Basham* [1987] 1 All ER 405, was applied and *Taylor v Dickens* [1998] 3 FCR 455 not followed. See also *Layton v Martin* [1986] 2 FLR 227 and *Jones v Watkins* [1987] CA Transcript 1200.

5 *Re Basham* [1987] 1 All ER 405. The claimant worked for many years, without payment, for her stepfather in the expectation of inheriting his estate; the stepfather died intestate. It was held that since her expectation had been encouraged by the deceased and she had acted to her detriment in reliance on that belief, she was entitled to the estate.

II.   GENERAL POINTS

[43.2]

Life interest acquired under will. Where possession has been acquired ostensibly under a testamentary disposition creating a life interest in property to which the testator had no title, and the person so taking possession subsequently obtains against the true owner a title under the Limitation Act, he is estopped from setting up that title against the person or persons interested in remainder under the same will.[1] This estoppel binds all persons who are privy in estate to such tenant for life, so that anyone claiming under the intestacy of the tenant for life is estopped against the remainderman or those claiming under him from denying that the will is valid.[2]

1   *Hawksbee v Hawksbee* (1853) 11 Hare 230; *Anstee v Nelms* (1856) 1 H & N 225 at 232; *Asher v Whitlock* (1865) LR 1 QB 1; *Board v Board* (1872) LR 9 QB 48; *Dalton v Fitzgerald* [1897] 2 Ch 86; *Kemaghan v M'Nally* (1861) 12 I Ch R 89 (where the devise was to trustees in trust for beneficiaries and it was held that the effect of the Statute of Limitations was to vest the legal estate in the trustees).
2   See n 1 supra.

[43.3]

Testator with good title for life but no power of testamentary disposition. On the other hand, when the testator has a good title to the property in his lifetime but no power of testamentary disposition, and purports to devise such property, a person entering under such devise or as entitled on the intestacy of the testator is not estopped from setting up a title under the Limitation Act against the person properly entitled or those claiming under him;[1] nor is the tenant for life under an invalid devise, or those claiming under him, estopped from disputing the title of the remainderman under the same invalid devise,[2] because the devise itself, and not merely the title, is invalid and defective and of no effect. It would appear that when the testator neither had a good title nor in fact purported to devise the property, but a person enters ostensibly under the will or under a settlement purporting to be made in pursuance of the will, that person is estopped from setting up a title under the Limitation Act.[3]

1   *Paine v Jones* (1874) LR 18 Eq 320; *Re Anderson, Pegler v Gillatt* [1905] 2 Ch 70; *Re Coole, Coole v Flight* [1920] 2 Ch 536.
2   *Re Stringer's Estate, Shaw v Jones-Ford* (1877) 6 Ch D 1 at 10; *Re Tennent's Estate* [1913] 1 IR 280.
3   *Dalton v Fitzgerald* [1897] 2 Ch 86 at 91.

[43.4]

Approbation and reprobation. The principle that a man may not both approbate and reprobate has already been referred to[1] in considering questions of election, and a similar question arises on the binding effect of probate proceedings. A person who, though not a party to the proceedings and not bound by the judgment therein, knowing all the circumstances and deliberately taking the benefit of the judgment, has stood by when he might have taken steps, by becoming a party or otherwise, to controvert it, cannot afterwards raise the question determined by the proceedings a second time.[2] This applies both to decisions relating to the construction of a will[3] and to decisions relating to the validity of the will.[4]

1   See Chapter 42.
2   *Re Lart, Wilkinson v Blades* [1896] 2 Ch 788 at 795; *Re King, Jackson v A-G* [1917] 2 Ch 420 (legatee accepting result of compromise of probate action).
3   *Re Lart, Wilkinson v Blades* [1896] 2 Ch 788 at 795. An order appointing a person to represent a class does not affect one of the class who claims a distinct and independent right so far as concerns that right: ibid at 793.
4   *Wytcherley v Andrews* (1871) LR 2 P & D 327, and see *Priestman v Thomas* (1884) 9 PD 210; *Young v Holloway* [1895] P 87; *Ritchie v Malcolm* [1902] 2 IR 403. A person who appears in a probate action as a party in his own right cannot afterwards contend that he was not cited to appear in a particular capacity: *Beardsley v Beardsley* [1899] 1 QB 746, and see *Concha v Concha* (1886) 11 App Cas 541. See n 3, as to person representing a class. But an administrator in an originating summons against him cannot challenge the fact that he is administrator and therefore may subsequently apply to have the grant of administration revoked and a grant of probate made to him: *Dooley v Dooley* [1927] IR 190.

[43.5]
Condition non-performance of which favours executor. It has already been pointed out that an executor is not obliged to tell a legatee of a condition attached to his gift and that, if he fails to perform the condition, the executor himself will benefit.[1]

1   See para **[30.32]** supra.

[43.6]
Hotchpot clause. If, in connection with a hotchpot clause, the testator sets out in his will the amounts of the advances made, the beneficiaries are bound by it though the stated amounts may be erroneous[1] even though the amount stated is too small.[2] But in a statement concerning a loan to be repaid or in course of repayment or where the will states that so much thereof as remains unpaid is to be brought into account, the true state of the accounts may be ascertained.[3]

1   *Re Wood, Ward v Wood* (1886) 32 Ch D 517; *Re Aird's Estate, Aird v Quick* (1879) 12 Ch D 291, not followed in *Re Kelsey, Woolley v Kelsey* [1905] 2 Ch 465.
2   *Burrowes v Lord Clonbrock* (1891) 27 LR IR 538.
3   *Re Taylor's Estate, Tomlin v Underhay* (1881) 22 Ch D 495; *Re Kelsey, Woolley v Kelsey* [1905] 2 Ch 465.

CHAPTER 44

Satisfaction

[44.1]

Different cases of satisfaction. Satisfaction is the donation of a thing with the intention that it shall be taken either wholly or partly in extinguishment of some prior claim of the donee.[1] It may occur (i) when a covenant to settle property is followed by a gift by will or settlement in favour of the person entitled beneficially under the covenant;[2] (ii) when a testamentary disposition is followed during the testator's lifetime by a gift or settlement in favour of the devisee or legatee;[3] and (iii) when a legacy is given to a creditor.[4] In all these cases the question of satisfaction is one of the intention of the settlor or testator;[5] and, if he expressly declares that the later disposition is to be in satisfaction of the earlier obligation or disposition, the matter is governed by this expression of his intention, and effect is given to the later disposition accordingly.[6] In the absence of such expression, certain presumptions as to his intention are raised in equity, and evidence, intrinsic and, in certain cases, extrinsic, may be used to rebut or to support such presumptions.[7] A case of satisfaction only arises where the person who makes the payment is himself the party bound to pay, or is the owner of the estate charged with the payment;[8] or is exercising a power of appointment.[9] The three cases stated above are shortly described as (i) satisfaction of portions by legacies or subsequent portions; (ii) ademption of legacies by portions; and (iii) satisfaction of debts by legacies. In the first two cases the court leans in favour of satisfaction; in the third case it leans against it.[10]

1   See the definition in 2 White & Tud LC (9th edn) p 326, adopted by Lord Romilly in *Lord Chichester v Coventry* (1867) LR 2 HL 71 at 95. The rule or presumption against double portions has been developed by judge-made law and is founded in good sense and adapted to the ordinary transactions of mankind which will change over time; per Lindsay J in *Re Cameron, Phillips v Cameron* [1999] 2 All ER 924 at 949; see para **[44.3]**, nn 3 and 4. It has no application where the prior claim has been paid: *Re Mark* (1921) 64 DLR 516.
2   See *Hinchcliffe v Hinchcliffe* (1797) 3 Ves 516; *Weall v Rice* (1831) 2 Russ & M 251; *Lady Thynne v Earl of Glengall* (1848) 2 HL Cas 131; *Scott (Scott's Trustees)* (1912) 50 SLR 299.
3   *Ex p Pye, Ex p Dubost* (1811) 18 Ves 140; *Pym v Lockyer* (1841) 5 My & Cr 29. This, though similar in its effect to satisfaction, is strictly ademption *Lord Chichester v Coventry* (1867) LR 2 HL 71 at 90; *Re Moore's Rents* [1917] 1 IR 244; see the rule stated in *Trimmer v Bayne* (1802) 7 Ves 508 at 515. The settlement may be by way of covenant to pay: *Cooper v MacDonald* (1873) LR 16 Eq 258.
4   *Talbott v Duke of Shrewsbury* (1714) Prec Ch 394.
5   This was emphasised by Lindsay J in *Re Cameron, Phillips v Cameron* [1999] 2 All ER 924 at 941, (discussed para **[44.3]**, nn 3 and 4) citing *Montefiore v Guedalla* (1859) 1 De GF & J 93; *Pym v Lockyer* (1841) 5 My & Cr 29 and *Re Vaux* [1938] 4 All ER 703, amongst others. See also *Weall v Rice* (1831) 2 Russ & M 251 at 265; *Hopwood v Hopwood* (1859) 7 HL Cas 728 at

737; *Lord Chichester v Coventry* (1867) LR 2 HL 71 at 82. Hence regard must be paid to the circumstances at the date of the instrument alleged to constitute satisfaction, and not to the actual result: *Cartwright v Cartwright* [1903] 2 Ch 306. And see *Warner v Latouche* (1855) 8 Ir Jur 34; *Leneham v Wall* [1922] 1 IR 59.

6   *Davis v Chambers* (1857) 7 De GM & G 386; see *Twisden v Twisden* (1804) 9 Ves 413; *Hardingham v Thomas* (1854) 2 Drew 353; *Scott (Scott's Trustees)* (1912) 50 SLR 299; *Re Eardley's Will, Simeon v Freemantle* [1920] 1 Ch 397. But a direction that portions are to be deemed to be satisfied by subsequent advances made by a specified person during his life is not operative as regards benefits passing under his will: *Cooper v Cooper* (1873) 8 Ch App 813; or on his intestacy: *Twisden v Twisden* (1804) 9 Ves 413; and see *Cooper v Cooper* (1873) 8 Ch App 813, as to certain inconsistencies in the earlier cases. When the testator states in his will that annuities given after his will are to be taken as satisfied by similar bequests, an annuity given before the will is not taken as so satisfied especially where the annuity given by the will is not so advantageous to the beneficiary: *Re Van den Bergh's Will Trusts, Van den Bergh v Simpson* [1948] 1 All ER 935.

7   See Chapter 57.

8   *Samuel v Ward* (1856) 22 Beav 347 at 350.

9   *Re Ashton, Ingram v Papillon* [1897] 2 Ch 574; revsd on other grounds [1898] 1 Ch 142, CA; but see *Re Eardley's Will, Simeon v Freemantle* [1920] 1 Ch 397.

10   *Lady Thynne v Earl of Glengall* (1848) 2 HL Cas 131 at 153. A question as to presumption against double gifts arises also where legacies are left to the same person by different testamentary instruments, or different legacies by the same instrument; as to this, see *Ridges v Morrison* (1784) 1 Bro CC 389 at 393; *Coote v Boyd* (1789) 2 Bro CC 521; *Benyon v Benyon* (1810) 17 Ves 34; *Currie v Pye* (1811) 17 Ves 462; *Hurst v Beach* (1821) 5 Madd 351; *Yockney v Hansard* (1844) 3 Hare 620; *Lee v Pain* (1845) 4 Hare 201; *Roch v Callen* (1848) 6 Hare 531; *Whyte v Whyte* (1873) LR 17 Eq 50.

[44.2]
Presumption of satisfaction of portion by legacy and legacy by portion. In the cases of a portion followed by a legacy, and of a legacy followed by a portion, where the gifts are substantially of the same nature and in favour of the same person, there arises a presumption of satisfaction (i) where the settlor and testator is the parent of the donee, or has placed themselves in loco parentis to the donee;[1] or (ii) where the first disposition is expressed to be made for a specific purpose, and the second disposition effects that purpose. In the first case the presumption is founded on the leaning of the court against double portions;[2] in the second it is founded upon the intention of the testator or settlor as appearing from the instruments and from the circumstances of the later disposition.[3] The presumption arises also as regards two dispositions, both expressed to be made for the purpose of satisfying the same moral obligation.[4]

1   If a child has to account on the footing of satisfaction, persons claiming under him are under the same liability. *Re Scott, Langton v Scott* [1903] 1 Ch 1. But the liability of children taking the share of their deceased parent is not on the footing of the parent's indebtedness to the testator: *Re Binns, Public Trustee v Ingle* [1929] 1 Ch 677. In the modern law the rule is expressed as applying to the parent not just the father of a child; see *Re Cameron, Phillips v Cameron* [1999] Ch 386, [1999] 2 All ER 924; see discussed para **[44.3]**, nn 3 and 4. The rule against double portions to children does not apply in Scotland: *Johnstone v Haviland* [1896] AC 95.

2   See *Ex p Pye, Ex p Dubost* (1811) 18 Ves 140 at 151, per Lord Eldon LC; *Weall v Rice* (1831) 2 Russ & M 251 at 267; *Lord Chichester v Coventry* (1867) LR 2 HL 71 at 86; *Montagu v Earl of Sandwich* (1886) 32 Ch D 525 at 534, CA; *Re Lacon, Lacon v Lacon* [1891] 2 Ch 482 at 492, CA, per Lindley LJ; at 497, per Bowen LJ.

3   See *Monck v Lord Monck* (1810) 1 Ball & B 298 at 303, per Lord Manners LC; and cf *Roome v Roome* (1744) 3 Atk 181 at 183; *Powel v Cleaver* (1789) 2 Bro CC 499; *Re Smythies, Weyman v Smythies* [1903] 1 Ch 259; *Re Furness, Furness v Stalkartt* [1901] 2 Ch 346 at 349; *Re Corbett, Corbett v Lord Cobham* [1903] 2 Ch 326; *Re Jupp, Harris v Grierson* [1922] 2 Ch 359. But there is no satisfaction where the dispositions are expressed to have different objects:

Re Aynsley, Kyrle v Turner [1915] 1 Ch 172. In *Pankhurst v Howell* (1870) 6 Ch App 136, a legacy of a sum of money to the testator's wife to be paid within ten days of his death was not adeemed by a gift of the same amount made during his last illness in order that she might have money in hand on his death, but as to debt to the wife paid off in the testator's lifetime, see *Re Fletcher, Gillings v Fletcher* (1888) 38 Ch D 373 at 377. A legacy is not satisfied by a subsequent gift to the legatee expressed in a letter to be in substitution for the legacy if the letter is not communicated to the legatee in the testator's lifetime: *Re Shields, Corbould-Ellis v Dales* [1912] 1 Ch 591. There is no presumption of satisfaction of a *donatio mortis causa* by a bequest of the same amount contained in a will executed after the gift: *Hudson v Spencer* [1910] 2 Ch 285.

4   *Re Pollock, Pollock v Worrall* (1885) 28 Ch D 552, followed in *Re Sparrow* [1967] VR 739 (testamentary gift of income to a spouse, intended to be for her maintenance, was adeemed by a provision for her maintenance in a subsequent separation agreement). In *Re Jupp, Harris v Grierson* [1922] 2 Ch 359, no moral obligation was specified.

[44.3]
Ademption of a legacy by an inter vivos portion. This presumption has been fully stated by the Earl of Selborne LC as follows.[1]

'Where a testator gives a legacy to a child, or to any other person towards whom he has taken on himself parental obligations, and afterwards makes a gift or enters into a binding contract in his lifetime in favour of the same legatee, then (unless there be a distinction between the nature and conditions of the two gifts, of a kind not in this case material) there is a presumption prima facie that both gifts were made to fulfil the same natural or moral obligation of providing for the legatee; and consequently that the gift inter vivos is either wholly or in part a substitution for, or an "ademption" of the legacy'.[2]

It has been held in a recent case that for the purpose of the rule against double portions, a gift for the benefit of a child is capable of being a portion, if it was made by either parent.[3] Moreover, while the rule required there to be two portions which benefited the same person, a gift could be for a person's benefit even though it did not come into his hands, so that a gift by a grandparent for the benefit of a grandchild could be taken to be for the benefit of the grandchild's parent.[4]

1   *Re Pollock* (1885) 28 Ch D 552 at 555.
2   Thus this category is more properly termed an 'ademption' rather than a 'satisfaction', see *Montefiore v Guedalla* (1859) 1 De GF & J 93 at 100 and should perhaps more properly be distinguished from the cases of satisfaction as being possibly subject to different rules. See the full exposition and examination of the case law on the topic by Lindsay J in *Re Cameron, Phillips v Cameron* [1999] Ch 386, [1999] 2 All ER 924, discussed at nn 3 and 4.
3   *Re Cameron, Phillips v Cameron* [1999] Ch 386, [1999] 2 All ER 924 per Lindsay J; an interesting and informative case where most of the previous authorities on this presumption were reviewed and considered.
4   *Re Cameron, Phillips v Cameron* [1999] Ch 386, [1999] 2 All ER 924. By her will a mother left her residuary estate to her four sons equally. Payments were made by the mother's attorneys under an enduring power of attorney towards the cost of the education of the son of the defendant—who was one of the mother's sons. Held, the payments were in the nature of portions and as such adeemed pro tanto that son's share in his mother's residuary estate.

[44.4]
Both gifts must be in nature of portions. The presumptions of satisfaction of both portions by legacies and legacies by portions, only arise when the two gifts are in the nature of portions.[1] A portion is a sum of money given to a child by

way of advancement, on marriage or for the purpose of establishing him in business,[2] or to pay for education[3] and in general it is only such a gift which will operate as a satisfaction of a prior gift.[4] Though it has been said that where a large sum has been given and nothing is known as to the circumstances, it will be treated as raising the presumption of satisfaction,[5] it has also been held that where the inference from the will is that the gift is mere bounty, the burden is on those setting up satisfaction to prove it.[6] It follows that gifts of small sums,[7] or payments of an annuity during the lifetime of the testator,[8] will not raise the presumption. Moreover, in the case of ademption the gift must be subsequent to the date of the will.[9]

1   *Re Lacon, Lacon v Lacon* [1891] 2 Ch 482 at 498, per Bowen LJ. There is no presumption of satisfaction where two portions are derived from different estates: *Douglas v Willes* (1849) 7 Hare 318 at 328. But a sum appointed under a special power may be a portion within the presumption of satisfaction: *Montague v Montague* (1852) 15 Beav 565; *Re Peel's Settlement, Biddulph v Peel* [1911] 2 Ch 165. See *Re Ashton, Ingram v Papillon* [1897] 2 Ch 574 at 579; *Re Newton King* [1953] NZLR 245.

2   *Taylor v Taylor* (1875) LR 20 Eq 155 at 158, per Jessel MR: see *Schofield v Heap* (1858) 27 Beav 93; *Re Lacon, Lacon v Lacon* [1891] 2 Ch 482, CA; *Re Watney, Watney v Gold* (1911) 56 Sol Jo 109; *Barry v Harding* (1844) 7 I Eq R 313. And it must be a benefit provided by the settlor, not merely a liability which he has incurred to the child—for example, by breach of trust: *Crichton v Crichton* [1895] 2 Ch 853 at 859.

3   See *Re Cameron, Phillips v Cameron* [1999] Ch 386r, [1999] 2 All ER 924, where provisions (in effect) by a grandmother to pay for the education of a grandchild were held to be portions benefiting the child's parent, ie the donor's son. See further discussed in para **[44.3]**, nn 3 and 4.

4   *Re Scott, Langton v Scott* [1903] 1 Ch 1. Formerly, money provided by a father to pay his son's debts was treated as an advance: *Boyd v Boyd* (1867) LR 4 Eq 305; *Re Blockley, Blockley v Blockley* (1885) 29 Ch D 250; but the view of Jessel MR in *Taylor v Taylor* (1875) LR 20 Eq 155, has prevailed, and the provision of sums for such a purpose does not raise a presumption of satisfaction: *Re Scott, Langton v Scott* [1903] 1 Ch 1. In *Re George's Will Trusts, Barclay's Bank Ltd v George* [1949] Ch 154, [1948] 2 All ER 1004, a gift of farming stock which had been valued in money and the taking over of the lease of the farm was held to be in the nature of a portion.

5   *Leighton v Leighton* (1874) LR 18 Eq 458 at 468; *Re Scott, Langton v Scott* [1903] 1 Ch 1 at 13, 16. And where a testator becomes of unsound mind after directing by his will advances out of surplus income to be brought into hotchpot, the court has a discretion as to enforcing this requirement: *Re Merrall, Greener v Merrall* [1924] 1 Ch 45.

6   *Re Livesey's Settlement Trusts, Livesey v Livesey* [1953] 2 All ER 723, [1953] 1 WLR 1114 (gifts of mortgage debts substantial in amount accompanied by other gifts held not to be a satisfaction unless facts were proved to show that intention).

7   *Schofield v Heap* (1858) 27 Beav 93; *Watson v Watson* (1864) 33 Beav 574; *Re Peacock's Estate* (1872) LR 14 Eq 236 at 240. The court has never added up small sums in order to show that if the child claims those sums as well as the larger provision made for him by the parent, he would be taking a double portion: *Suisse v Lowther* (1843) 2 Hare 424 at 434, per Wigram V-C. As to evidence whether a cheque is given as a gift or a loan, see *Re England, England v Garnett* (1912) 134 LT Jo 29.

8   See *Hatfield v Minet* (1878) 8 Ch D 136, CA.

9   Gifts made before the date of the will cannot operate as a satisfaction (*Re Peacock's Estate* (1872) LR 14 Eq 236; *Taylor v Cartwright* (1872) LR 14 Eq 167 at 176; *Leighton v Leighton* (1874) LR 18 Eq 458) unless so agreed by the donee; *Upton v Prince* (1735) Cas temp Talb 71.

[44.5]

Satisfaction pro tanto. The doctrine of satisfaction does not require that the second provision should be equal in value to or greater than the first; a smaller provision will, in a case which is otherwise suitable for raising the presumption, be a satisfaction pro tanto of the earlier provision;[1] and, in the case of ademption, a later smaller provision does not destroy altogether the provision in the will; it only destroys it pro tanto.[2] The value of the provision given by a subsequent settlement must be ascertained as at the date of the settlement, and the amount deducted from the legacy.[3]

1 *Warren v Warren* (1783) 1 Bro CC 305; *Lady Thynne v Earl of Glengall* (1848) 2 HL Cas 131 at 154; *Edgeworth v Johnston* (1878) IR 11 Eq 326; *Re Moore's Rents* [1917] 1 IR 244.
2 *Re Cameron, Phillips v Cameron* [1999] Ch 386r, [1999] 2 All ER 924, where the cases cited in this note were applied. There was at one time an impression that ademption by a smaller gift might destroy the provision in the will entirely (*Ex p Pye, Ex p Dubost* (1811) 18 Ves 140 at 151), but the cases were reviewed by Lord Cottenham LC in *Pym v Lockyer* (1841) 5 My & Cr 29, and he held that in such a case the ademption took effect only pro tanto, and this has been accepted as the settled rule: *Kirk v Eddowes* (1844) 3 Hare 509; *Re Pollock, Pollock v Worrall* (1885) 28 Ch D 552; *Re Jupp, Harris v Grierson* [1922] 2 Ch 359.
3 *Watson v Watson* (1864) 33 Beav 574; *Re Innes, Barclay v Innes* (1908) 125 LT Jo 60. And similarly the value of settled funds to be brought into account under a hotchpot clause in a will is the value at the date of the settlement, and not at the date of the will: *Re Crocker, Crocker v Crocker* [1916] 1 Ch 25.

[44.6]
Double portions and inheritance tax. Where a gift contained in a will is held to be adeemed by a gift inter vivos made to the same beneficiary, with the consequence that the gift inter vivos has to be brought into account against the gift made in the will, then it is thought that the gift inter vivos is to be brought in at its value after the payment of any inheritance tax payable by the donee.[1] Similarly the value of the residuary estate, against which the gift inter vivos is to be brought in, is the net value, after deduction of inheritance tax.[2] The position is different however where the advances have to be brought into hotchpot against a fund which bears its own tax.[3]

1 By reason of the gift being made within seven years of the death. Analogous to the position under estate duty; see *Re Beddington, Micholls v Samuel* [1900] 1 Ch 771; *Re Crocker, Crocker v Crocker* [1916] 1 Ch 25.
2 Likewise analogous to the position under estate duty; see *Re Turner's Will Trusts, Westminster Bank Ltd v Turner* [1968] 1 All ER 321, [1968] 1 WLR 227 (the gift by will was a share of residue which was bequeathed out of a net fund; the testator left no realty and estate duty on free personalty was a testamentary expense) following *Re Beddington, Micholls v Samuel* [1900] 1 Ch 771.
3 *Re Tollemache, Forbes v Public Trustee* [1930] WN 138 (where the advances were directed to be taken into account against the gross value of the settled fund); *Re Slee, Midland Bank Executor and Trustee Co Ltd v Slee* [1962] 1 All ER 542, [1962] 1 WLR 496.

[44.7]
In case of satisfaction of obligation, donee may elect. In a case of ademption the beneficiary has no choice as to whether he will take the earlier or the later provision. The earlier depends solely on the bounty of the testator, and the ademption operates by way of revocation of the bounty, either wholly or in part.[1] Where, however, a settlor has by a settlement undertaken an obligation, he has not the right of terminating that obligation by the substitution of a different provision by his will or by a later settlement.[2] Hence where such different provision would operate as satisfaction, so that the beneficiary cannot take both provisions, he is entitled to elect between the two.[3]

1   As was the effect of the pro tanto ademption in *Re Cameron, Phillips v Cameron* [1999] Ch 386, [1999] 2 All ER 924, discussed in para **[44.3]**, nn 3 and 4.

2   Without the consent of those entitled under the settlement he may have chosen to substitute the benefits he may have chosen to confer by his will for those which he had already secured by deed: *Lord Chichester v Coventry* (1867) LR 2 HL 71 at 87, per Lord Cranworth.

3   *Lord Chichester v Coventry* (1867) LR 2 HL 71 at 91, per Lord Romilly MR; see *Hinchcliffe v Hinchcliffe* (1797) 3 Ves 516 at 528; *Lady Thynne v Earl of Glengall* (1848) 2 HL Cas 131 at 155; and cf *Pole v Lord Somers* (1801) 6 Ves 309.

[44.8]

Person in loco parentis. The presumption against double portions arises when the provisions are made by a parent of[1], or by a person in loco parentis to, the donee.[2] A person is in loco parentis when he has placed himself in the situation of the lawful parent of the donee,[3] so far as such situation relates to the duty of the parent to make provisions for the donee.[4] Whether a person has placed himself in this relation is a question of fact as to which parol evidence is admissible.[5] The relation will be readily inferred where the donee resides with, and is maintained by, the donor;[6] or if the donee is an orphan and is maintained by the donor, though not residing with him.[7] But a donor may be in loco parentis to a donee where the donee has a father living, and resides with and is maintained by the father, especially if the donor contributes to the family income.[8] The mere leaving of a legacy does not show an intention on the part of the testator to place himself in loco parentis to the legatee.[9] A grandfather or a collateral relation is in the position of a stranger for the purpose of the rule, and evidence must be given of his intention to put himself in loco parentis.[10] It used to be held that a father was in a similar position in respect of his illegitimate child;[11] but in such a case there is an obvious duty to make provision for the child, and probably the presumption would now arise without evidence.[12] Though the gifts are construed as portions, if the object is to bring the donees upon an equal footing, the presumption against double portions is not applicable.[13]

1   The previous view that only a provision by a father could amount to a portion, no longer represents the law; see *Re Cameron, Phillips v Cameron* [1999] 2 All ER 924 at 939, applying *Pym v Lockyer* (1841) 5 My & Cr 29 at 35; *Watson v Watson* (1864) 33 Beav 574 at 575; *Parkhurst v Howell* (1870) 6 Ch App 136 at 137; *Re Pollock* (1885) 28 Ch D 552 at 555 and *Re Furness, Furness v Stalkartt* [1901] 2 Ch 346 at 348

2   See *Suisse v Lord Lowther* (1843) 2 Hare 424 at 435; cf *Powel v Cleaver* (1789) 2 Bro CC 499. Where an advance is made to one of the residuary legatees to whom the testator stands in loco parentis, it has been held not to have to be brought into account if the testator does not stand in loco parentis to the other residuary legatees: *O'Callaghan v Coady* (1912) 11 ELR 63. Where a father deposited £500 in a savings bank for each of his daughters, it was held to be in satisfaction of their share under his will: *Re Mills* [1952] SASR 274.

3   *Ex p Pye, Ex p Dubost* (1811) 18 Ves 140 at 154.

4   *Powys v Mansfield* (1837) 3 My & Cr 359; *Fowkes v Pascoe* (1875) 10 Ch App 343 at 350. The rule is best stated as including provisions by a parent or a person in loco parentis, and in the modern law the word 'parent' should not be restricted to 'father', on the basis that it is only on him that the duty of making provision for the child prima facie falls; see Lindsay J in *Re Cameron, Phillips v Cameron* [1999] 2 All ER 924 at 939 and para **[44.3]**, nn 3 and 4. The judge pointed out that the first instance decision in *Re Ashton, Ingram v Papillon* [1897] 2 Ch 574 ,which is often cited as confining the duty to make provision for a child to a father,was reversed without discussion of the law involved: [1898] 1 Ch 142. A mother can place herself in loco parentis see; *Re Ware, Re Rouse, Ware v Rouse* (1926) 70 Sol Jo 691. But see *Bennet v Bennet* (1879) 10 Ch D 474 and *Re Eyre, Johnson v Williams* [1917] 1 Ch 351 to the contrary.

It may be that in such a case the question of ademption of a gift by will by a subsequent settlement has to be determined by considering the intention apart from presumption: *Re Eardley's Will, Simeon v Freemantle* [1920] 1 Ch 397; *Re Ware, Re Rouse, Ware v Rouse* (1926) 70 Sol Jo 691.

5   Strictly the evidence is of intention by the donor to put himself in loco parentis; from such intention the presumption against double portions arises, and parol evidence is admissible to prove or disprove the facts upon which the presumption is to depend, namely, whether, in the language of Lord Eldon in *Ex p Pye, Ex p Dubost* (1811) 18 Ves 140, he had meant to put himself in loco parentis: per Lord Cottenham LC in *Powys v Mansfield* (1837) 3 My & Cr 359 at 370; see *Booker v Allen* (1831) 2 Russ & M 270, 299.

6   *Watson v Watson* (1864) 33 Beav 574. In *Twining v Powell* (1845) 2 Coll 262, the testatrix also referred to the legatee as her adopted child.

7   *Booker v Allen* (1831) 2 Russ & M 270.

8   *Powys v Mansfield* (1837) 3 My & Cr 359. 'A rich unmarried uncle', said Lord Cottenham LC in that case,

> 'taking under his protection the family of a brother, who has not the means of adequately providing for them, and furnishing through the father to the children the means of their maintenance and education, may surely be said to intend to put himself, for the purpose in question, in loco parentis to the children, although they never leave their father's roof.'

9   *Shudal v Jekyll* (1743) 2 Atk 516; *Lyddon v Ellison* (1854) 19 Beav 565; *Re Smythies, Weyman v Smythies* [1903] 1 Ch 259.

10   As to a grandfather, see *Roome v Roome* (1744) 3 Atk 181 at 183; *Powel v Cleaver* (1789) 2 Bro CC 499 at 517; *Perry v Whitehead* (1801) 6 Ves 544 at 547, 548; *Lyddon v Ellison* (1854) 19 Beav 565 at 572; *Re Dawson, Swainson v Dawson* [1919] 1 Ch 102; cf *Ellis v Ellis* (1802) 1 Sch & Lef 1. But a provision by a grandparent, for example the payment of education fees for a grandchild, could be regarded as being (directly or indirectly) a provision for the parent of the child and thus be a portion; see *Re Cameron, Phillips v Cameron* [1999] Ch 386r, [1999] 2 All ER 924, discussed para **[44.3]**, nn 3 and 4. As to collaterals, see *Shudal v Jekyll* (1743) 2 Atk 516.

11   *Grave v Earl of Salisbury* (1784) 1 Bro CC 425; *Perry v Whitehead* (1801) 6 Ves 544; *Ex p Pye, Ex p Dubost* (1811) 18 Ves 140.

12   In *Re Lawes, Lawes v Lawes* (1881) 20 Ch D 81 at 86 Jessel MR treated a father as being in loco parentis towards his illegitimate son. See now the Family Law Reform Act 1987.

13   *Elders Trustee and Executor Co Ltd v Eastoe* [1963] WAR 36.

[44.9]

Strength of presumption of satisfaction in different cases. The rule against double portions is only a rule of presumption, and the presumption is liable to be rebutted. The strength of the presumption varies according to the nature of the instruments and the order in which they are executed. The presumption is strongest in the case where a testamentary provision for a child is followed by a settlement. Here both provisions are still under the testator's control when he executes the later instrument. The presumption is less strong where a settlement, which creates an obligation remaining unperformed, is followed by a testamentary provision. The testator is not free from the obligation of the settlement when he makes his will, and it is not so readily presumed that he meant the latter to take the place of the former.[1] And where the settlement precedes the will, a direction in the will to pay debts may be held to include the liability under the settlement so as to rebut the presumption of satisfaction;[2] but only if the liability is of such a nature as properly to constitute a debt.[3] The strength of the presumption is further reduced when the double provision is contained in consecutive settlements, since in the case of a will the testator is supposed to be disposing of the whole of his property and distributing it among the different objects of his bounty;[4] but not so in the case of a settlement. And if the first settlement contains a power of revocation which is not exercised, this will be an indication that the provisions are intended to be cumulative.[5]

1   *Lord Chichester v Coventry* (1867) LR 2 HL 71 at 87; *Re Tussaud's Estate, Tussaud v Tussaud* (1878) 9 Ch D 363; and as to this distinction, see *Dawson v Dawson* (1867) LR 4 Eq 504 at 512; *Cooper v MacDonald* (1873) LR 16 Eq 258 at 268. See *Re Poyser* (1908) [1918] 1 Ch 573n.

2   *Lord Chichester v Coventry* (1867) LR 2 HL 71 at 85, 88; *Dawson v Dawson* (1867) LR 4 Eq 504; see *Lethbridge v Thurlow* (1851) 15 Beav 334; *Re Franklin, Franklin v Franklin* (1907) 52 Sol Jo 12. Where the will precedes the settlement, a direction to pay debts can have no such effect: *Trimmer v Bayne* (1802) 7 Ves 508; *Dawson v Dawson* (1867) LR 4 Eq 504; *Cooper v MacDonald* (1873) LR 16 Eq 258.

3   *Bennett v Houldsworth* (1877) 6 Ch D 671; *Re Vernon, Garland v Shaw* (1906) 95 LT 48.

4   *Palmer v Newell* (1855) 20 Beav 32; on appeal (1856) 8 De GM & G 74.

5   *Palmer v Newell* (1856) 8 De GM & G 74 at 78; and see *Cartwright v Cartwright* [1903] 2 Ch 306, where satisfaction was rebutted by the differences in the limitations.

[44.10]
Slight differences do not rebut presumption. Slight differences between the two provisions—that is, such as in the opinion of the judge leave the two provisions of substantially the same nature—do not rebut the presumption against double portions.[1] Thus the presumption is not rebutted by slight differences as to the time of payment of the two portions,[2] and sums agreed to be advanced may be satisfied pro tanto by a share of residue;[3] and similarly a bequest of a share of residue may be adeemed pro tanto by a subsequent advance of a specific sum.[4] Satisfaction by a residue and ademption of a residue cannot for this purpose be distinguished.[5]

1   *Weall v Rice* (1831) 2 Russ & M 251 at 268; *Re Newton King* [1953] NZLR 245.

2   *Hartopp v Hartopp* (1810) 17 Ves 184; cf *Lethbridge v Thurlow* (1851) 15 Beav 334.

3   *Schofield v Heap* (1858) 27 Beav 93.

4   *Lady Thynne v Earl of Glengall* (1848) 2 HL Cas 131.

5   *Montefiore v Guedalla* (1859) 1 De GF & J 93 at 101. But where the residue is left to other persons jointly with the children, advances to the children are brought into account only so as to increase the share of residue going to the children (*Meinertzagen v Walters* (1872) 7 Ch App 670); and if the residue is left between a stranger and a single child, the presumption of satisfaction is not admitted at all, since the effect would be to compel the child to bring advances into account for the benefit of the stranger, but not vice versa: *Re Heather, Pumfrey v Fryer* [1906] 2 Ch 230.

[44.11]
The gifts must be ejusdem generis. But the second portion must be ejusdem generis with the first.[1] Thus a pecuniary legacy is not adeemed by the father afterwards taking his son into partnership and giving him an interest in the business stock.[2] If, however, the father himself sets a pecuniary value on the property given or gives it with reference to its pecuniary value, it ceases to be of a different nature for this purpose.[3] Similarly, land is not to be taken in satisfaction for money, nor money for land,[4] unless the testator estimates the value of the land at a fixed sum, and desires it to be made up to a particular amount[5] and an annuity given by will is not ejusdem generis with a government annuity purchased during the testator's lifetime.[6] An interest subject to a contingency will not be a satisfaction of a vested interest,[7] unless the contingency is so remote that it may be disregarded.[8] Where the residuary estate is given to be distributed in the absolute discretion of the trustees, the rule does not apply to a pecuniary bequest earlier in the will or to a gift of shares by a settlement subsequent to the will.[9]

1   *Re Aynsley, Kyrle v Turner* [1915] 1 Ch 172 at 176; *Re Chirnside* (1903) 29 VLR 4; *Parker v Dowling* (1916) 16 SRNSW 234; *Leneham v Wall* [1922] 1 IR 59.
2   *Holmes v Holmes* (1783) 1 Bro CC 555. *Re Jaques, Hodgson v Braisby* [1903] 1 Ch 267; dissenting from *Re Vickers, Vickers v Vickers* (1888) 37 Ch D 525, where North J considered *Holmes v Holmes*, overruled by the observations of Jessel MR in *Re Lawes, Lawes v Lawes* (1881) 20 Ch D 81 at 87.
3   *Bengough v Walker* (1808) 15 Ves 507; *Re Lawes, Lawes v Lawes* (1881) 20 Ch D 81; *Re George's Will Trusts, Barclay's Bank Ltd v George* [1949] Ch 154, [1948] 2 All ER 1004 (farming stock and taking over of lease valued).
4   *Bellasis v Uthwatt* (1737) 1 Atk 426 at 428; and see *Davys v Boucher* (1839) 3 Y & C Ex 397.
5   *Lord Chichester v Coventry* (1867) LR 2 HL 71 at 96, per Lord Romilly MR, referring to *Bengough v Walker* (1808) 15 Ves 507.
6   *Re Garnett Estate, Armstrong v Garnett* (1954) 12 WWRNS 617.
7   *Bellasis v Uthwatt* (1737) 1 Atk 426; *Hanbury v Hanbury* (1788) 2 Bro CC 352.
8   *Powys v Mansfield* (1837) 3 My & Cr 359 at 374.
9   *Re Vaux, Nicholson v Vaux* [1939] Ch 465, [1938] 4 All ER 297, 703.

[44.12]

Difference in limitations. Differences between the limitations in the two provisions will only exclude the rule against double portions where they are so great as to indicate that the donor did not intend the later to be in satisfaction of the earlier.[1] Satisfaction is compatible with greater differences of limitation when the will precedes the settlement, since the testator is at liberty to vary as he pleases the bounty given by his will. Thus, where a father has by his will given a portion to his daughter absolutely, this may well be satisfied by a settlement under which she takes a life interest. It is simply such a settlement as she might be expected herself to make if she received the portion under the will.[2] In accordance with the principle already stated,[3] however, where the settlement precedes the will greater weight is given to differences in the limitations. The testator is already under an obligation to dispose of property in the manner defined by the settlement, and his will is no satisfaction unless, in making it, he could have supposed himself to be satisfying that obligation.[4]

1   See Lindsay J in *Re Cameron, Phillips v Cameron* [1999] 2 All ER 924 at 944 who stated: 'Where there is real difference between the two gifts by way of portion the question of ademption or not becomes a question of whether the donor might reasonably have supposed the two gifts, despite the differences between them, to be, very broadly, the same.' Citing *Lord Chichester v Coventry* (1867) LR 2 HL 71 at 88. See also *Trimmer v Bayne* (1802) 7 Ves 508 at 515; *Re Newton King* [1953] NZLR 245 (absolute gifts and gifts by settlement of substantial difference in amount held not to rebut presumption).
2   *Lord Chichester v Coventry* (1867) LR 2 HL 71 at 88; *Stevenson v Masson* (1873) LR 17 Eq 78; see *Re Innes, Barclay v Innes* (1908) 125 LT Jo 60; and a legacy given absolutely to a son may be ademed by a subsequent settlement of money on the marriage of the son: *Hopwood v Hopwood* (1859) 7 HL Cas 728. This is not necessarily prevented by a later codicil expressly declaring other portions to be in satisfaction of legacies, but not referring to the legacy in question. Similarly, where the will settles a sum on a daughter and her children, a subsequent settlement on the daughter and her children will be an ademption, notwithstanding differences in the trusts: *Re Furness, Furness v Stalkartt* [1901] 2 Ch 346.
3   See para **[44.9]** supra.
4   *Lord Chichester v Coventry* (1867) LR 2 HL 71 at 89. The three leading cases on this subject are *Earl of Durham v Wharton* (1836) 3 Cl & Fin 146; *Lady Thynne v Earl of Glengall* (1848) 2 HL Cas 131; and *Lord Chichester v Coventry* (1867) LR 2 HL 71. In *Earl of Durham v Wharton*, supra, where the will preceded the settlement, there were substantial differences in the trusts; in particular by the will £10,000 was given in trust for the testator's daughter and her children; under the settlement £15,000 was to be paid to the husband who at the same time made provision for the daughter and for younger children. But the rule against double portions

prevailed: see *Re Furness, Furness v Stalkartt* [1901] 2 Ch 346. In *Lady Thynne v Earl of Glengall* (1848) 2 HL Cas 131, the settlement preceded the will, and the chief differences were that, by the settlement, the power of appointment among children was given to husband and wife jointly, under the will to the wife alone; under the settlement, the children of the marriage, under the will, the daughter's children generally, were objects of the power. It was held that these were not differences which negatived the presumption of satisfaction. The limitations of the will were in effect a fulfilment of the obligations of the settlement. In *Lord Chichester v Coventry* (1867) LR 2 HL 71, also, the settlement (which was by covenant to pay £10,000 on demand) preceded the will, but it was held that there was no satisfaction, partly on the ground that a direction to pay debts contained in the will included the obligation under the settlement, which might at any time have been turned into a present debt by demand; but also because the differences between the limitations of the £10,000 in the settlement and those of the will were so marked as to be sufficient to overcome any presumption against a double provision; see *Re Tussaud's Estate, Tussaud v Tussaud* (1878) 9 Ch D 363; *Re Vernon, Garland v Shaw* (1906) 95 LT 48; *Re Franklin, Franklin v Franklin* (1907) 52 Sol Jo 12. But where a portion is, by the effect of the settlement, charged on all the settlor's real estate, and he subsequently by will makes such provision for the donee as to raise the presumption of satisfaction, this is not rebutted by the circumstances that he devises his real estate 'subject to the charges and encumbrances thereon': *Montagu v Earl of Sandwich* (1886) 32 Ch D 525. In *Re Stibbe, Cleverley v Stibbe* (1946) 175 LT 198, a first wife was entitled to a settled annuity of £300 under a settlement entered into on divorce. The husband left her an unsettled annuity of £400 by will. It was held that the annuity in the will was not in satisfaction of that under the settlement because (i) of the difference in amount, (ii) the difference in limitation, and (iii) a direction to pay debts out of residue and the liability under the settlement was a debt subject to which the annuity in the will was given.

[44.13]

Difference in beneficiaries. A provision by will may be adeemed in whole or in part by a subsequent advance, although the persons mentioned in the will and those to whom the advance is made are not the same. This difference is a matter to be considered in determining whether or not there is ademption; but if the decision is in favour of ademption, the ademption is final, and affects all the persons within the scope of the testamentary provision.[1] Satisfaction of a settlement by a will is different, and may operate as to certain persons benefited by the settlement, and not as to others. Consequently those who benefit both under the settlement and under the will are put to their election; but a beneficiary under the settlement who does not take under the will—as where a daughter's husband take a life interest under the settlement but not under the will[2]—cannot be put to election, and he retains his right under the settlement.[3] Conversely, if there are beneficiaries under the will who are not within the settlement, the beneficiaries under both settlement and will must elect. If they elect to take under the will, the provision of the will is substituted for that in the settlement, and the beneficiaries mentioned only in the will are let in to share in the whole property; if they elect against the will, then they cannot benefit under the will without compensating the beneficiaries under the will alone for the loss thus caused to them.[4]

1   *Lord Chichester v Coventry* (1867) LR 2 HL 71 at 90; *Twining v Powell* (1845) 2 Coll 262.
2   See *Mayd v Field* (1876) 3 Ch D 587.
3   See *Re Cameron, Phillips v Cameron* [1999] 2 All ER 924 , where the point was considered (see para **[44.3]**, nn 3 and 4). In *Lord Chichester v Coventry* (1867) LR 2 HL 71 at 92, 93, 95, Lord Romilly MR commented:
    'If a father, on the marriage of his daughter, should settle £10,000 on her for life, remainder to the children of the marriage, a bequest of £10,000 to that daughter would satisfy her life interest in the £10,000 but would not satisfy or touch the interests of her children.'

In *McCarogher v Whieldon* (1867) LR 3 Eq 236, a father, on the marriage of his son, covenanted to give, by will or otherwise, one-fifth of his real and personal estate at his death on trust for the son for a protected life interest, then for the wife and issue of the marriage. By his will he gave his real and personal estate to all his children living at his death. There were five such children. This gift did not operate as a satisfaction as regards the wife and children, and they retained their rights under the settlement; but it operated as a satisfaction as regards the son, and he had to elect whether to take his life interest under the settlement or one-fifth of the residue remaining after satisfaction. of the covenant. He elected to take under the will. This meant that he was cut out of the covenant, and the life estate of his wife thereunder was accelerated; see *Mayd v Field* (1876) 3 Ch D 587; and cf *Bethell v Abraham* (1874) 3 Ch D 590n, 31 LT 112. It will be appreciated that this is a case on satisfaction and not on the doctrine of election, discussed in Chapter 42, ante. The kind of election referred to in *McCarogher v Whieldon*, supra, is not concerned with compensation at all but merely with ensuring that the beneficiary does not take both benefits: *Re Gordon's Will Trusts, National Westminster Bank Ltd v Gordon* [1978] 2 All ER 969 at 977, per Buckley LJ. In general, where the will follows the settlement, the circumstance that certain persons included in the settlement are not included in the testamentary provision precludes the presumption: *Re Tussaud's Estate, Tussaud v Tussaud* (1878) 9 Ch D 363 at 368; and see *Hall v Hill* (1841) 1 Dr & War 94; *Re Vernon, Garland v Shaw* (1906) 95 LT 48. But see *Re Blundell, Blundell v Blundell* [1906] 2 Ch 222.

Moreover, where the settlement follows the will, the presumption will not arise (in the absence of express direction) if the persons taking under the several instruments are altogether different. Thus a legacy in favour of a daughter and her children is not adeemed by a subsequent gift in favour of her husband absolutely: *Cooper v MacDonald* (1873) LR 16 Eq 258 at 269; see *Baugh v Read* (1790) 1 Ves 257; and cf *Twinning v Powell* (1845) 2 Coll 262.

4   This would have been the case in *Lady Thynne v Earl of Glengall* (1848) 2 HL Cas 131, had there been children of a second marriage (see the hypothesis worked out by Lord Romilly MR in *Lord Chichester v Coventry* (1867) LR 2 HL 71 at 93).

[44.14]

Admission of parol evidence. Parol evidence cannot be admitted to add to or vary a written instrument;[1] but where from two written instruments, taken in conjunction with the surrounding circumstances, the court raises a presumption of satisfaction, then parol evidence is admissible to rebut the presumption, and therefore also to support it.[2] In the case of a will and a settlement, the rule is the same whether the will precedes or follows the settlement.[3] And where a disposition has been made by one written instrument, parol evidence may be given of the circumstances of a subsequent transaction which has not been reduced to writing, for the purpose of showing an intention on the part of the donor that it should be a satisfaction.[4]

1   But it may be given to explain the surrounding circumstances; see Chapter 57.
2   *Trimmer v Bayne* (1802) 7 Ves 508; *Kirk v Eddowes* (1844) 3 Hare 509, and cases there referred to: *Monck v Lord Monck* (1810) 1 Ball & B 298; *Hall v Hill* (1841) 1 Dr & War 94; *Curtin v Evans* (1875) IR 9 Eq 553 at 557; *Montagu v Earl of Sandwich* (1886) 32 Ch D 525 at 535; *Griffith v Bourke* (1888) 21 LR Ir 92; *Re Scott, Langton v Scott* [1903] 1 Ch 1 (where the presumption was rebutted); see *Debeze v Mann* (1789) 2 Bro CC 519. Where a testatrix bequeathed a sum for a church building fund and later subscribed nearly the same amount during her lifetime, evidence was admitted of statements by her to show that the subscriptions were not intended by her to be in reduction of the bequest: *Re Leggatt, Griffith v Calder* [1908] VLR 385. In such cases the evidence is not admitted on either side for the purpose of proving, in the first instance, with what intent either writing was made, but for the purpose only of ascertaining whether the presumption which the law has raised be well or ill founded: *Kirk v Eddowes* (1844) 3 Hare 509 at 517, per Wigram V-C; *Re Shields, Corbould-Ellis v Dales* [1912] 1 Ch 591 at 601. In *Weall v Rice* (1831) 2 Russ & M 251; Leach MR at 268, treated extrinsic evidence as being admissible both to raise and to rebut the presumption, and in *Booker v Allen* (1831) 2 Russ & M 270, he admitted extrinsic evidence to raise the presumption where the provisions of the instruments were so different as to prevent it from being raised by intrinsic

evidence. But the other authorities cited show that the presumption must first be raised on the language of the instruments, and on the relationship of the parties as one of the surrounding circumstances, before parol evidence of intention against or for satisfaction can be admitted. Otherwise the parol evidence would be admitted simply to vary the written instrument: *Re Tussaud's Estate, Tussaud v Tussaud* (1878) 9 Ch D 363 at 374. It can be noted that the Administration of Justice Act 1982, s 21, see Chapter 57, which makes new provisions for the admission of extrinsic evidence contains no reference to the admission of such evidence to rebut these equitable presumptions and it is thought that the existing case law as discussed above remains applicable.

3   *Re Tussaud's Estate, Tussaud v Tussaud* (1878) 9 Ch D 363 at 373.
4   *Kirk v Eddowes* (1844) 3 Hare 509.

[44.15]

Satisfaction of debt by legacy. Where a testator, being at the time of making his will,[1] indebted, leaves to his creditor a legacy of a sum equal to or greater than the debt, the legacy is presumed to be a satisfaction of the debt, and the creditor cannot have both his debt and the legacy,[2] and if the debt is discharged before the testator's death the legacy will not be payable.[3] But this is a presumption which is not favoured by the court, and it will be rebutted by slight circumstances whether appearing on the will or incident to the nature of the debt and of the legacy, which suggest that the testator did not intend the legacy to operate as a satisfaction.[4] Thus it will be rebutted where the will contains a direction for the payment of debts and legacies,[5] and even where the direction is only for payment of debts,[6] or where the will states a particular motive for the legacy other than satisfaction of the debt.[7] The presumption will also be rebutted where the legacy is so different as not to be a proper equivalent for the debt; as where it is payable at a later time than the debt, so as to be less advantageous to the creditor,[8] or where it is different in kind.

Such difference may exist either in the things themselves, as where they are not ejusdem generis—thus a devise of land is not a satisfaction of a debt[9]— or in their incidents, as where the legacy is either contingent[10] or of uncertain amount.[11] And the presumption may be excluded by differences in the title to the debt and legacy, as where the debt belongs to a married woman for her separate use and the legacy is not given;[12] or the debt and legacy are secured by different charges on property;[13] or the debt is secured and the legacy unsecured;[14] or the debt and the legacy are vested in different trustees;[15] or the debt is due on a negotiable instrument.[16] Where a testator is liable as trustee for a breach of trust, a bequest of money for the purposes of the trust will prima facie be a satisfaction of the breach of trust,[17] and sums charged on the testator's estate may be satisfied by a legacy to the owner of the charge.[18] A declaration in the will that certain legacies are in satisfaction of debts will assist to rebut the presumption of satisfaction in the case of a debt not so mentioned.[19]

1   A legacy will not be presumed to be a satisfaction of a debt not existing at the date of the will, since an intention to that effect cannot be imputed to the testator: *Fowler v Fowler* (1735) 3 P Wms 353; *Thomas v Bennet* (1725) 2 P Wms 341; *Haynes v Mico* (1781) 1 Bro CC 129 at 131; *Plunkett v Lewis* (1844) 3 Hare 316 at 330; and the fact that the debt is created contemporaneously with the will is a strong reason against satisfaction: *Horlock v Wiggins, Wiggins v Horlock* (1888) 39 Ch D 142.
2   *Talbott v Duke of Shrewsbury* (1714) Prec Ch 394; *Re Rattenberry, Ray v Grant* [1906] 1 Ch 667; *Ellard v Phelan* [1914] 1 IR 76 (bequest to a servant held to be a satisfaction of wages due at time of testator's death); *Buckley v Buckley* (1888) 19 LR Ir 544 (debt of business advances on a current account). The rule applies notwithstanding that there is interest then due and unpaid

(*Fitzgerald v National Bank Ltd* [1929] 1 KB 394), but a legacy of less amount than the debt is not a satisfaction pro tanto; *Atkinson v Webb* (1704) 2 Vern 478; *Crammer's Case* (1701) 2 Salk 508; *Eastwood v Vinke* (1731) 2 P Wms 613 at 616; *Lady Thynne v Earl of Glengall* (1848) 2 HL Cas 131 at 153; see *Graham v Graham* (1749) 1 Ves Sen 262; *Bor v Bor* (1756) 3 Bro Parl Cas 167 at 179, unless there is evidence that the legacy was intended as part payment and that the creditor assented; *Hammond v Smith* (1864) 33 Beav 452. There is only satisfaction where the creditor and the legatee are the same; hence there is no satisfaction where the debt is due to the husband and the legacy is given to his wife (*Hall v Hill* (1841) 1 Dr & War 94), or where the debt is due from the testator as trustee and the legacy is to one of the beneficiaries: *Fairer v Park* (1876) 3 Ch D 309; see *Smith v Smith* (1861) 3 Giff 263 at 272; *Haylion v Trotter* (1892) 10 NZLR 543 (bequest to children of debtor). A legacy given in satisfaction of a debt is liable to abate with other legacies: *Re Wedmore, Wedmore v Wedmore* [1907] 2 Ch 277; *Re Whitehead, Whitehead v Street* [1913] 2 Ch 56. As to a gift of residue to creditors in proportions corresponding to their debts, see *Philips v Philips* (1844) 3 Hare 281, and as to a gift of residue to a creditor not being a satisfaction: see *Lahay v Brown* [1957] OWN 210.

3   *Re Fletcher, Gillings v Fletcher* (1888) 38 Ch D 373.

4   *Lady Thynne v Earl of Glengall* (1848) 2 HL Cas 131. The presumption is founded on the maxim *debitor non presumitur donare*—or, that a man should be just before he is bountiful; but of course there is in principle no room for such maxims where the debtor leaves sufficient to pay both debts and legacies (*Chancey's Case* (175) 1 P Wms 408; *Fowler v Fowler* (1735) 3 P Wms 353; *Mathews v Mathews* (1755) 2 Ves Sen 635), and while it is settled that where there is a debt due in the testator's life, and nothing but a plain general legacy of equal or greater amount given to the creditor, the presumption will prevail, yet the court will not go further, and it will avail itself of slight circumstances to exclude the presumption (*Richardson v Greese* (1734) 3 Atk 65 at 68; *Hinchcliffe v Hinchcliffe* (1797) 3 Ves 516 at 529; *Re Horlock, Calham v Smith* [1895] 1 Ch 516 at 519); it will 'rely on the minutest shade of difference to escape from that false principle': *Hassell v Hawkins* (1859) 4 Drew 468 at 470. There is no difference in this respect between debts due to children of the testator and debts due to strangers; *Tolson v Collins* (1799) 4 Ves 483; see also *Stocken v Stocken* (1831) 4 Sim 152; on appeal (1838) 4 My & Cr 95. But see *Ross v Ross* [1930] 1 WWR 375 and *Re Haldorson Estate* (1953) 9 WWRNS 145. See also *Re Pottruff* (1972) 27 DLR (3d) 405.

5   *Chancey's Case* (1725) 1 P Wms 408; *Richardson v Greese* (1743) 3 Atk 65; *Field v Mostin* (1778) 2 Dick 543; *Jefferies v Michell* (1855) 20 Beav 15; *Hassell v Hawkins* (1859) 4 Drew 468; *Russell v White* (1895) 16 NSW Eq 158; *Burne v Knowles* (1892) 11 NZLR 98; *Sparrow v Royal Trust Co* [1932] 1 WWR 379 (direction to pay debts and thereafter legacies); *Re Trider* (1978) 84 DLR (3d) 336. But where the will contains such a direction, and the testator subsequently contracts a debt and then by codicil leaves an equal or greater legacy to the creditor, the presumption is not rebutted: *Gaynon v Wood* (1759) 1 Dick 331 at 332.

6   *Re Huish, Bradshaw v Huish* (1889) 43 Ch D 260; see *Cole v Willard* (1858) 25 Beav 568; *Pinchin v Simms* (1861) 30 Beav 119; *Dawson v Dawson* (1867) LR 4 Eq 504 at 514; *Atkinson v Littlewood* (1874) LR 18 Eq 595 at 604; *Glover v Hartcup* (1864) 34 Beav 74; *Lord Chichester v Coventry* (1867) LR 2 HL 71. It had previously been held that the mere direction to pay debts was not enough to rebut the presumption: *Edmunds v Low* (1857) 3 K & J 318, though it was an element to be considered in regard to the question of intention: *Rowe v Rowe* (1848) 2 De G & Sm 294 at 298. The direction to pay debts covers the testator's indebtedness on a covenant in favour of his wife or other beneficiary, although payment under the covenant is not to be made till after his death: *Cole v Willard* (1858) 25 Beav 568; *Atkinson v Littlewood* (1874) LR 18 Eq 595 at 605; *Re Stibbe, Cleverley v Stibbe* (1946) 175 LT 198; *Re Manners, Public Trustee v Manners* [1949] Ch 613, [1949] 2 All ER 201 (bequest of a sum much more than enough to purchase an annuity of the same amount as one given by covenant and gift over of the residue of the sum so provided); see *Lord Chichester v Coventry* (1867) LR 2 HL 71 at 85; contra, *Wathen v Smith* (1819) 4 Madd 325, though in the circumstances of the case it may appear that the testator did not intend the liability on the covenant to his wife to be treated as a debt within the direction to pay debts, and then it is discharged by the bequest: *Re Hall, Hope v Hall* [1918] 1 Ch 562. Where there is no direction to pay debts, an annuity given by the will of the same amount as that covenanted to be paid to a first wife in compromise of a claim for maintenance is a satisfaction: *Re Haves, Haves v Haves* [1951] 2 All ER 928.

7   See *Matthews v Mathews* (1755) 2 Ves Sen 635.

8   Thus, where the debt is due at the testator's death, the legacy must not be made payable at a fixed date after the death (*Nicholls v Judson* (1742) 2 Atk 300; *Clark v Sewell* (1744) 3 Atk 96; *Re Roberts, Roberts v Parry* (1902) 50 WR 469); and where the debt is due at a fixed date after

the death, the legacy must not be made payable at a later date: *Haynes v Mico* (1781) 1 Bro CC 129; see *Jeacock v Falkener* (1783) 1 Bro CC 295 at 297. Moreover, if the debt is due at a fixed date after death, and the legacy is given without a fixed date, there is no satisfaction, since the legacy is not, according to the ordinary rule, payable for a year (*Re Horlock, Calham v Smith* [1895] 1 Ch 516); and similarly where an annuity given by deed is payable at a fixed date within the year and an annuity is given by will generally (*Re Dowse, Dowse v Glass* (1881) 50 LJ Ch 285, and *Re Stibbe, Cleverley v Stibbe* (1946) 175 LT 198), or different fixed times are settled for the two annuities: *Atkinson v Webb* (1704) 2 Vern 478; *Hales v Darell* (1840) 3 Beav 324. But if the debt is payable at the death, and the legacy is given generally, the fact that the legacy may not be paid for a year does not rebut the presumption of satisfaction (*Re Rattenberry, Ray v Grant* [1906] 1 Ch 667); and since a legacy so given in satisfaction of a debt carries interest from the death (*Clark v Sewell* (1744) 3 Atk 96 at 99), there is no difference as to interest which will rebut the presumption: *Re Rattenberry, Ray v Grant,* supra. An acceleration in the date of payment is consistent with satisfaction: *Wathen v Smith* (1819) 4 Madd 325 at 332. It has been recognised that the exceptions, equally with the rule, are unsatisfactory: *Re Horlock, Calham v Smith* [1895] 1 Ch 516. A gift of residue was held no satisfaction for a mortgage debt in *Re Keogh's Estate* (1889) 23 LR Ir 257. A legacy is no satisfaction for a debt on an account current or open at the date of the testator's death; *Buckley v Buckley* (1888) 19 LR Ir 544; *Webb v Webb* (1900) 21 NSW Eq 245.

9   *Eastwood v Vinke* (1731) 2 P Wms 613, 616; *Byde v Byde* (1761) 1 Cox Eq Cas 44 at 48; see *Forsight v Grant* (1791) 1 Ves 298; *Richardson v Elphinstone* (1794) 2 Ves 463.

10 *Crompton v Sale* (1729) 2 P Wms 553; *Tolson v Collins* (1799) 4 Ves 483; *Crichton v Crichton* [1895] 2 Ch 853; on appeal [1896] 1 Ch 870; *Coates v Coates* [1898] 1 IR 258 (life interest in house and furniture).

11 Thus a residue or a share of residue is not a satisfaction of a debt: *Barret v Beckford* (1750) 1 Ves Sen 519; *Devese v Pontet* (1785) 1 Cox Eq Cas 188 at 192; *Lady Thynne v Earl of Glengall* (1848) 2 HL Cas 131 at 155. There may be satisfaction of a debt of unascertained amount (*Edmunds v Low* (1857) 3 K & J 318 at 323; *Smith v Smith* (1861) 3 Giff 263 at 269) unless it is on an open account in respect of which nothing, so far as the testator knows, may be owing: *Rawlins v Powel* (1718) 1 P Wms 297.

12 *Bartlett v Gillard* (1827) 3 Russ 149 at 156; *Fourdrin v Gowdey* (1834) 3 My & K 383 at 410; *Rowe v Rowe* (1848) 2 De G & Sm 294 at 298; *Fairer v Park* (1876) 3 Ch D 309 at 314; *Burne v Knowles* (1892) 11 NZLR 98; contra, *Atkinson v Littlewood* (1874) LR 18 Eq 595, and see *Edmunds v Low* (1857) 3 K & J 318, as to the effect of the marriage of a woman who was creditor-legatee, whereby the debt might formerly become payable to her husband.

13 *Barlett v Gillard* (1827) 3 Russ 149; *Hales v Darell* (1840) 3 Beav 324; *Re Gleeson, Smyth v Gleeson* [1911] 1 IR 113; but see *Atkinson v Littlewood* (1874) LR 18 Eq 595.

14 *Re Stibbe, Cleverley v Stibbe* (1946) 175 LT 198; and cf *Coates v Coates* [1898] 1 IR 258.

15 *Pinchin v Simms* (1861) 30 Beav 119.

16 *Carr v Eastabrooke* (1797) 3 Ves 561; *Re Roberts, Roberts v Parry* (1902) 50 WR 469.

17 *Bensusan v Nehemias* (1851) 4 De G & Sm 381. See *Sealy v Stawell* (1876) IR 2 Eq 499.

18 *Shadbolt v Vanderplank* (1861) 29 Beav 405.

19 *Atkinson v Webb* (1704) Prec Ch 236; *Jeacock v Falkener* (1783) 1 Bro CC 295 at 297; *Charlton v West* (1861) 30 Beav 124.

[44.16]

Parol evidence. Since the presumption of satisfaction of a debt by a legacy is opposed to the language of the will, parol evidence is admissible, as in other cases of satisfaction, to rebut it and also to affirm it.[1]

1   See *Plunkett v Lewis* (1844) 3 Hare 316 at 323; *Hall v Hill* (1841) 1 Dr & War 94 at 122. In *Fowler v Fowler* (1735) 3 P Wms 353, such evidence was considered not admissible, but it is only to be rejected when the intention in favour of satisfaction is expressed in the will itself: see *Hall v Hill* (1841) 1 Dr & War 94. In *Wallace v Pomfret* (1805) 11 Ves 542, this distinction was overlooked.

[44.17]

Debt from parent to child. Where a debt exists from a parent to a child, an advancement, in the parent's lifetime, upon the child's marriage or on some other occasion, of a portion equal to or exceeding the debt is prima facie a satisfaction of the debt.[1] The presumption may be rebutted by circumstances showing that satisfaction was not intended;[2] but it will not be rebutted merely because the gift is expressed to be in consideration of natural love and affection, or, in the case of a gift on the marriage of a daughter, because her husband was ignorant of her right.[3]

1   *Plunkett v Lewis* (1844) 3 Hare 316; *Reade v Reade* (1881) 9 LR Ir 409; see *Wood v Briant* (1742) 2 Atk 521; *Seed v Bradford* (1750) 1 Ves Sen 501; *Chave v Farrant* (1810) 18 Ves 8; cf *Hardingham v Thomas* (1854) 2 Drew 353. The advancement must be subsequent to the debt: *Plunkett v Lewis* (1844) 3 Hare 316 at 330.
2   As where the gift is of less amount, or uncertain or contingent in its nature: *Crichton v Crichton* [1895] 2 Ch 853. And as to the circumstances which will rebut the presumption, see *Crichton v Crichton* [1896] 1 Ch 870.
3   *Plunkett v Lewis* (1844) 3 Hare 316.

CHAPTER 45

Acceptance of a gift

[45.1]

Acceptance presumed. Acceptance, unless the will prescribes some act, election, or writing[1] by which the donee is required to show his acceptance, is generally inferred from the acts of the donee,[2] usually acts amounting to ownership of the property given.[3] Except where the will requires some definite act of acceptance, the donee will be presumed to have accepted the gift unless he disclaims it.[4] In the case of a gift of land, the assent of the personal representative is now requisite in order to vest the legal estate in the donee, but the absence of an assent would not, where the donee intended to accept the gift and the personal representative did not require the property for administration expenses, prevent the donee becoming entitled in equity and acceptance will be presumed.[5]

1   Wills seldom prescribe any special form of acceptance except where they confer an option. For a will requiring an acceptance in writing, see *Evans v Stratford* (1864) 2 Hem & M 142. Where a beneficiary has not been heard of for some time and it is uncertain whether he is still alive, a will sometimes requires a claim to be made within a specified time, see para **[35.48]** ante.

2   *Doe d Chidgey v Harris* (1847) 16 M & W 517 at 524.

3   *Bence v Gilpin* (1868) LR 3 Exch 76. Mere acts of preservation are not an acceptance; *A-G v Andrew* (1798) 3 Ves 633; *Stacey v Elph* (1833) 1 My & K 195.

4   *Townson v Tickell* (1819) 3 B & Ald 31 at 36, 37; *Re Arbib and Class's Contract* [1891] 1 Ch 601. If the donee is ignorant of the gift acceptance which would involve him in liability, is not presumed: *Houghton v Bell* (1892) 23 SCR 498 at 508.

5   *Re Hodge, Hodge v Griffiths* [1940] Ch 260 (where the gift was subject to the payment of annuities and was also to the executor of the will); *Re Lester, Lester v Lester* [1942] Ch 324, [1942] 1 All ER 646.

[45.2]

Acceptance means acceptance of burdens, benefits and conditions. Acceptance, however, must be subject to all the burdens incident to the gift and with all the benefits attached to it.[1] If the testator validly attaches a condition to a gift, the donee on accepting the gift must perform the condition.[2] If the condition requires the donee to incur some expense, even though he incurs a loss thereby,[3] he must fulfil the condition.[4] There are, however, two exceptions to this rule. The gift may, on its proper construction, be one of which the donee is only to have the enjoyment so long as he performs the condition, eg he is to receive the income so long as he performs the condition but is at liberty at any time to cease performing the condition and then is no longer entitled to the income.[5] On the other hand, the condition may be such that, once having accepted the gift, he cannot cease to perform the condition but is bound to continue to perform it.[6]

The liability of the beneficiary to perform the condition is a personal liability[7] and has been said to be on the footing of an implied contract.[8] It has also been enforced under the doctrine of estoppel.[9]

1   *Messenger v Andrews* (1828) 4 Russ 478 (plaintiff claiming property otherwise than under the will); *Hickling v Boyer* (1851) 3 Mac & G 635 (conditions). As to acceptance by trustee, see Chapter 27, ante. If the condition requires the donee to convey land to a third party, the donee after conveyance has no lien on that land for his legacy: *Barker v Barker* (1870) LR 10 Eq 438.

2   *Pitman v Crum Ewing* [1911] AC 217; *Re Tremblay* (1920) 56 DLR 281. The condition must be testamentary, ie in the will, unless the person to be so charged has been instrumental in causing the testator to omit it: *Peace v Hains* (1853) 11 Hare 151.

3   *A-G v Christ's Hospital* (1790) 3 Bro CC 165.

4   *Re Williames, Andrew v Williames* (1885) 54 LT 105; *Earl Northumberland v Lord Egrement* (1768) Amb 657 (release of all claims against estate); *Messenger v Andrews* (1828) 4 Russ 478 (to pay testator's debts); *Re Cowley, Souch v Cowley* (1885) 53 LT 494 (same, but debts charged on legacy and legatee not personally liable); *Welby v Rockcliffe* (1830) 1 Russ & M 571 (payment of annuity); *Rees v Engelback* (1871) LR 12 Eq 225 (same); *Bennett v Colley* (1833) 2 My & K 225 (renewal of lease); *Egg v Devey* (1847) 10 Beav 444 (legatee not to bring proceedings for breach of trust in administration of father's will); *Gregg v Coates* (1856) 23 Beav 33 (conditions to keep property in repair: reinstatement after fire); *Hickling v Boyer* (1851) 3 Mac & G 635 (conditions to keep property in repair); *Re Skingley* (1851) 3 Mac & G 221 (same); *Dingle v Coppen* [1899] 1 Ch 726 (same); *Re Loom, Fulford v Reversionary Interest Society Ltd* [1910] 2 Ch 230 (same); *Joliffe v Twyford* (1858) 26 Beav 227 (same, but repair does not include completion of unfinished building); *Vandeleur v Sloane* [1919] 1 IR 116 (assumption of name and arms).

5   *Re Robinson, Wright v Tugwell* [1892] 1 Ch 95 (gift to church on an 'abiding condition' that a black gown should be worn in the pulpit); *Re Da Costa, Clarke v Church of England Collegiate School of St Peter* [1912] 1 Ch 337 (accounts to be published annually).

6   *Blackmore v White* [1899] 1 QB 293 (condition to repair); *Dingle v Coppen* [1899] 1 Ch 726 at 733 (similar condition).

7   *Rees v Engleback* (1871) LR 12 Eq 225 at 237; *Re Loom, Fulfor v Reversionary Interest Society Ltd* [1910] 2 Ch 230 at 233; *Re M'Mahon, M'Mahon v M'Mahon* [1901] 1 IR 489.

8   *Gregg v Coates* (1856) 23 Beav 33 at 38; *Blackmore v White* [1899] 1 QB 293 at 304; *Batthyany v Walford* (1887) 36 Ch D 269 at 281.

9   *Egg v Devey* (1847) 10 Beav 444; *Robertson v Junkin* (1896) 26 SCR 192.

CHAPTER 46

Disclaimer of gift

[46.1]
How disclaimer made. Disclaimer[1] may be made in the case of a person sui juris by informal acts as well as by deed,[2] and this was so even though the gift conferred a legal estate upon the donee,[3] but now the donee can obtain the legal estate only by the assent of the personal representative.[4] Where the gift is subject to burdens or requires the performance of conditions, the disclaimer relieves the donee from those burdens and conditions.[5] The disclaimer affects only the interest of the donee and does not affect any other right or interest given by the will, eg a charge on the property or a trust.[6] A beneficiary who is one of the objects of a discretionary power under which trustees may or may not decide to make a gift in his favour, has a right to renounce his interest.[7] A putative beneficiary under the will or intestacy of a living person has no interest in the deceased's estate which can be the subject of a disclaimer and so a purported inter vivos disclaimer by such a beneficiary has no effect.[8]

1   The disclaimer here dealt with is the disclaimer of a gift by will; see *Townson v Tickell* (1819) 3 B & Ald 31 at 36; and Ventris J in *Thompson v Leach* (1690) 2 Vent 198; see also *Perpetual Executors and Trustees Association of Australia Ltd v Probate Duties Comr* [1981] VR 91 at 101, where this Chapter is referred to. As to disclaimer by trustees: see Chapter 27. As to renunciation by executors, see Chapter 25. It now seems to be settled by the decision in *Re Scott, Widdows v Friends of the Clergy Corpn* [1975] 2 All ER 1033, [1975] 1 WLR 1260 (where the point was assumed and not argued; see Goodhart 40 Conv 292) that an interest acquired on intestacy can be disclaimed at least up to the time of making of the assent (see J L Pinkerton 42 Conv 213). If an interest on intestacy is disclaimed then, on the reasoning in *Re Scott*, the property will not pass to the Crown as bona vacantia but will pass to the other persons entitled on intestacy as if the disclaimer had not survived; *Re Scott, Widdows v Friends of the Clergy Corpn* [1975] 2 All ER 1033, [1975] 1 WLR 1260. But the reasoning in *Re DWS, Re EHS, TWGS v JMG* [2000] 2 All ER 83; affirmed [2001] 1 All ER 97, CA (although not overruling *Re Scott*) casts doubts on this. In that case the intestate beneficiary did not disclaim but was prevented from taking because he had murdered the testator. The court applied the Administration Act 1925, ss 46 and 47 literally, so that a person cannot take where he belongs to a category in relation to which s 46 or s 47 provides that its members only take in the event of a prior category (which includes the person who has disclaimed his interest or murdered the intestate) not surviving the intestate. But a person can do so where he belongs to a category in relation to which s 46 or s 47 provides that its members take in the event of the members of the prior category 'not attaining a vested interest'. This can mean that in some situations disclaimed property will go to the Crown as bona vacantia even where there are persons who could take on intestacy, ie ones who are in a category which can only take where the category in which the disclaiming person or murdered falls, have predeceased the intestate. See also para **[46.5]**, n 2 and Chapter 48, para **[48.8]** infra. *Re Scott, Widdows v Friends of the Clergy Corpn* [1975] 2 All ER 1033, [1975] 1 WLR 1260 was applied in *Re Simmons Estate* (1990) 56 SASR 1 where the text, 6th Edition, Vol 2, p 1342, was applied.
2   *Townson v Tickell* (1819) 3 B & Ald 31; *Begbie v Crook* (1835) 2 Bing NC 70; *Re Birchall, Birchall v Ashton* (1889) 40 Ch D 436; *Re Clout and Frewer's Contract* [1924] 2 Ch 230; *Re*

Moss (1977) 77 DLR (3d) 314. A deed is certainly advisable as evidence of the disclaimer, especially where the gift is to a trustee, though the matter might now be satisfactorily completed by an assent in writing to the person becoming entitled on disclaimer by the donee, supported by the curtain provision of the Administration of Estates Act 1925, s 36(7). Disclaimer by informal acts is more readily presumed where it is to the manifest disadvantage of the beneficiary to retain the gift and will not be readily presumed where it is to his advantage to retain it: *Harris v Watkins* (1856) 2 K & J 473.

3   See the cases cited in n 2. Disclaimers are excepted from conveyances of land which must be by deed: Law of Property Act 1925, s 52(2); 37 *Halsbury's Statutes* (4th edn 192. Where a deed, purporting to be a disclaimer, disclaimed a share held in joint tenancy, it was held that the deed was not a disclaimer but a release: *Re Schar, Midland Bank Executor and Trustee Co Ltd v Damer* [1951] Ch 280, [1950] 2 All ER 1069.

4   Administration of Estates Act 1925, s 36(4); 17 *Halsbury's Statutes* (4th edn) 442; but this would not be so where the personal representative was the same person as the donee or as the trustee.

5   *Silcock v Roynon* (1843) 2 Y & C Ch Cas 376; *Manson v Ross* (1884) 1 BCR (pt 2) 49 (disclaimer of partly paid-up shares).

6   *Wilson v Wilson* (1847) 1 De G & Sm 152; *Mallott v Wilson* [1903] 2 Ch 494 at 501.

7   *Re Gulbenkian's Settlement Trusts (No 2), Stevens v Maun* [1970] Ch 408, [1969] 2 All ER 1173.

8   *Re Smith, Smith v Smith* [2001] 3 All ER 552, even if the disclaimer was made by deed.

[46.2]

Acceptance of the gift. Acceptance[1] of a gift, or any part of it, is inconsistent with an intention to renounce or disclaim, and so the right to disclaim a gift is extinguished as soon as any benefit has been received under it.[2]

1   See Chapter 45.
2   *Re Hodge, Hodge v Griffiths* [1940] Ch 260; *Re Wimperis, Wicker v Wilson* [1914] 1 Ch 502.

[46.3]

Disclaimer of onerous property. If a donee is given two distinct properties, he is in general entitled to disclaim one and take the other[1] even when the two are included under the same words of gift,[2] but it may be, upon the proper construction of the will, that the two properties are intended to be taken together or not at all, and in the latter case there is no option to disclaim one of them.[3] Where there is a single undivided gift, such as a gift of residue, the whole must be taken or none.[4] It seems that, where one gift is a leasehold known to the testator to be onerous and bequeathed in order to free the testator's general estate from the burden, the right to disclaim that gift and accept another will not be readily inferred.[5] Where the donee is not sui juris the court may disclaim on his behalf.[6] A married woman restrained from anticipation could disclaim.[7] It is no objection to a disclaimer that the disclaiming beneficiary will take on the intestacy arising thereunder and on more beneficial terms.[8]

1   *Andrew v Trinity Hall, Cambridge* (1804) 9 Ves 525 at 534; *Warren v Rudall, ex p Godfrey* (1860) 1 John & H 1; *Long v Kent* (1865) 6 New Rep 354 (gift of shares disclaimed); *Aston v Wood* (1874) 43 LJ Ch 715 (a similar case); *Re Loom, Fulford v Reversionary Society* [1910] 2 Ch 230. In *Moffett v Bates* (1857) 3 Sm & G 468, an infant on coming of age repudiated a gift of bank shares. The bank had become insolvent and a large debt was due from the estate, but it was held that the infant could disclaim and the debt was thrown on residue and not on a gift of realty which the infant accepted. In this case the executors had assented to the gift of shares and received dividends.

2   *Syer v Gladstone* (1885) 30 Ch D 614, explained in *Frewen v Law Life Assurance Society* [1896] 2 Ch 511 at 516; *Re Hotchkys, Freke v Calmady* (1886) 32 Ch D 408; *Re Kensington,*

Earl of Longford v Kensington [1902] 1 Ch 203. In *Re Lysons, Beck v Lysons* (1912) 107 LT 146, a gift of a leasehold house together with furniture was held to be two independent gifts, but in *Re Joel, Rogerson v Joel* [1943] Ch 311, [1943] 2 All ER 263, a similar gift was held to be one gift and a disclaimer could only be made of both house and furniture. It was argued that the lease was an onerous gift and the furniture not an onerous gift and that separated the gift so that it became two independent gifts. The Court of Appeal held, however, that this was not the case and there was nothing in *Syer v Gladstone* (1885) 30 Ch D 614, that compelled it to come to that decision.

3   Fry LJ said in *Guthrie v Walrond* (1883) 22 Ch D 573 at 577:

'It appears to me plain that when two distinct legacies or gifts are made by will to one person, he is, as a general rule, entitled to take one and disclaim the other, but that his right to do so may be rebutted if there is anything in the will to show that it was the testator's intention that that option should not exist.'

Applied in *Re Skinner* (1970) 12 DLR (3d) 227 (beneficiary could not disclaim simply for one year; must disclaim whole, cannot disclaim a part); see also *Re Metcalfe* (1973) 29 DLR (3d) 60 (university waiving scholarships because of conditions attached thereto); *Moffett v Bates* (1857) 3 Sm & G 465; *Re Pearce* [1926] NZLR 698.

4   *A-G v Brackenbury* (1863) 1 H & C 782 at 791; *Green v Britten* (1872) 42 LJ Ch 187; *Hawkins v Hawkins* (1880) 13 Ch D 470; *Parnell v Boyd* [1896] 2 IR 571; but see *Re Coulson* (1977) 78 DLR (3d) 435.

5   *Talbot v Earl of Radnor* (1834) 3 My & K 252; *Re Sitwell, Worsley v Sitwell* [1913] WN 261.

6   *Re Marriott* (1808) 2 Mol 516 (person of unsound mind); *Wolverhampton and Staffordshire Banking Co v George* (1883) 24 Ch D 707 (infant).

7   *Re Wimperis, Wicken v Wilson* [1914] 1 Ch 502; but no question of a married woman's capacity to disclaim or of the effect of a restraint on anticipation can now arise: Law Reform (Married Women and Tortfeasors) Act 1935, and Married Women (Restraint upon Anticipation) Act 1949.

8   *Re Sullivan, Dunkley v Sullivan* [1930] 1 Ch 84 (where a beneficial life tenant avoided royalties being treated as capital).

[46.4]

How far disclaimer may be retracted. A disclaimer by a person sui juris is in general final and cannot be retracted; but where the rights of other parties are not prejudiced and they have not altered their position on the faith of the disclaimer, and the disclaimer has been made without consideration, a disclaimer may be retracted.[1] A tenant for life who has refused to receive the income for some time may, so long as there has been no change in the position of other parties claiming under the will, change his mind and decide to receive the income in future.[2] Further a donee who has in the first instance claimed the property under a higher title, may change his mind, and take it as donee.[3]

1   *Re Cranstoun, Gibbs v Home of Rest for Horses* [1949] Ch 523, [1949] 1 All ER 871; *Re Young, Fraser v Young* [1913] 1 Ch 272.

2   *Re Young, Fraser v Young* [1913] 1 Ch 272. A life tenant merely refusing to take possession of onerous leaseholds is entitled to the income of the proceeds of sale: *Earl of Lonsdale v Countess of Berchtoldt* (1857) 3 K & J 185.

3   *Doe d Smyth v Smyth* (1826) 6 B & C 112 at 117; but a legatee could not disclaim a gift by will to him under a general power of appointment in order to take in default of appointment and so escape legacy duty on the gift: *A-G v Brackenbury* (1863) 1 H & C 782; *HM Advocate v Routledge's Trustees* (1907) 44 SLR 305 at 309. See, however, para **[46.3]**, n 6.

[46.5]

Effect of disclaimer. A disclaimer does not act positively as an assignment or disposition of property, but acts negatively by preventing the property from vesting at all.[1] Thus Walton J commented in *Re Scott, Widdows v Friends of the Clergy Corpn.*[2]

'The effect of a disclaimer is not to throw the property onto the scrap heap, but to refuse to accept it in the first place, leaving the ownership with the people or the interest or the estate, or whatever, from which it was derived in the first place.'

In many cases the effect of a disclaimer will be to accelerate a subsequent interest, and this is dealt with later.[3]

1   *Townson v Tickell* (1819) 3 B & Ald 31; see *Re Jung* (1979) 99 DLR (3d) 65.
2   [1975] 2 All ER 1033 at 1045. But see also *Re DWS, Re EHS, TWGS v JMG* [2000] 2 All ER 83 ;affirmed [2001] 1 All ER 97, where (in a different context) the court held the next available class under intestacy was entitled to take; but the conclusion in *Re DWS* is based on different reasoning to that in *Re Scott*; see para **[46.1]**, n 1 and Chapter 104. *Re Stratton's Deed of Disclaimer* [1958] Ch 42, [1957] 2 All ER 594; *Re Parsons* [1942] Ch 335; *Sembaliuk v Sembaliuk* (1985) 15 DLR (4th) 303.
3   See Chapter 48.

[46.6]

Tax advantages. Disclaimers can be used in appropriate circumstances to achieve tax advantages. Under the Inheritance Tax Act 1984 if a testamentary or intestate benefit is disclaimed by an instrument in writing within two years of the death, the disclaimer is not treated as a transfer of value, and the disclaimed benefit is treated as never having been conferred.[1] A somewhat similar, but more limited provision applies to capital gains tax by virtue of the Taxation of Chargeable Gains Act 1992, s 62(6)–(10).[2] It is possible that a disclaimer is not a settlement for the purposes of the Income and Corporations Taxes Act 1988, ss 660A and 660B, or the Taxation of Chargeable Gains Act 1992, s 77, so that, for example, where the disclaimer is in favour of unmarried minor children, the income is not treated as the income of the disclaiming parent.[3]

1   Inheritance Tax Act 1984, ss 17(a), 142(1) Similar advantages are achieved by a variation. See Vol 2, Part F, paras **[241.1]–[241.15]**.
2   See Vol 2, para **[241.17]**.
3   A variation is a settlement within the sections but there is no decided view on the effect of a disclaimer for this purpose. See, further, Vol 2 para **[241.16]**.

CHAPTER 47

Lapse

I. NATURE OF LAPSE

[47.1]
Meaning of 'lapse'. The term 'lapse' is generally applied to the failure of a testamentary gift owing to the death of the devisee or legatee in the testator's lifetime;[1] whether before or after the date of the will.[2] When used in a will it may have a wider significance and may refer to the failure of a testamentary gift in any other way.[3] Similarly the word 'lapse' when used, in the original wording , of the Wills Act 1837 (WA 1837), s 18A was not confined to the strict technical meaning of failure by reason of the legatee's death in the lifetime of the testator but included failure for other reasons, such as divorce, as provided by that section.[4] As a rule a devisee or legatee must survive the testator[5] in order that he or his estate may have the benefit of the gift,[6] and a confirmation by codicil of a gift in a will to a legatee who has died since the date of the will does not prevent a lapse.[7]

1   *Elliott v Davenport* (1705) 1 P Wms 83. A gift to an incorporated or unincorporated body may lapse when the body has ceased to exist. A gift to a friendly society all of whose members had been struck off the roll of members and its registry cancelled and held to lapse: *Walker v Irish Law Clerks Benefit Society* [1946] IR 222.
2   *Maybank v Brooks* (1780) 1 Bro CC 84 (where it was held that parol evidence was inadmissible to prove that the testator knew at the date of his will that the legatee was dead); *Clarke v Clemmans* (1866) 36 LJ Ch 171. A provision in a will against lapse of legacies given by 'this my will' will extend to legacies given by a codicil: *Re Smith, Prada v Vandroy* [1916] 2 Ch 368. As to simultaneous death of testator and beneficiary, see Chapter 70.
3   *Re Fox's Estate, Dawes v Druitt* [1937] 4 All ER 664, where the word 'lapse' in a homemade will was held to apply not only to death in the testator's lifetime, but also to failure of a gift by reason of a person having no children. This construction was reached upon the rule in *Jones v Westcomb* (1711) Prec Ch 316; see para **[93.9]** infra.
    A somewhat similar result was reached in *Aspinall v Duckworth* (1866) 35 Beav 307, and *Re Wand, Escritt v Wand* [1907] 1 Ch 391, where the word 'lapse' was used with reference to class gifts.
4   *Re Sinclair, Lloyds Bank plc v Imperial Cancer Research Fund* [1984] 3 All ER 362, [1984] 1 WLR 1240; affd [1985] Ch 446, [1985] 1 All ER 1066, CA. '... the word "lapse" is, in an appropriate context, perfectly apt to cover the happening of any event in a testator's lifetime which prevents the intended legatee from being entitled to the legacy and thus to mean nothing more than "fail"'; per Slade LJ at 1070. See also *Re Gillis Estate* [1988] 6 WWR 726. But the Wills Act 1837, s 18A has been amended (as a result of the *Sinclair* case) in relation to deaths on or after 1 January 1996 so as no longer to use the word 'lapse': see paras **[47.2]** and **[47.3]** infra.
5   See Chapter 9, paras **[9.2]** et seq, and for exceptions from the doctrine of lapse, see para **[47.10]** infra.
6   *Elliott v Davenport* (1705) 1 P Wms 83. The rule applies: (i) to a gift by the will of A upon the trusts of the will of a deceased person, and the gift fails as regards those devisees under the

latter will who predecease A: *Culsha v Cheese* (1849) 7 Hare 236 at 245; *Re Currie's Settlement, Re Rooper, Rooper v Williams* [1910] 1 Ch 329; (ii) to the forgiveness of a charge upon property: *Re MacDonnell, Colgan v MacDonnell* [1927] 1 IR 213; (iii) where a settlement covenants to pay sums to legacies and such sums are not payable if the beneficiaries predecease the testator: *Re Hall's Settlement Trusts, Samuel v Lamont* [1937] Ch 227, [1937] 1 All ER 571.

7   *Drinkwater v Falconer* (1755) 2 Ves Sen 623; *Hutcheson v Hammond* (1790) 3 Bro CC 128; *Maybank v Brooks* (1780) 1 Bro CC 84; see para [20.4] supra.

II.   THE EFFECT OF DISSOLUTION OR ANNULMENT OF MARRIAGE ON WILLS

[47.2]

The new s 18A. This was enacted by the Administration of Justice Act 1982 (AJA 1982), s 18(2) and was inserted into the WA 1837 as s 18A.[1] It provides for the effect of dissolution or annulment of marriage on wills and the prerequisites for the operation of the section are: that the testator should have made a will, and that subsequently his marriage should have been dissolved or annulled or declared void.[2] As originally enacted it provided that the will is to take effect as if any appointment of the former spouse as an executor or trustee had been omitted, and 'any devise or bequest to the former spouse shall lapse', both points being subject to a contrary intention appearing in the will.[3] This was found to be unsatisfactory because, despite an earlier first instance decision to the contrary,[4] the Court of Appeal[5] held that this provision did not have the effect of treating the former spouse as predeceasing the testator (if he or she did not actually do so) so as to bring into operation an alternative gift in the will. Accordingly, s 18A(1) is amended for deaths on or after 1 January 1996 so that it deems the testator's former spouse to have died on the date on which the marriage was dissolved or annulled for the purposes of any provision of the testator's will which confers a power of appointment on the spouse, appoints the spouse as an executor, or which relates to the devolution of property which, or an interest in which, was devised or bequeathed to the spouse.[6] This means that any gift, or provision appointing executors or conferring a power of appointment, which was included in the testator's will and which was to take effect in the alternative to a provision in favour of the testator's then spouse in the event of the spouse predeceasing the testator, will now also take effect in the event of the marriage to that spouse having been dissolved or annulled. These provisions are without prejudice to the right of a former spouse to apply for financial provision under the Inheritance (Provision for Family and Dependants) Act 1975.[7] However it must be remembered that orders for financial provision in favour of former spouses are limited to 'such financial provision as it would be reasonable in all the circumstances of the case for the applicant to receive for his maintenance',[8] and also that, in view of the wide powers of the court to make capital adjustments between divorced spouses as ancillary relief in divorce proceedings, successful claims by former spouses under the Inheritance (Provision for Family and Dependants) Act 1975 will be rare.[9]

The provisions will only apply where the will is made before the dissolution or annulment and thus care is needed with reference to subsequent codicils which will, generally, have the effect of republishing the will.[10] In many cases divorce or annulment will be followed by remarriage and this will, of course, have the effect of revoking the previous will in any event.[11]

1   50 *Halsbury's Statutes* (4th edn) 587. See Vol 2, Part G, para **[244.18]**. The original provisions
     apply to the wills of testators who die on or after 1 January 1983; s 73(6); s 76(11). The
     provisions were based on the recommendations of the Law Reform Committee, 22nd Report on
     The Making and Revocation of Wills, 1980, Cmnd 7902; see paras **[3.26]–[3.38]** supra.
2   Wills Act 1837, s 18A(1) as originally enacted.
3   Wills Act 1837, s 18A(1) as originally enacted.
4   *Re Cherrington* [1984] 2 All ER 285, [1984] 1 WLR 772.
5   *Re Sinclair* [1984] 3 All ER 362, [1984] 1 WLR 1240; affd [1985] Ch 446, [1985] 1 All ER
     1066; testator bequeathing entire estate to wife and in the event of the wife predeceasing him or
     failing to survive him for one month estate to pass to research fund. Marriage was dissolved
     before the testator's death and wife survived him. Held not to pass to research fund; passed as
     property undisposed of to the person entitled on an intestacy; *Re Cherrington* [1984] 2 All ER
     285, [1984] 1 WLR 772, overruled. The correctness of this ruling was confirmed by s 18A(3)
     designating the consequences for a gift in remainder, as if the spouse had predeceased, thus
     indicating that the word 'lapse' in s 18A(1)(b) was not intended to have that effect; see
     para **[47.3]** infra. But see now the amendment to the section; n 4.
6   Wills Act 1837, s 18A(1), as amended by the Law Reform (Succession) Act 1995, s 3(1); For
     further discussion, and the practical consequences, see Vol 2, the Preliminary Note to C2,
     para **[224.1]** et seq and Vol 2, Part G, para **[244.130]** for the amended text. See the Law Reform
     (Succession) Act 1995, s 3(2) (Vol 2, Part G, para **[244.130]**); the commencement of this
     amendment is in relation to any will made by a person dying on or after 1 January 1996,
     regardless of the date of the will and the date of the dissolution or annulment of the marriage.
7   Wills Act 1837, s 18A(2); see para **[105.10]** infra.
8   See the Inheritance (Provision for Family and Dependants) Act 1975, s 1(2)(b), see Chapter
     105.
9   See *Re Fullard* [1982] Fam 42, [1981] 2 All ER 796, and discussion at para **[105.10]** infra.
10   See Chapter 10.
11   See Chapter 17. In many cases it will be regarded as more appropriate for an existing will to be
     expressly revoked on divorce and a new will made. Where a re-marriage is contemplated the
     new will should either be expressed to be in expectation of the marriage or, preferably, made
     after the marriage.

[47.3]
Gifts in remainder. Many testamentary gifts to a spouse are gifts for life with
remainder. The WA 1837, s 18A as originally enacted provided, in subsection
(3), that where the gift to the spouse was deemed to lapse by virtue of the
section, ... the interest in remainder shall be treated as if it had not been subject
to the life interest, and if it was contingent upon the termination of the life
interest, as if it had not been so contingent'.[1] This resulted in an acceleration of
the remainder interests. Where those interests were to a class then the operation
of the class closing rules would likewise be accelerated since, it is submitted, the
situation was analogous to where the life tenant predeceases the testator.[2] This
provision is repealed in relation to the wills of testators dying on or after 1
January 1996.[3] The amendments to the WA 1837, s 18A(1) discussed above,
which deem the former spouse to have predeceased the testator, have the effect
of accelerating the remainders upon a life interest given to the former spouse,
and the specific provision for this purpose formerly in s 18A(3) is no longer
needed.

1   WA 1837, s 18A(3).
2   See para **[66.16]**. The modern cases of *Re Kebty-Fletcher's Will Trusts, Public Trustee v Swan
     and Snowden* [1969] 1 Ch 339, [1967] 3 All ER 1076 and *Re Harker's Will Trusts, Kean v
     Harker* [1969] 3 All ER 1, [1969] 1 WLR 1124, declining to accept an acceleration of the class
     closing rules where the prior life interest was disclaimed or released and assigned can be
     distinguished, see Chapter 66.
3   By the Schedule to the Law Reform (Succession) Act 1995.

III. EFFECT OF LAPSE

[47.4]

General principles. The usual result of the lapse of a specific gift is that it falls into residue[1] and, if there is no residuary gift, the lapsed gift passes as on an intestacy.[2] Before 1926, when different rules regulated the descent of realty and the distribution of personalty, it was necessarily of importance to distinguish real from personal property, but, since 1925 when this distinction was ended, this is immaterial unless there are separate residuary gifts for realty and personalty or the will creates both a particular and general residue. Where there is a residuary gift and it fails in whole or in part, there is an intestacy.

1   See, for example, *Re Leitch* [1997] 1 NZLR 38.
2   See *Re Sinclair, Lloyds Bank plc v Imperial Cancer Research Fund* [1985] 1 All ER 1066, CA; affirming [1984] 3 All ER 362.

[47.5]

Lapsed devises or bequests. A lapsed specific devise[1] or specific bequest[2] falls into residue. A lapsed gift of residue or a share of residue or a lapsed general gift of property[3] passes as on an intestacy.[4]

1   Wills Act 1837, s 25; 50 *Halsbury's Statutes* (4th edn) 594; Vol 2, Part G, para **[244.25]**, which assimilated the law as to residuary devises to that of residuary gifts of personal property: *Carter v Haswell* (1857) 3 Jur NS 788 at 790. If there is no residuary gift, the lapsed gift passes as on intestacy: *Cogan v Stephens* (1835) 1 Beav 482n; *Amyot v Dwarris* [1904] AC 268.
2   *Cambridge v Rous* (1802) 8 Ves 12.
3   Some wills contain only a general gift of all property to a universal legatee and the failure of such a gift causes an intestacy upon the same principle as the failure of a residuary gift.
4   *Bagwell v Dry* (1721) 1 P Wms 700; *Sykes v Sykes* (1868) 3 Ch App 301; *Re Watson* [1927] 4 DLR 626. As to where there are two residuary clauses, see *Johns v Wilson* [1900] 1 IR 342; *Re Isaac, Harrison v Isaac* [1905] 1 Ch 427; *Re Smith and McKay* (1994) 116 DLR (4th) 308. As to the doctrine of acceleration and lapse, see Chapter 48, paras **[48.4]** and **[48.5]** infra. As to application of assets and a lapsed share, see Vol 2, para **[214.1]** et seq.

[47.6]

Particular residue. The law supposes that a testator has in mind the distinct properties or parcels of land which he holds, but in the case of personalty there is no such supposition and it is generally regarded as one composite mass of property. For this reason a particular residuary gift of real property is specific and, in so far as it fails, will lapse. Thus if a testator disposes of certain real property in a named place or parish and then disposes of all the remaining real property there, the latter gift is a gift of a particular residue and is specific and will not carry a lapsed share of the first gift.[1] It is otherwise, however, where the first gift is a general gift of all real property in a certain parish, for such a gift will carry a further lapsed gift of property in the same parish.[2] In the case of personal property, however, there is no such assumption and a particular residue of personalty passes such property not previously given or in respect of which the gift has lapsed.[3] The question of appointed property is dealt with elsewhere.[4]

1   *Springett v Jenings* (1871) 6 Ch App 333; *Re Brown* (1855) 1 K & J 522.
2   *Re Davies, Thomas v Thomas-Davies* [1928] Ch 24 (where the testator after making his will acquired further property in the same parish and specifically disposed of it by codicil and the

gift in the codicil failed: the further property passed under the general gift which was not revoked by the codicil and not under a general residuary gift of real and personal property).

3   *De Trafford v Tempest* (1856) 21 Beav 564 (particular chattels in residence to A and remainder of chattels there to B with a general residuary gift to C: lapsed share of A's gift passed to B and not to C); *Champney v Davy* (1879) 11 Ch D 949 (particular residuary gift not affected by presence or absence of general residuary gift and there is no distinction between lapsed and invalid gifts); *Re Larking, Larking v Larking* (1887) 37 Ch D 310 (bequest of policy moneys subject to payment of two debts: debts paid off). See also *De Quetteville v De Quetteville* (1905) 93 LT 579 (payment of estate duty out of particular estate), and see *Re Whitrod, Burrows v Base* [1926] Ch 118.
4   See paras **[47.36]–[47.39]** infra.

[47.7]

Charge on lapsed property. Where property is given or appointed by will to one person charged with an annual or lump sum in favour of another, the charge is not affected by the death of the donee of the property before the testator,[1] though it would be destroyed if the gift to the donee were revoked;[2] but if the chargee dies in the testator's lifetime[3] or the charge fails for illegality,[4] the charge as a general rule[5] sinks for the benefit of the devisee. Similarly, where personal property, including a particular fund,[6] is bequeathed subject to a charge, and the chargee dies before the testator, his interest lapses for the benefit of the legatee.[7] The same principle applies where the object for which the charge was created fails for illegality.[8]

1   *Oke v Heath* (1748) 1 Ves Sen 135; see *Re Kirk, Kirk v Kirk* (1882) 21 Ch D 431, where land was charged to a creditor subject to his releasing a debt and the creditor predeceased the testator.
2   *Cowper v Mantell* (1856) 22 Beav 223.
3   *Re Cooper's Trusts, ex p Sparks* (1853) 4 De GM & G 757; *Re Clulow's Trust* (1859) 1 John & H 639; *Sutcliffe v Cole* (1855) 3 Drew 135; *Tucker v Kayess* (1858) 4 K & J 339; *Re Kirk, Kirk v Kirk* (1882) 21 Ch D 431.
4   *Cooke v Stationers' Co* (1831) 3 My & K 262; *Blight v Hartnoll* (1883) 23 Ch D 218 at 222.
5   The will may show an intention that the money charged shall be raised in any event; see *Tregonwell v Sydenham* (1815) 3 Dow 194 at 211; and compare *Re Clarke, Sheldon v Redrup* [1942] Ch 434, [1942] 2 All ER 294 (direction to set aside a fund to provide an annuity). For cases where the money charged was not disposed of by the will, see *Sidney v Shelley* (1815) 19 Ves 352; *Heptinstall v Gott* (1862) 2 John & H 449.
6   *Scott v Salmond* (1833) 1 My & K 363.
7   *Tucker v Kayess* (1858) 5 K & J 339 at 342.
8   *Re Rogerson, Bird v Lee* [1901] 1 Ch 715.

[47.8]

Exception out of lapsed property. A distinction must, however, be drawn between a devise subject to a charge and a devise or bequest with an exception out of it. In the latter case, if the gift of the excepted property lapses or fails for any reason, it falls as a rule into residue.[1]

1   *Re Jupp, Gladman v Jupp* (1903) 87 LT 739; *Sutcliffe v Cole* (1855) 3 Drew 135. See also *Tucker v Kayess* (1858) 5 K & J 339; *Heptinstall v Gott* (1862) 2 John & H 449; *Simmons v Pitt* (1873) 8 Ch App 978; *Wainman v Field* (1854) Kay 507; *Blight v Hartnoll* (1883) 23 Ch D 218 at 222; *Re Tilden, Coubrough v Royal Society of London* (1938) 82 Sol Jo 334. A gift of the 'remainder' of a residuary fund may be either a gift of the balance of the fund after previous gifts or a gift of the whole fund subject to the previous gifts. In the latter case, but not in the former, the gift of the fund carries with it any previous gift which fails; *Re Parnell, Ranks v Holmes* [1944] Ch 107; distinguished on the facts in *Re Fry Estate* (1957) 40 MPR 71.

[47.9]

Lapse of charitable legacies. Legacies to charitable institutions ceasing to exist in the testator's lifetime lapse, or are applicable cy-près, according as the gift is construed to be for the benefit of the particular institution or to import a general charitable intention.[1]

1   See Chapter 103.

IV.   STATUTORY EXCEPTIONS FROM LAPSE

[47.10]

Statutory provisions applicable. The Wills Act 1837, s 33 as originally enacted will apply to determine the effect of gifts to children who predecease the testator, in wills of testators who die before 1 January 1983. However, a new s 33 of the WA 1837 has been substituted by the Administration of Justice Act 1982, s 19[1] and this section, which extends and to some extent clarifies, the exemption from lapse will be applicable to gifts in wills of testators who die on or after 1 January 1983.[2] This new provision effects a true substitution in favour of issue and applies to class gifts as well as to gifts to individuals. The section as originally enacted will be shortly considered first. The Wills Act 1837, s 32, which applies to entails has been prospectively repealed by the Trusts of Land and Appointment of Trustees Act 1996.[3]

1   See Vol 2, Part G, para **[244.95]**.
2   AJA 1982, ss 73(6), and 76(11).
3   See para **[47.19]** infra.

[47.11]

The original WA 1837, s 33. In the absence of a contrary intention in the will[1] a devise or bequest of real or personal property to a child or other issue of the testator for any estate or interest not determinable at or before the death[2] of such child or issue did not lapse if the devisee or legatee predeceased the testator, leaving issue who were living at the death of the latter but took effect as if the devisee or legatee had died immediately after the testator,[3] and became disposable under the will[4] of the devisee or legatee, or as part of his estate if he died intestate;[5] and if the testator intended a gift to go over in the event of his child predeceasing him, he had to expressly so provide.[6] The rule was applicable in the case of a gift to a child dead at the date of the will,[7] or where the issue surviving the testator was not living at the death of the beneficiary, being issue of issue of the beneficiary, eg a grandchild.[8] The gift had to be to the legatee as a persona designata.[9] The rule was not applicable where the gift was to a class not ascertainable until the death of the testator,[10] even where that happened to be only one member of the class.[11] Nor was the statutory provision applicable to the lapse of a gift in joint tenancy where both the donees predeceased the testator and one or both left issue.[12]

1   As to which, see *Re Morris, Corfield v Waller* (1916) 86 LJ Ch 456; *Re Wilson, Lothian v Wilson* (1920) 89 LJ Ch 216; *Re Meredith, Davies v Davies* [1924] 2 Ch 552, but see *Re McNeill* (1980) 109 DLR (3d) 109.

2   The statutory provision did not apply to collateral relations of the testator: *Re Gresley's Settlement, Willoughby v Drummond* [1911] 1 Ch 358. Nor did it apply where the gift was contingent on the attainment of a specified age, eg 25, and the beneficiary died under that age although he or she would have attained that age if he or she had died immediately after the testator; *Re Wolson, Wolson v Jackson* [1939] Ch 780, [1939] 3 All ER 852, such a gift being one 'determinable at the death' of the beneficiary within the section. But where the gift was to children *nominatim* at 21 and one attained that age his share was saved from lapse: *Re Wilson, Lothian v Wilson* (1920) 89 LJ Ch 216.

3   Wills Act 1837, s 33; 50 *Halsbury's Statutes* (4th edn) 599. See *Re Scott* [1901] 1 KB 228 at 240.

4   *Johnson v Johnson* (1953) 3 Hare 157; *Re Mason's Will* (1864) 34 Beav 494. If the child died bankrupt, the share went to the trustee in bankruptcy: *Re Pearson, Smith v Pearson* [1920] 1 Ch 247.

5   *Skinner v Ogle* (1845) 1 Rob Eccl 363; *Re Peerless, Peerless v Smith* [1901] WN 151. The legatee's estate was administered according to the law at the true date of his death and not at the date he was deemed to have died: *Re Hurd, Stott v Stott* [1941] Ch 196, [1941] 1 All ER 238.

6   *Re More's Trust* (1851) 10 Hare 171.

7   *Mower v Orr* (1849) 7 Hare 473; *Wisden v Wisden* (1854) 2 Sm & G 396.

8   *Re Parker's Goods* (1860) 1 Sw & Tr 523 (where the legatee, a daughter, died leaving a child who also predeceased the testatrix, leaving a child who survived the testatrix).

9   *Re Stansfield, Stansfield v Stansfield* (1880) 15 Ch D 84 (where a gift was to 'my nine children' and was held not to be to a class but to named persons); *Re Morris, Corfield v Waller* (1916) 86 LJ Ch 456 (surviving children).

10   *Olney v Bates* (1855) 3 Drew 319; *Browne v Hammond* (1858) John 210; *Re Jackson, Shiers v Ashworth* (1883) 25 Ch D 162 at 164.

11   *Re Harvey's Estate, Harvey v Gillow* [1893] 1 Ch 567.

12   *Re Butler, Joyce v Brew* [1918] 1 IR 394.

[47.12]

Effect of child's decease. A gift to a child,[1] though dependent on the fact of there being issue of the devisee or legatee living at the testator's death, was not a gift to such issue, but took effect exactly as if the actual death of the devisee or legatee had happened immediately after the death of the testator (ie the gift was subject to the legatee's will (if any) or passed on his intestacy) and with all the consequences thereof;[2] and it devolved subject to any burden[3] or condition[4] which under the will would have been imposed on the devisee or legatee if he had survived the testator. Where a married woman, a legatee under her father's will, died in his lifetime and in that of her husband, leaving issue, and the husband also predeceased the father, the estate of that married woman was distributed to those entitled thereto at the date of her death, so that, in the circumstances stated, the husband took on the intestacy of the married woman, the interest of a surviving spouse.[5] The sole object of the Wills Act 1837, s 33[6] was to give effect to the parent's will and prevent lapse. The section was not intended to alter the devolution of the beneficiary's estate by imputing a fictitious date for his or her death as though he or she had immediately died after the testator.[7]

1   Child here includes a legitimated person: *Re Brodie, Barclays Bank Ltd v Dallas* [1967] Ch 818, [1967] 2 All ER 97.

2   *Johnson v Johnson* (1843) 3 Hare 157; *Eager v Furnivall* (1881) 17 Ch D 115 at 118. If the legatee was bankrupt, the gift passed to the trustee: *Re Pearson, Smith v Pearson* [1920] 1 Ch 247.

3   *Pickersgill v Rodger* (1876) 5 Ch D 163 at 172, where the estate of the legatee were put to their election whether to take under the will or against it.

4   *Re Hone's Trusts* (1883) 22 Ch D 663. A legacy so saved from lapse, however, was not caught by an after-acquired property clause to settle property acquired during coverture: *Pearce v Graham* (1863) 1 New Rep 507; *Re Blundell, Blundell v Blundell* [1906] 2 Ch 222 at 229.

5   *Re Basioli, Re Depaoli* [1953] Ch 367, [1953] 1 All ER 301, not following *Re Councell's Goods* (1871) LR 2 P & D 314, and *Re Allen's Trusts* [1909] WN 181, and applying the decision in *Re Hurd, Stott v Stott* [1941] Ch 196, [1941] 1 All ER 238; see also *Re Hone's Trusts* (1883) 22 Ch D 663.
6   See Vol 2, Part G, para **[244.33]** et seq.
7   *Re Basioli, Re Depaoli* [1953] Ch 367, [1953] 1 All ER 301. See also *Re Hensler, Jones v Hensler* (1881) 19 Ch D 612.

[47.13]

Gift under power of appointment. A gift under a general power of appointment to a child predeceasing the testator and leaving issue was preserved from lapse,[1] but not a gift under a special power,[2] or a power of charging given under a will to a tenant for life who died before the testator.[3]

1   *Eccles v Cheyne* (1856) 2 K & J 676; and see paras 47.36 to 47.39, post.
2   *Griffiths v Gale* (1844) 12 Sim 327; *Freeland v Pearson* (1867) LR 3 Eq 658; *Holyland v Lewin* (1884) 26 Ch D 266.
3   *Griggs v Gibson (No 2)* (1866) 35 LJ Ch 458.

[47.14]

The substituted WA 1837, s 33. The Administration of Justice Act 1982[1] has substituted a new provision for the Wills Act 1837, s 33 applicable to the wills of testators who die on or after 1 January 1983.[2] The section applies to both gifts to individual children[3] and to gifts to classes of children.[4] In the case of the former the section applies where: first, the will contains a devise or bequest to a child or remoter descendant of the testator; secondly, the intended beneficiary dies before the testator leaving issue; and thirdly, issue of the intended beneficiary are living at the testator's death. In these cases it is provided that ... the devise or bequest shall take effect as a devise or bequest to the issue living at the testator's death'.[5] In this way, in contrast to the effect of the original s 33, the provision effects a simple and true substitution in favour of issue, per stirpes, unless a contrary intention appears by the will.[6] The old s 33 did not apply to a class gift since in such a case the share of a deceased member of the class did not lapse, but accrued to the other members of the class. In the case of a gift to children as a class this had the effect of benefiting the brothers and sisters of the deceased child even if he or she left issue. The new s 33 contains an important extension of the previous law to remedy this situation. Where a will contains a gift to the testator's children (or remoter descendants) as a class, and a member of the class dies before the testator leaving issue who are living at the testator's death, then it is provided that the gifts, ... shall take effect as if the class included the issue of its deceased member living at the testator's death'. Again, this construction can be excluded if a contrary intention appears by the will.[7]

Where the section operates, the substituted issue take through all degrees per stirpes in equal shares if more than one, and in the usual way, they take the gift or share which their parent would have taken. There can of course be no possibility of such issue taking whose parent is living at the testator's death and so capable of taking.[8]

1   AJA 1982, s 19; 50 *Halsbury's Statutes* (4th edn) 599. See Vol 2, Part G, para **[244.34]**.
2   AJA 1982, ss 73(6), 76(11).
3   WA 1837, s 33(1).

4   Wills Act 1837, s 33(2). It is possible that the new provision would apply to gifts to persons as joint tenants because of the absence of any reference to the exclusion of interests ceasing on death (which the old s 33 contained and thus excluded gifts to joint tenants). However, it could be argued that a gift to joint tenants discloses a contrary intention within the section.

5   It will be noticed that in contrast to the previous formulation the new WA 1837, s 33 contains no reference to 'lapse'; see Michael Wheeler QC in *Re Sinclair, Lloyd's Bank plc v Imperial Cancer Research Fund* [1984] 3 All ER 362 and 365.

6   Contrast the effect of the old WA 1837, s 33, noted above at para **[47.11]** supra. Cases such as *Re Basioli, McGahey v Depaoli* [1953] Ch 367, [1953] 1 All ER 301 would now be decided differently if the facts were to recur with reference to a post-1982 death.

7   AJA 1982, s 19; new WA 1837, s 33(2); Vol 2, Part G, para **[244.34]**.

8   AJA 1982, s 19; new WA 1837, s 33(3).

[47.15]

Illegitimate children. The new provision expressly declares that 'the illegitimacy of any person is to be disregarded'[1] and thus such persons take under the section, whereas previously they were included by the effect of an amendment to the WA 1837 by the Family Law Reform Act 1969.[2]

1   WA 1837, s 33(4)(*a*).
2   Family Law Reform Act 1969, s 16, which is now repealed in respect of deaths on or after 1 January 1983; AJA 1982, s 75(1); s 73(6).

[47.16]

Children en ventre sa mere. The better view under the old WA 1837, s 33 was that a child en ventre sa mere at the death did not qualify.[1] It is now expressly provided that ... a person conceived before the testator's death and born living thereafter is to be taken to have been living at the testator's death'.[2]

1   *Elliot v Lord Joicey* [1935] AC 209; disapproving *Re Griffiths' Settlement, Griffiths v Waghorne* [1911] 1 Ch 246.
2   WA 1837, s 33(4)(*b*).

[47.17]

Contingent gifts. The application and effect of the new WA 1837, s 33 on contingent gifts is not clear. The first problem is whether the new WA 1837, s 33 applies at all where the gifts to a child or children or other descendant or descendants of the testator is contingent, and the second problem is, assuming the section does apply, whether the interests of the persons who take by statutory substitution are subject to the same contingency. If a gift to a specific child or descendant is contingent on the child or descendant surviving the testator (or surviving him by a specified period), that will usually be combined with there being some other gift of the same subject-matter which will take effect if he does not so survive. If so, that would seem to be an expression of a contrary intention excluding the operation of the new WA 1837, s 33(1), although the contrary might be arguable if the alternative gift were a general gift of residue (where there was no specific reference to it taking effect on the failure of the gift to the child or descendant).

If a gift to a specific child or descendant is contingent on attaining a specified age and the child or descendant attains that age and dies before the testator it seems that (in the absence of express provision in the will for what is to happen in that event) the new WA 1837, s 33(1) will apply just as the former s 33 did.[1]

The former s 33 did not apply where the child or descendant died before the testator without having attained the age on the attaining of which the gift was contingent,[2] but that was because of the presence of wording (the exception from the effect of the section for any estate or interest determinable at or before the death of the child or issue and the provision that a gift within the section 'shall not lapse') in the old s 33 which is not repeated in the new version. It seems that the new WA 1837, s 33 may well apply in these circumstances if there is no provision in the will to take effect if the child or descendant fails to attain the age on attaining which the gift is contingent, even though there would be no such substitution if he died without attaining a vested interest after the death of the testator.[3]

As regards the second problem mentioned above, it would seem that in the case of a gift to a specific child or descendant there is really nothing in s 33(1) to import into the statutory substitutional gift any contingency to which the primary gift was subject.

1   See *Re Wilson, Lothian v Wilson* (1920) 89 LJ Ch 216.
2   See *Re Wolson, Wolson v Jackson* [1939] Ch 780, [1939] 3 All ER 852.
3   In the case of a class gift it is arguable that the new WA 1837, s 33 will not apply to anyone who dies without fulfilling any contingency to which the gift is expressly subject. The point here is that a gift to, for example, such of the testator's children as shall survive him and attain the age of 21 years, is arguably a gift to a class which consists of the testator's children who survive him and attain 21, not one which consists of the testator's children. If that is right, the WA 1837, s 33(2) will not apply where a child predeceases the testator without having attained 21 but leaving issue, because he was not 'a member of the class' within the meaning of paragraph (b) of s 33(2). This construction would mean that s 33(2) does not apply to most class gifts, and it is probably not a result which was intended. It would seem particularly absurd if the only contingency to which a gift was expressly subject was surviving the testator, but less absurd in relation to a contingency such as surviving to a specified age. A liberal construction, whereby the class in the above example would be treated as being the testator's children, is possible.

[47.18]
Professional practice and substitutional gifts. It is suggested that the WA 1837, s 33 does not obviate the desirability of including express substitutional clauses in wills. Such a clause can clarify the uncertainties relating to contingency gifts noted above. Further s 33 only applies to issue and in all other gifts, eg to brothers, an express clause will be required. It is a requirement of the application of s 33 that the issue should predecease the testator and the section does not apply where the child survives the testator but dies before satisfying a condition or contingency. Finally it will usually be regarded as preferable to have the clause of substitution within the will rather than contained in an extraneous statutory provision.

[47.19]
Estate tail. Entailed interests cannot be created after 1 January 1997[1] and any purported attempt to create an entail takes effect as an absolute interest.[2] Where there is an entail existing at that date and no intention to the contrary is contained in the will, a devise of an estate tail or a quasi-estate tail does not lapse if the devisee dies in the lifetime of the testator leaving issue capable of inheriting under the entail. The devise in such case takes effect as if the death of the devisee had occurred immediately after the death of the testator.[3]

1   The date when the Trusts of Land and Appointment of Trustees Act 1996 (TLATA 1996) came into force.
2   TLATA 1996, s 2, Sch 1, para 5.
3   Wills Act 1837, s 32; 50 *Halsbury's Statutes* (4th edn) 599. The section is prospectively repealed by the TLATA 1996, s 25(2), Sch 4 but so as not to affect any entailed interests created before the commencement of the TLATA 1996.

V.   OTHER EXCEPTIONS FROM LAPSE

(a)   Moral obligation

[47.20]

Gifts in pursuance of moral obligation. The doctrine of lapse does not apply, although the legatee predeceases the testator, where the legacy is given with the intention of discharging a moral obligation,[1] whether legally binding or not, which is recognised by the testator and is existing at his death.[2] The fact that the gift is made in pursuance of a covenant by the testator does not, however, protect it from lapse.[3]

1   In this class of obligation are debts which are unenforceable by action, such as statute-barred debts: *Williamson v Naylor* (1838) 3 Y & C Ex 208; *Philips v Philips* (1844) 3 Hare 281; or debts barred by a discharge in bankruptcy; *Re Sowerby's Trusts* (1856) 2 K & J 630; *Turner v Martin* (1857) 7 De GM & G 429, but in *Coppin v Coppin* (1725) 2 P Wms 291, legacies of released debts were treated as ordinary bounty. There has been some question as to the extent of the application of the doctrine of moral duty.
2   *Stevens v King* [1904] 2 Ch 30; *Re Leach, Chatterton v Leach* [1948] Ch 232, [1948] 1 All ER 383 (legacy to deceased creditor of debt of deceased son).
3   *Re Brookman's Trust* (1869) 5 Ch App 182.

[47.21]

Gift of debt. A bequest of a debt to the debtor or to him, his executors and administrators, coupled with a direction to hand over securities, lapses like an ordinary legacy.[1]

1   *Elliott v Davenport* (1705) 1 P Wms 83; *Toplis v Baker* (1787) 2 Cox Eq Cas 118; *Maitland v Adair* (1796) 3 Ves 231; *Izon v Butler* (1815) 2 Price 34; *A-G v Holbrook* (1823) 3 Y & J 114; applied in *Stamp Duties Comr v Bone* [1977] AC 511, [1976] 2 All ER 354. See p 262, ante. In *Re Wedmore, Wedmore v Wedmore* [1907] 2 Ch 277, the forgiveness to sons of their debts secured by any bond, bill, note or other security was held to amount to a specific legacy which did not abate with other legacies; distinguished in *Re McClintock* (1976) 70 DLR (3d) 175 (executors given power to forgive debt). In *Sibthorp v Moxom* (1747) 3 Atk 580, and *South v Williams* (1842) 12 Sim 566, bequests of debts were treated as not subject to lapse but in these cases there was a direction to deliver over the securities to be cancelled.

(b)   Substituted gifts

[47.22]

Alternative gifts. Where it is clear that, in the event of the legatee or devisee predeceasing the testator, an alternative bequest is intended to be substituted, such alternative gift takes effect notwithstanding the death of the original legatee in the testator's lifetime; but if the intention is merely to signify that the legatee is to take a vested and transmissible interest, the legacy lapses in the ordinary way.[1] Thus, the mere addition to the name of the devisee[2] or legatee[3] of words of limitation such as 'executors', or the like, or a declaration that a devise or legacy shall not lapse, if unaccompanied by a gift by way of substitution,[4] or a declaration that a gift shall vest as from the date of the will, even though words of limitation are added to the name of the legatee or devisee,[5] does not prevent a lapse. On the other hand, a declaration that, if any of certain named legatees should die in the lifetime of the testator leaving issue living at his death, the benefits given to the legatees so dying should not lapse, but should take effect as if such legatees had died immediately after the testator, prevents a lapse, and the benefits of such legatees pass to their respective legal personal representatives as part of their estates.[6]

1   *Re Porter's Trust* (1857) 4 K & J 188 at 193; *Re Main* (1953) 30 MPR 313. But the alternative gift may be based upon the legatee predeceasing some person other than the testator and then this rule does not apply and the gift lapses; see *Re Graham, Graham v Graham* [1929] 2 Ch 127. See also discussion in Chapter 68.

2   *Hutton v Simpson* (1716) 2 Vern 722; *Goodright v Wright* (1717) 1 P Wms 397.

3   *Re Currie's Settlement, Re Rooper, Rooper v Williams* [1910] 1 Ch 329 at 333.

4   *Sibley v Cook* (1747) 3 Atk 572; *Pickering v Lord Stamford* (1797) 3 Ves 492; *Johnson v Johnson* (1841) 4 Beav 318; *Underwood v Wing* (1855) 4 De GM & G 633.

5   *Browne v Hope* (1872) LR 14 Eq 343.

6   *Re Greenwood, Greenwood v Sutcliffe* [1912] 1 Ch 392, following *Re Clunies-Ross, Stubbings v Clunies-Ross* (1912) 106 LT 96, and distinguishing *Re Gresley's Settlement, Willoughby v Drummond* [1911] 1 Ch 358, and *Re Scott* [1901] 1 KB 228. But an appointment by testatrix in favour of her husband, whether she survives or predeceases him, does not, if he predeceases her, operate in favour of his estate and there is a lapse; *Re Ladd, Henderson v Porter* [1932] 2 Ch 219.

[47.23]
Legacy to executors of deceased legatee. A legacy can be given to the executors or administrators of a deceased person as an original gift,[1] or to the executors or administrators of the legatee as a substitutional gift in case he predeceases the testator.[2] Such a substitutional gift prevents a lapse by the death of the legatee in the lifetime of the testator, and while the gift does not actually become part of the legatee's estate,[3] it is held by his personal representatives in trust to administer it as if it were part of his estate.[4] Moreover, while the gift does not lapse by the death before the testator of the persons who were the executors or administrators at the date of the will, it lapses by the death before the testator of the beneficiary who would take it under the legatee's will or on his intestacy,[5] including a personal representative who is himself sole beneficiary.[6]

1   *Trethewy v Helyar* (1876) 4 Ch D 53; *Newton's Trusts* (1867) LR 4 Eq 171 (where a gift of personalty to heirs and assigns of a deceased person was treated as a gift to statutory next of kin).

    In the following cases lapse was prevented: *Sibley v Cook* (1747) 3 Atk 572 (bequest to legatee his executors or administrators with declaration against lapse); *Long v Watkinson* (1852) 17 Beav 471 (to A and in the case of his death to his executors or administrators); *Hewitson v Todhunter* (1852) 22 LJ Ch 76 (legacy not to lapse but to go to personal representatives); *Re Wilder's Trusts* (1859) 27 Beav 418 (express words of substitution); *Maxwell v Maxwell* (1868) IR 2 Eq 478 (or executors); *Lord Advocate v Bogie* [1894] AC 83 (bequest to legatees failing them by their predeceasing the testator to their several and respective executors and representatives whomsoever 'whom I hereby appoint to be my residuary legatees'; *Re Bosanquet, Unwin v Petre* (1915) 85 LJ Ch 14 (to personal representative as part of personal estate); *Re Cousen's Will Trusts, Wright v Killick* [1937] Ch 381, [1937] 2 All ER 276 (where the substituted legatee also predeceased the testator and the gift lapsed). The principal authorities are discussed in the last case. See also *Re Hickman's Will Trusts* [1950] 2 All ER 285.

2   In the following cases there was a lapse, there being no intention to substitute an alternative gift: *Smith v Oliver* (1848) 11 Beav 494 (gift to legatee and in case of his death, 'not having received his legacy', to his children); *Tidwell v Ariel* (1818) 3 Madd 403 (legacy to a legatee or his heir) but see *Re Porter's Trust* (1857) 4 K & J 188 (where it was said that this form of limitation prevented lapse); *Bone v Cook* (1824) 13 Price 332 (distinction between gift to children and a gift to executors or administrators in event of legatee predeceasing); *Leach v Leach* (1866) 35 Beav 185 (gift to named persons or their executors administrators or assigns); *Re Masterson, Trevanion v Dumas* [1902] WN 192 (gift to legatee or his heirs). A gift in remainder to a legatee or his personal representatives has been held to lapse on the death of the legatee in the testator's lifetime where the will did not show a clear intention that the gift to the personal representatives was substitutional; *Re Matthews* [1958] VR 194.

3   This appears to be so where the gift is to the executors or administrators as part of his estate, as in *Re Seymour's Trusts* (1859) John 472; *Re Bosanquet, Unwin v Petre* (1915) 85 LJ Ch 14; *Re Cousen's Will Trusts, Wright v Killick* [1937] Ch 381, [1937] 2 All ER 276.

4   *Lord Advocate v Bogie* [1894] AC 83; *Re Cousen's Will Trusts, Wright v Killick* [1937] Ch 381, [1937] 2 All ER 276.

5   *Re Bosanquet, Unwin v Petre* (1915) 85 LJ Ch 14.

6   *Re Cousen's Will Trusts, Wright v Killick* [1937] Ch 381, [1937] 2 All ER 276.

(c)   Settled shares

[47.24]

Settled shares. A bequest of an absolute interest in a fixed share of residue to a named person followed by a direction settling such share does not lapse by reason of the legatee's death in the lifetime of the testator.[1] It is otherwise where the original gift is to a class[2] or where the share of residue cannot be regarded as fixed.[3]

1   *Re Speakman, Unsworth v Speakman* (1876) 4 Ch D 620; *Re Pinhorne, Moreton v Hughes* [1894] 2 Ch 276; *Re Powell, Campbell v Campbell* [1900] 2 Ch 525, and see *Re Whitmore, Walters v Harrison* [1902] 2 Ch 66; *Re Walter, Turner v Walter* (No 2) (1912) 56 Sol Jo 632; *Re Harward, Newton v Bankes* [1938] Ch 632, [1938] 2 All ER 804.

2   *Stewart v Jones* (1859) 3 De G & J 532; *Re Taylor, Taylor v Taylor* [1931] 2 Ch 237.

3   *Re Roberts, Tarleton v Bruton* (1885) 30 Ch D 234 (where there was an accruer clause).

[47.25]

Future gifts. A legacy to become vested at the expiration of six years from the death of the testator may fail if the legatee does not survive the period.[1] If, however, a testator directs payment of the income of a fund for three years after his death to one person followed by a gift of the capital to another, the gift of the capital does not lapse by the latter's death before the expiration of the three years;[2] nor does the death of a prospective tenant for life in the lifetime of the testator cause the gift in remainder to lapse,[3] nor does it cause a contingent limitation over to lapse.[4] The gift over may lapse from other causes.[5] A gift over following an absolute gift commonly fails on the ground that it is repugnant to the original gift, but it may be rendered valid by the lapse of the original gift.[6]

1   *Bruce v Charlton* (1842) 13 Sim 65; *Re Eve, Belton v Thompson* (1905) 93 LT 235, and see *Re Laing, Laing v Morrison* [1912] 2 Ch 386.

2   *Re Boam, Shorthouse v Annibal* (1911) 56 Sol Jo 142.

3   *Habergham v Ridehalgh* (1870) LR 9 Eq 395 at 401.
4   *Rackham v De La Mare* (1864) 2 De GJ & Sm 74 (gift to A for life, then for her children and then over if no child attained a vested interest and A died in the lifetime of the testator); *Re Green's Estate* (1860) 1 Drew & Sm 68.
5   *Williams v Jones* (1826) 1 Russ 517.
6   *Re Lowman, Devenish v Pester* [1895] 2 Ch 348; *Re Dunstan, Dunstan v Dunstan* [1918] 2 Ch 304.

(d)   Gifts in joint tenancy or tenancy in common

[47.26]

Joint tenancy. Where property is given to joint tenants and one dies in the lifetime of the testator, the doctrine of survivorship prevents a lapse occurring, and either a sole survivor takes the whole or the survivors take the whole as joint tenants.[1] Similarly, if the interest of one of the joint tenants is revoked, the others take the whole and there is no lapse.[2]

1   *Morley v Bird* (1798) 3 Ves 628.
2   *Sykes v Sykes* (1867) LR 4 Eq 200.

[47.27]

Tenancy in common. In the case of a gift to persons in common, not being a gift to a class,[1] the doctrine of survivorship does not apply, unless a contrary intention is shown in the will,[2] and the share of one dying before the testator lapses.[3] The revocation of a share also occasions a lapse.[4] It seems, however, that if one of the persons named as tenants in common has been previously referred to in the will as dead, the fund is divisible among the others and there is no lapse.[5]

1   As to class gifts, see para **[47.28]** infra.
2   *Re Radcliffe, Young v Beale* (1903) 51 WR 409 (gift to four named persons as tenants in common with gift over if only one survived the testatrix to that one, and three survived; held that there was no lapse); *Re Woods, Woods v Creagh* [1931] 2 Ch 138; *Watson v Donaldson* [1915] 1 IR 63.
3   *Re Bentley, Podmore v Smith* (1914) 110 LT 623; *Re Whitrod, Burrows v Base* [1926] Ch 118; *Griffith v Chomley* (1868) 5 WW & A'B (Eq) 186; *Re Forbes* (1916) 28 DLR 787. The settlement of a share to which a child is or shall become entitled does not prevent lapse where the child predeceases the testator: *Re Taylor, Taylor v Taylor* [1931] 2 Ch 237.
4   *Ramsay v Shelmerdine* (1865) LR 1 Eq 129; *Sykes v Sykes* (1868) 3 Ch App 301; *Re Forrest, Carr v Forrest* [1931] 1 Ch 162; *Re Midgley, Barclays Bank Ltd v Midgley* [1955] Ch 576, [1955] 2 All ER 625. The will may, however, show a contrary intention: *Vaudrey v Howard* (1853) 2 WR 32; *M'Kay v M'Kay* [1900] 1 IR 213; *Re Whiting, Ormond v De Launay* [1913] 2 Ch 1.
5   *Clarke v Clemmans* (1866) 36 LJ Ch 171; *Re Sharp, Maddison v Gill* [1908] 1 Ch 372.

(e)   Class gifts

[47.28]

Class gifts. Class gifts differ from other gifts in respect of lapse in that no person is definitely a member of the class until the time arrives for ascertaining who are included in it and who are excluded from it. For example, if a class has to be ascertained at the death of the testator, persons who die in his lifetime are never within it and no question of lapse can arise.[1] Where a member of a class is precluded from participation expressly by exception or revocation,[2] or by his attesting the will,[3] or by the felonious killing of the testator,[4] there is no lapse, and the property is divided among those members capable of taking. The rule is not, however, applicable where an appointment is made under a power to objects and non-objects; in such a case the part invalidly appointed goes as in default of appointment.[5] Where the class consists of children or remoter descendants of the testator, the Wills Act 1837, s 33[6] will apply in the absence of a contrary intention.[7]

1   The rule applies whether the number of members of the class increases or decreases: *Dimond v Bostock* (1875) 10 Ch App 358. The class is automatically expanded or contracted: *Re Dunster, Brown v Heywood* [1909] 1 Ch 103; *M'Kay v M'Kay* [1900] 1 IR 213. The survivors take the whole: *Leigh v Leigh* (1854) 17 Beav 605; *Cruse v Howell* (1858) 4 Drew 215; *FitzRoy v Duke of Richmond* (1859) 27 Beav 186; *Re Stanhope's Trusts* (1859) 27 Beav 201; *Re Banks' Will, Public Trustee v Eaves* (1901) 20 NZLR 436.
2   *Re Jackson, Shiers v Ashworth* (1883) 25 Ch D 162; *Re Dunster, Brown v Heywood* [1909] 1 Ch 103; *Re Woods, Woods v Creagh* [1931] 2 Ch 138 (gift to named persons or such as shall be living at testator's death), followed in *Re Walker, Clarke v Walker* [1973] 1 NZLR 449.
3   *Fell v Biddolph* (1875) LR 10 CP 701; *Re Coleman and Jarrom* (1876) 4 Ch D 165. See Chapter 9.
4   *Re Peacock, Midland Bank Executor and Trustee Co Ltd v Peacock* [1957] Ch 310, [1957] 2 All ER 98,
5   *Re Farncombe's Trusts* (1878) 9 Ch D 652.
6   As substituted by the AJA 1982, s 19.
7   See para **[47.14]** supra. The effect of the section is to substitute issue of the deceased child, rather than an accrual to the other members of the clan.

[47.29]
Provision against lapse. A provision in a class gift that the share of any member predeceasing the testator and leaving issue shall not lapse but go to his executors does not cause the share of a member dying without issue to lapse so as to exclude the other members of the class from taking such share.[1]

1   *Aspinall v Duckworth* (1866) 35 Beav 307.

[47.30]
Meaning of 'class gift'. In general a class gift is a gift to a class of persons included or comprehended under some general description and bearing a certain relation to the testator or some other person.[1] Where a testator divides his residue into as many shares as he shall have children surviving him or predeceasing him leaving issue, and gives a share to or in trust for each such child, the gift is a class gift.[2] The class may also be of persons answering one or other alternative descriptions, as 'the children of A and the children of B',[3] or 'the children of A who attain twenty-one and the issue of such as die under that age'.[4] A gift to the issue of A and B per stirpes and not per capita is divisible into as many parts as there are families of issue living at the death of the testator.[5]

1   *Kingsbury v Walter* [1901] AC 187; applied in *Re Green* [1975] 1 NZLR 475. As to the words 'or some other person', see *Re Featherstone's Trusts* (1882) 22 Ch D 111 at 121. See also *Pearks v Moseley* (1880) 5 App Cas 714 at 723, and *Re Chaplin's Trusts* (1863) 3 New Rep 192, upon which the statement in *Kingsbury v Walter* [1901] AC 187, is based. Difference in

relationship may prevent the formation of a class: *Watson v Donaldson* [1915] 1 IR 63 (a relative, two friends and two servants), but see *Kekewich v Barker* (1903) 88 LT 130.

2   *Re Dunster, Brown v Heywood* [1909] 1 Ch 103; *Re Gibson's Will* [1922] VLR 165. Where the testator wrongly stated the number of children and excepted those in a mental institution, the gift was held to be a class gift for the remainder of the children: *Re Telfer* [1964] 1 OR 373.

3   *Kingsbury v Walter* [1901] AC 187; *Best v Stonehewer* (1865) 2 De GJ & Sm 537.

4   *Pearks v Moseley* (1880) 5 App Cas 714 at 722.

5   *Re Dering, Neall v Beale* (1911) 105 LT 404; *Re Alexander, Alexander v Alexander* [1919] 1 Ch 371. See *Re Wilson, Parker v Winder* (1883) 24 Ch D 664, and *Re Fraser* (1986) 29 DLR (4th) 88 at 96 where the text is referred to.

[47.31]
Class gifts and gifts to individuals. Gifts to persons described only by relationship are sometimes construed as class gifts[1] and sometimes as gifts to individuals.[2] A gift may be none the less a gift to a class because some of the members are referred to by name,[3] or because a person who would otherwise fall within the class is excluded by name.[4] On the other hand, a gift to an individual and the children of another individual is not regarded as a class gift,[5] unless there is something in the context to show that the testator intended to form a class;[6] and gifts to several persons designated by name[7] or number[8] or by reference[9] are not class gifts, and are liable to lapse unless a joint tenancy is created,[10] or words are added implying a contingency.[11] Where the residuary estate is given to named persons it is not a gift to a class and a lapsed gift passes as on an intestacy.[12]

1   *Re Hannam, Haddelsey v Hannam* [1897] 2 Ch 39 at 216 (to my brothers and sisters in equal shares), following *Thornhill v Thornhill* (1819) 4 Madd 377 (nephews and nieces); *Ive v King* (1852) 16 Beav 46 at 53, and *King v Cleaveland)* (1858) 26 Beav 26 (nephews and nieces). See also *Doe d Stewart v Sheffield* (1811) 13 East 526 (gift to the children of A); *Shuttleworth v Greaves* (1838) 4 My & Cr 35 (brothers and sisters); *Re Scorer, Burtt v Harrison* (1924) 94 LJ Ch 196; *Re Gillespie* [1955] QSR 330 (such nieces being daughters of named brothers and sisters as shall survive me).

2   *Havergal v Harrison* (1843) 7 Beav 49 (brother and sister of A and my brothers and sisters); *Smith v Smith* (1837) 8 Sim 353 (children); *Jones v Frewin* (1864) 3 New Rep 415 (nephews and nieces); *Leach v Leach* (1843) 2 Y & C Ch Cas 495 (A and the other children of his brother B); *Habergham v Ridehalgh* (1870) LR 9 Eq 395 (H and all and every his brothers and sisters).

3   *Kingsbury v Walter* [1901] AC 187; *Shaw v M'Mahon* (1843) 4 Dr & War 431 (to all my children including A and B); *Re Stanhope's Trusts* (1859) 27 Beav 201 (to four named daughters, and all after-born daughters); *Re Jackson, Shiers v Ashworth* (1883) 25 Ch D 162 (similar case); *Re Mervin, Mervin v Crossman* [1891] 3 Ch 197 (similar case).

4   *Re Jackson, Shiers v Ashworth* (1883) 25 Ch D 162; *Dimond v Bostock* (1875) 10 Ch App 358.

5   *Re Wood's Will* (1862) 31 Beav 323; *Re Chaplin's Trusts* (1863) 3 New Rep 192; *Re Allen, Wilson v Atter* (1881) 44 LT 240; *Re Venn, Lindon v Ingram* [1904] 2 Ch 52.

6   *Kinsbury v Walter* [1901] AC 187 at 193; *Aspinall v Duckworth* (1866) 35 Beav 307; *Kekewich v Barker* (1903) 88 LT 130 (for A, B and children now living of C, is a class gift); *Re Collishaw* [1953] 3 DLR 829 (gift to one and children of another is not a class gift). Where residue was given one-quarter to the testator's mother and three-quarters to the brothers, sisters and nephew of the testator, the gift of the three-quarters was held to be a class gift: *Re McLeod's Will* [1923] VLR 218.

7   *Bain v Lescher* (1840) 11 Sim 397 (children of A, namely B, C, and D); *Re Ramadge* [1969] NI 71 (my four cousins A, B, C & D; *Spencer v Wilson* (1873) LR 16 Eq 501 (four children naming them); *Burrell v Baskerfield* (1849) 11 Beav 525 (twelve cousins by name, but naming eleven only as testator believed the other to be dead); *Sykes v Sykes* (1867) LR 4 Eq 200 (children by name); *Re Bentley, Podmore v Smith* (1914) 110 LT 623 (gift to all my nephews and nieces naming them); *Re Whiston, Whiston v Woolley* [1924] 1 Ch 122 (children named); and see *Watson v Donaldson* [1915] 1 IR 63.

8   *Jacob v Catling* [1881] WN 105 (four nephews and nieces); *Re Smith's Trusts* (1878) 9 Ch D 117 (five daughters); *Orford v Orford* [1903] 1 IR 121; *Re Selby* [1952] VLR 273 (gift to four named nephews); *Re Griffith* [1951] 1 DLR 551 (four named brothers); but see *Re Stansfield, Stansfield v Stansfield* (1880) 15 Ch D 84 (all my children except A).

9   *Re Gibson's Trusts* (1861) 2 John & H 656 (to all before-mentioned legatees); *Nicholson v Patrickson* (1861) 3 Giff 209 (similar case); *Barber v Barber* (1838) 3 My & Cr 688 (to executors herein named); The principle does not apply where the gift is to executors in their official capacity: *Knight v Gould* (1833) 2 My & K 295; *Parsons v Saffery* (1821) 9 Price 578; *Re Maxwell, Eivers v Curry* [1906] 1 IR 386.

10   *Morley v Bird* (1798) 3 Ves 628; *Sykes v Sykes* (1867) LR 4 Eq 200.

11   *Sanders v Ashford* (1860) 28 Beav 609 (to great nieces equally 'if more than one'); *Re Spiller, Spiller v Madge* (1881) 18 Ch D 614 (persons living at date of will); *Re Hornby's Wills* (1859) 34 LTOS 6 (to a person if living); *Re Midgley, Barclays Bank, Ltd v Midgley* [1955] Ch 576, [1955] 2 All ER 625 (gift to six persons by name with substitution of issue of those predeceasing testator and for accruer of any dying leaving no issue living at testator's death); *Re Peacock, Midland Bank Executor and Trustee Co Ltd v Peacock* [1957] Ch 310, [1957] 2 All ER 98 (gift to such of three named persons as shall survive me and attain 21, and if more than one as tenant in common and if only one then all to that one); *Re Gillespie* [1955] QSR 330.

12   *Re Stuart Estate* (1964) 47 WWR 500.

[47.32]

Issue of deceased child. The Wills Act 1837, s 33, as originally enacted did not apply to class gifts.[1] The substituted provision does however extend to gifts to a class.[2] A testator may by appropriate words expressly effect a substitution of the issue of a member of the class for their parent.[3]

1   See para **[47.10]** supra. *Olney v Bates* (1855) 3 Drew 319; *Browne v Hammond* (1858) John 210, *Re Harvey's Estate, Harvey v Gillow* [1893] 1 Ch 567 (where there was only one member of the class); *Re Morris, Corfield v Waller* (1916) 86 LJ Ch 456; *Re Coleman and Jarrom* (1876) 4 Ch D 165.

2   See the Administration of Justice Act 1982, s 19; Vol 2, Part G, para **[244.95]**; see also para **[47.14]** supra.

3   *Aspinall v Duckworth* (1866) 35 Beav 307; *Re Greenwood, Greenwood v Sutcliffe* [1912] 1 Ch 392.

[47.33]

Time when class ascertained. This matter is considered later.[1]

1   See Chapter 65 and 66.

[47.34]

Vesting. In class gifts the interest of all the members must vest at the same time, that is to say that the gift must vest in interest at the same time although the rules for the ascertainment of the class allow the class to be enlarged by the birth of children after the date for vesting in interest.[1]

1   *Kingsbury v Walter* [1901] AC 187 at 194.

VI.   APPLICATION TO POWERS

[47.35]

General position. The doctrine of lapse applies to powers created by will. In this connection there are three matters to be considered: (i) that the doctrine applies to all powers in that they will lapse if the donee of the power dies before the testator;[1] (ii) as regards powers of appointment (and this is the power with which practically all authority on this subject is concerned), it is possible not only for the power to lapse by the death of the donee in the life of the testator creating the power, but also, where the exercise of the power is by will, for the appointment to lapse by the death of the appointee in the lifetime of the donee (ie the testator exercising the power); (iii) the operation of the doctrine is in some respects different in the case of a general power from what it is in the case of a special power of appointment.

1   It applies to a power of appointment: *Jones v Southall (No 2)* (1862) 32 Beav 31; *Re Baker, Steadman v Dicksee* [1934] WN 94, and to a power of charging: *Griggs v Gibson (No 2)* (1866) 35 LJ Ch 458; *Sharpe v M'Call* [1903] 1 IR 179. The fact that the will was in express exercise of the power and contained the words 'to the intent that this will shall take effect whether I survive or predecease my husband' did not prevent a power lapsing: *Re Ladd* [1932] 2 Ch 219.

[47.36]

Lapse of power of appointment. A power of appointment lapses by the death of the donee of the power in the lifetime of the testator.[1] The power may also be defeated in part by the death of one of its objects during the lifetime of the testator creating the power. This is the special case where the appointment is to be among a number of named persons and, in default of appointment, the property is given to them individually and not as a class and as tenants in common. In such a case, if one or more of the objects of the power predecease the testator creating the power, then the gift in default of appointment lapses as to the share or shares of the object or objects so dying and the power is defeated pro tanto,[2] but the power is unaffected if one or more of the objects dies after the death of that testator but before the death of the donee of the power.[3] The death of the donee of the power in the lifetime of the testator creating the power does not by itself affect the gift over in default of appointment.[4]

1   *Jones v Southall (No 2)* (1862) 32 Beav 31. But the interests in default of appointment do not fail: *Nichols v Haviland* (1855) 1 K & J 504; *Edwards v Saloway* (1848) 2 Ph 625; *Hardwick v Thurston* (1828) 4 Russ 380; *Kellett v Kellett* (1871) IR 5 Eq 298.
2   *Reade v Reade* (1801) 5 Ves 744; *Re Turner, Hudson v Turner* [1932] 1 Ch 31; see *Re Ware, Cumberlege v Cumberlege-Ware* (1890) 45 Ch D 269.
3   *Re Ware, Cumberlege v Cumberlege-Ware,* supra. See also *Boyle v Bishop of Peterborough* (1791) 1 Ves 299; *Ricketts v Loftus* (1841) 4 Y & C Ex 519; *Woodcock v Renneck* (1842) 1 Ph 72.
4   See n 1.

[47.37]

Lapse of appointment by will. Where a power of appointment however created is exercised by will, it is in general necessary that the appointee shall survive the appointor (ie the donee of the power) if the appointment is not to lapse,[1] and this applies where the appointment is made in pursuance of a covenant to settled contained in marriage articles.[2] There is an exception, however, where an appointment is made to one person as trustee for another, for then the death of the trustee in the lifetime of the appointor does not cause the beneficiary's interest to lapse.[3] The appointment cannot be saved from lapse by providing that it shall take effect whether or not the appointees survive the appointor,[4] but in the case of a special power a substitutional appointment to persons who are objects of the power is good provided the substituted persons survive the appointor.[5] A power to appoint to an individual cannot be exercised by an appointment to that individual or his executors if he predeceases the appointor for his executors are not objects of the power.[6] An appointment under a special power, unlike an appointment under a general power, is rarely saved from lapse by the operation of the residuary gift. In order to prevent lapse the residuary gift must be within the scope of the power and an intention to exercise it must appear in the will itself.[7] Special powers are not within the Wills Act 1837, s 33,[8] so that they are not saved when made in favour of a child who predeceases the testator (ie the appointor) leaving issue.[9] Where objects of a power survive and no appointment is made and there is no gift in default of appointment, the surviving objects may take by implication.[10] Where the appointment is made in discharge of a moral or legal obligation it does not lapse.[11]

1   *Freeland v Pearson* (1867) LR 3 Eq 658; *Kennedy v Kingston* (1821) 2 Jac & W 431; *Duke of Marlborough v Lord Godolphin* (1750) 2 Ves Sen 61; *Re Susanni's Trusts* (1877) 47 LJ Ch 65. As to the saving of general powers by a residuary gift, see para 47.39, post.
2   *Re Brookman's Trust* (1869) 5 Ch App 182; *Jervis v Wolferstan* (1874) LR 18 Eq 18.
3   *Oke v Heath* (1748) 1 Ves Sen 135.
4   *Re Ladd, Henderson v Porter* [1932] 2 Ch 219.
5   *Maddison v Andrew* (1747) 1 Ves Sen 57; *Butcher v Butcher* (1812) 1 Ves & B 79. In *Ex p Williams* (1819) 1 Jac & W 89, a husband by his will gave his wife a power of appointment among his children and their issue and the wife by her will appointed to the then surviving children and to their children in case they predeceased her and the appointment was held good.
6   *Re Susanni's Trusts* (1877) 47 LJ Ch 65, but as to general powers, see para **[47.39]**, n 6.
7   *Re Hunt's Trusts* (1885) 31 Ch D 308. See Wills Act 1837, s 27; Vol 2, Part G, para **[244.27]**; and Chapter 39.
8   As substituted by the Administration of Justice Act 1982, s 19; see para **[47.14]** supra.
9   *Griffiths v Gale* (1844) 12 Sim 327; *Freeland v Pearson* (1867) LR 3 Eq 658; *Holyland v Lewin* (1884) 26 Ch D 266; *Re Turner* [1932] 1 Ch 31.
10   See Chapter 101.
11   *Stevens v King* [1904] 2 Ch 30, and see para **[47.20]** supra.

[47.38]
General powers. A general power of appointment and an appointment thereunder lapses by the death of the donee or the death of the appointee as above stated but the appointment is generally saved by the Wills Act 1837, s 27,[1] and is executed by the residuary gift.[2] An appointment under a general power of property to A in trust for B will not altogether fail on account of B's death before that of the appointor, for A will hold the property on the same trusts as if it had been the appointor's own property.[3] An appointment under a general power may also be saved from lapse by the operation of the Wills Act 1837, s 33[4] where it is in favour of a child who predeceases the appointor leaving issue,[5] and under a general power an appointment may be made to A or his personal representatives, provided the intention to avoid lapse is shown and the substituted appointees are definitely designated and the expression used does not amount merely to words of limitation.[6]

1   50 *Halsbury's Statutes* (4th edn) 595. See Vol 2, Part G, para **[244.27]**.
2   *Re Spooner's Trust* (1851) 2 Sim NS 129; *Bush v Cowan* (1863) 32 Beav 228. See also *Gale v Gale* (1856) 21 Beav 349; *Re Dowsett, Dowsett v Meakin* [1901] 1 Ch 398, where the appointed

property was sold under a power to sell and re-invest and it was held that the substituted property passed under the residuary gift.

3   *Re Davies' Trusts* (1871) LR 13 Eq 163.
4   As substituted by the Administration of Justice Act 1982, s 19; see para **[47.14]** supra.
5   *Eccles v Cheyne* (1856) 2 K & J 676.
6   *Browne v Hope* (1872) LR 14 Eq 343; *Stevens v King* [1904] 2 Ch 30.

CHAPTER 48

Failure of gift

I. MODES OF FAILURE OF A GIFT

[48.1]

In general. A gift may fail for reasons personal to the donee, as, for example, that the donee does not exist to benefit by the gift, and then the gift lapses.[1] The failure may result from the attestation of the will by the donee or his spouse,[2] or through the revocation of the gift by codicil,[3] or by the operation of a forfeiture clause,[4] or by the effect of divorce.[5] The donee may disclaim the gift.[6] The gift may also fail by reason of a title paramount to that of the donee, for example, that of the executors or administrators.[7] Again, the property purported to be given by the testator may not be his own property, but the property of some other person.[8]

1 See Chapter 47.
2 See Chapter 18.
3 See Chapter 20.
4 See Chapter 99.
5 See Chapter 46.
6 See Chapter 47.
7 The gift may be required for the payment of tax, debts or administration expenses. For this reason the gift may wholly fail or only partly fail. In the latter case it will become subject to abatement; see Chapter 31.
8 In some cases this may lead to the true owner being put to his election between taking a benefit under the will and insisting on his own title to the property in question: see Chapter 42.

[48.2]

Acts of testator. Acts of the testator prior to the date of the will may cause a gift to fail, in the sense that the gift takes effect not as a gift, but in entire or part satisfaction of a liability undertaken by the testator prior to and existing at the date of the will. In certain cases a presumption arises as to the satisfaction, in whole or in part, by gifts in a will, of portions already covenanted to be paid, or of debts already owing to creditors at the date of the will, in which cases, unless the presumption is displaced by evidence or the context of the will, the petitioner or creditor is bound to elect.[1]

1 See Chapter 42.

[48.3]

Subsequent gift to donee. A gift may be adeemed, or taken away from the donee, because it is deemed to be satisfied by benefits conferred by the testator on the donee subsequently to the date of the will. Thus, in certain cases a presumption arises that a gift by will for a particular purpose, or to a child or person to whom the testator stood in loco parentis, is adeemed by a subsequent gift inter vivos by the testator for the same purpose or to the same child or person.[1]

1   See Chapter 41.

II.   EFFECT OF FAILURE OF A GIFT

[48.4]

Effect on subject of gift. A general residuary gift includes all interests, not themselves interests in the general residue, which are otherwise undisposed of or which fail in any manner, unless the testator provides otherwise and, therefore, upon the failure of a gift, the subject-matter thereof falls into residue.[1] There may be a particular residuary gift, or a gift of the residue of a particular description of property, a specific part of which is the subject of a prior gift, and it may appear that on the failure of such latter gift the subject-matter is to fall into the particular residue.[2] Where the interest which fails is an interest in the general residue, such interest will pass as on an intestacy.[3] Where the failure of the beneficial interests leads to a total intestacy, the executor does not take beneficially, but in the absence of persons entitled by relationship under the provisions of the Administration of Estates Act 1925,[4] the Crown takes the property, both real and personal.[5] In order to prevent an intestacy the will should include a comprehensive substitutional gift or gift over to cover the possibility of failure of the gift of residue.[6] The gift over will be strictly construed and must in terms comprehend the cause of the failure of the residuary gift, so that if it is merely expressed in terms of 'predecease' and the donee does not predecease but the gift fails for other reasons, the gift over will not take effect and there will be an intestacy.[7]

1   As to residuary gifts, see Chapter 38. A specific legacy passes on disclaimer under the residuary gift: *Re Backhouse, Westminster Bank Ltd v Shaftesbury Society and Ragged School Union* [1931] WN 168. As to failure due to the rule against perpetuities, see Chapter 94; as to failure due to lapse, see Chapters 47 and 48.
2   See *Malcolm v Taylor* (1832) 2 Russ & M 416; *De Trafford v Tempest* (1856) 21 Beav 564; *Burke Irwin's Trust, Barrett v Barrett* [1918] 1 IR 350.
3   *Kelley v A-G* [1917] 1 IR 183; *Hughes v McNaull* [1923] 1 IR 78; *Re Watson* [1927] 4 DLR 626.
4   Administration of Estates Act 1925, s 46; see Vol 2, Part G, para **[244.60]**; see discussion in Chapter 104.
5   Administration of Estates Act 1925, s 46(1)(vi).
6   For suitable clauses see Vol 2.
7   *Re Sinclair* [1985] Ch 446 (gift of residue failed by reason of divorce; gift over limited to predecease did not apply); but note the effect of the 1995 amendment, see Chapter 47, para **[47.2]** et seq. Applied in *Re Jones, Jones v Midland Bank Trust Co Ltd* [1997] 3 FCR 697 (gift of residue failed by reason of the forfeiture rule; gift over limited to predecease did not apply).

[48.5]

Acceleration of subsequent interests. The effect of the failure of a prior life interest or other limited interest through the donee of that interest being dead or prevented by law from taking the gift or by the disclaimer thereof may be to accelerate the subsequent interests limited to take effect on the regular determination of that prior interest.[1] The rule applies to both real and personal property[2] and to the failure of the prior interest in any manner.[3] The rule is one of construction and it does not permit the misconstruction of the words of the will to give effect to the rule nor must the application of the rule have the effect of misconstruing the will.[4] It is not true to say that the rule is confined to cases where the life interest which fails must be followed by an absolutely vested remainder[5] and the rule has been applied to a remainder vested but liable to be divested. In such a case distribution must be deferred until it is ascertained whether or not the divestment operates.[6] In some cases there can be a gap during which the income falls to be paid to the remainderman[7] provided his estate is vested[8] or falls into residue[9] or is applied as on an intestacy[10] until a contingency is determined and acceleration takes place on such determination.[11] There is in respect of such income no application as on an intestacy where the testator has made a complete disposition of the estate or of the specific gift.[12] The rule cannot be applied where the interest to be accelerated is an executory limitation not taking effect on the determination of the prior interest;[13] and subsequent gifts cannot be accelerated where the persons who are to take under them are only ascertainable at a future date.[14]

However, acceleration has been applied where the interest was contingent on some personal qualification, such as attaining twenty-one or marrying, differentiating cases where the contingency related to the words of futurity or the determination of the prior interest.[15] At one time different considerations were applied to legal and to equitable limitations but, with the restriction on the number of legal limitations in 1925, this distinction is no longer applicable.[16]

1   *Re Kebty-Fletcher's Will Trusts, Public Trustee v Swan* [1969] 1 Ch 339, [1967] 3 All ER 1076. See *Re Hartigan* [1989] 2 Qd R 401, where several of the English cases cited on this page are referred to. 'From and after the death of all the said annuitants' was construed as meaning after the determination for any reason of the interests granted to the annuitants, so that the remainders would be accelerated by the surrender of the last annuity to subsist; applied in *Collins v Equity Trustees* [1997] 2 VR 166.

2   *Re Dunstan, Dunstan v Dunstan* [1918] 2 Ch 304. It was suggested in *Eavestaff v Austin* (1854) 19 Beav 591 at 592, that different rules apply according to the nature of the property but this view has not been accepted. See also *Harman v Anderson* [1930] NZLR 67.

3   *Jull v Jacobs* (1876) 3 Ch D 703 at 712; *Re Johnson, Danily v Johnson* (1893) 68 LT 20; *Re Crother's Trusts* [1915] 1 IR 53.

4   *Re Taylor, Lloyds Bank Ltd v Jones* [1957] 3 All ER 56, [1957] 1 WLR 1043. The rule gives way to a clear expression of intention in the will: *Re Blathwayt's Will Trusts, Blathwayt v Blathwayt* [1950] 1 All ER 582. See further proceedings, *Blathwayt v Lord Cawley* [1976] AC 397, [1975] 3 All ER 625; *Re Flower's Settlement Trusts* [1957] 1 All ER 462 at 468, the court declined to accelerate the gift as that would have involved an extraordinary departure from anything that the settlor could have intended. Jenkins LJ also thought at 465 that it may well be more difficult in the case of a settlement, to collect the intention necessary to bring the doctrine of acceleration into play. See also *Re Young's Settlement Trusts, Royal Exchange Assurance v Taylor-Young* [1959] 2 All ER 74, where there was no acceleration. It seems that the words of the will must be capable of meaning 'subject to the trusts aforesaid': *Re Dawson's Settlement, Lloyds Bank Ltd v Dawson* [1966] 3 All ER 68, [1966] 1 WLR 1456.

5   *Re Taylor, Lloyds Bank Ltd v Jones* [1957] 3 All ER 56. *Re Flower's Settlement Trusts, Flower v IRC* [1957] 1 All ER 462 at 465, 467, per Jenkins LJ. *Lainson v Lainson* (1854) 5 De GM & G 754; applied in *Re Brannan* (1991) 83 DLR (4th) 106.

6   *Jull v Jacobs* (1876) 3 Ch D 703; *Re Taylor, Lloyds Bank Ltd v Jones* [1957] 3 All ER 56, [1957] 1 WLR 1043; *Re Bogstie Estate* [1963] 42 WWR 702.

7   *Re Hatfield* [1958] Ch 469, [1957] 2 All ER 261; *Re Conyngham, Conyngham v Conyngham* [1921] 1 Ch 491; *Re Brooke, Brooke v Dickson* [1923] 2 Ch 265.

8   *Re Conyngham* [1921] 1 Ch 491 at 502, 503.
9   *Greene v Tribe* (1878) 9 Ch D 231.
10 *Re Townsend's Estate, Townsend v Townsend* (1886) 34 Ch D 357.
11 *Re Hatfield* [1958] Ch 469, [1957] 2 All ER 261. The will may, however, provide for such gap and then there is no acceleration: *Re Blathwayt's Will Trusts, Blathwayt v Blathwayt* [1950] 1 All ER 582.
12 *Re Conyngham, Conyngham v Conyngham* [1921] 1 Ch 491; *Re Blathwayt's Will Trusts, Blathwayt v Blathwayt* [1950] 1 All ER 582; *Re Hatfield* [1958] Ch 469, [1957] 2 All ER 261. In *Re Scott, Scott v Scott* [1911] 2 Ch 374, it was held that there was a complete disposition where the income fell into residue. This case is not now followed on other grounds; see *Re Hatfield* [1957] 2 All ER 261 at 264, 265.
13 *Sidney v Wilmer* (1858) 25 Beav 260; *M'Carthy v M'Carthy* (1878) 1 LR IR 189; *Kearney v Kearney* [1911] 1 IR 137. It is a question of construction whether there is a succession of limitations or whether there is a new contingency.
14 *Re Townsend's Estate, Townsend v Townsend* (1886) 34 Ch D 357; applied in *Re Scott, Widdows v Friends of the Clergy Corpn* [1975] 2 All ER 1033, [1975] 1 WLR 1260; *Re Vernon, Garland v Shaw* (1906) 95 LT 48; *Re Cooper, Townend v Townend* (1917) 86 LJ Ch 507. In such cases the income falls into residue or, if it arises out of residue, then it must be applied as on an intestacy. Where the trust for sale was to arise on the death of life tenants and the gift to such life tenants was revoked, the trust for sale arose immediately on the death of the testator although the life tenants survived him: *Re Johnson, Danily v Johnson* (1893) 68 LT 20. Where a protected life tenant had power to release her life interest 'for the purpose only of accelerating the vesting of the capital thereof in possession' in two children of the settlor or their respective issue, it was held that the power could not be exercised when the interests of the children were contingent, since the release would not have the immediate effect of bringing forward the date when the reversions fell into possession: *Re Shand Kydd's Settlement Trusts, Shand Kydd v Shand Kydd* (1970) 114 Sol Jo 789.
15 *Re Dawson's Settlement, Lloyds Bank v Dawson* [1966] 3 All ER 68, [1966] 1 WLR 1456; *Re Scott, Widdows v Friends of the Clergy Corpn* [1975] 2 All ER 1033 at 1039, 1041, per Walton J.
16 See *Re Hatfield's Will Trusts, Hatfield v Hatfield* [1958] Ch 469 at 475, [1957] 2 All ER 261 at 264, 265.

[48.6]
Acceleration and the class closing rules. If the subsequent gift is a class gift to which the class closing rules[1] are applicable, then the assignment or release of the prior gift does not accelerate the closing of the class entitled to take the subsequent gift.[2] Thus, where a life tenant released and assigned his interest to the trustees to the intent that the income should be held on the trusts applicable thereto as if he were dead, it was held that this did not accelerate the interests conferred by the testator on the subsequent class; nor did it alter the composition of the class of children intended to take and accordingly, the class remained open to include subsequently born members of the class.[3] Where a life tenant released, surrendered, and assigned his life interest to the trustees to the intent that his interest should cease, merge and be extinguished in the reversionary interests of the subsequent class, it was held that the life interest had been destroyed and that the interests of the class had vested in possession; but that the application of the class closing rules had not been accelerated and so the class remained open until the death of the former life tenant.[4] However, where the prior interest terminates, not by reason of the act of the donee, but by reason of the act of the testator[5] or by operation of law[6] then it might be that the operation of the class closing rules is accelerated.[7]

1   See full discussion in Chapter 66.
2   *Re Kebty-Fletcher's Will Trusts, Public Trustee v Swan* [1969] 1 Ch 339, [1967] 3 All ER 1076; *Re Harker's Will Trusts, Kean v Harker* [1969] 3 All ER 1, [1969] 1 WLR 1124; *Re*

Davies, Davies v Mackintosh [1957] 3 All ER 52, [1957] 1 WLR 922 (gift to A for life followed by a direction for a division equally between his issue; A disclaimed the life interest; held, that the disclaimer operated to accelerate the gift to issue) doubted in *Re Kebty-Fletcher's Will Trusts*, not followed in *Re Harker's Will Trusts, Kean v Harker*, notwithstanding that it had been approved in *Re Taylor, Lloyd's Bank Ltd v Jones* [1957] 3 All ER 56, [1957] 1 WLR 1043; *Re Chartres, Farman v Barrett* [1927] 1 Ch 466, [1927] All ER Rep 408 distinguished in both cases. See also *Jull v Jacobs* (1876) 3 Ch D 703; *Re Johnson, Danily v Johnson* (1893) 68 LT 20, and *Re Townsend's Estate, Townsend v Townsend* (1886) 34 Ch D 357.

3   *Re Kebty-Fletcher's Will Trusts, Public Trustee v Swan* [1969] 1 Ch 339, [1967] 3 All ER 1076.
4   *Re Harker's Will Trusts, Kean v Harker* [1969] 3 All ER 1, [1969] 1 WLR 1124. In this case the life interest had been destroyed and so the interests of the subsequent class had been accelerated; there can be no logical distinction in this respect between a surrender and a disclaimer and so *Re Davies, Davies v Mackintosh* [1957] 3 All ER 52, [1957] 1 WLR 922, was not followed. However, the assignment in *Re Kebty-Fletcher's Will Trusts, Public Trustee v Swan* [1969] 1 Ch 339, [1967] 3 All ER 1076, could be said to have merely changed the trusts of the life interest, and *Re Davies* could be distinguished. It will accordingly be appreciated that *Re Harker's Will Trusts* is a more far-reaching decision than *Re Kebty-Fletcher's Will Trusts*. See both cases further discussed in Chapter 66, see also *Re Syme* [1980] VR 109.
5   Where, for example the gift is revoked by codicil; *Re Johnson, Danily v Johnson* (1893) 68 LT 20; *Eavestaff v Austin* (1854) 19 Beav 591.
6   Where, for example, the Wills Act 1837, s 15 renders the gift void; *Jull v Jacobs* (1876) 3 Ch D 703; see also *Re Crother's Trusts* [1915] 1 IR 53.
7   Stamp J in *Re Kebty-Fletcher's Will Trusts, Public Trustee v Swan* [1969] 1 Ch 339, [1967] 3 All ER 1076, seemed to accept this distinction; [1967] 3 All ER 1076 at 1080–1081.

[48.7]
Acceleration where beneficiary attests the will. Where a tenant for life whose interest would have taken effect on the death of the testator was an attesting witness[1] and the remaindermen were in existence at that time, the interests in remainder were accelerated.[2] Where the interests in remainder were contingent on the tenant for life dying without leaving issue living at his death, there was no acceleration. The income was undisposed of until the birth of a child to the life tenant and then the remainders would take effect.[3] A gift to A or her children is an absolute gift to A if she is alive to take or to her children if she is then dead; and if A's husband is an attesting witness the gift to her fails and if she is alive and could take at the time the gift vests in possession the children take nothing.[4] The will should be treated as though it did not contain the disposition to the attesting witness at all, except in so far as it is necessary to look at it for the purpose of ascertaining what is the nature of other gifts in the will, or in what event other gifts are intended to take effect.[5]

1   As to such attestation, see Chapter 12.
2   *Jull v Jacobs* (1876) 3 Ch D 703; *Re Clark, Clark v Randall* (1885) 31 Ch D 72; *Burke v Burke* (1899) 18 NZLR 216.
3   *Re Townsend's Estate, Townsend v Townsend* (1886) 34 Ch D 357.
4   *Aplin v Stone* [1904] 1 Ch 543.
5   *Re Doland, Westminster Bank Ltd v Phillips* [1970] Ch 267, [1969] 3 All ER 713 (gift over if any of the previous trusts should 'fail'; certain of the previous trusts were in favour of a beneficiary whose wife witnessed the will; held, that the will must be read as if it contained no such trusts, and so, as there was no trust, it followed that the trust could not 'fail' and the gift over could not take effect).

[48.8]
Acceleration on disclaimer. The effect of a disclaimer is in general to accelerate the next interest in remainder[1] but where such next interest is not capable of taking at the time of the disclaimer (eg being an unborn person) the

next remainder takes the income until the happening of the contingency even though that remainder be an absolute interest.[2] If the interests are vested subject to defeasance, they are given effect subject to the defeasance.[3] Where a testatrix appointed a fund to her mother but, if the mother predeceased her, she appointed part of the fund but left the rest unappointed, and the mother disclaimed all interest under the will and the appointment, the disclaimer did not accelerate the subsequent gifts of the appointment since they were contingent on the mother predeceasing the testatrix. The result being an intestacy, the mother took under the intestacy despite the disclaimer.[4] If persons primarily entitled on intestacy disclaim, then the property does not pass to the Crown as bona vacantia, but is distributable among the next class entitled under the intestacy as if the disclaimers had not survived.[5]

1   *Re Scott, Scott v Scott* [1911] 2 Ch 374 at 377; *Re Hodge* [1943] Ch 300, [1943] 2 All ER 304; *Re Jacques* (1985) 16 DLR (4th) 472 (doctrine of acceleration should not be applied to defeat the testator's intention). As to acceleration upon disclaimer in the case of a settlement, see *Re Young's Settlement Trusts* [1959] 2 All ER 74, and *Re Penton's Settlements, Humphreys v Birch Reynardson* [1968] 1 All ER 36, [1968] 1 WLR 248.
2   *Re Willis, Crossman v Kirkaldy* [1917] 1 Ch 365; *Re Hatfield, Hatfield v Hatfield* [1958] Ch 469, [1957] 2 All ER 261. As to the effect of a widow repudiating a gift under the will and electing to take her just relictae, see *Muirhead v Muirhead v Crellin* (1890) 15 App Cas 289.
3   *Re Taylor, Lloyds Bank Ltd v Jones* [1957] 3 All ER 56, [1957] 1 WLR 1043 (where two remaindermen took equally subject to losing their share on death during the lifetime of the person disclaiming).
4   *Re Speedy, Guardian Trust and Executors Co of New Zealand Ltd v Speedy* [1964] NZLR 961.
5   This is based on the reasoning in *Re Scott, Widdows v Friends of the Clergy Corpn* [1975] 2 All ER 1033 at 1045, per Walton J but see also *Re DWS, Re EHS, TWGS v JMG* [2000] 2 All ER 83; affd [2001] 1 All ER 97, CA. The reasoning in *Re DWS* could arguably contradict the reasoning in *Re Scott*, and suggests that the disclaimed property would go as bona vacantia in some circumstances, eg, where a parent disclaims an interest in the estate of a child of his who has died intestate without issue. See para **[46.1]**, n 1, where the point is discussed.

[48.9]
Acceleration on revocation of gift. Where the remainder is to take effect 'from and immediately after the decease of' the tenant for life, immediate acceleration results if the gift is revoked[1] but such acceleration may have to await the birth of a remainderman entitled to take.[2] Where the survivor of life tenants is to take absolutely on the failure of the remainders, such an absolute interest takes effect on the revocation of the remainders.[3] The revocation may, however, extend to the interest in remainder.[4]

1   *Lainson v Lainson* (1854) 5 De GM & G 754; *Eavestaff v Austin* (1854) 19 Beav 591; *Re Whitehorne, Whitehorne v Best* [1906] 2 Ch 121.
2   *Green v Tribe* (1878) 9 Ch D 231.
3   *Re Stephenson, Stephenson v Stephenson* (1885) 54 LJ Ch 928.
4   *Re Jermingham Trusts, Gormanstown v Nicholl* [1922] 1 IR 115.

[48.10]
Acceleration on lapse. Where the will devised land in tail with remainders over and the devisee in tail predeceased the testator, it was held that the next remainder took effect and the issue of the devisee in tail took nothing.[1] Where property was given absolutely to a beneficiary subject to a provision that whatever remained at his death should be given to a charity and the beneficiary

predeceased the testator, the charity took the gift under the principle of acceleration.[2] Where a sum was to be set aside to provide an annuity and on the cesser of the annuity to go to a charity and the annuitant predeceased the testator, it was held that such a sum must be set aside and handed to the charity.[3]

1   *Fuller v Fuller* (1595) Cro Eliz 422.
2   *Re Dunstan, Dunstan v Dunstan* [1918] 2 Ch 304; see also *Re Lowman, Devenish v Pester* [1895] 2 Ch 348 (where the facts were very complicated but the same principle was applied).
3   *Re Clarke, Sheldon v Redrup* [1942] Ch 434, [1942] 2 All ER 294.

[48.11]
Acceleration on forfeiture. Where the forfeiture declares the forfeited interest to be utterly void and that interest is an estate tail, the accelerated interest is determined on the birth of a child to the donee in tail.[1] Where the forfeiture arose on bankruptcy there was no acceleration where the interest was to cease as if the beneficiary was then 'actually dead' but the income passed as on an intestacy.[2]

1   *Blathwayt v Lord Cawley* [1976] AC 397, [1975] 3 All ER 625; overruling Wynn-Perry J's earlier conclusion in *Re Blathwayt's Will Trusts, Blathwayt v Blathwayt* [1950] 1 All ER 582.
2   *Re Cooper, Townend v Townend* (1917) 86 LJ Ch 507, and see *Craven v Brady* (1869) 4 Ch App 296 (where the forfeiture was brought about by a second marriage).

[48.12]
Acceleration on election under will. Where a daughter had a life interest under a settlement and also under the will if she so elected and she elected against the will, subsequent interests under the will were not accelerated.[1]

1   *Re Vernon, Garland v Shaw* (1906) 95 LT 48.

[48.13]
Acceleration on gift being void for remoteness. By the Perpetuities and Accumulations Act 1964, a disposition is not to be treated as void for remoteness by reason only that the interest disposed of is ulterior to or dependent on an interest under a disposition which is so void, and the vesting of an interest is not prevented from being accelerated on the failure of a prior interest by reason only that the failure arises because of remoteness.[1] Where this statute does not apply there is no acceleration.[2]

1   Perpetuities and Accumulations Act 1964, s 6; 33 *Halsbury's Statutes* (4th edn) 1086. This section overrules the decisions in *Re Hubbard's Will Trusts, Marston v Angier* [1963] Ch 275, [1962] 2 All ER 917, and *Re Buckton's Declaration of Trust, Public Trustee v Midland Bank Executor and Trustee Co Ltd* [1964] Ch 497, [1964] 2 All ER 487; though it may be that the second part of the section was recognised in *Re Coleman, Public Trustee v Coleman* [1936] Ch 528, [1036] 2 All ER 225.
2   *Re Buckton's Declaration of Trust, Public Trustee v Midland Bank Executor and Trustee Co Ltd* [1964] Ch 497, [1964] 2 All ER 487.

[48.14]
Acceleration on divorce. Where a widow's life interest failed because the parties were divorced, the interests of children were accelerated subject to a special power of appointment by the divorced wife.[1] Where by virtue of the original wording of the Wills Act 1837, s 18A[2] a gift to a spouse for life lapsed

because of subsequent divorce or annulment, the interest in remainder ... shall be treated as if it had not been subject to the life interest and, if it was contingent upon the termination of the life interest, as if it had not been so contingent'.[3]

1   *Re Dawson's Settlement, Lloyds Bank Ltd v Dawson* [1966] 3 All ER 68, [1966] 1 WLR 1456.
2   Added by the Administration of Justice Act 1982, s 18(2) (in respect of deaths on or after 1 January 1983); 50 *Halsbury's Statutes* (4th edn) 587. See Vol 2, Part G, para **[244.18]**. WA 1837, s 18A is amended for deaths on or after 1 January 1996 by Law Reform (Succession) Act 1995, s 3 so that the former spouse is deemed to have died instead of the gift being declared to lapse: see Chapter 47, para **[47.2]** supra.
3   WA 1837, s 18A(3); see *Re Sinclair, Lloyds Bank plc v Imperial Cancer Research Fund* [1985] Ch 446, [1985] 1 All ER 1066, CA. Applied in *Re Jones, Jones v Midland Bank Trust Co Ltd* [1997] 3 FCR 697 (gift failed by forfeiture rule). Section 18A(3) is repealed for deaths on or after 1 January 1996 by the Schedule to Law Reform (Succession) Act 1995, but there is still acceleration in these circumstances because the divorced etc spouse is deemed to have died: see Chapter 47, para **[47.2]** supra.

[48.15]
Contingent gifts over. Where a gift is liable to fail upon a contingent event[1] and is followed by a gift over then, upon the contingency happening, the prior gift is divested, although, owing to lapse or some rule of law, the gift over fails to take effect according to its tenor in favour of the donee;[2] and the residuary donee or the person entitled on intestacy takes, as the case may be. The entire contingency suspending the vesting of the gift over must occur in such cases.[3] It is otherwise, however, where the gift over is a substitutionary gift to children. In such a case there is a partial divesting sufficient to let in the remaindermen;[4] as is the case where it is to be inferred that the testator intended divesting not to take place unless the gift over is effective, or where the gift over is void for uncertainty.[5] Where the contingency on which the prior gift is to fail may happen in two ways, and there is a gift over only if it happens in one way, there will be an implied gift over if it happens in the other way, provided that in the circumstances this is in accordance with the intention of the testator.[6]

1   The contingency must be such as the law allows as a condition precedent to the vesting of the gift over. Thus, prior to the Perpetuities and Accumulations Act 1964, s 6—that is to say, in an instrument taking effect before 16 July 1964—it could not be void as a perpetuity. If it is, the prior gift is not divested. The prior limitation may be invalid as offending the perpetuity rule and then the ultimate trust is valid if it is not dependent on the earlier limitation: *Re Hay* [1932] NI 215; *Re Canning's Will Trusts, Skues v Lyon* [1936] Ch 309; *Re Coleman, Public Trustee v Coleman* [1936] Ch 528, [1936] 2 All ER 225; *Re Allan's Will Trusts, Curtis v Nalder* [1958] 1 All ER 401, [1958] 1 WLR 220.
2   *Doe d Blomfield v Eyre* (1848) 5 CB 713 (gift over rendered ineffective by invalid apportionment under power); *Robinson v Wood* (1858) 27 LJ Ch 726 (gift to charity void); *O'Mahoney v Burdett* (1874) LR 7 HL 388 (lapse); *Re Bold, Banks v Hartland* (1926) 95 LJ Ch 201 (gift over on death without issue living at his death: failure of gift over did not indefeasibly vest prior gift, which must in any case fail on death without issue); *Re White* [1965] VR 250 (gift over to take effect on death without issue). Where the gift over infringes the perpetuity rule, a prior absolute gift is not divested: *Re Pratt's Settlement Trusts, McCullum v Phipps-Hornby* [1943] Ch 356, [1943] 2 All ER 458.
3   For example, a combined contingency of the coming into existence of a class and death without children of life tenant: *Jackson v Noble* (1838) 2 Keen 590; or a gift over on a contingent event (which happens) to the survivor of a number of persons. If no survivor exists the prior gift is not divested: *Jones v Davies* (1880) 28 WR 455; *Re Deacon's Trusts, Deacon v Deacon* (1906) 95 LT 701.
4   *Re Rooke's Will Trusts, Taylor v Rooke* [1953] Ch 716, [1953] 2 All ER 110, applying dictum in *Hurst v Hurst* (1882) 21 Ch D 278 at 293, and distinguishing *Doe d Blomfield v Eyre* (1848)

5 CB 713. A share of residue was given after the death of the tenant for life to certain relatives or their respective issue. One relative survived the testator but predeceased the tenant for life. That relative was a spinster. The gift to issue was treated as substitutionary and therefore failed but the vested gift in the spinster remained and her personal representatives were entitled to her share.

5   *Re Archer* (1907) 14 OLR 374 at 377, citing *O'Mahoney v Burdett* (1874) LR 7 HL 388 at 407.
6   *Re Fox's Estate, Dawes v Druitt* [1937] 4 All ER 664; *Re Graham, Graham v Graham* [1929] 2 Ch 127; *Re Riggall, Wildash v Riggall* [1949] WN 491.

Construction of wills: general principles

CHAPTER 49

Functions of the court of construction

[49.1]

General principle. The first and great rule to which all others must bend is that effect must be given to the intention of the testator;[1] but the intention here in question is not the intention in the mind of the testator at the time he made his will, but that declared and apparent in his will.[2] The application of the rule resolves itself into two questions of construction: first, what is the intention of the testator disclosed by the will; and secondly, how can effect be given to that intention.[3]

1   *Baker v Baker* (1858) 6 HL Cas 616 at 622; *Hickling v Fair* [1899] AC 15 at 27.
2   *Papillon v Voice* (1728) Kel W 27 at 32; *Earl of Scarborough v Doe d Savile* (1836) 3 Ad & El 897.
3   *Doe d Hickman v Haslewood* (1837) 6 Ad & El 167 at 174.

[49.2]

Ascertaining the intention of the testator. The court of construction must ascertain the language of the will, read the words used and ascertain the intention of the testator from them.[1] The court's duty is not to ascertain what the actual mental intentions were.[2] The only question for the court of construction is what is the meaning of the words used,[3] and the expressed intention in all cases is considered to be actual intention;[4] the court cannot give effect to any intention which is not expressed or employed in the will.[5] Though this principle is not in any way questioned, it is still possible for judges to disagree upon what intention the words show.[6]

1   *Re Freeman, Hope v Freeman* [1910] 1 Ch 681 at 691; *Re Mellor, Dodgson v Ashworth* (1912) 28 TLR 473. As to extrinsic evidence, see Chapter 57.
2   *Doe d Gwilliam v Gwilliam* (1833) 5 B & Ad 122 at 129.
3   *Grey v Pearson* (1857) 6 HL Cas 61 at 106; *Roddy v Fitzgerald* (1858) 6 HL Cas 823 at 876; *Waring v Currey* (1873) 22 WR 150.
4   *Simpson v Foxon* [1907] P 54 at 57.
5   *Scalé v Rawlins* [1892] AC 342 at 343, 344; *Livesey v Livesey* (1849) 2 HL Cas 419; *Re James's Will Trusts, Peard v James* [1962] Ch 226 at 235; per Buckley J: 'It is not the function of a court of construction to be officious in curing defects in a testator's dispositions, but merely to ascertain, as Rolphe B once said, *quod voluit* by interpreting *quod dixit: Grover v Burnigham* (1850) 5 Exch 184 at 193.' See to the same effect Rhind J in *Ng Chi-fong v Hui Ho Pui-fun* [1987] HKLR 462 at 485: 'The court must limit itself to the "expressed intentions... What is totally impermissible for the court is to conjecture that the testator probably had a particular intent and then go stretching the words of the will in an attempt to give that supposed intent. That type of a priori reasoning is wrong'. Citing this paragraph of the text.
6   *Re Rowland, Smith v Russell* [1963] Ch 1, [1962] 2 All ER 837. This passage of the text was referred to in *Mardulyn v Lee Yee Hung* [1992] 2 HKC 164 at 171 and on other points at 174, 178.

[49.3]

Questions involved. In ascertaining the intention there are three questions: (i) what words has the testator used to express his intention;[1] (ii) what is the meaning of such words in relation to the persons and things described, who are the specific persons to be identified as donees and what are the specific things to be identified as the subjects of disposition;[2] and (iii) what is the meaning of the words in relation to the disposition of the property among the donees.[3] There are differences in the evidence admissible to establish these matters of construction.[4]

1   As to evidence of words used, see Chapter 57.
2   *Webber v Stanley* (1864) 16 CBNS 698. As to evidence of identification, see Chapter 57.
3   As to evidence for this purpose, see Chapter 57.
4   See Chapter 57.

[49.4]

Distinction between rules of law and rules of construction. There are two classes of rules which operate in the construction of a will. The first class are called rules of law and are such rules as the proper words by which estates may be limited (ie what words will create an estate in fee simple or in tail or a life interest), or the rule against perpetuities or, formerly, the law of mortmain. These take effect in any event and are not subject to alteration according to the intention of the testator. In fact they may operate to defeat the clearly expressed intention of the testator altogether and any intention of the testator whether express or implied which is contrary to such rules cannot be given effect to in any circumstances.[1] The other class of rules are called rules of construction and generally they have not to be applied in any event.[2] If the intention of the testator is clear, rules of construction will not in the ordinary case prevail to override that clear intention. Such rules are in general resorted to where the intention is not clear upon the face of the will. The first thing a court of construction has to do is to look at the will and, if a clear enunciation of the testator's intentions is found, none of the technical rules of construction has anything to do with its proper construction.[3]

1   *Re Coward, Coward v Larkman* (1887) 57 LT 285; affd (1888) 60 LT 1; *Re Bedson's Trusts* (1885) 28 Ch D 523. The intention must prevail provided it is not inconsistent with any rules of law and can be enforced without breaking any such rule: *Sayer v Masterman* (1757) Wilm 386; *Doe d Long v Laming* (1760) 2 Burr 1100; *Tothill v Pitt* (1766) 1 Madd 488; *Roe d Dodson v Grew* (1767) Wilm 272; *Hodgson v Ambrose* (1780) 1 Doug KB 337 (the intention must first be determined, for until then it cannot be said that the intention involves a breach of the rules of law); *Thellusson v Woodward* (1799) 4 Ves 227; *Re Wynch's Trusts, ex p Wynch* (1854) 5 De GM & G 188; *Green v Gascoyne* (1865) 4 De GJ & Sm 565; *Ferguson v Ferguson* (1878) 2 SCR 497; *Re Denton* (1912) 4 DLR 626; *Re Cuming* [1943] SASR 336.
2   See Goulding in *Re Edmonson's Will Trusts, Baron Sandford v Edmondson* [1971] 3 All ER 1121 at 1126, [1971] 1 WLR 1652 at 1658.
3   *Limpus v Arnold* (1884) 15 QBD 300 at 302.

[49.5]

Rules of construction should be adhered to. The courts have recognised the necessity for adhering to general rules in the construction of wills[1] and that settled rules should not be departed from upon a finding of minute differences in language.[2] A system of construction which has existed for a long time should not be departed from.[3] It has been laid down as a principle to guide people whose duty it is to construe wills[4] and can be departed from only where the testator has expressed a different intention by the words which he has used, for then such rules do not apply.[5]

1   *Perrin v Morgan* [1943] 1 All ER 187 at 197.
2   *Doe d Clarke v Ludlam* (1831) 7 Bing 275; *Wake v Varah* (1876) 2 Ch D 348; *Kirby-Smith v Parnell* [1903] 1 Ch 483.
3   *A-G v Jeffreys* [1908] AC 411.
4   *A-G v Jeffreys* [1908] AC 411; *Re Inman, Inman v Rolls* [1893] 3 Ch 518.
5   *Singleton v Tomlinson* (1878) 3 App Cas 404; *Limpus v Arnold* (1884) 15 QBD 300; *Re Bedson's Trusts* (1885) 28 Ch D 523; *Barraclough v Cooper* (1905) [1908] 2 Ch 121n at 124n, where Lord Halsbury said: 'I repudiate the invocation of any canon of construction here, beyond the fact that I find enough in the language of this instrument to show what was the meaning of the testator; and I propose to give effect to what, in my view, the testator meant.'

[49.6]

Court of construction. The construction of a will is a matter for a court of construction which has historically been the Chancery Court. The Chancery Court also has jurisdiction over contentious probate actions.[1] Where the value of the estate does not exceed the county court limit the county court has jurisdiction.[2] All non-contentious probate jurisdiction is vested in the Family Division which exercises the jurisdiction through the principal or district registries.[3]

1   See now the Supreme Court Act 1981, s 25 (probate jurisdiction of High Court); 11 *Halsbury's Statutes* (4th edn) 1063; s 62 and Sch 1 (contentious probate to Chancery Division and non-contentious probate to Family Division). The jurisdiction was assigned in this way by the Administration of Justice Act 1970, s 1(4); 11 *Halsbury's Statutes* (4th edn) 892, a change which eliminated the previous dual function of the (old) Court of Probate and the Court of Chancery. See, for example, *Re Morris, Lloyds Bank Ltd v Peake* [1971] P 62, [1970] 1 All ER 1057. If under the former jurisdiction the Court of Probate found it necessary to make a limited construction of the will, then the Chancery Court was not bound thereby: *Re Hawksley's Settlements, Black v Tidy* [1934] Ch 384; *Re Thomas's Estate, Public Trustee v Davies* [1939] 2 All ER 567. In *Re Berger* [1989] 1 All ER 591. Sir Denys Buckley (at 602) reiterated the differing functions of the probate court and the court of construction. Once the identity of the deceased's testamentary papers has been determined and they have been admitted to probate, all questions of construction arising in the administration of the estate concern only the court of administration.
2   County Courts Act 1984, ss 32, 33; 11 *Halsbury's Statutes* (4th edn) 720, 721; reference should be made to the current monetary jurisdiction of the county court, which is a figure liable to change.
3   See n 2, supra.

[49.7]

Necessity for grant. It is necessary that in respect of every will there should be obtained a grant of probate or of administration with the will annexed.[1] The grant, however, is conclusive of the testamentary nature of the instrument, and the validity of the will as regards the capacity of the testator, form and execution.[2] This applies even where the will itself is forged[3] or obtained by fraud.[4] It can be set aside only by showing that the probate itself was forged,[5] or obtained by fraud,[6] or that the alleged testator was living at the time of the grant,[7] or that the court by which it was granted had not sufficient jurisdiction.[8] Probate is not conclusive of the right of the testator to dispose of the property concerned[9] or other collateral matters,[10] such as the domicile of the deceased,[11] nor even of the death of the testator.[12] The court of construction assumes that all documents admitted to probate are testamentary and that they constitute the whole of the testamentary dispositions of the testator.[13]

1 See *Tristram and Coote's Probate Practice* (28th edn); *Yates v Thomson* (1835) 3 Cl & Fin 544 at 575; *Tucker v Inman* (1842) 4 Man & G 1049; *Price v Dewhurst* (1838) 4 My & Cr 76.

2 *Thornton v Curling* (1824) 8 Sim 310; *Hewson v Shelley* [1914] 2 Ch 13. But see *Dansereau v Berget* [1954] AC 1, [1953] 2 All ER 1058.

3 *R v Vincent* (1721) 1 Stra 481.

4 *Kerrich v Bransby* (1727) 7 Bro Parl Cas 437.

5 *Noell v Wells and Page* (1668) 1 Lev 235; *Allen v Dundas* (1789) 3 Term Rep 125.

6 *Barnesly v Powel* (1749) 1 Ves Sen 284 at 287.

7 *Allen v Dundas* (1789) 3 Term Rep 125 at 129.

8 *Allen v Dundas* (1789) 3 Term Rep 125; *Young v Elworthy* (1833) 1 My & K 215.

9 *Smart v Tranter* (1890) 43 Ch D 587 at 593.

10 *Blackham's Case* (1709) 1 Salk 290.

11 *Whicker v Hume* (1858) 7 HL Cas 124 at 144; *Bradford v Young* (1884) 26 Ch D 656; *Concha v Concha* (1886) 11 App Cas 541.

12 *Moons v De Bernales* (1826) 1 Russ 301 at 307; *Allen v Dundas* (1789) 3 Term Rep 125 at 129. A grant has under exceptional circumstances been admitted as evidence of death; *French v French* (1755) 1 Dick 268; *Loyd v Finlayson* (1797) 2 Esp 564. The grant is conveyancing evidence of the death in the absence of suspicion. As to a grant of administration being evidence that the administrator is next of kin of the intestate, see *Re Ivory, Hankin v Turner* (1878) 10 Ch D 372; *Barrs v Jackson* (1845) 1 Ph 582; *Mohan v Broughton* [1900] P 56 at 58.

13 *Re Barrance, Barrance v Ellis* [1910] 2 Ch 419 at 421 (the court is bound to assume that all documents admitted to probate are testamentary and its duty is to construe them in order to ascertain the testator's intention and within the limits allowed by law to give effect to that intention: in this case a list of names with sums of money against each name but with no words of gift was admitted to probate as a codicil); *Bradford v Young* (1885) 29 Ch D 617 at 625 (unsigned will in Scottish form); *Re Price, Tomlin v Latter* [1900] 1 Ch 442 (holograph will recognised as valid by being admitted to probate in England); *Re Walker, MacColl v Bruce* [1908] 1 Ch 560 (similar case).

[49.8]

Attempts to oust the jurisdiction of the court. The jurisdiction of the court is not ousted by the fact that the will is in a foreign language, or has to be construed by foreign rules of construction;[1] or by direction of the testator that questions of construction are to be decided by the trustees or by arbitration;[2] and a direction that a beneficiary seeking to have the will construed by the court shall lose his benefits under the will is inoperative.[3] The question of what conditions of this nature may be valid is considered elsewhere.[4]

1 *Di Sora v Phillipps* (1863) 10 HL Cas 624; *Re Bonnefoi, Surrey v Perrin* [1912] P 233.

2 *Re Wynn* [1952] Ch 271, [1952] 1 All ER 341 (decision of trustee to bind all persons – not valid); *Massy v Rogers* (1883) 11 LR Ir 409; *Price v Dewhurst* (1837) 8 Sim 279 (decision of an executor set aside as fraudulent); *Re Walton's Estate* (1856) 8 De GM & G 173; *Re Bronson* [1958] OR 367; *Re Tuck's Settlement Trusts, Public Trustee v Tuck* [1976] Ch 99, [1976] 1 All ER 545; affd [1978] Ch 49, [1978] 1 All ER 104, CA. Acts done in good faith under a determination by the tribunal set up by the testator are valid it seems, not only to protect the executors or trustees, but for all purposes: *Re Thompson's Will, Brahe v Mason* [1910] VLR 251 at 255; *Re Raven, Spencer v National Association for the Prevention of Consumption and other Forms of Tuberculosis* [1915] 1 Ch 673 (direction that identity of legatees be decided by trustees whose decision was to be final held contrary to public policy and void for repugnancy). It is thought that the better practice is not in any way to attempt to oust the jurisdiction of the court or, indeed, to forfeit the interests of beneficiaries who dispute the will, but to relieve trustees from all liability if they act upon the opinion of counsel.

3 *Rhodes v Muswell Hill Land Co* (1861) 29 Beav 560 at 604; *Massy v Rogers* (1883) 11 LR Ir
   409. The persons claiming under the testator may agree upon arbitration: *Ridout v Pain* (1747)
   3 Atk 486.
4 See para **[35.38]** supra.

[49.9]
Court's duty to construe. Where the rights under a will are in dispute and a
meaning can be attached to the words of the will, the court has a duty to construe
it and must declare its meaning,[1] subject to two qualifications: (i) it is not bound
to answer a question arising on a contingency which has not yet happened;[2] and
(ii) it has a duty not to answer a contingent question unless it has before it a
representative of every interest which may in any event be affected.[3] Rather
different considerations arise when the question is whether the court will force a
title under the will on a purchaser from those where the question is purely one of
the rights of beneficiaries.[4] If the doubts on a title arise upon a question
connected with the general law, the court is the judge whether the general law on
the point is or is not settled, and, if it be not settled, or if the doubts as to the title
may be affected by extrinsic circumstances, which neither the purchaser nor the
court can satisfactorily investigate, the court will not force the title on a
purchaser.[5]

1 *Crofts v Beamish* [1905] 2 IR 349 at 362, 363; *Dormer v Phillips* (1855) 4 De GM & G 855 at
   859.
2 The declaration sought should be such as to settle the litigation between the parties. See *Re
   Freme's Contract* [1895] 2 Ch 256; affd [1895] 2 Ch 778, CA; *Bright v Tyndall* (1876) 4 Ch D
   189; *Coleman v Bloomfield* (1884) 2 NZLR 49.
3 But in *Johnson v Clarke* [1928] Ch 847, it was held that the court is bound to decide a question
   of law on the construction of a document even though the decision may not bind a third party
   interested.
4 Where the title depends on the construction of a will the court generally treats the title as
   doubtful and will not enforce it, but this is not the case where the difficulty can be solved by the
   application of general rules of construction or if it depends on the general law of the land:
   Radford v Willis (1871) 7 Ch App 7 (construction); *Wrigley v Sykes* (1856) 21 Beav 337 (power
   of sale of executors); *Osborne v Rowlett* (1880) 13 Ch D 774 (limitations of freeholds);
   Hamilton v Buckmaster (1866) LR 3 Eq 323 (land purchased after will made); *Forster v
   Abraham* (1874) LR 17 Eq 351 (validity of appointment of new trustees).
5 *Pyrke v Waddingham* (1852) 10 Hare 1.

CHAPTER 50

General principles of construction

I. IN GENERAL

[50.1]

Intention collected from whole will. It has already been stated that the first principle of construction is to give effect to the intention of the testator as expressed in the words of the will.[1] The intention is collected from the whole will[2] with such evidence as the rules already stated allow[3] and the meaning of the will and every part of it is determined according to that intention.[4] A will is construed in the same way as any other document subject to this, that, if the intention is shown, the mode of expression of that intention and the form and language of the will are unimportant.[5] The want of technical words which are necessary in some instruments for the purpose of giving expression to the intention,[6] or any inaccuracy in grammar[7] or any want or inaccuracy in punctuation marks is immaterial so long as the intention is clear.[8] In all such cases a benevolent construction is adopted.[9] Consideration is given to the fact whether the will is drafted by a skilled lawyer or by the testator himself.[10]

1 *Roberts v Roberts* (1613) 2 Bulst 123 (the intention of the testator is plainly collected out of the very words of the will); *Lowen v Cocks* (1627) Het 63; *Bowen v Lewis* (1884) 9 App Cas 890; *Beaudry v Barbeau* [1900] AC 569; *Re Ackland Trust* [1944] 2 WWR 56; *Ng Chi-fong v Hui Ho Pui-fun* [1987] HKLR 462 at 485, applying Lord Halsbury LC in *Leader v Duffy* (1888) 13 App Cas 294. See also *Mardulyn v Lee Yee Hung* [1992] 2 HKC 164 at 171 and 174, where the text is referred to. *Re Golan Estate* [1996] 2 WWR 614. See also *Gibson Estate v Ashbury College Inc* (1999) 179 DLR (4th) 557 at 562. The rule first applied to a will is to give words their ordinary meaning: see *Roddy v Fitzgerald* (1858) 6 HL Cas 823 at 876; *Gorringe v Mahlstedt* [1907] AC 225 at 227, but see paras **[50.10]** and **[50.11]** infra.
2 *Baddeley v Leppingwell* (1764) 3 Burr 1533; *Thellusson v Woodford* (1799) 4 Ves 227 at 329; *Martin v Lee* (1861) 14 Moo PCC 142 at 153; *Crumpe v Crumpe* [1900] AC 127; *Marchuk v Marchuk* (1965) 52 WWR 652; *Re Welsh* (1980) 111 DLR (3d) 390; *Re Huffman* (1979) 101 DLR (3d) 365.
3 *Stanley v Stanley* (1862) 2 John & H 491; *Re Cozens, Miles v Wilson* [1903] 1 Ch 138. Although the will may be plain and unambiguous on the face of it, yet extrinsic circumstances may show the words are not to have their ordinary meaning: *Crook v Whitley* (1857) 7 De GM & G 490 at 495 (a gift to children where there were only grandchildren); *Re Shaw, Shaw v Shaw* [1955] QSR 284 (all surrounding circumstances to be kept in mind); and although the words of the will are plain and can be given full effect to, a consideration of the whole will may lead the court to insert a word which it is clear the testator has omitted. Thus where the will said 'all the nephews and nieces of my late sister L', the court upon a consideration of the whole will and evidence of the state of the family inferred that the word 'children' had been omitted and the clause was intended to read 'all my nephews and nieces children of my late sister L': *Re Birkin, Heald v Millership* [1949] 1 All ER 1045. See also *Re Smith, Veasey v Smith* [1948] Ch 49, [1947] 2 All ER 708, but in *Re Hurring* [1950] NZLR 948, the court refused to construe the words 'grandnieces and grandnephews' otherwise than literally although there were no such at

the date of the will nor of the death but there were many nieces and nephews. As to insertion of words, see para **[52.3]** infra.

4   The intention, when legitimately proved, is competent not only to fix the sense of ambiguous words, but to control the sense even of clear words and to supply the place of express words, in cases of difficulty or ambiguity: *Re Haygarth, Wickham v Haygarth* [1913] 2 Ch 9 at 15, citing *Hawkins on Wills* (2nd edn) p 6; *Re Patterson, Dunlop v Greer* [1899] 1 IR 324. It has been said, however, that nothing is more fallacious than first endeavouring to find the intention of the testator and then to construe the words of the will with reference to the supposed intention: *Taaffe v Conmee* (1862) 10 HL Cas 64 at 85; see similarly *Ng Chi-fong v Hui Ho Pui-fun* [1987] HKLR 462, per Rhind J, at 485 (cited in para **[51.1]**, n 1) where the text is referred to.

5   *Ralph v Carrick* (1879) 11 Ch D 873 at 876; *Cave v Cave* (1762) 2 Eden 139 at 144; *Hull v Carpenter* [1920] NZLR 361.

6   *Ralph v Carrick* (1879) 11 Ch D 873; *Taylor v Shaw, Re Jones* (1920) 89 LJPC 124.

7   *Re Norman's Trust* (1853) 3 De GM & G 965; *Eden v Wilson* (1852) 4 HL Cas 257 at 284; *Hall v Warren* (1861) 9 HL Cas 420 at 427. The ordinary meaning must not be departed from upon a mere suggestion of false grammar: *Gorringe v Mahlstedt* [1907] AC 225 at 227.

8   *Gordon v Gordon* (1871) LR 5 HL 254 at 276; *Gauntlett v Carter* (1853) 17 Beav 586; *Re Campbell, M'Cabe v Campbell* [1918] 1 IR 429.

9   *Jones v Price* (1841) 11 Sim 557 at 565; *Lang v Pugh* (1842) 1 Y & C Ch Cas 718 at 725; *Edgeworth v Edgeworth* (1869) LR 4 HL 35 at 41; *Re Speakman, Unsworth v Speakman* (1876) 4 Ch D 620 at 625.

10 *Richards v Davids* (1862) 13 CBNS 69; affd (1863) 13 CBNS 861; *Re Dayrell, Hastie v Dayrell* [1904] 2 Ch 496; *Blathwayt v Lord Cawley* [1976] AC 397, [1975] 3 All ER 625. This guides the court as to the force to be given to technical words: *Thellusson v Lord Rendelsham* (1859) 7 HL Cas 429 at 486. In a home-made will words may be given a popular sense rather than a legal sense: *Forth v Chapman* (1720) 1 P Wms 663 at 666; *Re Taylor, Taylor v Tweedie* [1923] 1 Ch 99 at 105. The principles of construction are, however, the same in all cases: *Weale v Ollive (No 2)* (1863) 32 Beav 421 at 423; but technically rules of construction will not be strictly applied in the case of a home-made will: *Re Crocombe* [1949] SASR 302. See further para **[50.6]**, n 3.

[50.2]

General rule for ascertaining the meaning of words. For the purpose of ascertaining the intention, the will is read in the first place without reference or regard to the consequences of any rule of law or canon of construction.[1] Words are given the meaning which is rendered necessary by the context of the whole will,[2] the particular passage being taken together with whatever is relevant in the rest of the will to explain it.[3] Where the court finds on the face of the will a clear, general or paramount intention to which effect can be given, and a particular or subordinate intention to which, by reason of some rule of law, the court cannot wholly or partially give effect, or which is inconsistent with or does not carry out all the intentions which the testator has or is presumed to have, then the particular intention must be rejected or modified, and the general intention of the testator carried into effect.[4] A void limitation may be referred to in explanation of the testator's intention,[5] but it is said that less weight should be given to an indication in an inoperative clause.[6] The will itself is taken as the dictionary from which the meaning of the words is ascertained,[7] however inaccurate such meaning would be in ordinary or legal use. The only qualification on the application of this general principle is that a clear context is required in order to exclude the usual meaning of a word.[8] Relative terms and other terms needing a context to make them intelligible can be explained only by the context.[9]

1   *Earl of Scarborough v Doe d Savile* (1836) 3 Ad & El 897 at 963; *De Beauvoir v De Beauvoir* (1852) 3 HL Cas 524 at 545; *Macpherson v Stewart* (1858) 28 LJ Ch 177; *Green v Gascoyne*

(1865) 4 De GJ & Sm 565 at 569; *Re Parker, Parker v Osborne* [1897] 2 Ch 208 at 213; *Aplin v Stone* [1904] 1 Ch 543; *Comiskey v Bowring-Hanbury* [1905] AC 84 at 89; *Edwards v Edwards* [1909] AC 275 at 277; applied in *Hayes v National Heart Foundation of Australia* [1976] 1 NSWLR 29.

2   *Towns v Wentworth* (1858) 11 Moo PCC 526 at 543; *King v Rymill* (1898) 67 LJPC 107; *Seale-Hayne v Jodrell* [1891] AC 304 at 306; *Re Pinhorne, Moreton v Hughes* [1894] 2 Ch 276.

3   *Higgins v Dawson* [1902] AC 1; *Jenkins v Hughes* (1860) 8 HL Cas 571 at 588; *Re Bourke's Will Trusts, Barclays Bank Trust Co Ltd v Canada Permanent Trust Co* [1980] 1 All ER 219, [1980] 1 WLR 539 (court will put the same construction on the same word when it occurs twice or more in the same will).

4   *Doe d Blanford v Applin* (1790) 4 Term Rep 82; *Doe d Bosnall v Harvey* (1825) 4 B & C 610; *Doe d Bills to Hopkinson* (1843) 5 QB 223; *Monypenny v Dering* (1852) 2 De GM & G 145 at 173; *Habergham v Ridehalgh* (1870) LR 9 Eq 395 at 400; *Hampton v Holman* (1877) 5 Ch D 183 at 190; *Re Sharp, Maddison v Gill* [1908] 2 Ch 190 at 196; *Re Elton, Elton v Elton* [1917] 2 Ch 413.

5   *Martin v Martin* (1866) LR 2 Eq 404 at 414; *Re Wright, Mott v Issott* [1907] 1 Ch 231.

6   *Re Watkins, Maybery v Lightfoot* (1913) 108 LT 237 at 239; as explained in *Re Johnson, Pitt v Johnson* (1913) 30 TLR 200.

7   *Hill v Crook* (1873) LR 6 HL 265 at 285; see *Re Gibb* [1984] 1 NZLR 708 and *Re Sparrow* [1984] 1 NZLR 750. *Re Horner, Eagleton v Horner* (1887) 37 Ch D 695 at 703; *Re Jodrell, Jodrell v Seale* (1890) 44 Ch D 590 at 606; *Re Parker, Parker v Osborne* [1897] 2 Ch 208 at 213; *Re Birks, Kenyon v Birks* [1900] 1 Ch 417 at 419; *Re Wood, Wood v Wood* [1902] 2 Ch 542 at 546; *Re Kiddle, Gent v Kiddle* (1905) 92 LT 724 at 725; *Re Lynch, Lynch v Lynch* [1943] 1 All ER 168.

8   *Towns v Wentworth* (1858) 11 Moo PCC 526 at 543.

9   For example, 'residue': *Singleton v Tomlinson* (1878) 3 App Cas 404 at 418; *Higgins v Dawson* [1902] AC 1; 'survivor': *Inderwick v Tatchell* [1903] AC 120 at 123. As to evidence in such cases, see Chapter 57. The expression 'subject thereto' does not necessarily refer only to what has gone before; its effect must be discovered by an examination of the whole scheme of the will: *Re Colvile, Colvile v Martin* (1911) 105 LT 622.

II.   SCOPE OR PURPOSE OF WILL CONSIDERED IN DOUBTFUL CASES

[50.3]

Words ambiguous in context. Where a context is sufficient to control the meaning of the words, but the words in such context are ambiguous, contradictory, or obscure, or where the words have no special meaning given to them by context, but have two meanings in ordinary use,[1] the court adopts that construction which it considers that the testator probably meant by the words,[2] taking into account the general scope of the will and the general purpose of the testator.[3] The construction of the will is not decided in such cases on mere conjecture or belief,[4] but on judicial persuasion[5] of what the intention of the testator is, either expressly declared or collected by just reasoning from the words of the will or evidenced by the surrounding circumstances where they can be called in aid.[6]

1   This rule can be applied only where there is a choice between two interpretations; *Giles v Melsom* (1873) LR 6 HL 24 at 31; *Gibbons v Gibbons* (1881) 6 App Cas 471 at 481; *Re Boden, Boden v Boden* [1907] 1 Ch 132 at 145. It is not applied where the normal meaning of the words offers no difficulty: *Re Boden, Boden v Boden*.

2   *Key v Key* (1853) 4 De GM & G 73 at 84, considered in *Re Dolands Will Trusts, Westminster Bank Ltd v Phillips* [1970] Ch 267, [1969] 3 All ER 713; *Tunaley v Roch* (1857) 3 Drew 720 at 724; *Re James's Will Trusts, Peard v James* [1962] Ch 226, [1960] 3 All ER 744; *Re Wootton's Will Trusts, Trotter v Duffin* [1968] 2 All ER 618, [1968] 1 WLR 681.

3   *Coard v Holderness* (1855) 20 Beav 147 at 152; *Prescott v Barker* (1874) 9 Ch App 174 at 187; *Re Whiteley, Bishop of London v Whiteley* [1910] 1 Ch 600. As to this rule in executory trusts

where the testator has not been his own conveyancer, see *Sackville-West v Viscount Holmesdale* (1870) LR 4 HL 543 at 559.

4   *Giles v Melsom* (1873) LR 6 HL 24; *Re Elliot, Kelly v Elliot* [1896] 2 Ch 353 at 356; *Inderwick v Tatchell* [1903] AC 120 at 122; *Walford v Walford* [1912] AC 658 at 664.

5   *A-G v Grote* (1827) 2 Russ & M 699; *Barksdale v Gilliat* (1818) 1 Swan 562 at p 565.

6   *Doe d Brodbelt v Thomson* (1858) 12 Moo PCC 116 at 127; *Lady Langdale v Briggs* (1856) 8 De GM & G 391 at 429. As to evidence admissible, see Chapter 57.

[50.4]

Inferences from the scope of the will. The court makes any reasonable inference from a particular passage, comparing that inference with what is apparent in other parts of the will.[1] This power of inference, however, is limited; a general intention not carried out by appropriate words in the will itself cannot give the court the right to place the words there for the testator,[2] and a priori reasoning upon what the testator would naturally intend cannot be allowed to weigh against the proper construction of the words used.[3] The court cannot conjecture what the testator would have said if a particular state of things had been presented to his mind which it is apparent, from the language he had used, had not occurred to him and for which it cannot be supposed that he intended to make any provision.[4] Where, however, the words are conflicting, the court attempts to reconcile successive provisions without unduly straining the language and to make the whole consistent with the apparent general intention of the testator.[5]

1   *Law Union and Crown Insurance Co v Hill* [1902] AC 263 at 265; *Jenkins v Hughes* (1860) 8 HL Cas 571 at 588.

2   *Hunter v A-G* [1899] AC 309 at 315, 317; *Re Evans, Public Trustee v Evans* [1920] 2 Ch 304.

3   *Coltsmann v Coltsmann* (1868) LR 3 HL 121 at 130.

4   *Martin v Holgate* (1866) LR 1 HL 175 at 186; *Inderwick v Tatchell* [1903] AC 120 at 122.

5   *Re Bedson's Trusts* (1885) 28 Ch D 523 at 525; *Taylor v Sturrock* [1900] AC 225 at 232; *Shields v Shields* [1910] 1 IR 116 at 120. As to inconsistencies, see Chapter 52.

III.   WORDS GIVEN THEIR USUAL MEANING

[50.5]

Grammatical and ordinary meaning. It is a general rule applicable to all kinds of documents[1] that the words used in it are in the first place to be given ordinary grammatical meaning;[2] but, despite all that has been said as to the universality of the rule,[3] it is by no means a hard and fast rule which is subject to no exception.[4] As has already been stated even the ordinary meaning of words give way to some different or modified meaning required by the context[5] or by a consideration of the whole will.[6] Where a word has two proper and recognised meanings, this rule, if it applies to all, must be greatly modified, and in such cases the meaning of the words in a particular passage must be decided by the context and the surrounding circumstances.[7] A word will not, however, be given an artificial, secondary or technical meaning unless it is shown that it cannot without propriety receive its ordinary meaning.[8]

1   *Re Levy, ex p Walton* (1881) 17 Ch D 746 at 751; *Caledonian Rly Co v North British Rly Co* (1881) 6 App Cas 114 at 131; *Spencer v Metropolitan Board of Works* (1882) 22 Ch D 142 at 148. See generally the House of Lords judgments in *Perrin v Morgan* [1943] AC 399.

2   *Thellusson v Woodford* (1799) 4 Ves 227 at 329, adopted in *Villar v Sir Walter Gilbey* [1907] AC 139 at 147. The rule has been enunciated in a very large number of cases; see for example *Hamilton v Ritchie* [1894] AC 310 at 313; *Higgins v Dawson* [1902] AC 1 at 12; *Gorringe v Mahlstedt* [1907] AC 225 at 227; *Tarbutt v Nicholson* (1920) 89 LJPC 127; *Lynch v Johnson* (1878) 4 VLR 263; *Crawford v Broddy* (1896) 26 SCR 345; *De Robeck v Lord Cloncurry* (1871) IR 5 Eq 588; *Church Property Trustees v Public Trustee* (1907) 27 NZLR 354; *Re Stalker's Executor's, Petitioners* 1977 SLT (Notes) 4: *Re Rowland, Smith v Russell* [1963] Ch 1 (contrast the approach of Lord Denning MR in a dissenting judgment at 9, 10).

3   There is the well-known dictum of Kindersley V-C in *Re Crawford's Trusts* (1854) 2 Drew 230 ('a rule of universal application, which admits of no exception, and which ought never under any circumstances to be departed from'). The dictum in *Gether v Capper* (1855) 24 LJCP 69 at 71, is perhaps nearer the truth: 'The most general of rules; a rule of great utility.' The rule applies to all wills: *Smith v Butcher* (1878) 10 Ch D 113 at 116.

4   *Hamilton v Ritchie* [1894] AC 310 at 313 (unless the context of the instruments shows that he intended to use the words with some other than the conventional meaning); *Gordon v Gordon* (1871) LR 5 HL 254 at 271 (to the same effect). In practice, the rule is entirely subservient to the context of the will: *Seale-Hayne v Jodrell* (1891) AC 304 at 306.

5   See para **[50.3]** supra.

6   See para **[50.1]** supra.

7   See *Cave v Horsell* [1912] 3 KB 533 at 543, 544.

8   *Walker v Tipping* (1852) 9 Hare 800; *Crook v Whiteley* (1857) 7 De GM & G 490; *Lowther v Bentinck* (1874) LR 19 Eq 166; *Re Jackson's Will* (1879) 13 Ch D 189; *Re Benn, Benn v Benn* (1885) 29 Ch D 839; *Re Bennett, Henderson v Bennett* (1903) 21 NZLR 113.

[50.6]

Legal and technical words. These words are to receive their legal or technical meaning,[1] unless it clearly appears that they are intended to bear some other meaning.[2] The legal meaning of words is not necessarily applied where the testator has drawn his own will without legal advice,[3] and conversely in a will drawn by a lawyer legal expressions will be more strictly construed.

1   *Roddy v Fitzgerald* (1858) 6 HL Cas 823; *Giles v Melsom* (1873) LR 6 HL 24 at 31; *Van Grutten v Foxwell* [1897] AC 658; *Re Keane's Estate* [1903] 1 IR 215; *Re Simcoe, Vowler-Simcoe v Vowler* [1913] 1 Ch 552 at 557; *Davy v Redington* [1917] 1 IR 250; *Re Cook, Beck v Grant* [1948] Ch 212, [1948] 1 All ER 231.

2   *Gibbons v Gibbons* (1881) 6 App Cas 471; *Re Simcoe, Vowler-Simcoe v Vowler* [1913] 1 Ch 552; *Re Rooney* [1950] SASR 67 ('predecease me' read as dying before the date of distribution); *Re Taylor, Read v Carr* [1957] NZLR 647.

3   *Read v Backhouse* (1831) 2 Russ & M 546; *Lewis v Rees* (1856) 3 K & J 132; *Re Taylor, Taylor v Tweedie* [1923] 1 Ch 99; *Hall v Warren* (1861) 9 HL Cas 420. See also para **[50.1]**, n 9.

[50.7]

Usual rules of grammar applied. In general the grammatical construction of a will must prevail,[1] and where the necessity arises particular grammatical rules, such as the rule that a relative pronoun is referable to the last antecedent, will be applied.[2]

1   *Grey v Pearson* (1857) 6 HL Cas 61; *Roddy v Fitzgerald* (1858) 6 HL Cas 823; *Re Harrison, Turner v Hellard* (1885) 30 Ch D 390 at 393. The rule applies to foreign wills: *Re Harman, Lloyd v Tardy* [1894] 3 Ch 607. As to use of tenses in describing a contingency, see *Donald, Royal Exchange Assurance v Donald* [1947] 1 All ER 764.

2   *Castledon v Turner* (1745) 3 Atk 257; *Adshead v Willetts* (1861) 29 Beav 358 at 363.

[50.8]

When usual sense adhered to. Where the words interpreted according to their usual meaning are clear in reference to the surrounding circumstances,[1] that is to say, where these circumstances do not deprive the words of all reasonable application when so interpreted,[2] this sense must be adhered to;[3] but, where that course would lead to an absurdity or some repugnancy or inconsistency with the intentions of the testator,[4] collected from the whole will, the grammatical and ordinary or technical sense of the words may be modified, so far only as is necessary to avoid the absurdity or inconsistency.[5] There must, in any such case, be sufficient to satisfy a judicial mind that the words were meant to be used by the testator in some other sense.[6] The burden of proof in such a case lies on those who attribute to the words other than their usual sense.[7]

1   As to admission of evidence of surrounding circumstances, see Chapter 57.
2   *Shore v Wilson* (1842) 9 Cl & Fin 355 at 525.
3   *Croker v Marquis of Hertford* (1844) 4 Moo PCC 339 at 364; *Re Cope, Cross v Cross* [1908] 2 Ch 1; *Swifte v A-G for Ireland (No 2)* [1912] 1 IR 133 at 140. It is an erroneous method of construction to give to language which on its natural meaning is capable of a sensible interpretation and does not occasion any absurdity or give rise to any consequence which is an affront to common sense, some other meaning which the words are less appropriate to bear merely because, if the language is construed in accordance with its natural meaning, some part of it can be shown to be otiose: per Buckley LJ in *Re Priestley's Will Trusts, Hambros Bank Executors and Trustee Co Ltd v Robagliati* [1971] Ch 858 at 867, 858, [1971] 2 All ER 817 at 824. See also *Re Jones* [1971] NZLR 796.
4   This does not mean that evidence of the testator's intention other than the words of the will and the surrounding circumstances can be considered: *Re Atkinson's Will Trusts, Atkinson v Hall* [1978] 1 All ER 1275, [1978] 1 WLR 586 (neither a letter nor an undated memorandum was admissible to show the testatrix's intention; the letter was a statement of the intentions of the draftsman and not the testatrix, whilst the memorandum merely showed that the testatrix had used the term 'worthy causes' in a special sense on a particular occasion, and was not evidence of the surrounding circumstances in which the will was made or of any habitual sense in which the testatrix used the term); see para **[50.1]** supra.
5   See Lord Denning MR in *Re Allsop, Cardinal v Warr* [1968] Ch 39 at 47, [1967] 2 All ER 1056 at 1058, CA; and Buckley J in *Re Doland's Will Trusts, Westminster Bank Ltd v Phillips* [1970] Ch 267 at 272, 274, [1969] 3 All ER 713 at 715, 717. *Hicks v Sallitt* (1854) 3 De GM & G 782; *Nockolds v Locke* (1856) 3 K & J 6; *Thelluson v Lord Rendlesham* (1859) 7 HL Cas 429 at 494; *Rhodes v Rhodes* (1882) 7 App Cas 192 at 205; *Re Boden, Boden v Boden* [1907] 1 Ch 132; *Re Evans, Public Trustee v Evans* [1920] 2 Ch 304; *Re Thomas, Trustee Executors and Agency Co Ltd v Thomas* [1925] VLR 488. If the law places a certain signification on the words which the testator has used, they must, in the absence of a controlling context, be construed in that sense, no matter how he may possibly have meant them to be understood, unless so to do would lead to some palpable absurdity or violate some rule of law: *Palmer v Orpen* [1894] 1 IR 32.
6   *Roddy v Fitzgerald* (1858) 6 HL Cas 823 at 877; *Van Grutten v Foxwell* [1897] AC 658 at 672; *Re Segelman* [1995] 3 All ER 676 at 693.
7   *Re Crawford's Trusts* (1854) 2 Drew 230 at 233.

[50.9]
Effect of context and circumstances in excluding rule. There are few words, if any, which bear a meaning so exact that the reader can disregard the surrounding circumstances and the context in ascertaining the sense in which they are employed.[1] If, therefore, the intention of the testator can be collected with reasonable certainty from the whole will, with the aid of extrinsic evidence of a kind properly admissible, that intention must have effect given to it beyond and even against the literal and ordinary sense of particular words and expressions, and the court is not bound to adhere to the ordinary or legal meaning in such a case.[2]

1   *Cave v Horsell* [1912] 3 KB 533 at 543.
2   *Doe d Andrew v Lainchbury* (1809) 11 East 290; *Key v Key* (1853) 4 De GM & G 73; *Pride v Fooks* (1858) 3 De G & J 252; *Rhodes v Rhodes* (1882) 7 App Cas 192; and see para **[50.8]**, n 5.

[50.10]
Determination of the meaning of technical terms. These terms for the purpose of the determination of their meaning by evidence or otherwise are divided into two classes: technical terms of English law and technical terms of foreign law and of science and art. Technical terms of English law are questions of law and fall to be determined by the court with the aid, in certain cases, of the established canons of construction; and, in a technically drawn will, the court regards the practice of conveyancers as not wholly irrelevant though not binding.[1] Technical terms of foreign law, on the other hand, are questions of fact and fall, therefore, to be determined by evidence, ie the evidence of experts skilled in the law of the country in question.[2] The meaning of technical terms of art and science are also questions of fact and are determined by the evidence of experts in the particular subjects.[3]

1   'I feel strongly the importance of adhering to the rule that technical expressions and words of known legal import shall receive their ordinary legal meaning': Lord Davey in *Van Grutten v Foxwell* [1897] AC 658 at 684; *Re Athill, Athill v Athill* (1880) 16 Ch D 211 at 223; *Re Edwards, Edwards v Edwards* [1894] 3 Ch 644; *Villar v Sir Walter Gilbey* [1907] AC 139 at 152; *Gemmell v Gemmell* (1892) 18 VLR 781; *Davy v Redington* [1917] 1 IR 250; *Re Fetherston-Haugh-Whitney's Estate* [1924] 1 IR 153. What are 'usual' clauses is a question of fact on which the evidence of conveyancers may be accepted: *Re Maddy's Estate, Maddy v Maddy* [1901] 2 Ch 820 at 822. As to technical words of English law, see *Leach v Jay* (1878) 9 Ch D 42; *Parr v Parr* (1833) 1 My & K 647; *Gibbons v Gibbons* (1881) 6 App Cas 471; *Re Simcoe, Vowler-Simcow v Vowler* [1913] 1 Ch 552. Technical expressions of English law will be liberally construed in the case of a home-made will: see para **[50.6]**, n 3.
2   *Re Cliffe's Trusts* [1892] 2 Ch 229 at 232; *Re Manners, Manners v Manners* [1923] 1 Ch 220.
3   *Goblet v Beechey* (1829) 3 Sim 24; *Clayton v Gregson* (1836) 5 Ad & El 302. This rule extends to particular expressions used with a special meaning by groups or bodies of persons: *Share v Wilson* (1842) 9 Cl & Fin 355 ('godly persons' as used by members of a dissenting body); but see *Re How, How v How* [1930] 1 Ch 66 (where the words 'good works' used by a member of the Plymouth Brethren was not confined to religious works), distinguished in *Re Atkinson's Will Trusts, Atkinson v Hall* [1978] 1 All ER 1275, [1978] 1 WLR 586; see para **[50.8]**, n 4.

[50.11]
Ordinary meaning of words. The ordinary meaning of a word is the meaning given to it by the ordinary society,[1] that is, the testator's society, of that class and period in which he lived and moved.[2] If, therefore, the testator belonged to a district, trade or business in which a particular word has a certain meaning given to it by an existing custom, then the ordinary meaning of the word under the rule is this customary meaning, and not the meaning given to it by general English usage.[3] There can be no fixed meaning of a word which the courts adopt as the 'legal meaning' as opposed to the popular meaning. There is no necessary opposition between the proper meaning and the popular meaning and, where a word has several meanings, the only correct meaning is that ascertained without prejudice between various usual meanings as the correct interpretation of the particular will.[4]

1   *Shore v Wilson* (1842) 9 Cl & Fin 355; *Parker v Marchant* (1843) 1 Ph 356 at 360; *Re How, How v How* [1930] 1 Ch 66.
2   See Goulding J in *Re Barnes' Will Trusts, Prior v Barnes* [1972] 2 All ER 639 at 644, [1972] 1 WLR 587 at 593 (judge's own knowledge of the contemporary meaning of the word 'money'); see also para **[64.35]** et seq; *M'Hugh v M'Hugh* [1908] 1 IR 155 (any archaic or obsolete meaning is ignored).

3   *Barksdale v Morgan* (1693) 4 Mod Rep 185; *Re Steel, Wappett v Robinson* [1903] 1 Ch 135.
     Whether a word has a customary meaning is a question of fact: *Simpson v Margitson* (1847) 11
     QB 23 at 32.
4   *Perrin v Morgan* [1943] AC 399 at 408, [1943] 1 All ER 187 at 191; *Re Cooper* [1946] Ch 109,
     [1946] 1 All ER 28.

[50.12]

Etymological meaning. The ordinary meaning of a word is not necessarily the etymological meaning,[1] though there have been cases where the court has been guided by that meaning.[2] The court is generally guided by the meaning given to the word by dictionaries of repute, and may receive evidence of the meaning ordinarily given to the word.[3]

1   *Shore v Wilson* (1842) 9 Cl & Fin 355 at 527.
2   *Parr v Parr* (1833) 1 My & K 647 (construing the word 'devolve').
3   *A-G v Cast Plate Glass Co* (1792) 1 Anst 39 at 42; *Shore v Wilson* (1842) 9 Cl & Fin 355 at
     568; *Re Rayner, Rayner v Rayner* [1904] 1 Ch 176; *Marquis of Camden v IRC* [1914] 1 KB 641
     (any literary help); see Buckley LJ in *Re Priestley's Will Trusts, Hambros Bank Executors and
     Trustee Co Ltd v Rabagliati* [1971] Ch 858 at 866, [1971] 2 All ER 817 at 824. But compare
     Lord Denning MR in *Re Rowland* [1963] Ch 1 at 10, [1962] 2 All ER 837 at 841: 'In order to
     discover the meaning which he intended, you will not get much help by going to a dictionary. It
     is very unlikely that he used a dictionary, and even less likely that he used the same one as you.'
     But see *Re O'Brien* (1977) 77 DLR (3d) 397 where seven dictionaries were referred to for the
     meaning of 'establish'.

[50.13]

Meaning may change in course of time. It is common knowledge that the meaning of a word varies from time to time and, therefore, there are occasions when it has to be decided what was the ordinary meaning of a word at the time when the testator used it, and such inquiry may on occasions have to extend to the discovery of the secondary meanings which it could have had at that time.[1] It follows that the decided cases on the meaning of any word are not always applicable to the will under consideration and, because the meaning is dependent on the context and the circumstances, even modern cases are not a reliable guide to the precise meaning in any particular case, though they may be useful to show what meanings have been allowed to a particular word.[2]

1   *Cave v Horsell* [1912] 3 KB 533; *Pigg v Clarke* (1876) 3 Ch D 672; and see as to changes in the
     meaning of 'money' and on this subject generally *Perrin v Morgan* [1943] AC 399; and *Re
     Barnes' Will Trusts, Prior v Barnes* [1792] 2 All ER 639.
2   See *Perrin v Morgan* [1943] AC 399, where the earlier authority is referred to: As to the
     practical necessity for rules of construction and their strict observance, see *Perrin v Morgan*
     [1943] 1 All ER 187 at 197, per Lord Russell of Killowen and per Lord Romer.

[50.14]

Regard to punctuation. Different views have been taken as to the importance of punctuation. It has been said that it is to be disregarded[1] but the modern view seems to be in favour of having regard to punctuation marks.[2]

1   *Sandford v Raikes* (1816) 1 Mer 646; *Gordon v Gordon* (1871) LR 5 HL 254; *Re Campbell,
     M'Cabe v Campbell* [1918] 1 IR 429.
2   See Wood V-C in *Oppenheim v Henry* (1853), as reported in a note to *Walker v Tipping* (1852)
     9 Hare 800, 803; Sir John Romilly MR in *Gauntlett v Carter* (1853) 17 Beav 586 at 589, 590;

Knight Bruce LJ, note to *Manning v Purcell* (1855) 24 LJ Ch 522, 523; Lord Finlay LC in *Houston v Burns* [1918] AC 337 at 342; and Roxburgh J in *Re Jeffrey* [1948] 2 All ER 131 at 131. See also *Re Patton* (1971) 19 DLR (3d) 497 (mark not considered as a period); *Re Steel, Public Trustee v Christian Aid Society* [1979] Ch 218, [1978] 2 All ER 1026.

IV.   EFFECT TO BE GIVEN TO EVERY WORD

[50.15]
The rule. A will must be so construed that effect is given to every word.[1] The court has no right to disregard a word provided some meaning can be given to it,[2] and that meaning is not contrary to some intention plainly expressed in other parts of the will.[3] The court does not as a rule import to the testator that he uses additional words without some additional purpose or without any purpose at all.[4]

1   *Parker v Tootal* (1865) 11 HL Cas 143 at 159; *Best v Stonehewer* (1865) 2 De GJ & Sm 537 at 541; *Massy v Rowen* (1869) LR 4 HL 288 at 301 (the purpose for which a testator introduced the word into his disposition must be ascertained); *Re Sanford, Sanford v Sanford* [1901] 1 Ch 939 at 943; *Rickerby v Nicolson* [1912] 1 IR 343 at 347.
2   *Re Croxon, Croxon v Ferrers* [1904] 1 Ch 252 at 258 ('lawfully' in a name and arms clause); *Heasman v Pearse* (1871) 7 Ch App 275 at 283.
3   *Doe d Bladwin v Rawding* (1819) 2 B & Ald 441 at 448; *Constantine v Constantine* (1801) 6 Ves 100 at 102.
4   *Oddie v Woodford* (1821) 3 My & Cr 584 at 614; *Quarm v Quarm* [1892] 1 QB 184 at 186.

[50.16]
Rule subject to previous rules. The rule is not inflexible.[1] According to the context[2] or by reasoning from the scope of the will[3] words may be rejected,[4] or may be regarded as merely explanatory, expressing what would otherwise have been true under the will.[5] There need be no departure made from the rule giving words their usual meaning merely because they are in that sense only surplusage,[6] or because other words, inconsistent with their use in that sense but insufficient to give them any other sense, may have to be rejected.[7] The objection of surplusage has weight only when the presence of the word or phrase would be unusual or unaccountable if it were not specifically inserted for the purpose of altering the meaning of the sentence.[8]

1   *Sayer v Bradley* (1856) 5 HL Cas 873 at 899 (not to be departed from unless by adhering to it some intention gathered from the context is defeated); *Martin v Holgate* (1866) LR 1 HL 175; *Clarke v Colls* (1861) 9 HL Cas 601 at 613.
2   See para **[50.5]** supra.
3   See para **[50.5]** supra.
4   See Chapter 52.
5   *M'Lachlan v Taitt* (1860) 2 De GF & J 449 at 454; *Re Walton's Estate* (1856) 8 De GM & G 173 at 175; *Hicks v Sallitt* (1854) 3 De GM & G 782.
6   *Monk v Mawdsley* (1827) 1 Sim 286; *Taylor v Beverley* (1844) 1 Coll 108; *Craik v Lamb* (1844) 1 Coll 489; *Re Kirkbride's Trusts* (1866) LR 2 Eq 400; *Giles v Melsom* (1873) LR 6 HL 24 at 33; *Palmer v Orpen* [1894] 1 IR 32; *Roberts v Bishop of Kilmore* [1902] 1 IR 333 at 339.
7   See *Jesson v Wright* (1820) 2 Bligh 1; *Roddy v Fitzgerald* (1858) 6 HL Cas 823. These cases concern the rejection of technical legal words where inconsistent with the general intention. Where clearly shown to be inconsistent with the testator's meaning such words may be rejected, but unless there is something apparent on the face of the will, the rules of construction must prevail.
8   *Re Boden, Boden v Boden* [1907] 1 Ch 132 at 143.

V.   APPROPRIATE RULES OF CONSTRUCTION TO BE APPLIED

[50.17]

Use and purpose of rules of construction. The court applies certain established rules of construction[1] in cases where they are respectively appropriate. These rules seek to lay down what inferences ought in doubtful cases to be drawn, as a general rule, from particular indications of intention;[2] some more specially determine what meaning should be given to particular words and expressions which have acquired a technical or quasi-technical nature;[3] and others determine in what manner particular common forms of disposition are to be effectuated, where the testator has not fully and unambiguously disclosed his intention.[4]

1   *Ralph v Carrick* (1879) 11 Ch D 873 at 876. Rules of construction have been established by the courts and they should be followed not only as a matter of precedent but so that the draftsman may have reasonable certainty as to the construction which will be placed upon his words: see *Perrin v Morgan* [1943] AC 399 at 407, [1943] 1 All ER 187 at 191; *Re Bedson's Trusts* (1885) 28 Ch D 523; *Kirby-Smith v Parnell* [1903] 1 Ch 483; *Re MacMillan* (1977) 80 DLR (3d) 54 (the application of the rules of construction must be consistent with the testator's intention).
2   Examples are the rules as to the effect of a gift over on failure of issue and the rules as to application of limitations: see Chapter 101.
3   *Davenport v Coltman* (1842) 12 Sim 588; *Grey v Pearson* (1857) 6 HL Cas 61 at 79; *Greville v Brown* (1859) 7 HL Cas 689 at 703; *Re Bawden National Provincial Bank of England v Cresswell, Bawden v Cresswell* [1894] 1 Ch 693; *Barraclough v Cooper* [1908] 2 Ch 121n.
4   *Re Jodrell, Jodrell v Seale* (1890) 44 Ch D 590. See eg, the rule in *Andrews v Partington* (1791) 3 Bro CC 401, Chapter 66, and the rule in *Wild's Case* (1599) 6 Co Rep 166, Chapter 76.

[50.18]

Conflict of laws. The system of rules of construction, whether English or foreign, applied by the court varies according to the circumstances and the testator's intention.[1] A testator may expressly or impliedly show an intention that his meaning is to be ascertained according to some known system of jurisprudence; and such intention, if the provisions of the will and the circumstances admit, has effect given to it, irrespective of the domicile or nationality of the testator.[2] Similarly, the fact that the testator uses the English language, with or without the use of technical terms borrowed from the law of England, is considered in discovering the testator's intention even when the property dealt with and the validity and effect of his dispositions of that property are affected by a foreign law.[3] Where the will is to be construed by English law, but is written in a foreign language, the court only looks at the effect of that language in order to ascertain what are the equivalent expressions in English.[4]

1   The general principles apply to all wills whether English or foreign: *Di Sora v Phillipps* (1863) 10 HL Cas 624; *Re Harman, Lloyd v Tardy* [1894] 3 Ch 607.
2   *Raphael v Boehm* (1852) 22 LJ Ch 299; *Bradford v Young* (1885) 29 Ch D 617; *Re Price, Tomlin v Latter* [1900] 1 Ch 442.
3   *Studd v Cook* (1883) 8 App Cas 577; *Re Baker's Settlement Trusts, Hunt v Baker* [1908] WN 161; *Re Bonnefoi, Surrey v Perrin* [1912] P 233. The doctrines of the English Chancery Court are not imported into such a will: *McGibbon v Abbott* (1885) 10 App Cas 653; *Re Miller, Bailee v Miller* [1914] 1 Ch 511.
4   *Reynolds v Kortright* (1854) 18 Beav 417; *Baring v Ashburton* (1886) 54 LT 463.

[50.19]
Foreign law. What foreign law is to be applied is dealt with elsewhere.[1] The court may be informed of the appropriate foreign rules of construction by evidence.[2]

1   See Chapter 24.
2   See Chapter 57, para **[57.6]** infra.

VI.   APPLICATION OF RULES OF CONSTRUCTION

[50.20]
The rules of construction of wills in English law are not lightly departed from in cases where they are applicable;[1] but, on the other hand, it has been suggested in a recent case that the traditional rules of construction are not adhered to as rigidly as they have been observed in the past,[2] and are followed only where the testator has not clearly expressed his own intention and has not given any other guide to the court.[3] All these rules are therefore of the nature of presumptions only,[4] and are subject to any contrary intention[5] disclosed by the will, as construed in accordance with the principles already stated.[6] Thus, if the language of the will can be read in its ordinary and natural sense[7] so as to be sensible with respect to the surrounding circumstances, no rule of construction is applicable to ascertain the intention,[8] and no reliance can be placed on former decisions of the court on similar or even identical words in other wills.[9]

1   *Perrin v Morgan* [1943] AC 399 at 420, [1943] 1 All ER 187 at 197 (they should be strictly observed, but ought to be applied in a reasonable way). The ground on which these rules are followed has been stated in different terms from time to time and no doubt each suggestion is one element of the whole reason. It has been stated that the rules are followed for certainty in judicial decisions: *Jesson v Wright* (1820) 2 Bligh 1 at 56; *Doe d Clarke v Ludham* (1831) 7 Bing 275 at 279; *Morrall v Sutton* (1845) 1 Ph 533 at 536; *Grey v Pearson* (1857) 6 HL Cas 61 at 108; *Roddy v Fitzgerald* (1858) 6 HL Cas 823 at 884; or that the rules make it possible to advise confidently on titles: *Roddy v Fitzgerald* (1858) 6 HL Cas 823 at 875; or that it is to be assumed that lawyers draw instruments according to the known state of the law which includes the rules from time to time adopted by the court in the construction of wills, and the testator must be supposed to have used his words in the sense so fixed: *Re Bawden, National Provincial Bank of England v Cresswell, Bawden v Cresswell* [1894] 1 Ch 693 at 697; *Kingsbury v Walter* [1901] AC 187 at 189. These matters were for the most part confirmed by Lord Romer in *Perrin v Morgan* [1943] AC 399 at 421. He said that they should be regarded as a dictionary by which all parties including the courts are bound, but recourse must not be had to this dictionary until it has been ascertained from the language of the whole will, when read in the light of surrounding circumstances, whether the testator has indicated his intention of using a word or phrase in other than its dictionary meaning, ie whether the testator has been his own dictionary.
2   *Re Henderson's Trusts, Schreiber v Baring* [1969] 3 All ER 769 at 770, [1969] 1 WLR 651 at 654, per Harman LJ, referring to the class closing rules.
3   *Limpus v Arnold* (1884) 15 QBD 300 at 302; *Re Coward, Coward v Larkman* (1887) 57 LT 285; *Re Hamlet, Stephen v Cunninghame* (1888) 39 Ch D 426; *Re Stone, Baker v Stone* [1895] 2 Ch 196 at 200; and see the statement of Lord Romer digested at the conclusion of n 1, supra.
4   That is, an inference in favour of a given construction of particular words: *Lee v Pain* (1845) 4 Hare 201 at 216.
5   *Singleton v Tomlinson* (1878) 3 App Cas 404 at 423.
6   Thus the rules of construction are to be applied rationally and not in such a way as to produce an absurd or capricious result: per Stamp J in *Re Cockle's Will Trusts, Moreland v Draffen* [1967] Ch 690 at 706, [1967] 1 All ER 391 at 395.

7   See paras **[50.5]**–**[50.14]** supra.
8   *Leader v Duffey* (1888) 13 App Cas 294; *Inderwick v Tatchell* [1903] AC 120 at 122; *Comiskey v Bowring-Hanbury* [1905] AC 84 at 88.
9   *Re Tredwell, Jeffray v Tredwell* [1891] 2 Ch 640 at 653; *Re Morgan, Morgan v Morgan* [1893] 3 Ch 222 at 228; *Re Palmer v Answorth* [1893] 3 Ch 369 at 373; *Macculloch v Anderson* [1904] AC 55 at 60; *Chapman v Perkins* [1905] AC 106 at 108; *Gorringe v Mahlstedt* [1907] AC 225; *Re Cope, Cross v Cross* [1908] 2 Ch 1. See also infra.

[50.21]
How far the court is bound by previous decisions. It has been said that the true way to construe a will is to form an opinion as to its meaning and construction apart from the cases, and then see whether the cases require a modification of this opinion.[1] Previous decisions, particularly where the question relates to real property, are considered by the court,[2] but, except in so far as they lay down some rule of construction[3] applicable to the will to be construed, they are given little weight.[4] The court may follow a previous decision on another will where there is identity of language and where no real distinction exists between the cases,[5] but the mere fact of similarity of language does not bind the court to adopt a similar construction.[6] A different conclusion may be rendered necessary by the surrounding circumstances.[7] It is the principle of construction exemplified rather than the particular decisions themselves which are followed.[8] One judge is not bound to follow another on questions of mere verbal interpretation,[9] and even when the established rules of construction are applied, two minds may honestly differ and reach different conclusions.[10] On a question of mere construction the decision of the Court of Appeal on similar grounds is not binding on another court, and much less on a court of equal jurisdiction.[11]

1   *Re Tredwell, Jeffray v Tredwell* [1891] 2 Ch 640 at 659; *Re Blantern, Lowe v Cooke* [1891] WN 54; *Re Sanford, Sanford v Sanford* [1901] 1 Ch 939; *Re Williams, Metcalf v Williams* [1914] 1 Ch 219 at 222.
2   *Miles v Harford* (1879) 12 Ch D 691 at 698; *Morgan v Thomas* (1882) 9 QBD 643; *Re Bright-Smith, Bright-Smith v Bright-Smith* (1886) 31 Ch D 314 at 318. The fact that the testator's intention is defeated by these rules does not prevent the court giving effect to his intention as regards his personal estate: *White v Summers* [1908] 2 Ch 256 at 264.
3   *Re Jackson's Will* (1879) 13 Ch D 189; *Re Jodrell, Jodrell v Seale* (1890) 44 Ch D 590 at 610; *Re Morgan, Morgan v Morgan* [1893] 3 Ch 222 at 232; *Walford v Walford* [1912] AC 658 at 664.
4   *Re Masson, Morton v Masson* (1917) 86 LJ Ch 753 at 756; *Ashton v Adamson* (1841) 1 Dr & War 198; and see the cases cited in n 1.
5   *Roddy v Fitzgerald* (1858) 6 HL Cas 823 at 875; *Thorpe v Thorpe* (1862) 1 H & C 326 at 336; *Lightfoot v Burstall* (1863) 1 Hem & M 546 at 549. Scottish cases are authorities, for the general principles of construction are the same in both countries: *Young v Robertson* (1862) 4 Macq 314; *Hickling v Fair* [1899] AC 15 at 26; but it cannot be said that every rule of construction is common to the two countries; *Hickling v Fair* [1899] AC 15 at 25. The general position as to previous decisions being authorities is summed up in the sentence 'Cases can be of little use, for the words of one will are seldom the same as those of another': *Rhodes v Rhodes* (1882) 7 App Cas 192 at 206; or more caustically in *Smith v Coffin* (1795) 2 Hy Bl 444 at 450 ('The nonsense of one man cannot be guide for that of another').
6   *Slingsby v Grainber* (1859) 7 HL Cas 273 at 284.
7   The position is thus stated by Lord Wensleydale in *Grey v Pearson* (1857) 6 HL Cas 61 at 108: 'We are bound by decided cases, for the sake of securing as much certainty in the administration of the law as the subject is capable of. But when the decision is not upon some rule or other, and when the proper construction is so varied by the peculiar circumstances of each case, it seldom happens that the words of one will are a sure guide for the construction of words resembling them of another.'

8   *Re Booth, Booth v Booth* [1894] 2 Ch 282 at 285; *Waite v Littlewood* (1872) 8 Ch App 70 at 73 (decided cases show only the application of the principles of reasonable construction by judges of high authority).

9   *Re Veale's Trusts* (1876) 4 Ch D 61 at 68.

10   *Vickers v Pound* (1858) 6 HL Cas 885 at 899. For a case where different decisions have been reached applying the same established principle of construction, see *Re Chapman, Perkins v Chapman* [1904] 1 Ch 431.

11   *Hack v London Provident Building Society* (1883) 23 Ch D 103 at 111.

CHAPTER 51

Presumptions

I. AGAINST INTESTACY

[51.1]

Doubtful cases. A testator may well intend to die partly intestate; and, when he makes a will, he is testate only so far as he has expressed himself in his will.[1] Where, however, the construction of the will is doubtful, the court acts on the presumption that the testator did not intend to die either totally or partly intestate, provided that on a fair and reasonable construction there is no ground for a contrary conclusion.[2] In pursuance of an intention to avoid intestacy found in a will, or in pursuance of this presumption, the court does not give an unnatural meaning to a word or construe plain words otherwise than according to their plain meaning.[3] The application of the presumption is dependent on the context and the circumstances.[4]

1   *Re Edwards, Jones v Jones* [1906] 1 Ch 570 at 574 (where to avoid an intestacy it would have been necessary to construe a gift contingent on attaining twenty-one as a gift vesting at birth). The court should not in all cases lean too heavily against a construction which involves a partial intestacy: *Re Wragg, Hollingsworth v Wragg* [1959] 2 All ER 717 at 722; *Ng Chi-fong v Hui Ho Pui-fun* [1987] HKLR 462, see Rhind J at 485 (where the text is cited) '... but this does not mean that the court can give an unnatural meaning to a word or construe plain words otherwise than according to their plain meaning, unless there are good reasons for doing so'.

2   See *Re Harrison, Turner v Hellard* (1885) 30 Ch D 390 at 393, per Lord Esher MR; There is one rule of construction, which to my mind is a golden rule, viz, that when a testator has executed a will in solemn form you must assume that he did not intend to make it a solemn farce—that he did not intend to die intestate when he has gone through the form of making a will. You ought, if possible, to read the will so as to lead to a testacy, not an intestacy'; cited in *Re Johnston* (1982) 138 DLR (3d) 392 at 400; see also *Re MacDonnell* (1982) 133 DLR (3d) 128; *Edgeworth v Edgeworth* (1869) LR 4 HL 35 at 40; *Re Redfern, Redfern v Bryning* (1877) 6 Ch D 133 at 136; *Kirby-Smith v Parnell* [1903] 1 Ch 483 at 489; *Fell v Fell* (1922) 31 CLR 268; *Re Messenger's Estate, Chaplin v Ruane* [1937] 1 All ER 355; *Re Turner, Carpenter v Staveley* [1949] 2 All ER 935; *Re Lady Monck's Will, Monck v Croker* [1900] 1 IR 56; *Re Biln Estate* (1967) 61 DLR (2d) 535 and *Re Crone* (1969) 5 DLR (3d) 317; *Jankowski v Pelek Estate* (1995) 131 DLR (4th) 717. The text was cited in *Re Gray* (1990) 73 DLR (4th) 161 at 165.

3   *Re Benn, Benn v Benn* (1885) 29 Ch D 839; *Re Edwards, Jones v Jones* [1906] 1 Ch 570 at 574; *Re Powell, Bodvel-Roberts v Poole* [1918] 1 Ch 407; *Re McEwen Estate* (1967) 62 WWR 277.

4   The fact that the objects benefited are the wife and all the children shows an intention to dispose of the whole estate: *Hall v Hall* [1892] 1 Ch 361 at 367. The presumption applies especially to property which the testator has at the date of the will, but is not so strong in the case of after-acquired property: *Re Methuen and Blore's Contract* (1881) 16 Ch D 696 at 698; *Re Grazebrook, Chase v Layton* [1928] VLR 75. As to the distinction between 'after the death of A' and 'subject to A's interest' (A being a person having a limited interest) see *Re Wragg, Hollingsworth v Wragg* [1959] 2 All ER 717, explaining the decision in *Re Shuckburgh's Settlement, Robertson v Shuckburgh* [1901] 2 Ch 794; *Re Jobson, Jobson v Richardson* (1889) 44 Ch D 154; *Re Burden, Mitchell v St Luke's Hostel Trustees* [1948] Ch 160, [1948] 1 All ER 31.

[51.2]

Gap in interests created. Where the will shows an intention to dispose of all his property, but as regards the interests created the will admits of two constructions, according to one of which the will operates as a complete disposition of the whole, but according to the other the will leaves a gap in the interests created, the court inclines to the view that the former sense is the sense intended by the testator.[1] This construction is adopted where there is an ambiguity and one of the alternative constructions creates a gift which is illegal and void. If the result of such illegality is that a partial intestacy arises, then this presumption is adopted in order, if possible to avoid the intestacy by adopting the construction avoiding such illegality.[2]

1   *Philipps v Chamberlaine* (1798) 4 Ves 51 at 59; *Booth v Booth* (1799) 4 Ves 399 at 407; *Milson v Awdry* (1800) 5 Ves 465 at 466; *Goodman v Goodman* (1847) 1 De G & Sm 695 at 699; *Wiggins v Wiggins* (1852) 2 Sim NS 226 at 233; *Gosling v Gosling* (1859) John 265 at 274; *Fay v Fay* (1880) 5 LR Ir 274 at 282; *Re Ragdale, Public Trustee v Tuffill* [1934] Ch 352; *Re Messenger's Estate, Chaplin v Ruane* [1937] 1 All ER 355; *Re Hill* [1951] OR 619; *Re Rogers* [1955] SASR 211; *Re Campbell* (1963) 40 DLR (2d) 681. All these cases state that where there is a residuary gift, the presumption applies. The terms of the residuary gift may, however, prevent the presumptions: *Re Wragg, Hollingsworth v Wragg* [1959] 2 All ER 717. As to inference of residuary gift where gift has no statement of the subject matter, see *Fell v Fell* (1922) 31 CLR 268; *Re Messenger's Estate, Chaplin v Ruane* [1937] 1 All ER 355; *Re Turner, Carpenter v Staveley* [1949] 2 All ER 935; *Re Stevens* [1952] Ch 323, [1952] 1 All ER 674; *Re Swanson Estate* [1941] 1 WWR 641; *Re McKenzie* (1968) 67 DLR (2d) 105.
2   *Taylor v Frobisher* (1852) 5 De G & Sm 191: *Re Edmondson's Estate* (1868) LR 5 Eq 389; *Re Bevan's Trusts* (1887) 34 Ch D 716 at 718; *Re Coppard's Estate, Howlett v Hodson* (1887) 35 Ch D 350, as explained in *Re Wenmoth's Estate, Wenmoth v Wenmoth* (1887) 37 Ch D 266 at 270.

[51.3]

Limits of the presumption. This presumption, however, gives no assistance to the court where the contest is not between testacy and intestacy, but between two gifts in the same will.[1] It is not enough to satisfy the court that intestacy was not intended.[2] To oust the title of the persons claiming on intestacy it must be distinctly shown that there are words in the will sufficient to constitute a gift of property in question,[3] expressly or by implication to some particular donee,[4] and the burden of proof is on the alleged donee to that extent.[5] It is a rule of law[6] and not merely a rule of construction that those entitled on intestacy are not to be deprived of their statutory rights otherwise than by express words or necessary implication in the will.[7] That is to say, the will must clearly and unambiguously show the intention of the testator to leave his property to someone else and in such a way that there is certainty both in the subjects and objects of the gifts, and in the manner in which the gift takes effect.[8] A gift uncertain in any of these respects is void.[9]

1   *Re Price, Price v Newton* [1905] 2 Ch 55.
2   *Doe d Wall v Langlands* (1811) 14 East 370 at 372; *Pocock v Bishop of Lincoln* (1821) 6 Moore CP 159; *Hughes v Pritchard* (1877) 6 Ch D 24 at 27.
3   *Enohin v Wylie* (1862) 10 HL Cas 1 at 18.
4   *Hall v Warren* (1861) 9 HL Cas 420 at 433; *Drake v Drake* (1860) 8 HL Cas 172 at 180; *Re Hobson, Barwick v Holt* [1912] 1 Ch 626 (an intention to avoid an intestacy must not be considered as something which the testator had in contemplation, but it must appear from the words of the will that he had that intention); *Re Brown Estate* [1920] 2 WWR 226; *Re Johnstone Estate, Royal Trust Co v Vogler and Lawson* (1966) 55 WWR 167.

5   *Wilce v Wilce* (1831) 7 Bing 664 at 672; *Hall v Warren* (1861) 9 HL Cas 420 at 435.

6   *Doe d Hick v Dring* (1814) 2 M & S 448. The rule was mainly in favour of the heir and may
     have lost some of its force since 1925, but it seems to apply to those entitled on intestacy after
     1925. This proposition is a rule of law and not a rule of construction.

7   *Fitch v Weber* (1848) 6 Hare 145; *Milsome v Long* (1857) 3 Jur NS 1073; *Hall v Hall* [1892] 1
     Ch 361 at 365.

8   *Flint v Warren* (1847) 15 Sim 626; *Re Viscount Exmouth, Viscount Exmouth v Praed* (1883) 23
     Ch D 158; *Buckley v Buckley* (1888) 19 LR Ir 544; *Re Moore, Prior v Moore* [1901] 1 Ch 936;
     but see *Fell v Fell* (1922) 31 CLR 268 (will a mere list of eleven beneficiaries construed as a
     gift of the whole estate to those named beneficiaries); *Re Turner, Carpenter v Staveley* [1949] 2
     All ER 935 (a similar case); *Re Messenger Estate, Chaplin v Ruane* [1937] 1 All ER 355
     (similar case).

9   As to uncertainty, see Chapter 53.

II. LEGALITY AND KNOWLEDGE OF THE LEGAL EFFECT OF WORDS

[51.4]

No departure from plain words to escape illegality. The construction of the
will is in the first place considered quite apart from the question of the legality
of its provisions.[1] If the words of the will are plain, they cannot be struck out[2] or
taken in a sense different from that which they plainly bear[3] for the purpose of
escaping from the consequences of invalidity under some rule of law, or even
because it appears that the testator may have misunderstood the legal effect of
the various species of gifts, and may have used language the legal interpretation
of which may not carry out the intentions he had in his mind.[4] Where a will has
been read over to the testator, there is no unyielding rule that all inquiry as to his
knowledge and approval of it is shut out,[5] and the court may find as a fact that it
was not read over in a proper way;[6] but strong evidence is required to show that
some part of it is not his will.[7] Where the meaning of the will is ambiguous, and
it appears according to one construction to offend against some rule of law and
to be in part invalid, but is fairly capable of another construction which avoids
that objection, the latter is presumed to be the intention of the testator.[8] The
court has an inclination to believe, if reasonably possible, that the testator did
not intend to transgress the law.[9]

1   *Re Wynch's Trusts, ex p Wynch* (1854) 5 De GM & G 188; *Green v Gascoyne* (1865) 4 De GJ
     & Sm 565; *Re Parker, Parker v Osborne* [1897] 2 Ch 208; *Aplin v Stone* [1904] 1 Ch 543;
     Comiskey v Bowring-Hanbury [1905] AC 84 at 89; *De Beauvoir v De Beauvoir* (1852) 3 HL
     Cas 524 at 545.

2   *Heasman v Pearse* (1871) 7 Ch App 275; *Re Coyte, Coyte v Coyte* (1887) 56 LT 510.

3   *Mainwaring v Beevor* (1849) 8 Hare 44; *Speakman v Speakman* (1850) 8 Hare 180; *Pearks v
     Moseley* (1880) 5 App Cas 714; *Tatham v Drummond* (1864) 4 De GJ & Sm 484; *Re Hume,
     Public Trustee v Mabey* [1912] 1 Ch 693. This passage of the text was applied in *Re Mayhew*
     (1989) 63 DLR (4th) 198 at 201. Testator left entire estate to his wife and son 'share and share
     alike', but directed that at his wife's death her share was to be the property of the son. Held gift
     to wife for life remainder to the son.

4   *Higgins v Dawson* [1902] AC 1 at 11; *Egerton v Earl of Brownlow* (1853) 4 HL Cas 1 at 159;
     Nunn v Hancock (1868) 16 WR 818.

5   *Fulton v Andrew* (1875) LR 7 HL 448; *Re Morris, Lloyds Bank Ltd v Peake* [1971] P 62, [1970]
     1 All ER 1057.

6   *Garnett-Botfield v Garnett-Botfield* [1901] P 335.

7   *Gregson v Taylor* [1917] P 256; *Guardhouse v Blackburn* (1866) LR 1 P & D 109.

8   *Martelli v Holloway* (1872) LR 5 HL 532 at 548 (rule against perpetuities); *Pearks v Moseley*
     (1880) 5 App Cas 714 at 719 (same: this rule applies only where there is ambiguity, and cannot

be applied where the words are clear); *Von Brockdorff v Malcolm* (1885) 30 Ch D 172 at 179 (construction to preserve will rather than it should be a nullity); *Re Pounder, Williams v Pounder* (1886) 56 LJ Ch 113 at 114 (same); *Re Sanford, Sanford v Sanford* [1901] 1 Ch 939 (same); *Re Mortimer, Gray v Gray* [1905] 2 Ch 502 (perpetuity rule—one particular illegal intent is struck out if it leaves another lawful intent consonant with the general intention); *Re Stamford and Earl of Warrington, Payne v Grey* [1912] 1 Ch 343 (same).

9   *Leach v Leach* (1843) 2 Y & C Ch Cas 495 at 499.

[51.5]

What rules of law considered. For the purposes of ascertaining the intention those rules which prevailed at the time when the will was made, and with reference to which the will may fairly be presumed to have been framed, must be considered[1] except in cases where the testator by his will expressly or impliedly refers to the law as existing at his death.[2] An act of Parliament passed after the date of the will does not usually affect the ascertainment of the testator's intentions,[3] although it may affect the legal operation of those intentions.[4]

1   *Re March, Mander v Harris* (1884) 27 Ch D 166 at 169.
2   See *Re Bridger, Brompton Hospital for Consumption v Lewis* [1894] 1 Ch 297; *Re Rayer, Rayer v Rayer* [1903] 1 Ch 685; *Re Turnbull, Skipper v Wade* [1905] 1 Ch 726.
3   *Jones v Ogle* (1872) 8 Ch App 192 at 195.
4   *Re Rayer, Rayer v Rayer* [1903] 1 Ch 685; *Re Baroness Llanover, Herbert v Freshfield (No 2)* [1903] 2 Ch 330; *Re Yates' Estate* [1919] P 93.

[51.6]

Legal effect of words. The fact that when the testator desires to produce a particular disposition he shows himself able to do so and to choose words clearly apt to produce that result gives rise to a presumption that, where he uses other words of doubtful import, he does not wish to produce the same result.[1] The expression of that which, even if not expressed, would be implied by law has no independent legal effect on the interests created; but as, in discovering the intention of the testator, the whole will is considered, such expressions may be of importance in that respect.[2]

1   *Langston v Langston* (1834) 2 Cl & Fin 194 at 242; *Martin v Welstead* (1848) 18 LJ Ch 1 at 5; *Welland v Townsend* [1910] 1 IR 177; *Jury v Jury* (1882) 9 LR Ir 207.
2   See *Lee v Pain* (1844) 4 Hare 201 at 221.

III.   WILL RATIONAL AND NOT CAPRICIOUS

[51.7]

Testator's right to be capricious. A testator has a right to be capricious if he chooses.[1] If the words used by the testator are unambiguous in the context, the sense given to the words by the context cannot be departed from, and the court cannot put a meaning on them different from that which it judicially determines to be their meaning on account of any difficulty or inconvenience in carrying out the intention,[2] or because they lead to consequences which are generally considered capricious,[3] unusual,[4] unjust,[5] harsh or unreasonable.[6] The testator's bounty, except as now liable to be varied in favour of dependants,[7] is absolute and without control as to motive.[8]

1 *Hart v Tulk* (1852) 2 De GM & G 300 at 315; *Boosey v Gardener* (1854) 5 De GM & G 122 at 124; *Varley v Winn* (1856) 2 K & J 700 at 707; *Jenkins v Hughes* (1860) 8 HL Cas 571 at 589; *Re Hamlet, Stephen v Cunningham* (1888) 39 Ch D 426 at 434; *Bird v Luckie* (1850) 8 Hare 301 at 306; *Re James's Will Trusts, Peard v James* [1962] Ch 226 at 234, [1960] 3 All ER 744 at 747.

2 *Driver d Frank v Frank* (1814) 3 M & S 25 at 30; *Martineau v Briggs* (1875) 45 LJ Ch 674; *Re Seal, Seal v Taylor* [1894] 1 Ch 316 at 321.

3 *Wharton v Barker* (1858) 4 K & J 483 at 503; *Abbott v Middleton* (1858) 7 HL Cas 68 at 89; *Selby v Whittaker* (1877) 6 Ch D 239 at 245; *Hickling v Fair* [1899] AC 15 at 33; *Re Whitmore, Walters v Harrison* [1902] 2 Ch 66.

4 *Van Grutten v Foxwell* [1897] AC 658 at 678.

5 *Inderwick v Tatchell* [1903] AC 120 at 123.

6 *Abbott v Middleton* (1858) 7 HL Cas 68; *Bathurst v Errington* (1877) 2 App Cas 698. See also *Mason v Robinson* (1825) 2 Sim & St 295 (irrational dispositions); *Re Pollard's Estate* (1863) 3 De GJ & Sm 541 (unusual and eccentric dispositions); *Graves v Bainbrigge* (1792) 1 Ves 562 (intention absurd); *Martin v Holgate* (1866) LR 1 HL 175 at 189; *Re James's Will Trusts, Peard v James* [1962] Ch 226 (capricious, eccentric, fanciful or even harsh).

7 See the Inheritance (Provision for Family and Dependants) Act 1975, discussed in Chapter 105.

8 *Occleston v Fullalove* (1874) 9 Ch App 147.

[51.8]
Presumption in ambiguous cases. Without some clear intention on the part of the testator, however, the court does not attribute to him a capricious intention,[1] or a whimsical or harsh result to his dispositions,[2] where the words of the will can be read otherwise. Accordingly, if the language used in a will admits of two constructions, according to one of which the property will go in a rational, convenient and ordinary succession, and according to another in an irrational and inconvenient course, such that the court is driven to the conclusion that the testator is acting capriciously, without any intelligible motive, and contrary to the ordinary mode in which men act in similar cases, the court leans towards the former as what was intended, although a meaning is thereby given to the words different from their ordinary meaning.[3]

1 *Hillersdon v Lowe* (1843) 2 Hare 355 at 366; *Hart v Tulk* (1852) 2 De GM & G 300 at 313; *Thellusson v Lord Rendlesham* (1859) 7 HL Cas 429 at 497; *Re Doland's Will Trusts, Westminster Bank Ltd v Phillips* [1970] Ch 267 at 272, [1969] 3 All ER 713 at 715, per Buckley J: 'But the point may be reached at which apparent caprice does become a warning signal that something may have gone awry with the testator's true expression of his intention.' See also Stamp J in *Re Cockle's Will Trusts, Re Pittaway, Moreland v Draffen, Risdon v Public Trustee* [1967] Ch 690 at 708, [1967] 1 All ER 391 at 396; Lord Denning MR in *Re Allsop, Cardinal v Warr* [1968] Ch 39 at 47, [1967] 2 All ER 1056 at 1059; *Blathwayt v Lord Cawley* [1975] 3 All ER 625 at 641, per Lord Cross, and at 648, per Lord Edmund-Davies. But compare Buckley J in *Re James's Will Trusts, Peard v James* [1962] Ch 226, [1960] 3 All ER 744.

2 *Barraclough v Cooper* [1908] 2 Ch 121n; *Vickers v Pound* (1858) 6 HL Cas 885 at 897; *Bathurst v Errington* (1877) 2 App Cas 698.

3 *Atkinson v Holtby* (1863) 10 HL Cas 313 at 330; *Gordon v Gordon* (1871) LR 5 HL 254 at 279; *Re Hudson, Hudson v Hudson* (1882) 20 Ch D 406 at 417; *Bowman v Bowman* [1899] AC 518 at 528; *Hordern v Hordern* [1909] AC 210 at 215; *Re Jones, Lewis v Lewis* [1910] 1 Ch 167 at 172.

IV. FAVOURING RELATIVES AND PERSONS WITH A CLAIM ON TESTATOR

[51.9]
Children. There is no presumption in the case of a will, as there is in the case of a marriage settlement, that all the children of the testator are intended to be

provided for or to have equal shares,[1] and the only guide to the court in this respect is the language of the will.[2]

1   *Re Jodrell, Jodrell v Seale* (1890) 44 Ch D 590 at 605, CA; affd sub nom *Seale-Hayne v Jodrell* [1891] AC 304, HL.
2   *Abbott v Middleton* (1858) 7 HL Cas 68 at 93; *Tucker v Harris* (1832) 5 Sim 538 at 543 (there is no presumption that anyone is to be beneficiary except those named or described in the will as such, and it is only in the case of ambiguous gifts that any presumption can arise).

[51.10]

Express but ambiguous provisions for family. If the words of the will expressly providing for the family are ambiguous,[1] the court, so far as it can, prefers that construction which will most benefit the family generally, on the ground that this must more nearly correspond with the intention.[2] Thus, the court construes the will so as to include as many children as possible,[3] and to vest their interests on attaining twenty-one,[4] and so as not to make the interests of children dependent on surviving the parents, according to the presumption especially applicable to portions in a settlement.[5]

1   *Bright v Rowe* (1834) 3 My & K 316 at 322.
2   *Farrant v Nichols* (1846) 9 Beav 327; *Blythsea v Blythsea* (1854) 23 LJ Ch 1004; *Re Hamlet, Stephen v Cunningham* (1888) 39 Ch D 426.
3   *Bouverie v Bouverie* (1847) 2 Ph 349; *Lee v Lee* (1860) 1 Drew & Sm 85; *White v Hill* (1867) LR 4 Eq 265; *Williams v Haythorne* (1871) 6 Ch App 782.
4   *Re Hamlet, Stephen v Cunningham* (1888) 39 Ch D 426; *Waller v Stevenson* (1912) 56 Sol Jo 666.
5   *Jackson v Dover* (1864) 2 Hem & M 209; *Re Knowles, Nottage v Buxton* (1882) 21 Ch D 806; *Re Hamlet, Stephen v Cunningham* (1888) 39 Ch D 426 at 433; *Re Roberts, Percival v Roberts* [1903] 2 Ch 200 at 204 (the reason being that the child may make provision for his family); *Duffield v M'Master* [1906] 1 IR 333. The difference between a will and a settlement is a circumstance to be considered in applying the rule: *Farrer v Barker* (1852) 9 Hare 737; *Tucker v Harris* (1832) 5 Sim 538 (there is no supposition in a will that any but the persons described as takers can take); *Abbott v Middleton* (1858) 7 HL Cas 68 (a settlement has to be construed as a document intended to make provision for the children of the marriage and the courts are justified in so construing the settlement to give effect to that intention, but in a will the only guide is the words of the will).

[51.11]

Relatives and persons intimate with testator. Where the words of a will are ambiguous, the court sometimes is assisted by the presumptions that, in the absence of special circumstances, relatives of equal degree are of equal importance to the testator as recipients of his bounty,[1] and that as a rule a testator does not pass over a near relative for the purpose of benefiting more remote relatives, or over any relative or other persons having a claim on him,[2] or with whom he was intimate,[3] for the purpose of benefiting relatives having no claim on him or strangers. The latter presumption, however, gives no assistance to the court in a contest between persons related in equal degree to the testator,[4] nor are any of these presumptions applicable unless their application will accord with the actual words of the will.[5]

1   *Swift v Swift* (1863) 1 New Rep 353; *Jenkins v Hughes* (1860) 8 HL Cas 571 (transmission of property to grand-nephews of the testator); *Heasman v Pearse* (1871) 7 Ch App 275; *Selby v Whittaker* (1877) 6 Ch D 239 at 249; *Re Walbran, Milner v Walbran* [1906] 1 Ch 64; *Re Prosser, Prosser v Griffith* [1929] WN 85.
2   *Re Gregory's Settlement and Will* (1865) 34 Beav 600 (testator's godson preferred to his brother, the description applying to both).

3   *Careless v Careless* (1816) 1 Mer 384; *Murphy v Donnelly* (1871) IR 6 Eq 203. See also Chapter 57.
4   *Re Price, Price v Newton* [1905] 2 Ch 55.
5   *Beaudry v Barbeau* [1900] AC 569 at 575.

[51.12]
Persons entitled on intestacy. In certain cases of ambiguity in construction the first person entitled on intestacy is favoured by the court.[1] This appears only to be the case where it is desired to avoid holding the will void for uncertainty.[2] The general rule is that persons entitled on intestacy take, not under any presumed intention of the testator, but for want of any clear indication that anyone else is to take.[3]

1   This rule refers to the 'heir or head of a family in order of inheritance'. Since the abolition of descent, the rule may perhaps be stated as in the text, but the word 'heir' is retained to describe equitable interests in real estate and it might be that the rule ought to be transcribed with regard to this reservation in the statute. It was at one time a principle of public policy to favour the heir, but it seems doubtful whether this is so any longer. See *Thellusson v Rendlesham* (1859) 7 HL Cas 429 ('nearest' of family). See also *Power v Quealy* (1878) 2 LR Ir 227 (nearest and most deserving male cousin); *Doe d Winter v Perratt* (1843) 6 Man & G 314. The context of the will may show that the testator did not intend the order of inheritance: *Thomason v Moses* (1842) 5 Beav 77.
2   As to uncertainty, see Chapter 53.
3   *Mills v Farmer* (1815) 19 Ves 483.

V.   UNINTENDED LIFE INTEREST

[51.13]
Administration of Justice Act 1982. An unintended life interest is sometimes created by wills using language such as 'I leave everything to my wife and after her death to my children'. To meet such cases the Administration of Justice Act 1982 provides[1] that, except where a contrary intention is shown, it shall be presumed that if a testator devises or bequeaths property to his spouse in terms which in themselves would give an absolute interest to the spouse, but by the same instrument purports to give his issue an interest in the same property, the gift to the spouse is absolute notwithstanding the purported gift to the issue.[2]

1   Administration of Justice Act 1982, s 22; 50 *Halsbury's Statutes* (4th edn) 617. See Vol 2, Part G, para **[244.96]**, following the recommendations of the Law Reform Committee 19th Report 1973, Cmnd 5301, paras 60–62.
2   This provision applies to wills (whenever made) of testators who die on or after 1 January 1983; Administration of Justice Act 1982, s 73(6), s 76(11).

CHAPTER 52

Inconsistencies and transposition and rejection of words

[52.1]
Clear words are not controlled by subsequent ambiguous words. Subject to the intention shown by the whole will,[1] words clear and unambiguous in themselves cannot be qualified by other words, unless the latter show a very clear exposition of the meaning of the testator;[2] nor can the effect of such words be set aside because there is reason to suppose that they do not produce the effect which the testator intended they should produce;[3] and, in the endeavour to read the will as a consistent whole, and to reconcile the various clauses with each other,[4] a prior gift is not disturbed by a later gift in the same or a subsequent testamentary instrument, further than is necessary to give effect to the later gift.[5]

1   *Re Bagshaw's Trusts* (1877) 46 LJ Ch 567 (absolute interest cut down to life estate by subsequent provisions). If particular provisions are inconsistent with the main purpose and intention as gathered from the whole will, such expressions must be discarded: *Tonks v Crockett* (1907) 25 NZLR 572; *Smidmore v Smidmore* (1905) 3 CLR 344; *Re Carson Estate* (1921) 62 DLR 263; see *Re Jolley* (1985) 36 SASR 204 at 206 where this Chapter of the text is referred to.
2   *Boughton v Boughton* (1848) 1 HL Cas 406 at 434 (it cannot be said that any words can be so strong as to preclude the qualification of them by other parts of the will, but it would be very hazardous to permit terms perfectly unambiguous in themselves to be so qualified by anything short of a very clear exposition of testator's meaning); *Doe d Hearle v Hicks* (1832) 8 Bing 475 (to revoke a clear devise, the intention to revoke must be clear as the devisee); *Bickford v Chalker* (1854) 2 Drew 327 (obscure and partly inconsistent clause as to vesting where original clause clear); *Goodwin v Finlayson* (1858) 25 Beav 65 (a leading principle of construction that plain and distinct words are not to be controlled except by words equally plain and distinct); *Kerr v Baroness of Clinton* (1869) LR 8 Eq 462 (subsequent disposition only by necessary implication does not revoke prior express disposition); *Conmy v Cawley* [1910] 2 IR 465; *Re Smeltzer* (1976) 72 DLR (3d) 280. This passage of the text was cited in *Ng Chi-fong v Hui Ho Pui-fun* [1987] HKLR 462 at 492.
3   *Earl of Hardwick v Douglas* (1940) 7 Cl & Fin 795 at 185 (clear and unambiguous words cannot be set aside because there is reason to think that they do not produce the effect the testator intended). The inconsistent words are discarded or modified in such a way as to give effect to the intention: *Smidmore v Smidmore* (1905) 3 CLR 344; *Re Carson Estate* (1921) 62 DLR 263.
4   See Chapter 50, para **[50.3]** supra.
5   This part of the text was cited with approval by Jacobs J in *Re Jolley* (1985) 36 SASR 204 at 206.

[52.2]
Alterations in words. The Administration of Justice Act 1982 (AJA 1982) has now conferred jurisdiction on the court, in clearly defined circumstances, to rectify wills.[1] This jurisdiction, which is applicable to the wills of testators who

die on or after 1 January 1983[2] is in addition to two established powers to omit or add words. First, a court of probate has power, in exceptional circumstances, to omit words from the probate,[3] and secondly, the court of construction has, in effect, assumed a limited power to read words into a will in order to sensibly construe the will.[4] In view of the power to rectify, this latter jurisdiction will now be invoked less often in the case of post-1982 deaths,[5] but the jurisdiction can be shortly considered here. The limited nature of the power must be noted, thus no alteration will be made unless it is necessary[6] nor will any alteration be made purely upon a conjectural hypothesis of the intention of the testator, however reasonable, in opposition to the plain and obvious sense of the instrument.[7] No change can be made unless the court, even though satisfied that there has been an omission, can also see clearly what has been omitted or wrongly inserted and what words will truly correct the error.[8] No change can be made to assist a forfeiture.[9]

1   AJA 1982, s 20; 50 *Halsbury's Statutes* (4th edn) 615. See Vol 2, Part G, para [**244.96**]; see full discussion in Chapter 6.
2   AJA 1982, s 73(6); s 76(11).
3   See Chapter 6. For example, where words have been inserted without knowledge and approval, see *Re Morris, Lloyds Bank Ltd v Peake* [1971] P 62, [1970] 1 All ER 1057, and *Re Reynette-James, Wightman v Reynette-James* [1975] 3 All ER 1037, [1976] 1 WLR 161.
4   See *Re Whitrick, Sutcliffe v Sutcliffe* [1957] 2 All ER 467, [1957] 1 WLR 884; para [**52.3**] infra.
5   The power to rectify applies only to the wills of testators who die on or after 1 January 1983, see n 2.
6   *Eden v Wilson* (1852) 4 HL Cas 257; *Peacock v Stockford* (1853) 3 De GM & G 73; *Abbott v Middleton* (1858) 7 HL Cas 68.
7   *Abbott v Middleton* (1858) 7 HL Cas 68; *Hope v Potter* (1857) 3 K & J 206; *Re Mitchell, Mitchell v Mitchell* (1913) 108 LT 180.
8   *Re Follett, Barclays Bank Ltd v Dovell* [1955] 2 All ER 22; *Re Cochrane's Settlement Trusts* [1955] 1 All ER 222; *Re Thurlow, Riddick v Kennard* [1972] Ch 379 at 385, [1972] 1 All ER 10 at 14 (no alteration made because impossible to say what word the testatrix intended to use when she used the word 'descendants') following *Re Whitrick, Sutcliffe v Sutcliffe* [1957] 2 All ER 467, CA; *Re Gilbertstone* [1975] 2 NZLR 298.
9   *Re Murray, Martins Bank Ltd v Dill* [1955] Ch 69, [1954] 3 All ER 129.

[52.3]
Insertion of additional words. The court will not insert additional words unless it can see clearly what are the words or trusts which have been omitted[1] and, even though satisfied that there has been an inadvertent omission, no addition will be made where a literal construction is possible and it is not clear what words have been omitted or what words will truly correct the error.[2] A common case for such insertion is where two clauses of the will run parallel to each other (as in clauses settling the separate shares of the donees) except for a difference which may have been caused by the omission of some words or other mistake in copying.[3] Words have been supplied on the clear intention of the testator[4] and in cases of difficulty or ambiguity.[5] Where it is a question of supplying a word or rejecting part of the will, the word is supplied[6] and if there is a choice of alterations, that is chosen which was the most probable intention of the testator.[7] The following insertions have been made: 'after her death';[8] 'without children';[9] 'and other sons' in successive estates tail,[10] 'attain that age or [marry]',[11] 'son' inserted in substitutionary gift,[12] 'or his wife' where previous provision provided for persons predeceasing the testator or his wife;[13] 'as she shall appoint' a power

of appointment;[14] the words 'as such child as mine so dying shall appoint and in default of appointment upon trust for the children of the child of mine so dying';[15] and the words 'in any such event' have been enlarged to give effect to the intention;[16] and 'such share of' has been inserted before the words 'my residuary estate'.[17] Where the wife disposed of her property if her husband predeceased her or survived for less than one month but made no provision for the event of her husband surviving her for more than one month, the court supplied a provision for him to take absolutely in that event[18] and so where a wife in the case of mutual wills failed to provide for her husband predeceasing her.[19] Where shares were given to certain companies 'and any successor thereto', these words were added in another similar bequest.[20]

1   *Re Cochrane's Settlement Trusts* [1955] Ch 309, [1955] 1 All ER 222 (where a wife forfeited her life interest on ceasing to reside with her husband and then survived the husband thus creating a gap in the limitations).
2   *Re Follett, Barclays Bank Ltd v Dovell* [1955] 2 All ER 22 (accidental omission where will was following a recognised precedent: omission supplied): *Re Whitrick, Sutcliffe v Sutcliffe* [1957] 2 All ER 467, CA; *Re Thurlow, Riddick v Kennard* [1972] Ch 379; *Crawford's Trustees v Fleck* 1910 SC 998; *Re Craig* (1976) 74 DLR (3d) 442 (words not supplied); compare *Central and Nova Scotia Trust Co v Freeman* (1975) 58 DLR (3d) 541 (words supplied), and *Re Hawkinson and Hawkinson* (1977) 80 DLR (3d) 390 (words supplied where error or omission by typist).
3   *Re Redfern, Redfern v Bryning* (1877) 6 Ch D 133; *Phillips v Rail* (1906) 54 WR 517.
4   *Langston v Langston* (1834) 2 Cl & Fin 194; see also *Re Morris, Lloyds Bank Ltd v Peake* [1971] P 62, [1970] 1 All ER 1057 (probate court no power to add words in contrast to the court of construction).
5   *Re Haygarth, Wickham v Haygarth* [1913] 2 Ch 9.
6   *Re Le Blanc Estate* (1955) 16 WWR 389.
7   *Mason v Baker* (1856) 2 K & J 567; *Wills v Wills* (1875) LR 20 Eq 342.
8   *West Australian Trustee etc Co Ltd v Young* (1958) 59 WALR 42.
9   *Doe d Leach v Micklem* (1805) 6 East 486.
10 *Abbott v Middleton* (1858) 7 HL Cas 68.
11 *Parker v Tootal* (1865) 11 HL Cas 143.
12 *Re Hunt, Davies v Hetherington* (1890) 62 LT 753.
13 *Re Wroe, Frith v Wilson* (1896) 74 LT 302.
14 *Re Jones* [1955] NZLR 917.
15 *Re Riley's Will Trusts, Riley v Riley* [1962] 1 All ER 513, [1962] 1 WLR 344.
16 *Re Cory, Cory v Morel* [1955] 2 All ER 630.
17 *Re Doland's Will Trusts, Westminster Bank Ltd v Phillips* [1970] Ch 267 at 274, [1969] 3 All ER 713 at 718.
18 *Re Smith* [1948] Ch 49, [1947] 2 All ER 708.
19 *Re Whitrick, Sutcliffe v Sutcliffe* [1957] 2 All ER 467. In *Re Harmer* [1964] 1 OR 367; affd in [1965] SCR 24 sub nom *Kilby v Meyers,* a will of a wife provided expressly for the case of the wife dying at the same time as the husband and added 'I declare that my will shall take effect as if my husband had predeceased me'. It was held that these words should not be omitted or anything added to the words and the husband having predeceased the wife, the will took effect according to its terms. In *Re McEwen Estate* (1967) 62 WWR 277, a testator had provided for his daughter predeceasing his widow, but not for his widow predeceasing his daughter and the court refused to supply such a provision.
20 *Re Whelan* [1961] VR 706.

[52.4]

Change of words. Obvious errors may be corrected by changing words eg the name of a donee has been changed;[1] a reference to a wrong schedule has been corrected;[2] 'estate' has been changed to 'C estate';[3] 'or' has been changed to 'of';[4] 'hereinbefore' to 'hereinafter';[5] 'surviving' changed to 'deceased'.[6] The change of 'and' to 'or' and vice versa is dealt with separately.[7]

1   *Dent v Pepys* (1822) 6 Madd 350.
2   *Hart v Tulk* (1852) 2 De GM & G 300.
3   *Re Northen's Estate* (1884) 28 Ch D 153.
4   *Re Dayrell, Hastie v Dayrell* [1904] 2 Ch 496.
5   *Ellard v Phelan* [1914] 1 IR 76.
6   *Re Allen* [1950] VLR 405.
7   See Chapter 56.

[52.5]

Transposition of words. The court has power to transpose words though it has been rarely exercised.[1] Thus where the will was otherwise void and insensible,[2] or where the parts of the will are not in their regular order.[3] Similarly where a gift to a wife was interposed between the gift to the children and the trusts relating to the gift to the children.[4]

1   *Key v Key* (1855) 1 Jur NS 372.
2   *Chambers v Brailsford* (1816) 19 Ves 652.
3   *Hudson v Bryant* (1845) 1 Coll 681.
4   *Re Bacharach's Will Trusts, Minden v Bacharach* [1959] Ch 245, [1958] 3 All ER 618.

[52.6]

Rejection of words. No word can be rejected unless it is clear that the word or words in question are contrary to the intention expressed in the will,[1] but where that is shown there may be rejection on the ground of repugnance,[2] surplusage,[3] invalidity as to realty,[4] mistake or ignorance,[5] inconsistency,[6] words senseless in the context,[7] or by inadvertence not deleted.[8]

1   *Doe d Baldwin v Rawding* (1819) 2 B & Ald 441; *Jennings v Newman* (1839) 10 Sim 219.
2   *Smith v Pybus* (1804) 9 Ves 566.
3   *Langley v Thomas* (1856) 6 De GM & G 645.
4   *Jones v Price* (1841) 11 Sim 557 (word 'respective' rejected).
5   *Sherratt v Bentley* (1834) 2 My & K 149; *Sims v Doughty* (1800) 5 Ves 243.
6   *Re Peacock* [1958] NZLR 374; *Smith v Crabtree* (1877) 6 Ch D 591; *Re Barnett's Will* [1919] VLR 524; *Smidmore v Smidmore* (1905) 3 CLR 344.
7   *Re Macandrew's Will Trusts, Stephens v Barclays Bank Ltd* [1964] Ch 704, [1963] 2 All ER 919.
8   *Re Kennedy's Will* [1954] Tas LR 64.

[52.7]

Where gifts irreconcilable, last prevails. If in the same will,[1] there are two inconsistent and irreconcilable gifts, the rule is that, if the court can find nothing else to assist in determining the question,[2] the later clause is to prevail, as being the last expression of the testator's wish.[3] If the operation of this rule is to cause an intestacy, the former clause is preferred if that avoids an intestacy,[4] and, if the intention is shown that each beneficiary is to have a moiety, this rules does not apply, but each takes a moiety of the subject-matter.[5]

1   As to revocation of separate wills on ground of inconsistency, see Chapter 18. If there are two wills of the same date and it cannot be shown which was the later, both are void for uncertainty, so far as they are irreconcilable: *Phipps v Earl of Anglesey* (1751) 7 Bro Parl Cas 443 and see *Townsend v Moore* [1905] P 66.
2   *Doe d Leicester v Biggs* (1809) 2 Taunt 109 at 113; *Re Bywater, Bywater v Clarke* (1881) 18 Ch D 17 at 24.
3   *Paramour v Yardley* (1579) 2 Plowd 539; *Sherratt v Bentley* (1834) 2 My & K 149; *Morrall v Sutton* (1845) 1 Ph 533; *Brocklebank v Johnson* (1855) 20 Beav 205; *Re Hammond, Hammond*

v *Treharne* [1938] 3 All ER 308 (legacy in words and then a greater amount in figures, the latter prevailed); *Briant v Edrick* (1870) 1 VLR 35; *Re Swayzie* [1912] 3 DLR 631; *Re Fingland Estates* [1920] 1 WWR 473; *Re McCaul v Mason* (1909) 27 NZLR 65; *Re Girvin Estate* (1932) 40 Man LR 481; *Re Calt* [1957] 12 DLR 140.
4   *Piper v Piper* (1886) 5 NZLR 135.
5   *Re Alexander's Will Trust* [1948] 2 All ER 111.

[52.8]

Limits of rule. This rule, however, is used only as a last resort, when all attempts to reconcile the various provisions of the will have failed,[1] and it is subject, for example, to the application of the rule that a prior gift should not be disturbed further than is necessary for the purpose of giving effect to the later disposition.[2] Thus, if there are two absolute gifts, one of all the testator's property or all his property of a certain description, and the other of portions of that property, the more general gift is confined to the residue of that property;[3] and, if there is a clear, unambiguous gift, and a subsequent clause, in terms applying to this gift, or to this and other gifts, and as so applied inconsistent with the intention taken as a whole, the subsequent clause is neglected, or applied only to other gifts with which it is not inconsistent.[4]

1   *Press v Parker* (1825) 2 Bing 456; *White v Parker* (1835) 1 Bing NC 573; *Chapman v Gilbert* (1853) 4 De GM & G 366.
2   *Munro v Henderson* [1907] 1 IR 440; affd [1908] 1 IR 260 Ir CA; *Kerr v Baroness Clinton* (1869) LR 8 Eq 462.
3   *Coke v Bullock* (1604) Cro Jac 49; *Roe d Snape v Nevill* (1848) 11 QB 466. If the more general gift is for life, the other gift may take effect on its determination: *Young v Burdett* (1724) 5 Bro Parl Cas 54.
4   *Doe d Spencer v Pedley* (1836) 1 M & W 662; *Baker v Baker* (1847) 6 Hare 269; *Bickford v Chalker* (1854) 2 Drew 327; *Re Bellamy's Trust* (1862) 1 New Rep 191; *Re Hughes* [1956] NZLR 892 (gift subject to gift over on remarriage. Subsequent absolute gift also construed subject to gift over).

[52.9]

Two residuary gifts in the same will. If there are two gifts in the same instrument, each sufficient to include the residuary estate, in cases where lapsed shares of the first gift would leave something for the second gift to operate on, the first of the two gifts is preferred.[1] The context may show, however, that the second residuary gift is to include all lapsed legacies.[2] Where one gift is in the will and the other in a codicil, the court can conclude that there is a revocation of the gift in the will.[3]

1   *Davis v Bennett* (1861) 30 Beav 226; *Re Spencer, Hart v Manston* (1886) 54 LT 597; *Johns v Wilson* [1900] 1 IR 342; *Re Isaac, Harrison v Isaac* [1905] 1 Ch 427; *Kilvington v Parker* (1872) 21 WR 121; *Bristow v Masefield* (1882) 52 LJ Ch 27.
2   *Re Jessop* (1859) 11 I Ch R 424, as explained in *Re Isaac, Harrison v Isaac* [1905] 1 Ch 427; *Re Gare, Filmer v Carter* [1952] Ch 80, [1951] 2 All ER 863; *Re Iverson Estate* [1950] 2 WWR 1021; *Re Robertson* [1966] VR 196.
3   *Earl of Hardwicke v Douglas* (1840) 7 Cl & Fin 795; *Re Stoodley, Hooson v Locock* [1916] 1 Ch 242; *Pennefather v Lloyd* [1917] 1 IR 337.

[52.10]

Gifts of the same subject-matter. In certain cases, where the inconsistency lies in a gift to one person and a subsequent gift in the same instrument of the same thing to another person, it has been held, in order to reconcile the gifts, that both donees take the gift, either altogether as joint tenants or tenants in common,[1] or in succession,[2] according to the nature of the gift.

1 *Ridout v Pain* (1747) 3 Atk 486. This view is criticised in *Sherratt v Bentley* (1834) 2 My & K 149 at 161; *L'Estrange v L'Estrange* [1902] 1 IR 372; *Re Alexander's Will Trust* [1948] 2 All ER 111 (where each took a moiety of a bracelet which was easily divisible).
2 *Gravenor v Watkins* (1871) LR 6 CP 500; *Re Bagshaw's Trusts* (1877) 46 LJ Ch 567.

[52.11]

Effect of recitals. If there are in a will no words amounting to a gift, or other indication of an intention to confer a bounty but merely words of erroneous recital or recognition of indebtedness or affection, the court considers that no intention of making a gift is disclosed by the will.[1] A recital showing that the testator considered that some person possessed a title to property independent of his own, prima facie gives rise to the inference that the testator did not intend to make an actual disposition in favour of that person.[2] On the other hand, a recital showing that the testator is under the impression that he has made a certain disposition is evidence of an intention inadvertently not expressed to make that gift.[3] Accordingly in such a case the court may give effect to such intention if the other provisions of the will allow that course;[4] and the inference from such recital may be sufficient to overcome and correct the terms of an express gift to the person in question,[5] provided[6] that the court is satisfied that there has been a mistake in carrying out the testator's intention; otherwise the recital is treated as erroneous and neglected.[7] A recital unless obviously erroneous may be referred to by way of explanation of a gift in itself doubtful or ambiguous.[8] Where the testator wrongly assumed that his wife was entitled to jus relict' and expressly disposed of the other half of his estate, there was an implication that the wife should take what she would have been entitled to under the doctrine of jus relict'.[9]

1 *Re Rowe, Pike v Hamlyn* [1898] 1 Ch 153 at 160; *Dashwood v Peyton* (1811) 18 Ves 27.
2 *Adams v Adams* (1842) 1 Hare 537; *Ralph v Watson* (1840) 9 LJ Ch 328; *A-G v Dillon* (1862) 13 I Ch R 127 at 133; *Re Lee, Gibbon v Peele* (1910) 103 LT 103, and see *Re Maber, Armsby v Maber* (1896) 12 TLR 267 (recital that testator not possessed of property given); *Harris v Harris* (1869) 17 WR 790 (such recital sufficient to take the property out of residue and cause an intestacy).
3 *Adams v Adams* (1842) 1 Hare 537 at 541; *Re Smith* (1862) 2 John & H 594 at 598. But see *Vaughan v Foakes* (1836) 1 Keen 58 (where that recital was obviously erroneous), and *Wylie v Wylie* (1860) 1 De GF & J 410 (recital saying only that dispositions had been made and no reference to gift of specific property in question).
4 *Bibin v Walker* (1768) Amb 661; *Farrer v St Catharine's College, Cambridge* (1873) LR 16 Eq 19 at 24; *Re Yates, Singleton v Povah* (1922) 128 LT 619; *Re Bagot, Paton v Ormerod* [1893] 3 Ch 348; *Langan v Bergin* [1896] 1 IR 331; *A-G v Dillon* (1862) 13 I Ch R 127.
5 *Jordan v Fortescue* (1847) 10 Beav 259; *Re Margitson, Haggard v Haggard* (1882) 48 LT 172.
6 The court must see very clearly that there is nothing in the will to which the recital can refer before it is turned into a distinct bequest: *Smith v Fitzgerald* (1814) 3 Ves & B 2 at 8.
7 *Gordon v Hoffmann* (1834) 7 Sim 29; *Mann v Fuller* (1854) Kay 624; *Re Arnold's Estate* (1863) 33 Beav 163 at 171; *Mackenzie v Bradbury* (1865) 35 Beav 617; *Ives v Dodgson* (1870) LR 9 Eq 401.
8 *Darley v Martin* (1853) 13 CB 683; *Grover v Raper* (1856) 28 LTOS 215; *Re Venn, Lindon v Ingram* [1904] 2 Ch 52. Where the operative part is clear, it is not cut down by a recital: *Culsha v Cheese* (1849) 7 Hare 236; *Savile v Kinnaird* (1865) 11 LT 687.
9 *Re Angus's Will Trusts, Hall v Angus* [1960] 3 All ER 835.

CHAPTER 53

Uncertainty

[53.1]
Reluctance of court to hold gift void for uncertainty. To avoid a will on the ground of uncertainty it is not enough that the dispositions in it are so absurd and irrational that it is difficult to believe that they could have been intended by the testator. The will must be incapable of any clear meaning.[1] Where the result of holding a gift void for uncertainty is to create an intestacy, the presumption against such a result[2] is a ground for making every effort to give some meaning to the gift;[3] and the court adopts the benevolent rule that, if there is ever so little reason in favour of one construction of an ambiguous gift more than another, this is at least nearer the intention of the testator than that the whole disposition should be void and the persons entitled on intestacy let in.[4] In some cases uncertainty is avoided by the admission of extrinsic evidence, but it must be remembered that, if the evidence offered, even though it solves the uncertainty, is inadmissible under the rules governing the admission of such evidence,[5] the gift must inevitably be declared void however reluctant the court may be to arrive at such a decision.[6] A similar result is reached where the evidence though admissible is insufficient to resolve the ambiguity or uncertainty.[7]

1   *Mason v Robinson* (1825) 2 Sim & St 295; *Adams v Jones* (1852) 9 Hare 485 (gift not avoided if the court can arrive at a reasonable degree of certainty); *Cradock v Cradock* (1858) 32 LTOS 48 (uncertain parts valid if they can be construed with remainder to make a consistent whole); *Bentley v Oldfield* (1854) 19 Beav 225; see *Re Hopkins* (1982) 132 DLR (3d) 671 at 677 where this sentence of the text was cited with approval.
2   As to presumption against intestacy, see Chapter 52, paras **[51.1]**–**[51.3]** supra.
3   The antiquity of this rule is shown by *Inchley and Robinson's case* (1587) 2 Leon 41. See also *Boys v Bradley* (1853) 10 Hare 389.
4   *Doe d Winter v Perratt* (1843) 6 Man & G 314 at 359; *Bristow v Bristow* (1842) 5 Beav 289 at 292; *Oddie v Woodford* (1821) 3 My & Cr 584; *Doe d Angell v Angell* (1846) 9 QB 328 at 354; *Stephens v Powys* (1857) 1 De G & J 24.
5   See *Re Atkinson's Will Trusts, Atkinson v Hall* [1978] 1 All ER 1275, [1978] 1 WLR 586; see *Re Tepper's Will Trusts, Kramer v Ruda* [1987] Ch 358, [1987] 1 All ER 970. As to the admission of such evidence, see Chapter 67.
6   *Thomas d Evans v Thomas* (1796) 6 Term Rep 671; *Richardson v Watson* (1833) 4 B & Ad 787; *Blundell v Gladstone* (1844) 14 Sim 83; *Drake v Drake* (1860) 8 HL Cas 172; *Re Stephenson, Donaldson v Bamber* [1897] 1 Ch 75.
7   *Asten v Asten* [1894] 3 Ch 260.

[53.2]
Application of legal maxims for the avoidance of uncertainty. There are two well-known legal maxims which are sometimes instrumental in avoiding the lack of certainty in a disposition. The first is the maxim: *Id certum est quod*

certum reddi potest.[1] Indefinite words added to a gift do not render it uncertain where the gift is substantially ascertained from the nature of the case,[2] and no objection can arise where, though the amount of the gift is indefinite, it is stated to be for a particular purpose and the court can by inquiry ascertain what is the sum sufficient or necessary to answer the purpose.[3] A power of selection is another case where this principle applies,[4] but a power of selection which amounts to a total delegation of the testator's testamentary power is void,[5] except in the case of charitable gifts.[6] The other maxim is: *Ut res magis valeat quam pereat.* Where words are capable of two constructions, even in the case of a deed, and much more in the case of a will, it is just and reasonable that such construction should be adopted as tends to make the document effective[7] and the rule is to construe a will according to this maxim, giving effect as far as possible to every word,[8] and giving effect to the gift if it is possible to do so rather than to declare it void for uncertainty and so defeat the testator's intention.[9]

1   *Adams v Jones* (1852) 9 Hare 485; see *Re Tuck's Settlement Trusts, Public Trustee v Tuck* [1976] Ch 99, [1976] 1 All ER 545, applied in *Re Tepper's Will Trusts, Kramer v Ruda* [1987] Ch 358, [1987] 1 All ER 970.

2   *Oddie v Brown* (1859) 4 De G & J 179 ('or thereabouts' added to a definite sum of money); *Re Hunter's Settlement Trust, Elliot v Hunter* (1939) 83 Sol Jo 339.

3   *Dundee Magistrates v Morris* (1858) 3 Macq 134; *Broad v Bevan* (1823) 1 Russ 511n; *Jackson v Hamilton* (1846) 3 Jo & Lat 702 at 709; *Edwardes v Jones (No 2)* (1866) 35 Beav 474.

4   *Re Conn, Conn v Burns* [1898] 1 IR 337 (gift of portions to daughters to be determined by the testator's wife and executors according to the value of their services to the family and, in case of marriage, according to the match the daughter might make); *Broseau v Dor* (1904) 35 SCR 205 (gift to brothers and sisters or nephews and nieces whom trustees think to be most in need). As to selection by the donee, see para **[8.7]** supra. It has been held that a devise in two in such shares 'as shall be determined by——' (the name of the person to make the determination being left blank in the will) makes the devisees tenants in common in equal shares: *Robinson v Wheelwright* (1856) 21 Beav 214, but the general rule of law is that if a person to make a selection is not shown, or, if shown, it becomes impossible for him to act (as where he has died) or he refuses to act, the gift fails): *Boyce v Boyce* (1849) 16 Sim 476; *Re Madge, Pridie v Bellamy* (1928) 44 TLR 372. It must, too, be remembered that the right of selection rests with the testator and, unless he gives it to someone else, no one has the right to exercise it and the gift fails: see *Asten v Asten* [1894] 3 Ch 260; but, apparently it is sufficient if the testator in his will instead of giving a particular property gives 'one of' several properties of the same description to a legatee for then there is a reasonable inference that the testator intended the legatee to select or, in other words, there is an implied delegation; *Re Fenwick, Burns v Fenwick* [1957] NZLR 709 (gifts of 50 acres for wild duck lake sanctuary; exact location at discretion of trustee).

5   *Houston v Burns* [1918] AC 337 at 342; *Buckie v Bristow* (1864) 5 New Rep 7; *Re Matthews* [1920] NZLR 135; *Re Flavel's Will Trusts, Coleman v Flavel* [1969] 2 All ER 232, [1969] 1 WLR 444; *Re Abraham's Will Trusts, Caplan v Abrahams* [1969] 1 Ch 463, [1967] 2 All ER 1175, see Cross J at 474, 475; and at 1184; *Lutheran Church of Australia etc v Farmers Cooperative Executors and Trustees* (1969–70) 121 CLR 628. See also *Re Manisty's Settlement, Manisty v Manisty* [1974] Ch 17, [1973] 2 All ER 1203. See para **[8.7]** supra.

6   As to charitable gifts, see Chapters 102 and 103.

7   *Atkinson v Hutchinson* (1734) 3 P Wms 258; *Thellusson v Woodford* (1799) 4 Ves 227.

8   *Re Pounder, Williams v Pounder* (1886) 56 LJ Ch 113; *Re Sanford, Sanford v Sanford* [1901] 1 Ch 939.

9   *Von Brockdorff v Malcolm* (1885) 30 Ch D 172; *Re Hobson's Estate, Hobson v Sharp* [1907] VLR 724; *Re Parnell Estate* [1924] 1 DLR 15.

[53.3]

Kinds of gifts which are void for uncertainty. The following are examples of gifts which are void for uncertainty.

    (1)   Gifts which are wanting in particularity of expression, as to the subject[1] or object[2] of the gift, where no person is nominated by the testator or other means provided for giving particularity[3] or such means fail,[4] and no rule of construction assists the court;[5]

    (2)   Gifts which depend upon an infinite number of things;[6]

    (3)   Gifts which may have two or more alternative meanings, where there is nothing in the context or the admissible evidence[7] or any rule of construction,[8] to assist the court in resolving the ambiguity;[9]

    (4)   Gifts which are to be applied in perpetuity for purposes which are not in law charitable gifts,[10] and which include, without the possibility of severance, purposes for which a perpetual gift is not allowed.[11]

1   See para **[53.4]** infra.
2   See para **[53.5]** infra.
3   *Re Wolff* (1958) 16 DLR (2d) 527 (gift to senior members of staff is uncertain and lapses), but see para **[53.2]**, n 4.
4   *Boyce v Boyce* (1849) 16 Sim 476 (selector dead); *Jerningham v Herbert* (1828) 4 Russ 388 (lunacy of testatrix preventing particularisation).
5   As to such rules, see supra. See also *Re Bassett's Estate, Perkins v Fladgate* (1872) LR 14 Eq 54, and *Re Byrne's Will* (1898) 24 VLR 832, where the presumption against intestacy supplied the omission of any description of the subject matter, but in *Mohun v Mohun* (1818) 1 Swan 201, such omission made the gift void.
6   *Re Moore, Prior v Moore* [1901] 1 Ch 936 ('all the persons living at my death'). But the formula to avoid the perpetuity rule ('death of the last survivor of all lineal descendants of her late Majesty Queen Victoria living at the testator's death') was held not void for uncertainty: *Re Villar, Public Trustee v Villar* [1929] 1 Ch 243; *Re Leverhulme, Cooper v Leverhulme (No 2)* [1943] 2 All ER 274.
7   As to admissibility of evidence, see Chapter 57.
8   In *Webber v Corbett* (1873) LR 16 Eq 515, one of the donees was described clearly in another part of the will and the presumption that the same words in different passages of the will have the same meaning was applied; cf *Healy v Healy* (1875) IR 9 Eq 418. As to legitimate persons only taking: *Re Fish, Ingham v Rayner* [1894] 2 Ch 83; but see *Re Jackson, Beattie v Murphy* [1933] Ch 237 (presumption not applicable where there are two legitimate persons).
9   See para **[8.7]**, n 3, as to selection. Where a primary gift of income fails and the extent of the gift is not sufficiently defined, a gift of the balance has been held to fail: *Re Porter, Porter v Porter* [1925] Ch 746.
10 As to charitable gifts, see Chapters 102 and 103.
11 See Chapter 94.

[53.4]
Uncertainty of subject-matter of gift. Examples of this case are: 'some of my best linen';[1] 'a handsome gratuity';[2] 'a small portion of what is left';[3] bequest of unspecified legacy or share;[4] a bequest of 'whatever she can transfer to go to her daughters' after a gift to the mother for life.[5] Indefinite words of amount, as 'thereabouts' or 'as near as may be' have not generally been held uncertain[6] and where the amount of a gift has been stated in an alternative form, the legatee has been held entitled to the larger sum.[7] A gift of a sum not exceeding a stated amount has been construed as a gift of the stated amount.[8] A direction to allow a beneficiary to receive a 'reasonable income' is not void for uncertainty. It directs an objective determinant of amount which, if necessary, the court could apply.[9]

1   *Peck v Halsey* (1726) 2 P Wms 387.
2   *Jubber v Jubber* (1839) 9 Sim 503.
3   *White v White* (1908) 28 NZLR 129, but see Chapter 83, as to a gift of what remains after a life interest.

4   Where no subject-matter was mentioned at all but merely the names of beneficiaries, it was held
     that they took the whole in equal shares: *Fell v Fell* (1922) 31 CLR 268; *Re Messenger's
     Estate, Chaplin v Ruane* [1937] 1 All ER 355; *Re Turner, Carpenter v Staveley* [1949] 2 All ER
     935; *Re Stevens* [1952] Ch 323, [1952] 1 All ER 674; *Re Williams, Wiles v Madgin* [1985] 1 All
     ER 964 (will listing 25 names in three separate groups with no indication as to purpose of
     grouping, estate divided equally between the 25 named persons).

5   *Flint v Hughes* (1843) 6 Beav 342; but see para **[83.6]** infra, as to gift of what remains after a
     life interest.

6   *Oddie v Brown* (1859) 4 De G & J 179; *Re Hunter's Settlement Trust* (1939) 83 Sol Jo 339;
     Wood v Drew (1864) 33 Beav 610.

7   *Seale v Seale* (1715) 1 P Wms 290.

8   *Thompson v Thompson* (1844) 1 Coll 381; *Gough v Bult* (1848) 16 Sim 45.

9   *Re Golay, Morris v Bridgewater* [1965] 2 All ER 660, [1965] 1 WLR 969; *Talbot v Talbot*
     [1968] Ch 1, [1967] 2 All ER 920, CA (a testamentary option to purchase land at a reasonable
     valuation is not void for uncertainty).

[53.5]

Uncertainty as to donee. While in general the testator has the widest field from
which to choose his donees and is not restricted to those in existence at the date
of the will, yet the donee must always be described with certainty, so that the
donee can be definitely ascertained from the words of the will[1] or from those
words aided by such evidence as is admissible for their identification.[2] One of
the commonest forms of uncertainty in this respect is where the gift provides for
selection from a number of persons or bodies and does not state who is to make
the selection or how it is to be made.[3] Examples of this form of uncertainty are
the following: a gift to twenty of the poorest of the testator's kindred,[4] or to the
heirs male of any of the testator's sons or next of kin,[5] or to one of the sons of a
named person who has more than one son.[6] Then a gift may be void because no
definite meaning can be given to the words. In this class are gifts to a 'family' or
to the 'younger branches of a family'.[7] Where the testator makes a residuary gift
and does not in any way specify the legatee, the gift is void;[8] but if the gift is not
residuary, it falls into residue.[9] A gift over to a person's heirs and nearest
relations of her grand-aunt W of the W blood is void for uncertainty.[10] A gift to
my nephews and nieces, the said A and B, was held void because the use of the
plural in each case showed that there was intended to be more than one of each
class.[11] In another gift to nephews and nieces the will excluded A and a codicil
excluded B as in the will directed. The exclusion in this case was held void for
uncertainty and all took.[12] A gift to the children of a deceased son failed where
at the date of the will there were three sons fulfilling the description.[13] A gift to
such of the children as from time to time should appear to the executors to be
most in need of assistance and if none is in need of such assistance to all equally
is not void for uncertainty.[14]

1   Thus a gift of income to the person who would succeed to a peerage on the death of the present
     holder is ineffective since that person cannot be ascertained until such death: *Re Earl of
     Midleton's Will Trusts, Whitehead v Earl of Midleton* [1969] 1 Ch 600, [1967] 2 All ER 834.

2   As to such evidence, see Chapter 57. If a class can be ascertained, the fact that its ascertainment
     may involve difficulty, time or expense does not make it uncertain: *Re Connor Estate* (1970) 10
     DLR (3d) 5 (residue to be divided 'among my close friends'); *Re Denley's Trust, Holman v H
     H Martyn & Co Ltd* [1969] 1 Ch 373, [1968] 3 All ER 65 (trust for the employees of a company
     held not to be void for uncertainty).

3   Thus it is said that a gift to 'one of the sons' of A (who has several sons) is bad and cannot be
     explained by oral evidence: *Sir Litton Strode v Lady Russel and Lady Falkland* (1707) 2 Vern

621; *Dowset v Sweet* (1753) Amb 175. But a gift to 'the son of' A (who has several sons) may be explained by oral evidence to mean the son the testator had reason for preferring or with whom he was more intimate or whom he had shown an intention to benefit. Where, however, at the date of the will there is no person who satisfies the description, the expression may be construed to mean the first such person who comes into existence: *Bate v Amherst and Norton* (1663) T Raym 82; *Blackburn v Stables* (1814) 2 Ves & B 367; *Powell v Davies* (1839) 1 Beav 532; *Ashburner v Wilson* (1850) 17 Sim 204; *Radford v Willis* (1871) 7 Ch App 7; *Re Hickman* [1948] 2 All ER 303.

4   *Webb's Case* (1607) 1 Roll Abr 609.

5   *Beal v Wyman* (1650) Sty 240. Where there was a gift to A or if he be dead to his heirs executors administrators or assigns and A died before the testator, the gift was held void for uncertainty as 'heir' meant a person designated by descent and assigns meant a person designated by act of the legatee: *Waite v Templer* (1829) 2 Sim 524.

6   See n 3.

7   *Re Connor Estate* (1970) 10 DLR (3d) 5 (direction to divide residue 'among my close friends', void for uncertainty).

8   *Baker v Newton* (1839) 2 Beav 112. This is so where residue is given to be distributed as trustees in their absolute discretion think fit: *Re Brown* [1953] SASR 341; *Re White, Perpetual Trustees Estate and Agency Co Ltd v Milligan* [1963] NZLR 788. And the same result was arrived at where the gift was to brothers and sisters and any near relative according to urgent needs, *Re Tucker Estate* (1954) 13 WWRNS 351; *Salvesen's Trustees v Wye* 1954 SC 440; *Tatham v Huxtable* (1951) 81 CLR 639 (such as in the opinion of the executor had rendered service meriting consideration). *Re Pugh's Will Trusts, Marten v Pugh* [1967] 3 All ER 337, [1967] 1 WLR 1262 ('in accordance with any letters or memoranda which I may leave with this my will'; no such letters or memoranda left). A wide general power of appointment limited to 10 years is not void: *Re McEwan* [1955] NZLR 575. A specific gift to a beneficiary is good although the expression used is that the testator desires the trustees to make it: *Re Altson* [1955] VLR 281.

9   *Re Philp* [1952] OWN 783.

10 *Yearwood v Yearwood* (1846) 9 Beav 276.

11 *Greig v Martin* (1859) 33 LTOS 41.

12 *Cope v Henshaw* (1866) 35 Beav 420.

13 *Re Stephenson, Donaldson v Bamber* [1897] 1 Ch 75.

14 *Magee v Magee* [1936] 3 All ER 15, applied in *Kilroy and Callan v Parker and McGavran* [1966] IR 309 (possible fluctuation amongst class of 'necessitous nieces and nephews' did not make the trust void for uncertainty); and see *Re Wong Kee Kit* (1956) 7 DLR 124.

[53.6]

Uncertainty as to the persons to whom a fund may be appointed. In considering this matter there are two quite different kinds of powers: (a) a power in the nature of a trust or coupled with a duty usually called a fiduciary power, and (b) powers not of this nature. The simplest example of a power in the nature of a trust is one where the fund or property is given to named or a class of beneficiaries and the power is to decide only in what shares they are to take.[1] In such cases the intention to benefit the class is mandatory and in cases of default the beneficiaries can compel the trustees to execute the trust, by an application to the court if necessary. The court adopts the principle as to trusts that it will not permit the trustee's negligence, accident or other circumstances to disappoint the interests of those for whose benefit he is called upon to execute it.[2] Once that proposition is established, then it follows that since the court might be required to execute the trust it is essential that the beneficiaries should be known, in the sense of its being possible to draw up a definitive and complete list of all the persons within the class of beneficiaries.[3] If in the case of a fixed, as opposed to a discretionary, trust it is not possible to ascertain the beneficiaries at the date of the document declaring the donor's intentions (in the case of a will, his death) in any case with that precision, then the trust fails for uncertainty.[4] However, the position with regard to powers is quite different: the court (except in the case of a mala fide exercise) has little interest in the exercise of a power, and if it is not exercised the fund goes to those entitled in default under the settlement, or on a resulting trust, as the case may be. The only duty on which the court could insist is that the trustees should consider exercising the power and in particular consider a request from a person within the ambit of the power that the power should be exercised in his favour.[5] Further, since the court might be required to assess the validity of any proposed appointment, to prevent an invalid appointment, it is necessary that the court should be able to say with certainty, whether any particular person is, or is not, within the permissible class of objects, and this is the degree of certainty of the objects necessary for a power of appointment.[6] This rule is equally applicable to special and intermediate or hybrid powers of appointment.[7]

This rule, previously only applicable to powers, has now been held to be also applicable to discretionary trusts, so that such a trust is valid if it can be said with certainty that any given individual is or is not a member of the class.[8] Thus a discretionary trust exercisable in favour of employees and former employees of a company and their relatives and dependants was upheld notwithstanding the argument that the class was so large and arbitrary that the trustees could not reasonably estimate the membership or know how to set about instituting inquiries which would reveal the membership.[9]

1   *Brown v Higgs* (1801) 8 Ves 561; *IRC v Broadway Cottages Trust* [1955] Ch 20, [1954] 3 All ER 120.
2   Per Lord Eldon in *Brown v Higgs* (1801) 8 Ves 561.
3   *Re Ogden, Brydon v Samuel* [1933] Ch 678, [1933] All ER Rep 720 (associations in the United Kingdom having liberal principles); *IRC v Broadway Cottages Trust* [1955] Ch 20, [1954] 3 All ER 120; *Re Sayer Trust, MacGregor v Sayer* [1957] Ch 423, [1956] 3 All ER 600 (employees, their children and dependent relatives). In *Re Eden, Ellis v Crampton* [1957] 2 All ER 430 (employees employed or previously employed by a company at a certain date), and in *Re Hain's Settlement, Tooth v Hain* [1961] 1 All ER 848, [1961] 1 WLR 440 (past, present and future employees of a company) it was held that the whole range of beneficiaries was ascertainable or at least it was not proved that it was not ascertainable.
4   *Re Saxone Shoe Co, Ltd's Trust Deed, Re Abbott's Will Trusts, Abbott v Pearson* [1962] 2 All ER 904, [1962] 1 WLR 943 (where the expression 'employees or dependants' was held to be too vague). See also cases cited in n 3 and *Re Leek, Darwen v Leek* [1967] Ch 1061, [1961] 2 All ER 1160 (wife, children or other issue or such persons as had a 'moral claim' on deceased); *Re Wootton's Will Trusts, Trotter v Duffin* [1968] 2 All ER 618, [1968] 1 WLR 681 (trust for such other organisation or body not being registered as a charity but in the opinion of the trustees having charitable objects).
5   *Re Manisty's Settlement, Manisty v Manisty* [1974] Ch 17, [1973] 2 All ER 1203; see also *Re Hay's Settlement Trusts* [1981] 3 All ER 786, [1981] 1 WLR 202 where Sir Robert Megarry V-C stated the duties of trustees in exercising a hybrid power under four heads; *Re Manisty's Settlement* and the *Baden* trust deed cases, applied; see also *Turner v Turner* [1984] Ch 100, [1983] 2 All ER 745.
6   *Re Gulbenkian's Settlement Trusts, Hacobian v Maun* [1968] Ch 126, [1967] 3 All ER 15, CA; affd sub nom *Re Gulbenkian's Settlement Trusts, Whishaw v Stevens* [1970] AC 508, [1968] 3 All ER 785, HL (power to appoint to 'persons by or with whom G may be residing'); *Re Gestetner, Barnett v Blumka* [1953] Ch 672, [1953] 1 All ER 1150 (settlor's relatives and employees and their wives or widows); *Re Coates, Ramsden v Coates* [1955] Ch 495, [1955] 1 All ER 26 (friends nominated by the widow); *Re Sayer Trust, MacGregor v Sayer* [1957] Ch 423, [1956] 3 All ER 600; *Re Gibbard, Public Trustee v Davis* [1966] 1 All ER 273 (any of my old friends—not uncertain); *Re Barlow's Will Trusts* [1979] 1 All ER 296, [1979] 1 WLR 278; *Re Manisty's Settlement, Manisty v Manisty* [1974] Ch 17, [1973] 2 All ER 1203.
7   *Re Manisty's Settlement, Manisty v Manisty* [1974] Ch 17, [1973] 2 All ER 1203.

8   *McPhail v Doulton* [1971] AC 424, [1970] 2 All ER 228, HL, overruling, at least with respect
    to discretionary trusts, *IRC v Broadway Cottages Trust* [1955] Ch 20, [1954] 3 All ER 120. In
    the case of a trust power, if the trustees do not exercise it, the court will do so in the manner
    best calculated to give effect to the settlor's or testator's intentions. See *Re Locker's Settlement
    Trusts, Meachem v Sachs* [1978] 1 All ER 216, [1977] 1 WLR 1323 (court directed
    discretionary trustees to repair their failure and to distribute the retained fund in shares
    according to the trustees' discretion) dictum of Lord Wilberforce in *McPhail v Doulton* [1971]
    AC 424 at 457, [1970] 2 All ER 228 at 247, applied. See also *Blausten v IRC* [1972] Ch 256,
    [1972] 1 All ER 41, which was not followed in *Re Hay's Settlement Trusts* [1981] 3 All ER
    786, [1981] 1 WLR 202.
9   *Re Baden's Deed Trusts (No 2), Baden v Smith* [1973] Ch 9, [1972] 2 All ER 1304, applied in
    Re Manisty's Settlement, Manisty v Manisty [1974] Ch 17, [1973] 2 All ER 1203.

[53.7]

Uncertainty and the perpetuity rule. Mere difficulty in ascertaining the class
does not amount to uncertainty. Thus the formula for avoiding the perpetuity
rule by reference to the survivor of all descendants now living of a sovereign has
been held to be not void for uncertainty.[1] There are, however, limits to the
amount of uncertainty and a trust 'for the longest period allowed by law that is
to say, until the period of twenty-one years from the death of the last survivor of
all persons living at my death' is void for uncertainty.[2] It has been said that the
trust is still valid although the whole of the fund will be spent in ascertaining the
possible beneficiaries.[3]

1   *Re Villar, Public Trustee v Villar* [1929] 1 Ch 243.
2   *Re Moore, Prior to Moore* [1901] 1 Ch 936.
3   *Re Eden, Ellis v Crampton* [1957] 2 All ER 430 at 435.

CHAPTER 54

Context and meaning of words

I. TIME TO WHICH WILL REFERS

[54.1]

General rule. It is a matter of construction of the whole will whether a particular clause is intended to speak from the death of the testator, or the date of the will[1] or other time.[2]

---

1 *Re Chapman, Perkins v Chapman* [1904] 1 Ch 431 at 440; *Re McIntyre Estate* [1950] 2 WWR 682; *Re Creighton Estate* [1950] 2 WWR 529. By statute a will has to be construed as to the property comprised in it as at the death of the testator: Wills Act 1837, s 24; see Vol 2, Part G, para **[244.24]** (see more fully discussed, Chapter 58), but this has no application to the description of donees: *Bullock v Bennett* (1855) 7 De GM & G 283; *Amyot v Dwarris* [1904] AC 268; *Re Creighton Estate* [1950] 2 WWR 529.
2 *Re Bayliss' Trust* (1849) 17 Sim 178 (where the other time was the date at which the legacies were payable); *Broomfield v Summerfield* (1876) 2 VLR (Eq) 174. Where a codicil to the will is executed, it is a question of the intention of the testator whether the will is to be read as if made at the date of the codicil: *Royal Trust Co v Shimmin* [1933] 3 DLR 718.

[54.2]

Words of futurity. When the testator uses words of futurity[1] without showing clearly the time which he is contemplating, those words must in the first place be read, as speaking from the date of the will and not as from the date of his death.[2] But this rule is not applicable when it is a question of the property comprised in the will, for by statute that must be ascertained as at the date of death.[3] Where the context in a case not concerned with the property comprised in the will shows that the testator could not have had the time of making the will in mind, then the will must be taken as speaking from the date of the testator's death.[4]

---

1 Future words are not always given their precise grammatical meaning. Thus 'shall die in my lifetime' has often been construed as 'shall have died in my lifetime': *Loring v Thomas* (1861) 1 Drew & Sm 497 at 516; *Re Lambert, Corns v Harrison* [1908] 2 Ch 117; *Re Kirk, Wethey v Kirk* (1915) 85 LJ Ch 182; *Re Taylor* [1957] NZLR 647. 'Shall live to attain 21' has been held to include a child who had attained twenty-one at the date of the will: *Re Rayner, Couch v Warner* (1925) 134 LT 141; but see n 2, infra.
2 *Bullock v Bennett* (1855) 7 De GM & G 283; *Re Chapman, Perkins v Chapman* [1904] 1 Ch 431 at 436. Thus a person dead at the date of a will is not included in such a gift: *Gorringe v Mahlsedt* [1907] AC 225; *Re Cope, Cross v Cross* [1908] 2 Ch 1; *Re Karch* (1921) 64 DLR 541; *Guardian Trust and Executors Co Ltd v Smith* [1923] NZLR 1284; *Re Strombeck Estate* (1956) 2 DLR (2d) 109. The words 'shall die in my lifetime' introducing a substitutionary gift for children or issue must be construed, where the gift is to a class, as not including a person already dead at the date of the will unless there is some context to show that the words were not used in their literal sense: *Re Brown, Leeds v Spencer* [1917] 2 Ch 232; *Re Walker, Walker v Walker* [1930] 1 Ch 469; but this rule does not apply to a gift to named persons: *Re Booth's*

Will Trusts, Robbins v King (1940) 163 LT 77. The rule also applies to the construction of conditions: *Re Hewitt, Hewitt v Hewitt* [1926] Ch 740 ('unless she shall take the veil' refers to such taking after the date of the will and not only after the death of the testator); *Re Patton* [1929] 3 DLR 459 (condition relating to religion); but see *Re Chapman, Perkins v Chapman* [1904] 1 Ch 431, where a condition relating to marriage was construed as relating only to marriage after the testator's death; and cf *Aird's Executors v Aird* 1949 SC 154. 'Predecease me' has been read as die before the date of distribution: *Re Rooney* [1950] SASR 67.

3   Wills Act 1837, s 24; 50 *Halsbury's Statutes* (4th edn) 593, see Vol 2, Part G, para [**244.24**]. See Chapter 59.

4   *Re Davies, Scourfield v Davies* [1925] Ch 642 (gift of the proceeds of sale of such parts of the property as shall have been sold).

[54.3]
Descriptions of donees. Descriptions of persons in a will must be construed as referring to the descriptions of those persons at the date of the will, unless the words of the will clearly show that the person in question is to be ascertained at some future time.[1] Where the context shows that the person is to be ascertained in the future, but does not fix any specific time, then the first person to answer the description is presumed to be intended.[2]

1   *Bullock v Bennett* (1855) 7 De GM & G 283.
2   *Radford v Willis* (1871) 7 Ch App 7; *Re Daniels, London City v Midland Executor and Trustee Co Ltd v Daniels* (1918) 87 LJ Ch 661, and see para [**53.5**], n 3.

[54.4]
New statute passed after execution of will. In this case the will is in general construed according to the law at the date when it was made and the new statute does not affect it,[1] but a new statute enlarging the testator's power of disposition has the effect of making it apply to larger subject-matter than it previously would have done.[2] Where a statute is passed before the execution of a codicil and the codicil confirms the will, the testator is presumed to know the law and, therefore, to mean that his will shall be construed according to the new statute.[3]

1   *Jones v Ogle* (1872) 8 Ch App 192; *Re March, Mander v Harris* (1884) 27 Ch D 166; *Re Rayer, Rayer v Rayer* [1903] 1 Ch 685; *Re Turnbull, Skipper v Wade* [1905] 1 Ch 726.
2   *Re Bridger, Brompton Hospital for Consumption v Lewis* [1894] 1 Ch 297; *Re Rayer, Rayer v Rayer* [1903] 1 Ch 685; *Re Turnbull, Skipper v Wade* [1905] 1 Ch 726; *Re Yate's Estate* [1919] P 93.
3   *Hasluck v Pedley* (1874) LR 19 Eq 271.

II.   USE OF SAME WORDS IN DIFFERENT PARTS OF THE WILL

[54.5]
How far presumed to have same meaning. The force of the context may give different meanings to the same word when used in different parts of the same will, and the court does not, merely because a word bears a special meaning in one clause, necessarily give to it the same meaning in another clause of that will, in itself clear, and not connected with the first clause.[1] In all cases the context must be considered.[2] There is a presumption, however, that a word used in one part of a will with some clear and definite meaning is intended to mean the same thing in another part of the will, where its meaning is not clear.[3] Having regard, however, to the rule that the words of a will must be construed with reference to

the subject-matter,[4] a different meaning may be given to the same word when used with reference to real and personal property in a will, even in the same sentence.[5]

1   *Dalzell v Welch* (1828) 2 Sim 319 ('issue'); *Carter v Bentall* (1840) 2 Beav 551 ('issue'); *Head v Randall* (1843) 2 Y & C Ch Cas 231 ('issue'); *Williams v Teale* (1847) 6 Hare 239 at 250 ('issue'); *Neathway v Reed* (1853) 3 De GM & G 18 at 22 ('surviving'); *Gill v Barrett* (1860) 29 Beav 372 ('then').

2   *Doe d Stopford v Stopford* (1804) 5 East 501; *Right d Compton v Compton* (1808) 9 East 267; *Carter v Bentall* (1840) 2 Beav 551; *Neathway v Reed* (1853) 3 De GM & G 18.

3   *Re Birks, Kenyon v Birks* [1900] 1 Ch 417 at 418; *Edwards v Edwards* (1849) 12 Beav 97 ('issue'); *Rhodes v Rhodes* (1859) 27 Beav 413 ('issue'); *Re Buckle, Williams v Marson* [1894] 1 Ch 286 ('deductions'); *Ridgeway v Munkittrick* (1841) 1 Dr & War 84; *Edyvean v Archer, Re Brooke* [1903] AC 379 at 384; *Leeming v Sherratt* (1842) 2 Hare 14 ('survivors'). The rule, however, is not one of universal application: *Re Hickey, Beddoes v Hodgson* (1917) 86 LJ Ch 385; *Edyvean v Archer, Re Brooke, supra; Clifford v Koe* (1880) 5 App Cas 447. Where a word is used inaccurately in one place, it will not necessarily mean the same when used in another: *Re Ridge, Hancock v Dutton* (1933) 149 LT 266.

4   *Williams v Jeckyl* (1755) 2 Ves Sen 681 at 683.

5   *Forth v Chapman* (1720) 1 P Wms 663 at 667; *Doe d Chattaway v Smith* (1816) 5 M & S 126 at 132. At one time the words 'without leaving issue' were, in the case of real property, given a meaning different from that given to them in case of personal property, but since the Wills Act 1837, s 29; 50 *Halsbury's Statutes* (4th edn) 597, Vol 2, Part G, para **[244.29]**, came into force the same meaning has to be given to them in each case; see Chapter 98.

III.   EJUSDEM GENERIS RULE

[54.6]

This has already been dealt with.[1]

1   See para **[38.10]** ante.

CHAPTER 55

Meaning of particular words

[55.1]
Scope of Chapter. A large number of the particular words whose possible meaning in a will has been considered by the courts are connected with the description of donees or the description of the property which they are to take. The decisions on these words are collected elsewhere.[1] Another matter which, perhaps, falls under this heading is the change of the word 'and' to 'or' and vice versa and this is also dealt with as a separate subject.[2] The meaning of the word 'etc' and words commonly introducing an expression subject to the ejusdem generis rule has already been dealt with.[3] This Chapter considers words not included in these classes which have been considered by the court in some cases on several occasions. It must be remembered that decisions of the nature here referred to cannot be binding upon a court of construction and, at the highest, they show only what meanings have been ascribed to those words on various occasions and it is for the practitioner to consider whether any such decision can have any bearing upon the particular case under consideration.

1   As to particular descriptions of donees, see Chapters 65–81. As to particular words in the description of subject-matter of a gift, see Chapters 59–64.
2   See Chapter 56.
3   See para **[38.10]** supra.

[55.2]
General rule as to words of more than one meaning. There is no hard and fast rule that a particular word having two or more proper and recognised meanings has to bear what is called its primary meaning.[1] The meaning of such a word in any particular case is that which, according to the context and upon a consideration of all the provisions of the will or codicil, appears to be the sense in which the testator used it.[2]

1   *Seale-Hayne v Jodrell* [1891] AC 304 at 306; *Cave v Horsell* [1912] 3 KB 533 at 543.
2   *Seale-Hayne v Jodrell* [1891] AC 304 at 306; *Cave v Horsell* [1912] 3 KB 533 at 543.

[55.3]
'Entitled'. Clearly according to the context, this word may mean entitled in interest[1] or entitled in possession.[2] This word may also have a special meaning when used in a shifting clause.[3]

1   *Re Gryll's Trusts* (1868) LR 6 Eq 589.
2   *Chorley v Loveband* (1863) 33 Beav 189, *Umbers v Jaggard* (1870) LR 9 Eq 200; *Abbiss v Burney, Re Finch* (1880) 17 Ch D 211. For a case where the words were 'entitled as aforesaid',

see *Re Whiter, Windsor v Jones* (1911) 105 LT 749, but there the construction was clearly indicated by the context.

3   See para **[35.38]** supra.

[55.4]

Legacy or bequest. Generally these words and the word 'bequeath' are applied to a gift of personal property and the word 'devise' is reserved for a gift of land, but these words are wide enough to include land and interests therein where the context or the will as a whole requires such wider meaning.[1] 'Legacy' will usually include the gift of an annuity, but a will sometimes distinguishes between these two classes of gift.[2] Possibly a gift of residue is not a legacy, though a person taking the residue or a part thereof is properly described as a residuary legatee.[3]

1   *Beckley v Newland* (1723) 2 P Wms 182; *Griffyn v Griffyn* (1740) Barn Ch 391; *Hope d Brown v Taylor* (1757) 2 Keny 9; *Brady v Cubitt* (1778) 1 Doug KB 31; *Hardacre v Nash* (1794) 5 Term Rep 716; *Whicker v Hume* (1851) 14 Beav 509; *Gyett v Williams* (1862) 2 John & H 429; *Re Shepherd, Mitchell v Loram* (1914) 58 Sol Jo 304. Although leaseholds are personalty, the word 'devise' was almost universally used for testamentary gifts of such property until recent times.

2   *Sibley v Perry* (1802) 7 Ves 522; *Cornfield v Wyndham* (1845) 2 Coll 184; *Heath v Weston* (1853) 3 De GM & G 601; *Ward v Grey* (1859) 26 Beav 485; *Mullins v Smith* (1860) 1 Drew & Sm 204; *Gaskin v Rogers* (1866) LR 2 Eq 284; *Re Feather, Harrison v Tapsell* [1945] Ch 343, [1945] 1 All ER 552. In the Administration of Estates Act 1925, s 55(1)(ix); 17 *Halsbury's Statutes* (4th edn) 467, a 'pecuniary legacy' is defined as including an annuity.

3   *Ward v Grey* (1859) 26 Beav 485.

[55.5]

'Minority'. In the absence of a definition or of any indication of a contrary intention, the expressions 'full age', 'infant', 'minor', 'minority' and similar expressions in a will made on or after 1 January 1970, shall be construed with reference to the general rule that a person attains full age on attaining the age of eighteen years.[1] In the case of pre-1970 wills such expressions should be construed with reference to the age of twenty-one years.[2] But a testator may provide for a person to be kept out of the full control of his property subject in all cases to the operation of the perpetuity rule and to statutory provision,[3] until a later age and the word 'minority' has on occasion been construed to mean the period until that later age (usually twenty-five years) has been attained.[4]

1   Family Law Reform Act 1969, s 1(2); 6 *Halsbury's Statutes* (4th edn) 121.

2   *Maddison v Chapman* (1858) 4 K & J 709; *Fraser v Fraser* (1863) 1 New Rep 430.

3   Law of Property Act 1925, s 163; repealed in respect of instruments taking effect after 15 July 1964 by the Perpetuities and Accumulations Act 1964 s 4(6); s 15(5); Vol 2, Part G, para **[246.62]**; see Chapter 94.

4   *Milroy v Milroy* (1844) 14 Sim 48; *Re Sumner's Will Trusts, Midland Bank Executor and Trustee Co Ltd v Sumner* [1969] 1 All ER 779, [1969] 1 WLR 373 (restriction on interest vesting before twenty-one).

[55.6]

'Unmarried'. This word is flexible in its meaning[1] and may be construed according to the context to mean 'never having been married'[2] or simply not having a husband or wife living at a particular time[3] or without leaving a widow.[4] A gift to unmarried children may mean children unmarried at the date of the will[5] or unmarried at the death of the testator.[6] The word 'sole' in a will has no fixed meaning but, if such is contended, must be shown to have some other than its strict technical meaning of excluding the material right of the husband,[7] and 'sole and unmarried' has been held to mean 'not having a husband at the particular time'.[8]

1   *Coventry v Lauderdale* (1846) 7 LTOS 467; *Re Sanders' Trusts* (1866) LR 1 Eq 675; *Re Sergeant, Mertens v Walley* (1884) 26 Ch D 575; *Re Fanshawe's Trusts* (1904) 48 Sol Jo 525 (where the view is suggested that in a home-made will the word generally means 'never having been married'); *Re Collyer, Collyer v Back* (1907) 24 TLR 117.

2   *Coventry v Lauderdale* (1846) 7 LTOS 467; *Hall v Robertson* (1853) 1 Eq Rep 245; *Re Thistlethwayte's Trust* (1855) 24 LJ Ch 712; *Dalrymple v Hall* (1881) 16 Ch D 715; *Re Sergeant, Mertens v Walley* (1884) 26 Ch D 575; *Gonne v Cook* (1867) 15 WR 576 (in the two last-mentioned cases 'never having been married' is said to be the primary sense); *Re Fanshawe's Trusts* (1904) 48 Sol Jo 525; *Re Hall-Dare, Le Marchant v Lee Warner* [1916] 1 Ch 272; *Roberts v Bishop of Kilmore* [1902] 1 IR 333.

3   *Re Gratton's Trusts* (1857) 26 LJ Ch 648; *Day v Barnard* (1860) 1 Drew & Sm 351; *Re Sanders' Trusts* (1866) LR 1 Eq 675; *Re Sergeant, Mertens v Walley* (1884) 26 Ch D 575; *Re King, Salisbury v Ridley* (1890) 62 LT 789; *Re Fanshawe's Trusts* (1904) 48 Sol Jo 525 *Re Jones, Last v Dobson* [1915] 1 Ch 246 (where the word was used in its secondary sense of 'widower', since otherwise the words 'and without lawful issue' were superfluous).

4   *Re Chant, Chant v Lemon* [1900] 2 Ch 345; *Carolin v Carolin* (1881) 17 LR Ir 25n.

5   *Hall v Robertson* (1853) 4 De GM & G 781.

6   *Jubber v Jubber* (1839) 9 Sim 503.

7   *Massy v Rowen* (1869) LR 4 HL 288. The technical meaning is now obsolete and it seems essential that some other meaning must now be given to the word, if used.

8   *Re Lesingham's Trusts* (1883) 24 Ch D 703.

[55.7]

'Testamentary expenses'. This term is ordinarily synonymous with the less usual term 'executorship expenses'[1] and signifies expenses incident to the proper performance of the duty of the executor.[2] Costs in proceedings properly brought to administer the estate are included[3] including inquiries as to the persons entitled to a legacy where the difficulty is caused by the language used by the testator.[4] Earlier authorities established that estate duty payable in respect of the deceased's personal estate in Great Britain including any leasehold property[5] and interests in expectancy[6] forming part of such estate which passed to the executor as such was payable as a testamentary expense, that is, out of the residue of the estate.[7] It is thought that before there was specific legislation on the point the position was similar with reference to capital transfer tax. If the property did not pass to the executor as such, such as property appointed under a general power of appointment,[8] or subject to a *donatio mortis causa*[9] or a gift inter vivos,[10] then the tax was probably not a testamentary expense. The traditional attitude has been that duty or tax on real estate is not a testamentary expense.[11] The initial statutory provisions appeared to preserve this rule with reference to capital transfer tax.[12] However it was held in the Scottish case of *Re Dougal*[13] that in Scotland capital transfer tax on realty was a testamentary expense and thus payable out of residue. This raised some uncertainties in the law regarding the position in England and to remove these doubts legislation provided that capital transfer tax on UK fee estate devolving on the executors including realty was to be treated as a testamentary expense payable out of the residue instead of being borne by the beneficiary of the property in question, subject to any expression of a contrary intention.[14] The expenses of executing the trusts,[15] and the fees of the Public Trustee or a trust corporation[16] are testamentary expenses.

1   *Sharp v Lush* (1879) 10 Ch D 468 at 470 (executorship expenses); *Harland-Peck, Hercy v Mayglothling* [1941] Ch 182, [1940] 4 All ER 347, CA (funeral and testamentary expenses); *Re Beaumont's Will Trusts, Walker v Lawson* [1950] Ch 462, [1950] 1 All ER 802 (funeral and testamentary expenses and debts); all three cases applied in *Re Taylor's Estate and Will Trusts, Taylor v Taylor* [1969] 2 Ch 245, [1969] 1 All ER 113 (testamentary and administration expenses could not be segregated and the reference to testamentary expenses was wide enough to embrace both).

2   *Sharp v Lush* (1879) 10 Ch D 468.

3   *Morrell v Fisher* (1851) 4 De G & Sm 422; *Miles v Harrison* (1874) 9 Ch App 316; *Penny v Penny* (1879) 11 Ch D 440; *Re Taylor's Estate and Will Trusts, Taylor v Taylor* [1969] 2 Ch 245, [1969] 1 All ER 113.

4   *Re Groom, Booty v Groom* [1897] 2 Ch 407; *Re Hall-Dare, Le Marchant v Lee Warner* [1916] 1 Ch 272.

5   *Re Culverhouse, Cook v Culverhouse* [1896] 2 Ch 251, and see the Law of Property Act 1925, s 16(6), as amended by the Finance Act 1975, Sch 13 and the Trusts of Land and Appointment of Trustees Act 1996, s 25(1), Sch 3, para 4(4).

6   *Re Avery, Pinsent v Avery* [1913] 1 Ch 208.

7   *Re Clemow, Yeo v Clemow* [1900] 2 Ch 182; *Re Jolley* (1901) 17 TLR 244; *Re Morrison, Morrison v Morrison* (1910) 102 LT 530; *Re Avery, Pinsent v Avery* [1913] 1 Ch 208.

8   *O'Grady v Wilmot* [1916] 2 AC 231.

9   *Re Hudson, Spencer v Turner* [1911] 1 Ch 206.

10 *Re Payne, Poplett v A-G* [1940] Ch 576.

11 See cases on estate duty, *Re Williams, Williams and Glyn's Trust Co Ltd v Williams* [1974] 1 All ER 787, [1974] 1 WLR 754; *Re Sharman, Wright v Sharman* [1901] 2 Ch 280; *Re Spencer Cooper, Poe v Spencer Cooper* [1908] 1 Ch 130; affd post-1925, *Re Owers, Public Trustee v Death* [1941] Ch 17; *Re Rosenthal, Schwarz v Bernstein* [1972] 3 All ER 552.

12 Finance Act 1975, s 28 and Sch 4, para 20; 45 *Halsbury's Statutes* (3rd edn) 810, 1872.

13 [1981] STC 514.

14 Finance Act (No 2) 1983, s 13; 42 *Halsbury's Statutes* (4th edn) 606. See now the Inheritance Tax Act 1984, s 211; 42 *Halsbury's Statutes* (4th edn) 849 and Vol 2, Part G, para **[246.83]**.

15 *Lord Brougham v Lord Poulett* (1855) 19 Beav 119.

16 *Re Hicklin, Public Trustee v Hoare* [1917] 2 Ch 278.

CHAPTER 56

Change of 'or' into 'and' and vice versa

I. 'OR' CHANGED INTO 'AND'

[56.1]
Absolute interest with gift over on death without children or under twenty-one. If there is a gift to a named person in fee simple or, in the case of personal property, absolutely with a gift over if that person dies without children or under the age of twenty-one[1] to other donees, the word 'or' is read 'and', and the gift over does not take effect unless both events happen.[2] This rule of construction depends on the presumed intention of the testator to benefit the children of the beneficiary directly or indirectly, an intention which would be defeated if the devisee died under twenty-one leaving children and the word 'or' was construed disjunctively.[3] The change is made even though the sentence as changed contains a condition repugnant to the character of the estate given.[4] A similar rule holds good as to gifts over if the donee in question dies before a life tenant under a previous gift or without issue.[5] This rule also applies where the prior gift is contingent on the donee leaving issue[6] or on his attaining twenty-one,[7] provided that the prior gift is absolute or in fee simple.

1   In view of the reduction in the age of majority by the Family Law Reform Act 1969, s 1; 6 *Halsbury's Statutes* (4th edn) 121, the age of eighteen years might be specified in post-1970 wills. The rule will no doubt apply to such provisions although the justification of the rule will not be as cogent.

2   *Fairfield v Morgan* (1805) 2 Bos & PNR 38; *Eastman v Baker* (1808) 1 Taunt 174 at 182; *Right d Day v Day* (1812) 16 East 67; *Doe d Herbert v Selby* (1824) 2 B & C 926; *Morris v Morris* (1853) 17 Beav 198; *Mahaffy v Rooney* (1853) 5 Ir Jur 245; *Imray v Imeson* (1872) 26 LT 93. As to the application of the rule to personal estate, see *Wright v Marsom* [1895] WN 148; *Weddell v Mundy* (1801) 6 Ves 341; *Mytton v Boodle* (1834) 6 Sim 457. See also *Re Hudson* (1971) 14 DLR (3d) 79 at 86, where this and the following two pages of the text are referred to.

3   *Re Crutchley, Kidson v Marsden* [1912] 2 Ch 335 at 337 (where the rule in its modern form is stated). The rule was treated as established in *Grey v Pearson* (1857) 6 HL Cas 61, but some doubts were there (at p 80) expressed as to its necessity. Where the gift over is expressed in the form 'without issue or making a disposition of the property' it has been said that the change is unnecessary: *Stretton v Fitzgerald* (1889) 23 LR Ir 466 at 472.

4   *Incorporated Society in Dublin v Richards* (1841) 1 Dr & War 258 at 283 (without issue or intestate); *Green v Harvey* (1842) 1 Hare 428 (die without heir or will); *Greated v Greated* (1859) 26 Beav 621 at 627 ('before having heirs of their body or making a particular disposition of his or her property'); *Re Crutchley, Kidson v Marsden*, supra ('dying intestate, childless or under the age of 21 but not otherwise'); *Beachcroft v Broome* (1791) 4 Term Rep 441 (without settling or disposing of same or without issue); *Cuthbert v Purrier* (1822) Jac 415 (death under twenty-one or afterwards without heirs and intestate); *Stretton v Fitzgerald* (1889) 23 LR Ir 466 (without issue or making a particular disposition of the property).

5   *Denn d Wilkins v Kemeys* (1808) 8 East 366; *Wright d Burrill v Kemp* (1789) 3 Term Rep 470.

6   *Johnson v Simcock* (1861) 7 H & N 344.
7   *Mytton v Boodle* (1834) 6 Sim 457; *Wright v Marsom* [1895] WN 148.

[56.2]
Gift for life or in tail with similar gift over. Where the prior donee takes for life only, and his issue take absolute interests, and there is a similar gift over, this change cannot be made so as to defeat the interests of subsequent takers.[1] Where a prior donee takes in tail,[2] or takes for life only with remainder to his issue in tail as purchasers,[3] a gift over on his death under age or on the failure of his issue may be read without alteration of the 'or' into 'and', but even in this case a death under the specified age does not in general carry the estate over, unless there is a failure of issue, since the gift over would not be read so as to defeat any issue in tail,[4] while a death without issue, although after attaining that age, may carry the estate over by way of remainder or otherwise.[5]

1   *Cooke v Mirehouse* (1864) 34 Beav 27. Such a change would defeat the intentions of the testator and tend to an intestacy (supra at 29).
2   *Woodward v Glasbrook* (1700) 2 Vern 388; *Brownsword v Edwards* (1751) 2 Ves Sen 243 at 249; *Mortimer v Hartley* (1851) 6 Exch 47; *Grey v Pearson* (1857) 6 HL Cas 61 at 93.
3   *Hasker v Sutton* (1824) 9 Moore CP 2.
4   *Grey v Pearson* (1857) 6 HL Cas 61; and see *Monkhouse v Monkhouse* (1829) 3 Sim 119 at 126 (where a gift over on death or want of issue was construed as a gift over on death and want of issue).
5   *Brownsword v Edwards* (1751) 2 Ves Sen 243; *Hasker v Sutton* (1824) 9 Moore CP 2.

[56.3]
Gift over on death before full age or marriage. On the same principle[1] or to avoid inconsistency,[2] where a prior gift is absolute, or contingent on attaining a certain age, or on marriage, or on a specified age or marriage as alternative events, a gift over in any of these cases on the death of the donee before attaining that age or marriage is read as if 'or' was 'and'.

1   The ground for the rule is stated in *Re Clegg's Estate, ex p Evans* (1862) 14 I Ch R 70; *Re Cantillon's Minors* (1864) 16 I Ch R 301; *Butler v Trustees, Executors and Agency Co Ltd* (1906) 3 CLR 435 at 443.
2   This reason for the construction was stated in *Grant v Dyer* (1813) 2 Dow 73 at 87; *Malcolm v O'Callaghan* (1833) Coop *temp* Brough 73 at 76 (contingent on marriage with consent). See also *Thackeray v Hampson* (1825) 2 Sim & St 214; *Grimshawe v Pickup* (1839) 9 Sim 591; *Thompson v Teulon* (1852) 22 LJ Ch 243; *Collett v Collett* (1866) 35 Beav 312.

[56.4]
Gift over on death before life tenant or under age. In cases where the interest of a donee is postponed to a life interest, but is contingent only on his attaining a certain age, and not on his surviving the life tenant, a gift over on his death before the life tenant or under the specified age, is construed as if 'or' was 'and'.[1]

1   *Miles v Dyer* (1832) 5 Sim 435; followed as laying down an established rule of construction in *Bentley v Meech* (1858) 25 Beav 197.

[56.5]

Gifts expressed in the alternative. Where there is a gift to A or B and no contingency is expressed or implied,[1] then, if A and B are mutually exclusive,[2] the gift will be void for uncertainty.[3] This is obviously a result which the court will try to avoid, and one way in which the result may be avoided is to read the word 'or' as 'and', and the court will do so if such change can be justified by the context.[4] The change, however, will not be made where the gift can be read as substitutional and not as alternative.[5]

1   When it is known who A and B are and in what relation, if any, the person or persons represented by B stand to that or those represented by A, it may be possible to imply a contingency as involved in the word 'or' upon which B is to take: *Re Roberts, Percival v Roberts* [1903] 2 Ch 200 at 203; *Re Sibley's Trusts* (1877) 5 Ch D 494 □at 499; see, further, Chapter 68. In the case of a gift to 'A or heirs' or 'A or his personal representatives', the 'or' has often been changed to 'and' and the words treated as words of limitation: *Read v Snell* (1743) 2 Atk 642; *Wright v Wright* (1750) 1 Ves Sen 409; *Harris v Davis* (1844) 1 Coll 416; *Polley v Polley* (1861) 29 Beav 134; but not where the gifts are substitutional: see para **[56.7]**, n 4.
2   Gifts to 'heirs of next of kin' apply to one class and are not alternative: *Re Thompson's Trusts* (1878) 9 Ch D 607; *Lowndes v Stone* (1799) 4 Ves 649. If B is a general term for a large class (eg descendants) and A is a selected few of the class, or a sub-class (such as children) and the gift is to 'each of A or B', the gift is not void but includes all B and there is no need to change 'or' to 'and': *Solly v Solly* (1858) 5 Jur NS 36; *Clay v Pennington* (1835) 7 Sim 370.
3   *Richardson v Spraag* (1718) 1 P Wms 434; *Longmore v Broom* (1802) 7 Ves 124 at 218; *Flint v Warren* (1847) 15 Sim 626 at 629. If the gift is to charity and there is a general charitable intention, it will not be void but will be made the subject of a scheme; see Chapter 102. If the gift is by way of power of appointment, it may be saved by the implication of a trust in favour of objects of an unexercised power. For this to be so there must be a power to appoint to certain objects, no express gift to those objects and no gift over in default of appointment: *Longmore v Broom* (1802) 7 Ves 124; *Penny v Turner* (1848) 2 Ph 493; *Re White's Trusts* (1860) John 656.
4   *Richardson v Spraag* (1718) 1 P Wms 434; *Eccard v Brooke* (1790) 2 Cox Eq Cas 213; *Horridge v Ferguson* (1822) Jac 583; *Parkin v Knight* (1846) 15 Sim 83; *Lachlan v Reynolds* (1852) 9 Hare 796; *Shand v Kidd* (1854) 19 Beav 310; *Re Turney, Turney v Turney* [1899] 2 Ch 739. In *Re Hayden, Pask v Perry* [1931] 2 Ch 333, 'or their issue' was changed into 'and their issue' and an estate tail was implied. An estate tail can no longer be created by virtue of the TLATA 1996, s 2, Sch 1, para 5.
5   *Penley v Penley* (1850) 12 Beav 547; *Speakman v Speakman* (1850) 8 Hare 180; *Blundell v Chapman* (1864) 33 Beav 648; *Wingfield v Wingfield* (1878) 9 Ch D 658.

[56.6]

General reasons for which the court will make the change. The above cases are the most usual in which the court has made the change, but the court has made the change where it is necessary in order to arrive at a reasonable construction of the whole will and to avoid inconsistency where it is not possible to do so otherwise,[1] or to effectuate the intention of the testator,[2] or where the context clearly requires it.[3] In general the court is much more willing to change 'or' to 'and' than to make the contrary change.[4]

1   *Read v Snell* (1743) 2 Atk 642 (gift to daughter or heirs of her body). This is also a good reason for the contrary change of 'and' to 'or'.
2   *Wright d Burrill v Kemp* (1789) 3 Term Rep 470; *Maude v Maude* (1856) 22 Beav 290; *White v Supple* (1842) 2 Dr & War 471.
3   *Nichols v Tolley* (1700) 2 Vern 388 (gift to issue living at death of testator, his wife or survivor); *Green v Harvey* (1842) 1 Hare 428 (death without heir or will); *Greated v Greated* (1859) 26 Beav 621 (donee dying before having heirs of his body or making a disposition of the property); *Re Heard* [1956] VLR 102 ('survive me or my said wife').
4   See para **[56.7]** infra.

II.   CHANGE OF 'AND' INTO 'OR'

[56.7]

This change not generally made. In general, the court is unwilling to change the conjunction 'and' into 'or' in a gift over on several events connected by 'and', where the words may have their ordinary sense, since the effect would be to divest the prior gift in events other than the compound event which the testator has provided for.[1] Thus, after a gift to a donee absolutely,[2] or in tail,[3] or for life with remainder to his children,[4] a gift over on the donee dying under full age and without issue is read in its ordinary sense, and is not read as if 'and' were 'or' merely for the possible benefit of issue. Where a gift after a life tenancy was to three persons or such of them as should be then living and attaining twenty-one or marry, the court refused to change the 'and' after 'living' to 'or' so as to let in a person dying in the lifetime of a tenant for life.[5] The court has refused to construe 'and' as 'or' in the words 'charitable and benevolent'.[6]

1   *Doe d Usher v Jessep* (1810) 12 East 288 at 293; *Key v Key* (1855) 1 Jur NS 372; *Re Sanders' Trusts* (1866) LR 1 Eq 675; *Reed v Braithwaite* (1871) LR 11 Eq 514. See also *Gonne v Cook* (1867) 15 WR 576; *Brown v Walker* (1824) 2 LJOS Ch 82 (where there was said to be a balance of intention upon the words of the will); *Re Sharpe* [1946] Tas SR 13 (die unmarried and without lawful issue, change not made).
2   *Coates v Hart* (1863) 32 Beav 349; but see *Else v Else* (1872) LR 13 Eq 196. As to dying without issue and without making appointment, see *Barker v Young* (1864) 33 Beav 353.
3   *Doe d Usher v Jessep* (1810) 12 East 288, approved in *Grey v Pearson* (1857) 6 HL Cas 61.
4   *Malcolm v Malcolm* (1856) 21 Beav 225.
5   *Malden v Maine* (1855) 2 Jur NS 206.
6   *Caldwell v Caldwell* (1921) 91 LJPC 95, and the reason for so doing has been strengthened by the decision in *Chichester Diocesan Fund and Board of Finance Inc v Simpson* [1944] AC 341, [1944] 2 All ER 60.

[56.8]

When this change is made. 'And' may, however, be construed 'or' where one member of the sentence includes the other, so that by construing the words literally one member of the sentence would be rendered unnecessary, and the change is made in order to give effect to each member of the sentence.[1] The change, however, is not made if, by giving to that member of the sentence some less usual meaning, effect can be given to every word.[2] Thus, if, after a gift to a person absolutely or for life and afterwards to his children, there is a gift over on his death 'unmarried and without issue', it can be read as if 'and' were 'or' in cases where the word 'unmarried' is necessarily given its meaning of 'never having been married';[3] but as a rule, if in such a gift over 'unmarried' can be given the meaning 'without leaving a spouse',[4] so as to give effect to all the words without changing the conjunction, this construction is adopted rather than that the words should be altered.[5] It is an additional objection to this change that any part of the sentence thereby becomes inoperative.[6] A similar construction was approved where the gift over was dependent on death under twenty-one and before the testator's widow.[7] In the case of an alternative gift the word 'and' may be changed to 'or' where the context requires that it shall be substitutional and not original, and this construction is aided by the desire of the court to avoid an uncertainty or an infringement of the rule against perpetuities.[8] In a gift to a person entitled to an estate, the words 'freehold and inheritance' were construed in the alternative.[9]

1   *Day v Day* (1854) Kay 703 at 708. In a provision for the maintenance of a daughter and her children, 'and' has been read 'or' so that the daughter might be maintained after the death of her child: *Bethune v Bethune* [1944] Que SC 14; but see *Re Hamilton* [1953] QSR 48; *Re Sharpe* [1946] Tas SR 13.
2   See Chapter 50, para [50.5] supra.
3   *Wilson v Bayly* (1760) 3 Bro Parl Cas 195; *Hepworth v Taylor* (1784) 1 Cox Eq Cas 112; *Maberly v Strode* (1797) 3 Ves 450 at 454; *Bell v Phyn* (1802) 7 Ves 453 at 459; *Long v Lane* (1885) 17 LR Ir 11; *Carolin v Carolin* (1881) 17 LR Ir 25n; *Roberts v Bishop of Kilmore* [1902] 1 IR 333. See also *Mackenzie v King* (1848) 17 LJ Ch 448 ('nor' read 'or not'). Where the gift over was on death under twenty-four and unmarried, the court read 'unmarried' as meaning 'never having been married' and refused to change 'and' into 'or': *Gonne v Cook* (1867) 15 WR 576.
4   See Chapter 50, para [50.6] supra.
5   *Seccombe v Edwards* (1860) 28 Beav 440; *Re Sanders' Trusts* (1866) LR 1 Eq 675; *Re King, Salisbury v Ridley* (1890) 62 LT 789; *Re Chant, Chant v Lemon* [1900] 2 Ch 345 at 348; *Re Jones, Last v Dobson* [1915] 1 Ch 246 ('unmarried and without lawful issue' held to mean 'without leaving a widow'). See also *Dillon v Harris* (1830) 4 Bli NS 321 at 365, where marriage with consent was intended. After an absolute gift of realty or personalty, or a gift for life, followed by a gift to the donee's children, a gift over on a prior donee dying an infant unmarried and without issue prima facie is construed as given on a single contingency, and the words are not to be read disjunctively, unless the context so requires. For this purpose, the word 'unmarried' is taken to mean 'without leaving a spouse': *Doe d Everett v Cooke* (1806) 7 East 269 at 272, and cf *Framlingham v Brand* (1746) 3 Atk 390 (on death during minority and unmarried or without issue). Such a word as 'unmarried' in such a context cannot be struck out or left inoperative: *Doe d Baldwin v Rawding* (1819) 2 B & Ald 441. See also Chapter 55, para [55.6] supra.
6   *Key v Key* (1855) 1 Jur NS 372; *Re Kirkbride's Trusts* (1866) LR 2 Eq 400 at 403.
7   *Hetherington v Oakman* (1843) 2 Y & C Ch Cas 299.
8   *Maynard v Wright* (1858) 26 Beav 285; and see *Hurry v Hurry* (1870) LR 10 Eq 346 at 348; *Re Coulden, Coulden v Coulden* [1908] 1 Ch 320 at 325.
9   *Stapleton v Stapleton* (1852) 2 Sim NS 212 (the person who would take had a life interest only); but where a power of sale was given at the request of the person entitled to the freehold and inheritance, the change was not made and the sale could not be had at the request of the tenant for life: *Malmesbury v Malmesbury* (1862) 31 Beav 407.

[56.9]

Reasons for the change. The court is guided by much the same reasons whichever way the change is made and the reasons given for making the change from 'and' to 'or' have been: to make a consistent construction of the whole will,[1] to effectuate the intention of the testator,[2] and to avoid uncertainty and remoteness.[3] This change, however, will be made only in a case of necessity[4] and not when no inconvenience arises from making the change[5] or a reasonable construction is possible without the change.[6] It will be made to favour the vesting of a legacy and not to divest it.[7]

1   *Haws v Haws* (1747) 1 Ves Sen 13; *Burleigh v Pearson* (1749) 1 Ves Sen 281; *Maberley v Strode* (1797) 3 Ves 450.
2   *Jackson v Jackson* (1749) 1 Ves Sen 217; *Stubbs v Sargon* (1837) 2 Keen 255; *White v Supple* (1842) 2 Dr & War 471.
3   *Maynard v Wright* (1858) 26 Beav 285. See *Caldwell v Caldwell* (1921) 91 LJPC 95, where the court refused to make the change for this reason.
4   *Re Sanders' Trusts* (1866) LR 1 Eq 675.
5   *Doe d Usher v Jessep* (1810) 12 East 288.
6   *Key v Key* (1855) 1 Jur NS 372.
7   *Re Hamilton* [1953] QSR 48.

CHAPTER 57

Evidence admissible in a court of construction – extrinsic evidence

I. INTRODUCTION

[57.1]
The Administration of Justice Act 1982 (AJA 1982). The traditional approach of English law to the construction of wills has been to adopt a literal approach, looking mainly to the words of the will largely to the exclusion of extrinsic evidence. Factual evidence of surrounding circumstances has been admitted for the purpose of identification of persons or things but extrinsic evidence relating to the testator's dispositive intentions has been excluded, except to resolve latent ambiguities. Although this approach has been apparent for over a century the formulation of the rules regarding the admission of extrinsic evidence was not clear and many of the cases were open to charges of inconsistency and anomaly.[1]

The need for some legislative clarification, and relaxation, to match the prevalent judicial mood for a wider search for the testator's intention and a less rigid adherence to strict rules of construction, was apparent and found expression in the AJA 1982, s 21.[2] This provision sets out in short general terms the rules governing the admission of extrinsic evidence in the interpretation of wills and provides for the wider admission of evidence of the testator's intention. These new rules apply to the wills of testators who die on or after 1 January 1983[3] and the traditional rules remain applicable to earlier deaths. Further the new rules clearly owe something to the old formulations and for these reasons it is necessary to consider both the case law principles and the statutory provisions. But first the status and function of the probate must be considered.

1   See Law Reform Committee, 19th Report, 'Interpretation of Wills', Cmnd 5301. It was the recommendations of this committee that formed the basis of the legislative changes enacted in the Administration of Justice Act 1982; see Vol 2, Part G, para **[244.92]**.
2   50 *Halsbury's Statutes* (4th edn) 616.
3   AJA 1982, s 73(6); s 76(11); 50 *Halsbury's Statutes* (4th edn) 622.

II. THE PROBATE COPY

[57.2]
Nature of the evidence. Before a will comes before the court of construction the question of the documents forming the will and how far those documents are testamentary has already been determined. The court of construction receives a

document or documents admitted to probate, that is, documents duly executed as a will and made by a person of proper testamentary capacity and from which have been excluded any words which are for any reason not testamentary. In the case of the wills of testators who die on or after 1 January 1983 the power of rectification is available, in defined circumstances, to correct the will.[1] Where this jurisdiction has been invoked then it will be the will as rectified that the court of construction will construe. The question before the court of construction is the meaning of the document or documents thus preferred to it, all questions of the existence of an operative will and to what extent such will represents the testamentary dispositions of the testator having already been finally decided.[2] The meaning of the will is dependent upon the intention of the testator and in the court of construction the primary evidence of the testator's intention is the will itself,[3] but extrinsic evidence of circumstances may be given the nature and effect of which is to explain what the testator has written,[4] but not what he intended to write.[5] Thus, extrinsic evidence is admissible to make intelligible something in the will which without that evidence would not be intelligible.[6] This applies to both English and foreign wills and is independent of the statutory requirements as to form and execution.[7]

1   AJA 1982, s 20; 50 *Halsbury's Statutes* (4th edn) 615, see Vol 2, Part G, para **[244.96]**; see fully discussed Chapter 6.
2   *Reffell v Reffell* (1866) LR 1 P & D 139 at 141; *Re Hawksley's Settlements Black v Tidy* [1934] Ch 384.
3   *Doe d Gwillim v Gwillim* (1833) 5 B & Ad 122; *Earl Scarborough v Doe d Savile* (1836) 3 Ad & El 897; *Doe d Hiscocks v Hiscocks* (1839) 5 M & W 363; *Dormer v Phillips* (1855) 4 De GM & G 855; *Smith v Osborne* (1857) 6 HL Cas 375; *Roddy v Fitzgerald* (1858) 6 HL Cas 823; *Taylor v Graham* (1878) 3 App Cas 1287; *Singleton v Tomlinson* (1878) 3 App Cas 404; *Tatham v Drummond* (1864) 4 De GJ & Sm 484; *Bowen v Lewis* (1884) 9 App Cas 890; *Beaudry v Barbeau* [1900] AC 569.
4   *Thomson and Baxter v Hempenstall* (1849) 1 Rob Eccl 783; *Re Overhill's Trust* (1853) 1 Sm & G 362; *Slingsby v Grainger* (1859) 7 HL Cas 273; *Grant v Grant* (1870) LR 5 CP 727; *Robertson v Flynn* [1920] 1 IR 78; *Re Dickson* (1865) 49 DLR (2d) 289.
5   *Re Mayo, Chester v Keirl* [1901] 1 Ch 404, *Re Trimmer, Crundwell v Trimmer* (1904) 91 LT 26; *Re Hodgson, Nowell v Flannery* [1936] Ch 203. This sentence was referred to with approval by Hollingworth J in *Re Ohorodnyk* (1979) 97 DLR (3d) 502 at 510.
6   *Clemenston v Gandy* (1836) 1 Keen 309 at 316; *Re Glassington, Glassington v Follett* [1906] 2 Ch 305 at 314, explaining *Higgins v Dawson* [1902] AC 1.
7   *Yates v Thomson* (1835) 3 Cl & Fin 544; *Re Scholefield, Scholefield v St John* [1905] 2 Ch 408.

[57.3]
Probate generally evidence of words of will. As to the exact words of the will the court of construction accepts the probate as showing the state in which the will was at the time of its execution,[1] and as containing the whole will to be construed.[2]

1   *Lynn v Beaver* (1923) Turn & R 63; *Thornton v Curling* (1824) 8 Sim 310.
2   *Lynn v Beaver* (1823) Turn & R 63; *Re Berger* [1990] Ch 118, [1989] 1 All ER 591.

[57.4]
When original will looked at. The court may in all cases look at the original will in order to settle any question arising on punctuation,[1] or as to the effect of erasures[2] or of blanks in the will,[3] and generally in order to see whether any light is thrown on the construction of the will by its form.[4] This may be of

considerable importance where a printed form has been used as the basis of the will.[5] The court may also look at a document which is incorporated in the will,[6] though not admitted to probate.[7] Where the will is in a foreign language and the probate copy is a translation, the original may be looked at to ascertain the original foreign words and to consider whether they have a technical meaning.[8]

1   *Re Steel, Public Trustee v Christian Aid Society* [1979] Ch 218, [1978] 2 All ER 1026 (where the original will was holograph and probate was granted of a typewritten copy, the original will referred to to establish punctuation) *Child v Elsworth* (1852) 2 De GM & G 679; *Thellusson v Woodford* (1799) 4 Ves 227 (words put in a parenthesis); *Re Dorigan's Will* (1962) 40 WWR 505 (if clear and not confusing). As to the importance of punctuation, see para **[50.14]** supra.

2   *Manning v Purcell* (1855) 7 De GM & G 55 at 66; *Re Baynham, Hart v Mackenzie* (1891) 7 TLR 587; *Re Battie-Wrightson, Cecil v Battie-Wrightson* [1920] 2 Ch 330 (where the erasures omitted in the probate left later words insensible, but were clear having regard to the unintended effect of the erasure). In the case of photo-copies, this can now rarely be of importance. See also *Re Wyatt, Furniss v Phear* (1888) 36 WR 521. As to alterations and erasures generally, see Chapter 14.

3   *Re Harrison, Turner v Hellard* (1885) 30 Ch D 390 at 393, 394; *Re Cliff's Trusts* [1892] 2 Ch 229.

4   See *Shea v Boschetti* (1854) 18 Beav 321; *Oppenheim v Henry* (1853) 9 Hare 802n (to explain but not to contradict); *Compton v Bloxham* (1845) 2 Coll 201; *Gann v Gregory* (1854) 3 De GM & G 777; *Phillips v Chamberlaine* (1798) 4 Ves 51; *Lunn v Osborne* (1834) 7 Sim 56; *Wordsworth v Wood* (1847) 1 HL Cas 129; *Milsome v Long* (1857) 3 Jur NS 1073; *Thompson v Whitelock* (1859) 4 De G & J 490 (alteration of figure making figure intended doubtful); *Jull v Jacobs* (1876) 3 Ch D 703 (frame of will); *Munro v Henderson* [1907] 1 IR 440 at 443; affd [1908] 1 IR 260.

5   *Re Messenger's Estate, Chaplin v Ruane* [1937] 1 All ER 355; *Re Turner, Carpenter v Staveley* [1949] 2 All ER 935.

6   *Dillon v Harris* (1830) 4 Bli NS 321 at 350; *Quihampton v Going* (1876) 24 WR 917; *Singleton v Tomlinson* (1878) 3 App Cas 404 at 413; *University of North Wales v Taylor* [1908] P 140; *Re Deprez, Henriques v Deprez* [1917] 1 Ch 24 (entries in account books); *Re White, Knight v Briggs* [1925] Ch 179. Where the memorandum was expressly stated not to form part of the will, it was not admitted in evidence: *Re Louis, Louis v Treloar* (1916) 32 TLR 313. A gift on the trusts of a deed which does not become operative fails: *Re Hurdle, Blakeney v Hurdle* [1936] 3 All ER 810. Where a gift is by reference to an existing ascertainable document or future substituted document, as evidence of the latter is not admissible, the testator's intention as a whole cannot be ascertained, and therefore, evidence of the former document cannot be admitted and fails for uncertainty: *Re Jones* [1942] Ch 328, [1942] 1 All ER 642; distinguished in *Re Edward's Will Trusts, Dalgleish v Leighton* [1948] Ch 440, [1948] 1 All ER 821. See also *Re Bateman's Will Trusts, Brierley v Perry* [1970] 3 All ER 817, [1970] 1 WLR 1463.

7   *Quihampton v Going* (1876) 24 WR 917.

8   *L'Fit v L'Batt* (1718) 1 P Wms 526; *Re Cliff's Trusts* [1892] 2 Ch 229; *Re Manners, Manners v Manners* [1923] 1 Ch 220.

[57.5]
Where writing or language not easily understood. Where the characters in which a will is written are difficult to decipher,[1] or the language is a foreign language not understood by the court,[2] or is the language of a business or locality with which the testator was acquainted,[3] the evidence of experts is admissible to inform the court of the proper meaning of the will;[4] but evidence cannot be given to explain words or symbols which are not the language of a trade, locality or business, and are known only to the testator himself,[5] unless the will itself refers to the subject of such evidence as the means of identifying them.[6] In order to discover the ordinary meaning of a word, the court may refer to dictionaries of good reputation,[7] or other contemporary literary sources,[8] and also, in the case of words describing property, by evidence of the ordinary

meaning given to such words by those dealing in such property.[9] Evidence cannot, however, be given as a general rule to show the meaning of common words as understood by the testator or other persons[10] where that meaning is not the ordinary meaning of the words in the testator's society.[11]

1   *Masters v Masters* (1718) 1 P Wms 421 at 425 (illegible writing); *Goblet v Beechey* (1829) 3 Sim 24; on appeal (1831) 2 Russ & M 624 (obscurely written words of technical meaning). In both these cases expert evidence was held admissible.
2   *Re Cliff's Trusts* [1892] 2 Ch 229 at 232; *Reynolds v Kortright* (1854) 18 Beav 417 at 425. This may be necessary because the probate is a translation: *L'Fit v L'Batt* (1718) 1 P Wms 526. Where the words are technical legal expressions foreign lawyers may be called to explain the meaning: *Re Cliff's Trusts* [1892] 2 Ch 229: *Re Manners, Manners v Manners* [1923] 1 Ch 220.
3   *Kell v Charmer* (1856) 23 Beav 195 (private markings denoting prices); *Goblet v Beechey* (1829) 3 Sim 24; on appeal (1831) 2 Russ & M 624 (where the trade expert and a handwriting expert disagreed); *Shore v Wilson* (1842) 9 CL & Fin 355 at 525 (local language); *Re Rayner, Rayner v Rayner* [1904] 1 Ch 176 (meaning of 'securities').
4   See n 2.
5   *Goblet v Beechey* (1829) 3 Sim 24; on appeal (1831) 2 Russ & M 624; *Clayton v Lord Nugent* (1844) 13 M & W 200 (where donees were described by letters explained by separate card index. The card index was not admitted in evidence, not having been incorporated in the will, though an attempt had been made to do so).
6   See *East v Twyford* (1853) 4 HL Cas 517.
7   *Re Rayner, Rayner v Rayner* [1904] 1 Ch 176 at 178; see para **[50.12]** ante.
8   *Marquis of Camden v IRC* [1914] 1 KB 641; *Shore v Wilson* (1842) 9 CL & Fin 355; *Re Rayner, Rayner v Rayner* [1904] 1 Ch 176.
9   *Re Rayner, Rayner v Rayner* [1904] 1 Ch 176 at 188; *Re Herring, Murray v Herring* [1908] 2 Ch 493 (debenture stock: evidence of practice of company); *Brannigan v Murphy* [1896] 1 IR 418 at 426.
10 *King v Badeley* (1834) 3 My & K 417 (where the court refused to read 'contingent interests' as expectancies); *Shore v Wilson* (1842) 9 Cl & Fin 355 at 558; *Barrow v Methold* (1855) 26 LT 56 ('premium of insurance' used instead of policy and bonus).
11 *O'Donnell v O'Donnell* (1878) 1 LR Ir 284.

[57.6]

Foreign will. If a will is made in a foreign language the court must be furnished with an authenticated translation made by a qualified translator. It is that translation, not the text in the foreign language which is admitted to probate. It is from the document admitted to probate together with any other relevant testamentary instruments that an English court will ascertain the testator's testamentary intentions and determine their effect and validity.[1] Evidence may be admitted to prove (i) the translation of the words; (ii) the technical meaning of the words which are of a technical description or which have a peculiar meaning different from that which, literally translated into English, they would bear; and (iii) any established principle of construction of the particular instrument by the corresponding tribunal in the foreign country in question.[2]

The following guidance has been given, where the will contains foreign elements:[3]

'If a testator, who at all relevant times has been domiciled in England and whose movable property accordingly falls to be distributed in accordance with English law has made a will which, or some part of which, is in a foreign language and perhaps used technical terms inappropriate to English law but appropriate to a foreign system of law, an English court administering his estate must ascertain what the testator intended by ordinary processes of construction, including expert evidence of the meaning and effect of those technical terms in the relevant foreign law and possibly of how a court within that system of foreign law would give effect to that document. The English court in the light of all the admissible evidence will determine what the testator intended and will give effect to that intention so far as it is valid and effectual by English law. In so doing the English court is applying English law and has recourse to evidence of foreign law merely for the purpose of ascertaining the testator's intention. The English court would not refer any question arising on the meaning or effect of the foreign document for decision by a court in the foreign jurisdiction. This would, I think, be the case even if the testator were to provide expressly that any such question must be decided by a court of the foreign jurisdiction. To hold otherwise must, I think, conflict with the English law that the devolution and distribution of the movable property of such a testator shall be governed by the lex domicilii.'

1   Per Sir Denys Buckley in *Re Berger* [1989] 1 All ER 591 at 602.
2   *Mostyn v Fabrigas* (1775) 1 Cowp 161 at 174; *Di Sora v Phillipps* (1863) 10 HL Cas 624 at 633; *Re Fenston's Settlement, Max-Muller v Simonson* [1971] 3 All ER 1092, [1971] 1 WLR 1640 and see para **[57.5]** supra.
3   See n 1, *Re Berger* [1989] 1 All ER 591 at 602.

III.   THE TRADITIONAL RULES APPLICABLE TO DEATHS BEFORE 1983

[57.7]
General rule applied. Though it can be shown by evidence that the intention of the testator was different from that shown by the language of the will, the language of the will, if clear, must prevail and settle the rights of the parties.[1] Where the language of the will is ambiguous, evidence of surrounding circumstances is admitted in order to avoid attributing to the testator a capricious intention.[2]

1   *Higgins v Dawson* [1902] AC 1; followed in *Re Walker* [1973] 1 NZLR 449; *Merchant Taylor's Co v A-G* (1871) 6 Ch App 512 at 519. But see *Haidl v Sacher* (1980) 106 DLR (3d) 360. Evidence is not admitted where the only difficulty is in the construction of the sentence in which the words occur. For instance to decide to which antecedent a relative pronoun refers: *Castledon v Turner* (1745) 3 Atk 257, or to rebut a presumption which arises from the words as words: *Coote v Boyd* (1789) 2 Bro CC 521 at 526. But a gift to A or B where A and B represent persons ascertained by description cannot be construed until the contingency involved by the use of the word 'or' has been resolved: *Re Roberts, Percival v Roberts* [1903] 2 Ch 200 (gift to tenants for life and then for their children or legal representatives. The resolution of this difficulty does not involve the admission of extrinsic evidence). This paragraph of the text was referred to in *Re Laird* [1982] NZLR 325 at 328.
2   *Belaney v Belaney* (1867) 2 Ch App 138; *Hensman v Fryer* (1867) 3 Ch App 420; *Roddy v Fitzgerald* (1858) 6 HL Cas 823 at 876; *Gordon v Gordon* (1871) LR 5 HL 254 at 273; *Leslie v Earl of Rothes* [1894] 2 Ch 499. Where the general intent of the testator in creating an executory trust for a settlement is in question the court is not confined to the language of the will, it may refer to the motives which led to the will, to its general object and purpose collected from instruments to which the will refers, and to any circumstances which may have influenced the mind of the testator: *Sackville-West v Viscount Holmesdale* (1870) LR 4 HL 543.

[57.8]
Evidence of intention excluded. Where the words of the will aided by evidence of material facts (or of intention where admissible)[1] are insufficient to determine

the testator's meaning, no evidence is admissible to explain what the testator intended,[2] and the gift is void for uncertainty.[3]

1   In cases of latent ambiguity; see Chapter 57.
2   *Herbert v Reid* (1810) 16 Ves 481.
3   *Thomas d Evans v Thomas* (1796) 6 Term Rep 671; *Richardson v Watson* (1833) 4 B & Ad 787; *Blundell v Gladstone* (1844) 14 Sim 83; *Drake v Drake* (1860) 8 HL Cas 172; *Asten v Asten* [1894] 3 Ch 260; *Re Stephenson, Donaldson v Bamber* [1897] 1 Ch 75; *Baker v Newton* (1839) 2 Beav 112 (residuary gift to unspecified person); *Yearwood v Yearwood*(1846) 9 Beav 276 (gift to indefinite number).

[57.9]

No variation of terms of will. No evidence can be given in a court of construction in order to complete an incomplete will,[1] or to add to,[2] vary[3] or contradict[4] the terms of the will, or generally to prove any testamentary intentions of the testator not found in the will.[5] Such evidence is not admissible to reconcile two contradictory clauses, and declare which of the two was the testator's real intention.[6] No evidence is admissible to prove any intention or wish of the testator not contained in a duly executed instrument,[7] but undisclosed trusts within the limits imposed by the doctrine affecting them and duly incorporated documents are exceptions to this rule.[8] Where the will is in execution of a power, evidence is admissible as to the property of the testator.'[9]

1   A total blank in a will cannot be filled up: *Baylis and Church v A-G* (1741) 2 Atk 239; *Hunt v Hort* (1791) 3 Bro CC 311; *Taylor v Richardson* (1853) 2 Drew 16. A charitable gift with blanks in it is saved by the *cy-près* doctrine: *Pieschel v Paris* (1825) 2 Sim & St 384.
2   A gift omitted by mistake of the draftsman cannot be the subject of evidence: *Newburgh v Newburgh* (1820) 5 Madd 364; *Selwin v Brown* (1735) 3 Bro Parl Cas 607; *Langston v Langston* (1834) 8 Bli NS 167 at 214.
3   Inadmissible evidence of this class would be directed to changing the name or description of a legatee: *Del Mare v Rebello* (1792) 3 Bro CC 446; *Daubeny v Coghlan* (1842) 12 Sim 507; *Drake v Drake* (1860) 8 HL Cas 172; *Re Ely, Tottenham v Ely* (1891) 65 LT 452; the inclusion of a legatee among those referred to in a condition: *Lord Cheyney's Case* (1591) 5 Co Rep 68a; or by varying the terms of a legacy; *Lowfield v Stoneham* (1746) 2 Stra 1261; or by adding conditions to a legacy: *Lawrence v Dodwell* (1699) 1 Ld Raym 438.
4   *Clementson v Gandy* (1836) 1 Keen 309; *Brown v Langley* (1731) 2 Barn KB 118.
5   *Bertie v Falkland* (1698) 1 Salk 231; *Bennett v Davis* (1725) 2 P Wms 316. Thus in the case of a complete will ie duly executed and attested, no reference can be made to a draft: *Marchuk v Marchuk* (1965) 52 WWR 652.
6   *Re Bywater, Bywater v Clarke* (1881) 18 Ch D 17.
7   *Irvine v Sullivan* (1869) LR 8 Eq 673 at 678; *Briggs v Penny* (1849) 3 De G & Sm 525; on appeal (1851) 3 Mac & G 546. A document expressly directed not to form part of a will and excluded from probate was refused consideration by the court of construction: *Re Louis, Louis v Treloar* (1916) 32 TLR 313. A gift on the trusts of a deed which has never become operative fails: *Re Hurdle, Blakeney v Hurdle* [1936] 3 All ER 810.
8   See Chapter 36, as to secret trusts, and Chapter 15, as to incorporation documents.
9   See Chapter 39.

[57.10]

Incorporation of unattested documents. Evidence can be given of a document duly incorporated in a will, though unattested.[1] Except in the case of duly incorporated documents and evidence of secret trusts,[2] no evidence of any instrument not duly attested as a will or codicil or of any oral disposition can be given,[3] except to explain a latent ambiguity.[4]

1   See Chapter 15, where the conditions of such incorporation are stated.
2   See Chapter 36.
3   *Johnson v Ball* (1851) 5 De G & Sm 85 at 91; *Re Fane, Fane v Fane* (1886) 2 TLR 510; *Re Hyslop, Hyslop v Chamberlain* [1894] 3 Ch 522, *Re Walsh, Keenan v Brown* (1911) 30 NZLR 1166; *Re Keen, Evershed v Griffiths* [1937] Ch 236, [1937] 1 All ER 452; *Re Cooper, Le Neve Foster v National Provincial Bank Ltd* [1939] Ch 580, [1939] 2 All ER 192; *Re Jones, Jones v Jones* [1942] Ch 328, [1942] 1 All ER 642; *Re Edwards' Will Trusts, Dalgleish v Leighton* [1948] Ch 440, [1948] 1 All ER 821.
4   *Dillon v Harris* (1830) 4 Bli NS 321; *Re Battie-Wrightson, Cecil v Battie-Wrightson* [1920] 2 Ch 330; *Re White, Knight v Briggs* [1925] Ch 179; and see para **[57.19]** infra.

IV.   EVIDENCE FOR THE PURPOSE OF IDENTIFICATION OF PERSONS OR THINGS: DEATHS BEFORE 1983

[57.11]

Facts and circumstances of family, etc. Since the words of a will necessarily refer to facts and circumstances respecting the testator's property and his family and similar matters, the meaning and application of his words cannot be ascertained without evidence of such facts and circumstances.[1] Such evidence is therefore necessarily admissible so far as it corresponds to the facts and circumstances referred to in the will.[2] Such evidence is that adduced to show the persons and property referred to in the will, but it is admissible only after it is shown that the words of the will are insufficient for its proper construction.[3]

1   *Doe d Hiscocks v Hiscocks* (1839) 5 M & W 363 at 367; *Anstee v Nelms* (1856) 1 H & N 225; *Charter v Charter* (1874) LR 7 HL 364; *Doe d Le Chevalier v Huthwaite* (1820) 3 B & Ald 632 (state of family inquired into to identify donee); *Re Gregson's Trusts* (1864) 2 Hem & M 504 (donees described by surname only); *Re Ingle's Trusts* (1871) LR 11 Eq 578 (donee stated to be dead but in fact alive); *Re Heidenreich, Cole v Heidenreich* [1981] 27 SASR 455. *Charter v Charter* (1874) LR 7 HL 364 was applied in *Layer v Burn Philp Trustee Co Ltd* (1986) 6 NSWLR 60. See also *Re Allen* [1988] 1 Qd R 1; *Re Clinton* [1988] ILRM 80 and *Kernahan v Hanson* (1990) 73 DLR (4th) 286: where the will is unambiguous no extrinsic evidence is admissible.
2   *Sherratt v Mountford* (1873) 8 Ch App 928 at 929; *Sanford v Raikes* (1816) 1 Mer 646 at 653 (subject of gift described by reference to an extrinsic fact, evidence of that fact must be received to ascertain the subject of the gift); *Doe d Preedy v Holtom* (1835) 4 Ad & El 76 at 82; *Hedges v Aldworth* (1851) 13 I Eq R 406.
3   *Re Seal, Seal v Taylor* [1894] 1 Ch 316 at 322, 323. The words of the will must be construed first and then the extrinsic evidence is looked at to see whether there is anything which the words of the will fit.

[57.12]

Words generally insensible. Where the words of the will are insensible and have no reasonable application to the circumstances proved, further evidence is admitted to discover a meaning of the words so that the will may have effect.[1]

1   *Doe d Hiscocks v Hiscocks* (1839) 5 M & W 363 at 368; *Re Glassington, Glassington v Follett* [1906] 2 Ch 305; *Re Ray, Cant v Johnstone* [1916] 1 Ch 461; *Re Vear, Vear v Vear* (1917) 62 Sol Jo 159. In *Robertson v Flynn* [1920] 1 IR 78, the instructions for the will were referred to.

[57.13]

Evidence admissible. For the purpose of ascertaining the object of the testator's bounty, or the subject of the disposition, or the quantity of interest given, or the persons or things described by the will, and the facts and circumstances there referred to, a court of construction must[1] inquire into every material particular relating to the person or things said to be identified by that description.[2]

1   *Anstee v Nelms* (1856) 1 H & N 225 at 232.
2   *Doe d Le Chevalier v Huthwaite* (1820) 3 B & Ald 632 (suggested mistake in name of beneficiary); *Doe d Gore v Langton* (1831) 2 B & Ad 680; *Dashwood v Magniac* [1891] 3 Ch 306; *Bunbury v Doran* (1874) IR 8 CL 516. Such evidence included earlier wills in *Re Tetsall, Foyster v Testall* [1961] 2 All ER 801.

[57.14]
Evidence of testator's knowledge—arm-chair rule. For the purposes stated in the immediately preceding paragraph evidence is received which will enable the court to ascertain all the persons and facts known to the testator at the time when he made his will[1] and thus to place itself in the testator's position – or, as it is said, in the testator's arm-chair.[2] This rule cannot apply where the subject-matter of the gift was not in existence at the date of the will.[3] Evidence of this nature is closely related to evidence of the testator's intention which is inadmissible, except in the case of a latent ambiguity.[4] The distinction is that the court, having arrived at a conclusion of the testator's intention from the words of the will, requires this evidence to assure itself that such conclusion is in accordance with the circumstances by which he was surrounded at the time when he made that will.[5]

1   *Thomson and Baxter v Hempenstall* (1849) 1 Rob Eccl 783; *Grant v Grant* (1870) LR 5 CP 727; *Kingsbury v Walter* [1901] AC 187; *Re Thomas, Smith v Thomas* (1915) 34 NZLR 1110 (knowledge of boundary of property). As to circumstances when will made, see *Beaumont v Fell* (1723) 2 P Wms 141; *Re De Rosaz's Goods* (1877) 2 PD 66 (identity of executor).
2   *Boyes v Cook* (1880) 14 Ch D 53 at 56; *Clifford v Koe* (1880) 5 App Cas 447 at 462; *Fitzgerald v Ryan* [1899] 2 IR 637 at 658; *Re Vaughan, Scott v British and Foreign School Society* (1901) 17 TLR 278; *Re Sykes, Sykes v Sykes* [1909] 2 Ch 241 at 251; *Re Wills, Wills v Wills* [1909] 1 IR 268 at 276; *Robertson v Flynn* [1920] 1 IR 78. See also *Re Overhill's Trusts* (1853) 1 Sm & G 362 at 366; *Kingsbury v Walter* [1901] AC 187; *Re Eve, Edwards v Burns* [1909] 1 Ch 796 at 799; *Gibbs, Martin v Harding* [1907] 1 Ch 465 at 469; *Re Langley, Sissons v Public Trustee* [1972] NZLR 218; *Ng Chi-fong v Hui Ho Pui-fun* [1987] HKLR 462 at 472 where the text is referred to.
3   *Re Price, Price v Newton* [1905] 2 Ch 55.
4   See Chapter 57; and see *Re Byrne's Will, Byrne v Byrne* (1898) 24 VLR 832; *St Hill v St Hill* (1906) 26 NZLR 1105; *Free Church of Scotland Trustees v Maitland* (1887) 14 R 333.
5   *Blackwell v Pennant* (1852) 9 Hare 551 at 552.

[57.15]
Testator's knowledge of particular matters. The following are examples of the items of knowledge on the part of the testator which have been considered material and of which extrinsic evidence has been received. His knowledge of persons having a certain Christian name[1] or surname,[2] or even just the name of a person.[3] His knowledge that a person who might take under the description of the donee was dead at the time when he made his will.[4] His knowledge of the state of his own family or some other family.[5] His knowledge of the fact that one member of a family was amply provided for, as showing a good reason for making a disposition excepting that member.[6] Evidence of the testator's knowledge of or friendship with a person alleged to be the donee or of his intimacy with such persons has been admitted.[7] Similarly, evidence of the

manner in which the testator practised his faith so as to give meaning to the phrase 'Jewish faith' in his will.[8]

1   *Re De Rosaz's Goods* (1877) 2 PD 66 (where the surname was omitted).
2   *Re Gregson's Trusts* (1864) 2 Hem & M 504 (where the Christian name was omitted); *Gregory v Smith* (1852) 9 Hare 708.
3   *Bradshaw v Bradshaw* (1836) 2 Y & C Ex 72; *Lord Camoys v Blundell* (1848) 1 HL Cas 778.
4   *Re Whorwood, Ogle v Lord Sherborne* (1887) 34 Ch D 446 at 450; *Stringer v Gardiner* (1859) 4 De G & J 468; *Re Walker* [1924] 1 DLR 719; *Re Perry* [1941] 2 DLR 690.
5   *Doe d Thomas v Benyon* (1840) 12 Ad & El 431; *Goodinge v Goodinge* (1749) 1 Ves Sen 231; *Re Gregory's Settlement and Will* (1865) 34 Beav 600; *Re Taylor, Cloak v Hammond* (1886) 34 Ch D 255; *Re Fowler* [1963] VR 639 (testator's knowledge that beneficiary was unmarried).
6   *Hodgson v Clarke* (1860) 1 De GF & J 394. It has been said that the knowledge of a cousin's or remoter relative's family is not presumed: *Crook v Whitley* (1857) 7 De GM & G 490 at 496; *Re Herbet's Trusts* (1860) 1 John & H 121.
7   *Careless v Careless* (1816) 1 Mer 384 (two nephews of same name); *King's College Hospital v Wheildon* (1854) 18 Beav 30 (charitable bequest); *Re Feltham's Will Trusts* (1855) 1 K & J 528 (where there was a misdescription); *Re Gregory's Settlement and Will* (1865) 34 Beav 600 (where one claimant was testator's godson); *Re Noble's Trusts* (1870) IR 5 Eq 140 (misnomer); *Phelan v Slattery* (1887) 19 LR Ir 177 ('my nephew' where more than one); *Re Wyatt, Furniss v Phear* (1888) 36 WR 521 (blanks in description of legatee); *Re Twohill's Goods* (1879) 3 LR Ir 21 (misnomer of executor); *Re Brake's Goods* (1881) 6 PD 217 (misnomer of executor); *Re Chappell's Goods* [1894] P 98 (address partly in error); *Re Beale, Beale v Royal Hospital for Incurables* (1890) 6 TLR 308 (misdescription of charity); *Re Jeffrey, Nussey v Jeffrey* [1914] 1 Ch 375 (reference to 'daughter' where there were several daughters).
8   *Re Tepper's Will Trusts, Kramer v Ruda* [1987] Ch 358, [1987] 1 All ER 970. But is this evidence of circumstance or of intention? The testator died in 1959 and thus the 1982 Act provisions were not applicable.

[57.16]
Evidence of mistake. Evidence is not admissible in a court of construction directly to prove a mistake in a will in describing property or a donee,[1] but where on the face of the will it is clear that there is a mistake, evidence of surrounding circumstances[2] is admissible to prove how the mistake arose in order to identify the true object.[3]

1   See Chapter 5, para **[5.6]** et seq.
2   *Re Ray, Cant v Johnstone* [1916] 1 Ch 461; *Re Nicholl, Re Perkins, Nicholl v Perkins* (1920) 125 LT 62. Evidence that a name has been changed or omitted by the draftsman is inadmissible.
3   *Lindgren v Lindgren* (1846) 9 Beav 358; *Findlater v Lowe* [1904] 1 IR 519; *Re Perry* [1941] 2 DLR 690 (where, unless there was a mistake as to the brother named, there would have been a lapse of which the testator would have been aware); *Re Bowen* [1965] VR 113; *Re Skinner* [1965] VR 660.

[57.17]
Habits of the testator. The following are examples of this kind of evidence: the habit of the testator to call a person by a nickname[1] or other name by which he was not usually known,[2] but by which he is described in the will.[3] Similarly, property may be shown to be described by a name which the testator commonly used with regard to it and that he thought that an accurate description of it.[4] However, the limits of this admissibility must be noted. It has been said[5] that it is one thing to adduce evidence of the surrounding circumstances in which a will was made, or to adduce evidence of the habitual sense in which a testator used particular words, but quite another thing to adduce evidence that when the testator came to make his will he then stated that he was using a word in a

particular sense, or accepted the view of somebody else that the words held that special sense.

1   *Edge v Salisbury* (1749) Amb 70; *Goodinge v Goodinge* (1749) 1 Ves Sen 231; *Dowset v Sweet* (1753) Amb 175.
2   *Mostyn v Mostyn* (1854) 5 HL Cas 155 at 168; *Re Feltham's Will Trusts* (1855) 1 K & J 528; *Lee v Pain* (1845) 4 Hare 201; *Andrews v Andrews* (1885) 15 LR Ir 199; *Re Ofner, Samuel v Ofner* [1909] 1 Ch 60. Such names in a will must be explained in the same way as a will written in a foreign language; *Doe d Hiscocks v Hiscocks* (1839) 5 M & W 363 at 368. See also *Re Holosko's Will, Patrick and Patek v Hanewich* (1968) 63 WWR 125, where evidence of a foreign language was admitted to show that 'sisters' meant first cousins. This type of evidence should not be relied upon where there is sufficient evidence of other circumstances to make the will intelligible: *Lord Camoys v Blundell* (1848) 1 HL Cas 778 at 785.
3   For pre-1970 cases concerning the habitual reference to illegitimate children as children, see *Laker v Hordern* (1876) 1 Ch D 644; *Ellis v Houston* (1878) 10 Ch D 236. Wills made on or after 1 January 1970 are governed by the Family Law Reform Act 1969, s 15. See now the Family Law Reform Act 1987, ss 1 and 19 replacing the Family Law Reform Act 1969, s 15 with effect from 4 April 1988. See Vol 2, Part E; see Chapter 72.
4   *Doe d Beach v Earl of Jersey* (1825) 3 B & C 870; *Ricketts v Turquand* (1848) 1 HL Cas 472; *Webb v Byng* (1855) 1 K & J 580; *Castle v Fox* (1871) LR 11 Eq 542; *Jennings v Jennings* (1877) 1 LR Ir 552; *Re Vear, Vear v Vear* (1917) 62 Sol Jo 159.
5   Per Megarry V-C in *Re Atkinson's Hill Trusts, Atkinson v Hall* [1978] 1 All ER 1275 at 1278, [1978] 1 WLR 586 at 590, evidence to show that worthy causes meant charitable causes excluded.

[57.18]
Exclusion of further evidence except in case of latent ambiguity. When the result of the admission of such evidence is to discover a donee who or property which is not only within the words of the will but exhausts them, the court accepts that interpretation and no further evidence is admissible,[1] unless it is shown that another interpretation also exhausts the words.[2] In such a case there is a latent ambiguity, often described as an equivocation.[3] Evidence of the mere improbability that the 'testator intended to benefit certain persons is not admitted unless it is first proved that there are other persons who could take under the description.[4] Where, after the admission of the evidence of the material circumstances, the language of the testator remains obscure or ambiguous then, except in the case of a latent ambiguity,[5] no further evidence is admitted (whether of the testator's intention, or of a mistake in description or in the copying of the will or otherwise) and the gift is void for uncertainty.[6]

Thus, declarations by the testator as to the persons or property he meant to include under a particular description, or expressions of testamentary intentions in favour of particular person who might be so described, are inadmissible.[7] In a court of probate, however, such evidence was admissible in a doubtful or ambiguous case.

1   *Webb v Byng* (1855) 1 K & J 580 at 585; *Re Millar, Barnard v Mahoney* (1898) 17 NZLR 160.
2   *Sherratt v Mountford* (1873) 8 Ch App 928.
3   See para **[57.21]** infra. The term 'equivocation' seems to be falling into disuse, though still occasionally found in reports.
4   *Sherratt v Mountford* (1873) 8 Ch App 928 at 931.
5   See n 3.
6   *Doe d Hayter v Joinville* (1802) 3 East 172; *Drake v Drake* (1860) 8 HL Cas 172; *Richardson v Watson* (1833) 4 B & Ad 787; *Sullivan v Sullivan* (1870) IR 4 Eq 457; *Re Stephenson, Donaldson v Bamber* [1897] 1 Ch 75; *Re Livingston, Irving v Irving* [1923] SASR 387. But where the gift shows a general charitable intention, the gift may be administered *cy-près:*

Re Clergy Society (1856) 2 K & J 615; *Re Bateman, Wallace v Mawdsley* (1911) 27 TLR 313.

7   *Doe d Hiscocks v Hiscocks* (1839) 5 M & W 363; *Martin v Drinkwater* (1840) 2 Beav 215; *Douglas v Fellows* (1835) Kay 114; *Bernasconi v Atkinson* (1853) 10 Hare 345; *Drake v Drake* (1860) 8 HL Cas 172; *Sullivan v Sullivan* (1870) IR 4 Eq 457; *Re Ely, Tottenham v Ely* (1891) 65 LT 452; *Re Whorwood; Ogle v Lord Sherborne* (1887) 34 Ch D 446; *Re Cheadle, Bishop v Holt* [1900] 2 Ch 620; *M'Hugh v M'Hugh* [1908] 1 IR 155; *Re Fleck* (1923) 55 OLR 441.

V.   AMBIGUITIES: DEATHS BEFORE 1983

[57.19]
Words of will unambiguous. Where the words of the will are not on the face of them ambiguous, the court will not admit any further evidence unless it appears that that evidence will show that the words were in fact ambiguous when applied to the facts of the particular case.[1] In such a case the evidence may or may not prove an ambiguity. If it does, further evidence is admissible to resolve the ambiguity.[2] If it does not, then no further evidence is admissible.[3] Where it is not shown that the words equally, or with a negligible variation, be applicable to some other subject-matter, no further evidence is admissible[4] whether it be to show that the testator meant some person or property different from that to which his words plainly and unambiguously refer, such as evidence of the testator's fuller knowledge of or intimacy with other persons,[5] or his want of knowledge of the person so described,[6] or his habit of describing any other person in the same terms;[7] or the state of value generally of the testator's property[8] where the will itself does not make the state or value of importance;[9] or his knowledge or management,[10] or the history,[11] of the property or any part of it; or the testator's habits of describing other property in the same terms.[12]

1   *Josiak v Setler* (1971) 16 DLR (3d) 490, where a non-testamentary document was not admissible as extrinsic evidence because no ambiguity had been shown; see also *Re Cargill* (1977) 79 DLR (3d) 726. As soon as it is shown that such evidence may be material, it is generally admitted reserving the question of its materiality: *Sayer v Sayer* (1849) 7 Hare 377 at 381. But where there is a donee perfectly described in the will, that donee takes, see Chapter 58.

2   If there are existing persons or things which fit the words of the will, no evidence is needed or admissible: *Horwood v Griffith* (1853) 4 De GM & G 700 at 708; *Millard v Bailey* (1866) LR 1 Eq 378; *Re Seal, Seal v Taylor* [1894] 1 Ch 316; *Re Trimmer v Crundwell v Trimmer* (1904) 91 LT 26; *Re Livingston, Irving v Irving* [1923] SASR 387. The fact that there is no person or thing fitting the words does not necessarily make evidence admissible, for the testator may have made the gift not knowing or caring whether any such persons existed: *Del Mare v Rebello* (1792) 1 Ves 412 (gift to children of a woman who was a nun); *Daubeny v Coghlan* (1842) 12 Sim 507 at 518. These, however, are exceptional cases. The fact that the descriptions fit more persons than one does not let in evidence if it is clear which one is intended: *Doe d Westlake v Westlake* (1820) 4 B & Ald 57. Where a legatee is once correctly described, and the same name is mentioned again, evidence is not admissible to show that a different person is intended: *Webber v Corbett* (1873) LR 16 Eq 515. Where there is a legitimate and an illegitimate person of the same name, no evidence was admissible to prove the latter is to take: *Re Fish, Ingham v Rayner* [1894] 2 Ch 83; *Re Jackson, Beattie v Murphy* [1933] Ch 237; but the court received evidence where one illegitimate nephew claimed against two legitimate nephews: *Re Jackson, Beattie v Murphy*; see now Family Law Reform Act 1987, ss 1 and 19, replacing the Family Law Reform Act 1969, s 15 with effect from 4 April 1988; 6 *Halsbury's Statutes* (4th edn), 354, 356, Vol 2, Part G, paras **[245.70]**, **[245.72]**; and see Chapter 72.

3   *Shore v Wilson* (1842) 9 Cl & Fin 355 at 365; *Re Overhill's Trusts* (1853) 1 Sm & G 362 at 366; *Re Hurring* [1950] NZLR 948; *Hulks v Wills* (1949) 50 SRNSW 74.

4   *Sherratt v Mountford* (1873) 8 Ch App 928 (the only safe rule is that when persons have been found sufficiently answering the description in the will, the court goes no further unless it is

shown that there is another class of persons also sufficiently answering the description, in which case the court goes on to receive further evidence as to which of the two classes was intended).

5   *Holmes v Custance* (1806) 12 Ves 279; *Wilson v Squire* (1842) 1 Y & C Ch Cas 654.

6   *Re Corsellis, Freeborn v Napper* [1906] 2 Ch 316.

7   *Green v Howard* (1779) 1 Bro CC 31; *Ellis v Houston* (1878) 10 Ch D 236 at 245; *Re Parker, Bentham v Wilson* (1881) 17 Ch D 262; *Re Fish, Ingham v Rayner* [1894] 2 Ch 83.

8   *Hensman v Fryer* (1867) 3 Ch App 420 at 424; *Re Grainger, Dawson v Higgins* [1900] 2 Ch 756 at 768.

9   Such evidence is admissible where the words of the will are unintelligible without it: *Colpoys v Colpoys* (1822) Jac 451; *Boys v Williams* (1831) 2 Russ & M 689; *Hensman v Fryer* (1867) 3 Ch App 420; *Watson v Arundell* (1876) IR 11 Eq 53 at 75. The testator may make gifts by reference to the amount of his property: *Barksdale v Gilliat* (1818) 1 Swan 562; *Druce v Denison* (1801) 6 Ves 385; *Re Skillen, Charles v Charles* [1916] 1 Ch 518 (to explain a gift of 'money'); *Grealey v Sampson* [1917] 1 IR 286 (evidence not admissible where the question was one of construction only).

10 *Doe d Preedy v Holtom* (1835) 4 Ad & El 76; *Horwood v Griffith* (1853) 4 De GM & G 700 at 708. The rule applies where property is described by its local situation: *Doe d Browne v Greening* (1814) 3 M & S 171; *Doe d Tyrell v Lyford* (1816) 4 M & S 550 at 555; *Doe d Templeman v Martin* (1833) 4 B & Ad 771; *Miller v Travers* (1832) 8 Bing 244; *Homer v Homer* (1878) 8 Ch D 758 at 774.

11 *Millard v Bailey* (1866) LR 1 Eq 378.

12 *Doe d Oxenden v Chichester* (1816) 4 Dow 65; *Evans v Angell* (1858) 26 Beav 202 at 207; *King v King* (1885) 13 LR Ir 531; *Re Vear, Vear v Vear* (1917) 62 Sol Jo 159.

[57.20]

Words of will ambiguous. Where, after the admission of the evidence of the material circumstances, the language of the testator remains obscure or ambiguous, then, except in the case of a latent ambiguity,[1] no further evidence is admitted[2] (whether of the testator's intention, or of a mistake in description or in the copying of the will or otherwise) and the gift is void for uncertainty.[3] Thus, declarations by the testator as to the persons or property he meant to include under a particular description, or expressions of testamentary intentions in favour of particular persons who might be so described, are inadmissible.[4]

1   See para [57.19] supra.

2   *Sherratt v Mountford* (1873) 8 Ch App 928 at 931.

3   See the cases in para [57.19], n 6.

4   See the cases in para [57.19], n 7.

[57.21]

Latent ambiguity or equivocation. Where a latent ambiguity is shown and evidence of the surrounding circumstances is insufficient to resolve the ambiguity, then evidence has been admitted to prove the testator's declaration as to which of the persons or things was meant by him.[1] A latent ambiguity in this sense arises when the description in the will, considered in the light of the context, is on the face of it apt to describe and determine, unambiguously and without obscurity at the time when the subject is to be ascertained,[2] any of two or more different subjects, either accurately,[3] or subject to inaccuracies which are blanks in the description or which have to be rejected as a false description not applying to anyone[4] or are otherwise negligible.[5] There is no latent ambiguity where part of the description applies to one subject and another part to another subject,[6] or in cases where from the context of the whole will,[7] or by the aid of any canon of construction applicable to the will,[8] or from the circumstances of the case properly admissible in evidence,[9] it can be gathered which of the different subjects was intended. Nor is there a latent ambiguity where the description is on the face of it indefinite, and not apt to determine any subject, eg a devise to one of the sons of a named person who has more than one son. In such cases no evidence is admissible to resolve the patent ambiguity.[10] The declarations of the testator which are admissible in the case of a latent ambiguity may be contemporaneous with the making of the will or prior to or subsequent to that date, but the weight to be given to them varies according to the time and the circumstances in which they are made.[11] If no such evidence is available to resolve the latent ambiguity, the gift is void.[12]

1 Such evidence is called evidence of intention; *Doe d Morgan v Morgan* (1832) 1 Cr & M 235; *Doe d Gord v Needs* (1836) 2 M & W 129; *Fleming v Fleming* (1862) 1 H & C 242; *Phelan v Slattery* (1887) 19 LR Ir 177; *Re Jeffrey, Nussey v Jeffrey* [1914] 1 Ch 375; *Re Mayo, Chester v Keirl* [1901] 1 Ch 404 at 406; *Re Battie-Wrightson, Cecil v Battie-Wrightson* [1920] 2 Ch 330; *Re Dear* [1975] 2 NZLR 254.

2 As to time when property has to be ascertained, see Chapter 60, and as to time when persons have to be ascertained, see Chapter 65. It has been held that where a donee is described by name and there has been a person in existence known to the testator answering to the exact description of the donee, while at the date of the will or the death of the testator there is no such person, evidence is admissible to prove not only the testator's intimacy with a person who exists and to whom a sufficient part of the description is applicable, but even his intention to make the gift to that person: *Re Halston, Ewen v Halston* [1912] 1 Ch 435, not following *Re Ely, Tottenham v Ely* (1891) 65 LT 452; see also *Re Ofner, Samuel v Ofner* [1909] 1 Ch 60 at 63 and *Re Mayo, Chester v Keirl* [1901] 1 Ch 404 at 406.

3 Where the person is described by a Christian name and two persons are found, one having that name only, and the other having that name with others, this has been treated as an accurate description under this rule, and an equivocation has been held to arise: *Bennett v Marshall* (1856) 2 K & J 740; *Re Wolverton Mortgaged Estates* (1877) 7 Ch D 197 at 199, where, however, the decision is also sufficiently grounded on evidence of material circumstances. See also *Re Halston, Ewen v Halston* [1912] 1 Ch 435. Where two persons fit the description, no evidence is admissible that any other person who does not fully correspond with the description is the donee: *Re Millar, Barnard v Mahoney* (1898) 17 NZLR 160; *Re Carson* [1956] St R Qd 466. In *Re Alexander's Will Trust* [1948] 2 All ER 111, there was but one object to satisfy two bequests framed in different terms. Evidence was admitted. *Paykel v Guardian Trust and Executors Co of New Zealand Ltd* [1963] NZLR 168 (it is not sufficient that the language employed is inaccurate or its meaning doubtful, followed in *Re Jones* [1971] NZLR 796 (evidence admitted).

4 *Price v Page* (1799) 4 Ves 680 (blank); *McMurray v Dilworth, Re Dilworth* (1904) 22 NZLR 125 (plan said to be annexed, not annexed); *Still v Hoste* (1821) 6 Madd 192 (name wrong); *Careless v Careless* (1816) 1 Mer 384 ('to Robert C my nephew son of Joseph C', when the testator had two nephews of the name of Robert, but no brother Joseph). The decisions in these three cases are explained in *Doe d Hiscocks v Hiscocks* (1839) 5 M & W 363 at 370. See also *Garner v Garner* (1860) 29 Beav 114; *Re Hubbuck's Estate* [1905] P 129; *Re Ray, Cant v Johnstone* [1916] 1 Ch 461; *Re Walker Hanewich* (1968) 63 WWR 125 (gift to 'my sisters'; testator had no sisters but evidence admitted that first cousins intended); *Re Newman* [1967] VR 201. Where the amounts of legacies were left blank, no evidence was admissible: *Kennedy v Kelly* (1862) 14 Ir Jur 326; but such blanks where there is no residuary gift may result in the legatees taking the whole in equal shares: see para **[52.7]**, n 5.

5 *Henderson v Henderson* [1905] 1 IR 353 (inaccuracy as understood by the testator); *Re Taylor, Taylor v Baker* [1931] NZLR 352.

6 *Doe d Hiscocks v Hiscocks* (1839) 5 M & W 363; *Bernasconi v Atkinson* (1853) 10 Hare 345 at 348, 349; *Charter v Charter* (1874) LR 7 HL 364; *Re Chappell's Goods* [1894] P 98; *Re Ray, Cant v Johnstone* [1916] 1 Ch 461; *Re Linklater, Trustees and Executors Agency Co Ltd v Laidlaw* [1926] VLR 456; *Re James* [1965] VR 569.

7 *Doe d Westlake v Westlake* (1820) 4 B & Ald 57 (to MW by brother and SW my brother's son, there being two persons SW, sons of brothers of the testator. It was held that it was clear that the son of MW was the person to take).

8 In *Webber v Corbett* (1873) LR 16 Eq 515, one of the persons was described clearly in another part of the will, and the presumption as to repeated words (see para **[54.5]** supra) was applied:

cf *Healy v Healy* (1875) IR 9 Eq 418. In *Doe d Morgan v Morgan* (1832) 1 Cr & M 235, a similar case, this presumption was not alluded to, and evidence of intention was admitted; and in *Phelan v Slattery* (1887) 19 LR Ir 177, it was excluded by the context, and evidence of intention was admitted. In *Re Fish, Ingham v Rayner* [1894] 2 Ch 83, one of the persons claiming was illegitimate; the presumption as to legitimacy (see Chapter 72) was applied, and evidence of intention was excluded; but see *Re Jackson, Beattie v Murphy* [1933] Ch 237; and *Re Fleming, McNamara v Fleming* [1963] VR 17 (where the question arose between a son and a stepson). In *Re Ashton's Goods* [1892] P 83, this presumption was excluded by the terms of the will; the description was accordingly held applicable to both the legitimate and illegitimate claimants, and evidence of intention was held admissible, see now Family Law Reform Act 1987, ss 1 and 19, replacing the Family Law Reform Act 1969, s 15 with effect from 4 April 1988; 6 *Halsbury's Statutes* (4th edn) 354, 356; Vol 2, Part G, para **[245.70]**. In *Wells v Wells* (1874) LR 18 Eq 504 at 506, and in *Merrill v Morton* (1881) 17 Ch D 382 at 386, the decision in *Grant v Grant* (1870) LR 5 CP 380, was dissented from on the question of the meaning of 'nephew' on the ground that it was not given its ordinary meaning.

9   *Douglas v Fellows* (1853) Kay 114 at 120, citing *Fox v Collins* (1761) 2 Eden 107 (bequest to said A where the will had already mentioned two of the names mentioned); *Healy v Healy* (1875) IR 9 Eq 418 (court must be satisfied that ambiguity cannot be removed by application of ordinary rules); *Re Cheadle, Bishop v Holt* [1900] 2 Ch 620 (bequest of 'my 140 shares' where testatrix had 240 partly paid and 40 fully paid shares).

10   *Sir Litton Strode v Lady Russel* (1707) 2 Vern 621 at 624. See *Re Hubbuck's Estate* [1905] P 129; and *Re Morris, Lloyds Bank Ltd v Peake* [1971] P 62 at 82, [1970] 1 All ER 1057 at 1068, per Latey J.

11   *Doe d Allen v Allen* (1840) 12 Ad & El 451 at 455; and see *Price v Page* (1799) 4 Ves 680; *Langham v Sanford* (1816) 19 Ves 641 at 649; *Dwyer v Lysaght* (1812) 2 Ball & B 156 at 162; *Doe d Gord v Needs* (1836) 2 M & W 129; *Charter v Charter* (1874) LR 7 HL 364; *Re Halston, Ewen v Halston* [1912] 1 Ch 435; *Re Taylor, Cloak v Hammond* (1886) 34 Ch D 255. Such evidence may include a revoked will: *Re Nesbitt's Will Trusts, Dr Barnardo's Homes National Inc Association v United Newcastle-upon-Tyne Hospitals Board of Governors* [1953] 1 All ER 936, [1953] 1 WLR 595.

12   *Re Jackson, Beattie v Murphy* [1933] Ch 237 at 242; *Re Evans* [1950] VLR 60.

VI.   THE ADMISSIBILITY OF EXTRINSIC EVIDENCE: POST-1982 DEATHS

[57.22]
The Administration of Justice Act 1982 (AJA 1982). The admissibility of extrinsic evidence to aid the interpretation of the wills of testators who die on or after 1 January 1983 is governed by the provisions in the Administration of Justice Act 1982, s 21.[1] The section lays down general rules which are, presumably, intended to constitute a comprehensive list of the circumstances in which extrinsic evidence can be looked at to resolve difficulties of interpretation.[2] However, where extrinsic evidence is admissible under the general law which goes beyond that permitted by the section, as for example with reference to the equitable presumptions,[3] then there seems no reason why such evidence should not continue to be admissible.

The section provides that extrinsic evidence, including evidence of the testator's intention, may be admitted to assist in the interpretation of a will in three situations, as follows:

'(a) in so far as the language of any part of it [ie *the will*] is meaningless;
(b) in so far as the language used in any part of it is ambiguous on the face of it;
(c) in so far as evidence, other than evidence of the testator's intention, shows that the language used in any part of it is ambiguous in the light of surrounding circumstances'.

Under the case law extrinsic evidence other than evidence of the testator's intention was admissible in the circumstances specified in all three paragraphs, but evidence of the testator's intention was never admissible in the circumstances specified in paragraphs (a) and (b), and was only sometimes admissible in the circumstances specified in para (c).[4] Each of the three paragraphs will be considered in turn.

1   50 *Halsbury's Statutes* (4th edn) 616. See Vol 2, Part G, para [244.97]; the commencement provisions are the AJA 1982, s 73(6); and s 76(11).
2   The section implements the majority recommendations of the Law Reform Committees 19th Report on the Interpretation of Wills (1973) Cmnd 5301.
3   See para [57.23] infra.
4   The Administration of Justice Act 1982, s 21 has been considered in two unreported cases in which divergent views have been expressed as to the circumstances in which extrinsic evidence of intention is admissible. In *Re Freeman's Will Trusts* (10 July 1987, unreported), ChD, Sir Nicolas Browne-Wilkinson V-C rejected the submission that the section could only apply in a case where it would be impossible otherwise to decide the meaning of the will and expressed the view that extrinsic evidence of intention was admissible both under the old law and under the statute not only in cases where it was otherwise impossible to determine the testator's intention but also in cases where it was difficult to do so. By contrast Millett J in *Cook v Saxlova* (18 October 1988, unreported), ChD, expressed the view that the admissibility of extrinsic evidence of intention under the AJA 1982 (as under the former law) did not depend on the difficulty of the question to be answered; nor was it enough that the language used might be capable of more than one meaning or that it might be differently construed by different judges. It was essential in his view that the language of the will 'must still have more than one meaning after the process of construction is complete'. (The decision of Millett J was reversed on appeal, but the issue as to the admissibility of extrinsic evidence of intention was not considered by the Court of Appeal.) It is submitted that the views expressed by Millett J in *Cook v Saxlova* are in accordance with the cases under the former law (see, eg, *Re Cheadle, Bishop v Holt* [1900] 2 Ch 620, CA), none of which appear to have been cited to the Vice-Chancellor in *Re Freeman*. There remains a possibility, however, that a more liberal approach to the construction of s 21 might still be adopted by the courts on the basis that the old law has been superseded: see the cases referred to in para [57.24], nn 1 and 2 and *Watson v National Children's Homes* [1995] 37 LS Gaz R 24.

[57.23]
'Any part of it is meaningless' (para (a)). The case law and textbook learning on the extrinsic evidence rules does not in terms refer to meaningless as a category of case in which extrinsic evidence is admissible, whereas paras (b) and (c) of the AJA 1982, s 21(1) are immediately recognisable as resembling categories to be found in the existing law. Paragraph (a) was presumably added because there might be cases where an expression was unintelligible but not really capable of being characterised as ambiguous (the term used in paras (b) and (c)).

It might be questioned whether an expression which really was meaningless could ever become less so by reference to extrinsic evidence, but it seems that what is referred to by para (a) is any part of a will which is meaningless when the will is taken by itself, before any regard is had to extrinsic evidence. Thus the cases which would in practice come under this heading would mostly be ones where an expression unintelligible as ordinary English can be elucidated as some technical or personal linguistic usage of the testator.[1]

It may also be that vague expressions such as 'Ashford Hall Estate'[2] or 'my old pals' could be classified under paragraph (a) of the AJA 1982, s 21(1), although these could perhaps be thought of as ambiguous rather than meaningless.

Extrinsic evidence other than direct evidence of the testator's intention was admissible under the general law to assist in the construction of apparently meaningless expressions before this section came into force, and what is new about the section in relation to para (a) cases is that it admits evidence of the testator's intention. It remains to be seen how much difference the admission of evidence of the testator's intention will make in these cases. For example, how far would the court allow an expression to bear a private meaning which the testator intended to bestow on it in his will and nowhere else? It would be a considerable departure from the principles of the Wills Act 1837 to construe a will which consisted of the words 'There's glory for you' as meaning 'I leave all my real and personal property to my wife' in a case where the evidence showed that that is what the testator intended the words to mean.

1   An example would be *Kell v Charmer* (1856) 23 Beav 195, where a jeweller left a legacy of the sums of 'ixx' and 'oxx' and evidence was admitted to show that these were private marks used by him for £100 and £200 respectively.
2   See *Ricketts v Turquand* (1848) 1 HL Cas 472.

[57.24]
'The language used in any part of it is ambiguous on the face of it' (para (b)). This resembles the category of 'patent ambiguity' in the existing law, where evidence of surrounding circumstances, but not direct evidence of the testator's intention, was admissible. Examples are a gift of 'one thousand pounds (£10,000)' and a gift to 'the son of A' where the will itself shows that A has several sons. The effect of the section is that direct evidence of the testator's intention will now be admissible in this type of case. This change in the law is clearly capable of making a considerable difference to the outcome in many cases. Evidence of surrounding circumstances alone will often be incapable of resolving ambiguities of this kind in circumstances where direct evidence of the testator's intention can do so. Thus such evidence may assist to show which of two or more meanings a testator was attaching to a particular word or phrase, such as 'my effects' or 'my money'.[1] But the section cannot assist where the alleged meaning is one which the word or phrase cannot bear; in carrying out a process of construction the court cannot declare that meaning to be the meaning of the word or phrase. Such a conclusion, varying or contradicting the language used would amount to rewriting the will which can only be done under the limited powers of rectification provided by the AJA 1982, s 20.[2]

1   See Nicholls J in *Re Williams, Wiles v Madgin* [1985] 1 All ER 964 at 969.
2   See Nicholls J in *Re Williams, Wiles v Madgin* [1985] 1 All ER 964 at 969. In that case the will listed twenty-five names in three separate groups with no indication as to the purpose of the grouping. The question arose as to whether a letter written by the testatrix to her solicitors referring to the division in the will could be admitted in evidence to assist in the construction. It was held that the will was ambiguous on the face of it and that the letter could be admitted under the AJA 1982, s 21(1)(b) but that in fact the letter provided no assistance in the construction of the will. Nicholls J then construed the will without reference to the letter and came to the somewhat surprising decision that the estate should be divided equally between the twenty-five named persons. It is interesting that Nicholls J took a rather broad view of what constitutes an ambiguity for the purpose of the section. The alternative would have been to say that the provision in the will was 'meaningless' within the AJA 1982, s 21(1)(a) and to admit the letter as an aid to construction under that paragraph. A similarly liberal approach was adopted in *Re Benham's Will Trusts, Lockhart v Harker, Read and The Royal National Lifeboat Institution* [1955] STC 210.

[57.25]

'Evidence, other than evidence of the testator's intention, shows that the language used in any part of it is ambiguous in the light of surrounding circumstances' (para (c)). The admission of extrinsic evidence, including evidence of intention, in cases of latent ambiguities or equivocations is already established. The principle has been expressed as follows, that 'where the object of a testator's bounty, or the subject of disposition is described in terms which are applicable indifferently to more than one person or thing, evidence is admissible to prove which of the persons or things so described was intended by the testator'.[1] The case law illustrations of this principle are well known. Thus in *Re Jackson, Beattie v Murphy,*[2] the testator made a disposition to 'my nephew Arthur Murphy' and since this name was applicable to more than one legitimate nephew, evidence was admitted, which in fact established that it was an illegitimate nephew of that name who was intended. Similarly when the testator simply devises his house to a beneficiary and he owns more than one.

It is thought that para (c) has the effect of admitting evidence of the testator's intention in a wider class of cases than the latent ambiguity rule did. The conditions which had to be fulfilled for the latent ambiguity rule to apply[3] were more stringent. For example, it did not apply if the ambiguity could be resolved by the application of a rule of construction, or by the construction of the will as a whole, or from evidence of surrounding circumstances other than the testator's intention. It is thought that none of these restrictions would apply in relation to para (c), and that in general evidence of the testator's intention is no longer a last resort to be used only when all other methods of interpretation have failed (although it still cannot be admitted to show that there is an ambiguity if none is apparent from the will itself or the surrounding circumstances). Also, para (c) is not restricted, as the latent ambiguity rule apparently was, to ambiguity in descriptions (usually of persons or property), although other kinds of latent ambiguity in wills must be unusual.

It will be noticed that evidence of the testatrix's intention is not admissible to establish the ambiguity, but only to resolve an ambiguity that has been established by factual evidence.[4]

1   Wigram, *Admission of Extrinsic Evidence in Aid of the Interpretation of Wills.*
2   [1933] Ch 237.
3   See Chapter 57.
4   Following the majority of the Law Reform Committee, 19th Report on the Interpretation of Wills (1973, cmnd 5301).

[57.26]

The limits of the AJA 1982, s 21. The section only admits evidence to assist in the interpretation of any part of a will to which the section applies. It does not enable the court to give effect to the testator's intention if the words used are not capable of bearing the meaning he intended (in which case, however, the new remedy of rectification may be available), or if he has failed to put his intentions into writing at all (eg the name of the donee is left blank).[1]

1   See *Re Williams, Wiles v Madgin* [1985] 1 All ER 964.

VII.   EVIDENCE OF SECRET TRUSTS

[57.27]
The admissibility of such evidence is dealt with elsewhere.[1]

1   See Chapter 36.

VIII.   EVIDENCE IN SUPPORT OF RECTIFICATION

[57.28]
Where there is an application for rectification of a will under the Administration of Justice Act 1982, s 20(1) convincing evidence in support of the claim that there has either been a clerical error or a failure to carry out instructions, will need to be adduced.[1] Such evidence, particularly in relation to the latter, will be primarily extrinsic.[2]

1   The jurisdiction to rectify wills is fully discussed in Chapter 6.
2   See *Walker v Geo H Medlicott & Sons (a firm)* [1999] 1 All ER 685, where the evidence was insufficient.

IX.   CONDITIONAL WILL

[57.29]
The court has refused to admit extrinsic evidence to show that a will which was unconditional on its face was subject to a condition precedent.[1] For a conditional will to be effective the condition must appear in the will itself.[2]

1   *Corbett v Newey* [1998] Ch 57, [1996] 2 All ER 914; conditional wills are fully discussed in Chapter 1, para **[1.10]** supra.
2   *Re Govier* [1950] P 237 (in which extrinsic evidence of intention was admitted but only to resolve an ambiguity in the wording of the contingency in the will itself). See also *O'Leary v Douglass* (1879) 3 LR Ir 323.

X.   EVIDENCE TO SUPPORT OR REBUT PRESUMPTION OF FACT

[57.30]
Equitable doctrines. These rules apply only in the case of the equitable doctrines against double portions and the satisfaction of portions by legacies,[1] and of legacies by portions.[2] In the case of these presumptions evidence is admissible to rebut the presumption and on the other hand to support it,[3] but, if the presumption arises only on the words of the will, no evidence is admitted.[4] Such evidence is admissible as providing some obligation on the part of the donee apart from the will and outside it.[5] This principle also applies to resulting trusts and to constructive trusts,[6] and to the claim of an executor against the Crown[7] but not as against the statutory beneficiaries on intestacy.[8]

1   See Chapter 44.
2   See Chapter 44.

3   *Hurst v Beach* (1821) 5 Madd 351; *Hall v Hill* (1841) 4 I Eq R 27; *Kirk v Eddowes* (1844) 3 Hare 509 at 517; *Barrs v Fewkes* (1865) 6 New Rep 355; *Re Tussaud's Estate, Tussaud v Tussaud* (1878) 9 Ch D 363.

4   *Coote v Boyd* (1789) 2 Bro CC 521. Evidence is not admissible to raise such a presumption of fact: *Re Tussaud's Estate, Tussaud v Tussaud* (1878) 9 Ch D 363 at 373.

5   *Fowkes v Pascoe* (1875) 10 Ch App 343; *Re Shields, Corbould-Ellis v Dates* [1912] 1 Ch 591; *Hall v Hill* (1841) 1 Dr & War 94.

6   *Cook v Hutchinson* (1836) 1 Keen 42.

7   *Re Bacon's Will, Camp v Coe* (1886) 31 Ch D 460.

8   *Love v Gaze* (1845) 8 Beav 472.

[57.31]

Special position of executor. Where a testator has expressed outside his will an intention to forgive the debt of, or to make a gift of personal property to his executor, the intention continuing unchanged until his death, the executor is, it seems, entitled to hold the property for his own benefit, and extrinsic evidence is admissible to prove the intention;[1] but the rule is not extended to a mere promise to make such a gift on a future occasion.[2]

1   *Strong v Bird* (1874) LR 18 Eq 315; *Re Applebee, Leveson v Beales* [1891] 3 Ch 422; *Re Stewart, Stewart v McLaughlin* [1908] 2 Ch 251 at 255 (where the grounds of the rule are stated). The headnote in this case is considered and explained in *Re Freeland, Jackson v Rodgers* [1952] Ch 110, [1952] 1 All ER 16; *Re Pink, Pink v Pink* [1912] 2 Ch 528; *Re Goff, Featherstonehaugh v Murphy* (1914) 111 LT 34; *Re Stoneham, Stoneham v Stoneham* [1919] 1 Ch 149. Evidence to forgive the debt by will is inadmissible: *Selwin v Brown* (1735) 3 Bro Parl Cas 607.

2   *Re Innes, Innes v Innes* [1910] 1 Ch 188; *Re Freeland* [1952] Ch 110.

CHAPTER 58

Inaccuracy of description – *falsa demonstratio*

[58.1]
Description accurate. If all the terms of the description fit some particular property,[1] the whole of that property and nothing more passes; the description will not be enlarged so as to include anything which part of those terms does not accurately fit,[2] nor will it be restricted so as not to include some part of the property accurately described.[3] The accurate use in a will of the name of an individual or society, while it may not exclude further inquiry as to the person intended, creates a strong presumption that the person or society so described is the donee intended by the testator.[4]

1   *Re Seal, Seal v Taylor* [1894] 1 Ch 316 ('taking the words of the will in their natural sense there is a property which answers every word of the description, and that being so the argument *ab inconvenienti* has no application'); *Re Bright-Smith, Bright-Smith v Bright-Smith* (1886) 31 Ch D 314 at 317; *Gallagher v Adams* (1887), 13 VLR 948.

2   *Webber v Stanley* (1864) 16 CBNS 698; *Hardwick v Hardwick* (1873) LR 16 Eq 168 at 175 (no extrinsic evidence admissible to enlarge property); *Whitfield v Langdale* (1875) 1 Ch D 61 at 74; *Re Seal, Seal v Taylor* [1894] 1 Ch 316; *Re Davis, Tuxford v Davis* (1906) 7 SRNSW 71; *Re McPhee Estate* [1948] 1 WWR 65. Where a description is certain, additional words do not affect it, but it is otherwise where the first description is uncertain, for in that case additional words may remove the uncertainty: *Doe d Harris v Greathed* (1806) 8 East 91.

3   *Down v Down* (1817) 1 Moore CP 80 (property accurately described and then stated to be leased to A, but small part excepted from lease); *Pullin v Pullin* (1825) 10 Moore CP 464 (land described as under mortgage, part not under mortgage excluded); *Doe d Templeman v Martin* (1833) 4 B & Ad 771; *Corballis v Corballis* (1882) 9 LR Ir 309; *Re Milner-Gibson- Cullum, Cust v A-G* [1924] 1 Ch 456 (painting said to be wrongly described, but clearly the painting intended by the will); *Re Charleson* [1968] VR 252 (land of 128 acres in area held to be intended by gift of and described as '105 acres or thereabouts').

4   *National Society for the Prevention of Cruelty to Children v Scottish National Society for the Prevention of Cruelty to Children* [1915] AC 207; *Robertson v Flynn* [1920] 1 IR 78 (gift to sister, married name wrong).

[58.2]
Description inaccurate. On the other hand, if the words of description when examined do not fit any property or donee with accuracy, and if there must be some modification of them[1] in order to place a sensible construction on the will, then the whole must be looked at fairly in order to see what are the leading words of description and what is the subordinate matter, and generally how the subject intended by the testator can be identified[2] and for this purpose evidence of extrinsic facts may be regarded.[3] In such cases the words are presumed to be a misdescription of a subject existing and with regard to which the will may validly operate.[4] Where, however, the context shows that the testator was not merely misdescribing an actually existing subject, but was under an erroneous

impression that the subject actually did exist as described, or that he could dispose of it, the gift may fail.[5] It is not enough for the court to be satisfied what the testator would have wished to happen to his property; the court must be satisfied that the words which have been used, construed in the light of the admissible evidence, achieve that result.[6] The court cannot make a will for the testator on the basis of evidence as to what the testator would have done had he had in mind the true position which he did not have in mind when he made his will.[7]

1   As to modification of words of will, see Chapter 6.
2   *Doe d Humphreys v Roberts* (1822) 5 B & Ad 407; *Re Ofner, Samuel v Ofner* [1909] 1 Ch 60 (name of grand-nephew wrong aided by reading instructions for will); applied in *Re Bell* [1969] VR 597 (evidence admitted to explain words in the will which, as they stood could have no operation).
3   *Hardwick v Hardwick* (1873) LR 16 Eq 168; *Re Bright-Smith, Bright-Smith v Bright-Smith* (1886) 31 Ch D 314 at 317 (from which the text above is taken); *Re Skude Estate* [1950] 3 DLR 494 (north half section described as west half); *Re Wilton* [1958] Qd R 559 (name of institution for blind); *Re Arnal Estate* (1967) 60 WWR 317 (mistake in disposition of land).
4   The presumption is that a designation in general words of the property intended to be affected by a will refers prima facie to that property only upon which it is capable of operating: *Maxwell v Maxwell* (1852) 2 De GM & G 705 at 715; *Baring v Ashburton* (1886) 54 LT 463 (will incapable of operating on French realty).
5   Property erroneously believed by the testator to be owned by him or intended to be acquired: *Evans v Tripp* (1821) 6 Madd 91; *Waters v Wood* (1852) 5 De G & Sm 717; *Millar v Woodside* (1872) IR 6 Eq 546; *Re Mulder, Westminster Bank Ltd v Mulder* [1943] 2 All ER 150 (testator believing that he possessed whole business, but in fact entitled only to a share. Dispositions such as could only be applied to the whole); *Re Sykes, Skelton and Dyson v Sykes* [1940] 4 All ER 10 (gift of 'all my horses' held not to pass testator's part share in three racehorses; evidence not admitted to show that stator owned no other horses either at date of will or date of death). Persons imagined to exist but not in fact in existence: *Del Mare v Rebello* (1792) 1 Ves 412; *Daubeny v Coghlan* (1842) 12 Sim 507; *Re Evans* [1950] VLR 60.
6   Cross J in *Re Tetsall, Foster v Tetsall* [1961] 2 All ER 801 at 803–804, [1961] 1 WLR 938 at 942; applied by Scott J in *Re Lewis's Will Trusts, Lewis v Williams* [1984] 3 All ER 930 at 934, distinguishing *Re Mulder, Westminster Bank Ltd v Mulder* [1943] 2 All ER 150.
7   See *Re Tetsall*, n 6 supra.

[58.3]
Falsa demonstratio non nocet. This rule of construction, which applies to all written instruments and not to wills alone, is commonly known as the rule of *Falsa demonstratio*, but though generally known by this shorter title, the full rule or maxim is *Falsa demonstratio non nocet cum de copore constat* and the additional words are an essential part of the rule.[1] There have been many renderings of the rule in English and the following is the rendering of the rule as applicable to all instruments. Whenever there is in the first place a sufficient certainty and demonstration, and afterwards an accumulative description, and it fails in point of accuracy, it will be rejected.[2] In the case of wills the following is the statement of the rule which has been most commonly accepted: if of various terms used to describe a subjectmatter, whether a person or a property, some are sufficient to ascertain the subject-matter with certainty, but others add a description which is not true, these other terms are not allowed to vitiate the gift.[3] A more modern version of this statement is: where the description is made up of more than one part, and one part is true and the other false, then, if the part which is true describes the subject-matter or the object of the gift with sufficient certainty, the untrue part will be rejected and will not vitiate the gift.[4] But the

rule as thus stated is not the full doctrine of *falsa demonstratio*, for there is a second rule of no less importance than the first. This second rule is: *Non accipi debent verba in demonstrationem falsam quae competunt in limitation—veram.* In English this second rule can be rendered thus: Additional words are not rejected as importing a false description if they can be read as words of restriction.[5] The characteristic of cases within the rule of *falsa demonstratio* is that the description so far as it is false applies to no subject at all, and so far as it is true applies to one only.[6] The false description must be superadded to what is otherwise clear,[7] but it need not come at the end of the description[8] and it is immaterial in what part of the description the *falsa demonstratio* occurs.[9]

1   *Re Brocket, Davies v Miller* [1908] 1 Ch 185 at 194.
2   *Doe d Smith v Galloway* (1833) 5 B & Ad 43 at 51.
3   *Travers v Blundell* (1877) 6 Ch D 436 at 442; *Re Livingstone* [1951] OWN 385; *Re Beauchamp* (1975) 56 DLR (3d) 644.
4   *Re Brocket, Davies v Miller* [1908] 1 Ch 185; and see *Morrell v Fisher* (1849) 4 Exch 591.
5   *Morrell v Fisher* (1849) 4 Exch 591 at 604; *West v Lawday* (1865) 11 HL Cas 375.
6   *Re Rayer, Rayer v Rayer* [1903] 1 Ch 685.
7   *Thomas d Evans v Thomas* (1796) 6 Term Rep 671 at 676; *Doe d Hubbard v Hubbard* (1850) 15 QB 227 (the words of the devise, independently of the *falsa demonstratio*, must be sufficient of themselves to describe the property intended to pass).
8   *Cowen v Truefitt Ltd* [1899] 2 Ch 309 at 311.
9   *Cowen v Truefitt Ltd* [1899] 2 Ch 309 at 311.

[58.4]
Description wholly wrong, but subject-matter certain. A false description does not affect a gift if it is clear what is described.[1] Thus, where the description of either property or donee or any person or thing mentioned in the will[2] is wholly false, so that no known existing person or thing satisfies the description, but the context of the will and the circumstances of the case[3] show unambiguously who or what the testator meant, the description is rejected and the intention of the testator effectuated.[4] Examples of this proposition as applied to descriptions of donees are as follows. Where a legatee's name was badly misspelt, evidence was received to ascertain who was intended,[5] misdescription of a corporation;[6] description of legatee as 'rector' instead of 'vicar';[7] gift to 'three remaining children of uncle A B' where there was an uncle and a cousin of the same name and the uncle had three grandchildren and the cousin three children answering the description: the decision was in favour of the children of the cousin;[8] a bequest to 'Miss Sarah Jameson': testator was acquainted with a Mrs Sarah Jameson and her daughter, Miss Frances Ann Jameson; the daughter was held entitled to the bequest;[9] misdescription of the father of the children to whom a legacy was given;[10] gift to resident 'apothecary' where there was only a resident dispenser;[11] gift to children of person described as dead at the date of the will: person described still alive at the date of the will, but another of the same family but with different Christian names then dead;[12] gift to the children of A may take effect as a gift to the children of B provided that the context and circumstances show that such a gift may have been intended;[13] gift to two brothers naming them where there was no brother of one name but a cousin of that name.[14] Examples of this proposition as applied to the description of property and things are as follows. Bequest of 'money on deposit receipt' in a

named bank held to pass shares in the bank;[15] debentures passing under a description of shares;[16] bequest of 'debts owing from my late husband's estate' held to include money due on an IOU and on a promissory note which were unenforceable for want of consideration;[17] shares in a railway company wrongly named;[18] a devise held to pass the interest in the proceeds of sale of the land;[19] Exchequer Bonds passing under the description of 'my War Loans';[20] 'War Loan' may also pass Conversion Stock and Treasury Bonds;[21] 'War Savings Certificates' may pass National Savings Certificates;[22] misdescription of stock;[23] misdescription of house or land;[24] misdescription of house subject to a special power of appointment;[25] a devise of vacant land properly described will pass although built upon before testator's death;[26] bequest of jewellery where no piece exactly fits the description though two or more are described with minor inaccuracies.[27] However in the most recent case to consider this principle a bequest of 'my freehold farm' was held not to cover the testator's holding of three-quarters of the issued shares of a family company which owned a farm and other assets.[28]

1   *Evans v Tripp* (1821) 6 Madd 91; and see examples infra.
2   Any matter in the will is subject to the rule: eg *Re Rayer, Rayer v Rayer* [1903] 1 Ch 685 (the principle applied to direction to pay duty where the duty had been abolished as to particular legacies given).
3   As to admission of extrinsic evidence in such cases, see Chapter 57.
4   *Morrell v Fisher* (1849) 4 Exch 591; *Cowen v Truefitt Ltd* [1899] 2 Ch 309.
5   *Masters v Masters* (1718) 1 P Wms 421; *Beaumont v Fell* (1723) 2 P Wms 141.
6   *A-G v Rye Corpn* (1817) 7 Taunt 546. For misdescription in gifts to charities, see Chapter 103.
7   *Hopkinson v Ellis* (1842) 5 Beav 34.
8   *Bristow v Bristow* (1842) 5 Beav 289.
9   *Lee v Pain* (1845) 4 Hare 201.
10   *Douglas v Fellows* (1853) Kay 114.
11   *Ellis v Bartnum (No 2)* (1857) 25 Beav 109.
12   *Re Waller, White v Scoles* (1899) 68 LJ Ch 526.
13   *Braidwin v Harpur* (1759) Amb 374; *Bristow v Bristow* (1842) 5 Beav 289; *Lord Camoys v Blundell* (1848) 1 HL Cas 778. As to illegitimate persons, see Chapter 72.
14   *Re Evans* [1950] VLR 60.
15   *Re Cranfield, Mosse v Cranfield* [1895] 1 IR 80.
16   *Re Weeding, Armstrong v Wilkin* [1896] 2 Ch 364.
17   *Re Rowe, Pike v Hamlyn* [1898] 1 Ch 153.
18   *Flood v Flood* [1902] 1 IR 538.
19   *Re Glassington, Glassington v Follett* [1906] 2 Ch 305.
20   *Re Ionides, London County Westminster and Parr's Bank Ltd v Craies* (1922) 38 TLR 269.
21   *Re Price, Trumper v Price* [1932] 2 Ch 54; followed in *Re Gifford, Gifford v Seaman* [1944] Ch 186, [1944] 1 All ER 268, where, however, it was also held that 'war bonds' would not pass National Savings Certificates nor Defence Bonds bought after the date of the will.
22   *Re Lamb, Marston v Chauvet* (1933) 49 TLR 541.
23   *Re Anderson, Public Trustee v Bielby* (1928) 44 TLR 295; and see *Bruce v Bruce's Trustees* (1875) 2 R 775 (purchase-price of stock wrongly stated).
24   *Re Mathews, Ballarat Trustees, Executors and Agency Co Ltd v Mathews* [1917] VLR 1; *Keogh v Keogh* (1874) IR 8 Eq 179; *Moore v Phelan* [1920] 1 IR 232 (seven houses instead of eight).
25   *Re Nicholl, Re Perkins, Nicholl v Perkins* (1920) 125 LT 62.
26   *Burns Philp Trust Co Ltd v Stott* (1955) 72 WNNSW 322.
27   *Re Scott, Scott v Scott* [1914] 1 Ch 847.
28   *Re Lewis's Will Trusts* [1984] 3 All ER 930, not following *Re Glassington, Glassington v Follett* [1906] 2 Ch 305, or *Re Gifford, Gifford v Seaman* [1944] Ch 186, [1944] 1 All ER 268, the court preferred to rewrite the testator's will to make it accord with what he owned.

Part J   Construction of wills: general principles

[58.5]

Description partly wrong but applicable only to one subject. If there is in any part of a description a sufficient description of the subject-matter with convenient certainty of what was intended, any erroneous addition or error in part of the description does not vitiate the gift.[1] The characteristic of cases within this rule is that the description so far as it is false applies to no subject at all, and so far as it is true applies to one only.[2]

1   *Morrell v Fisher* (1849) 4 Exch 591 at 604; *Goodright d Lamb v Pears* (1809) 11 East 58; *Anderson v Berkeley* [1902] 1 Ch 936 at 940; *Gallagher v Adams* (1887) 13 VLR 948; *Re Carvill* (1913) 15 DLR 206.
2   *Morrell v Fisher* (1849) 4 Exch 591; *Cowen v Truefitt Ltd* [1899] 2 Ch 309 at 312.

[58.6]

Description wholly true as to one subject, partly true as to another. If it is doubtful upon the words of the will whether they import a false reference or demonstration, or whether they are words of restriction which limit the generality of the former words, the court never presumes error or falsehood, and the latter construction is preferred.[1] If there exists some subject to which all the description is true, and some as to which part is true and part is false, the words are considered to be words of true restriction, so that they refer to that subject only as to which all the description is true;[2] but it is a matter of construction of the will as a whole, for if the whole property is clearly given, the apparently restrictive words will not prejudice the general gift, nor on the other hand will clearly restrictive words be overruled by an apparently general gift.[3]

1   This rule has already been referred to as the second rule. For statements of this rule, see *Morrell v Fisher* (1849) 4 Exch 591 at 604; *Doe d Ashforth v Bower* (1832) 3 B & Ad 453 at 459; *Nightingall v Smith* (1848) 1 Exch 879 at 886; *Re Brocket, Dawes v Miller* [1908] 1 Ch 185 at 190. When the rule is applied all the words must be wholly true as to the restricted part, and there must be no clear intention that the whole should pass: see para **[58.7]** infra.
2   *Ridge v Newton* (1842) 2 Dr & War 239; *Slingsby v Grainger* (1859) 7 HL Cas 273; *Gilliat v Gilliat* (1860) 28 Beav 481; *Pedley v Dodds* (1866) LR 2 Eq 819; *O'Connor v O'Connor* (1870) IR 4 Eq 483; *Millar v Woodside* (1872) IR 6 Eq 546; *Re Bennett, ex p Kirk* (1877) 5 Ch D 800. Applications of the rule to matters of tenure are: *Doe d Conolly v Vernon and Vyse* (1804) 5 East 51; *Doe d Brown v Brown* (1809) 11 East 441; *Stone v Greening* (1843) 13 Sim 390; *Hall v Fisher* (1844) 1 Coll 47 (but see, as to the last two cases, the decisions in *Re Bright-Smith, Bright-Smith v Bright-Smith* (1866) 31 Ch D 314, and *Hallett v Hallett* (1898) 14 TLR 420; the latter is said to overrule *Hall v Fisher*); *Quennell v Turner* (1851) 13 Beav 240; *Mathews v Mathews* (1867) LR 4 Eq 278.
    Applications of the rule to occupation are: *Doe d Parkin v Parkin* (1814) 5 Taunt 321; *Morrell v Fisher* (1849) 4 Exch 591; *Doe d Renow v Ashley* (1847) 10 QB 663; *Doe d Hubbard-Hubbard* (1850) 15 QB 227; *Whitfield v Langdale* (1875) 1 Ch D 61 at 80; *Homer v Homer* (1878) 8 Ch D 758; *Re Seal, Seal v Taylor* [1894] 1 Ch 316.
    Applications of the rule to locality are: *White v Vitty* (1826) 2 Russ 484; *Moser v Platt* (1844) 14 Sim 95; *Attwater v Attwater* (1853) 18 Beav 330; *Evans v Angell* (1858) 26 Beav 202; *Webber v Stanley* (1864) 16 CBNS 698; *Lambert v Overton* (1864) 11 LT 503; *Smith v Ridgway* (1866) LR 1 Exch 331; *Keogh v Keogh* (1874) IR 8 Eq 179.
    Applications of the rule to mode of acquisition or title are. *Wilkinson v Bewicke* (1853) 3 De GM & G 937; *Cave v Harris* (1887) 57 LJ Ch 62; *Norman v Norman* [1919] 1 Ch 297.
    The rule was applied to donees in *Wrightson v Calvert* (1860) 1 John & H 250 (gift to two grand-children living near B. Testator had three grand-children but only two lived near B and the third was not entitled). As to enumeration of donees, see para **[58.8]** infra.
3   *Stanley v Stanley* (1862) 2 John & H 491 (court looks at the nature and circumstances of the property and at the value of the subject-matter of the various gifts, and, if the whole will

608

discloses an intention inconsistent with restrictive words, those words are rejected as *falsa demonstratio*); *West v Lawday* (1865) 11 HL Cas 375 (entirety expressly and definitely given is not prejudiced by the imperfect enumeration of particulars, nor a clear enumeration of particulars overruled by an apparently general devise); *Re Brocket, Dawes v Miller* [1908] 1 Ch 185 (the construction depends upon the terms in which the enumeration of the particulars are introduced, whether or not they substitute a definite and precise statement for an antecedent generality. There is no rule that where there are two complete descriptions, the first is to prevail).

[58.7]
Description partly true as to each of two or more subjects. If the description is not strictly applicable to any person or thing, but is applicable partly to one person or thing and partly to another, the court may inquire into the material circumstances of the case for the purpose of deciding whether the testator intended to make the gift applicable to the one or the other.[1]

1   *Bernasconi v Atkinson* (1853) 10 Hare 345 at 349 (the presumption is that the testator intended some existing person or thing. This was a gift to Vincent B, son of testator's late uncle Peter B. There was a George Vincent B whom testator called Vincent and with whom he was friendly, but he was not the son of Peter B); *Bradshaw v Bradshaw* (1836) 2 Y & C Ex 72 (Robert, second son of A, when Robert was in fact the eldest son. Description held right and name mistaken); *Adams v Jones* (1852) 9 Hare 485 (mistake in name more probable than in description); *Re Hooper, Hooper v Warner* (1902) 88 LT 160 (where both name and description were wrong, but error in name slight and an understandable one). See designation of donee, infra.

[58.8]
Enumeration of particulars. Where some subject-matter is given under a denomination applicable to the whole, and then words are added, on the principle of enumeration, which do not completely enumerate and exhaust all the particulars which are included under the antecedent denomination, the question is which is the predominant description.[1] If the subsequent description is meant to substitute a definite and precise statement for an antecedent generality, the subsequent description must be read as explanatory and if necessary as restrictive of the prior general description,[2] otherwise the general description is given its full effect.[3]

1   *West v Lawday* (1865) 11 HL Cas 375; *Travers v Blundell* (1877) 6 Ch D 436 at 441; *Hardwick v Hardwick* (1873) LR 16 Eq 168. See para **[58.6]**, n 3.
2   *Re Brocket, Dawes v Miller* [1908] 1 Ch 185 at 195 (devise of all property to which testatrix was entitled under a will, 'namely' certain parcels, omitting one property at a distance from the rest. Held that property did not pass). See also *D'Aglie v Fryer* (1841) 12 Sim 1; *Glanville v Glanville* (1863) 33 Beav 302; *Re Short* [1929] 1 DLR 454 (bequest to one child; residue to 'all' with enumeration omitting first donee, first donee not included in beneficiaries of residuary gift).
3   *West v Lawday* (1865) 11 HL Cas 375; *Matthews v Maude* (1830) 1 Russ & M 397 (a bonus increase included as manifestly intended by general description); *Reeves v Baker* (1854) 18 Beav 372 (all property whether freehold or personal); *Re Roberts, Kiff v Roberts* (1886) 55 LT 498 (all property leasehold and freehold included personalty); *Roberts v Thorp* (1911) 56 Sol Jo 13 (all my property followed by specific items but not including realty passed realty); *Re Aird Estate* [1954] 2 DLR 473; *Re Bingley Estate* (1953) 7 WWRNS 507; *Re Murray, Clarke v Wakem* [1964] NZLR 627 (testator who had a leasehold interest in 138 acres and a freehold interest in 52 acres gave all his estate and interest consisting of 52 acres. It was held that this passed both the leasehold and freehold interest).

[58.9]
Designation by name or description. A donee has often been sufficiently designated by a nick-name or erroneous name proved to have been used by the testator, or by a name gained by reputation and known to the testator;[1] and property may be sufficiently described by the description the testator was wont to use.[2]

1   *River's Case* (1737) 1 Atk 410 (illegitimate sons described as 'my sons'); *Gynes v Kemsley* (1677) Freem KB 293 (devise to Margaret where name was Margery); *Dowset v Sweet* (1753) Amb 175 (legacy to John where real name was James. In this case the legacy was to J and B, the sons of JS); *Andrews v Andrews* (1885) 15 LR Ir 199 (issue of two marriages); *Re Taylor, Cloak v Hammond* (1886) 34 Ch D 255 (cousin held to include wife of cousin).
2   *Doe d Beach v Jersey* (1825) 3 B & C 870 ('my Briton Ferry Estate', not situated in Briton Ferry); *Doe d Hiscocks v Hiscocks* (1839) 5 M & W 363.

[58.10]
Designation by both name and description. Where the donee is designated by name and description, if there is a person who has the name, and the description is incorrect for him and all others, the description is neglected,[1] so long as it is not shown that the gift was obtained by the fraud of the beneficiary.[2] There is no rule, however, that, without any evidence to prove an error of description, the mere name should prevail; in order that the rule may be applicable it is necessary first to show that there is an error in the description.[3] In similar cases, where a description is correct and sufficient an incorrect name may be neglected.[4] In cases where either the name alone or the description alone is sufficient to identify a subject, and they do not identify the same subject, then, according to the circumstances of the case, the description and not the name,[5] or the name and not the description,[6] may prevail. The name is in fact only a description,[7] and the question is to determine which portion of the whole description is to prevail.[8] A test often adopted by the court in such a case is to inquire whether the testator was in the circumstances more liable to err when he described the donee by name or when he attempted to point him out by some further adjunct; and the court adopts that description which in each instance appears to be least open to error.[9]

Examples of the application of this rule to the description of donees are as follows. A gift to 'EA, a natural daughter of' a named person, where the name and sex were incorrect;[10] or to a niece of a named person where the only child was a nephew;[11] a gift to a named person if he should survive a person wrongly named;[12] a gift to 'my niece ES' where a great-grandniece, EJS took;[13] a gift to 'my wife Caroline' where the testator had a wife Mary who survived him but was living with a woman named Caroline with whom he had gone through an invalid ceremony of marriage;[14] a gift to 'the children of my late nephew M' who was in fact still living, but a brother of the same name .was dead: the children of the nephew took;[15] a legatee described as 'the son of SE by MJ, or M, or E, his wife': there was no doubt as to the person intended, the gift was good and the question whether the legatee was born in lawful wedlock was immaterial;[16] a gift to person entitled in possession to a named house under a deed of entail: no such deed in existence and the heir, entitled in possession, took;[17] a gift to 'A's wife L', where A was living with a woman named L, who was reputed to be his wife but in fact he had not been married to her;[18] a gift to a person whose Christian name is wrongly given but is otherwise correctly described;[19] wrong address at date of death stated but donee has resided there for many years;[20] donee unnamed but gift given for years of companionship, assistance and help.[21]

Examples of the application of this rule to the description of property are as follows. A devise of all freehold houses in a named place where the testator has none but leasehold houses passes the leaseholds;[22] a gift to stock wrongly named but correct as to the amount;[23] a gift of stock stated to be in the name of the testator but in fact in the name of trustees;[24] bequest of bank stock as invested by a named stockbroker held to pass government stock invested by the named person;[25] a gift of stock said to be standing in the testator's name where the stock had been purchased but not transferred;[26] a gift of stock stated to be in joint names in fact standing in the name of the testator;[27] a devise of land correctly described but stated to be purchased from a named person when in fact part was purchased from another person;[28] references to parishes, streets, or other localities may be rejected if the rest of the description is sufficiently certain.[29]

1   *Giles v Giles* (1836) 1 Keen 685; *Doe d Gains v Rouse* (1848) 5 CB 422; *Ford v Batley* (1853) 23 LJ Ch 225.

2   *Re Posner, Posner v Miller* [1953] P 277, [1953] 1 All ER 1123 ('my wife RP'. It was shown that RP was not the legal wife of the testator but no fraud was alleged). Where the legatee described as the testator's wife, knew at the time of her pretended marriage that she had a husband living, the gift was void; *Wilkinson v Joughlin* (1866) LR 2 Eq 319.

3   *Drake v Drake* (1860) 8 HL Cas 172 at 179; *Charter v Charter* (1874) LR 7 HL 364 at 380. The court does not conjecture that an error exists: *Mostyn v Mostyn* (1854) 5 HL Cas 155.

4   *Pitcairne v Brase* (1679) Cas *temp* Finch 403; *Dowset v Sweet* (1753) Amb 175; *Stockdale v Bushby* (1815) Coop G 229.

5   *Garth v Meyrick* (1779) 1 Bro CC 30 (residue to six grandchildren, name of one repeated and one omitted, all took); *Smith v Coney* (1801) 6 Ves 42 (Christian name wrong); *Doe d Le Chevalier v Huthwaite* (1820) 3 B & Ald 632 (left to jury to say whether error in name or description); *Lord Camoys v Blundell* (1848) 1 HL Cas 778 (devisee unnamed); *Adams v Jones* (1852) 9 Hare 485 (description more likely to be correct than the name: donee described as wife of A); *Bradshaw v Bradshaw* (1836) 2 Y & C Ex 72 (description accepted); *Re Feltham's Will Trusts* (1855) 1 K & J 528 (JT of R named TT of R); *Hodgon v Clarke* (1860) 1 De GF & J 394 (eldest son wrongly named); *Re Nunn's Trusts* (1875) LR 19 Eq 331 ('my housekeeper'); *Re Hooper, Hooper v Warner* (1902) 88 LT 160 ('son of A'). In general, it may be said that, if there is a person for whom the name is accurate but with whom the testator was not intimate and another person for whom the name is inaccurate but the description is sufficient to identify him and the testator was intimate with him, the latter is entitled to the gift: *Charter v Charter* (1874) LR 7 HL 364; *Re Brake's Goods* (1881) 6 PD 217; *Re Chappell's Goods* [1894] P 98; *Re Blake's Trusts* [1904] 1 IR 98.

6   *Newbolt v Pryce* (1844) 14 Sim 354; *Garner v Garner* (1860) 29 Beav 114; *Gillett v Gane* (1870) LR 10 Eq 29; *Farrer v St Catherine's College, Cambridge* (1873) LR 16 Eq 19; *Garland v Beverley* (1878) 9 Ch D 213; *Re Taylor, Cloak v Hammond* (1886) 34 Ch D 255.

7   A description of legatees as those named in the will, although primarily referring to those mentioned by name may denote persons merely specified or mentioned by another description: *Bromley v Wright* (1849) 7 Hare 334; *Re Holme's Trusts* (1853) 1 Drew 321; *Seale-Hayne v Jodrell* [1891] AC 304 at 306.

8   *Bernasconi v Atkinson* (1853) 10 Hare 345 at 351.

9   *Bernasconi v Atkinson* (1853) 10 Hare 345 at 351; *Re Fry's Estate, Matthews v Greenman* (1874) 31 LT 8; *Re Lord Blayney's Trust* (1875) IR 9 Eq 413; *Re Lyon's Trusts* (1879) 48 LJ Ch 245. This paragraph of the text was adopted and applied by Kaye J in *Re Edwards, Turner v Roberts* [1981] VR 794 at 797.

10   *Ryall v Hannam* (1847) 10 Beav 536.

11   *Re Rickit's Trusts* (1853) 11 Hare 299.

12 *Ford v Batley* (1852) 23 LJ Ch 225. This was an annuity given to a man who was living with the woman wrongly named. It was proved that the testator had often visited the parties and given them money and had given the named person gifts of money since the death of the woman.

13 *Stringer v Gardiner* (1859) 4 De G & J 468.

14 *Doe d Gains v Rouse* (1848) 5 CB 422. For similar cases, see *Pratt v Mathew* (1856) 22 Beav 328; *Re Petts* (1859) 27 Beav 576; *Re Howe's Goods* (1884) 48 JP 743.

15 *Re Ingle's Trusts* (1871) LR 11 Eq 578.

16 *Thomson v Eastwood* (1877) 2 App Cas 215.

17 *Re Marquess of Bute, Marquess of Bute v Ryder* (1884) 27 Ch D 196.

18 *Anderson v Berkley* [1902] 1 Ch 936. In this case the testator had been told that there had been a marriage.

19 *Re Hooper, Hooper v Warner* (1902) 88 LT 160.

20 *Re Alleyn* [1965] SALR 22.

21 *Re Fabro's Estate* [1965] SASR 69.

22 *Day v Trig* (1715) 1 P Wms 286.

23 *Door v Geary* (1749) 1 Ves Sen 255; *Burbey v Burbey* (1867) 15 LT 501. See also *Rowlatt v Easton* (1863) 2 New Rep 262 (where the name of the stock was incorrect and the amount slightly incorrect).

24 *Mackinley v Sison* (1837) 8 Sim 561; *Quennell v Turner* (1851) 13 Beav 240; *Power v Lencham* (1838) 2 Jo Ex Ir 728 (where the stock stood in the name of the mother of the testatrix, of whom she was the executrix and sole residuary legatee).

25 *Drake v Martin* (1856) 23 Beav 89.

26 *Ellis v Eden (No 2)* (1858) 25 Beav 482.

27 *Coltman v Gregory* (1870) 40 LJ Ch 352.

28 *Norman v Norman* [1919] 1 Ch 297.

29 Street wrong: *Newton v Lucas* (1836) 1 My & Cr 391; *Armstrong v Buckland* (1854) 18 Beav 204; *Tann v Tann* (1863) 2 New Rep 412; *Harman v Gurner* (1866) 35 Beav 478; *Re Mayell, Foley v Wood* [1913] 2 Ch 488. Parish wrong: *Homer v Homer* (1878) 8 Ch D 758; *Keogh v Keogh* (1874) IR 8 Eq 179. County wrong: *Doe d Beach v Earl of Jersey* (1818) 1 B & Ald 550; lot numbers wrong: *Re Davidson* (1979) 101 DLR (3d) 372.

[58.11]
Effect of change of circumstances between date of will and death.
Descriptions must be construed according to the usual rules as to the circumstances taken into account;[1] but where a person or body who once satisfied the description no longer existed at the date of the will, another person or body existing at the date of the will and satisfying the description inaccurately but sufficiently, may, nevertheless, be entitled to the gift.[2] An accurate description of a donee by name is not as a rule affected in the case of a person by his changing his name before the testator's death or, in the case of a society, corporation or body by a change of name or reorganisation, if the donee substantially exists in the same nature as at the date of the will.[3] By the terms of the will, however, the use of a specified name[4] at the death of the testator,[5] or at the time of payment or vesting,[6] or at some other time[7] may be a condition of the gift taking effect at all.

1 In the case of property, see Chapter 59; in the case of persons, see Chapter 65.

2 *Dowsett v Sweet* (1753) Amb 175; *Dooley v Mahon* (1877) IR 11 Eq 299. It has been held that where a donee is described by name, and there has been a person in existence and known to the testator answering the exact description of the donee, while at the date of the will or of the death of the testator there is no such person, evidence is admissible to prove not only the testator's intimacy with a person who exists to whom a sufficient part of the description is applicable, but even his intention to make such gift to that person: *Re Halston, Ewen v Halston* [1912] 1 Ch 435, not following *Re Ely, Tottenham v Ely* (1891) 65 LT 452, as being disapproved by Farwell J, in *Re Ofner, Samuel v Ofner* [1909] 1 Ch 60 at 63, and following *Re Blackman* (1852) 16 Beav 377; see also *Re Mayo, Chester v Keirl* [1901] 1 Ch 404.

3   *Re Joy, Purday v Johnson* (1888) 60 LT 175 (amalgamation of societies); *Re Wedgwood, Sweet
     v Cotton* [1914] 2 Ch 245 (charitable work carried on at or in connection with the same home
     though transferred from one association to another); *Re Donald, Moore v Somerset* [1909] 2 Ch
     410 (change of volunteer units to Territorial Army); *Re Andrews, Dunedin Corpn v Smyth*
     (1910) 29 NZLR 43 (effect of introduction of compulsory service); *Re Dawson's Will Trusts,
     National Provincial Bank Ltd v National Council of YMCA Inc* [1957] 1 All ER 177, [1957] 1
     WLR 391 (amalgamation to two charities so that new society was old society under a new
     name, the objects being practically identical). But see *Re Recher's Will Trusts, National
     Westminster Bank Ltd v National Anti-Vivisection Society Ltd* [1972] Ch 526, [1971] 3 All ER
     401 (gift to a non-charitable unincorporated body which had been dissolved; held, gift could not
     be construed as one to a different unincorporated society with which it had amalgamated). See
     also the charities cases, *Re Stemson's Will Trusts, Carpenter v Treasury Solicitor* [1970] Ch 16,
     [1969] 2 All ER 517; *Re Fingers Will Trusts, Turner v Ministry of Health* [1972] Ch 286,
     [1971] 3 All ER 1050; *Re Vernon's Will Trusts, Lloyd's Bank Ltd v Group 20, Hospital
     Management Committee (Coventry)* [1972] Ch 300n, [1971] 3 All ER 1061n, fully discussed in
     para **[103.5]** infra.
4   See paras **[35.39]**–**[35.44]** supra. The word 'name' may mean stock, see *Pyot v Pyot* (1749) 1
     Ves Sen 335 (where a change of name by marriage did not exclude the donee).
5   *Bon v Smith* (1596) Cro Eliz 532 (marriage before testator's death: not entitled); *Jobson's Case*
     (1597) Cro Eliz 576 (marriage after testator's death: entitled).
6   *Doe d Wright v Plumptre* (1820) 3 B & Ald 474.
7   For instance, at birth so that the name is the family name: *Barlow v Bateman* (1735) 2 Bro Parl
     Cas 272; *Leigh v Leigh* (1808) 15 Ves 92.

[58.12]
Accuracy of generic description of property. A gift which accurately
describes property of a generic nature[1] belonging to the testator at the date of the
will does not fail where the description is sufficiently apt to indicate particular
property belonging to the testator at his death, though as a description of such
property it is inaccurate; and the latter property accordingly passes under the
gift,[2] the inaccuracy being then of no importance. A bequest of 'any leasehold
house', has been held to pass the subsequently acquired freehold interest in the
house.[3] Where out of several properties alleged to satisfy the description at the
death one only is accurately described,[4] that property only passes under the gift.[5]
Where no property at all is sufficiently described by the words of the will at the
death of the testator the gift fails,[6] except that in cases where the testator had
neither at the date of will nor at his death property accurately described by the
words of the will, the court may from circumstances be able to infer what was
meant to be described, and the gift does not necessarily fail;[7] in the case of
bequests of personal property, the gift may take effect as a general legacy.[8]

1   Something which may increase or diminish between the date of the will and the death: *Re
     Slater, Slater v Slater* [1906] 2 Ch 480 at 485.
2   *Cooch v Walden* (1877) 46 LJ Ch 639.
3   *Re Fleming's Will Trusts, Ennon v Hampstead Old People's Housing Trusts Ltd* [1974] 3 All
     ER 323, [1974] 1 WLR 1552 (the test of 'merger' was not a satisfactory one to apply; the court
     had to look to the intention of the testator), applying, *Struthers v Struthers* (1857) 5 WR 809;
     Miles v Miles (1866) LR 1 Eq 462; *Cox v Bennett* (1868) LR 6 Eq 422; *Saxton v Saxton* (1879)
     13 Ch D 359; but see *Emuss v Smith* (1848) 2 De G & Sm 722.
4   That is, the description is wholly true as to one property and partly true as another: see
     para **[58.6]** supra.
5   *Re Portal and Lamb* (1885) 30 Ch D 50 ('my cottage and all my land at S.' Subsequent
     purchase of a large house at S near the above. Not included); *Cave v Harris* (1887) 57 LJ Ch 62
     ('which I have lately purchased' restricted the property to that purchased before the will and a
     subsequent purchase did not pass); *Re Potter, Stevens v Potter* (1900) 83 LT 405 (land occupied
     in connection with certain property); *Webb v Byng* (1855) 1 K & J 580 (where testatrix had

coined a description of the property and after-acquired property was held not to be within the description); *Re Willis, Spencer v Willis* [1911] 2 Ch 563 ('where I now reside' held mere additional description which did not limit the gift).

6   *Barber v Wood* (1877) 4 Ch D 885 (no property of the kind in the place named and undivided shares in an adjoining place did not pass); *Re Knight, Knight v Burgess* (1887) 34 Ch D 518 (gift of lease of house in which testator should be living at his death. Testator subsequently bought and lived in a freehold house, which was held not to pass under the gift).

7   *Re Jameson, King v Winn* [1908] 2 Ch 111 (amalgamation of banks); *King v Wright* (1845) 14 Sim 400 (bequest copied from earlier will); *Flood v Flood* [1902] 1 IR 538 (misdescription of company).

8   *Lindgren v Lindgren* (1846) 9 Beav 358 (stock sold before will); *Finlater v Lowe* [1904] 1 IR 519.

[58.13]

Accuracy of specific descriptions. In the case of a specific property existing at the date of the will, the whole of that property may pass under the gift, notwithstanding that the description at the date of the death applies accurately to part only of the property.[1]

1   *Re Evans, Evans v Powell* [1909] 1 Ch 784 (erection of further houses on described land).

Construction of wills: particular rules relating to property

CHAPTER 59

Descriptions of property—will speaks from death

[59.1]

Will speaks from death. A will must be construed with reference to the property comprised within it,[1] to speak and take effect as if it has been executed immediately before the death of the testator,[2] and as if the condition of things to which it refers in this respect is that existing immediately before the death of the testator,[3] unless a contrary intention appears by the will. This rule, however, does not affect a description of some specific thing existing at the date of the will.[4]

1   Including property subject to a general power exercised by the will unless a contrary intention appears in the will: Wills Act 1837 (WA 1837), ss 24, 27; 50 *Halsbury's Statutes* (4th edn) 593, 595. See Vol 2, Part G, paras **[244.24]** and **[244.27]**; see *Re Hayes, Turnbull v Hayes* [1900] 2 Ch 322, and see paras **[39.11]–[39.15]** supra. It is doubtful if this principle applies to special powers: *Re Well's Trusts, Hardisty v Wells* (1889) 42 Ch D 646; *Re Hayes, Turnbull v Hayes* [1901] 2 Ch 529; *Doyle v Coyle* [1895] 1 IR 205.
2   Wills Act 1837, s 24; *Cole v Scott* (1849) 1 H & Tw 477; *Re Bridger, Brompton Hospital for Consumption v Lewis* [1894] 1 Ch 297; *Treadwell v Hitchings* [1925] NZLR 519. This section does not say that a will is to be construed in every respect as if it were made on the day of testator's death. Where there is a question as to which clause of a will carries the property, the WA 1837 does not say which clause is to outweigh the other, but only what property is to be comprised in the will: *Re Portal and Lamb* (1885) 30 Ch D 50 at 55, and *Re Gillins, Inglis v Gillins* [1909] 1 Ch 345 at 349. A release of debts to a specified person is within the statutory provision: *Everett v Everett* (1877) 7 Ch D 428; see also *Re Mitchell, Freelove v Mitchell* [1913] 1 Ch 201; *Re Williams, James v Williams* (1910) 26 TLR 307.
3   *Re Well's, Trusts, Hardisty v Wells* (1889) 42 Ch D 646; *Higgins v Dawson* [1902] AC 1 at 7.
4   *Douglas v Douglas* (1854) Kay 400. The section (Wills Act 1837, s 24) has, however, an application to specific gifts as well as residuary gifts: *Lady Langdale v Briggs* (1856) 8 De GM & G 391 at 436; *Re Ord, Dickinson v Dickinson* (1879) 12 Ch D 22 at 25.

[59.2]

Generic descriptions. In a case where the thing given is generic,[1] and may increase, diminish or otherwise change during the testator's life, so that the description may from time to time apply to different amounts of property of like nature or to different objects, then the effect of the presumption is that the property answering the description at the death of the testator passes under the gift.[2] Thus a general gift of all property of a certain description passes property of that description acquired after the date of the will.[3] So also in the case of a release of debts,[4] and in a gift of a share of a partner where the testator bought out the other partners,[5] and a gift of leaseholds has passed an after-acquired freehold reversion[6] and a gift of all lands at a specified place.[7]

1   This word is explained as applying to subject-matter capable of increase or decrease in *Re Slater, Slater v Slater* [1906] 2 Ch 480 at 485.

2   *Lady Langdale v Briggs* (1856) 8 De GM & G 391. The WA 1837 applies to both residuary and
     specific gifts: *Re Ord, Dickinson v Dickinson* (1879) 12 Ch D 22 at 25.

3   *Lady Langdale v Briggs* (1856) 8 De GM & G 391 (land); *Trinder v Trinder* (1866) LR 1 Eq
     695 (shares in a railway company); *Re Warren* (1922) 52 OLR 127 (shares in company
     subsequently amalgamated); *Re Slater, Slater v Slater* [1906] 2 Ch 480 (shares in water
     company taken over by Metropolitan Water Board); *Re Jenkins, Jenkins v Davies* [1931] 2 Ch
     218 (stock of harbour trustees taken over by railway company); *Lysaght v Edwards* (1876) 2 Ch
     D 499 (general gift of real estate). As to all lands at a stated place, see n 7; *Re Gillins, Inglis v
     Gillins* [1909] 1 Ch 345 (gift of 25 shares passed only those still owned at death; but this has
     been explained as a general legacy, see *Re Clifford* [1912] 1 Ch 29 at 31).

4   *Everett v Everett* (1877) 7 Ch D 428 (includes debts contracted after will).

5   *Re Russell, Russell v Chell* (1882) 19 Ch D 432.

6   *Saxton v Saxton* (1879) 13 Ch D 359; *Re Fleming's Will Trusts, Ennion v Hampstead Old
     People's Housing Trust Ltd* [1974] 3 All ER 323, [1974] 1 WLR 1552. See para **[58.12]**, n 3.

7   *Doe d York v Walker* (1844) 12 M & W 591; *Re Ord, Dickinson v Dickinson* (1879) 12 Ch D
     22; *Re Bridger, Brompton Hospital for Consumption v Lewis* [1894] 1 Ch 297. A gift of the
     proceeds of sale includes all the proceeds of sale of land sold up to date of death: *Re Davies,
     Scourfield v Davies* [1925] Ch 642. Additional property passes although specifically given by a
     codicil if the gift by codicil fails: *Re Davies, Thomas v Thomas-Davies* [1928] Ch 24.

[59.3]

Contrary intention. No contrary intention is shown by the mere use of a
possessive adjective[1] in the case of such a generic gift;[2] nor by a description of
the property as being that of which the testator is seised or possessed.[3] A
description of the property as that which the testator 'now' owns or occupies,
according to the circumstances,[4] may, but, it appears, prima facie does not[5],
show such a contrary intention as to exclude after-acquired property of the
generic nature. The statutory rule, however, does not affect a description of
some specific thing existing at the date of the will.[6] Where specific provision is
made for subsequent happenings there is a contrary intention.[7]

1   *Goodlad v Burnett* (1855) 1 K & J 341; *Ferguson v Ferguson* (1872) IR 6 Eq 199; *Re Ord,
     Dickinson v Dickinson* (1879) 12 Ch D 22; *Re Russell, Russell v Chell* (1882) 19 Ch D 432; *Re
     Bancroft, Bancroft v Bancroft* [1928] Ch 577; *Re Kidman* [1953] SASR 28; *Re Holmes, Villiers
     v Holmes* [1917] 1 IR 165 ('my shares in different securities' did not pass shares forming part
     of an estate to which testatrix was entitled as one of the beneficiaries); *Ferguson v Ferguson*
     (1872) IR 6 Eq 199 'my stock-in-trade and debts accruing therefrom' includes stock-in-trade
     and debts at death).

2   Such a possessive adjective may show that the gift is not generic: *Goodlad v Burnett* (1855) 1 K
     & J 341 at 348, and more particularly, where the gift is of a specific thing existing at the date of
     the will as 'my 1000 NBR shares'; 'my Holy Family' (*Re Gibson, Mathews v Foulsham* (1866)
     LR 2 Eq 669, 672); 'my cottage and land' (*Re Portal and Lamb* (1885) 30 Ch D 50); 'my
     piano' (*Re Sikes, Moxon v Crossley* [1927] 1 Ch 364; 'all the shares I have that are absolutely
     my own' (*Blake v Blake* [1923] 1 IR 88).

3   *Doe d York v Walker* (1844) 12 M & W 591. A devise of 'my house and land known as R
     wherein I now reside' did not include adjoining fields purchased after the will; *Re Fowler,
     Fowler v Wittingham* (1915) 139 LT Jo 183. 'Land now held by me' (*Re Horton, Lloyd v
     Hatchett* [1920] 2 Ch 1).

4   *Cole v Scott* (1849) 1 Mac & G 518, where the testator distinguished certain property which
     should be vested in him at his death; *Hutchinson v Barrow* (1861) 6 H & N 583 ('lands now
     occupied by me'); *Williams v Owen* (1863) 2 New Rep 585 ('house I now live in'); *Re
     Edwards, Rowland v Edwards* (1890) 63 LT 481 ('now reside'); *Noone v Lyons* (1862) 1 W &
     W (Eq) 235; *Re Whitby, Public Trustee v Whitby* [1944] Ch 210, [1944] 1 All ER 299
     (jewellery now deposited at a stated place; contrary intention sufficiently expressed). See also
     next following n 5.

5   *Wagstaff v Wagstaff* (1869) LR 8 Eq 229 ('which I now possess' said to be the same as 'which I
     possess'); *Hepburn v Skirving* (1858) 32 LTOS 26 ('now' must by reason of the statute refer to
     the death); *Re Midland Rly Co, Re Otley and Ilkey Branch* (1865) 34 Beav 525 ('now reside':

garden purchased and attached to residence after will); *Re Ashburnham, Gaby v Ashburnham* (1912) 107 LT 601 ('all my effects at present at A'). 'In which I now reside' have been treated as mere additional description and not as a vital or essential part of the description cutting down earlier words, and have been rejected: *Re Champion, Dudley v Champion* [1893] 1 Ch 101; *Re Willis* [1911] 2 Ch 563; *Re Horton, Lloyd v Hatchett* [1920] 2 Ch 1. 'Subject to an annuity now charged thereon' only means that the beneficiary is to bear the charge upon it and are a mere indication of a particular charge and do not affect the earlier description of the property nor prevent that description being applied to the date of death: *Re Ord, Dickinson v Dickinson* (1879) 12 Ch D 22.

6   *Emuss v Smith* (1848) 2 De G & Sm at 733 (where the subject is discussed); *Douglas v Douglas* (1854) Kay 400 (money 'charged' on certain lands included only money actually charged at the date of will, not money already spent and later charged nor money later spent and subsequently charged); *Re Gibson, Mathews v Foulsham* (1866) LR 2 Eq 669 at 672 ('my 1000 NBR shares'; 'my Holy Family'. If a sale is effected of these specific things, there is an ademption and a contrary intention shown); *Re Portal and Lamb* (1885) 30 Ch D 50 ('my cottage and land' no contrary intention shown, but on the language of the will, the gift did not include the after-acquired property); *Cave v Harris* (1887) 57 LJ Ch 62 ('which I have lately purchased' held to limit the gift, and after-acquired land occupied with one of the cottages did not pass); *Re Evans, Evans v Powell* [1909] 1 Ch 784 ('house and effects known as C Villa'. Part of a property divided off and houses erected on separated part. Held, all passed); *Re Alexander, Bathurst v Greenwood* [1910] WN 94 (express provision for replacement); *Re Whitby, Public Trustee v Whitby* [1944] Ch 210 (jewellery now deposited at a stated place; sufficient contrary intention); *Re Rudd, Rudd v Leitch* (1914) 33 NZLR 1446 (land in specified place); *Fuller v Taylor* (1897) 15 NZLR 229 ('the same real estate'). Where land is sold and the purchase money is payable by instalments, a specific devise does not carry the instalments unpaid at the death of the testator: *Church v Hill* [1923] SCR 642. As to devise of 'my dwelling-house' where the place of residence was changed between will and death, see *Re Georgetti's Will, Georgetti v Georgetti* (1900) 18 NZLR 849. A gift of shares in a company in addition to shares 'already held' by certain beneficiaries refers to the time of distribution and not to the date of the will and 'held' referred to beneficial and not registered ownership: *Fowler v Fowler* (1952) 69 WNNSW 283.

7   *Re Alexander, Bathurst v Greenwood* [1910] WN 94; *Re Farrelly, Howard v Shelley* [1941] IR 261 (if stock shall mature and be redeemed).

CHAPTER 60

General descriptions of property

[60.1]

All testator's interests included. A description of property of any kind in a general manner, such as 'lands', 'personal estate' or the like, not identifying any particular items of such property, prima facie[1] includes all interests, legal or equitable,[2] vested or contingent,[3] in possession, reversion, remainder or expectancy,[4] in property of that kind,[5] capable of being so disposed of[6] by the will of the testator; and general descriptions of property are prima facie construed in their general sense,[7] but are capable of being controlled by the context, for example, under the ejusdem generis rule.[8] A gift of the proceeds of sale of land will pass the fee if the land remains unsold.[9]

1   For an example of the expression of a contrary intention in the will as a whole, see *Teatt v Strong* (1760) 3 Bro Parl Cas 219, where the question was whether a reversion of a settled estate was included. In *Doe d Pell v Jeyes* (1830) 1 B & Ad 593 at 600, it is said that the rule of law is that a reversion will pass by general words, unless it distinctly appear that the settlor or testator intended to exclude it. That is that the absence of any expression to include it is not sufficient. There must be a positive intention to exclude it: *Doe d Lord and Lady Cholmondeley v Weatherby* (1809) 11 East 322 at 333; *Doe d Howell v Thomas* (1840) 1 Man & G 335 at 344; *Alliston v Chapple* (1806) 2 LT 110; *Tennent v Tennent* (1844) 1 Jo & Lat 379; *O'Reilly v Smith* (1851) 17 LTOS 280.

2   Every equitable interest is included even the interest of a purchaser who has entered into a binding agreement to purchase the property where such contract has not been completed by a conveyance: *Atcherley (or Acherley) v Vernon* (1723) 10 Mod Rep 518; *Greenhill v Greenhill* (1711) 2 Vern 679; *Holmes v Barker* (1816) 2 Madd 462; *Potter v Potter* (1750) 1 Ves Sen 437; *Capel v Girdler* (1804) 9 Ves 509. The position is the same where the testator gives an option to purchase all his property in a certain place. The option extends to property in that place which the testator has contracted to purchase: *Re Fison's Will Trusts, Fison v Fison* [1950] Ch 394, [1950] 1 All ER 501. Similarly in the case of legacy vested but not paid: *Re Cotter* (1918) 42 OLR 99.

3   *Ingilby v Amcotts* (1856) 21 Beav 585 (interest dependent on death of testator without issue). As to reversions see n 1; these interests will be vested but not in possession.

4   *Reversions in personalty. Re Egan, Mills v Penton* [1899] 1 Ch 688 (money in my possession at my death passed reversionary interest falling in possession after death); *Re Capel, Arbuthnot v Capel* (1914) 59 Sol Jo 177 (rest of my money passed reversionary interest), and see also *Re Woolley, Cathcart v Eyskens* [1918] 1 Ch 33 (as similar case). The term 'die possessed of' has been said not to be applicable to reversionary aliquot interest in stock and shares: *Re Lucas-Tooth, Lucas-Tooth v Public Trustee* (1923) 156 LT Jo 382.
    Reversions in realty. In the case of a general gift a clear intention not to exclude the reversion must appear in the will though not in express terms: see note 1, supra, and cases there cited. See also *Ridout v Pain* (1747) 3 Atk 486; *Doe d Phillips v Phillips* (1786) 1 Term Rep 105. A reversion in fee as the ultimate trust under a settlement may pass by a gift of 'lands not settled': *Glover v Spendlove* (1793) 4 Bro CC 337; *A-G v Vigor* (1803) 8 Ves 256; *Jones v Skinner* (1835) 5 LJ Ch 87; *Incorporated Society in Dublin v Richards* (1841) 4 1 Eq R 177; and such a reversion may pass under the words 'property not included in the settlement': *O'Reilly v Smith*

(1851) 17 LTOS 280; *Re Green, Walsh v Green* (1893) 31LR Ir 338. These expressions, however, are ambiguous and may mean the lands comprised in the settlement or so much of the whole interest in the land as is not subject to the settlement: *Ford v Ford* (1848) 6 Hare 486 at 494; *Incorporated Society in Dublin v Richards* (1841) 4 I Eq R 177 at 280; *Goodtitle d Daniels v Miles* (1805) 6 East 494; *Re Mather, Mather v Mather* (1926) 71 Sol Jo 142 (where a gift of all property real and personal which the testator had not settled, mortgaged or made any disposition of by any deed or instrument passed all equities of redemption and all reversions expectant on determination of leases). As to the accruing possessory interest of a squatter, see *Heward v Heward* (1868) 15 Gr 516.

5   As to mortgages and leaseholds, see para **[64.32]** infra. As to growing crops, see para **[64.20]**, n 2. As to charges on real estates not included in devise of the land, see *Davy v Redington* [1917] 1 IR 250; *Vallance v Vallance* (1863) 2 New Rep 229.

6   *Wentworth v Cox* (1882) 6 Madd 363; *Maxwell v Maxwell* (1852) 2 De GM & G 705; *Whateley v Whateley* (1867) 14 Gr 430.

7   See Chapter 50.

8   For this rule, see para **[38.10]** supra.

9   *Re Mercer* [1953] OWN 765 (gift of right to live in flat rent free for life or until sale and if sold a certain sum to be paid to life tenant and remainder to grandson. Grandson took the fee if no sale during the life of the life tenant).

[60.2]

Limitations applicable to one kind of property only. A description of property which in its usual sense is apt to include both real and personal property is not made applicable to real estate only because the limitations are more applicable to that kind of property, or are even inapplicable to any but that kind of property,[1] although that is an indication to be considered in connection with the whole context,[2] for real estate will not pass by the words 'all estate, effects and property whatsoever and wheresoever' when the trusts and general context point to personal estate only and afford no index to show that real estate was present to the mind of the testator when he made his will.[3]

1   In the following cases residuary gifts were construed to include real estate although the limitations were applicable to personalty only: *Doe d Burkitt v Chapman* (1789) 1 Hy Bl 223; *Morgan d Surman v Surman* (1808) 1 Taunt 289; *Newland v Marjoribanks* (1813) 5 Taunt 268; *Dunnage v White* (1820) 1 Jac & W 583; *Marks v Marks* (1833) 2 LJ Ch 110; *Ackers v Phipps* (1835) 3 Cl & Fin 665 (great force has been given to general bequests of all residue real and personal. Such a gift has been held to be sufficient to pass real estate, though accompanied by limitation utterly inapplicable to any but personal estate); *Barclay v Collett* (1838) 4 Bing NC 658; *Morrison v Hoppe* (1851) 4 De G & Sm 234; *D'Almaine v Moseley* (1853) 1 Drew 629; *Fullerton v Martin* (1853) 1 Eq Rep 224; *O'Toole v Browne* (1854) 3 E & B 572; *Re Greenwich Hospital Improvement Act* (1855) 20 Beav 458; *Streatfield v Cooper* (1859) 27 Beav 338; *Hamilton v Buckmaster* (1866) LR 3 Eq 323; *Stein v Ritherdon* (1868) 37 LJ Ch 369; *Lloyd v Lloyd* (1869) LR 7 Eq 458; *Longley v Longley* (1871) LR 13 Eq 133. In *Doe d Spearing v Buckner* (1796) 6 Term Rep 610, a gift to trustees 'their executors administrators and assigns' did not pass a freehold despite an introductory clause: 'as to all his estate and effects both real and personal'. *Doe d Hurrell v Hurrell* (1821) 5 B & Ald 18 (a similar case). In *Hunter v Pugh* (1839) 1 Hare 308n a contrary conclusion was reached on the context, and a similar decision was reached in *Kirby-Smith v Parnell* [1903] 1 Ch 483. A devise of messuages or tenements with appurtenances with limitations applicable only to freehold property will compromise leasehold property where a clear intention to that effect can be collected from the circumstance of the leasehold property having been blended in enjoyment with the freehold: *Hobson v Blackburn* (1833) 1 My & K 571, and see *Lane v Earl of Stanhope* (1795) 6 Term Rep 345 (gift of 'farm' partly freehold and leasehold always let as one entire farm). See also n 2.

2   *Fullerton v Martin* (1853) 1 Eq Rep 224; *Prescott v Barker* (1874) 9 Ch App 174; *Kirby-Smith v Parnell* [1903] 1 Ch 483; *Newland v Marjoribanks* (1813) 5 Taunt 268; *Doe d Hurrell v Hurrell* (1821) 5 B & Ald 18; *Coard v Holderness* (1855) 20 Beav 147. *Doe d Spearing v Buckner* (1796) 6 Term Rep 610, was doubted in *Fullerton v Martin*, and *Pogson v Thomas* (1840) 6 Bing NC 337, was doubted in *Stein v Ritherdon* (1868) 37 LJ Ch 369. Such indications

are of much less weight where there is a direction for sale and distribution: *O'Toole v Browne* (1854) 3 E & B 572 (discussing *Sanderson v Dobson* (1847) 1 Exch 141); *Streatfield v Cooper* (1859) 27 Beav 338; *Dobson v Bowness* (1868) LR 5 Eq 404.

3   *Coard v Holderness* (1855) 20 Beav 147, explained in *Re Greenwich Hospital Improvement Act* (1855) 20 Beav 458.

CHAPTER 61

Accessories follow principal gift

[61.1]
Accessories follow the principal gift. A rule which applies both to wills and to deeds is that, along with the subject-matter of any gift there impliedly go as accessory to the main gift all rights and benefits which are essential[1] to the reasonable enjoyment of the subject-matter in the state in which it is given.[2] This implication does not necessarily arise from construction, but from the circumstance of necessary dependence shown by the facts of the case; and when all the surrounding circumstances which may legitimately be inquired into are known the result may be different or the extent of the implied gift controlled.[3] The following accessories have been considered: accumulation of income;[4] contingent preference dividend;[5] right to surplus income after cesser of accumulation;[6] repaid income tax on accumulations during minority;[7] accretions to shares of a company;[8] bonus on insurance policy;[9] gift of money secured by bond;[10] growing crops;[11] timber;[12] plant on manufacturing premises;[13] rentcharges;[14] lease and renewal;[15] life policy securing an interest determining with the life;[16] cost of raising charge given by will;[17] copyright includes film rights;[18] right to compensation on compulsory acquisition;[19] bonus consideration on grant of lease of petroleum and natural gas rights passes to tenant for life under a gift for life of all proceeds received from petroleum and natural gas leases;[20] stud fees of a horse;[21] wool in store not included in bequest of sheep;[22] surrounding land reasonably necessary where use of house given.[23] 'Appurtenances' are considered separately[24].

---

1   *Palmer v Fletcher* (1663) 1 Lev 122. But it must be essential in the state in which the property is given. A way used when two properties were in one ownership does not necessarily go with the gift of one in severalty: *Pheysey v Vicary* (1847) 16 M & W 484; *Ewart v Cochrane* (1861) 5 LT 1.
2   *Pearson v Spencer* (1863) 3 B & S 761; *Phillips v Low* [1892] 1 Ch 47 at 51; *Milner's Safe Co Ltd v Great Northern and City Rly Co* [1907] 1 Ch 208 at 219; *Taws v Knowles* [1891] 2 QB 564; *Re Livingstone, Livingstone v Durell* (1917) 61 Sol Jo 384 ('moneys which shall arise from sale of land in Ireland' held to include statutory bonuses).
3   *Phillips v Low* [1892] 1 Ch 47 at 50; *Birmingham, Dudley and District Banking Co v Ross* (1888) 38 Ch D 295 at 308.
4   *Loscombe v Wintringham* (1849) 12 Beav 46 (not included: accumulations pending contingency); *Re Woolf, Public Trustee v Lazarus* [1920] 1 Ch 184 (not included); *Re Mellor, Alverez v Dodgson* [1922] 1 Ch 312 (not included); *Re Blackwell, Blackwell v Blackwell* [1926] Ch 223 (included); *Harvey v Cooke* (1827) 4 Russ 34 (not included unless it appears their non-inclusion was a clerical error); *Pursell v Elder* (1865) 4 Macq 992 (residuary gift). Where a tenant for life on her own initiative accumulated certain dividends the accumulations did not pass under an appointment of the shares which she was entitled to make: *Tugman v Hopkins* (1842) 4 Man & G 389.

5   *Re Marjoribanks, Marjoribanks v Dansey* [1923] 2 Ch 307 (included).

6   *Re Thornber, Crabtree v Thornber* [1937] Ch 29, [1936] 2 All ER 1594 (such surplus income was the subject of a partial intestacy but was not subject to the provisions of the will under the Administration of Estates Act 1925, s 49; 17 *Halsbury's Statutes* (4th edn) 462 (see Vol 2, Part G, para **[244.64]**, but was undisposed of and fell into residue, which in the circumstances was undisposed of. What wholly fails is not part of the will for the purposes of s 49). A similar result was reached in *Re Lushington* [1964] NZLR 161.

7   *Re Fulford, Fulford v Hyslop* [1930] 1 Ch 71 (beneficiary absolutely entitled to such repaid tax).

8   *Included in gift: Matthews v Maude* (1830) 1 Russ & M 397; *French v Craig* (1858) 8 I Ch R 142; *Re Buxton, Buxton v Buxton* [1930] 1 Ch 648; *Re Carson, Carson v Carson* [1915] 1 IR 321 (where a bonus was distributed partly in shares and partly in cash, the shares being an accretion to capital and the cash treated as income of the estate); *Re Henderson, Henderson v Henderson* [1926] NZLR 766; but a specific gift of the dividends and proceeds has been held not to include a bonus declared before the death of the testator: *Lock v Venables* (1859) 27 Beav 598; *Re Tetsall, Foyster v Tetsall* [1961] 2 All ER 801, [1961] 1 WLR 938. As a general rule the dividends on shares specifically bequeathed is appropriate as at the testator's death: *Pollock v Pollock* (1874) LR 18 Eq 329, though a declaration that the 'whole income derived from' shares shall be paid to a beneficiary is an express stipulation to the contrary: *Re Meredith, Stone v Meredith* (1898) 67 LJ Ch 409.

9   *Simpson v Mountain* (1835) 4 LJ Ch 221; *Harington v Moffat* (1853) 4 De GM & G 1; *Roberts v Edwards* (1863) 33 Beav 259.

10 Carries interest on bond: *Harcourt v Morgan* (1838) 2 Keen 274; *Kent v Tapley* (1847) 17 LJ Ch 99; *Re Jacob, M'Coy v Jacob* [1919] 1 IR 134.

11 *Spencer's Case* (1622) Win 51; *Cooper v Woolfitt* (1857) 2 H & N 122; *Cudney v Cudney* (1874) 21 Gr 153; *Re Burgin's Will* [1922] VLR 686. These cases show that the devisee takes except where there are words in the will to the contrary. For a case where such words were included, see *Cox v Godsalve* (1699) 6 East 604n.

12 Where the testator expressly gave timber along with personal estate, the devise of the realty carried the underwood: *Butler v Borton* (1820) 5 Madd 40.

13 *Wood v Gaynon* (1761) Amb 395 (plant of brewery).

14 Where on a conveyance in fee to a purchaser certain rentcharges were conveyed to trustees for him and he subsequently devised the property without mentioning the rentcharges, the property passed free from the rentcharges: *Vallance v Vallance* (1863) 2 New Rep 229. See also *Kilkelly v Powell* [1897] 1 IR 457.

15 *Abney v Miller* (1743) 2 Atk 593.

16 *Hamilton v Baldwin* (1852) 15 Beav 232 (policy excluded). See also *Simpson v Mountain* (1835) 4 LJ Ch 221 (policy specifically included did not include bonuses), and *Harington v Moffat* (1853) 4 De GM & G 1.

17 *Re Buckely's Trust* (1853) 17 Beav 110.

18 *Re Bancroft, Bancroft v Bancroft* [1928] Ch 577.

19 *Young v Midland Rly Co* (1892) 16 OR 738 (not included).

20 *Re Rigney Estate* (1954) 12 WWRNS 171.

21 *Arnold v Ennis* (1853) 2 I Ch R 601.

22 *Re Hawker* [1939] SASR 426.

23 *Re Mercer* [1953] OWN 765.

24 See Chapter 64.

CHAPTER 62

Unlimited gifts of income or unlimited charges

[62.1]

Unlimited gifts of income. An unlimited devise of the rents and profits of land is prima facie a gift of the land itself,[1] and an unlimited bequest of the income or produce of personal estate of a mixed fund is prima facie a gift of the capital or corpus thereof.[2] It has been said that once it is found that the gift is unlimited, it gives the corpus and is not subject to the intention of the will,[3] but the rule has been held to be excluded where the will shows that the donee is not to take the land or the capital,[4] as where the donee is to take an interest for life only,[5] and the rule does not apply where the gift of income is not unlimited,[6] or where the gift is not of all the benefits from the property;[7] but merely of a particular benefit[8] or a benefit to be enjoyed by the donee personally.[9] It makes no difference whether the income is given to the donee directly or through the intervention of trustees.[10] The principle does not apply to a charity as a charity continues in perpetuity and effect can be validly given to a perpetual trust of income.[11]

1   *Murthwaite v Jenkinson* (1824) 2 B & C 357 (where the property was in fact given to trustees, but on this point see, also, *Adshead v Willetts* (1861) 29 Beav 358; *Stewart v Garnett* (1830) 3 Sim 398 (such a gift passes everything necessary to the enjoyment of the estate); *Doe d Goldin v Lakeman* (1831) 2 B & Ad 30 (where the gift of the rents and profits was conditional on a prior devisee not returning to England); *Plenty v West* (1848) 6 CB 201; *Blann v Bell* (1852) 2 De GM & G 775; *Bignall v Rose* (1854) 24 LJ Ch 27 (gift of rents of leaseholds carries the leaseholds); *Mannox v Greener* (1872) LR 14 Eq 456 (where it was held that the gift need not necessarily be of the 'rents and profits', but might be of the 'income'); *Re Martin, Martin v Martin* [1892] WN 120; *Sheridan v O'Reilly* [1900] 1 IR 386; *Baker v Blount* [1917] 1 IR 316; *Malcolmson v Malcomson* (1851) 17 LTOS 44; *Re Baker's Will, Baker v Hutchinson* [1905] VLR 416; *Re Churchill* [1919] 3 WWR 557 (farm proceeds); *Re Jenkins, Jenkins v May* (1954) 2 DLR 268; *Re Steinberg Will* (1968) 63 WWR 649; *Torney v Lawrence* (1967) 61 WWR 510; contrast *Re Parsons* (1968) 67 DLR (2d) 685. Where a will directed the conversion of the estate into money and the payment of a monthly sum to a son during his life and made no other gift, the son took the corpus and the direction to pay the monthly sum was ineffective; *Re McGrath Estate* (1952) 5 WWRNS 637.

2   *Stretch v Watkins* (1816) 1 Madd 253; *Clough v Wynne* (1817) 2 Madd 188; *Haig v Swiney* (1823) 1 Sim & St 487; *Jenings v Baily* (1853) 17 Beav 118; *Cooney v Nicholls* (1881) 7 LR Ir 107; *Davidson v Kimpton* (1881) 18 Ch D 213; *Re L'Herminier, Mounsey v Buston* [1894] 1 Ch 675 (rule applied to a power of appointment); *Wiley v Chanteperdrix* [1894] 1 IR 209; *Tredennick v Tredennick* [1900] 1 IR 354; *Sheridan v O'Reilly* [1900] 1 IR 386; *Re Lawes-Wittewronge, Maurice v Bennett* [1915] 1 Ch 408 (gift of net profits in 'all my commercial undertakings' held to carry shares in company but not debentures); *Re Willcocks* [1959] Qd R 349; *Buick v Equity Trustees Executors and Agency Co Ltd* (1957) 97 CLR 599; *Re Florent Estate* [1927] 3 DLR 946; *Re Jones* [1927] 2 DLR 113; *Public Trustee v Wilson* [1916] NZLR 798; *Lyndon v Lyndon* [1930] NZLR 76 (where the unlimited gift of income was to children after a life interest to the mother); *Re Macdonald* [1931] 4 DLR 920. This passage of the text, and several others, was referred to in *Ng Chi-fong v Hui Ho Pui-fun* [1987] HKLR 462 at 470.

3   *Congregational Union of New South Wales v Thistlethwayte* (1952) 87 CLR 375.
4   *Re Morgan, Morgan v Morgan* [1893] 3 Ch 222 at 227; *Re Rawlins' Trusts* (1890) 45 Ch D
     299, on appeal sub nom; *Scalé v Rawlins* [1892] AC 342; *Baker v Smith* (1853) 1 WR 490
     (testator distinguishing between capital and income); *Re Mason, Mason v Mason* [1910] 1 Ch
     695 (gift over); *McKenzie v McKenzie* [1925] 1 DLR 373; *Re Williams, Bendigo and Northern
     District Base Hospital of Bendigo v A-G* [1955] VLR 65; *Re Dumaresq Will* (1967) 58 WWR
     172.
5   *Wynne v Wynne* (1837) 2 Keen 778 at 791; *Blann v Bell* (1852) 2 De GM & G 775 at 781
     (where the donee took the same interest as another donee who took for life only); *Re Maw
     Estate* (1952) 6 WWRNS 609.
6   *Buchanan v Harrison* (1861) 8 Jur NS 965 at 967; *Re Mason, Mason v Mason* [1910] 1 Ch 695
     at 700; *Re Orr, M'Dermott v Anderson* [1915] 1 IR 191 (diminution of interest on re-marriage).
7   See para **[62.3]**, nn 1 and 2, and text thereto.
8   Devise of use and occupation of land; see para **[64.32]** infra.
9   The fact that the donee was a married woman and the income was given to her for her separate
     use was not sufficient to exclude the rule: *Tawney v Ward* (1839) 1 Beav 563; *Humphrey v
     Humphrey* (1851) 1 Sim NS 536; *Watkins v Weston* (1863) 3 De GJ & Sm 434; *Epple v Stone*
     (1906) 3 CLR 412; *Royal Trust Co v Moore* (1955) 16 WWR 204 (gift only during occupation
     by husband and wife).
10   *Haig v Swiney* (1823) 1 Sim & St 487 at 490.
11   *Re Levy, Barclays Bank Ltd v Board of Guardians and Trustees for the Relief of the Jewish
     Poor* [1960] Ch 346, [1960] 1 All ER 42. See, however, to the contrary *Congregational Union
     of New South Wales v Thistlethwayte* (1952) 87 CLR 375 (disapproving *Re Wright's Will*
     [1917] VLR 127); *Re Burnham* (1958) 17 DLR (2d) 298; *Re Levy* [1960] Ch 346, [1960] 1 All
     ER 42 was followed in *Re Clark, Horwell v Dent* [1961] NZLR 635 and also in *Re Flannagan,
     Bealty v A-G* [1962] NZLR 480 so that in New Zealand the English rule applies that a perpetual
     gift of income to a charity does not carry the corpus. in *Re Beesty's Will Trusts, Farrar v Royal
     Alfred Merchant Seaman's Society* [1966] Ch 223, [1964] 3 All ER 82, however, the will
     showed that the estate should be wound up and a gift of the net revenue of an estate was held to
     carry the capital. In *Re Inman* [1965] VR 238 it was held that the will showed that no charity
     was to take any part of the corpus but that the annual income was to be divided among them.

[62.2]
Unlimited charge. A charge upon the rents and profits of land or upon income
of personalty indefinitely may be a charge on the property itself in similar
cases.[1]

1   *Phillips v Gutteridge* (1862) 3 De GJ & Sm 332 at 336; *Metcalfe v Hutchinson* (1875) 1 Ch D
     591 at 594 (will may show contrary intention); *Re Green, Baldock v Green* (1888) 40 Ch D 610
     (where the rule was excluded by the context of the gift was for payment of debts); *Re Young,
     Brown v Hodgson* [1912] 2 Ch 479; *Ramsay v Lowther* (1912) 16 CLR 1 (gifts of rents not
     indefinite). As to charges upon income as distinguished from charges on capital; see
     para **[33.30]** supra.

[62.3]
Gifts until marriage. Where there is a gift of income until marriage followed by
a gift over, the gift does not confer an absolute interest.[1] On the other hand if
there is a gift over the interest is absolute.[2]

1   *Re Mason, Mason v Mason* [1910] 1 Ch 695 at 700; *Re Henry Will Trust, Mussett v Smith*
     [1953] 1 All ER 531, [1953] 1 WLR 376 (where the cases are considered. In this case there was
     not a true gift over but on marriage the capital was to be settled on the donee for her benefit as
     the trustees should think fit).
2   *Rishton v Cobb* (1839) 5 My & Cr 145 (a case which has been commented on in *Re
     Boddington, Boddington v Clairat* (1884) 25 Ch D 685 at 689, and in *Re Mason, Mason v
     Mason* [1910] 1 Ch 695 at 697); *Re Howard, Taylor v Howard* [1901] 1 Ch 412 (gift to widow
     of £200 payable £3 monthly so long as she did not re-marry or until £200 exhausted. Held,
     absolute gift of £200). *Re Barklie* [1917] 1 IR 1 (annuity until marriage with gift of capital sum
     on marriage, held to be an annuity for life or until marriage).

[62.4]

Gifts of rents of property let. If a testator, being entitled to land subject to a lease, devises the 'rent', or 'the ground rent', of the land, without expressly disposing of his reversion, the devise prima facie includes not only the rent payable during the lease, but the whole interest of the testator in the land.[1]

---

1   *Kaye v Laxon* (1780) 1 Bro CC 76; *Walker v Shore* (1815) 19 Ves 387; *Ashton v Adamson* (1841) 1 Dr & War 198; *Cuthbert v Lemprière* (1814) 3 M & S 158. But if the testator only has a lease, the whole leasehold interest passes: *Watkins v Weston* (1863) 3 De GJ & Sm 434.

CHAPTER 63

Description by locality

[63.1]

General principles applicable. A description of property by its locality does not include property in any other locality at the death of the testator,[1] unless the restriction to that locality is to be rejected as *falsa demonstratio*.[2] If, however, the property described is movable, the intention is inferred, unless the context is to the contrary,[3] that the gift includes a property which is usually in that situation and has been removed merely temporarily[4] or of necessity for its preservation,[5] or, it seems, tortiously,[6] but not in general property otherwise permanently removed.[7] Since choses in action are not considered localised, a general description of property in a certain locality prima facie[8] does not include any choses in action due, payable or recoverable there, or represented by documents, other than Bank of England notes or other notes treated as cash,[9] which are kept there,[10] unless the locality is a place where such documents are usually kept.[11] A description of chattels in a certain receptacle does not ordinarily include articles in the specified place which are mere accessories to things in another place,[12] but may include such a sum of money[13] as may ordinarily be found there.[14]

The following matters are decided upon the principles already stated but are collected for convenience.

1 *Heseltine v Heseltine* (1818) 3 Madd 276; *Colleton v Garth* (1833) 6 Sim 19; *Houlding v Cross* (1855) 25 LTOS 29; *Spencer v Spencer* (1856) 21 Beav 548; *Blagrove v Coore* (1859) 27 Beav 138; *Wilkins v Jodrell* (1863) 11 WR 588. This principle applies although the property is acquired or brought to the locality after the date of the will: *Gayre v Gayre* (1705) 2 Vern 538; *Sayer v Sayer* (1714) Gilb Ch 87; but goods in transit to the locality do not pass: *Duke of Beaufort v Lord Dundonald* (1716) 2 Vern 739; *Lord Brooke v Earl of Warwick* (1848) 2 De G & Sm 425; *Lane v Sewell* (1874) 43 LJ Ch 378. But see *Arkell v Fletcher* (1839) 10 Sim 299. For a case where the restriction to locality applied only to part of a gift, see *Norris v Norris* (1846) 2 Coll 719; *Domvile v Taylor* (1863) 32 Beav 604. A gift of the 'contents' of a residence includes in the ordinary case everything that could, as between landlord and tenant, be removed by the testator from the residence: *Re Oppenheim, Oppenheim v Oppenheim* (1914) 111 LT 937, but furniture in a house has been held not to include that in a detached garage: *Re Smith* [1956] NZLR 841. Such a gift does not include a car: *Re Leslie* [1954] OWN 472, but may include a business article (cash register): *Re Smith* and has been held to include shares and stock represented by certificates in the house: *Re Rodger* (1966) 60 DLR (2d) 666.
2 *Norreys v Franks* (1875) IR 9 Eq 18; *Re Brimble, Brimble v Brimble* (1918) 144 LT Jo 217, and see Chapter 58.
3 *Re Earl of Stamford, Hall v Lambert* (1906) 22 TLR 632; *McAfee v Kerr* (1918) 52 ILT 178.
4 *Lord Brooke v Earl of Warwick* (1848) 2 De G & Sm 425; *Spencer v Spencer* (1856) 21 Beav 548; *Cardigan v Curzon-Howe* (1870) 23 LT 642; *Rawlinson v Rawlinson* (1876) 3 Ch D 302; *Re McCalmont, Rooper v McCalmont* (1903) 19 TLR 490; *Re Lea, Wells v Holt* (1911) 104 LT 253; *Re Baroness Zouche, Dugdale v Baroness Zouche* [1919] 2 Ch 178. In *Re Lea, Wells v Holt*, it was held, among other points, that £50 taken from the house and deposited at the bank without the instructions of the testatrix was not in the house, but in *Re Heilbronner, Nathan v*

Kenny [1953] 2 All ER 1016, [1953] 1 WLR 1254, money drawn from the bank for a temporary purpose was held to be money at the bank.

5   *Chapman v Hart* (1749) 1 Ves Sen 271 (goods in ship, original situation temporary and precarious); *Moore v Moore* (1781) 1 Bro CC 127; *Re Johnson, Cockerell v Earl of Essex* (1884) 26 Ch D 538 (jewellery sent to bankers); *Re Baxendale, Baxendale v Baxendale* (1919) 148 LT Jo 139 (plate sent to bankers).

6   *Earl of Shaftsbury v Countess of Shaftsbury* (1716) 2 Vern 747 at 748 (furniture removed on surrender of leasehold. The point on tortious removal is dictum).

7   Removal adeems the gift: *Green v Symonds* (1730) 1 Bro CC 129n. Removal by an authorised agent, though unknown to the testator, is an ademption, even if approval of the acts of the agent is subsequent to the removal; *Earl of Shaftsbury v Countess of Shaftsbury* (1716) 2 Vern 747. It has been held that there is no ademption when an account is moved from one bank to another: *Re Brems* [1963] 1 OR 122.

8   But intention to the contrary may be shown: *Scorey v Harrison* (1852) 20 LTOS 302 (promissory note due to testator in England but person in South Africa); *Earl of Tyrone v Marquis of Waterford* (1860) 1 De GF & J 613 (debts due in the county of N); *Guthrie v Walrond* (1883) 22 Ch D 573 (debts due from persons in Mauritius); *Re Prater, Desinge v Beare* (1888) 37 Ch D 481 (shares deposited at bank in Paris); *Re Robson, Robson v Hamilton* [1891] 2 Ch 559 (gift of contents including promissory notes and similar choses in action); *Re Clark, McKecknie v Clark* [1904] 1 Ch 294 (where of two localities, that of the bond debtor and that of the certificate, the latter was preferred); *Young v Bain, Re Young* (1902) 21 NZLR 503 (debtors must reside in locality at time of testator's death).

9   *Popham v Lady Aylesbury* (1748) Amb 68 (bank notes); *Brooke v Turner* (1836) 7 Sim 671 (contents of house includes Bank of England notes and cash, but not country bank notes, promissory notes or a mortgage); *Re Robson, Robson v Hamilton* [1891] 2 Ch 559 (bank notes and coin); *Mahoney v Donovan* (1863) 14 I Ch R 388 (bank notes in house); *Re Abbott* [1944] 2 All ER 457 ('contents of home or at bank' did not include choses in action even though the certificates were in the home or at the bank); *Thorne v Thorne* (1903) 33 SCR 309 (debt).

10 *Chapman v Hart* (1749) 1 Ves Sen 271 (goods on board ship pass though removed and not on board at testator's death. Goods in a house only pass where properly in possession, and choses in action except bank notes will not pass. Ready money if not an extraordinary sum and just received passes); *Moore v Moore* (1781) 1 Bro CC 127 (bond); *Jones v Lord Sefton* (1798) 4 Ves 166 (bond for arrears of rent); *Nisbett v Murray* (1799) 5 Ves 149 (bond); *Fleming v Brook* (1804) 1 Sch & Lef 318 (all property in A except a particular chose in action; other choses in action there do not pass despite the exception); *Stuart v Marquis of Bute* (1806) 11 Ves 657; *Brooke v Turner,* supra (promissory notes and mortgage); *Marquis Hertford v Lord Lowther* (1843) 7 Beav 1 (Polish certificates and Neopolitan bordereaux); *Rhodes v Rhodes* (1874) 22 WR 835 (balance at bank); *Thorne v Thorne* (1903) 33 SCR 309 (debt); *Lazarus v Lazarus* (1919) 88 LJ Ch 525 (estate situated in Great Britain: bonds certificate and share scrip of corporations not localised in Great Britain although the documents themselves were in Great Britain did not pass). In *Re O'Brien, O'Brien v O'Brien* [1906] 1 IR 649, the context was held to exclude cash in the house; *Re Harvey, Jenkinson v McWatters* [1962] NZLR 524 ('house and contents' does not include choses in action kept there).

11 As, for instance, a bureau desk, box or bank, where documents and money are usually kept; *Roberts v Kuffin* (1741) 2 Atk 112; *Re Robson, Robson v Hamilton* [1891] 2 Ch 559. A gift of box or other receptacle does not generally include securities which it contains: *Re Hunter, Northey v Northey* (1908) 25 TLR 19; *Joseph v Phillips* [1934] AC 348 (gift of desk with contents did not include pass books and promissory notes in the desk); followed in *Re Jones* (1973) 34 DLR (3d) 479 (bequest of 'my personal wallet', cash content not included). As to gift of the contents of a room, see *Re Neilson, Cumming v Clyde* (1929) 73 Sol Jo 765 (autograph letters).

12 As, for instance, title deeds or the key to another receptacle: *Brooke v Turner* (1836) 7 Sim 671 at 681; *Re Robson, Robson v Hamilton* [1891] 2 Ch 559 at 565; *Re Craven, Crewdson v Craven* (1908) 99 LT 390 (gift of a house and its contents: bonds and securities were excluded).

13 *Swinfen v Swinfen (No 4)* (1860) 29 Beav 207.

14 *Chapman v Hart* (1749) 1 Ves Sen 271 at 272 (if an extraordinary sum and just received).

[63.2]

County. Misdescription of the county has been held immaterial where there is sufficient otherwise to identify the land;[1] but this principle has been applied apparently with reluctance and lands outside the county have often been excluded.[2]

1   *Hastead v Searle* (1679) 1 Ld Raym 728; *Mosley v Massey* (1806) 8 East 149; *Doe d Beach v Earl of Jersey* (1818) 1 B & Ald 550 (description of estate devised).
2   *Webber v Stanley* (1864) 16 CBNS 698 ('property in the county of H devised to me by my late husband'; only property in county passed); *Moser v Platt* (1844) 14 Sim 95 (property in the city of H in the county of H: no property not in the city passed although it was in the county); *Church Property Trustees v Public Trustee* (1907) 27 NZLR 354 (property in borough within county not included because by local statute boroughs were not included in counties).

[63.3]

Parish. Lands described as in one parish have sometimes passed although in fact the lands extend into adjoining parishes,[1] but there are many cases where the contrary has been held.[2]

1   *Anstee v Nelms* (1856) 1 H & N 225 (lands reputed to be in named parish); *Hardwick v Hardwick* (1873) LR 16 Eq 168 (lands outside named parish only accessible from those in parish: error of description lay in accessory words); *Homer v Homer* (1878) 8 Ch D 758 (fields just over the boundary, the occupation of which was correctly described; but in this case land correctly described as in parish of G did not pass where the occupation was wrongly described); *Whitfield v Langdale* (1875) 1 Ch D 61 (real description in name of property). *Re Bassett* [1961] VR 51 (parish and township).
2   *Tuttesham v Roberts* (1603) Cro Jac 22 (lands usually occupied together); *Attwater v Attwater* (1853) 18 Beav 330 (lands at C in the parish of S; other property not situated at C but in the same parish did not pass); *Evans v Angell* (1858) 26 Beav 202 (lands in adjoining parish usually let together did not pass); *Pedley v Dodds* (1866) LR 2 Eq 819 (occupied as one farm, but only land in named parish passed). See *Keogh v Keogh* (1874) IR 8 Eq 179; *Doe d Tyrrell v Lyford* (1816) 4 M & S 550; *Doe d Dell v Pigott* (1817) 7 Taunt 553; *Pogson v Thomas* (1840) 6 Bing NC 337; *Barber v Wood* (1877) 4 Ch D 885.

[63.4]

Street. Where houses are said to be in a named street, they may include others in a lane entered from the street[1] or joined by a covered passage[2] or situated at the rear,[3] but it has been held that 'at in or near' does not include houses 400 yards off.[4] Neighbouring property rightly described may pass where there is no such property owned by testator in the named street,[5] but not where the description is fulfilled by the property in the named street.[6] Property abutting on two streets may pass although said to abut on one street and that the less important of the two.[7] A case where the numbers of the houses were correct but the name of the street was wrong was treated as *falsa demonstratio* and the houses passed under the will.[8] Houses in 'Bullen Court, Strand and Maiden Lane' are to be read separately and houses in each of these streets pass.[9] A gift of property on the west side of the street has been held to pass only property on that side although held together with property on the east side.[10]

1   *Doe d Humphreys v Roberts* (1822) 5 B & Ad 407.
2   *Newton v Lucas* (1836) 1 My & Cr 391.
3   *Armstrong v Buckland* (1854) 18 Beav 204. See also *Re Anderson* [1916] 12 Tas LR 71.
4   *Doe d Ashforth v Bower* (1832) 3 B & Ad 453 (where the houses were also described as purchased from a named vendor and those 400 yards away were so purchased and conveyed to testator under one conveyance).
5   *Tann v Tann* (1863) 2 New Rep 412.
6   *Lambert v Overton* (1864) 11 LT 503.
7   *Harman v Gurner* (1866) 35 Beav 478.

8   *Re Mayell, Foley v Wood* [1913] 2 Ch 488.
9   *Gauntlett v Carter* (1853) 17 Beav 586.
10   *Smith v Ridgway* (1866) LR 1 Exch 331.

[63.5]

Estate. The description of the estate may prevail over a description by the county in which it is situate,[1] and an estate in a named county may pass all testator's land in the county[2] and this is aided by the fact that by his acts and dealings the testator generally considered such lands as one estate.[3] Lands which have become known by a special description may pass though formerly known by other names.[4]

1   *Doe d Beach v Earl of Jersey* (1818) 1 B & Ald 550.
2   *Ricketts v Turquand* (1848) 1 HL Cas 472.
3   See cases cited in nn 1 and 2, and *Webb v Byng* (1855) 1 K & J 580.
4   *Whitfield v Langdale* (1875) 1 Ch D 61.

[63.6]

'Elsewhere'. By the use of the words 'and elsewhere' widely separated property may pass;[1] but 'elsewhere' added to a dwelling-house may be restricted to the testator's dwelling-house wherever it may be at the time of his death.[2] The word 'elsewhere' may be restricted by a recital of certain lands.[3]

1   *Freeman v Duke of Chandos* (1775) 1 Cowp 363 ('elsewhere in the United Kingdom'); *Pinney v Marriott* (1863) 32 Beav 643 ('Dorset and elsewhere', passed estate in Norfolk).
2   *Turner v Turner* (1880) 14 Ch D 829.
3   *Doe d Harris v Greathed* (1806) 8 East 91 (where a settlement was recited and the lands were confined to the settled lands).

[63.7]

Occupation. Generally where the description is by reference to occupation, only the part so occupied passes,[1] but the description of the land may prevail, the mention of the occupation being transposed if necessary to refer only to the part so occupied.[2] Where the description by reference to occupation states that the property is in the testator's own occupation, then the land includes not only that in the testator's sole occupation, but that in his joint occupation with others[3] and part used for business purposes is also included.[4] Generally such words 'as now in my occupation' do not restrict the gift otherwise accurately described,[5] and it may be that the description by reference to occupation or possession in the case of goods is the controlling description.[6]

1   *Doe d Hubbard v Hubbard* (1850) 15 QB 227; *Wellington v Shepherd* (1872) 27 LT 832 (where the description of the part occupied was incorrect); *Doe d Campton v Carpenter* (1850) 16 QB 181; *Cosby v Millington* (1869) 38 LJCP 373; *Homer v Homer* (1878) 8 Ch D 758; *Re Fuller, Arnold v Chandler* (1915) 59 Sol Jo 304.
2   *Marshall v Hopkins* (1812) 15 East 309; *Goodtitle d Radford v Southern* (1813) 1 M & S 299 (evidence that devise extended to more than part designated by occupation); *Hardwick v Hardwick* (1873) LR 16 Eq 168 (words referring to occupation treated as secondary description not overriding the main description).
3   *Mirrel v Nicholls* (1611) 1 Bulst 117.
4   *Doe d Clements v Collins* (1788) 2 Term Rep 498.
5   *Goodright d Lamb v Pears* (1809) 11 East 58; *White v Birch* (1867) 36 LJ Ch 174.
6   *Re Seal, Seal v Taylor* [1894] 1 Ch 316; *Doe d Parkin v Parkin* (1814) 1 Marsh 61. As to gift of house 'in which I now reside' or 'in which I shall be living at my death', see *Re Fowler, Fowler*

v Wittingham (1915) 139 LT Jo 183; *Re Knight, Knight v Burgess* (1887) 34 Ch D 518. 'Farm on which I now reside': *Lewis & Sons, Ltd v Dawson* [1934] SCR 676 (includes 'wood lot' 50 miles from farm, the general gift prevailing).

[63.8]

Source from which obtained. It is a question of construction whether the testator introduces words descriptive of the purchase or inheriting of the property as mere explanatory comment or as defining and restricting the extent of the gift. Such words have often been treated as merely explanatory or erroneous,[1] but may be treated as a restriction.[2] Property descended from an ancestor includes not only that directly descended, but that descended through the niece of that ancestor,[3] and property received by the death of B includes all that to which the testator was entitled in possession during his lifetime though not received until after his death.[4] Necessarily property received by 'inheritance' does not include property received under a deed of gift 'inter vivos' and this is so although it would have come to the testator by inheritance.[5]

1   *Doe d Tyrrell v Lyford* (1816) 4 M & S 550; *Welby v Welby* (1813) 2 Ves & B 187; *Doe d Hawthorn v Nickliss* (1840) 4 Jur 660; *Norman v Norman* [1919] 1 Ch 297. As to possession, see *Stark's Trustees v Stark* 1948 SC 41 (motor car ordered but not delivered).
2   *Re Jackson, Wilson v Donald* (1881) 44 LT 467; *Purchase v Shallis* (1850) 2 H & Tw 354 gift of annuity of £21 purchased by JG. Only annuity so purchased one of £46 subject to a premium of £25 leaving a net income of £21. This annuity passed under the will).
3   *Doe d Newton v Taylor* (1827) 7 B & C 384.
4   *Girdlestone v Creed* (1853) 10 Hare 480.
5   *Wilkinson v Bewicke* (1853) 3 De GM & G 937.

[63.9]

Reference to tenure. Freeholds may pass where the location of the property is correctly described although the nature of the property is mistakenly described as leasehold,[1] and a gift of 'all the terms and interest' in leasehold property may pass the fee where the testator has, after the date of his will, acquired the reversion.[2] Where the gift is of mortgaged property in a certain place, stated to be charged to a named mortgagee to secure a certain sum only the mortgaged property will pass and other property of the same or a different tenure in the same place does not pass.[3] Where the gift was of freehold and copyhold messuages, farms, lands, tenements, hereditaments and real estate situate in a named place, leaseholds held for a 1,000-year term passed where the testator had no freeholds or copyholds.[4] A testator devised his four leasehold messuages in a named place when in fact he had in that place five such messuages held under four leases. It was held that the five passed.[5]

1   *Denn d Wilkins v Kemeys* (1808) 8 East 366.
2   *Saxton v Saxton* (1879) 13 Ch D 359; *Miles v Miles* (1866) LR 1 Eq 462; *Hallett v Hallett* (1898) 14 TLR 420 (subsequent enlargement); *Re Fleming's Will Trust, Ennion v Hampstead Old People's Housing Trust Ltd* [1974] 3 All ER 323, [1974] 1 WLR 1552; see para **[59.2]**, n 6.
3   *Pullin v Pullin* (1825) 3 Bing 47.
4   *Nelson v Hopkins* (1851) 21 LJ Ch 410; but as to what passes under 'lands' see paras **[64.32]**– **[64.33]** infra.
5   *Sampson v Sampson* (1869) LR 8 Eq 479.

CHAPTER 64

Particular descriptions of property

[64.1]

Annuity. This word may in the construction of a will include annual payments whether they are of a sum certain or uncertain such as a balance of rents and profits.[1]

1   *Re Fitch's Will Trusts* (1928) 139 LT 556; affd sub nom *Shaw v Public Trustee* (1929) 141 LT 465; and Chapter 33.

[64.2]

Appurtenances. Lands do not usually pass under the word 'appurtenances' with reference to other land, in its strict sense,[1] but they do pass if it appears that the word is used in a larger sense.[2] Land has been held to pass under this word where there is a gift of a house with its appurtenances.[3] There has been a distinction between a gift of land with appurtenances and a gift with the land appertaining thereto, for the latter clearly carries land.[4] A chose in action does not ordinarily pass as appurtenant to other property.[5]

1   *Kaye v Laxon* (1780) 1 Bro CC 76; *Walker v Shore* (1815) 19 Ves 387; *Ashton v Adamson* (1841) 1 Dr & War 198; *Cuthbert v Robinson* (1882) 51 LJ Ch 238. For cases where the strict sense was applied, see *Smith v Ridgway* (1866) LR 1 Exch 331; *Doe d Renow v Ashley* (1847) 10 QB 663; *Pheysey v Vicary* (1847) 16 M & W 484; *Evans v Angell* (1858) 26 Beav 202; *Lister v Pickford* (1865) 34 Beav 576. The original doctrine was that land could not be 'appurtenant' to land and 'appurtenances' only included incorporeal hereditaments such as rights of way: *Lister v Pickford*.
2   *Buck d Whalley v Nurton* (1797) 1 Bos & P 53 at 57.
3   *Blackborn v Edgley* (1719) 1 P Wms 600 (gift of house and appurtenances passes only house and garden or orchard, but gift of a house with land appertaining passes land usually occupied therewith); *Doe d Lempriere v Martin* (1777) 2 Wm Bl 1148 (land occupied with house passed under appurtenances though held for a different term); *Ongley v Chambers* (1824) 1 Bing 483 (devise of rectory with messuages, lands, tenements, tithes, hereditaments and all and singular other the premises thereto belonging included land separately acquired but for long occupied with the rectory); *Hobson v Blackburn* (1833) 1 My & K 571 (appurtenances to freehold property will include leasehold property where there is a context justifying such inclusion); *Leach v Leach* [1878] WN 79 (three meadows adjoining house); *Cuthbert v Robinson* (1882) 51 LJ Ch 238 (devise to trustees).
4   *Blackborn v Edgley* (1719) 1 P Wms 600.
5   *Finch v Finch* (1876) 45 LJ Ch 816 ('appurtenances' to factory do not include outstanding loans); *Re McCalmont, Rooper v McCalmont* (1903) 19 TLR 490.

[64.3]

Articles of domestic use or ornament. Under this heading have been included books;[1] plants;[2] drawings[3] and a motor car.[4] Under a comprehensive clause of this nature specifically mentioning 'articles of *vertu*' a sheriff's chain of office was held to be included as under the specific heading, which would include any type of article which a virtuoso or connoisseur might collect for its artistic merit or the beauty of its workmanship,[5] but not merely for its archaeological interest.[6]

1   *Cornewall v Cornewall* (1841) 12 Sim 298.
2   *Re Owen, Peat v Owen* (1898) 78 LT 643 (valuable orchids of which some were brought into the house for ornament. Enquiry as to those so brought in which passed as 'articles of domestic use or ornament'). For a case of a collection of animals and birds, see *Re Fothergill, Horwood v Fothergill* (1916) 51 L Jo 169.
3   *Re Du Maurier, Millar v Coles* (1916) 32 TLR 579.
4   *Deans v Rees* [1954] NZLR 877 (where the car was registered as a business car and insurance premium was paid by a company of which the testator was a member). As to motor cars see also para **[64.8]** infra.
5   *Re Coxen, McCallum v Coxen* [1948] Ch 747, [1948] 2 All ER 492; *Re Tomline's Will Trusts, Pretyman v Pretyman* [1931] 1 Ch 521.
6   *Re Tomline's Will Trusts, Pretyman v Pretyman* [1931] 1 Ch 521 (prehistoric axe-head or Egyptian mummy not articles of *vertu*); but a gift of a cabinet of curiosities did not pass personal ornaments occasionally shown with it: *Cavendish v Cavendish* (1784) 1 Bro CC 467.

[64.4]

Belongings. This word by itself has been held sufficient to include freeholds,[1] though it will clearly include every other form of property whether used by itself or with the word 'personal' added.[2]

1   *Re Price* [1950] Ch 242, [1950] 1 All ER 338; *Re Schott's Will Trust, Prause v Malmcrantz* (1968) 112 Sol Jo 335 ('the rest and residue of all my belongings' included all the residuary estate including real as well as personal property).
2   *Re Bradfield* [1914] WN 423; *Re Mills' Will Trusts* [1937] 1 All ER 142. In these cases belongings was given to a very wide interpretation, but it did not appear in either case that there were any freeholds in the estate.

[64.5]

Bonds. This word is not applicable to a debenture the certificate of which is not under seal,[1] nor is it applicable to inscribed stock,[2] and shares in a company will not strictly pass under a gift of bonds or securities.[3] What are in fact bonds will not pass under the description 'promissory notes'[4] and under foreign bonds' colonial bonds will not pass,[5] and where the estate includes bonds properly so described, it cannot be enlarged to cover other government stock.[6]

1   *Re Manners, Manners v Manners* [1923] 1 Ch 220.
2   *Re Manners, Manners v Manners* [1923] 1 Ch 220, but compare *Re Alleyn* [1965] SALR 22, where bonds were held to include Treasury Bonds, Inscribed Stock and Debenture Stock, but not money on deposit.
3   *Hudleston v Gouldsbury* (1847) 10 Beav 547. As to bonds passing under such terms as 'funds', 'investments', 'securities', 'shares', see those headings, on paras **[64.23]**, **[64.30]**, **[64.53]** and **[64.54]** infra.
4   *Re Gee* [1928] 3 DLR 54 (debenture bonds).
5   *Hull v Hill* (1876) 4 Ch D 97.
6   *Re Edwards* [1964] VR 551.

[64.6]

Books. Under 'books' there have been passed the bound manuscript notes of a physician,[1] bound manuscript music,[2] a manuscript log-book of a ship[3] and a stamp collection.[4] Under a bequest of a law library all books appertaining to legal questions pass.[5]

1   *Willis v Curtois* (1838) 1 Beav 189 (in this case, however, a pocket-book carried about the person of the testator did not pass under the heading 'personal ornaments').
2   *Re Plowden, Plowden v Plowden* (1908) 24 TLR 883.
3   *Re Barratt, Barratt v Coates* (1915) 31 TLR 502.
4   *Re Fortlage, Ross v Fortlage* (1916) 60 Sol Jo 527, but see *Re Masson, Morton v Masson* (1917) 86 LJ Ch 753, to the contrary.
5   *Wallace v Bayldon* (1825) 4 LJOS Ch 74.

[64.7]
'Business'. The first question is whether the gift of a business carries the land or premises occupied by the business and the answer to this question has generally been a negative one.[1] The bequest will include the capital of a business and capital may include a debt due to the testator[2] and book debts,[3] but a gift of a business, goodwill and the premises in which it was carried on did not include the capital and stock-in-trade.[4] A bequest of a business includes all assets treated as part of the business but is subject to trade liabilities where it is clear that the business is to be carried on;[5] but a gift of 'any business or interest in business' does not include any holdings in companies unless the testator has an active interest in the management.[6] A gift of the goodwill of a solicitor's practice includes the testator's share of capital and undrawn profits.[7] A gift of the 'business and plant' has been held to include the balance at the bank,[8] and a gift of business assets may include money at the bank,[9] but a bequest of the 'effects used in a business and all book debts and the benefit of all contracts' does not include such a balance.[10] A gift of 'plant' does not include stock-in-trade.[11] A gift of profits of commercial undertakings has been held to include shares in a company but not debentures.[12] Where a testator assumed in his will that a business was his and his stepson was a salaried manager and the fact was that they were partners, it was held that the dispositions could not be given effect to as gifts of a share in a partnership and the bequest failed together.[13] Where a testator bequeathed his business and directed the formation of a company but a company was formed in his lifetime, the shares passed to the legatee.[14]

1   *Doe d Page v Page* (1851) 17 LTOS 123 (land on which shop stood, not included); *Re Henton, Henton v Henton* (1882) 30 WR 702 (direction to transfer business to son on attaining majority did not include the freehold shop in which the business was carried on); *Re Hawkins, Hawkins v Argent* (1913) 109 LT 969 (bequest of business and plant included house); *Rogers v Rogers* (1910) 11 SRNSW 38 (half-share in business included real estate, capital stock-in-trade and book debts); *Re Rhagg, Easten v Boyd* [1938] Ch 828, [1938] 3 All ER 314 (premises where solicitor's practice carried on included); *Re Betts, Burrell v Betts* [1949] 1 All ER 568 (in absence of a strong indication to the contrary a bequest of the goodwill and specified corporeal assets does not include the freehold house in which the business is carried on). Land which forms part of the assets is included: *Hall v Fennell* (1875) IR 9 Eq 615 at 618; *Devitt v Kearney* (1883) 13 LR Ir 45.
2   *Bevan v A-G* (1863) 4 Giff 361 (debt included); *Re Beard, Simpson v Beard* (1888) 57 LJ Ch 887 (debt not included); *Re Betts, Burrell v Betts* [1949] 1 All ER 568 ('debts due in respect of the business' means primarily debts due from trade debtors); *Re Hunter's Estate* [1957] SASR 194 (cash in business bank account excluded from 'business' and thus a loan from that account was excluded); *Re Jacobson* [1970] VR 180, a gift of 'the goodwill of my business and all stock-in-trade, plant and equipment ...' was held not to include the premises of, or the debts due to, the business, nor to be subject to the debts due to the business.
3   *Re Stevens, Stevens v Keily* [1888] WN 110; *Re Deller's Estate, Warman v Greenwood* [1888] WN 62; *Re Hawkins, Hawkins v Argent* (1913) 109 LT 969; *Re Spence, Wilkinson v Arlow* [1939] NI 83 (includes stock-in-trade and book debts); *Toplis v Vonder Heyde* (1840) 4 Y & C Ex 173 (bequest of all 'book debts' includes debts due to partnership); *Rogers v Rogers* (1910)

11 SRNSW 38. A bequest of a business and book debts did not include certain hire contracts, *Re Broad* [1953] VLR 49.

4   *Delany v Delany* (1885) 15 LR Ir 55. A gift of 'goodwill' may include the benefit of the provisions in articles for the testator's family: *Re England, England v Bayles* [1906] VLR 94.

5   *Re White, McCann v Hull* [1958] Ch 762, [1958] 1 All ER 379.

6   *Re Firn, Firn v Firn* [1962] NZLR 668.

7   *Re Barfield, Goodman v Child* (1901) 84 LT 28 (based on the consideration that goodwill is practically non-existent in the case of a solicitor's practice).

8   *Re Hawkins, Hawkins v Argent* (1913) 109 LT 969.

9   *Re Beecham, Woolley v Beecham* (1919) 63 Sol Jo 430.

10   *Re Haigh's Estate, Haigh v Haigh* (1907) 51 Sol Jo 343. In *Pinder v Pinder* (1870) 18 WR 309, 'effects belonging to' a business passed the fixtures.

11   *Blake v Shaw* (1860) John 732.

12   *Re Lawes-Wittewronge, Maurice v Bennett* [1915] 1 Ch 408. When introduced as a proviso to a general gift it did not include the residue or any interest in residue: *Re Kinchington* [1958] Qd R 136.

13   *Re Mulder, Westminster Bank Ltd v Mulder* [1943] 2 All ER 150; cf *Re Sykes, Skelton and Dyson v Sykes* [1940] 4 All ER 10 (gift of 'all my horses' held not to pass testator's part interest in three racehorses).

14   *Re Quibell's Will Trusts, White v Reichert* [1956] 3 All ER 679, [1957] 1 WLR 186; contrast *Re Lewis's Will Trusts, Lewis v Williams* [1984] 3 All ER 930, [1985] 1 WLR 102 (gift of 'my freehold farm and premises' did not pass testator's shareholding in company which owned farm).

[64.8]

Car. In most cases motor cars will be periodically changed by the owner and for this reason care is needed when drafting a specific bequest of a car in order to avoid ademption. Thus a gift 'my car' is prima facie specific and refers to the car owned at the date of the will and the gift is thus liable to ademption.[1] It is possible that such a gift would be saved by the Wills Act 1837, s 24,[2] so as to pass the car owned at the date of death but, of course, a particular description, or even perhaps a possessive adjective qualifying a specific rather than a generic gift, can amount to a contrary intention so as to exclude the section.[3] To avoid these difficulties such bequests should include a formula such as ... or any other car which I may own at my death'.[4] If the car is not made the subject of a specific or generic bequest then problems can arise as to whether it is included in other general words. 'Personal chattels' as defined by the Administration of Estates Act 1925, s 55(1)(x),[5] includes 'motor cars and accessories (not used for business purposes)'. 'Household furniture and effects' has likewise been construed as including motor cars.[6] A bequest of 'carriages' may pass a motor car.[7]

1   *Re Sikes, Moxon v Crossley* [1927] 1 Ch 364 (a specific bequest of 'my piano' held to refer to the piano which T possessed at the date of her will and thus when that piano was sold and another one acquired the gift was adeemed). See also *Goodlad v Burnett* (1855) 1 K & J 341; *Re Gibson, Mathews v Foulsham* (1866) LR 2 Eq 669 at 672. Compare *Re Smith's Will, Watson v Smith* [1916] VLR 540 (gift of 'my house and land in Urquhart Street, Coburg').

2   50 *Halsbury's Statutes* (4th edn) 593. See Vol 2, Part G, para **[244.24]**.

3   See para **[59.3]**, nn 1 and 2.

4   Provision should also be made for second cars, perhaps exclusively used by the wife or another member of the family, but in fact owned by the testator, and for cars used for business purposes whether or not owned by the business.

5   17 *Halsbury's Statutes* (4th edn) 467. Likewise the Statutory Will Forms 1925, Form 2; see Vol 2.

6   See para **[64.27]**, n 15.

7   *Denholm's Trustees v Denholm* 1908 SC 43 (included); *Re Dennis, Dennis v Dennis* (1908) 24 TLR 499 (where there was also the question as to which of the testator's two houses the car was

'in or about'); *Re Hall, Watson v Hall* (1912) 107 LT 196 (where the car did not pass owing to context); *Re White, White v White* [1916] 1 Ch 172 (where the car did not pass under 'carriages' but passed under 'furniture and all other articles of personal, domestic or household use'); *Re Sivewright, Law v Fenwick* (1922) 128 LT 416 (where the car passed under the bequest); *Stark's Trustees v Stark* 1948 SC 41 (where the gift was of 'any car I possess at the date of my death' and it was held this did not include one ordered but not delivered). Where a car is ordered but not paid for or delivered it will not pass subject to a charge of the price. The purchase price is payable out of residue: *Re Coxen* [1948] Ch 747, [1948] 2 All ER 492. A gift of a garage, house and personal effects does not include a car: *Re Parish* (1964) 42 DLR (2d) 212. See para **[64.3]**, n 1.

[64.9]

Chattels. 'Chattels' is one of the widest words known to law in its relation to personal property,[1] and its primary meaning extends to any kind of personal property.[2]

1   Per Fry LJ in *Robinson v Jenkins* (1890) 24 QBD 275 at 279.
2   *Re Givan, Rees v Green* [1966] 3 All ER 393, [1966] 1 WLR 1378.

[64.10]

Contents. A bequest of an antique bureau with its contents has been held to include money in loose bank notes contained in the bureau.[1] The construction of the phrase 'contents of a house', has already been considered.[2]

1   *Speaker's Executor v Spicker* 1969 SLT (Notes) 7 (OH); *Re Fisher, Canada Permanent Trust Co v Fisher* (1976) 74 DLR (3d) 680; *Re Bannister* [1985] 2 Qd R 246 but hidden money did not pass under a disposition of house contents.
2   See para **[63.1]**, n 1.

[64.11]

Debentures. Under a gift of debentures debenture stock will pass[1] and even a policy of insurance has passed.[2] Conversely, 'debenture stock' will carry debentures, especially if there is no issue of debenture stock.[3] A bequest of 'shares' does not ordinarily carry debentures or debenture stock,[4] but may do so where the testator has no shares in the named company.[5] A bequest of 'securities' carries debentures or debenture stock.[6]

1   *Re Herring, Murray v Herring* [1908] 2 Ch 493; *Re Lane, Luard v Lane* (1880) 14 Ch D 856, to contrary, has been doubted; see *Dillon v Arkins* (1885) 17 LR Ir 636. See para **[64.54]**, n 7.
2   *Phillips v Eastwood* (1835) L & G *temp* Sugd 270 at 291.
3   *Re Nottage, Jones v Palmer (No 2)* [1895] 2 Ch 657.
4   *Re Bodman, Bodman v Bodman* [1891] 3 Ch 135; *Re Connolly, Walton v Connolly* (1914) 110 LT 688; *Dillon v Arkins* (1885) 13 LR Ir 557; *Re Humphreys, Wren v Ward* (1915) 114 LT 230.
5   *Re Weeding, Armstrong v Wilkin* [1896] 2 Ch 364.
6   *Re Beavan, Beavan v Beavan* (1885) 53 LT 245.

[64.12]

Debts. See Money due or owing.

[64.13]

Devise. The inclusion of this word strengthens an apparent intention to include realty.[1]

1   *Marchuk v Marchuk* (1965) 52 WWR 652.

[64.14]

Dividends. A bequest of dividends due at the testator's death will not pass bonds which have been issued as capitalised arrears of dividends.[1] A plain bequest of dividends only passes those accruing due after his death. Those which have accrued due in his lifetime are part of the general personal estate,[2] but a bequest of 'current dividends' may in the context mean the dividends already earned at the date of death, but declared afterwards.[3] A gift of shares upon trust to hold 'all dividends bonuses benefits and rights' for a life tenant gives the life tenant the right to the proceeds of sale of a right to take up additional shares but bonus shares are not included in the gift and form part of the capital.[4] A bequest of dividends included redeemable preference shares subject to immediate redemption where such shares represented undistributed profits.[5]

1   *Ricketts v Harling* (1870) 23 LT 760.
2   *Shore v Weekly* (1849) 3 De G & Sm 467; *Re Jacob, M'Coy v Jacob* [1919] 1 IR 134.
3   *Re Raven, Spencer v Raven* (1914) 111 LT 938.
4   *Re Sears* (1951) 53 WALR 57.
5   *Re Carson* (1963) 37 DLR (2d) 292.

[64.15]

Effects—general meaning. This word used simpliciter, will carry the whole personal estate, as a gift 'of all my effects' without more, but when used in a restricted sense, it means 'goods and movables', as in the common expression of 'furniture and effects'. In every case the court has to collect from the context the particular sense in which the testator has intended to use it.[1] The word per se will not include real estate[2], but real property may pass under this word if the intention that it shall pass is expressed in the will.[3]

1   *Michell v Michell* (1820) 5 Madd 69; *Doe d Haw v Earles* (1846) 15 M & W 450; *Parker v Marchant* (1842) 1 Y & C Ch Cas 290.
2   *Hall v Hall* [1891] 3 Ch 389. See also *Doe d Hick v Dring* (1814) 2 M & S 448 (heir not to be disinherited except by plain and cogent inference from the words of the will); *Doe d Nixon v French* (1850) 15 LTOS 93; *Vertannes v Robinson* (1927) LR 54 Ind App 276.
3   *Denn d Franklin v Trout* (1812) 15 East 394; *Doe d Turner v Ash* (1852) 18 LTOS 239; *Marquis Titchfield v Horncastle* (1838) 7 LJ Ch 279, and see para **[64.16]** infra.

[64.16]

Effects—passing realty. The fact that the word 'effects' is coupled with the word 'devise' is not sufficient to include realty[1] nor would the further words 'whatsoever the same may be',[2] but coupled with the words 'whatsoever the same may be and wheresoever the same may be situate' is a sufficient context to pass realty, and is strengthened by a subsequent reference to the things included as 'property'.[3] A gift of 'all the residue of my effects real and personal' includes realty.[4] A sufficient indication of the intention to include realty may be found from the fact that the testator is contemplating a disposition of all his property[5] or is dealing with his real estate.[6] The inference is not necessarily negatived by the use of the word 'personal' with 'effects'.[7] The inclusion of realty may be prevented by the application of the ejusdem generis rule.[8] A gift of 'effects' as a gift of residue has already been considered.[9]

1   *Hall v Hall* [1891] 3 Ch 389; *Doe d Hick v Dring* (1814) 2 M & S 448; *Hammill v Hammill* (1884) 9 OR 530; *Pitcairn v Pitcairn* (1870) 8 M 604.
2   *Hall v Hall* [1891] 3 Ch 389. It must be noticed that in this case there was a gift under the words 'give devise and bequeath' and the subject-matter of the gift was furniture, goods and chattels and effects that the testator might be possessed of at his death, whatsoever the same might be and wheresoever the same might be situated. See also, *Doe d Hick v Dring* (1814) 2 M & S 448.
3   *Hall v Hall* [1891] 3 Ch 389; *Re Wass, Re Clarke* (1906) 95 LT 758, but see *Camfield v Gilbert* (1803) 3 East 516 (where the words were followed by 'except wearing apparel and plate' and a clear distinction had been made between real and personal property).
4   *Jackson v Hogan* (1776) 3 Bro Parl Cas 388; *Lord Torrington v Bowman* (1852) 22 LJ Ch 236.
5   *Phillips v Beal* (1858) 25 Beav 25; *Smyth v Smyth* (1878) 8 Ch D 561 (sheep and all the rest, residue, moneys, chattels and all other effects).
6   *Doe d Chillcott v White* (1800) 1 East 33 (where the testator was dealing with land and the word 'effects' referred back to a gift of all the rest and residue of his goods, etc, and also his lands).
7   See *Re Wass, Re Clark* (1906) 95 LT 758 ('personal estate and effects').
8   *Cross v Wilks* (1866) 35 Beav 562.
9   See para **[38.7]** ante.

[64.17]
Effects—restricted to personalty. Where there are no other words applicable to a general residuary gift of personalty, the word 'effects' will generally pass such residue,[1] but not where there is an express gift of residue.[2] A gift of the money to arise from the sale of 'my effects' has been held not to include residue.[3] In many cases the ejusdem generis rule has been applied and the 'effects' included are only those of a like nature with the property particularly specified in the gift.[4] A gift of personal effects contained in a drawer or other receptacle will not generally include such things as pass books and promissory notes.[5] The restricted sense of goods and movables is particularly applicable where other parts of the personal estate are separately disposed of,[6] or where there is a separate gift of the residue of the personal estate.[7]

1   *Hodgson v Jex* (1876) 2 Ch D 122; *Re Fitzpatrick, Deane v De Valera* (1934) 78 Sol Jo 735; *Re Wolfe's Goods* [1919] 2 IR 491; *Malone v Malone* [1925] 1 IR 140; *Moodie v Commins* (1904) 22 NZLR 510. But not where the ejusdem generis rule has to be applied: *Re Curling's Goods* [1928] IR 521.
2   *Howse v Seagoe* (1854) 2 WR 597.
3   *Re O'Loughlin's Goods* (1870) LR 2 P & D 102.
4   *Rawlings v Jennings* (1806) 13 Ves 39; *Gibbs v Lawrence* (1860) 30 LJ Ch 170 (household furniture, plate, linen, china, pictures and other goods, chattels and effects in or about a dwelling-house did not include a sum of money therein); *Campbell v M'Grain* (1875) IR 9 Eq 397 (a similar case); *Cross v Wilks* (1866) 35 Beav 562 (where the ejusdem generis rule prevented the inclusion of realty); *Re Miller, Daniel v Daniel* (1889) 61 LT 365 ('furniture and effects' did not include banknotes, securities and jewellery); *Re Hammersley, Heasman v Hammersley* (1899) 81 LT 150 ('furniture, books, pictures, paintings, engravings, plate, linen, china and other effects' limited to things of the same kind as previously enumerated and jewellery did not pass, but carriages and horses did pass under the gift); *Re Curling's Goods* [1928] IR 521 (jewellery, linen, silver and electroplated articles, all furniture, china, books, pictures and other effects did not carry residue).
5   *Joseph v Phillips* [1934] AC 348.
6   *Rawlings v Jennings* (1806) 13 Ves 39 at 46.
7   *MacPhail v Phillips* [1904] 1 IR 155.

[64.18]
Effects—personal effects. These words mean physical chattels having some personal connection with the testator.[1]

1   *Hodgson v Jex* (1876) 2 Ch D 122; followed in *Re Cuthbertson, Cuthbertson v Cuthbertson*
[1979] Tas SR 93 (included uncompleted yacht built as a hobby; tools and a motor car). Articles
of domestic use or ornament, not money or securities for money: *Joseph v Phillips* [1934] AC
348, and cf *Re Robson, Robson v Hamilton* [1891] 2 Ch 559; *Re Collins' Will Trusts, Donne v
Hewetson* [1971] 1 All ER 283, [1971] 1 WLR 37 (included stamp and coin collections and a
car). See also *Joseph v Phillips* [1934] AC 348. But in a suitable context, personal effects may
include the residuary personal estate: *Re Wolfe's Goods* [1919] 2 IR 491; or even real property:
Re Wass, Re Clarke (1906) 95 LT 758, but *Re O'Shea* [1953] VLR 43; *Re Dalzell* (1958) 26
WWR 215 proceeds of sale of realty), are to the contrary. Where a testator made specific gifts
of his library etchings and mountain photographs, these did not pass as effects: *Re Mengel's
Will Trusts, Westminster Bank Ltd v Mengel* [1962] Ch 791, [1962] 2 All ER 490.

[64.19]
Estate. This word is a word of general import and will of its own proper force
without the aid of context or implication of intention carry both real and
personal property and is not to be confined and restricted to personalty only
unless it is clearly so expressed in the will, as gathered from the whole will, or
from the way it is used in the particular part of the will where the contested use
arises.[1] It has been said, however, not to be a technical word and may therefore
be governed by the context.[2] When it refers to real property, it will carry the fee
simple or the whole interest of the testator unless restrained by other
expressions,[3] but where it is not used in the operative clause of the devise itself,
but is introduced into another part of the will referring to it, it cannot be
construed as having the effect of extending the meaning of the operative clause,
whether prior or subsequent.[4] The word in the first instance will pass the real
estate and it lies upon those who contend the contrary to prove the restriction.[5]
Realty has been held to pass although the terms of the gift to trustees and the
trusts were applicable to personalty only.[6] In a residuary clause, the words 'all
estate and effects' pass realty as well as personalty[7] but a gift of 'the whole of
my estate and all my household goods and all other my personal property' has
been held to exclude freehold property.[8]

1   *Hamilton Corpn v Hodsdon* (1847) 6 Moo PCC 76. The word is *genus genealissimum* and
includes all things real and personal: *Countess of Bridgewater v Duke of Bolton* (1704) 6 Mod
Rep 106; *Roe d Urry v Harvey* (1770) 5 Burr 2638; *Muddle v Fry* (1822) 6 Madd 270;
Robinson v Stuart (1891) 12 NSW Eq 47; *Cameron v Harper* (1891) 21 SCR 273.
2   *Basset v St Levan* (1894) 71 LT 718 at 720.
3   *Doe d Pottow v Fricker* (1851) 6 Ex Ch 510 (the meaning given to the word 'estate' is primarily
the thing devised and secondarily the interest in that thing). See also *Chester v Painter* (1725) 2
P Wms 335; *Goodwyn v Goodwyn* (1748) 1 Ves Sen 226. It will in a proper context include
property over which the testator has a power of appointment: *Re Plumb Estate* [1947] 1 WWR
666.
4   *Doe d Burton v White* (1848) 2 Exch 797.
5   *Midland Counties Rly Co v Oswin* (1844) 1 Coll 74; *Patterson v Huddart* (1853) 17 Beav 210.
6   *Stein v Ritherdon* (1868) 37 LJ Ch 369.
7   *Fullerton v Martin* (1853) 1 Eq Rep 224; *O'Toole v Browne* (1854) 3 E & B 572; *Meeds v
Wood* (1854) 19 Beav 215; *Hawksworth v Hawksworth* (1858) 27 Beav 1.
8   *Molyneux v Rowe* (1856) 8 De GM & G 368.

[64.20]
Farm; farming stock. A gift of a farm has been held to mean the land and
buildings.[1] A gift of 'farming stock' will include growing crops[2] and gathered
crops.[3] A gift of live and dead stock in or about a farm includes everything

belonging to the farm at the time of the testator's death.[4] A gift of live and dead stock passes growing crops.[5]

1   *Re Verdonk* (1979) 106 DLR (3d) 450 and not including partnership interest in cattle, equipment, milk quota, co-operative shares and bank operating account. But a gift of 'my freehold farm' did not pass the testator's three-quarters majority shareholding in a family company which owned the farm and other assets: *Re Lewis's Will Trusts, Lewis v Williams* [1984] 3 All ER 930, [1985] 1 WLR 102.

2   *West v Moore* (1807) 8 East 339; *Vaisey v Reynolds* (1828) 5 Russ 12 (only includes crops on the ground when the gift is to include all personal estate); *Burbidge v Burbidge* (1867) 37 LJ Ch 47; *Re Roose, Evans v Williamson* (1880) 17 Ch D 696.

3   *Harvey v Harvey* (1863) 32 Beav 441; *Re Rayner* [1907] SALR 129.

4   *Burbidge v Burbidge* (1867) 37 LJ Ch 47.

5   *Blake v Gibbs* (1825) 5 Russ 13n; *Burbidge v Burbidge* (1867) 37 LJ Ch 47; *Rudge v Winnall* (1849) 12 Beav 357; and see *Re Bowick* [1926] NZLR 79 (bales of wool).

[64.21]

Fixtures. Whether these pass under a devise must be determined from the terms of the will.[1]

1   *Re Murray, Clarke v Wakem* [1964] NZLR 627. See also para **[64.27]**.

[64.22]

Freeholds. A devise of freeholds will carry leaseholds where the testator has leaseholds and no freeholds, and this is more readily conceded where the situation of the property is stated and is obviously correct.[1] Where freeholds and leaseholds are intermixed and generally treated as freeholds, the better view now seems to be that, if it in any way appears to have been the intention of the testator, both freeholds and leaseholds pass.[2]

1   *Day v Trig* (1715) 1 P Wms 286; *Doe d Dunning v Cranstoun* (1840) 7 M & W 1.

2   *Re Bright-Smith, Bright-Smith v Bright-Smith* (1886) 31 Ch D 314; *Hallett v Hallett* (1898) 14 TLR 420; *Mathews v Mathews* (1867) LR 4 Eq 278. For earlier decisions to the contrary, see *Stone v Greening* (1843) 13 Sim 390; *Hall v Fisher* (1844) 1 Coll 47; *Morrell v Fisher* (1849) 4 Exch 591; *Doe d Parsey v Hemming* (1851) 17 LTOS 89. This matter is a question of *falsa demonstratio*: see Chapter 58.

[64.23]

Funds. Standing alone and without any context, this word or the words 'Stock in the Public Funds' is applied to the various investments forming part of the National Debt of the United Kingdom[1] and has been held not to refer to securities which are closely associated with such funds, eg East India Stock;[2] Bank Stock;[3] Exchequer Bills;[4] a government annuity;[5] foreign government bonds guaranteed by the English government[6] or colonial stock[7] and deposits in a trustee savings bank.[8] 'Foreign stock or funds' includes all foreign securities for which the faith of the foreign country is pledged.[9] The context may, however, show that a wider meaning is to be given.[10] Similar expressions considered elsewhere are 'debentures', 'securities', 'stock', 'shares'.[11]

1   *Slingsby v Grainger* (1859) 7 HL Cas 273 at 280 ('government funds' or 'public funds'); *Essington v Vashon* (1817) 3 Mer 434; *Re Parrott, Parrott v Parrott* (1885) 53 LT 12 (where a gift of 'all stock standing in my name in various companies with all bonds' carried public funds); *Montresor v Montresor* (1845) 1 Coll 693 ('any other funds' after 'Dutch funds' included English funds). A gift of funds does not carry funds standing in joint names: *Poole v Odling* (1862) 10 WR 591.

2   *Brown v Brown* (1858) 4 K & J 704; *Johnson v Digby* (1829) 8 LJOS Ch 38; *Mills v Mills* (1835) 7 Sim 501 (stock in public funds).

3   *Slingsby v Grainger* (1859) 7 HL Cas 273; but see *Mangin v Mangin* (1852) 16 Beav 300 (Irish Bank Stock passed as funded property). A bequest of 'bank stock and foreign securities' has passed three and a quarter per cent where there was nothing else to answer the description, 'as invested by' a named stockbroker being added: *Drake v Martin* (1856) 23 Beav 89.

4   *Johnson v Digby* (1829) 8 LJOS Ch 38.

5   *Kerr v Middlesex Hospital* (1852) 2 De GM & G 576.

6   *Burnie v Getting* (1845) 2 Coll 324 (Greek bonds guaranteed by England).

7   *Re Hamilton, Bazeley v Royal National Hospital for Consumption (President and Governors)* (1890) 6 TLR 173.

8   *Re Galway Inc Cripples' Institute, Peoples' Palace and Homes of Rest* [1944] NI 28 (bequest of British Government Securities).

9   *Ellis v Eden* (1857) 23 Beav 543.

10 *Mangin v Mangin* (1852) 16 Beav 300; *Cadett v Earle* (1877) 5 Ch D 710; *Re Dutton, Herbert v Harrison* (1869) 20 LT 386.

11 For 'debentures', see para **[64.1]** supra; for 'securities', see para **[64.53]** infra; for 'shares', see para **[64.54]** infra; for 'stock' see para **[64.57]** infra.

[64.24]

Furniture. The cases are dealt with under 'household furniture'.

[64.25]

Goods. This expression or 'goods and chattels' is sufficient to include the whole personal estate[1] and a will is more readily so construed where there are other descriptions added to goods, such as 'furniture, ready money, debts and securities' or 'effects'.[2] If there is a gift of residue, then the word 'goods' must be restricted so that effect may be given to the residuary gift[3] and restriction may be put upon the word by the operation of the ejusdem generis rule.[4] There are early cases holding that leaseholds, being chattels real, will not be included,[5] but 'all my worldly goods' has passed land[6]. An exception of goods 'now deposited at a safe deposit' excludes only the goods deposited at the named safe deposit at the time of the making of the will or codicil in which such words occur.[7]

1   *Stuart v Marquis of Bute* (1806) 11 Ves 657; *Kendall v Kendall* (1828) 4 Russ 360. As to chattels or fixtures, see paras **[64.9]** and **[64.21]** supra. As to household goods, see para **[64.27]** infra.

2   *Avison v Simpson* (1859) John 43; *Parker v Marchant* (1842) 1 Y & C Ch Cas 290; *Harris v James* (1864) 12 WR 509.

3   *Woolcomb v Woolcomb* (1731) 3 P Wms 112; *Lamphier v Despard* (1842) 2 Dr & War 59.

4   *Crichton v Symes* (1743) 3 Atk 61 (goods and wearing apparel); *Manton v Tabois* (1885) 30 Ch D 92 (furniture, goods and chattels).

5   *Anon* (1550) Bro NC 69; *Portman v Willis* (1593) Cro Eliz 386; *Re Foley* (1952) 53 SRNSW 31 (realty).

6   *Wright v Shelton* (1853) 18 Jur 445; *Re Young, Young v Young* [1951] Ch 344, [1950] 2 All ER 1245 ('wordly goods and chattels both real and personal').

7   *Re Whitby, Public Trustee v Whitby* [1944] Ch 210, [1944] 1 All ER 299.

[64.26]

House or building. Though the words used in the will describe merely the house or building, they may, according to the context or the circumstances, include land occupied and enjoyed with it, especially if such land is necessary for its convenient use or enjoyment.[1] A house according to its nature and the standing of those intended to occupy it must include a garden, pleasure grounds, proper approaches and outbuildings such as a garage or stables and coachhouse.[2]

The word 'house' is often accompanied by further words, such as 'and premises'[3] or 'and appurtenances'[4] and then something further than the actual building must be included, and this may extend to land commonly enjoyed with the house.[5] A house may be included in a gift of land on the principle that a gift of the land carries everything upon it[6] and a gift of a house includes chattels affixed and used for the decoration and convenience of the house called fixtures.[7] Premises, being a wide word, will sometimes carry to the remainderman all the property whether real or personal given to the tenant for life in the earlier part of the gift.[8]

1   *Smith v Martin* (1672) 2 Wms Saund 394; *Smith v Ridgway* (1866) LR 1 Exch 331 at 333 (land so intimately connected with the use of the building that without it the building would be useless).

2   *Lombe v Stoughton* (1849) 17 Sim 84; *Thomas v Lane* (1680) 2 Cas in Ch 26; *Heach v Pritchard* [1882] WN 140.

3   *Lethbridge v Lethbridge* (1862) 4 De GF & J 35; *Re Willis, Spencer v Willis* [1911] 2 Ch 563 at 569; *Ross v Veal* (1855) 1 Jur NS 751. See also *Doe d Norton v Norton* (1846) 8 LTOS 160 ('outbuildings thereto adjoining'); *Kennedy v Keily* (1860) 28 Beav 223 (land with all buildings); *Roe d Walker v Walker* (1803) 3 Bos & P 375 (where there are two gifts, one for life and one in remainder. Since one expressly included lands and the other made no mention of lands, the land was excluded from the latter); and cf with this case *Borrows v Ellison* (1871) LR 6 Exch 128 (a similar case where the second gift was in a codicil); *Keating v O'Hagan* (1922) 56 ILT 157.

4   See para **[64.2]** ante.

5   *Blackborn v Edgley* (1719) 1 P Wms 600; *Gulliver d Jeffereys v Poyntz* (1770) 2 Wm Bl 726; *Doe d Hemming v Willetts* (1849) 7 CB 709; *Hibon v Hibon* (1863) 1 New Rep 532; *Mocatta v Mocatta* (1883) 49 LT 629 (additional property held under distinct lease); *Re Fuller, Arnold v Chandler* (1915) 59 Sol Jo 304 (additional land now in the occupation of a stranger); *Barfoot v Lee* (1905) 50 Sol Jo 44 (adjoining plot of land); *Read v Read* (1866) 15 WR 165 (exclusion of yard and premises where business carried on did not include house in which business carried on); *Re Rayner's Will* (1929) 23 Tas LR 41 ('home' included 5« acres of orchard occupied with the house).

6   *O'Connor v O'Connor* (1870) IR 4 Eq 483.

7   *Re Whaley, Whaley v Roehrich* [1908] 1 Ch 615.

8   *Doe d Biddulph v Meakin* (1801) 1 East 456; *Sanford v Irby* (1825) 4 LJOS Ch 23.

[64.27]
Household furniture. A gift of household furniture is confined to articles of domestic use.[1] Books were often held not to pass as furniture[2] unless the house was not to be dismantled but kept up for the family,[3] but in recent times there is a tendency to infer an intention to include books unless they are rare books.[4] Fixtures are not furniture,[5] but china,[6] pictures,[7] plate and linen,[8] and wireless cabinets[9] and a cash register[10] have been held to pass under the word 'furniture'; wine[11] and coins and trinkets[12] do not pass. Under a gift of 'fixed furniture' chimney glasses passed but not a movable bookcase and it was doubted if carpets tacked to the floor were included.[13] The addition of the word 'and effects' to furniture will make it comprise all property placed there for use or ornament or consumption[14] including motor cars,[15] but will not include articles exclusively of personal ornament;[16] jewellery;[17] ornamental snuffboxes;[18] farming stock and implements;[19] literary notes;[20] fixtures where the house in which they are is directed to be sold;[21] stamp collection.[22] Where the added words are very wide (such as 'all other movable goods') the residue of the personal property may pass.[23]

Part K   Construction of wills: particular rules relating to property

1   *Le Farrant v Spencer* (1748) 1 Ves Sen 97 (not for trade); *Manning v Purcell* (1855) 7 De GM
& G 55 (where there was furniture both in a private house and on business premises, but only so
much of that on the business premises as was kept by the testator for his domestic or personal
use passed under the gift); but cf *Re Seton-Smith, Burnand v Waite* [1902] 1 Ch 717
(innkeeper). As to right of selection, see para **[8.7]** supra.

2   *Allen v Allen* (1729) Mos 112; *Bridgman v Dove* (1744) 3 Atk 201; *Kelley v Powlet* (1763)
Amb 605; *Porter v Tournay* (1797) 3 Ves 311; *Cremorne v Antrobus* (1829) 5 Russ 312;
Finney v Grice (1878) 10 Ch D 13; *Re Seton-Smith, Burnand v Waite* [1902] 1 Ch 717; *Re
Baroness of Zouche, Dugdale v Baroness of Zouche* [1919] 2 Ch 178 (rare books and MSS.). As
to 'books', see para **[64.6]** supra.

3   *Ouseley v Anstruther* (1847) 10 Beav 453; *Hutchinson v Smith* (1863) 1 New Rep 513. As to a
gift of a 'home', see *Re Rayner's Will* (1929) 23 Tas LR 41 (house and land occupied therewith
and all household goods, implements and curios).

4   *Re Holden* (1903) 5 OLR 156; *Re Baroness of Zouche, Dugdale v Baroness of Zouche* [1919] 2
Ch 178 (where only rare books and MSS were excluded. These might pass as articles of *vertu*).
No doubt books pass more readily where the word 'furniture' is accompanied by further words
such as 'and effects' or 'and other movable goods'. See *Burnside v Burnside* (1921) 56 ILT 20.
As to 'books', see para **[64.6]** supra.

5   *Allen v Allen* (1729) Mos 112 (marble slabs and chimney-pieces affixed to the freehold); *Finney
v Grice* (1878) 10 Ch D 13 (tenant's fixtures in a leasehold house); *Re Seton-Smith, Burnand v
Waite* [1902] 1 Ch 717 (tenant's and trade fixtures).

6   *Hele v Gilbert* (1752) 2 Ves Sen 430; *Kelly v Powlet* (1763) Amb 605.

7   *Kelly v Powlet* (1763) Amb 605; *Cremorne v Antrobus* (1829) 5 Russ 312; *Re Londesborough,
Bridgeman v Fitzgerald* (1880) 50 LJ Ch 9.

8   *Kelly v Powlet* (1763) Amb 605; *Cremorne v Antrobus* (1829) 5 Russ 312. See *Holden v
Ramsbottom* (1863) 4 Giff 205 (plated articles); *Fraser v Croft* (1898) 25 R 496.

9   *Re Willey, Goulding v Shirtcliffe* (1929) 45 TLR 327.

10 *Re Smith* [1956] NZLR 841.

11 *Porter v Tournay* (1797) 3 Ves 311; but 'wine' will not pass as 'household effects'. *Re Bourne,
Bourne v Brandreth* (1888) 58 LT 537, and see n 14 infra.

12 *Cremorne v Antrobus* (1829) 5 Russ 312.

13 *Birch v Dawson* (1834) 2 Ad & El 37.

14 *Cole v Fitzgerald* (1827) 3 Russ 301; *Miller's Trustees v Miller* 1907 SC 833 (wine); *Re Tweed,
Buckmaster v Moss* (1902) 46 Sol Jo 634 (wine and furniture stored on premises for business
purposes but where the business had no interest in the premises or the wine); *Beresford v
Preston* (1920) 54 ILT 48 (consumable goods); *Re Wavertree, Rutherford v Hall-Walker* [1933]
Ch 837 (consumable goods); *Minton v Minton* (1853) 21 LTOS 40 (medals in frame); *Re
Wavertree, Rutherford v Hall-Walker*, supra (garden implements and movable plants); *Re
Seton-Smith, Burnand v Waite* [1902] 1 Ch 717 (where testator was an innkeeper and all
furniture, china, glass and plate of the inn passed as well as household furniture, but not tenant's
fixtures); *Re McLuckie, Perpetual Executors and Trustees Association of Australia Ltd v
Honeycombe* [1943] VLR 137 ('furniture and personal belongings' included furniture of a
maisonette let furnished, and motor car, radio sets, electric refrigerators and fire-proof safe, but
not cactus plants and gardening implements).

15 *Re Howe, Ferniehough v Wilkinson* [1908] WN 223; *Re Sim* [1917] NZLR 169; *Re Johnson*
[1931] 2 DLR 987; *Re Wavertree, Rutherford v Hall-Walker* [1933] Ch 837; *Re McLuckie,
Perpetual Executors and Trustees Association of Australia Ltd v Honeycombe* [1943] VLR 137.
In *Re White, White v White* [1916] 1 Ch 172, a car passed as 'furniture and all other articles of
personal domestic or household use', but not under a gift of 'carriages'. As to 'carriages and
horses', see *Watson v Arundel* (1877) IR 10 Eq 299. Where the gift was of 'furniture and effects
in the house in which I now residue', a car kept in a garage about 30 yards from the house was
held not to pass: *Re Tormey, Tormey v Tormey* [1935] VLR 300, the car was excluded where
the gift was of 'all household goods, furniture, jewellery and personal effects', including certain
clothing: *Re Lappin* [1945] 1 DLR 241. In *Re Liverton* [1954] NZLR 612, a car passed under a
gift of 'household and personal effects' where its use for business purposes was not so
considerable as to exclude its inclusion in that category and in *Re Pridham* [1953] 1 DLR 782, a
car passed under a gift of 'household goods and effects' and similarly in *Johnston v Doak*
[1953] VLR 678. In *Re Collins' Settlement Trusts, Donne v Hewetson* [1971] 1 All ER 283,
[1971] 1 WLR 37, stamp and coin collections and a motor car were included in the description
'articles of furniture and personal effects'; applied in *Re Cuthbertson, Cuthbertson v
Cuthbertson* [1979] Tas SR 93 ('articles of furniture and personal effects' included car).

644

16 *Tempest v Tempest* (1856) 2 K & J 635; *Re Pettitt, Flaxman v Pettitt* (1894) 38 Sol Jo 531
    (clothes); *Re Tweed, Buckmaster v Moss* (1902) 46 Sol Jo 634 (clothes).
17 *Northey v Paxton* (1888) 60 LT 30.
18 *Field v Peckett (No 2)* (1861) 29 Beav 573.
19 *Bradish v Ellames* (1864) 11 LT 470; *Re Labron, Johnson v Johnson* (1885) 1 TLR 248
    (horses, cows and sheep); but horses and carriages used for pleasure and shopping are
    household effects: *Re Howe, Ferniehough v Wilkinson* [1908] WN 223.
20 *Re Pettitt, Flaxman v Pettitt* (1894) 38 Sol Jo 531 (the notes included a plot of a play and notes
    as to plots and scenes).
21 *Re Tweed, Buckmaster v Moss* (1902) 46 Sol Jo 634.
22 *Re Masson, Morton v Masson* (1917) 86 LJ Ch 753 (this did not pass as 'household effects', nor
    as 'pictures and prints', nor as 'books'); contrast *Re Collins' Settlement Trusts, Donne v
    Hewetson* [1971] 1 All ER 283, [1971] 1 WLR 37, a stamp and coin collection included in the
    phrase 'personal effects'.
23 *Re Johnson, Sandy v Reilly* (1905) 92 LT 357. Money passed in *Swinfen v Swinfen (No 4)*
    (1860) 29 Beav 207; *Lowry v Patterson* (1874) 8 LR Ir 372.

[64.28]
Household goods. These include plate,[1] articles of this nature though not used
by the testator nor kept in the house[2] and clocks.[3] It has been held that beer and
similar victuals are not 'household goods'[4] nor are guns and pistols.[5] A gift of
the 'contents of a house' includes goods and valuable articles temporarily sent
away for exhibition or for security in time of war, but not articles normally kept
at the bank though occasionally brought to the house for exhibition,[6] and a gift
of the contents does not include stocks bonds securities or a savings account.[7]
'All other contents of my house or at the bank' cannot be construed as a
residuary gift[8] and in any case does not include choses in action even though the
certificates were at the bank or in the house.[9]

1   *Lillcott v Compton* (1708) 2 Vern 638; *Stapleton v Conway* (1750) 3 Atk 727.
2   *Pellew v Horsford* (1856) 25 LJ Ch 352.
3   *Slanning v Style* (1734) 3 P Wms 334; *Pellew v Horsford* (1856) 25 LJ Ch 352.
4   *Slanning v Style* (1734) 3 P Wms 334.
5   *Slanning v Style* (1734) 3 P Wms 334.
6   *Re Eumorfopoulos, Ralli v Eumorfopoulos* [1944] Ch 133, [1943] 2 All ER 719.
7   *Re Brownell* (1858) 41 MPR 171.
8   *Re Abbott, Public Trustee v St Dunstan's British Home and Hospital for Incurables and
    Trustees of Western Ophthalmic Hospital and Lady Dugan* [1944] 2 All ER 457.
9   *Re Abbott, Public Trustee v St Dunstan's British Home and Hospital for Incurables and
    Trustees of Western Ophthalmic Hospital and Lady Dugan* [1944] 2 All ER 457.

[64.29]
Insurance policies. A gift of the proceeds payable under a policy includes a
refund or premiums[1] and a gift of 'policies of insurance' will not carry shares in
an insurance company although the company is named and the testator had no
policy with the company but had shares therein.[2]

1   *Re Devorkin* [1951] OWN 913.
2   *Waters v Wood* (1852) 5 De G & Sm 717.

[64.30]
Investments. This word includes stocks whether of a government or of a
company[1] and shares of companies,[2] but does not include money on deposit at a
bank,[3] nor money deposited with an employer;[4] but in certain circumstances
money on deposit may be an investment.[5] Generally, the word will refer to stock

exchange investments and such securities as debentures, but it will not include life policies or their proceeds.[6]

1   *Arnould v Grinstead* (1872) 21 WR 155.
2   *Arnould v Grinstead* (1872) 21 WR 155.
3   *Archibald v Hartley* (1852) 21 LJ Ch 399; *Re Price, Price v Newton* [1905] 2 Ch 55 ('pecuniary investments').
4   *Re Sudlow, Smith v Sudow* (1914) 59 Sol Jo 162.
5   *Re Lewis's Will Trusts, O'Sullivan v Robbins* [1937] Ch 118, [1937] 1 All ER 227 (gift of securities 'or investments representing the same'. Security redeemed: the redemption moneys placed on deposit at the bank and with A and N Stores: the deposited moneys were invested within the meaning of the will).
6   *Re Lilly's Will Trusts, Public Trustee v Johnstone* [1948] 2 All ER 906; applied in *Re Ledger* [1983] Qd R 176, where this passage of the text is referred to.

[64.31]
Jewellery. The following have been held not to pass as 'jewels' or 'jewellery': a watch;[1] a gold-headed cane;[2] coins.[3] Gold masonic orders, set with jewels, have been held to pass under this description.[4] 'Personal jewellery' is restricted to articles used or worn personally.[5] Cut unmounted diamonds pass under the description of jewellery.[6]

1   *Allen v Allen* (1729) Mos 112.
2   *Allen v Allen* (1729) Mos 112.
3   *Sudbury v Brown* (1856) 27 LTOS 260.
4   *Lord Brooke v Earl of Warwick* (1848) 2 De G & Sm 425.
5   *Re Pulley, Midland Bank v Carter* (1948) 92 Sol Jo 181; *Re Resch's Will Trusts, Le Cras v Perpetual Trustee Co Ltd, Far West Children's Health Scheme v Perpetual Trustee Co Ltd* [1969] 1 AC 514, [1967] 3 All ER 915, PC (valuable jewellery held not to be included in a gift of specific items and 'other personal jewellery'; phrase to be construed ejusdem generis with the descriptions that preceded them).
6   *Re Whitby, Public Trustee v Whitby* [1944] Ch 210, [1944] 1 All ER 299.

[64.32]
Land–general devises. By the Wills Act 1837, s 26,[1] a devise of the testator's land, or of the testator's land in any place,[2] or in the occupation of any person named in the will, or otherwise in a general manner, or any other general devise[3] which would describe a leasehold estate if the testator had no freehold estate which could be described by it, must be construed to include the leasehold estates of the testator, or such of those estates or any of them as are within such description, as the case may be, as well as freehold estates, unless a contrary intention appears by the will.[4] A devise of 'real estate' may be such a devise[5], but it appears is more readily given its technical meaning,[6] and, whether or not it is a devise within the section, where there is no real estate, it may pass leaseholds.[7] A gift of land in a named place does not in its technical sense[8] include incorporeal hereditaments[9] issuing out of the land in that locality. Also included in the description is money held upon trust for investment in land, as to which no effective election has been made to reconvert the property[10], but where the money is to be invested in land generally, the money will not pass under a devise of land in a particular locality.[11] A devise of land ordinarily includes whatever estate or interest the testator has in the land,[12] except mortgage debts charged on the land or any interest therein,[13] but the latter may pass where the intention to include them is shown,[14] or if there is no other estate or interest to

which the description can refer,[15] as in the case where the testator, at the date of the will and at the date of his death,[16] was a mortgagee in possession of the land[17] with no other interest in the land.[18] The mortgage money does not in general pass under a gift of the land where the testator, after the date of his will, sells the land and takes a mortgage to secure part of the purchase money.[19] A gift of a house of which the testator is described as the owner and occupier is satisfied if the testator would be rateable as occupier, though not himself actually resident there,[20] and a gift of a house the title of which is in fact in the name of the devisee is good where the testatrix is entitled under foreclosure proceedings to have the title put in her name.[21]

1 50 *Halsbury's Statutes* (4th edn) 595. See Vol 2, Part G, para **[244.26]**. It would seem that as a result of the changes made in the nature of an undivided share of land by the Trusts of Land and Appointment of Trustees Act 1996, a general devise of land will apparently now include an undivided share in land. See para **[41.18]** supra.

2 It must be noticed that the word is 'land' and is not 'real estate'. The section, it has been said, does not apply to a gift of 'real estate': see n 15. As to land in a named place, see *Wilson v Eden* (1852) 16 Beav 153 (lands at or near W in the county of D, and at B in the county of Y ... and all other 'his real estates' in the counties of D and Y and elsewhere). Again the word is 'land' and not 'lands' in the plural. For a suggestion that there may be a distinction between the singular and the plural, see *Re Lory's Will Trusts, Lambrick v Kenya Protectorate Public Trustee* [1950] 1 All ER 349 at 351.

3 This second branch was intended to cover certain cases that might not be covered by the first branch, but there must be found in the will containing a general devise some description which points to a particular property or interest in property: *Butler v Butler* (1884) 28 Ch D 66 at 72.

4 *Wilson v Eden* (1852) 16 Beav 153 (no contrary intention by the addition of 'all other my real estate' nor by the limitations being such as were applicable only to real estate—ie to C and D and their heirs). Contrary intention is shown by a separate gift of leasehold property: *Re Guyton and Rosenberg's Contract* [1901] 2 Ch 591; or of all personal estate wheresoever situated; *Butler v Butler* (1884) 28 Ch D 66; but not by a mere gift of personal estate simply or by a specific gift of a specified leasehold: *Re Davison, Greenwell v Davison* (1888) 58 LT 304. The addition of the words 'rents and profits' may show a contrary intention: *Craig v Wheeler* (1860) 29 LJ Ch 374. The section was intended to abolish the technical rule (established by *Rose v Bartlett* (1633) Cro Car 292) which generally defeated the intention, and not to substitute another technical rule in its place. If, therefore, on the fair construction of the will, there are indications of an intention that leaseholds should not pass by the devise of lands, they will be excluded: *Prescott v Barker* (1874) 9 Ch App 174. It must be noted that the rule in *Rose v Bartlett* (1633) Cro Car 292, is not that a devise of lands can never pass leaseholds, but that it will not pass leaseholds where the testator has other land in the same place, or as stated in *Knotsford v Gardiner* (1742) 2 Atk 450, if a man has lands in fee and for years and devises all his lands, the fee simple passes only; and if he has a lease for years and no fee simple, the lease for years passes, for otherwise the will would be void. Also under the old rule it was permitted to show that the will as a whole expressed an intention that leaseholds should be included: *Swift v Swift* (1859) 1 De GF & J 160 at 170.

5 *Moase v White* (1876) 3 Ch D 763, observed upon in *Butler v Butler* (1884) 28 Ch D 66 at 75; *Re Davison, Greenwell v Davison* (1888) 58 LT 304; *Re Uttermare, Leeson v Foulis* [1893] WN 158; *Hester v Trustees, Executors and Agency Co Ltd* (1892) 18 VLR 509. See, however, the next note, and different views have been expressed as to the result of all the cases.

6 *Butler v Butler* (1884) 28 Ch D 66, approving *Wilson v Eden* (1848) 11 Beav 237; *Prescott v Barker* (1874) 9 Ch App 174 (where the limitations were in strict settlement but made no provision against leaseholds vesting absolutely in the first tenant in tail at his birth); *Turner v Turner* (1852) 21 LJ Ch 843.

7 *Re Holt, Holt v Holt* [1921] 2 Ch 17 (where there was one devise of 'personal property' and another of 'real estate and property'. It was held that the second devise was not within the section, but the leaseholds passed under it upon the principle in *Rose v Bartlett* (1633) Cro Car 292.

8 The results may be otherwise where the testator has no land in the named place, so that the words can have no effect given to them in the technical sense and the provision would become

void. This was a reason for including leaseholds: *Knotsford v Gardiner* (1742) 2 Atk 450. See *Inchley v Robinson* (1587) 3 Leon 165 (land in A included tithes); *Ritch v Sanders* (1651) Sty 261 (tithes included); *Meredith v Webber* (1666) O Bridg 560 (where testator gave 'all his fee simple land wheresoever' to A and his heirs and from one part of the will it was necessarily inferred that the word 'lands' must comprise tithes, the same construction of the word 'lands' shall be applied to another part which would not alone have supported the same inference); *Ashton v Ashton* (1735) 3 P Wms 384 (no land in stated place, only tithes); *Re Lory's Will Trusts, Lambrick v Kenya Protectorate Public Trustee* [1950] 1 All ER 349 (tithes and where it was also held that redemption annuity also passed); *Re Hodgson, Taylor v Hodgson* [1898] 2 Ch 545 (advowson).

9   *Westfaling v Westfaling* (1746) 3 Atk 460; but as stated in the last preceding note, incorporeal hereditaments pass if there is no land, or if the surrounding circumstances or the presumed intention of the testator admit of such a construction: *Re Hodgson, Taylor v Hodgson* [1898] 2 Ch 545. Incorporeal hereditaments pass where the description is 'tenements and hereditaments': *Westfaling v Westfaling* (1746) 3 Atk 460. Although with the abolition of descent and heir the word hereditaments has ceased to have its proper meaning, its continued use may be more than justified where incorporeal hereditaments are or may be concerned or affected.

10   As to conversion and reconversion, see Chapter 37. See *Re Gosselin* [1906] 1 Ch 120.

11   See para [63.1] supra.

12   For instance, his interest under an existing trust for sale: *Re Lowman, Devenish v Pester* [1895] 2 Ch 348; *Re Glassington, Glassington v Follett* [1906] 2 Ch 305; his interest in a term of years where he also has the freehold reversion: *Mathews v Mathews* (1867) LR 4 Eq 278; *Re Guyton and Rosenberg's Contract* [1901] 2 Ch 591; or in rentcharges *Re Lory's Will Trust, Lambrick v Kenya Protective Public Trustee,* supra, even though these are merely kept on foot for his benefit and protection: *Vallance v Vallance* (1863) 2 New Rep 229; *Latham v Travers* [1912] 1 IR 140.

13   *Casborne v Scarfe* (1738) 1 Atk 603; *Bowen v Barlow* (1872) 8 Ch App 171 (mortgage of leasehold); *Davy v Redington* [1917] 1 IR 250.

14   *Mackesy v Mackesy* [1896] 1 IR 511; *Kilkelly v Powell* [1897] 1 IR 457.

15   *Re Lowman, Devenish v Pester* [1895] 2 Ch 348.

16   *Re Clowes* [1893] 1 Ch 214 at 218.

17   *Woodhouse v Meredith* (1816) 1 Mer 450; *Burdus v Dixon* (1858) 4 Jur NS 967; *Re Carter, Dodds v Pearson* [1900] 1 Ch 801.

18   *Bowen v Barlow* (1872) 8 Ch App 171, *Re Clowes* [1893] 1 Ch 214.

19   *Moor v Raisbeck* (1841) 12 Sim 123; *Farrar v Earl of Winterton* (1842) 5 Beav 1; *Re Clowes* [1893] 1 Ch 214.

20   *Re Garland, Eve v Garland* [1934] Ch 620 (where the testator shortly after purchasing a residence became insane and was removed to a mental home).

21   *Re Szczutkowski Estate* (1955) 14 WWR 396; affd (1956) 15 WWR 480.

[64.33]

Lands and tenements. The word 'tenements' has generally been restricted to freeholds,[1] but its meaning may be affected by the addition of other words, for where the additional words are applicable either to the description of leasehold property or to the description of the interests given which are applicable only to leasehold property, then leaseholds may, but only upon a fair construction of the whole will, be included.[2]

1   *Pistol d Rendal v Riccardson* (1784) 3 Doug KB 361; *Thompson v Lady Lawley* (1800) 2 Bos & P 303; *Arkell v Fletcher* (1839) 10 Sim 299. In the last two cases the word 'messuages' was included in the description.

2   *Hobson v Blackburn* (1833) 1 My & K 571 (making a distinction between 'lands and tenements' and 'messuages or tenements'); *Wilson v Eden* (1848) 11 Beav 237. *Thompson v Lady Lawley* (1800) 2 Bos & P 303, is to much the same effect.

[64.34]

Messuages. This word has sometimes aided the inclusion of leaseholds when used with other words usually descriptive of freeholds,[1] but it has more often

been considered as to the extent of the land to be included in the devise.[2]
Appurtenances have already been considered.[3]

1   See para **[64.33]**, nn 1 and 2.
2   *Carden v Tuck* (1588) Cro Eliz 89 (without any additional words carries garden and curtilage); *Borrows v Ellison* (1871) LR 6 Exch 128 (where an orchard enjoyed with the farmhouse passed, but no part of the farm).
3   See para **[64.2]** supra.

[64.35]
Money. The word 'money' has no strict technical meaning[1] and is a word of flexible meaning.[2] In order to construe the word, the court is obliged to apply its own knowledge of the ordinary use of the English language in the light of such context and circumstances as might assist it.[3] It was at one time said that this word is to be construed as meaning cash under the immediate control of the testator, unless there is a context to show otherwise,[4] but this statement of the position has been departed from,[5] though the extent of the departure is a little uncertain.[6] A comparatively slight context will, however, enlarge the strict meaning of the word,[7] and in a home-made will it may be treated less strictly than in a will drawn by a skilled lawyer.[8] Apart from any context sufficient to extend the meaning, the word includes cash and notes in hand,[9] money immediately payable to the testator at call,[10] and money at the bank on current account, or on deposit account when no long notice of withdrawal is required.[11] A testator gave the proceeds of a sale of certain real estate describing them as 'moneys which I have separately invested'. In fact such moneys though identifiable were paid into a current account. The moneys passed under the gift which was not void for uncertainty nor incorrectly described.[12] 'All moneys held by me' includes money on current account and in savings banks but not Treasury Bonds or shares in a company or an amount due for rent.[13] Without some context or qualifying word,[14] it does not include sums not immediately payable to the testator,[15] stock or shares[16] or other choses in action,[17] or the general estate of the testator,[18] or indeed, of the general personal and real estate of the testator.[19] The addition of qualifying words naturally affects the meaning of 'money' and 'moneys deposited in the Post Office Savings Bank' may also pass government stock purchased through that bank;[20] 'money deposited or invested in banks or institutions' has passed Consols.[21] Other words passing stock are 'remaining sum or sums of money',[22] 'surplus money',[23] 'balance',[24] 'all moneys'.[25] Money except money at the bank or in the funds or placed on security, does not include foreign stock and shares.[26] A direction may be given that stock or shares are to be considered as 'ready money'.[27]

1   *Perrin v Morgan* [1943] AC 399, [1943] 1 All ER 187 (the court is not bound in the absence of special circumstances to adopt a fixed meaning of the word as being its 'legal' meaning as opposed to its 'popular' meaning, but must ascertain as between its various usual meanings which is the correct interpretation of the particular document in the light of the context and other relevant circumstances); *Re Cadogan, Cadogan v Palagi* (1883) 25 Ch D 154 at 157; *Re Shaw, Mountain v Mountain* [1929] WN 246; *Re Bramley's Goods* [1902] P 106.
2   *Re Townley, Townley v Townley* (1884) 53 LJ Ch 516, where it is said that a more or less extended meaning must be given to the word, according to the facts of the case and the terms of the will. This part of the decision seems to be confirmed by the decision in *Perrin v Morgan* [1943] AC 399, [1943] 1 All ER 187; but the further statement that the court is bound to put upon the word its ordinary and literal meaning unless the context shows that a larger meaning

should be put upon it has been departed from. In every case the court may select, from the usual meanings of the word, the one most appropriate in all the circumstances of the case. This part of the decision of the House of Lords received little acceptance from Lord Russell of Killowen and practically none from Lord Romer, who emphasised the necessity for some rule not only to guide the court but also the draftsman and those who have to administer estates.

3   *Re Barnes' Will Trusts, Prior v Barnes* [1972] 2 All ER 639 at 644, per Goulding J; applying *Perrin v Morgan* [1943] AC 399, [1943] 1 All ER 187.

4   *Re Taylor, Taylor v Tweedie* [1923] 1 Ch 99 at 105; *Re Gates, Gates v Cabell* [1929] 2 Ch 420; *Re Putner, Putner v Brooke* (1929) 45 TLR 325; *Re Allan, Roberts v Robinson* (1933) 77 Sol Jo 448; *Re Hodgson, Nowell v Flannery* [1936] Ch 203; *Re Townley, Townley v Townley* (1884) 53 LJ Ch 516.

5   *Perrin v Morgan* [1943] AC 399, [1943] 1 All ER 187. See n 2.

6   *Perrin v Morgan* [1943] AC 399, [1943] 1 All ER 187. In this case Lord Russell of Killowen, and more particularly Lord Romer, seemed reluctant to go the whole way with the other noble Lords, but did not dissent from the decision. Lord Russell said that the meaning of the word is not restricted by any hard and fast rule but depends on the context. Lord Romer said that the rule was a salutary one and it would be a pity if it was altogether negatived. The real difficulty in the case lies in the fact that the Court of Appeal could find no context to modify the meaning of the word whereas the House of Lords have found such context but have not stated what or where the context is. See *Re Barnes' Will Trusts, Prior v Barnes* [1972] 2 All ER 639.

7   *Re Skillen, Charles v Charles* [1916] 1 Ch 518 at 521, and cases cited in n 4.

8   *Re Shaw, Mountain v Mountain* [1929] WN 246, and see para **[50.1]**, n 10.

9   *Re Hunter, Northey v Northey* (1908) 25 TLR 19 (money in the house or at the bank); *Downing (or Downes) v Townsend* (1755) Amb 280 (notes); *Barrett v White* (1855) 24 LJ Ch 724 (fund set apart for annuities). Money orders have also been treated as cash: *Re Windsor, Public Trustee v Windsor* (1913) 108 LT 947.

10 *Byrom v Brandreth* (1873) LR 16 Eq 475 (where the general position is stated); *Re Friedman, Friedman v Friedman* (1908) 8 SRNSW 127 (money on current account or in Savings Bank of New South Wales, but not money on fixed deposit).

11 *Manning v Purcell* (1855) 7 De GM & G 55 (balances at bank in both current and deposit accounts: deposit withdrawable at call); *Ogle v Knipe* (1869) LR 8 Eq 434 (money advanced on mortgage included in money and securities for money); *Byrom v Brandreth* (1873) LR 16 Eq 475 (cash at bankers); *Re Hunter, Northey v Northey* (1908) 25 TLR 19 (money in hands of agents); *Re Glendinning, Steel v Glendinning* (1918) 88 LJ Ch 87 (money on deposit at 7 day's notice); *Re Collings, Jones v Collings* [1933] Ch 920 (money on deposit account); *Re Barnes' Will Trusts, Prior v Barnes* [1972] 2 All ER 639, [1972] 1 WLR 587 (deposit account at a bank: sums, on deposit with the Post Office Savings Bank, in share account with a building society encashable without prior notice, in national developments bonds which could be withdrawn on one month's notice, and in premium savings bonds which could be cashed without notice, all included in a bequest of 'any money I may leave'); *Re Reed, Reed v Reed* [1911] VLR 232 (money on deposit not included, but moneys in Savings Bank at short notice included. 'Money on current account' can pass money on deposit in a case where the testator never had a current account: *Re Vear, Vear v Vear* (1917) 62 Sol Jo 159, but money 'to my account' means money on a drawing account and does not include money in the hands of trustees: *Re Bradfield, Bradfield v Bradfield* [1914] WN 423. 'Money in any banks' includes money on deposit for four years: *Harper's Trustee v Bain* (1903) 5 F 716; 'money' includes in addition to the matters above mentioned, an uncashed cheque: *Re Gates, Gates v Cabell* [1929] 2 Ch 420. Where the testator's deceased wife had deposited money in a bank and testator had a life interest in that sum the interest upon that sum accumulated at the bank did not pass under 'all money in the bank, War Stock, club money along with any money in hand'; *Re Lowe's Estate, Swann v Rockley* [1938] 2 All ER 774.

12 *Re Honeyfield, Honeyfield v Honeyfield* [1961] NZLR 1049.

13 *Re Ross, Carrail v Tilley* [1963] SASR 32.

14 As to securities for money, see para **[64.53]** infra.

15 Such as mortgage money vested in trustees and subject to legacy (*Ogle v Knipe* (1869) LR 8 Eq 434); apportioned part of an annuity to date of death and interest on bank balance (*Byrom v Brandreth* (1873) LR 16 Eq 475; and see *Re Lowe's Estate, Swann v Rockley* [1938] 2 All ER 774); apportioned part of dividends (*Re Beavan, Beavan v Beavan* (1885) 53 LT 245); National Savings Certificates and War Stock (*Re Hodgson, Nowell v Flannery* [1936] Ch 203).

16 *Gosden v Dotterill* (1832) 1 My & K 56 (Consols); *Willis v Plaskett* (1841) 4 Beav 208 (stock); *Hewit v Bredin* (1865) 17 Ir Jur 85 (Consols); *Lowe v Thomas* (1854) 5 De GM & G 315

(money in the funds: *Re Sutton, Stone v A-G* (1885) 28 Ch D 464 (Consols); *Re Gliddon, Smith v Gliddon* [1917] 1 Ch 174 (reversionary interest in investments); *Turner v Turner* (1852) 21 LJ Ch 843 (shares); *Re Dutton, Herbert v Harrison* (1869) 20 LT 386 (shares); *Re Gates, Gates v Cabell* [1929] 2 Ch 420 (stocks and shares); *Ogle v Knipe* (1869) LR 8 Eq 434 (bank stock); *Collins v Collins* (1871) LR 12 Eq 455 (building society shares and Consols); *Re Adkins, Solomon v Catchpole* (1908) 98 LT 667, and *Re Mann* [1912] 1 Ch 388 (Consols purchased through a Savings Bank account); *Beales v Crisford* (1843) 13 Sim 592 (government securities); *Dunally v Dunally* (1857) 6 I Ch R 540 (government securities); but in *Brennan v Brennan* (1868) IR 2 Eq 321, and *Boardman v Stanley* (1873) 21 WR 644, stock passed under 'money in the Bank of Ireland' in the first case and under 'money' in the second case where the gift was treated as residuary; and see *Re Cranfield, Mosse v Cranfield* [1895] 1 IR 80, where stock passed under 'money on deposit receipt' in the A bank, there being nothing else to which the gift could refer. Where 'money' can refer to nothing else, it will pass investments: *Re Jenkins, Tucker v Jenkins* (1901) 46 Sol Jo 13; *Re Taylor, Taylor v Tweedie* [1923] 1 Ch 99; *Re Hand's Goods* (1849) 7 Notes of Cases 59; *Chapman v Reynolds* (1860) 28 Beav 221; *Re Clifford Estate* (1953) 9 WWRNS 454.

17   Generally speaking choses in action are not cash or money. The following are examples: promissory notes: *Beales v Crisford,* supra: legacy to testatrix not acknowledged to be at her disposal: *Byrom v Brandreth* (1873) LR 16 Eq 475, amount deposited with stakeholder for a bet: *Manning v Purcell* (1855) 7 De GM & G 55; reversionary interest in stock: *Cowling v Cowling* (1859) 26 Beav 449, unpaid legacy: *Re Mason's Will* (1865) 34 Beav 494; fine on grant of lease: *Dillon v M'Donnell* (1881) 7 LR Ir 335. Mortgage debt, arrears of rent and dividends due were included in *Hewit v Bredin* (1865) 17 Ir Jur 85, but money in the hands of a land agent was excluded in *De Robeck v Lord Cloncurry* (1871) IR 5 Eq 588.

18   *Collet v Lawrence* (1791) 1 Ves 268; *Ommanney v Butcher* (1823) Turn & R 260; *Larner v Larner* (1857) 3 Drew 704; *Re Aston's Goods* (1881) 6 PD 203; *Hastings v Hane* (1833) 6 Sim 67; *Eaton v A-G* (1865) 13 WR 424; *Collins v Collins* (1871) LR 12 Eq 455; *Williams v Williams* (1878) 8 Ch D 789 (separate residuary bequest); *Re Townley, Townley v Townley* (1884) 53 LJ Ch 516; *Hart v Hernandez* (1885) 52 LT 217; *Lloyd v Lloyd* (1886) 54 LT 841; *Re Gliddon, Smith v Gliddon* [1917] 1 Ch 174; but 'money' with some small addition may well pass the residuary personal estate: *Legge v Asgill* (1818) 3 Hare 194n ('money left unemployed'); *Dowson v Gaskoin* (1837) 2 Keen 14 (whatever remains of money); *Waite v Combes* (1852) 5 De G & Sm 676 ('all moneys'); *Stocks v Barre* (1859) John 54 (in the absence of any other residuary bequest, a bequest of 'money' which may remain after payment of debts passes the residuary estate); *Cowling v Cowling* (1859) 26 Beav 449 ('moneys'); *Montagu v Earl of Sandwich* (1863) 33 Beav 324 ('residue of money': will commencing with general bequest of everything); *Patrick v Yeathered* (1864) 3 New Rep 367 ('all the remainder of my money'); *Stooke v Stooke* (1866) 35 Beav 396 ('remainder of my money in whatever it may be'); *Re Gammon, Shelton v Williams* [1986] CLY 3547 'remainder of money'; *Re Fisher's Goods* (1869) 20 LT 684 ('moneys of every kind'); *Prichard v Prichard* (1870) LR 11 Eq 232 ('money' held to pass personal estate including leaseholds, but not freeholds); *Re Pringle, Walker v Stewart* (1881) 17 Ch D 819 ('all the rest of my money however invested', though followed by specific gifts); *Re White's Goods* (1882) 7 PD 65 ('whole residue of money'); *Re Cadogan, Cadogan v Palagi* (1883) 25 Ch D 154 ('money'); *Re Buller, Buller v Giberne* (1896) 74 LT 406 ('all of my money' included reversionary interests); *Re Bramley's Goods* [1902] P 106 ('all the rest of my money'); *Re Capel, Arbuthnot v Capel* (1914) 59 Sol Jo 177 ('the rest of my money' preferred as a residuary gift to 'anything which I have not devised'); *Re Skillen, Charles v Charles* [1916] 1 Ch 518 ('money'); *Re Woolley, Cathcart v Eyskens* [1918] 1 Ch 33 ('moneys' passed residuary personal estate including reversionary interest); *Re Mellor, Porter v Hindsley* [1929] 1 Ch 446 ('remainder of any monies' passed residue of both real and personal estate); *Re Smithers, Watts v Smithers* [1939] Ch 1015, [1939] 3 All ER 689 ('remainder of my money' after provision for payment of debts includes residuary personal estate); *Re Samson* (1966) 59 DLR (2d) 132 ('the balance of my money').

19   *Re Mellor, Porter v Hindsley* [1929] 1 Ch 446; *Re Shaw, Mountain v Mountain* [1929] WN 246. The Administration of Estates Act 1925, has made real and personal property liable pari passu for debts, and therefore where a testator makes provision for the payment of his debts and then says the rest of the money is to be given to a certain beneficiary, it is possible to say that this expression includes both real and personal estate: *Re Mellor, Porter v Hindsley* [1929] 1 Ch 446, but this does not affect the proposition that money means cash or the equivalent of cash: *Re Emerson, Morril v Nutty* [1929] 1 Ch 128. It seems that, in general, 'money' will not include the real estate: *Re Tribe, Tribe v Truro Cathedral (Dean and Chapter)* (1915) 85 LJ Ch 79, and

see *Re Emerson, Morrill v Nutty* [1929] 1 Ch 128. The word 'all' by itself may pass real estate: *Re Shepherd, Mitchell v Loram* (1914) 58 Sol Jo 304; but in *Re Jennings, Caldbeck v Stafford and Lindmere* [1930] 1 IR 196 'all my money' did not carry real estate although it carried every kind of personal estate, and in *Re Recknell, White v Carter* [1936] 2 All ER 36, 'all other money invested or in the A Bank' was construed as being a gift of 'all other money', so that the words 'invested or in the A Bank' were words of enumeration and not qualifying words. 'All other money' was a residuary gift, but as there was no realty, no question of its inclusion arose; 'Any money I may leave' see *Re Barnes' Will Trusts, Prior v Barnes* [1972] 2 All ER 639, [972] 1 WLR 587, n 11. 'Money' does not in general carry real estate; *Re Bangs Estate* (1962) 38 DLR (2d) 99.

20   *Re Adkins, Solomon v Catchpole* (1908) 98 LT 667; but see the opposite conclusion in *Re Mann, Ford v Ward* [1912] 1 Ch 388 ('money standing to my credit at Post Office Savings Bank').

21   *Re Harding, Drew v St Thomas's Hospital* (1910) 27 TLR 102.

22   *Grosvenor v Durston* (1858) 25 Beav 97.

23   *Newman v Newman* (1858) 26 Beav 218.

24   *Hill v Mason* (1820) 2 Jac & W 248 (balance of money in hands of agent at death of testator afterwards invested).

25   *Re Ward's Estate* [1957] SASR 125 (included debentures).

26   *Ludlow v Stevenson* (1857) 1 De G & J 496.

27   *Knight v Knight* (1861) 2 Giff 616.

[64.36]
Money—reasons for giving a wide meaning. One of the most potent factors in influencing the court in giving a wide meaning to the word 'moneys' is the presumption against intestacy.[1] Again, where a testator has provided for the raising out of his general estate of a fund for the payment of debts, it has seemed reasonable to suppose that a gift of 'all other money' or 'the remainder of my money' is a general gift of the remainder of that fund.[2] The fact that there is a separate gift of residue will generally rebut an inference that a gift of 'money' is residuary,[3] and so sometimes will the fact that a specific gift follows what the court is asked to construe as a residuary gift,[4] but this has often been ignored.[5] The suggestion[6] that where the contest is not between residue and intestacy, but between one legatee and another, the word should be construed in accordance with the older more restrictive decisions, has been rejected.[7]

1   *Lowe v Thomas* (1854) Kay 369 at 377; *Boardman v Stanley* (1873) 21 WR 644; *Re Cadogan, Cadogan v Palagi* (1883) 25 Ch D 154 at 157; *Re Derbyshire, Webb v Derbyshire* [1906] 1 Ch 135; *Re Buller, Buller v Giberne* (1896) 74 LT 406; *Re Adkins, Solomon v Catchpole* (1908) 98 LT 667; *Re Harding, Drew v St Thomas's Hospital* (1910) 27 TLR 102.

2   *Ommanney v Butcher* (1823) Turn & R 260; *Stooke v Stooke* (1866) 35 Beav 396; *Re Mellor, Porter v Hindsley* [1929] 1 Ch 446; *Re Diver Estate* (1962) 34 DLR (2d) 667 ('any money remaining' is a general gift of residue).

3   *Willis v Plaskett* (1841) 4 Beav 208 at 210; *Williams v Williams* (1878) 8 Ch D 789; *Re Mann, Ford v Ward* [1912] 1 Ch 388 at 391; but see *Re Capel, Arbuthnot v Capel* (1914) 59 Sol Jo 177.

4   *Lowe v Thomas* (1854) Kay 369.

5   *Re Pringle* (1881) 17 Ch D 819; *Re Townley* (1884) 50 LT 394; *Re Maclean* (1894) 11 TLR 82.

6   *Per* Lord Russell in *Perrin v Morgan* [1943] AC 399 at 419, [1943] 1 All ER 187 at 197.

7   Goulding J in *Re Barnes' Will Trusts, Prior v Barnes* [1972] 2 All ER 639, [972] 1 WLR 587, where there was a residuary gift and yet the wider meaning of the word as stated in *Perrin v Morgan* [1943] AC 399, [1943] 1 All ER 187, was followed. See also *Re Brooks* (1969) 4 DLR (3d) 694 ('half my money' meant 'half my estate').

[64.37]
Money at bank. A bequest of money or cash at the bank includes all money there, whether in a current account or on deposit,[1] and a gift of 'money' simply

or 'moneys in hand' will pass money at the bank on current account.[2] A gift of 'my bank deposit at the M Bank' includes money there on current or deposit account but not certificates deposited there.[3] Money at the bank will pass under a bequest of 'money due and owing' to the testator,[4] and has been held to include bonds[5] but not State Savings Bank Deposit Stock.[6] A gift of money 'left in the bank' may mean what is left after providing for pecuniary legacies.[7] A gift of a 'bank book' carries the money in the account.[8] That a gift of 'money' includes money in the bank has already been dealt with.[9]

1   *Re Glendinning, Steel v Glendinning* (1918) 88 LJ Ch 87; *Manning v Purcell* (1855) 7 De GM & G 55; *Langdale v Whitfield* (1858) 4 K & J 426; *Liddle v Kebbells* (1915) 34 NZLR 593; *Masson v Smellie* (1903) 6 F 148 (sum paid into bank without the knowledge of the testator). Where the testatrix had only a deposit account, a gift of money in her 'current account' passed the deposit account: *Re Vear, Vear v Vear* (1917) 62 Sol Jo 159. In *Re Patterson* [1940] 1 DLR 802, bequest of 'all money in the bank' was held to pass securities there for safe keeping; but a bequest of 'any moneys that I have in the bank' was held to include only the current balance and certain uncashed travellers' cheques which were in the house and not to include National Savings Certificates, share certificates, post-war credits and a ring: *Re Trundle, Emanuel v Trundle* [1961] 1 All ER 103, [1960] 1 WLR 1388; *Re Mugford, Brenne v Bangs* (1975) 56 DLR 758; *Re Plant* [1974] Qd R 203. See also *Re Barnes' Will Trusts, Prior v Barnes* [1972] 2 All ER 639, [972] 1 WLR 587, para **[64.35]**, n 11. As to money in transit to bank, see *Re Lloyd, Lloyd v Chambers* (1894) 38 Sol Jo 235.
2   *Re Hunter, Northey v Northey* (1908) 25 TLR 19; *Re Gates' Goods* [1928] P 128; *Vaisey v Reynolds* (1828) 5 Russ 12; *Re Cox* (1927) 60 OLR 426; *Re Nicholas' Will* [1923] VLR 461.
3   *Re Heilbronner, Nathan v Kenny* [1953] 2 All ER 1016, [1953] 1 WLR 1254 (this was a home-made will and the doctrine that temporary removal did not affect the gift was applied).
4   *Carr v Carr* (1811) 1 Mer 541n; *Re Derbyshire, Webb v Derbyshire* [1906] 1 Ch 135 (whether on deposit or current account); *Re Stevens, Stevens v Keily* [1888] WN 110.
5   *Re Swindlehurst* [1952] 3 DLR 561; *Re Clark Estate* (1954) 13 WWRNS 79 (where the gift was of 'my bank balance'); *Re Cowan and Barry* (1977) 82 DLR (3d) 419 ('money in the banks and in cash' included bonds).
6   *Re Broad* [1953] VLR 49.
7   *Re Humfrey* [1944] 2 DLR 476.
8   *Re Dalzell* (1958) 26 WWR 215.
9   See para **[64.37]** supra.

[64.38]
Money—bequest of cash. A bequest of 'cash' will not pass a promissory note, government stock or bonds.[1] 'All cash moneys available in my estate' passes only assets of which the testator can demand immediate payment and does not include Dominion bonds or annuities, household furniture or realty.[2] 'Cash at bankers' may include money on deposit provided it is withdrawable without notice.[3] 'Cash in the house' has been held to include money orders of which it was the habit of the testator to keep a considerable amount in the house.[4] A gift of 'money' includes cash in the house.[5] A bequest of a balance in the hands of an agent will pass all moneys in the agent's hand though there are some which the testator has directed the agent to invest provided he has not so invested them.[6]

1   *Beales v Crisford* (1843) 13 Sim 592.
2   *Re Bennett* [1955] OWN 211; see also *Re Stinson* (1973) 30 DLR (3d) 519 ('balance of cash'); *Re Puczka* (1970) 10 DLR (3d) 339 ('cash deposited in my name in the XY Bank', not adeemed by change of bank); *Re Parker* (1982) 139 DLR (3d) 292 (all remaining cash a residuary bequest passing all personal property not specifically disposed of).

3   *Re Boorer, Boorer v Boorer* [1908] WN 189; *Re Stonham, Lloyds Bank Ltd v Maynard* [1963] 1
     All ER 377, [1963] 1 WLR 238 (bequest of 'cash in Lloyds Bank' included money on current
     and deposit account).
4   *Re Windsor, Public Trustee v Windsor* (1913) 108 LT 947.
5   *Byrom v Brandreth* (1873) LR 16 Eq 475.
6   *Hill v Mason* (1820) 2 Jac & W 248.

[64.39]
Money due or owing. A bequest of 'money due' will pass a judgment;[1] money
at bank;[2] testator's interest in the estate of a deceased person although the
amount is unascertained at the time of the testator's death;[3] damages recovered
by the executors in respect of a breach of contract in the lifetime of the testator;[4]
but not the apportioned part of dividends declared after the testator's death.[5]
Money due or owing on account of a business include Treasury Bonds deposited
as security for advances for the purposes of the business.[6] Money 'due or which
may become due' will include a reversionary interest.[7] Money 'due and owing'
will not pass unearned freight;[8] or an unascertained interest in a deceased's
estate;[9] or a sum charged on real estate.[10] A bequest of a debt can (in the absence
of express wording to this effect) include arrears of interest outstanding at the
testator's death; the authorities do not provide an explicit guiding principle, but a
possible reconciliation of them is that a gift of '£N which X owes me' or similar
does not include such arrears of interest,[11] and a gift of 'the debt which X owes
me of £N' or similar does include such arrears.[12] It has also been held that a gift
of 'all my interest and claim on household property in [*address of property*] on
which I have a mortgage of £1,500' included arrears of unpaid interest at the
testator's death.[13] It is submitted that where the debtor is being released from the
debt by the testator there is a stronger implication that such arrears are included
than where a debt owing to the testator is the subject of a specific gift to a third
party.[14] A bequest of sums due on mortgage will not pass a sum secured by a
settlement term of years.[15] Where a debt is due to the testator and payment is
made by cheque immediately before his death but such cheque is not presented
for payment until after his death but is in fact then paid, the debt is the amount
due at the death and passes to the legatee all moneys due and payable under a
named security.[16]

1   *Stenhouse v Mitchell* (1805) 11 Ves 352.
2   *Carr v Carr* (1811) 1 Mer 541n. If the expression used is 'money owing', it will be immaterial
     whether or not the money is on deposit: *Re Derbyshire, Webb v Derbyshire* [1906] 1 Ch 135;
     Re Stevens, Stevens v Keily [1888] WN 110.
3   *Bainbridge v Bainbridge* (1838) 9 Sim 16; but money 'owing' or money 'due and owing' will
     not pass an interest in an estate to which no grant has been taken: *Collins v Doyle* (1826) 1 Russ
     135; or an interest the amount of which is quite undetermined: *Martin v Hobson* (1873) 8 Ch
     App 401.
4   *Bide v Harrison* (1873) LR 17 Eq 76.
5   *Re Burke, Wood v Taylor* [1914] 1 IR 81.
6   *Re O'Shea* [1953] VLR 43.
7   *Re Maberly's Settlement Trusts* (1871) 24 LT 262.
8   *Stephenson v Dowson* (1840) 3 Beav 342.
9   See n 3.
10   *Brown v Brown* (1858) 4 K & J 704.
11   *Hawley v Cutts* (1677) Freem Ch 24; *Roberts v Kuffin* (1741) 2 Atk 112.
12   *Hawley v Cutts* (1677) Freem Ch 24; *Harcourt v Morgan* (1838) 2 Keen 274.
13   *Gibbon v Gibbon* (1853) 13 CB 205.

14   The only case on whether arrears of interest were included in the forgiveness of a debt, as opposed to a bequest of a debt to someone other than the debtor, seems to be *Hawley v Cutts* (1677) Freem Ch 24; it neither supports nor contradicts this submission.
15   *Earl of Poulett v Hood* (1866) 35 Beav 234.
16   *Ashby v Hayden* (1931) 31 SRNSW 324 (where the debt was a mortgage debt and the cheque was cashed on the day of death but after the precise time of death).

[64.40]

Money—ready money. Ready money in its ordinary sense includes money on current account at a bank,[1] or in the hands of an agent acting as banker[2] and money on deposit account at a bank where no notice of withdrawal is required;[3] but it does not ordinarily include money on deposit where a substantial notice of withdrawal is required according to the usual course of business.[4] It does not include choses in action[5] other than bank notes which have always been regarded as cash.[6]

1   *Taylor v Taylor* (1837) 1 Jur 401; *Fryer v Ranken* (1840) 11 Sim 55; *Re Powell's Trust* (1858) John 49 (savings bank deposit of which notice requiring payment had been given before death); *Parker v Marchant* (1843) 1 Ph 356; *Tallent v Scott* (1868) 18 LT 900 (balance at bank which included dividends actually received). It must be money due and payable: *Re Andrews' Will, Andrews v O'Mara* (1899) 25 VLR 408.
2   *Fryer v Ranken* (1840) 11 Sim 55; and see *Cooke v Wagster* (1854) 2 Sm & G 296.
3   *Stein v Ritherdon* (1868) 37 LJ Ch 369; *Mayne v Mayne* [1897] 1 IR 324; *Re Rodmell, Safford v Safford* (1913) 108 LT 184.
4   *Mayne v Mayne* [1897] 1 IR 324 (deposit receipts, withdrawable on demand, 'ready money': otherwise if previous notice is necessary); *Re Wheeler, Hankinson v Hayter* [1904] 2 Ch 66 (not ready money where 14 days' notice required); waiver of the notice does not make deposited money ready money: *Mayne v Mayne* [1897] 1 IR 324, unless it is the usual course of business: *Re Rodmell, Safford v Safford* (1913) 108 LT 184; *Re Barnes' Will Trusts, Prior v Barnes* [1972] 2 All ER 639, [1972] 1 WLR 587 (national development bonds included even though required one month's notice. A mere power to require notice where the ordinary practice is to pay on demand has been said not to be sufficient: *Re Cosgrove's Estate, Wills v Goddard* (1909) Times, 3 April, but see *Re Friedman, Friedman v Friedman* (1908) 8 SRNSW 127. In *Re Price, Price v Newton* [1905] 2 Ch 55, it was said that more than 24 hours' notice was a necessary condition to prevent a deposit being 'ready money'.
5   *Re Powell's Trust* (1858) John 49 (money due on note of hand); *Smith v Butler* (1846) 3 Jo & Lat 565 (money with agent not acting as banker); *Fryer v Ranken* (1840) 11 Sim 55 (rent of house and sum due on mortgage); *May v Grave* (1849) 3 De G & Sm 462 (unreceived dividends); *Stein v Ritherdon* (1868) 37 LJ Ch 369 (proportionate part of pensions, of dividends and of rent is not ready money); *Enohin v Wylie* (1862) 10 HL Cas 1 (government and other stock); *Re Andrews' Will, Andrews v O'Mara* (1899) 25 VLR 408 (share in another testator's residue); *Bevan v Bevan* (1880) 5 LR Ir 57 (government stock). As to dividends actually received, see *Tallent v Scott* (1868) 18 LT 900.
6   See para [63.1], n 10; *Re Bannister* [1985] 2 Qd R 246 (passed hidden cash).

[64.41]

Motor cars. When this will pass has been considered under 'car'.[1]

1   See para [64.8] supra.

[64.42]

Movables. A gift was described as 'all the remainder of my furniture and movables not hereby specifically disposed of not consisting of mortgages shares bonds or securities of any kind'. The exception of mortgages etc, did not extend the meaning of the word 'movables' so as to include anything beyond movable chattels and the gift did not include money in the bank, money payable under an insurance policy or other sums due to the testator at the time of his death.[1]

1   *Re Walsh, Walsh v Walsh* [1953] Ch 473, [1953] 1 All ER 982.

[64.43]

Partnership. A gift of one-half share in a partnership carries the half share in the capital of the partnership but not money standing to the credit of the partner in the current account of the partnership.[1] A bequest of the testator's 'estate and interest' in a partnership includes declared but undrawn profits and undeclared profits.[2] A gift of all the testator's real estate and all his livestock passed his interest in a partnership where he had no other such property.[3] Where a partnership deed provides that if either partner died the other was to succeed to his share, this was a contractual clause and not testamentary as each had a vested interest at the date of the agreement.[4] If the clause was testamentary, the agreement should have been executed as a will.

1   *Re Lanyon* [1957] SASR 135.
2   *Re Gartside* [1956] VLR 15. See *Re Miller* [1991] 1 Qd R 359 where this paragraph in the 4th Edition of the text, pp 481–482 was cited with approval, at 361.
3   *Hendry v Perpetual Executors and Trustees Association of Australia Ltd* (1961) 106 CLR 256.
4   *Bubnich, Marcan v Bubnich* [1965] WAR 138.

[64.44]

Personal chattels. These are for the purpose of an intestacy defined by the Administration of Estates Act 1925, s 55(1)(x),[1] and the definition has sometimes been incorporated in a will and the same definition (with a very minor addition) is also used in the Statutory Will Forms 1925.[2] These generally exclude anything used for business.[3] The meaning of some of the words used has been considered elsewhere,[4] these words include a motor yacht used for pleasure purposes,[5] and a stamp collection kept by the testator as his principal hobby.[6]

1   17 *Halsbury's Statutes* (4th edn) 467; Vol 2, Part G, para **[246.52]**.
2   See Vol 2, para **[238.7]** et seq.
3   *Re Ogilby, Ogilby v Wentworth-Stanley* [1942] Ch 288, [1942] 1 All ER 524 (herd of animals).
4   As to 'furniture', see para **[64.24]** supra; as to 'jewellery', see para **[64.31]** supra; as to 'plate', see para **[64.47]** infra; as to 'books', see para **[64.6]** supra.
5   *Re Chaplin, Royal Bank of Scotland v Chaplin* [1950] Ch 507, [1950] 2 All ER 155.
6   *Re Reynold's Will Trusts, Dove v Reynolds* [1965] 3 All ER 686, [1966] 1 WLR 19 followed in *Re Collins' Settlement Trusts, Donne v Hewetson* [1971] 1 All ER 283, [1971] 1 WLR 37; see para 64.45, note 10 infra; *Re Crispin's Will Trusts, Arkwright v Thurley* [1975] Ch 245, [1974] 3 All ER 772 (overruling the first-instance decision, [1973] 2 All ER 141) a collection of clocks held to be within the definition since a clock was, in the ordinary sense of the word, an article of furniture and it was immaterial where it was kept, what use, if any, it was put to, or whether it formed part of a collection of personal chattels.

[64.45]

Personal estate and property. Such expressions as 'personal estate', 'personal property', 'personal estate and effect', etc, are ordinarily construed to include only personal estate in the legal sense,[1] and leaseholds pass under such a description rather than under 'messuages and tenements'[2]. From the earliest times, however, it has been held that it may be properly assumed that what the testator meant by such words was not what is ordinarily understood by them, but that he intended to include freeholds, his words meaning 'all property owned by me personally'.[3] A gift of 'monetary and personal possessions' includes realty where the realty is acquired after the date of the will.[4] They have been held to pass shares in a navigation company though by Act of Parliament these were to lose all their freehold rights on conveyance.[5] A gift of 'personal belongings' may in the context either include the whole personal estate[6] or be restricted so as not to include stocks, shares and bank balances which would make the clause a residuary gift,[7] and such a gift may be defined by an enumeration of the classes of articles intended to be included.[8] 'Articles of personal use' do not include a piano or motor car.[9] A gift of 'personal effects' has been held to include a valuable stamp and coin collection, and a motor car.[10]

1   *Buchanan v Harrison* (1861) 1 John & H 662; *Belaney v Belaney* (1867) 2 Ch App 138; *Ex p Yates* (1869) 20 LT 940; *Re Noble* [1927] 1 DLR 1078; *Re Gangell* (1912) 8 Tas LR 120 (hay); *Re Way* (1903) 6 OLR 614 (mortgage); *Marchuk v Marchuk* (1965) 52 WWR 652. As a result of the changes made to the technical nature of an undivided share of land by the Trusts of Land and Appointment of Trustees Act 1996, a general gift of personalty in the strict sense will apparently now include an undivided share in land. See para **[41.18]** supra.
2   *Arkell v Fletcher* (1839) 10 Sim 299.
3   *Doe d Tofield v Tofield* (1809) 11 East 246; *Lines v Lines* (1869) 22 LT 400; *Re Smalley, Smalley v Smalley* (1883) 49 LT 662; *Re Wass, Re Clarke* (1906) 95 LT 758; *Re Banham, Westminister Bank Ltd v A-G* (1931) 47 TLR 376; *Re Batchelor* (1915) 34 NZLR 379; *Re Creamer Estate* [1932] 3 WWR 621. See also *Re Andrew's Estate, Creasey v Graves* (1902) 50 WR 471, where there was a devise of realty and personalty for life but the gift in remainder mentioned only personalty and it was held that the gift in remainder carried realty. This may be so where the word 'devise' is included in the gift: *Marchuk v Marchuk* (1965) 52 WWR 652.
4   *Re East* [1964] Qd R 42.
5   *Cadman v Cadman* (1872) LR 13 Eq 470 (shares held to be equitable converted under the Act, but it was held that they would have passed in any case).
6   *Re Bradfield, Bradfield v Bradfield* [1914] WN 423; *Re Mills' Will Trusts, Marriot v Mills* [1937] 1 All ER 142; but in *Re Price* [1950] Ch 242, [1950] 1 All ER 338, the word 'belongings' by itself was held not to include freeholds.
7   *Re Hynes, Knapp v Hynes* [1950] 2 All ER 879; *Re Stone* [1954] NZLR 1170 ('any of my personal belongings' not a residuary gift).
8   *Re Gebhardt* [1943] SASR 380.
9   *Re McFetridge, Speakman v McFetridge* [1950] NZLR 176 (such articles must bear some relation to the articles of personal adornment with which the testatrix associates them in her will).
10 *Re Collins' Settlement Trusts, Donne v Hewetson* [1971] 1 All ER 283; applied in *Re Cuthbertson, Cuthbertson v Cuthbertson* [1979] Tas SR 93; see also *Re Crispin's Will Trusts, Arkwright v Thurley* [1975] Ch 245, [1974] 3 All ER 772.

[64.46]

Pictures. Miniatures pass under a gift of 'pictures'.[1] Whether a stamp collection passes under this description is the subject of differing opinions.[2] There may be a question as to what is a 'portrait'.[3]

1   *Re Craven, Crewdson v Craven* (1908) 99 LT 390; *Re Marchioness Conyngham, Ramsden v Conyngham* (1908) 24 TLR 789.
2   *Re Fortlage, Ross v Fortlage* (1916) 60 Sol Jo 527 (where it passed); *Re Masson, Morton v Masson* (1917) 86 LJ Ch 753 (to the contrary).
3   See *Duke of Leeds v Lord Amherst* (1843) 13 Sim 459.

[64.47]

Plate. Under this description the following articles do not pass: watch,[1] gold-headed cane,[2] plated goods, but recently this view has been relaxed,[3] 'black jacks' (silver-mounted jugs).[4] Ornamental snuffboxes have passed under a gift of plate, china and other household effects.[5]

1   *Allen v Allen* (1729) Mos 112.
2   *Allen v Allen* (1729) Mos 112.
3   *Holden v Ramsbottom* (1863) 4 Giff 205; but in *Re Grimwood, Trewhella v Grimwood* [1946] Ch 54, [1945] 2 All ER 686, Sheffield plate and electro-plate passed under 'all my plate'.
4   *Re Lewis, Prothero v Lewis* (1909) 26 TLR 145.
5   *Field v Peckett (No 2)* (1861) 29 Beav 573.

[64.48]
Possessions. 'Any possessions I may have' include the whole personal estate of the testator.[1] 'Personal possessions' means 'personal effects'.[2]

1   *Re Brace, Gurton v Clements* [1954] 2 All ER 354; and see *Re East* [1964] Qd R 42.
2   *Re Leury* [1975] VR 601 applying *Joseph v Phillips* [1934] AC 348.

[64.49]
Premises. This word has already been considered in dealing with 'house'.[1]

1   See para **[64.26]** supra.

[64.50]
Presents. A house has been held not to be within the expression 'small presents'.[1]

1   *Re Osburn* (1969) 113 Sol Jo 387; In *Re Steel, Public Trustee v Christian Aid Society* [1979] Ch 218, [1978] 2 All ER 1026; there was a reference to 'small amounts' this was held to be an uncertain and provocative phrase.

[64.51]
Property. This is a wide term and includes all the testator's real and personal estate and all his interest therein,[1] but when joined with words peculiar to personalty, it may be restricted to that form of property[2] and the exception of an item of a particular kind of property may exclude others of the same kind.[3]

1   *Doe d Wall v Langlands* (1811) 14 East 370; *Jones v Skinner* (1835) 5 LJ Ch 87; *Thomas v Phelps* (1828) 4 Russ 348 at 351; *Saumarez v Saumarez* (1839) 4 My & Cr 331 at 338; *Morrison v Hoppe* (1851) 4 De G & Sm 234; *Re Greenwich Hospital Improvement Act* (1855) 20 Beav 458; *Lloyd v Lloyd* (1869) LR 7 Eq 458; *Cameron v Harper* (1891) 21 SCR 273; *Fitzgerald v Smith* (1889) 15 VLR 467.
2   *Doe d Bunny v Rout* (1816) 2 Marsh 397; *Re Fetherston-Haugh-Whitney's Estate* [1924] 1 IR 153; *Jauncey v A-G* (1861) 3 Giff 308 (gift to charity confined to such property as charity could take).
3   *Fleming v Brook* (1804) 1 Sch & Lef 318 (exception to chose in action in A excepted other choses in action found at A).

[64.52]
Real estate. Estates or interests in land or immovable property, including houses or other property situated thereon, are real property.[1] A lease of minerals has been held to be real estate and the rent therefrom to be applicable as the proceeds of a sale of real estate.[2] The strict meaning of the term does not include leaseholds.[3]

1 See also 'land' paras **[64.32]**–**[64.33]** supra.
2 *Re Montreal Trust Co's Application (Cleveland Estate)* (1962) 41 WWR 193.
3 As to the inclusion of an undivided share of land, see para **[64.32]** supra. It is submitted that realty or real estate includes equitable beneficial interests in freehold land; it seems that before 1926 an equitable interest in land descended to the heir on intestacy, *Re Somerville and Turner's Contract* [1903] 2 Ch 583.

[64.53]
Securities. The word 'securities' or 'securities for money', according to its literal meaning, includes such moneys as are secured on property[1] or on personal security[2] (including promissory notes[3] and bills of exchange)[4] and any stock or other investment which, by the terms of its creation, is a security for the payment of money;[5] but it does not include moneys for which a mere acknowledgement of indebtedness has been given,[6] nor is it the ordinary description of stock and shares in a public company.[7] The word 'securities' is, however, often used to describe investments or property dealt with on the Stock Exchange, and this meaning may readily be attributed to the word,[8] and even wider meanings have been given to it according to the context of the will and the circumstances of the case.[9]

1 *Ogle v Knipe* (1869) LR 8 Eq 434 (mortgage; cf real securities in the Trustee Act 1925, s 1(1)(*b*), and s 68(13)); *Duchess of Buccleuch v Hoare* (1819) 4 Madd 467 (Scottish heritable bond); *Cust v Goring* (1854) 18 Beav 383 (Scottish heritable bond); *Wilkes v Collin* (1869) LR 8 Eq 338 (reversionary interest in mortgage); *Callow v Callow* (1889) 42 Ch D 550 (agreement for sale of land with provision for mortgage securing instalments). A vendor's lien has been held to be not a security (*Goold v Teague* (1858) 32 LTOS 251) but that was doubted in *Callow v Callow* (1889) 42 Ch D 550. 'Securities' implies a right to resort to some property or fund in the event of default: *Boyd v Cowell* [1952] VLR 288.
2 *Bacchus v Gilbee* (1863) 3 De GJ & Sm 577 (bond); *Re Beavan, Beavan v Beavan* (1885) 53 LT 245 at 247 (railway debenture); *Puxley v Puxley* (1863) 1 New Rep 509 (judgment debt); *Lawrence v Galsworthy* (1857) 30 LTOS 112 (policy of assurance); *Re Lilly's Will Trusts, Public Trustee v Johnstone* [1948] 2 All ER 906 (policy of life assurance); *MacLaren v MacLaren* (1907) 15 OLR 142 (policy of insurance).
3 *Re Beavan, Beavan v Beavan* (1885) 53 LT 245; but for the purposes of an investment clause, a promissory note is not a security: *Stiles v Guy* (1832) 4 Y & C Ex 571.
4 *Barry v Harding* (1844) 7 I Eq R 313; but bank-notes are regarded as cash and not as securities: *Southcot v Watson* (1745) 3 Atk 226.
5 *Bescoby v Pack* (1823) 1 Sim & St 500 (stock in public funds); *Buckman v Ives* (1837) 6 LJ Ch 197 (stock in public funds); *Re Smithers, Watts v Smithers* [1939] Ch 1015, [1939] 3 All ER 689 (government bonds and stock); *Re Mayne, Stoneham v Woods* [1914] 2 Ch 115 (foreign government's bonds to bearer not securities); *Re Johnson, Greenwood v Greenwood* (1903) 89 LT 520 (India stock); *Re Maitland, Chitty v Maitland* (1896) 74 LT 274 (India stock); *Ferguson v Ogilby* (1842) 2 Dr & War 548 ('foreign bonds and other securities' did not pass British funds); *Hudleston v Gouldsbury* (1847) 10 Beav 547 (shares in canal company); *Re Rayner, Rayner v Rayner* [1904] 1 Ch 176 (railway stock and shares. It is here said that the primary meaning of security is 'money secured on property', but in its popular sense it includes stocks and shares); *Re Scorer, Burtt v Harrison* (1924) 94 LJ Ch 196 (securities given same meaning as investments); *Turner v Turner* (1852) 21 LJ Ch 843 (where insurance company share did not pass under 'securities'); *Re Beavan, Beavan v Beavan* (1885) 53 LT 245 (railway debenture stocks); *M'Donnell v Morrow* (1889) 23 LR Ir 591 (debenture stocks).
6 *Vaisey v Reynolds* (1828) 5 Russ 12 (money at bank passed as money in hand and not as money out on securities); *Re Beavan, Beavan v Beavan* (1885) 53 LT 245 (IOU); *Barry v Harding* (1844) 7 I Eq R 313 (IOU given for goods sold); *Hopkins v Abbott* (1875) LR 19 Eq 222 (banker's deposit notes); *Re Mason's Will* (1865) 34 Beav 494 (debt due to testator being an unpaid legacy bequeathed to testator); *Re Saxby, Saxby v Kiddell* [1890] WN 171 (money in Post Office Savings Bank).
7 In considering the following reference must also be made to n 8. *Harris v Harris* (1861) 29 Beav 107 (power to invest upon the security of the fund of any company incorporated by Act of

Parliament did not permit investment in preference shares of a railway company); *Ogle v Knipe* (1869) LR 8 Eq 434 (bank stock); *M'Donnell v Morrow* (1889) 23 LR Ir 591 (shares in companies); *Re Kavanagh, Murphy v Doyle* (1892) 29 LR Ir 333 (partly paid bank shares excluded from investment clause); *Re Maitland, Chitty v Maitland* (1896) 74 LT 274 (shares of Glove Telegraph Trust Co); *Re Smithers, Watts v Smithers* [1939] Ch 1015, [1939] 3 All ER 689 (not sufficient context to allow 'securities' to be read 'stock and shares in companies' and the word restricted to government stock secured on the revenues of the governments); *Re Hutchinson, Crispin v Hadden* (1919) 88 LJ Ch 352 (stocks and shares not included in will made as long ago as 1880).

8   *Re Lilly's Will Trusts* [1948] 2 All ER 906 (proceeds of life assurance policies); *Dicks v Lambert* (1799) 4 Ves 725 (securities properly so called insufficient to pay legacies charged on securities); *Re Rayner, Rayner v Rayner* [1904] 1 Ch 176 (investment clause of widest description with power to leave any moneys invested at my death in or upon the same securities); *Re Johnson, Greenwood v Greenwood and Robinson* (1903) 89 LT 520 (where a list of investments was found headed 'securities' and included shares in companies); *Re Scorer, Burtt v Harrison* (1924) 94 LJ Ch 196 (home-made will); *Re Mort, Perpetual Trustee Co Ltd v Bisdee* (1904) 4 SRNSW 760 (shares included); *Re J H* (1911) 25 OLR 132 (shares included). A description of 'all moneys, shares and securities at my bankers' does not pass stocks of which only stock receipts and inscription receipts are at the bank: *Re Hay Drummond, Halsey v Pechell* (1922) 128 LT 621; nor securities of which the bank holds no document of title though it has a power of attorney to receive the dividends and to sell the security: *Re Maitland, Chitty v Maitland* (1896) 74 LT 274; *Re Douglas's Will Trusts, Lloyds Bank Ltd v Nelson* [1959] 2 All ER 620, [1959] 1 WLR 744 (such securities as the trustee may think fit without being responsible for any loss or for the failure of any banker, broker or other person).

9   *Dicks v Lambert* (1799) 4 Ves 725; *Re Gent and Eason's Contract* [1905] 1 Ch 386 (power to vary securities included power to sell real estate). The word may be qualified by additional words in the description, eg 'securities standing in my name': *Re Mayne, Stoneham v Woods* [1914] 2 Ch 115 (bonds to bearer not included); *Re Johnson, Greenwood v Greenwood and Robinson*, supra ('securities held by bank') *Re Maitland, Chitty v Maitland* (1896) 74 LT 274 (bank must hold documents of title); *Re Palmer, National Provincial Bank Ltd v Barwell* [1945] Ch 8, [1944] 2 All ER 406 (testatrix becoming of unsound mind and stock transferred into court); applied in *Re Holland's Estate* [1950] 2 DLR 135, where the securities (government bonds) were purchased by the committee. In *Re Ellis Estate, Bond and Kirby (Ellis Estate) v Bond and Ellis* (1961) 33 DLR (2d) 594 'all my shares, bonds and securities of every kind whatsoever' was held to include the deceased's interest as vendor on a sale of land. In *Re Leigh's Will Trusts, Handyside v Durbridge* [1970] Ch 277, [1969] 3 All ER 432, a gift of 'all shares which I hold and any other interest or assets, which I may have' in a named company, included shares which the testatrix was entitled to as administrix of her husband's estate but which had not been transferred to her.

[64.54]

Shares. A bequest of 'shares' may be a gift of all the shares in a company owned by the testator and clearly if the testator owns shares, properly so called, in the company, all will pass though they be shares of different kinds, such as preference, ordinary or deferred shares of any other of the many descriptions of shares which limited companies issue. A gift of all testator's shares will include both shares purchased before those purchased after the date of the will.[1] 'Shares' in its primary sense means the shares of a limited company,[2] but its meaning may be widened by the context.[3] Where, however, a testator bequeaths a certain number of shares which is less than his total holding and his holding is of different classes of shares, then the donee may have a power of selection[4] or the gift might even be void for uncertainty.[5] The word 'shares', however, has been given a wider meaning and will include stock which is of the same nature as the shares and identical in substance with them,[6] but not generally stock issued as security, eg debenture stock.[7] Shares will include stock into which shares existing at the date of the will have been converted on an amalgamation of companies[8] and where the testator has no shares in the named company, but has stock in that company, such stock will pass.[9] Shares in a mining company can include shares in a slate quarry which was originally a mining company.[10] A subsequent subdivision of shares will not affect the bequest.[11] A bequest of 'my shares in different securities' does not carry an interest which the testator has as a beneficiary on intestacy in shares and stock forming part of an intestate's estate.[12] A bequest of the testator's share and interest in an assurance company will not pass policy moneys of or bonuses on a policy with the company.[13] A gift of all shares of a building society and all moneys standing to my credit in the society at my death passed moneys on deposit being the moneys which has become due on redemption of the shares.[14]

1   *Re Kidman* [1953] SASR 28 (but it was held that 'share' could not be construed as a share in a residuary estate).
2   *Re Everett, Prince v Hunt* [1944] Ch 176, [1944] 2 All ER 19 (the natural meaning of 'stocks and shares' is stocks and shares in a limited company and there was nothing in the circumstances of the case to extend the meaning).
3   *Re Purnchard's Will Trusts, Public Trustee v Pelly* [1948] Ch 312, [1948] 1 All ER 790 (where the circumstances justified the widest construction and the words included all forms of investment dealt with on stock exchanges).
4   See para [8.7] supra; and *Re Tetsall, Foyster v Tetsall* [1961] 2 All ER 801.
5   See Chapter 53.
6   *Morrice v Aylmer* (1875) LR 7 HL 717; overruling *Oakes v Oakes* (1852) 9 Hare 666 (where it was not to include stock in the same company); *Re Cruse, Gass v Ingham* [1930] WN 206. Where company issued both shares and investment certificates and the testatrix had some of both, the word 'shares' did not pass the investment certificates: *Re Kennedy Estate, Kennedy Estate Executors v Jickling* [1936] 1 WWR 204.
7   *Re Bodman, Bodman v Bodman* [1891] 3 Ch 135; *Re Connolly, Walton v Connolly* (1914) 110 LT 688; *Re Humphreys, Wren v Ward* (1915) 114 LT 230; *Dillon v Arkins* (1885) 17 LR Ir 636, but where a testatrix had no shares at all in the two specified companies but only debentures, the debentures were held to pass: *Re Weeding, Armstrong v Wilkin* [1896] 2 Ch 364.
8   *Re Loveman, Watson v Watson* (1879) 48 LJ Ch 565; *Re Humphreys, Wren v Ward* (1915) 114 LT 230; *Re Knaggs, Knaggs v Knaggs* (1905) 49 Sol Jo 314; *Oakes v Oakes* (1852) 9 Hare 666 but not necessarily a bonus issue; see *Re Tetsall, Foyster v Tetsall* [1961] 2 All ER 801.
9   *Re Weeding, Armstrong v Wilkin* [1896] 2 Ch 364.
10 *Dowager Duchess of Cleveland v Meyrick* (1867) 37 LJ Ch 125.
11 *Re O'Brien, Little v O'Brien* (1946) 115 LJ Ch 340; *Re Greenberry, Hops v Daniell* (1911) 55 Sol Jo 633; *Re Clifford, Mallam v McFie* [1912] 1 Ch 29; *Re M'Afee, Mack v Quirey* [1909] 1 IR 124; *Corley v Corley* (1912) 31 NZLR 887; and see para [64.53] supra. As to issue of bonus shares, see *Re O'Brien, Little v O'Brien*, and para [61.1] supra, and see *Re Speir* [1924] 1 Ch 359.
12 *Re Holmes, Villiers v Holmes* [1917] 1 IR 165; *Re Kidman* [1953] SASR 28.
13 *Harington v Moffat* (1853) 4 De GM & G 1.
14 *Re Foley* [1955] NZLR 535.

[64.55]
Sporting equipment. In a New Zealand case, the words, 'all my personal sporting equipment' were held apt to include a boat, trailer and two outboard motors used by the testator solely for recreational fishing.[1]

1   *Re Lowit* [1967] NZLR 883.

[64.56]
Stamps. A gift of 'stamps of Great Britain and of such of the British Colonies except Malta' is construed according to the meaning ascribed to such words by philatelists.[1]

1   *Re Van Lessen, National Provincial Bank Ltd v Beamont* [1955] 3 All ER 691; see also *Re Collins' Settlement Trusts, Donne v Hewetson* [1971] 1 All ER 283, [1971] 1 WLR 37.

[64.57]
Stock. A bequest of 'stock' will not in the ordinary way include shares,[1] but, when coupled with other words (such as 'funds or securities whatsoever'), the word may include shares.[2] Stock will pass under a bequest of shares.[3] Apart from stock in a company, the word may in a suitable context mean stock in trade[4] or farming stock.[5]

1   *Re Willis, Spencer v Willis* [1911] 2 Ch 563 (shares of a like description not included). As to debenture stock, see *Re Bodman, Bodman v Bodman* [1891] 3 Ch 135: *Re Weeding, Armstrong v Wilkin* [1896] 2 Ch 364: *Re Connolly, Walton v Connolly* (1914) 110 LT 688; *Re Humphreys, Wren v Ward* (1915) 114 LT 230.
2   *Re Inman, Inman v Inman* [1915] 1 Ch 187.
3   See para **[64.54]** supra.
4   *Elliott v Elliott* (1841) 9 M & W 23. See also *Wilson v Wilson* (1847) 1 De G & Sm 152.
5   *Brooksbank v Wentworth* (1743) 3 Atk 64; *Creagh v Creagh* (1862) 13 I Ch R 28; *Randall v Russell* (1817) 3 Mer 190 (where two kinds of 'stock' were given: 'all stock of cattle, horses and carriages' and 'his farm and stock and crops thereon'. It was held that the stock on the farm also passed under the earlier description). As to 'farming stock' see para **[64.20]** supra.

[64.58]
War loan and similar securities. A gift of 'War Loans' includes Exchequer Bonds issued under the War Loan Act 1919.[1] Where a specific investment was described as 'War Loan' but in fact consisted of 'national War Bonds' which had been converted into Conversion Stock and Treasury Bonds, these last were held to pass under the gift.[2] A gift of 'War Bonds' will pass war stock[3] and consolidated stock into which War Bonds have been converted.[4] 'War Savings Certificates' will not pass National Savings Certificates,[5] and National Savings Certificates and Defence Bonds purchased after the date of the will do not pass under a gift of 'War Loan'.[6] National Savings Certificates and War Stock have been held not to pass under a gift of money,[7] and under a gift of 'all my bonds',[8] but this is necessarily a matter of construction.

1   *Re Ionides, London County Westminster and Parr's Bank Ltd v Craies* (1922) 38 TLR 269.
2   *Re Price, Trumper v Price* [1932] 2 Ch 54.
3   *Re Balchin, Havenhand v Perugia* (1922) 38 TLR 868.
4   *Re Gifford, Gifford v Seaman* [1944] Ch 186, [1944] 1 All ER 268.
5   *Re Lamb, Marston v Chauvet* (1933) 49 TLR 541.
6   *Re Gifford, Gifford v Seaman* [1944] Ch 186, [1944] 1 All ER 268.
7   *Re Hodgson, Nowell v Flannery* [1936] Ch 203.
8   *Re O'Mullane* [1955] VLR 217.

Construction of wills: particular rules relating to persons

CHAPTER 65

Time for ascertaining the donees

[65.1]

General considerations. The ascertainment of the donee is an element in the ascertainment of the vesting of the gift, and, accordingly, the presumption of early vesting[1] has been invoked, in doubtful cases, to assist in determining which of various persons was intended by a description which was capable of denoting any of them.[2] In general, however, this presumption does not assist in finding out whom the testator intended as the objects of his bounty.[3] An express direction as to vesting (for example, at a specified age) or a gift over is in general immaterial in ascertaining a class,[4] unless it alters the description of the class.[5]

1   See Chapter 93. A court of equity will not presume that a party not *in esse* is intended to take unless such an intention is made clear and put beyond dispute by the words of the will, and it is only following out the same principle to hold that a person to whom a legacy is given in a particular character and by a particular description shall not be entitled to it unless he be clothed with that character and answer that description at the moment when the legacy vest in possession: *Bartleman v Murchison* (1831) 2 Russ & M 136.
2   *Radford v Willis* (1871) 7 Ch App 7. The rules of convenience (see Chapter 66) are said to be directed to make the gift vest as early as possible: *Gimblett v Purton* (1871) LR 12 Eq 427.
3   It does no more than suggest the most desirable method of carrying that intention into effect when those objects are ascertained, assumed that they can be ascertained: *Doe d Smith v Fleming* (1835) 2 Cr M & R 638 at 654.
4   *Williams v Haythorne* (1871) 6 Ch App 782; *Re Payne* (1858) 25 Beav 556.
5   *Williams v Russell* (1863) 10 Jur NS 168; *Re Knowles, Nottage v Buxton* (1882) 21 Ch D 806.

[65.2]

Individuals. Where the donee is designated by a description which may at different times apply to different individuals[1] and the context does not point to any future time as the time at which the donee has to be ascertained, then prima facie the only person who is entitled to take is the one satisfying the description at the date of the will,[2] if there is anyone to the knowledge of the testator who then satisfied it.[3] Where the context shows that the donee is to be ascertained in the future, but does not show at what specific time, then the first person to satisfy the description is presumed to be identified.[4] The context may, however, show that the donee in each case is to be ascertained at the death of the testator, or some other definite future time.[5] Where the will made an alternative gift 'in case he shall have married', this included marriage after the will as well as after the death of the testator.[6]

1   Such as eldest son or the holder of an office. As to 'wife', see Chapter 80, and as to 'servants', see para **[30.23]** supra.

2   The provisions of the Wills Act 1837, s 24 (see Vol 2, Part G, para **[244.24]**), do not apply to the objects of the bounty but only to the property comprised: see Chapter 59, and *Bullock v Bennett* (1855) 7 De GM & G 283; *Gibson v Gibson* (1852) 1 Drew 42.

3   *Lomax v Holmden* (1749) 1 Ves Sen 290 (first son means eldest at the material time); *Thompson v Thompson* (1844) 1 Coll 381 (similar case where the material time was the date of a codicil); *Re Whorwood, Ogle v Lord Sherborne* (1887) 34 Ch D 446 (holder of title: at date of will); *Re Laffan and Downes' Contract* [1897] 1 IR 469 (superioress of a convent); *Amyott v Dwarris* [1904] AC 268 (eldest son); *Re Devling* [1955] VLR 238 (gift to wife who was divorced after the date of the will and testator executed a codicil appointing a new executor but otherwise confirmed his will. The wife took). As to gifts to the holder of an office, see Chapter 81.

4   *Radford v Willis* (1871) 7 Ch App 7 (gift to husband of person unmarried at date of will); *Re Hickman's Will Trust, Hickman v Hickman* [1948] Ch 624, [1948] 2 All ER 303 (gift to wife of my grandson. Grandson not married at death of testatrix, but twice married later, the first marriage being dissolved. The first (divorced) wife took the gift); *Re Daniels, London City and Midland Executor and Trustee Co Ltd v Daniels* (1918) 87 LJ Ch 661 ('Lord Mayor for the time being': holder of office at death of testator held entitled). As to gifts to 'eldest son', see para **[81.2]** infra. An uncertain description has been satisfied by selecting the first person to fulfil it: *Ashburner v Wilson* (1850) 17 Sim 204 (a son of my nephew: firstborn son selected).

5   *Re Earl Cathcart* (1912) 56 Sol Jo 271 (a gift to successor to title).

6   *Re Fentem* [1950] 2 All ER 1073.

[65.3]

Groups of individuals. If the gift is immediate and is a separate bequest of specific amount (as a gift of so much apiece) to each one of a group of certain children, who (though generally described in the same words as a class) are to take as individuals and not as a class, prima facie only those in existence at the death of the testator can take, and those coming into existence afterwards are excluded.[1] The fact that at the date of the will or of the death of the testator there are no members of the group in existence does not render future members admissible.[2] If such a gift is postponed, all those who come into existence before the time of distribution are let in.[3] The rule is founded on the inconvenience of postponing distribution until all the children who might be born and the total amount of their bequests could be ascertained,[4] and accordingly it does not apply where by the provisions of the will this inconvenience does not exist,[5] or is expressly contemplated by the testator.[6]

1   *Garbrand v Mayot* (1689) 2 Vern 105 (gift of £20 apiece to all the children of testator's sister); *Storrs v Benbow* (1833) 2 My & K 46 (similar gift to children 'who may be born' to certain persons on attaining 21 does not include child born after testator's death, but a child *en ventre* took); *Townsend v Early* (1860) 3 De GF & J 1 (children who may be born); *Butler v Lowe* (1839) 10 Sim 317 (children begotten or to be begotten); *Peyton v Hughes* (1842) 7 Jur 311; *Mann v Thompson* (1854) Kay 628 (to all and every the child and children); *Rogers v Mutch* (1878) 10 Ch D 25 (to each of the children who shall live to attain 21); *Re Thompson's Will, Brahe v Mason* [1910] VLR 251 (to each child who shall attain 21).

2   *Mann v Thompson* (1854) Kay 628 at 644; *Rogers v Mutch* (1878) 10 Ch D 25.

3   *A-G v Crispin* (1784) 1 Bro CC 386 (bequest subject to life interest).

4   *Mann v Thompson* (1854) Kay 628; *Rogers v Mutch* (1878) 10 Ch D 25. Where there is no person to satisfy the description at the death of the testator, but more than one at a time of distribution, the first person to satisfy the description takes: see para **[66.1]** infra.

5   For example, where a fund is set apart out of which alone the legacies are payable: *Evans v Harris* (1842) 5 Beav 45.

6   *Defflis v Goldschmidt* (1816) 1 Mer 417 (a gift of £2,000 each to sister's children now born or hereafter to be born and direction for setting apart a fund shows intention to benefit children born after death of testator).

[65.4]
Class gifts. The rules applicable to these gifts are dealt with separately.[1]

1   As to time of ascertainment of class, see Chapter 66. As to what is a class, see paras **[47.28]–[47.34]** supra.

[65.5]
Survivors. This subject is dealt with as a whole.[1]

1   See Chapter 67.

[65.6]
Alternative donees. The rules applicable to these gifts are dealt with separately.[1]

1   See Chapter 68.

Class gifts – rules of convenience

I. TIME FOR ASCERTAINMENT FIXED BY THE CONTEXT

[66.1]
Context clear. The words of the will may clearly indicate the point of time at which the class[1] is to be ascertained and in all such cases there is no room for the application of any rules of construction. Thus, a gift to all children 'now living' includes only those in existence at the date of the will, and those born after that date are excluded.[2] In the case of a gift to children living at the death of the testator or any other person[3] or at any particular future time[4] or to children now born or to be born during the lifetime of their named parent,[5] the time of ascertaining the class is fixed by the express words of the will. So where life interests are given to several persons in succession and, on the death of the last, there is a gift to a class of persons then living, the word 'then' is generally to be taken as referring grammatically to the death of that last-named person even when such death takes place before the death of the testator and before one or more of the other life tenants.[6] The word 'then' may in some cases refer to the death of the testator or other period of distribution.[7] The court will not, in order to close a class, presume a woman is past child bearing.[8]
A gift to all the children of A and B who attain twenty-one where A and B are husband and wife includes all children of both parties and the class is not closed when the particular marriage is determined.[9]

1   As to what are class gifts and what are gifts to individuals as *personae designatae* see paras **[47.28]**–**[47.34]** supra.
2   *James v Richardson* (1678) Freem KB 472. It has been held that a will referred only to all sisters living at the date of the will and so excluded the issue of a sister then dead although the provision was for issue of sisters who 'may have predeceased me': *Mackintosh (or Miller) v Gerrard* [1947] AC 461.
3   *Barker v Lea* (1814) 3 Ves & B 113; *Jennings v Newman* (1839) 10 Sim 219 (including a donee of a life interest); *Turner v Hudson* (1847) 10 Beav 222 (where parents and children were to be classed together); *Re Helsby, Neate v Bozie* (1914) 84 LJ Ch 682 (gift to next of kin at death of tenant for life, a so-called artificial class); *Re Bulcock, Ingham v Ingham* [1916] 2 Ch 495 (a similar case, but the class was of a more peculiar nature). Where a class consisting of next of kin is to be ascertained at a date subsequent to the testator's death, the next of kin are ascertained on the assumption that the testator died at that time: *Re Mellish, Day v Withers* [1916] 1 Ch 562; *Hutchinson v National Refuges for Homeless and Destitute Children* [1920] AC 795.
4   *Hughes v Hughes* (1807) 14 Ves 256 (when youngest grandson attains twenty-one); *Dodd v Wake* (1837) 8 Sim 615 (gift to children of daughter when eldest (ie eldest for the time being) should attain twenty-four; then void for remoteness); *Boughton v Boughton* (1848) 1 HL Cas 406; *Hodson v Micklethwaite* (1854) 2 Drew 294 (children born during life of named husband and nine months later); *Stuart v Cockerell* (1870) 5 Ch App 713; *Re Deighton's Settled Estates*

(1876) 2 Ch D 783 (sale to take place and class to be determined after death of wife and all children had attained full age); *Wylie's Trustees v Bruce* 1919 SC 211 (gifts to heirs of A after life estate); *Conolly v Brophy* (1920) 54 ILT 41 (gift to surviving children when youngest attains twenty-one); *Re Wilson* [1954] NZLR 880.

5   *Scott v Earl of Scarborough* (1838) 1 Beav 154; cf *Hodson v Micklethwaite* (1854) 2 Drew 294.

6   *Archer v Jegon* (1837) 8 Sim 446; *Re Milne, Grant v Heysham* (1887) 56 LJ Ch 543; *Palmer v Orpen* [1894] 1 IR 32.

7   *Gaskell v Holmes* (1844) 3 Hare 438; *Widdicombe v Muller* (1853) 1 Drew 443.

8   See para [66.3] infra.

9   *Re Pilkington, Pilkington v Pilkington* (1892) 29 LR Ir 370.

[66.2]

Class to take on a contingency. Where there is a gift to a class on a contingent event, the time of the happening of the contingency is not imported into the description of the individuals composing the class.[1] This circumstance is, however, to be taken into consideration in combination with indications of the testator's intention to be found in other parts of the will,[2] and, on the whole of the will, the description of the class may be varied and the contingency applied to the class.[3]

1   *Boulton v Beard* (1853) 3 De GM & G 608 at 612; *Hickling v Fair* [1899] AC 15 at 35; *Re Walker, Dunkerly v Hewerdine* [1917] 1 Ch 38; *Re Sutcliffe, Alison v Alison* [1934] Ch 219. Hence the contingency that there shall be issue living at the time of distribution is not imported into the description of the issue who are to take, so as to exclude issue who have died before the date of distribution: *Re Sutcliffe, Alison v Alison* (where distribution was at the death of the last survivor of testator's children and the estates of deceased grandchildren took a share). See *Re Fraser* (1986) 29 DLR (4th) 88, at p 101 where the text was referred to.

2   *Selby v Whittaker* (1877) 6 Ch D 239 at 250.

3   *Selby v Whittaker* (1877) 6 Ch D 239 at 250. Thus a gift to all children of a named person if he shall leave any child is not restricted to the children he leaves: *Boulton v Beard* (1853) 3 De GM & G 608; *M'Lachlan v Taitt* (1860) 2 De GF & J 449; but it is otherwise if the gift is to 'such' children, for then only those surviving take: *Sheffield v Kennett* (1859) 4 De G & J 593; *Re Watson's Trusts* (1870) LR 10 Eq 36, or the gift is to 'vest' (used in its legal sense, see Chapter 93) at the death of the parent; *Selby v Whittaker* (1877) 6 Ch D 239; or there is a gift over, if no 'such' issue; *Wilson v Mount* (1854) 19 Beav 292.

II.   PRESUMPTION AND EVIDENCE AS TO FUTURE PARENTHOOD – WHEN WOMAN PAST CHILD-BEARING

[66.3]

Although the law has always been averse to assuming for perpetuity purposes that a woman was past child-bearing or to fixing a date at which it can be said that a woman was no longer able to become the mother of children[1] the Court of Chancery would in a clear case give trustees or others engaged in the administration of an estate permission to distribute on the footing that a woman was past child-bearing[2] and it has in practice been assumed that a woman who has attained 54 is past child-bearing.[3] However, it is now possible, by the application of techniques developed for the treatment of infertility, for a woman well over the age of 54 to bear a child, and the existing case law on the assumptions which the court will make must be treated with caution. Under the rule against perpetuities no presumption was ever made at common law. Now by the Perpetuities and Accumulations Act 1964, s 2 the rule has been modernised, but this amendment only applies where the question arises in proceedings regarding the application of the rule against perpetuities in an instrument taking effect after 15 July 1964.[4]

1   *Re Dawson, Johnston v Hill* (1888) 39 Ch D 155; *Ward v Van der Loeff* [1924] AC 653. In *Re Blake, Berry v Geen* [1938] 2 All ER 362 at 367, Lord Maugham LC said: 'I do not think it necessary ... to express any opinion as to the decision in *Re Deloitte, Griffiths v Deloitte* [1926] Ch 56. That authority, which turned on the refusal of the court to presume a woman aged 65 to be past child-bearing for the purposes of the case, might require consideration in this House at some future time and I think it better to leave open the question which it involves'. And see *Figgs v Clarke* [1997] STC 247.

2   Danckwerts J said in *IRC v Bernstein* [1960] Ch 444 at 454, [1960] 1 All ER 697 at 702; 'It is quite true that the Court of Chancery as a practical matter and as a matter of administration, on being satisfied by reason of age or for medical reasons that a woman is past the age of child-bearing, will allow the distribution of a fund, thus exonerating the trustees of a will or settlement from what otherwise might be a breach of trust'.

3   The cases for and against this presumption are collected in 22 English and Empire Digest (Reissue), pp 190–192. It would seem that apart from special reasons, the relevant age was 54. The Perpetuities and Accumulations Act 1964, s 2: 33 *Halsbury's Statutes* (4th edn) 1080, see Vol 2, Part G, para **[246.60]**, fixes the age of 55. The matters to be taken into consideration have been thus stated by Wilberforce J in *Re Westminster Bank Ltd's Declaration of Trust* [1963] 2 All ER 400n at 401: 'I think that the courts would now be rather cautious in accepting [the decided cases] as laying down any sort of rule as to any particular age. It seems to me that at this time one must take into account the physiological changes in human beings as a result of improvements in health and also the different circumstances of family planning. Moreover, it should be borne in mind that more accurate medical evidence is nowadays available, and ought to be put before the court.' See also *Re Whichelow, Bradshaw v Orpen* [1953] 2 All ER 1558, [1954] 1 WLR 5.

4   In the case of a will the testator must have died after 15 July 1964. See Vol 2, Part G, para **[246.60]** for the Perpetuities and Accumulations Act 1964, s 2.

III.   FIRST RULE OF CONVENIENCE

[66.4]

Applicable only where time for ascertaining class uncertain. Where it cannot be gathered, from the context and the circumstances of the case, what time is referred to for ascertaining a class, the court acts upon certain rules of construction, which have been framed for the convenience of the donees and of the administration of property, and have accordingly been called rules of convenience.[1] They are admittedly not founded on any view of the testator's intention,[2] and are artificial.[3] The rules both as to real and personal property are said to be founded on the presumption that only persons in being are intended to take.[4]

1   *Re Emmet's Estate, Emmet v Emmet* (1880) 13 Ch D 484; *Re Powell, Crosland v Holliday* [1898] 1 Ch 227 at 230.

2   *Re Emmet's Estate, Emmet v Emmet* (1880) 13 Ch D 484 at 490; *Re Roberts v Repington v Roberts-Gawen* (1881) 19 Ch D 520 at 527.

3   *Leake v Robinson* (1817) 2 Mer 363 at 383; *Re Chartres, Farman v Barrett* [1927] 1 Ch 466.

4   *Crone v Odell* (1811) 1 Ball & B 449 at 459; *Bartleman v Murchison* (1831) 2 Russ & M 136 at 140.

[66.5]

First rule of convenience. A class[1] is prima facie composed of those members (if any) existing ascertainable and capable of taking[2] at the death of the testator,[3] but where the period of distribution is at a later date, the class opens so as to let in all those members coming into existence before the period of distribution.[4] Apart from the letting in of additional members, the postponement of the gift does not otherwise postpone the time of ascertainment of the class,[5] and, on the one hand, persons who come into existence after the period of distribution are excluded,[6] and, on the other hand, those in existence at the death of the testator take an immediate vested interest, so that, if they die before the date of distribution, their share passes to their personal representatives.[7] Where, however, the gift is immediate, but at the death of the testator no member has yet come into existence, then all the members of the class who are born at any future time prima facie are intended to take under the gift.[8]

1   As to kinds of classes subject to the rules, see para **[66.19]** infra.
2   *Fell v Biddolph* (1875) LR 10 CP 701 at 709 (where two possible members of the class had attested the will); *Re Coleman and Jarrom* (1876) 4 Ch D 165 at 169 (the class does not include those who are incapable of taking whether by dying in the testator's lifetime or by attesting the will or by some other operation of law).
3   *Viner v Francis* (1789) 2 Bro CC 658; *Norman v Norman* (1830) Beat 430; *Re Winn, Brook v Whitton* [1910] 1 Ch 278 (where the testator has contemplated a class some of whom may die before a certain time and others survive that time, that time is naturally, if not more specifically designated, the death of the testator); *Re Singh* (1974) 50 DLR (3d) 628. (This rule applies to an immediate gift 'or so many of them as shall be living' at a postponed time: *Trelawney v Molesworth* (1701) Colles 163. A gift to 'unmarried' children is to such as are unmarried at the death of the testator and subsequent marriage is immaterial: *Jubber v Jubber* (1839) 9 Sim 503; *Blagrove v Coore* (1859) 27 Beav 138; but in *Hall v Robertson* (1853) 4 De GM & G 781, a gift to son and unmarried daughters meant unmarried daughters at the date of the disposition, in this case a codicil. Where the gift is revoked as to some members of the class, the effect is to increase the shares of others: *Watson v Donaldson* [1915] 1 IR 63. But this rule is not applicable to similar gifts of income: *Re Carter, Walker v Litchfield* (1911) 30 NZLR 707. *Ng Chi-fong v Hui Ho Pui-fun* [1987] HKLR 462 at 473 where the text is referred to.
4   *Middleton v Messenger* (1799) 5 Ves 136; *Oppenheim v Henry* (1853) 10 Hare 441; *Browne v Hammond* (1858) John 210; *Re Wood, Moore v Baily* (1880) 43 LT 730; *Re Walker, Dunkerly v Hewerdine* [1917] 1 Ch 38; *Re Thompson's Will, Brahe v Mason* [1910] VLR 251. The rule is applicable in Scotland: *Wood v Wood* (1861) 23 D 338; *Hickling v Fair* [1899] AC 15; *Cunningham's Trustees v Blackwell* 1909 SC 219. Where there is a direction to accumulate until all grandchildren attain twenty-one and then a gift to all grandchildren, all grandchildren take: *Re Stevens, Trustees, Executors and Agency Co Ltd v Teague* [1912] VLR 194. See also *Re Hudson* (1971) 14 DLR (3d) 79 at 86, where this paragraph of the text was applied and *Re Roberts* (1978) 82 DLR (3d) 591.
5   *Lee v Lee* (1860) 1 Drew & Sm 85 at 87 (gift to next of kin who must be ascertained at testator's death apart from some special provision).
6   *Hill v Chapman* (1791) 3 Bro CC 391; *Re Roberts, Repington v Roberts-Gawen* (1881) 19 Ch D 520.
7   *Middleton v Messenger* (1799) 5 Ves 136; *Watson v Watson* (1840) 11 Sim 73; *Pattison v Pattison* (1855) 19 Beav 638; *Browne v Hammond* (1858) John 210 (where the rule is stated). See also *Hickling v Fair* [1899] AC 15.
8   *Weld v Bradbury* (1715) 2 Vern 705; *Shepherd v Ingram* (1764) Amb 448; *Odell v Crone* (1815) 3 Dow 61; *Leake v Robinson* (1817) 2 Mer 363 at 383; *Harris v Lloyd* (1823) Turn & R 310; *Armitage v Williams* (1859) 27 Beav 346.

[66.6]
Effect of death before testator or distribution. As regards members of a class who die before the testator, the class is ascertained independently of them, and there is no question of lapse of their shares,[1] and they are not included.[2] In the case where such persons are issue of the testator, they do not take by leaving issue living at the death of the testator,[3] even where the class consists of but one person.[4] As regards members of a class taking under a postponed gift, the death

of one of them who has survived the testator before the period of distribution does not defeat his interest,[5] provided that the contingency of surviving that period is not part of the description of the class.[6] Objects among whom the property becomes ultimately divisible are those members of the class who may be living at the period of distribution, and the representatives of such as may have died before that period having survived the testator.[7]

1   There is no gift to them and there can therefore be no lapse: *Christopherson v Naylor* (1816) 1 Mer 320; *Gowling v Thompson* (1868) LR 11 Eq 366n.
2   *Fitz Roy v Duke of Richmond* (1859) 27 Beav 186.
3   *Olney v Bates* (1855) 3 Drew 319; *Browne v Hammond* (1858) John 210 (both these cases stating that the Wills Act 1837, s 33 (as now substituted by the Administration of Justice Act 1982; see Vol 2, Part G, para **[244.34]**) has no application to such a case); *Re Harvey's Estate, Harvey v Gillow* [1893] 1 Ch 567 (where the class consisted of only one person); *Re Kinnear, Kinnear v Barnett* (1904) 90 LT 537; *Cockburn's Trustees v Dundas* (1864) 4 M 1185.
4   *Re Harvey's Estate, Harvey v Gillow* [1893] 1 Ch 567.
5   See cases cited in para **[66.5]**, n 7. Such persons are said to take vested interests subject to being divested in quantity by the birth of further members of the class (*Stanley v Wise* (1788) 1 Cox Eq Cas 432; *Baldwin v Rogers* (1853) 3 De GM & G 649), but 'vested' then means 'transmissible' and 'divested' means merely 'diminished'. As to the meanings of the word 'vested', see Chapter 93. A provision in the final limitation requiring a beneficiary to survive the tenant for life is not reflected back into the earlier part of the gift: thus where the income was given to the testator's children for life and then the capital to each child's share of income to each child's children who should then have attained twenty-one or should thereafter attain twenty-one, a grandchild who attained twenty-one but died in his mother's lifetime took a share: *Re Stephens* [1927] 1 Ch 1.
6   *Parr v Parr* (1833) 1 My & K 647 (where the will required property to be settled on a daughter so as on her death to 'devolve' on her children, if she had any. The word 'devolve' means to pass from a dead person to a living person and so the children had, on the proper construction of the will, to survive the parent if they were to take). The interest of the child thus taking a transmissible interest on the death of the testator may be defeated by the insertion of a gift over or a substitutionary gift: *Pope v Whitcombe* (1827) 3 Russ 124; *Re Miles, Miles v Miles* (1889) 61 LT 359; *Re Shaw, Williams v Pledger* (1912) 56 Sol Jo 380.
7   *Re Roberts, Percival v Roberts* [1903] 2 Ch 200 at 202.

[66.7]
The period of distribution. The period of distribution may be postponed either by some prior gift, or by the nature of the property given, or by the conditions of the gift.[1]

1   Where a testator used the words 'period of distribution' in his will and the will granted a number of annuities out of residue, the period of distribution was at the determination of the last annuity remaining payable: *Re Hill* [1958] SASR 269. See *Re Emmet's Estate, Emmet v Emmet* (1880) 13 Ch D 484 at 489, CA, per Hall V-C; *Re Willoughby, Willoughby v Decies* [1911] 2 Ch 581 at 598, CA, per Buckley LJ; and *Re Cockle's Will Trusts* [1967] Ch 690, [1967] 1 All ER 391; per Stamp J at 701; at 394.

[66.8]
Postponement by life interests. In cases where the gift is postponed to a life interest, the period of distribution is usually, but not necessarily, the determination of the life interest,[1] but the existence of a mere charge on the fund, for example an annuity charged on it, does not necessarily affect the time for ascertaining the period of distribution,[2] except where distribution is impossible until the death of an annuitant or the survivor of annuitants.[3]

1   *Ayton v Ayton* (1787) 1 Cox Eq Cas 327; *Middleton v Messenger* (1799) 5 Ves 136; *Barnaby v Tassell* (1871) LR 11 Eq 363; *Re Knapp's Settlement, Knapp v Vassall* [1895] 1 Ch 91; *Re Rhodes* [1961] NZLR 65.
2   *Hill v Chapman* (1791) 3 Bro CC 391 (annuities); *Singleton v Gilbert* (1784) 1 Cox Eq Cas 68 (terms and annuities); *Watson v Watson* (1840) 11 Sim 73 (annuities); *Coventry v Coventry* (1865) 2 Drew & Sm 470 (accumulation); *Bortoft v Wadsworth* (1864) 12 WR 523 (annuity); *Re Whiteford, Inglis v Whiteford* [1903] 1 Ch 889 (annuity).
3   *Re Hiscoe, Hiscoe v Waite* (1883) 48 LT 510.

[66.9]

Gifts postponed by determinable life interests. If there is a prior life interest determinable by bankruptcy and there is no extension of the class let in, the class is fixed at the time of the bankruptcy,[1] but where the limitation over to the class after the life interest postpones payment until the death of the life tenant,[2] or expressly directs the property to be applicable in the same manner as if the life tenant were dead,[3] this extends the class so as to let in those coming into existence until the death.

1   *Re Smith* (1862) 2 John & H 594 (class must close when fund divisible); *Re Aylwin's Trusts* (1873) LR 16 Eq 585; *Re Curzon, Martin v Perry* (1912) 56 Sol Jo 362 (class closes on adjudication).
2   *Brandon v Aston* (1843) 2 Y & C Ch Cas 24.
3   *Re Bedson's Trusts* (1885) 28 Ch D 523 ('in the same manner as if he were naturally dead'). See the effect of acceleration, para [66.15] infra.

[66.10]

Re-marriage. In certain cases where a life interest has been determinable on re-marriage, and the gift over expressly referred only to the death of the life tenant, but the court construed the gift over as impliedly intended to take effect on re-marriage,[1] the class of children has been held to be ascertained at the re-marriage, although expressly described to the ascertained at the death.[2]

1   As to this rule of construction, see para [93.20] infra.
2   *Bainbridge v Cream* (1852) 16 Beav 25; *Stanford v Stanford* (1886) 34 Ch D 362; *Re Tucker* (1887) 56 LJ Ch 449; *Re Dear, Helby v Dear* (1889) 58 LJ Ch 659; *Re Crother's Trusts* [1915] 1 IR 53; *Re Warner, Watts v Silvey* [1918] 1 Ch 368.

[66.11]

Gifts of reversionary property. Where the property is reversionary the period of distribution may be postponed until the reversion falls into possession,[1] but there is no postponement in the case of a gift of residue which includes a reversionary interest with other property.[2]

1   *Walker v Shore* (1808) 15 Ves 122 at 125; *Harvey v Stracey* (1852) 1 Drew 73 at 123.
2   *Hagger v Payne* (1857) 23 Beav 474; *Coventry v Coventry* (1865) 2 Drew & Sm 470.

IV.   SECOND RULE OF CONVENIENCE

[66.12]

Postponement by attaching condition. This rule applies to the case where a gift of capital is postponed by conditions attached to the gift, as where payment is to be made on the attainment of a certain age by the donee,[1] or on his or her marriage,[2] or in any case, it seems, where the condition is of a nature personal to the donee.[3] The rule is that the period of distribution arrives and the class is closed as soon as the condition is so far performed that some one member of the class would be entitled to the enjoyment of his share, if the class were then not susceptible to increase.[4] Thus, where there is an immediate gift to a class, to be paid on their attaining a specified age, the period of distribution is the death of the testator if any member of the class has then attained the specified age,[5] and if not, then it is the time when a member first attains that age[6] and also where the gift to the class takes effect only on the determination of a prior interest and there is no member of the class in existence at such determination.[7] At that time the class closes and persons born after that date are excluded except for one case, that is, where the child is already *en ventre sa mère* at that date.[8]

1   As to gifts of income, see para **[66.21]** infra. Though the class closes at the testator's death, it includes a child *en ventre sa mère* that date (see n 8).

2   Where a class takes at birth, a gift over on the members failing to attain a specified age does not postpone the period of distribution: *Davidson v Dallas* (1808) 14 Ves 576.

3   *Barrington v Tristram* (1801) 6 Ves 345; *Dawson v Oliver-Massey* (1876) 2 Ch D 753.

4   *Re Emmet's Estate, Emmet v Emmet* (1880) 13 Ch D 484; *Re Bedson's Trusts* (1885) 28 Ch D 523; *Re Knapp's Settlement, Knapp v Vassall* [1895] 1 Ch 91; *Re Courtenay, Pearce v Foxwell* (1905) 74 LJ Ch 654; *Re Long* [1938] 1 DLR 344. The rule is an exemplification of the principle that all possible objects existing at the date of distribution of a trust fund are to be included, but because inconvenience would arise if those born after that event were to be included. They are excluded, see Stamp LJ in *Re Chapman's Settlement Trusts, Jones v Chapman* [1978] 1 All ER 1122 at 1125, referring to *Ellison v Airey* (1748) 1 Ves Sen 111; *Hoste v Pratt* (1798) 3 Ves 730; and *Barrington v Trustsam* (1801) 6 Ves 345. But the rule lets in a child *en ventre* when the eldest attains twenty-one: *Trustees, Executors and Agency Co Ltd v Sleeman* (1899) 25 VLR 187.

5   *Picken v Matthews* (1878) 10 Ch D 264; *Gillman v Daunt* (1856) 3 K & J 48. As to the words 'period of distribution' being a misnomer, see *Re Cockle's Will Trusts* [1967] 1 All ER 391 at 394.

6   *Andrews v Partington* (1791) 3 Bro CC 401; *Re Mervin, Mervin v Crossman* [1891] 3 Ch 197; *Re Knapp's Settlement, Knapp v Vassell* [1895] 1 Ch 91; *Crane v Crane* (1949) 80 CLR 327; *Re Murray, Perpetual Trustees (Canberra) Ltd v Lathom* [1963] ALR 68. The rule is known as the rule in *Andrews v Partington*, where it was treated as established; the rule is probably founded on the earlier case of *Ellison v Airey* (1748) 1 Ves Sen 111; see Sir R Evershed MR in *Re Bleckly, Bleckly v Bleckly* [1951] Ch 740 at 747, 750. The rule has been much criticised, but could hardly be departed from now. Where the gift is to children who shall attain 21, a child who has already attained that age at the date of the will is not excluded, but takes: *Re Rayner, Couch v Warner* (1925) 134 LT 141; but words of futurity are generally construed strictly: *Re Walker, Walker v Walker* [1930] 1 Ch 469; *Re Crosse, Crosse v Crosse* [1933] WN 36.

7   *Re Bleckly, Bleckly v Bleckly* [1951] Ch 740, [1951] 1 All ER 1064.

8   *Trustees, Executors and Agency Co Ltd v Sleeman* (1899) 25 VLR 187; *Re Bruce, Tasmanian Permanent Executors and Trustees Association v MacFarlane* [1979] Tas SR 110; and see Chapter 73.

[66.13]
When rule applied. The rule is adopted to reconcile the inconsistent directions of the will that all children should take and that the fund should be divided at a time when the class could not be ascertained.[1] Further, it has been stated in two modern cases that the rule should only be applied to gifts which disclose such inconsistent intentions.[2] It is not applied unless it is necessary,[3] or unless it fits in with the other provisions of the will, but the expressions 'all' or 'all and every' added to the words 'child or children of a person' do not exclude the rule.[4] The rule is not applied where the will contains provisions which are inconsistent with

the first child receiving its share on attaining the specified age,[5] as in cases where distribution is postponed until the youngest child attains twenty-one years of age,[6] where there is no one in existence at the testator's death who is entitled to a share absolutely vested in interest and possession,[7] or there is an effective direction to accumulate the income for a period extending beyond the time when a child attains the specified age or satisfies the conditions.[8] Where the period of accumulation is longer than that allowed by law, the class closes at the end of the permitted accumulation.[9]

1   *Re Stephen's, Kilby v Betts* [1904] 1 Ch 322 at 328. *Re Drummond's Settlement, Foster v Foster* [1988] 1 All ER 449, per Buckley LJ at p 454. See also *Re Tom's Settlement, Rose v Evans* [1987] 1 All ER 1081, [1987] 1 WLR 1021. The rule does not apply in Scotland where all the children are included: *Hope Johnstone v Sinclair's Trustees* (1904) 7 F 25.

2   *Re Kebty-Fletcher's Will Trusts, Public Trustee v Swan* [1969] 1 Ch 339, [1967] 3 All ER 1076; *Re Harker's Will Trusts, Kean v Harker* [1969] 3 All ER 1, [1969] 1 WLR 1124. See also Sir Robert Megarry V-C in *Re Clifford's Settlement Trusts, Heaton v Westwater* [1981] Ch 63 at 66, [1980] 1 All ER 1013 at 1015, 1016.

3   *Re Stephens, Kilby v Betts* [1904] 1 Ch 322; *Williamson v Williamson* [1974] NI 92 (rule not applied as testator has provided means whereby the beneficiaries' presumptive shares could be distributed as each attained the age of 25). The rule has been applied to similar gifts in a voluntary settlement (*Re Knapp's Settlement, Knapp v Vassall* [1895] 1 Ch 91, but in the case of a marriage settlement the rule is that all the children take: *Mann v Thompson* (1854) Kay 628 at 642). The rule may be excluded where the income of the property has been divided between two tenants for life: *Re Faux, Taylor v Faux* (1915) 84 LJ Ch 873. The rule was discussed in *Re Chartres, Farman v Barrett* [1927] 1 Ch 466 (where the class became definite by the release of a power of appointment), and see *Re Paul's Settlement Trusts, Paul v Nelson* [1920] 1 Ch 99.

4   See *Andrews v Partington* (1791) 3 Bro CC 401; *Prescott v Long* (1795) 2 Ves 690, ('and all every'); *Re Bleckly, Bleckly v Bleckly* [1951] Ch 740, [1951] 1 All ER 1064 ('all or any'); *Re Emmet's Estate, Emmet v Emmet* (1880) 13 Ch D 484, CA; *Re Canney's Trusts, Mayers v Strover* (1910) 101 LT 905; and *Singleton v Gilbert* (1784) 1 Cox Eq Cas 68 ('all and every'); *Re Wernher's Settlement Trusts, Lloyds Bank Ltd v Mountbatten* [1961] 1 All ER 184, [1961] 1 WLR 136 ('all children whether now living or hereafter to be born'); but the rule is excluded by the phrase 'whenever born'; see *Re Edmondson's Will Trusts, Sandford v Edmondson* [1972] 1 All ER 444, [1972] 1 WLR 183, CA. See also *Re Chapman's Settlement Trusts, Jones v Chapman* [1978] 1 All ER 1122, [1977] 1 WLR 1163; and *Re Clifford's Settlement Trusts* [1981] Ch 63, [1980] 1 All ER 1013 both more fully discussed at para **[66.20]** infra. The last three mentioned cases were applied in *Re Tom's Settlement, Rose v Evans* [1987] 1 All ER 1081, [1987] 1 WLR 1021.

5   *Re Kipping, Kipping v Kipping* [1914] 1 Ch 62 (absolute power to postpone sale of property); *Macculloch v Anderson* [1904] AC 55 at 61 (direction for payment on death of all children); *Re Bukowski* [1954] QSR 286. See the effect of maintenance and advancement clauses, see para **[66.14]** infra.

6   *Smith v Jackson* (1823) 1 LJOS Ch 231; *Re Manners, Public Trustee v Manners* [1955] 3 All ER 83.

7   *Re Ransome's Will Trusts, Moberley v Ransome* [1957] Ch 348, [1957] 1 All ER 690.

8   *Watson v Young* (1885) 28 Ch D 436; *Re Pilkington, Pilkington v Pilkington* (1892) 29 LR Ir 370; *Re Stephens, Kilby v Betts* [1904] 1 Ch 322; *Re Steven's Trustees, Executors and Agency Co Ltd v Teague* [1912] VLR 194; *Re Watt's Will Trusts, Watt v Watt* [1936] 2 All ER 1555. This may not be effective where the beneficiaries have the right to end the accumulations: *Curtis v Curtis* (1821) 6 Madd 14; *Coventry v Coventry* (1865) 2 Drew & Sm 470.

9   *Re Hart, Smith v Clarke* [1963] NSWR 627. But see *Re Ransome's Will Trusts, Moberley v Ransome* [1957] Ch 348, [1957] 1 All ER 690; *Berry v Green* [1938] AC 575, [1938] 2 All ER 362 HL; *Re Deloitte, Griffiths v Deloitte* [1926] Ch 56.

[66.14]

Maintenance and advancement. A direction to allow maintenance or advancement out of vested shares may likewise exclude the application of the rule,[1] but not where the direction is as to presumptive shares only or is a mere power and not a direction.[2] The mere incorporation of the statutory powers of maintenance and advancement contained in the Trustee Act 1925, ss 31, 32,[3] will not have the effect of excluding the rule.[4]

1   *Gardner v James* (1843) 6 Beav 170; *Bateman v Foster* (1844) 1 Coll 118; *Mainwaring v Beevor* (1849) 8 Hare 44; *Iredell v Iredell* (1858) 25 Beav 485; *Armitage v Williams* (1859) 27 Beav 346; *Bateman v Gray* (1868) LR 6 Eq 215 (advancement out of vested or presumptive shares); *Re Courtenay, Pearce v Foxwell* (1905) 74 LJ Ch 654 (advancement out of vested shares). *Re Henderson's Trusts, Schreiber v Baring* [1969] 3 All ER 769, CA (power of advancement out of vested or presumptive shares); applied in *Re Chapman's Settlement Trusts, Jones v Chapman* [1978] 1 All ER 1122, [1977] 1 WLR 1163. See also *Re Manners, Public Trustee v Manners* [1955] 3 All ER 83.
2   *Gimblett v Purton* (1871) LR 12 Eq 427.
3   See Vol 2, Part G, para **[246.26]**. The Trustee Act 1925, s 32 has been amended with effect from 1 January 1997 by the Trusts of Land and Appointment of Trustees Act 1996, s 25(1), Sch 3, para 3(8).
4   *Re Edmondson's Will Trusts, Sandford v Edmondson* [1972] 1 All ER 444, [1972] 1 WLR 183, CA. In this case there was no reference to 'presumptive shares' thus distinguishing *Re Henderson's Trusts, Schreiber v Baring* [1969] 3 All ER 769, CA. A reference in the power to vested and presumptive shares would seem to be crucial to exclude the rule, because such a situation cannot arise if the rule applies. The rule may also be defeated by a provision for postponement of conversion at the absolute discretion of the trustee, and where the trustees are empowered to carry on a business until such time as they deem a sale beneficial: *Permanent Trustee Co of New South Wales v R* (1929) 30 SRNSW 318.

[66.15]
Acceleration. When a remainder to a class is accelerated because the preceding life interest is for some reason void ab initio the application of the class closing rules is likewise accelerated.[1] But if the prior life interest is assigned and released,[2] or released surrendered and assigned, then the application of the class closing rules to the class in remainder, is not accelerated.[3]

1   *Re Chartres, Farman v Barrett* [1927] 1 Ch 466, [1927] All ER Rep 408 (release of power of appointment); *Eavestaff v Austin* (1854) 19 Beav 591 (revocation of preceding life interest); *Jull v Jacobs* (1876) 3 Ch D 703 (failure of prior interest because donee had witnessed will); *Re Crother's Trusts* [1915] 1 IR 53 (conditional gift); *Re Johnson, Danily v Johnson* (1893) 68 LT 20 (revocation of prior interest).
2   *Re Kebty-Fletcher's Will Trusts, Public Trustee v Swan* [1969] 1 Ch 339, [1967] 3 All ER 1076.
3   *Re Harker's Will Trusts, Kean v Harker* [1969] 3 All ER 1, [1969] 1 WLR 1124; both cases distinguishing, *Re Chartres, Farman v Barrett* [1927] 1 Ch 466, [1927] All ER Rep 408; *Re Davies, Davies v Mackintosh* [1957] 3 All ER 52, [1957] 1 WLR 922 not followed and doubted. But see *Re Syme* [1980] VR 109, whether or not a gift is accelerated is a matter of intention and surrenders in that case did not affect an acceleration.

[66.16]
Failure of gift as result of rule. Where the application of the rule would cause the gift to be obnoxious to the rule against perpetuities and so void, the court will not apply the rule but adopt an alternative construction, provided the adoption of that alternative will save the gift from becoming void.[1] This practice is also adopted where the gift affected is not the actual gift in question but an associated gift and is not confined to cases where the gift fails under the rule against perpetuities but is applied in any case where the gift would fail.

1   *Elliott v Elliott* (1841) 12 Sim 276; *Re Coppard's Estate, Howlett v Hodson* (1887) 35 Ch D 350; *Re Pilkington, Pilkington v Pilkington* (1892) 29 LR Ir 370; *Re Mervin, Mervin v*

Crossman [1891] 3 Ch 197; *Re Stevens, Clark v Stevens* (1896) 40 Sol Jo 296; *Re Cockle's Will Trusts* [1967] Ch 690, [1967] 1 All ER 391, applied in *Re Deeley's Settlement, Batchelor v Russell* [1974] Ch 454, [1973] 3 All ER 1127. See also *Re Ransome's Will Trusts, Moberley v Ransome* [1957] Ch 348, [1957] All ER 690.

[66.17]
Prior life interest. The rule is applied notwithstanding that there is a prior life interest,[1] unless the testator shows that the expiration of that life interest is intended by him to be the period of distribution.[2]

1   In both *Clarke v Clarke* (1836) 8 Sim 59, and *Re Emmet's Estate, Emmet v Emmet* (1880) 13 Ch D 484, no children had attained the specified age at the death of the life tenant.
2   *Kevern v Williams* (1832) 5 Sim 171, followed in *Berkely v Swinburne* (1848) 16 Sim 275, and explained in *Re Emmet's Estate, Emmet v Emmet* (1880) 13 Ch D 484.

[66.18]
Direction not excluding rule. The rule applies both where the gift and direction as to payment are distinct, so that the gift is not contingent,[1] and where the gift is contingent upon attaining the specified age[2] or other event, or subject to a gift over in any such event.[3]

1   *Andrews v Partington* (1791) 3 Bro CC 401; see *Re Mervin, Mervin v Crossman* [1891] 3 Ch 197 at 203.
2   *Whitbread v Lord St John* (1804) 10 Ves 152 (gift over on death of all under 21); *Balm v Balm* (1830) 3 Sim 492 (gifts to be transferable at 21 in the case of males and 21 or marriage in the case of females, if all die except one, the fund to be transferred to that one subject to being 21 or, being female, 21 or married); *Locke v Lamb* (1867) LR 4 Eq 372; *Gimblett v Purton* (1871) LR 12 Eq 427.
3   *Barrington v Tristram* (1801) 6 Ves 345 (gift over of share of child dying under 21 without leaving issue).

V.   CLASSES AND GIFTS SUBJECT TO RULES

[66.19]
Classes subject to the rules. These rules of convenience apply to class gifts which disclose inconsistent intentions, ie where the testator has indicated, firstly, an intention to include all the potential members of the class, but has, secondly, indicated a period of distribution at a time when all those persons are not necessarily in existence.[1] Thus the rules will not in general apply to gifts solely to the testator's own children or to the children of the tenant for life, or of a deceased person, since in such cases the class will be incapable of increasing after the period of distribution.[2] But the rules will apply to the children of any other person,[3] and it appears, to any other description of a class[4] which in the context and circumstances of the case does not point out some other mode of ascertaining the class.[5]

1   *Re Kebty-Fletcher's Will Trusts, Public Trustee v Swan* [1969] 1 Ch 339, [1967] 3 All ER 1076; *Re Harker's Will Trusts, Kean v Harker* [1969] 3 All ER 1, [1969] 1 WLR 1124.
2   *Re Harker's Will Trusts, Kean v Harker* [1969] 3 All ER 1, [1969] 1 WLR 1124.
3   *Viner v Francis* (1789) 2 Bro CC 658 (gift to children of a deceased sister of the testator construed to mean children living at the death of the testator).
4   Examples are: grandchildren; *Mainwaring v Beevor* (1849) 8 Hare 44; *Gimblett v Purton* (1871) LR 12 Eq 427; grandchildren and great-grandchildren of A and B; *Wetherell v Wetherell* (1863)

1 De GJ & Sm 134; son, daughter-in-law and grandchildren: *Coventry v Coventry* (1865) 2 Drew & Sm 470; cousins: *Baldwin v Rogers* (1853) 3 De GM & G 649; a fluctuating body: *Cocks v Manners* (1871) LR 12 Eq 574; *Re Delany's Estate* (1882) 9 LR Ir 226; *Re Laffan and Downes' Contract* [1897] 1 IR 469; *Re Smith, Johnson v Bright-Smith* [1914] 1 Ch 937. The rule applies to a class described as living at the death of a person in the lifetime of the testator: *Lee v Pain* (1844) 4 Hare 201; *Dimond v Bostock* (1875) 10 Ch App 358; or living at the date of the will: *Leigh v Leigh* (1854) 17 Beav 605. In these cases the class consists of those living at the death of the testator.

5   In the case of a gift to issue where it is clear that the settlor could not have intended all the generations of issue born at any time to take, the class closing rules are not applied; *Re Deeley's Settlement, Batchelor v Russell* [1974] Ch 454, [1973] 3 All ER 1127; *Re Edmondson's Will Trusts, Sandford v Edmondson* [1972] 1 All ER 444, [1972] 1 WLR 183 applying *Surridge v Clarkson* (1866) 14 WR 979, and *Re Cockle's Will Trusts* [1967] Ch 690, [1967] 1 All ER 391.

[66.20]

Exclusion of the rules. The rules are nevertheless applicable although the class may be described as 'begotten or to be begotten', 'born or to be born', 'now born or who shall be born hereafter',[1] 'whether now living or hereafter to be born'[2] or in like words[3] where no future period is fixed by the will;[4] and although the gift is postponed to a life interest given to a named person who by these rules takes as a member of the class.[5] But the rules will be excluded if the phrase 'whenever born' is appended to the class of children;[6] likewise the phrases, 'at whatever time they may be born', 'whenever in the lifetime of their respective parents born'[7] or 'hereafter born during the lifetime of their parents'.[8]

It has been said[9] that it is not enough that emphatic words have been used 'unless one finds that the emphasis is expressed in such a way that it is impossible to make it march in step with the application of the rule'. Sir Robert Megarry V-C has stated the principle as follows:[10]

'... it is not enough to find provisions which merely point to the exclusion of the rule if they nevertheless are capable of operating in conformity with it. There must be an inescapable incompatibility with the operation of the rule'.

Thus the mere fact that the rule could not apply to part of a compound class was not sufficient to demonstrate any incompatibility of the rule with the other part or with the gift as a whole.[11] Nor was it sufficient to show that the application of the rule would reduce the second limb of the clause defining the class to circumstances which were improbable but not impossible.[12] But the rules were held to be excluded where there was an express reference in the deed to future great-grandchildren 'living at the closing date' which clearly showed an intention that the class was to remain open until the defined date and not to close when a beneficiary attained the age of 18.[13]

1   *Re Chapman's Settlement Trusts, Jones v Chapman* [1978] 1 All ER 1122, [1977] 1 WLR 1163.
2   *Re Wernher's Settlement Trusts, Lloyds Bank Ltd v Earl Mountbatten* [1961] 1 All ER 184, [1961] 1 WLR 136.
3   *Sprackling v Ranier* (1761) 1 Dick 344 (to be begotten); *Whitbread v Lord St John* (1804) 10 Ves 152 (born or to be born); *Gilbert v Boorman* (1805) 11 Ves 238 (all other children hereafter to be born); *Clarke v Clarke* (1836) 8 Sim 59 (all and every); *Butler v Lowe* (1839) 10 Sim 317 (begotten or to be begotten); *Iredell v Iredell* (1858) 25 Beav 485 (to all my grandchildren whether born in my lifetime or after my death). The words in question are held to provide for the birth of children between the making of the will and the death of the testator (*Storrs v Benbow* (1833) 2 My & K 46 at 48; *Dias v De Livera* (1879) 5 App Cas 123 at 135).
4   *Scott v Earl of Scarborough* (1838) 1 Beav 154 ('during the lifetime of their respective parents').

5   *Elmsley v Young* (1835) 2 My & K 780; *King v Tootel* (1858) 25 Beav 23; *Reay v Rawlinson*
     (1860) 29 Beav 88; *Almack v Horn* (1863) 1 Hem & M 630.
6   *Re Edmondson's Will Trusts, Sandford v Edmondson* [1972] 1 All ER 444, [1972] 1 WLR 183,
     CA.
7   *Re Edmondson's Will Trusts, Sandford v Edmondson* [1972] 1 All ER 444, [1972] 1 WLR 183,
     CA.
8   *Scott v Earl of Scarborough* (1838) 1 Beav 154; distinguished in *Re Chapman's Settlement
     Trusts, Jones v Chapman* [1978] 1 All ER 1122, [1977] 1 WLR 1163: see also *Hodson v
     Micklewaite* (1854) 2 Drew 294 ('together with every other child hereafter to be born of the said
     (wife) during the life of the said husband or within nine months after his decease').
9   *Re Wernher's Settlement Trusts, Lloyds Bank Ltd v Earl Mountbatten* [1961] 1 All ER 184,
     [1961] 1 WLR 136, per Buckley J at 188; at 140, 141; approved in *Re Chapman's Settlement
     Trusts, Jones v Chapman* [1978] 1 All ER 1122, [1977] 1 WLR 1163; and applied in *Re
     Clifford's Settlement Trusts, Heaton v Westwater* [1981] Ch 63, [1980] 1 All ER 1013.
10   In *Re Clifford's Settlement Trusts, Heaton v Westwater* [1981] Ch 63, [1980] 1 All ER 1013; at
     1016; at 67; 'In determining what expressions suffice to exclude the application of the rule, I
     think that the standard is high'.
11   *Re Clifford's Settlement Trusts, Heaton v Westwater* [1981] Ch 63, [1980] 1 All ER 1013 (gift
     to compound class of children of settlor's son '... born in the settlor's lifetime or after his death
     who before the expiration of the period of twenty-one years from the death of the survivor of
     the settlor and [the son] shall attain the age of twenty-five years and the other children or child
     of [the son] living at the expiration of such period'. Held, class of persons entitled to a share
     under the settlement closed when the son's eldest child attained 25 years).
12   *Re Clifford's Settlement Trusts, Heaton v Westwater* [1981] Ch 63, [1980] 1 All ER 1013.
13   *Re Tom's Settlement, Rose v Evans* [1987] 1 All ER 1081, [1987] 1 WLR 1021, where the cases
     in the last three footnotes were applied.

[66.21]

Gifts subject to the rule. The rules of convenience apply to gifts of the capital
of personal estate,[1] or of a mixed fund of real and personal estate[2] but not to
contingent interests.[3] The rule does not apply to gifts of income alone.[4] The class
taking any particular payment is as a rule to be ascertained so as to let in all
members coming into existence before the time for that payment[5] and the class
is not to be closed finally for all subsequent payments at the time when the right
to receive payment first accrues to any member of the class, except in cases
where other considerations require it.[6]

1   Personal estate includes real estate or a mixed fund held upon trust for sale and investment:
     Hoste v Pratt (1798) 3 Ves 730; *Re Mervin, Mervin v Crossman* [1891] 3 Ch 197.
2   *Andrews v Partington* (1791) 3 Bro CC 401; *Re Emmet's Estate, Emmet v Emmet* (1880) 13 Ch
     D 484; *Dawson v Oliver-Massey* (1876) 2 Ch D 753; *Re Edmondson's Will Trusts, Sandford v
     Edmondson* [1972] 1 All ER 444, [1972] 1 WLR 183, CA.
3   *Re Ransome's Will Trusts, Moberley v Ransome* [1957] Ch 348, [1957] 1 All ER 690 (the court
     has never applied the rules to permit the artificially early closing of a class of beneficiaries
     except where there is someone in existence who, on the proper construction of the will, is
     entitled to a share absolutely vested in interest and possession. Fund to be applied to
     maintenance of great grandchildren until youngest attained 21, and then to be held for the great-
     grandchildren then living. The class was not closed on the youngest great-grandchild living at
     the death of the testatrix attaining 21).
4   *Re Ward's Will Trusts, Ward v Ward* [1965] Ch 856, [1964] 3 All ER 442.
5   *Re Wenmoth's Estate, Wenmoth v Wenmoth* (1887) 37 Ch D 266; *Re Stephens, Kilby v Betts*
     [1904] 1 Ch 322; *Re Carter, Walker v Litchfield* (1911) 30 NZLR 707; *Re Bullen, Bowman v
     Bowman* (1915) 17 WALR 73; *Re Mair, Public Trustee v Mair* [1925] NZLR 436; *Re Morley,
     Morley v Williams* (1935) 35 SRNSW 102; *Ross etc v Dunlop* (1878) 5 R 833; *Re Ward's Will
     Trusts, Ward v Ward* [1965] Ch 856, [1964] 3 All ER 442.
6   *Re Stephens, Kilby v Betts* [1904] 1 Ch 322; *Re Powell, Crosland v Holliday* [1898] 1 Ch 227,
     which appears to be to the contrary can be explained on the footing that, if subsequent payments
     had been let in, those payments should have been void under the rule against perpetuities. But

this case was not followed in *Re Ward's Will Trusts, Ward v Ward* [1965] Ch 856, [1964] 3 All ER 442.

VI.   GIFTS OF REAL ESTATE ALONE

[66.22]
Immediate gifts. If the gift to the class is construed to be immediate upon the death of the testator, that is the time when the class is ascertained if any members of the class have then come into existence.[1] A devise not otherwise postponed to 'all and every' the children of a person is construed as immediate and the class is ascertained at the death of the testator.[2]

1   *Singleton v Gilbert* (1784) 1 Cox Eq Cas 68; *Doe d Thwaites v Over* (1808) 1 Taunt 263; *Crone v Odell* (1811) 1 Ball & B 449. See also *Re Johnson, Danily v Johnson* (1893) 68 LT 20, where life interests were revoked and a trust for sale became effective immediately on the death of the testator.
2   *Scott v Harwood* (1821) 5 Madd 332.

[66.23]
Future gifts. The class closing rules apply even if the only property settled is land.[1] In a gift not otherwise postponed, a description of a class of children as 'born or to be born' or 'begotten or to be begotten', may cause the gift to take effect as an executory devise, and accordingly all the children, whether in existence at the death of the testator or otherwise, may take under the gift.[2] In an executory devise to the class on the death of any person or on any other postponed event which does not import contingency in the class, the donees are prima facie ascertained so as to let in all who come into existence and satisfy the description before the event.[3] In a gift to a class, not postponed otherwise than by the fact that the description may refer to persons yet to come into existence and that no member of the class has come into existence at the death of the testator, all members of the class coming into existence at any time are let in.[4] The rule applies to land held upon trust for sale.[5]

1   *Re Edmondson's Will Trusts, Sandford v Edmondson* [1972] 1 All ER 444, [1972] 1 WLR 183, CA applying *Re Canney's Trusts, Mayers v Strover* (1910) 101 LT 905; *Re Curzon, Martin v Perry* (1912) 56 Sol Jo 362 (in both of which cases the rules of convenience were applied), and *Re Chapman, Charley v Lewis* (1922) 56 ILT 32. *Blackman v Fysh* [1892] 3 Ch 209, to the effect that the rules do not apply to an executory devise to a class of children who attain a specified age, dismissed in *Re Edmondson's Will Trusts, Sandford v Edmondson* [1972] 1 All ER 444, [1972] 1 WLR 183, CA, as an unsatisfactory authority.
2   *Mogg v Mogg* (1815) 1 Mer 654; *Gooch v Gooch* (1853) 3 De GM & G 366 (devises of rents and profits only). The rule referring such words to the interval between the date of the will and the death of the testator applies only to personal estate and not to the income of real estate: *Dias v De Livera* (1879) 5 App Cas 123 at 130; *Cook v Cook* (1706) 2 Vern 545; *Eddowes v Eddowes* (1862) 30 Beav 603. See, however, *Woodhouse v Herrick* (1855) 1 K & J 352.
3   *Crone v Odell* (1811) 1 Ball & B 449; *Browne v Hammond* (1858) John 210; *Holland v Wood* (1870) LR 11 Eq 91; *Re Canney's Trusts, Mayers v Strover* (1910) 101 LT 905.
4   *Shepherd v Ingram* (1764) Amb 448.
5   *Re Edmondson's Will Trusts, Sandford v Edmondson* [1972] 1 All ER 444, [1972] 1 WLR 183, CA. The argument that the power to postpone sale in such cases was inconsistent with the right to demand a share at the period of distribution, was rejected.

CHAPTER 67

Survivorship

[67.1]

Meanings of 'survive'. The word 'survive' and its derivatives are, following the general rule, ordinarily given their strict and proper meaning and refer to the longest in duration of lives running concurrently.[1] They may, however, refer not to the concurrent lives, but to the fact of living after a named event or person.[2] There is no rule of construction as to the period to which survivorship refers apart from the context,[3] nor can the words receive any other meaning,[4] even though adhering to the strict meaning may lead to fanciful or harsh results.[5]

1   *Re Delany, Delany v Delany* (1895) 39 Sol Jo 468 (the common meaning of 'survivor' implies two or more lives running together); *Taaffe v Conmee* (1862) 10 HL Cas 64 (the longest liver of those named); *Gee v Liddell* (1866) LR 2 Eq 341 (imports that the survivor must be living at the time of the event which he is to survive); *Heath, Jackson v Norman* (1904) 48 Sol Jo 416; *Re Wilson* (1900) 19 NZLR 406.
2   *Re Clark's Estate* (1864) 3 De GJ & Sm 111 ('survive me' means 'be living after me'); *Mellor v Daintee* (1886) 33 Ch D 198 (may mean surviving a particular person or a particular period of time); *Re Sing, Sing v Mills* [1914] WN 90 (outliving particular person); *Re Hodgson* [1952] 1 All ER 769 (child or children of A who shall survive me); *Re Allsop, Cardinal v Warr* [1968] Ch 39, [1967] 2 All ER 1056, CA, (the ordinary meaning of the word 'survive' requires that the person who is to survive shall be living at the time of the writer's death and shall continue living afterwards); referred to in *Re Arndt's Will* [1990] WAR 5, another case in which 'survive' was held to have its ordinary meaning, so that it referred only to persons born (or conceived) before the testator's death; *Re Wilson* (1900) 19 NZLR 406 ('then remaining living'); *Knight v Knight* (1912) 14 CLR 86 ('outlive'); *Re Lawrence* [1943] Tas LR 33; *Re Crawley* (1976) 68 DLR (3d) 193. Prima facie a gift to a class 'surviving' an individual means a class living at his death and does not extend to persons coming into existence after that date, but where the requirement is that two events shall be survived (eg predeceasing the testator or being dead on the happening of a later event), the class will include persons who survive the second event although born after the first: *Re Castle, Public Trustee v Floud* [1949] Ch 46, [1948] 2 All ER 927, and see *Brennan v Permanent Trustee Co* [1945] ALR 411 ('survive me' included persons born after testator's death).
3   *Re Benn, Benn v Benn* (1885) 29 Ch D 839; *Inderwick v Tatchell* [1903] AC 120.
4   *Auger v Beaudry* [1920] AC 1010; *Gilmour v MacPhillamy* [1930] AC 712; *Re Keep's Will* (1863) 32 Beav 122; *Hodge v Foot* (1865) 34 Beav 349; *Re Usticke* (1866) 35 Beav 338; *Inderwick v Tatchell* [1903] AC 120.
5   *Re James's Will Trusts, Peard v James* [1962] Ch 226, [1960] 3 All ER 744; *Re Allsop, Cardinal v Warr* [1968] Ch 39, [1967] 2 All ER 1056, CA (the words 'as shall survive me' which in their plain and ordinary meaning point to those born in the testator's lifetime, cannot be construed as meaning 'shall not pre-decease me').

[67.2]

Ascertainment of survivors at period of distribution. In cases where there is a gift to a number of persons and survivors[1] and survivor of them, or with the benefit of survivorship, or in like words,[2] or where there is a postponed gift to persons 'surviving', the survivorship is, in default of any expressed intention of the testator,[3] prima facie referred to the period of distribution.[4] Thus, the time in question, where the gift is immediate, is the death of the testator, and where the gift is postponed to a life interest, is the death of the tenant for life[5] or the death of the testator, whichever last happens;[6] and this applies whether the gift is of real or of personal property.[7] However the construction will be governed by the wording of the will. Thus in a case where the gift was to 'heirs and surviving issue' it was held that 'surviving issue' meant surviving children and not surviving issue of all degrees, and that the word 'surviving' meant surviving the praepositus.[8] The will may show by its wording that 'survivors' means survivors inter se so that when one dies the other will take.[9]

1   A gift to 'survivors' may vest in a sole survivor: *Hearn v Baker* (1865) 2 K & J 383 (one survivor surviving period of distribution takes all where gift is to five or the survivors of them). Since 1925 the plural indicates the singular and vice versa in all instruments including wills: s 61 (c) of the Law of Property Act 1925; 37 *Halsbury's Statutes* (4th edn) 199; see Vol 2, Part G, para **[246.40]**.

2   *Wiley v Chanteperdrix* [1894] 1 IR 209 at 215; but such words must not be words which can be construed as words of limitation: see para **[67.8]** infra.

3   *Blackmore v Snee* (1857) 1 De G & J 455. A gift, after a life interest, to testator's then surviving children will exclude children dead on the death of the life tenant: *Wordsworth v Wood* (1847) 1 HL Cas 129. A gift to two and if either should die in the lifetime of the tenant for life to the survivor of them absolutely gives the survivor an indefeasible interest on the death of one in the lifetime of the tenant for life: *White v Baker* (1860) 2 De GF & J 55. On the other hand where the testator expressly adds a clause providing for those who do not survive him, the word 'survivors' may be referred to the testator's death; see *Rogers v Towsey* (1845) 2 Holt Eq 270.

4   *Cripps v Wolcott* (1819) 4 Madd 11 at 15; *Vorley v Richardson* (1856) 8 De GM & G 126 at 129; *Young v Robertson* (1862) 4 Macq 314; *Re Douglas's Will Trusts, Lloyds Bank Ltd v Nelson* [1959] 3 All ER 785, [1959] 1 WLR 1212; *Re Green, MacKenzie v Stringer* [1963] NZLR 148; *Re Krause* (1985) 18 DLR (4th) 631 (word 'surviving' means that the person who is to survive must be living at the time of the event which he is to survive). But see *Re Andrews* [1985] 2 Qd R 161.

5   *Cripps v Wolcott* (1819) 4 Madd 11; *Re Benn, Benn v Benn* (1885) 29 Ch D 839 at 844; *Re Poultney, Poultney v Poultney* [1912] 2 Ch 541; *Re Belfast Town Council, ex p Sayer* (1884) 13 LR Ir 169; *Outerbridge v Hollis* [1951] WN 318; *Re Helmcken Estate, Helmcken v Bullen* [1924] 3 WWR 172; *Moir v Graham* (1894) 12 NZLR 42; *Re Kearney* [1957] VLR 56; *Re Stone* [1958] SASR 246; *Davis v Lister* [1964] NSWR 1240. If there is more than one tenant for life, the time is the death of the last living tenant for life. Thus, where there is a gift to A for life, then to B for life and to the surviving brothers and sisters of the testator and of his wife, the survivors, if B predeceases A, are taken at the death of A: *Howard v Collins* (1868) LR 5 Eq 349. If B survives A, then the time would be the death of B. A gift to three persons or the survivors or survivor of them postponed to a life interest fails if none survives the tenant for life: *Re Douglas's Will Trusts, Lloyds Bank Ltd v Nelson*, supra. This is so only where the gift must be construed as a joint tenancy. It is otherwise if, by the addition of such words as 'in equal shares', there is a tenancy in common, when the personal representatives of each person take: see *Edmunds v Bisson* (1950) 50 SRNSW 28, and also where the final gift is to next of kin as on an intestacy: *Re Stillman* (1965) 52 DLR (2d) 601.

6   *Spurrell v Spurrell* (1853) 11 Hares 54 (where the tenant for life predeceased the testatrix).

7   *Re Gregson's Trust Estate* (1864) 2 De GJ & Sm 428 (real estate); *Buckle v Fawcett* (1845) 4 Hare 536 (mixed fund but no trust for sale); *Howard v Collins* (1868) LR 5 Eq 349 (residue); but see the older attitude, *Doe d Long v Prigg* (1828) 8 B & C 231.

8   *Re Bourke's Will Trusts, Barclays Bank Trust Co Ltd v Canada Permanent Trust Co* [1980] 1 All ER 219, [1980] 1 WLR 539, where it was held that the gift comprehended two separate, albeit overlapping categories and thus distinguishing *Re Kilvert, Midland Bank Executor and Trustee Co Ltd v Kilvert* [1957] Ch 388, [1957] 2 All ER 196.

9   *Re Wood, Hardy v Hull* (1923) 130 LT 408 (gift after death of tenant for life to two persons in equal shares, and, if either of them was then dead, to the survivor. Both died in the lifetime of the tenant for life. The personal representatives of the survivor took).

[67.3]
Survivorship on contingent event. In cases where there is a gift to several persons, followed by an express contingent gift over on any event to the survivors or survivor, the survivorship may be independent of both the contingent event and the period of distribution,[1] or on the other hand, may refer to the period of distribution[2] or to the contingent event,[3] according to the context in the particular case. The court leans against a construction involving a gift of the whole to the last survivor, particularly where there are words indicating a tenancy in common, and it attempts to discover a time to which survivorship is to be referred,[4] but no such attempt can be made where the last survivor is expressly stated to take the whole.[5] An accruer clause in favour of 'my surviving children' fails if there is a sole survivor of the children since there are then no surviving children to take under the clause and this is so even if there are grandchildren living at the death of the last survivor. In such a case there is an intestacy.[6]

---

1 In this case the gift will refer only to survivorship between the named persons: *White v Baker* (1860) 2 De GF & J 55; *Re Wood, Hardy v Hull* (1923) 130 LT 408.
2 *Cambridge v Rous* (1858) 25 Beav 409; *Re Pickworth, Snaith v Parkinson* [1899] 1 Ch 642.
3 *Crowder v Stone* (1829) 3 Russ 217.
4 *Cambridge v Rous* (1858) 25 Beav 409 at 415.
5 See, for example, *Re Barrat, Body v Barrat* [1929] 1 Ch 336.
6 *Re James's Will Trusts, Peard v James* [1962] Ch 226, [1960] 3 All ER 744.

[67.4]
Other meanings of 'survivors'. Where certain brothers and sisters were named in the will followed by a gift to surviving brother and sisters, only the survivors of the named brothers and sisters took.[1] In a set of dispositions in favour of several persons and their children and issue, the words may be used in a sense in which the element of survivorship involves not a survivorship between the named persons, but the subsistence of a line of children or issue or of vested estates and interests,[2] or the words may be used as meaning 'others'.[3] Such words may receive one of these constructions where the context requires it, but not otherwise.[4] Thus, after a gift to several children in tail, a gift over on the death of any of them without issue indefinitely to the survivors in tail is construed as a gift to the 'others', creating cross remainders.[5] Where the gift is to several persons equally for their respective lives and after the death of any to his children, but if any die without children to the survivors for life,[6] with remainder to their children, without more,[7] only children of survivors in the ordinary sense can, as a rule, take under the gift over.[8] Where, however, to similar gifts there is added a limitation over if all the tenants for life die without children, then the children of a predeceased tenant for life may participate in the share of one who dies without children after their parent;[9] but children of predeceased tenants for life do not take merely on account of a direction that accruing shares are to be taken in the same manner as original shares.[10] In the first case where there is no such limitation over, a contrary intention in favour of issue may be shown by a substantial gift, but the word 'survivors' may nevertheless have its original meaning[11] and, in such a case, without construing 'survivors' as 'others', the word 'their issue' may mean issue of all the children.[12]

1   *Re McFadden, Wright v Dowds* [1963] NZLR 289.
2   *Re Friend's Settlement, Cole v Allcot* [1906] 1 Ch 47.
3   *Wilmot v Wilmot* (1802) 8 Ves 10 (gift to three at specified age with accruer clause. One attained the age and died. Then another died under the age. The third attained the age: – Held, gift vested in equal shares in the first and third); *Leake v Robinson* (1817) 2 Mer 363 (gift to grandchildren with survivorship); *Smith v Osborne* (1857) 6 HL Cas 375 (gift to two in tail and on failure of issue to surviving devisee); *O'Brien v O'Brien* [1896] 2 IR 459; *Powell v Hellicar* [1919] 1 Ch 138 (accruer clause).
4   *Davidson v Dallas* (1808) 14 Ves 576; *Winterton v Crawfurd* (1830) 1 Russ & M 407 (where it was suggested that different meanings might be required in different parts of the will); *Cromek v Lumb* (1839) 3 Y & C Ex 565 (where 'survivors and survivor' were taken in their usual sense and considered as referring to survivors in each class of grandchildren); *Leeming v Sherratt* (1842) 2 Hare 14 ('survivors construed in natural sense and not as meaning others and the same construction applied throughout the will); *Stead v Platt* (1853) 18 Beav 50 ('survivors or survivor' not read as 'others or other'); *Mann v Thompson* (1854) Kay 628 (impossible to construe 'survivor' to allow a child to be entitled to the share of a person who died before the child in question was born); *Greenwood v Percy* (1859) 26 Beav 572 (devise to two as tenants in common in tail with gift to survivor on death of one without issue: 'survivor' must have ordinary meaning and not be read in the sense of 'other'); *Nevill v Boddam* (1860) 28 Beav 554 (accruer clause having reference to death of each donee); *De Gargagnol v Liardet* (1863) 32 Beav 608 ('survivor' cannot be construed 'other' where the gift over is to persons whose interests are not given over. In this case shares of daughters dying without children went over to sons and daughters).
5   *Doe d Watts v Wainwright* (1793) 5 Term Rep 427; *Smith v Osborne* (1857) 6 HL Cas 375. Cf *Cole v Sewell* (1848) 2 HL Cas 186, and *Re Tharp's Estate* (1863) 1 De GJ & Sm 453, where the gift over was after limitation in strict settlement.
6   If, in such a case the survivors take absolutely, there may be ground for reading survivor, in respect of the last, as the longest liver: *Maden v Taylor* (1876) 45 LJ Ch 569; *Davidson v Kimpton* (1881) 18 Ch D 213; *Re Roper's Estate, Morrell v Gissing* (1889) 41 Ch D 409. But in some cases the gift has passed into residue or is undisposed of: see *King v Frost* (1890) 15 App Cas 548; *Re Mortimer, Griffiths v Mortimer* (1885) 54 LJ Ch 414; *Askew v Askew* (1888) 57 LJ Ch 629.
7   For the position where there is a gift over, see para **[67.6]** infra.
8   This is known as the first rule in *Re Bowman, Re Lay, Whytehead v Boulton* (1889) 41 Ch D 525, and is more usually stated in this form: Where there is a gift to A, B and C equally for their respective lives, and after the death of any of his children, but, if any die without children, to the survivors for life with remainder to their children, only children of the survivors can take under the gift over. For other decisions in the same line, see *Re Usticke* (1866) 35 Beav 338; *Re Horner's Estate, Pomfret v Graham* (1881) 19 Ch D 186; *Re Dunlevy's Trusts* (1882) 7 LR Ir 525; *Re Rubbins, Gill v Worrall* (1898) 79 LT 313.
9   This is the second rule in *Re Bowman, Re Lay, Whytehead v Boulton* (1889) 41 Ch D 525. See also *Harrison v Harrison* [1901] 2 Ch 136 at 142; *O'Brien v O'Brien* [1896] 2 IR 459. The inference made from the gift over, in pursuance of the presumption against intestacy, is that the previously named donees shall take between them in the entire estate in every state of circumstances consistent with the gift over taking effect, *O'Brien v O'Brien* [1896] 2 IR 459 at 466.
10 *Harrison v Harrison* [1901] 2 Ch 136; *Inderwick v Tatchell* [1901] 2 Ch 738; on appeal [1903] AC 120, HL, where a rule to the contrary in *Re Bowman, Re Lay, Whytehead v Boulton* (1889) 41 Ch D 525, is disapproved, and in each of these cases it was said that there is no hard and fast rule when the literal construction is to be followed and when departed from. It is a matter of the intention of the testator to be gathered from the whole will.
11 *Willetts v Willetts* (1848) 7 Hare 38.
12 *Re Corbett's Trusts* (1860) John 591 at 598; *Re Bowman, Re Lay, Whytehead v Boulton* (1889) 41 Ch D 525 at 529.

[67.5]
Stirpital survivorship. If all the shares in the property are settled, and there is a general clause of accruer on the death of each tenant for life without children, all the accrued shares being settled in the same way as the original shares, and if

these dispositions are followed by a gift over in the event of all dying without issue,[1] this may show an intention, not to use the word 'survivors' in its proper sense, but to use it in the sense of those who survive either in person or figuratively in issue.[2] The fact that some only of the shares are settled[3] or that the ultimate gift over is on the death without issue of some only of the first takers,[4] is not sufficient to give this meaning to the word 'survivor'. In general, however, the word 'survivor' is taken in its natural sense.[5]

1   The absence of a gift over of the entire fund is not conclusive to show that the word 'survivor' is to be taken in the literal sense: *Powell v Hellicar* [1919] 1 Ch 138.
2   *Re Benn v Benn* (1885) 29 Ch D 839 at 844, explaining *Waite v Littlewood* (1872) 8 Ch App 70; *Wake v Varah* (1876) 2 Ch D 348; *Re Bilham, Buchanan v Hill* [1901] 2 Ch 169; *Lamont (or Chearnley) v Millar* [1921] WN 334. For a discussion and explanation of earlier cases, see *Re Bilham, Buchanan v Hill* [1901] 2 Ch 169 at 175; *Waite v Littlewood* (1872) 8 Ch App 70 at 73, 74 and *Wake v Varah* (1826) 2 Ch D 348 at 358. The construction has not been adopted in Ireland: *O'Brien v O'Brien,* supra, has been described as 'forced and fanciful' in the House of Lords: *King v Frost* (1890) 15 App Cas 548 at 553, and it is not clear that this construction can be adopted unless the limitations are expressly framed to produce this result: *Re Hobson, Barwick v Holt* [1912] 1 Ch 626 at 632. It was however, in a Scottish decision: *Mackenzie's Trustees v Mackenzie's Executors* 1947 SC 161.
3   *Lucena v Lucena* (1877) 7 Ch D 255.
4   *Re Hobson, Barwick v Holt* [1912] 1 Ch 626.
5   *Auger v Beaudry* [1920] AC 1010; *Gilmour v MacPhillamy* [1930] AC 712. 'Benefit of survivorship in the same family' was considered in *Re Sadler, Furniss v Cooper* (1915) 60 Sol Jo 89.

[67.6]

Gift over to 'others'. A gift over to 'others'[1] or to those 'remaining'[2] of a number of persons after a gift to each or one of them, is not read as meaning 'survivors', unless the context makes this necessary.[3]

1   *Re Chaston, Chaston v Seago* (1881) 18 Ch D 218 (meaning children other than children who die or have died without leaving issue), followed in *Re Crosse* [1933] WN 36; see also *Heron v Ulster Bank Ltd* [1974] NI 44. 'Others surviving' may mean 'then surviving'; *Beckwith v Beckwith* (1876) 46 LJ Ch 97; or 'others': *Re Arnold's Trusts* (1870) LR 10 Eq 252, but this case has been largely dissented from in subsequent cases: see *Harrison v Harrison* [1901] 2 Ch 136, and the case of *Inderwick v Tatchell* in the Court of Appeal [1901] 2 Ch 738.
2   *Re Speak, Speak v Speak* (1912) 56 Sol Jo 273, not following *Sheridan v O'Reilly* [1900] 1 IR 386.
3   *Re Hagen's Trusts* [1877] 46 LJ Ch 665; *Stanley v Bond* [1913] 1 IR 170.

[67.7]

Divesting. If there is a gift after a life interest to a number of persons in equal shares or alternatively to such of them as survive the life tenant, the survivorship clause is prima facie a divesting clause only, and if none of the donees survives the life tenant, their representatives take in equal shares.[1] A similar rule applies in other cases where, after a gift to a number of persons, there is a gift in any contingency to the survivor of them. The divesting is construed as conditional on his surviving the life tenant or some specified event and if none survives, the shares are vested and all take.[2] On the other hand, this rule is not adopted where, in the context of the will, a gift to the survivor of a number of persons is construed as referring to survivorship inter se and not as conditional on his surviving the life tenant; in such a case the longest liver takes the gift, although all die in the lifetime of the life tenant,[3] nor does the rule operate where the condition as to surviving the life tenant applies to the original gift.[4] Where there is a gift after a life interest to a number of persons and if none survives the life tenant to a named person then if none of the first class survives the life tenant, the named person takes although he does not survive the life tenant.[5]

1   *Browne v Lord Kenyon* (1818) 3 Madd 410 (gift after life interests to C and D in equal shares or whole to survivor, both predeceased life tenants and both estates took equally); *Sturgess v Pearson* (1819) 4 Madd 411 (where the gift in remainder was to three or such as should be living at the death of the life tenant. All three predeceased life tenant and all three estates took); *Belk v Slack* (1836) 1 Keen 238 (similar case); *Wiley v Chanteperdrix* [1894] 1 IR 209; *Re Pickworth, Snaith v Parkinson* [1899] 1 Ch 642; *Penny v Railways Comr* [1900] AC 628; *Ward v Brown* [1916] 2 AC 121; *Re Laurie* [1970] NZLR 710. See also *Re Douglas's Will Trusts, Lloyds Bank Ltd v Nelson* [1959] 3 All ER ER 785, [1959] 1 WLR 1212 (where this rule was not applicable but the matter was discussed).
2   *Harrison v Foreman* (1800) 5 Ves 207; *Maddison v Chapman* (1861) 1 John & H 470; *Marriott v Abell* (1869) LR 7 Eq 478; *Re Deacon's Trusts, Deacon v Deacon* (1906) 95 LT 701.
3   *Scurfield v Howes* (1790) 3 Bro CC 90; *White v Baker* (1860) 2 De GF & J 55; *Re Wood, Hardy v Hull* (1923) 130 LT 408, but see *Edmunds v Bisson* (1950) 50 SRNSW 28.
4   *Willis v Plakett* (1841) 4 Beav 208; and see para **[66.6]** supra.
5   *Re Bourke* [1952] VLR 216.

[67.8]

'Survivors' as word of limitation. An absolute gift to a number of persons and the 'survivors' of them or 'with benefit of survivorship' is a gift in joint tenancy,[1] but a gift for joint lives and then to the survivor is a tenancy in common for life with a contingent remainder in fee to the survivor.[2] In the first case, it is immaterial that the named persons take originally as tenants in common.[3]

1   *Doe d Borwell v Abey* (1813) 1 M & S 428; *Haddesley v Adams* (1856) 22 Beav 266 (with benefit of survivorship); *Re Schofield, Baker v Cheffins* [1918] 2 Ch 64.
2   *Quarm v Quarm* [1892] 1 QB 184; *Re Legh's Settlement Trusts, Public Trustee v Legh* [1938] Ch 39, [1937] 3 All ER 823.
3   *Doe d Borwell v Abey* (1813) 1 M & S 428; *Haddesley v Adams* (1856) 22 Beav 266.

CHAPTER 68

Alternative donees

[68.1]
Gifts expressed in the alternative. Two or more gifts may be made to take effect alternatively in certain mutually exclusive events.[1] Thus, a gift to A or B where A and B are donees, described or named, and mutually exclusive,[2] is an alternative gift. In such a gift there is generally a contingency implied, even if not expressed, on the happening of which the alternative gift is to take effect, and the circumstances of the gift must be ascertained before the contingency can be determined.[3] Usually it refers to the death of the first donee before some particular period; for example, the death of the testator or some period of distribution; and it is inferred that the intention of the testator is that the first donee shall take if then alive, while that the second is to take if the first does not survive the particular period.[4] Thus a gift to a named person with a substitutional gift to his children or issue takes effect on favour of that person if he is alive at the date of distribution,[5] but in favour of his children or issue if he is then dead.[6] The contingency of the death of one of the alternative donees in the lifetime of the tenant for life may sometimes be implied.[7] If such a contingency is not expressed or implied, then, if A and B are mutually exclusive, the gift[8] will be void for uncertainty,[9] unless either it is charitable, in which case the court is able to determine the mode in which the gift is to take effect,[10] or is made by way of power of appointment.[11]

---

1 The first question in all such cases is whether the second gift takes effect in succession to the first or is alternative to it: *Ware v Watson* (1855) 7 De GM & G 248 at 258 (a proviso with respect to sons dying without issue has different meanings in different wills, according to the intention of the testator. It may take effect by way of substitution or by way of limitation, and, if by way of limitation, it may be intended to operate generally or only in the period of the testator's lifetime); *Hatch v Hatch* (1855) 20 Beav 105 (successive gifts and not alternative). There is sometimes a question whether a gift is one single gift or two gifts for the purpose of the application of the rule against perpetuities. If it is one gift it may be wholly void, whereas if it is two, one may be valid and the other void: see Chapter 94.

2 Gift to 'heirs or next of kin' may be gifts to one class of donees and not to two classes alternatively: *Lowndes v Stone* (1799) 4 Ves 649 (next of kin or heir-at-law); *Re Thompson's Trusts* (1878) 9 Ch D 607 (gift of personalty to heirs or next of kin: held a gift to next of kin according to the Statute). There is no need to change 'or' to 'and': *Solly v Solly* (1858) 5 Jur NS 36; *Clay v Pennington* (1835) 7 Sim 370. As to change of 'or' to 'and', see Chapter 56.

3 In the case of a gift 'to A or B' it is necessary first to ascertain in what relation, if any, the person or persons represented by A stand to that or those represented by B, so as to supply what is the contingency to be understood as involved in the word 'or': *Re Roberts, Percival v Roberts* [1903] 2 Ch 200 at 203; *Re Sibley's Trusts* (1877) 5 Ch D 494 at 499.

4 *Re Sibley's Trusts* (1877) 5 Ch D 494 (all and every the children of F or their issue: issue of children deceased in lifetime of testator took); *Salisbury v Petty* (1843) 3 Hare 86 at 93 (gifts to B, C and D or their issue: alternative gifts); *Carey v Carey* (1857) 6 I Ch R 255; *Walmsley v*

Foxhall (1863) 1 De GJ & Sm 605; *Re Pearce, Eastwood v Pearce* (1912) 56 Sol Jo 686. Cf *Bowman v Bowman* [1899] AC 518 at 523 (the point to be ascertained is at what period of time testator must be held to have held it in view that the right of the first donee should cease if he was not then alive, and that the right of the alternative donee should take effect. This is a matter of reasonable inference from the will). In *Re Lewis, Goronwy v Richards* [1942] Ch 424, [1942] 2 All ER 364, there was a gift to A and/or B, where A and B were husband and wife and both survived the testator. It was held that they took as joint tenants.

5   *Montagu v Nucella* (1826) 1 Russ 165; *Jones v Torin* (1833) 6 Sim 255; *Whitcher v Penley* (1846) 9 Beav 477; *Chipchase v Simpson* (1849) 16 Sim 485; *Penley v Penley* (1850) 12 Beav 547; *Sparks v Restal* (1857) 24 Beav 218; *Margiston v Hall* (1864) 9 LT 755; *Holland v Wood* (1870) LR 11 Eq 91.

6   *Davenport v Hanbury* (1796) 3 Ves 257; *Girdlestone v Doe* (1828) 2 Sim 225; *Salisbury v Petty* (1843) 3 Hare 86 at 93; *Re Porter's Trusts* (1857) 4 K & J 188.

7   *Re Fisher, Robinson v Eardley* [1915] 1 Ch 302.

8   That is provided the gift must be read without alteration, but the 'or' will be changed to 'and' if that can be done in accordance with the whole will and the gift thus saved from being void: *Richardson v Spraag* (1718) 1 P Wms 434; *Eccard v Brooke* (1790) 2 Cox Eq Cas 213; *Horridge v Ferguson* (1822) Jac 583; *Parkin v Knight* (1846) 15 Sim 83; *Re Turney, Turney v Turney* [1899] 2 Ch 739 at 745; *Re Hayden, Pask v Perry* [1931] 2 Ch 333. The change is not made if the gift can be read as substitutional on some contingency: *Speakman v Speakman* (1850) 8 Hare 180.

9   *Richardson v Spraag* (1718) 1 P Wms 434 at 434; *Longmore v Broom* (1802) 7 Ves 124 at 128; *Flint v Warren* (1847) 15 Sim 626 at 629. See further, Chapter 53.

10 By direction of a scheme: see Chapter 103.

11 *Longmore v Broom* (1802) 7 Ves 124. In such a case where there is no appointment and no gift in default of appointment, the property goes to the objects of the power equally: *Penny v Turner* (1848) 2 Ph 493; *Re White's Trusts* (1860) John 656.

[68.2]

Original and substitutional gifts. Whether an alternative gift is original or substitutional is always a matter of construction.[1] At one time it was said that a gift preceded by 'and' was an original gift and one preceded by 'or' was substitutionary,[2] but this view has been departed from.[3] The gift is original where there is a direct gift to the second donee, although it is only to take effect if the contingency happens; it is substitutional where the second donee takes no direct gift, but only takes, on the contingency happening, the benefit which has been already given to the first donee. Thus, the gift is substitutional where the interest which the alternative donee is to take is by a prior clause in the will given to the first donee, so that the second donee merely stands in the place of the first if the latter is not capable of taking on the particular contingency in contemplation. A gift is original where the interest which the donee is to take is not by a prior clause given to the first donee.[4] The distinction may be illustrated thus. In the case of a gift for life and then to the sons or other relatives then living and to the issue of such as are then dead the issue to take only the parent's share, there is no gift to the relative who is not then living, and the issue of such person take an original gift because there is no gift to which it can be substitutional.[5] On the other hand, if the gift is not to a class of persons then living, but to the class simply with the addition that, if any be then dead, the issue of such shall take their share, the issue take a substitutional gift.[6] The difference is that the person whose issue are to take is in the first instance not included in the class and in the second case he is so included. In the case of a gift to a person and his heirs,[7] or to a person and the heirs of his body,[8] or a bequest to a person, his executors or administrators,[9] the additional words are words of limitation and the gifts are not substitutional. On the death of the person in the life of the testator, the whole gift goes and the personal representatives take nothing.[10] Where there is an immediate gift to a person or his personal representatives, the personal representatives take by substitution if the legatee dies in the lifetime of the testator,[11] but, where the gift is postponed, that expression is treated as a way of giving the legatee a vested interest on the testator's death. There is no substitutional gift and; if the legatee dies in the lifetime of the testator, the personal representatives take nothing.[12] In the case of a postponed gift to A or his heirs, the word 'heirs' may in some cases be used to mean those entitled on intestacy and then such persons take as personae designatae.[13] Where the persons referred to as 'personal representatives' are intended to take beneficially, they take by substitution.[14]

1   *Re Sibley's Trusts* (1877) 5 Ch D 494 at 499; *Re Bourke's Will Trusts, Barclays Bank Trust Co Ltd v Canada Permanent Trust Co* [1980] 1 All ER 219, [1980] 1 WLR 539.
2   *Re Merrick's Trusts* (1866) LR 1 Eq 551.
3   *Hurry v Hurry* (1870) LR 10 Eq 346 at 348; *Re Coulden, Coulden v Coulden* [1908] 1 Ch 320. In the latter case proceeds of sale of realty and personalty were to be equally divided among the 'then surviving children and their respective issue'. It was held that 'their issue' were not words of limitation, and that the issue of the surviving children could not compete with their parents and took nothing, while 'issue' was extended to children of deceased children, who took the share which their parent would have taken; see also *Re Whitcher* [1982] 2 NZLR 416. In the ordinary way, however, in a gift to a person and his issue, the issue take in competition with the named donee: *Re Hammond, Parry v Hammond* [1924] 2 Ch 276.
4   *Lamphier v Buck* (1865) 2 Drew & Sm 484 at 494; *Re Bentley's Trusts* (1935) 9 MPR 271; *Re Grasett* (1969) 31 DLR (3d) 153; *Re Taylor* (1972) 28 DLR (3d) 257.
5   *Re Taylor* (1972) 28 DLR (3d) 257.
6   *Re Taylor* (1972) 28 DLR (3d) 257; *Martin v Holgate* (1866) LR 1 HL 175; *Re Woolley, Wormald v Woolley* [1903] 2 Ch 206; *Attwood v Alford* (1866) LR 2 Eq 479; *Burt v Hellyar* (1872) LR 14 Eq 160; *Re Earle's Settlement Trusts, Reiss v Norrie* [1971] 2 All ER 1188, [1971] 1 WLR 1118 ('Such issue taking ... his ... parent's share only'). The word 'share' in a substitutionary gift cannot be construed to refer to a specific gift of a company's shares in a case where it can refer to the share of a gift some deceased person would have taken: *Re Hinton* [1953] NZLR 607.
7   *Brett v Rigden* (1568) 1 Plowd 340; *Warner v White* (1782) 3 Bro Parl Cas 435.
8   *Hutton v Simpson* (1716) 2 Vern 722; *Denn d Radclyffe v Bagshaw* (1796) 6 Term Rep 512; *Doe d Turner v Kett* (1792) 4 Term Rep 601.
9   *Elliott v Davenport* (1705) 1 P Wms 83.
10   See 'lapse', Chapter 47.
11   *Gittings v M'Dermott* (1834) 2 My & K 69.
12   *Re Porter's Trust* (1857) 4 K & J 188 at 193, 198; *Thompson v Whitelock* (1859) 4 De G & J 490; *Re Turner* (1865) 2 Drew & Sm 501.
13   *Re Porter's Trust* (1857) 4 K & J 188 at 193. Generally as to a gift to a person or his heirs; see Chapter 78.
14   *Wing v Wing* (1876) 34 LT 941.

[68.3]
Effect of time of death of prior donee. The effect of the time of the death of the prior donee in ascertaining the rights of the donees under the substitutional gift varies according as the primary gift is to a named person or a group of named persons[1] or to a class, and, if it is to a class, then according as the gift takes effect immediately on the death of the testator or is postponed to a subsequent date,[2] as stated in the next following paragraphs.

1   That is a number of persons taking not as a class but as individuals. Often the only indication that persons take as individuals is that they are given so much each or 'apiece', whereas, in a class gift, there is a stated sum or property for the whole class. Further upon the proper

construction of the will the substitution may be limited to the case of a donee predeceasing the testator may not apply to the case of that donee predeceasing one who survives the testator; see *Union Trustee Co of Australia Ltd v Pettit* (1958) 76 WNNSW 110.

2   See *Ive v King* (1852) 16 Beav 46 at 53, 54, and text at paras **[68.7]** and **[68.8]** infra.

[68.4]

Primary gift to individuals. If the primary gift is to a named person or a group of named persons, the substitutional gift takes effect on the death of the primary donee, whether the primary donee dies before the date of the will, or after the date of the will and before the death of the testator, or after the death of the testator and before the date of distribution.[1] Although the death of the primary legatee occurs before the death of the testator, the gift over takes effect on the presumption that such ulterior legatee was substituted in order to prevent a lapse of the legacy.[2] There is no distinction between the case of a gift to a person known to be alive, and in the event of his death to his children, and a gift to a person whom the testator may suppose to be alive but who is in fact dead, with a gift over to his children on his death.[3] It makes no difference whether the primary donee dies before or after the testator, so long as he dies before the tenant for life or other period of distribution.[4]

1   *Re Main* (1953) 30 MPR 313.
2   *Ive v King* (1852) 16 Beav 46 at 54.
3   See *Ive v King* (1852) 16 Beav 46 at 55, 56. As to death of the primary legatee before the date of the will, see *Hannam v Sims* (1858) 2 De G & J 151; *Re Booth's Will Trusts, Robins v King* (1940) 163 LT 77. As to death between the date of the will and the death of the testator, see *Le Jeune v Le Jeune* (1837) 2 Keen 701; *Ive v King* (1852) 16 Beav 46 at 54; *Ashling v Knowles* (1856) 3 Drew 593; *Hodgson v Smithson* (1856) 8 De GM & G 604; *Re Faulding's Trust* (1858) 26 Beav 263; *Jones v Frewin* (1864) 3 New Rep 415.
4   *Ashling v Knowles* (1856) 3 Drew 593.

[68.5]

Primary gift to individuals, substitutional gift to class. Where the substitutional gift is to a class, the following rules apply. Where the substitutional gift takes effect either before the date of the will or after that date and before the death of the testator, the class consists of those who are living at the death of the testator; and, where the substitutional gift takes effect after the death of the testator and before the date of distribution, the class consists of those living at the death of the primary donee.[1]

1   *Ive v King* (1852) 16 Beav 46 at 57.

[68.6]

Gifts to classes—in general. If the original gift is to a class, a person who was dead at the date of the will is not included in it,[1] and consequently no one can take in his place by way of substitution; for, in order to claim under the will, the substituted legatees must point out the original legatees in whose place they demand to stand,[2] and the substitutional gift fails where the corresponding member of the primary class was dead at the date of the will, and therefore, could not have taken as a member of the class under the will.[3] Thus, if the original donees are a class of parents, and there is a substitutional gift of each parent's share to his children, the children of a parent dead at the date of the will cannot take.[4]

1   In using words applicable only to a class, the testator must be taken to be referring to living persons, and persons dead at the date of the will cannot be included: *Re Hotchkiss's Trusts* (1869) LR 8 Eq 643 at 649; *Re Musther, Groves v Musther* (1890) 43 Ch D 569 at 572; *Re Brown, Leeds v Spencer* [1917] 2 Ch 232; *Re Walker, Walker v Walker* [1930] 1 Ch 469; *Re Booth's Will Trusts, Robins v King* (1940) 163 LT 77; *Mackintosh (or Miller) v Gerrard* [1947] AC 461. This rule excludes those dead at the date of the will and does not finally determine those who are to constitute the class or those who may be let in.

2   *Christopherson v Naylor* (1816) 1 Mer 320 at 326.

3   *Coulthurst v Carter* (1852) 15 Beav 421 at 427; *Ive v King* (1852) 16 Beav 46 at 53; *Congreve v Palmer* (1853) 16 Beav 435; *Re Wood's Will* (1862) 31 Beav 323.

4   *Butter v Ommaney* (1828) 4 Russ 73; *Gray v Garman* (1843) 2 Hare 268; *Atkinson v Atkinson* (1872) IR 6 Eq 184; *Kelsey v Ellis* (1878) 38 LT 471; *Re Barker, Asquith v Saville* (1882) 51 LJ Ch 835; *Re Webster's Estate, Widgen v Mello* (1883) 23 Ch D 737; *Re Chinery, Chinery v Hill* (1888) 39 Ch D 614; *Re Offiler, Offiler v Offiler* (1901) 83 LT 758; *Gorringe v Mahlstedt* [1907] AC 225; *Re Cope, Cross v Cross* [1908] 2 Ch 1; *Re Kirkpatrick, Ferguson v Kirkpatrick* (1912) 12 SRNSW 282; *Re Umpherson* [1918] SALR 147; *Public Trustee v Bolton* [1918] NZLR 908; *Re Fleming's Trusts* [1951] QSR 179; *Re McPherson* [1968] VR 368. This paragraph, and the paragraph on the next page headed 'Gifts to children', were referred to in *Re Davison* (1980) 99 DLR (3d) 80 at 88.

[68.7]

Gifts to classes—immediate gift. Where the primary gift to a class is immediate, ie not preceded by a life or other limited interest, a substitutional gift on the death of a member of the class takes effect on the death in the lifetime of the testator of any person who was living at the date of the will, and who, if he had survived, would have taken as a member of the class.[1]

1   *Re Hayward, Creery v Lingwood* (1882) 19 Ch D 470. The substituted class will be determined by the ordinary rules: see Chapter 66.

[68.8]

Gifts to classes—postponed gift. Where the gift is postponed, the testator is considered to be providing for the death of members of the class between his own death, or the time of ascertainment of the class, and the period of distribution, or the time when the gift is to come into possession.[1] Accordingly, it is prima facie only in respect of persons who are ascertained as members of the class and capable of taking under the gift that substitution is effected.[2] As to those who die before the testator or before the time when the class is to be ascertained, the substitutional gift fails.[3] If, however, there is no gap between the time of ascertainment of the class and the time of distribution, a person substituted for donees dying in the lifetime of the testator, even before the date of the will, may be let in.[4] On the other hand a gift postponed to a life interest to all brothers and sisters prima facie does not include a brother or sister dead at the date of the will.[5] Where there is a substitutionary clause for children of any brother or sister being then dead of the share the parent would have taken if living, the children of a brother or sister who dies before the date of the will do not take but in the case of any brother or sister living at the date of the will but predeceasing the tenant for life, the children will take as joint tenants.[6]

1   *Re Gilbert, Daniel v Matthews* (1886) 54 LT 752.

2   *Re Porter's Trust* (1857) 4 K & J 188 at 191 (to determine whether the substitutional gift is to take effect on the death of a particular member, it must be determined whether he was a

member of the class at all); *Re Earl's Settlement Trusts, Reiss v Norrie* [1971] 2 All ER 1188, [1971] 1 WLR 1118 (issue of primary class who were dead at the date of the settlement were excluded; further, the substituted issue had to survive their own parent and the date of substitution in order to take); applied in *Re Auerbach's Estate, Union Fidelity Trustee Co of Australia Ltd v Procter* [1974] NSWLR 57; *Re Manly's Will Trusts, Burton v Williams* [1969] 3 All ER 1011, [1969] 1 WLR 1818 (issue must survive the primary donee if they were to take).

3   *Thornhill v Thornhill* (1819) 4 Madd 377; *Neilson v Monro* (1879) 41 LT 209; *Re Hannam, Haddelsey v Hannam* [1897] 2 Ch 39; *Re Ibbetson, Ibbetson v Ibbetson* (1903) 88 LT 461 (to the child or children of J and H 'or their heirs', these last words being treated as substitutional); *Bank's Trustees v Bank's Trustees* 1907 SC 125.

4   *King v Cleaveland* (1858) 26 Beav 26; affd (1859) 4 De G & J 477 (gift after life interests to testator's nephews and nieces then living or their legal personal representatives: representatives, in this case the next of kin, of nephews and nieces dying in the lifetimes of the tenants for life took shares); *Re Philps' Will* (1868) LR 7 Eq 151 (life interest for wife and then to be divided among 'children then living or their heirs': two of the children were dead at the date of will, three survived testator and died in the lifetime of the wife: next of kin of these five shared in the fund).

5   *Re Brooke's Will Trusts, Jubber v Brooke* [1953] 1 All ER 668.

6   *Re Brooke's Will Trusts, Jubber v Brooke* [1953] 1 All ER 668. The class of brothers and sisters included those dying between the date of the will and the death of the testator because of the words 'if living'. If restricted to those dying during the life tenancy the words would have been unnecessary because the interests vested on the death of the testator.

[68.9]

Gifts to children. The exclusion of children from taking under a gift under which the parent cannot take[1] will be avoided where the gift can be construed as original and not as substitutional. Thus, the gift to the children may not be alternative to the gift actually made to the parent. It may be a gift of a share to be computed on the hypothesis that there had been a gift to the parent. A testator may so express himself as to cause the child or a deceased child to represent and be substituted for that deceased child, though he never intended a share for the deceased child.[2] This is an original gift to the children and does not fail, for the reason that the parent could not have taken.[3] Even where the children are expressed to take only their parent's share, the class of children, according to the construction of the whole will, may be ascertained, not by reference to those parents only who take under the original gift to parents, but by reference to all parents, whether eventually capable of taking or not. This again is an original gift to such children.[4] It has been suggested that in this respect there may be a distinction between a gift to children of the testator and a gift to nephews and nieces or more remote relatives, in which cases the testator might not know the state of the family.[5]

1   For example, for the reason that the parent dies in the lifetime of the testator or other similar reason.

2   *Loring v Thomas* (1861) 1 Drew & Sm 497 (proviso that if child dies in testator's lifetime leaving children who attain twenty-one, the children of such child shall 'represent and stand in the place of' the deceased parent and be entitled to the same share as the deceased parent); *Re Taylor* [1957] NZLR 647.

3   *Loring v Thomas* (1861) 1 Drew & Sm 497; *Barraclough v Cooper* [1908] 2 Ch 121n, followed in *Re Grassett* (1969) 31 DLR (3d) 153; *Re Chapman's Will* (1863) 32 Beav 382; *Re Woolrich, Harris v Harris* (1879) 11 Ch D 663; *Re Lambert, Corns v Harrison* [1908] 2 Ch 117; *Re Metcalfe, Metcalfe v Earle* [1909] 1 Ch 424; *Re Williams, Metcalf v Williams* [1914] 2 Ch 61; *Re Kirk, Wethey v Kirk* (1915) 85 LJ Ch 182; *Re Birchall, Re Valentine, Kennedy v Birchall* [1940] Ch 424, [1940] 1 All ER 545; *Re Lusher, Lusher v Lusher* [1928] NZLR 73; *Re Hansen Estate* (1951) 4 WWRNS 358 ('in the event of the death of any one or more of my children during my lifetime leaving lawful issue such issue to take the share to which the father or

mother would have been entitled'). In *Re Hickey, Beddoes v Hodgson* [1917] 1 Ch 601, there was a legacy 'to the descendants of' A or 'their descendants living at my death' and it was held that this was a direct gift to 'their descendants living' at the death of the testator, so that the grandchildren took as an original gift the share of a child who died in the lifetime of the testator: *Loring v Thomas* (1861) 1 Drew & Sm 497, is not affected by *Gorringe v Mahlstedt* [1907] AC 225; see *Re Lambert, Corns v Harrison* [1908] 2 Ch 117 at 121.

4   *Jarvis v Pond* (1839) 9 Sim 549 (in case of the decease of 'any' of my said children, the surviving children to have their parents' share. Some violence was said to be done in assigning a share to the parents); *Loring v Thomas* (1861) 1 Drew & Sm 497; *Re Sibley's Trusts* (1877) 5 Ch D 494 at 501 (where it is said that 'all and every' the parents must mean more than 'two' and that an ordinary man knowing he had but two surviving relatives of a particular kind would not use the words 'all and every' when speaking of them). As to gift with a proviso that if any donees should die in the lifetime of a tenant for life leaving issue, such issue were to have their parent's share, see *Smith v Smith* (1837) 8 Sim 353; *Habergham v Ridehalgh* (1870) LR 9 Eq 395. These gifts are framed on the hypothesis that the persons for whom the donees were alternative were ascertained members of the class of first donees, and accordingly it was held that these alternative donees might take in such a case, although the members of the class of first donees predeceased the testator. 'Any of the said children' has been said to exclude a substitution for a child dead at the date of the will: *Martin v Martin* [1953] QSR 54.

5   *Re Metcalfe, Metcalfe v Earle* [1909] 1 Ch 424 at 426.

[68.10]

Composite class of parents and issue. In cases where the gift is framed as a gift to a composite class, formed of a class of parents living at a certain period and a class of children of parents then dead, then it is a matter of construction whether such a gift is an original or a substitutional gift. If there is an independent and original gift to the latter class of children, then the children of parents who were dead before the date of the will may take,[1] as well as children of parents who died after the date of the will but before the testator.[2] But if the gift is held to be substitutionary then issue of the primary class who were dead at the date of the settlement would be excluded.[3] If a parent dies without issue, he or she takes if he or she survives the testator.[4]

1   *Tytherleigh v Harbin* (1835) 6 Sim 329; *Giles v Giles* (1837) 8 Sim 360; *Rust v Baker* (1837) 8 Sim 443; *Bebb v Beckwith* (1839) 2 Beav 308; *Gaskell v Holmes* (1844) 3 Hare 438; *Etches v Etches* (1856) 3 Drew 441.

2   *Baldwin v Rogers* (1835) 3 De GM & G 649; *Etches v Etches* (1856) 3 Drew 441; *Re Faulding's Trust* (1858) 26 Beav 263; *Re Jordan's Trusts* (1863) 2 New Rep 57; *Heasman v Pearse* (1871) 7 Ch App 275.

3   *Re Earl's Settlement Trust, Reiss v Norrie* [1971] 2 All ER 1188, [1971] 1 WLR 1118, not following *Etches v Etches* (1856) 3 Drew 441, since Goff J thought that a finding that the gift was immediately vested was inconsistent with the view that the gift to the issue was original; at 1194.

4   *Re Rooke's Will Trusts, Taylor v Rooke* [1953] Ch 716, [1953] 2 All ER 110.

[68.11]

Conditions attaching to alternative gifts. Conditions attaching to a gift do not prima facie attach to a gift alternative to it, whether original or substitutional,[1] although in the case of substitutional gifts it may much more easily be inferred that they attach than in the case of alternative original gifts.[2] Thus, it is not in general necessary, unless the testator so provides, that an alternative donee shall survive the period of distribution in order to take, whether the gift is original,[3] or substitutional;[4] nor, in an original and alternative gift, is it necessary, unless the testator so provides, that the alternative donee should survive the person for whom he is the alternative.[5] If the gift is substitutional, the substituted issue must survive their parent and the date of substitution, which may be the same or different, and which may or may not be the period of distribution.[6] Where the gift is to children of a stirps, a direction that, if the founder of the stirps be dead at a given time leaving children, the children shall take the parent's share, does not involve that the children must be living at the date of distribution. The children take a vested interest although the amount is uncertain until the given time arrives.[7] This construction, however, is inappropriate where the alternative gift is to issue construed as not restricted to children, because there may be substitutions not only of a child of the founder of the stirps, but of remoter issue for the child. This is a contingent gift to the remoter issue which is subject to the contingency of surviving the date of distribution.[8]

1   *Martin v Holgate* (1866) LR 1 HL 175. For cases where the contingency of the first applied to the alternative gift, see *Re Kirkman's Trusts* (1859) 3 De G & J 558; *Bennett v Merriman* (1843) 6 Beav 360; *Smith v Palmer* (1848) 7 Hare 225; *Macgregor v Macgregor* (1845) 2 Coll 192. In so far as these cases do not depend on the context, they were disapproved in the House of Lords in *Martin v Holgate* (1866) LR 1 HL 175.
2   *Martin v Holgate* (1866) LR 1 HL 175 at 187.
3   *Thompson v Clive* (1857) 23 Beav 282; *Martin v Holgate* (1866) LR 1 HL 175; *Re Woolley, Wormald v Woolley* [1903] 2 Ch 206; *Campbell's Trusts v Dick* 1915 SC 100.
4   *Masters v Scales* (1850) 13 Beav 60; *Re Battersby's Trusts* [1896] 1 IR 600; *Re Bradbury, Wing v Bradbury* (1904) 73 LJ Ch 591; *Re Langlands, Langlands v Langlands* (1917) 87 LJ Ch 1.
5   *Lyon v Coward* (1846) 15 Sim 287; *Lanphier v Buck* (1865) 2 Drew & Sm 484 at 498; *Heasman v Pearse* (1871) 7 Ch App 275; *Re Woolley, Wormald v Woolley* [1903] 2 Ch 206. For a contrary intention shown by the will, see *Barker v Barker* (1852) 5 De G & Sm 753.
6   *Re Earle's Settlement Trust, Reiss v Norrie* [1971] 2 All ER 1188, [1971] 1 WLR 1118 (time for substitution was the death of the husband, and the gift over was to the issue living at the date of the death of the husband through all degrees per stirpes of each parent living at the date of the settlement and who predeceased the husband); *Thompson v Clive* (1857) 23 Beav 282; *Crause v Cooper* (1859) 1 John & H 207; *Lanphier v Buck* (1865) 2 Drew & Sm 484; *Re Turner* (1865) 2 Drew & Sm 501; *Re Merrick's Trusts* (1866) LR 1 Eq 551 at 560; explained in *Re Woolley, Wormald v Woolley* [1903] 2 Ch 206 at 209.
7   *Mousley v Rigby* [1955] Ch 139, [1954] 3 All ER 553; applied in *Re Earle's Settlement Trust, Reiss v Norrie* [1971] 2 All ER 1188, [1971] 1 WLR 1118; *Re Green, McKenzie v Stringer* [1963] NZLR 148.
8   *Mousley v Rigby* [1955] Ch 139, distinguishing *Martin v Holgate* (1866) LR 1 HL 175, applying *Re Embury* (1913) 109 LT 511, and not following *Re Orton's Trust* (1866) LR 3 Eq 375. See also Chapter 88.

[68.12]
Ascertainment of class. Subject to the above considerations, the class of substituted donees is ascertained according to the usual rules.[1]

1   See Chapter 66. Thus, the class is ascertained at the testator's death: *Ive v King* (1852) 16 Beav 46 (children); *Re Philps' Will* (1868) LR 7 Eq 151 at 154 (heirs in the sense of next of kin); *Wingfield v Wingfield* (1878) 9 Ch D 658 (heirs); subject, in the case of a postponed gift, to letting in members coming into existence before the period of distribution: *Re Sibley's Trusts* (1877) 5 Ch D 494; *Re Jones' Estate, Hume v Lloyd* (1878) 47 LJ Ch 775; not following *Hobgen v Neale* (1870) LR 11 Eq 48.

[68.13]
Concurrent interests. Whether the members of classes taking under original and substituted gifts may take concurrently depends on the correspondence between the members of those classes respectively. A gift to a class of parents or their children, or parents or their issue, is construed as substituting for each

parent his own children or issue, wherever the context allows that construction.[1] Thus, when there are words denoting an intention to divide the property into shares for the purpose of substitution,[2] the parents surviving the period of distribution and the children or issue of parents dying before that period then take concurrently.[3] Otherwise, where the original and substitutional gifts are both to classes, and there is nothing indicative of a substitution for a member of the original class or a corresponding member of the substituted class,[4] the gifts are mutually exclusive, and, if any member of the original class survives the period of distribution, no member of the substituted class can taken.[5] In the absence of a contrary intention being shown,[6] the substituted donees as between themselves are joint tenants,[7] even where the original donees are tenants in common, and, therefore, as between original donees and substituted donees taking with them there is a tenancy in common. Where there are words of severance in the gift to the substituted donees (such as 'to take equally between them' or 'to take per stirpes in equal shares if more than one') then they take as tenants in common.[8]

1   *Re Coley, Gibson v Gibson* [1901] 1 Ch 40 at 44; *Re Alderton, Hughes v Vanderspar* [1913] WN 129.
2   *Re Gilbert, Daniel v Matthews* (1886) 54 LT 752; *Re Miles, Miles v Miles* (1889) 61 LT 359.
3   If all the original class survive, the substituted class is excluded because there is no case for substitution: *Re Coley, Gibson v Gibson* [1901] 1 Ch 40 at 43.
4   As, for example, gifts to children 'or their heirs': *Finlayson v Tatlock* (1870) LR 9 Eq 258.
5   *Re Coley, Gibson v Gibson* [1901] 1 Ch 40.
6   See *Lyon v Coward* (1846) 15 Sim 287; *Hodges v Grant* (1867) LR 4 Eq 140; *A-G v Fletcher* (1871) LR 13 Eq 128; *Re Horner, Eagleton v Horner* (1887) 37 Ch D 695 at 711 (where there were double words of severance sufficient to apply to the sustained donees). As to distribution per capita or per stirpes in such cases, see Chapter 87.
7   *Davenport v Hanbury* (1796) 3 Ves 257; *Heasman v Pearse* (1871) 7 Ch App 275 at 284; *Re Yates, Bostock v D'Eyncourt* [1891] 3 Ch 53; *Re Brooke's Will Trusts, Jubber v Brooke* [1953] 1 All ER 668; *Re Battersby's Trusts* [1896] 1 IR 600; *Rowe and Brown v Public Trustee* [1928] NZLR 51.
8   *Crosthwaite v Dean* (1879) 40 LT 837; *Re Froy, Froy v Froy* [1938] 2 All ER 316; *Re Gransloser's Will Trusts* [1952] Ch 30, [1951] 2 All ER 936; *Re Kilvert, Midland Bank Executor and Trustee Co Ltd v Kilvert* [1957] Ch 388, [1957] 2 All ER 196.

[68.14]
Failure of alternative gift. In cases where the alternative gift fails by reason of the event not having happened on which it is to take effect, then the prior gift to the first donee may take effect although he was not living at the period of distribution,[1] because the alternative gift operates as a divesting gift only.[2]

1   *Gray v Garman* (1843) 2 Hare 268; *Salisbury v Petty* (1843) 3 Hare 86 at 93.
2   As to divesting, see Chapter 96.

[68.15]
Extent of alternative gift. In the case of a gift to a group or class, a substitutional gift of the shares of such as die leaving issue to their issue does not affect the shares of those who die without leaving issue.[1]

1   *Baldwin v Rogers* (1853) 3 De GM & G 649; *Strother v Dutton* (1857) 1 De G & J 675 at 676.

CHAPTER 69

Descriptions of donees by number

[69.1]

Number erroneous. The testator's statement of the number of donees is sometimes inconsistent with the number of persons satisfying the description.[1] Where there is a gift to a number of persons designated by a class or group description, with a statement of the number of the donees, which is either greater or less[2] than the actual number of persons who fit the description at the death of the testator – as in the case of a gift to the four children of A who at the death of the testator is shown to have five children – then unless it appears that all persons so designated were intended to take, independently of their number,[3] the court considers[4] with how many of such persons the testator was acquainted at the date of his will, and, if the number corresponds with the number in the will, may thus be able to identify the particular persons described.[5] Those in existence at the date of the will are preferred to those coming into existence after that date and take as personae designatae.[6]

1   *Lord Selsey v Lord Lake* (1839) 1 Beav 146 ('her five daughters' where there were five sons and a daughter: only the daughter took under the gift); *Lane v Green* (1851) 4 De G & Sm 239 (gift to the four sons of A, who had three sons and a daughter, who all took).
2   *Re Sharp, Maddison v Gill* [1908] 2 Ch 190 (number whether greater or less is rejected where dominant intention is to benefit the persons who answer the description).
3   *Mathews v Foulsham* (1864) 4 New Rep 500; *Re Sharp, Maddison v Gill* [1908] 2 Ch 190; *Bryce's Trustee* (1878) 5 R (Ct of Sess) 722, and see para **[69.2]** infra.
4   See now the AJA 1982, s 21; Vol 2, Part G, para **[244.97]**; see Chapter 6.
5   *Newman v Piercey* (1876) 4 Ch D 41 (the rule that a gift to persons misdescribed in number is a gift to all persons answering that description does not apply where from admissible evidence it is possible to say which of the class were meant); *Re Mayo, Chester v Keirl* [1901] 1 Ch 404 (bequest to three children of A before her marriage. There were in fact four but testator had only acknowledged paternity of the three youngest: onus on eldest child to prove intention to include her). A child *en ventre sa mère* and not known to the testator may be excluded: *Re Emery's Estate, Jones v Emery* (1876) 3 Ch D 300; *Re Smiley* (1908) 28 NZLR 1; *Re McNeill, Wright v Johnstone* [1909] 9 SRNSW 220.
6   *Re Murray, Clarke v Wakem* [1964] NZLR 627.

[69.2]

Rejection of number. There are cases, however, where the court can arrive at the conclusion that all the persons satisfying a particular description are intended to be benefited, and, if there has been an inaccurate statement of the number of the persons composing the class, the court rejects the number.[1] Thus, if it appears that at the date of the will the fact was, and the testator knew, that the number of persons who then answered the description was greater or less than the number shown by the will,[2] or if the number could not then, in fact and to the knowledge of the testator, be ascertained[3], or if (in cases where the gift would otherwise be void for uncertainty) there is no evidence at all of the testator's knowledge or other admissible evidence to enable the court to determine who were meant by the description,[4] the court may reject the number as a mistake.

1   *Re Stephenson, Donaldson v Bamber* [1897] 1 Ch 75 at 81, 85 (rejection of number only where will shows intention to benefit all); *Re Sharp, Maddison v Gill* [1908] 2 Ch 190; *Re Dutton, Plunkett v Simeon* [1893] WN 65; *Re Groom, Booty v Groom* [1897] 2 Ch 407; *Re Burgess* (1968) 67 DLR (2d) 526 (bequest 'to the two children (boy and girl) of C $1,000 each'; C in fact had six children; held, that the dominant intention of the will was to benefit the children of C as a class and the testator's numerical mistake would be disregarded). This rule, however, does not apply where the persons are described by name; see *Re Whiston, Whiston v Woolley* [1924] 1 Ch 122 (where a named child had been killed in the war but the father refused to believe him dead).

2   *Daniell v Daniell* (1849) 3 De G & Sm 337; *Spencer v Ward* (1870) LR 9 Eq 507; *Lee v Lee* (1864) 10 Jur NS 1041.

3   *Sleech v Thorrington* (1754) 2 Ves Sen 560 (to the two servants living with me at my death: in fact at that time she had three: all took).

4   *Garvey v Hibbert* (1812) 19 Ves 125; *Harrison v Harrison* (1829) 1 Russ & M 71; *Lee v Pain* (1844) 4 Hare 201 at 249; *Morrison v Martin* (1846) 5 Hare 507; *Wrighton v Calvert* (1860) 1 John & H 250 at 251; *McKechnie v Vaughan* (1873) LR 15 Eq 289; *Re Bassett's Estate, Perkins v Fladgate* (1872) LR 14 Eq 54; *Re Sharp, Maddison v Gill* [1908] 2 Ch 190.

CHAPTER 70

Commorientes

[70.1]
Common law. Although it may be thought the law relating to simultaneous deaths is a comparatively modern development of the law, the reported cases on the subject go back to at least as early as 1793 when it was said that it was more fair and reasonable to consider the parties as all dying at the same instant rather than to resort to some fanciful supposition of survivorship on account of degrees of robustness.[1] In what is generally regarded as the leading case[2] on the law apart from statute the statement runs thus. There is no presumption of law arising from age or sex as to survivorship among persons whose death is occasioned by one and the same cause. Nor is there any presumption of law that all died at the same time. The question is one of fact depending wholly on evidence and, if the evidence does not establish the survivorship of anyone, the law will treat it as a matter incapable of being determined and the onus is on the person asserting the affirmative.

1   *Wright v Netherwood* (1793) 2 Salk 593n.
2   *Wing v Angrave* (1860) 8 HL Cas 183. For cases before the statutory enactment of 1925 see *Re Johnson's Goods* (1897) 78 LT 85; *Re Bruce and Bruce's Estate* (1910) 26 TLR 381. In this respect the common law differed from the Roman Law and the Code Napoleon.

[70.2]
Statutory law. Statute, however, has introduced a presumption in such cases.[1] Now in all cases where after 1 January 1926, two or more persons have died in circumstances rendering it uncertain which of them survived the other or others, such deaths shall (subject to any order of the court), for all purposes affecting the title to property, be presumed to have occurred in order of seniority and accordingly the younger shall be deemed to have survived the elder. It was contended that this section required a court to find first that the deaths did not occur at the same time and that the court was unable to say which death occurred first. In short that it did not apply to truly simultaneous deaths; but the House of Lords decided by a majority upon a common-sense construction of the section, that is to say that the presumption applies to any case where it is impossible to say which person died first whether the deaths were simultaneous or consecutive.[2] Simultaneous death means death in such circumstances that the ordinary man would infer death was simultaneous.[3] To rebut this statutory presumption there must be evidence leading to a defined and warranted conclusion that one died before the other.[4]

A man and his wife were lost at sea, there being no survivors and nothing known as to how the ship was lost. The husband had made a will providing for the event of his wife predeceasing him or her death coinciding with his. Coinciding meant occurring at the same point of time and not on the same occasion or in the same calamity and, as there was no evidence to prove that the wife's death preceded or coincided with that of the husband, the presumption provided by the Law of Property Act 1925, s 184 applied and the wife being the younger, she must be presumed to have survived her husband.[5]

1   See Law of Property Act 1925, s 184; 37 *Halsbury's Statutes* (4th edn) 349; Vol 2, Part G, para **[244.56]**.

2   *Hickman v Peacey* [1945] AC 304, [1945] 2 All ER 215; see per Lord Macmillan at 324 and 323.

3   *Re Pringle, Baker v Matherson* [1946] Ch 124, [1946] 1 All ER 89; *Re Bate, Chillingworth v Bate* [1947] 2 All ER 418.

4   *Re Bate, Chillingworth v Bate* [1947] 2 All ER 418. For case where such a conclusion was reached see *Re Howard, Howard v Treasury Solicitor* [1944] P 39. For cases where it was held that the deaths were not simultaneous but that presumption applied, see *Re Lindop, Lee-Barber v Reynolds* [1942] Ch 377, [1942] 2 All ER 46; *Re Mercer, Tanner v Bulmer* [1944] 1 All ER 759; see also *Re Dixon's Estate* (1969) 90 (Pt 1) WNNSW 469 not followed in *Halbert v Mynar* [1981] 2 NSWLR 659.

5   *Re Rowland, Smith v Russell* [1963] Ch 1, [1962] 2 All ER 837; *Re Loy* [1984] 1 Qd R 396.

[70.3]

Intestacy. For the different rule applicable to husbands and wives on intestacy, see the Administration of Estates Act 1925, s 46(3), and Chapter 104. It can be noted that the case of a death of a person intestate on or after 1 January 1996, the rights of the intestate's spouse are contingent on the spouse surviving the intestate by 28 days.[1]

1   Administration of Estates Act 1925, s 46(2A), inserted by the Law Reform (Succession) Act 1995, s 1(1). This will obviate the need to apply any fictitious presumptions in such cases.

[70.4]

Commorientes provisions. For precedents of commorientes clauses and for a statement of the inheritance tax provisions relevant to such clauses, see Vol 2, paras **[219.1]** to **[219.13]** and **[224.1]** et seq.

CHAPTER 71

Relationship by blood and affinity

[71.1]
Half-blood included. A description by relationship prima facie refers only to persons related by blood, but includes the half-blood,[1] though not those related by affinity only.[2] The description includes only those in the exact relationship prescribed by the will,[3] but by the force of the context of the will[4] or the circumstances of the case[5] the description may be extended to include persons related only by affinity,[6] or in the same or a different degree of distance in relationship.[7] The mere fact that in a prior part of the will a person is described as a relative does not alone admit to a share in a subsequent gift to relatives of that degree either the named person,[8] or other persons of like degree with him;[9] but this fact is an indication in that direction,[10] to be taken into consideration along with the context of the whole will and the circumstances of the case admissible in evidence.[11]

1 *Grieves v Rawley* (1852) 10 Hare 63 ('niece'); *Re Hammersley, Kitchen v Myers* (1886) 2 TLR 459 ('all nephews and nieces'); *Re Cozens, Miles v Wilson* [1903] 1 Ch 138 ('my own nephews and nieces'); *Ward v Van der Loeff* [1924] AC 653 ('my brothers and sisters' not confined to those existing at the date of the will or to those of the whole blood); *Re Stark* [1969] 2 OR 881. But who are included is dependent on the will and the circumstances of the case: *Re Cozens, Miles v Wilson* [1903] 1 Ch 138; *Re Dowson, Dowson v Beadle* (1909) 101 LT 671 ('my own brothers and sisters' excluded the half-blood); *Re Reed* (1888) 57 LJ Ch 790 (the context must be overruling to exclude the half-blood); *Norris v Norris* (1839) 2 D 220; *Lynneberg v Kildahl* [1948] NZLR 207 (use of 'aunt' in singular where there was one aunt of the whole blood and two aunts of the half-blood excluded the half-blood).
2 *Hibbert v Hibbert* (1873) LR 15 Eq 372; *Hussey v Berkeley* (1763) 2 Eden 194 (widow of grandson is not a grandchild); *Smith v Lidiard* (1857) 3 K & J 252 (nieces of the late husband of the testatrix); *Merrill v Morton* (1881) 17 Ch D 382 (nieces by affinity excluded).
3 See *Re Cozens, Miles v Wilson* [1903] 1 Ch 138, where the decisions in *Seale-Hayne v Jodrell* [1891] AC 304; *Smith v Lidiard* (1857) 3 K & J 252; *Wells v Wells* (1874) LR 18 Eq 504, and *Merrill v Morton* (1881) 17 Ch D 382, are considered.
4 See *Seale-Hayne v Jodrell* [1891] AC 304.
5 See *Re Cozens, Miles v Wilson* [1903] 1 Ch 138, and as to *falsa demonstratio*, see Chapter 58.
6 *Frogley v Phillips* (1861) 3 De GF & J 466; *Re Gue, Smith v Gue* (1892) 61 LJ Ch 510. In order to save the gift from failing altogether where the testator has no blood relations of the kind described and none can come into existence, relatives by affinity, ie by marriage, may take: *Hogg v Cook* (1863) 32 Beav 641; *Adney v Greatrex* (1869) 38 LJ Ch 414; *Sherratt v Mountford* (1873) 8 Ch App 928. Where it is shown that the testator has treated a relative by affinity as his own relative, and did not know of the existence of the blood relation, the relative by affinity may take: *Grant v Grant* (1870) LR 5 CP 380, on appeal LR 5 CP 727. 'Cousin' has been held to include the wife of a cousin: *Re Taylor, Cloak v Hammond* (1886) 34 Ch D 255.
7 See, as to extended meaning of cousins, para **[71.4]** infra; and see, as to 'nieces', para **[71.5]** infra.
8 Where a husband's niece is described as 'my niece A' she does not necessarily take under a subsequent gift to 'my nephews and nieces'; *Smith v Lidiard* (1857) 3 K & J 252; *Wells v Wells*

(1874) LR 18 Eq 504; *Merrill v Morton* (1881) 17 Ch D 382. These cases were criticised in *Re Gue, Smith v Gue* (1892) 61 LJ Ch 510, and in *Re Cozens, Miles v Wilson* [1903] 1 Ch 138, but followed in *Re Green, Bath v Cannon* [1914] 1 Ch 134; see also *Re Tylor, Barclays Bank Ltd v Norris* (1968) 112 Sol Jo 486. Where a grand-nephew is described as my 'nephew A', he does not necessarily take under a gift to 'all my nephews and nieces': *Thompson v Robinson* (1859) 27 Beav 486; *Re Blower's Trusts* (1871) 6 Ch App 351.

9   *Re Winn, Burgess v Winn* (1916) 86 LJ Ch 124 (wife's niece called 'my niece' did not make her included in residuary gift to 'all my nephews and nieces'); *Re Ridge, Hancock v Dutton* (1933) 149 LT 266 (grand-nephew called nephew did not take grand-nephews share in a gift to nephews).

10   *Hussey v Berkeley* (1763) 2 Eden 194 (great granddaughter described as 'my granddaughter'); *James v Smith* (1844) 14 Sim 214 ('my niece M daughter of my nephew T' admitted to share in gift to 'my nephews and nieces').

11   *Re Cozens, Miles v Wilson* [1903] 1 Ch 138.

[71.2]
Children. This description is considered separately.[1]

1   See Chapter 74.

[71.3]
Grandchildren. Where there are persons who satisfy the description taken in its ordinary sense, and there is nothing in the will or the circumstances to give any other sense to the word,[1] 'grandchildren' does not include great-grandchildren.[2] Grandchildren of any degree will include descendants of any degree other than children.[3] The widow of a grandson is not included in the description 'granddaughter'.[4] The description 'children' may include grandchildren.[5] In a gift to grandchildren where the testator has only one child and he is illegitimate, the legitimate children of that child take.[6] Illegitimacy in connection with grandchildren is considered elsewhere.[7]

1   For case where the will showed a contrary intention and children of a step-child were included, see *Re Davidson, National Provincial Bank Ltd v Davidson* [1949] 2 All ER 551, but an adopted child of a child of the testator has been held not to be grandchild: *Re Boyington* (1953) 8 WWRNS 206. Where in a woman's will there is a gift to grandchildren and she has none and cannot have children of her own ,the gift is to grandchildren of her husband by a former wife: *Re Harmer* (1964) 42 DLR (2d) 321. A gift to my living grandchildren has been held to mean grandchildren living at the date of distribution; *Re Duckworth* [1958] OWN 236.
2   *Earl of Orford v Churchill* (1814) 3 Ves & B 59. It was said in *Hussey v Berkeley* (1763) 2 Eden 194, that great-grandchildren were included unless the intention was to the contrary.
3   *Re Hall, Hall v Hall* [1932] 1 Ch 262.
4   *Hussey v Berkeley* (1763) 2 Eden 194.
5   See Chapter 74.
6   *Cocker v Dingey* [1963] Tas SR (NC) 20.
7   See Chapter 72.

[71.4]
Cousins. In general, 'cousins' include only first cousins,[1] and 'first cousins or cousins german' does not include the descendants of first cousins;[2] 'second cousins' does not include first cousins once removed, that is, children of first cousins or a fortiori grandchildren of first cousins[3] and 'half cousins' includes first cousins once removed and second cousins;[4] 'first and second cousins' has in various contexts been held to include first cousins once or twice removed, and other relations not more remote than second cousins,[5] and 'second cousins' has been held to include first cousins once or twice removed where no true second cousins existed.[6]

1   *Stoddart v Nelson* (1855) 6 De GM & G 68. *Stevenson v Abington* (1862) 31 Beav 305; *Burbey v Burbey* (1862) 6 LT 573; *Copland's Executors v Milne* 1908 SC 426; *Re Powell* [1956] OR 522.
2   *Sanderson v Bayley* (1838) 4 My & Cr 56.
3   *Bridgnorth Corpn v Collins* [1847] 15 Sim 538; *Re Parker, Bentham v Wilson* (1881) 17 Ch D 262.
4   *Re Chester, Servant v Hills* [1914] 2 Ch 580.
5   *Mayott v Mayott* (1786) 2 Bro CC 125 (great-niece included); *Silcox v Bell* (1823) 1 Sim & St 301; *Charge v Goodyer* (1826) 3 Russ 140; *Wilks v Bannister* (1885) 30 Ch D 512; *Re Colahan, Molloy v Hara* [1967] IR 29.
6   *Re Bonner, Tucker v Good* (1881) 19 Ch D 201; *Slade v Fooks* (1838) 9 Sim 386; *Bennett v Marshall* (1856) 2 K & J 740; *Drylie's Factor v Robertson etc* (1882) 9 R 1178.

[71.5]
Nephews and nieces. The description 'nephews and nieces' does not include great-nephews or great-nieces,[1] nor will it include grandchildren,[2] but extrinsic evidence may be admissible to show what relation was intended.[3] 'Niece' has been held to mean 'nephew';[4] and a gift to 'my niece A', who was dead, has been held to go to a great-great-niece of a similar name.[5] 'Nephews and nieces' has also been held to include the widower of a niece, the niece of a husband of the testatrix but not the husband of a niece of the husband of the testatrix.[6] A gift to 'all nephews and nieces of my late sister' has been construed as 'all nephews and nieces children of my late sister'.[7] A gift of a business to brothers and nephews was not confined to brothers and nephews associated with the testator in the business.[8] A gift to grand-nieces and grand-nephews will not be construed as a gift to nieces and nephews,[9] but where a list of names were said to be nephews and nieces and some were grand-nephews and grand-nieces, the named persons took.[10] A gift to testator's nephews and nieces where the testator had no natural nephews and nieces has been held to include his sister's step-daughter.[11]

Legacies given to grand-nephews and grand-nieces as a class vest at the testator's death and no one born thereafter (unless *en ventre sa mère*) can take.[12]

1   *Falkner v Butler* (1765) Amb 514; *Williamson v Moore* (1862) 8 Jur NS 875; *Weeds v Bristow* (1866) LR 2 Eq 333; *Re Blower's Trusts* (1871) 6 Ch App 351; *Shelley v Bryer* (1821) Jac 207; *Crook v Whitley* (1857) 7 De GM & G 490; *Re Dall* [1918] NZLR 755; *Re Ridge, Hancock v Dutton* (1933) 149 LT 266; *Re Waines' Estate* [1947] 2 DLR 746.
2   *Campbell v Bouskell* (1859) 27 Beav 325; *McHugh v McHugh* [1908] 1 IR 155 where the evidence showed that the real nephews and nieces were not the donees, but there was nothing to show who were).
3   *James v Smith* (1844) 14 Sim 214 (great-nephews and nieces included); *Re Ray, Cant v Johnstone* [1916] 1 Ch 461; *Re Stark* (1970) 7 DLR (3d) 313 (nephews and nieces of the half blood included). For a gift to 'male nephews', see *Lucas v Cuday* (1876) IR 10 Eq 514.
4   *Re Rickit's Trusts* (1853) 11 Hare 299.
5   *Stringer v Gardiner* (1859) 4 De G & J 468.
6   *Re Daoust, Dobell v Dobell* [1944] 1 All ER 443; but see *Re Tylor, Barclays Bank Ltd v Norris* (1968) 112 Sol Jo 486.
7   *Re Birkin* [1949] 1 All ER 1045.
8   *Re Gartside* [1956] VLR 15.
9   *Re Hurring* [1950] NZLR 948.
10   *Re Dickson* (1965) 49 DLR (2d) 289.
11   *CIBC Trust Corporation v Peebles* (1999) 180 DLR (4th) 720.
12   *Re MacEwen* [1963] 2 OR 490.

CHAPTER 72

Illegitimacy of donees

[72.1]

Introduction. The position with regard to the entitlement of illegitimate donees has been affected by the Family Law Reform Act 1969 (FLRA 1969),[1] in respect of dispositions made on or after 1 January 1970[2] and by the Family Law Reform Act 1987 (FLRA 1987), with effect from 4 April 1988.[3] It is necessary to consider the position, first, with reference to the traditional common law rules which apply to the construction of gifts in dispositions made before 1 January 1970 and to dispositions made after that date which manifest an intention to exclude the 1969 Act provisions; second, with reference to the position under the FLRA 1969, which continues to apply to wills made between 1 January 1970 and 4 April 1988, even though the testator dies after the latter date. Third, wills made after 4 April 1988 will be governed by the FLRA 1987. For this purpose it is provided that a will or codicil executed before that date is not to be treated for the purposes of the FLRA 1987, as made on or after that date by reason only that the will or codicil is confirmed by a codicil executed on or after that date.

1   FLRA 1969, s 15. See Vol 2, Part G, para **[245.39]**.
2   Notwithstanding any rule of law, a disposition made by will or codicil executed before this date shall not be treated for the purposes of the section as made on or after that date by reason only that the will or codicil is confirmed by a codicil executed on or after that date; FLRA 1969, s 15(8).
3   Again a will executed before that date is not to be treated as made after that date by reason of a codicil.

I.   THE TRADITIONAL COMMON LAW RULES

[72.2]

Legitimate relations only included. A reference to relationship to the testator or to any other person (as in the case of gifts to children, issue, and the like) is presumed to refer only to legitimate and not to illegitimate relatives.[1]

The rule applies to all descriptions of donees, including the children,[2] nephews,[3] nieces,[4] cousins,[5] or relations generally[6] of the person concerned. This meaning is adhered to and no mere conjecture, however probable, based on the testator's knowledge of or intimacy with the illegitimate relations can exclude the rule,[7] and the illegitimate relatives do not satisfy the description,[8] unless either from the circumstances[9] it is impossible that any legitimate relative can satisfy it,[10] or an intention to include illegitimate relatives appears in the will.[11] Where there are no legitimate children in existence, the testator must in the circumstances be presumed to have contemplated the illegitimate relatives as satisfying the description and being able to take under an immediate gift[12] but there is no such inference where, although no legitimate children were in existence at the date of the will, the testator may have contemplated future children coming into existence who might be legitimate and might satisfy the description in the gift.[13] The impossibility of legitimate children coming into existence where a woman is past child-bearing or a testator of his own knowledge knows that he is incapable of having any more children may be sufficient to include the illegitimate children in the case of an immediate gift.[14] Where in a gift the testator uses a plural word, such as children, when to his knowledge there is only one person who could properly take under the gift, an illegitimate child may be included to make the description sensible.[15] The use of the plural word, however, is not sufficient to include illegitimate persons if there are legitimate persons sufficient to satisfy the description in its ordinary sense, and there are no other indications of an intention to include illegitimate persons,[16] or, if, supposing them to be included, the description would still remain unsatisfied.[17] If the property is divided into a number of shares corresponding to the total number of legitimate and illegitimate children, that may be a sufficient indication that illegitimate claimants are to be included.[18] A gift by an unmarried person to his or her own children must take effect in favour of illegitimate children.[19] There is no rule that illegitimate children cannot in any circumstances participate with legitimate children in the benefit of a gift to children generally.[20]

1   *Cartwright v Vawdry* (1800) 5 Ves 530; *Hill v Crook* (1873) LR 6 HL 265 at 283; *Dorin v Dorin* (1875) LR 7 HL 568; *Re Ayles' Trusts* (1875) 1 Ch D 282; *Ellis v Houston* (1878) 10 Ch D 236; *Re Eve, Edwards v Burns* [1909] 1 Ch 796; *Re Fish, Ingham v Rayner* [1894] 2 Ch 83; *Gentle's Trustees v Bunting* 1908 16 SLT 437; *Re Deakin, Starkey v Eyres* [1894] 3 Ch 565 (power to wife to appoint to her 'relations': wife in fact illegitimate to knowledge of testator: relations determined as if the wife had been legitimate); *Re Pearce, Alliance Assurance Co Ltd v Francis* [1914] 1 Ch 254 (if illegitimate relations are to be treated as legitimate they must be brought within one of the two classes laid down in *Hill v Crook* (1873) LR 6 HL 265, that is (i), there are no legitimate relatives to satisfy the description, or (ii) an intention to include illegitimate relatives appears in the will); *Re Nicholls* (1973) 32 DLR (3d) 683. As to capacity of illegitimate children to take under a will, see para **[9.24]** supra. As to inclusion of legitimated children, see para **[72.11]** infra.
2   *Swaine v Kennerley* (1813) 1 Ves & B 469; *Re Wells' Estate* (1868) LR 6 Eq 599; *Hill v Crook* (1873) LR 6 HL 265; *Dorin v Dorin* (1875) LR 7 HL 568; *Re Pearce, Alliance Assurance Co Ltd v Francis* [1914] 1 Ch 254; *Re Hall, Hall v Hall* [1932] 1 Ch 262 (it is a sound rule that in an English will the word 'lawful' must be presumed to exist before such words as 'children', 'grandchildren' and 'issue', and the illegitimate persons cannot be included in a gift otherwise than nominatim or by a description sufficient to identify them).
3   *Re Byron, Drummond v Leigh* (1885) 30 Ch D 110; *Re Hall, Branston v Weightman* (1887) 35 Ch D 551; *Re Jackson, Beattie v Murphy* [1933] Ch 237. *Re H Smith v Public Trustee* [1956] NZLR 48; *Scott Trustees v Smart* 1954 SC 12 (where the testator knows of the illegitimacy, it is to be expected that he will mention it).
4   *Re Fish, Ingham v Rayner* [1894] 2 Ch 83.
5   *Seale-Hayne v Jodrell* [1891] AC 304.
6   *Re Deakin, Starkey v Eyres* [1894] 3 Ch 565.
7   *Hill v Crook* (1873) LR 6 HL 265 at 276; *Re Pearce, Alliance Assurance Co Ltd v Francis* [1914] 1 Ch 254.
8   The rule applies to both direct gifts and to gifts over; *Smith v Jobson* (1888) 59 LT 397.
9   The circumstances at the date of the will are considered, and, if the intention is shown thereby that illegitimate children are included, the construction is not varied by subsequent events, such as the circumstances existing at the date of a confirmatory codicil: *Wilkinson v Adam* (1823) 12

Price 470; *Mortimer v West* (1827) 3 Russ 370. But ambiguity as to legitimate relatives may make extrinsic evidence admissible as to the family and as to the person intended: *Re Jackson, Beattie v Murphy* [1933] Ch 237.

10   *Hill v Crook* (1873) LR 6 HL 265 at 283.

11   *Hill v Crook* (1873) LR 6 HL 265; *Holt v Sindrey* (1868) LR 7 Eq 170, as explained in *Re Pearce, Alliance Assurance Co Ltd v Francis* [1913] 2 Ch 674 at 687; *Re Bleckly, Sidebotham v Bleckly* [1920] 1 Ch 450; *Re Hogbin Estate* [1950] 3 DLR 843; *Re Brand* (1957) 7 DLR (2d) 579; *Re Langley, Sissons v Public Trustee* [1972] NZLR 218.

12   *Beachcroft v Beachcroft* (1816) 1 Madd 430; *Woodhouselee v Dalrymple* (1817) 2 Mer 419 (children of deceased person); *Wilkinson v Adam* (1813) 1 Ves & B 422 at 468; *Dilley v Matthews* (1865) 12 LT 488; *Savage v Robertson* (1868) LR 7 Eq 176 (description of mother by maiden name); *Laker v Hordern* (1876) 1 Ch D 644; *Re Haseldine, Grange v Sturdy* (1886) 31 Ch D 511; *Re Frogley's Estate* [1905] P 137; *O'Loughlin v Bellew* [1906] 1 IR 487.

13   *Dorin v Dorin* (1875) LR 7 HL 568; *Re Brown, Penrose v Manning* (1890) 63 LT 159; *Re Dieppe, Millard v Dieppe* (1915) 138 LT Jo 564.

14   *Paul v Children* (1871) LR 12 Eq 16 (future gift to her child or children: existing illegitimate children not entitled); *Re Eve, Edwards v Burns* [1909] 1 Ch 796 (immediate gift: existing illegitimate children held entitled where no possibility of legitimate children: woman sixty-eight and a widow living with testatrix); *Re Brown, Penrose v Manning* (1890) 63 LT 159 (illegitimate children excluded though woman fifty years of age); *Re Wohlgemuth, Public Trustee v Wohlgemuth* [1949] Ch 12, [1948] 2 All ER 882 (man with illegitimate children only and incapable of having further children).

15   *Gill v Shelley* (1831) 2 Russ & M 336; *Leigh v Byron* (1853) 1 Sm & G 486; *Tugwell v Scott* (1857) 24 Beav 141; *Re Embury, Bowyer v Page (No 2)* (1914) 111 LT 275.

16   *Edmunds v Fessey* (1861) 29 Beav 233.

17   *Hart v Durand* (1796) 3 Anst 684.

18   *Cartwright v Vawdry* (1800) 5 Ves 530; *Re Wells' Estate* (1868) LR 6 Eq 599.

19   *Clifton v Goodbun* (1868) LR 6 Eq 278. An illegitimate child adopted out of the family has been excluded; *Re Searle's Estate* [1963] SASR 303.

20   *Owen v Bryant* (1852) 2 De GM & G 697; *Evans v Davies* (1849) 7 Hare 498; *Hill v Crook* (1873) LR 6 HL 265 at 283; *Ebbern v Fowler* [1909] 1 Ch 578; *Re Pearce, Alliance Assurance Co Ltd v Francis* [1914] 1 Ch 254 at 267.

[72.3]

Indications that illegitimate persons included. A common indication on the face of the will to include illegitimate relatives in a description is the fact that in other clauses of the will they, or other relatives of theirs, are referred to in terms showing that the testator treated the illegitimate claimants in question[1] as legitimate, particularly where it is shown that the testator knew of the illegitimacy, and therefore could not be using his language in its ordinary sense;[2] but this indication may be rebutted by a special and distinct provision for the illegitimate relatives, or other similar indications that the testator drew a distinction between them and the legitimate relatives.[3] It must be the actual claimants who are treated as legitimate, and it is not sufficient that there are indications of other illegitimate persons being treated as legitimate.[4] This fact may, indeed, be a ground for an inference against the claimant.[5] Examples of persons being treated as legitimate are where the parents are spoken of as husband and wife,[6] or the illegitimate person is mentioned as 'son', 'daughter' or 'child' of his or her natural parent, or is otherwise considered as having relatives (which strictly could not exist) in such a way as impliedly to include the illegitimate persons among the description in question.[7] Such indications have not been conclusive where there are other indications.[8] It seems that there is no definite rule of construction that the mere description of a person as a relative in a previous part of the will shows that that person is included in a general description of relatives in a latter part of the will, but that in all such cases the context of the will and the evidence property admissible (that is, evidence of the surrounding circumstances) must be considered.[9]

1   The testator must show by the will that he treats the actual claimants of the gift in question as legitimate and it is not sufficient that he treats other illegitimate persons as illegitimate: *Mortimer v West* (1827) 3 Russ 370; *Re Wells' Estate* (1868) LR 6 Eq 599. Indeed, this fact may raise an inference against the inclusion of the claimant: *Kelly v Hammond* (1858) 26 Beav 36 (where one illegitimate person was named and the other was included in a bequest to A and her daughters).

2   *Re Herbert's Trusts* (1860) 1 John & H 121 at 124; *Hill v Crook* (1873) LR 6 HL 265; *Re Horner, Eagleton v Horner* (1887) 37 Ch D 695; *Re Cullum, Mercer v Flood* [1924] 1 Ch 540 (ultimate limitation to 'own right heirs': testatrix illegitimate but no evidence that she knew of her illegitimacy); *Re Taylor, Hockley v O'Neal* [1925] Ch 739 (ignorance of illegitimacy). Knowledge of illegitimacy is immaterial where the words of description are sensible in their ordinary sense: *Godfrey v Davis* (1901) 6 Ves 43; *Warner v Warner* (1850) 20 LJ Ch 273. The testator's ignorance of the illegitimacy and belief that the parents were married may in a case where there are legitimate issue negative the inference that the children of such parents were to take: *Re Pearce, Alliance Assurance Co Ltd v Francis* [1914] 1 Ch 254.

3   *Megson v Hindle* (1880) 15 Ch D 198; *Re Hall, Branston v Weightman* (1887) 35 Ch D 551 at 557; *Gill v Bagshaw* (1866) LR 2 Eq 746.

4   See n 1.

5   *Kelly v Hammond* (1858) 26 Beav 36.

6   *Lepine v Bean* (1870) LR 10 Eq 160; *Hill v Crook* (1873) LR 6 HL 265; *Perkins v Goodwin* [1877] WN 111; *Re Horner, Eagleton v Horner* (1887) 37 Ch D 695; *Re Lowe, Danily v Platt* (1892) 61 LJ Ch 415; *Re Harrison, Harrison v Higson* [1894] 1 Ch 561.

7   *Meredith v Farr* (1843) 2 Y & C Ch Cas 525 (children); *Worts v Cubitt* (1854) 19 Beav 421 (daughter); *Clifton v Goodbun* (1868) LR 6 Eq 278 (gift by unmarried woman to her children); *Savage v Robertson* (1868) LR 7 Eq 176 (similar case); *Re Humphries, Smith v Millidge* (1883) 24 Ch D 691 (daughter); *Re Bryon, Drummond v Leigh* (1885) 30 Ch D 110 ('daughter of my nephew'); *Re Hastie's Trusts* (1887) 35 Ch D 728 (children: recognition by testator of illicit connection with mother); *Seale-Hayne v Jodrell* [1891] AC 304 (illegitimate persons, previously described in will as 'cousins', held entitled to take under gift to 'relatives hereinbefore mentioned'); *Re Deakin, Starkey v Eyres* [1894] 3 Ch 565 (bequest to wife's 'relations': wife known by testator to be illegitimate); *Re Walker, Walker v Lutyens* [1897] 2 Ch 238 ('niece' and 'daughter'); *Re Plant, Griffith v Hill* (1898) 47 WR 183 ('children' wrongly believed by testatrix to have been legitimated); *Re Wood, Wood v Wood* [1902] 2 Ch 542 (legitimate and illegitimate children treated as a class); *Re Smilter, Bedford v Hughes* [1903] 1 Ch 198 (son of a nephew: earlier reference in will to the sons of such nephew expressly including illegitimate son); *Re Kiddle, Gent v Kiddle* (1905) 92 LT 724 ('my son'); *Re Corsellis, Freeborn v Napper* [1906] 2 Ch 316 (bequest to 'all my nephews and nieces' by son of parents who were never married); *Re Mitchell, Ballarat Trustees, Executors and Agency Co Ltd v National Trustees, Executors and Agency Co of Australasia Ltd* [1929] VLR 95 (child referred to as niece included in residuary gift to all children of brothers and sisters of the testator).

8   *Bagley v Mollard* (1830) 1 Russ & M 581; *Megson v Hindle* (1880) 15 Ch D 198; *Re Hall, Branston v Weightman* (1887) 35 Ch D 551; *Re Helliwell, Pickles v Helliwell* [1916] 2 Ch 580 (nephews and nieces and then children held to include legitimate descendants of testator's natural sister); *O v D* [1916] 1 IR 364 ('children' held to include illegitimate child described as 'my daughter' elsewhere in will).

9   *Re Jodrell, Jodrell v Seale* (1890) 44 Ch D 590; *Re Cozens, Miles v Wilson* [1903] 1 Ch 138; *Re Dicker, Crallan v Tomlinson* [1947] Ch 248, [1947] 1 All ER 317.

[72.4]

Gifts to illegitimate children of man. Where the gift is to the children of a man,[1] or children of a man by a certain woman,[2] and is such that in the circumstances existing illegitimate children are denoted, the gift is construed as referring to those who at the date of the will have acquired the reputation[3] of being the named man's children.

706

1   *Laker v Horden* (1876) 1 Ch D 644 at 650.
2   *Wilkinson v Adam* (1813) 1 Ves & B 422; affd (1823) 12 Price 470, but as to this case, see *Warner v Warner* (1850) 15 Jur 141 at 142.
3   Reputation in such cases does not mean mere rumour or gossip, but acknowledgment of the relationship either express or implied from conduct or living as a family: *Occleston v Fullalove* (1874) 9 Ch App 147 at 164.

[72.5]
Future gifts to illegitimate children. The rule of law forbidding gifts to future illegitimate children[1] may affect the way in which any such gift takes effect; and, in particular, in the case of a gift expressly or by implication to all the illegitimate children of a person as a class, the class is restricted to those in esse or *en ventre sa mère* at the testator's death.[2]

1   See para **[9.24]** supra.
2   *Holt v Sindrey* (1868) LR 7 Eq 170; *Hill v Crook* (1873) LR 6 HL 265 at 285, 286; *Ebbern v Fowler* [1909] 1 Ch 578 (a settlement case overruling *Re Shaw, Robinson v Shaw* [1894] 2 Ch 573).

[72.6]
Grandchildren. The same rules apply to grandchildren but illegitimate children of a legitimate child[1] and legitimate children of an illegitimate child[2] have been allowed to take.

1   *Re Couturier, Couturier v Shea* [1907] 1 Ch 470; *Public Trustee v Leslie* [1917] NZLR 841; *Kinnaird v Allen* (1898) 24 VLR 609.
2   *Allen v Webster* (1860) 2 Giff 177; *Re Kiddle, Gent v Kiddle* (1905) 92 LT 724.

[72.7]
Legitimacy is determined by law of domicile. The question of legitimacy is in all cases of this nature decided according to the law of the domicile of the person by reference to whom the relationship of the donees is described, whether the gift is a bequest of personalty,[1] a specific devise of real estate,[2] or a devise of land upon trust for sale and to apply the proceeds of sale as personalty.[3] Children of a polygamous marriage are legitimate if they are so by the law of the domicile.[4]

1   *Re Andros, Andros v Andros* (1883) 24 Ch D 637; *Re Bischoffsheim* [1948] Ch 79, [1947] 2 All ER 830.
2   *Re Grey's Trusts, Grey v Stamford* [1892] 3 Ch 88.
3   *Skottowe v Young* (1871) LR 11 Eq 474. In *Boyes v Bedale* (1863) 1 Hem & M 798, the law of testator's domicile was taken.
4   *Bamgbose v Daniel* [1955] AC 107, [1954] 3 All ER 263.

[72.8]
Presumption of legitimacy. Every child born during the subsistence of a marriage is prima facie legitimate and so is a child born within nine months of the death of a husband and if the wife has remarried such child is presumed to be the legitimate child of the deceased husband.[1] Where it was shown that the conception can be after the decree nisi but before decree absolute the presumption operates both as to the date of conception and the paternity of the father so that the child is a child of the marriage of the parties to the divorce proceedings.[2]

707

1   *Re Overbury, Sheppard v Matthews* [1955] Ch 122, [1954] 3 All ER 308.
2   *Knowles v Knowles* [1962] P 161, [1962] 1 All ER 659.

[72.9]
Voidable marriage. Where a decree of nullity in respect of a voidable marriage is granted any child who would have been the legitimate child of the parties to the marriage if it had been dissolved instead of being annulled at the date of the decree shall be deemed to be their legitimate child notwithstanding the annulment.[1] A child of a void marriage whenever born is treated as legitimate if at the time of intercourse or at the time of the marriage if later, both or either of the parties reasonably believed the marriage to be valid.[2]

1   Matrimonial Causes Act 1973, s 16; 27 *Halsbury's Statutes* (4th edn) 947; *Re Adams, Sursham v Farquharson* [1951] Ch 716, [1951] 1 All ER 1037. Where parties intended to submit to the Italian law, the marriage must conform to that law and, if it does not, it is void. Husband domiciled in Poland married during service with Polish forces in Italy: *Lazarewicz (otherwise Fadanelli) v Lazarewicz* [1962] P 171, [1962] 2 All ER 5.
2   Legitimacy Act 1976, s 1; see Vol 2, Part G, para **[245.44]**, and *Sheward v A-G* [1964] 2 All ER 324, [1964] 1 WLR 724.

II.   THE FAMILY LAW REFORM ACT 1969

[72.10]
Illegitimate children included. In any disposition[1] made on or after 1 January 1970 and before 4 April 1988, any express or implied reference to the child or children of any person shall (unless the contrary intention appears) be construed as (or as including) a reference to any illegitimate child of that person and any reference to a person or persons related in some other manner to another person shall (again unless the contrary appears) be construed as (or as including) a reference to anyone who would be so related if he, or some person through whom the relationship is deduced, had been born legitimate.[2] But this applies only where the reference in question is to a beneficiary under the disposition[3] or, for the purpose of designating a beneficiary, to someone else to or through whom that person is related. The construction of the word 'heir' or 'heirs' is unaffected.[4] Special provisions apply to property limited to devolve with a dignity or title of honour.[5] A post-1970 disposition in favour of illegitimate children not in being when the disposition is made is no longer in danger of being held void as contrary to public policy.[6]

1   Widely defined in the FLRA 1969, s 15(8). See Vol 2, Part G, para **[245.39]**.
2   FLRA 1969, s 15. See Vol 2, Part G, para **[245.39]**.
3   It seems therefore that a gift to 'my children' would include illegitimate children, but an appointment of 'my children as executors and trustees', would not.
4   FLRA 1969, s 15(2).
5   FLRA 1969, s 15(5).
6   FLRA 1969, s 15(7).

[72.11]
Legitimated and adopted children. The entitlement generally of legitimated children is noted in the following paragraph but one point must be mentioned here. The Legitimacy Act 1976 (LA 1976)[1] provides that where a disposition

depends on the date of birth of a child who was born illegitimate and who is legitimated (or, if deceased, is treated as legitimated), the general provision of the LA 1976 (which states that a legitimated child shall be deemed to have been born on the date of legitimation for the purposes of dispositions which depend on the date of birth of a child),[2] does not effect entitlement under the Family Law Reform Act 1969.[3] Likewise where a disposition depends on the date of birth of an adopted child who is legitimated (or, if deceased, is treated as legitimated).[4] These provisions cover, for example, the situation where a testator dies in 1976 bequeathing a legacy to his eldest grandchild living at a specified time. The testator's daughter has an illegitimate child in 1977 who is the first grandchild. His married son has a child in 1978 and subsequently the illegitimate child is legitimated. In such a case the daughter's child remains the eldest grandchild of the testator throughout.[5] Exactly similar provisions are contained in the Adoption Act 1976[6] so that notwithstanding the general provisions of the Act,[7] the subsequent adoption of an illegitimate child does not affect the child's entitlement under the Family Law Reform Act 1969, under a bequest depending on the date of birth of the child.[8]

1   LA 1976, s 6; see Vol 2, Part G, para **[245.49]**. The LA 1976 came into force on 22 August 1976. Deaths prior to that date were governed by the Legitimacy Act 1926; 1 *Halsbury's Statutes* (3rd edn) although the provisions of the Legitimacy Act 1976 were initially contained in the Children Act 1975, Sch 1; see Vol 2, Part G, para **[245.54]**, which came into force on 1 January 1976.
2   LA 1976, s 6(1).
3   LA 1976, s 5(4).
4   LA 1976, s 6(2).
5   LA 1976, s 6(3).
6   6 *Halsbury's Statutes* (4th edn) 211. The Adoption Act 1976 came into force on 1 January 1988 by the Children Act 1975 and the Adoption Act 1976 (Commencement No 2) Order 1987, SI 1987/1242.
7   Adoption Act 1976, s 42.
8   Adoption Act 1976, s 43.

[72.12]
Protective trusts. In any disposition made on or after 1 January 1970, the Trustee Act 1925, s 33[1] (which sets out the trusts which arise when income is directed to be held 'on protective trusts' for the benefit of any person) shall have effect as if (i) the reference to the children or more remote issue of the principal beneficiary included a reference to any illegitimate child of the principal beneficiary and to anyone who would rank as such issue if he, or some other person through whom he is descended from the principal beneficiary, had been legitimate, and (ii) the reference to the issue of the principal beneficiary included a reference to anyone who would rank as such issue if he or some other person through whom he is descended from the principal beneficiary, had been legitimate.[2]

1   Trustee Act 1925, s 33(3) has been amended by the Trustee Act 2000, Sch 2, para 22.
2   Trustee Act 1925, s 15(3).

[72.13]
Later codicil. These provisions only apply to dispositions made after the coming into force of the Trustee Act 1925, and it is expressly provided that the

rule that wills or codicils may be treated as having been made on the date of a confirmatory codicil is not to apply for this purpose.[1]

1   Trustee Act 1925, s 15(8).

III.   THE FAMILY LAW REFORM ACT 1987

[72.14]

The Family Law Reform Act 1987 (FLRA 1987) replaces the Family Law Reform Act 1969 (FLRA 1969), Part II, governing the property entitlement of illegitimate persons. The main provisions of the FLRA 1987 including all the provisions which relate to wills and intestacies came into force on 4 April 1988.[1]

The fundamental provision in the FLRA 1987, s 1 on which the Act is based, provides that, unless the contrary intention appears, in enactments and instruments made after 4 April 1988, references (however expressed) to any relationship between two persons shall be construed without regard to whether or not the father and mother of either of them, or the father and mother of any person through whom the relationship is deduced, have or had been married to each other at any time. Thus the terms 'legitimate' and 'illegitimate' should cease to be used as legal terms at all. This provision gives effect to the Law Commission's recommendations.[2] The special status of legitimated and adopted children is recognised and preserved by the FLRA 1987, s 1(3).

Provisions in wills or codicils which are made after 4 April 1988 which contain references to any relationship between two persons are to be construed in accordance with the fundamental principle set out above in the FLRA 1987, s 1: s 19(1).

This construction applies now to 'heirs' or to any expression which is used to create an entailed interest in real or personal property: FLRA 1987, s 19(2).[3]

Where property is limited to devolve along with a dignity or title of honour then the section does not operate to sever the property, or any interest in it, from the dignity or title: FLRA 1987, s 19(4).

It is to be noted that the Family Law Reform Act 1969, s 15 continues to apply to wills made between 1 January 1970 and 4 April 1988 even though the testator dies after the latter date. And it is provided that notwithstanding any rule of law, a disposition made by will or codicil executed before the date on which this section comes into force shall not be treated for the purposes of this section as made on or after that date by reason only that the will or codicil is confirmed by a codicil executed on or after that date: FLRA 1987, s 19(7).

The FLRA 1987, s 18 contains important provisions governing the entitlement of illegitimate persons to succeed on intestacy, and these are considered, post.[4]

Personal representatives formerly enjoyed a special protection by virtue of the FLRA 1969, s 17 regarding distributions which were made without notice of the entitlement of any illegitimate person but this provision now ceases to have effect: FLRA 1987, s 20. Accordingly, personal representatives will have to rely exclusively on the usual protection afforded by a notice under the Trustee Act 1925, s 27,[5] which is unaffected.

The entitlement to probate is governed by the FLRA 1987, s 21 as follows:

'For the purpose of determining the person or persons who would in accordance with probate rules be entitled to a grant of probate or administration in respect of the estate of a deceased person, the deceased shall be presumed, unless the contrary is shown, not to have been survived –

(i)   by any person related to him whose father and mother were not married to each other at the time of his birth; or

(ii)   by any person whose relationship with him is deduced through such a person as is mentioned in paragraph (i) above.'[6]

1   Family Law Reform Act 1987 (Commencement No 1) Order 1988 (SI 1988/425). For the text of the relevant provisions of the FLRA 1987, see Vol 2, Part G, para [245.69] et seq.
2   Law Com no 118, 1982 and Law Com no 157, 1986.
3   The FLRA 1987, s 19(2) has been slightly amended by the Trusts of Land and Appointment of Trustees Act 1996, s 25(1), Sch 3, para 25. Contrast the FLRA 1969, s 15(2), para [72.10] supra.
4   Chapter 104.
5   As amended by the Trusts of Land and Appointment of Trustees Act 1996, s 25(1), Sch 3, para 3(7).
6   As to the effect of this provision see *Practice Direction* [1988] 2 All ER 308, [1988] 1 WLR 610.
        It can be noted in this connection that new Non-Contentious Probate Rules 1987, came into force on 1 January 1988 (SI 1987/2024) replacing the previous 1954 Rules.

IV.   LEGITIMATION

[72.15]
Legitimation. Prior to 1927 English law did not allow legitimation by subsequent marriage except as a branch of private international law. The position was changed by the Legitimacy Act 1926 (LA 1926), s 3[1] which provided that a legitimated person and his spouse, children or issue were entitled to take any interest in the estate of an intestate dying after the date of legitimation or under any disposition inter vivos or by will coming into operation after the date of the legitimation. The LA 1926 has been repealed and the statutory provisions are consolidated in the Legitimacy Act 1976 (LA 1976).[2] The LA 1976 provides for three basic circumstances whereby a child can be legitimated. First, the child of a void marriage, whenever born, is treated as the legitimate child of his parents, if at the time of the act of intercourse, resulting in the birth (or at the time of the celebration of the marriage if later), both or either of the parties reasonably believed that the marriage was valid.[3] This provision has been amended as from 4 April 1988 by the Family Law Reform Act 1987 to include a reference to a child born as a result of artificial insemination.[4] Further it is now to be presumed that one of the parties to the void marriage reasonably believed at the time of the insemination resulting in the birth, or where there was no such insemination, the time of conception, or at the time of the celebration of the marriage, if later, that the marriage was valid.[5] Second, where the parents of an illegitimate person marry one another, the marriage shall, if the father of the illegitimate person is at the date of marriage domiciled in England and Wales, render that person, if living, legitimate from the date of the marriage.[6] Third, where the parents of an illegitimate person marry one another and the father of an illegitimate person is not at the time of the marriage domiciled in England and Wales but is domiciled in a country by the law of which the illegitimate person became legitimated by virtue of such subsequent marriage, that person, if living, shall in England and Wales be

recognised as having been so legitimated from the date of the marriage notwithstanding that, at the time of his birth, his father was domiciled in a country the law of which did not permit legitimisation by subsequent marriage.[7] Further, if an illegitimate person (or a person adopted by one of his natural parents) dies, or has died before 22 August 1976, and, after his death his parents marry or have married and the deceased would, if living, at the date of the marriage have become a legitimated person then his spouse, children or remoter issue are entitled under the LA 1976, as if he had been legitimated by virtue of the marriage.[8]

1   Vol 2, Part G, para **[245.8]**, as amended by Legitimacy Act 1959. For a discussion of the provision of this Act, see the 4th edn, pp 523, 524 of this work.
2   6 *Halsbury's Statutes* (4th edn) 202. The LA 1976 came into force on 22 August 1976. The provisions of the Act had previously, very largely been contained in the Children Act 1975, Sch 1; see Vol 2, Part G, para **[245.54]**.
3   LA 1976, s 1(1). Considered in *Re Spence, Spence-Dennis* [1990] Ch 197, [1989] 2 All ER 679; affd [1990] Ch 652, [1990] 2 All ER 827, CA. The relevant death occurred before the coming into force of the Family Law Reform Act 1987, which would now produce a different result. This section only applies where the father of the child was domiciled in England and Wales at the time of the birth or, if he died before the birth, was so domiciled immediately before his death, s 1(2).
4   FLRA 1987, s 28; 6 *Halsbury's Statutes* (4th edn) 358; Vol 2, Part G, para **[245.75]**.
5   LA 1976, s 76(4), added by the FLRA 1987.
6   Legitimacy Act 1976, s 2. An adopted child can be legitimated under this provision if either natural parent is the sole adoptive parent: LA 1976, s 4(1). See also s 4(2) of the LA 1976 for necessary consequential amendments to the adoption rules where an adopted child is legitimated.
7   Legitimacy Act 1976, s 3.
8   Legitimacy Act 1976, s 5(6).

[72.16]
Property rights of legitimated children. The provisions of the LA 1976 noted below apply to any instrument coming into force on or after 1 January 1976 so far as the instrument contains a disposition of property.[1] For this purpose provisions of the law of intestate succession are treated as if contained in an instrument executed by the deceased immediately before his death.[2] The fundamental provision is that a legitimated person is entitled to take any interest as if the legitimated person had been legitimate.[3] By virtue of this provision a legitimated child will thus take under intestacy or under a will providing for a class.

The LA 1976 provides for the situation where a disposition depends on the date of birth of a child, as where for example, the gift is to a class 'living' at a certain time. In such cases the LA 1976 provides that the disposition is to be construed as if the legitimated child had been born on the date of legitimation.[4] If two or more legitimated children were legitimated on the same date then they will be deemed to have been born on that date in the order of their actual births.[5] Thus if there is a gift to the children or grandchildren of a person 'living at my death',[6] or 'born within twenty-one years of my death', legitimated children will qualify or not depending not on their actual date of birth but on the date of legitimation.[7] Similar provisions would apply where the gift is a class gift to which the class closing rules apply.[8] When the first member of the class attains a vested interest and closes the class, the children then in existence will take, which in the case of legitimated children must mean those children then legitimated. Children then born and subsequently legitimated would not take.[9] However, as noted above these provisions affecting the construction of dispositions depending on the birth of a child[10] who was born illegitimate[11] and who is legitimated do not affect entitlement under the FLRA 1969, Part II.[12] The LA 1976 provisions will therefore usually govern dispositions to which the FLRA 1969 is inapplicable because of the date of the instrument, or the expression of a contrary intention.[13] The same point is relevant to a disposition to A for life 'until he has a child'[14] and then to his child or children. The LA 1976 provides that the child shall be deemed to have been born on the date of legitimation but, again, if the FLRA 1969 is applicable an illegitimate child would be entitled on birth.

These provisions attributing an artificial date of birth to a legitimated person apply only where the disposition depends on the date of birth of a child. They do not affect any reference to the age of the child.[15] Thus if a testator makes a gift to 'those children of A now born or born within five years of my death who attain 21' and one year after the testator's death a five-year old illegitimate child of A is legitimated, that child will be included in the class, but he will attain a vested interest in sixteen year's time, not 21 years. More difficult problems arise if the gift is to the 'youngest' or 'eldest' of a class. Thus if a testator makes a gift to 'the eldest of A's children now born or born within five years of my death who attain 21'. Assume that A has one ten-year old legitimate child at the date of the death and one year later legitimates a 16-year old illegitimate child.[16] If the FLRA 1969 is not applicable[17] the situation is not expressly covered by the LA 1976, but it is submitted that the better view is that the 16-year old child remains the 'eldest'.[18]

1 LA 1976, s 5(1). See also s 10(1) defining existing instruments and s 10(3) which has the effect that the Act applies to a will or codicil if the testator died on or after 1 January 1976, even if he made the will or codicil before that date.
2 LA 1976, s 5(2).
3 LA 1976, s 5(3).
4 LA 1976, s 5(4)(a).
5 LA 1976, s 5(4)(b).
6 LA 1976, s 5(5), example 1.
7 Likewise a gift to children of A 'living at my death or born afterwards before any one of such children for the time being in existence attains a vested interest, and who attains the age of 21 years', LA 1976, s 5(5), example 2.
8 See Chapter 66.
9 See Chapter 66.
10 LA 1976, s 5(4).
11 See para **[72.11]** supra,'Legitimated and adopted children'.
12 LA 1976, s 6(1).
13 See para **[72.11]** supra.
14 LA 1976, s 5(5), example 4.
15 LA 1976, s 5(4).
16 The example assumes that the FLRA 1969 has been excluded so that illegitimate children are not included in the class by the effect of that Act.
17 Ditto. If the FLRA 1969 applies, the situation is provided for by ss 6(1), 6(3) of the Legitimacy Act 1976, noted in para **[72.11]** supra.
18 This construction is supported by the example in s 6(3) of the LA 1976 and also it is suggested by the provision that two or more legitimated children legitimated on the same date are deemed to have been born on that date in the order of their actual births, s 5(4)(b). It is also suggested that 'eldest' and 'younger' situations could come within the exclusion in s 5(4) 'but this (ie the artificial date of birth) does not affect any reference to the age of the child'.

[72.17]

Protection of trustees and personal representatives. The LA 1976 provides that a trustee or personal representative is not under a duty, by virtue of the law relating to trusts or the administration of estates, to enquire, before conveying or distributing any property, whether any person could be legitimated (or if deceased be treated as legitimated), if that fact could affect entitlement to the property.[1] Similarly if a conveyance or distribution has been made without regard to a legitimation then a trustee or personal representative is not liable therefor unless he has received notice of the fact before the conveyance or distribution.[2]

1 LA 1976, s 7(1).
2 LA 1976, s 7(2). The section does not prejudice the right of a person to follow the property, or any property representing it, into the hands of another person, other than a purchaser, who has received it, s 7(3).

[72.18]

Human Fertilisation and Embryology Act 1990 (HFEA 1990). The HFEA 1990, ss 27–29 came into force on 1 August 1991 and make provision for who is treated as father and mother of a child produced by means (such as artificial insemination or in vitro fertilisation) regulated by the Act.[1]

1 HFEA 1990, ss 28–30. See fully discussed in Chapter 74.

CHAPTER 73

Persons *en ventre sa mère*

[73.1]

Treated as actually born. In certain cases persons *en ventre sa mère* are treated as actually born.[1] There may in the first place be a direct gift to a child *en ventre sa mère*.[2] It has been adopted as a rule of construction for giving effect to a presumed intention,[3] that, in a gift or condition referring to persons of a named relationship to the testator or other propositus who are born at or living at a particular time,[4] the description includes a person *en ventre sa mère* at that time provided he or she is afterwards born alive,[5] and would have come under the description if he had been actually born or living, provided that this construction is for the benefit of the unborn person,[6] and that there is no context in the will indicating a contrary intention.[7] The qualification 'born at' or 'living at' the particular time may be expressly made by the words of the will, or impliedly made under the rules for the ascertainment of the class; thus, the rule applies where the gift is to 'children' simply, where the class is ascertained during the gestation of the unborn person.[8] However the will may show or the circumstances may show that by the description in the will the testator meant to describe persons actually known to him[9] or that he had no thought of a child *en ventre sa mère* as the recipient of his bounty.[10] The rule is commonly stated with respect to gifts to children,[11] but it applies to other descriptions of relatives of the propositus,[12] and to descriptions of persons in conditions as well as in gifts.[13] In order to be capable of taking under this rule the person must be capable of having been legitimately begotten before the period of distribution.[14] The proviso that the rule is only applied where it is for the benefit of the unborn person admits of an exception in certain cases where there is a question of applying the rule against perpetuities.[15] Moreover, in the case of a limitation of real estate to a person and his children, where that person has a child *en ventre sa mère* but has no other child at the death of the testator, that child does not take concurrently with the parent,[16] and the usual rule of construction in similar cases where children are alive was not applied.[17]

---

1   *Elliot v Joicey* [1935] AC 209. The rule of construction is adopted in many cases other than the construction of wills: eg on intestacy, see Administration of Estates Act 1925, s 55(2); 17 *Halsbury's Statutes* (4th edn) 467; and in the rule against perpetuities. 'Within due time after my death' refers to the period of gestation: *Re Watson, Culme-Seymour v Brand* [1930] 2 Ch 344. The rule applies generally; see *Trustees, Executors and Agency Co Ltd v Sleeman* (1899) 25 VLR 187; *Aldwell v Aldwell* (1875) 21 Gr 627; *Murray's Trustee v Murray* 1919 SC 552; *Cox's Trustees v Cox* 1950 SC 117. See also *Re MacEwen* [1963] 2 OR 490 and *Wesley v Wesley* (1998) 71 SASR 1.

2   *Marsh v Kirby* (1634) 1 Rep Ch 76; *Burdet v Hopegood* (1718) 1 P Wms 486 (gift over if no
    son did not take effect on account of birth of a posthumous son); *Mogg v Mogg* (1815) 1 Mer
    654; *Blackburn v Stables* (1814) 2 Ves & B 367.
3   *Clarke v Blake* (1788) 2 Bro CC 319; *Trower v Butts* (1823) 1 Sim & St 181 at 184.
4   The instant the child is born he is considered by retrospect as born during the parent's lifetime:
    Doe d Lancashire v Lancashire (1792) 5 Term Rep 49; *Cox's Trustees v Cox* 1950 SC 117.
5   See *Re Wilmer's Trusts, Moore v Wingfield* [1903] 1 Ch 874 at 879 (the principle that a child *en
    ventre sa mère* is a life in being is of general application and is not restricted to cases where it is
    to the advantage of, or immaterial to, the infant to apply it), and in *Doe d Clarke v Clarke*
    (1795) 2 Hy Bl 399, Eyre CJ said that such a child was living independently of intention. This
    was followed in *Re Burrows, Cleghorn v Burrows* [1895] 2 Ch 497. But this was not the general
    opinion: see *Trower v Butts* (1823) 1 Sim & St 181 (not because it can be considered as living
    but because the potential existence of such a child places it plainly within the reason and motive
    of the gift); and this was approved in *Elliot v Joicey* [1935] AC 209, where *Re Burrows,
    Cleghorn v Burrows* [1895] 2 Ch 497 was overruled.
6   *Villar v Gilbey* [1907] AC 139 (there is no fixed rule which compels a court to hold that a child
    was born in the lifetime of the testator because it was at that time *en ventre sa mère*. That
    peculiar rule is limited to cases where that construction of the word 'born' is necessary for the
    benefit of the child. Rule not applied to a condition cutting down the interest of a tenant in tail
    to a life estate); *Pearce v Carrington* (1873) 8 Ch App 969 (where the benefit was that the
    divesting of the unborn person's interest under another clause was prevented); *Blasson v
    Blasson* (1864) 2 De GJ & Sm 665 (rule applies only for the purpose of enabling the unborn
    child to take a benefit which, if born, it would be entitled to). The rule is not applied where the
    result is to benefit the parent's interest and not that of the child directly: *Elliot v Joicey* [1935]
    AC 209. See also *Re Brown, Brown v Brown* [1933] NZLR 115.
7   The subject is fully considered in the opinion of Lord Russell of Killowen in *Elliot v Joicey*
    [1935] AC 209. Subject to any special context in the document to be construed words referring
    to children or issue 'born' before or 'living' at or 'surviving' a particular point of time or event
    will not in their ordinary or natural meaning include a child *en ventre sa mère* at the relevant
    date. The ordinary or natural meaning may be departed from, and a fictional construction
    applied to them so as to include therein a child *en ventre sa mère* at the relevant date and
    subsequently born alive if, but only if, that fictional construction will secure to the child a
    benefit to which it would have been entitled if it had been actually born at the relevant date. The
    only justification for applying such a fictional construction is that where a person makes a gift
    to a class of children or issue described as 'born' before or 'living' at or 'surviving' a particular
    point of time or event, a child *en ventre sa mère* must necessarily be within the reason and
    motive of the gift. That being the only justification for applying the fictional construction, it
    follows that, if the person who uses the words under consideration confers no gift on the
    children or issue, but confers the gift on someone else, it is impossible (except in the light of
    subsequent events) to affirm either that the fictional construction will secure to the child *en
    ventre sa mère* a benefit to which, if born, it would be entitled, or that child *en ventre sa mère*
    must necessarily be within the reason and motive of the gift made. In these circumstances the
    words used must bear their ordinary or natural meaning: *Elliot v Joicey* [1935] AC 209. The
    rule is also applied in Scotland: *Elliot v Joicey* [1935] AC 209, but that case was distinguished
    in *Johnstone's Trustees v Johnstone* 1936 SC 706.
8   *Northey v Strange* (1716) 1 P Wms 340; *Storrs v Benbow* (1833) 2 My & K 46, further
    proceedings reported in (1853) 3 De GM & G 390 (gift 'to each child that may be born' to
    certain persons); *Mogg v Mogg* (1815) 1 Mer 654; *Re Hallett, Hallett v Hallett* [1892] WN 148.
9   *Millar v Turner* (1748) 1 Ves Sen 85.
10 *Roper v Roper* (1867) LR 3 CP 32 at 35; *Re Emery's Estate, Jones v Emery* (1876) 3 Ch D 300.
11 *Hale v Hale* (1692) Prec Ch 50; *Clarke v Blake* (1788) 2 Bro CC 319; *Doe d Clarke v Clarke*
    (1795) 2 Hy Bl 399; *Rawlins v Rawlins* (1796) 2 Cox Eq Cas 425; *Whitelock v Heddon* (1798) 1
    Bos & P 243 ('to any son ... begotten and born' at certain time); *Trower v Butts* (1823) 1 Sim &
    St 181; *Re Salaman, De Pass v Sonnenthal* [1908] 1 Ch 4.
12 *Storrs v Benbow* (1853) 3 De GM & G 390; *Re Salaman, De Pass v Sonnenthal*, supra; *Re
    Hallett, Hallett v Hallett*, supra.
13 *Gibson v Gibson* (1698) 2 Eq Cas Abr 184 (bond for sum to be paid in case the obligor should
    have no son living at his decease); *Burdet v Hopegood* (1718) 1 P Wms 486 (devise in case
    testator had no son at the time of his death); *Pearce v Carrington* (1873) 8 Ch App 969 (if
    daughter living five years after death of wife and should not then have had any child or

children). In *Villar v Gilbey* [1907] AC 139, also a case of condition (any third or other son born in testator's lifetime), the rule was excluded on the ground of want of benefit.

14   *Re Corlass* (1875) 1 Ch D 460, cited in para **[73.1]**, n 4.
15   The perpetuity period is a life in being and twenty-one years thereafter with the addition, where gestation actually exists, of a period or periods of gestation: *Cadell v Palmer* (1833) 1 Cl & Fin 372, and this is so whether or not it is for the benefit of the unborn child: *Re Wilmer's Trusts, Moore v Wingfield* [1903] 1 Ch 874 at 888, and, on appeal [1903] 2 Ch 411 at 421, CA.
16   *Roper v Roper* (1867) LR 3 CP 32.
17   That was the rule in *Wild's Case* (1599) 6 Co Rep 16b, which has practically ceased to be operative now that entailed interests can be created only by the same words as in a deed: Law of Property Act 1925, s 130(1); 37 *Halsbury's Statutes* (4th edn) 288; see Chapter 85.

[73.2]

Wills Act 1837, s 33. It is now expressly provided[1] that, for the purposes of the Wills Act 1837, s 33 in respect of deaths on or after 1 January 1983,[2] a person conceived before the testator's death and born living thereafter is to be taken to have been living at the testator's death.[3] Such persons had been held to be excluded under the original wording of the section.[4]

1   Administration of Justice Act 1982 (AJA 1982), s 19, substituting a new s 33 for the original in the Wills Act 1837; 50 *Halsbury's Statutes* (4th edn) 599; Vol 2, Part G, para **[244.95]**; see Chapter 47, para **[47.10]** et seq.
2   AJA 1982, s 73(6); s 76(11).
3   New Wills Act 1837, s 33(4), as substituted by the AJA 1982, s 19.
4   *Elliot v Joicey* [1935] AC 209; to the contrary, *Re Griffiths' Settlement, Griffiths v Waghorne* [1911] 1 Ch 246.

CHAPTER 74

Gifts to children

[74.1]
'Children'. The description 'children' of a named person[1] in its ordinary sense[2] refers to the first generation only of legitimate[3] descendants, by any marriage,[4] and does not include any grandchildren[5] or remoter descendants;[6] but it may be extended by the context and the circumstances of the case admissible in evidence[7] to such other generations of descendants,[8] to the whole line capable of inheriting from the named person[9] or to step-children,[10] or adopted children.[11] In the case of dispositions made on or after 1 January 1970, illegitimate children are prima facie included, but are prima facie excluded in dispositions made before that date.[12] Children by any marriage[13] are included even though a second marriage is not in the contemplation of the testator,[14] and a reference to a present or future husband has been held not to exclude a deceased husband's children;[15] but children of a prior marriage may be excluded by the context,[16] or by words inconsistent with their inclusion.[17] 'Children' may include grandchildren where the context shows that the testator has used the word in an extended sense[18] or where the circumstances admissible in evidence give rise to a similar inference, for example, in a case of a legacy to the children of a deceased person where at the date of the will there are to the knowledge of the testator, no children, but only grandchildren, alive,[19] but there is no fixed rule that where a legacy is given to 'children' of a person known by the testator to be dead at the date of the will and to have no child then living, grandchildren will take.[20] It seems that the meaning grandchildren cannot be given where the parent of the children is alive[21] or where the context draws a distinction between children and grandchildren,[22] and there is more difficulty where there is a gift to the children of several persons, some of whom have children and some grandchildren only.[23] If the meaning extends children, it seems that great-grandchildren are also included.[24]

---

1   The time of ascertainment of a class of children is considered in Chapter 66, ante. 'Children' will at least include all children born before the death of the testator: *Goodwyn v Goodwyn* (1748) 1 Ves Sen 226; *Re Garnock, Garnock v Garnock* (1909) 10 SRNSW 51; *Re Charlton Estate* [1919] 1 WWR 134; *Re Chapman, Charley v Lewis* (1922) 56 ILT 32.
2   *Re Kirk, Nicholson v Kirk* (1885) 52 LT 346; *McPhail v McIntosh* (1887) 14 OR 312. It will be remembered that words must in the first instance be given their ordinary meaning: see Chapter 50, para **[50.5]** et seq; and see *Re Smiley* (1908) 28 NZLR 1 ('children' includes everyone who in the ordinary course would be included in that term). 'Remaining children' means children not otherwise dealt with: it does not mean surviving children unless there is a context to justify the meaning: *Re Speak, Speak v Speak* (1912) 56 Sol Jo 273.
3   See Chapter 72. As to legitimated childen, see Chapter 72. As to adopted children see Chapter 75.

4   See nn 14–17.

5   See nn 18–24.

6   *Re Kirk, Nicholson v Kirk* (1885) 52 LT 346, but see nn 18, 20, for cases where this rule has been departed from.

7   See Chapter 57, as to admissible evidence.

8   See para **[74.8]** infra.

9   For direct gift, see *Bowen v Lewis* (1884) 9 App Cas 890 (a gift to A and his children construed as an estate tail); for a gift over, see *Doe d Smith v Webber* (1818) 1 B & Ald 713 (gift to A and her heirs with gift over on death without children); *Re Synge's Trusts* (1854) 3 I Ch R 379. There is no definite rule that in a gift over on death without leaving children, children must be construed 'issue'. It is always a question of context and construction: *Re Milward's Estate, ex p Midland Rly Co* [1940] Ch 698. As to 'children' as a word of limitation and as to limitations to a person and his children, see Chapter 85.

10 *Re Jeans, Upton v Jeans* (1895) 72 LT 835, where it was shown that the testator, who had no children of his own, was accustomed to refer to his stepchildren by the word 'children'; *Re Connolly* [1935] 2 DLR 465 (not included); *Re Jamieson Estate* (1959) 29 WWR 650 (included), likewise in *Re Ahchay* (1997) 6 Tas R 369.

11 See Chapter 75. In *Barnes Estate v Wilson* (1992) 91 DLR (4th) 22 a child adopted after testator's death held entitled as 'grandchild' under postponed gift.

12 Family Law Reform Act 1969, s 15. See Vol 2, Part G, para **[245.39]**. See para **[72.10]** supra.

13 Children of a polygamous marriage are legitimate if they are so by the law of their domicile: *Bamgbose v Daniel* [1955] AC 107, [1954] 3 All ER 263.

14 *Braithwaite v Braithwate* (1685) 1 Vern 334; *Champion v Pickax* (1737) 1 Atk 472; *Barrington v Tristram* (1801) 6 Ves 345 (subsequent marriage); *Ex p Earl of Ilchester* (1803) 7 Ves 348; *Critchett v Taynton* (1830) 1 Russ & M 541; *Nash v Allen* (1889) 42 Ch D 54 at 59 ('respective marriages'); *Whittet's Trustees v Whittet* (1892) 19 R 975; *Buchan v Porteous* (1879) 7 R 211 (former marriage); *Re Lewis's Will Trusts, Phillips v Bowkett* [1937] 1 All ER 556 (child of a former marriage excluded). In a case where both husband and wife had children by former marriages and there was a gift to 'our children', it was held that all the children of all marriages took: *Re Zehr* [1944] 2 DLR 670.

15 *Pasmore v Huggins* (1855) 21 Beav 103 (a woman with husband at the date of the will and fund given to her children 'by her then present or any future husband'; children by former husband not excluded); *Re Pickup's Trusts* (1861) 1 John & H 389 (similar case); *Re Potter's Will Trusts, Re Thomson's Settlement Trusts, Eckford v Thomson* [1944] Ch 70, [1943] 2 All ER 805 (fund to be settled on daughter and 'any children she might have' includes children of all marriages).

16 Where some of the children by a former marriage were specifically named and others omitted, the latter did not take: *Stavers v Barnard* (1843) 2 Y & C Ch Cas 539. In *Stopford v Chaworth* (1845) 8 Beav 331, a provision was made for a married daughter and her then husband naming him and 'her' children, and it was held that children of her second marriage took nothing.

17 In *Lovejoy v Crafter* (1865) 35 Beav 149, children of a first marriage were excluded from a residuary gift where they had been specifically provided for in the earlier part of the will. In *Re Parrott, Walter v Parrott* (1886) 33 Ch D 274, the provision made by a father was in form at least a marriage settlement and confined to the husband of that particular marriage and his children. In *Re Baynham, Hart v Mackenzie* (1891) 7 TLR 587, a bequest to 'my wife' for life and then for 'our children' was confined to children of that marriage and, although there were none, children of an earlier marriage not let in. See also *Boyd v Martin* (1840) 2 Dr & Wal 355 ('our three children').

18 *Royle v Hamilton* (1799) 4 Ves 437; *Reeves v Brymer* (1799) 4 Ves 692 at 698 ('children may mean grandchildren where there can be no other construction, but not otherwise'); *Radcliffe v Buckley* (1804) 10 Ves 195 (only from necessity); *Thellusson v Woodford* (1829) 5 Russ 100 (privilege of residing in mansion house confined to sons though grandson presumptively entitled to share at the expiration of a period of accumulation); *Loring v Thomas* (1861) 1 Drew & Sm 497 at 508 (where it was a question of letting in a grandchild as an original donee and not as a substituted donee); *Re Crawhall's Trust* (1856) 8 De GM & G 480; *Re Blackman* (1852) 16 Beav 377 (where the beneficiaries were named); *Heinbigner v Heinbigner* (1972) 23 DLR (3d) 218 ('my children aforementioned').

19 *Re Smith, Lord v Hayward* (1887) 35 Ch D 558; *Fenn v Death* (1856) 23 Beav 73; *Pride v Fooks* (1858) 3 De G & J 252 at 275; *Berry v Berry* (1861) 3 Giff 134. But there is no fixed rule that in such circumstances the grandchildren will take: it is always a matter of construction: *Re Atkinson, Pybus v Boyd* [1918] 2 Ch 138.

20 *Re Atkinson, Pybus v Boyd* [1918] 2 Ch 138; *Re Moyle, Howie v Moyle* [1920] VLR 147.
21 The authority given for this is *Moor v Raisbeck* (1841) 12 Sim 123, but there the context was relied on.
22 *Loring v Thomas* (1861) 1 Drew & Sm 497 at 509.

23 *Radcliffe v Buckley* (1804) 10 Ves 195; *Re Smith, Lord v Hayward* (1887) 35 Ch D 558.
24 *Pride v Fooks* (1858) 3 De G & J 252 at 275–279, but see *Fenn v Death* (1856) 23 Beav 73, where great-grandchildren were excluded.

[74.2]

Children of A and B. A gift to 'the children of A and B', where A and B are two named persons, and have not, and are not capable of having children together,[1] has been held to mean grammatically a gift to B and to the children of A;[2] and prima facie the gift is construed accordingly. The context or surrounding circumstances may require a different construction;[3] and it has been said that the strict construction has been adopted only where it was in complete accordance with the context and the intention of the testator.[4] Where both classes of children exist, it may be that the gift is to the children of A and the children of B,[5] and the fact that either A or B had no children,[6] or that A was dead and B alive at the date of the will[7] or at the date contemplated by the gift,[8] or that A and B were relatives of the testator of the same degree,[9] or that there are special reasons for B personally being a beneficiary and not his children,[10] or that the dispositions of the will point to provision being made for the children of B,[11] may affect the construction of the gift.[12] The division will usually be between all the donees per capita.[13]

1 *Re Walbran, Milner v Walbran* [1906] 1 Ch 64 at 66. Where A and B are married and have children, the gift does not include the children of one of them by a former marriage: *Re Lewis's Will Trusts, Phillips v Bowkett* [1937] 1 All ER 556. For a gift to A and her children and to B and his children where A and B were husband and wife, see *Biggar, Biggar v Stinson* (1884) 8 OR 372.
2 *Peacock v Stockford* (1853) 3 De GM & G 73 at 78; *Hawes v Hawes* (1880) 14 Ch D 614; *Re Featherstone's Trusts* (1882) 22 Ch D 111; *Re Walbran, Milner v Walbran* [1906] 1 Ch 64; *Re Dale, Mayer v Wood* [1931] 1 Ch 357; *Re Cossentine, Philip v Wesleyan Methodist Local Preacher's Mutual Aid Association Trustees* [1933] Ch 119; *Re Birkett, Holland v Duncan* [1950] Ch 330, [1950] 1 All ER 316; *Re Durdin's Estate* [1957] SASR 199; *Canada Permanent Trust Co v Share* (1958) 25 WWR 638; *Re Sutton* [1952] NZLR 93, and see *Re Harper, Plowman v Harper* [1914] 1 Ch 70 at 73.
3 *Stummvoli v Hales* (1864) 34 Beav 124 at 126; *Re Walbran, Milner v Walbran* [1906] 1 Ch 64 at 66 (the facts about A and B must be ascertained).
4 *Re Dale, Mayer v Wood* [1931] 1 Ch 357 at 367.
5 *Mason v Baker* (1856) 2 K & J 567 (where A and B were given equal legacies in an earlier part of the will); *Re Davies' Will* (1860) 29 Beav 93; *Re Murray, Perpetual Trustees (Canberra) Ltd v Lathom* [1963] ALR 68; *Bruyn v Perpetual Trustee* (1974) 131 CLR 387.
6 *Stummvoli v Hales* (1864) 34 Beav 124.
7 *Lugar v Harman* (1786) 1 Cox Eq Cas 250 (where the omission of 'of' before the name of the living person was thought significant).
8 *Peacock v Stockford* (1853) 3 De GM & G 73 at 78.
9 *Re Walbran, Milner v Walbran* [1906] 1 Ch 64; *Re Prosser, Prosser v Griffith* [1929] WN 85.
10 *Re Harper, Plowman v Harper* [1914] 1 Ch 70 (gift to doctor in recognition of his kindness).
11 *Re Dale, Mayer v Wood* [1931] 1 Ch 357.
12 *Re Ingle's Trusts* (1871) LR 11 Eq 578 (reference in codicil to legacy to B).
13 *Mason v Baker* (1856) 2 K & J 567; *Re Davies' Will* (1860) 29 Beav 93; *Re Harper, Plowman v Harper* [1914] 1 Ch 70 (notwithstanding the word 'equally' is used); *Re Dale, Mayer v Wood* [1931] 1 Ch 357. In *Re Walbran, Milner v Walbran* [1906] 1 Ch 64, followed in *Re Prosser, Prosser v Griffith* [1929] WN 85, the division was into moieties, the persons taking each moiety

as joint tenants. In *Re Birkett, Holland v Duncan* [1950] Ch 330, [1950] 1 All ER 316, the division was in moieties because the testatrix was under some obligation to the adult legatee, having lived with her as a 'paying guest', and in *Re Hare* (1959) 61 DLR 774, the distribution was held to be stirpital because the court considered from the will as a whole that the testator intended to give more to the individual donee than to the children. Where there is no family relationship between the parties, the court leans against a stirpital distribution: *Re Hall, Parker v Knight* [1948] Ch 437. Affidavit evidence has been admitted to show testator's real intention in such circumstances: *Canada Permanent Trust Co v Share* (1958) 25 WWR 638.

[74.3]
Child born as a result of fertilisation techniques. The Human Fertilisation and Embryology Act 1990 (HFEA 1990) contains provisions identifying the persons who are to be treated as the mother and the father of a child born as a result of *in vitro* fertilisation or artificial insemination and governing the status of any such child. The HFEA 1990 also contains consequential provisions modifying the intestacy rules and the rules governing the construction of written instruments, including wills.

[74.4]
Child born as a result of artificial insemination. The Family Law Reform Act 1987 (FLRA 1987) anticipated these provisions with regard to a child born as a result of artificial insemination, on or after 4 April 1988. The FLRA 1987, s 27 provides that where after 1 April 1988 a child was born in England and Wales as the result of artificial insemination of a woman who was at the time of the insemination a party to a subsisting marriage and was artificially inseminated with the semen of some person other than the other party to that marriage, unless it is proved to the satisfaction of any court by which the matter has to be determined that the other party to that marriage did not consent to the insemination, the child should be treated in law as the child of the parties to that marriage and shall not be treated as the child of any person other than the parties to that marriage.[1] It has been held that a child being the product of his father's semen and his mother's ovum, implanted in the mother's womb subsequent to the death of his father is upon birth entitled to a right of inheritance afforded by law.[2]

1   FLRA 1987, s 27(1). The provision does not apply to unmarried couples, so that such a child would not be treated as the child of the male cohabitant.
2   *In the Estate of K* (1996) 5 Tas R 365.

[74.5]
Human Fertilisation and Embryology Act 1990. The relevant provisions are now to be found in the HFEA 1990, ss 27 to 29. These sections were brought into force on 1 August 1991 and have effect only in relation to children born as a consequence of in vitro fertilisation or artificial insemination carried out after that date.

The HFEA 1990, s 27, which defines the 'mother' of a child for the purposes of the Act, provides by subsection (1) as follows: 'The woman who is carrying or has carried a child as a result of the placing in her of an embryo or of sperm and eggs, and no other woman, is to be treated as the mother of the child'. This means that for the purposes of the HFEA 1990 a woman may be treated as the mother of a child with whom she is not genetically connected.

The HFEA 1990, s 28, which defines the 'father' for the purposes of the Act, applies where a child is being or has been carried by a woman as the result of the placing in her of an embryo or of sperm and eggs or of her artificial insemination. Subsection (2) provides that if (a) at the time of the placing in her of the sperm and eggs or of her insemination, the woman was a party to a marriage, and (b) the creation of the embryo carried by her was not brought about with the sperm of the other party to the marriage, then that other party is to be treated as the father of the child unless it is shown that he did not consent. This means that for the purposes of the HFEA 1990 a man may be treated as the father of a child with whom he is not genetically connected. Indeed having regard to the terms of the HFEA 1990, s 27 the child contemplated by s 28 might not be genetically connected with the wife either.

The effect of the HFEA 1990, ss 27 and 28 is spelled out in s 29. The HFEA 1990, s 29(1) provides that: 'Where by virtue of section 27 or 28 a person is to be treated as the mother or father of a child, that person is to be treated in law as the mother or, as the case may be, the father of the child for all purposes'. Neither s 28 nor s 27 provides in terms that a child born to a married couple in the circumstances contemplated by section 27 is to be treated as the legitimate child of that marriage, but this must surely follow from the principle established by the HFEA 1990 that each party to the marriage is to be treated in law as the child's parent. This view is impliedly confirmed by the saving contained in s 27(5) for any child who would be treated as the legitimate child of the parties at common law (eg a child born as a consequence of the prescribed medical techniques but in circumstances where the egg was provided by the wife and the sperm by the husband).

[74.6]
The construction of wills' retrospective effect. The HFEA 1990, s 29(3) provides that where s 29(1) applies, 'references to any relationship between two people in any enactment, deed or other instrument or document (*whenever passed or made*) are to be read accordingly' (emphasis supplied). The retrospective effect of the HFEA 1990, s 29(3) introduced by the words in brackets is thought to be unique. In the past a statutory provision modifying the rules of construction affecting references to children and issue have been limited in their operation to deaths occurring or instruments made after the commencement of the provision. The HFEA 1990, s 29(3) represents a significant departure from this practice. The effect of this is that a child born after 1 August 1991 as a result of fertilisation techniques will be included in a settlement or will coming into force before 1969 which creates continuing trusts for the settlor's or testator's issue and not containing any provisions modifying the rules of construction affecting references to children and issue, although an illegitimate child conceived naturally would not be.[1]

As regards the rules of intestacy the HFEA 1990, s 29(3) will in practice operate only prospectively, as the next of kin of a deceased person are all identified at the date of his death and the HFEA 1990 does not affect the status of persons born before the commencement of ss 27 to 29.[2]

---

1   Because the provisions of the FLRA 1969 are not retrospectively applied to wills executed before 1 January 1990, whereas the provisions of the HFEA 1990 are. An example will illustrate the point. Suppose that in 1993 an illegitimate child is born to a granddaughter of the

settlor of the testator, such a child, though genetically connected with the settlor or testator, will not be eligible to benefit as a member of the class. On the other hand if that granddaughter is married and in 1993 has a child with her husband's consent in consequence of the implantation of another woman's egg, that child would by force of the HFEA 1990 be eligible to benefit as the granddaughter's lawful child, even though not genetically connected with the settlor or testator.

2   Nor does the Family Law Reform Act 1987, s 27 relating to children born as a result of artificial insemination. The FLRA 1987, s 1 relating to the general entitlement of illegitimate persons, is of course, expressed to be subject to a contrary intention.

[74.7]
Modifying or excluding the Act. The HFEA 1990 does not expressly contain a provision stating that the effects of the HFEA 1990 can be excluded by a contrary intention expressed in the will. But it is thought that the provisions can be excluded by express wording, if that is thought to be desirable. A simple statement that the will should be construed as if the HFEA 1990 had not been enacted should suffice.

[74.8]
'Descendants'. 'Descendants' ordinarily refers to children, grandchildren, and other issue,[1] of every degree of remoteness[2] in descent; and although the word may be confined to mean children by a sufficiently strong context,[3] the court does not restrict the word to that sense merely because the testator speaks of the descendants taking their parents' share.[4] The class of descendants taking under a gift are ascertained according to the ordinary rules for ascertaining a class.[5] The descendants, when ascertained, prima facie take per capita and not per stirpes,[6] but in a gift to a group of persons or their descendants, the latter prima facie take by way of substitution only, and not in competition with their parents, if living at the time of distribution.[7] Where the gift is to descendants 'living at my death', these words govern the whole gift.[8]

1   *Oddie v Woodford* (1821) 3 My & Cr 584 at 617 ('descendants' must mean posterity of all kinds); *Re Thurlow, Riddick v Kennard* [1972] Ch 379, [1972] 1 All ER 10. See also *Sydall v Castings Ltd* [1967] 1 QB 302, CA, [1966] 3 All ER 770, now affected by the Family Law Reform Acts, 1969 and 1987; see Vol 2, Part G, para **[245.37]** et seq and para **[245.69]** et seq. A gift to a donee and the descendants of his branch of the family did not before 1926 create an estate tail: *Re Brownlie, Brownlie v Muaux* [1938] 4 All ER 54, and now could not do so; see Chapter 84.
2   Such a description is not void for uncertainty: *Pierson v Garnet* (1786) 2 Bro CC 38.
3   *Smith v Pepper* (1859) 27 Beav 86 (in proportions under the Statute); *Williamson v Moore* (1862) 8 Jur NS 875 (my nephews and nieces being descendants of my brothers and sisters); *Legard v Haworth* (1800) 1 East 120 (restricted to children and grandchildren). Collateral and relatives may be included by the context or the circumstances: *Best v Stonehewer* (1864) 34 Beav 66; *Craik v Lamb* (1844) 1 Coll 489 (gift to relations by lineal descent by person having no wife or issue when will made or afterwards: cousins entitled), but both cases were distinguished in *Re Thurlow, Riddick v Kennard* [1972] Ch 379, [1972] 1 All ER 10.
4   *Ralph v Carrick* (1879) 11 Ch D 873, where the rule in *Sibley v Perry* (see Chapter 76) was not applied.
5   *Tucker v Billing* (1856) 27 LTOS 132; *Re Roberts, Repington v Roberts-Gawen* (1881) 19 Ch D 520.
6   *Re Flower, Matheson v Goodwyn* (1890) 62 LT 216. In *Rowland v Gorsuch* (1789) 2 Cox Eq Cas 187, the context required a stirpital distribution. See also *Re Rawlinson, Hill v Withall* [1909] 2 Ch 36.
7   *Jones v Torin* (1833) 6 Sim 255; *Dick v Lacy* (1845) 8 Beav 214; *Re Flower, Matheson v Goodwyn* (1890) 62 LT 216; *Re Morgan, Morgan v Morgan* [1893] 3 Ch 222. The same rule applies to a gift to a group of individuals or their descendants: *Tucker v Billing* (1856) 27 LTOS 132.
8   *Re Hickey, Beddoes v Hodgson* [1917] 1 Ch 601.

[74.9]

Male descendants. Under a gift to 'male descendants' as purchasers, males claiming as descendants of males or females, can take.[1] This construction is in contrast to the meaning of the phrase 'male issue' where considerations relating to the creation of entails are relevant.[2]

1   *Re Drake's Will Trusts, Drake v Drake* [1971] Ch 179, [1970] 3 All ER 32, CA (a male descended through females held entitled to share in a gift ... between such of the male descendants of my father ...'), explaining *Oddie v Woodford* (1821) 3 My & Cr 584 ('his eldest male lineal descendants'; held, that phrase inapplicable to a descendant claiming through a female); overruling *Bernal v Bernal* (1838) 3 My & Cr 559 ('male descendants' meant descendants claiming through males only).
2   See Chapter 76.

CHAPTER 75

Adopted children

[75.1]
Position prior to 1976. Before 1 January 1950,[1] adoption, whether under an order of the court or otherwise, gave the adopted child no right to share in the property of the members of the adopting family, but, on the other hand, it did not deprive the child of any of its rights to share in the property of its original family to which it would have been entitled apart from the adoption.[2] This applied to all dispositions of property and to the rights upon intestacy.[3] This position was reversed by the Adoption of Children Act 1949 which provided that adopted persons were to be regarded as the children of the adopters, and of no other persons, for the purposes of intestacies, wills and settlements.[4] This basic provision has been re-enacted, with extensions and clarification in subsequent Acts. The governing legislative provisions can be stated thus:

(i) deaths on or after 1 January 1950: Adoption Act 1950;[5]
(ii) deaths on or after 1 April 1959: Adoption Act 1958;[6]
(iii) deaths on or after 1 January 1976: Children Act 1975;[7]
(iv) deaths on or after 1 January 1988: Adoption Act 1976 (AA 1976).[8]

This discussion will refer to the AA 1976 provisions; the position under the earlier Adoption Acts can be found in previous editions of this text.[9]

1 The date when the Adoption of Children Act 1949 came into force.
2 Adoption of Children Act 1926, s 5(2), repealed by the Adoption of Children Act 1949.
3 Adoption of Children Act 1926, s 5(2), repealed by the Adoption of Children Act 1949. Disposition includes assurance inter vivos as well as by will or codicil: Adoption of Children Act 1926, s 5(4).
4 Adoption of Children Act 1949, ss 9, 10.
5 Adoption Act 1950, ss 13, 14, Sch 5, para 4, proviso; see Vol 2, Part G, para **[245.18]**; which replaced the Adoption of Children Act 1949 with effect from the same commencement date.
6 Adoption Act 1958, ss 16, 17; see Vol 2, Part G, para **[245.26]**; which repealed the Adoption Act 1950.
7 The provisons were contained in the Children Act 1975, then replaced by the Adoption Act 1976. The provisions of the Children Act 1975 applied from 1 January 1976 but were repealed with retrospective effect by the same provisions in the Adoption Act 1976, from 1 January 1976. See the Children Act 1975 and the Adoption Act 1976 (Commencement No 2) Order 1987, SI 1987/1242 which brought the latter Act into force on 1 January 1988.
8 6 *Halsbury's Statutes* (4th edn) 211; see Vol 2, Part G, para **[245.55]** et seq, replacing the Children Act 1975.
9 For the pre-1976 rules, see the 4th edn of this work, pp 555–557.

[75.2]
The adoption order. Under the AA 1976 adoption means adoption by an 'adoption' order;[1] by an order made under the Children Act 1975, the Adoption

Act 1958, the Adoption Act 1950, or any enactment repealed by the Adoption Act 1950;[2] or by an order made in Scotland, Northern Ireland, the Isle of Man, or in any of the Channel Islands.[3] Also included are overseas adoptions[4] and an adoption recognised by the Law of England and Wales and effected under the law of any other country.[5] The AA 1976 applies subject to any contrary intention, for the construction of enactments or instruments passed or made before the adoption or later,[6] and has effect as respects things done or events occurring after the adoption or after 31 December 1975, whichever is the later.[7]

1   AA 1976, s 38(1)(a); see Vol 2, Part G, para [**245.57**].
2   AA 1976, s 38(1)(b).
3   AA 1976, s 38(1)(c).
4   AA 1976, s 38(1)(d).
5   AA 1976, s 38(1)(e)
6   AA 1976, s 39(6)(a).
7   AA 1976, s 39(6)(b).

[75.3]
Adopted children. The basic proposition is that an adopted child is to be treated in law, where the adopters are a married couple, as if he had been born as a child of the marriage (whether or not he was in fact born after the marriage was solemnised).[1] Where the child is adopted by a person who is not married then he will be regarded as if he had been born to the adopter in wedlock (but not as a child of any actual marriage of the adopter).[2] The AA 1976 expressly states that an adopted child is not to be treated in law as if he were the child of any person other than the adopters or adopter,[3] and thus ensures that an adopted child is not regarded as illegitimate.[4]

An adoption does not affect the descent of any peerage or dignity or title of honour nor the devolution of any property limited, expressly or not, to devolve along with any peerage or dignity or title of honour.[5] Nor does the AA 1976 prejudice any interest vested in possession in the adopted child before the adoption or any interest expectant (whether immediately or not) upon an interest so created.[6] Finally, the AA 1976 does not affect entitlement to a pension which is payable to or for the benefit of a child and is in payment at the time of his adoption.[7]

1   AA 1976, s 39(1)(*a*); see Vol 2, Part G, para [**245.58**].
2   AA 1976, s 39(1)(b).
3   AA 1976, s 39(2).
4   AA 1976, s 39(4).
5   AA 1976, s 44. Similarly with the old Family Law Reform Act 1969, s 15(5). See the new FLRA 1987, Chapter 72, para [**72.14**] et seq.
6   AA 1976, s 42(4).
7   AA 1976, s 48.

[75.4]
Wills. For the purposes of the AA 1976 the death of the testator is the date at which a will or codicil is to be regarded as made.[1] The new provisions reproduce the established law in so far as unless there is a contrary intention, an express or implied reference in the will to a child or children will include a reference to the adopted child.[2] This presumably extends to persons claiming through adopted children, eg a gift to a class of grandchildren will include children who are the issue of adopted children, and adopted children of natural children of the donor.[3]

If there is a gift to children with a substitutional gift to grandchildren, then again an adopted 'grandchild' will presumably be able to take his deceased parents' share.[4] But wills can present more difficult problems where, for example, the disposition depends on the date of birth of a child, as where the gift is to a class 'living' at a certain time. To meet these problems the AA 1976 provides that the disposition shall be construed as if the adopted child had been born on the date of the adoption,[5] thus giving the child an artificial date of birth. If two or more children had been adopted on the same date, then they will be deemed to have been born on that date in the order of their actual births.[6] Thus, if there is a gift to the children of A 'living at my death, or born afterwards'[7] or, 'born within twenty-one years of my death', adopted children will qualify or not, depending not on their actual date of birth but on the date of adoption. Similar constructions will apply where the gift is a class gift,[8] to which the class closing rules apply.[9] When the first member of the class attains a vested interest and closes the class, those children then in existence will take, which in the case of adopted children, must mean those children then adopted.[10] Children then born and subsequently adopted would not take. The provisions of the AA 1976 also apply to a conditional bequest eg 'to A for life, until he has a child, and then to his child or children'. The adoption of a child would satisfy the condition and the child would be deemed to have been born on the date of the adoption.[11]

So far as perpetuities are concerned the effect of the provision would seem to be that a 'parent' of the class of beneficiaries would only be a life in being for the purposes of the Perpetuities and Accumulations Act 1964, s 3, if he was adopted at the date when the instrument takes effect.[12] Thus, if the gift was to 'A's grandchildren to attain 21' and A had two existing natural born children at the date of the gift, they would be lives in being under s 3(5)(c). If subsequently he adopted a third child who was alive at the date of the instrument containing the gift but not then adopted, presumably he could not be a life in being for the purposes of the Perpetuities and Accumulations Act 1964.

1   AA 1976, s 46(3). Vol 2, Part G, para **[245.64]**.
2   AA 1976, s 39(1).
3   AA 1976, s 41 provides that 'parent' or any other term not qualified by the word 'adoptive' can be treated as including an adoptive relative.
4   AA 1976, s 41. Presumably adopted children would rank as 'issue' for the purposes of the Wills Act 1837, s 33.
5   AA 1976, s 42(2)(a).
6   AA 1976, s 42(2)(b). These are rules of construction which will yield to a contrary intention.
7   AA 1976, s 42(3), example 1. Likewise a gift to children of A 'living at my death or born afterwards before any one of such children for the time being in existence attains a vested interest and who attain the age of 21'; s 42(3), example 2.
8   See paras **[66.19]–[66.21]** supra.
9   See Chapter 66.
10   AA 1976, s 42(2), example 3. Presumably if the adopted child is the first member to attain a vested interest, he will close the class which might result in the class being closed earlier than the testator anticipated.
11   AA 1976, s 42(3), example 4.
12   In order to be a life in being under the Perpetuities and Accumulations Act 1964, a person must be 'in being and ascertainable at the commencement of the perpetuity period', s 3(4)(a).

[75.5]
References to age. The provisions noted above attributing an artificial date of birth to an adopted person apply only where the disposition depends on the date

of birth of a child. They do not affect any reference to the age of the child.[1] Thus suppose a testator makes a gift to 'those children of A now born or born within five years of my death at 21, [or majority]'. if one year after the testator's death A adopts a three-year-old child, that child will be included in the gift but will attain a vested interest 18 years later, not 21, AA 1976, s 42(2), (3). More difficult problems arise if the gift is to the 'youngest' or the 'eldest' of a class. In such cases it might be that an adopted child should be considered by reference to his actual age not his 'adopted' age. This is not expressly stated by the Act but it can be argued that 'references to the age of a child' include phrases such as 'eldest' and 'youngest'. There are, however, two contrary indications in the AA 1976. Firstly, it is difficult to see the relevance of the provision that 'two or more children adopted on the same date [shall be regarded as if they] had been born on that date in the order of their actual births', unless it applies to an 'eldest' or 'youngest' situation.[2] Secondly, although the example in s 43(1) is ambiguous, it could suggest that the artificial date of birth rule applies generally in the 'eldest' or 'youngest' situations. Whatever be the general rule, by virtue of s 43 it is quite clear that the artificial date of birth of a child who was born illegitimate and who was adopted by one of the natural parents as sole adoptive parent does not affect entitlement, s 43(1). Consider for example, the situation where a testator dies in 1976 bequeathing a legacy to his eldest grandchild living at a specified time. Suppose his daughter has an illegitimate child in 1977 who is the first grandchild but the testator's married son has a legitimate child in 1978. Subsequently the illegitimate child is adopted by the mother as the sole adoptive parent. In this case, the daughter's child remains the eldest grandchild of the testator throughout.[3]

1   AA 1976, s 42(2).
2   AA 1976, s 42(2)(b). Perhaps it applies in commorientes cases to which the Law of Property Act 1925, s 184 applies. This section raises the same problem if an adopted child is killed simultaneously with a natural child: is the true or the adopted age of the former to be considered? It is suggested that the true age should apply.
3   AA 1976, s 43(2).

[75.6]
Disposition. The references to 'dispositions' in the AA 1976 include the conferring of a power of appointment and any other disposition of an interest in, or right over, property and include an oral disposition as if contained in an instrument.[1] Also included are dispositions by the creation of an entailed interest.[2]

1   AA 1976, s 46(1), (2).
2   AA 1976, s 46(5); repealed by the Trusts of Land and Appointment of Trustees Act 1996 (TLATA 1996), s 25(2), Sch 4. This repeal does not affect entailed interests created before the commencement of the TLATA 1996, s 25(4).

[75.7]
Contrary intention. It will be noticed that the statutory provisions relating to the status conferred by adoption[1] and the rules of construction for instruments concerning property[2] apply 'subject to any contrary intention'. Cases under the previous law will no doubt continue to be relevant in this context. It was

established under the Adoption Act 1958 that the contrary intention might appear not only in the instrument in question, but also from any surrounding circumstances which carry conviction to the court; but the effect of surrounding circumstances, if relied on to establish a contrary intention, must be really gent and convincing.[3] Thus it had been held that the history of the testator's testamentary dispositions was admissible including the fact that at some time after a prior will but before the effective will, the testator had referred to an adopted person as being entitled to share.[4]

1   AA 1976, s 39(6)(a).
2   AA 1976, s 42(1).
3   *Re Jones's Will Trusts, Jones v Hawtin-Squire* [1965] Ch 1124, [1965] 2 All ER 828. See also *Re Fletcher, Barclays Bank Ltd v Ewing* [1949] Ch 473, [1949] 1 All ER 732; *Re Gilpin, Hutchinson v Gilpin* [1954] Ch 1, [1953] 2 All ER 1218; and *Re Jebb, Ward-Smith v Jebb* [1966] Ch 666, [1965] 3 All ER 358.
4   *Re Jones's Will Trusts, Jones v Hawtin-Squire* [1965] Ch 1124, [1965] 2 All ER 828. See also *Re Fletcher, Barclays Bank Ltd v Ewing* [1949] Ch 473, [1949] 1 All ER 732; *Re Gilpin, Hutchinson v Gilpin* [1954] Ch 1, [1953] 2 All ER 1218; and *Re Jebb, Ward-Smith v Jebb* [1966] Ch 666, [1965] 3 All ER 358.

[75.8]
Intestacy. The AA 1976 provides that for the purposes of the Act, provisions of the law of intestate succession applicable to the estate of a deceased person shall be treated as if contained in an instrument executed by him, while of full capacity, immediately before his death.[1] Thus if an intestate dies after 31 December 1976,[2] adopted children will be entitled to share in the estate as if they had been born in lawful wedlock.

1   AA 1976, s 46(4).
2   The date when the Children Act 1975 came into force.

[75.9]
Protection of trustee and personal representative. The AA 1976 contains useful provisions to protect trustees and personal representatives. A trustee or personal representative is not under a duty, by virtue of the law relating to trusts or the administrations of estates to enquire, before distributing any property, whether any adoption has been effected or revoked, if that fact could affect entitlement to the property.[1] Furthermore such a person is not liable for any conveyance or distribution of the property made without regard to any such fact if he has not received notice of the fact before the conveyance or distribution.[2] However, this does not prejudice the right of any person to follow the property or any property representing it, into the hands of another person, other than a purchaser who has received it.[3] The AA 1976 also contains a provision relating to future parenthood analogous to the Perpetuities and Accumulations Act 1964 presumptions.[4] To protect trustees and personal representatives it is provided that where it is necessary to determine for the purposes of a disposition of property affected by an instrument whether a woman can have a child it shall be presumed that once a woman has attained the age of 55 years, she will not adopt a child after execution of the instrument and notwithstanding the provisions of

the AA 1976, if she does so, that child is not to be treated as her child or as the child of her spouse (if any) for the purposes of the instrument.[5]

1   AA 1976, s 45(1).
2   AA 1976, s 45(2).
3   AA 1976, s 45(3).
4   See Chapter 94.
5   AA 1976, s 42(5).

CHAPTER 76

Gifts to 'issue'

[76.1]

As word of limitation. The word 'issue' in its legal sense means descendants of every degree.[1] In a devise of real estate to a person 'and his issue', especially where at the date of the will he has no issue,[2] the word is ordinarily a word of limitation,[3] and the gift created an estate tail in the devisee.[4] The word was treated as equivalent to 'heir of the body',[5] but the context of the will might show that 'issue' was a word of description and not of limitation, for the word was one of flexible meaning.[6] Since 1925, however, an entailed interest can be created only by the use of words which, if used in a deed, would create such an interest, so that this doctrine does not now apply.[7]

1   *Edyvean v Archer, Re Brooke* [1903] AC 379; *Re Burnham, Carrick v Carrick* [1918] 2 Ch 196; *Re Swain, Brett v Ward* [1918] 1 Ch 399; *Re Sutcliffe* [1934] Ch 219; *Re Hipwell, Hipwell v Hewitt* [1945] 2 All ER 476; *Walsh v Johnston* [1899] 1 IR 501; *Re Taylor's Trusts, Taylor v Blake* [1912] 1 IR 1; *Turner's Trustees v Turner* (1897) 24 R 619; *Re Harding* [1956] NZLR 482; *Re Patterson Estate* (1958) 66 Man R 416; *Re Matthews* [1960] VLR 3; *Re Green, McKenzie v Stringer* [1963] NZLR 148; *Re Linklater Estate* (1967) 66 DLR (2d) 30; 'It is conceded that in ordinary parlance the word "issue" means children and only children and does not include grandchildren or great-grandchildren, but in the language of lawyers and only in that language it means descendants'; *Ralph v Carrick* (1879) 11 Ch D 873 at 883; *Kernahan v Hanson* (1990) 73 DLR (4th) 286.
2   The old rule in *Wild's Case* (1599) 6 Co Rep 16b, is considered in Chapter 85.
3   *Roddy v Fitzgerald* (1858) 6 HL Cas 823; *Pelham-Clinton v Duke of Newcastle* [1902] 1 Ch 34; *Re Adams, Adams v Adams* (1906) 94 LT 720; *Re Gouk, Allen v Allen* [1957] 1 All ER 469, [1957] 1 WLR 493. When the word 'issue' is qualified, however, it becomes a word of purchase, eg 'eldest issue male'; *Lovelace v Lovelace* (1585) Cro Eliz 40; *Sheridan v O'Reilly* [1900] 1 IR 386; but see *Re Cosby's Estate* [1922] 1 IR 120 (where 'eldest issue male' gave an estate tail). In *Re Hobbs, Hobbs v Hobbs* [1917] 1 Ch 569, estates were limited to 'sons and their sons successively' and it was said that it was very significant in that case that (quite apart from what seemed a definition in the devise itself to sons and their sons as the persons meant by issue male) there were in the devises following those to the first donee and his descendants several distinct references to the estates limited to his sons and their sons successively. This was ample to amount to at least an explanation within the cases of the phrases 'male issue' as meaning sons and sons of sons.
4   *Re Simcoe, Vowler-Simcoe v Vowler* [1913] 1 Ch 552; *Walsh v Johnston* [1899] 1 IR 501. For cases where 'or' was changed into 'and', see *Re Clerke, Clowes v Clerke* [1915] 2 Ch 301; *Re Hayden, Pask v Perry* [1931] 2 Ch 333.
5   *Kavanagh v Morland* (1853) Kay 16; *Roddy v Fitzgerald* (1858) 6 HL Cas 823; *Re Adams, Adams v Adams* (1906) 94 LT 720. In a gift to a person for life with a remainder limited to his 'issue', the word was one of limitation: *King v Melling* (1671) 1 Vent 225.
6   *M'Gregor v M'Gregor* (1859) 1 De GF & J 63; *Re Birks, Kenyon v Birks* [1900] 1 Ch 417; *Young's Trustees v M'Nab etc* (1883) 10 R 1165. The word 'issue' is said to be more flexible than 'heirs of the body': *Kavanagh v Morland* (1853) Kay 16; *Slater v Dangerfield* (1846) 15 M & W 263; *Roddy v Fitzgerald* (1858) 6 HL Cas 823 at 881.

7   Law of Property Act 1925, s 130(1), (2); 37 *Halsbury's Statutes* (4th edn) 288. Entailed
    interests can no longer be created by virtue of the Trusts of Land and Appointment of Trustees
    Act 1996.

[76.2]
As word of purchase. In the case of direct gifts to issue[1] as purchasers, the
word may mean either lineal descendants, in accordance with its ordinary
meaning, or children or some particular class of descendants ascertained by
reference to some particular time or event.[2] The meaning is not necessarily
restricted to children by a context containing a gift to children couched in similar
terms,[3] or by gifts referring to 'issue' as meaning 'children';[4] but a gift to the
'issue of our marriage' is confined to children and grandchildren are excluded.[5]

1   As to gifts over in default of issue, see Chapter 98.
2   *Slater v Dangerfield* (1846) 15 M & W 263 at 272; *Sandes v Cooke* (1888) 21 LR Ir 445; *Re
    Burnham, Carrick v Carrick* [1918] 2 Ch 196; *Re Cust, Glasgow v Campbell* [1919] VLR 221;
    Re Downer [1957] SASR 207. The usual meaning of all descendants was adhered to in
    Dodsworth v Addy (1842) 11 LJ Ch 382 (gift over to issue on death before share payable); *Re
    Jones' Trusts* (1857) 23 Beav 242 (similar gift).
3   *Waldron v Boulter* (1856) 22 Beav 284; *Buick v Equity Trustees etc Co Ltd* (1957) 97 CLR 599;
    Re Rhodes [1961] NZLR 65; *Re Marsh* [1960] NZLR 294.
4   Issue has been construed with different meanings in different passages in the same will; see
    Carter v Bentall (1840) 2 Beav 551; *Louis v Louis* (1863) 7 LT 666; *Re Warren's Trusts* (1884)
    26 Ch D 208.
5   *Re Noad* [1951] Ch 553, [1951] 1 All ER 467.

[76.3]
Contexts confining 'issue' to children. The following are examples of contexts
from which the court has inferred that the word 'issue' has been used by the
testator as meaning 'children'.[1]

(1)   Where the testator in a later part of his will or in a codicil speaks of the
      gift in question as a gift to children,[2] or otherwise defines the issue taking
      under the gift as children.[3]
(2)   Where the testator expressly or impliedly limits the word 'issue' in other
      clauses of the same will to mean 'children', and the restriction, in the
      opinion of the court, applies throughout the will.[4]
(3)   Until recently, the so called rule in *Sibley v Perry*[5] was treated as a
      general rule of construction,[6] though it has been said that Lord Eldon did
      not in that case intend to lay down any general rule of construction but to
      deal only with the language of the particular will. Where in an original
      gift to issue the person whose issue is designated, or in a substitutional
      gift the first taker, is spoken of as the 'parent', 'father', or 'mother' of the
      issue,[7] for example, where the gift to the issue is contained in a direction
      that they shall take the share their parent would have taken if living at the
      time of distribution, and the reference to the parent is construed as a
      reference to the first taker. This rule of construction, however, may be
      controlled by the general effect and scope of the will; for example, by the
      use of the word 'issue' in other parts of the will in such a sense as to
      enlarge this construction and restore the word to its original
      comprehensive meaning.[8] Thus, the court is disinclined to apply the rule
      where there is a gift over on general failure of issue,[9] or where the result
      of its application would in certain events be an entire or partial

intestacy.[10] The rule has been further weakened by a decision to the effect that the rule does not constitute any exception to the general principle that a will must be construed as a whole, and that the word 'issue' when used in a substitutional gift referable to the parent of issue, or to the issue of a parent, bears its ordinary meaning of descendants generally and not children alone.[11]

(4)   Where the testator speaks of the 'issue of such issue', or uses other phrases showing that he contemplated issue of yet further degrees of remoteness not included in the 'issue' in question.[12]

(5)   Where the property is directed to be settled on a person and his 'issue'.[13]

1   The construction has also been applied to a gift to 'issue' of deceased members of a class: *Bennett v Houldsworth* (1911) 104 LT 304. When 'issue' are spoken of as 'begotten' by the named person, this does not necessarily confine the meaning to children: *Caulfield v Maguire* (1845) 2 Jo & Lat 141 at 176; *Haydon v Wilshire* (1789) 3 Term Rep 372; *Evans v Jones* (1846) 2 Coll 516; *Maddock v Legg* (1858) 25 Beav 531.

2   *Goldie v Greaves* (1844) 14 Sim 348; *Baker v Bayldon* (1862) 31 Beav 209; *M'Gregor v M'Gregor* (1859) 1 De GF & J 63; *Re Hobbs, Hobbs v Hobbs* [1917] 1 Ch 569; *Re Harrison's Estate* (1879) 3 LR Ir 114; *Harris v Loftus* [1899] 1 IR 491. This is an application of the general rule that the testator makes his own dictionary: see Chapter 50.

3   *Peel v Catlow* (1838) 9 Sim 372 (to issue 'in like manner' to previous gift); *Farrant v Nichols* (1846) 9 Beav 327 (gift to 'all and every the respective issues' of testator's daughters, 'either sons or daughters', followed by the frequent use in a subsequent part of the will of the word 'issue'); *Re Dean, Worland v Dickinson* (1923) 67 Sol Jo 768 (gift to issue 'who being a son ... or being a daughter'). A similar case is where there is a gift to issue, if more than one in equal shares, and if only one 'to such one child': *Bryden v Willett* (1869) LR 7 Eq 472; *Re Birks, Kenyon v Birks* [1900] 1 Ch 417; *Re Hopkins' Trusts* (1878) 9 Ch D 131.

4   *Cursham v Newland* (1838) 4 M & W 101 (remainder to issue of sons and daughters in tail general, with benefit of survivorship to and amongst the issue as tenants in common and not as joint tenants); *Ridgeway v Munkittrick* (1841) 1 Dr & War 84; *Edwards v Edwards* (1849) 12 Beav 97; *Re Harrison's Estate* (1879) 3 LR Ir 114 (where the term 'issue' has been clearly and frequently limited to 'children' and nowhere used as necessarily equivalent to descendants, the court would not put an extended construction upon the word, especially where interests vest at birth and are not contingent on surviving a tenant for life); *Re Birks, Kenyon v Birks* [1900] 1 Ch 417; *Re Cockle's Will Trusts; Re Pittaway, Moreland v Draffen; Risdon v Public Trustee* [1967] Ch 690, [1967] 1 All ER 391 (confined to children); *Re Bourke's Will Trusts, Barclays Bank Trust Co Ltd v Canada Permanent Trust Co* [1980] 1 All ER 219, [1980] 1 WLR 539, 'issue' meant 'children' consistent with an earlier reference in the same sentence to 'issue of my marriage', following *Re Noad, Noad v Noad* [1951] Ch 553, [1951] 1 All ER 467. See also *Re Crabtree* [1954] VLR 492; *Re Hudson* (1971) 14 DLR (3d) 79 ('issue' confined to grandchildren) and *GE v KM* [1995] 1 VR 471.

5   (1802) 7 Ves 522. The rule in *Sibley v Perry* (1802) 7 Ves 522 was discussed in *Perpetual Trustee Co Ltd v Wright, Re Cox's Will* (1987) 9 NSWLR 18. See also *Re Kernahan* (1990) 68 DLR (4th) 150, where 'issue' was capable of more than one meaning in the will and extrinsic evidence was admitted to resolve the ambiguity.

6   See *Ralph v Carrick* (1879) 11 Ch D 873 at 882. In *Re Spencer* (1973) 42 DLR (3d) 127 it was said that the rule in *Sibley v Perry* (1802) 7 Ves 522 was no longer in effect and instead of placing a prima facie meaning on particular words in such a case the whole will must be examined and so construed in its context.

7   For modern examples, see *Lanphier v Buck* (1865) 2 Drew & Sm 484; *Martin v Holgate* (1866) LR 1 HL 175; *Heasman v Pearse* (1871) 7 Ch App 275; *Re Judd's Trusts* [1884] WN 206; *Re Timson, Smiles v Timson* [1916] 2 Ch 362; *Black v Campbell* (1864) 14 I Ch R 92; *Re Sinclair* (1963) 37 DLR (2d) 103; *Re Austin* [1962] NZLR 516. In *Re Campbell* [1952] NZLR 214, the rule was applied although there was no substitutional gift to issue of children who might die.

8   *Maynard v Wright* (1858) 26 Beav 285; *Berry v Fisher* [1903] 1 IR 484; *Re Embury, Page v Bowyer* (1913) 109 LT 511; *Re Johnson, Pitt v Johnson* (1913) 30 TLR 200; affd (1914) 111 LT 130; *Re Swain, Brett v Ward* [1918] 1 Ch 399; *Re Langlands, Langlands v Langlands* (1917) 87 LJ Ch 1; *Re Hipwell, Hipwell v Hewitt* [1945] 2 All ER 476; *Eastern Trust Co v Stairs* [1955] 1 DLR 280.

9   *Ross v Ross* (1855) 20 Beav 645, and see *Ralph v Carrick* (1879) 11 Ch D 873; *Re Heard, McDonald v Edney* [1942] VLR 199.
10 *Ross v Ross* (1855) 20 Beav 645 at 651; *Ralph v Carrick* (1879) 11 Ch D 873 at 882.
11 *Re Manly's Will Trusts, Burton v Williams* [1969] 3 All ER 1011, [1969] 1 WLR 1818 (issue taking 'their deceased parent's share', not confined to children); see *Re Manly's Will Trusts (No 2) Tickle v Manly* [1976] 1 All ER 673, for further litigation on this will.
12 *Pope v Pope* (1851) 14 Beav 591; *Fairfield v Bushell* (1863) 32 Beav 158.
13 *Thompson v Simpson* (1841) 1 Dr & War 459; *Baker v Bayldon* (1862) 31 Beav 209; *Re Dixon's Trusts* (1869) IR 4 Eq 1; *Harris v Loftus* [1899] 1 IR 491; *Re Bromhead's Trusts* [1922] 1 IR 75.

[76.4]

Ascertainment of class of issue. The class of issue is ascertained according to the declared intention of the testator,[1] and where this is not otherwise shown, then, according to the ordinary rules, at the testator's death,[2] letting in issue coming into existence before the period of distribution,[3] every degree of issue taking concurrently with the descendants. In the ordinary way they take per capita,[4] and in the absence of words of severance or other inconsistent context,[5] as joint tenants.[6]

1   *Waldron v Boulter* (1856) 22 Beav 284 (issue of each grandchild ascertained at his death).
2   See Chapter 66.
3   *Clay v Pennington* (1835) 7 Sim 370; *Hobgen v Neale* (1870) LR 11 Eq 48; *Re Corlass* (1875) 1 Ch D 460; *Berry v Fisher* [1903] 1 IR 484; *Re Taylor's Trusts, Taylor v Blake* [1912] 1 IR 1.
4   *Davenport v Hanbury* (1796) 3 Ves 257; *Re Jones' Trusts* (1857) 23 Beav 242; *Weldon v Hoyland* (1862) 4 De GF & J 564.
5   *Weldon v Hoyland* (1862) 4 De GF & J 564; *Law v Thorp* (1858) 27 LJ Ch 649 ('with benefit of survivorship and accruer of shares').
6   *Davenport v Hanbury* (1796) 3 Ves 257.

[76.5]

Male issue. Under a gift to 'issue male'[1] or 'male heirs'[2] as purchasers, prima facie[3] only males claiming as descendants of males and not of females can take.[4] This rule is in contrast to the construction of the expression 'male descendants' where males claiming as descendants of males or females can take.[5] The reason for this distinction is to be found in the law relating to the creating of entails. Before the enactment of the Law of Property Act 1925, s 130, a testamentary disposition to 'A and his issue male (or male issue)' was equivalent to 'A and the heirs male of his body', ie an entail male in A. Thus the expression governed not only the sex of the beneficiaries but also the sex of the line of descent.[6]

1   *Lywood v Kimber* (1860) 29 Beav 38; *Lambert v Peyton* (1860) 8 HL Cas 1; *Re Du Cros Settlement* [1961] 3 All ER 193. The technical construction was applied to a New South Wales will executed in 1923 and 'male issue' meant males tracing their descent through males: *Allen v Crane* [1953] ALR 959, 'without leaving male issue' in a divesting clause excludes male issue through a female: *Re Forsyth* (1963) 37 DLR (2d) 379.
2   *Doe d Angell v Angell* (1846) 9 QB 328.
3   The following are cases where the prima facie rule was overborne by the context: *Sayer v Bradly* (1856) 5 HL Cas 873 ('nearest of kin in the male line' is not restricted to males claiming through males); *Trevor v Trevor* (1847) 1 HL Cas 239 ('in tail male' is a description of the estate taken and the first taker may be a female).
4   *Re Du Cros Settlement* [1961] 3 All ER 193, [1961] 1 WLR 1252.
5   See *Re Drake's Will Trusts, Drake v Drake* [1971] Ch 179, [1970] 3 All ER 32, CA. See para **[74.8]** supra.

6   See Chapter 84, and *Re Du Cros Settlement* [1961] 3 All ER 193, [1961] 1 WLR 1252 and
    Russell LJ in *Re Drake's Will Trusts, Drake v Drake* [1971] Ch 179 at 199, [1970] 3 All ER 32,
    at 43; *Allen v Crane* (1953) 89 CLR 152. Entailed interests can no longer be created by virtue of
    the Trusts of Land and Appointment of Trustees Act 1996.

[76.6]

'Offspring'. This word, like 'issue' extends in the ordinary way to any degree of
lineal descendants,[1] but may similarly be restricted or varied in meaning.[2]

1   *Thompson v Beasley* (1854) 3 Drew 7; *Young v Davies* (1863) 2 Drew & Sm 167; *Bradshaw v
    Bradshaw* [1908] 1 IR 288.
2   *Lister v Tidd* (1861) 29 Beav 618 (restricted to children by a direction to settle); *Tabuteau v
    Nixon* (1899) 15 TLR 485.

CHAPTER 77

Gifts to next of kin

[77.1]

General meaning. Under a gift to the next of kin of any person,[1] simply and without reference to the Statutes of Distribution, now replaced by the rules of distribution under the Administration of Estates Act 1925 (AEA 1925),[2] the donees are considered to be the nearest kindred in blood.[3] The same meaning is prima facie given to descriptions of donees similar to next of kin.[4] In a gift to the next of kin of two persons, the donees are prima facie a class composed of the next of kin of one together with the next of kin of the other,[5] but, according to the context, may be such persons as are common to the two classes of next of kin.[6] Such persons prima facie take as joint tenants.[7]

1 If the testator does not show distinctly to whose next of kin he is referring, the context may show that he is not referring to his own next of kin: *Robson v Ibbs* (1837) Donnelly 226.
2 See AEA 1925, ss 46, 47, as amended in the case of deaths intestate on or after 1 January 1996, by the Law Reform (Succession) Act 1995, s 1; the amendments do not affect the meaning of next of kin; 17 *Halsbury's Statutes* (4th edn) 452, 457. Vol 2, Part G, para **[244.129]**.
3 *Avison v Simpson* (1859) John 43; *Halton v Foster* (1868) 3 Ch App 505; *Re Bulcock, Ingham v Ingham* [1916] 2 Ch 495. The half-blood are included: *Cotton v Scarancke* (1815) 1 Madd 45; *Re Fergusson's Will* [1902] 1 Ch 483. See also *Gutheil v Ballarat Trustees, Executors and Agency Co Ltd* (1922) 30 CLR 293; *Rutherford's Trustee v Dickie* 1907 SC 1280; *Re Young* [1928] 2 DLR 966. In the case of a power of appointment, a power to appoint amongst 'her own family or next of kin' was held to include any relative: *Snow v Teed* (1870) LR 9 Eq 622. 'Nearest of kin' in the will of a domiciled Englishman means nearest of kin by English law: *Re Fergusson's Will* [1902] 1 Ch 483. Next of kin include children and grandchildren of the testator: *Fasken v Fasken* [1953] 2 SCR 10 (where it was argued that since lineal descendants are 'kin' they could not be 'next of kin').
4 *Harris v Newton* (1877) 46 LJ Ch 268 ('legal or next of kin'); *Halton v Foster* (1868) 3 Ch App 505 ('next of kin in blood'); *Sayer v Bradly* (1856) 5 HL Cas 873 ('nearest of kin in male line'); *Williams v Ashton* (1860) 1 John & H 115 ('nearest of kin by way of heirship': heir entitled); *Tucker v Ellick* (1883) cited in 49 LT at 674 ('next male kin'); *Re Chapman, Ellick v Cox* (1883) 49 LT 673 (next male kin).
5 *Re Soper, Naylor v Kettle* [1912] 2 Ch 467.
6 *Pycroft v Gregory* (1829) 4 Russ 526.
7 *Re Aspinall's Settlement Trusts* (1861) 30 LJ Ch 321; *Re Gansloser's Will Trusts* [1952] Ch 30, [1951] 2 All ER 936; *Re Kilvert, Midland Bank Executor and Trustee Co Ltd v Kilvert* [1957] Ch 388, [1957] 2 All ER 196.

[77.2]

Reference to rules of distribution. If the will describes the donees by reference to the statutory rules for the distribution of the estate of an intestate, either expressly or impliedly,[1] the distribution may be under the former law or under the new law. References to any Statutes of Distribution in a will coming into operation after 1925 are to be construed as references to the new rules of distribution; and references in such a will to the statutory next of kin are to be construed, unless the context otherwise requires, as referring to the persons who would take beneficially under those rules; and trusts declared in a will which come into operation before 1926 by reference to the old Statutes of Distribution are to be construed as references to the earlier Acts.[2] Hence, in general, the old law applies where the trust is created by the will of a testator who died before 1926,[3] even though the event which brings the trust into effect occurs after 1925;[4] and also where the will, although coming into operation after 1925, declares trusts by reference to a settlement made before 1926.[5] Prima facie,[6] a wife[7] or husband[8] were not included in the next of kin, either apart from the Statutes of Distribution or under them, but where the donees were the persons who by virtue of the statute would be entitled to the testator's property, the widow was included,[9] but there is no such distinction for the purposes of the new rules of distribution.[10]

1   The following are cases of implied reference: *Garrick v Lord Camden* (1807) 14 Ves 372 ('as if I had died intestate'); *Edwards v Saloway* (1848) 2 Ph 625 ('as in case of intestacy'). For distribution to be made according to the statute, there must be a distinct indication to that effect in the will: *Halton v Foster* (1868) 3 Ch App 505 (where it was held that a reference to 'death unmarried' contained no such implication). In one case a reference to the Statutes of Distribution was treated as equivalent to 'by law' and the heir was held entitled to realty: *Re Hughes, Loddiges v Jones* [1916] 1 Ch 493.

2   Administration of Estates Act 1925, s 50(1), (2), this section should now be read in the light of the Law Reform (Succession) Act 1995, s 1(4) (minor amendment). References to the AEA 1925, s 50(1) in wills or codicils coming into operation on or after 4 April 1988 will be construed subject to the provisions of the Family Law Reform Act 1987, ss 1 and 18; see Chapter 72, para **[72.14]** supra. 17 *Halsbury's Statutes* (4th edn) 556. See Vol 2, Part G, para **[245.70]**.

3   *Edwards v Saloway* (1848) 2 Ph 625; *Bullock v Downes* (1860) 9 HL Cas 1; *Nichols v Haviland* (1855) 1 K & J 504; *Re Hughes, Loddiges v Jones* [1916] 1 Ch 493.

4   *Re Sutcliffe, Sutcliffe v Robershaw* [1929] 1 Ch 123 (where the testator died in 1875 and the property was on the death of a life tenant to be held in trust for the next of kin under the statute at his decease if he had then died intestate); *Re Sutton, Evans v Oliver* [1934] Ch 209 ('if I were to die immediately after the death of my wife intestate'; wife died in 1933 but old law applied where will came into operation before 1926); *Re Jackson, Holiday v Jackson* (1943) 113 LJ Ch 78 (similar case).

5   *Re Walsh, Public Trustee v Walsh* [1936] 1 All ER 327; *Re Hooper's Settlement, Phillips v Lake* [1943] Ch 116, [1943] 1 All ER 173 (a reference to the statute by itself is not a sufficient indication of a contrary intention: it required some such words as 'for the time being in force', either express or implied, to show a contrary intention).

6   But the context may justify her inclusion: *Re Collins' Trust* [1877] WN 87.

7   *Garrick v Lord Camden* (1807) 14 Ves 372 at 385; *Lee v Lee* (1860) 1 Drew & Sm 85; *Re Parry, Leak v Scott* (1888) 4 TLR 696; *Re Fitzgerald* (1889) 58 LJ Ch 662; *Re Gray's Settlement, Akers v Sears* [1896] 2 Ch 802; *Queensland Trustees Ltd v Robertson* [1911] St R Qd 172; *Re Richardson* [1956] QSR 485. But see *Re Gilligan's Goods* [1950] P 32, [1949] 2 All ER 401, 'next of kin under the statute of distributions' in (original) s 18, Wills Act 1837; see Vol 2, Part G, para **[244.15]**, held to include a widow.

8   *Milne v Gilbart* (1852) 2 De GM & G 715; *Walker v Cusin* [1917] 1 IR 63.

9   *Martin v Glover* (1844) 1 Coll 269; *Jenkins v Gower* (1846) 2 Coll 537. But the widow might be excluded by the class of the next of kin being ascertained at a date later than the death of the testator and his widow: see *Godkin v Murphy* (1843) 2 Y & C Ch Cas 351, but this case was doubted in *Jenkins v Gower* and see *Starr v Newberry* (1857) 23 Beav 436; *Lee v Lee* (1860) 1 Drew & Sm 85.

10   Administration of Estates Act 1925, s 50(1); see Vol 2, Part G, para **[244.65]**.

[77.3]

Ascertainment of class. Whatever may be the time of distribution, where there is a gift to the next of kin of a testator, without more, the class prima facie has to be ascertained as at the death of the testator,[1] and where there is a gift to the next of kin of any other person, the class prima facie has to be ascertained at that person's death if he survived the testator,[2] and, if not, at the testator's death.[3] This prima facie rule can be displaced by the terms of the will. Thus where a will made it clear that the testator did not intend 'next of kin' to include his two daughters, who were his sole next of kin at the date of the will and at his death, the class of next of kin was to be ascertained at the death of the survivor of his two daughters.[4] In a gift to a class of next of kin of the testator, or his nearest relatives, or similar class, living at a future period of distribution, the entire class is ascertained at the death of the testator, but only those take who survive the period of distribution.[5] It is always possible for the testator to say that the class is to be ascertained at some later time, eg he may give property after the death of a tenant for life to the persons who shall then be his next of kin, and then, apart from any reference to the Statutes of Distribution, the class is to be ascertained at the death of the tenant for life in accordance with the express words of the will.[6]

1   *Wharton v Barker* (1858) 4 K & J 483; *Bird v Luckie* (1850) 8 Hare 301 (where the sole next of kin took a prior life interest); *Gorbell v Davison* (1854) 18 Beav 556 (where two of the next of kin had prior life interests); *Lee v Lee* (1860) 1 Drew & Sm 85 (one of the next of kin had a prior life interest); *Re Ford, Patten v Sparks* (1895) 72 LT 5 (where the life tenants were restricted from alienating their interests); *Re Maher, Maher v Toppin* [1909] 1 IR 70. In all cases the class had to be ascertained at the death of the testator. See also *Re Blyth, Trustees, Executor and Agency Co Ltd v Malcolm* [1925] VLR 633; *Re Maine, Union Trustee Co of Australia Ltd v Maine* [1927] VLR 82; *Re Jermyn* [1965] VR 376; *Re Campbell* [1928] 4 DLR 797; *Re Wright* [1955] 5 DLR 213; *Re Richardson* [1956] QSR 485.
2   *Gundry v Pinniger* (1852) 1 De GM & G 502; *Wharton v Barker* (1858) 4 K & J 483; *Jacobs v Jacobs* (1853) 16 Beav 557; *Re Goldie* [1952] NZLR 928; *Coles v Blakeley* [1955] SCR 508. See *Re Gansloser's Will Trusts* [1952] Ch 30, [1951] 2 All ER 936, where a contrary conclusion was reached on the construction of the will; see also *Re Bourke's Will Trusts, Barclays Bank Trust Co Ltd v Canada Permanent Trust Co* [1980] 1 All ER 219, [1980] 1 WLR 539; *Re Johnston* (1982) 138 DLR (3d) 392; and *Re Verdonk* (1979) 106 DLR (3d) 450, at 457 where this sentence is cited.
3   *Philps v Evans* (1850) 4 De G & Sm 188; *Wharton v Barker* (1858) 4 K & J 483; *Re Philps' Will* (1868) LR 7 Eq 151; *Rees v Fraser* (1879) 26 Gr 233. For a case of contrary intention, see *Re Rees, Williams v Davies* (1890) 44 Ch D 484 (where a widow gave her personal estate to 'such persons as would have become entitled to my husband's personal estate had he died intestate and without leaving any widow him surviving': the persons entitled had to be ascertained at the death of the husband and the share of any who died in the widow's lifetime lapsed), and *Trustees etc Co Ltd v Engelbert* (1951) 51 SRNSW 244 (the persons who upon the deaths of the wife and daughter are entitled as the testator's next of kin according to the law relating to intestate's estates: class ascertained at death of survivor of wife and daughter).
4   *Re Clanchy's Will Trusts, Lynch v Edwards* [1970] 2 All ER 489, distinguishing *Re Winn, Brook v Whitton* [1910] 1 Ch 278, infra; *Re Tuckett's Will Trusts, Williams v National Provincial Bank* (1967) 111 Sol Jo 811 (next of kin ascertained after the life tenant's death).
5   *Spink v Lewis* (1791) 3 Bro CC 355; *Re Nash, Prall v Bevan* (1894) 71 LT 5; *Re Winn, Brook v Whitton* [1910] 1 Ch 278 (next of kin living at the time of the trust failing). In every case of a gift 'to my next of kin' or 'my nearest relations' or any gift of that kind, the prima facie rule is, and it is not only a rule but the natural meaning of the words, that the class is to be ascertained at the death of the testator. When the testator dies, certain people answer the description of his relatives, or his next of kin, or his nearest in blood, or any of those expressions, and it is difficult to see, where he is contemplating a class some of whom may die before a certain time and others may survive that time, at what other time the class is to be ascertained than at the testator's death. Thus the most natural construction is that the gift is a gift to the next of kin to

be ascertained at the testator's death, but that any one of the class so ascertained, in order to take under the gift, must survive the time stated in the will: *Re Winn, Brook v Whitton* [1910] 1 Ch 278 at 286; *Re McRae, McDonald v Creer* (1928) 28 SRNSW 447. This rule is not affected by the fact that the gift comprises the proceeds of sale of realty as well as personal property: *Cusack v Rood* (1876) 24 WR 391.

6   *Re Winn, Brook v Whitton* [1910] 1 Ch 278; *National Trustee Co Ltd v Fleury* [1965] SCR 817 (property given to a person for life who was the sole next of kin at his death and then for his next of kin); *Re Butler* (1965) 50 DLR (2d) 210; *Re Treble* (1966) 56 DLR (2d) 402; but, if there is a reference to the Statutes of Distribution, see the cases in para **[77.4]**, n 1.

[77.4]
Ascertainment of class described by reference to Statutes of Distribution.
Where the gift was to the testator's next of kin entitled by virtue of the Statutes of Distribution, even though they were to be so entitled at some future time,[1] the class was prima facie ascertained as at the death of the testator.[2] The context, however, might require them to be ascertained as if the testator had died at some other period.[3] The same rules apply to the ascertainment of persons entitled under the new rules of distribution.[4]

1   *Re Winn, Brook v Whitton* [1910] 1 Ch 278. The ordinary rule which would have ascertained the class at the time referred to is rebutted, because of the necessity for every person who claims under the gift to prove his title by virtue of the statute.
2   *Bullock v Downes* (1860) 9 HL Cas 1 (in such cases the word 'then' is treated as referring only to the time when the persons entitled would come into possession of what had been bequeathed to them); *Mortimore v Mortimore* (1879) 4 App Cas 448; *Re Wilson, Wilson v Batchelor* [1907] 1 Ch 450 (a case where the tenant for life was the sole next of kin).
3   *Wharton v Barker* (1858) 4 K & J 483; *Clowes v Hilliard* (1876) 4 Ch D 413; *Sturge and Great Western Rly Co* (1881) 19 Ch D 444 (in such cases the class is said to be an artificial class); *Re McFee, McFee v Toner* (1910) 103 LT 210 (gift of annuity with a gift of accumulations of income on cesser of annuity); *Re Helsby, Neate v Bozie* (1914) 84 LJ Ch 682 (class to be ascertained at death of daughter of testatrix); *Re Mellish, Day v Withers* [1916] 1 Ch 562 (class to be ascertained after expiration of two life interests and to the next of kin of the first life tenant); *Hutchinson v National Refuges for Homeless and Destitute Children* [1920] AC 795 (class to be ascertained on failure of trusts); *Re Krawitz's Will Trusts, Krawitz v Crawford* [1959] 3 All ER 793, [1959] 1 WLR 1192 (a similar case).
4   *Re Bridgen, Chaytor v Edwin* [1938] Ch 205, [1937] 4 All ER 342.

[77.5]
Shares in which next of kin take. In the case of a gift to the next of kin under or according to the old rules of distribution, they take as tenants in common in the shares fixed by the statute in cases where either the will in terms refers to the statutory mode of distribution,[1] or is silent on the subject;[2] but if, for example, the testator directs that they are to take equally, effect must be given to such direction.[3] A gift to persons entitled under the new rules of distribution would, it seems, have a similar effect.[4]

1   *Holloway v Radcliffe* (1857) 23 Beav 163; *Fielden v Ashworth* (1875) LR 20 Eq 410 ('as the law directs').
2   Such a gift describes not only the persons but their interests; *Martin v Glover* (1844) 1 Coll 269 at 272.
3   *Re Richards, Davies v Edwards* [1910] 2 Ch 74.
4   *Re Bridgen, Chaytor v Edwin* [1938] Ch 205, [1937] 4 All ER 342.

[77.6]
Next of kin excluding certain persons. In the case of a gift of this kind the next of kin are ascertained as if these persons were dead at the time in question, but without any other difference from the above rule.[1]

1   *White v Springett* (1869) 4 Ch App 300; *Re Taylor, Taylor v Ley* (1885) 52 LT 839; *Lee v Lee* (1860) 1 Drew & Sm 85; *Lindsay v Ellicott* (1876) 46 LJ Ch 878. Where expressions of this kind are now used it is very common to create a special class: eg as if a named person had died at a certain time, intestate, a spinster or bachelor and without leaving a parent.

[77.7]
Next of kin as executors think fit. Where the residue is to be disposed of as the executors think fit, the executors take in trust for the persons entitled on intestacy.[1]

1   *Re Carville, Shone v Walthamstow Borough Council* [1937] 4 All ER 464.

CHAPTER 78

Gifts to 'heir'

[78.1]
'Heir'. This word has lost much of its importance since 1925 when descent to the heir on intestacy was abolished[1] and this finally destroyed the conception which had lingered so long in the law that the right of a person to dispose of his land by will was an encroachment upon the rights of the heir. The modern view of complete freedom of testamentary disposition has not, however, altogether prevailed, for that right has since been in effect curtailed by statute.[2] But, although descent was abolished, the word 'heir' was necessarily retained for certain purposes.[3] The principal of these was the use of the word when creating entailed interests, which were still created by the use of the same expressions as before 1926.[4] The importance of this has been much reduced by the Trusts of Land and Appointment of Trustees Act 1996 (TLATA 1996) which provides that no new entailed interest can be created after 1 January 1997.[5]

The word can also be used in a will to create interests where the heir takes, as it is said, by purchase, that is, otherwise than by descent on the death of a person intestate. Thus, a gift of real estate may still be made either immediately or as a remainder to the 'heir' or the 'heirs' of a named person and the person to take will be ascertained according to the old rules governing the descent of real estate under the Inheritance Act 1833.[6] A gift to the 'heir' or 'heirs' of any person will take effect in favour of the person or persons who satisfy that description at some particular time;[7] and in a gift to 'the heir of the body' of any person or 'heirs of the body' of any person, the words have a similar meaning.[8] A devise to the heirs of the body of a deceased person previously created an estate tail, the first of such heirs who becomes entitled taking by purchase.[9] A devise to 'my own right heirs except' A, where A is in fact the heir, is ineffectual.[10]

---

1 Administration of Estates Act 1925, s 45(1)(a); 17 *Halsbury's Statutes* (4th edn) 450.
2 Inheritance (Provision for Family and Dependants) Act 1975; 17 *Halsbury's Statutes* (4th edn) 505; see Chapter 105.
3 The word 'heir' may still be used for the purpose of creating equitable interests in an heir taking by purchase, that is, otherwise than by descent: Law of Property Act 1925, ss 130, 132 (37 *Halsbury's Statutes* (4th edn) 288, 292), as affected by the TLATA 1996. The construction of the word 'heir', or 'heirs' is unaffected by the provisions of the Family Law Reform Act 1969, s 15(2); see Vol 2, Part G, para **[245.39]** but is subject to the construction in the Family Law Reform Act 1987, s 19(2) (slightly amended by the TLATA 1996, s 25(1), Sch 3, para 25), see Vol 2, Part G, para **[246.111]**. Cf *Paton's Trustees v Paton* 1947 SC 250; *Rushbrook v Pearman* (1913) 32 NZLR 680; *Macleay v Treadwell* [1937] AC 626, [1937] 2 All ER 38.
4 The words used must be the same as those used in a deed before 1926, see Chapter 84.
5 TLATA 1996, s 2(6),Sch 1, para 5.

6   Law of Property Act 1925, s 132; 37 *Halsbury's Statutes* (4th edn) 292; *Re Bourke's Will Trusts, Barclays Bank Trust Co Ltd v Canada Permanent Trust Co* [1980] 1 All ER 219, [1980] 1 WLR 539.
7   *Evans v Evans* [1892] 2 Ch 173; *Skinner v Gumbleton* [1903] 1 IR 36.
8   *Van Grutten v Foxwell* [1897] AC 658; *Wesslbenyi v Jamieson* [1907] AC 440.
9   *Mandeville's Case* (1328) Co Litt 26b. As stated entailed interests can no longer be created after 1 January 1997 by virtue of the TLATA 1996, s 2, Sch 1, para 5.
10 *Re Smith, Bull v Smith* [1933] Ch 847, following *Pugh v Goodtitle* (1787) 3 Bro Parl Cas 454. A devise to 'right heirs' was construed in Tasmania as a devise to the eldest son: *Re Wescombe* (1944) Tas LR 35.

[78.2]

Heir of living person. In cases of a direct gift to the heir, where the ancestor is living, since no one can be the heir of a living person, the technical meaning may be displaced, and the person who is heir presumptive may be designated.[1] Otherwise the heir is prima facie ascertained at the death of the ancestor, whether the latter is the testator or any other person and whether the gift is immediate or future.[2] The context may make the heir ascertainable at the time of the death of a tenant for life,[3] or, where such a person predeceases the testator, as if the testator had died at the time of the death of such person.[4] The heir may also be ascertainable at the time a gift over takes effect.[5]

1   *Doe d Winter v Perratt* (1843) 6 Man & G 314 at 363; *Dormer v Phillips* (1855) 4 De GM & G 855; *Re Hooper, Hooper v Carpenter* [1936] Ch 442, [1936] 1 All ER 277.
2   *Doe d Pilkington v Spratt* (1833) 5 B & Ad 731; *Rawlinson v Wass* (1852) 9 Hare 673; *Re Frith, Hindson v Wood* (1901) 85 LT 455; *Re Maher, v Maher v Toppin* [1909] 1 IR 70; *Re Allan* [1939] 1 DLR 766; *Re Mackenzie* (1958) 15 DLR (2d) 113.
3   *Lightfoot v Maybery* [1914] AC 782; *Re Hooper, Hooper v Carpenter* [1936] Ch 442, [1936] 1 All ER 277; *Wylie's Trustees v Bruce* 1919 SC 211.
4   *Re Hooper, Hooper v Carpenter* [1936] Ch 442, [1936] 1 All ER 277; and see *Lucas-Tooth v Lucas-Tooth* [1921] 1 AC 594 (bequest of stock for life and then 'to the heir of the baronetcy at present held by Sir R L': heir ascertained at death of survivor of brothers).
5   *Doe d King v Frost* (1820) 3 B & Ald 546.

[78.3]

Heir of particular character. Unless some other form of heirship is specified in the will, the heir is ascertained under the Inheritance Act 1933.[1] The will may specify heirs of the testator's name.[2] A gift to heirs of a particular character, unless referring merely to the descent of an estate tail,[3] takes effect only in favour of heirs general, conditionally on their possessing that character, unless the intention of the testator is shown to the contrary.[4]

1   *Re Higham, Higham v Higham* [1937] 2 All ER 17. As to 'nearest male heir', see *Re McIlrath* [1959] VR 720.
2   *Wrightson v Macaulay* (1845) 14 M & W 214; *Thorpe v Thorpe* (1862) 1 H & C 326.
3   This may be the case where a devise to 'heirs male' is construed as 'heirs male of the body'; See Chapter 84.
4   See *Wrightson v Macaulay* (1845) 14 M & W 214 at 231; *Silcocks v Silcocks* [1916] 2 Ch 161; *Re Watkins, Maybery v Lightfoot* [1912] 2 Ch 430 at 436.

[78.4]

Bequest to the heir. Where the gift is of a personal estate or of a mixed fund of real and personal estate, the word 'heir' prima facie retains its usual meaning, and unless there is something in the will to show a contrary intention, the particular person filling the description of heir-at-law takes the property as a persona designata.[1] In a gift of personal estate alone, 'heirs' has been construed as meaning either next of kin,[2] the widow taking her share,[3] or executors and administrators.[4] The context may, however, give other meanings to the word such as children,[5] and it may have several meanings in one will,[6] and now heirs may properly be used for limitations of personal as well as real property, and the person designated as heir will be ascertained in accordance with the general law in force before 1926.[7] Thus a limitation of real and personal property to 'heirs and surviving issue' was construed as a gift to the person or persons who, if the general law immediately before 1 January 1926 had remained unaffected, would have answered the description of heir of the deceased in respect of his freehold land either at the date of death of the deceased or at the time named in the limitation.[8]

1   *Hamilton v Mills* (1861) 29 Beav 193; *Smith v Butcher* (1878) 10 Ch D 113; *Keay v Boulton* (1883) 25 Ch D 212 at 215; *Skinner v Gumbleton* [1903] 1 IR 36. In a gift to the successors in a person's titles, the intention is to make an absolute gift of the property to the person who should succeed the testator in either title: *Re Earl of Cathcart* (1912) 56 Sol Jo 271. Formerly, the heir might take the real estate and the next of kin the personal estate and a mixed gift was sometimes severed for this reason but this is not now necessary as one set of persons are entitled on intestacy to proceeds of sale of all the estate.
2   *Low v Smith* (1856) 2 Jur NS 344; *Doody v Higgins* (1856) 2 K & J 729; *Re Gamboa's Trusts* (1858) 4 K & J 756; *Re Preston's Trusts* (1863) 1 New Rep 470; *Re Jeaffreson's Trusts* (1866) LR 2 Eq 276; *Re Philps' Will* (1868) LR 7 Eq 151; *Walker v Cusin* [1917] 1 IR 63. A gift of personal estate to a person's 'heirs and assigns' is a gift to those entitled on intestacy at that person's death: *Re Newton's Trusts* (1867) LR 4 Eq 171.
3   *Re Stevens' Trusts* (1872) LR 15 Eq 110.
4   *Lachlan v Reynolds* (1852) 9 Hare 796 at 798 (a case where 'or' was changed to 'and', so that the gift read 'and their heirs'). A gift of personal property to a person and his heirs or assignees is an absolute gift to that person: *Re Fergusson* (1914) 34 NZLR 70.
5   *Loveday v Hopkins* (1755) Amb 273; *Symers v Jobson* (1848) 16 Sim 267 (heirs of the body); *Pattenden v Hobson* (1853) 1 Eq Rep 28; *Bull v Comberbach* (1858) 25 Beav 540.
6   *Powell v Boggis* (1866) 35 Beav 535, where the word occurred seven times in the will and was construed 'executors and administrators' in three places, 'next of kin' in two places, had its proper meaning of heir-at-law in one place and in the last place meant personal representatives and assigns.
7   Law of Property Act 1925, s 132; 37 *Halsbury's Statutes* (4th edn) 292.
8   *Re Bourke's Will Trusts, Barclays Bank Trust Co v Canada Permanent Trust Co* [1980] 1 All ER 219, [1980] 1 WLR 539, applying s 132, Law of Property Act 1925; 'heirs' was construed in its strict pre-1926 sense. The obiter observation of Roxburgh J in *Re Kilvert, Midland Bank Executor and Trustee Co Ltd v Kilvert* [1957] Ch 388 at 393–394, [1957] 2 All ER 196 at 199 to the effect that, in the case of a gift to a class of persons or their heirs both realty and personalty would be distributed in accordance with the present law of intestate succession, making no distinction between realty and personalty, was doubted. See also *Ng Chi-fong v Hui Ho Pui-fun* [1987] HKLR 462 at p 474, where the text is referred to.

[78.5]
To a person 'or his heirs'. In the case of personalty a gift to a named person 'or his heirs' is in the ordinary way substitutional, the word 'heirs' being read as 'next of kin'.[1] If a legacy is given to A 'or his heirs', A, if he survives the stator, will be entitled to take, but, if A dies in the lifetime of the testator, the word 'heirs' is introduced to prevent a lapse, and therefore if the first legatee, ie A, does not take, the same person will take as would have taken after him, if there had been no lapse, and the devolution of the legacy follows that of the personal

estate.² In a devise to a person or his heirs, the word 'or' is changed to 'and' and the devisee takes the fee.³ But in a direct gift in a deed of personal estate to 'the heir' of a named person, the words are in the ordinary case treated as descriptive and not substitutional, and the gift takes effect in favour of the person who is the named person's heir.⁴

1   *Re Ibbetson, Ibbetson v Ibbetson* (1903) 88 LT 461; *Re Whitehead, Whitehead v Hemsley* [1920] 1 Ch 298 at 304; *Re Roberts' Will* (1929) 29 SRNSW 562; and see *Re Marshall Estate* [1944] 3 DLR 178; *Re Collishaw* [1953] 3 DLR 829; *Re Hinkson* [1959] VR 686. Compare *Re Hollis's Estate* (1968) 66 DLR (2d) 369 ('and his heirs' construed as words of limitation); and *Tottrup v Patterson* (1970) 9 DLR (3d) 314 (gift of residue to a donee 'his heirs, executors, and administrators absolutely and forever'; held to be words of limitation).

2   *Hamilton v Mills* (1861) 29 Beav 193 at 198; *Finlason v Tatlock* (1870) LR 9 Eq 258. As to a postponed gift, see para [68.2] supra.

3   This was the construction adopted before the Wills Act 1837: *Read v Snell* (1743) 2 Atk 642 at 645; *Wright v Wright* (1750) 1 Ves Sen 409, and this construction was continued after that Act: *Harris v Davis* (1844) 1 Coll 416; *Greenway v Greenway* (1860) 2 De GF & J 128; *Re Boyer, Neathercoat v Lawrence* [1935] Ch 382. On the question whether the Wills Act 1837, s 29 (Vol 2, Part G, para [244.29]) altered the construction of changing 'or' into 'and', see *Re Clerke, Clowes v Clerke* [1915] 2 Ch 301; *Re Whitehead, Whitehead v Hemsley* [1920] 1 Ch 298; *Re Hayden, Pask v Perry* [1931] 2 Ch 333.

4   *Hamilton v Mills* (1861) 29 Beav 193. In a gift over of leasehold on the death of the donee 'without lawful heirs', it was held on the context that this meant without next of kin being children or descendants: *Gray v Gray* (1889) 23 IR 399. A gift of personal property to a donee and his heirs confers on him an absolute interest: *Re McElligott* [1944] Ch 216, [1944] 1 All ER 441, and similarly a gift to a donee his heirs executors and assigns without 'or' or 'and' is absolute: *Re Little* [1952] OWN 732.

[78.6]
To persons or their heirs and successors. The gift being one of residue comprising both realty and personality, it was held that the property was to be divided in equal shares between the parties, but one party being dead at the testator's death, the persons entitled under the law of intestacy applicable at the death of the testator took as joint tenants the share the deceased would have taken had he survived the testator.¹ However where in a similar gift there was no single category to which the words in the will could refer it was held that there was a gift to two separate categories of beneficiary, namely heirs, and surviving issue; but since there was nothing indicating a severance they took as joint tenants.² Further both categories were ascertained at the date of the death of the relevant praepositus.³ Where no personality was involved a gift over to 'my children and their heirs' operated in Saskatchewan where there was only one child who had died during the life interest as a gift of one third to the widow and two thirds to the children per stirpes.⁴ In the case of a mixed residue a gift to 'my own and my wife's natural heirs' after life interest, the heirs were to be determined at the death of the last life tenant.⁵

1   *Re Kilvert, Midland Bank Executor and Trustee Co Ltd v Kilvert* [1957] Ch 388, [1957] 2 All ER 196.

2   *Re Bourke's Will Trusts, Barclays Bank Trust Co Ltd v Canada Permanent Trust Co* [1980] 1 All ER 219, [1980] 1 WLR 539, *Re Kilvert, Midland Bank Executor and Trustee Co Ltd v Kilvert* [1957] Ch 388, [1957] 2 All ER 196, distinguished.

3   *Re Bourke's Will Trusts, Barclays Bank Trust Co Ltd v Canada Permanent Trust Co* [1980] 1 All ER 219, [1980] 1 WLR 539, and thus not at the date of ultimate distribution.

4   *Re Voice Estate, Voice v Voice* (1964) 48 DLR (2d) 558.
5   *Re McKinnon* [1966] 1 OR 663.

[78.7]
Bequest to 'my heirs and assigns'. This is a gift to the next of kin.[1]

1   *Re McKinnon* (1955) 55 DLR (2d) 20.

CHAPTER 79

Gifts to 'family', to 'relations', and to 'representatives'

I. 'FAMILY'

[79.1]

General meaning. A gift in the will of a married man to his family, or a gift of personalty[1] to the family of any person, is in the ordinary way a gift to his children,[2] who would take as joint tenants,[3] or, if there are no children, to all such persons as would be entitled on intestacy.[4] The primary meaning of 'family' in a will is 'children'[5] and other relatives are excluded.[6] Formerly, in the case of a gift of a mixed fund of realty and personalty, the word might be used to denote persons entitled on intestacy to the property, that is, the heir as to real estate and the next of kin as to the personalty,[7] but for such purposes the distinction between realty and personalty has been abolished.[8]

1   Including a gift of realty on trust for sale: *Woods v Woods* (1836) 1 My & Cr 401 at 408. The same rule may be applicable to mixed realty and personalty: *Barnes v Patch* (1803) 8 Ves 604; or to real estate alone: *Reay v Rawlinson* (1860) 29 Beav 88; *Burt v Hellyar* (1872) LR 14 Eq 160.
2   *Pigg v Clarke* (1876) 3 Ch D 672; *Re Hutchinson and Tenant* (1878) 8 Ch D 540; *Re Muffett, Jones v Mason* (1886) 55 LT 671; *Re Mulqueen's Trusts* (1881) 7 LR Ir 127; *Re Hobbs* [1929] 4 DLR 433; *Re McGrath's Will* (1899) 20 NSWLR (B & P) 55; *Re Allen* [1933] SASR 122; *Re M'Cann, Donnelly v Moore* [1916] 1 IR 255.
3   *Beales v Crisford* (1843) 13 Sim 592; *Gregory v Smith* (1852) 9 Hare 708 at 712; but *Owen v Penny* (1850) 14 Jur 359, is to the contrary.
4   *Doe d Chattaway v Smith* (1816) 5 M & S 126 at 130; *Grant v Lynam* (1828) 4 Russ 292; *Re Maxton* (1858) 4 Jur NS 407.
5   *Re M'Cann, Donnelly v Moore* [1916] 1 IR 255.
6   *Woods v Woods* (1836) 1 My & Cr 401; *Burt v Hellyar* (1872) LR 14 Eq 160; *Re Battersby's Trusts* [1896] 1 IR 600; *Searey's Trustees v Allbuary* 1907 SC 823. As to ascertainment of class, see *Re Parkinson's Trust, ex p Thompson* (1851) 1 Sim NS 242.
7   *White v Briggs* (1848) 2 Ph 583.
8   Administration of Estates Act 1925, s 45; 17 *Halsbury's Statutes* (4th edn) 450.

[79.2]

'Family'. This is a word of the most loose and flexible description,[1] and according to the circumstances, has been held to mean a man's wife and children,[2] or his household consisting of his wife, children, and servants;[3] of his next of kin[4] and his genealogical stock.[5] Where used to denote the objects of a power of appointment, the word may denote any relative whatever, or descendants of every degree.[6] Where the family is indicated merely by its surname, the court will ascertain from the surrounding circumstances of the case what family of that name was best known to the testator, and the persons to take will be determined accordingly.[7] Where none of these meanings can be given consistently with the words of the will, the gift may be void for uncertainty,[8] or the word may be rejected.[9] The word 'family' may on occasion be treated as a word of limitation.[10]

1   *Green v Marsden* (1853) 1 Drew 646 at 651; *Morton v Tewart* (1842) 2 Y & C Ch Cas 67 at 81.
2   *Blackwell v Bull* (1836) 1 Keen 176; *Re Drew, Drew v Drew* [1899] 1 Ch 336 at 342; *James v Lord Wynford* (1854) 2 Sm & G 350; *Re Hewitt* [1945] SASR 102; *Gibson Estate v Ashbury College Inc* (1999) 179 DLR (4th) 557 (family meant children). Where there are no children, relatives must be meant and the relationship may be restricted by a provision for equal division: *Re Edwardes* (1951) 95 Sol Jo 382.
3   *Blackwell v Bull* (1836) 1 Keen 176; *Pig v Clarke* (1876) 3 Ch D 672 at 674.
4   *Cruwys v Colman* (1804) 9 Ves 319.
5   *Lucas v Goldsmid* (1861) 29 Beav 657 at 660; *Re Macleay* (1875) LR 20 Eq 186.
6   *Grant v Lynam* (1828) 4 Russ 292 (power to appoint to such of his family or relations as he shall think fit, but, if the power was not exercised, the gift went to the next of kin); *Snow v Teed* (1870) LR 9 Eq 622 ('her own family' not confined to next of kin); *Re Keighley, Keighley v Keighley* [1919] 2 Ch 388 (power to appoint to 'my people': will exercise power in favour of a child of the illegitimate daughter of the donor's mother); *Lambe v Eames* (1871) 6 Ch App 597 (gift to illegitimate descendant held good); *Williams v Williams* (1851) 1 Sim NS 358 (descendants of every degree); *Doe d King v Frost* (1820) 3 B & Ald 546 ('younger branches of the family'); *Re Barlow's Will Trusts* [1979] 1 All ER 296, [1979] 1 WLR 278, ('family' held to mean all blood relations of the testatrix). In *Doe d Smith v Fleming* (1835) 2 Cr M & R 638, a gift to the 'younger branches of the family' was construed as void for uncertainty. See also *Armstrong v Armstrong* (1888) 21 LR Ir 114; and *Re Perowne* [1951] Ch 785, [1951] 2 All ER 201, where a gift to widows of deceased brothers of a testatrix was held excessive and void under a power to appoint for the benefit of my family.
7   *Gregory v Smith* (1852) 9 Hare 708; *Charitable Donations and Bequests Comrs v Deey* (1891) 27 LR Ir 289.
8   *Harland v Trigg* (1782) 1 Bro CC 142; *Doe d Hayter v Joinville* (1802) 3 East 172; *Yeap Cheah Neo v Ong Cheng Neo* (1875) LR 6 PC 381; *Re Cullimore's Trusts* (1891) 27 LR Ir 18.
9   *Robinson v Waddelow* (1836) 8 Sim 134; but see *Re Parkinson's Trust, ex p Thompson* (1851) 1 Sim NS 242 at 245.
10 A gift for the benefit of the testator's brothers and sisters and their respective families gives each brother and sister who survives the testator an absolute interest in his or her share at the death of the testator whether or not he or she then has any family or is married, and a brother or sister who predeceases the testator gets nothing; *Re Hill, Public Trustee v O'Donnell* [1923] 2 Ch 259.

[79.3]
Dependants. The definition of 'dependants' for the purposes of the Inheritance (Provision for Family and Dependants) Act 1975,[1] and any illustrative cases thereon, will no doubt have a considerable influence on the construction of the word when used in a will. It has been held in a Scottish case that the word 'dependants' is too uncertain in its meaning to be given any context in a testamentary deed.[2]

1   Inheritance (Provision for Family and Dependants) Act 1975, s 1(1), (3); see Vol 2, Part G, para **[247.2]**
2   *Robertson's Judicial Factor v Robertson* 1968 SLT 32, OH.

II. 'RELATIONS'

[79.4]
Operation of gift. The primary sense of the word 'relations'[1] extends to relations of every degree of relationship,[2] however remote, and where donees are

thus described, this effect is given to the word wherever it is possible,[3] for instance, in cases where the gift is a power of selection and appointment among relations,[4] or is to poor relations by way of perpetual charity.[5] In general, however, this meaning cannot be given to the word in a direct gift to relations, or in a gift to them under a power of distribution, on account of the uncertainty[6] in a number of persons designated,[7] and therefore the court in such a case formerly presumed that the testator intended his next of kin according to the Statutes of Distribution;[8] and there would be the like presumption in favour of the persons entitled under the new rules of distribution.[9] The rule that a disposition to the 'relations' of the testator will be restricted to the testator's next of kin is an artificial rule designed to prevent the failure of a bequest for uncertainty and the rule does not apply if the effect of the disposition is not uncertain.[10] A power in favour of relations which is a power of distribution, sometimes called a non-exclusive power, can only be exercised by appointing amongst the statutory next of kin,[11] the class being ascertained as at the death of the donee of the power.[12] But if the power authorises selection, ie an exclusive power, the word 'relation' is not restricted to next of kin, but extends to relations generally.[13] If, however, the power is not exercised, then, in the absence of a gift over, the class is in either case limited to the statutory next of kin, and the division among them is per capita and not per stirpes.[14] On the context illegitimate children may be included as 'relatives'.[15]

1   Since such words as 'relations' have a tendency to uncertainty the court has at times adopted a restriction upon the class intended, see infra. Similarly, in a gift to 'relations and friends', the word 'friends' has been restricted to relations to save the gift from uncertainty: *Gower v Mainwaring* (1750) 2 Ves Sen 87; *Re Caplin's Will* (1865) 2 Drew & Sm 527; *Coogan v Hayden* (1879) 4 LR Ir 585. A gift to brothers-in-law and sisters-in-law does not include a spouse of a brother or sister of testatrix's deceased husband: *Re Richards, Cawley v Dacey* (1940) 162 LT 47.

2   See *Pyot v Pyot* (1749) 1 Ves Sen 335; but the meaning is generally restricted; see infra.

3   *Bennett v Honywood* (1772) Amb 708.

4   *Supple v Lowson* (1773) Amb 729, and see note 11, infra.

5   Such cases, however, are confined to the statutory next of kin unless the will shows a contrary intention: *Carr v Bedford* (1678) 2 Rep Ch 146; *Griffith v Jones* (1686) 2 Rep Ch 394; and such gifts are confined to relations who are in fact poor: *Mahon v Savage* (1803) 1 Sch & Lef 111. An inquiry may be directed as to who are poor relations: *A-G v Price* (1810) 17 Ves 371; *A-G v Sidney Sussex College* (1865) 34 Beav 654; *Re Scarisbrick* [1951] Ch 622, [1951] 1 All ER 822. See also the Irish case, *Kilroy and Callan v Parker and McGauran* [1966] IR 309, where a gift to 'necessitous nieces and nephews' was not void for uncertainty since the word meant necessitous according to the circumstances in life of the individual whose eligibility fell for consideration.

6   As to uncertainty, see Chapter 53. 'Such of my relatives as are living at or in the vicinity of a named place' has been held uncertain: *Re Hannah's Will, Shields v A-G* (1939) 34 Tas LR 45; and in a forfeiture clause 'relations' has been restricted to blood relations: *Re Winzar* (1953) 55 WALR 35.

7   *Brandon v Brandon* (1819) 3 Swan 312 at 319.

8   *Re Aspinall's Settlement Trusts* (1861) 30 LJ Ch 321; *Re Greenwood's Will* (1861) 3 Giff 390; *Re Knox* (1910) 29 NZLR 1179; *Ross v Ross* (1894) 25 SCR 307; *Reid v Swan* [1911] 1 IR 405, 410; *Re Gun, Sheehy v Nugent* [1915] 1 IR 42; *Hibbert v Hibbert* (1873) LR 15 Eq 372 (where an illegitimate relative was excluded). *Re Shield's Will Trusts, Bache v Shield* [1974] Ch 373 at 376, [1974] 2 All ER 274 at 276: 'It is not disputed that in the absence of some indication of different intention a gift to relations in order to save its validity, is construed as a gift to the statutory next-of-kin of whoever is the person concerned.' See also *Re Gansloser's Will Trusts* [1951] 2 All ER 936. In *Re Kilvert, Midland Bank Executor and Trustee Co Ltd v Kilvert*

[1957] Ch 388, [1957] 2 All ER 196, the word 'successors' in the phrase 'or their heirs and successors was similarly saved from uncertainty by confining the persons intended to those who would take on intestacy; but they took as joint tenants.

9   See *Re Bridgen, Chaytor v Edwin* [1938] Ch 205, [1937] 4 All ER 342; *Re Fox* [1997] 1 Qd R 43 ('blood relations' meant persons who would have taken under intestacy).

10   Thus the rule was not applied in *Re Poulton's Will Trusts, Smail v Litchfield* [1987] 1 All ER 1068, [1987] 1 WLR 795 where the testatrix's daughter was empowered by will to divide the estate among her own 'relatives' at her discretion. This created a power of appointment (not coupled with a trust in favour of the class of objects of the power) and as such a definitive enumeration of the beneficiaries was not required. It would suffice if it was possible to say of any given person whether they were or were not within the class. Accordingly 'relatives' was construed in its ordinary meaning as extending to all persons related to the praepositus and an appointment by the daughter in favour of her cousin's three daughters was valid. *Re Gansloser's Will Trusts, Chartered Bank of India, Australia and China v Chillingworth* [1951] 2 All ER 936, see discussed in Chapter 77. *Re Deakin, Starkey v Eyres* [1894] 3 Ch 565, not followed.

11   *Pope v Whitcombe* (1810) 3 Mer 689; *Lawlor v Henderson* (1877) IR 10 Eq 150; *Re Patterson, Dunlop v Greer* [1899] 1 IR 324.

12   *Finch v Hollingworth* (1855) 21 Beav 112.

13   *Harding v Glyn* (1739) 1 Atk 469 (and see the statement of this case in 5 Ves 501); *Salmsbury v Denton* (1857) 3 K & J 529; *Reid v Swan* [1911] 1 IR 405, and see *Re Griffiths, Griffiths v Griffiths* [1926] VLR 212; *Brown v Gregg* [1945] IR 224.

14   *Pope v Whitcombe* (1810) 3 Mer 689; *Birch v Wade* (1814) 3 Ves & B 198; *Grant v Lynam* (1828) 4 Russ 292; *Lawlor v Henderson* (1877) IR 10 Eq 150; *Reid v Swan* [1911] 1 IR 405.

15   *Re Deakin, Starkey v Eyres* [1894] 3 Ch 565 (inclusion of illegitimate relations); *Hibbert v Hibbert* (1873) LR 15 Eq 372 (exclusion of such relations).

[79.5]

'Nearest relations'. A gift to 'nearest relations' is confined to next of kin within the Statutes of Distribution, even where a charitable purpose is shown.[1]

1   *Edge v Salisbury* (1749) Amb 70; *Goodinge v Goodinge* (1749) 1 Ves Sen 231; *Smith v Campbell* (1815) 19 Ves 400.

[79.6]

Ascertainment of class. A class of relations is ascertained as a rule as if it were a class of next of kin,[1] and in the ordinary way they take per capita[2] and as joint tenants.[3] Where there is a gift to the relations of two different people, the date or dates at which the class or classes of the relatives are to be ascertained depend on the terms of the particular will.[4]

1   See Chapter 79; *Pearce v Vincent* (1836) 2 Keen 230; *Bishop v Cappel* (1847) 1 De G & Sm 411; *Eagles v Le Breton* (1873) LR 15 Eq 148; *Tiffin v Longman* (1852) 15 Beav 275 (where the class was ascertained at the death of life tenant).

2   *Re Shield's Will Trusts, Bache v Shield* [1974] Ch 373, [1974] 2 All ER 274; *Thomas v Hole* (1728) Cas *temp* Talb 251; *Tiffin v Longman* (1852) 15 Beav 275; *Fielden v Ashworth* (1875) LR 20 Eq 410 (where there was a context to the contrary).

3   *Eagles v Le Breton* (1873) LR 15 Eq 148; *Re Gansloser's Will Trusts* [1951] 2 All ER 936.

4   *Re Shield's Will Trusts, Bache v Shield* [1974] Ch 373, [1974] 2 All ER 274 (gift to 'my relations also my wife's relations'; held class to be ascertained as to testator's relations and widow's relations at the widow's death; the other alternatives being that both classes be ascertained at the testator's death or that the testator's relations be ascertained at his death, and the widow's at her death). *Re Gansloser's Will Trusts* [1951] 2 All ER 936, distinguished where the relations were ascertained at the testator's death. The normal rule per Pennycuick VC in *Re Shield's Will Trusts, Bache v Shield* [1974] Ch 373, [1974] 2 All ER 274 at 376, 276, is that the class is ascertained at the death of the person referred to.

III. 'REPRESENTATIVES'

[79.7]
Bequest of personal property. In a bequest of personal property to the 'representatives' of any person, whether simply or with the added qualification of 'legal' or 'personal' or 'legal personal', the description is taken in its ordinary sense and prima facie designates the executors or administrators of that person.[1] Therefore, a gift to a person for life and then for his personal representatives is an absolute gift.[2] The term, however, is capable of being interpreted in any sense required by the context,[3] and this may show that the description means descendants,[4] or next of kin according to the Statutes of Distribution,[5] or where it is otherwise shown that the donees were to take beneficially and not in any fiduciary capacity.[6] The circumstance that the gift is to the person or his representatives immediately on the death of the testator, and not after a life interest, is not a reason for giving to 'executors and administrators' the meaning of next of kin.[7]

1   *Re Brooks, Public Trustee v White* [1928] Ch 214; *Mocatta v Mocatta* (1915) 19 CLR 515.
2   *Re Brooks, Public Trustee v White* [1928] Ch 214.
3   *Re Crawford's Trusts* (1854) 2 Drew 230 at 233. The mere appointment of executors, or references to executors and administrators, showing that they are distinguished from personal representatives, may, but will not necessarily, give a different sense to the words: *Re Ware, Cumberlege v Cumberlege-Ware* (1890) 45 Ch D 269 at 278; *Walter v Makin* (1833) 6 Sim 148 (next of kin intended); *Re Thompson, Machell v Newman* (1886) 55 LT 85 (use of the words 'executors and administrators' in another gift a reason for giving 'legal personal representatives' a different meaning); *Burkitt v Tozer* (1889) 17 OR 587 (needs but a slight context to turn the meaning to next of kin).
4   *Atherton v Crowther* (1854) 19 Beav 448; *Re Horner, Eagleton v Horner* (1887) 37 Ch D 695 at 710; *Re Knowles, Rainford v Knowles* (1888) 59 LT 359; *Re Bromley, Wilson v Bromley* (1900) 83 LT 315. In the case of a gift of real property this word was held to mean 'heirs': *Mallinson v Siddle* (1870) 39 LJ Ch 426.
5   *Booth v Vicars* (1844) 1 Coll 6; *Smith v Palmer* (1848) 7 Hare 225 (division intended); *Atherton v Crowther* (1854) 19 Beav 448 (where personal representatives were to take per stirpes).
6   *King v Cleaveland* (1859) 4 De G & J 477 at 481.
7   *Re Brooks, Public Trustee v White* [1928] Ch 214, following *Re Crawford's Trusts* (1854) 2 Drew 230, and overruling *Bridge v Abbot* (1791) 3 Bro CC 224, and *Cotton v Cotton* (1839) 2 Beav 67.

CHAPTER 80

'Gifts to wife' and 'husband'

I. 'WIFE'

[80.1]

When wife by subsequent marriage included. Where the donee is described as the wife of a person, and that person is married at the date of the will, then, in the absence of a context to the contrary, the wife existing at the date of the will is prima facie the person to take, and not any subsequent wife.[1] The fact that the interest conferred is only during widowhood, after a life interest to the husband,[2] or that it is expressed to be given for the support of the wife and her husband and his children,[3] does not of itself show any contrary intention. The context or the circumstances may show that the description, 'wife', is intended to include a subsequent wife,[4] a person not married to the testator or other person whose wife she is said to be,[5] or a betrothed woman.[6] Where a person is not married at the date of the will, prima facie the donee is the first person to answer the description in the will.[7]

1   *Garratt v Niblock* (1830) 1 Russ & M 629; *Re Drew, Drew v Drew* [1899] 1 Ch 336 at 339; *Re Coley, Hollinshead v Coley* [1903] 2 Ch 102; *Re D'Oyley, Swayne v D'Oyley* (1921) 152 LT Jo 259. In *Marks v Marks* (1908) 40 SCR 210, the gift was held to be in favour of a mistress with whom he was living at the date of the will rather than a former wife. In this case it was assumed that the former wife had been validly married to the testator. Where a remainder was defeasible if a son was born to a life tenant, defeasance was held to occur on the birth of a son by any wife for the time being; but 'son' meant son and not grandson or more remoter issue: *Re Jennings* (1954) 33 UPR 230. See also *Re Devling* [1955] VLR 238; *Re Bassett* [1961] VR 51 (later wife not known to testator); *Re Herlichka* (1969) 3 DLR (3d) 700 (wife benefited rather than mistress).
2   *Re Coley, Hollinshead v Coley* [1903] 2 Ch 102 at 104.
3   On this there is some conflict of authority: *Boreham v Bignall* (1850) 8 Hare 131, which supports the text was followed in *Re Burrow's Trusts* (1864) 10 LT 184, and *Firth v Fielden* (1874) 22 WR 622, but not followed in *Re Lyne's Trust* (1869) LR 8 Eq 65. The last case was followed in *Re Lory* (1891) 7 TLR 419, but has since been departed from in *Re Griffiths' Policy* [1903] 1 Ch 739; *Re Coley, Hollinshead v Coley* [1903] 2 Ch 102.
4   In both *Longworth v Bellamy* (1871) 40 LJ Ch 513; and *Re Drew, Drew v Drew* [1899] 1 Ch 336, a discretionary trust, after a determinable life interest, for the benefit of the donee, his wife and children was held sufficient to rebut the prima facie meaning that wife was confined to the wife living at the date of the will. Where the donee was not married at the date of the will, a second wife has been included: *Peppin v Bickford* (1797) 3 Ves 570. In *Re Hardyman, Teesdale v McClintock* [1925] Ch 287, the testator made a codicil after the second marriage and it was held that the codicil brought the will down to its date. There is a rule that where the person is not married at the date of the will, the first person to answer the description takes: *Re Hickman's Will Trust, Hickman v Hickman* [1948] Ch 624, [1948] 2 All ER 303; and cf *Radford v Willis* (1871) 7 Ch App 7; *Blount v Crozier* [1917] 1 IR 461. As to effect of divorce, see para **[80.3]** infra.

5   A partner to an invalid marriage has been held to be described by the word 'wife': see infra. For
     cases where a mistress has been referred to as 'wife' see *Re Davenport's Trust* (1852) 1 Sm &
     G 126 (gift void); *Turner v Brittain* (1863) 3 New Rep 21 (gift held good); *Re Lowe, Danily v
     Platt* (1892) 61 LJ Ch 415 (gifts held good except for illegitimate child born after date of will);
     Anderson v Berkeley [1902] 1 Ch 936 (gift held good); *Re Brown, Golding v Brady* (1910) 26
     TLR 257 (gift held good); *Re Gale, Gale v Gale* [1941] Ch 209, [1941] 1 All ER 329 (gift bad
     because given to 'widow'); *Re Lynch, Lynch v Lynch* [1943] 1 All ER 168 (gift upheld because
     testator had provided his own dictionary).
6   Applied in *Re Brechin* (1973) 38 DLR (3d) 305. See also *Schloss v Stiebel* (1833) 6 Sim 1
     (where the will recited the intended marriage); *Re Brown, Golding v Brady* (1910) 26 TLR 257
     (a mistress).
7   See cases cited in n 5.

[80.2]
Wife during 'widowhood'. If the gift is to the wife, who is accurately so
described, expressly 'during widowhood' the latter words form a condition as to
the beginning and ending of her interest, so that the effect of a subsequent
divorce before the gift takes effect is that she is disentitled to the gift, since she
does not then become a widow.[1] If she is not accurately so described, that is
where the marriage is for some reason invalid, the words 'until death or re-
marriage' may be read 'until death or marriage subsequent to the death of the
testator'[2] and a similar construction may be put upon the word 'widowhood'.[3] A
gift to a wife 'so long as she remains my widow' gives a determinable life
interest and not a determinable fee simple.[4]

1   *Re Boddington, Boddington v Clairat* (1884) 25 Ch D 685; *Re Kettlewell, Jones v Kettlewell*
     (1907) 98 LT 23.
2   *Re Wagstaff, Wagstaff v Jalland* [1908] 1 Ch 162; *Re Smalley, Smalley v Scotton* [1929] 2 Ch
     112 ('to my wife EAS', where the marriage was bigamous); *Re McInerney* [1966] VR 263.
3   *Re Hammond, Burniston v White* [1911] 2 Ch 342; but see para **[80.6]** infra, for cases where
     there has been no marriage; and see infra under 'widow'.
4   *Re Dietrich* (1963) 36 DLR (2d) 17.

[80.3]
Effect of divorce. A decree absolute of dissolution of marriage finally dissolves
the marriage and the parties cannot thereafter be properly described as
'husband', 'wife' or 'widow';[1] but where a testatrix described herself as the wife
of V and left her estate to the said husband, V, the husband took although the
testatrix subsequently divorced him.[2] Where a power of appointment is given to
appoint a life or less interest to any wife who may survive the appointor, a wife
who is divorced from the appointor cannot take under an appointment because
she is not a wife who survives the appointer.[3] The effect of the new provision
enacted as the Wills Act 1837, s 18A by the Administration of Justice Act 1982[4]
has been noted above.[5] As originally enacted the section provides that where,
after a testator has made a will, a decree of a court dissolves or annuls his
marriage or declares it void then ... any devise or bequest to the former spouse
shall lapse',[6] and the will takes effect as if any appointment of the former spouse
as an executor or as the executor and trustee of the will were omitted.[7] In
relation to the wills of testators dying on or after 1 January 1996, s 18A deems
for these purposes the former spouse to have died when the marriage was
dissolved or annulled.[8] These provisions are subject to a contrary intention
appearing by the will.[9]

1   *Re Morrieson, Hitchins v Morrieson* (1888) 40 Ch D 30; *Re Slaughter Trustees Corpn Ltd v Slaughter* [1945] Ch 355, [1945] 2 All ER 214; *Re Newcombe, Cresswell v Newcombe* [1938] NZLR 98; and see the settlement cases, *Bosworthick v Clegg* (1929) 45 TLR 438; *Re Williams' Settlement, Greenwell v Humphries* [1929] 2 Ch 361. A wife remains a wife until the decree absolute and if the husband dies the day before the decree is made absolute the decree absolute is a nullity and the wife is properly described as his widow: *Re Seaford* [1968] P 53, [1968] 1 All ER 482, CA; see also *Re Kindl* (1982) 140 DLR (3d) 92. But the word may possibly be held upon the context to be a sufficient description: see *N v M* (1885) 1 TLR 523; *Bullmore v Wynter* (1883) 22 Ch D 619. In *Re Devling* [1955] VLR 238, the testator after divorce executed a codicil appointing a new executor but otherwise confirmed his will and it was held that divorced wife took; in *Couper's Judicial Factor v Valentine* 1976 SLT 83 a divorced wife took under a gift 'to my wife, Mrs DC'.
2   *Re Vine* [1955] VLR 200.
3   *Re Allan, Allan v Midland Bank Executor and Trustee Co Ltd* [1954] Ch 295, [1954] 1 All ER 646. A power was given to appoint by deed executed in contemplation of marriage or by will or codicil a life or less interest in a settled fund to any wife who may survive the appointor. Upon its proper construction the condition of being a wife and also that of being a wife surviving the appointor applied both to exercise by deed and by will.
4   50 *Halsbury's Statutes* (4th edn) 587. See Vol 2, Part G, para **[244.17]**.
5   See Chapter 47, para **[47.2]** supra.
6   Wills Act 1837, s 18A(1)(b); see *Re Sinclair, Lloyds Bank plc v Imperial Cancer Research Fund* [1985] Ch 446, [1985] 1 All ER 1066, CA.
7   Wills Act 1837, s 18A(1)(a). This wording applies to wills of testators dying before 1 January 1996: see next note.
8   Wills Act 1837, s 18A is so amended by Law Reform (Succession) Act 1995, s 3 for deaths on or after 1 January 1996.
9   Wills Act 1837, s 18A(3). And without prejudice to the right of such a spouse to apply for financial provision under the Inheritance (Provision for Family and Dependants) Act 1975; 17 *Halsbury's Statutes* (4th edn) 505. See Chapter 105.

[80.4]

Widow. Widow prima facie means the surviving wife (ie legal wife) until death or re-marriage. Therefore, a wife who is divorced cannot become a widow,[1] but there are cases where a person not legally married has been held sufficiently described as 'widow'.[2] Widowhood normally ends on re-marriage, but if the remarriage should be annulled the widowhood does not cease on such remarriage or at least she is a widow after the decree absolute of annulment.[3] Where, after the date of the will, the testator's own marriage was declared null and void, the wife was held not to be entitled to any annuity payable 'so long as she shall continue my widow'.[4] It has been said that a 'spinster mistress' cannot become a widow.[5]

1   *Re Williams' Settlement, Greenwell v Humphries* [1929] 2 Ch 361; *Bosworthick v Clegg* (1929) 45 TLR 438; and *Re Seaford, Seaford v Seifert* [1968] P 53, [1968] 1 All ER 482, CA.
2   *Re Wagstaff, Wagstaff v Jalland* [1908] 1 Ch 162; *Re Hammond, Burniston v White* [1911] 2 Ch 342. Compare *Re Lynch, Lynch v Lynch* [1943] 1 All ER 168.
3   *Re Dewhirst, Flower v Dewhirst* [1948] Ch 198, [1948] 1 All ER 147; *Re Eaves, Eaves v Eaves* [1940] Ch 109, [1939] 4 All ER 260; followed in *Re d'Altroy's Will Trusts, Crane v Lowman* [1968] 1 All ER 181, [1968] 1 WLR 120; compared *Re Rodwell, Midgley v Rumbold* [1970] Ch 726, [1969] 3 All ER 1363. But a transaction which has been carried into execution on the assumption of the validity of the marriage either immediately before the marriage and in expectation of it or during the marriage and before the decree of nullity, cannot be set aside; *Re Eaves, Eaves v Eaves*.
4   *Re Boddington, Boddington v Clairat* (1884) 25 Ch D 685. But it seems that the principle that widowhood is not ended by a re-marriage which is subsequently annulled no longer applies if the nullity decree is granted on or after 1 August 1971, on the ground that the marriage is voidable: the Matrimonial Causes Act 1973, s 16; 27 *Halsbury's Statutes* (4th edn) 947.

5   *Re Gale, Gale v Gale* [1941] Ch 209, [1941] 1 All ER 329; *Re Lynch, Lynch v Lynch* [1943] 1
     All ER 168 (in this case the judge held that the testator had made his own dictionary and upheld
     the gifts).

[80.5]

Surviving spouse. Where a disposition is limited to the time of the death of the
survivor of a person and his or her spouse (that person being a person in being at
the commencement of the perpetuity period) and that time has not arrived at the
end of the perpetuity period, this disposition is treated for all purposes as if
limited to the time immediately before the end of the perpetuity period, if so
doing would prevent it from being void for remoteness. As far as wills are
concerned this provision only applies where a person in being at the testator's
death marries a person then unborn.[1]

1   Perpetuities and Accumulations Act 1964, s 5; see Vol 2, Part G, para **[246.63]**.

[80.6]

Partner in invalid marriage. The circumstances may show that the word 'wife'
refers to a partner in an invalid marriage whether or not the parties know of the
invalidity.[1] The fact that the description is false does not affect the validity of the
gift, so long as the testator is not deceived for the purpose of obtaining the gift.[2]

1   *Re Wagstaff, Wagstaff v Jalland* [1908] 1 Ch 162 (where the parties were aware of the
     invalidity); *Re Hammond, Burniston v White* [1911] 2 Ch 342 (where the parties, though they
     were aware of the remote possibility of the invalidity, thought the marriage valid and it was not
     found to be invalid until some years after the testator's death); *Re Smalley, Smalley v Scotton,*
     supra (where the invalidity was known, but the reputed wife was in effect named); *Doe d Gains
     v Rouse* (1848) 5 CB 422 (a similar case); *Pratt v Mathew* (1856) 22 Beav 328 (marriage with
     deceased wife's sister then invalid: 'wife' could not refer to future wife because a future
     marriage would have revoked the will). See now as to voidable marriages, Matrimonial Causes
     Act 1973, s 16; 27 *Halsbury's Statutes* (4th edn) 947.
2   *Giles v Giles* (1836) 1 Keen 685; *Turner v Brittain* (1863) 3 New Rep 21 (gift to mistress of
     testator's son, whom testator believed to be married to him: legacy valid because deception of
     testator not for purpose of obtaining the legacy); *Anderson v Berkley* [1902] 1 Ch 936 (a similar
     case where it was said that the court could not speculate on the motive of the testator in making
     the gift. The donee was named); *Re Petts* (1859) 27 Beav 576 (wife assumed that former
     husband dead at time of marriage to testator upon no very satisfactory evidence, but gift held
     valid because evidence showed fraud on her part); *Re Posner, Posner v Miller* [1953] P 277,
     [1953] 1 All ER 1123 (gift to my wife R P is good although it is shown that the beneficiary is
     not the legal wife if the gift is not obtained by fraud on the part of the beneficiary). But in
     Wilkinson v Joughin (1866) LR 2 Eq 319, a wife knowing her husband was still alive married
     testator without disclosing that fact. A gift in these circumstances was held to have been
     obtained by fraud of the legatee and void.

II.   A 'HUSBAND'

[80.7]

Generally speaking the decisions on the description of 'wife' apply mutatis
mutandis in the case of 'husband'. In general, therefore, 'husband' means the
husband at the date of the will and not an after-taken husband.[1] Where the
person whose husband is referred to in the will is unmarried at the date of the
will, the first husband she takes is the person referred to and he takes the gift for
the interest given.[2] A divorced husband cannot be a surviving husband.[3]

1   *Franks v Brooker* (1860) 27 Beav 635 (but in this case, there was a gift to five daughters (the wives of persons the testator named) and afterwards to their respective husbands, so that as the husbands were named, the context made the reference one to a named person); *Re Bryan's Trust, ex p Darnborough* (1851) 2 Sim NS 103.

2   *Radford v Willis* (1871) 7 Ch App 7; *Blount v Crozier* [1917] 1 IR 461: and cf *Re Hickman's Will Trusts, Hickman v Hickman* [1948] Ch 624, [1948] 2 All ER 303 (wife of grandson).

3   *Bosworthwick v Clegg* (1929) 45 TLR 438; *Bullmore v Wynter* (1883) 22 Ch D 619, to the contrary, was decided on the context and in so far as it states a general principle was dissented from in *Re Morrieson, Hitchens v Morrieson* (1888) 40 Ch D 30.

III.   INHERITANCE TAX

[80.8]

The exemption for gifts to spouses. A transfer of value between spouses is ordinarily exempt from inheritance tax to the extent of the value of property which thereby becomes comprised in the spouse's estate, or, where no property becomes so comprised to the extent that the spouse's estate is thereby increased.[1]

1   See now the Inheritance Tax Act 1984, s 18; 42 *Halsbury's Statutes* (4th edn) 692.

CHAPTER 81

Other descriptions of donees

[81.1]
'Begotten'. The words 'begotten' and 'to be begotten' generally refer to both the past and the future and include both children already begotten and those to be begotten in the future.[1] The context, however, may displace this usual meaning and the words may have their strict grammatical meaning.[2]

1   *Hewet v Ireland* (1718) 1 P Wms 426; *Doe d James v Hallett* (1813) 1 M & S 124; *Almack v Horn* (1863) 1 Hem & M 630 at 633; *Harrison v Harrison* (1876) IR 10 Eq 290; *Palmer v Palmer* (1886) 18 LR Ir 192; *Browne v Groombridge* (1819) 4 Madd 495 ('begotten' includes after-born children).
2   *Locke v Dunlop* (1888) 39 Ch D 387.

[81.2]
First or eldest son and younger children. The description 'first son' or 'eldest son' of a certain person in the strict sense means the first-born son,[1] and similarly for other sons.[2] The circumstances of the case and the context of the will may, however, show that the testator intended the eldest son of the person at the date of the will, and this is the ordinary sense of the words where the strict sense is inapplicable,[3] or his eldest son for the time being[4] or the son taking the family estate.[5] Where the provision is one providing portions, the eldest son or the one taking the family estate is generally excluded and the expression 'younger children' in such case means the children other than the one taking the estate.[6] It is possible for an eldest son to take under a limitation to 'second and other sons',[7] but this cannot be so where the context of the will excludes him.[8]

1   *Livesey v Livesey* (1849) 2 HL Cas 419; *Bathhurst v Errington* (1877) 2 App Cas 698 at 709; *Bennett v Bennett* (1864) 2 Drew & Sm 266; *Meredith v Treffry* (1879) 12 Ch D 170.
2   *Tafford v Ashton* (1710) 2 Vern 660 (second son); *Lyddon v Ellison* (1854) 19 Beav 565 (younger in order of birth). See *Crofts v Beamish* [1905] 2 IR 349 ('next eldest brother'). In *Re Smiley* (1908) 28 NZLR 1, there was a bequest to 'my three youngest daughters'. These did not include a posthumous child.
3   *Amyot v Dwarris* [1904] AC 268 (eldest at date of will).
4   *Matthews v Paul* (1819) 3 Swan 328; *King v Bennett* (1838) 4 M & W 36; *Stevens v Pyle* (1861) 30 Beav 284; *Caldbeck v Caldbeck* [1911] 1 IR 144; *Re Malin's Will and Estate* [1905] VLR 270.
5   *Collingwood v Stanhope* (1869) LR 4 HL 43; *Ellison v Thomas* (1862) 1 De GJ & Sm 18. 'Eldest' means eldest in right of primogeniture: *Thellusson v Lord Rendlesham* (1859) 7 HL Cas 429.
6   *Chadwick v Doleman* (1705) 2 Vern 528. When the eldest child is a daughter, she is a younger child for this purpose: *Beale v Beale* (1713) 1 P Wms 244; *Pierson v Garnet* (1786) 2 Bro CC 38.

7   *Clements v Paske* (1784) 2 Cl & Fin 230n; *Langston v Langston* (1834) 2 Cl & Fin 194; *Re Blake's Estate* (1871) 19 WR 765; *Tavernor v Grindley* (1875) 32 LT 424; *Grattan v Langdale* (1883) 11 LR Ir 473.
8   *Locke v Dunlop* (1888) 39 Ch D 387. See also *Tuite v Bermingham* (1875) LR 7 HL 634, where the eldest son was expressly excluded from the limitation.

[81.3]

Protestant. This word has been held to mean a member of a church, religious body or sect which separated from the Roman Communion in the sixteenth century or any subsequent offshoot thereof which professes Christianity.[1]

1   *Re Winzar, Public Trustee v Winzar* (1953) 55 WALR 35.

HOLDERS OF AN OFFICE

[81.4]

Right to beneficial interest. The mere description of a donee as the holder of an office is not in itself sufficient to raise the inference that the gift is for the benefit of the office and not for the holder personally,[1] unless the context and circumstances show that the holder for the time being was intended.[2] A gift to a person either described as, or known to the testator as, the holder of the office, 'or his successor', or a gift to the holder of the office for the time being, is for the benefit of the office or the association or body in which the office is held.[3]

1   *Doe d Phillips v Aldridge* (1791) 4 Term Rep 264; *Donnellan v O'Neill* (1870) Ir 5 Eq 523; *Re Barclay, Gardner v Barclay* [1929] 2 Ch 173 (gift to superior of a religious order).
2   *Re Corcoran, Corcoran v O'Kane* [1913] 1 IR 1.
3   *Smart v Prujean* (1801) 6 Ves 560 at 567; *Re Fowler, Fowler v Booth* (1914) 31 TLR 102; *Re Ray's Will Trusts, Public Trustee v Barry* [1936] Ch 520, [1936] 2 All ER 93. As to gift to executor, see Chapter 83.

[81.5]

Employees and servants. This form of legacy has already been considered.[1]

1   See Chapter 30, paras **[30.23]–[30.29]** supra.

Construction of wills: particular rules relating to beneficial interests

CHAPTER 82

Quantity of interest given

I. IN GENERAL

[82.1]

No presumption as to quantity. A testator gives such interest as he thinks fit, consistently with the law,[1] and there is no presumption that he means to give one quantity of interest rather than another. The subject, being mere bounty can be known only from the words in which it is given.[2] If an intention of bounty towards a particular donee is apparent on the face of the will, and the will is ambiguous as to the manner in which the gift is to take effect with regard to the property given, or the interest created therein, the court, in absence of all other means of ascertaining the intention[3] leans to the construction which is most favourable to the donee.[4] The gift is in the nature of a grant and is subject to the principle that the grantor must not derogate from his grant.[5] When any specific thing is given, it must be taken that the gift is meant to take effect in its entirety and without derogation.[6] There is a presumption against an intention to charge land specifically devised, and a contrary intention is not shown by a mere charge on all testator's land,[7] but may be shown by a sufficient context.[8] Where a question arises upon what property a charge of debts is to operate, the court inclines to a construction which gives the creditors a charge on the larger amount of property.[9] Where there is a devise of specific real property forming part of the assets of a partnership in which the testator is a partner, and where the other partnership property is more than sufficient to pay the partnership debts, as between the beneficiaries claiming under the will the devisee prima facie takes free from the liability to contribute to those debts,[10] but, if the partnership liabilities exhaust the assets, the devise fails;[11] though it seems that a bequest of the goodwill and assets of a business does not in general carry the liability to discharge the obligations of the business which are payable as general debts of the testator.[12]

---

1 As to what interests may be created by will, see Chapter 8. All a testator's bounty must, of course, be subject to the due payment of his debts, taxes and administration expenses.
2 *Blackburn v Stables* (1814) 2 Ves & B 367 at 370; *Coward v Larkman* (1888) 60 LT 1; *Doe d Brodbelt v Thomson* (1858) 12 Moo PCC 116 (no presumed intention that devisee over should take same estate as prior devisee).
3 For example, the principles of giving words their ordinary meaning , or giving effect to every word , see Chapter 50.
4 Except where the donee must give way to creditors: *Noel v Weston* (1813) 2 Ves & B 269.
5 *Cooper v Woolfitt* (1857) 2 H & N 122 at 125. As to rights of selection, see para **[8.7]** supra. As to grant of an option to purchase, see Chapter 92.

6   *Conron v Conron* (1858) 7 HL Cas 168; but it has been held that a gift of 'one-third of my one-third' interest in a mortgage is not increased by the testator becoming entitled to a greater interest: *Re Lamb* [1954] OWN 31.
7   *Spong v Spong* (1829) 1 Dow & Cl 365.
8   *Bank of Ireland v McCarthy* [1898] AC 181.
9   *Noel v Weston* (1813) 2 Ves & B 269.
10 *Re Holland, Brettell v Holland* [1907] 2 Ch 88.
11 *Farquhar v Hadden* (1871) 7 Ch App 1.
12 *Re Timberlake, Archer v Timberlake* (1919) 63 Sol Jo 286; *Re Beecham, Woolley v Beecham* (1919) 63 Sol Jo 430.

[82.2]

Clear gifts not cut down. It is a settled rule of construction that a clear gift in a will is not cut down by anything subsequent in the will which does not with reasonable certainty indicate the intention of the testator to cut it down.[1] The rule is commonly stated, however, in the form that an absolute interest is not to be cut down except by clear words.[2] The rule does not mean that the court is to institute a comparison between the two clauses in a will as to lucidity,[3] but it has been frequently stated that words which cut down a gift clearly must be as clear as the words which confer it or that the subsequent words must be equally clear as the first.[4] But it is an integral part of the rule that where the cutting down is reasonably consistent with the intention of the testator as ascertained from the whole will, then the first interest is cut down.[5] Where the subsequent words are fairly capable of being construed in two ways, and one construction will be consistent with the gift given in the first instance, the court will struggle to adopt that construction.[6] Thus where personal property is given in terms which confer an absolute interest on a named donee, and then further interests are given merely on the termination of the donee's interest, and not in defeasance of it, the absolute interest is not cut down and the further interests fail,[7] and an absolute interest is not cut down by a precatory trust unless the trust creates an imperative obligation.[8]

1   *Abbot v Middleton* (1858) 7 HL Cas 68 at 84; *Randfield v Randfield* (1860) 8 HL Cas 225; *Crozier v Crozier* (1873) LR 15 Eq 282; *Re Jones, Richards v Jones* [1898] 1 Ch 438; *Re Roberts, Percival v Roberts* [1903] 2 Ch 200; *Re Freeman, Hope v Freeman* [1910] 1 Ch 681; *Shields v Shields* [1910] 1 IR 116; *Re Mitchell, Mitchell v Mitchell* (1913) 108 LT 180.
2   *Adshead v Willets* (1861) 29 Beav 358; *Doe d Hearle v Hicks* (1832) 8 Bing 475; *Kiver v Oldfield* (1859) 4 De G & J 30; *Leslie v Earl of Rothes* [1894] 2 Ch 499; *Re Foss Estate* [1940] 4 DLR 791.
3   *Randfield v Randfield* (1860) 8 HL Cas 225 at 235.
4   See cases cited in n 3.
5   *Randfield v Randfield* (1860) 8 HL Cas 225.
6   *Re Roberts, Percival v Roberts* [1903] 2 Ch 200.
7   *Hoare v Byng* (1844) 10 Cl & Fin 508 (to B 'and afterwards', to others); *Re Percy, Percy v Percy* (1883) 24 Ch D 616 (gift to wife and 'afterwards' to go to another legatee), followed in *Hyndman v Hyndman* [1895] 1 IR 179 (gift to named persons and 'at their death' to others, in this case their children); *Re Robinson Estate* [1931] 1 DLR 289; *Yarnie v Panchyshyn* [1952] 3 DLR 693; *Ritchie v Magree* (1964) 114 CLR 173; *Re Gouk, Allen v Allen* [1957] 1 All ER 469 (gift of residue to a named person and thereafter to her issue is an absolute gift); *Re Smith* (1956) 20 WWR 254 (absolute gift to wife so long as she remains the widow with further provisions on her death is an absolute gift); *Re Keroack Estate* (1957) 24 WWR 145; *Re Ingram Estate* (1961) 36 WWR 536 (gift to D of half share in home and all I die possessed of. At her death to be sold and equally divided between grandchildren, is an absolute gift to D). As the absolute interests with gift over in case of death which may in the circumstances be construed a death in the testator's lifetime or death at any time, see Chapter 83.
8   *Re Johnson, Public Trustee v Calvert* [1939] 2 All ER 458.

[82.3]
Intention of testator governs construction. The intention of the testator as shown by the context of the whole will must in every case govern the construction and may cut down an apparent absolute interest to a life interest[1] or make it subject to defeasance;[2] and a life interest may, on the other hand, be extended to an absolute interest[3] or may be reduced to an interest until marriage or re-marriage or other event.[4] An absolute interest is not cut down to a life interest unless the contingency cutting it down happens,[5] and an absolute interest subject to an executory gift over on a contingency remains absolute if the contingency does not happen.[6]

1   *Sherratt v Bentley* (1834) 2 My & K 149 (where the latter part of the will was held to prevail). The following were gifts to one person without any words showing what interest he or she is to take followed by a gift over after his or her death: *Joslin v Hammond* (1834) 3 My & K 110; *Hayes v Hayes* (1836) 1 Keen 97; *Re Bagshaw's Trusts* (1877) 46 LJ Ch 567 (where the gift in question was of personalty, but was accompanied by a gift of realty to the same person (the wife) for life); *Re Russell* (1885) 52 LT 559; *Re Sanford, Sanford v Sanford* [1901] 1 Ch 939 (a complicated will and codicil, but held that there were no words of limitation in the gift to the wife).
   The following were gifts either in terms absolute or with limitations which would normally give an absolute interest followed by a gift after the death of the donee: *Morrall v Sutton* (1842) 5 Beav 100; *Johnston v Antrobus* (1856) 21 Beav 556; *Re Lupton's Estate* [1905] P 321; *Re Houghton, Houghton v Brown* (1884) 53 LJ Ch 1018 (an unlimited gift of rents). Where there is a gift to A for life, with remainder to B with remainder to C, B takes only a life interest: *Earl of Lonsdale v Countess of Berchtoldt* (1854) Kay 646.
2   *Bird v Webster* (1853) 1 Drew 338 (gift of personalty to persons and 'their descendants'. This gave an estate tail, but, being personalty, that became an absolute interest).
3   A gift of personal estate for life and afterwards to the donee's executors and administrators gives an absolute interest: *Re Brooks, Public Trustee v White* [1928] Ch 214. As to gift with a superadded power, see para **[83.8]** infra. As to unlimited gifts of income, see Chapter 62.
4   *Meeds v Wood* (1854) 19 Beav 215 (to A for life and if she should marry to B: B takes on marriage of A or on death of A, if she does not marry. B's interest is vested independently of A's marriage); *Lancaster v Varty* (1826) 5 LJOS Ch 41 (re-marriage). On the other hand where there is a gift to a widow until re-marriage with a gift over to A when he attains twenty-three, the widow, whether or not she re-marries, takes the property until A attains twenty-three: *Doe d Dean of Westminster v Freeman* (1786) 1 Term Rep 389; *Re Cabburn, Gage v Rutland* (1882) 46 LT 848.
5   *Re Watson, Clume-Seymour v Brand* [1930] 2 Ch 344.
6   *Watkins v Weston* (1863) 3 De GJ & Sm 434; *Re Bourke's Trusts* (1891) 27 LR Ir 573; *Parnell v Boyd* [1896] 2 IR 571; *Re Lady Monck's Will, Monck v Crocker* [1900] 1 IR 56; but see *Re Cohen's Will Trusts, Cullen v Westminster Bank Ltd* [1936] 1 All ER 103 (gift subject to the provisions and directions hereinafter contained).

[82.4]
Rule in *Lassence v Tierney*. A further application of this doctrine is to be found in the rule usually referred to as the rule in *Lassence v Tierney*,[1] that where the court finds, on consideration of the whole will, an absolute gift to a donee in the first instance,[2] and trusts are engrafted or imposed on the absolute interest[3] which fail, either for lapse or invalidity or any other reason, then the absolute gift takes effect so far as the trusts have failed, to the exclusion of the residuary donee or persons entitled on intestacy as the case may be.[4] Examples of such gifts are: a gift settled on a daughter and her children where the daughter never marries or marries and has no children;[5] and an absolute gift with restrictions upon the mode of user for securing certain objects for the benefit of the legatee, where those objects fail.[6] The principle applies where the ultimate limitations are

void for remoteness or, in the case of an appointment under a special power, where the appointment is in excess of the power.[7] The principle applies to real as well as personal estate[8] and applies equally to accrued shares as to original shares.[9] If, however, there is a direction for distribution of lapsed shares according to the law of intestacy, there is no failure of the trusts and the rule does not apply[10] and the same result was held to be the effect where a share which failed was subject to an accruer clause.[11]

1   (1849) 1 Mac & G 551. The most modern statement of the rule is in *Hancock v Watson* [1902] AC 14 at 22.
2   *McKenna v McCarten* [1915] 1 IR 282; *Re Cohen, Cohen v Cohen* (1915) 60 Sol Jo 239. For cases where the rule could not be applied in the absence of an absolute gift in the first instance, see *Scawin v Watson* (1847) 10 Beav 200 (limited bequest in first instance); *Savage v Tyers* (1872) 7 Ch App 356 (gift for life on attaining 21 which might materialise into an absolute gift on marriage); *Re Orr, M'Dermott v Anderson* [1915] 1 IR 191; *Re Cohen's Will Trusts, Cullen v Westminster Bank Ltd* [1936] 1 All ER 103 (absolute gift subject to provisions and directions which did not dispose of the whole interest).
3   As distinct from a clause not merely modifying the enjoyment under the absolute gift, but diminishing that estate or totally substituting a new gift for it: *Gompertz v Gompertz* (1846) 2 Ph 107; *Re Richards, Williams v Gorvin* (1883) 50 LT 22; *Re Wilcock, Kay v Dewhurst* [1898] 1 Ch 95 (where modification was by codicil); *Re Goold's Will Trusts, Lloyds Bank Ltd v Goold* [1967] 3 All ER 652 (no absolute gift on which the trusts conferring a life interest could be said to be grafted, therefore rule inapplicable).
4   *Hancock v Watson* [1902] AC 14 at 22; *Lassence v Tierney* (1849) 1 Mac & G 551 at 561; *Re Marshall, Graham v Marshall* [1928] Ch 661, [1928] All ER Rep 694; *Fisher v Wentworth* (1925) 32 Argus LR 129; *Stephens v Tolley* [1954] SASR 97; *Russell v Perpetual Trustee Co Ltd* [1956] ALR 952. See also *Re Rauckman* (1970) 8 DLR (3d) 494.
5   *Hulme v Hulme* (1839) 9 Sim 644; *Mayer v Townsend* (1841) 3 Beav 443; *Campbell v Brownrigg* (1843) 1 Ph 301; *Re Burton Settlement Trusts, Public Trustee v Montefiore* [1955] Ch 348, [1955] 1 All ER 433 (where there were two daughters who both died spinsters); *Dally v Dally* [1954] Tas LR 12; *Re Jones, Jones v McConkey* [1962] NZLR 460.
6   *Re Richards, Williams v Gorvin* (1883) 50 LT 22 (where this application of the rule is stated, but in fact there was in that case a clause diminishing the absolute gift); *Re Connell's Settlement, Re Bennett's Trusts, Fair v Connell* [1915] 1 Ch 867 (where this application was admitted as to part of the property).
7   *Ring v Hardwick* (1840) 2 Beav 352; *Stephens v Gadsden* (1855) 20 Beav 463; *Cooke v Cooke* (1887) 38 Ch D 202; *Re Boyd, Nield v Boyd* (1890) 63 LT 92; *Hancock v Watson* [1902] AC 14 at 22; *Guy v Guy* (1911) 30 NZLR 383; *Russell v Perpetual Trustee Co* [1956] ALR 952.
8   *Moryoseph v Moryoseph* [1920] 2 Ch 33.
9   *Re Litt's Will Trusts, Parry v Cooper* [1946] Ch 154, [1946] 1 All ER 314 (where in the same will it was applied both to the original gift and to the gift in the accruer clause).
10   *Re Cowlishaw* [1959] Qd R 67.
11   *Duncan v Equity Trustees etc Co Ltd* (1958) 32 ALJR 238.

II.   EXPRESSION OF TESTATOR'S MOTIVE OR PURPOSE

[82.5]
Effect of stated purpose. If the purpose of the testator in making a gift is stated, and it relates to the mode of application of the gift for the benefit of certain objects and is not merely personal to the donee (for example, a gift to a person for the benefit of his children,[1] or of himself and his children),[2] such purpose, if the context requires, may become binding on the donee by way of trust[3] or condition,[4] but, if the context allows,[5] the purpose is treated merely as the motive of the testator in making the gift, which is intended to increase the funds of the donee to enable him to accomplish the purpose,[6] and the donee takes an

unfettered interest.[7] A gift for the benefit of the donee and his children may give the donee a beneficial interest in the entire fund subject to a trust to apply a sufficient part for the support of children, with or without some discretion in the application of it,[8] and the court will not interfere with such application of the fund if the discretion is exercised in good faith,[9] although the parent may be liable to account.[10] The gift may, however, be merely subject to a personal obligation of the donee to maintain the children from that or some other source and with no liability to account so long as the obligation is fulfilled.[11] Where an obligation, charge, or trust is created, the court may direct an inquiry as to the proper amount to be applied.[12] Where the children take beneficially, they take according to the context either concurrently with the parent[13] or in succession to him.[14] Whether the purpose becomes binding on the donee as a trust or condition is decided by the construction of the gift as to whether the words create a gift for a particular purpose only, or are a gift subject to the performance of a particular purpose.[15] The inference that an unfettered interest is intended may be drawn from the absence of any expression excluding the donee from taking beneficially[16] or the difficulty in ascertaining the amount intended to be applied for the purposes specified in every possible state of circumstances,[17] or from the fact that the specified object necessarily depends on the choice of the named person, although he may desire it for his own convenience,[18] or that apart from the will, the donee is already under an obligation to the specified object.[19]

1   Such a gift may make the donee a mere trustee without beneficial interest: *Blakeney v Blakeney* (1833) 6 Sim 52; *Wetherell v Wilson* (1836) 1 Keen 80; *Barnes v Grant* (1856) 26 LJ Ch 92; *Wainford v Heyl* (1875) LR 20 Eq 321; *Re De la Hunty, O'Connor v Butler* [1907] 1 IR 507; *Re Hickey, Hickey v Hickey* [1913] 1 IR 390, so that the benefit of the children does not fail by the death of the parent in the lifetime of the testator: *Ford v Fowler* (1840) 3 Beav 146; *Hodgson v Green* (1842) 11 LJ Ch 312. Though a mere trustee, the donee is entitled to obtain a transfer of the fund: *Cooper v Thornton* (1970) 3 Bro CC 96; *Robinson v Tickell* (1803) 8 Ves 142; and to dispose of it (*Wood v Richardson* (1840) 4 Beav 174; *McIsaac v Beaton* (1905) 38 NSR 60).
2   See nn 8–19, and text thereto.
3   See *Hayes v National Heart Foundation of Australia, New South Wales Division* [1976] 1 NSWLR 29. (... on the understanding that ...' created a trust). If the trust affects only part of the property, the donee may take the remainder beneficially: *Re Foord, Foord v Conder* [1922] 2 Ch 519. A trust may be created by a secret memorandum or instruction (see Chapter 36, ante) and in such a case also, if no instruction is found, the donee may take beneficially: *Re Barton, Barton v Bourne* (1932) 48 TLR 205.
4   See n 15.
5   See nn 16–19.
6   *Thorp v Owen* (1843) 2 Hare 607 at 614; *Benson v Whittam* (1831) 5 Sim 22; *Re Lord Llangattock, Johnson v Central Board of Finance of the Church of England* (1918) 34 TLR 341.
7   *Thorp v Owen* (1843) 2 Hare 607; *Mackett v Mackett* (1872) LR 14 Eq 49; *Farr v Hennis* (1881) 44 LT 202; *Re Adams and Kensington Vestry* (1884) 27 Ch D 394; *Re Hill, Public Trustee v O'Donnell* [1923] 2 Ch 259 ('for the benefit of themselves and their respective families' held to be absolute gift); *Re Lysiak* (1975) 55 DLR (3d) 161.
8   *Raikes v Ward* (1842) 1 Hare 445; *Longmore v Elcum* (1843) 2 Y & C Ch Cas 363; *Crockett v Crockett* (1848) 2 Ph 553.
9   *Costabadie v Costabadie* (1847) 6 Hare 410; *Hart v Tribe* (1854) 18 Beav 215.
10 *Woods v Woods* (1836) 1 My & Cr 401 at 409.
11 *Hadow v Hadow* (1838) 9 Sim 438; *Leach v Leach* (1843) 13 Sim 304; *Browne v Paull* (1850) 1 Sim NS 92; *Re Robertson's Trusts* (1858) 6 WR 405; *Lambe v Eames* (1871) 6 Ch App 597.
12 *Hamley v Gilbert* (1821) Jac 354 (although there were express exceptions from liability in the will); *Re Booth, Booth v Booth* [1894] 2 Ch 282; *K'Eogh v K'Eogh* [1911] 1 IR 396.

13   *Jubber v Jubber* (1839) 9 Sim 503; *Wilson v Maddison* (1843) 2 Y & C Ch Cas 372; *Re Nolan, Sheridan v Nolan* [1912] 1 IR 416; *Re Campbell, M'Cabe v Campbell* [1918] 1 IR 429.
14   *Chambers v Atkins* (1823) 1 Sim & St 382; *Re Whitty, Evans v Evans* (1881) 43 LT 692.
15   *King v Denison* (1813) 1 Ves & B 260; *Croome v Croome* (1888) 59 LT 582; *Re West, George v Grose* [1900] 1 Ch 84. For cases where the condition, if any, is introduced by such words as 'subject to', 'paying', or 'on condition that', see Chapter 91. For such words as 'in trust on the understanding that', see *Re Dulson* (1929) 140 LT 470; or 'knowing that he will carry out my wishes', see *Re Gardner, Huey v Cunnington* [1920] 2 Ch 523; or 'knowing that he is fully aware of my intentions', see *Re Williams, Williams v All Souls, Hastings (Parochial Church Council)* [1933] Ch 244, distinguishing *Re Falkiner, Mead v Smith* [1924] 1 Ch 88; *Hayes v National Heart Foundation of Australia, New South Wales Division* [1976] 1 NSWLR 29.
16   *Thorp v Owen* (1843) 2 Hare 607; but the word 'absolutely' does not of necessity define the beneficial interest: it may define the interest the trustees are to take subject to the trust: *Re Rees, Williams v Hopkins* [1950] Ch 204, [1949] 2 All ER 1003.
17   *Re Rees, Williams v Hopkins* [1950] Ch 204, [1949] 2 All ER 1003; *Cowman v Harrison* (1852) 10 Hare 234.
18   *Barrs v Fewkes* (1864) 2 Hem & M 60.
19   *Byne v Blackburn* (1858) 26 Beav 41; *Re St Vincent Estate* (1953) 9 WWRNS 274.

[82.6]
Bequest of chattels. A convenient and popular device is for a testator to leave chattels to a person, often the spouse, absolutely, and couple such bequest with a non-binding request to distribute the same in accordance with any memorandum left by the testator with his papers.[1] For inheritance tax purposes the distribution made by the legatee will be treated as made by the testator if the distribution is made within two years of the testator's death.[2]

1   See Vol 2, Form B4.9, para **[204.23]**.
2   Inheritance Tax Act 1984, s 143; 43 *Halsbury's Statutes* (4th edn) 803.

III.   GIFTS FOR PARTICULAR PURPOSES

[82.7]
Gift for benefit of donee in a particular manner. If a gift is of specified amount, and the purpose is to benefit the donee personally in a particular manner, it is a question of construction of the particular will whether the primary object of the testator is to make the specified gift to the donee, or to have the specified purpose accomplished.[1] In the ordinary way in a gift otherwise unconditional, the primary object is to make the specified gift; and the gift is unaffected by the purpose expressed[2] and takes effect although the satisfaction of the purpose of the testator does not exhaust the whole fund or becomes impossible through no act or default of the donee, or has already been accomplished;[3] and the donee, if sui juris, or his representative after his death,[4] is prima facie entitled to payment without the testator's executors being bound to see to the application of the gift.[5] Where, however, the specified purpose is the primary object of the gift, the donee is entitled to the gift, but only so far as applicable to that purpose,[6] and for no other purpose;[7] and the gift may be so expressed that the cost of accomplishing the purpose may have to be paid out of the estate of the testator although the primary fund is sufficient.[8] In such cases, so far as the purpose cannot be accomplished, or becomes impossible, the gift fails.[9]

1   As to legacy made in satisfaction of a moral obligation, see *Re Pollock, Pollock v Worrall* (1885) 28 Ch D 552.

2   *Cope v Wilmot* (1772) Amb 704 (advancement in business); *Isherwood v Payne* (1800) 5 Ves 677 ('for any purpose she thinks proper'); *Paice v Archbishop of Canterbury* (1807) 14 Ves 364 at 370 (for such purposes as the donee shall think fit); *Leche v Lord Kilmoreywk* (1823) Turn & R 207 (to purchase army commission); *Lord Amherst v Duchess of Leeds* (1842) 12 Sim 476 (to pay rent of donee's residence); *Hutchison v Rough* (1879) 40 LT 289 (to establish donee in profession); *Re O'Mullane* [1955] VLR 217 (gift for education of grandchildren); *Re Osoba, Osoba v Osoba* [1979] 2 All ER 393, [1979] 1 WLR 247 (bequest for the maintenance of his widow, 'and for the training of my daughter A up to university grade'; held an absolute gift to the widow and daughter as joint tenants, the references to their maintenance and education being no more than an indication of motive), *Re Sanderson's Trust* (1857) 3 K & J 497, applied; *Dowling v Dowling* [1902] 1 IR 79 at 83; *Re Harbison, Morris v Larkin* [1902] 1 IR 103. If the purpose is one which the legatee is bound to perform (eg education of his children) the gift is absolute; *Re St Vincent Estate* (1953) 9 WWRNS 274.

3   *Lockhart v Hardy* (1846) 9 Beav 379 (to pay off mortgage foreclosed in testator's lifetime); *Adams v Lopdell* (1890) 25 LR Ir 311 (gift for benefit of children); *Hammond v Neame* (1818) 1 Swan 35 (maintenance of children who did not come into existence); *Parsons v Coke* (1858) 27 LJ Ch 828 (to carry on business sold by testator); *Palmer v Flower* (1871) LR 13 Eq 250 (purchase of army commission: right of purchase abolished); *Re Segelcke, Ziegler v Nicol* [1906] 2 Ch 301 (gifts of legacy to make gifts to donee up to an amount already exceeded). For gifts for purposes at the discretion of the donee, see *Gough v Bult* (1847) 16 Sim 45 at 54; *Re Harbison, Morris v Larkin* [1902] 1 IR 103. For gifts to apprentice an infant, see *Barlow v Grant* (1684) 1 Vern 255 (infant dead); *Nevill v Nevill* (1701) 2 Vern 431 (donee entitled to payment before specified age); *Barton v Cooke* (1800) 5 Ves 461 (entitled though not apprenticed); *Re Lee* [1955] OWN 984 (gift for education of nephew and nephew to have balance on graduation. Nephew entitled to balance though not proceeding to graduation); but in *Re Collishaw* [1953] 3 DLR 829, the gift failed; *Morrison v Mills* (1961) 31 DLR (2d) 159 (gift for education of grandson at university. Any surplus to be paid to grandson. Grandson not attending any university entitled to gift).

4   *Barlow v Grant* (1684) 1 Vern 255; *Lewes v Lewes* (1848) 16 Sim 266.

5   *Apreece v Apreece* (1813) 1 Ves & B 364 (gift to buy a ring); *Re Skinner's Trusts* (1860) 1 John & H 102 (printing a book); *Knox v Lord Hotham* (1845) 15 Sim 82 (purchase of house); *Noel v Jones* (1848) 16 Sim 309 (education of infant); *Dowling v Dowling* [1902] 1 IR 79 (purchase of house). The fact that a third party would benefit if the legacy were applied for the specified purpose does not affect the legatee's right: *Adams v Lopdell* (1890) 25 LR Ir 311; *Earl Mexborough v Savile* (1903) 88 LT 131 (gift to pay estate duty).

6   *Re Black, Falls v Alford* [1907] 1 IR 486 (capital and income, to be applied to education of infants).

7   *Dick's Trustees v Dick* 1911 48 SLR 325 (gift for education of donee in profession. Special diploma not included).

8   *Milner v Milner* (1748) 1 Ves Sen 106 (miscalculation of sum needed to make daughter's fortune to named amount); *Re Sanderson's Trust* (1857) 3 K & J 497 (to apply whole or part for support of testator's brother. Whole income not applicable unless it is proved that the application of the whole is necessary for the purpose).

9   *Re De Crespigny, De Crespigny v De Crespigny* [1886] WN 24; *Re Ward's Trusts* (1872) 7 Ch App 727.

[82.8]

Gift at discretion of a named person. Where a clear gift is made, and the application is left to the discretion of another person, and his discretion is not exercised, the donee is entitled to the gift irrespective of its application.[1] On the other hand, the donee is not entitled where the discretion extends to deciding the amount of the gift and whether it shall be given at all.[2]

1   *Gough v Bult* (1847) 16 Sim 45; *Beevor v Partridge* (1840) 11 Sim 229; *Re Johnston, Mills v Johnston* [1894] 3 Ch 204; *Gude v Worthington* (1849) 3 De G & Sm 389.

2   *Cowper v Mantell (No 2)* (1856) 22 Beav 231; *Re Sanderson's Trust* (1857) 3 K & J 497; *Re Ward's Trusts* (1872) 7 Ch App 727; *Mansen v Nash* [1954] 3 DLR 496.

[82.9]

Gift to benefit particular property. Where a fund is given, without specifying any donee, for particular purposes for the benefit of certain property (for example, to plant trees on an estate), the fund belongs to the persons entitled to that property.[1]

1   *Earl of Lonsdale v Countess of Berchtoldt* (1857) 3 K & J 185; *Re Bowes, Earl of Strathmore v Vane* [1896] 1 Ch 507; *Re Colson's Trusts* (1853) Kay 133; *Cox v Sutton* (1856) 25 LJ Ch 845 (gift as fund for repairs for the benefit of the persons in possession of an estate); *Kennedy v Kennedy* [1914] AC 215.

CHAPTER 83

Absolute and life interests

I. ABSOLUTE INTERESTS

[83.1]
Interest taken where no words of limitation. Where any real estate is devised
to any person without any word of limitation, such devise is construed to pass
the fee simple or other the whole estate or interest which the testator had power
to dispose of by his will in such real estate,[1] unless a contrary intention appears
by the will.[2] The contrary intention must appear from the whole will[3] and is not
shown merely by the use of words of limitation in other gifts.[4] This rule is
applicable only to real estate which exists and belongs to the testator at the time
of his death, over which he has then power to dispose, and does not apply to a
particular interest in real estate, or an annuity or rentcharge which the testator is
about to create for the first time by his will.[5] A gift of personal estate to a donee
and his heirs or without any context restricting his interest confers on him an
absolute interest.[6] Where the donee is given an interest until a specified age and
the remainder of the will is worded on the assumption that he takes absolutely at
that age, he takes an absolute interest though the will does not give it to him in
express terms.[7]

1 As to the interests which a general devise will pass apart from this rule, see Chapter 60.
2 Wills Act 1837, s 28; 50 *Halsbury's Statutes* (4th edn) 597. See Vol 2, Part G, para **[244.28]**.
   This rule was confined to testamentary instruments until 1926, but has been extended to
   conveyances executed after 1925 by the Law of Property Act 1925, s 60; 37 *Halsbury's Statutes*
   (4th edn) 198.
3 *Crumpe v Crumpe* [1900] AC 127 at 131; *Pelham-Clinton v Duke of Newcastle* [1902] 1 Ch 34;
   Gravenor v Watkins (1871) LR 6 CP 500; *Quarm v Quarm* [1892] 1 QB 184; *Re Gannon,
   Spence v Martin* [1914] 1 IR 86. The creation of successive estates after the gift in question
   shows a contrary intention but not necessarily an intention to create life interests only: *Re
   Pennefather, Savile v Savile* [1896] 1 IR 249 at 260; and a restriction on alienation may show a
   contrary intention: *Re Sanford, Sanford v Sanford* [1901] 1 Ch 939.
4 *Wisden v Wisden* (1854) 2 Sm & G 396.
5 *Nichols v Hawkes* (1853) 10 Hare 342.
6 *Re McElligott, Grant v McElligott* [1944] Ch 216, [1944] 1 All ER 441 (gift to donee and his
   heirs). See also *Re Ottewell* (1970) 9 DLR (3d) 314. As to creation of limited interests in
   personalty, see paras **[8.3]** and **[8.4]** supra. As to a tenant in tail taking an absolute interest in
   personalty, see Chapter 84.
7 *Re Tottenham, Public Trustee v Tottenham* (1946) 115 LJ Ch 170.

[83.2]
Interest defined by powers of disposition. The interest to be taken by the
donee may be defined by the powers of disposition or rights of enjoyment

conferred on him. A power of disposition may be itself equivalent to the property in the subject-matter of the power, or it may be merely a power of appointment.[1] Independently of the context, there is nothing in the word 'disposal' essentially indicating power rather than property,[2] and where real or personal property is given to a person to be at his disposal, or in words to the like effect,[3] and where the context does not refer to a power or trust,[4] the effect is to create a fee simple in real estate, and an absolute interest in personal estate.[5] Where a husband or wife is appointed sole personal representative and trustee and is given the residue with full power to employ income and capital for his or her own use and benefit, the gift is an absolute one.[6] An absolute interest has been similarly inferred even where the testator contemplated dispositions made only by the will of the donee,[7] or subject to other restrictions,[8] or where the gift is of a sum of money to be paid at the death of the donee.[9]

1   *Re Armstrong, ex p Gilchrist* (1886) 17 QBD 521; *Tremayne v Rashleigh* [1908] 1 Ch 681.
2   *Nowlan v Walsh* (1851) 4 De G & Sm 584; *Hixon v Oliver* (1806) 13 Ves 108 (power is a restraint on property and is never to be implied from the word disposal); *Re Armstrong, ex p Gilchrist* (1886) 17 QBD 521 (distinction between power and property).
3   *Hixon v Oliver* (1806) 13 Ves 108 (absolute gift with power of disposition by will); *Nowlan v Walsh* (1851) 4 De G & Sm 584 (life interest with power of disposition after death gives life interest only); *Re Maxwell's Will* (1857) 24 Beav 246 (gift for life and then for donee's children with liberty to dispose of it if no children is an absolute interest); *Parnell v Boyd* [1896] 2 IR 571; *Re Bogle, Bogle v Yorstoun* (1898) 78 LT 457; *Reid v Carleton* [1905] 1 IR 147.
4   Gift to be disposed of at discretion of trustees: *Re Booth, Hattersley v Cowgill* (1917) 86 LJ Ch 270; *Metcalfe v O'Kennedy* (1904) 4 SRNSW 175; *Re Bourk's Will, Cunningham v Rubenach* [1907] VLR 171.
5   *Alexander v Alexander* (1856) 6 De GM & G 593; *Re Maxwell's Will* (1857) 24 Beav 246; *Kellett v Kellet* (1868) LR 3 HL 160. This construction was adopted where the gift was for use as the widow thought fit during her lifetime: *Re Murray* [1958] VR 4; and see cases cited in n 6.
6   *Re Schuker's Estate, Bromley v Reed* [1937] 3 All ER 25; *Re Baskin* [1954] 2 DLR 748.
7   *Glover v Hall* (1849) 16 Sim 568 at 571; but see *Johnston v Rowlands* (1848) 2 De G & Sm 356; *Evans v Evans* (1865) 33 LJ Ch 662; *Weale v Ollive (No 2)* (1863) 32 Beav 421; *Reigh v Kearney* [1936] 1 IR 138.
8   *Bull v Kingston* (1816) 1 Mer 314 (certain disposition prohibited); *Comber v Graham* (1830) 1 Russ & M 450.
9   *Hixon v Oliver* (1806) 13 Ves 108.

[83.3]
Gift to executor. An executor will take beneficially property which is directly given to him to be at his disposal;[1] but in the absence of a direct gift, these words do not give the executor a beneficial interest, and, if the subject of the disposition is the residue, the executor will hold it in trust for the persons entitled on intestacy.[2] The executor must show a distinct intention in the words of the will that he is to take beneficially and the onus is on him to prove that intention.[3] Under a gift to the executors of another person, whether directly or by way of substitution for him, prima facie they take the gift as part of the estate,[4] but the will may show that they were to take beneficially.[5] Where the residue was given beneficially to two persons also appointed executors and one predeceased the testator, the gift was to two named persons and not to a class and the survivor took one half and the other half passed as on an intestacy[6].

1   *Re Howell, Re Buckingham, Liggins v Buckingham* [1915] 1 Ch 241.
2   *Re Chapman, Hales v A-G* [1922] 2 Ch 479; *Re Pugh's Will Trusts, Marten v Pugh* [1967] 3 All ER 337 (trust void for uncertainty, residuary estate to be held for those entitled on intestacy).

3   *Juler v Juler* (1860) 29 Beav 34; *Love v Gaze* (1845) 8 Beav 472; *Williams v Arkle* (1875) LR 7
      HL 606; *Re Selman Estate* (1957) 23 WWR 349.
4   *Stocks v Dodsley* (1836) 1 Keen 325; *Long v Watkinson* (1852) 17 Beav 471; *Leak v Macdowall
      (No 2)* (1863) 33 Beav 238; *Trethewy v Helyar* (1876) 4 Ch D 53; *Re Valdez's Trusts* (1888) 40
      Ch D 159.
5   *Saunders v Franks* (1817) 2 Madd 147; *Wallis v Taylor* (1836) 8 Sim 241.
6   *Mitchell v Arblaster* [1964–5] NSWR 119; *Re Melvin* (1972) 24 DLR (3d) 240.

[83.4]
Gifts of income only. A gift of income only may amount to an absolute interest as already shown.[1]

1   See Chapter 62.

[83.5]
Gift of an annuity. While a gift of an annuity is generally for life only, it may be for a longer period, but this matter has already been dealt with.[1]

1   See Chapter 33.

II.   LIFE INTEREST

[83.6]
Rights of enjoyment. The interest taken by the donee may be defined by the rights of enjoyment attached to it.[1] Thus, a gift of the use,[2] or of the free use and occupation[3] of a house or land is generally a gift of the rents and profits at all events during the life of the donee,[4] and prima facie the donee under such a gift need not personally reside in the house or on the land, but may let or dispose of the property during his lifetime.[5] An intention that occupation shall be personal may be shown by a gift over on the donee ceasing to occupy[6] or by the context.[7] Even in these cases the right of occupation, previously, made the donee a tenant for life under the Settled Land Act 1925,[8] and he or she could exercise the right of sale provided the right to occupy was exercised.[9] The exercise of such right of sale will defeat the gift over[10] and the requirement of residence is void in so far as it is a fetter on the statutory right of sale.[11] The testator, however, can oblige a tenant for life to reside in a house until it is disposed of under the statutory power of sale and failure to comply with this condition can be enforced by a forfeiture clause.[12] A personal right of residence rent free does not entitle the donee to the rents and profits in case of non-residence.[13] A person given the option of becoming a lessee at a rent is not a tenant for life.[14] A gift of the possession or use and enjoyment of chattels prima facie gives the donee a life interest,[15] and the donee may let the goods on hire.[16]

1   Where property is given 'freely to be possessed and enjoyed', the authorities are conflicting as
     to whether these words are sufficient to pass the fee. The principal authority giving only a life
     estate under these words is *Bromitt v Moor* (1851) 9 Hare 374, and it seems that, if it is
     necessary to carry out the wishes expressed in the will, the fee will pass: *Lloyd v Jackson*
     (1867) LR 2 QB 269. For cases giving a fee, see *Loveacres d Mudge v Blight* (1775) 1 Cowp
     352; *Thomas v Phelps* (1828) 4 Russ 348; *Gilham v Walker and Walker* [1919] St R Qd 9. For
     cases giving a life interest, see *Goodright d Drewry v Barron* (1809) 11 East 220; *Doe d Ashby
     v Baines* (1835) 2 Cr M & R 23; *Re Richer* (1920) 50 DLR 614. For a case where a donee was
     given the 'full and entire' enjoyment of a leasehold, see *Harvey v Harvey* (1842) 5 Beav 134.

2   *Cook v Gerrard* (1668) 1 Saund 180 (passes fee); *Green v Marsden* (1853) 1 Drew 646 (passes fee).

3   *Mannox v Greener* (1872) LR 14 Eq 456; *Coward v Larkman* (1888) 60 LT 1; *Re Waugh* [1955] NZLR 1129 (undisturbed possession and occupation gave interest *pur autre vie* and merged with interest in remainder).

4   As to whether a gift in perpetuity can be inferred, see *Coward v Larkman* (1888) 60 LT 1 (life interest only); *Public Trustee v Edmond* (1912) 32 NZLR 202; *Holland v McKenzie* [1932] NZLR 1153; *Re Edwards* [1950] NZLR 516.

5   *Clive v Clive* (1854) 2 Eq Rep 913; *Rabbeth v Squire* (1859) 4 De G & J 406; *Mannox v Greener* (1872) LR 14 Eq 456; *National Trustees, Executors and Agency Co Ltd v Keast* (1896) 22 VLR 447.

6   *Maclaren v Stainton* (1858) 27 LJ Ch 442; *Stone v Parker* (1860) 1 Drew & Sm 212; *Moore v Royal Trust Co* [1956] SCR 880 (use and enjoyment gave mere licence to occupy).

7   *Re Varley, Thornton v Varley* (1893) 62 LJ Ch 652 (where the life interest was given to another person subject to the right of residence); *Re Stewart, Stewart v Hislop* (1905) 23 NZLR 797; *Re Richardson* [1951] OR 130.

8   *Re Anderson, Halligey v Kirkley* [1920] 1 Ch 175 (to use and occupy for own personal use and occupation: no right to let but only licence to occupy, and only when the donee informed the trustees of her desire to occupy could she exercise the powers of a tenant for life: not entitled to income from proceeds of sale of furniture); *Re Gibbons, Gibbons v Gibbons* [1920] 1 Ch 372 (option to occupy exercised); *Re Acklom, Oakeshott v Hawkins* [1929] 1 Ch 195 (permission to reside for life or during pleasure: donee gave up residence, let property and subsequently sold it: powers of tenant for life properly exercised and right to interest in proceeds of sale not forfeited); distinguished in *Re Rosar* (1975) 60 DLR (3d) 615; *Re Patten, Westminster Bank v Carlyon* [1929] 2 Ch 276 (use given for life or during pleasure without power to sub-let and on ceasing to occupy, house to be sold: prohibition of sub-letting void: interest not determined if property sold or leased under the Settled Land Act powers, but would be determined if occupation ceased otherwise than by the exercise of such powers). As to powers with right to occupy settled land being a tenant for life or rather a person having the powers of a tenant for life, see *Re Baroness Llanover's Will, Herbert v Freshfield* [1903] 2 Ch 16; *Re Gibbons, Gibbons v Gibbons* [1920] 1 Ch 372; *Re Acklom, Oakeshott v Hawkins* [1929] 1 Ch 195; *Re Patten, Westminster Bank v Carlyon* [1929] 2 Ch 276. Note that no new settlements can be created under the Settled Land Act 1925 after 1 January 1997, by virtue of the Trusts of Land and Appointment of Trustees Act 1996, s 2(1). Thus the Settled Land Act 1925 can no longer render ineffective conditions in trusts created on or after that date.

9   *Re Anderson, Halligey v Kirkley* [1920] 1 Ch 175; *Re Gibbons, Gibbons v Gibbons* [1920] 1 Ch 372.

10   *Re Paget's Settled Estates* (1885) 30 Ch D 161; *Re Dalrymple, Bircham v Springfield* (1901) 49 WR 627; *Re Adair and Settled Land Act* [1909] 1 IR 311.

11   *Re Trenchard, Trenchard v Trenchard* [1902] 1 Ch 378.

12   *Re Haynes, Kemp v Haynes* (1887) 37 Ch D 306; *Re Edwards' Settlement* [1897] 2 Ch 412; *Re Patten, Westminster Bank v Carlyon* [1929] 2 Ch 276.

13   *Parker v Parker* (1863) 1 New Rep 508; *May v May* (1881) 44 LT 412; *Re Denton* [1956] NZLR 104; but see *Re Acklom, Oakeshott v Hawkins* [1929] 1 Ch 195, and *Re Patten, Westminster Bank v Carlyon* [1929] 2 Ch 276, as to obtaining the right by acting under the Settled Land Act powers. But see n 8.

14   *Re Catling, Public Trustee v Catling* [1931] 2 Ch 359 (where the rent was a purely nominal one of £1 per annum).

15   *Low v Carter* (1839) 1 Beav 426; *Espinasse v Luffingham* (1846) 3 Jo & Lat 186 (plate). A contrary intention may, however, be shown, eg where the use of book debts or capital in a business is given, the donee takes an absolute interest: *Terry v Terry* (1863) 33 Beav 232; and the donee also takes an absolute interest where the bequest is of consumable goods: *Montresor v Montresor* (1845) 1 Coll 693.

16   *Re Williams, Murray v Williamson* (1906) 94 LT 813; *Rabbeth v Squire* (1859) 4 De G & J 406.

[83.7]
Determinable interest. A gift until bankruptcy, alienation, marriage or other event which must happen, if at all, during the life of the donee, prima facie creates a determinable life interest only,[1] but such a gift,[2] or a gift 'so long as

certain circumstances continue'³ (even, for example, a gift so long as the donee remains unmarried),⁴ may create an estate in fee simple or absolute interest determinable on those circumstances ceasing to exist.

1   *Banks v Braithwaite* (1863) 1 New Rep 306 (alienation); *Re Boddington, Boddington v Clairat* (1884) 25 Ch D 685 (so long as she continues my widow); *Re Mason, Mason v Mason* [1910] 1 Ch 695 (marriage); *Re Wiltshire, Eldred v Comport* (1916) 142 LT Jo 57 (during spinsterhood). A gift during widowhood determines on re-marriage and it is an open question whether the widowhood is restored on that marriage being annulled: see para **[80.2]** ante. A divorced wife is not and cannot become a widow: *Re Williams' Settlement, Greenwell v Humphries* [1929] 2 Ch 361; *Bosworthwick v Clegg* (1929) 45 TLR 438. A woman who is a 'spinster mistress' cannot become a widow: *Re Gale, Gale v Gale* [1941] Ch 209, [1941] 1 All ER 329, but see *Re Lynch* [1943] 1 All ER 168. Where the gift over on re-marriage was to a son when he should attain twenty-three years, the devise gave the widow the property until the son attained the age of twenty-three years though she should marry before that time: *Doe d Dean of Westminster v Freeman* (1786) 2 Chit 498. As to effect of divorce, see Chapter 47, para **[47.2]** et seq.
2   *Rishton v Cobb* (1839) 5 My & Cr 145, criticised in *Re Boddington, Boddington v Clairat* (1884) 25 Ch D 685 at 689, and explained in *Re Mason, Mason v Mason* [1910] 1 Ch 695 at 698; *Re Barklie, McCalmont v Barklie* [1917] 1 IR 1, and see *M'Culloch v M'Culloch* (1862) 3 Giff 606; *Price v Boustead* (1863) 8 LT 565.
3   Eg a gift so long as persons live together: *Sutcliffe v Richardson* (1872) LR 13 Eq 606 (annuity so long as widow and son lived together: annuity did not cease on death of son).
4   *Re Howard, Taylor v Howard* [1901] 1 Ch 412; *Re Rowland, Jones v Rowland* (1902) 86 LT 78; *M'Culloch v M'Culloch* (1862) 3 Giff 606; *Re Taylor* (1914) 28 WLR 630 (re-marriage).

III.   GIFTS WITH SUPERADDED POWERS OR PROVISIONS

[83.8]

Executory gifts over. It has already been stated that a gift which is apparently absolute can be made subject to defeasance, or can be cut down to a life interest.¹ On the other hand, a life interest may have attached to it a power of disposition of the corpus. Thus, a gift of real property, or of personal property for an interest which prima facie is absolute, may be made subject to an executory gift over; but a gift over which conflicts with the right of disposition attached to the gift is not permitted. Thus, a restriction on the donee's right of alienation of an interest clearly given to him is repugnant to the gift and void,² and a gift over on breach of the restrictions cannot take effect.³ A gift over if the donee dies without having disposed of the property,⁴ or of so much as the donee does not dispose of,⁵ is also treated as void. A gift over in the event of death may be confined to death in the lifetime of the testator.⁶

1   See Chapter 82.
2   See Chapter 99.
3   It is the same where the gift over attempts to interfere with the devolution of the property on death: *Shaw v Ford* (1877) 7 Ch D 669 (various dispositions on death after a gift in fee of real property to four sons); *Weale v Ollive (No 2)* (1863) 32 Beav 421 (indefinite bequest of residue held to amount to absolute interest and, therefore, a gift over if they should omit to make a will was void); *Re Ashton, Ballard v Ashton* [1920] 2 Ch 481 (gift over if person, to whom property is absolutely given, dies mentally unfit). The same applies to a gift over if a person dies intestate.
4   *Gulliver v Vaux* (1746) 8 De GM & G 167n; *Re Yalden* (1851) 1 De GM & G 53.
5   *Watkins v Williams* (1851) 3 Mac & G 622; *Perry v Merritt* (1874) LR 18 Eq 152; *Re Dixon, Dixon v Charlesworth* [1903] 2 Ch 458. In such cases (ie where on the construction of the will the first gift is absolute) the court does not treat the restrictions as forming a context clearly cutting down the prior gift: *Re Jones, Richards v Jones* [1898] 1 Ch 438 at 441; *Lloyd v Tweedy*

[1898] 1 IR 5. If the first donee predeceased the testator, the doctrine of repugnancy does not apply, and the gift over takes effect: *Re Dunstan, Dunstan v Dunstan* [1918] 2 Ch 304 (where there are in a will a series of absolute gifts of personal property in favour of several persons absolutely the first of those persons who survives the testator takes absolutely, although he would have taken nothing if any previous legatee had survived and taken. This principle applies also to real property); *Re Dawson's Estate* [1941] 1 WWR 177; *Re Keroak Estate* (1957) 24 WWR 145 (cases where the beneficiary had to be paid by instalments).

6   *Re Blackstock Estate* (1957) 10 DLR (2d) 192 (where the evidence that the will was made when the testator was on his death bed and there was no possibility of his wife (the beneficiary) dying before him was held not admissible).

[83.9]
Clear absolute gift in the first instance. Where there is a clear absolute gift followed by words purporting to confer a power of disposition[1] with a gift over if the power is not exercised, the absolute gift takes effect, and the gift over is inconsistent with it and void.[2] A devise in fee simple to a wife with the intention that she may enjoy the same during her life and by her will dispose of the same as she thinks proper gives her a fee simple estate[3] nor is an absolute gift cut down by an expression of a wish as to how she shall dispose of the property.[4] An absolute gift is not necessarily cut down by a direction for settlement.[5] A gift over in default of disposition by an absolute owner is void.[6] An absolute gift of property followed by a gift of so much of that property as the first donee shall not have disposed of is an absolute gift in the first instance and the gift over is void.[7] The main difficulty in these cases is that what is apparently an absolute gift in the first instance may by reason of subsequent provisions in the will be held to be cut down to a life interest, and the following are examples of such cases. The gift is so cut down (i) where the gift at the death of the first donee of what remains of the estate can be construed as a gift over of the residue after payment of debts;[8] (ii) if such an expression appears in a codicil so that an intention is shown to vary the absolute interest given by the will, the first donee will take a life interest, with a power of disposition either inter vivos, or by will only, or generally;[9] (iii) where there is a doubt as to what interest the first donee takes raised by inconsistent provisions in the will such as a restriction on alienation,[10] to merely a gift over on death,[11] or a gift over on the donee disposing,[12] or failing to dispose,[13] of the property.

1   *Comber v Graham* (1830) 1 Russ & M 450; *Brook v Brook* (1856) 3 Sm & G 280; *Howorth v Dewell* (1860) 29 Beav 18; *McKenna v McCarten* [1915] 1 IR 282; *Lambe v Eames* (1871) 6 Ch App 597 (to be at her disposal in any way she may think best for the benefit of herself and family: an absolute gift); *Re Hutchinson and Tenant* (1878) 8 Ch D 540.
2   *Re Mortlock's Trusts* (1857) 3 K & J 456 applied in *Re Paithouski* (1976) 71 DLR (3d) 60; *Doe d Herbert v Thomas* (1835) 3 Ad & El 123; *Re Iversen* (1956) 19 WWR 524.
3   *Doe d Herbert v Thomas* (1835) 3 Ad & El 123.
4   *Re Humphrey's Estate* [1916] 1 IR 21; *Ostrom v Bendall* (1956) 5 DLR (2d) 419.
5   *Re Bannister, Heys-Jones v Bannister* (1921) 90 LJ Ch 415. As to the rule in *Lassence v Tierney* (1849) 1 Mac & G 551, see para **[82.4]** supra.
6   See Chapter 34, as to conditions generally.
7   *Bowes v Goslett* (1857) 27 LJ Ch 249; *Re Jones, Richards v Jones* [1898] 1 Ch 438; *Re Dunstan, Dunstan v Dunstan* [1918] 2 Ch 304; *Re Ferguson* [1957] VLR 635; *Re White* (1962) 33 DLR (2d) 185; *Ritchie v Magree* [1964] ALR 649; *Re Burton, Public Trustee v Burton* [1965] NZLR 712. This sentence was referred to with approval by Hollingworth J in *Re Ohorodnyk* (1979) 97 DLR (3d) 502 at 514.
8   *Constable v Bull* (1849) 3 De G & Sm 411; *Bibbens v Potter* (1879) 10 Ch D 733 (absolute gift in will: codicil giving property remaining on death of first donee); *Re Sheldon and Kemble*

(1885) 53 LT 527 (desire that, at death of wife, what might remain should be equally divided between children); *Re Brooks' Will* (1865) 2 Drew & Sm 362 (gift of 'residue' at decease of wife); *Re Adams' Trust* (1865) 13 LT 347 (codicil wishing all remaining to be for benefit of certain donees); *Re Holden, Holden v Smith* (1888) 57 LJ Ch 648 (for widow as long as she might live and remainder which then exists); *Re Dixon, Dixon v Dixon* (1912) 56 Sol Jo 445 (residue to be divided between brothers and sisters); *Re Gate* [1923] NZLR 419; *Re Bennett* [1956] NZLR 304.

9   *Re Pounder, Williams v Pounder* (1886) 56 LJ Ch 113 (absolute gift in will revoked in codicil which gave residue to wife for her own absolute use and benefit and disposal but without prejudice to absolute power of disposal, a gift over of what remained: life interest with power to dispose inter vivos but not by will); *Re Sanford, Sanford v Sanford* [1901] 1 Ch 939 (similar gift: life interest with general power of appointment). In *Borton v Borton* (1849) 16 Sim 552, there was a subsequent clause in the will in case the donee should die under age without disposing of it: life interest with power of disposition by will. Cf, however, this with cases in para **[83.5]**, n 8. If there is no absolute disposition in the first place, the principle of these cases is not required: *Roberts v Thorp* (1911) 56 Sol Jo 13.

10 *Mortimer v Hartley* (1851) 6 Exch 47; *Re Banks' Trust, ex p Hovill* (1855) 2 K & J 387; *Magee v Martin* [1902] 1 IR 367. The fact that a testator has the idea that he can make property perpetually inalienable will have the opposite effect, for then the limitations he expresses must receive their legal interpretation: *Britton v Twining* (1817) 3 Mer 176, where the testator desired the capital to be kept always intact, but used words which gave an estate tail in personalty, then the equivalent of an absolute interest.

11 *Re Last's Estate* [1958] P 137, [1958] 1 All ER 316; *Re Moren* [1953] 4 DLR 138.

12 *Crumpe v Crumpe* [1900] AC 127.

13 *Re Stringer's Estate, Shaw v Jones-Ford* (1877) 6 Ch D 1 (first gift absolute but cut down by later words to life estate with power of appointment, and as power of appointment had not been exercised, the gift over took effect); *Comiskey v Bowring-Hanbury* [1905] AC 84 (absolute gift to wife held to be subject to executory gift over so far as she had not disposed of estate in their favour); *Shearer v Hogg* (1912) 46 SCR 492; *Re Burke* (1959) 20 DLR 396.

[83.10]

Absolute gift to a spouse. Non-professional wills sometimes include a gift to a spouse in terms such as 'I leave everything to my wife and after her death to my children'. The intention in such cases is probably that the wife should have full power to dispose of capital and income but if anything was left over on her death it should go to the children. However such wording might result in the spouse obtaining no more than a life interest with remainder to the children.[1]

The Administration of Justice Act 1982,[2] contains a provision in s 22 to the effect that in such cases, except where a contrary intention is shown it shall be presumed that the gift to the spouse is absolute notwithstanding the purported gift to issue.

1   See the Law Reform Committee's 19th Report on the Interpretation of Wills 1973, Cmnd 5301, paras 60–62.

2   See Vol 2, Part G, para **[244.98]**.

[83.11]

Clear gift for life in the first instance. Where the gift is expressly for life, though after the death of the donee to be at his disposal, he will not in general take more than a life interest[1] and even a right of absolute disposal during his life may not enlarge his interest to an absolute interest.[2] If, however, the words of disposition can be referred to property rather than to power[3] they may have this effect.[4] A bequest to a donee for his absolute enjoyment during his life, and to be disposed of as he thinks fit after his death, is equivalent to a gift for life with a general power of appointment by deed or will, and upon the power being exercised in his own favour[5] the donee is entitled to the bequest absolutely.[6] If there is no right of disposition on death, the donee has a general power of appointment inter vivos,[7] and the unappointed part will pass under the gift over.[8] A gift for life and a further disposition if anything is left over is an absolute gift.[9]

1 *Nowlan v Walsh* (1851) 4 De G & Sm 584. Where there is a gift apparently of an absolute interest but all other gifts to that donee are of income only, then the gift is of income only: *Re Patane* [1957] QSR 529.
2 *Bradly v Westcott* (1807) 13 Ves 445 (gift for life to be at his full, free, and absolute disposal during life: life interest with power of disposition during life); *Reith v Seymour* (1828) 4 Russ 263 (although the power of disposal was by will or otherwise); *Re Burkitt, Handcock v Studdert* [1915] 1 IR 205 (life interest and at her death to be disposed of as she wishes); *Scott v Josselyn* (1859) 26 Beav 174 (for life with power to dispose of capital during life and to appoint by will); *Pennock v Pennock* (1871) LR 13 Eq 144 (donee with power to apply capital for own benefit); *Re Thomson's Estate, Herring v Barrow* (1880) 14 Ch D 263. Cf *Henderson v Cross* (1861) 29 Beav 216 (life interest with power to spend capital or any part thereof was construed as an absolute gift); *Re Cameron* (1967) 62 DLR (2d) 389 (life interest only).
3 See Chapter 82.
4 *Nowlan v Walsh* (1851) 4 De G & Sm 584 at 586; *Hoy v Master* (1834) 6 Sim 568; *Reid v Carleton* [1905] 1 IR 147; *Re Rogers* [1955] SASR 211 (gift of house 'to live in or let during her lifetime but not to sell it' is a gift of the fee simple); see also *Goodtitle d Pearson v Otway* (1753) 2 Wils 6; *Re Maxwell's Will* (1857) 24 Beav 246 at 251.
5 See *Re Stringer's Estate, Shaw v Jones-Ford* (1877) 6 Ch D 1, as to failure to exercise the power.
6 *Re David's Trusts* (1859) John 495 at 500; *Harvey v Harvey* (1842) 5 Beav 134.
7 *Re Ryder, Burton v Kearsley* [1914] 1 Ch 865; *Re Richards, Uglow v Richards* [1902] 1 Ch 76, applied in *Re Saunders and Halom* (1986) 32 DLR (4th) 503; the trustees had power to provide capital out of the estate for the proper care and maintenance of the testator's widow, who had a life interest in the estate and was sole trustee—held not to be a general power.
8 *Re Thomson's Estate, Herring v Barrow* (1880) 14 Ch D 263; *Pennock v Pennock* (1871) LR 13 Eq 144; *Re Rowland, Jones v Rowland* (1902) 86 LT 78 (as to the gift of £400).
9 *Re Minchell's Will Trusts* [1964] 2 All ER 47.

[83.12]
Gift for life with added power of disposition. If a life interest is first given and a power of disposition by deed or will added, this is not an absolute gift vesting the property in the donee but a life interest with such added power of disposition as is stated in the gift.[1] This rule applies although the first gift is on the face of it absolute and is only cut down by the subsequent words.[2] It is, however, in every case a question of construction and it has been suggested that the express mention of the life interest is merely a mention of one of the advantages attached to the absolute interest passing under the gift,[3] and it must be shown whether or not the power has been effectively exercised.[4]

1 *Bradly v Westcott* (1807) 13 Ves 445; *Reith v Seymour* (1828) 4 Russ 263; *Nannock v Horton* (1802) 7 Ves 391; *Archibald v Wright* (1838) 9 Sim 161; *Scott v Josselyn* (1859) 26 Beav 174; *Re Thomson's Estate, Herring v Barrow* (1880) 14 Ch D 263 (where a power of disposition by will was held not to be given, though in *Re Lawry, Andrew v Coad* [1938] Ch 318, [1937] 4 All ER 1, this power was held to be given by a somewhat similar disposition); *Pennock v Pennock* (1871) LR 13 Eq 144; *Re Burkitt, Handcock v Studdert* [1915] 1 IR 205; *Young v Young* (1918) 52 ILT 40; *Re Keighley, Keighley v Keighley* [1919] 2 Ch 388; *Re Richards, Uglow v Richards* [1902] 1 Ch 76; *Re Lawry, Andrew v Coad* [1938] Ch 318, [1937] 4 All ER 1 (life interest with full power to deal with the property as the donee's own. This gives the donee a life interest with a general power of appointment by deed or will); *Stadder v Canadian Bank of Commerce* [1929] 3 DLR 651; *Lister v Gilbert* (1938) 12 MPR 566; *Re Rohatynski Estate* [1948] 2 WWR 618. It is otherwise where the power of appointment is by the will alone: see *Re Comstock* [1949] 3 DLR 677; *Re Berwick Estate* [1948] SCR 151. If the power is not exercised the property falls into residue: *Mansen v Nash* [1954] 3 DLR 496.

2   *Re Stringer's Estate, Shaw v Jones-Ford* (1877) 6 Ch D 1; *Re Pounder, Williams v Pounder* (1886) 56 LJ Ch 113.
3   *Reid v Atkinson* (1871) IR 5 Eq 373 at 382.
4   Where the proceeds of the estate were placed in the beneficiary's own personal banking account the power was exercised: *Re Box Estate* (1957) 7 DLR (2d) 478; but, where shares were transferred into the beneficiary's own name but not applied to her maintenance, there was insufficient exercise: *Mansen v Nash* [1954] 3 DLR 496.

[83.13]
Indefinite gift in first instance with added power. Where there is an indefinite gift with an added power of disposition by deed or will, the property vests in the donee absolutely at once[1] and this is so although the first gift is a gift of income only, provided it is unlimited in point of time.[2]

1   *Re Jones, Richards v Jones* [1898] 1 Ch 438; *Howarth v Dewell* (1860) 29 Beav 18; *Doe d Herbert v Thomas* (1835) 3 Ad & El 123; *McKenna v McCarten* [1915] 1 IR 282; *Pratt v Church* (1830) 4 Beav 177; *Ex p Shaw* (1836) 8 Sim 159; *Re Berryman, Berryman v Berryman* [1913] 1 IR 21.
2   *Southouse v Bate* (1851) 16 Beav 132; *Weale v Ollive (No 2)* (1863) 32 Beav 421; *Re L'Herminier, Mounsey v Buston* [1894] 1 Ch 675 (power to appoint income without limit is power to appoint capital); *Townshend v Ashcroft* [1917] 2 Ch 14 (gift for life of £30 per annum charged on land with power of 'leaving it' is a general power to appoint a perpetual rentcharge of that amount).

[83.14]
Gift for life with direction to trustees to apply capital at donee's request. Where the testator gave his widow a life interest in the residue and directed his trustees to allow her to use so much of it as she might wish during her lifetime, this did not authorise the trustees to turn over the capital to the widow but the widow on asking for any portion of the capital or the whole thereof was required only to express the purpose for which she required it and was under no obligation to demonstrate the actual need.[1]

1   *Re Claman Estate* (1963) 42 DLR (2d) 670.

[83.15]
Gift of income with liberty to use capital. A gift of income for life, with liberty to use the capital if the income is not sufficient, gives a general power of appointment by deed or writing, but probably not by will, over the capital. The word 'sufficient' means sufficient for the desires of the beneficiary, and is not restricted to his needs.[1] Where there was a protected life interest under a discretionary trust and the trustees were given uncontrolled discretion to apply capital for the general benefit of the beneficiary, it was held that the trustees must consider it for such benefit before they could hand over the capital.[2]

1   *Re Richards, Uglow v Richards* [1902] 1 Ch 76; *Re Pedrotti's Will* (1859) 27 Beav 583; *Re Ryder, Burton v Kearsley* [1914] 1 Ch 865 (gift of income to A for life with authority so long as he shall be entitled to the income to apply such part of the capital as he shall think fit for his own use and benefit creates a general power of appointment inter vivos over the capital); *Re McIntosh* [1933] IR 69 (gift of a limited interest in all property with power to utilise it for the benefit of his daughters held not to confer any power to apply the capital for their benefit); *Re Banko Estate* (1958) 12 DLR (2d) 515 (resort to capital in discretion of trustees); *Re Mayer Estate* [1950] 2 WWR 858; *Re McFarland* (1963) 36 DLR (2d) 689; *Re Ward's Estate* [1957] SASR 125 (where the gift over was to charity).
2   *Re Powles, Little v Powles* [1954] 1 All ER 516.

[83.16]

Gifts of property with added limitations in favour of personal representatives. A gift of property to one for life, with remainder as he shall appoint, with remainder to his executors and administrators, is an absolute gift to him if he does not exercise the power.[1] The result is still the same though the power be testamentary only[2] and whether it is contained in a will or settlement.[3] If the ultimate limitation is to the personal representatives of the donee, this (whether in a will or deed) apart from an expression to the contrary, is to them in their representative capacity.[4] If the ultimate limitation is to the next of kin, or if, the limitation being to the personal representatives, these words are on construction of the particular document read as equivalent to next of kin, the donee only takes an interest for life with a power of disposition.[5]

1   See Chapter 83.
2   *Holloway v Clarkson* (1843) 2 Hare 521; *Devall v Dickens* (1845) 9 Jur 550; *Page v Soper* (1853) 11 Hare 321; *Gardiner v Young* (1876) 34 LT 348; *Re Onslow, Plowden v Gayford* (1888) 39 Ch D 622; *Re Davenport, Turner v King* [1895] 1 Ch 361.
3   *Daniel v Dudley* (1841) 1 Ph 1.
4   *Re Crawford's Trusts* (1854) 2 Drew 230; *Re Wyndham's Trusts* (1865) LR 1 Eq 290; *Alger v Parrott* (1866) LR 3 Eq 328; *Re Best's Settlement Trusts* (1874) LR 18 Eq 686; *Re Brooks, Public Trustee v White* [1928] Ch 214.
5   *Anderson v Dawson* (1808) 15 Ves 532; *Baines v Ottey* (1832) 1 My & K 465; *Daniel v Dudley* (1841) 1 Ph 1; *Briggs v Upton* (1872) 7 Ch App 376. But the donee can, if the power is a general power, exercise it in his own favour and is then entitled to a transfer of the property: *Re Templeton Estate, Templeton v Royal Trust Co* [1936] 3 DLR 782.

[83.17]

When powers testamentary. A power to a person to appoint real or personal property after his own death is not rendered testamentary only by the mere reference to his death[1] but, if the words are used which are inapplicable to an execution by writing inter vivos, or if an intention otherwise appears to confine the exercise of the power to an execution by will, it is testamentary only.[2]

1   *Re David's Trusts* (1859) John 495; *Humble v Bowman* (1877) 47 LJ Ch 62; *Re Jackson's Will* (1879) 13 Ch D 189; but see *Freeland v Pearson* (1867) LR 3 Eq 658 (to the contrary).
2   *Doe d Thorley v Thorley* (1809) 10 East 438; *Walsh v Wallinger* (1830) 2 Russ & M 78; *Paul v Hewetson* (1833) 2 My & K 434.

[83.18]

Gift over in default of exercise of power. A gift over in default of the exercise of a power, not being a mere residuary gift, is evidence of an intention to create a power and not to give an absolute interest[1] as is the fact that the donee is under some disability which the donor cannot remove.[2]

1   *Re Maxwell's Will* (1857) 24 Beav 246; *Healy v Donnery* (1853) 3 ICLR 213; *Re Brierley, Brierley v Brierley* (1894) 43 WR 36; *Re Weekes' Settlement* [1897] 1 Ch 289; *Re Combe, Combe v Combe* [1925] Ch 210.
2   *Reid v Carleton* [1905] 1 IR 147.

[83.19]

Life estate severed from power. If the life estate is severed from the power of appointment for the purpose of introducing other distinct and separate contingent estates which never in fact arise, the court may infer that the donee takes, not a life estate with a power of appointment but an absolute interest.[1]

1   *Re Maxwell's Will* (1857) 24 Beav 246; *Nowlan v Walsh* (1851) 4 De G & Sm 584.

[83.20]

Absolute gift with power and gift over. Where there is an absolute gift, whether of real or personal property, followed by words sounding like a power, whether general or special, and whether exercisable by deed or will, with a gift over if not exercised, the gift over is repugnant and void and the donee takes absolutely.[1]

1   *Re Mortlock's Trust* (1857) 3 K & J 456; *Bull v Kingston* (1816) 1 Mer 314. It may be doubtful whether this applies in the case where the power is testamentary only.

CHAPTER 84

Entailed interests

[84.1]
Entailed interests after 1 January 1997. By virtue of the provisions in the Trusts of Land and Appointment of Trustees Act 1996 (TLATA 1996), it is not possible to create entailed interests on or after 1 January 1997.[1] Where a person purports by instrument to create an entailed interest after that date the instrument will take effect as a declaration that the property is held in trust absolutely for the grantee.[2] Entails created before that date will continue until barred or the property is disposed of under the Law of Property Act 1925.[3] The discussion which follows in this chapter refers accordingly to entails created before 1 January 1997 and which are continuing.

1 TLATA 1996, s 2(6), Sch 1, para 5.and Sch 4, repealing, inter alia, the Law of Property Act 1925, s 130 (1), (2), (3) and (6).
2 TLATA 1996, s 5(1).
3 Under the Law of Property Act 1925, s 176.

[84.2]
Law after 1925 and before 1 January 1997 as to creation of estates tail. By the Law of Property Act 1925 (LPA 1925),[1] the law relating to estates tail was altered as follows: (1) an estate tail was an equitable interest which could be created only by way of trust, and was described as an entailed interest;[2] (2) the creation of entailed interests was extended to personal property; (3) an entailed interest could be created only by the like expressions which before 1926 a similar interest could have been created by deed (not being an executory instrument) in freehold land;[3] (4) informal expressions occurring in a will coming into operation after 1925, which formerly would have created an estate tail, could no longer have that effect, but operated in equity, in regard to property real or personal, to create absolute, fee simple, or other interests corresponding to the interests which would formerly have been created by similar expressions in personal estate.[4] It was not essential for this purpose that the words 'heirs of the body' should be actually used. The word 'heirs'[5] would be sufficient if, on the construction of the will, it meant 'heirs of the body'. Thus, while a devise to a person and his heirs usually gave a fee simple,[6] the context could show that by 'heirs' was meant 'heirs of the body'.[7] So that only an entailed interest was created; and a devise over on the donee's death without heirs of the body[8] could have the effect of cutting down the fee simple to an entailed interest.[9] A direction that the donee was made the testator's heir,[10] or other expressions indicating an intention that the donee could be recognised as filling the character which would entitle him by law to the whole of the

testator's real property might give him an estate in fee simple or other inheritable estate.[11] This could have been so where he was made the testator's executor as to a freehold.[12] In such cases it seemed that, since the gift in the will was, upon its construction, to the heirs of the body, an entailed interest could still have been created.

1 See the LPA 1925, s 130. The LPA 1925, s 130(1)–(3) and (6) are repealed by the TLATA 1996, Sch 4. Thus the rules set out in this and para **[84.3]** infra state the position under the LPA 1925 and will no longer apply after the commencement of the TLATA 1996, see para **[84.1]** supra. For the pre-1925 law see the seventh edition of this text.

2 LPA 1925, s 130(1); 37 *Halsbury's Statutes* (4th edn) 288. By the LPA 1925, s 130(7), the expression 'entailed interest' included an estate tail created before 1926.

3 LPA 1925, s 130(2). Where personal estate (including the proceeds of sale of land directed to be sold and chattels to be held as heirlooms) was directed to be enjoyed or held with, or upon trusts corresponding to trusts affecting land in which, either before 1926 or after 1925, an entailed interest had been created or was subsisting, such direction was deemed sufficient to create a corresponding entailed interest in such personal estate: LPA 1925, s 130(3); 37 *Halsbury's Statutes* (4th edn) 288. Repealed by the TLATA 1996, Sch 4; see n 1. For this purpose, however, the actual words of the subsection should be used; *Re Jones, Public Trustee v Jones* [1934] Ch 315 (where the trust was to pay the income to the beneficiary in possession of the P estate under another will. This was not within the section and the first tenant in possession would take the property absolutely under the law before 1926).

4 LPA 1925, s 130(2); 37 *Halsbury's Statutes* (4th edn) 288. Repealed by the TLATA 1996, Sch 4; see n 1.

5 As to this word, see, further Chapter 78.

6 This might before 1926 have been assisted by the rule in *Shelley's Case*: see *Re Norrington, Norrington v Norrington* (1923) 40 TLR 96; *Re Hack, Beadman v Beadman* [1925] Ch 633. On the other hand, a word defining the interest the heir was to take gave him a separate interest and made him a new stock of descent: *Re Hussey and Green's Contract, Re Hussey, Hussey v Simper* [1921] 1 Ch 566 (where the word 'absolutely' was added and was held to make him a designated taker by purchase).

7 *Cowper v Scott* (1731) 3 P Wms 119; *Roe d James v Avis* (1792) 4 Term Rep 605; *Doe d Jearrad v Bannister* (1840) 10 LJ Ex 33; *Biddulph v Lees* (1859) EB & E 289, 308 (where a shifting clause in the event of any daughter becoming a nun cut down the estate given by 'heirs' to an estate tail); *Re Thompson, ex p Thompson* (1864) 16 I Ch R 228 ('always to go in the male line'); *O'Hanlon v Unthank* (1872) IR 7 Eq 68 ('heirs being issue').

8 *Wallop v Darby* (1612) Yelv 209; *Jenkins v Herries* (1819) 4 Madd 67; *Jenkins v Hughes* (1860) 8 HL Cas 571.

9 *Nottingham v Jennings* (1700) 1 P Wms 23; *Re Ross* (1901) 1 SRNSW 1; *King v Evans* (1895) 24 SCR 356; *Doe d Hatch v Bluck* (1816) 6 Taunt 485; *Simpson v Ashworth* (1843) 6 Beav 412; *Hancock v Clavey* (1871) 25 LT 323. As to the gift over being dependent on the existence of a collateral heir, see *Re Waugh, Waugh v Cripps* [1903] 1 Ch 744 (the rule is stated in this case at p 747). In *Harris v Davis* (1844) 1 Coll 416, the rule was applied where some but not all of the devisees were capable of being collateral heirs. The rule was confined to these cases; see *A-G v Gill* (1726) 2 P Wms 369 (devise over to charity); *Preston v Funnell* (1739) 7 Mod Rep 296 (testator's nearest of kindred, who were not necessarily capable of inheriting from the donee, his son); *Tilburgh v Barbut* (1748) 1 Ves Sen 89 (first devisee's half-brother, who could not then inherit from him).

10 *Spark v Purnell* (1615) Hob 75; *Taylor v Web (or Webb)* (1651) Sty 301.

11 *Parker v Nickson* (1863) 1 De GJ & Sm 177.

12 *Doe d Gillard v Gillard* (1822) 5 B & Ald 785; *Doe d Hickman v Haslewood* (1837) 6 Ad & El 167; *Doe d Pratt v Pratt* (1837) 6 Ad & El 180; *Murphy v Donnelly* (1870) IR 4 Eq 111. The context could exclude this construction; *Shelton v Watson* (1849) 13 Jur 203 (direction for settlement); *Stratford v Powell* (1807) 1 Ball & B 1 ('sole heiress for life'). The word 'inherit' could be used in the sense of 'take in succession' to the last taker: *Stratford v Powell*.

[84.3]

Heirs taking by purchase. A limitation of real or personal property in favour of the heir, either general or special, of a deceased person which, if limited in respect of freehold land before 1926, would have conferred on the heir an estate in the land by purchase, operated to confer a corresponding equitable interest in the property on the person who would, if the general law in force immediately before the commencement of the LPA 1925 had remained unaffected, have answered the description of heir, either general or special, of the deceased in respect of his freehold land, either at the death of the deceased or at any time named in the limitation, as the case might require.[1] The word 'heir' might formerly be a word of limitation, or it could be descriptive of the donee himself and then it was a word of purchase. The question whether the word was a word of limitation was equivalent to the question whether the word was plural, 'heirs', was used for the purpose of defining the interest the heir was to take.[2]

1   LPA 1925, s 132; 37 *Halsburys Statutes* (4th edn) 292.
2   *Harvey v Towell* (1847) 7 Hare 231 at 234.

[84.4]
Quasi-inheritable gifts of personal property. Before 1926 a disposition of personal property by words which showed an intention to give and inheritable estate in it to a donee gave him an absolute interest.[1] Thus, a donee took an absolute interest under a bequest of personal property to him and his heirs[2] or to him and the heirs of his body,[3] or to him and the heirs male of his body,[4] or under other expressions showing an intention that his issue throughout the whole of their line should take after him by descent.[5] The intention might be inferred by implication from a gift over on failure of his heirs of the body or failure of issue generally.[6] This rule of construction was applied even in cases where the donee was expressly given only a life interest,[7] and the inheritable interest arose by virtue of or by analogy to the application of the rule in *Shelley's Case* to the limitations,[8] in spite of the fact that the rule in *Shelley's Case* was not strictly applicable to personal property.[9] Even in the case of real property the rule in *Shelley's Case* was not invariably applied. It would not be applied if the result was to defeat entirely the intention of the testator appearing from the whole will and capable, without violation of the rules of law, of being carried into effect,[10] in a case, for example, where the word 'heirs' might describe particular persons intended to take by purchase.[11] If the gift were for life and then for the issue of the donee for life, prima facie the first donee took for life only, and the issue took on his death.[12] If, in such a case, the gift were one of blended real and personal property, the donee might take an estate tail in the real property and a life interest in the personal property.[13]

1   *Re Hope's Will Trust, Hope v Thorp* [1929] 2 Ch 136. The rule was commonly stated in the form 'words which create an estate tail in realty will give an absolute interest in personal property'; *Audsley v Horn* (1859) 1 De GF & J 226 at 236; *Williams v Lewis* (1859) 6 HL Cas 1013 at 1020; *Re Barker's Trusts* (1883) 52 LJ Ch 565; *Re Lowman, Devenish v Pester* [1895] 2 Ch 348 at 361. The rule was not to be taken absolutely for in that case it would conflict with the rule in *Forth v Chapman* (1720) 1 P Wms 663; see *Re Jeaffreson's Trusts* (1866) LR 2 Eq 276.
2   *Anstruther v Chalmer* (1826) 2 Sim 1; *Re Banks' Trusts, ex p Hovill* (1855) 2 K & J 387. In these cases there was a preliminary question whether, upon the whole will and considering that the property was personal and not real property, the words were thus used in their usual sense; *Re Jeaffreson's Trusts* (1866) LR 2 Eq 276 at 280. Upon a consideration of the whole will it might appear that the words 'heirs of the body' and the like, described particular persons (see

Dakin v Nicholson (1837) 6 LJ Ch 329). The question in the first place, therefore, was not whether or not the testator intended the donee to have an absolute interest but whether the words of limitation were used in a sense different from their usual sense; *Garth v Baldwin* (1755) 2 Ves Sen 646 at 661.

3   *Garth v Baldwin* (1755) 2 Ves Sen 646; *Crooke v De Vandes* (1803) 9 Ves 197; *Crawford v Trotter* (1819) 4 Madd 361; *Widdison v Hodgkin* (1823) 2 LJOS Ch 9 ('heirs' in the context meaning 'heirs of the body').

4   *Leventhorpe v Ashbie* (1635) 1 Roll Abr 831, pl 1; *Seale v Seale* (1715) 1 P Wms 290.

5   *Re Wynch's Trusts, ex p Wynch* (1854) 5 De GM & G 188 at 206; *Re Barker's Trusts* (1883) 48 LT 573 ('heirs of his body in equal proportions'); *Earl Tyrone v Marquis of Waterford* (1860) 1 De GF & J 613 (his children in succession); *Britton v Twining* (1817) 3 Mer 176 (the heir of his body and so on in succession to the heir-at-law male or female); *Re Commercial Railway Act, ex p Harrison* (1838) 3 Y & C Ex 275 (gift of leasehold house to H for life, then to H's eldest son or daughter and next heir male or female until expiration of lease held to be an absolute gift); *Young v Davies* (1863) 2 Drew & Sm 167 (to my surviving daughters and their lawful offspring); *Atkinson v L'Estrange* (1885) 15 LR Ir 340 (to A for life and to her heirs after her); *Bearer v Nowell* (1858) 25 Beav 551 (to A for life and then to be divided among all her children and their lawful issue).

6   *Campbell v Harding* (1831) 2 Russ & M 390; *Dunk v Fenner* (1831) 2 Russ & M 557; *Simmons v Simmons* (1836) 8 Sim 22; *Re Andrew's Will* (1859) 27 Beav 608; *Re Sallery* (1861) 11 I Ch R 236.

7   *Britton v Twining* (1817) 3 Mer 176; *Atkinson v L'Estrange* (1885) 15 LR Ir 340; *Re Score, Tolman v Score* (1887) 57 LT 40.

8   The rule in *Shelley's Case* was applied in *Douglas v Congreve* (1838) 1 Beav 59; *Harvey v Towell* (1847) 7 Hare 231; *Ousby v Harvey* (1848) 17 LJ Ch 160; *Williams v Lewis* (1859) 6 HL Cas 1013; *Comfort v Brown* (1878) 10 Ch D 146; *Re Score, Tolman v Score* (1887) 57 LT 40. In the following cases personal property was settled by reference to real property, to which the rule in *Shelley's Case* was applicable: *Brouncker v Bagot* (1816) 1 Mer 271; *Tate v Clarke* (1838) 1 Beav 100, and see cases cited in n 3. The rule in *Shelley's Case* was abolished for all instruments coming into operation after 1925, by the Law of Property Act 1925, s 131.

9   *Herrick v Franklin* (1868) LR 6 Eq 593 at 596; *Re Jeaffreson's Trusts* (1866) LR 2 Eq 276 at 281.

10 *Audsley v Horn* (1859) 1 De GF at J 226 at 236; *Dodds v Dodds* (1860) 11 I Ch R 374.

11 *Symers v Jobson* (1848) 16 Sim 267; *Bull v Comberbach* (1858) 25 Beav 540 at 543.

12 *Re Wynch's Trusts, ex p Wynch* (1854) 5 De GM & G 188; *Goldney v Crabb* (1854) 19 Beav 338; *Waldron v Boulter* (1856) 22 Beav 284; *Jackson v Calvert* (1860) 1 John & H 235; *Bannister v Lang* (1867) 17 LT 137; *Foster v Wybrants* (1874) IR 11 Eq 40; *Re Cullen's Estate* [1907] 1 IR 73.

13 *Jackson v Calvert* (1860) 1 John & H 235; *Re Longworth, Longworth v Campbell* [1910] 1 IR 23.

CHAPTER 85

Gifts to a person and his children or to a person and his issue

I. TO A PERSON AND HIS CHILDREN

[85.1]

Rule of construction. A gift to a donee 'and his children'[1] – the last words in the phrase were capable of being used as words of limitation or words of description of persons to take either concurrently with or in succession to the named donee,[2] or in substitution for him.[3] In such cases the construction was determined before 1926 by the rule in *Wild's Case*.[4]

1 See para **[85.2]** infra, for gifts to a donee and 'his issue'.
2 *Lampley v Blower* (1746) 3 Atk 396.
3 See Chapter 68.
4 (1599) 6 Co Rep 16 b, 17 a. The rule has lost its importance since entailed interests could be created only by the same words as in a deed and cannot now be created at all; see Chapter 84.

[85.2]

Rule in *Wild's Case*. Where there was an immediate[1] devise of real estate[2] to a person and his children, and he had at the date of the will[3] no child, then prima facie the word 'children' was taken to be a word of limitation and the named person took an estate tail;[4] but the context might show that the unborn children were to take as purchasers.[5] On the other hand, if he had a child or children at the time of the devise, then the will was prima facie construed as giving a joint estate to him and his children as purchasers,[6] but even in the latter case the context might show that the word was a word of limitation and that an estate tail was intended,[7] or that the children took in succession to their parents and as purchasers.[8] It seems that for the purpose of these rules of construction an only child *en ventre sa mère* was not regarded as in existence.[9] The rule applied only where the testator had not sufficiently indicated his intention,[10] and the court always considered itself at liberty to disregard it in both its branches where an adherence to it would have defeated the intention shown by the will as a whole[11].

1 The devise must be immediate and the rule was inapplicable unless the interests of the parent and children were both concurrent. As stated in *Wild's Case* (1599) 6 Co Rep 16 b, 17 a, the intent of the testator is manifest and certain that his children or issue should take and they cannot take as immediate devisees since they are not in existence nor can they take as remaindermen for that was not the testator's intent. The only solution is that the parent takes an estate tail.
2 The rule was a rule applicable to real estate and strictly had no application to personal estate.
3 *Seale v Barter* (1801) 2 Bos & P 485; *Clifford v Koe* (1880) 5 App Cas 447. The Wills Act 1837 did not affect the rule in this respect: *Grieve v Grieve* (1867) LR 4 Eq 180.

4   *Wild's Case* (1599) 6 Co Rep 16 b, 17 a, as stated in *Byng v Byng* (1862) 10 HL Cas 171 at 178;
   Sweetapple v Bindon (1705) 2 Vern 536; *Cook v Cook* (1706) 2 Vern 545; *Wharton v Gresham*
   (1776) 2 Wm Bl 1083 (to A and his sons in tail male gave A an estate tail); *Trevor v Trevor*
   (1847) 1 HL Cas 239 (an executory trust where the issue took as purchasers).

5   *Re Moyles' Estate* (1878) 1 LR Ir 155 (words of limitation applying to children's interest). The
   addition of words of limitation did not affect the rule so long as they could be read as referring
   to the first donee and as describing his interest: *Wharton v Gresham* (1776) 2 Wm Bl 1083;
   Cormack v Copous (1853) 17 Beav 397 at 401. A devise to a named person and after his death
   to his children although he had no children at the time of the devise was yet a remainder to
   every child he might have: *Wild's Case* (1599) 6 Co Rep 16 b, 17 a; *Ginger d White v White*
   (1742) Willes 348 (to children of J successively ... and to their heirs); *Doe d Liversage v
   Vaughan* (1822) 5 B & Ald 464.

6   *Wild's Case* (1599) 6 Co Rep 16 b, 17 a; *Oates d Hatterley v Jackson* (1742) 2 Stra 1172.

7   *Wood v Baron* (1801) 1 East 259; *Webb v Byng* (1856) 2 K & J 669 (inferences against rule
   drawn from name and arms clause and the fact that heirlooms would be enjoyed jointly if the
   rule applied); *Earl of Tyrone v Marquis of Waterford* (1860) 1 De GF & J 613 at 624 ('children
   in succession'); *Ward v Ward* [1921] 1 IR 117 (devise to J 'with remainder to her and her
   children for ever': children here a limitation and J took an estate tail general).

8   *Jeffrey v Honywood* (1819) 4 Madd 398 (where words of limitation were added to the limitation
   to the issue: devise to M. and to all and every the child and children whether male or female of
   her body lawfully issuing and unto his her or their heirs as tenants in common); *Bowen v
   Scowcroft* (1837) 2 Y & C Ex 640 at 661; and see *Webb v Byng* (1856) 2 K & J 669; and *Grant
   v Fuller* (1902) 33 SCR 34 (gift over if no children).

9   *Roper v Roper* (1867) LR 3 CP 32.

10 *Re Jones, Lewis v Lewis* [1910] 1 Ch 167 at 175; *Re Buckmaster's Estate* (1882) 47 LT 514.

11 *Byng v Byng* (1862) 10 HL Cas 171 at 178; *Clifford v Koe* (1880) 5 App Cas 447 at 453. As to
   exclusion of rule in the case of a gift of furniture with real estate, see *Grieve v Grieve* (1867)
   LR 4 Eq 180 ; doubted in *Clifford v Koe* (1880) 5 App Cas 447 at 461.

[85.3]

Bequests of personal property. The above rule had strictly no application to
personal property,[1] and, if in a bequest to a named person and his children the
word 'children' was used as a word of limitation, the named person took and
still takes an absolute interest.[2] In general, however, the word is not one of
limitation,[3] and under such a bequest the parent and the children take
concurrently[4] and as joint tenants.[5] The class of children is ascertained according
to the usual rules,[6] and no child born after the death of the testator can take in the
case of an immediate gift,[7] though, in the case of a postponed gift, after-born
children are let in.[8] The context, however, may point to a construction not giving
such concurrent interests,[9] and slight circumstances have been held by the
courts[10] as enabling them to come to the conclusion that successive interests, ie a
gift for life for the named person and after his death to his children, were
intended.[11] The interests are presumed to be successive, for example where all
the children of the donee, whether born before or after the death of the testator
are intended to take,[12] or where there is a gift over on failure of issue of the
parent or other provision showing that the property is contemplated as still
subsisting undivided at the death of the parent,[13] or otherwise inconsistent with
the parent taking an interest in the capital together with the children.[14]

1   *Audsley v Horn* (1859) 1 De GF & J 226 at 236 (where, however, a gift over assisted the
   construction of the gift as creating successive interests); *Re Jones, Lewis v Lewis* [1910] 1 Ch
   167; *Stokes v Heron* (1845) 12 Cl & Fin 161 at 183, 198.

2   *Doe d Gigg v Bradley* (1812) 16 East 399 (where a child existed at the date of the will); *Cape v
   Cape* (1837) 2 Y & C Ex 543; *Re MacDougall* [1927] 3 DLR 464.

3   *Buffar v Bradford* (1741) 2 Atk 220.

4   *Mason v Clarke* (1853) 17 Beav 126 (where the construction is stated); *Alcock v Ellen* (1692) Freem Ch 186; *Buffar v Bradford* (1741) 2 Atk 220 (where the parent predeceased the testator and the one child took absolutely); *Pync v Franklin* (1832) 5 Sim 458 (where no children at the time gift is to be paid, the parent takes absolutely); *De Witte v De Witte* (1840) 11 Sim 41; *Sutton v Torre* (1842) 6 Jur 234; *Beales v Crisford* (1843) 13 Sim 592 (B and 'his family' construed as B and 'his children'); *Bustard v Saunders* (1843) 7 Beav 92; *Newill v Newill* (1872) 7 Ch App 253.

5   The general rule is that they take as joint tenants: see cases in n 4 and *Queensland Trustees Ltd v Gray* [1927] St R Qd 68; but the context may require that they shall take as tenants in common: *Eccard v Brooke* (1790) 2 Cox Eq Cas 213; *Lenden v Blackmore* (1840) 10 Sim 626 (equally divided); *Paine v Wagner* (1841) 12 Sim 184 (equally divided); *Cunningham v Murray* (1847) 1 De G & Sm 366 (to be divided in equal shares); *Salmon v Tidmarsh* (1859) 5 Jur NS 1380 (equally divided).

6   See Chapter 66.

7   *De Witte v De Witte* (1840) 11 Sim 41.

8   *Cook v Cook* (1706) 2 Vern 545; *Read v Willis* (1844) 1 Coll 86; *Lenden v Blackmore* (1840) 10 Sim 626; but see *Scott v Scott* (1845) 15 Sim 47 (where the gift was a postponed gift and there were no children at the death of the testator, though there were children at the death of the life tenant, the parent took absolutely); and *Read v Willis* (1844) 1 Coll 86, and *Cape v Cape* (1837) 2 Y & C Ex 543 (similar cases).

9   *Caffary v Caffary* (1844) 8 Jur 329 (subsequent reference to fund as given to parent). The fact that the parent is the testator's wife and the gift is to her and his children does not exclude the ordinary rule that they take concurrently: *Newill v Newill* (1872) 7 Ch App 253; and cf *Re Seyton, Seyton v Satterthwaite* (1887) 34 Ch D 511; *Re Davies' Policy Trusts* [1892] 1 Ch 90; not following *Re Adam's Policy Trusts* (1883) 23 Ch D 525. The rule applies in the case of a gift to a person, his wife and children, though formerly this was subject to the rule that a husband and wife counted as only one person in such a case: *Gordon v Whieldon* (1848) 11 Beav 170. Formerly, where the gift was to a married woman for her separate use and her children, a succession of interests was indicated, for otherwise the separate use could not be applied to the whole fund: *French v French* (1840) 11 Sim 257; *Bain v Lescher* (1840) 11 Sim 397; *Jeffery v De Vitre* (1857) 24 Beav 296.

10   *Re Wilmot, Wilmot v Betterton* (1897) 76 LT 415 at 417; *Crockett v Crockett* (1848) 2 Ph 553 at 555; *Newill v Newill* (1872) 7 Ch App 253 at 256; *Re Jones, Lewis v Lewis* [1910] 1 Ch 167 at 172.

11   *Newman v Nightingale* (1787) 1 Cox Eq Cas 341 (to A and her children for ever); *Crawford v Trotter* (1819) 4 Madd 361 (legacy to S and her heirs); *Cator v Cator* (1851) 14 Beav 463 (addition to a previous settled legacy). A direction that the fund is to be secured for their use or similar direction has been considered a direction to settle; *Vaughan v Marquis of Headfort* (1840) 10 Sim 639; *French v French* (1840) 11 Sim 257; *Combe v Hughes* (1872) LR 14 Eq 415; *Re Mills, Mills v Mills* (1902) 22 NZLR 425; *Yates v Yates* (1905) 25 NZLR 263; although a gift to the named person in trust for himself and his children is not sufficient: *Newill v Newill* (1872) 7 Ch App 253 at 258; *Young v Young* (1918) 52 ILT 40. A separate gift to the two eldest sons affected the decision in *Re Owen's Trusts* (1871) LR 12 Eq 316 (gift of residue to A and all her children, separate gift to A and her children except her two eldest sons and separate gift to two eldest sons). As to creation of a power of appointment among the children, see *Ward v Grey* (1859) 26 Beav 485 at 494; *Bradshaw v Bradshaw* [1908] 1 IR 288 ('she has a right to divide the above possessions among her offspring which may be descendants of mine').

12   *Morse v Morse* (1829) 2 Sim 485; *Froggatt v Wardell* (1850) 3 De G & Sm 685; *Jeffery v De Vitre* (1857) 24 Beav 296; *Audsley v Horn* (1858) 26 Beav 195; *Ward v Grey* (1859) 26 Beav 485 ('A and her children' spoken of as 'A and her family' in a codicil).

13   *Gawler v Cadby* (1821) Jac 346; *Dawson v Bourne* (1852) 16 Beav 29; *Audsley v Horn* (1858) 26 Beav 195 at 235 (gift over if children died without issue); *Re Jones, Lewis v Lewis* [1910] 1 Ch 167 at 173; *Conyngham v Tripp* [1925] 1 IR 27.

14   *Garden v Pulteney* (1765) 2 Eden 323 (if there should be but one younger son, the whole to him); *Parsons v Coke* (1858) 4 Drew 296 (issue to take parent's share); *Newill v Newill* (1872) 7 Ch App 253 (direction that children should take shares in whole fund).

II.   TO A PERSON AND HIS ISSUE

[85.4]

Gift of real estate. In a devise to a person and his issue the word 'issue' is generally a word of limitation,[1] but it may be a description of the persons to take.[2] In the former case the devise was before 1926 treated as equivalent to a devise to the donee and the heirs of his body, and he took an estate tail.[3] Particularly, the word 'issue' in such a gift was a word of limitation if there were no issue at the date of the will.[4] 'Issue' does not now, however, create an entail, and under such a gift the donee takes the fee simple.[5] Where the context shows that the issue are to take as purchasers then prima facie they take as joint tenants with the named person.[6]

1   *Tate v Clarke* (1838) 1 Beav 100; *Slater v Dangerfield* (1846) 15 M & W 263.
2   See Chapter 76.
3   *Roddy v Fitzgerald* (1858) 6 HL Cas 823 at 872; *Martin v Swannell* (1840) 2 Beav 249; *Re Coulden, Coulden v Coulden* [1908] 1 Ch 320 at 324; *Re Hammond, Parry v Hammond* [1924] 2 Ch 276. In a gift to a person 'or' his issue, the word 'or' might be changed to 'and', whereupon the donee took an estate tail: *Re Clerke, Clowes v Clerke* [1915] 2 Ch 301; *Re Hayden, Pask v Perry* [1931] 2 Ch 333 (but see now para **[84.1]** ante); or, on the construction of the whole will, a fee simple: *W Gardiner & Co v Dessaix* [1915] AC 1096.
4   *Campbell v Bouskell* (1859) 27 Beav 325; *Underhill v Roden* (1876) 2 Ch D 494, at 499. This is the rule in *Wild's Case* (1599) 6 Co Rep 16 b, 17 a: see para **[85.2]** supra. A devise to A for life with remainder to his issue used to operate a gift of the fee simple under the rule in *Shelley's Case*.
5   See para **[85.2]** supra.
6   *Re Wilmot, Wilmot v Betterton* (1897) 76 LT 415; *Re Hammond, Parry v Hammond* [1924] 2 Ch 276. The context may require the issue to take in succession to their parent: eg to A and his issue if more than one as tenants in common: *Doe d Gilman v Elvey* (1803) 4 East 313; or to A and her issue in strict settlement: *Trevor v Trevor* (1847) 1 HL Cas 239; *Re Lord Lawrence, Lawrence v Lawrence* [1915] 1 Ch 129.

[85.5]
Bequest of personal property. In a gift of personal property to a person and his issue[1] prima facie all (that is, including the parent) take by purchase[2] and concurrently as joint tenants, the issue taking in competition with the parent,[3] but the context and the circumstances may show an intention to the contrary. Thus, gifts of personal property to a person and his issue have in several cases conferred an absolute interest on him,[4] particularly where there was a gift over on failure of issue generally.[5] In such cases the context showed that the words were used as words of limitation, but whether they are or not is purely a question of the construction of each particular will, and the court is not fettered by any general rule.[6] In several cases under such a gift the issue have taken alternatively only, in case their ancestor was not in existence at the time of distribution, either by way of substitution[7] or by way of original gift[8] or has taken in succession to their parent.[9] Since 1925 the word 'issue' in such a case cannot create an estate tail, so that wherever the court construes the word as a word of limitation, the donee will take an absolute interest. Where the word is not one of limitation, the principles set out above remain unaltered.

1   As to bequests of personal property to a person for life and then to his issue, see para **[85.3]** supra.
2   *Re Longworth, Longworth, v Campbell* [1910] 1 IR 23; *Re Taylor's Trusts, Taylor v Blake* [1912] 1 IR 1.
3   *Re Wilmot, Wilmot v Betterton* (1897) 76 LT 415 at 417. See also *Law v Thorp* (1858) 27 LJ Ch 649 (gift to children and their issue with benefit of survivorship).
4   *Butter v Ommaney* (1827) 4 Russ 70 (pecuniary legacy to be paid twelve months after testator's death); *Donn v Penny* (1815) 1 Mer 20 (personal property to A and his male issue and for want of male issue after him to B and his male issue: A took absolute interest in personal property);

Lyon v Mitchell (1816) 1 Madd 467 (bequest for four sons and their respective issue, each son took an absolute interest subject to the accruer clause contained in the will); *Samuel v Samuel* (1845) 2 Coop *temp* Cott 119 (money to be settled for the sole use of daughters and their lawful issue).

5   *Donn v Penny* (1815) 1 Mer 20; *Beaver v Nowell* (1858) 25 Beav 551; *Re Andrew's Will* (1859) 27 Beav 608.

6   *Re Coulden, Coulden v Coulden* [1908] 1 Ch 320. In such cases by the holding of the word 'issue' to be a word of limitation and thus giving the donee an absolute interest the issue are deprived of all direct benefit under the will, ibid, and see *Re Hammond, Parry v Hammond* [1924] 2 Ch 276.

7   *Butter v Ommaney* (1827) 4 Russ 70; *Pearson v Stephen* (1831) 5 Bli NS 203; *Dick v Lacy* (1845) 8 Beav 214; *Re Stanhope's Trusts* (1859) 27 Beav 201.

8   *Re Coulden, Coulden v Coulden* [1908] 1 Ch 320.

9   *Parsons v Coke* (1858) 4 Drew 296.

CHAPTER 86

Concurrent gifts – joint tenancy and tenancy in common

[86.1]
Trusts of Land and Appointment of Trustees Act 1996 (TLATA 1996).
Dispositions to tenants in common or as joint tenants of real estate no longer
take effect as trusts for sale but are held on simple trusts of land and take effect
in trust for the persons interested in the land.[1] The personal representatives will
hold the land on trust for the beneficial tenants in common or joint tenants
without a trust for sale[2] but they can require the beneficiaries to accept a transfer
of the land.[3]

1   TLATA 1996, s 5(1), Sch 2 paras 3 and 4, with effect from 1 January 1997 amending the Law
    of Property Act 1925 (LPA 1925), ss 34 and 36.
2   With effect from 1 January 1997 the trusts imposed by the LPA 1925, ss 34 (tenants in
    common) and 36 (joint tenants) are amended and s 3(1)(b) and s 35 (statutory trust for sale) of
    the LPA 1925 are repealed by the TLATA 1996.
3   TLATA 1996, s 6(2).

[86.2]
Gifts in joint tenancy. Where property is given to several persons concurrently,
the questions whether those persons take as joint tenants or tenants in common,[1]
and in the latter case in what shares they take,[2] depend on the context of the
whole will. Prima facie they take as joint tenants,[3] but it has been said that, in
considering the context, anything in the slightest degree indicating an intention
to divide the property negatives the idea of a joint tenancy,[4] and in a case of
ambiguity the court leans to the construction which creates a tenancy in common
in preference to that which creates a joint tenancy.[5] Where a gift creates original
and substitutional shares, words of severance can apply to each set of shares;[6]
but this construction is dependent upon a finding that the will uses a kind of
shorthand so that the words of severance in the principal gift apply also to the
substitutional gift. Unless this is so, the ordinary rule applies and the
substitutional donees take as joint tenants where there are no words of severance
in their gift. Thus 'children taking the share their parent would have taken'
creates a joint tenancy;[7] but 'to be divided among my children then living or the
issue of any deceased child' gives the latter a tenancy in common.[8]

1   A simple gift to A and B without more is a joint tenancy and it is upon those setting up a
    tenancy in common to show from the context that the words are not to have that meaning:
    Crooke v De Vandes (1803) 9 Ves 197. On the other hand anything which in the slightest
    degree indicates an intention to divide the property must be held to abrogate the idea of a joint
    tenancy and to create a tenancy in common: *Robertson v Fraser* (1871) 6 Ch App 696, and the
    court has favoured a tenancy in common rather than a joint tenancy: *Billing v Billing* (1895) 11
    TLR 502.

2   *Robertson v Fraser* (1871) 6 Ch App 696 at 700; *Fisher v Anderson* (1879) 4 SCR 406, at 419.
    Formerly a husband and wife were regarded as one person in reckoning such shares: *Re Jeffrey,*
    Nussey v Jeffrey [1914] 1 Ch 375; but now they are treated as two persons for all purposes of
    the acquisition of property: Law of Property Act 1925, s 37; 37 *Halsbury's Statutes* (4th edn)
    166.
3   *Morley v Bird* (1798) 3 Ves 628; *Stuart v Bruce* (1798) 3 Ves 632; *Ritchie's Trustees v*
    M'Donald 1915 SC 501; *Re Clarkson, Public Trustee v Clarkson* [1915] 2 Ch 216; *Re Bancroft,*
    Eastern Trust Co v Calder [1936] 4 DLR 571. See also *Re Boyd* (1969) 6 DLR (3d) 110. A gift
    to A and/or B was construed as a joint tenancy: *Re Lewis, Goronwy v Richards* [1942] Ch 424,
    [1942] 2 All ER 364.
4   See n 1; *Re Woolley, Wormald v Woolley* [1903] 2 Ch 206. The mere fact that the interest is to
    be divided is not sufficient to make a tenancy in common of the capital: *Crooke v De Vandes*
    (1803) 9 Ves 197 at 206. A description of the donees as 'joint tenants', although a technical
    description, is not necessarily fatal to a tenancy in common: *Booth v Alington* (1857) 27 LJ Ch
    117; and the words 'equally as joint tenants' have been held to create a tenancy in common:
    Rentoul v Rentoul [1944] VLR 205. As to expressions indicative of a tenancy in common, see
    Re Dunn, Carter v Barrett [1916] 1 Ch 97; *Re Ward, Partridge v Hoare–Ward* [1920] 1 Ch
    334; and *Re Peter's Will* (1967) 63 WWR 180.
5   *Jolliffe v East* (1789) 3 Bro CC 25; *Re Woolley, Wormald v Woolley* [1903] 2 Ch 206 at 211;
    Bennett v Houldsworth (1911) 104 LT 304; *Re Fisher, Robinson v Eardley* [1915] 1 Ch 302.
6   *Crosthwaite v Dean* (1879) 40 LT 837; *Re Froy, Froy v Froy* [1938] Ch 566, [1938] 2 All ER
    316.
7   *Re Brooke's Will Trusts, Jubber v Brooke* [1953] 1 All ER 668, [1953] 1 WLR 439.
8   *Re Froy, Froy v Froy* [1938] Ch 566, [1938] 2 All ER 316.

[86.3]

Joint estates for life with separate remainders. In some cases, to give effect to
the whole will, the severance in interest is made to commence at a future time.
Thus, joint estates for life and separate remainders may be created, for example,
in gifts of real property to several persons, who cannot marry, and the heirs of
their bodies,[1] or in other cases on a sufficient context, for example, where the
heirs taking the inheritance are defined by reference to the respective donees.[2]

1   *Barker v Gyles* (1727) 3 Bro Parl Cas 104; *Forrest v Whiteway* (1849) 3 Exch 367; *Edwards v*
    Champion (1853) 3 De GM & G 202 at 216.
2   *Re Atkinson, Wilson v Atkinson* [1892] 3 Ch 52; *Re Tiverton Market Act, ex p Tanner* (1855) 20
    Beav 374; *Doe d Littlewood v Green* (1838) 4 M & W 229.

[86.4]

Effect of vesting at different times. There is no necessity in the case of a gift
by will for the application of the rule in the case of conveyances operating at
common law,[1] that there can be no joint tenancy where the co-tenants come into
existence at different times, or their joint interests vest at different times,[2]
although in both cases the joint tenants must take the same quantity of interest,[3]
but the fact that the vesting of a gift in a will must take place at different times
otherwise than by the donees coming into existence at different times has been
treated as an indication of a tenancy in common.[4]

1   In the case of wills, the fourth unity, ie that the interest of the joint tenants must vest at the same
    time, is not essential: *Oates d Hatterley v Jackson* (1742) 2 Stra 1172; *Kenworthy v Ward*
    (1853) 11 Hare 196; *Morgan v Britten* (1871) LR 13 Eq 28; *Billing v Billing* (1895) 11 TLR
    502; *Surtees v Surtees* (1871) LR 12 Eq 400 at 406. A remainder which is to vest only in such
    of a class as attain 21 years cannot be a joint tenancy: *Woodgate v Unwin* (1831) 4 Sim 129;
    Hand v North (1863) 3 New Rep 239.
2   *M'Gregor v M'Gregor* (1859) 1 De GF & J 63 at 73, and the case cited in n 1.

3   *Woodgate v Unwin* (1831) 4 Sim 129, explained in *M'Gregor v M'Gregor* (1859) 1 De GF & J 63.
4   See the last part of n 1.

[86.5]

Particular words of severance. Any words indicating in the slightest degree an intention to divide the property abrogates the idea of a joint tenancy and creates a tenancy in common.[1] The following words have been held sufficient for the purpose: 'between';[2] 'divided';[3] 'equally';[4] 'equal proportions';[5] 'equal shares';[6] 'equally to be divided';[7] 'share and share alike';[8] and 'among'.[9] A personal obligation imposed on each of the co-owners may be sufficient to indicate a tenancy in common and negative a joint tenancy.[10]

1   *Robertson v Fraser* (1871) 6 Ch App 696; *Billing v Billing* (1895) 11 TLR 502.
2   *Lashbrook v Cock* (1816) 2 Mer 70; *A-G v Fletcher* (1871) LR 13 Eq 128; *Marshall v Marshall* (1912) 31 NZLR 1120; *Cobban's Executors v Cobban* 1915 SC 82. Though the word 'between' may be taken to apply to a division between two persons, it has been applied to more than two: *Re O'Mullane* [1955] VLR 217; *Campbell's Trustee v Welsh* 1952 SC 343, and see Chapter 87.
3   *Swan v Holmes* (1854) 19 Beav 471; *Garland v Brown* (1864) 10 LT 292; *Crosthwaite v Dean* (1879) 40 LT 837.
4   *Harcourt v Harcourt* (1857) 26 LJ Ch 536; *Evans v Walker* (1876) 3 Ch D 211; *Re Woolley, Wormald v Woolley* [1903] 2 Ch 206; *Fraser v Fraser* (1896) 26 SCR 316; *Webb v Hodge* [1925] NZLR 22; *Paxton's Trustees v Cowie* (1886) 13 R 1191.
5   *Hansley v Wills* (1866) 14 LT 162; *Re Whitehead, Whitehead v Hemsley* [1920] 1 Ch 298.
6   *Brown v Oakshot* (1857) 24 Beav 254; *Pearce v Edmeades* (1838) 3 Y & C Ex 246 (not controlled by any context); *Re Davies, Public Trustee v Davies* [1950] 1 All ER 120.
7   *Shaw v Ford* (1877) 7 Ch D 669; *Re Smith* (1889) 58 LJ Ch 661.
8   *Jones v Jones* (1881) 44 LT 642; *Re Yates, Bostock v D'Eyncourt* [1891] 3 Ch 53; *Re Pryor, Woods v Pryor* [1923] SASR 199.
9   *Richardson v Richardson* (1845) 14 Sim 526; *Re Wylde's Estate* (1852) 2 De GM & G 724; *Krull v Bradey* (1885) 4 NZLR 369.
10 *Re North* [1952] Ch 397, [1952] 1 All ER 609 (where property was given to two sons on condition that they agreed to pay in equal shares to the widow during her life the sum of 10s. per week). This paragraph of the text and the next paragraph, were cited with approval by Rae J in *Re Woodward* (1975) 64 DLR (3d) 364 at 369, 370.

[86.6]

Tenants in common for life. In a gift to A, B and C during their respective lives and after the death of the survivor of the whole property is given over, the court implies cross-remainders for life to the survivors of A, B and C[1] and these parties take as tenants in common and not as joint tenants[2] so that if the interest is land, the land was formerly subject to a trust for sale and was not settled land.[3]

1   *Re Hobson* [1912] 1 Ch 626; *Re Tate* [1914] 2 Ch 182; *Re Davies* [1950] 1 All ER 120; *Re Richerson (No 2)* [1893] 3 Ch 146. See also *Re Stanley's Settlement* [1916] 2 Ch 50 (where the words were: 'for and during their natural lives as tenants in common and not as joint tenants').
2   *Re Hobson* [1912] 1 Ch 626.
3   *Re Davies* [1950] 1 All ER 120.

[86.7]

'Survivors' as a word of limitation. In a gift to a number of persons, and the 'survivors' of them, or 'with the benefit of survivorship', these words may be used as words of limitation creating a joint tenancy, even where the named persons take originally as tenants in common.[1]

1   *Doe d Borwell v Abey* (1813) 1 M & S 428; *Wisden v Wisden* (1854) 2 Sm & G 396; *Haddelsey v Adams* (1856) 22 Beav 266, approved in *Taaffe v Conmee* (1862) 10 HL Cas 64 at 83; *Wiley v Chanteperdrix* [1894] 1 IR 209 at 220, and see *Gooch v Gooch* (1853) 3 De GM & G 366, explained in *Re Ashforth, Sibley v Ashforth* [1905] 1 Ch 535.

[86.8]

Shares prima facie equal. If there is to be a sharing, the shares must prima facie be equal.[1]

1   *Robertson v Fraser* (1871) 6 Ch App 696 at 700; *Fisher v Anderson* (1879) 4 SCR 406 at 419. As to concurrent interests of members of a class, see Chapter 68, para **[68.13]** supra.

CHAPTER 87

Distribution per capita and per stirpes

[87.1]
Usually per capita. In a gift to a number of donees (for example, to the children of several persons), whether taking as a class or combination of classes or not, the distribution between them may be intended to be made per capita, in which case each donee takes a share equal in amount to the share of each other donee, or per stirpes, in which case each family or stock takes an equal share with every other family or stock, and such share is then subdivided equally between the members of such family or stock. Prima facie the distribution is made per capita and not per stirpes.[1] A number of words and expressions indicating the taking of equal shares have been said to show an intention that the division shall be per capita.[2] The following are examples of these expressions: 'equally';[3] 'share and share alike';[4] 'in equal shares';[5] 'equally divided';[6] 'divide';[7] 'for and equally between';[8] 'evenly distributed';[9] 'divided between'.[10] The prima facie rule is applicable, subject to a contrary intention appearing in the will,[11] to a number of class gifts;[12] gifts to a combination of classes;[13] gifts to a number of named persons taking as individuals together with a class;[14] and a gift to a number of persons taking as individuals and not as a class.[15] The rule is applied although the bequest is to persons who, under the statutory rule of distribution on the testator's intestacy, would take per stirpes,[16] and the fact that the persons taking are living relatives of the testator and the children of deceased relatives of the same relationship does not ordinarily take the case out of the rule.[17] Where the new Wills Act 1837, s 33 (substituted by the Administration of Justice Act 1982)[18] applies, the substituted class take per stirpes.[19] The word 'between' although originally referring to two, has been extended to more than two.[20]

---

1 *Re Alcock, Bonser v Alcock* [1945] Ch 264, [1945] 1 All ER 613 (the prima facie rule of distribution is per capita); *Re Jeffrey, Welch v Jeffrey* [1948] 2 All ER 131; *Re Adams Estate* [1957] OWN 568. See *Re Verdonk* (1979) 106 DLR (3d) 450; *Haidl v Sacher* (1979) 106 DLR (3d) 360. See *King v Perpetual Trustee Co Ltd* (1955) 94 CLR 70, where the authorities are discussed. There may be an express proviso that the distribution is to be per stirpes and not per capita; *Re Cockle's Will Trusts* [1967] Ch 690, [1967] 1 All ER 391.
2 *Mattison v Tanfield* (1840) 3 Beav 131 (the cases seem to show that the word 'equally' or the words 'share and share alike' would have the effect of making the division per capita).
3 *Butler v Stratton* (1791) 3 Bro CC 367; *Mattison v Tanfield* (1840) 3 Beav 131: *Rickabe v Garwood* (1845) 8 Beav 579; *Dugdale v Dugdale* (1849) 11 Beav 402; *Pattison v Pattison* (1855) 19 Beav 638; *Mason v Baker* (1856) 2 K & J 567; *Weldon v Hoyland* (1862) 4 De GF & J 564; *Re Jeffrey, Welch v Jeffrey* [1948] 2 All ER 131, *Houghton v Bell* (1892) 23 SCR 498; *Re Davies* (1913) 10 DLR 164.
4 *Phillips v Garth* (1790) 3 Bro CC 64; *Paine v Wagner* (1841) 12 Sim 184; *Abbay v Howe* (1847) 1 De G & Sm 470; *Boughton v Farrer* (1855) 3 WR 495; *Mitchison v Buckton* (1875) 32

LT 11; *Re Bossi* [1897] 5 BCR 446; *Anderson v Bell* (1883) 8 AR 531; *Re Baulderstone* [1928] SALR 262.

5   *Pearce v Edmeades* (1838) 3 Y & C Ex 246; *Cunningham v Murray* (1847) 1 De G & Sm 366; *Baker v Baker* (1847) 6 Hare 269; *Rook v A-G* (1862) 31 Beav 313; *Payne v Webb* (1874) LR 19 Eq 26; *Re Taylor, Taylor v Ley* (1885) 52 LT 839; *Kekewich v Barker* (1903) 88 LT 130; *Re Jones, Harris v Jones* [1910] VLR 306; *Re McKinnon* (1966) 55 DLR (2d) 20.

6   *Abrey v Newman* (1853) 16 Beav 431; *Re Fox* (1865) 35 Beav 163; *Swabey v Goldie* (1875) 1 Ch D 380; *Re Stone, Baker v Stone* [1895] 2 Ch 196; *Re Alcock, Bonser v Alcock* [1945] Ch 264, [1945] 1 All ER 613; *Re Foster's Will Trusts, Smith v Foster* (1967) 111 Sol Jo 685.

7   *Amson v Harris* (1854) 19 Beav 210.

8   *Re Richards, Davies v Edwards* [1910] 2 Ch 74.

9   *Re Foster* [1946] Ch 135, [1946] 1 All ER 333.

10   *Re Cossentine, Philp v Wesleyan Preachers' Association* [1933] Ch 119: *Cunningham's Trustees v Blackwell* 1909 SC 219; *Campbell's Trustee v Welsh* 1952 SC 343; *Equity, Trustees, Executors and Agency Co v Green* (1895) 21 VLR 618; but see *Re Heather* (1958) 13 DLR (2d) 587 (between my husband and my two sisters: husband took half).

11   The prima facie rule is very easily displaced: *Re Hall, Parker v Knight* [1948] Ch 437, and is displaced where the donees are of different generations and there is a reason arising from friendship or obligation for a stirpital distribution: *Re Birkett, Holland v Duncan* [1950] Ch 330, [1950] 1 All ER 316; *Canada Permanent Trust Co v Share* (1958) 25 WWR 638.

12   The following are examples of the class gifts held to be within the rule: to the children of A and B: *Weld v Bradbury* (1715) 2 Vern 705; descendants of A and B: *Lady Lincoln v Pelham* (1804) 10 Ves 166; nephews and nieces and issue of deceased nephews and nieces: *Tomlin v Hatfield* (1841) 12 Sim 167; parents and children 'to be classed together': *Pattison v Pattison* (1885) 19 Beav 638; children of brother and of sister equally: *Mason v Baker* (1856) 2 K & J 567; children of A and B for their education in equal shares: *Armitage v Williams* (1859) 27 Beav 346; testator's and his wife's next of kin in equal shares: *Rook v A-G* (1862) 31 Beav 313; issue of a deceased person equally to be divided between them: *Weldon v Hoyland* (1862) 4 De GF & J 564; to be equally divided between the children of the aforesaid share and share alike: *Re Stone, Baker v Stone* [1895] 2 Ch 196.

13   The following are examples of such combinations of classes: children and grandchildren: *Northey v Strange* (1716) 1 P Wms 340; the families of A and B: *Barnes v Patch* (1803) 8 Ves 604; testator's next of kin both maternal and paternal: *Dugdale v Dugdale* (1849) 11 Beav 402; children and issue: *Cancellor v Cancellor* (1862) 2 Drew & Sm 194; surviving brothers and sisters and their children: *Re Fox's Will* (1865) 35 Beav 163; see also *Re Hughes* [1968] VR 28.

14   In a case where such persons took as a single class, see *Kekewich v Barker* (1903) 88 LT 130. For cases where they were not made a single class, see *Paine v Wagner* (1841) 12 Sim 184; *Rickabe v Garwood* (1845) 8 Beav 579; *Cunningham v Murray* (1847) 1 De G & Sm 366; *Baker v Baker* (1847) 6 Hare 269; *Amson v Harris* (1854) 19 Beav 210; *Tyndale v Wilkinson* (1856) 23 Beav 74; *Re Harper, Plowman v Harper* [1914] 1 Ch 70; *Re Gill* [1959] Qd R 373.

15   *Cooke v Bowen* (1840) 4 Y & C Ex 244 (five nephews and nieces two shares each and their children one share each: children including all living at testator's death and those born in the lifetime of tenant for life and all took per capita, each nephew and niece (all of whom survived testator) taking a double share).

16   *Lady Lincoln v Pelham* (1804) 10 Ves 166 at 176.

17   *Blackler v Webb* (1726) 2 P Wms 383; *Amson v Harris* (1854) 19 Beav 210; *Payne v Webb* (1874) LR 19 Eq 26; *Evans v Turner* (1904) 23 NZLR 825.

18   Administration of Justice Act 1982, s 19; see Vol 2, Part G, para [**244.95**]; see Chapter 47.

19   New Wills Act 1837, s 33(3), which applies to deaths on or after 1 January 1983: Administration of Justice Act 1982, s 73(6); s 76(11).

20   *Re Cossentine, Philp v Wesleyan Preachers' Association* [1933] Ch 119; following *Re Harper, Plowman v Harper* [1914] 1 Ch 70, and distinguishing *Re Walbran, Milner v Walbran* [1906] 1 Ch 64; and see *Re Hall, Parker v Knight* [1948] Ch 437; *Cobban's Trustees v Cobban* 1915 SC 82; *Re McNeil Estate* (1959) 43 MPR 357.

[87.2]

Inference from contexts in favour of distribution per stirpes. The context of the whole will may require stirpital distribution,[1] as, for instance, where the number of shares is mentioned and is equal to the number of parents[2] or the words imply a further subdivision of a share[3] or there is a reference to the

Statutes of Distribution.[4] An intention that the distribution shall be stirpital is shown where the gift is to a number of parents and their children in such a manner that the children are substituted for[5] or take on the death of their respective parents.[6] No presumption in favour of distribution per stirpes arises in the case of an original alternative gift to issue,[7] but the description of issue by reference to 'respective' parents,[8] or a direction that the issue are to take their parent's share[9] are indications of distribution per stirpes. The word 'respective' in such cases points to a stirpital distribution.[10] Gifts to several parents and at, or after, their deaths to their children, or to their issue, have received this construction as meaning at or after their respective deaths.[11] Where, however, the children of all the parents are mentioned together as forming a single group or class to take under a single gift without any other indication of distribution per stirpes, the children take per capita.[12] If the gift is postponed to the death of all the parents, then, where the intermediate income after the death of any parent is given to or is to be applied for the benefit of his children per stirpes, this fact is an element to be considered in favour of distribution of the capital per stirpes,[13] but does not rebut a clear direction that the distribution is to be per capita.[14] If a stirpital distribution is indicated in one part of the will, the court leans to a stirpital construction throughout.[15] Cases of stirpital distribution are cases of family distribution and cases of capital distribution are not cases of family distribution.[16]

1 *Brett v Horton* (1841) 4 Beav 239 (equal disposition of income pending vesting of gift); *Nettleton v Stephenson* (1849) 18 LJ Ch 191 (gift over to others of the class per stirpes); *Archer v Legg* (1862) 31 Beav 187 (gift over to children after gift to parents as tenants in common); *Baird's Trustee v Crombie* 1926 SC 518 (children to take parent's share); *Re Hickey, Beddoes v Hodgson* [1917] 1 Ch 601 ('to descendants to A or their descendants living at my death').

2 *Overton v Banister* (1841) 4 Beav 205.

3 *Davis v Bennett* (1862) 4 De GF & J 327.

4 *Mattison v Tanfield* (1840) 3 Beav 131; *Lewis v Morris* (1854) 19 Beav 34.

5 *Alker v Barton* (1842) 12 LJ Ch 16; *Congreve v Palmer* (1853) 16 Beav 435; *Palmer v Crutwell* (1862) 8 Jur NS 479; *Timins v Stackhouse* (1858) 27 Beav 434; *Gowling v Thompson* (1868) LR 11 Eq 366 n; *Re Daniel, Jones v Michael* [1945] 2 All ER 101; *Re Jeeves, Morris- Williams v Haylett* [1949] Ch 49, [1948] 2 All ER 961; *Re Young, Trustees, Executors and Agency Co Ltd v Wilson* [1925] VLR 672; *Sumpton v Downing* [1947] ALR 513 (life interests to A and B and subject thereto capital to the children of A and of B with substitutional gift in the case of a child dying before the mother). See also *Re Moore's Will* [1963] VR 168; *Re Carter* (1909) 20 OLR 127, but see *Atkinson v Bartrum* (1860) 28 Beav 219 (where there were no surviving parents and the children took per capita).

6 In such cases the word 'respective' points to a stirpital division: *Archer v Legg* (1862) 31 Beav 187 at 191; *Re Campbell's Trusts* (1886) 31 Ch D 685; affd (1886) 33 Ch D 98, CA; *Hunt v Dorsett* (1855) 5 De GM & G 570; *McDonnell v Neil* [1951] AC 342 ('issue if any taking per stirpes'). See also *Ayscough v Savage* (1865) 13 WR 373 (gift to be divided at the respective deaths of the parents).

7 *Abbay v Howe* (1847) 1 De G & Sm 470; but not where the issue are specifically named: thus in a gift to two named brothers and E and G equally, where E and G were the children of a deceased brother, the division was per capita: *Re Jeffrey* [1948] 2 All ER 131. As to substituted gifts, see Chapter 68.

8 *Re Coulden, Coulden v Coulden* [1908] 1 Ch 320.

9 *Shand v Kidd* (1854) 19 Beav 310.

10 See cases in nn 6 and 8, but the rule was departed from in *Re McNeil Estate* (1959) 43 MPR 357, where the word 'among' instead of 'between' was held to show a division per capita.

11 *Re Hutchinson's Trusts* (1882) 21 Ch D 811; *Re Errington, Gibbs v Lassam* [1927] 1 Ch 421 (where the rule is stated and where it was held to apply to substituted gifts); *Wills v Wills* (1875) LR 20 Eq 342; *Baranaby v Tassell* (1871) LR 11 Eq 363; but see *Van Grutten v Foxwell* [1897]

AC 658 at 686, and *Re Browne's Will Trusts, Landon v Brown* [1915] 1 Ch 690; *Re Foster* [1946] Ch 135, [1946] 1 All ER 333.

12   *Pearce v Edmeades* (1838) 3 Y & C Ex 246 (income to E and G for their respective lives and after the death of E and G upon trust for all the children of E and G: held to give income to E and G, then on death of E all income to G and upon G's death to all the children of E and G in equal shares per capita; *Stevenson v Gullan* (1854) 18 Beav 590 (gift to surviving children of two named life beneficiaries); *Swabey v Goldie* (1875) 1 Ch D 380 (clear words requiring distribution per capita on death of survivor of life tenants not defeated by the inconvenience of keeping part of the income in suspense awaiting the death of such survivor though in some cases where the language was very concise and obscure, the court has held the share of each of the tenants for life divisible on his death among his own children exclusively).

13   *Brett v Horton* (1841) 4 Beav 239 at 242; *Re Campbell's Trusts* (1886) 31 Ch D 685; *Bradshaw v Melling* (1853) 19 Beav 417 (where the issue of a life tenant were to receive the income the life tenant had received until time of final distribution: issue took per stirpes and the members of each stirpes took equally). It has been said that such a fact is of itself insufficient to warrant stirpital distribution: *Re Stone, Baker v Stone* [1895] 2 Ch 196 at 200, and certainly a mere discretionary trust is insufficient: *Nockolds v Locke* (1856) 3 K & J 6 (after death of each life tenant income to be distributed at absolute discretion of trustees to children and all capital and undistributed income to be divided on death of last life tenant: issue took per capita.)

14   *Re Stone, Baker v Stone* [1895] 2 Ch 196; *Re Parish* (1964) 42 DLR (2d) 212 (the fact that beneficiaries are of different generations may warrant a stirpital distribution).

15   *Re Smythe, Guinness v Smythe* [1932] IR 136.

16   *Re Hall, Parker v Knight* [1948] Ch 437 (division between sister and niece and her children: sister took half and niece and her children the other half). As to gifts to A and the children of B, see Chapter 74, para **[74.2]** supra.

[87.3]

Substitution of issue. In the case of a gift where issue are substituted for or take after their respective ancestors, the members of each set of issue prima facie take per capita as between themselves the share which is distributed per stirpes to them,[1] but the context may show that the substitution is distributive throughout and a distribution per stirpes is intended.[2] A characteristic of distribution per stirpes is that remote descendants do not take in competition with a living immediate ancestor of their own who takes under the gift.[3]

1   *Armstrong v Stockham* (1843) 7 Jur 230; *Birdsall v York* (1859) 5 Jur NS 1237; *Gowling v Thompson* (1868) LR 11 Eq 366 n; *Barnaby v Tassell* (1871) LR 11 Eq 363; *Re Sibley's Trusts* (1877) 5 Ch D 494. As to shares of substituted donees, see Chapter 68.

2   *Re Earle's Settlement, Reiss v Norrie* [1971] 2 All ER 1188, [1971] 1 WLR 1118; *Ross v Ross* (1855) 20 Beav 645; *Re Orton's Trust* (1866) LR 3 Eq 375; *Gibson v Fisher* (1867) LR 5 Eq 51.

3   *Pearson v Stephen* (1831) 2 Dow & Cl 328; *Dick v Lacy* (1845) 8 Beav 214; *Amson v Harris* (1854) 19 Beav 210; *Re Bennett's Trust* (1857) 3 K & J 280; *Palmer v Crutwell* (1862) 8 Jur NS 479; *Gibson v Fisher* (1867) LR 5 Eq 51; *Re Rawlinson, Hill v Withall* [1909] 2 Ch 36.

[87.4]

Determination of stocks. The determination of the persons forming the stocks from which the stirpes are to spring is a matter of construction of each will. It appears that, in the ordinary case, the stock should be persons who might themselves take under the gift, as, for example, the original takers for whom the stirpes are substituted,[1] and not the ancestors of such takers.[2]

1   *Re Wilson, Parker v Winder* (1883) 24 Ch D 664; *Re Dering, Neall v Beale* (1911) 105 LT 404; *Re Alexander, Alexander v Alexander* [1919] 1 Ch 371; *Re Karkalatos Estate* [1962] SCR 390. See also *Robinson v Shepherd* (1863) 4 De GJ & Sm 129.

2   *Gibson v Fisher* (1867) LR 5 Eq 51 (where the context required such a determination of the stocks). But the matter is one for determination on the consideration of the whole will for there is no reason why the stocks should be found among the takers and not among the ancestors: *Sidey v Perpetual Trustees Estate and Agency Co of New Zealand Ltd* [1944] AC 194, [1944] 2 All ER 225. See also *Re Sinclair Estate* (1996) 136 DLR (4th) 427.

CHAPTER 88

Cumulative and substituted gifts

[88.1]
Gifts clearly cumulative. A testator may well intend to give to the same donee two or more gifts, of equal or unequal amounts, and where the intention to do so is clear, effect is given to it.[1] The intention is collected from the whole will.[2] The court has refused to cut down the additional gift where an intention was expressed to make up the earlier gift to a certain amount, in fact less than the earlier gift.[3] Where one of the gifts is non-testamentary, there may be a presumption against double portions.[4]

1   *Burkinshaw v Hodge* (1874) 22 WR 484; *Re Dyke, Dyke v Dyke* (1881) 44 LT 568.
2   *Guy v Sharp* (1833) 1 My & K 589.
3   *Re Segelcke, Ziegler v Nicol* [1906] 2 Ch 301.
4   See Chapter 44.

[88.2]
Presumption where gifts in the same instrument. Where two legacies are given by the same testamentary instrument to the same person described in the same terms in each case,[1] and are of the same specific thing or of the same specified amount, the second is presumed to be merely a repetition of the first,[2] and the legatee is entitled to only one such legacy; but, if such legacies are of different specified amounts,[3] or have substantially different incidents,[4] or if one is a residuary gift and the other a specific or pecuniary legacy,[5] the second legacy is presumed to be additional or, as it is said, cumulative, and, apart from some special context, the legatee takes both.[6]

1   In considering whether testamentary instruments are the same a decision of the probate court that they are the same was binding on a court of construction: *Baillie v Butterfield* (1787) 1 Cox Eq Cas 392; *Brine v Ferrier* (1835) 7 Sim 549. It is sufficient that the probate treats the instruments as the same. For a case where two codicils of the same date were held to be one and same instruments, see *Re Mitchell, Thomas v Hoskins* [1929] 1 Ch 552.
2   *Garth v Meyrick* (1779) 1 Bro CC 30; *Holford v Wood* (1798) 4 Ves 76 at 86; *Heming v Clutterbuck* (1827) 1 Bli NS 479 (where the judgment is based on an alleged finding of the Ecclesiastical Court that the two instruments were one will: see *Brine v Ferrier* (1835) 7 Sim 549).
3   *Hooley v Hatton* (1773) 1 Bro CC 390n; *Curry v Pile* (1787) 2 Bro CC 225; *Brennan v Moran* (1866) 16 I Ch R 126; *Re Liddle, Shrewsbury v McGuffie* (1915) 34 NZLR 962.
4   *Mackinnon v Peach* (1838) 2 Keen 555; *Inglefield v Coghlan* (1845) 2 Coll 247; *Thompson v Teulon* (1852) 22 LJ Ch 243; *Wildes v Davies* (1853) 1 Sm & G 475. In *Manning v Thesiger* (1835) 3 My & K 29, the amounts were the same but the times of payment very slightly different and this was held insufficient to render the legacies cumulative and the legatee was entitled to one legacy only.
5   *Kirkpatrick v Bedford* (1878) 4 App Cas 96; *Gordon v Anderson* (1858) 4 Jur NS 1097; *Ball v Church of the Ascension (Rector and Churchwardens)* (1883) 5 OR 386.

6   For a case where the context was sufficient for a contrary conclusion, see *Yockney v Hansard* (1844) 3 Hare 620, where an annuity of £800 was given to the testator's wife and an annuity of £200 to his daughter and then it was provided that on the death of the wife the daughter was to have £400 a year and it was held that, after the death of the wife, the daughter was entitled to £400 a year only.

[88.3]

Gifts in different testamentary instruments. If the same specific thing is given by two different testamentary instruments[1] to the same person, the second gift is presumed to be a mere repetition of the first.[2] In general, however, if by different testamentary instruments two legacies, whether of the same or different amounts, are given to the same person, they are presumed to be additional to each other.[3] Such presumption is strengthened by any substantial difference between the gifts.[4]

1   See para **[88.2]**, n 1.
2   *Duke of St Albans v Beauclerk* (1743) 2 Atk 636 at 640; *Hooley v Hatton* (1773) 1 Bro CC 390n; *Re Bagnall, Scale v Willett* [1949] LJR 1; *Coote v Boyd* (1789) 2 Bro CC 521; *Re Michell, Thomas v Hoskins* [1929] 1 Ch 552.
3   *Foy v Foy* (1785) 1 Cox Eq Cas 163; *Bartholomew and Brown v Henley* (1820) 3 Phillim 317; *Lee v Pain* (1844) 4 Hare 201 (unless the plain effect of the separate gifts is contradicted by the construction of the later instruments or by presumption of law. Repetition in the later instrument of some legacies and not of others strengthens the case that the legacies were cumulative); *Townshend v Mostyn* (1858) 26 Beav 72; *Johnstone v Earl of Harrowby* (1859) 1 De GF & J 183; *Cresswell v Cresswell* (1868) LR 6 Eq 69 at 76; *Re Davies, Davies v Mackintosh* [1957] 3 All ER 52, [1957] 1 WLR 922 (legacy of £350 by will. Codicil giving £1,000 'thus increasing the sum of £350 as mentioned in my said will, in appreciation', etc. Held: no context to displace rule that such legacies were cumulative and legatee was entitled to £1,350); *Henderson v Fraser* [1923] SCR 23; *Re Armstrong, Ayne v Woodward* (1893) 31 LR Ir 154; *Bryce's Trustee* (1878) 5 R 722.
4   *Suisse v Lord Lowther* (1843) 2 Hare 424 (differences in character and amount or a further motive or reason assigned in the instrument: in this case the particular difference was in amount); *Lee v Pain* (1844) 4 Hare 201 at 223 (circumstances that legacies carry interest from different dates).

[88.4]

Inferences from the context. The context in these cases may lead to contrary conclusions. The fact that other legacies in the same will are given in terms expressly making them cumulative is some indication that legacies not so described are substitutional,[1] but is of slight importance in rebutting a presumption applicable to the case[2] and the fact that legacies are given in terms making them substitutional, does not make other legacies not so described substitutional, where the presumption that they are cumulative is otherwise applicable.[3]

The later gift is prima facie merely a repetition of the first where the later gift is of the same specified amount as the earlier,[4] and is expressed to be given for the same cause or motive.[5] No presumption of repetition is raised if in either instrument there is no motive or no motive other than the testator's bounty[6] or a different motive expressed, although the sums are the same, or where the same motive is expressed in both and the legacies are of different amounts.[7] Generally, whatever the amounts of the legacies, the later instrument may explain,[8] repeat,[9] or be in substitution for[10] the earlier instrument in respect of the gift, or otherwise be the final declaration of the testator's intentions,[11] and then the later gift supersedes the other. These rules are applicable only to cases where there is no internal evidence of intention in the instruments themselves.[12] Where two wills are admitted to probate, it is not open to the court of construction to say that the second revoked the first in toto, but the two wills must be construed side by side and effect given to the intention of the testator shown by the two wills as a whole.[13]

1   *Allen v Callow* (1796) 3 Ves 289; *Barclays v Wainwright* (1797) 3 Ves 462; *Russell v Dickson* (1842) 2 Dr & War 133.
2   *Mackenzie v Mackenzie* (1826) 2 Russ 262 at 273; *Suisse v Lord Lowther* (1843) 2 Hare 424. In *Wray v Field* (1822) 6 Madd 300, the following reasons are assigned for the legacies not being cumulative: substitution evidently intended from the character of the second instrument; the expressions used; the same sum given twice; the same motive for the gift expressed in both instruments, but these reasons are not exhaustive.
3   *Re Armstrong, Ayne v Woodward* (1893) 31 LR Ir 154.
4   *Duke of St Albans v Beauclerk* (1743) 2 Atk 636; *Wray v Field* (1822) 6 Madd 300; *Marquis of Hertford v Lord Lowther* (1845) 4 LTOS 450.
5   *Benyon v Benyon* (1810) 17 Ves 34; *Hurst v Beach* (1821) 5 Madd 351 (the court is here said to require the double coincidence, the same sum and the same motive); *Wray v Field* (1822) 6 Madd 300.
6   *Suisse v Lord Lowther* (1843) 2 Hare 424 at 432.
7   *Hurst v Beach* (1821) 5 Madd 351.
8   *Moggridge v Thackwell* (1792) 1 Ves 464 at 473.
9   *Moggridge v Thackwell* (1792) 1 Ves 464 (simple repetition, where it is exact and punctual, has been regarded as sufficient proof that legacies are not cumulative); *Tatham v Drummond* (1864) 4 De GJ & Sm 484 (same legacies in first and second codicils not cumulative); *Hubbard v Alexander* (1876) 3 Ch D 738 (where two similar codicils were shown to be but one instrument); *Re Resch's Will Trusts, Le Cras v Perpetual Trustee Co Ltd, Far West Children's Health Scheme v Perpetual Trustee Co Ltd* [1969] 1 AC 514, [1967] 3 All ER 915, PC (legacies not cumulative in view of a consistent scheme of benefit indicated by the testamentary instruments). Many legacies may be given to the same persons in the same or nearly the same words as in the prior instrument: *Coote v Boyd* (1789) 2 Bro CC 521 (legacies not doubled); *Barclay v Wainwright* (1797) 3 Ves 462 (legatees all the same except those dead or who had quitted the testator's service); *Whyte v Whyte* (1873) LR 17 Eq 50 (instruments of the same date and contents). In *Wilson v O'Leary* (1872) 7 Ch App 448, there was not sufficient in the context and circumstances to rebut the presumption that the legacies were cumulative. The original reason for the rule is that prima facie there is no reason why the second instrument should be made unless the intention was to add to the first: *Moggridge v Thackwell* (1792) 3 Bro CC 517.
10 *Kidd v North* (1846) 2 Ph 91; *Duncan v Duncan (No 2)* (1859) 27 Beav 392; *Tuckey v Henderson* (1863) 33 Beav 174; *Bell v Park* [1914] 1 IR 158; *Grealey v Sampson* [1917] 1 IR 286; *Re Michell, Thomas v Hoskins* [1929] 1 Ch 552 and *Re Bagnall* [1949] LJR 1.
11 *Russell v Dickson* (1853) 4 HL Cas 293 (recital that codicil made because there was no time to alter the will); *Sawrey v Rumney* (1852) 5 De G & Sm 698 (alteration by further codicil of a legacy in a will already altered by a previous codicil); *Re Picton, Porter v Jones* [1944] Ch 303 (codicil giving legacies in lieu of revoked legacies).
12 *Kidd v North* (1846) 2 Ph 91 at 97.
13 *Re Plant* [1952] Ch 298, [1952] 1 All ER 78n.

CHAPTER 89

Successive interests

[89.1]
Donees named together. The context of a will may show that persons named together as donees were intended to take successively,[1] either in the order of their names,[2] or according to seniority of age,[3] whichever is appropriate to the context and the circumstances of the case. Without such a context a gift to persons named together as donees is prima facie not construed to give them interest in succession.[4] If the testator gives one of a number of like things to each of several donees, it appears that prima facie the legatees exercise their right of selection according to the priority of the gifts,[5] and, if there is no indication of priority, then they must draw lots.[6]

1 See *Re Green, Fitzwilliam v Green* (1916) 50 ILT 179 (bequest to widow during her life to be held in the interest of grandson held a gift to widow for life and then for grandson).
2 *Stratford v Powell* (1807) 1 Ball & B 1. Cf the principle that donees with a right of selection select in the order in which they are named: *Duckmanton v Duckmanton* (1860) 5 H & N 219 at 222; *Asten v Asten* [1894] 3 Ch 260.
3 *Ongley v Peale* (1712) 2 Ld Raym 1312 (in a devise to A and his brothers successively for their lives without mention of order of succession they take in order of seniority if A is the eldest); *Lewis d Ormond v Waters* (1805) 6 East 336 (gift for first and other sons); *Young v Sheppard* (1847) 10 Beav 207 (gift to eldest for life to devolve in succession on remaining children); *Honywood v Honywood* (1905) 92 LT 814 (first and other sons); *Re Harcourt, Fitzwilliam v Portman* [1920] 1 Ch 492 (devise on death of eldest son without issue to every other son, other than a son entitled to the barony, every such son to take for life with remainder to his sons in tail). In the case of real property, a direction for settlement on children in succession may be an epitome of a strict settlement (*Doe d Phipps v Lord Mulgrave* (1793) 5 Term Rep 320 at 324; *Earl of Tyrone v Marquis of Waterford* (1860) 1 De GF & J 613 at 623; *Re Brown and Slater* (1903) 5 OLR 386). The rule applies to deeds as well as wills: *Re Gosset's Settlement, Gribble v Lloyds Bank Ltd* [1943] Ch 351, [1943] 2 All ER 515.
4 *De Windt v De Windt* (1866) LR 1 HL 87 (gift to sons of A); *Surtees v Surtees* (1871) LR 12 Eq 400 (gift to every son); *Re Roberts, Repington v Roberts-Gawan* (1881) 19 Ch D 520 (in a gift to a class for life, there is no right to import the word 'successively' or 'for the time being' or any words of that kind); but see *Allgood v Blake* (1873) LR 8 Exch 160 at 169 ('all and every' do not import that 'all and every' are to take at the same time but are well satisfied by all taking in succession).
5 See n 2.
6 See *Re Knapton, Knapton v Hindle* [1941] Ch 428, [1941] 2 All ER 573.

[89.2]
Cy-près doctrine. In some cases a gift of a succession of interests in real property to donees, some of whom were not allowed by law to take as purchasers, has been construed under the *cy-près* doctrine to be a gift of an entailed interest to one of them, where that interest if allowed to descend unbarred would carry the property to the donees and no others, and words

referring to successive generations have been held to be descriptive of the descent of an estate tail and used as words of limitation.[1] This principle can now have no application since an entailed interest cannot now be created after 1 January 1997.[2]

1   See Chapter 84.
2   Trusts of Land and Appointment of Trustees Act 1996; see Chapter 84. As to the previous position see the Law of Property Act 1925, s 130(1); 37 *Halsbury's Statutes* (4th edn) 288.

CHAPTER 90

Accruer clauses

[90.1]
Prima facie extends only to original share. A clause of accruer, which divests and disposes of the share of a donee dying before a particular time, or in particular circumstances, prima facie refers only to the original share of that donee, and does not extend to shares which have accrued under such clause.[1] A similar construction applies in other cases where the description of the property subject to the clause of accruer is not necessarily comprehensive both of the donee's original share and of his other shares, or of his whole interest under the gifts in question, including the clauses of accruer,[2] but this construction does not apply where the clause clearly refers to the donee's whole interest in the fund,[3] or to a plurality of shares of a single donee.[4] The word 'share' alone, or a similar word, may also be explained by the context to mean the donee's whole interest.[5] For example, by any expression directing the accrued shares to devolve in a similar way to the original shares,[6] or by a context treating the accrued and original shares as blended, or as developing together,[7] or treating the whole property as subject to a gift over in an aggregate mass.[8]

---

1   *Re Scaife, ex p West* (1784) 1 Bro CC 575; *Crowder v Stone* (1829) 3 Russ 217 at 233; *Rickett v Guillemard* (1841) 12 Sim 88; *Re Lybbe's Will Trusts, Kildahl v Bowker* [1954] 1 All ER 487, [1954] 1 WLR 573 (there must be a context to extend the word 'share' to mean other than the original share).

2   *Woodward v Glasbrook* (1700) 2 Vern 388 (his part or share: what goes over on one's child's death shall not go over again a second time); *Perkins v Micklethwaite* (1714) 1 P Wms 274 (portion); *Bright v Rowe* (1834) 3 My & K 316 (his, her, or their portion or portions); *Rickett v Guillemard* (1841) 12 Sim 88 (his, her, or their shares); *Jones v Hall* (1849) 16 Sim 500 (his share and portion); *Maddison v Chapman* (1858) 4 K & J 709 at 716 (the part of the deceased; nothing said about any share that might come to her by accretion); *Goodwin v Finlayson* (1858) 25 Beav 65 (the word 'share' of itself is not sufficient to carry over accrued shares); *Evans v Evans* (1858) 25 Beav 81 ('share' not sufficient to carry over accrued share). A description of the property subject to the clause of accruer in terms such as 'his, her, or their share or shares', may be read *reddendo singula singulis*, shares being related to 'their' and not to 'his' or 'her' and therefore as not denoting a plurality of the shares of a single donee: *Bright v Rowe* (1834) 3 My & K 316; *Rickett v Guillemard* (1841) 12 Sim 88; *Wilmot v Flewitt* (1865) 13 LT 90; *Sutton v Sutton* (1892) 30 LR Ir 251; *Ganapathy Pillay v Alamaloo* [1929] AC 462; *Campbell's Trustee v Dick* 1915 SC 100.

3   *Goodman v Goodman* (1847) 1 De G & Sm 695 (the interest and capital of a child dying); *Douglas v Andrews* (1851) 14 Beav 347 (the part and parts, share and shares and interest of him her or them); *Re Crawhall's Trust* (1856) 8 De GM & G 480 (with benefit of survivorship); *Re Henrique's Trusts* [1875] WN 187 (part share and interest); *Re Sadler, Furniss v Cooper* (1915) 60 Sol Jo 89 (with benefit of survivorship in the same family); *Re Morris, Corfield v Waller* (1916) 86 LJ Ch 456 (substitutional gift of share of child predeceasing testator held not to carry accrued share under same provision).

4   *Re Chaston, Chaston v Seago* (1881) 18 Ch D 218 (such parts to be divided between the others or other of them); *Clifton v Crawford* (1900) 27 AR 315 (words used contemplating a plurality of shares in one person).
5   *Doe d Clift v Birkhead* (1849) 4 Exch 110.
6   *Giles v Melsom* (1873) LR 6 HL 24 (a proviso placed at the end of all the devises must be applicable to all and not be read as applicable as if placed at the end of one); *Eyre v Marsden* (1839) 4 My & Cr 231 (property treated as aggregated); *Leeming v Sherratt* (1842) 2 Hare 14 (share to be divided among survivors).
7   *Milsom v Awdry* (1800) 5 Ves 465 (shares to go equally to and among the survivors or survivor); *Douglas v Andrews* (1851) 14 Beav 347 (intention shown to keep the fund 'aggregate' and unsevered).
8   *Barker v Lea* (1823) Turn & R 413; *Eyre v Marsden* (1838) 2 Keen 564 at 575; *Sillick v Booth* (1842) 1 Y & C Ch Cas 117 at 121; *Doe d Clift v Birkhead* (1849) 4 Exch 110; *Dutton v Crowdy* (1863) 33 Beav 272; *Re Henrique's Trusts* [1875] WN 187; *Re Allan, Dow v Cassaigne* [1903] 1 Ch 276; *Bartholomew's Trustees v Bartholomew* (1904) 6 F 322; *Re Slater* (1964) 46 DLR (2d) 359.

[90.2]
Conditions applicable to accrued share. The conditions applicable to the original share are not generally applicable to the accrued share under such a clause.[1] An intention that they shall apply can be expressly shown or be inferred from the context.[2] They may be held applicable in order to prevent the accruing shares from becoming void under the rule against perpetuities.[3] Where the accruing share would under the rules for ascertaining classes vest in a different class from that in which the original share vests it may be that the class in each case is that in which the original share vests.[4]

1   *Gibbons v Langdon* (1833) 6 Sim 260; *Ranelagh v Ranelagh* (1841) 4 Beav 419 (original gift for life, but accrued share absolute); *Jones v Hall* (1849) 16 Sim 500 (tenancy in common of original gift: accrued shares held in joint tenancy); *Leigh v Mosley* (1851) 14 Beav 605 (similar case); *Ware v Watson* (1855) 7 De GM & G 248 (direction for settlement applied only to original share); *Carver v Burgess* (1853) 18 Beav 541 (original gift to all sisters except one, accruer to 'surviving sisters' includes the one excepted in the original gift).
2   *Milson v Awdry* (1800) 5 Ves 465 (in manner aforesaid); *Cursham v Newland* (1839) 2 Beav 145 (in the same manner as original shares); *Re Jarman's Trusts* (1865) LR 1 Eq 71 (separate use attached to original and accrued shares); *Giles v Melsom* (1873) LR 6 HL 24 (life estate 'in hereditaments so specifically devised' following accruer clause); *Sutton v Sutton* (1892) 30 LR Ir 251 at 260; *Hayes v Hayes* [1917] 1 IR 194. The reference to separate use is now obsolete.
3   *Trickey v Trickey* (1832) 3 My & K 560 (where a condition expressly applied to original shares was also applied to the accrued shares to avoid invalidity under the perpetuity rule).
4   *Re Ridge's Trusts* (1872) 7 Ch App 665.

[90.3]
To whom accruings hare may pass. Upon the construction of an accruer clause, a share may pass to the representatives of an original donee, provided that the condition (such as dying leaving a child or children surviving him) was fulfilled,[1] and this may be so although the donee has been paid his share in his lifetime.[2]

1   *Murphy v Paxton* (1930) Argus LR 389, and see *Re Walter's Will's Trusts, Stuart v Pitman* [1949] Ch 91, [1948] 2 All ER 955.
2   *Re Huntingdon's Settlement Trusts, Struthers v Mayne* [1949] Ch 414, [1949] 1 All ER 674 (this decision turned on the question whether by payment the share had 'failed or determined').

[90.4]
Right of last survivor to accrued shares. Generally on the death of the last survivor, the accrued shares pass as his or her property, but this may be a matter

of construction[1] and the accruer may be to shares and not in individuals so that on the death of the last survivor there is an accruer to shares of deceased beneficiaries.[2]

1   *Re Litt's Will Trust, Parry v Cooper* [1946] Ch 154, [1946] 1 All ER 314.
2   *Re Walter's Will's Trust, Stuart v Pitman* [1949] Ch 91, [1948] 2 All ER 955; distinguished in *Heron v Ulster Bank Ltd* [1974] NI 44.

[90.5]

All original beneficiaries dying without issue. Where shares are given absolutely and trusts are then engrafted on the shares and all beneficiaries die without leaving issue, then under the usual form of an accruer clause the personal representatives of each of the beneficiaries take the share given to such beneficiary upon the footing that the engrafted trusts have failed and the original absolute gift alone takes effect.[1] This however does not prevent the accruer of the income during the lives or life of the survivors or survivor.[2]

1   *Re Atkinson's Will Trusts, Prescott v Child* [1957] Ch 117, [1956] 3 All ER 738. The accruer clause can be so worded as to provide for this particular event.
2   Ibid.

[90.6]

Accruing share accrues to other shares equally. Although the original shares may not be equal shares, an accruing share will accrue to them equally and not in the proportions which the original shares bear to one another unless the will or settlement otherwise provides.[1]

1   *Re Bower's Settlement Trusts, Bower v Ridley-Thompson* [1942] Ch 197, [1942] 1 All ER 278; considered by Megarry VC in *Re Steel, Public Trustee v Christian Aid Society* [1979] Ch 218, [1978] 2 All ER 1026, who thought that he might have reached the opposite conclusion, on the facts, in favour of proportionate shares.

CHAPTER 91

Conditional gifts

[91.1]
Condition must be clear. Where the testator has by any means[1] clearly attached conditions or obligations to his gifts, his expressed intention is paramount[2] but where the will is not clear, it is a settled rule of construction that words are not construed as importing a condition, in particular a condition of forfeiture, if they are fairly capable of another construction.[3] Words expressing a condition may be treated as being words of limitation[4] or as creating a trust,[5] or a charge.[6]

1 Equitable obligations, whether trusts or conditions, can be imposed by any words clear enough to show an intention to impose an obligation, provided those words are definite enough to enable a court to ascertain what the precise obligation is and in whose favour it is to be performed: *Re Williams, Williams v Williams* [1897] 2 Ch 12 at 18; applied in *Re Singh* [1995] 2 NZLR 487. As to certainty in conditions, see Chapter 34.
2 The intention is that expressed in the words of the will: *Bastin v Watts* (1840) 3 Beav 97 (gift confined to vested shares although it should obviously have extended to the share of a child which did not vest by reason of his dying under twenty-one). See also *Archbold v Austin-Gourlay* (1880) 5 LR Ir 214.
3 *Edgeworth v Edgeworth* (1869) LR 4 HL 35 at 41; *Wright v Wilkin* (1862) 2 B & S 259; *Re Gregory, How v Charrington* (1935) 52 TLR 130 (gift to charity if not subsidised by local authority).
4 See Chapter 34.
5 See Chapter 34.
6 See para **[91.2]** infra.

[91.2]
Gift subject to payment. A gift upon condition that the donee makes certain payments for the benefit of other persons,[1] or a gift subject to such payments,[2] is generally construed, in a case where in the circumstances existing at the date of the will some surplus could remain out of the property after making the payments, as constituting those payments a charge on the property given,[3] and in a case where no substantial surplus could remain after making the payments at the date of the will, as constituting the donee a trustee of the property.[4] The refusal to perform the condition, or the death of the donee, does not disappoint those entitled under the condition,[5] but, where the effect of the condition is to create a mere charge, they may be disappointed by the operation of the Limitation Acts 1939 and 1980.[6] When the surplus is appropriated to a purpose which may or may not require the whole of it to be applied, the question is one of construction of the particular will.[7] The condition for the payment of the sum may, however, be in the terms not sufficient to create a charge upon the property and then the payment is only a personal obligation on the legatee to make the payments.[8] The question whether the words of the will create a charge or a

personal obligation is one of construction in every case.[9] There seems to be no difference between such payments being a personal obligation and being a trust.

1   *Hodge v Churchward* (1847) 16 Sim 71 (gift of freeholds and copyholds, paying £10 a year to A for life); *Cunninghame v Foot* (1878) 3 App Cas 974 (devise subject to payment of legacies); *Re Oliver, Newbald v Beckett* (1890) 62 LT 533 (devise subject to payment of legacies, donee not liable to account for rents and profits); *Re Hazlette* [1915] 1 IR 285 (legacy charged on land).

2   *Hughes v Kelly* (1843) 5 I Eq R 286 (legacy charged on land); *Jacquet v Jacquet* (1959) 27 Beav 332 (charge of debts not a trust); *Proud v Proud* (1862) 32 Beav 234 (land charged with legacies); *Re Cowley, Souch v Cowley* (1885) 53 LT 494 (leaseholds charged with debts does not make donee liable to pay debts since they are merely a charge); *Re Murray Scott, Scott v Scott (No 2)* (1915) 31 TLR 505 (devise subject to payment of pensions and allowances).

3   As to annuity out of income, see Chapter 33.

4   *Wright v Wilkin* (1860) 2 B & S 232; affd (1862) 2 B & S 259; *A-G v Wax Chandlers' Co (Master, Wardens, etc)* (1873) LR 6 HL 1; *Bird v Harris* (1870) LR 9 Eq 204; *Re Corcoran, Corcoran v O'Kane* [1913] 1 IR 1 at 7; *Re Smith* [1957] VLR 683.

5   *Re Kirk, Kirk v Kirk* (1882) 21 Ch D 431.

6   *Jacquet v Jacquet* (1959) 27 Beav 332; *Proud v Proud* (1862) 32 Beav 234.

7   *A-G v Wax Chandlers' Co (Master, Wardens, etc)* (1873) LR 6 HL 1.

8   *Rees v Engleback* (1871) LR 12 Eq 225 (where the question of there being a charge was apparently not decided); *Re Hodge, Hodge v Griffiths* [1940] Ch 260 (no charge because legacy 'in consideration of' certain payments); *Re Cowley, Souch v Cowley* (1885) 53 LT 494 (a charge in addition to personal liability if the legatee is named as the person to make the payment).

9   *Re Lester, Lester v Lester* [1942] Ch 324, [1942] 1 All ER 646. If the legatee is not named as the person to make the payments, the latter are on a charge on the property rather than a personal obligation (ibid, at 647); applied in *Re Walker* (1971) 13 DLR (3d) 688. See also *Re Porter, Logan v Northern Bank Ltd* [1975] NI 157, where the text was referred to.

[91.3]

Alteration of conditions. As in the case of the other provisions of a will, the conditions of a gift may be altered so as to be in accordance with the rest of the will, where this is clearly required by the context.[1] The court does this with reluctance, and words are not readily inserted which will prevent vesting.[2]

1   *Lunn v Osborne* (1834) 7 Sim 56 (gift over on certain children not leaving issue omitted); *Doe d Leach v Micklem* (1805) 6 East 486 (gift to A for life 'or if she should survive B and C' over read 'and after her death or'); *Perrin v Lyon* (1807) 9 East 170 (gift over 'if my daughter were dead' read 'as if she were dead under age and unmarried').

2   *Walker v Mower* (1852) 16 Beav 365; *Hope v Potter* (1857) 3 K & J 206; *Re Litchfield, Horton v Jones* (1911) 104 LT 631.

[91.4]

Conditions attached to a series of gifts. A condition attached to the first of a series of gifts may attach to that one alone or to the whole series. For example, where there is a condition that the share of a female beneficiary shall be settled, this was held to apply both to a gift of the residue of personal property and to a gift of the produce of realty,[1] but a gift over on death without issue was applied only to gifts for life and not to a gift of plain terms of the fee simple.[2] A gift commencing with the word 'likewise' can be held to be subject to the same contingency as the preceding gifts;[3] and although each of two gifts commences with the words 'as to', a gift over, attached apparently only to the second gift, may be held to apply to both.[4]

1   *Cockerill v Pitchforth* (1845) 1 Coll 626.
2   *Doe d Bailey v Sloggett* (1850) 5 Exch 107; cf *Gower v Towers* (1858) 25 Beav 81 (gifts to same person in successive sentences, only the second with added words 'for life' and those words applied only to the second gift).
3   *Paylor v Pegg* (1857) 24 Beav 105, distinguishing *Boosey v Gardener* (1854) 5 De GM & G 122.
4   *Gordon v Gordon* (1871) LR 5 HL 254. See also *Child v Elsworth* (1852) 2 De GM & G 679.

[91.5]
Gifts by reference. In a gift expressly made 'in the same manner as' another gift, the reference may be to the conditions attached by the testator[1] to the mode of enjoyment only[2] and not to the mode of settlement, if any, of that gift,[3] or other restrictions,[4] or the words may refer to all interests, including gifts over, into which, under the principal gift, the absolute interest was to be divided.[5]

1   The true rule is not to look out for any conditions which may be affixed by law to the estates given by the will, but to conditions attached thereto by documents such as wills and settlements: *Ord v Ord* (1866) LR 2 Eq 393 at 396.
2   Examples are in gifts to married women where the reference was held not to refer to the quantity of the interest given but to the fact that the gift was to be for the donee's separate use (*Shanley v Baker* (1799) 4 Ves 732; *Judd v Wyatt* (1805) 11 Ves 483); in a gift to a number of persons the words of reference may import a tenancy in common from a prior gift (*Lumley v Robbins* (1853) 10 Hare 621; *Re Wilder's Trusts* (1859) 27 Beav 418); a condition as to marriage may be so imported into a further gift by codicil: *Younge v Furse* (1857) 8 De GM & G 756.
3   *Eames v Anstee* (1863) 33 Beav 264 (where 'in equal shares' referred only to the shares in which children of a deceased nephew were to take in the case of a gift to a niece, nephew and children of a deceased nephew); *Re Green's Will, Crowson v Wild* [1907] VLR 284.
4   *Yardley v Yardley* (1858) 26 Beav 38 (restriction that donee living at death of testator not imported); *Pigott v Wilder* (1858) 26 Beav 90 (original gift to six of eight children, gift by reference held to be for all the eight children); *Re Wilder's Trusts* (1859) 27 Beav 418; *Swift v Swift* (1863) 1 New Rep 353 (gift to children living at decease of parent. Condition requiring that the donee should be living at death of parent incorporated into another gift by reference).
5   *Ross v Ross* (1845) 2 Coll 269 (words indicated the manner in which and the persons in favour of whom the absolute interest was to be carved and divided); *Re Liverpool Docks Acts, Re Colshead's Will Trusts* (1852) 2 De G & J 690 (gift 'precisely in the same way' all limitations imported); *Auldjo v Wallace* (1862) 31 Beav 193 ('during her life' in an additional gift did not restrict it to an increase in the legacy during the life of the life tenant only, but increased the legacy for her and her children after her); *Re Shirley's Trusts* (1863) 32 Beav 394 ('and otherwise' incorporated a gift over); *Ord v Ord* (1866) LR 2 Eq 393. There is no flexible rule on the subject: *Pigott v Wilder* (1858) 26 Beav 90.

[91.6]
Cumulative and substitutional legacies. Legacies given expressly[1] or impliedly[2] in addition to or in substitution for a legacy previously given, so as to vary the amount of the legacy[3] are prima facie subject to the like conditions, if any, as are imposed on the original legacy,[4] in respect of the mode of enjoyment of that legacy.[5] The context or the circumstances may however, exclude this rule[6] and it does not apply unless the context so requires,[7] to cases where its application would alter the interests in the property;[8] or where the character of the gifts is entirely different,[9] or, in general, where in the case of a substitutional gift the legatee of the substituted legacy is not the same as the legatee of the original legacy,[10] though it may apply in this case also.[11]

1   The rule applies especially to cases of an express declaration and the presumption is that the testator intended to alter the amount of the legacy only and not to alter the conditions and

limitations affecting the legacy. This is the general rule but it is not adopted where its effect would be to introduce such limitations as would convert a gift its terms absolute into one of a life estate only: *Re Boden, Boden v Boden* [1907] 1 Ch 132.

2 *Johnstone v Earl of Harrowby* (1859) 1 De GF & J 183 (implication that legacy payable out of same fund and upon the same conditions).

3 The rule is not confined to questions of amount but may apply where the substituted legatee is different from the original legatee: *Re Backhouse, Salmon v Backhouse* [1916] 1 Ch 65; *Re Joseph, Pain v Joseph* [1908] 2 Ch 507 at 512. See also *Barry v Crundall* (1835) 7 Sim 430 (change of trustees only); *Fenton v Farington* (1856) 2 Jur NS 1120 (alteration of fund provided for payment).

4 *Leacroft v Maynard* (1791) 3 Bro CC 233 (charged on same fund): *Crowder v Clowes* (1794) 2 Ves 449 (raisable out of same property); *Cooper v Day* (1817) 3 Mer 154 (incidence of legacy duty); *Earl of Shaftesbury v Duke of Marlborough* (1835) 7 Sim 237 (same); *Martin v Drinkwater* (1840) 2 Beav 215 (separate use); *Day v Croft* (1842) 4 Beav 561 (separate use); *Bristow v Bristow* (1842) 5 Beav 289 (charged on same fund); *Warwick v Hawkins* (1852) 5 De G & Sm 481 (separate use); *Giesler v Jones* (1858) 25 Beav 418 (payment postponed to death of tenant for life of original legacy); *Duncan v Duncan (No 2)* (1859) 27 Beav 392 (provision for increase not applying to original legacy); *Johnstone v Earl of Harrowby* (1859) 1 De GF & J 183 at 191 (out of same fund, free of duty); *Duffield v Currie* (1860) 29 Beav 284 (same time of payment); *Re Smith* (1862) 2 John & H 594 at 600 (determination on insolvency); *Re Boddington, Boddington v Clairat* (1884) 25 Ch D 685 (condition as to widowhood); *Re Benyon, Benyon v Grieve* (1884) 53 LJ Ch 1165 (condition of remaining in testator's service); *Re Colyer, Millikin v Snelling* (1886) 55 LT 344 (payment postponed to death of tenant for life of original legacy); *Re Boden, Boden v Boden* [1907] 1 Ch 132 (annuities charged alike on income alone); *Re Crichton's Settlement, Sweetman v Batty* (1912) 106 LT 588 (limited gift during spinsterhood).

5 Conditions as to the mode of settlement are not generally imported. The rule is applied where the original legacy is absolute or subject to defeasance, but not in other cases: *Re More's Trust* (1851) 10 Hare 171; *Mann v Fuller* (1854) Kay 624; *Cooney v Nicholls* (1881) 7 LR Ir 107 (cases where the original legacy was settled and the donee was tenant for life); *Re Joseph, Pain v Joseph* [1908] 2 Ch 507 (where the original gift was an absolute one and the substituted gift a settled one the rule was not applicable).

6 *Re More's Trust* (1851) 10 Hare 171; *Overend v Gurney* (1834) 7 Sim 128 (original legacy immediate, other out of proceeds of sale after a life interest); *Goodman v Goodman* (1847) 1 De G & Sm 695 (restriction on alienation: presumption against intestacy); *King v Tootel* (1858) 25 Beav 23 (donee taking as specifically name and as member of a contingent class).

7 *Re Freme's Contract* [1895] 2 Ch 778.

8 *Alexander v Alexander* (1842) 5 Beav 518; *Re More's Trust* (1851) 10 Hare 171; *Re Gibson's Trust* (1861) 2 John & H 656; *Hargreaves v Pennington* (1864) 34 LJ Ch 180; *Hill v Jones* (1868) 37 LJ Ch 465; *Re Joseph, Pain v Joseph* [1908] 2 Ch 507. But the context may attach the trusts of the original legacy to the substituted legacy: *Cookson v Hancock* (1836) 2 My & Cr 606.

9 *Alexander v Alexander* (1842) 5 Beav 518 (pecuniary substituted for residue); *Tibbs v Elliot* (1865) 34 Beav 424 (residue not subject to contingent gift over in original gift); *Re Howe, Wilkinson v Ferniehough* (1910) 103 LT 185.

10 *Chatteris v Young* (1827) 2 Russ 183; *Haley v Bannister* (1857) 23 Beav 336; *Re Joseph, Pain v Joseph* [1908] 2 Ch 507.

11 *Re Backhouse, Salmon v Backhouse* [1916] 1 Ch 65.

CHAPTER 92

Option to purchase

[92.1]
When personal to the donee. An option to purchase may be personal to the donee so that it must be exercised by him[1] or it may be transmissible to his personal representatives so that they can exercise it after his death.[2] Whether or not it is so is purely a question of construction of the will. The absence of words negativing assignability is not necessary to prevent its assignability[3] but, if on the construction of the will it is held to be assignable, the personal representatives will be strictly bound by any conditions attached to the option.[4]

1   *Earl of Radnor v Shafto* (1805) 11 Ves 448; *Doe d Davies v Davies* (1851) 16 QB 951; *Re Cousins, Alexander v Cross* (1885) 30 Ch D 203; *Skelton v Younghouse* [1942] AC 571, [1942] 1 All ER 650 (where the cases are reviewed by the House of Lords). An option to purchase within 3 years of the testator's death was held to be personal: *Re Taylor's Estate* (1950) 51 SRNSW 16. After the option is effectively exercised, the obligation to pay is not personal to the donee: *McKendrick v Lewis* (1889) 15 VLR 450.
2   *Taylor v Cooper* (1846) 10 Jur 1078; *Belshaw v Rollins* [1904] 1 IR 284; *Re Avard, Hook v Parker* [1948] Ch 43, [1947] 2 All ER 548.
3   *Skelton v Younghouse* [1942] AC 571, [1942] 1 All ER 650, explaining *Wright v Morgan* [1926] AC 788 (where it was said that any vested interest is assignable unless there is something in the nature of the interest which contradicts its assignability. An option to purchase until exercised appears to be a conditional interest); applied in *Re Zerny's Will Trusts, Symons v Zerny* [1968] Ch 415, [1968] 1 All ER 686, CA (option held to be personal); and in *Re Seldon* (1970) 10 DLR (3d) 306. An option to purchase given to B has been held to direct an absolute devise to A: *Oliver v Oliver* [1958] ALR 609.
4   *Re Avard, Hook v Parker* [1948] Ch 43, [1947] 2 All ER 548.

[92.2]
Bounty or sale. The option may be mere bounty, that is where the beneficiary is to purchase at less than the full value of the property[1] or it may be for full value when it will create the relationship of vendor and purchaser between the testator's estate and the beneficiary.[2] In the former case the beneficiary will not be entitled to an abstract of title[3] and would be liable under the former law to pay estate duty on the difference between the price paid and the value of the property.[4] If the donee has to pay the full value he is entitled to a conveyance free from encumbrances[5] and, if the stated price is fixed having regard to existing encumbrances, then to a conveyance free from encumbrances created after the death of the testator.[6]

1   *Brooke v Garrod* (1857) 2 De G & J 62; *Re Lander, Lander v Lander* [1951] Ch 546, [1951] 1 All ER 622.
2   *Re Wilson, Wilson v Wilson* [1908] 1 Ch 839; *Givan v Massey* (1892) 31 LR Ir 126.
3   *Re Davison and Torrens* (1865) 17 I Ch R 7; *Brooke v Garrod* (1857) 2 De G & J 62.

4   *Re Lander, Lander v Lander* [1951] Ch 546, [1951] 1 All ER 622.
5   *Re Wilson, Wilson v Wilson* [1908] 1 Ch 839; *Givan v Massay* (1892) 31 LR Ir 126; *Waite v Morland* (1866) 14 LT 649.
6   *Re Fison's Will Trusts, Fison v Fison* [1950] Ch 394, [1950] 1 All ER 501.

[92.3]
The price. Such an option may be at a price fixed by the testator in his will[1] or to be fixed by the trustees,[2] or to be arrived at by valuation[3] or arbitration[4] or under the former law, 'at the value for estate duty purposes'.[5] Where the purchaser is to be at a valuation by a named person or in some other particular way, it is a question whether that provision is of the essence of the gift or is merely a subsidiary provision. In the former case the court will not aid the valuation if the named person dies before valuation or refuses to proceed with the valuation or for any reason the particular method of valuation cannot be carried out. In the latter case the court will fix or cause to be fixed a fair value.[6]

1   *Evans v Stratford* (1864) 2 Hem & M 142 (followed in *Re Stewart* [1976] 1 NZLR 661); *Lord Lilford v Keck* (1862) 30 Beav 295; *Re Fison's Will Trusts, Fison v Fison* [1950] Ch 394, [1950] 1 All ER 501. For precedents, see Vol 2, Form B.9, para **[209.1]** et seq.
2   *Earl of Radnor v Shafto* (1805) 11 Ves 448; *Edmonds v Millett* (1855) 20 Beav 54.
3   *Waite v Morland* (1866) 12 Jur NS 763; *Talbot v Talbot* [1967] 1 All ER 601; on appeal [1968] Ch 1, [1967] 2 All ER 920, CA, 'at a reasonable valuation', price ascertained by the court as at the time of the testator's death; applied in *Re Malpass, Lloyds Bank Ltd v Malpass* [1985] Ch 42, [1984] 2 All ER 313.
4   *Austin v Tawney* (1867) 2 Ch App 143.
5   See under the former law relating to estate duty, *Re Dowse, Dowse v Dowse* [1951] 1 All ER 558n. In *Re De Lisle's Will Trusts, White v De Lisle* [1968] 1 All ER 492, [1968] 1 WLR 322 it was held that an option to purchase a house 'at the valuation agreed for probate' meant the valuation ultimately agreed with the estate duty office. It would seem that the duty of the personal representatives in agreeing the estate duty valuation is no higher than usual: *Re Hayes' Will Trusts, Pattinson v Hayes* [1971] 2 All ER 341, [1971] 1 WLR 758.
6   *Sudbrook Trading Estate Ltd v Eggleton* [1983] 1 AC 444, [1982] 3 All ER 1; *Re Malpass, Lloyds Bank Ltd v Malpass* [1985] Ch 42, [1984] 2 All ER 313; *Richardson v Smith* (1870) 5 Ch App 648; *Cameron v Cuddy* [1914] AC 651.

[92.4]
Time for exercise of the option. If the will fixes any time for the exercise of the option, such time must be strictly observed[1] and difficulty in ascertaining the proper construction of the will does not extend the time.[2] If no time is fixed by the will, the exercise of the option must be within a reasonable time.[3] If the price has to be fixed, the time cannot run until that has been done[4] and communicated to the donee.[5] The date for the exercise of the option must be within the perpetuity rule.[6] The same rule as to strict observance applies to any other conditions attached to the option.

1   *Master v Willoughby* (1705) 2 Bro Parl Cas 244; *Dawson v Dawson* (1837) 8 Sim 346; *Re Stewart* [1976] 1 NZLR 661; compare *Re Goldsmith, Brett v Bingham* [1947] Ch 339, [1947] 1 All ER 451, and the cases there cited.
2   *Re Avard, Hook v Parker* [1948] Ch 43, [1947] 2 All ER 548.
3   *Huckstep v Matthews* (1685) 1 Vern 362; *Oliver v Oliver* [1958] ALR 609 (six months held reasonable).
4   *Lord Lilford v Keck* (1862) 30 Beav 295.
5   *Austin v Tawney* (1867) 2 Ch App 143.
6   *Re Gibson* [1952] NZLR 875.

[92.5]

Option taking effect on death of life tenant. Lands are sometimes devised for a life estate and after the termination of that estate option is given to a donee to purchase. In such a case if the lands have been sold during the subsistence of the life interest, the donee of the option upon exercising it and paying any stipulated sum is entitled to the proceeds of sale[1] and similarly if, during the subsistence of the life interest, the lands have been compulsorily purchased.[2] Where, however, there was a mere power to trustees to sell at a stated price to a beneficiary after the termination of a life interest, it was held upon the construction of the will that the trustees were not obliged to sell the land to the son when its value had increased tenfold.[3] Where there was no life interest and the lands were sold in a creditor's action, the beneficiary was held entitled to the surplus value.[4]

If the intended life tenant predeceases the testator the option does not arise and is not exercisable.[5] Though the whole estate of the testator is subject to a trust for sale, yet if a beneficiary other than the person entitled to the proceeds of sale is given an option to purchase, that option takes precedence over the trust of sale.[6]

1 *Re Armstrong's Will Trusts, Graham v Armstrong* [1943] Ch 400, [1943] 2 All ER 537.
2 *Re Cant's Estate* (1859) 4 De G & J 503.
3 *Re Noble* [1955] SASR 92.
4 *Re Kerry* (1889) 5 TLR 178.
5 *Re Hammersley* [1965] Ch 481, [1965] 2 All ER 24 (followed in [1976] 1 NZLR 661); the rule in *Jones v Westcomb* (1711) Prec Ch 316 (see Chapter 93) does not apply to options.
6 *Cox v Archer* [1964] ALR 782.

[92.6]

Perpetuities and Accumulations Act 1964 (PAA 1964) and options to purchase. By the PAA 1964, s 9 in the case of an option to acquire for valuable consideration the perpetuity period is now 21 years and the new law under which a period of 80 years or less may be prescribed does not apply in such a case nor does the period of life in being and 21 years. This does not apply to a right of pre-emption given to a public or local authority in respect of land used for religious purposes where the right becomes exercisable only on the land ceasing to be used for such purposes. By virtue of the PAA 1964, s 3(3) any exercise of the right within 21 years is valid although the provision giving the right does not limit it within that period, but in no case can the option be exercised after a period of 21 years from its creation.

CHAPTER 93

Vesting

I. PRESUMPTION OF EARLY VESTING

[93.1]

Meaning of 'vest'. The proper legal meaning of the word 'vest' is to vest in interest,[1] and when a testator uses this word by directing, for example, that the gift is to vest on a certain event, it must in general be given its proper legal meaning, and the gift is then contingent until the happening of that event.[2] This is so whether the gift is of real or personal property.[3] The context may show by indications that the donee is to take a vested interest before the specified event, that the word 'vest' is used in some other sense, for example, in the sense of 'fall into possession',[4] or 'become payable',[5] or 'be indefeasibly vested'.[6] In the last case the gift may be vested, subject only to be divested if the event does not happen. A direction with regard to vesting of a gift to a class may, on the construction of a particular will, even introduce a new category of beneficiaries to share in the gift.[7]

1 *Re Arnold's Estate* (1863) 33 Beav 163; *Re Baxter's Trusts* (1864) 4 New Rep 131; *Hale v Hale* (1876) 3 Ch D 643; *Re Mudie's Will, Beattie v Mudie* [1916] VLR 265; *Creeth v Wilson* (1882) 9 LR Ir 216 at 223; *Re Morrissey's Trusts* [1952] SR Qd 98.
2 *Re Morse's Settlement* (1855) 21 Beav 174; *Rowland v Tawney* (1858) 26 Beav 67; *Wakefield v Dyott* (1858) 32 LTOS 121; *Re Arnold's Estate* (1863) 33 Beav 163; *Richardson v Power* (1865) 19 CBNS 780; *Lushington v Penrice* (1868) 18 LT 597; *Creeth v Wilson* (1882) 9 LR Ir 216; *Re Whistson, Whiston v Woolley* [1924] 1 Ch 122; *Parkes (or Keswick) v Parkes (or Keswick)* [1936] 3 All ER 653 (contest between a general clause and a particular clause as to vesting: declaration that bequests to vest at the dates when they should become due and payable did not prevent vesting at time of testator's death); *Re Wrightson, Battie-Wrightson v Thomas* [1904] 2 Ch 95 (where the testator drew a distinction between vesting and falling into possession). A provision for maintenance out of 'vested or expectant' shares does not alter the meaning of the word 'vest': *Bull v Pritchard* (1847) 5 Hare 567 at 572; *Re Thatcher's Trusts* (1859) 26 Beav 365; *Pickford v Brown* (1856) 2 K & J 426.
3 *Re Featherstone's Trusts* (1882) 22 Ch D 111 at 114.
4 *Simpson v Peach* (1873) LR 16 Eq 208.
5 *Williams v Haythorne* (1871) 6 Ch App 782. In *Ellis v Maxwell* (1841) 3 Beav 587, a distinction was drawn in the will itself between vesting and payment.
6 *Berkeley v Swinburne* (1848) 16 Sim 275; *Taylor v Frobisher* (1852) 5 De G & Sm 191; *Poole v Bott* (1853) 11 Hare 33; *Barnet v Barnet* (1861) 29 Beav 239; *Re Baxter's Trusts* (1864) 4 New Rep 131; *Re Edmondson's Estate* (1868) LR 5 Eq 389; *Re Parr's Trusts* (1871) 41 LJ Ch 170; *Armytage v Wilkinson* (1878) 3 App Cas 355.
7 *Williams v Russell* (1863) 10 Jur NS 168 (where children who attained 21 but predeceased the life tenant were entitled to share); *Draycott v Wood* (1856) 28 LTOS 196 (where the class was determined notwithstanding the declaration as to the vesting); *Sheffield v Kennett* (1859) 4 De G & J 593 (where those who predeceased the life tenant took no share). As to the time when a class gift vests for the purposes of perpetuity see *Re Drummond's Settlement, Foster v Foster* [1988] 1 All ER 449, [1988] 1 WLR 234 discussed in Chapter 66.

[93.2]

Presumption in favour of vesting. In cases where there is a doubt as to the time of vesting, the presumption is in favour of early vesting of the gift and accordingly it vests at the death of the testator[1] or at the earliest moment after that date which is possible in the context,[2] whether the gift is of real or personal property.[3] It is presumed that the testator intended the gift to be vested rather than to remain in suspense.[4] A bequest making no reference to the time of vesting takes effect at the testator's death unless this date would disturb provisions already made in the will, or unless an intention that the bequest shall operate at a later date clearly appears.[5] Since the will is ambulatory until death, the testator cannot make a gift vest at a date earlier than his death: eg at the date of the will, and a provision to that effect does not prevent lapse.[6] The presumption is especially applicable in cases where the interest created is a remainder,[7] or where the donees are the children of a named person as a class,[8] or where the gift is of residuary personal or of residuary real and personal property.[9]

1   *Hamilton v Ritchie* [1894] AC 310; *Bernard v Walker* (1921) 55 ILT 73; *Re Taylor* (1972) 28 DLR (3d) 257; *Melnik v Sawycky* (1977) 80 DLR (3d) 371.
2   *Re Blakemore's Settlement* (1855) 20 Beav 214 at 217; *Darley v Perceval* [1900] 1 IR 129; *Ward v Brown* [1916] 2 AC 121. Since the will is ambulatory until death, a testator cannot make a gift vest at the date of the will and an attempt to do so will not prevent lapse: *Browne v Hope* (1872) LR 14 Eq 343.
3   For cases of real property, see *Re Wrightson, Battie-Wrightson v Thomas* [1904] 2 Ch 95; *Re Blackwell, Blackwell v Blackwell* [1926] Ch 223 at 233; *Bickersteth v Shanu* [1936] AC 290, [1936] 1 All ER 227. For cases of personal property, see *Re Merrick's Trusts* (1866) LR 1 Eq 551 at 557; *Rhodes v Rhodes* (1882) 7 App Cas 192 at 211; *Parkes (or Keswick) v Parkes (or Keswick)* [1936] 3 All ER 653.
4   *Taylor v Graham* (1878) 3 App Cas 1287; *Hickling v Fair* [1899] AC 15 at 30; *Re Grove, Public Trustee v Dixon* [1919] 1 Ch 249; *Yule's Trustees v Deans* 1919 SC 570; *Lees' Trustees v Lees* 1927 SC 886; *Re Peter's Estate* [1952] 4 DLR 259.
5   See n 1.
6   See n 2.
7   *Driver d Frank v Frank* (1814) 3 M & S 25; *Re Watkins, Maybery v Lightfoot* (1913) 108 LT 237 at 240, CA (the case was reversed sub nom *Lightfoot v Maybery* [1914] AC 782, HL). The reason given is that keeping the remainder contingent might in many cases exclude the issue of a person intended to take in tail, by the parents dying before the remainder became vested.
8   *M'Lachlan v Taitt* (1860) 2 De GF & J 449; *Selby v Whittaker* (1877) 6 Ch D 239 at 249; *Re Ransome's Will Trusts, Moberley v Ransome* [1957] Ch 348, [1957] 1 All ER 690 (where the limits of the application of this doctrine on the closing of a class is stated, see Chapter 66). There may be no reason for the application of the presumption in the case of a child if all the testator's descendants living at the period of distribution are provided for: *Re Deighton's Settled Estates* (1876) 2 Ch D 783.
9   *Oddie v Brown* (1859) 4 De G & J 179; *Pearman v Pearman* (1864) 33 Beav 394; *West v West* (1863) 4 Giff 198. As to when such gifts carry the intermediate interest whether vested or contingent, see Chapter 32.

[93.3]

Conditions precedent or subsequent. The presumption of early vesting may assist in the determining whether a condition is to be construed as precedent or subsequent, but it is only where upon the construction of the will that the court is left in doubt whether the condition is precedent or subsequent that the presumption in favour of early vesting applies,[1] and the condition is treated as subsequent.[2]

1   *Hickling v Fair* [1899] AC 15 at 27. As to the general considerations that distinguish conditions
     precedent from conditions subsequent, see Chapter 34.
2   *Egerton v Earl Brownlow* (1853) 4 HL Cas 1 at 182; *Woodhouse v Herrick* (1855) 1 K & J 352 at
     359; *Lady Langdale v Briggs* (1856) 8 De GM & G 391; *Re Greenwood, Goodhart v Woodhead*
     [1903] 1 Ch 749; *Re Blackwell, Blackwell v Blackwell* [1926] Ch 223; *Bickersteth v Shanu* [1936]
     AC 290, [1936] 1 All ER 227; *Sifton v Sifton* [1938] AC 656, [1938] 3 All ER 435.

II.   CIRCUMSTANCES AFFECTING VESTING

[93.4]

Nature of the postponement. In addition to the general presumption in favour
of early vesting, there are particular circumstances which affect the question
whether or not a gift is vested. Thus, where a condition can be fairly read as
postponing merely the right to possession or of obtaining the payment, transfer
or conveyance, so that there is an express or implied distinction between the
time of vesting and the time of enjoyment, the gift is held to be vested, if the rest
of the context allows.[1] This construction is particularly applicable where the
postponement is for convenience of the testator's estate,[2] or is occasioned by the
gift of some prior interest filling up the interval.[3] Examples are: postponement
for the payment of debts;[4] for investment as directed;[5] for performance of trusts.[6]
Postponement by trustees of a sale of property given on trust for sale does not
postpone the vesting of the interests in the proceeds of sale.[7] In these cases the
nature of the provision shows that it is merely the enjoyment which is
postponed. On the other hand there may be an intention clearly expressed[8] to
suspend until such time as the payment of debts is completed,[9] or the sale for the
division of the estate is had and the estate got in.[10] In these cases effect must be
given to the intention however inconvenient the result may be.[11] Similarly,
although if the context is clear, vesting of a legacy may be postponed until actual
payment,[12] in a case of doubt, the court interprets a gift, apparently vesting on
payment, as vesting when the legacy becomes payable.[13]

1   As to real estate, see *Duffield v Duffield* (1829) 1 Dow & Cl 268 at 311; *Snow v Poulden* (1836)
     1 Keen 186 (residue directed to be invested in land: donee 'not to be of an age to receive this
     until 25'); *Peard v Kekewich* (1852) 15 Beav 166 at 171; *Dennis v Frend* (1863) 14 I Ch R 271
     (donee not to become entitled to or take the estate until 23). As to personal estate, see 93.24,
     post, and *Re Panter, Panter-Downes v Bally* (1906) 22 TLR 431 (to go to him when he is
     married and has a house of his own). As to a mixed fund, see *M'Lachlan v Taitt* (1860) 2 De
     GF & J 449 (children to become beneficially interested on death of parent).
2   See text at para **[93.4]**, n 11 infra. See also *Re Moore* [1931] 4 DLR 668.
3   See para **[93.10]** infra.
4   *Tewart v Lawson* (1874) LR 18 Eq 490; *Marshall v Holloway* (1820) 2 Swan 432 at 446; *Bacon
     v Proctor* (1822) Turn & R 31 at 40.
5   *Sitwell v Bernard* (1801) 6 Ves 520.
6   *Birds v Askey* (1857) 24 Beav 615.
7   *Parker v Sowerby* (1853) 1 Drew 488; *Re Raw, Morris v Griffiths* (1884) 26 Ch D 601.
8   In such cases the legatees are not prejudiced by delay on the part of executors or trustees:
     Gaskell v Harman (1805) 11 Ves 489; *Bernard v Mountague* (1816) 1 Mer 422; *Astley v Earl of
     Essex* (1871) 6 Ch App 898.
9   *Bernard v Mountague* (1816) 1 Mer 422; *Tewart v Lawson* (1874) LR 18 Eq 490 at 495; *Re
     Bewick, Ryle v Ryle* [1911] 1 Ch 116.
10   *Elwin v Elwin* (1803) 8 Ves 547 (to named persons, if living at time of sale); *Blight v Hartnoll*
     (1881) 19 Ch D 294 (class of grandchildren living at time of sale).

11   *Gaskell v Harman* (1805) 11 Ves 489.
12   *Gaskell v Harman* (1805) 11 Ves 489, and the position is the same both in the case of pecuniary and of residuary legacies.
13   *Gaskell v Harman* (1805) 11 Ves 489; *Re Kirkley, Halligey v Kirkley* (1918) 87 LJ Ch 247. Cf cases on gifts over on death before payment, Chapter 96.

[93.5]

Contingency in description of donee. An interest must remain contingent until there is a donee in existence having all the qualifications which the testator requires and completely answering the description of the object of his bounty given in the will.[1] Particular examples of such qualifications are: the first son of A that shall be bred a clergyman;[2] such children as shall attain twenty-one;[3] such son as shall attain a stated age.[4]

1   As to gifts to a person living at a particular time, see Chapter 65, and *Cooper v Macdonald* (1873) LR 16 Eq 258 ('then living' held to include persons whose issue shall be then living); *Re Laing* [1912] 2 Ch 386 (gift to person provided she was a widow at death of life tenant. The person died a widow in the lifetime of the life tenant and took nothing). As to gifts to 'survivors', see Chapter 67. A gift to a survivor imports contingency and is necessarily contingent until it is known who is the survivor: *Whitby v Von Luedecke* [1906] 1 Ch 783; *Re Legh's Settlement Trusts, Public Trustees v Legh* [1938] Ch 39, [1937] 3 All ER 823.
2   *Proctor v Bishop of Bath and Wells* (1794) 2 Hy Bl 358.
3   *Duffield v Duffield* (1829) 1 Dow & Cl 268; *Re Astor, Astor v Astor* [1922] 1 Ch 364.
4   *Leake v Robinson* (1817) 2 Mer 363 (to donee on attaining 25).

[93.6]

Gift at specified age. A gift to a person 'at', 'if', 'as soon as', 'when', or 'provided' he attains a certain age may or may not mean that the gift is not to vest until that age is attained. Such a gift, without further context to govern the meaning of the words, is contingent,[1] this being a quality or description which the donee must possess in order to claim under the gift.[2] Where the gift is to a class, the specified age in general determines the persons who may claim as members of the class.[3] Where, however, there is a context, these words have been held not to import a contingency in the sense of a condition precedent to vesting, but to have the effect of a proviso or condition subsequent operating as a defeasance of a vested interest.[4]

1   As to real estate: *Re Francis, Francis v Francis* [1905] 2 Ch 295; *Love v Love* (1881) 7 LR Ir 306; *Phipps v Ackers* (1842) 9 Cl & Fin 583; *Re Dwyer's Will* [1916] VLR 114; *Re Scott* [1919] SALR 134; *Re Galbraith Estate* [1919] 2 WWR 193; *Re Osmond, Cummings v Gallaway* (1911) 30 NZLR 65.
       As to personal estate: *Mair v Quilter* (1843) 2 Y & C Ch Cas 465; *Re Edwards, Jones v Jones* [1906] 1 Ch 570; *Re Kirkley, Halligey v Kirkley* (1918) 87 LJ Ch 247 (to be paid if and when they attain 21: held contingent); *Re Shurey, Savory v Shurey* [1918] 1 Ch 263; *Re Blackwell, Blackwell v Blackwell* [1926] Ch 223; *Re Pfrimmer Estate* [1945] 3 DLR 518.
       In *Fast v Van Vliet* (1965) 51 WWR 65 a gift 'to be paid' on the beneficiary attaining 25 was held contingent.
2   *Leake v Robinson* (1817) 2 Mer 363 at 385. A gift to a class at 21 may be affected by an alternative gift, if there is but one member of the class, to that member at birth, or vice versa; *Judd v Judd* (1830) 3 Sim 525 (where the age was 25 and it was held that they were not intended to take until 25 and the gift, under the law then in force, was void); *Hunter v Judd* (1833) 4 Sim 455 (testator made it perfectly plain no child was to take until 25); *Walker v Mower* (1852) 16 Beav 365 (gift over on death of parent without leaving a child: only child took at birth); *Johnson v Foulds* (1868) LR 5 Eq 268 (gift over if no such child or all such children should die before attaining vested interest: only child took at birth); *Re Fletcher, Doré*

v Fletcher (1885) 53 LT 813 (gift over if no child lived to attain vested interest; only child, dying before 21, did not take).

3   As to real estate: *Duffield v Duffield* (1829) 1 Dow & Cl 268; *Newman v Newman* (1839) 10 Sim 51; *Kennedy v Sedgwick* (1857) 3 K & J 540; *Re Astor, Astor v Astor* [1922] 1 Ch 364; *Re Fulton* (1978) 85 DLR (3d) 291.
   As to personal estate: *Leake v Robinson* (1817) 2 Mer 363; *Chance v Chance* (1853) 16 Beav 572; *Merlin v Blagrave* (1858) 25 Beav 125; *Thomas v Wilberforce* (1862) 31 Beav 299; *Bowyer v West* (1871) 24 LT 414; *Re Williams, Spencer v Brighouse* (1886) 54 LT 831.

4   *Andrew v Andrew* (1875) 1 Ch D 410; *Re James' Settled Estates* (1884) 51 LT 596; *Re Campbell, Cooper v Campbell* (1919) 88 LJ Ch 239; *Bickersteth v Shanu* [1936] AC 290, [1936] 1 All ER 227; *Re Tegler Estate* [1929] 1 DLR 445; *Singer v Singer* [1932] SCR 44. This passage of the text was cited with approval in *Re Monroe Estate* (1995) 9 WWR 372 at 375.

[93.7]
Contingency in the subject-matter of the gift. An estate or interest remains contingent until the property, the subject-matter of the gift,[1] and the precise extent of the interest therein of the donee,[2] becomes ascertainable.

1   *Wood v Drew* (1864) 33 Beav 610; *Redington v Browne* (1893) 32 LR Ir 347 at 356; *Re Coulson's Trusts, Prichard v Coulson* (1907) 97 LT 754.
2   *Re Thompson, Thompson v Thompson* [1906] 2 Ch 199. The most common example is the case of a gift to a class where the amount each is to take is determined by the number of the other members when finally determined: *Cattlin v Brown* (1853) 11 Hare 372; *Hale v Hale* (1876) 3 Ch D 643.

[93.8]
Contingencies in successive gifts. A contingency which is a condition precedent to vesting of a particular interest applies to all interest dependent on that interest or limited in immediate succession to that interest as a continuous series,[1] but not to other limitations.[2] If the gifts follow other gifts – if, for example, all are contingent on a certain event[3] – the court may infer from the will, taken as a whole, that it is a mere inaccuracy of expression, and that the contingency is only meant to apply to such of the subsequent trusts and limitations as necessarily depend for their existence on the happening of the event in question.[4]

1   *Cattley v Vincent* (1852) 15 Beav 198; *Paylor v Pegg* (1857) 24 Beav 105; *Gray v Golding* (1860) 2 LT 198; *Crosse v Eldridge* (1918) 53 L Jo 52. For cases where a contrary intention was inferred from the scope of the will, see *Sheffield v Earl of Coventry* (1852) 2 De GM & G 551; *Boosey v Gardener* (1854) 5 De GM & G 122.
2   *Partridge v Foster (No 2)* (1866) 35 Beav 545. A contingency affecting a gift by will to a parent is not extended to a gift to his issue, which is an independent bequest; and the court will construe such a gift as vested if the words will at all permit of that construction: *Re Applebee's Trusts* (1873) 28 LT 102.
3   *Pearson v Rutter* (1853) 3 De GM & G 398 at 406; *Sheffield v Earl of Coventry* (1852) 2 De GM & G 551; *Boosey v Gardener* (1854) 5 De GM & G 122; *Duffield v M'Master* [1906] 1 IR 333.
4   *Quicke v Leach* (1844) 13 M & W 218 (devises preceded by 'in case my son J shall attain 25 and I shall have any other child ... living at ... my death': some such devises took effect although the testator had no other child); *Eaton v Hewitt* (1862) 2 Drew & Sm 184; *Re Blight, Blight v Hartnall* (1880) 13 Ch D 858.

[93.9]
Gift over on particular event taking effect generally. If an ultimate gift is made to take effect on the failure of a preceding gift in a particular manner, but the court can gather that the meaning of the testator is that the ultimate limitation

should take effect on the failure of the preceding gift in any manner whatever, then, although the language in which the ultimate gift is expressed does not in terms apply to the event which has happened, the ultimate gift takes effect, and the particular manner of failure of the preceding gift is not a condition precedent to the vesting.[1] The same rule applies where the prior donees are a class,[2] and it appears to apply to a gift by way of substitution where the events giving rise to the substitution do not happen.[3] The fact that the prior gift fails by reason of some rule of law, such as the law of mortmain, may not, however, prevent the gift over from taking effect according to this principle.[4] This principle does not, however, enable a gift over to take effect on an event not provided for where the prior donees come into existence and satisfy the conditions of their gift during the lifetime of the testator, and the failure of the prior gift is due to lapse by the deaths of the prior donees in the lifetime of the testator.[5] For instance, where the gift over is on the death of the prior donee before attaining twenty-one, or satisfying some other condition which is satisfied during the testator's lifetime.[6] It has been stated in a modern case[7] that the general rule of construction of a conditional gift requires the condition to be strictly observed, and that the rule in *Jones v Westcomb*[8] is but a limited exception operating where, from the condition attached to the gift, it is possible to infer that the testator must have intended the gift over to take effect on another event not express but implicit in the condition. The rule cannot apply where that would involve contradicting the express terms of the condition precedent for the gift over.[9]

1   This is known as the rule in *Jones v Westcomb* (1711) Prec Ch 316 (gift over based on the condition that the wife was enceinte at the date of the will which condition proved to be based on a mistake); *Re Fox's Estate, Dawes v Druitt* [1937] 4 All ER 664 (gift to daughter and her children; gift over in case of lapse: daughter survived but had no children: gift over took effect under rule and construing 'lapse' in a wider sense); *Re Bowen, Treasury Solicitor v Bowen* [1949] Ch 67, [1948] 2 All ER 979 (gift to mother for life and after her death to uncle: if uncle died in mother's lifetime, to uncle's children: both mother and uncle predeceased testator: held, uncle's children took); *Prestwidge v Groombridge* (1833) 6 Sim 171 (provision for event of sons being 'settled' in lifetime of testatrix: sons survived testatrix but died under 21: gift over took effect); *Lenox v Lenox* (1839) 10 Sim 400 (when an ultimate limitation is to take effect on the failure of the preceding gift and the language which describes the preceding gift happens to be not in terms applicable, then the meaning is clear that the gift over should take effect); *Wing v Angrave* (1860) 8 HL Cas 183 (where the prior gift did not take effect); *Re Chappell's Trusts* (1862) 6 LT 643 (gift over if son insane at death of tenant for life, son dying insane in lifetime of tenant for life). There may be a difficulty in applying this rule where the will has been confirmed by a codicil after the happening of a particular event; *Re May, Cockerton v Jones* [1944] Ch 1, [1943] 2 All ER 604.

2   *Brookman v Smith* (1872) LR 7 Exch 271; approving *Tarbuck v Tarbuck* (1835) 4 LJ Ch 129. *Brookman v Smith*, was distinguished in *Re May, Cockerton v Jones* [1944] Ch 1, [1943] 2 All ER 604 (gift over if no child attained 21; though one child attained that age, the gift over took effect because that child died and the will was confirmed by codicil after that event); see also *Re Andrews* [1980] Qd R 317, apparently misinterpreting this passage of the text.

3   *Hannam v Sims* (1858) 2 De G & J 151 at 154.

4   *Hall v Warren* (1861) 9 HL Cas 420.

5   *Varley v Winn* (1856) 2 K & J 700; *Re Gaitskell's Trust* (1873) LR 15 Eq 386; *Chapman v Perkins* [1905] AC 106.

6   *Cox v Parker* (1856) 22 Beav 168; *Re Graham, Graham v Graham* [1929] 2 Ch 127; *Kellett v Kellett* (1871) IR 5 Eq 298 at 305 (where the cases were fully considered); *Re Bailey* [1951] Ch 407, [1951] 1 All ER 391 (gift over if A predeceased B, but A survived B and died in testator's lifetime: gift over did not take effect).

7   Per Peter Gibson J in *Re Koeppler's Will Trusts, Barclays Bank Trust Co v Slack* [1984] 2 All ER 111 at 128; not affected by Court of Appeal [1985] 2 All ER 869.

8   (1711) Prec Ch 316.
9   Under the express terms of the gift over to a named Oxford college the condition precedent for
    the gift over, namely that Wilton Park had ceased to exist in a particular form at the date of the
    testator's death, had not been fulfilled; *Re Bailey, Barrett v Hyder* [1951] Ch 407, [1951] 1 All
    ER 391, applied; *Hall v Warren* (1861) 9 HL Cas 420, and *Re Fox's Estate, Phoenix Assurance
    Co Ltd v Fox* [1937] 4 All ER 664, distinguished; *Jones v Westcomb* (1711) Prec Ch 316 not
    applied. Similarly in *Re Sinclair, Lloyds Bank plc v Imperial Cancer Research Fund* [1985] Ch
    446, [1985] 1 All ER 1066, CA, where there was a gift over if the wife should predecease the
    testator and it was held that the gift over did not operate where the gift to the wife 'lapsed' by
    reason of a divorce and the effect of the Wills Act 1837, s 18A; the property was regarded as
    undisposed of and passed on an intestacy. See Chapter 47, para **[47.2]** et seq. *Jones v Westcomb*
    (1711) Prec Ch 316, was applied in *Re Jolley* (1985) 36 SASR 204.

III.   VESTING OF REMAINDERS

[93.10]

Former rule as to remainders. Formerly it was a rule of law that a legal
limitation which in its inception could operate as a remainder should be allowed
to do so,[1] and, apart from statute,[2] should not operate as an executory devise.
The rule did not apply to equitable limitations, and accordingly it became
obsolete when future interests ceased to be capable of subsisting at law.[3]

1   The rule in *Purefoy v Rogers* (1671) 2 Wms Saund 380. A contingent remainder was originally
    liable to destruction if the contingency did not happen before the determination of the preceding
    estate.
2   Contingent Remainders Act 1877, whereby every contingent remainder valid as a springing or
    shifting use or executory devise was capable of taking effect as such where there was no
    sufficient estate to support it as a contingent remainder.
3   Law of Property Act 1925, s 1; 37 *Halsbury's Statutes* (4th edn) 124.

[93.11]

Rule in *Boraston's Case*. A future interest, though expressed to take effect on a
contingent event, may be construed to be a vested remainder, taking effect in its
natural order on the determination of the previous interest.[1] Thus, where real
estate is devised to a devisee when, or until, or, it seems, if[2] he shall attain a
certain age, and a prior interest is limited to endure pending his attainment of
that age, the attainment of that age is not the time when the interest is to vest, but
is an event on which the interest, already vested, is to come into possession, and
even if the donee dies without having attained that age, the gift is not divested,
but the property devolves as part of his estate.[3]

1   *Phipps v Ackers* (1842) 9 Cl & Fin 583 at 591. The happening of the event in such a case is not
    a condition precedent any more than other words stating that a remainderman shall not take
    until after the determination of the previous estate.
2   In *Doe d Wheedon v Lea* (1789) 3 Term Rep 41 at 43, it was said that 'if' would make a
    condition precedent, but in *Phipps v Ackers* (1842) 9 Cl & Fin 583, Tindal CJ included 'if' as
    attracting the rule. See also para **[93.12]**, n 1.
3   *Boraston's Case* (1587) 3 Co Rep 19a; *Doe d Wheedon v Lea* (1789) 3 Term Rep 41; *Re
    Townsend* (1970) 7 DLR (3d) 270.

[93.12]

Prior interest essential. It is essential that a prior interest should be limited. If it
is not, the rule in *Boraston's Case* does not apply and words of contingency then

have their natural effect and create only a contingent interest.[1] The prior interest may be given to some person, either for the benefit of the donee himself, for instance, for his education and maintenance,[2] or for the benefit of the prior donee or other persons.[3]

1   *Re Blackwell, Blackwell v Blackwell* [1926] Ch 223 (an immediate gift for the eldest of the testator's sons, if any, 'who shall be living at my death absolutely upon his attaining the age of 21 years' held to be contingent on his attaining that age). In such a case no distinction can be drawn between 'when' and 'if': *Re Francis, Francis v Francis* [1905] 2 Ch 295 at 298.
2   *Doe d Cadogan v Ewart* (1838) 7 Ad & El 636 at 663; *Jackson v Marjoribanks* (1841) 12 Sim 93; *Greene v Potter* (1843) 2 Y & C Ch Cas 517 at 522; *Milroy v Milroy* (1844) 14 Sim 48; *Bird v Bird* (1842) 11 LJ Ch 390; *Re Mottram* (1864) 10 LT 866. In *Milroy v Milroy*, the gift was of a blended fund.
3   *Boraston's Case* (1587) 3 Co Rep 19a; *Parkin v Knight* (1846) 15 Sim 83 at 86; *James v Lord Wynford* (1852) 1 Sm & G 40; *Re Radford, Jones v Radford* (1918) 62 Sol Jo 604.

[93.13]
Gifts in default of issue. The words 'in default of issue' or 'in default of such issue' introducing a gift after an estate tail are apt words to use for introducing a remainder, and are not words of contingency,[1] and they may be so used even after gifts for life only to the issue,[2] and the gift may take effect although issue has come into existence and failed.[3] But a devise, after a prior gift for life, to a child of the life tenant or other donee if attaining a specified age is not made vested merely by the fact that it is expressed to take effect 'from and after' the death of the life tenant,[4] although this expression may be of importance if there are other indications of such intention[5].

1   *White v Summers* [1908] 2 Ch 256 at 271; *Leadbeater v Cross* (1876) 2 QBD 18.
2   *Goodright d Lloyd v Jones* (1815) 4 M & S 88.
3   *Doe d Baroness Dacre v Dowager Lady Dacre* (1798) 1 Bos & P 250; *Lewis d Ormond v Waters* (1805) 6 East 336; *Ashley v Ashley* (1833) 6 Sim 358 at 363.
4   *Alexander v Alexander* (1855) 16 CB 59; *Re Williams, Spencer v Brighouse* (1886) 54 LT 831; *Re Jobson, Jobson v Richardson* (1889) 44 Ch D 154.
5   *Andrew v Andrew* (1875) 1 Ch D 410 (where, as pointed out in *Re Jobson, Jobson v Richardson* (1889) 44 Ch D 154 at 158, there was a gift over in default of the tenant for life having a son); *Re James' Settled Estates* (1884) 51 LT 596. In *Simmonds v Cock* (1861) 29 Beav 455, the condition as to age was held in the context to be a condition subsequent and the infant was entitled to the rents until she attained 21.

[93.14]
Extension of the rule in *Boraston's Case* to personal property. The rule in *Boraston's Case* is applicable to real estate, but it applies also to personal property which is directed to be converted into land,[1] and where personalty and land are given together, with a direction to invest the personalty in the purchase of land, the rule applies to the personalty.[2]

1   See *Snow v Poulden* (1836) 1 Keen 186, but though this was said to be within the principle of *Boraston's Case* (1587) 3 Co Rep 19a, there was no prior interest and the vested estate, an estate tail, was subject to be divested if the donee did not attain 25; and see *Attwater v Attwater* (1853) 18 Beav 330.
2   *Jackson v Marjoribanks* (1841) 12 Sim 93 at 98.

[93.15]
Subject to prior interests. With regard both to real and personal property there is a rule, analogous to the rule in *Boraston's Case*, under which words

apparently of condition do not prevent vesting. Thus, words which, though in the form of a condition, merely denote that the gift is to come into possession on the failure or at the determination of prior interests, do not as a general rule form a condition precedent to vesting.[1] The principle may be applied not only where the contingency is a condition subsequent for the determination of the previous gift, but where it is a condition precedent to that gift.[2] In order, however, that a gift in such terms may be vested, the condition upon which the gift is dependent must involve no incident but such as is essential to the failure or determination of the interests previously limited,[3] and must be equivalent to 'subject to the interests previously given';[4] if any superadded condition, not connected with the previous limitation, is imposed by the testator, that condition must be fulfilled prior to vesting.[5]

1 Thus in *Pearsall v Simpson* (1808) 15 Ves 29, there was a gift for life, then of the capital for the children, and if there was a child, for the husband for life, and after his death, if he should become entitled, to other persons. There was no child, and, since the husband died in the lifetime of the life tenant, he never became entitled, yet the ultimate gift to other persons took effect. It was not a condition precedent, but a provision fixing the time at which the gift over took effect, (1808) 15 Ves 29 at 33, and see *Maddison v Chapman* (1858) 4 K & J 709 at 719; applied in *Permanent Trustee Co of New South Wales Ltd v D'Apice* (1967–1968) 118 CLR 105; *Edgeworth v Edgeworth* (1869) LR 4 HL 35 at 41 'in case A should come to the possession of the said estate' and should die leaving issue, gift to issue: A died leaving a son, but did not come into possession, nevertheless the gift to the son took effect); *Webb v Hearing* (1617) Cro Jac 415 (if their daughters, or either of them, should outlive prior donees, they were to take, with remainder over; 'this was no limitation contingent, but shows when it shall commence, which is well enough performed'); this assumes that they did not outlive, but according to the report only two of them predeceased the prior donees; *Massey v Hudson* (1817) 2 Mer 130 (in case E should survive the life tenant); *Hillersdon v Lowe* (1843) 2 Hare 355 at 359; *Key v Key* (1853) 4 De GM & G 73 at 79 (in case annuitants or any of them should survive A); *Re Smith's Trusts* (1865) LR 1 Eq 79 (in case of the death of A during the life of B); *Chellew v Martin* (1873) 28 LT 662 at 664; *Leadbeater v Cross* (1876) 2 QBD 18 at 22; *Yule's Trustees v Deans* 1919 SC 570.
2 *Re Sanforth's Will* [1901] WN 152. A gift in default of appointment is not contingent: it is vested subject to being divested by the exercise of the power.
3 *Maddison v Chapman* (1858) 4 K & J 709 at 719; *M'Kay v M'Kay* [1901] 1 IR 109 at 120.
4 The true test of limitations of this nature is whether the words which in form import the contingency can be read as equivalent to: 'subject to the interests previously limited': *Maddison v Chapman* (1858) 4 K & J 709; *Re Martin, Smith v Martin* (1885) 53 LT 34 at 35; *Re Shuckburgh's Settlement, Robertson v Shuckburgh* [1901] 2 Ch 794 at 798, or whether the contingency is after the happening of some event, eg the death of a named person: *Re Wragg, Hollingsworth v Wragg* [1959] 2 All ER 717, [1959] 1 WLR 922, which was applied in *Re Nash, Miller v Allen* [1965] 1 All ER 51, [1965] 1 WLR 221 (where after three annuities the estate was given to a niece and a nephew or their heirs. These were future vested interests).
5 *Maddison v Chapman* (1858) 4 K & J 709; *Edgeworth v Edgeworth* (1869) LR 4 HL 35 at 40; *Merchants Bank of Canada v Keefer* (1885) 13 SCR 515 ('if then living' adds a contingency because they are otherwise redundant).

IV.   EFFECT OF GIFT OVER ON VESTING

[93.16]
Contingent gift over. Where property is devised to a devisee 'if' or 'when' he attains a certain age, and there is a gift over in the event of his failing to attain that age, with or without other contingencies, the attainment of that age is held to be a condition subsequent, and not precedent, and the gift is vested

immediately subject to be divested if the devisee dies under the specified age.[1] This rule (known as the rule in *Phipps v Ackers*[2]) applies to all kinds of property and is based on the principle that the subsequent gift over, in the event of the devisee dying under the specified age, sufficiently shows the meaning of the testator to have been that the first devisee should take whatever interest the part claiming under the devisee over is not entitled to, which of course gives him the immediate interest subject only to the chance of its being divested on a future contingency[3]. For the rule to apply there must be an express gift over which spells out the conditions on which the gift over will take place and includes amongst those conditions the counterparts, though no necessarily identical counterparts, of the conditions applicable to the prior gift.[4] The rule does not apply where there is an express direction as to vesting,[5] and it is not required where vesting is implied from a trust for maintenance out of intermediate income.[6] Though the rule may be negatived by the express terms of the will, it will not now be negatived because there may be some disparity between the primary gift and the gift over.[7] There is no difference in this respect with regard to devises to individuals or to classes[8] and the rule applies to personal as well as real property.[9] The rule has been applied where the original gift was apparently contingent on surviving a life tenant, but there was a gift over if the donee should die in the lifetime of the life tenant without leaving issue.[10] The rule appears to have been established with a view to the prevention of gifts in remainder being liable to destruction as contingent remainders owing to there being no legal estate to support them before they fell into possession, and for this purpose the language was strained.[11] In this view the rule should have been confined to legal remainders, but it applied to equitable remainders,[12] to executory trusts,[13] and to gifts of residuary real and personal estate, and to personalty alone.[14]

1   *Phipps v Ackers* (1842) 9 Cl & Fin 583, where the opinion of the judges was delivered to the House of Lords by Tindal CJ; the rule is based on intention ascertained as a matter of construction, per Ungoed-Thomas J in *Re Penton's Settlements, Humphreys v Birch-Reynardson* [1968] 1 All ER 36 at 43, [1968] 1 WLR 248 at 256; see also *McGredy v IRC* [1951] NI 155, where the nature and history of the rule is discussed. The original justification of the rule is, no longer operative by virtue of the changes effected by the Trustee Act 1925, s 31; 48 *Halsbury's Statutes* (4th edn) 487, Vol 2, Part G, para **[246.26]**, and the Law of Property Act 1925, s 175; 37 *Halsbury's Statutes* (4th edn) 342, Vol 2, Part G, para **[244.52]**. The chief case in which it makes a difference now is the case of a contingent legacy by a person not in loco parentis to the legatee, per Cross J in *Re Kilpatrick's Policies Trusts, Kilpatrick v IRC* [1966] Ch 730 at 738, [1965] 2 All ER 673 at 678.
2   (1842) 9 Cl & Fin 583, sometimes also known as the rule in *Edwards v Hammond* (1684) 3 Lev 132.
3   *Phipps v Ackers* (1842) 9 Cl & Fin 583 at 592; *Bull v Pritchard* (1847) 5 Hare 567 at 571; *Boulton v Beard* (1853) 3 De GM & G 608 at 613. In *Phipps v Ackers* (1842) 9 Cl & Fin 583, the devise was in trust to convey to A when and so soon as he should attain 21, but, in case he should die before attaining 21 without issue, then over. It was held that an equitable estate in fee vested in A immediately on the testator's death, liable to be divested in the event of the death of A under 21 without leaving issue of his body. The text was cited in connection with the rule in *Phipps v Ackers* (1835) 3 Cl & Fin 702 in *Re Targa* (1986) 43 SASR 234 at 240 where an illiterate will was confirmed as conferring a life interest on the principal named beneficiary with a vested interest in remainder to her two children in equal shares as tenants in common.
4   Per Templeman J in *Re Mallinson Consolidated Trusts, Mallinson v Gooley* [1974] 2 All ER 530 at 534; faced with a prior gift which creates a condition precedent followed by a gift over which creates a condition subsequent in relation to the same events, the court being in favour of

early vesting resolves the dilemma by accepting the condition subsequent which achieves early vesting. The terms of the gift over alter the construction of a prior gift and convert what would otherwise be a contingent interest into a vested interest liable to be divested.

5 *Russel v Buchanan* (1836) 7 Sim 628.

6 *Re Astor, Astor v Astor* [1922] 1 Ch 364 at 368.

7 *McGredy v IRC* [1951] NI 155.

8 *Doe d Roake v Nowell* (1813) 1 M & S 327; affd sub nom *Randoll v Doe d Roake* (1817) 5 Dow 202 (remainder to donee's children equally at 21, but, if only one child should live to attain 21, to him or her at 21, and if donee died without lawful issue or all such issue died under 21, then over); *Farmer v Francis* (1826) 2 Sim & St 505 (gift of residue in remainder after life estates to A and B to children of the survivor of A and B equally when and as they respectively reached the age of 24 but, if no such issue or all should die without lawful issue under 24, then over); *Doe d Dolley v Ward* (1839) 9 Ad & El 582 (remainder to such of a woman's children as she now has or may have, sons at 23, daughters at 21, in fee, and if any die, sons under 23 or daughters under 21, over to the survivors; and if only one child to such child so attaining such age).

9 *Whitter v Bremridge* (1866) LR 2 Eq 736 (gift of residuary real and personal property upon trust for sale); *Re Heath, Public Trustee v Heath* [1936] Ch 259 (personal property only); *Re Kilpatrick's Policies Trusts, Kilpatrick v IRC* [1966] Ch 730, [1965] 2 All ER 673; on appeal [1966] Ch at 747, [1966] 2 All ER 149 (personal property ie insurance policies).

10 *Finch v Lane* (1870) LR 10 Eq 501 (life interest to wife, and after her death to H if living at death of wife, but if H should die in lifetime of wife without leaving issue then over); followed in *Re Penton's Settlements, Humphreys v Birch-Reynardson* [1968] 1 All ER 36, [1968] 1 WLR 248. A gift over on the death of the donee before the tenant for life, simply and without any further contingency, does not raise the same inference of vesting: *Doe d Planner v Scudamore* (1800) 2 Bos & P 289 (devise to G for life and then to C if she outlives G but not otherwise and if she predecease G, then to G, his heirs and assigns for ever: devise to C was a contingent remainder); *Re Symons* [1949] SASR 289 (residue to children after death of widow and attainment of full age of infant daughter. Interests of children dying in testator's or widow's lifetime given over. Widow only given an annuity. Children's interests vested subject to widow's annuity); *Re Heard* [1956] VLR 102 (a similar case where widow had a life interest. Gift to son held to be vested on death of testator); see also *Kotsar v Shattock* [1981] VR 13. As to the effect of gifts at a specified age followed by a gift over on death under that age without issue, see para **[93.20]** infra.

11 *Pearks v Moseley* (1880) 5 App Cas 714 at 721; *Re Astor, Astor v Astor* [1922] 1 Ch 364 at 385. As to the abolition of this rule, see nn 1 and 2, para **[93.10]** ante.

12 *Phipps v Ackers* (1842) 9 Cl & Fin 583.

13 *Phipps v Ackers* (1842) 9 Cl & Fin 583 at 600; *Stanley v Stanley* (1809) 16 Ves 491.

14 See n 4.

[93.17]

Contingency part of description. The rule does not apply where the contingency is part of the description of the donee, for instance, where the gift is to such children as attain or who attain the specified age.[1] The difference is to be noted[2] between a gift in this form, which is contingent, and a gift to certain persons at the specified age, which is vested, there being in each case a gift over.[3] Nor does the rule apply where the gift over is contingent on an event which cannot happen until after the death of the first taker,[4] or has no relation to the first taker's interest.[5]

1 *Duffield v Duffield* (1829) 3 Bli NS 260 at 333; *Festing v Allen* (1843) 12 M & W 279 (devise to M for life and after her decease to all her children who shall attain 21 as tenants in common); *Re Astor, Astor v Astor* [1922] 1 Ch 364 (gift of lands and a house and its contents upon trust, in fee simple or absolutely, for such son (living at the death of the testator) of his son WA as first or alone attains 21, or, failing any such son, then upon trust as part of the residuary estate: held, assuming that the final gift was a gift over, and not an alternative gift, that the interests of the grandsons were contingent and not vested); and see *Holmes v Prescott* (1864) 3 New Rep 559; *Price v Hall* (1868) LR 5 Eq 399 at 402; *Re Williams, Spencer v Brighouse* (1886) 54 LT 831.

2   *Doe d Dolley v Ward* (1839) 9 Ad & El 582 at 605; *Holmes v Prescott* (1864) 10 Jur NS 507 at 513; *Re Hume, Public Trustee v Mabey* [1912] 1 Ch 693 at 699.
3   *Farmer v Francis* (1824) 2 Bing 151; *Farmer v Francis* (1826) 2 Sim & St 505; *Doe d Dolley v Ward* (1839) 9 Ad & El 582; *Attwater v Attwater* (1853) 18 Beav 330; and see para [93.16] supra.
4   *L'Estrange v L'Estrange* (1890) 25 LR Ir 399 at 417.
5   *Price v Hall* (1868) LR 5 Eq 399 at 403 (the contingency which is introduced does not fit in with the prior interest).

[93.18]
Application of gift over to omitted events. The gift over may take effect not only on the events specified in the will, but also on events not specified, if the will and the nature of the provision show an indication of the intention of the testator of this effect.[1] The event on which the gift over is alleged to come into operation, as well as on the events expressly mentioned in the will, must be an event implied by, if not expressly indicated by the will.[2]

1   *Re Tredwell, Jeffray v Tredwell* [1891] 2 Ch 640 at 656; *Eastwood v Lockwood* (1867) LR 3 Eq 487 at 492; *Pride v Fooks* (1858) 3 De G & J 252 at 267; *Chia Khwee Eng v Chia Poh Choon* [1923] AC 424. As to destination of accumulations of income prior to vesting, see *Re Woolf, Public Trustee v Lazarus* [1920] 1 Ch 184; *Re Ussher, Foster v Ussher* [1922] 2 Ch 321.
2   *Underwood v Wing* (1855) 4 De GM & G 633; *M'Carthy v M'Carthy* (1878) 1 LR Ir 189 at 196.

[93.19]
Examples of application. Where there is a conditional limitation over of an estate defeating a prior absolute interest, and the latter is by any means out of the way, nevertheless the subsequent limitation may take effect.[1] Again, where there is a prior particular interest given, with remainder to a person unborn, and on the death of the donee in remainder, or on his death under age, there is a gift over, then, though the unborn person never came into existence[2] and so could not literally fulfil the condition of dying, or dying under age, it is inferred that the gift over is to take effect,[3] whenever it can do so in immediate succession to the prior limitation in the manner of a remainder.[4] In cases where a gift is made with an obligation imposed on the donee to do some act, with a gift over in default of performance, it is inferred that the gift over is also to take effect if the donee fails to come into existence[5] or dies in the testator's lifetime without having performed the condition.[6]

1   *Re Sheppard's Trust* (1855) 1 K & J 269 at 276 (gift to three as tenants in common with accruer if any die under 21 and unmarried. One died prior to the date of the will; held the survivors took: in conditional limitations the rule is that, if the precedent limitation by any means whatsoever is out of the case, the subsequent limitation takes effect); *Barnes v Jennings* (1866) LR 2 Eq 448 at 451; *Edgeworth v Edgeworth* (1869) LR 4 HL 35 at 40 (where an estate has been plainly given, it is not, from the use of subsequent words, to be treated as given on a condition, if those subsequent words are capable of being interpreted, not as a condition imposed, but as a mere description of the event upon which the gift is to come into existence. 'In case A should come into possession' of the estate hereinbefore limited to him prefaced to a provision stating how his children should take, did not make it a condition of the children taking, that A should actually come into possession); *Re Green's Estate* (1860) 1 Drew & Sm 68 (gift to go over if donee who had gone to Australia did not claim it within three years: donee in fact died in testator's lifetime: no lapse but gift over takes effect); *Re Smith's Trusts* (1865) LR 1 Eq 79 at 83 (life interest to A, then to B, and then, in case B dies in the lifetime of A, to C, and then on deaths of both B and C over: C takes although B does not die in lifetime of A). In all these cases reference is expressly or impliedly made to the old leading case of *Avelyn v Ward* (1750) 1 Ves Sen 420, and to the statement there made that, if the prior gift be by any means whatsoever taken out of the case ... then the subsequent gift takes effect.

2   *Foster v Cook* (1791) 3 Bro CC 347 (child still-born: gift over literally took effect).
3   *Jones v Westcomb* (1711) Prec Ch 316 (to child testator's wife was then enceinte with, there
    being no such child); *Re Fox's Estate, Dawes v Druitt* [1937] 4 All ER 664, where the rule is
    stated. So where the prior donees are a class: *Meadows v Parry* (1812) 1 Ves & B 124; *Doe d
    Evers v Challis* (1852) 18 QB 224; *Lanphier v Buck* (1865) 2 Drew & Sm 484; *Beardsley v
    Beynon* (1865) 12 LT 698; *Re Riggall, Wildash v Riggall* [1949] WN 491.
4   In *Evers v Challis* (1859) 7 HL Cas 531 at 555, the case of *Gulliver v Wickett* (1745) 1 Wils
    105, is explained as based on the doctrines relating to contingent remainders and the gift in
    Evers v Challis, was held valid and able to take effect as a contingent remainder. The doctrine
    does not apply to a gift over by way of executory devise, the contingencies in which cannot be
    split so as accurately to correspond with the events which have happened; *Hancock v Watson*
    [1902] AC 14. It applies, however, to limitations of personal estate which may take effect
    immediately on the termination of prior limitations in the manner of a remainder: *Jones v
    Westcomb* (1711) Prec Ch 316.
5   *Scatterwood v Edge* (1697) 1 Salk 229 (devise to issue of A who had none).
6   *Avelyn v Ward* (1750) 1 Ves Sen 420 (devise on condition that prior devisee gave a release, and,
    if he neglected, then over); *Doe d Wells v Scott* (1814) 3 M & S 300 (devise on condition of
    assuring certain lands in a certain manner, and, on default, over); *Underwood v Wing* (1855) 4
    De GM & G 633 at 662 (where a gift was dependent on the event of the testator surviving his
    wife, the donee was not entitled simply because the gift to the wife failed to have any practical
    operation).

[93.20]

Gift over on marriage or death interchangeably. Where a testator makes a
gift to a woman of an interest for her life if she so long remains unmarried, and
then directs that, in the event of her marrying, the property shall go over to
another, without more, then the gift over takes effect on the determination of her
estate, whether she marries again or not.[1] Conversely, where the first gift is
during widowhood, and the gift over is on death, the court infers that the gift is
to take effect on remarriage.[2] Where there is no gift over, it seems still to be the
law that the donee takes absolutely on the footing that there is an indefinite gift
of income which amounts to a gift of the corpus.[3] Where there was a gift until
marriage and a direction to settle the capital on the donee on marriage and no
gift over and the donee died a spinster, the capital fell into residue.[4]

1   *Brown v Jarvis* (1860) 2 De GF & J 168; *Walpole v Laslett* (1862) 1 New Rep 180; *Eaton v
    Hewitt* (1862) 2 Drew & Sm 184; *Wardroper v Cutfield* (1864) 33 LJ Ch 605; *Underhill v
    Roden* (1876) 2 Ch D 494 at 497; *Re Mason, Mason v Mason* [1910] 1 Ch 695; *Re Cane, Ruff v
    Sivers* (1890) 60 LJ Ch 36; *O'Donoghue v O'Donoghue* [1906] 1 IR 482; *Re Griffith's Estate,
    Morgan v Stephens* [1917] P 59. This principle was held not to extend to a gift over to a woman
    with other persons on her remarriage: *Pile v Salter* (1832) 5 Sim 411 (gift for widowhood: on
    remarriage one-third to widow and two-thirds to nieces: on widow's death without remarriage
    property undisposed of), but this case was said to be wrongly decided in *Underhill v Roden*,
    supra, and was not followed in *Wardroper v Cutfield* (1864) 33 LJ Ch 605, and *Scarborough v
    Scarborough* (1888) 58 LT 851.
2   *Bainbridge v Cream* (1852) 16 Beav 25; *Stanford v Stanford* (1886) 34 Ch D 362; *Re Dear,
    Helby v Dear* (1889) 58 LJ Ch 659; *Stanier v Hodgkinson* (1903) 73 LJ Ch 179; *Re Warner,
    Watts v Silvey* [1918] 1 Ch 368; *Re Main, Official Solicitor v Main* [1947] 1 All ER 255 (where
    it was thought that mention of the second event was due to clumsy drafting); *Re Carleton*
    (1909) 28 NZLR 1066. As to ascertainment of a class on such events, see Chapter 66, ante.
3   *Rishton v Cobb* (1839) 5 My & Cr 145; *Re Howard, Taylor v Howard* [1901] 1 Ch 412; *Re
    Henry Will Trust, Mussett v Smith* [1953] 1 All ER 531 at 532–534.
4   *Re Henry Will Trust, Mussett v Smith* [1953] 1 All ER 531. See also *Re Davies* [1954] NZLR 520.

[93.21]

Bankruptcy or death interchangeably. In the same way, where a gift to a
person for life or until some event, such as bankruptcy, is followed by a gift over

on such event, but those events are ignored by the testator, the court infers that the gift over is to take effect on death or on the other events, when that inference is consistent with the whole will.[1]

1   *Etches v Etches* (1856) 3 Drew 441 (gift until bankruptcy: gift over on death implied); *Re Seaton, Ellis v Seaton* [1913] 2 Ch 614 (gift to daughter until she should receive a legacy: gift for life); *Re Akeroyd's Settlement, Roberts v Akeroyd* [1893] 3 Ch 363 (gift over on bankruptcy implied), distinguishing *Re Tredwell, Jeffray v Tredwell* [1891] 2 Ch 640. The distinction in all these cases is between a limitation for a definite period with a gift over on some of the events defining that period, when the above rules may apply, and a limitation followed by an executory gift over on any collateral contingency, which is to determine the first estate sooner than it would otherwise be determined: *Sheffield v Lord Orrery* (1745) 3 Atk 282 at 285; *Walpole v Laslett* (1862) 1 New Rep 180.

[93.22]
Inferences from gifts over or other clauses. A gift over or other clause may be an indication of intention more or less valuable according to the context and the circumstances.[1] Ambiguous words in an original gift may be explained by unambiguous words in a gift over[2] or other subsequent clause,[3] but where the words in an original gift are plain and unambiguous taken by themselves, a gift over confined to one particular event does not compel the court to place a forced construction upon the original gift.[4] A gift to a donee at a specified age, followed by a gift over on his death before that age without issue, is prima facie vested independently of that age.[5]

1   *Boughton v James* (1844) 1 Coll 26 at 44.
2   *Ralph v Carrick* (1879) 11 Ch D 873 at 884; *Re Swain, Brett v Ward* [1918] 1 Ch 399 (construction of 'issue'); *Re Manly's Will Trusts, Burton v Williams* [1969] 3 All ER 1011, [1969] 1 WLR 1818; *Re Rawson, Rigby v Rawson* (1920) 90 LJ Ch 304 (condition of living at testator's death: direction for retention until expiration of six months after declaration of peace).
3   *Vivian v Mills* (1839) 1 Beav 315 (advancement clause); *Harrison v Grimwood* (1849) 12 Beav 192 (maintenance and advancement clauses); *Walker v Simpson* (1855) 1 K & J 713 (advancement clause and construction against intestacy): *Re Turney, Turney v Turney* [1899] 2 Ch 739 (provision for interest on respective portions of children until 25, and gift over of share of a child not attaining 25 to a stranger).
4   *Re Rawlinson, Hill v Withall* [1909] 2 Ch 36 at 39; *Walker v Mower* (1852) 16 Beav 365. Where remainders vested on the death of the testator a gift over if any of the 'shares should fail' did not take effect: *Thompson v Ahern* [1958] Qd R 504.
5   *Bland v Williams* (1834) 3 My & K 411 at 417; *Mytton v Boodle* (1834) 6 Sim 457; *Phipps v Ackers* (1842) 9 Cl & Fin 583; *Wetherell v Wetherell* (1863) 1 De GJ & Sm 134; *Whitter v Bremridge* (1866) LR 2 Eq 736 (residue: gift over a donee not attaining specified age or leaving male issue); *O'Reilly v Walsh* (1872) 6 IR Eq 555; *Re Bateman's Trust* (1873) LR 15 Eq 355. The rule was applied to a gift of pure personalty in *Re Heath, Public Trustee v Heath* [1936] Ch 259. For a case where such a gift was contingent, see *Freeborn's Trustees v Bennett* 1940 SC 517.

[93.23]
Exclusion of those entitled on intestacy. When a will shows an intention that persons claiming under the testator as on his intestacy shall not take in any event[1] but the testator has only expressly provided for other persons to take in certain contingencies, the restriction to such contingencies may sometimes be disregarded, and the gifts in the will take effect in all events.[2] Except in such cases, however, the title of persons claiming on a failure of a gift or for want of disposition by the testator is not excluded merely by reason of the fact that the

testator has not contemplated all contingencies; such persons take on every event which the testator has not provided for.[3]

1   *Re Wynn, Landolt v Wynn* [1983] 3 All ER 310, [1984] 1 WLR 237.
2   *Bradford v Foley* (1779) 1 Doug KB 63 (heir-at-law). For the differences in the rules respecting realty and personalty, see per Lord Greene MR in *Re Morgan* [1942] Ch 345 at 347, [1942] 2 All ER 30 at 33.
3   *Amtherst v Lytton* (1729) 5 Bro Parl Cas 254; *Sheffield v Lord Orrery* (1745) 3 Atk 282 at 285; *Doe d Vessey v Wilkinson* (1788) 2 Term Rep 209 at 218; *Shuldham v Smith* (1818) 6 Dow 22; *Dicken v Clarke* (1837) 2 Y & C Ex 572.

V.   LEGACIES PAYABLE OUT OF PERSONAL PROPERTY

(a)   In general

[93.24]
Property to which the rules apply. The following rules apply to specific legacies of personal property, including leaseholds[1] and the proceeds of sale of real property held on trust for sale,[2] and to general legacies so far as they are charged on personal property. When freeholds are given together with leaseholds or other personal property, under a single description in terms such that, according to the rules above stated, there is a vested interest conferred in the freeholds, the interest in the leaseholds or other personal property may also be considered as vested, although, according to the rules stated below, they would be regarded as contingent.[3]

1   *Ingram v Suckling* (1859) 33 LTOS 89; *Re Hudson's Minors* (1843) Drury *temp* Sug 6.
2   *Re Hart's Trusts, ex p Block* (1858) 3 De G & J 195; *Bellairs v Bellairs* (1874) LR 18 Eq 510 at 514.
3   *Farmer v Francis* (1826) 2 Sim & St 505 (residue); *Tapscott v Newcombe* (1842) 6 Jur 755; *Riley v Garnett* (1849) 3 De G & Sm 629; *James v Lord Wynford* (1852) 1 Sm & G 40 at 59.

[93.25]
Distinction between vesting and payment. In all cases of legacies given on any future event, whether certain to happen or not, the question of vesting is whether the gift is wholly dependent on that event,[1] so that it must have happened before any part of the testator's bounty can attach to the legatee,[2] or whether the time of payment only is postponed to that event. In the latter case the legatee may take a vested interest at once subject to such postponed payment.[3]

1   In such cases the question is whether the testator meant to make the happening of the event a condition of the legacy: *Monkhouse v Holme* (1783) 1 Bro CC 298 at 300.
2   *May v Wood* (1792) 3 Bro CC 471 at 473; *Leeming v Sherratt* (1842) 2 Hare 14 at 19.
3   This rule has been adopted from the civil law: *Maddison v Andrew* (1747) 1 Ves Sen 57 at 59; *Monkhouse v Holme* (1783) 1 Bro CC 298 at 300; *Re Crother's Trusts (No 2)* [1917] 1 IR 356. If the legatee dies after the testator but before payment his representatives are entitled as the interest is a vested one: *Bateman v Roach* (1724) 9 Mod Rep 104; *Re Hay* (1912) 2 DLR 152; *Finlay's Trustees v Finlay* (1886) 13 R 1052; *Durand v Durand Manor* [1920] NZLR 489; *Re Livingstone's Estate (No 2)* [1923] 1 WWR 358. Where the gift is vested, payment cannot be postponed beyond the age of 18, Trustee Act 1925, s 31(2), as amended by Family Law Reform Act 1969, s 1(3) and by the Trustee Act 2000, Sch 2, para 21; 48 *Halsbury's Statutes* (4th edn) 487. See Vol 2, Part G, para **[246.26]**.

(b)   Direction as to payment

[93.26]
Gift contained wholly in direction to pay. Where there is a simple gift on a future event, or from a future event, or it is contained wholly in direction to pay, or to divide or to transfer, at or from and after a future event, so that there is no gift except in the direction to pay or transfer, the vesting is prima facie postponed until the event happens, and consequently, if the legatee dies before the event, his representatives are prima facie not entitled to payment.[1] Thus, a legacy to a named person at a certain definite time, without more, is prima facie contingent, and he or his representatives take no interest if he dies before that time.[2] A gift, however, to a class upon a contingency does not prima facie render the contingency applicable to the description of the class.[3]

1   *Stapleton v Cheales* (1711) Prec Ch 317 (the second rule in this case); *Morgan v Morgan* (1851) 4 De G & Sm 164 (direction to pay on marriage); *Gardiner v Slater* (1858) 25 Beav 509 (direction to pay at 21 or marriage); *Chance v Chance* (1853) 16 Beav 572 (direction to pay at 25); *Re Wrangham's Trust* (1860) 1 Drew & Sm 358 (gift on attaining 21); *Locke v Lamb* (1867) LR 4 Eq 372 (gift to class who attain 21); *Johnston v O'Neill* (1879) 3 LR Ir 476 at 482; *Wilson v Knox* (1884) 13 LR Ir 349.
2   *Smell v Dee* (1707) 2 Salk 415; *Bruce v Charlton* (1842) 13 Sim 65 at 68; *Re Eve, Belton v Thompson* (1905) 93 LT 235. For cases where there was a context leading to a contrary decision, see note 5, infra. In *Edmunds v Waugh* (1858) 4 Drew 275, a testator bequeathed a sum of Bank Annuities to such child of A, a bachelor, as attained 21 and directed the sum to be transferred to the child at that age, and, if no child attained that age, then over to residue. It was held that the dividends from the testator's death to the birth of a child of A fell into residue.
3   See Chapter 66.

[93.27]
Express distinction between gift and time of payment. If the words of the gift express a distinction between the gift itself and the event denoting the time of payment, division, or transfer,[1] and this time is the attainment by the donee of the age of twenty-one years[2] or other age,[3] or is any other event which, assuming the requisite duration of life, must necessarily happen at a determinable time,[4] then the gift is prima facie[5] not contingent in respect of the event.[6] The personal representative of the donee is accordingly entitled to the gift, even if the donee dies before attaining the specified age or before the happening of the named event, but is prima facie not entitled to payment before the donee himself would have been entitled,[7] unless there is a direction for the payment of the whole interest on the legacy in the meantime. In the latter case the personal representative will be entitled to immediate payment, even before the time when the donee would himself have been entitled to payment,[8] but a direction to allow maintenance, not amounting to a gift of the whole interest on the legacy, has not this effect.[9] This presumption as to vesting does not arise where the gift is on an event, such as the marriage of the donee, which will not necessarily happen at all however long the donee or the other person concerned lives.[10] In such a case, however, other indications as mentioned below may be present to show that the vesting is independent of the named event.[11] Even where the gift and direction to pay are distinct, the context may show that the gift is contingent.[12] A mere direction for accumulation until payment, however, is not sufficient,[13] and even an express contingency attached to payment may not be sufficient to make the vesting contingent.[14]

1   *Re Bartholomew's Trust* (1849) 1 Mac & G 354; *Locke v Lamb* (1867) LR 4 Eq 372 at 380; *Williams v Clark* (1851) 4 De G & Sm 472; *Shum v Hobbs* (1855) 3 Drew 93; *Merry v Hill* (1869) LR 8 Eq 619 (where it was held that no distinction existed: gift to children of M living at testator's death to be equally divided if more than one when they should attain 21 and if there should be but one should attain 21, then the whole to that child). In the case of a gift for life and afterwards to sell and divide the produce amongst all the children, to be paid as and when they respectively attain 21, there is a clear distinction between the gift and the time of payment. It is to be divided among all, but is to be paid as and when such children attain 21. The postponement of the payment does not postpone the vesting. If in addition there is a direction that the interest is to be applied in maintenance, education or support until they attain 21, the interests are clearly vested: *Shrimpton v Shrimpton* (1862) 31 Beav 425.

2   *Skey v Barnes* (1816) 3 Mer 335; *Vivian v Mills* (1839) 1 Beav 315 (to four children to be paid when and if they attain 21); *Williams v Clark* (1851) 4 De G & Sm 472; *Shrimpton v Shrimpton* (1862) 31 Beav 425.

3   *Farmer v Francis* (1826) 2 Sim & St 505; *Blease v Burgh* (1840) 2 Beav 221; *Saumarez v Saumarez* (1865) 34 Beav 432. Such postponement of enjoyment after the attainment of his majority may be voidable by the donee unless there is a gift over: see *Saunders v Vautier* (1841) Cr & Ph 240; *Wharton v Masterman* [1895] AC 186 at 192; *Re Couturier, Couturier v Shea* [1907] 1 Ch 470 at 473; *Re Hendy's Will, Hayes v Hendy* [1913] VLR 559; *Re Marsh* [1960] NZLR 294.

4   *Chaffers and Abell v Abell* (1839) 3 Jur 578 (when youngest attained 21); *Jackson v Jackson* (1749) 1 Ves Sen 217 (after death of third party). The following are cases of gifts to be paid at a certain fixed time after the death of the testator: *Sheldon v Sheldon* (1739) 9 Mod Rep 211 (two years); *Bromley v Wright* (1849) 7 Hare 334 (ten years after death of survivor of testator and wife); *Oppenheim v Henry* (1853) 10 Hare 441; *Lucas v Carline* (1840) 2 Beav 367; *Re Eve, Belton v Thompson* (1905) 93 LT 235; *Re Boam, Shorthouse v Annibal* (1911) 56 Sol Jo 142; *Re Jeffery, Nussey v Jeffery* [1914] 1 Ch 375.

5   In the following cases the context displaced the presumption: *Oseland v Oseland* (1795) 3 Anst 628; *Heath v Perry* (1744) 3 Atk 101; *Knight v Cameron* (1807) 14 Ves 389 (where the gift was also contingent on the donee being then living).

6   *Stapleton v Cheales* (1711) Prec Ch 317 (first rule); *Jackson v Jackson* (1749) 1 Ves Sen 217 (gifts to be paid at stated times); *Wadley v North* (1797) 3 Ves 364 (gift to children, each receiving his share at 21); *Bolger v Mackell* (1800) 5 Ves 509 (to be paid at 21 or marriage); *Clutterbuck v Edwards* (1832) 2 Russ 8 M 577. This rule does not apply to real property or legacies charged on real property: *Maddison v Andrew* (1747) 1 Ves Sen 57; *Mackell v Winter* (1797) 3 Ves 536 at 543. See para **[93.44]** infra.

7   *Chester v Painter* (1725) 2 P Wms 335; *Roden v Smith* (1744) Amb 588; *Maher v Maher* (1877) 1 LR Ir 22.

8   *Fonnereau v Fonnereau* (1748) 1 Ves Sen 119; *May v Wood* (1792) 3 Bro CC 471 at 474; *Hanson v Graham* (1801) 6 Ves 239.

9   *Harrison v Buckle* (1719) 1 Stra 238.

10 *Atkins v Hiccocks* (1737) 1 Atk 500; *Ellis v Ellis* (1802) 1 Sch & Lef 1; *Morgan v Morgan* (1851) 4 De G & Sm 164 at 167; *Re Cantillon's Minors* (1864) 16 I Ch R 301 at 308. In *Maher v Maher* (1877) 1 LR Ir 22, the principle was applied where payment was directed at 21 or marriage with consent.

11 *Booth v Booth* (1799) 4 Ves 399 (residue and whole interest given in the meantime); *Vize v Stoney* (1841) 1 Dr & War 337 at 349 (legacies payable on respective marriage day with interest thereon from death to testator); *Re Wrey, Stuart v Wrey* (1885) 30 Ch D 507 (income from stocks and shares until marriage and transfer on marriage); *M'Cutcheon v Allen* (1880) 5 LR Ir 268; *Corr v Corr* (1873) IR 7 Eq 397 (day of marriage or on becoming a nun: legacies contingent).

12 *Knight v Cameron* (1807) 14 Ves 389, (legacy at 21 and in case she shall live to that age and not otherwise; or upon marriage with consent: in case of death before 21 or marriage without consent, over. The legacy was contingent, but having married without consent, one executor being dead and the other abroad, there was but a single effective contingency of attaining 21); *Judd v Judd* (1830) 3 Sim 525 (expressly stated to become transmissible at 25 and gift over if no child fulfilling the condition expressly; reconsidered in *Hunter v Judd* (1833) 4 Sim 455); *Chevaux v Aislabie* (1842) 13 Sim 71 (provision to raise and pay all or any part of presumption share); *Merry v Hill* (1869) LR 8 Eq 619 (direction for maintenance and accumulation of surplus income).

13 *Stretch v Watkins* (1816) 1 Madd 253; *Bull v Johns* (1830) Taml 513; *Josselyn v Josselyn* (1837) 9 Sim 63; *Blease v Burgh* (1840) 2 Beav 221; *Saunders v Vautier* (1841) 4 Beav 115; *Re*

Bragger, Bragger v Bragger (1887) 56 LT 521; *Re Thompson, Griffith v Thompson* (1896) 44 WR 582; *Re Couturier, Couturier v Shea* [1907] 1 Ch 470. A donee having a vested interest subject to postponement by such accumulation, may put an end to the accumulation and claim payment or transfer the moment he has attained his majority and is by law entitled to give a receipt: *Re Couturier, Couturier v Shea.*

14 *Massey v Hudson* (1817) 2 Mer 130 (12 months from the death of B if B should happen to survive testator's wife); *Clutterbuck v Edwards* (1832) 2 Russ & M 577 (on decease of testator's wife if he shall then have attained 12); *Wright v Wright* (1852) 21 LJ Ch 775 (if donees of competent understanding: this did not make gift conditional and, though both donees were of unsound mind on attaining majority, the gifts were vested); *Re Shannon* [1968] NZLR 852 (interest given by will, though contingent, may be transmissible, though the beneficiary dies before the contingency takes place).

[93.28]

Implied distinction between the gift and time of payment. The context may also show that the gift is vested, even where there is no express distinction between the gift and a direction as to the time of payment. Thus, it may appear that the reason for the postponement of the gift is on account of prior interests given in the meantime, or on account of the nature of the property and the convenience of administration.[1] In such a case the gift prima facie vests independently of the postponement of enjoyment.[2]

1 See para **[93.1]** supra.
2 *Packham v Gregory* (1845) 4 Hare 396 at 398; *Bromley v Wright* (1849) 7 Hare 334 at 342; *Re Bennett's Trust* (1857) 3 K & J 280 at 283; *Adams v Robarts* (1858) 25 Beav 658 at 661; *Re Couturier, Couturier v Shea* [1907] 1 Ch 470 at 472; *Browne v Moody* [1936] AC 635, [1936] 2 All ER 1695; applied in *Re Thompson* (1973) 41 DLR (3d) 305; *Greenwood v Greenwood* [1939] 2 All ER 150; *Re Rauckman Estate* (1970) 8 DLR (3d) 494; *Re Oswell* (1982) 136 DLR (3d) 672 and *Tanner v New Zealand Guardian Trustee Co* [1992] 3 NZLR 74; distinguished in *Re Dawson* [1987] 1 NZLR 580. See also *Re Fraser* (1986) 29 DLR (4th) 88, at p 96 where the text is referred to; and *Re Jacques* (1985) 16 DLR (4th) 472.

[93.29]

Postponement to a life interest. Prima facie no contingency is imported by the fact that the legacy is given after a life interest in the property bequeathed,[1] and this rule applies to classes of, as well as named, remaindermen.[2] Where a legacy is given to a donee contingently on the attainment of a specified age, the fact that the legacy is also postponed to a life interest prima facie does not render it contingent on the donee surviving the tenant for life,[3] while the fact that the interest is given to another person pending his attaining that age may be an indication of a vested gift.[4] Where the shares of residue were postponed to life interests and the only gift after the life interest was in a direction to divide the residue equally among a class of beneficiaries, that class gift vested on testator's death subject to letting in subsequently born members of the class, and personal representatives of those dying during the life interest took.[5]

1 *Cochrane v Wiltshire* (1847) 16 LJ Ch 366; *Re Bright's Trusts* (1855) 21 Beav 67; *Re Bennett's Trust* (1857) 3 K & J 280; *Strother v Dutton* (1857) 1 De G & J 675; *Adams v Robarts* (1858) 25 Beav 658; *Hickling v Fair* [1899] AC 15; *Re Crother's Trusts (No 2)* [1917] 1 IR 356; *Browne v Moody* [1936] AC 635, [1936] 2 All ER 1695: overruling *Busch v Eastern Trust Co* [1928] 3 DLR 834; *Re MacFarlane* [1934] 3 DLR 457; applied in *Re Duffield* (1971) 16 DLR (3d) 7. See also *Re Kiddle* [1951] VLR 415; *Congregational Union of New South Wales v Thistlethwayte* (1952) 87 CLR 375; *Re Hamilton* [1953] QSR 48; *Re Heard* [1956] VLR 102;

Re MacInnes [1958] OR 592; *Goguen v Godwin* (1978) 82 DLR (3d) 547. For a context to the contrary, see *Willis v Plaskett* (1841) 4 Beav 208.

2   *Ross v National Trust Co* [1939] 4 DLR 653; *Re Simpson* [1945] 1 DLR 478; *Re Brooke's Will Trusts, Jubber v Brooke* [1953] 1 All ER 668, [1953] 1 WLR 439; *Re Skinner* [1965] VR 660.

3   *Hallifax v Wilson* (1809) 16 Ves 168; applied in *Re Cohn, National Westminster Bank Ltd v Cohn* [1974] 3 All ER 928 (beneficiary took a vested interest); *Walker v Main* (1819) 1 Jac & W 1; *Cousins v Schroder* (1830) 4 Sim 23; *Jones v Jones* (1843) 13 Sim 561; *Mendham v Williams* (1866) LR 2 Eq 396; *Re Amodeo* [1958] NZLR 787. For a context to the contrary, see *Billingsley v Wills* (1745) 3 Atk 219.

4   *Lane v Goudge* (1803) 9 Ves 225.

5   *Re Wilson* [1954] NZLR 880, and see *Re Heard* [1956] VLR 102.

[93.30]
Postponement until youngest attains specified age. A gift to a class of children when the youngest attains a specified age confers a vested interest on all who attain that age, whether they are living or dead at the time of payment.[1] Prima facie those who do not attain that age do not take a vested interest,[2] unless there are other provisions in the will from which a contrary inference may be drawn, as, for instance, by gift of the intermediate income generally or by way of maintenance to each member of the class[3] or by a distinction between the gift and the direction as to time of payment,[4] but a gift of maintenance during minority to each member is insufficient,[5] as is a gift for maintenance of the whole class as a common fund.[6] Where a testatrix had bequeathed a fund in trust to use the income at the trustee's discretion towards the education of a named person's child or children, accumulating any surplus income, until the youngest child should attain 21 years, and then to divide the fund and its accumulations amongst such of the children 'as should then be living', it was held that the interest of a child who had attained twenty-one was still contingent, because the words of the gift restricted it to those children who would be living when the youngest attained 21, and until that time the class remained open.[7] In the case of a similar gift to individuals, and not to a class, prima facie they take vested interests although dying before the specified age.[8]

1   *Leeming v Sherratt* (1842) 2 Hare 14; *Re Smith's Will* (1855) 20 Beav 197; *Brocklebank v Johnson* (1855) 20 Beav 205; *Kennedy v Sedgwick* (1857) 3 K & J 540. Children may be expressly required by the will to survive distribution: *Castle v Eate* (1844) 7 Beav 296; *Re Hunter's Trusts* (1865) LR 1 Eq 295. Special provisions relating to the time of payment were considered in the following: *Beckton v Barton* (1859) 27 Beav 99 (where the time of payment was in the first place when the youngest attained 21 but was to be postponed, if the widow was then still alive, to the date of her death); *Evans v Pilkington* (1839) 10 Sim 412 (trust for accumulation ceasing on account of deaths under 21). See also *Re Nicholson, Stace v Nicholson* (1904) 24 NZLR 633; *Re Osmond, Cummings v Gallaway* (1911) 30 NZLR 65; *Public Trustee v Bowyern* [1929] NZLR 438.

2   *Ford v Rawlins* (1823) 1 Sim & St 328; *Leeming v Sherratt* (1842) 2 Hare 14 at 23; *Parker v Sowerby* (1853) 1 Drew 488 at 496; *Lloyd v Lloyd* (1856) 3 K & J 20 at 25. There is, however, no general principle of construction in the case of gifts to classes at a specified age that children must attain that age in order to obtain vested interests: *Re Lodwig, Lodwig v Evans* [1916] 2 Ch 26, where this requirement was negatived.

3   *Re Grove's Trusts* (1862) 3 Giff 575; *Boulton v Pilcher* (1861) 29 Beav 633.

4   *Knox v Wells* (1864) 2 Hem & M 674.

5   *Lloyd v Lloyd* (1856) 3 K & J 20; *Coldicott v Best* [1881] WN 150.

6   *Re Hunter's Trusts* (1865) LR 1 Eq 295.

7   *Re Ransome's Will Trusts, Moberley v Ransome* [1957] Ch 348, [1957] 1 All ER 690.

8   *Cooper v Cooper* (1861) 29 Beav 229; *Re Radford, Jones v Radford* (1918) 62 Sol Jo 604.

(c)   Direction as to maintenance

[93.31]

Gift of interim interest. Where a postponed gift is accompanied by a gift of the whole interim interest of the fund to the donee[1] it is presumed, unless the context is to the contrary,[2] that the testator meant a single immediate vested gift.[3] In order to raise this inference the gift of interim income must be free from contingency,[4] except in cases where the gift would be vested in every event except the named contingency causing postponement.[5] It does not arise, therefore, where the capital and income of the legacy are given in a single gift[6] so that the same contingency applies to them both.

1   For questions as to interest on legacies generally, see Chapter 32.
2   For cases where on the context the gift of capital was nevertheless held contingent, see *Vawdry v Geddes* (1830) 1 Russ & M 203 at 208 (gift over in case of death of legatee before particular period, but this case has been criticised in this respect). See, also, *Mills v Robarts* (1830) Taml 476 (gift provided the legatee attained 21); *Re Bulley's Trust Estate* (1865) 13 LT 264 (class of donees clearly contingent).
3   *Vawdry v Geddes* (1830) 1 Russ & M 203 (putting the matter on the ground that for the purpose of interest the legacy must be immediately separated from the testator's estate); *Saunders v Vautier* (1841) Cr & Ph 240 at 248; *Re Jacob's Will* (1861) 29 Beav 402; *Dundas v Wolfe Murray* (1863) 1 Hem & M 425; *Re Bunn, Isaacson v Webster* (1880) 16 Ch D 47; *Re Wrey, Stuart v Wrey* (1885) 30 Ch D 507; *Scotney v Lomer* (1886) 31 Ch D 380. In so far as *Batsford v Kebbell* (1797) 3 Ves 363, and *Spencer v Wilson* (1873) LR 16 Eq 501, depend on treating gifts of capital and income as separate gifts, they have not been followed: see *Re Holt's Estate, Bolding v Strugnell* (1876) 45 LJ Ch 208; and n 1. An intention to make such separate gifts may, however, be shown: *Re Peek's Trusts* (1873) LR 16 Eq 221 (gift over as to capital only, if not attaining specified age). It has been suggested that the true principle is that where there is one gift of capital and income as parts of a whole, a gift otherwise contingent will be vested, but where they are separate gifts, one of capital and one of income, not necessarily going together, the gift will not be deemed vested: *Brennan v Brennan* [1894] 1 IR 69 at 73.
4   *Re Thruston's Will Trusts* (1849) 17 Sim 21.
5   *Hammond v Maule* (1844) 1 Coll 281 (trust for A for life, and at her death for her daughter B in case she should then have attained 21, but if B has not attained that age at death of A for payment of interest as maintenance of B until 21).
6   *Knight v Knight* (1826) 2 Sim & St 490 (legacy to a person as soon as he attains 21 with interest. Nothing payable until legatee attains 21 and then legacy payable with interest from one year after death of testator); *Morgan v Morgan* (1851) 4 De G & Sm 164 (interest to be accumulated); *Re Kirkley, Halligey v Kirkley* (1918) 87 LJ Ch 247 (legacy 'if and when' legatee attains a certain age); *Locke v Lamb* (1867) LR 4 Eq 372 (direction for accumulation); *Breedon v Tugman* (1834) 3 My & K 289 (where the construction making the same contingency apply to both was avoided).

[93.32]

Kind of interim gift sufficient. The fact that the income and capital of the subject-matter are given subject to annuities or life interests is immaterial. Howsoever the capital may be charged, if the income of that capital less the charge is given, the rule is satisfied.[1] It is not sufficient, however, that the income of property equal in amount to that which is the subject of the gift should be directed to be paid to the legatee, where the severance of the property is to take place only at the future time of payment,[2] or that an annuity of amount equal to the interest on the sum given should be given to the donee pending the event, but not as interest on capital.[3]

1   *Potts v Atherton* (1859) 28 LJ Ch 486 (annuity); *Jones v Mackilwain* (1826) 1 Russ 220 (annuity).

2   *Batsford v Kebbell* (1797) 3 Ves 363 (on the ground that the gift of income and capital were
      distinct); explained and commented on in *Re Hart's Trusts, ex p Block* (1858) 3 De G & J 195
      at 202, and in *Re Wrey, Stuart v Wrey* (1885) 30 Ch D 507 at 510.
3   *Watson v Hayes* (1839) 5 My & Cr 125; *Merlin v Blagrave* (1858) 25 Beav 125.

[93.33]

To what contingent legacies applicable. This presumption of vesting arising
from gifts of income fails if the context is to the contrary,[1] but when that
presumption applies, it applies whatever the nature of the contingent event
denoting the time of payment of the capital of the legacy.[2]

1   See para **[93.31]**, n 1.
2   *Booth v Booth* (1799) 4 Ves 399; *Vize v Stoney* (1841) 1 Dr & War 337 at 350; *Re Wrey, Stuart
      v Wrey* (1885) 30 Ch D 507 (marriage).

[93.34]

Gift of interim maintenance. When provision is made for the maintenance of
the legatee in the meantime, the question arises whether it is a distinct gift from
the legacy in question, or is merely a direction as to the mode of application of
the interest.[1] If maintenance is given as the distinct gift it has no effect in making
the legacy vested,[2] as, for instance, a gift of a fixed annual sum for maintenance,
even when payable out of the interest of the legacy,[3] or a gift of a 'handsome
allowance',[4] or a gift of a yearly sum not to exceed the interest on the legacy.[5]

1   *Watson v Hayes* (1839) 5 My & Cr 125 at 133.
2   *Pulsford v Hunter* (1792) 3 Bro CC 416 at 419; *Leake v Robinson* (1817) 2 Mer 363 at 386. The
      passage in *Pulsford v Hunter,* supra, was questioned in *Fox v Fox* (1875) LR 19 Eq 286 at 289,
      but it seems to be the correct view: *Wilson v Knox* (1884) 13 LR Ir 349 at 356.
3   *Livesey v Livesey* (1830) 3 Russ 542; *Watson v Hayes* (1839) 5 My & Cr 125; *Boughton v
      Boughton* (1848) 1 HL Cas 406 at 434.
4   *Tawney v Ward* (1839) 1 Beav 563.
5   *Rudge v Winnall* (1849) 12 Beav 357.

[93.35]

Gifts to individuals. Where the donee is an individual, or is one of the group of
persons taking as individuals and not as a class,[1] the fact that the gift is to carry
interest, and that the whole interest or income of the gift is directed to be applied
for maintenance, or in some other manner for the benefit of the donee until the
happening of the contingent event on which the legacy itself is given, is an
indication[2] that vesting is independent of the contingency.[3] This inference in
favour of vesting is not necessarily excluded by the fact that the mode of
application of the interest may come to an end before the specified event; for
instance, where the interest is to be applied only to education[4] or where interest
is payable only during legal minority, but capital is payable only at an age
greater than majority.[5] In general, however, if there necessarily occurs an
interval which separates the gift of income from the capital, the latter gift is not
vested[6] unless there are other indications to that effect.[7]

1   As to the distinction between a group of individuals and a class, see para 65.3, ante.
2   A gift of interim maintenance does not make a gift vested which is clearly contingent on the
      whole context: *Butcher v Leach* (1843) 5 Beav 392; *Re Coleman* (1888) 39 Ch D 443. A
      provision for the payment of the income of the fund to the mother of the legatee for his
      'advancement and education' is not sufficient to make the gift vested in face of the prima facie

contingency and is not a gift of the entirety of the income of the fund: *Re Rogers, Lloyds Bank Ltd v Lory* [1944] Ch 297, [1944] 2 All ER 1.

3   *Rose v Sowerby* (1830) Taml 376; *Lister v Bradley* (1841) 1 Hare 10 at 13 (interest payable to mother of legatees for support and education); *Brocklebank v Johnson* (1855) 20 Beav 205 at 211; *Re Hart's Trusts, ex p Block* (1858) 3 De G & J 195; *Shrimpton v Shrimpton* (1862) 31 Beav 425 at 427; *Re Holt's Estate, Bolding v Strugnell* (1876) 45 LJ Ch 208; *Re Bunn, Isaacson v Webster* (1880) 16 Ch D 47; *Re Byrne, Byrne v Kenny* (1889) 23 LR Ir 260 (gift to each of a group); *Brennan v Brennan* [1894] 1 IR 69 at 73; *Re Williams, Williams v Williams* [1907] 1 Ch 180 at 183.

4   *Dodson v Hay* (1791) 3 Bro CC 405 at 409.

5   *Davies v Fisher* (1842) 5 Beav 201; *Harrison v Grimwood* (1849) 12 Beav 192; *Tatham v Vernon* (1861) 29 Beav 604, though in these cases other indications were also relied on. 'Minority' may mean a conventional minority up to the time of payment of capital: *Milroy v Milroy* (1844) 14 Sim 48 at 55.

6   *Hanson v Graham* (1801) 6 Ves 239 at 250; *Tawney v Ward* (1839) 1 Beav 563; *Thomas v Wilberforce* (1862) 31 Beav 299 at 302; *Pearson v Dolman* (1866) LR 3 Eq 315 at 321 (gift defeasible on alienation).

7   *Pearman v Pearman* (1864) 33 Beav 394 at 396.

[93.36]

Gifts to classes. In the case of a gift to a class at a specified age, with a direction to apply each share of the whole interest for the maintenance or benefit of the corresponding member of the class, the whole class in general take vested interests irrespective of their attaining the age,[1] even if the trustees have a discretion as to the mode of application of such share of the interest.[2] This rule, however, does not hold good where the gift for maintenance is not out of each share of the fund for the benefit of the corresponding member of the class, but is a general gift for maintenance of the whole class out of the whole undivided interest in the fund.[3]

1   *Dodson v Hay* (1791) 3 Bro CC 405; *Bell v Cade* (1861) 2 John & H 122; *Re Campbell, Cooper v Campbell* (1919) 88 LJ Ch 239.

2   *Perrott v Davies* (1877) 38 LT 52 (direction to apply income for the respective maintenance of children, as trustees should think proper, construed as referring to respective shares). As to a discretion as to the amount to be so applied, see paras **[93.37]** and **[93.38]** infra.

3   *Re Ashmore Trusts* (1869) LR 9 Eq 99 (not affected on this point by *Fox v Fox* (1875) LR 19 Eq 286); *Re Parker, Barker v Barker* (1880) 16 Ch D 44; *Re Grimshaw's Trusts* (1879) 11 Ch D 406; *Re Morris, Salter v A-G* (1885) 52 LT 840; *Re Martin, Tuke v Gilbert* (1887) 57 LT 471; *Re Mervin, Mervin v Crossman* [1891] 3 Ch 197 at 201; *Re Hume, Public Trustee v Mabey* [1912] 1 Ch 693 at 699 (where a full statement of the law is made). *Jones v Mackilwain* (1826) 1 Russ 220, is explained in a manner to reconcile the decision with the above lines of cases in *Lloyd v Lloyd* (1856) 3 K & J 20. *Parker v Golding* (1843) 13 Sim 418, is a decision to the contrary effect.

[93.37]

Discretionary trust or power to make interim payments of income—other than class gift. Where the donee is a single person, the legacy becomes vested none the less because, in the direction to pay the whole interest in the meantime, there is a superadded direction that the trustees shall pay the whole or such part of that interest as they shall think fit for the maintenance of the donee.[1] A similar rule prevails as to gifts to a number of persons as a group, and not as a class, if the direction applies to their respective shares or interests.[2]

1   *Re Parker, Barker v Barker* (1880) 16 Ch D 44 at 46, followed in *Re Williams, Williams v Williams* [1907] 1 Ch 180; *Re Ussher, Foster and Ussher* [1922] 2 Ch 321. In *Re Sanderson's*

Trust (1857) 3 K & J 497 at 507, a direction to apply 'the whole or any part' of the income in maintenance was considered not discretionary, and therefore, as coming within the ordinary rule; see para **[93.34]** supra. See also *Re Eichardt, Brebrer v O'Meara* (1905) 25 NZLR 374.

2   *Re Gossling, Gossling v Elcock* [1903] 1 Ch 448; *Re Barnshaw's Trusts* (1867) 15 WR 378 (where the interests were held not to be vested); *Re Benjamin, Mason v Benjamin* [1926] VLR 378 (part not applied to be accumulated: share not vested).

[93.38]

Discretionary trust—class gift. Even in a case where a gift to a class at a specified age is accompanied by a trust or direction to apply the income of the presumptive share of each member, or so much of such income as the trustees think proper, for his maintenance until payment, it is possible[1] to draw the inference that the members take vested interests independently of attaining that age,[2] at all events if the context not only does not show the contrary,[3] but assists the inference.[4] A trust that, at the discretion of the trustees, a sufficient part of the income of the presumptive shares shall be applied in maintenance has been considered insufficient to render the gift of capital a vested gift where there is an alternative trust for accumulation[5] or where the will contains an advancement clause.[6] In general the distinction for this purpose between gifts to named persons as individuals and a gift to a class appears to be that a gift to a named person, though in terms contingent, is vested if there is a direction to pay interest to him in the meantime; and none the less when there is a superadded direction that the trustees shall pay the whole or such part of the interest as they think fit. In the case of a class gift, however, which in terms is contingent on the donee attaining a specified age, a direction to apply the whole of the fund in the meantime for the maintenance of the class does not vest an interest in the member of the class who does not attain the specified age.[7]

1   *Re Hume, Public Trustee v Mabey*[1912] 1 Ch 693 at 699; *Price v St Hill* (1914) 33 NZLR 1096.
2   *Fox v Fox* (1875) LR 19 Eq 286 at 290. This decision has been much discussed and though doubted in some cases, has been followed or supported in *Re Turney, Turney v Turney* [1899] 2 Ch 739; *Re Campbell, Cooper v Campbell* (1919) 120 LT 562 at 564; *Re Eichardt, Brebner v O'Meara* (1905) 25 NZLR 374; *Re Levy, Cohen v Cohen* (1907) 7 SRNSW 885; *Re Usshet, Foster v Ussher* [1922] 2 Ch 321.
3   The inference is obviously excluded where the class is clearly a contingent class, with the specified age forming part of the description of the class: *Re Ricketts, Ricketts v Ricketts* (1910) 103 LT 278; *Re Hume, Public Trustee v Mabey* [1912] 1 Ch 693; *Re Harding* [1956] NZLR 482; *Re Michaels* [1958] NZLR 476.
4   In *Fox v Fox* (1875) LR 19 Eq 286, the construction in favour of vesting was aided by a gift over: see para **[93.41]** infra.
5   *Vawdry v Geddes* (1830) 1 Russ & M 203 at 207.
6   *Boreham v Bignall* (1850) 8 Hare 131.
7   *Re Mervin, Mervin v Crossman* [1891] 3 Ch 197 at 201; *Bowyer v West* (1871) 24 LT 414.

[93.39]

Where gift remains contingent. A mere discretionary power in like terms is not sufficient[1] to vest the gift, whether the donee is a class,[2] an individual,[3] or a group of persons taking not as a class,[4] and whether there is[5] or is not,[6] a direction to accumulate the income not so applied for the benefit of persons who ultimately attain a vested interest. Where the gift is a specific or general legacy, and interest is given for maintenance pending the donee arriving at a specified age, but under the provisions of the will there is no possibility of the separation of the subject-matter of the gift from the rest of the testator's estate, the inference is that the gift remains contingent.[7]

1   In *Re Turney, Turney v Turney* [1899] 2 Ch 739, a power of maintenance out of the income of an expectant share was considered to point in the direction of vesting, and in *Fox v Fox* (1875) LR 19 Eq 286, a trust for maintenance was treated as a power.

2   *Leake v Robinson* (1817) 2 Mer 363; applied in *Re Carlson* (1975) 55 DLR (3d) 616; *Marquis of Bute v Harman* (1846) 9 Beav 320 (corrected in *Southern v Wollaston* (1852) 16 Beav 166; *Re Thatcher's Trusts* (1859) 26 Beav 365; *Dewar v Brooke* (1880) 14 Ch D 529; *Re Wintle, Tucker v Wintle* [1896] 2 Ch 711; *Re Ricketts, Ricketts v Ricketts* (1910) 103 LT 278; *Re Hume, Public Trustee v Mabey* [1912] 1 Ch 693.

3   *Russell v Russell* [1903] 1 IR 168.

4   *Wilson v Knox* (1884) 13 LR Ir 349; *Re Rogers, Lloyds Bank Ltd v Lory* [1944] Ch 297, [1944] 2 All ER 1 (gift of income to mother for 'maintenance and education' of the legatee held not a gift of the entirety of the income).

5   *Pickford v Brown* (1856) 2 K & J 426; *Merry v Hill* (1869) LR 8 Eq 619; *Re Hume, Public Trustee v Mabey* [1912] 1 Ch 693.

6   *Re Wintle, Tucker v Wintle* [1896] 2 Ch 711.

7   *Re Lord Nunburnholme, Wilson v Nunburnholme* [1912] 1 Ch 489; and see *Cromek v Lumb* (1839) 3 Y & C Ex 565 at 576, where *Batsford v Kebbell* (1797) 3 Ves 363, is explained. See para **[93.32]**, n 2.

(d)   Severance from the estate

[93.40]
Separation aids vesting. The circumstance that the testator has expressly or impliedly directed the legacy fund, immediately or after any intermediate event, to be severed for the purpose of the gift from his general estate is also prima facie sufficient to show that the further postponement of enjoyment is not for the purpose of making the gift contingent.[1] It is a sufficient separation for this purpose that the trustees must properly, as a matter of book-keeping or physically, set apart the property as being property to which no one but the donee has any right to look, subject, if necessary, to the right to resort to such property to satisfy the testator's debts.[2]

1   *Saunders v Vautier* (1841) Cr & Ph 240 at 248 (a positive direction to separate the legacy from the estate and to hold it upon trust for the legatee when he attains a stated age); *Lister v Bradley* (1841) 1 Hare 10 (direction for immediate separation); *Greet v Greet* (1842) 5 Beav 123 (severance at a stated time); *Dundas v Wolfe Murray* (1863) 1 Hem & M 425 (the severance must be connected with the legacy itself); *Brennan v Brennan* [1894] 1 IR 69.

2   *Re Lord Nunburnholme, Wilson v Nunburnholme* [1912] 1 Ch 489 at 497.

(e)   Effect of gift over

[93.41]
Gifts over. The circumstances of a gift of property being followed by a gift over to another donee on a certain contingency does not, of itself and without more, prevent the first vesting in the meantime, and, although it may be called in aid of other circumstances for that purpose,[1] the effect of the gift over may be to vest the first gift,[2] though this result does not follow irrespective of other contingencies attached to the gift.[3]

1   *Skey v Barnes* (1816) 3 Mer 335 at 340; *Davies v Fisher* (1842) 5 Beav 201 at 214; *Hardcastle v Hardcastle* (1862) 1 Hem & M 405 at 412; *Re McGarrity, Ballance and Benson v M'Garrity* (1912) 46 ILT 175; *Re Campbell, Cooper v Campbell* (1919) 88 LJ Ch 239.
2   See para [93.16] supra.
3   *Malcolm v O'Callaghan* (1833) Coop *temp* Brough 73 (to daughters on their marriage with consent; give over on death under 25 or (read as 'and') before marriage without consent: held not to be vested at 25; but in *Re Thomson's Trusts* (1870) LR 11 Eq 146, where the gift over was in the event of one person surviving another or attaining 21, the gift was held to be vested at 21, and in *Re Gunning's Estate* (1884) 13 LR Ir 203, where the gift was to a person when he attained 25 with a gift over on death under 21, the gift was held vested at 21).

[93.42]

Failure to attain specified age. If a gift is made to an individual donee in terms which prima facie make it contingent on the donee attaining a specified age, and a gift over is made in the event of the donee failing to attain that age, the gift over is treated as showing that the first gift is vested,[1] and where there are indications in favour of the original gift being vested independently of the specified age, this confirms that the mere gift over does not prevent vesting.[2] If the original gift is to a class, and the gift over refers to the shares of those dying under the age, the inference is that the original gift is vested. If the gift over is to a stranger and not to other members of the class, the inference is that the person not attaining the specified age is nevertheless to take a share as a member of the class,[3] and if the gift over is an accruer clause[4] in favour of other members of the class, the inference is the same, so that the accruer clause may not be worthless.[5] In the case of a gift to a class, the gift over may show that a person not attaining the specified age is nevertheless to take, or to be treated as taking, a share as a member of the class, and that such share is given over in the specified events. Accordingly, the attainment of the specified age is not then a condition precedent to vesting.[6]

1   See para [93.16] supra.
2   *Davies v Fisher* (1842) 5 Beav 201 at 214 (gift to A for life and after his death in trust for his children as they severally attain 25 years the income to be applied during minority for maintenance with a gift over in case no child should attain 25 gives the children a vested interest); *Hardcastle v Hardcastle* (1862) 1 Hem & M 405 at 412 (a similar case but with a gift of income to such children pending the attainment of the age of 25 or dying thereunder leaving issue); *Re Baxter's Trusts* (1864) 4 New Rep 131. In *Bland v Williams* (1834) 3 My & K 411, and *Harrison v Grimwood* (1849) 12 Beav 192, a gift over on death under a specified age did not prevent vesting.
3   See Chapter 66, ante.
4   See Chapter 90.
5   *Re Edmondson's Estate* (1868) LR 5 Eq 389; *Re Gunning's Estate* (1884) 13 LR Ir 203.
6   *Berkeley v Swinburne* (1848) 16 Sim 275; *Taylor v Frobisher* (1852) 5 De G & Sm 191; *Fox v Fox* (1875) LR 19 Eq 286; *Re Turney, Turney v Turney* [1899] 2 Ch 739.

[93.43]

Gift over on parent's death without issue. Where a gift is made to the children generally of a named person at a specified age (and therefore prima facie contingently on attaining that age), a gift over on the parent dying without issue does not of itself render the gift vested without regard to the attainment of that age,[1] but in cases of gifts to a class of children surviving the parent at such an age, a similar gift over has sometimes given rise to the inference that the attainment of that age was not a condition precedent.[2]

1 *Walker v Mower* (1852) 16 Beav 365 (gift to children of A to assign to them at 21 with gift over if no child: an only child dying under 21 did not have a vested interest); *Re Wrangham's Trust* (1860) 1 Drew & Sm 358 (gift to children at 21, gift over in event of no children, gift contingent on attaining 21); *Kidman v Kidman* (1871) 40 LJ Ch 359; *Re Edwards, Jones v Jones* [1906] 1 Ch 570 (gift for children who attained 21, gift over if no such children: one child dying under 21: interest contingent; gift over did not take effect and there was an intestacy). Cf *Re Campbell, Cooper v Campbell* (1919) 88 LJ Ch 239 (where the words 'expectant share or interest' in a maintenance clause were construed as a reference to a vested share liable to be divested).

2 *Bree v Perfect* (1844) 1 Coll 128; followed in *Ingram v Suckling* (1859) 33 LTOS 89, and in *Re Bevan's Trusts* (1887) 34 Ch D 716, although the case is said to be not always accepted as correct: *Re Edwards, Jones v Jones* [1906] 1 Ch 570 at 572.

VI. LEGACIES CHARGED ON REAL PROPERTY

[93.44]

Time of vesting. Legacies, so far as they are charged on real property, prima facie[1] do not vest until the time fixed for payment,[2] and fail if the donee dies before that time, even though interest is given in the meantime.[3] If, however, the payment is clearly postponed, not for reasons personal to the donee, but for benefit of the estate,[4] or merely in order to let in a prior life or other limited interest,[5] then the legacies vest at once. This rule applies generally, whether the land is the primary or the auxiliary fund, and whether the gift is for a portion or is merely a general legacy, and whether the donee is a child or a stranger.[6]

1 This prima facie rule was rebutted in *Watkins v Cheek* (1825) 2 Sim & St 199 (express direction for vesting on death of testator); *Brown v Wooler* (1843) 2 Y & C Ch Cas 134 (time of payment fixed as 12 months after youngest legatee attained 21 but power in the discretion of devisee to pay as each legatee attained 21); *Hudson v Forster* (1841) 2 Mont D & De G 177 (request to legatee to allow legacy to remain in hands of executors until her marriage and then to be paid in instalments).

2 *Duke of Chandos v Talbot* (1731) 2 P Wms 601 at 610; *Hall v Terry* (1738) 1 Atk 502; *Davidson v Proctor* (1848) 19 LJ Ch 395; *Bolton v Bolton* (1861) 12 I Ch R 233; *Taylor v Lambert* (1876) 2 Ch D 177.

3 *Parker v Hodgson* (1861) 1 Drew & Sm 568; *Smith v Smith* (1688) 2 Vern 92; *Boycot v Cotton* (1738) 1 Atk 552 at 555.

4 *Murkin v Phillipson* (1834) 3 My & K 257; *Goulbourn v Brooks* (1837) 2 Y & C Ex 539; *Goodman v Drury* (1852) 21 LJ Ch 680; *Remnant v Hood* (1860) 2 De GF & J 396; *Evans v Scott* (1847) 1 HL Cas 43; *Haverty v Curtis* [1895] 1 IR 23 at 34.

5 *King v Withers* (1735) Cas *temp* Talb 117; *Dawson v Killet* (1781) 1 Bro CC 119; *Bayley v Bishop* (1803) 9 Ves 6; *Poole v Terry* (1831) 4 Sim 294.

6 *Duke of Chandos v Talbot* (1731) 2 P Wms 601 at 612.

VII. LEGACIES CHARGED ON MIXED FUND

[93.45]

Time of vesting. Formerly where legacies were charged on both real and personal estate, then prima facie the personal estate was applied first towards payment, and the real estate only in aid of it. The vesting of the legacies, so far as personal estate was applied towards payment was governed by the ordinary rules[1] applying to bequests of pure personal estate alone.[2] So far as it was necessary to resort to the real estate, the vesting was governed by the rules[3] applying to legacies charged on real estate alone.[4] Now, where the testator's real and personal estate have been given as a mixed fund for payment of legacies, these are, in the absence of a contrary intention, borne by the real and personal estate rateably, and it is thought that the distinction as to the part borne by the real estate is obsolete and the whole position is governed by the rules applicable to legacies payable out of personal estate.

1   See para **[93.24]** supra.
2   *Re Hudson's Minors* (1843) Drury *temp* Sug 6.
3   See para **[93.44]** supra.
4   *Duke of Chandos v Talbot* (1731) 2 P Wms 601 at 612; *Prowse v Abingdon* (1738) 1 Atk 482; *Van v Clarke* (1739) 1 Atk 510; *Parker v Hodgson* (1861) 1 Drew & Sm 568. Where the legatee died before payment, his personal representatives might be entitled so far as personal estate was concerned: *Richardson v Greese* (1743) 3 Atk 65 at 69; *Van v Clarke*.

CHAPTER 94

Perpetuities

I. PERIOD ALLOWED

[94.1]
Statement of the rule apart from statute. Every future interest in property of any kind[1] must be such that, at the time when the instrument creating it comes into operation,[2] it can be predicated that, if the estate or interest vests at all, it must necessarily vest not later than at the end of 21 years if no life in being is ascertained by the instrument or, if a life in being is ascertained by the instrument, then the period is the life of that person or of the survivor of any number of persons in being at the time the instrument comes into operation and 21 years from the dropping of that life or the life of the last survivor.[3]

1 The rule applies to all property governed by, or, in the case of dominion, or colonial property, by reference to, English law; see *Yeap Cheah Neo v Ong Cheng Neo* (1875) LR 6 PC 381. As to Crown grants, see *Cooper v Stuart* (1889) 14 App Cas 286. Execution of the will under the Wills Act 1861, now replaced by the Wills Act 1963, does not render valid a limitation infringing the rule: *Re Grassi, Stubberfield v Grassi* [1905] 1 Ch 584. The rule does not apply to immovable property in Scotland or in foreign countries or to money bequeathed to be invested in such property, limited or to be settled in a manner valid by the law of the place where the immovable property is situated although invalid by English law: *Fordyce v Bridges* (1848) 2 Ph 497.
2 In the case of a will this will be the death of the testator.
3 As to added period or periods of gestation, see para **[94.4]** infra.

[94.2]
Common law lives in being. The choice of the life in being may be quite arbitrary.[1] It is immaterial that such persons take no interest in the property[2] and are not connected with the persons having an interest therein.[3] There is no limit to their number.[4] They must all be persons[5] who are or will necessarily[6] be ascertainable and in existence or in gestation[7] at the time from which the instrument speaks[8] so that their lives are running concurrently,[9] and that, in effect there is but one life to consider, that of the longest liver of them[10] and that they must be such that the determination of their lives may be proved without difficulty.[11] Where the persons chosen are not practically ascertainable or their deaths are not ascertainable, the limitation, though theoretically within the proper limits, is void for uncertainty.[12] It has been suggested that what may have been sufficiently certain at one time may now have become uncertain.[13] In a will the persons must necessarily be persons living at the death of the testator,[14] and though no definite life is chosen, it is sufficient if the clause or gift must take effect during the life of a person living at the testator's death.[15]

1   *Caddell v Palmer* (1833) 1 Cl & Fin 372.
2   *Caddell v Palmer* (1833) 1 Cl & Fin 372; *Proctor v Bishop of Bath and Wells* (1794) 2 Hy & Bl 358.
3   *Cadell v Palmer* (1833) 1 Cl & Fin 372.
4   *Caddell v Palmer* (1833) 1 Cl & Fin 372, where there were in fact 28 lives.
5   It has been generally assumed that the lives must be human lives and if there is anything in *Re Dean, Cooper-Dean v Stevens* (1889) 41 Ch D 552, to suggest that the lives of animals may be taken, that has been generally thought to be wrong.
6   *Gooch v Gooch* (1853) 3 De GM & G 366 at 385.
7   See para **[94.4]** infra.
8   *Thellusson v Woodford* (1805) 11 Ves 112. In a will this is the testator's death.
9   *Low v Burron* (1734) 3 P Wms 262 at 265; *Gooch v Gooch* (1853) 3 De GM & G 366 at 384. As it was said in *Goring v Bickerstaff* (1662) Poll 31, 'the candles are all lighted at once'.
10 *Scatterwood v Edge* (1697) 1 Salk 229.
11 *Thellusson v Woodford* (1805) 11 Ves 112; *Re Villar, Public Trustee v Villar* [1929] 1 Ch 243; followed in *Hardabol v Perpetual Trustee Co Ltd* [1975] 1 NSWLR 221; *Re Leverhulme, Cooper v Leverhulme (No 2)* [1943] 2 All ER 274. If there is sufficient certainty at the date of the testator's death, subsequent events cannot make the limitations void.
12 *Re Viscount Exmouth, Viscount Exmouth v Praed* (1883) 23 Ch D 158; *Re Moore, Prior v Moore* [1901] 1 Ch 936 (all persons living at the death of testatrix).
13 See *Re Villar, Public Trustee v Villar* [1929] 1 Ch 243; *Re Leverhulme, Cooper v Leverhulme (No 2)* [1943] 2 All ER 274.
14 *Gooch v Gooch* (1853) 3 De GM & G 366 at 385; *Re Backhouse, Findlay v Backhouse* [1921] 2 Ch 51. They will be living for this purpose, if en ventre sa mère: *Thellusson v Woodford* (1805) 11 Ves 112; and see Chapter 73.
15 *Re Grotrian, Cox v Grotrian* [1955] Ch 501, [1955] 1 All ER 778 (gift to son if he should survive testator and the then war with Germany. This did not offend the rule because the clause must take effect in the son's lifetime).

[94.3]

The addition of twenty-one years. This period has no necessary connection with the minority of any particular person.[1] It may be denoted by the minority of any person, who may be the person in whom the interest is to vest,[2] or any other person, whether taking an interest in the property[3] or not.[4]

1   *Cadell v Palmer* (1833) 1 Cl & Fin 372.
2   *Taylor d Smith v Biddall* (1677) 2 Mod Rep 289.
3   *Massenburgh v Ash* (1684) 1 Vern 234 at 304; *Maddox v Staines* (1727) 2 P Wms 421.
4   *Beard v Westcott* (1813) 5 Taunt 393 (where the person took an interest void under the rule); *Packer v Scott* (1864) 33 Beav 511 (vesting taking effect at majority of an unborn child of a living person); *Shaw v Rhodes* (1835) 1 My & Cr 135 (when youngest grandchild of the testator attains 21).

[94.4]

The period of gestation. This does not add automatically an additional nine months to the period. In the first place the addition is made only where gestation actually exists and ends upon the birth of the child alive.[1] In the second place, it applies to the life in being as well as to the twenty-one years after that life.[2] Thus a person en ventre sa mère at the death of the testator and afterwards born alive is a life in being for the purposes of the rule, and on the other hand the period of twenty-one years can be extended to let in a person who is en ventre sa mère at the expiration of the period. This branch of the rule is not subject to the doctrine that the period of gestation is allowed only where it is for the advantage of the infant, and is applied whether or not it is for his advantage or benefit.[3]

1   *Cadell v Palmer* (1833) 1 Cl & Fin 372.
2   *Cadell v Palmer* (1833) 1 Cl & Fin 372, where it was held that two periods of gestation were allowable. It has been suggested that there may be three such periods, that of the living person, of his child, and of the donee, see *Smith v Farr* (1839) 3 Y & C Ex 328.
3   *Re Wilmer's Trusts, Moore v Wingfield* [1903] 1 Ch 874.

[94.5]
Period where no lives are chosen. In this case the period is twenty-one years and no more, for there is no allowance here for any period of gestation.[1] It also applies where all the lives chosen or indicated by the will have predeceased the testator. In certain cases, however, where terms of years exceeding twenty-one years were settled in trust and for persons in succession, whose interests under the trusts were valid with respect to the rule, provisions for recouping the beneficiaries in each case at the end of the term, out of other property for the capital value lost by not selling the term have been treated as valid.[2] Where a testatrix provided for the distribution of her estate to charity at the time when the residue was realised in the event of the legatees predeceasing her, and the legatees did predecease her, there was no infringement of the rule against perpetuities since the time when the estate was realised meant the usual completion of administration or the end of the executor's year.[3] Thus where there was a gift of the proceeds of sale of a farm, to be divided equally among a class of beneficiaries living at the date of the completion of the sale, it was held that the gift was not void for perpetuity since the sale and thus the vesting must take place within one year of the death.[4]

1   *Palmer v Holford* (1828) 4 Russ 403; *Speakman v Speakman* (1850) 8 Hare 180; *Crooke v De Vandes* (1805) 11 Ves 330. A gift over 'after the end of the present war' is void as it could not be said that the war would end within 21 years: *Re Engels, National Provincial Bank Ltd v Mayer* [1943] 1 All ER 506; *Re Miller* [1938] 2 DLR 765 (80 years).
2   *Re Gardiner, Gardiner v Smith* [1901] 1 Ch 697; *Re Hurlbatt, Hurlbatt v Hurlbatt* [1910] 2 Ch 553; but these cases are more concerned with accumulation periods: see Chapter 95.
3   *Re Petrie, Lloyds Bank Ltd v Royal National Institute for the Blind* [1962] Ch 355, [1961] 3 All ER 1067.
4   *Re Atkin's Will Trusts, National Westminster Bank Ltd v Atkins* [1974] 2 All ER 1, [1974] 1 WLR 761. Although in determining whether a gift was void for perpetuity and court had to take into account the possibility of delay in consequence of physical causes, it could not properly take into account the possibility that a breach of trust by the trustees might delay the vesting of the beneficiaries' interests beyond the perpetuity period, ibid, applying *Re Petrie, Lloyds Bank Ltd v Royal National Institute for the Blind* [1962] Ch 355, [1961] 3 All ER 1067.

[94.6]
The new statutory period. The perpetuity period stated in the above paragraphs still stands but a new period is added by the Perpetuities and Accumulations Act 1964, s 1, being such number of years not exceeding 80 as is specified in that behalf in the instrument. Thus a testator may provide in his will that for the purposes of this will the perpetuity period shall be 80 years or some shorter period which the testator may prefer.[1] As the principal reason for this enactment is to provide some certain period for the rather uncertain period known as the 'royal lives' period, it is unlikely that testators will choose any period much less than 80 years since the reason for choosing a 'royal lives' period was to ensure as long a perpetuity period as possible. This as stated above is purely an additional provision and, in the case of an ordinary will, the limit will still in

general be the attaining of the age of 21 years by grandchildren of the testator or the creator of the power.

In the case of a special power of appointment, the already existing distinction between the creation of the power and its exercise is retained by the Perpetuities and Accumulations Act 1964, s 1(2), that is to say that the exercise of a special power must be 'read back' into the instrument creating it. Thus, assuming a period of 80 years is chosen, the instrument creating the special power can specify that as the perpetuity period, but in construing the instrument exercising the power, the period of 80 years must be reckoned from the date of the instrument creating the power and not from the date of the instrument exercising it.

1   See *Re Green's Will Trusts, Fitzgerald-Hart v A-G* [1985] 3 All ER 455 where it was held that a period of 43 11/12 years had been specified within the Perpetuities and Accumulations Act 1964, s 1(1), since the disposition had unambiguously identified and made clear a period from the date of the testator's death, 1 February 1970 to 1 January 2020.

[94.7]

Rule directed to the vesting of interests. The rule is directed to ensure that interests shall vest within the period allowed by the rule, and if an interest is immediately vested or must necessarily vest within the period allowed, its validity cannot be questioned so far as this rule is concerned.[1] An interest becomes vested[2] when, first, the person or persons or corporation or body of persons to whom or to which it is limited is or are ascertained and in existence and capable of taking,[3] secondly, the quantum of the interest is ascertained, and thirdly, all other events have happened to enable the interest to come into possession at once, subject to the determination at any time of the prior interests. Where property is to be accumulated, it is sufficient if within the period there is a person in existence entitled to take the property whatever its value or amount[4] if the limitation is vested in other respects; but where the direction for accumulation is a condition precedent to the interest, and that accumulation may extend beyond the legal limits and cannot be stopped and the fund disposed of by the beneficiary, the direction is void.[5]

1   *Oddie v Brown* (1859) 4 De G & J 179 at 196; *Redington v Browne* (1893) 32 LR Ir 347.
2   As to vesting of interests, see Chapter 93.
3   That the donee is himself under disability is ignored in questions of perpetuity: *Re Earl of Stamford and Warrington, Payne v Grey* [1912] 1 Ch 343 at 355; *Ferrand v Wilson* (1845) 4 Hare 344.
4   *Oddie v Brown* (1859) 4 De G & J 179; *Re Swain, Monckton v Hands* [1905] 1 Ch 669.
5   *Curtis v Lukin* (1842) 5 Beav 147 at 154; *Smith v Cunninghame* (1884) 13 LR Ir 480.

[94.8]

Duration of limitations. So long as the interest vests in interest within the period, it is immaterial that it will extend beyond the period even though it is a limited interest.[1] Thus, a life interest may be given to an unborn person[2] or an interest until marriage,[3] or until any other event provided it must vest if at all within the period. There may thus be a limitation to a succession of unborn persons whose interests vest within the period[4] or to a number of persons for life who may be unborn at the testator's death,[5] but no limitation can be made directly to the survivor of a number of unborn persons.[6]

1   *Wainwright v Miller* [1897] 2 Ch 255.
2   *Stuart v Cockerell* (1870) 5 Ch App 713; *Hampton v Holman* (1877) 5 Ch D 183; *Re Ashforth, Sibley v Ashforth* [1905] 1 Ch 535 at 540.
3   *Re Gage, Hill v Gage* [1898] 1 Ch 498; *Re Crichton's Settlement, Sweetman v Batty* (1912) 106 LT 588.
4   *Cadell v Palmer* (1833) 1 Cl & Fin 372; *Garland v Brown* (1864) 10 LT 292; *Re Hargreaves, Midgley v Tatley* (1889) 43 Ch D 401.
5   *Williams v Teale* (1847) 6 Hare 239; *Gooch v Gooch* (1853) 3 De GM & G 366. In these cases the limitation is valid without reference to the validity of subsequent limitations (which may or may not be rendered invalid by the insertion of such a limitation); see *Hampton v Holman* (1877) 5 Ch D 183 at 188; *Re Roberts, Repington v Roberts-Gawen* (1881) 19 Ch D 520.
6   *Courtier v Oram* (1855) 21 Beav 91; *Garland v Brown* (1864) 10 LT 292; *Re Ashforth, Sibley v Ashforth* [1905] 1 Ch 535; *Whitby v Von Luedecke* [1906] 1 Ch 783; *Re Samuda's Settlement Trusts, Horne v Courtenay* [1924] 1 Ch 61; *Re Legh's Settlement Trusts, Public Trustee v Legh* [1938] Ch 39, [1937] 3 All ER 823.

[94.9]
Postponement of possession. The rule does not prescribe any limit within which interests must come into possession. It requires only that the interest shall be vested within the proper limits.[1] A limitation subsequent to an estate for life of an unborn person is not valid under the rule unless the vesting is postponed beyond the period.[2] The contingency on which the vesting is to take place must not depend on the death of an unborn tenant for life.[3]

1   *Montgomerie v Woodley* (1800) 5 Ves 522; *Dennis v Frend* (1863) 14 I Ch R 271.
2   *Evans v Walker* (1876) 3 Ch D 211; *Re Norton, Norton v Norton* [1911] 2 Ch 27; *Re Coleman, Public Trustee v Coleman* [1936] Ch 528, [1936] 2 All ER 225.
3   *Re Merrick's Trusts* (1866) LR 1 Eq 551.

II.   APPLICATION OF THE RULE: THE COMMON LAW RULES

[94.10]
Time for ascertaining the facts. In the case of a will the time for ascertaining the facts is the death of the testator.[1] After that date regard must be had, not to the events which have actually happened, but to the events which might have happened.[2] If the limitations are such that the rule might have been infringed, then the limitations fail, although in the events which have actually happened the rule has not been infringed.

1   *Vanderplank v King* (1843) 3 Hare 1; *Williams v Teale* (1847) 6 Hare 239; *Re Fane, Fane v Fane* [1913] 1 Ch 404.
2   *Re Wilmer's Trusts, Moore v Wingfield* [1903] 1 Ch 874; *Re Lowman, Devenish v Pester* [1895] 2 Ch 348; *Re Beale's Settlement, Barrett v Beales* [1905] 1 Ch 256. But not only are actual events excluded but also events which would be contrary to statute law; see *Re Gaite's Will Trust, Banks v Gaite* [1949] 1 All ER 459.

[94.11]
Admissibility of evidence. Evidence of the facts existing at the time of the testator's death are admissible on the question whether the limitations are or are not void under the rule,[1] but not evidence of what actually happened after that time, nor can the court act upon evidence of opinion or even of probability of the highest degree.[2] No evidence can be given that a woman is past child-bearing, nor does the court act upon any inference to that effect however advanced her age.[3]

1   *Re Wood, Tullett v Colville* [1894] 3 Ch 381 (distinguished in *Re Atkin's Will Trusts, National Westminster Bank Ltd v Atkins* [1974] 2 All ER 1, [1974] 1 WLR 761; see para **[94.12]**, n 1); *Re Thompson, Thompson v Thompson* [1906] 2 Ch 199. Evidence to prove a child *en ventre sa mère* at death of testator is admissible; *Storrs v Benbow* (1853) 3 De GM & G 390.

2   *Jee v Audley* (1787) 1 Cox Eq Cas 324 (refusal to assume person of 70 years of age not capable of having children. The probability of mines and quarries being worked out by a certain date will not be assumed: *Re Wood, Tullett v Colville* [1894] 3 Ch 381.

3   *Re Dawson, Johnston v Hill* (1888) 39 Ch D 155; *Rachstraw v Douglas* 1917 SC 284; *Ward v Van der Loeff* [1924] AC 653.

[94.12]
Remoteness in description of the donee. The description of the donee where he is not a living person may require him to survive a particular event or to be ascertained at the death of a particular person or class of persons, and such descriptions render the gift void as not being ascertainable within the perpetuity period.[1] If the person at whose death the donee is to be ascertained is unborn or possibly unborn, the gift is invalid.[2] Again the survivor of a class of persons which includes unborn persons cannot be a direct donee.[3] On the other hand, the limitation is valid where all the persons at the death of the survivor of whom the donee is to be ascertained are alive or en ventre sa mère.[4] So, too, a gift to an unborn person is invalid if he is to acquire some personal qualification which need not necessarily be acquired during his minority.[5]

1   *Jee v Audley* (1787) 1 Cox Eq Cas 324 (to daughters of A and B, his wife, living at the failure of C's issue); *Gooding v Read* (1853) 4 De GM & G 510 (when youngest child of A attains 25, but see now para **[94.16]** et seq); *Re Bowles, Page v Page* [1905] 1 Ch 371 (determinations of trusts); *Re Hart's Will Trusts, Public Trustee v Barclays Bank Ltd* [1950] Ch 84, [1949] 2 All ER 898 (gift to persons entitled on intestacy on determination of trusts after life interests, the decision being based on the fact that under the Administration of Estates Act 1925, s 47 (17 *Halsbury's Statutes* (4th edn) 457) the interests of persons entitled on intestacy may be contingent). A gift of a perpetual investment fund for all the lawful descendants of three named persons is void as perpetuity: *Re Compton* [1946] 1 All ER 117; compare *Re Symm's Will Trusts* [1936] 3 All ER 236.

2   *Courtier v Oram* (1855) 21 Beav 91 (to testator's grandchildren living at the death of each of his present or future grandchildren); *Gooch v Gooch* (1853) 3 De GM & G 366 (grandchildren); *Hodson v Ball* (1845) 14 Sim 558; *Lett v Randall* (1855) 3 Sm & G 83; *Buchanan v Harrison* (1861) 1 John & H 662; *Re Taylor's Trusts, Taylor v Blake* [1912] 1 IR 1 (husbands of children); *Re Bowles, Page v Page* [1905] 1 Ch 371.

3   *Courtier v Oram* (1855) 21 Beav 91; *Re Hargreaves, Midgley v Tatley* (1889) 43 Ch D 401; *Re Ashforth, Sibley v Ashforth* [1905] 1 Ch 535; *Whitby v Von Luedecke* [1906] 1 Ch 783; *Re Samuda's Settlement Trusts, Horne v Courtenay* [1924] 1 Ch 61; *Re Ramadge's Settlement, Hamilton v Ramadge* [1919] 1 IR 205.

4   *Long v Blackall* (1797) 7 Term Rep 100; *Thellusson v Woodford* (1805) 11 Ves 112; *Re Roberts, Repington v Roberts-Gawen* (1881) 19 Ch D 520.

5   *Re Gage, Hill v Gage* [1898] 1 Ch 498 (gift to unborn person on marriage).

[94.13]
Remoteness apart from the description of the donee. Apart from the description of the donee, there may be events which must happen in order to render the interest ready to come into possession at once, subject to the determination of prior interests, and which are such that they may not necessarily happen within the perpetuity period.[1] The question of uncertainty must be kept distinct from the question of remoteness. The uncertainty of the donee existing at all,[2] or the uncertainty of the other events on which the limitation is contingent happening at all, is immaterial on the question of

remoteness. If existing at all, the donee must of necessity be ascertained, and, if happening at all, the events must be such as will of necessity happen within the perpetuity period.[3]

1   *Chamberlayne v Brockett* (1872) 8 Ch App 206 at 212; *London and South Western Rly Co v Gomm* (1882) 20 Ch D 562; *Tyrrell v Naylor* (1892) 11 NZLR 118; *Re Bowen, Lloyd Phillips v Davis* [1893] 2 Ch 491 (establishment of a government system); *Re Lord Stratheden and Campbell, Alt v Lord Stratheden and Campbell* [1894] 3 Ch 265 (on appointment of next officer to a corps); *Re Wood, Tullett v Colville* [1894] 3 Ch 381; distinguished in *Re Atkin's Will Trusts, National Westminster Bank Ltd v Atkins* [1974] 2 All ER 1, [1974] 1 WLR 761 (delay owing to physical causes distinguished from the possibility of delay owing to breach of trust on the part of the trustee concerned); *Re Kingham, Kingham v Kingham* [1897] 1 IR 170; *Re Bewick, Ryle v Ryle* [1911] 1 Ch 116 (when estate clear of charges); *Re Whiteford, Whiteford v Whiteford* [1915] 1 Ch 347; *Re Peel's Release* [1921] 2 Ch 218, followed in *Re Talbot, Jubb v Sheard* [1933] Ch 895; *Re Johnson's Settlement Trusts, McClure v Johnson* [1943] Ch 341, [1943] 2 All ER 499 (recourse to capital on net income falling below a stated amount); *Re Jones, Midland Bank Executor and Trustee Co Ltd v Welldoers League* [1950] 2 All ER 239 (on realisation of foreign estate).
2   *Thellusson v Woodford* (1799) 4 Ves 227 at 309; *Smithwick v Hayden* (1887) 19 LR Ir 490 at 495.
3   *Cadell v Palmer* (1833) 1 Cl & Fin 372.

[94.14]
How far will construed to avoid perpetuity. If the words of the will are plain, their meaning is arrived at as if there was no rule against perpetuity and as if the whole intention expressed by the words could lawfully take effect, without regard to the consequences arising from the application of the rule.[1] The definition of the parties may make the rule applicable. Thus if trustees are defined to include the trustees for the time being, this will prevent a clause being limited to the lives of the present trustees.[2] Words cannot be struck out because their inclusion offends against the rule.[3] Where words are ambiguous, however, and one construction will avoid invalidity under the rule while another would render the will ineffective, the former construction may be adopted on the ground that the testator must be presumed not to intend to transgress the law,[4] but the former construction must be in accordance with the general intention of the will.[5] Where the testator has introduced in his will words such as, 'so far as the law will allow' or similar words, effect may be given to them only in the case of an ambiguous will.[6]

1   *Pearks v Moseley* (1880) 5 App Cas 714 at 719; *Hutchinson v Tottenham* [1898] 1 IR 403 at 418; *Re Wrightson, Battie-Wrightson v Thomas* [1904] 2 Ch 95; *Edwards v Edwards* [1909] AC 275 at 277; *Re Hume, Public Trustee v Mabey* [1912] 1 Ch 693; *Re Mervin, Mervin v Crossman* [1891] 3 Ch 197; *Re Ramadge's Settlement, Hamilton v Ramadge* [1919] 1 IR 205; *Re Rhodes* [1961] NZLR 65; *Re Schwartz* (1975) 59 DLR (3d) 161.
2   *Innes v Harrison* [1954] 1 All ER 884, [1954] 1 WLR 668 (where trustees were directed to distribute at such time or times as they in their discretion think fit and the trustees were defined as the trustees for the time being).
3   *Heasman v Pearse* (1871) 7 Ch App 275 at 283.
4   *Pearks v Moseley* (1880) 5 App Cas 714; *Re Turney, Turney v Turney* [1899] 2 Ch 739; *Re Deeley's Settlement, Batchelor v Russell* [1974] Ch 454, [1973] 3 All ER 1127.
5   *Martelli v Holloway* (1872) LR 5 HL 532 at 548; *Re Mortimer, Gray v Gray* [1905] 2 Ch 502; *Re Earl of Stamford and Warrington, Payne v Grey* [1912] 1 Ch 343 at 365; *Re Hume, Public Trustee v Mabey* [1912] 1 Ch 693.
6   See para **[94.15]** infra.

[94.15]

'As far as the law admits'. These and similar words have no effect in a will except in the case of executory trusts.[1] Where the gift is direct and unambiguous these words have no effect whatever, but as stated above, where the will is ambiguous, and these words are present, they aid the court to choose a construction which will render the will operative rather than void.[2] In one case an appointment on the trusts of a previous instrument or such of them as were 'capable of taking effect' took effect with the trusts excluded which would have been void under the rule.[3] Executory trusts, though subject to the rule in common with other trusts,[4] are executed by the court in such a way as to preclude the objection arising from the rule and are moulded so as to carry out the intention of the testator so far as the rules of law admit.[5] Provisions which offend against the rule are omitted,[6] modified,[7] or confined within the rule,[8] unless the creator of the trust has specifically or by necessary implication directed the inclusion of such provisions,[9] or the trust is wholly incapable of being executed so as to avoid the objection arising from the rule.[10] It follows, therefore, that in the case of executory trusts the court will in the ordinary way be prepared to give effect to a direction by a testator that the provisions of his will are to take effect only so far as the law allows or will admit. Where property is settled or directed to be settled in a particular course of succession, so far as the rules of law will admit, or with other words to the same effect, then, according to the intention shown, the qualification may refer to the quality of the property, to which the course of succession may be inapt (as in the case of personal property settled to follow real estate)—this being the ordinary sense of the words in such a case[11]—or to the length of time that the property is to be tied up, having regard to the rule against perpetuities. In the first case, no executory trust is necessarily created, nor are the interests deemed to be settled to the limits of time allowed by the rule.[12] In the second case, if the intention is that the property is to be tied up as long as possible, then an executory trust may be created, but such trust must be executed by prolonging the settlement, not to the farthest limit possible in any event under the rules, but to that convenient limit which will enable the primary purpose of the instrument to be carried out.[13] In such a case the court inclines to give life interests only to all persons, becoming entitled under the limitations, who are in existence at the date of the death of the testator creating the limitations.[14]

1   *Christie v Gosling* (1866) LR 1 HL 279; *Re Viscount Exmouth, Viscount Exmouth v Praed* (1883) 23 Ch D 158; *Portman v Viscount Portman* [1922] 2 AC 473.
2   See cases cited in n 1; and *Re Vaux, Nicholson v Vaux* [1939] Ch 465, [1938] 4 All ER 297 (power to trustees to deal with capital and income as they think best within limits prescribed by law); *Re Craig* [1955] VLR 196 (where land was not to be sold until such time or times as the law directs. Held to be a direction that the sale must take place at the end of the perpetuity period).
3   *Re Finch and Chew's Contract* [1903] 2 Ch 486.
4   *Duke of Marlborough v Earl Godolphin* (1759) 1 Eden 404; *Blackburn v Stables* (1814) 2 Ves & B 367.
5   *Christie v Gosling* (1866) LR 1 HL 279; *Re Beresford-Hope, Aldenham v Beresford-Hope* [1917] 1 Ch 287.
6   *Miles v Harford* (1879) 12 Ch D 691; distinguished in *Re Flavel's Will Trusts, Coleman v Flavel* [1969] 2 All ER 232, [1969] 1 WLR 444.
7   *Lord Dorchester v Earl Effingham* (1813) 10 Sim 587n: *Woolmore v Burrows* (1827) 1 Sim 512.

8   *Bankes v Le Despencer* (1840) 10 Sim 576; *Lyddon v Ellison* (1854) 19 Beav 565; *Shelley v Shelley* (1868) LR 6 Eq 540.

9   *Sackville-West v Viscount Holmesdale* (1870) LR 4 HL 543; compare *IRC v Williams* [1969] 3 All ER 614 ('upon such trusts as shall not impinge the rule against perpetuities'). See also *Re Earl of Coventry's Indentures, Smith v Earl of Coventry* [1974] Ch 77, [1973] 3 All ER 1, where the words 'due regard being had to the law relating to perpetuities' were ineffective to save a void appointment, since the purpose of the words was merely to remind the trustees to think carefully before exercising the powers conferred on them, rather than to cut down the period during which the power could be exercised.

10   *Tregonwell v Sydenham* (1815) 3 Dow 194.

11   *Countess of Lincoln v Duke of Newcastle* (1806) 12 Ves 218; *Christie v Gosling* (1866) LR 1 HL 279.

12   *Lord Deerhurst v Duke of St Albans* (1820) 5 Madd 232; *Re Hill, Hill v Hill* [1902] 1 Ch 807.

13   *Williams v Teale* (1847) 6 Hare 239; *Shelley v Shelley* (1868) LR 6 Eq 540; *Re Beresford-Hope, Aldenham v Beresford-Hope* [1917] 1 Ch 287; *Pole v Pole* [1924] 1 Ch 156.

14   *Woolmore v Burrows* (1827) 1 Sim 512 at 526; *Bankes v Le Despencer* (1840) 10 Sim 576; *Williams v Teale* (1847) 6 Hare 239.

III.   THE PERPETUITIES AND ACCUMULATIONS ACT 1964

[94.16]

The statutory law. The common law rules discussed above have been considerably modified by the provisions of the Perpetuities and Accumulations Act 1964 (PAA 1964),[1] which governs dispositions in instruments taking effect after 16 July 1964. The common law rules however remain important since many of the provisions of the Act are only applicable if the disposition would otherwise be void at common law.

1   33 *Halsbury's Statutes* (4th edn) 1078. See Vol 2, Part G, para **[246.59]**.

[94.17]

Wait and see. The most striking change introduced by the PAA 1964 is the abrogation of the common law rule that possible, rather than actual events, should be considered, by the introduction of a 'wait and see' rule. Where a disposition would be void at common law on the ground that the interest disposed of might not become vested until too remote a time, then the disposition shall be treated until such time (if any) as it becomes established that the vesting must occur, if at all, after the end of the perpetuity period,[1] as if the disposition were not subject to the rule against perpetuities. In other words one can wait and see whether the interest does in fact vest within the period, rather than conjecturing at the outset the most adverse possibilities. Where the wait and see provisions are applicable the perpetuity period is either the statutory number of years, by virtue of the PAA 1964, s 1, or alternatively the duration of statutory lives in being as specified in s 3(5), plus 21 years.[2]

1   PAA 1964, s 3(1); see Vol 2, Part G, para **[246.61]**.

2   PAA 1964, s 3(4). Before the PAA 1964 a limitation to a class who should be living at the death of a husband or his widow whichever should last happen, was subject to the 'unborn widow trap' and was void at common law; see *Re Frost, Frost v Frost* (1889) 43 Ch D 246; *Re Garnham, Taylor v Baker* [1916] 2 Ch 413. The PAA 1964, s 5 specifically validates such gifts.

[94.18]
Presumptions and evidence as to future parenthood. The PAA 1964 seeks to remove some of the anomalies of the common law refusal to recognise de facto limits as to the age of parenthood. The PAA 1964 introduces presumptions to the effect that a male can have a child at the age of 14 years or over, but not under that age, and that a female can have a child at the age of twelve years or over, but not under that age or over the age of 55 years; but in the case of a living person evidence may be given to show that he or she will not be able to have a child at the time in question.[1]

1   PAA 1964, s 2. These presumptions are equally applicable to adoption and legitimation: PAA 1964, s 2(4).

[94.19]
Reduction of age. A limitation by reference to the attainment by any person or persons of a specified age exceeding 21 years, where it is or becomes apparent that the disposition would be void for remoteness but it would not be so if the age specified had been 21, is to be treated for all purposes as if it had been limited to the age nearest to that age which would, if specified instead, have prevented it from being void.[1] Thus where the age specified is 25 years and the disposition would be valid if limited to 23 years, the age need only be reduced to 23 years and it is not necessary to reduce it to 21 years. Where different ages are specified in respect of different persons each age may be reduced so far as necessary to prevent remoteness.[2] Where the inclusion of potential members of class or unborn persons would under the disposition be void for remoteness, such members or persons are to be excluded.[3] Where this becomes apparent at the time the disposition is made or afterwards such members are to be excluded unless their exclusion would exhaust the class.[4] The operation of this section does not affect anything done by way of advancement or application of intermediate income before it becomes clear that the disposition is void for remoteness.[5]

1   PAA 1964, s 4(1). This section applies to dispositions taking effect after 16 July 1964. In the case of wills of a testator dying after 1925, the Law of Property Act 1925, s 163 provided for the reduction of excessive ages to 21, where to do so would validate the gift for perpetuities.
2   PAA 1964, s 4(2).
3   PAA 1964, s 4(3).
4   PAA 1964, s 4(4).
5   PAA 1964, s 4(5).

[94.20]
Condition relating to death of surviving spouse. This has already been considered.[1]

1   See Chapter 80.

IV.   CLASS GIFTS

[94.21]
The common law rules. A limitation to such members of a class as are living at an event not necessarily within the period, where the class consists partly of

possibly unborn persons, is void,[1] but a limitation to such of a class entirely composed of living persons, who survive a certain event, must vest during the lifetime of one of them, if the limitation is to take effect at all, and is accordingly valid.[2] A limitation to a class of persons answering a given description, of which any member may possibly have to be ascertained or be ascertainable for the first time at a period exceeding the time allowed by the rule, is wholly void, even as to those members of the class who are ascertainable within the period[3], since the quantum of the interest of each member is not so ascertainable.[4] The principle has been expressed as follows in a recent case:[5]

'So long as the proportions in which members of the class are to participate remain uncertain, it seems that no member of the class is to be regarded as having an interest vested in possession in any part of the subject matter, notwithstanding that it may have become clear that some member or members of the class must ultimately become entitled to at least an ascertained minimum share or shares. This is presumably on the ground that, until the precise share of the subject matter which any particular member of the class is to receive is known, what is to vest in him cannot be identified, so that there can be no vesting.'

The judge expressed some doubts about the logic of this proposition but was prepared to accept it for the purposes of his judgment.

'It follows that, until all potential participants are known to have qualified to participate, the interest of no potential participant can vest in him although he may have already qualified. On this basis, so long as any potential participant's interest may vest in possession later than the end of any appropriate perpetuity period, the whole class gift will be void.'

Where the class is defined as part of a larger class (as those of a class who attain a certain age or survive a certain event or satisfy any other condition or description), it is of no avail that the larger class is wholly ascertainable within the period, and the minimum interest of a member of the class ascertained in consequence.[6] A limitation can be well made to such of the unborn children of a living person who attain 21,[7] and this limitation may be extended to include in the class the children of any child who should die under twenty-one leaving issue at death,[8] so that their interests would arise at birth, and all shares would necessarily be ascertained within due limits of time. But this further addition of grandchildren cannot be made when the grandchildren are only to take if they attain 21, so that the condition of attaining that age is to apply to both children and grandchildren forming the composite class.[9] In this case the gift to the children cannot be severed from that to the grandchildren, nor can a limitation be made generally to children of a living person whenever born. The last limitation is valid, however, in a will where the class of children is expressly or impliedly closed at the death of the testator.[10] Where the gift is not a true class gift but what is called a gift to a group of individuals, it may be good as to those individuals ascertained within the period. Thus, a gift of a given sum of money or amount of property to each member of a class of persons where the gift to each is wholly independent of the similar gift to every other member, and can be neither augmented nor diminished whatever the number of takers may turn out to be, the gift is good as to those members of the class (or, more strictly speaking, of the group of individuals, for the gift is not a gift in the proper legal sense of that term) who are in fact ascertained within the period.[11]

1   *Jee v Audley* (1787) 1 Cox Eq Cas 324; *Palmer v Holford* (1828) 4 Russ 403; *Dodd v Wake* (1837) 8 Sim 615; *Re Harvey, Peek v Savory* (1888) 39 Ch D 289; *Re Bence, Smith v Bence* [1891] 3 Ch 242; *Re Johnson* (1963) 37 DLR (2d) 185.

2   *Lachlan v Reynolds* (1852) 9 Hare 796; *Re Watkins, James v Cordey* (1889) 37 WR 609.

3   *Jee v Audley* (1787) 1 Cox Eq Cas 324; *Leake v Robinson* (1817) 2 Mer 363; *Cattlin v Brown* (1853) 11 Hare 372; *Hancock v Watson* [1902] AC 14.

4   See previous note.

5   *Re Drummond's Settlement, Foster v Foster* [1988] 1 All ER 449, per Buckley LJ at p 453. The decision of Foster J [1986] 3 All ER 45 was reversed. No perpetuity because the daughters were lives in being at the date of the settlement and the interests in each share due to the daughters' issue, had to vest within 21 years from the death of the last surviving daughter.

6   *Smith v Smith* (1870) 5 Ch App 342; *Hale v Hale* (1876) 3 Ch D 643; *Pearks v Moseley* (1880) 5 App Cas 714.

7   *Knapping v Tomlinson* (1864) 34 LJ Ch 3. So where the gift is to children of a class of persons all ascertained at the death of the testator on attaining 21, the gift is valid: *Re Chinnery's Estate* (1877) 1 LR Ir 296; *Re Hobson's Estate, Hobson v Sharp* [1907] VLR 724. This was the limit in a will where the living person is not the testator himself, but now a period of 80 years can be used; see para **[94.6]** supra.

8   *Pearks v Moseley* (1880) 5 App Cas 714 at 719; considered in *Re Drummond's Settlement, Foster v Foster* [1988] 1 All ER 449.

9   *Seaman v Wood* (1856) 22 Beav 591; *Re Moseley's Trusts* (1879) 11 Ch D 555. See, however, *Re Gaite's Will Trusts, Banks v Gaite* [1949] 1 All ER 459.

10 *Re Watkins, James v Cordey* (1889) 37 WR 609; *Re Powell, Crossland v Holliday* [1898] 1 Ch 227; *Re Hobson's Estate, Hobson v Sharp* [1907] VLR 724 (children of named persons only intended); *Re Roberts, Repington v Roberts-Gawen* (1881) 19 Ch D 520 (class of descendants to be ascertained at death of tenant for life).

11 *Storrs v Benbow* (1853) 3 De GM & G 390; *Cattlin v Brown* (1853) 11 Hare 372; *Wilkinson v Duncan* (1861) 30 Beav 111. A characteristic gift of this kind is a gift to a class (say, nephews) of so much apiece.

[94.22]

The PAA 1964. The common law rule that 'the vice of remoteness affects the class as a whole, if it may affect an unascertained number of its members'[1] has been abrogated. The PAA 1964 enables the class in such circumstances to be split; where there is a gift to a class some members of which are ascertained within the perpetuity period but where other members of the class will not be ascertained within the period, the Act enables the gift to the void members to be severed and those takers excluded, leaving the gift to the unobjectionable class to take effect.[2]

1   Per Lord Selborne LC in *Pearks v Moseley* (1880) 5 App Cas 714 at 723.

2   PAA 1964, s 4(4); see Vol 2, Part G, para **[246.62]**. It is now necessary to approach class gifts in the following way; firstly to ascertain whether the gift is void at common law—if it is then the statutory lives in being should be identified and 'wait and see'; secondly the relevance of the age reduction provisions and the presumptions as to future parenthood should be considered; thirdly, if the gift is still invalid the offending members of the class should be excluded. At each stage the application of the class closing rules (see Chapter 66) should be considered.

[94.23]

Fund in separate shares. Where a time is fixed at which a fund is to be divided into separate shares, and that time is not obnoxious to the rule, then each share stands separate from the others, and the limitation takes effect or not according as the dispositions of that share do or do not violate the rule, and the valid gift of one share is not made void by the invalidity of the dispositions of another share or part of a share.[1]

1   *Bentinck v Duke of Portland* (1877) 7 Ch D 693 at 698; *Re Russell, Dorrell v Dorrell* [1895] 2 Ch 698; *Re Morrison's Will Trusts, Walsingham v Blathwayt* [1940] Ch 102, [1939] 4 All ER 332.

[94.24]
Substitutionary clause. Where the limitation is first of all to a class of children or other issue absolutely, who are themselves ascertainable within the rule, and a substitutionary clause is added giving the share of each one dying before distribution to a class of his or her issue not necessarily ascertainable within the rule, then, provided the substitutionary clause is separated from the first absolute gift, the latter stands good, and the substitutionary clause only fails,[1] but, if there is no absolute gift in the first place, the whole is void.[2]

1   *Goodier v Johnson* (1881) 18 Ch D 441. The substitutionary gift is valid if the issue are necessarily ascertainable within the period: *Pearks v Moseley* (1880) 5 App Cas 714 at 719. For cases where an apparent substitutionary gift was not a true substitution but merely added members to the original class, see *Re Lord's Settlement, Martins Bank Ltd v Lord* [1947] 2 All ER 685; *Re Hooper's Settlement Trusts, Bosman v Hooper* [1948] Ch 586, [1948] 2 All ER 261.
2   *Whitehead v Bennett* (1853) 1 Eq Rep 560; *Webster v Boddington* (1858) 26 Beav 128.

[94.25]
Direction for settlement. A direction for the settlement of each share is severable among the shares, and takes effect as to those members of the class living at the time when the instrument comes into operation[1] though void as to other members. There must be an absolute gift of each share in the first place.[2]

1   *Wilson v Wilson* (1858) 28 LJ Ch 95; *Re Boyd, Nield v Boyd* (1890) 63 LT 92; *Re Russell, Dorrell v Dorrell* [1895] 2 Ch 698.
2   *Lassence v Tierney* (1849) 1 Mac & G 551; *Hancock v Watson* [1902] AC 14.

[94.26]
Forfeiture clause. This is severable in the same way as a direction for settlement.[1]

1   *Hodgson v Halford* (1879) 11 Ch D 959.

[94.27]
Limitations to a series of persons. Where there is a limitation to a series of persons answering a given description, and the first member of the series intended to take is excluded by the rule, then no person whatever can take under the limitation.[1] If the first members of the series are not excluded by the rule, they make take, provided that their interests are severable.[2]

1   *Lord Dungannon v Smith* (1846) 12 Cl & Fin 546; *Cattlin v Brown* (1853) 11 Hare 372.
2   *Lord Dungannon v Smith* (1846) 12 Cl & Fin 546.

[94.28]
Alternative independent limitations. An alternative limitation expressed to take effect independently of any other limitation may take effect although the

other is void.[1] A single gift expressed to be limited contingently on one or other of two or more separate events, of which one is too remote under the rule, and the other not, may take effect on the latter contingency,[2] although void so far as it depends upon the former.

1   *Crompe v Barrow* (1799) 4 Ves 681; *Re Davey, Prisk v Mitchell* [1915] 1 Ch 837.
2   *Leake v Robinson* (1817) 2 Mer 363 at 394; *Minter v Wraith* (1842) 13 Sim 52; *Goring v Howard* (1848) 16 Sim 395; *Monypenny v Dering* (1852) 2 De GM & G 145 at 181; *Cambridge v Rous* (1858) 25 Beav 409; *Re Bowles, Page v Page* [1905] 1 Ch 371; *Earl Bandon v Moreland* [1910] 1 IR 220; *Re Davies and Kent's Contract* [1910] 2 Ch 35. But the addition of the words 'whichever shall last happen' does not always make a gift refer to only one of two events: *Re Curryer's Will Trusts, Wyly v Curryer* [1938] Ch 952, [1938] 3 All ER 574 (if one such gift is void, the decision must be delayed until it is seen which event happens before it is decided that the gift is void.).

[94.29]
Limitations valid if power exercised in a certain way. There may be an alternative independent gift to a class valid if a power of appointment is exercised in a certain way. Where there is a gift to children with power to appoint life interests to a husband or wife and an ultimate gift to grandchildren living at the determination of the prior interests, including that appointed to such husband or wife, the gift to the grandchildren is valid if the power has not been exercised, because then the class of grandchildren will be ascertained on the death of the child, that is, in due time within the rule. On the other hand the gift to the grandchildren may be invalidated if there is an appointment to a husband or wife not born in the lifetime of the testator. If, instead of a power to appoint interests to a husband or wife, life interests had been given to husband or wife, and the class of children to take had not to be ascertained until the death of the survivor of the husband and wife, the whole gift would be bad for perpetuity, and there would be no independent valid alternative gift.[1]

1   *Re Bowles, Page v Page* [1905] 1 Ch 371. See *Re Norton, Norton v Norton* [1911] 2 Ch 27; *Re Boulton's Settlement Trust, Stewart v Boulton* [1928] Ch 703.

V.   EFFECT OF GIFT BEING VOID UNDER THE RULE

[94.30]
General effect. In general an instrument takes effect as if a void limitation and all limitations dependent on it were omitted from it.[1] Where a prior limitation is defeasible by a limitation which is found to be void, it takes effect free from it and may become indefeasible,[2] but a prior limitation is not in itself affected by the failure of a limitation arising on the expiration of the prior estate.[3] In a series of limitations, every part which is valid in itself and can be separated from those parts which are void is upheld.[4] The estate or interest which is the subject of the void limitation in the case of a will devolves as in case of the failure of an interest from any other cause.[5] Every limitation on the failure, or expectant on the determination, or in defeasance, of a limitation void under the rule, is void.[6] This applies although the subsequent limitation is to a person in esse, who would otherwise take a vested interest,[7] and although such person only takes an interest for his own life.[8] In every case it is a question of construction whether the prior

contingency is expressly or impliedly imported into the subsequent limitations.[9] If it is, it is void; but if not they take effect as independent or alternative limitations and may be valid.[10] Limitations in default of appointment are thus unaffected by a void power of appointment.[11]

1   *Re Backhouse, Findlay v Backhouse* [1921] 2 Ch 51; *Re Coleman, Public Trustee v Coleman* [1936] Ch 528, [1936] 2 All ER 225.
2   *Goodier v Johnson* (1881) 18 Ch D 441; *Re Baillie, Faithful v Sydney Industrial Blind Institution* (1907) 7 SRNSW 265; *Re Tyrrell's Estate* [1907] 1 IR 292.
3   *Garland v Brown* (1864) 10 LT 292; *Re Coleman, Public Trustee v Coleman* [1936] Ch 528, [1936] 2 All ER 225; *Re Allan's Will Trusts, Curtis v Nalder* [1958] 1 All ER 401, [1958] 1 WLR 220.
4   *Gooding v Read* (1853) 4 De GM & G 510; *Congregational Union of New South Wales v Thistlethwayte* (1952) 87 CLR 375.
5   See Chaper 48.
6   *Proctor v Bishop of Bath and Wells* (1794) 2 Hy Bl 358; *Re Rhodes* [1959] NZLR 458.
7   *Monypenny v Dering* (1852) 2 De GM & G 145 at 181; *Re Thatcher's Trusts* (1859) 26 Beav 365.
8   *Monypenny v Dering* (1852) 2 De GM & G 145; *Re Norton, Norton v Norton* [1911] 2 Ch 27; *Re Hewett's Settlement, Hewett v Eldridge* [1915] 1 Ch 810.
9   *Re Abbott, Peacock v Frigout* [1893] 1 Ch 54; *Re Coleman, Public Trustee v Coleman* [1936] Ch 528, [1936] 2 All ER 225. See also n 1.
10 *Willson v Cobley* [1870] WN 46 (trust to take effect 'on failure of' a trust); *Re Davey, Prisk v Mitchell* [1915] 1 Ch 837; *Re Canning's Will Trusts, Skues v Lyon* [1936] Ch 309; *Re Mill's Declaration of Trust, Midland Bank Executor and Trustee Co Ltd v Mill* [1950] 2 All ER 292; *Re O'Brien, Prytz v Trustee, Executors and Agency Co Ltd* (1898) 24 VLR 360; *Re Hubbard's Will Trusts, Marston v Angier* [1963] Ch 275, [1962] 2 All ER 917 (accruer provision taking effect only on exhaustion of objects of the preceding trusts is dependent on them and expectant of their failure and void when the preceding trusts offend the rule against perpetuities. But a clause may be divided into two parts so that one fails, but the other is good). But in *Re Robinson's Will Trusts, Public Trustee v Gotto* [1963] 1 All ER 777, [1963] 1 WLR 628 it was held that where the accruer was to take effect on the 'failure or determination' of a prior gift it was sufficient to cover a total or partial failure on the ground of perpetuity and the accrual took effect. *Re Hubbard's Will Trusts, Marston v Angier* [1963] Ch 275, [1962] 2 All ER 917, was followed in *Re Buckton's Settlement of Trusts, Public Trustee v Midland Bank Executor and Trustee Co Ltd* [1964] Ch 497, [1964] 2 All ER 487, but see para **[94.32]** infra as to the statutory variation of these decisions so far as England and Wales are concerned.
11 *Woollaston v King* (1869) LR 8 Eq 165; *Webb v Sadler* (1873) 8 Ch App 419; *Re Coulman, Munby v Ross* (1885) 30 Ch D 186; *Re Abbott, Peacock v Frigout* [1893] 1 Ch 54.

[94.31]
Void restrictions on a valid limitation. If there is a direction to settle on trusts which fail for remoteness, the direction to settle is inoperative and may be rejected, so long as there is a good absolute gift to the person in the first instance,[1] but not where there is no such absolute gift.[2]

1   *Cooke v Cooke* (1887) 38 Ch D 202; *Re Boyd, Nield v Boyd* (1890) 63 LT 92; *Hancock v Watson* [1902] AC 14.
2   *Lassence v Tierney* (1849) 1 Mac & G 551.

[94.32]
Statutory variation. By the Perpetuities and Accumulations Act 1964, s 6, a disposition is not treated as void for remoteness by reason only that the interest disposed of is ulterior to or dependent upon an interest under a disposition which is so void, and the vesting of an interest shall not be prevented from being

accelerated on the failure of a prior interest by reason only that the failure arises because of remoteness.

VI. INTERESTS SUBJECT TO THE RULE

[94.33]
Interests in real estate. The following have been held subject to the perpetuity rule: executory devises;[1] springing and shifting uses;[2] legal contingent remainders[3] and certain rights of re-entry on breach of a condition subsequent.[4] Legal remainders in land have since 1925 taken effect as equitable interests if previously valid as legal interests.[5] A legal contingent remainder where the particular estate was limited to a person or persons in being, might be valid whatever the contingency on which it depended, though it might be invalid as an executory devise.[6] In such a case the nature of the remainder afforded a guarantee against remoteness, because the remainder, unless ready to take effect *eo instanti* on the determination of the particular estate, could never take effect at all as a remainder.[7] Where such a remainder was limited by will, however, there was a doubt whether the effect of the Land Transfer Act 1897, was to provide a sufficient estate in the personal representative to save it from the doctrine of abeyance of the seisin.[8] By statute (now repealed) a legal remainder, limited on a contingency not too remote under the rule, which would, therefore, be valid if limited as an executory devise, might take effect notwithstanding the determination of the particular estate before the contingent vested.[9]

1 *Thellusson v Woodward* (1805) 11 Ves 112; *Cadell v Palmer* (1833) 1 Cl & Fin 372.
2 *Blandford v Thackerell* (1793) 2 Ves 238; *Savill Bros Ltd v Bethell* [1902] 2 Ch 523; *Re Ramadge's Settlement, Hamiton v Ramadge* [1919] 1 IR 205.
3 *Re Frost, Frost v Frost* (1889) 43 Ch D 246; *Re Ashforth, Sibley v Ashforth* [1905] 1 Ch 535.
4 See para **[94.34]** infra.
5 Law of Property Act 1925, s 1; 37 *Halsbury's Statutes* (4th edn) 124.
6 *Jack d Westby v Fetherstone* (1829) 2 Hud & B 320; *Doe d Winter v Perratt* (1843) 9 Cl & Fin 606; *Cole v Sewell* (1848) 2 HL Cas 186; *Symes v Symes* [1896] 1 Ch 272.
7 This rule did not apply where the determination was caused by forfeiture surrender or merger.
8 See *Re Robson, Douglass v Douglass* [1916] 1 Ch 116. Though saved from failure for this reason, the limitation may yet be too remote: *Re Finch, Abbiss v Burney* (1880) 17 Ch D 211.
9 Contingent Remainders Act 1877, s 1.

[94.34]
Common law conditions. Rights of entry by a grantor or his heirs,[1] under or on breach of a common law condition subsequent, have been held to be subject to the rule, at all events in cases where the legal estate, to be defeated by the right, arises by will or the Statute of Uses.[2]

1 The difference between a condition properly so called and conditional limitation or executory devise is that, in the case of a condition, the estate reverts to the grantor or his heirs; in an executory devise, it is given over to other persons: *Re Dugdale, Dugdale v Dugdale* (1888) 38 Ch D 176 at 179. The rule applies to a shifting use.
2 *Dunn v Flood* (1883) 25 Ch D 629; *Re Da Costa, Clarke v Church of England Collegiate School of St Peter* [1912] 1 Ch 337; *Re Peel's Release* [1921] 2 Ch 218; *Re Talbot, Jubb v Sheard* [1933] Ch 895. The matter is, however, one of great difference of opinion.

[94.35]
Personal property. Executory limitations of personal property are subject to the rule.[1]

1   *Maddox v Staines* (1727) 2 P Wms 421.

[94.36]
Equitable interests. Equitable interests of all kinds, including contingent remainders of equitable interests, are subject to the rule. The mode of creation of the interest, whether by will or otherwise, is immaterial.[1]

1   *London and South Western Rly Co v Gomm* (1882) 20 Ch D 562.

[94.37]
Trusts for sale. Trusts for sale whether created before or after 1 January 1997 now become trusts of land.[1] Such trusts, like a trust for sale, under the previous law, cannot be directed to commence at a time beyond the perpetuity period,[2] but where the trust was mere machinery for effecting a division of the property between the persons entitled, the equitable interests would be given effect to as if the trust for sale had been omitted.[3]

1   Trusts of Land and Appointment of Trustees Act 1996, ss 1 and 4.
2   *Re Wood, Tullett v Colville* [1894] 3 Ch 381; *Re Davies and Kent's Contract* [1910] 2 Ch 35; *Re Bewick, Ryle v Ryle* [1911] 1 Ch 116; *Re Allott, Hanmer v Allott* [1924] 2 Ch 498.
3   *Goodier v Edmunds* [1893] 3 Ch 455; *Re Daveron, Bowen v Churchill* [1893] 3 Ch 421; *Re Appleby, Walker v Lever* [1903] 1 Ch 565. See also *Goodier v Edmunds* [1893] 3 Ch 455; *Re Appleby, Walker v Lever* [1903] 1 Ch 565; *Re Garnham, Taylor v Baker* [1916] 2 Ch 413; *Re Bewick, Ryle v Ryle* [1911] 1 Ch 116; *Re Allott, Hanmer v Allott* [1924] 2 Ch 498; *Tregonwell v Sydenham* (1815) 3 Dow 194 and *Newman v Newman* (1839) 10 Sim 51.

[94.38]
Trusts for indefinite duration. The rule does not affect validly created trusts lasting a possibly indefinite period where the interests are vested and the beneficiaries may, apart from disability, put an end to the trust,[1] but an indefinite trust where the interests may not be vested within the perpetuity period, and the trust is therefore not determinable, is subject to the rule.[2] A discretionary trust of the income of a fund for the maintenance of a class of persons, some unborn, which may possibly last longer than the period is void.[3] On the other hand, a trust of income which is not discretionary for the maintenance of the children of a living person, in equal shares, where the interest of each child is fixed, is not void even though the trust may terminate after the period.[4] A gift rendering capital inalienable for an indefinite period is void.[5]

1   See para **[95.12]** infra.
2   *Mainwaring v Baxter* (1800) 5 Ves 458; *Thomson v Shakespear* (1860) 1 De GF & J 399; *Smith v Cunninghame* (1884) 13 LR Ir 480; *Trustees, Executors and Agency Co v Bush* (1908) 28 NZLR 117.
3   *Re Blew, Blew v Gunner* [1906] 1 Ch 624, not following *Re Wise, Jackson v Parrott* [1896] 1 Ch 281; *Re Watson, Cox v Watson* (1892) 27 LJNC 174; *Re Hyne* [1958] Qd R 431.
4   *Gooding v Read* (1853) 4 De GM & G 510; *Williams v Papworth* [1900] AC 563.
5   *Re Wightwick's Will Trusts* [1950] Ch 260, [1950] 1 All ER 689 (gift of income of fund until vivisection shall be made a punishable offence void as tending to a perpetuity, and as it could not be postulated when the gift would determine a gift over to a charity also failed. See also *Re*

Mander [1950] Ch 547, [1950] 2 All ER 191 (gift to be retained until a candidate for priesthood comes forward); *Re Jones* [1950] 2 All ER 239 (capital sums to be paid when realisation of estate possible).

[94.39]

Enforcement of rentcharges. The rule does not apply to any powers or remedies for recovering or compelling the payment of an annual sum to which the Law of Property Act 1925, s 121 or 122 applies, or otherwise becoming exercisable or enforceable on the breach of any condition or other requirement relating to that sum.[1]

1   PAA 1964, s 11; see Vol 2, Part G, para **[246.68]**.

[94.40]

Possibilities of reverter, conditions subsequent, exceptions and reservations. In the case of a possibility of reverter on the determination of a determinable fee simple or a possibility of a resulting trust on the determination of any other determinable interest in property, the rule shall apply in relation to the provision causing the interest to be determinable as it would apply if that provision were expressed in the form of a condition subsequent giving rise, on the breach thereof, to a right of re-entry or an equivalent right in the case of property other than land and where the provision falls to be treated as void for remoteness the determinable interest shall become an absolute interest.[1] Where a disposition is subject to any such provision, or to any such condition subsequent or to any exception or reservation, the disposition shall be treated for the purposes of the Perpetuities and Accumulations Act 1964, as including a separate disposition of any rights arising by virtue of the provision, condition subsequent, exception or reservation.[2]

1   PAA 1964, ss 12(1), 15.
2   PAA 1964, s 12(2).

VII.   POWERS OF APPOINTMENT AND THE RULE AGAINST PERPETUITIES

[94.41]

Remoteness. Objections to the validity of a power of appointment in its creation are based on the contention either that the persons to exercise it or the time fixed for its exercise or the objects or the subject-matter of the power may not be ascertained within the time allowed by the perpetuity rule.[1] Such an objection, if well founded, is fatal to the power from the time of its creation and it can never be effectively exercised.[2] Objection based on the rule may also be taken to the disposition exercising the power, but even if such objection is found to be valid, its effect can be only that the particular disposition is void. The perpetuity period must in the case of a special power of appointment always be reckoned from the creation of the power, but in the case of a general power the period for ascertaining the validity of an exercise of the power is reckoned from the time of its exercise and not from the time of its creation.[3]

857

1   That is, the interest must vest in interest within a life or lives in being and twenty-one years and a possible period of gestation afterwards, or if it so expressly stated, within a period of not more than 80 years: PAA 1964, s 1; see Vol 2, Part G, para **[246.59]**. The gestation period is allowed only in cases where there is a gestation. This, so far as concerns wills of persons dying after 15 July 1964, is modified by the new wait and see rule.
2   The exercise of a power of appointment by will is ambulatory, until the death of the testator, and events which happen between the date of the will and the death of the testator, though in a sense subsequent, are not subsequent for this purpose.
3   See para **[94.43]** infra.

[94.42]
Perpetuities and Accumulations Act 1964. The application of the Perpetuities and Accumulations Act 1964 to powers of appointment is consistent with these rules.[1] If a special power is created by an instrument taking effect before 15 July 1964, then the common law perpetuity rules will be applicable to determine the validity of both the creation and the exercise of the power. But if the power is created by an instrument taking effect after that date then the provisions of the PAA 1964 will be applicable to both the creation and the exercise of the power. The exercise of a general power, however, will be subject to the provisions of the PAA 1964 if it is exercised in an instrument taking effect after 15 July 1964, whether created before or after that date. If the power is exercised before that date, it will be governed by the common law rules. It is accordingly necessary to differentiate between the common law rules and the provisions of the PAA 1964, and the former will be stated first.

1   PAA 1964, s 15(5); see Vol 2, Part G, para **[246.73]**.

Common law rules

[94.43]
Donees. In the case both of a general and a special power of appointment the donees of the power must be ascertainable within the perpetuity period reckoned from the time of the creation of the power.[1] A power conferred on persons living at the time of the creation of the power or on the survivor of any number of such persons[2] is valid. The donee may even be unborn at the time, so long as it is certain, as in the case of a living person, that he will be in existence and ascertainable within the proper period, at all events where the power is equivalent to absolute ownership,[3] but, if the donee will not necessarily be in existence and ascertainable within the proper period, for example if he is the survivor of a class of persons not then in existence, the power is void.[4]

1   *Re Hargreaves, Midgley v Tatley* (1889) 43 Ch D 401.
2   *Robinson v Hardcastle* (1786) 2 Bro CC 22 at 30.
3   *Bray v Hammersley* (1830) 3 Sim 513.
4   *Re Hargreaves, Midgley v Tatley* (1889) 43 Ch D 401 (the longest liver of living persons and all their children). See also *Re Legh's Settlement Trusts* [1938] Ch 39, [1937] 3 All ER 823; *Re Abbott, Peacock v Frigout* [1893] 1 Ch 54 at 60; *Attenborough v Attenborough* (1855) 1 K & J 296 (power given to trustees). See *Re De Sommery, Coelenbier v De Sommery* [1912] 2 Ch 622, where two separate powers were vested in trustees for the time being, one of which was held good and the other bad under the rule.

[94.44]
Contingency on which power is exercisable. This contingency must also be within the perpetuity period.[1] Under the common law rules, a general power of appointment conferred on an unborn person who must necessarily be in existence within the proper period, for example the child of a living person, exercisable by deed or will (but not when exercisable by will only) being equivalent to absolute ownership, is not invalid,[2] except in cases where other restrictions, such as the necessary consent of trustees, introduce an element of uncertainty which may not be resolved within the period.[3] A power exercisable only by the will of a person unborn at the date of the creation of the power is invalid, since such person could not make a valid will until he was twenty-one and the property would be tied up until his death, and, therefore, beyond the perpetuity period.[4] Where, however, the donee of such a power is alive at the creation of the power, there can be no objection on the ground of perpetuity.[5] A power which can be exercised 'at any time' is good if it can be exercised only by ascertained persons, but it is bad if it is exercisable by unascertained persons, eg unborn persons or the successors of present trustees.[6]

1 *Blight v Hartnoll* (1881) 19 Ch D 294.
2 *Bray v Hammersley* (1830) 3 Sim 513; *Re Teague's Settlement* (1870) LR 10 Eq 564; *Re Meredith's Trusts* (1876) 3 Ch D 757. In *Re Hargreaves, Midgley v Tatley* (1889) 43 Ch D 401, the donee might not be ascertained within the period. See *Re Abbott, Peacock v Frigout* [1893] 1 Ch 54.
3 *Webb v Sadler* (1873) 8 Ch App 419.
4 *Wollaston v King* (1869) LR 8 Eq 165; *Cooke v Cooke* (1887) 38 Ch D 202; *Whitby v Mitchell* (1889) 42 Ch D 494; *Hutchinson v Tottenham* [1899] 1 IR 344; *Tredennick v Tredennick* [1900] 1 IR 354. A person can now make a valid will at 18 years (Family Law Reform Act 1969, s 3(1); 50 *Halsbury's Statutes* (4th edn 613) and so, in view of the post-1964 'wait and see' provisions, such a power could not be valid.
5 *Phipson v Turner* (1838) 9 Sim 227; *Morse v Martin* (1865) 34 Beav 500; *Slark v Dakyns* (1874) 10 Ch App 35 (all cases where a special power was exercised by an appointment in favour of a child, alive at the creation of the power, for life and after his death as he should by will appoint).
6 *Re Watson's Settlement Trusts, Dawson v Reid* [1959] 2 All ER 676; *Re Bowles, Page v Page* [1905] 1 Ch 371; *Re Davies and Kent's Contract* [1910] 2 Ch 35.

[94.45]
Contingency on which appointment is to take effect. The contingency on which the appointment is to take effect must also be confined to the perpetuity period. In so far as the contingency is prescribed by the creator of the power, the period is calculated from the time of the creation of the power.[1] Thus, a power given by will to a lady unmarried at the death of the testator to appoint generally in default of her future issue taking vested interests under the previous gifts is valid,[2] but the power is not valid where the children are to take vested interests at an age greater than twenty-one.[3] A power for an unborn person to appoint so that the appointment takes effect on his death is invalid;[4] and so is a power to appoint so that the appointment takes effect on his marriage, for in such cases marriage is as uncertain as death with regard to the time when it is to take place.[5]

1 *Re Norton, Norton v Norton* [1911] 2 Ch 27.
2 It must be known within 21 years from the death of the donee of the power whether the children take under the gift to them at 21.

3   *Trustees Executors and Agency Co Ltd v Jenner* (1897) 22 VLR 584; *Re O'Brien, Prytz v Trustees, Executors and Agency Co Ltd* (1898) 24 VLR 360. Cf *Massey v Barton* (1844) 7 I Eq R 95. In England and Wales, such provisions are now to be read as if the gift vested at the nearest age which would have prevented the disposition being void: Law of Property Act 1925, s 163; see Vol 2, Part G, para **[246.41]**, as varied by the Perpetuities and Accumulations Act 1964, s 4; 33 *Halsbury's Statutes* (4th edn) 1084.
4   See cases cited in para **[94.44]**, n 5.
5   *Morgan v Gronow* (1873) LR 16 Eq 1; *Re Finch and Chew's Contract* [1903] 2 Ch 486.

[94.46]
Objects. Special powers are subject to restrictions due to the fact that the class of objects in favour of whom the power may be exercised is limited by the creator of the power. If this class is to be ascertainable on a contingency, the contingency must be one which must necessarily occur within the perpetuity period, reckoning from the date of the creation of the power.[1] The power is void if the contingency upon which the class of objects is to be ascertained is or may be beyond the perpetuity period, even although the class forms part of a larger class, every member of which must be so ascertained. The rule requires the ascertainment not only of the extreme limits of the class of persons who may take, but of the very persons who are to take.[2]

1   Eg shares in property to be taken by persons living at a certain time, such as a sale of the property. Sale to be had beyond perpetuity period: *Blight v Hartnoll* (1881) 19 Ch D 294; *Re Norton, Norton v Norton* [1911] 2 Ch 27 (gift over on death of survivor of unborn persons); *Re Bowles, Page v Page* [1905] 1 Ch 371; *Re Staveley, Dyke v Staveley* (1920) 90 LJ Ch 111 (gift over on contingency which will not necessarily happen within the period allowed by the rule).
2   *Blight v Hartnoll* (1881) 19 Ch D 294 at 300. The rule is aimed at the practical object of ascertaining who can deal with the property; and, if it is not known who are entitled to the property but only who may become entitled to it, it is practically tied up.

[94.47]
Class comprising valid and invalid objects. Where the class of objects is defined by such a description that, if any of the class exist at all, some at all events of the class must necessarily be ascertained within the proper period, although the whole class may not be, as in the case of a power to appoint to issue generally of a living person, then the power is valid, although within the terms an appointment may be made which is too remote. In such a case the only question that can arise will be as to how in fact the power has been exercised.[1] In creating such a power as last mentioned, therefore, it is not necessary to insert words limiting the objects to persons born within a particular time, or otherwise taking vested interests within the proper period;[2] the insertion of such a restriction has no influence in rendering valid an appointment, even so far as the appointees are within the restriction.[3]

1   *Griffith v Pownall* (1843) 13 Sim 393 at 396; *Slark v Dakyns* (1874) 10 Ch App 35; *Re Warren's Trusts* (1884) 26 Ch D 208; *Davy v Clarke* [1920] 1 IR 137; *Re Dowling, Thompson v Union Trustee Co of Australia Ltd* [1961] VR 615.
2   It is, however, a desirable practice to refer to the rule by way of reminder to the parties. See *Re Vaux, Nicholson v Vaux* [1939] Ch 465, [1938] 4 All ER 297.
3   *Kampf v Jones* (1837) 2 Keen 756 at 761; *Whitby v Mitchell* (1889) 42 Ch D 494 at 500; *Hutchinson v Tottenham* [1898] 1 IR 403; affd [1899] 1 IR 344.

[94.48]
Remoteness in the appointees. In the case of a general power the perpetuity period for the purpose of the exercise of the power is calculated not from the

time of the creation of the power, but from the time of its exercise, and in such a case no question can arise at the time of the creation of such a power as to any remoteness in the appointees. Indeed it is the very nature of the general power that the donee has an unfettered choice of appointees, although, of course, when he comes to exercise the power the rule will apply to his appointment; but then, in the case of a general power, the perpetuity period must be calculated not from the time of the creation of the power but from the time of its exercise.[1] This is so although the power is made exercisable by will only.[2] In order for an exercise of a general power to qualify for this fresh start for perpetuity purposes, it must be one which is equivalent to a vested interest in the subject-matter to which the power extends, in the donees thereof.[3] If it is not so equivalent, then vesting of the subject matter to which the power extends must be postponed and can only take effect, if at all, under and by virtue of an exercise of the power.[4] Thus, the distinction between general and special powers in this respect is that in the case of special powers the validity of the exercise of the power is tested by calculating the perpetuity period from the time of its creation.[5] The exercise of a special power of appointment takes effect as a selection among the objects, and as a delegated disposition by the creator of the power. The donee may not, by exercising the power, create interests which the creator of the power could not himself in like circumstances have created by some other disposition instead of creating the power.[6] In other words, while the circumstances in which the power of appointment is made are considered and taken into account, the perpetuity period is reckoned from the time of the creation of the power, and a convenient test of the validity of any appointment is to place the interests created in the place of the power itself as if the instrument creating the power and the instrument exercising it were one instrument.[7] In adopting this test the language of the appointment should neither be written literally into the instrument creating the power—for in that case contradictions of time would be introduced[8]—nor be translated into the language which the creator of the power would have used at the time of the creation to describe the appointees or to fix the times of vesting of their interests.[9] The appointment should be read into the prior instrument with reference to all its attendant circumstances at the time when it took effect.[10] It is as if the creator had left a blank in the limitations or succession of interests in the instrument creating the power and had himself at the date and in the circumstances existing when the appointment took effect filled the blank. An appointment by will is ambulatory until the death of the testator, and an appointment may be valid at the time of his death although it would have been invalid at the time he made his will.[11] This may be put in another and perhaps simpler form. If, in the circumstances existing at the death of the appointer,[12] the property is bound, under the appointment actually made, to vest absolutely within 21 years after the death of the appointor or of any other person who was in fact alive at the date of the creation of the power, the appointment will be good, although if read back into the instrument creating the power the actual appointment would then be bad.[13]

1 *Rous v Jackson* (1885) 29 Ch D 521.
2 *Rous v Jackson* (1885) 29 Ch D 521; *Re Flower, Edmonds v Edmonds* (1885) 55 LJ Ch 200; *Stuart v Babington* (1891) 27 LR Ir 551.

3   *Bray v Bree* (1834) 2 Cl & Fin 453; *Re Earl of Coventry's Indentures, Smith v Earl of Coventry* [1974] Ch 77, [1973] 3 All ER 1.

4   *Bray v Bree* (1834) 2 Cl & Fin 453; *Re Earl of Coventry's Indentures, Smith v Earl of Coventry* [1974] Ch 77, [1973] 3 All ER 1.

5   *Re Boyd, Nield v Boyd* (1890) 63 LT 92; *Tredennick v Tredennick* [1900] 1 IR 354; *Whitby v Von Luedecke* [1906] 1 Ch 783; *Re Ramadge's Settlement, Hamilton v Ramadge* [1919] 1 IR 205; *Re Samuda's Settlement Trusts, Horne v Courtenay* [1924] 1 Ch 61; *Re McLean, Bullen v Paton* [1926] VLR 21; *IRC v Williams* [1969] 3 All ER 614 (appointment void because it included person born after the date of the creation of the special power by the settlement and not saved by a clause restricting the objects to such as would not infringe the perpetuity period). Likewise, *Re Earl of Coventry's Indentures, Smith v Earl of Coventry* [1974] Ch 77, [1973] 3 All ER 1, where it was held that a joint power of appointment was, for the purposes of the rule against perpetuities, to be regarded as special and so had to be read back to the creating instrument, and was void for perpetuities, the 1964 Act not being applicable. Nor was the appointment saved by the inclusion of the clause 'due regard being had to the law relating to perpetuities' in the appointing instrument.

6   *Whitting v Whitting* (1908) 53 Sol Jo 100.

7   *Re Thompson, Thompson v Thompson* [1906] 2 Ch 199; *Re Paul, Public Trustee v Pearce* [1921] 2 Ch 1.

8   *Re Thompson, Thompson v Thompson* [1906] 2 Ch 199 at 205.

9   *Re Hallinan's Trusts* [1904] 1 IR 452.

10   *Von Brockdorff v Malcolm* (1885) 30 Ch D 172; *Re Hallinan's Trusts* [1904] 1 IR 452; *Re Thompson, Thompson v Thompson* [1906] 2 Ch 199; *White v Stamps Comr* (1908) 8 SRNSW 287. *Re Vaux, Nicholson v Vaux* [1939] Ch 465, [1938] 4 All ER 297; *Re Abrahams' Will Trusts, Caplan v Abrahams* [1969] 1 Ch 463, [1967] 2 All ER 1175; *Re Earl of Coventry's Indentures, Smith v Earl of Coventry* [1974] Ch 77, [1973] 3 All ER 1. This is commonly called 'reading back' the appointment into the prior instrument.

11   *Re Thompson, Thompson v Thompson* [1906] 2 Ch 199 at 205; *Re Fane, Fane v Fane* [1913] 1 Ch 404.

12   That is, the testator exercising the power of appointment.

13   *Re Thompson, Thompson v Thompson* [1906] 2 Ch 199; *Re Paul, Public Trustee v Pearce* [1921] 2 Ch 1; *Re Liverton* [1951] NZLR 351. For other cases illustrating the common law rules applicable to powers see *Slark v Dakyns* (1874) 10 Ch App 35; *Wollaston v King* (1869) LR 8 Eq 165; *Whitby v Mitchell* (1889) 42 Ch D 494; *Re Coulman, Munby v Ross* (1885) 30 Ch D 186; *Re Legh's Settlement Trusts, Public Trustee v Legh* [1938] Ch 39, [1937] 3 All ER 823, and cf *Re Johnson's Settlement Trusts, McClure v Johnston* [1943] Ch 341, [1943] 2 All ER 499 (power to resort to capital if income deficient); *Cooke v Cooke* (1887) 38 Ch D 202; *Re Oliphant's Trusts, Re Dixon's Will, Phillips v Phelps* (1916) 86 LJ Ch 452; *Re Staveley, Dyke v Staveley* (1920) 90 LJ Ch 111; *Morgan v Gronow* (1873) LR 16 Eq 1 at 11; *Webb v Sadler* (1873) 8 Ch App 419; *Re Abbott, Peacock v Frigout* [1893] 1 Ch 54; *Lambert v Thwaites* (1866) LR 2 Eq 151 at 155; *Re Master's Settlement, Master v Master* [1911] 1 Ch 321 (right to income pending exercise of power); *Re Bowles, Page v Page* [1905] 1 Ch 371; *Re Nash, Cook v Frederick* [1910] 1 Ch 1; *Re Edwards* (1959) 20 DLR (2d) 755.

[94.49]

'Wait and see' rule. Generally speaking at common law there was no 'wait and see' rule. The law of perpetuities dealt with possibilities and not with probabilities or actual events, as was said by Wigram V-C in *Vanderplank v King:*[1] '... it is clear that for the purpose of determining whether the whole of the class can take, I must look at the events as they existed at the death of the testator. I cannot wait for subsequent events'. But in some cases it had been held that if in the circumstances existing at the death of the appointor, the property was bound, under the appointment actually made, to vest absolutely within 21 years after the death of the appointor, or any other person who also was in fact alive at the date of the creation of the power, the appointment was good, although if read back into the instrument creating the powers the actual appointment would be bad. The last case upon this point before the PAA 1964 was *Re Paul, Public Trustee v Pearce*[2] but that was founded on cases decided as far back as 1861. In *Re Witty, Wright v Robinson,*[3] Cozens-Hardy MR said: 'The principle seems to be that you must wait and see in a case of appointment', so that at any rate in dealing with appointments under special powers there was a 'wait and see' rule before enactment of the PAA 1964.

1   (1843) 3 Hare 1 at 13.
2   [1921] 2 Ch 1.
3   [1913] 2 Ch 666.

Perpetuities and Accumulations Act 1964.

[94.50]
Application of the PAA 1964. For the purpose of the PAA 1964 a 'disposition' includes the conferring of a power of appointment and any other disposition of an interest in or right over property, and a power of appointment includes any discretionary power to transfer a beneficial interest in property without the furnishing of valuable consideration.[1] Accordingly the PAA 1964 applies to both the creation and the exercise of powers of appointment, subject to the dates of the instruments as stated at the beginning of this section.[2]

1   PAA 1964, s 15(2); see Vol 2, Part G, para **[246.73]**.
2   See para **[94.41]** supra.

[94.51]
Fixed perpetuity period. The alternative fixed perpetuity period, not exceeding 80 years, provided for by the PAA 1964 can be specified in the instrument creating a power of appointment, in which case it will govern both the creation and the exercise of the power.[1] But if not so specified it cannot be invoked for the exercise of a special power.[2]

1   See para **[94.6]** supra.
2   PAA 1964, s 1(2); see Vol 2, Part G, para **[246.59]**.

[94.52]
Special power. For the purposes of the PAA 1964 a power of appointment shall be treated as special unless, firstly, in the instrument creating the power it is expressed to be exercisable by one person only, and secondly, it could, at all times during its currency when that person is of full age and capacity, be exercised by him so as immediately to transfer to himself the whole of the interest governed by the power without the consent of any other person or compliance with any other condition,[1] not being a formal condition relating only to the mode of exercising the power: provided that for the purpose of applying the perpetuity rule to an appointment made under a power of appointment exercisable by will only the power shall be treated as general if it would have been so treated had it been exercisable by deed.[2]

1   Thus a 'joint' power of appointment would for the purposes of this section be special; *Re Earl of Coventry's Indentures, Smith v Earl of Coventry* [1974] Ch 77, [1973] 3 All ER 1.
2   PAA 1964, s 7; see Vol 2, Part G, para **[246.65]**.

[94.53]
Wait and see. Under the PAA 1964, s 3, where a disposition may be void as not becoming vested until too remote a time, it is to be treated as valid until it is established that the vesting must occur, if at all, at a time beyond the perpetuity period—that is, beyond the ordinary period of a life in being and 21 years or the special period of 80 years or less if the instrument creating the power so provides. So long as it can be so treated as valid, provisions as to advancement and application of intermediate income and so forth can be exercised and will be binding on all parties provided they are exercised before it becomes clear that the interest cannot vest within the perpetuity period.[1]

Where, in the case of a general power, the power might become exercisable within the perpetuity period, it is to be treated as valid until such time as it is certain that it cannot be exercised within the perpetuity period.[2]

Any power option or other right is to be treated as not subject to the rule against perpetuities in the case of any exercise thereof within the perpetuity period and is to be treated as invalid on the ground of perpetuity only if and so far as the power or right is not fully exercised within that period.[3]

Certain limitations are put upon the rule.[4] These concern only cases where the period is for a life and 21 years and not those where the testator has specified a definite number of years (80 or less) as the perpetuity period nor options to acquire an interest in land. These limitations concern the lives that are to be taken into account in determining the perpetuity period.

Where the person making the disposition is alive at the commencement of the perpetuity period, only the duration of his or her life is to be considered. Where there is a disposition to a person or in his favour then the life or lives to be considered are: (i) any members or potential member of a class; (ii) where conditions have to be satisfied, any person satisfying some and likely to satisfy the remainder afterwards; (iii) in the case of a special power exercisable in favour of a class any member or potential member; (iv) where the special power is exercisable in favour of one person only, that person or, if the person has to satisfy conditions, any person satisfying some of the conditions and likely to satisfy the remainder afterwards. Cases (i) to (iv) above include a person having a child or grandchild or whose children or grandchildren if subsequently born would by virtue of descent fall within these sub-paragraphs. Where a disposition is limited to take effect on the failure or determination of a prior interest, the life to be considered is the life of the person given such prior interest.[5]

1   PAA 1964, s 3(1); see Vol 2, Part G, para **[246.61]**.
2   PAA 1964, s 3(2).
3   PAA 1964, s 3(3).
4   PAA 1964, s 3(4).
5   PAA 1964, s 3(5).

CHAPTER 95

Accumulations

[95.1]
What is an accumulation. An accumulation is a setting aside of money that is to be kept intact until the end of a specified period.[1] It involves the addition of income to capital, thus increasing the estate in favour of those entitled to capital and against the interests of those entitled to income.[2] A direction that property shall not be diminished[3] or one where the money is at all times free and available for the payment of sums which become due[4] is not an accumulation.

1   *Re Robertson* [1953] 2 SCR 1 at 9. As to the effect of a power to accumulate on the previous capital transfer tax charge, see *Pearson v IRC* [1981] AC 753, [1980] 2 All ER 479.
2   *Re Earl of Berkeley, Inglis v Countess Berkeley* [1968] Ch 744, [1968] 3 All ER 364; per Harman LJ at 772; at 378.
3   Eg a direction to keep up an assurance policy: *Re Gardiner, Gardiner v Smith* [1901] 1 Ch 697.
4   Eg provision of a reserve fund: *Re Hurlbatt, Hurlbatt v Hurlbatt* [1910] 2 Ch 553; *Re Robertson* [1953] 2 SCR 1.

[95.2]
Limits of period of accumulation. For all practical purposes the restriction on accumulation is now statutory, but it is at times necessary to remember that the ordinary perpetuity rule applies to accumulation and no trust for accumulation to which the statutory provisions do not apply can be valid unless it restricts the accumulation within the perpetuity rule.[1]

1   *Harrison v Harrison* (1787) cited in *Thellusson v Woodford* (1799) 4 Ves 227 at 286, 338; *Wilson v Wilson* (1851) 1 Sim NS 288. Even this limitation, however, does not apply to accumulation for the payment of debts or incumbrances: *Lord Southampton v Marquis of Hertford* (1813) 2 Ves & B 54; *Re Earl of Stamford Warrington, Payne v Grey* [1912] 1 Ch 343 at 355. This limitation may still render a direction wholly void: see n 1, para **[95.8]** infra and the text thereto.

[95.3]
Periods under the Law of Property Act 1925. The statute[1] allows four periods during which accumulation is permitted, but the first of these does not apply to wills. The four periods are: (a) the life of the grantor or settlor, and this obviously has no application to wills; (b) a term of twenty-one years from the death of the grantor, settlor or testator; (c) the minority of respective minorities of any person or persons living or *en ventre sa mère* at the death of the grantor, settlor or testator; and (d) the minority or respective minorities only of any person or persons who, under the limitations of the instrument directing the accumulations, would for the time being, if of full age, be entitled to the income

directed to be accumulated. The periods are alternative and one only can be chosen; two or more cannot be made consecutive periods of accumulation.[2] If the testator has not by the terms of his will selected one of three periods open to him, the period applicable has to be determined by reference to the language of the will.[3]

1   Law of Property Act 1925, s 164, replacing Accumulations Act 1800; 37 *Halsbury's Statutes* (4th edn) 336. See Vol 2, Part G, para **[246.42]**. The fourth rule is applicable only where the persons would be entitled to the income and is not applicable where the intermediate income might go to persons other than those entitled to receive the capital: *Re Bourne's Settlement Trusts, Bourne v Mackay* [1946] 1 All ER 411.
2   *Re Lady's Rosslyn's Trust* (1848) 16 Sim 391; *Jagger v Jagger* (1883) 25 Ch D 729; *Re Errington, Errington-Turbutt v Errington* (1897) 76 LT 616. Any shorter period may be chosen. In the case of the fourth period, time need not begin at the death of the testator and the period applies to the minority of persons born after the testator's death: *Re Cattell, Cattell v Cattell* [1907] 1 Ch 567.
3   *Jagger v Jagger* (1883) 25 Ch D 729; *Re Watt's Will Trusts, Watt v Watt* [1936] 2 All ER 1555 at 1562; *Re Ransome's Will Trusts, Moberley v Ransome* [1957] Ch 348 at 361, [1957] 1 All ER 690 at 696.

[95.4]
Additional periods. The following additional periods are added to those specified in the Law of Property Act 1925, s 164, by the Perpetuities and Accumulations Act 1964, s 13.

(i)   A term of twenty-one years from the date of the instrument making the disposition.
(ii)   The duration of the minority or respective minorities of any person or persons in being at that date.

It is also declared the restrictions on the power to accumulate income apply whether or not there is a duty to exercise that power[1] and that they apply whether or not the power extends to income produced by the investment of income previously accumulated. References to 'minority' in these provisions now means under age 18,[2] but this change shall not invalidate any direction for accumulation in a settlement or other disposition made by a deed, will or other instrument which was made before 15 July 1969.[3]

The new rules about the presumptions as to future parenthood apply to any question as to the right of beneficiaries to put an end to accumulations of income as they apply to the questions arising on the rule against perpetuities. It will be remembered that a person or persons having the whole beneficial interest in the property being sui juris of full age and not having encumbered the property or made it subject to subsidiary trusts can always stop accumulations.[4]

1   Thus giving statutory effect to the decision in *Re Robb's Will Trusts, Marshall v Marshall* [1953] Ch 459, [1953] 1 All ER 920.
2   Family Law Reform Act 1969, s 1(2); 6 *Halsbury's Statutes* (4th edn) 121.
3   Family Law Reform Act 1969, s 1(4), and Sch 3, para 7.
4   *Saunders v Vautier* (1841) Cr & Ph 240.

[95.5]
Accumulation for purchase of land. Where the accumulation is directed wholly or partly for the purchase of land, the only period allowed is the fourth period stated above.[1] This provision does not apply to accumulations to be held

as capital money for the purposes of the Settled Land Act 1925, whether or not the accumulations are to be primarily laid out in the purchase of land.[2]

1   Law of Property Act 1925, s 166(1); 37 *Halsbury's Statutes* (4th edn) 340. See Vol 2, Part G, para **[246.44]**.
2   Law of Property Act 1925, s 166(2). These provisions do not render the whole direction void but only prohibit the accumulation of income: *Robertson's Trustees* 1933 SC 639. But note that this provision can now have much less impact since no new settlements under the Settled Land Act 1925 can be created after 1 January 1997 by virtue of the Trusts of Land and Appointment of Trustees Act 1996 (TLATA 1996), s 2(1). The TLATA 1996 makes significant amendments to the Settled Land Act 1925; see Sch 3.

[95.6]
Accumulation during minority under statute. When a statute or the general law require excess income to be accumulated during a minority, the period for which such accumulations are made is not to be taken into account in determining the periods for which accumulations are permitted under the statutory rules. Accordingly an express trust for accumulation for any other permitted period is not invalidated by reason of accumulations also having been made, as aforesaid, during such minority.[1]

1   Law of Property Act 1925, s 165; 37 *Halsbury's Statutes* (4th edn) 340. See Vol 2, Part G, para **[246.43]**; *Re Maber, Ward v Maber* [1928] Ch 88 (period of accumulations during minority not counted in ascertaining the 21-year period after testator's death).

[95.7]
Express direction for accumulation not necessary. Where the testator by any form of expression shows that he intends the whole part of the income of property to be separated from the ownership of that property so as either to form, or to be an accretion to, the capital of any fund or so as to be a postponement of and restriction on the beneficial enjoyment of the property, such expression is a sufficient direction for accumulation and an express direction to accumulate is not necessary.[1] But where annuitants have a continuing charge on income of residue and are entitled to call on the trustees to preserve income in so far as necessary to make the annuities secure, then this retention of income to protect the annuitants is not an accumulation within the Law of Property Act 1925, s 164.[2]

1   *Webb v Webb* (1840) 2 Beav 493 (direction to add dividends to capital): *Mathews v Keble* (1868) 3 Ch App 691 (to invest income to form a subsequent gift); *Re Walker, Walker v Walker* (1886) 54 LT 792 (similar gift); *Re Mason, Mason v Mason* [1891] 3 Ch 467 (similar gift); *Re Cox, Cox v Edwards* [1900] WN 89 (retain and set apart income); *Re Swain, Monckton v Hands* [1905] 1 Ch 669 (form a reserve fund); *Tench v Cheese* (1855) 6 De GM & G 453 (property given upon such contingencies that there must be accumulation for more than 21 years).
2   *Re Earl of Berkeley, Inglis v Countess of Berkeley* [1968] Ch 744, [1968] 3 All ER 364, CA, considering *Re Earle, Tucker v Donne* (1923) 131 LT 383, not following dictum of Romer LJ in *Re Coller's Deed Trusts, Coller v Coller* [1939] Ch 277 at 282, [1937] 3 All ER 292, CA; overruling *Re Robb's Will Trusts, Marshall v Marshall* [1953] Ch 459, [1953] 1 All ER 920; and *Re Nash, Miller v Allen* [1965] 1 All ER 51, [1965] 1 WLR 221.

[95.8]
Excessive direction for accumulation. Where accumulation is directed for any period longer than the statutory periods, then, if the period may exceed the

perpetuity period, the direction is entirely void;[1] but, if it does not exceed the perpetuity period, or is necessarily determinable by the beneficiaries within that period, the direction is not entirely void, but is invalid only to the extent by which it exceeds one of the four statutory periods.[2]

1   *Lord Southampton v Marquis of Hertford* (1813) 2 Ves & B 54; *Marshall v Holloway* (1820) 2 Swan 432; *Turvin v Newcome* (1856) 3 K & J 16; *Smith v Cuninghame* (1884) 13 LR Ir 480.
2   *Griffiths v Vere* (1803) 9 Ves 127; *Blease v Burgh* (1840) 2 Beav 221; *Re Lady Rosslyn's Trust* (1848) 16 Sim 391; *Re Errington, Errington-Turbutt v Errington* (1897) 76 LT 616; *Inne's Trustees v Bowen* 1920 SC 133; *Re Watt's Will Trusts, Watt v Watt* [1936] 2 All ER 1555.

[95.9]

Portions. The restrictions do not apply to provisions for raising portions for any child, children or remoter issue of the testator or any child, children or remoter issue of a person taking any interest under the will or to whom any interest is thereby limited.[1] A pecuniary legacy or annuity directed to be accumulated may be a portion.[2] A portion is not constituted by a provision directing additions of income to capital merely for the purpose of making one gift of an aggregate fund.[3] In such a case, in which the accumulation is simply to increase the amount of the fund, there is no portion where the fund is the whole estate of the testator[4] or is the residuary estate or share of a residuary estate of the testator,[5] or is a specific or general legacy to named persons.[6] An accumulated fund held for a parent for life and then for his children is not a portion, even though the eldest son is excluded;[7] nor where the fund is set apart to provide annuities for the parents and then given to the children;[8] nor where the child has only a power of appointment,[9] or only takes the interest of the fund.[10] The use of the word 'portion' is immaterial.[11]

1   Law of Property Act 1925, s 164(2); 37 *Halsbury's Statutes* (4th edn) 336, but these provisions must still not be void under the ordinary perpetuity rule. The fund must under the terms of the will be applicable for portions and it is not sufficient that trustees have a discretion so to apply it or not: *Re Bourne's Settlement Trusts, Bourne v Mackay* [1946] 1 All ER 411.
2   *Beech v Lord St Vincent* (1850) 3 De G & Sm 678; *Re Stephens, Kilby v Betts* [1904] 1 Ch 322; *Colquhoun's Trustees v Colquhoun* 1907 SC 346. A portion is a sum of money secured to a child out of property either coming from or settled upon its parents and may benefit all children including the eldest: *Re Stephens, Kilby v Betts*. The question of what is not a portion was discussed in *Re Elliott, Public Trustee v Pinder* [1918] 2 Ch 150 and in *Re Cameron* [1999] 2 All ER 924.
3   *Eyre v Marsden* (1838) 2 Keen 564; *Bourne v Buckton* (1851) 2 Sim NS 91; *Re Clulow's Trust* (1859) 1 John & H 639.
4   *Wildes v Davies* (1853) 1 Sm & G 475; *Edwards v Tuck* (1853) 3 De GM & G 40 at 57.
5   *Eyre v Marsden* (1838) 2 Keen 564; *Pride v Fookes* (1840) 2 Beav 430; *Edwards v Tuck* (1853) 3 De GM & G 40; *Mathews v Keble* (1868) 3 Ch App 691; *Cain v Watson* [1910] VLR 256; *Carroll v Perpetual Trustee Co Ltd* (1916) 22 CLR 423. But an independent fund may be given out of residue and be a portion: *Re Walker, Walker v Walker* (1886) 54 LT 792.
6   *Morgan v Morgan* (1851) 4 De G & Sm 164.
7   *Watt v Wood* (1862) 2 Drew & Sm 56.
8   *Webb v Webb* (1840) 2 Beav 493; *Drewett v Pollard* (1859) 27 Beav 196; *Re Walker, Walker v Walker* (1886) 54 LT 792; *Re Elliott, Public Trustee v Pinder* [1918] 2 Ch 150.
9   *Re Clulow's Trust* (1859) 1 John & H 639 at 646.
10 *Mackay's Trustees v Mackay* 1909 SC 139 at 143.
11 *Halford v Stains* (1849) 16 Sim 488; *Bourne v Buckton* (1851) 2 Sim NS 91.

[95.10]

Who are children, etc. The children referred to in the statute include children born after the death of the testator.[1] It is only since 1925 that the exception has been extended to issue; formerly it applied to children only.

1   *Beech v Lord St Vincent* (1850) 3 De G & Sm 678. If there is a failure of children or issue, the accumulation is void after the appropriate period: *Edwards v Tuck* (1853) 3 De GM & G 40; *Re Clulow's Trust* (1859) 1 John & H 639.

[95.11]

Parent's interest. The interest which must be taken by the parent may be any interest, however small, taken under the will in any property, not necessarily in that the income of which is to be accumulated.[1]

1   *Barrington v Liddell* (1852) 2 De GM & G 480; *Re Stephens, Kilby v Betts* [1904] 1 Ch 322.

[95.12]

Right to stop accumulations. There is a rule of law that the person or persons entitled to the whole equitable interest in the property the subject of the accumulation (being sui juris and of full age) can always stop accumulations. For this to be so, of course, there must be no charge of any kind upon the interests and none of them have been in any way settled or subjected to trusts by the beneficiary or beneficiaries.[1] Now by section 14 of the Perpetuities and Accumulations Act 1964, the provisions of section 2 of that Act relating to the presumption against child-bearing are to apply to the question of the right to stop accumulations.[2]

1   *Wharton v Masterman* [1895] AC 186; *Re Swain, Monckton v Hands* [1905] 1 Ch 669; *Re Knapp, Spreckley v A-G* [1929] 1 Ch 341.
2   See Chapter 94.

[95.13]

Invalid direction to accumulate. In this case the income for the excess period devolves as on a lapse of an interest held for the void excess and therefore, if not itself income of the residuary estate, falls into residue,[1] and forms part of the income of the residue.[2] If the direction is for the accumulating of the residuary estate or there is no residuary gift, the income for the excess period passes as on an intestacy.[3] Where accumulations of income ceased during the life of a tenant for life, it was held that the residuary gift was vested and the income was divisible between the residuary legatees living from time to time in the proportions to which they were entitled to the residue at the date of each distribution of income[4] but where a gift to a local authority was not vested, the surplus income fell into residue.[5] A direction to accumulate, even if invalid, is an expression of a contrary intention excluding the statutory powers of advancement and maintenance.[6]

1   *Re Parry, Powell v Parry* (1889) 60 LT 489; *Re Pope, Sharp v Marshall* [1901] 1 Ch 64; *Re Deloitte, Griffiths v Deloitte* [1926] Ch 56.
2   *Re Hawkins, White v White* [1916] 2 Ch 570; *Re Garside, Wragg v Garside* [1919] 1 Ch 132.
3   *Berry v Geen* [1938] AC 575; *Re Robb's Will Trusts, Marshall v Marshall* [1953] Ch 459, [1953] 1 All ER 920; *Re J Hart, Smith v Clarke* [1963] NSWR 627.

4   *Re Benor* (1963) 39 DLR (2d) 122.
5   *Re Lushington* [1964] NZLR 161.
6   *Re Erskine's Settlement Trusts, Hollis v Pigott* [1971] 1 All ER 572, [1971] 1 WLR 162.

[95.14]
Accumulation and maintenance trusts. Considerable inheritance tax advantages are conferred on accumulations and maintenance trust which satisfy the requirements of section 71 of the Inheritance Tax Act 1984.[1]

1   Previously the Finance Act 1975, Sch 5, para 15(1), as subsequently amended.

CHAPTER 96

Divesting

[96.1]
In general. The court in a doubtful case[1] leans against the divesting of vested interests,[2] and favours that construction which leads to the vesting indefeasibly of the property as early as possible.[3] In general, therefore, subject to the intention of the testator shown by the will as a whole,[4] divesting conditions are construed strictly.[5] The principle applies to the divesting not only of vested interests but also of contingent interests.[6] Where there is a gift to children of a named parent, followed by a gift over if all the children die in the lifetime of the parent, and where some but not all survive their parent, all take.[7] Where there is a prior vested gift, and then a clause divesting the gift on a specified contingency, the court does not hold the gift divested unless the precise contingency referred to occurs, and does not introduce other contingencies unless the context requires that course.[8]

1   See n 4, and text thereto.
2   *Maddison v Chapman* (1858) 4 K & J 709; *Re Wood, Moore v Bailey* (1880) 43 LT 730; *Re Roberts, Percival v Roberts* [1903] 2 Ch 200 at 204.
3   *Minors v Battison* (1876) 1 App Cas 428; *Re Teale, Teale v Teale* (1885) 53 LT 936.
4   *Lady Langdale v Briggs* (1856) 8 De GM & G 391. Shifting clauses, if not to be construed strictly, are at all events not to receive a construction which will carry them beyond the purpose for which they are introduced (1856) 8 De GM & G 391 at 429. See para **[35.39]** supra, where name and arms clauses are considered.
5   *Kiallmark v Kiallmark* (1856) 26 LJ Ch 1; *Blagrove v Bradshaw* (1858) 4 Drew 230 at 235. Where there was a gift over in the event of death before 'participating' in residue, there is no divesting where the legatee survives the testator but dies before the residue is distributed: *Re Graham's Estate* [1946] 1 DLR 357.
6   *Blagrove v Bradshaw* (1858) 4 Drew 230.
7   *Bromhead v Hunt* (1821) 2 Jac & W 459; *Gordon v Hope* (1849) 3 De G & Sm 351; *Templeman v Warrington* (1842) 13 Sim 267 (gift over, if but one child at parent's decease, to that one); *Re Firth, Loveridge v Firth* [1914] 2 Ch 386 (divesting provisions not given any further operation than is necessitated by the actual terms of the provision); *Re Stephens, Tomalin v Tomalin's Trustee* [1927] 1 Ch 1 (inclusion of child attaining 21 but dying in lifetime of the parent).
8   *Tarbuck v Tarbuck* (1835) 4 LJ Ch 129; *Cox v Parker* (1856) 22 Beav 168; *Potts v Atherton* (1859) 28 LJ Ch 486 (cases where a donee survived 21 but died before distribution); *Re Kirkbride's Trusts* (1866) LR 2 Eq 400 (death in lifetime of testator); *Re Pickworth, Snaith v Parkinson* [1899] 1 Ch 642 (gift to survivor where there was no survivor because both donees were dead); *Re Searle, Searle v Searle* [1905] WN 86; *Re Solomons' Estate* [1957] SASR 240 (proviso if son died married and before death of life tenant).

[96.2]
Gift over on death 'without leaving children'. Where there is a gift to a named person for life, and after his death to his children, either generally, or on

attaining any age, or other event,[1] in terms which give the children a vested absolute interest independently of whether the children survive their parent or not,[2] followed by a gift over if the parent dies 'without leaving children' these words are construed so as not to destroy any prior vested interest,[3] and are read as 'without having children',[4] or 'without having had children',[5] or 'without leaving children who have attained vested interests',[6] according to the context.

1   As in cases where the interests of the children are to vest at birth: *Treharne v Layton* (1875) LR 10 QB 459; *Re Bradbury, Wing v Bradbury* (1904) 73 LJ Ch 591; *Re Goldney, Re Dighton, Clarke v Dighton* (1911) 130 LT Jo 484. As to cases where their interests are to vest at 21: *Maitland v Chalie* (1822) 6 Madd 243; *Re Thompson's Trust, ex p Oliver* (1852) 5 De G & Sm 667. As to cases where their interests are to vest at 21 or marriage: *Casamajor v Strode* (1843) 8 Jur 14; or when youngest attains 21: *Kennedy v Sedgwick* (1857) 3 K & J 540; or any similar events, if only the vesting is without reference to surviving the parent: *Barkworth v Barkworth* (1906) 75 LJ Ch 754 at 756.

2   The rule is inapplicable where the interests of the children are contingent on their surviving their parents: *Bythesea v Bythesea* (1854) 23 LJ Ch 1004; *Sheffield v Kennett* (1859) 4 De G & J 593; *Re Watson's Trusts* (1870) LR 10 Eq 36. A non-exclusive power of appointment by the parent, however, does not exclude the rule: *Re Jackson's Will* (1879) 13 Ch D 189; *Barkworth v Barkworth* (1906) 75 LJ Ch 754 (gift to two daughters for life with remainder to their children as they should appoint with a provision if they died without leaving a child or no child who should attain 21); *Re Simmons, Dennison v Orman* (1902) 87 LT 594 (gift over held not to displace appointment under a power).

3   *Re Cobbold, Cobbold v Lawton* [1903] 2 Ch 299; *Chunilal Parvatishankar v Bai Samrath* (1914) 30 TLR 407; but the court has refused to apply these cases to a case where the disposition is in a settlement and in the exercise of the power of appointment in that settlement by will: *Re Milling's Settlement, Peake v Thom* [1944] Ch 263, [1944] 1 All ER 541, and in a case where the will provided that beneficiaries were not entitled to receive any part of the estate during the life of the widow: *Re Underwood Estate* (1959) 19 DLR (2d) 65. As to vesting of such remainders, see Chapter 93.

4   *Re Buckinghamshire Rly Co, Re Tookey's Trust, ex p Hooper* (1852) 1 Drew 264; *Kennedy v Sedgwick* (1857) 3 K & J 540; *White v Hill* (1867) LR 4 Eq 265; *Re Brown's Trust* (1873) LR 16 Eq 239; *Re Jackson's Will* (1879) 13 Ch D 189 (the rule is that a clear gift is not to be cut down by the words 'without leaving' if they can properly mean 'without having').

5   *Marshall v Hill* (1814) 2 M & S 608 at 615; *Bryden v Willett* (1869) LR 7 Eq 472 at 476; *Treharne v Layton* (1875) LR 10 QB 459 at 461.

6   *Re Cobbold, Cobbold v Lawton* [1903] 2 Ch 299 (now well-settled principle that, where there is a gift to A for life, and after his death to his children in terms which give the children an absolute interest in A's lifetime, followed by a gift over if 'A dies without leaving children', the word 'leaving' is so to be construed as not to destroy any prior vested interest: that is to say, 'without leaving children' should be read as 'without leaving children who have attained vested interests' and this rule of construction is not affected by the circumstance that testator knew of the existence of a child of A and that such knowledge appears on the face of the will).

[96.3]
Without leaving male issue. In a divesting clause these words are narrowly construed and mean a son of the propositus. Male issue through a female are excluded.[1]

1   *Re Forsyth* (1963) 37 DLR (2d) 379.

[96.4]
Extent of rule. This rule is not confined to a case in which the tenant for life stands in loco parentis to the donee in remainder, but extends to a case in which the tenant for life is a complete stranger,[1] and, it seems, to a case in which the children mentioned in the gift over take no interest, but there is an interest in their parent,[2] or in any one else,[3] independent of the children surviving their

parent, and where the result of reading the words in their ordinary sense would be to divest interests which, it is inferred, the testator intended to remain vested. The rule is not affected by the circumstance that the testator knew of the existence of a child of the named person, and that such knowledge appears on the face of the will itself;[4] but it is inapplicable where the context shows that the prior vested interests were intended to be destroyed in accordance with the plain meaning of the words,[5] or where the subject-matter of the gift is an annuity bequeathed so as to involve the notion of personal enjoyment by each of the successive donees.[6]

1 *Casamajor v Strode* (1843) 8 Jur 14.
2 *Re Bogle, Bogle v Yorstoun* (1898) 78 LT 457 (where the gift was to the parent for life and then to his executors and administrators contingently on his attaining 21).
3 *Re Jackson's Will* (1879) 13 Ch D 189 at 194. See, however, *Armstrong v Armstrong* (1888) 21 LR Ir 114 at 120.
4 *Re Cobbold, Cobbold v Lawton* [1903] 2 Ch 299. See n 6, para **[96.2]** supra.
5 *Re Ball, Slattery v Ball* (1888) 40 Ch D 11. See, however, *Barkworth v Barkworth* (1906) 75 LJ Ch 754 at 756, where it is suggested that this sentence should not appear in the report of *Re Ball, Slattery v Ball*, and cf *Hedges v Harpur* (1858) 3 De G & J 129 at 141; *Clay v Coles* (1887) 57 LT 682 at 683; *Re Hamlet, Stephen v Cunningham* (1888) 39 Ch D 426. Therefore the rule does not generally apply to a gift to a person absolutely followed by a gift over on his death without leaving issue: *Armstrong v Armstrong* (1888) 21 LR Ir 114; *Re Ball, Slattery v Ball*, disapproving *White v Hight* (1879) 12 Ch D 751. See also *Hambleton, Hamilton v Hambleton* [1884] WN 157, and *Re Bogle, Bogle v Yorstoun* (1898) 78 LT 457.
6 *Re Hemingway, James v Dawson* (1890) 45 Ch D 453 at 456.

[96.5]
Change of 'or' into 'and' and vice versa. This has already been considered.[1]

1 See Chapter 56.

[96.6]
Survivorship clauses. These are considered elsewhere.[1]

1 See Chapter 67.

[96.7]
Time of operation. The time of operation of a divesting provision may be limited by the context,[1] for example, by a direction for payment, transfer, or conveyance to the donee, or for the doing of any such act on any specified event. Subject to such a clause, a divesting clause operates when the contingency happens on which it is to take effect.[2] The court considers that the trustees or executors could not conveniently obey such a direction if divesting were intended to take place after that event.[3]

1 *Vulliamy v Huskisson* (1838) 3 Y & C Ex 80 (vested at 21: clause settling gift on donee's marriage held confined to marriage under 21); *Lloyd v Davies* (1854) 15 CB 76.
2 *Witham v Witham* (1861) 3 De GF & J 758. The following gifts over are considered infra: gift over the event of death, gift over on death with contingencies, limitations on failure of issue, gift over or forfeiture on alienation, see the next Chapter.
3 *Woodburne v Woodburne* (1850) 3 De G & Sm 643; *Glyn v Glyn* (1857) 26 LJ Ch 409; *O'Mahoney v Burdett* (1874) LR 7 HL 388; *Re Luddy, Peard v Morton* (1883) 25 Ch D 394; *Re Kerr's Estate* [1913] 1 IR 214. This indication of intention may be overborne: *Martineau v Rogers* (1856) 8 De GM & G 328 at 333.

CHAPTER 97

Gift over on death

I. GIFT OVER ON DEATH SIMPLY

[97.1]

Absolute gift. A gift over of property, given to a person absolutely, in the event of his death is construed as a gift over in the event of his death before the period of distribution or vesting, unless some other period is indicated by the context.[1] If, therefore, the gift is immediate, and there is a gift over in case of the donee's death, as a contingency, the gift over takes effect only in the case of the donee dying in the lifetime of the testator, as an alternative gift,[2] and, if the gift is postponed to a life interest, the gift over prima facie takes effect only on the death before the tenant for life, as an alternative gift,[3] or, if the context so requires, the gift over may be construed as referring to death before vesting.[4]

1   *Penny v Railways Comr* [1900] AC 628 at 634; *Hodgson v Smithson* (1856) 8 De GM & G 604; *O'Mahoney v Burdett* (1874) LR 7 HL 388 at 395. The rule is based on the ground that death is so inevitable that it cannot be deemed a contingency, and therefore the testator could not have intended merely to provide for the case of the donee dying at any time. It is also based on the presumption in favour of vesting: *Home v Pillans* (1833) 2 My & K 15 at 20, but where the gift over was subject to his predeceasing a named person the gift over took effect: *Re Tyrrell* [1959] OR 248.
2   *Gee v Manchester Corpn* (1852) 17 QB 737; *Crigan v Bains* (1834) 7 Sim 40; *Clarke v Lubbock* (1842) 1 Y & C Ch Cas 492; *Howard v Howard* (1856) 21 Beav 550; *Taylor v Stainton* (1856) 2 Jur NS 634; *Re Neary's Estate* (1881) 7 LR Ir 311; *Elliott v Smith* (1882) 22 Ch D 236; *Re Valdez's Trusts* (1888) 40 Ch D 159; *Re Reeves, Edwards v Reeves-Hughes* (1907) 51 Sol Jo 325; *Re Fisher, Robinson v Eardley* [1915] 1 Ch 302; *Dilnot v Hinkley* (1888) 14 VLR 702; *Re Hall's Estate* [1944] IR 54.
3   *Hervey v M'Laughlin* (1815) 1 Price 264; *Galland v Leonard* (1818) 1 Swan 161; *Green v Barrow* (1853) 10 Hare 459; *Bolitho v Hillyar* (1865) 34 Beav 180.
4   *Penny v Railways Comr* [1900] AC 628; *Re Kerr's Estate* [1913] 1 IR 214. It may on occasion have the effect of giving the first taker a life interest only: see Chapter 83.

[97.2]

Life interest. Where the first donee takes only a life interest, or the second donee takes in succession to the first, the second donee then takes on the death of the first donee at any time.[1] A gift to one person in the event of the death of another is treated as a gift in remainder or succession only when the first taker takes for life only,[2] but many gifts on the face of them absolute are construed as life interests.[3] Death is regarded as a contingency only from necessity and where the words import no other contingency.[4]

1   *Lord Douglas v Chalmer* (1795) 2 Ves 501 (gift to the use of A and in case of her decease to the use of her children is a life interest to A and capital to her children on her decease); *Nowlan v*

Nelligan (1785) 1 Bro CC 489 (gift to wife, but in case of her death testator desired his executors to take care of his daughter); *Smart v Clark* (1827) 3 Russ 365 ('if he should die' construed as 'when he should die'); *Tilson v Jones* (1830) 1 Russ & M 553 (meaning of 'in case of death' depends on context); *Jones v Morris* (1922) 91 LJ Ch 495 (after life estate to wife gift to daughter then a widow, but in case of her death or second marriage or cohabitation with any man, then over: daughter took only life interest). These matters are all matters of construction and the weight to be given to various matters is considered in *Taylor v Stainton* (1856) 2 Jur NS 634, where a gift to a married woman for her own proper use and benefit and in case he should die for her children was held to give her an absolute interest in the first instance which was not cut down by the following provisions. There is no general rule that a prior gift is always cut down to a life interest by a gift over after the death of the first taker: *Re Lady Monck's Will, Monck v Croker* [1900] 1 IR 56 at 66.

2   *Penny v Railways Comr* [1900] AC 628 at 635.
3   See n 2.
4   *Woodroofe v Woodroofe* [1894] 1 IR 299 at 302; *Gawler v Cadby* (1821) Jac 346 at 348. As to death coupled with a contingency, see para **[97.4]** infra.

[97.3]
Gift at the death of prior donee. In a gift to one donee indefinitely followed by a gift at the death of that donee or after his death, the gift over prima facie takes effect at death, not as on a contingent event, by way of succession, and the first donee takes a life interest only.[1]

1   *Joslin v Hammond* (1834) 3 My & K 110; *Constable v Bull* (1849) 3 De G & Sm 411; *Re Adam's Trusts* (1865) 13 LT 347; *Waters v Waters* (1857) 26 LJ Ch 624; *Bibbens v Potter* (1879) 10 Ch D 733; *Re Russell* (1885) 52 LT 559. Cf with the cases cited in Chapter 89.

II.   ON DEATH WITH CONTINGENCIES

[97.4]
Contingency happening in testator's lifetime. Whenever there is an interest validly limited by will, either by way of remainder, or by way of executory interest and all the preceding estates have failed or determined, and the events on which the interest is limited have taken effect, it is in general immaterial whether this has happened in the lifetime of the testator or after his decease.[1] Thus, in the case of a gift over on a prior named individual donee dying in any contingent circumstances,[2] or dying before any specified event,[3] the gift over as a rule takes effect if the prior donee so dies in the lifetime of the testator.[4] A gift on a prior donee dying without having attained a vested interest takes effect if that prior donee dies in the lifetime of the testator, although he otherwise satisfies the conditions of the prior gift.[5] The will, however, on its true construction may refer only to events taking place after the death of the testator, or other time.[6]

1   *Varley v Winn* (1856) 2 K & J 700 at 705.
2   Examples are: gift over on death under 21 and the prior donee dies under 21 in the lifetime of the testator: *Ledsome v Hickman* (1708) 2 Vern 611; *Perkins v Micklethwaite* (1714) 1 P Wms 274 (death before 21 or marriage); *Willing v Baine* (1731) 3 P Wms 113; gift over on death without issue: *Mackinnon v Peach* (1838) 2 Keen 555 at 560; *Varley v Winn* (1856) 2 K & J 700 (gift over on death without issue who become entitled under an intermediate gift); *Rackham v De La Mare* (1864) 2 De GJ & Sm 74 (gift to daughter for life and then for her children with accruer clause to other daughters and their children: share of daughter dying without issue in testator's lifetime does not lapse but accrues to the other shares). Another example is a gift over on death leaving issue: *Rheeder v Ower* (1791) 3 Bro CC 240 (gift to sisters and if any died

leaving issue to such issue at 21. One sister died in the lifetime of the testator leaving issue and it was held that the issue took and there was no lapse).

3   Examples are: gift over death before payment: *Ive v King* (1852) 16 Beav 46; gift over on death before division of estate: *Bretton v Lethulier* (1710) 2 Vern 653; gift over on death before legacy becomes payable: *Darrel v Molesworth* (1700) 2 Vern 378; *Walker v Main* (1819) 1 Jac & W 1; *Humphreys v Howes* (1830) 1 Russ & M 639.

4   The effect of the failure of an interest is considered in Chapter 48.

5   *Re Gaitskell's Trust* (1873) LR 15 Eq 386 (legacy on attaining 21 or on death under that age leaving issue and in case of death without attaining vested interest over. Legatee died in testator's lifetime after attaining 21. The gift over took effect).

6   *Chapman v Perkins* [1905] AC 106; *Smith v Stewart* (1851) 4 De G & Sm 253.

[97.5]

Apart from context. Where the gift over is on death coupled with some contingency, such as on the death of the donee without leaving issue, or without leaving issue living at the time of his death, then prima facie the gift over takes effect on the death of the donee at any time and not merely on his death before the date of distribution, if the rest of the contingency is fulfilled at his death.[1] No difference is made by the fact that the donees under the gift over are children of the first taker,[2] and the rule is the same as to real and personal estate,[3] and whether there is a previous life interest[4] or not.[5]

1   *Ingram v Soutten* (1874) LR 7 HL 408 (dying without issue living at his death); *O'Mahoney v Burdett* (1874) LR 7 HL 388 (dying unmarried and without children); *Woodroofe v Woodroofe* [1894] 1 IR 299; *Re Richardson's Trusts* [1896] 1 IR 295; *Re Schnadhorst, Sandkuhl v Schnadhorst* [1902] 2 Ch 234 (gift over of shares of class dying leaving issue); *Duffill v Duffill* [1903] AC 491 (dying without leaving issue); *Smith v Stewart* (1851) 4 De G & Sm 253 (dying with issue where death in testator's lifetime was excluded); *Smith v Spencer* (1856) 6 De GM & G 631 (gift over on beneficiary dying under 21 without issue, but the gift was also given by reference to the trusts of other property as to which there was a gift over on death without issue: held the gift over took effect as a divesting on death without issue after attaining 21); *Drake v Collins* (1869) 20 LT 970 (gift defeasible in event of death without children); *Re Parry and Daggs* (1885) 31 Ch D 130 (gift of land defeasible on death without issue at any time and gift over held void); *Re Williams' Will Trusts, Rees v Williams* [1949] 2 All ER 11 (if daughter die without issue her surviving, her share to devolve on her own children 'then' surviving and the issue of such as may be 'then' dead: held to refer to death of daughter at any time and not confined to death in the lifetime of the tenant for life); *Re Gleeson, Gleeson v Gleeson* [1910] VLR 181; *Re Farrell* [1953] NZLR 147; *Re Holt Will* [1952] 3 DLR 426 (not returning from overseas and in the event of his death).

2   *Home v Pillans* (1833) 2 My & K 15 at 22; *Re Schnadhorst, Sandkuhl v Schnadhorst* [1901] 2 Ch 338 at 343. The general rule applies to the contingency of death leaving issue: *Johnstone v Antrobus* (1856) 21 Beav 556; *Bowers v Bowers* (1870) 5 Ch App 244; *Re Stuckey, Executor, Trustee and Agency Co of South Australia Ltd v Stuckey* [1915] SALR 190.

3   *Slaney v Slaney* (1864) 33 Beav 631.

4   In *Edwards v Edwards* (1852) 15 Beav 357, four so-called rules were enunciated for the following four classes of gifts: (1) to A and if he shall die to B; (2) to A and if he shall die without children to B; (3) to X for life with remainder to A and if he shall die to B; (4) to X for life with remainder to A and if he shall die without leaving children to B. It was stated that in (1) the contingency has reference to the death of the testator; in (2) to the death of A and in (3) and (4) to the death of X the tenant for life. The fourth rule has been much criticised and was disapproved in *O'Mahoney v Burdett* (1874) LR 7 HL 388. In the following cases where the rule was followed it may be that the decisions can be supported on the contexts of the wills in question: *Beckton v Barton* (1859) 27 Beav 99; *Slaney v Slaney* (1864) 33 Beav 631; *Wood v Wood* (1866) 35 Beav 587.

5   *Child v Giblett* (1834) 3 My & K 71; *Smith v Stewart* (1851) 4 De G & Sm 253; *Edwards v Edwards* (1852) 15 Beav 357 at 363; *Cotton v Cotton* (1854) 23 LJ Ch 489; *Randfield v Randfield* (1860) 8 HL Cas 225; *Bowers v Bowers* (1870) 5 Ch App 244.

[97.6]

Exclusion by context. On the context of the will, however, the contingency may be confined to a death during the lifetime of the tenant for life,[1] or during the lifetime of the testator,[2] or before distribution, or some other event.[3] In particular, it may appear that the gift over is not an executory limitation defeating the prior gift at any time, but a substantial gift, and the death with a contingency is confined to the period within which substitution takes place,[4] or there may be alternative gifts over, whether the death takes place with or without a failure of issue or other contingent event.[5]

1 *Besant v Cox* (1877) 6 Ch D 604 (gift over to survivors of a class leaving issue), following *Olivant v Wright* (1875) 1 Ch D 346 (a direction after the death of the tenant for life to divide the property is a sufficient indication of a contrary intention in the will to take the case out of the rule established by *O'Mahoney v Burdett* (1874) LR 7 HL 388, and *Ingram v Soutten* (1874) LR 7 HL 408); *McCormick v Simpson* [1907] AC 494 ('in case of death without such male issue as aforesaid' construed to mean death before the death of the tenant for life); *Re Mitchell, Mitchell v Mitchell* (1913) 108 LT 180 (construction of whole will pointed to death of tenant for life); *Re Roberts, Roberts v Morgan* [1916] 2 Ch 42 (similar case); *Christian v Taylor* [1926] AC 773. *Besant v Cox* (1877) 6 Ch D 604 and *Re Smaling, Johnston v Smaling* (1877) 37 LT 392, may be thought to be of doubtful authority: *Woodroofe v Woodroofe* [1894] 1 IR 299.
2 *Re Luddy, Peard v Morton* (1883) 25 Ch D 394.
3 *Clark v Henry* (1871) 6 Ch App 588; *Brotherton v Bury* (1853) 18 Beav 65; *Hordern v Hordern* [1909] AC 210 at 216. Where on a particular event the fund is directed to be divided, or the receipt of the donee is directed to be a good discharge, the death without issue is confined to the period prior to division or payment, for otherwise the direction could not be carried out: *Galland v Leonard* (1818) 1 Swan 161; *Baker v Cocks* (1843) 6 Beav 82; *Wheable v Withers* (1849) 16 Sim 505; *Johnston v Antrobus* (1856) 21 Beav 556; *Re Anstice* (1856) 23 Beav 135; *O'Mahoney v Burdett* (1874) LR 7 HL 388 at 403; *Lewin v Killey* (1888) 13 App Cas 783; *Re Mackinlay, Scrimgeour v Mackinlay* (1911) 56 Sol Jo 142; *Re Mitchell, Mitchell v Mitchell* (1913) 108 LT 180.
4 *Re Hayward, Creery v Lingwood* (1882) 19 Ch D 470. As to substitutional gifts, see Chapter 68, ante. If the substitutionary gift fails, the original gift remains vested, see *Re Rooke's Will Trusts, Taylor v Rooke* [1953] Ch 716, [1953] 2 All ER 110.
5 *Clayton v Lowe* (1822) 5 B & Ald 636 (gifts over both on death without children and on death leaving children); *Gee v Manchester Corpn* (1852) 17 QB 737 at 745. The reason given for the decision in these cases (namely, that the addition of all the contingencies amounted to a certainty) was dissented from in *Cooper v Cooper* (1855) 1 K & J 658 at 662; *Bowers v Bowers* (1870) 5 Ch App 244 at 248, and in *Gosling v Townsend* (1853) 22 LTOS 125, but it seems to have been approved in *O'Mahoney v Burdett* (1874) LR 7 HL 388 at 397. See also *Galland v Leonard* (1818) 1 Swan 161; *Woodburne v Woodburne* (1853) 23 LJ Ch 336; *Re Brailsford, Holmes v Crompton and Evans' Union Bank* [1916] 2 Ch 536; *Re Colles' Estate* [1918] 1 IR 1.

[97.7]

Gift over on death before payment. A gift over can be well made, as a rule, on the donee dying before he actually receives his legacy or on his becoming disentitled to receive it before actual payment. Such a gift may be expressed so as not to be void for uncertainty,[1] at all events in the case of non-residuary gifts,[2] or in the case of any gift where the gift over is of the part of the property which has not been received.[3] Such a gift over, or a gift over before execution of all or any of the trusts of the will,[4] in the case of a residuary gift, and applying to the whole fund, whether paid over to the donee or not, may, as it stands in a particular will, be void for uncertainty.[5] The court, however, inclines to construe such gifts over so that the period over which the operation of the gift over is to extend shall not continue beyond the time at which the legacy is by law receivable,[6] that is, in general, where the gift is not otherwise postponed, at a year from the death of the testator,[7] and in other cases at the death of the tenant for life or other period of distribution.[8]

1   *Johnson v Crook* (1879) 12 Ch D 639, approved in *Re Chaston, Chaston v Seago* (1881) 18 Ch D 218; *Re Wilkins, Spencer v Duckworth* (1881) 18 Ch D 634; *Re Goulder, Goulder v Goulder* [1905] 2 Ch 100, disapproving *Martin v Martin* (1866) LR 2 Eq 404.
2   *Whitman v Aitken* (1866) LR 2 Eq 414; *Re Kenny, Read v Isaacs* [1921] NZLR 537.
3   *Re Chaston, Chaston v Seago* (1881) 18 Ch D 218; *Re Goulder, Goulder v Goulder* [1905] 2 Ch 100.
4   A gift over on death during the continuance of the trusts was held valid in case of a specific gift in *Re Teale, Teale v Teale* (1885) 53 LT 936.
5   *Hutcheon v Mannington* (1791) 1 Ves 366 (although on the construction adopted the gift over was on death the gift was receivable) see *Johnston v Crook* (1879) 12 Ch D 639; *Martin v Martin* (1866) LR 2 Eq 404; *Bubb v Padwick* (1880) 13 Ch D 517; *Minors v Battison* (1876) 1 App Cas 428 (accepting *Bubb v Padwick*, and *Martin v Martin*, as authorities on this point); *Roberts v Youle* (1880) 49 LJ Ch 744; *Re Hudson* [1912] VLR 140. There is no objection to postponing the vesting of a residuary gift until actual receipt: *Gaskell v Harman* (1805) 11 Ves 489 at 497 (explaining *Hutcheon v Mannington* (1791) 1 Ves 366), and there appears to be no reason for a different rule in the case of the postponement of divesting if the intention is clearly shown. Though inconvenient, effect may be given to such intention: see Chapter 53.
6   *Re Sampson, Sampson v Sampson* [1896] 1 Ch 630 at 635 (early indefeasible vesting is favoured as it is undesirable that rights and interests should depend on the diligence of executors and trustees); *Whiting v Force* (1840) 2 Beav 571 ('receiving' construed with its correlative 'pay' in original gift); *Rammell v Gillow* (1845) 15 LJ Ch 35. In particular cases an enquiry may be directed as to when the property could have been got in: *Law v Thompson* (1827) 4 Russ 92; *Re Arrowsmith's Trust* (1860) 29 LJ Ch 774.
7   *Re Arrowsmith's Trust* (1860) 29 LJ Ch 774; *Re Collison, Collison v Barber* (1879) 12 Ch D 834; *Re Wilkins, Spencer v Duckworth* (1881) 18 Ch D 634 (residue: gift over before final division of testator's estate); *Barnes v Whittaker* (1893) 14 NSW Eq 148; *Hunt v Hunt* (1902) 2 SRNSW (Eq) 72; *Re Ramsden* (1974) 46 DLR (3d) 758.
8   *Re Dodgson's Trusts* (1853) 1 Drew 440; *Minors v Battison* (1876) 1 App Cas 428; *Re Chaston, Chaston v Seago* (1881) 18 Ch D 218; *Wilks v Bannister* (1885) 30 Ch D 512.

[97.8]
Gift over on death before legacy is payable. A gift over on the death of the donee before the gift becomes due or payable is valid, and may take effect on the death of the donee in the lifetime of the testator.[1] The time referred to depends on the period of distribution contemplated by the will,[2] but is susceptible of a variety of interpretations according to the context.[3] In a gift to children, where the time for payment is after a life interest on their attaining their majority or other qualification, their shares prima facie become vested when they are wanted (for example in the case of sons at majority, and in the case of daughters at majority or marriage), and the gift is not read as making the provision for a child contingent on surviving both or either of its parents unless the intention is clearly so expressed.[4] A gift over on death before the gift becomes payable is confined to a death before attaining majority or other qualification, 'payable' in such a case being construed as 'vested', and accordingly the share of a child who attains his majority and dies in the lifetime of his parent is not divested.[5]

1   *Willing v Baine* (1731) 3 P Wms 113; *Humberstone v Stanton* (1813) 1 Ves & B 385; *Walker v Main* (1819) 1 Jac & W 1; *Humphreys v Howes* (1830) 1 Russ & M 639.
2   On the death of the tenant for life where the legacy is given after a life interest: *Crowder v Stone* (1829) 3 Russ 217; *Creswick v Gaskell* (1853) 16 Beav 577. In the case of immediate gifts, the death of the testator was considered to be denoted in *Collins v Macpherson* (1827) 2 Sim 87; *Cort v Winder* (1844) 1 Coll 320; *Whitman v Aitken* (1866) LR 2 Eq 414 at 417. The expiration of the executor's year may be adopted in particular cases where the context does not

otherwise provide: compare last paragraph, and see *Hunt v Hunt* (1902) 2 SRNSW (Eq) 72; *Hamilton v Hart* (1919) 47 DLR 231.

3   *Cort v Winder* (1844) 1 Coll 320 at 322.

4   See Chapter 52, para **[52.1]**, n 1.

5   *Schenck v Legh* (1803) 9 Ves 300; *Powis v Burdett* (1804) 9 Ves 428 (in spite of expressions referring to 'leaving children'); *Hallifax v Wilson* (1809) 16 Ves 168; *Walker v Main* (1819) 1 Jac & W 1 (death before legacy 'due and payable'); *Hayward v James* (1860) 28 Beav 523; *Haydon v Rose* (1870) LR 10 Eq 224; *Partridge v Baylis* (1881) 17 Ch D 835; *Wakefield v Maffet* (1885) 10 App Cas 422; but cf *Re Williams* (1849) 12 Beav 317.

[97.9]
Gift over on death before becoming entitled. In the case of a gift over on the death of the donee before becoming entitled, this word has no definite legal meaning, and may mean either entitled in interest[1] or entitled in possession,[2] according to the context.

1   *Re Crosland, Craig v Midgley* (1886) 54 LT 238.

2   *Re Maunder, Maunder v Maunder* [1902] 2 Ch 875; *Turner v Gosset* (1865) 34 Beav 593; *Re Noyce, Brown v Rigg* (1885) 31 Ch D 75; *Re Whiter, Windsor v Jones* (1911) 105 LT 749. *Charitable Donations and Bequests Comrs v Cotter* (1841) 1 Dr & War 498, followed in *Henderson v Kennicot* (1848) 2 De G & Sm 492, was said in *Re Maunder, Maunder v Maunder* [1902] 2 Ch 875, at 879, to be founded on *Doe d Long v Prigg* (1828) 8 B & C 231, which was disapproved on other grounds in *Wordsworth v Wood* (1847) 1 HL Cas 129 at 154, and in *Re Gregson's Trust Estate* (1864) 2 De GJ & Sm 428. A gift over on death before 'being entitled in possession' has been construed by force of the context, 'entitled in interest'; *Re Yates's Trust* (1851) 21 LJ Ch 281.

[97.10]
Gift over on death before vesting. A gift over on the prior donee's death before attaining a vested interest prima facie refers to death before vesting in the technical sense.[1] But, if the context requires, it may refer to death before taking possession,[2] or before having the right to possession.[3]

1   *Parkin v Hodgkinson* (1846) 15 Sim 293; *Bull v Jones* (1862) 31 LJ Ch 858 at 861; *Richardson v Power* (1865) 19 CBNS 780 at 802 (remainder in fee simple); *Reid v Wishart* (1898) 16 NZLR 218. The gift over took effect on a class of prior donees failing to come into existence in *Beardsley v Benyon* (1865) 12 LT 698.

2   *King v Cullen* (1848) 2 De G & Sm 252 at 254 (where the will showed that a death after vesting, in the technical sense, was within the testator's meaning); *Re Morris* (1857) 26 LJ Ch 688; *Young v Robertson* (1862) 4 Macq 314 (gift over to survivors).

3   *Sillick v Booth* (1841) 1 Y & C Ch Cas 117 at 121.

III.   STATUTORY PROVISION

[97.11]
Restriction on executory limitations. Where a person is entitled to an equitable interest in land in fee simple or for any less interest not being an entailed interest, or any interest in personalty not being an entailed interest, with an executory limitation over on default or failure of all or any of his issue, whether within or at any specified period of time or not, that executory limitation shall be or become void and incapable of taking effect, if and as soon as there is living any issue who has attained the age of eighteen years of the class on default or failure whereof the limitation over was to take effect.[1]

1   Law of Property Act 1925, s 134 (37 *Halsbury's Statutes* (4th edn) 293), replacing and
extending Conveyancing Act 1882, s 10; 18 years substituted for 21 years by the Family Law
Reform Act 1969, s 1(3), Sch 1, Pt I; 6 *Halsbury's Statutes* (4th edn) 121, 125. This provision
from 1 January 1883 to 31 December 1925, applies only to land (including leaseholds) but from
1 January 1926, applies to all property except entailed interests. Where the gift over is if the
donee shall die without ever having had a child, this provision does not apply: *Re Booth,
Pickard v Booth* [1900] 1 Ch 768.

CHAPTER 98

Limitations on failure of issue

[98.1]

Statutory provision. By the Wills Act 1837, s 29,[1] in a gift by will of real or of personal property the words 'die without issue' or 'die without leaving issue' or 'have no issue' or any other words which may import either a want or failure of issue of any person in his lifetime, or at the time of his death, or an indefinite failure of issue shall be construed to mean a want or failure in the lifetime or at the time of the death of such person, and not an indefinite failure of issue, unless a contrary intention shall appear by the will, by reason of such person having a prior estate tail or of a preceding gift being (without any implication arising from such words) a limitation of an estate tail to such person or issue, or otherwise, provided that the Act shall not extend to cases where such words as aforesaid import if no issue described in a preceding gift shall be born, or if there shall be no issue who shall live to attain the age, or otherwise answer the description required for obtaining a vested interest by a preceding gift to such issue. This provision has been applied to gifts on death 'without leaving male issue',[2] but not to like gifts in terms of 'heirs of the body' or 'heirs', even though coupled with words of procreation.[3] It has been suggested that the statutory provision has no application to words such as 'in default of issue' or 'on failure of issue', not containing in themselves or by inference from the context, any reference to the death of the person failure of whose issue is spoken of;[4] but the contrary has also been both stated and assumed.[5] The fact that the provision contemplates words which may import a failure of issue in the lifetime of the named person appears to be inconsistent with the suggestion.[6] It has been questioned whether the Wills Act applies to the case of any but an entire failure of issue.[7]

---

1   50 *Halsbury's Statutes* (4th edn) 597. See Vol 2, Part G, para **[244.29]**. There is also a restriction placed on the creation of executory interests to take effect on failure of issue by the Law of Property Act 1925, s 134; 37 *Halsbury's Statutes* (4th edn) 293. See para **[97.11]** supra.
2   *Re Edwards, Edwards v Edwards* [1894] 3 Ch 644; *Upton v Hardman* (1874) IR 9 Eq 157; *Neville v Thacker* (1888) 23 LR Ir 344.
3   *Harris v Davis* (1844) 1 Coll 416 (in case of there being no heir); *Re Sallery* (1861) 11 I Ch R 236; *Dawson v Small* (1874) 9 Ch App 651; *Re Leach, Leach v Leach* [1912] 2 Ch 422.
4   *Shand v Robinson* (1898) 19 NSW Eq 85 at 88.
5   *Neville v Thacker* (1888) 23 LR Ir 344 at 357; *Green v Green* (1849) 3 De G & Sm 480 (contrary assumed).
6   *Morris v Morris* (1853) 17 Beav 198 at 202, where it is suggested that the provision did not apply to cases where the words referring to dying without issue were combined with other words, such as 'dying under 21' which had been the subject of judicial decision.
7   *Re Conbay's Estate* [1916] 1 IR 51; *Re Thomas, Thomas v Thomas* [1921] 1 Ch 306.

[98.2]

Contrary intention. This may be shown by the fact that the person whose failure of issue is spoken of has a prior estate tail, or that a preceding gift is, without any implication arising from the words in question,[1] a limitation of an estate tail to that person or issue[2] or otherwise generally by the context of the will.[3] The effect of the statutory provision is that a limitation which *can* be construed to mean a failure of issue in the lifetime or at the death of any person, must be so construed, but if the words of the will must mean an indefinite failure, then the statute has no effect upon their construction.

1 *Re O'Bierne* (1844) 1 Jo & Lat 352.
2 *Fay v Fay* (1880) 5 LR Ir 274; *Greenway v Greenway* (1860) 2 De GF & J 128 at 130; *Re Clerke, Clowes v Clerke* [1915] 2 Ch 301. An entailed interest can now be created only by such words as would have that effect in a deed; see Chapter 84.
3 *Green v Green* (1849) 3 De G & Sm 480; *Green v Giles* (1855) 5 I Ch R 25; *Neville v Thacker* (1888) 23 LR Ir 344; *Weldon v Weldon* [1911] 1 IR 177, followed in *Cowan and Johnson v Ball* [1933] NI 173.

[98.3]

Reference to issue taking under prior gifts. As already stated the statutory presumption does not apply to cases where the words of the gift import if no issue described in a preceding gift shall be born, or if there shall be no issue who shall live to attain the age or otherwise answer the description required for obtaining a vested estate by a preceding gift to such issue.[1] Where, after gifts to particular descriptions of issue, the gift over is 'in default of such issue', the word 'such' cannot, as a general rule, be rejected,[2] but, where the particular descriptions of issue are to take in tail, especially if their estates are shown to be estates tail to each of them successively, the words 'such issue' may be explained to mean their issue, so that the subsequent limitations take effect as remainders.[3] In other cases the word 'such', when the will is considered as a whole, may have to be rejected in order to give the first son an estate tail.[4] The same construction may have to be adopted when the gift over is in default of issue 'as aforesaid'.[5] The rule is excluded, if the failure of issue, expressly or by inference from the will taken as a whole, is ascertained at a specified death[6] or is indefinite.[7] Thus, words referring to failure of issue of a person in a gift over following a devise to the children of such person, or other special class of his issue, either in fee simple or in fee tail, prima facie mean in default of such children, or other special class of issue, and the gift takes effect only on failure of the previous gifts.[8] A similar rule holds good in cases of bequests of personalty or of a mixed fund, where the prior gift is an absolute bequest to children or other special class of issue, not being a contingent class.[9]

1 *Re Bence, Smith v Bence* [1891] 3 Ch 242.
2 *Foster v Earl of Romney* (1809) 11 East 594; *Ryan v Cowley* (1835) L & G *temp* Sugd 7; *Boydell v Golightly* (1844) 14 Sim 327; *Ashburner v Wilson* (1850) 17 Sim 204; *Bridge v Ramsey* (1835) 10 Hare 320.
3 *Lewis d Ormond v Waters* (1805) 6 East 336; *Biddulph v Lees* (1859) EB & E 289.
4 See para **[83.20]** supra, and *Evans d Brooke v Astley* (1764) 3 Burr 1570; *Parker v Tootal* (1865) 11 HL Cas 143.
5 *Malcolm v Taylor* (1832) 2 Russ & M 416; *Walker v Petchell* (1845) 1 CB 652. See Chapter 101, as to implied gifts.

6   *Westwood v Southey* (1852) 2 Sim NS 192 at 203; *Re Edwards, Jones v Jones* [1906] 1 Ch 570, disapproving *Kidman v Kidman* (1871) 40 LJ Ch 359.
7   *Bowen v Lewis* (1884) 9 App Cas 890.
8   *Bamfield v Popham* (1703) 1 P Wms 54 (corrected at p 760); *Goodright v Dunham* (1779) 1 Doug KB 264; *Baker v Tucker* (1850) 3 HL Cas 106; *Cormack v Copous* (1853) 17 Beav 397; *Foster v Hayes* (1855) 4 E & B 717; *Towns v Wentworth* (1858) 11 Moo PCC 526 at 547; *Smyth v Power* (1876) IR 10 Eq 192 at 199.
9   *Salkeld v Vernon* (1758) 1 Eden 64; *Pride v Fooks* (1858) 3 De G & J 252 at 280; *Re Wyndham's Trusts* (1865) LR 1 Eq 290; *Re Sanders' Trusts* (1866) LR 1 Eq 675; *Re Merceron's Trusts, Davies v Merceron* (1876) 4 Ch D 182.

[98.4]

Prior gift contingent. It is more difficult, though not impossible,[1] to refer the issue to those taking under the prior gifts where the prior limitation is on contingent events,[2] or is a contingent class, such as sons attaining twenty-one or surviving a life tenant, so that there may be issue who may not take under it,[3] or where the prior limitation is to a definite number of the children,[4] or if the issue taking under previous gifts take for life only.[5]

1   *Bryan v Mansion* (1852) 5 De G & Sm 737 at 742 (where, however, in the context 'issue' meant 'children'); *Sanders v Ashford* (1860) 28 Beav 609 (where the gift over was in default of issue attaining 21); *Re Merceron's Trusts, Davies v Merceron* (1876) 4 Ch D 182 (issue living at parent's death); *Hutchinson v Tottenham* [1898] 1 IR 403; affd [1899] 1 IR 344 (children born in lifetime of testatrix). It seems that the fact that the issue take merely as the objects of a power of appointment does not prevent the construction by reference to such issue, objects of the power, as are living at the death of the appointor: *Target v Gaunt* (1718) 1 P Wms 432; *Hockley v Mawbey* (1790) 3 Bro CC 82; *Ryan v Cowley* (1835) L & G *temp* Sugd 7; *Leeming v Sherratt* (1842) 2 Hare 14; *Eastwood v Avison* (1869) LR 4 Exch 141.
2   *Andree v Ward* (1826) 1 Russ 260 (if ancestor married a woman of specified fortune); *Campbell v Harding* (1831) 2 Russ & M 390 (if ancestor married); *Franks v Price* (1838) 5 Bing NC 37.
3   *Doe d Rew v Lucraft* (1832) 1 Moo & S 573 (prior issue taking at 21); *Pride v Fooks* (1858) 3 De G & J 252 at 280.
4   *Langley v Baldwin* (1707) 1 Eq Cas Abr 185, pl 29 (first six sons only); *A-G v Sutton* (1721) 1 P Wms 754 (first and second sons only); *Stanley v Lennard* (1758) 1 Eden 87 (eldest son only); *Key v Key* (1853) 4 De GM & G 73 (eldest surviving son).
5   *Parr v Swindels* (1828) 4 Russ 283.

[98.5]

Gift over on death of stranger. In cases where there is a third period (other than an indefinitely distant time or the death of the person) to which the failure of issue may refer (for example, the death of any other person), the statutory presumption does no more than exclude the construction which gives an indefinitely distant failure of issue.[1]

1   *Jarman v Vye* (1866) LR 2 Eq 784 at 787; *Dunn v Morgan* (1915) 84 LJ Ch 812 ('die without issue' held to mean without leaving issue him surviving, and not an indefinite failure of issue), distinguishing *Crowder v Stone* (1829) 3 Russ 217; *Jarman v Vye*.

[98.6]

Recognised rules. There are certain recognised rules applicable to wills which are subject to the statutory provision.

[98.7]

Gift on death without leaving issue. A gift on a death 'without leaving issue' is, where the subject-matter is personal estate, prima facie confined to a failure of issue at death;[1] where the subject-matter is real estate, the gift prima facie[2] extends to an indefinite failure of issue;[3] where both real and personal property are comprised in the same gift, the words are construed differently according to the subject-matter.[4]

1   *Forth v Chapman* (1720) 1 P Wms 663; *Radford v Radford* (1836) 1 Keen 486; *Daniel v Warren* (1843) 2 Y & C Ch Cas 290; *Mansell v Grove* (1843) 2 Y & C Ch Cas 484; *Hawkins v Hamerton* (1848) 16 Sim 410; *Re Synge's Trusts* (1854) 3 I Ch R 379; *Sealy v Stawell* (1868) IR 2 Eq 326; *Auger v Beaudry* [1920] AC 1010; *Re Patterson Estate* (1958) 66 Man R 416.
2   The following are instances to the contrary: *Porter v Bradley* (1789) 3 Term Rep 143 ('leaving ... behind him'); *Roe d Sheers v Jeffrey* (1798) 7 Term Rep 589 (gift over of life estates to living persons). These cases have been much criticised but are not apparently overruled; see *Van Tassel v Frederick* (1896) 27 OR 646 at 648.
3   *Walter v Drew* (1723) 1 Com 373; *Bamford v Lord* (1854) 14 CB 708; *Feakes v Standley* (1857) 24 Beav 485; *Biss v Smith* (1857) 2 H & N 105; *Richards v Davies* (1862) 13 CBNS 69; affd (1863) 13 CBNS 861; *Re Thomas, Thomas v Thomas* [1921] 1 Ch 306.
4   *Forth v Chapman* (1720) 1 P Wms 663; *Sheffield v Lord Orrery* (1745) 3 Atk 282; *Radford v Radford* (1836) 1 Keen 486; *Greenway v Greenway* (1860) 2 De GF & J 128 at 137. In *Porter v Bradley* (1789) 3 Term Rep 143 at 146, and in *Roe d Sheers v Jeffrey* (1798) 7 Term Rep 589, this rule is criticised because it construes the same word in different senses according to the subject-matter in a single gift of a blended fund, but these criticisms have been disapproved: *Crooke v De Vandes* (1803) 9 Ves 197 at 203; *Elton v Eason* (1812) 19 Ves 73 at 79; *Doe d Cadogan v Ewart* (1838) 7 Ad & El 636 at 655.

[98.8]
Gift of property in possession on failure of issue of testator. A gift of property to which the testator is entitled in possession, to take effect on failure of his own issue, not preceded by any other gift, is not a future gift, but is a gift in possession at the testator's death, in the event of there being at that time a failure of his issue.[1]

1   *French v Cadell* (1765) 3 Bro Parl Cas 257; *Wellington v Wellington* (1768) 4 Burr 2165; *Lytton v Lytton* (1793) 4 Bro CC 441; *Sanford v Irby* (1820) 3 B & Ald 654.

[98.9]
Gift of property in remainder on failure of issue taking under prior interests. When the testator under the limitations of another instrument is entitled in remainder or reversion on failure of the issue, or the issue male or female, of any person, and the testator makes a gift of the property not preceded by any other limitation, then on the failure of that issue, these words do not make the gift a future gift, but are merely a description of the testator's interest.[1] The question in such cases is whether the issue referred to in the will is the same as or is different from the issue inheritable under the other instrument.[2]

1   *Badger v Lloyd* (1699) 1 Ld Raym 523; *Lytton v Lytton* (1793) 4 Bro CC 441; *Egerton v Jones* (1830) 3 Sim 409.
2   *Morse v Lord Ormonde* (1826) 1 Russ 382; *Sanford v Irby* (1820) 3 B & Ald 654; *Eno v Eno* (1847) 6 Hare 171; *Lewis v Templer* (1864) 33 Beav 625 (in these cases the issue was the same); *Lady Lanesborough v Fox* (1733) Cas *temp* Talb 262; *Jones v Morgan* (1774) 3 Bro Parl Cas 323; *Bankes v Holme* (1821) 1 Russ 394n (in these cases the issue was different).

[98.10]
Personal provisions on failure of issue. Where the court finds an intention that the persons entitled under the gift over are to enjoy the benefits of their gift as a

personal provision during their lives, and are not merely to take interests which are not vested in possession though vested in right, this fact leads to the inference that the failure of issue is confined to the lives of those persons.[1] For instance where the gift over provides for a charge of a legacy intended as a personal provision[2] or where the gift over is to such of a number of named persons or described persons as are living at the time of failure.[3] The inference also arises where the gift over is to survivors of the persons, failure of whose issue is spoken of, in cases where 'survivors' is used in its ordinary sense of surviving the failure of issue,[4] but does not arise where 'survivor' means the 'longest liver'[5] or 'surviving stirps' or 'other'.[6] So, too, where the only interest taken under the gift over is an interest for life, or succession of interests for lives, it can be inferred that the failure of issue is confined to the lives of the donees under the gift over.[7] This is not the case, however, where life interests are not the only interests arising under the gift over. The mere fact that the next interest under the gift over is a life interest is insufficient.[8]

1   *Doe d Smith v Webber* (1818) 1 B & Ald 713 at 721.
2   *Nichols v Hooper* (1712) 1 P Wms 198; *Doe d Smith v Webber* (1818) 1 B & Ald 713. The mere fact that a legacy is given on failure of issue is insufficient: *Doe d Todd v Duesbury* (1841) 8 M & W 514.
3   *Murray v Addenbrook* (1830) 4 Russ 407 at 419; *Greenwood v Verdon* (1854) 1 K & J 74 at 81.
4   *Hughes v Sayer* (1718) 1 P Wms 534; *Ranelagh v Ranelagh* (1834) 2 My & K 441 at 448; *Turner v Frampton* (1846) 2 Coll 331; *Westwood v Southey* (1852) 2 Sim NS 192 at 201; *Massey v Hudson* (1817) 2 Mer 130 (where a substitutional gift to personal representatives of the survivor excluded the presumption).
5   *Chadock v Cowley* (1624) Cro Jac 695.
6   See Chapter 87.
7   *Trafford v Boehm* (1746) 3 Atk 440 at 449; *Roe d Sheers v Jeffrey* (1798) 7 Term Rep 589 (where failure was said to be confined to the life of the prior donee, but see *Lepine v Ferard* (1831) 2 Russ & M 378 at 398).
8   *Boehm v Clarke* (1804) 9 Ves 580 at 582; *Barlow v Salter* (1810) 17 Ves 479 at 482; *Doe d Jones v Owens* (1830) 1 B & Ad 318 at 320.

[98.11]
Personal events coupled with failure of issue. Where after a devise to a person and his heirs,[1] or after a bequest to a person absolutely,[2] there is a gift over on his dying under or over a certain age without issue, the compound event is restricted to his dying under or over that age without issue living at his death.

1   *Toovey v Bassett* (1809) 10 East 460; *Right d Day v Day* (1812) 16 East 67; *Glover v Monckton* (1825) 3 Bing 13; *Doe d Johnson v Johnson* (1852) 8 Exch 81; *Gwynne v Berry* (1875) IR 9 CL 494. The devise would now be in fee simple.
2   *Pawlett v Dogget* (1688) 2 Vern 86; *Martin v Long* (1690) 2 Vern 151 (leaseholds); *Morris v Morris* (1853) 17 Beav 198 (gift over if prior donee should die without issue or before 21, where 'or' was construed 'and' as if would have been before the Wills Act 1837); *Re Morgan* (1883) 24 Ch D 114.

[98.12]
Gift over on death without heir. A devise over on death without having or leaving an heir or male heir or heirs of the body[1] prima facie[2] refers to a failure of such heirs at any time.[3]

1   This expression is not subject to the Wills Act 1837, s 29; see Vol 2, Part G, para **[244.29]**; see para **[98.1]**, n 3.

2   The contrary was shown in *Polley v Polley* (1861) 29 Beav 134; *Coltsmann v Coltsmann* (1868) LR 3 HL 121; *Re Leach, Leach v Leach* [1912] 2 Ch 422.
3   *Nottingham v Jennings* (1700) 1 P Wms 23; *A-G v Hird* (1782) 1 Bro CC 170; *Crooke v De Vandes* (1803) 9 Ves 197.

[98.13]
Gift over on death without children. A devise over of real property on a death without children either after a prior gift in fee or generally without words of limitation, may be construed, in order not to disappoint more remote generations of issue, as taking effect on death or failure of issue, either indefinitely[1] or within a limited time, for example before the death of the named ancestor,[2] according to the context.[3] A similar gift of personal property prima facie refers to a failure of children at the death of the named parent,[4] but the words are not construed to mean a failure of issue indefinitely if the effect is to defeat the intention of the testator, and especially in bequests of personal property, the ordinary meaning of 'children' is adhered to.[5] A gift over on death 'without having children' is construed as if on death 'without having had children', and fails to take effect if the parent has any child, though no such child survives him.[6] Where the testator provides for the event of a son or daughter predeceasing him but in fact there is no issue of the marriage, the court reads the appropriate words into the will to prevent an intestacy.[7]

1   *Bifield's Case* (1600), cited in 1 Vent 231, and apparently reported sub nom *Milliner v Robinson* (1600) Moore KB 682 (to A and, if he dies not having a son, over); *Doe d Blesard v Simpson* (1842) 3 Man & G 929 at 954; *Bacon v Cosby* (1851) 4 De G & Sm 261. For a contrary decision, see *Re Galligan, Galligan v Galligan* (1913) 13 SRNSW 291.
2   *Doe d Smith v Webber* (1818) 1 B & Ald 713; *Parker v Birks* (1854) 1 K & J 156; *Richards v Davies* (1862) 13 CBNS 69 at 87; *Re Thomas, Vivian v Vivian* [1920] 1 Ch 515.
3   To say that 'children' is read as 'issue' is too wide a statement; the rule is that the court has a discretion to construe the word 'children' as 'issue' but will do so only if satisfied that the word was used with that meaning and that to construe it strictly would defeat the true intent of the will: *Re Milward's Estate, ex p Midland Rly Co* [1940] Ch 698.
4   *Hughes v Sayer* (1718) 1 P Wms 534; *Pleydell v Pleydell* (1721) 1 P Wms 748; *Thicknesse v Liege* (1775) 3 Bro Parl Cas 365; *Re Booth, Pickard v Booth* [1900] 1 Ch 768 (where *Jeffreys v Conner* (1860) 28 Beav 328, is explained); *Re Raphael, Permanent Trustee Co of NSW Ltd v Lee* (1903) 3 SRNSW 196.
5   *Studholme v Hodgson* (1734) 3 P Wms 300; *Stone v Maule* (1829) 2 Sim 490; *Mathews v Gardiner* (1853) 17 Bev 254; *Jeffreys v Conner* (1860) 28 Beav 328. In the context of the wills considered in some cases a similar rule to that in the case of real property may be applied to personal property: *Re Synge's Trusts* (1854) 3 I Ch R 379.
6   *Weakley d Knight v Rugg* (1797) 7 Term Rep 322; *Bell v Phyn* (1802) 7 Ves 453; *Wall v Tomlinson* (1810) 16 Ves 413; *Jeffreys v Conner* (1860) 28 Beav 328; and see the following cases of gifts over on death without having 'issue': *M'Kay v M'Allister* (1912) 46 ILT 88; *Chunilal Parvatishankar v Bai Samrath* (1914) 30 TLR 407.
7   *Re Kallil* [1957] NZLR 10.

CHAPTER 99

Restriction on alienation and forfeiture clause

[99.1]
Conditions restricting the donee's right of alienation. Where a donee is clearly given an interest in property, whether in possession or reversion, any restriction on his right of alienation is void as repugnant to the gift;[1] and, where he takes an absolute interest, a gift over on his failure to dispose at his death of the property or to dispose then of whatever part of the property he has not disposed of during his life is void.[2] There may, however, be cases where there is doubt as to the interest which the donee takes, and then, if he is restrained from alienating the property,[3] or there is a gift over on his disposing of it,[4] or on his failing to dispose of it,[5] or a gift over of what is remaining at his death,[6] this restriction may lead to the inference that the gift is not an absolute one, but a life or other limited interest to which an absolute power of disposition does not attach.[7] A gift in such a form may, however, give the donee a power of appointment over the property.[8] Where the donee has an unrestricted right of enjoyment in specie during his life and a power of disposition either both during the life and on his death or only on his death, he takes an absolute interest.[9] Where the donee has no such right of disposition on death, but the testator himself in his will provides for the destination of so much of the property as shall not have been disposed of by the donee, then the donee takes only a life interest with such powers of disposition during his life as the will gives him.[10] A direction against the alienation of a life interest where there is no provision for its termination or a gift over is invalid.[11]

1   *Ludlow v Bunbury* (1865) 35 Beav 36; *Hood v Oglander* (1865) 34 Beav 513; *Re Jones' Will* (1870) 23 LT 211; *Hunt-Foulston v Furber* (1876) 3 Ch D 285; *Re Wolstenholme, Marshall v Aizlewood* (1881) 43 LT 752; *Corbett v Corbett* (1888) 14 PD 7; *W Gardiner & Co Ltd v Dessaix* [1915] AC 1096. The restriction is not rendered valid by being limited in point of time: *Blackburn v McCallum* (1903) 33 SCR 65 (limit of twenty-five years); *James v Gard* (1887) 13 VLR 908; *Re Dunn, Dunn v McCowan* [1927] St R Qd 265; *Doherty v Doherty* [1936] 2 DLR 180; *Re Brodribb, Queensland Trustees Ltd v Brodribb* (1942) QSR 263; *Re Malcolm* [1947] 4 DLR 756; *Re Goode* [1960] VR 117. In New Zealand it has been held that a total restriction on alienation is legal in the case of a charity: *Re Clark, Horwell v Dent* [1961] NZLR 635 following *Caldwell v Fleming* [1927] NZLR 145. The rule applies to vested interests only, see para **[99.3]** infra.
2   *Watkins v Williams* (1851) 3 Mac & G 622; *Perry v Merritt* (1874) LR 18 Eq 152; *Re Dixon, Dixon v Charlesworth* [1903] 2 Ch 458. The restrictions in such cases do not cut down the prior clear gift: *Re Jones, Richards v Jones* [1898] 1 Ch 438; *Lloyd v Tweedy* [1898] 1 IR 5.
3   *Mortimer v Hartley* (1851) 3 De G & Sm 328 n; *Re Banks' Trusts, ex p Hovill* (1855) 2 K & J 387; *Banks v Braithwaite* (1863) 1 New Rep 306; *Magee v Martin* [1902] 1 IR 367. The fact that the testator thought that he could make the property perpetually inalienable does not alter the construction of words he has used in describing the donees and their interests; *Britton v Twining* (1817) 3 Mer 176 at 183.

4   *Crumpe v Crumpe* [1900] AC 127.
5   *Re Stringer's Estate, Shaw v Jones-Ford* (1877) 6 Ch D 1; *Comiskey v Bowring-Hanbury* [1905] AC 84.
6   *Re Adam's Trusts* (1865) 13 LT 347; *Re Sheldon and Kemble* (1885) 53 LT 527; *Bibbens v Potter* (1879) 10 Ch D 733; *Roberts v Thorpe* (1911) 56 Sol Jo 13; *Shearer v Hogg* (1912) 46 SCR 492. Where in the context apart from such words, a life estate only would be created, this life estate is not increased by these words to a larger interest: *Constable v Bull* (1849) 3 De G & Sm 411 at 413.
7   *Re Sanford, Sanford v Sanford* [1901] 1 Ch 939; *Re Pounder, Williams v Pounder* (1886) 56 LJ Ch 113 at 114.
8   See *Scott v Josselyn* (1859) 26 Beav 174; *Re Thomson's Estate, Herring v Barrow* (1880) 14 Ch D 263; *Pennock v Pennock* (1871) LR 13 Eq 144; *Re Richards, Uglow v Richards* [1902] 1 Ch 76; *Reid v Atkinson* (1871) IR 5 Eq 373 at 382, and the cases cited in nn 6 and 7.
9   *Re David's Trusts* (1859) John 495 at 500; *Re Jones, Richards v Jones* [1898] 1 Ch 438.
10 *Re Thomson's Estate, Herring v Barrow* (1880) 14 Ch D 263; *Pennock v Pennock* (1871) LR 13 Eq 144; *Re Colyer, Millikin v Snelling* (1886) 55 LT 344; *Re Sanford, Sanford v Sanford* [1901] 1 Ch 939; *Re Richards, Uglow v Richards* [1902] 1 Ch 76; *Re Rowland, Jones v Rowland* (1902) 86 LT 78; *Rosenberg v Sraggs* (1900) 19 NZLR 196; *Yates v Yates* (1905) 25 NZLR 263. See also *Re Holden, Holden v Smith* (1888) 57 LJ Ch 648; *Re Dixon, Dixon v Dixon* (1912) 56 Sol Jo 445. It is no doubt difficult to reconcile all these decisions and the task is not made easier by the fact that all the provisions of the will must be taken into account in each case. Further many of the wills here considered had been drafted without professional advice.
11 *Re Jennings* (1954) 33 UPR 230.

[99.2]
Partial restraint on alienation. A restraint which allows alienation with the consent of the executors is void.[1] A restraint which allows alienation to certain named persons or certain classes of persons has been the subject of conflicting decisions, but as the law stands at present it seems that, if the persons to whom alienation is allowed are at the commencement of the restraint few in number and that number must in course of time necessarily diminish, the restraint is void and can be disregarded, but if the number of such persons is large and indeterminate and will increase in course of time, the restraint is not void and effect will be given to it.[2] There has been a short line of conflicting decisions on this subject. It is clear a prohibition of alienation to one named person and his heirs or issue is not a void prohibition.[3] It must be noticed that such a condition allows alienation to everyone except a named person. The common form of the condition, however, is to allow alienation to named persons and not any one else. The first case of this kind[4] restrained the devisee from alienating the property to anyone but one person. This was held void: it seems chiefly on account of the fact that the testator could select a person who would not or could not purchase the property. Where the testator gave lands to two of his five daughters as tenants in common on condition that, in case they or either of them should have no issue, they or she having no issue should have no power to dispose of their share except to her sister or sisters or their children, this condition against alienation was held to be valid.[5] A restriction never to sell the property out of the family but, if sold at all, to be sold to one of the beneficiary's brothers, was held invalid.[6] Where the restriction was that, if any of the testator's four sons should execute any assurance or mortgage whereby but for that provision the share or the income of the share or any part thereof would or might become vested in or payable to any person or persons other than a brother or brothers of such son, then the share of that son was to be held on certain trusts in

the form of protective trusts. This was held to amount in substance to a total prohibition of alienation and to be void.[7]

1   *Re O'Mullane* [1955] VLR 217.
2   *Re Brown, District Bank Ltd v Brown* [1953] 2 All ER 1342 at 1348; *Re Mavromatis* [1964] VR 612 (permitted alienees a small contracting class: prohibition void).
3   Coke upon Littleton, Charles Butler edn, Vol 2, s 361.
4   *Muschamp v Bluet* (1617) J Bridg 132.
5   *Doe d Gill v Pearson* (1805) 6 East 173.
6   *Attwater v Attwater* (1853) 18 Beav 330, not following *Doe d Gill v Pearson* (1805) 6 East 173. In *Re Macleay* (1875) LR 20 Eq 186, the condition again was not to sell the property out of the family and after criticising the decision in *Attwater v Attwater*, Sir George Jessel MR held the condition a good one, partly on the ground that it was a condition against selling and not against disposing. This decision in *Re Macleay*, was in its turn much criticised in *Re Rosher, Rosher v Rosher* (1884) 26 Ch D 801, where the property was not to be sold during the lifetime of the testator's widow without first offering it to her at a figure which was in fact one-fifth of its value. This condition was held to be void.
7   *Re Brown, District Bank Ltd v Brown* [1953] 2 All ER 1342.

[99.3]
Rules apply to vested interest only. These rules restraining alienation apply only to vested interests which include vested life interests.[1] In the case of settled land, there was a statutory prohibition of conditions which conflict with a life tenant's right of sale under the provisions of the Settled Land Act.[2] There are, however, methods of restraining a life tenant from parting with his or her interest which are dealt with below.[3] A married woman could under the doctrine of restraint upon anticipation be prevented from assigning or charging a vested interest during coverture, but this power has been negatived by statute.[4] The rule does not apply to contingent interests before the contingency happens and until that time any condition against alienation operates according to its terms. Thus where interests were contingent on the youngest child attaining twenty-one and, on proof of one of the children having sold or parted with his share or interest, his share was to accrue to the others, a share was forfeited by one of the children assigning his share on bankruptcy before the contingency happened, ie the youngest child attaining twenty-one years of age.[5] Similarly where a child mortgaged her share before vesting,[6] and also where a reversionary share though vested was liable to be divested.[7] But if the restriction against assignment is so generally worded as to be applicable to both absolute and contingent interests, it cannot be split and is void.[8]

1   *Brandon v Robinson* (1811) 18 Ves 429; *Metcalfe v Metcalfe* (1889) 43 Ch D 633.
2   See Settled Land Act 1925, s 106; *Re Jeffreys, Finch v Martin* [1939] Ch 205, [1938] 4 All ER 120. But note that no new settlements can be created under the Settled Land Act 1925 after 1 January 1997, by virtue of the Trusts of Land and Appointment of Trustees Act 1996, s 2(1).
3   See para **[99.4]** infra.
4   Married Women (Restraint upon Anticipation) Act 1949; 27 *Halsbury's Statutes* (4th edn) 741.
5   *Churchill v Marks* (1844) 1 Coll 441.
6   *Re Payne* (1858) 25 Beav 556.
7   *Re Porter, Coulson v Capper* [1892] 3 Ch 481.
8   *Re Smith, Smith v Smith* [1916] 1 Ch 369.

[99.4]
Forfeiture clause. A clause giving a life interest but making it subject to forfeiture on alienation or on bankruptcy or on similar events, is construed to

preserve the life interest and nothing else.[1] A total restraint on alienation is as repugnant and void in the case of a life interest as in the case of an absolute interest,[2] but a life interest may be made determinable on voluntary alienation either by being given until alienation[3] or by a gift over or by a clause for forfeiture on alienation,[4] and also on involuntary alienation such as bankruptcy, taking in execution and the like.[5] A common method of preserving the trust fund from bankruptcy or alienation is to put the property upon 'protective trusts'. Under such a trust the interest of the principal beneficiary is made determinable on bankruptcy or attempted alienation and thereupon a discretionary trust arises in favour of himself and a related class of beneficiaries. These trusts can be expressly created or, more commonly, the protective trusts set out in the Trustee Act 1925, s 33 are incorporated.[6] The courts have always shown a dislike for forfeitures, but in the case of forfeiture clauses the rule has been relaxed to some extent because the purpose of such a clause is to preserve the benefit of the settled funds for beneficiaries under the settlement rather than that they should be dissipated by one of them.[7] In general, therefore, while such clauses will be construed strictly so that nothing is an alienation within their meaning which is not fully covered by the words of the clause, yet, once a transaction is within that meaning, the clause is effective. Thus a forfeiture clause is effective although the beneficiary against whom it is to be enforced is ignorant of its existence[8] but, on the other hand, the onus is on those who allege a forfeiture to prove it.[9] Where the forfeiture is upon alienation, there is no forfeiture in the case of a transaction not intended to effect an alienation nor in the case of an ineffectual attempt at alienation,[10] and there must be something on which the forfeiture can operate, so that, if the bankruptcy is annulled before any sum is payable to the beneficiary, there is no forfeiture,[11] nor where an assignment of a dividend is withdrawn before any dividend is due.[12] In all cases the exact terms of the forfeiture clause is most material in deciding whether forfeiture has been incurred. Where a receiver is appointed by the Court of Protection in the case of a person mentally disordered such receiver is the person to receive the income and any equitable charge on the income by the beneficiary after such appointment and during the continuance of the receivership is null and void and cannot work a forfeiture[13].

1   That is to say, the court will enforce the forfeiture only when the acts proved fall within the description given in the clause of the acts which are to cause the forfeiture. Thus in *Re Mair, Williamson v French* [1909] 2 Ch 280 at 282, it was said that the court must look at the object of these forfeiture clauses. It cannot help knowing that the object is to preserve the life interest and nothing else. It may be that in some cases words are used which compel the court to hold that a forfeiture has been incurred, though the life interest has been preserved. In that case the condition was 'until some event shall happen whereby if the same income belonged absolutely to her she would be deprived of the personal enjoyment thereof or any part thereof'. The life tenant asked the trustee to pay certain dividends when they became due to one of her creditors, but before such dividends became due she discharged the debt out of other moneys. It was held that the assignment, which was cancelled before it became really effective, did not operate to cause a forfeiture. These matters, of course, depend almost wholly on the wording of the forfeiture clause. See also *Re Sheward, Sheward v Brown* [1893] 3 Ch 502 (document appearing to be a charge but not intended as such); *Re Oppenheim's Will Trusts, Westminster Bank Ltd v Oppenheim* [1950] Ch 633, [1950] 2 All ER 86 (forfeiture if beneficiary unable to give a personal discharge; appointment of receiver in lunacy no forfeiture). The interest must be vested in the beneficiary at the time the forfeiture is alleged to have taken place: see *Re Walker, Public Trustee v Walker* [1939] Ch 974, [1939] 3 All ER 902.

2   *Brandon v Robinson* (1811) 18 Ves 429.

3   *Carter v Carter* (1857) 3 K & J 617.

4   *Hurst v Hurst* (1882) 21 Ch D 278 (a case where the forfeiture operated although the chargee under the charge causing the forfeiture did not enforce it and ultimately disclaimed it and there were no objects to take under the gift over).

5   As to validity of a gift to cease on the bankruptcy, see *Mackintosh v Pogose* [1895] 1 Ch 505; *Heenan v Heenan* (1894) 12 NZLR 111. A gift can be made to cease on the bankruptcy of the alienee. The other branch of the rule that a disposition cannot be made to cease on the bankruptcy of the donor necessarily has no application to gifts by a testator. The interest of the beneficiary has in some cases ceased upon his becoming an enemy under the Trading with the Enemy Act 1939: *Re Gourju's Will Trusts, Starling v Custodian of Enemy Property* [1943] Ch 24, [1942] 2 All ER 605 (where the statutory protective trusts were incorporated and there was an event which prevented the receipt of the income); *Re Hatch, Public Trustee v Hatch* [1948] Ch 592, [1948] 2 All ER 288 (where the beneficiary was deprived of the 'personal enjoyment'); but in other cases the court has decided against forfeiture: *Re Hall, Public Trustee v Montgomery* [1944] Ch 46, [1943] 2 All ER 753 (a thing occurring by operation of law is not something 'permitted or suffered'); *Re Harris, Cope v Evans* [1945] Ch 316, [1945] 1 All ER 702 (where it was further held that the beneficiary had not suffered 'a process'); *Re Pozot's Settlement Trusts* [1952] Ch 427, [1952] 1 All ER 1107 (the interest did not vest in the custodian though payment had to be made to him) overruling *Fraenkel v Whitty* [1948] Ch 55, [1947] 2 All ER 646. A court order creating an equitable charge (eg to secure payment of maintenance on divorce) can cause a forfeiture: *Re Richardson's Will Trusts, Public Trustee v Llewellyn-Evans' Trustees* [1958] Ch 504, [1958] 1 All ER 538; but see *General Accident Fire and Life Assurance Corpn Ltd v IRC* [1963] 3 All ER 259, [1963] 1 WLR 1207 (an order of the Divorce Court held not to effect a forfeiture) and as to the application of this case to a pension fund payment, see *Edmonds v Edmonds* [1965] 1 All ER 379n, [1965] 1 WLR 58.

   Where both the testatrix and her husband were undischarged bankrupts and the wife left the income of her estate upon discretionary trusts for the husband, the court refused to accept the surrender of the trustee's discretion but would be prepared to give directions for its exercise in any particular case. Apart from this the trustees must unanimously decide within a reasonable time how they would apply the income: *Re Allen-Meyrick's Will Trusts, Magnall v Allen-Meyrick* [1966] 1 All ER 740, [1966] 1 WLR 499.

6   See Vol 2, Part G, para **[246.28]**. Illegitimate children and more remote issue are now included, see Family Law Reform Act 1987, s 1, Vol 2, Part G, para **[245.70]**. See Chapter 72, para **[72.15]** supra.

7   *Samuel v Samuel* (1879) 12 Ch D 152.

8   *Carter v Carter* (1857) 3 K & J 617. As to general rule that ignorance of a condition is no excuse for non-compliance, see Chapter 34, para **[34.24]** supra.

9   *Cox v Bockett* (1865) 35 Beav 48 at 51, and any ambiguity will be construed so as to prevent a forfeiture: *Durran v Durran* (1904) 91 LT 819; *Samuel v Samuel* (1879) 12 Ch D 152 (where mortgages by a remainderman were paid off in the lifetime of the tenant of life and the mortgages were stated to be subject to the proviso or condition in the will); *Re Sheward, Sheward v Brown* [1893] 3 Ch 502 (where a charge on a life interest was not intended as such, and, if it amounted to such, would have been set aside on the ground of fraud or mistake). As to where an attempt to charge or alienate is made a ground of forfeiture, see infra. An alienation by a married woman restrained from anticipation being void, did not effect a forfeiture: *Re Wormald, Frank v Muzeen* (1890) 43 Ch D 630, but the abolition of such restraint makes this precise decision now immaterial.

10 See infra and *Re Greenwood, Sutcliffe v Gledhill* [1901] 1 Ch 887 (garnishee order on income accrued due); *Re Westby's Settlement* [1950] Ch 296, [1950] 1 All ER 479 (lunacy percentage charged on estate of lunatic) overruling *Re Custance's Settlement, Keppel v Douglas* [1946] Ch 42, [1945] 2 All ER 441; and followed in *Re Oppenheim's Will Trust* [1950] Ch 633, [1950] 2 All ER 86; *Re Tancred's Settlement* [1903] 1 Ch 715 (settlement under which the beneficiary was still to receive the income). If a doubt arises whether a document of alienation is intended to deal with income already accrued due or to deal with future income, the court favours a construction not causing a forfeiture: *Cox v Blockett* (1865) 35 Beav 48 (security for debt not proved to exceed arrears due to chargor); *Durran v Durran* (1904) 91 LT 819 (sufficient moneys accrued due to pay sum asked to be paid to debtor). See also *Irwin v Tyson* [1966] ALR 117.

11 *Re Parnham's Trusts* (1876) 46 LJ Ch 80; *Metcalfe v Metcalfe* [1891] 3 Ch 1; *Re Forder, Forder v Forder* [1927] 2 Ch 291, [1927] All ER Rep 324; *Re Walker, Public Trustee v Walker* [1939] Ch 974, [1939] 3 All ER 902.

12   *Re Mair, Williamson v French* [1909] 2 Ch 280; see also *Re Longman, Westminster Bank Ltd v Hatton* [1955] 1 All ER 455.
13   *Re Marshall, Marshall v Whateley* [1920] 1 Ch 284.

[99.5]
Attempt to assign. A clause against attempting to assign or anticipate is not broken by abortive negotiations for an assignment;[1] nor by the execution of a document which is in an equitable assignment if it can be shown that the document was not intended as an assignment and could upon proper proceedings being brought have been set aside,[2] but an assignment in a settlement though inoperative in law has been held to be an attempt.[3] Unless the forfeiture clause extends to prohibit an attempted assignment an attempt does not cause a forfeiture.[4]

1   *Graham v Lee* (1857) 23 Beav 388. An 'attempt' must be an act which, but for the clause of forfeiture, or some rule of law, would operate as an alienation (ibid). For the application of this rule to interests of married women restrained from anticipation, see *Re Wormald, Frank v Muzeen* (1890) 43 Ch D 630; *Re Wolstenholme, Marshall v Aizlewood* (1881) 43 LT 752, but this particular application has now no importance.
2   *Re Sheward, Sheward v Brown* [1893] 3 Ch 502.
3   *Re Porter, Coulson v Capper* [1892] 3 Ch 481.
4   *Re Wormald, Frank v Muzeen* (1890) 43 Ch D 630; *Re Adamson, Public Trustee v Billing* (1913) 108 LT 179.

[99.6]
Definite act by donee required. Where the clause does not go on to prohibit matters suffered or permitted by the donee, it requires a definite act of alienation by him to cause a forfeiture and acts done by others do not cause a forfeiture.[1]

1   *Re Kelly's Settlement, West v Turner* (1888) 59 LT 494 (charging order); *Campbell v Campbell and Davis* (1895) 72 LT 294 (appointment of receiver); *Lear v Leggett* (1830) 1 Russ & M 690; *Pym v Lockyer* (1841) 12 Sim 394 (bankruptcy petition by person other than donee). For cases where the petition was filed by the donee himself see *Re Griffiths* [1926] Ch 1007; *Re Moon, ex p Dawes* (1886) 17 QBD 275; *Re Gates* (1895) 39 Sol Jo 331; *Re Cotgrave* [1903] 2 Ch 705. The last case was criticised in *Re Griffiths*.

[99.7]
Clause contemplating events in which donee is a passive or unwilling party. A clause not only prohibiting the doing of acts but going on to prohibit the suffering or permitting of acts will be operative in the case of acts of other parties such as proceedings in bankruptcy,[1] charging orders,[2] registration of a judgment.[3] But even in such cases the terms of the clause must be fulfilled and where the clause requires the property to vest in another, the proceedings must have that result before a forfeiture is caused.[4]

1   *Re Throckmorton, ex p Eyston* (1877) 7 Ch D 145; *Re Sartoris's Estate, Sartoris v Sartoris* [1892] 1 Ch 11; *Re Laye, Turnbull v Laye* [1913] 1 Ch 298.
2   *Roffey v Bent* (1867) LR 3 Eq 759.
3   *Re Moore* (1885) 17 LR Ir 549.
4   *Re Moon, ex p Dawes* (1886) 17 QBD 275 (filing of bankruptcy petition not followed by adjudication); *Re Ryan* (1887) 19 LR Ir 24 (execution on cattle). See also *Re James, Clutterbuck v James* (1890) 62 LT 545 (Scottish sequestration. No forfeiture because no vesting of property in another. The beneficiary does not permit any act or any process whereby the income becomes payable to another person when he becomes an enemy by operation of the Trading with the Enemy Act 1939: *Re Hall, Public Trustee v Montgomery* [1944] Ch 46, [1943] 2 All ER 753; *Re Harris, Cope v Evans* [1945] Ch 316, [1945] 1 All ER 702.

[99.8]

Clause providing for no loss of beneficial enjoyment. The common form of clause provides for forfeiture on the doing or attempting to do or suffering or permitting something which, if the interest belonged absolutely to the beneficiary, it would become vested in or payable to some person or persons other than the beneficiary. An assignment to trustees for the benefit of the assignor does not create a forfeiture under this clause[1] and where the beneficiary gave a written authority to pay to creditors the dividend to be declared at a stated time and in fact the company paid no dividend there was no forfeiture.[2] A bona fide power of attorney which is a mere authority to receive the income and not a colourable transaction amounting to an equitable assignment does not cause a forfeiture under this clause.[3] The forfeiture is not incurred so long as the beneficiary has the right to be paid the income as it falls due[4] and there is no vesting in any other person of the right to receive it;[5] but it is incurred where a person become an enemy by residence in enemy territory during a war.[6]

1 *Lockwood v Sikes* (1884) 51 LT 562 (marriage settlement of life interest by beneficiary); *Re Selby, Church v Tancred* [1903] 1 Ch 715 (power of attorney to receive income to trustees of settlement of such income, the settler being entitled under his settlement to receive such income during his life); *Re Swannell, Morice v Swannell* (1909) 101 LT 76 (power of attorney to receive income and apply it for benefit of beneficiary).
2 *Re Longman, Westminster Bank Ltd v Hatton* [1955] 1 All ER 455, [1955] 1 WLR 197.
3 *Avison v Holmes* (1861) 1 John & H 530; *Re Swannell, Morice v Swannell* (1909) 101 LT 76; *Smith v Perpetual Trustee Co Ltd and Delohery* (1910) 11 CLR 148; and for cases where there was an assignment, see *Wilkinson v Wilkinson* (1819) 2 Wils Ch 47; *Oldham v Oldham* (1867) LR 3 Eq 404; *Smith v Perpetual Trustee Co Ltd and Delohery*.
4 *Re Sampson, Sampson v Sampson* [1896] 1 Ch 630; *Re Jenkins, Williams v Jenkins* [1915] 1 Ch 46; *Re Clark, Clark v Clark* [1926] Ch 833.
5 *Re Brewer's Settlement, Morton v Blackmore* [1896] 2 Ch 503 (loan of trust fund to tenant for life who spent it; income not vested in another); *Re Dash, Darley v King* (1887) 57 LT 219 (conviction: no administrator appointed); *Re Beaumount, Woods v Beaumont* (1910) 79 LJ Ch 744 (appointment of receiver: no vesting in another person); *Re Mordaunt, Mordaunt v Mordaunt* (1914) 49 L Jo 225 (debt, though postponed until capital fell into possession, also charged on present income); *Re Crother's Trusts* [1915] 1 IR 53. As to clause of forfeiture on interest being taken in execution, see *Blackman v Fysh* [1892] 3 Ch 209 (judgment creditor obtaining the appointment of a receiver); *Re Baring's Settlement Trusts, Baring Bros & Co Ltd v Liddle* [1940] Ch 737, [1940] 3 All ER 20 (sequestration causes a forfeiture where clause provides for forfeiture when income payable to some other person). Cf however, *Re James, Clutterbuck v James* (1890) 62 LT 545 (Scottish sequestration); *Re Vaughan, Vaughan v MacIvor* [1926] IR 67 (suffering judgment against beneficiary).
6 *Re Hatch, Public Trustee v Hatch* [1948] Ch 592, [1948] 2 All ER 288, in which case the person was resident in the Channel Islands. It is otherwise in the case of a prisoner of war: *Vandyke v Adams* [1942] Ch 155, [1942] 1 All ER 139.

[99.9]

Clause refers to alienation by anticipation. The beneficiary is entirely free to assign or otherwise deal with the income which has already accrued due under the gift in the will and the clause is confined to dispositions of income to accrue due in the future.[1] Thus an assignment by way of security of all money due but not any future income is good;[2] and an assignment not referring to future income was held good where there were sufficient arrears to cover the debt;[3] a letter to the receiver of the estate to pay a creditor a certain sum when in fact the receiver had that sum in hand already accrued due to the beneficiary although the letter was worded 'to deduct from any sum that might become due';[4] garnishee order on income accrued due is not a ground for forfeiture.[5]

1   *Re Stulz's Trusts, ex p Kingsford and Stulz* (1853) 4 De GM & G 404; *Re Greenwood, Sutcliffe v Gledhill* [1901] 1 Ch 887 (where it is suggested that a prohibition of assignment of money accrued due is repugnant to the gift and void). As to dealing with both money accrued and to accrue due, see *Re Jenkins, Williams v Jenkins* [1915] 1 Ch 46 (where a mortgage was held valid so far as the sums had accrued due and invalid as to sums accruing due).
2   *Re Stulz's Trusts, ex p Kingsford and Stulz* (1853) 4 De GM & G 404.
3   *Cox v Bockett* (1865) 35 Beav 48 (apparently on the ground that a case of forfeiture is *strictissimi juris* and the court will not find one where it can avoid doing so).
4   *Durran v Durran* (1904) 91 LT 819.
5   *Re Greenwood, Sutcliffe v Gledhill* [1901] 1 Ch 887.

[99.10]
Where interest of beneficiary is reversionary. Where the interest of the beneficiary is reversionary a charge on it before it falls into possession does not cause a forfeiture the charge is got rid of before the interest vests in possession.[1] At what time thereafter the charge may be got rid of so as to avoid a forfeiture is a question on which the authorities are not unanimous. It has been said that it is sufficient if the charge is got rid of before any income is actually receivable;[2] or, in another case, before the time for distribution arrives[3] or a further view makes forfeiture dependent upon whether the chargee has taken any steps to enforce his security.[4] A forfeiture results where the charge is created after the interest has fallen into possession.[5]

1   *Re Parnham's Trusts* (1876) 46 LJ Ch 80; *Samuel v Samuel* (1879) 12 Ch D 152; *Hurst v Hurst* (1882) 21 Ch D 278. In *Re Loftus-Otway, Otway v Otway* [1895] 2 Ch 235, there was an act of bankruptcy before the interest fell into possession but the receiving order was made after that time. There was held to be a forfeiture.
2   *White v Chitty* (1866) LR 1 Eq 372: *Re Parnham's Trusts* (1876) 46 LJ Ch 80; *Robertson v Richardson* (1885) 30 Ch D 623; *Re Broughton, Peat v Broughton* (1887) 57 LT 8; *Metcalfe v Metcalfe* [1891] 3 Ch 1; *Re Forder, Forder v Forder* [1927] 2 Ch 291 (where the bankruptcy was not got rid of before income was actually received by the trustees but before the trustees actually decided to make any payment thereof, the forfeiture clause operated). Cf *Re Walker, Public Trustee v Walker* [1939] Ch 974, [1939] 3 All ER 902 (bankruptcy order before vesting of interest to be discharged as from a date after the vesting of the interest).
3   *Samuel v Samuel* (1879) 12 Ch D 152.
4   *Lloyd v Lloyd* (1866) LR 2 Eq 722; *Robertson v Richardson* (1885) 30 Ch D 623; *Re Broughton, Peat v Broughton* (1887) 57 LT 8.
5   *Hurst v Hurst* (1882) 21 Ch D 278; *Re Baker, Baker v Baker* [1904] 1 Ch 157.

CHAPTER 100

Hotchpot clauses

[100.1]

Purposes of the clause. A hotchpot clause in a will may be required both for the purpose of equalising the benefits which beneficiaries may receive under the exercise of a power of appointment as well as the benefits which may be conferred on them either by advances by the testator in his lifetime or by the release by provision in the will of debts owing to the testator.[1] The analogous presumption against double portions can also be referred to in this context.[2] The previous requirement to account for advancements in an intestacy, which also had some analogy with the matters discussed in this Chapter, has now been abolished.[3]

1   The ordinary hotchpot clause in settlements does not apply to advances: *Re Fox, Wodehouse v Fox* [1904] 1 Ch 480. See Vol 2, paras **[217.41]** to **[217.46]**.
2   See Chapter 44. The recent decision in *Re Cameron* [1999] Ch 386, [1999] 2 All ER 924 contains a full review of the cases and principles applicable to the analogous presumption of ademption of a legacy by a portion, to which reference can usefully be made.
3   By the Law Reform (Succession) Act 1995, s 1(2), whereby ss 47(1)(iii) and 49 (1)(aa), (a), (2) and (3), of the Administration of Estates Act 1925, cease to have effect after 1 January 1996.

[100.2]

Shares of fund under a power of appointment. The hotchpot clause in this case is designated to preclude appointees of a share of the fund subject to a power of appointment from receiving both under an exercise of the power of appointment and under the provisions in default of appointment which allow the beneficiaries to take in so far as any appointment does not extend. No beneficiary in whose favour an appointment has been made ought to participate in the unappointed part of the fund without bringing into account the appointed shares on the footing that they are received in or towards satisfaction of the shares to which he or she is entitled on the fund going in default of appointment.[1] If the power extends to issue more remote than children, the clause should be made to apply expressly to such issue.[2] The hotchpot clause applies to appointments of life or reversionary interests. Thus, if A and B are in default of appointment entitled to a fund in equal shares and by an appointment A takes a life interest and B takes a life interest on the death of A but in fact dies before A, then A's estate has to bring in the value of her life interest, but B's estate brings in nothing for his interest has been defeated.[3] Such a life interest has to be brought into account at the actuarial value of such interest determined at the date it falls into possession[4] and even if before any actual valuation is made such life tenant dies and its value could be precisely calculated in the events which have happened, it still has to be brought in on such actuarial valuation above stated.[5] In a later case a power of appointment was exercised by appointing one-third to each of two daughters for life with remainder to their children who should attain twenty-one or being female marry under that age and in default of any such children for such persons as the daughter should by will appoint. The remaining one-third share was left to pass in default of appointment. At the time of distribution one daughter had three infant children and the other, who had been married but a short time, had no children. It was held that in this case the daughters had to bring into hotchpot only the value of their life interests in the one-third shares and that the contingent interests of the children should be ignored although the hotchpot clause required to be bought into account 'the share or shares or interest appointed to him or her or his or her issue'.[6] Such life or reversionary interests must be valued for the purpose in the best way possible, and, if the parties cannot agree as to such valuation, an inquiry to determine such value will be ordered.[7]

1   In the absence of a hotchpot clause the appointee of a share in a fund is entitled to share in the unappointed residue of the fund: *Wilson v Piggott* (1794) 2 Ves 351; *Alloway v Alloway* (1843) 4 Dr & War 380; *Walmsley v Vaughan* (1857) 1 De G & J 114; *Foster v Cautley* (1855) 6 De GM & G 55; *Re Alfreton's Trust Estates* (1883) 52 LJ Ch 745; *Close v Coote* (1880) 7 LR Ir 564, and where a beneficiary is given a certain sum at the age of 21 which is called an advance and a larger sum at a later age and there is no hotchpot clause, the beneficiary is entitled to the larger sum in full without bringing the earlier payment into account: *Re Cross Estate* (1965) 51 WWR 377. The rule may, however, be excluded by clear expression of intention on the part of the appointor: *Fortescue v Gregor* (1800) 5 Ves 553; *Foster v Cautley*, or by the appointee agreeing to take under the appointment in lieu of his share in the unappointed property: *Clune v Apjohn* (1866) 17 I Ch R 25; *Armstrong v Lynn* (1875) IR 9 Eq 186. Where the appointor states that he makes no appointment of the unappointed part in order that it may pass directly to the other objects of the power, this does not prevent the appointee sharing in the unappointed part: *Re Jack, Jack v Jack* [1899] 1 Ch 374; *Langslow v Langslow* (1856) 21 Beav 552. The fact that the appointment is made and stated to be 'as his share' does not prevent the appointee sharing the unappointed part: *Wilson v Piggott* (1794) 2 Ves 351; *Wombwell v Hanrott* (1851) 14 Beav 143; *Walmsley v Vaughan* (1857) 1 De G & J 114. The hotchpot clause may be in the will creating the power or in the will exercising the power.
2   *Langslow v Langslow* (1856) 21 Beav 552; *Hewitt v Jardine* (1872) LR 14 Eq 58.
3   *Re West, Denton v West* [1921] 1 Ch 533.
4   *Re Westropp* (1903) 37 ILT Rep 183.
5   *Re Thomson Settlement Trusts, Robertson v Makepeace* [1953] Ch 414, [1953] 1 All ER 1139, and compare *Re Heathcote, Trench v Heathcote* [1891] WN 10; *Re West, Denton v West* [1921] 1 Ch 533; *Re North Settled Estates, Public Trustee v Graham* [1946] Ch 13.
6   *Re Gordon, Public Trustee v Bland* [1942] Ch 131, [1942] 1 All ER 59.
7   *Rücker v Scholefield* (1862) 1 Hem & M 36; *Eales v Drake* (1875) 1 Ch 217, but see *Williamson v Jeffreys* (1854) 18 Jur 1071.

[100.3]
Application where two settled funds. If two distinct funds are settled for the same purpose by two distinct instruments, each containing a hotchpot clause, each hotchpot clause applies only to the fund settled by the instrument containing it,[1] and where an instrument declared express trusts of one fund with a hotchpot clause referring to that fund, the hotchpot clause was not incorporated with reference to the second and distinct fund by a general reference to the trusts, powers, provisos, and agreements expressed in reference to the former fund.[2] An instrument may, however, contain an express provision that the clause

shall apply to all funds, and, even in the absence of such a clause, a clear intention may be shown that it shall apply to all funds thereby settled.[3]

1   *Montague v Montague* (1852) 15 Beav 565; *Lady Wellesley v Earl of Mornington* (1855) 2 K & J 143. A power of appointment over an original share operates on an accruing share which become subject to the same trusts, powers and provisos as the original share: *Re Hutchison's Settlement, ex p Drum* (1852) 5 De G & Sm 681.
2   *Re Marquis of Bristol, Earl Grey v Grey* [1897] 1 Ch 946; *Re Cavendish's Settlement, Grosvenor v Butler* [1912] 1 Ch 794; *Re Wood, Wodehouse v Wood* [1913] 1 Ch 303.
3   *Hutchinson v Tottenham* [1898] 1 IR 403; *Re Perkins, Perkins v Bagot* [1893] 1 Ch 283.

[100.4]

Prior advances. A hotchpot clause[1] directing past advances or other sums or property to be brought into account is construed so as to give effect to the whole will,[2] and, as in the case of other divesting provisions,[3] is in general construed strictly.[4] Such a clause is not, of itself, a release from the personal liability, if any, of the donee to repay such advances.[5] Where the debts of a legatee to the testator are greater than his benefits under the will, he is not released as to the excess unless the will so provides.[6]

1   The object of such a clause is to produce equality as between the donees, taking into consideration past gifts: see *Fox v Fox* (1870) LR 11 Eq 142 (effect as notional increase of testator's estate); *Smith v Crabtree* (1877) 6 Ch D 591 (exclusion of set-off of debt against specific legacy); *Wheeler v Humphreys* [1898] AC 506 (reversionary interest (which was contingent) brought in not under hotchpot clause but under directions in will). The clause does not operate as a release of personal liability: see infra. An advance to a tenant for life of a settled share may have to be brought into account against the stirps: *Re Sparkes, Kemp-Welch v Kemp-Welch* (1911) 56 Sol Jo 90. A child is not liable to bring into account his parent's debt against the estate: *Re Binns, Public Trustee v Ingle* [1929] 1 Ch 677.
2   *Brocklehurst v Flint* (1852) 16 Beav 100 (where the clause was that any advances made were to be brought into account, it was held that it referred only to the unappointed part of a fund given to the four persons); *Stares v Penton* (1867) LR 4 Eq 40 (clause ceasing to operate after one member entitled to payment); *Stewart v Stewart* (1880) 15 Ch D 539 (applied only to children and not to widow); *Re Arbuthnot, Arbuthnot v Arbuthnot* [1915] 1 Ch 422 (covenant to pay trustees of marriage settlement not within clause); *Nugee v Chapman* (1860) 29 Beav 288 (direction to bring purchase price of property into account: contract rescinded before testator's death: direction inoperative).
3   See Chapter 96.
4   Even where the person to account has obtained a benefit, the clause is not extended to advances to persons other than those contemplated by the will, eg the husband of a daughter; *M'Clure v Evans* (1861) 29 Beav 422; *Silverside v Silverside* (1858) 25 Beav 340 (children of the legatee); *Douglas v Willes* (1849) 7 Hare 318 (assignees of legatee under an assignment before advance); *Hewitt v Jardine* (1872) LR 14 Eq 58 (unless necessarily implied); *White v Turner* (1858) 25 Beav 505 (wife and children who were given interests in a son's share); *Re Haygarth, Wickham v Haygarth* [1913] 2 Ch 9 (where an obvious blunder was made in the clause and it was corrected to make it a consistent whole).
5   *Re Warde, Warde v Ridgway* (1914) 111 LT 35; *Re Young, Young v Young* [1914] 1 Ch 581; *Re Barker, Gilbey v Barker* [1918] 1 Ch 128; and this is so even where there is a deficiency of assets and the hotchpot clause becomes inoperative: *Re Horn, Westminster Bank Ltd v Horn* [1946] Ch 254, [1946] 2 All ER 118.
6   *Re Horn, Westminster Bank Ltd v Horn* [1946] Ch 254, [1946] 2 All ER 118, disapproving *Re Trollope, Game v Trollope* [1915] 1 Ch 853; *Re Clark, Cross v Hillis* [1924] WN 75.

[100.5]

Methods of accounting. Apart from a special direction,[1] there are two methods of bringing the advances into account. The first is to value the estate at the time fixed by the will for the distribution;[2] to that value is added for computation the amount of the advances; the total is then divided into the required number of shares and the advances are deducted from the advanced shares respectively. The income is then divided on the footing that these shares represent the shares of the persons interested in the residuary estate.[3] The second method is to defer the valuation until the period of actual distribution. Meanwhile to the actual income of the estate is added for the purpose of computation a sum equivalent to 4 per cent on the amount of the advances. The income thus notionally arrived at is divided into the required number of shares, and interest at the rate of 4 per cent[4] on the advances is deducted from the shares of that income of the advanced beneficiaries respectively.[5] The first method has been adopted in recent years.[6] The second method has been adopted when, from the nature of the estate or a substantial part of it, it is not practicable to make a fair and proper valuation at the time fixed for distribution,[7] or it appears from the will as a whole that the testator did not contemplate that there would in fact be an actual distribution at that time;[8] and this is the rule which should be generally adopted.[9] Only by taking the value at the date of distribution is the postulated equality reached and the rules and practice of the court assume and require due diligence in administration.[10] It appears, however, that each donee bears a share of any annuities charged on the estate, according to his aliquot share as determined by the will apart from hotchpot.[11] It was held under the former law relating to estate duty that it was the net value of both the advance[12] and the estate[13] that was relevant where the advances had to be brought into account against the net residuary estate.[14]

1   *Re Willoughby, Willoughby v Decies* [1911] 2 Ch 581 (direction for securing equality of portions held to refer only to capital).

2   Whether this date is that of the death of the testator: *Hilton v Hilton* (1872) LR 14 Eq 468; *Field v Seward* (1877) 5 Ch D 538; *Re Lambert, Middleton v Moore* [1897] 2 Ch 169; *Re Whiteford, Inglis v Whiteford* [1903] 1 Ch 889, or other later period: *Andrewes v George* (1830) 3 Sim 393; *Re Rees, Rees v George* (1881) 17 Ch D 701; *Re Dallmeyer, Dallmeyer v Dallmeyer* [1896] 1 Ch 372. The effect of a charge on the fund, such as an annuity secured on part of the fund does not alter the date of distribution for this purpose: *Re Whiteford, Inglis v Whiteford*; *Re Willoughby, Willoughby v Decies* [1911] 2 Ch 581. Settled funds must be brought into account at the value at the date of settlement: *Re Crocker, Crocker v Crocker* [1916] 1 Ch 25.

3   *Re Hargreaves, Hargreaves v Hargreaves* (1903) 88 LT 100; *Re Gilbert, Gilbert v Gilbert* [1908] WN 63; *Re Hart, Hart v Arnold* (1912) 107 LT 759; *Re Mansel, Smith v Mansel* [1930] 1 Ch 352.

4   Under neither mode is interest charged up to the death of the testator: *Re Willoughby, Willoughby v Decies* [1911] 2 Ch 581; *Re Whiteford, Inglis v Whiteford* [1903] 1 Ch 889, or other time fixed for distribution: *Re Dallmeyer, Dallmeyer v Dallmeyer* [1896] 1 Ch 372; *Re Willoughby v Decies*; *Re Forster-Brown, Barry v Forster-Brown* [1914] 2 Ch 584. Interest, however, runs from the time fixed for distribution until actual distribution: *Re Dallmeyer, Dallmeyer v Dallmeyer*. The rate was usually 4 per cent per annum: *Re Cooke, Randall v Cooke* [1916] 1 Ch 480; *Re Hillas-Drake, National Provincial Bank v Liddell* [1944] Ch 235, [1944] 1 All ER 375. But for the current rate of interest on general legacies, see Chapter 32, para **[32.4]**, n 1.

5   *Re Mansel, Smith v Mansel* [1930] 1 Ch 352. As to deduction of income tax, see *Re Foster, Hunt v Foster* [1920] 1 Ch 391; *Re Hillas-Drake, National Provincial Bank v Liddell* [1944] Ch 235, [1944] 1 All ER 375.

6   *Re Mansel, Smith v Mansel* [1930] 1 Ch 352, where the cases in which the two modes have been applied is discussed.

7   *Re Craven, Watson v Craven* [1914] 1 Ch 358; *Re Cooke, Randall v Cooke* [1916] 1 Ch 480; *Re Forster-Brown, Barry v Forster-Brown* [1914] 2 Ch 584; *Re Tod, Bradshaw v Turner* [1916] 1 Ch 567.

8   *Re Poyser, Landon v Poyser* [1908] 1 Ch 828.

9   *Re Wills, Dulverton v Macleod* [1939] Ch 705, [1939] 2 All ER 775 (where the subject was
    reviewed); *Re Hillas-Drake, National Provincial Bank v Liddell* [1944] Ch 235, [1944] 1 All
    ER 375; not following *Re Gunther's Will Trusts, Alexander v Gunther* [1939] Ch 985, [1939] 3
    All ER 291; *Re Oram, Oram v Oram* [1940] Ch 1001, [1940] 4 All ER 161; *Re Slee, Midland
    Bank Executor and Trustee Co Ltd v Slee* [1962] 1 All ER 542, [1962] 1 WLR 496; *Re
    Rudderham* (1971) 21 DLR (3d) 457.
10 *Re Hillas-Drake, National Provincial Bank v Liddell* [1944] Ch 235 at 240, [1944] 1 All ER
    375 at 377.
11 *Re Hargreaves, Hargreaves v Hargreaves* (1902) 86 LT 43; on appeal (1903) 88 LT 100, CA.
    See also *Re Poyser, London v Poyser* (1908) 99 LT 50 at 53, where some doubt was expressed
    on this point, but the rule is apparently settled: see *Re Hargreaves, Hargreaves v Hargreaves*
    (1903) 88 LT 100 at 101.
12 *Re Beddington, Micholls v Samuel* [1900] 1 Ch 771; *Re Crocker, Crocker v Crocker* [1916] 1
    Ch 25.
13 *Re Turner's Will Trusts, Westminster Bank Ltd v Turner* [1968] 1 All ER 321; compare *Re
    Tollemache, Forbes v Public Trustees* [1930] WN 138.
14 See *Re Slee, Midland Bank Executor and Trustee Co Ltd v Slee* [1962] 1 All ER 542 at 508,
    [1962] 1 WLR 496 at 550, 551, for the position where the advance was not itself liable to estate
    duty and the advanced beneficiary had to bring the advance into hotchpot, against a fund which
    bore its own duty.

[100.6]

What are advances. The word 'advances' primarily means advances of money,
whether by way of loan or by payment at the request of the legatee.[1] It may
include debts which are statute-barred[2] or the balance of a debt after deducting
dividends received in the legatee's bankruptcy;[3] but, if the clause directs
hotchpot, not of the sums advanced, but of the debts owing, the effect of a
composition or bankruptcy or of the Limitation Act is to render the clause
inoperative as to those sums.[4] It does not ordinarily include payments made after
death, even in discharge of liabilities undertaken during the life of the testator on
behalf of the legatee,[5] or other kinds of property given during the life of the
testator,[6] but it may include all gifts during his life, and advances made by the
trustees or executors after the death of the testator are included where such
advances are contemplated by the will.[7] If the hotchpot clause relates to
advances made by any person in his lifetime, without more, a gift by the will of
that person,[8] or an interest taken under his intestacy,[9] is not within the clause.
Advances must in the ordinary way be made early in life, be sufficiently large to
give rise to a presumption that they are a permanent provision for the
beneficiary, and perhaps form a relatively large part of the estate of the person
making the advance.[10]

1   *Re Jaques, Hodgson v Braisby* [1903] 1 Ch 267 at 274; *Re Clarke, Clarke v Sturt* [1929] VLR
    249 (not payments in lieu of sums due under settlement). See also *Re Cameron* [1999] Ch 386,
    [1999] 2 All ER 924, where it was held that a payment (in effect) by a grandmother towards the
    cost of a grandchild's education could be a portion to the child's father, within the presumption
    against double portions.
2   *Poole v Poole* (1871) 7 Ch App 17.
3   *Auster v Powell* (1863) 1 De GJ & Sm 99; *Re Ainsworth, Millington v Ainsworth* [1922] 1 Ch
    22.
4   *Golds v Greenfield* (1854) 2 Sm & G 476 (composition); *Re Jolly, Gathercole v Norfolk* [1900]
    2 Ch 616 (Limitation Act).
5   *Auster v Powell* (1863) 1 De GJ & Sm 99; *Re Whitehouse, Whitehouse v Edwards* (1887) 37 Ch
    D 683.
6   *Douglas v Willes* (1849) 7 Hare 318; *Re Jacques, Hodgson v Braisby* [1903] 1 Ch 267 (an
    advance of money is commonly spoken of and the expression is perfectly intelligible, but an

advance of a house or a chattel would not be understood, without explanation, by anyone but a lawyer).

7   *Re Whiteford, Inglis v Whiteford* [1903] 1 Ch 889 (where *Hilton v Hilton* (1872) LR 14 Eq 468 is corrected); *Re Prittie* [1940] 1 DLR 795. The payment by the testator of a premium for a son is not an 'advance' to be accounted for: *Re Watney, Watney v Gold* (1911) 56 Sol Jo 109 (fee paid to architect to learn the business).
8   *Cooper v Cooper* (1873) 8 Ch App 813 (where earlier cases are discussed and criticised).
9   *Twisden v Twisden* (1804) 9 Ves 413 at 427.
10 *Re Hayward, Kerrod v Hayward* [1957] Ch 528, [1957] 2 All ER 474; applied in *Hardy v Shaw* [1975] 2 All ER 1052 at 1056, rejecting a narrow construction of 'advancement' in favour of including, 'anything which may fairly be described as a permanent provision'.

[100.7]
Recitals relating to advances. In cases where the testator states by recital in his will the sum advanced, a mistake in the amount is immaterial if the hotchpot clause clearly directs hotchpot of the sum received to have been advanced,[1] but if the clause directs hotchpot of that sum or so much thereof as remains unpaid, the intention is inferred that only the amount actually owing is to be brought into account, and the mistake may be corrected.[2] In such a recital or in his will the testator may refer to non-testamentary documents even made subsequent to the will and such documents may be referred to as evidence of the advances made,[3] but cannot be used for the purpose of varying the terms of the will.[4]

1   *Re Wood, Ward v Wood* (1886) 32 Ch D 517.
2   *Re Taylor's Estate, Tomlin v Underhay* (1881) 22 Ch D 495 at 500; *Re Kelsey, Woolley v Kelsey* [1905] 2 Ch 465.
3   *Whateley v Spooner* (1857) 3 K & J 542. In *Smith v Conder* (1878) 9 Ch D 170, and *Re Coyte* (1887) 56 LT 510, it was said that subsequent unattested letters or entries in a book could not be referred to, but it appears that this is so only for the purpose of admitting them to probate. In *Quihampton v Going* (1876) 24 WR 917, the entries were made previously to the date of the will. See also *Kirk v Eddowes* (1844) 3 Hare 509 at 518 and *Re Deprez, Henriques v Deprez* [1917] 1 Ch 24.
4   *Smith v Conder* (1878) 9 Ch D 170; *Whateley v Spooner* (1857) 3 K & J 542.

CHAPTER 101

Gifts by implication

[101.1]

Basis of implication. In certain cases limitations and gifts can be implied. The doctrine of implication of limitations is based, not on necessity, but on so strong a probability of intention to benefit the persons in question that a contrary intention cannot be supposed;[1] and this probability of intention to benefit must arise out of the words of the will.[2] Implication has been said to be founded on two grounds. It may either arise from an elliptical form of expression which involves and implies something else as contemplated by the person using the expression, or the implication may be founded on the form of the gift, or upon a direction to do something which cannot be carried into effect without, of necessity, involving something else in order to give effect to that direction, or something else which is a consequence necessarily resulting from that direction.[3] Thus it arises in a case which on the words of the will was obviously within the intention of the testator, but for which he has made no express provision,[4] and there is a gap to be filled in.[5] The court will supply the defect by implication and thus mould the language of the testator so as to carry into effect, as far as possible, the intention of the testator, provided always that the court is of opinion that such intention which is to be so implied is sufficiently declared in the will itself.[6] A construction which leads to an intestacy should be avoided unless the language of the will necessarily leads to this result.[7] An interest will not be implied in favour of any person for whom it cannot be said that the testator intended to provide.[8]

1   *Wilkinson v Adam* (1813) 1 Ves & B 422 at 466 (not natural necessity but so strong probability that intention to the contrary impossible); *Crook v Hill* (1871) 6 Ch App 311 at 315 (approval of statement in *Wilkinson v Adam*).
2   *Scalé v Rawlins* [1892] AC 342.
3   *Parker v Tootal* (1865) 11 HL Cas 143 at 161; *Hall v Leitch* (1870) LR 9 Eq 376.
4   *Re Redfern, Redfern v Bryning* (1877) 6 Ch D 133; *Mellor v Daintree* (1886) 33 Ch D 198 at 206; *Lillicrap v Sinclair* [1919] NZLR 194.
5   *Watkins v Frederick* (1865) 11 HL Cas 358 at 374; *Saunders v Lowe* (1775) 2 Wm Bl 1014 (gift to trustees during lives of four daughters and survivors upon trust for the survivor and the children of such daughters as should first die); *Re Morton, M'Auley v Harvey* (1919) 53 ILT 105 (gift on marriage).
6   *Towns v Wentworth* (1858) 11 Moo PCC 526 at 543, followed in *Sweeting v Prideaux* (1876) 2 Ch D 413 at 416.
7   *Re Ragdale, Public Trustee v Tuffill* [1934] Ch 352.
8   *Monnypeny v Dering* (1852) 2 De GM & G 145 at 174; *Re Rising, Rising v Rising* [1904] 1 Ch 533; *Re Mortimer, Gray v Gray* [1905] 2 Ch 502 (all cases in which this principle placed a limit on the application of the *cy-près* doctrine to the construction of limitations). See also *Law's Trustee v Gray* 1921 SC 455.

[101.2]
Nature of implication. The term is applied to the inference of gifts to persons not mentioned in the will. Thus from a declared intention to provide for posthumous children, it may in some contexts be inferred that the testator intended to provide for children born in his lifetime after the date of the will,[1] but this inference will not be made in all cases.[2] Words of exclusion may imply a gift to others not expressly excluded, for instance, where it is directed that certain persons entitled on intestacy are not to take any benefit in the testator's estate, this may be a sufficient gift to the others so entitled.[3] A mere exclusion from benefits under the will is not sufficient, since such persons claim outside the will.[4] A recital that a certain person is entitled to a certain interest has sometimes constituted a gift of that interest.[5] There may, also, be an inference of an extension or modification of the interests of persons who are mentioned as the objects of the testator's bounty, so as to give them interests which the words of the will making gifts to them would not create if taken by themselves.[6] Where if the daughter died before the widow, her issue were to be entitled to an absolute interest, but no provision was made for her surviving the widow and dying leaving issue though every other contingency was provided for, there was implied a gift to the issue in equal shares if the daughter survived the widow and died leaving issue.[7]

1   *White v Barber* (1771) 5 Burr 2703 (devise to son then living and if he die under 21 and wife enceinte at his death with other child or children, then to such at 21. Two children born in lifetime of testator but after the date of the will took); *Goodfellow v Goodfellow* (1854) 18 Beav 356; *Re Lindsay* (1852) 5 Ir Jur 97.
2   *Doe d Blakiston v Haslewood* (1851) 10 CB 544, where the Court of Common Pleas refused to follow *White v Barber* (1771) 5 Burr 2703, but subsequently in Ireland a preference was stated for the earlier decision, though it was not in the particular case necessary to act upon it: *Re Lindsay* (1852) 5 Ir Jur 97. As to implication of gifts to children or issue from gifts in default of children or issue, see para **[101.10]** infra.
3   *Vachell v Breton* (1706) 5 Bro Parl Cas 51; *Bund v Green* (1879) 12 Ch D 819; *Re Wynn, Landolt v Wynn* [1983] 3 All ER 310, followed in *Re Jacques* (1985) 16 DLR (4th) 472 and in *Re Sharpe* (1985) 18 DLR (4th) 421.
4   *Re Holmes, Holmes v Holmes* (1890) 62 LT 383; *Bateman v Bateman* [1941] 3 DLR 762.
5   See Chapter 52.
6   See implication from gifts on failure of issue, para **[101.10]** infra. Where a will provided for simultaneous deaths and made no provision for the husband surviving for more than one month, an absolute gift to the husband was implied: *Re Smith, Veasey v Smith* [1948] Ch 49, [1947] 2 All ER 78.
7   *Re Brown* (1962) 31 DLR (2d) 477.

[101.3]
Implication more than mere construction. The term 'implication' is not applied to the construction of gifts where the only question is the manner in which the words of the will are to be read, and no interest is inferred which the words of the gift taken in some sense or other would not create.[1] Thus, a gift to a person in trust for his children after his death, or to him to be distributed or disposed of by his will in a certain manner, may give that person a life estate expressly and not by implication.[2] Nor is it a case of implication where words are altered or supplied as being erroneously written or omitted, so long as the quantum of interest conferred on the donees under the will is unchanged,[3] nor can there be any estate raised by implication in a gift of another man's property

under the doctrine of election,[4] or, in general, by a mere erroneous recital of a right which the testator considers to belong to the person claiming the implied interest.[5]

1   *Tunaley v Roch* (1857) 3 Drew 720 at 725; *Crumpe v Crumpe* [1900] AC 127 at 132 (it is not a gift by implication, but it is an explanation of what he has done before).

2   *Ramsden v Hassard* (1791) 3 Bro CC 236; *Acheson v Fair* (1843) 3 Dr & War 512 at 527; *Greenwood v Greenwood* (1877) 5 Ch D 954.

3   See Chapter 52. In certain cases limitations have been inspired in dispositions: *Mellor v Daintree* (1886) 33 Ch D 198 (though in this case it was spoken of as an implication); *Phillips v Rail* (1906) 54 WR 517.

4   *Dashwood v Peyton* (1811) 18 Ves 27 at 48.

5   *Dashwood v Peyton* (1811) 18 Ves 27, discussing *Tilly v Tilly* (1743), cited in that case at p 43, and the decision in which is said to be to the contrary.

[101.4]
Implication of life interest from gift over on death. A life interest has been impliedly conferred on a person where the will contains a gift after the death of that person, and the court has from the context of the will inferred an intention on the part of the testator that the person should enjoy the property in the meantime.[1] In general, however, a gift after the death of any person does not by implication confer on him any interest.[2]

1   *Roe d Bendall v Summerset* (1770) 2 Wm Bl 692 (gift to A after the death of B implies a life interest in B; a strong probable implication is sufficient, it need not be a necessary implication); *Bird v Hunsdon* (1818) 3 Swan 342 (income to be paid to M while single and without child implied a gift to M while married and having a child where no gift until her death); *Townley v Bolton* (1832) 1 My & K 148 (interest given for joint lives of husband and wife, surviving husband took for the remainder of his life where no other interest created until 'after their decease'); *Re Smith's Trusts* (1865) LR 1 Eq 79 (gift after death of J to E for life but if E died during lifetime of J to M for life and after decease of both E and M over: M took for life although E did not die in the lifetime of J); *Re Blake's Trust* (1867) LR 3 Eq 799 (husband given life estate if children, but not provided for if no children, but as the gift over in the latter case only took effect on death of both husband and wife, gift implied of life estate for husband as he survived the wife); *Blackwell v Bull* (1836) 1 Keen 176 (life interest for wife implied where property given over on her death): *Cockshott v Cockshott* (1846) 2 Coll 432 (similar case where wife took only so long as she was a widow); *Re Lindley, Lindley v Lindley and Union Trustee Co of Australia Ltd* [1911] SR Qd 96 (property given to wife to be divided between children on wife's death). The principle of these cases was not applied in *Barnet v Barnet* (1861) 29 Beav 239, and *Ralph v Carrick* (1877) 5 Ch D 984, but seems to have been applied in *Re Willatts, Willatts v Artley* [1905] 1 Ch 378, where, however, the order was by consent. The court, it appears, must find a context in order to apply the principle of the above cases.

2   *Dyer v Dyer* (1816) 1 Mer 414; *Re Drakeley's Estate* (1854) 19 Beav 395; *Swan v Holmes* (1854) 19 Beav 471; *Cranley v Dixon* (1857) 23 Beav 512 (will giving immediate annuities, codicil postponing annuities to death of wife); *Barnet v Barnet*, supra (to E for life but no division to be made until death of E and her husband: husband took no interest by implication); *Isaacson v Van Goor* (1872) 42 LJ Ch 193; *Round v Pickett* (1878) 47 LJ Ch 631; *Ralph v Carrick* (1879) 11 Ch D 873 (decided on the point that though a life estate will be implied where the gift is to A and then to the testator's heir or next of kin, it will not be implied where the gift over is to the heir or next of kin along with other persons: see next following paragraph).

[101.5]
Gift over on death to testator's successor on intestacy. Before 1926 where a will contained a devise of real estate from the death of A (a named person) to the heir-at-law of the testator, but there was no express disposition of the property during A's life, a gift to A for his life was implied.[1] Since descent to the heir is

abolished, the rule in its original form cannot now be applied to real property. All property both real and personal undisposed of by the will becomes subject to a trust (with power of sale, previously a trust for sale),[2] and the net residue after payment of debts and expenses goes to the persons entitled under the new rules of distribution.[3] It would appear, however, that the rule is still applicable where property, real or personal, is given after the death of A to the person who is solely entitled, or who are all the persons, with or without the exclusion of the named person, entitled under these new rules. It is, of course, open to the court to decline to apply this technical rule of construction to these new circumstances.

1   For a full discussion of this rule see the third edition of this work, p 649, 650.
2   Administration of Estates Act 1925, s 33; 17 *Halsbury's Statutes* (4th edn) 437. Vol 2, Part G, para **[244.58]**. This section has been amended by the Trusts of Land and Appointment of Trustees Act 1996 with the effect of substituting a simple trust for the previous trust for sale and conversion. See Chapter 104, para **[104.2]** infra, on the previous trust for sale and the present trust with power to sell on intestacy.
3   Administration of Estates Act 1925, ss 46, 47; 17 *Halsbury's Statutes* (4th edn) 452, 457. See Vol 2, Part G, paras **[244.60]**, **[244.61]**.

[101.6]
Gift over after death of survivor of life tenants. Where property is given to named persons for their respective lives, either generally or expressly as tenants in common, and is given over after the death of the survivor,[1] or after 'their' death,[2] the survivors and survivor are held to take estates for life, subject to any contrary intention shown by the context.[3]

1   The reason for the rule is either that the gift over modifies the previous words, showing an intention to create a joint tenancy, or that the implication is necessary to effectuate the intention: *Armstrong v Eldridge* (1791) 3 Bro CC 215; *Doe d Borwell v Abey* (1813) 1 M & S 428; *Re Richerson, Scales v Heyhoe (No 2)* [1893] 3 Ch 146; *Re Buller, Buller v Giberne* (1896) 74 LT 406; *Jennings v Hanna* [1904] 1 IR 540; *Re Telfair, Garrioch v Barclay* (1902) 86 LT 496; *Re Hobson, Barwick v Holt* [1912] 1 Ch 626; *Re Tate, Williamson v Gilpin* [1914] 2 Ch 182 (where the rule was applied notwithstanding that there was a clause substituting issue for their deceased parents); *Re Hey's Settlement Trusts and Will Trusts, Hey v Nickell-Lean* [1945] Ch 294, [1945] 1 All ER 618 (following the last case); *Re Stanley's Settlement, Maddocks v Andrews* [1916] 2 Ch 50. As to gifts 'at their deaths', see *Malcolm v Martin* (1790) 3 Bro CC 50; *Alt v Gregory* (1856) 8 De GM & G 221; *Townley v Bolton* (1832) 1 My & K 148; *Moffatt v Burnie* (1853) 18 Beav 211 (with remainder to my grandchildren). As to distributive construction where different properties are given and the gift over is on death of all, see para **[101.14]** infra. As to gift of shares in the same property, see *Round v Pickett* (1878) 47 LJ Ch 631. There is no such implication from a gift on the death of a tenant for life to two persons with a gift over if neither of them is then living: *Baxter v Losh* (1851) 14 Beav 612.
2   *Re Ragdale, Public Trustee v Tuffill* [1934] Ch 352 ('from and after their decease'); *Re Pringle, Baker v Matheson* [1946] Ch 124, [1946] 1 All ER 88 (after the 'deaths of these two named'); both cases followed in *Re McKay* [1968] NZLR 131; *Re Foster* [1946] Ch 135, [1946] 1 All ER 333 ('after their death'); *Re Pritchard, Hamblin v Pritchard* (1906) 6 SRNSW 353; *Re Moran* [1950] SASR 209. This is not so where the life interests are gifts of income only: *Re Bassett* [1961] VR 51.
3   *Hawkins v Hammerton* (1848) 16 Sim 410 (express gift in one contingency to survivors and their issue); *Doe d Partick v Royle* (1849) 13 QB 100 (after the death of either of them); *Re Hobson, Barwick v Holt* [1912] 1 Ch 626 (provision for some of the ultimate takers during lives of first takers); *Re Tate* [1914] 2 Ch 182 (to pay the income to their issue if any of them; die before the others of them), *Re Davies* [1950] 1 All ER 120 (after the death of all children); *Re Clancy* [1953] OWN 741 (gift of income from one third of residue to each of A, B and C. Upon death of the survivor of A and B, residue to be divided among children of C B having died, the income from his third was undisposed of during the life of A but it was held as there was no limitation on the gift of income to B, the income until A's death belonged to B's estate).

[101.7]
Implication of absolute interests from gifts over. Implication of an absolute interest often arises from a gift over, where after a prior gift[1] the property given is directed to go over in a particular event, and it is taken to have been intended that it was not to go over in any other event.[2] Thus, where there is a gift to the donee until he attains a certain age, followed by a gift over to other persons on his failure to attain that age, the donee takes by implication absolutely if he attains that age.[3] Such a gift is not implied, however, in a case where the gift over and the period for which the property is held in suspense do not correspond.[4] Although a gift to trustees for a person until he attains a certain age, without a gift over, does not always give that person the absolute interest, it may do so if there are other indications that such is the intention[5] and that the trust is only to point out the mode of taking.[6]

1   There is no such implication where there is no prior gift: *James v Shannon* (1868) IR 2 Eq 118.
2   *Re Harrison's Estate* (1870) 5 Ch App 408 at 411; *Re Thomson's Trusts* (1870) LR 11 Eq 146; *Lock v Lock* (1915) 15 SRNSW 287; *Re Branton* (1910) 15 SRNSW 287.
3   *Tomkins v Tomkins* (1743), cited in 1 Burr at 234; *Goodright d Hoskins v Hoskins* (1808) 9 East 306; *Doe d Wright v Cundall* (1808) 9 East 400; *Gardiner v Stevens* (1860) 7 Jur NS 307; *Cropton v Davies* (1869) LR 4 CP 159; *Re Cotter* (1915) 24 DLR 289; *Re Walker, Romilly v Robinson* [1905] St R Qd 74; *Re Vicker's Will* [1912] VLR 385; *Re Eichardt, Brebner v O'Meara* (1905) 25 NZLR 374.
4   *Savage v Tyers* (1872) 7 Ch App 356 at 364 (first gift of a life estate); *Fitzhenry v Bonner* (1853) 2 Drew 36 (first gift to wife for her and her son's support until he attained 21).
5   Such a gift was held to give the absolute interest in *Newland v Shephard* (1723) 2 P Wms 194 (where no gift over occurred), but this case was disapproved in *Fonnereau v Fonnereau* (1745) 3 Atk 315 at 317, and *Peat v Powell* (1760) Amb 387 (where at 21 the trust was to cease). Further authorities on this point are *Cropton v Davies* (1869) LR 4 CP 159; *Wilks v Williams* (1861) 2 John & H 125 at 128. In *Re Hedley's Trusts* (1877) 25 WR 529, the gift was held not to pass the absolute interest, but see *Re Vicker's Will* [1912] VLR 385.
6   *Hale v Beck* (1764) 2 Eden 229; *Atkinson v Paice* (1781) 1 Bro CC 91.

[101.8]
Other implications of absolute interests. From the fact that some person is appointed trustee for another person simply, in circumstances such that the trustee takes an absolute interest or estate in fee simple, it is inferred that the second is intended to have the life interest,[1] or from the fact that the testator has given a life interest upon a condition it may be in some cases inferred that he intends an absolute gift where the condition is unfulfilled and the will makes no disposition of the property after the life interest.[2] In all cases the court must find in the will a context requiring such an implication. Where there is no such context no such implication can be made. Thus a gift to individuals until attaining the age of twenty-five is a gift of income till that age is attained, and the capital then falls into residue or passes on intestacy as the case may require.[3]

1   *Peat v Powell* (1760) Amb 387; *Davis v Davis* (1830) 1 Russ & M 645; *Wilks v Williams* (1861) 2 John & H 125.
2   *Re Lane's Estate, Meagher v National Gallery of Ireland (Governors and Guardians) and Heaven* [1946] 1 All ER 735.
3   *Re Arnould, Arnould v Lloyd* [1955] 2 All ER 316, [1955] 1 WLR 539, not followed and disapproved of, in *McClymont v Hooper* (1973) 47 ALJR 222, HC of A. But a gift in trust for an infant until he shall attain 21 has been held to give an absolute gift if there is no further gift of the property: *Re Muller* [1950] QWN 33.

[101.9]

Implication in favour of objects of power of appointment. Where there is a power to appoint among certain objects, but no gift to those objects and no gift over in default of appointment,[1] the court implies a trust for or a gift to those objects equally if the power is not exercised,[2] and the rule is the same whether there is a gift over in default of objects of the power or not,[3] and although the donee of the power has power to exclude one class entirely, if there is an intention to give the property to those objects.[4] There must, however, be a clear intention that the donor intended the power to be in the nature of a trust, and any contrary intention defeats an implied gift.[5] Where there is a gift over in default of appointment to the objects of the power or to other persons, the words of the power cannot operate to vest any interest in the objects of it by implication if there is no appointment.[6] If the instrument itself gives the property to a class, but gives to a named person a power to appoint in what shares and in what manner the members of the class shall take, the property vests in all the members of the class until the power is exercised, and they all take in default of appointment[7], and the fact that the power is exercisable by will only does not postpone the period of vesting.[8] If the instrument does not contain a gift to any class, but only a power to a third person to appoint as he chooses among a class, those take by implication only in default of appointment who might have taken under an exercise of the power, and the court implies an intention to give the property in default of appointment to those only to whom the donee of the power might have given it.[9] Where there is an implied gift to members of a class in default of appointment which takes effect, the whole class takes equally[10]. The court adopts any rule laid down by the donor of the power as to the manner of disposition.[11]

1   A residuary gift is not equivalent to a gift in default: *Re Hall, Sheil v Clark* [1890] 1 IR 308; *Re Brierley, Brierley v Brierley* (1894) 43 WR 36.
2   *Brown v Higgs* (1799) 4 Ves 708; *Re White's Trusts* (1860) John 656; *Re Caplin's Will* (1865) 2 Drew & Sm 527; *Re Hargrove's Trusts* (1873) IR 8 Eq 256; *Butler v Gray* (1869) 5 Ch App 26; *Carthew v Enraght* (1872) 26 LT 834; *Ahearne v Ahearne* (1881) 9 LR Ir 144; *Moore v Ffolliott* (1887) 19 LR Ir 499; *Re Brierley, Brierley v Brierley* (1894) 43 WR 36; *Re Patterson, Dunlop v Greer* [1899] 1 IR 324; *Re Coppley* [1940] 3 DLR 535. A gift over in tail has been implied from a gift to A, B and C and their lawful issue in such proportions as X shall appoint: *Martin v Swannell* (1840) 2 Beav 249; but a merely permissive power is not enough: *Brook v Brook* (1856) 3 Sm & G 280.
3   *Witts v Boddington* (1789) cited in 5 Ves at 503; *Roddy v Fitzgerald* (1858) 6 HL Cas 823 at 856; *Butler v Gray* (1869) 5 Ch App 26; *Wilson v Duguid* (1883) 24 Ch D 244.
4   *Longmore v Broom* (1802) 7 Ves 124; *Penny v Turner* (1848) 2 Ph 493; *Re White's Trusts* (1860) John 656; *Carthew v Enraght* (1872) 26 LT 834 .
5   *Healy v Donnery* (1853) 3 ICLR 213; *Re Eddowes* (1861) 1 Drew & Sm 395; *Carberry v McCarthy* (1881) 7 LR Ir 328; *Re Weekes' Settlement* [1897] 1 Ch 289; followed in *Re Combe, Combe v Combe* [1925] Ch 210, where Tomlin J stated that there was no inflexible rule that, if a testator conferred a power to appoint among a class but made no gift over in default of appointment, the court would imply a gift to the class in equal shares if the power was not exercised. See also *Re Scarisbrick, Cockshott v Public Trustee* [1951] Ch 622, [1951] 1 All ER 822; and *Re Wills' Trusts Deeds, Wills v Godfrey* [1964] Ch 219, [1963] 1 All ER 390; *Re Manning* (1976) 84 DLR (3d) 715. The words of the will must be imperative and must indicate clearly the class to be benefited: *Re Perowne* [1951] Ch 785, [1951] 2 All ER 201 (where 'my family' did not sufficiently define the class to take).
6   *Pattison v Pattison* (1855) 19 Beav 638; *Re Sprague, Miley v Cape* (1880) 43 LT 236; *Richardson v Harrison* (1885) 16 QBD 85. A gift over to take effect upon an event which does not happen has no effect and does not prevent the implication of a grant arising from the power: *Kennedy v Kingston* (1821) 2 Jac & W 431.

7 *Doe d Willis v Martin* (1790) 4 Term Rep 39; *Lambert v Thwaites* (1866) LR 2 Eq 151; *Bradley v Cartwright* (1867) LR 2 CP 511; *Wilson v Duguid* (1883) 24 Ch D 244; *Re Master's Settlement, Master v Master* [1911] 1 Ch 321. A vested interest in objects entitled in default can be divested only by a valid exercise of the power: *Vanderzee v Aclom* (1799) 4 Ves 771 at 787.

8 *Heron v Stokes* (1842) 2 Dr & War 89; *Brown v Pocock* (1833) 6 Sim 257. If the power is contingent on the donee leaving children, no one can take by implication if no child survives: *Winn v Fenwick* (1849) 11 Beav 438; *Stolworthy v Sancroft* (1864) 33 LJ Ch 708.

9 *Kennedy v Kingston* (1821) 2 Jac & W 431; *Lambert v Thwaites* (1866) LR 2 Eq 151; *Sinnott v Walsh* (1880) 5 LR Ir 27; *Re Susanni's Trusts* (1877) 47 LJ Ch 65.

10 *Doyley v A-G* (1735) 4 Vin Abr 485, pl 16; *Salusbury v Denton* (1857) 3 K & J 529.

11 *Gower v Mainwaring* (1750) 2 Ves Sen 87; *A-G v Price* (1810) 17 Ves 371; *Mahon v Savage* (1803) 1 Sch & Lef 111.

[101.10]

No implications in bequests from gift over on failure of children. In cases where there is a bequest to a parent, either indefinitely or for life, followed by a bequest over if he dies without having or leaving children, or by a life bequest over referring to issue, the court does not, on the parents' death leaving children, imply a gift to those children[1], unless there are other matters in the will raising an inference in their favour.[2]

1 *Scalé v Rawlings* [1892] AC 342, approving *Kinsella v Caffrey* (1860) 11 I Ch R 154; *Neighbour v Thurlow* (1860) 28 Beav 33; *Re Hayton's Trusts* (1864) 4 New Rep 55; *Dowling v Dowling* (1866) 1 Ch App 612; *Seymour v Kilbee* (1879) 3 LR Ir 33; *Champ v Champ* (1892) 30 LR Ir 72; *Re Murray, Brownrigg v Murray* [1951] Tas SR 38.

2 *Kinsella v Caffrey* (1860) 11 I Ch R 154; *Wetherell v Wetherell* (1862) 4 Giff 51; *M'Lean v Simpson* (1887) 19 LR Ir 528; *Re Macdonald Estate* (1956) 5 DLR (2d) 175.

[101.11]

Implied estate tail. Though there could be an estate tail by construction after 1925, there could be no such interest by implication, for the Law of Property Act 1925[1] forbade any such implication. In cases where there would have been such implication in a will coming into operation before 1926, the gift after 1925, took effect as a gift of the fee simple.[1] Entailed interests cannot be created after 1 January 1997.[2] Where a person purports by an instrument coming into operation after that date, to grant to another person an entailed interest in real or personal property, the instrument operates as a declaration that the property is held in trust absolutely for the person to whom an entailed interest in the property was purportedly granted.[3]

1 Law of Property Act 1925, s 130 (2); 37 *Halsbury's Statutes* (4th edn) 288.

2 Trusts for Land and Appointment of Trustees Act 1996, s 2.

3 Trusts for Land and Appointment of Trustees Act 1996, Sch 1, para 5.

[101.12]

Implication of cross-remainders. Since, before 1925, cross-remainders would not be implied in a deed,[1] they cannot now be implied in a will where the testator died after 1925.[2]

1 *Edwards v Alliston* (1827) 4 Russ 78; *Doe d Clift v Birkhead* (1849) 4 Exch 110 at 124.

2 Law of Property Act 1925, s 130.

[101.13]

Implication of cross executory limitations. Cross executory limitations[1] are similarly implied to fill up a hiatus in the limitations, which seems from the context to have been contrary to the intention of the testator,[2] but they cannot be implied to divest an interest given by the will.[3] Thus in a gift to several persons contingently on satisfying a specified condition or description as tenants in common, with a gift over on all failing to satisfy that condition or description, cross-limitations are implied on the death of each of them failing to attain that description.[4] According as the context requires, the persons between whom the cross-limitations are implied in such a case may be the original stocks, or their respective issues taking under the will[5] or both.[6] Although the existence of other cross-limitations between the different persons does not prevent the implication,[7] yet, where such express cross-limitations are in favour of the very persons to whom the implied cross-limitations would convey the property, that circumstance is of weight in determining the intention.[8]

1   This paragraph substantially states the rules given by Kay J in *Re Hudson, Hudson v Hudson* (1882) 20 Ch D 406 at 415, and again considered in *Re Hart's Will Trusts, Public Trustee v Barclays Bank Ltd* [1950] Ch 84, [1949] 2 All ER 898.
2   *Re Ridge's Trusts* (1872) 7 Ch App 665; *Coates v Hart* (1863) 3 De GJ & Sm 504 at 516; *Re Mears, Parker v Mears* [1914] 1 Ch 694. For a case where the second of two tenants for life took the income for the rest of her life after the death of the other tenant for life, see *Re Riall, Westminster Bank Ltd v Harrison* [1939] 3 All ER 657. There must, however, be words in the will which, despite the reluctance to find an intestacy, point so strongly to the making of the implication, that the contrary cannot be supposed: *Re Sedgeley* [1961] NZLR 394. See also *Re Dawson* [1968] NZLR 115.
3   In the case of personal property, if a share once vests, though liable to be divested on a contingency, the question of reciprocal survivorship or succession can never arise; *Skey v Barnes* (1816) 3 Mer 335 at 343; *Baxter v Losh* (1851) 14 Beav 612; *Beaver v Nowell* (1858) 25 Beav 551; *Re Clark's Trusts* (1863) 2 New Rep 386. For a settlement case, see *Re Bickerton's Settlement, Shaw v Bickerton* [1942] Ch 84, [1942] 1 All ER 217.
4   As, for instance, contingently on attaining 21: *Scott v Bargeman* (1722) 2 P Wms 69 (gift over on death before legacies payable); or on attaining 21 or marriage: *Re Clark's Trusts* (1863) 2 New Rep 386; or in the event of surviving a named person: *Graves v Waters* (1847) 10 I Eq R 234.
5   *Atkinsons v Holtby* (1863) 10 HL Cas 313.
6   *Roe d Wren v Clayton* (1805) 6 East 628; *Horne v Barton* (1815) 19 Ves 398.
7   *Re Clark's Trusts* (1863) 2 New Rep 386.
8   *Rabbeth v Squire* (1859) 4 De G & J 406; *Sutton v Sutton* (1892) 30 LR Ir 251; *Re Hart's Will Trusts, Public Trustee v Barclays Bank Ltd* [1950] Ch 84, [1949] 2 All ER 898.

[101.14]

Cases of distributive construction. Cases where particular property is given to one person for life, and after his death that property with other property is given to other persons, and the question is what is to happen to the latter property during that person's life, are to be distinguished from cases of implication. In these cases the question is rather whether the words alluding to the time of death are to be referred distributively to the property given and not to the time of the gift taking effect, in which event the ultimate donees will take an immediate interest in the property in question.[1] Similarly where several properties are given to various donees for life, and there is a general gift over of all the properties on the deaths of all the previously named donees, the gift over may take effect, on a distributive construction, as to each property on the death of the tenant for life of that property.[2] If the words cannot be read distributively, the persons entitled on intestacy cannot be excluded.[3]

1   *Doe d Annandale v Brazier* (1821) 5 B & Ald 64; *Lill v Lill* (1857) 23 Beav 446, distinguished in *Jennings v Hanna* [1904] 1 IR 540; *Rhodes v Rhodes* (1882) 7 App Cas 192 at 217.

2   *Re Browne's Will Trusts, Landon v Brown* [1915] 1 Ch 690; *Swan v Holmes* (1854) 19 Beav 471; *Sarel v Sarel* (1856) 23 Beav 87; *Re Motherwell, Keane v Motherwell* [1910] 1 IR 249.

3   *R v Ringstead (Inhabitants)* (1829) 9 B & C 218 at 233; *Attwater v Attwater* (1853) 18 Beav 330; *Davenport v Coltman* (1842) 9 M & W 481; *Stevens v Pyle* (1860) 28 Beav 388. As to cases regarding donees, see *Round v Pickett* (1878) 47 LJ Ch 631.

Charities

CHAPTER 102

Charities: gifts for charitable purposes

[102.1]

Charitable trusts are in a privileged position and enjoy fiscal advantages over non-charitable trusts with reference to income tax,[1] capital gains tax,[2] corporation tax,[3] and inheritance tax.[4] They are also favourably treated by the law and enjoy a relaxed 'certainty'[5] rule; certain exemptions from the perpetuity rule[6] and from the rule against perpetual trusts;[7] and of course the application of the *cy-près* rule will mitigate the principles of lapse and will prevent many charitable trusts from failing.[8] If a trust is held to be charitable then it automatically enjoys all these privileges. However, it has been stated that the fiscal advantages should be confined to a more restrictive class of trusts[9] since charitable status is often claimed primarily in order to claim these privileges.[10] This factor might influence the courts to take a more restrictive attitude to the entitlement to charitable status.[11] It can be noted that where land is held on charitable, ecclesiastical and public trusts it no longer takes effect as settled land but is instead held on a trust of land.[12]

1 Income and Corporation Taxes Act 1988, s 505; 44 *Halsbury's Statutes* (4th edn) 815; see *George Drexler Ofrex Foundation (Trustees) v IRC* [1966] Ch 675, [1965] 3 All ER 529; *IRC v Education Grants Association Ltd* [1967] Ch 993, [1967] 2 All ER 893; *Campbell v IRC* [1970] AC 77, [1968] 3 All ER 588.
2 Taxation of Chargeable Gains Act 1992, s 263.
3 Income and Corporation Taxes Act 1988, s 9(4); 44 *Halsbury's Statutes* (4th edn) 38.
4 There is exemption from inheritance tax; see now the Inheritance Tax Act 1984, s 23 (gifts to charities); s 24 (gifts to political parties); s 25 (gifts for national purposes); s 26 (gifts for public benefit); s 27 (gifts of maintenance funds for historic buildings), consolidating the previous legislation, in this case principally the Finance Act 1975, Sch 6, paras 10–15, as amended. See *Guild v IRC* [1992] 2 AC 310, [1992] 2 All ER 10, HL, a case on capital transfer tax. Gifts to charities made on or after 15 March 1983 are exempt without limit on the amount or value of the property: Finance (No 2) Act 1983, s 19; gifts after 9 March 1982 were subject to a limit of £250,000, raising the previous figure of £200,000: Finance Act 1982, s 92(2)(3); figures liable to change. The limit was originally £100,000: Finance Act 1975, Sch 6, para 10(1); see now the Inheritance Tax Act 1984, s 23. The Local Government Finance Act 1988, s 47 provides discretionary relief from local taxes save for places of religious worship and property used by disabled persons, which are exempt, Local Government Finance Act 1988, s 51.
5 See para **[102.18]** infra.
6 See para **[102.25]** infra.
7 See para **[102.25]** infra.
8 See para **[103.18]** infra.
9 Per Lord Cross in *Dingle v Turner* [1972] AC 601 at 624, [1972] 1 All ER 878 at 889–890. But see the reservations of Lords Dilhorne, MacDermott and Hodson on this point, at 614; at 880–881.
10 Per Lord Upjohn in *Scottish Burial Reform and Cremation Society v Glasgow City Corpn* [1968] AC 138 at 153, [1967] 3 All ER 215 at 222, HL.

11   Per Lord Cross in *Dingle v Turner* [1972] AC 601 at 624, [1972] 1 All ER 878 at 889–890. For precedents of charitable gifts see Volume 2 pp 1260–1277.
12   Under the Trusts of Land and Appointment of Trustees Act 1996 (TLATA 1996), see Sch 1, para 4. The trustees' administrative powers under that Act are subject to the powers of the court and the Charity Commissioners and cannot be excluded or restricted by the terms of the disposition, TLATA 1996, s 6(6). Charitable trusts are also subject to incidental changes effected by the Trustee Act 2000 which will not be specifically noted here; see Chapter 27.

I.   CHARITABLE PURPOSES

[102.2]
Charity. A charity is now defined as any institution, corporate or not, which is established for charitable purposes and is subject to the control of the High Court[1] in the exercise of its jurisdiction with respect to charities.[2] There is now provision for the registration of endowed charities and any registered charity is by the Charities Act 1993 (CA 1993), s 4(1) for all purposes other than rectification of the register, a charity.[3] Neither the Charities Act 1960 nor the CA 1993, defines charitable purposes and these are, therefore, ascertained according to the previous law.

1   Considered in *Construction Industry Training Board v A-G* [1973] Ch 173, [1972] 2 All ER 1339.
2   CA 1993, s 96(1); 5 *Halsbury's Statutes* (4th edn) 1051.
3   Previously Charities Act 1960, s 5(1).*Wynn v Skegness UDC* [1966] 3 All ER 336, [1967] 1 WLR 52; *Finch v Poplar Borough Council* (1967) 66 LGR 324. If an institution is registered under the Charities Act 1960, and so conclusively presumed to be a charity by virtue of s 5(1), and its purposes are shown to have been the same for a certain period prior to registration, it will be presumed to have been a charitable institution during that period also; *Re Murawski's Will Trusts, Lloyds Bank Ltd v Royal Society for the Prevention of Cruelty to Animals* [1971] 2 All ER 328, [1971] 1 WLR 707. See also *Construction Industry Training Board v A-G* [1973] Ch 173, [1972] 2 All ER 1339; and *Childs v A-G* [1973] 2 All ER 108, [1973] 1 WLR 497.

[102.3]
General nature of charitable purposes. The words have a special legal meaning which is much narrower in its scope than that popularly given to them.[1] Whilst all the purposes which are in law charitable would be within the popular meaning of the word, there are many things which are included in their popular significance which are not within their legal meaning. The purposes are strictly those mentioned in the preamble of a statute of the reign of Elizabeth I[2] or analogous to them,[3] but many there mentioned have little significance in the modern world and a more recent definition groups them under the following four heads, namely: (i) relief of poverty; (ii) advancement of education; (iii) advancement of religion; and (iv) other purposes beneficial to the community, not falling within the preceding heads.[4] A purpose regarded in one age as charitable may in another, by a change in social habits and needs, be regarded differently.[5] It is no objection that the persons to be benefited are resident outside the jurisdiction provided the other conditions relating to charitable gifts are satisfied.[6] A gift on charitable trusts is good although it is subject to a proviso which is void as infringing the perpetuity rule.[7]

1   See Sachs LJ in *Incorporated Council of Law Reporting for England and Wales v A-G* [1972] Ch 73 at 90, [1971] 3 All ER 1029 at 1038–1039; and Lord Hailsham LC in *IRC v McMullen* [1980] 1 All ER 884 at 890. Where however the intention is to set up a charitable trust and where there is an ambiguity, a benign construction should be given if possible.

2   Stat 43 Eliz I, c 4. Though this statute has been repealed, the preamble has been expressly preserved for the purpose of defining charitable purposes; *Scottish Burial Reform and Cremation Society Ltd v Glasgow City Corpn* [1968] AC 138, [1967] 3 All ER 215, HL, per Lord Upjohn at 151; at 221. The Scots Law, however, gives a wider meaning to 'charity'; *Blair v Duncan* [1902] AC 37; *Verge v Somerville* [1924] AC 496 at 502.

3   Usually referred to as the 'spirit and intendment' of the statute, alternatively as 'the equity of the statute': see *Incorporated Council of Law Reporting for England and Wales v A-G* [1972] Ch 73, [1971] 3 All ER 1029, per Russell LJ at 88; at 1035–36, and Sachs LJ at 1037. 'The purposes in question to be charitable must be shown to be for the benefit of the public or the community, in a sense or manner within the intendment of the preamble to the statute', per Lord Wilberforce in *Scottish Burial Reform and Cremation Society Ltd v Glasgow Corpn* [1968] AC 138, [1967] 3 All ER 215 at 223. The courts have endeavoured to keep the law as to charities moving according as new social needs arise or old ones become obsolete or satisfied; ibid and Lord Hailsham LC in *IRC v McMullen* [1980] 1 All ER 884 at 890, 891.

4   *Income Tax Special Purposes Comrs v Pemsel* [1891] AC 531. But it should be noted that this formulation, firstly, is a classification of convenience, so that there may be purposes which do not fit neatly into one or other of the headings. Secondly, that the words used must not be given the force of a statute to be construed. Thirdly, that the law of charities is a moving subject which may well have evolved even since 1891; per Lord Wilberforce in *Scottish Burial Reform and Cremation Society Ltd v Glasgow Corpn* [1968] AC 138 at 154, [1967] 3 All ER 215 at 223; see cases referred to by Slade J in *McGovern v A-G* [1981] 3 All ER 493 at 503. The fourth heading has been described as a 'portmanteau' which is incapable of further definition per Lord Upjohn in *Scottish Burial Reform and Cremation Society Ltd v Glasgow Corpn* [1968] AC 138 at 150, [1967] 3 All ER 215 at 220.

5   *National Anti-Vivisection Society v IRC* [1948] AC 31 at 74, [1947] 2 All ER 217 at 238.

6   *Re Robinson, Besant v German Reich* [1931] 2 Ch 122; *Re Masoud* [1961] OR 583.

7   *George Drexler Ofrex Foundation Trustees v IRC* [1966] Ch 675, [1965] 3 All ER 529.

[102.4]

Relief of the aged. At one time it was said to be doubtful whether a gift for the aged was charitable unless there was an element of poverty[1] but more recent decisions have favoured the view that poverty is not essential, and that the words 'aged impotent and poor' in the preamble to the Elizabeth Act are to be construed disjunctively.[2] Further, essential to the charitable purpose is that it should relieve aged, impotent and poor people.[3] The word 'relief' implies that the persons in question have a need attributable to their condition as aged, impotent or poor persons which requires alleviating and which those persons could not alleviate, or would find difficulty in alleviating, themselves from their own resources.[4] Thus a trust to provide dwellings for aged persons was held to be charitable notwithstanding that they operated by way of bargain rather than by way of bounty; that the benefits could not be withdrawn once provided even if the beneficiary subsequently ceased to qualify and even though it was possible for the beneficiary to make a profit on his or her capital contribution.[5] A trust for persons not under 50 years of age is a good charitable gift for the benefit of 'aged' persons,[6] and also a gift for the 'oldest respectable inhabitants' of a district.[7]

1   *Re Lucas, Rhys v A-G* [1922] 2 Ch 52, [1922] All ER Rep 317; *A-G v Haberdashers' Co* (1834) 1 My & K 420 at 428.

2   *Joseph Rowntree Memorial Trust Housing Association Ltd v A-G* [1983] 1 All ER 288, referring to *Re Robinson, Davis v Robinson* [1951] Ch 198 [1950] 2 All ER 1148; *Re Bradbury,*

Needham v Reekie [1950] 2 All ER 1150n; *Re Glyn's Will Trusts* [1950] 2 All ER 1150n; *Re Lewis, Public Trustee v Allen* [1955] Ch 104, [1954] 3 All ER 257 and *Re Cottam's Will Trusts, Midland Bank Executor and Trustee Co Ltd v Huddersfield Corpn* [1955] 3 All ER 704, [1955] 1 WLR 1299, which support the view that it is a sufficient charitable purpose to benefit the aged, or the impotent, without more. But Peter Gibson J in the *Rowntree* case preferred the approach adopted in *Re Neal, Barclays Bank Ltd v Neal* (1966) 110 Sol Jo 549 and in *Re Resch's Will Trusts, Le Cras v Perpetual Trustee Co Ltd* [1969] 1 AC 514, [1967] 3 All ER 915 that there must be a need which is to be relieved by the charitable gift, such need being attributable to the aged or impotent conditions or the person to be benefited. See also *Re Finkle* (1977) 82 DLR (3d) 445; *Re Bingham, Public Trustee v New Plymouth Council for Social Services Inc* [1951] NZLR 491; *McGovern v A-G* [1981] 3 All ER 493 at 503.

3   *Joseph Rowntree Memorial Trust Housing Association Ltd v A-G* [1983] 1 All ER 288 at 295.
4   *Joseph Rowntree Memorial Trust Housing Association Ltd v A-G* [1983] 1 All ER 288 at 295.
5   *Joseph Rowntree Memorial Trust Housing Association Ltd v A-G* [1983] 1 All ER 288 at 295, referring to *Re Cottam's Will Trusts, Midland Bank Executor and Trustee Co Ltd v Huddersfield Corpn* [1955] 3 All ER 704, [1955] 1 WLR 1299, and *Re Resch's Will Trusts, Le Cras v Perpetual Trustee Co Ltd* [1969] 1 AC 514, [1967] 3 All ER 915, and to cases on fee paying schools, such as *Abbey Malvern Wells Ltd v Ministry of Local Government and Planning* [1951] Ch 728, [1951] 2 All ER 154. See also *Re Estlin, Prichard v Thomas* (1903) 72 LJ Ch 687 (gift for the provision of homes of rest for lady teachers at a rent).
6   *Re Wall, Pomeroy v Willway* (1889) 42 Ch D 510; *Re Dudgeon, Truman v Pope* (1896) 74 LT 613 (where the age was 60). But in *Re Martin* (1977) 121 Sol Jo 828, a trust to create a home for old people with a right for either or both of the testator's daughters to reside there was held not to be a valid charitable trust.
7   *Re Lucas, Rhys v A-G* [1922] 2 Ch 52, [1922] All ER Rep 317.

[102.5]

Relief of the impotent. A gift for the relief of the impotent without any reference to poverty is a good charitable gift.[1] A gift for the blind is a good charitable gift under this heading[2] and so are gifts for disabled or wounded members of the forces[3] and for a home of rest for those in need of it[4] and a nursing home for those of moderate means although they might have to pay some part of the expense.[5]

1   *Re Roadley, Iveson v Wakefield* [1930] 1 Ch 524; *Re Elliot, Raven v Nicholson* (1910) 102 LT 528; *Re Fraser, Yeates v Fraser* (1883) 22 Ch D 827.
2   *Re Elliot, Raven v Nicholson* (1910) 102 LT 528; *Re Lewis, Public Trustee v Allen* [1955] Ch 104, [1954] 3 All ER 257.
3   *Re Hillier, Dauncey v Finch* [1944] 1 All ER 480; *Re Simmonds* [1933] NZLR Supp 172; *Re Robinson, Besant v German Reich* [1931] 2 Ch 122 (disabled soldiers of former enemy); *Muir v Open Brethren* (1956) 96 CLR 166.
4   *Re Estlin, Prichard v Thomas* (1903) 72 LJ Ch 687; *Re James, Grenfell v Hamilton* [1932] 2 Ch 25, [1932] All ER Rep 452; *Re Chaplin, Neame v A-G* [1933] Ch 115.
5   *Re Clarke, Bracey v Royal National Lifeboat Institution* [1923] 2 Ch 407, and see para **[102.6]**, n 3.

[102.6]

Relief of poverty. 'Poor' is a relative term and is not confined to the destitute.[1] While the relief to the poor must be given by way of bounty and not by way of bargain,[2] it is not an absolute objection that the beneficiaries are required to contribute some part of the cost of the benefits.[3] The gift to the poor may be general and indefinite[4] or confined to the inhabitants of some particular place[5] or some particular religious sect[6] or the members of a regiment[7] or some particular section or class of the public.[8] A common form of charity is provision for the victims of a particular disaster.[9] A gift for such poor persons as the executor should consider deserving of assistance has been upheld as a good charitable gift.[10] The relief of poverty is still charitable although it is effected indirectly.[11] Thus, the establishment, maintenance, and support of institutions or funds for the relief of various forms of poverty or distress is charitable,[12] and this includes gifts to religious communities having for their object the relief of the sick and poor.[13] A gift for the working classes generally or restricted to a particular district is not charitable,[14] nor for members of a trade union.[15] A gift for the provision of religious services and instruction and for the social and physical training and recreation for persons of insufficient means otherwise to enjoy the advantages provided is not charitable.[16]

1   *Mary Clark Home (Trustees) v Anderson* [1904] 2 KB 645; *Re Estlin, Prichard v Thomas* (1903) 72 LJ Ch 687; *Re Gardom, Le Page v A-G* [1914] 1 Ch 662; *Shaw v Halifax Corpn* [1915] 2 KB 170; *Re Clarke, Bracey v Royal National Lifeboat Institution* [1923] 2 Ch 407; *Re De Carteret, Forster v De Carteret* [1933] Ch 103, [1932] All ER Rep 355; *Jones v Executive Officers of T Eaton Co Ltd* (1973) 35 DLR (3d) 97 (trust for the benefit of 'needy or deserving' members of a club held to be charitable; 'poverty' is a relative term which extends to include those of moderate means). In *Re Drummond, Ashworth v Drummond* [1914] 2 Ch 90, persons earning a weekly wage of fifteen shillings were held not to be poor within the meaning of the statute but no doubt regard must now be had to the change in the cost of living. 'Eleemosynary charity' covers all charities directed to the relief of individual distress whether due to age, poverty, sickness or other similar afflictions: *Re Armitage, Ellam v Norwich Corpn* [1972] Ch 438, [1972] 1 All ER 708.
2   *IRC v Society for Relief of Widows and Orphans of Medical Men* (1926) 136 LT 60 at 65.
3   *Re Estlin, Prichard v Thomas* (1903) 72 LJ Ch 687; *Re Clarke, Bracey v Royal National Lifeboat Institution* [1923] 2 Ch 407; *Re Chaplin, Neame v A-G* [1933] Ch 115; *A-G v M'Carthy* (1885) 12 VLR 535; *Re Monk, Giffen v Wedd* [1927] 2 Ch 197, [1927] All ER Rep 157; *Re Cottam's Will Trusts* [1955] 3 All ER 704; *Re Payling's Will Trusts, Armstrong v Payling* [1969] 3 All ER 698, [1969] 1 WLR 1595; *Joseph Rowntree Memorial Trust Housing Association Ltd v A-G* [1983] Ch 159, [1983] 1 All ER 288.
4   *A-G v Matthews* (1676) 2 Lev 167; *Nash v Morley* (1842) 5 Beav 177; *Re Darling, Farquhar v Darling* [1896] 1 Ch 50.
5   *A-G v Exeter Corpn* (1826) 2 Russ 45; (1827) 3 Russ 395; *A-G v Bovill* (1840) 1 Ph 762; *A-G v Blizard* (1855) 21 Beav 233; *Dillon v Reilly* (1873) IR 10 Eq 152; *Re Roadley, Iveson v Wakefield* [1930] 1 Ch 524 (poor of a parish); *Re Robinson, Davis v Robinson* [1951] Ch 198, [1950] 2 All ER 1148 (poor of parish over 65); *Re Lucas, Rhys v A-G* [1922] 2 Ch 52 (poor of a town); *Re Lousada, Bacon v Bacon* (1887) 82 LT Jo 358 ('London poor'); *Re Lambeth Charities* (1853) 22 LJ Ch 959; *Re St Alphage, London Wall* (1888) 59 LT 614; *Bristow v Bristow* (1842) 5 Beav 289 (on a particular estate); but see *Browne v King* (1885) 17 LR Ir 488 (poor tenantry not charitable); *Bruce v Deer Presbytery* (1867) LR 1 Sc & Div 96 (poor of a presbytery).
6   *Re Wall, Pomeroy v Willway* (1889) 42 Ch D 510 (Unitarians); *A-G v Mathieson* [1907] 2 Ch 383 (Jews); *A-G v Wansay* (1808) 15 Ves 231 (Presbyterians); *Income Tax Special Purposes Comrs v Pemsel* [1891] AC 531 (Moravians); *A-G v Shore* (1843) 11 Sim 592 (Unitarians); *A-G v Lawes* (1849) 8 Hare 32 (Irvingite ministers persecuted or in poverty); *Dawson v Small* (1874) LR 18 Eq 114 (Methodists); *Canada Permanent Trust Co v MacFarlane* (1972) 27 DLR (3d) 480 (Protestant homes or institutions for the care and welfare of children).
7   *Re Donald, Moore v Somerset* [1909] 2 Ch 410.
8   *A-G v Power* (1809) 1 Ball & B 145; *Re Estlin, Prichard v Thomas* (1903) 72 LJ Ch 687; *Mary Clarke Home (Trustees) v Anderson* [1904] 2 KB 645; *Re Gardom, Le Page v A-G* [1914] 1 Ch 662; *Shaw v Halifax Corpn* [1915] 2 KB 170; *Re Campbell* [1930] NZLR 713 (all charities for poor gentlewomen); *Re Young, Young v Young* [1951] Ch 344, [1950] 2 All ER 1245 (distressed gentlefolk); *Re Clarke, Bracey v Royal National Lifeboat Institution* [1923] 2 Ch 407 (persons of moderate means); *Re De Carteret, Forster v De Carteret* [1933] Ch 103, [1932] All ER Rep 355 (persons of limited means); *Re Central Employment Bureau for Women and Students' Careers Association* [1942] 1 All ER 232 (persons not self-supporting); *A-G v Pearce* (1740) 2 Atk 87 (housekeepers); *Re White's Trusts* (1886) 33 Ch D 449 (tradesmen); *Thompson v Thompson* (1844) 1 Coll 381 at 395 (unsuccessful literary men); in *Re Payling's Will Trusts, Armstrong v Payling* [1969] 3 All ER 698, [1969] 1 WLR 1595 (rent-free accommodation for

the aged); *Reeve v A-G* (1843) 3 Hare 191; *Loscombe v Wintringham* (1850) 13 Beav 87 (servants); *Re Gosling, Gosling v Smith* (1900) 48 WR 300 (old clerk of a firm); *Re Rayner, Cloutman v Regnant* (1920) 89 LJ Ch 369 (poor or incapacitated employees); *Gibson v South American Stores (Gath and Chaves) Ltd* [1950] Ch 177 [1949] 2 All ER 985 (necessitous employees of a limited company and their dependants): *Re Drummond, Ashworth v Drummond* [1914] 2 Ch 90, [1914–15] All ER Rep 223 (contributions to the holiday expenses of employees not charitable); *Re Coulthurst, Coutts & Co v Coulthurst* [1951] Ch 661, [1951] 1 All ER 774 (dependants of bank officers); *Milne's Executors v Aberdeen University Court* (1905) 7 F 642 (poor struggling youths of merit); *Barclay v Maskelyne* (1858) 32 LTOS 205 (poor emigrants); *Re Tree, Idle v Tree* [1945] Ch 325, [1945] 2 All ER 65 (persons descending from residents in a particular borough in a particular year desirous of emigrating); *Re Wedge* (1968) 67 DLR (2d) 433 (needy displaced family of European origin); *Re Morrison, Wakefield v Falmouth* (1967) 111 Sol Jo 758 (relief of refugees); *A-G v Vint* (1850) 3 De G & Sm 704 (inmates of a workhouse); *Waldo v Caley* (1809) 16 Ves 206; *Re Friends of the Clergy's Charter, Friends of the Clergy v A-G* [1921] 1 Ch 409 (widows and orphans of poor clergymen); *Powell v A-G* (1817) 3 Mer 48 (seamen of a particular port); *Russell v Kellett* (1855) 3 Sm & G 264 (widows and orphans of a particular parish); *Weir v Crum-Brown* [1908] AC 162 (indigent bachelors and widowers interested in science). As to poor relations, and poor employees, see paras **[102.13]** and **[102.14]** infra.

9   *Pease v Pattinson* (1886) 32 Ch D 154; *Re Hartley Colliery Accident Relief Fund, Plummer v Jordan* (1908) 102 LT 165n; *Cross v Lloyd-Greame* (1909) 102 LT 163; *Re North Devon and West Somerset Relief Fund Trusts, Hylton v Wright* [1953] 2 All ER 1032, [1953] 1 WLR 1250; *Re Gillingham Bus Disaster Fund* [1958] Ch 300, [1958] 1 All ER 37.

10   *Brett v A-G* [1945] IR 526; *Re Angell Estate* (1955) 16 WWR 342; *Re Ward's Estate* [1957] SASR 125.

11   *A-G v Minshull* (1798) 4 Ves 11; *A-G for Northern Ireland v Forde* [1932] NI 1; *Re Dean's Will Trusts, Cowan v St Mary's Hospital, Paddington, Board of Governors* [1950] 1 All ER 882.

12   *Biscoe v Jackson* (1887) 35 Ch D 460 (soup kitchens); *Re Welsh Hospital (Netley) Fund, Thomas v A-G* [1921] 1 Ch 655 (hospital); *Re Clarke, Bracey v Royal National Lifeboat Institution*, supra (nursing home); *IRC v Roberts Marine Mansions Trustees* (1926) 43 TLR 270 (seaside boarding-house for business people needing rest); *IRC v Peeblesshire Nursing Association* 1927 SC 215 (nursing association); *Harbin v Masterman* (1871) LR 12 Eq 559 (asylum); *Re Whiteley, Bishop of London v Whiteley* [1910] 1 Ch 600 (alm-houses); *Re Estlin, Prichard v Thomas* (1903) 72 LJ Ch 687, and *Re James, Grenfell v Hamilton* [1932] 2 Ch 25 (homes for teachers); *Rolls v Miller* (1884) 27 Ch D 71 (homes for working girls); *Hall v Derby Sanitary Authority* (1885) 16 QBD 163 (orphanages); *Re Lacy, Royal General Theatrical Fund Association v Kydd* [1899] 2 Ch 149 (homes for impoverished actors); *Re Bernstein's Will Trusts, National Westminster Bank Ltd v Board of Governors of the United Liverpool Hospital* (1971) 115 Sol Jo 808 (extra comforts for the nursing staff); in *Re Niyazi's Will Trusts* [1978] 3 All ER 785, [1978] 1 WLR 910, it was held that a gift for a working men's hostel in Famagusta was charitable as being for the relief of poverty in a place where housing was in short supply. A gift of income for the general benefit and welfare of children in a children's home established by a local authority under the (then) Children Act 1948, s 15 has been held to be not charitable as it may be applied to non-charitable purposes: *Re Cole, Westminster Bank Ltd v Moore* [1958] Ch 877, [1958] 3 All ER 102.

13   *Cocks v Manners* (1871) LR 12 Eq 574; *Re Delany, Conoley v Quick* [1902] 2 Ch 642. A gift to establish a sanatorium or hospital is charitable: *Kytherian Association of Queensland v Sklavos* (1958) 101 CLR 56.

14   *Re Sanders' Will Trusts, Public Trustee v McLaren* [1954] Ch 265, [1954] 1 All ER 667.

15   *Re Mead's Trust Deed* [1961] 2 All ER 836, [1961] 1 WLR 1244 (where an element of self-help loomed large).

16   *Baddeley v IRC* [1953] Ch 504, [1953] 2 All ER 233; affd on this point in the House of Lords [1955] AC 572, [1955] 1 All ER 525.

[102.7]

Education. The phrase 'advancement of education'[1] has consistently been taken to be an enlargement of the phrase 'advancement of learning' and the latter is included in the former.[2] An extended view of the meaning of education has been taken in a recent House of Lords decision consistent with modern concepts of what is educationally valuable so that the provision of sporting facilities limited to students at universities and schools was held to be charitable.[3] Charitable gifts for the purposes of education include the establishment and support of educational institutions of all kinds,[4] gifts to learned societies,[5] gifts for the education of special classes of persons,[6] and instruction in special subjects.[7] The institution and maintenance of a library for the study of a learned subject or a science, is within the phrase whatever be the age of those frequenting it.[8] Likewise, the provision of books forming the raw material for that study.[9] A students' union existing to further the educational purposes of a school of learning which is charitable has been held to be charitable,[10] notwithstanding the personal benefit conferred on the union members.[11] These trusts, however, must benefit a section of the public and be of public nature.[12] A trust for the promotion of the religious social and physical well-being of persons by the provision of facilities for religious services and instruction and for social and physical training and recreation is not a trust for education.[13] Nor does a trust for the mere promotion of a particular sport or sports qualify as charity under this head[14] but a gift to a particular educational establishment for the purpose of improving the sporting facilities available to the pupils there does so qualify,[15] and likewise the provisions of facilities in schools and universities generally.[16] But an overriding trust for charitable purposes is good though there is a non-charitable proviso which is void as infringing the perpetuity rule.[17]

1   As used by Lord Macnaghten in *Income Tax Special Purposes Comrs v Pemsel* [1891] AC 531.
2   Per Sachs LJ in *Incorporated Council of Law Reporting for England and Wales v A-G* [1972] Ch 73 at 92, [1971] 3 All ER 1029 at 1040.
3   *IRC v McMullen* [1981] AC 1, [1980] 1 All ER 884, where the Education Act 1944 was referred to. See also Dillon J in *Barralet v A-G* [1980] 3 All ER 918 at 927 who pointed out that the authorities show that the term 'education' is to be construed very widely, adopting Buckley LJ's view that this head ... should be regarded as extending to the improvement of a useful branch of human knowledge and its public dissemination', *Re Hopkins' Will Trusts, Naish v Francis Bacon Society Inc* [1965] Ch 669 at 680, [1964] 3 All ER 46 at 52. In *Re Koeppler's Will Trusts, Barclays Bank Trust Co Ltd v Slack* [1984] Ch 243, [1984] 2 All ER 111, Peter Gibson J at 122 referred to 'the broad and evolving concept of education in the law of charity'.
4   Colleges: *Walsh v Gladstone* (1843) 1 Ph 290; *Aberdeen University v Irvine* (1868) LR 1 Sc & Div 289; *Wallis v New Zealand Solicitor-General* [1903] AC 173; schools: *Re Gilchrist Educational Trust* [1895] 1 Ch 367; *Smith v Kerr* [1902] 1 Ch 774; *Re Hawkins, Walrond v Newton* (1906) 22 TLR 521; *Brighton College v Marriott* [1926] AC 192; *Re Woodhams, Lloyds Bank Ltd v London College of Music* [1981] 1 All ER 202, [1981] 1 WLR 493 (music colleges); professorships: *Yates v University College, London* (1875) LR 7 HL 438; *Re Buckland, Buckland v Bennett* (1887) 22 LJNC 7; fellowship: *Jesus College Case* (1615) *Duke on Charitable Uses* ed Bridgman, 363; lectureship: *A-G v Cambridge Margaret and Regius Professors* (1682) 1 Vern 55; *Re Freeston's Charity, Sylvester v University College Oxford* [1978] 1 All ER 481, [1978] 1 WLR 120; affd [1979] 1 All ER 51, CA (alteration of beneficial interests); scholarships: *University College of North Wales v Taylor* [1908] P 140; *Re Williams, Taylor v University of Wales* (1908) 24 TLR 716; *Wilson v Toronto General Trustees Corpn* [1954] 3 DLR 136; educational bursary: *Re Evans* [1957] SR Qd 345; prizes: *Farrer v St Catherine College, Cambridge* (1873) LR 16 Eq 19; schoolmaster's house: *Sills v Warner* (1896) 27 OR 266; British School of Egyptian Archaeology where it was held no bar that a contributor was entitled to certain printed books: *Re British School of Egyptian Archaeology, Murray v Public Trustee* [1954] 1 All ER 887. Now that secondary education must be provided free of charge a bequest to assist pupils to obtain such education is void as incapable of performance: *Re Mackenzie, Moir v Angus County Council* [1962] 2 All ER 890, [1962] 1 WLR 880; distinguished in *Re Leitch* [1965] VR 204 (a scholarship is not limited to money to assist scholars financially to continue their education); *Construction Industry Training Board v A-G* [1973] Ch 173, [1972] 2 All ER 1339 (Industrial Training Board); *Re Koeppler's Will Trusts,*

Barclays Bank Trust Co Ltd v Slack [1986] Ch 423, [1985] 2 All ER 869 (conference centre; but the mere organisation and conduct of conferences albeit dealing with topics of public interest, would not necessarily constitute a charitable activity. Charitable as advancement of education here).

5   *Beaumont v Oliveira* (1869) 4 Ch App 309; *Royal Society of London and Thompson* (1881) 17 Ch D 407; *Thomas v Howell* (1874) LR 18 Eq 198; *Re Lopes, Bence–Jones v Zoological Society of London* [1931] 2 Ch 130; *Re Bland-Sutton's Will Trusts, National Provincial Bank Ltd v Middlesex Hospital Medical School Council* [1951] Ch 70, [1950] 2 All ER 466.

6   Testator's descendants: *A-G v Sidney Sussex College* (1865) 34 Beav 654; *Re Lavelle, Concannon v A-G* [1914] 1 IR 194; daughters of missionaries: *German v Chapman* (1877) 7 Ch D 271; persons of particular religious faith: *Income Tax Special Purposes Comrs v Pemsel* [1891] AC 531; *Walsh v Gladstone* (1843) 1 Ph 290; *Carbery v Cox* (1852) 3 I Ch R 231n; *Re Michel's Trust* (1860) 28 Beav 39; *Re Doering* [1949] 1 DLR 267; children of employees of a company: *Re Rayner, Cloutman v Regnart* (1920) 89 LJ Ch 369, but this case was disapproved in *Oppenheim v Tobacco Securities Trust Co Ltd* [1951] AC 297, [1951] 1 All ER 31, but not compulsory training of employees of a company: *Re Leverhulme, Cooper v Leverhulme* [1943] 2 All ER 143; *Davies v Perpetual Trustee Co Ltd* [1959] AC 439, [1959] 2 All ER 128 (education of Presbyterians, descendants of those settled in New South Wales hailing from or born in Northern Ireland).

7   *A-G v Flood* (1816) Hayes & Jo App xxi at p xxxviii (Irish language); *Re Berridge, Berridge v Turner* (1890) 63 LT 470 (economics); *Re Allsop, Gell v Carver* (1884) 1 TLR 4 (art); *IRC v Glasgow Musical Festival Association* 1926 SC 920 (music); *Re Shakespeare Memorial Trust, Earl of Lytton v A-G* [1923] 2 Ch 398 (drama); *Yates v University College, London* (1873) 8 Ch App 454 (archaeology); *A-G v Stepney* (1804) 10 Ves 22; *Scottish Woollen Technical College v IRC* 1926 SC 934; *Royal North Shore Hospital of Sydney v A-G for New South Wales* (1938) 60 CLR 396. A gift to the Simplified Spelling Society has been held not charitable: *Hunter (Sir GB) (1922) C Trusts (Trustees) v IRC* (1929) 45 TLR 344. See also *Re Dupree's Deed Trusts, Daley v Lloyds Bank* [1945] Ch 16, [1944] 2 All ER 443 (chess tournaments and prizes); *Re Hopkinson, Lloyds Bank Ltd v Baker* [1949] 1 All ER 346; *Re Shaw's Will Trusts* [1952] Ch 163, [1952] 1 All ER 49 (teaching, promotion, and encouragement of appreciation of the fine arts, and also of self-control, elocution, oratory, deportment, and the arts of personal contact, social intercourse and public, private, professional and business life—held a charitable trust); *Re Ogden, Taylor v Sharp* (1909) 25 TLR 382 (trust for art students, held not charitable); *Re Koettgen's Will Trusts, Westminster Bank Ltd v Family Welfare Association Trustees Ltd* [1954] Ch 252, [1954] 1 All ER 581 (higher commercial education giving preference to employees of a company and members of their families); *Re Webber, Barclays Bank Ltd v Webber* [1954] 3 All ER 712 (Boy Scouts); *Re Hopkins' Will Trusts, Naish v Francis Bacon Society Inc* [1965] Ch 669, [1964] 3 All ER 46 (trust to help find the Bacon-Shakespeare manuscripts); *Baldry v Feintuck* [1972] 2 All ER 81, [1972] 1 WLR 552 (educational purposes can include research, discussion, debate and reaching a corporate conclusion on social and economic problems): *Re Koeppler's Will Trusts, Barclays Bank Trust Co Ltd v Slack* [1986] Ch 423, [1985] 2 All ER 869 (conferences for the formation of informal international public opinion and the promotion of greater co-operation in Europe and the West; held by the Court of Appeal to be exclusively for the advancement of education and charitable); *Barralet v A-G* [1980] 3 All ER 918, [1980] 1 WLR 1565 (dissemination of ethical principles: educational).

8   *A-G v Marchant* (1866) LR 3 Eq 424 (Trinity College Oxford library); *Re Mason* [1971] NZLR 714 (Law Society's library in some respects charitable); *Carne v Long* (1860) 2 De GF & J 75 (library for the benefit of subscribers not charitable).

9   *Incorporated Council of Law Reporting for England and Wales v A-G* [1972] Ch 73 at 93, [1971] 3 All ER 1029 at 1040, per Sachs LJ. Accordingly, the publication of the law reports is charitable because their virtually exclusive purpose is to further the study of law.

10   *London Hospital Medical College v IRC* [1976] 2 All ER 113 applying *Re Mariette, Mariette v Aldenham School Governing Body* [1915] 2 Ch 284; *Re Coxen, McCallum v Coxen* [1948] Ch 747, [1948] 2 All ER 492; *Neville Estates Ltd v Madden* [1962] Ch 832, [1961] 3 All ER 769; in *Baldry v Feintuck* [1972] 2 All ER 81, [1972] 1 WLR 552, the point was conceded; *A-G v Ross* [1985] 3 All ER 334.

11   The union was held to further educational purposes of the college, rather than existing for the benefit of its members: Brightman J [1976] 2 All ER 113 at 120; distinguishing *IRC v Glasgow City Police Athletic Association* [1953] AC 380, [1953] 1 All ER 747; applying *IRC v Yorkshire Agricultural Society* [1928] 1 KB 611, [1927] All ER Rep 536.

12 *Re Compton* [1945] Ch 123, [1945] 1 All ER 198; *Oppenheim v Tobacco Securities Trust Co Ltd* [1951] AC 297, [1951] 1 All ER 31; *Re Mead's Trust Deed* [1961] 2 All ER 836, [1961] 1 WLR 1244. But see now *Dingle v Turner* [1972] AC 601, [1972] 1 All ER 878, HL; see para **[102.14]** infra. In *Re Shaw's Will Trusts* [1952] Ch 163, [1952] 1 All ER 49, it is said that where trusts are not only educational, but are educational in the sense that they benefit the public, no evidence of benefit to the community is required; applied in *Re Macdonald* (1971) 18 DLR (3d) 521 (part of residue 'to be used in collecting of historical objects for showing and presentation').

13 *IRC v Baddeley* [1955] AC 572, [1955] 1 All ER 525 (and such trusts were not exclusively for religious purposes).

14 *Re Nottage, Jones v Palmer* [1895] 2 Ch 649.

15 *Re Mariette, Mariette v Aldenham School Governing Body* [1915] 2 Ch 284.

16 *IRC v McMullen* [1981] AC 1, [1980] 1 All ER 884.

17 *George Drexler Ofrex Foundation (Trustees) v IRC* [1966] Ch 675, [1965] 3 All ER 529.

[102.8]

Religious purposes. The words 'advancement of religion' mean the promotion of spiritual teaching in a wide sense and the maintenance of the doctrines on which it rests and of the observances that serve to promote and manifest it,[1] but the gift must tend directly or indirectly to the instruction or edification of the public.[2] It has been said that a trust for the purpose of any kind of monotheistic theism would be a good charitable trust.[3] Religion is concerned with man's relations with God and the two essential attributes of religion are faith and worship; faith in a god and worship of that god.[4] Such gifts will include gifts for the saying of masses,[5] for missionary purposes,[6] provision and support of the clergy,[7] building or repair of buildings used for religious purposes[8] and graveyards[9] and burial places.[10] Such gifts when in general terms must, however, be confined to religious purposes and are not charitable where they include social or other non-charitable purposes.[11] The fact that a religious community opens its doors to those of all creeds and to those who have no creed, does not prevent its being a valid charity.[12] They may, however, include a gift for the choir;[13] for the organ and organist,[14] or for the provision of religious books.[15]

1 *Keren Kayemeth Le Jisroel Ltd v IRC* [1931] 2 KB 465 at 477, CA; affd [1932] AC 650, HL. See *Re Brooks* (1969) 4 DLR (3d) 694 ('the work of the Lord') and *Re Barker's Will Trusts, Barker v Crouch* (1948) 64 TLR 273 ('for God's work'); *Re Le Cren Clarke, Funnell v Stewart* [1996] 1 All ER 715 (faith healing).

2 *Cocks v Manners* (1871) LR 12 Eq 574 at 585; *Re Delany, Conoley v Quick* [1902] 2 Ch 642 at 648; *Re Williams, Public Trustee v Williams* [1927] 2 Ch 283 at 287; *Gilmour v Coats* [1949] AC 426, [1949] 1 All ER 848; see *Holmes v A-G* (1981) Times, 12 February.

3 Per Lord Parker of Waddington in *Bowman v Secular Society Ltd* [1917] AC 406 at 448–450.

4 Per Dillon J in *Barralet v A-G* [1980] 3 All ER 918 at 924; thus a society for the dissemination of ethical principles and cultivation of rational belief was not for religious purposes since ethics are concerned with man's relation with man, referring to *United Grand Lodge of Ancient Free and Accepted Masons of England v Holborn Borough Council* [1957] 3 All ER 281, [1957] 1 WLR 1080 (freemasonry not charitable as religious purposes).

5 *Re Hetherington* [1990] Ch 1, [1989] 2 All ER 129. *Re Caus, Lindeboom v Camille* [1934] Ch 162 followed, *Bourne v Keane* [1919] AC 815, and *Gilmour v Coats* [1949] AC 426, and other cases cited under this heading in the text, considered. The Vice-Chancellor Sir Nicholas Browne-Wilkinson considered that a gift for the saying of masses was prima facie charitable as being for a religious purpose. The necessary public benefit was found in the fact that the masses were to be celebrated in public and that the gift would contribute to the stipends of priests.

6 The term 'missionary' purposes is ambiguous and may comprise non-charitable objects: *Re Rees* [1920] 2 Ch 59; *Scott v Browrigg* (1881) 9 LR Ir 246; *A-G v Becher* [1910] 2 IR 251. See also for cases where purposes were charitable: *Dunne v Duignan* [1908] 1 IR 228; *Allan's Executors v Allan* 1908 SC 807.

7   *Dundee Magistrates v Dundee Presbytery* (1861) 4 Macq 228; *Pennington v Buckley* (1848) 6 Hare 451; *Re Maguire* (1870) LR 9 Eq 632; *Re Macnamara, Hewitt v Jeans* (1911) 104 LT 771; *Re Williams, Public Trustee v Williams* [1927] 2 Ch 283. See also *A-G v Parker* (1747) 1 Ves Sen 43 (pension for a perpetual curate); *Re Manuel* [1958] OWN 194 (gift to minister good though church acceded to another denomination); *Touchet and Touchet v Blais* (1963) 40 DLR (2d) 961 (gift to named bishop 'for his works as would aid French Canadians in his Diocese'); *Re Clark, Horwell v Dent* [1961] NZLR 635 (a gift of an annuity to the wife of the minister for the time being of a specified church is not a charitable gift and is void as infringing the perpetuity rule).

8   *Re Church Estate Charity, Wandsworth* (1871) 6 Ch App 296; *A-G v Dartmouth Corpn* (1883) 48 LT 933; *Re St Alphage, London Wall* (1888) 59 LT 614; *Re Manser, A-G v Lucas* [1905] 1 Ch 68; *Re Williams, James v Williams* (1910) 26 TLR 307; *Maguire v A-G* [1943] IR 238 (founding a convent); *Re Beresford* (1966) 57 DLR (2d) 380 (gift to 'build a church edifice of luxurious and beautiful appearance', sufficient general intention to devote to charity and could be used to renovate the crypt of a church for use as a church hall).

9   *Re Vaughan, Vaughan v Thomas* (1886) 33 Ch D 187; *Re Douglas, Douglas v Simpson* [1905] 1 Ch 279; *A-G v Blizard* (1855) 21 Beav 233.

10 *Re Manser, A-G v Lucas* [1905] 1 Ch 68.

11 *Oxford Group v IRC* [1949] 2 All ER 537 (expenditure on subsidiary purposes), and see *Re Morton Estate, Summerfield and London and Western Trusts Co Ltd v Phillips* [1941] WWR 310; *Munster and Leinster Bank v A-G* [1940] IR 19 (Catholic Young Men's Society); *Re Lloyd* [1958] VLR 523. If the social activities are merely ancillary to the religious purposes they do not prevent the gift being charitable: *Neville Estates Ltd v Madden* [1962] Ch 832, [1961] 3 All ER 769.

12 *Re Banfield, Lloyds Bank Ltd v Smith* [1968] 2 All ER 276, [1968] 1 WLR 846 (community received and assisted those members of the public who needed help for a variety of reasons, eg drug addiction, drink, having been in prison or loneliness; and members went out to offer help where required). Alternatively, if the community was not a religious charity, the gift was valid as being for a public purpose within the fourth heading in *Pemsel's Case*.

13 *Re Royce, Turner v Wormald* [1940] Ch 514, [1940] 2 All ER 291.

14 *Carbery v Cox* (1852) 3 I Ch R 231n.

15 *Re Anderson* [1943] 4 DLR 268.

[102.9]

Purposes beneficial to the community. While all charitable gifts must be for the benefit of the public as distinct from private individuals,[1] the gifts now to be considered are essentially for the benefit of the general public. It is not enough that the trust should be for the public benefit, it must also be beneficial in a way which the law regards as a charitable trust.[2] The question whether the purposes are for the benefit of the general public need not be considered where the gift is exclusively for the relief of poverty, for educational or religious purposes or for purposes analogous to those purposes, but the ambit of the purposes must not be so wide as to include purposes which the law considers as not charitable.[3] The question of the public nature of the trusts arises when the primary class of eligible persons is ascertained. If this primary class is sufficiently wide, the fact that the trustees are bound to give priority to a narrower class does not destroy the essential public and charitable nature of the trust,[4] but where the class is confined not only to a particular area but also to be selected from within it by reference to a particular creed it is not charitable.[5] The question whether or not the potential beneficiaries of a trust can fairly be said to constitute a section of the public is a question of degree and cannot be by itself decisive of the question whether the trust is a charity: much will depend on the purpose of the trust.[6] These gifts which are extremely various in their nature may for convenience be classified as follows: gifts encouraging patriotism or national feeling;[7] gifts for public works;[8] gifts for public instruction or recreation;[9] gifts promoting the efficiency of the Army;[10] gifts for the improvement of agriculture;[11] gifts for the protection of animals;[12] gifts for the care of the sick;[13] gifts for the spread of certain principles;[14] gifts to foster promote and increase public interest in dramatic art[15] or music.[16] The question whether the promulgation of a particular doctrine or principle is for the benefit of the public is to be answered by the court on the evidence before it.[17] A gift of this nature is none the less charitable if it benefits only a section of the public[18] or a particular locality or the inhabitants of a particular locality[19] but not members of a particular creed in a particular locality.[20]

1   *Peggs v Lamb* [1994] Ch 172, [1994] 2 All ER 15; citing *Williams' Trustees v IRC* [1947] AC 447, [1947] 1 All ER 513.
2   The importance of this aspect of charitable gifts came before the courts in *Re Compton, Powell v Compton* [1945] Ch 123, [1945] 1 All ER 198, and has been much discussed since that decision; see *Re Tree, Idle v Tree* [1945] Ch 325, [1945] 2 All ER 65; *Re Hobourn Aero Components Ltd's Air Raid Distress Fund, Ryan v Forrest* [1946] Ch 194, [1946] 1 All ER 501; *National Anti-Vivisection Society v IRC* [1948] AC 31, [1947] 2 All ER 217; *Gibson v South American Stores (Gath and Chaves) Ltd* [1950] Ch 177, [1949] 2 All ER 985; *Oppenheim v Tobacco Securities Trust Co Ltd* [1951] AC 297, [1951] 1 All ER 31; *Keren Kayemeth Le Jisroel Ltd v IRC* [1932] AC 650; *Williams' Trustees v IRC* [1947] AC 447, [1947] 1 All ER 513; *Re Scarisbrick* [1951] Ch 622, [1951] 1 All ER 822 (poor relations); *IRC v Glasgow City Police Athletic Association* [1953] AC 380, [1953] 1 All ER 747 (to encourage athletic sports connected with city police force not charitable); *Incorporated Council of Law Reporting for England and Wales v A-G* [1972] Ch 73, [1971] 3 All ER 1029; the publication of the Law Reports is a purpose beneficial to the community). See also *Scottish Burial Reform and Cremation Society Ltd v Glasgow City Corpn* [1968] AC 138, [1967] 3 All ER 215, HL.
3   *IRC v Baddeley* [1955] AC 572, [1955] 1 All ER 525. The question whether a trust set up by a will was charitable because it was of public benefit stood or fell by the law and character of the objects of the trust at the date of the testator's death, *Re Bushnell, Lloyds Bank Ltd v Murray* [1975] 1 All ER 721, [1975] 1 WLR 1596, distinguishing *Scottish Burial Reform and Cremation Society Ltd v Glasgow City Corpn* [1968] AC 138, [1967] 3 All ER 215, HL.
4   *Re Koettgen's Will Trust, Westminster Bank Ltd v Family Welfare Association Trustees Ltd* [1954] Ch 252, [1954] 1 All ER 581 (trust for commercial education generally with a preference for employees of a company and members of their families).
5   *IRC v Baddeley* [1955] AC 572, [1955] 1 All ER 525.
6   Per Lord Cross in *Dingle v Turner* [1972] AC 601 at 624, [1972] 1 All ER 878 at p 889, 'sections of the public' include, for example, the ratepayers in the Royal Boroughs of Kensington and Chelsea, the blind; applied in *Re Denison* (1974) 42 DLR (3d) 652; the descendants of Gladstone and the employees of a small company are a private class: *Davies v Perpetual Trustee Co Ltd* [1959] AC 439, [1959] 2 All ER 128.
7   *Re Smith, Public Trustee v Smith* [1932] 1 Ch 153 (gift 'to my country England'); *Nightingale v Goulbourn* (1848) 2 Ph 594 (gift for benefit of country to be applied by the Chancellor of the Exchequer); *A-G v Bushby* (1857) 24 Beav 299 (for relief of taxes); *Thellusson v Woodford* (1805) 11 Ves 112 (for reduction of National Debt); *Newland v A-G* (1809) 3 Mer 684 (same); *Ashton v Lord Langdale* (1851) 4 De G & Sm 402 (same); *Re Bell, Ballarat Trustees, Executors and Agency Co Ltd* [1943] VLR 103 (person rendering in any year the greatest benefit to humanity); *Re Strakosch, Temperley v A-G* [1949] Ch 529, [1949] 2 All ER 6 (strengthen unity of mother country with South Africa: not charitable); *Re Spensley's Will Trusts, Barclays Bank Ltd v Staughton* [1954] Ch 233, [1954] 1 All ER 178 (residence of High Commissioner: not charitable); *Re Elgar* [1957] NZLR 556 (patriotism); *Gray Estate v Yule* (1990) 73 DLR (4th) 162, gift to 'the German people' held charitable.
8   *A-G v Day* [1900] 1 Ch 31 (repair of highways); *Forbes v Forbes* (1854) 18 Beav 552 (building bridges); *Wilson v Barnes* (1886) 38 Ch D 507 (protection of coast); *Jones v Williams* (1767) Amb 651 (provision of water); *A-G v Eastlake* (1853) 11 Hare 205 (provision of public lighting); *Re Spence, Barclays Bank Ltd v Stockton-on-Tees Corpn* [1938] Ch 96, [1937] 3 All ER 684 (public hall for borough); *Re Bones, Goltz v Ballarat Trustees, Executors and Agency Co Ltd* [1930] VLR 346 (improvement of city); *Re Knowles* [1938] 3 DLR 178 (beautifying a street); *Re Bobier* [1949] 4 DLR 288 (hospital); *Re List, List v Prime* [1949] NZLR 78

(convalescent home for children); *Public Trustee v Nolan* (1943) 43 SRNSW 169 (to erect carillon: not charitable); *Re Wokingham Fire Brigade Trusts* [1951] Ch 373, [1951] 1 All ER 454 (provision of fire brigade); *Re Mair* [1964] VR 529 (gift of public park: charitable); *Scottish Burial Reform and Cremation Society Ltd v Glasgow City Corpn* [1968] AC 138, [1967] 3 All ER 215, HL (provision of crematorium and promotion of cremation).

9   *Re Scowcroft, Ormrod v Wilkinson* [1898] 2 Ch 638 (public library); *Re Holburne, Coates v Mackillop* (1885) 53 LT 212 (museum); *Re Scowcroft, Ormrod v Wilkinson* (reading-room); *Harrison v Southampton Corpn* (1854) 2 Sm & G 387 (botanical garden and observatory); *Re Jacobs, Westminster Bank v Chinn* (1970) 114 Sol Jo 515 (planting of a grove of trees in Israel); *Shillington v Portadown Urban Council* [1911] 1 IR 247 (recreation); *Re Hadden, Public Trustee v More* [1932] 1 Ch 133 (public recreation); *Taylor v Taylor* (1910) 10 CLR 218 (scientific research); *Re Vernon Estate, Boyle v Battye* [1948] 2 WWR 46 (community hall). A gift for the encouragement of mere sport is not charitable: *Re Jacques* (1967) 63 DLR (2d) 673 (residue to be distributed 'to finance some community project', possibly swimming pool: held, not charitable); *Re Gray, Todd v Taylor* [1925] Ch 362 (regimental sports: charitable); *Baddeley v IRC* [1953] 2 All ER 233 at 251; *Re Morgan, Cecil–Williams v A-G* [1955] 2 All ER 632 (public recreation ground); *Kearins v Kearins* [1957] SRNSW 286; *Alexandra Park Trustees v Haringey London Borough* (1967) 66 LGR 306 (public park and sports ground); *Royal College of Surgeons of England v National Provincial Bank Ltd* [1952] 1 All ER 984 (promotion of surgery); *Royal College of Nursing for England and Wales v St Marylebone Corpn* [1959] 3 All ER 663 (promotion of nursing); *General Nursing Council v St Marylebone Borough Council* [1959] 1 All ER 325 (regulation of nursing profession not charitable); *Re Lysaght, Hill v Royal College of Surgeons of England* [1966] Ch 191, [1965] 2 All ER 888 (gift for medical studentship: not void because Roman Catholics and Jews excluded there being a general charitable intent); *Re Pinion, Westminster Bank Ltd v Pinion* [1965] Ch 85 at 98, [1964] 1 All ER 890 (gift of studio paintings and old furniture to form exhibition not charitable where the few pieces of any educational value were not sufficient to make the whole charitable and the collection was directed by the will to be kept intact); *Incorporated Council of Law Reporting for England and Wales v A-G* [1972] Ch 73, [1971] 3 All ER 1029 (publication of Law Reports).

10   *Re Lord Stratheden and Campbell, Alt v Lord Stratheden and Campbell* [1894] 3 Ch 265 (volunteer corps); *Re Stephens, Giles v Stephens* (1892) 8 TLR 792 (teaching shooting); *Re Good, Harrington v Watts* [1905] 2 Ch 60, and *Re Donald, Moore v Somerset* [1909] 2 Ch 410 (officer's mess); *Re Gray, Todd v Taylor* [1925] Ch 362 (regimental fund for sport); *Re Barker, Sherrington v St Paul's Cathedral (Dean and Chapter)* (1909) 25 TLR 753 (prize for cadets); *Re Driffill, Harvey v Chamberlain* [1950] Ch 92, [1949] 2 All ER 933 (defence from air attack). A gift for training boys to become officers in the Navy or the mercantile marine is charitable: *Re Corbyn, Midland Bank Executor and Trustee Co Ltd v A-G* [1941] Ch 400, [1941] 2 All ER 160. See also *Whitmore v Regina Branch of Canadian Legion of British Empire Service League* [1940] 3 WWR 359 (returned soldiers); *Re Elgar* [1957] NZLR 556; *Re Gillespie* [1965] VR 402 (gift for any organisation for ex-members of forces, the choice is to be in the discretion of the trustee. Restriction to protestant members of British descent).

11   *IRC v Yorkshire Agricultural Society* [1928] 1 KB 611; *Re Pleasants, Pleasants v A-G* (1923) 39 TLR 675; *London University of Yarrow* (1857) 1 De G & J 72. As to gift to promote natural history, see *Re Benham* [1939] SASR 450. A gift of residue to found a bank for the purpose of granting loans to assist planters and agriculturalists at a low rate of interest, but compatible with the proper operation of the bank is not a valid charitable trust because the loans might not be applied by the planters or agriculturalists for agricultural purposes and restrictive words are not to be imported into a trust which without them is invalid: *Hadaway v Hadaway* [1955] 1 WLR 16.

12   See para **[102.12]** infra.

13   *Re Resch's Will Trusts, Le Cras v Perpetual Trustee Co Ltd, Far West Children's Health Scheme v Perpetual Trustee Co Ltd* [1969] 1 AC 514, [1967] 3 All ER 915 (gift to a private hospital which charged fees, poor sometimes treated without payment). A gift for the purpose of a hospital is prima facie a good charitable trust; it is not a condition of validity of a trust for the relief of the sick that it should be limited to the poor sick; if a bequest is made on trusts requiring it to be applied for a particular purpose which is charitable, it is immaterial that some of the general purposes of the recipient body may not be charitable. See also *Re Adams, Gee v Barnet Group Hospital Management Committee* [1968] Ch 80, [1967] 3 All ER 285; *Re Smith's Will Trusts, Barclays Bank Ltd v Merchantile Bank Ltd* [1962] 2 All ER 563, [1962] 1 WLR 763.

14   *Re Scowcroft, Ormrod v Wilkinson* [1898] 2 Ch 638 (Conservative principles combined with mental and moral improvement); *Re Hood, Public Trustee v Hood* [1931] 1 Ch 240 (Christian principles); *Re Price, Midland Bank Exor and Trustee Co Ltd v Harwood* [1943] Ch 422, [1943] 2 All ER 505 (teaching of Steiner); and see *Barralet v A-G* [1980] 3 All ER 918, [1980] 1 WLR 1565 (whole of society's objects were for the mental and moral improvement of man and thus for purposes beneficial to the community). But the trust must not be political; see *McGovern v A-G* [1982] Ch 321, [1981] 3 All ER 493, and next section. *Re Trusts of Arthur McDougall Fund* [1956] 3 All ER 867 (advancement of education or other charitable purposes connected with the art and science of government is charitable and not invalidated by the fact that the trustees must be members of the Proportional Representation Society); *Re Shaw, Public Trustee v Day* [1957] 1 All ER 745 (reform of alphabet); *Re Davis, Watts v Davis and Westralian Farmers Co-operative Ltd* [1965] WAR 25 (a gift to the directors of the company to apply the income in perpetuity for the expansion of co-operation and the co-operative movement held invalid); *Re Shapiro* (1980) 107 DLR (3d) 133.

15   *Associated Artists Ltd v IRC* [1956] 2 All ER 583, [1956] 1 WLR 752.

16   *Royal Choral Society v IRC* [1943] 2 All ER 101; *Re Levien, Lloyds Bank Ltd v Worshipful of Musicians* [1955] 3 All ER 35; *Re Delius' Will Trusts, Emanuel v Rosen* [1957] Ch 299, [1957] 1 All ER 854.

17   *Re Hummeltenberg, Beatty v London Spiritualistic Alliance Ltd* [1923] 1 Ch 237; *Re Grove-Grady, Plowden v Lawrence* [1929] 1 Ch 557; *National Anti-Vivisection Society v IRC* [1948] AC 31, [1947] 2 All ER 217, disapproving *Re Foveaux, Cross v London Anti-Vivisection Society* [1895] 2 Ch 501, where it was stated that where the merits of a particular object are controversial the court stands neutral.

18   *Re Hummeltenberg, Beatty v London Spiritualistic Alliance Ltd* [1923] 1 Ch 237. The part of the public to be benefited must be substantial enough to give it a public character: *Shaw v Halifax Corpn* [1915] 2 KB 170; *Hall v Derby Borough Urban Sanitary Authority* (1885) 16 QBD 163, and may be a class of the inhabitants of a particular locality: *Mitford v Reynolds* (1842) 1 Ph 185 (native inhabitants of Dacca); *Re Norwich Town Close Estate Charity* (1888) 40 Ch D 298 (freemen of a borough); *Re Mellody, Brandwood v Haden* [1918] 1 Ch 228 (schoolchildren of a town); *Re Koetten's Will Trusts, Westminster Bank Ltd v Family Welfare Association Trustees Ltd* [1954] Ch 252, [1954] 1 All ER 581 (employees of a company). A gift to a parish council is not necessarily charitable and where the object was described as 'some useful memorial' of the testator it was held not charitable and too uncertain to be enforced: *Re Endacott, Corpe v Endacott* [1960] Ch 232, [1959] 3 All ER 562.

19   *A-G v Earl Lonsdale* (1827) 1 Sim 105 (county); *A-G v Dartmouth Corpn* (1883) 48 LT 933 (town); *Re St Nicholas Acons (Parish)* (1889) 60 LT 532 (parish); *Schellenberger v Trustees etc Co* (1952) 86 CLR 454 (gift to add to the beauty and advancement of a town); *Goodman v Saltash Corpn* (1882) 7 App Cas 633; *Peggs v Lamb* [1994] Ch 172, [1994] 2 All ER 15.

20   *IRC v Baddeley* [1955] AC 572, [1955] 1 All ER 525; *Re Lipinski's Will Trusts, Gosschalk v Levy* [1976] Ch 235, [1977] 1 All ER 33 (trust for the Hull Judeans (Maccabi) Association, founded as a cricket club and subsequently provided social, cultural and sporting activities for Jewish youths who were members, held not charitable because essentially a sports club for the benefit of its members).

[102.10]

Trusts for political purposes. Trusts of a political nature even if appearing to fall within the spirit and intendment of the preamble to the Statute of Elizabeth are not regarded as charitable.[1] A useful review of the law can be found in *McGovern v A-G*[2] where the Amnesty International Trust was found to be of essentially a political nature and refused registration. Slade J[3] categorised such trusts as those where a direct or principal purpose is either:

(i)   to further the interests of particular political party,[4] or
(ii) to procure changes in the laws of this country,[5] or
(iii) to procure changes in the laws of a foreign country,[6] or
(iv) to procure a reversal of government policy or of particular decisions of governmental authorities in this country,[7] or

(v) to procure a reversal of government policy or of particular decisions of government authorities in a foreign country.[8]

However if the main objects of the trust are exclusively charitable the mere fact that the trustees had incidental powers under the trust to employ political means to further non-political purposes of the trust would not deprive the trust of its charitable status.[9] This analysis was referred to in *Re Koeppler's Will Trusts*[10] where the trust was concerned with the promotion of greater co-operation in Europe and the West. Slade LJ following his own previous decision in *McGovern*[11] held that the trust was educational rather than political, noting that no activities of a party political nature were involved and the aim was not to procure change in the laws or governmental policy of England or other countries.

1   See Lord Parker in *Bowman v Secular Society Ltd* [1917] AC 406 at 422; *National Anti-Vivisection Society v IRC* [1948] AC 31 at 49–50 [1947] 2 All ER 217 at 224, per Lord Wright; and at 62–63 and 232 per Lord Simonds.
2   [1982] Ch 321, [1981] 3 All ER 493.
3   [1982] Ch 321, [1981] 3 All ER 493 at 509.
4   *Bonar Law Memorial Trust v IRC* (1933) 49 TLR 220 (Conservative); *Re Ogden, Brydon v Samuel* [1933] Ch 678 (Liberal); *Re Hopkinson, Lloyds Bank Ltd v Barker* [1949] 1 All ER 346 (Labour principles but the court found that the object of the gift was to advance the cause of the party by improving its methods of propaganda and electoral efficiency and held the trust not a valid charitable trust as being for the attainment of political objects); applied in *Re Bushnell, Lloyds Bank Ltd v Murray* [1975] 1 All ER 721, [1975] 1 WLR 1596 (testator trying to promote by education his own theory of 'socialised medicine' rather than to educate the public to choose for themselves, starting from neutral information, accordingly essential object of trust was political and not an educational one); *Russell v Jackson* (1852) 10 Hare 204 (socialism); *Bacon v Pianta* [1966] ALR 1044 (Communist Party of Australia).
5   *National Anti-Vivisection Society v IRC* [1948] AC 31, [1947] 2 All ER 217 (anti-vivisection: this is not charitable where total abolition is sought because then the detriment to medical research outweighs the public benefit. A society whose main object is the promotion of legislation is political and not charitable); applied in *Re Bushnell, Lloyds Bank Ltd v Murray* [1975] 1 All ER 721, [1975] 1 WLR 1596; *Re Hood, Public Trustee v Hood* [1931] 1 Ch 240 (temperance); *IRC v Falkirk Temperance Cafe Trust* 1927 SC 261 (same); *IRC v Temperance Council of Christian Churches of England and Wales* (1926) 136 LT 27 (same but promotion by political means is not charitable); *Re Corbett* (1921) 17 Tas LR 139 (improvement of relations between employers and employed).
6   *McGovern v A-G* [1982] Ch 321, [1981] 3 All ER 493, thus attempting to procure the abolition of torture or inhumane or degrading treatment or punishment (including capital and corporal punishment) necessarily involved procuring reforming legislation whether in the United Kingdom or elsewhere and so was not charitable.
7   *Baldry v Feintuck* [1972] 2 All ER 81, [1972] 1 WLR 552 (campaign of protest against the government's policy of ending the supply of free milk to school children is not charitable).
8   *McGovern v A-G* [1982] Ch 321, [1981] 3 All ER 493, attempting to secure release of prisoners of conscience which involved the application of moral prèsure on foreign governments or authorities.
9   *McGovern v A-G* [1982] Ch 321, [1981] 3 All ER 493 at 509.
10 *Re Koeppler's Will Trusts, Barclays Bank Trust Co Ltd v Slack* [1986] Ch 423, [1985] 2 All ER 869, reversing Peter Gibson J [1984] 2 All ER 111.
11 *McGovern v A-G* [1982] Ch 321, [1981] 3 All ER 493.

[102.11]

Recreational charities. The Recreational Charities Act 1958 (RCA 1958)[1] provides that it shall be, and be deemed always to have been charitable, to provide, or assist in the provision of, facilities for recreation or other leisure-time occupation, if the facilities are provided in the interests of social welfare.[2] There must be some deprivation, although not necessarily financial deprivation, which falls to be alleviated[3] and the facilities have to be provided with the object of improving the conditions of life for the persons for whom the facilities are primarily intended, and either those persons have need of such facilities by reason of their youth,[4] age, infirmity or disablement, poverty or social and economic circumstances,[5] or the facilities are to be available to the members or female members of the public at large.[6] For facilities to be provided within the RCA 1958 it is not necessary that the persons for whom the facilities were primarily provided be confined to those who had need of them by one of these forms of social deprivation.[7] It is sufficient if the facilities are provided with the object of improving the conditions of life for members of the community generally.[8] The object of the RCA 1958 is to give statutory recognition to the charitable nature of the trusts and institutions in question, without enlarging the definition of charity or encroaching on the existing authorities. In particular it is specifically provided that the RCA 1958 applies to the provision of facilities at village halls, community centres and women's institutes, and to the provision and maintenance of grounds and buildings to be used for purposes of recreation or leisure-time occupation, and extends to the provision of facilities for those purposes by the organising of any activity.[9] The provision of a holiday centre for North Derbyshire miners and their families in need of a change of air, has been held to be within the RCA 1958.[10]

1   5 *Halsbury's Statutes* (4th edn) 893.
2   RCA 1958, s 1(1). See also *IRC v McMullen* [1979] 1 All ER 588, CA; revd [1981] AC 1, [1980] 1 All ER 884, HL, but without reference to the Court of Appeal's comments on the RCA 1958.
3   *IRC v McMullen* [1978] 1 All ER 230 at 241, per Walton J, who did not think the Football Association Youth Trust satisfied this condition since it was impossible for the court to say that, as a class, pupils at schools and universities were 'deprived' (affd [1979] 1 All ER 588; revsd, [1981] AC 1, [1980] 1 All ER 884, HL).
4   However Walton J in *IRC v McMullen,* see n 3 supra, did think that notwithstanding the presence of many mature students it would be possible to regard the trust as intended primarily to benefit the young.
5   RCA 1958, s 1(2)(b)(ii).
6   RCA 1958, s 1(2)(b)(ii).
7   The RCA 1958 was prompted by the House of Lords decision in *IRC v Baddeley* [1955] AC 572, [1955] 1 All ER 525, HL, where it was held that a trust for the promotion of the moral, social and physical well-being of persons, resident in a particular area, by the provision of facilities for moral, social and physical training and recreation and by promoting and encouraging all forms of such activities as were calculated to contribute to the health and well-being of such persons, was not charitable. It is doubtful whether the provisions of the Act would in fact have validated this very wide trust. *Guild v IRC* [1992] 2 AC 310, [1992] 2 All ER 10, HL.
8   *IRC v Baddeley* [1955] AC 572, [1955] 1 All ER 525, HL, dictum of Bridge LJ in *IRC v McMullen* [1979] 1 All ER 588, CA at 597–598 approved; dictum of Walton J in *IRC v McMullen* [1978] 1 All ER 230 at 241, disapproved. It was held that a gift of residue left 'to the Town Council of North Berwick for the use in connection with the Sports Centre in North Berwick or some similar purpose in connection with sport' was charitable as within s 1 of the 1958 Act. The House thought that a benignant approach should be adopted to the Act which favoured finding the gift charitable, rather than void. Dicta by Lord Loreburn LC in *Weir v Crum-Brown* [1908] AC 162 at 16; and of Lord Hailsham LC in *IRC v McMullen* [1980] 1 All ER 884 at 890 applied.
9   RCA 1958, s 1(3); see *IRC v McMullen,* see n 3 supra.

10 *Wynn v Skegness UDC* [1966] 3 All ER 336, [1967] 1 WLR 52. Compare the pre-Act case of *IRC v Glasgow City Police Athletic Association* [1953] AC 380, [1953] 1 All ER 747, HL (provision of recreation facilities for members of a police force not charitable); distinguished in *London Hospital Medical College v IRC* [1976] 2 All ER 113, [1976] 1 WLR 613 (students union held charitable on grounds of education; no decision on RCA 1958).

[102.12]

Benefit to animals. A trust for the benefit of animals is charitable not upon the ground that it benefits the animals, but upon the ground that it produces some benefit to mankind, that is, it is calculated to develop the finer side of human nature.[1] The objects of such a trust are not charitable even though for the benefit of animals if, on balance, the object is detrimental to the public benefit, as, for example, hindering medical research.[2] On these principles trusts for the prevention of cruelty to animals have been upheld.[3]

1 *Re Grove-Grady, Plowden v Lawrence* [1929] 1 Ch 557; *National Anti-Vivisection Society v IRC* [1948] AC 31, [1947] 2 All ER 217; *Re Moss, Hobrough v Harvey* [1949] 1 All ER 495; *Re Weaver* [1963] VR 257; *Re Salterthwaite's Will Trusts* [1966] 1 All ER 919, [1966] 1 WLR 277.

2 *National Anti-Vivisection Society v IRC* [1948] AC 31, [1947] 2 All ER 217.

3 *Re Murawski's Will Trusts, Lloyds Bank v Royal Society for the Prevention of Cruelty to Animals* [1971] 2 All ER 328, [1971] 1 WLR 707; *Re Wedgwood, Allen v Wedgwood* [1915] 1 Ch 113; *Re Grove-Grady, Plowden v Lawrence* [1929] 1 Ch 557; *Re Joy, Purday v Johnson* (1888) 60 LT 175; *Re Dean, Cooper-Dean v Stevens* (1889) 41 Ch D 552; *Re Moss, Hobrough v Harvey* [1949] 1 All ER 495; followed in *Re Green's Will Trusts, Fitzgerald-Hart v A-G* [1985] 3 All ER 455 (gift to trustees to set up foundation for rescue, maintenance and benefit of cruelly treated animals). Many of the cases are discussed in the House of Lords decision in *National Anti-Vivisection Society v IRC* [1948] AC 31, [1947] 2 All ER 217.

[102.13]

Poor relations. Perpetual trusts for the benefit of poor relations are charitable[1] unless confined to statutory next of kin and such trusts are so confined unless a contrary intention appears from the will.[2] Poor relations who become rich must not participate[3] and a trust for poorest relations must not benefit persons in fact rich.[4]

1 *A-G v Price* (1810) 17 Ves 371; *Bernal v Bernal* (1838) 3 My & Cr 559; *A-G v Duke of Northumberland* (1877) 7 Ch D 745; *Mahon v Savage* (1803) 1 Sch & Lef 111; *Re Compton, Powell v Compton* [1945] Ch 123, [1945] 1 All ER 198; *Re Cohn* [1952] 3 DLR 833; *Re McEnery, O'Connell v A-G* [1941] IR 323 (where trust was held invalid); *Re Scarisbrick, Cockshott v Public Trustee* [1951] Ch 622, [1951] 1 All ER 822; in this field the distinction between a public or charitable trust and a private trust depends on whether as a matter of construction the gift was for the relief of poverty amongst a particular description of poor people or was merely a gift to particular poor persons, the relief of poverty among them being the motive of the gift. The fact that the gift took the form of a perpetual trust would no doubt indicate that the intention of the donor could not have been to confer private benefits on particular people whose possible necessities he had in mind; but the fact that the capital of the gift was to be distributed at once did not necessarily show that the gift was a private trust. See *Dingle v Turner* [1972] AC 601 at 617, [1972] 1 All ER 878 at 883. *Re Scarisbrick, Cockshott v Public Trustee* [1951] Ch 622, [1951] 1 All ER 822 ('in needy circumstances') was followed in *Re Cohen, Cowan v Cohen* [1973] 1 All ER 889, [1973] 1 WLR 415 ('relations of mine whom my trustees shall consider to be in special need', held to be charitable and not confined to persons living at the death of the testatrix); *Re Mills* (1981) 27 SASR 200. See also *Re Segelman* [1995] 3 All ER 676 at 687–692 (gift of fund on trusts for a period of 21 years for the assistance of 'the poor and needy' members of a class consisting of six named persons and their issue held to be charitable).

2   *Carr v Bedford* (1678) 2 Rep Ch 146.
3   *Mahon v Savage* (1803) 1 Sch & Lef 111.
4   *A-G v Duke of Northumberland* (1877) 7 Ch D 745.

[102.14]
Poor employees. The 'poor relations' cases, although of long-standing are an anomalous exception to the general requirement of public benefit and the courts seemed reluctant to extent the exception to include trusts for other groups.[1] However, it has now been decided that 'poor employees' and 'poor members' trusts are a natural development from the 'poor relations' cases and enjoy a similar exemption from the requirement of public benefit.[2] But a trust to wind up the fund applying any surplus for such a purpose and in such a manner for the benefit of employees or ex-employees as the trustees think most appropriate in the circumstances then existing is too vague and uncertain as it is impossible to ascertain the class entitled to benefit.[3]

1   *Re Compton, Powell v Compton* [1945] Ch 123, [1945] 1 All ER 198; *Oppenheim v Tobacco Securities Trusts Co Ltd* [1951] AC 297, [1951] 1 All ER 31; *Re Hobourn Aero Components Ltd's Air Raid Distress Fund, Ryan v Forrest* [1946] Ch 194, [1946] 1 All ER 501; *Re Cox, Baker v National Trust Co Ltd* [1955] AC 627, [1955] 2 All ER 550; *Davies v Perpetual Trustee Co Ltd* [1959] AC 439, [1959] 2 All ER 128.
2   *Dingle v Turner* [1972] AC 601, [1972] 1 All ER 878, applying *Re Gosling, Gosling v Smith* (1900) 48 WR 300, and *Gibson v South American Stores (Gath and Chaves) Ltd* [1950] Ch 177, [1949] 2 All ER 985. See also *Re Scarisbrick, Cockshott v Public Trustee* [1951] Ch 622, [1951] 1 All ER 822; and *Re Young's Will Trusts, Westminster Bank Ltd v Sterling* [1955] 3 All ER 689.
3   *Re Sayer Trust, MacGregor v Sayer* [1957] Ch 423, [1956] 3 All ER 600.

[102.15]
Poor members. Funds held on trust for the relief of poverty among members of a voluntary association have been held charitable, the funds in each case, being derived in part from subscriptions made by the members and in part from donations or bequests by well-wishers.[1]

1   *Spiller v Maude* (1881) 32 Ch D 158n; *Pease v Pattinson* (1886) 32 Ch D 154, [1886–1890] All ER Rep 507; *Re Buck, Bruty v Mackey* [1896] 2 Ch 727, [1895–99] All ER Rep 366. It does not appear to have been argued in these cases that the fact that the benefits were confined to persons who were linked by the common tie of membership of an association prevented the trusts from being charitable, see *Dingle v Turner* [1972] AC 601 at 617, [1972] 1 All ER 878 at 883.

[102.16]
Gifts for 'parish' etc work. The following gifts have been considered in this connection: gift to trustees of parish church for any purpose authorised by trust deed;[1] mission work;[2] gift to Vicar for his work in the parish;[3] for his benevolent work;[4] for purposes in connection with the church;[5] for such objects connected with the church as he shall think fit;[6] such parochial institutions or purposes as he shall select;[7] for benefit of work of cathedral;[8] for work connected with Roman Catholic church;[9] gift to archbishop for helping church in Wales as he thinks best;[10] a gift to an archbishop as he in his absolute discretion should think fit;[11]; bequest to editors of missionary periodical to be applied as they think fit;[12] bequest to bishop to dispose in best interests of religion.[13] A gift to trustees of a church 'to help in any good work' is not charitable[14] but a gift to be used by the bishop for the time being as he thinks fit in his diocese is charitable.[15]

1   *Re Lawton, Lloyds Bank Ltd v Longfleet St Mary's Parochial Church Council* [1940] Ch 984 (no charitable intention).
2   *Re Moon's Will Trusts, Foale v Gillians* [1948] 1 All ER 300 (valid).
3   *Re Simson, Fowler v Tinley* [1946] Ch 299, [1946] 2 All ER 220 (valid).
4   *Re Simson, Fowler v Tinley* [1946] Ch 299, [1946] 2 All ER 220 (invalid).
5   *Re Eastes, Pain v Paxton* [1948] Ch 257, [1948] 1 All ER 536 (valid, following *Re Bain, Public Trustee v Ross* [1930] 1 Ch 224) and also, a gift merely for 'St Peter's Church, Staines': see *Re Gare* [1952] Ch 80, [1951] 2 All ER 863.
6   *Re Bain, Public Trustee v Ross* [1930] 1 Ch 224 (valid).
7   *Re Stratton, Knapman v A-G* [1931] 1 Ch 197 (invalid).
8   *Re Martley, Simpson v Cardinal Bourne* (1931) 47 TLR 392 (valid).
9   *Re Davies, Lloyds Bank Ltd v Mostyn* (1932) 48 TLR 539 (invalid).
10 *Re Jackson, Midland Bank Executor and Trustee Co Ltd v Archbishop of Wales* [1930] 2 Ch 389 (invalid).
11 *Re Flinn, Public Trustee v Flinn* [1948] Ch 241, [1948] 1 All ER 541 (valid).
12 *Re Norman, Andrew v Vine* [1947] Ch 349, [1947] 1 All ER 400 (valid). As to this case and that in the preceding note, see also *Re Spensley's Will Trusts* [1952] Ch 886, [1952] 2 All ER 49.
13 *Re Howley, Naughton v Hegarty* [1940] IR 109 (valid).
14 *Re Ashton* [1955] NZLR 192; applied in *Re White, Perpetual Trustee Estate and Agency Co Ltd v Milligan* [1963] NZLR 788.
15 *Re Rumball, Sherlock v Allan* [1956] Ch 105, [1955] 3 All ER 71; *Touchet and Touchet v Blais* (1963) 45 WWR 246.

[102.17]

Charges for services. Objects which are otherwise charitable do not cease to be charitable merely because beneficiaries are required to make payments for what they receive.[1] Even if public demand for the kind of services which the charity provides becomes so large that there is room for a commercial undertaking to come in and supply similar services on a commercial basis, the objects and activities of a non-profitable charitable organisation do not cease to be charitable.[2] If a body is established for a charitable purpose, it will be not the less a charity because the pursuit of that purpose will or may confer incidental benefits upon the members of a profession.[3]

1   *Scottish Burial Reform and Cremation Society Ltd v Glasgow City Corpn* [1968] AC 138 at 156, [1967] 3 All ER 215 at 224, HL; *Joseph Rowntree Memorial Trust Housing Association Ltd v A-G* [1983] Ch 159, [1983] 1 All ER 288.
2   *Scottish Burial Reform and Cremation Society Ltd v Glasgow City Corpn* [1968] AC 138 at 147, per Lord Reid, [1967] 3 All ER 215 at 218; see also Sachs LJ in *Incorporated Council of Law Reporting for England and Wales v A-G* [1972] Ch 73 at 90, [1971] 3 All ER 1029 at 1038: 'It is clear that the mere fact that charges on a commercial scale are made for services rendered by an institution does not itself bar that institution from being held to be charitable—so long, at any rate, as all the profits must be retained for its purposes, and none can enure to the benefit of its individual members'.
3   Per Buckley LJ in *Incorporated Council of Law Reporting for England and Wales v A-G* [1972] Ch 73 at 103, [1971] 3 All ER 1029 at 1044, referring to *Royal College of Surgeons of England v National Provincial Bank Ltd* [1952] AC 631, [1952] 1 All ER 984, and *Royal College of Nursing v St Marylebone Corpn* [1959] 3 All ER 663. The fact that the law reports enable the lawyer to earn his livelihood, is incidental to, or consequential on, the primary scholastic function of advancing and disseminating knowledge of the law.

II.   CREATION OF CHARITABLE TRUST

[102.18]
Technical language unnecessary. A charitable trust may be created by informal as well as by technical language, provided that the intention of the testator to

devote the property to charity is clear. Thus, precatory or recommendatory words have frequently been held to create trusts where the intention of the testator has been considered imperative.[1] Provisions in which the word 'condition' occurs may create a trust.[2] A secret trust may be established in favour of a charity provided it is clear that the testator intended the property to be applied to charitable purposes and the ordinary law applicable to such trusts applies equally to charitable trusts as to ordinary private trusts.[3]

1   *A-G v Davies* (1802) 9 Ves 535; *Kirkbank v Hudson* (1819) 7 Price 212; *Pilkington v Boughley* (1841) 12 Sim 114.
2   A trust is created where the condition is that the whole property is to be devoted to the purposes to the exclusion of any beneficial interest in the donee: *Merchant Taylors' Co v A-G* (1871) 6 Ch App 512, or where the condition is that a fixed and definite sum shall be applied in a specified charitable way: *Re Richardson, Shuldham v Royal National Lifeboat Institution* (1887) 56 LJ Ch 784.
3   See Chapter 36.

[102.19]
Application to charity usually binding on donee. An old equitable doctrine forbids any person to acquire an interest with notice of a charitable trust without being bound by it, and the donee of an interest subject to a charge in favour of a charity is a trustee for the charity unless and until separate trustees of the charge are appointed.[1] Once money is effectually dedicated by will to charity, whether in pursuance of a general or particular intent, the testator's next of kin or residuary legatees are for ever excluded and no question of subsequent lapse, or anything analogous to lapse, between the date of the testator's death and the time when the money becomes available for actual application to the testator's purpose could affect the matter so far as they are concerned. It makes no difference whether the money is to be paid over to other persons or bodies to be applied to the charitable purpose or is to be so applied by the trustees of the will.[2] Property may be given by will to make certain payments to a charity which do not exhaust the whole estate.[3] In those cases where the testator has not shown a general intention to devote the whole property to charity, the donee takes beneficially subject only to the specific appropriation,[4] unless it appears that he was intended to take only as trustee, in which case a resulting trust in favour of the testator's estate arises.[5]

1   *Charitable Donations and Bequests Comrs v Wybrants* (1845) 2 Jo & Lat 182.
2   *Re Wright, Blizard v Lockhart* [1954] Ch 347, [1954] 2 All ER 98. For this reason the proper date for ascertaining the practicability of the purpose is the death of the testator: *Re Wright*, applying *Re Slevin, Slevin v Hepburn* [1891] 2 Ch 236, and see *Re White's Will Trusts, Barlow v Gillard* [1955] Ch 188, [1954] 2 All ER 620.
3   *Merchant Taylors' Co v A-G* (1871) 6 Ch App 512; *A-G v Cordwainers' Co* (1833) 3 My & K 534; *A-G v Trinity College, Cambridge* (1856) 24 Beav 383.
4   *A-G v Wax Chandlers' Co (Master, Wardens, etc)* (1873) LR 6 HL 1.
5   *Re Stanford, Cambridge University v A-G* [1924] 1 Ch 73.

[102.20]
Ademption. The ordinary law of ademption applies to gifts for charity, subject only to the doctrine of general charitable intention.[1]

1   *Twining v Powell* (1845) 2 Coll 262; *Makeown v Ardagh* (1876) IR 10 Eq 445; *Re Corbett, Corbett v Lord Cobham* [1903] 2 Ch 326.

[102.21]

Requisites of creation. The established rule is that no testamentary gift is deemed charitable unless the testator has in express terms, or by necessary implication signified a clear intention to devote the property to charity.[1] To ascertain such intention a fair interpretation must be put upon the whole will.[2] Purposes which are not defined or indicated are not presumed to be charitable,[3] except where a general intention to give to charity is to be gathered from the will taken as a whole, in which case a general indefiniteness as to the particular mode of execution does not invalidate the gift.[4] A charitable intention cannot be deducted from the mere fact that the trustee is a charitable society,[5] or holds a religious or charitable office,[6] if the gift is made in plain language admitting non-charitable objects.[7] A recital of a charitable intention does not render charitable a trust for objects which are not charitable, but such a recital may have effect where the objects are ambiguous.[8] A charitable intention which is expressed to be conditional fails if the condition is not satisfied.[9] A charitable intention may be revoked by codicil by necessary implication.[10] If a testator revokes legacies by codicil stating a reason for revocation which turns out to be untrue, the revocation is inoperative,[11] but, where the mistake is one of law or based on a doubt as to facts, it stands.[12] An expression of intention made in the testator's lifetime to devote certain funds to charity is not, in the absence of a binding contract, effective after death.[13] If the amount of a gift purporting to be made in favour of a charity cannot be ascertained, the gift fails.[14] A gift not exceeding a named figure is construed as a gift of the named sum,[15] and a gift of such sum as shall be necessary to endow a bed in a hospital is good even though there is no recognised scheme for such purpose and although the hospital has been nationalised.[16] Where the testator gives a part of a fund to charity and the rest to non-charitable objects or to objects which fail, the court makes any necessary apportionment.[17] Where a fund is to be applied to a named purpose and the surplus is to be applied to charity, then, if the first purpose is unlawful and is also so indefinite that the amount required cannot be reasonably ascertained, the gift fails entirely.[18] The result is the same where the amount for the first purpose is ascertained but the testator gives his executors a discretion to exceed it.[19] Where, however, the amount necessary for the first purpose can be reasonably ascertained, the gift of the surplus to charity is good.[20] In some cases relating to the repair of tombs,[21] where a fund is given to trustees to pay out of income the cost of keeping a tomb in repair[22] and as to the residue,[23] surplus,[24] balance,[25] or remainder,[26] upon trust for charity, the gift is construed as a gift of the whole fund charged with a gift which fails, and not as a gift of the residue after a void gift, and accordingly the whole fund, including the amount necessary to satisfy the invalid object, is applicable to the valid charitable object.[27]

---

1 *Hunter v A-G* [1899] AC 309.
2 *Hunter v A-G* [1899] AC 309 at 320.
3 *Buckle v Bristow* (1864) 5 New Rep 7.
4 *Mills v Farmer* (1815) 1 Mer 55 at 65; *Re Willis, Shaw v Willis* [1921] 1 Ch 44, and see Chapter 103.
5 *Re Freeman, Shilton v Freeman* [1908] 1 Ch 720; *Re White, White v White* [1893] 2 Ch 41.
6 *Re Davidson, Minty v Bourne* [1909] 1 Ch 567; *Dunne v Byrne* [1912] AC 407; *Re Moore, Moore v His Holiness Pope Benedict XV* [1919] 1 IR 443.

7   Where the language is ambiguous, admitting either charitable or non-charitable objects, the character of the trustee has sometimes been held to afford an indication of the testator's intention: *Re Kenny, Clode v Andrews* (1907) 97 LT 130; *Re Rees, Jones v Evans* [1920] 2 Ch 59; *Re Williams, Public Trustee v Williams* [1927] 2 Ch 283.

8   *A-G v Jesus College, Oxford* (1861) 29 Beav 163.

9   *Thomas v Howell* (1874) LR 18 Eq 198 (testator under a misapprehension as to the amount of his estate).

10   *Wheeler v Sheer* (1730) Mos 288.

11   *Thomas v Howell* (1874) LR 18 Eq 198.

12   *A-G v Lloyd* (1747) 1 Ves Sen 32, questioned in *Thomas v Howell* (1874) LR 18 Eq 198; *A-G v Ward* (1797) 3 Ves 327.

13   *Re Hudson, Creed v Henderson* (1885) 54 LJ Ch 811.

14   *Hartshorne v Nicholson* (1858) 26 Beav 58 (amount left blank); *Ewan v Bannerman* (1830) 2 Dow & Cl 74; *Cherry v Mott* (1836) 1 My & Cr 123. A gift for establishing a hospital for a hundred boys is sufficiently certain though no amount is mentioned: *Dundee Magistrates v Morris* (1858) 3 Macq 134.

15   *Thompson v Thompson* (1844) 1 Coll 381; *Gough v Bult* (1848) 16 Sim 45.

16   *Re Mills, Midland Bank Executor and Trustee Co Ltd v United Birmingham Hospital Board of Governors* [1953] 1 All ER 835, [1953] 1 WLR 554 (where it was shown that the hospital had on request named a bed where a gift of £1,000 had been made to the general funds of the hospital. The gift construed as a gift of £1,000).

17   *Re Rigley's Trusts* (1866) 36 LJ Ch 147; *Re Vaughan, Vaughan v Thomas* (1886) 33 Ch D 187; *Salusbury v Denton* (1857) 3 K & J 529; *Public Trustee v Smith* (1944) 44 SRNSW 348. It is immaterial whether the non-charitable objects are definite or indefinite: *Re Clarke, Bracey v Royal National Lifeboat Institution* [1923] 2 Ch 407.

18   *Re Taylor, Martin v Freeman* (1888) 58 LT 538; *Re Porter, Porter v Porter* [1925] Ch 746 (on the ground that if the purpose were lawful and the entire fund might have been applied to it, there is no ascertainable residue for the charitable purpose).

19   *Limbrey v Gurr* (1819) 6 Madd 151.

20   *Dundee Magistrates v Morris* (1858) 3 Macq 134; *Mitford v Reynolds* (1842) 1 Ph 185.

21   See para **[9.28]** supra.

22   The repair or upkeep of a tomb is a charitable purpose where the tomb is part of the fabric of a church: *Re Barker, Sherrington v St Paul's Cathedral (Dean and Chapter)* (1909) 25 TLR 753.

23   *Fisk v A-G* (1867) LR 4 Eq 521; *Re Vaughan, Vaughan v Thomas* (1886) 33 Ch D 187.

24   *Hoare v Osborne* (1866) LR 1 Eq 585; *Dawson v Small* (1874) LR 18 Eq 114; *Re Williams* (1877) 5 Ch D 735.

25   *Hunter v Bullock* (1872) LR 14 Eq 45. As to what constitutes a residuary gift to charity, see *Harbin v Masterman* (1871) LR 12 Eq 559.

26   *Re Birkett* (1878) 9 Ch D 576.

27   *Re Rogerson, Bird v Lee* [1901] 1 Ch 715.

[102.22]

Application to charity must be obligatory. The gift to charity is only valid if its application to charity is obligatory. If trustees are allowed an alternative application of the fund which is not charitable, the trust can not be maintained.[1] Thus a gift of residue to 'worthy causes' was void for uncertainty because the term could not be confined within the bounds of charity, there being many causes which could properly be called 'worthy' without being charitable.[2] Gifts for charitable or other purposes,[3] or gifts expressed in alternative terms admitting non-charitable objects[4] are not charitable, for they might be executed without any part of the gift being applied to charity. The fact that the trustees have decided to apply the gift to the charitable purpose does not save the gift, for the question must be decided at the death of the testator.[5] In cases of this nature where no clear intention appears to devote some portion of the property to charity, there can be no apportionment.[6] Gifts where the conjunction is 'and' and not 'or', such as 'charitable and benevolent' purposes[7] and similar gifts[8] have been held good on the ground that any object to be benefited must possess both characteristics, but where upon the true construction of the gift words are so conjoined as to create not cumulative characteristics but cumulative classes of objects, the trust is invalid,[9] unless it appears from the context that the word which would otherwise admit non-charitable objects bore in the particular will a restricted meaning admitting only such objects of the kind which it indicated as were also charitable.[10] Activities of an organisation which were ultra vires and non-charitable were irrelevant to determining whether the main purpose of an organisation was or was not charitable.[11]

1   *Re Macduff, Macduff v Macduff* [1896] 2 Ch 451; *Re Douglas, Obert v Barrow* (1887) 35 Ch D 472; *Re Davidson, Minty v Bourne* [1909] 1 Ch 567; *Re MacKay Estate* [1948] SCR 500; *Re Ashton, Gordon v Siddall* [1950] NZLR 42 (in any good work); *Re Resch's Will Trusts, Le Cras v Perpetual Trustee Co Ltd, Far West Children's Health Scheme v Perpetual Trustee Co Ltd* [1969] 1 AC 514, [1967] 3 All ER 915 (income had to be used for purposes of the hospital, and immaterial that the general property of the recipient was applicable for non-charitable purposes); *Re Wootton's Will Trusts, Trotter v Duffin* [1968] 2 All ER 618, [1968] 1 WLR 681 (not exclusively charitable). It is not open to one charity to subscribe to the funds of another charity unless the recipient charity was an object or purpose of the donor charity; *Baldry v Feintuck* [1972] 2 All ER 81, [1972] 1 WLR 552. It is not what the intended recipient (in this case a diocesan authority) says he will do with the bequest, but what the terms of the will empower, if not oblige, him to do with it that determines whether or not it is a charitable gift; *Re Delaney Estate, Canada Trust Co v Roman Catholic Archiepiscopal Corpn of Winnipeg* (1957) 12 DLR (2d) 23. The Charity Commissioners have refused to register a charity where the objects were expressed to be 'for the benefit of any charitable object or purpose that the trustees may deem proper', coupled with additional extremely wide powers. Such a charity is not saved by a proviso that nothing contained in the deed should 'either expressly or by implication authorise the application of any part of the income or capital of the trust fund for any object or purpose which is not a charitable object or purpose'. See Report of the Charity Commissioners for England and Wales 1971, paras 76–79.

2   *Re Atkinson's Will Trusts, Atkinson v Hall* [1978] 1 All ER 1275, [1978] 1 WLR 586; applying dictum of Harman J in *Re Gillingham Bus Disaster Fund* [1958] Ch 300, [1958] 1 All ER 37 at 39. See also *Brewster v Foreign Mission Board of Baptist Convention of Maritime Provinces* (1900) 2 NB Eq Rep 172; *Planta v Greenshields* [1931] 2 DLR 189; *Re Aydt Estate, Bergermann v Aydt* (1965) 54 DLR (2d) 771.

3   *Ellis v Selby* (1836) 1 My & Cr 286; *Re Chapman, Hales v A-G* [1922] 2 Ch 479 (for charitable purposes or for such objects as the executor in his discretion may select); *Chichester Diocesan Fund and Board of Finance Inc v Simpson* [1944] AC 341, [1944] 2 All ER 60 (charitable or benevolent purposes); *Ellis v IRC* (1949) 31 TC 178 (permissible application to non-charitable objects); *Re Edwards* [1952] SASR 67 (benevolent institutions and institutions for relief of poor); *Brewer v McCauley* [1954] SCR 645 (charitable, religious, educational or philanthropic purposes); *Re Wootton's Will Trusts, Trotter v Duffin* [1968] 2 All ER 618, [1968] 1 WLR 681 (gift to charitable institutions or bodies or such other organisations as in the trustees' opinion had charitable objects); *Re Lipinski's Will Trusts, Gosschalk v Levy* [1976] Ch 235, [1977] 1 All ER 33 (despite the additions of some charitable objects the benefited association was essentially a sports club for the benefit of its members and not confined to exclusively charitable objects, so not charitable); *Re Koeppler's Will Trusts, Barclays Bank Trust Co Ltd v Slack* [1986] Ch 423, [1985] 2 All ER 869.

4   *Vezey v Jamson* (1822) 1 Sim & St 69 (charitable or public purposes or otherwise as the law admits); *Re Davis, Thomas v Davis* [1923] 1 Ch 225 (charitable or public institution in Wales); *Blair v Duncan* [1902] AC 37 (charitable or public purposes as my trustee thinks proper); *Langham v Peterson* (1903) 87 LT 744 (charity or works of public utility); *Houston v Burns* [1918] AC 337 (public, benevolent or charitable purposes); *Re Riland's Estate, Phillips v Robinson* [1881] WN 173 (charitable or benevolent purposes); *Chichester Diocesan Fund and Board of Finance Inc v Simpson* [1944] AC 341, [1944] 2 All ER 60 (charitable or benevolent purposes). See also *Wink's Executors v Tallent* 1947 SC 470; *A-G for New Zealand v Brown* [1917] AC 393; *Teele v Federal Commission of Taxation* (1940) 63 CLR 201; *Re Davidson, Minty v Bourne* [1909] 1 Ch 567; *Re Macduff, Macduff v Macduff* [1896] 2 Ch 451; *Campbell's*

Trustees v Campbell 1921 SC (HL) 12; *Symmer's Trustees v Symmers* 1918 SC 337; *Rintoul's Trustees v Rintoul* 1949 SC 297; *Re Sidney, Hingeston v Sidney* [1908] 1 Ch 488; *Re Gillingham Bus Disaster Fund, Bowman v Official Solicitor* [1958] Ch 300, [1958] 1 All ER 37; *Re Harpur's Will Trusts, Haller v A-G* [1962] Ch 78, [1961] 3 All ER 588 (institutions with both charitable and non-charitable objects). It has been held in Victoria, however, that 'benevolent' does not include anything not charitable in law: *Re Parker, Ballarat Trustees, Executors and Agency Co Ltd* [1949] VLR 133. In some cases the word 'or' has been treated as used conjunctivally or as introducing synonymous words: *Rickerby v Nicholson* [1912] 1 IR 343 (religious or charitable purposes); *Re Salter, Rea v Crozier* [1911] 1 IR 289 (charitable or religious purposes); *Re Sinclair's Trust* (1884) 13 LR Ir 150 (any charitable or religious purposes he may please); *McPhee's Trustees v McPhee* 1912 SC 75 (religious or charitable purposes); *Re Tomkinson, M'Crea and Bell v A-G of the Duchy of Lancaster* (1929) 74 Sol Jo 77 (such charities or such religious bodies); *A-G of the Cayman Islands v Wahr-Nansen* [2001] 1 AC 75, [2000] 3 All ER 642 ('or any organisations or institutions operating for the public good'; invalid).

5   *Re Jarman's Estate, Leavers v Clayton* (1878) 8 Ch D 584 at 587.
6   *Re Davis, Thomas v Davis* [1923] 1 Ch 225.
7   *Re Best, Jarvis v Birmingham Corpn* [1904] 2 Ch 354; *Caldwell v Caldwell* (1921) 91 LJ PC 95.
8   *Re Lloyd Greame v A-G* (1893) 10 TLR 66 (religious and benevolent); *Re Sutton, Stone v A-G* (1885) 28 Ch D 464 (charitable and deserving); *Blair v Duncan* [1902] AC 37 at 44 (charitable and public); *Re Scowcroft, Ormrod v Wilkinson* [1898] 2 Ch 638 (Conservative principles and religious and moral improvement).
9   *Re Eades, Eades v Eades* [1920] 2 Ch 353 (religious charitable and philanthropic); *Williams v Williams* (1835) 5 Cl & Fin 111n (benevolent charitable and religious purposes); *A-G v Dartmouth Corpn* (1883) 48 LT 933 (charitable, needful and necessary). *A-G of the Bahamas v Royal Trust Co* [1986] 3 All ER 423, [1986] 1 WLR 1001, (education and welfare).
10 *Dolan v MacDermot* (1868) 3 Ch App 676; *Re Bennett, Gibson v A-G* [1920] 1 Ch 305; *Re Ludlow, Bence-Jones v A-G* (1923) 93 LJ Ch 30.
11 *A-G v Ross* [1985] 3 All ER 334; on this basis a students' union was held to be charitable since its authorised and primary activities were charitable and the non-charitable activities which by its constitution the union was authorised to carry on were as a matter of degree merely the ancillary means by which the overall charitable purpose could be pursued.

[102.23]
Charitable Trusts (Validation) Act 1954 (CT(V)A 1954).[1] The CT(V)A 1954 deals with the position of certain imperfect trust provisions of a charitable nature which are contained in an instrument taking effect before 16 December 1952. The imperfect trust provision is one declaring objects for which property is to be held or applied and so describing those objects that, consistently with the terms of the provision, the property could be used exclusively for charitable purposes[2] but could nevertheless be used for purposes which are not charitable.[3] Such a trust or any covenant to create such a trust is to be applied to the objects which are exclusively charitable,[4] but if the trust took effect before 16 December 1952 (the date of publication of the Nathan Report), then it is to have effect as to the period before 30 July 1954, as if all the declared objects were charitable but as to the period after 30 July 1954 (the date of commencement of the CT(V)A 1954), only in so far as the objects are charitable.[5] There are savings for transactions completed before the commencement of the CT(V)A 1954 and a disposition creating more than one interest in the same property is to be treated as a separate disposition of each of the interests created.[6] A trust is not validated by the CT(V)A 1954 where it is a private discretionary trust (ie for the application of income and capital for the benefit of a class of persons in any way thought fit) as distinct from a trust for purposes which, though wider than charitable, includes purposes which are charitable in law.[7]

935

1   5 *Halsbury's Statutes* (4th edn) 888.
2   Compare *Re Wykes' Will Trusts* [1961] Ch 229, [1961] 1 All ER 470, which did satisfy this
    requirement, with *Vernon v IRC* [1956] 3 All ER 14, [1956] 1 WLR 1169, which did not.
3   The Act is intended to correct the position both where there are alternative purposes, one set of
    which are charitable and the other non-charitable, and where there is a composite purpose
    including both charitable and non-charitable objects. Such cases are exemplified by *Chichester
    Diocesan Fund and Board of Finance Inc v Simpson* [1944] AC 341, [1944] 2 All ER 60 and
    Oxford Group v IRC [1949] 2 All ER 537, and *Leahy v A-G for New South Wales* [1959] AC 457,
    [1959] 2 All ER 300. See also *Re Chitty's Will Trusts, Ransford v Lloyds Bank Ltd* [1970] Ch 254,
    [1969] 3 All ER 1492; *Re Flavel's Will Trusts, Coleman v Flavel* [1969] 2 All ER 232, [1969] 1
    WLR 444 (superannuation and bonus fund for employees of a company not saved by the Act).
4   Charitable Trusts (Validation) Act 1954, s 2(1).
5   Cross J observed in *Re Harpur's Will Trusts* [1961] Ch 38 at 49, [1960] 3 All ER 237 at 243,
    understand, validates retrospectively a limited number of dispositions which had already failed.
    'The Act leaves the law untouched for the future but, for some reason which I do not pretend to
    I do not know on what principle these particular dispositions were selected for favourable
    treatment, and so I see no reason for construing this Act liberally'. The effect of s 1 has been the
    subject of some discussion in *Re Gillingham Bus Disaster Fund* [1958] Ch 300, [1958] 1 All
    ER 37, on appeal, [1959] Ch 62, [1958] 2 All ER 749, CA; *Re Harpur's Will Trusts* [1961] Ch
    38 at 49, [1960] 3 All ER 237; affd [1962] Ch 78, [1961] 3 All ER 588, CA. *Re Wyke,
    Riddington v Spencer* [1961] Ch 229, [1961] 1 All ER 470; *Re Mead's Trust Deed, Briginshaw
    v National Society of Operative Printers and Assistants* [1961] 2 All ER 836, [1961] 1 WLR
    1244. It was first suggested that one of the purposes of the trust must be a legal charitable
    purpose, but it now seems sufficient that the trust can be confined to legal charitable purposes.
6   Charitable Trusts (Validation) Act 1954, s 2(2), (3).
7   *Re Saxone Shoe Co Ltd's Trust Deed, Re Abbott's Will Trusts, Abbott v Pearson* [1962] 2 All
    ER 904, [1962] 1 WLR 943.

[102.24]

Indefinite purposes. A power to trustees to distribute an indefinite sum in charity is not enforced,[1] nor a trust to distribute a fund among such persons[2] or purposes[3] as may appear just to the trustees, if no charitable intention is manifested. Where the application of the fund is held to be precatory and not mandatory there is no charitable gift[4] and the gift may be void for uncertainty.[5] If, however, there is an overriding intention that at least some part of the fund shall be applied to charity, the gift may be good though some of the objects or alternative methods of applying the fund are non-charitable[6] or even illegal.[7]

1   *Coxe v Basset* (1796) 3 Ves 155.
2   *Harris v Du Pasquier* (1872) 26 LT 689.
3   *Fowler v Garlike* (1830) 1 Russ & M 232; *Buckle v Bristow* (1864) 5 New Rep 7.
4   *Re Warre's Will Trusts, Wort v Salisbury Diocesan Board of Finance* [1953] 2 All ER 99,
    [1953] 1 WLR 725, but in this case the gift also failed for uncertainty and as lacking the
    necessary public benefit. But see para **[102.25]**, n 2.
5   *Re Warre's Will Trusts, Wort v Salisbury Diocesan Board of Finance* [1953] 2 All ER 99,
    [1953] 1 WLR 725; *Re Boland* [1950] QSR 45 (gift to any deserving Roman Catholic
    institution).
6   *Hunter v A-G* [1899] AC 309 at 323; *Wilkinson v Lindgren* (1870) 5 Ch App 570; *Pocock v A-G*
    (1876) 3 Ch D 342; *Re Douglas, Obert v Barrow* (1887) 35 Ch D 472; *Re Hurley, Nichols v
    Pargiter* (1900) 17 TLR 115; *Re Allen, Hargreaves v Taylor* [1905] 2 Ch 400; *Re Hood, Public
    Trustee v Hood* [1931] 1 Ch 240.
7   *Carter v Green* (1857) 3 K & J 591.

III.   RULE AGAINST PERPETUITIES

[102.25]

Rule against perpetuities. A perpetual trust is void unless it is charitable and perpetual gifts to non-charitable institutions, or for non-charitable objects, are void.[1] A legacy to a perpetual non-charitable institution is valid if, when paid, it will not become subject to any trust preventing the members from spending it as they please.[2] On the other hand, a gift of income for an unlimited period to a non-charitable institution, where there is no intention, express or implied, that the donee is to take the corpus, is void for perpetuity[3] and an indefinite gift of income to a charity does not carry the corpus without clear words to that effect.[4] A charity cannot be a trustee for a perpetual non-charitable purpose,[5] and, if the terms of a gift require a portion of a fund to be applied for a non-charitable purpose for ever, the gift will, at any rate to the extent of the sum required, be void as a perpetuity.[6] Where, however, a charitable trust has once come into operation, the rule is not applicable,[7] and a charitable trust may be made to last for any period, whether perpetual, indefinite or limited.[8] The rule has no application to a gift over from one charity to another,[9] but does not apply where either the original gift or the gift over is to an individual or individuals,[10] although the other gift may be to a charity. Thus, the perpetuity rule applies in cases where (1) an immediate gift to private individuals is followed by a gift over to a charity,[11] or (2) an immediate gift to a charity is followed by a gift over to private individuals. A gift over to residue on failure of a charitable trust is not void as a perpetuity as the gift falls into residue in any case by operation of law.[12] A charitable trust which may, but need not, take effect within the time allowed by the rule is void[13] unless the prior limitation is also charitable,[14] and a future gift which is subject to a condition precedent which need not be fulfilled within the period fails.[15] So also a trust for the benefit of a charity is void if limited to take effect after an indefinite failure of issue,[16] or upon alienation,[17] but the fact that the particular application of a charitable gift is postponed indefinitely does not render it void where the gift as distinct from the application of it is immediate.[18] Where at the expiration of twenty-one years properties were to be sold and the proceeds applied to the erection of buildings, it being a condition precedent that such buildings should be named in a particular way, such provision for the gifts of corpus was void for remoteness.[19]

1   *Re Dutton, ex p Peake* (1878) 4 Ex D 54; *Re Norwich Town Close Estate Charity* (1888) 40 Ch D 298 at 307.
2   *Cocks v Manners* (1871) LR 12 Eq 574; *Re Clarke, Clarke v Clarke* [1901] 2 Ch 110; *Re Smith, Johnson v Bright-Smith* [1914] 1 Ch 937; *Re Drummond, Ashworth v Drummond* [1914] 2 Ch 90; *Bourne v Keane* [1919] AC 815 at 874; *Leahy v A-G for New South Wales* [1959] AC 457, [1959] 2 All ER 300; *Re Barwick Estate* (1951) 11 DLR (2d) 341; *Re Governor* [1965] NSWR 723; *Re Recher's Will Trusts, National Westminster Bank Ltd v National Anti-Vivisection Society Ltd* [1972] Ch 526, [1971] 3 All ER 401; *Re Grant's Will Trusts* [1979] 3 All ER 359.
3   *Re Swain, Phillips v Poole* (1908) 99 LT 604; *Re Clifford, Mallam v McFie* [1912] 1 Ch 29.
4   *Re Levy, Barclays Bank Ltd v Board of Guardians and Trustees for Relief of Jewish Poor* [1960] Ch 346, [1960] 1 All ER 42; *Re Beesty's Will Trusts, Farrar v Royal Alfred Merchant Seamen's Society* [1966] Ch 223, [1964] 3 All ER 82 (where the trust was to be wound up in a certain event, it carried the capital).
5   *Re Tyler, Tyler v Tyler* [1891] 3 Ch 252; *Re Freeman, Shilton v Freeman* [1908] 1 Ch 720.
6   *Re Tyler, Tyler v Tyler* [1891] 3 Ch 252 at 259.
7   *Chamberlayne v Brockett* (1872) 8 Ch App 206 at 211; *A-G v Webster* (1875) LR 20 Eq 483 at 491.
8   *Re Randell, Randell v Dixon* (1888) 38 Ch D 213 at 218; *Re Bowen, Lloyd Phillips v Davis* [1893] 2 Ch 491 at 494; *Re Robinson* (1976) 75 DLR (3d) 532.
9   *Christ's Hospital v Grainger* (1849) 1 Mac & G 460; *Re Tyler, Tyler v Tyler* [1891] 3 Ch 252; *Royal College of Surgeons of England v National Provincial Bank* [1952] AC 631, [1952] 1 All ER 984 (and it makes no difference that a charity is incorporated by royal charter or other means).

10 *Re Bowen, Lloyd Phillips v Davis* [1893] 2 Ch 491; *Re Barnett, Waring v Painter-Stainers' Co* (1908) 24 TLR 788; *Re Peel's Release* [1921] 2 Ch 218. But where the first gift is to charity, it can continue indefinitely: *Re Bawden's Settlement, Besant v London Hospital Board of Governors* [1953] 2 All ER 1235.

11 *Re Spensley's Will Trusts, Barclays Bank Ltd v Staughton* [1952] Ch 886, [1952] 2 All ER 49.

12 *Re Blunt's Trusts, Wigan v Clinch* [1904] 2 Ch 767.

13 *Re Roberts, Repington v Roberts-Gawen* (1881) 19 Ch D 520; *Re White's Trusts* (1886) 33 Ch D 449; *Re Swain, Monckton v Hands* [1905] 1 Ch 669.

14 *Re Tyler, Tyler v Tyler* [1891] 3 Ch 252.

15 *Re Lord Stratheden and Campbell, Alt v Lord Stratheden and Campbell* [1894] 3 Ch 265.

16 *Re Johnson's Trusts* (1886) LR 2 Eq 716 at 720.

17 *Pewterers Co v Christ's Hospital (Governors)* (1683) 1 Vern 161.

18 *Re Gyde, Ward v Little* (1898) 79 LT 261; *Wallis v Solicitor-General for New Zealand* [1903] AC 173 at 186; *Jewish Home for Aged of British Columbia v Toronto General Trusts Corpn* [1961] SCR 465.

19 *Re Kagan* [1966] VR 538.

[102.26]

Undisposed-of interests. These do not come within the rule. A sum of money given to a charity so long as it remains endowed, falls by operation of law into residue (or passes as on an intestacy where there is no residuary gift) on the charity ceasing to be endowed,[1] and this is so although there is an express provision that it shall fall into residue.[2]

1 *Re Randell, Randell v Dixon* (1888) 38 Ch D 213.

2 *Re Randell, Randell v Dixon* (1888) 38 Ch D 213; *Re Blunt's Trusts, Wigan v Clinch* [1904] 2 Ch 767; *Lyons Corpn v Advocate-General of Bengal* (1876) 1 App Cas 91.

[102.27]

Accumulations. The statutory restrictions on accumulations[1] are applicable to charity funds directed to be accumulated,[2] and the ordinary rule applies that a charity absolutely entitled can stop the accumulation and require immediate payment of the fund.[3] Where there is a general charitable intention, the transgression of this rule will not defeat the gift and a scheme will be directed.[4]

1 See Chapter 95.

2 *Martin v Margham* (1844) 14 Sim 230; *Re Swain, Monckton v Hands* [1905] 1 Ch 669.

3 *Wharton v Masterman* [1895] AC 186; *Re Travis, Frost v Greatorex* [1900] 2 Ch 541. The direction, however, should prima facie be carried out by the trustees: *Re Knapp, Spreckley v A-G* [1929] 1 Ch 341 at 344.

4 *Re Monk, Giffen v Wedd* [1927] 2 Ch 197; *Re Bradwell's Will Trusts, Goode v Board of Trustees for Methodist Church Purposes* [1952] Ch 575, [1952] 2 All ER 286; *Re Burns Estate* (1960) 25 DLR (2d) 427; *Jewish Home for Aged of British Columbia v Toronto General Trusts Corpn* [1961] SCR 465.

CHAPTER 103

Charitable gifts; construction and *cy-près*

I. CONSTRUCTION OF CHARITABLE GIFTS

[103.1]

General charitable intention. Where a clear intention is expressed that a fund or other property shall be applied to charity, it is immaterial that the objects are not defined.[1] The general intention will be carried into effect, if necessary by means of a scheme, notwithstanding that the particular objects are not stated.[2] The principle is that the court treats charity as the substance and the particular disposition as the mode of the gift,[3] and draws a distinction between the charitable intention, which must be clear, and the mode of executing it, which, though vague and indefinite, does not affect the validity of the gift. The existence of such a general intention is a matter of construction, and is not dependent on the issue of any particular words,[4] but is deemed to exist wherever a testator intended the subject-matter of the gift to be applied in charity, notwithstanding the failure of the particular object or mode of application indicated.[5] The distinction to be drawn is between, on the one hand, the case where the scheme prescribed by the will can be regarded as the mode by which a general charitable purpose is to be effected, in which case the mode is not the substance of the gift, and, on the other, the case where no part of the scheme in the will can be disregarded as inessential without frustrating the testator's intention.[6] A declaration to give the whole estate to charity will prevail although only part is specifically given to charity,[7] and precatory recommendations in favour of particular charities do not prevent partial applications in other ways.[8] A charitable intention is not inferred from the fact that the trustees are a charitable society and given a wide discretion.[9] A gift to trustees to apply it in any manner in their absolute discretion in furtherance of the testator's 'general charitable intention' is not sufficient to validate an intention or purpose which is not in itself charitable in law.[10] A gift to a legatee 'for the charitable purposes agreed between us' does not imply a general charitable intention, but only an intention limited to the purposes agreed[11] and evidence is admissible to show that the purposes are, but not to limit the amount of the gift.[12] The rule of general charitable intention is applicable where the testator has neither specified the objects nor the particular way of carrying out his intention as in bequests for charitable purposes generally[13] or in relief of poverty[14] or for advancement of education[15] or religion[16] generally. It also applies where the testator states the class of objects to be benefited but does not prescribe the particular way in which his intention is to be carried out, as in gifts to the poor of a particular

939

place,[17] or the clergy of a particular sect.[18] Effect is given to gifts where the testator omits the names of the charities he wishes to benefit,[19] or the gift is for the benefit of such charities as he shall direct and he makes no direction.[20]

1 *Moggridge v Thackwell* (1803) 7 Ves 36; *Re White, White v White* [1893] 2 Ch 41; *Re Forester, Jervis v Forester* (1897) 13 TLR 555; *Re Pyne, Lilley v A-G* [1903] 1 Ch 83; *Re Gott, Glazebrook v Leeds University* [1944] Ch 193, [1944] 1 All ER 293 (charitable trust cannot fail for uncertainty so long as there is a general or specific charitable intention).

2 *Re Gott, Glazebrook v Leeds University* [1944] Ch 193, [1944] 1 All ER 293.

3 *Lyons Corpn v Advocate General of Bengal* (1876) 1 App Cas 91 at 113; *Re Spence's Will Trusts, Ogden v Shackleton* [1979] Ch 483, [1978] 3 All ER 92, per Megarry V-C at 101, ' ... the court is nevertheless able to see a clear general charitable intention underlying the particular mode of carrying it out that the testator has laid down', applying *Biscoe v Jackson* (1887) 35 Ch D 460.

4 *Mills v Farmer* (1815) 1 Mer 55 at 95.

5 *Clark v Taylor* (1853) 1 Drew 642 at 644.

6 *Re Woodhams, Lloyds Bank Ltd v London College of Music* [1981] 1 All ER 202, [1981] 1 WLR 493; referring to *Mills v Farmer* (1815) 19 Ves 483; *Re Rymer, Rymer v Stanfield* [1895] 1 Ch 19; *Re Wilson, Twentyman v Simpson* [1913] 1 Ch 314; *Re Willis, Shaw v Willis* [1921] 1 Ch 44; *A-G for New South Wales v Perpetual Trustee Co Ltd* (1940) 63 CLR 209; and *Re Lysaght, Hill v Royal College of Surgeons of England* [1966] Ch 191, [1965] 2 All ER 888, applied. A useful test was formulated by Vinelott J in *Re Woodhams*, supra (at pp 210 and 501), as follows: 'one way of approaching the question whether a prescribed scheme or project which has proved impracticable is the only way of furthering a desirable purpose that the testator or settlor contemplated or intended is to ask whether a modification of that scheme or project, which would enable it to be carried into effect at the relevant time, is one which would frustrate the intention of the testator or settlor as disclosed by the will or trust instrument interpreted in the light of any admissible evidence of surrounding circumstances'. In the case the testator had bequeathed gifts of residue to music colleges for music scholarships for orphans from named charitable homes. There were in fact adequate public grants available for the musical education of such orphans and thus the gift was regarded as impractical in its stated form. A *cy-près* scheme was directed. See also *Re Machin* (1980) 101 DLR (3d) 438; *Re Jung* (1980) 99 DLR (3d) 65.

7 *Beverley Corpn v A-G* (1857) 6 HL Cas 310 at 318.

8 *Moggridge v Thackwell* (1803) 7 Ves 36.

9 *Re Freeman, Shilton v Freeman* [1908] 1 Ch 720. A gift to charitable society is construed as a gift for the purposes of the society: *Re White, White v White* [1893] 2 Ch 41.

10 *Re Sanders' Will Trusts, Public Trustee v McLaren* [1954] Ch 265, [1954] 1 All ER 667.

11 *Re Huxtable, Huxtable v Crawfurd* [1902] 2 Ch 793.

12 *Blackwell v Blackwell* [1929] AC 318.

13 *Miller v Rowan* (1837) 5 Cl & Fin 99 at 109.

14 *A-G v Rance* (1728) cited in (1762) Amb at 422.

15 *Whicker v Hume* (1858) 7 HL Cas 124.

16 *Re White, White v White* [1893] 2 Ch 41 at 52.

17 *A-G v Wilkinson* (1839) 1 Beav 370.

18 *A-G v Gladstone* (1842) 13 Sim 7.

19 *Re White, White v White* [1893] 2 Ch 41.

20 *Pocock v A-G* (1876) 3 Ch D 342; *Re Pyne, Lilley v A-G* [1903] 1 Ch 83.

[103.2]

Charity by association. It the will gives the residue among a number of charities with kindred objects, but one of the apparent charities does not, in fact, exist, the court will be ready to find a general charitable intention and so apply the share of the non-existent charity *cy-près*.[1] In such cases the court views the testator as having shown the general charitable intention of giving his residue to promote charities with that type of kindred objects, and then, when he comes to dividing the residue, as casting around for particular charities with that type of objects to name as donees. If one or more of these are non-existent, then the general intention will suffice for a *cy-près* application.[2]

940

1   Per Megarry V-C in *Re Spence's Will Trusts, Ogden v Shackleton* [1978] 3 All ER 92 at 100.
2   Per Megarry V-C in *Re Spence's Will Trusts, Ogden v Shackleton* [1978] 3 All ER 92 at 100,
    referring to *Re Satterthwaite's Will Trusts, Midland Bank Executor and Trustee Co Ltd v Royal
    Veterinary College* [1966] 1 All ER 919, [1966] 1 WLR 277 (residuary gift to nine charitable
    bodies which were all concerned with kindness to animals, but the gifts to two of them failed as
    no bodies could be found which sufficiently answered the descriptions in the will, held general
    charitable intention): and *Re Knox Fleming v Carmichael* [1937] Ch 109, [1936] 3 All ER 623
    (residuary gift in quarters to two named infirmaries, a named nursing home and Dr Barnardo's
    Homes, no institution answering the description of the nursing home, held general charitable
    intention and '*cy-près*').

[103.3]

Charity wrongly named or having ceased to exist. A charitable gift does not
fail because the institution cannot be identified[1] or has never existed;[2] but it must
be clear from the description of the institution that the testator intended to
benefit a charitable purpose.[3] A gift to an institution which has ceased to exist in
the testator's lifetime, whether before or after the date of the will, lapses[4] unless
a general intention can be shown.[5] There is no lapse where the institution has not
wholly ceased to exist;[6] nor where there has merely been a change of name,[7] nor
where the institution is named merely as the channel for carrying out the
charitable intention.[8] A gift to an institution carried on by the testator which
ceased at his death is construed as a gift for the purposes of that institution[9] and
similarly a gift to an institution properly described for purposes which have
ceased to be exercised by that institution by reason of a profession ceasing to
adopt a method of practice is good and possibly subject to a trust to apply to
such purposes as far as possible.[10] If the charity ceases to exist after the death of
the testator but before payment, the gift still takes effect.[11] Where the premises
of the charity were before the execution of the will closed down on the
expiration of the lease under which they were held but the charity was continued
by a scheme, it was held that a gift by way of addition to the endowment of the
charity and not merely for the upkeep of the particular premises of the charity
did not fail.[12] Where the testator's intention was to benefit the charity generally
the gift was not affected by the fact that he had referred to the address at which it
was carried on at the date of his will, although the work at that address had been
closed down before his death and transferred elsewhere.[13] A gift to a hospital
does not lapse where its specified work is transferred to a general hospital and its
funds are to be applied to such special work in the general hospital,[14] but where
the hospital closed down and its work was carried on by the Australian Red
Cross, the gift could not be treated as a gift to that society because the will said
that the receipt of the treasurer of the hospital was to be a sufficient discharge.[15]

1   *Gibson v Coleman* (1868) 18 LT 236; *Re Kilvert's Trusts* (1871) 7 Ch App 170. As to the
    jurisdiction of the court to order a scheme in such a case, see para **[103.19]** infra.
2   *Re Davis, Hannen v Hillyer* [1902] 1 Ch 876 at 884; *Re Clergy Society* (1856) 2 K & J 615;
    Daly v A-G (1860) 11 I Ch R 41; *Re Geary's Trusts* (1890) 25 LR Ir 171; *Re Mann, Hardy v A-
    G* [1903] 1 Ch 232; *Re Songest, Mayger v Forces Help Society and Lord Roberts Workshops*
    [1956] 2 All ER 765.
3   *Re Parkes, Cottrell v Parkes* (1909) 25 TLR 523. From *Re Bailey, Bailey v Working Ladies
    Guild* (1931) 75 Sol Jo 415, it might appear that the court requires only that there shall be no
    evidence to contradict the charitable intention shown by the name given by the testator to a
    society which has never existed. See also *Re Forshaw, Wallace v Middlesex Hospital* (1934) 51
    TLR 97; *Re Nesbitt's Will Trusts* [1953] 1 All ER 936; *Re Kerr* [1957] QSR 292. In *Re
    Goldschmidt* [1957] 1 All ER 513, the gift was given to an institution not capable of

identification and, the ultimate gift being to a charity, it passed under the ultimate gift. See also *Re Jacobsen* (1977) 80 DLR (3d) 122.

4 It is more difficult to find a general charitable intention where the gift is to a body which existed at the date of the will but ceased to exist before the testator died than it is to find the intention when the body never did exist: per Megarry V-C in *Re Spence's Will Trusts, Ogden v Shackleton* [1978] 3 All ER 92 at 100; *Re Ovey, Broadbent v Barrow* (1885) 29 Ch D 560 (ceasing to exist before date of will); *Re Rymer, Rymer v Stanfield* [1895] 1 Ch 19 (ceasing after date of will); *Re Joy, Purday v Johnson* (1888) 60 LT 175; *Makeown v Ardagh* (1876) IR 10 Eq 445; *Re Tharp, Longrigg v People's Dispensary for Sick Animals of the Poor Inc* [1942] 2 All ER 358; revsd on another point [1943] 1 All ER 257 (there is a lapse where the gift is to the particular society and not for the particular purpose); *Re Lucas, Sheard v Mellor* [1948] Ch 175 [1947] 2 All ER 773; *Re Stemson's Will Trusts, Carpenter v Treasury Solicitor* [1970] Ch 16, [1969] 2 All ER 517; *Re Rowell, Public Trustee v Bailey* (1982) 31 SASR 36.

5 *Clark v Taylor* (1853) 1 Drew 642; *Marsh v A-G* (1860) 2 John & H 61. It is difficult to find a general intention where the testator has taken care to identify the particular charity: *Re Harwood, Coleman v Innes* [1936] Ch 285; applied in *Re Spence, Ogden v Shackleton* [1979] Ch 483, [1978] 3 All ER 92 (a gift for the benefit of patients at a specified home; at the date of the will there were such patients but at the death of the testatrix there was no longer any home, or any patients there, or any possibility of them, held gift failed), distinguishing *Re Finger's Will Trusts, Turner v Ministry of Health* [1972] Ch 286, [1971] 3 All ER 1050. See also *Re Broadbent* [2001] 28 LS Gaz R 44.

6 *Re Waring, Hayward v A-G* [1907] 1 Ch 166 (school closed on weekdays, but used on Sundays); *Re Bradfield* (1892) 8 TLR 696 (closing of branch); *Re Faraker, Faraker v Durell* [1912] 2 Ch 488; *Re Scott Estate* (1957) 11 DLR (2d) 223 (cesser in named town but continuing elsewhere); applied in *Re Roberts, Stenton v Hardy* [1963] 1 All ER 674 (gift for the purposes of an institution not so correlated with the physical premises where the institution was located that it failed when those premises ceased to exist); *St Dunstan's University v Canada Permanent Trust Co* (1976) 67 DLR (3d) 480; *Re Bezpalko* (1980) 106 DLR (3d) 290; *Re Machin* (1980) 101 DLR (3d) 438.

7 *Re Donald, Moore v Somerset* [1909] 2 Ch 410; *Re Magrath, Histed v Queen's University of Belfast* [1913] 2 Ch 331; *Re Gray, Todd v Taylor* [1925] Ch 362; *Re Gordon* (1965) 52 DLR (2d) 197.

8 *Marsh v A-G* (1860) 2 John & H 61; *Re Ovey, Broadbent v Barrow* (1885) 29 Ch D 560 at 565; *Loscombe v Wintringham* (1850) 13 Beav 87; *Re Watt, Hicks v Hill* [1932] 2 Ch 243n.

9 *Re Mann, Hardy v A-G* [1903] 1 Ch 232; *Re Webster, Pearson v Webster* [1912] 1 Ch 106.

10 *Sydney Homoeopathic Hospital v Turner* [1959] ALR 782.

11 *Re Slevin, Slevin v Hepburn* [1891] 2 Ch 236; *Re Wright, Blizard v Lockhart* [1954] 2 All ER 98 (where the purpose became impracticable after the testator's death); *Re Morrison, Wakefield v Falmouth* (1967) 111 Sol Jo 758; *Re Hunter* (1973) 34 DLR (3d) 602.

12 *Re Lucas, Sheard v Mellor* [1948] Ch 424, [1948] 2 All ER 22; distinguished in *Re Spence's Will Trusts, Ogden v Shackleton* [1978] 3 All ER 92, where, having regard to the fact that the testatrix had provided for the gift to be for the benefit of the patients of a specified home, the gift could not be added to the association's general endowment but was to be restricted by way of the scheme, to being used for the benefit of the patients for the time being of the specified home.

13 *Re Hutchinson's Will Trusts, Gibbons v Nottingham Area No 1, Hospital Management Committee* [1953] Ch 387, [1953] 1 All ER 996; *Re Abbott* (1974) 45 DLR (3d) 478; *Re MacAulay* (1971) 18 DLR (3d) 726; and *Re Boyd* (1969) 6 DLR (3d) 110.

14 *Re Boyd* (1969) 6 DLR (3d) 110.

15 *Re Slatter's Will Trusts, Turner v Turner* [1964] Ch 512, [1964] 2 All ER 469.

[103.4]

Charity companies. Although traditionally charities are created as trusts, it is also possible for a charity to be constituted as a registered company.[1] A bequest to an incorporated body including a company charity prima facie, takes effect simply as a gift to that body beneficially as part of its general funds and without imposition of any trust.[2] If the body is incorporated for exclusively charitable purposes so that none of its funds could be used otherwise than for charitable purposes, then a change in the charity's mechanical aspect will not involve the charity ceasing to exist. In such case the law regards the charity, an abstract conception distinct from the institutional mechanism provided for holding and administering the fund of the charity, as the legatee, and so long as the charity as so conceived continues to exist the bequest will not lapse.[3] However it is possible for a testator or donor to introduce positive or express words in the gift to a charity company, importing a trust. In these circumstances, the charity company becomes a trustee of the gift made on trust and does not hold the fund representing the gift as part of its general property.[4] If such a charity company wishes to change or add to its purposes then the assets held on trust can only be altered by a *cy-près* scheme and those of the assets which form corporate property can only be varied by a change in the memorandum of association.[5]

1   Charities Act 1993, s 63; 5 *Halsbury's Statutes* (4th edn) 1020. Although the section uses the word 'trusts' when referring to a charity it redefines it to include provisions which may not take effect by way of trust, see Charities Act 1993, s 45.

2   Per Buckley J in *Re Vernon's Will Trusts, Lloyds Bank Ltd v Group 20, Hospital Management Committee*, noted [1972] Ch 300n at 303, [1971] 3 All ER 1061n at 1064; followed in *Re Finger's Will Trusts, Turner v Ministry of Health* [1972] Ch 286, [1971] 3 All ER 1050 (gift to a corporate body failed since there was no context in the will from which to imply a trust for carrying on of the work of the body; however it was possible to find a general charitable intention and the gift was applied *cy-près*). Considered in *Re ARMS (Multiple Sclerosis Research) Ltd, Alleyne v Attorney General* [1997] 2 All ER 679 where it was held that it could not be implied from the fact that the bequest was made to a company established for charitable purposes that the testator intended the company to take as trustee for charitable purposes.

3   Per Buckley J in *Re Vernon's Will Trusts*, see n 2 supra, applying *Re Faraker, Faraker v Durell* [1912] 2 Ch 488, [1911–13] All ER Rep 488; and *Re Lucas, Sheard v Mellor* [1948] Ch 175, [1947] 2 All ER 773; revsd [1948] Ch 424, [1947] 2 All ER 773. Thus in *Re Vernon's Will Trusts, Lloyds Bank Ltd v Group 20, Hospital Management Committee*, noted [1972] Ch 300, [1971] 3 All ER 1061, a gift to a corporate body which was affected by the National Health Service Act 1946, and subsequently dissolved before the testatrix's death, did not fail but took effect in favour of the work of the charity as it was then being carried on; applied in *Liverpool and District Hospital for Diseases of the Heart v A-G* [1981] Ch 193, [1981] 1 All ER 994 (surplus assets of a charitable company applied *cy-près*).

4   Per Buckley J in *Re Vernon's Will Trusts*, see n 2 supra. See the Report of the Charity Commissioners for England and Wales 1971, paras 22–30. A similar situation can arise also from the particular words used in an appeal made to the public for funds and expressed to be for particular purposes of the charity company.

5   Report of the Charity Commissioners for England and Wales 1971, para 28. It is obviously important that both alterations should have the same effect so that the purposes for which all the charity's assets may be applied will have been changed in the same way.

[103.5]

Unincorporated bodies. Every bequest to an unincorporated charity by name without more must take effect as a gift for a charitable purpose.[1] If the named charity ceases to exist in the testator's lifetime the gift will only fail if the testator's intention is to make the gift dependent on the named charitable organisation being available at the time when the gift took effect to serve as the instrument for applying the subject matter of the gift to the charitable purposes for which it is by inference given.[2] But usually since the gift is per se a purpose trust, then if the work is still being carried on, effect will be given to it by way of a scheme, notwithstanding the disappearance of the donee in the lifetime of the testator.[3]

1   Per Buckley J in *Re Vernon's Will Trusts, Lloyds Bank Ltd v Group 20 Hospital Management Committee*, noted [1972] Ch 300n at 303, [1971] All ER 1061n at 1064; followed in *Re*

Finger's Will Trusts, Turner v Ministry of Health [1972] Ch 286, [1971] 3 All ER 1050; and in *Re Morrison, Wakefield v Falmouth* (1967) 111 Sol Jo 758. This is because no individual or aggregate of individuals would claim to take such a bequest beneficially.

2   Per Buckley J in *Re Vernon's Will Trusts*, see n 1 supra; see also *Re Ovey, Broadbent v Barrow* (1885) 29 Ch D 560; *Re Meyers, London Life Association v St George's Hospital* [1951] Ch 534, [1951] 1 All ER 538. Thus, in *Re Finger's Will Trusts, Turner v Ministry of Health* [1972] Ch 286, [1971] 3 All ER 1050, a gift to an unincorporated charity was a purpose trust for the work of the body which did not fail because there was no indication in the will to make that body of the essence of the gift and the work of the body had, since its dissolution, been carried on by the Secretary of State for Social Services; the gift was therefore valid and a scheme for its administration was settled; distinguishing *Re Harwood, Coleman v Innes* [1936] Ch 285, [1935] All ER Rep 918.

3   Per Goff J in *Re Finger's Will Trusts, Turner v Ministry of Health* [1972] Ch 286 at 295, [1971] 3 All ER 1050 at 1057.

[103.6]

Failure of particular intention. Where the intention is to benefit some particular charitable institution, or to accomplish some particular charitable purpose, then if circumstances render the carrying out impossible, the gift fails and no *cy-près*[1] application is possible.[2] Where subscriptions are made and no intention can be inferred that the money should be returned on failure of the purpose, the funds are applied *cy-près*[3] but where return is possible such subscriptions must be returned though in some cases return is impossible.[4]

1   See para **[103.19]** infra.
2   *Re Wilson, Twentyman v Simpson* [1913] 1 Ch 314; *Re Packe, Sanders v A-G* [1918] 1 Ch 437; *Re Stanford, Cambridge University v A-G* [1924] 1 Ch 73; *Re Blunt's Trusts, Wigan v Clinch* [1904] 2 Ch 767; *Re University of London Medical Sciences Institute Fund, Fowler v A-G* [1909] 2 Ch 1; *Re Good's Will Trusts, Oliver v Batten* [1950] 2 All ER 653; *Re Gwilym* [1952] VLR 282. But see *Re Hardy, Nelson v A-G* [1933] NI 150.
3   *Re Hillier, Hillier v A-G* [1954] 2 All ER 59.
4   *Re Ulverston and District New Hospital Building Trusts, Birkett v Barrow and Furness Hospital Management Committee* [1956] Ch 622, [1956] 3 All ER 164; *Re Gillingham Bus Disaster Fund, Bowman v Official Solicitor* [1958] Ch 300, [1958] 1 All ER 37. But see *Re West Sussex Constabulary's Widows, Children and Benevolent* (1930) *Fund Trusts, Barnett v Ketteringham* [1971] Ch 1, [1970] 1 All ER 544 (amalgamation of police force so that original purpose of benevolent fund could not be carried out. It was held that money contributed by members of the fund and money obtained through entertainments, raffles, sweepstakes and collecting boxes, was bona vacantia; money contributed by members of the public by donation and legacies, was held on resulting trusts for the donors and their estates).

[103.7]

Uncertain description of charity. Extrinsic evidence is admissible to prove that the charity as named exists[1] or to remove a latent ambiguity as to which of two societies a testator intends to benefit.[2] A trivial error in naming the charity is immaterial,[3] and if the institution is correctly described, a direction for the utilisation of the gift not applicable to the circumstances is immaterial.[4] If the testator names the locality of the charity, the legacy prima facie goes to the institution of a name resembling the testator's description in that locality rather than to one in another locality, though the latter has a name nearer to that used by the testator.[5] In any case the construction in such cases may be controlled by the context which may show that the description of the charity is exact and not loose[6] or that the testator did not intend to benefit institutions of a particular character.[7]

1   *Wilson v Squire* (1842) 1 Y & C Ch Cas 654.
2   *Re Kilvert's Trusts* (1871) 7 Ch App 170 at 173.
3   *Hopkinson v Ellis* (1842) 5 Beav 34 (vicar described as rector); *Re Kilvert's Trusts* (1871) 7 Ch
    App 170 (change of name but not of objects); *Makeown v Ardagh* (1876) IR 10 Eq 445; *Re
    Meikle Estate* [1943] 3 DLR 668; *Re Humfrey* [1944] 2 DLR 476; *Re Manning Estate* [1947] 2
    WWR 487; *Re Jacobs, Westminster Bank Ltd v Chinn* (1970) 114 Sol Jo 515 (gift to the Jewish
    National Fund was, on evidence of the testator's intention, held to be a gift to Keren Kayemeth
    Leisrael, which was commonly known by the former name).
4   *Smith v Ruger* (1859) 33 LTOS 282.
5   *Re Lycett, Riley v King's College Hospital* (1897) 13 TLR 373; *Bradshaw v Thompson* (1843) 2
    Y & C Ch Cas 295; *Re Clergy Society* (1856) 2 K & J 615; *Buxton v Blakiston* (1886) 2 TLR
    293; *Re Glubb, Barnfield v Rogers* (1897) 14 TLR 66. For cases where indications other than
    locality in the will prevailed, see *Re Morgan, Marriott v Society for Abolition of Vivisection*
    (1909) 25 TLR 303; *British Home and Hospital for Incurables v Royal Hospital for Incurables*
    (1904) 90 LT 601; *Re Thomson* [1956] SASR 188 (acts and statements of testator subsequent to
    making the will).
6   *Bradshaw v Thompson* (1843) 2 Y & C Ch Cas 295 (context showed that a general hospital was
    intended and not one for particular complaints, because where there testator intended to benefit
    the latter class of hospital he had said so in plain terms); *Re Alchin's Trusts, ex p Furley, ex p
    Earl of Romney* (1872) LR 14 Eq 230.
7   Eg rate-aided institutions: *Lechmere v Curtler* (1855) 3 Eq Rep 938; *Re Davies' Trusts* (1872)
    21 WR 154. As to nationalised institutions, see para **[103.10]** infra.

[103.8]
Closing of branch of society. The closing of one branch of a society does not
cause a legacy to it to lapse,[1] nor does the conversion of a chapel of ease into a
separate parish involve the forfeiture of a trust previously applied to the repair of
the chapel.[2]

1   *Re Bradfield* (1892) 8 TLR 696; *Re Wedgwood, Sweet v Cotton* [1914] 2 Ch 245.
2   *Re Cloudesley's Charity* (1900) 17 TLR 123.

[103.9]
Amalgamation of institutions. This does not affect the gift, which will be paid
to the amalgamated institutions;[1] but the amalgamated institution may be put
upon an undertaking to apply the gift for the purposes within the scope of the
institution named in the will.[2] Where there are gifts to each of the amalgamated
societies, the two legacies will be paid to the amalgamated institution[3] and
where the gift is to the society and not expressed to be for its purposes, the gift
can be applied by way of scheme or otherwise.[4] Although the objects of an
amalgamated society are not identical with those of the named society yet if the
general purposes of the named society are identifiable charitable purposes, then
the bequest may be applied to those purposes by scheme or otherwise.[5]

1   *Re Adams, Harle v Adams* (1888) 4 TLR 757; *Re Faraker, Faraker v Durell* [1912] 2 Ch 488;
    Re Pritt, Morton v National Church League (1915) 85 LJ Ch 166; *Re Kappele* [1955] 1 DLR 29
    (where the testator had executed several codicils after the amalgamation).
2   *Re Marchant, Weaver v Royal Society for the Prevention of Cruelty to Animals* (1910) 54 Sol
    Jo 425. It should be noted that in the case here cited the amalgamation took place 10 years
    before the date of the will. Most cases refer to amalgamations subsequent to the date of
    the will.
3   *Re Joy, Purday v Johnson* (1888) 60 LT 175. The fact that a dissolved society answers the
    testator's description better than an existing society does not prevent the latter taking so long as
    it sufficiently answers the description; *Coldwell v Holme* (1854) 2 Sm & G 31; *Re Magrath,
    Histed v Queen's University of Belfast* [1913] 2 Ch 331 (defunct institution reconstituted).

4   *Re Dawson's Will Trusts, National Provincial Bank Ltd v National Council of YMCA Inc*
    [1957] 1 All ER 177, [1957] 1 WLR 391.
5   *Re Roberts, Stenton v Hardy* [1963] 1 All ER 674, [1963] 1 WLR 406. See also *Re Bateman*
    1972 SLT (Notes) 78.

[103.10]

Effect of legislation. The fact that legislation causes an institution or body to adopt a different method of attaining its object does not cause a legacy to lapse.[1] It is otherwise where the testator has foreseen this possibility and has provided for it.[2] Where there was a gift of a share of residue to a teaching hospital which was still in existence at the testator's death, there was no lapse because the institution had not ceased to exist under the National Health Service Act 1946;[3] but where there was a proviso that if any of the funds had come under government control the gift was to go over to other institutions, the gift to the teaching hospital did not take effect.[4]

1   *Re Donald, Moore v Somerset* [1909] 2 Ch 410; *Re Morgan's Will Trusts, Lewarne v Ministry of Health* [1950] Ch 637, [1950] 1 All ER 1097 (hospital passing into public ownership under National Health Service Act 1946); *Re Hunter, Lloyds Bank v Girton College, Cambridge (Mistress and Governors)* [1951] Ch 190, [1951] 1 All ER 58; *Re White's Will Trusts, Tindall v Board of Governors of United Sheffield Hospitals* [1951] 1 All ER 528; *Re Meyers, London Life Association v St George's Hospital* [1951] Ch 534, [1951] 1 All ER 538. A gift to such hospital and/or hospitals and/or charitable institutions as a named person shall think fit is a good charitable gift since at the time when the bequest was made the testator must be taken as referring to voluntary hospitals which were charitable institutions; *Re Smith's Will Trusts, Barclays Bank Ltd v Mercantile Bank Ltd* [1962] 2 All ER 563.
2   See note 1, supra and *Re Bland-Sutton's Will Trusts, National Provincial Bank Ltd v Middlesex Hospital* [1951] Ch 485, [1951] 1 All ER 494 (gift to medical school to fail if hospital of which it forms part is nationalised; but it would be otherwise if the gift was conditioned to fail if the medical school were nationalised for such schools have not been nationalised); *Re Frere, Kidd v Farnham Group Hospital Management Committee* [1951] Ch 27, [1950] 2 All ER 513 (gift to fail if hospital nationalised, but the residue was given to the hospital unconditionally).
3   *Re Kellner's Will Trusts, Blundell v Royal Cancer Hospital* [1950] Ch 46, [1949] 2 All ER 774. See *Re Gartside, Coote and Eyre-Kaye v Lees* [1949] 2 All ER 546 (where, however, the estate had been fully administered).
4   *Re Buzzacott, Munday v King's College Hospital* [1953] Ch 28, [1952] 2 All ER 1011. See also cases arising out of the National Health Service Act 1946: *Re Perreyman, National Provincial Bank Ltd v Perreyman* [1953] 1 All ER 223; *Re Hayes' Will Trusts, Dobie v National Hospital Board of Governors* [1953] 2 All ER 1242; *Re Hayes' Will Trusts, Dobie v National Hospital Board of Governors* [1953] 2 All ER 1242, [1954] 1 WLR 22; *Re Bawden's Settlement, Besant v London Hospital Board of Governors* [1953] 2 All ER 1235, [1954] 1 WLR 33n; *Re Little, Barclays Bank Ltd v Bournemouth and East Dorset Hospital Management Committee* [1953] 2 All ER 852, [1953] 1 WLR 1132; *Re Bagshaw, Westminster Bank Ltd v Taylor* [1954] 1 All ER 227; *Re Vernon's Will Trusts, Lloyds Bank Ltd v Group 20, Hospital Management Committee* [1972] Ch 300n, [1971] 3 All ER 1061n; *Minister of Health v Fox* [1950] Ch 369, [1950] 1 All ER 1050; *Re Marjoribanks' Indenture, Frankland v Minister of Health* [1952] Ch 181, [1952] 1 All ER 191; *Re Lowry's Will Trusts, Barclays Bank Ltd v United Newcastle-on-Tyne Hospitals Board of Governors* [1967] Ch 638, [1966] 3 All ER 955.

[103.11]

Illegality or impossibility of purpose. Where a general charitable intention is expressed but the mode of carrying it out is illegal or impracticable, the intention is executed *cy-près*,[1] but if some of the purposes or some of the modes of application are illegal or impossible, the trust must be carried out for the purposes or in the modes not open to objection.[2] An immediate gift to charity is good although its application may not of necessity take effect within any reasonable limit of time, or may never take effect at all except on the occurrence of events in their essence contingent and uncertain.[3] Thus, bequests for building when the necessary sites have been obtained,[4] to endow a bishopric in case a bishop should be appointed,[5] to endow a church if erected,[6] or a bequest postponed until a licence in mortmain is obtained,[7] have been upheld. Where a gift is void as illegal or impossible, a secondary bequest for endowment of the charity also fails[8] unless there is a direction for its alternative application.[9] A gift to establish a charity on property not devoted to charity and of which the testator has no power to dispose, is void ab initio.[10] A gift with a total prohibition of sale or mortgage is valid in the case of a charity.[11]

1   *A-G v Vint* (1850) 3 De G & Sm 704 (legacy to provide intoxicating liquor); *Chamberlayne v Brockett* (1872) 8 Ch App 206 (legacy dependent on land being provided for almshouses); *Biscoe v Jackson* (1887) 35 Ch D 460 (violation of Mortmain Acts); *Bunting v Marriott* (1854) 19 Beav 163 (reduction of debt on chapel which was already paid off); *Re Wright, Blizard v Lockhart* [1954] Ch 347, [1954] 2 All ER 98 (founding a convalescent home); *Re Woodhams, Lloyds Bank Ltd v London College of Music* [1981] 1 All ER 202, [1981] 1 WLR 493, (music scholarship for orphans from named charitable homes already adequately provided for, applied *cy-près* by deleting restriction); *Re J W Laing Trust, Stewards' Co Ltd v A-G* [1984] Ch 143, [1984] 1 All ER 50.

2   *Hunter v A-G* [1899] AC 309 at 324; *Sinnett v Herbert* (1872) 7 Ch App 232; *Re Douglas, Obert v Barrow* (1887) 35 Ch D 472. 'If at any time it proves impracticable' includes an initial failure of the purpose: *Re Adams, Gee v Barnet Group Hospital Management Committee* [1968] Ch 80, [1967] 3 All ER 285, CA. If, however, the gift is repugnant to the Mortmain Act, it fails entirely; *Girdlestone v Creed* (1853) 10 Hare 480.

3   *Wallis v New Zealand Solicitor-General* [1903] AC 173; *Re Monk, Giffen v Wedd* [1927] 2 Ch 197; *Re Swan, Monkton v Hands* [1905] 1 Ch 669; *Re Pearse, Genn v Pearse* [1955] 1 DLR 801.

4   *Chamberlayne v Brockett* (1872) 8 Ch App 206 (almshouses); *Henshaw v Atkinson* (1818) 3 Madd 306 (school).

5   *A-G v Bishop of Chester* (1785) 1 Bro CC 444; *Society for Propagation of the Gospel v A-G* (1826) 3 Russ 142.

6   *Sinnett v Herbert* (1872) 7 Ch App 232.

7   *Abbott v Fraser* (1874) LR 6 PC 96.

8   *Edwards v Hall* (1853) 11 Hare 1; *Cramp v Playfoot* (1858) 4 K & J 479; *Re Taylor, Martin v Freeman* (1888) 58 LT 538; *Re Packe, Sanders v A-G* [1918] 1 Ch 437. But, if the principal gift is good and the secondary gift is void, the former stands: *A-G v Stepney* (1804) 10 Ves 22; *Blandford v Thackerell* (1793) 2 Ves 238.

9   *Faversham Corpn v Ryder* (1854) 5 De GM & G 350; *Dunn v Bownas* (1855) 1 K & J 596.

10   *A-G v Earl of Lonsdale* (1827) 1 Sim 105; *Hoare v Hoare* (1886) 56 LT 147; *Thomson v Shakespear* (1860) 1 De GF & J 399.

11   *Re Clark, Horwell v Dent* [1961] NZLR 635 following *Caldell v Fleming* [1927] NZLR 145.

[103.12]

Discrimination. Acts of discrimination against sections of the community[1] are now governed by the Race Relations Act 1976 (RRA 1976)[2] and the Sex Discrimination Act 1975 (SDA 1975).[3] For the purposes of the RRA 1976 a person discriminates against another if on the ground of colour, race or ethnic or national origins he treats that other, in any situation to which the RRA 1976 applies, less favourably than he treats or would treat other persons (and it is expressly declared that if a person is segregated from other persons he is treated less favourably than they are treated).[4] The RRA 1976 expressly refers to charities[5] and to a 'charitable instrument', which means an enactment or other instrument passed or made for charitable purposes or an enactment or other instrument so far as it relates to charitable purposes, which are purposes which are exclusively charitable according to the law of England and Wales.[6] With reference to provisions taking effect after the coming into operation of the RRA 1976, the Act differentiates between discrimination on the grounds of colour and discrimination on other grounds. A provision which is contained in a charitable instrument which provides for conferring benefits on persons of a class defined by reference to colour has effect for all purposes as if it provided for conferring the like benefits, (a) on persons of the class which results if the restriction by reference to colour is disregarded or, (b) where the original class is defined by reference to colour only, on persons generally.[7] Where a charitable instrument provides for conferring benefits on persons of a class defined by reference to colour has effect for all purposes as if it provided for conferring the like benefits, (a) on persons of the class which results if the restriction by reference to colour is disregarded or, (b) where the original class is defined by reference to colour only, on persons generally. Where a charitable instrument provides for conferring benefits on persons of a class defined otherwise than by reference to colour (including a class resulting from the operation of the provision noted above) then the RRA 1976 is not to be construed as affecting the provision[8] or as rendering unlawful an act which is done in order to give effect to such a provision.[9] Thus charitable trusts which discriminate on the grounds of colour will be affected by the legislation but not trusts which discriminate in favour of a class defined otherwise than by reference to colour. The SDA 1975 likewise safeguards charities by providing that the Act does not affect provisions in a charitable instrument conferring benefits on persons of one sex only.[10]

1   For examples of discriminatory trusts before the anti-discriminatory legislation, see *Re Dominion Students' Hall Trusts* [1947] Ch 183 (colour bar); and *Re Lysaght, Hill v Royal College of Surgeons of England* [1966] Ch 191, [1965] 2 All ER 888 (exclusion of Roman Catholic or Jewish Students from benefit).
2   7 *Halsbury's Statutes* (4th edn) 115, which came into force on 13 June 1977 by virtue of SI 1977/840.
3   7 *Halsbury's Statutes* (4th edn) 36.
4   RRA 1976, s 1; 7 *Halsbury's Statutes* (4th edn) 118.
5   RRA 1976, s 34; 7 *Halsbury's Statutes* (4th edn) 147.
6   RRA 1976, s 34(4).
7   RRA 1976, s 34(1).
8   RRA 1976, s 34(2)(a); 7 *Halsbury's Statutes* (4th edn) 147.
9   RRA 1976, s 34(2)(b); 7 *Halsbury's Statutes* (4th edn) 147.
10   SDA 1975, s 43; 7 *Halsbury's Statutes* (4th edn) 72. SI 1977/528 amends the Sex Discrimination Act 1975, s 43 in relation to 'charitable instrument' and re-defines the phrase to correspond with that used in the RRA 1976, s 34(4).

[103.13]

Surplus income. Where at the date of the bequest the property given is more than enough to satisfy the purposes specified in the will, and it also appears that the testator intended to give the whole property to charity, and was mistaken as to the amount only, the whole is applicable to the specified purposes[1] or may be applied *cy-près*.[2] Where, however, it appears on the face of the will that the testator knew that the value of his estate was or might be more than the amount of the specific appropriation, and he has expressed no intention of devoting the whole to charity, the surplus does not go to charity, but goes either to the donees to whom the property is given in trust for the charity[3] or results to the testator's

, rentcharge equal to the annual value of the land is given, any ,ent increase in the value of the land accrues to the charity.[5] If there is a .ection to make certain payments out of income, it is a question of construction whether the intention is to devote the whole to charity.[6] Where particular sums, not exhausting the entire income, are given to specified charities and the remainder to other charitable purposes, a question of construction may arise whether any increase of income is divisible pro rata among the specified and other objects or purposes[7] or whether the whole increase goes to the objects entitled to the remainder of the income.[8] Where the surplus income is directed to be applied in repairing the premises given to the charity, the whole property is available for the charity.[9]

1   *Re Monk, Giffen v Wedd* [1927] 2 Ch 197.
2   *Re Raine, Walton v A-G* [1956] Ch 417, [1956] 1 All ER 355.
3   *A-G v Skinners' Co* (1833) 5 Sim 596; *Merchant Taylor's Co v A-G* (1871) 6 Ch App 512 at 519.
4   *Re Stanford, Cambridge University v A-G* [1924] 1 Ch 73.
5   *A-G v Wilson* (1834) 3 My & K 362.
6   *A-G v Windsor (Dean and Canons)* (1860) 8 HL Cas 369 at 393.
7   *A-G v Caius College* (1837) 2 Keen 150.
8   *Re Avenon's Charity, A-G v Pelly* (1912) 56 Sol Jo 241; further consideration [1913] 2 Ch 261.
9   *Beverley Corpn v A-G* (1857) 6 HL Cas 310 at 324; *Merchant Taylors' Co v A-G* (1871) 6 Ch App 512; *A-G v Wax Chandlers' Co (Master, Wardens, etc)* (1873) LR 6 HL 1.

[103.14]

Surplus given to person charged with payments. If there is an express gift of the surplus income to the donee who is charged with the payments, this may be construed in two ways: (1) as a gift of the residue whatever it may amount to, in which case the donee is entitled to any increased income,[1] or (2) as a gift of an aliquot portion of the whole, in which case the donee shares rateably with the other donees in any increase.[2] Which construction is adopted is decided on a consideration of the will as a whole.[3] Such words as 'overplus', 'surplus' or 'residue' do not necessarily indicate that the gift is residuary.[4] An express gift of surplus will be disregarded where the intention of the testator would be defeated by giving effect to it.[5]

1   *Southmolton Corpn v A-G* (1854) 5 HL Cas 1; *Re Rowe, Merchant Taylors' Co v London Corpn* (1914) 30 TLR 528.
2   *A-G v Drapers' Co, Kendrick's Charity* (1841) 4 Beav 67.
3   *A-G v Windsor (Dean and Canons)* (1860) 8 HL Cas 369.
4   *Beverley Corpn v A-G* (1857) 6 HL Cas 310; *Southmolton Corpn v A-G* (1854) 5 HL Cas 1.
5   *Re Ashton's Charity* (1859) 27 Beav 115.

[103.15]

Income exhausted at date of gift. If there is no express gift of the surplus income, but the specific gifts exhaust the income at the time of the gift, any subsequent increase in the income is applicable to similar purposes and prima facie in similar proportions.[1] This rule is equally applicable whether the donor thought at the time that he was disposing of the entire income,[2] or there are words which might limit the extent of the charitable purpose had they stood alone, but such words are coupled with other words which show that the purpose was to give the whole fund.³

1 *Southmolton Corpn v A-G* (1854) 5 HL Cas 1; *Beverley Corpn v A-G* (1857) 6 HL Cas 310 at 320. But the court has the power within certain limits to vary the proportions: *A-G v Windsor (Dean and Canons)* (1860) 8 HL Cas 369; *A-G v Marchant* (1866) LR 3 Eq 424 at 430.
2 *A-G v Marchant* (1866) LR 3 Eq 424.
3 *A-G v Painter-Stainers' Co* (1788) 2 Cox Eq Cas 51 at 55.

[103.16]
Income not exhausted at date of gift. In this case if there is no express gift of the surplus, but there is a clear intention, express or implied, to attach a charitable trust to the whole property, then however deficient may be the appropriation of the whole income, the surplus will be applicable to charity, for the general intention will prevail.¹ The donees will not be entitled to the increase unless they are themselves a charity,² or there are other circumstances from which a contrary intention can be collected.³ If, however, there is no general intention to devote the whole to charity, the surplus income belongs to the parties who are charged with making the payments, and not the charities,⁴ notwithstanding that such specific payments, by lapse of time or otherwise, have become insufficient to satisfy the purposes for which they were originally made⁵ for the absence of any disposition of the surplus is an indication of an intention to benefit the donee.⁶

1 *Southmolton Corpn v A-G* (1854) 5 HL Cas 1; *Beverley Corpn v A-G* (1857) 6 HL Cas 310; *A-G v Windsor (Dean and Canons)* (1860) 8 HL Cas 369.
2 *A-G v Trinity College, Cambridge* (1856) 24 Beav 383 at 389.
3 *A-G v Drapers' Co* (1840) 2 Beav 508.
4 *A-G v Bristol Corpn* (1820) 2 Jac & W 294 at 307; *Merchant Taylors' Co v A-G* (1871) 6 Ch App 512 at 519. A gift of a specific sum of income to charity does not carry the whole income and more so where the class of beneficiaries is bound to come to an end at some future date; *Re Waite, Cox v New Zealand Insurance Co Ltd* [1964] NZLR 1034.
5 *A-G v Gascoigne* (1833) 2 My & K 647; *Charitable Donations Comrs v De Clifford* (1841) 1 Dr & War 245.
6 *A-G v Trinity College, Cambridge* (1856) 24 Beav 383 at 392.

[103.17]
Delegation of power to determine objects. Power to determine the particular object to be benefited may be delegated.¹ Thus, a direction to trustees to divide a fund at their discretion among such charitable institutions or objects as they may think expedient is valid.² If the person to whom such power is delegated does not exercise it, the gift does not fail on that account. Thus, a gift does not fail because a trustee fails to appoint,³ or an executor renounces,⁴ or because his appointment is revoked,⁵ or because the person given the power to nominate the beneficiary dies in the lifetime of the testator,⁶ or because the name of the nominator is left blank,⁷ or by the trustees or nominator refusing to act⁸ or dying without exercising the discretion.⁹ Where the discretion is sufficiently wide, the trustees need not exercise it in accordance with the known wishes of the testator.¹⁰ A bequest to a definite class of charitable objects, coupled with the appointment of a person to select the objects is not void for uncertainty,¹¹ but a gift of residue to the executor to be disposed of for worthy causes as he considers fit, is not a valid charitable gift.¹² A bequest to be applied to such

purposes as the donee may think fit does not give too wide a discretion where the donee takes virtue officii[13] but it is otherwise where the gift is to a donee taking virtute officii and another person.[14] The exercise of the power of delegation is sometimes subject to a condition limiting the time of such exercise.[15]

1   *A-G v National Provincial and Union Bank of England* [1924] AC 262 at 264; *Re Nilen's Will, Kidd v Nilen* [1908] VLR 332; *Manning v Robinson* (1898) 29 OR 483; *Blount v Viditz* [1895] 1 IR 42.

2   *Re Lea, Lea v Cooke* (1887) 34 Ch D 528; *Dick's Trustees v Dick* 1907 SC 953; affd sub nom *Dick v Audsley* [1908] AC 347. The discretion must, however, be clearly limited to charitable objects: *Blair v Duncan* [1902] AC 37.

3   *Re Douglas, Obert v Barrow* (1887) 35 Ch D 472.

4   *A-G v Fletcher* (1835) 5 LJ Ch 75. A power for executors to nominate is not exercisable by trustees subsequently appointed: *Hibbard v Lamb* (1756) Amb 309.

5   *White v White* (1778) 1 Bro CC 12; *Moggridge v Thackwell* (1803) 7 Ves 36 at 78.

6   *Moggridge v Thackwell* (1803) 7 Ves 36; *Re Willis, Shaw v Willis* [1921] 1 Ch 44, unless the personality of the chosen trustee is essential to a donor's charitable intention; *Re Lawton, Gartside v A-G* [1936] 3 All ER 378; *Re Lysaght, Hill v Royal College of Surgeons of England* [1966] Ch 191, [1965] 2 All ER 888; *Re Armitage, Ellam v Norwich Corpn* [1972] Ch 438, [1972] 1 All ER 708; *Re Tyler's Fund Trusts, Graves v King* [1967] 3 All ER 389, [1967] 1 WLR 1269.

7   *Baylis v A-G* (1741) 2 Atk 239; but *Angus's Executrix v Batchan's Trustees* 1949 SC 335, is to the contrary.

8   *Doyley v A-G* (1735) 2 Eq Cas Abr 194.

9   *A-G v Bucknall* (1742) 2 Atk 328.

10   *Re Squire's Trusts, Chester and Flower v Oxford and Cambridge Universities and A-G* (1901) 17 TLR 724. If the testator's wishes are clearly not regarded, the court may modify the selection: *A-G v Buller* (1822) Jac 407.

11   *Allan's Executors v Allan* 1908 SC 807.

12   *Planta v Greenshields* [1931] 2 DLR 189; *Re Aydit's Estate, Bergerman v Aydit* (1965) 54 DLR (2d) 771.

13   *Re Flinn* [1948] Ch 241, [1948] 1 All ER 541 (bequest to Archbishop of Westminster, who, it must be considered, would apply such gift to legal charitable purposes).

14   *Re Spensley's Will Trusts, Barclays Bank Ltd v Staughton* [1954] Ch 233, [1954] 1 All ER 178.

15   See para **[9.45]** supra.

II.   THE *CY-PRÈS* DOCTRINE

[103.18]

Inherent jurisdiction. Where a clear charitable intention is expressed, it will not be permitted to fail because the mode, if specified, cannot be executed, but the law will, by directing a scheme to be prepared, substitute another mode *cy-près*,[1] that is, as near as possible to the mode specified by the testator[2] but it seems to be always in the discretion of the court whether or not in all the circumstances of the case it will order a scheme.[3] There can be no application *cy- près* until it is clear that the mode specified by the donor cannot be carried out,[4] and that the donor had a general charitable intention,[5] where the particular mode of application was the essence of the testator's intention[6] or where the gift is for a limited time and purpose which fails.[7] A condition or requirement attached to the gift can be removed by an approved scheme where it is shown to be impractical or manifestly undesirable.[8] The *cy-près* doctrine may be applied in the case of a charitable gift which has failed where the residue is given to charity,[9] even if there is a gift over to a second charity[10] but the gift over will be allowed to take effect where any possible scheme will not give effect to the testator's wishes.[11] Trustees cannot on their own authority apply the doctrine of *cy-près*. They must apply to and obtain the direction of the court.[12]

1 *Re Woodhams, Lloyds Bank Ltd v London College of Music* [1981] 1 All ER 202, [1981] 1 WLR 493 (particular charitable purpose expressed in will impractical; *cy-près* scheme settled) *Moggridge v Thackwell* (1803) 7 Ves 36 at 69; *Chamberlayne v Brockett* (1872) 8 Ch App 206; *Re Mitchner* [1922] St R Qd 39; *Re Mulcahy, Butler v Meagher* [1931] IR 239.
2 *Re Avenon's Charity, A-G v Pelly* (1912) 106 LT 295.
3 *Re Hanbey's Will Trusts, Cutlers' Co v Christ's Hospital, London* [1956] Ch 264, [1955] 3 All ER 874.
4 *Re Weir Hospital* [1910] 2 Ch 124 at 132. This must be determined as at the testator's death; *Re Slevin, Slevin v Hepburn* [1891] 2 Ch 236, and *Re Wright, Blizard v Lockhart* [1954] Ch 347, [1954] 2 All ER 98.
5 *Biscoe v Jackson* (1887) 35 Ch D 460 at 465.
6 *Re Wilson, Twentyman v Simpson* [1913] 1 Ch 314 at 321; *Re Monk, Giffen v Wedd* [1927] 2 Ch 197 at 211; *Re Good's Will Trusts, Oliver v Batten* [1950] 2 All ER 653. As to subscriptions, see *Re Hillier, Hillier v A-G* [1954] 2 All ER 59; *Re Gillingham Bus Disaster Fund, Bowman v Official Solicitor* [1958] Ch 300, [1958] 1 All ER 37.
7 *Re Cooper's Conveyance Trusts, Crewdson v Bagot* [1956] 3 All ER 28, [1956] 1 WLR 1096.
8 *Re Robinson, Wright v Tugwell* [1923] 2 Ch 332; *Re Dominion Students' Hall Trusts, Dominion Students' Hall Trust v A-G* [1947] Ch 183; *Re Lysaght, Hill v Royal College of Surgeons* [1966] Ch 191, [1965] 2 All ER 888; *Re J W Laing Trust, Stewards Co Ltd v A-G* [1984] Ch 143, [1984] 1 All ER 50.
9 *Lyons Corpn v Advocate-General of Bengal* (1876) 1 App Cas 91 at 115.
10 *Re Cunningham, Dulcken v Cunningham* [1914] 1 Ch 427.
11 *Re Hanbey's Will Trusts, Cutlers' Co v Christ's Hospital, London* [1956] Ch 264, [1955] 3 All ER 874.
12 *A-G v Coopers' Co* (1812) 19 Ves 187; *Re Campden Charities* (1881) 18 Ch D 310; *Cross v Lloyd-Greame* (1909) 102 LT 163. See now Charities Act 1993, s 16 (Charities Act 1960, s 18) and as to the duty of trustees to apply for a scheme, see Charities Act 1993, s 13(5)): see para **[103.19]** infra.

[103.19]
Charities Act 1993: extended powers of applying property *cy-près*. The circumstances in which the original purposes of a charitable gift can be altered to allow the property given or part of it to be applied *cy-près* are as follows.[1] (a) Where the original purposes, in whole or in part, (i) have been as far as may be fulfilled, or (ii) cannot be carried out, or not according to the directions given and to the spirit of the gift; or (b) where the original purposes provide a use for part only of the property available by virtue of the gift; or (c) where the property available by virtue of the gift and other property applicable for similar purposes can be more effectively used in conjunction, and to that end can suitably, regard being had to the spirit of the gift, be made applicable to common purposes; or (d) where the original purposes were laid down by reference to an area which then was but has since ceased to be a unit for some other purpose, or by reference to a class of persons or to an area which has for any reason since ceased to be suitable, regard being had to the spirit of the gift, or to be practical in administering the gift;[2] or (e) where the original purposes, in whole or in part, have, since they were laid down, (i) been adequately provided for by other means; or (ii) ceased, as being useless or harmful to the community or for other reasons, to be in law charitable; or (iii) ceased in any other way to provide a suitable and effective method of using the property available by virtue of the gift,[3] regard being had to the spirit of the gift. The above do not affect the

conditions which must be satisfied in order that property given for charitable purposes may be applied *cy-près*, except in so far as those conditions require a failure of the original purposes. References to the original purposes of a gift are construed, where the application of the property given has been altered or regulated by a scheme or otherwise, as referring to the purposes for which the property is for the time being applicable.[4] Without prejudice to the above power to make schemes, the court may by scheme made under the court's jurisdiction with respect to charities, in any case where the purposes for which the property is held are laid down by reference to any local area, provide for enlarging that area.[5] A trust for charitable purposes places a trustee under a duty, where the case permits and requires the property or some part of it to be applied *cy-près*, to secure its effective use for charity by taking steps to enable it to be so applied.[6]

1   Charities Act 1993 (CA 1993), s 13 (Charities Act 1960, s 13); 5 *Halsbury's Statutes* (4th edn) 960; the Charities Act 1960 came into force on 1 January 1961 and the CA 1993 on 1 August 1993 (with a few exceptions). The CA 1993 is subject to some amendments by the Trustee Act 2000, which do not affect this discussion.
2   *Peggs v Lamb* [1994] Ch 172, [1994] 2 All ER 15, class enlarged from the freemen of the borough of Huntingdon, to the inhabitants as a whole.
3   *Re Lepton's Charity, Ambler v Thomas* [1972] Ch 276, [1971] 1 All ER 799 (direction in 1715 to pay £3 per annum; income now £791; scheme to pay £100 per annum approved); but see *Re J W Laing Trust, Stewards' Co Ltd v A-G* [1984] Ch 143, [1984] 1 All ER 50 (direction that fund be distributed within ten years of the settlor's death not part of the 'original purpose' of the gift within the meaning of the CA 1993, s 13(1) and thus not within jurisdiction conferred by s 13(1)(e)(iii) condition removed under inherent jurisdiction).
4   CA 1993, s 13 (Charities Act 1960, s 13(2), (3)).
5   CA 1993, s 13 (Charities Act 1960, s 13(4)).
6   CA 1993, s 13 (Charities Act 1960, s 13(5)).

[103.20]
Application *cy-près* of gifts of donors unknown or disclaiming. Property given for specific charitable purposes which fail is applicable *cy-près* as if given for charitable purposes generally, where it belongs – (a) to a donor who, after (i) the prescribed advertisements and inquiries have been published and made, and (ii) the prescribed period beginning with the publication of these advertisements has expired, cannot be identified or cannot be found; or (b) to a donor who has executed a disclaimer in the prescribed form of his right to have the property returned.[1] Where the prescribed advertisements and inquiries have been published and made by or on behalf of trustees with respect to any such property, the trustees shall not be liable to any person in respect of the property if no claim by him to be interested in it is received by them before the expiry of the period mentioned in the subsection above.[2] Property is conclusively presumed (without any advertisement or inquiry) to belong to donors who cannot be identified, in so far as it consists – (a) of the proceeds of cash collections made by means of collecting boxes or by other means not adapted for distinguishing one gift from another; or (b) of the proceeds of any lottery, competition, entertainment, sale or similar money-raising activity, after allowing for property given to provide prizes or articles for sale or otherwise to enable the activity to be undertaken. The court may by order direct that property shall be treated (without any advertisement or inquiry) as belonging to donors who cannot be identified, where it appears to the court either – (a) that it would be

unreasonable, having regard to the amounts likely to be returned to the donors, to incur expense with a view to returning the property; or (b) that it would be unreasonable, having regard to the nature, circumstances and amounts of the gifts, and to the lapse of time since the gifts were made, for the donors to expect the property to be returned.[3] Where property is thus applied *cy-près* the donor is deemed to have parted with all his interest at the time when the gift was made; but where property is so applied as belonging to donors who cannot be identified or cannot be found, and is not applied as above – (a) the scheme shall specify the total amount of that property; and (b) the donor of any part of that amount shall be entitled, if he makes a claim not later than six[4] months after the date on which the scheme is made, to recover from the charity for which the property is applied a sum equal to that part, less any expenses properly incurred by the charity trustees after that date in connection with claims relating to his gift; and (c) the scheme may include directions as to the provision to be made for meeting any such claim.

Charitable purposes are deemed to 'fail' where any difficulty in applying property to those purposes makes that property or the part not applicable *cy-près*, available to be returned to the donors.[5]

1   As amended by the Charities Act 1992, s 15, now the CA 1993, s 14.
2   Added as s 1A by the Charities Act 1993, s 15. See now the CA 1993, s 14.
3   CA 1993, s 14 (1960 Act, s 14(1)–3(3)). For the pre-Act position see *Re Hillier, Hillier v A-G* [1954] 2 All ER 59; *Re North Devon and West Somerset Relief Fund Trusts, Hylton v Wright* [1953] 2 All ER 1032, [1953] 1 WLR 1260; *Re Gillingham Bus Disaster Fund* [1958] Ch 300, [1958] 1 All ER 37; affd [1959] Ch 62, [1958] 2 All ER 749, CA.
4   As amended by the CA 1993.
5   CA 1993, s 14 (Charities Act 1960, s 14(4), (5)); 5 *Halsbury's Statutes* (4th edn) 962.

[103.21]

Charities Acts 1992 and 1993. The Charities Act 1992 (CA 1992), now consolidated into the provisions of the Charities Act 1993 (CA 1993), is an important addition to the law of charities but it is concerned mainly with administrative and regulatory aspects of the law which are beyond the scope of this text to discuss in detail. The CA 1993 reflects the increased size and activities of the charitable sector and the problems that have become apparent as charities have become more involved with the mainstream of social welfare provision. The CA 1993 strengthens the supervisory role of the Charity Commissioners, and includes measures to control the activities of professional fund raisers and for the control of public charitable collections. The two sections of the consolidating CA 1993 which are most relevant to this text are s 14,[1] which is concerned with the application of property *cy-près* which amends the Charities Act 1960, s 14 (these changes have been noted above[2]) and s 43,[3] which is concerned with small charities and the power to transfer all of the property or to modify their objects if that is thought necessary. This section in effect replaces the Charities Act 1985,[4] which is wholly repealed by the CA 1992 and CA 1993.

The Charities Act 1985 which sought to address the problems of small charities, ie local charities with an income of less than £200 per annum, was found in practice to be too restricted and was of little use. The CA 1993 in s 74 seeks to further the objectives of the Charities Act 1985 but to render the provisions more effective by widening the range of charities to which it is applicable. The details of the legislation need not be set out here but reference can be made to the fact that the previous limit income of £200 has now been increased to £5,000 per annum. The previous restriction to local charities which are at least 50 years old, has been removed. There is an additional requirement that the charity must not hold any land on trusts which stipulate that the land is to be used for any particular purposes of the charity.[5] If a small charity satisfies these two requirements the charity trustees of the charity may resolve on the following actions. First, that all the property of the charity should be transferred to such other charity as is specified in the resolution being either a registered charity or a charity which is not required to be registered. Second, that all the property of the charity should be divided in such manner as is specified in the resolution between such two or more charities as are so specified, being in each case either a registered charity, or a charity which is not required to be registered. Third, that the trusts of the charity should be modified by replacing all or any of the purposes of the charity with such other purposes being in law charitable as are specified in the resolution. Fourth, any provision of the trusts of the charity relating to any of the powers exercisable by the charity trustees in the administration of the charity or regulating the procedure to be followed in any respect in connection with the administration, can be modified in like manner as is specified in the resolution.[6] The regulations governing the resolutions have been simplified in subsequent provisions of the CA 1993, s 43.[7]

1   CA 1993.
2   See para **[103.21]** supra.
3   CA 1993, previously the CA 1992, s 21.
4   As to the Charities Act 1985 see the sixth edition of this text, p 797.
5   CA 1993, s 43(1)(a), (b).
6   CA 1993, s 86(3). Section 86(2)(b) has been repealed by the Trustee Act 2000, Sch 2, para 2 without affecting this discussion.
7   CA 1993, s 86(1).

PART O

Intestacy

CHAPTER 104

Intestacy

[104.1]

Intestacy in general. Intestacy is either total or partial. Total intestacy occurs when a person makes no effective testamentary disposition of any property of which he is competent to dispose by will.[1] Partial intestacy occurs where a person makes testamentary dispositions which are ineffectual as to part or as to some interest in all or part of the property of which he is competent to dispose by will.[2] If a testator does not by his will make an effective disposition of the whole of his disposable property, such property as he does not dispose of must be distributed at the time when the partial intestacy occurs[3] as if no will had been made, but it devolves on the executor or administrator with will annexed and no further grant is necessary.[4] If the testator gives property to a beneficiary and it is clear that the beneficiary is to hold the property in trust for others and the trust fails, then, in the absence of a residuary gift, the donee in trust will hold that property in trust for those entitled on intestacy.[5]

It is beyond the scope of this book to discuss the statutory provisions governing total intestacy in detail,[6] but a brief outline of the main features of the law is included.

1   Where all the provisions of a will fail, including the appointment of executors, there is a total intestacy: *Re Ford, Ford v Ford* [1902] 2 Ch 605; *Re Cuffe, Fooks v Cuffe* [1908] 2 Ch 500. At common law, the appointment of executors had to fail as well as the dispositions, because prima facie they took the personal estate by virtue of their appointment, but it has now been decided that where the dispositions fail but not the appointment of executors, the latter hold upon trust for the statutory beneficiaries under the Administration of Estates Act 1925, s 46; 17 *Halsbury's Statutes* (4th edn) 452. See Vol 2, Part G, para **[244.60]**; *Re Skeats, Thain v Gibbs* [1936] Ch 683, [1936] 2 All ER 298. Where residue is given to executors to dispose of as they think fit and the executors have already been given a pecuniary legacy, they hold such residue upon trust for the statutory beneficiaries on intestacy: *Re Carville, Shone v Walthamstow Borough Council* [1937] 4 All ER 464. See *Re Basham* [1987] 1 All ER 405, [1986] 1 WLR 1498 where the statutory entitlement was held to have been displaced by the application of the doctrine of proprietary estoppel.
2   Partial intestacy is now subject to the Administration of Estates Act 1925, Vol 2, Part G, para **[244.57]**, which requires that there must be some part of the testator's property disposed of by his will and part undisposed of: see para **[104.10]** infra. Section 49, is amended by the Intestates' Estates Act 1952, s 3, and the Law Reform (Succession) Act 1995, s 1;
3   *Re McKee, Public Trustee v McKee* [1931] 2 Ch 145, not followed on one point in *Re Bowen-Buscarlet's Will Trusts, Nathan v Bowen-Buscarlet* [1972] Ch 463, [1971] 3 All ER 636; see para **[104.10]** infra.
4   That is provided the grant is a general grant, which carries all property in which the testator has an interest not ceasing at his death, or a grant save and except where the partial intestacy occurs in respect of the property not excepted.
5   *Muckleston v Brown* (1801) 6 Ves 52.

Part O Intestacy

6   As to which see Sherrin and Bonehill, *Law and Practice of Intestate Succession* (2nd edn). It
    can be noted that the provisions governing intestacy in the Administration of Estates Act 1925,
    Part III have been most recently amended by the Trusts of Land and Appointment of Trustees
    Act 1996 by which s 33 has been amended to substitute simple trust with power of sale for trust
    for sale, see s 5, Sch 2, para 5. Important amendments have been made to ss 46, 47 and 49 by
    the Law Reform (Succession) Act 1995; these amendments have been noted in the following
    paragraphs. The statutory provisions governing intestate succession are printed in Vol 2, Part G,
    paras [244.57] to [244.74] and [244.82] to [244.92].

I. TOTAL INTESTACY

[104.2]
Entitlement: the spouse. The succession to real and personal estate on intestacy
is governed by the table of distribution in the Administration of Estates Act 1925
(AEA 1925), s 46.[1] In the case of the death of a person intestate on or after 1
January 1996 all the rights of the intestate's spouse are contingent on the spouse
surviving the intestate by 28 days.[2] There is no such contingency where the
death occurs before that date. Where the intestate leaves a husband or wife[3] and
no issue, no parent or brother or sister of the whole blood or issue of a brother or
sister of the whole blood, then the residuary estate is held in trust for the
surviving husband or wife absolutely.[4] Where the intestate leaves a husband or
wife and issue then the surviving husband or wife takes the personal chattels
absolutely;[5] a fixed net sum, currently of £125,000,[6] and subject thereto the
residuary estate is held as to one-half upon trust for the surviving husband or
wife during his or her life; and subject thereto on the statutory trusts for the issue
of the intestate;[7] and as to the other half, on the statutory trusts for the issue of
the intestate.[8] Where the intestate leaves a husband or wife, no issue, but either a
parent, or a brother or sister of the whole blood or issue of a brother or sister of
the whole blood, then the surviving husband or wife takes the personal chattels
absolutely;[9] a fixed net sum, currently of £200,000[10] and subject thereto the
residuary estate is held as to one-half in trust for the surviving husband or wife
absolutely:[11] and as to the other half, where the intestate leaves one or both
parents then in trust for the parent absolutely or, as the case may be, for the two
parents in equal shares absolutely;[12] or where the intestate leaves no parent, on
the statutory trusts for the brothers and sisters of the whole blood of the
intestate.[13]

1   As amended in the case of deaths on or after 1 January 1953 by the Intestates' Estates Act 1952;
    in the case of deaths on or after 1 January 1967 by the Family Provision Act 1966; in the case
    of deaths on or after 1 January 1970 by the Family Law Reform Act 1969 and in the case of
    deaths on or after 1 January 1996 by the Law Reform (Succession) Act 1995. The amount of
    the fixed net sum or statutory legacy has been progressively increased subsequent to 1967 by
    statutory instrument.
2   AEA 1925, s 46(2A) inserted by Law Reform (Succession) Act 1995, s 1(1) and printed in
    Vol 2, Part G, para [244.129].
3   The presumption in the Law of Property Act 1925, s 184 does not apply so that in a
    commorientes situation neither party is presumed to have survived the other; AEA 1925,
    s 46(3): see Vol 2, Part G, para [244.60]. In relation to deaths on or after 1 January 1996 this
    provision is largely superseded by the 28-day survivorship contingency (see above).
4   AEA 1925, s 46(1)(i)(1).
5   See para [104.3] infra.

6 See para **[104.4]** infra; see *Re Collens, Royal Bank of Canada (London) Ltd v Krogh* [1986] Ch 505, [1986] 1 All ER 611 concerning the entitlement of the spouse to the statutory legacy where he/she was also entitled to movable property in another jurisdiction.
7 See para **[104.5]** infra.
8 AEA 1925, s 46(1)(i), (2).
9 See para **[104.3]** infra.
10 See para **[104.4]** infra.
11 AEA 1925, s 46(1)(i), (3)(a).
12 AEA 1925, s 46(1)(i), (3)(b)(i).
13 AEA 1925, s 46(1)(i), (3)(b)(ii).

[104.3]
Personal chattels. The personal chattels are defined in the AEA 1925, s 55(1)(x) as follows:

'Personal chattels" means carriages, horses, stable furniture and effects (not used for business purposes), motor cars and accessories (not used for business purposes), garden effects, domestic animals, plate, plated articles, linen, china, glass, books, pictures, prints, furniture, jewellery, articles of household or personal use or ornament, musical and scientific instruments and apparatus, wines, liquors and consumable stores, but do not include any chattels used at the death of the intestate for business purposes nor money or securities for money.'

It will be noticed that the definition includes a number of specific items and a general phrase 'articles of household or personal use or ornament'. Of the former the following have been the subject of judicial decision; horses,[1] jewellery,[2] furniture,[3] and animals.[4] Articles of personal use have been held to include watches,[5] a stamp collection,[6] a motor yacht,[7] and a motor car.[8]

1 *Re Hutchinson, Holt v Hutchinson* [1955] Ch 255.
2 *Re Whitby, Public Trustee v Whitby* [1944] Ch 210, [1944] 1 All ER 299, CA.
3 *Re Crispin's Will Trusts, Arkwright v Thurley* [1975] Ch 245, [1974] 3 All ER 772, CA.
4 *Re Ogilby, Ogilby v Wentworth-Stanley* [1942] Ch 288, [1942] 1 All ER 524.
5 *Re Crispins Will Trusts, Arkwright v Thurley* [1975] Ch 245, [1974] 3 All ER 772, CA.
6 *Re Reynolds' Will Trusts, Dove v Reynolds* [1965] 3 All ER 686, [1966] 1 WLR 19; see also *Re Collins's Settlement Trusts, Donne v Hewetson* [1971] 1 All ER 283, [1971] 1 WLR 37 (stamp and coin collections and a motor car included in a bequest of 'personal effects' which phrase was held to be synonymous with 'personal chattels').
7 *Re Chaplin, Royal Bank of Scotland v Chaplin* [1950] Ch 507, [1950] 2 All ER 155.
8 *Re White, White v White* [1916] 1 Ch 172.

[104.4]
The fixed net sum. The amount to which the spouse is entitled as a fixed net sum was initially fixed in 1925 as £1,000.[1] The Intestate's Estates Act 1952 increased the amount to £5,000, where there were issue surviving, and to £20,000, where there were no issue but specified relatives, with effect from 1 January 1953.[2] The Family Provision Act 1966 increased the amounts further, to £8,750 and to £30,000 respectively, with effect from 1 January 1967 and provided that henceforth the amounts should be increased by statutory instrument.[3] This has been done on four subsequent occasions; in the case of deaths on or after 1 July 1972 the entitlement was to £15,000 and £40,000 respectively;[4] in the case of deaths on or after 15 March 1977, the entitlement was to £25,000 and to £55,000 respectively;[5] in respect of deaths on or after 1

March 1981 the entitlement was to £40,000 and to £85,000 respectively;[6] in respect of deaths on or after 1 June 1987 to £75,000 and £125,000 respectively.[7] The current figures in respect of deaths on or after 1 December 1993 are £125,000 and £200,000 respectively.[8] The absolute entitlement (in effect) to the statutory legacy (or the fixed net sum as it is more properly called) is often used to effect an appropriation of the matrimonial home under the Intestates' Estates Act 1952, Second Schedule, and the fixed net sum has been increased in line with the value of dwelling houses since 1981.[9] The sum carries interest at 6 per cent per annum from the date of death.[10]

1   AEA 1925, s 46(1)(i). In all cases, which was itself an increase on the £500 entitlement under the Intestates' Estates Act 1890.
2   AEA 1925, s 1(2).
3   Family Provision Act 1966, s 1.
4   Family Provision (Intestate Succession) Order 1972, SI 1972/96.
5   Family Provision (Intestate Succession) Order 1977, SI 1977/415.
6   Family Provision (Intestate Succession) Order 1981, SI 1981/255.
7   Family Provision (Intestate Succession) Order 1987, SI 1987/799.
8   Family Provision (Intestate Succession) Order 1993, SI 1993/2906.
9   As to possible double entitlement where a foreign domicile is involved see *Re Collens, Royal Bank of Canada (London) v Krogh* [1986] Ch 505, [1986] 1 All ER 611 applying *Re Rea, Rea v Rea* [1902] 1 IR 451 and *Re Ralston* [1906] VLR 689.
10   Intestate Succession (Interest and Capitalisation) Order 1983 (Amendment) Order 1983, SI 1983/1374 with effect from 1 October 1983. The rate was previously 7 per cent with effect from 15 September 1977, SI 1977/1491; and before that date it was 4 per cent per annum, Intestate's Estates Act 1952, reducing the original rate of 5 per cent in the AEA 1925, in respect of deaths on or after 1 January 1953.

[104.5]
Redemption and appropriation. Where the surviving husband or wife is entitled to a life interest in part of the residuary estate, he or she may elect to have the life interest purchased or redeemed by the personal representatives and thus receive the capitalised value instead.[1] The Intestates' Estates Act 1952[2] conferred a right on the surviving spouse to require the personal representatives to appropriate[3] the matrimonial home in or towards satisfaction of any absolute interest in the intestacy.[4]

1   AEA 1925, s 47A, added by the Intestates' Estates Act 1952, s 2(b); 17 *Halsbury's Statutes* (4th edn) 459. For the method of ascertaining the capital value, see Intestate Succession (Interest and Capitalisation) Order 1977, SI 1977/1491.
2   See Second Schedule to the Intestates' Estates Act 1952.
3   In exercise of the power in the Administration of Estates Act 1925, s 41.
4   See *Re Phelps, Wells v Phelps* [1980] Ch 275, [1979] 3 All ER 373; *Robinson v Collins* [1975] 1 All ER 321, sub nom *Re Collins, Robinson v Collins* [1975] 1 WLR 309.

[104.6]
Entitlement of issue. Where the intestate leaves a surviving spouse and issue then the spouse has the primary entitlement as set out above.[1] Subject to the spouse's entitlement to the personal chattels, and to the fixed net sum, and to a life interest in one-half of the residuary estate, the estate is held on the statutory trusts for the issue.[2] In the case of one-half of the estate this is an interest in remainder after the spouse's life interest; in the case of the other half it is an immediate interest.[3] Where the intestate leaves issue but no husband or wife, the residuary estate is held on the statutory trusts for the issue of the intestate.[4]

Leaving issue means leaving issue who attain an absolute vested interest.[5] Issue means children and grandchildren and more remote descendants,[6] and includes legitimated, adopted and illegitimate persons[7] and children en ventre sa mère at the death.[8]

1   See para [104.2] supra.
2   AEA 1925, s 46(1)(i), (2).
3   But possibly contingent, see para [104.10] infra.
4   AEA 1925, s 46(1)(ii).
5   AEA 1925, s 47(2)(c).
6   See Chapter 76.
7   Legitimacy Act 1976, s 5(2); Adoption Act 1976, s 46(4); and Family Law Reform Act 1987, ss 1 and 18 (replacing the more restricted provisions of Family Law Reform Act 1969, s 14), all of which are printed in Vol 2, Part G.
8   AEA 1925, s 55(2). It is not possible in this section to discuss the meaning of issue for the purposes of intestate succession in any greater detail; see Chapter 76.

[104.7]
The statutory trusts. Issue take on intestacy on the statutory trusts, which are defined in the AEA 1925, s 47. These trusts are not discussed in detail in this section but one or two points can be noted. First, children take in equal shares;[1] secondly, they take vested interests when they attain the age of eighteen years or marry under that age;[2] thirdly, issue take per stirpes, through all degrees, 'the share which their parent would have taken if living at the death of the intestate, and so that no issue shall take whose parent is living at the death of the intestate and so capable of taking'.[3] The statutory powers of maintenance and advancement apply.[4] In relation to deaths before 1 January 1996 children must account for any inter vivos advancements in order to achieve equality of total shares between the class of children.[5] This requirement is abolished in relation to deaths on or after that date.[6]

1   AEA 1925, s 47(1)(i).
2   AEA 1925, s 47(1)(i), as amended by the Family Law Reform Act 1969, s 3(2), in the case of deaths on or after 1 January 1970; in the case of deaths before that date issue took a vested interest at the age of 21 years.
3   AEA 1925, s 47(1)(i).
4   AEA 1925, s 47(1)(ii).
5   AEA 1925, s 47(1)(iii); grandchildren taking their parents' share must account for any advancements received by that child, but do not account for benefits made to them.
6   Law Reform (Succession) Act 1995, s 1(2)(a).

[104.8]
Entitlement of other relatives. It has been seen above that a parent or parents, or bother or sister of the whole blood or issue of a brother or sister of the whole blood, have some entitlement where there is also a surviving spouse.[1] In other cases the entitlement of relatives other than the spouse and issue is set out in the order prescribed by the AEA 1925, s 46(1).[2]

If the intestate leaves no husband or wife and no issue but both parents, then the residuary estate of the intestate is held in trust for the father[3] and mother in equal shares absolutely.

If the intestate leaves no husband or wife no issue but one parent, then the residuary estate of the intestate is held in trust for the surviving father[4] or mother absolutely.

If the intestate leaves no husband or wife and no issue and no parents, then the residuary estate of the intestate is held in trust for the following persons living at the death of the intestate, and in the following order and manner, namely:

First, on the statutory trusts for the brothers and sisters of the whole blood of the intestate; but if no person takes an absolutely vested interest under such trusts; then

Secondly, on the statutory trusts for the brothers and sisters of the half blood of the intestate; but if no person takes an absolutely vested interest under such trusts; then

Thirdly, for the grandparents of the intestate and, if more than one survive the intestate, in equal shares; but if there is no member of this class; then

Fourthly, on the statutory trusts for the uncles and aunts of the intestate (being brothers or sisters of the whole blood of a parent of the intestate); but if no person takes an absolutely vested interest under such trusts; then

Fifthly, on the statutory trusts for the uncles and aunts of the intestate (being brothers or sisters of the half blood of a parent of the intestate).

If the person or persons who are prima facie entitled in priority fails by reason of disclaimer,[5] or the public policy rule,[6] the persons entitled are the next class of qualifying relatives.

1   AEA 1925, s 46(1)(i), (3).
2   See the Family Law Reform Act 1987 in the case of deaths on or after 4 April 1988, n 7.
3   There is a rebuttable presumption that the father of an illegitimate person (or any person claiming through the father) predeceased him: Family Law Reform Act 1987, s 18(2): see Vol 2, Part G, para **[245.71]**.
4   See preceding note.
5   See *Re Scott, Widdows v Friends of the Clergy Corpn* [1975] 2 All ER 1033. The Crown does not take as bona vacantia if there are qualified surviving relatives.
6   See *Re DWS, Re EHS, TWGS v JMG* [2000] 2 All ER 83; affd [2001] 1 All ER 97. The disqualified person is not regarded as having predeceased. But note that the reasoning supporting the conclusion in *Re DWS* is different from that in *Re Scott, Widdows v Friends of the Clergy Corpn* [1975] 2 All ER 1033, which could result in a different conclusion, ie the possibility of the Crown taking as bona vacantia, in certain situations; see para **[46.1]**, n 1 where the point is discussed.

[104.9]
The Crown: bona vacantia. In default of the spouse of issue, or other relatives taking an absolute interest, then the residuary estate of the intestate belongs to the Crown or to the Duchy of Lancaster or to the Duke of Cornwall for the time being, as the case may be, as bona vacantia.[1] The Crown or the Duchy can make ex gratia payments out of the estate for dependants and other persons for whom the intestate might reasonably have been expected to make provision.[2]

1   AEA 1925, s 47(1)(vi). See further Ing, *Bona Vacantia* (1971) especially chapters 1–10.
2   AEA 1925, s 47(1)(vi). See further Ing, *Bona Vacantia* (1971) especially chapters 1–10.

II.   PARTIAL INTESTACY

[104.10]
Different result of partial intestacy arising at death or subsequently. Partial intestacy may result from the failure to make any effective disposition whatever in respect of some specific part of the estate,[1] or from failure to dispose of some

interest in the whole or part of the estate.[2] The first must occur at the death of the deceased, but the second may occur then or at any period subsequent to the death. The distinction is important since, of the two provisions made for partial intestacy in the AEA 1925, the first[3] applies only where the deceased fails to make any disposition whatever of a specific part of his estate. In other cases it is only the second provision of the AEA 1925[4] which need be considered in respect of a partial intestacy. The result of these considerations is that the statutory trust for sale affecting the property of a person who dies intestate applies only to the first form of partial intestacy.[5] That trust for sale does not arise where a testator fails to dispose of some interest in the whole or part of his property whether the failure arises immediately upon his decease or at some subsequent time.[6] In other words the statutory trust for sale on intestacy arises only in respect of an item of the estate of the testator belonging to him at the time of his death and in respect of which item he has made no effective disposition whatever, and not in respect of a beneficial interest which first comes into existence on his death by the operation of his will or the statutory provisions relating to intestacies.[7]

1   That is to say that, as to some specific property, the testator has made no testamentary disposition whatsoever.
2   That is to say that as to some property the testator has disposed, eg of a life interest therein but not the remainder, or, the more usual case, where the testator has failed to dispose of the income from the property for some period: *Re McKee, Public Trustee v McKee* [1931] 2 Ch 145.
3   AEA 1925, s 33, which subjects the estate to a trust for sale.
4   AEA 1925, ss 46, 47 which deal with the beneficial interests arising on intestacy and are applied to partial intestacy by s 49: see Vol 2, Part G, para **[244.60]** et seq.
5   *Re McKee, Public Trustee v McKee* [1931] 2 Ch 145 at 165; *Re Plowman, Westminster Bank Ltd v Plowman* [1943] Ch 269, [1943] 2 All ER 532.
6   *Re McKee, Public Trustee v McKee*, see n 5 supra. In this case the property is subject to the provisions of the will which may include a trust for sale, but then it will be the trust for sale and not the statutory trust to which all the testator's property is subjected.
7   See *Re McKee, Public Trustee v McKee* [1931] 2 Ch 145 at 160.

[104.11]
What is a partial intestacy. At common law a man did not die wholly intestate if the only effective part of his will was the appointment of executors.[1] Such a person, therefore, died partially intestate; but the present statutory provision[2] does not apply unless there is a will which effectively disposes of part of the property of the deceased.[3]

1   See para **[104.1]**, n 1.
2   Administration of Estates Act 1925, s 49: see Vol 2, Part G, para **[244.64]**.
3   *Re McKee, Public Trustee v McKee* [1931] 2 Ch 145, where the will failed to dispose of a reversionary interest. As already explained 'part of the property' may be an interest, such as a life interest or remainder in the whole or part of the estate, or it may be the whole beneficial interest in part of the estate.

[104.12]
Partial intestacy—general provisions. The personal representative holds the undisposed of estate, after payment of all liabilities and administration expenses, in trust for the persons entitled on an intestacy unless it appears from the will

that he is to take beneficially.¹ The onus is on the personal representative to show that he is so entitled, and this appears to be so even when the Crown is entitled under a partial intestacy.²

1   AEA 1925, s 49(1)(b). As to where executors take beneficially, see paras **[30.14]** and **[79.7]** supra. The provisions of the AEA 1925, Pt IV (that is, ss 45–52), but not those of Pt III (that is, ss 32–44) are applied to a partial intestacy by s 49. The provisions of s 46 are to be read into the will so far as the same is defective and so far as it is necessary to make a will for the testator where he has failed to make one for himself: *Re McKee, Public Trustee v McKee* [1931] 2 Ch 145 at 161; applying the principles stated by Lord Cairns in *Cooper v Cooper* (1874) LR 7 HL 53 at 66.
2   AEA 1925, s 49(1)(b). Apparently the Crown is one of the 'persons entitled under this Part of this Act'. A declaration in his will by the testator that he intended his property to pass according to law was, before the passing of the Executors Act 1830, sufficient to oust the executors in favour of the next of kin, and it would seem that after the passing of that Act, such a declaration would oust them in favour of the Crown: *Lord Cranley v Hale* (1807) 14 Ves 307. See the cases cited in n 1, para **[104.1]** supra.

[104.13]
Deaths before 1 January 1996—hotchpot provisions. The following hotchpot provisions apply in the case of the death partially intestate of a person before 1 January 1996:

   (i)   where the surviving spouse acquires any beneficial interests under the will of the deceased other than personal chattels specifically bequeathed, the fixed net sums¹ to which such spouse would be entitled are diminished by the value at the date of death of such beneficial interests and the interest thereon. The surviving spouse is entitled only to such sums as diminished and the interest on such sums as diminished. Accordingly if the value of interests taken under the will exceeds £125,000 or £200,00¹ as the case may be, the provisions on intestacy take effect as if references to the sums of £125,000 or £200,00¹ were omitted;²
   (ii) the issue of the deceased, but not other statutory beneficiaries, must bring into hotchpot the interests they take under the will.³ Any member of a family belonging to a certain branch must bring in everything that has been taken or acquired under the will by that branch;⁴ if a person takes no more than a life interest then the life or less interest must be brought in at an actuarial valuation.⁵ Where a child and his issue have interests which amount to the whole beneficial interest in a fund, then the capital value of the fund has to be brought into account.⁶ Apparently the issue have also to bring into account advances received from the intestate.⁷ These hotchpot provisions apply to foreign assets as well as English assets;⁸
   (iii) references to beneficial interests acquired under the will include beneficial interests acquired by the exercise by the will of a general power of appointment (including the statutory power to dispose of entailed interests) but not of a special power;
   (iv) personal representatives must employ a qualified valuer in any case where necessary for valuing an interest taken under (i) above;
   (v)   the references in the AEA 1925, s 47A(3) to property are references to property comprised in the residuary estate and, accordingly, where the will creates a life interest in property in possession, and the remaining

interest in that property forms part of the residuary estate, the references are references to that remaining interest (which, until determination of the life interest, is property not in possession).[9] These provisions take effect subject to the provisions of the will; but this means the provisions which remain operative and effective and do not include any provisions which are rendered inoperative by a disclaimer[10] or by the failure of the provision in the will such as a provision for accumulation.[11]

1   Family Provision (Intestate Succession) Order 1993, SI 1993, No 2906, with effect from 1 December 1993. The Intestate Succession (Interest and Capitalisation) Order 1983 (Amendment) Order 1983, SI 1983/1374, with effect from 1 October 1983 provides for a rate of interest of 6 per cent; previously with effect from 15 September 1977 (SI 1977/1491), the rate was 7 per cent. See para **[104.4]** ante for the amounts of the statutory legacy in respect of earlier deaths.
2   Intestates' Estates Act 1952, s 3, inserting a new AEA 1925, s 49(1)(aa).
3   AEA 1925, s 49(1)(a), not amended by the Intestates' Estates Act 1952. Here 'issue' means children or remoter issue: *Re Young, Young v Young* [1951] Ch 185, sub nom *Re Young's Will Trust, Young v Young* [1950] 2 All ER 1040.
4   *Re Young, Young v Young* [1951] Ch 185, sub nom *Re Young's Will Trust, Young v Young* [1950] 2 All ER 1040.
5   *Re Morton, Morton v Warham* [1956] Ch 644, [1956] 3 All ER 259.
6   *Re Grover's Will Trusts, National Provincial Bank Ltd v Clarke* [1971] Ch 168, [1970] 1 All ER 1185.
7   AEA 1925, s 47(1)(iii), not amended in 1952. See *Re Hayward, Kerrod v Hayward* [1957] Ch 528, [1957] 2 All ER 474.
8   *Re Osoba, Osoba v Osoba* [1978] 2 All ER 1099, [1978] 1 WLR 791.
9   These provisions (iv), (v) and (vi) were inserted by the Intestates' Estates Act 1952. Section 47A was also inserted by the Intestates' Estates Act 1952 and deals with the right of the surviving spouse to have his or her life interest redeemed.
10   *Re Sullivan, Dunkley v Sullivan* [1930] 1 Ch 84 (where by disclaiming a life interest under the will, the widow avoided the effect of a provision in the will that royalties should be treated as capital, and was held entitled to receive them as income under her life interest as on an intestacy); see AEA 1925, s 33(5), which, in effect, excludes the rules in *Howe v Earl of Dartmouth* (1802) 7 Ves 137 from the administration of an intestate's estate: see Chapter 38.
11   *Re Thornber, Crabtree v Thornber* [1937] Ch 29, [1936] 2 All ER 1594 (where the will directed accumulation of the surplus income of his residuary estate for the benefit of his children: this provision failed because he had no children and, there being a partial intestacy as to such surplus income, not only the gift to children failed but the direction for accumulation also).

[104.14]
Deaths on or after 1 January 1996. The hotchpot provisions referred to above do not apply and are repealed in relation to deaths on or after 1 January 1996.[1]

1   Law Reform (Succession) Act 1995, s 1(2)(b) and the Schedule.

[104.15]
Surviving spouse with life interest under will. There are two alternative views as to the position where the surviving spouse has under the will a life interest in the whole of the residuary estate but where the reversionary interest is undisposed of. Firstly, it has been held by the Court of Appeal that where in such circumstances the reversionary interests fail, the surviving spouse is not entitled to any further interest during his or her lifetime,[1] the reasoning being that, if the statutory provisions as to intestacy have to be read into the will in substitution for those which have failed,[2] then since the statutory life interest of the surviving spouse will only fall into possession after her death it can only

endure for the benefit of her estate.³ Therefore the surviving spouse has no right to have any reversionary interests under the statute sold and the debts and administration expenses or the statutory legacy (subject to deduction as above stated)⁴ paid out of the proceeds.⁵ The only right of the surviving spouse is that his or her personal representative shall receive on his or her death the personal chattels (if not already received under the terms of the will) and the statutory legacy (subject to deduction as above stated) with interest as from the death of the testator. However this authority has not been followed in a subsequent case⁶ where a widow was given a life interest in the estate but where there was no provision thereafter. It was held that the effect of the will and the statutory charge was to give the widow the right to the benefit of the charge and the right to the income; she therefore had an interest which was immediate and was entitled to be paid the statutory legacy forthwith.⁷

1   *Re McKee, Public Trustee v McKee* [1931] 2 Ch 145.
2   See para **[104.13]**, n 10.
3   If it is a case where on intestacy the surviving spouse takes the whole estate, then it would appear that his or her interest in reversion would merge with his or her life interest and he or she would be absolutely entitled to the whole at once.
4   See the provision (i) in para **[104.13]** supra.
5   The rules in *Howe v Earl of Dartmouth* (1802) 7 Ves 137; *Re Chesterfield's (Earl) Trusts* (1883) 24 Ch D 643, do not apply: *Re McKee, Public Trustee v McKee* [1931] 2 Ch 145. For these rules, see Chapter 38.
6   *Re Bowen-Buscarlet's Will Trusts, Nathan v Bowen-Buscarlet* [1972] Ch 463, [1971] 3 All ER 636.
7   Goff J felt at liberty to reconsider the question and not to follow *Re McKee, Public Trustee v McKee* [1931] 2 Ch 145, for the following reasons: firstly, because that particular point was not fully argued before the Court of Appeal; secondly, because the widow's position on a partial intestacy had been modified since that decision by the Intestates' Estates Act 1952, adding s 49(1)(aa) which requires the widow to bring into account an actuarial valuation of her life interest, rather than the actual value at her death; thirdly, because the decision in *Re McKee, Public Trustee v McKee* [1931] 2 Ch 145, had not been followed in *Re Douglas's Will Trusts, Lloyds Bank Ltd v Nelson* [1959] 2 All ER 620, where it was held that the widow was entitled to immediate payment of the statutory legacy. The abolition of hotchpot (see para **[104.14]** supra) will strengthen the case for immediate payment in future cases.

Family provision

CHAPTER 105

Family provision

[105.1]
Restriction of testamentary disposition. The complete freedom of testamentary disposition which had for a long time been a characteristic of English law was limited by the Inheritance (Family Provision) Act 1938.[1] An analogous jurisdiction was conferred by the Matrimonial Causes Act 1965, ss 26–28A[2] with respect to former spouses. Both of these Acts were repealed by the Inheritance (Provision for Family and Dependants) Act 1975[3] which now governs the situation where a dependant claims that the disposition of the deceased's estate fails to make adequate provision for him or her. The main changes were: the categories of applicant were extended, in particular so that a person maintained by the deceased at his death may make application; a surviving spouse was enabled to receive the same standard of provision as on divorce; and the property available from which provision can be made was extended to include certain property given inter vivos and property passing on the death of the deceased other than under his will. The first major amendment to it has been the addition of cohabitees to the categories of claimant, in relation to deaths on or after 1 January 1996.[4]

1   13 *Halsbury's Statutes* (3rd edn) 118. The Inheritance (Family Provision) Act 1938, as amended, still governs deaths before 1 April 1976.
2   17 *Halsbury's Statutes* (3rd edn) 197.
3   17 *Halsbury's Statutes* (4th edn) 504. Set out in Vol 2, Part G, para **[247.28]**. See the *Law Commission's Second Report on Family Property: Family Provision on Death* (Law Com no 61).
4   By virtue of amendments made by the Law Reform (Succession) Act 1995, s 2, following recommendations made in Law Com no 187. See para **[105.13]** et seq. The Act has also been amended by the Family Law Act 1996.

I.   THE JURISDICTION

[105.2]
Basic provision. Where after the commencement of the Inheritance (Provision for Family and Dependants) Act 1975 (I(PFD)A 1975) (1 April 1976) a deceased is survived by one of the specified class of persons, that person may apply to the court for various orders on the ground that the disposition of the deceased's estate effected by his will (including codicils) or the law relating to intestacy or the combination of his will and that law is not such as to make reasonable financial provision for the applicant.[1]

1   I(PFD)A 1975, s 1(1).

[105.3]

Intestacy. It will be noticed that the I(PFD)A 1975 also applies in cases of intestacy. Where the deceased's only dependants are his wife and children the rules of intestate succession are likely to ensure adequate provision, but they will not normally do so where he leaves dependants who can claim provision under the I(PFD)A 1975 by being in the new category of persons who can so claim by virtue of being maintained by the deceased immediately before his death.[1]

1 See *Re B* [2000] 1 All ER 665, CA, successful claim by a mother against her minor daughters intestate estate. See also the successful applications by a child of the family against intestate estates in *Re Leach, Leach v Lindeman* [1986] Ch 226, [1985] 2 All ER 754; and *Re Callaghan* [1985] Fam 1, [1984] 3 All ER 790.

[105.4]

The court. The Law Commission[1] recommended that the jurisdiction to hear family provision applications should be transferred to the Family Division, but this recommendation was not enacted. Instead applications in the High Court under the Act are assigned to the Chancery Division or the Family Division (the choice is the applicant's subject to transfer to the other division at a later stage if appropriate), and there is a code of procedure common to both divisions.[2] Although the County Court has unlimited jurisdiction;[3] a claim of which the value[4] is within the jurisdictional limits of the County Court should be heard there; and one of which the value exceeds that jurisdiction should be heard in the High Court, unless the court considering whether to transfer the proceedings decides otherwise having regard to certain criteria laid down in the legislation.[5] Applications in the High Court under the I(PFD)A 1975 are now frequently heard and disposed of by Masters or District Judges.[6]

1 Law Com no 61.
2 RSC Order 99, SI 1976/337. See *Practice Direction* [1976] 2 All ER 447. As to transfers between courts see County Courts Act 1984, ss 40,41 and 42 and County Court. See also the Civil Procedure Rules as to case management.
3 County Courts Act 1984, s 25, as amended by the High Court and County Courts Jurisdiction Order 1991 (SI 1991/724).
4 Ie the amount the applicant reasonably expects to recover or could reasonably state to be the financial worth of the claim to him (it is not clear which): SI 1991/724, art 9(1).
5 See SI 1991/724, art 7. The criteria relevant to transfer between courts are laid down in art 7(5), and include whether the action is of importance to persons who are not parties or raises questions of general public interest, the complexity of the facts, legal issues, remedies, or procedures involved, and whether transfer will bring a more speedy trial.
6 See *Practice Direction* [1978] 2 All ER 167, [1978] 1 WLR 585.

[105.5]

Time for application. Applications under the I(PFD)A 1975 should be made before the end of the period of six months from the date on which representation in regard to the estate of the deceased is first taken out.[1] The six months period was also applicable under the Inheritance (Family Provision) Act 1938 and some of the decisions on that Act might still assist under the I(PFD)A 1975. Thus it was decided that the six month period ran from the date of the grant of probate in common form and that no further period was initiated by a subsequent grant in solemn form.[2] If a grant of administration was revoked and a grant of probate made, the period ran from the date of the grant of probate.[3] Provided the originating summons was issued within six months, it was immaterial that it was not served within that time.[4] The court had power to order provision to be made as from a future date and could direct that the summons should stand over until a given date with liberty to all parties to apply in the meantime if circumstances should so require.[5] The court has however power to permit applications to be made after six months.[6] The circumstances in which the court will permit an application for financial provision under the I(PFD)A 1975, to be made out of time, were considered in *Re Salmon*.[7] In that case permission to apply out of time under the I(PFD)A 1975, s 4 was refused for the following reasons; first, the delay was substantial and was wholly the applicant's fault; second, there had been no negotiations with, and no warning to, the executor during the six months period; third, almost all the estate had been distributed; fourth, the applicant probably had a remedy in negligence against her solicitors: fifth, it would in the circumstances have been unjust to the beneficiaries to grant the extension.

A similar application was also dismissed in *Re Dennis*,[8] where the court thought that a crucial factor in such cases was whether the applicant was able to satisfy the court that he had an arguable case that he was entitled to reasonable financial provision out of the estate.

1   I(PFD)A 1975, s 4; which must mean time begins to run from the date on which effective or valid representation was first taken out; *Re Freeman* [1984] 3 All ER 906, [1980] 1 WLR 1419 (probate revoked and letters of administration granted). In *Re Johnson* [1987] CLY 3882 it was held that time ran under the I(PFD)A 1975, s 4, not from the date of a limited grant, but from the date of the general grant.
2   *Re Miller, Miller v de Courcey* [1968] 3 All ER 844, [1969] 1 WLR 583.
3   *Re Bidie, Bidie v General Accident, Fire and Life Assurance Corpn Ltd* [1949] Ch 121, [1948] 2 All ER 995.
4   *Re Chittenden, Chittenden v Doe* [1970] 3 All ER 562, [1970] 1 WLR 1618.
5   *Re Franks, Franks v Franks* [1948] Ch 62, [1947] 2 All ER 638.
6   Recognised as a power of the court in the I(PFD)A 1975, s 4.
7   *Re Salmon, Coard v National Westminster Bank Ltd* [1981] Ch 167, [1980] 3 All ER 532. For cases on the Inheritance (Family Provision) Act 1938, s 2(1A) see the previous edition of this work.
8   *Re Dennis, Dennis v Lloyds Bank Ltd* [1981] 2 All ER 140. See also *Re Longley* [1981] CLY 2885 and *Re Gonin, Gonin v Garmeson* [1979] Ch 16, sub nom *Re Gonin, Gonin v Garmeson* [1977] 2 All ER 720 (where the delay was two and a half years and permission was refused since the vital dates were under the control of the plaintiff). Extensions were granted in *Stock v Brown* [1994] 2 FCR 1125 (applicant had no independent advice and there was no prejudice to other beneficiaries; *Re W (a minor)* [1995] 2 FCR 689 (child would otherwise suffer); *Re C* [1995] 2 FLR 24; (substantial estate and very strong claim); *Re W (a minor)* [1995] 2 FCR 689; *Re Abram* [1996] 2 FLR 379 (six months late) and in *Re B* [2000] 1 All ER 665 (court of appeal followed exercise of discretion by master and judge).

[105.6]
Death of applicant. Where the applicant dies after commencing an action under the I(PFD)A 1975, the cause of action is not enforceable by the deceased applicant's personal representatives and the originating summons will be struck out.[1]

1   *Re R, R v O* [1986] Fam Law 58. To the same effect see *Whyte v Ticehurst* [1986] Fam 64, [1986] 2 All ER 158. The cause of action under the 1975 Act was personal to the applicant so that on the death of both parties to the marriage the right to claim against the deceased's spouse's estate ceased to exist. Followed in *Re Bramwell, Campbell v Tobin* [1988] 2 FLR 263, [1988] Fam Law 391. Where the applicant died after the award had been made but before an appeal could be heard, the order stood *Smith v Smith* [1991] 2 All ER 306.

[105.7]

Domicile. The I(PFD)A 1975 only applies to the estates of deceased persons dying domiciled in England and Wales.[1]

1   I(PFD)A 1975, s 1(1). The I(PFD)A 1975 does not extend to Scotland or Northern Ireland, s 27(2). The onus is on the applicant to prove this domicile: *Mastaka v Midland Bank Executor and Trustee Co Ltd* [1941] Ch 192, sub nom *Re White, Mastaka v Midland Bank Executor and Trustee Co Ltd* [1941] 1 All ER 236.

[105.8]

Forfeiture Act 1982. It would seem that in cases to which the Forfeiture Act 1982 does not apply,[1] a person who is precluded by the rule of public policy from benefiting under the deceased's will or intestacy, because that person was responsible for the unlawful killing of the deceased, would likewise be unable to apply under the I(PFD)A 1975 for provision out of the estate.[2] This is because the absence of reasonable financial provision for such a person stems not from the deceased's will or intestacy but solely by the operation of the rule of public policy.[3] The Forfeiture Act 1982 expressly provides in s 3 that the forfeiture rule shall not be taken to preclude any application under the I(PFD)A 1975.[4] At first sight this would seem to enable successful applications by persons subject to the public policy rule to be brought under the I(PFD)A 1975. However there are indications in *Re Royse*[5] that this would not necessarily be the case since such persons would still not be able to satisfy the preconditions in the I(PFD)A 1975, s 2.[6] A preliminary application invoking the jurisdiction under the Forfeiture Act 1982[6] may be necessary to enable an application to be made under the I(PFD)A 1975 alleging that the will or intestacy fails to make reasonable financial provision for the application.[7]

1   The Forfeiture Act 1982 came into operation on 13 October 1982.
2   *Re Royse, Royse v Royse* [1985] Ch 22, [1984] 3 All ER 339, applicant convicted of the manslaughter of her husband in 1979. Furthermore the alternative of applying for relief under the Forfeiture Act 1982 was not open to her since the Act was not in force when she commenced proceedings and the time bar in s 2(3) was fatal to any application under the Forfeiture Act 1982.
3   *Re Royse, Royse v Royse* [1985] Ch 22, [1984] 3 All ER 339.
4   Forfeiture Act 1982, s 3(2)(a). It is noticeable that the section does not expressly amend the I(PFD)A 1975, s 2 which is strictly necessary if the problem discussed here is to be avoided. This point has been more fully discussed, para **[9.19]** supra.
5   *Re Royse, Royse v Royse* [1985] Ch 22, [1984] 3 All ER 339; see Ackner LJ at 343; Slade LJ at 344, 345. Ie that the failure to provide reasonable provision is due to the will or the intestacy provisions, and not simply consequential to the operation of the forfeiture rule.
6   As to which see para **[9.19]** supra. An order modifying the effects of the rule so that the beneficiary is not disentitled to his or her testate or intestate share and can thus point to that entitlement as inadequate.
7   If this is correct then the Forfeiture Act 1982, s 3 has a limited scope.

II.   THE APPLICANTS

[105.9]

The spouse. The specified class of persons who have locus standi to apply under the I(PFD)A 1975 includes 'the wife or husband of the deceased'.[1] The applicant would thus have to prove that he or she was the deceased's spouse under a subsisting marriage at the date of the death. A judicially separated spouse can apply under this heading but provision is limited to maintenance.[2] Also included is a person who, in good faith, entered into a void marriage with the deceased, unless either the marriage of the deceased and that person was dissolved or annulled during the lifetime of the deceased, or that person has during the lifetime of the deceased entered into a later marriage.[3] Likewise, a party to a voidable marriage which has not been annulled before the death of the party is included.[4] In *Re Sehota, Surjit Kaur v Gian Kaur,*[5] the deceased had contracted two marriages at a time when all parties concerned had had Indian domiciles of origin and both marriages were valid under Indian law. The deceased had left the whole of his residuary estate to his second wife and it was held that the first wife was entitled to claim under the I(PFD)A 1975 despite the fact that the marriage was polygamous.

The I(PFD)A 1975 makes an important change in the law so far as the standard of provision for a spouse is concerned. The Inheritance (Family Provision) Act 1938 set the standard of 'reasonable provision for the maintenance' of the applicant, whereas in divorce proceedings the court is not limited to any such standard.[6]

The Law Commission[7] recommended that the surviving spouse should have a claim upon the family assets at least equivalent to that of a divorced spouse. Accordingly, the I(PFD)A 1975, s 1(2)(a) provides:

'In this Act "reasonable financial provision"—
(a) in the case of an application made by virtue of subsection (1)(a) above by the husband or wife of the deceased (except where the marriage with the deceased was the subject of a decree of judicial separation and at the date of death the decree was in force and the separation was continuing), means such financial provision as it would be reasonable in all the circumstances of the case for a husband or wife to receive, whether or not that provision is required for his or her maintenance.'

The court is instructed to have regard to what provision would have been awarded in divorce proceedings,[8] but this is not to be regarded as the sole criterion. The overriding consideration is what is reasonable in the circumstances.[9] Further it has been pointed out in a later case that the amount that might be awarded under the Matrimonial Causes Act 1973 is not analogous to the position on death, since an award under the former would have to take into account the husband's likely future needs.[10] Nevertheless this stated requirement of the Act in determining the level of provision for a surviving spouse, has been applied by the Court of Appeal. The intention of the Act was that the acceptable minimum posthumous provision for a surviving spouse should correspond as closely as possible to the inchoate rights enjoyed by that spouse during the deceased's lifetime under matrimonial law.[11]

1 I(PFD)A 1975, s 1(1)(a).
2 I(PFD)A 1975, s 1(2)(a).
3 I(PFD)A 1975, s 25(4).
4 Law Com no 62, p 8.
5 *Re Sehota Surjit Kaur v Gian Kaur* [1978] 3 All ER 385, [1978] 1 WLR 1506.
6 Matrimonial Causes Act 1973, ss 23–25, and see *Wachtel v Wachtel* [1973] Fam 72, [1973] 1 All ER 829.
7 Law Com no 61, p 8.
8 I(PFD)A 1975, s 3(2).

9   *Re Besterman* [1984] Ch 458, [1984] 2 All ER 656 where, in the case of a very large estate
where the testator's only obligation was to his widow who was wholly blameless and incapable
of supporting herself, reasonable financial provision required that she should have access to a
sufficient lump sum to ensure beyond any reasonable doubt that she was relieved of any anxiety
for the future; capital sum of £378,000 awarded.
10 *Re Bunning, Bunning v Salmon* [1984] Ch 480, [1984] 3 All ER 1, wife not limited to the
amount she might have received under the Matrimonial Causes Act 1973 but given a lump sum
award giving her roughly half the spouse's total assets; see *Re Rowlands* [1984] Fam Law 280
(small award); *Stead v Stead* [1985] Fam Law 154; *Rajabally v Rajabally* [1987] 2 FLR 390;
Davis v Davis [1993] 1 FLR 54. See also *Re Krubert* [1997] Ch 97 where the approach in *Re
Besterman* [1984] Ch 458, [1984] 2 All ER 656 which minimised the relevance of the 'divorce
standard' was preferred to the approach in *Moody v Stevenson* [1992] Ch 486, sub nom *Re
Moody, Moody v Stevenson* [1992] 2 All ER 524 which emphasised the relevance of the
'divorce standard'.
11 *Moody v Stevenson* [1992] Ch 486, sub nom *Re Moody, Moody v Stevenson* [1992] 2 All ER
524 (widower awarded a settlement of the matrimonial home to enable him to continue living in
the house as long as he was willing and able to do so).

[105.10]

A former spouse. A 'former wife or husband of the deceased' who has not
remarried can apply.[1] Such a person was defined originally by the I(PFD)A 1975
as a person whose marriage with the deceased was during the deceased's
lifetime dissolved or annulled by a decree of divorce or of nullity of marriage
under the Matrimonial Causes Act 1973.[2] This definition excluded persons
whose marriages had been dissolved by alternative jurisdictions and the
Matrimonial and Family Proceedings Act 1984[3] redefines the category to
include a person whose marriage was dissolved or annulled 'under the law of
any part of the British Isles'[4] or in any country or territory outside the British
Isles by a divorce or annulment 'which is entitled to be recognised as valid by
the law of England and Wales'.[5]

'Remarriage' includes a marriage which is by law void or voidable and
includes a marriage where in relation to any party thereto his or her previous
marriage was void or voidable.

The I(PFD)A 1975 follows the Inheritance (Family Provision) Act 1938 by
setting the standard of provision for a former spouse or a judicially separated
spouse as 'such financial provision as it would be reasonable in all the
circumstances of the case for the applicant to receive for his maintenance'.[6] It
has been said that there will be few cases where an application under the
I(PFD)A 1975 by a divorced spouse for financial provision out of the former
spouse's estate, will be successful. The reasons for this have been explained by
the Court of Appeal in *Re Fullard, Fullard v King.*[7] First, the Family Court has
wide powers under the Matrimonial Causes Act 1973 to make orders affecting
the property of the parties on divorce and these orders are likely to pre-empt an
application under the I(PFD)A 1975. Second, where the deceased's estate is
small, the former spouse has a heavy onus of showing that inadequate
testamentary or intestate provision has been made. Third, the fact of divorce and
the financial arrangements made on the divorce are relevant matters for the court
to have regard to under the I(PFD)A 1975, s 3(1)(g) and where the financial and
property matters have been settled on divorce with legal advice, some
exceptional developments or conditions present at the death will need to be
shown, if an application is to be successful.

The circumstances in which an application by a former spouse might be
successful include the case where a long period has elapsed since the dissolution

of the marriage during which time the deceased has had a continuing responsibility for the maintenance of the former spouse, and on the death, the deceased is shown to have appreciable capital. Another possible case is where the death unlocks a substantial capital sum. But a mere accretion of wealth by the deceased spouse since the divorce would not of itself justify an application by a former spouse.[8]

1   I(PFD)A 1975, s 1(1)(b).
2   I(PFD)A 1975, s 25(1).
3   Matrimonial and Family Proceedings Act 1984, s 25(2), substituting a new s 25(1) and inserting a new s 15A in the I(PFD)A 1975.
4   Matrimonial and Family Proceedings Act 1984, s 25(2)(a); see n 3 supra.
5   Matrimonial and Family Proceedings Act 1984, s 25(2)(b); see n 3 supra.
6   I(PFD)A 1975, s 1(2)(b). However, exceptionally, where a party to a marriage dies within twelve months of a decree of divorce of nullity or judicial separation being made and no final order for financial provision has been made by the Family Court, then the court may apply the standard applicable to claims by a surviving spouse: s 14(1).
7   [1982] Fam 42, [1981] 2 All ER 796, where the application failed. See also *Re Crawford* (1982) 4 FLR 273; *Brill v Proud* [1984] Fam Law 59 and *Re O'Rourke* [1997] 1 FCR 188 (unsuccessful claim by a former spouse—no moral claim).
8   *Re Fullard, Fullard v King* [1982] Fam 42, [1981] 2 All ER 796. *In Re Farrow* [1987] 1 FLR 205, [1987] Fam Law 14 a former spouse made a successful application for provision out of her deceased former husband's estate. The parties obtained a decree nisi in 1973 but financial provision (£50,000 lump sum and £5,500 per annum periodical payments) was not finalised until 1978. Former husband died in 1979 intestate, and his considerable estate, which consisted mainly of a farm, was inherited by the two sons of the marriage. The former wife was awarded a lump sum of £15,000 to take account of the fact that for some seven years she was without periodical payments, and £5,500 per annum on the basis that there had been no 'clean break'. *Re Fullard, Fullard v King* [1982] Fam 42, [1981] 2 All ER 796 was distinguished on this ground.

[105.11]
Section 15 orders. It is possible for restriction orders to be imposed in divorce proceedings on future applications by the former spouse, under the I(PFD)A 1975. The original provision in the I(PFD)A 1975, s 15 enabled such orders to be made if the court considered it just to do so and if the parties to the marriage agreed. A new section has been substituted for the original s 15(1) by the Matrimonial and Family Proceedings Act 1984, s 8 which dispenses with the requirement of consent and states that an order precluding an application under the I(PFD)A 1975 can be made by a court on the grant of a decree of divorce, a decree of nullity of marriage, or a decree of judicial separation or at any time thereafter, if the court considers it just to do so on the application of either party to the marriage.[1] Further the Matrimonial and Family Proceedings Act 1984 adds, by s 25(3), a new s 15A to the I(PFD)A 1975 enabling the court to make a similar restrictive order in relation to an overseas divorce.[2]

1   The jurisdiction to make such orders was considered in *Whiting v Whiting* [1988] 2 All ER 275, [1988] 1 WLR 565. The Court of Appeal stated that the court had a duty under the I(PFD)A 1975, s 15(1) to consider whether it was 'just' to make an order depriving a divorced spouse of any opportunity to claim financial provision from the estate of the other spouse. In this case the court declined to make such an order because no evidence had been submitted of what the estate was likely to consist of or of the details of persons whom the applicant for the s 15 order might consider to have a prior claim to the estate on death.
2   Pursuant to an application under the Matrimonial and Family Proceedings Act 1984, s 17.

[105.12]
Administration of Justice Act 1982. The effect of the Wills Act 1837, s 18A[1] is to cause testamentary gifts to spouses who are subsequently divorced etc, to fail.[2] It is expressly stated that the effect of the provision is without prejudice to the right of the former spouse to apply for financial provision under the I(PFD)A 1975.[3]

1   Added by the Administration of Justice Act 1982, s 18(2) with effect from 1 January 1983; see para **[47.2]** ante.
2   Wills Act 1837, s 18A(1). In relation to deaths before 1 January 1996 such a gift is deemed to lapse, for deaths on or after that date s 18A(1) is amended by Law Reform (Succession) Act 1995, s 3 so that the former spouse is deemed to have died when the marriage was dissolved or annulled. This makes a difference to the operation of alternative gifts: see para **[47.2]** supra.
3   Wills Act 1837, s 18A(2).

[105.13]
Applications by cohabitees – deaths on or after 1 January 1996. A new category of applicant is added, in relation to persons dying on or after 1 January 1996, by the Law Reform (Succession) Act 1995.[1] A person is within this category of claimant if he or she is not the spouse or unremarried former spouse of the deceased and, during the whole of the period of two years preceding the deceased's death, he or she lived in the same household as the deceased and as the husband or wife of the deceased.[2]

The 'living as husband and wife' formula can be found in a number of other statutes,[3] and there is some case law on it.[4] A question which could arise in practice, particularly where the applicant and the deceased were elderly, is whether sexual intercourse must be proved (i) at some stage in the history of the relationship or (ii) during the two years preceding the deceased's death, for the applicant to qualify as falling in this category. It is submitted that the presence or absence of sexual relations will be an important but not decisive factor, along with other factors,[5] although it will be an unusual case (eg where there was physical incapacity) where an applicant is held to fall into this category and there is no history of a sexual relationship at all. That there should have been sexual intercourse during the two years before the deceased's death is fairly clearly not a requirement. For example, if the applicant and the deceased had had a sexual relationship, but sexual intercourse had ceased more than two years before the deceased's death as a result of age or illness, they could still be regarded as living together as husband and wife during the two years preceding the deceased's death.[6] A person of the same sex as the deceased, and a brother or sister of the deceased, will be ruled out as a claimant in this category, even if there have been sexual relations.[7]

The standard of provision for persons falling into this category is 'maintenance' rather than 'what it is reasonable for a husband or wife to receive'.[8]

Where it is not certain that an applicant was living with the deceased as his or her wife or husband, the case may be put in the alternative that the applicant qualifies for an order for provision under the I(PFD)A 1975 as someone who was wholly or partly maintained by the deceased[9] (if there is evidence to support such a claim), and it will be necessary to rely on the latter ground where the applicant and the deceased were together for less than two years preceding the deceased's death (or the applicant is of the same sex as or a sibling of the deceased). This new category of cohabitee applicants was introduced on the recommendations of the Law Commission to deal with the problems of proving dependence which sometimes arose in claims by cohabitees.[10]

1 See the I(PFD)A 1975, ss 1(1)(ba), (1A) and 3(2A), as inserted by Law Reform (Succession) Act 1995, s 2, and printed in Vol 2, Part G, paras **[247.2]** and **[247.4]**.

2 I(PFD)A 1975, s 1(1)(ba), (1A). See *Re Watson* [1999] 1 FLR 878, the test of living in the same household is objective.

3 Eg Fatal Accidents Act 1976, s 1(3)(b) (which was added to that Act for the first time by Administration of Justice Act 1982, s 3); Social Security Contributions and Benefits Act 1992, s 137, definition of 'unmarried couple'; Housing Act 1985, s 113; Domestic Violence and Matrimonial Proceedings Act 1976, s 1(2).

4 See the first case reported on the I(PFD)A 1975, s 1(1A), *Re Watson* [1999] 1 FLR 878; the correct approach is to ask whether a reasonable person with normal perceptions would regard them as having lived together as man and wife bearing in mind the multifarious nature pf marital relations. For cases on other statutes see *Adeoso v Adeoso* [1981] 1 All ER 107 (a case on Domestic Violence and Matrimonial Proceedings Act 1976, s 1); *Crake v Supplementary Benefits Commission* [1982] 1 All ER 498; *Westminster City Council v Peart* (1991) 24 HLR 389 (a case on the Housing Act 1985, s 113(1)).

5 For a summary of the practice in social security cases see *Crake v Supplementary Benefits Commission* [1982] 1 All ER 498 at 505f–h. See also *Thomas v Thomas* [1948] 2 KB 294 at 297.

6 See the remarks in *Crake v Supplementary Benefits Commission* [1982] 1 All ER 498 at 502g–h.

7 See *Fitzpatrick v Sterling Housing Association* [1998] Ch 304.

8 Ie I(PFD)A 1975, s 1(2)(b) applies. See para **[105.9]** supra, and contrast the provision for spouses discussed on para **[105.9]** supra.

9 Ie that he or she falls within the I(PFD)A 1975, s 1(1)(e). See para **[105.16]** infra.

10 *Distribution on Intestacy* (Law Com no 187). For the problems which have arisen see para **[105.16]** infra.

[105.14]

Applications by children. Under the Inheritance (Family Provision) Act 1938 children of the deceased who could apply for provision were limited to unmarried and disabled daughters and minor and disabled sons. The definition of 'son' and 'daughter' included both adopted and illegitimate children as well as posthumous children of the deceased. The I(PFD)A 1975 refers simply to 'a child of the deceased'.[1] This removes the age limit and any distinction between married and unmarried children and the relevance of any disability, so far as locus standi is concerned. 'Child' includes an illegitimate child and a child en ventre sa mère at the time of the death of the deceased.[2] The standard of provision for children is limited to 'such financial provision as it would be reasonable in all the circumstances of the case for the applicant to receive for his maintenance'.[3] What is proper 'maintenance' depends on all the facts and circumstances of the case[4] but it has been said that it connotes only payments which would directly or indirectly enable the applicant to discharge the recurring costs of his living expenses.[5] It has been stated that it is not the law that an adult child has to show exceptional circumstances to justify an award.[6] The element of mere obligation has been referred to as a criterion for determining whether a child should succeed in an application.[7] The case *Re Collins*,[8] decides three points relevant to applications by children. First, a child who may have been qualified to apply for family provision ceases to be so qualified if he is subsequently adopted by another person before the application is made.[9] Second, in considering a claim under the I(PFD)A 1975 the court may take into account the wishes of the deceased expressed before death including any indications of his intentions in an invalid will. Third, any receipts of social security benefits by the applicant are to be disregarded in considering the applicant's financial resources.[10]

1   I(PFD)A 1975, s 1(1)(c).
2   I(PFD)A 1975, s 25(1).
3   I(PFD)A 1975, s 1(2)(b).
4   *Re Coventry, Coventry v Coventry* [1980] Ch 461, [1979] 3 All ER 815 where an able-bodied 46-year-old son did not succeed in an application. The mere fact that it would have been reasonable for the deceased to make some provision was not sufficient; the applicant had to establish a moral claim to be maintained over and above the claim of a blood relationship. Not following *Re Christie, Christie v Keeble* [1979] Ch 168, [1979] 1 All ER 546. *Re Coventry* was followed in *Re Jennings* [1994] Ch 286, [1994] 3 All ER 27 in which the deceased's failure to support his son during his infancy was not of itself sufficient to justify an award. (See also *Harlow v National Westminster Bank* (3 January 1994, unreported), Fam D). But a successful claim was made by an adult son against his father's estate in *Re Goodchild* [1997] 3 All ER 63 where the award was justified on the basis of 'exceptional circumstances' arising from the fact that his parents had made similar (though not mutual) wills under which the son was the ultimate beneficiary of the joint estate, a consideration which was held to give rise to a 'moral obligation' to the son. See also *Re Abram* [1996] 2 FLR 379 where an application by a grown-up son succeeded. Likewise *Re Pearce* [1998] 2 FLR 705. In the following two cases on applications under para (d) as a 'child of the family' a more generous approach was also adopted: *Re Callaghan* [1985] Fam 1, [1984] 3 All ER 790, and *Re Leach, Leach v Lindeman* [1986] Ch 226, [1985] 2 All ER 754.
5   *Re Dennis, Dennis v Lloyds Bank Ltd* [1981] 2 All ER 140 where an adult son failed in an application for payment of tax out of the father's estate. The application was also out of time, see para **[105.5]** supra.
6   *Re Hancock (sub nom Snapes v Aram)* [1998] 2 FLR 346 (successful application by an adult daughter); *Re Debenham* [1986] 1 FLR 404, adult epileptic daughter received an award of £3,000 capital plus a periodical payments order of £4,500. Contrast *Williams v Johns* [1988] 2 FLR 475 where a claim by an adult daughter who had been delinquent, was refused. Claims succeeded in *Re Pearce* [1998] 2 FLR 705 (adult son) and *Espinosa v Bourke* [1999] 1 FLR 747 (adult daughter).
7   *Re Hancock*, sub nom *Snapes v Aram* [1998] 2 FLR 346.
8   [1990] Fam 56, [1990] 2 All ER 47.
9   This is consistent with the view taken in *Whyte v Ticehurst* [1986] Fam 64, [1986] 2 All ER 158, that the claim is neither an indefeasible right nor an interest expectant.
10   This is consistent with the view taken in *Re E, E v E* [1966] 2 All ER 44, [1966] 1 WLR 709, on a comparable point under the Inheritance (Family Provision) Act 1938.

[105.15]
Child of the family. The I(PFD)A 1975 includes a category of 'any person (not being a child of the deceased) who, in the case of any marriage to which the deceased was at any time a party, was treated by the deceased as a child of the family in relation to that marriage'.[1] This provision has been fully considered by the Court of Appeal in *Re Leach*[2] and at first instance in *Re Callaghan*.[3] The following points emerge. First, there is no doubt that an adult child can qualify. Second, the relevant treatment is the behaviour of the deceased towards the potential applicant. Third, the treatment must 'stem from' the marriage and the treatment of any applicant by a surviving spouse after the death of the other spouse may be relevant. Fourth, the mere display of affection, kindness or hospitality by a step-parent towards a step-child is not sufficient to bring the child within the section; what is needed is proof that the deceased has, as wife or husband, or widow or widower, under the relevant marriage, expressly or impliedly, assumed the position of a parent towards the applicant, with the attendant responsibilities and privileges of that relationship.[4] There is evidence

of a more generous judicial attitude to the sort of awards that can be made in such cases. In *Leach*[5] the Court of Appeal awarded a lump sum of £14,000, being approximately one-half of the net value of the residuary estate. In *Callaghan*[6] the award was a lump sum of £15,000 (again being approximately one-half of the net estate), that being the sum needed by the applicant to enable him to purchase his own house.[7]

1   I(PFD)A 1975, s 1(1)(d); analogous to the Matrimonial Causes Act 1973, ss 23 and 52(1), see Slade LJ in *Re Leach, Leach v Lindeman* [1986] Ch 226, [1985] 2 All ER 754.
2   *Re Leach, Leach v Lindeman* [1986] Ch 226, [1985] 2 All ER 754.
3   *Re Callaghan* [1985] Fam 1, [1984] 3 All ER 790.
4   Per Slade LJ in *Re Leach, Leach v Lindeman* [1986] Ch 226, [1985] 2 All ER 754. In that case a 55-year-old spinster obtained an award against her deceased step-mother's estate despite the fact that she had never lived in her deceased step-mother's household and was never maintained either wholly or partly by her. The factors in her favour were that there was evidence that the deceased had intended to make a will in the daughter's favour and that much of the step-mother's estate derived from the daughter's father. In *Re Callaghan* [1985] Fam 1, [1984] 3 All ER 790, a 47-year-old married step-son obtained an award against his deceased step-father's estate despite the fact that during the time the son lived with his mother and step-father the parties were not married. They married subsequent to the son's own marriage and he never lived with them as a married couple. After the mother's death, the son and his wife cared for the step-father during his serious illness. See also *Re A (child of the family)* [1998] 1 FLR 347 (grandchild) and *Carr v Carr* (23 June 1997, unreported), QBD, HHJ Roger Cooke (right of step daughter to adjourn claim).
5   Intestacy, and the deceased's brothers and sisters who had no strong moral claim, were the next of kin.
6   Intestacy, and deceased's sisters were next of kin. But can either award be strictly justified on the basis of 'such financial provision as it would be reasonable in all the circumstances of the case for the applicant to receive for his maintenance'? *Re Coventry* [1980] Ch 461, [1979] 3 All ER 815, was not discussed in detail. Although that case can clearly be distinguished, small estate and contest between a son and a spouse, the judicial attitude to the claims seems different.
7   In *Re Basham* [1987] 1 All ER 405, [1986] 1 WLR 1498 (discussed at para **[104.1]** supra) a step-daughter successfully claimed the whole of an intestate estate by invoking the principles of proprietary estoppel, thus illustrating an alternative approach to an application under the I(PFD)A 1975. Contrast *Layton v Martin* [1986] 2 FLR 227, [1986] Fam Law 212 where a former cohabitant failed to establish any claim to the estate on the grounds, inter alia, of proprietary estoppel.

[105.16]
Applications by other dependants. The most important extension made by the I(PFD)A 1975 to the categories of applicants who can make applications for provision is the class of applicants defined by s 1(1)(e) as follows 'any person (not being a person included in the foregoing paragraphs of this subsection) who immediately before the death of the deceased was being maintained, either wholly or partly, by the deceased'. This category is further defined in s 1(3) to the effect that 'a person shall be treated as being maintained by the deceased either wholly or partly as the case may be, if the deceased, otherwise than for full valuable consideration, was making a substantial contribution in money or money's worth towards the reasonable needs of that person'. The I(PFD)A 1975, s 3(4) provides that 'without prejudice to the generality of paragraph (g) of subsection (1) above, where an application for an order under section 2 of this Act is made by virtue of section 1(1)(e) of this Act, the court shall, in addition to the matters specifically mentioned in paragraphs (a) to (f) of that subsection, have regard to the extent to which and the basis upon which the deceased

assumed responsibility for the maintenance of the applicant and to the length of time for which the deceased discharged that responsibility'. These provisions have been fully considered in three decisions which provide useful guidance on the applications under paragraph (e).

The first case is the decision of Sir Robert Megarry V-C in *Re Beaumont, Martin v Midland Bank Trust Co Ltd.*[1] The plaintiff, a man who had lived with the deceased as man and wife for 36 years, applied for financial provision out of her estate as a dependant under the I(PFD)A 1975. Sir Robert Megarry V-C, decided that s 1(1)(e) was qualified by both ss 1(3) and 3(4) and that the plaintiff could only claim under that paragraph if he satisfied three conditions. First, it was necessary to show that he was being maintained 'immediately before' the death of the deceased with reference to the degree of maintenance normally and habitually existing under the arrangement. Second, the substantial contributions made towards the reasonable needs of the applicant must have been otherwise than for full valuable consideration which was not restricted to contributions supplied under a contract but extended to any contribution provided for full consideration.[2] Third, it had to be shown that the deceased had demonstrated an undertaking or assumption of responsibility for the applicant. This requirement was held not to have been satisfied on the facts of the case which indicated that the applicant was merely one of two people of independent means who had chosen to pool their individual resources to enable them to live together without either undertaking any responsibility for maintaining the other. The summons was accordingly struck out. The decision in *Re Beaumont*, was subsequently considered by the Court of Appeal in *Jelley v Iliffe*,[3] where a widower had been living with a widow in her house rent-free, for some eight years before her death. The parties had pooled their financial resources to pay living expenses and the widower had provided some furniture for the house, looked after the garden and done household jobs. The deceased widow, by her will, left all her property, including the house, to her children, which was consistent with an understanding she had had with them from whom she had acquired the house. The widower applied under the I(PFD)A 1975, s 1(1) for reasonable financial provision out of the deceased's estate on the ground that immediately before her death he was being maintained by her within s (1)(e) of the Act. The Court of Appeal held that the applicant satisfied the requirements of 'being maintained' in the I(PFD)A 1975, s 1(1)(e) as defined in s 1(3), applying *Re Beaumont*. Further that the fact of maintenance raised a presumption of 'assumed responsibility', and that it was not necessary to show a specific intention to this effect, not following *Re Beaumont*, on this point. In determining whether the deceased's contribution to the applicant's needs had been 'otherwise than for full valuable consideration' the court stated that a balance had to be struck between the benefits received, and those provided, by the applicant. On the facts of the case before them the Court of Appeal thought that the provision of rent-free accommodation was a significant contribution to a person's reasonable needs, particularly in the case of an old-age pensioner. Since it was not clear beyond doubt that the applicant's contribution had equalled or outweighed the benefit of the rent-free accommodation there was an arguable case and the issue was ordered to proceed to trial.

The Court of Appeal considered these cases in the more recent decision in *Bishop v Plumley*[4] where the applicant was the cohabitee of the deceased, living with him as his wife and described as waiting on him 'hand and foot' and doing everything for him. She had enjoyed in return rent-free accommodation in a house that he had purchased with an inheritance. The court thought that there was no difficulty in finding that the deceased had made a substantial contribution towards her reasonable needs. The difficulty centred on whether she had provided full valuable consideration in return and thus disentitled herself from applying under paragraph (e). The court held that she had not, and this aspect of the case is more fully discussed in the next section.

In the most recent case *Re B*[5] the Court of Appeal preferred the approach in *Jelley v Iliffe*[6] to the effect that the fact that one person has made a substantial contribution to another person's needs, in itself raised an inference of an assumption of responsibility for the latter. On that basis a claim by a mother against the intestate estate of her deceased (disabled) daughter succeeded where the Court of Protection had made substantial inter vivos payments to her as her daughter's receiver for the maintenance of the daughter,out of which she also (as mother/carer) had benefited.[7]

1 [1980] Ch 444, [1980] 1 All ER 266. But see *Re B* [2000] 1 All ER 665, CA, discussed above, where the comments in the third heading were doubted.
2 On this requirement see also the confirmation of Sir Robert Megarry V-C's view by the Court of Appeal in *Jelley v Iliffe* [1981] Fam 128, [1981] 2 All ER 29. See also *Kourkgy v Lusher* (1981) 4 FLR 65 where the evidence established that the deceased had abandoned cohabitation and maintenance of the applicant some months before his death, and the claim failed. Likewise in *Layton v Martin* [1986] 2 FLR 227, [1986] Fam Law 212, a former mistress of the deceased whose five-year relationship with him ended two years before his death had no claim to any interest in his property, at law, equity, or under the 1975 Act.
3 [1981] Fam 128, [1981] 1 All ER 29, provision of accommodation held to be a substantial benefit. Likewise in *Re Wilkinson, Neale v Newell* [1978] 1 All ER 221 (sister). See also *Graham v Murphy* [1997] 1 FLR 860; *Rees v Newberry, (sub nom Lankesheer)* [1998] 1 FLR 1041 and *Wayling v Jones* [1995] 2 FLR 1029 (homosexual relationship). *Jelley v Iliffe* [1981] Fam 128, [1981] 2 All ER 29 has been considered in *Kourkgy v Lusher* (1981) 12 Fam Law 86 where a claim by a cohabitee failed, and applied in *Re Kirby* (1982) 11 Fam Law 210. See also *Malone v Harrison* [1979] 1 WLR 1353 on assumption of responsibility and computation of lump sum award; *Harrington v Gill* (1983) 4 FLR 265, cohabitant held entitled to a lump sum and also the deceased's house settled on her for life; *Williams v Roberts* [1984] Fam Law 210 and *Re Watson* [1999] 1 FLR 878 (ten years cohabitation).
4 [1991] 1 All ER 236, [1991] 1 WLR 582. It will be appreciated that this was case, like many of those noted above, of an application by a cohabitee under the I(PFD)A 1975, s 1(1)(e), which would now be brought under s 1(1)(ba); see para **[105.13]** supra.
5 [2000] 1 All ER 665; reversing Jonathan Parker J [1999] 2 All ER 425 who had dismissed the claim. The Court of Appeal emphasised that the 'assumption of responsibility' in the I(PFD)A 1975, s 3(4) was not part of the threshold requirements of s1(1)(e) but was a factor to be taken into account, once the court was satisfied that the applicant had locus standi, in determining the merits of the claim and thus the exercise of the court's discretion. *Jelley v Iliffe* [1981] Fam 128, [1981] 2 All ER 29, was applied; *Re Beaumont, Martin v Midland Bank Trust Co Ltd* [1980] Ch 444, [1980] 1 All ER 266 was doubted. See also *Rees v Newbery and the Institute of Cancer Research* [1998] 1 FLR 1041 (immaterial that the maintenance of the applicant arose through a tenancy agreement)
6 *Jelley v Iliffe* [1981] Fam 128, [1981] 2 All ER 29.
7 The daughter had been severely disabled at birth owing to medical negligence and an award of £250,000 had been made to her. This money was controlled by the Court of Protection which applied it for the benefit and maintenance of the daughter which inevitably also benefited the mother who lived with and cared for the daughter. Thus the daughter had made a substantial provision in money or money's worth for the reasonable needs of the mother within the I(PFD)A 1975, s 1(1)(e) who could claim under that paragraph (as a dependant) against her daughter's estate.

[105.17]
Full valuable consideration. The requirement that the contribution by the deceased should be 'otherwise than for full valuable consideration' has caused difficulties. It was included, no doubt, in an excess of caution, to exclude persons such as live-in servants or housekeepers or occupants of a commercial nursing home, where the provision towards a person's reasonable needs is made pursuant to a contractual obligation. However, the section is not so limited, with the danger that a person who performs services, such as housekeeping or nursing, for the deceased, in return for board and lodgings, could be excluded from the class of persons with locus standi to apply under this paragraph. The requirement also had serious consequences for cohabitees or common law husbands and wives since such a person might perform the multitude of services provided by a husband or wife in return, in many cases, for fairly modest benefits of a material kind provided by the deceased; it has ceased to be a problem in relation to common law husbands or wives who are given a right to apply under the I(PFD)A 1975 where the death is on or after 1 January 1996.[1] When these respective benefits to the deceased were placed in the scales against the contributions received from the deceased, it was likely that the balance would come down to the advantage of the deceased. In other words, the surviving partner might have been taken to have provided full valuable consideration for the contributions received. These anomalies were the more pointed if financial costings were put upon the value of the services provided and the benefits received. The courts were anxious to avoid this consequence and have adopted a generous approach in favour of the applicant to the requirement. The courts may perhaps adopt a more restrictive approach in future in view of the introduction of the new category of cohabitee applicant, ie a person who lived with the deceased as his or her wife or husband.[2]
The first case to consider the effect of the qualification was *Re Wilkinson.*[3] The applicant, at the age of 61 years, left her employment as a housekeeper to live with her sister, the deceased, who was a childless widow. The deceased and the applicant had shared light household duties and the cooking and the deceased had paid all the household expenses. During the last few years of her life the applicant had had to care for and assist her sister with dressing, etc. Arnold J decided that the onus was on the claimant to show that immediately before her death the deceased was making a substantial contribution in money or money's worth towards the claimant's reasonable needs and that the deceased was making that contribution other than as full valuable consideration for the services rendered by the claimant. The sister was able to discharge that onus in the case since the court considered that the services which she performed were not a full valuable requital for the substantial contribution made by the deceased towards the claimant's needs. Accordingly, Arnold J decided that she was a person entitled to claim under the I(PFD)A 1975, s 1(1)(e) for provision out of her sister's estate.
The issue was further considered in *Jelley v Iliffe,*[4] which has been noted in the previous section. The approach adopted there was that the comparison of substantial contribution and full valuable consideration is factual and involves no exercise of discretion. If the flow of benefits from the one to the other is broadly commensurate, full valuable consideration will be demonstrated; if there

is an obvious imbalance in favour of the applicant, he or she will have surmounted the first hurdle.

But Lord Justice Griffiths continued:[5]

'In striking this balance the court must use common sense and remember that the object of Parliament in creating this extra class of persons who may claim benefit from an estate was to provide relief for persons of whom it could truly be said that they were wholly or partially dependent on the deceased. It cannot be an exact exercise of evaluating services in pounds and pence. By way of example, if a man was living with a woman as his wife and providing the house and all the money for their living expenses she would clearly be dependent on him, and it would not be right to deprive her of her claim by arguing that she was in fact performing the services that a housekeeper would perform and it would cost more to employ a housekeeper than was spent on her and indeed perhaps more than the deceased had available to spend on her. Each case will have to be looked at carefully on its own facts to see whether common sense leads to the conclusion that the applicant can fairly be regarded as a dependant.'

This approach was followed in *Bishop v Plumley*[6] where Lord Justice Butler-Sloss thought that one must look at the problem in the round, apply a commonsense approach, and avoid fine balancing computations involving the normal exchange of support in the domestic sense. The conclusion in the case in support of the cohabitee was as follows:

'I do not consider that her evidence that she did everything for him over a period of years can be assessed in isolation from the mutuality of the relationship. If a man or a woman living as man and wife with a partner gives the other extra devoted care and attention, particularly when the partner is in poor health, is he or she to be in a less advantageous position on an application under the Act than one who may be less loving and give less attention to the partner? I do not accept that this could have been the intention of Parliament in passing this legislation. In the case of this applicant, she is now 64, herself in poor health, with no assets, on supplementary benefit from which she is repaying overpayments to the Department of Social Security and, if unsuccessful to this claim, homeless. In that regard, the Registrar found that, although the circumstances of the beneficiaries were modest, the applicant's needs were greater than theirs'.[7]

1   See the I(PFD)A 1975, s 1(1)(ba) and (1A), added by the Law Reform (Succession) Act 1995, s 2, and discussed at para **[105.13]** et seq.
2   See previous note.
3   *Re Wilkinson, Neale v Newell* [1978] Fam 22, [1978] 1 All ER 221. Followed in *Re Viner, Kreeger v Cooper* [1978] CLY 3091 (the plaintiff was the 71-year-old widowed sister of the deceased). See also *Re C* [1995] 2 FLR 24 (common law wife entitled under the I(PFD)A 1975, s 1(1)(e) to a lump sum): and *Re McC's Estate* (1978) 9 Fam Law 26 (family unit order made).
4   [1981] Fam 128 at 141, [1981] 2 All ER 29 at 38. Applications by cohabitees would now be brought under the new I(PFD)A 1975, s 1(1)(ba) (see para **[105.13]** supra) and the problems centering on consideration would not arise.
5   *Jelley v Iliffe* [1981] Fam 128, [1981] 2 All ER 29
6   [1991] 1 All ER 236 at 242.
7   The Lord Justice thought that the Registrar and the Judge (who had decided against the applicant) had fallen into error in their approach to the test to be applied under s 1(3). Neither

had appeared to take into account Griffiths LJ's view in *Jelley v Iliffe* [1981] Fam 128, [1981] 2 All ER 29, cited in the text above. The case was remitted to the Registrar for consideration of what order should be made in the applicant's favour.

III. THE DISCRETION

[105.18]

Where an application is made for an order under the I(PFD)A 1975 the court will have to decide two issues: firstly, whether the disposition of the deceased's estate effected by his will and/or the law relating to intestacy is such as to make reasonable financial provision for the applicant; secondly, if satisfied that reasonable provision has not been made, the court will then have to consider whether any, and if so what, provision should be made for the applicant.[1] To assist in deciding these questions, which lie in the discretion of the court, the I(PFD)A 1975 provides a list of matters to which the court should have regard. This list bears some resemblance to the factors mentioned in the Matrimonial Causes Act 1973, s 25 which govern the exercise of the court's discretion when ordering financial provision in connection with the decree of divorce, nullity or judicial separation.

1   *Re Coventry, Coventry v Coventry* [1979] 3 All ER 815.

[105.19]

All applicants. With reference to all applicants the court, under the I(PFD)A 1975, s 3(1), has regard to:

   (a)   the financial resources and financial needs which the applicant has or is likely to have in the foreseeable future;
   (b)   the financial resources and financial needs which any other applicant for an order under the I(PFD)A 1975, s 2 has or is likely to have in the foreseeable future;
   (c)   the financial resources and financial needs which any beneficiary of the estate of the deceased has or is likely to have in the foreseeable future.
   (d)   any obligations and responsibilities which the deceased has towards any applicant or towards any beneficiary of the estate of the deceased;
   (e)   the size and nature of the net estate of the deceased;
   (f)   any physical or mental disability of any applicant or any beneficiary of the estate of the deceased;
   (g)   any other matter, including the conduct of the applicant or any other person, which in the circumstances of the case the court may consider relevant.

[105.20]

Financial position of the parties. The relative financial position of the parties is relevant so that the court will have regard to the standard of living previously enjoyed by a widow.[1] However so far as children and applicants other than a spouse are concerned, the jurisdiction is only to provide maintenance and the mere fact that an adult son finds himself in necessitous circumstances cannot by itself render it unreasonable that no provision has, in the events which have happened, been made for his maintenance.² Where the property-owning partner in an unmarried relationship dies, the court recognises the fact that the provision of rent-free accommodation for the survivor is a significant contribution to a person's reasonable needs.³ The court should have regard to the deceased's entire estate, including foreign property, when considering whether the estate made reasonable provision for the applicant.⁴

1   *Re Besterman* [1984] Ch 458, [1984] 2 All ER 656, where the widow of a millionaire was awarded substantial provision; see also *Re Bunning, Bunning v Salmon* [1984] Ch 480, [1984] 3 All ER 1 and *Re Krubert* [1997] Ch 97; discussed above, para **[105.9]** supra.
2   Per Oliver J in *Re Coventry, Coventry v Coventry* [1980] Ch 461, [1979] 2 All ER 408 at 419 who analysed, in a very cautious way, the approach of the court to the exercise of the discretion; see also *Re Dennis, Dennis v Lloyds Bank Ltd* [1981] 2 All ER 140; but see *Re Callaghan* [1984] 3 All ER 790 and *Re Leach, Leach v Lindeman* [1986] Ch 226, [1985] 2 All ER 754 where a different attitude seems evident with reference to claims by 'a child of the family'; para **[105.15]** supra.
3   *Jelley v Iliffe* [1981] Fam 128, [1981] 2 All ER 29; see also *Re Beaumont, Martin v Midland Bank Trust Co Ltd* [1980] Ch 444, [1980] 1 All ER 266. For cases on the Inheritance (Family Provision) Act 1938 under this heading, which might provide some guidance to the jurisdiction of the I(PFD)A 1975, see previous editions of this text.
3   *Bheekhun v Williams* [1999] 2 FLR 229.

[105.21]
Objective test. Whether the provision is reasonable or not is to be determined on the facts known at the date of the hearing and not the death¹ and the test is objective rather than subjective.² This is made clear by the definition of reasonable provision in the I(PFD)A 1975, s 1(2) and cases under the Inheritance (Family Provision) Act 1938 had established the objective test for the purposes of that Act.³

1   I(PFD)A 1975, s 3(5). The court is not entitled to have regard to events subsequent to the hearing: *Re Coventry, Coventry v Coventry* [1979] 3 All ER 815.
2   *Re Coventry, Coventry v Coventry* [1979] 3 All ER 815; *Moody v Stevenson* [1992] Ch 486, sub nom *Re Moody, Moody v Stevenson* [1992] 2 All ER 524. Thus the court can remedy an accidental failure to make adequate provision for a dependant, as for example when the value of the residuary estate left to a wife falls in value after the date of the will, or where a beneficiary is excluded from benefiting because he or she witnessed the will.
3   Megarry J in *Re Goodwin, Goodwin v Goodwin* [1969] 1 Ch 283 at 278, [1968] 3 All ER 12 at 15, approved by Winn LJ in *Re Gregory, Gregory v Goodenough* [1971] 1 All ER 497 at 502, [1970] 1 WLR 1455 at 1461, and applied by Lord Denning MR in *Millward v Shenton* [1972] 2 All ER 1025 at 1028, [1972] 1 WLR 711 at 715. See also *Re Coventry, Coventry v Coventry* [1979] 2 All ER 408; *Moody v Stevenson* [1992] Ch 486 and *Re Jennings* [1994] 3 All ER 27.

[105.22]
Testator's state of mind. It was held that the testamentary capacity was not a matter that should be investigated on an application under the Inheritance (Family Provision) Act 1938 ¹ but the state of the deceased's mind may properly be regarded as relevant and material in cases, for instance in considering the weight to be attributed to any reason given for failing to make any provision.

1   *Re Blanch, Blanch v Henhold* [1967] 2 All ER 468, [1967] 1 WLR 987, per Buckley J considering *Practice Note* [1945] WN 210, based on a statement by Vaisey J after consultation with his judicial colleagues.

[105.23]
Testator's reasons. The deceased's reasons for making or not making provision
under his will were specifically mentioned as a factor to be taken into account
under the Inheritance (Family Provision) Act 1938.[1] This factor is not
specifically included under the I(PFD)A 1975 but can obviously still be regarded
under s 3(1)(g). Reasons if expressed whether orally or in any document are
admissible under the Civil Evidence Act 1968, s 2, by the I(PFD)A 1975, s 21.
The significance of such statements, however, has been reduced by the fact that
the test as to whether reasonable provision has been made is objective.[2]

1   Inheritance (Family Provision) Act 1938, s 1(7). See cases, *Williams v Johns* [1988] 2 FLR 475;
    Re Pugh, Pugh v Pugh [1943] Ch 387, [1943] 2 All ER 361; *Re Smallwood, Smallwood v
    Martins Bank* [1951] Ch 369, [1951] 1 All ER 372; *Re Gregory, Gregory v Goodenough* [1971]
    1 All ER 497, [1970] 1 WLR 1455; *Re Borthwick, Borthwick v Beauvais (No 2)* [1949] Ch 395,
    [1949] 1 All ER 472; *Re Clarke, Clarke v Roberts* [1968] 1 All ER 451, [1968] 1 WLR 415; *Re
    Preston, Preston v Hogarth* [1969] 2 All ER 961, [1969] 1 WLR 317; and *Millward v Shenton*
    [1972] 2 All ER 1025, [1972] 1 WLR 711; in the last two cases the testator's reasons for
    making no provision were overruled.
2   See *Re Collins* [1990] Fam 56, [1990] 2 All ER 47 and *Moody v Stevenson* [1992] Ch 486, sub
    nom *Re Moody, Moody v Stevenson* [1992] 2 All ER 524. For a precedent see Vol 2, Form
    B2.15, para **[202.40]**.

[105.24]
Spouses. Where the applicant is the spouse of the deceased the court will, under
the I(PFD)A 1975, s 3(2), consider the following additional factors:

(a)   the age of the applicant and the duration of the marriage;
(b)   the contribution made by the applicant to the welfare of the family of the
      deceased, including any contribution made by looking after the home or
      caring for the family;

and, in the case of an application by the wife or husband of the deceased, the
court will also, unless at the date of the death a decree of judicial separation was
in force and the separation was continuing, have regard to the provision which
the applicant might reasonably have expected to receive if on the day on which
the deceased died the marriage, instead of being terminated by death, had been
terminated by a decree of divorce.

So far as matrimonial conduct is concerned the approach under the Act is
analogous to that in the divorce court; Lord Denning MR in *Wachtel v Wachtel*[1]
held that if the conduct of one spouse was 'both obvious and gross' so that it
would be 'repugnant to anyone's sense of justice' to make an order against the
other party, the court was free to decline an order. However, he went on, 'short
of cases falling into this category, the court should not reduce its order for
financial provision merely because of what was formerly regarded as guilt or
blame'.[2]

1   [1973] Fam 72; see also *Re Besterman* [1984] Ch 458, [1984] 2 All ER 656 where the fact that
    the wife was blameless was referred to: See also *Moody v Stevenson* [1992] Ch 486, sub nom
    Re Moody, Moody v Stevenson [1992] 2 All ER 524 and *Re Krubert* [1997] Ch 97.
2   *Wachtel v Wachtel* [1973] Fam 72 at 90. The Law Commission (Law Com no 61, p 11)
    expressed the hope that this standard would likewise apply for family provision.

[105.25]
Cohabitees. Where a claim is by a paragraph (ba) applicant,[1] the court will
additionally have regard to the age of the applicant and the length of the period

during which the applicant lived as the husband or wife of the deceased and in the same household as the deceased, and to the contribution made by the applicant to the welfare of the family of the deceased, including any contribution made by looking after the home or caring for the family.[2]

1   Ie a cohabitee qualifying under the I(PFD)A 1975, s 1(1)(ba) and (1A), added by the Law Reform (Succession) Act 1995, s 2 in relation to deaths on or after 1 January 1996. See para [**105.13**] et seq.
2   I(PFD)A 1975, s 3(2A), added by the Law Reform (Succession) Act 1995, s 2.

[105.26]

Children. Where the applicant is a 'child' or a 'child of the family' the court will, under the I(PFD)A 1975, s 3(3), additionally have regard:

'(a) to whether the deceased had assumed any responsibility for the applicant's maintenance and, if so, to the extent to which and the basis upon which the deceased assumed responsibility and to the length of time for which the deceased discharged that responsibility;

(b) to whether in assuming and discharging that responsibility the deceased did so knowing that the applicant was not his own child;

(c) to the liability of any person to maintain the applicant'.[1]

1   See *Re Coventry, Coventry v Coventry* [1980] Ch 461, [1979] 2 All ER 408; *Re Callaghan* [1985] Fam 1, [1984] 3 All ER 790.

[105.27]

Other applicants. With reference to paragraph (e) applicants, the court will have regard to the extent to which, and the basis upon which, the deceased assumed responsibility for the maintenance of the applicant and to the length of time for which the deceased discharged that responsibility.[1]

1   I(PFD)A 1975, s 3(4); see *Re Beaumont, Martin v Midland Bank Trust Co Ltd* [1980] Ch 444, [1980] 1 All ER 266; *Jelley v Iliffe* [1981] Fam 128, [1981] 2 All ER 29; *Bishop v Plumley* [1991] 1 All ER 236, [1991] 1 WLR 582 and *Re B* [2000] 1 All ER 665; fully discussed above in para [**105.15**] supra.

IV.   THE ORDERS

[105.28]

If the court is satisfied that reasonable provision has not been, but should be, made for the applicant then the court has wide powers to make any appropriate order. The possible kinds of order which can be made under the I(PFD)A 1975 are more extensive than those the court was empowered to make under the Inheritance (Family Provision) Act 1938, even after the amendments which widened its scope. So far as the spouse is concerned it has been seen that, under the I(PFD)A 1975, the court can order a higher standard of provision than maintenance, and the powers available to the court have been significantly increased partly so that this might be achieved. The orders that can be made under the I(PFD)A 1975, set out in the I(PFD)A 1975, s 2, will be considered briefly in turn.

[105.29]

Periodical payments. 'An order for the making to the applicant out of the net estate of the deceased of such periodical payments for such terms as may be specified in the order'.[1]

Unlike the situation under the Inheritance (Family Provision) Act 1938 or the Matrimonial Causes Act 1973, these payments do not automatically terminate on the remarriage of a surviving spouse, but do so in the case of a judicially separated or former spouse.[2] Likewise, periodic payments in favour of children do not terminate on marriage or majority. However, of course, these circumstances could occasion a variation of the order under the I(PFD)A 1975, s 6.

If an order for periodical payments is made the court can order, under the I(PFD)A 1975, s 2(2):

'(a) payments of such amount as may be specified in the order,
(b) payments equal to the whole of the income of the net estate or of such portion thereof as may be so specified,
(c) payments equal to the whole of the income of such part of the net estate as the court may direct to be set aside or appropriated for the making out of the income thereof of payments under this section, or may provide for the amount of the payments or any of them to be determined in any other way the court thinks fit'.

Furthermore, the order may direct that such part of the net estate as may be so specified shall be set aside or appropriated for the making out of the income thereof of those payments; but no larger part of the net estate may be so set aside or appropriated than is sufficient, at the date of the order, to produce by the income thereof the amount required for the making of those payments.[3]

1 I(PFD)A 1975, s 2(1)(a). See *Re Debenham* [1986] 1 FLR 404 and *Re Collins* [1990] 2 All ER 47.
2 I(PFD)A 1975, s 19(2).
3 I(PFD)A 1975, s 2(3).

[105.30]

Lump sum payments. 'An order for the payment to the applicant out of the estate of a lump sum of such amount as may be so specified'.[1]

Previously, the court ordered lump sums by way of maintenance; now, vis à vis the surviving spouse, this power acquires greater significance. The order may provide for the payment of the lump sum by instalments of any amount,[2] and these instalments can be varied as to number, amount or date payable[3] but otherwise lump sum orders cannot be varied.

1 I(PFD)A 1975, s 2(1)(b); see *Re Besterman* [1984] Ch 458, [1984] 2 All ER 656; *Re Bunning , Bunning v Salmon* [1984] 3 All ER 1; *Re Callaghan* [1985] Fam 1, [1984] 3 All ER 790; *Re Leach, Leach v Lindeman* [1986] Ch 226, [1985] 2 All ER 754 and *Espinosa v Bourke* [1999] 1 FLR 747.
2 I(PFD)A 1975, s 7(1).
3 I(PFD)A 1975, s 7(2).

[105.31]

Transfers and settlement of property. 'An order for the transfer to the applicant of such property comprised in that estate as may be so specified'.[1]

'An order for the settlement for the benefit of the applicant of such property comprised in that estate as may be so specified'.[2]

These are extensions to the court's powers on family provision and are analogous to the powers contained in the Matrimonial Causes Act 1973, s 24, and thus consistent with the Law Commission's objective that the widow should be in no less advantageous position than the divorced wife. The powers have obvious relevance where the matrimonial home forms part of the estate but can be used with reference to any property. The power might be invoked where it is difficult or undesirable to realise an asset at that time in order to make a lump sum payment. I(PFD)A 1975, s 2(1)(d) orders cannot be varied.[3]

1   I(PFD)A 1975, s 2(1)(c).
2   I(PFD)A 1975, s 2(1)(d); see *Harrington v Gill* (1983) 4 FLR 265, and *Moody v Stevenson* [1992] Ch 486, sub nom *Re Moody, Moody v Stevenson* [1992] 2 All ER 524.
3   I(PFD)A 1975, s 6(9).

[105.32]
Purchase of property or other rights. 'An order for the acquisition, out of property comprised in the estate, of such property as may be so specified and for the transfer of the property so acquired to the applicant or for the settlement thereof for his benefit.'[1] This is useful where a home does not form part of the estate or where the applicant wishes to move to a smaller home. Such an order cannot be varied.[2]

1   I(PFD)A 1975, s 2(1)(e).
2   I(PFD)A 1975, s 6(9).

[105.33]
Variation of marriage settlements. The court can vary any ante- or post-nuptial settlement (including one made by will) which was made on the parties to a marriage of the deceased.[1] This variation must be for the benefit of the surviving party to that marriage, or any child of the marriage. Such an order cannot be subsequently varied.[2]

1   I(PFD)A 1975, s 2(1)(f).
2   I(PFD)A 1975, s 6(9).

[105.34]
Interim orders. The previous legislation provided for interim payments which are useful where, for example, a widow needs money to live on, to pay her rent or to make mortgage payments. This power is reproduced in the I(PFD)A 1975, s 5(1):

'Where on an application for an order under section 2 of this Act it appears to the court—
(a) that the applicant is in immediate need of financial assistance, but it is not yet possible to determine what order (if any) should be made under that section; and
(b) that property forming part of the net estate of the deceased is or can be made available to meet the need of the applicant;

the court may order that, subject to such conditions or restrictions, if any, as the court may impose and to any further order of the court, there shall be paid to the applicant out of the net estate of the deceased such sum or sums and (if more than one) at such intervals as the court thinks fit; and the court may order that, subject to the provisions of this Act, such payments are to be made until such date as the court may specify, not being later than the date on which the court either makes an order under the said section 2 or decides not to exercise its powers under that section.'

A personal representative who pays any sum under this power is not under any liability if it should transpire that the estate was not sufficient to make the payment, unless at the time of making the payment he had reasonable cause to believe that the estate was not sufficient.[1]

---

1   I(PFD)A 1975, s 20(2). For an interim order made under the Inheritance (Family Provision) Act 1938 see *Re Ralphs* [1968] 1 WLR 1522.

[105.35]
Anticipated needs. The I(PFD)A 1975, s 2(3), which provides that part of the net estate may be set aside to meet the periodical payments, continues: 'but no larger part of the net estate shall be set aside or appropriated than is sufficient at the date of the order, to produce by the income thereof the amount required for the making of those payments'. This provision severely restricts any possibility of setting aside sums in anticipation of future needs. The only way such needs can be provided for is by variation under s 6, but it will be seen that this power is limited to variation of 'relevant property' set aside to meet existing orders and cannot involve new property.

[105.36]
Consequential directions. If the court makes an order in a case where the deceased has effectively disposed of all his assets, then the burden or incidence of the award will have to be considered. It was decided under the Inheritance (Family Provision) Act 1938 that the court had power to allocate the burden of the award as between beneficiaries and that the residuary estate would not necessarily bear the award before division between the beneficiaries.[1]

The I(PFD)A 1975 enables the court to make such consequential and supplemental provisions as the court thinks necessary or expedient for the purpose of giving effect to the order, or for the purpose of securing that the order operates fairly as between one beneficiary and another; s 2(4). In particular the court can:

'(a) order any person who holds any property which forms part of the net estate of the deceased to make such payment or transfer such property as may be specified in the order;

(b) vary the disposition of the deceased's estate effected by the will or the law relating to intestacy, or by both the will and the law relating to intestacy in such manner as the court thinks fair and reasonable having regard to the provisions of the order and all the circumstances of the case;

(c) confer on the trustee of any property which is the subject of an order under this section such powers as appear to the court to be necessary or expedient.'

1   See *Re Preston, Preston v Hoggarth* [1969] 2 All ER 961, [1969] 1 WLR 317 and *Re Bunning, Bunning v Salmon* [1984] Ch 480, on the Inheritance (Family Provision) Act 1938, s 3(1) and (2).

V.   VARIATION AND DISCHARGE OF ORDERS

[105.37]

There is a strong argument based on certainty that all orders under family provision should be final. However, there is also the need to ensure that orders for family provisions may be varied to meet changes in circumstances. Thus the I(PFD)A 1975 provides that orders for periodical payments may be varied but that the other orders should not be (except for instalments of lump sum orders).[1] However, the power of variation can only affect the 'relevant property', defined as 'property the income of which is at the date of the order applicable wholly or in part for the making of periodical payments to any person who has applied for an order under the Act'.[2] Thus the order can only be varied within the limits of the property available. Any further order must be because of increased income available, or at the expense of some other beneficiary receiving periodic payments, or because of the death of another recipient of periodic payments. The limited power to vary reflects the compromise between certainty and finality in the administration of estates on the one hand, and the need for continuing justice between the dependants on the other. But within the scope of the 'relevant property' the court has wide powers, thus, under s 6(1):

> 'Subject to the provisions of this Act, where the court has made an order under section 2(1)(a) of this Act (in this section referred to as "the original order") for the making of periodical payments to any person (in this section referred to as "the original recipient"), the court, on an application under this section, shall have power by order to vary or discharge the original order or to suspend any provision of it temporarily and to revive the operation of any provision so suspended.'

In exercising the powers under this section the court has regard to all the circumstances of the case,[3] and the court may give such consequential directions as it thinks necessary or expedient having regard to the provisions of the order.[4]

1   I(PFD)A 1975, s 6. See *Smith v Smith* [1991] 2 All ER 306 (order made under the Matrimonial Causes Act 1973).
2   I(PFD)A 1975, s 6(6).
3   I(PFD)A 1975, s 6(7).
4   I(PFD)A 1975, s 6(8).

[105.38]
Extension of power to vary. Where there has been a family provision order for periodical payments, and the property set aside for making such payments has not been distributed, that property remains available for additional family provision and the court has power to make an order in favour of a new applicant.[1] This might be appropriate where the original recipient of the order no longer had need of it, because, for example, the wife has inherited a substantial estate from her parents.

Where, under an order for periodical payments, the payments are by the terms of the order to cease on a particular event, such as remarriage, the court now has power to vary the provision for cessation.[2]

An application for variation may be made by any person who by virtue of the I(PFD)A 1975, s 1(1) has applied, or would be entitled to apply but for the I(PFD)A 1975, s 4 (which refers to the time limit for applications), for an order under the I(PFD)A 1975, s 2, the personal representatives of the deceased, the trustees of any relevant property, and any beneficiary of the estate of the deceased.

'Beneficiary' means in relation to the estate of a deceased person, (a) a person who under the will of the deceased or under the law relating to intestacy is beneficially interested in the estate or would be so interested if an order had not been made under the I(PFD)A 1975, and (b) a person who has received any sum of money or other property which by virtue of the I(PFD)A 1975, s 8(1) or (2) is treated as part of the net estate of the deceased or would have received that sum or other property if an order had not been made under the Act.[3]

1   I(PFD)A 1975, s 6(2).
2   I(PFD)A 1975, s 6(3), (10).
3   I(PFD)A 1975, s 25(1).

VI.   NET ESTATE

[105.39]
The deceased's 'net estate' from which any order for financial provision under the I(PFD)A 1975 will be made is widely defined by the I(PFD)A 1975. The Inheritance (Family Provision) Act 1938 could be easily avoided by minimising the net estate left on death, thus effectively defeating applications under the Act, something the Law Commission were anxious to avoid. By virtue of the I(PFD)A 1975, s 25(1), net estate includes all property of which the deceased had power to dispose of by his will (otherwise than by virtue of a special power of appointment) less the amount of his funeral, testamentary and administration expenses, debts, and liabilities, including any capital taxes payable out of his estate on his death. Also included is any property in respect of which the deceased held a general power of appointment (not being a power exercisable by will) which has not been exercised.

By virtue of the I(PFD)A 1975, s 8(1) property which has been 'nominated' in accordance with any enactment is automatically treated for the purposes of the I(PFD)A 1975 as part of the net estate, and so is property subject to a donatio mortis causa.[1] Property which the deceased owned as joint tenant does not form part of the net estate for the purposes of administration but clearly must be brought in the net estate if the I(PFD)A 1975 is not to be easily avoided. Thus I(PFD)A 1975, s 9 provides that the court, for the purpose of facilitating the making of financial provision for the applicant, may order that the deceased's severable share of the property shall, to such extent as appears to the court to be just in all circumstances, be treated for the purposes of the I(PFD)A 1975 as part of the net estate of the deceased.[2] Presumably if the deceased's estate is sufficient to satisfy all applicants his share of jointly owned property will not be subject to an order for provision. This provision includes choses in action, such as a joint bank account.[3]

Finally, any property which is subject to an order under the I(PFD)A 1975, s 10 or s 11 is deemed to be part of the net estate. These provisions will be discussed in the next section.

1   I(PFD)A 1975, s 8(2); *Re Cairnes, Howard v Cairnes* (1982) 4 FLR 225 (money nominated under private pension scheme not within s 8).
2   *Re Crawford* (1982) 4 FLR 273; *Kourkgy v Lusher* (1981) 4 FLR 65.
3   See *Hanbury v Hanbury* [1999] 2 FLR 255, I(PFD)A 1975, s 9 applied to a joint bank account.

VII.   PREVENTION OF AVOIDANCE

[105.40]
The Law Commission were very conscious of the fact that, notwithstanding the extensions of the meaning of net estate noted above, the family provision legislation would only be truly effective if it tackled the problem of inter vivos dispositions, whether by way of gift, settlement or otherwise, made by the deceased shortly before death to a non-dependant with the intention of defeating an application under the I(PFD)A 1975. Under the Inheritance (Family Provision) Act 1938 the deceased could effectively settle all his property on himself for life with remainder to, eg, his mistress, and on his death there would be little if any net estate out of which to make provision for a dependant, however deserving. The I(PFD)A 1975, s 10 deals with this situation. Further, the decision in *Schaefer v Schuhmann*[1] had shown that the Inheritance (Family Provision) Act 1938 could also be effectively avoided by making inter vivos contracts to leave property to a beneficiary by will. The donee in such a case ranks as a creditor on the death and thus takes the property out of the estate before any question of provision for an applicant arises. That problem is dealt with by the I(PFD)A 1975, s 11.

1   [1972] AC 572, [1972] 1 All ER 621.

[105.41]
Inter vivos dispositions: I(PFD)A 1975, s 10. The section provides that the applicant may apply to the court for an order under subsection (2), which is in the following terms:

'Where on an application under subsection (1) above the court is satisfied—
(a)   that, less than six years before the date of the death of the deceased, the deceased with the intention of defeating an application for financial provision under this Act made a disposition, and
(b)   that full valuable consideration for that disposition was not given by the person to whom or for the benefit of whom the disposition was made (in this section referred to as "the donee") or by any other person, and
(c)   that the exercise of the powers conferred by this section would facilitate the making of financial provision for the applicant under this Act,
then, subject to the provisions of this section and of sections 12 and 13 of this Act, the court may order the donee (whether or not at the date of the order he holds any interest in the property disposed of to him or for his benefit by the deceased) to provide, for the purpose of the making of that financial

provision, such sum of money or other property as may be specified in the order.'[1]

The time limit of six years was chosen somewhat arbitrarily because of the difficulties of investigating a person's intention at remoter period of time. Attempts in Parliament to reduce the period were unsuccessful.

Valuable consideration does not include marriage or a promise of marriage.[2] The section does not apply to any disposition made before 1 April 1976.[3]

1   A successful invocation of the anti-avoidance provisions in the I(PFD)A 1975, s 10 was made in *Re Dawkins, Dawkins v Judd* [1986] 2 FLR 360, [1986] Fam Law 295. Deceased husband had made a will in 1980 whereby he left £8,000 and a life interest in the matrimonial home to his wife. In 1981 he transferred the home to the daughter of his previous marriage for £100 thus defeating the will since there were insufficient other assets to meet the £8,000 legacy and the wife had no remaining right to reside in the house. In 1982 the parties separated and he died shortly after. By a new will the whole estate was left to the daughter. Estate was insolvent but widow claimed under the I(PFD)A 1975, s 10 for payment to her of part of the sum realised by the sale of the former matrimonial home. The order was made and s 10 applied. The judge commented:
    'The conclusion that I have come to is that the widow should have a lump sum as a financial capital cushion against the vicissitudes of life, particularly the financial vicissitudes, and that figure I assess at £10,000.'
    See also on the I(PFD)A 1975, s 10 *Clifford v Tanner* [1987] CLY 3881 (release of a covenant to provide a home for testator and testator's wife held to be a 'disposition' within s 10). In *Hanbury v Hanbury* [1999] 2 FLR 255, the I(PFD)A 1975, ss 9 and 10 were applied where the deceased and his second wife had deliberately sought to reduce his apparent net estate to minimise any claim that his mentally handicapped daughter by his first marriage might make.
2   I(PFD)A 1975, s 25(1).
3   I(PFD)A 1975, s 10(8).

[105.42]

The property. The I(PFD)A 1975 differentiates between dispositions consisting of the payment of money and other property. Where the disposition consisted of a sum of money then the amount ordered to be provided under the section shall not exceed the amount of the payment by the deceased, less any capital transfer tax.[1] So, if the money was invested in shares which have increased in value or in interest-yielding investments, the donees does not need to account for any increase or any interest.

So far as property other than money is concerned the question of valuation is dealt with by the I(PFD)A 1975, s 10(4), as follows:

'Where an order is made under subsection (2) above as respects any disposition made by the deceased which consisted of the transfer of property (other than a sum of money) to or for the benefit of the donee, the amount of any sum of money or the value of any property ordered to be provided under the sub-section shall not exceed the value at the date of the death of the deceased of the property disposed of by him to or for the benefit of the donee (or if that property has been disposed of by the person to whom it was transferred by the deceased, the value at the date of that disposal thereof) after deducting therefrom any capital transfer tax borne by the donee in respect of the transfer of that property by the deceased.'

So if the property increases in value between the gift and the death the donee will have to return the increased value. But if the property has been disposed of by the person to whom it was transferred, then the amount shall not exceed the value at the date of disposal.[2] It can perhaps be emphasised that it is not necessary that the donee should still be owner of the property since, if he is not, the court can still order him to repay a sum of money.[3]

It thus seems clear that if the donor is determined to benefit the donee at the expense of the applicants he should, if possible, give wasting assets rather than appreciating assets.[4] It is worth noting that the I(PFD)A 1975 does not appear to include any provision to deal with 'associated operations' of the kind familiar in tax law. Thus there might be an advantage in making several gifts of parts of a whole, where the value of the whole greatly exceeds the value of the individual parts.

1   I(PFD)A 1975, s 10(3).
2   I(PFD)A 1975, s 10(4).
3   I(PFD)A 1975, s 10(1).
4   It has been suggested that a gift of travel tickets would be an effective way of benefiting the donee since because he would have used the tickets at the date of death the accountable value would be nil. However, it might be that the use of the tickets would be a disposal and the donee would have to account for the value at the time. Likewise with consumables, such as wine.

[105.43]
The donee. Orders can be made against the original donee but not against any subsequent owner of the property, other than a trustee.[1] It should be noted that 'trustee' for this purpose includes the trustee or trustees for the time being of the trust in question.[2] The Law Commission[3] considered but rejected the idea that property should be traced or followed into the hands of third parties. It was thought that such a power if conferred would lead to complexities and uncertainties. If the donee has parted with the property then he can be asked to provide 'such sum of money or other property as may be specified in the order'. If the donee is dead, then the court can proceed against his personal representatives, but once any property has been distributed by his personal representatives, no order can be made in respect of that property.[4]

The section also covers cases where the property was given in trust for the donee by reason of the words 'or for his benefit', and in such cases the order can be made against either the donee or the trustee. The liability of the trustee in such cases is governed by the I(PFD)A 1975, s 13, and is basically limited to such money or other property as is in his hands at the date of the order (whether the money or property originally given, or money or property which represents what was originally given).

If the donee is proceeded against by an applicant under the I(PFD)A 1975, s 10 then he can in turn show that there is *another* disposition made less than six years before the death, not for full valuable consideration, and ask the court to proceed against that disposition.[5]

1   I(PFD)A 1975, s 13.
2   I(PFD)A 1975, s 13(3).
3   Law Com no 61, p 62.
4   I(PFD)A 1975, s 12(4).
5   I(PFD)A 1975, s 10(5).

[105.44]
The discretion. In deciding whether to make an order under the section the court has regard to the circumstances in which the disposition was made and any

valuable consideration which was given thereof, the relationship, if any, of the donee to the deceased, the conduct and financial resources of the donee, and all the other circumstances of the case.[1]

The court can make such consequential directions as it thinks fit, for giving effect to the order or for securing a fair adjustment of the rights of the person effected thereby.[2] Thus, if a donee is ordered to transfer a specific item of property the court could order some payment to the donee out of the net estate and so make consequential adjustments of the rights of the beneficiaries.

1   I(PFD)A 1975, s 10(6).
2   I(PFD)A 1975, s 12(3).

[105.45]
The disposition. For the purposes of the I(PFD)A 1975, s 10, 'disposition' does not include any provision in a will, any such nomination as is mentioned in the I(PFD)A 1975, s 8(1) or any donatio mortis causa, or any appointment of property made, otherwise than by will, in the exercise of a special power of appointment. But subject to these exceptions, any payment of money (including the payment of a premium under a policy of assurance), any appointment or gift of property of any description, whether made by an instrument or otherwise, is included.[1]

1   I(PFD)A 1975, s 10(7). It will be noted that so far as assurance policies are concerned the premiums but not the capital sum payable on death are included. Thus, there might be an advantage for a donor determined to defeat his dependants to take out, and pay the premiums on, an assurance policy for his own life for the benefit of the donee on his death. It has also been suggested that use could be made of the fact that appointments of property in exercise of a special power of appointment do not constitute dispositions for the purposes of s 10, and the property subject to a special power is not within the definition of net estate. Thus, the donor could settle his property inter vivos on himself for life reserving a special power of appointment exercisable by deed or will which could be in favour of a wide class; see eg *Re Gulbenkian's Settlement, Hocobian v Maun* [1968] Ch 126, [1967] 3 All ER 15, and *Re Manisty's Settlement, Manisty v Manisty* [1974] Ch 17, [1973] 2 All ER 1203. Once six years had elapsed the settled property would not be available for financial provision under the I(PFD)A 1975, and this would probably be so even if the settlor had retained a power to revoke the settlement, provided that the power of revocation was exercisable only by deed.

[105.46]
The intention to defeat an application. The proof of the intention to defeat an application under the I(PFD)A 1975 is obviously going to present problems. The Law Commission's report provides little guidance and the only assistance in the I(PFD)A 1975 is s 12(1), to the effect that it must be proved on a balance of probabilities that the intention of the deceased, though not necessarily his sole intention, in making the disposition was to prevent an order for financial provision being made under the I(PFD)A 1975, or to reduce the amount of the provision that might otherwise be granted.

It is therefore a question of subjective intention, and the court will not be able to make an order in a case of an honest mistake as to whether a gift would leave enough property in the donee's hands to satisfy the claims of his dependants.[1]

There are certain consequences of this for someone about to make an inter vivos disposition. If there is a possibility that the disposition might not leave enough disposable estate to satisfy claims to financial provision which could arise on that person's death – for example the disposition is to be substantial or is not in favour of that person's immediate family or dependants – it will plainly be advisable to consider the amount of his disposable property and the moral claims on it. It is also going to be a good idea to keep a full record of the result of any deliberations, which would be important evidence of the intention behind the disposition if it ever called into question in an application for financial provision after his death. In trying to work out the effect of a disposition it will be important to take into account any capital tax the disposition will bear, and also the reduction in the potential net value of the retained estate on death which will occur as a result of the disposition provided of course the donor survives the required seven years. As already suggested it seems that if an honest mistake is made in this exercise, or there is a subsequent drastic fall in the value of the disposer's net estate, the disposition will not be liable to be reopened in financial provision proceedings on the death, unlike a mistake in drafting a will or a change in circumstances after a will is executed.

It can be noted that the Law Commission considered, but rejected, the idea of including a presumption of intention to defeat on the grounds that it would place too great a burden on the donee to discharge. There is such a presumption under the Matrimonial Causes Act 1973, s 37 where the disposition took place within three years of the application, and the I(PFD)A 1975 provides a presumption in s 12(2) where contracts, dealt with by the I(PFD)A 1975, s 11, are concerned.

1   One obvious difficulty is that the section specifically requires an intention to defeat an application 'under this Act', rather than a vaguer intention to reduce the estate to the detriment of the dependants, and this might be simply avoided by showing that the deceased was a lay man who had never heard of the Act and had no knowledge of the possibility of applications for family provision. Thus in *Re Kennedy, Kennedy v Official Solicitor to the Supreme Court* [1980] CLY 2820 an application for an order under the I(PFD)A 1975, s 10 failed. The decision indicates that in order to obtain such an order it is not essential to show that the deceased had the existence of or the provisions of the I(PFD)A 1975 present in his mind when he made the disputed transaction but there must be evidence that the deceased intended to defeat a claim made after his death against his estate. In the absence of any guidance in the I(PFD)A 1975 as to how this intention could be proved, perhaps some guidance could be obtained from cases on the somewhat analogous provisions of the Matrimonial Causes Act 1973, s 37 (eg *Jordan v Jordan* (1965) 109 Sol Jo 353), and the Law of Property Act 1925, s 172 (eg *Lloyds Bank Ltd v Marcan* [1973] 2 All ER 359, [1973] 1 WLR 339), now repealed by the Insolvency Acts 1985, 1986.

[105.47]

Contracts to leave property by will. The decision in *Schaefer v Shuhmann,*[1] illustrated how the family provision legislation could perhaps be avoided by inter vivos contract to leave property by will. The Law Commission thought that this loophole should be closed and the I(PFD)A 1975, s 11 enacts that recommendation. Where the deceased made a contract by which he agreed to leave by his will a sum of money or other property to any person then, if that contract was not made for full valuable consideration (which does not include marriage or a promise of marriage) and was made with the intention of defeating an application under the I(PFD)A 1975, the court can make one or more of the following orders if that would facilitate the making of financial provision under the I(PFD)A 1975:[2]

   '(i)   if any money has been paid or any other property has been transferred to or for the benefit of the donee in accordance with the contract, an order directing the donee to provide, for the purpose of the making of that financial provision, such sum of money or other property as may be specified in the order;

(ii) if the money or all the money has not been paid or the property or all the property has not been transferred in accordance with the contract, an order directing the personal representatives not to make any payment or transfer any further property, as the case may be, in accordance therewith or directing the personal representatives only to make such payment or transfer such property as may be specified in the order.'

The court has power to give consequential directions analogous to the I(PFD)A 1975, s 10 orders.[3]

The section only applies to a contract made on or after 1 April 1976, and in determining whether and in what manner to exercise its powers under this section, the court has regard to the circumstances in which the contract was made, the relationship, if any, of the donee to the deceased, the conduct and financial resources of the donee, and all the other circumstances of the case.[4]

There is no time limit within which the contract has to have been made as in the case of the six-year period in the I(PFD)A 1975, s 10. This is because with a contract the property will remain with the deceased until death. Similar problems will arise under the I(PFD)A 1975, s 11 relating to the proof the intention to defeat an application under the I(PFD)A 1975, as arise under s 10. It is necessary to prove on a balance of probabilities that the intention of the deceased, though not necessarily his sole intention, in making the contract was to prevent an order for financial provision being made under the I(PFD)A 1975, or to reduce the amount of the provision which might otherwise be granted by an order.[5]

Some assistance is provided by the I(PFD)A 1975, s 12(2) to the effect that where an application is made under the I(PFD)A 1975, s 11 with respect to any contract made by the deceased and no valuable consideration was given or promised by any person for that contract then, it shall be presumed, unless the contrary is shown, that the deceased made that contract with the intention of defeating an application for financial provision under the I(PFD)A 1975.[6]

1   [1972] AC 572, [1972] 1 All ER 621.
2   I(PFD)A 1975, s 11(2).
3   I(PFD)A 1975, s 13(3).
4   I(PFD)A 1975, s 11(4).
5   I(PFD)A 1975, s 12(1).
6   But, even so, it is doubtful if a contract such as the one in *Schaefer v Schuhmann* [1972] AC 572, [1972] 1 All ER 621, could be reviewed under the I(PFD)A 1975, s 11.

VIII.   SPECIAL PROVISIONS RELATING TO ORDERS, ETC MADE IN FAVOUR OF FORMER SPOUSES

[105.48]

Mention can be made of the I(PFD)A 1975, s 15, relating to restrictions imposed in divorce, etc, proceedings on applications under the I(PFD)A 1975,[1] s 16, relating to variation and discharge of orders under the Matrimonial Causes Act 1973, s 17, relating to variation and revocation of maintenance agreements; and s 18, relating to the availability of the court's powers under the I(PFD)A 1975 in applications under the Matrimonial Causes Act 1973, ss 31 and 36.

1   See the substituted I(PFD)A 1975, s 15(1), and the new s 15A, resulting from the Matrimonial and Family Proceedings Act 1984, discussed para **[105.11]** supra.

IX.   INHERITANCE TAX AND FAMILY PROVISION

[105.49]
The general provision is that if an order is made under the I(PFD)A 1975 then, for the purposes of inheritance tax charging provisions, the order shall have effect and be deemed to have had effect as from the deceased's death subject to the contrary provisions in the order.[1] Thus any disposition effected by the order is charged to inheritance tax as if it were an ordinary testamentary provision, so that if the order is made in favour of a spouse then the inheritance tax exemption applies. Further there is now a specific provision to the effect that compromise of claims under the I(PFD)A 1975 embodied in *Tomlin* orders are to the extent that the terms agreed could have been embodied in an order under the I(PFD)A 1975 treated as if it were provisions of such an order,[2] so that they will be treated as if taking effect on the death for tax purposes.[3] Out of court settlements are not within these provisions.[4] The Finance Act 1989 introduced an anti-avoidance provision in a new s 29A inserted in the Inheritance Tax Act 1984. If a claim under the I(PFD)A 1975 by, eg, a child or mistress of the deceased, is settled out of his own resources by a beneficiary, such as the deceased's widow or a charity, the deceased's gift to whom is exempt from inheritance tax, the exemption available for the deceased's gift to the beneficiary will be appropriately reduced. This new provision applies in relation to deaths on or after the passing of the Finance Act 1989. Its effect can be avoided by the widow or charity settling the claim out of property in the deceased's estate by an out of court settlement which is not treated as a disposition taking effect on the deceased's death under Inheritance Tax Act 1984, ss 142 or 146.

Where the powers under the I(PFD)A 1975, s 8 or 9 are invoked then, if nominated property is by virtue of section 8 treated as part of the net estate of the deceased, it is the net sum which is brought into the estate.[5] Likewise with reference to donatio mortis causa.[6] Similarly, when under s 9 the court orders a share of property held in joint tenancy to be treated for the purposes of the I(PFD)A 1975 as part of the net estate of the deceased, it is to have regard to any capital tax payable in respect of it.[7]

If the court sets aside any disposition intended to defeat applications made under the I(PFD)A 1975 pursuant to the powers in the I(PFD)A 1975, s 10, then it is the net amount of any sum of money or the value of any property which is brought into the estate, after deducting any capital tax borne by the donee in respect of that payment.[8] For further discussion reference should be made to Foster's Inheritance Tax, D4.41–46.

1   Inheritance Tax Act 1984, s 146(1); previously the Finance Act 1975, s 19(1); and the Finance Act 1976, s 122.
2   Inheritance Tax Act 1984, s 146(8), 42 *Halsbury's Statutes* (4th edn) 804, previously the Finance Act 1976, s 122(7A) introduced by the Finance Act 1980, s 92.

3   Under the Inheritance Tax Act 1984, s 146(1).
4   But may fall within the Inheritance Tax Act 1984, s 142 as an alteration or disposition taking effect on death.
5   I(PFD)A 1975, s 8(1); see also the Inheritance Tax Act 1984, s 146(4), (5).
6   I(PFD)A 1975, s 8(2).
7   I(PFD)A 1975, s 9(2); see also the Inheritance Tax Act 1984, s 146(4), (5).
8   I(PFD)A 1975, s 10(3) and (4). See the Inheritance Tax Act 1984, s 146(2) on refunding the tax.

Index

Index

Index

Grand-nephews and nieces
description of donees, and, **71**.5
Grants
foreign element wills, and
deceased domiciled in England & Wales,
23.19
deceased domiciled outside England &
Wales, **23**.20
Graves, gifts for upkeep of
capacity to benefit, and, **9**.29–9.30
Growing crops
and see **Description of property**
generally, **61**.1
Guardians, appointment of
appointees, **28**.3
appointers, **28**.2
before 14ᵗʰ October 1991, **28**.9
conditional, **28**.4
disclaimer, **28**.7
formalities, **28**.5
introduction, **28**.1
parental responsibility, **28**.2
revocation, **28**.6
transitional arrangements, **28**.8

Half-blood relatives
description of donees, and, **71**.1
Heirs
entailed interests, and, **84**.3
generally, **78**.1–78.7
living person, of, **78**.2
particular character, of, **78**.3
Heirs and assigns
description of donees, and, **78**.7
Heirs and successors
description of donees, and, **78**.6
HM Forces, entering
conditions, and, **35**.46
Holders of office
description of donees, and, **81**.4
Holograph will
generally, **10**.18
Hotchpot
estoppel, and, **43**.6
generally, **100**.1–100.7
partial intestacy, and
death after 1996, **104**.14
death before 1996, **104**.13
House
description of property, and, **64**.26
Household furniture
description of property, and, **64**.27
Household goods
description of property, and, **64**.28
Howe v. Dartmouth **rule**
adjustment of debts, **38**.26–38.28
generally, **38**.17–38.25
reversionary interests, **38**.22–38.23
Husband
and see **Spouse**
description of donees, and, **80**.7

Hybrid power of appointment
generally, **40**.5

Id certum est quod certum redid potest
uncertainty, and, **53**.2
Illegality
charitable gifts, and, **103**.11
creation of interests by will, and, **8**.2
Illegitimate children
capacity to benefit, and, **9**.24–9.26
description of donees, and
common law, **72**.2–72.9
introduction, **72**.1
legitimation, **72**.15–72.18
statute, **72**.10–72.14
lapse, and, **47**.15
legitimation, and, **72**.15–72.18
Illiterate testator
signature of wills, and, **11**.22
Immovable property
foreign element wills, and
construction, **24**.8
definitions, **23**.3–23.4
formalities, **23**.11–23.12
intestate succession, **23**.17
Implication, gifts by
generally, **101**.1–101.14
Implied election
generally, **42**.12
Impossibility
charitable gifts, and, **103**.11
effect, **34**.8
generally, **34**.7
Impotence, relief of
charitable purposes, and, **102**.5
In terrorem **conditions**
generally, **34**.13–34.16
In vitro fertilisation, children born by
capacity to benefit, and, **9**.27
generally, **74**.3–74.5
introduction, **72**.18
Inaccuracy of description
change of circumstances, and, **58**.11
description of property, and, **63**.1
descriptive designation, **58**.9
enumeration of particulars, **58**.8
general rule, **58**.3
generic description, **58**.12
introduction, **58**.2
name and descriptive designation, **58**.10
name designation, **58**.9
partly true as to each subject, **58**.7
partly true as to one subject, **58**.6
partly wrong but applicable to one subject,
58.5
specific description, **58**.13
wholly true as to one subject, **58**.6
wholly wrong but subject-matter certain, **58**.4
Income, gifts of
absolute interests, and, **83**.4
charge on rents and profits, **62**.2

1024